Dietary Reference Intakes: RDA, AI*

	Elements														
Life Stage Group	**Calcium (mg/d)**	**Chromium (μg/d)**	**Copper (μg/d)**	**Fluoride (mg/d)**	**Iodine (μg/d)**	**Iron (mg/d)**	**Magnesium (mg/d)**	**Manganese (mg/d)**	**Molybdenum (μg/d)**	**Phosphorus (mg/d)**	**Selenium (μg/d)**	**Zinc (mg/d)**	**Potassium (g/d)**	**Sodium (g/d)**	**Chloride (g/d)**
Infants															
0–6 mo	200*	0.2*	200*	0.01*	110*	0.27*	30*	0.003*	2*	100*	15*	2*	0.4*	0.12*	0.18*
6–12 mo	260*	5.5*	220*	0.5*	130*	**11**	75*	0.6*	3*	275*	20*	**3**	0.7*	0.37*	0.57*
Children															
1–3 y	**700**	11*	**340**	0.7*	**90**	**7**	**80**	1.2*	**17**	**460**	**20**	**3**	3.0*	1.0*	1.5*
4–8 y	**1,000**	15*	**440**	1*	**90**	**10**	**130**	1.5*	**22**	**500**	**30**	**5**	3.8*	1.2*	1.9*
Males															
9–13 y	**1,300**	25*	**700**	2*	**120**	**8**	**240**	1.9*	**34**	**1,250**	**40**	**8**	4.5*	1.5*	2.3*
14–18 y	**1,300**	35*	**890**	3*	**150**	**11**	**410**	2.2*	**43**	**1,250**	**55**	**11**	4.7*	1.5*	2.3*
19–30 y	**1,000**	35*	**900**	4*	**150**	**8**	**400**	2.3*	**45**	**700**	**55**	**11**	4.7*	1.5*	2.3*
31–50 y	**1,000**	35*	**900**	4*	**150**	**8**	**420**	2.3*	**45**	**700**	**55**	**11**	4.7*	1.5*	2.3*
51–70 y	**1,000**	30*	**900**	4*	**150**	**8**	**420**	2.3*	**45**	**700**	**55**	**11**	4.7*	1.3*	2.0*
>70 y	**1,200**	30*	**900**	4*	**150**	**8**	**420**	2.3*	**45**	**700**	**55**	**11**	4.7*	1.2*	1.8*
Females															
9–13 y	**1,300**	21*	**700**	2*	**120**	**8**	**240**	1.6*	**34**	**1,250**	**40**	**8**	4.5*	1.5*	2.3*
14–18 y	**1,300**	24*	**890**	3*	**150**	**15**	**360**	1.6*	**43**	**1,250**	**55**	**9**	4.7*	1.5*	2.3*
19–30 y	**1,000**	25*	**900**	3*	**150**	**18**	**310**	1.8*	**45**	**700**	**55**	**8**	4.7*	1.5*	2.3*
31–50 y	**1,000**	25*	**900**	3*	**150**	**18**	**320**	1.8*	**45**	**700**	**55**	**8**	4.7*	1.5*	2.3*
51–70 y	**1,200**	20*	**900**	3*	**150**	**8**	**320**	1.8*	**45**	**700**	**55**	**8**	4.7*	1.3*	2.0*
>70 y	**1,200**	20*	**900**	3*	**150**	**8**	**320**	1.8*	**45**	**700**	**55**	**8**	4.7*	1.2*	1.8*
Pregnancy															
14–18 y	**1,300**	29*	**1,000**	3*	**220**	**27**	**400**	2.0*	**50**	**1,250**	**60**	**12**	4.7*	1.5*	2.3*
19–30 y	**1,000**	30*	**1,000**	3*	**220**	**27**	**350**	2.0*	**50**	**700**	**60**	**11**	4.7*	1.5*	2.3*
31–50 y	**1,000**	30*	**1,000**	3*	**220**	**27**	**360**	2.0*	**50**	**700**	**60**	**11**	4.7*	1.5*	2.3*
Lactation															
14–18 y	**1,300**	44*	**1,300**	3*	**290**	**10**	**360**	2.6*	**50**	**1,250**	**70**	**13**	5.1*	1.5*	2.3*
19–30 y	**1,000**	45*	**1,300**	3*	**290**	**9**	**310**	2.6*	**50**	**700**	**70**	**12**	5.1*	1.5*	2.3*
31–50 y	**1,000**	45*	**1,300**	3*	**290**	**9**	**320**	2.6*	**50**	**700**	**70**	**12**	5.1*	1.5*	2.3*

Note: This table (taken from the DRI reports, see www.nap.edu) presents Recommended Dietary Allowances (RDAs) in **bold type** and Adequate Intakes (AIs) in ordinary type followed by an asterisk (*). An RDA is the average daily dietary intake level sufficient to meet the nutrient requirements of nearly all (97-98 percent) healthy individuals in a group. It is calculated from an Estimated Average Requirement (EAR). If sufficient scientific evidence is not available to establish an EAR, and thus calculate an RDA, an AI is usually developed. For healthy breastfed infants, an AI is the mean intake. The AI for other life stage and gender groups is believed to cover the needs of all healthy individuals in the groups, but lack of data or uncertainty in the data prevent being able to specify with confidence the percentage of individuals covered by this intake.

Dietary Reference Intakes: RDA, AI*

Life Stage Group	Vitamins Vitamin A (μg/d)[a]	Vitamin C (mg/d)	Vitamin D (μg/d)[b,c]	Vitamin E (mg/d)[d]	Vitamin K (μg/d)	Thiamin (mg/d)	Riboflavin (mg/d)	Niacin (mg/d)[e]	Vitamin B_6 (mg/d)	Folate (μg/d)[f]	Vitamin B_{12} (μg/d)	Pantothenic Acid (mg/d)	Biotin (μg/d)	Choline (mg/d)[g]
Infants														
0–6 mo	400*	40*	10	4*	2.0*	0.2*	0.3*	2*	0.1*	65*	0.4*	1.7*	5*	125*
6–12 mo	500*	50*	10	5*	2.5*	0.3*	0.4*	4*	0.3*	80*	0.5*	1.8*	6*	150*
Children														
1–3 y	**300**	**15**	**15**	**6**	30*	**0.5**	**0.5**	**6**	**0.5**	**150**	**0.9**	2*	8*	200*
4–8 y	**400**	**25**	**15**	**7**	55*	**0.6**	**0.6**	**8**	**0.6**	**200**	**1.2**	3*	12*	250*
Males														
9–13 y	**600**	**45**	**15**	**11**	60*	**0.9**	**0.9**	**12**	**1.0**	**300**	**1.8**	4*	20*	375*
14–18 y	**900**	**75**	**15**	**15**	75*	**1.2**	**1.3**	**16**	**1.3**	**400**	**2.4**	5*	25*	550*
19–30 y	**900**	**90**	**15**	**15**	120*	**1.2**	**1.3**	**16**	**1.3**	**400**	**2.4**	5*	30*	550*
31–50 y	**900**	**90**	**15**	**15**	120*	**1.2**	**1.3**	**16**	**1.3**	**400**	**2.4**	5*	30*	550*
51–70 y	**900**	**90**	**15**	**15**	120*	**1.2**	**1.3**	**16**	**1.7**	**400**	**2.4**[h]	5*	30*	550*
>70 y	**900**	**90**	**20**	**15**	120*	**1.2**	**1.3**	**16**	**1.7**	**400**	**2.4**[h]	5*	30*	550*
Females														
9–13 y	**600**	**45**	**15**	**11**	60*	**0.9**	**0.9**	**12**	**1.0**	**300**	**1.8**	4*	20*	375*
14–18 y	**700**	**65**	**15**	**15**	75*	**1.0**	**1.0**	**14**	**1.2**	**400**[i]	**2.4**	5*	25*	400*
19–30 y	**700**	**75**	**15**	**15**	90*	**1.1**	**1.1**	**14**	**1.3**	**400**[i]	**2.4**	5*	30*	425*
31–50 y	**700**	**75**	**15**	**15**	90*	**1.1**	**1.1**	**14**	**1.3**	**400**[i]	**2.4**	5*	30*	425*
51–70 y	**700**	**75**	**15**	**15**	90*	**1.1**	**1.1**	**14**	**1.5**	**400**	**2.4**[h]	5*	30*	425*
>70 y	**700**	**75**	**20**	**15**	90*	**1.1**	**1.1**	**14**	**1.5**	**400**	**2.4**[h]	5*	30*	425*
Pregnancy														
14–18 y	**750**	**80**	**15**	**15**	75*	**1.4**	**1.4**	**18**	**1.9**	**600**[j]	**2.6**	6*	30*	450*
19–30 y	**770**	**85**	**15**	**15**	90*	**1.4**	**1.4**	**18**	**1.9**	**600**[j]	**2.6**	6*	30*	450*
31–50 y	**770**	**85**	**15**	**15**	90*	**1.4**	**1.4**	**18**	**1.9**	**600**[j]	**2.6**	6*	30*	450*
Lactation														
14–18 y	**1,200**	**115**	**15**	**19**	75*	**1.4**	**1.6**	**17**	**2.0**	**500**	**2.8**	7*	35*	550*
19–30 y	**1,300**	**120**	**15**	**19**	90*	**1.4**	**1.6**	**17**	**2.0**	**500**	**2.8**	7*	35*	550*
31–50 y	**1,300**	**120**	**15**	**19**	90*	**1.4**	**1.6**	**17**	**2.0**	**500**	**2.8**	7*	35*	550*

Note: This table (taken from the DRI reports, see www.nap.edu) presents Recommended Dietary Allowances (RDAs) in **bold type** and Adequate Intakes (AIs) in ordinary type followed by an asterisk (*). An RDA is the average daily dietary intake level sufficient to meet the nutrient requirements of nearly all (97–98 percent) healthy individuals in a group. It is calculated from an Estimated Average Requirement (EAR). If sufficient scientific evidence is not available to establish an EAR, and thus calculate an RDA, an AI is usually developed. For healthy breastfed infants, an AI is the mean intake. The AI for other life stage and gender groups is believed to cover the needs of all healthy individuals in the groups, but lack of data or uncertainty in the data prevent being able to specify with confidence the percentage of individuals covered by this intake.

[a] As retinol activity equivalents (RAEs). 1 RAE = 1 μg retinol, 12 μg β-carotene, 24 μg α-carotene, or 24 μg β-cryptoxanthin. The RAE for dietary provitamin A carotenoids is two-fold greater than retinol equivalents (RE), whereas the RAE for preformed vitamin A is the same as RE.

[b] As cholecalciferol. 1 μg cholecalciferol = 40 IU vitamin D.

[c] Under the assumption of minimal sunlight.

[d] As α-tocopherol. α-Tocopherol includes RRR-α-tocopherol, the only form of α-tocopherol that occurs naturally in foods, and the 2R-stereoisomeric forms of α-tocopherol (RRR-, RSR-, RRS-, and RSS-α-tocopherol) that occur in fortified foods and supplements. It does not include the 2S-stereoisomeric forms of α-tocopherol (SRR-, SSR-, SRS-, and SSS-α-tocopherol), also found in fortified foods and supplements.

[e] As niacin equivalents (NE). 1 mg of niacin = 60 mg of tryptophan; 0–6 months = preformed niacin (not NE).

[f] As dietary folate equivalents (DFE). 1 DFE = 1 μg food folate = 0.6 μg of folic acid from fortified food or as a supplement consumed with food = 0.5 μg of a supplement taken on an empty stomach.

[g] Although AIs have been set for choline, there are few data to assess whether a dietary supply of choline is needed at all stages of the life cycle, and it may be that the choline requirement can be met by endogenous synthesis at some of these stages.

[h] Because 10 to 30 percent of older people may malabsorb food-bound B_{12}, it is advisable for those older than 50 years to meet their RDA mainly by consuming foods fortified with B_{12} or a supplement containing B_{12}.

[i] In view of evidence linking folate intake with neural tube defects in the fetus, it is recommended that all women capable of becoming pregnant consume 400 μg from supplements or fortified foods in addition to intake of food folate from a varied diet.

[j] It is assumed that women will continue consuming 400 μg from supplements or fortified food until their pregnancy is confirmed and they enter prenatal care, which ordinarily occurs after the end of the periconceptional period—the critical time for formation of the neural tube.

Bring your nutrition course

INTO FOCUS

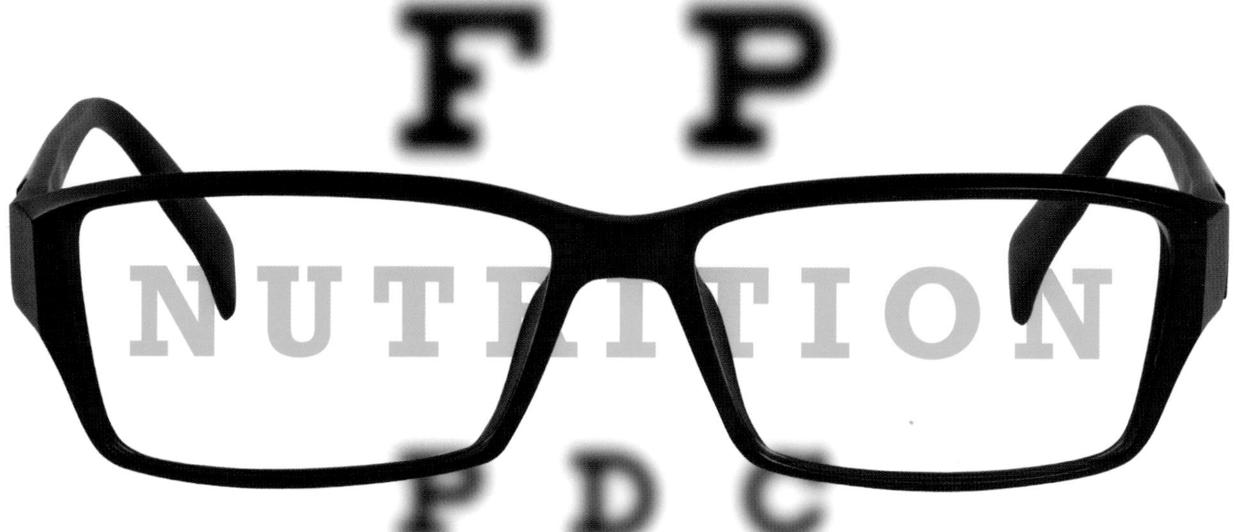

L P E D

An approach that focuses on

"I really like these and students appreciate them."
—Amy Frith, *Ithaca College*

***Nutrition: From Science to You,* Second Edition** provides the tools students need to understand the science of nutrition and successfully apply it in their personal lives and future careers.

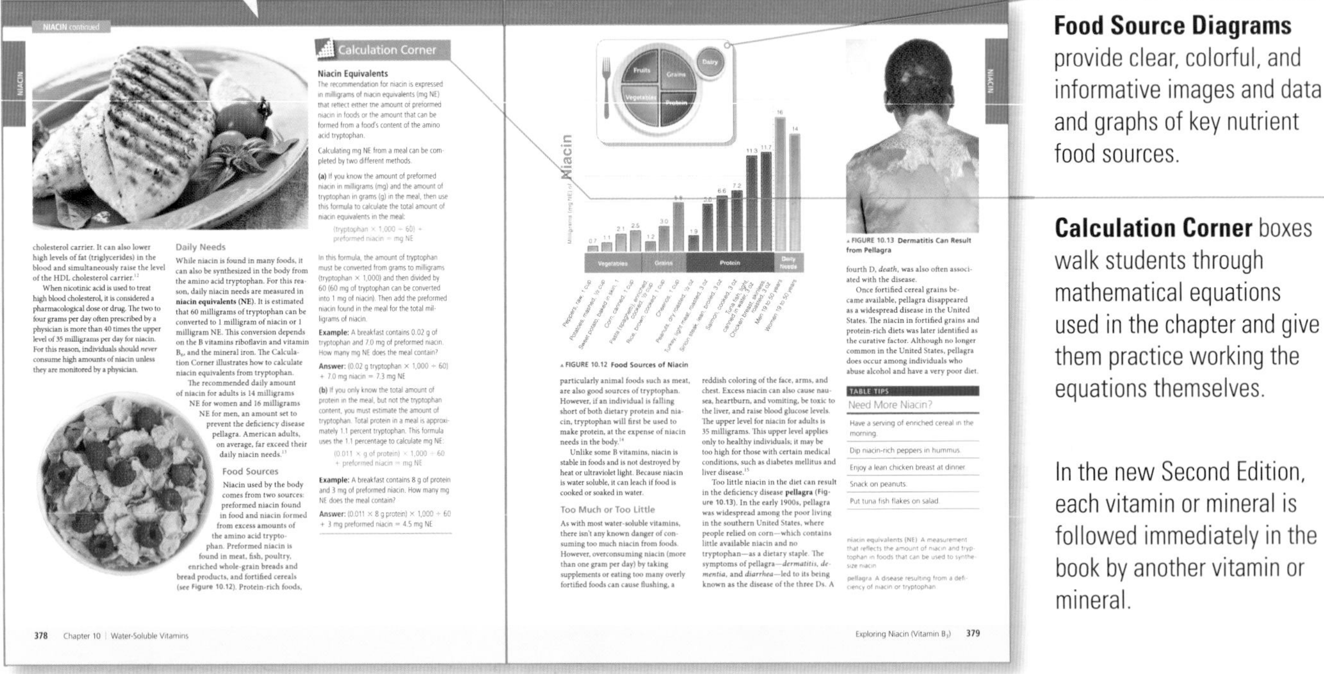

Food Source Diagrams provide clear, colorful, and informative images and data and graphs of key nutrient food sources.

Calculation Corner boxes walk students through mathematical equations used in the chapter and give them practice working the equations themselves.

In the new Second Edition, each vitamin or mineral is followed immediately in the book by another vitamin or mineral.

Exploring Micronutrients

These self-contained sections incorporate photos, illustrations, and text to present each vitamin and mineral. Each micronutrient is discussed using the same categories (forms, absorption and transport, functions, daily needs, food sources, toxicity and deficiency symptoms) for a consistent and easy-to-study format.

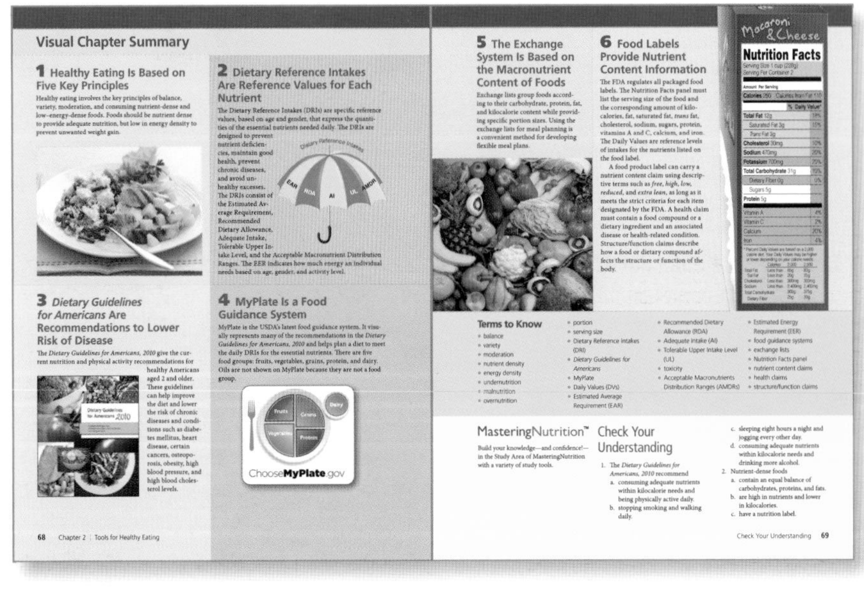

NEW! Visual Chapter Summaries

Structured to mirror the organization of the chapter content and the chapter objectives, these sections contain important art and photos from the main chapter text and serve as concise study and review tools.

STUDENT LEARNING

Praise for *Nutrition: From Science to You*

"I really like the vibrant look, feel, and style of the book. I find it easier to read and more engaging than some of the other texts out there."
—Heidi Wengreen, *Utah State University*

"The diagrams are excellent—making the concepts much easier to visualize than any other book I've used or reviewed."
—Eric Vlahov, *University of Tampa*

"The other nutrition faculty and I chose this text because we liked the level of detail and difficulty. ... It provides a solid reference for students to address [our course] goals."
— Julia L. Lapp, *Ithaca College*

Health Connection

Celiac Disease: An Issue of Absorption

Popcorn is a gluten-free snack that people with celiac disease can safely enjoy.

One of the more serious malabsorption conditions to occur in the small intestine is *celiac disease*. A healthy small intestine contains numerous villi and microvilli that efficiently and exhaustively absorb nutrients from food. But when a person has celiac disease, the lining of the small intestine flattens out, which reduces its ability to absorb nutrients. The flattening is caused by an abnormal reaction to the protein gluten, found in wheat, rye, and barley.

Celiac disease is most common among people of European descent. Though the exact cause of celiac disease is unknown, it is believed to be genetic. The most recent estimates suggest that 1 in 133 people (less than 1%) is affected by celiac disease in the United States. But when an individual has celiac disease, the incidence among close family members is estimated to be as high as 4.5 percent.[1] Because of this genetic link, celiac disease is classified as a lifelong disorder.

What Are the Symptoms of Celiac Disease?

Classic celiac symptoms include reoccurring abdominal bloating, cramping, diarrhea, gas, fatty and foul-smelling stools, weight loss, anemia, fatigue, bone or joint pain, and even a painful skin rash called dermatitis herpetiformis. Some people develop the symptoms of celiac disease in infancy or childhood. Others develop it later in life, after being misdiagnosed with irritable bowel syndrome or various food intolerances.

How Serious Is Celiac Disease?

Depending on the length of time between symptom development and diagnosis, the complications from celiac disease can be serious. Celiac patients have an increased incidence of osteoporosis from poor calcium absorption, diminished growth because of nutrient malabsorption, and even seizures due to inadequate folate absorption. Celiac disease also increases the risk of developing certain types of cancer, including esophageal cancer and melanoma.[2]

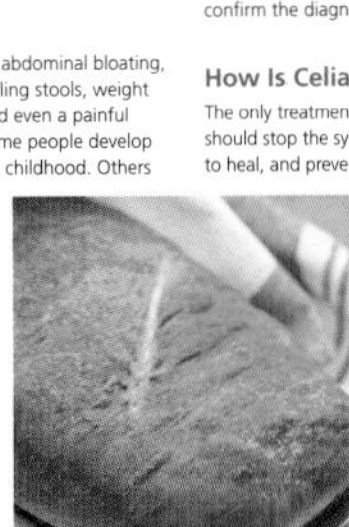

Bread and other foods containing wheat, barley, and rye must be avoided on a gluten-free diet.

How Is Celiac Disease Diagnosed?

In the past, diagnosing celiac disease was sometimes difficult because it resembles other similar malabsorption diseases. The contemporary method of diagnosis begins with a simple blood test.[3] If the test proves positive, the next step is a tissue biopsy of the small intestine to confirm the diagnosis.[2, 4]

How Is Celiac Disease Treated?

The only treatment for celiac disease is a gluten-free diet.[5] This should stop the symptoms from progressing, allow the intestine to heal, and prevent further damage. The symptoms often improve within a few days after beginning the gluten-free diet. If the diet is followed faithfully, the absorption area of the intestinal tract often returns to normal status within three to six months.

Adhering to a gluten-free diet, which means avoiding all gluten-containing foods, can be challenging. All breads, pasta, cereals, and other wheat-containing foods must be eliminated. Gluten-free foods such as meat, milk, eggs, fruit, and vegetables are permissible. Rice, potatoes, corn, and beans, as well as grains such as quinoa, amaranth, and millet do not contain gluten and are also acceptable. The Academy of Nutrition and Dietetics maintains a comprehensive list of foods allowed on a gluten-free diet on their website, www.eatright.org.[6]

Due to an increased awareness of celiac disease and gluten intolerance, the demand for gluten-free products has exploded. Gluten-free products are now easier to find in your local markets and

102 Chapter 3 | Digestion, Absorption, and Transport

NEW! Health Connection Features

These boxes highlight diseases and disorders in which nutrition plays a major role, as well as nutritional practices that offer unique health benefits.

Nutrition in Practice: Brendan

As a biology professor, Brendan's annual physical at the campus health center uncovered that his blood glucose levels classified him as having "prediabetes." According to his doctor, his blood glucose levels are higher than ideal but not high enough to be diagnosed as having full-fledged diabetes. Because his father and grandfather both developed diabetes later in their lives, the doctor explained that his family history and excess weight put Brendan at a higher risk for developing type 2 diabetes. Because of Brendan's daily one-hour drive to campus each way, his physical activity consists of parking his car in the faculty lot and walking less than one block to his office.

Brendan's doctor refers him to the campus Registered Dietitian for an appointment. Brendan is dreading meeting with the dietitian because as a bachelor, he doesn't enjoy cooking and is concerned that his diet of takeout foods, along with his sedentary lifestyle, is about to end. The dietitian meets with Brendan to discuss his diet and lifestyle habits and its effect on his blood glucose levels.

Brendan's Stats:

- Age: 45
- Height: 6 feet 1 inches
- Weight: 230 pounds
- BMI: 30
- Fasting Blood Glucose: 124 mg/dl

Critical Thinking Questions

1. How does Brendan's weight contribute to his elevated blood glucose levels?
2. What foods/beverages could be contributing to Brendan's weight and blood glucose levels and why?
3. How could increasing Brendan's daily physical activity improve his blood glucose levels and why?

Dietitian's Observation and Plan for Brendan:

- Discuss the need to lose weight. A weight loss of as little as 5 to 7 percent of a person's body weight can reduce the cells' resistance to insulin. This enables glucose to be taken up by the cells and improve his blood glucose levels.
- Increase his dietary fiber. Fiber has been shown to improve insulin sensitivity, or the use of insulin by the cells.
- Plan a well-balanced, kilocalorie-reducing diet that includes fruits, vegetables, whole grains, legumes, and low-fat dairy, along with some lean protein and healthy oils, to promote weight loss of approximately ½ to 1 pound weekly. Provide him with healthier choices when dining out and purchasing takeout foods.
- Increase physical activity to at least 2.5 hours weekly. Exercise improves the cells' sensitivity to insulin and lowers blood glucose levels.

Two weeks later, Brendan visits the dietitian again and is excited that he has lost 2 pounds. He is parking his car in a parking lot that is five blocks from his office so he walks more every day. A review of his food record shows that his diet is still too low in vegetables and fruit. The dietitian works with Brendan to increase his produce not only at meals but also as snacks. They also discuss ways that Brendan can walk during the day on campus to increase his daily physical activity.

Brendan's Food Log

Food/Beverage	Time Consumed	Hunger Rating*	Location
Donut and coffee with cream	8:30 am	2	Coffee shop
Hamburger, fries, and cola	1 pm	5	Fast-food eatery
Chocolate bar	4 pm	4	Vending machine in faculty lounge
Fried chicken, mashed potatoes, corn	6:30 pm	4	Picked up from supermarket takeout. Consumed at home.
Ice cream	9 pm	1	Home, watching TV

*Hunger Rating (1–5): 1 = not hungry; 5 = super hungry

Why Is Dietary Fiber So Important? 127

NEW! Nutrition in Practice Case Studies

Drawing upon Joan Salge Blake's experience as a dietitian working with actual clients, these case studies encourage critical thinking and emphasize the applicability of the content to students' own lives and future careers.

FOCUS FIGURES bring

NEW! Focus Figures teach students key concepts in nutrition. These full-page figures explore targeted and integrated topic areas through visual information displays that are bold, clear, and detailed. These figures also have corresponding tutorials in MasteringNutrition™.

NEW! Second Edition

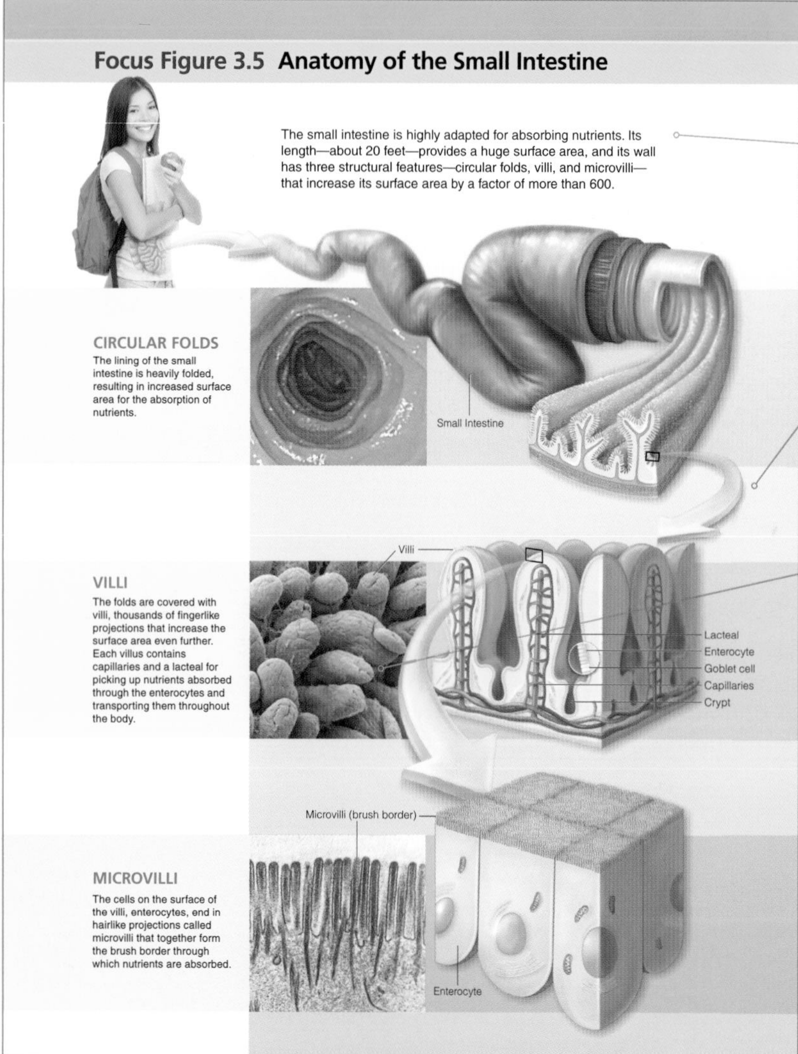

Focus Figure 3.5 Anatomy of the Small Intestine
The small intestine is highly adapted for absorbing nutrients. Its length—about 20 feet—provides a huge surface area, and its wall has three structural features—circular folds, villi, and microvilli—that increase its surface area by a factor of more than 600.
CIRCULAR FOLDS
The lining of the small intestine is heavily folded, resulting in increased surface area for the absorption of nutrients.
Small Intestine
VILLI
The folds are covered with villi, thousands of fingerlike projections that increase the surface area even further. Each villus contains capillaries and a lacteal for picking up nutrients absorbed through the enterocytes and transporting them throughout the body.
Villi
Lacteal
Enterocyte
Goblet cell
Capillaries
Crypt
MICROVILLI
The cells on the surface of the villi, enterocytes, end in hairlike projections called microvilli that together form the brush border through which nutrients are absorbed.
Microvilli (brush border)
Enterocyte

p. 79

Focus Figures are presented with introductory text that explains how the figure is key to other concepts students will learn in this chapter and future chapters.

Students get clear direction with **stepped out art** that guides the eye through complex processes, breaking them down into clear, manageable pieces that make concepts easier to teach and understand.

Pairing of dynamic art and actual photographs provide students with the visual reinforcement needed for concepts to come alive.

First Edition

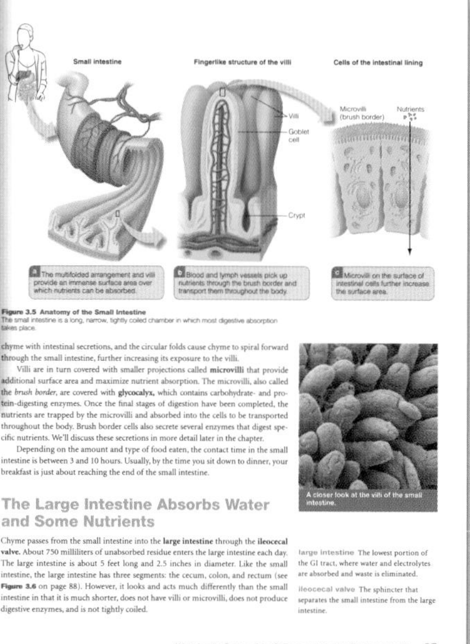

Figure 3.5 Anatomy of the Small Intestine
The small intestine is a long, narrow, tightly coiled chamber in which most digestive absorption takes place.

chyme with intestinal secretions, and the circular folds cause chyme to spiral forward through the small intestine, further increasing its exposure to the villi.

Villi are in turn covered with smaller projections called **microvilli** that provide additional surface area and maximize nutrient absorption. The microvilli, also called the *brush border*, are covered with **glycocalyx,** which contains carbohydrate- and protein-digesting enzymes. Once the final stages of digestion have been completed, the nutrients are trapped by the microvilli and absorbed into the cells to be transported throughout the body. Brush border cells also secrete several enzymes that digest specific nutrients. We'll discuss these secretions in more detail later in the chapter.

Depending on the amount and type of food eaten, the contact time in the small intestine is between 3 and 10 hours. Usually, by the time you sit down to dinner, your breakfast is just about reaching the end of the small intestine.

A closer look at the villi of the small intestine.

The Large Intestine Absorbs Water and Some Nutrients

Chyme passes from the small intestine into the **large intestine** through the **ileocecal valve.** About 750 milliliters of unabsorbed residue enters the large intestine each day. The large intestine is about 5 feet long and 2.5 inches in diameter. Like the small intestine, the large intestine has three segments: the cecum, colon, and rectum (see **Figure 3.6** on page 88). However, it looks and acts much differently than the small intestine in that it is much shorter, does not have villi or microvilli, does not produce digestive enzymes, and is not tightly coiled.

large intestine The lowest portion of the GI tract, where water and electrolytes are absorbed and waste is eliminated.

ileocecal valve The sphincter that separates the small intestine from the large intestine.

What Are the Organs of the GI Tract and Why Are They Important? 87

p. 87

clarity to tough topics

NEW! Second Edition

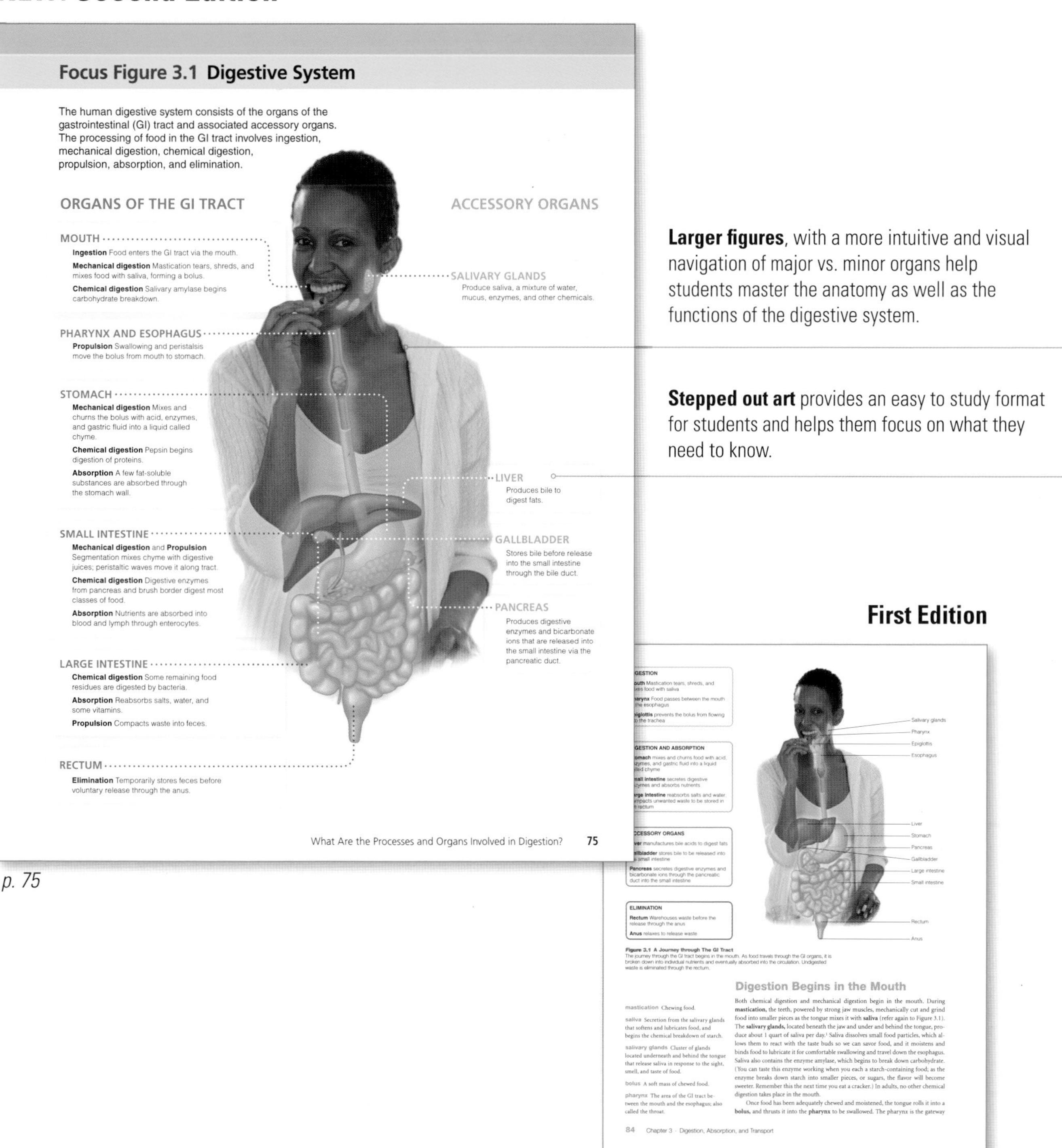

Focus Figure 3.1 Digestive System

The human digestive system consists of the organs of the gastrointestinal (GI) tract and associated accessory organs. The processing of food in the GI tract involves ingestion, mechanical digestion, chemical digestion, propulsion, absorption, and elimination.

ORGANS OF THE GI TRACT

MOUTH
Ingestion Food enters the GI tract via the mouth.
Mechanical digestion Mastication tears, shreds, and mixes food with saliva, forming a bolus.
Chemical digestion Salivary amylase begins carbohydrate breakdown.

PHARYNX AND ESOPHAGUS
Propulsion Swallowing and peristalsis move the bolus from mouth to stomach.

STOMACH
Mechanical digestion Mixes and churns the bolus with acid, enzymes, and gastric fluid into a liquid called chyme.
Chemical digestion Pepsin begins digestion of proteins.
Absorption A few fat-soluble substances are absorbed through the stomach wall.

SMALL INTESTINE
Mechanical digestion and **Propulsion** Segmentation mixes chyme with digestive juices; peristaltic waves move it along tract.
Chemical digestion Digestive enzymes from pancreas and brush border digest most classes of food.
Absorption Nutrients are absorbed into blood and lymph through enterocytes.

LARGE INTESTINE
Chemical digestion Some remaining food residues are digested by bacteria.
Absorption Reabsorbs salts, water, and some vitamins.
Propulsion Compacts waste into feces.

RECTUM
Elimination Temporarily stores feces before voluntary release through the anus.

ACCESSORY ORGANS

SALIVARY GLANDS
Produce saliva, a mixture of water, mucus, enzymes, and other chemicals.

LIVER
Produces bile to digest fats.

GALLBLADDER
Stores bile before release into the small intestine through the bile duct.

PANCREAS
Produces digestive enzymes and bicarbonate ions that are released into the small intestine via the pancreatic duct.

What Are the Processes and Organs Involved in Digestion? 75

p. 75

Larger figures, with a more intuitive and visual navigation of major vs. minor organs help students master the anatomy as well as the functions of the digestive system.

Stepped out art provides an easy to study format for students and helps them focus on what they need to know.

First Edition

ELIMINATION
Rectum Warehouses waste before the release through the anus
Anus relaxes to release waste

Figure 3.1 A Journey through The GI Tract
The journey through the GI tract begins in the mouth. As food travels through the GI organs, it is broken down into individual nutrients and eventually absorbed into the circulation. Undigested waste is eliminated through the rectum.

Digestion Begins in the Mouth

mastication Chewing food.

saliva Secretion from the salivary glands that softens and lubricates food, and begins the chemical breakdown of starch.

salivary glands Cluster of glands located underneath and behind the tongue that release saliva in response to the sight, smell, and taste of food.

bolus A soft mass of chewed food.

pharynx The area of the GI tract between the mouth and the esophagus; also called the throat.

Both chemical digestion and mechanical digestion begin in the mouth. During **mastication,** the teeth, powered by strong jaw muscles, mechanically cut and grind food into smaller pieces as the tongue mixes it with **saliva** (refer again to Figure 3.1). The **salivary glands,** located beneath the jaw and under and behind the tongue, produce about 1 quart of saliva per day.[1] Saliva dissolves small food particles, which allows them to react with the taste buds so we can savor food, and it moistens and binds food to lubricate it for comfortable swallowing and travel down the esophagus. Saliva also contains the enzyme amylase, which begins to break down carbohydrate. (You can taste this enzyme working when you each a starch-containing food; as the enzyme breaks down starch into smaller pieces, or sugars, the flavor will become sweeter. Remember this the next time you eat a cracker.) In adults, no other chemical digestion takes place in the mouth.

Once food has been adequately chewed and moistened, the tongue rolls it into a **bolus,** and thrusts it into the **pharynx** to be swallowed. The pharynx is the gateway

84 Chapter 3 · Digestion, Absorption, and Transport

p. 84

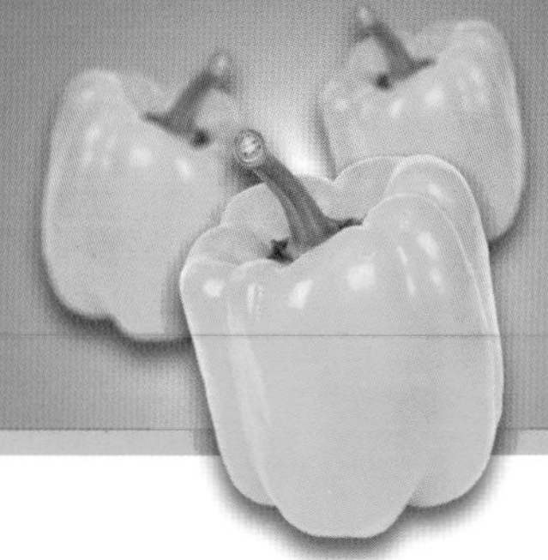

EASY TO GET STARTED,

MasteringNutrition™

www.masteringnutrition.pearson.com
www.pearsonmylabandmastering.com

Mastering is the most effective and widely used online homework, tutorial, and assessment system for the sciences. It delivers self-paced tutorials that focus on your course objectives, provide individualized coaching, and respond to each student's progress.

For Students

Proven, assignable, and automatically graded nutrition activities reinforce course learning objectives.

NutriTools Build-A-Meal Activities

These unique activities allow students to combine and experiment with different food options and learn firsthand how to build healthier meals.

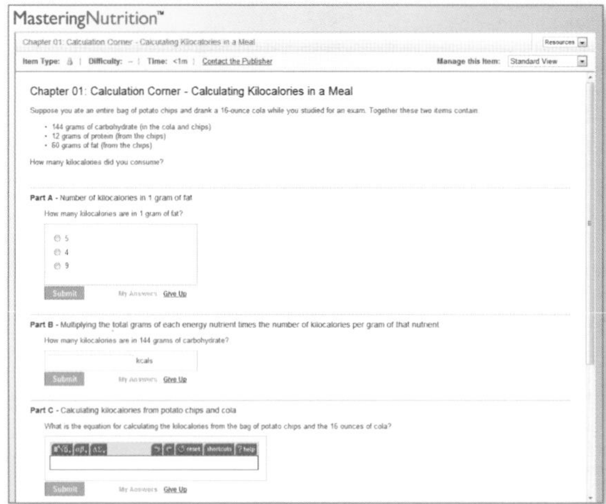

Calculation Corner Activities

New activities based on the text feature provide hands-on practice of important calculations to help students understand and apply the material, with helpful wrong-answer feedback.

Other automatically graded nutrition activities include:

- MyDietAnalysis Case Study Coaching Activities
- Reading Quizzes
- *ABC News* Videos
- Chapter MP3s
- Animations
- *Get Ready for Nutrition*

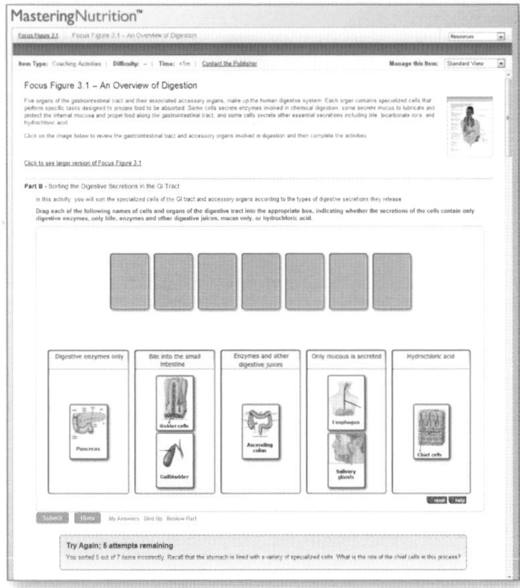

Focus Figure Coaching Activities

Coaching activities guide students through key nutrition concepts with interactive mini-lessons that provide hints and feedback.

use, and make your own

For Instructors

MasteringNutrition with MyDietAnalysis helps instructors maximize class time with easy-to-assign, customizable, and automatically graded assessments that motivate students to learn outside of class and arrive prepared for lecture or lab.

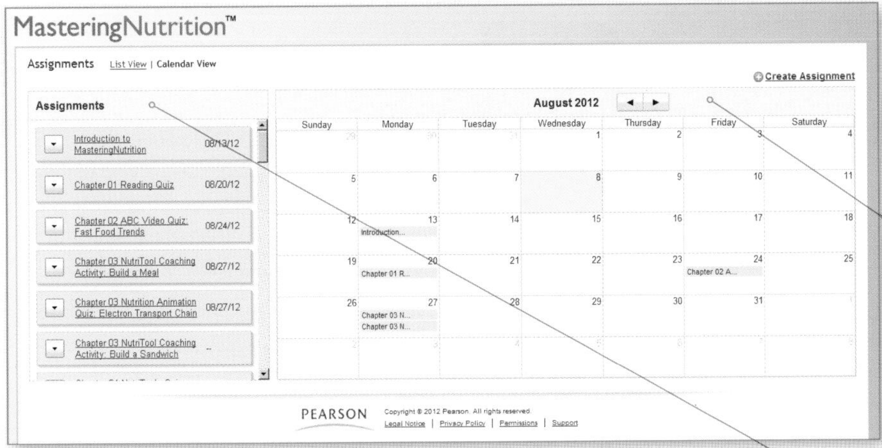

Calendar Feature for Instructors and Students

The Course Home default page now features a Calendar View displaying upcoming assignments and due dates.

- Instructors can schedule assignments by dragging and dropping the assignment onto a date in the calendar.
- The calendar view lets students see at-a-glance when an assignment is due, and resembles a syllabus.

Customize Publisher-provided Problems or Quickly Add Your Own

MasteringNutrition™ makes it easy to edit any questions or answers, import your own questions, and quickly add images or links to further enhance the student experience.

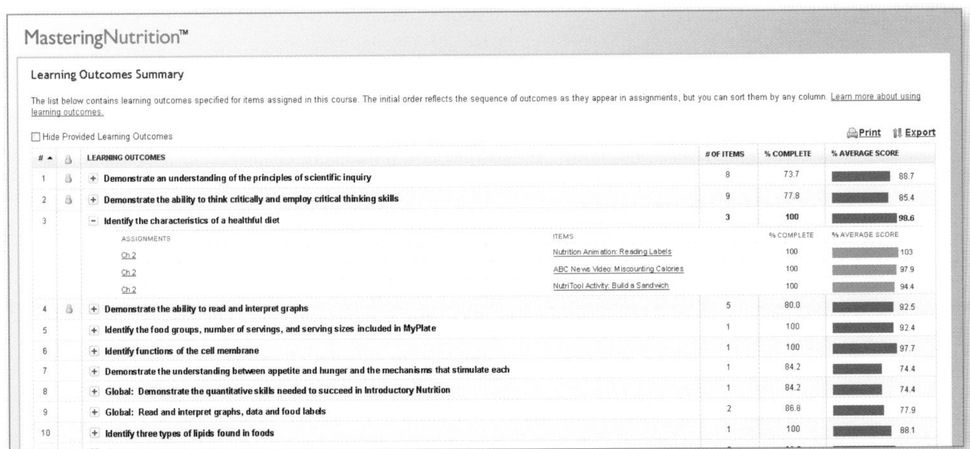

MasteringNutrition™

Learning Outcomes Summary

The list below contains learning outcomes specified for items assigned in this course. The initial order reflects the sequence of outcomes as they appear in assignments, but you can sort them by any column. Learn more about using learning outcomes.

Hide Provided Learning Outcomes — Print — Export

#	LEARNING OUTCOMES	# OF ITEMS	% COMPLETE	% AVERAGE SCORE
1	Demonstrate an understanding of the principles of scientific inquiry	8	73.7	88.7
2	Demonstrate the ability to think critically and employ critical thinking skills	9	77.8	85.4
3	Identify the characteristics of a healthful diet	3	100	98.6
	ASSIGNMENTS / ITEMS		% COMPLETE	% AVERAGE SCORE
	Ch 2 — Nutrition Animation: Reading Labels		100	103
	Ch 2 — ABC News Video: Miscounting Calories		100	97.9
	Ch 2 — NutriTool Activity: Build a Sandwich		100	94.4
4	Demonstrate the ability to read and interpret graphs	5	80.0	92.5
5	Identify the food groups, number of servings, and serving sizes included in MyPlate	1	100	92.4
6	Identify functions of the cell membrane	1	100	97.7
7	Demonstrate the understanding between appetite and hunger and the mechanisms that stimulate each	1	84.2	74.4
8	Global: Demonstrate the quantitative skills needed to succeed in Introductory Nutrition	1	84.2	74.4
9	Global: Read and interpret graphs, data and food labels	2	86.8	77.9
10	Identify three types of lipids found in foods	1	100	88.1

Learning Outcomes

Tagged to book content and tied to Bloom's Taxonomy, Learning Outcomes are designed to let Mastering do the work in tracking student performance against your learning outcomes. Mastering offers a data-supported measure to quantify students' learning gains and to share those results quickly and easily:

- Add your own or use the publisher-provided learning outcomes.
- View class performance against the specified learning outcomes.
- Export results to a spreadsheet.

Bring focus to your course with DYNAMIC SUPPLEMENTS

For Instructors

Instructor Resource and Support Manual

978-0-321-86384-3 | 0-321-86384-4

This resource includes outlines that summarize each chapter, author-provided ideas for hands-on group assignments, key terms, teaching tips, suggested source materials, "Two Points of View" interviews, Focus on Research assignments, and topics for discussion.

Printed Test Bank

978-0-321-86379-9 | 0-321-86379-8

This supplement provides multiple-choice, true/false, short answer, and essay questions for each chapter of the text.

Instructor Resource DVD (IR-DVD)

978-0-321-86383-6 | 0-321-86383-6

This valuable teaching resource offers everything you need to create lecture presentations and course materials, including JPEG and PowerPoint® files of all the art, tables, and selected photos from the text, and "stepped-out" art for selected figures from the text, as well as animations.

The IR-DVD also includes:

- PowerPoint® lecture outlines with embedded links to animations and *ABC News* Lecture Launcher Videos
- A Jeopardy-type quiz show
- The Instructor Manual
- Test Bank Microsoft® Word files
- Computerized Test Bank
- Questions for Classroom Response Systems (CRS) in PowerPoint format, allowing you to import the questions into your own CRS

Great Ideas: Active Ways to Teach Nutrition

978-0-321-59646-8 | 0-321-59646-3

This updated, revised booklet compiles the best ideas from nutrition instructors across the country on innovative ways to teach nutrition topics with an emphasis on active learning.

MyDietAnalysis

MyDietAnalysis Premium Website

www.mydietanalysis.com

MyDietAnalysis was developed by the nutrition database experts at ESHA Research, Inc. and is tailored for use in college nutrition courses. MyDietAnalysis is available as a single sign on to MasteringNutrition.

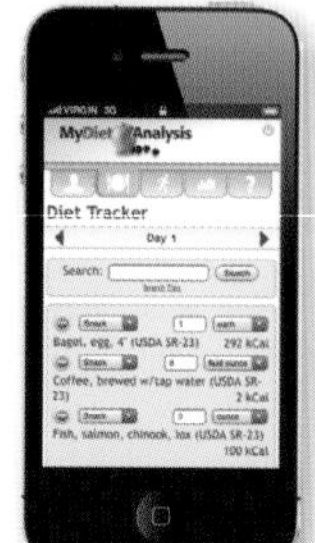

- **NEW FOR SPRING 2013!** For online users, a new mobile website version of MyDietAnalysis is available. Students can track their diet and activity intake accurately, anytime and anywhere, from their mobile device.

Food Composition Table

978-0-321-66793-9 | 0-321-66793-X

The USDA Nutrient Database for Standard Reference is provided as a new supplement, offering the nutritional values of over 1,500 separate foods in an easy-to-follow format.

NEW! MasteringNutrition™ with MyDietAnalysis and Pearson eText

See pages 6 & 7 for details.

For Students

Food Composition Table

978-0-321-66793-9 | 0-321-66793-X

See "For Instructors" for full description.

MasteringNutrition with MyDietAnalysis and Pearson eText Student Access Code Card

978-0-321-88351-3 | 0-321-88351-9

Nutrition

FROM SCIENCE TO YOU

Second Edition

Joan Salge Blake
BOSTON UNIVERSITY

Kathy D. Munoz
HUMBOLDT STATE UNIVERSITY

Stella Volpe
DREXEL UNIVERSITY

PEARSON

Boston Columbus Indianapolis New York San Francisco Upper Saddle River
Amsterdam Cape Town Dubai London Madrid Milan Munich Paris Montréal Toronto
Delhi Mexico City São Paulo Sydney Hong Kong Seoul Singapore Taipei Tokyo

Executive Editor: Sandra Lindelof
Project Editor: Kari Hopperstead
Director of Development: Barbara Yien
Editorial Manager: Susan Malloy
Development Editor: Marilyn Freedman
Art Editor: Kelly Murphy
Assistant Editor: Meghan Zolnay
Media Producers: Lee Ann Doctor, Joe Mochnick
Editorial Assistant: Briana Verdugo
Text Permissions Project Manager: Alison Bruckner
Text Permissions Specialist: Adrienne Matzen
Managing Editor: Deborah Cogan
Production Project Manager: Caroline Ayres
Production Management: S4Carlisle Publishing Services
Copyeditor: Anna Reynolds Trabucco
Compositor: S4 Carlisle Publishing Services
Design Manager: Mark Ong
Interior Designer: Gary Hespenheide
Cover Designer: Gary Hespenheide
Illustrator: Precision Graphics
Photo Permissions Management: PreMedia Global
Photo Researchers: Kristin Piljay, Steve Merland
Senior Manufacturing Buyer: Stacey Weinberger
Executive Marketing Manager: Neena Bali
Cover Photo Credit: Foodcollection RF/Getty Images

Library of Congress Cataloging-in-Publication data is available upon request.

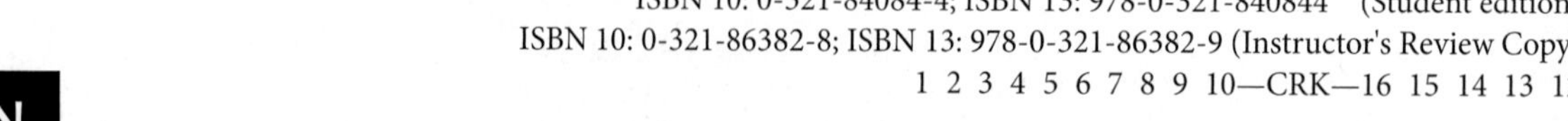
ISBN 10: 0-321-84084-4; ISBN 13: 978-0-321-840844 (Student edition)
ISBN 10: 0-321-86382-8; ISBN 13: 978-0-321-86382-9 (Instructor's Review Copy)
1 2 3 4 5 6 7 8 9 10—CRK—16 15 14 13 12

Manufactured in the United States of America.

Brief Contents

Contents

6 Proteins 206

7 Alcohol 250

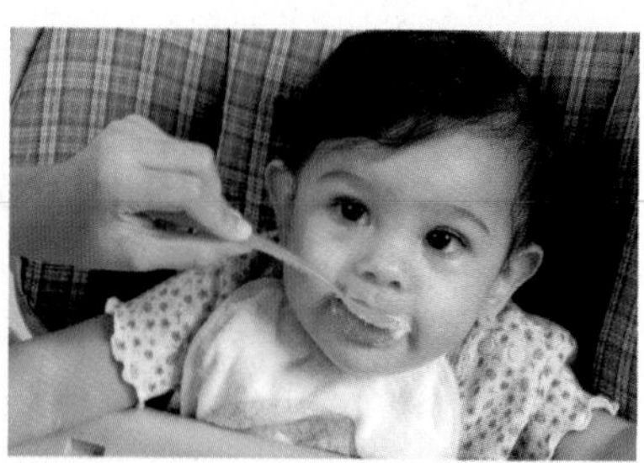

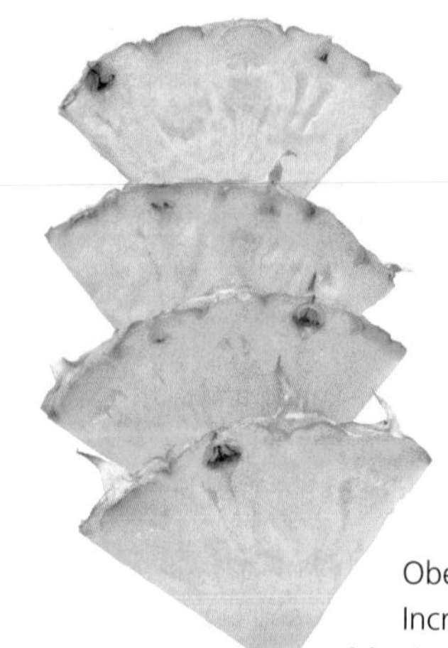

Appendices

Special Features

Focus Figure

Calculation Corner

Chemistry Boost

Examining the Evidence

Health Connection

Nutrition in Practice

Self-Assessment

SPOTLIGHT

TABLE TIPS

FITNESS TIPS

Two Points of View

About the Authors

Joan Salge Blake, MS, RD, LDN

Boston University

Joan Salge Blake is a Clinical Associate Professor and Dietetics Internship Director at Boston University's Sargent College of Health and Rehabilitation Sciences. She teaches both graduate and undergraduate nutrition courses. She received her MS from Boston University.

Joan is a member of the Academy of Nutrition and Dietetics (formerly the American Dietetic Association) and the Massachusetts Dietetic Association (MDA). She has been a presenter and Presiding Officer at both the AND Annual Meeting and the MDA Annual Convention and is a guest lecturer at both the Boston University Goldman School of Dental Medicine and the Boston University School of Medicine. She was previously named MDA's "Young Dietitian of the Year" and is the past Director of Education and Nominating Committee Chairperson for the MDA. She currently serves on the MDA board. Joan has received the Whitney Powers Excellence in Teaching award from Boston University and the Annie Galbraith Outstanding Dietitian award from the Massachusetts Dietetic Association.

In addition to teaching and writing, Joan has a private practice specializing in weight management and lifestyle changes. Joan is often asked to translate complex nutritional issues in popular terms. As an AND National Media Spokesperson she has conducted over 850 media interviews, and is a contributor of nutrition articles to a variety of magazines and news outlets.

Kathy D. Munoz, EdD, RD

Humboldt State University

Kathy D. Munoz is a professor emerita and professor of nutrition in the Department of Kinesiology and Recreation Administration at Humboldt State University. She teaches undergraduate introductory nutrition, exercise nutrition, and weight management courses, and teaching preparation in higher education courses in the Department of Education. She received her EdD from the University of Southern California in curriculum design and an MS in Foods and Nutrition with a minor in exercise physiology from Oregon State University.

Kathy is a member of the Academy of Nutrition and Dietetics and the California Dietetic Association. Her professional memberships include Dietitians in Integrative and Functional Medicine (DIFM), Sports, Cardiovascular, and Wellness Nutrition (SCAN), and Weight Management (WM).

Kathy has published articles in *Research Quarterly for Exercise and Sport, Children's Health Care,* the *Journal of Nutrition Education,* and the *International Journal of Sport Nutrition and Exercise,* and has co-authored a series of curriculum guides for elementary teachers. Kathy has also been recognized for her research in, and development of curriculum for, asynchronous learning.

Stella L. Volpe, PhD, RD, LDN, FACSM

Drexel University

Dr. Stella Lucia Volpe is Professor and Chair of the Department of Nutrition Sciences at Drexel University. She is also Co-Director of their newly established Center for Integrated Nutrition and Performance. Stella is Chair of the President's Council for Fitness, Sports and Nutrition. Stella is a nutritionist and exercise physiologist who has built a program of research focusing on three interrelated areas that traverse the lifespan: 1) obesity and diabetes prevention via mineral supplementation, 2) weight management through diet, exercise and educational programs, and 3) environmental change leading to weight management. She is presently conducting a randomized controlled trial on the effect of magnesium supplementation on the prevention of the metabolic syndrome. Stella has also become interested in studying the effects of the human-animal interaction on weight loss and health in children and older adults.

Prior to beginning her faculty appointment at Drexel University, Stella was on faculty at the University of Pennsylvania, and previous to that, she was on faculty at the University of Massachusetts, Amherst. Stella is both a Certified Clinical Exercise Specialist (American College of Sports Medicine [ACSM]), and a Registered Dietitian. She is a Fellow of the ACSM. Stella is a competitive athlete in field hockey, rowing and ice hockey. She enjoys being active with her family, which includes her German Shepherd dogs, Sasha and Bear.

Preface

Why We Wrote *Nutrition: From Science to You*

We wrote *Nutrition: From Science to You* to provide you with a solid foundation about nutrition and how it affects *you* and your nutritional needs, concerns, and questions.

Between the three of us, we have more than 50 years of experience teaching college-level nutrition. We've conducted and published research, studied the literature, and listened to and watched our students learn this science. We've made copious notes regarding students' questions, interests, concerns, and misunderstandings, both in and outside the classroom. These years of experience have culminated in a textbook that we believe translates the latest nutrition science into a readable format to provide you with information that you can easily incorporate into your life and the lives of others.

As a college student, you are exposed to a steady stream of nutrition and health information from the media, your family and friends, and the Internet. Although you may think Google has the answer to your nutrition questions, we have seen students frequently fall victim to misinformation found via a quick Web search. We designed *Nutrition: From Science to You* to be as user friendly as possible, and packed exclusively with sound nutrition information. The text goes beyond basic nutrition science and provides realistic advice and strategies to help you apply what you learn in your own life. The text is written to meet *your* nutritional concerns and answer *your* questions.

Remember, nutrition matters to *you!* What you eat today and tomorrow will affect you and your body for years to come. Just as important, what you learn about nutrition today will enable you to make a positive effect on the lives of others from now on.

New to This Edition

- **Focus Figures** teach key concepts in nutrition. These full-page figures explore targeted and integrated topic areas through visual information displays that are bold, clear, and detailed. These figures also have corresponding coaching activities in MasteringNutrition.
- **Visual Chapter Summaries** are structured to mirror the organization of the chapter content and numbered to correspond with the chapter objectives. They contain important art and photos from the main chapter text and serve as concise study and review tools.
- **Health Connection** features highlight diseases and disorders in which nutrition plays a major role, as well as nutritional practices that offer unique health benefits.
- **Examining the Evidence** features look at the latest research on hot topics in nutrition today. These features guide you to making better, informed choices in your personal nutrition, while also demonstrating the ways nutrition pro-

fessionals are constantly expanding and refining our understanding of nutritional science.

- **Nutrition in Practice case studies** draw upon Joan Salge Blake's experience as a dietitian working with actual clients. They encourage critical thinking and emphasize the applicability of the content to your own life and future career.
- **Content has been updated throughout** to be consistent with the *Dietary Guidelines for Americans, 2010* and other new guidelines, data, research, and trends.
- **Organizational changes** tie the learning objectives, chapter headings, and summary sections together to provide a strong pedagogical structure that promotes comprehension and facilitates study and review.
- **MasteringNutrition™**, the online homework, tutorial, and assessment system, delivers self-paced tutorials and activities that provide individualized coaching, focus on your course objectives, and are responsive to your personal progress. The Mastering system is the most effective and widely used online homework, tutorial, and assessment system for the sciences. It helps instructors maximize class time with customizable, easy-to-assign, and automatically graded assessments that motivate students to learn outside of class and arrive prepared for lecture. Learn more at www.masteringnutrition.pearson.com (or www.pearsonmylabandmastering.com).
- **MyDietAnalysis mobile website** is now available, so you can track your diet and activity intake accurately, anytime and anywhere, from your mobile device. Learn more at www.mydietanalysis.com.

Other Key Features

- **Exploring Micronutrients** within Chapters 9, 10, 12, and 13 are self-contained sections that incorporate photos, illustrations, and text to present each vitamin and mineral. Each micronutrient is discussed using the same categories (forms, absorption and transport, functions, daily needs, food sources, toxicity and deficiency symptoms) for a consistent and easy-to-study format.
- **Chemistry Boosts** review chemistry concepts within the context in which you need to know them.
- **Calculation Corners** walk through mathematical equations used in the chapter and give you practice working the equations themselves. These features also have corresponding tutorials in MasteringNutrition.
- **Two Points of View** features contain interviews with two experts representing differing viewpoints on a timely topic. These features encourage thinking critically about the arguments surrounding a given issue, and provide insight into career possibilities within the field of nutrition.
- **Myths and Misconceptions** pretests open each chapter with 10 true/false statements that help you realize that the things you think you know about nutrition aren't always accurate. Answers are given at the end of the chapter.
- **Table Tips** give practical ideas for incorporating adequate amounts of each nutrient into your diet using widely available foods.
- **Self-Assessments** throughout the book ask you to think about your own diet and behaviors and how well you are meeting your various nutrient needs.

Chapter-by-Chapter Updates

Nutrition research and applications continue to expand our understanding of this advancing and dynamic science. To keep pace, we've reorganized the content, visually improved the figures and tables to enrich student learning, and added new features to each chapter in the 2nd edition of *Nutrition: From Science to You.*

Chapter 1: What Is Nutrition?

- Updated obesity discussion and figure with latest statistics from the CDC
- Created a new table presenting *Healthy People 2020* objectives for nutrition and weight status
- Expanded the functional foods information to include zoochemicals
- Updated statistics on the leading causes of death in the United States
- Created a new Chemistry Boost on covalent bonds to help students connect the chemistry of nutrition to the application of nutrition concepts
- Created a new Calculation Corner on calculating kilocalories in a meal, for students to practice their basic computation skills used in nutrition
- Created a new Calculation Corner on converting pounds to kilograms
- Expanded the information on nutrigenomics and created a new figure to accompany it
- Replaced Top Ten Points to Remember with new Visual Chapter Summary correlated with Chapter Objectives

Chapter 2: Tools for Healthy Eating

- Streamlined the text information on the key principles of healthy eating
- Updated the Dietary Guidelines discussion to reflect *Dietary Guidelines for Americans, 2010* information and the most recent guidelines for achieving the dietary and lifestyle recommendations
- Replaced the text, tables, and figures about MyPyramid with new content based on MyPlate
- Replaced the dietary exchanges table with a new one explaining macronutrient breakdown of the exchange groups
- Replaced Top Ten Points to Remember with new Visual Chapter Summary correlated with Chapter Objectives

Chapter 3: Digestion, Absorption, and Transport

- Created a new Focus Figure 3.1, Digestive System
- Created a new Focus Figure 3.5, Anatomy of the Small Intestine
- Created a new Chemistry Boost explaining hydrolysis
- Revised and reordered the tables on digestive enzymes and GI secretions
- Added a new table presenting the hormones secreted by organs of the GI tract
- Created a new Examining the Evidence feature exploring probiotics and their effects on intestinal health
- Added a new Nutrition in Practice feature on irritable bowel syndrome, which introduces the student to the process of nutrition counseling and dietetics in a real-world setting
- Moved celiac disease coverage into a new Health Connection feature
- Replaced Top Ten Points to Remember with new Visual Chapter Summary correlated with Chapter Objectives

Chapter 4: Carbohydrates

- Added a new figure to the Chemistry Boost describing condensation reactions
- Moved lactose intolerance coverage into a new Health Connection feature
- Created a new Focus Figure 4.8, Carbohydrate Digestion and Absorption
- Created a new Focus Figure 4.10, Hormones Regulate Blood Glucose
- Added a new Nutrition in Practice feature on pre-diabetes
- Moved diabetes content into a new Health Connection feature and added a new figure on diabetes prevalence, a new table on interpreting blood glucose levels, and a new table of dietary recommendations for diabetes
- Integrated discussions of glycemic index, glycemic load, and hypoglycemia into the diabetes Health Connection feature
- Moved whole grains coverage into main text discussion of recommendations for carbohydrate intake
- Moved discussion of health effects of sugar into a new Health Connection feature
- Revised all carbohydrate food source diagrams to feature the new MyPlate connection
- Revised and updated figure showing the increase in consumption of sugar-free foods and beverages
- Revised and updated figure showing the per capita consumption patterns of refined sugar and high-fructose corn syrup
- Added coverage of the sugar substitutes rebaudioside A and tagalose
- Replaced summary pages and Top Ten Points to Remember with new Visual Chapter Summary correlated with Chapter Objectives

Chapter 5: Lipids

- Created a new figure showing the formation of bile acid from cholesterol
- Created a new Focus Figure 5.13, Lipid Digestion and Absorption
- Created a new Focus Figure 5.18, Lipoprotein Transport and Distribution
- Created a new figure on comparing saturated fat and *trans* fat content using food labels
- Revised all lipid food source diagrams to feature the new MyPlate connection
- Added a new Examining the Evidence feature on the Mediterranean Diet, including a figure of the Mediterranean Diet Pyramid
- Added a new Nutrition in Practice feature on elevated LDL cholesterol
- Combined coverage of heart disease and high blood cholesterol into a new Health Connection feature
- Replaced summary pages and Top Ten Points to Remember with new Visual Chapter Summary correlated with Chapter Objectives

Chapter 6: Proteins

- Created a new Focus Figure 6.7, Protein Digestion and Absorption
- Created a new Focus Figure 6.9, Protein Synthesis
- Created a new figure showing the chemical processes of deamination and transamination
- Moved the content on vegetarian diets into a new Health Connection feature
- Added a new Examining the Evidence feature on protein supplements, including shakes and powders, amino acid supplements, and protein bars and energy bars

- Revised all protein food source diagrams to feature the new MyPlate connection
- Added a new Nutrition in Practice feature on vegan diets
- Replaced summary pages and Top Ten Points to Remember with new Visual Chapter Summary correlated with Chapter Objectives

Chapter 7: Alcohol

- Added a new figure to the Chemistry Boost describing fermentation
- Revised the figure on alcohol metabolism in the liver to depict the processes and the coenzymes involved
- Created a new Calculation Corner on estimating blood alcohol concentration
- Revised the text discussion and figure on the effects of alcohol on the brain to emphasize the impact on different brain areas and their functions
- Moved content on alcohol abuse and alcoholism into a new Health Connection feature box and updated statistics on prevalence of different types of alcohol abuse
- Revised the figure on red wine and cardiovascular disease to explain how wine's components may contribute to reduced risk
- Replaced Top Ten Points to Remember with new Visual Chapter Summary correlated with Chapter Objectives

Chapter 8: Your Body's Metabolism

- Created a new Chemistry Boost on oxidation-reduction reactions in metabolism
- Revised the figures of metabolic pathways to specify the coenzymes being used
- Created a new figure showing the conversion of pyruvate to lactate
- Revised the discussions of glycolysis and the intermediate reaction to aid student understanding about the ways each of the macronutrients enter the pathways
- Revised the electron transport chain figure to clarify where in the mitochondria the process takes place
- Expanded the discussion of absorptive and postabsorptive states
- Created new Focus Figure 8.15, Metabolism during the Absorptive State
- Created new Focus Figure 8.16, Metabolism during the Postabsorptive State
- Added a new Health Connection feature with expanded discussion of inborn errors of metabolism
- Replaced Top Ten Points to Remember with new Visual Chapter Summary correlated with Chapter Objectives

Chapter 9: Fat-Soluble Vitamins

- Revised all fat-soluble vitamin food source diagrams to feature the new MyPlate connection
- Updated daily needs and tolerable upper intake levels of the fat-soluble vitamins to match *Dietary Guidelines for Americans, 2010*
- Revised the coverage of nutrition's role in cancer prevention as a Health Connection feature
- Moved the content on fortified foods and vitamin supplements into the main text discussion of sources of vitamins
- Added a new Nutrition in Practice feature on vitamin D deficiency
- Created two new Calculation Corners to teach students how to convert international units for vitamin D and for vitamin E
- Replaced Top Ten Points to Remember with new Visual Chapter Summary correlated with Chapter Objectives

Chapter 10: Water-Soluble Vitamins

- Revised all water-soluble vitamin food source diagrams to feature the new MyPlate connection
- Updated daily needs and tolerable upper intake levels of the water-soluble vitamins to match *Dietary Guidelines for Americans, 2010*
- Added a new Nutrition in Practice feature on vitamin B_{12} deficiency
- Replaced Top Ten Points to Remember with new Visual Chapter Summary correlated with Chapter Objectives

Chapter 11: Water

- Revised the figure on blood volume and blood pressure regulation to separate the different hormone processes
- Updated the Spotlight feature on bottled water versus tap water with information about "designer" beverages and about the environmental impact of bottled water
- Updated the Examining the Evidence feature on enhanced water with recent research
- Replaced summary pages and Top Ten Points to Remember with new Visual Chapter Summary correlated with Chapter Objectives

Chapter 12: Major Minerals

- Revised all major mineral food source diagrams to feature the new MyPlate connection
- Updated daily needs and tolerable upper intake levels of the major minerals to match *Dietary Guidelines for Americans, 2010*
- Separated discussion of chloride into its own section immediately following sodium coverage
- Revised the content on controlling hypertension into a Health Connection feature
- Added a new figure on bioavailability of calcium
- Revised the figure on hormone regulation of blood calcium levels to depict the feedback pathways involved
- Revised the content on bone mass and osteoporosis into a Health Connection feature
- Added a new Nutrition in Practice feature on calcium and bone density
- Replaced Top Ten Points to Remember with new Visual Chapter Summary correlated with Chapter Objectives

Chapter 13: Trace Minerals

- Revised all trace mineral food source diagrams to feature the new MyPlate connection
- Updated daily needs and tolerable upper intake levels of the trace minerals to match *Dietary Guidelines for Americans, 2010*
- Revised the content on iron-deficiency anemia into a Health Connection feature
- Added a new Nutrition in Practice feature on iron-deficiency anemia
- Updated the discussion of zinc gels and lozenges with recent research
- Replaced Top Ten Points to Remember with new Visual Chapter Summary correlated with Chapter Objectives

Chapter 14: Energy Balance and Body Composition

- Created a new Examining the Evidence feature on non-exercise activity thermogenesis
- Revised the figure on visceral and subcutaneous fat storage to depict the difference in location and quantity of fat between lean and overweight individuals
- Created a new Calculation Corner on using body volume and density to estimate percent body fat
- Created a new Calculation Corner on estimating percent body fat using BMI
- Replaced Top Ten Points to Remember with new Visual Chapter Summary correlated with Chapter Objectives

Chapter 15: Weight Management and Disordered Eating

- Updated all statistics about the prevalence of overweight and obesity
- Created a new figure describing the effects of hormones that regulate hunger and satiety
- Revised the Examining the Evidence feature on popular diets to address the distinctions among major diet types
- Created a new Calculation Corner on calculating energy density using food labels
- Added a new Nutrition in Practice feature on weight loss
- Revised and updated the content on very low-kilocarlorie diets, obesity medications, and bariatric surgery into a Health Connection feature
- Added a new Spotlight feature on body image and body dysmorphic disorder
- Replaced Top Ten Points to Remember with new Visual Chapter Summary correlated with Chapter Objectives

Chapter 16: Nutrition and Fitness

- Created a new Calculation Corner on target heart rate
- Expanded the table on health benefits of physical fitness to include information on reduced cancer risk and improved mental well-being
- Updated the table on American College of Sports Medicine (ACSM) fitness recommendations based on latest position stand
- Expanded the discussion to include more information on exercise metabolism and energy production
- Created a new Chemistry Boost on ATP and ADP
- Revised the figure on anaerobic energy metabolism to correspond with Chapter 8 figures on ATP
- Created a new figure on glucose utilization during exercise
- Created a new figure on fatty acid and glycerol utilization during exercise
- Revised the content on the female athlete triad into a Health Connection feature
- Updated the table on ACSM hydration recommendations
- Replaced Top Ten Points to Remember with new Visual Chapter Summary correlated with Chapter Objectives

Chapter 17: Life Cycle Nutrition: Pregnancy through Infancy

- Updated the figure and information on nutrient needs during pregnancy to reflect MyPlate and the *Dietary Guidelines for Americans, 2010*
- Created two new Table Tips on suggestions for healthy snacks to increase kilocalorie consumption during the second and third trimesters of pregnancy

- Added a new Nutrition in Practice feature on nutrient needs during pregnancy
- Updated Spotlight feature on breast-feeding at work
- Replaced Top Ten Points to Remember with new Visual Chapter Summary correlated with Chapter Objectives

Chapter 18: Life Cycle Nutrition: Toddlers through Adolescence

- Created a new Calculation Corner on reading growth charts
- Updated the information on nutrient needs for children at different stages of development to reflect MyPlate and the *Dietary Guidelines for Americans, 2010*
- Added a new Nutrition in Practice feature on the eating habits of a toddler
- Created a new Spotlight feature on the school lunch program
- Created a new Health Connection feature on the health effects of childhood obesity
- Replaced Top Ten Points to Remember with new Visual Chapter Summary correlated with Chapter Objectives

Chapter 19: Life Cycle Nutrition: Older Adults

- Added a Spotlight feature on the key indicators of older adult health
- Updated the figure and information on nutrient needs for older adults to reflect MyPlate and the *Dietary Guidelines for Americans, 2010*
- Created a new Calculation Corner on estimating energy requirmements
- Added a new Nutrition in Practice feature on heart disease risk
- Replaced Top Ten Points to Remember with new Visual Chapter Summary correlated with Chapter Objectives

Chapter 20: Food Safety, Technology, and Availability

- Created a new figure on the components of a food system from production to consumer
- Added coverage and Table Tips on avoiding chemical agents that may cause foodborne illness
- Created a new figure about pesticide risk assessment
- Added a section on sustainable food systems, including coverage of the environmental effects of food production
- Added a new figure of a sustainable food systems model
- Added a new figure looking at distances food travels to market
- Added a new figure of a food web
- Created a new Spotlight feature on farmers' markets
- Created a new Spotlight feature on container gardening
- Added coverage of labeling terms used with animal foods
- Replaced Top Ten Points to Remember with new Visual Chapter Summary correlated with Chapter Objectives

Chapter 21: Hunger at Home and Abroad

- Updated statistics about the prevalence of hunger and food insecurity
- Updated statistics about water and sanitation
- Replaced Top Ten Points to Remember with new Visual Chapter Summary correlated with Chapter Objectives

Supplements

MasteringNutrition™ with MyDietAnalysis with Pearson eText

www.masteringnutrition.pearson.com or www.pearsonmylabandmastering.com
The MasteringNutrition with MyDietAnalysis online homework, tutorial, and assessment system delivers self-paced tutorials that provide individualized coaching, focus on your course objectives, and are responsive to each student's progress. Set up your course in 15 minutes with proven, assignable, and automatically graded nutrition activities that reinforce your course's learning objectives.

- **Focus Figure Coaching Activities** guide students through key nutrition concepts with interactive mini-lessons.
- **MyDietAnalysis Case Study Coaching Activities** provide students with hands-on diet analysis practice that can also be automatically graded.
- **Reading Quizzes** (20 questions per chapter) ensure that students have completed the assigned reading before class.
- **28 *ABC News* Videos** bring nutrition to life and spark discussion on current hot topics in the nutrition field and include multiple-choice questions that provide wrong-answer feedback to redirect students to the correct answer.
- **40 animations** explain big-picture concepts that help students learn the hardest topics in nutrition. These animations have questions that provide wrong-answer feedback that address students' common misconceptions.
- **NutriTools Coaching Activities** allow students to combine and experiment with different food options and learn firsthand how to build healthier meals.
- **MP3s** relate to chapter content and come with multiple-choice questions that provide wrong-answer feedback.
- **Access to *Get Ready for Nutrition*** gives students extra math and chemistry study assistance.
- **The Study Area** is broken down into learning areas and includes videos, animations, MP3s, and much more.

MyDietAnalysis Premium Website

www.mydietanalysis.com
MyDietAnalysis was developed by the nutrition database experts at ESHA Research, Inc. and is tailored for use in college nutrition courses. MyDietAnalysis is available as a single sign-on to MasteringNutrition.

- View a classwide nutritional average. MyDietAnalysis will allow you to see a nutritional profile of your entire class, enabling you to base your lecture on your students' needs.
- Video help with associated quizzes cover the topics students struggle with most.
- **NEW FOR SPRING 2013!** For online users, a new mobile website version of MyDietAnalysis is available.

Food Composition Table

The USDA Nutrient Database for Standard Reference is provided as a new supplement, offering the nutritional values of over 1,500 separate foods in an easy-to-follow format.

Instructor Resource and Support Manual

This resource includes outlines that summarize each chapter, author-provided ideas for hands-on group assignments, key terms, teaching tips, suggested source materials, "Two Points of View" interviews, Focus on Research assignments, and topics for discussion.

Printed Test Bank and TestGen® Computerized Test Bank

The test bank provides multiple-choice, true/false, short answer, and essay questions for each chapter of the text in both print and computerized form.

Instructor Resource DVD (IR-DVD)

This valuable teaching resource offers everything you need to create lecture presentations and course materials, including JPEG and PowerPoint® files of all the art, tables, and selected photos from the text, and "stepped-out" art for selected figures from the text, as well as animations.

The IR-DVD also includes:

- PowerPoint® lecture outlines with embedded links to animations and *ABC News* Lecture Launcher videos
- A Jeopardy-type quiz show
- The Instructor Manual
- Test Bank Microsoft® Word files and Computerized Test Bank
- Questions for Classroom Response Systems (CRS) in PowerPoint format, allowing you to import the questions into your own CRS

Great Ideas: Active Ways to Teach Nutrition

This updated, revised booklet compiles the best ideas from nutrition instructors across the country on innovative ways to teach nutrition topics with an emphasis on active learning.

Acknowledgments

It takes a village, and then some, when it comes to writing a dynamic textbook. *Nutrition: From Science to You* is no exception. We personally want to extend our gratitude to all of those who passionately shared their expertise and support to make *Nutrition: From Science to You* better than we could have envisioned.

Beginning with the energetic staff at Pearson, we would like to thank Sandy Lindelof, who helped make our vision for this textbook into a reality. Marilyn Freedman's on-the-mark developmental editing improved *Nutrition: From Science to You* and made it more enjoyable to read. Revising a text of this nature takes a lot of coordination, and project editor Kari Hopperstead managed to keep us all on track while still applying her eagle eye to every aspect of the revision. Crackerjack assistant editor Meghan Zolnay and media producers Lee Ann Doctor and Joe Mochnick worked diligently to create the best supplements for *Nutrition: From Science to You*. Thanks also to editorial assistant Briana Verdugo for all of her behind-the-scenes work.

A very special thanks to Caroline Ayres, production supervisor extraordinaire, and Norine Strang, production coordinator at S4Carlisle Publishing Services, for all of their hard work shepherding this book through to publication. Our humble appreciation also goes to Kelly Murphy, art development editor, for developing our stunning new Focus Figures; to Stephen Merland and Kristin Piljay for obtaining the most vivid and unique photos available; to Gary Hespenheide, whose design made the text, art, and photos all come alive; and to design manager Mark Ong, who designed the exciting new Visual Chapter Summaries.

Marketing takes energy, and that's exactly what marketing manager Neena Bali and her team seem to generate nonstop. The many instructors who reviewed the first edition, as well as those who reviewed and class-tested early versions of this book, are listed on the following pages; we are grateful to all of them for helping in the development of *Nutrition: From Science to You.* The village also included loyal contributors who lent their expertise to specific chapters. They are: Tara Smith at East Carolina University, who solidified the nutrition and fitness chapter; Elizabeth Quintana at West Virginia University School of Medicine, who revised the three "life cycle" chapters; Heidi Wengreen at Utah State University, who overhauled and expanded the food safety and availability chapter; and Claire Alexander, who updated the hunger chapter.

Lastly, an endless thanks to our colleagues, friends, and especially our families. Joan would like to "thank my family, Adam, Brendan, and Craig for their love and support when I was working more than I should have been." Kathy sends a special thanks to "my husband Rich and our children Heather, Wes, and Ryan for keeping me sane and grounded, and my Mom, Dad, and sister Vicki for their steadfast support." Stella would like to acknowledge "my husband, Gary Snyder, for his constant support; and our wonderful dogs, Sasha and Bear, for always making me smile! And to my Mom and Dad, who both instilled in me a wonderful relationship with food, especially home grown and homemade food."

Reviewers

First Edition

Janet Anderson
Utah State University

Sandra Baker
University of Delaware

Gita Bangera
Bellevue College

Lisa Blackman
Tarrant County College, Northwest

Jeanne Boone
Palm Beach State College

John Capeheart
University of Houston-Downtown

Susan Chou
American River College

Nicole Clark
Indiana University of Pennsylvania

Susan Cooper
Montana State University-Great Falls College of Technology

Jessica Coppola
Sacramento City College

Lynn Monahan Couch
West Chester University of Pennsylvania

Wendy Cunningham
California State University, Sacramento

Jeannette Davidson
Bradley University

Holly Dieken
The University of Tennessee at Chattanooga

Johanna Donnenfield
Scottsdale Community College

Roberta Durschlag
Boston University

Brenda Eissenstat
The Pennsylvania State University

Sheryl L. Fuller-Espie
Cabrini College

Eugene J. Fenster
Metropolitan Community College, Longview

Alyce D. Fly
Indiana University

Sara Folta
Tufts University

Betty Forbes
West Virginia University

Sue Fredstrom
Minnesota State University, Mankato

Teresa Fung
Simmons College

Susan Gaumont
Chandler-Gilbert Community College

Jill Golden
Orange Coast College

Gloria Gonzalez
Pensacola State College

Donna Handley
The University of Rhode Island

William Helferich
University of Illinois at Urbana-Champaign

Catherine Howard
Texarkana College

Karen Israel
Anne Arundel Community College

Seema Jejurikar
Bellevue College

Jayanthi Kandiah
Ball State University

Vicki Kloosterhouse
Oakland Community College

Allen Knehans
The University of Oklahoma

Kathy Knight
The University of Mississippi

Shui-Ming Kuo
University at Buffalo

Robert D. Lee
Central Michigan University

Sharon Lemons
Tarrant County College, Northwest

Darlene Levinson
Oakland Community College

Rose Martin
Iowa State University

Mary Martinez
Central New Mexico Community College

George F. McNeil
Fort Hays State University

Monica Meadows
The University of Texas at Austin

Kathleen Melanson
The University of Rhode Island

Mithia Mukutmoni
Sierra College

Pat Munn
Metropolitan Community College, Longview

Megan Murphy
Southwest Tennessee Community College

Dan Neisner
Walla Walla Community College

Corin Nishimura
Leeward Community College

Anna Page
Johnson County Community College

Jill Patterson
The Pennsylvania State University

Janet Peterson
Linfield College

Gwendolyn Pla
Howard University

Roseanne Poole
Tallahassee Community College

Linda Pope
Southwest Tennessee Community College

Elizabeth Quintana
West Virginia University

Denise Russo
Cabrillo College

Kevin Schalinske
Iowa State University

Diana Spillman
Miami University

Sherry Stewart
Navarro College

Leeann Sticker
Northwestern State University

Susan Swadener
California Polytechnic State University, San Luis Obispo

Janelle Walter
Baylor University

Sandy Walz
West Chester University of Pennsylvania

Daryl Wane
Pasco-Hernando Community College

Garrison Wilkes
University of Massachusetts Boston

Jessie Yearwood
El Centro College

Gloria Young
Virginia State University

Maureen Zimmerman
Mesa Community College

Second Edition

Ellen Brennan
San Antonio College

Wendy Buchan
California State University, Sacramento

Nicole A. Clark
Indiana University of Pennsylvania

Mary Dean Coleman-Kelly
The Pennsylvania State University

Eugene J. Fenster
Metropolitan Community College, Longview

Karen Friedman-Kester
Harrisburg Area Community College

Amy Frith
Ithaca College

Susan Edgar Helm
Pepperdine University

Shanil Juma
Texas Woman's University

Allen Knehans
The University of Oklahoma Health Sciences Center

Julia L. Lapp
Ithaca College

John Radcliffe
Texas Woman's University

Nancy L. Shearer
Cape Cod Community College

Eric Vlahov
The University of Tampa

Heidi Wengreen
Utah State University

Class Testers

Janet Anderson
Utah State University

Jeanne Boone
Palm Beach State College

Jessica Coppola
Sacramento City College

Robert Cullen
Illinois State University

Gloria Gonzales
Pensacola State College

Jill Goode-Englett
University of North Alabama

Debra Head
University of Central Arkansas

Lenka Humenikova-Shriver
Oklahoma State University

Allen Knehans
The University of Oklahoma

Janet Levin
Pensacola State College

Darlene Levinson
Oakland Community College

Anna Miller
DeAnza College

Vijaya Narayanan
Florida International University

Anna Page
Johnson County Community College

Nancy Parkinson
Miami University

Renee Romig
Western Iowa Tech Community College

Janet Sass
Northern Virginia Community College, Annandale

Susan Swadener
California Polytechnic State University, San Luis Obispo

Janelle Walter
Baylor University

Suzy Weems
Baylor University

Jennifer Zimmerman
Tallahassee Community College

I am nothing without my ABCs.

Thanks.

—Joan Salge Blake

I dedicate this book to my family for their love and support that sustained me through the development of this book. And to my students, both present and past, for whom this book was written.

—Kathy D. Munoz

I would like to dedicate this book to my Mom, Felicetta Volpe, and my Dad, Antonio Volpe (in memory).

—Stella Lucia Volpe

1 What Is Nutrition?

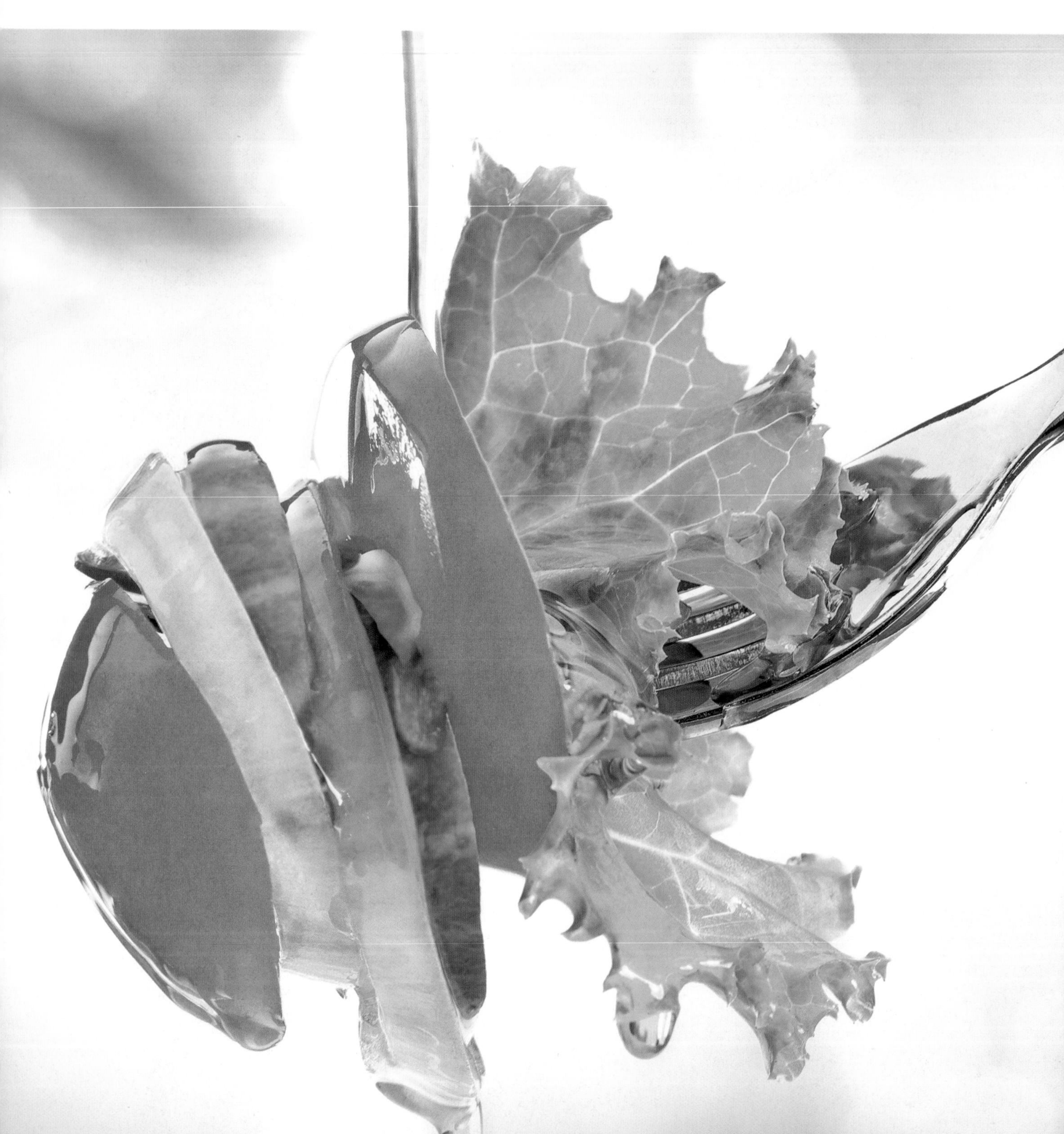

Chapter Objectives

After reading this chapter, you will be able to:

1. Discuss the factors that influence food choice.
2. Define the term nutrition and discuss why it is important to health.
3. Name the six classifications of essential nutrients found in food and explain their primary role in the body.
4. Identify the sources of reliable and accurate nutrition information.
5. Summarize the methods used to assess the nutrient status of individuals and populations.
6. Discuss the current nutritional state of the American diet.
7. Summarize the best dietary strategies to reduce the risk of developing chronic disease.

1. Food choices are driven primarily by flavor. T/F
2. Cancer is the leading cause of death in the United States. T/F
3. Eliminating all fat from the diet will improve health. T/F
4. Alcohol is a nutrient. T/F
5. The energy in foods is measured in kilocalories. T/F
6. Protein contains more energy per gram than fat. T/F
7. The most effective method of nutritional assessment is to ask a client to write down what he's eaten in the last 24 hours. T/F
8. You can get good nutrition advice from anyone who calls himself a nutritionist. T/F
9. The number of obese Americans is lower today than it was five years ago. T/F
10. As long as you take a vitamin pill, you don't have to worry about eating healthy food. T/F

See page 34 for answers to these Myths and Misconceptions.

During the course of a day, we make over 200 decisions about food, from when to eat, how much to eat, and what to eat, to how the food is prepared, and even what plate to use.[1] You make these decisions for reasons you may not even be aware of. If your dietary advice comes from media sound bites, you may receive conflicting information. Yesterday's news flash announced that eating more protein would help you fight a bulging waist. Last week's headline boldly announced you should minimize *trans* fats in your diet to avoid cardiovascular disease. This morning, the TV news lead was a health report advising you to consume more whole grains to live longer, but to cut back on sodium to avoid hypertension.

Though you may find it frustrating that dietary advice seems to change with the daily news, this barrage of nutrition news illustrates the inroads nutritional scientists are making toward a better understanding of what you eat and its effects on health. Today's research validates what nutrition professionals have known for decades: Nutrition plays an invaluable role in your health.

In addition to exploring the factors that can affect food choice, this chapter will introduce you to the study of nutrition. Let's begin with the basic concepts of why and what you eat, how you can identify credible sources of nutrition information, and why a healthy diet is important to your well-being.

What Drives Our Food Choices?

Have you ever considered what drives your food choices? Or are you on autopilot as you stand in line at the sub shop and squint at yet another menu board? Do you enjoy some foods and eat them often, while avoiding others with a vengeance? You obviously need food to survive, but beyond your basic instinct to eat are many other factors that affect your food choices. These factors include taste and enjoyment; culture and environment; social life and trends; weight concerns, body image, and health benefits; advertising; time, convenience, and cost; and habits and emotion (**Figure 1.1**).

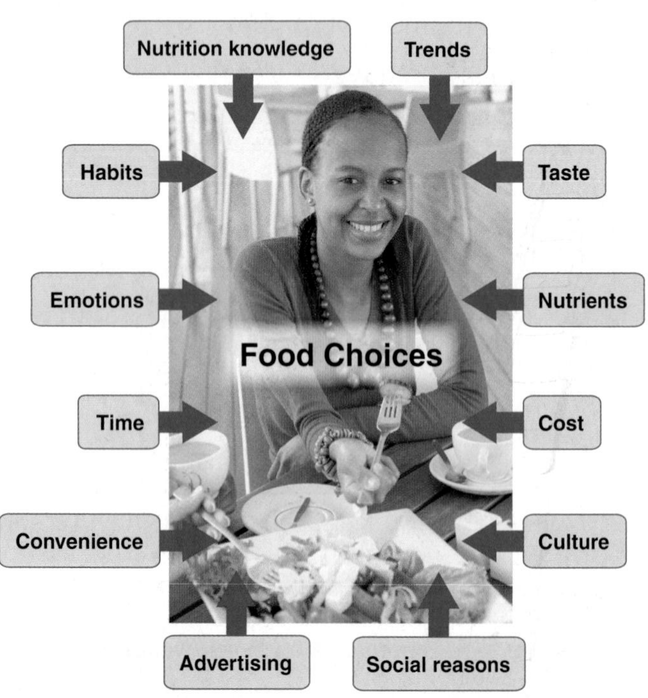

▲ **Figure 1.1 Many Factors Influence Your Food Choices**

Taste and Enjoyment

Research confirms that when it comes to making food choices, taste is the most important consideration.[2] This shouldn't be too much of a surprise, considering there are more than 10,000 taste buds in the mouth. These taste buds tell you that chocolate cheesecake is sweet, fresh lemon juice is sour, and a pretzel is salty. This preference for sweet or salty foods begins during infancy, may be influenced by our genes,[3] and changes as we age.[4]

We have a taste for fat, which may also be genetically linked, although a gene has not been found that supports this theory.[5] When fat is combined with sugar, such as in a sugar-laden doughnut, our taste for that food is even stronger.[6]

Texture also affects our likelihood of enjoying foods. We enjoy a flaky piecrust but dislike one that is tough; we prefer crunchy apples to mealy ones, and creamy rather than lumpy soups. Almost 30 percent of adults dislike slippery foods, such as oysters and okra.[7] Researchers have suggested that these preferences for sweetness, high fat, and specific textures may have begun early in life and this makes them resistant to change.[8]

Culture and Environment

Enjoying food is not just a physiological sensation. Other factors, such as our culture and the environment, also play a role in which foods we enjoy eating.[9] If you were a student in Mexico, you may regularly feast on corn tortillas and tamales, as corn is a staple of Mexican cuisines. In India, meals commonly include lentils and other legumes with rice and vegetables, whereas Native Americans often enjoy stews of mutton (sheep), corn, vegetables, and berries. And, in Asian countries, rice likely would be front and center on your plate.

One in four Americans is of Hispanic, Native American, Asian, or African descent. Cultural food preferences often influence food choices.

A culture's cuisine is significantly influenced by the environment in which its people live. This includes the climate and soil conditions as well as the native plants and animals, and the distance people live from rivers, lakes, or the sea. Foods that are available and accessible are more likely to be regularly consumed than foods that are scarce. For example, native Alaskans feast on fish because it is plentiful, but eat less fresh produce, which is difficult to grow locally. For most Americans, eating only locally available foods is less of an issue today than in the past, due to global food distribution networks. However, the tendency persists for some food items. People living in landlocked states may have less access to fresh fish, while those outside the south may not see collard greens or beignets on local store shelves as often as their Gulf State counterparts do.

Our food environment—the variety of food choices available, the size and shape of plates and glassware, the packaging of foods, and the types and amounts of food that are visible—has a strong influence on what and how much we consume. We eat more food when the serving plates are larger, or drink less when beverages are served in taller glassware. Environmental cues also affect eating patterns. You are more likely to linger over a meal when the light is dimmed, or quickly finish your meal when others at the table stop eating.[10]

Environmental factors including lighting at a meal, the size of a package, and the shape of a glass can influence the type and amount of food you eat.

Social Life and Trends

Every year on the fourth Thursday in November, over 95 percent of Americans gather with family and friends to consume close to 700 million pounds of turkey as they celebrate Thanksgiving.[11] A person is likely to eat more on Thanksgiving than on any other Thursday, and this is partly because of the number of people eating with them. Eating dinner with others has been shown to increase the size of the meal by over 40 percent, and the more people present at the meal, the more you'll eat.[12]

Eating is an important way to bond with others. Sharing a meal with family or friends stimulates conversation, creates traditions, and expands our food experiences. Although eating a quick meal in the campus cafeteria may not be the best choice for healthy food options, it will allow you to socialize with classmates.

For many people, activities such as watching a football game with fellow fans or going to a movie with friends often involve particular foods. More pizzas are sold on Super Bowl Sunday than on any other day of the year.[13] Movie theater owners bank on their patrons buying popcorn, candy, and beverages at the concession stand before heading in to watch the film, and moviegoers are more likely to buy these snacks if they're with a group of friends.[14]

Eating junk food while watching sports sometimes seems like an American way of life.

The USDA certifies that organic foods are grown without the use of pesticides, herbicides, or chemical fertilizers.

Food choices are also affected by popular trends. For instance, home cooks in the 1950s bought bags of "new-fangled" frozen vegetables in order to provide healthy meals in less time. A few decades later, vegetables went upscale and consumers bought them as part of ready-to-heat stir-fry mixes. Today, shoppers pay a premium for bags of fresh veggies, like carrots, that have been prewashed and peeled, sliced, or diced, and they pay even more of a premium if the food is labeled "organic." In 2010 alone, Americans spent more than $26 billion on organic foods.[15] Consumers also ate more plant-based products, especially from locally grown farmer's markets, and ate more foods with added benefits, such as eggs with more omega-3 fatty acids or calcium-fortified orange juice.[16]

Weight Concerns, Body Image, and Health Benefits

While the French take pleasure in cheese, bread, and high-fat desserts, Americans worry about fried eggs causing heart disease and butter-laden pastries leading to obesity. Hence, individuals may choose certain foods because they perceive them as being healthy, or avoid other foods that are associated with weight gain or loss.

Your perception of foods can be influenced by your current state of health. For example, if you are overweight, you are more likely to be aware of the kilocalorie content of foods and avoid foods that are high in fat and sugar.[17] This can have a positive effect on health as long as body image concerns don't become extreme or cause disordered eating patterns.

The more aware you are of the effects of food choices on health, the more likely you are to make an effort to improve your eating habits.[18] If you believe that low-sodium foods decrease blood pressure or eating yogurt with active cultures improves your digestion, you are more likely to choose these foods.

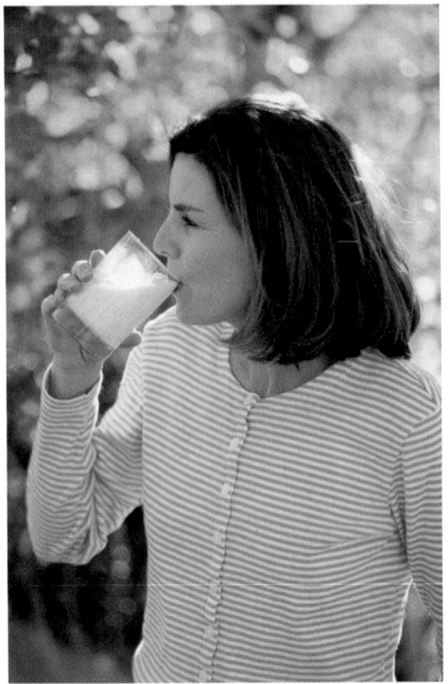
Rates of milk consumption increased after the *Got Milk?* advertising campaign.

Advertising

Manufacturers spend $10 billion to $15 billion annually on food advertising, with over $700 million each year spent to market breakfast cereals, candy, and gum. Another $500 million is spent to advertise carbonated soft drinks.[19] You probably saw at least a few processed food ads as you surfed online, watched TV, or drove to campus today. In comparison, when was the last time you saw an advertisement for broccoli? Have you ever seen an ad for broccoli?

Food companies spend these large sums on advertising for one reason: They work, especially on young people.[20] American children view up to 40,000 television commercials annually. On Saturday morning, more than half of the between-cartoon ads are for foods. Of these, over 40 percent are for items such as candy, soft drinks, chips, and sugary breakfast cereals.[21]

In contrast, commercials for fruits and vegetables are rare, which is unfortunate, because healthy foods can be successfully marketed. When the dairy industry noted a decline in milk consumption among Americans in 1994, it launched the *Got Milk?* ad campaign, which featured celebrities wearing milk mustaches. This campaign strove to make drinking milk sexy and it worked. Milk sales increased by nearly 1.5 billion pounds, which is the equivalent of about 45 pounds of milk being sold for each advertising dollar spent.[22]

Time, Convenience, and Cost

When it comes to putting together a meal, time is often at a premium. Americans, especially working women with families, spend less than 30 minutes preparing a meal, including cleanup.[23] Consequently, supermarkets are offering more prepared and partially prepared foods. If chicken is on the menu tonight, you can buy it uncooked at the meat counter in the supermarket, or you can go to the deli and buy it hot off the rotisserie, cooked and stuffed with bread crumbs, or grilled with teriyaki sauce. Rice or pasta side dishes and cooked vegetables are also available to complete the meal.

Convenience has also become more of a factor in food selection. Decades ago, the most convenient way to get a hot cup of coffee was to brew it at home. Today, Americans are more likely to get their latte or half-caff from one of the 17,000 coffee shops, carts, and kiosks across the United States.[24]

For reasons related to both time and convenience, people are eating out more often today than they did a few decades ago. In the 1970s, Americans spent about 25 percent of their household food budget on eating out, compared with almost 48 percent today.[25] Because cost is often an issue when considering where to eat out, most meals consumed away from home are fast food, which is often cheaper and quicker than more nutritious meals. Though cheap fast food may be easy on the pocketbook, it is taking its toll on the health of Americans. Epidemiological research suggests that low-cost, high-kilocalorie diets, such as those that incorporate lots of burgers, fries, tacos, and soft drinks, increase the risk of obesity, especially among those at lower socioeconomic levels.[26]

The good news is that cheaper food doesn't have to always mean fast food, and when healthy foods are offered at lower prices, people do buy them. Researchers have found that lowering the cost of fresh fruits, vegetables, and lower-fat snacks improves the consumption of these nutritious foods.[27,28] These studies demonstrate that price reductions are an effective strategy to increase the purchase of more-healthful foods. Results were consistent across various food types and populations.

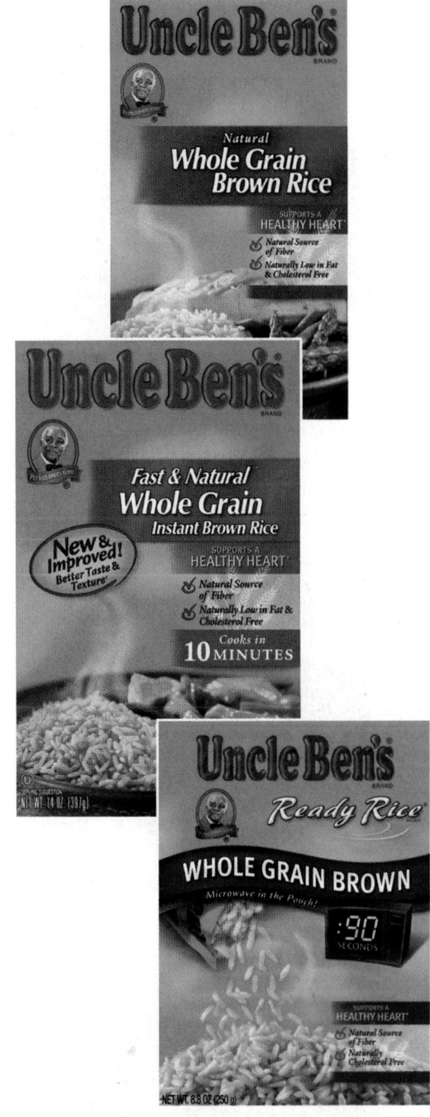

Although brown rice is a healthy whole-grain addition to any meal, it takes close to an hour to cook. For time-strapped consumers, food manufacturers have developed brown rice that cooks in 10 minutes, and a precooked, microwavable variety that reheats in less than 2 minutes.

Habits and Emotions

Your daily routine and habits often affect both when you eat and what you eat. For example, if you routinely start your day with a bowl of cereal and a glass of orange juice, you're not alone. Ready-to-eat cereals are the number-one breakfast food choice among Americans, and citrus juice is their top juice in the morning.[29] Many individuals regularly snack when watching television or sitting at the computer.[30]

For some individuals, emotions can sometimes drive food choice, and feeling happy or sad can trigger eating. In some cases, eating is suppressed during periods of sadness or depression. For many, food is used as an emotional crutch during times of stress, depression, or joy.

THE TAKE-HOME MESSAGE Taste and enjoyment are the primary reasons people prefer certain foods. Food availability makes it easier to become part of a culture, and many foods can be regularly eaten out of habit. Advertising, food trends, limited time, convenience, emotions, and the perception that foods are healthy or unhealthy also influence food choices.

What Is Nutrition?

The science of **nutrition** is the study of food and the nutrients we need to sustain life and reproduce. It also examines the way food nourishes the body and affects health. Since its inception, the science of nutrition has explored how

nutrition The science that studies how nutrients and compounds in foods nourish the body and affect body functions and overall health.

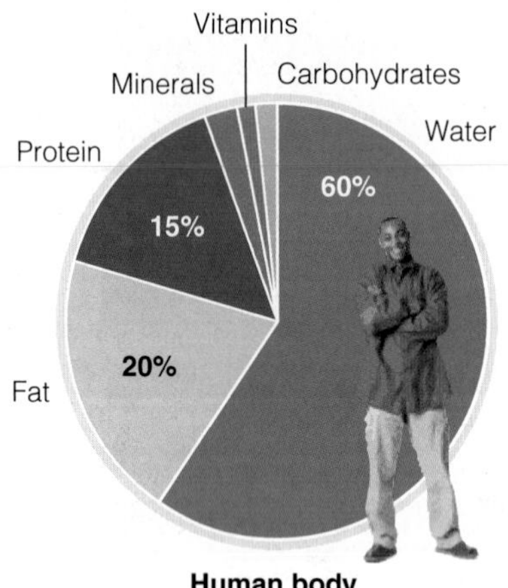

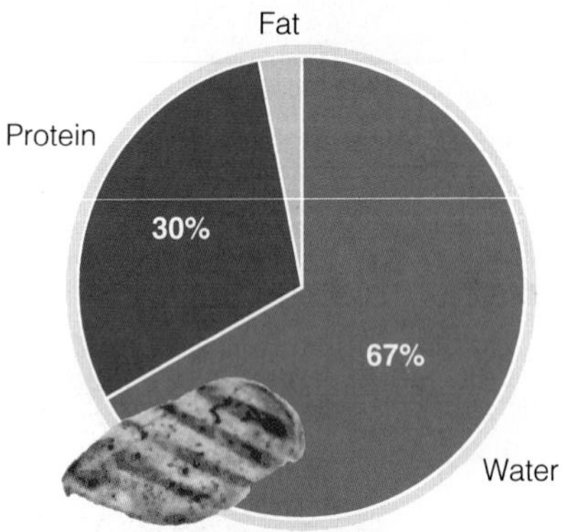

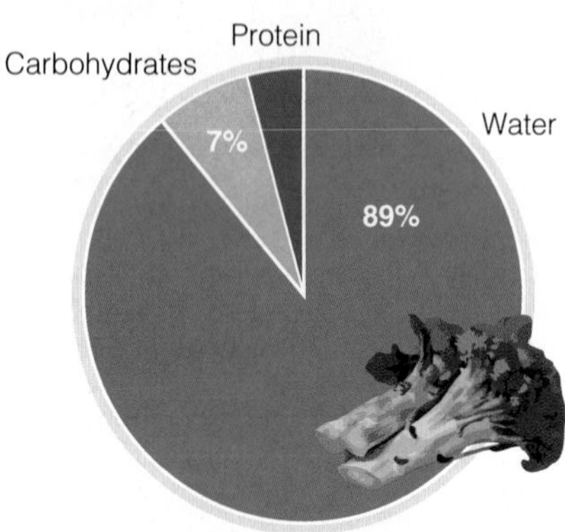

▲ **Figure 1.2 Nutrients in Foods and in the Body**
Water is the most abundant nutrient found in foods and in the body. Carbohydrates, fats, proteins, vitamins, and minerals make up the rest. Note that foods also contain nonnutritive compounds, such as phytochemicals and fiber.

nutrients Compounds in foods that sustain body processes. There are six classes of nutrients: carbohydrates, fats (lipids), proteins, vitamins, minerals, and water.

organic Describing compounds that contain carbon or carbon–carbon bonds.

inorganic Describing compounds that do not contain carbon.

food is digested, absorbed, transported, metabolized, and used or stored in the body. Nutritional scientists study how much we need of each nutrient, the factors that influence our needs, and what happens if we don't consume enough. As with any science, nutrition is not stagnant. The more we discover about the relationship between nutrition and well-being, the greater the impact will be on long-term health.

Nutrients Are Essential Compounds in Food

The body is one large organism made up of millions of cells that grow, age, reproduce, and die, all without your noticing. You slough off millions of skin cells when you towel off after a shower, yet your skin isn't noticeably thinner today than it was last week. Your body replaces skin cells at a rate fast enough to keep you covered, and it manufactures new cells using the same nutrients found in a variety of foods. As cells die, **nutrients** from food provide the building blocks to replace them. Nutrients also provide the energy we need to perform all body functions and processes, from maintaining heart beat to playing tennis.

There are six categories of nutrients found in foods and in the body: carbohydrates, lipids (fats), protein, vitamins, minerals, and water. Foods also often contain nonnutrient compounds, such as phytochemicals or zoochemicals, nondigestible fiber, and other chemicals added by food manufacturers to enhance color, flavor, or texture, or extend shelf life.

About 10 percent of plant foods are made up of carbohydrates, fats, protein, vitamins, and minerals (**Figure 1.2**). The rest is typically water, and plant foods contain more water (90 percent) than do animal foods (60 percent). The other 40 percent of animal foods consist of protein, lipids, vitamins, and minerals. One unique quality of animal foods is that they do not contain any carbohydrates by the time we consume them.

In comparison with plant products, a healthy human body is 60 percent water. The other 40 percent is made up of protein and fat, as well as a small amount of stored carbohydrates, minerals in the bone, and small amounts of vitamins. Thus, the old saying is true: *we are what we eat,* from the carbohydrates in broccoli to the proteins in meat; the six biochemical ingredients needed to sustain life are all provided by the foods in our diets.

Most Nutrients Are Organic

Carbohydrates, proteins, lipids, and vitamins are the most complex of the six classes of nutrients. These nutrients are **organic** because their chemical structures contain carbon. Organic nutrients also contain the elements hydrogen and oxygen, and in the case of proteins and some vitamins, nitrogen is also part of the molecule (**Figure 1.3**).

Minerals are the least complex of the nutrients and are **inorganic** because their chemical structure does not include carbon. Each mineral is an individual element, and its atoms are exactly the same whether found in food or in the body. For instance, the structure of zinc found in lean meats and nuts is the same as that found in a cell membrane or a hair follicle. Water, a three-atom molecule comprised of hydrogen and oxygen, is also inorganic.

Most Nutrients Are Essential

In general, nutrients are **essential** and must come from foods, because either they cannot be made in the body, or they cannot be made in sufficient amounts to meet the body's needs. A few **nonessential nutrients** can be made in sufficient quantities in the body. An example of this is vitamin D, which is synthesized in the skin upon exposure to sunlight. Under some circumstances, *nonessential* nutrients can

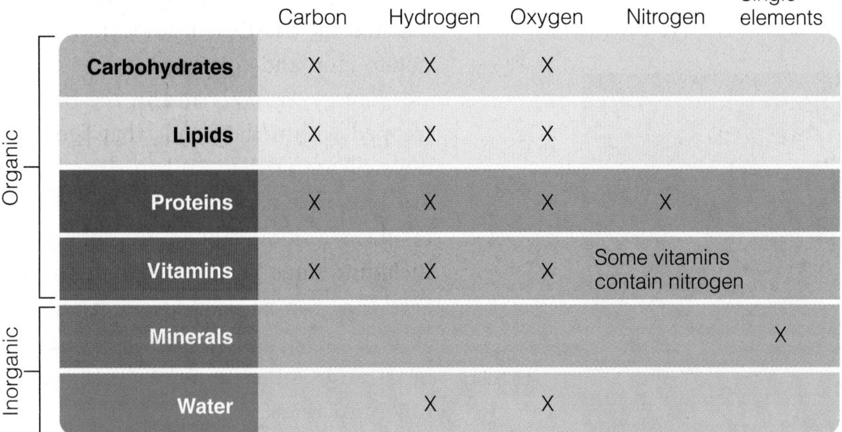

▲ **Figure 1.3 The Chemical Composition of the Six Classifications of Nutrients in Food**
Each nutrient contains a unique combination of chemical elements.

become *essential.* We refer to these nutrients as *conditionally essential.* In the case of vitamin D, if you are not exposed to enough sunlight, you will not be able to synthesize an adequate amount of the vitamin. You must then obtain vitamin D from foods.

Some Nutrients Provide Energy

All creatures need energy in order to function, and humans are no exception. **Energy** is defined as the capacity to do work and provides a source of heat. The body derives chemical energy from certain nutrients in foods, which store energy in their chemical bonds. During digestion and metabolism, the bonds are broken, and the energy is released. This chemical energy released when the foods are digested can be converted into a form the body can use called **adenosine triphosphate (ATP).** Carbohydrates, lipids (fats), and proteins are defined as the **energy-yielding nutrients** because they contribute energy to the body. Whereas alcohol also provides energy, it is not considered a nutrient because it doesn't serve a known function and it interferes with the repair and maintenance of the body.

Energy in foods is measured in kilocalories. A **kilocalorie** is the term used by scientists to quantify the amount of energy found in a food. The term kilocalorie (*kilo* = 1,000) is defined as the amount of energy needed to raise the temperature of one kilogram of water 1 degree Celsius. A kilocalorie is not the same as a *calorie* (with a lowercase "c"), which is a much smaller unit of measurement. (In fact, a "calorie" is so small that one slice of bread contains about 63,000 calories.) One kilocalorie is equal to 1,000 calories.

To add to the confusion, the term Calorie (with an uppercase "C") is used on nutrition labels to express the energy content of foods and is often used in science textbooks to mean kilocalories. This textbook will refer to the units of energy found in foods as kilocalories, abbreviated kcalories or kcals.

Each energy-yielding nutrient provides a set number of kilocalories per gram. Thus the number of kilocalories in one serving of a given food can be determined based on the amount (weight, in grams) of carbohydrates, protein, and fat in the food. Carbohydrates and protein provide 4 kilocalories per gram; so, for example, a food that contains 5 grams of carbohydrate and 3 grams of protein would have 32 kilocalories ($[5 \times 4] + [3 \times 4] = 32$). Fats yield 9 kilocalories per gram, more than twice the number of kilocalories in either carbohydrates or protein. Alcohol contains 7 kilocalories per gram, which must be taken into account when calculating the energy of alcohol-containing foods and beverages (**Figure 1.4**).

Chemistry Boost

Chemical Bonds

Most nutrients consist of carbon, hydrogen, and oxygen. These elements combine to form compounds through chemical reactions. An atom of each element can carry a positive or negative charge and can form a set number of bonds with other elements. For example, carbon can form bonds with four elements, hydrogen can form one bond, and oxygen can form two bonds, as illustrated below. When two atoms bond together to form a compound, they are called molecules. Molecules tend to be more stable than atoms, and, like atoms, can carry a positive or negative charge. Charged atoms or molecules are called *ions*.

```
    H
    |
H—C—H        H—O—H
    |
    H
```

Methane (CH_4)   Water (H_2O)

essential [nutrients] Nutrients that must be consumed from foods because they cannot be made in the body in sufficient quantities to meet its needs and support health.

nonessential nutrients Nutrients that can be made in sufficient quantities in the body to meet the body's requirements and support health.

energy The capacity to do work.

adenosine triphosphate (ATP) A compound that is broken down to produce energy for working muscles and other tissues.

energy-yielding nutrients The three nutrients that provide energy to the body to fuel physiological functions: carbohydrates, lipids, and protein.

kilocalorie The amount of energy required to raise the temperature of 1 kilogram of water 1 degree centigrade; used to express the measurement of energy in foods; 1 kilocalorie is equal to 1,000 calories.

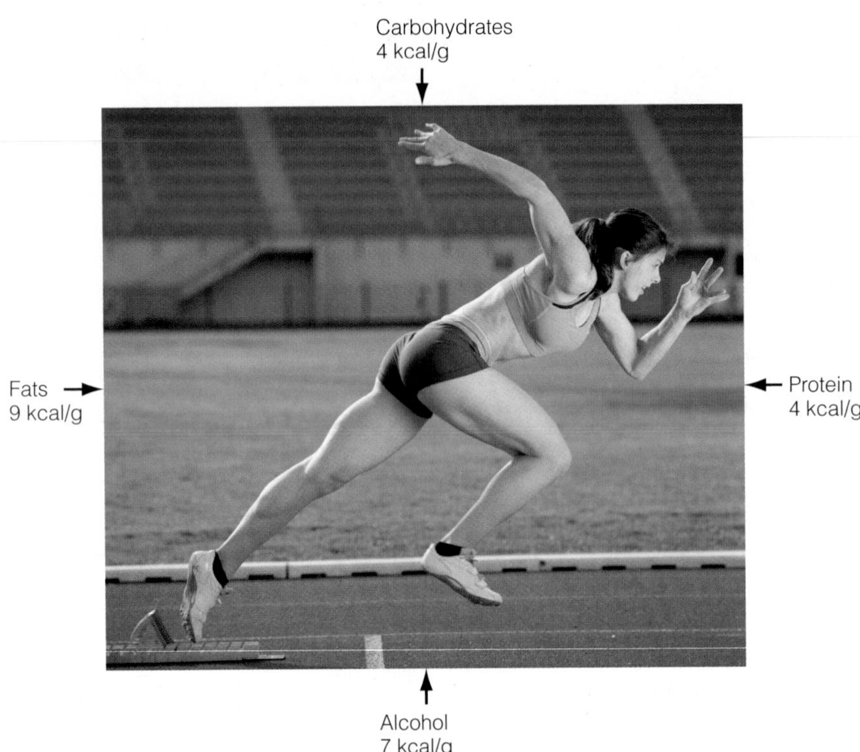

▲ **Figure 1.4 Nutrients and Alcohol Provide Kilocalories to Fuel the Body**
Carbohydrates, fats, protein, and alcohol provide energy, or kilocalories.

Use the Calculation Corner to determine the number of kilocalories in a potato-chip-and-cola snack.

Energy in foods and in the body is trapped within the bonds that keep the molecules together. When the bonds are broken during the process of metabolism, a significant amount of energy, including some heat, is released. The energy can then be used to digest and absorb the meal, contract muscles, fuel the heart, and synthesize new cells, as well as other functions.

People's energy needs vary according to their age, gender, and activity level. Males generally need more energy because they weigh more, and have more muscle mass (which requires more kilocalories to function) and less body fat. A younger person requires more energy than an older adult because he is still growing and is therefore synthesizing more new tissue. Physically active

Calculation Corner

Calculating Kilocalories in a Meal

Suppose you ate an entire bag of potato chips and drank a 16-ounce cola while you studied for an exam. Together these two items contain 144 grams of carbohydrate (in the cola and chips), 12 grams of protein (from the chips), and 60 grams of fat (also in the chips). How many kilocalories did you consume?

(a) To calculate the total kilocalories in this snack, multiply the total grams of each energy nutrient times the number of kilocalories per gram of that nutrient. Remember, a gram of carbohydrate and protein each contain 4 kilocalories and a gram of fat contains 9 kilocalories.

$$(144 \text{ g} \times 4 \text{ kcals/g}) + (12 \text{ g} \times 4 \text{ kcals/g}) + (60 \text{ g} \times 9 \text{ kcals/g}) = 1{,}164 \text{ kcals}$$

$$576 \text{ kcals} + 48 \text{ kcals} + 540 \text{ kcals} = 1{,}164 \text{ kcals}$$

In one sitting, you consumed more than 1,100 kilocalories, which for some people may be more than half of the amount they need to meet their daily energy requirement. If behaviors like this become habits, they can quickly result in weight gain.

(b) Another useful measure for assessing the nutritional quality of the snack is the percentage of fat, protein, and/or carbohydrate found in the food (you will learn in later chapters that there are ranges for each nutrient that are considered part of a healthy diet). For example, what percent of kilocalories in the chips and soda is from fat? To answer this question, divide the fat kilocalories by the total kilocalories in the food and multiply by 100:

$$(540 \text{ kcals} \div 1{,}164 \text{ kcals}) \times 100 = 46\% \text{ fat}$$

Almost half of the kilocalories in this snack are from fat. Do you think this is likely to be a desirable proportion?

For practice, complete the same calculations for carbohydrate and protein.

Chemistry Boost

Covalent Bonds

A chemical reaction unites two atoms by creating a covalent bond to form a new molecule. This covalent bond is formed when atoms share their electrons, as in the case of water. The oxygen atoms require two additional electrons and the hydrogen atoms need one electron to be stable. When these three atoms combine, the oxygen shares one electron with each of the hydrogen atoms and the hydrogen atoms share one electron with the oxygen atom. The atoms are held together because of their affinity to share each other's electrons. The covalent bond that is formed is strong and difficult to break. Trapped within the bonds is stored energy that is released when the bonds are broken.

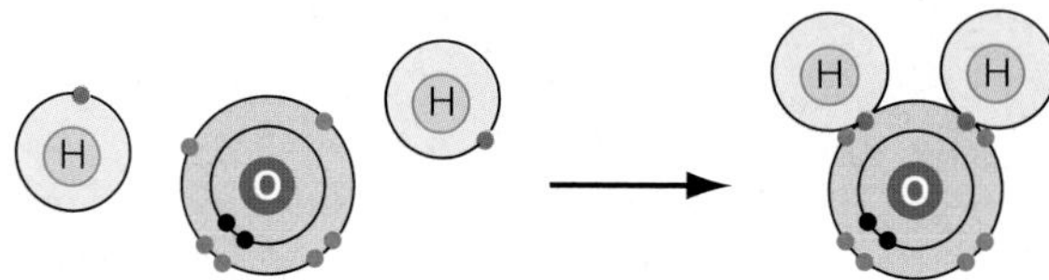

individuals require more energy than sedentary people to fuel their activities and meet their body's basic energy needs.

Energy that is not used to fuel the body will be rearranged into storage forms, predominantly as fat, for later use. If you regularly consume more kilocalories than you expend, you will accumulate stored fat in adipose tissue and gain weight. The opposite is also true. Eating fewer kilocalories than the body needs will result in the breakdown of stored energy and weight loss.

THE TAKE-HOME MESSAGE Nutrition is the science of how the nutrients and compounds in foods nourish the body. The body uses the nutrients found in foods to manufacture and replace cells, and produce energy. Carbohydrates, lipids, proteins, and vitamins are organic nutrients composed of the chemical elements carbon, hydrogen, oxygen, and sometimes nitrogen. Minerals and water are inorganic. Minerals are comprised of single atoms and water is made up of hydrogen and oxygen. Energy in foods is measured in kilocalories. The energy-yielding nutrients—carbohydrates (4 kilocalories per gram), lipids (9 kilocalories per gram), and proteins (4 kilocalories per gram)—provide fuel to be used by the body or stored for future use. Alcohol (7 kilocalories per gram) is not a nutrient but does provide energy.

Calculation Corner

Converting Pounds to Kilograms

Some of the calculations used in nutrition require conversion of body weight from pounds to kilograms (kg). For example, one common calculation for the recommended intake of protein uses kilograms (although there are also formulas using pounds).

Example: To determine how many kilograms a woman weighs, use her weight in pounds (125 pounds) and divide by the conversion factor 2.2:

$$125 \text{ lb} \div 2.2 = 56.8 \text{ kg}$$

Using your own body weight in pounds, calculate your weight in kilograms.

What Are the Primary Roles of the Individual Nutrients?

Individual nutrients serve unique roles in the body. They supply energy, regulate metabolism, and provide structure (Table 1.1). Some nutrients, including carbohydrates, lipids, proteins, and water, are called **macronutrients** (*macro* means large) because they are needed in much larger amounts to support normal functioning. Vitamins and minerals, though equally important to health, are considered **micronutrients** (*micro* means small) because they are required in smaller amounts to perform their key roles. Each of the six classifications of nutrients will be briefly introduced in this chapter, and then discussed in much greater detail later in the textbook.

macronutrients Organic nutrients, including the energy-containing carbohydrates, lipids, proteins, and water that the body needs in large amounts.

micronutrients Essential nutrients the body needs in smaller amounts: vitamins and minerals.

TABLE 1.1 Functions of the Major Nutrients by Type

	Nutrient	Provides Energy	Participates in Growth, Maintenance, Support, or Structure	Regulates Body Processes
Macronutrients	Carbohydrates	Yes	No	No
	Protein	Yes	Yes	Yes
	Fats	Yes	Yes	Yes
	Water	No	Yes	Yes
Micronutrients	Vitamins	No	Yes	Yes
	Minerals	No	Yes	Yes

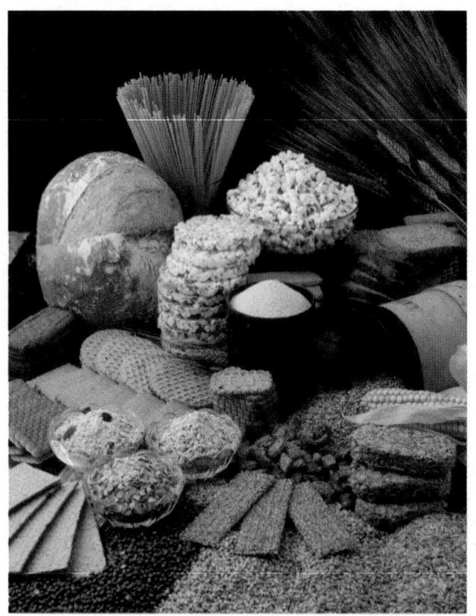

Carbohydrates are found in a variety of foods, including breads, grains, and pasta.

Carbohydrates Are the Primary Energy Source

Carbohydrates are the body's main source of energy. All forms of carbohydrates are composed of carbon (*carbo-*), hydrogen, and oxygen (*hydrate* means water). Carbohydrates supply the simple sugar, glucose, which is the primary source of energy for several body cell types, including red blood cells and brain cells. Carbohydrates are found in most foods. Breads, cereals, legumes, nuts, fruits, vegetables, and dairy products are all rich in carbohydrates. The only foods that do not provide significant amounts of carbohydrates are animal products other than dairy, such as eggs, meat, poultry, and fish. (Carbohydrates are covered in detail in Chapter 4.)

Lipids Also Provide Energy

The term lipid refers to a diverse group of organic compounds including fats (also called triglycerides), oils, phospholipids, and sterols that are insoluble in water. These nutrients contain the same chemical elements as carbohydrates, including carbon, hydrogen, and oxygen. The difference is that lipids are much more concentrated than carbohydrates and contain less oxygen and water.

Lipids in the form of triglycerides are an important energy source for the body, especially during rest and sleep. This is also the form in which the body stores excess energy. The stored energy makes up the adipose tissue beneath the skin, which insulates the body and cushions the organs. Triglycerides make up the majority of the lipids we eat and are found in margarine, butter, oils, and animal products. (Chapter 5 presents more information on lipids.)

Meats and dairy products are excellent sources of protein. Plant products, such as nuts, seeds, and legumes, also provide protein to the diet.

Proteins Provide the Building Blocks for Tissue Synthesis

Proteins can be used for energy but are usually not the primary energy source. Proteins are similar in composition to carbohydrates and lipids in that they contain carbon, hydrogen, and oxygen. But proteins are unique in that they all contain the element nitrogen, and some also contain sulfur.

Proteins contribute the basic building blocks, known as amino acids, to synthesize, grow, and maintain tissues in the body. The tissues in muscles, bones, and skin are primarily made up of protein. Proteins also participate as neurotransmitters in the complex communication network between the brain and the rest of the body, and they play a role in the immune system and as **enzymes** that catalyze chemical reactions.

Protein is found in a variety of foods, including meats, dairy products, and legumes such as soy, nuts, and seeds. Whole grains, vegetables, and some fruits contain smaller amounts of protein. (Chapter 6 covers protein in detail.)

A wide variety of fruits and vegetables are abundant sources of water-soluble vitamins.

Vitamins and Minerals Play Vital Roles in Metabolism

Vitamins and minerals do not provide energy, but they are involved in numerous key functions in the body. They are essential to help regulate metabolism, for example, and without them we would be unable to use carbohydrates, fats, and proteins for energy or to sustain numerous chemical reactions. A deficiency of vitamins and minerals can cause a cascade of ill health effects ranging from fatigue to stunted growth, weak bones, and organ damage. The metabolic fate of carbohydrates, protein, and fats in the body depends on consuming enough vitamins and minerals in the daily diet.

Vitamins

Many vitamins function as **coenzymes,** that is, they help enzymes catalyze reactions in the body. For example, the B vitamin thiamin attaches to and assists an enzyme involved in carbohydrate metabolism. Vitamins also activate enzymes that participate in building bone and muscle, energy production, fighting infections, and maintaining healthy nerves and vision.

There are 13 known vitamins, and each has a unique chemical structure. They are grouped into two classifications according to their **solubility,** which affects how they are absorbed, stored, and excreted. **Water-soluble vitamins,** which include vitamin C and the eight B-complex vitamins, are easily absorbed and excreted by the body, and need to be consumed daily. The **fat-soluble vitamins,** A, D, E, and K, are stored in the liver and other organs and thus don't need to be consumed on a daily basis. (Vitamins are described in Chapters 9 and 10.)

Minerals

Minerals are inorganic substances that assist in body processes and are essential to the structure of hard tissues, such as bone, and soft tissues, including the red blood cells. Minerals such as calcium and phosphorus work with protein-containing hormones and enzymes to maintain and strengthen teeth and bones. A deficiency of any of the minerals can cause disease symptoms. Falling short of daily iron needs, for example, can cause fatigue and interfere with the ability to function.

Minerals are classified by the amount needed in the diet and total content found in the body. **Major minerals** are needed in amounts of at least 100 milligrams per day, and are found in amounts of at least 5 grams in the body. Calcium and magnesium are two examples of major minerals. In addition to the structure of bones and teeth, some major minerals help maintain fluid balance, participate in energy production, and participate in muscle contractions. (Details on each individual major mineral are discussed in Chapter 12.)

Trace minerals are needed in amounts of less than 100 milligrams per day and are found in amounts of less than 5 grams in the body. Iron and zinc are two examples of trace minerals. Among other functions, trace minerals transport oxygen and carbon dioxide, participate in cell growth and development, control the metabolic rate, and play a role as an antioxidant. (Chapter 13 provides more specific detail on the role of these trace minerals.)

enzymes Proteins in living cells that act as catalysts and control chemical reactions.

coenzymes Substances, such as vitamins or minerals, that facilitate the activity of enzymes.

solubility The ability to dissolve into another substance.

water-soluble vitamins Vitamins that dissolve in water; they generally cannot be stored in the body and must be consumed daily.

fat-soluble vitamins Vitamins that dissolve in fat and can be stored in the body.

major minerals Minerals found in the body in amounts greater than 5 grams; also referred to as macrominerals.

trace minerals Minerals found in the body in amounts less than 5 grams; also referred to as microminerals.

Water Is Critical for Numerous Functions

Some of the essential roles of water in the body probably seem obvious, as it makes up the majority of all body fluids, including digestive secretions, blood, urine, and perspiration. Less obvious is the fact that water is part of every cell in the body, from muscle and bone cells to brain and nerve cells. Water is also vital to several key body functions. It is essential during metabolism, for example, because it provides the medium in which metabolic reactions take place. Water functions in digestion and absorption, and as a transport medium that delivers nutrients and oxygen to the cells and excretes waste products through the urine. Water helps maintain body temperature and acts as a lubricant for the joints, eyes, mouth, and intestinal tract. It surrounds vital organs and cushions them from injury. Because the body can't store water, it must be replenished every day to maintain hydration. (The role of water in the body is discussed in detail in Chapter 11.)

THE TAKE-HOME MESSAGE The six classes of essential nutrients, carbohydrates, lipids (fats), protein, vitamins, minerals, and water, each have specific roles in the body. Carbohydrates, fats, and protein provide energy, while vitamins, minerals, and water are needed to use the energy-producing nutrients and for various body processes.

What Is Credible Nutrition Research?

If you Google the word *nutrition*, you will get a list of about 103,000,000 entries in 0.25 seconds. Obviously, the world is full of nutrition information at our fingertips. But is it credible?

Anyone who has attempted to lose weight can probably tell you how hard it is to keep up with the latest diet advice—because it seems to keep changing. In the 1970s, waist watchers were told that carbohydrates were the bane of their existence and that a protein-rich, low-carbohydrate diet was the name of the game when it came to shrinking their waistline. A decade later, avoiding fat was the key to winning the battle of the bulge. By 2000, carbohydrates were being ousted again, and protein-rich diets were back in vogue. But recently protein-heavy diets seem to be less popular and high-carbohydrate diets are once again becoming the way to fight weight gain. So . . . are you frustrated yet?

Whereas diet trends and popular wisdom seem to change frequently, basic scientific knowledge about nutrition does not. Results from individual studies are often deemed newsworthy and publicized in the media, but the results of one report do not radically change expert opinion. Only when multiple affirming research studies have been conducted is a **consensus** reached about nutrition advice. News of the results of one study is just that: news. In contrast, advice from an authoritative health organization or committee, such as the American Heart Association or the Dietary Guidelines Committee, which is based on a consensus of research information, is sound information that can be trusted for the long term. (See Examining the Evidence: How Can I Evaluate Nutrition News? for tips on how to critically evaluate media headlines.)

Nutrition-related stories often lead in newspapers and magazines and on websites.

consensus Agreed-upon conclusion of a group of experts based on a collection of information.

EXAMINING THE EVIDENCE

How Can I Evaluate Nutrition News?

February 11, 2010

Sweet Science: The Health Benefits of Chocolate

Rachael Rettner, *LiveScience*

Did this headline grab your attention? If it did, you may be tempted to run out immediately and buy a couple of chocolate bars. However, you would be doing a disservice to your health if you didn't read beyond the tantalizing headline. Dramatic headlines are designed to grab your attention, but they can be misleading. Whether they're delivered via a magazine or newspaper, TV, or online, sensational headlines should always be considered with a critical eye. You need to analyze the evidence on which the headline is based.

Why do such headlines appear so regularly in our popular press? The media is routinely bombarded by press releases sent from medical journals, food companies, organizations, and universities about research being conducted or conferences being sponsored by these institutions. These releases are sent for one reason: to gain publicity. Rather than repeat them indiscriminately, reputable news organizations that report on these findings will seek out independent experts in the field to weigh in on the research and, just as importantly, explain how these findings relate to the public. Even with this added context, there's often much detail that's left out of the story. Here are some questions to consider when hearing or reading about a new study, finding, or claim in the mainstream media:

1. Was the Research Finding Published in a Peer-Reviewed Journal? You can be confident that studies published in a peer-reviewed journal have been thoroughly reviewed by experts in this area of research. In most cases, if there are flaws in the study, the study does not get published. If the research isn't published in a peer-reviewed journal, you have no way of knowing if the study was conducted in an appropriate manner and whether the findings are accurate. A study about the possible virtues of chocolate in fighting heart disease that is published in the *New England Journal of Medicine* has more credibility than a similar article published in a banking magazine.

2. Was the Study Done Using Animals or Humans? Experiments with animals are often used to study how a particular substance affects a health outcome. But if the study is conducted in rats, it doesn't necessarily mean that the substance will have the same effect if consumed by humans. This doesn't mean that animal studies are frivolous. They are important stepping-stones to designing and conducting similar experiments involving humans.

3. Do the Study Participants Resemble Me? When you read or hear about studies involving humans, you always want to find out more information about the individuals who took part in the research. For example, were the people in the chocolate studies college-aged or older individuals with heart disease and high blood pressure? If older adults were studied, then would these findings be of any benefit to young adults who don't have high blood pressure or heart disease?

4. Is This the First Time I've Heard about This? A single study in a specific area of research is a lonely entity in the scientific world. Is this the first study regarding the health benefits of chocolate? If the media article doesn't confirm that other studies have also supported these findings, this initial study may be the *only* study of its kind. Wait until you hear that these research findings are confirmed by a reputable health organization, such as the American Heart Association, before considering making any changes in your diet. These organizations will only change their advice based on a consensus of research findings.

In your lifetime, you are going to read thousands of newspaper and website headlines, as well as watch and listen to countless television and radio reports. Your critical thinking skill in evaluating the sources and information presented will be your best friend when it comes to deciding which blurbs to believe. This skill may also save you considerable money by helping you avoid nutrition gimmicks. When it comes to assessing nutrition information in the media, it's worth your time and effort to find out where it came from and why (or if) you should care.

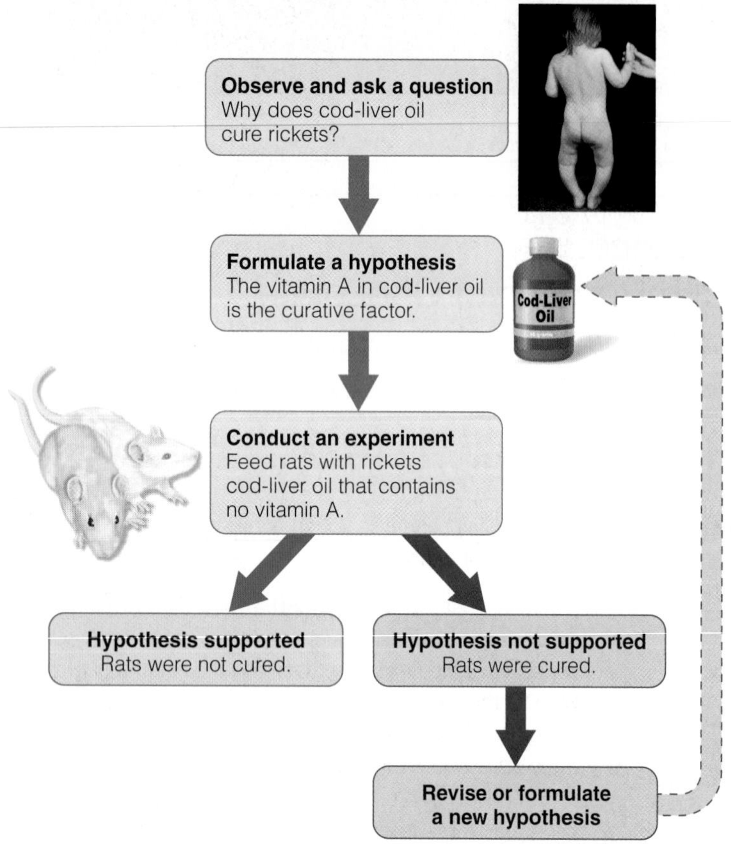
Observe and ask a question
Why does cod-liver oil cure rickets?
Formulate a hypothesis
The vitamin A in cod-liver oil is the curative factor.
Cod-Liver Oil
Conduct an experiment
Feed rats with rickets cod-liver oil that contains no vitamin A.
Hypothesis supported
Rats were not cured.
Hypothesis not supported
Rats were cured.
Revise or formulate a new hypothesis

▲ **Figure 1.5 Steps of the Scientific Method**
The scientific method is used to conduct credible research in nutrition and other scientific fields.

Sound Nutrition Research Begins with the Scientific Method

Sound research studies begin with a process called the **scientific method.** Scientists observe something in the natural world, ask questions, and propose an explanation (or **hypothesis**) based on their observations. They then test their hypothesis to determine if their idea is correct. There are many steps in the scientific method and many adjustments are made along the way before a scientist has gained enough information to draw a conclusion about his or her hypothesis. In fact, the entire process can take years to complete.

Let's walk through a nutrition-related study in which scientists used the scientific method to study rickets (**Figure 1.5**). Rickets is a disease in children in which the leg bones are so weakened that they cannot hold up the child's body weight. The legs bow as a result. In the early 1800s, parents often used cod-liver oil to treat rickets because it seemed to provide a miraculous cure.

Scientists noticed the cod-liver oil curing phenomenon and asked themselves why it cured rickets. In making note of the fact that cod-liver oil had an effect on rickets, and in asking why this was the case, these scientists were using the first step in the scientific method: observing and asking questions.

The second step of the scientific method is to formulate a hypothesis. Because cod-liver oil is very rich in vitamin A, scientists initially thought that this vitamin was the curative factor. To confirm this, scientists proceeded to the third step, which was to conduct an experiment.

The scientists altered the cod-liver oil to destroy its vitamin A. The altered oil was given to rats that had been fed a diet that caused rickets. Surprisingly, the rats were still cured of rickets. This disproved the scientists' original hypothesis that vitamin A was the curative factor. They then needed to modify their hypothesis, as it was obvious that there was something else in the cod-liver oil that cured rickets. They next hypothesized that it was the vitamin D that cured the rats, and conducted another experiment to confirm this hypothesis, which it did.

What good would it be to make such an important discovery if other scientists couldn't find out about it? Fortunately, scientists today share their findings by summarizing and submitting their research to a **peer-reviewed journal** (**Figure 1.6**). Other scientists (peers) review the researchers' findings to make sure that they are sound. If so, the research study is published in the journal. After that, it may be picked up by the popular press and relayed to the rest of the population. If the relationship between vitamin D and rickets was discovered today, it would probably be the lead story on CNN.

As more and more studies confirmed that vitamin D could cure and prevent rickets, a theory developed. By the 1920s, researchers knew with great certainty that vitamin D prevents rickets, and that a deficiency of vitamin D can cause deformed bones in children. Because of this, there is a consensus among health professionals as to the importance of vitamin D in the diets of children.

scientific method A process used by scientists to gather and test information for the sake of generating sound research findings.

hypothesis An idea or explanation proposed by scientists based on observations or known facts.

peer-reviewed journal A journal in which scientists publish research findings, after the findings have gone through a rigorous review process by other scientists.

Research Studies and Experiments Confirm Hypotheses

Scientists can use different types of experiments to test a hypothesis. A **laboratory experiment** is done within the confines of a lab setting, such as the rickets experiments with rats. Research conducted with humans is usually observational or experimental.

Observational research involves exploring factors in two or more groups of subjects to see if there is a relationship to a certain disease or health outcome. One type of observational research is **epidemiological research,** which looks at health and disease in populations of people. For example, scientists may notice that there is a higher incidence of rickets among children who live in Norway than among children who live in Australia. Through their observations, they may find a relationship between the lack of sun exposure in Norway and the high incidence of rickets there compared with sunny Australia. However, the scientists can't rule out that the difference in the incidence of rickets in these two populations may also be due to other factors in the subjects' diet or lifestyle. This type of research does not answer the question of whether one factor directly causes another.

Experimental research involves at least two groups of subjects. One group, the **experimental group,** is given a treatment, and another group, the **control group,** isn't. When scientists hypothesized that vitamin D cured rickets, they would have randomly assigned children with rickets to one of two groups (Figure 1.7). The scientists would have given the experimental group a vitamin D supplement but would have given the control group a **placebo,** which looked just like the vitamin D supplement but contained only sugar. If neither of the two groups of subjects knew which pill they received, then the subjects were "blind" to the treatment. If the scientists who gave the placebo and the vitamin D supplement also didn't know which group received which treatment, the experiment would be called a **double-blind placebo-controlled study.** The scientists would also have to make sure that the variables were the same or controlled for both groups during the experiment. For example, they couldn't let the control group go outside in the sunshine, since sunlight is known to allow humans to synthesize vitamin D, and at the same time keep the experimental group of subjects inside. The exposure to the sunshine would change the outcome of the experiment.

A double-blind placebo-controlled study is considered the "gold standard" of research because all of the variables are the same and controlled for the groups of subjects, and neither the subjects nor the researcher are biased toward one group.

In any scientific research, sample sizes must be large enough to ensure that differences found in the study are due to the treatment rather than to chance. Studying an entire population is usually impossible, because the population is too large, the study would be too expensive or time-consuming, or all members of the population do not want to participate. This was the case with the vitamin D and rickets study mentioned earlier. It would be virtually impossible to measure all children with rickets. Instead, a sample of children with rickets was used and a statistical comparison was done to estimate the effects on the population. Generally, the larger the sample size, the more confident the researchers are that the data reflects reliable differences that would most likely be seen in the population.

The beauty of science is that one discovery builds on another. Though this may seem frustrating when the findings of one research study contradict the results of another from just a few months before, conflicting findings actually help scientists formulate new questions. Though many hypotheses fail along the way, a great many discoveries are also made.

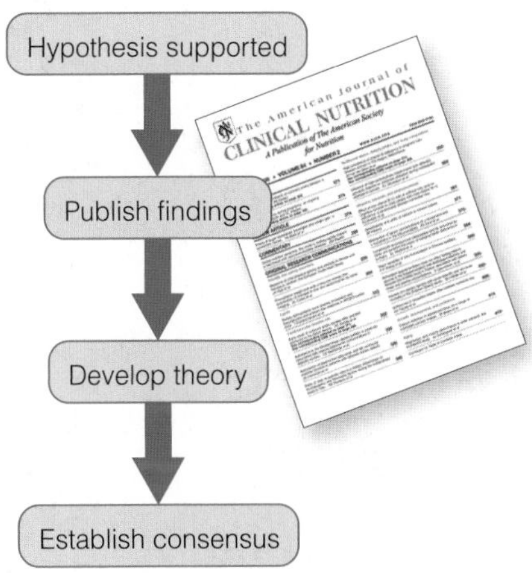

▲ **Figure 1.6 A Hypothesis Can Lead to a Scientific Consensus**
When a hypothesis is supported by research, the results are published in peer-reviewed journals. Once a theory has been developed and supported by subsequent experiments, a consensus is reached in the scientific community.

laboratory experiment A scientific experiment conducted in a laboratory. Some laboratory experiments involve animals.

observational research Research that involves systematically observing subjects to see if there is a relationship to certain outcomes.

epidemiological research Research that studies the variables that influence health in a population; it is often observational.

experimental research Research involving at least two groups of subjects receiving different treatments.

experimental group In experimental research, the group of participants given a specific treatment, such as a drug, as part of the study.

control group In experimental research, the group that does not receive the treatment but may be given a placebo instead; used as a standard for comparison.

placebo An inactive substance, such as a sugar pill, administered to a control group during an experiment.

double-blind placebo-controlled study An experimental study in which neither the researchers nor the subjects in the study are aware of who is receiving the treatment or the placebo.

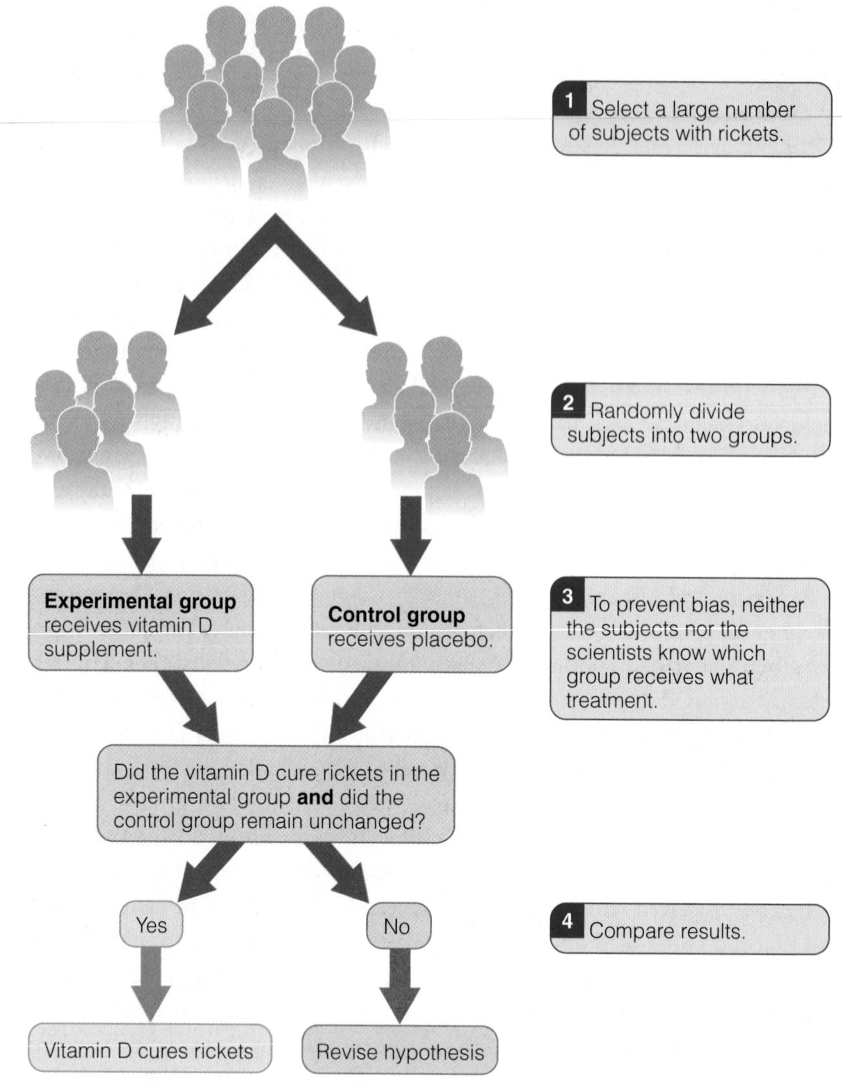
1 Select a large number of subjects with rickets.
2 Randomly divide subjects into two groups.
Experimental group receives vitamin D supplement.
Control group receives placebo.
3 To prevent bias, neither the subjects nor the scientists know which group receives what treatment.
Did the vitamin D cure rickets in the experimental group and did the control group remain unchanged?
Yes
No
4 Compare results.
Vitamin D cures rickets
Revise hypothesis

▲ **Figure 1.7 Controlled Scientific Experiments**
Scientists use experimental research to test hypotheses.

THE TAKE-HOME MESSAGE Sound nutrition advice is based on years of research using the scientific method. Several methods can be used to conduct nutrition research, including laboratory experiments (on animals), experimental research (on humans), and observational, particularly epidemiological, research. Double-blind placebo-controlled studies mean that neither the subjects nor the researchers are aware of who is receiving treatment, and such studies are therefore considered the gold standard of experimental research. Findings from observational and epidemiological research are only considered valid if the study was conducted with an adequate sample size of subjects.

How Do We Assess Nutritional Status?

How do you know if you are eating enough of the essential nutrients? A person's *state of nutrition* is usually described as either healthy or **malnourished.** Someone who lacks a specific nutrient, or isn't consuming enough energy, is

malnourished A condition that results when the body does not receive the right amount of essential nutrients to maintain health; overnourished and undernourished are forms of malnutrition.

TABLE 1.2 The ABCDs of Nutrition Assessment

Types of Assessment	Measurements	What They Determine
Anthropometric	Height Weight Body mass index Waist-to-hip ratio Waist circumference	Growth, obesity, changes in weight loss, and risk of developing chronic disease such as diabetes and heart disease
Biochemical	Blood, urine, and feces	Protein, mineral, and vitamin status and disease
Clinical	Observe hair, fingernails, skin, lips, mouth, muscles, joints, overall appearance	Signs of deficiencies and excesses of nutrients
Dietary Intake	Diet history Diet record Food frequency questionnaire 24-hour dietary recall	Usual nutrient intake, and deficiencies or excesses of various nutrients

undernourished, which means that person is at risk of losing too much weight or developing a disease related to a nutrient deficiency. In contrast, an individual who overconsumes a particular nutrient, or eats too many kilocalories, is described as being **overnourished.** This person runs the risk of becoming overweight, developing diseases such as diabetes or heart disease, and potentially accumulating toxic amounts of a specific nutrient in the body.

A variety of methods are used to assess both under- and overnutrition of individuals. No one measurement is sufficient to determine malnutrition, and thus a combination of tools is used (see the ABCDs in Table 1.2). If you suspect you may not be meeting all of your nutrient needs, or that you are suffering from a nutrition-related disease or condition, turn to a nutrition professional, such as a **Registered Dietitian (RD),** to determine your current nutrition status (see Spotlight: Obtaining Nutrition Advice: Who Are the Experts? Who Are the Quacks? on page 20). An RD will conduct a complete assessment to find out if you are getting too much, too little, or the right amount of a nutrient.

Assessing the Nutritional Status of Individuals

Part of evaluating a person's current nutrition status is to look at that person's health history, including any experiences with **acute** or **chronic** illness, and diagnostic procedures, therapies, or treatments that may increase nutrient needs or induce **malabsorption.** Does the patient have a family history of diabetes or heart disease? Has the patient been overweight or underweight in the past?

Registered Dietitians use a number of specialized methods to assess the nutrition status of individuals, including dietary intake assessments, collecting anthropometric data, conducting physical exams, and collecting laboratory data.

Assessing Dietary Intake through Questionnaires and Interviews

Questioning an individual about his or her dietary intake and diet history is an important aspect of a nutrition assessment. A detailed diet history is conducted by a skilled researcher who knows just what types of questions to ask to help a patient remember not only current food intake but food intake in the past.

undernourished A condition in which the individual lacks sufficient energy or is deficient in quality or quantity of essential nutrients.

overnourished The condition of having consumed excess energy or nutrients.

Registered Dietitian (RD) A health professional who is a food and nutrition expert; RDs obtain a college degree in nutrition from an Academy of Nutrition and Dietetics–accredited program, and pass a national exam to become a Registered Dietitian.

acute Describes a sudden onset of symptoms or disease.

chronic Describes a symptom or condition that lasts over a long period of time.

malabsorption A problem associated with the lack of absorption of nutrients through the intestinal tract.

Obtaining Nutrition Advice: Who Are the Experts? Who Are the Quacks?

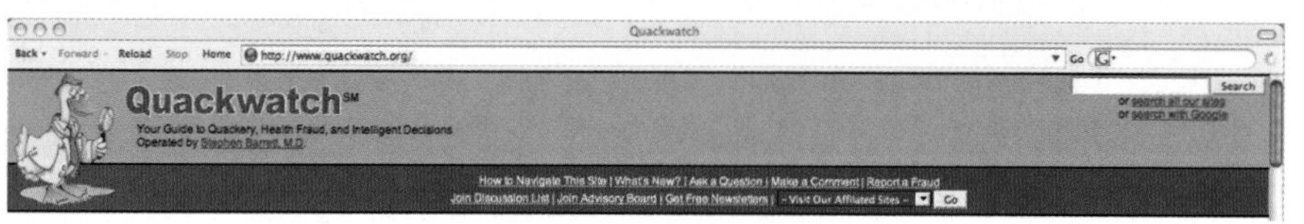

Screenshot from www.quackwatch.com. Reprinted with permission."

If you need legal advice, you seek the expertise of an attorney. If you need knee surgery, you go to an orthopedic surgeon. Whom do you consult for nutrition advice?

The Nutrition Experts

Who is a credible expert with training in the field of nutrition? Different health professionals have varying levels of nutrition training, but by far, the professional with the most nutrition training is the Registered Dietitian (RD). An RD has completed at least a bachelor's degree from a university or college accredited by the Academy of Nutrition and Dietetics and has passed the Commission on Dietetic Registration (CDR)–administered national exam. The Academy of Nutrition and Dietetics is the largest professional organization in the United States, with a membership of almost 67,000 nutrition experts. RDs must maintain registration with the national organization and participate in continuing professional education to remain current in the fast-changing world of nutrition, medicine, and health.

RDs are trained to administer **medical nutrition therapy** and work with patients to make dietary changes that can help prevent diseases such as heart disease, diabetes, stroke, and obesity. Patients are often referred to RDs for nutrition advice and guidance by their physicians. RDs work in hospitals and other health care facilities, private practice, universities, medical schools, professional athletic teams, food companies, and other nutrition-related businesses.

medical nutrition therapy The integration of nutrition counseling and dietary changes, based on individual medical and health needs, to treat a patient's medical condition.

public health nutritionists Individuals who may have an undergraduate degree in nutrition but who are not Registered Dietitians.

licensed dietitian (LD) An individual who has met specified educational and experience criteria deemed by a state licensing board necessary to be considered an expert in the field of nutrition. An RD would meet all the qualifications to be an LD.

nutritionist A generic term with no recognized legal or professional meaning. Some people may call themselves a nutritionist without having any credible training in nutrition.

quackery The promotion and selling of health products and services of questionable validity. A quack is a person who promotes these products and services in order to make money.

Some individuals other than RDs, including those with advanced degrees in nutrition, can also provide credible nutrition information. Some physicians have taken a nutrition course in medical school and gone on to get a master of science in public health (MPH), which involves some nutrition courses, or an MS in nutrition at an accredited university or college.

Some **public health nutritionists** may have an undergraduate degree in nutrition but didn't complete a supervised practice, so are not eligible to take the Academy of Nutrition and Dietetics exam. These individuals can work in the government organizing community outreach nutrition programs, such as programs for the elderly.

In order to protect the health of the public, over 40 states currently license nutrition professionals. A person who meets these qualifications is a **licensed dietitian (LD)** and so will have the letters "LD" after his or her name. Because RDs have completed the rigorous standards set forth by the Academy of Nutrition and Dietetics, they automatically meet the criteria for LD and often will have both "RD" and "LD" after their names.

Be careful when taking nutrition advice from a trainer at the gym or the person who works at the local health food store. Whereas some of these people may be credible, many are not, and thus, less likely to give you information based on solid scientific evidence. Anyone who calls himself or herself a **nutritionist** may have taken few or no accredited courses in nutrition.

Be a Quackwatcher

Whereas credible nutrition experts can provide highly useful nutrition guidance, people of questionable credentials often dole out misinformation, usually for the sake of turning a profit. These skilled salespeople specialize in health **quackery,** or fraud, introducing health fears and then trying to sell services and products to allay these newly created fears. Part of their sales pitch is to make unrealistic promises and guarantees.

In order to help people avoid falling for profit-motivated schemes, Dr. Stephen Barrett has developed a list of common deceptive statements made by health quacks.[1, 2] Be leery of infomercials, magazine ads, and websites that try to convince you that:

- Most Americans are not adequately nourished.
- Everyone should take vitamin supplements.
- You need supplements to relieve stress or give you energy.
- You can lose a lot of weight in a short amount of time.
- Their products can produce amazing results and cure whatever ails you.

- Your behavior is caused by your diet.
- Herbs are safe because they are natural.
- Sugar will poison you.
- A hair sample can identify nutrient deficiencies.
- Your MD or RD is a quack to whom you should not listen.
- There is no risk, as there is a money-back guarantee. (Good luck getting your money back!)

You Can Obtain Accurate Nutrition Information on the Internet

Many people turn to various websites when they have a question about health or nutrition. In fact, over 88 percent of American adult Internet users, or 175 million people, have surfed more than 3 million websites looking for health and medical information.[3] The good news is that you can find credible nutrition information online; you just need to evaluate every site with a critical eye. Remember that anyone with computer skills can put up a slick website, and there are many that promote misleading or false information.

To help evaluate the validity of websites, the National Institutes of Health (NIH) has developed ten questions to consider:[4]

1. **Who Runs the Site?** Credible websites are willing to show their credentials. For example, the National Center for Complementary and Alternative Medicine (www.nccam.nih.gov) provides information about its association with the NIH and its extensive ongoing research and educational programs.
2. **Who Pays for the Site?** Running a website is expensive, and finding out who's paying for a particular site will tell you something about the reliability of its content. Websites sponsored by the government (with URLs ending in .gov), a nonprofit organization (ending in .org), or an academic institution (.edu) are more reliable than many commercial websites (.com or .net). Some commercial websites, such as WebMD, carry articles that can be reliable if they are written by credible health professionals, but other websites may be promoting information to suit a company's own purposes. For example, if the funding source for the website is a vitamin and mineral supplement company, are all the articles geared toward supporting the use of supplements? Does the website have advertisers and do their products influence the content of the website?
3. **What Is the Purpose of the Site?** After you answer the first two questions, look for the "About This Site" link. This will help you understand the website's purpose. For example, at www.nutrition.gov, the purpose is to "provide easy access to the best food and nutrition information across the federal government." This website doesn't exist to sell anything, but to help you find reliable information.
4. **Where Does the Information Come From?** You should always know who wrote what you are reading. Is the author a qualified nutrition expert or did she or he interview qualified individuals? If the site obtained information from another source, was that source cited?
5. **What Is the Basis for the Information?** Is the article's information based on medical facts and figures that have references? For example, any medical news items released on the American Heart Association website (www.heart.org/HEARTORG) will include the medical journal from which the information came.
6. **How Is the Information Selected?** Check to see if the website has an editorial board of medical and health experts and if qualified individuals review or write the content before it is released.
7. **How Current Is the Information?** Once a website is on the Internet, it will stay there until someone removes it. Consequently, the health information that you read may not be the most up to date. Check the date; if it is over a year old, check to see if it has been updated.
8. **How Does the Site Choose Links to Other Sites?** Some medical sites don't like to link to other sites, as they don't have control over other sites' credibility and content. Others do link, if they are confident that these sites meet their criteria. Don't assume that the link is credible.
9. **What Information Is Collected about the Viewer and Why?** Websites track the pages consumers visit to analyze popular topics. Sometimes they elicit personal information such as gender, age, and health concerns, which can then be sold to interested companies. Credible sites should state their privacy policy and if they will or will not give or sell this information to other sources.
10. **How Does the Site Manage Interactions with Visitors?** Contact information of the website's owners should be listed in case readers have any concerns or questions that they want answered. If the site has a chat room or ongoing discussion group, how is it moderated? Read the discussion group dialogue before you jump in.

When obtaining information from the Internet, carefully peruse the site to make sure that it is credible and contains up-to-date information, and that its content isn't influenced by those who fund and support the website.

References

1. S. Barrett and V. Herbert. Revised 2008. *Twenty-Five Ways to Spot Quacks and Vitamin Pushers.* Available at www.quackwatch.org. Accessed January 2012.
2. S. Barrett. 2006. *How to Spot a "Quacky" Web Site.* Available at www.quackwatch.org. Accessed January 2012.
3. H. Taylor. 2010. *"Cyberchondriacs" on the Rise?* Available at www.harrisinteractive.com. Accessed January 2012.
4. National Center for Complementary and Alternative Medicine. 2006. *10 Things to Know About Evaluating Medical Resources on the Web.* Available at www.nccam.nih.gov. Accessed January 2012.

A handwritten food diary can be a useful tool for assessing nutritional status.

Two tools used to collect dietary intake data are questionnaires and interviews. Food frequency questionnaires (FFQs) and food records can be used to gather information about how often a specific food or category of food is eaten. A nutrition interview can reveal data about lifestyle habits, such as how many meals are eaten daily, where they are eaten, and who prepares them.

One of the easiest ways to determine an individual's intake of nutrients is to use the *food frequency questionnaire* (*FFQ*). This form of assessment provides evidence of consumption patterns over time. For example, if you wanted to determine the usual calcium intake over time of an older woman with osteoporosis, an FFQ could be used to indicate the number of servings "per day, per week, and per month," as well as whether she "seldom" or "never" consumes milk, cheese, or yogurt. The FFQ is a reasonably reliable, accurate, and inexpensive method to assess usual intake.[31]

This assessment tool is not as helpful in assessing the actual grams consumed of a nutrient, nor does it always accurately reveal usual intake. For that information, a food record or 24-hour dietary recall usually provides a better picture.

A *food record* is simply a diary of what foods and beverages are eaten, how much, and when they are eaten over a defined period of time. Food records are often kept for three to seven days and are considered by some to be one of the best methods for collecting diet information. There are drawbacks to this method. The accuracy depends on the individual's skill and commitment to keeping a valid record. Many people start out strong and then lose interest or simply forget to record the food. Or, they might alter their usual food intake to avoid feeling embarrassed about what they eat.

Food records can be kept in written form, such as a journal, or with an electronic diet analysis program. There are also new handheld devices being tested that may help improve the accuracy, ease, and evaluation of recording dietary intake.[32]

The FFQ or a diet record should be selected based on the specific information the assessor needs to know, such as iron intake over time and how much iron the individual eats daily, as well as the assessor's ability to complete the instrument accurately.[33] The information obtained from these tools is then compared with current dietary standards, which we will discuss in the next chapter.

The *24-hour dietary recall* method is a quick assessment conducted by a trained interviewer who asks a patient to recall all the food and drink, including snacks, eaten the previous day. This tool relies on the skills of the interviewer and the individual's ability to remember what he ate and drank the day before. Because dietary intake varies from one day to the next, one 24-hour period may not provide an accurate estimate of typical intake.

Collect Anthropometric Data to Help Assess Nutritional Status

Anthropometric data measures body size or body composition. In adults, this usually means measuring height, weight, **body mass index (BMI),** waist-to-hip ratios, and waist circumference. For children, growth charts have been developed that compare height to weight, as well as how a child's height and weight compare with others of the same age. All of these measurements are easily obtained with a scale and tape measure.

The BMI is a measure of weight relative to height, and waist circumference measures abdominal fat. Body composition measurements can provide data on an individual's lean body tissue and the percent body fat, depending on the tool used. These measurements can be assessed with specialized equipment, such as skin calipers, or more expensive equipment, such as the Bod Pod. (We discuss these measurements in greater detail in Chapter 14.)

body mass index (BMI) A measurement calculated using the metric formula of weight in kg divided by height in centimeters squared; used to determine whether an individual is underweight, at a healthy weight, or overweight or obese.

Data collected from anthropometric measurements is then compared with reference standards. Patterns and trends become evident when more than one measurement is taken over time and compared with the initial values. By combining the results of the BMI and waist circumference with other information gathered during the nutrition assessment, an individual's risk of developing diseases associated with obesity, such as diabetes and heart disease, can be determined.

Conduct a Physical Examination

A person who is malnourished will exhibit physical symptoms as the body adjusts to the lack or overaccumulation of nutrients. Therefore, several parts of the body can be inspected during a clinical exam for evidence of poor nutrition. Observing the hair, skin, eyes, fingernails, tongue, and lips of an individual can provide clues that point to under- or overnutrition. For example, cracks at the corners of the mouth can be evidence of B vitamin deficiencies, while small pinpoint hemorrhages on the skin may reflect a deficiency of vitamin C. Observations of physical symptoms should be followed up by more direct measurements, including laboratory assessments.

Collect Biochemical Data

Laboratory tests based on body fluids, including blood and urine, can be important indicators of nutritional status, but they are also influenced by nonnutritional factors. Biochemical tests assess nutritional status by measuring the nutrient levels in body fluids, how fast a nutrient is excreted through the urine, and the metabolic by-products of various nutrients found in urine. For example, low levels of albumin (a blood protein) in the serum reflect protein deficiency; low hemoglobin levels in the blood indicate iron-deficiency anemia; and a high fasting blood sugar level may suggest diabetes.

Assessing the Nutritional Status of a Population Group

Assessing the nutritional status of an individual in a clinical setting is one thing, but how do we determine the nutritional status of a population? What percentage of Americans is meeting the dietary recommendations for healthy eating? To find out, we collect dietary intake information on a large scale. Such information allows researchers to determine the adequacy of the current recommendations for different population groups, to evaluate and develop food assistance programs, and to assess risk.

Assessing groups of people involves gathering the same type of information used to evaluate individuals, usually through the use of surveys.

Conduct or Review National Surveys

Numerous national surveys have been developed by a variety of federal agencies to assess the health and nutritional status of Americans. These surveys, including the National Health and Nutrition Examination Survey (NHANES), the Behavioral Risk Factor Surveillance System (BRFSS), and the Framingham Heart Study, have collected and published reliable data that has been used to develop the current dietary recommendations.

The National Health and Nutrition Examination Survey (NHANES) is a series of surveys conducted by the National Center for Health Statistics (NCHS) and the Centers for Disease Control and Prevention (CDC). These surveys, which began in 1960, were established to determine the nutritional status of Americans of all ages and to monitor their risk behaviors over time. The intake of carbohydrates, lipids, protein, vitamins, minerals, and fiber has been collected using a 24-hour recall method and reported in the document *What We Eat In America*. For more information about the data collected during the eight NHANES surveys, visit the CDC website at www.cdc.gov/nchs/nhanes.htm.

The CDC began tracking the health behaviors of Americans in 1984 through the world's largest telephone survey, called the Behavioral Risk Factor Surveillance System, or BRFSS. With financial support from the CDC, the 50 state health departments develop surveys to assess the prevalence of specific health conditions, including chronic disease, injury, and infectious diseases. These surveys track health behaviors such as sedentary lifestyles, obesity, not using a seat belt, smoking, alcohol abuse, and lack of medical care that relate to the leading causes of death, including cardiovascular disease, cancer, stroke, diabetes, and injury. The data collected by each state is used to allocate state resources to plan and evaluate the health programs.

The term "risk factors" was first coined by the researchers of the 1948 Framingham Heart Study conducted in Framingham, Massachusetts. Fifty years later, these research pioneers had collected longitudinal data on two generations and more than 10,000 participants to establish the current recommendations for cardiovascular disease.

This study, supported by the National Heart, Lung, and Blood Institute, initially monitored participants as an epidemiological study. In the 1970s, advances in technology resulted in better testing methods, such as echocardiograms, exercise stress tests, and carotid artery ultrasounds. The current phase of the study, which began in the 1980s, is exploring the genetic connections to cardiovascular disease in a third generation of Framingham citizens.

The Framingham Heart Study had a major impact on the dietary intake of Americans. For instance, once the connection between blood cholesterol levels and heart disease was revealed, the common bacon-and-eggs breakfast eaten by most Americans in 1948 was replaced with whole grains and low-fat dairy.

THE TAKE-HOME MESSAGE An individual's nutritional status is assessed by gathering information from health history, dietary record, and anthropometric, clinical, and biochemical (laboratory) data. When the information from several tools is viewed together, a comprehensive picture of the individual's nutritional status can be determined. National surveys are used to determine the nutritional status of a large population. Two surveys conducted by the U.S. federal government are the National Health and Nutrition Examination Survey (NHANES) and the Behavioral Risk Factor Surveillance System (BRFSS), both supported by the Centers for Disease Control. The Framingham Heart Study, which is a project of the National Heart, Lung, and Blood Institute, has provided the foundation for the current dietary recommendations for heart health.

How Does the American Diet Stack Up?

The food supply in the United States provides an array of nutritious choices to meet the dietary needs of Americans. Fresh fruits and vegetables, whole grains, and lean meats, fish, and poultry are easily accessible and affordable through local grocery stores and farmer's markets. With such an abundance of healthy foods to choose from, are Americans adopting healthy diets?

The Quality of the American Diet

In general, Americans eat too much protein, sugar, sodium, and saturated fat, and too little fiber and some vitamins and minerals. Our low fiber intake is partly due to inadequate consumption of fruits and vegetables and overconsumption of refined grains.[34] While dietary fiber intakes are below recommended levels, added sugars account for almost 30 percent of carbohydrate intake. This is largely due to Americans' love of soft drinks and other sugary beverages.

The fat intake of most Americans ranges at the high end of the recommendation, at about 33 percent. The American diet contains too much saturated fat, but most Americans don't exceed the recommended dietary cholesterol intake limit of 300 milligrams per day.

American men meet their recommendations for most vitamins and minerals, but women fall short of many nutrients—iron, for example. Americans in general eat too much sodium, but not enough vitamin A, vitamin E, and calcium. In an attempt to balance our poor choice in foods, 40 percent of Americans take at least one vitamin or mineral supplement per day.[35]

The lack of a healthy diet may be due to where we eat. Today, many Americans eat their meals away from home. Some of us eat in the car, or buy prepared foods from the supermarket or take-out meals. When we eat at home, it's often in front of the television. Research reports that meals eaten while watching television are usually lower in fruits and vegetables and higher in fat and soft drinks. Only one-third of Americans eat family meals at least twice a week and almost 50 percent report never eating together as a family.

One positive habit is that almost 85 percent of Americans eat breakfast. Breakfast provides about 18 percent of the fiber and energy, and 25 percent of the vitamins A and C, folate, calcium, and iron, that we consume each day.

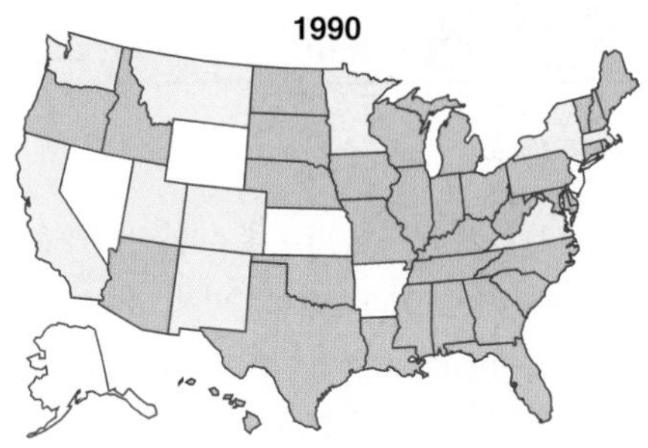

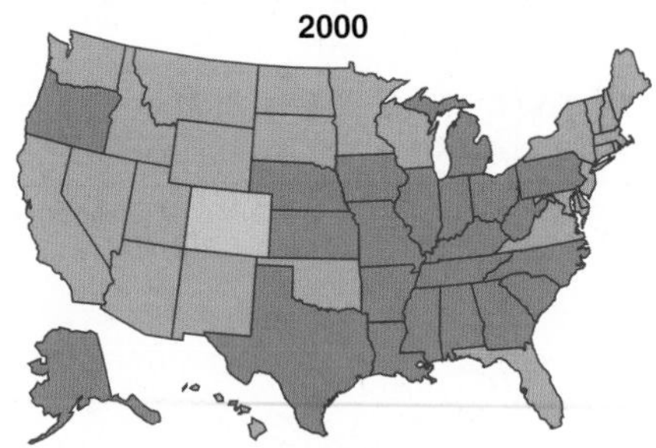

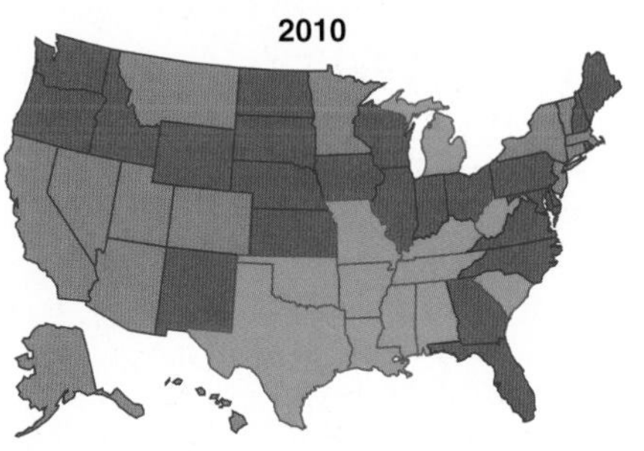

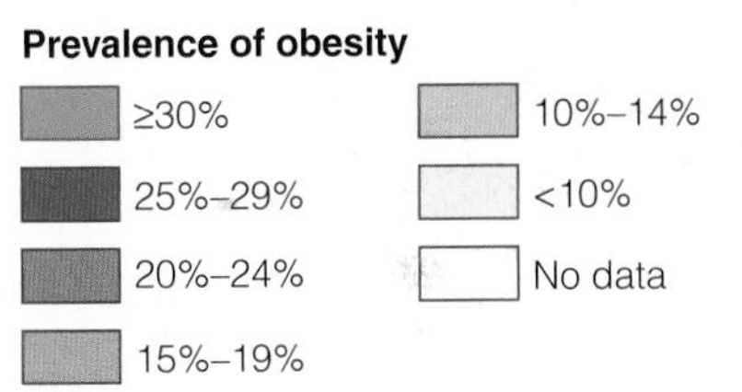

▲ **Figure 1.8 Obesity Trends among U.S. Adults**
Over the last two decades, rates of overweight and obesity have risen significantly in the United States.

Source: Centers for Disease Control. 2011. *U.S. Obesity Trends*. www.cdc.gov/obesity/data/trends.html.

Rates of Overweight and Obesity in Americans

As people take in more kilocalories than they burn, usually due to sedentary lifestyles, they create a recipe for poor health. This is reflected in the high rates of **overweight** and **obesity** in the United States (see **Figure 1.8**). Over 35 percent of American adults and 17 percent of children are obese regardless of their gender, age, race, ethnicity, socioeconomic status, education level, or geographical region.[36] These rates are too high, and reducing them is a top priority.

Along with the weight gain have come higher rates of type 2 diabetes, particularly among children, and increased rates of heart disease, cancer, and stroke.

Healthy People 2020

The U.S. Surgeon General has issued calls for a nationwide health improvement program since 1979. The latest edition of this report, ***Healthy People 2020***, contains a set of health objectives for the nation to achieve over the second decade of the twenty-first century.[37]

Healthy People 2020 focuses on several overarching goals:

- Attain high-quality, longer lives free of preventable disease, disability, injury, and premature death.
- Achieve health equity, eliminate disparities, and improve the health of all groups.
- Create social and physical environments that promote good health for all.
- Promote quality of life, healthy development, and healthy behaviors across every stage of life.

There are more than 35 topic areas in *Healthy People 2020,* ranging from ensuring that Americans have adequate access to health services to improvements in their diets and physical activity. Objectives are developed within each topic area.

overweight For adults, having a BMI greater than 25.

obesity For adults, having a BMI greater than 30.

Healthy People 2020 A set of disease prevention and health promotion objectives for Americans to meet during the second decade of the twenty-first century.

TABLE 1.3 *Healthy People 2020* **Nutrition and Weight Status Objectives**

Objectives	Target for Americans (%)	Status of Americans (%)
Increase the proportion of adults who are at a healthy weight	33.9	30.8
Reduce the proportion of adults who are obese	30.6	33.8
Reduce the proportion of children and adolescents who are considered obese	14.6	16.2
Increase the contribution of fruits to diets of the population age 2 years and older	0.9 cups/1,000 kcals	0.5 cups/1,000 kcals
Increase the variety and contribution of vegetables to the diets of the population age 2 years and older	1.1 cups/1,000 kcals	0.8 cups/1,000 kcals

Source: United States Department of Health and Human Services. 2010. *Healthy People 2020*. Available at www.HealthyPeople.gov. Accessed February 2012.

For example, current research indicates that Americans' body weights are increasing rather than decreasing.[38] Thus, "Nutrition and Weight Status" is one topic area. Its goal is to promote health and reduce chronic diseases associated with diet and weight. There are numerous objectives developed within this topic area that, if fulfilled, will help Americans improve their diet and reduce their weight. See Table 1.3 for a list of a few objectives in this area of focus.

As you can see from the table, consuming adequate amounts of fruits and vegetables is beneficial to managing one's weight. Americans should increase their intake of both of these food sources to help them improve their nutrition and weight status.

THE TAKE-HOME MESSAGE The American diet is too high in kilocalories, sodium, added sugar, and saturated fat, and too low in dietary fiber, vitamins A and E, calcium, and iron. Rates of overweight and obesity among Americans are too high. Incidences of overweight and obesity among Americans are prevalent, yet many people are falling short of some nutrient needs. *Healthy People 2020* is a set of health objectives for the nation to achieve over the second decade of the twenty-first century.

How Does Diet Impact Overall Health?

There is no question that the body requires all six classes of nutrients to function properly. A chronic deficiency of even one nutrient will impact the body's ability to function in the short term. Over time, chronic deficiencies, excesses, and imbalances will affect long-term health.

Good nutrition reduces the risk of four of the top ten leading causes of death in the United States, including the top two—heart disease and cancer—as well as stroke and diabetes (Table 1.4). Nutrition also plays an important role in preventing other diseases and conditions that can impede one's lifestyle. A healthy diet, for example, can keep bones strong and reduce the risk of developing osteoporosis. Eating well will also improve body weight, which in turn will reduce the risk of developing obesity, diabetes mellitus, and high blood pressure.

The relationship between food and health has changed drastically over several centuries. For example, the term *lime-juicer* was coined after one of the earliest reports of the British Navy supplying sailors in the 1600s with limes and citrus juice to prevent scurvy. During the 1700s, scientists recognized the value of what we eat in

TABLE 1.4 Leading Causes of Death in the United States

Disease/Cause of Death	Nutrition Related
1. **Heart Disease**	X
2. **Cancer**	X
3. Respiratory Diseases	
4. **Stroke**	X
5. Accidents	
6. Alzheimer's Disease	
7. **Diabetes**	X
8. Kidney Disease	
9. Influenza and Pneumonia	
10. Suicide	

Source: Centers for Disease Control. 2012. *National Vital Statistics Preliminary Data for 2010.* www.cdc.gov.

treating disease, so that by the early 1900s the concept of *essential nutrients* had been widely accepted. By the late nineteenth century, nutrition was becoming more quantitative, addressing the question of how much of each nutrient is required as well as accepting that individuals vary in their nutrient requirements. Nutrition epidemiology had been developed by the end of the twentieth century, and the advent of dietary surveys conducted by the government was used to further the science. Nutrition in the twenty-first century has evolved to developing new functional foods and nutraceuticals, and designing diets for longevity rather than just for preventing chronic disease. With the completion of the Human Genome Project in 2003 nutritionists and researchers are actively examining the synergistic effects of nutrition and genetics. These efforts may eventually result in more personalized, gene-driven diet plans.

Genetics and Nutrition Combine to Impact Health Risks

Most chronic diseases stem from the interplay between our genetic makeup, our environment, and our diet (**Figure 1.9**). Each one of us carries a unique combination of genes that were transferred from our parents. These genes are responsible for what we look like, our metabolism, and our susceptibility to disease. Some of our genes have variations in their codes, which make us more susceptible to diseases including cancer, cardiovascular disease, and diabetes, whereas other gene variants enhance our ability to resist chronic disease. Variants alone don't cause the disease, but rather increase the risk that the disease will develop given a conducive environment.

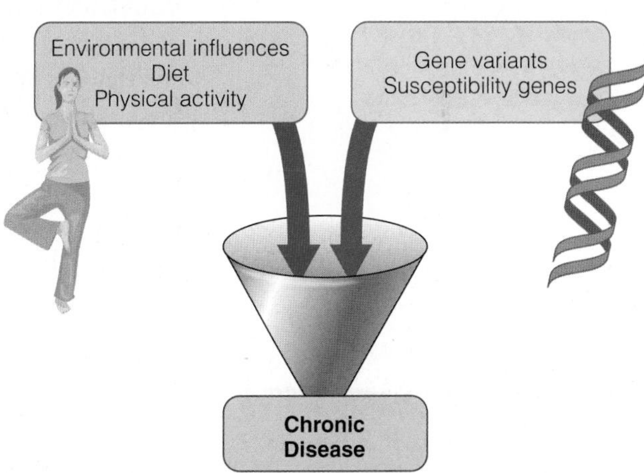

▲ **Figure 1.9 Chronic Disease Is a Mixture of Genetic Influences and Our Environment**

While the interaction is complex, scientific advances point to a variety of mechanisms in which the environment and genes interact to affect disease. Research suggests that the nutrients we eat attach to proteins that bind to DNA or to the cell surface. This reaction either increases or decreases **gene expression,** producing greater or smaller amounts of proteins, which in turn affects body function. For example, hypertension may be the result of gene variants that respond to a diet high in salt by raising blood pressure. When dietary salt is decreased, blood pressure drops.

gene expression The processing of genetic information to create a specific protein.

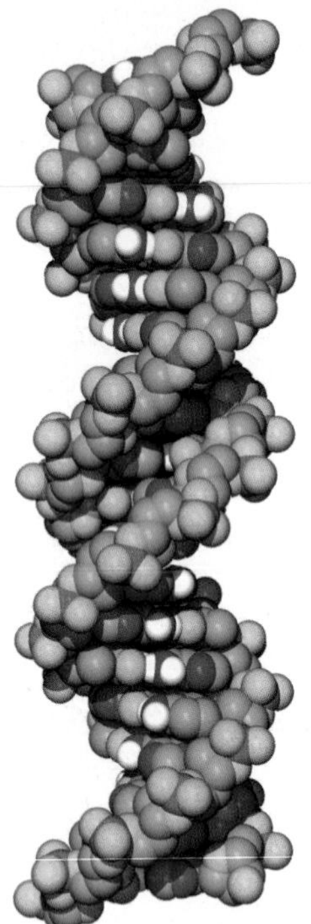

The study of nutritional genomics may one day allow individuals to tailor their diets based on their DNA.

Self-Assessment

How Healthy Is Your Family Tree?

You inherited your DNA from your parents, so the extent to which DNA affects health is largely hereditary. Does your family have a history of heart disease, diabetes, or obesity? What about other chronic diseases or conditions? Before you learn about the role that healthy eating plays in preventing chronic diseases, ask your parents and grandparents about your family's health history. If there are certain diseases or conditions that run in your family, you'll want to pay particular attention to these as you learn more throughout this book.

An easy way to gather information about your family's health history is by visiting My Family Health Portrait at http://familyhistory.hhs.gov. The site generates a family tree report according to the medical history you enter. Save a copy of the report for future reference.

Individuals without these gene variants are not salt sensitive and must rely on other means, including medications, to reduce hypertension.

The area of research that studies the relationship between gene expression, nutrition, and health, called **nutritional genomics,** may have far-reaching effects on health and disease. Until this new science emerged, nutrition research and the study of genetics contributed separately to the body of knowledge about chronic disease. Studied together, these two fields help us understand the interaction between genes and nutrients, and whether the genes are responding to the nutrients we eat (nutrigenetics), or whether the nutrients themselves influence genetic expression (nutrigenomics).

Recent advances in nutritional genomics have already yielded potential clinical applications. For example, research has shown a relationship between chronic inflammation and certain bioactive compounds found in food, including resveratrol in the skin of red grapes, theaflavins in tea, omega-3 fatty acids in flaxseed and fish, and lactones in chicory (a coffee substitute).[39] Adding foods to the diet that contain these compounds may regulate the genes that cause inflammation.

Nutritional genomics may have tremendous potential to provide personalized dietary recommendations based on an individual's genetic makeup. Ultimately, future Registered Dietitians may be able to use this information to recommend diet modifications that are specific to a patient's DNA.

The Best Way to Meet Nutrient Needs Is with a Well-Balanced Diet

Most credible nutrition experts will tell you that the best way to maintain nutritional health is to eat a variety of whole foods. Among the reasons for this recommendation is that many foods provide a variety of nutrients. For example, low-fat milk is high in carbohydrates and protein, and provides a small amount of fat. Milk is also a good source of the vitamins A, D, and riboflavin, as well as the minerals potassium and calcium, and is approximately 90 percent water by weight.

Whole foods and a well-balanced diet will also provide other dietary compounds, including phytochemicals, zoochemicals, and fiber, which have been shown to help fight many diseases. Further, whole foods almost always contain more than one beneficial compound.

nutritional genomics A field of study of the relationship between genes, gene expression, and nutrition.

Improving Health through Functional Foods, Phytochemicals, and Zoochemicals

Americans have been consuming **functional foods** to improve their health since the late 1920s, when iodine was first added to salt. Today's functional foods include whole foods such as oatmeal, genetically modified foods that are developed to have a higher nutrient content, and foods that have been fortified with **phytochemicals** and **zoochemicals.**

Phytochemicals are nonnutritive plant chemicals that can be added to foods to reduce your risk of developing certain diseases. At least 900 different phytochemicals have been identified in foods and more are likely to be discovered. The disease-fighting properties of phytochemicals may be due to more than the compounds themselves, and instead result from the interactions between the phytochemicals and fiber, nutrients, or unknown substances in foods. Thus, these compounds cannot be extracted from foods, put in a pill, and still produce the same positive health effect. Foods with phytochemicals added have the same appearance and taste as your favorites but provide added health benefits.

Zoochemicals are naturally occurring chemicals found in animal foods that have health-enhancing properties such as strong antioxidant benefits.[40] Examples include lutein and zeaxanthin found in egg yolks, which may protect against macular degeneration or the formation of cataracts.[41] Omega-3 fatty acids from fish, added to butter substitutes and eggs, may improve heart health and reduce inflammation, protecting us against heart disease, cancer, and a decline in cognitive function.[42]

functional foods Foods that may provide additional health benefits beyond the basic nutrient value.

phytochemicals Nonnutritive plant compounds, found in fruits and vegetables, that may play a role in fighting chronic diseases.

zoochemicals Nonnutritive animal compounds that play a role in fighting chronic diseases.

Some Nutrient Needs Can Be Met with a Supplement

Some individuals with diet restrictions or higher nutrient needs may benefit from taking a supplement if they cannot meet their nutrient requirements through whole foods alone. For example, someone who is lactose intolerant (has difficulty digesting milk products) has to meet his or her calcium needs from sources other than dairy products. A calcium-fortified food, such as orange juice, or a calcium supplement would be an option for such an individual. Pregnant women should take an iron supplement because their increased need for this mineral is unlikely to be met through a healthy diet alone.

Note that a well-balanced diet and dietary supplements aren't mutually exclusive. In some situations, the use of enriched and fortified foods can be partnered with dietary supplements as the best nutritional strategy for good health.

THE TAKE-HOME MESSAGE A well-balanced diet is the best way to meet all nutrient needs and also provide a variety of compounds that may help prevent chronic diseases. Nutritional genomics is an evolving scientific field that studies how diet may modify the way genes work, and how genetic makeup affects nutrient requirements. People who cannot meet their nutrient needs through food alone may benefit from taking a supplement or consuming functional foods high in phytochemicals and zoochemicals to reduce the risk of developing certain diseases.

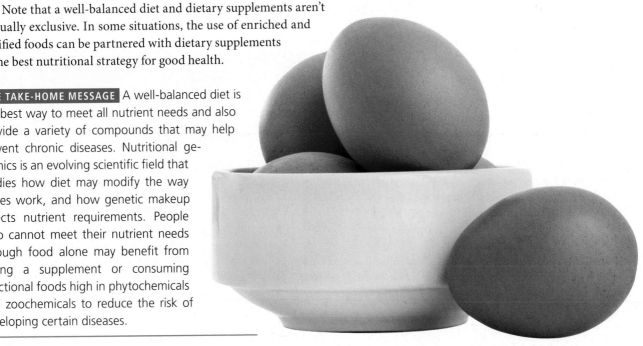

Visual Chapter Summary

1 Food Choices Are Influenced by Many Factors

Food choices are influenced by personal taste, culture, environment, social life, trends, weight concerns, body image, advertising, time, convenience, cost, and health beliefs. People often eat out of habit, in response to emotions, and, of course, because food is delicious.

2 Nutrition Is the Science of Food

Nutrition is the science that studies the nutrient components and health effects of food, as well as how food is digested, absorbed, and metabolized by the body. There are six categories of nutrients: carbohydrates, lipids, proteins, vitamins, minerals, and water.

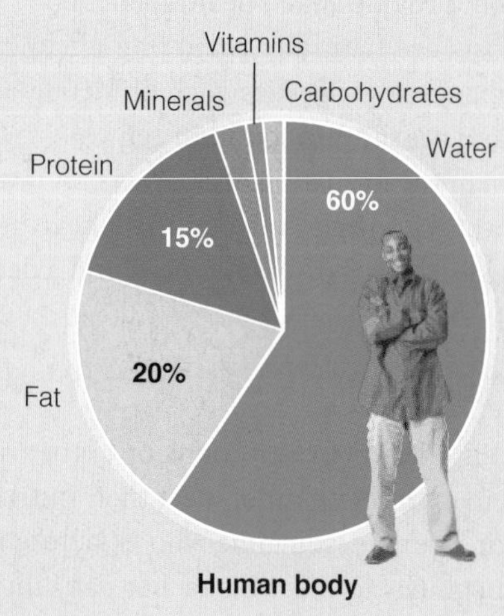

3 Individual Nutrients Have Primary Roles in the Body

Carbohydrates, fats (lipids), and proteins provide energy in the form of kilocalories. Carbohydrates are the body's preferred source of energy. Fats insulate the body and cushion internal organs. The primary role of dietary protein is to build and maintain body tissues. Protein also acts as enzymes that catalyze chemical reactions. Vitamins and minerals do not provide energy but are necessary to properly metabolize carbohydrates, fats, and protein. Many vitamins aid enzymes in the body. Water bathes the inside and outside of the cells, helps maintain body temperature, acts as a lubricant and protective cushion, and delivers nutrients and oxygen to the cells.

Carbohydrates and proteins each contain 4 kilocalories per gram, while fats contain 9 kilocalories per gram. Alcohol, though not a nutrient, also contains energy at 7 kilocalories per gram.

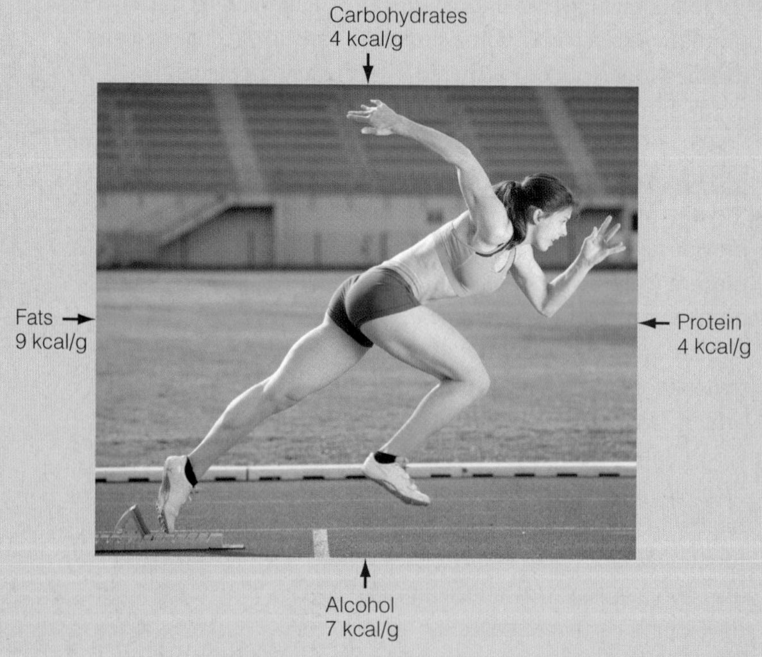

4 Credible Nutrition Research Is Found in Scientific Journals

Sound nutrition information is the result of numerous research studies based on the scientific method that are reviewed by the medical and scientific community.

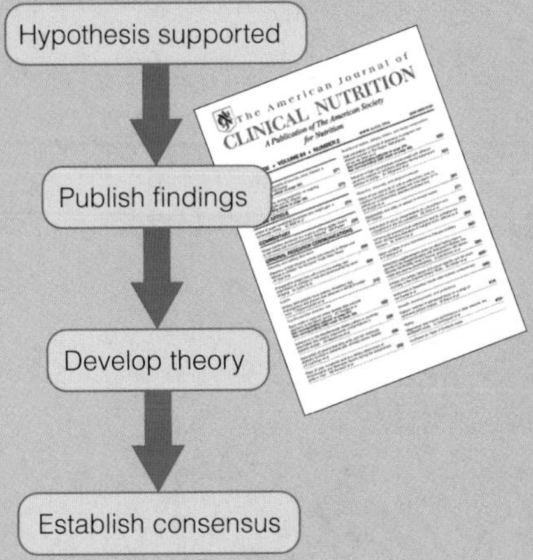

5 We Assess Nutritional Status Using the ABCD Method

Reliable nutrition information can be obtained from Registered Dietitians, licensed nutritionists, or professionals with advanced degrees in nutrition. Nutrient assessment methods for individuals include assessing health history, collecting anthropometric and biochemical laboratory data, clinical observation, and dietary intake surveys. The nutritional status of population groups is determined by national surveys, including the National Health and Nutrition Examination Survey (NHANES), the Behavioral Risk Factor Surveillance System (BRFSS), and the Framingham Heart Study.

6 The American Diet Doesn't Stack Up

Most Americans are not meeting all their nutrient needs without exceeding their kilocalorie requirements. The average American diet is high in protein, sugar, sodium, saturated fat, and kilocalories, but low in vitamin E, calcium, and fiber. In addition, the rates of overweight and obesity among Americans are too high.

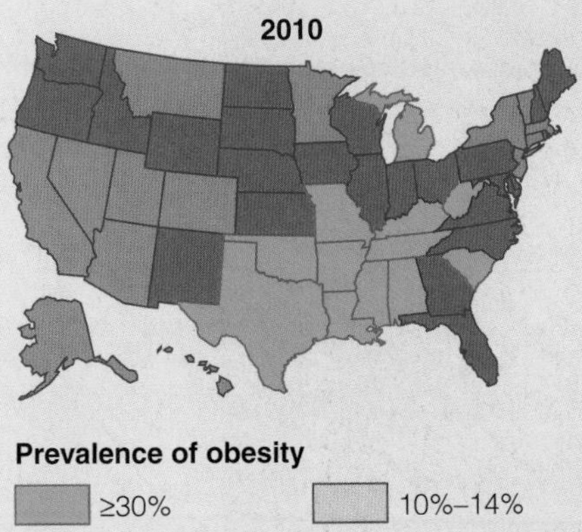

7 The American Diet Impacts Our Overall Health

Nutrition plays an important role in preventing many of the leading causes of death in the United States, including heart disease, cancer, stroke, and type 2 diabetes. Interactions between nutrition and disease are explored in the science of nutritional genomics, which studies how diet may modify the way genes work and how genetic makeup affects nutrient requirements.

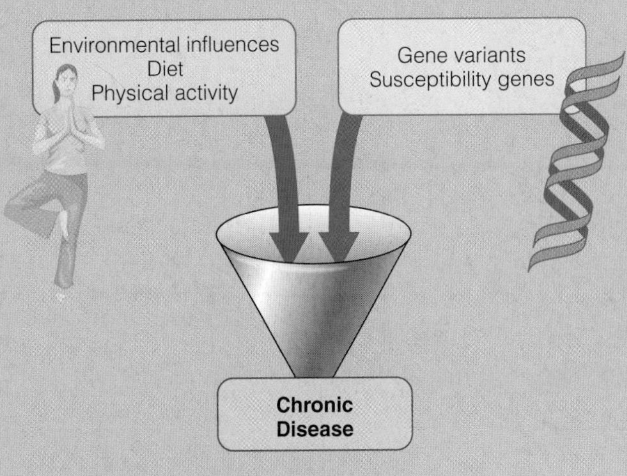

Terms to Know

- nutrition
- nutrients
- organic
- inorganic
- essential
- nonessential nutrients
- adenosine triphosphate (ATP)
- energy-yielding nutrients
- kilocalorie
- macronutrients
- micronutrients
- enzymes
- coenzymes
- water-soluble vitamins
- fat-soluble vitamins
- major minerals
- trace minerals
- scientific method
- malnourished
- undernourished
- overnourished
- Registered Dietitian (RD)
- *Healthy People 2020*
- gene expression
- nutritional genomics
- functional foods
- phytochemicals
- zoochemicals

MasteringNutrition™

Want extra practice with key terms in this chapter? Or, would you like additional questions to prep for an exam? Check out the Study Area of MasteringNutrition at www.masteringnutrition.pearson.com (http://pearsonmylabandmastering.com). There you'll find everything from pre-built flashcards that can be downloaded to your smartphone for studying on-the-go to chapter reading quizzes that assess your knowledge of the chapter—and so much more!

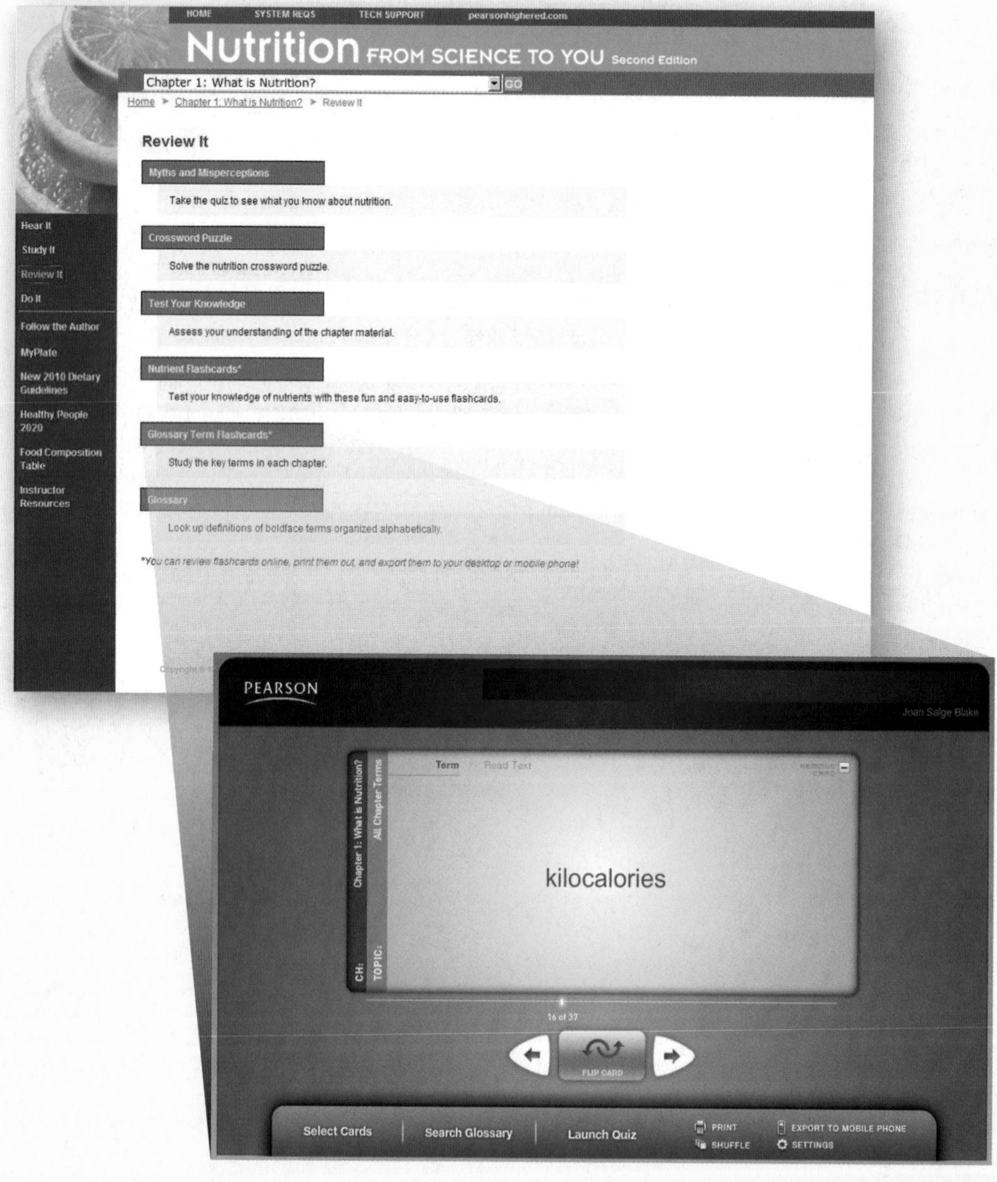

Check Your Understanding

1. Which of the following influences food choice?
   a. ethnic background
   b. time constraints
   c. emotions
   d. all of the above
2. Nutrition is
   a. the study of genes, how they function in the body, and the environment.
   b. the study of how the body functions.
   c. the study of nutrients and compounds in foods that nourish and affect body functions and health.
   d. the study of hormones and how they function in the body.
3. Minerals are considered an organic nutrient because they contain the element carbon.
   a. true
   b. false
4. Which of the following functions do nutrients perform in the body?
   a. Nutrients provide energy.
   b. Nutrients provide structure for bone, muscle, and other tissues.
   c. Nutrients facilitate metabolism.
   d. Nutrients perform all of the above functions.
5. A slice of whole-wheat bread contains 1 gram of fat, 18 grams of carbohydrate, and 4 grams of protein. How many kilocalories does it contain?
   a. 65 kilocalories
   b. 72 kilocalories
   c. 89 kilocalories
   d. 97 kilocalories
6. The first step in the scientific method is to
   a. make observations and ask questions.
   b. form a hypothesis.
   c. do an experiment.
   d. develop a theory.
7. When exploring a website that provides nutrition and health information, which of the following should you consider to assess its content?
   a. who wrote it
   b. when it was written
   c. when it was last updated
   d. all of the above
8. You want to lose weight and decide to seek the help of a professional to have your diet assessed. Which of the following individuals would be the most credible source of information?
   a. an employee at the local health food store
   b. a personal trainer at the gym
   c. a Registered Dietitian
   d. your aunt
   e. your roommate, who runs for the campus track team
9. The overarching goal of *Healthy People 2020* is
   a. to help Americans attain high-quality, longer lives free of preventable disease, disability, injury, and premature death.
   b. to increase the hours Americans sleep each night.
   c. to eliminate added sugars in school lunch programs across the nation.
   d. to reduce the cost of food for all Americans.
10. Dietary supplements are essential for an overall healthy diet.
    a. true
    b. false

Answers

1. (d) Food choices are influenced by many factors, including ethnic background, the limited time for food preparation and/or shopping, and emotions.
2. (c) Nutrition is the science related to how nutrients are used in the body and how they affect health. The study of genes is called genomics. Physiology is the study of how the body functions. The study of hormones is called endocrinology.
3. (b) Minerals are actually inorganic nutrients because they do not contain carbon. Nutrients that do contain carbon, including protein, carbohydrates, lipids, and vitamins, are classified as organic.
4. (d) Nutrients help perform numerous vital body functions. Carbohydrates, protein, and fats provide energy in the form of kilocalories; protein and some minerals help build body tissues; and several vitamins and minerals are essential during metabolic processes.
5. (d) A slice of bread contains 97 kilocalories: (18 g $\times$ 4 kcal) + (4 g $\times$ 4 kcal) + (1 g $\times$ 9 kcal).
6. (a) The scientific method begins with scientists observing and asking questions. From this step, a hypothesis follows. The scientists will then test their hypothesis using an experiment. After many experiments confirm their hypothesis, a theory will be developed.
7. (d) When reading nutrition and health information on the Internet, it is very important to make sure the source is qualified to provide the information. Because you also need to assess if the information is current, you should find out when it was written and if it has been or needs to be updated.
8. (c) Unless the health food store employee, personal trainer, your aunt, and your roommate are Registered Dietitians, they are not qualified to provide nutrition counseling.
9. (a) *Healthy People 2020* has set helping Americans attain high-quality, longer lives free of preventable disease, disability, injury, and premature death as one of four overarching goals. Increasing the amount of hours Americans sleep, eliminating added sugars from school lunches, and reducing the cost of food for Americans are not overarching goals of *Healthy People 2020*.
10. (b) Dietary supplements can be beneficial for individuals with diet restrictions or higher nutrient needs, but they are not essential. Consuming a diet rich in a variety of whole foods is the best way to achieve a healthy, well-balanced diet.

Answers to Myths and Misconceptions

1. **True.** Taste is the strongest motivating factor for choosing foods. However, numerous other factors, including culture, social setting, health, advertising, habit, emotion, time, cost, and convenience, also play a role in food choice.
2. **False.** Heart disease is the leading cause of death among Americans. The good news is that your diet can play an important role in preventing it.
3. **False.** Dietary fat is essential for several body functions, including its role in providing energy.
4. **False.** Whereas alcohol does provide kilocalories, eliminating it from the diet would not result in malnutrition. Therefore, alcohol is not a nutrient.
5. **True.** Kilocalories are the measure of energy in foods.
6. **False.** Like carbohydrate, protein provides 4 kilocalories per gram, while fat provides 9 kilocalories per gram. Therefore, fat provides more energy per gram than protein.
7. **False.** The 24-hour food record is one tool for gathering information about the quality of an individual's diet, but it doesn't reveal a complete picture. Long-term food records, interviews, and anthropometric data are additional tools that can help a dietitian assess an individual's eating habits.
8. **False.** There is no standard or legal definition of the word "nutritionist," so it does not convey expert status. In fact, anyone can call himself or herself a nutritionist.
9. **False.** The rate of obesity in American adults shows little sign of declining. In 2010, more than 35 percent of adult Americans were considered obese.
10. **False.** There is no replacement for whole foods in a healthy diet. A supplement can augment a healthy diet, but it can't replace it.

Web Resources

Examples of reliable nutrition and health websites include:

- Agricultural Research Service: www.ars.usda.gov
- American Cancer Society: www.cancer.org
- American College of Sports Medicine: www.acsm.org
- Academy of Nutrition and Dietetics: www.eatright.org
- American Medical Association: www.ama-assn.org
- Center for Science in the Public Interest: www.cspinet.org
- Centers for Disease Control and Prevention: www.cdc.gov
- Food and Drug Administration: www.fda.gov
- Food and Nutrition Information Center: www.nal.usda.gov/fnic
- National Institutes of Health: www.nih.gov
- Shape Up America!: www.shapeup.org
- Tufts University Health and Nutrition Newsletter: www.healthletter.tufts.edu
- Nutrition.gov: www.nutrition.gov
- Vegetarian Resource Group: www.vrg.org

References

1. Wansink, B. and J. Sobal. 2007. Mindless Eating: The 200 Daily Food Decisions We Overlook. *Environment and Behavior* 39:106–123.
2. Glanz, K., M. Basil, E. Maibach, J. Goldberg, and D. Snyder. 1998. Why Americans Eat What They Do: Taste, Nutrition, Cost, Convenience, and Weight Control Concerns as Influences on Food Consumption. *Journal of the American Dietetic Association* 98:1118–1126.
3. Keskitalo, K., A. Knaapila, M. Kallela, A. Palotie, M. Wessman, S. Sammalisto, L. Peltonen, H. Tuorila, and M. Perola. 2007. Sweet Taste Preferences Are Partly Genetically Determined: Identification of a Trait Locus on Chromosome 16. *American Journal of Clinical Nutrition* 86:55–63.
4. Cooke, L. J. and J. Wardle. 2005. Age and Gender Differences in Children's Food Preferences. *British Journal of Nutrition* 93:741–746.
5. Keskitalo, K., et al. 2007. Sweet Taste Preferences.
6. Drewnowski, A. and M. R. Greenwood. 1983. Cream and Sugar: Human Preferences for High-Fat Foods. *Physiology & Behavior* 30:629–633.
7. Drewnowski, A. 1997. Taste Preferences and Food Intake. *Annual Review of Nutrition* 17:237–253.
8. Mennella, J. A. 2007. Sweet Taste and Development. In *Handbook of the Senses: Olfaction and Taste*. G. Smith, D. S. Firestein, and S. Firestein, eds. San Diego: Elsevier.
9. Sneijder, P. and H. F. Te Molder. 2005. Disputing Taste: Food Pleasure as an Achievement in Interaction. *Appetite* 45:51–61.
10. Wansink, B. 2004. Environmental Factors That Increase the Food Intake and Consumption Volume of Unknowing Consumers. *Annual Review of Nutrition* 24:455–470.
11. National Turkey Federation. 2004. *Turkey Facts and Trivia*. Available at www.eatturkey.com/consumer/history/history.html. Accessed January 2012.
12. Freeland-Graves, J. and S. Nitzke. 2002. Total Diet Approach to Communicating Food and Nutrition Information. *Journal of the American Dietetic Association* 102:100–108.
13. Coomes, S. 2006, February. Pizza Marketplace. Personal communication.
14. Mintel International Group. 2005. Cinemas and Movie Theaters—United States. *Mintel Reports-USA, Leisure-USA*. Available at www.reports.mintel.com. Accessed January 2012.
15. Organic Trade Association. 2011. *2011 Organic Industry Survey*. Available at www.ota.com/organic/mt/business.html. Accessed January 2012.
16. Agricultural Marketing Resource Center. 2011. *Food Consumption Trends*. 2008. Available at www.agmrc.org. Accessed January 2012.
17. Carels, R. A., K. Konrada, and J. Harper. 2007. Individual Differences in Food Perceptions and Calorie Estimation: An Examination of Dieting Status, Weight, and Gender. *Appetite* 49:450–458.
18. Kolodinsky, J., J. R. Harvey-Berino, L. Berlin, R. K. Johnson, and T. W. Reynolds. 2007. Knowledge of Current Dietary Guidelines and Food Choice by College Students: Better Eaters Have Higher Knowledge of Dietary Guidance. *Journal of the American Dietetic Association* 107:1409–1413.
19. Gallo, A. 1999. Food Advertising in the United States. In *America's Eating Habits: Changes and Consequences*. Edited by Economic Research Service. Available at www.ers.usda.gov. Accessed January 2012.
20. Linn, S. and C. L. Novosat. 2008. Calories for Sale: Food Marketing to Children in the Twenty-First Century. *Annals of the American Academy of Political and Social Science* 615:133–155.
21. Story, M. and S. French. 2004. Food Advertising and Marketing Directed at Children and Adolescents in the U.S. *International Journal of Behavioral Nutrition and Physical Activity* 1:1–17.

22. Blisard, N. 1999. Advertising and How We Eat: The Case of Dairy Products. In *America's Eating Habits: Changes and Consequences.* Edited by Economic Research Service.
23. Economic Research Service. 2011. *How Much Time Do Americans Spend on Food?* Available at www.ers.usda.gov/Publications/EI886. Accessed January 2012.
24. Speciality Coffee Association. *Retail in the USA 2004–2007.* Available at www.scaa.org. Accessed January 2012.
25. U.S. Department of Agriculture. 2011. *Table 12 in Food CPI, Prices and Expenditure Tables: Food Expenditure Table.* Available at www.ers.usda.gov/data-products/food-expenditures.aspx. Accessed January 2012.
26. Drewnowski, A. and N. Darmon. 2005. The Economics of Obesity: Dietary Energy Density and Energy Cost. *American Journal of Clinical Nutrition* 82:265S–273S.
27. Abusabha, R., D. Namjoshi, and A. Klein. 2011. Increasing Access and Affordability of Produce Improves Perceived Consumption of Vegetables in Low-Income Seniors. *Journal of the American Dietetic Association* 111:1549–1555.
28. French, S. A. 2003. Pricing Effects on Food Choices. *Journal of Nutrition* 133:841S–843S.
29. Mintel International Group. 2008. *Breakfast Foods: The Consumer—US.* Available at www.marketresearch.com. Accessed January 2012.
30. Cleland, V. J., M. D. Schmidt, T. Dwyer, and A. J. Venn. 2008. Television Viewing and Abdominal Obesity in Young Adults: Is the Association Mediated by Food and Beverage Consumption during Viewing Time or Reduced Leisure-Time Physical Activity? *American Journal of Clinical Nutrition* 87:1148–1155.
31. Osowski, J. M., T. Beare, and B. Specker. 2007. Validation of a Food Frequency Questionnaire for Assessment of Calcium and Bone-Related Nutrient Intake in Rural Populations. *Journal of the American Dietetic Association* 107:1349–1355.
32. Wang, D., M. Kogashiwa, and S. Kira. 2006. Development of a New Instrument for Evaluating Individuals' Dietary Intakes. *Journal of the American Dietetic Association* 106:1588–1593.
33. Briefel, R. R. 2007. Dietary Methodology: Advancements in the Development of Short Instruments to Assess Dietary Fat. *Journal of the American Dietetic Association* 107:744–749.
34. U.S. Department of Agriculture, Agricultural Research Service. 2008. *Nutrient Intakes from Food: Mean Amounts Consumed per Individual, One Day, 2005–2006.* Available at www.ars.usda.gov/ba/bhnrc.fsrg. Accessed January 2012.
35. Abbot, J. M. and C. Byrd-Bredbenner. 2007. The State of the American Diet: How Can We Cope? *Topics in Clinical Nutrition* 22: 202–233.
36. Centers for Disease Control. 2012. *U.S. Obesity Trends.* Available at www.cdc.gov. Accessed July 2012.
37. U.S. Department of Health and Preventative Services. 2010. *Healthy People 2020.* Available at www.healthypeople.gov/2020/about/default.aspx. Accessed January 2012.
38. Centers for Disease Control. *U.S. Obesity Trends.*
39. Afman, L. and M. Muller. 2007. Nutrigenomics: From Molecular Nutrition to Prevention of Disease. *Journal of the American Dietetic Association* 106:569–576.
40. deGoede, J., J. Geleijnse, et al. 2010. Marine (Ω-3) Fatty Acids, Fish Consumption, and the 10-year Risk of Fatal and Nonfatal Coronary Heart Disease in a Large Population of Dutch Adults with Low Fish Intake. *Journal of Nutrition* 140:1023–1028.
41. Ma, L. and X. M. Lin. 2010. Effects of Lutein and Zeaxanthin on Aspects of Eye Health. *Journal of Science and Food Agriculture* 90:2–12.
42. Danthir, V., N. R. Burns, T. Nettelbeck, C. Wilson, and G. Wittert. 2011. The Older People, Omega-3, and Cognitive Health (EPOCH) Trial Design and Methodology: A Randomised, Double-blind, Controlled Trial Investigating the Effect of Long-chain Omega-3 Fatty Acids on Cognitive Ageing and Wellbeing in Cognitively Healthy Older Adults. *Nutrition Journal* 10:117. Available at http://www.nutritionj.com/content/10/1/117. Accessed January 2012.

2 Tools for Healthy Eating

Chapter Objectives

After reading this chapter, you will be able to:

1. Describe the key principles of a healthy diet, and define the terms nutrient density and energy density.
2. Discuss the differences between the EAR, AI, RDA, UL, and AMDR.
3. Describe the principles in the 2010 *Dietary Guidelines for Americans*.
4. Define the food groups, number of servings or portion sizes, and typical foods represented in the MyPlate food guide.
5. Describe how the exchange system can be used as a guide to plan a balanced diet.
6. Identify the required components of a food label, and determine the nutritional adequacy of a food based on the food label and Nutrition Facts panel.

1. Having a balanced diet means eating the same number servings from each food group. T/F
2. Nutrient density refers to foods that are lower in weight relative to volume. T/F
3. The current Dietary Reference Intakes for vitamins and minerals are set at the amount you should consume daily to maintain good health. T/F
4. The Recommended Dietary Allowance of a nutrient is based on an estimated average requirement, or EAR. T/F
5. According to the USDA, there are five basic food groups. T/F
6. If you follow the advice in the *Dietary Guidelines for Americans* you can reduce your risk of dying from chronic diseases such as heart disease, high blood pressure, and diabetes mellitus. T/F
7. Americans typically have a good sense of portion sizes. T/F
8. All packaged foods must contain a food label. T/F
9. A nutrient claim on the food label boasts that the food contains a significant source of a specific nutrient. T/F
10. Exchange lists are similar to MyPlate except the foods are based on the carbohydrate, protein, fat, and kilocalorie contents. T/F

See page 70 for answers to these Myths and Misconceptions.

Many Americans believe that to eat a healthful diet means giving up their favorite foods. Nothing could be farther from the truth! With a little planning, you can still occasionally eat almost any food even if it contains added sugars and fat and is high in kilocalories. All it takes are the right tools to balance those higher kilocalorie foods with more nutritious choices each day.

The good news is that a number of tools are available to help you achieve a healthful, balanced eating plan. In this chapter we will learn how to use these tools in a positive, consistent manner that over time will lead to better eating habits while still enjoying those comfort foods. Let's begin with a discussion on what is healthy eating.

A meal that contains foods from every food group is part of a balanced, healthy diet.

What Is Healthy Eating?

Healthy eating involves the key principles of **balance, variety,** and **moderation.** As a student, you are probably familiar with these principles from other areas of your life. You balance your time between work, school, family, and friends. You engage in a variety of activities to avoid being bored, and enjoy each in moderation, as spending too much time on one activity (like working) will disrupt the amount of time you can spend on others (like studying or socializing). A chronic imbalance of any one of these activities will affect the others. If you regularly forgo sleep in order to work extra hours at a job, sleep deprivation will affect your ability to stay awake in class, which will hamper your studies. Your unbalanced life would soon become unhealthy and unhappy. Likewise, your diet must be balanced, varied, and moderate in order to be healthy. Two additional principles that are essential to healthy eating are the concepts of **nutrient density** and **energy density.**

balance The diet principle of providing the correct proportion of nutrients to maintain health and prevent disease.

variety The diet principle of consuming a mixture of different food groups and foods within each group.

moderation The diet principle of providing reasonable but not excessive amounts of foods and nutrients.

nutrient density A measurement of the nutrients in a food compared with the kilocalorie content; nutrient-dense foods are high in nutrients and low in kilocalories.

energy density A measurement of the kilocalories in a food compared with the weight (grams) of the food.

undernutrition A state of inadequate nutrition whereby a person's nutrient and/or energy needs aren't met through the diet.

malnutrition The long-term outcome of consuming a diet that is either lacking in the essential nutrients or contains excess energy; an imbalance of nutrients in the diet.

overnutrition The state of consuming excess nutrients or energy.

Healthy Eating Involves Balance between Food Groups

A balanced diet includes healthy proportions of all nutrients and is adequate in energy. A diet that lacks balance can cause **undernutrition.** For instance, a student subsisting largely on bread, bagels, muffins, crackers, chips, and cookies might be eating too much carbohydrate and fat but too little protein, vitamins, and minerals. If the diet lacks a particular nutrient, such as protein, over time the body suffers from **malnutrition.** A meal that contains foods from the grain, vegetable, fruit, meat, and dairy groups, such as a lunch of a turkey-and-cheese sandwich with lettuce and tomato plus an apple, provides the proper proportion of foods from each of the food groups. This balancing act prevents **overnutrition** of a specific nutrient, such as fat,[1] or too many kilocalories, which can lead to overweight and obesity. Consuming adequate amounts of all essential nutrients is key to avoiding nutrient deficiencies, and, in many cases, chronic disease.

Healthy Eating Means Consuming a Variety of Foods

Choosing a variety of foods will improve the quality of the diet because the more varied the food choices, the better the chance of consuming adequate amounts of all the essential nutrients.[2] Even within one food group, the nutrient composition of foods can vary dramatically. For example, while broccoli is a good source of folate, it has less than half the vitamin A of a carrot. Similarly, if the only fruit you eat is bananas, your diet would include an excellent source of potassium, but little vitamin C. Because no single food or food group contains everything you need to be healthy, you should choose a variety of foods from within each food group and among food groups each day to achieve a healthy diet. This is the basic principle of the *Fruits & Veggies—More Matters* campaign developed by the Produce for Better Health Foundation and the Centers for Disease Control and Prevention.[3] This campaign promotes eating a variety of colorful fruits and vegetables, which are rich in vitamins, minerals, fiber, and phytochemicals, each day to help reduce the risk of cancer and heart disease, and slow the effects of aging.

Healthy Eating Means Moderate Intake of All Foods

According to many Registered Dietitians, "there are no good or bad foods, just good or bad habits." What they mean is that all foods—even less nutritious foods—can be part of a healthy diet, as long as they are consumed in moderation. Foods such as sweets and fried or packaged snack foods should be eaten only in small amounts to avoid consuming too much sugar and fat. Eating too much of these foods can also mean taking in more energy than you need, potentially resulting in weight gain. Finally, these foods can displace more nutrient-rich choices, resulting in a diet that lacks essential nutrients. Even some healthy foods, such as nutrient-dense nuts, can be high in kilocalories and should be consumed in moderation. Healthy eating doesn't mean you can't enjoy your favorite foods. It simply means eating those foods in moderation by limiting the **portion** size and number of servings you eat.

Many people overestimate the appropriate portion sizes of foods. An entire body of research is devoted to studying factors that affect how much we put on our plates (see "Portion Distortion" for more on this topic). The important point is that, in general, we consume two or more portions of a given food at a given meal. Fortunately, one easy way to tell if you are helping yourself to too much of a food is to use a visual that represents a standard **serving size** of the food, such as a cup of vegetables, three ounces of meat, or 1 tablespoon of salad dressing. See **Figure 2.1** for examples of visuals you can use to estimate portion sizes.

portion The quantity of a food usually eaten at one sitting.

serving size A recommended portion of food that is used as a standard reference on food labels.

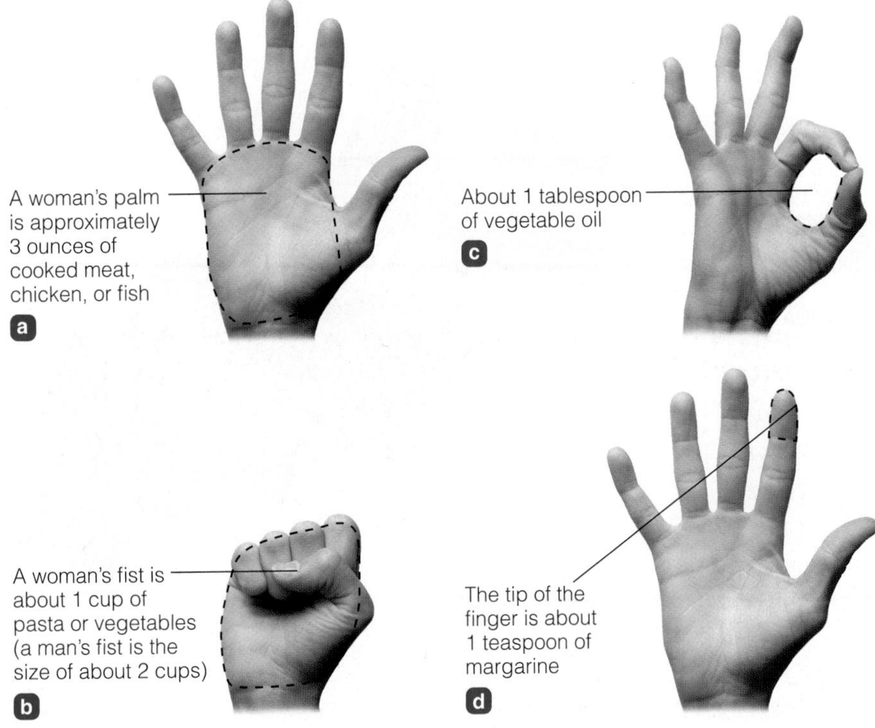
A woman's palm is approximately 3 ounces of cooked meat, chicken, or fish
a
About 1 tablespoon of vegetable oil
c
A woman's fist is about 1 cup of pasta or vegetables (a man's fist is the size of about 2 cups)
b
The tip of the finger is about 1 teaspoon of margarine
d

◂ **Figure 2.1 What's a Portion Size? Eat with Your Hands!**
Your hands can help you estimate the appropriate portion size of foods.

SPOTLIGHT

Portion Distortion

Portion distortion, or perceiving larger portions of food as appropriate sizes, may be contributing to obesity. These larger-than-recommended portion sizes, which are viewed as typical by Americans today, add more kilocalories to our diets and may contribute to weight gain.

The typical portion of pasta (left) is often much larger than the recommended serving size (right).

Portion versus Serving Size: What's the Difference?

The USDA defines a portion as the amount of food eaten at one sitting rather than a standard size of the food. In contrast, a serving size (a term that's only used on nutrient labels) is a standard amount of food for which the nutrient composition is presented. We can illustrate the difference with a food that people often pile on their plates, such as spaghetti. A generous helping of cooked spaghetti that spills over the edge of a plate is probably equal to about 3 cups. According to MyPlate, a standard serving size of pasta is ½ cup. A portion of 3 cups of cooked pasta is therefore six servings, which contains more than 600 kilocalories!

Unfortunately, many of us frequently underestimate the portion sizes we put on our plates, and therefore overconsume foods during snacks and mealtimes.[1] The table below illustrates several foods that people commonly consume in oversized portions.

How Have Portion Sizes Changed?

If your great-grandmother treated herself to a Hershey's chocolate bar when it was first introduced, at the beginning of the last century, she would have paid a small amount of money for about 0.6 ounce of chocolate. Today the same milk chocolate bar is sold in 0.75-, 1.6-, 2.6-, 4.0-, 7.0-, and 8.0-ounce weights. When McDonald's first introduced french fries in 1954, the standard serving weighed 2.4 ounces. Although a small 2.4-ounce size is still on the menu, you can also choose the medium french fries weighing 5.3 ounces or the large at 6.3 ounces. Twenty years ago, a cup of coffee was 8 ounces and just 45 kilocalories with added milk and sugar. Today, consumers enjoy 16-ounce lattes on their way to work, to the tune of 350 kilocalories.[2]

The restaurant industry has appealed to Americans' interest in getting more food for less money with larger portion sizes at relatively low costs.[3] Americans eat out more often than they did in the past, and are offered a wide variety of inexpensive choices sold in larger-than-normal portion sizes that often exceed the standards defined by the federal

Comparison of Portion Sizes of Common Foods

Food	Typical Portion	Recommended Serving Size	FDA Label
Cooked pasta	2.9 cups	0.5 cup	1.0 cup
French fries	5.3 oz	10 fries	2.5 oz
Bagel	4.4 oz	1.0 oz	2.0 oz
Muffin	6.5 oz	1.5 oz	2.0 oz
Cookie, chocolate chip	4.0 oz	0.5 oz	1.1 oz

Source: Adapted from L. R. Young and M. Nestle. 2003. "Expanding Portion Sizes in the U.S. Marketplace: Implications for Nutrition Counseling." *Journal of the American Dietetic Association* 103:231–234.

Hershey's milk chocolate bars now come in several sizes, including 0.75-, 1.6-, 2.6-, 4.0-, 7.0-, and 8.0-ounce versions.

government.[4] And most people are unaware of the changes in their portion sizes.[5] Though getting more food for the money may be beneficial on the wallet, the health costs may be higher than Americans realize.

In addition to restaurant and packaged foods, home-cooked meals have also bulked up over the past few decades. If you were to measure your grandmother's favorite dinner plates, they would likely be much smaller, about 9 inches in diameter, than the plates in your cupboard, which probably measure closer to 11.5 inches across. The bigger the plate, the more food you are likely to add to it. Further, the larger portions you put on your plate influence your perception of what is normal. Thus, a large plate covered with pasta appears to be normal, whereas the ½ cup of pasta suggested by the MyPlate guide seems small.

Another adverse result of oversized portions is that the larger the portion, the less we are able to estimate kilocalorie intake. For example, eating potato chips directly from the bag, rather than taking a handful out of the bag and only eating that portion, will likely mean consuming significantly more kilocalories.

Controlling Portion Size

When You Are	Do This
At Home	■ Measure your food until you develop an "eye" for correct portion sizes ■ Use smaller plates so portions appear larger ■ Plate your food at the counter before sitting down at the table or in front of the television ■ Store leftover foods in portion-controlled containers ■ Don't eat snacks directly from the box or bag; measure a portion first, then eat only that amount ■ Cook smaller quantities of food so you don't pick at the leftovers ■ Keep tempting foods, such as high-sugar or -kilocalorie foods, out of sight
Eating Out	■ Ask for half orders when available ■ Order an appetizer as your entrée ■ Don't be compelled to "clean your plate"; stop eating when you're full and take the rest home
Buying Groceries	■ Divide a package of snacks into individual portion sizes and consume only one portion at any one sitting ■ Be aware of the number of servings in a package; read the labels ■ Buy foods that are already divided into portion sizes, such as 1 oz sliced cheese or lunch meat ■ Avoid "mini" sizes of crackers, cookies, etc.; just because they're small doesn't mean you can eat the whole box!

Health Effects of Increased Portion Size

Research has shown that even slight changes in the portion sizes of typical foods can lead to increased energy intake and weight gain.[6] As body weight increases, the risk of developing cardiovascular disease, diabetes, joint problems, and some cancers also increases.[7]

Tips for Controlling Portion Size

According to recent studies, young adults have distorted views of what a correct portion size should be.[8] To reduce overconsumption of fat and kilocalories, and therefore the likelihood for an unhealthy body weight, consumers need to recognize healthy portion sizes, which are based on serving sizes. Steps that can help reduce oversized portions include buying smaller or single-portion packages of foods, or dividing larger packages into individual portion sizes. In restaurants, order one meal to share with your companion, or split the food in half and take the other half home. In your cupboard, replace larger glasses and plates with smaller versions.

References

1. National Institutes of Health. 2007. *Portion Distortion.* Available at http://hp2010.nhlbihin.net/portion/index.htm.
2. H. Smiciklas-Wright, D. C. Mitchell, S. Mickle, J. Goldman, and A. Cook. 2003. "Foods Commonly Eaten in the United States, 1989–1991 and 1994–1996: Are Portion Sizes Changing?" *Journal of the American Dietetic Association* 103:41–47.
3. L. R. Young and M. Nestle. 2003. "Expanding Portion Sizes in the U.S. Marketplace: Implications for Nutrition Counseling." *Journal of the American Dietetic Association* 103:231–234.
4. N. Diliberti, P. L. Bordi, M. T. Conklin, and B. J. Rolls. 2004. "Increased Portion Size Leads to Increased Energy Intake in a Restaurant Meal." *Obesity Research* 12:562–568.
5. S. J. Nielsen and B. M. Popkin. 2003. "Patterns and Trends in Food Portion Sizes, 1977–1998." *Journal of the American Medical Association* 289:450–453.
6. B. Rolls, L. S. Roe, and J. S. Meengs. 2006. "Larger Portion Sizes Lead to a Sustained Increase in Energy Intake Over 2 Days." *Journal of the American Dietetic Association* 106:543–549.
7. Centers for Disease Control. 2005. *Overweight and Obesity: Obesity Trends.* Available at www.cdc.gov.
8. J. Schwartz and C. Byrd-Bredbenner. 2006. "Portion Distortion: Typical Portion Sizes Selected by Young Adults." *Journal of the American Dietetic Association* 106:1412–1418.

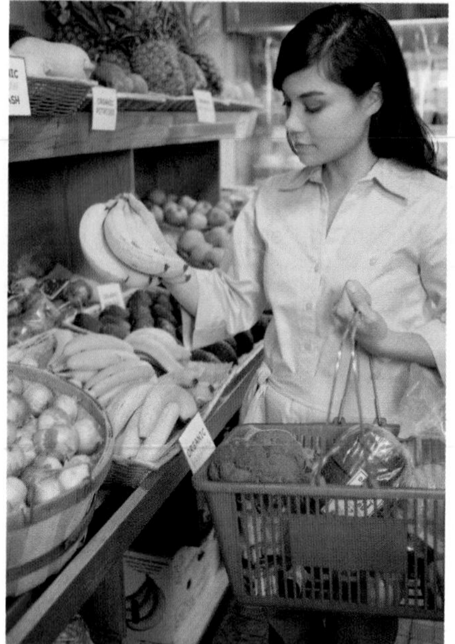

Choosing nutrient-dense foods you enjoy is a key ingredient for eating a healthy diet.

Healthy Eating Involves Nutrient-Dense Foods

Healthy eating includes not only choosing foods based on these key principles of balance, moderation, and variety, but also choosing foods that are nutrient dense. Being nutrient dense means that foods are high in nutrients, such as vitamins and minerals, but low in energy (kilocalories). Nutrient-dense foods provide more nutrients per kilocalorie (and in each bite) than less nutrient-dense foods.[4] Fresh fruits and vegetables, for example, are nutrient dense because they are high in B vitamins, vitamin C, minerals such as calcium and magnesium, and fiber, while usually providing fewer than 60 kilocalories per serving.

Nutrient-dense foods are also low in fat and added sugars. To illustrate this concept, compare the nutrient density of two versions of the same food: a baked potato and potato chips (**Figure 2.2**). Although a medium baked potato and one ounce of potato chips have about the same number of kilocalories, the baked potato provides much higher amounts of vitamins and minerals than the deep-fried chips.

Though many foods, such as broccoli and carrots, are clearly nutrient dense, and other foods, such as potato chips and doughnuts, are clearly not, not all foods fit neatly into these two categories. Items such as dried fruits, nuts, peanut butter, and avocados are high in kilocalories, but they are also excellent sources of important nutrients, including polyunsaturated fatty acids, calcium, and iron. Other foods, such as whole milk or yogurt, contain the same nutrients, but higher amounts of fat and kilocalories than their nonfat or low-fat counterparts. These higher fat versions still provide significant amounts of calcium, riboflavin, vitamins A and D, and protein. Some foods, such as fruit-flavored yogurt and some fortified cereals, contain added sugars in addition to several essential nutrients. Do you think these foods can be considered nutrient dense?

In all of these scenarios, the answer is yes. Whereas nutrient dense usually means high in nutrients and low in energy, foods that are high in nutrients and high in energy can also be considered nutrient dense. The key is to be aware of the extra kilocalories and make up for them elsewhere in the diet. If you don't like skim milk and won't drink it, but do enjoy the taste of whole milk, then drinking whole milk is preferable to drinking non-calcium-containing beverages, such as soda. Just remember that unless you compensate for the extra kilocalories (by cutting that nighttime cookie, for example), you may gain weight.

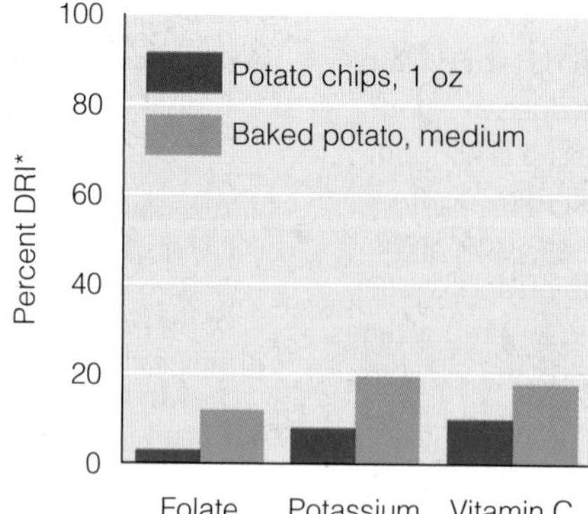

▲ **Figure 2.2 Which Is the Healthier Way to Enjoy Potatoes?**
Whereas one ounce of potato chips and one medium baked potato have similar amounts of kilocalories, their nutrient content is worlds apart. A baked potato contains more folate, potassium, and vitamin C, and fewer fat kilocalories, than its fried counterpart. The baked potato is therefore more nutrient dense than potato chips.

*Note: Based on the percentage of the DRI for 19-to-50-year-old males. All these percentages apply to females in the same age range, except for vitamin C. Females have lower vitamin C needs than males, so a baked potato provides over 20 percent of the DRI of this vitamin for women.

Healthy Eating Involves Low-Energy-Dense Foods

In contrast to nutrient density, energy density refers to foods that are high in energy but low in weight or volume, such as that potato chip. A serving of deep-fried chips weighs much less than a plain baked potato, but is considerably higher in fat and kilocalories. Therefore, the chip contains more energy per gram. A big, leafy green salad, on the other hand, is large in volume but low in energy density, due to its high water content.

Most high-fat foods are considered energy dense.[5] This is because fat has 9 kilocalories per gram and is thus 2.25 times more energy dense than either carbohydrates or protein at 4 kilocalories per gram. Individuals who choose low-energy-dense foods will generally have diets that are lower in fat and higher in nutrient content.

Eating a low-energy-dense diet can sometimes be the key to weight loss. Recent studies have found that leaner individuals ate more low-energy-dense foods and fewer kilocalories, while consuming a greater volume of food, compared with their obese counterparts.[6] Eating low-density foods means larger portions for the same number of kilocalories.

Even modest changes in dietary intake may promote and help maintain weight loss[7] over time.[8] One reason for this may be improved satiety and appetite control.[9] Eating a larger volume of low-energy foods improves satiety and decreases hunger. In other words, low-energy foods will "fill you up before they fill you out."

If you are trying to maintain your current weight, or lose weight, you are probably on a limited energy budget and need to choose foods that are nutrient dense and low in kilocalories. Use the guide in Table 2.1 to help stretch your energy budget while consuming the most nutrient-dense foods.

TABLE 2.1 Bargain Shopping on an Energy Budget

Use the following guidelines when choosing energy-dense foods.

Foods	Energy Density	Are They an Energy Bargain?
Soups Fruits Vegetables	0.0 to 0.6 kcal/g	**Great Bargain:** Eat as much of these low-energy-density foods as you want on a low-energy budget; however, take care that soups don't contain too much sodium, and are broth rather than cream based.
Starchy fruits and vegetables Lean meats Beans and legumes	0.6 to 1.5 kcal/g	**Good Bargain:** Consume healthy portions of these foods on a low-energy budget.
Cheese Salad dressings Snack foods Desserts	1.5 to 4.0 kcal/g	**More Expensive Choices:** These foods should be chosen carefully and consumed in moderation.
Chocolates Deep-fat fried foods Nuts Chips Candy	4.0 to 9.0 kcal/g	**Very Expensive Choices:** Eat less of these foods and be aware of the portion size to avoid over-consuming kilocalories.

Source: Adapted from B. Rolls. 2007. *Volumetrics Eating Plan.* New York: HarperCollins.

▸ **Figure 2.3 Dietary Recommendations and Implementation Tools**
The *Dietary Guidelines for Americans* serve as the basis for several tools that guide Americans in choosing healthy diets.

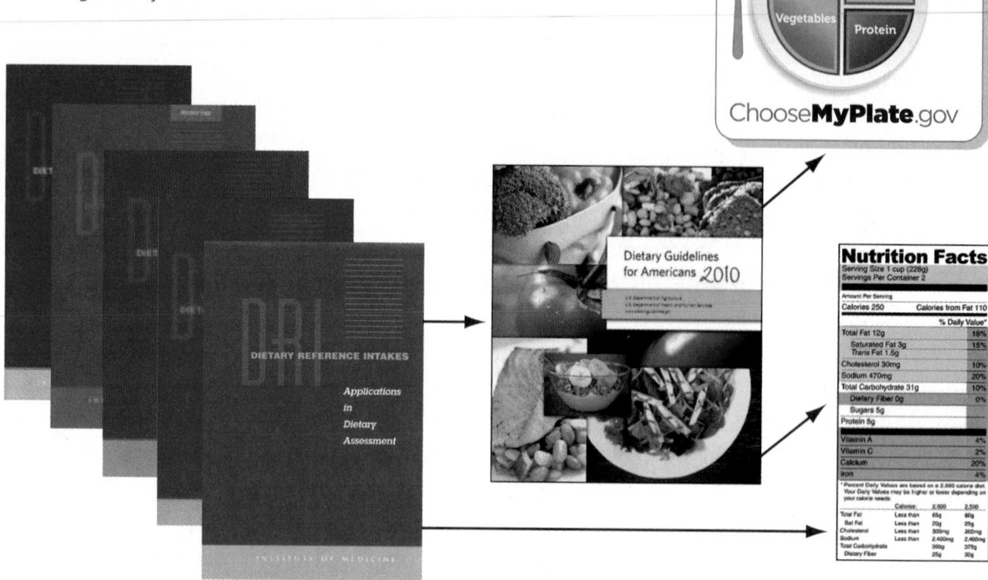

Resources for Planning a Healthy Diet

Do you think all this advice for planning a healthy diet is hard to keep straight? If so, you're not alone. Luckily, there are several resources available to help guide you. Two of these are the **Dietary Reference Intakes (DRIs)** and the ***Dietary Guidelines for Americans.***

The DRIs were developed to improve Americans' intake of individual nutrients (see **Figure 2.3**).[10] They form the basis of the *Dietary Guidelines for Americans*, which provide broad dietary and lifestyle advice.

Two more resources, the **MyPlate** food guidance system and the **Daily Values (DVs),** help implement the DRI recommendations for the purpose of selecting and comparing specific foods. MyPlate reflects recommendations from the DRIs and the advice in the *Dietary Guidelines*. The *Nutrition Facts panel* on food labels contains the Daily Values. Their purpose is to help consumers decide which foods to buy. Together, these reference values, guidelines, and tools can help people plan a varied, moderate, and balanced diet.

Dietary Reference Intakes (DRIs) Reference values for nutrients developed by the Food and Nutrition Board of the Institute of Medicine, used to plan and evaluate the diets of healthy people in the United States and Canada. It includes the Estimated Average Requirement (EAR), the Recommended Dietary Allowance (RDA), the Adequate Intake (AI), and the Tolerable Upper Intake Level (UL).

Dietary Guidelines for Americans Guidelines published every five years by the Department of Health and Human Services and the United States Department of Agriculture that provide dietary and lifestyle advice to healthy individuals aged 2 and older to maintain good health and prevent chronic diseases. They are the basis for the federal food and nutrition education programs.

MyPlate A food guidance system that illustrates the recommendations in the *Dietary Guidelines for Americans* and the Dietary Reference Intakes (DRIs) nutrient goals.

Daily Values (DVs) Reference values developed by the Food and Drug Administration and used on nutrition labels to describe the amount of a nutrient provided in one serving of the food.

THE TAKE-HOME MESSAGE Healthy eating emphasizes consuming the right amount of food from a variety of food groups to provide an adequate intake of nutrients and a moderate level of energy. Choosing nutrient-dense and low-energy-dense foods ensures a diet high in nutrient content and low enough in energy to prevent weight gain. Reference values, guidelines, and tools have been developed to help individuals make healthy choices.

What Are the Dietary Reference Intakes?

The DRIs are specific reference values for each nutrient issued by the Food and Nutrition Board (FNB) of the National Academy of Sciences' Institute of Medicine. The DRIs are the specific amounts of each nutrient that one needs to consume to maintain good health, prevent chronic diseases, and avoid unhealthy excesses.[11] The Institute of Medicine periodically organizes committees of U.S. and Canadian scientists and health experts to update these recommendations based on the latest scientific research.

The DRIs Suggest an Intake Level for Each Nutrient

Individuals have different **nutrient requirements** during different life stages, such as during pregnancy or older age, and men and women vary in some of their nutrient requirements due to the physiological differences of their bodies.[12] In other words, a teenager may need more of a specific nutrient than a 55-year-old (and vice versa) and women need more of certain nutrients during pregnancy and lactation. Since the 1940s, the DRIs have been updated ten times.

In the 1990s, nutrition researchers identified expanded roles for many nutrients. Though nutrient deficiencies were still an important issue, research suggested that higher amounts of some nutrients could play a role in disease prevention. Also, as consumers began using more dietary supplements and fortified foods, committee members grew concerned that excessive consumption of some nutrients might be as unhealthy as, or even more dangerous than, not consuming enough. Hence the Food and Nutrition Board convened a variety of committees between 1997 and 2004 to take on the enormous task of reviewing the research on vitamins, minerals, carbohydrates, fats, protein, water, and other substances such as fiber, and developing the current DRI reference values for all the nutrients. As research evolves, changes are made in the DRIs.

The DRIs Encompass Several Reference Values

The DRIs cover five reference values: the Estimated Average Requirement (EAR), the Recommended Dietary Allowance (RDA), the Adequate Intake (AI), the Tolerable Upper Intake Level (UL), and the Acceptable Macronutrient Distribution Range (AMDR) (**Figure 2.4**). Each of these values is unique, and serves a different need in planning a healthy diet. Only three of these values, the RDA or AI (not both), the AMDR, and the UL, are used to assess the quality of meals.

The EAR is the starting point in the process of determining the other values. Let's look at how the values are determined.

▲ **Figure 2.4 The Dietary Reference Intakes**
Of the reference values that comprise the DRIs, the RDAs or AIs and the AMDRs are most useful for diet planning. Individuals should avoid consuming the UL of any nutrient.

Estimated Average Requirements

The DRI committee members begin by reviewing a variety of research studies to determine the **Estimated Average Requirement (EAR)** for a nutrient. The committee members may look at studies that investigate the consequences of eating a diet too low in the nutrient and the associated side effects or physical changes that develop, as well as how much of the nutrient should be consumed to correct the deficiency. They may also review studies that measure the amount a healthy individual absorbs, stores, and maintains daily. Additionally, they look at research studies that address the role the nutrient plays in reducing the risk of associated chronic diseases, such as heart disease. After a thorough review process, the EAR for the nutrient is determined.

The EAR is the amount of a nutrient projected to meet the needs of 50 percent of healthy Americans by age and gender.[13] The EAR is a good starting point to determine the amount of a nutrient individuals should consume daily for good health.

Let's use **Figure 2.5** to locate the EAR for Nutrient X. As you can see from the figure, the EAR for Nutrient X is about 40 units. If the recommended reference value for Nutrient X was set at 40 units, then half of the individuals would either meet or exceed their needs, while the other half would not.

nutrient requirements The amounts of specific nutrients needed to prevent malnutrition or deficiency; reflected in the DRIs.

Estimated Average Requirement (EAR) The average daily amount of a nutrient needed by 50 percent of the individuals in a similar age and gender group.

▸ **Figure 2.5 The DRIs in Action**
(a) The EAR is the average amount of a nutrient that is likely to meet the daily needs of half of the healthy individuals in a specific age and gender group. **(b)** The RDA, which is higher than the EAR, will meet the needs of approximately 97 to 98 percent of healthy individuals in a specific group. Consuming more than the RDA but less than the UL is safe for individuals. **(c)** The UL is the highest amount of a nutrient that is unlikely to pose any risk of adverse health effects even if consumed daily. As the intake of a nutrient increases above the UL, the risk of toxicity increases.

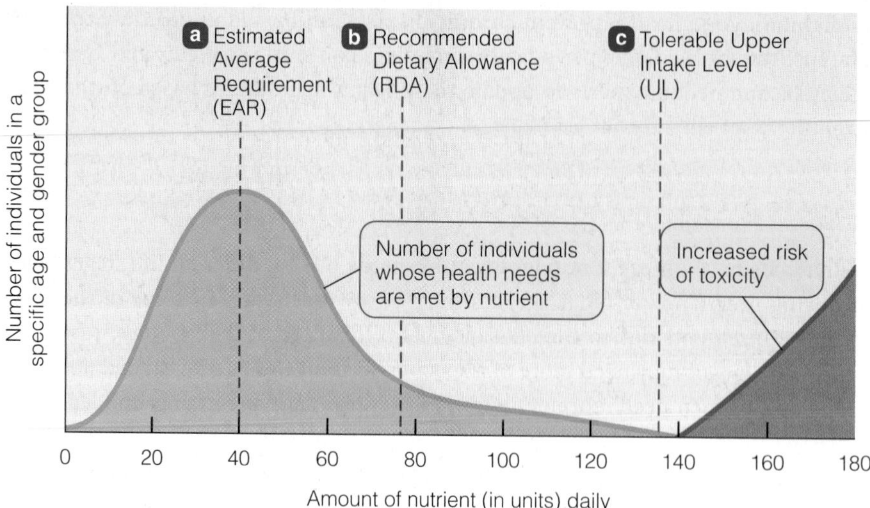

An EAR for each nutrient is established based on a measurement that indicates whether an individual is at risk of a deficiency. For example, the EAR for iron for a 19-year-old female uses hemoglobin concentrations in the blood to determine if iron intake is adequate. The measurement differs from nutrient to nutrient. For vitamin A, dark adaptation is used to determine the EAR, while researchers use enzyme activity to recommend thiamin requirements.[14] If there aren't enough studies or collected data to develop an appropriate measurement for a nutrient, an EAR or requirement for that nutrient is not established. Once the EAR has been set for each nutrient, the Recommended Dietary Allowances (RDAs) can be calculated.

Recommended Dietary Allowances

The **Recommended Dietary Allowance (RDA)** is based on the EAR, but it is set higher. It represents the amount for each nutrient that should meet the needs of nearly all (97 to 98 percent) of the individuals in a specific gender and age group. We can again use iron to illustrate the relationship between the EAR and the RDA. After careful review of the latest research on iron metabolism, the EAR for iron was set at 6 milligrams per day for both men and women over all age groups.[15] The amount is increased to an RDA of 18 milligrams per day to cover the needs of 97 to 98 percent of females aged 19 to 30. For 19-to-30-year-old males, the RDA for iron is 8 milligrams daily. The RDA for each nutrient according to age and gender is presented in the front of the textbook.

Although the RDA is a valuable reference for healthy eating, researchers have not established RDAs for all nutrients. If there is insufficient evidence to determine an EAR for a nutrient, the RDA can't be calculated. For nutrients for which no RDA has been established (such as calcium), the Adequate Intake (AI) can provide an alternative guideline.

Recommended Dietary Allowance (RDA) The recommended daily amount of a nutrient that meets the needs of nearly all individuals (97 to 98 percent) in a similar age and gender group. The RDA is set higher than the EAR.

Adequate Intake (AI) The *approximate* daily amount of a nutrient that is sufficient to meet the needs of similar individuals within a population group. The Food and Nutrition Board uses AIs for nutrients that do not have enough scientific evidence to calculate an RDA.

Adequate Intakes

Adequate Intake (AI) is a formal reference value that is estimated based on the judgment of the members of the FNB, according to the latest research. The AI is the next best scientific estimate of the amount of a nutrient that groups of similar individuals should consume to maintain good health.

There are several differences between the RDAs and the AIs. First, the RDAs are based on EARs, whereas the AIs are set without having established a requirement. If a nutrient has an AI, then more research must be done to accurately set an RDA. Second, the RDAs should cover the needs of 97 to 98 percent of the population, but the AIs do not estimate how many people will be covered because the EAR is not available. However, if you consume an amount equal to the AIs you will likely exceed the EARs or RDAs.[16] Finally, for infants, AIs are the only estimations for nutrients to evaluate dietary adequacy. This is because conducting the types of studies necessary to determine more specific information would be unethical.

The nutrients with AIs are noted in the DRI tables in the front of your textbook and include some vitamins and minerals, such as biotin, pantothenic acid, and vitamins D and K, and the minerals calcium and potassium.

Tolerable Upper Intake Level

Because consuming too much of some nutrients can lead to harmful side effects, the FNB developed the **Tolerable Upper Intake Level (UL),** which refers to the highest amount of a nutrient that is unlikely to cause harm if consumed daily. The higher the consumption above the UL, the higher the risk of **toxicity.** These reference values became necessary because of individuals' increased interest in consuming dietary supplements and fortified foods in pursuit of supposed health benefits. Unfortunately, many individuals are unaware that consuming too much of some nutrients can have a deleterious effect.

Not all nutrients have UL values. This doesn't mean that high intakes of those nutrients are safe, however. Because there aren't any known benefits for a healthy adult to consume a higher amount than the UL, people should aim to consume less than the UL and avoid the risk of health problems. The UL for selected nutrients according to age and gender is presented in the front of the textbook.

Acceptable Macronutrient Distribution Ranges

To ensure that intake of the energy nutrients is adequate and proportionate to physiological needs, recommended ranges of carbohydrates, fats, and proteins have been developed and are called the **Acceptable Macronutrient Distribution Ranges (AMDRs).** The AMDRs are as follows:

- Carbohydrates should comprise 45 to 65 percent of your daily kilocalories
- Fat should comprise 20 to 35 percent of your daily kilocalories
- Proteins should comprise 10 to 35 percent of your daily kilocalories

Consuming these nutrients in these ranges will ensure that kilocalorie and nutrient needs are met, while the risk of developing chronic diseases such as heart disease and obesity is reduced.[17] Practice calculating the AMDR using the Calculation Corner. (We will cover this in greater detail in Chapter 14.)

Estimated Energy Requirements

Although dietary recommendations have been established for carbohydrate, fat, protein, vitamins, and minerals that meet the optimal intake of nutrients, no DRI has been established for energy (kilocalorie) intake.[18] The method used to determine the amount of energy you need, or your **Estimated Energy Requirement (EER),** uses a different approach than the RDAs or AIs. The EER is calculated based on age, gender, height, weight, and activity level, and indicates the amount of energy needed to maintain energy balance. Individuals who consume more energy than they need will gain weight. Equations have been designed for males and females to provide a general estimate of energy needs. You can find the approximate amount of energy you require daily in Table 2.2.

Tolerable Upper Intake Level (UL) The maximum daily amount of a nutrient considered safe in a group of similar individuals.

toxicity The level of nutrient intake at which exposure to a substance becomes harmful.

Acceptable Macronutrient Distribution Ranges (AMDRs) A healthy range of intakes for the energy-containing nutrients—carbohydrates, proteins, and fats—expressed as a percentage of total daily energy. The AMDRs for adults are 45 to 65 percent carbohydrates, 10 to 35 percent protein, and 20 to 35 percent fat.

Estimated Energy Requirement (EER) The amount of daily energy to maintain a healthy body weight and meet energy needs based on age, gender, height, weight, and activity level.

TABLE 2.2 How Many Kilocalories Do You Need Daily?

The amount of kilocalories needed daily to maintain a healthy weight is based upon age, gender, and activity level.*

Males				Females			
Age	**Sedentary***	**Moderately Active**	**Active**	**Age**	**Sedentary**	**Moderately Active**	**Active**
16–18	2,400	2,800	3,200	**18**	1,800	2,000	2,400
19–20	2,600	2,800	3,000	**19–20**	2,000	2,200	2,400
21–25	2,400	2,800	3,000	**21–25**	2,000	2,200	2,400
26–30	2,400	2,600	3,000	**26–30**	1,800	2,000	2,400
31–35	2,400	2,600	3,000	**31–35**	1,800	2,000	2,200
36–40	2,400	2,600	2,800	**36–40**	1,800	2,000	2,200
41–45	2,200	2,600	2,800	**41–45**	1,800	2,000	2,200
46–50	2,200	2,400	2,800	**46–50**	1,800	2,000	2,200

*These kilocalorie levels are based on the Institute of Medicine's Estimated Energy Requirements from the *Dietary Reference Intakes: Macronutrients Report,* 2002. Sedentary: Partaking in less than 30 minutes a day of moderate physical activity in addition to daily activities. Moderately Active: Partaking in at least 30 minutes and up to 60 minutes a day of moderate physical activity in addition to daily activities. Active: Partaking in 60 or more minutes a day of moderate physical activity in addition to daily activities.

Source: U.S. Department of Agriculture. 2011. *Dietary Guidelines for Americans, 2010.* Available at www.health.gov/dietaryguidelines.

Calculation Corner

Calculating AMDR

Use the following scenario to calculate the AMDR for carbohydrate and fat:

Suppose a woman needs 2,150 kcal per day to maintain her current healthy weight.

The AMDR for carbohydrate is 45 to 65 percent of total daily kilocalories. To determine the number of kilocalories she needs to obtain daily from carbohydrate, we run the following equations:

$$2{,}150 \text{ kcal} \times 45 \text{ percent carbohydrates} = 2{,}150 \times 0.45 = 968 \text{ kcal}$$

$$2{,}150 \text{ kcal} \times 65 \text{ percent carbohydrates} = 2{,}150 \times 0.65 = 1{,}398 \text{ kcal}$$

Thus, of the 2,150 kcal the woman eats each day, 968 to 1,398 kcal should be from carbohydrates.

The AMDR for fat is 20 to 35 percent of daily kilocalories. Therefore:

$$2{,}150 \text{ kcal} \times 20 \text{ percent fats} = 2{,}150 \times 0.20 = 430 \text{ kcal}$$

$$2{,}150 \text{ kcal} \times 35 \text{ percent fats} = 2{,}150 \times 0.35 = 753 \text{ kcal}$$

Of the 2,150 kcal the woman eats each day, 430 to 753 kcal should be from fat.

Can you calculate the AMDR for your daily intake of kilocalories?

The DRIs Can Be Used to Plan a Quality Diet

You can use the DRIs to make healthy food choices and plan a quality diet. To meet your needs, your goal should be to achieve the RDA or the AI of all nutrients, but not exceed the UL. Table 2.3 summarizes how to use the DRIs to plan a quality diet. (You will also find the DRIs for all nutrients on the inside front cover of this textbook.)

Each chapter in this textbook will further explain what each nutrient is, why it is important, how much (based on the DRIs) you need to consume, and how to get enough, without consuming too much, in your diet.

TABLE 2.3 The Do's and Don'ts of the DRIs	
Reference Value	**When Planning Your Diet**
Estimated Average Requirement (EAR)	**Don't** use this amount.
Recommended Dietary Allowance (RDA)	**Do** aim for this amount!
Adequate Intake (AI)	**Do** aim for this amount if an RDA isn't available.
Tolerable Upper Intake Level (UL)	**Don't** exceed this amount on a daily basis.
Acceptable Macronutrient Distribution Range (AMDR)	**Do** follow these guidelines regarding the percentage of carbohydrates, protein, and fat in the diet.

THE TAKE-HOME MESSAGE The Dietary Reference Intakes (DRIs) are specific reference values that help individuals determine daily nutrient needs to maintain good health, prevent chronic diseases, and avoid unhealthy excesses. The reference values include the EAR, RDA, AI, UL, and AMDR. The EER can help determine the appropriate amount of energy needed to maintain a healthy body weight given one's age, gender, height, weight, and activity levels. You should try to meet your RDA or AI and consume below the UL for each nutrient daily while maintaining sufficient energy intake.

What Are the *Dietary Guidelines for Americans*?

Whereas the DRIs were released to prevent undernutrition, the *Dietary Guidelines for Americans* were developed out of concern over the incidence of overnutrition among Americans. By the 1970s, research had shown that Americans' overconsumption of foods rich in fat, saturated fat, cholesterol, and sodium was increasing their risk for chronic diseases such as heart disease and stroke.[19] In 1977, the U.S. government released the *Dietary Goals for Americans,* which were designed to improve the nutritional quality of Americans' diets and to try to reduce the incidence of overnutrition and its associated health problems.[20]

Amid controversy over the scientific validity of the goals, the government asked scientists to lend credence to the goals and provide dietary guidance. Their work culminated in the 1980 *Dietary Guidelines for Americans,* which emphasized eating a variety of foods to obtain a nutritionally well-balanced daily diet. Since 1990, the U.S. Department of Agriculture (USDA) and the Department of Health and Human Services (DHHS) have been mandated by law to update the guidelines every five years. The guidelines serve as one governmental voice to shape all federally funded nutrition programs in areas such as research and labeling, and to educate and guide consumers about healthy diet and lifestyle choices.[21]

The *Dietary Guidelines* encourage consumption of a variety of fruits and vegetables.

The *Dietary Guidelines for Americans, 2010* reflect the most current nutrition and lifestyle advice for good health. They are designed to help individuals aged 2

TABLE 2.4 The *Dietary Guidelines for Americans* at a Glance

Balance Kilocalories to Manage Weight	■ Prevent and/or reduce overweight and obesity through improved eating and physical activity behaviors. ■ Control total kilocalorie intake to manage body weight. For people who are overweight or obese, this will mean consuming fewer kilocalories from foods and beverages. ■ Increase physical activity and reduce time spent in sedentary behaviors. ■ Maintain appropriate kilocalorie balance during each stage of life—childhood, adolescence, adulthood, pregnancy and breast-feeding, and older age.
Reduce these Foods and Food Components	■ Reduce daily sodium intake to less than 2,300 mg and further reduce intake to 1,500 mg among persons who are 51 and older and those of any age who are African-American or have hypertension, diabetes, or chronic kidney disease. The 1,500-mg recommendation applies to about half of the U.S. population, including children, and the majority of adults. ■ Consume less than 10 percent of kilocalories from saturated fatty acids by replacing them with monounsaturated and polyunsaturated fatty acids. ■ Consume less than 300 mg per day of dietary cholesterol. ■ Keep *trans* fatty acid consumption as low as possible by limiting foods that contain synthetic sources of *trans* fats, such as partially hydrogenated oils, and by limiting other solid fats. ■ Reduce the intake of kilocalories from solid fats and added sugars. ■ Limit the consumption of foods that contain refined grains, especially refined grain foods that contain solid fats, added sugars, and sodium. ■ If alcohol is consumed, it should be consumed in moderation—up to 1 drink per day for women and 2 drinks per day for men—and only by adults of legal drinking age.
Increase these Foods and Nutrients	■ Increase vegetable and fruit intake. ■ Eat a variety of vegetables, especially dark green and red and orange vegetables and beans and peas. ■ Consume at least half of all grains as whole grains. Increase whole-grain intake by replacing refined grains with whole grains. ■ Increase intake of fat-free or low-fat milk and milk products, such as milk, yogurt, cheese, or fortified soy beverages. ■ Choose a variety of protein foods, which include seafood, lean meat and poultry, eggs, beans and peas, soy products, and unsalted nuts and seeds. ■ Increase the amount and variety of seafood consumed by choosing seafood in place of some meat and poultry. ■ Replace protein foods that are higher in solid fats with choices that are lower in solid fats and kilocalories and/or are sources of oils. ■ Use oils to replace solid fats where possible. ■ Choose foods that provide more potassium, dietary fiber, calcium, and vitamin D, which are nutrients of concern in American diets. These foods include vegetables, fruits, whole grains, and milk and milk products.
Build Healthy Eating Patterns	■ Select an eating pattern that meets nutrient needs over time at an appropriate kilocalorie level. ■ Account for all foods and beverages consumed and assess how they fit within a total healthy eating pattern. ■ Follow food safety recommendations when preparing and eating foods to reduce the risk of foodborne illnesses.

Source: Report of the Dietary Guidelines Advisory Committee on the *Dietary Guidelines for Americans, 2010*. Available at www.cnpp.usda.gov/DGAs2010-DGACReport.htm. Accessed February 2012.

and over improve the quality and content of their diet and lifestyle to lower their risk of chronic diseases and conditions, such as high blood pressure, high blood cholesterol levels, diabetes mellitus, heart disease, certain cancers, and osteoporosis.

These most recent guidelines are different from previous reports, as they address the obesity epidemic that is occurring among Americans.[22] Table 2.4 provides an overview of the current major goals, along with helpful dietary and lifestyle recommendations.

THE TAKE-HOME MESSAGE The *Dietary Guidelines* consist of key recommendations and lifestyle advice designed to help Americans lead a healthy lifestyle. They are updated every five years.

What Is the MyPlate Food Guidance System?

Illustrated graphics called **food guidance systems** are often used to summarize guidelines for healthy eating. MyPlate is the most recent food guidance system developed by the USDA for Americans. Released in 2011, MyPlate is a tool that reflects the recommendations in the *Dietary Guidelines for Americans, 2010.* Its online component, ChooseMyPlate.gov, is a Web-based communication and education initiative that provides information, tips, and tools to help people build a healthier diet based on the latest nutrition and health recommendations from the Dietary Guidelines Advisory Committee Report and the DRIs. Also available is an interactive food guidance system that is based on the USDA Food Patterns, which provides a personalized food plan based on the latest nutrition and health recommendations.

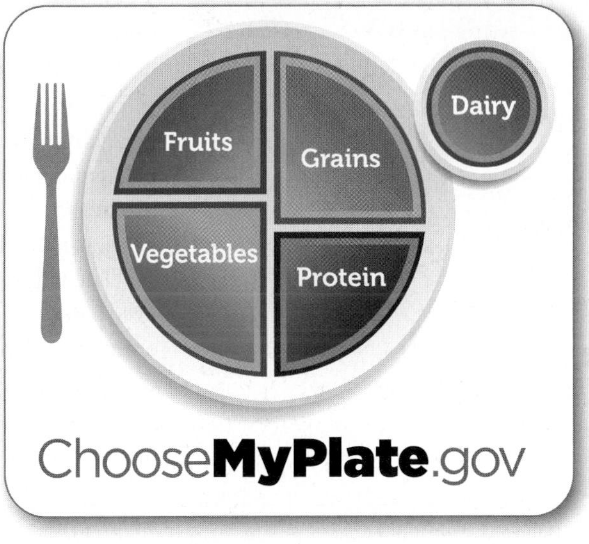

▲ **Figure 2.6 Anatomy of MyPlate**
The MyPlate icon reinforces important concepts of meal planning, healthful choices, proportionality, and moderation to be used in planning a healthful diet.

Source: U.S. Department of Agriculture. 2011. ChooseMyPlate.gov. Available at www.ChooseMyPlate.gov.

MyPlate Emphasizes Changes in Diet, Eating Behaviors, and Physical Activity

MyPlate shows five food groups in relative proportion using the familiar mealtime visual of a place setting. It serves as an icon to remind consumers to eat healthfully. In addition, the tool MyPlate and the supporting information at ChooseMyPlate.gov promote proportionality, moderation, variety, and personalization. As you can see in **Figure 2.6**, MyPlate shows a place setting split into sections, with each colored section representing one of five food groups: fruits, vegetables, grains, protein, and dairy. Whereas oils are an important part of a healthy diet, they are not represented on the plate, as they are not considered a food group.

You can now easily see **proportionality** in how these food groups should dominate your diet. Half of your plate should be devoted to waist- and heart-friendly vegetables and fruits, with a smaller portion for grains (preferably whole grains) and lean protein foods such as fish, skinless poultry, lean meats, dried beans, and peas. The blue circle next to the plate is a visual reminder to make sure that fat-free and low-fat dairy foods such as milk should not be forgotten at mealtimes. With the majority of Americans overweight, this shift of food proportionality on your plate can have a dramatic effect on your kilocalorie intake. Devoting more than half of the surface of the plate to low-kilocalorie fruits and vegetables should crowd out higher kilocalorie grains and protein food choices. Take the Self-Assessment on page 52 to see how well-proportioned your diet is.

Several important nutrition messages at ChooseMyPlate.gov are based on three general areas of recommendation from the current *Dietary Guidelines*:

1. Balance kilocalories
   - Enjoy your food, but eat less.
   - Avoid oversized portions.
2. Increase the following foods
   - Make half your plate fruits and vegetables.
   - Make at least half your grains whole grains.
   - Switch to fat-free or low-fat (1%) milk.
3. Reduce the following foods
   - Compare sodium in foods like soup, bread, and frozen meals—and choose the foods with lower numbers.
   - Drink water instead of sugary drinks.

food guidance systems Visual diagrams that provide a variety of food recommendations to help a person create a well-balanced diet.

proportionality The relationship of one entity to another. Vegetables and fruits should be consumed in a higher proportion than dairy and protein foods in the diet.

Self-Assessment

Does Your Diet Have Proportionality?

Answer "yes" or "no" to the following questions:

1. Are grains the main food choice at all your meals?

   Yes ☐ **No** ☐

2. Do you often forget to eat vegetables?

   Yes ☐ **No** ☐

3. Do you typically eat fewer than three pieces of fruit daily?

   Yes ☐ **No** ☐

4. Do you often have fewer than three cups of milk daily?

   Yes ☐ **No** ☐

5. Is the portion of meat, chicken, or fish the largest item on your dinner plate?

   Yes ☐ **No** ☐

Answer

If you answered "yes" to three or more of these questions, it is very likely that your diet lacks proportionality. You can use the information in this chapter to help improve the proportionality of your diet.

These messages emphasize not only that you should balance your kilocalories daily to better manage your weight but also that you should choose mostly nutrient-dense foods from each food group.

Individuals who choose high-nutrient-dense and low-energy-dense foods will generally have diets that are lower in solid fats and added sugars and higher in nutrient content. **Figure 2.7** helps you compare some nutrient-dense food choices to less healthy food choices in each food group.

Eating a variety of foods among and within the food groups highlighted in MyPlate will increase your chances of consuming all 40 of the nutrients your body needs. Because no single food or food group provides all the nutrients, a varied diet of nutrient-dense foods is the savviest strategy. **Figure 2.8** provides tips on how to choose a variety of foods from each food group.

Lastly, physical activity is an important component in the successful implementation of the intention behind MyPlate. Being physically active (see Table 2.5) helps you stay fit and reduce your risk of chronic diseases such as heart disease and cancer. Advice regarding physical activity can also be found at ChooseMyPlate.gov.

How to Use MyPlate

You now know to eat a variety of nutrient-dense foods to be healthy, and that MyPlate helps you select a diverse group of foods, but you may be wondering how much from each food group a person should be eating. The ChooseMyPlate.gov interactive website will give you the exact numbers of servings to eat from each food group based on your daily kilocalorie needs. If you cannot go to the website, you can obtain similar information by using Tables 2.2 and 2.6 in this chapter. Table 2.6 on page 54 will tell you the quantity from each food group you should consume to healthfully obtain the daily kilocalories you need.

For a moderately active female who needs 2,000 kilocalories daily, a healthy daily diet would consist of the following:

- 6 servings from the grains group
- 2½ cups of dark green, orange, starchy, and other vegetables, and some legumes
- 2 cups of fruits
- 3 cups of fat-free or low-fat milk and yogurt
- 5½ ounces of lean meat, poultry, and fish, or the equivalent in meat alternatives such as beans
- 6 teaspoons of vegetable oils

▾ **Figure 2.7 Nutrient-Dense Food Choices**
Choose nutrient-dense foods more often to build a well-balanced diet.

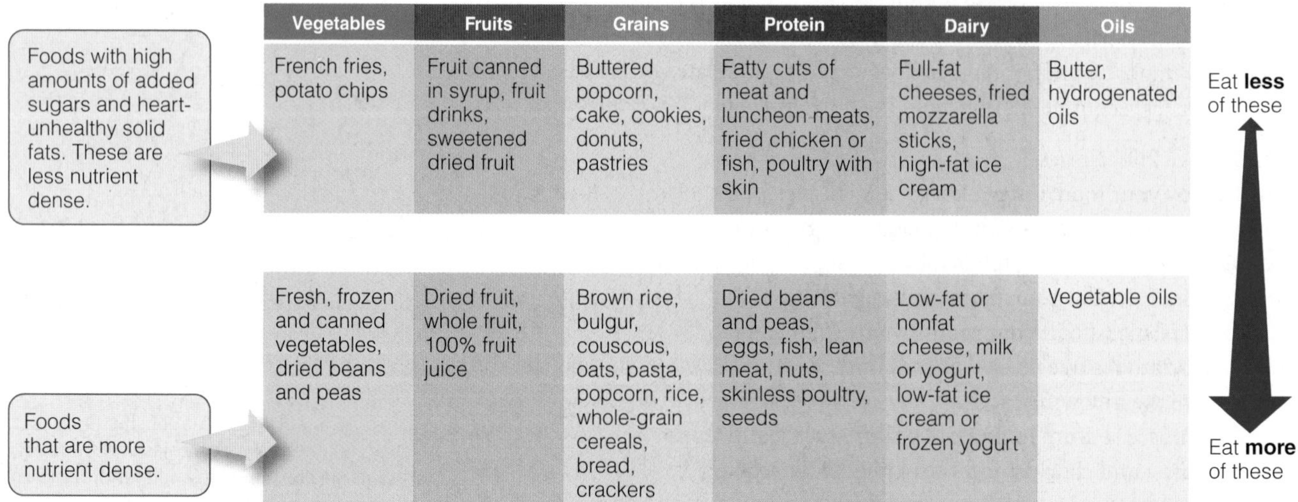

Vegetables
Fruits
Grains
Protein
Dairy
Oils
Foods with high amounts of added sugars and heart-unhealthy solid fats. These are less nutrient dense.
French fries, potato chips
Fruit canned in syrup, fruit drinks, sweetened dried fruit
Buttered popcorn, cake, cookies, donuts, pastries
Fatty cuts of meat and luncheon meats, fried chicken or fish, poultry with skin
Full-fat cheeses, fried mozzarella sticks, high-fat ice cream
Butter, hydrogenated oils
Eat **less** of these
Foods that are more nutrient dense.
Fresh, frozen and canned vegetables, dried beans and peas
Dried fruit, whole fruit, 100% fruit juice
Brown rice, bulgur, couscous, oats, pasta, popcorn, rice, whole-grain cereals, bread, crackers
Dried beans and peas, eggs, fish, lean meat, nuts, skinless poultry, seeds
Low-fat or nonfat cheese, milk or yogurt, low-fat ice cream or frozen yogurt
Vegetable oils
Eat **more** of these

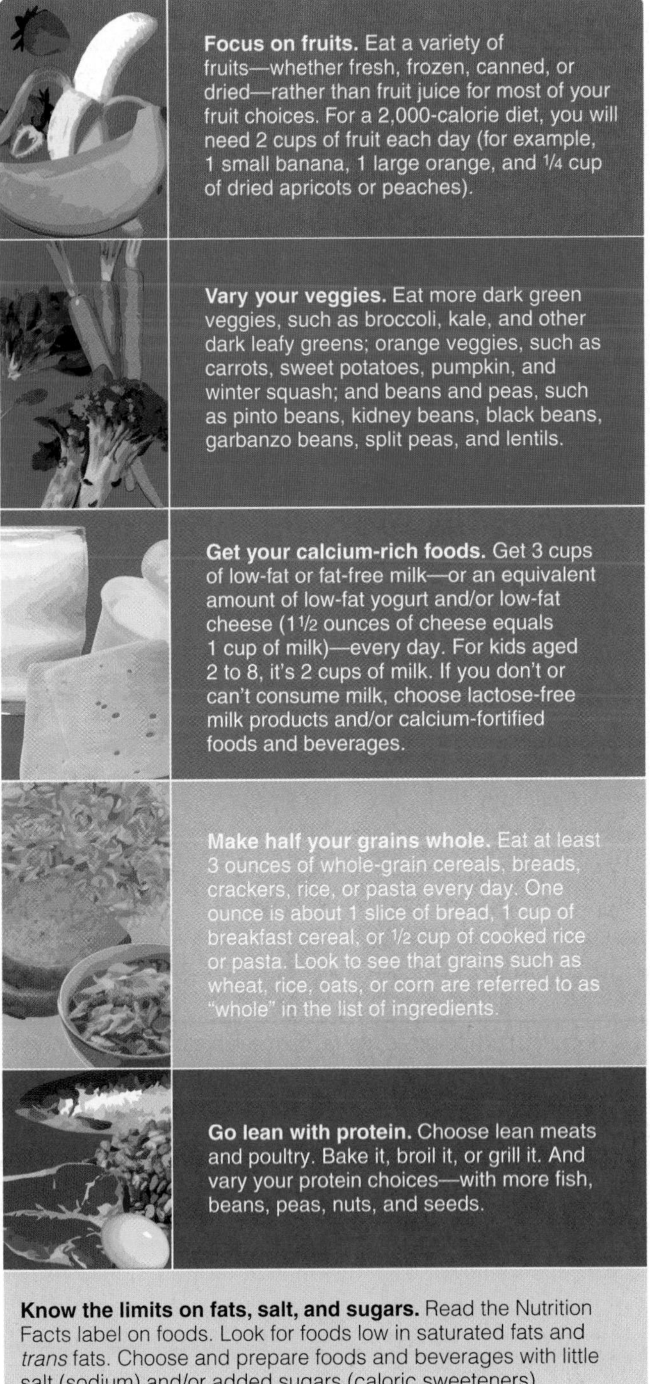

Focus on fruits. Eat a variety of fruits—whether fresh, frozen, canned, or dried—rather than fruit juice for most of your fruit choices. For a 2,000-calorie diet, you will need 2 cups of fruit each day (for example, 1 small banana, 1 large orange, and 1/4 cup of dried apricots or peaches).
Vary your veggies. Eat more dark green veggies, such as broccoli, kale, and other dark leafy greens; orange veggies, such as carrots, sweet potatoes, pumpkin, and winter squash; and beans and peas, such as pinto beans, kidney beans, black beans, garbanzo beans, split peas, and lentils.
Get your calcium-rich foods. Get 3 cups of low-fat or fat-free milk—or an equivalent amount of low-fat yogurt and/or low-fat cheese (1 1/2 ounces of cheese equals 1 cup of milk)—every day. For kids aged 2 to 8, it's 2 cups of milk. If you don't or can't consume milk, choose lactose-free milk products and/or calcium-fortified foods and beverages.
Make half your grains whole. Eat at least 3 ounces of whole-grain cereals, breads, crackers, rice, or pasta every day. One ounce is about 1 slice of bread, 1 cup of breakfast cereal, or 1/2 cup of cooked rice or pasta. Look to see that grains such as wheat, rice, oats, or corn are referred to as "whole" in the list of ingredients.
Go lean with protein. Choose lean meats and poultry. Bake it, broil it, or grill it. And vary your protein choices—with more fish, beans, peas, nuts, and seeds.
Know the limits on fats, salt, and sugars. Read the Nutrition Facts label on foods. Look for foods low in saturated fats and *trans* fats. Choose and prepare foods and beverages with little salt (sodium) and/or added sugars (caloric sweeteners).

◂ **Figure 2.8 Mix Up Your Choices within Each Food Group**

Source: USDA Consumer Brochure. 2005. *Finding Your Way to a Healthier You.* Based on the *Dietary Guidelines for Americans.*

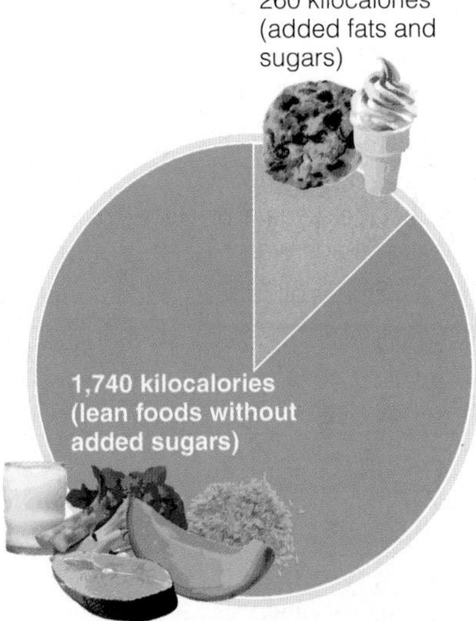

▴ **Figure 2.9 How Solid Fats and Added Sugars Fit into a Balanced Diet**

If you select mostly nutrient-dense, lean foods that contain few solid fats and added sugars, you may have leftover kilocalories to "spend" on extra helpings or a sweet dessert.

The kilocalorie levels and distribution of food groups in daily food plans are calculated using the leanest food choices with no added sugar. If all food selections are low in fat and added sugar, this menu will provide a total of about 1,740 kilocalories (**Figure 2.9**). If you pour whole milk (high in fat) over your sweetened cereal (added sugar) instead of using skim milk (fat free) to drench your shredded wheat (no added sugar), the extra fat and sugar kilocalories add up quickly to reach 2,000 kilocalories (Table 2.7 on page 55).

Figure 2.10 shows how servings from the various food groups can create well-balanced meals and snacks throughout the day. Although this particular menu is balanced and the foods are nutrient dense, it is unlikely that every day will be this ideal. Fortunately, nutrient needs are averaged over time. If an individual eats insufficient

TABLE 2.5 What Is Moderate and Vigorous Activity?

Moderate Activities (Expend 3.5 to 7 Kilocalories per Minute):	Vigorous Activities (Expend More Than 7 Kilocalories per Minute):
Brisk walking	Jogging or running
Bicycling 5 to 9 mph	Bicycling more than 10 mph
Shooting hoops	Playing competitive sports like basketball, soccer, or lacrosse
Using free weights	Rowing on a machine vigorously
Yoga	Karate, judo, or tae kwon do
Walking a dog	Jumping rope

Adapted from the Centers for Disease Control and Prevention. 2011. *Physical Activity for a Healthy Weight.* Available at www.cdc.gov/healthyweight/physical_activity/index.html. Accessed February 2012.

TABLE 2.6 How Much Should You Eat from Each Food Group?

The following are suggested amounts to consume daily from each of the basic food groups and the oils based on daily kilocalorie needs. Remember that most food choices should be fat free or low fat and contain little added sugar.

Kilocalorie Level	Grains (oz eq)	Vegetables (cups)	Fruits (cups)	Oils (tsp)	Dairy (cups)	Protein (oz eq)
1,400	5	1.5	1.5	4	2	4
1,600	5	2	1.5	5	3	5
1,800	6	2.5	1.5	5	3	5
2,000	6	2.5	2	6	3	5.5
2,200	7	3	2	6	3	6
2,400	8	3	2	7	3	6.5
2,600	9	3.5	2	8	3	6.5
2,800	10	3.5	2.5	8	3	7

Grains: Includes all foods made with wheat, rice, oats, cornmeal, or barley, such as bread, pasta, oatmeal, breakfast cereals, tortillas, and grits. In general, 1 slice of bread, 1 cup of ready-to-eat cereal, or ½ cup of cooked rice, pasta, or cooked cereal is considered 1 ounce equivalent (oz eq) from the grains group. *At least half of all grains consumed should be whole grains such as whole-wheat bread, oats, or brown rice.*

Vegetables: Includes all fresh, frozen, canned, and dried vegetables, and vegetable juices. In general, 1 cup of raw or cooked vegetables or vegetable juice, or 2 cups of raw leafy greens, is considered 1 cup from the vegetable group.

Fruits: Includes all fresh, frozen, canned, and dried fruits, and fruit juices. In general, 1 cup of fruit or 100% fruit juice, or ½ cup of dried fruit, is considered 1 cup from the fruit group.

Oils: Includes vegetable oils such as canola, corn, olive, soybean, and sunflower oil, fatty fish, nuts, avocados, mayonnaise, salad dressings made with oils, and soft margarine.

Dairy: Includes all fat-free and low-fat milk, yogurt, and cheese. In general, 1 cup of milk or yogurt, 1½ ounces of natural cheese, or 2 ounces of processed cheese is considered 1 cup from the dairy group.

Proteins: In general, 1 ounce of lean meat, poultry, or fish, 1 egg, 1 tablespoon peanut butter, ¼ cup cooked dry beans, or ½ ounce of nuts or seeds is considered 1 ounce equivalent (oz eq) from the protein group.

Source: U.S. Department of Agriculture. 2011. www.ChooseMyPlate.gov.

servings of one food group or a specific nutrient one day, he or she can make up for it the next day. For example, if you did not eat enough fruit one day, but did eat an extra serving of grains, you could adjust your diet the next day by cutting back on your grain servings and adding an extra serving of fruit.

Should you worry about *when* you eat? Read more about the time of day you should eat in Examining the Evidence: Does the Time of Day You Eat Impact Your Health? on page 56.

TABLE 2.7 Choose Right

As you can see, your daily food plan can include solid fats and added sugars depending on food choices.

Choosing . . .	Over . . .	Will Cost You
Whole milk (1 cup)	Fat-free milk (1 cup)	65 kilocalories
Roasted chicken thigh with skin (3 oz)	Roasted chicken breast, skinless (3 oz)	70 kilocalories
Glazed doughnut, (three ¾″ diameter)	English muffin (one muffin)	165 kilocalories
French fries (one medium order)	Baked potato (one medium)	299 kilocalories
Regular soda (one can, 12 fl oz)	Diet soda (one can, 12 fl oz)	150 kilocalories

Source: U.S. Department of Agriculture. 2011. Available at www.choosemyplate.gov/supertracker-tools/empty-calories-chart.html. Accessed February 2012.

▼ **Figure 2.10 A Healthy Daily Food Plan**
A variety of foods from each food group creates a well-balanced diet.

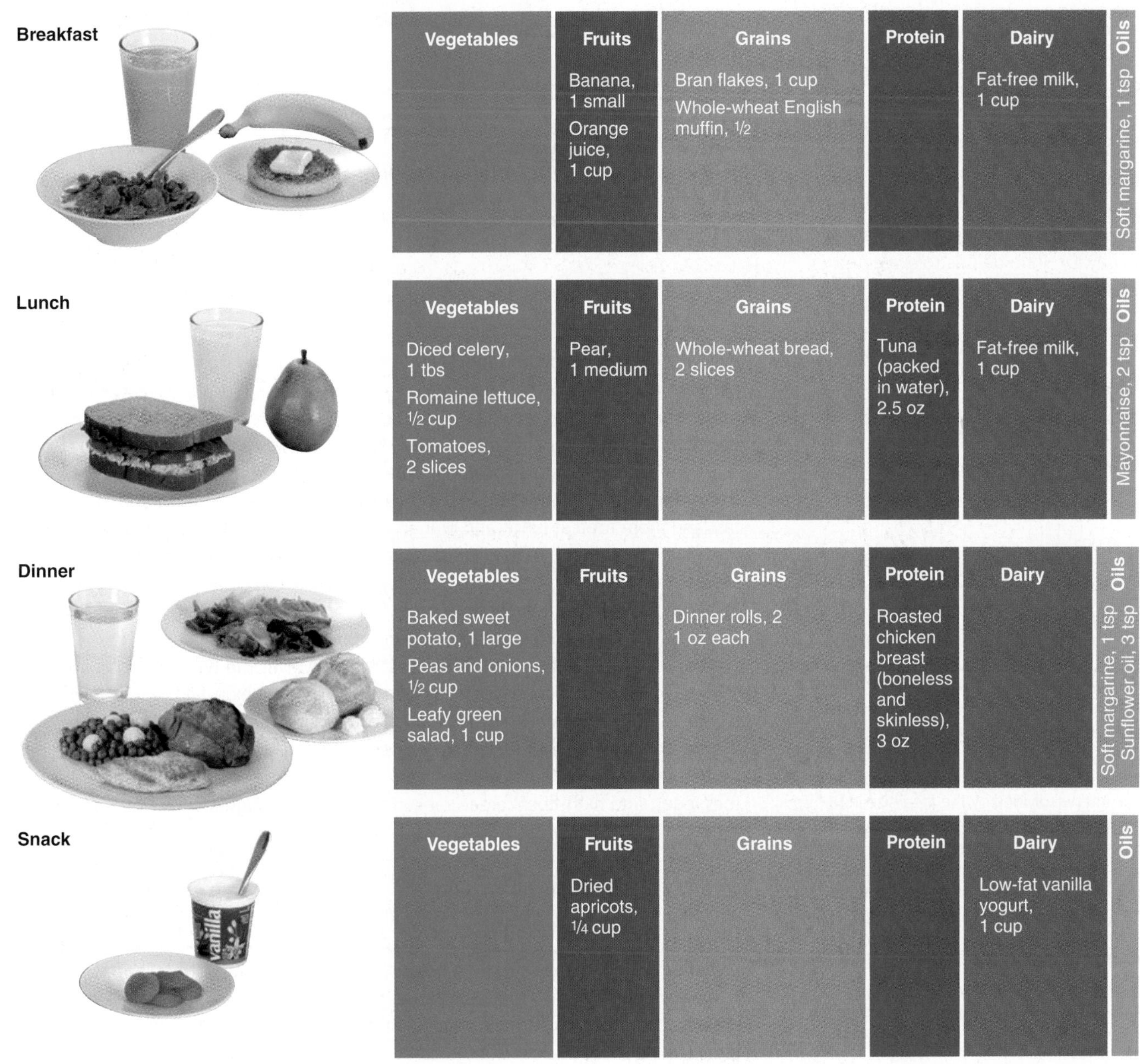

Breakfast
Vegetables
Fruits
Banana, 1 small
Orange juice, 1 cup
Grains
Bran flakes, 1 cup
Whole-wheat English muffin, 1/2
Protein
Dairy
Fat-free milk, 1 cup
Soft margarine, 1 tsp Oils
Lunch
Vegetables
Diced celery, 1 tbs
Romaine lettuce, 1/2 cup
Tomatoes, 2 slices
Fruits
Pear, 1 medium
Grains
Whole-wheat bread, 2 slices
Protein
Tuna (packed in water), 2.5 oz
Dairy
Fat-free milk, 1 cup
Mayonnaise, 2 tsp Oils
Dinner
Vegetables
Baked sweet potato, 1 large
Peas and onions, 1/2 cup
Leafy green salad, 1 cup
Fruits
Grains
Dinner rolls, 2
1 oz each
Protein
Roasted chicken breast (boneless and skinless), 3 oz
Dairy
Soft margarine, 1 tsp
Sunflower oil, 3 tsp Oils
Snack
vanilla
Vegetables
Fruits
Dried apricots, 1/4 cup
Grains
Protein
Dairy
Low-fat vanilla yogurt, 1 cup
Oils

EXAMINING THE EVIDENCE

Does the Time of Day You Eat Impact Your Health?

We are all creatures of habit. Some of these habits, such as the time of day we eat, can either enhance or detract from overall health. Do you typically eat breakfast? Do you often snack after dinner or late at night? Do you overload on high-fat or fried foods, or drink a lot of alcohol, when you go out on the weekends? The choice to skip breakfast, eat later in the day, or overeat on the weekend can impact your nutrient intake, appetite, and body weight.

Eating Breakfast Means More Energy and Fewer Kilocalories Throughout the Day

You probably know that grabbing a latte on the way to your morning class is not a healthy breakfast, but do you understand how such a habit impacts your overall nutrient intake? For one thing, skipping breakfast may affect the total number of kilocalories you consume the rest of the day. Dr. John de Castro evaluated the timing of food intake in 867 people over a seven-day period and found that people who ate a larger proportion of food earlier in the day had a significantly lower intake of total kilocalories (Figure 1).[1] In other words, if you eat breakfast, you are more likely to eat less by the end of the day than if you skip this important meal.

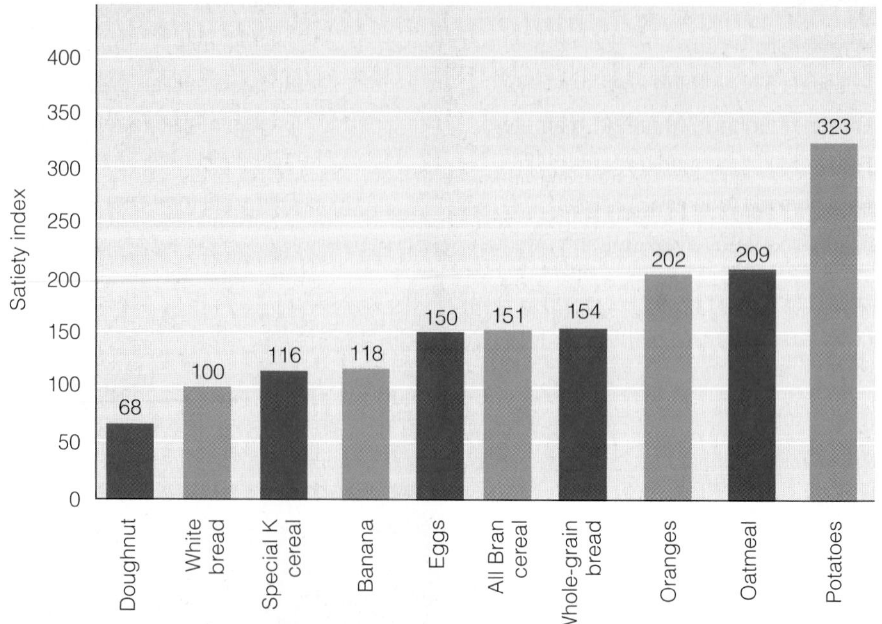

▲ **Figure 2 Satiety Index of Different Foods**
Subjects were asked to rate their feelings of hunger every 15 minutes for 2 hours after eating 240-kilocalorie portions of specific foods. All foods were compared with white bread, which scored a satiety index of 100.

Data from S. H. Holt, J. C. Miller, P. Petocz, and E. Farmakalidis. 1995. "A Satiety Index of Common Foods." *European Journal of Clinical Nutrition* 49:675–690.

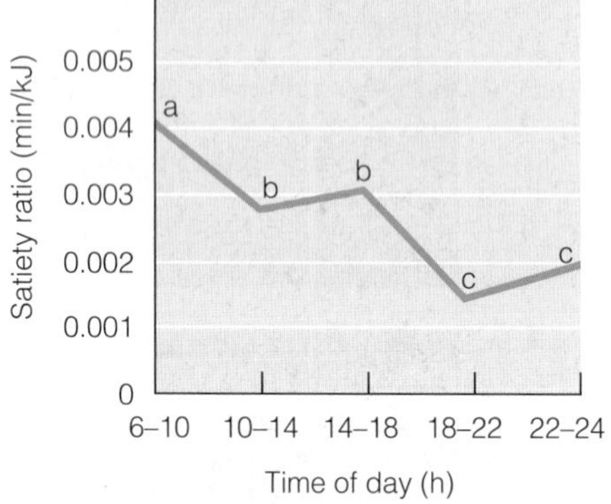

▲ **Figure 1 Satiety Ratios Based on Time Between Meals and Energy Content**
Satiety ratios were calculated during five 4-hour periods of the day reported in 7-day diet diaries and were calculated as the duration of the after-meal interval divided by the meal size in kJ.* To be considered a meal, there had to be at least 15 minutes from the preceding or following meal. Meal **(a)** contained 15 minutes and 209 kJ; **(b)** 45 minutes and 209 kJ or **(b)** 45 minutes and 418 kJ; and **(c)** 45 minutes and 837 kJ or **(c)** 90 minutes and 209 kJ. Values are means, $n = 867$; pooled SEM = 0.00007. Means without a common letter differ; $p < 0.05$.

*Note: The International System uses kilojoules (kJ) to define energy in foods. One kilocalorie equals 4.184 joules.

The reduction in total kilocalories when you eat breakfast may be due to the size of the meal and how satisfied you feel. Most of us eat smaller meals at breakfast and more food at lunch and dinner. We also appear to spend less time eating breakfast than other meals. In Dr. de Castro's study, both of these factors affected satiety. Satiety ratios, or the time between meals based on the size of the previous meal, decreased over the day from breakfast through late-evening snacks.[2] Thus, a more substantial breakfast is more satiating than the evening meal.

One reason breakfast may be more satiating involves the types of foods consumed. Holt and colleagues investigated the effects of a high-fat breakfast versus a high-carbohydrate meal on the amount of snacking reported later in the day (Figure 2).[3] If the breakfast included higher fiber foods, such as cereal, and a good protein source, the subjects ate less later in the day. Breakfast foods including potatoes, eggs, and high-fiber cereals ranked higher than doughnuts or white bread for satiety.

What if you skip breakfast? Not only will you eat more during the day, chances are you will choose less-nutrient-dense foods. Those who eat breakfast, lunch, and dinner tend to have higher calcium and iron intakes than individuals who skip breakfast.[4, 5]

Eating breakfast may also be a good strategy for weight control. Several studies have reported higher BMIs and body weight in subjects who don't consistently eat breakfast compared with their breakfast-eating counterparts.[6] In addition, eating breakfast helps maintain weight loss.[7]

Eating More during Evenings and Weekends Can Lead to Overconsumption of Kilocalories

Do you eat after 7:00 p.m.? Most young adults do, especially during the weekend.[8] For most students, eating schedules are influenced by hunger, pressures from work and school, convenience, and social habits. Regardless of why you eat at various times, the timing of your meals can affect body weight, the level of hormones in the blood, body temperature, and blood pressure.[9] Because eating later is less satisfying, you are likely to eat more food, and hence consume more kilocalories, particularly from carbohydrates, fat, and alcohol, in the evening hours.

Though there is no current evidence that eating later in the day increases BMI or the risk of obesity,[10] timing of meals may impact changes in body composition during a weight-loss program. In a controlled metabolic ward study, overweight women who ate the bulk of their kilocalories in the morning hours had a slightly greater weight loss than when the bulk of the kilocalories was consumed later in the day. However, when they ate more of their kilocalories later in the day, they retained more lean muscle mass.[11] More research is needed before any strong conclusions can be drawn from these results.

Weekend eating patterns can also influence overall dietary intake. Haines reports that people in their study ate an average of 82 kilocalories more per day on Friday, Saturday, and Sunday compared with weekdays. These increases in kilocalories were mostly due to an increase in fat (approximately 0.7 percent) and alcohol (1.4 percent); carbohydrates decreased by 1.6 percent.[12] Over time, this increase in kilocalorie intake may lead to weight gain.

Recommendations

Based on the current research on eating and time of day, it is recommended that you:

- Start your day with a nutrient-dense breakfast as part of a healthy eating pattern. Many breakfast foods, such as dry whole-grain cereals, fresh fruit, or whole-grain toast or bagels with low-fat cream cheese, can be eaten on the go. You'll have more energy and will most likely eat fewer total kilocalories by the end of the day.
- Choose breakfast foods that are more satisfying to improve your appetite control throughout the day. Enjoy foods such as whole-grain cereals and whole fruits, which are higher in fiber, protein, and water, and lower in fat and sugar.
- Control kilocalorie intake on nights and weekends. Monitor your weekend eating habits to maintain a consistent balance of carbohydrates, fats, and proteins and to reduce alcohol consumption.

References

1. J. M. de Castro. 2003. "The Time of Day of Food Intake Influences Overall Intake in Humans." *Journal of Nutrition* 134:104–111.
2. Ibid.
3. S. H. Holt, J. C. Miller, P. Petocz, and E. Farmakalidis. 1995. "A Satiety Index of Common Foods." *European Journal of Clinical Nutrition* 49:675–690.
4. J. M. Kerver, E. Yang, S. Obayashi, L. Bianchi, and W. Song. 2006. "Meal and Snack Patterns Are Associated with Dietary Intake of Energy and Nutrients in U.S. Adults." *Journal of the American Dietetic Association* 106:46–54.
5. N. K. A. Stockman, T. C. Schenkel, J. N. Brown, and A. Duncan. 2005. "Comparison of Energy and Nutrient Intakes among Meals and Snacks of Adolescent Males." *Preventive Medicine* 41:203–210.
6. Ibid.
7. H. R. Wyatt, G. K. Grunwald, C. L. Mosca, M. L. Klem, R. R. Wing, and J. O. Hill. 2002. "Long-Term Weight Loss and Breakfast in Subjects in the National Weight Control Registry." *Obesity Research* 10:78–82.
8. R. H. Striegel-Moore, D. L. Franko, D. Thompson, S. Affenito, and H. C. Kraemer. 2006. "Night Eating: Prevalence and Demographic Correlates." *Obesity* 14:139–147.
9. F. Halberg. 1989. "Some Aspects of the Chronobiology of Nutrition: More Work Is Needed on 'When to Eat.'" *Journal of Nutrition* 119:333–343.
10. N. K. A. Stockman, et al. 2005. "Comparison of Energy and Nutrient Intakes."
11. N. L. Keim, M. D. Van Loan, W. F. Horn, T. F. Barbieri, and P. L. Mayclin. 1997. "Weight Loss Is Greater with Consumption of Large Morning Meals and Fat-Free Mass Is Preserved with Large Evening Meals in Women on a Controlled Weight Reduction Program." *Journal of Nutrition* 127:75–82.
12. P. S. Haines, M. Y. Hama, D. K. Guilkey, and B. M. Popkin. 2003. "Weekend Eating in the United States Is Linked with Greater Energy, Fat, and Alcohol Intake." *Obesity Research* 11:945–949.

THE TAKE-HOME MESSAGE MyPlate depicts the five food groups using the familiar mealtime visual of a place setting. It is part of the USDA's Web-based initiative at ChooseMyPlate.gov, providing information, a food guidance system, and a personalized daily food plan to help you build a healthy diet based on the 2010 *Dietary Guidelines for Americans*. You want to consume nutrient-dense foods—fruits, vegetables, whole grains, and lean dairy and protein foods—but limit energy-dense foods, which provide kilocalories from solid fats and added sugars but little nutrition. Daily physical activity is encouraged to better manage your weight and health.

What Is the Exchange System?

The **exchange lists** for meal planning were designed in 1950 to give people with diabetes a structured, balanced eating plan. The lists are still in use today. Unlike some of the other dietary guides, the exchange lists group foods according to their carbohydrate, protein, and fat composition and provide specific portion sizes for each food. This assures that each food in the group contributes a similar amount of kilocalories per exchange (see Table 2.8 part 1).

This system of exchanges is organized into six food groups: starch, fruit, milk, vegetable, meat, and fat. You might be surprised to find some foods located in unexpected places. For example, in MyPlate, cheese is in the milk group because of its calcium content. In the exchange system, cheese is in the meat group because it has less carbohydrate than milk or yogurt but contains levels of protein and fat similar to those found in chicken or meat. Potatoes are not found in the vegetable list, but in the starch list; bacon is considered a fat exchange because it contains more fat than protein; and peanut butter is found in both the high-fat meat list and the fat list because it is high in both protein and fat.

Using the exchange lists is a convenient method for designing a flexible meal plan. Because of their similar macronutrient composition, foods within each group can be exchanged or swapped with each other. The flexibility of this meal plan makes it a useful tool for controlling proportions of carbohydrate, protein, and fat intake. Table 2.8 part 2 presents the number of exchanges in healthy, balanced diets of different kilocalorie levels that consist of fifty-five percent carbohydrate, twenty percent protein, and twenty-five percent fat. For example, using these percentages of macronutrients, a daily menu that contains approximately 1,800 kilocalories would include nine starch, four fruit, two low-fat milk, five non-starchy vegetable, five lean meat or meat substitute, and six fat exchanges. As you can see from the table, the higher the kilocalorie intake, the greater the number of exchanges allowed.

THE TAKE-HOME MESSAGE The Exchange System is a convenient tool for creating meal plans based on the macronutrient content and total kilocalories of foods. The plan contains six food groups: starch, fruit, milk, vegetables, meat, and fat. Foods within each group can be exchanged or swapped to add variety to meals and snacks.

What Information Is on the Food Label?

Although most people probably do not pay close attention to the food labels of items they purchase at the supermarket, the information on labels can be tremendously useful when it comes to planning a healthy diet.

Food Labels Are Strictly Regulated by the FDA

To help consumers make informed food choices, the Food and Drug Administration (FDA) regulates the labeling of all packaged foods in the United States. Since the 1930s, the FDA has mandated that every packaged food be labeled with:

exchange lists A diet planning tool that groups foods together based on their carbohydrate, protein, and fat content. One food on the list can be exchanged for another food on the same list.

TABLE 2.8 Part 1: Macronutrients per Exchange by Food Group

Food Group	Carbohydrate (grams)	Protein (grams)	Fat (grams)	Kilocalories
Carbohydrate Group				
Starch	15	3	0–1	80
Fruit	15	0	0	60
Milk				
Nonfat, low-fat	12	8	0–3	100
Reduced fat	12	8	5	120
Whole	12	8	8	160
Sweets, desserts, and other carbohydrates	15	Varies	Varies	Varies
Non-starchy vegetables	5	2	0	25
Meat and Meat Substitutes Group				
Lean	0	7	0–3	100
Medium-fat	0	7	4–7	130
High-fat	0	7	8+	150
Fat Group	0	0	5	45

Part 2: Number of Exchanges per Day by Kilocalorie Intake

Food Group	1,500 kcal	1,800 kcal	2,000 kcal	2,200 kcal	2,400 kcal
Starch	8	9	10	11	12
Fruit	3	4	4	4	5
Milk, low-fat	2	2	3	3	3
Non-starchy vegetables	4	5	6	6	7
Meat and meat substitutes, lean	3	5	5	6	7
Fat	5	6	6	7	7

Note: Check Appendix C for the variation in macronutrient and kilocalorie content per exchange based on the food chosen from each food group.

- The name of the food
- The net weight, which is the weight of the food in the package, excluding the weight of the package or packing material
- The name and address of the manufacturer or distributor
- A list of ingredients in descending order by weight, with the heaviest item listed first

New labeling laws have been enacted to further benefit the consumer.[23] In 1990, the Nutrition Labeling and Education Act (NLEA) began mandating that labels include uniform nutrition information, serving sizes, and specific criteria for health claims. Additional requirements for food labels have since been passed to require that labels now also show:

- Nutrition information, which lists total kilocalories, kilocalories from fat, total fat, saturated fat, *trans* fats, cholesterol, sodium, total carbohydrate, dietary fiber, sugars, vitamin A, vitamin C, calcium, and iron
- Serving sizes that are uniform among similar products, which allows for easier comparison shopping
- An indication of how a serving of the food fits into an overall daily diet
- Uniform definitions for descriptive label terms such as "light" and "fat free"
- Health claims that are accurate and science based, if made about the food or one of its nutrients

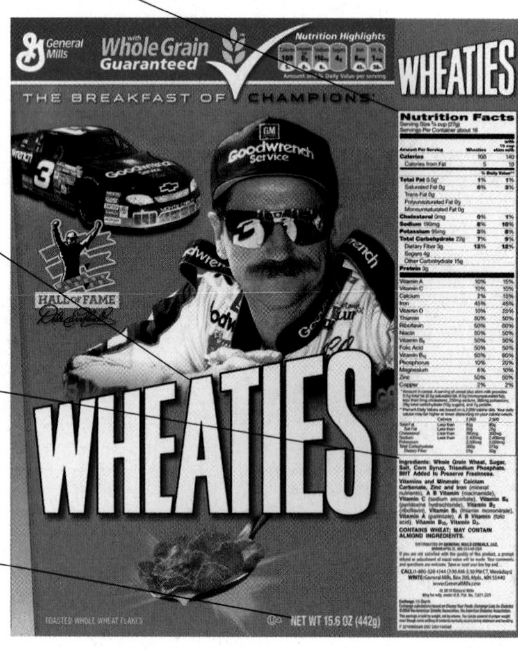

The **Nutrition Facts panel** lists standardized serving sizes and specific nutrients, and shows how a serving of the food fits into a healthy diet by stating its contribution to the percentage of the Daily Value for each nutrient. The old cereal box doesn't contain this information.

The **name** of the product must be displayed on the front label.

The **ingredients** must be listed in descending order by weight. This format is missing in the old box. Whole-grain wheat is the predominant ingredient in the current cereal box.

The **net weight** of the food in the box must now be located at the bottom of the package.

▲ **Figure 2.11 Out with The Old and In with the New**
(a) A cereal box from the 1920s carried vague nutrition information. **(b)** Today, manufacturers must adhere to strict labeling requirements mandated by the FDA.

Compare the two food labels in **Figure 2.11**. Note that the amount and type of nutrition information on the 1925 box of cereal is vague and less informative than the more recent version, which meets the FDA's current labeling requirements.

Very few foods are exempt from carrying a Nutrition Facts panel on the label. Such foods include plain coffee and tea; some spices, flavorings, and other foods that don't provide a significant amount of nutrients; deli items, bakery foods, and other ready-to-eat foods that are prepared and sold in retail establishments; restaurant meals; and foods produced by small businesses (companies that have total sales of less than $500,000).[24]

Whereas raw fruits and vegetables and fresh fish typically don't have a label, these foods fall under the FDA's voluntary, point-of-purchase nutrition information program. Under the guidelines of this program, at least 60 percent of a nationwide sample of grocery stores must post the nutrition information of the most commonly eaten fruits, vegetables, and fish near where the foods are sold. The FDA surveys a sample of nationwide grocery stores every two years. The latest findings show that over 70 percent of stores surveyed are in compliance with the program.[25]

Although a similar voluntary program is in place for meat and poultry, the USDA (which regulates meat and poultry) is considering mandating labels on these foods. This is because less than 60 percent of meat and poultry retailers and manufacturers have provided the information voluntarily.[26, 27]

The Nutrition Facts Panel Indicates Nutrient Values

One area of the food label in particular, the **Nutrition Facts panel,** provides a nutritional snapshot of the food inside a package. As mentioned earlier, by law, the panel must list amounts of specific nutrients. If an additional nutrient such as vitamin E or vitamin B_{12} has been added, or if the product makes a claim about a nutrient, then that nutrient must also be listed. Other nutrients, such as additional vitamins and minerals, can be voluntarily listed by the manufacturer. The majority of packaged foods contain this nutrition information.

We can use **Figure 2.12** to walk through a sample Nutrition Facts panel for a box of macaroni and cheese. At the top of the panel is the serving size. By law, the serving size must be listed both by weight in grams (less useful to you) and in common household measures, such as cups and ounces (more useful to you). Because serving sizes are

Nutrition Facts panel The area on the food label that provides a list of specific nutrients obtained in one serving of the food.

standardized among similar food products, consumers can compare one brand of macaroni and cheese with a different brand to assess which one better meets their needs.

The rest of the information on the panel is based on the listed serving size (in this case, one cup) of the food. For example, if you ate two servings (two cups) of this macaroni and cheese, which is the number of servings in the entire box, you would double the nutrient information on the label to calculate the kilocalories as well as the fat and other nutrients. The servings per container are particularly useful for portion control.

Below the serving size is listed the kilocalories per serving. The kilocalories from fat listing gives you an idea of what proportion of the food's kilocalories comes from fat. In this box of macaroni and cheese, 110 out of a total of 250 kilocalories—that is, nearly half—are from fat.

Next are the nutrients that should be limited or added to the diet. Americans typically eat too much fat, including saturated fat, *trans* fat, and cholesterol, and too much sodium. In contrast, they tend to fall short in dietary fiber, vitamins A and C, and iron. These are on the label to remind consumers to make sure to eat foods rich in these substances. The Nutrition Facts panel can be your best shopping guide when identifying and choosing foods that are low in the nutrients you want to limit (like saturated fat) and high in the nutrients that you need to eat in higher amounts (like fiber).

Are you wondering what determines if a food contains a "high" or "low" amount of a specific nutrient? That's where the Daily Values come into play.

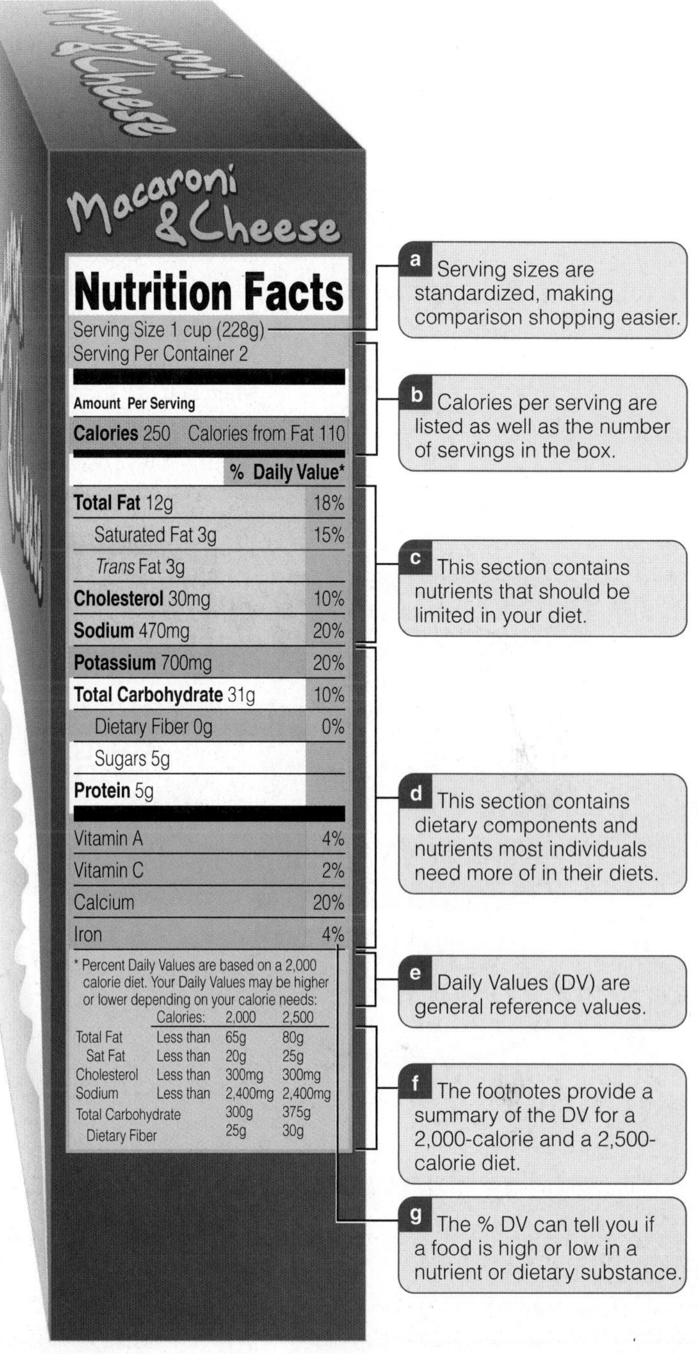

▲ **Figure 2.12 The Anatomy of the Nutrition Facts Panel**

Source: U.S. Food and Drug Administration. Protecting and Promoting Your Health. 2012. *How to Understand and Use the Nutrition Facts Label.* Available at www.fda.gov/Food/ResourcesForYou/Consumers/NFLPM/ucm274593.htm. Accessed February 2012.

The Daily Values Help Compare Packaged Foods

Unlike the DRIs, which are precise recommended amounts for each nutrient, the Daily Values (DVs), listed on the Nutrition Facts panel, are general reference levels for the nutrients listed on the food label. The DVs give a general idea of how the nutrients in the food fit into the overall diet. The DVs are based on older reference levels and are not as current as the DRIs. For example, whereas the DRIs recommend an upper level of dietary sodium of no more than 2,300 milligrams daily, the DVs use less than 2,400 milligrams as the reference level.

There are no DVs listed on the label for *trans* fat, sugars, and protein. For *trans* fat and sugars there isn't enough information available to set reference values for these nutrients. Although there are reference values for protein, consuming adequate amounts of protein isn't a health concern for most Americans over age 4, so listing the percent of the DV for this nutrient isn't warranted on the label. The DV for protein will only be listed if the product, such as a jar of baby food, is being marketed for children under the age of 4, or if a claim is made about the food, such as that it is "high in protein."[28]

The DVs on the food label are based on a 2,000-kilocalorie diet. Individuals who need more or fewer than 2,000 kilocalories daily may have DV values that are higher or lower than those listed on the Nutrition Facts panel.

If a serving provides 20 percent or more of the DV for a given nutrient, it is considered high in that nutrient. A serving of the macaroni and cheese (refer again to Figure 2.12) is high in sodium and calcium. If a serving provides 5 percent or less of the DV for a nutrient, it is considered low in that nutrient. A serving of macaroni and cheese doesn't provide much fiber, vitamin A, vitamin C, or iron.

Lastly, depending on the size of the food package, there may be a footnote at the bottom of the label. This provides a summary of the DVs for a 2,000-kilocalorie diet as well as a 2,500-kilocalorie diet. This area of the panel is something of a "cheat sheet" when you are shopping so that you don't have to memorize the values. As you can see from the footnote, you should try to keep your sodium intake to less than 2,400 milligrams daily. Because you know that this macaroni and cheese is high in sodium,

a Because this can of chicken noodle soup displays the "low sodium" nutrient claim, it can't provide more than 140 milligrams of sodium in a serving.

b This can of soup has more than 25 percent less sodium than the classic version, so the term "less" can be displayed on its label.

c The classic variety of chicken noodle soup has the most sodium per serving.

▲ **Figure 2.13 Soup's On!**
Nutrient claims on the food label must conform to strict criteria.

providing 470 milligrams, or 20 percent of the DV, you should try to keep the sodium in your remaining food choices during the day to less than 2,000 milligrams.

The Nutrition Facts panel on the side or back of the package can help you make healthier food choices, and some foods carry claims on their front labels that may also influence your decision to buy.

Label Claims Can Reveal Potential Health Benefits

In the 1980s, the Kellogg Company ran an ad campaign for its fiber-rich All Bran cereal reminding the public of the National Cancer Institute's recommendation to eat low-fat, high-fiber foods, fresh fruits, and vegetables to maintain a healthy weight. According to the FDA, sales of high-fiber cereals increased over 35 percent within a year.[29] Manufacturers realized that putting nutrition and health claims on labels was effective in influencing consumer purchases. Supermarket shelves were soon crowded with products boasting various claims.

The FDA mandates that all claims on labels follow strict guidelines. Currently, the FDA allows the use of three types of claims on food products: (1) **nutrient content claims,** (2) **health claims,** and (3) **structure/function claims.** All foods displaying these claims on the label must meet specified criteria.

nutrient content claims Claims on the food label that describe the level or amount of a nutrient in the food. Terms such as *free, high, reduced,* or *lite* are examples of nutrient content claims.

health claims Claims on food labels that describe a relationship between a food, food component, dietary ingredient, or dietary supplement and a disease or health-related condition.

structure/function claims Claims on the label that describe the role of a nutrient or dietary compound that is proposed to influence the structure or function of the human body. For example, "Calcium builds strong bones" is a structure/function claim.

Nutrient Content Claims

A food product can make a claim about the amount of a nutrient it contains (or doesn't contain) by using descriptive terms such as *free* (fat-free yogurt), *high* (high-fiber crackers), *low* (low saturated fat cereal), *reduced* (reduced-sodium soup), and *extra lean* (extra lean ground beef) as long as it meets the strict criteria designated by the FDA. These terms can help identify at a glance the food items that best meet your needs. For instance, if you want to decrease or limit the amount of sodium in your diet, you could look for low-sodium claims on labels.

Look at the labels of the canned soups in **Figure 2.13**. Note that the "low-sodium" version of the chicken soup cannot contain more than 140 milligrams of sodium per serving. In contrast, the soup with the term "less sodium" on the label contains 450 milligrams of sodium per serving, which is at least 25 percent less sodium than the regular variety. The can of classic chicken soup contains almost 900 milligrams for a serving, which is likely the same or even more sodium than the average American consumes at dinner. Table 2.9 on page 64 provides some of the most common nutrient claims on food labels, and the specific criteria that each claim must meet as mandated by the FDA.

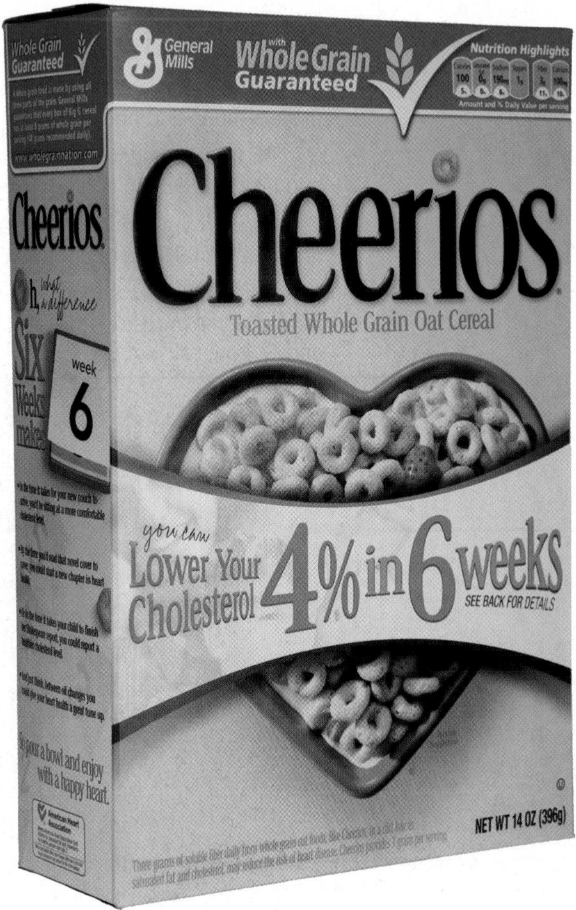

Cheerios uses an authorized health claim stating that soluble fiber reduces the risk of heart disease.

Health Claims

Suppose you are sitting at your kitchen table eating a bowl of Cheerios in skim milk, and staring at the cereal box. You notice a claim on the front of box that states: "The soluble fiber in Cheerios, as part of a heart-healthy diet, can help lower your cholesterol." Do you recognize this as a health claim that links Cheerios with better heart health?

A health claim must contain two important components: (1) a food or a dietary compound, such as fiber, and (2) a corresponding disease or health-related condition that is associated

TABLE 2.9 What Does That Labeling Term Mean?

Nutrient	Free	Low	Reduced/Less	Light
Calories	<5 kilocalories (kcal) per serving	<40 kcal per serving	At least 25% fewer kcal per serving	If the food contains 50% or more of its kcal from fat, then the fat must be reduced
Fat	<0.5 grams (g) per serving	<3 g per serving	At least 25% less fat per serving	Same as above
Saturated fat	<0.5 g per serving	<1 g per serving	At least 25% less saturated fat per serving	N/A
Cholesterol	<2 milligrams (mg) per serving	<20 mg per serving	At least 25% less cholesterol per serving	N/A
Sodium	<5 mg per serving	<140 mg per serving	At least 25% less sodium per serving	If the sodium is reduced by at least 50% per serving
Sugars	<0.5 g	N/A	As least 25% less sugar per serving	N/A

Other Labeling Terms

Term	Definition
"High," "Rich in," or "Excellent source of"	The food contains 20% or more of the DV of the nutrient in a serving. Can be used to describe protein, vitamins, minerals, fiber, or potassium.
"Good source of"	A serving of the food provides 10–19% of the DV of the nutrient. Can be used to describe protein, vitamins, minerals, fiber, or potassium.
"More," "Added," "Extra," or "Plus"	A serving of the food provides 10% of the DV. Can only be used to describe vitamins, minerals, protein, fiber, and potassium.
"Lean"	Can be used on seafood and meat that contains less than 10 g of fat, 4.5 g or less of saturated fat, and less than 95 mg of cholesterol per serving.
"Extra lean"	Can be used on seafood and meat that contains less than 5 g of fat, less than 2 g of saturated fat, and less than 95 mg of cholesterol per serving.
"Healthy"	Low in fat and saturated fat; limited in cholesterol content; sodium content can't exceed 360 mg for individual foods or 480 for meal-type foods; contains 10% of the DV of one or more of vitamins A and C, iron, calcium, protein, or fiber.

N/A = not applicable

with the substance.[30] In the Cheerios example, the soluble fiber (the dietary compound) that naturally occurs in oats has been shown to lower blood cholesterol levels (the corresponding health-related condition), which can help reduce the risk of heart disease.

There are three types of health claims: (1) authorized health claims, (2) health claims based on authoritative statements, and (3) qualified health claims. The differences between them lie in the amount of supporting research and agreement among scientists about the strength of the relationship between the food or dietary ingredient and the disease or condition. See Table 2.10 for a definition and examples of each type of health claim.

Structure/Function Claims

The last type of label claim is the structure/function claim, which describes how a nutrient or dietary compound affects the structure or function of the human

TABLE 2.10 Sorting Out the Label Claims

Type of Claim	Definition	Examples
Authorized health claims (well established)	Claims are based on a well-established relationship between the food or compound and the health benefit. Food manufacturers must submit a petition to the FDA and provide the scientific research that backs up the claim. If there is significant agreement in the supporting research and a consensus among numerous scientists and experts in the field that there is a relationship between the food or dietary ingredient and the disease or health condition, the FDA will allow an authorized health claim. Specified wording must be used.	The FDA has approved 12 authorized health claims. 1. Calcium and osteoporosis 2. Sodium and hypertension 3. Dietary fat and cancer 4. Dietary saturated fat and cholesterol and risk of coronary heart disease 5. Fiber-containing grain products, fruits, and vegetables and cancer 6. Fruits, vegetables, and grain products that contain fiber, particularly soluble fiber, and the risk of coronary heart disease 7. Fruits and vegetables and cancer 8. Folate and neural tube defects 9. Dietary sugar, alcohol, and dental caries 10. Soluble fiber from certain foods and risk of coronary heart disease 11. Soy protein and risk of coronary heart disease 12. Plant sterol/stanol esters and risk of coronary heart disease
Health claims based on authoritative statements (well established)	Claims based on statements made by a U.S. government agency, such as the Centers for Disease Control and Prevention (CDC) and the National Institutes of Health (NIH). If the FDA approves a claim submitted by the manufacturer, the wording of the claim must include "may," as in "whole grains may help reduce the risk of heart disease," to illustrate that other factors in addition to the food or dietary ingredient may play a role in the disease or condition. This type of health claim can only be used on food and cannot be used on dietary supplements.	■ Whole-grain foods and risk of heart disease and certain cancers ■ Potassium and the risk of high blood pressure
Qualified health claims (less well established)	Claims based on evidence that is still emerging. However, the current evidence to support the claim is greater than the evidence suggesting that the claim isn't valid. These claims are allowed in order to expedite the communication of potential beneficial health information to the public. They must be accompanied by the statement "the evidence to support the claim is limited or not conclusive" or "some scientific evidence suggests. . . ." Many experts, including the Academy of Nutrition and Dietetics, don't support this type of health claim, as it is based on emerging evidence. Qualified health claims can be used on dietary supplements if approved by the FDA.	■ Selenium and cancer ■ Antioxidant vitamins and cancer ■ Nuts and heart disease ■ Omega-3 fatty acids and coronary heart disease ■ B vitamins and vascular disease ■ Monounsaturated fatty acids from olive oil and coronary heart disease

▲ **Figure 2.14 A Structure/Function Label Claim**
A structure/function claim describes how a nutrient or substance, such as the antioxidants that have been added to this cereal, support a function in the body, such as the immune system.

body (**Figure 2.14**).[31] The claims "calcium (nutrient) builds strong bones (body structure)" and "fiber (dietary compound) maintains bowel regularity (body function)" are examples of structure/function claims. Structure/function claims cannot state that the nutrient or dietary compound can be used to treat a disease or a condition.[32] These claims can be made on both foods and dietary supplements. Unlike the health claims, structure/function claims don't need to be preapproved by the FDA. They do need to be truthful and not misleading, but the manufacturer is responsible for making sure that the claims are accurate.

Structure/function claims can be a source of confusion. Shoppers can easily fall into the trap of assuming that one brand of a product with a structure/function claim on its label is superior to another product without the claim. For instance, a yogurt that says "Calcium builds strong bones" on its label may be identical to another yogurt without the flashy label claim. The consumer has to recognize the difference between claims that are supported by a significant amount of solid research and approved by the FDA, and structure/function claims that don't need prior approval for use.

Dietary supplements that use structure/function claims must display a disclaimer on the label stating that the FDA did not evaluate the claim and that the dietary supplement is not intended to "diagnose, treat, cure or prevent any disease." Manufacturers of foods bearing structure/function claims do not have to display this disclaimer on the label.

Although keeping the types of health claims and the structure/function claims straight can be challenging, here's one way to remember them: Authorized health claims and health claims based on authoritative statements are the strongest, as they are based on years of accumulated research or an authoritative statement. Qualified health claims are made on potentially healthful foods or dietary ingredients but because the evidence is still emerging, the claim has to be "qualified" as such. All health claims provide information on how the food or dietary ingredient can help reduce your risk of a condition or a disease.

Structure/function claims are the weakest claims, as they are just statements or facts about the role the nutrient or dietary ingredient plays in the body. They can't claim how the food or dietary ingredient lowers the risk of developing a chronic disease such as heart disease or cancer. In general, label claims with less established scientific evidence behind them have the weakest wording.

THE TAKE-HOME MESSAGE The FDA regulates the labeling on all packaged foods. Every food label must contain the name of the food, its net weight, the name and address of the manufacturer or distributor, a list of ingredients, and standardized nutrition information. The FDA allows and regulates the use of nutrient content claims, health claims, and structure/function claims on food labels. Any foods or dietary supplements displaying these label claims must meet specified criteria and the claims must be truthful.

TABLE TIPS

Tips for an Adequate, Balanced, Varied, and Moderate Diet

Keep healthy snacks such as whole-grain crackers in your dorm room and combine them with protein-rich peanut butter or low-fat yogurt.

Pop a snack-pack size of *light* microwave popcorn for a portion-controlled whole-grain snack while you study.

Adopt a multicolor code to guide your food choices. Add tomato slices and a low-fat cheese slice to your whole-grain sandwich and carrots to your tossed green salad to ensure that your choices are adequate and varied.

Pack your own snack-sized portions of dried fruit, trail mix, whole-wheat crackers, baby carrots, or salt-free pretzels to carry in your backpack. Snack-sized bags of nuts and seeds are a nutritious way to help you avoid the vending machine and eat smaller, more moderate portions.

Keep your sweets to no more than about 100 kilocalories.

Putting It All Together

Healthy eating involves the key principles of balance, variety, and moderation. Nutrient density, energy density, and portion size also need to be taken into account when making food choices. Though implementing this advice may seem difficult at first, scientifically sound reference values and tools have been developed to make healthy eating much easier. These include the DRIs, the 2010 *Dietary Guidelines for Americans*, MyPlate, exchange lists for creating healthy menus with a variety of foods, and the Nutrition Facts panels on food labels. Table 2.11 provides a comparison of these tools, showing some of the unique features of each.

TABLE 2.11 Putting It All Together: Tools for Healthy Eating

	DRIs	*Dietary Guidelines for Americans, 2010*	MyPlate	Nutrition Facts Panel	Exchange Lists for Healthy Eating
What Are They?	Specific reference values for each nutrient by age and gender	Reflect the most current nutrition and physical activity recommendations for good health	A representational icon that depicts five food groups using the familiar mealtime visual of a place setting	Contains important nutrition information to be used to compare food products	Exchange lists are organized into food groups by their carbohydrate, protein, fat, and kilocalorie contents.
How Do They Guide You in Healthy Eating?	DRIs provide recommendations to prevent malnutrition and chronic diseases for each nutrient. The upper level is designed to prevent overnutrition or toxicity.	The *Dietary Guidelines* emphasize healthy food choices, maintaining healthy weight, and physical activity. Guidelines for types of foods, moderate alcohol intake, and food safety are also included.	MyPlate is the focal point for the Web-based ChooseMyPlate.gov initiative, which provides information to build a healthy diet based on the *Dietary Guidelines for Americans, 2010*.	You can use the Nutrition Facts panel to compare the nutrient density of foods.	It's easy to plan healthy menus with a variety of foods. The exchanges are based on specific food portion sizes plus various fat levels in foods.
What Are They Made Up Of?	EARs, RDAs, AIs, ULs, and AMDRs	Divided into nine categories: 1. Adequate nutrients 2. Weight management 3. Physical activity 4. Food groups 5. Fats 6. Carbohydrates 7. Sodium and potassium 8. Alcoholic beverages 9. Food safety	Recommendations are made for physical activity as well as five food groups, plus oils: 1. Vegetables 2. Fruits 3. Grains 4. Protein 5. Dairy 6. Oils	Information is presented about: ■ Serving size ■ Servings per package ■ Total kilocalories and kilocalories from fat ■ Macronutrients ■ Vitamins and minerals ■ % Daily Values	Exchange lists consist of six food groups: 1. Starch 2. Meat 3. Vegetables 4. Fruit 5. Milk 6. Fat

Visual Chapter Summary

1 Healthy Eating Is Based on Five Key Principles

Healthy eating involves the key principles of balance, variety, moderation, and consuming nutrient-dense and low–energy-dense foods. Foods should be nutrient dense to provide adequate nutrition, but low in energy density to prevent unwanted weight gain.

2 Dietary Reference Intakes Are Reference Values for Each Nutrient

The Dietary Reference Intakes (DRIs) are specific reference values, based on age and gender, that express the quantities of the essential nutrients needed daily. The DRIs are designed to prevent nutrient deficiencies, maintain good health, prevent chronic diseases, and avoid unhealthy excesses. The DRIs consist of the Estimated Average Requirement, Recommended Dietary Allowance, Adequate Intake, Tolerable Upper Intake Level, and the Acceptable Macronutrient Distribution Ranges. The EER indicates how much energy an individual needs based on age, gender, and activity level.

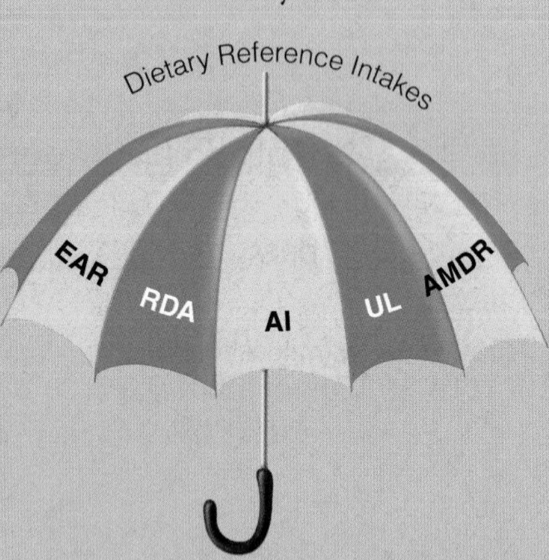

3 *Dietary Guidelines for Americans* Are Recommendations to Lower Risk of Disease

The *Dietary Guidelines for Americans, 2010* give the current nutrition and physical activity recommendations for healthy Americans aged 2 and older. These guidelines can help improve the diet and lower the risk of chronic diseases and conditions such as diabetes mellitus, heart disease, certain cancers, osteoporosis, obesity, high blood pressure, and high blood cholesterol levels.

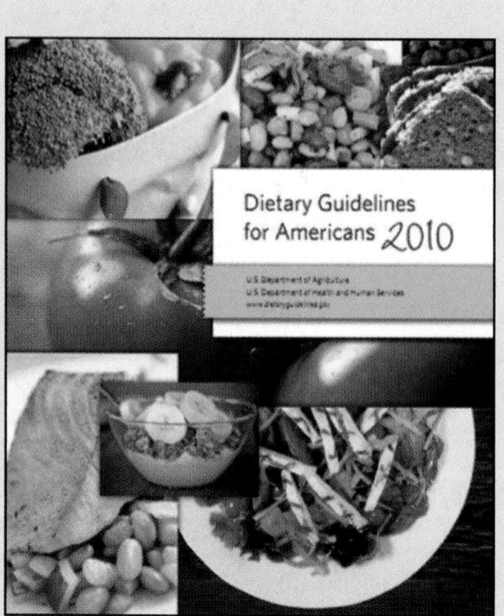

4 MyPlate Is a Food Guidance System

MyPlate is the USDA's latest food guidance system. It visually represents many of the recommendations in the *Dietary Guidelines for Americans, 2010* and helps plan a diet to meet the daily DRIs for the essential nutrients. There are five food groups: fruits, vegetables, grains, protein, and dairy. Oils are not shown on MyPlate because they are not a food group.

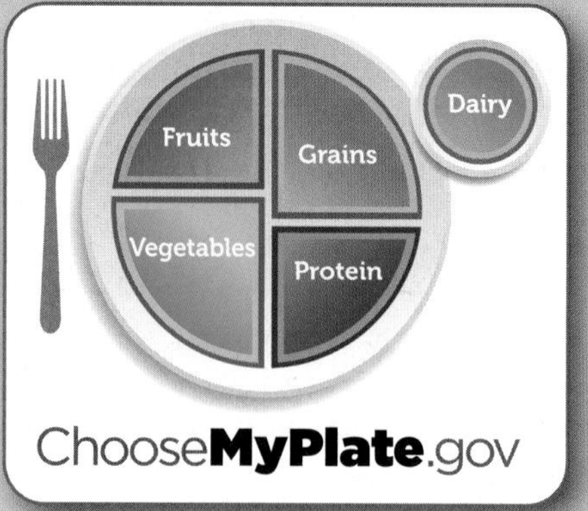

5 The Exchange System Is Based on the Macronutrient Content of Foods

Exchange lists group foods according to their carbohydrate, protein, fat, and kilocalorie content while providing specific portion sizes. Using the exchange lists for meal planning is a convenient method for developing flexible meal plans.

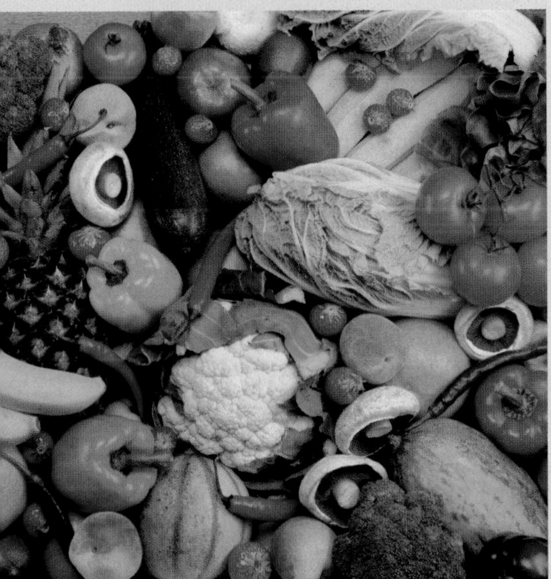

6 Food Labels Provide Nutrient Content Information

The FDA regulates all packaged food labels. The Nutrition Facts panel must list the serving size of the food and the corresponding amount of kilocalories, fat, saturated fat, *trans* fat, cholesterol, sodium, sugars, protein, vitamins A and C, calcium, and iron. The Daily Values are reference levels of intakes for the nutrients listed on the food label.

A food product label can carry a nutrient content claim using descriptive terms such as *free, high, low, reduced,* and *extra lean*, as long as it meets the strict criteria for each item designated by the FDA. A health claim must contain a food compound or a dietary ingredient and an associated disease or health-related condition. Structure/function claims describe how a food or dietary compound affects the structure or function of the body.

Macaroni & Cheese

Nutrition Facts

Serving Size 1 cup (228g)
Serving Per Container 2

Amount Per Serving	
Calories 250 Calories from Fat 110	
	% Daily Value*
Total Fat 12g	18%
Saturated Fat 3g	15%
Trans Fat 3g	
Cholesterol 30mg	10%
Sodium 470mg	20%
Potassium 700mg	20%
Total Carbohydrate 31g	10%
Dietary Fiber 0g	0%
Sugars 5g	
Protein 5g	
Vitamin A	4%
Vitamin C	2%
Calcium	20%
Iron	4%

* Percent Daily Values are based on a 2,000 calorie diet. Your Daily Values may be higher or lower depending on your calorie needs:

	Calories:	2,000	2,500
Total Fat	Less than	65g	80g
Sat Fat	Less than	20g	25g
Cholesterol	Less than	300mg	300mg
Sodium	Less than	2,400mg	2,400mg
Total Carbohydrate		300g	375g
Dietary Fiber		25g	30g

Terms to Know

- balance
- variety
- moderation
- nutrient density
- energy density
- undernutrition
- malnutrition
- overnutrition
- portion
- serving size
- Dietary Reference Intakes (DRI)
- *Dietary Guidelines for Americans*
- MyPlate
- Daily Values (DVs)
- Estimated Average Requirement (EAR)
- Recommended Dietary Allowance (RDA)
- Adequate Intake (AI)
- Tolerable Upper Intake Level (UL)
- toxicity
- Acceptable Macronutrients Distribution Ranges (AMDRs)
- Estimated Energy Requirement (EER)
- food guidance systems
- exchange lists
- Nutrition Facts panel
- nutrient content claims
- health claims
- structure/function claims

MasteringNutrition™

Build your knowledge—and confidence!—in the Study Area of MasteringNutrition with a variety of study tools.

Check Your Understanding

1. The *Dietary Guidelines for Americans, 2010* recommend
   a. consuming adequate nutrients within kilocalorie needs and being physically active daily.
   b. stopping smoking and walking daily.
   c. sleeping eight hours a night and jogging every other day.
   d. consuming adequate nutrients within kilocalorie needs and drinking more alcohol.
2. Nutrient-dense foods
   a. contain an equal balance of carbohydrates, proteins, and fats.
   b. are high in nutrients and lower in kilocalories.
   c. have a nutrition label.

d. have greater weight than volume.
3. The Dietary Reference Intakes (DRIs) are reference values for nutrients and are designed to
   a. only prevent a nutritional deficiency.
   b. provide a general range of nutrient needs.
   c. prevent nutritional deficiencies by meeting nutrient needs and prevent the consumption of excessive and dangerous amounts of nutrients.
   d. apply only to infants and children.
4. The Estimated Average Requirement (EAR) is
   a. the estimated amount of a nutrient that should be consumed daily to be healthy.
   b. the amount of a nutrient that meets the average needs of 50 percent of individuals in a specific age and gender group.
   c. the maximum safe amount of a nutrient that should be consumed daily.
   d. the amount of a nutrient that meets the needs of 99 percent of the population.
5. MyPlate is a food guidance system that can
   a. help implement the recommendations in the DRIs.
   b. help individuals use the advice in the *Dietary Guidelines for Americans.*
   c. provide personalized food choices among a variety of food groups to help create a balanced diet.
   d. do all of the above.
6. Which of the following are the food groups in MyPlate?
   a. grains, vegetables, dairy, sweets, and meat and beans
   b. grains, fruits, alcohol, sweets, and protein
   c. grains, vegetables, fruits, dairy, and protein
   d. grains, vegetables, sweets, milk, and protein
7. Which of the following foods is most nutrient dense?
   a. an orange ice pop
   b. an orange
   c. orange-flavored punch
   d. orange sherbet
8. By law, which of the following MUST be listed on the food label?
   a. kilocalories, fat, and potassium
   b. fat, saturated fat, and vitamin E
   c. kilocalories, fat, and saturated fat
   d. kilocalories, sodium, and vitamin D
9. Bran cereal that carries a "high-fiber" claim on its label is an example of a
   a. nutrient claim.
   b. structure/function claim.
   c. health claim.
   d. density claim.
10. A yogurt that states that a serving provides 30 percent of the Daily Value for calcium contains a ____________ amount of calcium.
   a. high
   b. medium
   c. low
   d. negligible

Answers

1. (a) The *Dietary Guidelines for Americans* recommend a balanced diet to meet nutrient needs without overconsuming kilocalories, and that individuals be physically active daily. Walking or jogging are wonderful ways to be physically active. Though the *Dietary Guidelines* do not specifically address stopping smoking, this is a habit worth kicking. Sleeping eight hours a night isn't mentioned in the *Dietary Guidelines* but is another beneficial lifestyle habit. Many people should abstain from alcohol, and those who choose to drink should do so only in moderation.
2. (b) Nutrient-dense foods are high in nutrients, such as vitamins and minerals, but low in energy (kilocalories).
3. (c) The DRIs recommend the amount of nutrients needed to prevent deficiencies, maintain good health, and avoid toxicity.
4. (b) The EAR is the amount of a nutrient that would meet the needs of half of the individuals in a specific age and gender group. The EAR is used to obtain the Recommended Dietary Allowance (RDA), which is the amount of a nutrient that should be consumed daily to maintain good health. The Tolerable Upper Intake Level (UL) is the maximum amount of a nutrient that can be consumed on a regular basis that is unlikely to cause harm.
5. (d) MyPlate is a food guidance tool that helps individuals create a balanced diet. It is designed to help meet the nutrient needs recommended in the DRIs and also implement the advice in the *Dietary Guidelines for Americans.*
6. (c) Grains, vegetables, fruits, dairy, and protein are the five basic food groups in MyPlate. Sweets and alcohol are not food groups and should be limited in the diet.
7. (b) Though an orange ice pop or orange sherbet may be a refreshing treat on a hot day, the orange is by far the most nutrient-dense food among these choices. The orange-flavored punch is a sugary drink.
8. (c) The Nutrition Facts panel on the package must indicate the amounts of kilocalories, fat, and saturated fat per serving. Vitamins E and D do not have to be listed unless they have been added to the food and/or the product makes a claim about them on the label.
9. (a) This high-fiber cereal label boasts a nutrient claim.
10. (a) A product with 20 percent or more of the Daily Value for a nutrient is considered "high" in that nutrient. If a food provides 5 percent or less of the Daily Value for a nutrient, it is considered "low" in that nutrient.

Answers to Myths and Misconceptions

1. **False.** Eating a balanced diet means not eating too much of any one food.
2. **False.** Nutrient density refers to foods that are high in nutrients but low in energy or kilocalories.
3. **True.** The Dietary Reference Intakes are specific reference values for each nutrient according to age, gender, and life stage. Their main focus is to maintain good health and reduce the risk of developing chronic diseases and avoid unhealthy excesses.

4. **True.** If there is adequate scientific evidence to establish an Estimated Average Requirement (EAR) for a nutrient, then an RDA can be calculated. Some nutrients have not been sufficiently researched to provide an EAR and therefore an Adequate Intake is recommended.
5. **True.** The five food groups are grains, vegetables, fruits, dairy, and protein.
6. **True.** These guidelines are the latest recommendations for nutrition and physical activity for healthy Americans over the age of 2.
7. **False.** Many people overconsume a food at any one sitting by piling two or more portions of it on their plate.
8. **True.** The FDA requires a food label on all packaged food items, and specific information must be included.
9. **False.** A nutrient content claim can be made for a nutrient that is present in low or reduced amounts, as well as for one that is present in significant amounts. Specific terms approved by the FDA must be used.
10. **True.** Exchange lists allow you to swap foods within each food group while still controlling the amount of carbohydrate, protein, fat, and kilocalories you ingest.

Web Resources

- For more tips and resources for MyPlate, visit www.ChooseMyPlate.gov
- For details on the *Dietary Guidelines for Americans, 2010,* visit www.cnpp.usda.gov/DietaryGuidelines.htm

References

1. Simpson, K. M., E. R. Morris, and J. D. Cook. 1981. The Inhibitory Effect of Bran on Iron Absorption in Man. *American Journal of Clinical Nutrition* 34:1469–1478.
2. Murphy, S., J. Foote, L. Wilkens, P. Basiotis, A. Carlson, K. White, and K. Yonemoriet. 2006. Simple Measures of Dietary Variety Are Associated with Improved Dietary Quality. *Journal of the American Dietetic Association* 106:425–429.
3. Produce for Better Health Foundation. 2012. *Fruits and Vegetables, More Matters.* Available at www.fruitsandveggiesmorematters.org. Accessed February 2012.
4. Ledikwe, J. H., H. M. Blanck, L. K. Khan, M. K. Serdula, J. D. Seymour, B. C. Tohill, and B. J. Rolls. 2006. Low-Energy-Density Diets Are Associated with High Diet Quality in Adults in the United States. *Journal of the American Dietetic Association* 106:1172–1180.
5. Bell, E. A. and B. J. Rolls. 2001. Energy Density of Foods Affects Energy Intake Across Multiple Levels of Fat Content in Lean and Obese Women. *American Journal of Clinical Nutrition* 73:1010–1018.
6. Ledikwe, J. H., H. M. Blanck, L. K. Khan, M. K. Serdula, J. D. Seymour, B. C. Tohill, and B. J. Rolls. 2006. Dietary Energy Density Is Associated with Energy Intake and Weight Status in U.S. Adults. *American Journal of Clinical Nutrition* 83:1362–1368.
7. Ledikwe, J. H., B. J. Rolls, H. Smiciklas-Wright, D. C. Mitchell, J. D. Ard, C. Champagne, N. Karanja, P. Lin, V. J. Stevens, and L. J. Appel. 2007. Reductions in Dietary Energy Density Are Associated with Weight Loss in Overweight and Obese Participants in the PREMIER Trial. *American Journal of Clinical Nutrition* 85:1212–1221.
8. Greene, L., C. Z. Malpede, C. S. Henson, K. A. Hubbert, D. C. Heimburger, and J. D. Ard. 2006. Weight Maintenance 2 Years After Participation in a Weight Loss Program Promoting Low-Energy-Density Foods. *Obesity* 14:1795–1801.
9. Rolls, B. J., E. A. Bell, V. H. Castellanos, M. Chow, C. L. Pelkman, and M. L. Thorwart. 1999. Energy Density but Not Fat Content of Foods Affected Energy Intake in Lean and Obese Women. *American Journal of Clinical Nutrition* 69: 863–871.
10. U.S. Department of Agriculture. 2011. *Dietary Guidance.* Available at http://fnic.nal.usda.gov. Accessed February 2012.
11. Institute of Medicine. 2003. Dietary Reference Intakes: Applications in Dietary Planning. Washington, DC:The National Academies Press.
12. Barr, S. I., S. P. Murphy, T. D. Agurs-Collins, and M. I. Poose. 2003. Planning Diets for Individuals Using the Dietary Reference Intakes. *Nutrition Reviews* 61:352–360.
13. Tarasuk, V. 2006. Use of Population-Weighted Estimated Average Requirements as a Basis for Daily Values on Food Labels. *American Journal of Clinical Nutrition* 83:1217S–1222S.
14. Institute of Medicine. 2001. *Dietary Reference Intakes for Vitamin A, Vitamin K, Arsenic, Boron, Chromium, Copper, Iodine, Iron, Manganese, Molybdenum, Nickel, Silicon, Vanadium, and Zinc.* Washington, DC: The National Academies Press.
15. Ibid.
16. Shils, M. E., M. Shike, A. C. Ross, B. Caballero, and R. J. Cousins. 2006. *Modern Nutrition in Health and Disease,* 10th ed. Baltimore: Lippincott Williams & Wilkins.
17. U.S. Department of Agriculture. 2011. [Q10] *Dietary Guidance.* Available at http://fnic.nal.usda.gov. Accessed February 2012.
18. Institute of Medicine. 2002. *Dietary Reference Intakes for Energy, Carbohydrate, Fiber, Fat, Fatty Acids, Cholesterol, Protein, and Amino Acids.* Washington, DC: The National Academies Press.
19. Davis, C. and E. Saltos. 1999. Dietary Recommendations and How They Have Changed Over Time, in *America's Eating Habits: Changes and Consequences.* E. Frazo, ed. *Agriculture Information Bulletin No. AIB750.*
20. Lee, P. R. 1978. Nutrition Policy: From Neglect and Uncertainty to Debate and Action. *Journal of the American Dietetic Association* 72:581–588.
21. U.S. Department of Agriculture. 2005. The Report of the Dietary Guidelines Advisory Committee on *Dietary Guidelines for Americans, 2005.* Available at www.health.gov/dietaryguidelines/dga2005/report. Accessed February 2012.
22. U.S. Department of Agriculture, 2011. *Dietary Guidelines for Americans, 2010.* Available at www.cnpp.usda.gov/DGAs2010-PolicyDocument.htm. Accessed February 2012.
23. Center for Food Safety and Applied Nutrition. 2009. *A Food Labeling Guide.* Available at www.fda.gov/Food/GuidanceCompliance RegulatoryInformation/Guidance Documents/FoodLabelingNutrition/default.htm. Accessed February 2012.
24. Food and Drug Administration. 2011. *Food Labeling and Nutrition.* Available at www.fda.gov/Food/LabelingNutrition. Accessed February 2012.
25. Ibid.
26. United States Department of Agriculture. 2002. Food Labeling: Guidelines for Voluntary Nutrition Labeling of Raw Fruits, Vegetables, and Fish; Identification of the 20 Most Frequently Consumed Raw Fruits, Vegetables, and Fish. *Federal Register* 67:12918–12937.
27. Food Safety and Inspection Service. 2009. *Nutrition Labeling of Single-Ingredient Products and Ground or Chopped Meat and Poultry Products.* Available at www.fsis.usda.gov. Accessed February 2012.
28. Center for Food Safety and Applied Nutrition. 2012. *How to Understand and Use the Nutrition Facts Label.* Available at www.fda.gov/Food/ResourcesForYou/Consumers/NFLPM/ucm274593.htm. Accessed February 2012.
29. Kurtzweil, P. 1998. Staking a Claim to Good Health. *FDA Consumer.* Available at www.fda.gov. Accessed February 2012.
30. Center for Food Safety and Applied Nutrition. 2003. *Guidance for Industry: Interim Procedures for Qualified Health Claims in the Labeling of Conventional Human Food and Human Dietary Supplements.* Available at www.fda.gov. Accessed February 2012.
31. Hasler, C. M., et al. 2004. Position of the American Dietetic Association: Functional Foods. *Journal of the American Dietetic Association* 104: 814–826.
32. Institute of Food Technologists. 2005. *Expert Report on Functional Foods: Opportunities and Challenges, Executive Summary.* Available at www.ift.org. Accessed February 2012.

3 Digestion, Absorption, and Transport

Chapter Objectives

After reading this chapter, you will be able to:

1. Describe the gastrointestinal tract organs and accessory organs involved in digestion and their primary functions.
2. Explain how peristalsis and segmentation move food through the gastrointestinal tract.
3. Explain the role of enzymes in digestion, and list the main carbohydrate-, protein-, and fat-digesting enzymes and the tissues that secrete them.
4. Describe the four mechanisms of absorption in the small intestine.
5. Identify the hormones involved, and explain how they work with the nervous system to regulate digestion.
6. Explain how the circulatory and lymphatic systems transport absorbed nutrients throughout the body.
7. Describe the symptoms and causes of the most common digestive disorders.

1. Saliva can alter the taste of food. T/F
2. Without mucus, the stomach would digest itself. T/F
3. The major function of bile is to emulsify fats. T/F
4. Acid reflux is caused by gas in the stomach. T/F
5. The primary function of the large intestine is to absorb water. T/F
6. Feces contain a high amount of bacteria. T/F
7. The lymphatic system transports all nutrients through the body once they've been absorbed. T/F
8. Hormones play an important role in digestion. T/F
9. Diarrhea is always caused by bacterial infection. T/F
10. Irritable bowel syndrome is caused by an allergy to gluten. T/F

See page 107 for answers to these Myths and Misconceptions.

The digestion of food begins even before you take that first bite. Just the smell of warm bread fresh out of the oven or the sight of homemade apple pie stimulates saliva to be released in the mouth. The secretion of saliva and other digestion juices sets in motion a cascade of events that prepares the body to digest that delicious morsel.

When digestion works properly, these complex processes go unnoticed. You consciously chew and swallow the warm apple pie, but you don't feel the muscular contractions that propel it through the GI tract organs. Nor is it obvious when the pancreas and small intestine release secretions, or when the single molecules of nutrients are absorbed into the intestinal cell wall. Unless you feel a few grumblings of **borborygmus** when gas and air pockets form as stomach contents are pushed through the GI tract, the entire process goes unnoticed until about 48 hours after eating, when the body is ready to eliminate waste through the rectum.

The body digests food *chemically*, by actions of digestive secretions such as **enzymes** (which we'll discuss in detail later in the chapter), and *mechanically*, by the actions of the teeth and powerful muscular contractions of the GI tract. We will explore the processes of both **chemical digestion** and **mechanical digestion** in this chapter, and learn more about absorption and transport of digested nutrients, the organs involved, and the other biological mechanisms that regulate our bodies' processing of food and nutrients. We'll also discuss the causes and treatments of some common gastrointestinal conditions and disorders.

What Are the Processes and Organs Involved in Digestion?

For the nutrients in food to be absorbed, the bonds that link the nutrients together must be broken down in the **gastrointestinal (GI) tract** (digestive tract). **Digestion** is the process that breaks the bonds and reduces food into individual molecules. The particles that result are small enough to pass through the cells of the small intestinal wall by **absorption.** Once the nutrients have been absorbed, they undergo **transport** through the circulatory system to the liver and various tissues throughout the body. Those nutrients that aren't digested or absorbed are excreted as waste (feces) by **elimination.** Figure 3.1 illustrates the organs and processes of the digestive system.

The Organs of the GI Tract

The GI tract is a 23-foot-long muscular tube that extends from the mouth to the anus. Stretched vertically, the tube would be about as high as a two-story building. It provides a barrier between the food we eat (external) and the body cells (internal). This barrier regulates which nutrients enter the body based on need, and which nutrients pass through the GI tract unabsorbed.

The five organs that make up the digestive tract—the mouth, esophagus, stomach, small intestine, and large intestine—contain numerous specialized cells involved in the digestive process. Cells in the lining of the small intestine, for example, secrete enzymes involved in chemical digestion, while specialized muscles of the stomach mechanically digest and propel food through the tract.

Various **sphincters** along the way allow food to pass from one organ to the next. These muscular rings act like one-way doors, allowing the mixture of food and digestive juices to flow into one organ but not back out.

Outside the GI tract are **accessory organs**, the liver, pancreas, and gallbladder, which aid in digestion by secreting digestive juices through ducts into the

borborygmus Grumbling of the stomach caused by air pockets formed as food is pushed through the GI tract.

enzymes Substances, mostly proteins, that increase the rate of chemical changes or catalyze chemical reactions; also called biological catalysts.

chemical digestion Breaking down food through enzymatic reactions.

mechanical digestion Breaking down food by chewing, grinding, squeezing, and moving food through the GI tract by peristalsis and segmentation.

gastrointestinal (GI) tract A long tube comprised of the organs of the digestive tract. It extends from the mouth through the esophagus, stomach, and small and large intestines to the anus.

digestion A process that breaks down food into individual molecules small enough to be absorbed through the intestinal wall.

absorption The process of moving nutrients from the GI tract into the circulatory system.

transport The process of moving absorbed nutrients throughout the body through the circulatory and lymph systems.

elimination Excretion of undigested and unabsorbed food through the feces.

sphincter A circular ring of muscle that opens and closes in response to nerve input.

accessory organs Organs that participate in digestion but are not considered part of the GI tract. They include the liver, pancreas, and gallbladder.

Focus Figure 3.1 Digestive System

The human digestive system consists of the organs of the gastrointestinal (GI) tract and associated accessory organs. The processing of food in the GI tract involves ingestion, mechanical digestion, chemical digestion, propulsion, absorption, and elimination.

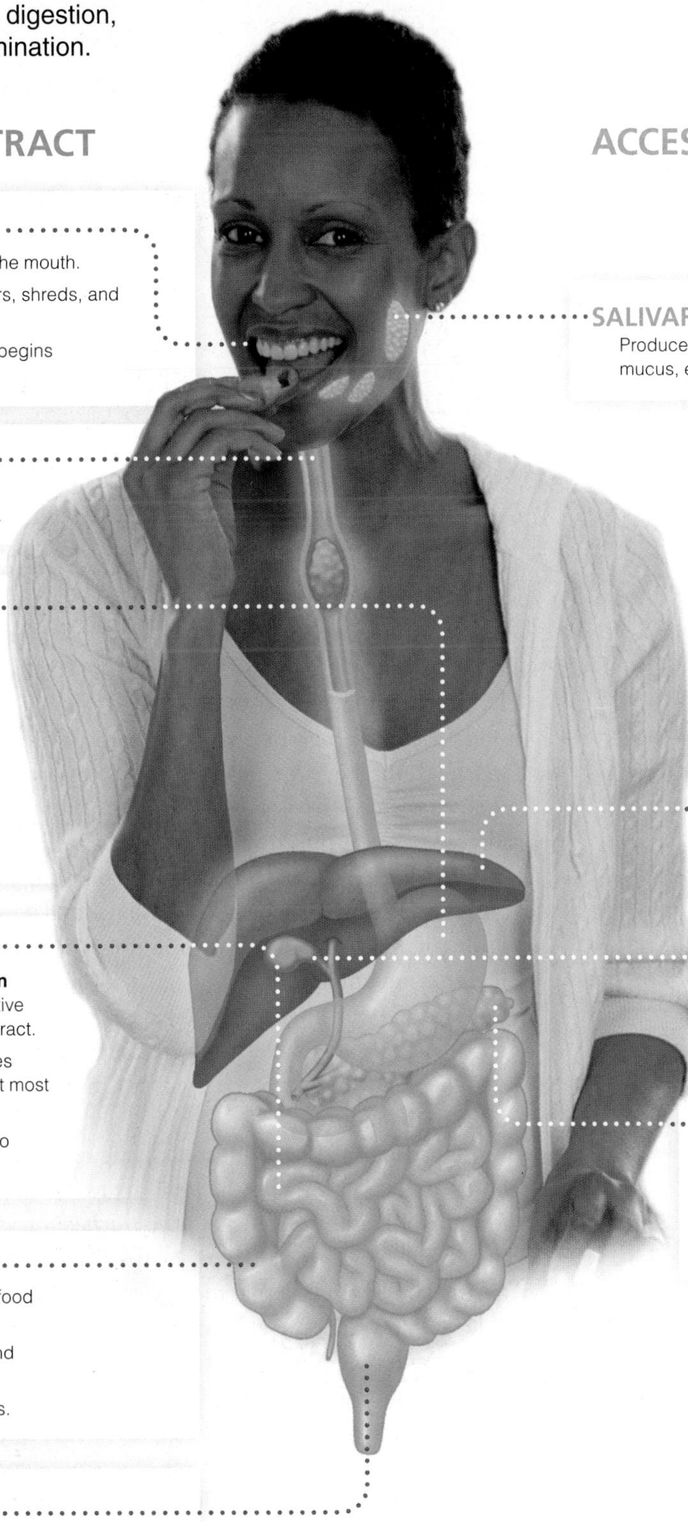

ORGANS OF THE GI TRACT

MOUTH

Ingestion Food enters the GI tract via the mouth.

Mechanical digestion Mastication tears, shreds, and mixes food with saliva, forming a bolus.

Chemical digestion Salivary amylase begins carbohydrate breakdown.

PHARYNX AND ESOPHAGUS

Propulsion Swallowing and peristalsis move the bolus from mouth to stomach.

STOMACH

Mechanical digestion Mixes and churns the bolus with acid, enzymes, and gastric fluid into a liquid called chyme.

Chemical digestion Pepsin begins digestion of proteins.

Absorption A few fat-soluble substances are absorbed through the stomach wall.

SMALL INTESTINE

Mechanical digestion and **Propulsion** Segmentation mixes chyme with digestive juices; peristaltic waves move it along tract.

Chemical digestion Digestive enzymes from pancreas and brush border digest most classes of food.

Absorption Nutrients are absorbed into blood and lymph through enterocytes.

LARGE INTESTINE

Chemical digestion Some remaining food residues are digested by bacteria.

Absorption Reabsorbs salts, water, and some vitamins.

Propulsion Compacts waste into feces.

RECTUM

Elimination Temporarily stores feces before voluntary release through the anus.

ACCESSORY ORGANS

SALIVARY GLANDS

Produce saliva, a mixture of water, mucus, enzymes, and other chemicals.

LIVER

Produces bile to digest fats.

GALLBLADDER

Stores bile before release into the small intestine through the bile duct.

PANCREAS

Produces digestive enzymes and bicarbonate ions that are released into the small intestine via the pancreatic duct.

Digestion converts whole foods into individual nutrients that can be used by the body's cells.

small intestine. The following discussion explores the structure and function of the individual GI tract organs, and the succeeding discussion covers the accessory organs.

Digestion Begins in the Mouth

Both chemical digestion and mechanical digestion begin in the mouth. During **mastication,** the teeth, powered by strong jaw muscles, mechanically cut and grind food into smaller pieces as the tongue mixes it with **saliva**. The **salivary glands,** located beneath the jaw and under and behind the tongue, produce about 1 quart of saliva per day.[1] Saliva dissolves small food particles, which allows them to react with the taste buds so we can savor food, and it moistens and binds food to lubricate it for comfortable swallowing and travel down the esophagus. Saliva also contains the enzyme amylase, which begins to break down carbohydrate. (You can taste this enzyme working when you eat a starch-containing food; as the enzyme breaks down starch into smaller pieces, or sugars, the flavor becomes sweeter. Remember this the next time you eat a cracker.) In adults, no other chemical digestion takes place in the mouth.

Once food has been adequately chewed and moistened, the tongue rolls it into a **bolus,** and thrusts it into the **pharynx** to be swallowed. The pharynx is the gateway to the **esophagus,** as well as to the *trachea* (or windpipe, the tube that connects to the lungs). Normally, a flap of cartilage called the **epiglottis** closes off the trachea during swallowing, so that food doesn't accidentally "go down the wrong pipe" (see Figure 3.2). When the epiglottis doesn't work properly, food can get lodged in the trachea and potentially result in choking.

The esophagus has only one function—to transport food and fluids from the mouth to the stomach. As food passes through the pharynx, the **upper esophageal sphincter** opens, allowing the bolus to enter the esophagus. After swallowing, rhythmic muscular contractions, with the help of gravity, move the bolus toward the stomach. The esophagus narrows at the bottom (just above the stomach) and ends at the **lower esophageal sphincter (LES)** (Figure 3.3). Under normal conditions, when the bolus reaches the stomach, the LES relaxes and allows food to

mastication Chewing food.

saliva Secretion from the salivary glands that softens and lubricates food, and begins the chemical breakdown of starch.

salivary glands Cluster of glands located underneath and behind the tongue that release saliva in response to the sight, smell, and taste of food.

bolus A soft mass of chewed food.

pharynx The area of the GI tract between the mouth and the esophagus; also called the throat.

esophagus Tube that connects the mouth to the stomach.

epiglottis Cartilage at the back of the tongue that closes off the trachea during swallowing.

upper esophageal sphincter The muscular ring located at the top of the esophagus.

lower esophageal sphincter (LES) The muscular ring located between the base of the esophagus and the stomach.

pass into the stomach. The stomach also relaxes to comfortably receive the bolus. After food enters the stomach, the LES closes to prevent the stomach contents from regurgitating backward into the esophagus.

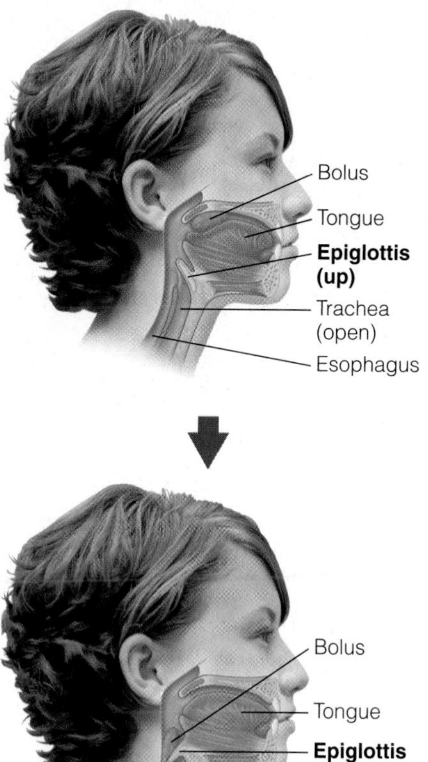

▲ **Figure 3.2 The Role of the Epiglottis**
The epiglottis prevents food from entering the trachea during swallowing.

The Stomach Stores, Mixes, and Prepares Food for Digestion

The primary function of the **stomach** is to mix food with various gastric juices to chemically break it down into smaller and smaller pieces (**Figure 3.4**). The stomach lining includes four layers. The innermost layer contains **goblet cells** and **gastric pits** or ducts, which contain gastric glands that secrete a variety of critical digestive juices. Various other cells in the stomach lining, among them **parietal cells, chief cells,** and mucous neck cells, secrete other gastric juices and mucus.

Mechanical digestion in the stomach occurs as the *longitudinal, circular,* and *diagonal* muscles that surround the organ forcefully push, churn, and mix the contents of the stomach with the gastric juices. These powerful muscles can also stretch to accommodate different volumes of food. Stomach capacity is a little less than a cup when it's empty but it can expand to hold up to 1 gallon (4 liters).[2] For several hours, food is continuously churned and mixed in the stomach.

By the time the mixture reaches the lower portion of the stomach it is a semi-liquid mass called **chyme,** which contains digestive secretions plus the original food. As the chyme accumulates near the pyloric sphincter, between the stomach and the small intestine, the sphincter relaxes and the chyme gradually enters the small intestine. You eat much faster than you can digest and absorb food, so the stomach also acts as a holding tank for chyme until it can be released into the small intestine. The numerous folds of the stomach lining, which stretch out after a large meal, make it an ideal site for temporarily storing chyme. Approximately 1 to 5 milliliters (1 teaspoon) of chyme is released into the small intestine every 30 seconds.[3] The pyloric sphincter prevents chyme from exiting the stomach too soon, and blocks the intestinal contents from returning to the stomach.

Most Digestion Occurs in the Small Intestine

As chyme passes through the pyloric sphincter, it enters the long, coiled chamber of the **small intestine.** This organ consists of three segments—the duodenum, jejunum, and ileum—and extends from the pyloric sphincter to the ileocecal valve at the beginning of the large intestine. The first segment, the duodenum, is approximately 10 inches long. The second area, the jejunum, measures about 8 feet long,

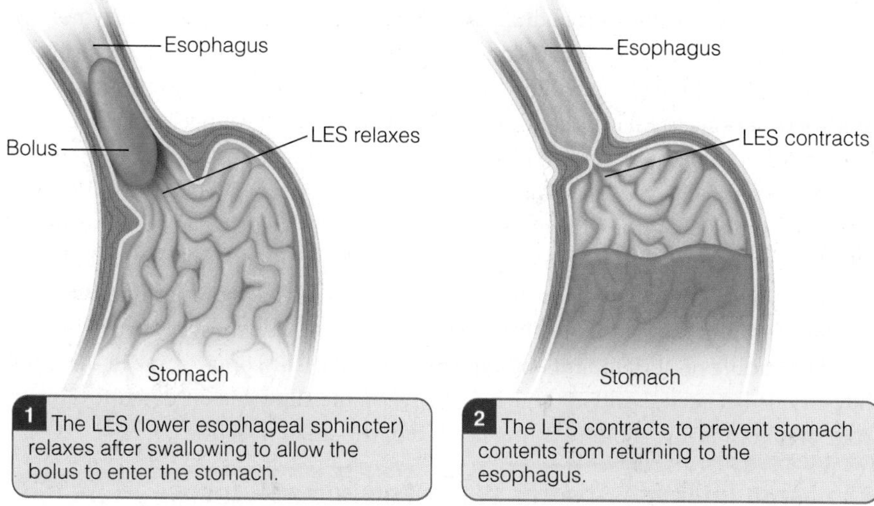

▲ **Figure 3.3 Sphincters at Work**
Sphincters control the passage of food by contracting or relaxing.

stomach A J-shaped muscular organ that mixes and churns food with digestive juices and acid to form chyme.

goblet cells Cells throughout the GI tract that secrete mucus.

gastric pits Indentations or small pits in the stomach lining where the gastric glands are located; gastric glands produce gastric juices.

parietal cells Specialized cells in the stomach that secrete the gastric juices hydrochloric acid and intrinsic factor.

chief cells Specialized cells in the stomach that secrete an inactive protein-digesting enzyme called pepsinogen.

chyme The semi-liquid, partially digested food mass that leaves the stomach and enters the small intestine.

small intestine The long coiled chamber that is the major site of digestion of food and the absorption of nutrients.

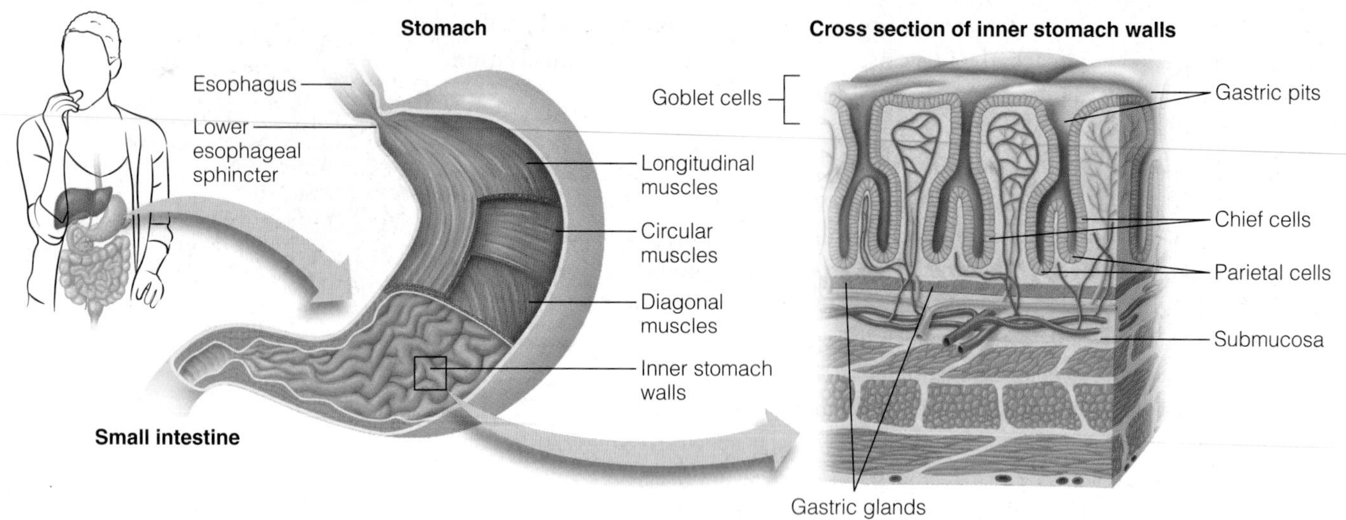

▲ **Figure 3.4 Anatomy of the Stomach**
The cross section of the stomach illustrates the gastric cells that secrete digestive juices.

and the final region, the ileum, is about 12 feet long. The "small" in "small intestine" refers to its diameter (about 1 inch), not its extended length.

As in the stomach, both mechanical and chemical digestion occur in the small intestine. Muscular contractions allow the organ to squeeze chyme forward while digestive secretions from the pancreas, gallbladder, and intestinal lining chemically break down the nutrients.

The small intestine is lined with numerous fingerlike projections, called **villi,** that help increase its surface area to maximize absorption (**Figure 3.5**). Each villus contains capillaries and lymphatic vessels called *lacteals* that pick up digested nutrients during absorption. The villi extend about 1 millimeter into the interior (or *lumen*), creating a velvety appearance, and are arranged into hundreds of overlapping, circular folds. Scattered along the villi are goblet cells whose sole function is to secrete lubricating mucus into the intestine.

Villi are covered by epithelial cells called **enterocytes** that have smaller projections called **microvilli,** which provide additional surface area and maximize nutrient absorption. The microvilli, also called the *brush border,* are covered with **glycocalyx,** which contains carbohydrate- and protein-digesting enzymes. Once the final stages of digestion have been completed, the nutrients are trapped by the microvilli and absorbed into the cells to be transported throughout the body. Brush border cells also secrete several enzymes that digest specific nutrients. We'll discuss these secretions in more detail later in the chapter.

Around the base of the villi lie glands called **crypts** that secrete intestinal juice. Within the crypts, stem cells continually divide, producing younger cells that travel up the villi to replace mature cells when they die. A constant source of nutrients is needed to replace these cells and maintain a healthy absorptive surface. Without the proper nutrients, the villi deteriorate and flatten, resulting in malabsorption. In addition to providing increased surface area, the villi help mix the partially digested chyme with intestinal secretions, and the circular folds cause chyme to spiral forward through the small intestine, further increasing its exposure to the villi.

Depending on the amount and type of food eaten, the contact time in the small intestine is between 3 and 10 hours. Usually, by the time you sit down to dinner, your breakfast is just about reaching the end of the small intestine.

villi Small, fingerlike projections that line the interior of the small intestine.

enterocytes Absorptive epithelial cells that line the walls of the small intestine.

microvilli Tiny projections on the villi in the small intestine.

glycocalyx Substance on the microvilli that contains protein- and carbohydrate-digesting enzymes.

crypts Glands at the base of the villi; they contain stem cells that manufacture young cells to replace the cells of the villi when they die.

large intestine The lowest portion of the GI tract, where water and electrolytes are absorbed and waste is eliminated.

ileocecal valve The sphincter that separates the small intestine from the large intestine.

The Large Intestine Absorbs Water and Some Nutrients

Chyme passes from the small intestine into the **large intestine** through the **ileocecal valve.** Almost 750 milliliters of unabsorbed residue enters the large intestine each

Focus Figure 3.5 Anatomy of the Small Intestine

The small intestine is highly adapted for absorbing nutrients. Its length—about 20 feet—provides a huge surface area, and its wall has three structural features—circular folds, villi, and microvilli—that increase its surface area by a factor of more than 600.

CIRCULAR FOLDS

The lining of the small intestine is heavily folded, resulting in increased surface area for the absorption of nutrients.

VILLI

The folds are covered with villi, thousands of fingerlike projections that increase the surface area even further. Each villus contains capillaries and a lacteal for picking up nutrients absorbed through the enterocytes and transporting them throughout the body.

MICROVILLI

The cells on the surface of the villi, enterocytes, end in hairlike projections called microvilli that together form the brush border through which nutrients are absorbed.

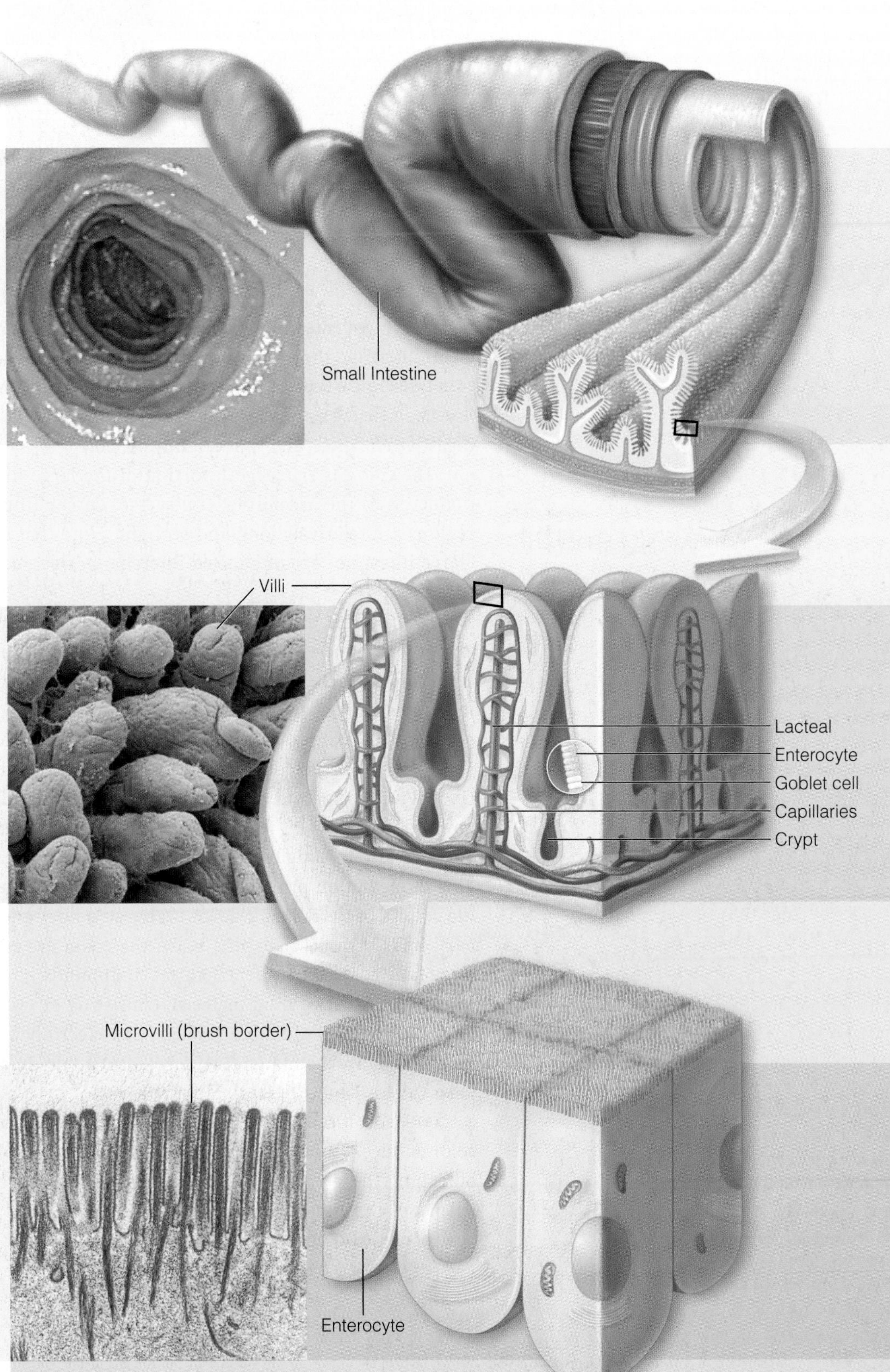

▸ **Figure 3.6 Anatomy of the Large Intestine**
By the time chyme reaches the large intestine, most of its nutrients have been absorbed. However, water and some electrolytes are absorbed in the colon. The final waste products of digestion pass out of the body through the anus.

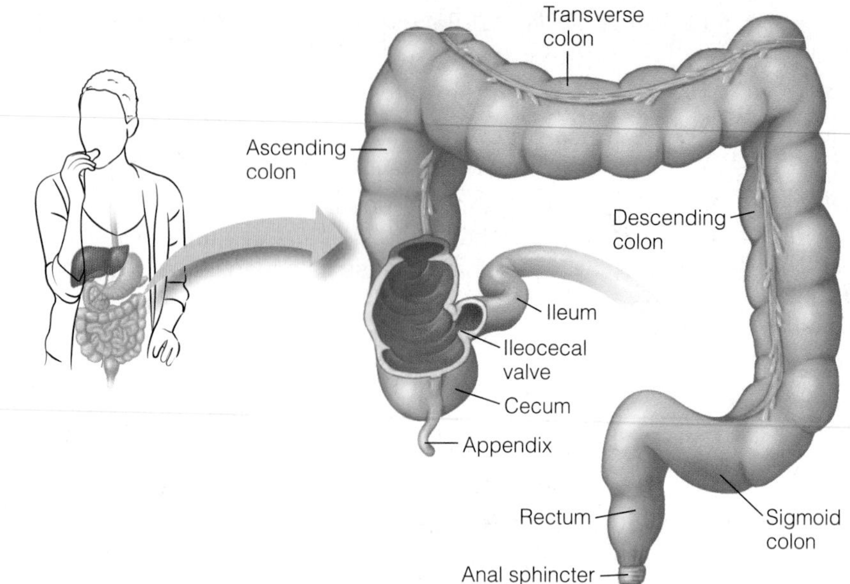

day. The large intestine is about 5 feet long and 2.5 inches in diameter. Like the small intestine, the large intestine has three segments: the cecum, colon, and rectum (see **Figure 3.6**). However, it looks and acts much differently than the small intestine in that it is much shorter, does not have villi or microvilli, does not produce digestive enzymes, and is not tightly coiled.

The colon is the largest portion of the large intestine, and it is further subdivided into the ascending, transverse, descending, and sigmoid regions. These regions are relatively long and straight. Note that though the terms "colon" and "large intestine" are often used interchangeably, technically they're not the same thing.

By the time chyme enters the large intestine, the majority of the nutrients, except water and the electrolytes sodium, potassium, and chloride, have been absorbed. The cells of the large intestine absorb water and these electrolytes much more efficiently than the cells of the small intestine. The large intestine also produces mucus that protects the cells and acts as a lubricant for fecal matter.

Bacteria in the colon produce some vitamins, including vitamin K, thiamin, riboflavin, biotin, and vitamin B_{12}. Only biotin and vitamin K can be absorbed, however. Bacteria also **ferment** some of the undigested and unabsorbed dietary carbohydrates into simpler compounds, methane gas, carbon dioxide, and hydrogen. This fermentation process is the major source of intestinal gas. Similarly, some of the colon's bacteria break down undigested fiber and produce various short-chain fatty acids. Amino acids that reach the colon are converted to hydrogen, sulfide, some fatty acids, and other chemical compounds.

About 1 liter of fluid material, consisting of water, undigested or unabsorbed food particles, indigestible residue, and electrolytes, passes into the colon each day. Gradually, the material is reduced to about 200 grams of brown fecal matter (also called **stool,** or feces). Stool consists of the undigested food residue, as well as sloughed-off cells from the GI tract, and a large quantity of bacteria. The brown color is due to unabsorbed iron mixing with a yellowish-orange substance called bilirubin. The greater the iron content, the darker the feces. The intestinal matter passes through the colon within 12 to 70 hours, depending on a person's age, health, diet, and fiber intake.

ferment To metabolize sugar into carbon dioxide and other gases.

stool Waste produced in the large intestine; also called *feces*.

Stool is propelled through the large intestine until it reaches the final 8-inch portion called the **rectum.** The **anus** is connected to the rectum and controlled by two sphincters: an internal and an external sphincter. Under normal conditions, the anal sphincters are closed. When stool distends the rectum, the action stimulates stretch receptors that in turn stimulate the internal anal sphincters to relax, allowing the stool to enter the anal canal. This causes nerve impulses of the rectum to communicate with the rectum's muscles, resulting in defecation. The final stage of defecation is under voluntary control and influenced by age, diet, prescription medicines, health, and abdominal muscle tone.

The Accessory Organs Secrete Digestive Juices

There are three organs that food does not pass through during digestion, but that are still key to the digestive process (**Figure 3.7**). These organs, the liver, gallbladder, and pancreas, secrete digestive secretions such as bile and enzymes that help transport and break down nutrients.

Weighing in at about three pounds, the **liver** is the largest organ in the body. It is located just beneath the rib cage, and functions as a major player in the digestion, absorption, and transport of nutrients. The liver plays an essential role in carbohydrate metabolism, produces proteins, and manufactures bile salts used to digest fats. The bile produced by the liver is secreted into the gallbladder for storage. The liver is also the site for alcohol metabolism and removes and degrades toxins and excess hormones from the circulation.

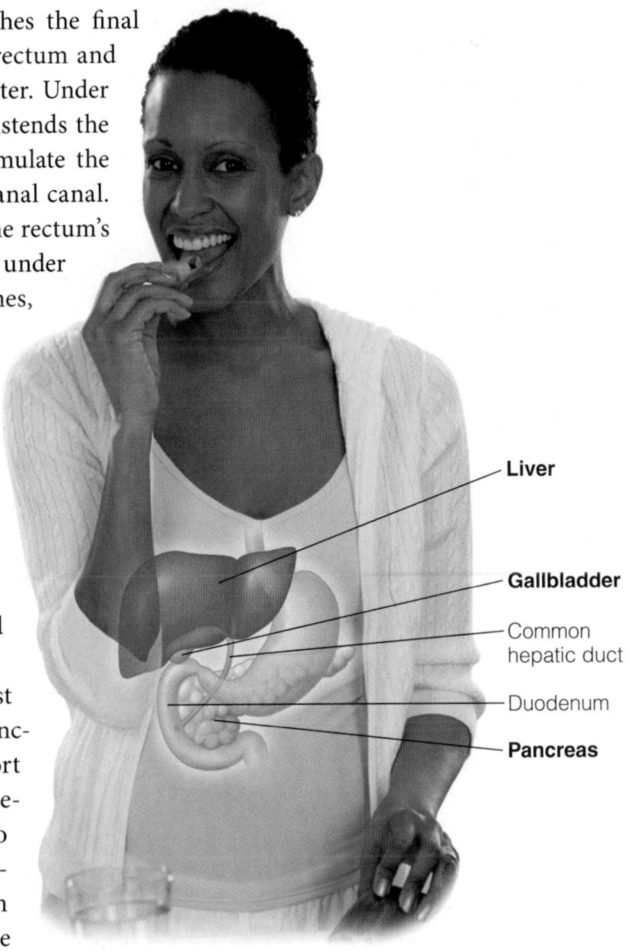

▲ **Figure 3.7 The Accessory Organs**
The liver, gallbladder, and pancreas produce digestive secretions that flow into the duodenum through various ducts.

The **gallbladder** is located beneath the right side of the liver. This pear-shaped organ receives bile from the liver through the common hepatic duct, concentrates it, and secretes bile into the small intestine through the common bile duct.

The **pancreas** is a flat organ about 10 to 15 centimeters long that hides behind the stomach and snugly fits in the bend of the duodenum. The function of the pancreas is both *endocrine* (*endo* = inside) and *exocrine (exo* = outside). As an endocrine organ, the pancreas releases hormones to maintain blood glucose levels. As an exocrine organ, the pancreas produces and secretes digestive enzymes into the small intestine.

THE TAKE-HOME MESSAGE Digestion, which takes place in the GI tract, breaks the molecular bonds in food so that nutrients can be absorbed and transported throughout the body. Saliva mixes with and moistens food in the mouth, making it easier to swallow. Once a bolus of food mixes with gastric juices in the stomach, it becomes chyme. Maximum digestion and absorption occur in the small intestine. Undigested residue enters the large intestine, where water is removed from the chyme as it is prepared for elimination. Eventually, the remnants of digestion reach the anus and exit the body in the feces. The liver, gallbladder, and pancreas are important accessory organs. The liver produces bile and the gallbladder concentrates and stores it. The pancreas produces enzymes and hormones.

rectum Final 8-inch portion of the large intestine.

anus The opening of the rectum, or end of the GI tract.

liver The largest organ in the body, located in the upper abdomen. This organ aids digestion by secreting bile.

gallbladder A pear-shaped organ located behind the liver. The gallbladder stores bile produced by the liver and secretes the bile through the common bile duct into the small intestine.

pancreas A large gland located behind the stomach that releases digestive enzymes after a meal. The pancreas also secretes the hormones insulin and glucagon, which control blood glucose.

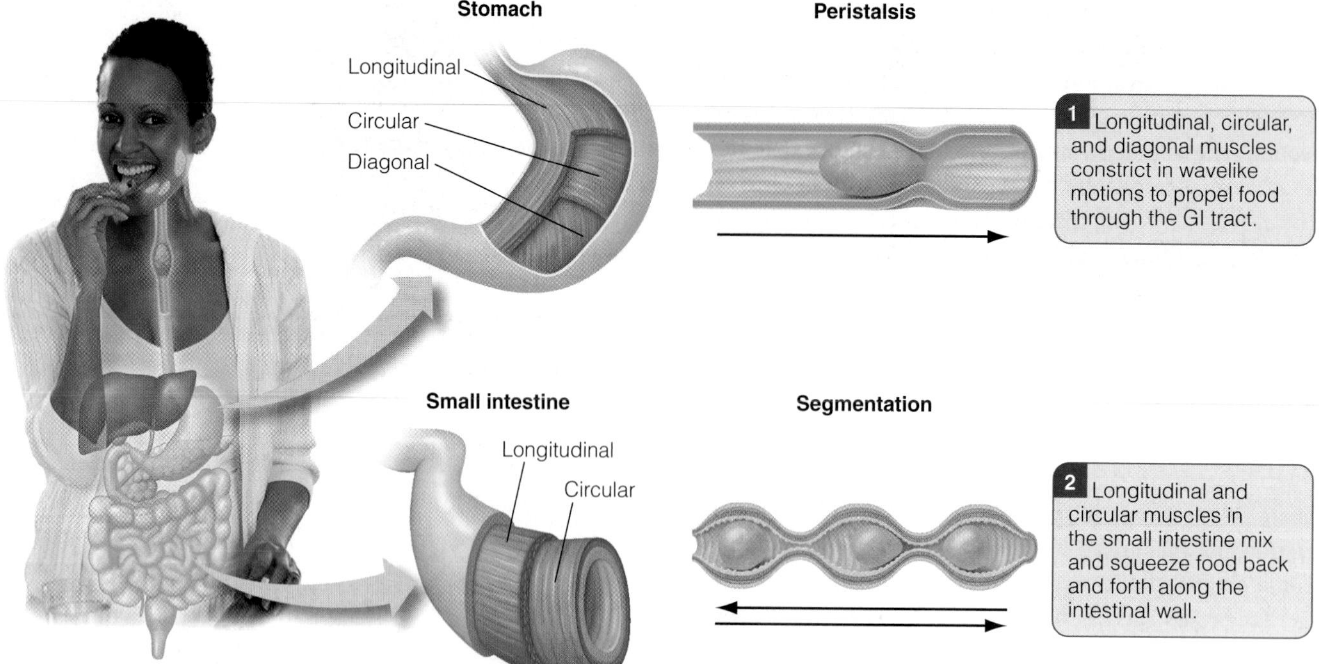
Stomach
Longitudinal
Circular
Diagonal
Peristalsis
1 Longitudinal, circular, and diagonal muscles constrict in wavelike motions to propel food through the GI tract.
Small intestine
Longitudinal
Circular
Segmentation
2 Longitudinal and circular muscles in the small intestine mix and squeeze food back and forth along the intestinal wall.

▲ **Figure 3.8 Peristalsis and Segmentation**

How Is Food Propelled through the GI Tract?

Wavelike movements of the muscles throughout the GI tract propel food and liquid forward. The two primary types of contractions, called **peristalsis** and **segmentation,** depend upon coordination between the muscles, nerves, and hormones in the digestive tract (**Figure 3.8**). As food moves down the GI tract, the muscles help mechanically digest the food by mixing and pushing it at just the right pace through each organ.

Peristalsis Squeezes Food Forward

The circular muscles that contract during peristalsis in the esophagus prevent food from moving backward. A second wave of contractions follows as the circular muscles relax and the longitudinal muscles push the food forward.

In the stomach, circular, longitudinal, and diagonal muscles move the food from the top of the stomach toward the pyloric sphincter at the base of the stomach. The waves of contractions in the stomach are slower than in other GI organs, as peristalsis mixes and churns the stomach contents with gastric juices until the food is liquefied.

Segmentation Shifts Food along the Intestinal Wall

As the partially digested food leaves the stomach, the second form of mechanical digestion, called segmentation, helps break down the mass of food into smaller pieces while mixing it with the chemical secretions of the intestine. Segmentation differs from peristalsis in that food is shifted (rather than squeezed) back and forth along the intestinal walls to increase the time food is in contact with the surface of the small intestine. This shifting action moves food through the small intestine at a rate of 1 centimeter per minute.[4]

peristalsis The forward, rhythmic motion that moves food through the digestive system. Peristalsis is a form of mechanical digestion because it influences motion, but it does not add chemical secretions.

segmentation Muscular contractions of the small intestine that move food back and forth, breaking the mixture into smaller and smaller pieces and combining it with digestive juices.

Segmentation contractions in the large intestine are much stronger and slower as the chyme moves through the colon, allowing for the maximum amount of water to be absorbed. Three or four times a day, these slow but powerful muscular contractions force the waste products toward the rectum. These contractions often occur shortly after eating and are stronger when the diet contains more fiber.

THE TAKE-HOME MESSAGE Food is propelled through the GI tract by strong muscular contractions. Peristalsis in the esophagus, stomach, and small intestine squeezes the food and propels it forward, while segmentation in the small and large intestines shifts food back and forth along the intestinal walls, moving it further down the intestinal tract.

How Is Food Chemically Digested?

While food travels through the organs of the GI tract during digestion, specific chemicals break down the food into nutrients. How do these chemicals work and what regulates the process? Chemical digestion is accomplished with the aid of digestive enzymes and other substances, and is regulated by a series of hormones. The chemicals generally complete their activities by the time the food reaches the large intestine.

Enzymes Drive the Process of Digestion

Enzymes are proteins that catalyze or speed up **hydrolysis** (*hydro* = water, *lysis* = break), the chemical reaction that uses water to split the bonds of all digestible foods, and produces single molecules small enough to be absorbed by the intestines. During hydrolysis, the hydroxyl (OH) group from water is added to one of the molecules, while the hydrogen ion (H) is incorporated into the other molecule, forming two new molecules. This is illustrated in the Chemistry Boost. Enzymes aren't changed in the reaction and can thus be used over and over again.

Chemistry Boost

Hydrolysis

Most food molecules are digested by the process known as hydrolysis. This process involves water and a specific enzyme for the molecule being digested. In the figure below, a molecule of sucrose (sugar) is digested by the enzyme sucrase when it breaks the bond with the addition of water by adding a hydroxyl group (OH) to form glucose and hydrogen (H) to form fructose.

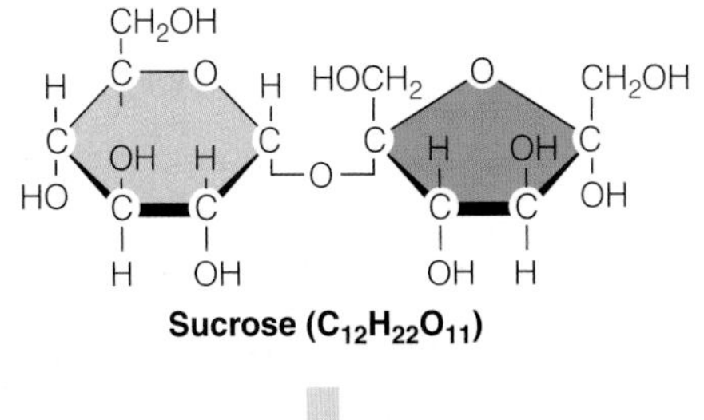

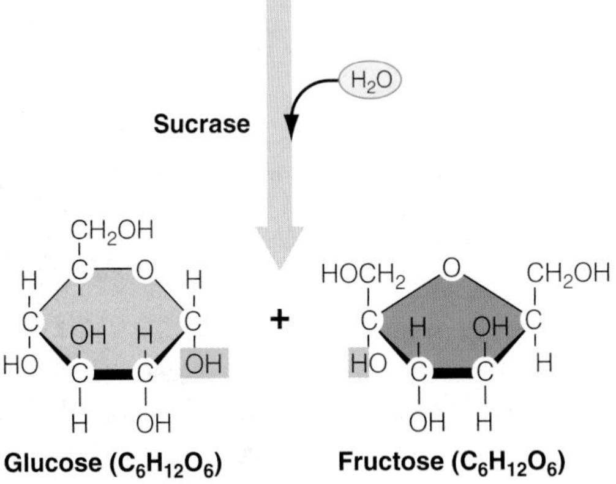

hydrolysis A chemical reaction that breaks the bond between two molecules with water. A hydroxyl group is added to one molecule and a hydrogen ion is added to the other molecule.

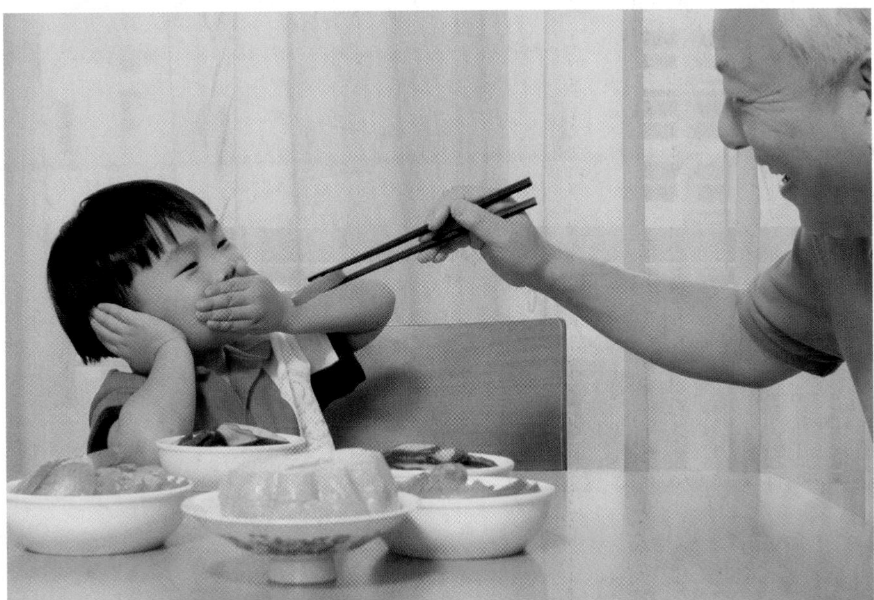

Once food enters the mouth, enzymes begin to chemically break the bonds that bind the nutrients.

In order for enzymes to catalyze hydrolytic reactions, three conditions must be present.

1. The compatible enzyme and nutrient must both be present.
2. The pH of the surrounding environment falls in the correct range.
3. The temperature of the environment is optimal.

Enzymes Are Specific in Their Action

First, enzymes are compatible only with a specific compound or nutrient, referred to as a **substrate.** Each enzyme has a binding site that only fits certain substrates, much like a key fits a specific lock. When the substrate binds to the active site of the enzyme, the bond is hydrolyzed. This reaction is illustrated in **Figure 3.9**.

Enzymes are often named according to the type of substrate they act upon, plus the suffix *-ase*. For example, sucr*ase* hydrolyzes the sugar sucrose, and malt*ase* hydrolyzes maltose. Some enzymes, such as the protein enzyme pepsin, were named before this new nomenclature was developed and don't follow these naming rules.

Enzymes and pH Range

The second condition that must be met involves the **pH** of the surrounding environment. Enzymes are the most active and efficient when the fluid environment falls within a certain range of acidity or alkalinity (see the Chemistry Boost). When the pH falls outside of that range, the activity of the enzyme is decreased or even halted. For example, saliva has a pH of about 6.4, which is optimal for the starch-digesting enzymes in the mouth. When the bolus containing the salivary enzymes reaches the stomach, where the pH is closer to 1, the salivary enzyme activity is stopped. However, another enzyme, pepsin, becomes activated in this acidic environment. As chyme continues to travel through the GI tract, various organs secrete digestive juices that produce the optimal range of pH for the enzymes to function.

substrate A substance or compound that is altered by an enzyme.

pH A scale of measurement that indicates the acidity or alkalinity of a solution.

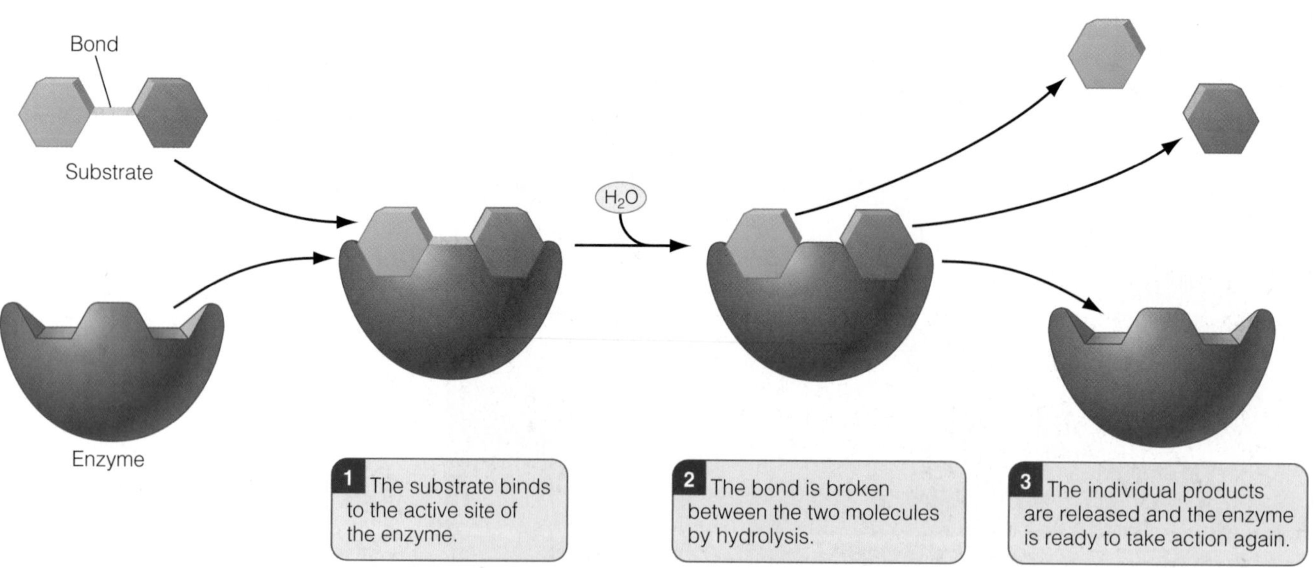
Bond
Substrate
Enzyme
H_2O
1 The substrate binds to the active site of the enzyme.
2 The bond is broken between the two molecules by hydrolysis.
3 The individual products are released and the enzyme is ready to take action again.

▲ **Figure 3.9 An Enzyme in Action**
Enzymes increase the rate of digestion without altering their shape.

Chemistry Boost

Acids and Bases

The pH is a measure of the concentration of hydrogen ions (H^+) in a solution. When acidic compounds dissociate or break apart in water, they produce more H^+. The more H^+ produced, the stronger the acid. For example, the acidic gastric juice hydrochloric acid breaks down into hydrogen and chloride ions:

$$HCl \rightarrow H^+ + Cl^-$$

Basic compounds dissociate in a solution and release hydroxide ions (OH^-). The more OH^- in the solution, the stronger the base. For example, sodium hydroxide breaks down into sodium and hydroxide ions:

$$NaOH \rightarrow Na^+ + OH^-$$

An acidic solution can be buffered by adding a base, such as NaOH, to the solution. When the NaOH breaks apart, the OH^- reacts with the H^+ to form water and reduce the acidity or number of H^+ ions present. One of the main buffers in the blood is carbonic acid (HCO_3). This acid is formed when carbon dioxide dissolves in the blood:

$$H^+ + HCO_3^- \leftrightarrow H_2CO_3 \leftrightarrow H_2O + CO_2$$

Acidity level is expressed using a pH scale that measures the hydrogen ion concentration. The range of a pH scale is 0 to 14, with 7 considered a neutral pH. A solution that has a pH lower than 7 is considered acidic (0 is the most acidic); one higher than 7 is basic (14 is the most basic).

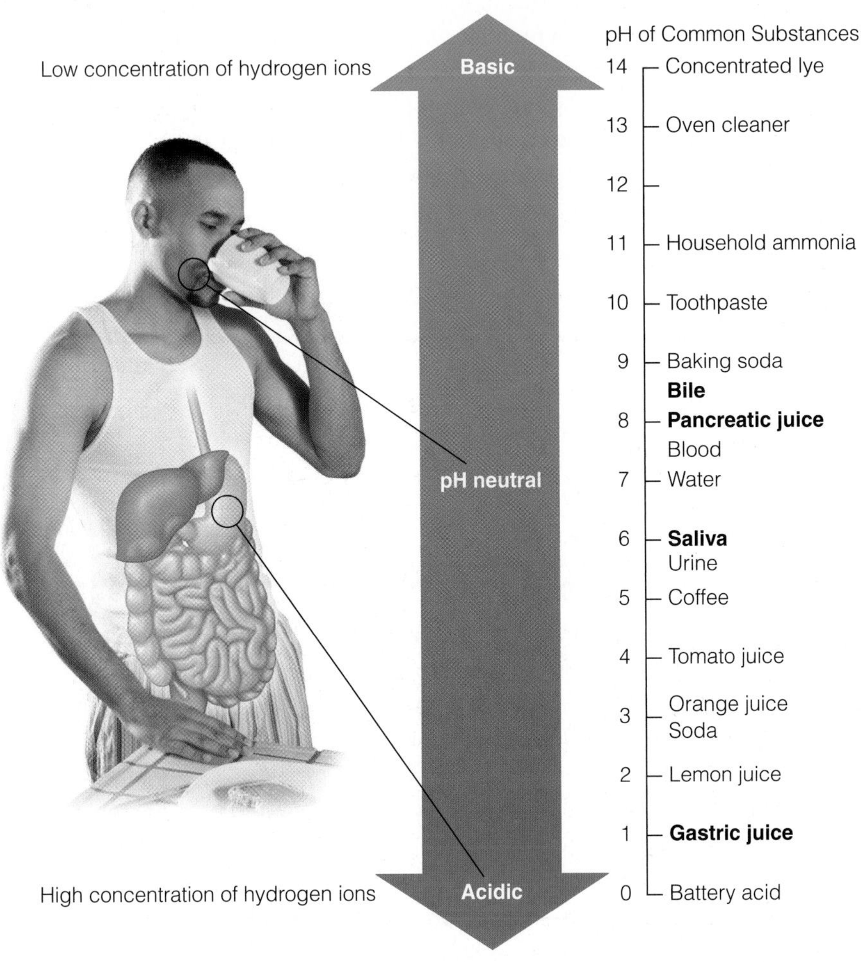

Enzymes and Temperature

The third and final condition is temperature. As temperature falls below optimal levels, enzyme activity slows. If the temperature becomes too high, the enzyme is inactivated. In the body, the optimal temperature for enzymatic activity is 98.6°F (35.7°C), which is considered normal body temperature. Temperature also controls enzyme activity in foods. Cooling food in a refrigerator or freezing it in a freezer slows down enzymes, and cooking food completely inactivates any enzymes it contains.

Digestive enzymes are secreted all along the GI tract, but most are produced in the pancreas. The pancreas secretes digestive enzymes into the duodenum through the pancreatic duct. The last of the digestive enzymes is released by the brush border of the small intestine. Table 3.1 summarizes the digestive enzymes, the organs that secrete them, and their actions.

Other Secretions Essential for Digestion

Enzymes and other essential compounds are often contained in fluids that are secreted throughout the digestion process. These secretions, including saliva, the gastric juices, bile, and bicarbonate ions, provide optimal conditions for digestion to occur.

Saliva

Saliva is 99 percent water and rich in **mucus,** electrolytes, salivary amylase, and antibacterial compounds. Saliva functions mostly as a lubricant, but it also helps protect teeth and sanitize the mouth. It contains an antiseptic enzyme called lysozyme, which destroys the cell membranes of oral bacteria. What's more, saliva contains bicarbonate, which neutralizes acids in the food. This change in pH is essential for optimal enzyme activity of salivary amylase.

mucus Secretion produced throughout the GI tract that moistens and lubricates food and protects membranes.

TABLE 3.1 Digestive Enzymes and Their Actions

Organ or Gland	Enzyme	Action	Nutrient
Salivary glands	Salivary amylase	Begins the digestion of starch	Carbohydrates
Stomach	Pepsinogen → Pepsin	Begins the hydrolysis of polypeptides	Protein
	Gastric lipase	Begins digestion of lipids	Lipids
Pancreas	Pancreatic amylase	Digests starch	Carbohydrates
	Trypsinogen → Trypsin	Catalyzes the hydrolysis of proteins in the small intestine to form smaller polypeptides	Protein
	Chymotrypsinogen → Chymotrypsin	Catalyzes the hydrolysis of proteins in the small intestine into polypeptides and amino acids	Protein
	Procarboxypeptidase → Carboxypeptidase	Hydrolyzes the carboxyl end of a peptide, releasing the last amino acid in the peptide chain	Protein
	Pancreatic lipase	Digests triglycerides	Lipids
Small Intestine	Sucrase	Digests sucrose	Carbohydrates
	Maltase	Digests maltose	Carbohydrates
	Lactase	Digests lactose	Carbohydrates
	Dipeptidase	Digests dipeptides	Protein
	Tripeptidase	Digests tripeptides	Protein
	Lipase	Digests monoglycerides	Lipids

Gastric Juices

The gastric juices secreted by the stomach are produced by the specialized parietal and chief cells introduced earlier in the chapter. When food enters the stomach, the parietal cells produce **hydrochloric acid (HCl)** and a protein called *intrinsic factor* (which is important for the absorption of vitamin B_{12} in the ileum).

Hydrochloric acid is unique in that it can destroy the activity of some proteins while activating others. It is essential for digestion because of its ability to change the acidity of digestive fluids to a pH close to 1.5. This acidic pH denatures proteins, which means it inactivates the protein by uncoiling its strands to enable **proteases,** or protein-digesting enzymes, to attack the bonds. Once the protein is denatured, the protease hydrolyzes the bonds into shorter chains. Denaturing applies to all proteins, including hormones, and to bacteria found in food, which are destroyed before they can be absorbed intact.

Hydrochloric acid can also activate proteins, such as pepsinogen, a protein-digesting enzyme secreted from the chief cells lining the gastric glands. In the presence of HCl, **pepsinogen** is converted to its active form, **pepsin,** which begins the digestion of protein. HCl also enhances the absorption of certain minerals, such as calcium. In addition to pepsinogen, the chief cells also secrete *gastric lipase*, which begins to digest fats, although this enzyme is not a particularly active digestive enzyme in adults.

You might think that an acid as strong as HCl would "digest" the stomach itself, but mucus secreted by the goblet cells and neck cells acts as a barrier between the HCl and the stomach lining, protecting the lining from irritation or damage. This slippery secretion is also produced in the mucous membranes lining the esophagus to lubricate food as it passes down the GI tract.

Bile

Bile, the yellowish-green substance synthesized in the liver, helps digest dietary fat. This dilute, alkaline liquid is stored in concentrated form—up to five times its original composition—in the gallbladder. Bile, which is comprised of water, bile salts, bile pigments, fat, and cholesterol, functions to **emulsify** fat by breaking down large fat globules into smaller globules, much like dishwashing detergent breaks up the grease in a frying pan. Emulsification increases the surface area of the fat globule. The increased surface raises the efficiency of fat digestion to more than 95 percent.

In addition to dietary fat, bile also increases the absorption of the fat-soluble vitamins A, D, E, and K. Because bile has an alkaline pH, it also helps neutralize excess HCl and exhibits antibacterial properties that destroy bacteria in food.

Unlike other digestive juices, bile can be reused. From the large intestine, bile is recycled back to the liver through **enterohepatic** (*entero* = intestine, *hepatic* = liver) **circulation.** This recycling allows bile to be reused up to 20 times.

Bicarbonate

Bicarbonate ions alter the pH of food at various points along the GI tract. The salivary glands produce enough bicarbonate to neutralize the food you eat and produce a favorable pH (between 6.5 and 7.5) for salivary enzymes to hydrolyze starch. The pancreas secretes bicarbonate ions that flow into the duodenum via the pancreatic duct. The bicarbonate helps neutralize chyme as it arrives in the small intestine. The alkaline pH (about 8) is critical to protect the cells lining the duodenum, which are not resistant to damage by HCl, and to provide a favorable pH for the pancreatic and brush border enzymes (sucrase, maltase, lactase).

hydrochloric acid (HCl) A strong acid produced in the stomach that aids in digestion.

proteases A classification of enzymes that catalyze the hydrolysis of protein.

pepsinogen The inactive protease secreted by the chief cells in the stomach; this enzyme is converted to the active form called pepsin in the presence of HCl.

pepsin The active protease that begins the digestion of proteins in the stomach.

bile A secretion produced in the liver and stored in the gallbladder. It is released through the common bile duct into the duodenum to digest dietary fat.

emulsify To break large fat globules into smaller droplets.

enterohepatic circulation The process of recycling bile from the large intestine back to the liver to be reused during fat digestion.

bicarbonate A negatively charged alkali ion produced from bicarbonate salts; during digestion, bicarbonate ions are released from the pancreas to neutralize HCl in the duodenum.

TABLE 3.2 Secretions of the GI Tract and Their Actions

Secretion	Secretion Pathway	Action(s)
Saliva	Secreted by salivary glands into mouth	Moistens food, eases swallowing; contains the enzyme salivary amylase
Hydrochloric acid (HCl)	Secreted by parietal cells into stomach	Denatures protein; activates pepsinogen → pepsin
Intrinsic factor	Secreted by parietal cells into stomach	Needed for vitamin B_{12} absorption
Mucus	Secreted by gastric glands into stomach	Lubricates and coats the internal mucosa to protect it from chemical or mechanical damage
Intestinal juice	Secreted by the crypts into small intestine	Contains enzymes that digest carbohydrate, protein, and lipid
Mucus	Secreted by intestinal glands into small intestine	Protects the intestinal cells
Bile	Secreted by liver into gallbladder for storage; released from gallbladder into small intestine via common bile duct	Emulsifies large globules of lipid into smaller droplets
Bicarbonate ions	Secreted by pancreas through the pancreatic duct into the small intestine	Raise pH and neutralize stomach acid

Table 3.2 summarizes the important digestive compounds and the organs that secrete them.

THE TAKE-HOME MESSAGE Foods are chemically digested by hydrolysis, which is catalyzed by enzymes. The three conditions that govern enzyme action are specific substrates (nutrients), pH, and optimal temperature. Other secretions produced in the GI tract, such as saliva, gastric juices, bile, and bicarbonate, contribute to the optimal environment for digestion to occur.

How Are Digested Nutrients Absorbed?

Digestion is the key to breaking down food. Absorption is the key to using food once it's digested. Some absorption occurs in the stomach and large intestine, but most nutrients are absorbed by specially designed cells along the small intestinal wall. Nutrients that are digested by the time they reach the duodenum are absorbed quickly. Nutrients that need more time to be disassembled are absorbed lower in the GI tract. The body is remarkably efficient when it comes to absorbing nutrients. Under normal conditions, you digest and absorb 92 to 97 percent of the nutrients in food.

Nutrients Are Absorbed through the Small Intestinal Lining

The remarkable surface area (enough to cover a tennis court) of the folds and crevices of the small intestine lining allows for continuous, efficient absorption of virtually all digested nutrients. The villi are covered with mature enterocytes, cells that absorb digested nutrients. These cells live only a few days before they are sloughed off into the lumen to be digested.

Nutrients move across cell membranes in the small intestine via one of four mechanisms: passive diffusion, facilitated diffusion, active transport, or endocytosis. **Figure 3.10** illustrates these four processes.

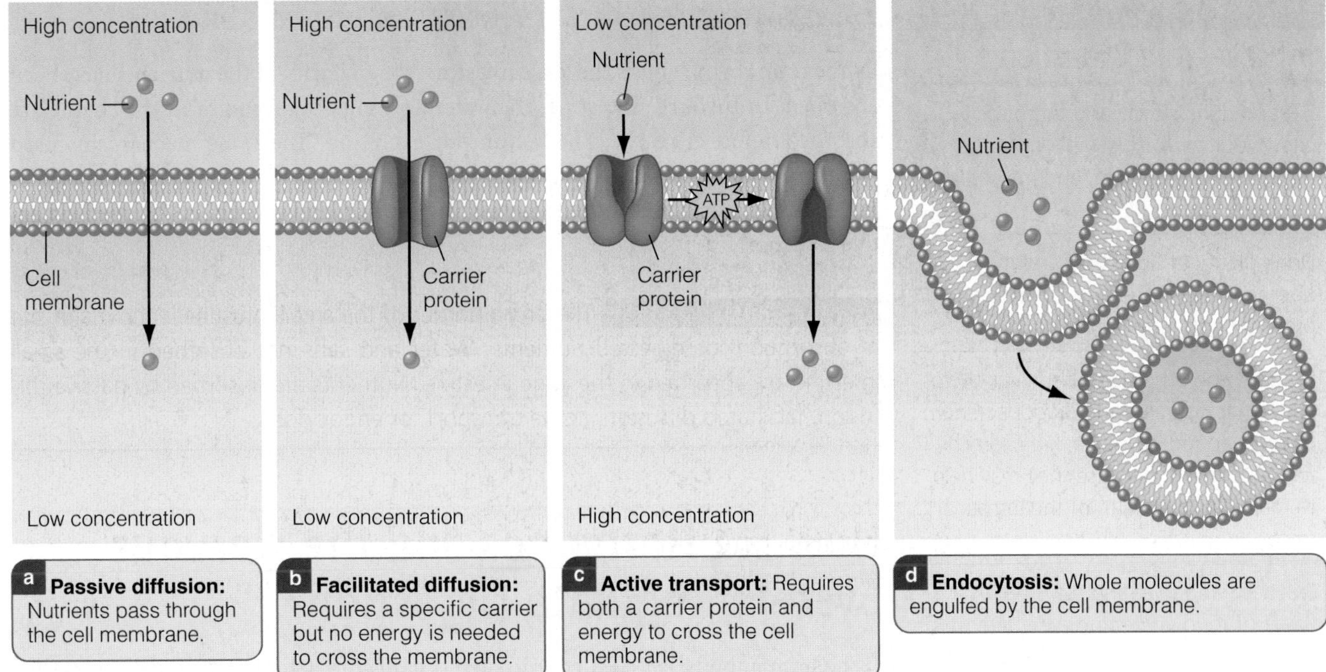

▲ Figure 3.10 **Four Methods of Nutrient Absorption in the Small Intestine**

Passive Diffusion

Passive diffusion is a process in which nutrients are absorbed due to a concentration gradient. When the concentration of a nutrient is greater in the GI tract than inside the enterocyte, the nutrient is forced across the cell membrane. Thus, the nutrient moves from a high concentration to a low concentration. This simple process requires neither energy nor a special carrier molecule. Water, small lipids, a few minerals, and vitamin C are examples of nutrients absorbed via passive diffusion.

Facilitated Diffusion

Enterocytes have a lipid layer that is impermeable to most nutrients. Thus, most nutrients require an alternate route for absorption: facilitated diffusion. In **facilitated diffusion,** nutrients are helped across the membrane by specific carrier proteins. This form of absorption is similar to passive diffusion in that it does not require energy and transport is from a higher to a lower concentration. Fructose is an example of a nutrient that needs a carrier to move across a membrane.

Active Transport

Active transport is the absorption of nutrients from a low to a high concentration that requires both a carrier molecule and energy in the form of ATP to shuttle nutrients across the cell membrane. This transport mechanism allows foods that are in short supply in the diet to be absorbed because the concentration outside the absorptive cell is lower than inside the cell. Glucose and amino acids are examples of nutrients absorbed by active transport.

Endocytosis

Endocytosis occurs when a cell forms a *vesicle* to surround and engulf a nutrient. Once inside the vesicle, the nutrient is dissolved in water; endocytosis is often referred to as "cell drinking." This type of absorption allows whole proteins, such as an immunoglobulin from breast milk, to be absorbed intact.

passive diffusion The process of absorbing nutrients freely across the cell membrane.

facilitated diffusion The process of absorbing nutrients with the help of a carrier molecule.

active transport The process of absorbing nutrients with the help of a carrier molecule and energy expenditure.

endocytosis A type of active transport in which the cell membrane forms an indentation, engulfing the substance to be absorbed.

TABLE TIPS

Improve Your Digestion

Eat and drink slowly and thoroughly chew your food. This will reduce the amount of air taken in, and may reduce the need for belching later on.

Drink plenty of fluids and add more fiber to increase the bulk of feces and prevent constipation.

Include probiotic bacteria such as *Lactobacillus acidophilus* and *Bifidobacterium bifidum*, found in yogurt, kefir, kimchi, and sauerkraut, because they may help to maintain the health of the intestinal tract.

Practice mindful eating. Savor the flavor of food and enjoy every bite to allow the brain time to receive signals from digestive hormones that you are becoming full. This reduces overeating and improves portion control.

Identify foods that cause irritation or sensitivities. Reduce or eliminate these foods if necessary to improve digestion.

Fluid Absorption Occurs in the Large Intestine

By the time chyme enters the large intestine, the majority of the nutrients have been absorbed. In the large intestine, the water and salts that remain in the chyme are absorbed before it reaches the rectum for excretion. The same mechanisms used to absorb water and salts in the small intestine are also used in the large intestine. For example, water is absorbed via passive diffusion and sodium is absorbed via active transport.

THE TAKE-HOME MESSAGE The brush border of the small intestine is the major site of absorption for digested nutrients. Water and salts not absorbed in the small intestine are absorbed in the large intestine. Nutrients are absorbed by passive diffusion, facilitated diffusion, active transport, or endocytosis.

How Do Hormones and the Nervous System Regulate Digestion?

The human body is a well-coordinated organism. Each of us eats, drinks, sleeps, and lives a normal existence without too much thought about what we are consuming. We don't have to worry about keeping ourselves nourished, or distributing nutrients to our cells, because numerous body systems do the work for us. Two important systems that control and coordinate the digestion, absorption, and excretion of waste products are the endocrine and nervous systems.

Digestion runs smoothly when the endocrine system communicates with the nervous systems built into the gastrointestinal tract. The endocrine glands in the GI tract are scattered throughout the lining of the stomach and the small intestine. These specialized cells secrete hormones when there is a stimulus present and stop secreting the hormones when the stimulus is gone. For example, when the food you eat reaches your the stomach, gastric hormones are released to signal the rest of the GI tract to prepare for digestion. When food is not present, these hormones are not released. The pancreas also secretes hormones that participate in digestion.

Digestion is also controlled by the enteric nervous system. The enteric nervous system is a meshwork of nerve fibers that innervate the GI tract, pancreas, and gallbladder. These nerves monitor the contractions of your stomach when you eat and the secretions of the cells of the GI tract.

Let's take a closer look at how these two systems communicate and ultimately control the digestive process.

Hormones in the GI Tract

Hormones secreted throughout the GI tract regulate digestion by controlling the release of gastric and pancreatic secretions, peristalsis, and enzyme activity. **Enterogastrones,** for example, are produced and secreted by the cells lining the stomach and small intestine. These hormones, including gastrin, secretin, cholecystokinin, and gastric inhibitory peptide (GIP), have a powerful influence on gastrointestinal motility, stomach emptying, gallbladder contraction, intestinal absorption, and even hunger.

The release of hormones is stimulated by the type of food passing through the digestive tract. For example, when a protein-containing bolus passes through the lower esophageal sphincter (LES), the hormone **gastrin** is secreted in the stomach and small intestine. This hormone causes the release of gastric secretions that

enterogastrones A group of GI tract hormones, produced in the stomach and small intestine, that controls gastric motility and secretions.

gastrin A hormone released from the stomach that stimulates the release of acid.

contain gastric lipase and stimulates the secretion of HCl. Gastrin also increases gastric motility and emptying, and increases the tone of the LES.

Secretin is released by the duodenum when the acidic chyme passes through the pyloric sphincter. The release of secretin in turn stimulates the pancreas to send bicarbonate ions through the pancreatic duct to neutralize the acid.

At the same time that secretin is stimulating the release of bicarbonate ions, another intestinal hormone, **cholecystokinin (CCK),** is secreted as partially digested protein and fat enter the duodenum. This powerful hormone stimulates the pancreas to release lipase and the gallbladder to contract and release bile, while it slows down gastric motility (which controls the pace of digestion) and contributes to meal satisfaction.

Gastric inhibitory peptide (GIP) also inhibits gastric motility and stomach secretions. This allows time for the digestive process to proceed in the duodenum before it receives more chyme.

This synchronized effort by the GI tract hormones ensures the efficiency of digestion and maintains homeostasis in the body. Refer to Table 3.3 for a summary of the individual hormones, the tissues that secrete them, and their actions.

The Role of the Nervous System in Digestion

The main role of the nervous system in digestion is to let you know when you need to eat and drink, and when to stop. The brain, with the help of hormones, has a central role in communicating and interpreting the message of hunger and encouraging you to seek food. Receptors within the walls of the GI tract organs respond to changes in the cells and communicate these changes to the brain.

Nervous System Receptors

Two types of nerves are involved in communicating and interpreting these changes: extrinsic and intrinsic nerves. The extrinsic nerves originate in the brain or the spinal cord; the intrinsic nerves are woven like a spider web into the linings of the esophagus, stomach, and the small and large intestines. These nerves communicate changes in the GI tract, which, in turn, affect motility and the release or inhibition of digestive juices.

Imagine that you walk by a bakery and smell freshly baked bread. The extrinsic nerves signal to the GI tract what your senses just experienced, and the intrinsic nerves interpret this signal and respond by stimulating the release of digestive juices. If you haven't eaten in the past few hours, the fact that your stomach is empty is communicated from the intrinsic nerves back to your brain. The result is a feeling of hunger.

secretin A hormone secreted from the duodenum that stimulates the stomach to release pepsin, the liver to make bile, and the pancreas to release digestive juices.

cholecystokinin (CCK) A hormone released by the duodenum that stimulates the gallbladder to release bile.

gastric inhibitory peptide (GIP) A hormone produced by the small intestine that slows the release of chyme from the stomach.

TABLE 3.3 Hormones of the GI Tract and Their Actions

Organ	Hormone	Secreted from	Action(s)
Stomach	Ghrelin	Gastric cells	Stimulates gastric motility; stimulates hunger
	Gastrin	Gastric cells	Stimulates parietal cells to release HCl
Small Intestine	Secretin	Duodenum	Stimulates the pancreas to release bicarbonate ions
	Cholecystokinin (CCK)	Intestinal wall	Stimulates the gallbladder to secrete bile and the pancreas to secrete bicarbonate ions and enzymes
	Gastric inhibitory peptide (GIP)	Duodenum	Stimulates secretions from the intestines and pancreas; inhibits stomach motility
	Peptide YY	Ileum	Slows stomach motility

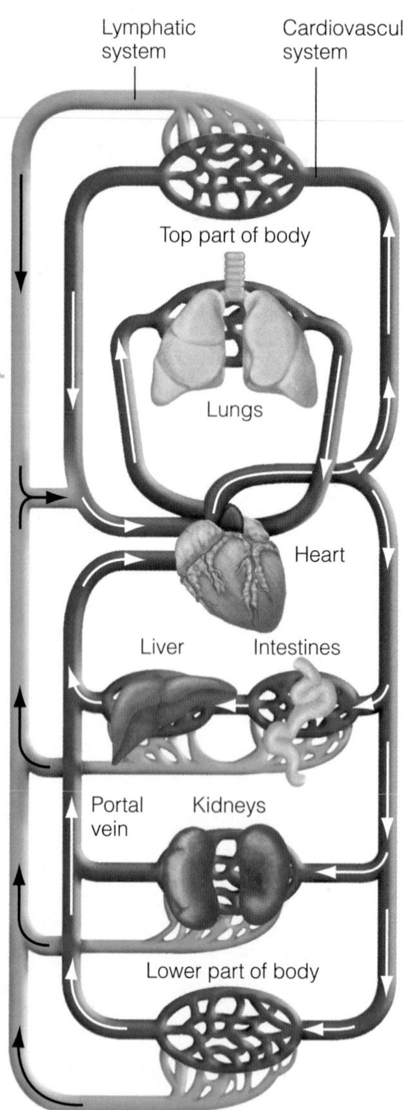

▲ **Figure 3.11 The Cardiovascular and Lymphatic Systems**
Blood and lymph circulate throughout the body to distribute nutrients to cells.

Hormones that Communicate with the Brain

Hormones, such as **ghrelin** and **peptide YY,** work together with the extrinsic and intrinsic nerves to communicate feelings of hunger or fullness. Ghrelin, which is referred to as the "hormone of hunger," is released from the gastric cells when the stomach is empty. Peptide YY signals the brain when you have eaten or are full.

After you eat that warm piece of fresh bread, the receptor cells lining the stomach stretch, and the hormone peptide YY is released. This hormone travels through the circulation to the brain and signals that you've eaten.

In addition, the extrinsic nerves excite the muscles stimulating peristalsis, pushing the food and digestive juices through the GI tract. Once the stomach has emptied, the release of hormones and digestive juices ceases and the process begins again.

THE TAKE-HOME MESSAGE The enterogastrones gastrin, secretin, cholecystokinin, and gastric inhibitory peptide regulate digestion by stimulating or inhibiting the release of secretions from the stomach, small intestine, pancreas, and gallbladder. They also influence gastric motility, which controls the pace of digestion. Extrinsic and intrinsic nerves communicate and interpret changes in the GI tract, which affects gastric motility, the release or inhibition of digestive juices, and hunger. Two hormones, ghrelin and peptide YY, communicate with the nervous system to help you decide when to eat and when to stop eating.

How Are Nutrients Transported throughout the Body?

Once the nutrients have been absorbed through the small intestinal mucosa, they are carried off either through the bloodstream or the lymphatic system to other parts of the body (**Figure 3.11**). These two transportation systems consist of varying levels of pathways that deliver nutrients to, and pick up waste products from, cells in a simple route that begins with the heart.

The Cardiovascular System Distributes Nutrients through Blood

The blood is the body's primary transport system, shuttling oxygen, nutrients, hormones, and waste products throughout the body. As the heart pumps blood, this closed system of vessels flows continuously through the hands and feet, up to the head, and back to the heart.

The heart is divided into four chambers, two upper atria and two lower ventricles. The oxygen-poor blood the heart receives from the body flows into the right atrium, through the right ventricle, and into the lungs, where it is replenished with oxygen. The oxygen-rich blood flows from the lungs to the left atrium and then into the left ventricle. As the left ventricle contracts, blood is pumped through the aorta and arteries to the capillaries, where it exchanges a variety of substances, including water, glucose, and amino acids, with the cells. These substances picked up by the blood are eventually returned via the veins as the blood completes its route. Carbon dioxide produced during metabolism is one example of a substance that is picked up from the cells and routed back to the lungs, to be exchanged for oxygen, and eventually expelled.

During digestion the blood travels through the arteries to the capillaries lining the intestinal tract. Water-soluble nutrients, including carbohydrates, amino acids, and water-soluble vitamins, are picked up by the capillaries in the GI tract and transported out of the intestine by way of the **hepatic portal vein** to the liver.

ghrelin A hormone produced in the stomach that stimulates hunger.

peptide YY A hormone produced in the small intestine that reduces hunger.

hepatic portal vein A large vein that connects the intestinal tract to the liver and transports newly absorbed nutrients.

The portal vein branches out into capillaries supplying all the liver cells with nutrient-rich blood. Blood leaves the liver and continues on its journey through the **hepatic vein** back to the heart. Thus, the liver plays a key role in nutrition—it is the first organ to receive water-soluble nutrients absorbed through the intestines via the hepatic portal vein.

The Lymphatic System Distributes Some Nutrients through the Lymph

The **lymphatic system** is a complex network of capillaries, small vessels, valves, nodes, and ducts that transport fat-soluble nutrients throughout the body. The lymphatic system, which is connected to the villi of the small intestine, collects fat-soluble vitamins, long-chain fatty acids, and some proteins too large to be transported via the capillaries. Unlike the cardiovascular system, the lymph system does not contain arteries, but rather the cells of the lymph capillary overlap one another, allowing the contents of the lymph vessels to seep out under pressure and circulate between the cells. The fat-soluble nutrients are transported from the lymph capillaries through the lymphatic vessels and eventually arrive at the thoracic duct. At the junction of the thoracic duct is a valve that allows the lymph fluid to flow into the subclavian vein, where it finally enters the blood. The nutrients can then be circulated by the blood to be picked up and used by cells.

The Excretory System Eliminates Waste

After the cells have gleaned the nutrients and other useful metabolic components they need from the blood, the rest is waste and is eliminated through the excretory system. For instance, the breakdown of proteins creates nitrogen-containing waste, such as urea, that must be eliminated. The kidneys filter the blood, allowing these waste products to be concentrated in the urine and excreted.

THE TAKE-HOME MESSAGE The cardiovascular and lymphatic systems transport absorbed nutrients throughout the body and deliver them to cells. Water-soluble nutrients, including carbohydrate, proteins (amino acids), and the water-soluble vitamins, are transported via the cardiovascular system; fat-soluble nutrients, including the fat-soluble vitamins and long-chain fatty acids, are transported via the lymphatic system. The excretory system filters the blood and eliminates waste.

What Are Some Common Digestive Disorders?

Generally, the digestive tract doesn't require tinkering or medications to be healthy. But sometimes the digestive tract gets "off track" and the resulting symptoms can quickly catch your attention. Some of the problems are minor, like occasional heartburn or indigestion; other problems such as ulcers or colon cancer are very serious and require medical treatment.

Esophageal Problems

Several minor esophageal problems can lead to annoying symptoms such as belching, hiccups, burning sensations, or uncomfortable feelings of fullness. More serious esophageal problems include cancer, obstruction from tumors, faulty nerve impulses, severe inflammation, abnormal sphincter function, and even death.

hepatic vein The vein that carries the blood received from the hepatic portal vein away from the liver.

lymphatic system A system of interconnected spaces and vessels between the tissues and organs that contains lymph and circulates fat-soluble nutrients throughout the body.

Being overweight and eating certain foods are two factors that can cause GERD.

Heartburn

One of the most common problems involving the esophagus is the burning sensation in the middle of the chest known as *heartburn* (also called indigestion or acid reflux). About 7 percent of the population experiences daily heartburn; about 20 percent of adults report frequent heartburn; and 25 to 35 percent of adults have occasional symptoms. Collectively, this adds up to millions of people experiencing heartburn symptoms.[5]

Heartburn generally occurs when the lower esophageal sphincter (LES) doesn't close properly, and HCl from the stomach flows back into the esophagus and irritates its lining. Chronic heartburn and the reflux of stomach acids are typical symptoms of **gastroesophageal reflux disease (GERD).**

Certain foods, including chocolate, fried or fatty foods, coffee, soda, onions, and garlic, seem to be associated with this condition.[6] Lifestyle factors also play a role. For example, smoking cigarettes, drinking alcohol, wearing tight-fitting clothes, being overweight or obese, eating large evening meals, and reclining after eating tend to cause or worsen the condition.

If dietary changes and behavior modification are insufficient to relieve heartburn, over-the-counter antacids or prescription drugs may help. In rare circumstances, surgical intervention is required to treat severe, unrelenting heartburn.

Esophageal Cancer

Esophageal cancer is another medical condition that has serious consequences. According to the National Cancer Institute, esophageal cancer is one of the most common cancers of the digestive tract, and the seventh leading cause of cancer-related deaths worldwide. In the United States, this type of cancer is typically found among individuals older than 50 years, men, those who live in urban areas, long-term smokers, and heavy drinkers. Treatments include surgery, radiation, and chemotherapy.[7]

Disorders of the Stomach

Stomach problems can range from the trivial, such as belching or an occasional stomachache, to life-threatening complications such as bleeding ulcers or stomach cancer. Common causes of stomachache include overeating, gastric bloating, or eating too fast. Other possible causes include eating foods that are high in fat or fiber, lactose intolerance, or swallowing air while eating.

Belching

Belching is usually caused by swallowing air. The air may distend the stomach, and then be expelled up through the esophagus and out through the mouth, to relieve abdominal discomfort. Swallowing large amounts of air (called *aerophagia*) is most often due to eating or drinking too fast, consuming carbonated beverages, or anxiety. However, aerophagia can occur without any act of swallowing, such as during chewing gum or smoking.

Stomach Flu and Foodborne Illness

A stomachache can be due to a number of causes, including stomach flu or foodborne illness. Despite its name, stomach flu, or **gastroenteritis,** is not caused by the influenza virus but rather by a variety of viruses (the most common being the rotavirus) that cause an inflammation of the stomach or intestines. Stomach flu symptoms include nausea, vomiting, diarrhea, and abdominal cramping. Sometimes the problem requires medical intervention, but usually rest, oral

gastroesophageal reflux disease (GERD) The backward flow of stomach contents into the esophagus due to improper functioning of the LES, resulting in heartburn.

gastroenteritis Inflammation of the lining of the stomach and intestines; also known as stomach flu.

rehydration therapy, and a soft-food diet will help with the symptoms of this type of illness.

Foodborne illnesses are usually contracted by eating food or drinking fluid that is contaminated with a pathogenic microbe such as the bacteria campylobacter, salmonella, or *E. coli*, or a calicivirus (also known as the Norwalk and Norwalk-like viruses). Symptoms such as vomiting, abdominal cramps, diarrhea, and fever occur when enough of the pathogen has been ingested to trigger the body's immune response. Most foodborne illnesses are self-limiting and require oral rehydration therapy and rest. More severe foodborne infections may require medical intervention. (You will read more about specific foodborne illnesses in Chapter 20.)

Ulcers

An **ulcer** is a sore or erosion in the lining of the lower region of the stomach or the upper part of the duodenum. Ulcers are named according to their location, such as gastric ulcers, duodenal ulcers, and esophageal ulcers. Whereas spicy foods and stress were once thought to cause most ulcers, researchers have since discovered that a bacterium, *Helicobacter pylori*, is often involved. The use of anti-inflammatory drugs, such as aspirin, ibuprofen, naproxen, and ketoprofen, may also cause or aggravate ulcers. These pain relievers inhibit the hormonelike substances that protect the stomach lining from HCl, which results in bleeding and ulceration. Nicotine increases the production of HCl, which increases the risk of developing an ulcer and slows the healing process of ulcers that have already developed. Both excess consumption of alcohol and stress can contribute to ulcer formations, although these factors may not be directly involved.

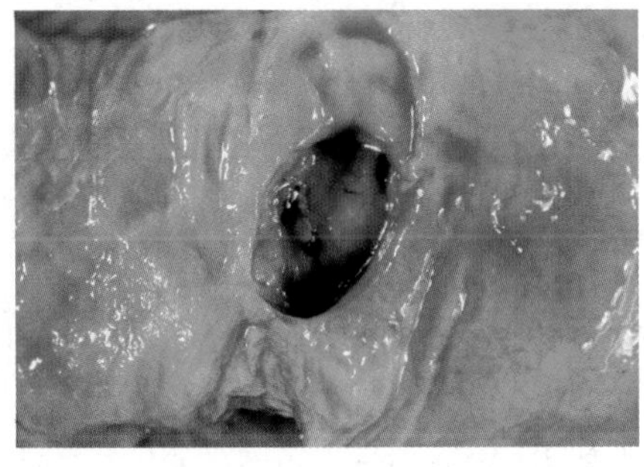

An ulcer is created when the mucosal lining of the GI tract erodes.

Burning pain is the most common symptom of an ulcer, along with vomiting, fatigue, bleeding, and general weakness. Medical treatments may consist of prescription drugs and dietary recommendations, such as limiting alcohol and caffeine-containing beverages, and/or restricting spices and acidic foods. Surgery is necessary only when an ulcer does not respond to drug treatment. Left untreated, ulcers can result in internal bleeding and perforation of the stomach or intestinal lining, causing peritonitis, or infection of the abdominal cavity. Scar tissue can also form in the GI tract, obstructing food and causing vomiting and weight loss. People who have ulcers caused by *H. pylori* have a greater risk of developing stomach cancer.

Gallbladder Disease

The incidence of gallbladder disease is high in the United States, especially in women and older Americans. Obesity is one of the major risk factors, and this risk is even greater following rapid weight loss.[8]

One common problem of an unhealthy gallbladder is the presence of **gallstones.** Most people with gallstones have abnormally thick bile, and the bile is high in cholesterol and low in bile acids. Over time, the high-cholesterol bile forms crystals, then sludge, and finally gallstones. Some individuals with gallstones experience no pain or mild pain. Others have severe pain accompanied by fever, nausea, vomiting, cramps, and obstruction of the bile duct.

The size and composition of gallstones vary.

Medical treatment for gallstones may involve surgery to remove the gallbladder, prescription medicine to dissolve the stones, shock-wave therapy (a type of ultrasound treatment) to break them up, or a combination of therapies. If surgery is required to remove the gallbladder, patients typically recover quickly. After gallbladder removal surgery, the anatomy of the biliary tract adapts. The liver continues to produce the bile and secretes it directly into the duodenum.

ulcer A sore or erosion of the stomach or intestinal lining.

gallstones Stones formed from cholesterol in the gallbladder or bile duct.

EXAMINING THE EVIDENCE Do Probiotics Improve Your Intestinal Health?

If you are like most people, the thought of eating food that contains live bugs is not very appealing. But did you know that consuming certain live microorganisms may improve your overall health? This is probably the reason the consumer attraction for foods that contain live microorganisms, called **probiotics** (*pro* = for, *bios* = life), has taken off in the United States. Sales of probiotic supplements and foods increased to almost $2 billion in 2011 and are projected to reach $31 billion by 2015.[1] What are probiotics and why are Americans clamoring to buy them?

What Are Probiotics?

Probiotics are defined as "live microorganisms, which when administered in adequate amounts, confer a health benefit on the host."[2] These live bacteria are similar to the more than 10 trillion microflora that colonize your colon. Medications, stress, diet, and illness can disrupt the balance of friendly microflora, and probiotics may bring them back into balance.

How Do Probiotics Work to Improve Health?

Probiotics function in the same way the native bacteria in your GI tract do—they produce organic acids that inhibit disease-causing bacteria from growing. The friendly bacteria compete with these pathogens for nutrients and receptor sites, keeping the population of harmful bacteria in check.

Specific strains of bacteria have different effects on our health.

- Several strains of probiotics, including *L. rhamnosus GG* and *Saccharomyces boulardii lyo,* may reduce diarrhea and constipation.[3]
- *Bifidobacterium lactis* DN-173 010, *Lactobacillus casei* reduces the transit time of chyme through the GI tract.[4] This results in fewer bouts of constipation.
- *L. acidophilus* BG2FO4 may alleviate lactose intolerance symptoms, including cramping and bloating, although studies are not conclusive.[5]
- *Lactobacillus reuteri* shows promise in the prevention of food allergy.[6]
- *Lactobacillus gasseri* PA 16/8, *Bifidobacterium longum* SP 07/3 and *B. bifidum* MF 20/5 have been shown to shorten duration of the common cold and reduced the severity of the symptoms.[7]
- *Lactobacillus reuteri* ATCC 55730 has been shown to reduce colic in infants.[8]

Where Do We Find Probiotics?

Probiotics are found in foods, such as fermented dairy and soy products, and in dietary supplements, and are known by a

Disorders of the Intestines

Disorders of the intestines can occur anywhere along the length of the small and large intestines. Common, temporary problems can include gassiness or constipation; more serious disorders include celiac disease and Crohn's disease.

Flatulence

Flatulence is an uncomfortable and sometimes embarrassing (but normal) condition that results from the formation of intestinal gas. Intestinal gas is produced for a variety of reasons, and most adults release it 10 to 20 times a day. Eating too fast, or drinking beverages with added air such as beer or carbonated beverages, can result in the intake of incidental air that makes its way through the digestive tract.

probiotics Live microorganisms, which, when administered in adequate amounts, confer a health benefit on the host.

flatulence Production of excessive gas in the stomach or the intestines.

Beneficial Bacteria

If You Have This Problem	Try This Probiotic	Found in These Foods and Dietary Supplements
Diarrhea	■ *Lactobacillus reuteri* 55730 ■ *Saccharomyces boulardii* yeast	■ BioGai tablets, drops and lozenges ■ Florastor dietary supplement
Constipation	■ *Bifidobacterium animalis* DN-173 010	■ Dannon Activia yogurt
Irritable bowel syndrome and overall digestion problems	■ *Bifidobacterium infantis* 35624	■ Align Supplement
Poor immune system	■ *Bifidobacterium lactis* Bb-12 ■ *Lactobacillus casei* Shirota ■ *Lactobacillus casei* DN-114 001	■ Yo-Plus Yogurt ■ Yakult Fermented dairy drink ■ Dannon's DanActive dairy drink
Vaginal infections	■ *Lactobacillus rhamnosus* GR-1 combined with *Lactobacillus reuteri*	■ Fem Dophilus dietary supplements

variety of names (see the table). Read the label carefully to learn the strain of the bacteria used, when the product expires, the suggested serving size, and how to store the product to make sure the bacteria are still alive when you eat it. A serving should contain at least one billion CFUs (a measure of live bacteria called colony-forming units) to provide the level of probiotics found to deliver health benefits.

Although there is a great deal we don't know about probiotics and the impact on our health, research does suggest that probiotics in the daily diet help maintain a healthy digestive system.

References

1. J. Townsend. 2011. *Probiotics Sales Proliferate at a Stunning Rate in 2011.* Available at http://newhope360.com/probiotics/probiotics-sales-proliferate-stunning-rate-2011. Accessed February 2012.
2. Food and Agriculture Organization of the United Nations. 2001, *Health and Nutritional Properties of Probiotics in Food Including Powder Milk with Live Lactic Acid Bacteria.* Available at www.who.int/foodsafety/publications/fs_management/en/probiotics.pdf. Accessed February 2012.
3. L V. McFarland. 2006. "Meta-Analysis of Probiotics for the Prevention of Antibiotic Associated Diarrhea and the Treatment of Clostridium Difficile Disease." *American Journal of Gastroenterology* 101:812–822.
4. A. Chmielewska and H. Szajewska. 2010. "Systematic Review of Randomised Controlled Trials: Probiotics for Functional Constipation." *World Journal of Gastroenterology* 16:69–75.
5. S. R. Hertzler and D. A. Savaiano. 1996. "Colonic Adaptation to Daily Lactose Feeding in Lactose Maldigesters Reduces Lactose Intolerance." *American Journal of Clinical Nutrition* 64:232–236.
6. T. R. Abrahamsson, T. Jakobsson, M. F. Böttcher, M. Fredrikson, M. C. Jenmalm, B. Björkstén, and G. Oldaeus. 2007. "Probiotics in Prevention of IgE-Associated Eczema: A Double-Blind, Randomized, Placebo-Controlled Trial." *The Journal of Allergy and Clinical Immunology* 119:1174–1180.
7. M. de Vrese, P. Winkler, P. Rautenber, T. Harder, C. Noah, C. Laue, S. Ott, J. Hampe, S. Schreiber, K. Heller, and J. Schrezenmeir. 2005. "Effect of Probiotic Bacteria *B. longum, B. bifidum, L. gasseri* Reduced the Duration of Colds in Healthy Adults." *Clinical Nutrition* 24:481–491.
8. F. Savino, E. Pelle, E. Palumeri, R. Oggero, and R. Miniero. 2007. "*L. reuteri* ATCC 55730 Reduced Infantile Colic." *Pediatrics* 119:124–130.

Foods like beans, lentils, and other legumes can lead to gas production because they contain indigestible carbohydrates that are fermented by intestinal bacteria. The bacteria produce the gas as a by-product. Lack of exercise and smoking have also been identified as culprits in flatulence.

The gas (or *flatus*) is a mixture of carbon dioxide, hydrogen, nitrogen, oxygen, and methane. The offending odor comes from gases that contain sulfur, chiefly hydrogen sulfide and methylmercaptan. Foods high in fiber and starches tend to produce more intestinal gas. Using products such as Beano or eating smaller meals will help reduce the amount of gas produced.

Diarrhea and Constipation

Two of the most common intestinal disorders are diarrhea and constipation. **Diarrhea** is the passage of watery, loose stools more than three times a day. Acute diarrhea lasts for up to two days and is usually the result of bacterial, viral, or parasitic infection. The infection results in the enterocytes becoming inflamed and secreting, rather than absorbing, fluid into the GI tract. The result is that food and fluids pass too quickly through the colon and out through the rectum.

Diarrhea can be potentially serious because of the loss of fluids and electrolytes. Whereas brief episodes of diarrhea may be a sign of infection or an adverse reaction to a specific food, medication, or other compound (such as the sugar substitute sorbitol), chronic diarrhea may be a sign of irritable bowel syndrome (see below) or colitis, two conditions that require medical treatment and must be diagnosed by a health care provider.

Diarrhea is generally treated with fluid and electrolyte replacement. Diarrhea that lasts for an extended period of time can lead to malabsorption of additional nutrients, which can in turn lead to malnutrition. Left untreated, diarrhea can lead to dehydration and potentially even death. The condition can be particularly dangerous for children and the elderly, who are more susceptible to dehydration.

Constipation can be prevented with a diet higher in fiber, fluid, and daily exercise.

Constipation is caused by excessively slow movements of the undigested residue through the colon, and is often due to insufficient fiber or water intake. Ignoring or putting off the need to defecate can also result in more absorption of water from fecal matter in the large intestine, leading to harder, drier stools. Stress, inactivity, cessation of smoking, or various illnesses can also lead to constipation.[9, 10]

Because fiber attracts water, adds bulk to stool in the colon, and stimulates peristalsis, constipation is often treated with a high-fiber, high-liquid diet. Daily exercise, establishing eating and resting routines, and using over-the-counter stool softeners are usually recommended to treat this condition without the use of laxatives or enemas.

If constipation persists, laxatives can provide some relief, but should be used sparingly. A variety of laxatives can be purchased over the counter, including bulk-forming laxatives, stool softeners, and stimulants. Bulk-forming or stool-softening laxatives trigger peristalsis by drawing water into the GI tract, which increases the bulk of the feces and stretches the circular muscles in the intestine. Stimulant laxatives, such as Ex-lax or Senokot, are the harshest form of laxative and work by irritating the lining of the GI tract to stimulate peristalsis. Because laxatives can cause dehydration, salt imbalances, and laxative dependency, they should not be used routinely unless under the supervision of a physician.

One harmful and unnecessary practice is colonic cleansing, which involves an enema to draw water or other fluids into the large intestine through the anus and rectum. The practice can interfere with the absorption of fat-soluble vitamins, and can be dangerous if the equipment used to administer the enema isn't sanitized, or if the bowel is perforated when the rubber tube is inserted. Other problems may result from electrolyte and water imbalance, and dependency.

Hemorrhoids

The term **hemorrhoid** refers to a condition in which pressure in the veins in the rectum and anus causes swelling and inflammation similar to varicose veins in the legs. Though the exact cause of hemorrhoids is not known, there are contributing factors that result in pressure buildup within the veins. These factors include straining to pass dry stools, pregnancy, constant constipation or diarrhea, and aging. Whatever the cause, the result is that the walls of the veins dilate, become thin, and bleed. As the pressure builds, the vessels protrude. The presence of hemorrhoids may not be noticed until they begin to bleed (following a bowel movement), itch, or become painful.

diarrhea The abnormally frequent passage of watery stools.

constipation The infrequent passage of dry, hardened stools.

hemorrhoid Swelling in the veins of the rectum and anus.

The most common treatment for hemorrhoids is the same as for constipation: Increase dietary fiber and fluid intake. Other symptoms, including itching and pain, can be relieved with over-the-counter creams, ice packs to relieve swelling, and soaking in a warm bath. In severe cases of hemorrhoids, surgery may be necessary.

More Serious Intestinal Disorders

Both diarrhea and constipation can be indicative of small- and large-intestine problems that involve nutrient malabsorption, which can cause severe health consequences. Celiac disease, gastroenteritis, duodenal ulcers, intestinal enzyme deficiencies, irritable bowel syndrome, ulcerative colitis, and Crohn's disease are examples of serious intestinal disorders. The symptoms of these diseases vary, but they include abdominal pain, nausea, vomiting, bloating, loss of appetite, diarrhea, anxiety, weight loss, and fatigue. The prevalence of some of these disorders may be increasing or it could be that these disorders are now being more readily recognized and documented.

Irritable Bowel Syndrome (IBS), Ulcerative Colitis, and Crohn's Disease

Although **irritable bowel syndrome (IBS)** is a general term used to describe changes in colon rhythm, not an actual disease, it causes a great deal of discomfort for the estimated 30 million North Americans who have it.[11] People with IBS do not have tissue damage, inflammation, or immunologic involvement of the colon. They do, however, overrespond to colon stimuli. This results in alternating patterns of diarrhea, constipation, and abdominal pain. The exact cause of IBS is unknown, but low-fiber diets, stress, consumption of foods that trigger the symptoms (such as alcohol, chocolate, and dairy products), and intestinal motility disorders are all suspected factors. Medical management includes increasing dietary fiber, stress management, and occasional use of prescription drugs.

Ulcerative colitis is a chronic inflammation of the large intestine that results in ulcers in the lining of the colon. This disorder of the large intestine usually begins between the ages of 15 and 30, occurs in both men and women, and tends to run in families, especially in Caucasians and people of Jewish descent. **Crohn's disease** is similar to ulcerative colitis except that the ulcers can occur throughout the gastrointestinal tract, from the mouth to the anus, not just in the colon.

The cause of ulcerative colitis and Crohn's disease is not known and there is no cure. Physical examinations, laboratory tests, and a colonoscopy are often used to distinguish between the two conditions. Treatment includes drug therapy; in severe cases, surgery may be required.

Celiac disease, also known as gluten-induced enteropathy, is a genetic disorder that causes damage to the small intestine when foods containing gluten are consumed. Health Connection: Celiac Disease: An Issue of Absorption on page 102 explains this intestinal disorder in greater detail.

irritable bowel syndrome (IBS) An intestinal disorder resulting in abdominal discomfort, pain, diarrhea, constipation, and bloating; the cause is unknown.

ulcerative colitis A chronic inflammation of the colon or large intestine that results in ulcers forming in the lining of the colon.

Crohn's disease A form of ulcerative colitis in which ulcers form throughout the GI tract and not just in the colon.

celiac disease Genetic disease that causes damage to the small intestine when gluten-containing foods are eaten.

Colon Cancer

Colon cancer is one of the leading forms of cancer and the third leading cause of cancer death.[12] Fortunately, colon cancer is one of the most curable forms of cancer, if it is detected in the early stages.

Colon cancer often begins with polyps on the lining of the colon. They vary in size from that of a small pea to that of a mushroom or plum. The good news is that polyps are often small and benign, and they can be removed surgically. If the polyps are not removed, or if they develop into cancerous tumors, colon cancer can be difficult to cure.

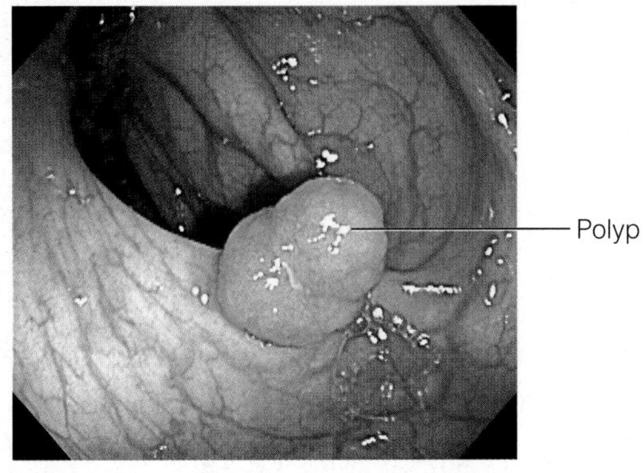

Polyps on the lining of the colon can be one of the first signs of colon cancer.

Individuals diagnosed with colon cancer may require radiation therapy, chemotherapy, and surgery to remove part or all of the colon. After

TABLE 3.4 Common Digestive Disorders

Site	Disorder	Symptoms	Cause	Treatment
Esophagus	GERD	Heartburn, nausea, and belching	Reflux of HCl into esophagus	Lifestyle changes including diet, exercise, and smoking cessation
Stomach	Gastroenteritis	Flulike symptoms	Virus or bacteria; irritation of the stomach lining	Soft-food diet and fluid
	Peptic ulcer	Abdominal pain, vomiting, bleeding, and general weakness	Drugs, alcohol, or *H. pylori* bacteria	Drug therapy and limiting alcohol, caffeine, and acidic foods
Gallbladder	Gallstones	Cramps, nausea, fever, vomiting	Bile high in cholesterol; obesity; rapid weight loss	Surgery and drug therapy
Small Intestine	Celiac disease	Malabsorption	Error of gluten metabolism	Gluten-free diet
Large Intestine	Diarrhea	Frequent loose, watery stools	Contaminated water or food; stress; excessive fiber intake	Water and electrolyte replacement
	Constipation	Cramping, bloating	Insufficient water and fiber intake; inactivity	High fiber, high fluid intake; exercise
	Irritable bowel syndrome (IBS)	Diarrhea, constipation, and abdominal pain	Unknown cause(s); stress worsens the condition	Self-management with increased dietary fiber, stress relief, good sleep habits
	Ulcerative colitis	Abdominal pain and bleeding	Unknown cause	Drug therapy
	Crohn's disease	Abdominal pain and bleeding	Unknown cause	Drug therapy
	Colon cancer	Often none detectable	Multiple causes (genetics, various colon diseases, smoking, dietary carcinogens)	Surgery, radiation, and chemotherapy

surgery, patients are given dietary advice regarding the foods that would be the most comfortable to eat. Survival rates vary depending on the individual's age, health, treatment response, and stage of cancer diagnosis.

THE TAKE-HOME MESSAGE Gastrointestinal diseases and digestive disorders include less serious conditions, like heartburn, GERD, and stomach flu, and more serious conditions, such as esophageal cancer and ulcers. Disorders of the small intestine can be the most dangerous, as they may result in malabsorption and/or malnutrition. Constipation, diarrhea, and irritable bowel syndrome are all disorders of the large intestine. Colon cancer typically begins with polyps on the intestinal lining. Table 3.4 summarizes the common digestive disorders.

Putting It All Together

You may be familiar with the saying, "Food is food, until you swallow it; and then it becomes 'nutrition.'" The digestive process prepares the food you eat to be absorbed out of the GI tract and into the circulation to be delivered to cells. Your body builds your health around the food choices you make.

The DRIs and MyPlate guidelines (presented in Chapter 2) are designed to help you make healthful food choices and ensure that you receive adequate amounts of the essential nutrients without taking in too many kilocalories. Food choice, however, is a multifaceted effort. What we should eat, actually eat, and prefer to eat are sometimes conflicting decisions. Hopefully, the more you learn, the more healthful your choices will be.

Nutrition in Practice: Emily

College senior Emily doesn't eat breakfast before her 10 a.m. nutrition class because she knows she's likely to feel uncomfortably full and bloated after. Lately, Emily has had frequent bouts of abdominal pain that are only relieved by a bowel movement, followed by several loose, watery stools. Her symptoms are worse when she eats large meals, and right before a midterm exam or a paper is due. For a few weeks at the beginning of the semester, her symptoms had subsided, and she actually became constipated. But lately, the abdominal pains and diarrhea returned and appear to be getting worse. She is experiencing difficultly falling asleep at night, which is causing her to become tired by midday. She decides to visit the campus health center.

After meeting with the doctor at the health center, Emily is told that she has irritable bowel syndrome (IBS) and is referred to the campus's Registered Dietitian for an appointment. The dietitian meets with Emily to discuss her diet and lifestyle habits.

Emily's Stats:

- Age: 21
- Height: 5 feet 4 inches
- Weight: 125 lbs
- Symptoms: Frequent bouts of abdominal pain; loose, watery stool

Critical Thinking Questions

1. What aspect of Emily's lifestyle may be contributing to her IBS symptoms?
2. What foods/beverages could be contributing to Emily's bouts of diarrhea and why?
3. How could exercise help Emily with her IBS?

Dietitian's Observation and Plan for Emily:

- Exercise 30 minutes daily to release stress, which is a trigger for IBS.
- Slowly reduce the caffeine (coffee, energy drinks) in her diet. Caffeine can increase jitteriness (anxiety), cause a spastic colon (diarrhea), and interfere with the ability to fall asleep (fatigue).
- Get 8 hours of sleep each night.
- Avoid large meals. Eat three smaller meals and two small snacks throughout the day.

Three weeks later, Emily visits the dietitian again and reports that she has reduced her caffeine intake by eliminating her daily energy drinks. She is walking every day and is sleeping better at night. Her symptoms have subsided somewhat, but she is experiencing more constipation than diarrhea. A dietary analysis of Emily's food intake reveals she is eating less than 30% of the recommended intake for fiber. The dietitian works with Emily to add fiber-rich whole grains, fruits, and vegetables along with adequate fluids to her diet to alleviate the constipation.

Emily's Food Log

Food/Beverage	Time Consumed	Hunger Rating*	Location	Feelings/Symptoms
Latte with whole milk, 24 oz	7:30 a.m.	1	Walking to class	Anxious about midterms
Pepperoni pizza, 3 slices	12 noon	5	Campus dining hall	Tired
Large cola	1 p.m.	1	Library	Some diarrhea
Energy drink, 12 oz	3 p.m.	1	Walking to dorm	Tired
Clam chowder	6 p.m.	2	In dorm	Stressed, stomach cramps; feeling bloated

*Hunger Rating (1–5): 1 = not hungry; 5 = super-hungry

You will learn more in the next few chapters about the metabolism of the absorbed nutrients, the individual categories of nutrients that make up a healthy diet, and their functions in the body. When you read about carbohydrates, fat, proteins, vitamins, minerals, and water, keep in mind that they are all digested in the GI tract, absorbed in the intestines, distributed throughout the body by the blood and lymph, provide energy to individual cells, and regulate numerous critical processes.

Health Connection

Celiac Disease: An Issue of Absorption

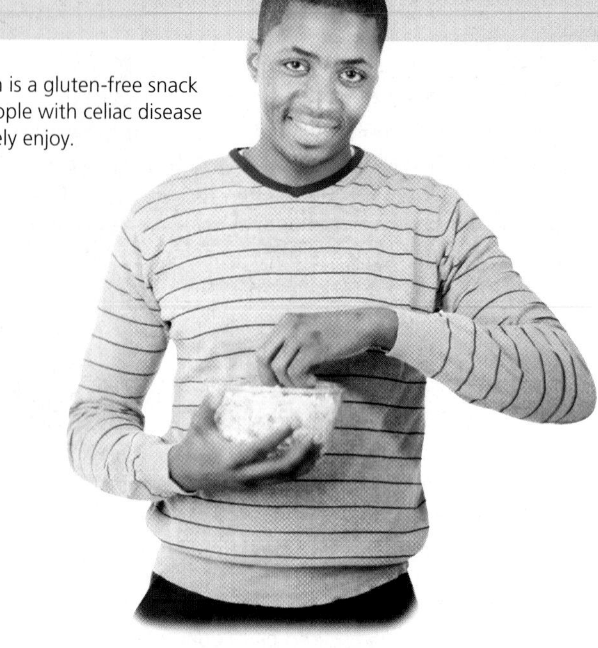

Popcorn is a gluten-free snack that people with celiac disease can safely enjoy.

One of the more serious malabsorption conditions to occur in the small intestine is *celiac disease*. A healthy small intestine contains numerous villi and microvilli that efficiently and exhaustively absorb nutrients from food. But when a person has celiac disease, the lining of the small intestine flattens out, which reduces its ability to absorb nutrients. The flattening is caused by an abnormal reaction to the protein gluten, found in wheat, rye, and barley.

Celiac disease is most common among people of European descent. Though the exact cause of celiac disease is unknown, it is believed to be genetic. The most recent estimates suggest that 1 in 133 people (less than 1%) is affected by celiac disease in the United States. But when an individual has celiac disease, the incidence among close family members is estimated to be as high as 4.5 percent.[1] Because of this genetic link, celiac disease is classified as a lifelong disorder.

What Are the Symptoms of Celiac Disease?

Classic celiac symptoms include reoccurring abdominal bloating, cramping, diarrhea, gas, fatty and foul-smelling stools, weight loss, anemia, fatigue, bone or joint pain, and even a painful skin rash called dermatitis herpetiformis. Some people develop the symptoms of celiac disease in infancy or childhood. Others develop it later in life, after being misdiagnosed with irritable bowel syndrome or various food intolerances.

How Serious Is Celiac Disease?

Depending on the length of time between symptom development and diagnosis, the complications from celiac disease can be serious. Celiac patients have an increased incidence of osteoporosis from poor calcium absorption, diminished growth because of nutrient malabsorption, and even seizures due to inadequate folate absorption. Celiac disease also increases the risk of developing certain types of cancer, including esophageal cancer and melanoma.[2]

Bread and other foods containing wheat, barley, and rye must be avoided on a gluten-free diet.

How Is Celiac Disease Diagnosed?

In the past, diagnosing celiac disease was sometimes difficult because it resembles other similar malabsorption diseases. The contemporary method of diagnosis begins with a simple blood test.[3] If the test proves positive, the next step is a tissue biopsy of the small intestine to confirm the diagnosis.[2, 4]

How Is Celiac Disease Treated?

The only treatment for celiac disease is a gluten-free diet.[5] This should stop the symptoms from progressing, allow the intestine to heal, and prevent further damage. The symptoms often improve within a few days after beginning the gluten-free diet. If the diet is followed faithfully, the absorption area of the intestinal tract often returns to normal status within three to six months.

Adhering to a gluten-free diet, which means avoiding all gluten-containing foods, can be challenging. All breads, pasta, cereals, and other wheat-containing foods must be eliminated. Gluten-free foods such as meat, milk, eggs, fruit, and vegetables are permissible. Rice, potatoes, corn, and beans, as well as grains such as quinoa, amaranth, and millet do not contain gluten and are also acceptable. The Academy of Nutrition and Dietetics maintains a comprehensive list of foods allowed on a gluten-free diet on their website, www.eatright.org.[6]

Due to an increased awareness of celiac disease and gluten intolerance, the demand for gluten-free products has exploded. Gluten-free products are now easier to find in your local markets and there is a wider range of choices. There are now smart phone apps to locate gluten-friendly restaurants, even while traveling to another country.

Until recently, oats had been considered a forbidden food for celiac patients. Recent studies suggest that moderate amounts, up to about ¼ cup of dry oats, may be safe for adults and children with celiac disease.[7] Concerns about adding oats to the gluten-free diet are related to the possibility that oats may be contaminated with hidden sources of gluten. Such concerns can be allayed by purchasing oats from companies that advertise gluten-free products and avoiding oats sold in bulk bins.

Be cautious of cross-contamination and additives from foods found in salad bars and buffets, medications and dietary supplements, and foods that contain vegetable gums or modified food starch. When you purchase any packaged food at the grocery store, be sure that you read the food labels carefully. Otherwise, you could be unpleasantly surprised by hidden gluten content.

Celiac disease is a manageable condition. Individuals with celiac disease can live normal lives by successfully implementing the guidelines for gluten-free diets, reading labels, and finding resources for gluten-free products. In the meantime, more research will be conducted to increase our understanding of the disease and lead to new treatments.[8]

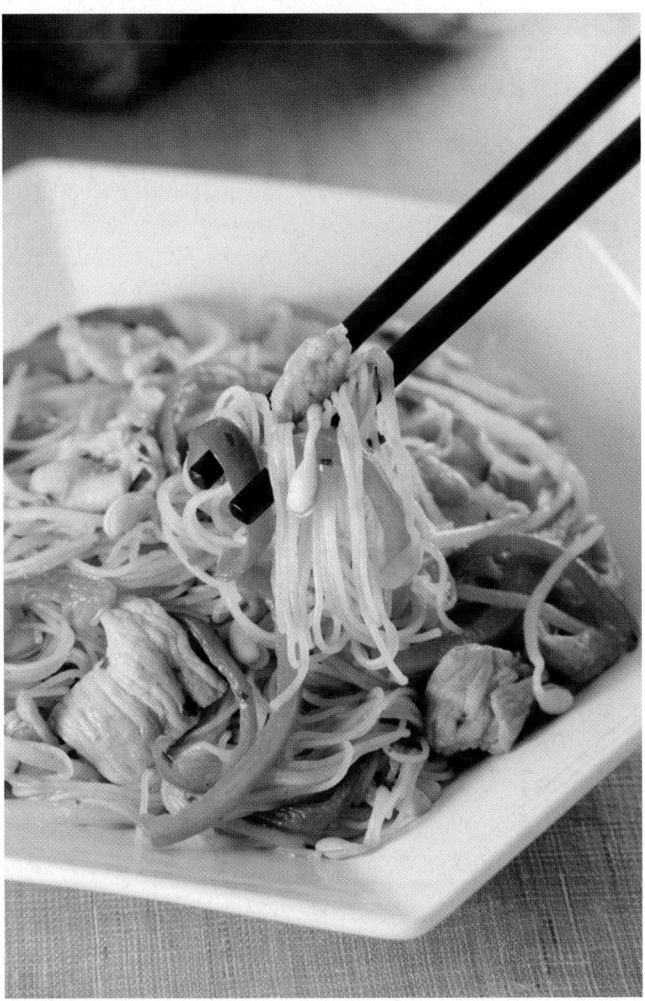

Rice noodles are a good gluten-free substitute for pasta.

TABLE TIPS

Eat Gluten-Free

Be a label reader to avoid products that contain all forms of wheat, barley, rye, triticale, or their hybrids.

Substitute whole wheat bread with gluten-free whole grains, such as quinoa, buckwheat, amaranth, sorghum, and millet.

If you like a hot cereal for breakfast try teff, a nutritious cereal grain from Ethiopia with a nutty, chewy texture.

Avoid packaged foods that contain modified food starch, dextrin, malt, or malt syrup, as they may be sources of gluten-containing grains.

Enjoy coffee, tea, sodas, fruit juices, and even fermented or distilled beverages, such as wine, sake, and distilled spirits on a gluten-free diet. But avoid coffee flavorings or creamers.

Look for either the GFCO or CSA Seal of Recognition marks on labels to assure the product is gluten-free.

Maintain a high fiber intake by incorporating gluten-free fresh fruits, vegetables, beans, peas, and lentils to your diet.

Consume calcium-rich dairy or calcium-fortified gluten-free products, such as orange juice, soy products, or non-milk beverages made from rice or nuts.

Snack on gluten-free nuts, fruits, popcorn, raisins, rice cakes, and fruit smoothies.

Enjoy homemade meals to control gluten intake and eat a variety of nutrient-dense foods.

References

1. A. Fasano, I. Berti, T. Gerarduzzi, et al. 2003. "Prevalence of Celiac Disease in At-Risk and Not-At-Risk Groups in the United States: A Large Multicenter Study." *Archives of Internal Medicine* 163:286–292.
2. D. P. Westerberg, J. M. Gill, B. Dave, M. J. DiPrinzio, A. Quisel, and A. Foy. 2006. "New Strategies for Diagnosis and Management of Celiac Disease." *The Journal of the American Osteopathic Association* 106:145–151.
3. P. A. Russo, L. J. Chartrand, and E. Seidman. 1999. "Comparative Analysis of Serologic Screening Tests for the Initial Diagnosis of Celiac Disease." *Pediatrics* 104:75–78.
4. D. A. van Heel and J. West. 2006. "Recent Advances in Celiac Disease." *Gut* 55:1037–1046.
5. A. Lee and J. Newman. 2003. "Celiac Diet: Its Impact on Quality of Life." *Journal of the American Dietetic Association* 103:1533–1535.
6. Academy of Nutrition and Dietetics. Available at www.eatright.org.
7. T. Thompson 2003. "Oats and the Gluten-Free Diet." *Journal of the American Dietetic Association* 103:376–379.
8. National Digestive Diseases Information Clearinghouse. 2007. *Celiac Disease.* Available at www.digestive.niddk.nih.gov/ddiseases/pubs/celiac/index.aspx. Accessed February 2012.

Visual Chapter Summary

1 The Organs of the GI Tract Are Involved in Digestion

Digestion is the process of breaking down whole food into absorbable nutrients. Digestion takes place in the GI tract, a long tube comprised of the mouth, esophagus, stomach, small intestine, and large intestine. Several sphincters control entry and exit of food and chyme through the various organs of the GI tract. Accessory organs, including the liver, gallbladder, and pancreas, secrete bile, hormones, and enzymes that help regulate and facilitate digestion.

The small intestine is the primary organ for the absorption of digested nutrients. The large intestine absorbs water and electrolytes before pushing waste through the colon and out of the body via the rectum.

Bile produced in the liver helps digest fat. The liver is the first organ to receive, process, and store absorbed nutrients. The pancreas and gallbladder are two other accessory organs that provide digestive fluids to the GI tract.

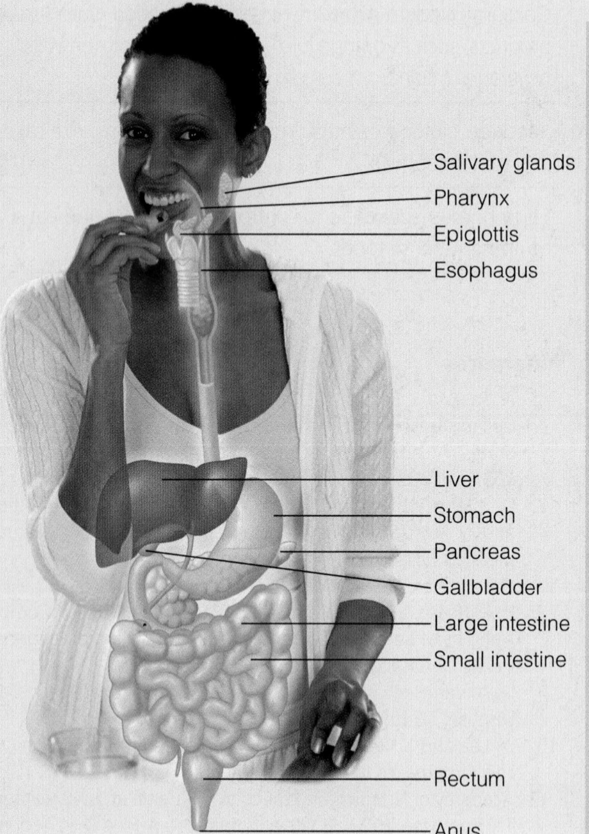

2 Peristalsis Propels Food through the GI Tract

Peristalsis moves food through the stomach and intestines by rhythmic contractions of longitudinal and circular muscles. Segmentation squeezes the mass of food into smaller pieces while mixing it with the chemical secretions of the intestine. Muscular contractions in the large intestine facilitate the absorption of water from the feces by compacting the mass and pushing it toward the rectum for excretion.

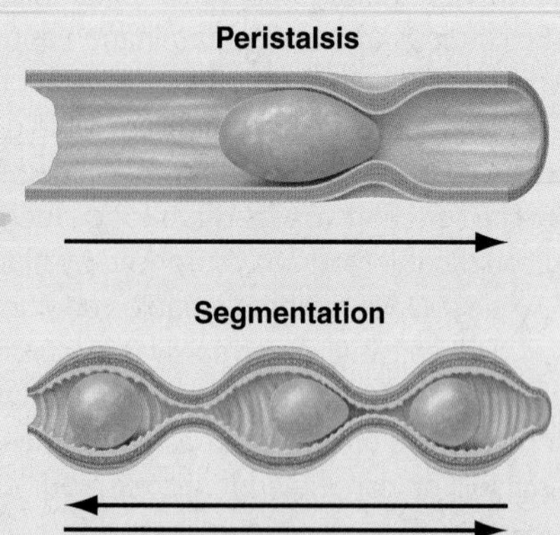

3 Food Is Chemically Digested by Enzymes

Chemical digestion involves mixing food with enzymes that break the bonds by adding water through hydrolysis. HCl also denatures protein and activates pepsinogen to initiate protein digestion. Bile from the gallbladder emulsifies large fat globules into smaller pieces to improve enzymatic action. Digestion is completed by the brush border enzymes maltase, sucrase, and lactase, and the proteases, breaking nutrients down into single molecules that can be absorbed into the small intestine lining.

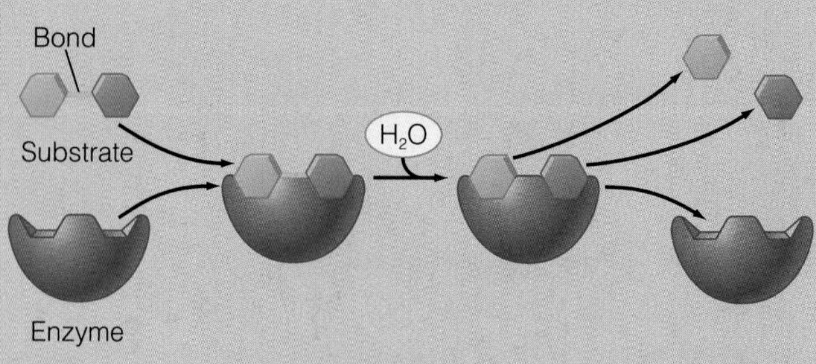

4 Digested Nutrients Are Absorbed through the Small Intestine

Nutrients pass through the small intestinal wall via passive diffusion, facilitated diffusion, active transport, or endocytosis.

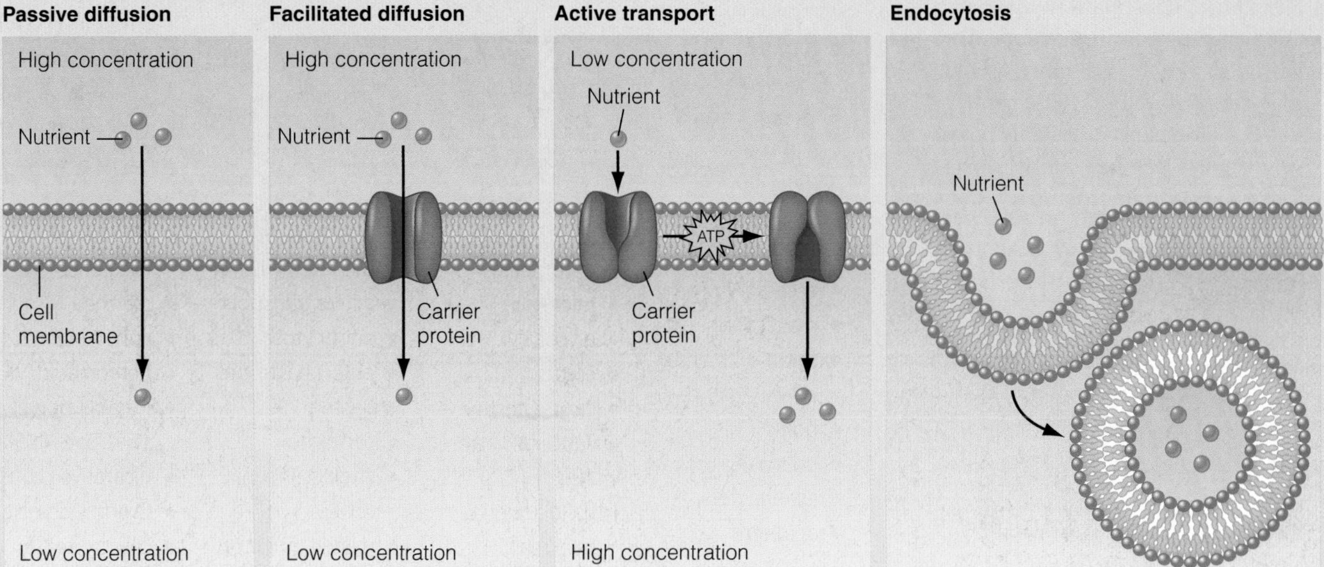

5 Digestion Is Regulated by Hormones and the Nervous System

Hormones, including gastrin, secretin, cholecystokinin, and gastric inhibitory peptide, are chemical messengers secreted from the GI tract that direct enzymes and the release of digestive secretions during digestion. The nervous system communicates signals of hunger and thirst.

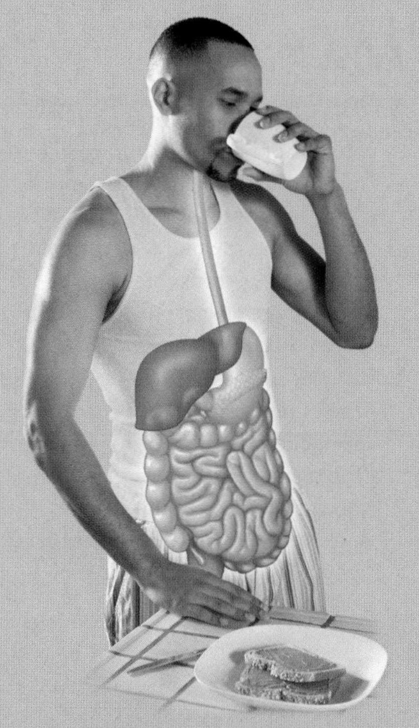

6 Nutrients Are Transported throughout the Body by the Circulatory System

Body systems other than the digestive system are involved in the body's digestion, absorption, and transport of nutrients. The circulatory system distributes water-soluble nutrients throughout the body and carries carbon dioxide and other waste products to be excreted through the lungs and the kidneys. The lymph system transports fat-soluble vitamins from the GI tract through the lymph system and into the circulatory system.

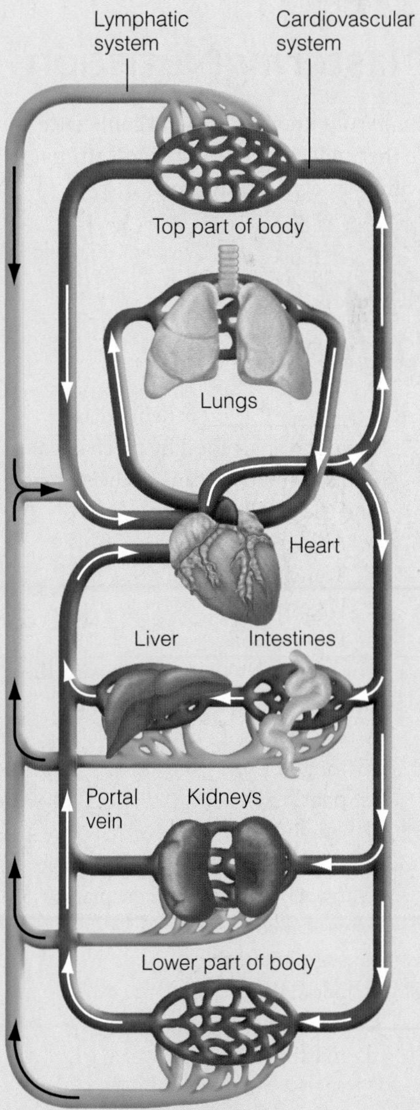

7 There Are Many Digestive Disorders

Heartburn, constipation, diarrhea, and hemorrhoids are common digestive disorders. The more serious digestive disorders include peptic ulcers, colon cancer, irritable bowel syndrome, ulcerative colitis, celiac disease and Crohn's disease.

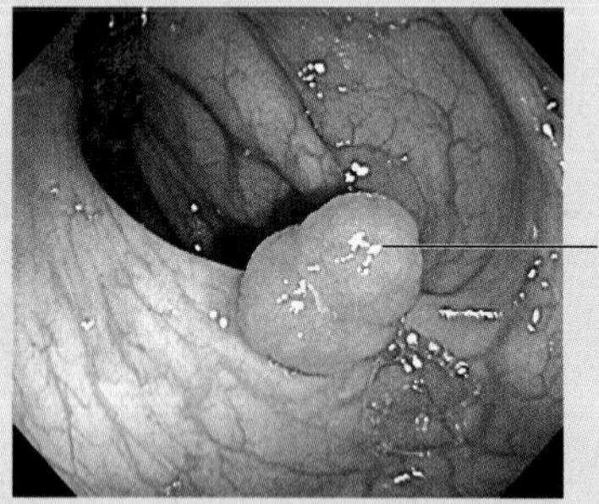

Colon polyp

Terms to Know

- chemical digestion
- mechanical digestion
- gastrointestinal (GI) tract
- digestion
- absorption
- sphincters
- accessory organs
- mastication
- saliva
- salivary glands
- bolus
- pharynx
- esophagus
- epiglottis
- upper esophageal sphincter
- lower esophageal sphincter
- goblet cells
- gastric pits
- parietal cells
- chief cells
- chyme
- small intestine
- villi
- enterocytes
- microvilli
- glycocalyx
- crypts
- large intestine
- ileocecal valve
- liver
- gallbladder
- pancreas
- peristalsis
- segmentation
- hydrolysis
- mucus
- hydrochloric acid (HCL)
- proteases
- pepsinogen
- pepsin
- bile
- emulsify
- bicarbonate
- passive diffusion
- active transport
- endocytosis
- enterogastrones
- gastrin
- secretin
- cholecystokinin (CCK)
- gastric inhibitory peptide (GIP)
- ghrelin
- peptide YY
- hepatic portal vein
- lymphatic system
- gastsroesophageal reflux disease (GERD)
- gastroenteritis
- ulcer
- gallstones
- flatulence
- diarrhea
- constipation
- hemorrhoid
- irritable bowel syndrome (IBS)
- ulcerative colitis
- Crohn's disease
- celiac disease

MasteringNutrition™

Build your knowledge—and confidence!—in the Study Area of MasteringNutrition with a variety of study tools.

Check Your Understanding

1. _______________ is defined as breaking apart food by mechanical and enzymatic means in the stomach and the small intestine.
   a. Absorption
   b. Transport
   c. Digestion
   d. Elimination
2. The protective tissue that covers the trachea during swallowing is the
   a. esophagus.
   b. tongue.
   c. pharynx.
   d. epiglottis.
3. Food is moved through the GI tract by rhythmic muscular waves called
   a. segmentation.
   b. peristalsis.
   c. bowel movement.
   d. mastication.
4. Which of the following secretions chemically breaks apart foods?
   a. bile
   b. bicarbonate ions
   c. cholecystokinin
   d. enzymes
5. What is the function of hydrochloric acid in the digestive process?
   a. activates pepsinogen to pepsin
   b. slows peristalsis
   c. neutralizes the pH in the stomach
   d. begins carbohydrates digestion.
6. Which of the following is true regarding the small intestine?
   a. It is shorter than the large intestine.
   b. It is the major organ for digestion and absorption.
   c. It has access to lymph tissue but not to the bloodstream.
   d. It is composed of the ileum, duodenum, and jejunum, in that order.
7. The emulsifying agent that is produced by the liver is
   a. pepsin.
   b. gastrin.
   c. cholecystokinin.
   d. bile.
8. Glucose is absorbed by
   a. passive diffusion.
   b. facilitated diffusion.
   c. active transport.
   d. osmosis.
9. Which of the following transports fat-soluble nutrients to the blood?
   a. hepatic portal vein
   b. lymph vessels
   c. red blood cells
   d. the kidneys
10. Celiac disease is caused by a reaction to gluten found in which foods?
    a. citrus fruits
    b. wheat, barley, and rye
    c. legumes, nuts, and seeds
    d. milk, cheese, and yogurt

Answers

1. (c) Digestion is defined as the process of breaking apart food by mechanical and enzymatic means. Once food is digested it can be absorbed into the blood or lymphatic system to be transported to the cells. Any waste products are eliminated through urine and feces.
2. (d) The epiglottis covers the trachea. The esophagus is a tube that connects the mouth with the stomach. The tongue is a muscle that pushes food to the back of the mouth into the pharynx, a chamber that food passes through before being swallowed.

3. (b) Peristalsis is the process that moves food through the stomach and small intestine. Segmentation squeezes chyme back and forth along the intestinal walls. A bowel movement involves peristalsis moving feces through the large intestine. Mastication is the process of chewing food.
4. (d) Enzymes secreted from the stomach, small intestine, and pancreas chemically break apart food. Bile emulsifies lipids. Bicarbonate ions neutralize acid. Cholecystokinin slows peristalsis.
5. (a) Hydrochloric acid produced in the stomach activates pepsinogen to pepsin, breaks down connective tissue in meat, and destroys some microorganisms. Cholecystokinin and gastric inhibitory hormones slow peristalsis. Bicarbonate ions neutralize pH in the duodenum. Amylase begins carbohydrate breakdown in the mouth.
6. (b) The small intestine is critical to digestion and absorption. With numerous villi and microvilli, it has a vast surface area to enhance absorption. It allows nutrients to pass into both blood and lymph. It consists of the duodenum, then the jejunum, and finally the ileum. It is much longer than the large intestine.
7. (d) The liver makes bile in a dilute, liquid form that is concentrated and stored in the gallbladder. Pepsin is the active form of a protease secreted by the chief cells in the stomach. Gastrin and cholecystokinin are GI tract hormones.
8. (c) Glucose and amino acids are absorbed by active transport.
9. (b) The fat-soluble nutrients are transported through the lymphatic vessels and eventually arrive at the thoracic duct, where they reach the blood. The hepatic portal vein transports water-soluble nutrients to the liver. Red blood cells transport oxygen. The kidneys filter the blood to remove and excrete waste into the urine.
10. (b) Wheat, barley, and rye contain gluten, which causes the symptoms associated with celiac disease. Fruits, vegetables, dairy, meat, nuts, legumes, and seeds are free of gluten and are safe to eat on a gluten-free diet.

Answers to Myths and Misconceptions

1. **True.** The enzyme salivary amylase, found in saliva, begins digesting carbohydrate during chewing; hence, starchy foods will begin to taste sweet as they are broken down.
2. **True.** The stomach secretes a powerful acid, HCl, that is critical to digestion. The acid is also strong enough to damage the stomach wall, so a thick layer of mucus protects it.
3. **True.** Bile emulsifies fat by breaking up the large globules into smaller fat droplets.
4. **False.** Acid reflux occurs when stomach contents pass back through the lower esophageal sphincter into the esophagus.
5. **True.** After food has been completely broken down and its nutrients absorbed in the small intestine, it passes into the large intestine, where water and electrolytes continue to be absorbed.
6. **True.** Fecal matter consists of 50 percent bacteria, while the rest is undigested food, water, and sloughed intestinal cells.
7. **False.** Lymph only transports fat-soluble components. Blood transports water-soluble materials.
8. **True.** Several hormones, including gastrin, secretin, cholecystokinin (CCK), and gastric inhibitory peptide help regulate digestion.
9. **False.** Though foodborne illness can cause diarrhea, the condition can also result from an adverse reaction to certain foods, medications, or other compounds.
10. **False.** The cause of irritable bowel syndrome is not known, but low-fiber diets, stress, consumption of irritating foods, and intestinal motility disorders are all suspected factors.

Web Resources

- To learn more about the various conditions related to digestion, absorption, and elimination, visit the Center for Digestive Health and Nutrition at www.gihealth.com
- Search the National Digestive Diseases Information Clearinghouse site for more information about various digestive diseases: http://digestive.niddk.nih.gov

References

1. Pedersen, A. M., A. Bardow, S. Jensen, and B. Nauntofte. 2002. Saliva and Gastrointestinal Functions of Taste, Mastication, Swallowing and Digestion. *Oral Diseases* 8:117–129.
2. Marieb, E. N. and K. Hoehn. 2007. *Human Anatomy and Physiology*. 7th ed. San Francisco: Benjamin Cummings.
3. Gropper, S. S., J. L. Smith, and J. L. Groff. 2005. *Advanced Nutrition and Human Metabolism*. 4th ed. Belmont, CA: Thomson Wadsworth.
4. Tortora, G. J. and N. P. Anagnostakos. 2008. *Principles of Anatomy and Physiology*. 12th ed. New York: Harper & Row.
5. Wong, W. and R. Pass. 2004. Extraesophageal and Atypical Manifestations of GERD. *Journal of Gastroenterology and Hepatology* 19:S33–S43.
6. Tytgat, G. N. J. 2002. Review Article: Treatment of Mild and Severe Cases of GERD. *Alimentary Pharmacology & Therapeutics* 16:73–78; Nelson, J. K., K. E. Moxness, M. D. Jensen, and C. F. Gastineau. 1994. *Mayo Clinic Diet Manual*. 7th ed. St. Louis: Mosby.
7. National Cancer Institute. 2012. Esophageal Cancer. Available at http://www.cancer.gov/cancertopics/types/esophageal. Accessed February 2012.
8. Fobi, M. 2002. Prophylactic Cholecystectomy with Gastric Bypass Operation: Incidence of Gallbladder Disease. *Obesity Surgery* 12:350–353.
9. Hajek, P., F. Gillison, and H. McRobbie. 2003. Stopping Smoking Can Cause Constipation. *Addiction*. 98:1563-1567.
10. Dukas, L., W. C. Willett, and E. L. Giovannucci. 2003. Association Between Physical Activity, Fiber Intake, and Other Lifestyle Variables and Constipation in a Study of Women. *American Journal of Gastroenterology* 98:1790–1796.
11. Saito, Y. A., P. Schoenfeld, and G. R. Locke. 2002. The Epidemiology of Irritable Bowel Syndrome in North America: A Systematic Review. *American Journal of Gastroenterology* 97:1910–1915.
12. National Cancer Institute. 2012. Colon and Rectal Cancer. Available at http://www.cancer.gov/cancertopics/types/colon-and-rectal. Accessed February 2012.

4 Carbohydrates

Chapter Objectives

After reading this chapter, you will be able to:

1. Compare and contrast the simple and complex carbohydrates: monosaccharides, disaccharides, polysaccharides, and oligosaccharides.
2. Explain the process of digesting and absorbing dietary carbohydrates.
3. List the functions of carbohydrates in the body.
4. Explain how the body regulates blood glucose levels and the hormones involved in the process.
5. Describe the role of fiber in promoting health and the potential health implications of consuming too little or too much dietary fiber.
6. Describe the guidelines for carbohydrate intake, including the AMDR for carbohydrates, the AI for fiber, and the recommendation for consuming simple sugars, and identify the best food sources for each type of carbohydrate.
7. Define type 1 and type 2 diabetes and explain how diabetes differs from hypoglycemia.
8. Describe the differences between natural sugars, added sugars, and alternative sweeteners used as sugar substitutes.

1. Carbohydrates are the least important macronutrient. T/F
2. Most babies are born lactose intolerant. T/F
3. Carbohydrates are a main cause of obesity. T/F
4. Sugar causes hyperactivity in children. T/F
5. Whole grains are more nutrient dense than refined grains. T/F
6. Sugar causes tooth decay. T/F
7. Aspartame causes cancer in humans. T/F
8. Americans do not consume enough fiber. T/F
9. Soda and other sugar-sweetened beverages play a big role in Americans' rising rate of obesity. T/F
10. Obese individuals are more likely to develop type 2 diabetes. T/F

See page 154 for answers to these Myths and Misconceptions.

Carbohydrates are essential macronutrients produced mainly in plants. These compounds, often referred to as *sugars*, can be as simple as a single sugar unit or as complex as a molecule containing 1,000 or more sugar units. Carbohydrates' main role in the body is to supply fuel, primarily in the form of glucose (*ose* = sugar), the predominant sugar in high-carbohydrate foods. Cells use glucose as the primary source of energy (ATP) to fuel the demands of the brain, red blood cells, and the nervous system. With such an important role in the body, it isn't surprising that foods high in carbohydrates are a big part of the diet, no matter what continent you live on.

Carbohydrate-rich foods, including rice, beans, fruits, tubers, and nuts, make up the foundation of diets the world over. In Asia, rice accounts for 80 percent of people's daily kilocalories. In Latin America, carbohydrate-laden bananas, chilies, beans, tubers, and nuts adorn most dinner plates. In the Mediterranean, grain-based pastas, breads, and couscous are plentiful, and here in the United States, many people consume the potato on a daily basis.[1]

In this chapter, you will learn about different types of carbohydrates and the functions they perform in the body. We will also discuss how we digest carbohydrates, and how the body metabolizes glucose and what happens when metabolic control fails, as in the disease diabetes mellitus. You will learn the role that certain types of carbohydrates can play in fighting obesity, heart disease, cancer, and diabetes. Finally, we will explore how to incorporate a rich balance of carbohydrates into your daily diet.

What Are Carbohydrates and How Are They Classified?

Carbohydrates originate in plants during a process called **photosynthesis** (**Figure 4.1**). During photosynthesis, plants use the **chlorophyll** in their leaves to absorb the energy in sunlight. The absorbed energy splits water in the plant into its component parts of hydrogen and oxygen. The hydrogen joins with carbon dioxide that the plant has taken in from the air to form **glucose.** Thus, carbohydrates are literally hydrated carbons. Plants use the glucose they produce directly for energy, store it, or combine it with minerals from the soil to make other compounds, including protein and vitamins. We then eat the plants and digest, absorb, and utilize the glucose.

All carbohydrates consist of strings of sugar units bound together. We classify carbohydrates according to how many of these units are in the string. **Simple carbohydrates** consist of either a single sugar unit called a **monosaccharide** (*mono* = one, *saccharide* = sugar) or two units bonded together as a **disaccharide** (*di* = two). **Oligosaccharides** (*oligo* = a few) are slightly longer and contain three to ten units. **Complex carbohydrates** include more than ten and up to hundreds or thousands of connected units. Such **polysaccharides** (*poly* = many) include **starch** and **fiber.**

photosynthesis A process by which plants create carbohydrates using the energy from sunlight.

chlorophyll The green pigment in plants that absorbs energy from sunlight to begin the process of photosynthesis.

glucose The most abundant carbohydrate in nature and the primary energy source for the body.

simple carbohydrates Carbohydrates that consist of one sugar unit (monosaccharides) or two sugar units (disaccharides).

monosaccharide Simple sugar that consists of a single sugar unit. There are three monosaccharides: glucose, fructose, and galactose.

disaccharide Simple sugar that consists of two sugar units combined. There are three disaccharides: sucrose, lactose, and maltose.

oligosaccharides Three to ten units of monosaccharides combined.

complex carbohydrates A category of carbohydrates that contain many sugar units combined. A polysaccharide is a complex carbohydrate.

polysaccharides Many sugar units combined. Starch, glycogen, and fiber are all polysaccharides.

starch The storage form of glucose in plants.

fiber A nondigestible carbohydrate that provides structural support to the cell walls in plants.

hexose A sugar that contains six carbons; glucose, galactose, and fructose are all hexoses.

Monosaccharides Are Single Sugar Units

There are three nutritionally important monosaccharides: glucose, fructose, and galactose. Glucose is the most common, but fructose and galactose are also found naturally in foods. All three simple sugars share the same molecular formula of six carbon atoms, twelve hydrogen atoms, and six oxygen atoms ($C_6H_{12}O_6$), referred to as a **hexose** (*hex* = six). The difference between the three monosaccharides lies in how their atoms are arranged (see **Figure 4.2**). Glucose and galactose are both six-sided ring structures that, at first glance, look identical to each other. Examine both structures carefully. The hydroxyl group (OH) and the hydrogen (H) of glucose are arranged in a specific way on the fourth carbon. Now look at the structure of galactose. You'll notice that the hydrogen (H) on the fourth carbon is shifted to the right side of the carbon, while the hydroxyl group (OH) is on the left. This slight

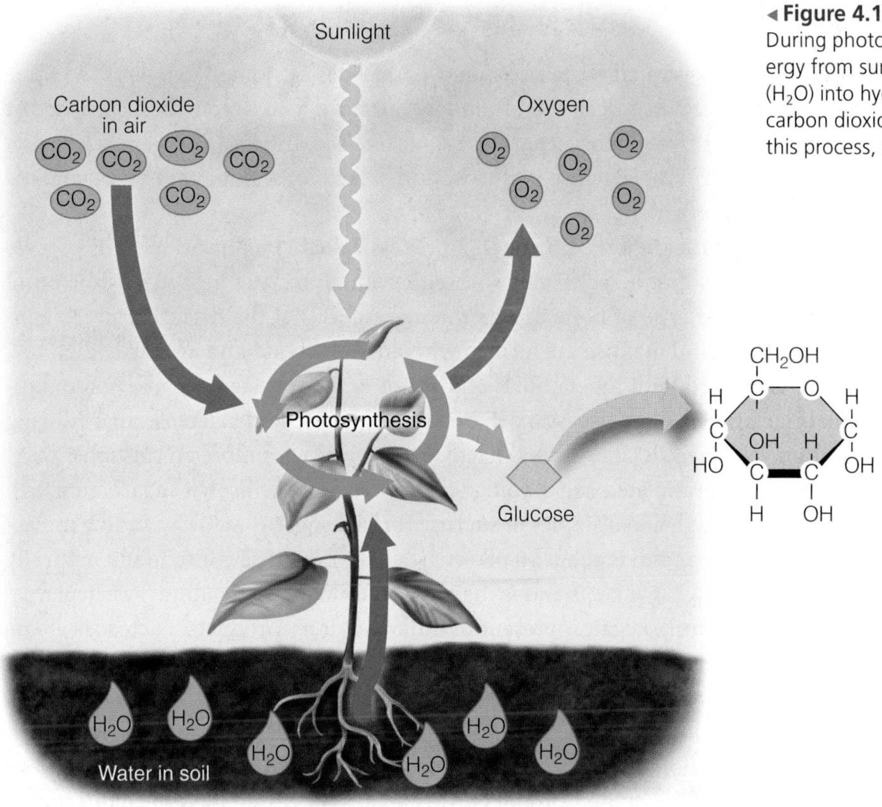

Figure 4.1 Photosynthesis: How Glucose Is Made
During photosynthesis, the leaves of green plants absorb energy from sunlight. The energy splits six molecules of water (H_2O) into hydrogen and oxygen. The hydrogen joins with carbon dioxide in the plant to create glucose ($C_6H_{12}O_6$). In this process, six molecules of oxygen are released into the air.

rearrangement of atoms makes a difference in the way the body metabolizes and uses these two monosaccharides.

Fructose contains the same number of carbon, hydrogen, and oxygen atoms as glucose and galactose but its molecular structure is arranged as a five-sided, rather than a six-sided, ring. However, fructose is still classified as a hexose because it contains six carbons (notice the location of all six carbons on the fructose molecule in Figure 4.2).

Glucose is the most abundant monosaccharide in foods. Glucose is also the most abundant monosaccharide in the body. The brain in particular relies on glucose (also known as blood glucose or blood sugar) as its main source of ATP, as do the red blood cells.

Galactose is seldom found on its own in nature; it is most commonly bound with glucose as part of the disaccharide lactose found in milk and milk products. Several plant products, including cereals, beans, nuts, seeds, and vegetables, contain slight amounts of galactose, but it is in a form that is resistant to digestion.

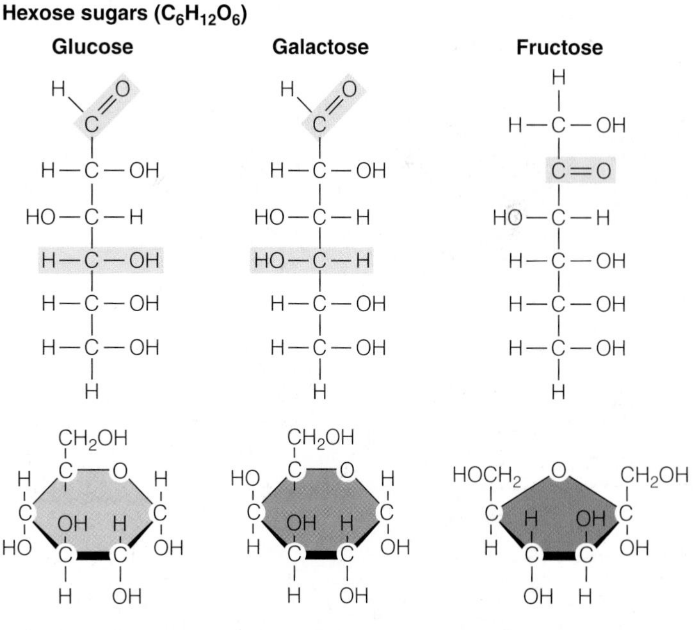

Fructose, the sweetest of the natural sugars, is found abundantly in fruits and is also known as fruit sugar. Fructose is part of high fructose corn syrup, a sweetener commonly used by the food industry in soft drinks and fruit beverages. Some U.S. health professionals have expressed concern that overconsumption of high fructose corn syrup may contribute to the obesity epidemic.[2] (See the Examining the Evidence feature on this topic on page 144.)

From the three monosaccharides, disaccharides and complex carbohydrates are created.

Figure 4.2 The Structural Differences between Glucose, Galactose, and Fructose
The three monosaccharides are shown in their linear form (as found in foods) and in the ring structure found in the body.

galactose A monosaccharide that links with glucose to create the sugar found in dairy foods.

fructose The sweetest of all the monosaccharides; also known as fruit sugar or levulose.

Disaccharides Consist of Two Sugar Units

A disaccharide is created when two monosaccharides are joined together. The three disaccharides, *sucrose, lactose*, and *maltose*, all have a common characteristic: At least one of their two monosaccharides is glucose. The disaccharide sucrose consists of glucose and fructose; lactose is glucose and galactose; and maltose is two glucose units linked together.

Disaccharides are joined through a process called **condensation.** This process chemically links monosaccharides with either an alpha or a beta **glycosidic bond** (**Figure 4.3**). The type of bond affects the digestibility of the disaccharide. For instance, sucrose and maltose are formed with an alpha bond and are easily digested. Lactose is formed with a beta bond and is not easily digested because some individuals lack the enzyme necessary to break the glucose and galactose apart during digestion. (See Health Connection: Lactose Intolerance for more on this topic.)

condensation A chemical reaction in which two molecules combine to form a larger molecule, and water is released.

glycosidic bond A bond that forms when two sugar molecules are joined together during condensation.

sucrose A disaccharide composed of glucose and fructose; also known as table sugar.

lactose A disaccharide composed of glucose and galactose; also known as milk sugar.

maltose A disaccharide composed of two glucose units joined together.

The white granulated sugar you add to coffee and the brown sugar you use to make cookie dough are examples of **sucrose** (brown sugar is made by adding molasses to refined sugar and is about 90 percent sucrose[3]). Sucrose is also found naturally in sugar cane and sugar beets and is the most commonly used natural sweetener.

Lactose, or milk sugar, is present in milk and dairy products. Lactose is a particularly important carbohydrate in the diets of newborn infants because it is the first and only carbohydrate they consume in breast milk.

Maltose, or malt sugar, is the least common of the disaccharides and is formed during the digestion of starch. Manufacturers add maltose as a sweetener and to improve the shelf life of their products. This makes processed food the main source

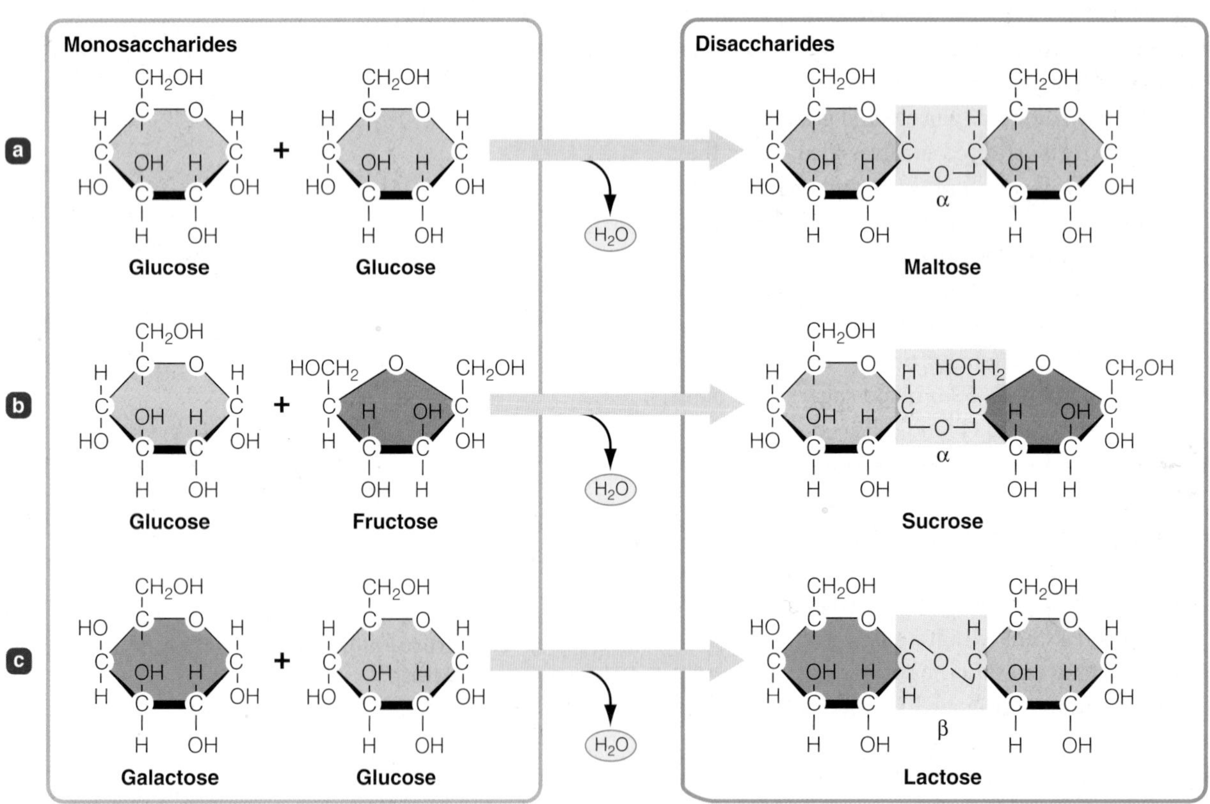

▲ **Figure 4.3 Condensation Reaction Links Monosaccharides to Form Disaccharides**
Through the process of condensation, monosaccharides join together to form disaccharides. **(a)** Two glucose units join together with an alpha bond to produce maltose. **(b)** The disaccharide sucrose is composed of a molecule of glucose linked to a molecule of fructose by an alpha bond. **(c)** The disaccharide lactose is composed of glucose and galactose. Lactose differs from sucrose and maltose in that the two monosaccharides are joined by a beta bond.

of maltose in our diets. Maltose is also formed during the fermentation of barley used to brew beer.

In general, simple carbohydrates are sweeter than complex carbohydrates (which we'll discuss next). Foods such as table sugar and fruit, which are high in fructose, are perceived as sweet compared with the carbohydrates found in starchy foods such as rice or bread. This perception is due to the structure of the molecule. The five-sided ring of fructose mixes with saliva and reacts with taste buds, signaling the brain that the food is sweet.

Some of us experience a stronger sense of sweetness than others do when we eat foods high in monosaccharides and disaccharides. For example, across all ethnic groups, females seem to crave sweetness more than males.[4,5] This ability to sense sweetness may be influenced by age or by health conditions, or may have a genetic component.[6]

Chemistry Boost

Condensation Reaction

A condensation reaction occurs when two smaller molecules join to form a larger molecule. When two monosaccharides join together, a hydroxyl group (—OH) from one sugar gains a hydrogen and forms a molecule of water. The OH group on the second sugar loses a hydrogen and links to the other molecule where the OH group was removed.

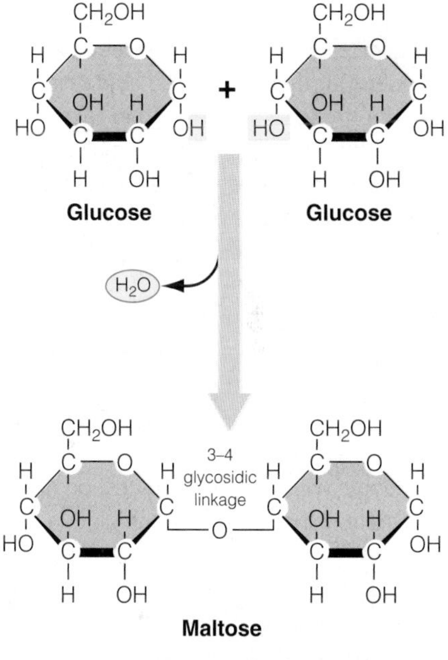

The Polysaccharides Consist of Many Sugar Units

Complex carbohydrates, or polysaccharides, consist of long chains and branches of glucose linked together. Some polysaccharides, such as starch and **glycogen,** serve as storage forms of glucose in plants and animals, while dietary fiber provides structure in plant cells.

Starch

Plants store glucose in chains of starch. These chains can be hundreds or even thousands of glucose units long. Straight chains are called **amylose,** and the branched chains are called **amylopectin** (**Figure 4.4**). Although plants contain both forms of these polysaccharides, about 60 percent of most starches is usually amylopectin,

a Two types of polysaccharides in starch are amylose (straight chain) and amylopectin (branched).

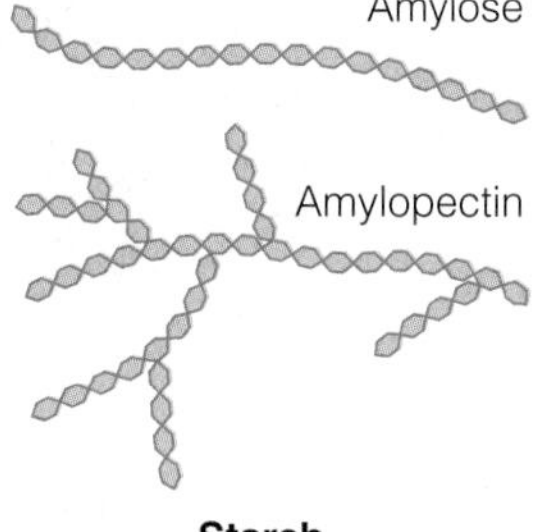

b Dietary fiber is a nondigestible polysaccharide found in the cell walls of plants. Most dietary fiber is in the form of cellulose, a straight chain of glucose units with a beta-glycosidic bond that humans lack the enzyme to digest.

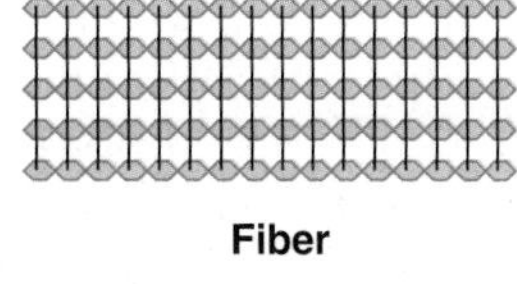

c Glycogen, the storage form of glucose in animals, including humans, is more branched than amylopectin. Each new glycogen needs a special protein to attach the glucose molecule.

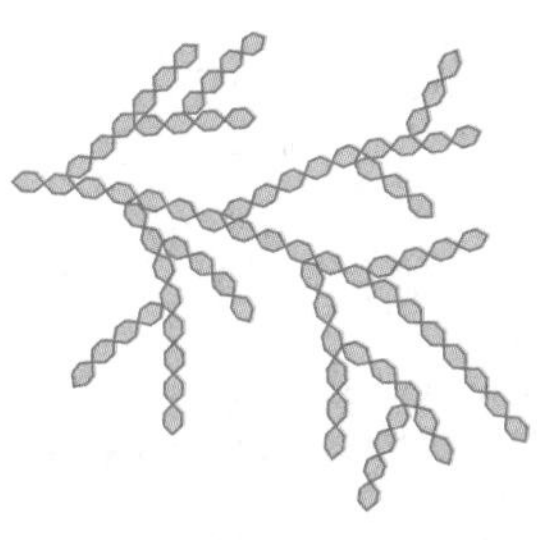

▲ **Figure 4.4 The Comparison of Starch, Fiber, and Glycogen**

glycogen The storage form of glucose in animals, including humans.

amylose A straight chain of polysaccharides found in starch.

amylopectin A branched chain of polysaccharides found in starch.

Health Connection

What Is Lactose Intolerance?

People with a deficiency of the brush border enzyme lactase cannot properly digest lactose, the principal carbohydrate found in dairy products. They may be diagnosed with **lactose maldigestion,** which can lead to distressing symptoms. For example, the undigested lactose can draw water into the digestive tract, causing diarrhea. Once the lactose reaches the colon, the bacteria in the colon ferment the sugar and produce various gases. For some lactose-sensitive individuals, bloating, flatulence, and cramps can sometimes be an unpleasant reminder that they ate lactose-containing foods. Individuals who develop these symptoms within two hours after eating or drinking foods that contain lactose may be **lactose intolerant.**[1]

Lactose maldigestion is a natural part of the aging process. In fact, as soon as a child stops nursing, his body makes less lactase. An estimated 25 percent of Americans, and 75 percent of adults around the world, maldigest lactose. Individuals of some specific ethnic origins, such as those from northern Europe, central Africa, and the Middle East, aren't as prone to developing lactose maldigestion. They appear to have a genetic predisposition to maintaining higher levels of lactase throughout their adult life.[2,3]

People with lactose maldigestion don't necessarily need to eliminate dairy foods from the diet. In fact, many people continue to eat milk, yogurt, and cheese without any problems or unpleasant side effects.[4,5] This is good news, as dairy products provide over 70 percent of the calcium in the diet.[6,7]

However, people with lactose intolerance have varying thresholds for tolerating lactose-containing foods and beverages (see the table). These thresholds can be raised depending upon how much of a lactose-containing food one eats at a time. Consuming smaller amounts of dairy foods throughout the day can be better tolerated than having a large amount at one time. Eating lactose-containing foods with a meal or snack, rather than by themselves, can also influence how much can be tolerated.[8,9]

lactose maldigestion The inability to digest lactose due to low levels of the enzyme lactase.

lactose intolerant When maldigestion of lactose results in symptoms such as nausea, cramps, bloating, flatulence, and diarrhea.

How Much Lactose Is in Your Foods?

Food	Amount	Lactose (grams)
Milk, whole, 1%, or skim	1 cup	11
Lactaid milk	1 cup	<1
Soy milk	1 cup	0
Ice cream	1/2 cup	6
Yogurt, low fat	1 cup	5
Sherbet	1/2 cup	2
Cottage cheese	1/2 cup	2
Swiss, Blue, Cheddar, or Parmesan cheese	1 oz	1
Cream cheese	1 oz	1

Don't Forget These Hidden Sources of Lactose

Baked goods
Baking mixes for pancakes, biscuits, and cookies
Bread
Breakfast drinks
Candies
Cereals, processed
Instant potatoes
Lunch meats (other than kosher meats)
Margarine
Salad dressings
Soups

Adapted from the American Dietetic Association, *Manual of Clinical Dietetics* (2000); food manufacturers; and the National Digestive Diseases Information Clearinghouse, "Lactose Intolerance," National Institutes of Health Publication No. 02-2751 (2002). National Institutes of Health. 2010. NIH Consensus Development Conference: Lactose Intolerance and Health. Available at http://consensus.nih.gov/2010/lactosestatement.htm. Accessed February 2012.

People respond differently to various dairy foods.[10,11] Whole milk tends to be tolerated better than skim milk. Cheese typically has less lactose than milk, especially hard, aged cheeses, as the amount of lactose remaining after the aging

with the remainder (about 40 percent) in the form of amylose. When we eat plant foods such as corn, rice, and potatoes, we consume the stored starch.

Some starch is resistant to digestion. In beans, half of the starch is digestible and the remainder is in the form of **resistant starch.** The amylose in starch is more resistant to digestion than is the amylopectin. Linear chains of amylose are

resistant starch A type of starch that is not digested in the GI tract but has important health benefits in the large intestine.

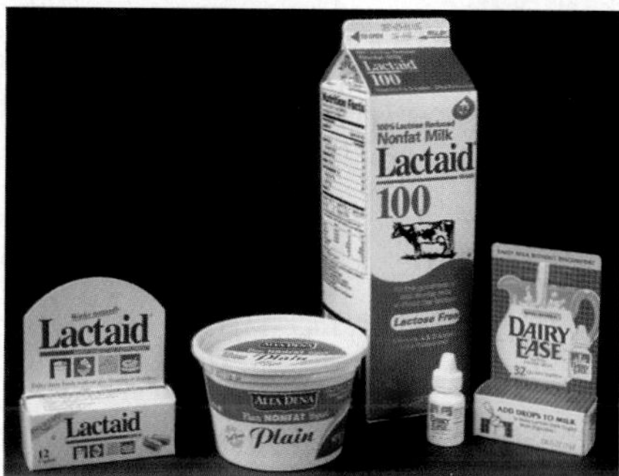

Many products are available to help those who are lactose intolerant enjoy dairy foods.

process is negligible. Yogurts that contain active cultures are better tolerated than skim or low-fat milk.

Consuming dairy foods regularly may improve lactose tolerance. The continuous exposure to undigested lactose promotes an acidic environment created by the fermenting of lactose by the bacteria in the colon, which inhibits further fermentation. Also, the constant presence of lactose in the colon perpetuates an increase in the growth of nongaseous bacteria and subsequent displacement of the gas-producing bacteria.[12]

For those who want to enjoy dairy foods without worrying about unpleasant side effects, there are lactose-reduced dairy products such as milk, cottage cheese, and ice cream in many supermarkets. Lactase pills or drops can also be used to break down lactose in foods before or while they are eaten. See the Table Tips for more ideas on improving your lactose tolerance.

Finally, note that lactose intolerance is not the same as having an allergy to milk. A milk allergy is a response by the immune system to one or more of the proteins in cow's milk. This condition typically affects only about 1 to 3 percent of children, and rarely occurs in adults.[13] (Food allergies are covered in Chapter 17.)

TABLE TIPS

Improving Lactose Tolerance

To determine the amount of milk you can tolerate, start with less than one cup and gradually increase the serving size until symptoms develop.

Choose aged hard cheeses such as Cheddar, Colby, and Parmesan over softer cheeses.

Drink one serving of milk with lunch and have an ounce of cheese as an afternoon snack, rather than having the milk and the cheese at the same time.

Drink that cup of milk along with a meal or snack, rather than by itself.

Try reduced-lactose yogurt or cottage cheese.

References

1. National Digestive Diseases Information Clearinghouse. 2002. *Lactose Intolerance*. National Institutes of Health Publication No. 02-2751.
2. McBean, L. and G. Miller. 1998. Allaying Fears and Fallacies About Lactose Intolerance. *Journal of the American Dietetic Association* 98:671–676.
3. Johnson, A., J. Semenya, M. Buchowski, C. Enwonwu, and N. Scrimshaw. 1993. Correlation of Lactose Maldigestion, Lactose Intolerance, and Milk Intolerance. *American Journal of Clinical Nutrition* 57:399–401.
4. Ibid.
5. Suarez, F., D. Savaiano, and M. Levitt. 1995. A Comparison of Symptoms After the Consumption of Milk or Lactose-Hydrolyzed Milk by People with Self-Reported Severe Lactose Intolerance. *New England Journal of Medicine* 333:1–4.
6. McBean, L. and G. Miller. 1998. Allaying Fears and Fallacies About Lactose Intolerance.
7. Putnam, J., J. Allshouse, and L. Kantor. 2002. U.S. Per Capita Food Supply Trends: More Calories, Refined Carbohydrates, and Fats. Economic Research Service, *Food Review* 25:2–15.
8. Suarez, F., D. Savaiano, P. Arbisi, and M. Levitt. 1997. Tolerance to the Daily Ingestion of Two Cups of Milk by Individuals Claiming Lactose Intolerance. *American Journal of Clinical Nutrition* 65:1502–1506.
9. Dehkordi, N., D. Rao, A. Warren, and C. Chawan. 1995. Lactose Malabsorption as Influenced by Chocolate Milk, Skim Milk, Sucrose, Whole Milk, and Lactic Cultures. *Journal of the American Dietetic Association* 95:484–486.
10. Hertzler, S., B. Huynh, and D. Savaiano. 1996. How Much Lactose Is Low Lactose? *Journal of the American Dietetic Association* 96:243–246.
11. Lee, C. and C. Hardy. 1989. Cocoa Feeding and Human Lactose Intolerance. *American Journal of Clinical Nutrition* 49:840–844.
12. Johnson, A., J. Semenya, M. Buchowski, C. Enwonwu, and N. Scrimshaw. 1993. Adaptation of Lactose Maldigesters to Continued Milk Intakes. *American Journal of Clinical Nutrition* 58:879–881.
13. McBean, L. and G. Miller. 1998. Allaying Fears and Fallacies About Lactose Intolerance.

harder to break down during digestion because the molecules stack together into tight granules, which hinders the ability of enzymes to reach and break down the bonds. The branched-chain shape of amylopectin makes it impossible to compact and therefore allows for much easier digestion. Unripe bananas, cooked and chilled pasta, raw potatoes, baked beans, and plantains are examples of foods with high levels of resistant starch.[7]

Plantains contain a fair amount of resistant starch.

Resistant starches are added to foods for health benefits.[8] Some researchers have reported that resistant starch may improve the health of the digestive tract by increasing bulk; improve glucose tolerance by lowering the glycemic impact on the blood and increasing insulin sensitivity[9]; and stimulate the growth of beneficial intestinal bacteria.[10]

Fiber

Most forms of dietary fiber are nondigestible polysaccharides and occur naturally as a structural component called **cellulose** in the cell walls of plants. Cellulose looks simple—just a straight string of glucose units (never branched like amylopectin) linked with beta-glycosidic bonds (**Figure 4.5**). When several strands stack together, like a wall of bricks, it gives the plant cell its structure and shape, which contributes to the texture of fruits and vegetables. **Lignin,** which is also a type of dietary fiber, is not a carbohydrate but acts as an adhesive in cell walls.

Foods high in carbohydrates are staples in many of the world's cultures.

As mentioned earlier, humans lack the digestive enzyme needed to break the beta form of the glycosidic bond, so for the most part, fiber cannot be digested, and passes through the intestines intact. This means that fiber does not provide energy. However, it performs numerous key roles in the body and is an essential component of a healthy diet.

Dietary fiber is sometimes classified according to its affinity for water. **Soluble fiber** dissolves in water, while **insoluble fiber** does not. Viscous, soluble fibers include pectins; beta-glucans; some gums, such as guar gum; and mucilages (for example, psyllium). Cellulose, lignin, and some hemicelluloses are considered insoluble, nonviscous fibers.[11, 12] Soluble fibers are more easily fermented by intestinal bacteria. Fruits and vegetables that are rich in pectin and hemicellulose can be hydrolyzed by these bacteria to form carbon dioxide, methane, and some fatty acids. Insoluble fibers, including cellulose found in grains, are not easily fermented.

Soluble fibers may have numerous health benefits. The gels formed by soluble fibers slow gastric emptying and may delay the absorption of some nutrients, which helps to reduce serum cholesterol, improve appetite control, and normalize blood glucose levels. The by-products produced by intestinal bacteria during fiber fermentation may also help protect against colon cancer.

Insoluble fibers may also have health benefits. In comparison with soluble fibers, less viscous, insoluble fibers increase the bulk of the stool. The greater stool

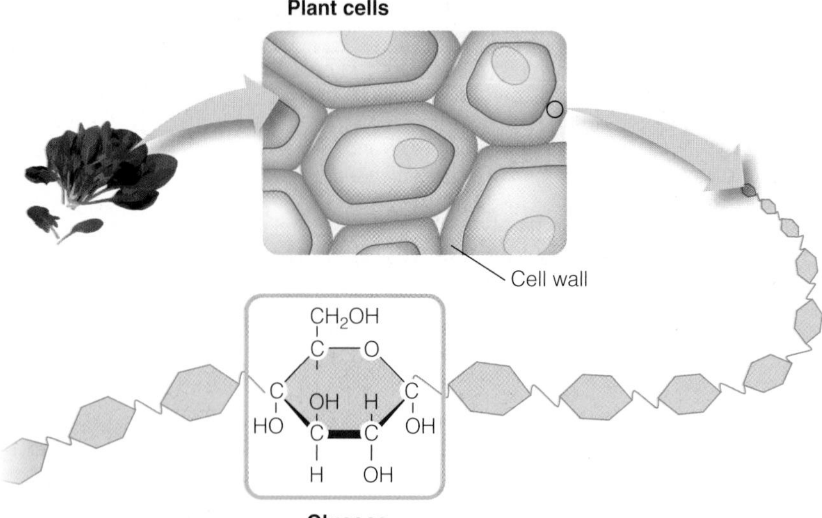

▲ **Figure 4.5 Plants Contain Cellulose**
Found in the cell walls of plants, cellulose is a polysaccharide composed of numerous glucose units linked together.

cellulose A nondigestible polysaccharide found in plant cell walls.

lignin A noncarbohydrate form of dietary fiber that binds to cellulose fibers to harden and strengthen the cell walls of plants.

soluble fiber A type of fiber that dissolves in water and is fermented by intestinal bacteria. Many soluble fibers are viscous and have thickening properties.

insoluble fiber A type of fiber that isn't dissolved in water or fermented by intestinal bacteria.

weight stimulates peristalsis, which speeds up the movement of the feces through the intestinal tract. This increase in movement, called transit time, relieves constipation and keeps the gastrointestinal tract healthy. There are exceptions to these statements because not all soluble fibers reduce serum cholesterol, and constipation may be relieved by some soluble fiber. At the end of the day, whether fiber is soluble is not as important as the overall dietary fiber intake, and the good news is that most plant foods contain both soluble and insoluble forms of dietary fiber (**Figure 4.6**). Animal products do not contain fiber.

Many compounds can be classified as both dietary fiber and functional fiber, depending on how they are used. **Functional fiber** is a type of fiber that has been extracted or isolated from a plant or manufactured by the food industry, and has been shown to have health benefits.[13] For example, psyllium, used in products such as Metamucil, is isolated from psyllium seed husks. Psyllium is high in soluble fiber and has been reported to reduce total cholesterol and LDL cholesterol. Synthetic or manufactured forms of functional fiber also include some forms of resistant starch. Together, dietary fiber and functional fiber contribute to the total fiber in the diet.

Table 4.1 summarizes the various types of fiber, some of their sources, and some of their health benefits.

▲ **Figure 4.6 Most Plant Foods Contain Both Soluble and Insoluble Fibers**
The skin of an apple is high in cellulose and insoluble fiber, while the pulp is high in pectin, a soluble fiber.

Glycogen

Whereas starch is the storage form of glucose in plants, glycogen is the storage form in animals, including humans. Molecules of glycogen are long, branched chains, similar to amylopectin, and are stored in muscle and in the liver. The branched structure enables the body to break glycogen down quickly and easily because there are so many sites where enzymes can attach. When blood glucose levels decrease, the liver breaks down the stored glycogen branches, one glucose molecule at a time, and releases the glucose into the blood. Muscle glycogen can similarly be broken down to glucose to provide ATP for the muscle. Because it breaks down quickly after an animal dies, animal products do not contain glycogen. In other words, eating meat or poultry will not provide glycogen.

Oligosaccharides

One carbohydrate class falls in between the definitions of simple and complex carbohydrates—the oligosaccharides. They are short chains of three to ten monosaccharides that are similar in length to simple carbohydrates (*oligo* = few). But they are also similar to polysaccharides because they make up part of the cellulose found in plant cell walls, and, like fiber, most of the oligosaccharides we consume escape digestion.[14] Oligosaccharides are found in legumes, beans, cabbage, brussels sprouts, and broccoli.

TABLE 4.1 Forms of Dietary Fiber and Their Health Benefits

Type	Found in These Foods	Reduces the Risk of
Insoluble Fiber		
■ Cellulose ■ Hemicellulose ■ Lignins	Whole grains, whole-grain cereals, bran, oats, fruit, vegetables, legumes	Constipation, diverticulosis, certain cancers, heart disease, obesity
Soluble Fiber		
■ Pectin ■ Beta-glucan ■ Gums ■ Psyllium	Citrus fruits, prunes, legumes, oats, barley, brussels sprouts, carrots	Constipation, heart disease, diabetes mellitus, obesity

functional fiber The nondigestible polysaccharides that are added to foods because of a specific desired effect on human health.

Raffinose

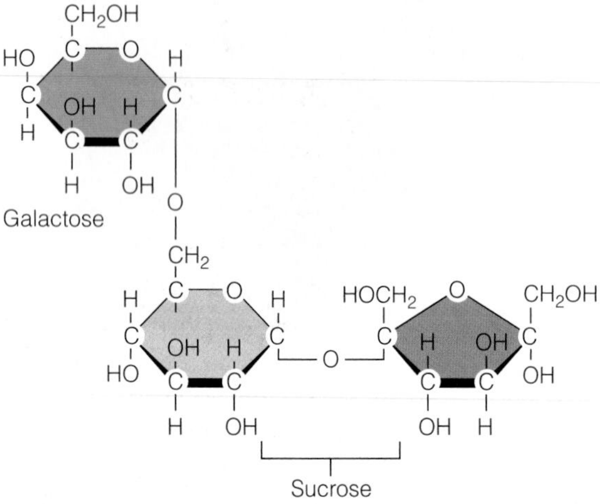

Galactose

Sucrose

▲ **Figure 4.7 The Structure of an Oligosaccharide**
The oligosaccharide raffinose consists of galactose connected to sucrose.

Two common oligosaccharides are raffinose (**Figure 4.7**) and stachyose. Humans lack the enzyme necessary to break apart the bonds in oligosaccharides and they pass undigested into the large intestine, where the intestinal microflora digest and ferment them. This fermentation may result in bloating, discomfort, and flatulence (gas). Taking a product such as Beano with a meal, which contains enzymes that digest oligosaccharides, can reduce the amount of flatulence produced.[15]

Oligosaccharides are also present in human breast milk. Even though these carbohydrates aren't digested, they may stimulate the immune system and increase the amount of healthy intestinal microflora in newborn infants.[16]

THE TAKE-HOME MESSAGE Carbohydrates are found primarily in plant-based foods and are needed by the cells for energy. Glucose is the preferred source of energy in the body. Glucose is stored in plants in the form of starch and fiber. Numerous cultures around the world rely on carbohydrate-based foods as staples in their diets. Simple carbohydrates include the monosaccharides and disaccharides. The monosaccharides glucose, fructose, and galactose combine to form the disaccharides sucrose, lactose, and maltose. The complex carbohydrates starch, fiber, and glycogen are all polysaccharides. The total fiber in the diet is a combination of both soluble and insoluble dietary fiber and functional fiber added to foods. Viscous, soluble fiber has thickening properties, can be fermented by intestinal bacteria, and moves slowly through the intestinal tract. Insoluble fiber typically moves quickly through the digestive system, reducing constipation. Oligosaccharides contain three to ten units and are part of cellulose in cell walls.

Beano helps reduce the production of gas in the large intestine.

How Do We Digest and Absorb Carbohydrates?

Disaccharides and starch are digested into monosaccharides that can be easily absorbed through the walls of the small intestine, whereas fiber generally passes through the GI tract undigested. Let's follow the carbohydrates from a typical sandwich through the digestive process, as illustrated in **Figure 4.8**.

Digestion of Carbohydrates Begins in the Mouth

The digestion of carbohydrates begins in the mouth, where the teeth grind the food and mix it with saliva, which contains the enzyme **salivary amylase** (recall that *ase* = enzyme). The amylase begins breaking down some of the amylose and amylopectin in the bread into the disaccharide maltose. The disaccharides and fiber are not altered in the mouth.

This food mixture, which now contains starch and amylase, along with the maltose, lactose, sucrose, and fiber, travels down the esophagus to the stomach. The amylase continues to break down the starch until the hydrochloric acid in the stomach deactivates this enzyme. There are no carbohydrate-digesting enzymes in the stomach; thus, little to no carbohydrate digestion takes place there.

The arrival of carbohydrates in the small intestine signals the pancreas to release an enzyme called pancreatic amylase. The pancreatic amylase breaks down the remaining starch units from the bread into maltose.

salivary amylase A digestive enzyme that begins breaking down carbohydrate (starch) in the mouth; other important enzymes during carbohydrate digestion include pancreatic amylase, maltase, sucrase, and lactase.

Focus Figure 4.8 Carbohydrate Digestion and Absorption

Carbohydrate digestion begins in the mouth and ends with the absorption of the monosaccharides glucose, fructose, and galactose in the small intestine.

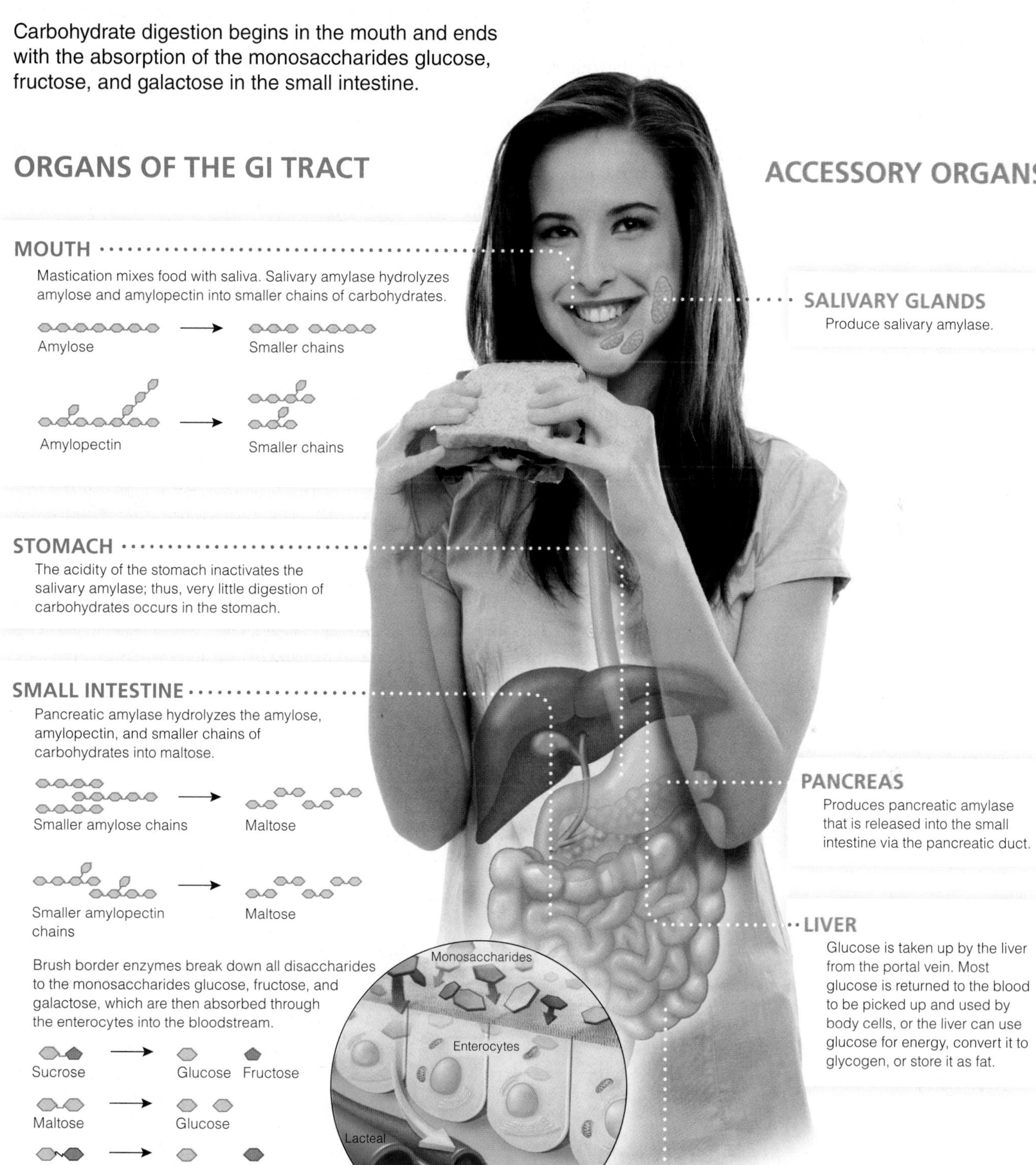

ORGANS OF THE GI TRACT

MOUTH

Mastication mixes food with saliva. Salivary amylase hydrolyzes amylose and amylopectin into smaller chains of carbohydrates.

STOMACH

The acidity of the stomach inactivates the salivary amylase; thus, very little digestion of carbohydrates occurs in the stomach.

SMALL INTESTINE

Pancreatic amylase hydrolyzes the amylose, amylopectin, and smaller chains of carbohydrates into maltose.

Brush border enzymes break down all disaccharides to the monosaccharides glucose, fructose, and galactose, which are then absorbed through the enterocytes into the bloodstream.

LARGE INTESTINE

All starches and simple sugars are broken down and absorbed in the small intestine; only fiber passes into the large intestine. Bacteria in the colon metabolize some of the fiber. The majority of fiber is eliminated in feces.

ACCESSORY ORGANS

SALIVARY GLANDS

Produce salivary amylase.

PANCREAS

Produces pancreatic amylase that is released into the small intestine via the pancreatic duct.

LIVER

Glucose is taken up by the liver from the portal vein. Most glucose is returned to the blood to be picked up and used by body cells, or the liver can use glucose for energy, convert it to glycogen, or store it as fat.

The disaccharides maltose, lactose, and sucrose will need further dismantling by the brush border enzymes, including maltase, lactase, and sucrase, housed in the microvilli of the small intestine. These enzymes break down the disaccharides into monosaccharides, specifically glucose, fructose, and galactose. The monosaccharides are now ready to be absorbed into the blood.

By the time the remnants of the sandwich reach the large intestine, all starch and simple sugars have been broken down and absorbed, and only the indigestible fiber remains. The bacteria in the colon can metabolize some of the fiber, producing water, gas, and some short-chain fatty acids. The colon uses these short-chain fatty acids for energy. The majority of the fiber is eliminated from the body in the feces. Resistant starch can also be metabolized by intestinal bacteria or excreted in the feces.

Carbohydrates Are Absorbed as Monosaccharides

After carbohydrate digestion, the monosaccharides glucose and galactose are absorbed into the intestinal cell mucosa by active transport, while fructose is absorbed by facilitated diffusion. Once glucose, galactose, and fructose are absorbed into the enterocyte, they are transported through the portal vein to the liver. Some fructose may be converted to glucose in the enterocyte before it enters the portal vein, but both glucose and galactose remain intact.

The fate of the monosaccharides once they've reached the liver depends on an individual's metabolic needs. Galactose and fructose are used mostly by the liver for energy, or they can be converted into glucose before entering the blood to circulate throughout the body. Any surplus glucose that is not used immediately for energy is stored as glycogen.

The process of converting excess glucose to glycogen is called **glycogenesis** and occurs mostly in the liver and muscle cells (see **Figure 4.9**). As you learned earlier in the chapter, this stored form of glucose can be used by the body when the diet lacks sufficient carbohydrate.

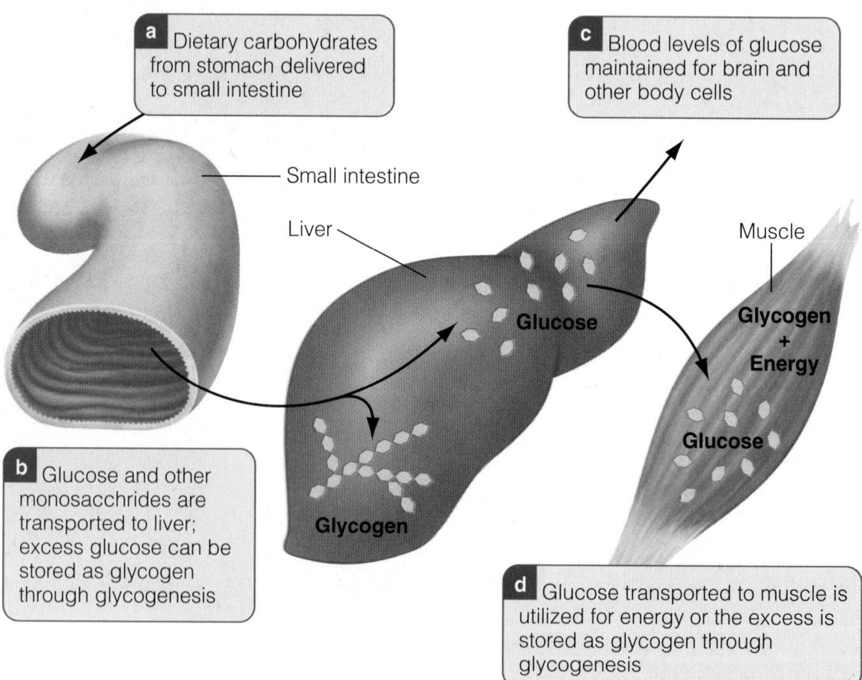
a Dietary carbohydrates from stomach delivered to small intestine
c Blood levels of glucose maintained for brain and other body cells
Small intestine
Liver
Muscle
Glucose
Glycogen + Energy
Glucose
Glycogen
b Glucose and other monosacchrides are transported to liver; excess glucose can be stored as glycogen through glycogenesis
d Glucose transported to muscle is utilized for energy or the excess is stored as glycogen through glycogenesis

▲ **Figure 4.9 Glucose Is Stored in the Liver and Muscle Cells as Glycogen**
Surplus glucose is stored in the liver and muscle cells. The liver glycogen can be used to supply the blood with glucose when the diet is deficient in carbohydrates. Muscle glycogen provides glucose to the muscle cell.

glycogenesis The process of assembling excess glucose into glycogen in the liver and muscle cells.

Once the glycogen stores are fully replenished and the diet contains sufficient kilocalories to meet energy needs, excess glucose will be converted into glycerol and fatty acids. These two are combined into a triglyceride and stored in the adipocytes (fat cells).

THE TAKE-HOME MESSAGE Digestion of carbohydrates begins in the mouth, where salivary amylase breaks down starch. Most carbohydrate digestion occurs in the small intestine. Pancreatic and small intestinal enzymes break down the carbohydrates into disaccharides and then monosaccharides so that they can be absorbed. All the monosaccharides are converted to glucose in the liver to be used as energy, or stored as glycogen in the liver and muscle cells. When glycogen stores are full and energy needs have been met, excess glucose is converted to glycerol and fatty acids and stored as fat. Fiber travels to the colon undigested and most of it is eliminated from the body.

What Functions Do Carbohydrates Perform in the Body?

Carbohydrates—primarily glucose—are the most desirable source of energy for the body. A complete discussion of the metabolism of glucose will be found in Chapter 8. This section briefly describes the overall functions of carbohydrates and the variety of health benefits they provide.

Carbohydrates Provide Energy and Maintain Blood Glucose Levels

Much of the energy we need to fuel our activities comes from a combination of glucose and fats. When you consume carbohydrate, whether it is in the form of a monosaccharide, disaccharide, or polysaccharide, the digested carbohydrate provides 4 kilocalories of energy per gram. Stored forms of both carbohydrates and fats come in handy between meals when you aren't eating but the body continues to need fuel.

In addition to providing energy, eating carbohydrate-rich foods helps maintain blood glucose levels. Under most conditions, glucose is the sole energy source for the brain, which requires a steady supply of glucose to function properly. If you haven't eaten for longer than four hours, blood glucose levels drop too low and the body will tap its glycogen stores by initiating **glycogenolysis** (*lysis* = loosening) to hydrolyze liver glycogen and supply glucose to the blood. Once liver glycogen stores are depleted, the body turns to other sources, such as amino acids and glycerol found in stored fat, to maintain blood glucose. Note that muscle glycogen cannot be used to raise blood glucose levels, because muscles lack the enzyme necessary to release glucose into the blood. Instead, muscle uses glycogen to fuel its own energy needs.

Carbohydrates Spare Protein

Glucose is the body's preferred fuel source, and as long as there is adequate glucose in the blood, protein can be spared for its many other essential functions. In times of carbohydrate deprivation, however, the body turns to noncarbohydrate sources, particularly amino acids (the building blocks of protein, which we will discuss in Chapter 6), to generate glucose. The process of creating glucose from noncarbohydrate sources is called **gluconeogenesis** (*gluco* = sugar/sweet, *neo* = new,

glycogenolysis The hydrolysis of glycogen to release glucose.

gluconeogenesis The creation of glucose from noncarbohydrate sources, predominantly protein.

genesis = origin). Gluconeogenesis primarily occurs in the liver, but can also take place in the kidneys, because these are the only organs that contain the enzymes needed for this process. The kidney is not an active site of gluconeogenesis except after long periods of fasting.

The body does not store extra protein to provide fuel during times of deprivation. Instead, the body dismantles protein from the muscles and organs to generate the needed glucose. Whereas gluconeogenesis can provide needed glucose to the blood, the use of muscle protein can have negative consequences for the body.

Carbohydrates Prevent Ketosis

After about 18 hours of fasting, liver glycogen is depleted and the body will begin to rely solely on fat breakdown to meet the body's energy needs and preserve muscle proteins. The by-products of the incomplete breakdown of fat, called **ketone bodies,** are created and spill out into the blood. Most ketone bodies are acids and reduce the pH of the blood, making it slightly acidic. After about two days of fasting, the number of ketone bodies in the blood doubles, which results in a state of **ketosis.** Individuals who fast or follow strict, low-carbohydrate diets are often in ketosis.

THE TAKE-HOME MESSAGE Glucose is the body's preferred source for energy, especially for the brain and red blood cells. Adequate carbohydrate intake helps maintain normal blood glucose levels, spares protein to be used for important functions other than energy production, and prevents ketosis.

How Do We Maintain Blood Glucose Levels?

Blood glucose levels are not constant—they rise and fall depending on the body's energy needs. Blood glucose levels also change following a carbohydrate-heavy meal. How does the body regulate blood glucose levels, given these changes in metabolic needs and dietary intake? The answer is: hormones. In fact, two hormones in particular, **insulin** and **glucagon,** secreted from the pancreas, maintain blood glucose levels between 70 and 110 mg/dl (**Figure 4.10**). Other hormones, including epinephrine, norepinephrine, cortisol, and growth hormone, also assist in the process.

Insulin Regulates Glucose in the Blood

After eating a carbohydrate-heavy meal, the blood is flooded with glucose, which cannot be used by the cells until it crosses the cell membrane. The high blood glucose levels stimulate the release of insulin from the beta cells of the pancreas. Insulin helps glucose enter cells by attaching to specific receptor sites on the cell membrane, which stimulates an increase in the number of glucose transporters found on the membrane surface. These transporters unlock the cell membrane and transport glucose inside the cell. As soon as glucose enters the cell, insulin stimulates the enzymes that will convert glucose to ATP or store it as glycogen for later use. This role of stimulating the uptake of glucose by the cells is what makes insulin so integral to blood glucose regulation. However, note that liver, kidney, and brain cells can use glucose without the aid of insulin.

In addition to helping glucose enter cells, insulin also helps convert glucose to glycogen if the amount of glucose in the blood exceeds the body's immediate energy needs. It does this by stimulating glycogenesis in both the liver and the muscle,

ketone bodies The by-products of the incomplete breakdown of fat.

ketosis The condition of increased ketone bodies in the blood.

insulin The hormone secreted from the beta cells of the pancreas that stimulates the uptake of glucose from the blood into the cells.

glucagon The hormone secreted from the alpha cells of the pancreas that stimulates glycogenolysis and gluconeogenesis to increase blood levels of glucose.

Focus Figure 4.10 Hormones Regulate Blood Glucose

Our bodies regulate blood glucose levels within a fairly narrow range to provide adequate glucose to the brain and other cells. Insulin and glucagon are two hormones that play a key role in regulating blood glucose levels.

HIGH BLOOD GLUCOSE

1 Insulin secretion: When blood glucose levels increase after a meal, the pancreas secretes the hormone insulin from the beta cells into the bloodstream.

2 Cellular uptake: Insulin travels to the tissues where it alters the cell membranes to allow the transport of glucose into the cells by increasing the number of glucose transporters on the cell membrane.

3 Glucose storage: Insulin also stimulates the storage of glucose in body tissues. Glucose is stored as glycogen in the liver and muscles (glycogenesis), and is stored as triglycerides in adipose tissue (lipogenesis).

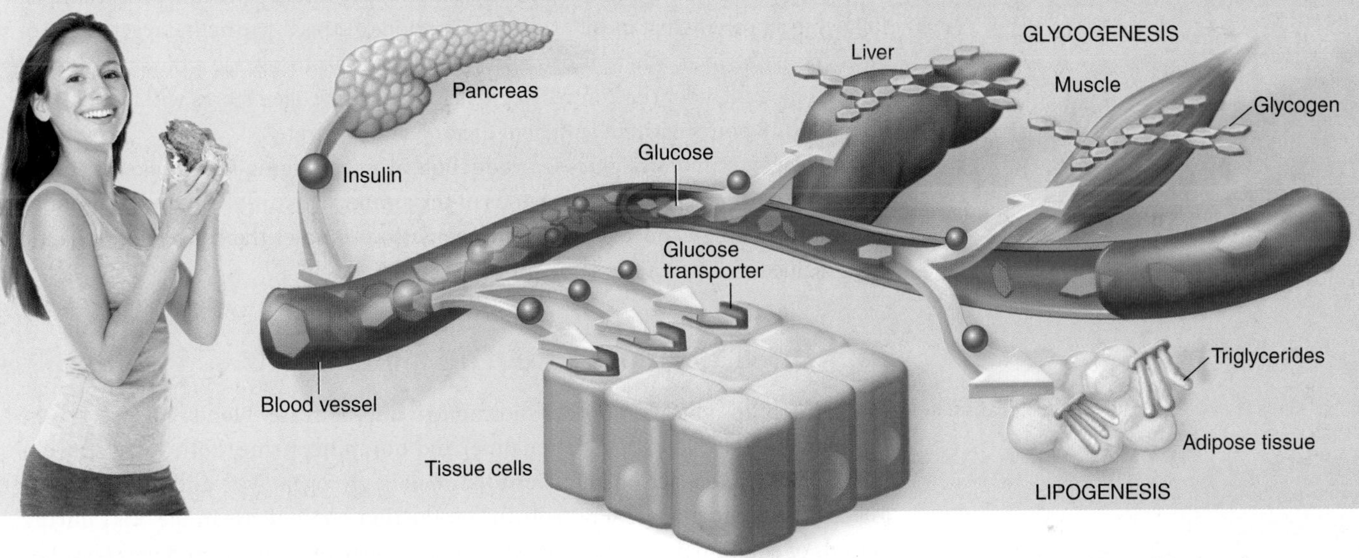

LOW BLOOD GLUCOSE

1 Glucagon secretion: When blood glucose levels are low, the pancreas secretes the hormone glucagon from the alpha cells into the bloodstream.

2 Glycogenolysis: Glucagon stimulates glycogenolysis in the liver to break down stored glycogen to glucose, which is released into the blood and transported to the cells for energy.

3 Gluconeogenesis: Glucagon also activates gluconeogenesis in the liver, stimulating the conversion of glucogenic amino acids to glucose.

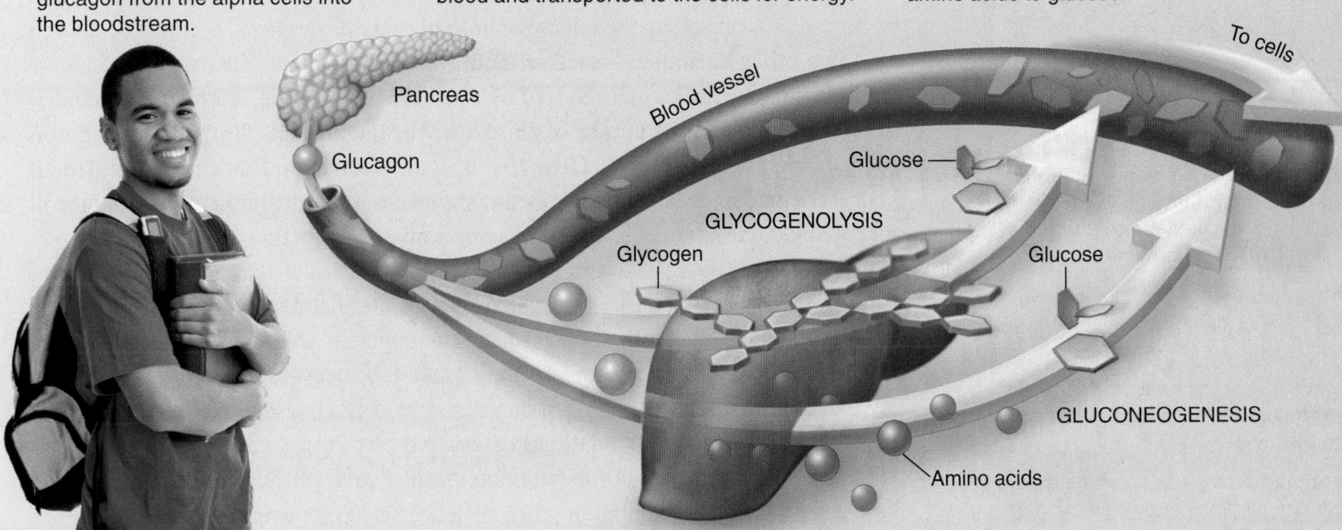

and by inhibiting the enzymes involved in glycogenolysis and gluconeogenesis. The body will store excess glucose as glycogen until it reaches its limit.

When glycogen stores are full, excess glucose may be converted into fatty acids in a process called **lipogenesis.** The method insulin uses to promote lipogenesis is similar to the way it promotes glycogenesis: by increasing the number of glucose receptors on the surface of the fat cell. Insulin also inhibits lipolysis (fat breakdown) by reducing the activity of the enzyme that hydrolyzes stored fat. The result of insulin's actions is that more fat is formed and fewer fatty acids are found in the blood.

Glucagon Regulates Liver Glycogenolysis

Glucagon has the opposite effect of insulin on blood glucose levels: It stimulates release of glucose into the blood (see Figure 4.10). The alpha cells of the pancreas release glucagon into the circulation when blood glucose levels are low—for example, following a protein-rich meal, or during a period of stress. The main target organ of glucagon is the liver, where it promotes glycogenolysis to release a burst of glucose into the blood. Under the control of glucagon, liver glycogen stores will be depleted after 10 to 18 hours without sufficient dietary carbohydrate.

Glucagon stimulates glucose production by encouraging the uptake of amino acids by the liver. The carbon skeletons of the amino acids are then used to produce glucose through gluconeogenesis. Glucagon also promotes the conversion of lactic acid to glucose through the same process.

Four Other Hormones Help Regulate Glucose Metabolism

In addition to glucagon, other hormones can increase blood glucose levels. **Epinephrine** (also known as adrenaline) and **norepinephrine,** both secreted from the adrenal glands, act on the liver to stimulate glycogenolysis and gluconeogenesis to raise blood glucose. Epinephrine production can increase in the body during periods of emotional and physical stress, such as fear, excitement, and bleeding. For example, if a ferocious dog was chasing you down the street, your body would be pumping out epinephrine to help provide the fuel you need to run. For this reason, epinephrine is also referred to as the "fight-or-flight" hormone.

A low blood glucose level can trigger the release of both epinephrine and norephinephrine. In fact, some of the symptoms that you may experience when your blood glucose level dips too low, such as anxiety, rapid heart beat, turning pale, and shakiness, are caused by the release of both of these hormones.

Two other hormones—**cortisol** and **growth hormone**—also regulate glucose metabolism. Cortisol, often referred to as the stress hormone, stimulates gluconeogenesis and reduces the uptake of glucose by the muscle cells. Both of these actions increase blood glucose levels. Growth hormone has the opposite effect of insulin: It conserves glucose by stimulating fat breakdown for energy, reducing the uptake of glucose by the muscle cells, and increasing glucose production in the liver.

THE TAKE-HOME MESSAGE Blood glucose levels are maintained by two hormones, insulin and glucagon, both secreted from the pancreas. When blood glucose levels rise, insulin is released to stimulate the uptake of glucose by the muscle and liver, lowering blood levels back to normal. When blood glucose levels fall below normal, glucagon is released to stimulate glycogenolysis of liver glycogen, raising blood glucose levels. Epinephrine, norepinephrine, cortisol, and growth hormone also raise blood glucose by stimulating either glycogenolysis or gluconeogenesis.

lipogenesis The process that converts excess glucose into fat for storage.

epinephrine A hormone produced by the adrenal glands that signals the liver cells to release glucose; also referred to as the "fight-or-flight" hormone.

norepinephrine A hormone produced by the adrenal glands that stimulates glycogenolysis and gluconeogenesis.

cortisol A hormone produced by the adrenal cortex that stimulates gluconeogenesis and lipolysis.

growth hormone A hormone that regulates glucose metabolism by increasing glycogenolysis and lipolysis.

Why Is Dietary Fiber So Important?

Even though fiber passes through the GI tract undigested, it can have many powerful health effects in the body. As mentioned earlier, fiber has been shown to help lower the risk of developing constipation and diverticulosis, as well as reduce the risk of obesity, heart disease, cancer, and diabetes. Let's look closely at how this works.

Dried fruits and nuts are excellent sources of fiber, though nuts can also contribute significantly to fat intake, and should be eaten in moderation.

Fiber Helps Prevent Constipation and Diverticulosis

Over 4 million Americans complain about being constipated, with pregnant women, children, and adults 65 years of age and older experiencing it more often than others.[17] Constipation is usually caused by sluggish muscle contractions in the colon that move stool along too slowly, which leads to too much water being reabsorbed along the way. This can create hard, dry stools that are more difficult and painful to expel.

A diet plentiful in insoluble fibers such as bran, whole grains, and many fruits and vegetables will reduce the transit time of food in the colon and decrease the likelihood of constipation. (Note: Some soluble fibers, such as psyllium, can also relieve constipation; psyllium's water-attracting capability allows the stool to increase in bulk and form a gel-like, soft texture, which makes it easier to pass.)

Chronic constipation can lead to a disorder called **diverticulosis** (*osis* = condition), in which increased pressure in the colon causes weak spots along its wall to bulge out and form pouches called **diverticula** (see **Figure 4.11**). Infection of the diverticula, a condition known as **diverticulitis** (*itis* = inflammation), can lead to stomach pain, fever, nausea, vomiting, cramping, and chills. Approximately 50 percent of Americans aged 60 to 80 and the majority of individuals over 80 years of age have diverticulosis.[18] The best way to prevent both diverticulosis and diverticulitis is to eat a diet that is adequate in fiber.

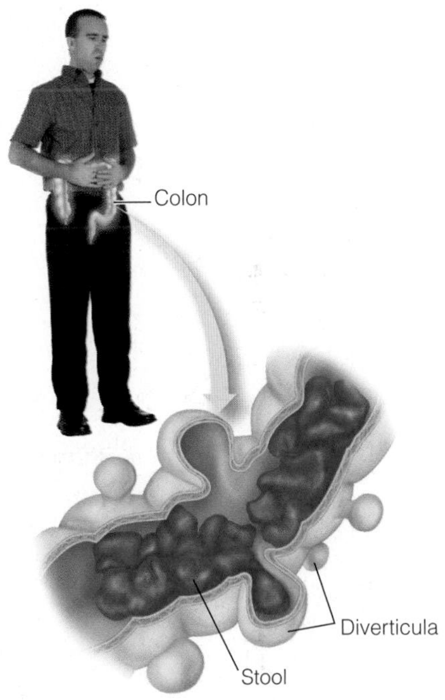

▲ **Figure 4.11 Diverticulosis**
Diverticulosis is a condition in which small pouches, or diverticula, bulge out along the colon. When stool gets trapped in these pouches, they can become inflamed, leading to diverticulitis.

Fiber Helps Prevent Heart Disease, Diabetes, and Cancer

A diet rich in fiber from whole grains, vegetables, and fruits is important to prevent or treat certain chronic diseases. Let's look at the role that fiber plays in reducing the risk of developing heart disease, diabetes, and cancer.

Heart Disease

Viscous, soluble fibers have been shown to help lower elevated blood cholesterol levels, which may decrease the risk of heart disease. Viscous fiber is believed to interfere with the reabsorption of bile acids in the intestines (**Figure 4.12**). Bile acids are high in cholesterol and are secreted into the intestine by the gallbladder to help with the digestion of fat. The bile acids are likely "grabbed" or sequestered by the fiber before they can be reabsorbed by the body. They end up being excreted along with the fiber in the feces. The liver then removes cholesterol from the blood to replace the bile acids that were lost. Blood cholesterol levels are lowered as a result.

Slow-moving, viscous, soluble fibers may also reduce the rate at which fat and carbohydrates are absorbed from meals. Delayed absorption can lower the surge of fat in the blood after a meal, and may help improve sensitivity to the hormone insulin. Both high levels of fat in the blood and a decreased sensitivity to insulin are considered risk factors for heart disease.

diverticulosis The existence of diverticula in the lining of the large intestine or colon.

diverticula Small bulges at weak spots in the colon wall.

diverticulitis Infection of the diverticula.

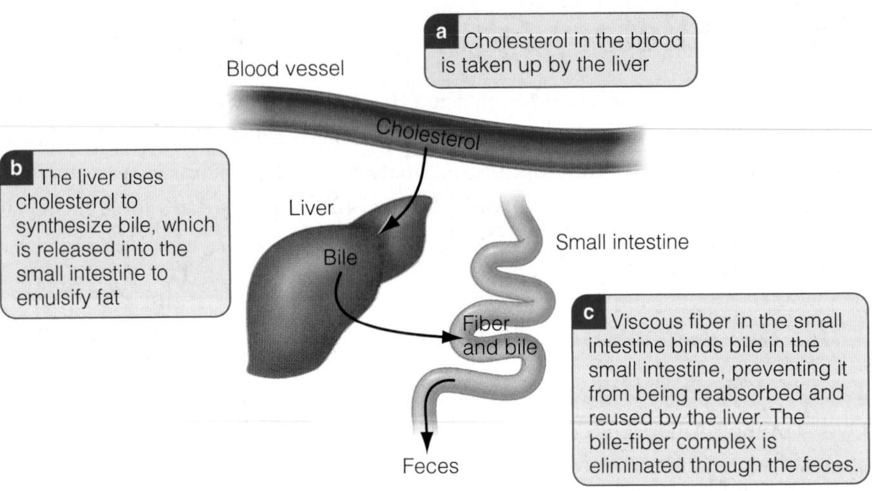

▲ **Figure 4.12 Dietary Fiber Reduces Blood Cholesterol Levels**
Dietary fiber acts as a bile acid sequestrant, as it binds the bile in the intestinal tract and carries it out in the feces.

While soluble fibers may decrease the risk for heart disease, insoluble fiber may also promote heart health. Several research studies have shown that cereal and grains, which contain insoluble fiber, may help to lower the risk of heart disease.[19, 20] A study that explored the dietary habits of over 65,000 women for 10 years found that the risk of developing heart disease was over 30 percent lower in those consuming the highest amount of cereal fiber.[21]

Diabetes

Research studies involving both men and women have shown that a higher consumption of fiber from cereals helped reduce the risk of developing certain types of diabetes mellitus.[22] Viscous, soluble fibers have also been shown to help individuals who already have diabetes mellitus manage the condition. Viscous fibers slow the release of food from the stomach, and thus slow down the digestion and absorption of glucose. This could help avoid a large spike in blood glucose after eating and help individuals with diabetes improve the long-term control of their blood glucose level.[23, 24] See Health Connection: What Is Diabetes? on page 128 for a complete discussion of diabetes, its prevalence, control, and prevention.

Cancer

Fiber is thought to have many positive and protective effects in the fight against certain cancers. Fiber from cereals has been shown to help lower the risk of breast cancer.[25, 26] This may be due to fiber's effect on reducing estrogen levels by excreting more through bile. The evidence is not conclusive but it is promising.

Research also suggests that as fiber consumption increases, the incidence of colorectal cancer is reduced.[27] This may be due to the increase in the bulk of stools, which can dilute cancer-promoting substances in the colon. Fiber helps keep things moving through the digestive tract so that potential cancer-promoting substances spend less time in contact with the intestinal lining. Fiber encourages the growth in the colon of friendly bacteria and their fermentation by-products, both of which may have cancer-fighting potential. Because an increased amount of bile acids in the colon is thought to be associated with colon and rectal cancer, fiber's ability to reduce the concentration of these acids is viewed as a cancer deterrent.[28]

Nutrition in Practice: Brendan

As a biology professor, Brendan's annual physical at the campus health center uncovered that his blood glucose levels classified him as having "prediabetes." According to his doctor, his blood glucose levels are higher than ideal but not high enough to be diagnosed as having full-fledged diabetes. Because his father and grandfather both developed diabetes later in their lives, the doctor explained that his family history and excess weight put Brendan at a higher risk for developing type 2 diabetes. Because of Brendan's daily one-hour drive to campus each way, his physical activity consists of parking his car in the faculty lot and walking less than one block to his office.

Brendan's doctor refers him to the campus Registered Dietitian for an appointment. Brendan is dreading meeting with the dietitian because as a bachelor, he doesn't enjoy cooking and is concerned that his diet of takeout foods, along with his sedentary lifestyle, is about to end. The dietitian meets with Brendan to discuss his diet and lifestyle habits and its effect on his blood glucose levels.

Brendan's Stats:

- □ Age: 45
- □ Height: 6 feet 1 inches
- □ Weight: 230 pounds
- □ BMI: 30
- □ Fasting Blood Glucose: 124 mg/dl

Critical Thinking Questions

1. How does Brendan's weight contribute to his elevated blood glucose levels?
2. What foods/beverages could be contributing to Brendan's weight and blood glucose levels and why?
3. How could increasing Brendan's daily physical activity improve his blood glucose levels and why?

Dietitian's Observation and Plan for Brendan:

- □ Discuss the need to lose weight. A weight loss of as little as 5 to 7 percent of a person's body weight can reduce the cells' resistance to insulin. This enables glucose to be taken up by the cells and improve his blood glucose levels.
- □ Increase his dietary fiber. Fiber has been shown to improve insulin sensitivity, or the use of insulin by the cells.
- □ Plan a well-balanced, kilocalorie-reducing diet that includes fruits, vegetables, whole grains, legumes, and low-fat dairy, along with some lean protein and healthy oils, to promote weight loss of approximately ½ to 1 pound weekly. Provide him with healthier choices when dining out and purchasing takeout foods.
- □ Increase physical activity to at least 2.5 hours weekly. Exercise improves the cells' sensitivity to insulin and lowers blood glucose levels.

Two weeks later, Brendan visits the dietitian again and is excited that he has lost 2 pounds. He is parking his car in a parking lot that is five blocks from his office so he walks more every day. A review of his food record shows that his diet is still too low in vegetables and fruit. The dietitian works with Brendan to increase his produce not only at meals but also as snacks. They also discuss ways that Brendan can walk during the day on campus to increase his daily physical activity.

Brendan's Food Log

Food/Beverage	Time Consumed	Hunger Rating*	Location
Donut and coffee with cream	8:30 am	2	Coffee shop
Hamburger, fries, and cola	1 pm	5	Fast-food eatery
Chocolate bar	4 pm	4	Vending machine in faculty lounge
Fried chicken, mashed potatoes, corn	6:30 pm	4	Picked up from supermarket takeout. Consumed at home.
Ice cream	9 pm	1	Home, watching TV

*Hunger Rating (1–5): 1 = not hungry; 5 = super hungry

Health Connection

What Is Diabetes?

Diabetes mellitus, or *diabetes*, is a condition related to an inadequate regulation of blood glucose, and it's becoming so common in the United States that it would be rare if you *didn't* know someone who has it. An estimated 25.8 million Americans—more than 8 percent of the population—have diabetes.[1] Of these individuals, 7 million have the disease, but don't know it yet (Figure 1). The incidence of adults being diagnosed with diabetes in the United States has more than doubled since the early 1990s. According to the CDC, if this trend continues, it is likely that one-third of Americans will develop diabetes in their lifetime, reducing their life expectancy, on average, by 10 to 15 years.[2]

The number of people who have diabetes is not only strikingly high; it's rising, particularly among children. Whereas the disease used to be common only in adults, in the last couple of decades there's been a steady increase among those under age 20. Approximately 215,000 people under the age of 20, or 0.26 percent, had been diagnosed with diabetes in the year 2010.

Over 200,000 Americans die from diabetic complications annually, and diabetes is the seventh leading cause of death in the United States. Diabetes is not only a deadly disease, but also an extremely costly one. Disability insurance payments, time lost from employment, and the medical costs associated with diabetes cost more than $170 billion annually in the United States.[3,4] This is an epidemic that is spiraling out of control.[5,6]

There are different types of diabetes, but they all result from the inability of the body to make or properly use the hormone insulin. Insulin directs glucose into the cells to be used as immediate energy or stored for later use. Diabetes develops when individuals either produce an inadequate amount of insulin and/or develop **insulin resistance,** such that their cells do not respond to the insulin when it arrives. In either case, the bloodstream is flooded with glucose that can't get into the cells. When this happens, the body shifts into fasting mode. The liver begins the process of breaking down its glycogen stores (glycogenolysis) and making glucose from noncarbohydrate sources (gluconeogenesis) in an attempt to provide glucose to the cells. This floods the blood with even more glucose. Eventually, the level of glucose builds up in the blood and some of it spills over into the urine.

At the same time, the body has called on its energy reserve—fat—to be used as fuel. The body needs glucose in order to thoroughly burn fat; otherwise, it makes ketone bodies. In poorly managed diabetes, when glucose is unable to get into the cells, acidic ketone bodies build up in the blood to dangerous levels, causing **ketoacidosis.** Diabetic ketoacidosis can cause nausea and confusion, and in some cases, if left untreated, could result in coma or death. (Note: Ketoacidosis occurs when insulin is lacking in the body, and is different from the condition of ketosis, which can develop in individuals who are fasting or consuming a low-carbohydrate diet; unlike diabetic ketoacidosis, ketosis is not life-threatening.)

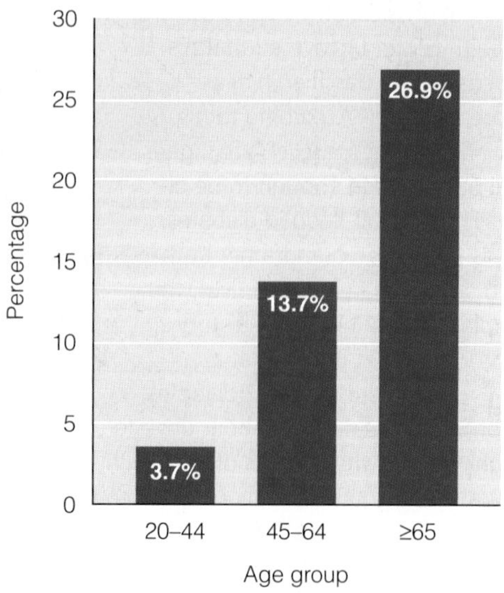

▲ **Figure 1 Diagnosed and Undiagnosed Diabetes in the United States by Age Group**
The estimated percentage of Americans aged 20 years or older with diagnosed and undiagnosed diabetes between 2005 and 2008.
Data from Centers for Disease Control. 2005–2008 National Health and Nutrition Examination Survey. Available at www.cdc.gov/diabetes/pubs/estimates11.htm. Accessed February 2012.

Individuals with diabetes must regularly monitor blood glucose levels.

Diabetes Types and Risk Factors

All forms of diabetes involve insulin and unregulated blood glucose levels. Some are due to insulin resistance, as just described, and others are due to a lack of insulin production. Still another version occurs only during pregnancy. The most prevalent types of diabetes are type 1 and type 2.

Type 1 Diabetes

Type 1 diabetes is considered an autoimmune disease and is the rarer of the two main forms.[7]

This form of diabetes usually begins in childhood or the early adult years and is found in 5 to 10 percent of the individuals with diabetes in the United States.[8] The immune system in people with type 1 diabetes destroys the insulin-producing cells in the pancreas. An obsessive, uncontrollable thirst (**polydipsia**), excessive urination (**polyuria**), and a strong desire to eat (**polyphagia**) are common symptoms associated with diabetes, due to the increased level of blood sugar. Other common symptoms are constant blurred vision, hunger, weight loss, and fatigue, because the glucose can't get into the cells of the body. If not treated with insulin, the person is susceptible to the dangers of ketoacidosis. Individuals with type 1 diabetes must monitor their glucose levels and inject insulin every day in order to live a normal life.

The hormone insulin is derived from the components of protein and is digestible by the GI tract, so it can't be taken orally. Therefore, most individuals have to inject insulin directly into their fat or muscle tissue with a syringe. Researchers are continually testing alternative, non-needle methods for those with diabetes to self-administer insulin. Insulin pens, insulin jet injectors, and insulin pumps are among the devices becoming available.

Type 2 Diabetes

Type 2 diabetes is more common than type 1, accounting for 90 to 95 percent of diagnoses of the disease. Being overweight increases the risk of developing type 2 diabetes.[9] People with type 2 diabetes typically produce insulin but have become insulin resistant. After several years of exhausting their insulin-producing cells in the pancreas, their production of insulin decreases to the point where they have to take medication and/or inject insulin to manage their blood glucose level.

One of the major problems with type 2 diabetes is that this condition can go undiagnosed for some time. Some people may have symptoms such as increased thirst; others may not. Consequently, diabetes can damage a person's vital organs without their being aware of it. Because of this, the American Diabetes Association (ADA) recommends that everyone 45 years of age and older undergo testing for diabetes every three years. However, if a person is at a higher risk for developing diabetes (such as those who are overweight or obese, or who are genetically predisposed), he or she shouldn't wait until age 45 to be tested. Overweight children should be screened when they turn 10 years old and repeat the screening every two years. (See the Self-Assessment on page 130 to determine whether you are at risk for type 2 diabetes.)

One predictor of type 2 diabetes is a disorder called metabolic syndrome, which is associated with insulin resistance. This syndrome is characterized by a cluster of symptoms found in cardiovascular disease, including elevated fasting blood glucose and blood lipids, high blood pressure, and obesity. The same risk factors of metabolic syndrome, such as eating a poor diet, obesity, and lack of exercise, are also risk factors for type 2 diabetes. In fact, a diagnosis of metabolic syndrome often precedes a diagnosis of type 2 diabetes.[10]

Prediabetes

A simple blood test at a physician's office can reveal if a person's blood glucose is higher than normal and whether he or she has **impaired glucose tolerance,** or *prediabetes*. The blood is typically drawn first thing in the morning after fasting overnight for 8 to 12 hours. A fasting blood glucose level of under 100 milligrams per deciliter (mg/dl) is considered "negative," and a fasting blood glucose of 126 mg/dl or higher is considered a "positive" test for diabetes (Table 1). A reading between 100 mg/dl and 126 mg/dl is classified as prediabetes. Individuals with prediabetes have a blood glucose level that is higher than it should be but not yet high enough to be classified as diabetic. About 79 million Americans over the age of 20 have prediabetes and are at a higher risk of developing not only diabetes, but also heart disease.[11] When a person is in this prediabetic state, damage may already be occurring to the heart and circulatory system.

TABLE 1 Interpreting Blood Glucose Levels

If a Fasting Blood Glucose Level Is	It Means That the Level Is Considered
<100 mg/dl	Normal
100 to 125 mg/dl	Prediabetic
126 mg/dl*	Diabetic

*There must be two "positive" tests, done on separate days, for an official diagnosis of diabetes.

Data from American Diabetes Association, "Diagnosis and Classification of Diabetes Mellitus," *Diabetes Care* 29 (2006): S43–S48.

Diabetes Can Result in Long-Term Damage

Constant exposure to high blood glucose levels can damage vital organs over time. Diabetes, especially if it is poorly managed, increases the likelihood of a multitude of health effects such as nerve damage, leg and foot amputations, eye diseases, blindness, tooth loss, gum problems, kidney disease, and heart disease.[12]

Nerve damage occurs in an estimated 50 percent of individuals with diabetes, and the longer the person has diabetes, the greater the risk of damage. Numbness in the toes, feet, legs, and hands, as well as changes in bowel, bladder, and sexual function are all signs of damage to nerves. This nerve damage can affect the ability to feel a change in temperature or pain in the legs and feet. A cut or sore on the foot could go unnoticed until it becomes

diabetes mellitus A medical condition whereby an individual either doesn't have enough insulin or is resistant to the insulin available, resulting in a rise in blood glucose levels. Diabetes mellitus is often called diabetes.

insulin resistance The inability of the cells to respond to insulin.

ketoacidosis The buildup of ketone bodies in the blood to dangerous levels, which can result in coma or death.

polydipsia The symptom of excessive thirst, common in diabetes mellitus.

polyuria The symptom of excessive urination, common in diabetes mellitus.

polyphagia The symptom of an excessive desire to eat, common in diabetes mellitus.

impaired glucose tolerance A condition whereby a fasting blood glucose level is higher than normal, but not high enough to be classified as having diabetes mellitus. Also called prediabetes.

Self-Assessment

Are You at Risk for Type 2 Diabetes?

Take the following quiz to assess if you are at risk for developing type 2 diabetes. Whereas this list contains the presently known risk factors for type 2 diabetes, there may be others. If you have questions or doubts, check with your doctor.

Do you have a body mass index (BMI) of 25 or higher*?

Yes ☐ **No** ☐

If you answered "no," you don't need to continue. If you answered "yes," continue.

1. Does your mom, dad, brother, or sister have diabetes?

   Yes ☐ **No** ☐

2. Do you typically exercise for less than 30 minutes daily?

   Yes ☐ **No** ☐

3. Are you of African-American, Alaskan Native, Native American, Asian-American, Hispanic, or Pacific Islander-American descent?

   Yes ☐ **No** ☐

4. Have you ever delivered a baby that weighed more than 9 pounds at birth?

   Yes ☐ **No** ☐

5. Have you ever had diabetes during pregnancy?

   Yes ☐ **No** ☐

6. Do you have a blood pressure of 140/90 millimeters of mercury (mmHg) or higher?

   Yes ☐ **No** ☐

7. Have you been told by your doctor that you have too much triglyceride (fat) in your blood (more than 250 mg/dl) or too little of the "good" HDL cholesterol (less than 35 mg/dl)?

   Yes ☐ **No** ☐

8. Have you ever had blood glucose test results that were higher than normal?

   Yes ☐ **No** ☐

9. Have you ever been told that you have vascular disease or problems with your blood vessels?

   Yes ☐ **No** ☐

10. Do you have metabolic syndrome**?

    Yes ☐ **No** ☐

Answers

If you are overweight and answered "yes" to any of the above 10 questions, you could benefit from speaking with your doctor.

*BMI is a measure of your weight in relationship to your height. See Chapter 14 for a chart to determine your BMI.

**Metabolic syndrome is a cluster of symptoms including elevated blood glucose and lipids, high blood pressure, and obesity. This disorder increases the risk of diabetes as well as of heart disease and stroke.

infected. The poor blood circulation common in diabetics can also make it harder for sores or infections to heal. Over time, an infection can infiltrate the bone, causing the need for an amputation.

Diabetes can also damage the tiny blood vessels in the retina of the eye, which can cause bleeding and cloudy vision, and eventually destroy the retina and cause blindness. A high blood glucose level can cause tooth and gum problems, including the loss of teeth, and damage to the kidneys. If the kidneys are damaged, protein can leak into the urine and, at the same time, cause a backup of wastes in the blood. Kidney failure could result.

Diabetes is a risk factor for heart disease. The excess amount of fat often seen in the blood in poorly managed diabetes is likely an important factor in this increased risk. Fortunately, good nutrition habits play a key role in both the prevention and management of diabetes.[13]

Control Is Key

For years, people with diabetes have been advised to keep their blood glucose level under control. In the early 1990s, the research community finally gathered the evidence to back up that advice. The groundbreaking Diabetes Control and Complications Trial (DCCT), conducted from 1983 to 1993, involved over 1,400 people with type 1 diabetes. It showed that controlling the level of blood glucose with an intense regimen of diet, insulin, and exercise, along with monitoring blood sugar levels and routinely visiting health care professionals, slowed the onset of some of the complications of diabetes. In this study, reducing high blood glucose was shown to help lower the risk of eye disease by 76 percent, and the risk of kidney and nerve disease by at least 50 percent. However, because some individuals experienced bouts of **hypoglycemia** (low blood glucose levels, discussed in the next section), this type of intense regimen

TABLE 2 Dietary Recommendations for Diabetes

- Carbohydrate intake and monounsaturated fat together should provide 60 to 70 percent of total daily energy intake.
- Foods containing soluble fiber, such as oats and bran, should be part of a healthy plan to lower blood glucose and cholesterol.
- Dietary cholesterol should be less than 300 mg per day; if LDL cholesterol levels are high, dietary cholesterol should be lowered to not more than 200 mg per day.
- Saturated fat intake should be less than 10 percent of total daily energy intake or less than 7 percent if evidence of heart disease is present.
- Polyunsaturated fat should be less than 10 percent of total daily energy intake.
- Whole grains, fruits, vegetables, and low-fat milk should be consumed as part of a healthy diet.
- Sugars do not need to be eliminated but should be eaten in moderation as part of a healthy diet.
- Protein intake of 15 to 20 percent of total daily energy intake is sufficient if kidney function is normal.
- The total amount of carbohydrate in meals or snacks is more important than the source or type.
- Vitamin and mineral supplements are not necessary to prevent or treat diabetes.
- Moderate alcohol consumption (1 drink per day for adult women, and 2 drinks for adult men) is considered safe for people with diabetes.

Data from American Diabetes Association, "Nutrition Principles and Recommendations in Diabetes," *Diabetes Care* 27 (2004): S36–S46.

is not recommended for children under age 13, people with heart disease or advanced complications of heart disease, older people, and those prone to frequent severe hypoglycemia.[14, 15] For all others, diligent and conscientious management of their blood glucose can minimize the devastating complications of diabetes often seen later in life.

The nutrition and lifestyle goals for individuals with type 1 or type 2 diabetes are the same: to minimize the complications of diabetes by adopting a healthy, well-balanced diet and participating in regular physical activity that maintains blood glucose levels in a normal or close-to-normal range.

Eat a Balanced Diet

The ADA recommends that individuals with diabetes consume a combination of predominantly high-fiber carbohydrates from whole grains, fruits, and vegetables, along with low-fat milk, adequate amounts of lean protein, and unsaturated fats.[16] The fat and fiber content of a food lowers the effect it has on blood glucose levels. This is often referred to as the glycemic index and may be beneficial for meal planning. Table 2 lists the ADA dietary recommendations for diabetics.

The terms **glycemic index** (GI) and **glycemic load** (GL) have been used to classify the effects of carbohydrate-containing foods on blood glucose and may be potentially helpful for those with diabetes. The GI refers to the measured upward rise, peak, and eventual fall of blood glucose following the consumption of a high-carbohydrate food. Some foods cause a sharp spike and rapid fall in blood glucose levels; others cause less of a spike and a more gradual decline.[17] The index ranks foods according to their effect on blood glucose levels compared with that of an equal amount of white bread or pure glucose (see Figure 2).

hypoglycemia A blood glucose level that drops to lower than 70 mg/dl.

glycemic index A rating scale of the likelihood of foods to increase the levels of blood glucose and insulin.

glycemic load The amount of carbohydrate in a food multiplied by the amount of the glycemic index of that food.

Foods	GI*
Rice, low amylose	126
Potato, baked	121
Cornflakes	119
Jelly beans	114
Green peas	107
Cheerios	106
Puffed wheat	105
Bagel, plain	103
White bread	100
Angel food cake	95
Ice cream	87
Bran muffin	85
Rice, long grain†	80
Brown rice	79
Oatmeal	79
Popcorn	79
Corn	78
Banana, overripe	74
Chocolate	70
Baked beans	69
Sponge cake	66
Pear, canned in juice	63
Custard	61
Spaghetti	59
Rice, long grain‡	58
Apple	52
Pear	47
Banana, underripe	43
Kidney beans	42
Whole milk	39
Peanuts	21

*GI = Glycemic Index
†Boiled for 25 minutes.
‡Boiled for 5 minutes.

▲ **Figure 2 The Glycemic Index of Commonly Eaten Foods**
The glycemic index is a ranking of foods that indicates their potential to raise insulin and glucose levels in the blood.

A problem with using the GI is that it doesn't take into account the amount of carbohydrate consumed. For example, two slices of white bread usually weighs about 60 grams, which would be over 5 cups of cereal, an amount that is unlikely to be eaten in one sitting. The glycemic load (GL) adjusts the GI to take into account the amount of carbohydrate consumed in a typical serving of a food, and in the case of puffed wheat cereal, the normal portion size has a dramatically lower effect on blood glucose.

The usefulness of the GI for disease prevention or weight management is controversial. Research suggests that high–glycemic index foods do not raise blood glucose levels as rapidly as once believed. In fact, blood glucose levels peak at about the same level regardless of the source of the carbohydrate.[18]

While the glycemic index may be a useful tool for diabetics to select carbohydrate foods, a less confusing approach to blood glucose control is to follow the current guidelines suggested by the American Diabetes Association (refer to Table 2). These guidelines follow the same basic principles for choosing low-glycemic foods, namely that the diet most effective at controlling blood sugar is based on high-fiber foods, such as whole grains, legumes, fruits and vegetables, and fresh over canned or processed foods.

Although sugar has a high glycemic index and was once thought of as a "diabetic no-no," it can now be part of a diabetic's diet. Research has found that eating sucrose doesn't cause a greater rise in a person's blood glucose level than starch does, so avoidance of sugar isn't necessary. However, because weight management is often a concern, especially for those with type 2 diabetes, there's little room for sweets and treats in a diabetic diet (or *anyone's* diet, for that matter).

Be Physically Active

Exercise is important for everyone, but especially for diabetics. Exercise on a regular basis increases insulin sensitivity, reduces body fat, and lowers blood pressure and blood lipids. Any exercise that raises your heart rate for at least 30 minutes a day helps control blood sugar levels.

Hypoglycemia: When Blood Sugar Is Too Low

Whereas a consistently high level of glucose in the blood isn't healthy, a blood glucose level that is too low (usually less than 70 mg/dl), or hypoglycemia, can be unpleasant and downright dangerous for some with diabetes. Individuals who experience hypoglycemia may feel hungry, nervous, dizzy, light-headed, confused, weak, and shaky, and even begin to sweat. Eating or drinking carbohydrate-rich foods, such as hard candies, juice, or soda, can relieve these symptoms quickly and raise the blood glucose level to a normal range.

Those with diabetes who need to use insulin and/or blood glucose–lowering medications daily are at risk of hypoglycemia if they skip meals and snacks or if they don't eat enough to cover the effects of the medication. If these individuals ignore their symptoms, their blood glucose level can drop so low that they could faint, or slip into a coma (see Figure 3).[19] This is why individuals with diabetes need to eat regularly, so as to maintain blood glucose levels that coincide with their medication. A change in activity or exercise level can also lower blood glucose, so individuals with diabetes need to check their blood glucose level before they exercise to determine if a snack is needed.

Though not common, people without diabetes may also experience bouts of *reactive hypoglycemia* within four hours after a meal. Reactive hypoglycemia can cause symptoms similar to hypoglycemia: shakiness, dizziness, hunger, and perspiration. A doctor can diagnose this condition by testing a person's blood glucose level while they are having these symptoms. Though the cause of reactive hypoglycemia is not known, one theory is that it is hormone related. Some people may be overly sensitive to epinephrine, which is released when the blood glucose level begins to drop. The hormone glucagon may also play a role. Eating smaller, well-balanced meals throughout the day can help avoid hypoglycemia.

Another type of hypoglycemia, called *fasting hypoglycemia*, can occur in the morning, after overnight fasting. It can also

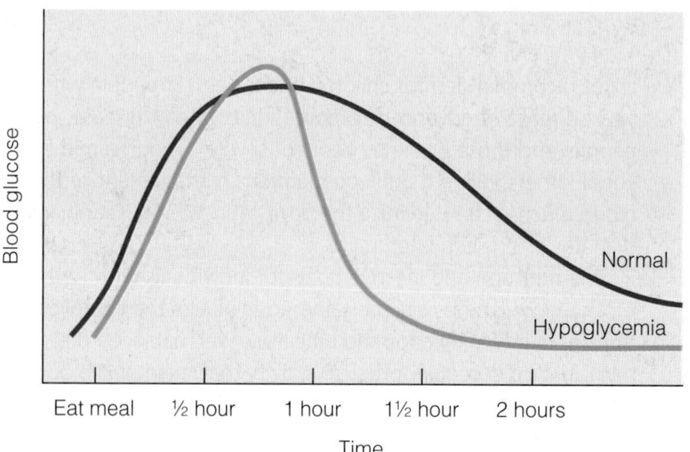

▲ **Figure 3 Change in Blood Glucose After Eating a High-Carbohydrate Meal**
An individual with hypoglycemia experiences a more rapid decline in blood glucose after a carbohydrate-rich meal.

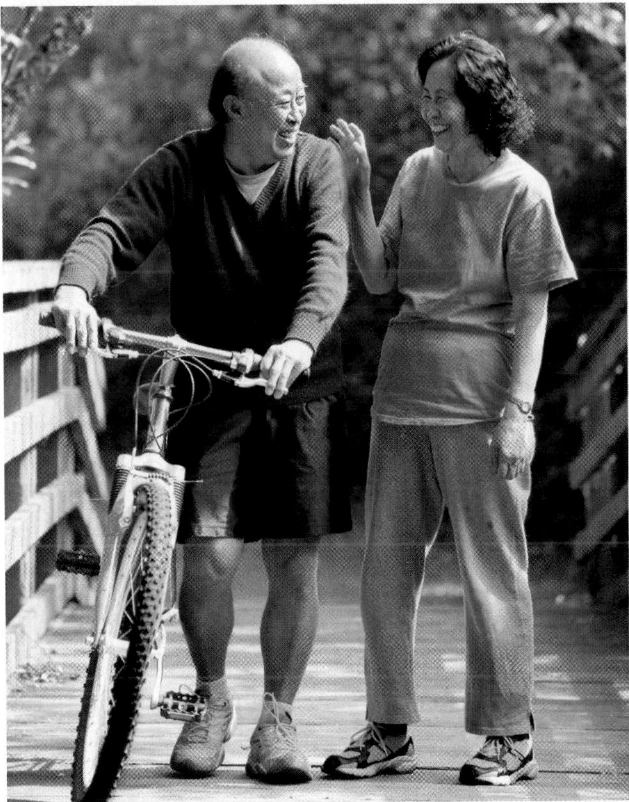

occur during long stretches between meals or after exercise. Some medications, illnesses, certain tumors, hormone imbalances, or drinking too much alcohol may cause this type of hypoglycemia.

Preventing Type 2 Diabetes

Recent research has suggested that shedding some excess weight, exercising regularly, and eating a balanced, high-fiber, healthy diet may be the best strategy to lower the risk of developing diabetes. A landmark study by the Diabetes Prevention Program of over 3,000 individuals with prediabetes showed that those who made changes in their lifestyle, such as losing weight, exercising several hours a week, eating a plant-based, heart-healthy diet, and meeting with a health professional for ongoing support and education, were 58 percent less likely to develop type 2 diabetes than those who did not undertake such intervention. When it comes to winning the battle against diabetes, a healthful diet and lifestyle is the best game plan.

References

1. Centers for Disease Control and Prevention. 2011. *Diabetes Successes and Opportunities for Population-Based Prevention and Control: At a Glance 2011.* Available at www.cdc.gov/chronicdisease/resources/publications/AAG/ddt.htm. Accessed November 2012.
2. Boyle, J., T. Thompson, E. Gregg, L. Barker, and D. Williamson. 2010. Projection of the Year 2050 Burden of Diabetes in the US Adult Population: Dynamic Modeling of Incidence, Mortality and Prediabetes Prevalence. *Population Health Metrics.* Available at www.pophealthmetrics.com/content/8/1/29. Accessed February 2012.
3. National Digestive Diseases Information Clearinghouse. 2005. *Diabetes Overview.* Available at www.niddk.nih.gov. Accessed February 2012.
4. Centers for Disease Control and Prevention. 2007. *Diabetes: Disabling Disease to Double by 2050.* Available at www.cdc.gov. Accessed February 2012.
5. National Digestive Diseases Information Clearinghouse. 2005. *Diabetes Overview.*
6. American Diabetes Association. 2006. Diagnosis and Classification of Diabetes Mellitus. *Diabetes Care* 29:S43–S48.
7. National Digestive Diseases Information Clearinghouse. 2005. *Diabetes Overview.*
8. Ibid.
9. Centers for Disease Control and Prevention. 2007. *Diabetes: Disabling Disease to Double by 2050.*
10. Laaksonen, D. E., H. M. Lakka, L. K. Niskanen, G. A. Kaplan, J. T. Salonen, and T. A. Lakka. 2002. Metabolic Syndrome and Development of Diabetes Mellitus: Application and Validation of Recently Suggested Definitions of the Metabolic Syndrome in a Prospective Cohort Study. *American Journal of Epidemiology 156:*1070–1077.
11. Centers for Disease Control and Prevention. 2011. *National Diabetes Fact Sheet: National Estimates and General Information on Diabetes and Prediabetes in the United States, 2011.* Available at www.cdc.gov/diabetes/pubs/factsheet11.htm. Accessed February 2012.
12. National Diabetes Information Clearinghouse. 2001. *Diabetes Control and Complications Trial (DCCT).* Available at www.diabetes.niddk.nih.gov. Accessed February 2012.
13. Wheeler, M. L., S. A. Dunbar, L. M. Jaacks, W. Karmally, E. J. Mayer-Davis, J. Wylie-Rosett, and W. S. Yancy. 2012. Macronutrients, Food Groups, and Eating Patterns in the Management of Diabetes. A Systematic Review of the Literature, 2010. *Diabetes Care* 35:434–445.
14. American Diabetes Association. 2002. Evidence-Based Nutrition Principles and Recommendations for the Treatment and Prevention of Diabetes and Related Complications. *Diabetes Care* 25:202–212.
15. Diabetes Prevention Program Research Group. 2002. Reduction in the Incidence of Type 2 Diabetes with Lifestyle Intervention or Metformin. *New England Journal of Medicine* 346:393–403.
16. Ibid.
17. Sheard, N., N. Clark, J. Brand-Miller, M. Franz, F. Pi-Sunyer, E. Mayer-Davis, K. Kulkarni, and P. Geil. 2004. Dietary Carbohydrate (Amount and Type) in the Prevention and Management of Diabetes. *Diabetes Care* 27:2266–2271.
18. Ibid.
19. National Digestive Diseases Information Clearinghouse. 2003. *Hypoglycemia.* National Institutes of Health Publication No. 03–3926.

The abundant fiber found in beans and legumes will help provide bulk to stool and may help with weight management.

TABLE TIPS

Increasing Daily Fiber Intake

Choose whole-grain breakfast cereals such as shredded wheat, bran flakes, raisin bran, and oatmeal.

Enjoy a lunchtime sandwich made with a whole-wheat pita or 100% whole-grain bread.

Have two pieces of whole fresh fruit daily.

Layer lettuce, tomatoes, or other vegetables on sandwiches.

Include plenty of root vegetables, such as carrots, turnips, and potatoes, at lunch and dinner.

Fiber Helps Prevent Obesity

A fiber-rich diet can be a key factor in the fight against obesity. High-fiber foods, such as whole grains, fruits, and vegetables, can help you feel fuller faster (recall the concept of *satiety* from Chapter 2), helping reduce overall caloric intake. Research studies have shown that obese men and women tend to consume lower amounts of dietary fiber daily than their leaner counterparts. This lends credence to the concept that fiber plays a role in weight management.[29, 30] Some weight-loss diets restrict carbohydrates, but these plans would work better if they *increased* high-fiber carbohydrates.

A twelve-year, longitudinal study of middle-aged women found that women who consume whole grains gained less weight over time than those who consumed higher amounts of refined grains. These results suggest that the intake of dietary fiber, especially whole grains, is a useful dietary tool to control body weight.[31] Similar results have been observed in men.[32]

A word of caution: Initially, a high-fiber diet can have negative side effects (flatulence and bloating). Consuming too much fiber may cause fluid imbalance or lead to mineral deficiencies by reducing the absorption and increasing the excretion of minerals such as iron and zinc, especially when the diet is low in these minerals or needs have temporarily increased, such as during pregnancy.[33] Gradually increase the fiber in your diet, rather than suddenly adding large amounts. This will allow your body to adjust to the increased amount of fiber and minimize these side effects. See the Table Tips for some easy ways to gradually introduce more fiber into your diet.

THE TAKE-HOME MESSAGE A diet high in fiber has been found to have numerous health benefits, including reduced risk for constipation, diverticulosis, heart disease, obesity, diabetes, and certain cancers.

What Is the Recommended Carbohydrate Intake and What Foods Provide It?

The body needs a minimum amount of carbohydrate daily to support brain and nerve function and to efficiently meet its energy needs. The latest Dietary Reference Intakes (DRIs) for carbohydrates recommend that adults and children consume a minimum of 130 grams of carbohydrate daily. This is based on the estimated minimum amount of glucose the brain needs to function efficiently. Though this may seem high, 130 grams is less than the amount found in the recommended daily servings for each food group in MyPlate, that is, six servings from the grain group, three servings each from the vegetable and dairy groups, and two servings from the fruit group.

In the United States, most adults consume well over the minimum DRI. Adult males consume, on average, over 300 grams of carbohydrates daily, whereas adult females eat over 200 grams daily.

The AMDR for carbohydrates is 45 to 65 percent of total daily kilocalories (see Chapter 2). Adults in the United States consume at least 50 percent of their kilocalories from carbohydrate-rich foods, so they are easily within this optimal range.

For fiber, the current DRIs recommend 14 grams of fiber for every 1,000 kilocalories consumed. The AI for fiber is 25 to 38 grams per day for adults, which is

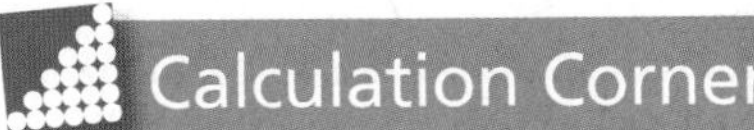

Calculation Corner

Daily Carbohydrate Intake

(a) Adam needs to eat approximately 4,000 kilocalories (kcals) daily to maintain his current weight, given his age, gender, height, weight, and activity level. Calculate how many kcals of carbohydrate Adam should eat each day to meet the AMDR.

$$4{,}000 \text{ (kcals)} \times 0.45 = 1{,}800 \text{ (kcals)}$$
$$4{,}000 \text{ (kcals)} \times 0.65 = 2{,}600 \text{ (kcals)}$$

Answer: If Adam ate between 1,800 and 2,600 kilocalories of carbohydrate each day, he would meet the AMDR for carbohydrates.

(b) How many grams of carbohydrate should Adam eat to equal 45 to 65 percent of his total kilocalories?

$$1{,}800 \text{ kcals} \div 4 \text{ kcals/gram} = 450 \text{ grams}$$
$$2{,}600 \text{ kcals} \div 4 \text{ kcals/gram} = 650 \text{ grams}$$

Answer: Adam should eat between 450 and 650 grams of carbohydrate each day.

(c) Would this intake of carbohydrate meet the minimum suggested intake?

Answer: Yes; Adam needs a minimum of 130 grams of carbohydrate.

TABLE 4.2 What Are Your Fiber Needs?

	Grams of Fiber Daily*	
	Males	**Females**
14 through 18 years old	38	36
19 through 50 years old	38	25
51 through 70+ years old	30	21
Pregnancy		28
Lactation		29

*Based on an Adequate Intake (AI) for fiber.

Data from Institute of Medicine, *Dietary Reference Intakes for Energy, Carbohydrate, Fiber, Fat, Fatty Acids, Cholesterol, Protein, and Amino Acids* (Washington, DC: The National Academies Press, 2002).

based on the amount needed to protect them from developing cardiovascular disease (see Table 4.2). Adults in the United States fall short of these recommendations and currently consume only about 12 to 18 grams per day. Thus, whereas most Americans consume an adequate amount of carbohydrate overall, they are getting less than the AI for dietary fiber, on average.

Whole Foods Are the Best Sources of Carbohydrates

The DRIs indicate the minimum amount of carbohydrate that individuals should consume daily, but it's important to note that all carbohydrates are not created equal, and some carbohydrate-rich foods are nutritionally better than others. Whole, intact foods, including grains, fruits, vegetables, and beans, deliver vitamins, minerals, fiber, and a host of phytochemicals. Refined, high-carbohydrate foods lack these nutrients and contain considerably higher amounts of kilocalories than others, which can lead to weight gain. Eating high-sugar foods that don't contain many other nutrients will provide kilocalories but not much else. If the high-carbohydrate foods are high in saturated fat, they can also be unhealthy for the heart. Therefore, the best food choices for meeting carbohydrate requirements include a range of nutrient-dense, low-saturated-fat foods, with low to moderate amounts of simple carbohydrates and higher amounts of fiber and other complex carbohydrates.

Choosing whole-grain rather than refined grain products, such as whole-grain cereal, provides more nutrition, including fiber, per bite.

Whole Grains

Whole grains (but not refined grains) are abundant in complex carbohydrates, including starch and dietary fiber, and they are an important staple in the diet. Moreover, whole grains are associated with a reduced risk of several chronic diseases.[34] In view of these potential health benefits, MyPlate recommends three servings per day from whole grains. Currently, Americans are consuming less than one serving of grains per day, most of which are refined rather than whole grains.[35] Select whole-grain breads and cereals that have at least 2 to 3 grams of total fiber per serving, such as whole-wheat (or whole-grain) bread, bulgur, brown rice, quinoa, and whole-grain pasta.

whole grains Grain foods that are made with the entire edible grain kernel: the bran, the endosperm, and the germ.

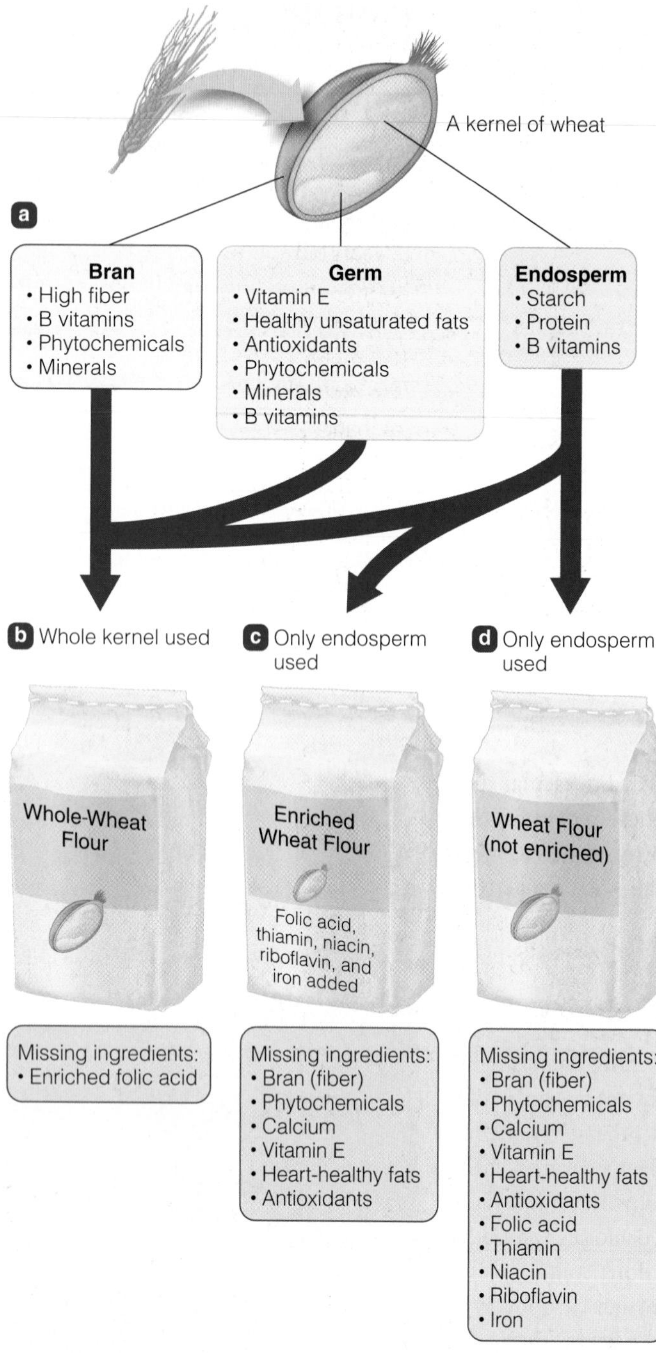

▲ **Figure 4.13 From Wheat Kernel to Flour**
(a) The wheat grain kernel has three parts: bran, germ, and endosperm. **(b)** Whole-wheat flour is made using the entire grain kernel. It is not enriched. **(c)** Enriched wheat flour doesn't contain the bran and germ, so it is missing nutrients and phytochemicals. Some nutrients, including folic acid, thiamin, niacin, riboflavin, and iron, are added back to the flour during an enrichment process. **(d)** Wheat flour that is not enriched lacks not only the bran and germ, but also many nutrients and phytochemicals.

TABLE TIPS

Ways to Enjoy Whole Grains

Choose whole-grain cereal such as shredded wheat, bran flakes, raisin bran, or oatmeal in the morning.

Combine a 100% whole-wheat English muffin and low-fat Cheddar cheese for a hearty breakfast cheese melt.

Enjoy your lunchtime sandwich made with a whole-wheat pita or 100% whole-grain bread.

Try instant brown rice for a quick whole grain at dinner.

Snack on popcorn or 100% whole-wheat crackers for a high-fiber filler in the afternoon.

What is a whole grain and why is it important? Before processing, a kernel of a grain, such as wheat or oats, includes three edible parts: the **bran**, the **endosperm**, and the **germ** (**Figure 4.13**). Whole-grain foods contain all three parts of the grain.

The grain kernel in **refined grains,** such as found in wheat or white bread and white rice, goes through a milling process that strips out the bran and germ, leaving only the endosperm of the kernel in the end product. As a result, some, though not all, of the B vitamins, iron, phytochemicals, and dietary fiber are removed. Refining also improves the digestibility of the carbohydrate in the endosperm, resulting in a more rapid rise in blood glucose and an increased demand for insulin.[36]

To restore some of the nutrition lost from refined grains, **enriched grains** have folic acid, thiamin, niacin, riboflavin, and iron added back after the milling process. This improves their nutritional quality somewhat, but the fiber and the phytochemicals are lost.

Whole grains are potential disease-fighting allies in the diet.[37] As little as one serving of whole grains daily may help lower the risk of dying from heart disease[38, 39] or cancer,[40] reduce the risk of stroke,[41] improve intestinal health,[42, 43] and improve body weight.[44] Several research studies have also shown that the fiber in whole grains may help reduce the risk of diabetes.[45, 46] Because whole grains are abundant with vitamins, minerals, fiber, and phytochemicals, it is uncertain which substances are the disease-fighting heroes or if some or all of them work in a complementary fashion to provide the protection.

bran The indigestible outer shell of the grain kernel.

endosperm The starchy inner portion of a cereal grain.

germ The vitamin-rich embryo, or seed, of a grain.

Low-Fat and Fat-Free Dairy Products

Milk and milk products, including cheese and yogurt, contain 1 to 17 grams of lactose per serving. Choose low-fat or fat-free dairy products whenever possible, for the sake of heart health. The lactose content is the same regardless of the fat content.

Fruits and Vegetables

Whole fruits, 100 percent fruit juices, and vegetables are naturally good sources of both simple and complex carbohydrates. The flesh of fruit is also rich in simple sugars, including fructose and glucose. Though you can also get simple sugars from processed foods and sweets, the higher kilocalorie and lower nutrient levels in these foods make them a less healthy option. The skins of many fruits contain the fiber cellulose, so eating an unpeeled fruit is preferable to eating a peeled fruit. Another type of fiber, pectin, is found in the flesh of fruit, and makes up about 15 to 30 percent of the fiber in fruit. Fruit overall contains about 2 grams of dietary fiber per serving.

When selecting fruit, fresh or frozen versions will provide more nutrients than canned versions, which lose some vitamins and minerals during processing. If canned fruit is the only option, be sure the product is packed in fruit juice, rather than heavy syrup, to cut down on added sugar and kilocalories.

Vegetables contain abundant amounts of complex carbohydrates, including starch and fiber. In general, starchy vegetables, such as corn and potatoes, contain more carbohydrate per serving than nonstarchy vegetables like green beans or carrots (**Figure 4.14**). Overall, a serving of vegetables contains approximately 2 grams of soluble and insoluble fiber. As with fruit, many vegetable skins are an excellent source of fiber, so consuming edible skins whenever possible will also increase fiber intake.

refined grains Grain foods that are made with only the endosperm of the kernel. The bran and germ have been removed during milling.

enriched grains Refined grain foods that have folic acid, thiamin, niacin, riboflavin, and iron added.

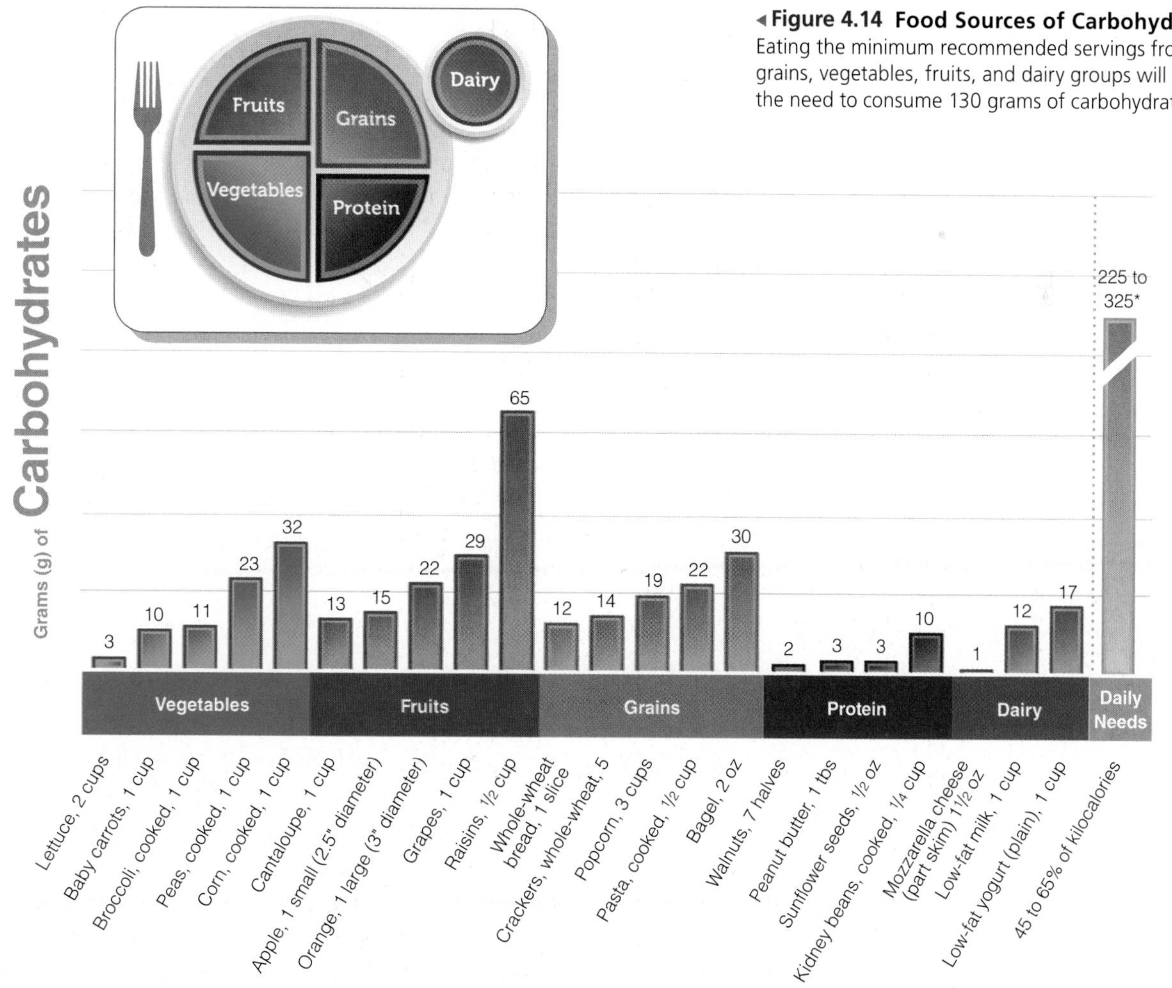

◂ **Figure 4.14 Food Sources of Carbohydrates** Eating the minimum recommended servings from the grains, vegetables, fruits, and dairy groups will meet the need to consume 130 grams of carbohydrate daily.

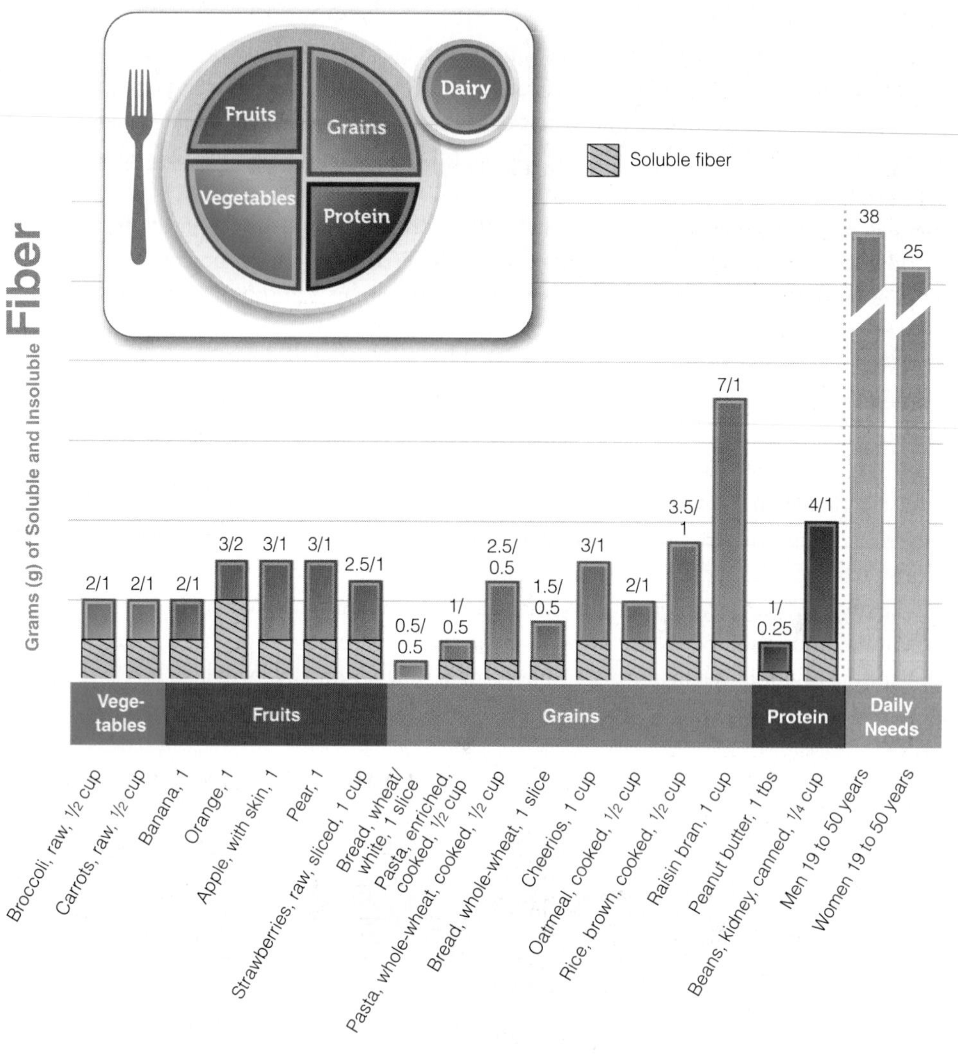

▸ **Figure 4.15 Food Sources of Fiber**

Adults need to consume about 25 to 38 grams of fiber daily.

Data from J. Anderson and S. Bridges, "Dietary Fiber Content of Selected Foods," *American Journal of Clinical Nutrition* 47 (1988): 440–447. USDA National Nutrient Database for Standard Reference, Release 25, www.ars.usda.gov/Services/docs.htm?docid=8964.

Legumes, Nuts, and Seeds

Legumes, such as black beans and peas, are a rich source of starch and dietary fiber (**Figure 4.15**). Legumes provide an average of 4 grams of fiber per serving, about half of which is in the form of hemicellulose.

Nuts and seeds contain very little starch but are good sources of fiber. Nuts provide over 1 gram of fiber in a half ounce or small handful. A half ounce of nuts is about 15 peanuts, 7 walnut halves, or 24 shelled pistachios.

Packaged Foods Can Be Good Sources of Carbohydrates

Packaged and processed foods, such as ready-to-eat cereals and baked crackers, can be good sources of starch and fiber, but can also contain high amounts of added sugar (which we'll discuss in depth later in this chapter), fat, kilocalories, and salt, and should generally be consumed in moderation. When selecting packaged foods, choose products that contain at least two grams of dietary fiber per serving, and be aware of the amounts of added sugar, fat, and total kilocalories. If you're buying snack items, aim for the baked, whole-grain crackers or low-fat pita bread rather

a

Nutrition Facts	
Serving Size 1 cup (30.0g)	
Amount Per Serving	
Calories 120	Calories from Fat 9
	% Daily Value*
Total Fat 1.0g	2%
Saturated Fat 0.2g	1%
Trans Fat 0.0g	
Polyunsaturated Fat 0.2g	
Monounsaturated Fat 0.5g	
Cholesterol 0mg	0%
Sodium 190mg	8%
Total Carbohydrates 26.5g	9%
Dietary Fiber 1.2g	5%
Sugars 13.0g	
Protein 1.0g	
Vitamin A	0%
Vitamin C	10%
Calcium	10%
Iron	25%

* Based on a 2,000 calorie diet.

b

Nutrition Facts		
Serving Size ½ cup (30g) Servings Per Container about 15		
Amount Per Serving	**Fiber One Cereal**	**with ½ cup skim milk**
Calories	60	100
Calories from Fat	10	10
		% Daily Value*
Total Fat 1g	1%	2%
Saturated Fat 0g	0%	0%
Trans Fat 0g		
Polyunsaturated Fat 0g		
Monounsaturated Fat 0g		
Cholesterol 0mg	0%	1%
Sodium 105mg	4%	7%
Potassium 180mg	5%	11%
Total Carbohydrate 25g	8%	10%
Dietary Fiber 14g	57%	57%
Soluble Fiber 1g		
Sugars 0g		
Other Carbohydrates 11g		
Protein 2g		
Vitamin A	0%	
Vitamin C	10%	
Calcium	10%	
Iron	25%	

* Based on a 2,000 calorie diet.

◂ **Figure 4.16 Dietary Fiber Content of Breakfast Cereals**
Nutrition labels list total carbohydrates, dietary fiber, and sugars per serving. Compare the two breakfast cereal labels. Which cereal provides more than 50 percent of the DV for fiber in just one serving? Which cereal is higher in sugar content per serving?

than the box of cookies or doughnuts. The amount of total carbohydrates, including starch, dietary fiber, and sugars, in a packaged food is listed on the nutrition label (see **Figure 4.16**).

THE TAKE-HOME MESSAGE Fresh fruits and vegetables, whole grains, legumes, and low-fat dairy products are the best food sources of carbohydrates. Whole grains, fruits, vegetables, legumes, nuts, and seeds are excellent sources of fiber. Packaged foods can be a good source of starch and fiber, but nutrition labels should be read carefully to avoid consuming too much added sugar, fat, or kilocalories.

What Is the Difference Between Natural Sugars, Added Sugars, and Artificial Sweeteners?

Finding the taste of sweet foods pleasurable is an innate response. You don't have to fight this taste for sweetness. A modest amount of sweet foods can easily be part of a well-balanced diet. However, some sources of sugar provide more nutrition than others.

Your taste buds can't distinguish between **naturally occurring sugars,** like the fructose and lactose found in fruit and dairy products, and **added sugars,** which are

naturally occurring sugars Sugars such as fructose and lactose that are found naturally in foods.

added sugars Sugars that are added to processed foods and sweets.

added by manufacturers to foods such as soda or candy. From a nutritional standpoint, however, there is a big difference between these sugar sources.

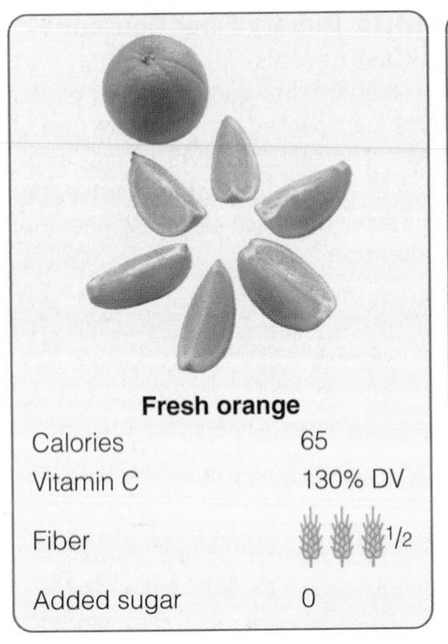

Fresh orange
Calories 65
Vitamin C 130% DV
Fiber 1/2
Added sugar 0
= 1 gram of fiber
= 1 tsp of added sugar

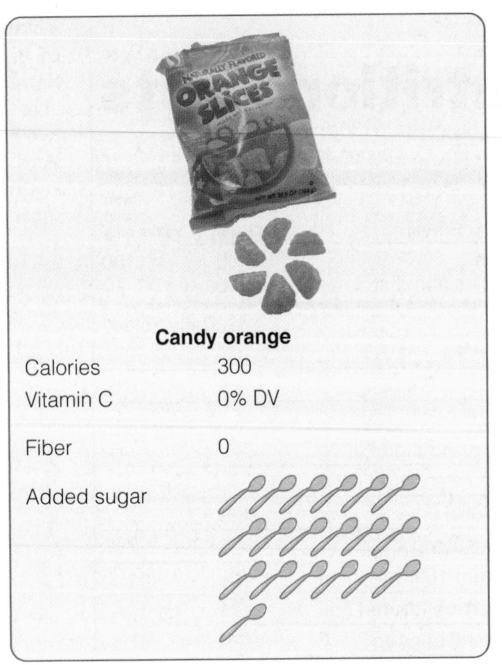

▲ **Figure 4.17 Slices of an Orange versus Orange Slices**
A fresh orange provides more nutrients for fewer kilocalories, and without any added sugars, compared with candy orange slices.

Foods with Natural Sugars Generally Provide More Nutrients for Fewer Kilocalories

Foods that contain naturally occurring sugar tend to be nutrient dense and thus provide more nutrition per serving. In contrast, foods that contain a lot of added sugar tend to provide high amounts of kilocalories but little else. The kilocalories in sugar-laden foods are often called **empty calories** because they provide so little nutrition.

Many fruits are among the most naturally sweet foods available. Just one bite into a ripe peach or navel orange will confirm that fruit can contain more than 15 percent sugar by weight. There are many nutritional advantages of satisfying a sweet tooth with fruit, such as a whole orange, rather than sweets with added sugar, such as a package of candy orange slices. Let's compare these two snacks (**Figure 4.17**).

For the 65 kilocalories in six slices of a navel orange, you get more than 100 percent of the daily value for vitamin C, and 3.5 grams of fiber, which is more than 10 percent of the amount of fiber that many adults should consume daily. These juicy slices of orange also provide fluid. In fact, *over 85 percent* of the weight of an orange is water. The hefty amounts of fiber and water make the orange a sweet snack that provides bulk. This bulk can increase satiety and reduce the likelihood that you'll need to eat a second or third orange to feel satisfied. Eating fruit not only meets the urge for something sweet but reduces the risk of overeating.

In contrast, for the 300 kilocalories found in six candy orange slices, you'll get about 19 teaspoons of added sugar and little else. Although the candy is quite energy dense, it provides no fiber and only negligible amounts of water, and it contains a concentrated amount of kilocalories in relationship to the volume of food in the serving. You wouldn't likely feel satiated after consuming six candy orange slices. To consume close to the 300 kilocalories found in the six pieces of candy, you would have to eat more than four oranges. It would be easier to overeat candy orange slices than fresh oranges.

Added Sugars Are Used during Food Processing

Sugars are added to foods for many reasons. In baked goods, they can hold onto water, which helps keep the product moist, and they help turn pastries a golden brown color. Sugars function as preservatives and thickeners in foods such as sauces. Fermenting sugars in dough produce the carbon dioxide that makes yeast breads rise. And of course, sugars make foods taste sweet. In the last several decades, Americans' increased consumption of processed foods has led to an increased consumption of added sugar. In fact, between 1970 and 2005 our yearly consumption of added sugars increased by more than 19 percent.[47]

empty calories Kilocalories that provide little nutrition, such as those found in candy.

Health Connection

Health Effects of Sugar: Fact vs. Fiction

Is sugar harming your health? Scientists, dietitians, doctors, and especially diet book authors have a variety of opinions about including carbohydrates in the form of sugar in the diet. Many popular publications have branded sugars as dietary evils—the cause of obesity, hyperactivity, and increased risk of developing serious medical complications, including diabetes mellitus. Are any of these allegations accurate?

Fact: Sugar Can Cause Dental Caries

Carbohydrates play a role in tooth decay. Sugars and starches contribute to **dental caries** because they provide an energy source for the bacteria in the mouth. As the bacteria grow, they produce acids that erode the enamel of the teeth. The stickier the carbohydrate, the longer it is in contact with the teeth and the more opportunity there is for the bacteria to produce their damaging acids. Hence hard candies that dissolve slowly in the mouth or dried fruits that can adhere to the teeth are potentially more harmful than foods that are quickly swallowed, such as whole fruits and vegetables. To avoid increased risk of dental caries, sugary snacks should be kept to a minimum, and whole fruits and raw vegetables should be chosen over candies or pastries as snacks.

Some foods may actually help reduce the risk of acid attacks on teeth. The texture of cheese, for example, stimulates the release of cleansing saliva. Cheese is also rich in protein, calcium, and phosphorus, all of which help buffer the acids in the mouth following a meal or snack. The calcium can also assist in **remineralization** of the teeth. Chewing sugarless gum encourages the production of saliva and provides a postmeal bath for your teeth.

Fiction: Sugar Causes Diabetes Mellitus

Contrary to popular belief, sugar does not cause diabetes mellitus. However, too much sugar in the diet can increase the blood level of triglycerides (the primary form of fat in the body, discussed in Chapter 5) and lower the "good" HDL cholesterol. Together, these two changes may increase risk for heart disease.[1] Luckily, a reduction in the amount of sugar coupled with an increase in dietary fiber can typically alleviate this problem.

dental caries Tooth decay.

remineralization Replacing the lost minerals in a decayed lesion or dental caries on a tooth.

Fact: Too Much Sugar Can Hinder Weight Loss

Consuming too much sugar can make weight management challenging. But eating sugar itself does not lead to weight gain or impede weight loss. However, it is easy to overeat energy-dense, sugary foods and quickly add excess kilocalories to the diet. If the increased consumption of kilocalories is not offset by increased exercise or physical activity, weight gain can occur.

Individuals on low-carbohydrate diets sometimes report initial success with weight loss. However, this loss is usually due to the reduced consumption of overall kilocalories, and is often short term. Once normal eating habits resume, the weight is regained. Research hasn't yet concluded what the long-term effects of eating few or no carbohydrates are. A diet that is low in carbohydrates can be high in heart-unhealthy fats or too high in protein.

Fiction: Sugar Is Addictive

Some people claim that sugar is addicting, but most experts agree that this is not the case. To be classified as an addiction, a substance must meet several requirements: It has to make you feel good; change the chemicals in the brain; trigger a physical dependence and irrepressible cravings; and, when removed from consumption, result in severe physical and psychological reactions. Sugar does not meet all of these criteria. Sugar has been shown, at least in rats, to increase the levels of dopamine in the brain. This neurotransmitter is responsible for feeling pleasure, which could be the reason you felt happy after eating that piece of dark chocolate cake.

Fiction: Sugar Causes Hyperactivity in Children

Adults often point to sugary foods as the culprit behind the overly excited behavior of children at parties and holidays. However, research does not support the theory that sugar makes kids hyperactive.[2] The behavior of the kids is more likely due to the excitement and festivities of the day than the sweets being consumed.

References

1. Howard, B. and J. Wylie-Rosett. 2002. Sugar and Cardiovascular Disease: A Statement for Healthcare Professionals from the Committee on Nutrition of the Council on Nutrition, Physical Activity, and Metabolism of the American Heart Association. *Circulation* 106:523–527.
2. American Dietetic Association. 1998. Position of the American Dietetic Association: Use of Nutritive and Nonnutritive Sweeteners. *Journal of the American Dietetic Association* 98:580–587.

a Sugar can be called a number of different names on ingredient lists and labels.

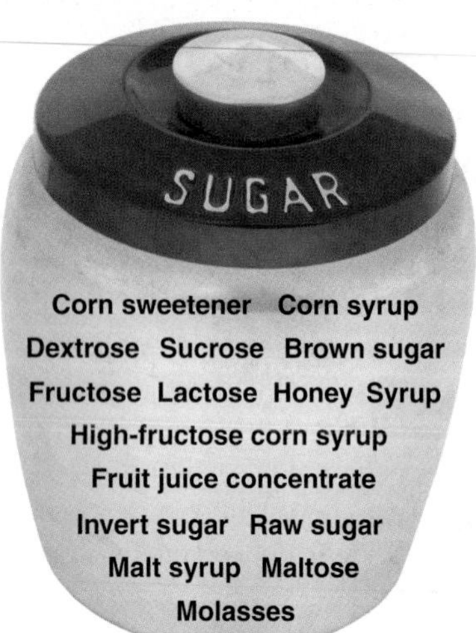

SUGAR
Corn sweetener Corn syrup
Dextrose Sucrose Brown sugar
Fructose Lactose Honey Syrup
High-fructose corn syrup
Fruit juice concentrate
Invert sugar Raw sugar
Malt syrup Maltose
Molasses

Ingredients: Granola (whole grain rolled oats, sugar, rice flour, whole grain rolled wheat, partially hydrogenated soybean and cottonseed oils* with TBHQ and citric acid added to preserve freshness and/or sunflower oil with natural tocopherol added to preserve freshness, whole wheat flour, molasses, sodium bicarbonate, soy lecithin, caramel color, barley malt, salt, nonfat dry milk), corn syrup, crisp rice (rice, sugar, salt, barley malt), semisweet chocolate chunks (sugar, chocolate liquor, cocoa butter, soy lecithin, vanillin [an artificial flavor]), sugar, corn syrup solids, glycerin, high fructose corn syrup, partially hydrogenated soybean and/or cottonseed oil*, sorbitol, fructose, calcium carbonate, natural and artificial flavors, salt, soy lecithin, molasses, water, BHT (a preservative), citric acid.

* Adds a dietarily insignificant amount of *trans* fat.

b You can also look on the Nutrition Facts panel to see the total grams of sugar.

Nutrition Facts
Serving Size 1 Bar (24g)
Servings Per Container 10

Amount Per Serving	
Calories 90	Calories from Fat 20
	% Daily Value*
Total Fat 2g	3%
Saturated Fat 0.5g	3%
Trans Fat 0g	
Sodium 80mg	3%
Total Carbohydrate 19g	6%
Dietary Fiber 1g	3%
Sugars 7g	
Protein 1g	
Calcium 8% • Iron 4%	

Not a significant source of Cholesterol, Vitamin A, Vitamin C

* Percent Daily Values are based on a 2,000 calorie diet. Your Daily Values may be higher or lower depending on your calorie needs:

	Calories:	2,000	2,500
Total Fat	Less than	65g	80g
Sat Fat	Less than	20g	25g
Cholesterol	Less than	300mg	300mg
Sodium	Less than	2,400mg	2,400mg
Total Carbohydrate		300g	375g
Dietary Fiber		25g	30g

▲ **Figure 4.18 Finding Added Sugars on the Label**
A food is likely to contain a large amount of sugar if added sugars appear first or second on the ingredients list and/or if there are many varieties of added sugars listed.

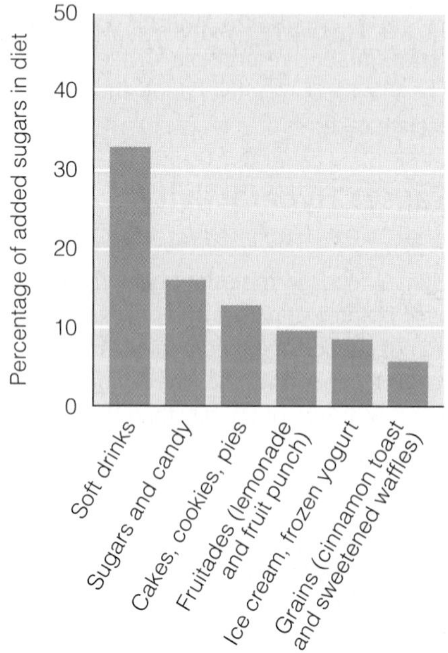

▲ **Figure 4.19 Where Are All the Added Sugars Coming From?**
Soft drinks are the number-one source of added sugars in the diets of Americans.

Added Sugars

While sucrose and fructose are the most common added sugars in our foods, sugars can appear on the food label under numerous different names (see **Figure 4.18**). To find the amount and type of added sugars in a food, read the ingredients list. If added sugars appear first or second on the list, or if the product contains many varieties of added sugars, it is likely high in sugar. Note, for example, that the ingredient label from the box of low-fat chocolate chip granola bars lists added sugars ten different times!

The Nutrition Facts panel that is currently used on food labels doesn't distinguish between naturally occurring and added sugars. For example, the nutrition labels on a box of raisin bran and a carton of milk list 21 grams of sugars for raisin bran and 12 grams for low-fat milk. This can be misleading, as the grams of sugars listed for the raisin bran include both the amount of naturally occurring sugars from the raisins and the sugars added to sweeten the cereal. For the milk, the sugar listed on the Nutrition Facts panel is just the naturally occurring sugar, lactose. With the growing concern about the rising levels of added sugars in the diets of Americans, various health professionals and organizations have pressured the FDA to require that all *added* sugars be disclosed on the food label. A final decision by the FDA is pending.

Americans don't eat the majority of the added sugars in their diets—they drink them (see **Figure 4.19**). The number-one source of added sugars in the United States is sweetened soft drinks, energy drinks, and sports drinks. This fact isn't too surprising when you look at the size of the sweetened beverages that Americans consume (see **Figure 4.20**). A classic (and rare) 8-ounce bottle of cola provides almost 7 teaspoons of added sugars. In today's vending machine, you are more likely to find a 12-ounce can or a 20-ounce bottle. Because people typically consume the entire can or bottle, regardless of its size, they consume more sugar. See the Table Tips for ways to cut down on your consumption of added sugars.

Since the 1970s, high fructose corn syrup (HFCS) has replaced sucrose in most sweetened beverages.[48] This sweetener has been implicated in many health-related problems, including obesity. However, most experts agree that high fructose corn syrup is no more harmful than sucrose. Both sweeteners are nutritionally equivalent and have similar metabolic responses. Once absorbed into the blood, these two sweeteners are impossible to tell apart. See Examining the Evidence: Is High Fructose Corn Syrup Causing the Obesity Epidemic? for more information on the health concerns associated with HFCS.

▲ **Figure 4.20 The Many Sizes of Soft Drinks**
A single soda can provide from 6 to 17 teaspoons of added sugars, depending upon the size of the container.

Sugar Substitutes Add Sweetness but Not Kilocalories

Because most people perceive eating too much sugar as unhealthy, food manufacturers often use artificially created **sugar substitutes** to provide the sweet taste of sugar for fewer kilocalories, and Americans' consumption of these products has increased steadily over the last two decades (see **Figure 4.21**). All sugar substitutes must be approved by the FDA and deemed safe for consumption before they are allowed in food products sold in the United States.[49]

Several sugar substitutes are presently available to consumers, including polyols, saccharin, aspartame, acesulfame-K, sucralose, rebaudioside A, and neotame. Alitame and cyclamate are two other sugar substitutes that are not yet approved for use in the United States, but are on the horizon. Polyols don't promote dental caries, and

TABLE TIPS

Lowering Consumption of Added Sugars

Mix chocolate milk with an equal amount of regular low-fat milk.

Mix equal amounts of sweetened cereal with an unsweetened variety for a breakfast cereal with half the added sugar.

Drink water rather than soda or sweetened beverages throughout the day.

Buy sweets such as candy and cookies packaged in individual serving sizes rather than in large packages. The less you buy, the less you'll eat.

Mix an ounce of 100% fruit juice with 10 ounces of sparkling water for a no-sugar-added "fruit" drink.

▲ **Figure 4.21 Growing Interest in Sugar-Free Foods and Beverages**
The use of sugar-free products has more than doubled since 1986.

Source: Figure from "Trends and Statistics" from Calorie Control Council website, 4 September 2012. Copyright © 2012 by Calorie Control Council. Reprinted with permission.

sugar substitutes Alternatives to table sugar that sweeten foods for fewer kilocalories.

EXAMINING THE EVIDENCE

Is High Fructose Corn Syrup Causing the Obesity Epidemic?

When high fructose corn syrup (HFCS) was first introduced in 1970, U.S. adults consumed approximately 85 pounds of sweeteners per year, most of which was refined sugar. Since 1970, the consumption of sweeteners has risen to nearly 100 pounds per person per year, mostly due to the increase in HFCS (34.3 pounds per person per year in 2011).[1] At the same time that our consumption of HFCS has increased, obesity rates among Americans have also skyrocketed.[2] Is this a coincidence or is HFCS to blame?

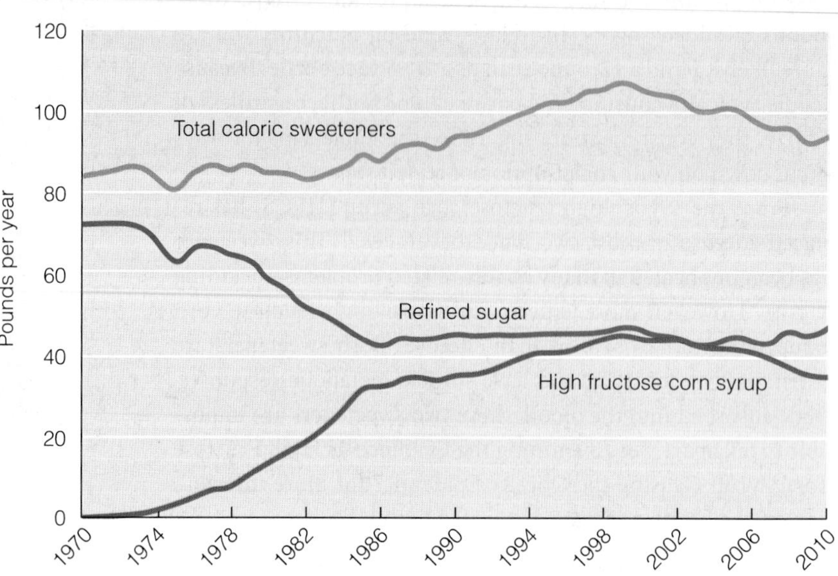

The Per Capita Consumption Patterns, in Pounds, of Sucrose and High Fructose Corn Syrup

Data from U.S. Department of Agriculture, Economic Research Service. 2011. Table 51—Refined Cane and Beet Sugar: Estimated Number of Per Capita Calories Consumed Daily, by Calendar Year; Table 52—High-Fructose Corn Syrup: Estimated Number of Per Capita Calories Consumed Daily, by Calendar Year; Table 53—Other Sweeteners: Estimated Number of Per Capita Calories Consumed Daily, by Calendar Year. *Sugars and Sweeteners Yearbook.*

What Is High Fructose Corn Syrup?

HFCS is a sweetener produced from modified corn and composed of glucose and fructose. Because glucose and fructose are in a "free" state, the syrup is stable and easy to handle in food processing—a plus for manufacturers. HFCS is less expensive than sucrose, which is probably the reason HFCS has replaced sucrose as the most common sweetener in processed foods, including baked goods, sweets, and soft drinks. In baked products, HFCS gives cookies and snacks their chewy, soft texture, and makes bread brown better. HFCS inhibits the growth of microbes by reducing the availability of water and thus improves freshness and extends the shelf life of many food products. It's no wonder that HFCS is estimated to represent the highest percentage—more than 40 percent—of added sugar in the food supply.[3] The question is, has our increased consumption of this particular sweetener led to our expanded waistlines?

Does HFCS Consumption Lead to Weight Gain?

Two theories have been proposed to explain the possible connection between weight gain and the increased consumption of HFCS. One theory suggests that HFCS is sweeter than sucrose, resulting in an increased consumption of kilocalories.[4] A second theory posits that the increase in HFCS means an increase in fructose consumption, which may stimulate appetite and alter insulin metabolism.[5] Research exploring both of these theories has yielded some interesting results.

HFCS Is Not Sweeter than Sugar

Monosaccharides and disaccharides vary in their level of sweetness. Fructose is the sweetest monosaccharide, and sucrose, because of its high fructose content, is the sweetest of the disaccharides.

Sucrose contains 50 percent glucose and 50 percent fructose—one molecule of glucose for every molecule of fructose. HFCS comes in two different forms: HFCS-42 and HFCS-55. HFCS-42 is 42 percent fructose and 58 percent glucose (see table). This version is used in bakery products, jams and jellies, canned fruit, and dairy products. HFCS-55 is 55 percent fructose and 45 percent glucose and is used to sweeten beverages, including soft drinks and sweetened teas. Essentially, HFCS has the same composition as sucrose. Thus, despite its name, HFCS is not dramatically higher in fructose than sucrose and therefore is not any sweeter than sucrose.

The Monosaccharide Composition and Sweetness Levels of Sucrose and High Fructose Corn Syrup

	HFCS-42	Sucrose	HFCS-55
Fructose	42%	50%	55%
Glucose	58%	50%	45%
Moisture	29%	5%	23%
Sweetness index	92	100	99

Data from G. L. Hein, M. L. Storey, and J. S. White, "The Highs and Lows of High Fructose Corn Syrup: A Report from the Center for Food and Nutrition Policy and Its Ceres Workshop," *Nutrition Today* 40 (2005): 253–256.

HFCS May Impact Satiation

Some researchers have suggested that HFCS may change our appetite control mechanisms, resulting in less satiation and a greater intake of kilocalories. This theory is based on earlier studies conducted with pure crystalline fructose (not HFCS), which reported that fructose ingestion resulted in a decrease in the hormones insulin and leptin. Both of these hormones increase satiety. Fructose does not increase insulin levels because it does not depend on insulin to enter the liver cell. Whereas glucose stimulates satiety, fructose does not.

This is significant in that insulin stimulates the release of leptin, a hormone that decreases appetite.[6] These two hormones also suppress the release of ghrelin, another hormone that stimulates our appetite. If insulin is reduced, then leptin is reduced and ghrelin is not suppressed, which leads to feeling hungry and eating more kilocalories. Thus, if pure fructose reduces the release of appetite-suppressing hormones, then does high fructose corn syrup increase appetite?

Based on research, the answer is no, because HFCS does not cause the same reaction as pure fructose does in the body. Remember, HFCS is approximately 50 percent fructose and 50 percent glucose. If HFCS did increase appetite, research subjects would report a decrease in satiety and an increase in kilocalorie intake compared with otherwise sweetened drinks. A recent study showed no significant differences in hunger or satiety ratings, or in the amount of kilocalories eaten at a later meal, when subjects drank a beverage sweetened with HFCS, low-fat milk, or orange juice.[7] Nor did a beverage with HFCS increase the amount of food eaten later in the day when compared with a beverage containing sucrose.[8]

How Does the Body Metabolize HFCS?

Because HFCS contains fructose and glucose, the metabolism of this sweetener is generally the same as the metabolism of each individual monosaccharide.

As soon as it is absorbed, fructose is transported through the portal vein and metabolized by the liver. During metabolism, fructose can be converted to intermediate substrates used by the liver for energy production or used as the starter molecules for lipogenesis or fat synthesis. If intake of fructose is high, there is a potential that the liver may accumulate higher than normal levels of stored triglyceride, reduce the sensitivity to insulin, and increase the formation of lipoproteins in the blood, leading to increased risk of cardiovascular disease.[9] The lack of glucose makes the absorption of pure fructose different from HFCS. Glucose appears to have a tempering effect on the metabolism of fructose.[10]

The current evidence suggests that HFCS and sucrose are metabolized in a similar way once the monosaccharides have been absorbed.[11]

Different Sweeteners and Insulin Production

Whether the sweetener is sucrose or HFCS, they both trigger an insulin response. Pure glucose stimulates the greatest release of insulin compared with pure fructose, which stimulates the least. Because HFCS and sucrose contain approximately the same ratio of glucose to fructose, they trigger a similar, intermediate release of insulin. Fructose is generally eaten as part of a food, such as fruit, or as part of a sweetener, such as sucrose or HFCS. The composition of the entire meal, rather than just the type of monosaccharide, also affects the release of insulin in the body.

The Bottom Line: Does HFCS Cause Obesity?

Currently, there is no evidence that HFCS consumption contributes more to obesity than do other sweeteners or energy sources.[12] In fact, obesity has increased sharply in countries where beverage consumption is lower than in the United States and HFCS is not a common sweetener.[13] One expert review of the research literature on the dietary role of HFCS found insufficient support for the theory that HFCS could play a role in obesity. The report states that there are many other "plausible explanations for rising overweight and obesity rates" in the United States, including a reduction in smoking, a decrease in physical activity, including reduced physical education programs in schools, an increase in technology, which leads to more sedentary activities, and watching television.[14]

Although HFCS may not be the main culprit in the dramatic rise in obesity, it likely does play a role in Americans' overall increased caloric intake, including from energy-dense sweets, snacks, and baked goods, which contain more kilocalories than nutrient-dense fruits and vegetables. The DRI recommends reducing all refined sugars, regardless of whether the sweetener is fructose, sucrose, or HFCS.

References

1. United States Department of Agriculture, Economic Research Service. 2012. Table 52—High Fructose Corn Syrup: Estimated Number of Per Capita Calories Consumed Daily, by Calendar Year. *Sugar and Sweeteners Yearbook 2011.*
2. Centers for Disease Control and Prevention. 2012. *Adult Obesity Facts.* Available at www.cdc.gov/obesity/data/adult.html. Accessed November 2012.
3. Bray, G. A., S. J. Nielsen, and B. M. Popkin. 2004. Consumption of High Fructose Corn Syrup in Beverages May Play a Role in the Epidemic of Obesity. *American Journal of Clinical Nutrition* 79:537–543.
4. Ibid.
5. Forshee, R. A., M. L. Storey, D. B. Allison, W. H. Glinsmann, G. L. Hein, D. R. Lineback, S. A. Miller, T. A. Nicklas, G. A. Weaver, and J. S. White. 2007. A Critical Examination of the Evidence Relating High Fructose Corn Syrup and Weight Gain. *Critical Reviews in Food Science and Nutrition* 47:561–582.
6. Melanson, K. J., L. Zukley, J. Lowndes, V. Nguyen, T. J. Angelopoulos, and J. M. Rippe. 2007. Effects of High Fructose Corn Syrup and Sucrose Consumption on Circulating Glucose, Insulin, Leptin, and Ghrelin and on Appetite in Normal-Weight Women. *Nutrition* 23:103–112.
7. Almiron-Roig, E. and A. Drewnowski. 2003. Hunger, Thirst, and Energy Intakes Following Consumption of Caloric Beverages. *Physiology of Behavior* 79:767–774.
8. Akhavan, T. and G. H. Anderson. 2007. Effects of Glucose-to-Fructose Ratios in Solutions on Subjective Satiety, Food Intake, and Satiety Hormones in Young Men. *American Journal of Clinical Nutrition* 86:1354–1363.
9. Bray et al. 2004. Consumption of High Fructose Corn Syrup in Beverages.
10. Melanson, K. J., et al. 2007. Effects of High Fructose Corn Syrup and Sucrose Consumption.
11. Schorin, M. 2005. High Fructose Corn Syrups, Part 1: Composition, Consumption, Metabolism. *Nutrition Today* 40:248–252.
12. Monsivais, P., M. Perrigue, and A. Drewnowski. 2007. Sugars and Satiety: Does the Type of Sweetener Make a Difference? *American Journal of Clinical Nutrition* 86:116–123.
13. Ibid.
14. Forshee, R. A., et al. 2007. A Critical Examination of the Evidence.

TABLE 4.3 Oh So Sweet!

Sweetener	Kilocalories/Gram	Trade Names	Sweetening Power	The Facts
Sucrose	4.0	Table sugar	—	Sweetens food, enhances flavor, tenderizes, and contributes browning properties to baked goods
Reduced-Kilocalorie Sweeteners				
Polyols (Sugar Alcohols)				
Sorbitol	2.6	Sorbitol	50% to 70% as sweet as sucrose	Found in foods such as sugarless chewing gum, jams, baked goods, and candy
Mannitol	1.6	Mannitol	50% to 70% as sweet as sucrose	Found in foods such as chewing gum, jams, and as a bulking agent in powdered foods. May cause diarrhea.
Xylitol	2.4	Xylitol	Equally sweet as sucrose	Found in foods such as chewing gum, candies; also in pharmaceuticals and hygiene products
Hydrogenated Starch Hydrolysates (HSH)	3.0	HSH	50% to 70% as sweet as sucrose	Found in confections and can be used as a bulking agent
Kilocalorie-Free Sweeteners				
Saccharin	0	Sweet 'N Low	200% to 700% sweeter than sucrose	Retains its sweetening power at high temperatures such as baking
Aspartame	4.0*	NutraSweet, Equal	Approximately 200% sweeter than sucrose	Sweetening power is reduced at high temperatures such as baking. Can be added at end stages of recipes such as cooked puddings if removed from heat source. Individuals with PKU need to monitor all dietary sources of phenylalanine, including aspartame.
Acesulfame-K	0	Sunette	200% sweeter than sucrose	Retains its sweetening power at high temperatures
Sucralose	0	Splenda	600% sweeter than sucrose	Retains its sweetening power at high temperatures
Rebaudioside A	0	Truvia, Sun Crystals, PureVia	200% sweeter than sucrose	Retains its sweetening power at high temperatures
Tagalose	1.5	Naturlose	92% as sweet as sugar	Texture and taste similar to sucrose
Neotame	0	Neotame	7,000% to 13,000% sweeter than sucrose	Retains its sweetening power at high temperatures

*Because so little aspartame is needed to sweeten foods, it provides negligible kilocalories.

they cause a slower rise in blood glucose than sugar. Saccharin, aspartame, acesulfame-K, sucralose, and neotame also don't promote dental caries and have the added advantage of not affecting blood glucose levels at all. These sugar substitutes are a plus for people with diabetes, who have a more challenging time managing their blood glucose levels. Additionally, all sugar substitutes are either reduced in kilocalories or are kilocalorie free. See Table 4.3 for a comparison of available sweeteners.

Sugar Alcohols

Polyols are often called sugar alcohols because they have the chemical structure of sugar, with an alcohol component added. Whereas polyols such as sorbitol, mannitol, and xylitol are found naturally in plants, they are also produced synthetically and are used as sweeteners in foods such as chewing gum and candies. They can be used tablespoon for tablespoon to substitute for sucrose. Sorbitol and mannitol are less likely to promote dental caries because the bacteria on the teeth metabolize them so slowly. (Humans lack the enzyme needed to ferment xylitol.) Their slower absorption means that they do not produce a spike in blood glucose, which is a benefit for those with diabetes.

Chewing gums and candies that contain sugar alcohols can be labeled "sugar free" and claim that they don't promote tooth decay. Keep in mind, however, that although these products are sugar free, they are not necessarily kilocalorie free. Even more important, because polyols are incompletely absorbed in the digestive tract, they can cause diarrhea. For this reason, they should be used in moderation.

Another type of polyol is hydrogenated starch hydrolysate (HSH), which is made by partially breaking down corn, wheat, or potato starch and adding hydrogen. The end product is a wide range of polyols, including those that can be strung together and used commercially. HSH adds sweetness, texture, and bulk to many sugarless products such as baked goods and candies.[50]

Saccharin

Consumers today often associate saccharin with the pink packets found on restaurant tables, but it's been in use for more than a century. Saccharin was first discovered in 1879, and was used as a sugar substitute in the United States and Europe during the two World Wars, when sugar was being rationed. It is used in more than 100 countries in foods, beverages, vitamins, and pharmaceuticals. Because saccharin is not metabolized by the body, it doesn't provide any kilocalories.

In 1977, the FDA banned saccharin due to reports from the research community that it could cause bladder cancer in rats. Congress immediately implemented an 18-month moratorium on this ban through the Saccharin Study and Labeling Act. This allowed the continued commercial use of saccharin, but required that any saccharin-containing products bear a warning label stating that saccharin was potentially hazardous to health as it caused cancer in laboratory animals.

In 2000, the National Toxicology Program (NTP) removed saccharin from the list of substances that could potentially cause cancer. After extensive review, the NTP determined that the observed bladder tumors in rats were actually from a mechanism that wasn't relevant to humans.[51] The lesson learned from this is that though you can safely consume saccharin in moderation, you shouldn't feed it to your pet rat.

Aspartame

In 1965, a scientist named James Schlatter was conducting research on amino acids in his quest to find a treatment for ulcers. To pick up a piece of paper in his laboratory, he licked his finger—and stumbled upon a sweet-tasting compound.[52] It was the "lick" that was soon to be "tasted" around the world. Schlatter had just discovered aspartame, a substance that has become one of the most-used sugar substitutes in the world.

Aspartame is composed of two amino acids: a modified aspartic acid and phenylalanine. Enzymes in the digestive tract break down aspartame into its components, and the amino acids are absorbed, providing 4 kilocalories per gram. Consequently, aspartame has the potential to provide kilocalories to foods as an added sweetener. However, as aspartame is 200 times sweeter than sucrose, only a small amount is needed to sweeten a food.

In 1981, the FDA approved aspartame for use in tabletop sweeteners such as Equal and NutraSweet, and for various other uses, such as to sweeten breakfast cereals, chewing gums, and carbonated beverages. The majority of the aspartame that is consumed in the United States is in soft drinks. In 1996, the FDA gave the food industry carte blanche to use aspartame in all types of foods and beverages. It is currently used as a sweetener in over 100 countries, and can now be found in over 6,000 foods, as well as pharmaceuticals and personal care products, sold in the United States.

Aspartame has undergone continual, vigorous reviews to ensure that it is safe for human consumption. The FDA considers it one of the most thoroughly studied and tested food additives approved by the agency. The FDA has reevaluated the safety of aspartame more than 25 times since it first came on the market and each time has concluded that it is safe to consume.[53]

Despite its intense evaluation, aspartame has been, and still is, blamed for ailments ranging from headaches to Gulf War Syndrome. Major health organizations such as the Academy of Nutrition and Dietetics, the American Medical Association, and the American Diabetes Association all support aspartame's use by healthy adults, children, and pregnant women in moderation as part of a well-balanced diet.[54] The FDA has set an acceptable daily intake (ADI) for aspartame at 50 milligrams per kilogram (mg/kg) of body weight. To exceed this ADI, a 150-pound person would need to consume almost sixteen 12-ounce cans of a "diet" (aspartame-containing) soda daily for a lifetime. Currently, the general public consumes an estimated 4 to 7 percent of the ADI, or 2 to 3.5 milligrams per kilogram of body weight daily.

Foods and beverages that contain aspartame must carry a label warning that phenylalanine is present.

Individuals with a rare, inherited disorder known as phenylketonuria (PKU) are unable to metabolize phenylalanine, one of the amino acids in aspartame, and must adhere to a special diet. PKU affects about 1 out of every 15,000 infants in the United States. It is usually the result of a deficiency of phenylalanine hydroxylase, an enzyme needed to properly metabolize phenylalanine.[55]

Because of the seriousness of this disorder, the FDA mandates that all food products that contain phenylalanine carry a label declaring its content. People with PKU need to control all dietary sources of this amino acid, including aspartame as well as protein-rich foods such as meat, milk, eggs, and nuts. These individuals do not necessarily have to avoid aspartame, but they need to monitor it as an additional source of phenylalanine in their diet.

Acesulfame-K

Although its name is less than sweet sounding, acesulfame-K (the K refers to the potassium component) is about 200 times sweeter than sucrose. It is available as a tabletop sweetener, called Sunette, and is currently used in chewing gum, candy, desserts, yogurt, and alcoholic beverages. The body does not metabolize acesulfame-K and it's excreted intact in the urine.[56]

Sucralose

Sucralose was developed in 1976 by slightly changing the structure of the sucrose molecule. Unlike sucrose, sucralose isn't digested or absorbed by the body—it passes through the GI tract and is excreted. In 1998, sucralose was approved as a tabletop sweetener, and it's available commercially as Splenda. Sucralose can be used in baking because it doesn't break down when it reaches high cooking temperatures.

A variety of sugar substitutes are available to consumers.

Rebaudioside A

One of the newest additions to the world of sugar substitutes is rebaudioside A, a combination of a sugar alcohol with an extract from the stevia plant. Extracts from the stevia plant, an herb native to Brazil and Paraguay, are currently used in the United States as an additive in beverages and foods as well as a dietary supplement you can sprinkle in your coffee. This zero-calorie sweetener is approximately 200 times sweeter than sugar and is available under trade names such as Truvia, Sun Crystals, and PureVia. It doesn't affect blood glucose levels, so it could be used by those with diabetes.

Tagalose

Tagalose is a low-kilocalorie sweetener derived from lactose that can be found naturally in some dairy products. This sweetener, marketed under the brand name Naturlose, has a natural taste and the texture of sugar, and is about 90 percent as sweet, with only a third of the kilocalories. Because tagalose is not completely absorbed, it has a minimal effect on blood glucose levels. The FDA-approved sweetener is used in a variety of foods and beverages but does not promote tooth decay.

Neotame

The newest addition to the world of sugar substitutes is neotame, which was approved by the FDA in 2002. Neotame comprises the same two amino acids—aspartic acid and phenylalanine—as aspartame, but they are joined together in such a way that the body cannot break them apart. Thus, individuals with PKU can use neotame without concern. Neotame is completely eliminated in either urine or stool. It has been approved as a sweetener and for a variety of uses such as chewing gum, frostings, frozen desserts, puddings, fruit juices, and syrups.[57]

THE TAKE-HOME MESSAGE Your taste buds can't distinguish between naturally occurring and added sugars. Foods with naturally occurring sugars, such as whole fruit, tend to provide more nutrition and satiation than empty-calorie sweets such as candy. Numerous names for sugar are found on food labels, and soft drinks are the number-one contributor of added sugars to Americans' diets. Millions of Americans consume reduced-kilocalorie or kilocalorie-free sugar substitutes. The FDA has approved polyols, saccharin, aspartame, acesulfame-K, sucralose, rebaudioside A, tagalose, and neotame to be used in a variety of foods. These sugar substitutes add sweetness to your food without the added kilocalories, do not promote dental caries, and can benefit those with diabetes who need to carefully manage their blood glucose.

Putting It All Together

Carbohydrates are an important part of a healthy diet; they are the main source of energy for cells. Whole grains, fruits, vegetables, and lean dairy products provide carbohydrates along with vitamins and minerals and should be the predominant source of carbohydrates in the diet. Whole grains, fruits, and vegetables are also good sources of fiber and phytochemicals. A diet that contains adequate amounts of these foods can help prevent many chronic diseases. Sugary foods also provide carbohydrates but often contain fewer nutrients, so should be eaten in moderation.

Visual Chapter Summary

1 Carbohydrates Are Energy Nutrients with Different Classifications

Carbohydrates are energy nutrients composed of carbon, hydrogen, and oxygen that are predominant in plant-based foods.

Carbohydrates are divided into two categories: simple and complex carbohydrates. Simple carbohydrates, or sugars, include monosaccharides and disaccharides. Complex carbohydrates include oligosaccharides and polysaccharides.

The three nutritionally important monosaccharides are: glucose, fructose, and galactose. Each monosaccharide is called a hexose ($C_6H_{12}O_6$). Monosacharides linked together with a glycosidic bond form disaccharides including sucrose, lactose, and maltose.

Starch and fiber are polysaccharides found in plants. Glycogen is the storage form of glucose in animals.

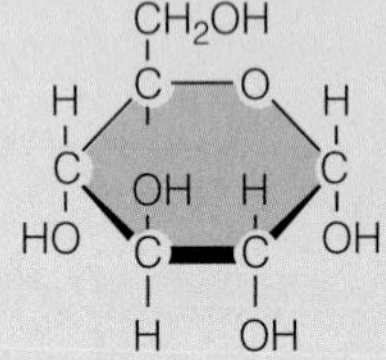

Glucose, a monosaccharide

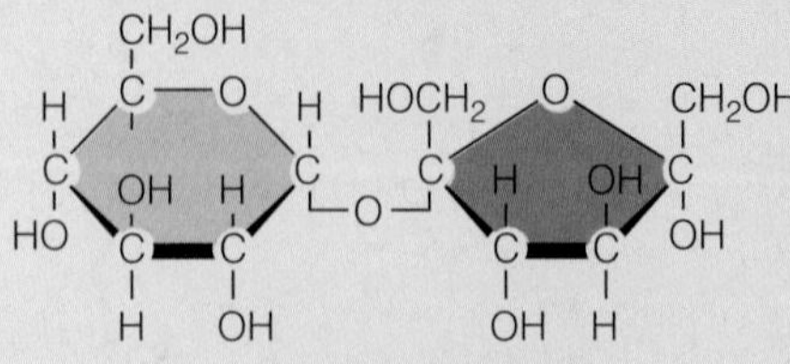

Sucrose, a disaccharide

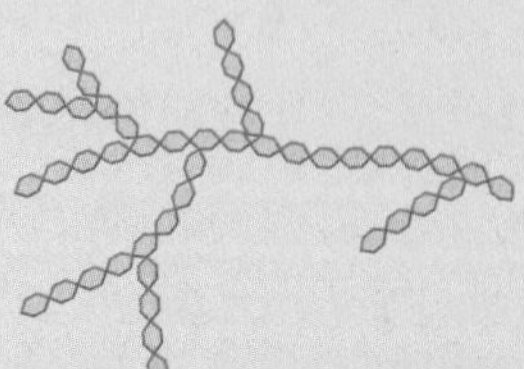

Starch, a polysaccharide

2 Carbohydrates Are Digested and Absorbed in the Mouth and Small Intestine

Salivary amylase begins digestion of carbohydrates in the mouth although most carbohydrate digestion occurs in the small intestine, facilitated by pancreatic amylase. Sucrose, maltose, and lactose are digested by small intestine enzymes. Fiber is nondigestible. Glucose, fructose, and galactose are absorbed directly into the portal vein.

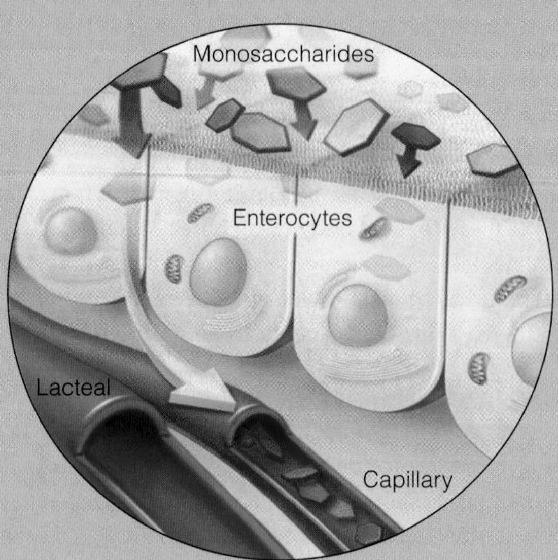

3 Energy Is the Key Function of Carbohydrates

The body uses carbohydrates, specifically glucose, for energy. Surplus glucose is converted to glycogen by glycogenesis, and stored in the liver and muscle. Carbohydrates spare protein from being used for energy and prevent the rapid breakdown of triglycerides (lipolysis).

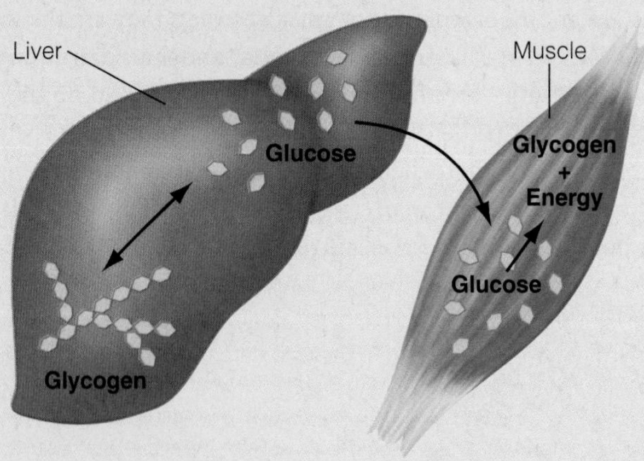

4 Hormones Control Blood Glucose Levels

The pancreatic hormones insulin and glucagon maintain the amount of glucose in the blood at 70 to 110 mg/dl. Insulin directs glucose into cells, which lowers the blood levels. Glucagon breaks down glycogen, a process called glycogenolysis, to raise blood glucose levels.

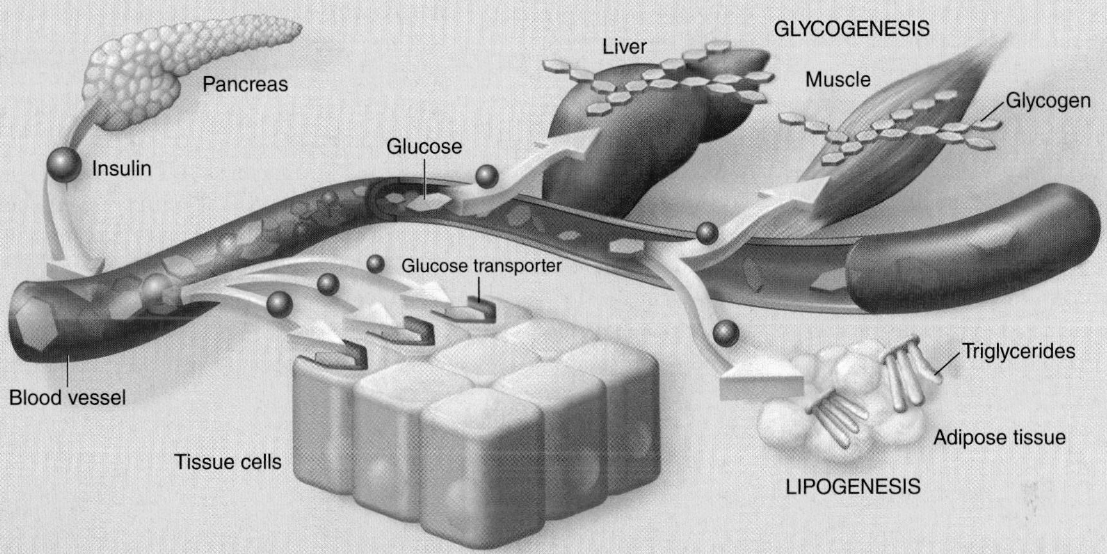

5 Fiber Has Many Health Benefits

Fiber may help lower the risk of developing constipation, diverticulosis, obesity, heart disease, cancer, and diabetes mellitus. Foods high in fiber can add to satiation. Viscous, soluble fibers help lower blood cholesterol levels. Insoluble fibers increase the bulk of the feces and reduce the risk of constipation and diverticulosis.

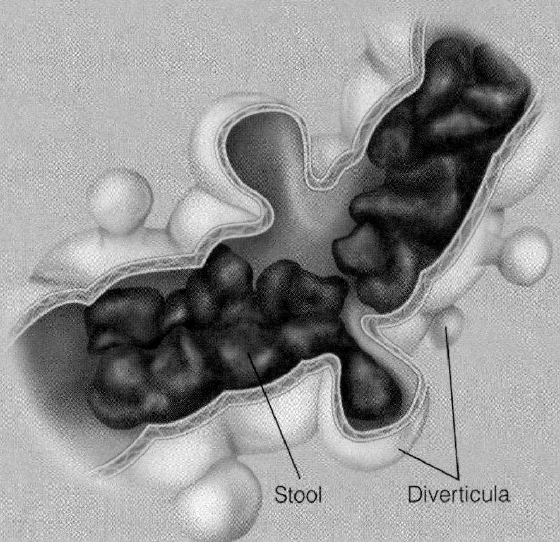

6 Not All Carbohydrates Are Created Equal

The latest Dietary Reference Intakes (DRIs) for carbohydrates recommend that adults and children consume a minimum of 130 grams daily. The AMDR for carbohydrates is 45 to 65 percent of total daily kilocalories.

The DRI for fiber is 14 grams per 1,000 kilocalories per day. A range of 20 to 38 grams per day is considered adequate to reduce the risk of cardiovascular disease in adults. No UL is set for dietary fiber.

Simple carbohydrates are found naturally in fruits, vegetables, and dairy foods or in processed foods. Soft drinks are the major source of dietary added sugar.

Complex carbohydrates are abundant in grains, whole fruits, and vegetables. Grains and potatoes provide starch, while fiber is found in whole grains, whole fruits, vegetables, legumes, nuts, and seeds.

7 Diabetes and Hypoglycemia Differ in Blood Glucose Levels

Individuals develop diabetes because they aren't producing enough insulin (type 1 diabetes) and/or they have developed insulin resistance (type 2 diabetes). Type 1 diabetes is an autoimmune disease and is not as common as type 2 diabetes. In both cases, hyperglycemia is the main characteristic. Poorly managed diabetes increases the likelihood of nerve damage, leg and foot amputations, eye diseases, tooth loss, gum problems, kidney disease, and heart disease. Diabetes can also damage the retina of the eye, which can cause bleeding, cloudy vision, and eventually blindness.

Hypoglycemia, or low blood sugar, can occur in individuals with diabetes, especially if they are taking medication and/or insulin and are not eating properly. People without diabetes may also experience reactive hypoglycemia or fasting hypoglycemia possibly due to over reactive hormones or hormone imbalance. The symptoms include shakiness, dizziness, lightheadedness, hunger, and perspiration.

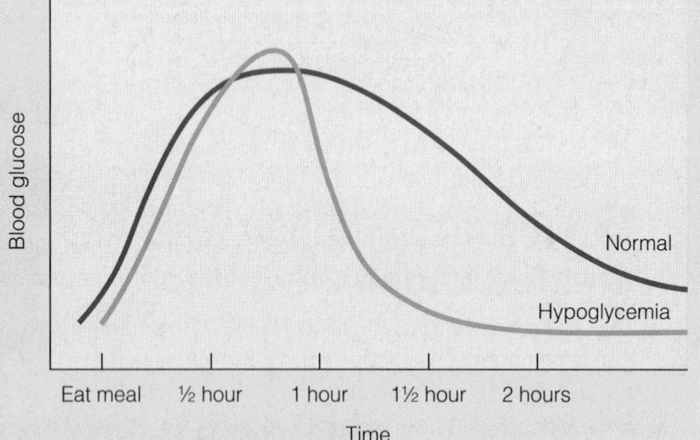

8 There Are Differences among Natural Sugars, Added Sugars, and Sugar Substitutes

Foods with naturally occurring sugars are more nutritious than foods with a lot of added sugar. A diet too high in added sugar may increase the level of body fat and decrease the level of "good" cholesterol in the blood.

Starch and sugary foods, especially sticky foods, can increase the risk of dental caries. Chewing sugarless gum and eating low-fat cheese may help reduce the risk of dental caries.

Polyols, saccharin, aspartame, acesulfame-K, sucralose, rebaudioside A, tagalose, and neotame are sugar substitutes currently deemed safe by the FDA.

Terms to Know

- glucose
- simple
- carbohydrates
- monosaccharides
- disaccharides
- complex carbohydrates
- polysaccharides
- oligosaccharides
- glucose
- fructose
- galactose
- hexose
- maltose
- sucrose
- lactose
- starch
- fiber
- glycogen
- insulin
- glycogenesis
- glucagon
- glycogenolysis
- diabetes
- insulin resistance
- glycosidic bond
- lactose maldigestion
- lactose intolerant
- amylose
- amylopectin
- resistant starch
- cellulose
- soluble fiber
- insoluble fiber
- functional fiber
- salivary amylase
- gluconeogenesis
- ketosis
- epinephrine
- norepinephrine
- cortisol
- diverticulosis
- diverticula
- diverticulitis
- ketoacidosis
- glycemic index
- glycemic load
- hypoglycemia

MasteringNutrition™

Build your knowledge—and confidence!—in the Study Area of MasteringNutrition with a variety of study tools.

Check Your Understanding

1. Sucrose is a
   a. monosaccharide.
   b. disaccharide.
   c. oligosaccharide.
   d. polysaccharide.
2. _____________ is the storage form of glucose in animals, including humans.
   a. Glucagon
   b. Glycogen
   c. Gluconeogenesis
   d. Glucose
3. Three brush border enzymes that hydrolyze carbohydrates in the small intestine are
   a. insulin, glucagon, and cortisone.
   b. salivary amylase, salivary lipase, and gastric lipase.
   c. maltase, lactase, and sucrase.
   d. fiber, starch, and glycogen.
4. The hormone that directs the breakdown of glycogen is
   a. galactose.
   b. glucagon.
   c. insulin.
   d. cortisol.
5. The minimum amount of carbohydrates needed daily is
   a. 75 grams.
   b. 100 grams.
   c. 120 grams.
   d. 130 grams.
6. Which of the following can help someone who is lactose intolerant enjoy dairy products?
   a. drinking Lactaid milk
   b. pouring milk over a cup of bran cereal
   c. enjoying cheese a little at a time, and building up to larger servings
   d. all of the above
7. Reducing consumption of which item would have the biggest impact on decreasing the amount of added sugars that Americans consume?
   a. watermelon
   b. candy
   c. soft drinks
   d. apples
8. Your blood cholesterol level is too high, so you would like to eat additional viscous, soluble high-fiber foods to help lower it. A good choice would be
   a. low-fat milk.
   b. chocolate chip cookies.
   c. hardboiled eggs.
   d. oatmeal.
9. Which of the following can help reduce your risk of type 2 diabetes?
   a. avoiding sugar
   b. eating a high-fiber, plant-based diet
   c. exercising regularly
   d. b and c.
10. An individual who has PKU should not consume which of the following sugar substitutes?
    a. sucralose
    b. acesulfame-K
    c. aspartame
    d. neotame

Answers

1. (b). Sucrose contains the two monosaccharides glucose and fructose, and is therefore a disaccharide. Oligosaccharides and polysaccharides contain more than two sugar units.
2. (b). Glycogen is stored in the liver and muscles and provides a ready-to-use form of glucose for the body. Glucagon is the hormone that directs the release of glucose from the stored glycogen. Gluconeogenesis is the creation of glucose from noncarbohydrate sources.
3. (c). The enzymes maltase, lactase, and sucrase are located in the brush border of the small intestine and hydrolyze the disaccharides maltose, lactose, and sucrose, respectively. Insulin, glucagon, and cortisone are hormones, not enzymes. Salivary amylase is an enzyme in the saliva that begins digesting starch, a form of complex carbohydrate.
4. (b). When the blood glucose level drops too low, glucagon is released from the pancreas to direct the breakdown of glycogen in the liver, which provides glucose to the blood. Insulin is a hormone that directs the uptake of glucose by cells. Cortisol is a stress hormone that stimulates the production of glucose from amino acids. Galactose is a monosaccharide found in dairy foods.
5. (d). The DRI for carbohydrate is to consume at least 130 grams daily. This is the minimum amount needed to supply the glucose that the body, particularly the brain and red blood cells, must have to function effectively.
6. (d). All of these can help improve lactose absorption. The Lactaid milk is pretreated to facilitate the breakdown of the lactose in the milk. Consuming lactose-containing foods with a meal or snack will improve the digestion of lactose. Gradually adding dairy foods to the diet will lessen the symptoms of lactose intolerance.
7. (c). Soft drinks are the number-one source of added sugars in the American diet, so reducing the intake of these sugary beverages would go a long way in reducing the amount of added sugars that Americans consume. Reducing the amount of candy would also help reduce the added sugars in the diet but not as much as soft drinks. Watermelon and apples contain only naturally occurring sugars.
8. (d). Oatmeal is rich in beta-glucan, a viscous fiber that can help lower cholesterol when eaten as part of a heart-healthy diet. Though nutrient dense, the hardboiled eggs and milk do not contain fiber. Cookies won't help lower cholesterol.
9. (d). Eating a high-fiber, plant-based diet and getting regular exercise, both of which will help you maintain a healthy weight, is the best approach, at present, to help reduce the

risk of developing type 2 diabetes. Eating sugar doesn't cause diabetes.

10. (c). Individuals diagnosed with PKU, or phenylketonuria, should not consume aspartame because it contains the amino acid phenylalanine.

Answers to Myths and Misconceptions

1. **False.** All macronutrients are essential for health, including carbohydrate, which is vital for numerous body functions.
2. **False.** In fact, infants have higher amounts of lactase, the enzyme necessary for lactose digestion, due to their initial diet of breast milk. As people get older, however, their bodies produce less of this enzyme, which can result in the condition of lactose intolerance.
3. **False.** Kilocalories, not carbohydrates, are the main culprit behind most weight gain. In fact, some high-fiber carbohydrates can actually help people lose weight.
4. **False.** There is insufficient evidence to suggest that eating sugar causes hyperactivity or other behavioral problems in children.
5. **True.** Whole grains contain more fiber and nutrients than refined grains, which have had much of the grain kernel removed during processing.
6. **True.** Simple carbohydrates, especially added sugars, encourage the growth of acid-producing bacteria in the mouth, which in turn promote dental caries.
7. **False.** There is no scientific evidence to support claims that aspartame causes cancer or other health problems in humans.
8. **True.** The average American consumes about half the amount of fiber that's recommended daily.
9. **True.** Much of the added sugars and excess kilocalories in the American diet come from sodas and other sugary beverages. Consuming more kilocalories than are necessary to meet energy needs causes weight gain.
10. **True.** Being overweight or obese can increase one's chances of developing type 2 diabetes.

Web Resources

- For more on fiber, visit the American Heart Association at www.americanheart.org
- For more on diabetes, visit the FDA's Diabetes Information site at www.fda.gov/diabetes or the American Diabetes Association website at www.diabetes.org
- For more on lactose intolerance, visit the National Institute of Diabetes and Digestive and Kidney Disease (NIDDK) at http://digestive.niddk.nih.gov/ddiseases/pubs/lactoseintolerance

References

1. Painter, J., J. Rah, and Y. Lee. 2002. Comparison of International Food Guide Pictorial Representations. *Journal of the American Dietetic Association* 102:483–489.
2. Bray, G. A., S. J. Nielsen, and B. M. Popkin. 2004. Consumption of High-Fructose Corn Syrup in Beverages May Play a Role in the Epidemic of Obesity. *American Journal of Clinical Nutrition* 79:537–543.
3. *Riegel's Handbook of Industrial Chemistry.* 2003. 10th ed. P. James and A. Kent, eds. New York: Kluwer Academic/Plenum Publishers.
4. Laeng, B., K. C. Berridge, and C. M. Butter. 1993. Pleasantness of a Sweet Taste During Hunger and Satiety: Effects of Gender and "Sweet Tooth." *Appetite* S21:247–254.
5. Zellner, D. A., A. Garriga-Trillo, E. Rohm, S. Centeno, and S. Parker. 1999. Food Liking and Craving: A Cross-Cultural Approach. *Appetite* 33:61–70.
6. Bretz, W. A., P. M. Corby, M. R. Melo, M. Q. Coelho, S. M. Costa, M. Robinson, N. J. Schork, A. Drewnowski, and T. C. Hart. 2006. Heritability Estimates for Dental Caries and Sucrose Sweetness Preference. *Archives of Oral Biology* 51:1156–1160.
7. Higgins, J. A., D. R. Higbee, W. T. Donahoo, I. L. Brown, M. L. Bell, and D. H. Bessesen. 2004. Resistant Starch Consumption Promotes Lipid Oxidation. *Nutrition and Metabolism.* Available at www.nutritionandmetabolism.com/content/pdf/1743-7075-1-8.pdf. Accessed March 2008.
8. Ibid.
9. Robertson, M. D., A. S. Bickerton, A. L. Dennis, H. Vidal, and K. N. Frayn. 2005. Insulin-Sensitizing Effects of Dietary Resistant Starch and Effects on Skeletal Muscle and Adipose Tissue Metabolism. *American Journal of Clinical Nutrition* 82:559–567.
10. Topping, D. L., M. Fukushima, and A. R. Bird. 2003. Resistant Starch as a Prebiotic and a Synbiotic: State of the Art. *Proceedings for the Nutrition Society* 62:171–176.
11. Kay, R. 1982. Dietary Fiber. *Journal of Lipid Research* 23: 221–242.
12. DeVries, J. W. 2003. On Defining Fibre. *Proceedings of the Nutrition Society* 62: 37–43.
13. Institute of Medicine. 2006. *Dietary Reference Intakes: The Essential Guide to Nutrient Requirements.* Washington, DC: The National Academies Press.
14. Osborn, H. and T. Kahn. 2000. *Oligosaccharides: Their Synthesis and Biological Role.* Oxford Chemistry Masters. Oxford, England: Oxford University Press.
15. Queiroz, K. S., A. C. de Oliveira, E. Helbig, S. M. Reis, and F. Carraro. 2002. Soaking the Common Bean in a Domestic Preparation Reduced the Contents of Raffinose-Type Oligosaccharides but Did Not Interfere with Nutritive Value. *Journal of Nutritional Science and Vitaminology* 48:283–289.
16. Boehm, G. and B. Stahl. 2007. Oligosaccharides from Milk. *Journal of Nutrition* 137:847S–849S.
17. National Digestive Diseases Information Clearinghouse. 2000. *Constipation.* Available at http://digestive.niddk.nih.gov/ddiseases/pubs/constipation. Accessed February 2012.
18. National Digestive Diseases Information Clearinghouse. 2002. *Diverticulosis and Diverticulitis.* Available at http://digestive.niddk.nih.gov/ddiseases/pubs/diverticulosis/index.htm. Accessed February 2012.
19. Rimm, E., A. Ascherio, E. Giovannucci, D. Spiegelman, M. Stampfer, and W. Willett. 1996. Vegetable, Fruit, and Cereal Fiber Intake and Risk of Coronary Heart Disease among Men. *Journal of the American Medical Association* 275:447–451.
20. Pietinen, P., E. Rimm, P. Korhonen, A. Hartman, W. Willet, D. Albanes, and J. Virtamo. 1996. Intake of Dietary Fiber and Risk of Coronary Heart Disease in a Cohort of Finnish Men: The Alpha-Tocopherol, Beta-Carotene Cancer Prevention Study. *Circulation* 94:2720–2727.
21. Wolk, A., J. Manson, M. Stampfer, G. Colditz, F. Hu, F. Speizer, C. Hennekens, and W. Willett. 1999. Long-Term Intake of Dietary Fiber and Decreased Risk of Coronary Heart Disease among Women. *Journal of the American Medical Association* 281:1998–2004.
22. Kocher, J., L. Djousse, and J. M. Gaziano. 2007. Breakfast Cereals and Risk of Type 2

Chapter Objectives

After reading this chapter, you will be able to:

1. Explain the differences in the structure of triglycerides, phospholipids, and cholesterol.
2. Describe how lipids are digested, absorbed, and transported in the body.
3. Describe the functions of lipids in the body.
4. Define the dietary recommendations for total fat, the essential fatty acids, cholesterol, and *trans* fat.
5. Identify the major food sources of the different types of fats, including the essential fatty acids, saturated fats, and *trans* fats.
6. Describe the development of atherosclerosis, including its role in the risk of heart disease, and explain how lifestyle factors can affect the risk of heart disease.

1. Cholesterol should be consumed daily to meet the body's needs. T/F
2. A healthy diet is fat free. T/F
3. Only commercially made fried foods and snack items contain *trans* fats. T/F
4. Saturated fat is a major dietary factor for elevated blood cholesterol. T/F
5. You can eat as many fat-free cookies as you want without gaining weight. T/F
6. A high level of HDL cholesterol in the blood is considered heart healthy. T/F
7. Butter is a healthier choice than margarine. T/F
8. Nuts are high in cholesterol. T/F
9. Taking fish oil supplements is the best way to consume adequate omega-3 fatty acids. T/F
10. Dietary LDL cholesterol is unhealthy for the heart. T/F

See page 204 for answers to these Myths and Misconceptions.

When you go shopping, what is on your grocery list? If you're like many Americans, you probably have the best intentions of filling your grocery cart with low-fat, nonfat, or cholesterol-free items to eat a more healthful diet. Even just saying the words *fat* or *cholesterol* brings up negative images of foods that we should avoid. The truth is, a small amount of dietary fat is essential to the body.

In this chapter, we will discuss the structure and functions of the different types of lipids, how they are handled in the body, and the amounts of each that should be consumed in a healthy diet. We will also explore the role of high-fat foods in the development of cardiovascular disease and other health conditions.

What Are Lipids and Why Are They Important?

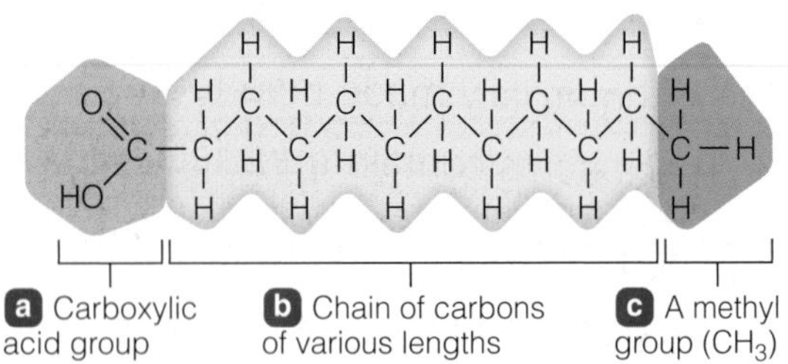

▲ **Figure 5.1 Chemical Structure of a Fatty Acid**
The basic chemical structure of a fatty acid is composed of three different parts.

When you think of the word **lipid,** you may think it's a synonym for fat. But that's only partly correct. *Lipo* means *fatty,* and lipids actually refer to a category of compounds that includes **triglycerides** (*fats* and *oils*), **phospholipids,** and **sterols.** These compounds all contain carbon, oxygen, and hydrogen, and they are all **hydrophobic** (*hydro* = water, *phobic* = fearing). In other words, they don't dissolve in water. If you were to drop lipids like butter or olive oil into a glass of water, you would see these substances rise to the top and sit on the water's surface. This repelling of water allows lipids to play a unique role in foods and in the body.

Whereas the popular press often portrays lipids as bad or unhealthy, the reality is that lipids serve several basic functions for maintaining health. In the body, lipids store and provide energy, provide insulation, help manufacture steroids and bile, and play a key role in transporting fat-soluble nutrients in the blood. They are also used to manufacture the major sex hormones, and one type of lipid is key to the structure of cell membranes.

We'll begin the discussion of lipids by introducing the chemical structure of the various forms, starting with fatty acids, the building blocks, and continuing with triglycerides, phospholipids, and sterols.

lipid A category of carbon, hydrogen, and oxygen compounds that are insoluble in water.

triglycerides A type of lipid commonly found in foods and the body; also known as fat. Triglycerides consist of three fatty acids attached to a glycerol backbone.

phospholipids A category of lipids that consist of two fatty acids and a phosphorus group attached to a glycerol backbone. Lecithin is an example of a phospholipid found in food and in the body.

sterols A category of lipids that contains four connecting rings of carbon and hydrogen. Cholesterol is the most common sterol.

hydrophobic "Water fearing." In nutrition, the term refers to compounds that are not soluble in water.

fatty acid The most basic unit of triglycerides and phospholipids; fatty acids consist of even numbers of carbon chains ranging from two to 80 carbons in length.

short-chain fatty acid A fatty acid with a chain of two to four carbons.

medium-chain fatty acids Fatty acids with a chain of six to 10 carbons.

long-chain fatty acids Fatty acids with a chain of 12 carbons or more.

Many Lipids Are Comprised of Fatty Acids

Triglycerides and phospholipids are built from a basic unit called a **fatty acid.** All fatty acids (**Figure 5.1**) are organic compounds that consist of chains of carbon and hydrogen atoms, with an acid group (called a carboxyl group, abbreviated as COOH) at one end, called the alpha end, and a methyl group (CH_3) on the other end, called the omega end. The carboxyl group consists of a carbon atom attached with a double bond to an oxygen atom and single bonded to a hydroxyl group (OH). The ratio of carbon and hydrogen to oxygen accounts for the higher number of kilocalories in fat (9 kilocalories per gram) than in carbohydrates and proteins (4 kilocalories per gram).

There are over 20 different fatty acids. They vary in structure by the length of the carbon chain, degree of saturation, and shape.

Length of Fatty Acids

The carbon chains of most naturally occurring dietary fatty acids contain two to 80 carbons (usually in even numbers), with the most common fatty acids containing 12 to 24 carbons. If the fatty acid is two to four carbons long, it is a **short-chain fatty acid.** The shortest fatty acid, acetic acid, contains two carbons and is illustrated in **Figure 5.2a**. Fatty acids with six to 10 carbons are called **medium-chain fatty acids,** and those with 12 or more carbons are called **long-chain fatty acids**. Long-chain fatty acids are the most common type of fatty acid found in foods.

The chain length of fatty acids is important because it affects the way we digest, absorb, and metabolize fatty acids. For example, long-chain fatty acids take longer

a Acetic acid (C2:0)

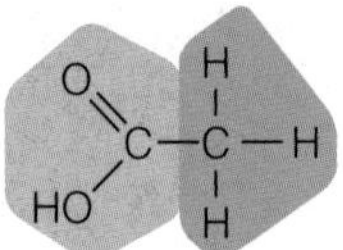

b Palmitic acid, a saturated fatty acid (C14:0)

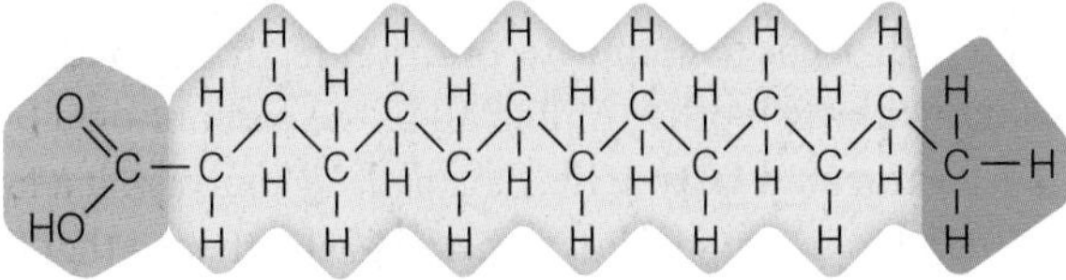

c Oleic acid, a monounsaturated fatty acid (C18:1)

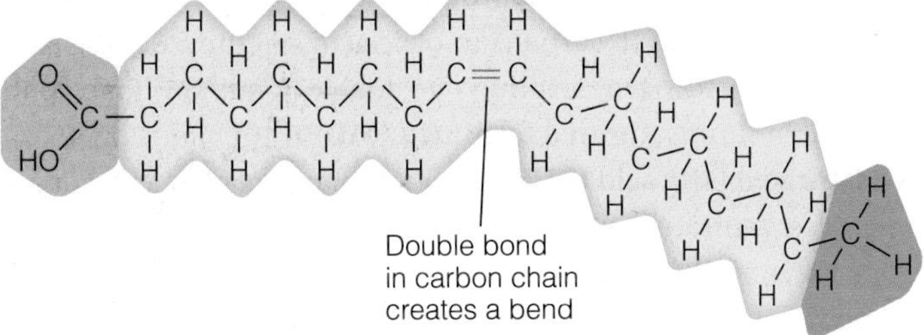

d Linoleic acid, a polyunsaturated fatty acid (C18:2)

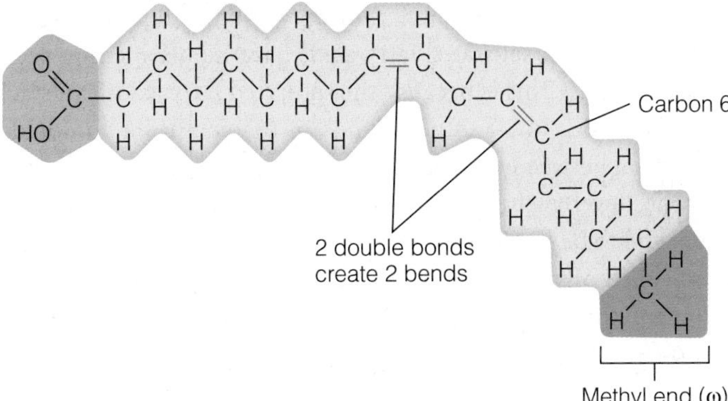

e Alpha-linolenic acid, a polyunsaturated, omega-3 fatty acid (C18:3)

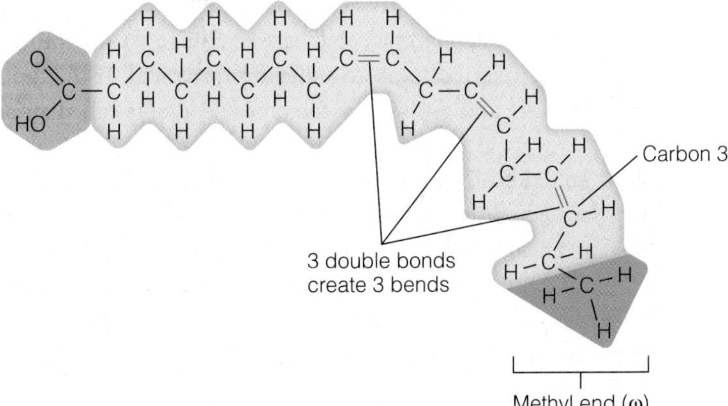

▲ **Figure 5.2 Fatty Acids Vary by Length, Degree of Saturation, and Shape**
Fatty acids differ by the number of carbons in the chain, whether or not the chain contains any double bonds (the saturation of the fatty acid), and the shape of the carbon chains on either side of the double bonds.

Due to their chemical properties, fats and oils don't dissolve in water.

a Saturated fatty acids

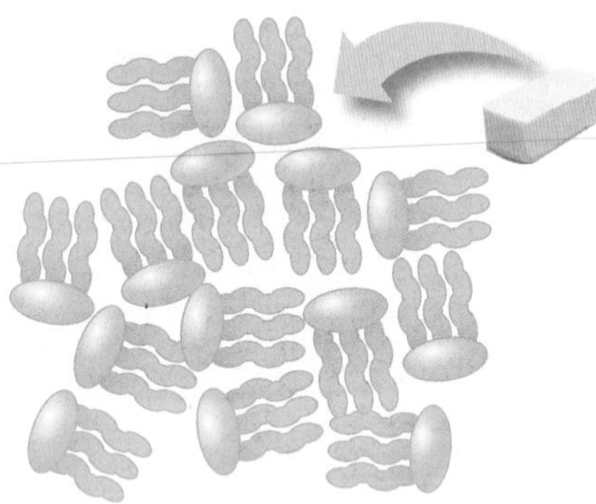

b Unsaturated fatty acids

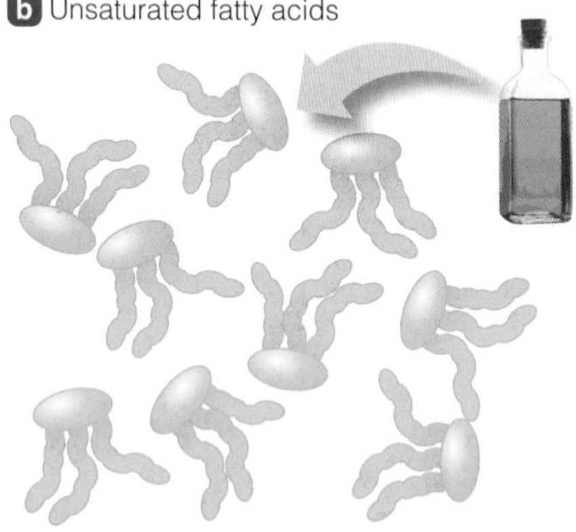

▲ **Figure 5.3 Saturated and Unsaturated Fatty Acids Help Shape Foods**
The straight chains of saturated fatty acids pack tightly together and are solid at room temperature. The double bonds in unsaturated fatty acids cause kinks in their shape and prevent them from packing tightly together, so they tend to be liquid at room temperature.

saturated fatty acid A fatty acid in which all of the carbons are bound with hydrogen.

unsaturated fatty acid A fatty acid in which there are one or more double bonds between carbons.

monounsaturated fatty acid (MUFA) A fatty acid that has one double bond.

polyunsaturated fatty acid (PUFA) A fatty acid with two or more double bonds.

oils Fats that are liquid at room temperature.

omega-3 fatty acid A family of polyunsaturated fatty acids with the first double bond located at the third carbon from the omega end.

omega-6 fatty acid A family of polyunsaturated fatty acids with the first double bond located at the sixth carbon from the omega end.

linoleic acid A polyunsaturated essential fatty acid; part of the omega-6 fatty acid family.

to digest and absorb than do short- or medium-chain fatty acids. Shorter chain fatty acids are more water soluble than those fatty acids with more carbons. The length of the chain changes the way the body transports the fatty acids. The details of fat digestion will be covered later in the chapter.

Saturation of Fatty Acids

The degree of saturation of a fatty acid is determined by whether the carbons are held together by a double or a single bond. Every carbon molecule has four bonds, and if there are not enough hydrogens to complete, or *saturate*, those bonds, then the carbons form a double bond with each other. When all of the carbons on a fatty acid are bound with hydrogen, a **saturated fatty acid** is formed. In contrast, if a fatty acid has carbons that are not bound to hydrogen, but rather to each other so that there are one or more double bonds, the structure is called an **unsaturated fatty acid.**

Palmitic acid (Figure 5.2b) is an example of a saturated fatty acid, because all of its 14 carbons are bound with hydrogen and none are double bound to each other. In contrast, two of the 18 carbons in oleic acid (Figure 5.2c) are paired with each other rather than hydrogen, forming one double bond. This lone double bond makes oleic acid a **monounsaturated fatty acid (MUFA)** (*mono* = one).

A **polyunsaturated fatty acid (PUFA)** (*poly* = many) contains two or more double bonds, and is less saturated with hydrogen. Linoleic acid, shown in Figure 5.2d, is an example of a polyunsaturated fatty acid.

Double bonds cause a kink in the chain of the fatty acid, which prevents fatty acids from packing together tightly. The length of the fatty acid chain and the presence of double bonds between carbons will also determine the melting point of a fat, or the temperature at which it changes from a solid to liquid (**Figure 5.3**). In general, straight, long-chain saturated fatty acids have higher melting points than do unsaturated fatty acids. This is because the saturated fatty acids can stack closer together and interact with one another. Bends in the chain due to double bonds reduce the interaction between the molecules and produce a fatty acid with a lower melting point. The lower melting points of shorter chain and unsaturated fatty acids mean they tend to be liquid at room temperature. Fats that are liquid at room temperature are called **oils.** The monounsaturated fatty acid oleic acid is found in olive oil, and the polyunsaturated fatty acids, linoleic acid and alpha-linolenic acid, are found in soybean oil.

Location of the Double Bond

The location of the first double bond from the methyl (or *omega*) end of the fatty acid chain also affects the properties of a fatty acid (see Figure 5.2d and 5.2e). If the first double bond in a polyunsaturated fat is located between the third and fourth carbon from the omega end, it is referred to as an **omega-3 fatty acid.** If the first double bond is between carbons six and seven from the omega end, it is called an **omega-6 fatty acid.**

Linoleic acid is an omega-6 fatty acid. It has 18 carbons with two double bonds, the first of which is located on the sixth carbon from the omega end. **Alpha-linolenic acid** is an omega-3 fatty acid, and is the same length as the omega-6 (18 carbons) but has three double bonds, with the first double bond on carbon three from the omega end. These two fatty acids are called **essential fatty acids** because they must be obtained from foods. Later in the chapter we will discuss the health benefits of omega fatty acids.

Shape of Fatty Acids

Unsaturated fatty acids form two different shapes based on the position of the hydrogen atoms around the double bond. If the hydrogen atoms are on the same side of the double bond, as illustrated in **Figure 5.4**, the fatty acid has a ***cis*** configuration.

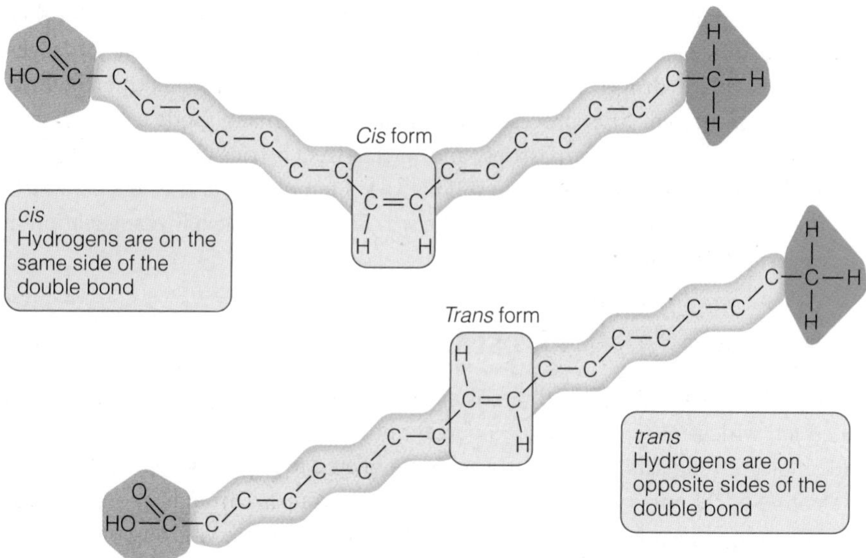

▲ **Figure 5.4 The *Cis* and *Trans* Configurations of Unsaturated Fatty Acids**

If the hydrogen atoms are on opposite sides of the double bond, it is a ***trans*** configuration.

Rancidity

Foods that contain unsaturated fatty acids can spoil and develop a bitter, pungent smell or taste when exposed to oxygen, a condition called **rancidity.** The rancidity reaction forms new compounds that cause the typical rancid taste and smell. The double bonds of an unsaturated fatty acid are the most reactive sites on the fatty acid chain. During the first step, a H^+ is extracted from the unstable fatty acid to form a free radical, as illustrated in **Figure 5.5**. Oxygen reacts with the unstable fatty acid, producing even more compounds in the chain reaction. At some point during this process, free radicals themselves combine to form compounds that eventually halt the reaction.

Because double bonds are less stable than single bonds, foods that contain unsaturated fatty acids become rancid faster than foods that contain saturated fatty acids. Similarly, polyunsaturated fatty acids are more susceptible to rancidity than monounsaturated fatty acids because they have more double bonds. Flax oil, which is rich in polyunsaturated fatty acids, is more susceptible to oxidation than corn oil, which contains more saturated and monounsaturated fatty acids. Saturated fatty acids have no double bonds, and are thus much less susceptible to oxidation.

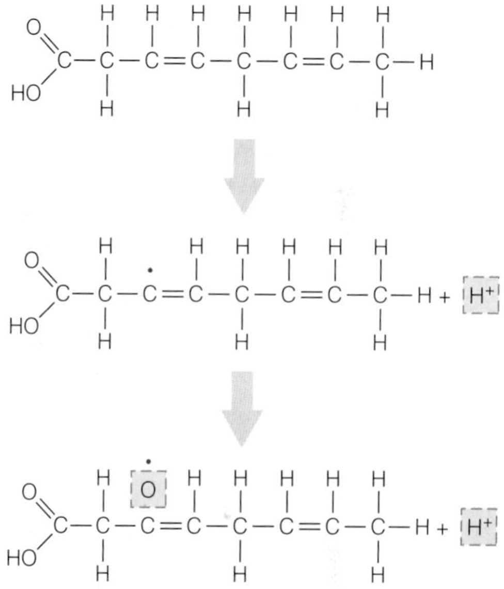

▲ **Figure 5.5 Rancidity Reaction of a Fatty Acid**
When fatty acids become oxidized, the chemical structure is altered, creating the off smell and flavors characteristic of rancid food.

Stability of Fatty Acids

Food manufacturers have tested various ways to reduce rancidity, including adding antioxidants to hinder the oxidation process. Antioxidants bond with the free radicals (more on antioxidants in Chapter 9), thereby preventing oxygen from attacking the double bonds. Vitamins such as C and E are natural antioxidants but lack the shelf life of synthetic antioxidants such as butylated hydroxyanisole (BHA) and butylated hydroxytoluene (BHT).

Rancidity can also be reduced by limiting the food's exposure to oxygen, heat, and light. Storing oils and fats in airtight containers, in a cool, dry, and dark location will lessen the formation of free radicals, which contribute to the rancidity of foods.

alpha-linolenic acid A polyunsaturated essential fatty acid; part of the omega-3 fatty acid family.

essential fatty acids The two polyunsaturated fatty acids that the body cannot make and therefore must be eaten in foods: linoleic acid and alpha-linolenic acid.

cis The configuration of a fatty acid in which the carbon chains on each side of the double bond are on the same side.

trans The configuration of a fatty acid in which the carbon chains are on opposite sides of the double bond.

rancidity The spoiling of fats through oxidation.

Another method used to stabilize unsaturated fatty acids is a process called **hydrogenation.** Hydrogenation involves heating oil and exposing it to hydrogen gas, which adds hydrogen to the carbons in the double bonds, making the fatty acids more saturated. This process gives crackers and snack foods a longer shelf life, improves the texture of pastries, and makes french fries crisper. Hydrogenation makes liquid oils become more solid at room temperature. It is less expensive and provides a "mouthfeel" like butter. We will discuss the use of hydrogenation in more detail later in the chapter.

Triglycerides Are the Most Common Lipid

The most common lipid in both foods and the body is the triglyceride, commonly called *fat*, which makes up about 95 percent of the lipids found in food. A triglyceride molecule consists of three fatty acids connected to a **glycerol** (*glyc* = sweet, *ol* = alcohol) backbone made of three alcohol (OH) groups. Through a condensation reaction, a hydrogen from the glycerol bonds with the hydroxyl group (OH) of the fatty acid, attaches the fatty acid to the glycerol (**Figure 5.6**). A molecule of water is released in the process. A variety of fatty acids can bond with the same glycerol backbone, so a triglyceride usually contains a mixture of fatty acids. For example,

hydrogenation Adding hydrogen to an unsaturated fatty acid to make it more saturated and solid at room temperature.

glycerol The three-carbon backbone of a triglyceride.

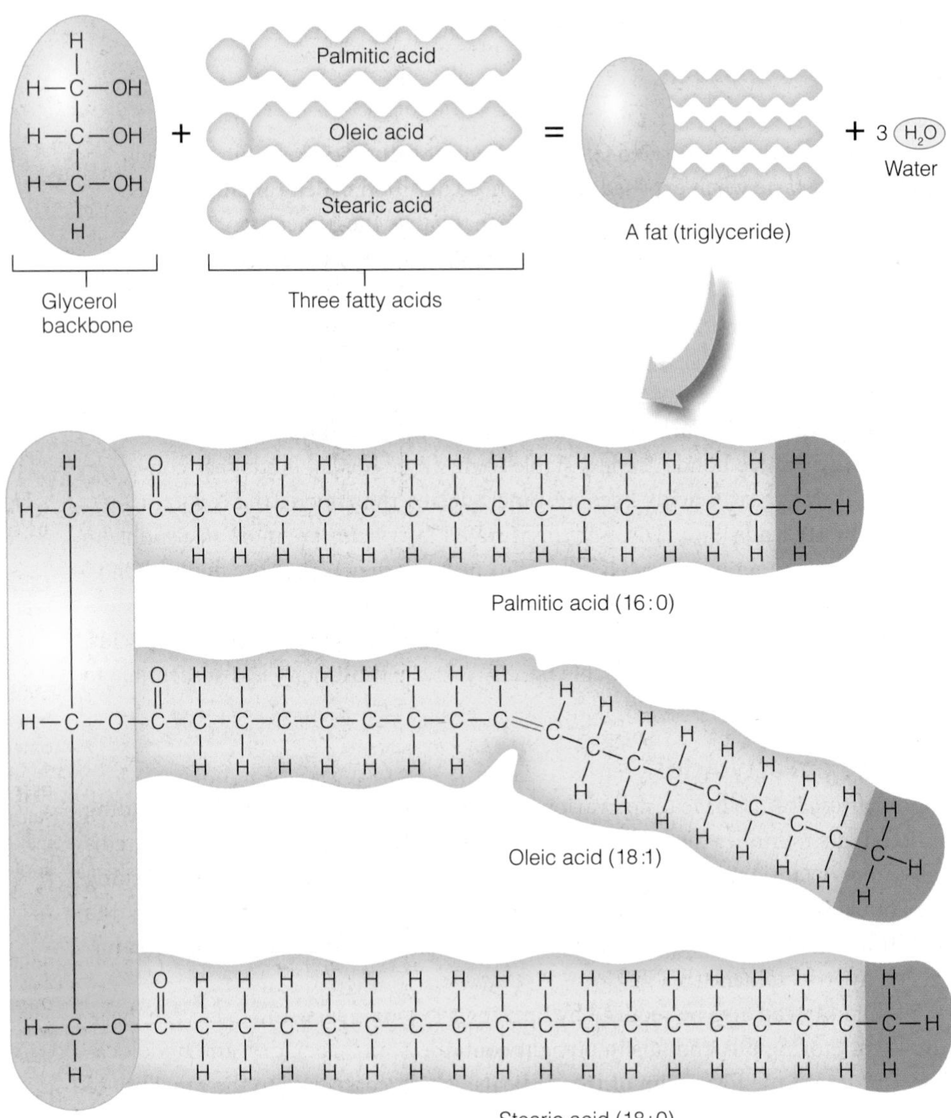

▸ **Figure 5.6 Structure of a Triglyceride**
A triglyceride is formed when three fatty acids attach to a glycerol backbone with a condensation reaction.

canola oil is not just composed of polyunsaturated fatty acids; there are also small amounts of saturated and monounsaturated fats present.

Triglycerides perform a variety of functions in food, including adding flaky texture to pie crusts and other baked goods, and making meat tender. Triglycerides are also important in food processing, particularly when it comes to preserving freshness.

In the body, triglycerides are carried through the blood and stored in the adipose tissue to provide a major source of available energy. Higher levels of triglycerides in the blood are a risk factor associated with heart disease. This topic will be covered later in the chapter.

Phospholipids Differ from Triglycerides

Like triglycerides, phospholipids contain a glycerol backbone, but instead of three fatty acids, the glycerol is linked to two fatty acids, a phosphate group, and different nitrogen-containing compounds such as choline (**Figure 5.7**). The glycerol backbone and phosphorus group form a polar head, which means it attracts charged particles, such as water. The fatty acid–containing tail is nonpolar and therefore soluble with other nonpolar molecules, such as fats. In other words, one end of the phospholipid is hydrophilic (*philic* = loving) and the other end is hydrophobic.

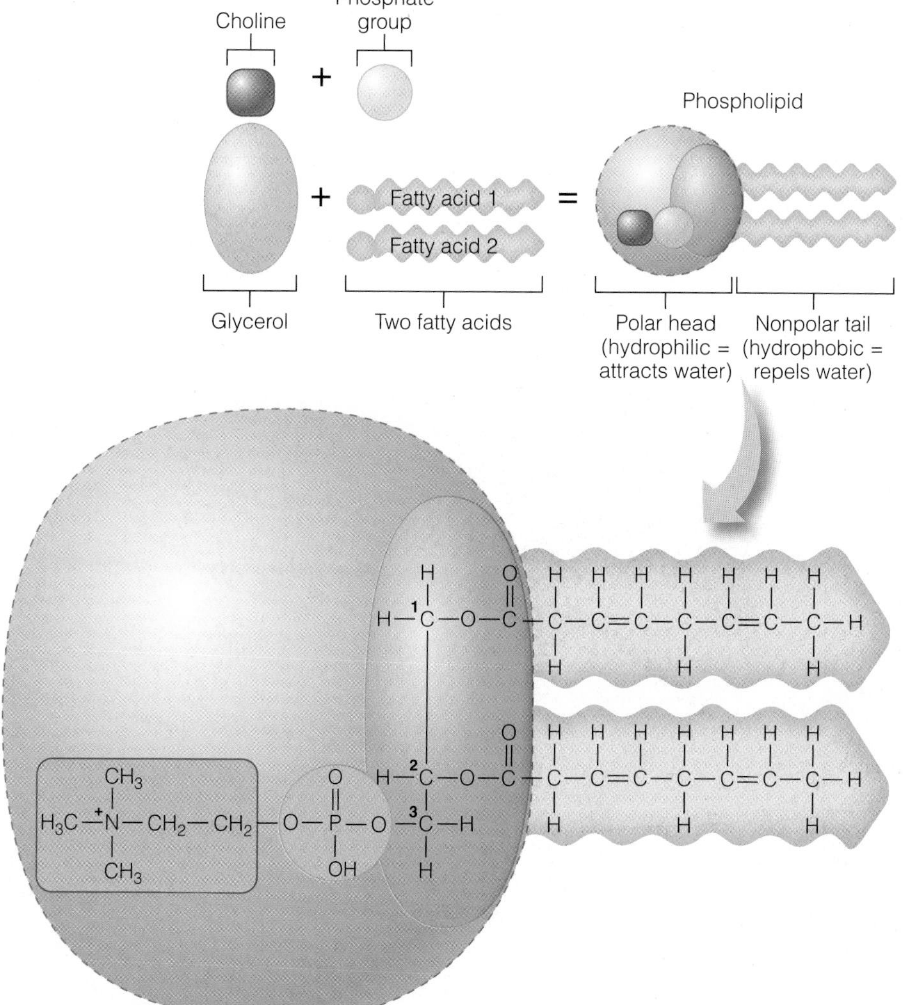

◂ **Figure 5.7 Phospholipids**
Phospholipids, such as the lecithin shown here, are similar in structure to triglycerides, but they have only two fatty acids and a phosphate group connected to the glycerol backbone. This configuration allows phospholipids to be attracted to both water and fat.

Phospholipids make up the phospholipid bilayer in cell membranes. Their hydrophilic polar heads are attracted to the watery fluids both outside and inside of the cells, and their hydrophobic tails line up with each other in the center, creating a phospholipid barrier that surrounds the cell (**Figure 5.8**). This structure of the cell membrane allows certain substances, such as water, to enter the cell but keeps others, like protein, from leaking out. Visualize this phospholipid layer as similar to a picket fence, protecting the cells as a gated fence would surround and protect a piece of property.

lecithin A phospholipid made in the body that is integral in the structure of cell membranes; also known as phosphatidylcholine.

choline A member of the B vitamin family that is a component of the phospholipid lecithin.

emulsifier A compound that keeps two incompatible substances, such as oil and water, mixed together.

cholesterol A common sterol found in animal products and made in the liver from saturated fatty acids; cholesterol is found in cell membranes and is used to make a variety of hormones.

phytosterols Naturally occurring sterols found in plants.

phytostanols A type of plant sterol similar in structure to cholesterol.

The major phospholipid in cell membranes is **lecithin.** As shown in Figure 5.8, lecithin, also called phosphatidylcholine, contains a **choline** group attached to the phosphate on the third carbon of the glycerol backbone. The fatty acids and the phosphate and choline give the phospholipid both fat-soluble and water-soluble properties, which allow it to shuttle other lipids across the cell membrane.

Even though lecithin plays an important role in the body, it does not need to be consumed in foods or in supplements. The liver is able to synthesize all phospholipids, including lecithin. In fact, dietary lecithin is digested in the GI tract, which means it does not reach the cell membranes intact.

Despite their frequent mention in the popular press, lecithin supplements, which are often marketed as a miracle solution for weight loss, fat metabolism, cardiovascular health, exercise performance, and arthritis relief, have not been scientifically proven to be effective in weight loss or improving health. In addition, the fatty acids present in dietary phospholipids (which, like all lipids, contain 9 kilocalories per gram) can add unwanted kilocalories.

▸ Figure 5.8 The Role of Phospholipids and Cholesterol in Cell Membranes
The two-layer cell membrane surrounding the cell is comprised of a polar head and nonpolar tail. Cholesterol keeps the phospholipids separate.

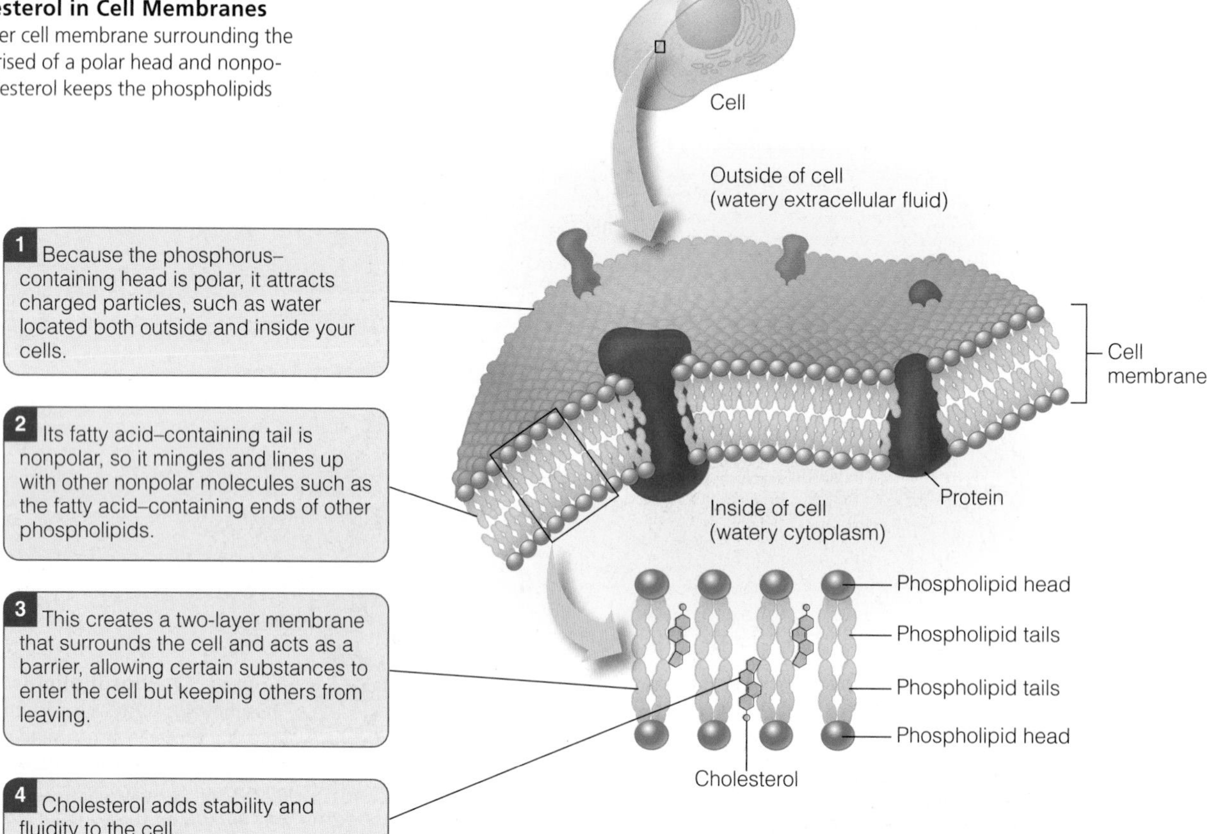
Cell
Outside of cell
(watery extracellular fluid)
1 Because the phosphorus-containing head is polar, it attracts charged particles, such as water located both outside and inside your cells.
Cell membrane
2 Its fatty acid–containing tail is nonpolar, so it mingles and lines up with other nonpolar molecules such as the fatty acid–containing ends of other phospholipids.
Protein
Inside of cell
(watery cytoplasm)
Phospholipid head
Phospholipid tails
3 This creates a two-layer membrane that surrounds the cell and acts as a barrier, allowing certain substances to enter the cell but keeping others from leaving.
Phospholipid tails
Phospholipid head
Cholesterol
4 Cholesterol adds stability and fluidity to the cell.

Because of its unique water- and fat-loving attributes, lecithin is used in many foods as an **emulsifier,** which helps keep incompatible substances, such as water and oil, mixed together. An emulsifier is sometimes added to commercially made salad dressings to prevent the fat from separating and rising to the top of the dressing (**Figure 5.9**). The emulsifier's nonpolar, fat-attracting tail surrounds the droplets of fat, which orients the polar, water-attracting head toward the watery solution of the dressing. This keeps the fat droplet suspended and allows the water and the oil to stay blended together.

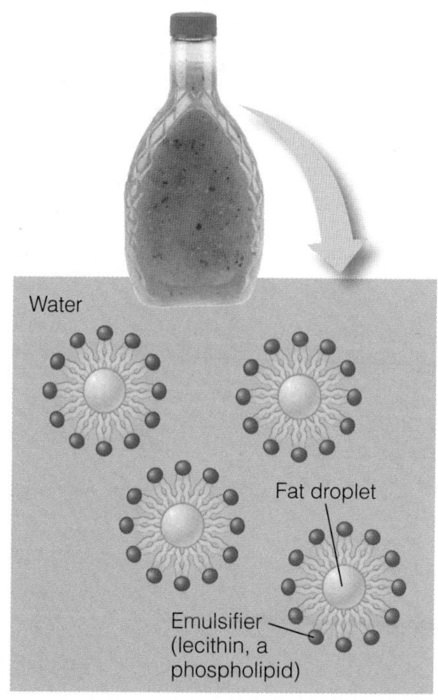

▲ **Figure 5.9 Keeping a Salad Dressing Blended**
Emulsifiers are often added to salad dressing to keep the oil part of the dressing blended in the watery solution. When a salad dressing does separate, it is usually because it doesn't contain an emulsifier.

Sterols Are More Complex than Triglycerides

Sterols are a much more complex molecule than phospholipids or triglycerides. They do not contain glycerol or fatty acids, but rather are composed mainly of four connecting rings of carbon and hydrogen (**Figure 5.10**). Unlike the other lipids, sterols do not provide energy.

The best-known sterol, **cholesterol,** is found in every cell in the body. It plays an important role as a structural component in cell membranes by improving cell fluidity. In cell membranes, cholesterol is interwoven with phospholipids to provide integrity to the cells (refer again to Figure 5.8). The unique shape of cholesterol makes the outer surface of the cell membrane less soluble to very small molecules that could pass too easily across the cell membrane. Without cholesterol, the membrane would lack firmness; the cells in the body would need a cell wall similar to that in plants to maintain their shape. Cholesterol also helps keep phospholipids separate from each other so that the tails or fatty acid chains of the phospholipids don't crystallize. In this way, cholesterol improves cell fluidity.

Cholesterol is also the precursor of some very important compounds. A key role of cholesterol is to serve as the starting material in the synthesis of steroid hormones, including the sex hormones estrogen and testosterone, and the adrenal corticoids such as cortisol and aldosterone. Cholesterol is used by the liver to manufacture bile (**Figure 5.11**), and a type of cholesterol in the skin is converted to a previtamin D by the ultraviolet rays of the sun.

The majority of sterols found in plants are **phytosterols** and **phytostanols,** which are similar in structure to cholesterol. While there are over 60 different types of phytosterols and phytostanols found in plants, the most common are sistanol, campesterol, and stigmasterol. Sitostanol and campestanol are more saturated than other plant sterols.

Figure 5.12 summarizes the three types of lipids.

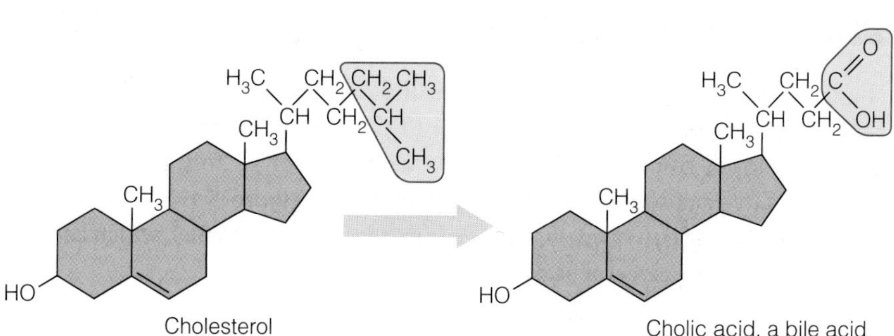

▲ **Figure 5.11 Bile Is Made from Cholesterol in the Liver**
Bile is made in the liver from cholesterol and stored in the gallbladder. It contains water, electrolytes, and a variety of *bile acids.* Cholic acid is one of the primary bile acids utilized for fat digestion.

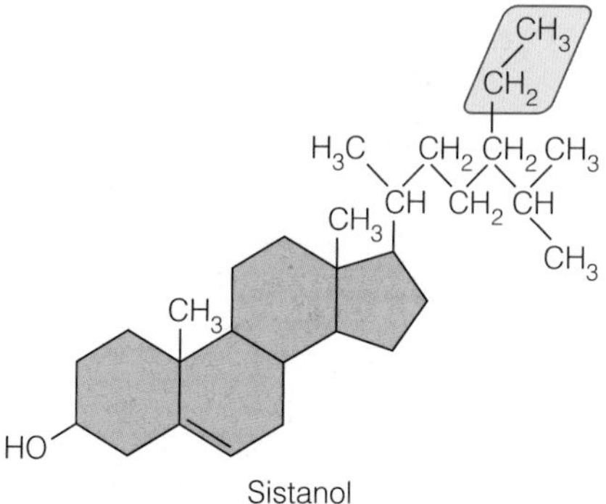

▲ **Figure 5.10 Structure of a Sterol**
Sterols have a carbon ring configuration with hydrogens and an oxygen attached. Cholesterol is the best-known sterol found in animal products. Sistanol is a common sterol found in plants.

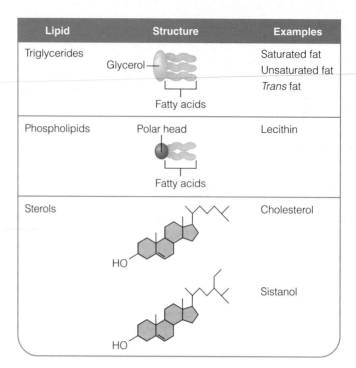

Lipid	Structure	Examples
Triglycerides	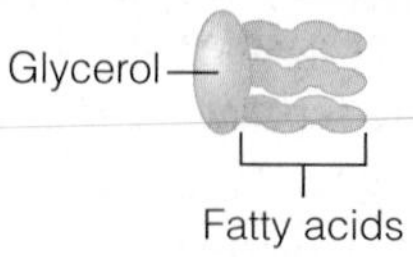 Glycerol; Fatty acids	Saturated fat Unsaturated fat *Trans* fat
Phospholipids	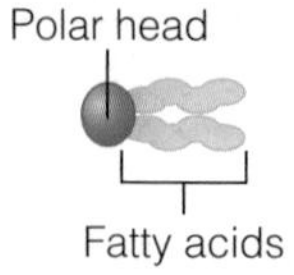 Polar head; Fatty acids	Lecithin
Sterols	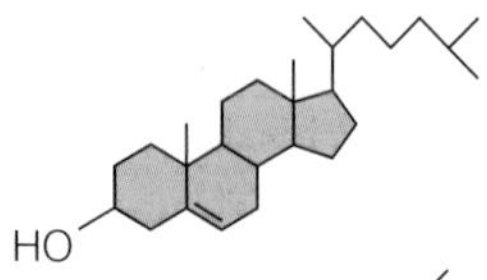 HO	Cholesterol
	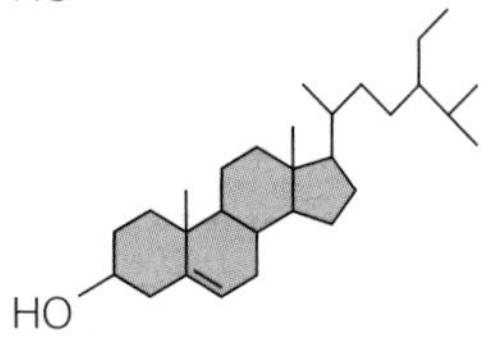 HO	Sistanol

▲ **Figure 5.12 Three Types of Lipids**
The three types of lipids vary in structure. Triglycerides and phospholipids are built from fatty acids, while sterols are composed of carbon rings.

THE TAKE-HOME MESSAGE Lipids are hydrophobic compounds made up of carbon, hydrogen, and oxygen. The three types of lipids are triglycerides, phospholipids, and sterols. Lipids provide and store energy for the body, transport fat-soluble nutrients, provide insulation, and are used to synthesize bile, sex hormones, and cell membranes. Fatty acids, which consist of a carbon and hydrogen chain, a carboxylic acid, and a methyl group, are the basic structural units of triglycerides and phospholipids. Fatty acids differ in chain length, degree of saturation, and shape. Triglycerides consist of three fatty acids attached to a glycerol backbone by condensation reactions. Triglycerides are found in blood, stored in the adipose tissue, and are a major source of energy to the body. Phospholipids are made of two fatty acids and a phosphate group attached to a glycerol backbone. Phospholipids are an important part of the structure of cell membranes. Sterols are made up of four connected rings of carbon and hydrogen. Sterols do not provide energy.

What Happens to the Lipids You Eat?

The lipids found in food are primarily in the form of fat (triglycerides) and, to a lesser extent, phospholipids and sterols. During the digestion of fat, the fatty acids are removed from the glycerol backbone by hydrolysis to form a combination of free fatty acids, glycerol, and monoglycerides (**Figure 5.13**). This action is accomplished by a group of enzymes called **lipases** (*-ase* = enzyme), which act on a specific site along the glycerol backbone.

Fat Digestion Begins in the Mouth and Stomach

The digestion of fat begins in the mouth as the warmth of the body begins to melt it. As chewing continues and food mixes with saliva, lingual lipase (secreted from the glands located at the base of the tongue) begins to hydrolyze the medium-chain fatty

lipases A group of lipid-digesting enzymes.

Focus Figure 5.13 Lipid Digestion and Absorption

Most lipid digestion occurs in the small intestine with the aid of bile and lipase enzymes. The absorbed lipids are transported via chylomicrons into the lymphatic system.

ORGANS OF THE GI TRACT

MOUTH

Mastication begins the mechanical digestion of food. Solid fat melts with the warmth of the body. Lingual lipase in the saliva begins the chemical digestion of triglycerides.

STOMACH

Peristalsis mixes and churns the fat-containing food with gastric juices. Gastric lipase hydrolyzes some triglycerides, creating diglycerides and free fatty acids. In infants, lingual lipase also continues hydrolyzing triglycerides in the stomach.

SMALL INTESTINE

Bile secreted from the gallbladder through the common bile duct into the duodenum emulsifies fat into smaller globules.

Pancreatic lipase hydrolyzes triglycerides into monoglycerides, glycerol, and free fatty acids.

Phospholipases hydrolyze phospholipids.

The products of lipid hydrolysis are packaged into micelles for transport to enterocytes of the intestinal wall.

As they are absorbed into enterocytes, micelles separate into their component parts. Short-chain fatty acids enter the bloodstream directly. Long-chain fatty acids, cholesterol, phospholipids, and other remnants are repackaged into chylomicrons for transport into the lymphatic system.

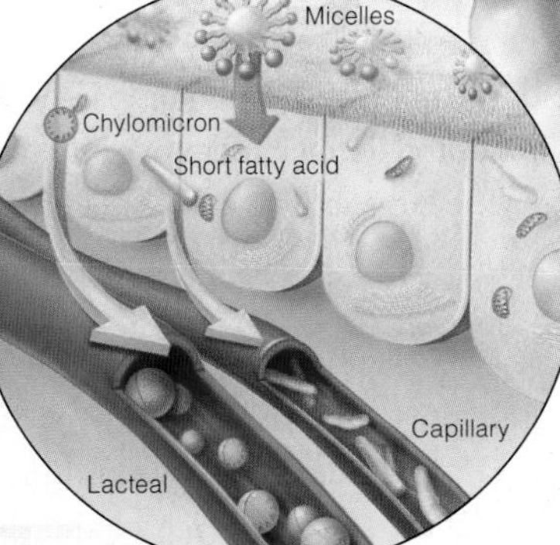

LARGE INTESTINE

Any lipids not digested and absorbed in the small intestine bind to fiber and move into the large intestine to be eliminated in the feces.

ACCESSORY ORGANS

SALIVARY GLANDS

Produce saliva.

LIVER

Produces bile, which is stored in the gallbladder.

GALLBLADDER

Upon stimulation by CCK, releases bile into the duodenum through the common bile duct.

PANCREAS

Produces pancreatic lipase and phospholipases, which are secreted into the small intestine via the pancreatic duct.

acids. Lingual lipase is structurally different from the other lipases found in the body, and it can hydrolyze fatty acids from any of the three carbons of the glycerol molecule. Lingual lipase travels with the bolus through the esophagus and into the stomach where it can function in the acid environment of the stomach before being inactivated.

Once the bolus enters the stomach, the hormone gastrin is released from the gastric pits lining the stomach. Gastrin in turn stimulates the release of gastric juices, rich in gastric lipase, from the chief cells. Fat mixes with the gastric lipase, and the enzyme hydrolyzes one fatty acid from the triglyceride, which produces a free fatty acid and a **diglyceride**.

Most Fat Is Digested and Absorbed in the Small Intestine

The majority of fat digestion occurs in the small intestine. Just as oil can't disperse in water without the help of an emulsifier, the fat globules in chyme tend to cluster together rather than disperse in the watery digestive juices. The first step in the digestion of fat begins by breaking up these fat globules with bile, the emulsifying greenish liquid made in the liver and stored in the gallbladder. When the fat in chyme enters the duodenum, the hormone cholecystokinin (CCK) is secreted, which in turn stimulates the gallbladder to release bile through the bile duct into the duodenum. Hydrophobic portions of bile combine with the fat while hydrophilic portions attract the water in the digestive juices (**Figure 5.14**). This action reduces the fat globules to smaller droplets that are surrounded by bile and phospholipids, preventing the smaller droplets of fat from remerging. Reducing the size of the fat globules provides more surface area to expose the bonds so the enzyme pancreatic lipase can more easily hydrolyze the fat. The result is a smaller lipid complex called a **micelle,** which easily disperses throughout the fluids, with the hydrophilic head of phospholipids projecting into the intestinal juices surrounding a variety of lipids at the hydrophobic center of the complex.

Micelles also help transport the triglyceride remnants to the intestinal walls for absorption into the bloodstream. As pancreatic lipase continues to hydrolyze the triglyceride into two free fatty acids and a **monoglyceride,** these components are added to the micelle and transported inside the enterocyte.

Phospholipids are also emulsified by bile during digestion. Phospholipids are hydrolyzed by a group of enzymes called *phospholipases*. These enzymes dismantle the phospholipids, producing two free fatty acids and the phospholipid remnant, which are part of the micelle complex transported through the intestinal wall.

Bile emulsifies sterols as well. Unlike triglycerides and phospholipids, however, sterols are not digested. Instead, they are absorbed intact in the center of the micelle through the intestinal wall.

If lipids are not digested and prepared for absorption in the small intestine, the undigested lipids bind to fiber and move into the large intestine, where they are eliminated in the feces. The large intestine does not have the enzymes necessary to digest lipids.

Chylomicrons Facilitate Lipid Absorption

Micelles transport digested fats and phospholipids from the GI tract inside the enterocyte. Once inside, the different lipids are absorbed based on their structure and the circulatory system. Glycerol and short- to medium-chain fatty acids can be absorbed into the bloodstream directly through the mucosa of the small intestine because they are more water soluble. They then enter the portal vein and go directly to the liver. Long-chain fatty acids must first be reassembled before being absorbed.

Inside the enterocyte, free long-chain fatty acids reattach to the glycerol molecule to reform a triglyceride. These fats, together with the other dietary lipids

diglyceride A remnant of fat digestion that consists of a glycerol with two attached fatty acids; also the form of fat used as an emulsifier in food production.

micelle Transport carrier in the small intestine that enables fatty acids and other compounds to be absorbed.

monoglyceride A remnant of fat digestion that consists of a glycerol with only one fatty acid attached to one of the three carbons.

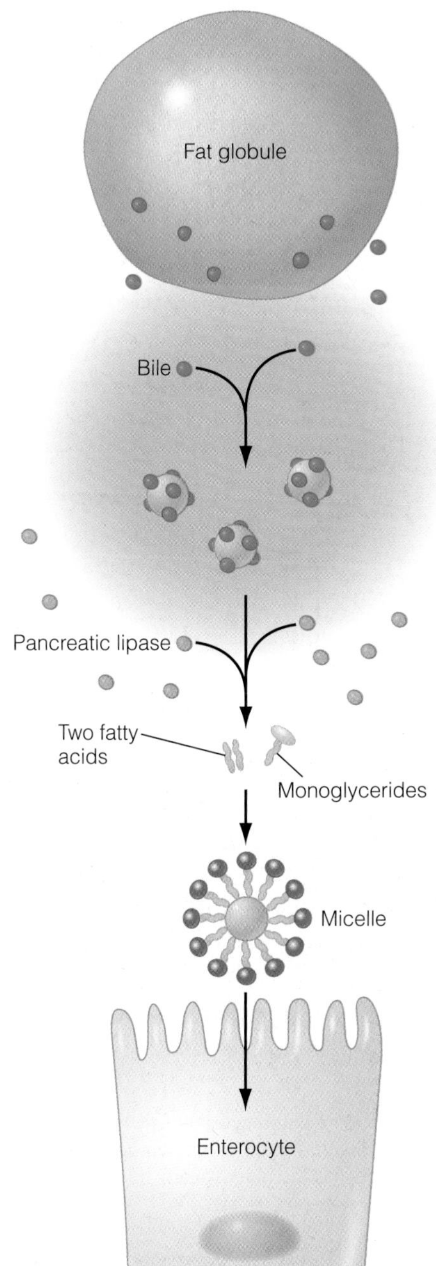

Fat globule
a Large fat globules are emulsified by bile salts into smaller fat droplets.
Bile
b Emulsified fat droplets repel each other as they are suspended in water.
Pancreatic lipase
Two fatty acids
Monoglycerides
c Pancreatic lipase hydrolyzes the triglycerides into two fatty acids and monoglycerides.
Micelle
Enterocyte
d Monoglycerides and fatty acids are absorbed into the enterocyte as micelles interact with the intestinal cell membranes.

◂ **Figure 5.14 Role of Bile in Emulsifying Fat**
As fat globules enter the small intestine, bile breaks them apart into smaller globules called micelles.

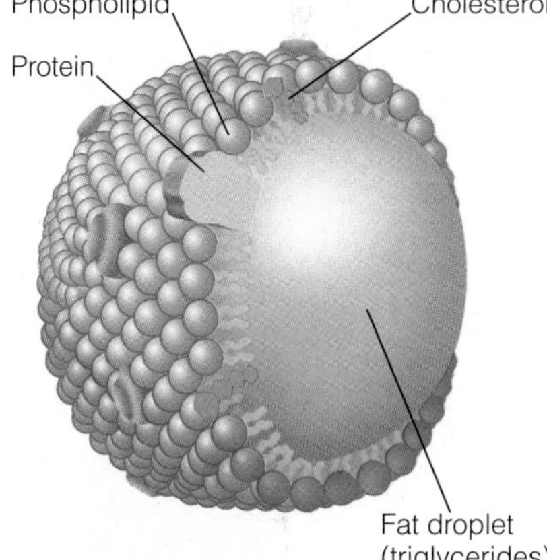

▴ **Figure 5.15 Structure of a Chylomicron**
A chylomicron contains a core of triglycerides and dietary lipids, surrounded by a coat of protein, phospholipids, and cholesterol.

including phospholipids and cholesterol, are combined into a protein-containing transport carrier (or **lipoprotein**) called a **chylomicron** (**Figure 5.15**) and released into the tiny vessels of the lymph system called *lacteals* that contain **lymph fluid** (**Figure 5.16**).

Chylomicrons are too large to be absorbed directly into the bloodstream, so they travel through the lymph system before entering the main circulation. They enter the bloodstream when the lymph fluid joins the blood through the thoracic duct located next to the heart. As the chylomicrons travel through the blood en route to the liver, they interact with the enzyme **lipoprotein lipase (LPL)** located in the walls of the capillaries. This enzyme hydrolyzes the triglycerides in the chylomicrons, separating the fatty acids from the glycerol backbone so they can be stored in the cells.

Fatty acids are used by the heart and muscles as energy, or stored as an energy reserve in the fat cells. After the fat is removed from the chylomicrons, the remnants of these lipoproteins travel to the liver to be dismantled.

lipoprotein Capsule-shaped transport carrier that enables fat and cholesterol to travel through the lymph and blood.

chylomicron A type of lipoprotein that carries digested fat and other lipids through the lymph system into the blood.

lymph fluid Fluid that circulates through the body in lymph vessels and eventually enters the bloodstream.

lipoprotein lipase (LPL) An enzyme that hydrolyzes triglycerides in lipoproteins into three fatty acids and glycerol.

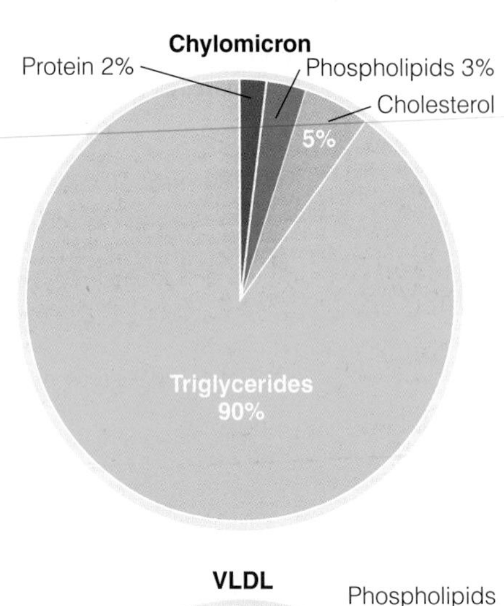

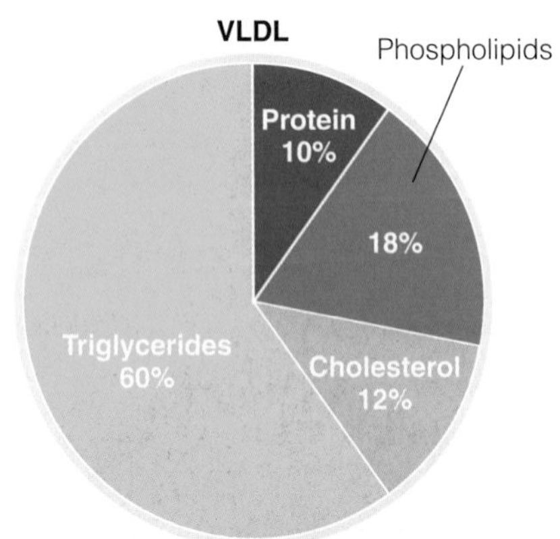

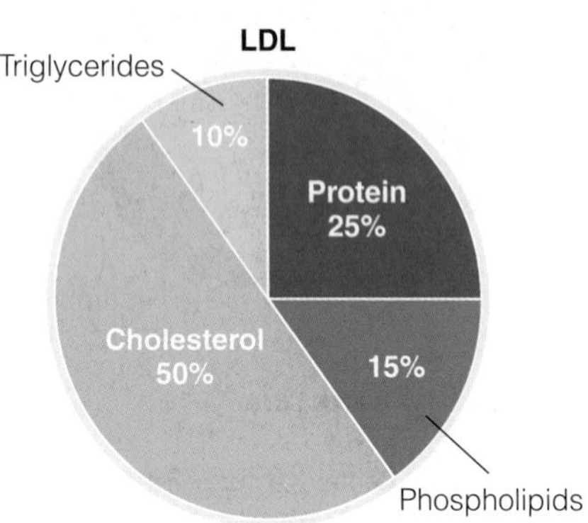

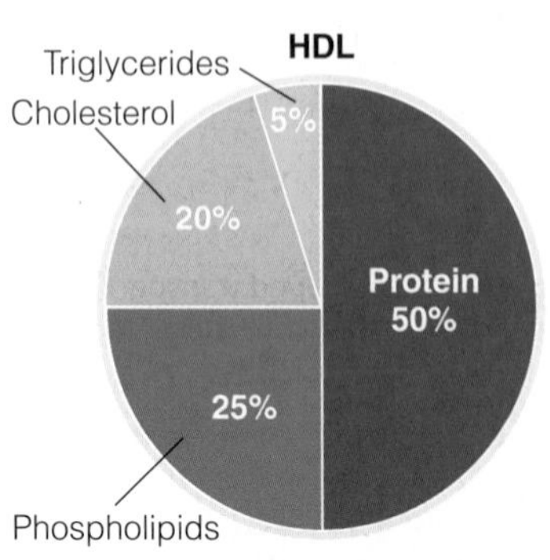

▲ **Figure 5.17 Lipoproteins**
The ratio of protein to lipid determines the density of the lipoprotein (as well as its name). Chylomicrons are the largest of the lipoproteins and contain the least amount of protein.

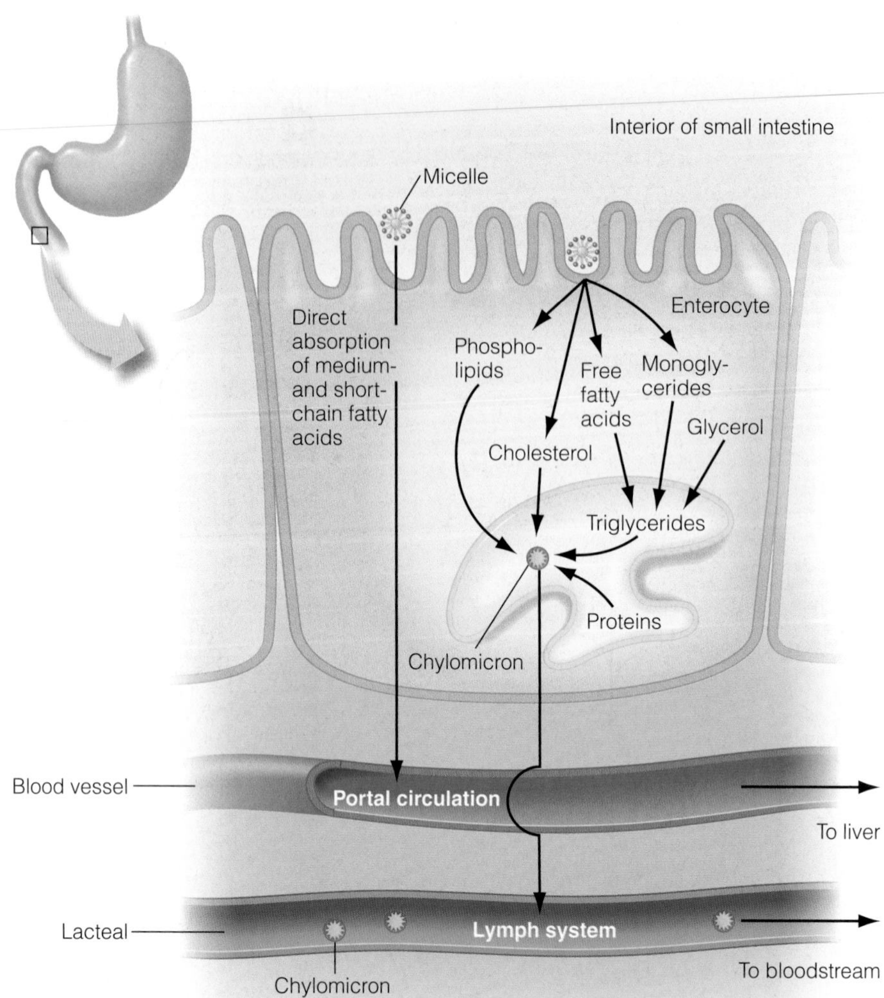

▲ **Figure 5.16 Absorption of Dietary Lipids**
Short- and medium-chain fatty acids are absorbed from the enterocytes directly into the bloodstream. Longer chain fatty acids, cholesterol, phospholipids, and other remnants are reassembled into chylomicrons and enter lymph before being routed into the bloodstream.

Lipoproteins Transport Fat

Chylomicrons are one form of lipoprotein made in the enterocytes. The liver produces three other lipoproteins important to the transport of fat in the body: **very low-density lipoproteins (VLDLs), low-density lipoproteins (LDLs),** and **high-density lipoproteins (HDLs).** These lipoproteins are globular molecules comprised of a lipid center surrounded by a plasma membrane (refer again to the similarly shaped chylomicron in Figure 5.15).

The density of each lipoprotein determines how it functions. Density is determined by the amount of lipid and protein each lipoprotein contains (**Figure 5.17**). The more protein in the lipoprotein, the higher its density. For example, chylomicrons and VLDLs are both composed mostly of triglycerides, but the VLDLs have more protein compared with lipid than chylomicrons do and are more dense. The opposite is true for HDLs. These lipoproteins are smaller and contain more protein than lipid, which makes them the most dense of the lipoproteins.

The role of the VLDLs is to transport triglycerides and cholesterol from the liver to the cells, where they interact with lipoprotein lipase (**Figure 5.18**).

Focus Figure 5.18 Lipoprotein Transport and Distribution

Dietary and endogenous lipids are transported in the body via several different lipoprotein compounds, such as chylomicrons, VLDLs, LDLs, and HDLs.

CHYLOMICRONS

Chylomicrons are produced in the enterocytes to transport lipids from a meal. Lipoprotein lipase, which is located on the surface of non-liver cells (mostly muscle and adipose cells), catalyzes the uptake of fatty acids into the cells through hydrolysis. The remaining chylomicron remnant is dismantled in the liver.

VLDLs

VLDLs (very-low-density lipoproteins), produced mainly in the liver, transport triglycerides to the cells. Lipoprotein lipase catalyzes the uptake of fatty acids into the cells, primarily those in muscle and adipose tissue, transforming VLDLs to LDLs (low-density lipoproteins).

LDLs

Low-density lipoproteins interact with receptor sites on body cells and release cholesterol into those cells. LDLs not taken up by cells degrade over time, releasing cholesterol that may then adhere to blood vessel walls.

HDLs

HDLs (high-density lipoproteins) produced by the liver and small intestine circulate in the blood, picking up cholesterol from cells. The cholesterol is returned to the liver and excreted through the bile, removing it from the bloodstream.

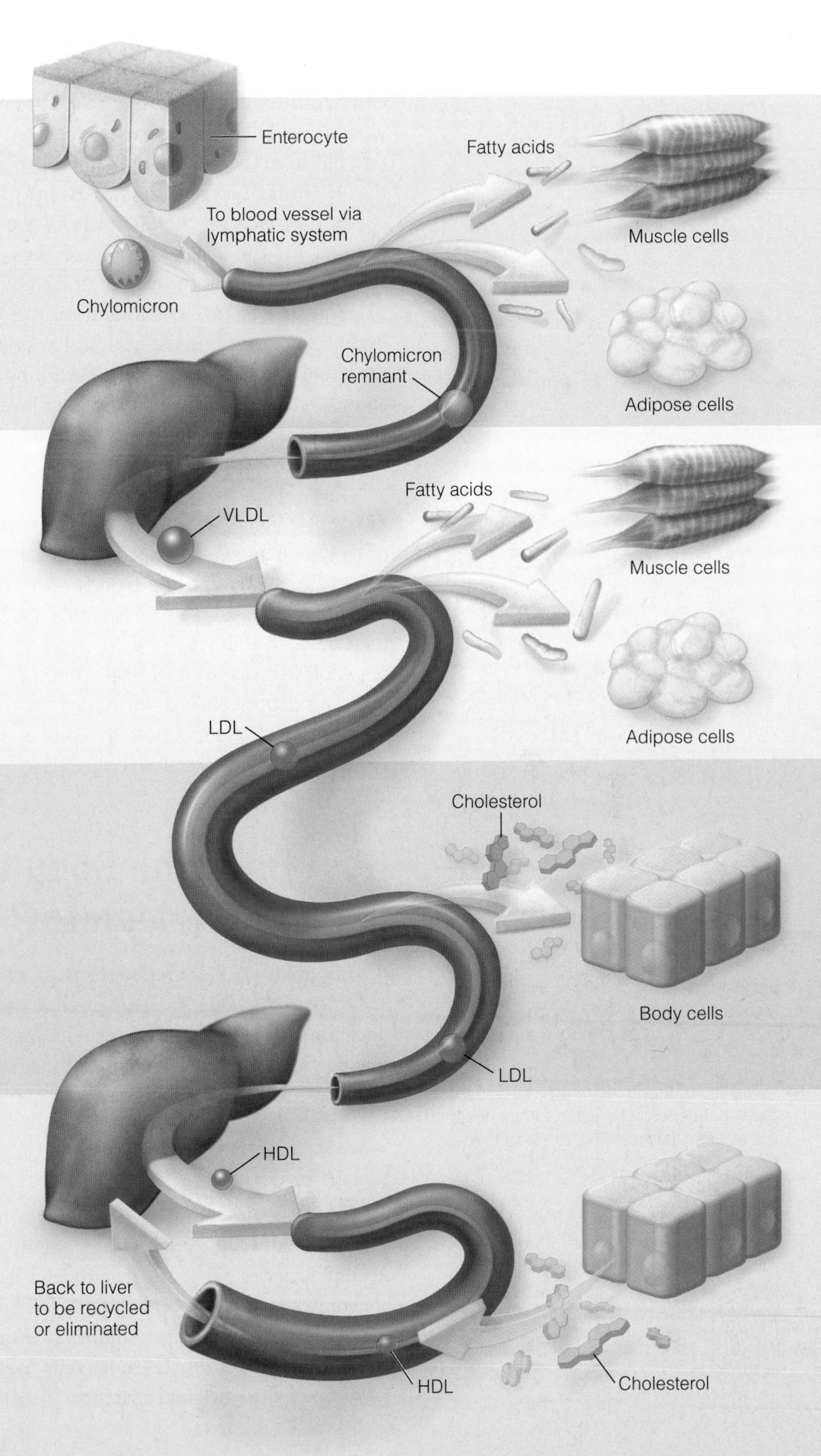

The enzyme lipoprotein lipase (LPL) resides on the surface of the cells and hydrolyzes the fatty acids and glycerol from the core of the lipoprotein. As fat is deposited in cells and tissues, the ratio of protein to lipid increases. What began as a VLDL becomes an LDL, which continues to transport triglycerides to the cells. The LDLs are often referred to as the "bad" cholesterol carriers because they deposit cholesterol in the walls of the arteries, which can lead to heart disease. To help remember this, think of the first "**L**" in **L**DL as being "**L**ousy."

The primary role of HDLs is to pick up cholesterol from the body cells and return it to the liver to be used to make bile, which is then either reabsorbed or excreted through the feces. In fact, approximately 25 percent of the cholesterol in blood is carried by HDLs back to the liver. Because of this function, HDLs are often referred to as the "good" cholesterol. An easy way to remember this is to think of the "**H**" in **H**DL as referring to "**H**ealthy." HDLs begin as high-density molecules, but as they pick up cholesterol from the cells, the percentage of lipid to protein changes and the density decreases. Thus, lipoproteins are constantly changing as they transport lipids throughout the body.

The level of LDL cholesterol relative to HDL cholesterol in the blood can be useful in determining the health of arteries. Essentially, the more HDL carriers in the blood, the harder the body is working to remove cholesterol from arterial cells and excrete it from the body. Higher levels of LDL carriers in the blood indicate that more fatty acids are being delivered to cells and deposited in the arterial walls, which may contribute to blockage.

THE TAKE-HOME MESSAGE Most fat is digested in the small intestine with the help of emulsifying bile and pancreatic lipase. Short- and medium-chain fatty acids are absorbed directly into the bloodstream. Longer chain fatty acids and other remnants of fat digestion are packaged as part of a chylomicron lipoprotein carrier, and then travel in the lymph before entering the bloodstream. Lipoproteins transport fat, cholesterol, and other lipids, through the lymph and bloodstream. The VLDLs and LDLs deposit cholesterol in the cells and the arterial walls. HDL cholesterol carriers remove cholesterol from the arteries and deliver it to the liver to be used in the synthesis of bile or excreted in the feces.

How Does the Body Use Fat and Cholesterol?

Once lipids are delivered to the tissues by lipoproteins, they serve several critical roles in the body. They are used as a source of energy, to form body structures (including cell membranes), regulate metabolism, enhance the absorption of fat-soluble vitamins, provide a layer of insulation to help regulate body temperature, and help cushion the major organs.

Fat Is Used as Energy

Fat is a powerful source of fuel because it provides a concentrated source of kilocalories, is easily stored, and is readily available when the body needs energy. At 9 kilocalories per gram, fat provides more than twice the energy of either carbohydrates or protein. In fact, fat is the body's main source of energy throughout the day. The body has an *unlimited* ability to store excess energy as fat in **adipocytes** (see **Figure 5.19**). These fat cells have the capacity to enlarge to as much as 1,000 times their original size. And if they fill to capacity, the body manufactures

very low-density lipoproteins (VLDLs) Lipoproteins that deliver fat made in the liver to the tissues. VLDL remnants are converted into LDLs.

low-density lipoproteins (LDLs) Lipoproteins that deposit cholesterol in the walls of the arteries. Because this can lead to heart disease, LDL is referred to as the "bad" cholesterol.

high-density lipoproteins (HDLs) Lipoproteins that remove cholesterol from the tissues and deliver it to the liver to be used as part of bile and/or to be excreted from the body. Because of this, HDL is known as the "good" cholesterol.

adipocytes Cells in adipose tissue that store fat; also known as fat cells.

more adipocytes. Though some fat is also stored in the muscle, and a small amount is found in blood plasma, the majority of it is in adipose tissue. The body stores more than 60 times the energy reserves in adipocytes as it stores energy in both liver and muscle glycogen combined.

Fat is deposited into adipose (and some muscle) cells from the chylomicrons and VLDLs that carry it through the blood. As mentioned earlier, the lipoprotein lipase enzyme located on the outside of adipocytes and muscle cells reacts with the lipoprotein carriers and cleaves the fatty acids from the triglyceride. This allows the fatty acid to move into the adipocyte and muscle cells to be stored for later use.

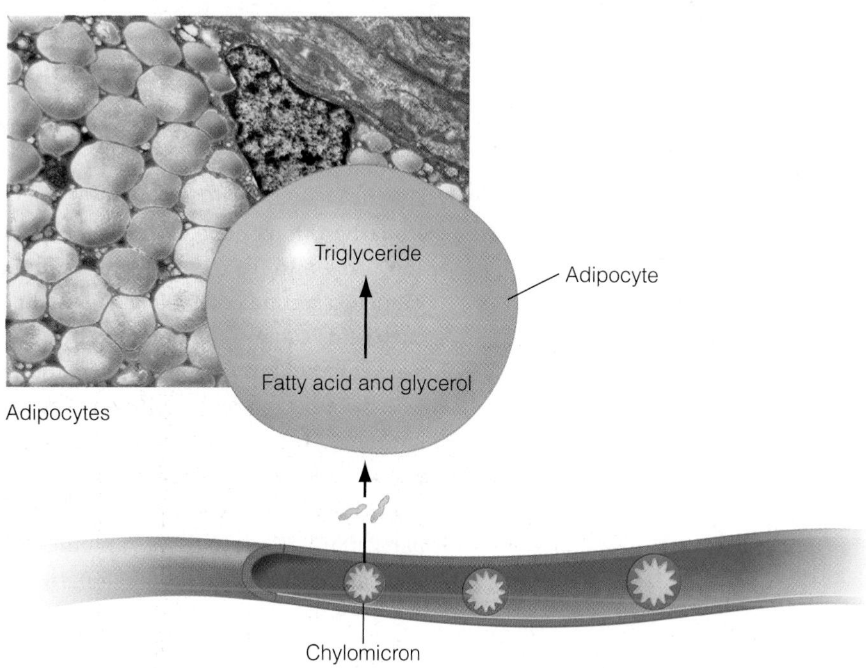

▲ **Figure 5.19 Adipocytes**
Excess triglycerides are stored in the adipocytes for later use. When the body needs energy, the enzyme lipoprotein lipase, located on the outside of the adipocyte, breaks off the fatty acids from the chylomicron or VLDL.

When blood glucose levels begin to decline, the hormone glucagon promotes the release of glucose from the liver and fat from adipocytes to provide additional energy for the body. The heart, liver, and resting muscles prefer fat as their fuel source, which spares glucose to be used by the central nervous system and red blood cells. The fat stored in the adipocytes provides a backup source of energy between meals.

In a famine situation, some individuals could last months without eating, depending upon the extent of their fat stores and the availability of adequate fluids. However, people can still die from starvation before their fat stores are depleted if they do not consume some glucose. Fat stores alone cannot sustain life because glucose cannot be made from fatty acids or ketone bodies. Glycerol is the only part of the stored triglycerides that can be used for gluconeogenesis.

Fat Helps Absorb Lipid Compounds

Several essential nutrients, including the fat-soluble vitamins A, D, E, and K, as well as carotenoids, cholesterol, phospholipids, and other lipid compounds, require dietary fat in order to be absorbed. Twenty grams of dietary fat is needed daily to stimulate the formation of the chylomicrons that transport the fat-soluble vitamins. Consuming less than this amount may impede fat-soluble vitamin absorption.

Fat Helps Insulate the Body and Protect Vital Organs

The fat that is located in the subcutaneous tissue, just under the skin, helps to insulate the body and maintain body temperature, especially during cold temperatures. However, excess body fat may actually hinder temperature regulation in hot weather, as the excess layer of fat prevents heat from flowing to the skin for release.

Fat also acts as a protective cushion against trauma for the bones and vital organs, including the brain, liver, kidneys, and spinal cord. Stored fat in the abdomen acts like a fatty apron protecting the liver and stomach from injury. However, too much stored fat eliminates the protective benefits because of the accompanying increased risk of heart disease, hypertension, and diabetes.

Essential Fatty Acids Manufacture Eicosanoids and Maintain Cell Membranes

The essential fatty acids discussed earlier in the chapter, linoleic acid and alpha-linolenic acid, are needed as precursors to form other compounds in the body. For instance, linoleic acid can be elongated and converted to **arachidonic acid,** a 20-carbon, four-double-bond polyunsaturated fatty acid. Alpha-linolenic acid is converted into the omega-3 fatty acid **eicosapentaenoic acid (EPA)** and then elongated to a second omega-3 fatty acid, **docosahexaenoic acid (DHA).** These omega-3 fatty acids can also be obtained by eating cold-water fish such as salmon, herring, tuna, and halibut. EPA and arachidonic acid are used to manufacture **eicosanoids,** which are hormonelike substances such as prostaglandins, thromboxanes, and leukotrienes. These compounds regulate the immune system, blood clotting, inflammation, and blood pressure.

Alpha-linolenic acid is also needed for the structure of healthy cell membranes, particularly in nerve tissues and the retina. A lack of this essential fatty acid in the diet can result in depression, impaired vision, and scaly skin.

Cholesterol Is Used to Make Bile, Hormones, and Vitamin D

When dietary cholesterol is consumed, it is absorbed along with other lipids and can perform the essential functions of cholesterol in the body. The body needs cholesterol both as a structural part of cell membranes and as the precursor for vitamin D and bile. Cholesterol is also the precursor for sex hormones such as estrogen and testosterone, which help to determine sexual characteristics.

Many people are confused about the merits of cholesterol. Though dietary cholesterol has been proclaimed as unhealthy, the cholesterol in the blood can be either good or bad cholesterol, as discussed earlier. How can one substance be both Dr. Jekyll and Mr. Hyde? Later in this chapter, we will look at the health effects of cholesterol and unravel this confusion. During the discussion keep in mind that dietary cholesterol isn't the only factor that determines the levels of cholesterol in the blood.

THE TAKE-HOME MESSAGE Fat is an energy-dense source of fuel for the body. Fat cushions and protects bones, organs, and nerves, and helps maintain body temperature. Fat also provides essential fatty acids and is needed for the absorption of fat-soluble vitamins and carotenoids. Essential fatty acids are precursors to EPA and DHA, which manufacture prostaglandins, thromboxanes, and leukotrienes, substances that regulate the immune system, blood clotting, inflammation, and blood pressure. Cholesterol is part of cell membranes and is needed to make vitamin D, bile, and sex hormones.

How Much Fat Do We Need Each Day?

Americans' fat consumption has gone up and down over the last century. In the 1930s, Americans were consuming about 34 percent of their kilocalories from fat; this number climbed to 42 percent in the mid-1960s. By 1984, fat consumption had declined to 36 percent of total kilocalories. The latest research indicates that our dietary fat intake is at 34 percent of total kilocalories.[1] However, while today's consumption levels are in line with the current recommendations, we can't break

arachidonic acid An omega-6 fatty acid formed from linoleic acid; it is used to synthesize the eicosanoids, including leukotrienes, prostaglandins, and thromboxanes.

eicosapentaenoic acid (EPA) and **docosahexaenoic acid (DHA)** EPA (C20:5n–3) and DHA (C22:6n–3) are omega-3 fatty acids that are synthesized in the body and found in cold-water fish. These compounds may be beneficial in reducing heart disease.

eicosanoids Hormonelike substances in the body. Prostaglandins, thromboxanes, and leukotrienes are all eicosanoids.

Two Points of View

Farmed Salmon vs Wild Salmon: Is One Healthier Than the Other?

Are there nutritional differences between farmed salmon and wild salmon? What does the research reveal? Two experts weigh in.

David O. Carpenter, MD

Professor; Director, Institute for Health and the Environment, State University of New York at Albany

Dr. David O. Carpenter, MD, is director of the Institute for Health and the Environment at SUNY–Albany. He was the founding dean of the university's School of Public Health, and has interests in disease prevention, reducing exposure to harmful chemicals, and healthy diets.

Q: Is there a nutritional difference between farmed and wild salmon? Is there a difference in methylmercury levels between the two?

A: We found that farmed salmon do have more of the omega-3 fatty acids because they carry more fat. In farmed salmon, about 15 percent of total body weight is fat, compared to about 5 percent for wild salmon. Neither type has elevated levels of mercury. But there are other contaminants to consider that have risks similar to those of mercury.

Q: What other differences exist between farmed and wild salmon, if any, and why?

A: The major findings of our research were that farmed salmon have much higher levels of toxic chemicals such as PCBs and certain pesticides. If a fish was higher in one contaminant, it was higher in all of them.

The contamination source in farmed fish is clearly fish oil and fishmeal in their feed. Salmon feed is made from small fish, and it's usually produced locally. Farmed salmon from northern Europe are more contaminated than those from North America, and North America is worse than South America. That tracks with human activity. Northern European waters have been subject to industrial pollution longer than North America, and North American waters longer than South America.

Q: Are any of these issues likely to change in the future?

A: I hope they are. The solution to the problem is that the industry has to stop feeding the salmon concentrated fish oil and fishmeal.

Q: How can consumers make the most healthful choices when it comes to eating fish?

A: Be cautious. I'm increasingly of the opinion that benefits of fish have been oversold. Many of the risks have not been adequately addressed by the nutrition community. Know where your fish comes from. Wild salmon carry fewer contaminants, but they still have some.

William S. Harris, PhD

Research Professor of Medicine, the Sanford School of Medicine, University of South Dakota, and Senior Scientist, Health Diagnostic Laboratory, Inc., Richmond, VA

William S. Harris, PhD, has conducted research on fish oils and cardiovascular disease. He was the principal investigator on five NIH grants studying omega-3 fatty acids and human lipid metabolism.

Q: Is there a nutritional difference between farmed and wild salmon? Is there a difference in methylmercury levels between the two?

A: As a source of the omega-3 fatty acids EPA and DHA, no, there is no substantial difference between wild and farmed salmon. Wild salmon can vary in omega-3 content more than farmed salmon, but on average the omega-3 levels are similar. All salmon are extremely low in methylmercury.

Q: What other differences exist between farmed and wild salmon, if any, and why?

A: Farmed tend to have more oil per serving than wild salmon (like beef from feedlot cattle has more fat than beef from grass-fed cattle). Since the percent of omega-3 is a bit lower in farmed salmon, the higher oil content per serving provides equal (or more) omega-3 per serving of farmed salmon.

Q: Are any of these issues likely to change in the future?

A: Levels of pesticide and herbicide residues were reported to be higher in farmed vs. wild salmon, but this report must be taken with a grain of salt. First, the most contaminated farmed salmon were from the northern seas around Scandinavia and Scotland. Second, the levels of PCBs—although higher in farmed salmon—were still well below FDA action levels and similar to levels in beef, butter, chicken, and pork. Third, the fish in this study were analyzed with the skin, where the PCB accumulates. But most people do not eat the skin.

Q: How can consumers make the most healthful choices when it comes to eating fish?

A: The healthiest fish are those that provide the long-chain omega-3 fatty acids EPA and DHA: for example, salmon, sardines, albacore tuna, herring, mackerel. But even the lower fat fish, which provide small amounts of omega-3 (such as cod, tilapia, catfish), are better choices than most beef or pork.

Calculation Corner

Calculating the AMDR for Fat

Approximately how many grams of total fat does an individual with a 2,000-kilocalorie energy requirement need to consume to meet the recommendations?

The AMDR recommends that 20 to 35 percent of daily kilocalories (kcal) come from fat, so the range for an individual who needs 2,000 kilocalories per day would be:

2,000 kcal × 0.20 (20%) = 400 kcal; 9 kcal/g = 44 g

2,000 kcal × 0.35 (35%) = 700 kcal; 9 kcal/g = 78 g

Answer: This person's range of fat intake should be 44 to 78 grams daily.

To find the maximum grams of saturated and *trans* fats that this person should consume daily, calculate 10 percent of total kcal:

2,000 kcal × 0.10 (10%) = 200 kcal; 9 kcal/g = 22 g

Answer: The total amount of saturated fat and *trans* fat should be no more than 22 grams daily.

out the hot fudge sundaes just yet. Measuring fat consumption as a percentage of total kilocalories, without including the absolute grams of fat, can be misleading.

The latest patterns of food intake by Americans indicate that the total grams of fat we consume daily has increased about 12 percent since the early 1990s, but the amount of total kilocalories has also increased about 15 percent.[2] In other words, Americans are eating more of both kilocalories and grams of fat, and the percentage of dietary fat has declined because the number of kilocalories has increased. The main source of this increase in total kilocalories is sweetened beverages, such as soft drinks, which are high in refined carbohydrates.[3,4]

Clearly, the overall consumption of fat in the United States is higher than it should be. But dietary fat is still essential for health. So, how much should you consume?

Fat Intake Is Based on a Percentage of Total Kilocalories

The current AMDR (Acceptable Macronutrient Distribution Range) recommendation is that 20 to 35 percent of daily kilocalories should come from all fats. For some individuals, especially those who are sedentary, overweight, or both, a very low-fat diet (providing less than 20 percent of daily kilocalories from fat) that is consequently high in carbohydrates may increase LDL cholesterol and triglyceride levels in the blood and lower HDL cholesterol—which is not a healthy combination for the heart. For others, consuming more than 35 percent of total daily kilocalories from fat could perpetuate obesity, which is a risk factor for heart disease.

The overconsumption of dietary fat doesn't increase overall body weight unless it's coupled with too many kilocalories. However, because dietary fat is more concentrated in kilocalories than either carbohydrates or protein, a diet high in fat is likely to result in eating too many kilocalories, and could make for a weight management problem. Numerous research studies have shown that reducing dietary fat can also reduce dietary kilocalories, which can result in weight loss.[5] Consequently, controlling fat intake may help control body weight.

For heart health, the recommendation is to consume no more than 10 percent of total kilocalories from saturated fats (and ideally less than 7 percent) and to limit *trans* fats to less than 1 percent.[6] Individuals are encouraged to use more monounsaturated and polyunsaturated fats to replace saturated fats. For example, if a person consumes 30 percent of his total kilocalories as fat, about 6 percent should be derived from saturated fats, 1 percent or less from *trans* fat, about 10 percent from polyunsaturated fats, and 13 percent from monounsaturated fats. This is because monounsaturated fats are the best at lowering LDL cholesterol and either maintaining or slightly increasing HDL cholesterol.

When it comes to keeping track of fat intake, counting grams of fat in foods is a good strategy. Table 5.1 provides a healthy range of recommended fat intake based on daily kilocalorie needs. (To figure out your approximate daily kilocalorie needs, see Chapter 2). Use the Self-Assessment to estimate how much total fat you currently consume daily.

Essential Fatty Acids Have Specific Recommendations

The only necessary dietary fats are the two essential fatty acids: linoleic acid and alpha-linolenic acid. The Adequate Intake (AI) of alpha-linolenic acid per day for men and women is 1.6 and 1.1 grams, respectively. The AI for linoleic acid is set much higher, at 17 grams per day for adult men and 12 grams per day for adult women.[7] Americans currently consume only about 0.1 to 0.2 grams of EPA and DHA in their daily diet.

The AMDR for linoleic acid is set at 5 to 10 percent of total kilocalories, while alpha-linolenic acid should make up 0.6 percent to 1.2 percent of total kilocalories. These recommended amounts are based on the estimated daily kilocalorie needs according to gender and age.

Based on randomized trials, the American Heart Association recommends that people diagnosed with heart disease consume about 1 gram of essential fatty acids

TABLE 5.1 Capping Your Fat Intake

Daily Energy Needs (Kilocalories)	Maximum Recommended Amount of Daily Dietary Fat Intake	
	Fat (g) (20% to 35% of Total Kilocalories)	Saturated Fat and *Trans* Fat (g) (< 10% of Total Kilocalories)
1,600	36–62	18
1,700	38–66	19
1,800	40–70	20
1,900	42–74	21
2,000	44–78	22
2,100	47–82	23
2,200	49–86	24
2,300	51–89	26
2,400	53–93	27
2,500	56–97	28
2,600	58–101	29
2,700	60–105	30
2,800	62–109	31

Sedentary women consume approximately 1,600 kilocalories daily. Teenage girls, active women, and many sedentary men need approximately 2,200 kilocalories daily. Teenage boys, many active men, and some very active women need about 2,800 kilocalories daily.

Self-Assessment

How Much Fat Is in Your Diet?

Are you consuming too much fat, saturated fat, *trans* fat, or all three? Use a diet analysis program, the food tables in the appendix, or food labels to track your fat consumption for a day and fill out the food log below. How does your actual intake compare with the amount recommended for you in Table 5.1?

Food Log

Meal	Food/Drink	Total Fat (g)	Saturated Fat (g)	*Trans* Fat (g)
Breakfast				
Snack				
Lunch				
Snack				
Dinner				
Snack				
Total				

EXAMINING THE EVIDENCE

Facts and Myths About Fats, Oils, and Cholesterol

Many people are confused about whether to embrace or avoid fat, which types they should aim to eat, and how much they need. Below, we address six common consumer (mis)perceptions about dietary fat with research-based answers.

Fact or Myth?

The amount of fat you eat is more important than the type of fat.

Myth. The type of fat matters more than the amount consumed when it comes to impacting the risk of certain diseases, including heart disease and cancer. Data from the Women's Health Initiative Dietary Modification Trial, which followed 50,000 women between ages 50 and 79 for eight years, showed that women who consumed a low-fat diet did not have a significant reduction in breast cancer compared with those who ate high-fat diets,[1] nor did low fat intake reduce the risk of developing colon cancer,[2] stroke, or cardiovascular disease.[3] However, intake of *trans* fats and saturated fats were correlated to an increased risk for cardiovascular disease, stroke, and cancer. Substituting or replacing hydrogenated fats, which are rich in *trans* fats, and saturated fats with monounsaturated and polyunsaturated fatty acids can lower the risk of developing heart disease and cancer, regardless of the amount consumed. (Remember though, that kilocalories count, and consuming more fat means consuming more kilocalories, thereby potentially resulting in weight gain.)

Fact or Myth?

Fat free means kilocalorie free.

Myth. To be considered fat free, a product must contain less than 0.5 gram of fat per serving, while the definition of kilocalorie free requires less than 5 kilocalories per serving. This means that a product that is low in fat or even fat free isn't necessarily lower in total kilocalories. Some fat-free foods, especially baked goods, may have reduced fat content, but have added carbohydrates to make up for the lost flavor, which adds back some kilocalories. For example, two fat-free fig cookies contain 90 kilocalories, which is not much different from the 110 kilocalories found in two regular fig cookies[4] (see table).

Consumers should be careful not to assume that fat-free foods are healthy, because they often aren't. Jelly beans are fat free, but they don't provide the vitamins and minerals found in, for example, naturally fat-free green beans. And while snacking on 4 ounces of fat-free chips will provide half of the 600 kilocalories found in the same amount of regular chips, the real problem is that the fat-free chips are displacing 300 calories of more nutritious foods, such as fruits, vegetables, and whole grains, elsewhere in the diet.

Fact or Myth?

Olive oil is the healthiest oil.

Myth. While it's true that olive oil has beneficial health effects because of its high content of monounsaturated fatty acids (especially oleic acid) and antioxidants (including vitamin E) and a low content of saturated fatty acids, that doesn't mean that other vegetable oils are less healthy. All plant oils contain the same number of fat grams and kilocalories per tablespoon. The difference lies in the type of fat they contain (see graph). Canola oil is less saturated than olive oil and contains more polyunsaturated fatty acids. Olive oil is higher in monounsaturated fatty acids. Sunflower, safflower, and corn oil are also lower in saturated fat and higher in polyunsaturated fatty acids than olive oil. Thus, olive oil is not the only healthy oil available to consumers; all these oils are considered healthy choices.

The American Heart Association recommends vegetable oils that contain no more than 2 grams of saturated fat per tablespoon.[5] Canola, corn, olive, safflower, sesame, soybean, and sunflower oils all fit the heart-healthy recommendations. Tropical oils such as coconut and palm oils should be used less often, as they contain higher levels of saturated fat.

Fact or Myth?

Eggs should be avoided in a heart-healthy diet.

Myth. Eggs have long been considered a villain in the fight against heart disease because of their cholesterol-containing yolks. However, this threat has largely been overstated. The reality is that dietary cholesterol does not have as big an impact on heart disease as blood cholesterol levels, which are affected more by

Fat Free Doesn't Equal Kilocalorie Free

	Serving Size (g)	Kilocalories	Fat (g)	Carbohydrates (g)	Kilocalories Saved
Fig Newtons (Nabisco)	2 (31 g)	110	2	22	
Fat-Free Fig Newtons (Nabisco)	2 (29 g)	90	0	22	20
Oatmeal Raisin Cookies (Archway)	1 (28 g)	120	3.5	20	
Fat-Free Oatmeal Raisin Cookies (Archway)	1 (31 g)	110	0	25	10
Fudgsicle Pop (Popsicle)	1 (1.65 fl oz)	60	1.5	12	
Fat-Free Fudgsicle Bar (Popsicle)	1 (1.75 fl oz)	60	0	13	0

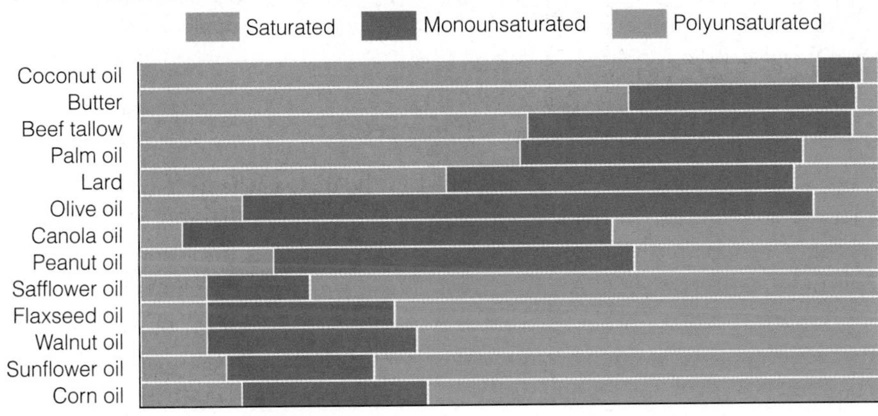

Composition of Various Oils
Oils used for cooking and in food preparation vary in their saturation.

saturated and *trans* fat intake than cholesterol intake. In a study of over 80,000 nurses, researchers found that increasing dietary cholesterol by about 200 milligrams per 1,000 kilocalories (about the amount in a large egg), didn't raise blood cholesterol levels.[6]

However, that's not to say that people should aim to eat more cholesterol-containing foods. High cholesterol intake is associated with an increased risk for heart disease. Because egg yolks tend to be a significant source of cholesterol in Americans' diets, the National Institutes of Health (NIH) recommends consuming no more than four egg yolks per week to help prevent heart disease. Given that eggs are also a source of many healthy nutrients, including protein, numerous B vitamins, and vitamins A, D, and E, some health professionals have suggested lifting the weekly cap on egg yolks for healthy individuals and focusing on keeping dietary cholesterol to no more 300 milligrams daily, regardless of the source.[7] Hence, egg yolks can be eaten more often if other sources of dietary cholesterol are low.

Fact or Myth?

Fish oil supplements are essential for health.

Myth. A daily dose of > 1 gram of both EPA and DHA is needed to achieve heart-healthy benefits. But though consuming some omega-3 fatty acids is good, more may not be better, and too much can produce harmful side effects. Taking omega-3 fatty acid supplements (fish oil supplements) increases the chance of consuming high doses of DHA and EPA, which can interfere with blood clotting. Consuming more than 3 grams, which typically only happens by taking supplements, could raise both blood glucose and LDL cholesterol levels, increase the risk of excessive bleeding, and cause other related side effects, including nausea and GI distress. Consuming large amounts of fish oil supplements can also leave a less-than-appealing fishy aftertaste in the mouth. Because of these potential adverse side effects, omega-3 fish oil supplements should only be consumed with the advice and guidance of a doctor.

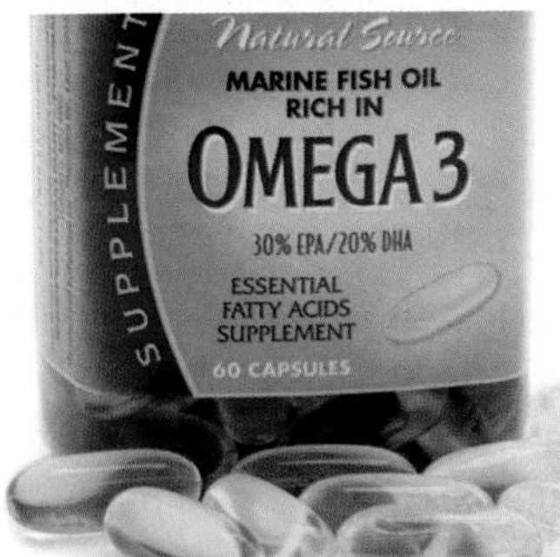

While fish oil supplements contain omega-3 fatty acids, excessive amounts can be unhealthy for some individuals.

Norwegian researchers report that omega-3 fatty acids are better absorbed from food than from fish oil supplements.[8] For healthy individuals who have not been diagnosed with coronary artery disease, increasing intake of omega-3 fatty acids through food is the preferred method.

Fact or Myth?

Shellfish is high in cholesterol.

It depends on the shellfish. A 3-ounce serving of scallops contains 34 milligrams of cholesterol, but the same size portion of shrimp contains five times more cholesterol (165 milligrams), half the recommended daily intake. Shrimp is also higher in cholesterol than 3 ounces of beef (80 milligrams). At first glance, it would seem that shellfish should not be included in a low-cholesterol diet. But though shrimp is high in cholesterol, it contains less than 0.25 gram of saturated fat and 0.4 gram, or 15 percent, of the omega-3 recommendation. Researchers have shown that eating shellfish, including shrimp, reduced the risk of dying from a heart attack by 20 percent.[9]

References

1. Prentice, R. L., B. Caan, R. T. Chlebowski, R. Patternson, L. H. Kuller, J. K. Ockene, K. L. Margolis, et al. 2006. Low-Fat Dietary Pattern and Risk of Invasive Breast Cancer: The Women's Health Initiative Randomized Controlled Dietary Modification Trial. *Journal of the American Medical Association* 295:629–642.
2. Beresford, S. A. A., K. C. Johnson, C. Ritenbaugh, N. L. Lasser, L. G. Snetselaar, G. Linda, H. R. Black, et al. 2006. Low-Fat Dietary Pattern and Risk of Colorectal Cancer: The Women's Health Initiative Randomized Controlled Dietary Modification Trial. *Journal of the American Medical Association* 295:643–654.
3. Howard, B. V., L. Van Horn, J. Hsia, J. E. Manson, M. L. Stefanick, S. Wassertheil-Smoller, L. H. Kuller, et al. 2006. Low-Fat Dietary Pattern and Risk of Cardiovascular Disease: The Women's Health Initiative Randomized Controlled Dietary Modification Trial. *Journal of the American Medical Association* 295:655–666.
4. United States Department of Agriculture. 2002. Fat-Free vs Regular Calorie Comparison. *FDA Consumer.* 36:23.
5. American Heart Association. 2008. *Fats and Oils.* Available at www.americanheart.org. Accessed March 2012.
6. Hu, F. B., E. B. Rimm, M. J. Stampfer, A. Ascherio, D. Spiegelman, and W. C. Willett. 1999. A Prospective Study of Egg Consumption and Risk of Cardiovascular Disease in Men and Women. *Journal of the American Medical Association* 281:1387–1394.
7. Ibid.
8. Elvevoll, E. O., H. Barstad, E. S. Breimo, J. Brox, K. E. Eilertsen, T. Lund, J. O. Olsen, and B. Osterud. 2006. Enhanced Incorporation of ω-3 Fatty Acids from Fish Compared with Fish Oils. *Lipids* 41:1109–1114.
9. Yuan, J., R. K. Ross, G. Yu-Tang, and M. C. Yu. 2001. Fish and Shellfish Consumption in Relation to Death from Myocardial Infarction among Men in Shanghai, China. *American Journal of Epidemiology* 154:809–816; Kris-Etherton, P. M., W. S. Harris, and L. J. Appel. 2002. Fish Consumption, Fish Oil, Omega-3 Fatty Acids, and Cardiovascular Disease. *Circulation* 106:2747–2757.

TABLE 5.2 How Much Cholesterol Is in Foods?

	Cholesterol (mg)
Liver, 3 oz	324
Breakfast biscuit with egg and sausage, 1	290
Egg, 1 large	186
Shrimp, canned, 3 oz	147
Fast-food hamburger, large, double patty	122
Ice cream, soft serve, vanilla, ½ cup	78
Beef, ground, cooked, 3 oz	77
Salmon, cooked, 3 oz	74
Chicken or turkey, breast, cooked, 3 oz	72
Lobster, cooked, 3 oz	61
Turkey, light meat, cooked, 3 oz	59
Egg noodles, 1 cup	53
Butter, 1 tbs	31
Cheddar cheese, 1 oz	30
Frankfurter, beef, 1	24
Milk, whole, 1 cup	24
Cheddar cheese, low fat, 1 oz	6
Milk, skim, 1 cup	4

Data from USDA. *National Nutrient Database for Standard Reference, Release 24.* Available at www.ars.usda.gov. Accessed March 2012.

each day. For those who have been diagnosed with **hypertriglyceridemia** (elevated blood triglycerides), 2 to 4 grams per day of EPA and DHA supplements may lower blood triglycerides.[8]

Dietary Cholesterol Is Not Essential

Cholesterol does not need to be consumed in the diet, as the liver synthesizes all that the body needs. The liver manufactures about 900 milligrams of cholesterol per day. This is three times greater than the 300 milligrams the average American consumes daily. However, if cholesterol is consumed, the body adjusts the amount it synthesizes. Normally, the total amount of cholesterol remains constant because the rate of cholesterol synthesis in the liver is under feedback control. When the dietary intake is high, liver synthesis is low; when intake is low, synthesis increases.

As mentioned earlier, dietary cholesterol should be limited to reduce the risk of developing cardiovascular disease. Healthy individuals over the age of 2 are advised to limit their dietary cholesterol to less than 300 milligrams (mg) daily, on average.[9] Adult males in the United States currently consume about 358 milligrams daily, whereas adult females take in slightly more than 237 milligrams of cholesterol daily, on average. Table 5.2 lists a variety of foods and their cholesterol content.

THE TAKE-HOME MESSAGE Dietary lipids, particularly the essential fatty acids, are key for a healthy diet, but intake of saturated fats, *trans* fats, and cholesterol should be limited. Dietary fat intake should range from 20 to 35 percent of total kilocalories. To meet essential fatty acid needs, 5 to 10 percent of total kilocalories should come from linoleic acid and 0.6 to 1.2 percent of total daily kilocalories should come from alpha-linolenic acid. Dietary intake of saturated fat should be limited to no more than 10 percent of total fat consumption, and less than 1 percent of fat consumption should be from *trans* fats. Dietary cholesterol should be limited to less than 300 milligrams per day.

Eggs are an excellent source of protein, but egg yolks are high in dietary cholesterol.

hypertriglyceridemia The presence of high levels of triglycerides in the blood. Defined as triglyceride levels between 400 and 1,000 milligrams per deciliter.

What Are the Best, Worst, and Alternative Food Sources for Fat?

Eating foods that contain unsaturated fats (which also contain essential fatty acids) is better for health than eating foods high in saturated fat, cholesterol, and/or *trans* fat. So, which foods contain the healthier fats?

The Best Food Sources Are Low in Saturated Fat

Unsaturated fats are abundant in vegetable oils, such as soybean, corn, and canola oils, as well as soybeans, walnuts, flaxseeds, and wheat germ. These foods are also all good sources of linoleic acid. Walnuts, flaxseeds, and canola oil also contain alpha-linolenic acid. **Figure 5.20** lists examples of foods that are excellent sources of unsaturated fats and essential fatty acids.

Fish are generally good sources of omega-3 fatty acids, and all fish contain EPA and DHA, with fatty fish being especially rich sources (**Figure 5.21**). Cod-liver oil is abundant in EPA and DHA but it is also very high in vitamin A, which can be detrimental. Eating fish, rather than taking cod-liver oil, is a safer way to obtain EPA and DHA, and has been shown to improve heart health.[10]

Individuals are sometimes hesitant to consume fish due to a concern about mercury levels. Although all fish and shellfish contain a trace of mercury, the levels

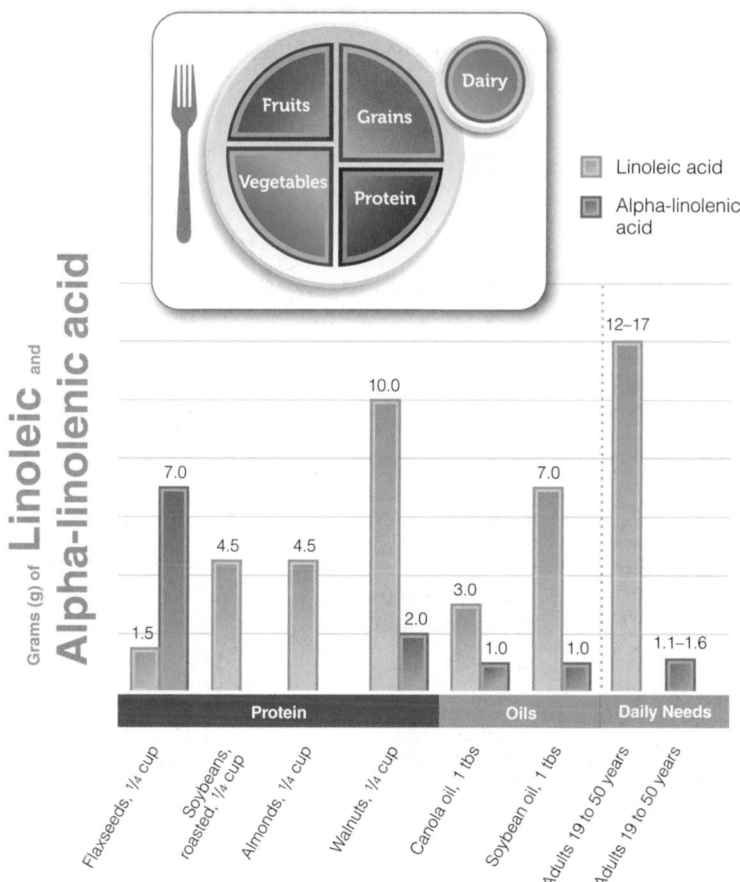

◂ **Figure 5.20 Food Sources of the Essential Fatty Acids**
Many oils and nuts are good sources of the two essential fatty acids.

of mercury are not considered a health risk for most people. More information is provided on this topic in "Spotlight: Mercury and Fish" on page 184.

Foods high in saturated fat should be limited in the diet. Most saturated fat comes from animal foods, such as fatty cuts of meat, whole-milk dairy products (including cheese, butter, and ice cream), and the skin on poultry. Certain vegetable oils, such as coconut, palm, and palm kernel oils, are also very high in saturated fat. These tropical oils are sometimes found in candies, commercially made baked goods, and gourmet ice cream. Reading the ingredient label on food packages is the best way to check for these oils.

While it's important to limit saturated fat in the diet, it's impossible to eliminate it entirely. All fats and oils contain a variety of fatty acids, some of which are bound to be saturated. Avoiding all fat-containing foods, or eliminating all oils during cooking, could lead to the unnecessary exclusion of healthy foods, such as soybean and canola oils, lean meats, fish, poultry, and low-fat dairy foods. The result may be an inadequate intake of important nutrients such as essential fatty acids, protein, and calcium. A better strategy is to consume lower fat versions of these foods, so you obtain the healthy nutrients while avoiding unnecessary, unhealthy fats. **Figure 5.22** helps compare high-fat and lower fat versions of several commonly eaten foods.

In the supermarket, read the Nutrition Facts panel to help you choose foods that are low in fat. The nutrition label of packaged foods can be used to compare the amount of total fat, the type of fat, and the

▾ **Figure 5.21 Food Sources of Omega-3 Fatty Acids**
Several types of fish, particularly fatty fish, are high in the heart-healthy omega-3 fatty acids.

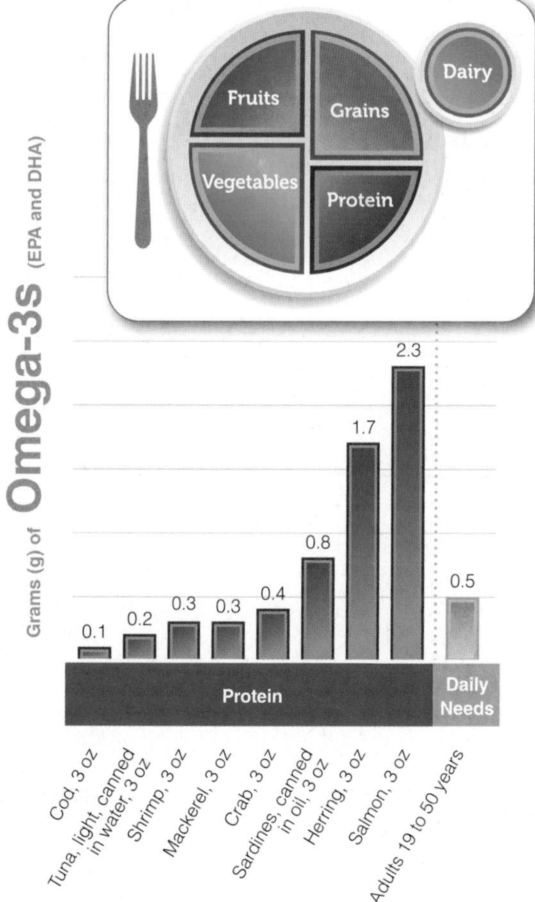

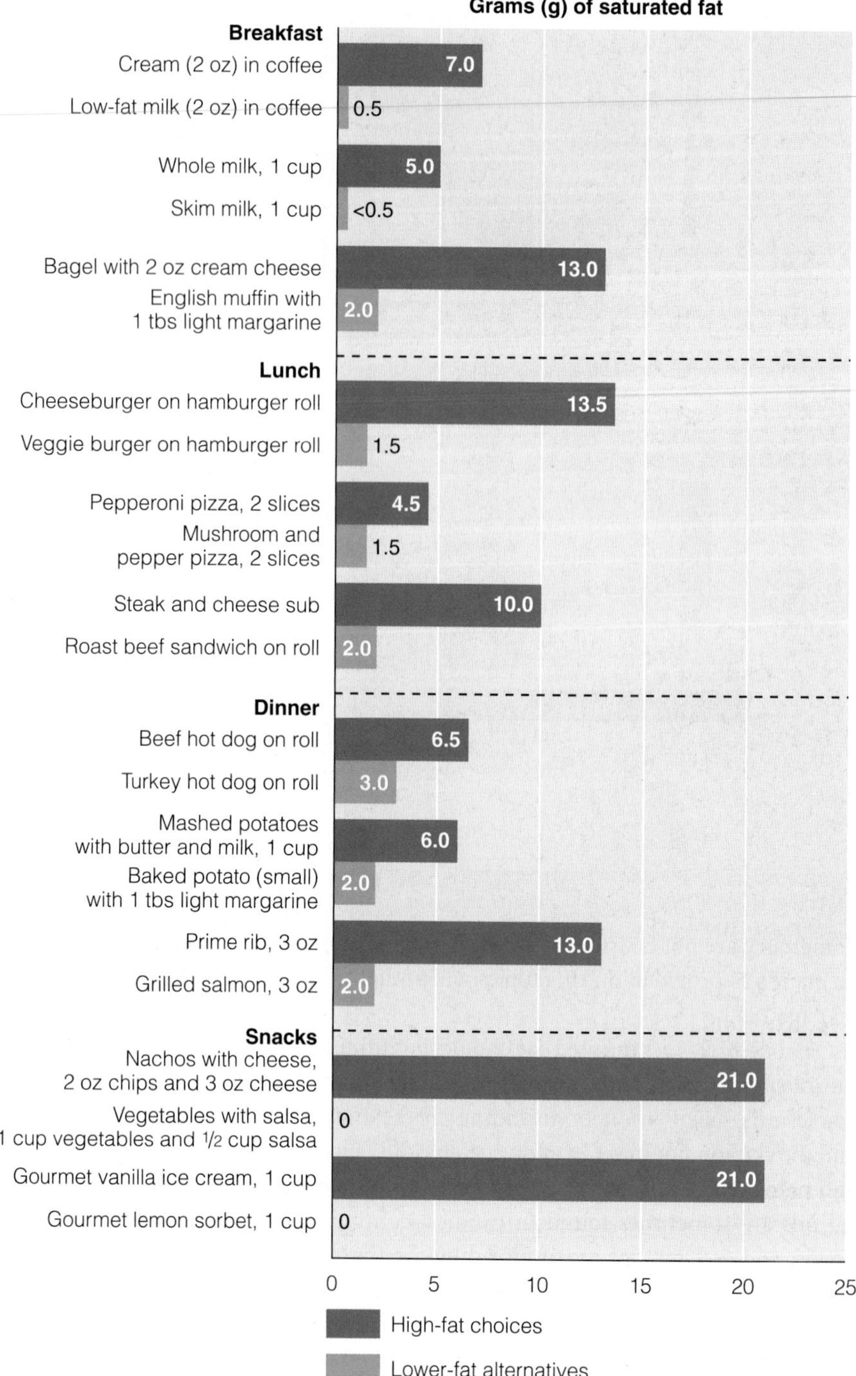

▲ **Figure 5.22 Where's the Saturated Fat in Foods?**
Choosing less-saturated-fat versions of foods can dramatically lower the amount of saturated fat consumed in the diet.

calories from fat per serving of a food, as illustrated in **Figure 5.23**. Scan the ingredient list to make sure the product has little or no partially hydrogenated oil.

Reduce Foods That Contain *Trans* Fat and Cholesterol

At one time, saturated fats from animal sources, like lard, and highly saturated tropical plant oils, like coconut and palm oils, were staples in home cooking and commercial food preparation. These saturated fats worked well in commercial products because they provided a rich, flaky texture to baked goods and were more resistant

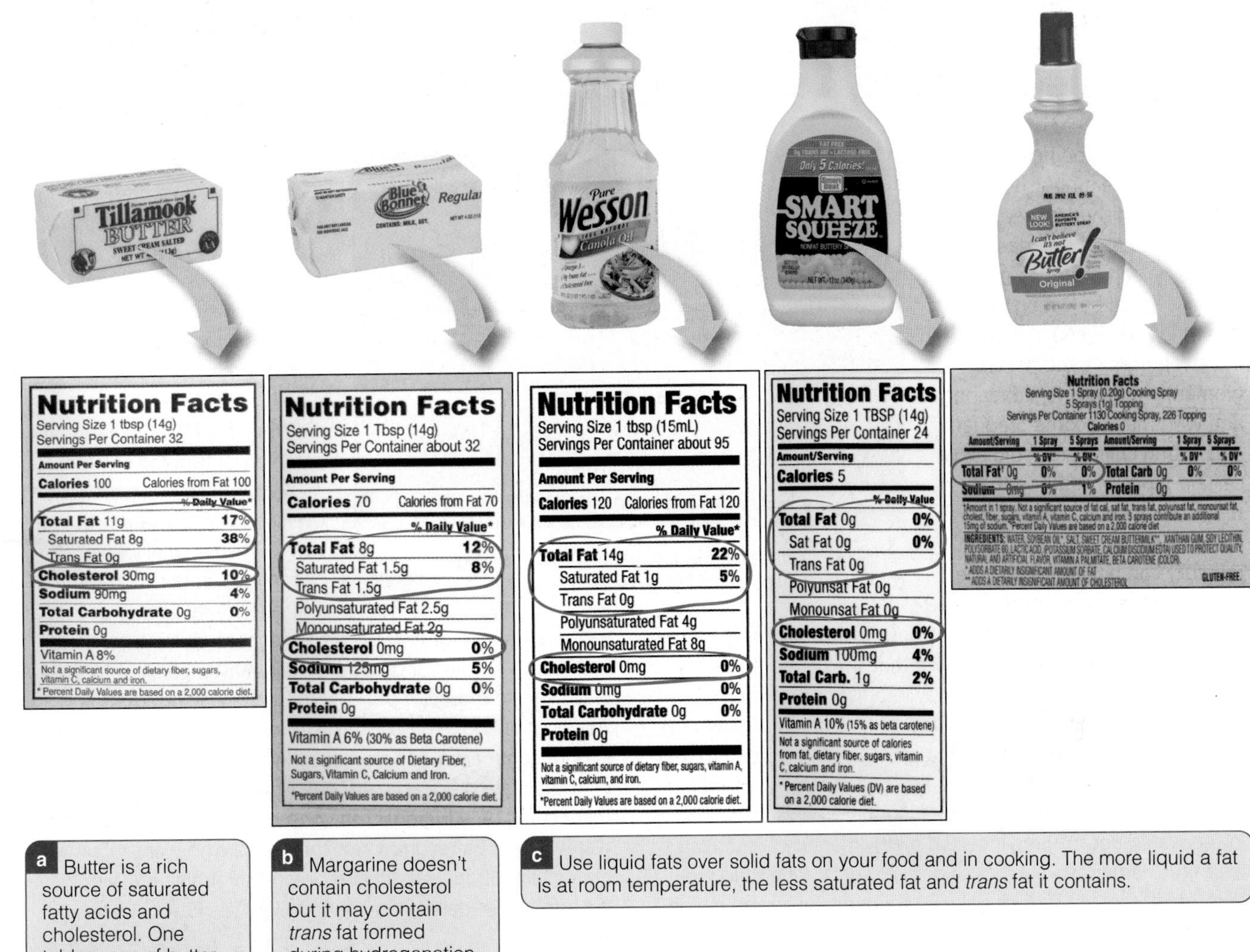

a Butter is a rich source of saturated fatty acids and cholesterol. One tablespoon of butter contains over 7 grams of saturated fat.

b Margarine doesn't contain cholesterol but it may contain *trans* fat formed during hydrogenation of vegetable oils.

c Use liquid fats over solid fats on your food and in cooking. The more liquid a fat is at room temperature, the less saturated fat and *trans* fat it contains.

▲ **Figure 5.23 Read Food Labels to Lower Saturated and *Trans* Fat Intake**

to rancidity than the unsaturated fats found in oils. Later, the technique of hydrogenation of oils and the use of *trans* fat performed a similar function without adding cholesterol to the diet.

Foods with *Trans* Fats

Similar to lard and animal fats, hydrogenated oils provide a richer texture, a longer shelf life, and better resistance to rancidity than unsaturated fats, so food manufacturers like to use them in many commercially made food products. Hydrogenated fats came into widespread commercial use when saturated fat fell out of favor in the 1980s. Research had confirmed that saturated fat played a role in increased risk of heart disease, so food manufacturers reformulated many of their products to contain less saturated fat. The easiest solution was to replace the saturated fat with hydrogenated fats. During the hydrogenation process, some of the unstable *cis* fatty acids are converted to *trans* fatty acids, increasing the level of ***trans* fat** found in processed foods. Everything from cookies, cakes, and crackers to fried chips and doughnuts used hydrogenated fats to maintain their texture and shelf life. Hydrogenated oils were also frequently used for frying at fast-food restaurants. Today, most fast-food companies are seeking alternatives to hydrogenated fats to reduce the level of *trans* fats in their products.

***trans* fat** Substance that contains mostly *trans* fatty acids, a result of hydrogenating an unsaturated fatty acid, causing a reconfiguring of some of its double bonds. A small amount of *trans* fatty acid occurs naturally in foods from animal sources.

SPOTLIGHT Mercury and Fish

Although the health benefits of eating fish are well established—they are excellent sources of omega-3 fatty acids and lean protein—not everyone should be eating unlimited amounts of *all* types of fish. In fact, pregnant and nursing women, women of childbearing age who may become pregnant, and young children should avoid certain types of seafood that may contain high amounts of *methylmercury*. This form of mercury can be harmful to the nervous system of unborn children, especially during the first trimester of pregnancy, a time when women may not even realize that they are pregnant.[1]

Large fish such as swordfish, shark, and tilefish are likely to contain high levels of methylmercury.

How does mercury make its way into fish? The airborne form of mercury accumulates on the surface of streams and oceans and is transformed by the bacteria in the water into the toxic form of methylmercury. The fish absorb the methylmercury from the water, or get it by eating the organisms that live in the water. Because the ingested methylmercury accumulates over time, larger fish, such as swordfish, shark, king mackerel, and tilefish (golden bass or golden snapper), will have the highest concentration of methylmercury; they have a longer life span and feed on other, smaller fish.

The Food and Drug Administration (FDA) recommends that women of childbearing age and young children avoid eating these four types of fish. Pregnant women and women of childbearing age can eat up to 12 ounces weekly of other types of cooked fish, including shellfish, and should choose from a variety of fish. Luckily, the ten most popular types of seafood (canned *light* tuna, shrimp, pollock, salmon, cod, catfish, clams, flatfish, crabs, and scallops) contain only low amounts of methylmercury. Canned albacore (white) tuna has more mercury than the light variety, so consumption should be limited to no more than 6 ounces weekly.[2]

While the FDA regulates all commercial fish, the Environmental Protection Agency (EPA) oversees all freshwater fish caught recreationally, such as by family members and friends. This agency recommends that all women who are or may become pregnant, nursing mothers, and young children should limit their consumption of freshwater fish to 6 ounces of cooked fish weekly for adults and 2 ounces of cooked fish weekly for children. Individuals who eat noncommercial fish from local waters should always check with the state or local health department for specific advice, as there could be additional fish consumption advisories for local waters. The EPA recommends that those who want to eat recreationally caught coastal and ocean fish also check with local or state health departments and follow the FDA guidelines above.[3]

References

1. Environmental Protection Agency. 2012. *Consumption Advice: Joint Federal Advisory on Mercury in Fish.* Available at http://water.epa.gov/scitech/swguidance/fishshellfish/outreach/factsheet.cfm. Accessed March 2012.
2. Ibid.
3. Ibid.

Despite the fact that the health effects of *trans* fats are now well known—research shows that *trans* fats raise LDL cholesterol levels and lower HDL cholesterol in the blood—these fats are still found in many foods. Processed foods, including commercially prepared baked goods, margarines, fried potatoes, snacks, shortenings, and salad dressings, are often major sources (**Figure 5.24**). About 15 to 20 percent of the *trans* fatty acids in the diet are naturally occurring in meat and dairy products. Ground beef, for example, contains approximately one gram of *trans* fats per 100 grams (3.5 ounces) of beef, while butter fat has double that amount.[11] Even some plant products contain small amounts of *trans* fatty acids. Pomegranates are low in fat but almost 70 percent of the fat they do contain is a *trans* fatty acid called punicic acid.[12] (However, pomegranates are still considered a healthy fruit.) *Trans* fat currently provides an estimated 2.5 percent of the daily kilocalories in the diets of American adults. Of this amount, about 25 percent of them are coming from naturally occurring *trans* fats.[13]

Research has suggested that *trans* fats pose a greater risk for heart health than saturated fat because they raise LDL cholesterol levels and lower HDL

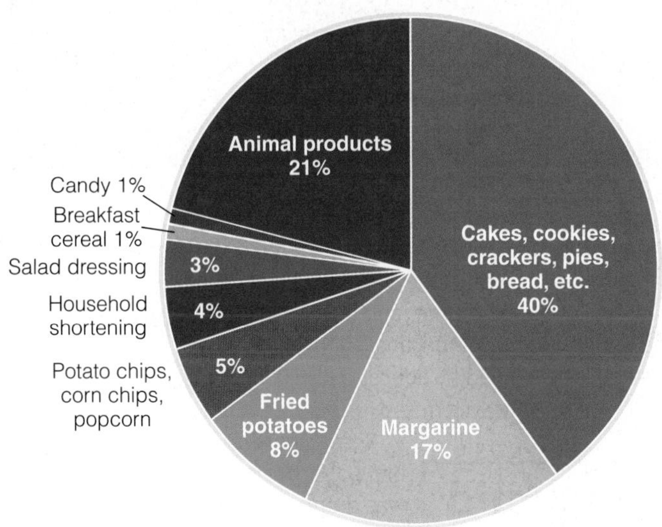

Figure 5.24 Major Food Sources of *Trans* Fat for American Adults
Commercially made baked goods and snack items are the major contributors of *trans* fat in the diet.

Data from FDA. 2003. "Questions and Answers About *Trans* Fat Nutrition Labeling."

cholesterol in the blood. Whether naturally occurring *trans* fats have the same heart-unhealthy effects as do those that are created through hydrogenation has yet to be determined. The bottom line is that *trans* fats should be kept as low as possible in the diet.

Trans Fats on Food Labels

To make consumers more aware of *trans* fat, the FDA mandates that most foods, and even some dietary supplements such as energy bars, list the grams of *trans* fats per serving.[14] Because the food label is also required to list the amount of saturated fat in foods, consumers can quickly calculate the saturated and *trans* fats in a given food and monitor the amount of these fats consumed.

Trans Fat in Foods

Food producers are testing new products to find a replacement for *trans* fatty acids in foods. The key objective is to produce oil that has the characteristics of *trans* fatty acids without increasing the risk of heart disease or otherwise compromising health. New methods being tested include genetically altering seeds to produce food products with new properties and hydrogenating oils and then altering them to change the *trans* fatty acid content. The process of **interesterification,** for example, rearranges the fatty acids on the triglyceride molecules found in plant oils. This improves the properties of the plant oils without changing the configuration to a *trans* fat. These altered fats can replace *trans* fats in pastries, margarines, shortening, and desserts.

The tropical palm kernel and coconut oils can be successfully changed using interesterification. Tropical oils have traditionally been shunned by the health community because of their high saturated fat content. The interesterification process alters the oils without using *trans* fats or increasing the saturated fat content.[15]

Cholesterol and Plant Sterols

Most of the dietary cholesterol we consume comes from animal products, such as meat, chicken, fish, shellfish, eggs, and dairy products. Some plants also produce cholesterol as part of the cell walls and oils in their leaves.[16] However, the quantity of cholesterol in plants is so small when it is expressed as a percent of the total lipid content (about 5 milligrams per 100 grams in plants, versus as much as 500 milligrams

interesterification The process that food manufacturers use to rearrange the fatty acids on the triglyceride molecule to improve the consistency and usefulness of processed food.

EXAMINING THE EVIDENCE

The Mediterranean Diet: What Do People Living in the Mediterranean Do Differently?

The Mediterranean diet doesn't refer to the diet of a specific country but to the dietary patterns found in several areas of the Mediterranean region, specifically Crete (a Greek island), other areas of Greece, and southern Italy, circa 1960. Researchers were drawn to these areas because the adults living there had very low rates of chronic diseases, such as heart disease and cancer, and a very long life expectancy. For example, the natives of Greece had a rate of heart disease that was 90 percent lower than that of Americans at that time.[1] Ironically, the people in Crete, in particular, were less educated and affluent, and less likely to obtain good medical care than were Americans, so their health successes could not be explained by education level, financial status, or a superior health care system.

Researchers found that compared with the diets of affluent Americans, the Cretans' diet was dramatically lower in foods from animal sources, such as meat, eggs, and dairy products, and higher in monounsaturated fats (mostly from olive oil and olives) and inexpensive grains, fruits, and vegetables.

Research continues to support the benefits of a Mediterranean-style diet. A study in Greece showed that greater adherence to a traditional Mediterranean diet was associated with greater longevity.[2] In another study, individuals who had experienced a heart attack, and then adopted a Mediterranean-style diet, had a 50 to 70 percent lower risk of recurrent heart disease compared with those following a more classic low-saturated-fat, low-cholesterol diet.[3, 4]

The newly updated Mediterranean Diet Pyramid shown here was designed to reflect these dietary patterns and lifestyle habits (see figure).[5]

The Healthy Mediterranean Diet Pyramid
A plant-based diet with minimal amounts of high-saturated-fat, high-sugar foods, coupled with daily physical activity, reflects the healthy habits of the Mediterranean lifestyle.

Mediterranean Lifestyle

The Mediterranean Diet Pyramid does not recommend any specific portion sizes for food. This purposeful omission portrays the relative importance and frequency of each group of foods as it contributes to the whole diet, rather than to a strict diet plan. It was designed to provide an overview of healthy food choices rather than dictate rigid amounts from each food group.[6]

Physical activity is front and center, at the base of this pyramid, reflecting the foundation for the Mediterranean way of life. This is an important concept, as the Mediterranean residents in the 1960s were very active and, not surprisingly, much leaner than Americans at that time. In addition to exercise, Mediterranean citizens enjoyed other lifestyle habits that have been known to promote good mental and physical health. They had a supportive community of family and friends, long relaxing family meals, and afternoon siestas (naps).[7] Exercising daily, resting, and relaxing with family and friends is good health advice for all, no matter what food pyramid you follow.

A Diet of Well-Seasoned Plant Foods, Olive Oil, Fish, and Dairy

Plant-based foods such as whole grains, fruits, vegetables, legumes, and nuts are the focus of the Mediterranean diet. In fact, more than 60 percent of the calories of the Cretans' diets in the 1960s were supplied by these high-fiber, nutritionally dense plant foods. In traditional Mediterranean-style eating, a combination of plant foods, such as vegetables and legumes ladled over couscous or pasta, was the focus of the meal.[8] Fresh bread, without margarine or butter, often accompanied the meal, and fruit was served as dessert.

More than 75 percent of the fat in the diets of the Cretans was supplied by olives and olive oil.[9] As previously discussed, vegetable oils are low in saturated fat, and olive oil in particular is high in monounsaturated fat. Heart-healthy meals featuring fish and seafood should be enjoyed at least twice a week, following the example of the Mediterraneans.

Nonfat milk and yogurt, and low- or reduced-fat cheeses can be enjoyed on a daily basis when eating a Mediterranean-style diet. A small amount of grated Parmesan cheese sprinkled over vegetables and a grain-based meal can provide a distinct Mediterranean flavor.

Occasional Poultry, Eggs, and Meat

Foods from animal sources were limited in the Cretan diet; local people consumed less than 2 ounces of meat and poultry daily.[10] No more than four eggs were eaten weekly, which included those used in cooking and baking. Following this trend, the Mediterranean Diet Pyramid suggests eating limited amounts of poultry and eggs weekly, but relegates red meat consumption to only occasionally.

Sweets, Water, and Wine

Historically, sweets were more prevalent during the holidays and fruit was the standard daily dessert.[11] Consequently, this pyramid recommends that consumption of honey- or sugar-based sweets remain modest. Water is recommended daily. The Cretans drank it all day long and with their meals. They also drank low to moderate amounts of wine, typically only with meals. Sometimes the wine was mixed with water, and many times women did not consume any alcohol. Though the pyramid depicts wine on a daily basis, it is actually considered optional and based on personal preferences, family and medical history, and social situations.

How Does the Mediterranean Diet Pyramid Compare with MyPlate?

There are many similarities between the Mediterranean Diet Pyramid and MyPlate. Both emphasize the importance of regular physical activity, and both encourage a plant-based diet rich in whole grains, fruits, and vegetables, and daily consumption of dairy products. Mediterranean-style eating encourages the use of olive oil, a fat source that is rich in heart-healthy, unsaturated fat, and fish and seafood. Vegetable oils are also encouraged on MyPlate, but more modestly. Whereas poultry, eggs, and meat are recommended more modestly in the Mediterranean Diet Pyramid than in MyPlate, both advise minimizing intake of sweets. Both tools can be used as a foundation for a healthy diet. The key is to stick to the recommendations.

References

1. Helsing, E. 1995. Traditional Diets and Disease Patterns of the Mediterranean, circa 1960. *American Journal of Clinical Nutrition* 61:1329S–1337S.
2. Kris-Etherton, P., R. H. Eckel, B. V. Howard, S. St. Jeor, and T. L. Bazzarre. 2001. Lyon Diet Heart Study: Benefits of a Mediterranean-Style, National Cholesterol Education Program/American Heart Association Step I Dietary Pattern on Cardiovascular Disease. *Circulation* 103:1823–1825.
3. Trichopoulou, A. N., T. Costacou, C. Bamia, and D. Trichopoulos. 2003. Adherence to a Mediterranean Diet and Survival in a Greek Population. *New England Journal of Medicine* 348:2599–2608.
4. de Loregil, M., P. Salen, J. L. Martin, I. Monjaud, J. Delaye, and N. Mamelle. 1999. Mediterranean Diet, Traditional Risk Factors, and the Rate of Cardiovascular Complications After Myocardial Infarction: Final Report of the Lyon Diet Heart Study. *Circulation* 99:779–785.
5. Willett, W. C., F. Sacks, A. N. Trichopoulou, G. Drescher, A. Ferro-Luzzi, E. Helsing, and D. Trichopoulos. 1995. Mediterranean Diet Pyramid: A Cultural Model for Healthy Eating. *American Journal of Clinical Nutrition* 61:1402S–1406S.
6. Ibid.
7. de Lorgeril, M. 1999. Mediterranean Diet.
8. Willet, W. C. 1995. Mediterranean Diet Pyramid; Nestle, M. 1995. Mediterranean Diets: Historical and Research Overview. *American Journal of Clinical Nutrition* 61:1313S–1320S.
9. Nestle, M. 1995. Mediterranean Diets: Historical and Research Overview.
10. Ibid.
11. Keys, A. 1995. Mediterranean Diet and Public Health: Personal Reflections. *American Journal of Clinical Nutrition* 61:1321S–1323S.

per 100 grams in foods from animal sources) that plant oils are considered cholesterol free. Thus the main lipid in plant fats and oils is a triglyceride.

Phytosterols (which lower LDL cholesterol levels by competing with cholesterol for absorption in the intestinal tract) and stanols occur naturally in soybean oil, many fruits, vegetables, legumes, sesame seeds, nuts, cereals, and other plant foods.[17] In addition, food manufacturers fortify foods such as margarine with plant sterols and stanols to help lower blood cholesterol.

Fat Substitutes Lower Fat in Foods

If you enjoy the taste and texture of creamy foods but don't want the extra fat, you're not alone. A research survey found that over 160 million Americans (79 percent of the adult population) chose lower fat foods and beverages. Respondents cited their health as the major reason they were actively shopping for these foods.[18] To meet this demand, food manufacturers introduced more than 1,000 reduced-fat or low-fat products, from margarine to potato chips, each year during the 1990s.[19] Today, with few exceptions, almost any high-fat food on the grocery store shelves will be sitting next to its lower fat counterpart. The keys to these products' lower fat content are **fat substitutes.**

Fat substitutes are designed to provide all the creamy properties of fat but with fewer kilocalories and total fat grams. Because fat has more than double the kilocalories per gram of carbohydrates or protein, fat substitutes have the potential to reduce kilocalories from fat by more than 50 percent without sacrificing taste and texture.

Carbohydrate-, Protein-, or Fat-Based Fat Substitutes

No single fat substitute works in all foods and with all cooking preparations, so several types of fat substitutes have been developed. Depending on their primary ingredient, fat substitutes fall into three categories: (1) carbohydrate-based substitutes, (2) protein-based substitutes, and (3) fat-based substitutes. Table 5.3 lists all three types of fat substitutes and their uses in foods.

- **Carbohydrate-Based Substitutes** The majority of fat substitutes are carbohydrate based and use plant polysaccharides such as fiber, starches, gums, and cellulose to help retain moisture and provide a fatlike texture.[20] For example, low-fat muffins might have fiber added to them to help retain the moisture that is lost when fat is reduced. Carbohydrate-based substitutes have been used for years and work well under heat preparations other than frying.
- **Protein-Based Substitutes** Protein-based fat substitutes are created from the protein in eggs and milk. The protein is heated and broken down into microscopic balls that tumble over each other during chewing, providing a creamy feel in the mouth that's similar to fat. Protein-based substitutes break down under high temperatures and lose their creamy properties, which makes them unsuitable for frying and baking.[21]
- **Fat-Based Substitutes** Fat-based substitutes are fats that have been modified to either provide the physical attributes of fat for fewer kilocalories than regular fat or to interfere with the absorption of fat.[22] Mono- and diglycerides are used as emulsifiers in products such as baked goods and icings to provide moistness and mouthfeel. These emulsifiers are used with water to replace part of the fat in bakery goods and ice creams. Though these remnants of fat have the same amount of kilocalories per gram as fat, less of them are needed to create the same effect, so the total amount of kilocalories and fat is reduced.

fat substitutes Substances that replace added fat in foods; they provide the creamy properties of fat for fewer kilocalories and total fat grams.

TABLE 5.3 The Lighter Side of Fat: Fat Substitutes

Name (trade names)	Kilocalories per Gram	Properties	Used For
Carbohydrate-Based			
Fibers from grains (Betatrim)	1–4	Gelling, thickener	Baked goods, meats, spreads
Fibers, cellulose (Cellulose gel)	0	Water retention, texture, mouthfeel	Sauces, dairy products, frozen desserts, salad dressings
Gums	0	Thickener, texture, mouthfeel, water retention	Salad dressings, processed meats
Polydextrose (Litesse)	1	Water retention, adds bulk	Baked goods, dairy products, salad dressings, cookies, and gum
Modified food starch (Sta-Slim)	1–4	Thickener, gelling, texture	Processed meats, salad dressings, frostings, fillings, frozen desserts
Protein-Based			
Microparticulated protein (Simplesse)	1–4	Mouthfeel	Dairy products, salad dressings, spreads
Fat-Based			
Mono- or diglycerides (Dur-Lo)	9*	Mouthfeel, moisture retention	Baked goods
Short-chain fatty acids (Salatrim)	5	Mouthfeel	Confections, baked goods
Olestra (Olean)	0	Mouthfeel	Savory snacks

*Less of this fat substitute is needed to create the same effect as fat, so the kilocalories are reduced in foods using this product.

Data from R. D. Mattes, "Fat Replacers," *Journal of the American Dietetic Association* 98 (1998): 463–468; J. Wylie-Rosett, "Fat Substitutes and Health: An Advisory from the Nutrition Committee of the American Heart Association," *Circulation* 105 (2002): 2800–2804.

One fat substitute, olestra (also known as Olean), is a mixture of sucrose and long-chain fatty acids. Unlike fat, which contains three fatty acids connected to a glycerol backbone, olestra contains six to eight fatty acids connected to sucrose. The enzymes that normally break apart fatty acids from their glycerol backbones during digestion cannot hydrolyze the fatty acids in olestra. Instead, olestra moves through the GI tract unabsorbed. Thus, this fat substitute has zero kilocalories. Olestra is very heat stable, so it can be used in baked and fried foods.

In 1996, the FDA approved olestra's use in salty snacks such as potato and corn chips. An ounce of potato chips made with olestra has half the kilocalories and none of the fat that an ounce of regular chips does. Because of its inability to be absorbed, there was concern about olestra's interference with the absorption of fat-soluble vitamins and carotenoids.[23] Consequently, the FDA has mandated that fat-soluble vitamins be added to olestra to offset these losses. There was also a concern that olestra may cause stomach cramps and loose stools. Though there have been anecdotal reports of individuals experiencing bouts of diarrhea and cramps after consuming olestra-containing products, controlled research studies don't seem to support the existence of such side effects.[24, 25] In a study of over 3,000 individuals, there was no significant difference in GI complaints between the group that consumed olestra-containing snacks and the individuals who ate regular snacks. Ironically, those who consumed the largest amount of *regular* chips actually complained more of loose stools and more frequent bowel movements than those consuming the olestra-containing chips. The FDA no longer requires a warning of the potential interaction with fat-soluble vitamins and carotenoids or the potential GI tract issues on the label. Even so, fat-soluble vitamins continue to be added to foods containing olestra.[26]

Foods made with fat substitutes aren't kilocalorie free.

Reduced-Fat Products

Despite their intended purpose, the use of fat substitutes doesn't seem to curb Americans' kilocalorie intake or help with weight management. One explanation for this may be that individuals feel a false sense of entitlement when eating low-fat and fat-free foods, and thus overeat. Research indicates that people who snack on olestra-containing products may be reducing their overall fat intake, but not their intake of total kilocalories.[27] As with sugar substitutes, consumers should recognize that using reduced-fat or fat-free products does not mean they can eat unlimited amounts of those foods. The foods still contain kilocalories, and overconsuming kilocalories leads to weight gain.

THE TAKE-HOME MESSAGE Lean meat and poultry, fish, low-fat or nonfat dairy products, and limited amounts of nuts and cheese are the best food sources to obtain the essential fatty acids and limit saturated and *trans* fats. Commercially prepared baked goods and snack items are high in kilocalories, saturated fat, and *trans* fats, and should be consumed rarely. Vegetable oils should be used in place of butter. *Trans* fats are found in many commercially prepared foods and must be listed on the food label. Cholesterol is found mostly in animal products, while plant products, such as vegetable oils, nuts, legumes, whole grains, fruits, and vegetables, contain mostly phytosterols. Fat substitutes can be carbohydrate-based, protein-based, or fat-based. Reduced-fat or fat-free foods still contain kilocalories and should be eaten in limited amounts.

Putting It All Together

How do lipids fit in with carbohydrates and the healthy eating tools when it comes to creating an overall healthy diet? As mentioned in the preceding chapter, your diet should include a proper balance of all nutrients, especially carbohydrates and fat, to meet daily energy needs and for optimal long-term health. There are different types of lipids, some essential and others not required from foods. Aim for a diet consisting mostly of unsaturated fats and limit the amount of saturated and *trans* fats. Use the MyPlate diagram and the DRIs to plan meals that are abundant in complex carbohydrates, fiber, and essential fatty acids. A plant-based diet plentiful in whole grains, fruits, and vegetables, with some low-fat dairy and lean meat, poultry, fish, and vegetable oils will be high in fiber and lower in saturated fats, *trans* fats, and dietary cholesterol.

Nutrition in Practice: Adam

Adam, a 20-year-old junior in finance, returned from spring break with a laboratory report from his doctor's office that showed that his blood cholesterol levels were too high. The note on the report stated that he should meet with a Registered Dietitian to see if he could change his diet to lower his levels. Both his mom and dad have high blood cholesterol, so Adam wasn't shocked by his own results. Because he has an unlimited meal plan at college, his mom suggested that he set up an appointment with the campus dietitian for nutrition counseling and advice about what to eat at the dining hall.

Adam's Stats:

- Age: 20
- Height: 5 feet 11 inches
- Weight: 170 pounds
- BMI: 23.7
- Total Cholesterol: 240 mg/dl
- LDL Cholesterol: 185 mg/dl
- HDL Cholesterol: < 40 mg/dl

Critical Thinking Questions

1. How could Adam's food and beverage choices potentially contribute to his high blood cholesterol level?
2. What foods could be added to Adam's diet that may help lower his cholesterol?
3. What lifestyle changes could Adam make to possibly increase his HDL cholesterol?

Dietitian's Observation and Plan for Adam:

- Discuss the need to reduce saturated fat to less than 10 percent of total kilocalories and dietary cholesterol to less than 300 milligrams (mg) per day. Use egg whites or an egg substitute when ordering an omelet, switch from whole to 2% milk, replace butter with tub margarine, and use reduced-fat Cheddar cheese instead of full-fat cheese. Order a turkey sandwich at lunch and skinless poultry or fish more often at dinner. Try to consume at least two fish meals weekly.
- Increase dietary fiber, especially soluble fiber. Try to have a soup or salad with meals and add beans from the salad bar. Add a piece of fruit to breakfast and snacks.
- Increase physical activity to at least 2.5 hours weekly. Exercise may help increase the HDL cholesterol.

Three weeks later, Adam visits the dietitian again. He has made the switch from whole milk to 2% milk and butter to margarine, added the soup and salad with his meals, and is walking on the treadmill at the gym. A review of his food record shows that his saturated fat is a little over 10 percent of his total calorie intake but his dietary cholesterol is less than 300 mg. He is having difficulty eating two fish meals weekly and eating fruit. The dietitian suggests that Adam consume tuna fish sandwiches at lunch at least twice a week and switch to 1% milk to decrease his saturated fat intake. She also recommends that he take a couple of pieces of fruit from the dining hall for a high-fiber evening snack.

Adam's Food Log

Food/Beverage	Time Consumed	Hunger Rating*	Location
3-egg omelet with cheese Wheat toast w/butter OJ	9:30 am	5	In dining hall
Ham & cheese sandwich Potato chips Whole milk	1:30 pm	3	In dining hall
Oreos and whole milk	3 pm	4	Studying in dorm room
Steak, mashed potatoes, peas	6:30 pm	4	In dining hall
Pretzels	11 pm	4	In dorm room

*Hunger Rating (1–5): 1 = not hungry; 5 = super hungry

Health Connection

What Is Heart Disease and What Factors Increase Risk?

Cardiovascular disease is a name that encompasses several disorders affecting the heart, including problems with heart valves, heartbeat irregularities, and infections. But the most common type of heart disease is *coronary heart disease,* which affects the blood vessels that serve the heart muscle, and can lead to a heart attack. That's the type we focus on in this chapter.

Heart disease has been the number-one killer of adults in the United States since 1918. Currently, one in six deaths among Americans is caused by heart disease. Though it was once believed to be more of a danger to males than females, heart disease actually poses somewhat more of a risk to women than to men. More than 267,000 American women die each year—about one every minute—from heart disease, or six times more than those who die from breast cancer. About 232,000 men lose their lives to heart disease annually.[1]

Heart Disease Begins with Atherosclerosis

Heart disease develops when the coronary arteries, the large blood vessels that lead to the heart, accumulate substances such as fat and cholesterol along their walls. As the artery narrows, blood flow is impeded, and less oxygen and nutrients are delivered to the heart. If the heart doesn't receive enough oxygen, chest pains can result.

Narrowed arteries increase the likelihood that a blood clot can get caught and block the vessel, leading to a **heart attack.** If the artery leads to the brain, a **stroke** can occur. Over 9 million Americans experience chest pains (a symptom of heart disease), and 8 million suffer a heart attack every year.[2]

The exact cause of the narrowed arteries, known as **atherosclerosis** (*athero* = porridge, *sclera* = hardening, *sis* = condition), is unknown, but researchers believe it begins with an injury to the lining of the arteries. Just as with a cut finger or sprained ankle, the injury results in inflammation. Inflamed arterial walls may develop weak areas that can rupture easily, increasing the risk of blood clots and a heart attack. High blood levels of cholesterol and fat, high blood pressure, and smoking likely contribute to this damage.

Over time, LDLs and other lipid substances infiltrate the injured artery wall.[3] The LDLs that accumulate become oxidized by reacting with free radicals and metal ions such as iron; attract macrophages (white blood cells), which become enlarged with cholesterol-laden LDLs; and develop into foam cells. The foam cells stick to the walls of the artery and build up, along with platelets (fragments of cells in the blood) and other substances, into **plaque.** The plaque narrows the passageway of the artery (see Figure 1).

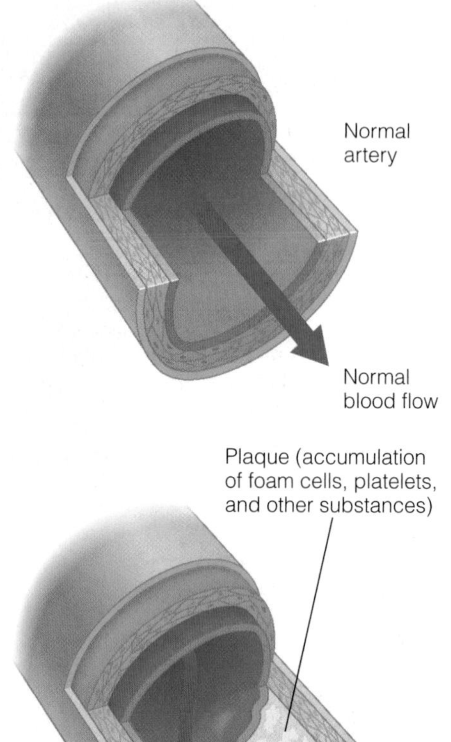

▲ **Figure 1 Atherosclerosis**
When plaque builds up in the coronary arteries, it narrows the passageway and causes a decreased flow of oxygen-rich blood to the heart. A clot, traveling in the blood, can partially or totally block the arteries to the heart, leading to a heart attack.

Risk Factors for Heart Disease

In addition to diet, there are several factors that affect the likelihood of developing heart disease (see Table 1). Some of these risk factors, such as age, gender, and heredity, cannot be controlled. Others, including exercise, smoking, and maintaining a healthy body weight, can be controlled.

Uncontrollable Risk Factors

Blood cholesterol, along with the risk of a heart attack, tends to rise with age until it stabilizes around age 65. Gender also plays a role. Up until menopause (usually around age 50), women tend to have a lower blood cholesterol level than men and a reduced risk of heart disease. After menopause, the blood cholesterol level in women tends to catch up and even surpass that of men of the same age.[4] About one in eight American women between 45 and 64 years of age has heart disease, but this increases to one out of every three women over the age of 65.

TABLE 1 Risk Factors for Heart Disease

Uncontrollable Risk Factors	Controllable Risk Factors	Emerging Risk Factors
Age	Type 2 diabetes mellitus	Blood levels of C-reactive protein
Gender	High blood pressure	High amount of homocysteine
Family history of heart disease	Smoking	Presence of *Chlamydia pneumoniae* in the blood
Type 1 diabetes mellitus	Physical activity	Lp(a) protein
	Excess body weight	Metabolic syndrome
	Low HDL blood cholesterol	
	High LDL blood cholesterol	

The decrease in the level of the hormone estrogen in postmenopausal women plays a part in the increased risk.[5]

Genetics can also be a risk factor for heart disease, as high LDL cholesterol levels can run in families.[6] An individual whose father or brother had early signs of heart disease before age 55, or whose mother or sister had them before age 65, is at a greater risk. This may be due to a genetic defect in the LDL receptor that regulates the amount of LDL cholesterol in the blood. Family members who have this defective gene have elevated LDL levels in the blood, which may produce premature atherosclerosis.[7]

Controllable Risk Factors

Diabetes is a significant risk factor for heart disease; an estimated 75 percent of adults with diabetes die due to heart disease and stroke. It's not surprising, then, that controlling diabetes can help dramatically lower the risk of heart disease.[8] Though the less common form of diabetes, type 1, is not preventable, the more prevalent form, type 2 diabetes, can be managed, and possibly even prevented, through diet, exercise, and other lifestyle changes.

Blood pressure (the force of blood against the walls of the arteries) can affect the risk of heart disease. Chronic high blood pressure, or **hypertension,** can damage the arteries and begin the progression of atherosclerosis. A **normal blood pressure** is considered less than 120 millimeters mercury (Hg) for the systolic pressure (the top number in the blood pressure reading) and less than 80 millimeters Hg for the diastolic pressure (the bottom number). A blood pressure reading of 140/90 or higher is considered hypertension.

Chronic high blood pressure thickens the arteries and causes them to become stiff and less flexible, which may initiate injury to the arterial walls and accelerate plaque buildup. Chronic high blood pressure also causes the heart to work harder than normal and can lead to an enlarged heart. (Chapter 12 contains a detailed discussion of hypertension and how a healthy diet can help lower high blood pressure.)

Smoking damages the walls of the arteries and accelerates atherosclerosis. In fact, women smokers are two to six times more likely to have a heart attack than female nonsmokers. Male smokers also increase their risk for heart disease.[9]

Regular exercise is one way to help lower LDL cholesterol, raise HDL cholesterol, and reduce hypertension. Only 30 minutes of moderate-level physical activity, such as brisk walking, bicycling, raking leaves, or gardening, most days of the week, is sufficient to provide a health benefit.

Because high HDL cholesterol can help protect against heart disease, having an HDL level of less than 40 milligrams per deciliter (mg/dl) increases risk. In contrast, having a high level of HDL cholesterol, 60 mg/dl or higher, is considered a negative risk factor. In other words, there is so much of this good cholesterol helping to protect against heart disease that it counteracts another risk factor on the list.

In addition to regular exercise, losing excess weight, consuming only moderate amounts of alcohol, and quitting smoking can help increase the levels of HDL cholesterol. Exercise can also help sustain a healthy body weight. Obesity correlates to thicker arterial walls and can raise the levels of LDL cholesterol.[10]

Emerging Risk Factors

Some individuals have normal levels of LDL cholesterol in their blood, yet still develop heart disease, which points to other factors that must be affecting their heart health. These other potential risk factors are referred to as emerging risk factors.

Researchers continually search for clues or blood markers other than cholesterol that indicate the presence of heart disease. One important marker is high blood levels of **C-reactive protein (CRP),** which is produced when there is inflammation.[11] Because of the critical link between inflammation and heart disease, measuring CRP levels can assist in predicting the risk of heart attacks.[12] Another blood marker associated with atherosclerosis is a high amount of the amino

heart attack Permanent damage to the heart muscle that results from a sudden lack of oxygen-rich blood; also called a myocardial infarction (MI).

stroke A condition caused by a lack of oxygen to the brain that could result in paralysis and possibly death.

atherosclerosis Narrowing of the coronary arteries due to buildup of debris along the artery walls.

plaque The hardened buildup of cholesterol-laden foam cells, platelets, cellular waste products, and calcium in the arteries that results in atherosclerosis.

hypertension High blood pressure; defined as a systolic blood pressure higher than 140 mm Hg and/or a diastolic blood pressure greater than 90 mm Hg.

normal blood pressure A systolic blood pressure less than 120 mm Hg (the top number) and a diastolic blood pressure less than 80 mm Hg (the bottom number). Referred to as 120/80.

C-reactive protein (CRP) A protein found in the blood that is released from the cells during inflammation; used as a marker for the presence of atherosclerosis.

acid *homocysteine*. High levels of this amino acid may injure the arteries, decrease their flexibility, and increase the likelihood of blood clots. The presence of *Chlamydia pneumoniae,* a bacterium that can cause pneumonia and respiratory infections, in the blood may also damage or inflame the vessel walls. Lastly, another lipoprotein, **Lp(a) protein,** is being investigated for its role in causing excessive blood clotting and exacerbating inflammation.

Metabolic syndrome refers to a cluster of risk factors that put some people at risk for heart disease regardless of their level of LDL cholesterol. The risk factors include abdominal obesity, high blood pressure, elevated blood levels of triglycerides and the slower clearance of this fat from the blood, a low level of HDL cholesterol, smaller and more dense LDL cholesterol particles, the higher likelihood of forming and maintaining blood clots, too much insulin, and, possibly, too much glucose in the blood.

The culprit behind this syndrome appears to be the resistance of the cells in the body to insulin. Being overweight and inactive increases the risk for insulin resistance. Exercise and weight reduction can help reduce all risk factors associated with this syndrome.[13]

TABLE 2 What Blood Cholesterol Levels* Indicate

If Total Cholesterol Level Is (mg/dl)	That Is Considered
< 200	Desirable
200–239	Borderline high
≥ 240	High
If LDL Cholesterol Level Is (mg/dl)	**That Is Considered**
< 100	Optimal
100–129	Near or above optimal
130–159	Borderline high
160–189	High
≥ 190	Very high
If HDL Cholesterol Is (mg/dl)	**That Is Considered**
> 60	Desirable
40–60	Adequate
< 40	Low

Note: *All lipoprotein levels are measured in milligrams of cholesterol per deciliter of blood (mg/dl).

Data from National Cholesterol Education Program, "Detection, Evaluation, and Treatment of High Blood Cholesterol in Adults (Adult Treatment Panel III)," National Institutes of Health Publication No. 01-3290 (2001).

How Can High Blood Cholesterol Levels Be Lowered?

The primary risk factor for heart disease is elevated blood lipids, especially the LDL cholesterol level.[14] Starting at age 20, individuals should have their blood tested at least once every five years to obtain a **blood lipid profile.** This profile includes tests for total cholesterol, HDL cholesterol, LDL cholesterol, and triglycerides. Often the profile will also include the cholesterol-to-HDL ratio or a risk score calculated from the lipid measurements, age, gender, and other risk factors.[15] Table 2 indicates the optimal blood levels for total cholesterol, LDL cholesterol, and HDL cholesterol.

The best way to impact blood levels of these lipids is through diet, exercise, and other lifestyle factors.

Consume Less Saturated and *Trans* Fat and Moderate Cholesterol Intake

In general, blood levels of LDL cholesterol increase on a high-saturated-fat diet, not a high-cholesterol diet. In fact, research has shown that foods high in cholesterol that are also low in saturated fat, such as egg yolks and shellfish, have a much lower effect on LDL cholesterol than high-saturated-fat diets alone.[16] Thus, replacing saturated fats in the diet with unsaturated fats will have a blood-cholesterol-lowering effect.

Flaxseed oil is low in saturated fat.

The Impact of Saturated Fatty Acids

It may not be just the total saturated fat intake that raises LDL cholesterol. The type of saturated fatty acid may have a greater influence. Saturated fatty acids such as myristic acid, which is high in butterfat and coconut oil, and palmitic acid both raise LDL cholesterol levels.[17] But the saturated fat stearic acid does not appear to do so.[18]

That stearic acid does not appear to raise LDL cholesterol levels is positive news for chocolate lovers.[19] Though the cocoa butter in chocolate is high in saturated fatty acids, the predominant fat is stearic acid. In addition to the stearic acid, chocolate contains high levels of antioxidant flavonoids, which also help reduce the risk of heart disease. Not all chocolates are created equal, however. Dark chocolate has four times the amount of flavonoids as milk chocolate, and white chocolate contains none. In spite of these benefits, keep in mind that chocolate is still high in kilocalories and shouldn't be

TABLE 3 The Cholesterol-Raising Effects of Popular Foods

Food	Total Fat (g)	Saturated Fat (g)	*Trans* Fat (g)	Total Cholesterol-Raising Fats (g) (Saturated Fats + *Trans* Fats)
Spreads				
Butter, 1 tbs	11	7.0	0.5	7.5
Margarine (stick), 1 tbs	11	2.0	3.0	5.0
Margarine (tub), 1 tbs	6.5	1.0	0.5	1.5
Commercially Prepared Foods and Snacks				
French fries, medium (fast food)	27	6.5	8.0	14.5
Doughnut, 1	18	4.5	5.0	9.5
Potato chips, small bag	11	2.0	3.0	5.0
Cookies, 3	6	1.0	2.0	3.0

Data from U.S. Food and Drug Administration. 2012. Talking About Trans Fat: What You Need to Know. Available at www.fda.gov/Food/ResourcesForYou/Consumers/ucm079609.htm. Accessed October 2012; U.S. Department of Agriculture. 2002. *National Nutrient Database for Standard Reference, Release 15.* Available at www.nal.usda .gov/fnic/foodcomp/search.

consumed in excessive amounts. Reducing saturated fat intake overall, regardless of the type of fatty acid in the molecule, will reduce LDL cholesterol and the risk of heart disease.

The Impact of *Trans* Fats

Per kilocalorie, *trans* fats appear to increase the risk of heart disease more than any other nutrient.[20] Controlled studies have shown that a diet containing *trans* fats raises levels of LDL cholesterol, lowers HDL cholesterol, and increases the ratio of total cholesterol to HDL cholesterol.[21] These fats also increase the blood levels of triglycerides and inflammation along the arterial wall.

Americans consume about five times more saturated fat than *trans* fat, and decreasing the *trans* fats in the diet while simultaneously increasing the saturated fat won't be healthy for the heart.[22] This was illustrated when, years ago, some consumers switched from using stick margarine, which is high in *trans* fat, to butter, thinking that butter was better for their blood cholesterol. As shown in Table 3, though butter has less *trans* fat than stick margarine, if you consider the saturated fat and *trans* fat in each spread, margarine would still be the better choice to lower blood cholesterol.

The best grocery list for lowering blood cholesterol levels includes foods that are low in saturated fats, *trans* fats, and cholesterol. Specifically, lean meats, fruits and vegetables, whole grains, fish, shellfish, and fat-free dairy products are healthy choices. Processed foods, such as snacks and bakery items that contain *trans* fats plus saturated fats, increase the risk of heart disease and therefore should be consumed in moderation or avoided entirely.

Fatty fish, such as salmon, are an excellent source of omega-3 fatty acids.

Eat More Fish and Plant Foods

The American Heart Association (AHA) encourages Americans to increase their fish and plant-based foods consumption as part of a heart-healthy diet. This dietary pattern increases omega-3 fatty acids, reduces saturated fat and LDL cholesterol, and adds soluble dietary fiber and heart-healthy phytochemicals.

Fish and Seafood

In general, seafood contains an abundance of healthy fats. It's true that some shellfish, such as shrimp, are high in cholesterol, but they are very low in saturated fat and contain some heart-healthy omega-3 fatty acids. Lobster has less than one-third the amount of cholesterol of shrimp and is very low in total fat. Unfortunately, the high price of shrimp and lobster limits their consumption for many people.

Over a decade ago, researchers suggested that the Greenland Eskimos' regular consumption of fatty fish (approximately 14 ounces a day), which is rich in EPA and DHA, played a key role in their low incidence of dying from heart disease.[23] Ongoing research continues to support the protective roles EPA and DHA may play to reduce the risk of heart disease and stroke. These omega-3 fatty acids may prevent an irregular heartbeat, reduce atherosclerosis, mildly lower blood pressure, decrease the clustering or clumping of platelets, lower the level of fat in the blood, and modestly increase the amount of good HDL cholesterol in the blood.[24] In fact, research studies have shown that eating an ounce or more of fish daily may help to reduce the risk of dying from heart disease, and that consuming even one fish meal per week may help reduce the risk of heart attack.[25]

The American Heart Association (AHA) recommends consuming at least two servings of fish (especially fatty fish) per week to obtain omega-3 fatty acids.[26] These recommendations should be met with baked, poached, or broiled fish. Fried fish that is commercially prepared tends to have few omega-3 fatty acids and is often fried in unhealthy fat. The Table Tips provide a few quick ways to add

Lp(a) protein A lipoprotein containing LDL cholesterol found in the blood; this lipoprotein has been correlated to increased risk of heart disease.

blood lipid profile A measurement of blood lipids used to assess cardiovascular risk.

TABLE TIPS

Easy Ways to Add Fish to the Diet

Flake canned salmon over a lunch or dinner salad.
Add tuna to cooked pasta and vegetables and toss with a light salad dressing for a quick pasta salad meal.
Order baked, broiled, or grilled fish when dining out.
Try a shrimp cocktail for added omega-3 fatty acids.

fish to your diet. Note some cautions regarding fish consumption in the Spotlight: Mercury and Fish on page 184.

Though consuming some omega-3 fatty acids is good, more may not be better. Because EPA and DHA interfere with blood clotting, consuming more than 3 grams, which typically only happens by taking supplements, could raise both blood glucose and LDL cholesterol levels, increase the risk of excessive bleeding, and cause other related problems such as hemorrhagic stroke (*hemo* = blood, *rhagic* = ruptured flow) in certain people.[27] Because of these potential adverse side effects, omega-3 fatty acid supplements (fish oil supplements) should only be consumed with the advice and guidance of a doctor. Eating one gram of EPA and DHA daily from fish may provide some protection against heart disease without any known adverse side effects.[28]

Plant Foods

The AHA also recommends consuming foods such as soybean and canola oils, walnuts, and flaxseeds that are high in alpha-linolenic acid.[29] Some alpha-linolenic acid is converted in the body to omega-3 fatty acids.[30]

Eating more plant foods high in viscous, soluble fiber may be one of the easiest ways to decrease LDL cholesterol levels. In reviewing over 65 studies, researchers found that each gram of viscous, soluble fiber consumed, in the range of 2 to 10 grams daily, lowered LDL cholesterol levels over 2.0 milligrams per deciliter on average.[31] While the DRI for fiber ranges from 20 to 38 grams daily, consuming about half of this amount, or 10 to 25 grams, can help decrease high LDL cholesterol levels.

Increasing soy consumption may also help reduce the risk of heart disease. In a review of over 35 studies, researchers found that soy protein lowered total cholesterol, LDL cholesterol, and triglycerides by approximately 10 percent each, on average.[32]

Plant sterols are effective in lowering LDL cholesterol. In a study of over 150 individuals with mildly high cholesterol levels, a margarine containing a plant sterol was shown to reduce LDL cholesterol levels by approximately 14 percent after one year of use.[33] Although the mechanism is still unclear, it appears that foods enriched with plant sterols reduce the absorption of cholesterol in the intestinal tract. Consuming 2 grams of plant sterols per day lowers LDL cholesterol levels by 10 percent and may cut heart disease risk up to 20 percent.[34] Products such as margarines, yogurt, cream cheese spreads, cereals, fruit juices, and soft-gel tablets that contain plant sterols are now available.

Benecol, a margarine made with plant sterols, may reduce LDL cholesterol levels in the blood.

Chemistry Boost

Fatty Acid Notations

Fatty acids are frequently represented by two different methods of notation. The first method, the delta (Δ) system, is often used by chemists (see figure below). In this form, the first number indicates the number of carbons in the chain. The second number, after the colon, notes how many double bonds are in the molecule. The two superscript numbers indicate the location of the two double bonds from the carboxyl end of the fatty acid.

The second method, called the omega (ω) system, is similar to the delta system. This system uses either the symbol w or the letter *n* after the number of double bonds. This symbol notes the position of the first double bond from the omega (methyl) end of the fatty acid. In polyunsaturated fatty acids, double bonds are usually separated by three carbons. Using this notation makes it easy to locate the rest of the double bonds in a fatty acid molecule. With linoleic acid, the first double bond is located on carbon 6, followed by the second double bond on carbon 9.

Delta system describing linoleic acid:

$$18{:}2\ \Delta^{9,12}$$

Omega system describing linoleic acid:

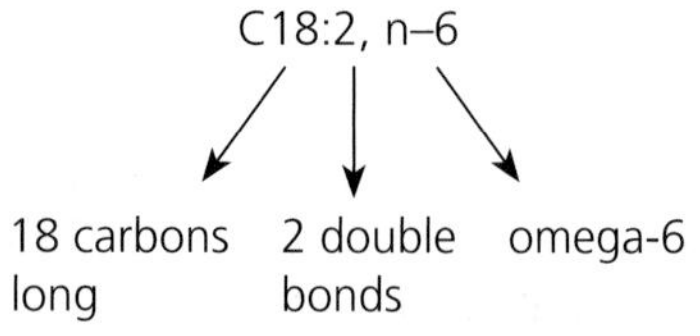

Consume Antioxidants and Phytochemicals

You might think that a substance that begins with the prefix "anti" couldn't be good for you. However, a diet rich in plants contains antioxidants and phytochemicals that protect tissues from oxidative damage (for more explanation on antioxidants, see Chapter 9). These potent chemicals neutralize free radicals that are formed during oxidative metabolism, stimulate your immune system to repair tissue damage, and reduce the risk of heart disease.

Antioxidants

Antioxidants, including the vitamins C and E, and beta-carotene, appear to protect LDL cholesterol from oxidation by inhibiting the formation of oxidants, intercepting them once they are created, or helping to repair any injury to cells due to these substances. Antioxidants may help LDL cholesterol become more resistant to oxidants.[35]

Antioxidant-rich foods contain many other vitamins and minerals, which are not only healthy for the heart in their own right, but may work with antioxidants. These foods are naturally low in saturated fat and *trans* fat and are cholesterol free, so they can displace heart-unhealthy foods in the diet. Nuts are one type of food that is rich in antioxidants, and they can have a positive effect on LDL cholesterol levels for other reasons. Research involving healthy men showed that a diet with 20 percent of the kilocalories coming from walnuts lowered LDL cholesterol by a little over 15 percent. A study of over 80,000 women showed that those who ate nuts frequently—an ounce of nuts at least five times a week—had approximately a 35 percent reduction in the risk of heart disease compared with women who hardly ever ate nuts.[36] Nuts are high in fiber, and contain plant sterols and folic acid, which has been shown to help reduce homocysteine levels in the blood.

Though high in kilocalories, nuts are an excellent source of antioxidants, have zero cholesterol, and are low in saturated fat.

The only disadvantage to nuts is that they're high in kilocalories. An ounce of nuts (about 24 almonds or 28 peanuts) can contribute 160 to 200 kilocalories to the diet. Without adjusting for these kilocalories elsewhere, weight gain will occur. The Table Tips on this page provide ideas on how to enjoy a moderate amount of nuts in the diet.

TABLE TIPS

Nuts About Nuts?

- Toss some nuts into a mealtime salad. Use less oil or salad dressing and more nonfat vinegar to adjust for the added kilocalories.
- Swap nuts for meat, like chicken or beef, in meals such as stir-fries. A third of a cup of nuts is equal to an ounce of red meat or chicken.
- Add a tablespoon of nuts to morning cereal, and use skim rather than reduced-fat milk to offset some of the extra kilocalories.
- Add a tablespoon of chopped nuts to an afternoon yogurt.
- Add a handful of peanuts to air-popped popcorn for a snack.

Phytochemicals

Other substances may provide an extra boost to heart health. Garlic has been found in some studies to reduce high blood cholesterol levels by inhibiting cholesterol synthesis in the body, decreasing the clustering of platelets, interfering with blood clotting, and helping to lower blood pressure. Sulfur-containing compounds, specifically allicin, that are abundant in garlic are believed to be the protective factor.[37] However, some researchers question whether adding garlic as part of a low-fat, low-cholesterol diet has a substantial cholesterol-lowering benefit.[38]

Black and green tea are high in **flavonoids,** phytochemicals similar to antioxidants that are believed to prevent LDL cholesterol from becoming oxidized in the body. In a study of over 800 elderly men, those who consumed the most flavonoids, predominantly from tea, cut their risk of dying from heart disease by about half compared with those who had low flavonoid consumption.[39] Drinking tea may be beneficial even if a person has already had a heart attack. In a study of 1,900 heart attack victims, researchers found that those who consumed large amounts of tea (> 14 cups weekly) had a 44 percent lower risk of dying from a heart attack during the three-and-a-half-year follow-up period than those who didn't consume any tea. Even those who drank moderate amounts of tea (< 2 cups weekly) fared better than tea abstainers, reducing their risk by 28 percent.[40]

When it comes to reducing the risk of heart disease, the whole diet may be greater than the sum of its parts. A study of over 45 adults with elevated total and LDL cholesterol levels illustrated that a diet "portfolio" consisting of a diet low in saturated fat and cholesterol and that was high in soluble fiber, soy protein, plant sterols, and nuts lowered LDL cholesterol levels by almost 30 percent. This impressive reduction was similar to that observed in the group that was given a cholesterol-lowering drug but was limiting *only* the saturated fat and cholesterol in their diet. (The latter group's diet did not include the other items in the portfolio diet.)[41] Hence, a dietary portfolio approach to eating may be a viable way for individuals to lower high cholesterol levels and avoid taking medication that could have potential side effects.[42] The Table Tips on the next page summarize several eating tips for a heart-healthy diet.

flavonoids Phytochemicals found in fruits, vegetables, tea, nuts, and seeds that have antioxidant properties and neutralize free radicals.

TABLE TIPS

Eating for a Healthy Heart

Choose only lean meats (round, sirloin, and tenderloin cuts) and skinless poultry, and keep portions to about 6 ounces daily. Eat fish at least twice a week.

Use two egg whites in place of a whole egg when baking.

Use reduced-fat or nonfat dairy products, such as low-fat or skim milk, reduced-fat cheese, and low-fat or nonfat ice cream. Sprinkle cheese on top of food rather than mixing it in, so as to use less. Be sure to keep ice cream servings small.

Substitute cooked beans for half the meat in chili, soups, and casseroles.

Use canola, olive, soybean, or corn oil, and *trans* fat–free margarine instead of butter or shortening.

Get Plenty of Exercise and Manage Your Weight

Routine exercise can help reduce LDL cholesterol levels, high blood pressure, insulin resistance, and excess weight, and raise HDL cholesterol levels.[43] A review of over 50 studies involving more than 4,500 people found that exercise training for more than 12 weeks increased HDL cholesterol levels by about 4.5 percent. Currently, the AHA recommends that healthy individuals partake in 30 minutes or more of moderate exercise on most days, if not every day. This amount of physical activity is considered sufficient to help reduce the risk of heart disease, but exercising longer than 30 minutes or at higher intensity could offer greater protection, especially when it comes to maintaining a healthy body weight.[44] Sedentary individuals should "move" and sedentary, overweight individuals should "move and lose" to lower their risk of heart disease. Table 4 summarizes the diet and lifestyle changes that can help lower LDL cholesterol levels and risk for heart disease.

TABLE 4 To Decrease Excess LDL Cholesterol

Dietary Changes	Lifestyle Changes
Consume less saturated fat	Lose excess body weight
Consume less *trans* fats	Exercise more
Consume less dietary cholesterol	
Consume more soluble fiber–rich foods	
Consume a more plant-based diet	

A Word about the Protective Effects of Red Wine and Alcohol

Some studies have shown that drinking alcohol in moderate amounts can reduce the risk of heart disease.[45] The heart-protective action of alcohol may occur through three different mechanisms. Alcohol can increase the level of the heart-protective HDL cholesterol. In fact, approximately 50 percent of alcohol's heart-protective effect is probably due to this positive effect on HDL cholesterol. Other studies have suggested that alcohol may decrease blood clotting by affecting the coagulation of platelets or by helping the blood to break up clots.[46] Still other research has suggested that the antioxidants in wine as well as in dark beer also contribute to the heart-protective aspects of alcohol.[47]

However, the health benefits of alcohol have only been shown to occur in middle-aged individuals and the problems associated with overconsumption far outweigh the health benefits of moderate consumption. In fact, individuals who consume three or more drinks per day *increase* their risk of dying prematurely.[48] (We will talk more about alcohol in Chapter 7.)

References

1. American Heart Association. 2011. Heart Disease and Stroke Statistics—2012 Update: A Report from the American Heart Association. *Circulation* 125: e2–e220.
2. Ibid.
3. American Heart Association. 2008. *Atherosclerosis.* Available at www.americanheart.org. Accessed March 2012.
4. National Heart, Lung, and Blood Institute. 2005. *High Blood Cholesterol: What You Need to Know.* NIH Publication No. 01-3290. Available at www.nhlbi.nih.gov/health/public/heart/chol/hbc_what.htm. Accessed March 2012.
5. Sandmaier, M. 2007. *The Healthy Heart Handbook for Women.* National Heart, Lung, and Blood Institute. NIH Publication No. 03-2720.
6. American Heart Association. 2007. *Know the Facts, Get the Stats 2007.*
7. Goldstein, J. L. and M. S. Brown. 1987. Regulation of Low-Density Lipoprotein Receptors: Implications for Pathogenesis and Therapy of Hypercholesterolemia and Atherosclerosis. *Circulation* 76:504–507.
8. American Heart Association. 2007. K*now the Facts, Get the Stats* 2007.
9. National Heart, Lung, and Blood Institute. 2003. *Quitting Smoking.* Available at www.nhlbi.nih.gov/hbp/prevent/q_smoke/q_smoke.htm. Accessed June 2008.
10. Pace, B., C. L. Lynn, and R. M. Glass. 2001. Alcohol Use and Heart Disease. *Journal of the American Medical Association* 285:2040.
11. Devaraj, S., S. Valleggi, D. Siegel, and I. Jialal. 2010. Role of C-Reactive Protein in Contributing to Increased Cardiovascular Risk in Metabolic Syndrome. *Current Atherosclerosis Reports* 12:110–118.
12. Windgassen, E. B., L. Funtowicz, T. N. Lunsford, et al. 2011. C-Reactive Protein and High-Sensitivity C-Reactive Protein: An Update for Clinicians. *Postgraduate Medicine* 123:114–119.
13. Grundy, S. M., N. Abate, and M. Chandalia. 2002. Diet Composition and the Metabolic Syndrome: What Is the Optimal Fat Intake? *American Journal of Medicine* 113:25S–29S.
14. Seo, T., Q. Kemin, C. Chang, Y. Liu, T. S. Worgall, R. Ramakrishnan, and R. J. Deckelbaum. 2005. Saturated Fat–Rich Diet Enhances

Selective Uptake of LDL Cholesteryl Esters in the Arterial Wall. *Journal of Clinical Investigation* 115:2214–2222.

15. D'Agostino, R. B., R. S. Vasan, and M. J. Pencina. 2008. General Cardiovascular Risk Profile for Use in Primary Care. The Framingham Heart Study. *Circulation* 117:743–753.
16. Howard, B. V., L. Van Horn, J. Hsia, J. E. Manson, M. L. Stefanick, S. Wassertheil-Smoller, L. H. Kuller, et al. 2006. Low-Fat Dietary Pattern and Risk of Cardiovascular Disease: The Women's Health Initiative Randomized Controlled Dietary Modification Trial. *Journal of the American Medical Association* 295:655–666.
17. de Roos, N. M., E. G. Schouten, and M. B. Katan. 2001. Consumption of a Solid Fat Rich in Lauric Acid Results in a More Favorable Serum Lipid Profile in Healthy Men and Women than Consumption of a Solid Fat Rich in *Trans*-Fatty Acids. *Journal of Nutrition* 131:242–245.
18. Sundram, K., T. Karupaiah, and K. C. Hayes. 2007. Stearic Acid–Rich Interesterified Fat and *Trans*-Rich Fat Raise the LDL/HDL Ratio and Plasma Glucose Relative to Palm Olein in Humans. *Nutrition and Metabolism* 4:1–12.
19. Ding, E., S. Hutfless, X. Ding, and S. Girotra. 2006. Chocolate and Prevention of Cardiovascular Disease: A Systematic Review. *Nutrition and Metabolism* 3:2.
20. Mozaffarian, D., M. B. Katan, A. Ascherio, M. J. Stampfer, and W. C. Willett. 2006. *Trans*-Fatty Acids and Cardiovascular Disease. *New England Journal of Medicine* 354:1601–1611.
21. Aroa, A., J. M. Antoineb, L. Pizzoferrantoc, O. Reykdald, and G. van Poppel. 1998. *Trans*-Fatty Acids in Dairy and Meat Products from 14 European Countries: The TRANSFAIR Study. *Journal of Food Composition and Analysis* 11:150–160.
22. Food and Drug Administration. 2011. Trans *Fat Now Listed with Saturated Fat and Cholesterol on the Nutrition Facts Label.* Available at www.fda.gov/Food/ResourcesForYou/Consumers/NFLPM/ucm274590.htm. Accessed March 2012.
23. Kramhout, D., E. B. Bosschieter, and C. Coulander. 1985. The Inverse Relation between Fish Consumption and 20-Year Mortality from Coronary Heart Disease. *New England Journal of Medicine* 312:1205–1209.
24. Institute of Medicine. 2002. *Dietary Reference Intakes for Energy, Carbohydrate, Fiber, Fat, Fatty Acids, Cholesterol, Protein, and Amino Acids.* Washington, DC: The National Academies Press.
25. Marckmann, P. and M. Grønbæk. 1999. Fish Consumption and Coronary Heart Disease Mortality. A Systematic Review of Prospective Cohort Studies. *European Journal of Clinical Nutrition* 53:585–590.
26. Kris-Etherton, P. M., W. S. Harris, and L. J. Appel. 2002. Fish Consumption, Fish Oil, Omega-3 Fatty Acids, and Cardiovascular Disease. *Circulation* 106:2747–2757.
27. Ibid.
28. Kris-Etherton, P. M. and A. M. Hill. 2008. N-3 Fatty Acids: Food or Supplements? *Journal of the American Dietetic Association* 108:1125–1130.
29. Kris-Etherton, P. M., D. S. Taylor, S. Yu-Poth, P. Huth, K. Moriarty, V. Fishell, R. L. Hargrove, G. Zhao, and T. D. Etherton. 2000. Polyunsaturated Fatty Acids in the Food Chain in the United States. *American Journal of Clinical Nutrition* 71:179S–188S.
30. Ibid.
31. Brown, L., B. Rosner, W. Willett, and F. Sacks. 1999. Cholesterol-Lowering Effects of Dietary Fiber: A Meta-Analysis. *American Journal of Clinical Nutrition* 69:30–42.
32. Anderson, J., B. Johnstone, and M. Cook-Newell. 1995. Meta-Analysis of the Effects of Soy Protein Intake on Serum Lipids. *New England Journal of Medicine* 333:276–282.
33. Katan, M. B., S. M. Grundy, P. Jones, M. Law, T. Miettinen, and R. Paoletti. 2003. Efficacy and Safety of Plant Stanols and Sterols in the Management of Blood Cholesterol Levels. *Mayo Clinic Proceedings* 78:965–978.
34. Anderson, J. W. 2003. Diet First, Then Medication of Hypercholesterolemia. *Journal of the American Medical Association* 290:531–533.
35. Tribble, D. L. 1999. AHA Science Advisory. Antioxidant Consumption and Risk of Coronary Heart Disease: Emphasis on Vitamin C, Vitamin E, and Beta-Carotene. *Circulation* 99:591–595.
36. Hu, F. B., M. J. Stampfer, J. E. Manson, E. B. Rimm, G. A. Colditz, B. A. Rosner, F. E. Speizer, C. H. Hennekens, and W. C. Willett. 1998. Frequent Nut Consumption and Risk of Coronary Heart Disease in Women: Prospective Cohort Study. *British Medical Journal* 317:1341–1345.
37. Spigelski, D. and P. J. Jones. 2001. Efficacy of Garlic Supplementation in Lowering Serum Cholesterol Levels. *Nutrition Reviews* 59:236–244.
38. Rahman, K. and G. M. Lowe. 2006. Garlic and Cardiovascular Disease: A Critical Review. *Journal of Nutrition* 136:736S–740S.
39. Mukamal, K. J., M. Maclure, J. E. Muffer, J. B. Sherwood, and M. A. Mittleman. 2002. Tea Consumption and Mortality After Acute Myocardial Infarction. *Circulation* 105:2476–2481.
40. Ibid.
41. Jenkins, D. J., C. W. Kendal, A. Marchie, D. A. Faulkner, J. M. Wong, R. de Souza, A. Emam, et al. 2003. Effects of a Dietary Portfolio of Cholesterol-Lowering Foods vs Lovastatin on Serum Lipids and C-Reactive Protein. *Journal of the American Medical Association* 290:502–510.
42. Anderson, J. W. 2003. Diet First.
43. Myers, J. 2003. Exercise and Cardiovascular Health. *Circulation* 107:e2–e5.
44. Thompson, P. D., D. Buchner, I. Pina, G. Balady, M. A. Williams, B. H. Marcus, K. Berra, et al. 2003. AHA Scientific Statement. Exercise and Physical Activity in the Prevention and Treatment of Atherosclerotic Cardiovascular Disease. A Statement from the Council on Clinical Cardiology (Subcommittee on Exercise, Rehabilitation, and Prevention) and the Council on Nutrition, Physical Activity, and Metabolism (Subcommittee on Physical Activity). *Circulation* 107:3109–3116.
45. Goldberg, I. J., L. Mosca, M. R. Piano, and E. A. Fisher. 2001. Wine and Your Heart: A Science Advisory for Healthcare Professionals from the Nutrition Committee, Council on Epidemiology and Prevention, and Council on Cardiovascular Nursing of the American Heart Association. *Circulation* 103:472–475.
46. Rimm, E. B. and R. C. Ellison. 1995. Alcohol in the Mediterranean Diet. *American Journal of Clinical Nutrition* 61:1378S–1382S.
47. Rimm, E. B., A. Klatsky, D. Grobbee, and M. J. Stampfer. 1996. Review of Moderate Alcohol Consumption and Reduced Risk of Coronary Heart Disease: Is the Effect Due to Beer, Wine or Spirits? *British Medical Journal* 312:731–736.
48. Mukamal, K. J., K. M. Conigrave, M. A. Mittleman, C. A. Camaro, M. J. Stampfer, W. C. Willett, and E. B. Rimm. 2003. Roles of Drinking Pattern and Type of Alcohol Consumed in Coronary Heart Disease in Men. *New England Journal of Medicine* 348:109–118.

Visual Chapter Summary

1 Lipids Are Organic Water Insoluble Compounds That Vary in Structure

Lipids refer to a category of carbon, oxygen, and hydrogen compounds that don't dissolve in water. There are three types of lipids: triglycerides, phospholipids, and sterols. Triglycerides and phospholipids are built from a fatty acid, which consist of a chain of carbon and hydrogen atoms with an acid group (COOH) at the *alpha* end and a methyl group (CH_3) at the *omega* end.

Short-chain fatty acids contain two to four carbons; medium-chain fatty acids have six to 10 carbons; and long-chain fatty acids have 12 or more carbons. A saturated fatty acid has all of its carbons bound with hydrogen. An unsaturated fatty acid that has one double bond is called a monounsaturated fatty acid. A polyunsaturated fatty acid contains two or more double bonds. If the first double bond is located between the third and fourth carbon from the omega end it is called an omega-3 fatty acid. The first double bond for an omega-6 fatty acid is between carbons six and seven from the omega end.

Unsaturated fatty acids have either a *cis* (hydrogen atoms are on the same side of the double bond) or *trans* configuration (one hydrogen atom is on the opposite side of the double bond).

Lipid	Structure
Triglycerides	Glycerol; Fatty acids
Phospholipids	Polar head; Fatty acids
Sterols	
Cholesterol	HO
Sistanol	HO

2 Lipids Are Digested and Absorbed in the Small Intestine

Most fat digestion occurs in the small intestine. Fat globules are emulsified by bile before pancreatic lipase hydrolyzes the fatty acids producing two free fatty acids and a monoglyceride. Sterols are absorbed intact. Phospholipids are hydrolyzed by phospholipases.

Glycerol and short- and medium-chain fatty acids enter the portal vein and go directly to the liver. Free long-chain fatty acids reattach to the glycerol molecule to reform a triglyceride in the enterocyte. These fats are combined into a chylomicron with other dietary lipids and released into the lymph fluid.

Chylomicrons transport dietary fat to the cells. Very low-density lipoproteins (VLDLs) and low-density lipoproteins (LDLs) carry lipids from the liver to the cells. High-density lipoproteins (HDLs) pick up cholesterol from the body cells and return it to the liver.

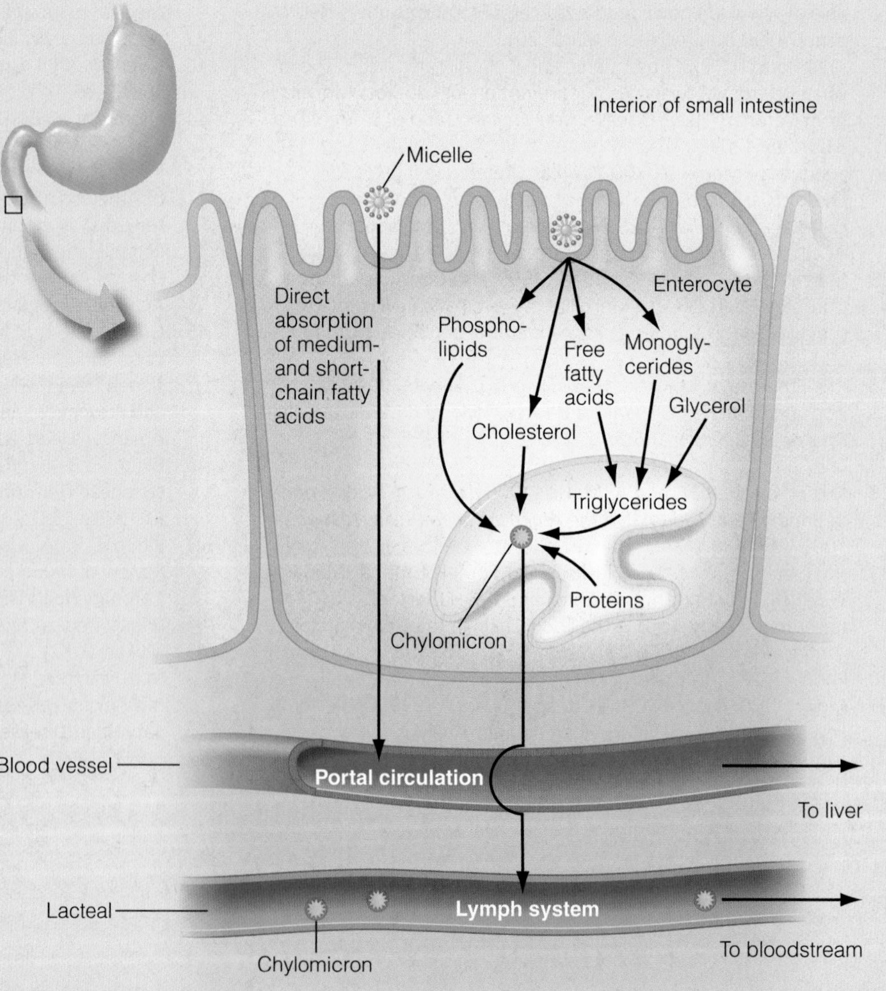

3 Fat Plays Many Key Roles in the Body

Fats provide essential fatty acids, enhance the absorption of the fat-soluble vitamins, provide a layer of insulation, and cushion the major organs. Fat is also an important source of energy, providing 9 kilocalories per gram.

Phospholipids and cholesterol make up the cell membranes. Cholesterol is also a precursor for vitamin D, bile, and sex hormones such as estrogen and testosterone.

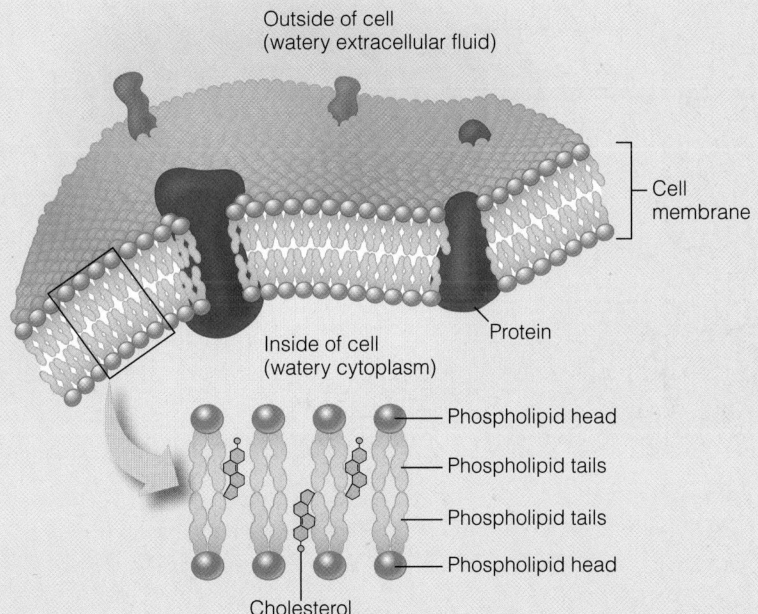

4 Moderate Consumption of Dietary Fat Is Essential for Health

The AMDR recommendation is for 20 to 35 percent of the daily kilocalories to come from fat, no more than 10 percent from saturated fat and less than 1 percent from *trans* fats. A minimum of 5 to 10 percent of the total kilocalories should come from linoleic acid and 0.6 to 1.2 percent from alpha-linolenic acid.

Men aged 19 to 50 need 17 grams and women need 12 grams of linoleic acid daily. Men aged 14 to 70 need 1.6 grams and women need 1.1 grams of alpha-linolenic daily.

Healthy individuals over the age of 2 are advised to limit their dietary cholesterol to under 300 milligrams daily.

5 The Best Food Sources of Fat Contain Unsaturated Fats and Essential Fatty Acids

Unsaturated fats are abundant in vegetable oils, soybeans, walnuts, flaxseeds, and wheat germ, and these are also all good sources of linoleic acid. Walnuts, flaxseeds, and canola oil are good sources of alpha-linolenic acid.

Most saturated fat comes from animal foods such as fatty cuts of meat, whole-milk dairy products, butter, ice cream, and the skin of poultry. Certain vegetable oils, such as coconut, palm, and palm kernel oils, are very high in saturated fat and are often found in candies, commercially made baked goods, and gourmet ice cream. *Trans* fats are mostly found in processed foods. Dietary cholesterol is found only in foods from animal sources including egg yolks, meats, and whole fat dairy.

6 Too Much Fat Can Lead to Heart Disease

Consuming too much dietary fat can lead to high blood cholesterol levels which is a major cause of heart disease. The goal is to lower the LDL level to less than 100 milligrams per deciliter (mg/dl) and raise the HDL level to greater than 40 mg/dl.

To lower LDL cholesterol, eat a well-balanced plant-based diet that contains lean meats and dairy foods with moderate amounts of heart-healthy unsaturated fat; limit commercially prepared baked goods, snack items, and fried foods to decrease *trans* fat intake; and eat more soluble fiber-containing foods such as oats, legumes, psyllium-containing cereal, soy protein, and plant sterols.

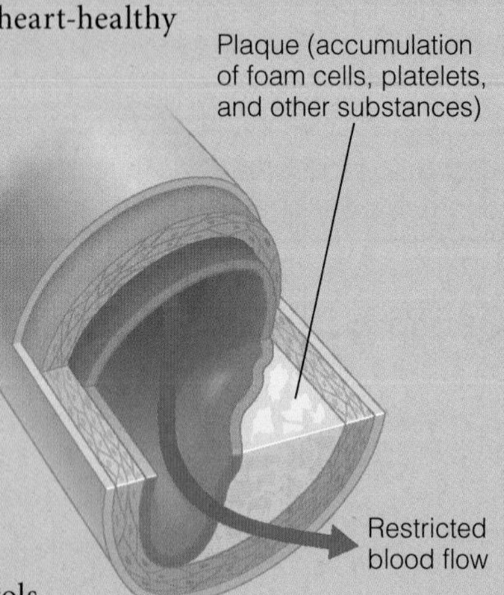

Terms to Know

- fatty acids
- short-chain fatty acids
- medium-chain fatty acids
- long-chain fatty acids
- saturated fatty acid
- unsaturated fatty acid
- monounsaturated fatty acid
- polyunsaturated fatty acid
- omega-3 fatty acid
- omega-6 fatty acid
- essential fatty acids
- linoleic acid
- alpha-linolenic acid
- *cis*
- *trans*
- rancidity
- glycerol
- triglyceride
- fat
- phospholipids
- sterols
- monoglyceride
- lipoprotein
- chylomicron
- lymph fluid
- very low-density lipoproteins (VLDLs)
- low-density lipoproteins (LDLs)
- high-density lipoproteins (HDLs)
- adipocytes

MasteringNutrition™

Build your knowledge—and confidence!—in the Study Area of MasteringNutrition with a variety of study tools.

Check Your Understanding

1. Which statement best describes the characteristics of a polyunsaturated fatty acid?
   a. They are solid at room temperature.
   b. They are higher in kilocalorie content than a saturated fatty acid.
   c. They tend to be liquid at room temperature.
   d. They are more stable than saturated fatty acids and resist oxidation.
2. Fatty acids are classified by
   a. the number of carbons in the fatty acid chain.
   b. the number of double bonds in the fatty acid chain.
   c. the shape of the fatty acid chain.
   d. all of the above.
3. The type of lipoprotein that carries absorbed dietary fat and other lipids through the lymph system is called
   a. Lp(a) protein.
   b. a VLDL.
   c. an LDL.
   d. a chylomicron.
4. Arachidonic acid and docosahexaenoic acid (DHA) are
   a. used to manufacture hormonelike substances called eicosanoids.
   b. stored as part of the subcutaneous tissue needed to insulate the body.
   c. the main fatty acids used to manufacture bile in the liver.
   d. used by the body to manufacture the essential fatty acids linoleic acid and alpha-linolenic acid.
5. The AMDR for dietary fat is
   a. 8 to 10 percent of daily kilocalories.
   b. 20 to 35 percent of daily kilocalories.
   c. 40 to 45 percent of daily kilocalories.
   d. under 300 milligrams to 500 milligrams daily.
6. At least two fish meals should be consumed weekly to obtain the heart-healthy omega-3 fatty acids. Examples of heart-healthy fish meals include
   a. a tuna fish sandwich and a Burger King fish sandwich.
   b. boiled or grilled shrimp and grilled salmon.
   c. fish and chips and flounder.
   d. fried fish sticks and steamed lobster.
7. Which of the following foods does not contain dietary cholesterol?
   a. steak
   b. chicken
   c. low-fat milk
   d. peanut butter
8. Which of the following foods are good sources of the essential fatty acids linoleic acid and alpha-linolenic acid?
   a. flaxseeds
   b. cheese
   c. butter
   d. oranges
9. The major dietary component that raises LDL cholesterol is
   a. viscous soluble fiber.
   b. dietary cholesterol.
   c. saturated fat.
   d. plant sterols.
10. To raise the level of HDL cholesterol,
    a. increase the viscous, soluble fiber in the diet.
    b. increase exercise.
    c. maintain a healthy body weight.
    d. do all of the above.

Answers

1. (c) The double bonds in polyunsaturated fatty acids prevent them from packing together tightly. This causes them to be liquid at room temperature, not solid. The double bonds are less stable and more easily oxidized compared with saturated fatty acids. All fatty acids, regardless of type, have 9 kilocalories per gram.
2. (d) The number of carbons in the chain determine whether a fatty acid is short chain, medium chain, or long chain. Fatty acids are either saturated or unsaturated, depending on the presence of double bonds, and they have either a *cis* or a *trans* shape, or configuration.
3. (d) Chylomicrons are capsule-shaped carriers that enable insoluble fat as well as cholesterol and phospholipids to travel through the watery lymph system to the bloodstream. Lp(a) protein contains cholesterol and is correlated with an increased risk for heart disease. VLDLs and LDLs are lipoproteins that transport fat and other lipids through the blood.
4. (a) Arachidonic acid and docosahexaenoic acid (DHA) are used to manufacture eicosanoids such as prostaglandins, thromboxanes, and leukotrienes, not to be stored in subcutaneous tissue, or used to synthesize cholesterol. These two compounds are made from the essential fatty acids linoleic acid and alpha-linolenic acid.
5. (b) The AMDR for daily fat intake is 20 to 35 percent of total daily kilocalories. Saturated fat and *trans* fat intake should be less than 10 percent of daily kilocalories and dietary cholesterol should be kept under 300 milligrams daily.
6. (b) While tuna fish is a wonderful way to enjoy fish at lunch, the commercially prepared fried fish sandwich, fish and chips, and fish sticks have little of the heart-healthy omega-3 fatty acids. Boiled shrimp and grilled salmon are much healthier ways to enjoy fish.
7. (d) Because plant sources are not a significant source of dietary cholesterol, peanut butter, which is made from peanuts and vegetable oils, is free of dietary cholesterol.
8. (a) Flaxseeds are a good source of essential fatty acids.
9. (c) Whereas dietary cholesterol raises LDL cholesterol, saturated fat is the bigger culprit behind elevated LDL cholesterol in the blood. Viscous, soluble fiber, such as psyllium, as well as plant sterols can help lower LDL cholesterol.
10. (b) Increasing exercise can help increase the HDL cholesterol level. Increasing soluble fiber intake and maintaining a healthy body weight can help lower the LDL cholesterol level but does not affect the level of HDL cholesterol.

Answers to Myths and Misconceptions

1. **False.** While the body *does* need cholesterol for important functions, it can be synthesized in the liver in sufficient amounts. Thus, consuming dietary cholesterol is not necessary.
2. **False.** Whereas too much dietary fat may cause weight gain, eating too little isn't healthy either. A diet low in fat but high in added sugars may increase the level of fat in the blood.
3. **False.** Though the majority of *trans* fats are made from hydrogenated oils that are found in commercially prepared, processed foods, *trans* fats also occur naturally in foods such as meat and dairy products.
4. **True.** A diet high in saturated fat can raise blood cholesterol.
5. **False.** Fat-free foods are not necessarily kilocalorie free. In fact, in most cases fat-free foods have the same amount of kilocalories, because of added carbohydrates, as their fat-containing counterparts.
6. **True.** High levels of HDL cholesterol can help reduce the risk of heart disease.
7. **False.** Although stick margarines can contain heart-unhealthy *trans* fats, butter has more total cholesterol-raising fats than margarine, and so is ultimately less healthy.
8. **False.** Because nuts are plant foods, they do not contain cholesterol but are rich sources of essential fatty acids.
9. **False.** Consuming too much fish oil can be unhealthy. The best source of omega-3 fatty acids is fresh fish.
10. **False.** LDL cholesterol is a lipoprotein carrier found in the blood and is not found in foods.

Web Resources

To learn more about lipids and health, visit

- National Cholesterol Education Program at www.nhlbi.nih.gov/about/ncep
- EPA Fish Advisories at www.epa.gov/waterscience/fish/advice
- American Heart Association at www.americanheart.org
- EFA Education at http://efaeducation.nih.gov
- National Heart, Lung, and Blood Institute at www.nhlbi.nih.gov/health/public/heart/index.htm
- Centers for Disease Control and Prevention, Physical Activity, Energize Your Life! at www.cdc.gov/nccdphp/dnpa/physical/index.htm
- Heart Healthy Women at www.hearthealthywomen.org
- WebMD Heart Health Center at www.webmd.com/heart/default.htm
- Lipid Corner for the Lipid Research Division of ASBMB at www.asbmb.org/lipidcorner
- MEDLINE Plus Health Information at www.nlm.nih.gov/medlineplus

References

1. Chanmugam, P., J. F. Guthrie, S. Cecilio, J. F. Morton, P. Basiotis, and R. Anand. 2003. Did Fat Intake in the United States Really Decline between 1989–1991 and 1994–1996? *Journal of the American Dietetic Association* 103:867–872.
2. Ibid.
3. Stephen, A. M. and N. J. Wald. 1990. Trends in Individual Consumption of Dietary Fat in the United States, 1920–1984. *American Journal of Clinical Nutrition* 52:457–469.
4. U.S. Department of Agriculture, Agricultural Research Service. 2008. *Nutrient Intakes from Food: Mean Amounts Consumed per Individual, One Day, 2005–2006.* Available at www.ars.usda.gov/ba/bhnrc/fsrg. Accessed January 2010.
5. Institute of Medicine. 2005. *Dietary Reference Intakes for Energy, Carbohydrate, Fiber, Fat, Fatty Acids, Cholesterol, Protein, and Amino Acids.* Washington, DC: The National Academies Press.
6. Ibid.
7. Institute of Medicine. 2006. *Dietary Reference Intakes: The Essential Guide to Nutrient Requirements.* Washington, DC: The National Academies Press.
8. Schuchardt, J. P., I. Schneider, H. Meyer, J. Neubronner, C. von Schacky, and A. Hahn. 2011. Incorporation of EPA and DHA into Plasma Phospholipids in Response to Different Omega-3 Fatty Acid Formulations—A Comparative Bioavailability Study of Fish Oil vs. Krill Oil. *Lipids in Health and Disease* 10:145.
9. Institute of Medicine. 2006. *Dietary Reference Intakes.*
10. Elvevoll, E. O., H. Barstad, E. S. Breimo, J. Brox, K. E. Eilertsen, T. Lund, J. O. Olsen, and B. Osterud. 2006. Enhanced Incorporation of ω-3 Fatty Acids from Fish Compared with Fish Oils. *Lipids* 41:1109–1114.
11. Aroa, A., J. M. Antoineb, L. Pizzoferratoc, O. Reykdald, and G. van Poppel. 1998. *Trans*-Fatty Acids in Dairy and Meat Products from 14 European Countries: The TRANSFAIR Study. *Journal of Food Composition and Analysis* 11:150–160.
12. Ibid.
13. Allison, D. B., S. K. Egan, L. M. Barraj, C. Caughman, M. Infante, and J. Heimbach. 1999. Estimated Intakes of *Trans* Fatty and Other Fatty Acids in the U.S. Population. *Journal of the American Dietetic Association* 99:166–174.
14. Food and Drug Administration. 2011. Trans *Fat Now Listed with Saturated Fat and Cholesterol on the Nutrition Facts Label.* Available at www.fda.gov/Food/ResourcesForYou/Consumers/NFLPM/ucm274590.htm. Accessed March 2012.
15. Upritchard, J. E., M. J. Zeelenberg, H. Huizinga, P. M. Verschuren, and E. A. Trautwein. 2005. Modern Fat Technology: What Is the Potential for Heart Health? *Proceedings of the Nutrition Society* 64:379–386.
16. Behrman, E. J. and V. Gopalan. 2005. Cholesterol and Plants. *Journal of Chemical Education* 82:1791–1793.
17. Law, M. 2000. Plant Sterol and Stanol Margarines and Health. *British Medical Journal* 320:861–864.

18. Calorie Control Council. 2012. *Fat Replacers.* www.caloriecontrol.org/sweeteners-and-lite/fat-replacers. Accessed October 2012.
19. Mattes, R. D. 1998. Fat Replacers. *Journal of the American Dietetic Association* 98:463–468.
20. Wylie-Rosett, J. 2002. Fat Substitutes and Health: An Advisory from the Nutrition Committee of the American Heart Association. *Circulation* 105:2800–2804.
21. Calorie Control Council. 2012. *Fat Replacers: Food Ingredients for Healthy Eating.* Available at www.caloriecontrol.org/sweeteners-and-lite/fat-replacers. Accessed March 2012.
22. Ibid.
23. Mattes, R. D. 1998. Fat Replacers.
24. Sandler, R. S., N. L. Zorich, T. G. Filloon, H. B. Wiseman, D. J. Lietz, M. H. Brock, M. G. Royer, and R. K. Miday. 1999. Gastrointestinal Symptoms in 3,181 Volunteers Ingesting Snack Foods Containing Olestra or Triglycerides: A 6-Week Randomized, Placebo-Controlled Trial. *Annals of Internal Medicine* 130:253–261.
25. Cheskin, L. J., R. Miday, N. Zorich, and T. Filloon. 1998. Gastrointestinal Symptoms Following Consumption of Olestra or Regular Triglyceride Potato Chips: A Controlled Comparison. *Journal of the American Medical Association* 279:150–152.
26. Food and Drug Administration. August 5, 2003. *Food Additives Permitted for Direct Addition to Food for Human Consumption; Olestra; Final Rules.* 21 CFR Part 172. *Federal Register.* Available at www.fda.gov/OHRMS/DOCKETS/98fr/03-19508.pdf. Accessed March 2012.
27. Patterson, R. E., A. R. Kristal, J. C. Peters, M. L. Neuhouser, C. L. Rock, L. J. Cheskin, D. Neumark-Sztainer, and M. D. Thornquist. 2000. Changes in Diet, Weight, and Serum Lipid Levels Associated with Olestra Consumption. *Archives of Internal Medicine* 160:2600–2604.

6 Proteins

Chapter Objectives

After reading this chapter, you will be able to:

1. Describe the basic structure of an amino acid, and classify amino acids as essential, nonessential, or conditionally essential.
2. Identify the key steps in digesting protein.
3. Explain the metabolism of amino acids and the role of the amino acid pool.
4. Identify the functions of protein in the body.
5. Calculate the amount of protein recommended for an individual based on the Dietary Reference Intakes.
6. Describe the best food sources of protein and the methods available to determine protein quality.
7. Explain the health consequences of consuming too little or too much protein.
8. Describe the benefits and risks of a vegetarian diet.

1. Proteins are chemically different from carbohydrates or lipids because they contain nitrogen. T/F
2. Proteins are made up of 20 essential amino acids. T/F
3. The first step in the chemical digestion of protein occurs in the mouth with the enzyme pepsin. T/F
4. Hydrochloric acid denatures protein in the stomach. T/F
5. The body can use protein as a source of glucose. T/F
6. The primary function of protein is to provide energy to the cells. T/F
7. Growing children are in a state of negative nitrogen balance. T/F
8. Animal products are a good source of incomplete protein. T/F
9. Eating too much protein is associated with high blood cholesterol levels. T/F
10. Consuming a diet inadequate in protein may lead to a disease called kwashiorkor. T/F

See page 249 for answers to these Myths and Misconceptions.

Proteins are the predominant structural and functional materials in every cell. In fact, protein alone makes up 50 percent of your body's dry weight. Proteins do most of the work of the cell and are necessary to facilitate movement in bones and muscles. Your protein-rich muscles enable you to swim, jog, walk, and hold your head up so you can read this textbook. Without adequate protein, you couldn't replace the skin cells that slough off when you shower or produce sufficient antibodies to fight off infections. Your hair wouldn't grow, your fingernails would be mere stubs, and you wouldn't be able to digest your food.

In this chapter we discuss the structure and roles of proteins and how they are digested, absorbed, and metabolized in the body. We will also cover the health risks associated with consuming too much or too little protein and the pros and cons of different eating patterns, including vegetarian diets.

Protein-rich muscles enable you to perform daily activities.

What Are Proteins?

Proteins are macronutrients found in each cell in the body. These diverse molecules play a role in virtually every cellular activity, from building, repairing and maintaining cells to storage, transport, and utilization of the nutrients you eat.

Hormones and enzymes, which control essential metabolic processes, are also made of proteins. These proteins direct how fast the body burns kilocalories, how quickly the heart beats, and possibly your attraction to another person.[1] In fact, proteins are involved in most of the body's functions and life processes, and without them, you wouldn't survive.

Proteins Differ Structurally from Carbohydrates and Lipids

In Chapters 4 and 5, you learned that dietary carbohydrates are chains of glucose units, while most dietary lipids contain chains of fatty acids (see **Figure 6.1**). Proteins are also made of chains, but in this case the units (or building blocks) are called **amino acids.** These chains of proteins are synthesized based on the individual's

proteins Large molecules, made up of chains of amino acids, that are found in all living cells; the sequence of amino acids is determined by the DNA.

amino acids The building blocks of protein. There are 20 different amino acids composed of carbon, hydrogen, oxygen, and nitrogen.

peptide A protein chain made up of fewer than 50 amino acids.

dipeptide A protein chain made up of two amino acids joined together by a peptide bond.

tripeptide A protein chain made up of three amino acids joined together by peptide bonds.

polypeptide A protein chain consisting of ten to more than a hundred amino acids joined together by peptide bonds.

Macronutrients	Composed of	Example
Carbohydrates	Monosaccharides	Glucose units
Lipids	Fatty acids	Triglyceride Fatty acids
Proteins	Amino acids	Amino acids

▲ **Figure 6.1 Structural Differences between Carbohydrates, Lipids, and Proteins**
Carbohydrates, some lipids, and proteins are similar in their chainlike structures. The main difference is that proteins contain nitrogen and carbohydrates and lipids do not. Carbohydrates are composed of glucose chains, triglycerides and phospholipids contain fatty acid chains, and proteins are made of chains of amino acids.

unique DNA. Unlike dietary carbohydrates and triglycerides, excess dietary protein cannot be stored in the body.

Chemically, the structure of protein is similar to carbohydrates and lipids in that all three nutrients contain atoms of carbon (C), hydrogen (H), and oxygen (O). Protein is unique, however, because 16 percent of each protein molecule is nitrogen (N), found in the amine group. In fact, protein is the only food component that provides the nitrogen the body needs for important processes, such as the synthesis of neurotransmitters. Some proteins found in eggs, meat, dairy products, nuts, and seeds also contain the mineral sulfur (S), which is not found in either carbohydrates or lipids.

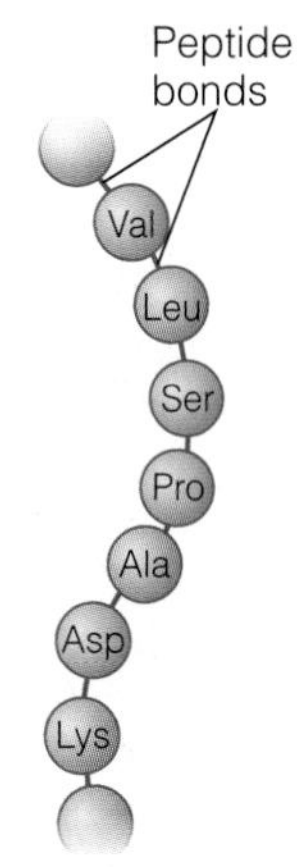

▲ **Figure 6.2 The Building Blocks of Proteins Are Amino Acids**
Proteins are composed of chains of amino acids linked together.

The Building Blocks of Proteins Are Amino Acids

All proteins in the body consist of a unique combination of 20 different amino acids and are classified according to the number of amino acids in the chain. Any amino acid chain that contains fewer than 50 amino acids is called a **peptide.** If a chain consists of two joined amino acids it is called a **dipeptide;** three joined amino acids form a **tripeptide;** more than 10 amino acids joined together is called a **polypeptide.** A polypeptide chain containing more than 50 amino acids is called a protein (**Figure 6.2**).

Proteins typically contain between 100 and 10,000 amino acids in a sequence. For instance, the protein that forms the hemoglobin in red blood cells consists of close to 300 amino acids. In contrast, collagen, a protein found in connective tissue, contains approximately 1,000 amino acids.

Amino acids are like numeric digits: Their specific sequence determines a specific function. Consider that telephone numbers, Social Security numbers, and bank PIN numbers are all made up of the same digits (0 to 9) arranged in different sequences of varying lengths. Each of these numbers has a specific purpose. Similarly, amino acids can be linked together to make unique sequences of varying lengths, each with a specific function.

Anatomy of an Amino Acid

As illustrated in **Figure 6.3**, each amino acid contains a central carbon (C) surrounded by four parts: a **carboxyl or acid group** (COOH), which is why it is called an amino "acid;" an **amine group** (NH_2) that contains the nitrogen; a hydrogen atom; and a distinctive **side chain,** also referred to as the R group. While each of the 20 amino acids contains the same four parts, it is the side chain that makes each amino acid unique.

Side chains can be as simple as a single hydrogen atom, as in the amino acid glycine, or they can be as complex as the ring structure in phenylalanine. Though each side chain is distinct, some have similar properties. For example, some side chains cause their amino acids to be basic, such as those found in arginine and histidine, while others, such as the side chain in aspartic acid, cause their amino acid to be acidic. Some side chains contain sulfur, including those of methionine and cysteine, and some side chains are branched, as in the case of leucine, isoleucine, and valine.

Side chains influence the function of each amino acid, whether the body can make the amino acid, and the metabolic pathway the amino acid follows after absorption. Side chains also influence the shape of the polypeptide due to their interactions with each other. Some side chains are attracted to other side chains; some are neutral; and some repel each other, causing the polypeptide to be globular in shape. It is the shape of the protein that determines its function in the body. Therefore, anything that alters the bonds between the side chains will alter the protein's shape and thus its function.

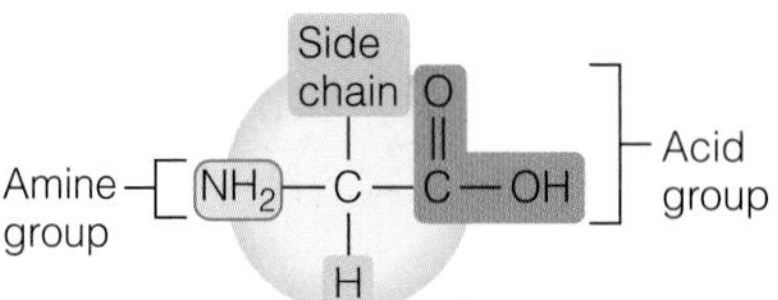

a Amino acid structure

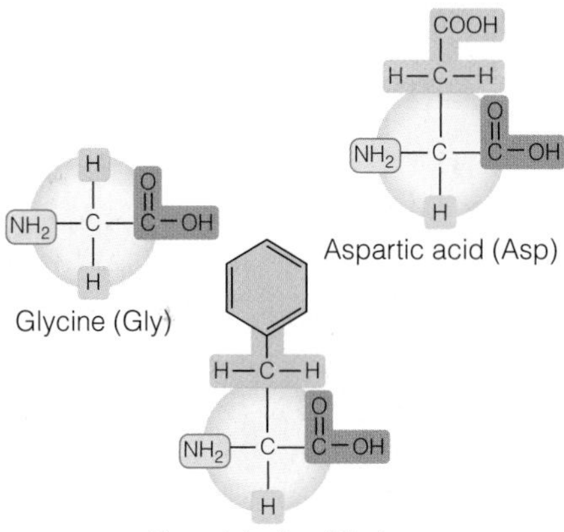

b Different amino acids, showing their unique side chains

▲ **Figure 6.3 The Anatomy of an Amino Acid**
(a) All amino acids contain a central carbon surrounded by carboxylic acid (COOH), a hydrogen, an amine group (NH_2), and **(b)** a unique side group that makes each amino acid different.

carboxyl or acid group The organic group attached to an amino acid that is composed of one carbon, one hydrogen, and two oxygen atoms (COOH).

amine group The nitrogen-containing part (NH_2) connected to the carbon of an amino acid.

side chain The part of an amino acid that provides it with its unique qualities; also referred to as the R group.

▸ **Figure 6.4 Condensation and Hydrolytic Reactions**

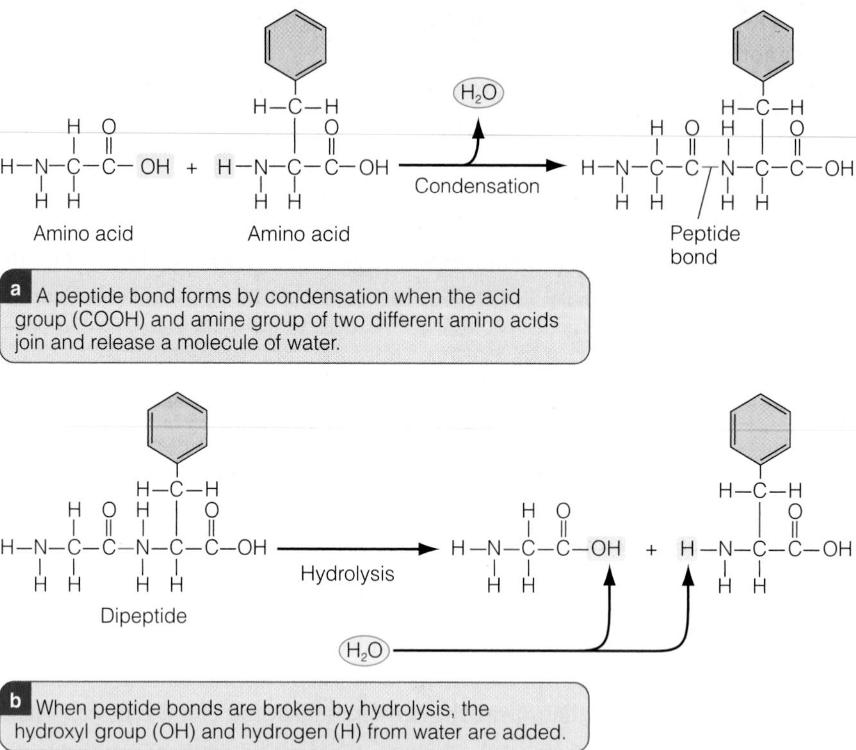

H₂O
Condensation
Amino acid
Amino acid
Peptide bond
a A peptide bond forms by condensation when the acid group (COOH) and amine group of two different amino acids join and release a molecule of water.
Dipeptide
Hydrolysis
H₂O
b When peptide bonds are broken by hydrolysis, the hydroxyl group (OH) and hydrogen (H) from water are added.

Peptide Bonds

Peptide bonds unite amino acids into unique chains. These bonds are formed when the carbon from the acid group (COOH) of one amino acid joins with the nitrogen atom from the amine group (NH_2) of a second amino acid by a condensation reaction (**Figure 6.4**), releasing a molecule of water. In contrast, peptide bonds are broken by hydrolysis, which is particularly important during digestion (see Figure 6.3). In this process, a molecule of water is used to split the bond, adding the hydroxyl (OH) group to one amino acid and a hydrogen to the other.

Essential, Nonessential, and Conditional Amino Acids

Nine of the 20 amino acids that the body combines to make protein are classified as **essential** amino acids. It is *essential* that the diet provide them because these amino acids either cannot be made by the body or cannot be made in sufficient quantities to sustain the body's needs. You have to consume protein to create protein in the body.

The remaining 11 amino acids are considered **nonessential** because they can be made by the body. It is not essential to consume them in the diet. Table 6.1 lists the 20 known, nutritionally important amino acids by their classification.

Some nonessential amino acids may become **conditionally essential** if the body cannot make them because of illness, or because the body lacks the necessary precursors or enzymes. In such situations, they are considered essential and must be consumed through food. An example of this is when premature infants are not able to make enough of the enzymes needed to create arginine, so they need to get this amino acid in their diet.

The Organization and Shape of Proteins Affect Their Function

Protein is composed of hundreds to thousands of amino acids linked in a specific order, the length and pattern determined by your genes. Every protein has four different levels of structure: primary, secondary, tertiary, and quaternary; each level must be complete in order for the protein to function (**Figure 6.5**).

peptide bonds The bonds that connect amino acids, created when the acid group of one amino acid is joined with the nitrogen-containing amine group of another amino acid through condensation.

essential [amino acids] The nine amino acids that the body cannot synthesize; they must be obtained through dietary sources.

nonessential [amino acids] The 11 amino acids the body can synthesize and that therefore do not need to be consumed in the diet.

conditionally essential [amino acids] Those nonessential amino acids, such as tyrosine and glycine, that become essential (and must be consumed in the diet) when the body cannot make them.

TABLE 6.1 The Mighty Twenty

Essential Amino Acids	Nonessential Amino Acids (Conditionally Essential[b] Amino Acids in Italics)
Histidine (His)[a]	Alanine (Ala)
Isoleucine (Ile)	*Arginine (Arg)*
Leucine (Leu)	Asparagine (Asn)
Lysine (Lys)	Aspartic acid (Asp)
Methionine (Met)	*Cysteine (Cys)*
Phenylalanine (Phe)	Glutamic acid (Glu)
Threonine (Thr)	*Glutamine (Gln)*
Tryptophan (Trp)	*Glycine (Gly)*
Valine (Val)	*Proline (Pro)*
	Serine (Ser)
	Tyrosine (Tyr)

[a] Histidine was once thought to be essential only for infants. It is now known that small amounts are also needed for adults.
[b] These amino acids can be "conditionally essential" if there are either inadequate precursors or inadequate enzymes available to create these in the body.

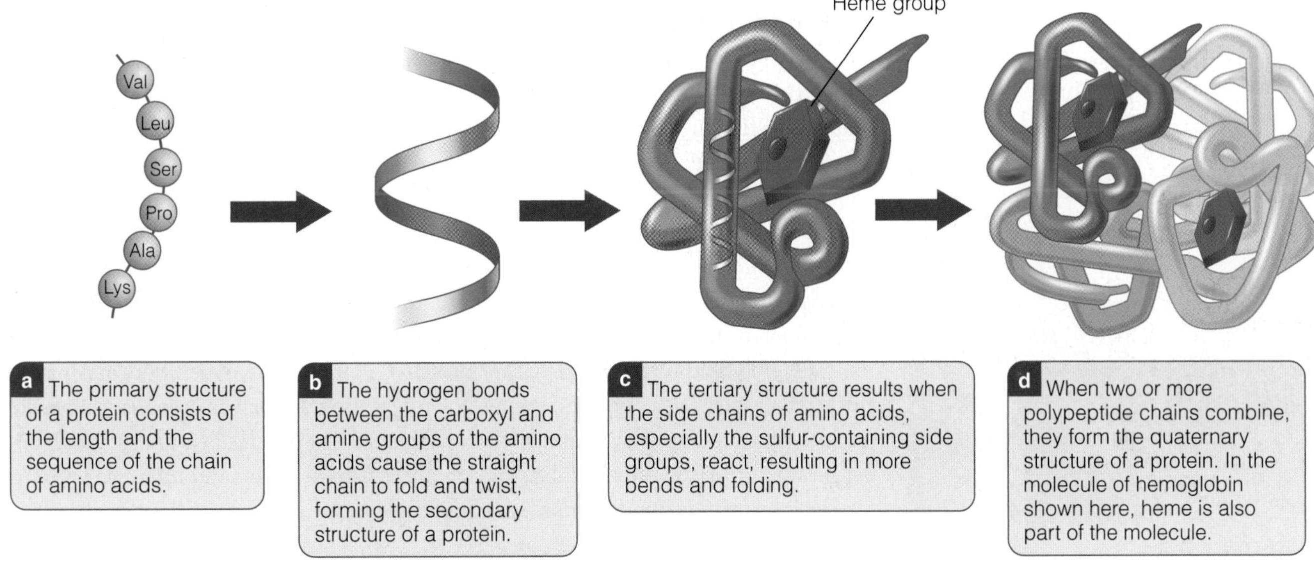

Heme group
Val
Leu
Ser
Pro
Ala
Lys
a The primary structure of a protein consists of the length and the sequence of the chain of amino acids.
b The hydrogen bonds between the carboxyl and amine groups of the amino acids cause the straight chain to fold and twist, forming the secondary structure of a protein.
c The tertiary structure results when the side chains of amino acids, especially the sulfur-containing side groups, react, resulting in more bends and folding.
d When two or more polypeptide chains combine, they form the quaternary structure of a protein. In the molecule of hemoglobin shown here, heme is also part of the molecule.

▲ **Figure 6.5 The Organization and Shape of Proteins**

The **primary structure** is the order of amino acids and the length of the polypeptide chain. The amino acids are held together by a peptide bond in a sequence that is unique to that protein. A change in the sequence of just one amino acid results in a dramatic change in the shape of the protein and, therefore, its function, similar to a telephone number with digits out of order or missing a number.

Once the sequence is formed, the amino acids will either be attracted to each other and form bonds or be repelled by each other. This formation of bonds between the amino acids creates the **secondary structure.** The hydrogen bonds between the carboxyl and amine groups cause the straight chain to fold, twist, and bend into a coil. Anything that alters the bonds between the amino acids or the sequence will change the shape and function of the protein.

In addition, side chains can be attracted to (*hydrophilic*) or repelled by (*hydrophobic*) water in the cells, which affects how they interact with their environment. This is especially true for sulfur-containing side chains. The hydrophobic side chains cluster together on the inside and combine to form a three-dimensional

primary structure The first stage of protein synthesis after transcription when the amino acids have been linked together with a peptide bond to form a simple linear chain.

secondary structure The geometric shape of a protein caused by the hydrogen ions of amino acids linking together with the amine group, causing the straight chain to fold and twist.

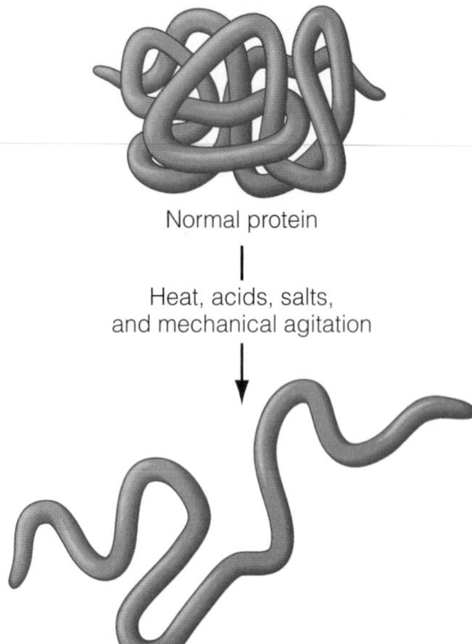

▲ **Figure 6.6 Denaturing a Protein**
A protein can be denatured, or unfolded, by exposure to heat, acids, or salts or by mechanical agitation. Any change in a protein's shape will alter its function.

Whipping egg whites denatures the protein.

tertiary structure The third geometric shape of a protein; occurs when the side chains of the amino acids, most often containing sulfur, form bridges, causing the protein to form even stronger bonds than in the secondary structure; these bonds form loops, bends, and folds in the molecule.

quaternary structure The fourth geometric pattern of a protein; formed when two or more polypeptide chains cluster together, forming a final ball-like structure.

denatured Having altered a protein's shape, generally the secondary, tertiary, or quaternary structure, which changes its function; the chains of amino acids remain linked together by peptide bonds.

globular shape called the **tertiary structure,** while the hydrophilic side chains assemble on the outside of the protein and interact with the watery portion of blood and other body fluids.

Finally, the **quaternary structure** of a protein forms when two or more polypeptide chains bond together with a hydrogen bond or there is a reaction between the sulfur-containing side chains of the amino acid cysteine. A good example of a quaternary structure of a protein is hemoglobin, as illustrated in Figure 6.5d. The iron-containing heme groups shown in red in the illustration assist in binding oxygen and are not part of the normal quaternary structure of proteins.

Denaturation of Proteins Changes Their Shape

Proteins can be unfolded or **denatured** (**Figure 6.6**) by heat, acids, bases, salts, or mechanical agitation. Denaturation doesn't alter the primary structure of the protein (the amino acids will still be in the same sequence), but does change the shape. As mentioned earlier, changing a protein's shape alters its function, sometimes permanently, until it is again denatured by HCL during digestion.

What happens during cooking to the protein found in eggs illustrates denaturation. When you apply heat to a raw egg, such as by frying it, the heat denatures the protein in both the yolk and the egg white. Heat disrupts the bonds between the amino acid side chains, causing the protein in the egg to uncoil. New bonds then form between the side chains, changing the shape and structure of the protein, and the texture of the egg. As the egg cooks, it solidifies; the change in the protein's shape and structure is permanent.

Similarly, mechanical agitation, such as beating egg whites when you prepare a meringue, can denature protein. Beating an egg white uncoils the protein, allowing the hydrophilic side chains to react with the water in the egg white, while the hydrophobic portions of the side chains form new bonds, trapping the air from the beating. The stiffer the peaks of egg white, the more denatured the protein. Again, the change in the protein's shape and structure is permanent.

Salts and acids can also denature proteins. For example, when you marinate a chicken breast or a steak before cooking, you might use salt (such as in soy sauce) or acid (such as wine or vinegar), which denatures its protein. The end result is juicier, more tender meat. During digestion, acidic stomach juices help denature and untangle proteins to reveal the peptide bonds. This allows digestive enzymes to break the bonds apart.

THE TAKE-HOME MESSAGE Proteins are chains of amino acids linked together with a peptide bond by condensation and broken down by hydrolysis. Amino acids, which contain carbon, hydrogen, oxygen, nitrogen, and, in some cases, sulfur, are comprised of a central carbon with a carboxyl group, a hydrogen, a nitrogen-containing amine group, and a unique side chain. There are 20 different side chains and therefore 20 unique amino acids. Eleven are classified as nonessential and nine are classified as essential. Under certain circumstances, some nonessential amino acids are considered conditionally essential. The attractions and interactions between the side chains cause the protein to fold into a precise three-dimensional shape that determines its function. Heat, mechanical agitation, acids, bases, and salts can denature a protein and alter its shape and function.

What Happens to the Protein You Eat?

When you eat a peanut butter sandwich, what happens to the protein in the peanut butter and the whole-wheat bread after it has been chewed and swallowed? How do proteins in food become body proteins?

Even before you eat the sandwich, the sight and smell of the food stimulates the mouth to produce saliva and the stomach to produce gastric juices to prepare for digestion. Let's take a closer look at protein digestion as presented in **Figure 6.7**.

Protein Digestion Begins in the Stomach

The peanut butter sandwich is prepared for digestion in the mouth, where teeth tear and shred the food, breaking the sandwich into smaller pieces while mixing it with saliva. This mechanical digestion helps make the food easy to swallow, and is the only digestion of protein that takes place in the mouth. No chemical or enzymatic digestion of proteins occurs in the mouth.

After you eat a meal, the hormone **gastrin** directs the release of hydrochloric acid (HCl) from the parietal cells in the stomach wall. Gastrin also directs the release of **pepsinogen,** an inactive protein enzyme, from the chief cells. Once the bolus enters the stomach, HCl begins to denature the protein strands. HCl also converts the pepsinogen to an active enzyme called **pepsin,** which begins breaking the polypeptides into shorter chains by hydrolysis. The strands are then propelled into the small intestine as part of the chyme.

Table 6.2 provides a complete list of enzymes that participate in protein digestion.

Protein Digestion Continues in the Small Intestine

When the polypeptides reach the small intestine, the intestinal cells release the hormone cholecystokinin into the blood. This hormone stimulates the pancreas to secrete **proteases,** which are protein-digesting enzymes including trypsin, chymotrypsin, and carboxypeptidase, through the pancreatic duct into the small intestine. Trypsin and chymotrypsin continue to break apart the peptide bonds in the center of the polypeptide chain, resulting in smaller and smaller peptide chains. What started out in the peanut butter as a very large protein molecule has now been reduced to tripeptides and dipeptides. Dipeptidases and tripeptidases help break down the smaller peptide chains into single amino acids.

Amino Acids Are Absorbed in the Small Intestine

Amino acids are absorbed across the small intestinal cell membranes. The single amino acids pool inside the enterocytes until they exit the cell, and are transported via the portal vein to the liver. After reaching the liver, amino acids can be used to synthesize new proteins, or can be converted to ATP, glucose, or fat. When other cells need to be replenished, the amino acids are released into the bloodstream and transported throughout the body.

gastrin A stomach hormone released after eating a meal that stimulates the release of hydrochloric acid.

pepsinogen The inactive precursor of pepsin; pepsinogen is stored in the gastric cells and is converted to pepsin by hydrochloric acid.

pepsin An enzyme in the stomach that begins the digestion of dietary protein.

proteases Protein-digesting enzymes that can break the peptide bonds linking amino acids together.

TABLE 6.2 Enzymes Involved in Protein Digestion

Digestive Enzyme	Where Released	Purpose
Pepsinogen	From chief cells in the stomach (activated to pepsin by HCL)	Breaks apart polypeptides into shorter polypeptide chains
Trypsin	From pancreas into small intestine	Breaks apart peptide bonds
Chymotrypsin	From pancreas into small intestine	Breaks apart peptide bonds
Carboxypeptidase	From pancreas into small intestine	Breaks free one amino acid at a time from the carboxyl end of a peptide chain
Aminopeptidase	Brush border of the small intestine	Breaks free the end amino acids from tri- and dipeptides into single amino acids
Tripeptidase	Brush border of the small intestine	Breaks tripeptides into single amino acids
Dipeptidase	Brush border of the small intestine	Breaks dipeptides into single amino acids

Focus Figure 6.7 Protein Digestion and Absorption

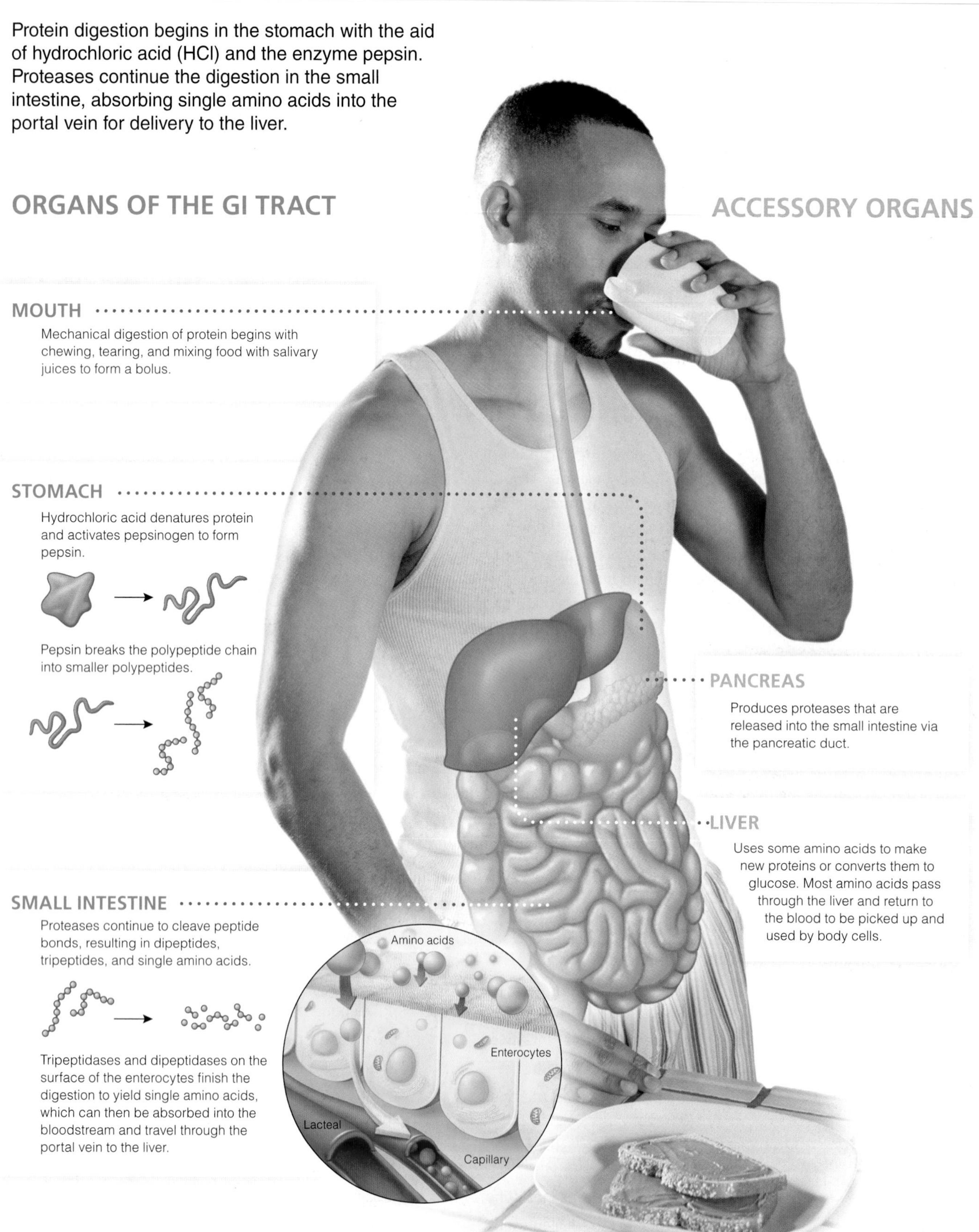

Protein digestion begins in the stomach with the aid of hydrochloric acid (HCl) and the enzyme pepsin. Proteases continue the digestion in the small intestine, absorbing single amino acids into the portal vein for delivery to the liver.
ORGANS OF THE GI TRACT
ACCESSORY ORGANS
MOUTH
Mechanical digestion of protein begins with chewing, tearing, and mixing food with salivary juices to form a bolus.
STOMACH
Hydrochloric acid denatures protein and activates pepsinogen to form pepsin.
Pepsin breaks the polypeptide chain into smaller polypeptides.
PANCREAS
Produces proteases that are released into the small intestine via the pancreatic duct.
LIVER
Uses some amino acids to make new proteins or converts them to glucose. Most amino acids pass through the liver and return to the blood to be picked up and used by body cells.
SMALL INTESTINE
Proteases continue to cleave peptide bonds, resulting in dipeptides, tripeptides, and single amino acids.
Tripeptidases and dipeptidases on the surface of the enterocytes finish the digestion to yield single amino acids, which can then be absorbed into the bloodstream and travel through the portal vein to the liver.
Amino acids
Enterocytes
Lacteal
Capillary

Almost all dietary proteins are digested, absorbed, and transported via the portal vein as single amino acids. However, there are some circumstances when whole proteins are absorbed intact, such as in the absorption of antibodies from breast milk or in the case of food allergies.[2]

How Is Protein Metabolized?

How the liver metabolizes newly absorbed amino acids depends on the needs of the body. For example, amino acids might be used to replace old proteins or synthesize new ones or, if necessary, they may be used as an energy source. If an individual is not eating sufficient carbohydrates, amino acids can be converted to glucose through a process called gluconeogenesis. However, most amino acids travel back out to the blood to be picked up and used by cells.

Amino Acid Pools Supply the Body's Ongoing Needs for Protein Synthesis

Proteins don't last indefinitely. The daily wear and tear on the body causes the breakdown of hundreds of grams of proteins each day. For example, the protein-rich cells in the skin are constantly sloughed off, and proteins help create a new layer of outer skin every 25 to 45 days.[3] Because red blood cells have a short life span—only about 120 days—new red blood cells must be continually regenerated. The cells that line the inner surfaces of the organs, such as the lungs and intestines, are recycled and replaced every three to five days, thanks to protein synthesis.

In addition to regular maintenance, extra protein is sometimes needed for emergency repairs. Protein is essential in healing, and a person with extensive wounds, such as severe burns, may have dietary protein needs that are more than triple his or her normal needs.

Newly absorbed amino acids are stockpiled in limited amounts in **amino acid pools** found in the blood and inside cells. When cellular proteins are degraded or broken down into their component parts, the resulting amino acids also enter the amino acid pools. The body can then use the amino acids in the pool to create proteins on demand. This process of degrading and synthesizing protein is called **protein turnover** (Figure 6.8). More than 200 grams of protein are turned over

amino acid pools Limited supplies of amino acids that accumulate in the blood and cells; amino acids are pulled from the pools and used to build new proteins.

protein turnover The continual process of degrading and synthesizing protein.

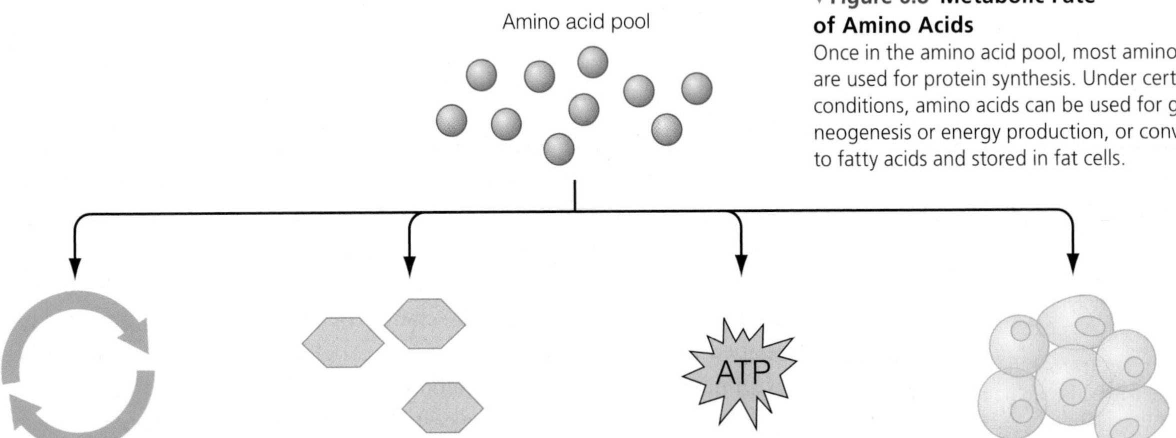
Amino acid pool
ATP
Protein turnover:
Proteins are constantly made and broken down, releasing their amino acids into the amino acid pool or using the amino acids for protein synthesis.
Gluconeogenesis:
Amino acids can be used to make glucose when glucose is limited.
Energy production:
Amino acids can be used for energy when the diet is deficient in kilocalories.
Fat cells:
Amino acids can be converted to fatty acids and stored as a triglyceride in the adipose tissue when kilocalorie intake is sufficient.

▾ Figure 6.8 Metabolic Fate of Amino Acids
Once in the amino acid pool, most amino acids are used for protein synthesis. Under certain conditions, amino acids can be used for gluconeogenesis or energy production, or converted to fatty acids and stored in fat cells.

daily. The proteins in the intestines and liver—two tissue types with rapid degradation and resynthesis rates—account for as much as 50 percent of this turnover. Some of the amino acids in the pools are also used to synthesize nonprotein substances, including thyroid hormones and melanin, the pigment that gives color to dark skin and hair.

Protein Synthesis Is Regulated by Your Genes

Red blood cells with normal hemoglobin are smooth and round, like the three similar ones. A person with sickle-cell anemia has red blood cells that are stiff and form a sickle (half-moon) shape when blood oxygen levels are low.

The body is made up of over 100,000 different proteins. When the body is ready to build new or repair old proteins, the cells receive a signal to begin the process of protein synthesis. This signal is communicated to a cell receptor by hormones, cell-to-cell contact, or neurotransmitters. Cells can "turn on" and "turn off" protein synthesis as needed, similar to controlling the light in a room with an electrical switch.

The exact code to create specific proteins is stored in your **genes** located within the cell's DNA. Because the DNA cannot leave the nucleus of the cell and protein is synthesized outside the nucleus in the cytoplasm, the code must be copied, translated, and reproduced to build the exact sequence of amino acids described in the code. Let's walk through the three steps of the process of protein synthesis (**Figure 6.9**).

1. **Transcription.** The first step in making a new polypeptide chain is to transcribe (or copy) the information contained in the DNA. The information contained in the DNA includes the sequence and number of amino acids in the chain and how to assemble the protein, similar to written instructions you follow when putting together a new bookshelf. The DNA transcribes the instructions by replicating itself, forming a new molecule called **messenger RNA (mRNA).**
2. **Translation.** Once the code has been transcribed from DNA to mRNA, the new mRNA detaches from the DNA, leaves the nucleus, and enters the cytoplasm to transfer this information to the ribosomes. This is the second phase of the process, called translation. During this stage, the ribosome moves along the mRNA, reading or translating the instructions.
3. **Elongation.** The sequence of the amino acids recorded in the mRNA is communicated to a second type of RNA called **transfer RNA (tRNA).** Based on the pattern copied from the DNA, tRNA collects and transports the amino acids to the ribosomes to build the polypeptide chain in the proper sequence. There is a unique tRNA for each of the 20 different amino acids. This gathering and building step is called elongation, and continues until the sequence has been completed and a new protein is released.

When the sequence of amino acids is changed, abnormalities occur and a serious medical condition can result. One such condition is **sickle-cell anemia.** The most common inherited blood disorder in the United States, sickle-cell anemia is caused by the abnormal formation of the protein hemoglobin. The displacement of just *one* amino acid, glutamine, with another amino acid, valine, in the polypeptide chains of hemoglobin causes the chains to stick to one another and form crescent-shaped structures rather than the normal globular ones. Whereas red blood cells with normal hemoglobin are smooth and round, those with this mutation are stiff and form a sickle shape under certain conditions, such as after vigorous exercise, when oxygen levels in the blood are low. These abnormal sickle cells are easily destroyed, which can lead to anemia, and they can build up in blood vessels, causing painful blockages and damage to tissues and organs. According to the National Institutes of Health (NIH), approximately one in 12 African-Americans and one in 100 Hispanics are carriers of the mutated gene that causes the disease.[4]

gene The basic biological unit in a segment of DNA that contributes to the function of a specific protein.

transcription The first stage in protein synthesis, in which the DNA sequence is copied from the gene and transferred to messenger RNA.

messenger RNA (mRNA) A type of RNA that copies the genetic information from the DNA and carries it from the nucleus to the ribosomes in the cell.

translation The second phase of protein synthesis; the process of converting the information in mRNA to an amino acid sequence in the ribosomes.

elongation The phase of protein synthesis in which the polypeptide chain grows longer by adding amino acids.

transfer RNA (tRNA) A type of RNA that transfers a specific amino acid to a growing polypeptide chain in the ribosomes during the processes of translation and elongation.

sickle-cell anemia A blood disorder caused by a genetic defect in the development of hemoglobin. Sickle-cell anemia causes the red blood cells to distort into a sickle shape and can damage organs and tissues.

Focus Figure 6.9 Protein Synthesis

Protein synthesis is the process by which the DNA code within a cell's nucleus directs the cell's production of specific proteins.

1 In the nucleus, DNA unwinds to allow a copy of the code, called messenger RNA (mRNA) to be made. This process is called **transcription**.

2 The mRNA leaves the nucleus and travels to the cytosol.

3 Once the mRNA reaches the cytosol, it binds to a ribosome.

4 The ribosome moves along the mRNA, reading the code. Transfer RNA (tRNA) brings specific amino acids to the ribosome based on the code. This begins the process of **translation**.

5 The ribosome then builds a chain of amino acids (the protein) in the proper sequence, based on the code in the mRNA. This process is called **elongation**.

6 When all the appropriate amino acids are added and the protein is complete, the protein is released from the ribosome.

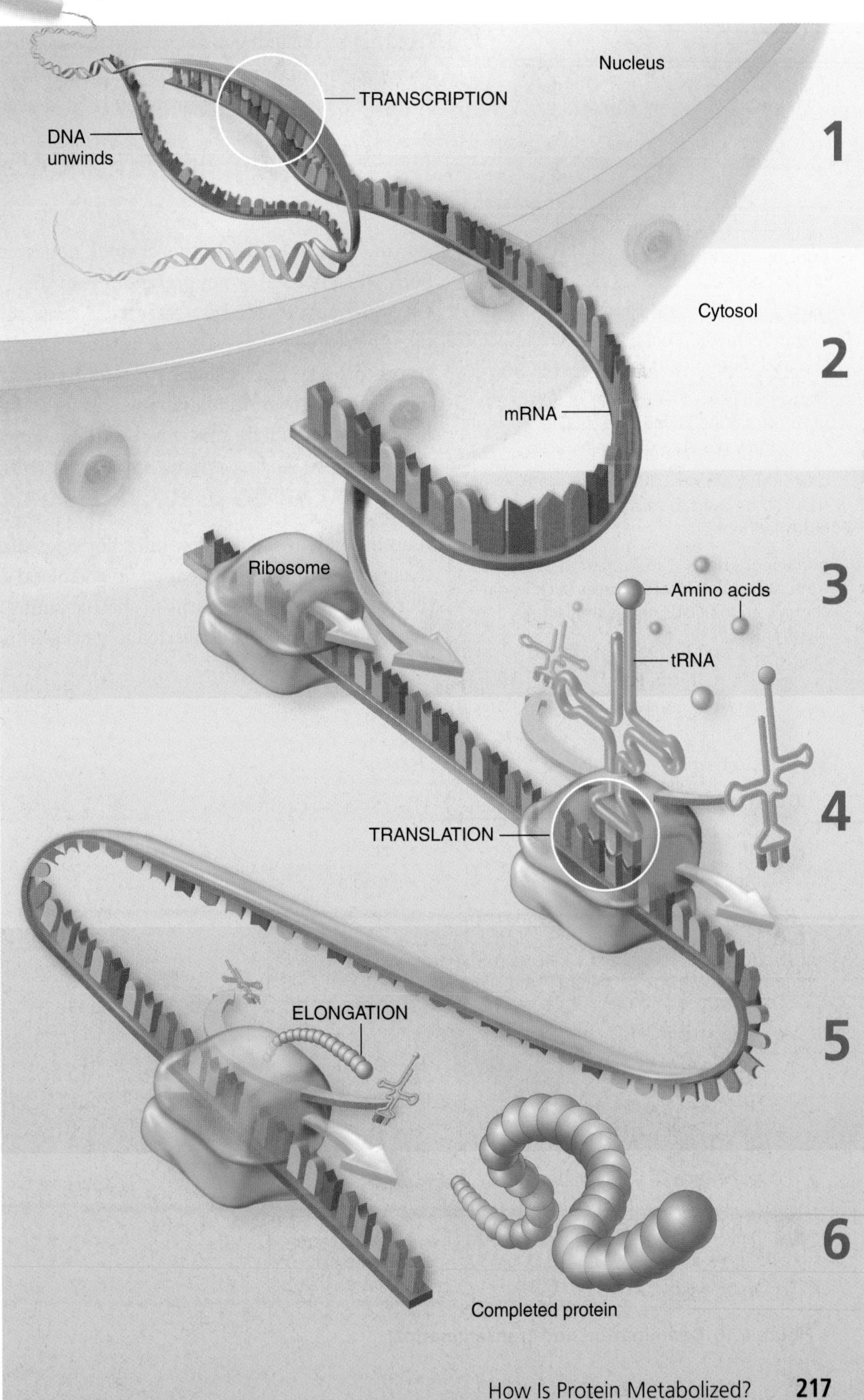

Deamination Removes the Amine Group from Amino Acids

What happens if amino acids in the pool aren't used for protein synthesis? As the amino acid pool reaches capacity, the amino acids that are not used to build proteins are broken down into their component parts. These component parts are used for other purposes, such as energy production, or stored in another form.

Before amino acids can be used for energy production or converted to other compounds, the amine group must be removed and converted to ammonia (NH_3) in a process called **deamination** (**Figure 6.10a**). Because ammonia in high amounts can be toxic to cells, the ammonia is sent through the bloodstream to the liver, where it is quickly converted to **urea,** CH_4N_2O, a waste product that is released into the blood, filtered out by the kidneys, and eventually excreted in urine. Once the nitrogen has been removed, the carbon-containing remnants of the amino acids are eventually converted to glucose, used as energy, or stored as fat, depending on the needs of the body.

Nonessential Amino Acids Are Synthesized through Transamination

deamination The removal of the amine group from an amino acid when amino acids are used for energy, fat synthesis, or gluconeogenesis.

urea A nitrogen-containing waste product of protein metabolism that is mainly excreted through the urine via the kidneys.

transamination The transfer of an amino group from one amino acid to a keto acid to form a new nonessential amino acid.

glucogenic amino acids Amino acids that can be used to form glucose through gluconeogenesis.

gluconeogenesis The formation of glucose from noncarbohydrate sources such as glucogenic amino acids, pyruvate, lactate, and glycerol.

As you learned earlier in this chapter, nonessential amino acids can be made in the body when needed or not present in your diet. These amino acids can be made from the nitrogen provided by essential amino acids or ammonia, and another compound referred to as a *keto acid* by the process called **transamination** (Figure 6.10b). In this process, the liver transfers the amino group to the keto acid, creating a new, nonessential amino acid and a new keto acid. This reaction requires vitamin B_6 to be complete. We'll discuss this reaction in greater detail in Chapter 8.

Protein Can Be Used for Gluconeogenesis

If an individual eats too few kilocalories or carbohydrates, the stores of glycogen in the liver and muscle will be used up and blood glucose levels will drop. To raise blood glucose levels, the body turns to specific amino acids called **glucogenic amino acids.** These amino acids are converted to glucose through the process of **gluconeogenesis,**

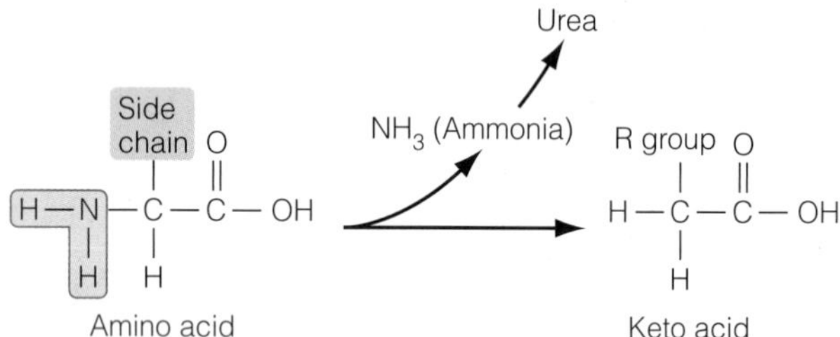

a Deamination: In the liver, the amine group is removed, producing ammonia and a keto acid. The ammonia is used to form urea, which is excreted in the urine.

Side chain A

Side chain B

Amino acid A + Keto acid A → Keto acid B + Amino acid B

b Transamination: An amine group from an essential amino acid is transferred to a keto acid, producing a nonessential amino acid and a new keto acid.

▲ **Figure 6.10 Deamination and Transamination**

the creation (*genesis*) of glucose (*gluco*) from new (*neo*) compounds other than carbohydrates. (Remember that the brain and nervous system need a minimum amount of glucose to function properly.)

Excess Protein Is Converted to Body Fat

If you add too much water to a swimming pool, the excess overflows. The same is true of an amino acid pool. When the diet contains sufficient carbohydrates, and protein intake exceeds requirements, the amino acid pool becomes saturated. The "overflow" amino acids are deaminated, and the remaining carbon remnants are converted to fatty acids and stored as triglycerides in adipose tissue.

THE TAKE-HOME MESSAGE During digestion, proteins are broken down into amino acids with the help of gastric juices, enzymes in the stomach and small intestine, and enzymes from the pancreas and small intestinal lining. A limited supply of amino acids exists in the amino acid pools, which act as a reservoir for protein synthesis. Surplus amino acids are deaminated, with the carbon-containing remnants used for glucose or energy, or stored as fat, depending on the body's needs. The nitrogen in the amine groups is eventually converted to the waste product urea and excreted in urine.

How Does the Body Use Protein?

Proteins play many important roles in the body, from providing structural and mechanical support and maintaining body tissues to functioning as enzymes and hormones and helping maintain acid-base and fluid balance. They also transport nutrients, assist the immune system, and, when necessary, are a source of energy. Let's examine each of these vital functions in more depth.

Proteins Provide Structural Support and Enable Movement

Proteins provide much of the structural and mechanical support that keeps the body upright, moving, and flexible. Collagen, the most abundant protein in the body, is found in all connective tissues, including the bones, tendons, and ligaments, that support and connect joints and other body parts. This fibrous protein is also responsible for the skin's elasticity and forms the scar tissue necessary to repair injuries.

The proteins actin and myosin provide mechanical support by contracting muscles during movement. They are also involved in nonmuscle movement when cells divide during mitosis or chemicals are transported in the nerve cells.

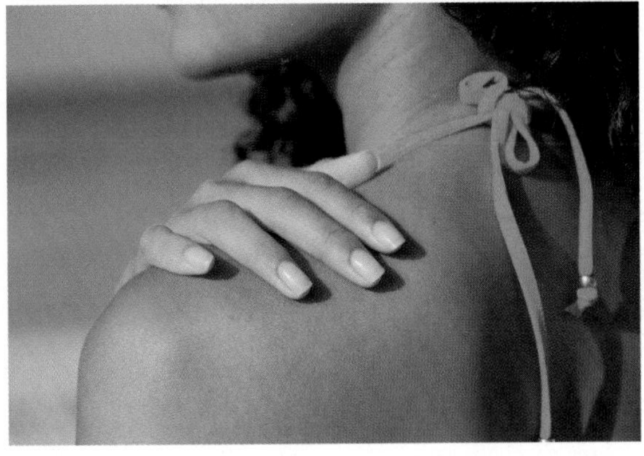

Proteins play an important role in keeping skin healthy and nails strong.

Proteins Act as Catalysts

When the body requires a reaction to take place promptly, such as breaking down carbohydrates after a meal, it calls upon enzymes, biological **catalysts** that speed up reactions. Most enzymes are proteins, although to be activated, some may also need a coenzyme, such as a vitamin. Without enzymes, reactions would occur so slowly that you couldn't survive.

Each of the thousands of enzymes in the body catalyzes a specific reaction. Some enzymes, such as digestive enzymes, are **catabolic** enzymes that break compounds apart. The enzyme lactase is needed to break down the milk sugar lactose (refer back to Chapter 4). Other enzymes are **anabolic,** and build substances. For

catalysts Substances that aid and speed up reactions without being changed, damaged, or used up in the process.

catabolic A metabolic process that breaks larger molecules into smaller parts.

anabolic A metabolic process in which smaller molecules are combined to form larger molecules.

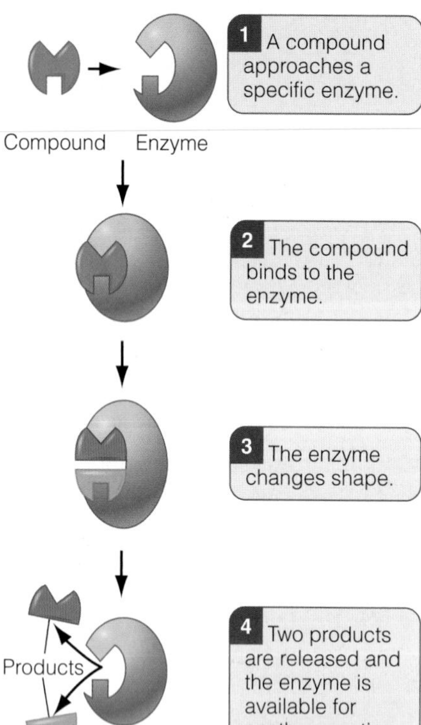

1 A compound approaches a specific enzyme.
Compound
Enzyme
2 The compound binds to the enzyme.
3 The enzyme changes shape.
Products
4 Two products are released and the enzyme is available for another reaction.

▲ **Figure 6.11 An Enzyme in Action**
Enzymes speed up reactions in the body, yet they aren't changed, damaged, or used up in the process.

example, the ability to store glucose as glycogen is stimulated by the anabolic enzyme glycogen synthetase. Without this enzyme, you wouldn't be able to maintain blood glucose levels during sleep. Enzymes aren't changed, damaged, or used up in the process of speeding up a particular reaction. Thus, an enzyme is available to catalyze additional reactions. **Figure 6.11** shows how an enzyme joins two compounds, yet isn't changed in the process.

Proteins Act as Chemical Messengers

While enzymes expedite reactions, **hormones** are messengers that regulate the actions carried out in the cells. Hormones direct or alter reactions, often by turning on or shutting off enzymes. Although many hormones are proteins (amino acid based), some hormones, such as steroids, are made from cholesterol (refer to Chapter 5). Hormones are released from tissues and organs and travel to target cells in another part of the body to direct an activity. There are over 70 trillion cells in the body, and all of these cells interact with at least one of over 50 known hormones.[5]

Consider an example of one peptide hormone in action. Under certain situations, such as dehydration, blood levels of salt (referred to as solutes) can become highly concentrated. Receptors in the blood vessels sense the change in concentration, and signal the hypothalamus to synthesize and release antidiuretic hormone (ADH) into the blood, a hormone that limits urine production. ADH travels to the kidneys and directs them to reabsorb more water, which, in turn, causes the kidneys to produce less urine, thus raising the blood volume and lowering the solute concentration. Once the blood concentration of solutes returns to normal, ADH levels are reduced.

Proteins Regulate Fluid Balance

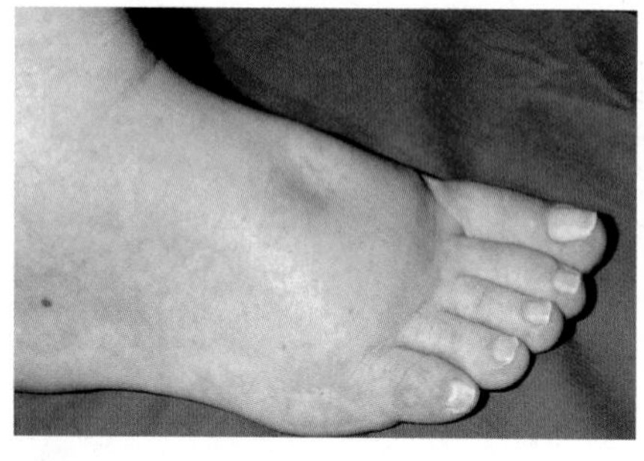

▲ **Figure 6.12 Edema**
Inadequate protein in the blood can cause edema.

The body is made up predominantly of water, which is distributed both outside (extracellular) and inside (intracellular) the cells. Fluid can generally flow easily in and out of cells. However, proteins are too large to move across the cell membranes and thus stay either within the cells or outside in the extracellular fluid. Normally, blood pressure forces the nutrient- and oxygen-rich fluids out of capillaries and into the spaces between the cells (called interstitial spaces). But protein remains in the blood, especially the protein **albumin.** As fluid is forced out of the blood, the concentration of albumin increases, which draws fluid from the interstitial spaces back into the blood by osmosis. Hence, protein plays an important role in moving fluids and keeping water dispersed evenly inside and outside of cells, which helps maintain a state of **fluid balance.** (Note: The mineral sodium, discussed in Chapter 12, also plays a major role in fluid balance.)

When fewer proteins are available to draw the fluid from between the cells back into the bloodstream, as during severe malnutrition, a fluid imbalance results. The interstitial spaces between the cells become bloated and the body tissue swells, a condition known as **edema** (**Figure 6.12**).

hormones Substances, usually protein- or lipid-based, that initiate or direct specific actions. Insulin, glucagons, ADH, and estrogen are examples of hormones in the body.

albumin A protein produced in the liver and found in the blood that helps maintain fluid balance.

fluid balance The difference between the amount of water taken into the body and the amount of water excreted.

edema The accumulation of excess water in the spaces surrounding the cells, which causes swelling of the body tissue.

Proteins Help Regulate Acid-Base Balance

Proteins can alter the **pH** of the body fluids. Normally, the blood has a pH of about 7.4, and the fluid in the cells has a pH of about 7.0. Even a small change in the pH of the blood in either direction can be harmful or even fatal. With a blood pH below 7.35, a condition called **acidosis** sets in, which can result in a coma. A blood pH above 7.45, known as **alkalosis,** can result in convulsions.

Proteins act as **buffers** and minimize the changes in acid-base levels by picking up hydrogen ions in the blood or donating hydrogen ions to the blood. Should the blood become too basic (contain too few hydrogen ions), the carboxyl groups of amino acids lower the pH of the blood by donating hydrogen ions; if blood becomes too acidic (too many hydrogen ions), the amine groups bind the excess hydrogen ions and restore the pH to an optimal level. This dual buffering role helps maintain the acid-base balance in the cells and the blood.

Proteins Transport Substances Throughout the Body

Transport proteins shuttle oxygen, waste products, lipids, some vitamins, and sodium and potassium through the blood and through cell membranes. For example, hemoglobin is a transport protein that carries oxygen to cells from the lungs; hemoglobin also picks up carbon dioxide for delivery to the lungs to be exhaled. Lipoproteins transport fat-soluble nutrients through the bloodstream (refer back to Chapter 5).

Some nutrients, such as vitamin A, are fat soluble, and need assistance to move through the water-based blood. Once in the blood, vitamin A attaches to the protein albumin for transport to the liver and other cells.

Other nutrients, such as essential minerals—for example, iron and zinc—have specialized transport proteins whose sole function is to escort them across the enterocytes to their intended locations.

Transport proteins in cell membranes form a doorway or channel that allows substances such as sodium and potassium to pass in and out of cells (**Figure 6.13**). Without these membrane proteins, cells would be unable to maintain an optimal concentration of nutrients or remove waste from the cell. Substances that are not fat soluble or that are too big to pass through the cell membrane also have to enter the cell through a protein channel. If your diet is deficient in essential amino acids, fewer transport proteins are produced, causing an unhealthy balance of nutrients inside and outside of the cell membrane.

Proteins Contribute to a Healthy Immune System

The immune system works like an army to protect the body from pathogens. Once pathogens, including bacteria and viruses, enter the cells, they can multiply rapidly, eventually causing illness. Specialized protein "soldiers," called **antibodies,** work

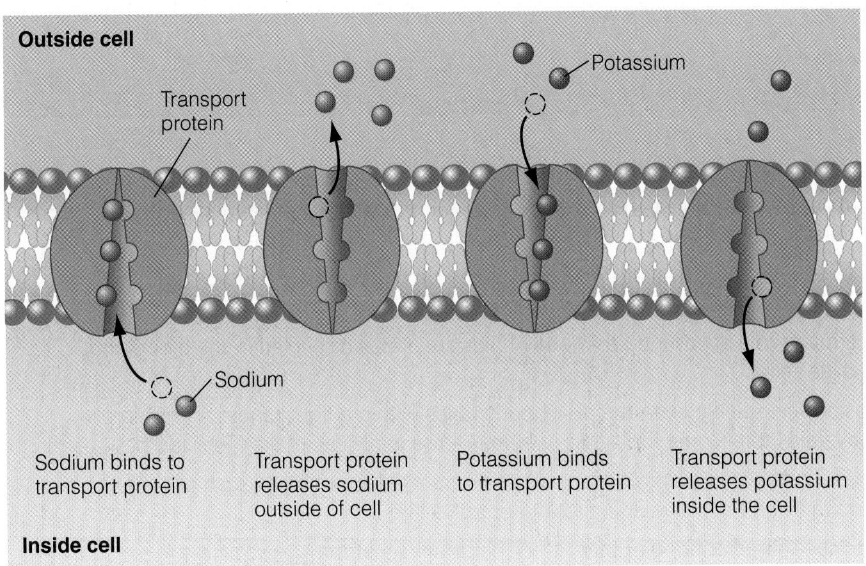

▲ **Figure 6.13 Proteins as Transport Channels**
Transport proteins form a channel through which substances such as sodium and potassium can move from one side of the cell membrane to the other.

pH A measurement of the concentration of hydrogen ions in the body fluid.

acidosis A condition in which the blood is more acidic than normal, generally due to excessive hydrogen ions.

alkalosis A condition in which the blood has a lower hydrogen ion concentration and a higher pH than is generally considered normal.

buffers Substances that help maintain the proper pH in a solution by attracting or donating hydrogen ions.

transport proteins Proteins that carry lipids (fat and cholesterol), oxygen, waste products, minerals, and vitamins through your blood to your various organs and tissues. Proteins can also act as channels through which some substances enter your cells.

antibodies Proteins that bind to and neutralize pathogens as part of the body's immune response.

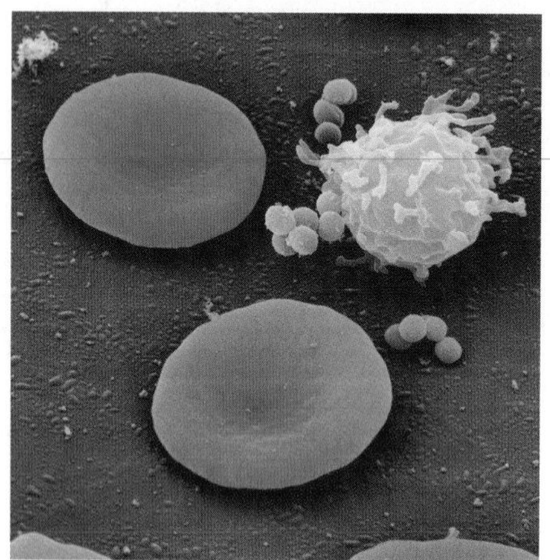

Specialized proteins, called antibodies, protect the body from disease-causing bacteria and viruses.

quickly to eliminate these potentially harmful substances before they have a chance to multiply.

Once the body knows how to create antibodies against a specific foreign substance, such as a particular virus, it stores that information and the body has **immunity** to that pathogen. The next time the invader enters the body, the body can respond very quickly (producing up to 2,000 precise antibodies per second!) to fight it.

Sometimes, the body incorrectly perceives a nonthreatening substance, such as a protein, as an intruder and attacks it. This perceived invader is called an **allergen.** Food allergens are proteins that are resistant to being broken down during cooking or digestion. Individuals who react to these allergens are diagnosed with food allergies.

Proteins Can Provide Energy

Because proteins provide 4 kilocalories per gram, they can be used as an energy source. After amino acids are deaminated, the remaining carbon remnants can enter the energy cycle to produce ATP. (We'll cover this process in depth when we talk about metabolism in Chapter 8.)

However, the last thing you want to do is use this valuable nutrient, which plays so many important roles in the body, as a regular source of fuel, because carbohydrates and fats are far better suited to providing energy. When the diet contains adequate amounts of kilocalories from carbohydrates and fat, proteins are spared and used for their more important roles. For optimal health, individuals need to eat enough protein daily to meet the body's needs, and enough carbohydrates and fats to prevent protein from being used as energy.

Table 6.3 summarizes the many structural and functional roles proteins play in the body.

Protein Improves Satiety and Appetite Control

immunity The state of having built up antibodies to a particular foreign substance so that when particles of the substance enter the body, they are destroyed by the antibodies.

allergen A substance, such as wheat, that causes an allergic reaction.

In addition to the structural and functional roles protein plays in the body, protein also improves satiety after a meal more than either carbohydrate or fat.[6,7] Eating a meal that contains a good source of protein will leave you more satisfied than will a high-carbohydrate meal with the same number of kilocalories. The satiety following a high-protein meal may be due to dietary protein suppressing the release of ghrelin.[8] Recall that ghrelin, which is produced in the stomach, stimulates the

TABLE 6.3 The Many Roles of Proteins

Role of Protein	How It Works
Structural and mechanical support and maintenance	Proteins are the body's building materials, providing strength and flexibility to tissues, tendons, ligaments, muscles, organs, bones, nails, hair, and skin. Proteins are also needed for the ongoing maintenance of the body.
Enzymes and hormones	Proteins are needed to make most enzymes that speed up reactions in the body and many hormones that direct specific activities, such as regulating blood glucose levels.
Fluid balance	Proteins play a major role in ensuring that body fluids are evenly dispersed in the blood and inside and outside cells.
Acid-base balance	Proteins act as buffers to help keep the pH of body fluids within a tight range. A drop in pH will cause body fluids to become too acidic, whereas a rise in pH can make them too basic.
Transport	Proteins shuttle substances such as oxygen, waste products, and nutrients (such as sodium and potassium) through the blood and into and out of cells.
Antibodies and the immune response	Proteins create specialized antibodies that attack pathogens that may cause illness.
Energy	Because proteins provide 4 kilocalories per gram, they can be used as fuel or energy.
Satiety	Protein increases satiety, which can help control appetite and weight.

hypothalamus to sense hunger. Including protein in each meal helps to control appetite, which in turn can help maintain a healthy weight.

THE TAKE-HOME MESSAGE Proteins play many important roles in the body: (1) the synthesis, repair, and maintenance of structural tissues, (2) helping facilitate muscular contraction, (3) catalyzing reactions as enzymes, (4) acting as hormones, (5) maintaining fluid balance, (6) maintaining acid-base equilibrium, (7) transporting nutrients throughout the body, (8) providing antibodies for a strong immune system, (9) providing energy when kilocalorie intake doesn't meet daily energy needs, and (10) promoting satiety and appetite control.

How Much Protein Do You Need?

Healthy, nonpregnant adults should consume enough dietary protein to replace the amount they use each day. However, pregnant women, people recovering from surgery or an injury, and growing children need more protein to supply the necessary amino acids and nitrogen to build new tissue. **Nitrogen balance** studies are often used to determine how much protein individuals need to replace or build new tissue.

Healthy Adults Should Be in Nitrogen Balance

A person's protein requirement can be estimated by using what we know about the structure of an amino acid. We know that 16 percent of every dietary protein molecule is nitrogen. And we know that this nitrogen is retained by the body during protein synthesis. It follows that we can assess a person's protein status by checking their nitrogen

Calculation Corner

Nitrogen Balance

(a) Using the fact that protein is 16 percent nitrogen, a common factor of 6.25 is used to calculate how much nitrogen is in a given amount of food (100/16 = 6.25).

We analyzed the food and beverages from a meal and found that it contained 73 grams (g) of protein. Divide this by 6.25 to determine the nitrogen content of the meal:

$$\text{Nitrogen} = \frac{73\text{g protein}}{6.25\text{g nitrogen}} = 11.6\text{g of nitrogen}$$

(b) Now calculate the amount of nitrogen lost from the body. First, nitrogen is lost in the urine as urea nitrogen, and in other nitrogen sources that are not part of the urea molecule. Because it's difficult to account for the non-urea sources directly, a factor of 0.2 grams × urinary urea nitrogen (UUN) is used to determine these losses. In this example, let's assume we analyzed the urine and found 8 grams of UUN. The total nitrogen lost in the urine would be calculated as follows:

$$8\text{ g UUN} + (0.2 \times 8\text{ g UUN}) = 9.6\text{ g nitrogen lost}$$

(c) Next, we must account for nitrogen lost through other means, including hair, skin, and feces—approximately 2 grams per day. Add this to the equation.

$$8\text{ g UUN} + (0.2 \times 8\text{ g UUN}) + 2\text{ g} = 11.6\text{ g nitrogen lost}$$

(d) Now let's put it all together with the equation:

$$\text{Nitrogen balance} = \text{nitrogen in} - \text{nitrogen out}$$

$$\text{Nitrogen balance} = (73\text{ g protein}/6.25) - (8\text{ g UUN} + [0.2 \times 8\text{ g UUN}] + 2\text{ g}) = 0\text{ g of nitrogen}$$

The calculation for nitrogen balance can be useful to dietitians as well as researchers to determine protein requirements.

nitrogen balance The difference between nitrogen intake and nitrogen excretion.

balance—measuring the amount of nitrogen they consume and subtracting the amount of nitrogen they excrete, mostly as urea. The goal is to achieve nitrogen balance. See the Calculation Corner for an example of the calculation done to assess nitrogen balance.

Once we know the amount of nitrogen consumed, we can compare that to the amount of nitrogen excreted to determine if an individual is in nitrogen balance. In other words, nitrogen balance equals nitrogen in minus nitrogen out. The concept is similar to a checking account: If you deposit the same amount of money that you spend, your account is balanced. If the nitrogen intake from dietary protein is equivalent to the amount of nitrogen excreted as urea in the urine, then a person is in nitrogen balance. Such an individual is consuming a balanced diet with adequate amounts of protein and excreting an equally balanced amount of nitrogen. Healthy, nonpregnant adults are typically in nitrogen balance.

A body that retains more nitrogen than it excretes is in positive nitrogen balance. Rapidly growing babies, children, or teenagers are all in positive nitrogen balance because their bodies excrete less nitrogen than they take in to incorporate into new tissues that aid growth, build muscles, and expand the supply of red blood cells. When a woman is pregnant, she, too, is in positive nitrogen balance because she is building a robust baby.

An individual is in negative nitrogen balance when their nitrogen losses are greater than their nitrogen intake, such as immediately following surgery, when fighting an infection, or when experiencing severe emotional trauma. These situations all increase the body's need for both kilocalories and protein. If the kilocalories and protein in the diet are inadequate to cover these increased demands, then proteins from tissues are broken down to meet the body's needs. **Figure 6.14** lists some of the situations that lead to nitrogen balance or imbalance in the body.

Not All Protein Is Created Equal

A high-quality protein is digestible, contains all the essential amino acids, and provides a sufficient quantity of protein to be used to synthesize the nonessential

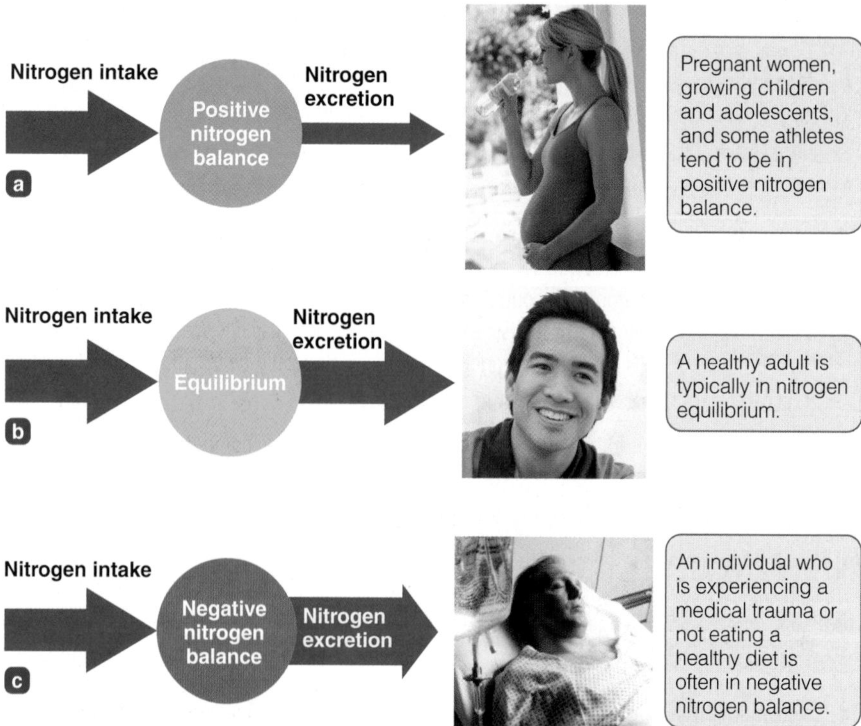

▲ **Figure 6.14 Nitrogen Balance and Imbalance**

amino acids and support the body's requirements for growth and maintenance. Thus, while it is important to eat enough protein, the quality of protein also matters.

The quality of the protein is determined by two factors: your body's ability to digest the protein and the types and amounts of amino acids that the protein contains. If a single essential amino acid is in low supply in the diet and thus in the amino acid pool, the ability to synthesize proteins will be limited.

Which protein is best? Several methods have been used to yield chemical scores to answer this question. These methods include the amino acid score, protein digestibility corrected amino acid score, and biological value.

Amino Acid Score

The quality of a food protein refers to its amino acid profile compared with a standard or reference protein. For example, egg white protein is used as a standard because it is known to have a balance of all of the essential amino acids needed to support growth. Other food proteins are compared with egg protein using an **amino acid score.** The Calculation Corner on page 226 provides an example of how to calculate this score for peanut butter using the information shown in Table 6.4.

The essential amino acid that has the lowest score is called the **limiting amino acid.** In the case of peanut butter, the limiting amino acid is methionine, with a score of 0.42. This score means that peanut butter contains 42 percent of the methionine found in egg protein.

The amino acid score is one method for comparing food proteins and their essential amino acid composition. Though it is a useful method of comparison, it doesn't take into consideration how protein is digested.

Protein Digestibility Corrected Amino Acid Score (PDCAAS)

The **protein digestibility corrected amino acid score (PDCAAS)** combines the chemical score with the digestibility of a food protein to give a more accurate indication of quality. This is important because only amino acids that are digested and absorbed can contribute to the amino acid pool and be used to build and maintain body proteins. An example of the PDCAAS calculation for peanut butter is presented in the Calculation Corner on page 227.

TABLE 6.4 Amino Acid Scores for Peanut Butter (mg/g)

Essential Amino Acid	Peanut Butter (mg/g)	Egg Protein (mg/g)	Amino Acid Score
Histidine	30	22	1.36
Isoleucine	40	54	0.74
Leucine	77	86	0.90
Lysine	39	70	0.56
Methionine plus cysteine	24	57	0.42
Phenylalanine plus tyrosine	108	93	1.16
Threonine	30	47	0.64
Tryptophan	12	17	0.71
Valine	46	66	0.71

Data from Institute of Medicine, *Dietary Reference Intakes for Energy, Carbohydrate, Fiber, Fat, Fatty Acids, Cholesterol, Protein, and Amino Acids* (Washington, DC: National Academies Press, 2002).

amino acid score The composition of essential amino acids in a protein compared with a standard, usually egg protein.

limiting amino acid An essential amino acid that is in the shortest supply, relative to the body's needs, in an incomplete protein.

protein digestibility corrected amino acid score (PDCAAS) A score measured as a percentage that takes into account both digestibility and amino acid score and provides a good indication of the quality of a protein.

Calculation Corner

Amino Acid Score

The formula used to calculate the amino acid score for any food is:

$$\text{Amino acid score} = \frac{\text{essential amino acid for protein (mg/g)}}{\text{essential amino acid for standard (mg/g)}}$$

We can use peanut butter to illustrate this calculation. Table 6.4 shows the essential amino acid content for peanut butter in column two. The third column shows the essential amino acid content for egg protein, which is most often used as the standard for this calculation. As you read across the table to column four, you can see the amino acid score. This means that peanut butter contains 136% of the histidine compared with egg protein. This is how you calculate the amino acid score. Begin with histidine and divide the amount of histidine in peanut butter by the amount found in egg protein:

$$30 \text{ mg/g} \div 22 \text{ mg/g} = 1.36$$

You continue the calculation for each of the amino acids. Each of the nine essential amino acid scores is calculated individually and presented in column four in Table 6.4. Now calculate the entire food of peanut butter compared with egg protein using the total mg/g for each as follows:

$$406 \text{ mg/g peanut butter} \div 674 \text{ mg/g egg protein} = 0.60 \text{ or } 60\%$$

This amino acid score means that overall, peanut butter contains 60 percent of the essential amino acids that egg protein does.

The digestibility of proteins varies, depending on their source. In general, animal proteins are more digestible than plant proteins. Some plant proteins, especially when consumed raw, are protected by the plant's cell walls and cannot be broken down by the enzymes in the intestinal tract, whereas 90 to 99 percent of the proteins from animal sources (cheese and other dairy foods, meat, poultry, and eggs) are digestible. Raw plant proteins, such as in oatmeal (86 percent digestible) and soybeans (78 percent digestible), are generally only 70 to 90 percent digestible.[9]

▾ **Figure 6.15 Protein on Nutrition Labels**
Protein is listed on nutrition labels in grams and as a percentage of the daily value if the manufacturer makes a health claim.

Milk protein, which is easily digested and meets essential amino acid requirements, has a PDCAAS of 1.00. In comparison, kidney beans garner a PDCAAS of 0.68, and wheat has a score of only 0.40. If your only dietary source of protein is wheat, you are not meeting your essential amino acid needs. However, when wheat is combined with another protein source, such as peanut butter, the protein quality of the meal is improved.

The PDCAAS is used by the Food and Drug Administration to calculate the % Daily Value of protein used on food labels. Manufacturers use 50 grams of protein as the standard to calculate the % Daily Value for a serving of a food for adults and children 4 or more years of age. As you can see in **Figure 6.15**, the serving of low-fat milk contains 21 percent of the daily value, or 10.5 grams of protein (0.21×50 grams = 10.5 grams), which the manufacturer has rounded up to 11 grams.

Not all labels are required to list the % Daily Value for protein. It is only required on a label if a protein claim is made for the product.

Biological Value

The **biological value** of a protein refers to how quickly the nitrogen from the absorbed protein can be synthesized into body protein. If the food contains all nine essential amino acids, the synthesis can proceed

Calculation Corner

PDCAAS

The digestibility of a food has a major impact on the protein quality. This calculation, called the Protein Digestibility Corrected Amino Acid Score (PDCAAS), compares the amino acid content of a food with the amino acid requirement for humans and then corrects for digestibility. This is how the calculation works:

1. First you need to know the amino acid score of the food. For this calculation you use the lowest amino acid score. From Table 6.4 you see that the lowest amino acid score for peanut butter is methionine plus cysteine, or 0.42.
2. Next, to determine the PDCAAS for peanut butter, multiply the score for its lowest limiting amino acid (0.42) by the protein digestibility of peanut butter (95%):

$$\text{PDCAAS for peanut butter} = 0.42 \times 0.95 = 0.40$$

In other words, because the protein in peanut butter is not completely digested, the amino acid score for methionine plus cysteine has been corrected from 0.42 to 0.40.

These calculations are used by the Food and Drug Administration to determine the Daily Values represented on food labels. For example, one serving (2 tbs) of peanut butter contains 8 grams (g) of protein. To calculate the % Daily Value, this number is multiplied by the PDCAAS:

$$8 \text{ g} \times 0.40 = 3.2$$

Next, divide this by 50 grams, which is the recommended intake of protein for adults used on the label:

$$3.2 \div 50 \text{ g} = 0.064 \text{ or } 6.4\%$$

In this example, a serving of peanut butter would represent 6.4 percent of the Daily Value for protein.

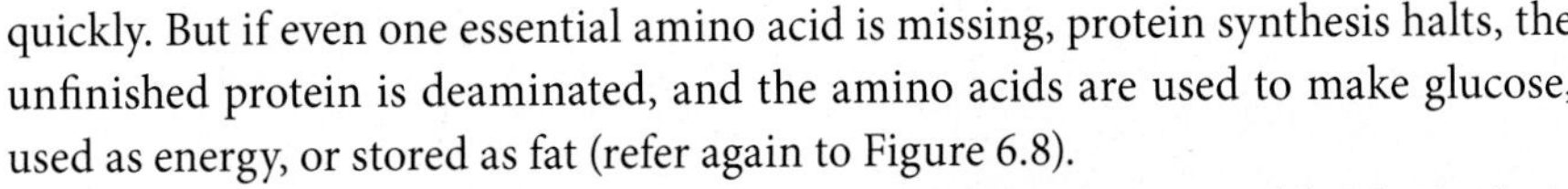

Egg protein has a biological value of 100, the highest quality protein in the diet.

quickly. But if even one essential amino acid is missing, protein synthesis halts, the unfinished protein is deaminated, and the amino acids are used to make glucose, used as energy, or stored as fat (refer again to Figure 6.8).

To calculate biological value, the amount of nitrogen retained by the body is divided by the amount consumed. Egg protein has a biological value of 100, which means that 100 percent of consumed nitrogen in egg protein is absorbed and retained for use by the body.

Complementary and Complete Proteins

Protein from animal products is considered a high-quality, **complete protein** based on higher chemical scores and nitrogen balance studies. Complete proteins provide all nine of the essential amino acids, along with some of the 11 nonessential amino acids. Plant proteins are considered an **incomplete protein** because plants are deficient in one or more essential amino acids. Two exceptions to this generalization are gelatin and soy. Gelatin, an animal protein, is not a complete protein because it is missing the amino acid tryptophan. Soy, a plant protein, has an amino acid profile that resembles the protein needs in the body, making it a complete protein by itself. Examining the Evidence: Does Soy Reduce the Risk of Disease? discusses a variety of soy products to incorporate into a vegetarian diet to improve the quality of your meals.

Does this mean that plant proteins are of less value in the diet? Absolutely not. When incomplete proteins are eaten with modest amounts of animal proteins or soy, or combined with other plant proteins that are rich in the incomplete protein's limiting amino acids, the incomplete protein is *complemented*. In other words, its

biological value The percentage of absorbed amino acids that are efficiently used to synthesize proteins.

complete protein A protein that provides all the essential amino acids, along with some nonessential amino acids. Soy protein and protein from animal sources are complete proteins.

incomplete protein A protein that is low in one or more of the essential amino acids. Proteins from plant sources tend to be incomplete.

EXAMINING THE EVIDENCE

Does Soy Reduce the Risk of Disease?

Soy consumption in the United States, in foods ranging from soy milk to soy burgers, has been increasing since the 1990s. From 1996 to 2010, the market for soy products has grown from $1 billion to $4.9 billion.[1] According to a survey conducted by the United Soybean Board, 81 percent of U.S. consumers perceive soy foods as being healthy and 37 percent of Americans consume soy foods or beverages once a month or more often.[2]

The popularity of soy foods is increasing among many age groups and ethnic groups, including baby boomers, who are more interested in good health and longevity than was their parents' generation; Asian populations in the United States looking for traditional soy-based foods; and young adults with an increasing interest in vegetarian diets.[3]

Soy is a high-quality protein source that is low in saturated fat and that contains **isoflavones,** which are naturally occurring phytoestrogens (*phyto* = plant). These plant **estrogens** have a chemical structure similar to human estrogen, a female sex hormone. Though they are considered weak estrogens (they have less than a thousandth the potential activity of estrogen), they may interfere with or mimic some of estrogen's activities in certain cells in the body.[4] Though isoflavones can also be found in other plant foods, such as grains, vegetables, and legumes, soybeans contain the largest amount found in food.

Soy and Your Health

Epidemiological studies, which look at health and disease in populations, have suggested that isoflavones may reduce the risk of chronic diseases, including heart disease and certain cancers. Some other studies suggest that isoflavones may help relieve menopausal symptoms.[5] At the same time, because isoflavones act as weak estrogens in the body, some concern exists that they may have a harmful impact on diseases such as breast cancer.[6]

Eating soy protein as part of a heart-healthy diet may reduce the risk of heart disease by lowering cholesterol levels. A review

What's on the Soy Menu?

Tofu ▸

- Cooked, pureed soybeans that are processed into a silken, soft, or firm texture; has a neutral flavor, which allows it to blend well
- Use the silken version in dips, soups, and cream pies. Use the firm variety in stir-fries or salads, or marinate it and then bake or grill it.

Soy Milk ▴

- A soy beverage made from a mixture of ground soybeans and water
- Use in place of cow's milk. Combine soy milk with ice and fruit in a blender for a soy shake.

Edamame ▴

- Tender young soybeans; can be purchased fresh, frozen, or canned
- Use in salads, grain dishes, stir-fries, and casseroles.

Soy Flour ▴

- Made from ground, roasted soybeans
- Use in baked goods such as pancakes, muffins, and cookies. It can also substitute for eggs in baked goods: Use 1 tbs soy flour combined with 1 tbs of water for each whole egg.

of over 35 research studies showed that soy protein lowered total cholesterol, the "bad" LDL cholesterol, and triglycerides all by about 10 percent.[7] However, recent findings suggest that the lowering effect may be a more modest 3 percent.[8, 9]

Numerous studies suggest that the isoflavones in soy may help reduce the risk of cancer, as these weak estrogens may have anticancer functions in the body. For example, isoflavones compete with the hormone estrogen for its binding site on specific cells. The isoflavone latches onto the cell and blocks the binding of the hormone. Because estrogen may increase the risk of breast cancer, inhibiting or blocking the actions of estrogen may help reduce the risk.[10]

Timing may be an important part of the preventive role that soy plays in breast cancer. A study of Chinese women revealed that those who ate the most soy during their adolescent years had a reduced risk of breast cancer in adulthood. Early exposure to soy foods may be protective by stimulating the growth of cells in the breast, enhancing the rate at which the glands mature, and altering the tissues in a beneficial way.[11]

However, this anticancer role of isoflavones may also be a detriment. There is some concern that once the isoflavones are bound to the estrogen receptors, they can initiate the production of cancer cells, which can *raise* the risk of breast cancer.[12] A review of over 200 research studies supports the safety of soy isoflavones when consumed as soy and soy products.[13] However, this issue of potentially increasing the risk of breast cancer, especially for those who are at high risk of developing it or who presently have breast cancer, isn't resolved yet. According to the American Cancer Society, women with breast cancer should consume a healthy, plant-based diet with only moderate amounts of soy foods and should avoid soy-containing pills, powders, and supplements with high levels of isoflavones.[14]

Soy can be an inexpensive, heart-healthy protein source that may also help modestly lower your blood cholesterol. While soy may help lower the risk of certain cancers, it is currently unclear if it is beneficial or harmful for individuals at high risk of developing breast cancer.

isoflavones Naturally occurring phytoestrogens, or weak plant estrogens, that function in a similar fashion to the hormone estrogen in the human body.

estrogen The hormone responsible for female sex characteristics.

Tempeh ▸
- Made from cooked whole soybeans that are condensed into a solid block
- Can be seasoned and used as a meat substitute.

Textured Soy Protein ▴
- Created from defatted soy flour that has been compressed and dehydrated
- Use as a meat substitute in foods such as meatballs, meatloaf, chili, tacos, and spaghetti sauce.

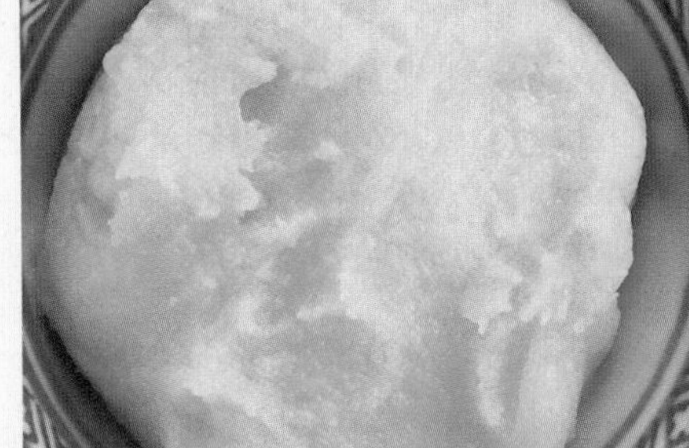

Miso ▴
- A flavorful paste of fermented soybeans used to season foods
- Use in soups, stews, and sauces.

Soy Meat Analogs ▴
- Products such as hot dogs, sausages, burgers, cold cuts, yogurts, and cheese that are made using soy
- Use as a meat substitute at meals and snacks.

References

1. Soyfoods Association of North America. 2010. *Sales and Trends.* Available at www.soyfoods.org/products/sales-and-trends. Accessed April 2012.
2. United Soybean Board. 2011. *Consumer Attitudes About Nutrition: Insights into Nutrition, Health, and Soyfoods.* Available at www.soyconnection.com/health_nutrition/pdf/Consumer Attitudes2012.pdf. Accessed April 2012.
3. Henkel, J. 2000. Soy: Health Claims for Soy Protein, Questions about Other Components. *FDA Consumer Magazine* 34:13–15, 18–20.
4. Munro, I. C., M. Harwood, J. J. Hlywka, A. M. Stephen, J. Doull, W. G. Flammn, and H. Adlercrutz. 2003. Soy Isoflavones: A Safety Review. *Nutrition Review* 61:1–33.
5. Ibid.
6. Maskarinec, G. 2005. Soy Foods for Breast Cancer Survivors and Women at High Risk for Breast Cancer. *Journal of the American Dietetic Association* 105:1524–1528.
7. Anderson, J. W., B. M. Johnstone, and M. E. Cook-Newell. 1995. Meta-Analysis of the Effects of Soy Protein Intake on Serum Lipids. *New England Journal of Medicine* 333:276–282.
8. Balk, E., M. Chung, P. Chew, S. Ip, G. Raman, B. Kupelnick, A. Tatsioni, Y. Sun, B. Wolk, D. Devine, and J. Lau. 2005. Effects of Soy on Health Outcomes, Summary, Evidence Report/ Technology Assessment No. 126. AHRQ Publication No. 05-E024-1. Rockville, MD: Agency for Healthcare Research and Quality.
9. Sacks, F., A. Lichtenstein, L. Van Horn, W. Harris, P. Kris-Etherton, M. Winston, and the American Heart Association Nutrition Committee. 2006. Soy Protein, Isoflavones, and Cardiovascular Health: An American Heart Association Science Advisory for Professions from the Nutrition Committee. *Circulation* 113:1034–1044.
10. Messina, M. J. and C. L. Loprinzi, 2001. Soy for Breast Cancer Survivors: A Critical Review of the Literature. *Journal of Nutrition* 131:3095S–3108S.
11. Shu, X. O., F. Jin, Q. Dai, W. Wen, J. D. Potter, L. H. Kushi, Z. Ruan, Y. Gao, and W. Zheng. 2001. Soyfood Intake during Adolescence and Subsequent Risk of Breast Cancer among Chinese Women. *Cancer Epidemiology, Biomarkers & Prevention* 10:483–488.
12. McMichael-Phillips, D. F., C. Harding, M. Morton, S. A. Roberts, A. Howell, C. S. Potten, and N. J. Bundred. 1998. Effects of Soy-Protein Supplementation on Epithelial Proliferation in the Histologically Normal Human Breast. *American Journal of Clinical Nutrition* 68:1431S–1436S.
13. Munro, I. C. 2003. Soy Isoflavones.
14. American Cancer Society. 2008. *Frequently Asked Questions about Nutrition and Physical Activity.* Available at www.cancer.org/docroot/ped/content/ped_3_2x_common_questions_about_diet_and_cancer.asp. Accessed May 2010; McMichael-Phillips, D. F. 1998. Effects of Soy-Protein Supplementation.

amino acid profile is upgraded to a complete protein. For example, when rice, which is low in lysine but high in methionine, is combined with beans, which provide a sufficient source of lysine, they complement each other and provide all nine essential amino acids. In addition, adding a small amount of cheese or meat to a plant protein, such as in macaroni and cheese or a shrimp stir-fry, provides the amino acid that is limited in the plant food.

Complementary proteins do not need to be consumed at the same meal to improve the quality of the protein source. As long as the foods are consumed in the same day, all the essential amino acids will be provided to meet your biological needs. Vegetarian diets can contain a sufficient quality as well as quantity of protein in carefully planned meals. Read more on this topic in Health Connection: What Is a Vegetarian Diet? on page 232.

Chickpeas are short of the limiting amino acid methionine. The addition of sesame seed paste, which has an abundance of methionine, completes the protein. Add garlic and lemon as seasonings for a *completely* delicious hummus.

You Can Determine Your Own Protein Needs

The RDA for protein has been established to provide adequate amounts of essential amino acids and nitrogen. This ensures the body will have the materials necessary to make the nonessential amino acids and body proteins necessary to meet daily needs.

There are two ways to determine protein intake in the diet. It can be measured as grams of protein eaten per day or as a percentage of total kilocalories.

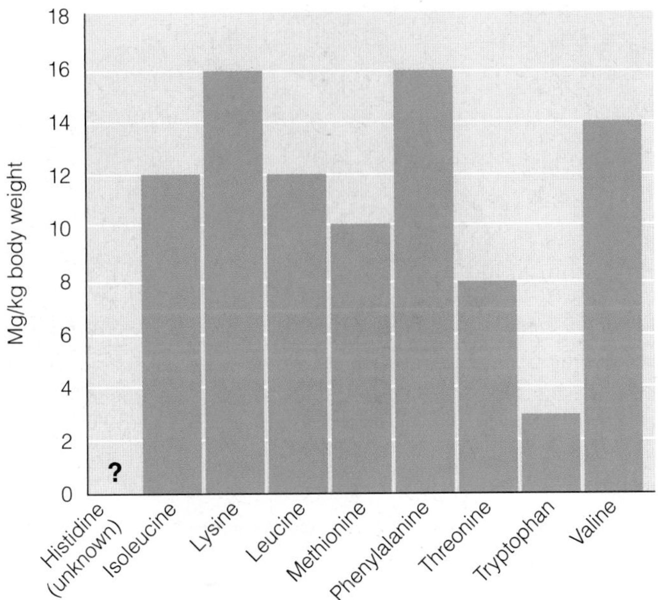

▲ **Figure 6.16 RDAs for Essential Amino Acids**
Recommended Dietary Allowances for the nine essential amino acids based on body weight.
Data from Institute of Medicine. *Dietary Reference Intakes for Energy, Carbohydrate, Fiber, Fat, Fatty Acids, Cholesterol, Protein, and Amino Acids.* (Washington, DC: National Academies Press, 2005).

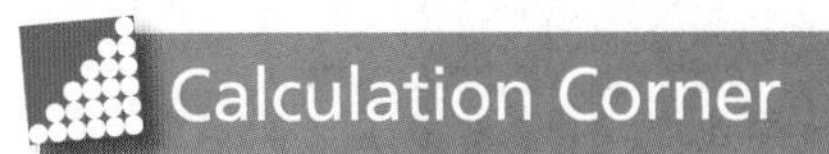

Protein Requirements

(a) To calculate protein requirements, the first step is to convert body weight in pounds to kilograms. The conversion factor is 2.2. For example, an adult who weights 176 pounds (lb) would weigh 80 kilograms (kg):

$$176 \text{ lb} \div 2.2 = 80 \text{ kg}$$

(b) Next, multiply weight in kilograms × 0.8 grams of protein. In this example, a healthy adult who weighs 80 kg should consume 64 grams (g) of protein per day.

$$80 \text{ kg} \times 0.8 \text{ g} = 64 \text{ g protein}$$

(c) How much protein should a healthy adult who weighs 130 pounds consume each day?

Data from Institute of Medicine, National Academy of Science, *Dietary Reference Intakes for Energy, Carbohydrate, Fiber, Fat, Fatty Acids, Cholesterol, Protein, and Amino Acids* (Washington, DC: The National Academies Press, 2002).

The RDA for Protein

The Recommended Dietary Allowances (RDAs) for the essential amino acids are illustrated in **Figure 6.16**. As you can see, the RDA per day for each of the nine essential amino acids is based on grams per kilogram of body weight.

The current RDA for protein is based on the age and weight of healthy individuals. Adults older than 19 years of age should consume 0.8 grams of protein for each kilogram of body weight. For individuals under the age of 19, the RDA is somewhat higher (see the tables in the front cover of this textbook).

In the United States, men aged 20 and older consume, on average, more than 100 grams of protein daily, and women on average consume more than 70 grams. In general, Americans are meeting, and even exceeding, their dietary protein needs. Follow the steps in the Calculation Corner to calculate your RDA for protein.

Adequate Protein

Total protein intake in the diet is also measured as a percentage of total kilocalories. The latest recommendation, based on data from numerous nitrogen balance studies, is to consume from 10 to 35 percent of total daily kilocalories from protein. Currently, adults in the United States consume about 15 percent of their daily kilocalories from protein, which falls within this range.

Even though many Americans are consuming more protein than they need, their percentage of daily kilocalories contributed by protein (15 percent) falls within the recommended range (10 to 35 percent). This is because Americans are consuming an abundant amount of kilocalories from carbohydrates and fats, which lowers the percentage of the total kilocalories coming from protein.

An overweight individual's protein needs are not much greater than those of a normal-weight person of similar height because the RDA for dietary protein is based on a person's need to maintain protein-dependent tissues, like lean muscle and organs, and to perform protein-dependent body functions. Because most overweight people carry most of their extra body weight as fat, not

Health Connection

What Is a Vegetarian Diet?

For many people, being a **vegetarian** is a lifestyle choice made for a particular reason. Whereas some vegetarians avoid foods from animal sources for ethical, religious, or environmental reasons, others choose a vegetarian lifestyle for health reasons.[1, 2] There are several types of vegetarians and associated ranges of acceptable foods. See Table 1 for a description of different vegetarian diets and the foods associated with each.

Because vegetarians avoid meat, which is high in complete protein, they need to be sure to get adequate protein from other food sources. Vegetarians can meet their daily protein needs by consuming a varied plant-based diet that contains meat alternatives such as soy, dried beans and other legumes, and nuts. Vegetarians who consume some animal products, such as milk, eggs, and/or fish, can use these foods to help meet their protein needs.

An estimated 3 percent of American adults, or about 6 million people, follow a vegetarian diet. In the United States, the vegetarian food market has become an over $1.5 billion industry as manufacturers accommodate this growing consumer demand with an array of new vegetarian products.[3]

Vegetarian Diets Carry Potential Benefits and Risks

A plant-based vegetarian diet can be rich in high-fiber whole grains, vegetables, fruits, legumes, and nuts, and naturally lower in saturated fat and cholesterol-containing foods. These qualities are fundamental for reducing the risk of heart disease, high blood pressure, diabetes, cancer, stroke, and obesity, assuming the diet is not limited or unbalanced in nutrients.

vegetarian A person who avoids eating animal foods. Some vegetarians only avoid meat, fish, and poultry, while others (vegans) avoid all animal products, including milk, eggs, and cheese.

Vegetarian food staples such as soy, nuts, and soluble fiber–rich foods including beans and oats have all been shown to reduce blood cholesterol levels. Research collected from numerous studies has shown that deaths from heart disease are about 25 percent lower among vegetarians than among nonvegetarians.[4, 5]

Vegetarians also tend to have lower blood pressure. The incidence of high blood pressure has been shown to be over two times higher in nonvegetarians.[6] High blood pressure is a risk factor not only for heart disease, but also for stroke.

Because you know from Chapter 4 that a plant-based diet can help reduce the risk of type 2 diabetes, you shouldn't be surprised to learn that vegetarians tend to have a lower risk of diabetes. Diabetes mellitus is also a risk for heart disease. For those with diabetes, the predominance of foods rich in fiber and low in saturated fat and cholesterol in a vegetarian diet can help them manage the disease.[7]

TABLE 1 The Many Types of Vegetarians

Type	Eats	Avoids
Lacto-vegetarian	Grains, vegetables, fruits, legumes, seeds, nuts, dairy foods	Meat, fish, poultry, and eggs
Lacto-ovo-vegetarian	Grains, vegetables, fruits, legumes, seeds, nuts, dairy foods, eggs	Meat, fish, and poultry
Ovo-vegetarian	Grains, vegetables, fruits, legumes, seeds, nuts, eggs	Meat, fish, poultry, dairy foods
Vegan	Grains, vegetables, fruits, legumes, seeds, nuts	Any animal foods, meat, fish, poultry, dairy foods, eggs
Semivegetarian	A vegetarian diet that occasionally includes meat, fish, and poultry	Meat, fish, and poultry on occasion

Vegetarian diets have been shown to reduce the risk of both prostate and colon cancer.[8] Though some of this may be due to the fact that many vegetarians are nonsmokers, nondrinkers, and physically active, much of it may also be due to their diet.[9] Respected health organizations, such as the American Institute for Cancer Research and the American Cancer Society, advocate a plant-based diet to reduce the risk of cancer.[10]

Also, a plant-based diet that contains mostly fiber-rich whole grains and low-kilocalorie, nutrient-dense vegetables and fruits tends to be one that "fills you up before it fills you out," which means that you are likely to eat fewer overall kilocalories. Consequently, eating the plant-based foods of a vegetarian diet can be a healthy and satisfying strategy for fighting the battle against obesity.[11]

The biggest risk of a vegetarian diet is underconsuming certain nutrients, such as protein and vitamin B_{12}. Vegetarian foods contain protein, but the amount per serving is lower than that found in animal sources. For example, 100 grams, or a serving, of kidney beans contains 7 grams of protein, whereas 100 grams of cooked chicken breast, or the size of a medium boneless chicken breast, contains 17 grams. Vitamin B_{12} is a concern in vegetarian diets because it is only found in animal foods.[12] Strictly avoiding meat, fish, poultry, and foods derived from animal sources can be unhealthy if these foods are not replaced with nutrient-dense alternatives. Thus, vegetarians need to carefully plan their meals to make sure they meet all of their nutrient needs.

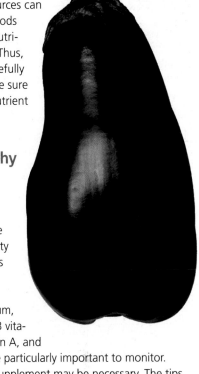

Planning a Healthy Vegetarian Diet

To avoid nutrient deficiencies, vegetarians must consume adequate amounts of a wide variety of foods. Some nutrients found in abundance in animal foods, including protein, iron, zinc, calcium, vitamin D, riboflavin (a B vitamin), vitamin B_{12}, vitamin A, and omega-3 fatty acids, are particularly important to monitor. A vitamin and mineral supplement may be necessary. The tips in Tables 2 and 3 can help vegetarians easily incorporate these nutrients into their diet.

TABLE 2 Suggested Servings for a Healthy Vegetarian Diet

Food Group	Number of Servings	Serving Size	Calcium-Rich Foods (8 servings daily)
Grains	6	Bread, 1 slice Cooked grain or cereal, ½ cup Ready-to-eat cereal, 1 oz	Whole wheat bread, 1 slice Calcium-fortified cereal, 1 oz
Legumes, nuts, and other protein rich foods	5	Cooked beans, peas, or lentils, ½ cup Tofu or tempeh, ½ cup Nut or seed butter, 2 tbs Nuts ¼ cup Meat analog, 1 oz Egg, 1	Cow's milk or yogurt, ½ cup Calcium-fortified soy milk, ½ cup Cheese ¾ oz
Vegetables	4	Cooked vegetables, ½ cup Raw vegetables, 1 cup Vegetable juice, ½ cup	Bok choy, collards, broccoli Chinese cabbage, kale, mustard greens, or okra; 1 cup cooked or 2 cups raw Calcium-fortified tomato juice, ½ cup
Fruits	2	Medium fruit, 1 Cut-up or cooked fruit, ½ cup; Fruit juice, ½ cup Dried fruit ¼ cup	Calcium-fortified fruit juice, ½ cup Figs, 5
Fats	2	Oil, 1 tsp Soft margarine, 1 tsp Mayonnaise, 1 tsp	

Adapted from V. Messina, V. Melina, and A. R. Mangels, "A New Food Guide for North American Vegetarians," *Journal of the American Dietetic Association* 103 (2003): 771–775.

TABLE 3 Nutrients That Could Be Missing in a Vegetarian Diet

Vegetarians need to take care in planning a diet that meets all their nutritional needs. Here are the nutrients that vegetarians could fall short of in their diet, some vegetarian food sources for these nutrients, and tips on how to enjoy these foods as part of a balanced diet.

Nutrient	Risks	Vegetarian Food Sources	Table Tips
Protein	Most plant foods do not contain complete protein. However, a vegetarian's protein needs can be met by consuming a *variety* of plant foods. A combination of protein-rich soy foods, legumes, nuts, or seeds should be eaten daily.	Soybeans, soy burgers, tofu, tempeh, nuts, peanuts, peanut butter, legumes, sunflower seeds, milk, soy milk, yogurt, cheese	■ Add nuts to your morning cereal. ■ Add beans to your salads, soups, and main entrées. ■ Have a soy burger for lunch. ■ Use tofu in stir-fries, rice and pasta dishes, and casseroles. ■ Snack on a soy milk and banana or berry shake.
Iron	The form of iron in plants is not as easily absorbed as the type in meat, milk, and poultry. Also, phytate in grains and rice and polyphenols in tea and coffee can inhibit iron absorption. The iron needs of vegetarians are about $1^1/_2$ times higher than those of nonvegetarians. Vitamin C enhances the absorption of the iron in plant foods.	Iron-fortified cereals, enriched grains, pasta, bread, oatmeal, potatoes, wheat germ, cashews and other nuts, sunflower seeds, legumes, soybeans, tofu, bok choy, broccoli, mushrooms, dried fruits	■ Make sure your morning cereal is iron fortified. ■ Add soybeans to your lunchtime salad. ■ Eat bread with your salad lunch or make a sandwich. ■ Pack a trail mix of dried fruits and nuts for a snack. ■ Add vitamin C–rich foods (broccoli, tomatoes, citrus fruits) to all your meals.
Zinc	The absorption of zinc is enhanced by animal protein. Eating a vegetarian diet means that you lose out on this benefit and are more likely to develop a deficiency. Phytate also binds zinc, making it unavailable to your body. A vegan's zinc needs may be as much as 50 percent higher than a nonvegetarian's.	Soybeans, soy milk, tofu, tempeh, fortified soy burgers, legumes, nuts, sunflower seeds, wheat germ, fortified ready-to-eat cereals, mushrooms, and low-fat or nonfat milk, yogurt, and cheese	■ Douse your morning cereal with low-fat milk. ■ Add low-fat cheese and soybeans to your lunchtime salad. ■ Snack on sunflower seeds. ■ Top an afternoon yogurt with wheat germ. ■ Add soybeans to your dinner rice.
Calcium	Calcium is abundant in lean dairy foods such as nonfat or low-fat milk, yogurt, and cheese, so obtaining adequate amounts shouldn't be difficult if you consume these foods. Calcium-fortified soy milk and orange juice as well as tofu can provide about the same amount of calcium per serving as is found in dairy foods.	Low-fat or nonfat milk, yogurt, and cheese, fortified soy milk, soy yogurt, and soy cheese, calcium-fortified orange juice, legumes, sesame tahini, tofu processed with calcium, bok choy, broccoli, kale, collard greens, mustard greens, okra	■ Add milk to your morning cereal and coffee. ■ Have at least one yogurt a day. ■ Have a glass of calcium-fortified orange juice with lunch. ■ Snack on low-fat cheese or yogurt in the afternoon. ■ Eat green vegetables often at dinner.

TABLE 3 Nutrients That Could Be Missing in a Vegetarian Diet *(continued)*

Nutrient	Risks	Vegetarian Food Sources	Table Tips
Vitamin D	Some vegetarians will need to consume vitamin D–fortified milk or soy products.	Low-fat or nonfat milk, egg yolk, fortified yogurt, soy milk, soy yogurt, ready-to-eat cereals; vitamin supplement	■ Have a glass of milk or soy milk at breakfast every day. ■ Make sure your morning cereal is vitamin D fortified. ■ Use fortified evaporated skim milk as a base for cream sauces. ■ Snack on fortified cereals. ■ Have a fortified yogurt each day.
Vitamin B_{12}	Animal foods are the only naturally occurring food source of B_{12}, so it is extremely important that vegetarians, especially strict vegans, look to fortified cereals and soy milk or a supplement to meet their daily needs.	Low-fat and nonfat milk, yogurt, or cheese, eggs, fortified soy milk, ready-to-eat cereals, soy burgers, egg substitutes; vitamin supplement	■ Make sure your morning cereal is fortified with vitamin B_{12}. ■ Drink a cup of milk or fortified soy milk with your meals. ■ Top an afternoon yogurt snack with a fortified cereal. ■ Try an egg substitute omelet for lunch. ■ Use fortified soy "meat" alternatives at dinner.
Vitamin A	Vitamin A is found only in animal foods. However, vegetarians can meet their needs by consuming the vitamin A precursor, beta-carotene.	Fortified low-fat or nonfat milk and soy milk, apricots, cantaloupe, mangoes, pumpkin, kale, carrots, spinach	■ Enjoy a slice or bowl of cantaloupe in the morning. ■ Snack on dried apricots. ■ Add spinach to your lunchtime salad. ■ Drink a glass of fortified milk or soy milk with dinner. ■ Try mangoes for a sweet dessert.
Omega-3 fatty acids	If your vegetarian diet doesn't include fish, you may not be consuming enough of the essential omega-3 fatty acid called alpha-linolenic acid.	Fish, especially fatty fish such as salmon and sardines, walnuts, flaxseed and flaxseed oil, soybean and canola oil	■ Add walnuts to baked breads and muffins. ■ Try canned salmon on top of your lunchtime salad. ■ Top your yogurt with ground flaxseeds. ■ Have fish regularly for dinner. ■ Cook with canola and flaxseed oil.

References

1. Pimentel, D. and M. Pimentel. 2003. Sustainability of Meat-Based and Plant-Based Diets and the Environment. *American Journal of Clinical Nutrition* 78:660S–663S.
2. Ginsberg, C. and A. Ostrowski. 2003. The Market for Vegetarian Foods. *The Vegetarian Resource Group*. Available at www.vrg.org/nutshell/market.htm. Accessed March 2012.
3. The Vegetarian Resource Group. 2009. How Many Vegetarians Are There? Available at www.vrg.org/nutshell/poll.htm. Accessed March 2012.
4. Appleby, P. N., M. Thorogood, J. I. Mann, and T. J. A. Key. 1999. The Oxford Vegetarian Study: An Overview. *American Journal of Clinical Nutrition* 70:525S–531S.
5. Sabate, J. 2003. The Contribution of Vegetarian Diets to Health and Disease: A Paradigm Shift? *American Journal of Clinical Nutrition* 78:502S–507S.
6. Fraser, G. E. 1999. Associations between Diet and Cancer, Ischemic Heart Disease, and All-Cause Mortality in Non-Hispanic White California Seventh-Day Adventists. *American Journal of Clinical Nutrition* 70:532S–538S.
7. Jenkins, D. J., C. Kendall, A. Marchie, A. L. Jenkins, L. Augustin, D. S. Ludwig, N. D. Barnard, and J. W. Anderson. 2003. Type 2 Diabetes and the Vegetarian Diet. *American Journal of Clinical Nutrition* 78:610S–616S.
8. Lewin, M. H., N. Bailey, T. Bandaletova, R. Bowman, A. J. Cross, J. Pollock, D. E. G. Shuker, and S. A. Bingham. 2006. Red Meat Enhances the Colonic Function of the DNA Adduct 0-Carboxymethyl Guanine: Implications for Colorectal Cancer Risk. *Cancer Research* 66:1859–1865.
9. Fraser, G. E. 1999. Associations between Diet and Cancer.
10. Ibid.
11. Burke, L. E., M. A. Styn, A. R. Steenkiste, E. Music, M. Warziski, and J. Choo. 2006. A Randomized Clinical Trial Testing Treatment Preferences and Two Dietary Options in Behavioral Weight Management: Preliminary Results of the Impact of Diet at 6 Months—PREFER Study. *Obesity* 14:2007–2017.
12. School, H. M. 2005. Are You Getting Enough of this Vitamin? If You're a Vegetarian or Over Age 60, You Need to be Concerned About Getting Enough Vitamin B_{12}. *Harvard Health Letter* 30:1–2.

muscle, they do not need to consume significantly more protein than normal-weight people.

The American College of Sports Medicine, the Academy of Nutrition and Dietetics, and other experts have advocated an increase of 50 to 100 percent more protein for competitive athletes participating in endurance exercise (marathon runners) or resistance exercise (weight lifters) to meet their needs.[10, 11] However, due to their active lifestyles, athletes typically have a higher intake of food and thus already consume higher amounts of both kilocalories and protein.

THE TAKE-HOME MESSAGE Protein quality is determined by the protein's digestibility and by the types and amounts of amino acids (essential versus nonessential) it contains. Protein from animal foods is more easily digested than protein from plant foods. A complete protein, which is typically found in animal foods and soy, provides a complete set of the essential amino acids, along with some nonessential amino acids. Plant proteins are typically incomplete, as they are missing or low in one or more of the essential amino acids. Plant proteins can be complemented with protein from other plant sources or animal sources to improve their protein quality. Adults should consume 0.8 gram of protein for each kilogram of body weight. In the United States, men typically consume more than 100 grams of protein daily, and women more than 70 grams—in both cases, far more than is needed.

What Are the Best Food Sources of Protein?

The content of protein varies in foods commonly consumed in the United States and other developed countries. Although fruits are an excellent dietary choice, most contain one gram or less of protein per serving. Other foods, especially animal products, can contribute substantial amounts of protein to the diet.

Eggs, Meat, Soy, and Dairy Contain Significant Amounts of Protein

Protein is particularly abundant in dairy foods, meat, fish, poultry, and meat alternatives such as dried beans, peanut butter, nuts, and soy (**Figure 6.17**). A 3-ounce serving of cooked meat, poultry, or fish provides 21 to 25 grams of protein, or about 7 grams per ounce. A serving size of 3 ounces, which is about the size of a deck of cards, is plenty of protein for one meal. Grains and vegetables are less robust protein sources, providing about 3 to 4 grams per serving, but as part of a varied, balanced diet, they can contribute significantly to daily needs.

Eating a wide variety of foods is the best approach to meeting protein needs. A diet that consists of the recommended servings from the five food groups based on 1,600 kilocalories (which is far less than most adults consume daily) will supply an adequate amount of protein for adult women and most adult men (Table 6.5 on page 240). In fact, many people have met their daily protein needs before they even sit down to dinner.

You Don't Need Protein Supplements

Some of the most popular supplements in the United States are protein and amino acids, often marketed especially to athletes (see Examining the Evidence: Protein

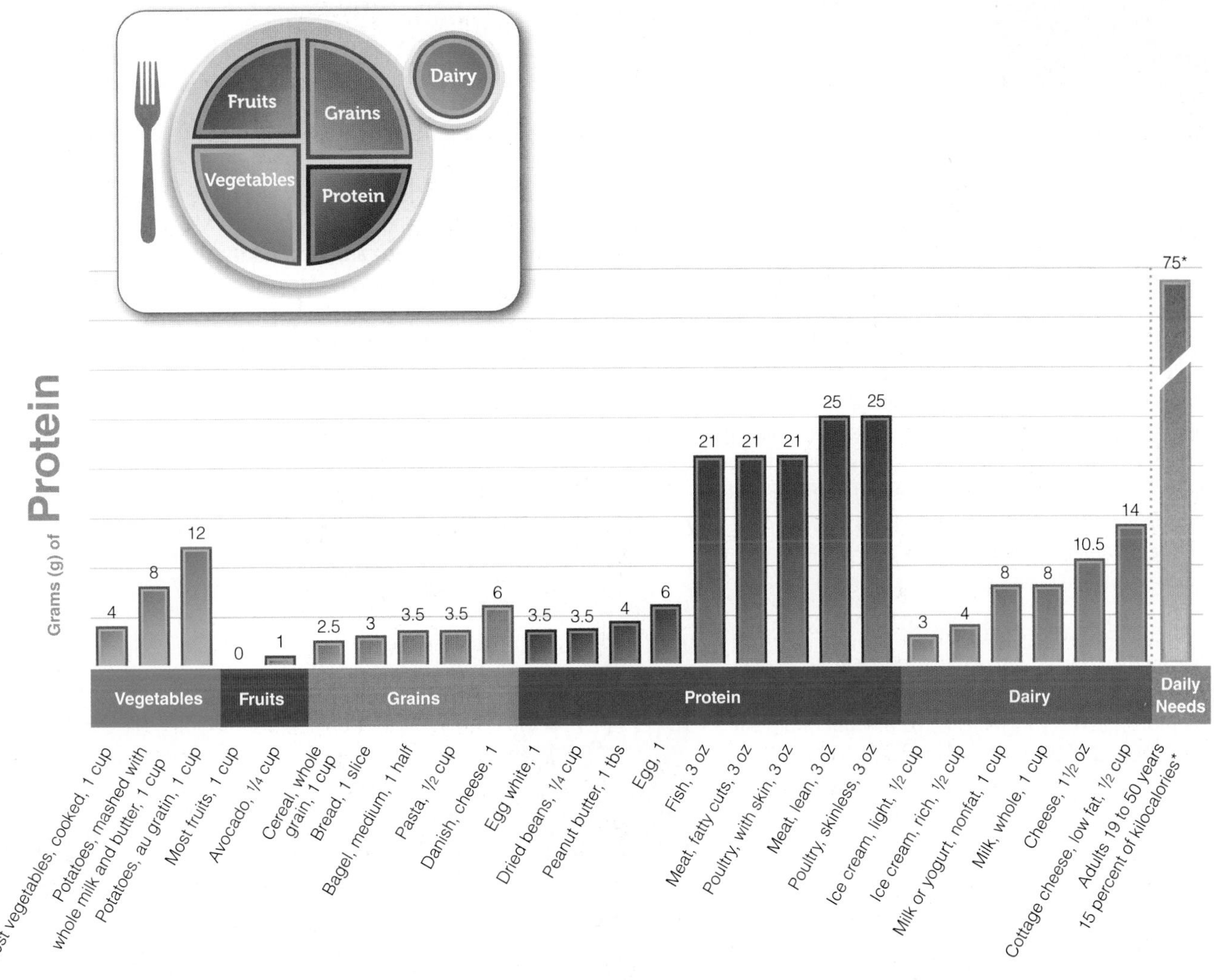

▲ **Figure 6.17 Food Sources of Protein**
Food choices from the meat, poultry, fish, meat alternative, and milk groups are the most abundant sources of dietary protein. Grains and vegetables provide less protein per serving, but as part of a varied, balanced diet can contribute to daily needs.
Data from *USDA National Nutrient Database for Standard Reference*. Available at www.nal.usda.gov/fnic.

Supplements: Are They Necessary?). Physically active people may take protein supplements as an ergogenic aid to increase muscle size and strength, and endurance performance. While the debate on the benefits of protein supplements (especially four amino acids with a branched side chain, referred to as *branched-chain amino acids*, or *BCAAs*) continues, you don't need to supplement your diet with protein. The DRIs for protein are based on healthy food choices and do not recommend additional protein in the form of supplementation. (We'll discuss protein and sport performance in greater detail in Chapter 16.)

THE TAKE-HOME MESSAGE A well-balanced diet can easily meet daily protein needs. The best food sources of proteins are found in animal products and include eggs, lean meats, and low-fat or fat-free dairy products. Plant proteins such as soy, grains, and vegetables also supply substantial proteins to the diet. Most people consume more than enough protein each day and thus protein supplements are not necessary.

EXAMINING THE EVIDENCE

Protein Supplements: Are They Necessary?

The sale of protein supplements has skyrocketed over the last decade, fueling an industry that now generates almost two billion dollars annually.[1] These products are enticing. They promise to give you an energy boost, help shed those unwanted pounds, build muscle, fight aging, and cure a host of health problems. With very few exceptions, purchasing and consuming these products is, at best, a waste of money, and at worst, exposure to potentially harmful heavy metals.

Protein supplement manufacturers use phrases such as "scientifically proven," "nutritious and time-saving snack or meal replacement," and "look years younger" as a promise to consumers. Unfortunately, dietary supplements do not go through a rigorous testing for screening or efficacy. So how do you know if these supplements contain what they say they contain, do what they say they do, and are safe? Is more protein always better? Let's examine the evidence.

Protein Shakes and Powder

Most protein shakes and powders use whey (concentrates, isolates, and hydrolysates), soy, or occasionally rice protein as a key ingredient. The amount of protein their label claims they contain ranges from10 to 40 grams of protein per serving, along with added vitamins and minerals. Muscle Milk® powder lists 40 grams of protein per serving and suggests 3 servings per day for a total of 120 grams of protein. This amounts to 150% of the RDA for protein for a male weighing 176 pounds (RDA = 80 grams per day). This does not account for the other foods consumed during the day.

Do these products actually contain what is listed on the label? Based on research conducted by ConsumerLab.com, twenty protein supplements tested did contain what the label claimed but two products were contaminated with lead (6 to 19 mcg per day) and one product contained an additional 4 grams of sugar not accounted for on the label.[2] Other labs report arsenic, cadmium, lead, and mercury in fifteen tested samples.[3] Chronic ingestion of these toxic metals can cause severe health consequences, including kidney and pulmonary damage, anemia, and osteoporosis. Exposure is avoidable because most consumers more than meet their daily protein requirements by choosing whole foods.

Protein intake does enhance muscle sythesis.[4] But athletes consume enough protein for muscle growth and repair in an average mixed diet. Whey protein used in protein supplements is abundant in milk and dairy products.[5] The additional protein consumed through powders and shakes not used for protein synthesis is either burned for energy or converted to a fatty acid and stored in the adipocyte. In fact, excessive amounts of protein can be unhealthy and produce undesirable results.

The key to increasing muscle weight is a well-designed strength-training program combined with additional calories from all three macronutrients. These calories allow dietary protein to be used for muscle synthesis instead of energy. Another important key is timing. Research suggests that ingestion of protein before and immediately after a workout combined with a carbohydrate source improves muscle synthesis.[6] Choose a glass of nonfat milk, rather than a protein supplement, before and after a workout. Milk provides both key amino acids and the carbohydrate to stimulate muscle growth.

Protein shakes and powders are also marketed as meal replacers to those interested in losing weight. Whereas dieters may lose weight using a high-protein meal replacer, the same results can be obtained with a kilocalorie-controlled meal of whole foods, without the risk. When it comes to losing weight, it's the total kilocalories that count.

There are instances where protein shakes and supplements may be a nutritionally sound approach. Older adults, who may have limited appetites and be less likely to consume adequate nutrients in foods, may benefit from ingesting a protein shake every day. However, these products should be used to *supplement* their meals, not replace them.

Amino Acid Supplements

Amino acid supplements, including those containing individual amino acids such as tryptophan and lysine, are marketed as remedies for a range of health issues, including pain, depression, insomnia, and certain infections. These supplements contain single amino acids often in amounts or combinations not found naturally in foods. Consuming single amino acids in unnatural doses can compete with other amino acids for absorption, possibly resulting in a deficiency of other amino acids. Further, overconsuming specific amino acids can lead to side effects such as nausea, light-headedness, vomiting, and drowsiness.

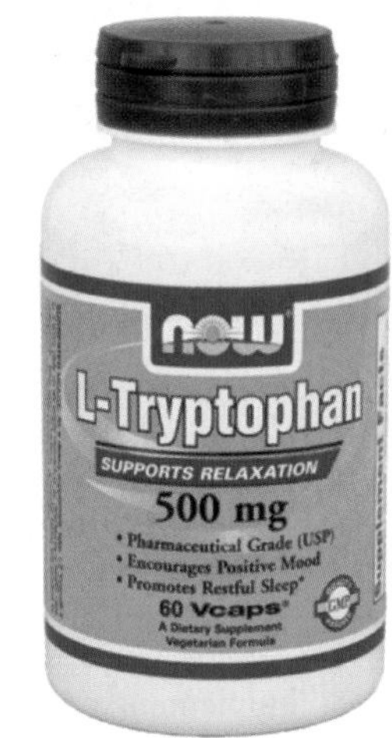

Protein Bars and Energy Bars

The sales of protein bars and energy bars have fueled an industry that now generates over a billion dollars annually. There are bars advertised for women, bars for men, bars for the elderly, and junior bars for children. When they emerged in the 1980s, these bars were marketed as a portable snack or a quick meal in a cellophane wrapper to help athletes stay fueled for long-distance or endurance outings.

As you learned from the previous two chapters, all foods provide kilocalories and therefore energy. Whether your kilocalories come from a balanced meal or a "balanced bar," your body will either use them for fuel or store them as body fat if they are not immediately needed. You also just learned that you can meet your daily protein needs by making wise food choices. Given this knowledge, what advantage, if any, do you think protein supplements provide?

Bar Hopping

Product	Price	Kilo-calories	Protein (g)	Total Carb. (g)	Total Fat (g)	Sat. Fat (g)	Sugars (tsp)	Fiber (g)
Peanut butter (1 tbs) on 2 slices whole-wheat bread	$0.22	234	9	29	11	2	<1 (5%)*	5
Atkins Advantage Chocolate Decadence	2.29	220	17	25	11	7	0	11
Carb Solutions Creamy Chocolate Peanut Butter	2.24	240	24	14	10	3.5	0.5 (3%)	1
Ensure Chewy Chocolate Peanut	1.13	230	9	35	6	4	6 (42%)	1
Genisoy Ultimate Chocolate Fudge Brownie	1.15	230	14	33	4.5	3	7 (49%)	2
Met-Rx Protein Plus Chocolate Roasted Peanut	2.57	320	31	29	9	4.5	0.5 (3%)	1
PowerBar ProteinPlus Chocolate Fudge Brownie	1.99	270	24	36	5	3	5 (38%)	2
PowerBar Pria Double Chocolate Cookie	0.94	110	5	16	3	2.5	2.5 ½ (36%)	0
Slim-Fast Meal Options Rich Chocolate Brownie	1.02	220	8	35	5	3	6 (44%)	2

Key: = 1 tsp sugar
= 1 g fiber
* = % of total kilocalories

Data from Adapted from *Consumer Reports* 68 (June 2003):19–21.

If convenience and portability are the main attractions of protein bars, then consider another convenient and portable food, the peanut butter sandwich. It can be made in a snap, and since it doesn't have to be refrigerated, it can travel anywhere. The table above lets you do some comparison shopping to see how a peanut butter sandwich stacks up to a protein bar.

From a price standpoint, a peanut butter sandwich is a bargain compared with bars that cost more than $2.50 each, or ten times as much as the sandwich. While the kilocalories and protein content of the sandwich are similar to that in many bars, the saturated fat and sugar contents are not. Some bars provide up to 7 grams of saturated fat, which is about one-third of the daily upper limit recommended for many adults. In contrast, the sandwich contains less saturated fat than all the bars listed. Because these bars can contain up to 7 teaspoons of sugar, which supplies up to 50 percent of the kilocalories in the bar, much of the "energy" is simply sugar. The bars with the most sugar tend to have the least amount of fiber. Ironically, most consumers need more fiber in their diet. Because the peanut butter sandwich has lower amounts of sugar and a higher amount of fiber than almost all of the bars, it's actually the healthier food choice.

References

1. Moo-ve Over Milk: Plant Alternatives Primed to Benefit from Protein Supplement Demand. 2012. *Euromoniter International.* Available at http://blog.euromonitor.com. Accessed March 2012.
2. Tests of Protein Powders and Shakes Contain Some Lead Contamination But No Melamine. 2012. Available from www.consumerlab.com/news/protein_powder_review/05_05_2010/. Accessed March 2012.
3. Alert! You Don't Need the Extra Protein or the Heavy Metals Our Tests Found. 2010. *Consumer Reports* 75:24.
4. Maughan, R. J. and S. M. Shirreffs. 2012. Nutrition for Sports Performance: Issues and Opportunities. *The Proceedings of the Nutrition Society* 71:112–119.
5. Graf, S., S. Egert, and M. Heer. 2011. Effects of Whey Protein Supplements on Metabolism: Evidence from Human Intervention Studies. *Current Opinion in Clinical Nutrition and Metabolic Care* 14:569–580.
6. Spillane, M., N. Schwarz, S. Leddy, T. Correa, M. Minter, V. Longoria, and D. S. Willoughby. 2011. Effects of 28 Days of Resistance Exercise while Consuming Commercially Available Pre- and Post-Workout Supplements, NO-Shotgun® and NO-Synthesize® on Body Composition, Muscle Strength and Mass, Markers of Protein Synthesis, and Clinical Safety Markers in Males. *Nutrition & Metabolism* 8:78.

TABLE 6.5 The Amount of Protein Found in a Typical Daily Menu

Food	Amount	Kilocalories	Protein (g)	Vegetable Group (servings)	Fruit Group (servings)	Grain Group (servings)	Protein Group (oz)	Dairy Group (servings)	Oil Group (tsp)
Breakfast									
Bran flakes	2 cups	256	**7.5**			2			
Milk, nonfat	1 cup	86	**8**					1	
Orange juice	8 oz	112	**2**		1				
Lunch									
Turkey and cheese sandwich:									
Turkey breast	2 oz	94	**11**				2		
Cheese, low fat	2 oz	98	**14**					1	
Whole-wheat bread	2 slices	138	**5**			2			
Tossed salad	3 cups	30	**2**	1.5					
Italian dressing	1 tbs	69	**0**						3
Snack									
Yogurt, vanilla	8 oz	160	**8**					1	
Banana	1	109	**1**		1				
Dinner									
Chicken breast, skinless	3 oz	189	**25**				3		
Brown rice	1 cup	216	**5**			2			
Broccoli, cooked	1 cup	52	**6**	1					
Margarine	2 tsp	68	**0**						2
Totals:		1,677	**94.5**	2.5	2	6	5	3	5

Note: A 140-pound adult needs 51 grams of protein daily. A 180-pound adult needs 65 grams of protein daily.

Data from MyPyramid.gov; J. Pennington and J. S. Douglass, *Bowes & Church's Food Values of Portions Commonly Used*, 18th ed. (New York: Lippincott Williams & Wilkins, 2005).

What Happens If You Eat Too Much or Too Little Protein?

Protein is essential to health and normal body function, and eating either too much or too little can be unhealthy. Most people in industrialized nations consume more than enough protein, while people from less developed countries may struggle to meet even the minimum requirements. Let's look at what happens to the human body when it gets too much or too little protein.

Eating Too Much Protein May Mean Too Much Heart-Unhealthy Fat and Weaker Bones

A diet high in protein has long been proposed to increase risk of heart disease, kidney stones, osteoporosis, and some types of cancer in normal, healthy people. Recent research provides some reassurance that eating too much protein (0.8 to 2.0 g/kg per day) may not be as bad as we once thought. However, consuming too much protein, to the point where it replaces other essential nutrients, also leads to an unbalanced diet.

Heart Disease

Recent research reports that the type of protein is more important in reducing the risk of heart disease than the quantity.[12] In the 26-year Nurses' Health Study, a diet low in red meat that contained nuts, low-fat dairy, poultry, or fish was associated with a 13 to 30 percent lower risk for heart disease than a diet high in red meat and high-fat dairy. In addition, low-carbohydrate diets that contained animal protein had a 23 percent higher mortality rate than plant-protein diets (20 percent lower mortality rate).

The high-red-meat diets may mean overloading on heart-unhealthy saturated fat (see **Figure 6.18**). Even lean meats and skinless poultry, which contain less saturated

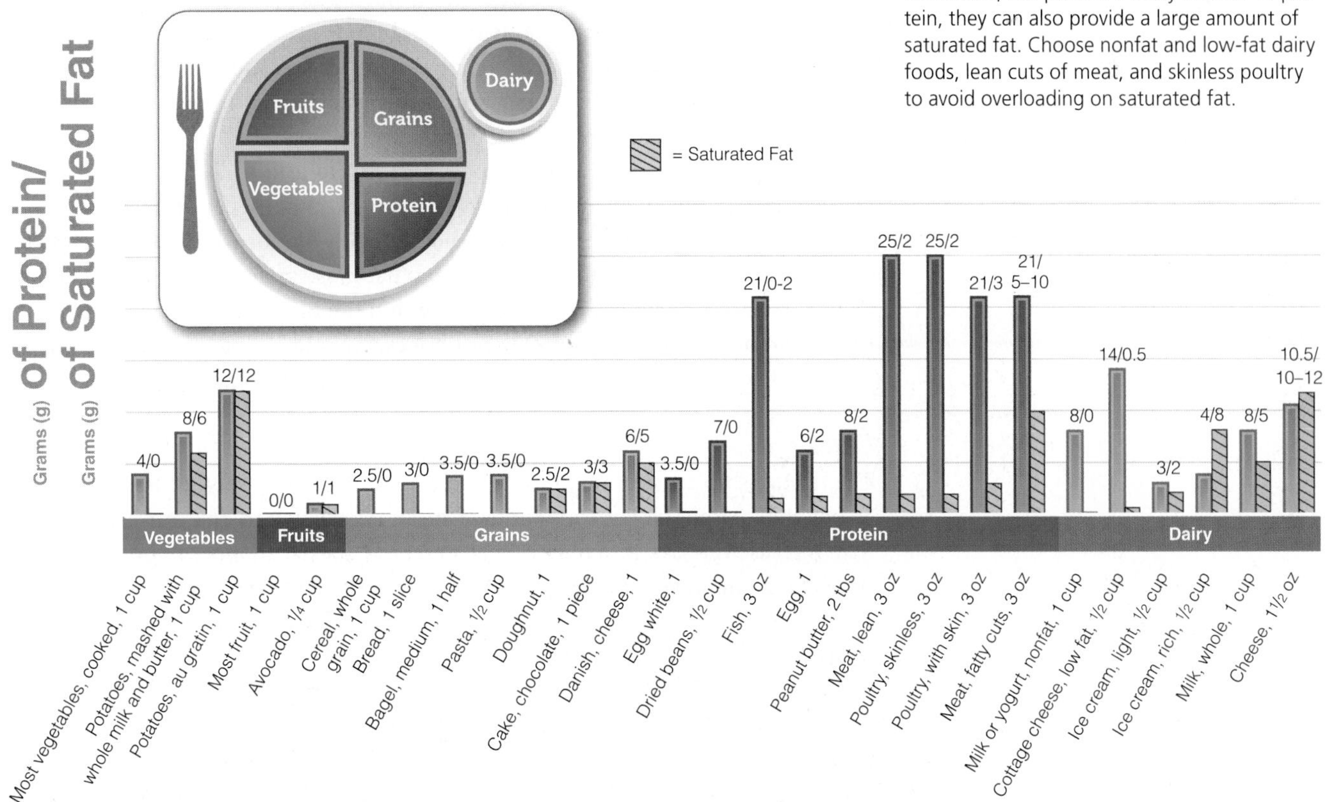

▾ **Figure 6.18 Where's the Protein and Saturated Fat in Foods?**
Though many foods, in particular dairy foods and meats, can provide a hefty amount of protein, they can also provide a large amount of saturated fat. Choose nonfat and low-fat dairy foods, lean cuts of meat, and skinless poultry to avoid overloading on saturated fat.

fat than some other cuts of meat, are not saturated fat free. A diet high in saturated fat can raise LDL ("bad") cholesterol levels in the blood, whereas lowering the saturated fat may lower the risk of heart disease. While the overall effect of a high protein intake on heart disease is still not clear, it is clear that eating a variety of plant proteins low in saturated fat and cholesterol is the best heart-healthy approach.

Kidney Stones

A high-protein diet may increase the risk of kidney stones. Eating a diet high in animal protein and low in carbohydrate lowers the pH of the urine, which raises the risk of developing kidney stones, especially in people who are more susceptible to the condition.[13] This change in pH may be due to higher levels of oxalates in the urine from oxalic acid; oxalic acid combines with other compounds, including calcium, to form kidney stones. The impact of protein on the change in pH may be the type of protein, not the amount of protein, consumed. A diet that contains plenty of fluid, a lower protein intake (not greater than 0.8 g/kg), and a balance of fruits and vegetables may be beneficial, especially for people who already have kidney disease.

Osteoporosis

Though still controversial, numerous studies have shown that bones lose calcium when a person's diet is too high in protein. The loss seems to occur because calcium is removed from bone to neutralize the acid generated when specific amino acids are broken down. In fact, in a study of individuals on a low-carbohydrate, high-protein diet, researchers observed a 50 percent loss of calcium in the subjects' urine. The calcium loss was not observed when these individuals were on a lower-protein diet, so the researchers concluded that it was due to the buffering effect.[14, 15]

More recent research suggests a more positive effect of a high protein intake on bone health.[16] In postmenopausal women, a high protein intake (between 1.6 and 2.0 g/kg) was associated with a reduction in hip fractures. Other research has been done to determine if calcium loss leads to osteoporosis when a high-protein diet includes an adequate amount of calcium. In fact, a higher dietary protein intake, especially if it is coming from foods such as low-fat milk, yogurt, and cheese, can add calcium to the diet.[17] Unfortunately, many American adults are falling short of their recommended calcium intake, and if their diets are also high in protein, the combination isn't healthy for their bones.

Eating too little protein has also been shown to lead to loss of bone mass. A study of more than 500 women over age 55 showed that higher protein consumption was associated with denser bone. Another study of more than 2,000 males and females, ranging in age from 50 to 89, found that those under the age of 70 who had a diet higher in protein had 65 percent fewer hip fractures than those with the lowest protein intake. When it comes to our bones, too much protein coupled with low calcium intake, or too little protein intake can both be unhealthy.[18, 19]

Cancer

The relationship between high-protein diets and cancer is another less-than-clear association. Although large amounts of meat, especially red and processed meats, may increase the risk for colon cancer, research doesn't support a connection between high amounts of total protein and increased colon cancer risk.[20]

Displacing Other Nutrients

An important health concern surrounding a high-protein diet is the displacement of other foods. If the diet is overloaded with high-protein meat, fish, and poultry, these will likely crowd out other nutrient- and fiber-rich foods. Because a diet that contains ample fiber and nutrient-rich foods can help reduce the risk of several chronic diseases, such as cancer, heart disease, diabetes, and stroke, filling up on meat and milk at meals and snacks could shortchange foods such as whole grains, fruits, and vegetables, which contain disease-fighting compounds.

Whereas many individuals have the luxury of worrying about consuming too much protein, others are desperately trying to meet their daily needs. Let's look at the serious health implications of chronically eating too little dietary protein.

Eating Too Little Protein Can Lead to Protein-Energy Malnutrition

Every day, almost 17,000 children around the world—approximately 6 million annually—die because they don't have access to enough food. These children's diets are inadequate in either protein or kilocalories or both, a condition known as **protein-energy malnutrition (PEM).** When kilocalories and protein are inadequate, dietary protein is used for energy rather than for its other roles in the body. Moreover, other important nutrients, such as vitamins and minerals, also tend to be in short supply, which further compounds PEM.

Many factors can lead to PEM, including poverty, poor food quality, insufficient food intake, unsanitary living conditions (causing diarrhea and infection), ignorance regarding the proper feeding of children, and the cessation of breast-feeding in the first few months of age.[21] Because they are growing, infants and children have higher nutritional needs for their size than adults. They are also dependent on others to provide them with food. For these reasons, PEM is more frequently seen in infants and children than in adults.

Because protein is needed for so many functions in the body, it isn't surprising that chronic protein deficiency can lead to numerous health problems. Without adequate dietary protein, cells lining the gastrointestinal tract aren't sufficiently replaced as they're sloughed off. The inability to regenerate these cells inhibits digestive function. Absorption of the little amount of food that may be available is reduced, and bacteria that normally stay in the intestines can get into the blood and poison it, causing septicemia. Malnourished individuals frequently have a compromised immune system, which can make fighting even a minor infection, such as a respiratory infection or diarrhea, impossible. Malnourished children have died after exposure to measles as well as after bouts of diarrhea.[22, 23]

Though deficiencies of kilocalories and protein often occur simultaneously, sometimes one may be more prevalent than the other. A severe deficiency of protein is called **kwashiorkor,** whereas a severe deficiency of kilocalories is called **marasmus.** A condition that is caused by a chronic deficiency of both kilocalories and protein is called marasmic kwashiorkor.

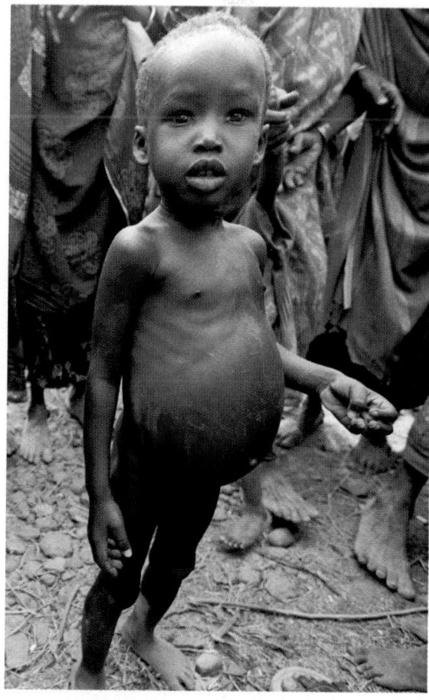

▲ **Figure 6.19 Kwashiorkor**
The edema in this child's belly is a classic sign of kwashiorkor.

Kwashiorkor

Kwashiorkor was first observed in the 1930s in tribes in Ghana (a republic of West Africa) when frequently a firstborn child became sick following the birth of a new sibling. Typically, the newborn displaced the first child from receiving their mother's nutritionally balanced breast milk. The first child was then relegated to an inadequate and unbalanced diet high in carbohydrate-rich grains but severely deficient in protein. This sets the stage for serious medical complications.

A classic symptom of severe kwashiorkor is edema in the legs, feet, and stomach (see **Figure 6.19**). Because protein plays an important role in maintaining fluid balance in the blood and around the cells, a protein deficiency can cause fluid to accumulate in the spaces surrounding the cells, causing swelling. The body wastes away as the muscle proteins are broken down to generate the amino acids needed to synthesize other proteins. Consequently, muscle tone and strength diminish. Those with kwashiorkor may have skin that is dry and peeling. Rashes or lesions can also develop. Their hair is often brittle and can be easily pulled out. Children with

protein-energy malnutrition (PEM) A lack of sufficient dietary protein and/or kilocalories.

kwashiorkor A state of PEM where there is a severe deficiency of dietary protein.

marasmus A state of PEM where there is a severe deficiency of kilocalories, which perpetuates wasting; also called starvation.

Nutrition in Practice: Erinn

After much reading about vegetarian diets, Erinn, a college sophomore, decided that she wanted to become a vegan. Unfortunately, after two months of following a vegan diet, she has lost 5 pounds, and her clothes are beginning to look "baggy." She also notices that she seems to always be hungry between meals. Although she eats tons of fruits, vegetables, and grains, she is finding it a challenge to add protein-rich, vegan choices at her lunch and dinner. She has a micro-fridge in her dorm room, so eats breakfast in her room. Her lunch and dinner are eaten in the campus dining hall. Erinn decides to seek the advice of the campus dietitian.

Erinn's Stats:

- □ Age: 19
- □ Height: 5 feet 4 inches
- □ Weight: 115 pounds
- □ BMI: 19.7

Critical Thinking Questions

1. Why do you think Erinn is so hungry between meals?
2. What foods could be added to Erinn's diet to increase her protein intake?
3. Based on her food log, which other food group is she falling short of?

Dietitian's Observation and Plan for Erinn:

- □ Discuss the need to add vegan protein sources at each meal to meet her daily needs. Add peanut butter to morning toast. Order a soy burger along with her salad bar lunch. Add tofu and beans to all dinners.
- □ Need to consume a vegan equivalent of dairy foods. Add a soy yogurt at breakfast and replace diet soda with soy milk at lunch and dinner.

A month later, Erinn returns for a follow-up visit with the dietitian. By incorporating all of the dietitian's suggestions, she has gained 1.5 pounds! A review of her food record shows that she is meeting her daily protein needs. However, she is still hungry late in the afternoon. The dietitian recommends that Erinn consume some nuts with her afternoon snack to increase her satiety.

Erinn's Food Log

Food/Beverage	Time Consumed	Hunger Rating*	Location
Whole-wheat bread with jelly Clementine	8 am	5	In dorm room
Salad bar salad: lettuce, tomato, carrots, peppers, and cucumbers with oil and red wine vinegar along with pita bread. Diet soda.	12:30 pm	5	In dining hall
Apple	3 pm	5	Studying in dorm room
Pasta with broccoli. Diet soda.	6:30 pm	5	In dining hall

*Hunger Rating (1–5): 1 = not hungry; 5 = super hungry

kwashiorkor often appear pale, sad, and apathetic, and cry easily. They are prone to infections, rapid heart beats, excess fluid in the lungs, pneumonia, septicemia, and water and electrolyte imbalances—all of which can be deadly.

Marasmus and Marasmic Kwashiorkor

The bloating seen in kwashiorkor is the opposite of the frail, emaciated appearance of marasmus (**Figure 6.20**). Because they are not consuming enough kilocalories, marasmic individuals literally look as though they are starving. They are often not even at 60 percent of their desirable body weight. Marasmic children's bodies use all available kilocalories to stay alive; thus, growth is interrupted. Such children are weakened and appear apathetic. Many can't stand without support. They look old beyond their years, as the loss of fat in their face—one of the last places that the body loses fat during starvation—diminishes their childlike appearance. Their hair is thin and dry and lacks the sheen found in healthy children. Their body temperature and blood pressure are both low, and they are prone to dehydration, infections, and unnecessary blood clotting.

Individuals with marasmic kwashiorkor have the worst of both conditions. They often have edema in their legs and arms, yet have a "skin and bones" appearance in other parts of the body. When these individuals are provided with medical and nutritional treatment, such as receiving adequate protein, the edema subsides and their clinical symptoms more closely resemble that of a person with marasmus.

Appropriate medical care and treatment can dramatically reduce the 20 to 30 percent mortality rate seen among children with severe PEM worldwide.[24] The treatment for PEM should be carefully and slowly implemented using a three-step approach. The first step addresses the life-threatening factors, such as severe dehydration and fluid imbalances, using electrolyte solutions. The second step is to restore the individual's depleted tissues by gradually providing nutritionally dense kilocalories and high-quality protein. The third step involves transitioning the person to solid foods and introducing physical activity. The only successful way to cure PEM is to eradicate it.

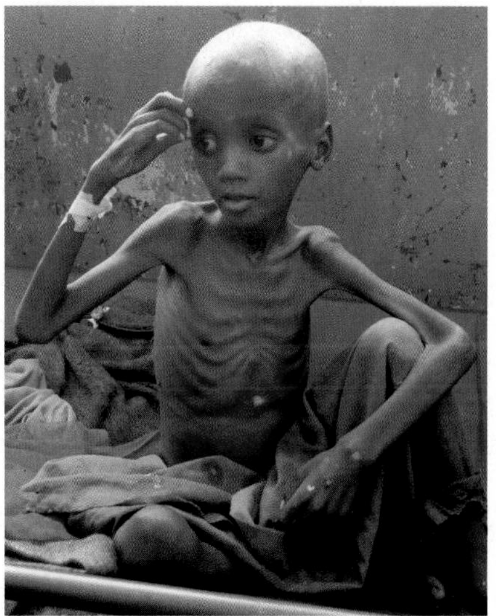

▲ **Figure 6.20 Marasmus**
The emaciated appearance of this child is a symptom of marasmus.

THE TAKE-HOME MESSAGE A high-protein diet may play a role in increasing the risk of heart disease, kidney problems, and calcium loss from bone. Consuming too much protein from animal sources can increase the amount of saturated fat in the diet. Too many protein-rich foods can displace whole grains, fruits, and vegetables, which have been shown to help reduce many chronic diseases. A low-protein diet has also been shown to lead to loss of bone mass. PEM is caused by an inadequate amount of protein, kilocalories, or both in the diet. A severe deficiency of protein is called kwashiorkor; a deficiency of kilocalories is called marasmus.

Putting It All Together

The majority of daily kilocalories should come from carbohydrate-rich foods; fat intake should be no more than about one-third of daily kilocalories; and protein should provide the rest. Table 6.6 provides a recap of the three energy-providing nutrients that we have discussed and their recommended proportions in a healthy diet.

The best plan for a healthy diet is to eat an abundance of grains (with at least half being whole grains), vegetables, and fruits. Eat only modest amounts of commercially made bakery and snack items, vegetables with creamy sauces or added butter, and sweets. Choose low-fat dairy products and lean meat, poultry, and fish to minimize the intake of heart-unhealthy saturated fat.

TABLE 6.6 The Macronutrient Makeup of a Healthy Diet

Nutrient	Current Adult Dietary Intake Recommendations (percent of total kilocalories)	Example of a Healthy Diet*
Carbohydrates	45–65	55
Fats	20–35	30
Proteins	10–35	15
Total		100

*Percent of total kilocalories

Visual Chapter Summary

1 Proteins Are Made of Amino Acids

Proteins are made up of 20 amino acids, 11 nonessential and nine essential. Nonessential amino acids can be made in the body and do not need to be consumed in the diet; essential amino acids cannot be made, or cannot be made in adequate amounts, in the body and must therefore be consumed in the diet. A third category, conditionally essential, are those amino acids that under certain conditions must be supplied by food.

Amino acids are composed of carbon, hydrogen, oxygen, nitrogen, and in some cases, sulfur. Every amino acid contains a central carbon, an acid group (COOH), an amine group (NH_2), a single hydrogen, and a unique side chain. The side chain varies for each amino acid and gives each its distinguishing qualities.

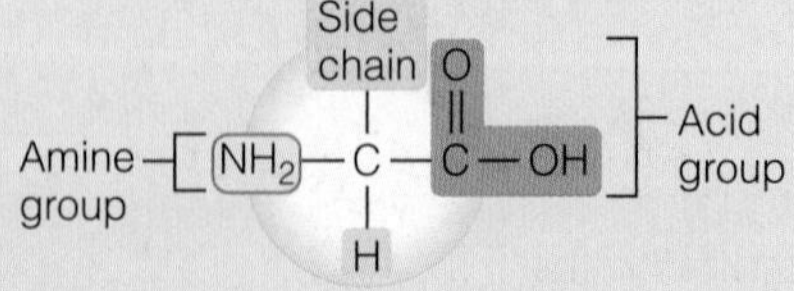

Amino acids are joined together by peptide bonds through condensation. Two amino acids joined together form a dipeptide, three amino acids form a tripeptide, and a polypeptide consists of many amino acids joined together.

2 Protein Digestion Occurs in the Stomach and Small Intestine

Enzymatic digestion of protein begins in the stomach. Hydrochloric acid denatures the protein, allowing the enzyme pepsin to access the peptide bonds. Digestion continues in the small intestine with the aid of pancreatic and small intestinal enzymes, which produce tripeptides, dipeptides, and single amino acids. Single amino acids are actively absorbed into the portal vein where they enter the amino acid pool to be utilized for protein synthesis or converted to energy, glucose, or fat after the nitrogen is removed by deamination. Transamination is used to synthesize nonessential amino acids.

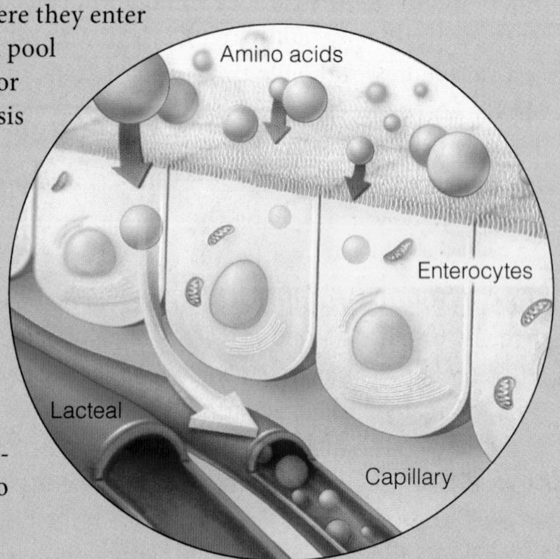

3 The Metabolism of Protein Is Based on the Body's Needs

Amino acids located in the amino acid pools throughout the body can be used to synthesize new proteins when needed, or excess amino acids can be deaminated and then transformed into ATP, or converted to glucose or fatty acids. When other cells need to be replenished, the amino acids are released into the bloodstream and transported throughout the body.

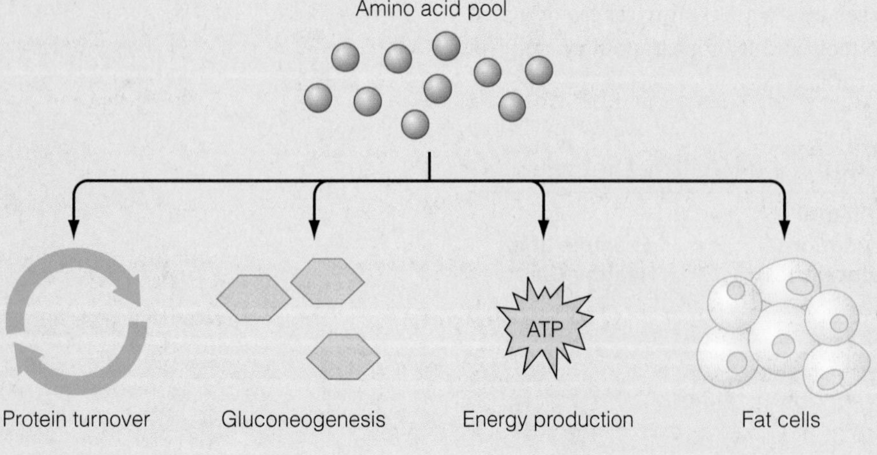

4 Protein Plays Key Roles in the Body

Proteins provide structural and mechanical support and help maintain body tissues. They build enzymes and hormones and help maintain fluid and acid-base balance. Proteins also transport substances throughout the body and act as channels in membranes. They assist antibodies and the immune response, provide energy, improve satiety, and help control appetite.

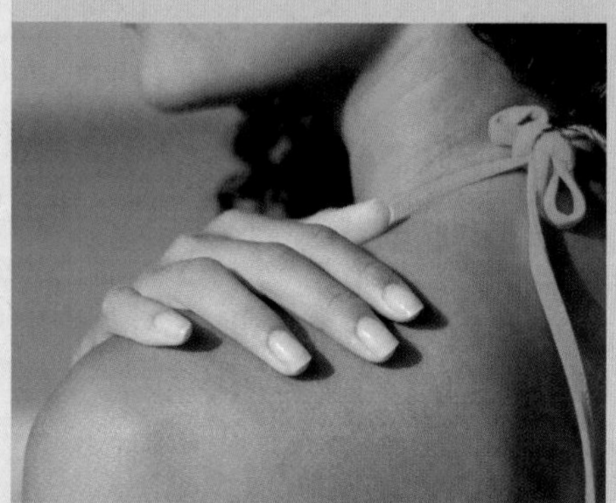

5 Protein Needs Are Determined by Nitrogen Balance Studies

For a healthy adult, the amount of dietary protein consumed every day should equal the amount of protein used. Nitrogen balance studies suggest adults over the age of 18 need 0.80 gram per kilogram of body weight daily. Men typically consume more than 100 grams of protein daily, and women more than 70 grams—in both cases, far more than is needed.

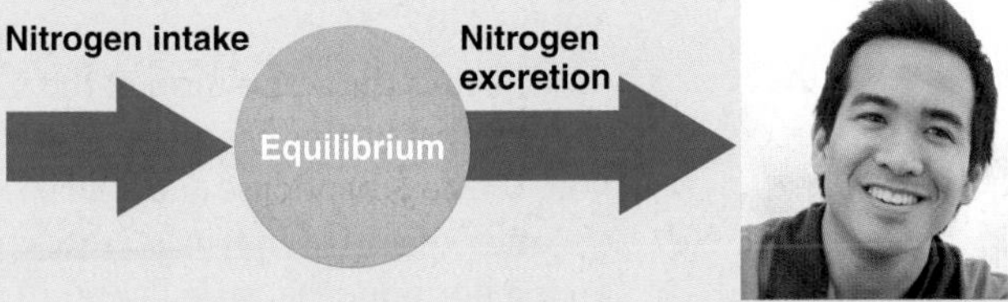

6 Not All Proteins Are Created Equal

Protein quality is determined by the body's ability to digest the protein and the essential or nonessential amino acids that the protein contains, called the chemical, or amino acid, score. A protein's digestibility and its amino acid score are combined to yield a protein digestibility corrected amino acid score (PDCAAS). The essential amino acid with the lowest score is called the limiting amino acid. Proteins with a higher PDCAAS are of higher quality. A complete protein, found in animal foods and soy, provides a complete set of the essential amino acids. Plant proteins are typically incomplete, as they are missing or low in one or more of the essential amino acids. Combining nonmeat protein sources can provide high quality protein and is particularly important for vegetarians.

7 Too Much or Too Little Protein Is Linked to Health Problems

A diet too high in protein is linked to health problems such as cardiovascular disease, kidney stones, osteoporosis, and some types of cancer. An excess of protein-rich foods can displace whole grains, fruits, and vegetables in the diet. Eating too little protein can also compromise bone health.

Diets that are inadequate in protein, kilocalories, or both lead to protein-energy malnutrition (PEM), also called marasmus and kwashiorkor. Marasmus is a disease caused by insufficient intake of kilocalories. Kwashiorkor occurs when a person consumes sufficient kilocalories but not sufficient protein. Symptoms of severe kwashiorkor include edema in the legs, feet, and stomach, dry and peeling skin, rashes or lesions, and brittle hair that can be easily pulled out. PEM can be improved with proper nutrition and treatment.

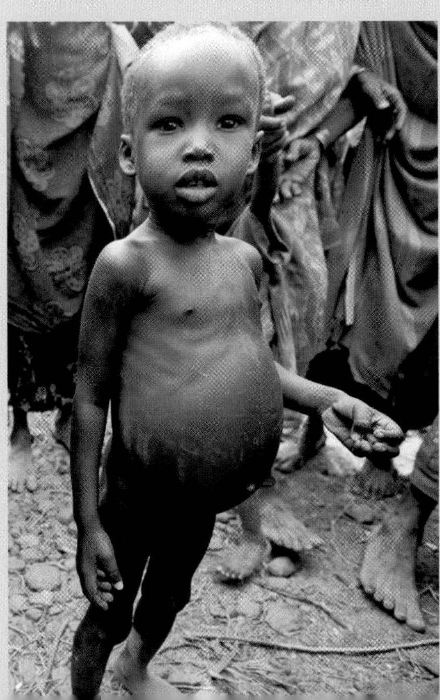

8 Vegetarian Diets Can Reduce the Risk of Certain Diseases

Healthy vegetarian diets can reduce the risk of heart disease, high blood pressure, diabetes, cancer, stroke, and obesity. All vegetarians must take care to eat a varied diet that meets all of their nutrient needs, especially for protein, iron, zinc, calcium, vitamin D, riboflavin (a B vitamin), vitamin B_{12}, vitamin A, and omega-3 fatty acids.

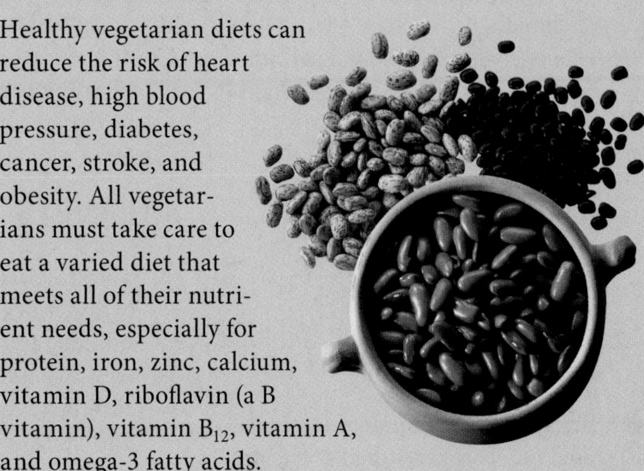

Terms to Know

- proteins
- amino acids
- nonessential amino acid
- essential amino acid
- acid group
- amine group
- side chain
- peptide bonds
- dipeptide
- tripeptide
- polypeptide
- denatured
- pepsin
- deamination
- transcription
- translation
- elongation
- nitrogen balance
- protein digestibility corrected amino acid score (PDCAAS)
- limiting amino acid
- protein-energy malnutrition (PEM)
- marasmus
- kwashiorkor

MasteringNutrition™

Build your knowledge—and confidence!—in the Study Area of MasteringNutrition with a variety of study tools.

Check Your Understanding

1. Proteins differ from carbohydrates and lipids because
   a. they contain carbon-carbon bonds.
   b. they contain nitrogen.
   c. they contain carbon, hydrogen, and oxygen.
   d. they have a longer chain length.
2. Which of the following nonessential amino acids can also be considered a conditional amino acid?
   a. alanine
   b. serine
   c. glutamic acid
   d. proline
3. The enzyme that begins the chemical digestion of protein in the stomach is
   a. carboxypeptidase.
   b. pepsin.
   c. ADH.
   d. ghrelin.
4. Gluconeogenesis is stimulated when
   a. the diet is high in carbohydrate.
   b. the diet is high in fat.
   c. the diet is low in protein.
   d. the diet is low in carbohydrate.
5. Which of the following will *not* denature a protein?
   a. grilling a chicken breast
   b. frying an egg
   c. marinating a steak in red wine
   d. refrigerating milk
6. Before an excess amino acid can be used for energy or stored as fat, it must first be
   a. deaminated.
   b. digested.
   c. denatured.
   d. deactivated.
7. Proteins play important roles in the body, such as
   a. helping fight the flu.
   b. contracting muscles.
   c. helping digest your lunch.
   d. all of the above.
8. Protein is found abundantly in
   a. fruits.
   b. milk, eggs, meat, and beans.
   c. vegetables and whole grains.
   d. oils and sugars.
9. Which of the following is a source of complete protein?
   a. kidney beans
   b. peanut butter
   c. soy milk
   d. pasta
10. Kwashiorkor is a type of PEM that develops when
    a. there is a severe deficiency of protein in the diet but an adequate amount of kilocalories.
    b. there are inadequate amounts of both protein and kilocalories in the diet.
    c. there is inadequate amount of animal protein in the diet.
    d. there are adequate amounts of both protein and kilocalories in the diet.

Answers

1. (b) Proteins differ from carbohydrates because they contain nitrogen found in the amine group. All three macronutrients contain carbon, hydrogen, and oxygen. The chains of glucose units or fatty acids vary in lengths similar to proteins.
2. (d) Proline can be a conditional amino acid under certain conditions.
3. (b) Pepsin is the active form of the enzyme that begins protein digestion. Carboxypeptidase and ADH are other digestive enzymes. Ghrelin is a hormone that stimulates appetite.
4. (d) If an individual does not eat an adequate amount of carbohydrates, the body can break down proteins to create glucose.
5. (d) Refrigeration does not alter the bonds between the amino acid side chains and therefore does not denature proteins. Heat (from frying or grilling) and acids (from marinating) will denature proteins.
6. (a) Before amino acids can be converted to glucose or fatty acids, or enter the energy cycle, the amine group must first be removed through deamination. Denaturing is the process of unfolding or changing the shape of proteins.
7. (d) The body needs adequate amounts of protein to fight infections such as the flu, to provide structural and mechanical support when contracting muscles, and to build enzymes that help digest foods.
8. (b) Animal foods and some plant-based proteins, such as beans, are protein-rich. There is some protein in vegetables, but little in fruits. Oils and sugars do not contain protein.
9. (c) Soy foods provide all the essential amino acids, and thus are a source of complete protein. Kidney beans, peanut butter, and pasta are missing adequate amounts of the essential amino acids and are considered incomplete proteins.

10. (a) Kwashiorkor occurs when protein is deficient in the diet even though kilocalories may be adequate. Marasmus occurs when kilocalories are inadequate in a person's diet. Protein from animal sources is not necessary because people can meet their protein needs from a combination of plant proteins. There doesn't need to be a balance between animal and plant proteins.

Answers to Myths and Misconceptions

1. **True.** Proteins are the only macronutrients that contain nitrogen.
2. **False.** Of the 20 amino acids that make up protein, nine are considered essential and 11 are nonessential.
3. **False.** Chemical digestion of protein begins in the stomach with the enzyme pepsin, which is secreted by the chief cells lining the stomach.
4. **True.** When proteins arrive in the stomach, hydrochloric acid uncoils them, revealing the peptide bonds that connect the amino acids.
5. **True.** Amino acids can be converted to glucose through gluconeogenesis.
6. **False.** The primary function of protein is to build new tissues and repair proteins that have been degraded or sloughed off in the body.
7. **False.** Growing children are in a state of positive nitrogen balance, which means that more nitrogen is being retained by the body than excreted in the urine.
8. **False.** Animal proteins are considered complete proteins because they contain all nine essential amino acids.
9. **False.** Protein itself doesn't raise blood cholesterol levels. It depends on the type of protein food you consume.
10. **True.** A diet that is inadequate in protein results in kwashiorkor, characterized by edema and body wasting..

Web Resources

- For information on specific genetic disorders, including those that affect protein use in the body, visit the National Human Genome Research Institute at www.nhgri.nih.gov
- For more information on protein bars and supplements, visit the Center for Science in the Public Interest at www.cspinet.org/nah/12_00/barexam.html
- For more information on vegetarian diets, visit the Vegetarian Resource Group at www.vrg.org

References

1. Savic, I., H. Berglund, B. Guylas, and P. Roland. 2001. Smelling of Odorous Sex Hormone-Like Compounds Causes Sex-Differentiated Hypothalamic Activations in Humans. *Neuron* 31:661–668.
2. Stevens, B. R. 1992. Amino Acid Transport in Intestine. In *Mammalian Amino Acid Transport: Mechanisms and Control.* M. S. Kilberg and D. Haussinger, eds., 149–164. New York: Plenum.
3. Marieb, E. N. 2004. *Human Anatomy and Physiology.* 6th ed. San Francisco: Benjamin Cummings.
4. National Human Genome Research Institute. 2011. *Learning About Sickle-Cell Disease.* Available at www.genome.gov. Accessed March 2012.
5. Murray, R. K., D. K. Granner, P. A. Mayes, and V. W. Rodwell. 2003. *Harper's Illustrated Biochemistry.* 26th ed. New York: Lange Medical Books/McGraw-Hill.
6. Tannous dit El Khoury, D., O. Obeid, S. T. Azar, and N. Hwalla. 2006. Variations in Postprandial Ghrelin Status Following Ingestion of High-Carbohydrate, High-Fat and High-Protein Meals in Males. *Annals of Nutrition & Metabolism* 50:260–269.
7. Halton, T. L. and F. B. Hu. 2004. The Effects of High-Protein Diets on Thermogenesis, Satiety and Weight Loss: A Critical Review. *Journal of the American College of Nutrition* 23:373–385.
8. Blom, W. A., A. Lluch, A. Stafleu, S. Vinoy, J. J. Holst, G. Schaafsma, and H. F. J. Hendriks. 2006. Effect of a High-Protein Breakfast on the Postprandial Ghrelin Response. *American Journal of Clinical Nutrition* 83:211–220.
9. Stipanuk, M. 2000. *Biochemical and Physiological Aspects of Human Nutrition.* Philadelphia: W. B. Saunders.
10. American Dietetic Association, Dietitians of Canada, and American College of Sports Medicine. 2000. Nutrition and Athletic Performance. *Journal of the American Dietetic Association* 100:1543–1556.
11. Eschbach, L. C. 2002. Protein and Creatine: Some Basic Facts. *ACSM Fit Society Page.*
12. Clifton, P. M. 2011. Protein and Coronary Heart Disease: The Role of Different Protein Sources. *Current Atherosclerosis Report* 13:493–498.
13. Giannini, S., M. Nobile, L. Sartori, L. D. Carbonare, M. Ciuffreda, P. Corro, A. D'Angelo, L. Calo, and G. Crepaldi. 1999. Acute Effects of Moderate Dietary Protein Restriction in Patients with Idiopathic Hypercalciuria and Calcium Nephrolithiasis. *American Journal of Clinical Nutrition* 69:267–271.
14. Allen, L. H., E. A. Oddoye, and S. Margen. 1979. Protein-Induced Calciuria: A Longer-Term Study. *American Journal of Clinical Nutrition* 32:741–749.
15. Lemann, J. 1999. Relationship Between Urinary Calcium and Net Acid Excretion as Determined by Dietary Protein and Potassium: A Review: *Nephron* 81:1–25.
16. Bonjour, J. P. 2011. Protein Intake and Bone Health. *International Journal of Vitamin Nutrition Research* 81:134–142.
17. Heaney, R. P. 1998. Excess Dietary Protein May Not Adversely Affect Bone. *Journal of Nutrition* 128:1054–1057.
18. Wengree, H. J., R. G. Munger, N. A. West, D. R. Cutler, C. D. Corcoran, J. Zhang, and N. E. Sassano. 2004. Dietary Protein Intake and Risk of Osteoporotic Hip Fracture in Elderly Residents of Utah. *Journal of Bone and Mineral Research* 19:537–545.
19. Promislow, J. H. E., D. Goodman-Gruen, D. J. Slymen, and E. Barrett-Connor. 2002. Protein Consumption and Bone Mineral Density in the Elderly. *American Journal of Epidemiology* 155:636–644.
20. Key, T. J., N. E. Allen, E. A. Spencer, and R. C. Travis. 2002. The Effect of Diet on Risk of Cancer. *The Lancet* 360:861–868.
21. World Health Organization. 2012. *WHO Global Database on Child Growth and Malnutrition Introduction.* Available at www.who.int/nutgrowthdb/en/. Accessed March 2012.
22. de Onis, M., M. Blossner, E. Borghi, A. Frongillo, and R. Morris. 2004. Estimates of Global Prevalance of Childhood Underweight in 1990 and 2015. *Journal of the American Medical Association* 291:2600–2606.
23. Caulfield, L. E., M. de Onis, M. Blossner, and R. E. Black. 2004. Undernutrition as an Underlying Cause of Child Deaths Associated with Diarrhea, Pneumonia, Malaria, and Measles. *American Journal of Clinical Nutrition* 80:193–198.
24. Shils, M. E., M. Shike, A. C. Ross, B. Caballero, and R. J. Cousins. 2006. *Modern Nutrition in Health and Disease.* 10th ed. Baltimore: Lippincott Williams & Wilkins.

7 Alcohol

Chapter Objectives

After reading this chapter, you will be able to:

1. Describe the sources of alcohol and the process used in alcohol fermentation.
2. Explain how alcohol is absorbed by and circulates throughout the body.
3. Explain the role of the liver and enzymes in the metabolism of alcohol.
4. Explain the effects of alcohol on the central nervous system.
5. Define the term "moderate drinking" and discuss the benefits of moderate alcohol consumption.
6. Describe the short-term and long-term consequences of heavy alcohol consumption.
7. Summarize the methods used to diagnose and treat alcohol abuse and alcoholism.

1. Alcohol is an essential nutrient. T/F
2. A shot of whiskey contains more alcohol than a can of beer. T/F
3. Red wine contains phytochemicals that are beneficial for the heart. T/F
4. Women feel the effects of alcohol sooner than men. T/F
5. The body can metabolize three alcoholic beverages per hour. T/F
6. The best way to cure a hangover is to drink a Bloody Mary. T/F
7. Alcohol provides 7 kilocalories per gram. T/F
8. Drinking too much alcohol can lead to malnutrition. T/F
9. Moderate drinking means consuming six or more drinks once a week. T/F
10. Alcoholism can be cured through counseling. T/F

See page 282 for answers to these Myths and Misconceptions.

Your body doesn't need alcohol to survive; therefore alcohol is not an essential nutrient. Alcohol provides only kilocalories to the diet and can put a dent in your budget. Ounce for ounce, alcohol can cost 100 times more than bottled water. It's legally sold in the United States, but supposedly off-limits to those who aren't adults, even though teenagers often feel under social pressure to consume it. Some medical reports say that in moderation, alcohol can provide health benefits, at least in older adults, while others tell you that drinking too much alcohol can be fatal.

In this chapter, we will discuss how the body handles alcohol, its positive and negative health effects, and how to tell if you or someone you know has become an alcohol abuser. We begin with the basic definition of alcohol.

What Is Alcohol and How Is It Made?

What is the first image that comes to mind when you hear the word **alcohol**? Do you envision a bottle of beer, a glass of wine, or a stiff martini? Technically, these beverages aren't alcohol by themselves, but they all contain a form of alcohol called *ethyl alcohol,* or **ethanol.**

Ethanol (C_2H_5OH) is one of a group of organic chemicals called alcohols, in which one or more hydroxyl (OH) groups are attached to the carbon atoms in place of hydrogen atoms (see **Figure 7.1**). In Chapter 5, we covered another type of alcohol, *glycerol,* that is found in food and the body as part of the triglyceride molecule. The difference between glycerol and ethanol is that glycerol has three hydroxyl groups (one attached to each of the three carbons that make up the glycerol backbone), while ethanol contains only one hydroxyl group.

Two other alcohol compounds, methanol (CH_3OH), used in antifreeze, and isopropanol (C_3H_7OH), used in rubbing alcohol, are both poisonous when ingested. Ethanol is considered safe for consumption, but it is not harmless. Consuming excessive amounts of ethanol can be toxic and damage the body. Too much can be lethal.

Alcohol compounds tend to be soluble in water because the OH is polar and attracts water. Ethanol is also a lipid solvent, which means it can dissolve lipids, including those that make up cell membranes. Although ethanol is the scientific name for the alcohol found in consumable beverages, the more common term "alcohol" will be used interchangeably with it throughout the chapter.

From Sugar to Alcohol

Ethanol is made through the **fermentation** of natural sugars in grains (glucose and maltose) and fruits (fructose and glucose) by different types of yeast. Yeasts are single-celled organisms that metabolize glucose into ethanol and carbon dioxide (see the Chemistry Boost). Alcoholic beverages, including mead, wine, beer, or distilled spirits such as rum and whiskey, all use yeast at some stage in their production.

alcohol A chemical class of organic substances that contain one or more hydroxyl groups attached to carbons. Examples include ethanol, glycerol, and methanol. Ethanol is often referred to as "alcohol."

ethanol The type of alcohol, specifically *ethyl alcohol* (C_2H_5OH), found in alcoholic beverages such as wine, beer, and liquor.

fermentation The process by which yeast converts sugars in grains or fruits into ethanol and carbon dioxide.

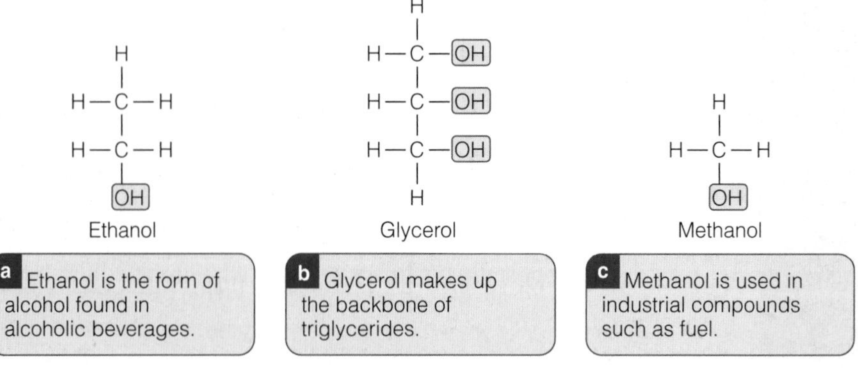

Ethanol
Glycerol
Methanol
a Ethanol is the form of alcohol found in alcoholic beverages.
b Glycerol makes up the backbone of triglycerides.
c Methanol is used in industrial compounds such as fuel.

▲ **Figure 7.1 Structure of Three Alcohols**

Chemistry Boost

Fermentation

The process of fermentation involves converting glucose ($C_6H_{12}O_6$) into alcohol (CH_3CH_2OH) and carbon dioxide gas (CO_2). The basic reaction of fermentation happens within the yeast as shown below.

$$C_6H_{12}O_6 \rightarrow 2\,(CH_3CH_2OH) + 2(CO_2) + 2ATP$$

Glucose → Ethyl alcohol + Carbon dioxide gas + Energy

Fermentation begins with glucose, the main energy source for yeast. The enzymes in the yeast convert the glucose first to pyruvate, which generates energy in the form of ATP. Once pyruvate is formed, the enzymes in the yeast convert it to acetaldehyde and carbon dioxide. In the final step of ethyl alcohol production, acetaldehyde is converted into ethanol. The hydrogen needed to convert the acetaldehyde to ethanol is provided by the coenzyme form of the B vitamin niacin NADH + H^+.

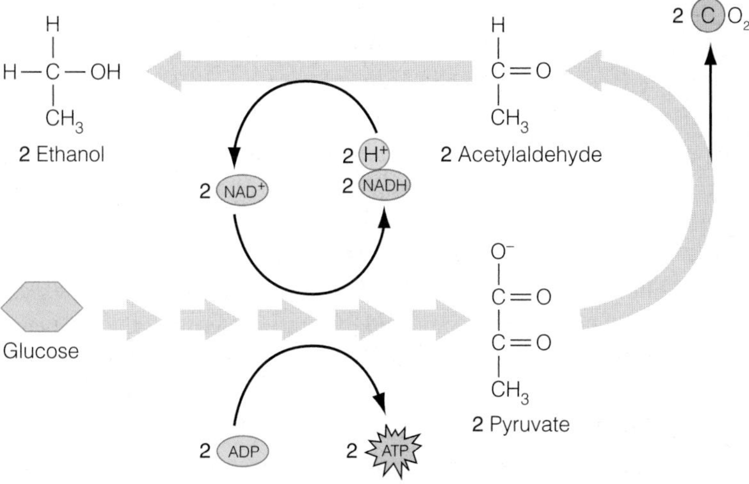

The most common form of yeast used to make alcohol, brewer's yeast, can tolerate up to about 5 percent alcohol. Beyond this level of alcohol, the yeast is unable to continue fermentation. Wine yeast is still active in 12 percent alcohol and some cultured strains of yeast can tolerate up to 21% alcohol. Depending on the type of yeast that is used, the fermentation reaction stops once the alcohol content reaches 11 to 14 percent because the enzymes involved in catalyzing the fermentation become inactive and the yeast itself dies. The carbon dioxide formed during fermentation bubbles through the liquid and evaporates, leaving an alcohol-containing beverage.

Wine is made by fermenting the sugars glucose and fructose in grapes and other fruits. The characteristics of wines—whether the wine is spicy, zesty, acidic, or sweet—vary depending on the types of grapes or fruit that are used, where they are grown, and the climate.

Malted cereal grains, such as barley, are used to make beer. Malting barley, which is the source of maltose that is used to ferment beer, allows the barley to partially germinate, releasing enzymes that hydrolyze the starch in the endosperm into smaller sugar molecules, or maltose. The brewer stops germination before the plant uses all the sugars to germinate new seeds. The maltose produced is further hydrolyzed into glucose by the brewing process, which then undergoes fermentation. The carbon dioxide is captured and used to carbonate the brew. The basic ingredients added to beer include hops for flavor, sugar, water, and different types of yeast, which account for the varying types of beer.

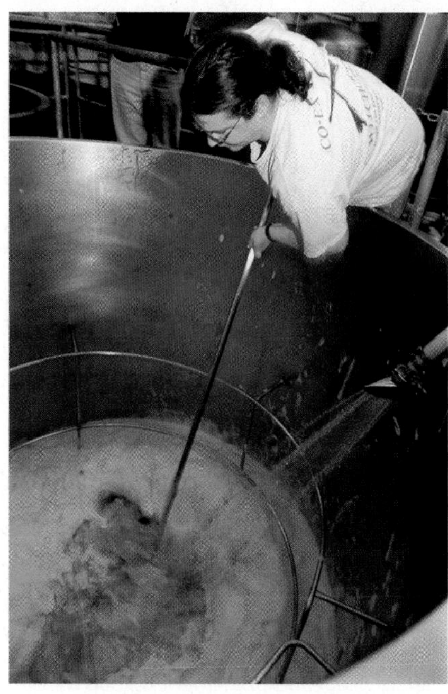

Beer is made when yeast converts the glucose in grain to ethyl alcohol and carbon dioxide gas.

Like beer and wine, liquors begin with the fermentation of sugars from an initial food item: Vodka begins with potatoes or grains, rum begins with molasses or sugarcane juice, and tequila begins with the blue agave plant. After fermentation, the alcoholic liquids go through a process of **distillation.** In this process, the liquid is heated, causing the ethanol to vaporize. The vapor is collected, cooled, and condensed into a concentrated beverage called *liquor* (or, more accurately, distilled spirits). The alcohol content of these beverages is indicated by its **proof,** a number that reflects twice the alcohol content in the beverage. For example, 80 proof vodka contains 40 percent alcohol.

Reasons for Drinking Alcohol

People around the world drink alcohol in many different forms and for many different reasons. The sake (rice wine) of Japan is used during tea and Shinto ceremonies, while the dark beer of the Irish is consumed by many pub patrons celebrating their favorite sport. The vodka of Russia and the chardonnay of Napa Valley are consumed for relaxation and pleasure. Wine is part of many religious traditions, including the Catholic Mass and the Jewish Sabbath, and in some cultures, it's the beverage of choice during the main meal of the day. For parts of human history, wine and beer were safer to drink than water.

In the United States, more than half of adults consume at least one alcoholic beverage per month.[1] Americans drink alcohol for many of the same reasons people in other parts of the world do—to relax, celebrate, and socialize. In college-aged students, alcohol is sometimes used to signify emerging adulthood.[2]

▲ **Figure 7.2 Alcohol Advertisements Target Young Adults**
Alcohol advertisements often portray people who drink as happy, successful, attractive, and popular.

distillation The evaporation and then collection of a liquid by condensation. Liquors are made using distillation.

proof A measure of the amount of ethanol contained in alcoholic beverages.

social drinking Moderate drinking of alcoholic beverages during social settings within safe limits.

moderate drinking According to the *Dietary Guidelines for Americans,* up to one drink per day for women and up to two drinks a day for men.

Alcohol is a drug that alters your conscious mind. Within minutes of sipping an alcoholic beverage, a person will feel more relaxed. After a few more sips, a mild, pleasant euphoria sets in and inhibitions begin to loosen. By the end of the first or second drink, a person will often feel more outgoing, happy, and social. This anxiety-reducing initial effect is why people seek out and continue to drink alcohol.[3]

Having a drink with another person also symbolizes social bonding.[4] When it comes to mingling with others or celebrating a special occasion, whether it's with friends, coworkers, or even strangers, pubs and parties are common gathering spots, and alcoholic drinks are commonly served. This is considered **social drinking,** which is defined as drinking patterns that are considered acceptable by society. Social drinking is not the same as moderate drinking (see the next section), as consuming too much alcohol, even in socially acceptable situations, can be harmful, even if it is only done on the weekends. Later in this chapter we discuss binge drinking, which often occurs in social settings.

Some researchers believe that advertising influences alcohol consumption. One need only drive down a major highway or turn on the television to see billboards and commercials for a beer or liquor brand. In some media, including popular magazines like *Rolling Stone* and *Sports Illustrated,* alcohol ads can outnumber nonalcohol ads by almost three to one.[5] Some studies have shown that advertisements for alcoholic beverages are associated with an increase of drinking among adolescents. Many ads tend to emphasize sexual and social stereotypes. When targeted to underage drinkers, this type of message has been shown to increase adolescents' desire to emulate those portrayed in the advertisements.[6] **Figure 7.2** illustrates the look of a typical alcohol advertisement that may appear in a magazine. These ads should be viewed with caution, as the messages in them are often misleading and in some cases blatantly false.

Moderate Alcohol Consumption May Have Health Benefits

Some people drink alcohol because of its health benefits. That's right. Some studies have suggested that moderate alcohol consumption may reduce the risk of heart disease, and the risk of dying in general, for middle-aged and older adults.[7, 8] **Moderate drinking** is considered the amount of alcohol that puts the individual and others at the lowest risk of alcohol-related problems. Moderation is defined in the latest *Dietary Guidelines for Americans* as up to one drink per day for women and up to two drinks a day for men. In order to be a moderate drinker, an individual must limit both the size of drinks and the frequency of drinking.

A standard drink, whether it's in a 12-ounce bottle of beer, a shot of liquor, or a 5-ounce glass of wine, contains about ½ ounce of alcohol (**Figure 7.3**). Sometimes, the drinks ordered at a local bar or restaurant appear to be a standard size, but are actually larger than that. If an 8-ounce wine glass gets filled to the brim, or if a mug of beer is the size of a pitcher, an individual can consume multiple standard drinks in one glass or mug (**Figure 7.4**). Mixed drinks also often contain more than one standard drink. A rum and coke, for example, could provide the equivalent of over 2½ alcoholic drinks.

Another very important point about drinking in moderation is that abstaining from alcohol for six days and then drinking 10 beers on the seventh day does not count as moderate drinking. There isn't any "banking" allowed when it comes to alcohol; drinking excessive quantities in a short amount of time is *binge drinking* (which we'll discuss in more detail later in the chapter).

If the old adage "an apple a day keeps the doctor away" still rings true, would it also be on the right track to state "a drink a day keeps the cardiologist at bay"? Research results are mixed. The question of whether moderate drinking conveys health benefits is undergoing rigorous study; factors such as age, body size, gender, and health status all impact whether an individual would benefit from moderate alcohol consumption.

Red wine contains resveratrol, a flavonoid and type of phytochemical, which acts as an antioxidant. (Dark beer also contains flavonoids.) Antioxidants help prevent the "bad" LDL cholesterol from becoming oxidized, which leads to its accumulation in the artery wall and atherosclerosis. Flavonoids help inhibit the stickiness of the platelets in the blood. Alcohol also helps inhibit the stickiness of blood platelets, similar to flavonoids, and increases the level of heart-protective "good" HDL cholesterol. Because of these potential heart-healthy attributes, alcohol and red wine have been in the media limelight since the 1990s.

There isn't enough evidence to support the theory that wine, whether red, white, or rosé, has any health superiority over beer and distilled spirits. In fact, some studies comparing various alcohol sources have found that the majority of heart-protective effects are attributable to the alcohol content regardless of the source. In other words, a beer, a glass of cabernet, or a shot of scotch all appear to have similar heart-protective effects. When it comes to the health benefits of alcohol, the source is unlikely to make much of a difference.

But before you crack open a beer to celebrate, be aware that the people who gain the health benefits from moderate alcohol consumption are women aged 55 and older and men aged 45 and older. Alcohol consumption by younger people has not been shown to provide many—if any—health benefits. In fact, drinking alcohol during your younger years increases the risk of injuries and violent, traumatic deaths, which offsets any possible health benefits from the alcohol. Read Examining the Evidence: Does Moderate Alcohol Consumption Provide Health Benefits? for more information.

Research is very clear that some people should abstain from alcohol to avoid adverse health effects. Individuals who should avoid alcohol include:

- Women of childbearing age who may become pregnant
- Pregnant and lactating women
- Children and adolescents, and anyone who is not yet of legal drinking age

▲ **Figure 7.3 What Is a Standard Drink?** One standard drink of beer, liquor, or wine contains about ½ ounce of alcohol.

▲ **Figure 7.4 Size Does Matter** Depending on the size, one drink may actually be the equivalent of 1½ to more than two standard drinks.

Does Moderate Alcohol Consumption Provide Health Benefits?

The popular press is notorious for publishing frequent reports on the health benefits of alcohol. Consumers, however, need to proceed with caution. The benefits from drinking moderate amounts of alcohol are not endorsed by the medical community because most, but not all, of the evidence supporting the beneficial effects are epidemiological in nature.[1, 2] Recall that epidemiological evidence does not prove cause and effect but shows a pattern of health effects when moderate alcohol is consumed. In addition, alcohol consumption is not endorsed because of the potential risks associated with drinking in excess. However, the question remains: Is alcohol beneficial for health? The answer may be yes, in moderation.

Moderate Consumption of Alcohol May Reduce Cardiovascular Risk in Older Adults

On November 17, 1991, the television news show *60 Minutes* aired a segment called "The French Paradox" touting the benefits of modest amounts of red wine to help reduce the risk of heart disease. The French Paradox is so called because the people of France have lower rates of heart disease even though their saturated fat intake mimics that of Americans. They also drink more red wine than Americans do, which is thought to be the differentiating factor. However, the French also consume fewer *trans* fats and have a less stressful lifestyle and better developed social networks, which can also contribute to their impressively lower risk of heart disease. Since the 1990s researchers have explored the possible relationship between wine consumption and heart disease. They report that drinking moderate amounts of alcohol, especially red wine, appears to reduce the incidence of heart disease. Chronic consumption of red wine has been reported to lower LDL cholesterol by 8 percent and raise HDL cholesterol concentrations by 17 percent in postmenopausal women with hypercholesterolemia.[3] Other reported positive effects include reducing the stickiness of platelets in the blood, which lowers the chance of developing blood clots, and reducing inflammation.[4] These benefits are not linear, however, but rather J shaped. A J-shaped relationship means that low to moderate amounts of alcohol may reduce cardiovascular risk, but higher intakes actually increase risk. Drinking less than 12 grams per day, or approximately 5 ounces of wine, a 12-ounce beer, or 1½ ounces of distilled liquor, is the level at which the risk is the lowest.[5]

Another factor may be the effect alcohol has on lowering hypertension.[6] Females who drink less than 14 drinks per week show a drop in blood pressure. However, when the number of drinks is greater than 15 per week, their blood pressure goes up. Even men who have been diagnosed with hypertension report a benefit with moderate alcohol intake.[7] Blood pressure rises, however, when more than four drinks per day are consumed (40–60 grams of alcohol).

Age may play a factor in the health benefits of alcohol. Until recently, it was believed that people who gain health benefits from moderate alcohol consumption were women aged 55 and older and men aged 45 and older. A recent study suggests that women as young as 45 may also benefit.[8] For people younger than 45, no beneficial effects have been found.[9] In fact, drinking heavily in college may lead to heart disease later in life. The current National Institute on Alcohol Abuse and Alcoholism guidelines suggest that older adults limit alcohol intake to one drink per day because they may be more susceptible to alcohol-related injury.[10] And for adults younger than 45, guidelines for moderate alcohol consumption should be followed.

One thing health professionals do agree on is that while moderate drinking may be useful to reduce the risk of coronary heart disease, there are other lifestyle measures that are just as effective, including exercise and a low-fat diet. Men who already follow heart-healthy practices and have a low-risk profile for cardiovascular risk show a reduction in risk with moderate alcohol consumption.[11]

Moderate Consumption May Reduce the Risk of Diabetes and Metabolic Syndrome

Another potential health benefit of drinking alcohol is the effect it has on glucose metabolism. In studies involving individuals with diabetes, alcohol has been shown to increase insulin sensitivity,[12] and does not appear to adversely affect glycemic control. However, these studies do not prove cause and effect. Until further research is presented, the American Diabetes Association recommendations for individuals with diabetes is to not start drinking if you don't already. People with diabetes who do consume alcohol should limit consumption to one (for women) or two (for men) drinks per day and be sure to drink alcohol with a meal to reduce the risk of hypoglycemia. Larger amounts may result in severe consequences in glucose metabolism, worsened diabetic eye disease, and nerve damage.

Alcohol consumption may also affect metabolic syndrome. An analysis of 8,125 people surveyed during the third NHANES found a significant relationship between consuming mild to moderate amounts of alcohol, especially beer and wine, and the reduced risk of symptoms related to an increased risk of cardiovascular disease, stroke, and diabetes. The results of the survey suggested a mild to moderate intake of alcohol lowered blood levels of triglycerides and glucose, reduced hypertension and waist circumference, and improved HDL cholesterol and insulin resistance.[13] There was a 30 percent reduction in risk in individuals who consumed 1 to 19 drinks of beer and wine per month. More than 20 drinks per month had the opposite effect and increased the risk of metabolic syndrome.

Moderate Consumption Is Associated with Longevity

Moderate drinkers appear to live longer.[14] In fact, the lowest death rate from any cause has been reported in those who drink one to two drinks per day. Meta-analysis research that reviewed 34 studies and over a million people from countries around the world reported that one to two drinks per day for women and two to four drinks per day for men increased life expectancy by two years when compared with mortality risk for those who don't drink at all. Once again, however, the risk of mortality increased when the number of alcoholic beverages was greater than moderate intake. When the individuals in the study also exercised and did not smoke, their chances of living longer increased significantly.

All Types of Alcohol May Have Some Benefit

The type of alcoholic beverage that increases longevity is still not known. Although not all health professionals agree, the results in the meta-analysis suggest that living longer is more closely related to wine than liquor.[15] This may be due to the fact that the health benefits of wine have been studied the most.

Other convincing evidence suggests that red wine and beer may both have some health benefits. For example, when red and white wine, beer, and liquor were compared, red wine and dark-colored beer showed the most health protection. Liquor, on the other hand, did not. Researchers suggested this was probably because liquor does not contain polyphenols, which appear to be the compounds in alcoholic beverages that contribute to the reduction of cardiovascular risk.[16]

The data among moderate red wine drinkers is encouraging. They appear to have a lower risk of heart disease than either nondrinkers or excessive drinkers, even if their diet is high in saturated fat.[17] Wine contains the polyphenol resveratrol. Large amounts of resveratrol and other polyphenols are found in the skins of the grape, and the bark, leaves, and twigs of the grapevine. When red wine is produced, the grape skins and other parts of the plant are included in the fermentation process. This is in contrast to white wine, which is fermented without the skins.

Though its nutrient content is still negligible, beer contains more protein and B vitamins (B_6 and folate) than wine, and a similar amount of antioxidants.[18] The type of flavonoid differs, however, because beer is made from barley and hops and wine is made mostly from grapes. Beer also contains more kilocalories and carbohydrates than wine.

The bottom line is, if you don't drink alcohol, don't start. If you do consume alcohol, regardless of whether it is beer, wine, or distilled liquor, be sure to drink no more than one drink per day if you are a female and no more than two drinks per day if you are a male.

References

1. Gronbaek, M., U. Becker, D. Johansen, A. Gottschau, P. Schnohr, H. O. Hein, G. Jensen, and T. I. Sorensen. 2000. Type of Alcohol Consumed and Mortality from All Causes, Coronary Heart Disease, and Cancer. *Annals of Internal Medicine* 133:411–419.
2. Naissaides, M., J. C. L. Mamo, A. P. James, and P. Sebely. 2006. The Effect of Chronic Consumption of Red Wine on Cardiovascular Disease Risk Factors in Postmenopausal Women. *Atherosclerosis* 185:438–445.
3. Ibid.
4. Kloner, R. A. and S. H. Rezkalla. 2007. To Drink or Not to Drink? That Is the Question. *Circulation* 116:1306–1317.
5. Klatsky, A. L., M. A. Armstrong, and G. D. Friedman. 1997. Red Wine, White Wine, Liquor, Beer, and Risk for Coronary Artery Disease Hospitalization. *American Journal of Cardiology* 80:416–420.
6. Nanchahal, K., W. D. Ashton, and D. A. Wood. 2000. Alcohol Consumption, Metabolic Cardiovascular Risk Factors and Hypertension in Women. *International Journal of Epidemiology* 29:57–64.
7. Beulens, J. W., E. B. Rimm, A. Ascherio, D. Spiegelman, H. F. J. Hendriks, and K. J. Mukamal. 2007. Alcohol Consumption and Risk for Coronary Heart Disease Among Men with Hypertension. *Annals of Internal Medicine* 146:10–19.
8. King, D. E., A. G. Mainous, and M. E. Geesey. 2008. Adopting Moderate Alcohol Consumption in Middle Age: Subsequent Cardiovascular Events. *American Journal of Medicine* 121:201–206.
9. Chick, J. 1998. Alcohol, Health, and the Heart: Implications for Clinicians. *Alcohol and Alcoholism* 33:576–591.
10. Mukamal, K. J., H. Chung, N. S. Jenny, L. H. Kuller, W. T. Longstreth, Jr., M. A. Mittleman, G. L. Burke, et al. 2006. Alcohol Consumption and Risk of Coronary Heart Disease in Older Adults: the Cardiovascular Health Study. *Journal of the American Geriatric Society* 54:30–37.

11. Mukamal, K., S. E. Chiuve, and E. B. Rimm. 2006. Alcohol Consumption and Risk for Coronary Heart Disease in Men with Healthy Lifestyles. *Archives of Internal Medicine* 166:2145–2150.
12. Wheeler, M. L., M. J. Franz, and J. C. Froehlich. 2004. Alcohol Consumption and Type 2 Diabetes. *DOC News* 1:7.
13. Freiberg, M. S., H. J. Cabral, T. C. Heeren, R. S. Vasan, and R. C. Curtis. 2004. Alcohol Consumption and the Prevalence of the Metabolic Syndrome in the U.S.: A Cross-Sectional Analysis of Data from the Third National Health and Nutrition Examination Survey. *Diabetes Care* 27:2954–2959.
14. Baglietto, L., D. R. English, J. L. Hopper, J. Powles, and G. G. Giles. 2006. Average Volume of Alcohol Consumed, Type of Beverage, Drinking Pattern and the Risk of Death from All Causes. *Alcohol and Alcoholism* 46:664–671.
15. Gronbaek, M. et al. 2000. Type of Alcohol Consumed and Mortality.
16. Mann, L. B. and J. D. Folts. 2004. Effects of Ethanol and Other Constituents of Alcoholic Beverages on Coronary Heart Disease: A Review. *Pathophysiology* 10:105–112.
17. Klatsky, A. L., M. A. Armstrong, and G. D. Friedman. 1990. Risk of Cardiovascular Mortality in Alcohol Drinkers, Ex-Drinkers and Nondrinkers. *American Journal of Cardiology* 66:1237–1242.
18. Denke, M. A. 2000. Nutritional and Health Benefits of Beer. *American Journal of the Medical Sciences* 320:320–326.

- Those taking medications, including prescription and over-the-counter medications, that can interact with alcohol.
- Those with specific medical conditions, such as stomach ulcers
- Those engaging in activities that require attention, skill, or coordination, such as driving a vehicle or operating machinery
- Those who cannot restrict their alcohol intake

THE TAKE-HOME MESSAGE Ethanol is an organic chemical form of alcohol produced by the fermentation of sugars by yeast, as in beer or wine, or by distillation, as with distilled spirits. Alcohol provides kilocalories but very little nutritional value. People drink alcohol to relax, celebrate, socialize, and to feel more "adult." The *Dietary Guidelines for Americans* emphasize moderation for those who choose to drink alcohol, defined as up to one drink a day for women and two drinks a day for men; a drink is defined as 12 ounces of beer, 5 ounces of wine, or 1½ ounces of spirits. One drink contains ½ ounce of alcohol. While the flavonoids in red wine and dark beer are thought to be beneficial compounds, the alcohol itself may also provide protective benefits such as increasing "good" HDL cholesterol levels.

What Happens to Alcohol in the Body?

The body treats alcohol differently from any other substance. Unlike carbohydrates and fats, the body cannot store alcohol. Because alcohol is a toxin that can stimulate pathological changes in the liver and brain, the body quickly works to metabolize and eliminate it.

Alcohol Is Absorbed in the Stomach and Small Intestine

Alcohol doesn't require digestion, so it can be absorbed by simple diffusion through the gastric mucosa into the bloodstream. About 20 percent of alcohol is absorbed through the stomach, while the majority is absorbed through the duodenum of the small intestine. As soon as alcohol enters the blood, it travels through the body and is distributed throughout the watery tissues (**Figure 7.5**). This means that it quickly

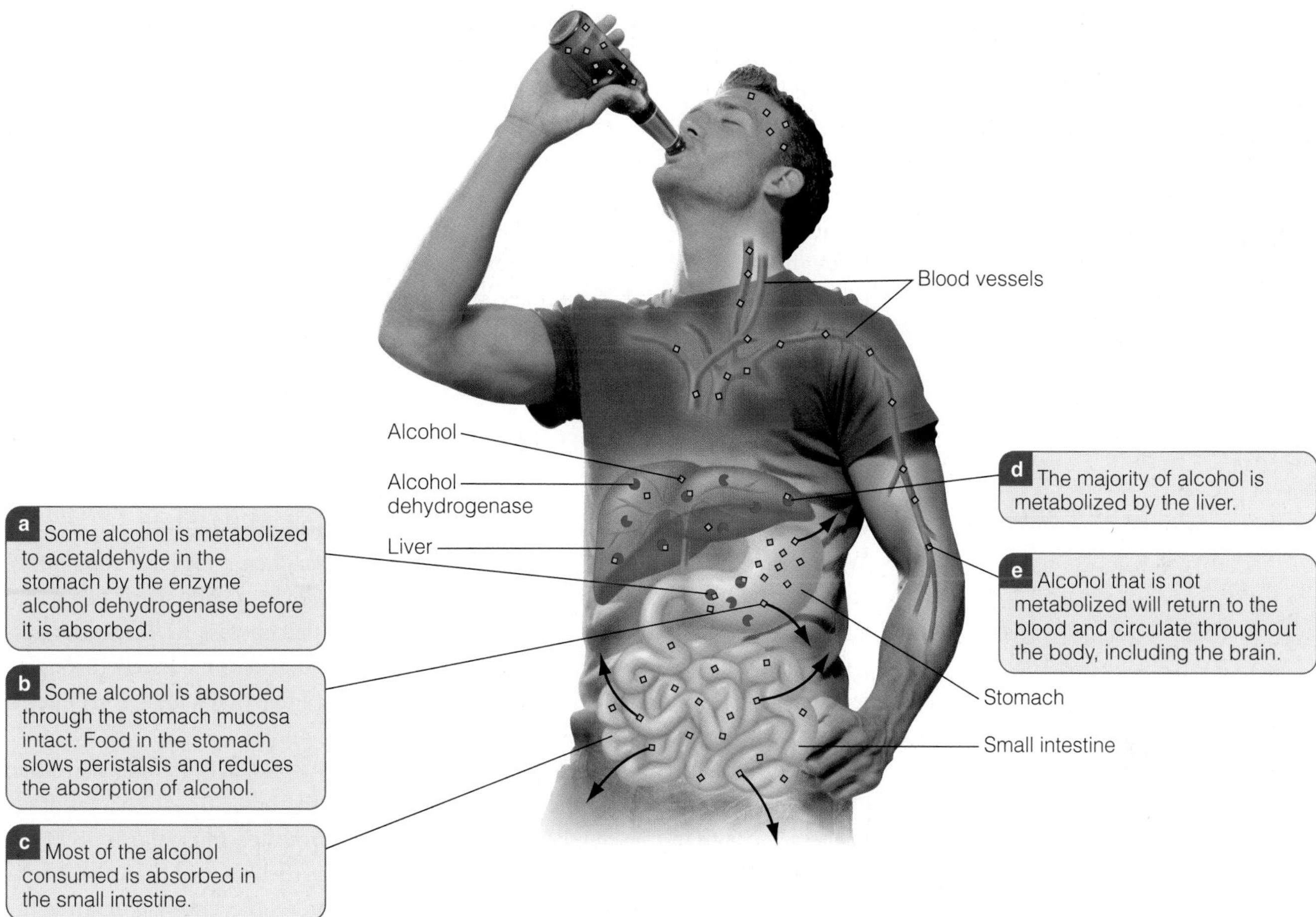
Blood vessels
Alcohol
Alcohol dehydrogenase
Liver
a Some alcohol is metabolized to acetaldehyde in the stomach by the enzyme alcohol dehydrogenase before it is absorbed.
b Some alcohol is absorbed through the stomach mucosa intact. Food in the stomach slows peristalsis and reduces the absorption of alcohol.
c Most of the alcohol consumed is absorbed in the small intestine.
d The majority of alcohol is metabolized by the liver.
e Alcohol that is not metabolized will return to the blood and circulate throughout the body, including the brain.
Stomach
Small intestine

▲ **Figure 7.5 The Absorption of Alcohol**

reaches the brain. Many factors, including the amount of food in the stomach, gender, age, ethnicity, and the amount of alcohol consumed, will affect how quickly alcohol is absorbed and metabolized.[9]

Some Alcohol Is Metabolized in the Stomach

The stomach gets the first pass at metabolizing alcohol before it is absorbed into the blood. Gastric cells secrete **alcohol dehydrogenase (ADH),** an enzyme that begins to metabolize alcohol. The reaction converts alcohol to acetaldehyde with the help of ADH and a form of the B vitamin niacin called NAD^+ (we will cover this reaction in more detail in Chapter 8). Acetaldehyde is further metabolized to acetate and released into the blood.

The rate at which alcohol is metabolized in the stomach is affected by how quickly the stomach empties into the duodenum. The longer alcohol lingers in the stomach, the more time ADH has to metabolize it,[10] and the less alcohol will directly enter the blood and eventually reach the brain.

Food in the Stomach Affects Alcohol Absorption

One factor controlling the rate at which the stomach empties is the amount and type of food in the stomach. If a swallow of beer chases a cheeseburger and fries, the alcohol will take longer to leave the stomach and enter the small intestine than if the beer were consumed on an empty stomach. This is partly due to the fact that a partially full or full stomach is more likely to keep the alcohol away from the stomach wall, thereby reducing the amount that diffuses through the gastric lining. Fat- and

alcohol dehydrogenase (ADH) One of the alcohol-metabolizing enzymes, found in the stomach and the liver, that converts ethanol to acetaldehyde.

Eating food while drinking alcohol affects the rate at which the alcohol is absorbed.

carbohydrate-containing foods have additional effects. Fat slows down peristalsis, and carbohydrates slow the absorption of alcohol through the stomach lining.[11] The result is a slow departure of food from the stomach. Hence, the large amount of fat in a burger meal will help delay the arrival of the alcohol in the small intestine and the carbohydrates will slow the absorption rate through the stomach lining.

Here lies the logic behind not drinking alcohol on an empty stomach. Without food in the stomach, alcohol has greater opportunity to react with and diffuse through the gastric cells, and be absorbed into the blood. In fact, a study showed that an alcoholic drink consumed after a meal was absorbed about three times more slowly than if it was consumed on an empty stomach.[12, 13]

Keep in mind, however, that while a full stomach will delay the arrival of alcohol in the small intestine, the alcohol will still eventually arrive there. If a person drinks several glasses of beer with dinner, the alcohol will be absorbed once the stomach starts emptying.

Gender, Age, and Ethnicity Affect Absorption of Alcohol

When females consume the same amount of alcohol as men, they have a higher alcohol concentration in the blood, even when the difference in body size is taken into account. This is because women have about 20 to 30 percent less ADH in their gastric mucosa than men, so more ethanol will enter the blood immediately through a female's gastric lining. In essence, every alcoholic beverage that a male consumes is equivalent to about $1^1/_3$ alcoholic beverages for a woman.

In addition to a reduced first-pass metabolism of alcohol in the stomach, women also have less muscle mass, and thus less body water, than men (recall that fat tissue has less water than muscle). Because alcohol mixes in water, muscular individuals are able to distribute more of the alcohol throughout their bodies than those who have more fat tissue and, consequently, less body water. So even if a woman is the same height and weight as a man, the female, drinking the same amount of alcohol, will have a higher concentration of alcohol in her blood than the male.

Because of these two factors—less gastric ADH and less body water in which to distribute the ingested alcohol—women will feel alcohol's narcotic effects sooner than men. Women take note: Females can't keep up, drink for drink, with their male friends.

Age and ethnicity may also influence the effects of alcohol. In men, ADH activity levels decrease with age, while females over the age of 40 have higher levels of ADH than they did when they were in their twenties or will have after the age of 60. Some ethnic groups, such as Asians, also have lower ADH activity levels and feel the effects of alcohol much sooner than Caucasians.[14, 15]

The Liver Metabolizes Alcohol

The liver is the main site for alcohol metabolism. The amount of alcohol that can be metabolized every hour is limited, and depends on body mass and liver size.

There are two pathways that metabolize alcohol in the liver. The majority of alcohol is metabolized by the enzyme alcohol dehydrogenase (ADH) with the help of the B vitamin niacin in the form of NAD^+. The second system of enzyme pathways is known as the MEOS, or microsomal ethanol oxidizing system, which uses niacin in the form of NADPH.

acetaldehyde One of the first compounds produced in the metabolism of ethanol. Eventually, acetaldehyde is converted to carbon dioxide and water and excreted.

acetaldehyde dehydrogenase (ALDH) An alcohol-metabolizing enzyme found in the liver that converts acetaldehyde to acetate.

The Alcohol Dehydrogenase (ADH) Pathway

The initial pathway to oxidize alcohol is an anaerobic, two-step enzyme process in the cytosol, or fluid portion of the cell. The enzyme ADH with the help of NAD^+ converts ethanol to **acetaldehyde** by removing two hydrogen atoms (**Figure 7.6**). During the second step, the enzyme **acetaldehyde dehydrogenase (ALDH)**

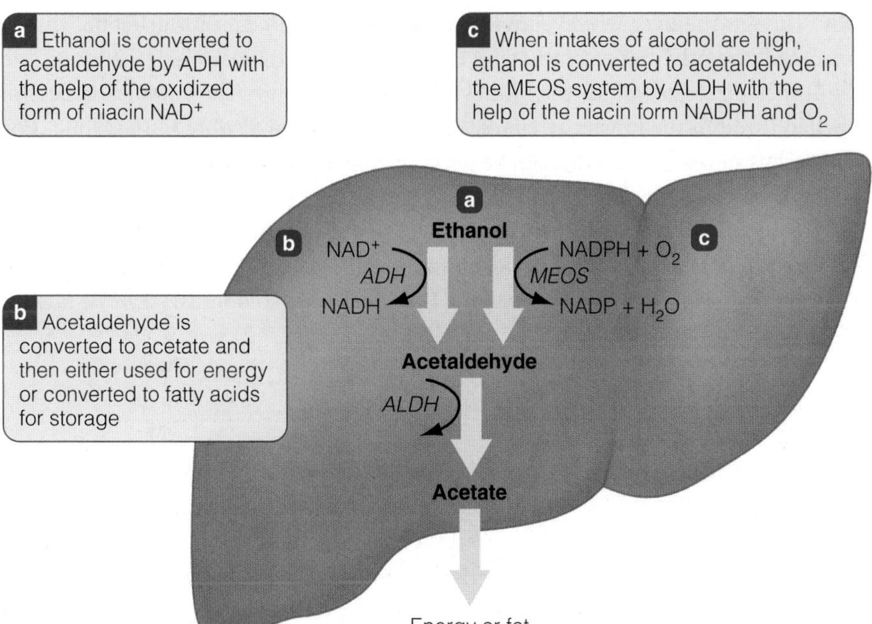
a Ethanol is converted to acetaldehyde by ADH with the help of the oxidized form of niacin NAD+
c When intakes of alcohol are high, ethanol is converted to acetaldehyde in the MEOS system by ALDH with the help of the niacin form NADPH and O2
a
Ethanol
b NAD+
ADH
NADH
NADPH + O2 c
MEOS
NADP + H2O
b Acetaldehyde is converted to acetate and then either used for energy or converted to fatty acids for storage
Acetaldehyde
ALDH
Acetate
Energy or fat

▲ **Figure 7.6 The Liver Metabolizes Alcohol**
The liver rapidly breaks down ethanol to acetyl CoA through either the ADH pathway or using the MEOS.

removes more hydrogen atoms from acetaldehyde to form acetate. Once the acetate is produced, it can continue through the metabolic pathways to produce energy or be converted to a fatty acid and stored as body fat in the adipocytes. (See Chapter 8 for more details on the metabolic pathways for alcohol.)

The Microsomal Ethanol Oxidizing System (MEOS)

When an individual consumes too much alcohol, the ADH enzymes become overwhelmed and can't keep up with the need to oxidize ethanol into acetaldehyde. Under these circumstances, a second major enzyme system in the liver—the **microsomal ethanol oxidizing system (MEOS)**—takes over. Chronic alcohol abuse increases the number of these enzymes, which in turn increases the rate of alcohol that can be metabolized. However, because the MEOS also metabolizes drugs (and other compounds foreign to cells), using it to metabolize alcohol may interfere with the body's ability to metabolize drugs. Alcohol takes precedence over drugs, so consuming drugs and alcohol together can result in the drugs building up to lethal levels while waiting for the MEOS to metabolize them.

As a result of the increase in liver enzymes in the MEOS, there is a small increase in the ability of the liver to metabolize alcohol, so that a larger dose of alcohol is needed to achieve the same effects. The more alcohol you drink, the more active the MEOS becomes, which can result in **alcohol tolerance.**

The difference between the MEOS and the ADH pathway is that the MEOS takes place in the **microsomes** of the cell rather than the cytosol, the fluid inside the cell. The reactions in these small vesicles use oxygen (aerobic) and produce water as a by-product; use a different form of niacin, NADPH, rather than NAD^+; and consume energy rather than produce it to convert ethanol to acetaldehyde.

microsomal ethanol oxidizing system (MEOS) The second major enzyme system in the liver that metabolizes alcohol.

alcohol tolerance When the body adjusts to long-term alcohol use by becoming less sensitive to the alcohol. More alcohol needs to be consumed in order to get the same euphoric effect.

microsomes Small vesicles in the cytoplasm of liver cells where oxidative metabolism of alcohol takes place.

Alcohol Circulates in the Blood

If the liver cannot metabolize alcohol as fast as it is consumed, some of the alcohol remains in the blood, and is continually circulated in the fluid portions of the

A Breathalyzer is used to measure a person's blood alcohol concentration (BAC).

body. Though the liver will eventually metabolize 95 percent of the alcohol that is consumed, the other 5 percent will be excreted intact either through the lungs, the skin in perspiration, and/or the kidneys through the urine. The amount of alcohol expelled through the lungs correlates with the amount of alcohol in the blood. For this reason, a Breathalyzer test can be used by police officers who suspect that a person has consumed too much alcohol.

The **blood alcohol concentration (BAC)** is the amount of alcohol in the blood measured in grams of alcohol per deciliter, usually expressed as a percentage. Because alcohol infiltrates the brain, as the BAC increases so does the level of mental impairment and intoxication.

Alcohol Affects the Brain

Alcohol is considered a *drug* because of its effects on the central nervous system and other systems of the body. Although many people think alcohol is a stimulant, because it has the effect of lowering inhibitions, it is actually a *depressant* of the central nervous system, which means it slows communication between neurons. The brain is part of the central nervous system and is very sensitive to alcohol, which can easily cross the blood–brain barrier. The depressant effect of alcohol on the brain is also what slows down a person's reaction time to stimuli (such as an oncoming car on the road) after drinking.

The more alcohol consumed, the more areas of the brain are affected. Look at Figure 7.7 and Table 7.1 to see how increasing alcohol levels impact specific areas of the brain, and how BAC rises with successive drinks; the Calculation Corner also provides one equation for estimating BAC. Keep in mind that if a person drinks enough alcohol in a short enough period of time, his or her BAC can continue to rise even after unconsciousness.

blood alcohol concentration (BAC) The amount of alcohol in the blood. BAC is measured in grams of alcohol per deciliter of blood, usually expressed as a percentage.

The area of the brain affected by alcohol first is the cerebral cortex, where you process information received from your senses, including sight, smell, and hearing. When alcohol reaches this part of the brain, individuals become more talkative and

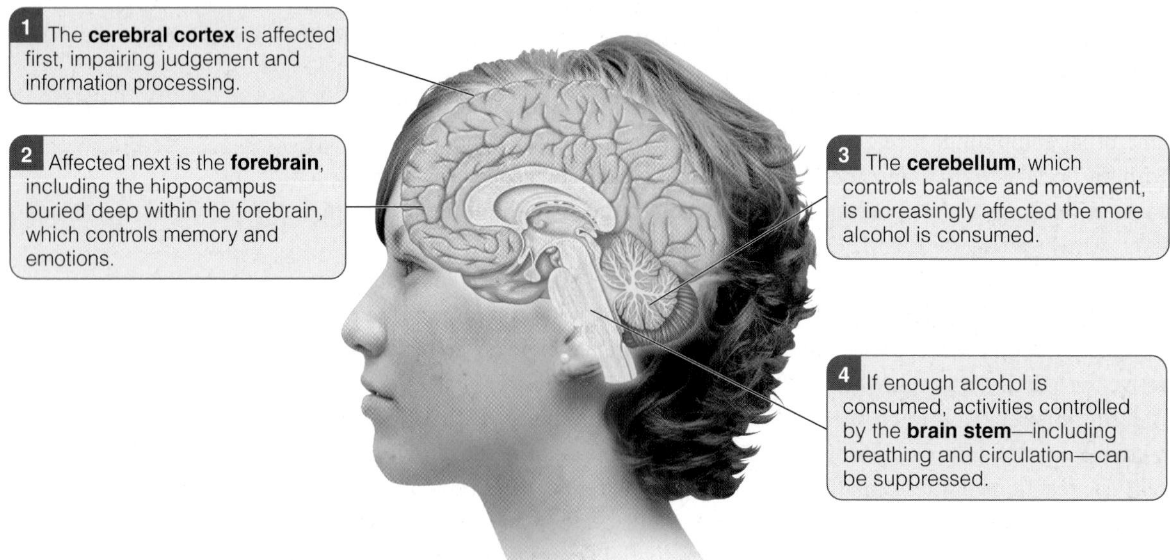

1 The **cerebral cortex** is affected first, impairing judgement and information processing.
2 Affected next is the **forebrain**, including the hippocampus buried deep within the forebrain, which controls memory and emotions.
3 The **cerebellum**, which controls balance and movement, is increasingly affected the more alcohol is consumed.
4 If enough alcohol is consumed, activities controlled by the **brain stem**—including breathing and circulation—can be suppressed.

▲ **Figure 7.7 The Brain and Alcohol**
As more alcohol is consumed, additional areas of the brain are affected. The cerebral cortex is affected first, followed by the forebrain, cerebellum, and brain stem. The greater the alcohol intake, the greater the physical and behavioral changes in the body.

TABLE 7.1 Blood Alcohol Concentration Tables

For Women
Body Weight in Pounds

Drinks Per Hour	100	120	140	160	180	200
1	0.05	0.04	0.03	0.03	0.03	0.02
2	0.09	0.08	0.07	0.06	0.05	0.05
3	0.14	0.11	0.10	0.09	0.08	0.07
4	0.18	0.15	0.13	0.11	0.10	0.09
5	0.23	0.19	0.16	0.14	0.13	0.11
6	0.27	0.23	0.19	0.17	0.15	0.14
7	0.32	0.27	0.23	0.20	0.18	0.16
8	0.36	0.30	0.26	0.23	0.20	0.18
9	0.08	0.34	0.29	0.26	0.23	0.20
10	0.45	0.38	0.32	0.28	0.25	0.23

For Men
Body Weight in Pounds

Drinks Per Hour	100	120	140	160	180	200
1	0.04	0.03	0.03	0.02	0.02	0.02
2	0.08	0.06	0.05	0.05	0.04	0.04
3	0.11	0.09	0.08	0.07	0.06	0.06
4	0.08	0.12	0.11	0.09	0.08	0.08
5	0.19	0.16	0.13	0.12	0.11	0.09
6	0.23	0.19	0.16	0.14	0.13	0.11
7	0.26	0.22	0.19	0.16	0.15	0.13
8	0.30	0.25	0.21	0.19	0.17	0.15
9	0.34	0.28	0.24	0.21	0.19	0.17
10	0.38	0.31	0.27	0.23	0.21	0.19

Notes: Shaded area indicates the condition of being mentally and physically impaired; the definition of legal intoxication. Blood alcohol concentrations are expressed as percent, meaning grams of alcohol per 10 milliliters (per deciliter) of blood. Tables are adapted from those of the Pennsylvania Liquor Control Board, Harrisburg, PA.

less inhibited, and have more confidence. The ability to think clearly or make good judgments is reduced. The higher the BAC, the more noticeable the effects.

The hippocampus, which is buried deep inside the forebrain and responsible for memory, is affected next. Alcohol prevents short-term memories from becoming long-term memories and may result in "blacking out." Even a small amount of alcohol can make you forget what you were doing (or learning) while drinking. The hippocampus also controls emotions. As alcohol intake is increased, feelings such as sadness, aggressiveness, and withdrawal become exaggerated.

The cerebellum controls your balance and movements such as walking and talking. The more alcohol consumed, the more difficult it is to control body movements and speech. The result is the inability to stand or walk in a straight line.

If enough alcohol has been consumed, the activities of the brain stem, which controls breathing and circulation, can be suppressed, impairing breathing and heart rate and ultimately causing death. A particular area at the top of the brain stem, called the *reticular activating system* (RAS), controls whether an individual is awake or asleep. Excessive quantities of alcohol can shut down the RAS, causing unconsciousness. This reaction to excessive alcohol may be a beneficial

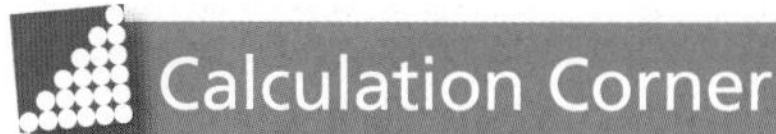

Calculation Corner

Estimate Blood Alcohol Concentration

The current BAC estimation calculators are based on the original equation developed by Widmark 80 years ago.[1] The estimation of BAC takes into account the amount of alcohol in a drink, the individual's metabolism rate of alcohol, the amount of body water (recall that males have more body water than females), and the time since alcohol was consumed and metabolized. In the equation below, use 7.5 for the gender constant for males and 9.0 for the gender constant for females. Body weight is in pounds (lbs), and 0.017 g/dl per hour is the average rate of alcohol metabolism.[2]

$$\text{BAC} = [(\text{\# of standard drinks} \div 2) \times (\text{gender constant} \div \text{body weight})] - (0.017 \times \text{hours})$$

Example #1: Calculate Mark's percent BAC if he weighs 175 lbs and drank 3 regular 12 oz beers in 2 hours.

Mark's estimate of BAC

$$= [(3 \div 2) \times (7.5 \div 175)] - (0.017 \times 2)$$
$$= [(1.5 \times 0.04)] - (0.03)$$
$$= 0.06 - 0.03$$
$$= 0.03$$

Does Mark's BAC indicate he would be legally impaired?

Example 2: Calculate Ruby's percent BAC if she weighs 120 lbs and drank 3 regular 12 oz beers in 2 hours.

Ruby's estimate of BAC

$$= [(3 \div 2) \times (9.0 \div 120)] - (0.017 \times 2)$$
$$= [(1.5 \times 0.075)] - (0.034)$$
$$= 0.11 - 0.034$$
$$= 0.08$$

Does Ruby's estimate of BAC indicate she would be legally impaired?

[1]Widmark, E. M. P. 1932. *Principles and Applications of Medicolegal Alcohol Determination*, translated into English by R. C. Baselt, Department of Pathology, University of California, Davis, 1981, p. 163.

[2]Hustad, J.T.P., and K. B. Carey. 2005. Using Calculations to Estimate Blood Alcohol Concentrations for Naturally Occurring Drinking Episodes: A Validity Study. *Journal of Studies on Alcohol* 66: 130-138.

mechanism that prevents drinking to the point that breathing and heart rate shut down.

THE TAKE-HOME MESSAGE Alcohol is absorbed in the stomach and small intestine and is metabolized primarily in the liver. A person's gender, age, and ethnicity; the amount of food in the stomach; and the quantity of alcohol consumed affect the rate of absorption and metabolism in the body. Chronic consumption of alcohol can disrupt liver function and damage the liver. The blood alcohol concentration (BAC) is the measurement of alcohol in the blood. Alcohol is a central nervous system depressant. Because the brain is sensitive to alcohol, alcohol affects brain function and behavior.

TABLE TIPS

Moderate Your Drinking

Never drink on an empty stomach. The alcohol will be absorbed too quickly, which will impair judgment and lower willpower to decline the next drink.

Keep track of how many beverages you drink using one of the free apps available for smart phones.

Make your first drink at a party a glass of water. This will help you pace yourself and reduce the chance that you will guzzle your first alcoholic drink because you are thirsty. Drink another glass of water before you have a second alcoholic drink.

Drink fun nonalcoholic drinks. Try a Virgin Mary (a Bloody Mary without the vodka), a tame frozen margarita (use the mix and don't add the tequila), or a Tom Collins without the gin.

Don't drink a lot of junk; drink a little of the good stuff. Rather than consume excessive amounts of cheap beer or jug wine, have a single microbrewed beer or one glass of fine wine.

Become the standing Designated Driver among your friends and make your passengers reimburse you for the cost of the gasoline.

How Can Alcohol Be Harmful?

Alcohol can have many harmful effects on the body and the brain caused mostly by the products of metabolism: acetaldehyde and acids. The more alcohol consumed, the more acetaldehyde is formed. These effects can be acute and short-term, occurring while an individual is intoxicated, or they can occur within 72 hours following intoxication. Or the effects can be long term, occurring over one or more years, due to chronic use of alcohol. Both acute, short-term and chronic, long-term effects of heavy drinking put individuals at risk for serious health consequences.

Overconsumption of Alcohol Can Have Numerous Short-Term Consequences

Alcohol is a toxin, and the body works quickly to eliminate it to avoid damage. Drinking in moderation allows the body time to eliminate the alcohol and to repair itself. Moderate drinkers probably will not experience short-term physiological consequences. Drinking in excess, in contrast, can have quick, dangerous physiological consequences, and also often puts personal safety at risk. However, even at low doses, alcohol can impair judgment and coordination.

Unintentional Injuries

Deaths and injuries from car accidents, falls, assaults, and other non-chronic-disease-related events are not uncommon when an individual is intoxicated. Each year nearly 600,000 students between the ages of 18 and 24 are unintentionally injured because of drinking, and close to 700,000 are hit or assaulted by another intoxicated student. Numerous instances of sexual abuse, unsafe sex, suicide attempts, drunk driving, and property damage also occur due to the influence of alcohol. More than 1,800 students die each year as a result of drinking alcohol.[16] What is the answer to reducing unintentional injuries and other consequences of drinking in young adults? Two experts present their views on the best approach to reduce college drinking and associated harm to students and others in Two Points of View: Should the Drinking Age Be Lowered?.

Drinking and driving can be deadly.

Sleep Disruption

Having a drink within an hour before bed may help an individual fall asleep sooner, but it will disrupt the sleep cycle, cause middle-of-night wakefulness, and make returning to sleep a challenge.[17] Even a moderate amount of alcohol consumed at dinner or even late in the afternoon during happy hour can disrupt that evening's sleep.

After a poor night's sleep, it's a bad idea to drink alcohol the next day. Studies have shown that a night of sleep disruption followed by even small amounts of alcohol the next day reduces reaction time and alertness in individuals performing a simulated driving test. Being tired and then drinking alcohol exacerbates alcohol's sedating effect.[18]

Hangovers

A **hangover** is the body's way of saying, "Don't do that to me again." After a bout of heavy drinking, individuals can experience hangover symptoms ranging from a pounding headache, fatigue, nausea, and increased thirst to a rapid heartbeat, tremors, sweating, dizziness, depression, anxiety, and irritability. A hangover begins within hours of the last drink, as the BAC begins to drop. The symptoms will appear in full force once all the alcohol is gone from the blood, and can linger for up to an additional 24 hours.[19] In other words, a few hours of excessive alcohol consumption on a Saturday night can not only ruin an entire Sunday, but even disrupt part of Monday morning.

Alcohol contributes to the symptoms of a hangover in several ways. Acetaldehyde, the intermediate by-product of alcohol metabolism, is mildly toxic. In large enough amounts, acetaldehyde can cause nausea, headache, fatigue, and irritability, all the symptoms of a hangover. But this is not the only cause of hangovers. Alcohol is also a diuretic, so it can cause dehydration, and thus, electrolyte imbalances. It inhibits the release of antidiuretic hormone from the pituitary gland, which in turn causes the kidneys to excrete water, as well as electrolytes, into the urine. Vomiting and sweating during or after excessive drinking will further contribute to dehydration and electrolyte loss. Dehydration also increases thirst and can cause feelings of lightheadedness, dizziness, and weakness. Increased acid production in the stomach and secretions from the pancreas and intestines can cause stomach pain, nausea, and vomiting.

Lastly, alcoholic beverages often contain compounds called **congeners,** which enhance their taste and appearance but may contribute to hangover symptoms. Congeners include tannins found in wine or acetaldehyde formed during the metabolism of alcohol.

Congeners can also be produced during the fermentation process or be added during production of the alcoholic beverages. The greatest amounts of congeners are found in red wine and darker liquors such as tequila, brandy, or bourbon. For example, bourbon has more than forty times the quantity of congeners that vodka does. Combining alcoholic beverages that contain different levels of congeners can cause severe hangover symptoms. Drinking beer that is carbonated along with liquor that contains congeners speeds up the absorption of the alcohol, which gives the body less time to eliminate the congeners.

Forget the old wives' tale of consuming an alcoholic beverage to "cure" a hangover. Drinking more alcohol, even if it is mixed with tomato or orange juice, during a hangover only prolongs the recovery time. Nor do caffeine, hot showers, and long walks improve the symptoms. The only cure for a hangover is time.

Whereas aspirin and other nonsteroidal anti-inflammatory medications, such as ibuprofen, can ease a headache, these medications can also contribute to stomachache and nausea. Taking acetaminophen (Tylenol) during and after alcohol consumption, when the alcohol is being metabolized, has been shown to intensify this pain reliever's toxicity to the liver and may cause liver damage in some cases.[20] The best strategy for dealing with a hangover is to avoid it by limiting the amount of alcohol consumed.

Staying hydrated by drinking water between alcoholic beverages can help you avoid the effects of a hangover.

hangover A collective term for the unpleasant symptoms, such as a headache and dizziness, that occur after drinking an excessive amount of alcohol; many of the symptoms are caused by high levels of acetaldehyde in the blood.

congeners Fermentation by-products or additives in alcohol that may contribute to hangover symptoms.

Two Points of View

Should the Drinking Age Be Lowered?

Two experts take opposing sides on the benefits and risks of lowering the legal age for alcohol consumption.

Ruth C. Engs, EdD

Professor Emeritus, Indiana University

Ruth C. Engs is professor emeritus, Applied Health Science, at Indiana University. She has published research on student drinking patterns and books on the cultural use of alcohol and its history, including *Clean Living Movements: American Cycles of Health Reform* (2000) and *Women: Alcohol and Other Drugs* (reprinted 2007).

Q: Do you believe the drinking age should be changed in the United States?

A: Yes, based upon research I think the drinking age should be lowered in certain circumstances. I advocate allowing youth to drink with their parents, and in controlled environments such as restaurants, campus pubs, and campus-sponsored parties. However, I am opposed to allowing youth to buy alcohol in retail stores and then going home to get drunk or sneaking it to very young individuals. This is not responsible drinking behavior. Youth could be required to take an alcohol education class before they could purchase alcohol in the controlled environment. After passing this class, their driver's licenses could have an endorsement that allows them to drink alcohol.

Q: What would be the consequences of lowering the drinking age?

A: The consequences would be increased moral responsibility and respect for society and its laws. A high proportion of university and college students consume alcohol even though it is illegal. This flouting of current laws has led to a "prohibition mentality" similar to the heavy drinking and disrespect of laws and social conventions in the 1920s.

Q: What research supports your position?

A: Most of the research studying university students, including my own, suggests that after the imposition of a mandatory 21-year-old purchase age in 1987, problems related to alcohol dramatically *increased* over the next decade. The decrease in fatal alcohol-related crashes—which began in the early 1980s before the mandatory laws were passed—was due to many factors, including designated driver programs, safer cars, and seat belt use, not just decreased per capita consumption. Compared to two decades ago, vandalism, fighting, alcohol intoxication, lower grades, and other personal and social

James C. Fell

Senior Director, Pacific Institute for Research and Evaluation

James C. Fell is a senior program director with the Pacific Institute for Research and Evaluation in Calverton, Maryland. Mr. Fell completed research on grants from the National Institute on Alcohol Abuse and Alcoholism and the Robert Wood Johnson Foundation that assessed the status and enforcement of the Minimum Legal Drinking Age 21 (MLDA 21) and the law's relationship to teenage traffic deaths.

Q: Do you believe the drinking age should be changed in the United States?

A: No, for the following four reasons:

1. The National Highway Traffic Safety Administration reports the MLDA 21 laws save approximately 600–700 lives each year and have saved close to 29,000 lives since their inception.
2. Medical research shows that excessive drinking by youth aged 20 and younger may cause brain damage and reduce brain function. Other studies show that the brain is not fully developed until about age 25.
3. Early onset of drinking before age 21 increases the risk for alcohol abuse, crash involvements, and assaults.
4. European countries with lower drinking ages report higher percentages of drinking, heavy drinking, and intoxication by adolescents aged 15 to 16.

Q: What would be the consequences of lowering the drinking age?

A: There would be substantial increases in motor vehicle crash fatalities, youth alcohol addiction, suicides, rapes, assaults, and robberies involving youths aged 15 to 20.

Q: What research supports your position?

A: Studies in the 1970s and 1980s showed increases in alcohol-related crashes involving youth aged 18 to 20 in states that lowered their drinking age from 21 to 18 or 19. Between 1982 and 2004, when all states adopted 21 for the drinking age, the number of drinking drivers under age 21 involved in fatal crashes decreased 62 percent. Drinking drivers aged 21 and older in fatal crashes decreased 33 percent in the same period. The MLDA 21 law accounted for the difference. According to a study in New Zealand in 2006, lowering the drinking age from 20

problems related to increased heavy drinking in an "underground" situation have leveled off. Studies suggest that European youth do not have these problems to the extent that American youth do because they drink openly in controlled environments and not on the sly. Alcohol is not seen as a "forbidden fruit" as it is in the United States.

Q: Would there be any health benefits or consequences to changing the law?

A: Yes. If youth were drinking in controlled environments where social pressure to conform to moderate drinking behavior is found, alcohol intoxication and its resulting personal, physical, and social health problems would likely begin to decrease. Of course, designated driver programs or campus buses to take students back to their residences should also be continued.

to 18 increased traffic crashes and injuries 12 percent for 18- to 19-year-old males and 14 percent for males aged 15 to 17. For females, rates increased 51 percent for 18- to 19-year-olds and 24 percent for 15- to 17-year-olds. Studies in the 1990s showed that raising the drinking age to 21 was associated with significant reductions in homicides, suicides and unintentional injuries to 18- to 20-year-olds.

Q: Would there be any health benefits or consequences to changing the law?

A: There would certainly be health consequences. According to the American Medical Association it takes less alcohol for a teenager to get drunk than it does for an adult. A normal adult's liver can process about 50 alcohol calories per hour (one ounce of 40 percent alcohol); a teenager's liver can only process half that amount. Youths who start drinking at age 18 compared to those who start at age 21 are 1.4 times more likely to become alcohol dependent, twice as likely to become intoxicated when they drink, and have a 50 percent greater chance of being injured while under the influence of alcohol.

Chronic Alcohol Abuse May Lead to Serious Health Consequences

The long-term effects of alcohol consumption are not completely understood. However, data suggests alcohol abuse may result in malnutrition, affect metabolism and hormones, and the increase the risk of developing cardiovascular disease and some cancers. **Figure 7.8** summarizes the many harmful effects of excessive drinking. The health consequences associated with abuse of and dependence upon alcohol are explored in Health Connection: What Are Alcohol Abuse and Alcoholism? on page 268.

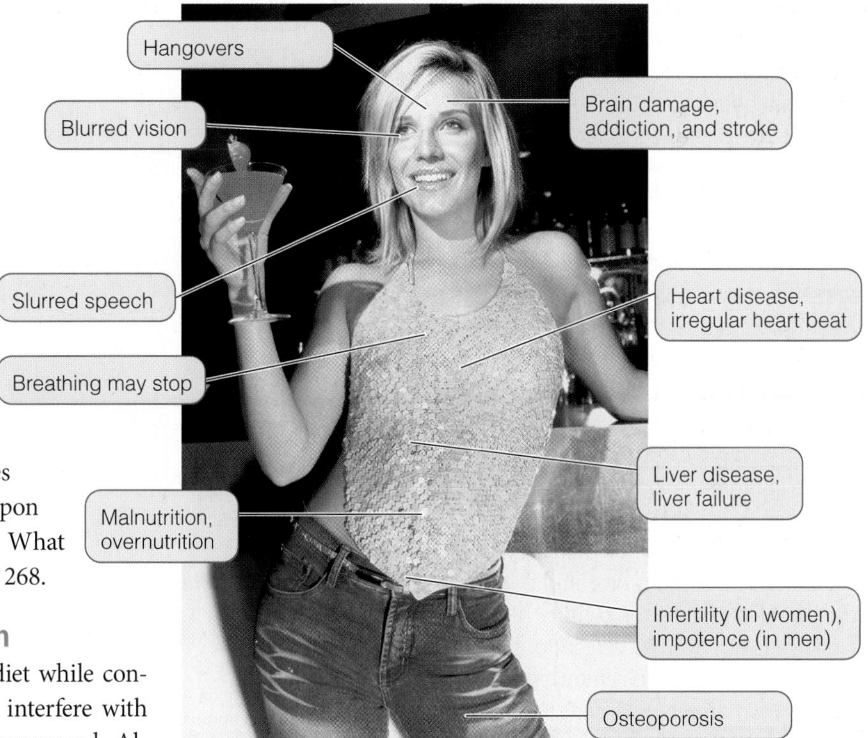

▲ **Figure 7.8 Effects of Alcohol on the Body**
Consuming more than a moderate amount of alcohol will lead to both short-term and long-term adverse health effects.

Impaired Digestion and Absorption

Even if an individual consumes a healthy diet while consuming too much alcohol, the alcohol can interfere with the digestion and absorption of nutrients consumed. Alcohol can inhibit chemical digestion of food by decreasing secretion of digestive enzymes from the pancreas, thereby inhibiting the breakdown of nutrients into usable molecules, for

Health Connection

What Are Alcohol Abuse and Alcoholism?

When people choose not to drink alcohol responsibly, they often end up abusing alcohol or suffering from a full-blown addiction. **Alcohol abuse** begins when a person allows alcohol to interfere with his or her life. He may have to call in sick to work or school due to a hangover, or she may have blank spots in her memory due to intoxication. At the extreme end of the spectrum is the disease of **alcoholism.** By the time a person is addicted to alcohol, he or she is no longer in control of drinking habits and is at serious risk of suffering long-term health damage. Approximately 17 percent of regular drinkers either abuse or are addicted to alcohol.[1]

Forms of Alcohol Abuse

When people continue to consume alcohol even though the behavior has created social, legal, and/or health problems for them, they are abusing alcohol. These problems can include binge drinking, driving while under the influence of alcohol, and underage drinking.

Binge Drinking

Binge drinking occurs when a male consumes five or more drinks and when a woman consumes four or more drinks in about two hours.[2]

Binge drinkers, the incidence of which is highest in individuals 18 to 24 years of age, report binge drinking more than four times per month and 7.9 drinks each time they binge.[3] College students who binge drink are more likely to miss classes, have hangovers, and experience unintentional injuries such as falling, motor vehicle accidents, and drowning, and may even die (see figure). Research also indicates that binge drinkers engage in more unplanned sexual activity and fail to use safe sex strategies more frequently than non–binge drinkers. Sexual aggression and assaults on campus increase when drinking enters the picture. Alcohol is involved with over 70 percent of the reported rapes on college campuses; victims are often too drunk to consent to or refuse the actions of the other person.

Binge drinking is associated with many health problems, such as hypertension, heart attack, sexually transmitted disease, suicide, homicide, and child abuse. Binge drinking can also cause **blackouts,** which are periods of time that a person cannot remember, even though he or she may have been conscious. A research study of over 700 college students found that more than half of them had blacked out from alcohol consumption at least once in their lives, and many found out after the fact that they had taken part in activities such as vandalism, unprotected sex, and driving a motor vehicle during the blackout period.[4]

Binge drinking can lead to **alcohol poisoning** as alcohol depresses the nerves involved in numerous actions in the body, such as breathing and heart rate (see table). Alcohol in the stomach and intestine will continue to be absorbed and the BAC will continue to rise even after an individual passes out.

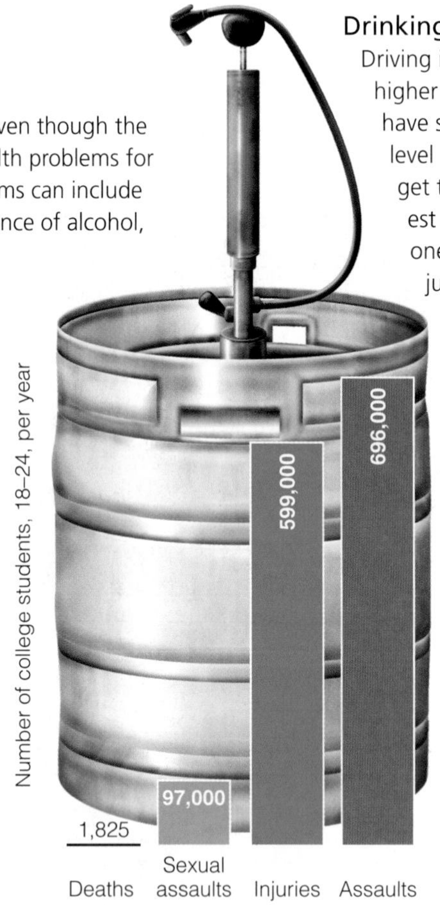

Consequences of College Binge Drinking

Alcohol use by college students results in numerous assaults, injuries, and deaths each year.

Source: National Institute on Alcohol Abuse and Alcoholism, based on information from R. Hingson, et al., "Magnitude of Alcohol-Related Mortality and Morbidity Among U.S. College Students Ages 18–24: Changes from 1998 to 2001," *Annual Review of Public Health* 26 (2005): 259–279.

Drinking and Driving

Driving in the United States with a BAC of 0.08 or higher is illegal (some states in the United States have set their legal limit even lower), but the level of alcohol in the blood doesn't need to get that high to impair driving. Even the lowest level of BAC, the level that occurs after one alcoholic beverage, will impair alertness, judgment, and coordination (see table). In 2004, more than 17,000 people died in automobile accidents that involved a driver with a BAC of 0.01 or higher.[5]

Underage Drinking

The average age of the first drink for Americans from 12 to 20 years of age is 14.[6] By the time they graduate from high school, over 30 percent of teenagers are binge drinking at least once a month.[7] Underage drinking not only increases the risk of violence, injuries, and other health risks as discussed earlier, but alcohol consumption at this age can also interfere with brain development and lead to permanent cognitive and memory damage in teenagers.

There is another danger in consuming alcohol at a young age. The earlier a person starts drinking, the higher the chances that alcohol will become a problem later in life. A person who starts drinking at age 15 is four times more likely to suffer from alcoholism than an individual who doesn't start drinking until age 20.[8]

Progressive Effects of Alcohol			
Blood Alcohol Concentration	**Changes in Feelings and Personality**	**Brain Regions Affected**	**Impaired Functions (continuum)**
0.01–0.05	Relaxation, sense of well-being, loss of inhibition	Cerebral cortex	Alertness; judgment
0.06–0.10	Pleasure, numbing of feelings, nausea, sleepiness, emotional arousal	Cerebral cortex and forebrain	Coordination (especially fine motor skills); visual tracking
0.11–0.20	Mood swings, anger, sadness, mania	Cerebral cortex, forebrain, and cerebellum	Reasoning and depth perception; appropriate social behavior
0.21–0.30	Aggression, reduced sensations, depression, stupor	Cerebral cortex, forebrain, cerebellum, and brain stem	Speech; balance; temperature regulation
0.31–0.40	Unconsciousness, coma, death possible	Entire brain	Bladder control; breathing
0.41 and greater	Death		Heart rate

Source: National Institute on Alcohol Abuse and Alcoholism. 2003. *Understanding Alcohol: Investigations into Biology and Behavior.* Available at http://science.education.nih.gov/supplements/nih3/alcohol/default.htm. Accessed April 2012.

Alcoholism Is a Disease

A person who suffers from alcoholism exhibits four classic symptoms of the disease; he or she:

1. Craves alcohol
2. Has developed a higher tolerance for it
3. Can't control or limit his or her intake once drinking starts
4. Has developed a dependency on alcohol because, if the person stops drinking, his or her body reacts to the withdrawal

An alcoholic's craving, loss of control, and physical dependence distinguishes him or her as an "alcoholic" rather than a person who abuses alcohol but doesn't have these three other characteristics.[9]

A family history of alcoholism—for example, you may have a father and grandfather who both died of cirrhosis due to alcoholism and a brother who drinks heavily—puts a person at a higher than average risk for alcoholism. Research has shown that approximately 50 percent of the risk for alcoholism is determined genetically.[10] However, this genetic risk alone does not mean an individual is destined to become an alcoholic. A person's risk for alcoholism is also influenced by his or her environment. Home life, the drinking habits of family and friends, social pressures, and access to alcohol all impact whether a person develops the disease. If a person's roommate and friends drink heavily, and he or she works part-time as a bartender, that person will be at greater risk of developing alcoholism. If she chooses to surround herself with acquaintances and a lifestyle that don't focus on alcohol, she can reduce her risk of following in her grandfather's, father's, and brother's footsteps.

There is no cure for alcoholism. However, it can be treated using a combined physical and psychological approach. The physical symptoms, such as the severe craving for alcohol, can be treated with medication that helps reduce the craving. Psychologically, self-help therapies and support groups can be invaluable to an alcoholic on the road to recovery. Because alcoholics can't limit their consumption once they start drinking, reducing the amount of alcohol consumed will not work for them. They must eliminate alcohol entirely from their lives in order to have a successful recovery.

alcohol abuse Continuing to consume alcohol even though the behavior has created social, legal, and/or health problems.

alcoholism A chronic disease characterized by craving for and elevated tolerance to alcohol, inability to control alcohol intake, and dependency on alcohol to prevent withdrawal symptoms; also referred to as *alcohol dependence*.

binge drinking The consumption of five or more alcoholic drinks by men, or four or more drinks by women, in about two hours.

blackouts Periods of time when an intoxicated person cannot recall part or all of an event.

alcohol poisoning When the BAC rises to the point that a person's central nervous system is affected and his or her breathing and heart rate are interrupted.

Self-Assessment

Red Flags for Alcohol Abuse

Complete the following self-assessment to see if you may be at increased risk for alcohol abuse.

1. Do you fail to fulfill major work, school, or home responsibilities because of your consumption of alcohol?

   Yes ☐ **No** ☐

2. Do you drink in situations that are potentially dangerous, such as while driving a car or operating heavy machinery?

   Yes ☐ **No** ☐

3. Do you experience repeated alcohol-related legal problems, such as being arrested for driving while intoxicated?

   Yes ☐ **No** ☐

4. Do you have relationship problems that are caused or made worse by alcohol?

   Yes ☐ **No** ☐

5. Do you try to hide your alcohol consumption from family or friends because you know they will tell you to stop?

   Yes ☐ **No** ☐

Answers

If you answered "yes" to any of these questions, you should speak with your health care provider. You may benefit from an alcohol abstinence program, or other guidance.

Adapted from Recovery Through Support.Com. 2008. Available at www.recoverythroughsupport.com/self-assessment.html. Accessed July 2008.

References

1. National Institute on Alcohol Abuse and Alcoholism. 2006. *National Epidemiologic Survey on Alcohol and Related Conditions: Selected Findings.* Available at http://pubs.niaaa.nih.gov. Accessed April 2012.
2. National Institute on Alcohol Abuse and Alcoholism. 2004. National Institute of Alcohol Abuse and Alcoholism Council Approves Definition of Binge Drinking. *NIAAA Newsletter.* Available at http://pubs.niaaa.nih.gov/publications/Newsletter/winter2004/Newsletter_Number3.htm. Accessed April 2012.
3. Centers for Disease Control and Prevention. 2012. *Vital Signs: Binge Drinking Prevalence, Frequency, and Intensity Among Adults—United States, 2010.* Available at www.cdc.gov/mmwr/preview/mmwrhtml/mm6101a4.htm?s_cid=mm6101a4_w. Accessed April 2012.
4. White, A. M., D. W. Jamieson-Drake, and H. S. Swartzwelder. 2002. Prevalence and Correlates of Alcohol-Induced Blackouts Among College Students: Results of an E-Mail Survey. *Journal of American College Health* 51:117–131.
5. National Highway Traffic Safety Administration. 2005. *Traffic Safety Facts: Crash Statistics on Alcohol-Related Fatalities in 2004.* Available at www.nhtsa.dot.gov. Accessed April 2012.
6. Chen, C. M., H. Yi, and V. B. Faden. 2011. *Trends in Underage Drinking in the United States, 1991–2009. Surveillance Report #91.* National Institute on Alcohol Abuse and Alcoholism. Available at pubs.niaaa.nih.gov/publications/surveillance91/Underage09.pdf. Accessed April 2012.
7. Ibid.
8. Ibid.
9. National Institute on Alcohol Abuse and Alcoholism. 2007. Alcohol Use Disorders. Available at www.niaaa.nih.gov/alcohol-health/overview-alcohol-consumption/alcohol-use-disorders. Accessed April 2012.
10. Villafuerte, S., M. M. Heitzeg, S. Foley, W-Y Wendy Yau, K. Majczenko, I-K Zubieta, R. A. Zucker, and M. Burmeister. 2011. Impulsiveness and Insula Activation During Reward Anticipation are Associated with Genetic Variants in GABRA2 in a Family Sample Enriched for Alcoholism. *Molecular Psychiatry,* DOI: 10.1038/mp.2011.33.

instance dietary triglycerides.[21] Alcohol also impairs nutrient absorption by damaging the cells lining the stomach and intestines and disabling transport of some nutrients into the blood. Because alcohol interferes with fat digestion, it also impairs the absorption and transport of fat-soluble vitamins. In addition, nutritional deficiencies themselves may lead to further absorption problems. For example, folate deficiency alters the cells lining the small intestine, which in turn impairs absorption of water and other essential nutrients such as glucose, sodium, and vitamins, including vitamin B_{12}.

Malnutrition

Individuals who consume large amounts of alcohol over the long term often have some form of malnutrition. Because alcohol provides kilocalories (7 kilocalories per gram) but very little nutritional value, people who drink large amounts can easily exceed their energy needs, and may gain weight. If these individuals compensate for the extra kilocalories by cutting nutritious foods from the diet, they can fall short of specific nutrient needs, and **primary malnutrition** may occur.

primary malnutrition A state of being malnourished due to lack of consuming essential nutrients.

Individuals who drink heavily tend to eat poorly, and a major concern is that alcohol's effects on the digestion of food and utilization of nutrients may shift a mildly malnourished person toward severe malnutrition. People who consume more than 30 percent of their daily kilocalories from alcohol tend to consume less protein, fiber, vitamins A, C, D, riboflavin, and thiamin, and the minerals calcium and iron.[22] A thiamin deficiency can affect brain function, including causing memory loss, and increase the risk of **Wernicke-Korsakoff syndrome,** a condition that includes mental confusion and uncontrolled muscle movement.

Specific nutrient deficiencies aren't surprising once you consider that if a person consuming 2,000 kilocalories daily devotes 600 (30 percent) of these kilocalories to alcohol, there would only be 1,400 kilocalories left to meet all of his or her nutrient needs. An adult diet routinely limited to 1,400 kilocalories daily is bound to have nutrient deficiencies.

Once in the body, alcohol can also interfere with nutrient metabolism, resulting in **secondary malnutrition.** Regularly drinking too much alcohol can interfere with the absorption and/or use of several nutrients, including protein, zinc, magnesium, and the B vitamins thiamin, folate, and B_{12}, as well as the fat-soluble vitamins A, D, E, and K.

Alcohol and Weight Gain

At 7 kilocalories per gram, alcohol provides less energy than fat (9 kilocalories per gram) but more than either carbohydrates or protein (4 kilocalories per gram). However, mixed drinks almost always contain more kilocalories than just those from the alcohol (Table 7.2). For example, a rum and coke contains the kilocalories from both the rum and the coke, making the drink more than three times as high in kilocalories as the rum itself. In many mixed drinks, depending on the mixers and other ingredients, the kilocalorie count can approach that of a meal. The popular mudslide, for example, made with vodka, Irish cream, coffee liqueur, ice cream, and cream, should be ordered from the dessert menu and served with a spoon. If high-kilocalorie "bar foods" are consumed with the drinks, the kilocalories can add up rapidly (**Figure 7.9**).

Wernicke-Korsakoff syndrome A severe brain disorder associated with chronic excessive alcohol consumption; symptoms include vision changes, loss of muscle coordination, and loss of memory; the cause is a thiamin deficiency.

secondary malnutrition A state of being malnourished due to interference with nutrient absorption and metabolism.

Dinner 1

5 12-oz beers

1,719 total kilocalories

8 BBQ chicken wings

1 handful Goldfish crackers

1 large serving nachos with cheese

Total fat (g) 51
Saturated fat (g) 16
Cholesterol (mg) 154

Dinner 2

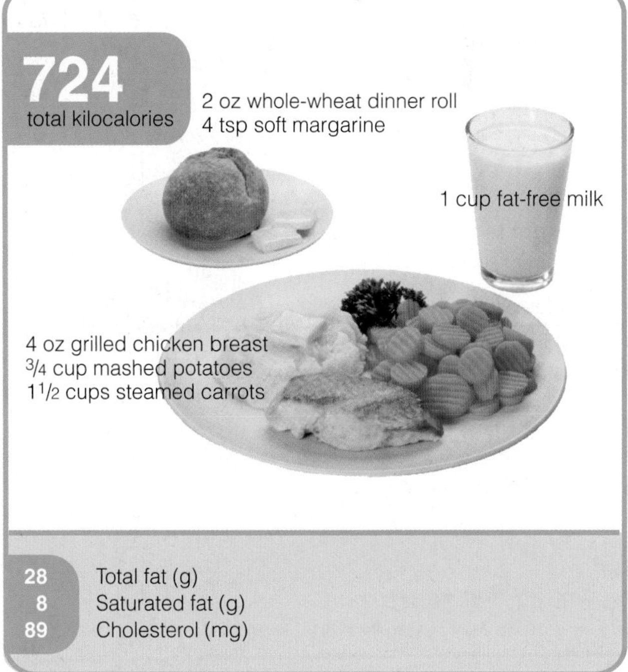

▲ **Figure 7.9 Too Much Alcohol Costs Good Nutrition**
A dinner of several alcoholic beverages and bar foods not only adds kilocalories, fat, and saturated fat to the diet, but displaces healthier foods that would provide better nutrition.

TABLE 7.2 Kilocalories in Selected Alcoholic Drinks

Drink	Serving size	Alcohol servings	Kilocalories per drink
Beer	12 oz	1	150
Light beer	12 oz	1	110
Mudslide	12 oz	4	820
Distilled spirits (whiskey, vodka, gin, rum)	1.5 oz	1	100
Bloody Mary	5.5 oz	1	97
Red or white wine	5 oz	1	100–105
Margarita	6.3 oz	3	327
Cosmopolitan	2.5 oz	1.7	131
Rum and Coke	12 oz	2.7	361

Note: Alcohol servings are per beverage.

Data from U.S. Department of Agriculture. 2010. *Dietary Guidelines for Americans, 2010.* Available at www.health.gov/dietaryguidelines/2010.asp#resources. Accessed April 2012.

Consistently adding extra kilocalories from alcoholic beverages—or any food or beverage source—to a diet that is already meeting daily energy needs will result in weight gain. However, recent research appears to indicate that alcohol itself does not cause weight gain. Epidemiological data from the National Health and Nutrition Examination Survey (NHANES) reported that alcohol consumption did not increase obesity. In fact, in the 10-year follow-up study, people who consumed alcohol did not gain weight but rather had more stable weight than those who didn't drink alcohol.[23] (Even consuming as much as two drinks or more a day did not appear to increase the risk of weight gain.) These results may be confounded by the amount of alcohol consumed. Research on college freshmen suggests that weight gain is related to increased alcohol consumption, at least in males.[24] Is this weight gain related to a "beer belly"? Because current research suggests that alcohol alone may not increase the waistline, alcohol does not appear to be the only factor influencing weight gain.[25]

Changes in Nutrient Metabolism

Excessive alcohol consumption can also affect how the body handles the essential nutrients once they are absorbed. Alcohol can prevent absorbed nutrients from being fully used by altering their transport, storage, and excretion. Decreased liver stores of vitamins such as vitamin A, and increased excretion of nutrients such as fat in the feces, indicate impaired use of nutrients by alcoholics.

Alcohol Can Interact with Hormones

When individuals who overindulge in alcohol don't eat enough while they are drinking, their body's glucose stores can become depleted, and their blood glucose levels can fall. Typically, the hormones insulin and glucagon would automatically be released to control blood glucose, but alcohol interferes with this process. Because the brain needs glucose to function properly, a low blood glucose level can contribute to the feelings of fatigue, weakness, mood changes, irritability, and anxiety often experienced during a hangover.[26, 27]

In addition to hormones that regulate blood glucose levels, alcohol can interfere with other hormones. Alcohol negatively affects parathyroid hormone and other bone-strengthening hormones, which can increase the risk of osteoporosis.[28, 29] Alcohol can also increase estrogen levels in women, which may increase the risk of breast cancer.[30] Drinking alcohol can affect reproductive hormones and is associated with both male and female sexual dysfunction and infertility.

Alcohol and Liver Disease

The liver bears the brunt of the impact of overconsumption of alcohol, so it's not surprising that individuals who drink in excess over a long period of time are likely to develop **alcohol liver disease,** a condition that kills more than 12,000 people each year.[31] The disease develops in three stages, although some stages can occur simultaneously.

Stage 1: The first stage is **fatty liver** (**Figure 7.10**), which can result from just a weekend or a few days of excessive drinking. Because alcohol metabolism takes top priority in the liver, the metabolism of other nutrients, including fats, will take a back seat to alcohol. The metabolic reactions of alcohol cause a buildup of NADH and NADP, which disrupts the breakdown of fatty acids for energy. Fatty acids that are not metabolized accumulate in the liver cells, resulting in fatty liver. The liver tries to reduce this accumulation of fatty acids by transporting them away from the liver into the blood. The result is *hyperlipemia*—an excess of fat in the blood, which contributes to atherosclerosis (see Chapter 5).

alcohol liver disease A degenerative liver condition that occurs in three stages: (1) fatty liver, (2) alcoholic hepatitis, and (3) cirrhosis.

fatty liver Stage 1 of alcohol liver disease, in which fat begins to build up in the liver cells.

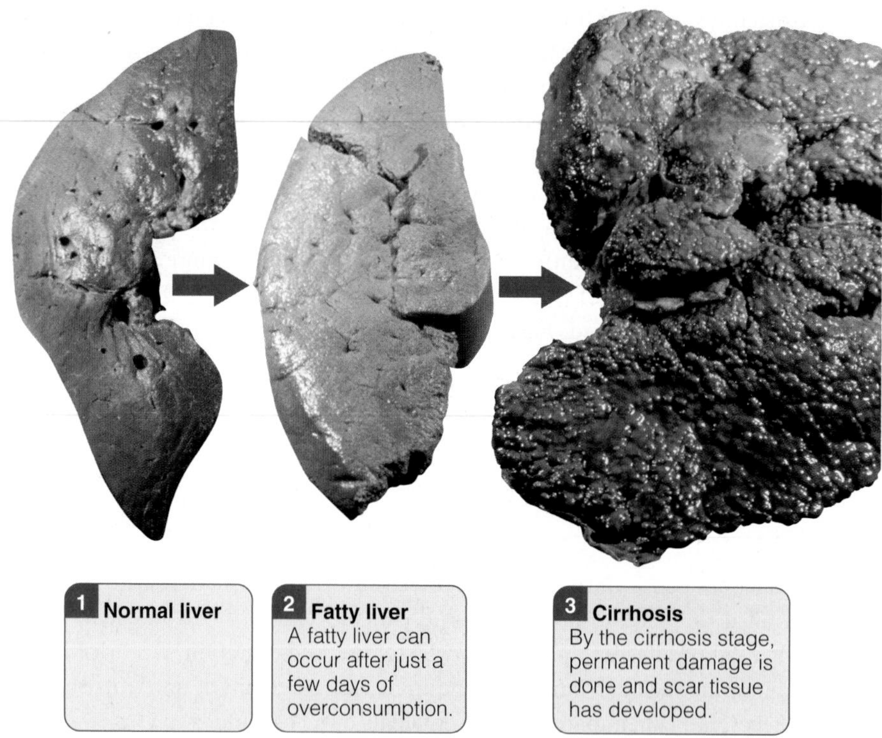

1 Normal liver
2 Fatty liver
A fatty liver can occur after just a few days of overconsumption.
3 Cirrhosis
By the cirrhosis stage, permanent damage is done and scar tissue has developed.

▲ Figure 7.10 **The Progression of Alcohol Liver Disease**

As fat accumulates in the liver, the liver's ability to perform vital functions is impaired. For example, the liver can't make bile for fat digestion, produce proteins needed for blood clotting, or remove dangerous toxins from the blood. In addition, the hydrogen ions created during the conversion of ethanol to acetaldehyde and acetaldehyde to acetate lower the pH, making the liver more acidic. The good news is that at this stage a fatty liver can reverse itself *if* the alcohol consumption is stopped.

Stage 2: If the drinking doesn't stop, the second stage of liver disease, **alcoholic hepatitis,** can develop. In alcoholic hepatitis, the various by-products of alcohol metabolism, such as acetaldehyde and free radicals (review the discussion of free radicals in Chapter 5), irritate the liver. Acetaldehyde inhibits liver function, while free radicals damage cells by reacting with their proteins, lipids, and DNA. Nausea, vomiting, fever, jaundice, and loss of appetite are signs of alcoholic hepatitis. Chronic, excessive amounts of alcohol may also impair the immune system, which can contribute to liver damage and increase the susceptibility to pneumonia and other infectious diseases.

Heavy drinking can also cause the increased passage of destructive **endotoxins,** which are released from bacteria in the intestines into the blood. Once an endotoxin arrives in the liver, it can cause the release of substances called **cytokines** that further damage healthy liver cells. Alcoholic hepatitis can last for years before progressing to the most serious stage of liver disease. If someone is diagnosed with alcoholic hepatitis, alcohol use must cease to reverse this condition or, in more advanced cases, prevent it from progressing to cirrhosis.

Stage 3: As many as 70 percent of individuals with alcoholic hepatitis develop **cirrhosis,** the final stage of alcohol liver disease. Cirrhosis occurs with continued bouts of heavy drinking, as chronic inflammation further injures and kills the liver

alcoholic hepatitis Stage 2 of alcohol liver disease, in which the liver becomes inflamed.

endotoxins Damaging products produced by intestinal bacteria that travel in the blood to the liver and initiate the release of cytokines.

cytokines Substances that damage liver cells and lead to scarring.

cirrhosis Stage 3 of alcohol liver disease, in which liver cells die and are replaced by scar tissue.

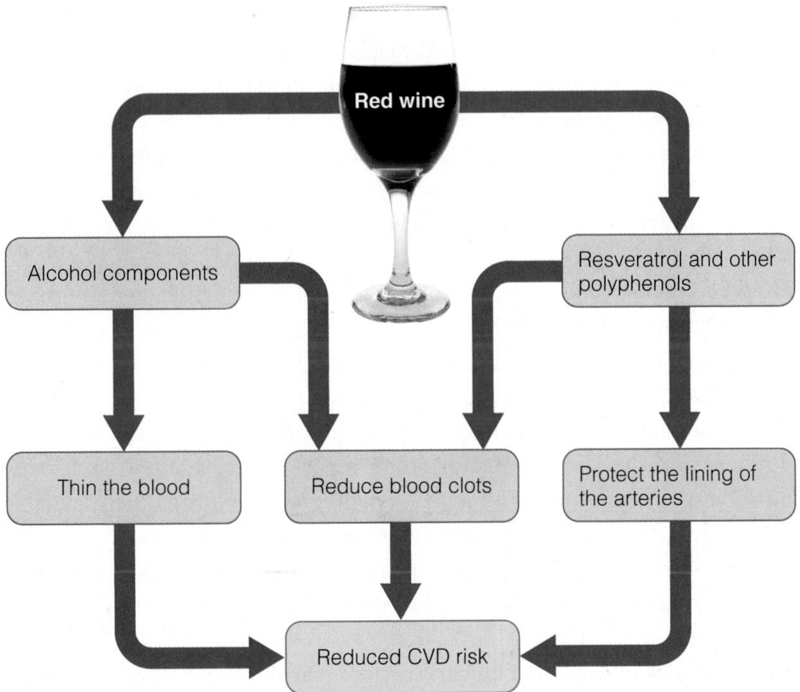

▲ **Figure 7.11 How Red Wine May Affect the Risk of Cardiovascular Disease**
Red wine may have a greater potential to reduce the risk of cardiovascular disease (CVD) than beer or spirits. Its phenolic compounds appear to be beneficial by reducing LDL oxidation; the alcohol itself affects the risk of CVD by thinning the blood.

Adapted from S. D. Wollin and P. J. H. Jones, "Alcohol, Red Wine and Cardiovascular Disease," *Journal of Nutrition* 131 (2001): 1401–1404.

cells and causes more scarring. The scar tissue prevents the liver from performing critical metabolic roles, such as filtering toxins and waste products in the blood and out of the body. If toxins and waste products build up, it can lead to mental confusion, nausea, tremors or shakiness, and even coma.

By the time scar tissue develops, the liver is permanently damaged, and only a liver transplant will cure the condition. Cirrhosis is the second leading cause of the need for liver transplants in the United States; liver damage due to hepatitis C virus is the most common reason. The survival rate for those with cirrhosis is grim: More than 50 percent of individuals with the condition die within four years.[32]

Alcohol and Cardiovascular Disease

Alcohol has both favorable and adverse effects on the risks associated with cardiovascular disease (CVD). Moderate alcohol intake (up to three drinks a day) may lower CVD risk by increasing the levels of HDL cholesterol, decreasing LDL cholesterol and lipoprotein(a), and/or reducing clot formations in both men and women.[33, 34] Numerous studies have reported a reduction of 25 to 40 percent risk of heart disease, stroke, and sudden death with a moderate intake of wine.[35] The research also reports that, because of the higher amounts of antioxidants called polyphenols in red wine, it may contribute a stronger positive benefit than either beer or spirits. As illustrated in **Figure 7.11**, the resveratrol and other polyphenols in red wine appear to protect the lining of the blood vessels from oxidation (discussed in Chapter 5). The polyphenols also appear to reduce *thrombosis,* or the formation of blood clots that are made inside a blood vessel and can block blood flow. The reduction in blood clots may be related more to the alcohol in wine than to polyphenols. Researchers hypothesize that red wine reduces levels of proteins involved in blood clotting, as well as reducing platelet stickiness, which results in thinning the blood. The benefits appear to be the same whether or not an individual has heart disease, type 2 diabetes, high blood pressure, or other forms of CVD.

However, higher intakes of alcohol (more than three drinks per day) have the opposite effect, and increase the risk of developing or dying from cardiovascular disease. Studies have reported that alcohol may stimulate the synthesis of cholesterol in the liver, which increases blood lipids such as cholesterol.[36]

Drinking more than two drinks a day is considered an important determinant of hypertension. The Nurses' Health Study reported that adult women between 30 and 55 years of age who drank more than 20 grams of alcohol per day (about 2 drinks) had an increase in hypertension.[37] In fact, compared with nondrinkers, both men and women drinking 6 to 8 drinks in one day had increased systolic blood pressure of more than 9 mm Hg, and their diastolic blood pressure went up more than 5 mm Hg.[38]

Excessive amounts of alcohol can trigger a **cardiac arrhythmia,** which likely plays a role in the sudden deaths of some alcoholics.[39] In addition, alcohol can cause **cardiac myopathy,** a condition in which the heart enlarges and becomes weak, thin, and unable to pump blood effectively throughout the body. Excessive drinking plus a poor diet can result in heart failure over time.

Alcohol Can Harm the Digestive Organs

Alcohol reduces the effectiveness of the lower esophageal sphincter in contracting and preventing stomach acids from refluxing back into the esophagus. The more alcohol consumed, the more acid that can reflux and damage the lining of the esophagus. Chronic inflammation can be a stepping stone to esophageal cancer.[40] Heavy drinkers also have increased incidences of **gastritis** (*gastr* = stomach, *itis* = inflammation) and stomach ulcers. Chronic consumption of alcohol can also cause pancreatitis, a painful inflammation of the pancreas.[41]

Alcohol and Cancer

In addition to the damaging effects of alcohol on the liver, heart, esophagus, and pancreas, alcohol consumption contributes to the risk of developing cancers, including cancers of the mouth, esophagus, liver, colon or rectum, and breast. Cancer of the mouth is six times greater in people who drink alcohol. Individuals who smoke while drinking alcohol increase their chances of developing esophageal cancer, as well as mouth and throat cancer, as the alcohol exacerbates the cancer-causing effects of cigarettes.[42] Alcohol is the primary cause of liver cancer, which is often preceded by cirrhosis of the liver. Breast cancer studies have shown a relationship to alcohol intake. The more alcohol consumed, the greater the risk. Some cancer studies have suggested a link of alcohol intake to colorectal cancer, but the evidence is not yet conclusive.

How alcohol contributes to cancer is not well understood, but it probably relates to the toxic effects of acetaldehyde. Research is currently being conducted to test whether or not folate supplements may reduce cancer risk in those who consume alcohol.

cardiac arrhythmia A disturbance in the beating and rhythm of the heart; can be caused by excessive alcohol consumption.

cardiac myopathy Condition in which the heart becomes thin and weak and is unable to pump blood throughout the body; also called disease of the heart muscle.

gastritis Inflammation of the lining in the stomach.

Alcohol Can Put a Healthy Pregnancy at Risk

When a pregnant woman drinks, she is never drinking alone—her fetus becomes her drinking partner. Alcohol easily crosses the placenta and enters the bloodstream of the fetus through the umbilical cord. Because the baby is developing, the alcohol isn't metabolized in the underdeveloped organs as quickly as in the mother's body. This results in the baby's BAC becoming higher and staying higher longer than the mother's, potentially causing serious damage to its central nervous system, particularly the brain. Because researchers do not fully understand when alcohol ingestion might be safe, zero alcohol ingestion during pregnancy is the only safe approach to ensure zero risk for the fetus.

Ultimately, a child exposed to alcohol in utero may be born with **fetal alcohol syndrome (FAS)** and exhibit numerous debilitating symptoms, including facial abnormalities such as eyes with very small openings and thin upper lips (**Figure 7.12**). They may not physically grow as normally as other children their age, and they are likely to have mental and behavioral difficulties, such as reduced attention span and memory, and learning disabilities.[43]

FAS is the leading cause of mental retardation and birth defects in the United States. Children with FAS often have problems in school and in interacting socially with others, poor coordination, low IQ, and problems with everyday living. Approximately 4 million infants each year in the United States experienced prenatal exposure to alcohol, and up to an estimated 6,000 babies are born with FAS.[44]

Recently a newer term, **fetal alcohol spectrum disorders (FASDs),** which includes FAS, has been adopted by major health organizations to describe a wide range of conditions that can occur in children exposed to alcohol in utero.[45] Not all children exposed to alcohol during pregnancy experience *all* of the physical, mental, and behavioral abnormalities seen in FAS, which is the severe end of the FASDs. However, no matter the degree of abnormalities, FASDs are permanent. The only proven, safe amount of alcohol a pregnant woman can consume is *none*. Women should avoid alcohol if they think they are, or could become, pregnant.

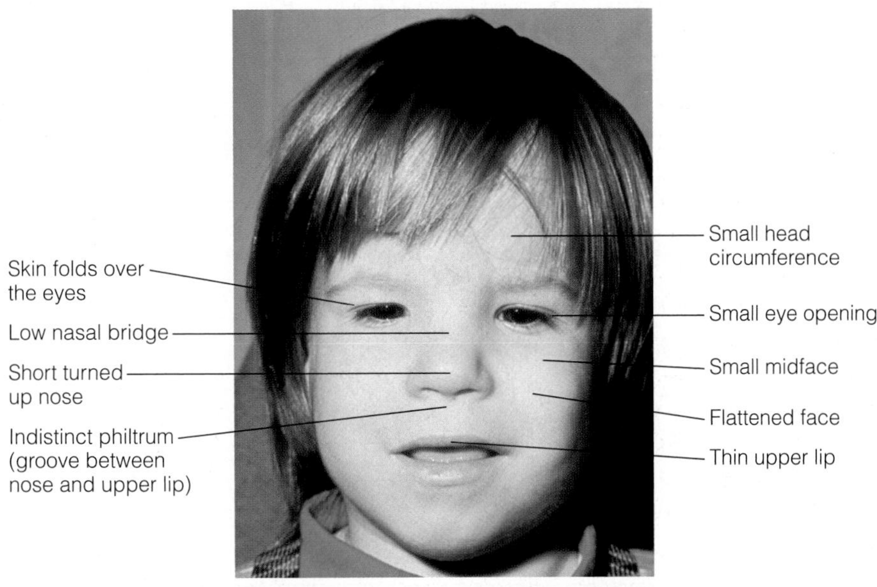

▲ **Figure 7.12 Fetal Alcohol Syndrome**
Children born with fetal alcohol syndrome often have facial abnormalities.

fetal alcohol syndrome (FAS) The most severe of the fetal alcohol spectrum disorders (FASDs); children with FAS will display physical, mental, and behavioral abnormalities.

fetal alcohol spectrum disorders (FASDs) A range of conditions that can occur in children who are exposed to alcohol in utero.

THE TAKE-HOME MESSAGE The short-term consequences of excessive drinking include unintentional injuries, disrupted sleep, hangovers, and the addition of extra kilocalories to the diet, which can lead to weight gain. Long-term consequences can include hormone imbalances; malnutrition; damage to the digestive organs, heart, and liver; increased risk of cancer and heart disease, and irreversible damage to a developing fetus during pregnancy. Individuals with alcohol liver disease can experience a fatty liver and deterioration of the liver that develops into alcohol-related hepatitis and cirrhosis.

Putting It All Together

Unlike carbohydrates, protein, fat, vitamins, minerals, and water, alcohol is not an essential nutrient, but it contributes kilocalories to the diet. Alcohol is not digested, but some is absorbed directly in the stomach and quickly enters the blood. Alcohol can displace essential nutrients and contribute extra kilocalories to the diet, which can help lead to weight gain. For some middle-aged and older adults, alcohol in moderation may help reduce the risk of certain diseases, such as heart disease. The *Dietary Guidelines* recommend that individuals who do not drink should not start, and those who choose to drink should do so only in moderation.

Visual Chapter Summary

1 Alcohol Is Produced by Fermentation of Sugars

Ethanol is the type of alcohol in alcoholic beverages. Ethanol isn't poisonous when ingested, but it can be toxic if consumed in excess. Alcohol is not an essential nutrient, having very little nutritional value, but it does provide kilocalories. In beer and wine production, alcohol is produced by the fermentation of sugars by yeast. In liquor, distillation is used to concentrate the alcohol produced by fermentation.

H
H—C—H
H—C—H
OH
Ethanol

2 Alcohol Is Absorbed in the Stomach and Small Intestine and Circulates in the Blood

Some alcohol is absorbed into the bloodstream directly in the stomach but most alcohol is absorbed in the small intestine. Alcohol mixes with water and is distributed in the watery tissues of the body. Some of the alcohol remains in the blood and is continually circulated in the fluid portions of the body until it is finally metabolized. A person's gender, age, ethnicity, the amount of food in the stomach, and the quantity of alcohol consumed affect the rate of absorption and metabolism in the body. Some alcohol in the blood is lost in the breath and urine.

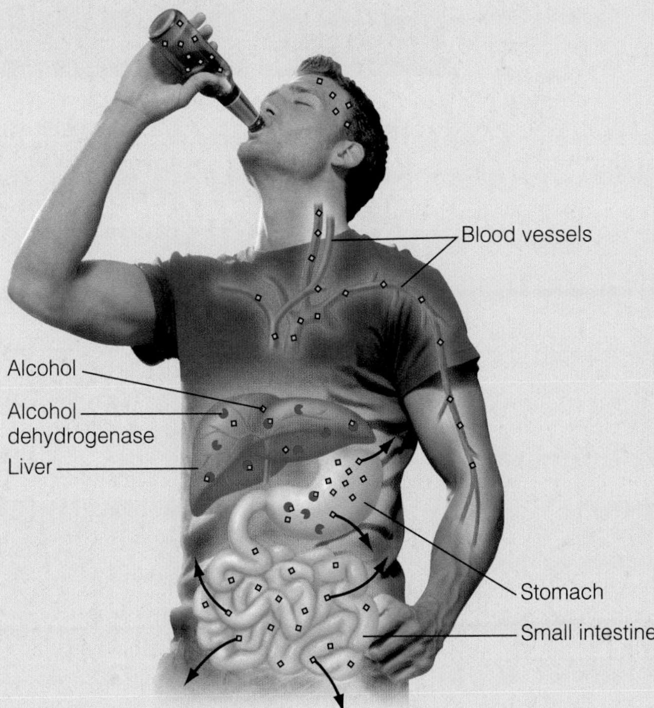

3 Alcohol Is Metabolized in the Stomach and the Liver

Some alcohol is metabolized in the stomach by the enzyme alcohol dehydrogenase before it can be absorbed. However, most of the alcohol is metabolized in the liver with another form of ADH and the enzyme acetaldehyde dehydrogenase (ALDH). The microsomal ethanol oxidizing system (MEOS) is a secondary pathway that takes over alcohol metabolism if the ALDH pathway is overwhelmed. MEOS is also the primary pathway for drugs and pharmaceuticals, but alcohol takes precedence over these substances.

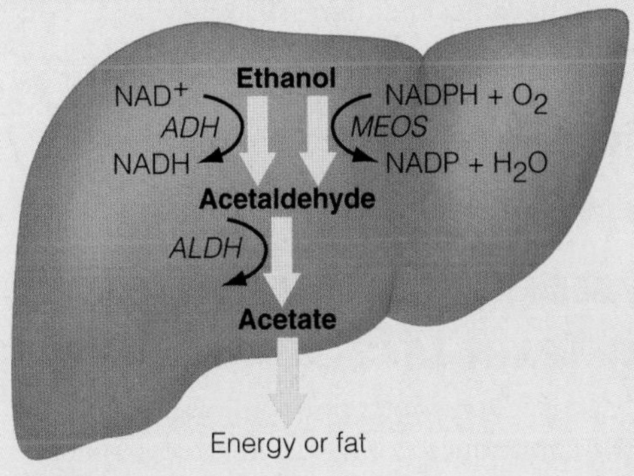

4 Alcohol Affects the Central Nervous System

Alcohol is a central nervous system depressant. The brain is sensitive to the effects of alcohol, and, depending on the amount consumed, alcohol can cause numerous mental, behavioral, and physical changes in the body. Alertness, judgment, and coordination will initially be affected. Higher BACs can cause impaired vision, speech, reasoning, and balance. Alcohol poisoning (usually at a BAC of 0.30 or higher) can result in impaired breathing and heart rate, and can ultimately lead to death.

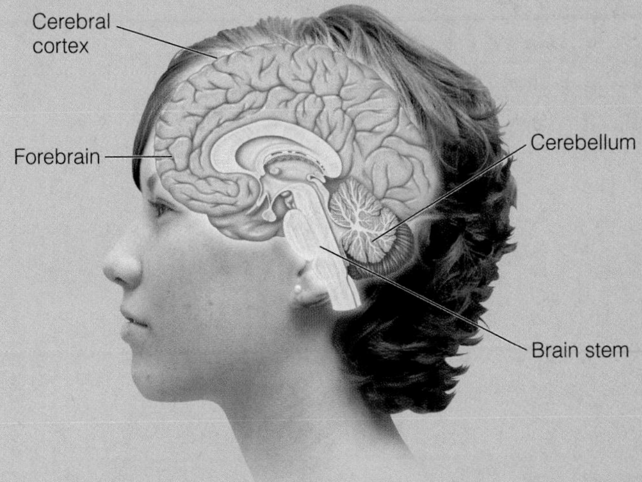

5 Alcohol Should Be Consumed Only in Moderation, and May Have Some Health Benefits

Moderate drinking is defined as the amount of alcohol that puts the individual and others at the lowest risk of alcohol-related problems. No one needs to drink alcohol, but those who choose to drink should do so in moderation, which is up to one drink a day for women and up to two drinks a day for men, with a standard drink containing ½ ounce of alcohol. Moderate alcohol consumption may reduce the risk of heart disease, diabetes and metabolic syndrome, and increase longevity in middle-aged to older adults. Alcohol consumption provides no health benefits for younger adults.

6 Alcohol Can Have Both Short-Term and Long-Term Effects on the Body and Brain

Alcohol can lead to unintentional injuries, disrupted sleep and hangovers; interfere with hormones; contribute to excess kilocalorie intake; and displace healthier food choices from the diet. Chronically consuming excessive amounts of alcohol can harm the digestive organs, heart, and liver and can lead to cancer. Alcohol can put a fetus at risk for fetal alcohol spectrum disorders.

The liver is damaged from excess alcohol consumption. The three stages of alcohol liver disease are fatty liver, alcoholic hepatitis, and cirrhosis. Many individuals die annually of alcohol-related liver disease

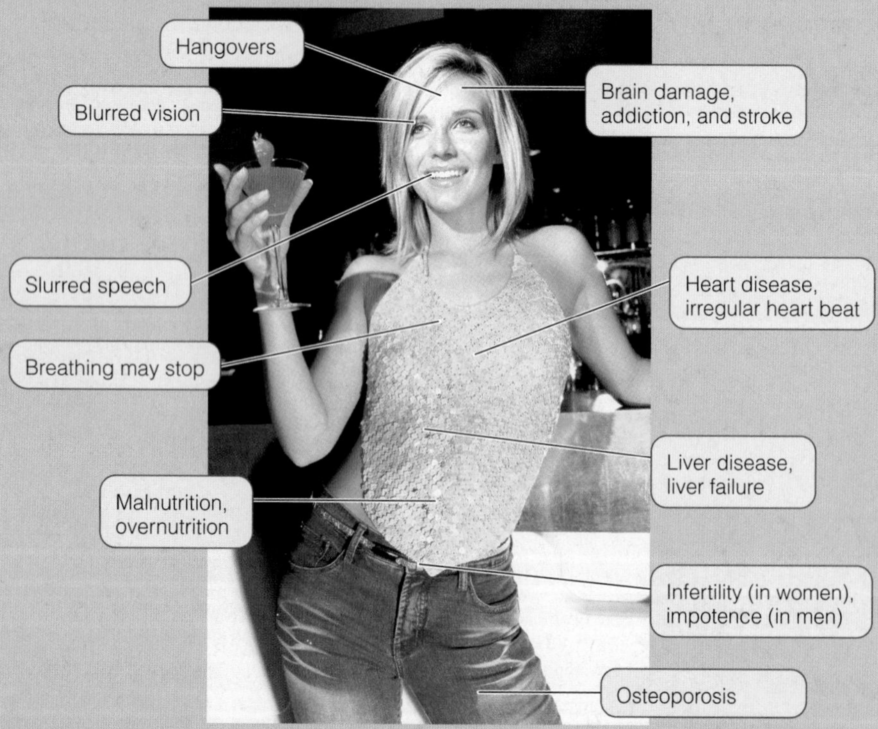

7 Alcohol Abuse and Alcoholism Negatively Affect One's Life and Health

Alcohol abuse, such as binge drinking, underage drinking, and drinking and driving, occurs when people continue to consume alcohol even though this behavior negatively affects their lives. Individuals who binge drink are at risk for blackouts and alcohol poisoning. Alcoholism is a disease characterized by four symptoms: a craving for alcohol, a higher tolerance for alcohol, the inability to control or limit its intake, and a physical dependence on it. Though alcoholism can't be cured, it can be treated with medical and psychological support.

Terms to Know

- ethanol
- fermentation
- distillation
- proof
- alcohol dehydrogenase (ADH)
- acetaldehyde
- acetaldehyde dehydrogenase (ALDH)
- microsomal ethanol oxidizing system (MEOS)
- alcohol tolerance
- microsomes
- hangover
- cirrhosis
- blood alcohol concentration (BAC)
- moderate drinking
- congeners
- Wernicke-Korsakoff syndrome
- alcohol liver disease
- fatty liver
- alcohol hepatitis
- cytokines
- cardiac arrhythmia

MasteringNutrition™

Build your knowledge—and confidence!—in the Study Area of MasteringNutrition with a variety of study tools.

Check Your Understanding

1. Alcohol, also known as ethanol, is made by the process known as
   a. distillation.
   b. fermentation.
   c. malting.
   d. germination.
2. A standard drink is
   a. a 12-ounce can of beer.
   b. a 5-ounce glass of wine.
   c. a shot (1.5 ounces) of liquor.
   d. any of the above.
3. The majority of alcohol is
   a. absorbed through the mucosa lining the mouth.
   b. absorbed slowly on an empty stomach.
   c. absorbed mainly through the small intestine into the blood.
   d. absorbed directly into the liver through the lymph system.
4. _______________ is the enzyme that begins metabolizing alcohol in the liver and the stomach.
   a. Sucrase
   b. Insulin
   c. Alcohol dehydrogenase (ADH)
   d. Ethanol
5. MEOS is
   a. the enzyme system found in the liver that metabolizes alcohol and drugs.
   b. an intermediate compound formed during the metabolism of alcohol.
   c. the chemical that causes the symptoms related to a hangover.
   d. a form of liver disease.
6. Which of the following statements is true?
   a. All areas of the brain are affected equally even when only a small amount of alcohol is consumed.
   b. Drinking an excessive amount of alcohol can shut down the reticular activating system (RAS) in the brain that controls consciousness.
   c. The more alcohol you consume, the greater the effect on the forebrain that controls walking and talking.
   d. Alcohol stimulates the central nervous system.
7. Individuals who chronically drink excessively are at increased risk for
   a. malnutrition.
   b. gastritis.
   c. inflammation of the esophagus.
   d. all of the above.
8. The four characteristics of alcoholism are (1) a craving for alcohol, (2) the development of a higher tolerance for alcohol, (3) the inability to control or limit the intake of alcohol, and (4) _______________.
   a. the inability to keep a stable job
   b. the inability to maintain social relationships
   c. the tendency to become violent
   d. the development of a dependency on alcohol
9. Short-term consequences of heavy alcohol consumption include
   a. unintentional injuries.
   b. sleep disruption.
   c. a hangover.
   d. all of the above.
10. Drinking four to five alcoholic beverages on one occasion in a span of two hours is called
    a. alcoholism.
    b. drunk driving.
    c. a blackout.
    d. binge drinking.

Answers

1. (b) Alcohol found in alcoholic beverages is made by fermentation of natural sugars in grains such as glucose and maltose and fruit sugar or fructose by yeast. After fermentation, liquors go through a distillation process, which concentrates the beverage. Beer is made by germinating cereal grains to convert starch into sugar, referred to as malting. The sugar is then fermented by yeast to make beer.
2. (d) All of these drinks contain ½ ounce of alcohol, so each is considered a standard drink.
3. (c) Most alcohol is absorbed through the small intestine into the blood, where it is taken up by the liver and metabolized. Some alcohol is also absorbed through the stomach on an empty stomach, but absorption is reduced after eating. Alcohol is water soluble and therefore is not absorbed through the lymph system. Alcohol is not absorbed through the mouth.
4. (c) ADH is the enzyme in the stomach and the liver that begins metabolizing alcohol. Sucrase is an enzyme that breaks down the sugar sucrose. Insulin is a hormone, not an enzyme, which regulates blood glucose levels. Ethanol is the chemical name for the form of alcohol found in alcoholic beverages.
5. (a) The term MEOS (microsomal ethanol oxidizing system) refers to a set of enzymes found in the liver that oxidize ethanol when the consumption is greater than the ADH enzymes can handle. This system also oxidizes drugs. The MEOS does not refer to an intermediate compound, or a compound that causes the symptoms of a hangover.
6. (b) Excessive alcohol can shut down the reticular activating system in the brain, causing unconsciousness. The more alcohol you consume, the more areas of the brain are affected. Alcohol affects the cerebellum, which controls walking, while the forebrain controls behavior. Alcohol is a depressant, not a stimulant.
7. (d) All of the above. When too much alcohol is chronically consumed, more nutritious foods are often displaced in the diet, increasing the risk of malnutrition. A constant intake of alcohol will not only cause irritation and inflammation of the esophagus, but also the stomach.
8. (d) The last characteristic of alcoholism is the development of a dependency on alcohol, such that a withdrawal will cause symptoms

in the body. Although alcoholism can have financial consequences such as job instability, interfere with personal relationships, and increase the risk of violence, not all individuals with alcoholism have these experiences.

9. (d) All of the above. Alcohol is a toxin. Drinking in excess can put your personal safety at risk, cause sleep disruptions, and result in an unpleasant hangover.
10. (d) Consuming that much alcohol in a very short time is considered binge drinking. Binge drinking can lead to alcoholism. Individuals who binge drink may experience blackouts or may drive while drunk.

Answers to Myths and Misconceptions

1. **False.** Although alcohol provides kilocalories, the body does not need it to function and it is therefore not an essential nutrient.
2. **False.** A straight shot of liquor may look and taste more potent than a can of beer, but they contain the same amount of alcohol.
3. **True.** Red wine does contain heart-healthy, phytochemical compounds.
4. **True.** Women have less body water and less of the enzyme that metabolizes alcohol in the stomach; they therefore respond more quickly to the narcotic effects of alcohol than do men.
5. **False.** In general, the body can only metabolize about one drink per $1^1/_2$ hours.
6. **False.** Drinking more alcohol isn't going to take away the ill effects of a hangover. The only cure for a hangover is time.
7. **True.** However, not all alcoholic beverages contain equal amounts of kilocalories. In fact, some mixed drinks can contain almost as many kilocalories as a meal.
8. **True.** Overconsumption of alcohol can lead to displacement of more nutritious foods, and diminish the body's ability to absorb or use some essential nutrients.
9. **False.** Moderate drinking is defined as up to one drink per day for women and up to two drinks per day for men. Drinking several alcoholic beverages in one sitting is binge drinking, not moderate drinking.
10. **False.** Although counseling is an important component of alcoholism recovery, there is no cure for alcoholism.

Web Resources

- For research-based information about alcohol abuse and binge drinking among college students, visit www.collegedrinkingprevention.gov
- For more information about alcohol and your health, visit the National Institute on Alcohol Abuse and Alcoholism (NIAAA) at www.niaaa.nih.gov
- For more information about alcohol consumption and its consequences, visit the National Center for Chronic Disease Prevention and Health Promotion, Alcohol and Public Health, at www.cdc.gov/alcohol/index.htm
- For an overview of the risks and benefits of alcohol, visit The Harvard School of Public Health, The Nutrition Source, *Alcohol: Balancing Risks and Benefits* at www.hsph.harvard.edu/nutritionsource/what-should-you-eat/alcohol-full-story/index.html

References

1. Centers for Disease Control and Prevention. 2011. *Alcohol Use and Health.* Available at www.cdc.gov. Accessed April 2012.
2. National Institute on Alcohol Abuse and Alcoholism. 2008. *Statistical Snapshot of College Drinking.* Available at www.niaaa.nih.gov. Accessed April 2012.
3. National Institute on Alcohol Abuse and Alcoholism. 2003. *Understanding Alcohol: Investigations into Biology and Behavior.* Available at http://pubs.niaaa.nih.gov. Accessed April 2012.
4. Mandelbaum, D. G. 1965. Alcohol and Culture. *Current Anthropology* 6:281–288.
5. Austin, E., and S. Hust. 2005. Targeting Adolescents? The Content and Frequency of Alcoholic and Nonalcoholic Beverage Ads in Magazine and Video Formats November 1999–April 2000. *Journal of Health Communications* 10:769–785.
6. Austin, E., M. Chen, and J. Grube. 2006. How Does Alcohol Advertising Influence Underage Drinking? The Role of Desirability, Identification, and Skepticism. *Journal of Adolescent Health* 38:376–384.
7. U.S. Department of Agriculture. 2010. *Report of the Dietary Guidelines Advisory Committee 2010.* Available at www.cnpp.usda.gov/Publications/DietaryGuidelines/2010/DGAC/Report/D-7-Alcohol.pdf. Accessed April 2012.
8. Goldberg, I. J., L. Mosca, M. R. Piano, and E. A. Fisher. 2001. Wine and Your Heart. A Science Advisory for Healthcare Professionals from the Nutrition Committee, Council on Epidemiology and Prevention, and Council on Cardiovascular Nursing of the American Heart Association. *Circulation* 103:472–475.
9. National Institute on Alcohol Abuse and Alcoholism. 2007. *Alcohol Metabolism: An Update.* Available at http://pubs.niaaa.nih.gov. Accessed April 2012.
10. Oneta, C., U. Simanowski, M. Martinez, A. Allali-Hassani, X. Pares, N. Homann, C. Conradt, et al. 1998. First-Pass Metabolism of Ethanol Is Strikingly Influenced by the Speed of Gastric Emptying. *Gut* 43:612–619.
11. Finnigan, F., R. Hammersley, and K. Millar. 1998. Effects of Meal Composition on Blood Alcohol Level, Psychomotor Performance and Subjective State after Ingestion of Alcohol. *Appetite* 31:361–375.
12. Jones, A. W. and K. A. Jonsson. 1994. Food-Induced Lowering of Blood-Ethanol Profiles and Increased Rate of Elimination Immediately After a Meal. *Journal of Forensic Sciences* 39:1084–1093.
13. Roine, R. P., R. T. Gentry, R. T. Lim, E. Helkkonen, M. Salaspuro, and C. S. Lieber. 1993. Comparison of Blood Alcohol Concentrations After Beer and Whiskey. *Alcoholism: Clinical and Experimental Research* 17:709–711.
14. Prakash, O. and S. Nelson. 2002. Alcohol and Liver Disease. *The Ochsner Journal* 4:241–244.
15. Dong, X., L. M. Hines, M. J. Stampfer, and D. J. Hunter. 2001. Genetic Variation in Alcohol Dehydrogenase and Myocardial Infarction. *New England Journal of Medicine* 345:221–222.
16. Wechsler, H. and T. F. Nelson. 2008. What We Have Learned from the Harvard School of Public Health College Alcohol Study: Focusing Attention on College Student Alcohol Consumption and the Environmental Conditions That Promote It. *Journal of Studies on Alcohol and Drugs* 69:481–490.
17. National Institute on Alcohol Abuse and Alcoholism. 1998. *Alcohol Alert: Alcohol and Sleep.* Available at http://pubs.niaaa.nih.gov. Accessed April 2012.

18. Roehrs, T., D. Beare, F. Zorick, and T. Roth. 1994. Sleepiness and Ethanol Effects on Simulated Driving. *Alcoholism: Clinical and Experimental Research* 18:154–158.
19. Swift, R. S. and D. Davidson. 1998. Alcohol Hangover: Mechanisms and Mediators. *Alcohol Health and Research World* 22:54–60.
20. Ibid.
21. Lieber, C. S. 2000. Alcohol: Its Metabolism and Interaction with Nutrients. *Annual Review of Nutrition* 20:394–430.
22. Ibid.
23. Liu, S., M. K. Serdula, D. F. Williamson, A. H. Modkad, and T. Byers. 1994. A Prospective Study of Alcohol Intake and Change in Body Weight Among US Adults. *American Journal of Epidemiology* 140:912–920.
24. Economos, C. D., M. L. Hildebrandt, and R. R. Hyatt. 2008. College Freshman Stress and Weight Change: Differences by Gender. *American Journal of Health Behavior* 32:16–25.
25. Tolstrup, J. S., J. Halkjaer, B. L. Heitmann, A. M. Tjonneland, K. Overvad, T. I. A. Sorensen, and M. N. Gronbaek. 2008. Alcohol Drinking Frequency in Relation to Subsequent Changes in Waist Circumference. *American Journal of Clinical Nutrition* 87:957–963.
26. National Institute on Alcohol Abuse and Alcoholism. 2003. *State of the Science Report on the Effects of Moderate Drinking.* Available at http://pubs.niaaa.nih.gov. Accessed April 2012.
27. National Institute on Alcohol Abuse and Alcoholism. 1998. *Alcohol Alert: Alcohol and Hormones.* Available at http://pubs.niaaa.nih.gov. Accessed April 2012.
28. Garcia-Sanchez, A., J. L. Gonzalez-Calvin, A. Diez-Ruiz, J. L. Casals, F. Gallego-Rojo, and D. S. Vatierra. 1995. Effect of Acute Alcohol Ingestion on Mineral Metabolism and Osteoblastic Function. *Alcohol* 30:449–453.
29. Perry, H. M., M. Horowitz, S. Fleming, F. E. Kaiser, P. Patrick, J. E. Morley, W. Cushman, et al. 1998. Effect of Recent Alcohol Intake on Parathyroid Hormone and Mineral Metabolism in Men. *Alcoholism: Clinical and Experimental Research* 22:1369–1375.
30. Fan, S., Q. Meng, B. Gao, J. Grossman, M. Yadegari, I. D. Goldberg, and E. M. Rosen. 2000. Alcohol Stimulates Estrogen Receptor Signaling in Human Breast Cancer Cell Lines. *Cancer Research* 60:5635–5639.
31. National Institute on Alcohol Abuse and Alcoholism. 2000. *Alcohol and the Liver: Research Update.* Available at http://pubs.niaaa.nih.gov. Accessed April 2012.
32. Ibid.
33. Srivastava, L. M., S. Vasisht, D. P. Agarwal, and H. W. Goedde. 1994. Relation Between Alcohol Intake, Lipoproteins and Coronary Heart Disease: The Interest Continues. *Alcohol* 29:11–24.
34. Agarwal, D. P. 2002. Cardioprotective Effects of Light–Moderate Consumption of Alcohol: A Review of Putative Mechanisms. *Alcohol* 37:409–415.
35. Goldberg, I. J., et al. 2001. Wine and Your Heart.
36. Visiolia, F., S. Montia, C. Colomboa, and C. Gallia. 1998. Ethanol Enhances Cholesterol Synthesis and Secretion in Human Hepatomal Cells. *Alcohol* 15:299–303.
37. Witteman, J. C., W. C. Willett, and M. J. Stampfer. 1990. Relation of Moderate Alcohol Consumption and Risk of Systemic Hypertension in Women. *American Journal of Cardiology* 65:633–637.
38. Klatsky, A. L., G. D. Friedman, and M. A. Armstrong. 1986. The Relationships Between Alcoholic Beverage Use and Other Traits to Blood Pressure: A New Kaiser Permanente Study. *Circulation* 73:628–636.
39. Rosenqvist, M. 1998. Alcohol and Cardiac Arrhythmias. *Alcoholism: Clinical and Experimental Research* 22:318s–322s.
40. National Institute on Alcohol Abuse and Alcoholism. 2005. *Finding May Explain Link Between Alcohol and Certain Cancers.* Available at http://pubs.niaaa.nih.gov. Accessed April 2012.
41. Lerch, M. M., E. Albrecht, M. Ruthenburger, J. Mayerle, W. Halangk, and B. Kruger. 2003. Pathophysiology of Alcohol-Induced Pancreatitis. *Pancreas* 27:291–296.
42. National Institute on Alcohol Abuse and Alcoholism. 2007. *Alcohol Alert: Alcohol and Tobacco.* Available at http://pubs.niaaa.nih.gov. Accessed April 2012.
43. Jones, K. and D. Smith. 1973. Recognition of the Fetal Alcohol Syndrome in Early Infancy. *The Lancet* 2:999–1001.
44. Ibid.
45. Centers for Disease Control. 2011. *Fetal Alcohol Syndrome Disorders.* Available at www.cdc.gov. Accessed April 2012.

8 Your Body's Metabolism

Chapter Objectives

After reading this chapter, you will be able to:

1. Define metabolism and provide examples of anabolic and catabolic reactions and the role of hormones regulating these reactions.
2. Explain the role of adenosine triphosphate (ATP) as an energy source for cells.
3. Compare and contrast the major metabolic pathways that carbohydrates, fatty acids, glycerol, and amino acids follow to produce ATP.
4. Explain how metabolism changes during the absorptive, postabsorptive, and starvation stages of food intake.
5. Describe the metabolism of alcohol.
6. Describe the causes, diagnosis, symptoms, and dietary treatments of the most common inborn errors of metabolism.

1. Metabolism takes place within cells. T/F
2. The body prefers to use carbohydrates for fuel because very little energy is needed to break them down during metabolism. T/F
3. Fructose is preferable to glucose as an energy source. T/F
4. Lactate buildup during exercise causes a burning sensation in the legs. T/F
5. Excess dietary protein is stored in the muscle and therefore increases muscle size. T/F
6. Fat is the main fuel used during high-intensity energy metabolism. T/F
7. Alcohol is converted to blood sugar during metabolism. T/F
8. B vitamins provide energy. T/F
9. Kilocalories consumed after 7:00 p.m. are automatically stored as fat and contribute to weight gain. T/F
10. Children with inborn errors of metabolism will outgrow such disorders when they reach puberty. T/F

See page 319 for answers to these Myths and Misconceptions.

Every second of every day, your cells produce a steady supply of energy from the foods you eat. There are hundreds of complex chemical reactions needed to transform energy-yielding macronutrients in food to a form of energy the cells can use. The cells then adjust to times when you feed and times when you aren't eating to provide a continuous, uninterrupted source of energy.

Understanding these intricate energy-producing reactions is an important aspect of the study of nutrition. This may seem a little daunting as you begin to study these processes, but remember that the process is not unlike assembling a jigsaw puzzle. Once the first pieces are in place, the larger picture begins to take shape and the later pieces are easier to understand.

In this chapter we'll discuss the chemical reactions within the pathways and how the individual nutrients—the pieces—flow into this larger metabolic puzzle. We will discuss how the body adapts to the day-to-day changes in dietary intake and what happens when metabolic processes fail to work properly.

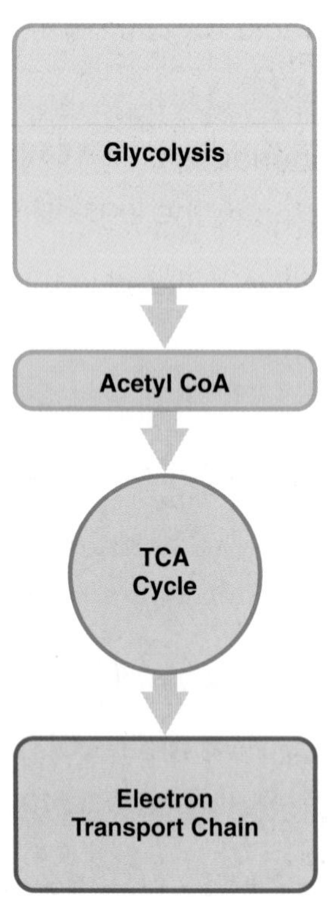

▲ **Figure 8.1 The Stages of Metabolism**
The chemical reactions of metabolism include glycolysis, the intermediate reaction of pyruvate to acetyl CoA, the TCA cycle, and the electron transport chain.

What Is Metabolism?

How does a kilocalorie from food transform into the energy required to throw a baseball, open a door, or think through a math equation? The answer can be summed up in one word: **metabolism.**

Metabolism is the sum of all the chemical reactions that take place within the 10 trillion cells in the body. These chemical reactions follow a **metabolic pathway** of reactions in which the product of one reaction is the starting substance for the next reaction. This chapter will focus on the metabolic pathways involved with energy production beginning with *glycolysis*, and follow the chemical reactions through the completion of the *electron transport chain.* **Figure 8.1** illustrates the big picture of the stages in which food is transformed into metabolic by-products and energy.

Each of the chemical reactions within these pathways produces a change in energy as a new bond is formed or old bonds are broken. For example, when glucose is stored as glycogen, new bonds form, which requires energy, whereas when glycogen is broken down to yield glucose, energy is released. The energy that is produced when the bonds are broken can be produced anaerobically (without oxygen) or aerobically (with oxygen), depending on the fuel that is available and the amount of oxygen within the cell.

Because the body constantly needs energy, metabolism never stops. The major energy nutrient, glucose, keeps metabolism flowing from the first stage through the final stage, much like electricity streaming through electrical wires. If the electricity stops, the lights go out. Other macronutrients—fatty acids and amino acids—contribute to metabolism as they are transformed into different substrates along the pathway. These metabolic processes continue to adapt and shift, whether you're in the middle of a meal or fasting during sleep, to maintain a continual source of energy for the cells.

Metabolism Takes Place within Cells

The chemical reactions involved in energy production and storage take place within the body's cells. Even though different cells perform different metabolic functions, their structure is similar (**Figure 8.2**). All cells have an outer envelope, called the *plasma membrane*, which holds in the cell's contents, and several specialized internal structures, called *organelles*. The organelles shown in Figure 8.3 include the ribosomes, nucleus, endoplasmic reticulum, and the mitochondria.

One particular organelle, the **mitochondrion** (plural: mitochondria), is referred to as the powerhouse of the cell. The mitochondria generate most of the cell's energy through aerobic metabolism. Almost all body cells contain mitochondria. The exception is the red blood cells, which produce energy anaerobically in the **cytosol,** or fluid portion of the cell.

metabolism The sum of all chemical reactions in the body.

metabolic pathway A sequence of reactions that convert compounds from one form to another.

mitochondrion A cellular organelle that produces energy from carbohydrates, proteins, and fats; *pl.* mitochondria.

cytosol The fluid portion of the cell where anaerobic metabolism takes place.

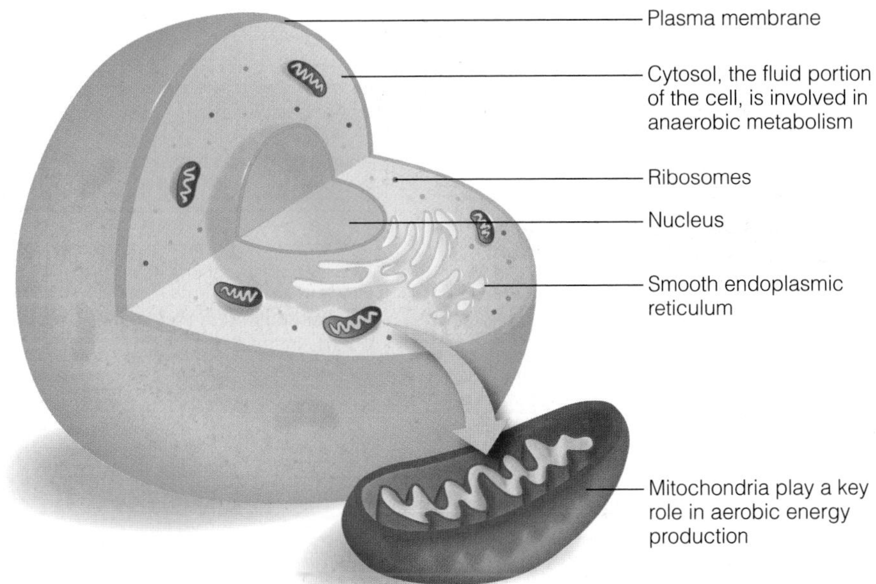

◂ **Figure 8.2 Metabolism Takes Place within Cells**
The mitochondrion is a metabolically active organelle located in the cytoplasm of a cell. Other cell structures involved in metabolism include the cytosol, where glycolysis takes place; the ribosomes, which help manufacture proteins; and the smooth endoplasmic reticulum, which produces lipids used by the organelles.

Other organelles also participate in metabolism. The ribosomes, for example, help to manufacture proteins (as you learned in Chapter 6), and the smooth endoplasmic reticulum produces lipids used by the other organelles.[1]

Metabolism allows the body to convert energy from foods into energy needed for physical activity.

The Liver Plays a Central Role in Metabolism

The most metabolically active organ in the body is the liver. Once nutrients have been absorbed, the liver is the first organ to metabolize, store, or send them through the blood to other tissues. In previous chapters you learned that the proteins, carbohydrates, and fats in foods are digested and absorbed as amino acids, monosaccharides, glycerol, and fatty acids, respectively. The liver splits these nutrients into different molecules through a series of chemical reactions to produce energy or to synthesize new compounds—for instance, converting essential amino acids into nonessential amino acids. The liver also stores these nutrients to use in the future, such as storing glucose as glycogen.

Metabolism Is a Series of Chemical Reactions

Metabolic reactions within each stage can be as simple as only two to three chemical reactions, or they can be much more complex and require many more reactions to complete each stage.

Anabolic Reactions

As mentioned earlier in the chapter, chemical reactions involved in metabolism either absorb energy for the reaction or they produce energy (**Figure 8.3**). **Anabolic reactions** generally use or absorb energy to combine simpler molecules into larger, more complex ones. For example, single amino acids join to form larger proteins, excess glucose molecules combine in a branched-chain structure to form glycogen for storage in the liver and muscle, and excess fatty acids attach to glycerol molecules and are stored as triglycerides in adipocytes.

anabolic reactions Metabolic reactions that combine smaller compounds into larger molecules.

Catabolic Reactions

Catabolic reactions are the opposite of anabolic processes: They provide the energy or ATP to fuel anabolic reactions. Catabolic processes break down large molecules

catabolic reactions Metabolic reactions that break large compounds into smaller molecules.

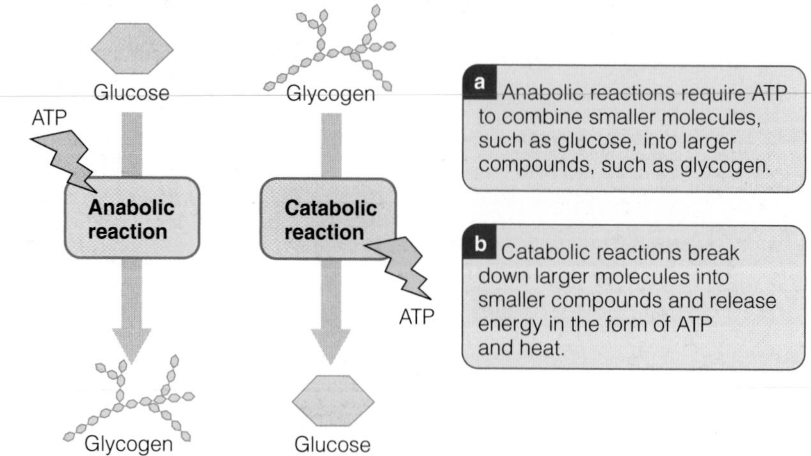

▲ **Figure 8.3 Anabolic and Catabolic Reactions**
Metabolic processes involve both anabolic and catabolic reactions.

into simple structures that can be used for energy, recycled for their individual parts, or excreted. For example, larger glycogen molecules can be hydrolyzed to yield smaller molecules of glucose, and triglycerides are disassembled to yield fatty acids and glycerol. The smaller glucose, fatty acid, and glycerol molecules are then transformed through the stages of metabolism to produce energy. In both catabolic and anabolic reactions, some of the energy is released as heat.

Enzymes and Hormones Regulate Metabolism

Enzymes and their assistant coenzymes enable the chemical reactions of metabolism to occur at fast enough rates to maintain normal body function. Nearly every metabolic reaction requires a specific enzyme to catalyze the reaction and, in some cases, the enzyme is assisted by a coenzyme, or helper, that is often a vitamin. For example, the B vitamin niacin in its coenzyme form NAD^+ and riboflavin in its coenzyme form FAD assist enzymes by accepting or donating electrons and hydrogen ions produced during oxidation-reduction reactions (see the Chemistry Boost).

Anabolic and catabolic reactions can also be regulated by hormones. When the endocrine system detects a change in the concentration of nutrients, such as when blood glucose levels rise, hormones are released that influence whether enzymes are

Chemistry Boost

Oxidation-Reduction Reactions

We obtain energy during metabolism by oxidation-reduction reactions (also called redox reactions), which involve the transfer of electrons. Oxidation reactions involve the loss of an electron, while reduction reactions gain an electron. These reactions happen in sets: When an oxidation reaction occurs and one molecule loses an electron, another molecule is reduced and gains an electron.

During glycolysis, glucose is oxidized to pyruvate by the coenzyme form of the B vitamin niacin (NAD^+), which acts as the oxidizing agent. Glucose loses an electron to NAD^+, which in turn is reduced to NADH.

Here is the oxidation-reduction reaction in glycolysis:

$$2\ NAD^+ + \text{glucose} \rightarrow 2\ \text{pyruvate} + 2\ NADH + 2\ H^+$$

TABLE 8.1 The Major Hormones That Control Metabolism

Hormone	Produced by	Type of Reaction	Control of Protein Metabolism	Control of Carbohydrate Metabolism	Control of Fat Metabolism
Insulin	Pancreas	Anabolic	Stimulates protein synthesis	Stimulates glycogen synthesis	No effect
Glucagon	Pancreas	Catabolic	Stimulates protein degradation	Stimulates glycogenolysis	Stimulates lipolysis
Epinephrine	Adrenal glands	Catabolic	No effect	Stimulates glycogenolysis	Stimulates lipolysis
Cortisol	Adrenal glands	Catabolic	Stimulates protein degradation	Stimulates gluconeogenesis	No effect

activated or deactivated to regulate the metabolic pathways. For instance, the hormone insulin lowers blood glucose levels by allowing the movement of glucose into the cells. Further, within the cells, insulin controls the metabolic fate of glucose. Three other hormones, namely glucagon, epinephrine, and cortisol, can also influence metabolism and result in an increase in blood glucose by stimulating glycogenolysis. Table 8.1 outlines the major hormones controlling anabolic and catabolic reactions.

THE TAKE-HOME MESSAGE Metabolism is the sum of all metabolic processes that occur in cells. Most of these reactions take place within the mitochondria. Metabolic processes use energy to build new substances through anabolic reactions or produce energy by breaking molecules apart through catabolic reactions. Enzymes catalyze the reactions involved in metabolism along with the aid of coenzymes, and hormones, including insulin, glucagon, epinephrine, and cortisol, regulate these reactions.

What Is the Energy Currency That Fuels Metabolism?

All body actions require energy, whether you're running a marathon or lying in bed. Further, the more difficult the action, the more energy the body needs to fuel it. For example, your body must produce much more energy to lift a 50-pound bag of dog food than to lift a 5-pound bag of flour. You know by now that the source of fuel for all this energy production is food.

However, before your body can use the energy in the cereal, fruit, and toast you ate for breakfast, it must first disassemble the macronutrients, build them into new compounds, and transform them into the high-energy molecule **adenosine triphosphate**, or **ATP**. Any source of macronutrients can be transformed into ATP, but some, such as energy drinks, are not always the best choices (read more in Examining the Evidence: Can Energy Drinks Alter Your Metabolism?).

Adenosine Triphosphate Is the Cell's Energy Currency

ATP is the only source of energy that can be used directly by cells. The process of disassembling food to create ATP actually requires some ATP to convert the food into energy and more ATP. (In other words, you have to "spend" ATP to make ATP.) The cells then use that ATP to fuel other metabolic processes.

ATP is made of adenine (a nitrogen-containing compound), ribose (a five-carbon sugar), and three phosphate groups (which contain phosphorus and oxygen). The energy is stored in the bonds that connect the phosphate groups to each other.

adenosine triphosphate (ATP) A high-energy molecule composed of adenine, ribose, and three phosphate molecules; cells use this to fuel all biological processes.

EXAMINING THE EVIDENCE

Can Energy Drinks Alter Your Metabolism?

In 2011, young adults in the United States spent over $9 billion on energy drinks, including brands such as Red Bull, Monster, and Hype.[1] Why are these drinks so popular, particularly with college-aged adults? The answer, at least in part, is that many people believe that energy drinks boost metabolism.

Energy Drinks Contain Caffeine

Energy drinks contain a combination of ingredients, including caffeine and an assortment of amino acids, herbs, sugar, and B vitamins. The main ingredient is caffeine, a well-known central nervous system stimulant that makes some people feel more alert and energized, and others jittery. In addition to its stimulating effects, caffeine has also been shown to promote lipolysis,[2] enhance the rate of fatty acid oxidation, and decrease the utilization of glycogen. In other words, when you ingest caffeine, you burn more fat to produce energy and spare glycogen stores.[3] Though this might sound like an easy recipe for weight loss, the reality is that consuming too much caffeine can have negative health effects. Until further research has been conducted, caffeine should not be considered a weight-loss aid.

Herbs such as guarana and ginseng are also frequent ingredients in energy drinks. In addition to putting extra caffeine into the beverage (guarana can add 40 milligrams of caffeine for every gram of guarana added to the drink), these substances may also enhance the effects of the caffeine.

Side Effects of Caffeine

Though people vary in their responses to caffeine, overall it is a strong stimulant, and the amount of caffeine contained in an energy drink is sufficient to boost heart rate and raise blood pressure. In some individuals, caffeine can cause anxiety and diminish the ability to concentrate, as well as impact sleep and cause insomnia. Whereas ingesting high amounts of caffeine may help you stay awake during an all-night study session, your classroom performance is actually more likely to suffer due to lack of adequate sleep.

Though it was once known as a diuretic, caffeine does not appear to be as dehydrating as researchers once thought.[4, 5] Caffeine does stimulate the kidneys to excrete more water, but the fluid intake from drinking a caffeinated beverage probably offsets the diuresis stimulated by the caffeine.

Most people should limit caffeine intake to no more than 300 milligrams of caffeine per day, the amount found in three 8-ounce cups of coffee or four cans of Red Bull (see table). This amount has not been found to cause health concerns for most individuals.

Energy Drinks and Alcohol

The rise in popularity of mixing energy drinks with alcoholic beverages, such as vodka, has been cause for concern in the last decade.[6, 7] Caffeine and alcohol affect the central nervous system in opposite ways: Ethanol acts as a depressant, while caffeine is a stimulant. The concern is that combining alcohol with caffeine may make you feel less intoxicated even though your reaction time is impaired.

To address these concerns, researchers tested volunteers using a double-blind study on motor coordination, visual reaction times, and feelings of intoxication after drinking either alcohol alone, alcohol mixed with a popular brand of energy drink, or the energy drink alone. The results suggested that drinking alcohol with an energy drink causes the same level of intoxication as alcohol alone, but the individual feels more energetic and less impaired than if he or she had only consumed alcohol.[8] The results also showed that drinking an energy drink with alcohol is likely to raise heart rate higher than drinking either the alcohol or the energy drink alone.[9]

Combining alcohol with caffeine is also more likely to result in injury. One study found that students who consume "energy drink cocktails" are at double the risk of injury, needing medical attention, and driving with intoxicated drivers as those who don't mix energy drinks with alcohol.[10]

Blending alcohol with caffeine can also have a negative impact on bone health. Excessive consumption of either alcohol or caffeine can reduce the mineralization of

Energy drinks claim to increase mental alertness and boost your metabolism.

Caffeine Content of Energy Drinks and Common Beverages

Beverage	Serving Size (fl oz)	Energy (kcal/8 oz)	Caffeine (mg/serving)	Other Ingredients
Starbucks brewed coffee	12	0	140.0	Water
5-Hour Energy	2.0	15	138.0	Taurine, vitamins
Rockstar Zero Calorie	8.0	10.0	120.0	Taurine, carnitine, Yerba Mate, vitamins, minerals
Wired	8.0	5.0	99.0	Inositol, vitamins
Monster Lo-Carb	8.3	100	80.0	Taurine, inositol, ginseng, guarana, carnitine, vitamins, minerals
Full Throttle	8.0	110	72.0	Taurine, guarana, carnitine, ginseng, vitamins
Amp	8.4	120	69.6	Taurine, guarana, ginseng, maltodextrin
Red Bull	8.3	109	66.7	Taurine, inositol, vitamins
Red Bull Sugarfree	8.3	0	64.7	Taurine, inositol, aspartame, vitamins
Mountain Dew MDX	12	120	48.2	Ginseng, taurine, guarana, maltodextrin
Tea (black)	12	0	45.0	Water
Coca-Cola Classic	12	140	34.0	High-fructose corn syrup
Pepsi	12	150	37.0	High-fructose corn syrup

bone. The combination of the two could pose an increased risk for osteoporosis for both men and women.[11]

The consumption of energy drinks alone, due to their caffeine content, should be limited as part of your total caffeine intake for the day. No more than 200 to 300 milligrams of caffeine should be consumed per day. Because the mix of energy drinks and alcohol can lead to serious health consequences, individuals are advised to abstain from this practice.

The impact of energy drinks on altering one's metabolism is still unclear. What is clear, however, is that the side effects of mixing energy drinks with alcohol can put your health at risk.

References

1. WTHITV. 2012. *Energy Drink Sales Skyrocket.* Available at www.wthitv.com/dpp/news/local/energy-drinks-sales-skyrocket. Accessed April 2012.
2. Servane, R., M. Ferruzzi, I. Cristiana, J. Moulin, K. Mace, K. Acheson, and L. Tappy. 2007. Effect of a Thermogenic Beverage on 24-Hour Energy Metabolism in Humans. *Obesity* 15:349–355.
3. Acheson, K. J., G. Gremaud, I. Meirim, F. Montigon, Y. Krebs, L. B. Fay, L. J. Gay, et al. 2004. Metabolic Effects of Caffeine in Humans: Lipid Oxidation or Futile Cycling? *American Journal of Clinical Nutrition* 79:40–46.
4. Armstrong, L. 2002. Caffeine, Body Fluid-Electrolyte Balance, and Exercise Performance. *International Journal of Sport Nutrition and Exercise Metabolism* 12:189–206.
5. Armstrong, L. E., A. C. Pumerantz, M. W. Roti, D. A. Judelson, G. Watson, J. C. Dias, B. Sokmen, et al. 2005. Fluid, Electrolyte, and Renal Indices of Hydration During 11 Days of Controlled Caffeine Consumption. *International Journal of Sport Nutrition and Exercise Metabolism* 15:252–265.
6. Ferreira, S. E., M. T. de Mello, M. V. Rossi, and M. Souza-Formigoni. 2006. Effects of Energy Drink Ingestion on Alcohol Intoxication. *Alcoholism: Clinical and Experimental Research* 30:598–605.
7. Oteri, A., F. Salvo, A. Caputi, and G. Calapai. 2007. Intake of Energy Drinks in Association with Alcoholic Beverages in a Cohort of Students of the School of Medicine of the University of Messina. *Alcoholism: Clinical and Experimental Research* 31:1677–1680.
8. Ferreira, S. E., et al. 2006. Effects of Energy Drink Ingestion.
9. Ferreira, S. E., M. T. de Mello, M. V. Rossi, and M. Formigoni. 2004. Does an Energy Drink Modify the Effects of Alcohol in a Maximal Effort Test? *Alcoholism: Clinical and Experimental Research* 28:1408–1412.
10. Wake Forest University Baptist Medical Center. 2007. Energy Drink "Cocktails" Lead to Increased Injury Risk, Study Shows. *Science Daily.* www.sciencedaily.com/releases/2007/11/071104191538.htm. Accessed April 2012.
11. Hansen, S. A., A. R. Folson, L. H. Kushi, and T. A. Sellers. 2002. Association of Fractures with Caffeine and Alcohol in Postmenopausal Women: The Iowa Women's Health Study. *Public Health Nutrition* 3:253–261.

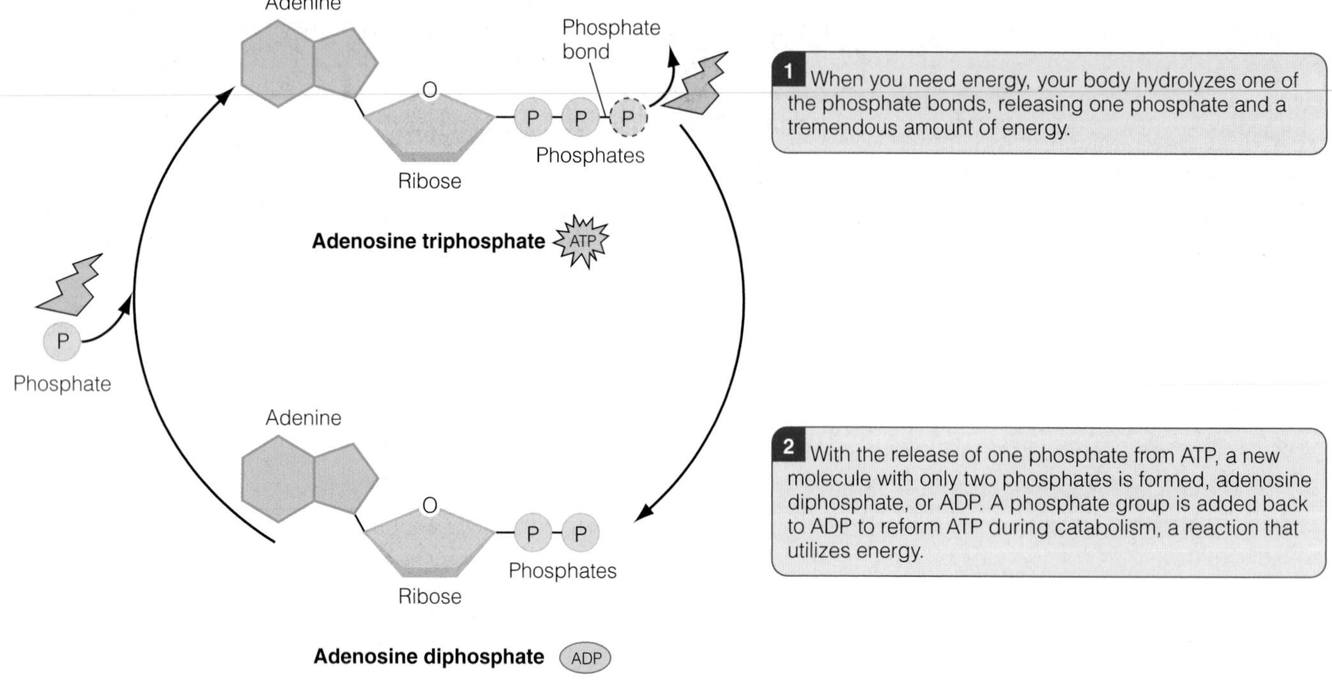
Adenine
Phosphate bond
O
P
P
P
Phosphates
Ribose
1 When you need energy, your body hydrolyzes one of the phosphate bonds, releasing one phosphate and a tremendous amount of energy.
Adenosine triphosphate
ATP
P
Phosphate
Adenine
O
P
P
Phosphates
Ribose
2 With the release of one phosphate from ATP, a new molecule with only two phosphates is formed, adenosine diphosphate, or ADP. A phosphate group is added back to ADP to reform ATP during catabolism, a reaction that utilizes energy.
Adenosine diphosphate
ADP

▲ **Figure 8.4 ATP to ADP**
The high-energy molecule adenosine triphosphate (ATP) releases energy to be used by the cells when the phosphate bond is broken, producing adenosine diphosphate (ADP).

As **Figure 8.4** illustrates, when you need energy, one of the bonds connecting the phosphate groups is hydrolyzed, which releases one phosphate *plus* a tremendous amount of energy. The new molecule that is formed is called **adenosine diphosphate,** or **ADP.**

At any given moment, cells only have 3 to 5 seconds' worth of ATP available for immediate use. Therefore, the body must continually produce ATP to provide a constant supply of energy.

ATP Can Be Regenerated from ADP and Creatine Phosphate

Regenerating ATP from ADP requires a source of phosphate. As illustrated in Figure 8.5, the phosphate produced from the initial breakdown of ATP is one source. However, this provides only 8 to 10 seconds of energy. Another source of phosphate is **creatine phosphate,** also called phosphocreatine, or **PCr.** PCr is a high-energy compound formed in muscle cells when creatine (an amino acid structure found in foods and produced in the body) combines with phosphate. This phosphate can be released from creatine phosphate and added to ADP to form ATP. In addition, when the phosphate bond is broken, energy is released, which provides the fuel needed to restore ATP. You may have heard of the supplement creatine monohydrate, which is marketed to athletes to maximize their PCr stores. Research shows that supplemental creatine can increase performance of short-duration, high-intensity activities but may also have side effects.[2] (We'll discuss creatine supplements more in Chapter 16.)

Once the available ATP and creatine phosphate in the muscle cell is exhausted, more ATP must be produced through anaerobic and aerobic metabolic processes. Anaerobic metabolism produces more ATP per minute than aerobic metabolism, but it is very limited in its use (it only provides about 1 to 1.5 minutes

adenosine diphosphate (ADP) A nucleotide composed of adenine, ribose, and two phosphate molecules; it is formed when one phosphate molecule is removed from ATP.

creatine phosphate (PCr) A compound that provides a reserve of phosphate to regenerate ADP to ATP.

of maximal activity). Activities that primarily involve anaerobic metabolism are high-intensity, short-duration activities such as sprinting or heavy weight lifting. Aerobic metabolism produces less ATP per minute than anaerobic metabolism, but it can continue indefinitely. Low-intensity, long-duration activities, such as walking or slow jogging, primarily involve aerobic metabolism. When the demand for ATP is greater than the rate at which metabolism can produce it, the activity slows down or stops completely. This is one reason why individuals who lift weights have to rest between sets; it gives the body time to form more ATP to be used for the next set of lifts.

The transformations that convert energy stored in protein, carbohydrate, and fat into ATP are tightly integrated and somewhat complex. To learn this material, we'll break down these integrated processes by stages.

THE TAKE-HOME MESSAGE ATP is the energy source cells use to fuel metabolic reactions. No ATP is stored, thus ATP must be regenerated from ADP and phosphate (which can be donated by creatine phosphate), or produced during anaerobic or aerobic metabolism.

How Do the Macronutrients Generate ATP?

All three macronutrients—carbohydrates, proteins, and fats—generate ATP by entering the metabolic pathway at some point in the stages of metabolism. Their metabolic fate is determined by the chemical reactions within each metabolic pathway (**Figure 8.5**).

Carbohydrates are unique in that they are oxidized anaerobically in **glycolysis** (stage 1) and the intermediate stage of converting **pyruvate** to **acetyl CoA** (stage 2) and also aerobically in the **tricarboxylic acid (TCA) cycle** (stage 3) to release electrons and hydrogen ions to generate ATP in the **electron transport chain** (stage 4). Fatty acids from triglycerides are only oxidized aerobically, which is slower than anaerobic metabolism in producing ATP. The fatty acids are split from the glycerol backbone before they are metabolized and converted to acetyl CoA, while glycerol enters metabolism through glycolysis.

When amino acids from proteins are needed for energy, they are converted to substrates in the first three stages, depending on the structure of their side groups. The glucogenic amino acids can be transformed to substrates in glycolysis or into glucose through gluconeogenesis when carbohydrate intake is low. Other amino acids can be converted to acetyl CoA and intermediate substrates in the TCA cycle.

Regardless of the stage in which energy nutrients enter metabolism, they eventually all converge at acetyl CoA. Let's take a closer look at each stage.

Glycolysis Transforms Glucose to Pyruvate

The first step in forming ATP from glucose begins with glycolysis (*glyco* = glucose, *lysis* = break apart), the universal pathway for glucose oxidation. Glucose metabolism is an essential energy source for all cells and particularly the brain and red blood cells. As you follow the metabolic pathway, illustrated in **Figure 8.6**, track the carbons through the process from beginning to end.

Glycolysis is a ten-step anaerobic catabolic pathway that takes place in the cytosol of the cells. It begins with one six-carbon glucose molecule and ends with

glycolysis The breakdown of glucose; for each molecule of glucose, two molecules of pyruvate and two ATP molecules are produced.

pyruvate A three-carbon molecule formed from the oxidation of glucose during glycolysis.

acetyl CoA A two-carbon compound formed when pantothenic acid combines with acetate.

tricarboxylic acid cycle (TCA) A cycle of aerobic chemical reactions in the mitochondria that oxidize glucose, amino acids, and fatty acids, producing hydrogen ions to be used in the electron transport chain, some ATP, and by-products carbon dioxide and water.

electron transport chain The final stage of energy metabolism when electrons are transferred from one complex to another, resulting in the formation of ATP and water.

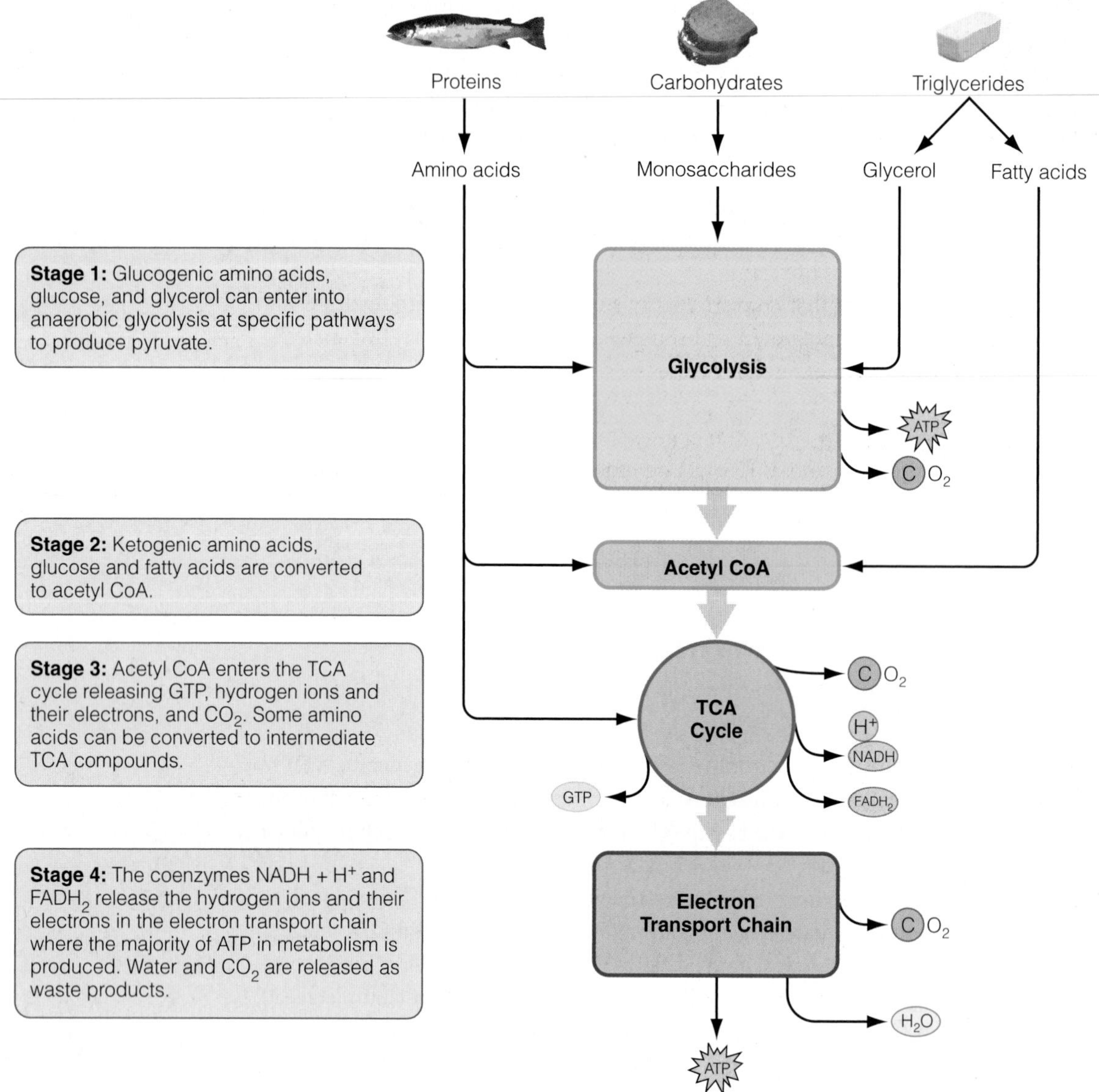

Proteins
Carbohydrates
Triglycerides
Amino acids
Monosaccharides
Glycerol
Fatty acids
Stage 1: Glucogenic amino acids, glucose, and glycerol can enter into anaerobic glycolysis at specific pathways to produce pyruvate.
Glycolysis
ATP
CO2
Stage 2: Ketogenic amino acids, glucose and fatty acids are converted to acetyl CoA.
Acetyl CoA
Stage 3: Acetyl CoA enters the TCA cycle releasing GTP, hydrogen ions and their electrons, and CO2. Some amino acids can be converted to intermediate TCA compounds.
TCA Cycle
CO2
H+
NADH
FADH2
GTP
Stage 4: The coenzymes NADH + H+ and FADH2 release the hydrogen ions and their electrons in the electron transport chain where the majority of ATP in metabolism is produced. Water and CO2 are released as waste products.
Electron Transport Chain
CO2
H2O
ATP

▲ **Figure 8.5 The Metabolic Fate of Food**
After the energy-containing nutrients have been absorbed through the small intestine, they can enter a metabolic pathway and be converted to energy, or be stored as fat for later use.

two three-carbon molecules of pyruvate and a net of two molecules of ATP.[3] The initial step absorbs or uses ATP. In this reaction, a phosphate is transferred from ATP to the sixth carbon of glucose as the glucose enters the cell, forming glucose 6-phosphate and ADP. Once glucose 6-phosphate is formed, it continues through nine more reactions until the anaerobic stage of glycolysis is complete and pyruvate is created. In addition to ATP, glycolysis also generates hydrogen ions (H^+). As you can see in Figure 8.6, the coenzyme NAD^+ picks up the hydrogen ion, changing its form to NADH, and carries the hydrogen ion to the final stage of energy production, the electron transport chain.

Fructose and Galactose

In addition to glucose, other monosaccharides, including fructose and galactose, can be used to produce ATP, but they are converted to substrates in glycolysis at different points. In muscle, fructose is first phosphorylated before it enters glycolysis

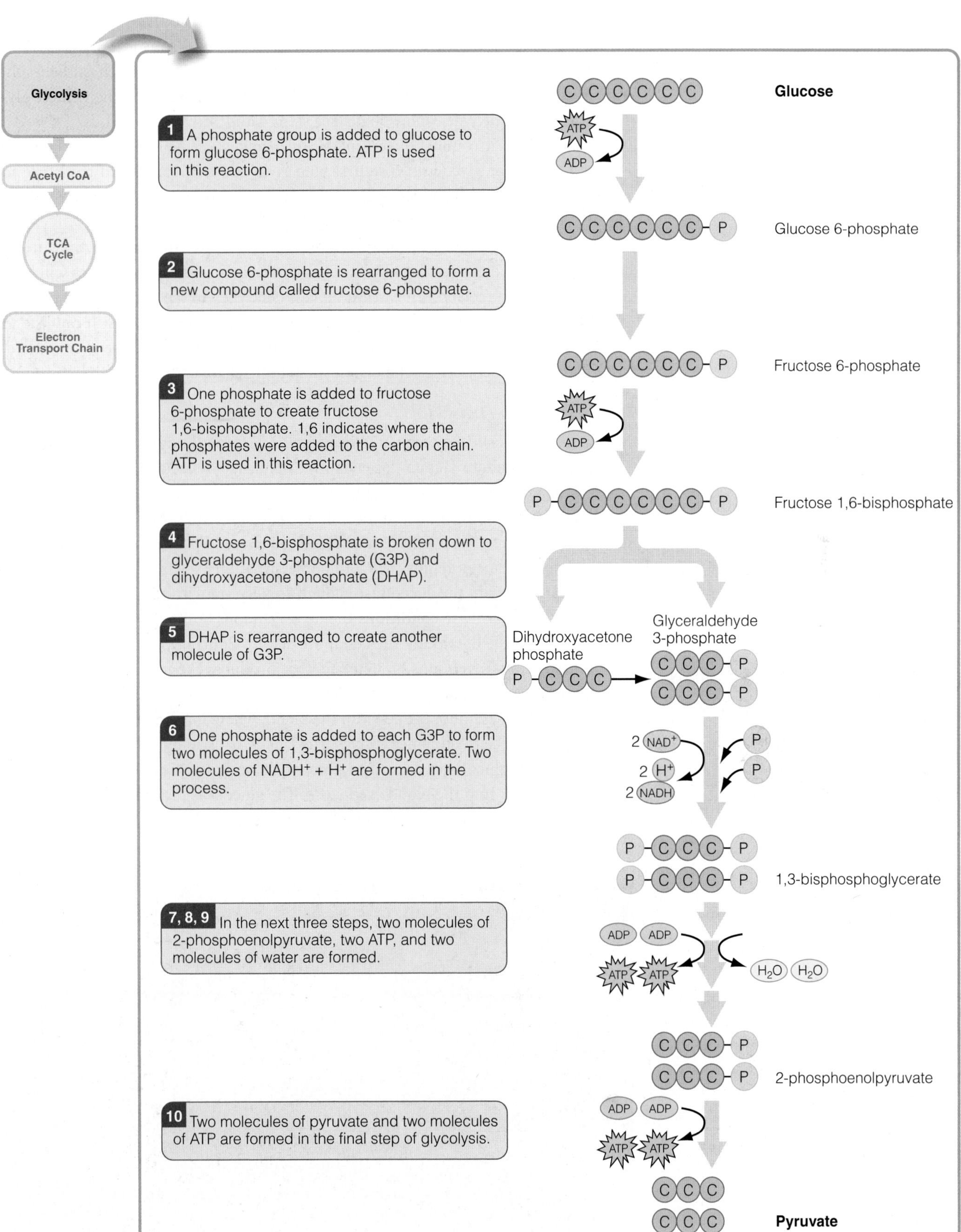

Glycolysis
Acetyl CoA
TCA Cycle
Electron Transport Chain
Glucose
1 A phosphate group is added to glucose to form glucose 6-phosphate. ATP is used in this reaction.
ATP
ADP
Glucose 6-phosphate
2 Glucose 6-phosphate is rearranged to form a new compound called fructose 6-phosphate.
Fructose 6-phosphate
3 One phosphate is added to fructose 6-phosphate to create fructose 1,6-bisphosphate. 1,6 indicates where the phosphates were added to the carbon chain. ATP is used in this reaction.
Fructose 1,6-bisphosphate
4 Fructose 1,6-bisphosphate is broken down to glyceraldehyde 3-phosphate (G3P) and dihydroxyacetone phosphate (DHAP).
5 DHAP is rearranged to create another molecule of G3P.
Dihydroxyacetone phosphate
Glyceraldehyde 3-phosphate
6 One phosphate is added to each G3P to form two molecules of 1,3-bisphosphoglycerate. Two molecules of NADH⁺ + H⁺ are formed in the process.
2 NAD⁺
2 H⁺
2 NADH
1,3-bisphosphoglycerate
7, 8, 9 In the next three steps, two molecules of 2-phosphoenolpyruvate, two ATP, and two molecules of water are formed.
H₂O H₂O
2-phosphoenolpyruvate
10 Two molecules of pyruvate and two molecules of ATP are formed in the final step of glycolysis.
Pyruvate

▲ **Figure 8.6 Glycolysis**
Glycolysis is a ten-step process that takes place in the cytosol of the cell; it converts glucose to pyruvate.

as fructose 6-phosphate (see step 3 in Figure 8.6). In the liver, fructose passes through a more complex conversion before it becomes a substrate in glycolysis. Fructose is first phosphorylated to form fructose 1-phosphate, which is then split into glyceraldehyde and dihydroxyacetone phosphate (DHAP), and then enters glycolysis as glyceraldehyde 3-phosphate (see steps 4 and 5 in Figure 8.6).

Galactose is also metabolized in the liver and must be converted to glucose before it can enter glycolysis. The first step is to add a phosphate to galactose to produce galactose 1-phosphate. After four more metabolic steps, galactose enters glycolysis as glucose 6-phosphate (see step 1 in Figure 8.6).

Each step of converting the monosaccharides into an intermediate substrate in glycolysis is directed by a specific enzyme. Deficiencies in any of these enzymes will have a distinct effect on metabolism. For example, a deficiency in the enzymes that convert galactose into glucose results in a condition known as galactosemia, which can lead to mental retardation and liver damage unless dietary intake of galactose is controlled. We will discuss genetic errors of metabolism in more detail at the end of this chapter.

Pyruvate to Lactate

Most people associate the term lactate with muscle, even though the metabolic conversion of pyruvate to lactate happens in any human cell. For this discussion we will use the muscle cell as an example.

When mitochondria lack sufficient oxygen (anaerobic metabolism), such as during intense exercise, pyruvate is reduced to **lactate** to prevent the buildup of hydrogen ions in the cell (**Figure 8.7**). In some situations, such as during strenuous exercise, lactate is not produced fast enough to keep up with the production of hydrogen ions. Under these conditions the hydrogen ions build up, which reduces the pH in the muscle cell, making the cell more acidic. Contrary to popular belief, it is the buildup of hydrogen ions, not lactate, that produces the uncomfortable "burning" sensation in the muscles after exercise.

Lactate diffuses out of the cell into the blood, where it is transferred to the liver. Once in the liver cells, enzymes convert the lactate back to pyruvate, which is then transformed by gluconeogenesis into glucose through the **Cori cycle** (**Figure 8.8**) and released back into the blood as glucose. The glucose is picked up by the muscle to begin glycolysis over again.[4] This gluconeogenic mechanism occurs mainly in

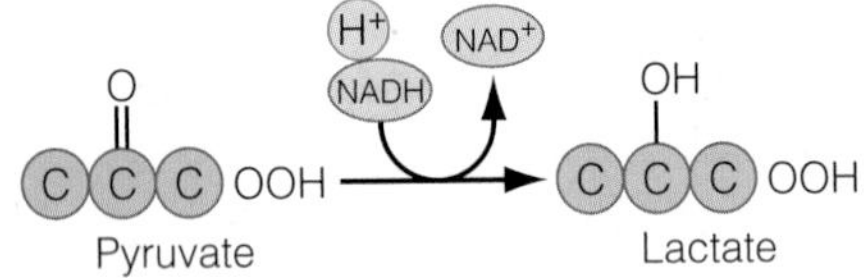

▲ **Figure 8.7 The Conversion of Pyruvate to Lactate**
Pyruvate is reduced to lactate during anaerobic metabolism and NADH is oxidized to NAD^+ that can be used in glycolysis.

Strenuous exercise can cause a buildup of hydrogen ions in the muscle.

lactate A three-carbon compound generated from pyruvate when mitochondria lack sufficient oxygen.

Cori cycle A series of metabolic reactions in liver cells that convert lactate to glucose; also called gluconeogenesis.

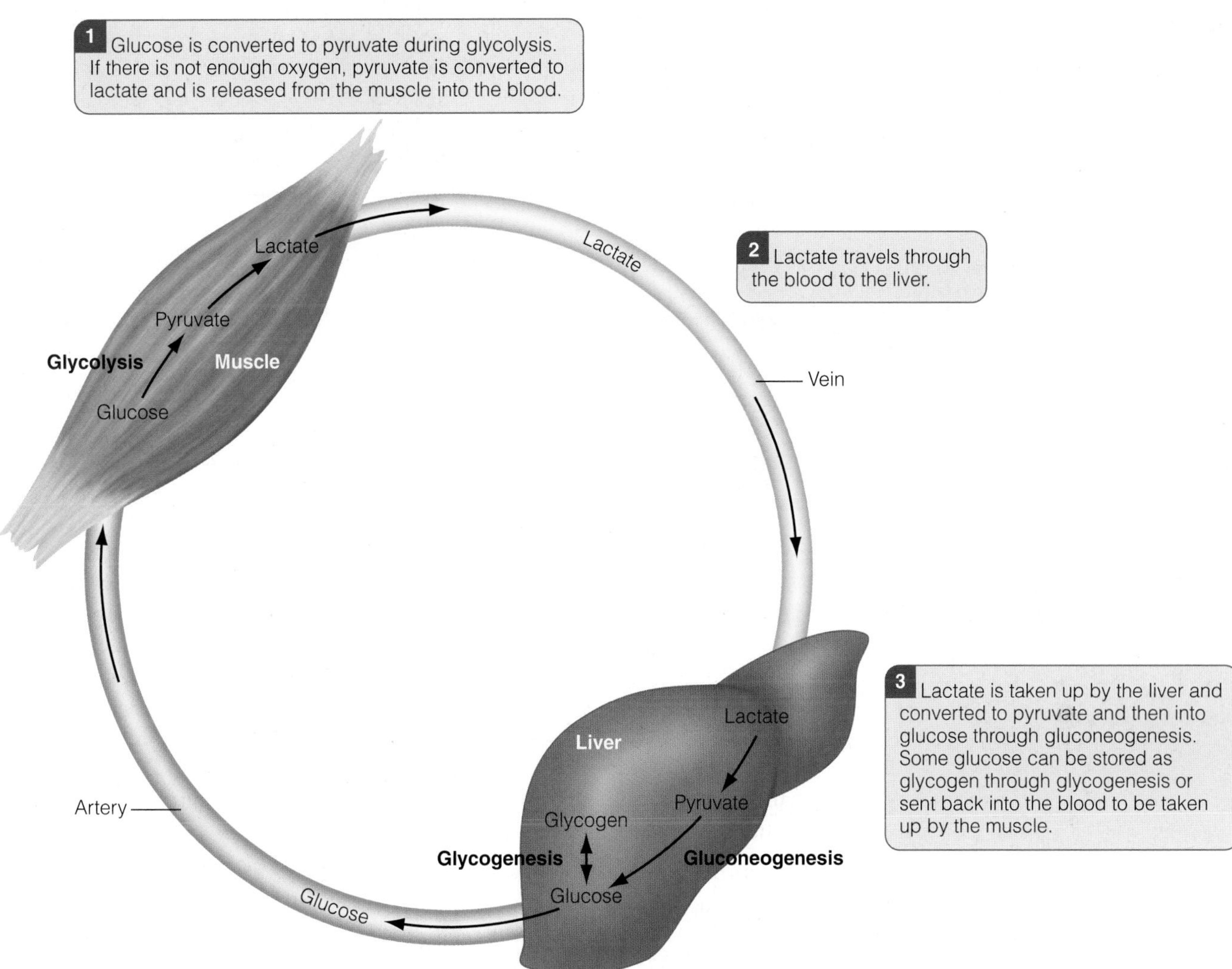

1 Glucose is converted to pyruvate during glycolysis. If there is not enough oxygen, pyruvate is converted to lactate and is released from the muscle into the blood.
Lactate
Pyruvate
Glycolysis
Muscle
Glucose
Lactate
2 Lactate travels through the blood to the liver.
Vein
3 Lactate is taken up by the liver and converted to pyruvate and then into glucose through gluconeogenesis. Some glucose can be stored as glycogen through glycogenesis or sent back into the blood to be taken up by the muscle.
Lactate
Liver
Pyruvate
Glycogen
Artery
Glycogenesis
Gluconeogenesis
Glucose
Glucose

▲ **Figure 8.8 The Cori Cycle**
The Cori cycle takes place in the liver and converts lactate to glucose.

the liver and to a lesser extent in the kidneys. The muscles do not contain the necessary gluconeogenic enzymes to catalyze the conversion of lactate to glucose.

Glucogenic Amino Acids to Pyruvate

Fourteen out of twenty amino acids are considered glucogenic because they can be transformed into pyruvate and other TCA cycle intermediates that enter gluconeogenesis and produce glucose. For six of these amino acids—alanine, serine, glycine, threonine, tryptophan, and cysteine—pyruvate is the entry point into metabolism. The others enter at points along the TCA cycle. These glucogenic amino acids, which come from food or the breakdown of proteins in the muscle, are a major source of blood glucose when the diet is lacking in carbohydrate. The glucose formed can enter glycolysis and continue through the later stages of metabolism to produce ATP. These conversions are shown in **Figure 8.9**.

Glycerol to Pyruvate

Dietary fat (triglycerides) is a more concentrated source of kilocalories and yields about six times more energy than either carbohydrates or proteins. Both glycerol and fatty acids can be used for fuel, but only the glycerol portion of the triglyceride is glucogenic and thus able to contribute to blood glucose levels. As an energy source, glycerol produces very little energy compared with glucose, amino acids, or fatty acids.

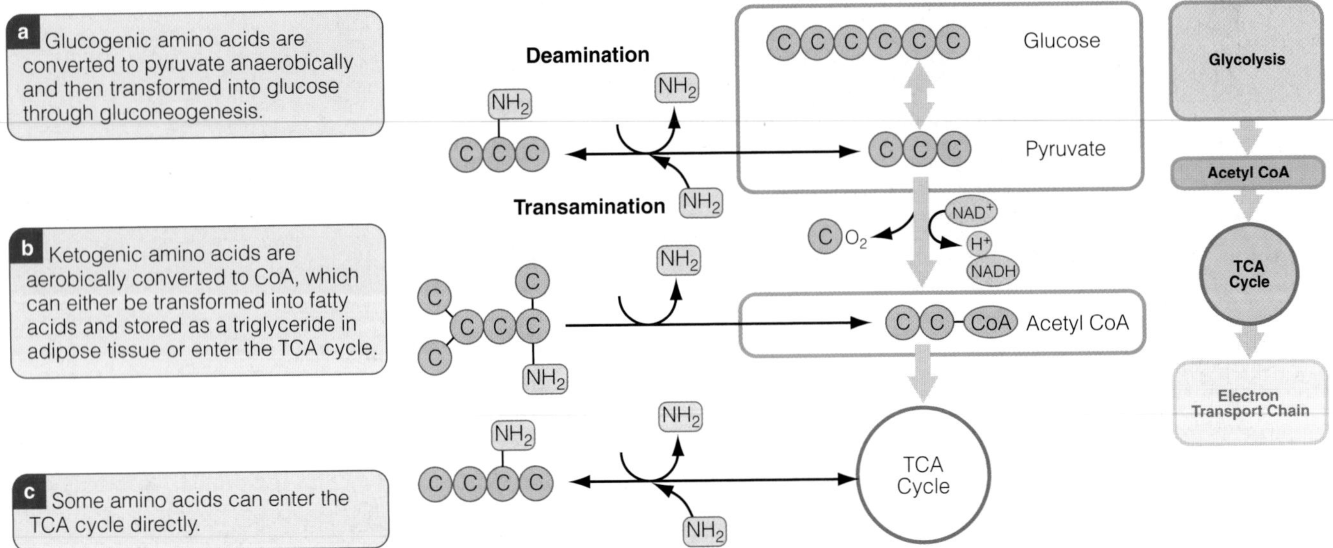

▲ **Figure 8.9 Glucogenic and Ketogenic Amino Acid Metabolism**

Glycerol can enter the main pathway at two distinct points. First, glycerol can be taken up by the liver cells and converted to glucose via gluconeogenesis. The first step in this pathway uses ATP to phosphorylate (add a phosphate group to) the three-carbon glycerol into DHAP (dihydroxyacetone phosphate), one of the intermediate substrates in glycolysis. Once glycerol is converted to DHAP it can be changed into glucose in one direction or it can follow a different series of chemical reactions to produce pyruvate, depending on the body's need for glucose.

Pyruvate Is Transformed into the Gateway Molecule Acetyl CoA

At the end of glycolysis, what began as one six-carbon molecule of glucose has produced two three-carbon molecules of pyruvate, a net of two ATP, two coenzyme molecules in the form of NADH, two hydrogen ions (which enter the electron transport chain), and two molecules of water. Now let's continue down the metabolic pathway with the newly formed pyruvate as it is transformed into acetyl CoA.

Acetyl CoA is often called the "gateway" molecule for aerobic metabolism because all energy-producing nutrients—glucose, amino acids, fatty acids, and glycerol—and even alcohol are usually transformed to acetyl CoA before entering the TCA cycle. Until this point along the metabolic pathway, energy is produced anaerobically. When cells contain an ample supply of oxygen, pyruvate continues down the aerobic energy pathway to create acetyl CoA. In the presence of oxygen, the two molecules of pyruvate formed during glycolysis cross the mitochondrial membrane and enter the mitochondria, where they each lose a carbon. Coenzyme A (which contains the B vitamin pantothenic acid) attaches to the remaining two carbons from each pyruvate molecule to form acetyl CoA. Thus a three-carbon pyruvate molecule is changed into a two-carbon acetyl CoA. The third carbon combines with oxygen to form carbon dioxide, and is expelled through the lungs as waste. This step is illustrated in **Figure 8.10**.

Once acetyl CoA is formed it can either continue down the pathway to enter the TCA cycle (if ATP is scarce) or it can be transformed into a fatty acid and through lipogenesis be stored as fat (if ATP is abundant). When ATP is scarce, acetyl CoA enters the TCA cycle (stage 3) where hydrogen ions are produced for use by the electron transport chain (stage 4).

Fatty Acids to Acetyl CoA

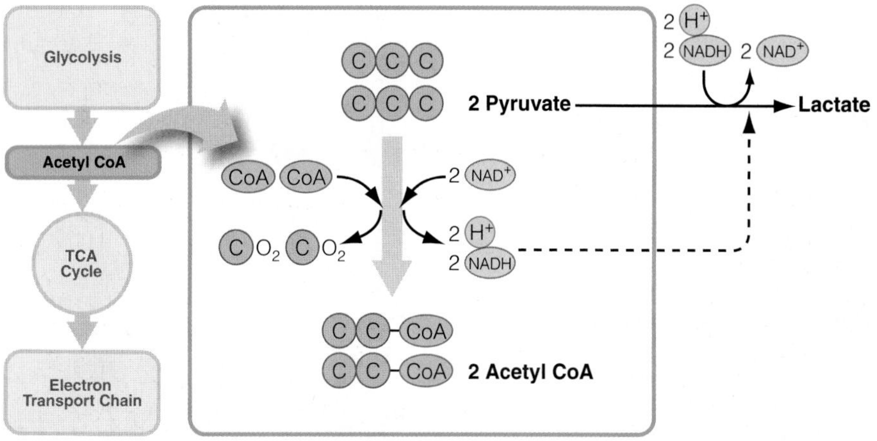

Fatty acids are hydrolyzed by lipolysis (*lipo* = fat, *lysis* = break apart) from triglycerides before they can be used for energy. An enzyme called **hormone-sensitive lipase** in the adipose tissue catalyzes the reaction, and the activity of this enzyme is stimulated by the hormone glucagon when blood glucose levels are low (as when the diet is low in carbohydrate or kilocalories), or by the adrenal hormones epinephrine or cortisol when an individual is under stress. Once the fatty acids are free, they are released into the blood and taken up by various tissues, including the muscle and the liver.

▲ **Figure 8.10 The Fate of Pyruvate**
At the end of glycolysis, two molecules of pyruvate are formed for every molecule of glucose. These three-carbon molecules can be converted to acetyl CoA and enter the TCA cycle or be transformed into lactate, which diffuses out of the cell into the blood.

Just as you put on a coat to prepare to step outside on a cold day, fatty acids are "prepared" or activated before they cross into the mitochondria. This step, which absorbs ATP, involves adding coenzyme A to the carboxylic end of the fatty acid chain. The resulting long-chain fatty acetyl CoA can then easily cross the mitochondrial membrane with the help of a carrier molecule.

The fatty acid is disassembled inside the mitochondrion by a series of chemical reactions called **beta-oxidation.** During beta-oxidation the fatty acid is taken apart two carbon fragments at a time, beginning at the carboxyl end of the molecule. The two-carbon pairs are joined with a molecule of CoA and converted to acetyl CoA. This process continues, forming a new acetyl CoA and a shorter fatty acid chain, until all of the carbons have been oxidized. **Figure 8.11** illustrates this process.

As each pair of carbons is cleaved off from the fatty acid chain, hydrogen and electrons are released. The hydrogen atoms are picked up by two coenzyme hydrogen carriers, NAD^+ and FAD, which then unload the hydrogen atoms in the electron transport chain.

Fatty acids are considered **ketogenic** (*keto* = ketone, *genic* = forming), not glucogenic, which means fatty acids can be used to produce ketone bodies, which are used as backup fuel for the brain and nerve functions when glucose is limited. (We will discuss this process later in the chapter.)

Amino Acids to Acetyl CoA

Recall that earlier in the chapter you learned that 14 of the 20 amino acids are considered glucogenic. What about the remaining six amino acids? Two of these six amino acids, leucine and lysine, are considered strictly ketogenic (refer to Figure 8.9b), while four of the six, isoleucine, tryptophan, phenylalanine, and tyrosine, can be both ketogenic and glucogenic.[5]

Leucine and lysine first undergo transamination with **alpha-ketoglutarate** accepting the amino group that is transferred (review Chapter 6 on the transamination reaction). After several more steps, leucine and lysine are ultimately converted to acetyl CoA. Both amino acids are considered ketogenic because once they have been transformed into acetyl CoA they can be converted into a fatty acid or acetoacetate and then into ketone bodies, depending on cellular needs.

Isoleucine and tryptophan are converted to acetyl CoA using the same pathway as leucine. Phenylalanine and tyrosine are transformed into acetoacetyl CoA first before they are converted to acetyl CoA.

Remember that acetyl CoA cannot be used to make glucose, so once these amino acids are transformed, they are committed to continue through the energy pathway or be converted to fatty acids and stored as a triglyceride in the adipocyte.

hormone-sensitive lipase The enzyme that catalyzes lipolysis of triglycerides.

beta-oxidation A series of metabolic reactions in which fatty acids are oxidized to acetyl CoA; also called *fatty acid oxidation*.

ketogenic Describing molecules that can be transformed into ketone bodies.

alpha-ketoglutarate A compound that participates in the formation of nonessential amino acids during transamination.

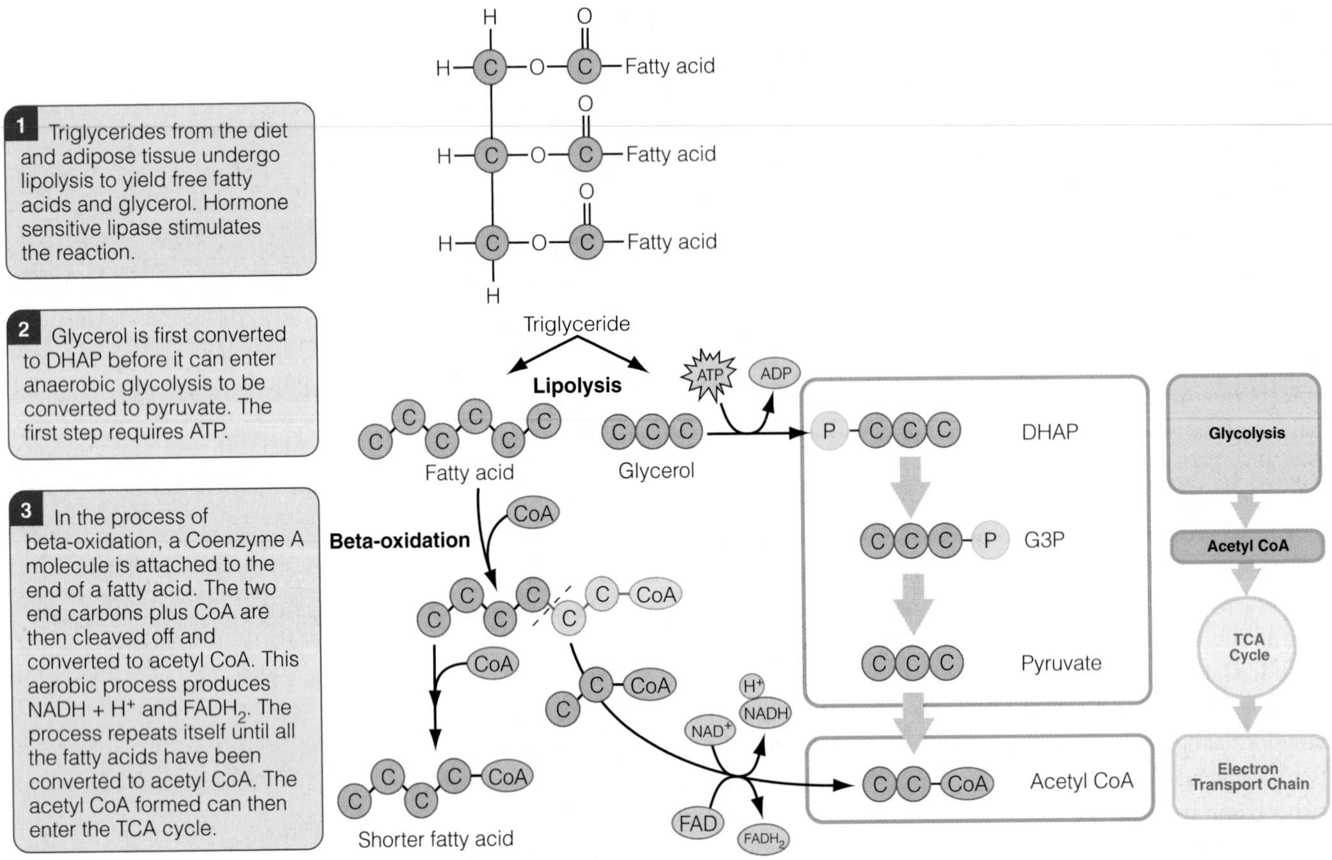
1 Triglycerides from the diet and adipose tissue undergo lipolysis to yield free fatty acids and glycerol. Hormone sensitive lipase stimulates the reaction.
2 Glycerol is first converted to DHAP before it can enter anaerobic glycolysis to be converted to pyruvate. The first step requires ATP.
3 In the process of beta-oxidation, a Coenzyme A molecule is attached to the end of a fatty acid. The two end carbons plus CoA are then cleaved off and converted to acetyl CoA. This aerobic process produces NADH + H+ and FADH2. The process repeats itself until all the fatty acids have been converted to acetyl CoA. The acetyl CoA formed can then enter the TCA cycle.
Fatty acid
Triglyceride
Lipolysis
ATP
ADP
Fatty acid
Glycerol
DHAP
G3P
Pyruvate
Acetyl CoA
Beta-oxidation
CoA
NAD+
NADH
H+
FAD
FADH2
Shorter fatty acid
Glycolysis
Acetyl CoA
TCA Cycle
Electron Transport Chain

▲ **Figure 8.11 Using Fatty Acids for Energy**
Stored triglycerides can be used for energy after the fatty acids are first hydrolyzed from the glycerol backbone.

Tricarboxylic Acid (TCA) Cycle Releases Hydrogen Ions

The tricarboxylic acid cycle (TCA), which occurs in the mitochondria, is the third stage for the oxidation of fuel molecules (**Figure 8.12**). These macronutrients enter the cycle as acetyl CoA, where most of the energy in the original molecule is now trapped. Remember that these fuel molecules are carbon-containing compounds that can lose electrons in the form of hydrogen ions during metabolism. During the TCA cycle, this stored energy is freed and the hydrogen ions are gathered up by NAD^+, forming NADH, and FAD, forming $FADH_2$, and carried to the electron transport chain. These hydrogen ions are what drives the production of ATP in the electron transport chain.

One molecule of acetyl CoA enters the cycle at a time. The first step is to remove the CoA and combine the two remaining carbons with a four-carbon molecule called **oxaloacetate.** Together, oxaloacetate and acetyl CoA form a new six-carbon compound called citrate. The cycle continues with seven more reactions, ending with oxaloacetate as the last molecule formed at the end of every turn of the TCA cycle. This brings us back to the beginning of the cycle. You'll notice as you track the carbons in Figure 8.12 that for every acetyl CoA that enters the TCA cycle, two carbons are lost as CO_2.

In addition to the two carbons, eight hydrogen atoms and their electrons are removed during each turn of the TCA cycle. For example, in the third step of the cycle, a hydrogen atom and electron is grabbed by the coenzyme carrier NAD^+. In the succeeding steps of the cycle, three more coenzymes are formed and six hydrogen ions are released, NADH in step 4 and step 8 and $FADH_2$ in step 6. In total, for

oxaloacetate The starting molecule for the TCA cycle.

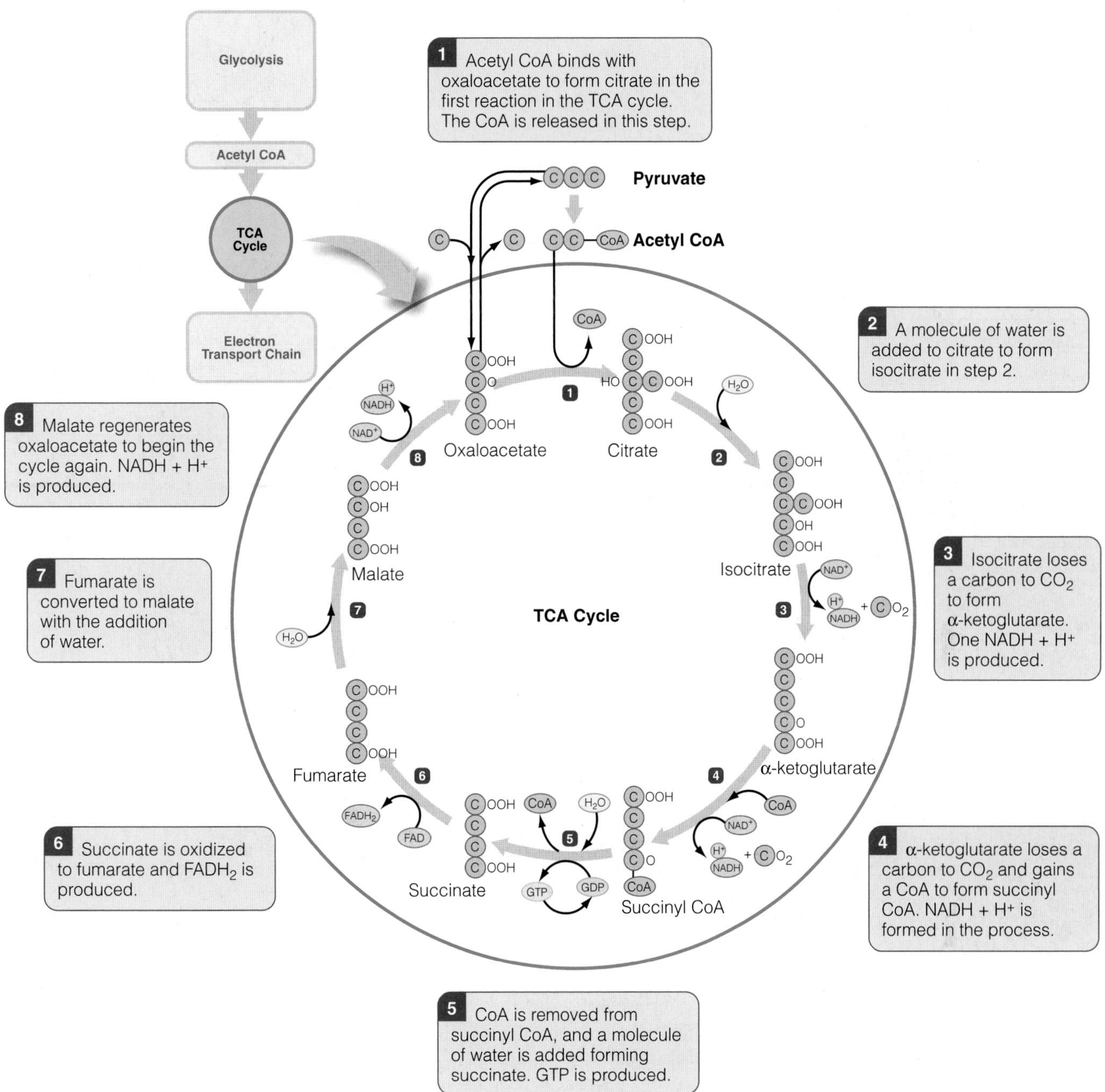

▲ **Figure 8.12 The TCA Cycle**
(**1**) The TCA cycle begins with oxaloacetate combining with acetyl CoA to form citrate. (**2–8**) The cycle continues through seven more steps, changing the molecules and releasing hydrogen atoms. Pyruvate can provide some oxaloacetate as a starting molecule for the cycle.

each turn of the TCA cycle, four molecules of coenzymes are released, along with carbon dioxide and water.

Also notice in step 5, a molecule called *guanasine triphosphate (GTP)* is generated. This energy molecule is readily converted to ATP.

The Electron Transport Chain Produces the Majority of ATP

The primary purpose of the electron transport chain is to assemble the majority of the ATP that cells need to fuel the body's actions. In fact, about 90 percent of the

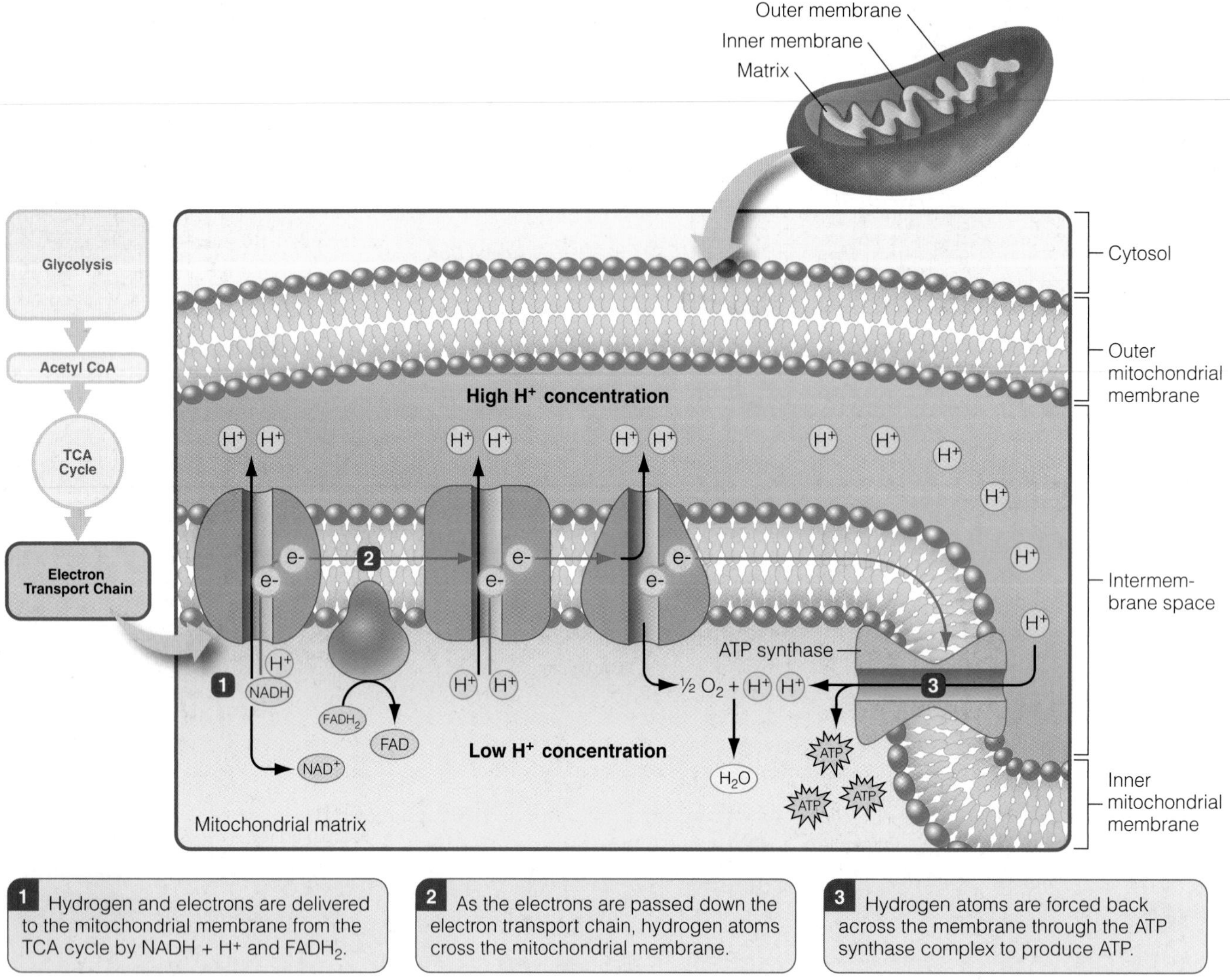

▲ **Figure 8.13 The Electron Transport Chain**

ATP you use every day for energy, growth, and maintenance is generated during this final stage of energy metabolism.[6] This step is illustrated in **Figure 8.13**.

The electron transport chain is comprised of a series of protein complexes located in the inner mitochondrial membrane. These protein complexes act as carrier molecules to transport the electrons and hydrogen ions generated during glycolysis, the TCA cycle, and fatty acid oxidation along the chain. The electrons are passed from one protein complex to the next until they reach oxygen. At the end of the chain, oxygen accepts the electron and binds with two molecules of hydrogen to form water. You can think of this process as being similar to a bucket brigade in a fire. If one person in the brigade drops the bucket, the entire process slows down. Likewise, if one electron is dropped during the electron transport chain, the production of ATP is slowed.

As the electrons are passed along the chain, the protons separate from the hydrogen atoms in the coenzymes and are pumped out of the inner mitochondria into the intermembrane space. As the protons accumulate, they are forced back across the mitochondrial membrane into the matrix. The hydrogen ions are used by the enzyme ATP synthase at the end of the chain to produce ATP. For every pair of hydrogen ions that crosses the inner mitochondrial membrane, one ATP is formed. The ATP is now ready to be used for energy.

The protein complexes that transfer the electrons through the electron transport chain are classified as **flavoproteins,** which contain the B vitamin riboflavin, and **cytochromes,** which contain the minerals iron and copper. If you are iron deficient, the cytochromes are less able to pass the electrons along the chain to complete the production of ATP. This is one of the reasons someone with inadequate iron intake will feel tired or fatigued. This illustrates the point that though vitamins and minerals do not provide energy, they are essential for energy production in the body.

Table 8.2 summarizes the role of individual nutrients in producing ATP, glycogen, nonessential amino acids, and fat, and **Figure 8.14** provides a detailed overview

flavoproteins Protein complexes that move electrons down the electron transport chain; they contain the B vitamin riboflavin.

cytochromes Protein complexes that move electrons down the electron transport chain; they contain the minerals iron and copper.

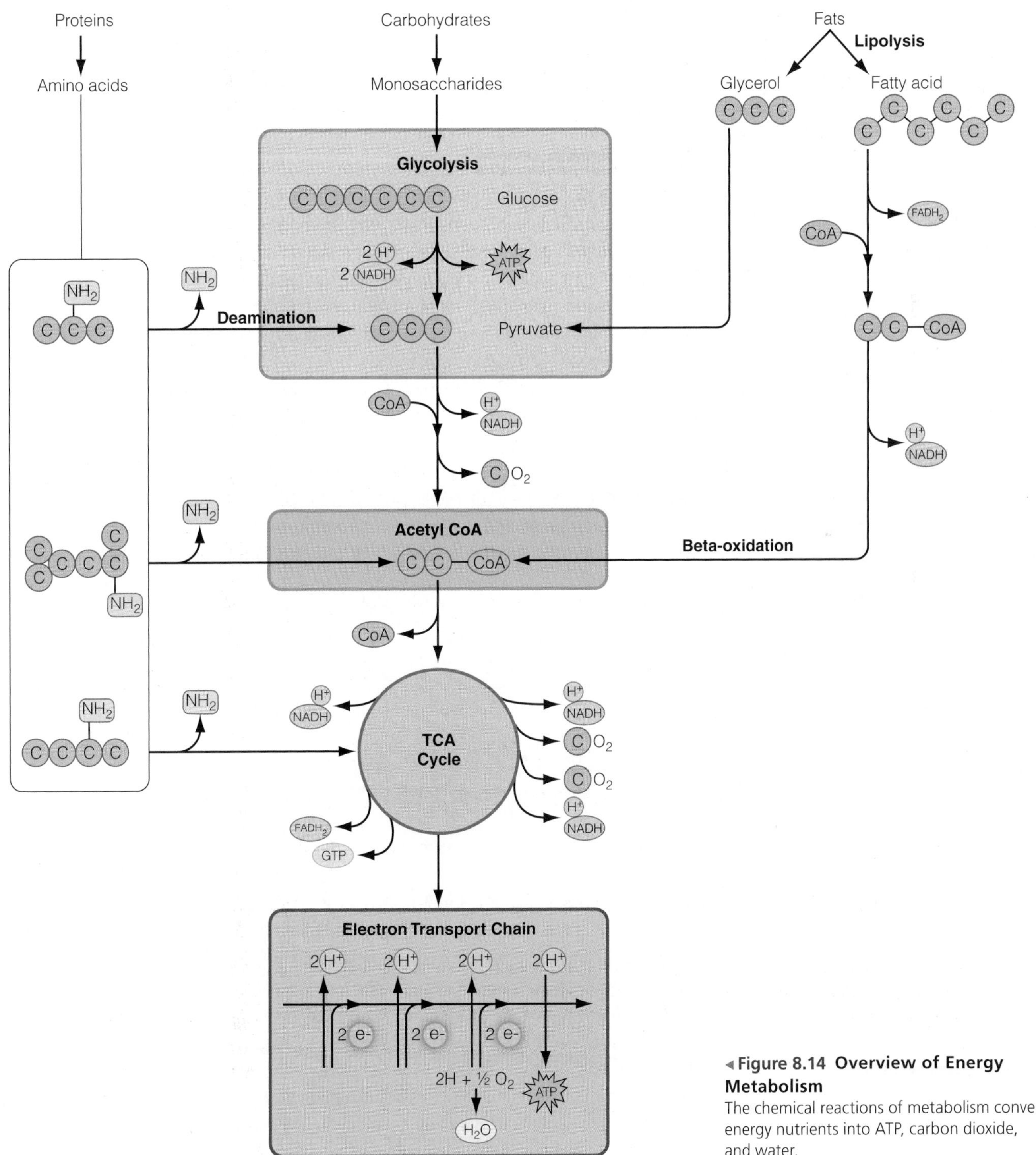

◂ Figure 8.14 Overview of Energy Metabolism
The chemical reactions of metabolism convert energy nutrients into ATP, carbon dioxide, and water.

TABLE 8.2 The Metabolic Fate of Energy-Producing Nutrients

Nutrient	Produces ATP?	Can Produce Glucose?	Can Be Used in Transamination (to produce amino acids)?	Excess Can Be Stored as Fat?
Glucose	Yes	Yes	Yes	Yes
Amino acid	Yes	Yes	Yes	Yes
Fatty acid	Yes	No	No	Yes
Glycerol	Yes	Yes	Yes	Yes
Alcohol	Yes	No	No	Yes

of all four stages of energy metabolism. Look at the figure closely; can you describe what's happening in each stage?

THE TAKE-HOME MESSAGE Carbohydrates provide energy to cells through glycolysis. Glucose undergoes a ten-step conversion to yield two molecules of pyruvate, a net of two ATP, two coenzymes, two hydrogen ions, and two molecules of water. Pyruvate can be reduced to lactate during anaerobic metabolism, or it can be converted to acetyl CoA during aerobic metabolism. Glycerol can produce energy by entering glycolysis or form glucose through gluconeogenesis and thus help maintain blood glucose levels. Fatty acids are ketogenic and cannot be used to form glucose. Fatty acids are broken down into two-carbon fragments to be converted into acetyl CoA through beta-oxidation. Amino acids can be used to produce energy and glucose or converted to fatty acids and stored as triglycerides. All of the energy nutrients come together in the gateway molecule acetyl CoA. Once acetyl CoA is formed, it combines with oxaloacetate to form citrate in the first step of the TCA cycle. One turn of the TCA cycle produces two coenzymes, one molecule of CO_2, and a small amount of energy in the form of guanasine triphosphate (GTP, the equivalent of a molecule of ATP). The electrons from hydrogen atoms in coenzymes enter the electron transport chain, where they are passed along the chain by protein complexes. During this process, the protons are used to form ATP and the hydrogen ions join with oxygen to make water, fatty acids, or ketone bodies.

How Does Metabolism Change during the Absorptive and Postabsorptive States?

After eating a meal, once food has been digested and absorbed, the amino acids, monoglycerides, and triglycerides are available to be used by the body. We refer to this as the **absorptive state,** or that period within four hours following a meal in which anabolic processes exceed catabolic processes. During the absorptive state, the body uses glucose as the primary source of energy. Later, when you need energy during sleep, between meals, or when you're too busy to eat, your body will use the glucose stored as glycogen, and the fatty acids and glycerol stored in triglycerides, for fuel. This is referred to as the **postabsorptive state,** or the period of time usually more than four hours after eating, such as during the late afternoon or overnight. Both the absorptive and postabsorptive states are regulated by hormones.

absorptive state The period after you eat when the stomach and small intestines are full and anabolic reactions exceed catabolic reactions.

postabsorptive state The period when you haven't eaten for more than four hours and the stomach and intestines are empty. Energy needs are met by the breakdown of stores.

During the Absorptive State, Metabolism Favors Energy Storage

Metabolism adjusts to either provide energy for immediate use or store it for later, depending on your energy needs and intake. In the normal process of eating, if you consume more kilocalories than you require for your immediate energy needs, your metabolism favors anabolic reactions for the sake of storing the excess kilocalories for later use. For instance, if you eat excess protein, the excess is converted to fatty acids and stored as a triglyceride. If you overconsume carbohydrates, the anabolic reactions include converting the excess carbohydrates to glycogen. Once the glycogen stores are full, carbohydrates are converted to fatty acids.

Take a close look at **Figure 8.15**, which illustrates the anabolic and catabolic pathways of the absorptive state.

Carbohydrates Are Stored as Glycogen

Although glucose is essential to red blood cells and the central nervous system, neither of these tissues can convert glucose to its storage forms, and both burn glucose readily. The red blood cells don't have mitochondria, which means that they can only use glucose anaerobically. The nervous system can't store glucose as glycogen, nor can it convert excess glucose to fat. The liver and muscles can convert excess glucose to glycogen, but only the liver can break down the glycogen and release it into the blood for red blood cells and the central nervous system to use when blood glucose levels are low.

Remember that dietary glucose arrives first at the liver from the portal vein. If glucose levels are high in the liver, glucose can be converted to glycogen through glycogenesis, or it can circulate to other tissues. Enzymes in the muscle can also convert excess glucose to glycogen. The body has a limited ability to store glycogen, however, and only about 1 percent of body weight is in the form of glycogen.

Liver glycogen plays an important role in maintaining glucose homeostasis. When intake of dietary carbohydrate is low, blood glucose levels drop. The glycogen stored in the liver can be converted to blood glucose through glycogenolysis. However, about 12 to 18 hours after eating, liver glycogen levels are nearly depleted.

Even though muscle has a larger storage capacity for glycogen, it lacks the enzyme that can release glucose into the blood. In essence, glucose is "trapped" in the muscle to be used by the muscle for energy or stored as glycogen and is not used to maintain blood glucose levels.

Excess Carbohydrates and Amino Acids Are Stored as Triglycerides

Carbohydrates are first stored as glycogen and only after those stores are full and energy needs are met will carbohydrates undergo transformation to a triglyceride. Once glucose has been oxidized to acetyl CoA it enters lipogenesis, forming fatty acids that are stored in the adipocytes. This conversion is very costly—almost 25 percent of the kilocalories must be spent to convert carbohydrates to fatty acids—and inefficient.

The same is true for excess amino acids. Protein is first used for the numerous functions it provides to the body before excess is converted to body fatty acids. Amino acids are first deaminated before the remaining carbons are converted to acetyl CoA and then formed into fatty acids. Both ketogenic and glucogenic amino acids can be catabolized and converted to fatty acids through pyruvate and acetyl CoA pathways, but the process is highly inefficient.

Fatty Acids Are Stored as Triglycerides

Excess kilocalories in any form will be stored as a triglyceride through the process known as lipogenesis, or fatty acid synthesis. Fatty acid synthesis begins with the two-carbon

Focus Figure 8.15 Metabolism during the Absorptive State

The absorptive (fed) state is generally an anabolic state: After digestion, absorption, and transport in the body, the end products of digestion can be synthesized into important biological compounds, used for energy, or converted to storage forms of energy.

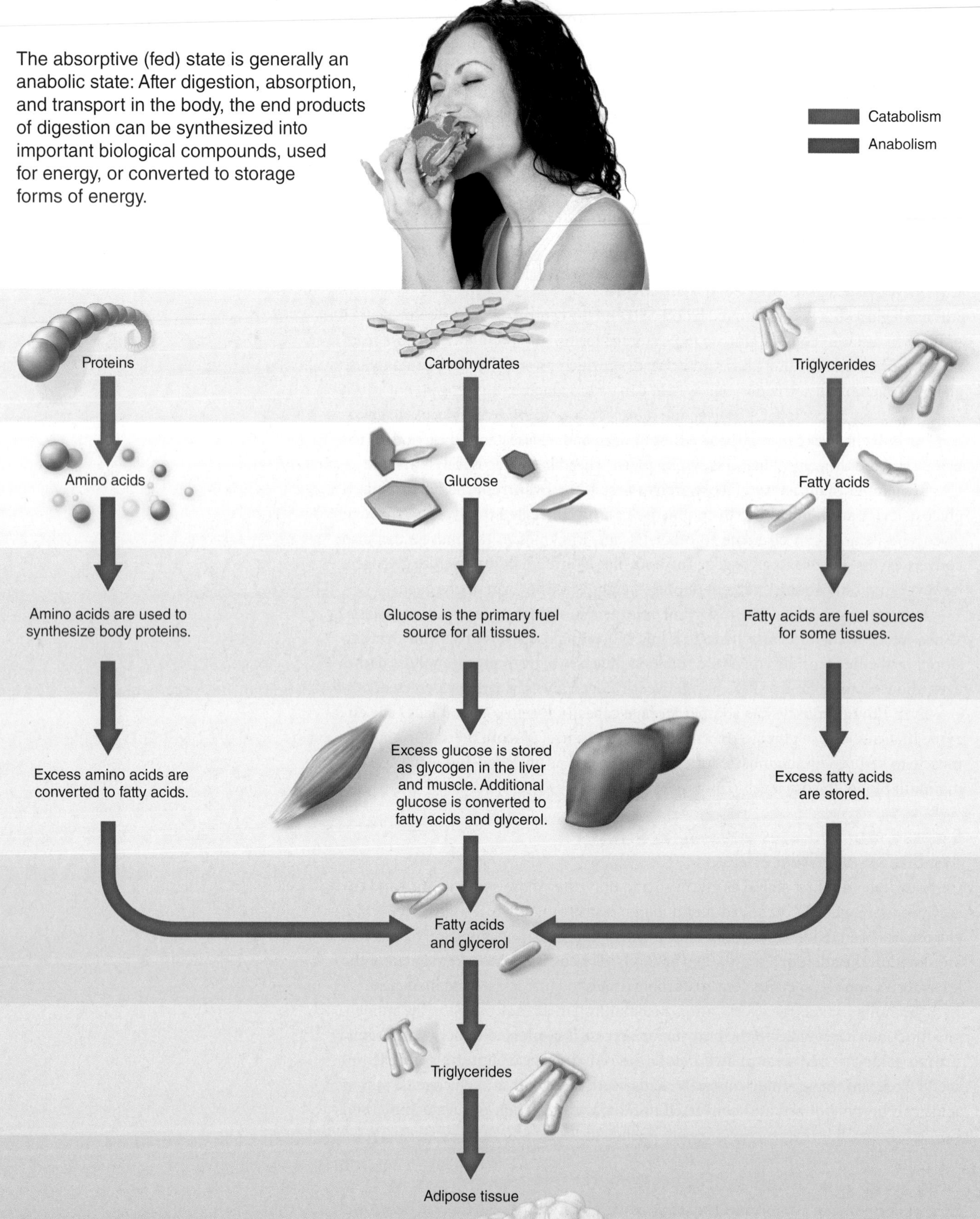

Catabolism
Anabolism
Proteins
Carbohydrates
Triglycerides
Amino acids
Glucose
Fatty acids
Amino acids are used to synthesize body proteins.
Glucose is the primary fuel source for all tissues.
Fatty acids are fuel sources for some tissues.
Excess amino acids are converted to fatty acids.
Excess glucose is stored as glycogen in the liver and muscle. Additional glucose is converted to fatty acids and glycerol.
Excess fatty acids are stored.
Fatty acids and glycerol
Triglycerides
Adipose tissue

gateway molecule acetyl CoA. This molecule eventually becomes a long-chain fatty acid that will attach to a glycerol backbone and be stored as a triglyceride in fat cells.

The metabolic pathway to store dietary fat requires little energy (only about 5 percent of the stored energy within the fatty acid) and only a few steps; therefore dietary fat is easier to store as body fat than are dietary carbohydrate or protein. Lipogenesis is a separate anabolic pathway that synthesizes fatty acids to be stored and is not just a reversal of the reactions involved in the breakdown of fat. In fact, the two processes take place in different parts of the cell. Fatty acids are made in the cytosol rather than in the mitochondria, where fats are oxidized. Lipogenesis also differs from fat oxidation in the way it's affected by glucagon and insulin. Glucagon stimulates lipolysis, which provides the fatty acids for beta-oxidation. Insulin has the opposite effect: It inhibits the breakdown of fat and promotes fatty acid synthesis.

During the Postabsorptive State, Metabolism Favors Energy Production

Many Americans consume more than enough kilocalories to meet their energy demands, which is reflected in the current obesity crisis. But what happens when the opposite is true? That is, you're too busy to consume enough food, or you choose not to eat? Regardless of the reason, when you do not consume enough kilocalories to meet your energy needs, your body will turn to stored energy to fuel itself. During this postabsorptive state—usually more than four hours after eating—the stomach and small intestine are empty and the need for energy is met from stored energy.

Take a look at **Figure 8.16**, which illustrates the metabolic pathways that are active during the postabsorptive state.

Stores Are Depleted during Fasting

Whereas glycogen stores will supply energy during short periods of fasting, such as overnight or between meals, the body will adapt differently if you go more than 18 hours without consuming carbohydrates. Initially, the body maintains blood glucose levels by tapping into liver glycogen through glycogenolysis. At the same time, an increase in lipolysis provides fatty acids for energy, thus reducing the use of glucose by the cell. In addition, once liver glycogen has been depleted, gluconeogenesis is initiated using amino acids, glycerol, pyruvate, and lactate to meet the body's glucose needs.

Fat reserves are broken down faster as fasting continues. The brain has quickly used up the glycogen reserves from the liver and must switch to an alternative source of energy—ketone bodies—derived from the fatty acids. A severe, prolonged fast, or starvation, depletes fat reserves and begins to break down muscle tissue to provide energy.

Ketogenesis Generates Energy during Prolonged Fasting

When deprived of carbohydrates, the body will depend less and less on glucose, and will resort to using ketone bodies instead. **Ketogenesis** (the formation of ketone bodies, illustrated in **Figure 8.17**) occurs when there is an excess buildup of acetyl CoA. Acetyl CoA accumulates because it is not being metabolized in the TCA cycle due to a reduced supply of oxaloacetate (which comes from pyruvate and, ultimately, glucose).

Ketogenesis reaches peak levels after an individual has fasted or consumed a limited-carbohydrate diet for three days. By the fourth day of a fast, the ketone bodies are providing almost half of the fuel used by the mitochondria.[7] The presence of ketone bodies is referred to as ketosis (described in Chapter 4). As you continue to fast, your brain will switch from glucose to ketone bodies for fuel to reduce the drain on blood glucose. Eventually, about 30 percent of the brain's energy will come from ketone bodies, with the rest provided by blood glucose.

ketogenesis The formation of ketone bodies from excess acetyl CoA.

Focus Figure 8.16 Metabolism during the Postabsorptive State

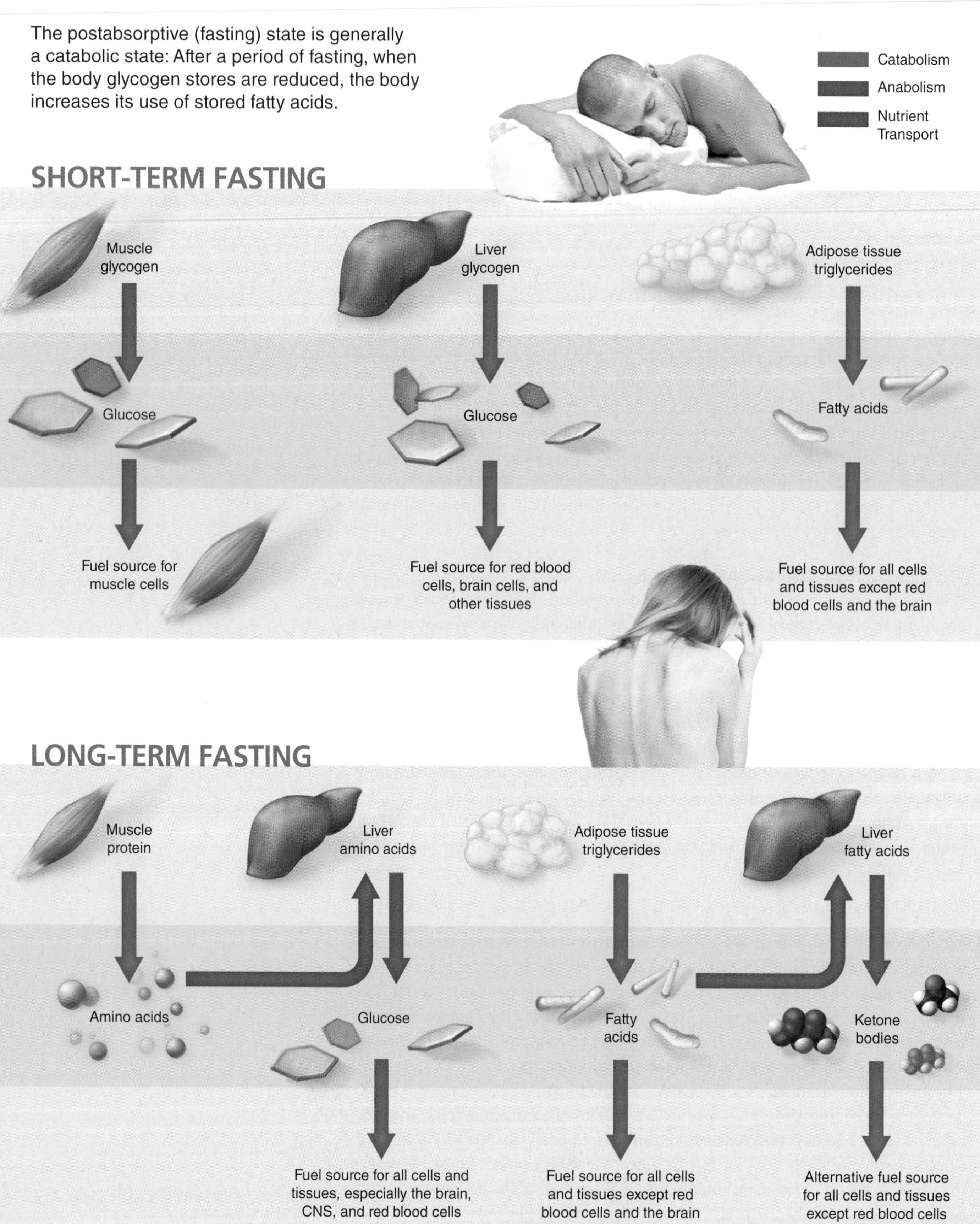
The postabsorptive (fasting) state is generally a catabolic state: After a period of fasting, when the body glycogen stores are reduced, the body increases its use of stored fatty acids.
Catabolism
Anabolism
Nutrient Transport
SHORT-TERM FASTING
Muscle glycogen
Liver glycogen
Adipose tissue triglycerides
Glucose
Glucose
Fatty acids
Fuel source for muscle cells
Fuel source for red blood cells, brain cells, and other tissues
Fuel source for all cells and tissues except red blood cells and the brain
LONG-TERM FASTING
Muscle protein
Liver amino acids
Adipose tissue triglycerides
Liver fatty acids
Amino acids
Glucose
Fatty acids
Ketone bodies
Fuel source for all cells and tissues, especially the brain, CNS, and red blood cells
Fuel source for all cells and tissues except red blood cells and the brain
Alternative fuel source for all cells and tissues except red blood cells

Ketogenesis is a normal metabolic response to fasting, and ketosis is not life-threatening. The kidneys will reabsorb ketone bodies to be used by other tissues for energy or excrete excess ketone bodies in the urine to maintain a balanced pH under normal conditions. There can be consequences, however, when ketosis advances to **ketoacidosis**. This condition can occur in individuals with untreated type 1 diabetes mellitus because of the lack of usable insulin, which lowers glucose availability to the cells. When ketone bodies accumulate, the blood pH drops. The body responds by increasing breathing to excrete more CO_2, which increases the pH. If the level of ketone bodies surpasses the kidneys' ability to reabsorb them, they spill into the urine. Severe diabetic ketoacidosis can lead to impaired heart activity, coma, and even death.

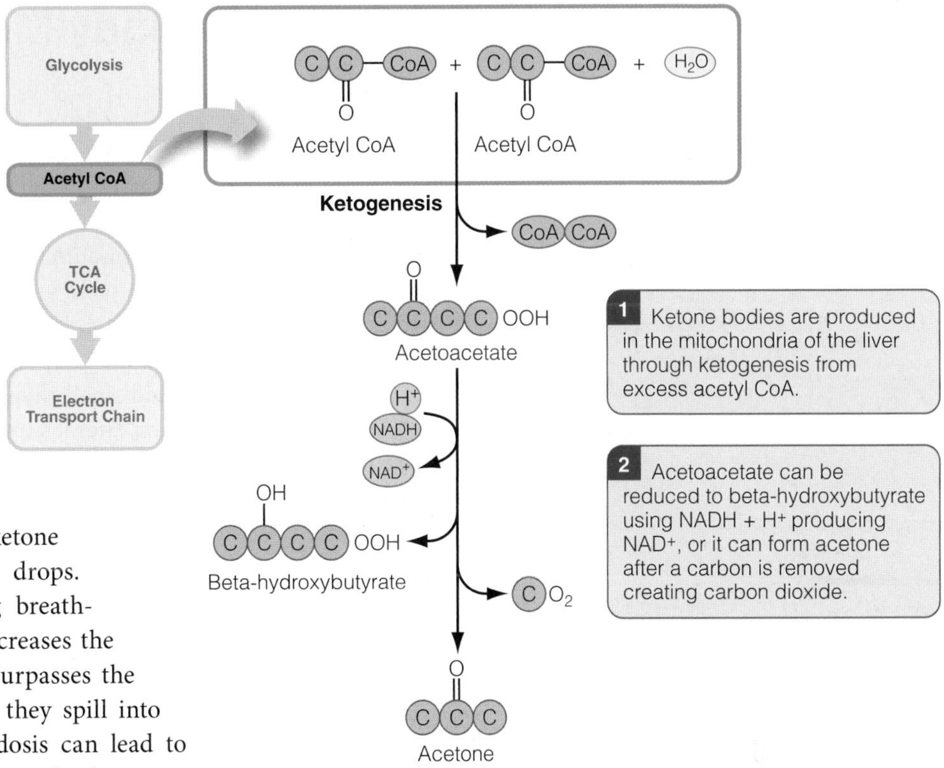

▲ **Figure 8.17 The Formation of Ketone Bodies**

THE TAKE-HOME MESSAGE The differences in metabolism between the absorptive, or feeding, state and the postabsorptive, or fasting, state are listed in Table 8.3. During the absorptive state, anabolic reactions are favored, as more kilocalories have been ingested than are immediately needed to produce energy. Regardless of whether the excess kilocalories are from carbohydrates, proteins, or fats, the excess energy can be converted to fat and stored. The metabolic pathways for storing excess kilocalories are more efficient at storing dietary fat. During the postabsorptive state, metabolism shifts to favor catabolic reactions. Fat is broken down to fatty acids to be used for ATP synthesis, while liver glycogen, glycerol, and amino acids are used to maintain blood glucose levels. As fasting continues, glycogen stores are depleted, and muscle is broken down to provide amino acids for energy and gluconeogenesis. A lack of sufficient glucose in the blood can lead to excess breakdown of fat and the synthesis of ketone bodies, which can be used by the brain and muscles for energy. If ketogenesis is prolonged, ketoacidosis can lead to serious conditions, including death.

ketoacidosis A form of metabolic acidosis, or pH imbalance due to excess acid, that occurs when excess ketone bodies are present in the blood; most often seen in individuals with untreated type I diabetes.

TABLE 8.3 Metabolism during Feeding and Fasting

	Feeding: Metabolism Following a Meal in the Absorptive State	Fasting: Metabolism Following a Meal in the Postabsorptive State	If Fasting Continues After Liver and Muscle Glycogen Stores Are Depleted
Proteins	Amino acids are used for protein synthesis or stored as a triglyceride in the adipose tissue		Amino acids are used for gluconeogenesis or catabolized for energy
Carbohydrates	Glucose is used for energy or stored as glycogen in the liver or muscle	Liver and muscle glycogen is broken down to provide glucose for energy	
Triglycerides	Fatty acids and glycerol are stored as a triglyceride in the adipose tissue	Triglycerides in adipose tissue are broken down to glycerol and fatty acids to be used for energy metabolism	Fatty acids are used to produce ketone bodies and oxidized for energy

How Does the Body Metabolize Alcohol?

Despite the fact that alcohol (ethanol) contains kilocalories, it adds no nutritional value to the diet, has no function in the human body, and is therefore not an essential nutrient. However, alcohol can be a significant source of energy. In fact, alcohol contains almost twice the amount of energy (7 kilocalories per gram) of an equal amount of carbohydrate or protein (4 kilocalories per gram).

Alcohol is also different from carbohydrates, proteins, and fats because it doesn't have to be digested before the body absorbs it. Rather, it's absorbed directly through the stomach mucosa and small intestine lining. This means that alcohol makes its way into the blood soon after it's ingested. Through the blood, alcohol is transported to the liver, where it is metabolized.

The body can easily metabolize about half an ounce of alcohol, the amount in a standard drink, in an hour and a half; however, when more than this amount is consumed in that period of time, the excess alcohol will circulate throughout the body until the liver enzymes can break it down.

The Enzymes That Metabolize Ethanol

Alcohol is metabolized through three distinct pathways. The primary pathway involves the oxidation of ethanol by the enzyme alcohol dehydrogenase (ADH) (described in Chapter 7), which is found in both the stomach and the liver. The liver contains enough ADH to metabolize alcohol efficiently. As you can see in **Figure 8.18**, as soon as the capillaries deliver the alcohol to the liver cells, it is converted to acetaldehyde. In this reaction, ADH removes hydrogen ions from alcohol, which are picked up by the coenzyme NAD^+. More hydrogens are removed as acetaldehyde is quickly changed to acetate by a similar enzyme called **acetaldehyde dehydrogenase (ALDH).** The final step converts acetate to acetyl CoA. The acetyl CoA can then either be used to produce energy in the TCA cycle if needed, or be transformed into fatty acids and stored as a triglyceride in the adipocyte.

The second pathway that can oxidize alcohol is the **microsomal ethanol oxidizing system (MEOS).** This system is not as significant as ADH for small amounts

acetaldehyde dehydrogenase (ALDH). The enzyme that converts acetaldehyde to acetate; this is the second step in oxidizing ethanol in the liver.

microsomal ethanol oxidizing system (MEOS) The second metabolic pathway for oxidizing ethanol, used at higher intakes of alcohol; it also participates in metabolizing drugs.

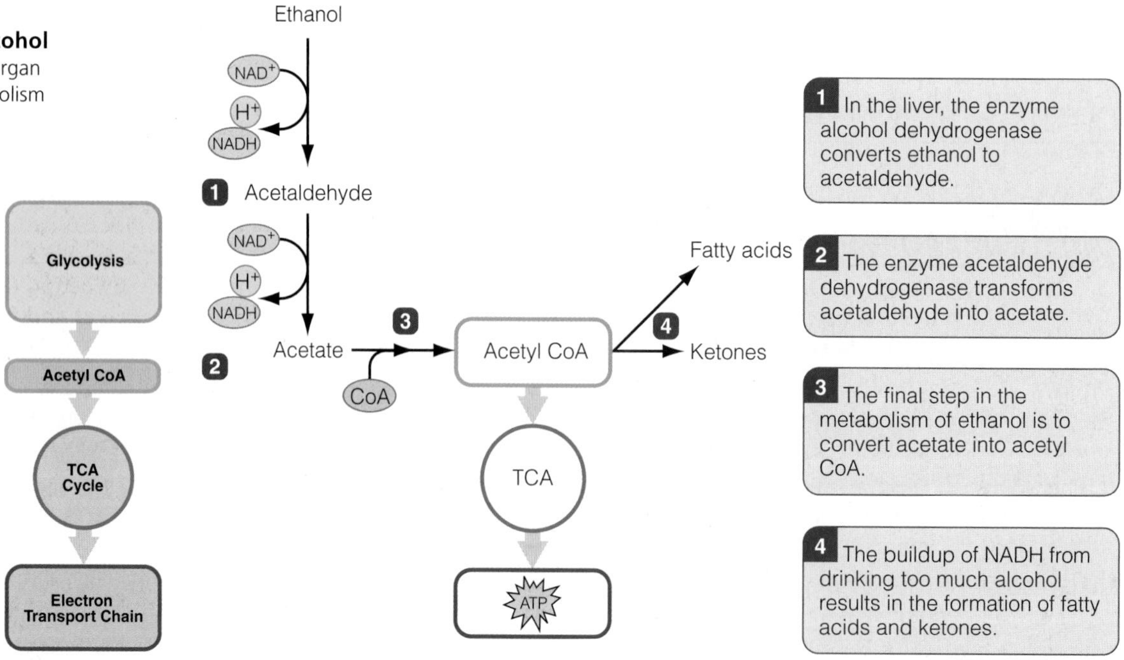

Figure 8.18 The Metabolism of Alcohol
The liver is the main organ involved in the metabolism of alcohol.

Ethanol
NAD^+
H^+
NADH
1 Acetaldehyde
NAD^+
H^+
NADH
2
Acetate
CoA
3
Acetyl CoA
4
Fatty acids
Ketones
TCA
ATP
Glycolysis
Acetyl CoA
TCA Cycle
Electron Transport Chain

1 In the liver, the enzyme alcohol dehydrogenase converts ethanol to acetaldehyde.

2 The enzyme acetaldehyde dehydrogenase transforms acetaldehyde into acetate.

3 The final step in the metabolism of ethanol is to convert acetate into acetyl CoA.

4 The buildup of NADH from drinking too much alcohol results in the formation of fatty acids and ketones.

of alcohol, but becomes more important with the chronic consumption of alcohol. This system also metabolizes many prescription and over-the-counter medications. If you drink alcohol while taking certain medications, the liver will metabolize the alcohol first, which causes the effects of the drugs to be felt over a longer period of time. This is the reason drugs and alcohol should never be taken together.

Not all alcohol is oxidized in the liver. A third metabolic pathway for alcohol takes place in the brain, where alcohol is oxidized to acetaldehyde by the enzyme catalase.[8] This pathway may be responsible for some of the psychological effects people experience, such as reduced inhibitions, when they consume alcohol.

Excess Alcohol Is Stored as Fat

Fat metabolism shifts after you drink alcohol. When alcohol is consumed, fewer fatty acids are used for energy. At the same time, the excess kilocalories in alcohol are metabolized and stored as fatty acids in the adipose tissue and liver. In chronic alcoholics, excess fatty deposits in the liver can result in cirrhosis (see the discussion of this dangerous condition in Chapter 7). Note that fat can begin to accumulate in the liver after a single bout of heavy drinking.[9]

THE TAKE-HOME MESSAGE Alcohol is primarily absorbed and metabolized in the liver by two enzyme systems. The most efficient enzyme system is ADH and ALDH, which convert the ethanol to acetaldehyde in the initial stages of metabolism, and ultimately to acetyl CoA. The MEOS system, which is used with chronic consumption of alcohol, also metabolizes drugs. A third system is found in the brain and metabolizes alcohol to acetaldehyde. Alcohol is not stored, but the excess kilocalories from alcohol not used for ATP production are converted to fatty acids and stored as a triglyceride.

Putting It All Together

A healthful eating plan for an active person provides enough protein, carbohydrate, fat, vitamins, minerals, and water to enable metabolism to work at an optimal level. Table 8.4 on page 315 summarizes the metabolism of the energy nutrients found in food.

If we consume more energy than we need, metabolism works to store the extra kilocalories as glycogen or triglycerides. Excess fat storage can lead to an increase in body weight and increased risk of developing chronic disease.

If the guidelines for healthy eating are not met, including consuming sufficient kilocalories, an imbalance in energy intake will cause a shift in metabolism to favor catabolic rather than anabolic reactions. While this shift occurs throughout the day during normal eating, chronic fasting or starvation can result in ketosis and a breakdown of protein to meet blood glucose needs.

The *Dietary Guidelines for Americans* include recommendations for moderate alcohol intake. Ethanol in moderate amounts can be quickly metabolized in the liver to acetyl CoA, which provides energy through the TCA cycle and the electron transport chain. However, an excessive intake can redirect the acetyl CoA to fatty acids to be stored as triglycerides in the liver and fat cells.

Balancing a nutrient-dense diet with irregular schedules can be challenging. However, the body's metabolism is flexible enough to adapt to moderate changes in eating and exercise patterns. The key is to provide adequate energy coupled with an optimal intake of vitamins, minerals, and water. This approach will provide the fuel metabolism needs to meet daily energy requirements, sustain blood glucose levels, and maintain adequate fat stores without increasing the risk of chronic disease.

TABLE TIPS

Important Advice for Maintaining Energy Levels

Eat breakfast! It's the most important meal and will help improve energy levels throughout the day by switching to an absorptive state and maintaining blood glucose levels rather than depleting glycogen stores in a postabsorptive state.

Don't skip meals; instead, be sure to eat at least three meals and one to two small snacks throughout the day.

Be sure each meal includes a combination of protein, carbohydrates, and some fat.

Enjoy carbohydrate-rich foods such as whole-grain crackers, baby carrots, grapes, string cheese, or nuts as snacks when you need a pick-me-up between meals.

Drink plenty of fluid, especially water, so you're sure to stay hydrated.

Health Connection

What Are Inborn Errors of Metabolism?

Healthy individuals are born with gene coding for all the enzymes they need to control metabolism and function properly (see the Two Points of View on page 314 for a discussion of nutritional genomics). However, some people inherit a genetic defect in a single gene that codes for the enzyme that controls a specific metabolic pathway. The lack of the appropriate enzyme prevents one substrate from being converted to another. The result is a buildup of abnormal by-products that can be toxic. Though such **inborn errors of metabolism** are rare and cannot be cured, they can be controlled through careful dietary treatment. We'll discuss some of the most common disorders involving protein and carbohydrate metabolism next.

inborn errors of metabolism Genetic conditions in which an individual lacks an enzyme that controls a specific metabolic pathway, resulting in the buildup of toxins.

phenylketonuria (PKU) A genetic disorder characterized by the inability to metabolize the essential amino acid phenylalanine.

hyperphenylalanemia Elevated levels of blood phenylalanine due to a lack of the enzyme phenylalanine hydroxylase.

Phenylketonuria (PKU)

A simple blood test at birth can detect **phenylketonuria (PKU),** a rare genetic disorder that causes serious health problems if untreated. Classic PKU is the most severe form of the genetic disorder, resulting in behavior problems and mental retardation before the child's first birthday. The mild to moderate conditions of PKU have a lower risk of mental retardation that can be prevented by following a prescribed, controlled diet.

Individuals with phenylketonuria (PKU) lack the enzyme *phenylalanine hydroxylase* that converts the essential amino acid phenylalanine to the nonessential amino acid tyrosine (see table). Under these conditions, phenylalanine accumulates in the blood, a condition called **hyperphenylalanemia.** The treatment for PKU is a controlled phenylalanine diet designed to maintain blood levels of phenylalanine and provide sufficient tyrosine, energy, and protein to grow and develop normally. Individuals with PKU must avoid high-protein foods and eliminate any products containing aspartame (the sugar substitute found in NutraSweet), which contains phenylalanine, from their diet.

Many diet sodas contain phenylalanine, a major ingredient in the artificial sweetener aspartame, also called Equal or NutraSweet.

Five Inborn Errors in Metabolism

Disorder	Incidence	Enzyme That Is Lacking	Examples of Acceptable Foods	Examples of Foods to Avoid
Phenylketonuria	1:15,000	Phenylalanine hydroxylase	Fruits, vegetables, breads, cereals, special formulas	Meat, chicken, fish, eggs, dairy, nuts, legumes
Maple syrup urine disease	1:300,000	Branched-chain alpha-keto acid dehydrogenase	Foods low in branched-chain amino acids, fruits, vegetables, breads, cereals, specialized formulas	Meats, eggs, dairy, nuts, legumes
Homocystinuria	1:300,000	Cystathionine beta-synthase	Fruits, vegetables, special formulas	Meats, eggs, dairy
Galactosemia	1:65,000	Galactose 1-phosphate uridyltransferase	Fruits, vegetables, breads, cereals, eggs, meats	Milk, cheese, milk chocolate, organ meats, legumes, hydrolyzed protein made from milk, casein, fermented soy products
Glycogen Storage Disease	1:50,000	Glucose 6-phosphatase	Corn starch and continuous overnight feeds	Milk, cheese, fruits

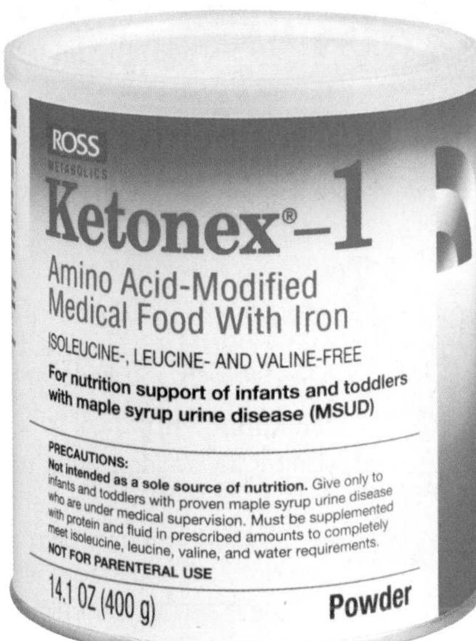

Special formulas and medically designed foods have been developed to meet the nutritional needs of children and adults with genetic disorders such as maple syrup urine disease.

Individuals must follow the diet strictly through adolescence and generally throughout their entire life.

Maple Syrup Urine Disease

Another protein-related disorder, **maple syrup urine disease (MSUD),** results from an inability to metabolize the branched-chain amino acids leucine, isoleucine, and valine. Babies with MSUD appear normal at birth but begin to show signs of the disease, such as a maple syrup smell to their urine (hence the name), within a few weeks. If left untreated, the condition can result in seizures, coma, and even death.[1] The prescribed diet includes specially designed formulas and avoidance of foods such as beef, chicken, fish, eggs, nuts, and legumes, which are high in the three affected amino acids.[2] Unfortunately, such a restrictive diet often means the child subsists solely on specially designed formulas or medically created foods.

Homocystinuria

Homocystinuria is an inherited genetic disorder that occurs when the enzyme cystathionine beta-synthase that converts homocysteine to cystathionine is lacking or not working properly. A diet rich in the essential amino acid methionine adds to the buildup of homocysteine because methionine is converted to homocysteine during metabolism. The prescribed treatment is a diet low in methionine, along with a supplement of B vitamins, including folate, vitamin B_6, and vitamin B_{12}, which are often low in individuals with homocystinuria.[3] The low-methionine diet must be followed for life. Homocysteine and certain amino acids, such as methionine, building up in the blood can result in dislocation of the lens in the eye,[4] nearsightedness, and blood clots in the veins and arteries.[5] In adults, the high rate of blood clots and atherosclerosis, especially in the carotid artery, could cause premature cardiovascular disease.[6]

Galactosemia and Glycogen Storage Disease

Two carbohydrate-related genetic disorders are **galactosemia** and **glycogen storage disease.** Galactosemia results in the inability to convert galactose to glucose due to the lack of the enzyme galactose 1-phosphate uridyltransferase and a buildup of galactose, which can damage the liver, brain, kidneys, and eyes if left untreated. The treatment focuses mainly on restricting dietary lactose and galactose, which means avoiding milk and all dairy products, and products that contain milk chocolate, whey protein or whey solids, casein, and dry milk solids, all of which may contain galactose.

Glycogen storage disease refers to the inability to break down glycogen due to a deficiency in the enzyme glucose 6-phosphatase. If glycogen is trapped in the liver or muscle, the body is unable to provide glucose for energy metabolism, or to maintain normal blood glucose levels between meals. To treat glycogen storage disease, foods that contain sucrose, lactose, galactose, and fructose are restricted because these carbohydrates are often stored as glycogen in the liver. Individuals diagnosed with glycogen storage disease follow the dietary recommendations for life.

maple syrup urine disease (MSUD) A genetic disorder characterized by the inability to metabolize branched-chain amino acids; symptoms include a maple syrup smell in the urine.

homocystinuria A genetic disorder characterized by the inability to metabolize the essential amino acid methionine.

galactosemia The genetic disorder characterized by high levels of galactose in the blood due to the inability to convert galactose to glucose.

glycogen storage disease A genetic disorder characterized by the inability to break down glycogen due to the lack of glucose 6-phosphatase.

References

1. Mitsubuchi, H., M. Owada, and F. Endo. 2005. Markers Associated with Inborn Errors of Metabolism of Branched-Chain Amino Acids and Their Relevance to Upper Levels of Intake in Healthy People: An Implication from Clinical and Molecular Investigations on Maple Syrup Urine Disease. *Journal of Nutrition* 135:1565S–1570S.
2. Shils, M. E., M. Shike, A. C. Ross, B. Caballero, and R. J. Cousins. 2006. *Modern Nutrition in Health and Disease.* 10th ed. Philadelphia: Lippincott Williams & Williams.
3. Robinson, K., E. Mayer, and D. W. Jacobsen. 1994. Homocysteine and Coronary Artery Disease. *Cleveland Clinic Journal of Medicine* 61:438–450.
4. Burton, M. J., K. J. Burton, and C. M. Chuka-Okosa. 2002. Plummeting Lenses in the TB Clinic. *The Lancet* 360:138.
5. Thambyrajah, J. and J. N. Townend. 2000. Homocysteine and Atherothrombosis—Mechanisms for Injury. *European Heart Journal* 21:967–974.
6. Robinson, K., E. Mayer, and D. W. Jacobsen. 1994. Homocysteine and Coronary Artery Disease. *Cleveland Clinic Journal of Medicine* 61:438–450.

Two Points of View

Can Genetics Be Used to Improve Nutritional Health?

Two experts in the field of nutritional genomics discuss the interaction between genetic variations and nutrition.

Ruth DeBusk, PhD, RD

Geneticist and Clinical Nutritionist

Ruth DeBusk is a private practitioner specializing in genetics, nutrition, and gene-based counseling. She has authored numerous books, textbook chapters, and peer-reviewed articles for scientific journals, and has served on journal editorial boards, scientific advisory boards, and grant review panels. Before entering private practice, she was on the genetic faculty at Florida State University, where her research focused on how genes regulate the absorption of dietary nutrients.

Q: What is nutritional genomics?

A: Nutritional genomics is a marriage between genetic technology and food and nutrition science and concerns the interaction between environmental factors and our genetic makeup. The field of nutritional genomics provides insight into how our individual set of genetic variations and the diet and lifestyle choices we make work together to determine whether we'll be well or ill and, ultimately, provides insight on how we might maximize our genetic potential.

Q: How will nutritional genomics potentially benefit nutrition research and the consumer?

A: The real promise of nutritional genomics is disease prevention. While we know that food and nutrition are keys to health, it's been difficult to get beyond general guidelines because everyone responds differently to the same foods, diets, and lifestyle experiences. Even identical twins, who have the same genetic material, can have distinctly different health outcomes. We now understand that these differences are the result of the interaction between our genes and our environment, specifically the nutritional epigenetic effects of diet and lifestyle choices on gene expression at key times during development and throughout life. In fact, current research suggests that, in addition to the diet and lifestyle choices we make, those of our parents and grandparents also significantly influence our health.

Q: What are the potential challenges of implementing the research to everyday practice?

A: I see two major challenges that I feel certain will resolve as this field develops. The first is the need for a strong foundation of nutritional genomics research. The second is the education and training of the researchers who will conduct the basic and clinical nutritional genomics research and for the clinicians who will translate the research findings into practical applications. No type of healthcare

Jim Kaput, PhD

Nestlé Institute of Health Sciences, Clinical Translation Unit

Jim Kaput, PhD, is the Head of the Clinical Translation Unit at the Nestlé Institute of Health Sciences, and the former director of the Division of Personalized Nutrition and Medicine at the Food and Drug Administration.* He is also co-founder of the international Nutrigenomics Society (NxS) and recently co-edited with Raymond Rodriguez *Nutritional Genomics: Discovering the Path to Personalized Nutrition*.

Q: What is nutritional genomics?

A: Nutrigenomics seeks to provide a genetic understanding for how common dietary chemicals (that is, nutrition) affect human physiology at the molecular level and how individual physiology affects the metabolism of nutrients. The basis for this new branch of genomic research can be summarized with the following five tenets:

- Common dietary chemicals act on the human genome to alter gene expression or structure.
- Under certain circumstances and in some individuals, diet can be a serious risk factor for a number of diseases.
- Some diet-regulated genes play a role in the onset, incidence, progression, and/or severity of chronic diseases.
- The degree to which diet influences the balance between healthy and disease states may depend on an individual's genetic makeup.
- Dietary intervention based on "individualized nutrition" can be used to prevent, mitigate, or cure chronic disease.

Q: How will nutritional genomics potentially benefit nutrition research and the consumer?

A: A comprehensive nutritional genomics approach will yield short- and long-term benefits to human health by (1) revealing nutrient–gene interactions, (2) developing new diagnostic tests for adverse responses to diets, (3) identifying specific populations with special nutrient needs, (4) improving the definitions and methodology related to dietary assessment, and (5) provid[ing] information for developing more nutritious foods and food formulations that promote health and prevent, mitigate, or cure disease.

*The views presented in this interview do not necessarily reflect those of the Food and Drug Administration.

professional is presently being trained in the basics of genomics in general, nutritional genomics in particular, and the applications of this science at the patient care level.

Q: How do you address these potential challenges?

A: The technology exists for developing the research foundation for nutritional genomics. What is needed is significant funding and trained researchers and technical personnel to design and execute the large studies that have sufficient statistical power to detect strong associations between genetic variations and specific functional outcomes. From this foundation will come clinically relevant approaches to disease management and disease prevention. The capacity gap is also beginning to be addressed. The Academy of Nutrition and Dietetics and university nutrition programs are playing a leadership role in incorporating nutritional genomics into undergraduate and graduate education. The Academy of Nutrition and Dietetics and university nutrition programs are playing a leadership role in incorporating nutritional genomics into undergraduate and graduate education.

Q: What are the potential challenges of implementing the research to everyday practice?

A: While the potential benefits of personalized health care are significant, research and applications face challenges based on human genetic heterogeneity, the complexity of foods, and physiological mechanisms that produce health or disease states. Another significant challenge is that association studies are based on population studies that yield the attributable fraction (AF)—"the proportional reduction in average disease risk over a specified time interval that would be achieved by eliminating the exposure of interest from the population"—while other factors remain unchanged.

Q: How do you address these potential challenges?

A: The most important components for addressing these challenges will be the development of research strategies that analyze individual responses rather than populations. A second strategy focuses on predicting how an individual responds to a metabolic challenge.

TABLE 8.4 Summary of Metabolic Processes in the Cells

Metabolic Pathway	Nutrient(s) Involved in the Pathway	Description of the Pathway	Major Tissues Involved	Type of Pathway
Glycolysis	Carbohydrates	Metabolism of glucose to produce pyruvate and two ATP	All cells	Catabolic and anabolic
Glycogenesis	Carbohydrates	Producing glycogen from excess glucose	Muscle and liver	Anabolic
Glycogenolysis	Carbohydrates	Breakdown of glycogen to glucose	Muscle and liver	Catabolic
Gluconeogenesis	Noncarbohydrates, including amino acids, glycerol, pyruvate, and lactate	Producing glucose from noncarbohydrate sources	Liver and kidneys	Anabolic
Beta-oxidation	Fatty acids	Fatty acid oxidation to acetyl CoA	Liver and muscle	Catabolic
Lipolysis	Fatty acids	Breakdown of triglycerides to yield fatty acids and glycerol	Adipose tissue and liver	Catabolic
Lipogenesis	Fatty acids	Synthesis of fatty acids and triglycerides	Adipose tissue and liver	Anabolic
Ketogenesis	Fatty acids and ketogenic amino acids	The conversion of fatty acids and ketogenic amino acids to acetyl CoA and to ketone bodies	Liver	Anabolic
Transamination	Amino acids	Formation of nonessential amino acids produced by transferring an amine group from one amino acid to an alpha-keto acid	Liver	Catabolic
TCA cycle	All nutrients	Oxidation of acetyl CoA to produce hydrogen ions, carbon dioxide, and GTP	All cells (except RBCs)	Catabolic and anabolic
Electron transport chain	All nutrients	Formation of ATP and water from hydrogen ions and protons generated during glycolysis and the TCA cycle	All cells (except RBCs)	Catabolic

Visual Chapter Summary

1 Metabolism Is the Sum of All Chemical Reactions in the Body

Metabolism is the term given to all chemical reactions in the cells. The mitochondria are the organelles within the cells that generate most of the cell's energy through aerobic metabolism. Metabolism balances anabolic reactions that create large molecules from smaller parts, such as glucose to glycogen, with catabolic reactions that break apart large molecules, such as triglycerides to glycerol and fatty acids, to produce energy and create building blocks for essential compounds. These reactions are turned on and off by hormones and are stimulated by enzymes and coenzymes.

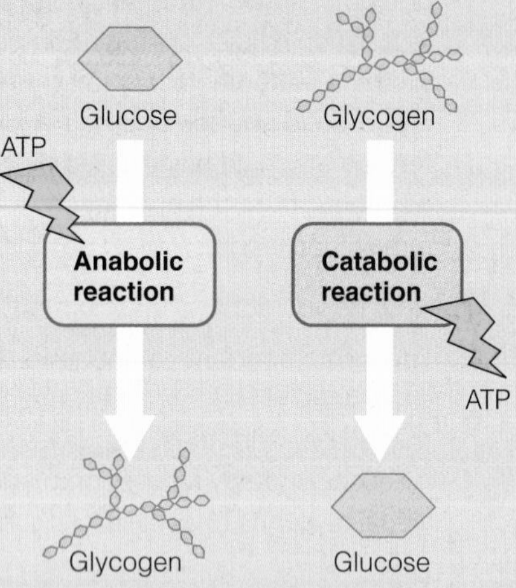

2 ATP Is the Energy Currency

Adenosine triphosphate or ATP is the energy currency that fuels metabolism. Energy is released when a phosphate bond is broken, producing adenosine diphosphate or ADP. This energy is used to fuel anabolic reactions. ATP is regenerated from ADP plus a phosphate molecule, which can be donated from creatine phosphate.

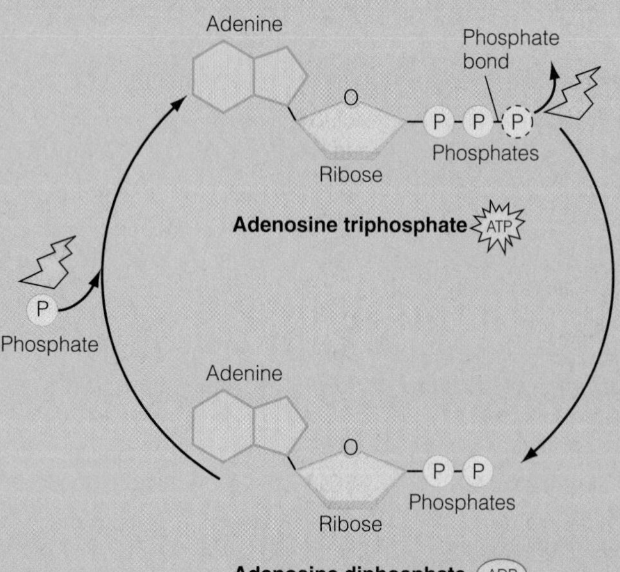

3 Carbohydrates, Triglycerides, and Amino Acids Follow Metabolic Pathways

Glucose, the main monosaccharide in metabolism, is oxidized in the cytosol through glycolysis to form pyruvate. If there is sufficient oxygen in the cell, pyruvate continues down the pathway to acetyl CoA and enters the TCA cycle.

Triglycerides are hydrolyzed to glycerol and fatty acids. Glycerol enters the metabolic pathway during glycolysis, while fatty acids undergo beta-oxidation to form acetyl CoA.

Deaminated amino acids can be oxidized in the TCA cycle. Glucogenic amino acids can be transformed into pyruvate and participate in gluconeogenesis. Ketogenic amino acids are converted to acetyl CoA and are either oxidized in the TCA cycle or turned into fatty acids and stored as triglycerides.

The TCA cycle, which occurs in the mitochondria, begins with acetyl CoA. Its products include hydrogen atoms and electrons that are transferred to the electron transport chain where the majority of ATP is generated.

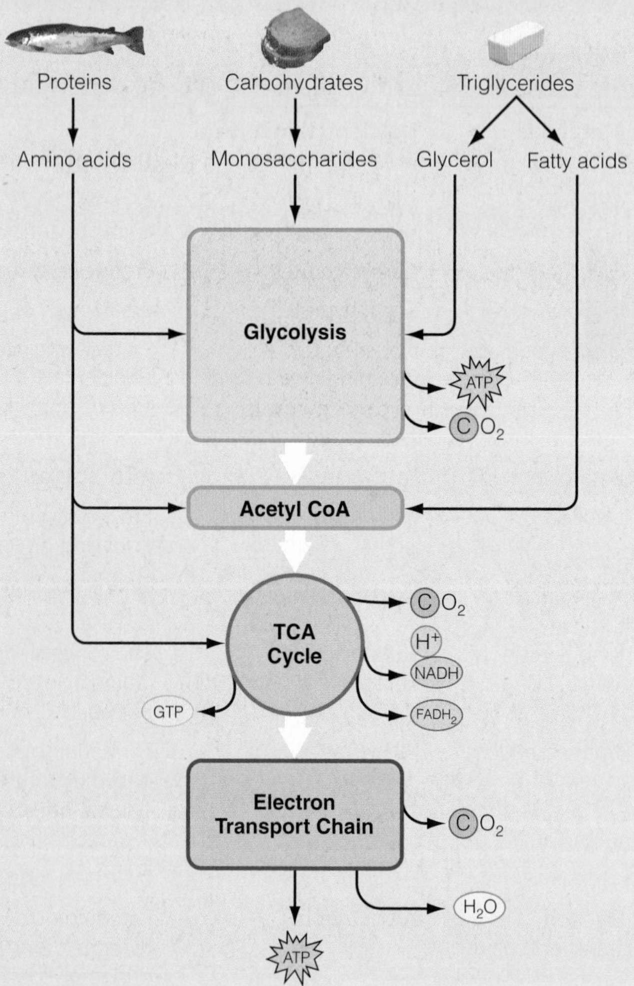

4 Metabolism Switches between Anabolic Processes and Catabolic Processes during the Absorptive State, Postabsorptive State, and Starvation

During the absorptive state, excess kilocalories stimulate fat synthesis and are stored as triglycerides. Excess carbohydrates can also be stored as glycogen.

Fasting during the postabsorptive state shifts the metabolism to catabolic reactions to maintain energy balance. The body uses stored glycogen and fatty acids from stored triglycerides in the early stages of fasting. As fasting continues, the body increases the breakdown of fats for energy and conversion to ketone bodies, which can be used by the brain and muscle. Blood glucose levels are maintained using amino acids, pyruvate, lactate, and glycerol as precursors in gluconeogenesis.

5 The Liver Metabolizes Alcohol

Alcohol is metabolized in the liver to acetyl CoA by the enzyme system ADH. The acetyl CoA enters the TCA cycle to produce energy. When an excess of alcohol builds up, the acetyl CoA is converted to fatty acids and can be stored as a triglyceride in the liver or sent out into the blood. The consumption of excess alcohol can result in the buildup of stored fat in the liver, leading to a condition called cirrhosis.

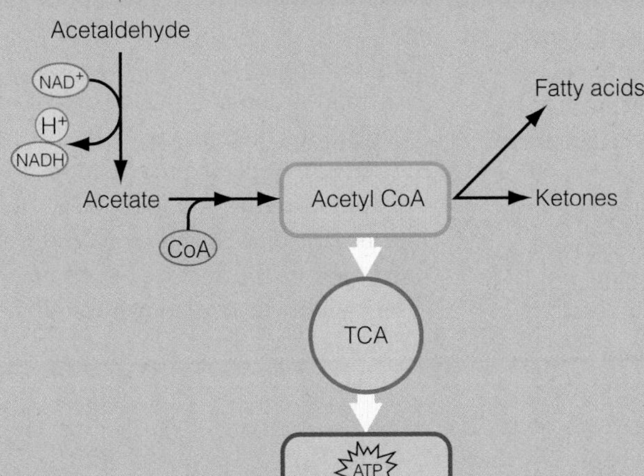

6 Inborn Errors of Metabolism Are Genetic

Inborn errors of metabolism are genetic disorders that can disrupt one or more metabolic pathways, due to the lack of an enzyme involved in either protein or carbohydrate metabolism. For infants with some genetic disorders, formulas are used to control the amount of specific nutrients consumed, such as with maple syrup urine disease.

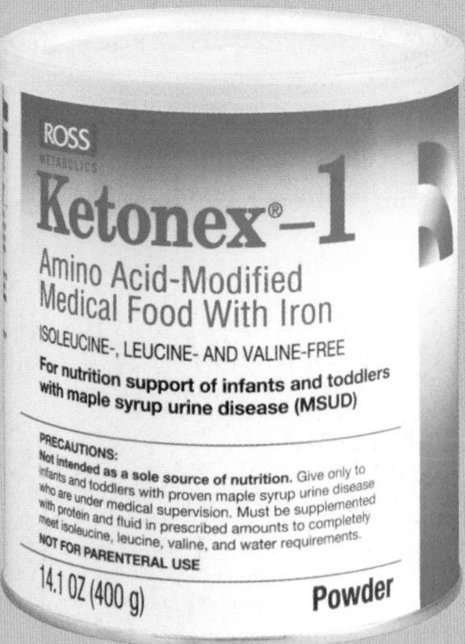

Terms to Know

- metabolism
- metabolic pathway
- mitochondrion
- cytosol
- anabolic reactions
- catabolic reactions
- adenosine diphosphate (ADP)
- creatine phosphate (PCr)
- glycolysis
- pyruvate
- acetyl CoA
- tricarboxylic acid (TCA) cycle
- electron transport chain
- lactate
- Cori cycle
- hormone-sensitive lipase
- beta-oxidation
- ketogenic
- alpha-ketoglutarate
- oxaloacetate
- flavoproteins
- cytochromes
- absorptive state
- postabsorptive state
- ketogenesis
- ketoacidosis
- aldehyde dehydrogenase
- microsomal ethanol oxidizing system (MEOS)
- inborn errors of metabolism
- phenylketonuria (PKU)
- hyperphenylalanemia
- maple syrup urine disease (MSUD)
- homocystinuria
- galactosemia
- glycogen storage disease

MasteringNutrition™

Build your knowledge—and confidence!—in the Study Area of MasteringNutrition with a variety of study tools.

Check Your Understanding

1. Metabolism is defined as
   a. the breakdown of large compounds into smaller particles.
   b. the synthesis of new compounds.
   c. the sum of all chemical reactions in the body.
   d. the storage of fat in the adipocyte.
2. Glycolysis is a metabolic pathway that breaks down glucose for energy. This is an example of a(n)
   a. anabolic reaction.
   b. catabolic reaction.
   c. redox reaction
   d. glucogenic reaction
3. Your metabolism is regulated by
   a. hormones such as insulin and glucagon.
   b. hydroxylase activity.
   c. the amount of creatine phosphate in your cells.
   d. all of the above.
4. The energy molecule that fuels metabolism is
   a. adenosine diphosphate.
   b. adenosine triphosphate.
   c. creatine phosphate.
   d. acetyl CoA.
5. The first stage in using glucose for energy metabolism is called
   a. beta-oxidation.
   b. the Cori cycle.
   c. glycolysis.
   d. the electron transport chain.
6. The compounds that can be used for gluconeogenesis include
   a. fatty acids.
   b. lactate.
   c. ketogenic amino acids.
   d. acetaldehyde.
7. Fatty acids cannot be used for gluconeogenesis because
   a. they lack sufficient carbons to form glucose.
   b. they are converted to acetyl CoA, which can't reform pyruvate.
   c. they are converted to oxaloacetate, which can't reform pyruvate.
   d. they enter the TCA cycle through citrate.
8. If your diet contains excess protein, the excess amino acids are
   a. deaminated and then converted to ATP or fatty acids.
   b. stored as glycogen in the liver.
   c. stored as protein in the muscle.
   d. subject to all of the above.
9. If you don't eat enough food, especially carbohydrates, to meet your body's energy needs,
   a. ketogenesis is stimulated.
   b. glycogenesis is stimulated.
   c. lipogenesis is stimulated.
   d. all of the above may occur.
10. Homocystinuria is a genetic disorder caused by
    a. a buildup of galactose.
    b. a lack of the enzyme cystathionine beta-synthase.
    c. the inability to break down glycogen.
    d. a deficiency in the amino acid methionine.

Answers

1. (c) Metabolism is defined as the sum of all chemical reactions in the body. This includes anabolic reactions that build larger compounds from smaller molecules, catabolic reactions that break molecules apart, or lipogenesis or storing fat in the adipocyte.
2. (b) Catabolic reactions are those that break apart larger molecules into smaller molecules. Anabolic reactions are the opposite and build larger molecules from smaller molecules. Redox reactions, or oxidation-reduction reactions, involve the transfer of electrons, and glucogenic reactions produce glucose.
3. (a) Metabolism is controlled by hormones, which are released in response to changes in ATP and enzyme activity.
4. (a) Adenosine triphosphate (ATP) is a high-energy molecule that, when hydrolyzed to adenosine disphosphate (ADP), provides energy to cells. ATP can be reformed by adding an inorganic phosphate to ADP donated from the initial reaction, or from creatine phosphate (PCr).
5. (c) Glycolysis is the first stage of carbohydrate metabolism. Eventually, the hydrogen atoms and electrons generated from glycolysis are carried to the electron transport chain. Beta-oxidation is the metabolic pathway used to convert fatty acids to acetyl CoA. At the end of glycolysis, pyruvate can be converted to lactate, which is converted into glucose through the Cori cycle in the liver.
6. (b) Lactate can be transformed into glucose through gluconeogenesis. Fatty acids, ketogenic amino acids, and acetaldehyde are not gluconeogenic substrates.
7. (b) Fatty acids contain sufficient carbons but they are converted to acetyl CoA, which is not able to form the pyruvate needed for gluconeogenesis.
8. (a) Because we can't store excess amino acids as protein, we have to either use them for ATP synthesis or convert them to fatty acids and store them as a triglyceride.
9. (a) If an individual does not eat sufficient kilocalories, the body will use other metabolic pathways, including ketogenesis, to provide energy. Glucogenesis and lipogenesis are metabolic pathways that are stimulated when an excess of kilocalories are consumed.
10. (b) Homocystinuria is caused by the lack or impaired function of the enzyme cystathionine beta-synthase that converts homocysteine to cystathionine. Homocysteine and certain amino acids, such as methionine, build up in the blood. Controlling methionine intake is essential to reducing the buildup of homocysteine. A buildup of galactose is called galactosemia and glycogen storage disease results in the inability to break down stored glycogen.

Answers to Myths and Misconceptions

1. **True.** All chemical reactions involved in metabolism take place within the mitochondria or the cytosol of cells.
2. **True.** The body metabolizes carbohydrates mostly as glucose through glycolysis, which produces more energy in the form of ATP than it uses, compared with amino acid and fatty acid metabolism.
3. **False.** Most fructose is converted to glucose before entering the metabolic pathway.
4. **False.** A burning sensation in muscles during strenuous exercise is caused by the reduction in pH due to the buildup of hydrogen ions, not the buildup of lactate.
5. **False.** Once protein and energy needs have been met, excess amino acids are converted to fatty acids through acetyl CoA and stored as triglycerides in adipocytes. Thus excess intake of dietary protein will not result in larger muscle.
6. **False.** Fatty acids are oxidized in the TCA cycle when cells contain sufficient oxygen. Under the anaerobic conditions of high-intensity exercise, a larger percentage of glucose, rather than fatty acids, is used for energy production.
7. **False.** During alcohol metabolism in the liver, ethanol is converted to acetyl CoA, which either enters the TCA cycle or is transformed into fatty acids. Acetyl CoA cannot be used to produce glucose.
8. **False.** Vitamins and minerals in foods do not provide energy. However, the B vitamins niacin and riboflavin are essential for energy production because of their roles as coenzymes during metabolism. As coenzymes, they accept hydrogen atoms and electrons produced during glycolysis and the TCA cycle, which are in turn used by the electron transport chain to produce energy.
9. **False.** Regardless of what time of day you eat, an excess of total kilocalories favors anabolic metabolism, which means you store the excess kilocalories as body fat or glycogen. If you consume fewer kilocalories than you need each day for metabolism, catabolic reactions are favored, resulting in a breakdown of triglycerides.
10. **False.** Inborn errors of metabolism are the result of a genetic mutation that causes a specific metabolic enzyme to be either missing or produced in inadequate amounts. The gene is not repaired during puberty, and the disorders cannot be outgrown.

Web Resources

- For general information on genetic disorders, visit the National Human Genome Research Institute at www.nhgri.nih.gov
- For more information on phenylketonuria, visit the National PKU Alliance at www.npkua.org
- For more information on galactosemia, visit the Galactosemia Foundation at http://galactosemia.org
- For more information from a peer-reviewed online journal, visit *Nutrition and Metabolism* at www.nutritionandmetabolism.com

References

1. Stipanuk, M. H. 2000. *Biochemical and Physiological Aspects of Human Nutrition.* Philadelphia: W. B. Saunders.
2. Schröder, H., N. Terrados, and A. Tramullas. 2005. Risk Assessment of the Potential Side Effects of Long-Term Creatine Supplementation in Team Sport Athletes. *European Journal of Nutrition* 44:255–261.
3. Tortora, G., B. Funke, and C. Case. 2007. *Microbiology: An Introduction.* San Francisco: Pearson Benjamin Cummings.
4. Berg, J. M., J. L. Tymoczko, and L. Stryer. 2001. *Biochemistry.* 5th ed. New York: W. H. Freeman and Company.
5. Ibid.
6. Ibid.
7. Shils, M. E., M. Shike, A. C. Ross, B. Caballero, and R. J. Cousins. 2006. *Modern Nutrition in Health and Disease.* 10th ed. Philadelphia: Lippincott Williams & Williams.
8. Zimatkin, S. M. and A. L. Buben. 2007. Ethanol Oxidation in the Living Brain. *Alcohol and Alcoholism* 42:529–532.
9. Berg, J. M. 2001. *Biochemistry.*

9 Fat-Soluble Vitamins

Chapter Objectives

After reading this chapter, you will be able to:

1. Explain the characteristics of vitamins, and classify the different vitamins according to their solubility.
2. Describe the differences between absorption and storage of fat-soluble and water-soluble vitamins.
3. Define the term "antioxidant" and explain which vitamins perform this function.
4. Describe the best sources of vitamins and the factors that affect the vitamin content of foods.
5. Describe the functions, recommended intakes, food sources, and the deficiency and toxicity effects of vitamin A.
6. Describe the functions, recommended intakes, food sources, and the deficiency and toxicity effects of vitamin D.
7. Describe the functions, recommended intakes, food sources, and the deficiency and toxicity effects of vitamin E.
8. Describe the functions, recommended intakes, food sources, and the deficiency and toxicity effects of vitamin K.
9. Explain the role that fat-soluble vitamins and antioxidants play in cancer risk and progression.

1. Vitamins provide the body with energy. T/F
2. Fat-soluble vitamins are found in fatty foods. T/F
3. Taking vitamin supplements is *never* harmful. T/F
4. Most people can meet their vitamin needs through food, so supplements are unnecessary. T/F
5. Steaming is the best cooking method to retain the vitamins in vegetables. T/F
6. Carrots, winter squash, and broccoli are good sources of vitamin A. T/F
7. The body makes vitamin D with the help of sunlight. T/F
8. Vitamin K is an anticoagulant. T/F
9. Vitamin E helps keep bones strong. T/F
10. Antioxidants are a magic pill that will prevent aging. T/F

See page 363 for answers to these Myths and Misconceptions.

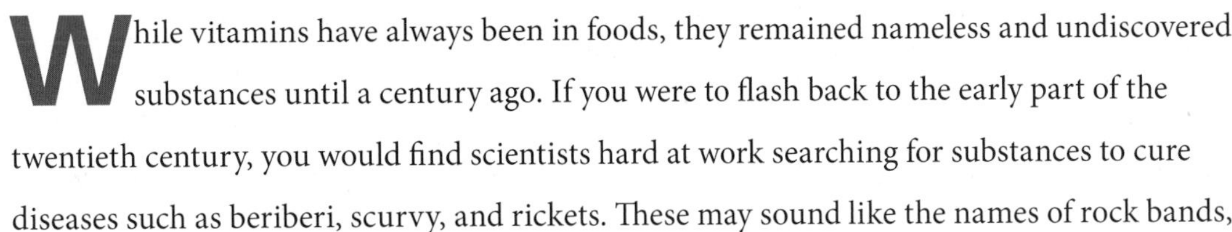

While vitamins have always been in foods, they remained nameless and undiscovered substances until a century ago. If you were to flash back to the early part of the twentieth century, you would find scientists hard at work searching for substances to cure diseases such as beriberi, scurvy, and rickets. These may sound like the names of rock bands,

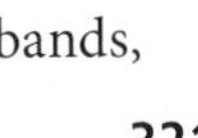

but they are actually devastating diseases caused by deficiencies of thiamin (for beriberi), vitamin C (for scurvy), and vitamin D (for rickets). Throughout the twentieth century, scientists discovered the vitamins that cured these and other diseases. By the 1940s, the U.S. government mandated that specific vitamins be added to grains and milk to improve the nation's health by improving people's diet.

Now flash forward to the latter part of the twentieth century, when an improved diet meant that vitamin deficiencies became less of an issue for most Americans. Scientists shifted their focus from using vitamins to cure disease to using them to prevent disease. Today, research is being done to find out how vitamins affect and prevent everything from birth defects to heart disease and cancer.

In this chapter, we begin with an overview of vitamins, followed by a discussion of differences between the fat-soluble and water-soluble vitamins. We'll then cover the four fat-soluble vitamins in detail, including their functions, recommended intakes, food sources, and the deficiency and toxicity effects. (The water-soluble vitamins will be discussed in Chapter 10.)

What Are Vitamins?

Vitamins (*vita* = vital, *amine* = contains nitrogen) are tasteless organic compounds the body requires in small amounts for normal metabolic functions. Vitamins act as coenzymes to regulate metabolism; assist the body to convert the energy in fat, carbohydrates, and protein into ATP; and promote growth and reproduction. Vitamins do not provide energy themselves. A deficiency of any vitamin can result in potentially serious symptoms.

Vitamins Were Discovered about One Hundred Years Ago

Though vitamin deficiency diseases have been around for millennia, vitamins themselves were largely undiscovered until about a hundred years ago. During the eighteenth century alone, an estimated 2 million sailors died of scurvy, the deficiency disease caused by a lack of vitamin C. The mottled skin and spongy gums that are symptomatic of the disease frequently occurred among men on long sea voyages, during which supplies of fresh foods would be depleted before the end of the trip. Eventually, the acid in citrus fruit was recognized as a curative factor, and British sailors came to be known as "Limeys" because of the British Navy's policy of issuing lime juice on board its ships to prevent scurvy. What they didn't recognize was that the citrus fruit provides vitamin C, which is the vitamin needed to ward off scurvy.

Two hundred years after the British Navy's use of lime juice on its ships, other vitamin deficiency diseases began to be recognized. During the early part of the

vitamins Thirteen essential, organic micronutrients that are needed by the body for normal functions, such as regulating metabolism and assisting in energy production, growth, reproduction, and overall health.

twentieth century, scientists were searching for substances to cure diseases such as beriberi and rickets.[1] Researchers eventually identified thiamin as the curative vitamin for beriberi, and vitamin D as the cure for rickets. As additional vitamins were associated with other diseases and conditions, scientists realized their value in promoting public health.

As each new vitamin was discovered, it was given a temporary name until its structure was isolated. Researchers started at the beginning of the alphabet with vitamins A, B, C, D, E, and K. The letters F, G, and H were dropped once those substances were found not to exist.

This nomenclature changed after vitamin B was found to have more than one physiological function, and chemists began adding a subscript number to each newly isolated role. Together, these vitamins became known as the B complex, with individual vitamins labeled B_1, B_2, and so forth. While vitamins B_6 and B_{12} still retain their numeric names, most of the B vitamins are now better known by their chemical names. For instance, vitamin B_1 is more commonly referred to as thiamin and vitamin B_2 is known as riboflavin.

There Are Criteria for Designating Vitamins

Vitamins are unique nutrients in that they are not the same in their chemical structure nor do they have similar functions. Whereas, as you learned from earlier chapters, amino acids each have a basic structure but differ in their side groups, this is not the case with vitamins. So how, then, are vitamins classified?

A compound is classified as a vitamin when it cannot be synthesized in ample amounts in the body. For instance, vitamin K and two of the B vitamins (niacin and biotin) can be made in the body, but not in amounts sufficient to meet the body's metabolic needs, so they must also be consumed in the diet. A second requirement for a compound to be called a vitamin is that a chronic deficiency of the compound is likely to cause physical symptoms, from fatigue or confusion to scaly skin or blindness. The symptoms disappear once the vitamin has been sufficiently restored to the diet and absorbed into the body, provided the deficiency has not caused permanent damage.

Based on these criteria, 13 compounds are classified as vitamins. The vitamins are further classified according to their solubility. There are eight water-soluble (hydrophilic) vitamins, including the B vitamin complex and vitamin C, and four fat-soluble (hydrophobic) vitamins: A, D, E, and K (see **Figure 9.1**). The distinction in solubility is important because it influences how the body digests, absorbs, transports, stores, and excretes these essential nutrients.

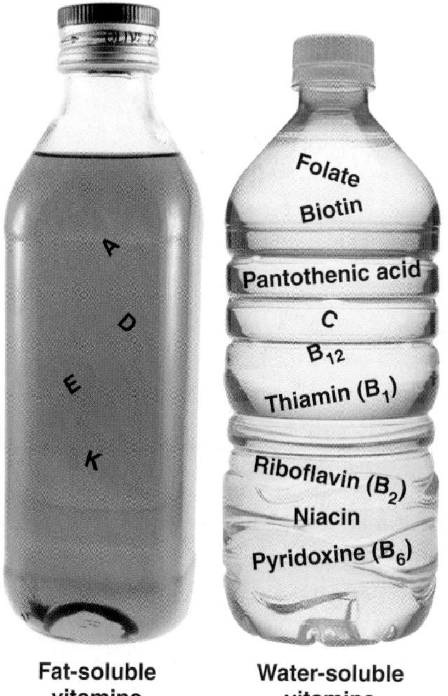

▲ **Figure 9.1 Categorizing the Vitamins: Fat-Soluble and Water-Soluble**
A vitamin is either fat-soluble or water-soluble, depending on how it is absorbed and handled in the body. Fat-soluble vitamins need dietary fat to be properly absorbed, while water-soluble vitamins are absorbed with water.

All Vitamins Are Organic, but Differ in Structure and Function

All vitamins are organic because they contain carbon. Vitamins also contain hydrogen and oxygen and, in some cases, nitrogen and sulfur. The chemical structure of each vitamin is unique. That is, unlike proteins, which consist of and vary by chains of amino acids, vitamins are singular units. For this reason, there are no bonds for the body to hydrolyze during digestion, and vitamins are absorbed intact into the intestinal wall.

Vitamins perform numerous essential functions in the body. Some, including thiamin, riboflavin, and niacin, participate in releasing energy from the macronutrients. Vitamin D helps regulate bone metabolism, while vitamins E and C donate

TABLE 9.1 The Many Roles of Vitamins in Maintaining Health

Metabolic Function	Vitamins That Play a Role
Antioxidants	Vitamin C, vitamin E, beta-carotene
Blood clotting and red blood cell synthesis	Folate, vitamin B_6, vitamin B_{12}, vitamin K
Bone health	Vitamin A, vitamin C, vitamin D, vitamin K
Energy production	Biotin, niacin (B_3), pantothenic acid, riboflavin (B_2), thiamin (B_1), vitamin B_6, vitamin B_{12}
Growth and reproduction	Vitamin A, vitamin D
Immune function	Vitamin A, vitamin C, vitamin D
Protein metabolism and synthesis	Folate, vitamin B_6, vitamin B_{12}

or accept electrons as an antioxidant. Several vitamins play more than one role in metabolism. Table 9.1 illustrates the variety of functions vitamins play in maintaining health.

Provitamins Can Be Converted to Active Vitamins by the Body

Provitamins are substances found in foods that are not in a form directly usable by the body, but that can be converted into an active form once they are absorbed. The most well-known example of this is beta-carotene, which is split into two molecules of vitamin A in the small intestinal cell wall or in the liver cells. Vitamins found in foods that are already in the active form, called **preformed vitamins,** do not undergo conversion.

Overconsumption of Some Vitamins Can Be Toxic

Vitamin **toxicity,** or **hypervitaminosis,** is very rare. This condition results from ingesting more of the vitamin than the body needs, to the point where tissues become saturated. The excess vitamin can damage cells, sometimes permanently. Vitamin toxicity does not occur by eating a normal balanced diet. It can result when individuals consume **megadose** levels of vitamin supplements, usually in the false belief that "more is better." Many individuals, for example, overload on vitamin C tablets to ward off a cold, despite the fact that there is no evidence that vitamin C prevents the common cold, and despite the fact that too much vitamin C in the body can lead to unpleasant side effects, including diarrhea.

To prevent excessive intake, the Dietary Reference Intakes include a tolerable upper intake level for most vitamins. Even though sufficient evidence to establish a UL is lacking for some vitamins, there still may be risks in taking them in megadose amounts.

THE TAKE-HOME MESSAGE Vitamins are essential nutrients needed in small amounts for growth, reproduction, and overall good health. All vitamins are either fat-soluble or water-soluble. Provitamins are converted to their active form before they can be directly used in the body. Vitamins, especially fat-soluble vitamins, can be toxic if taken in megadose amounts.

provitamin A vitamin precursor that is converted to a vitamin in the body.

preformed vitamins Vitamins found in food.

toxicity The accumulation of a substance to a harmful level.

hypervitaminosis A condition resulting from the presence of excessive amounts of vitamins in the body; also referred to as *vitamin toxicity*.

megadose An amount of a vitamin or mineral that's at least 10 times the amount recommended in the DRI.

How Do Vitamins Differ in Their Absorption and Storage?

All vitamins are absorbed in the small intestine, but fat-soluble vitamins are absorbed differently from water-soluble vitamins. They also differ in their bioavailability from foods. Let's look closer at these differences.

Vitamins Differ in Bioavailability

Not all of the vitamins consumed in foods are available to be used in the body. In other words, they are not 100 percent bioavailable. The **bioavailability** of individual vitamins varies according to several factors, including the amount of the vitamin in the food; whether the food is cooked, raw, or refined; how efficiently the food is digested and absorbed; the individual's nutritional status; and whether or not the vitamin is natural or synthetic. In general, if the body needs more vitamins, a greater percentage will be absorbed. For example, a young child or pregnant woman will absorb more ingested vitamins than will a nonpregnant adult.

The bioavailability of vitamins differs based on their solubility and the type of food. Fat-soluble vitamins are usually less bioavailable than water-soluble vitamins because fat-soluble vitamins require bile and the formation of a micelle in order to be absorbed. Vitamins in plant foods are typically less bioavailable than those in animal foods because plant fiber can trap vitamins.

Fat-Soluble Vitamins Are Stored after They Are Absorbed

Fat-soluble vitamins are often attached to food components, usually protein, in foods. To be absorbed, the vitamin must be released from the protein with the help of pepsin and hydrochloric acid (refer to Chapter 3). The freed fat-soluble vitamins are then ready to be absorbed, primarily in the duodenum (**Figure 9.2**). They are packaged with fatty acids and bile in micelles that transport

bioavailability The degree to which a nutrient is absorbed from foods and used in the body.

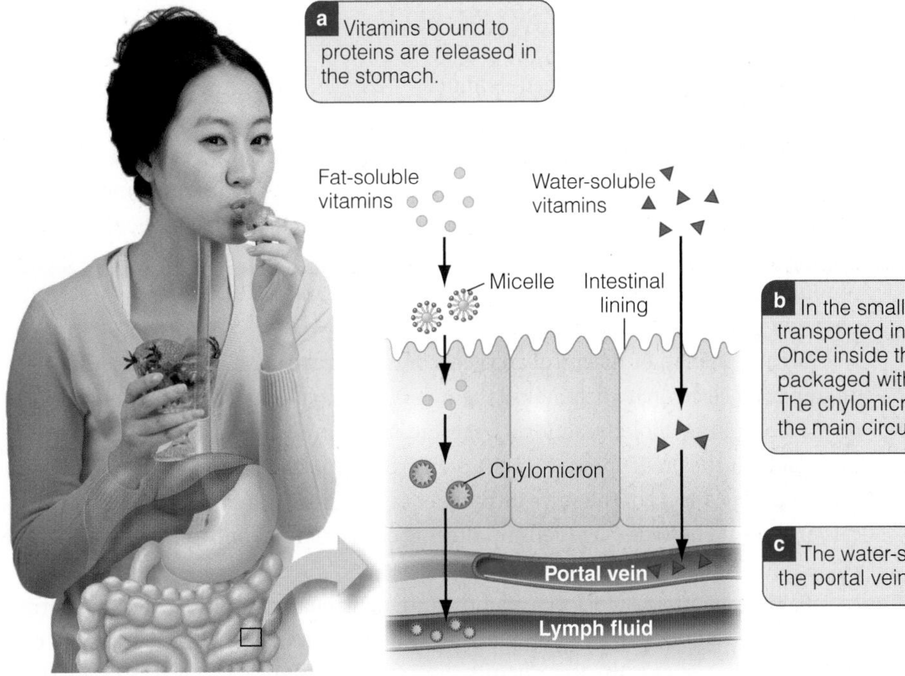
a Vitamins bound to proteins are released in the stomach.
Fat-soluble vitamins
Water-soluble vitamins
Micelle
Intestinal lining
Chylomicron
Portal vein
Lymph fluid
b In the small intestine, the fat-soluble vitamins are transported into the intestinal cells as part of micelles. Once inside the intestinal cells, fat-soluble vitamins are packaged with fat and other lipids into a chylomicron. The chylomicrons travel through the lymph system to the main circulation.
c The water-soluble vitamins are absorbed directly into the portal vein from the small intestine.

▲ **Figure 9.2 Digesting and Absorbing Vitamins**

them close to the intestinal mucosa. Once there, the fat-soluble vitamins travel through the cells in the intestinal wall, and are repackaged with fat and other lipids into chylomicrons. The vitamins then travel through the lymph system before they enter the bloodstream. Note that absorption of fat-soluble vitamins can be compromised in the absence of adequate fatty acids or bile. This is why having some fat in the diet is absolutely necessary to avoid fat soluble-vitamin deficiencies.

Fat-soluble vitamins are stored in the body and used as needed when dietary intake falls short of the body's needs. The liver is the main storage depot for vitamin A and to a lesser extent vitamins K and E, whereas vitamin D is mainly stored in fat and muscle tissues. Because they are stored in the body, large quantities of some of the fat-soluble vitamins, particularly A, can build up to the point of toxicity, causing harmful symptoms and conditions.

Water-Soluble Vitamins Are Not Stored after Absorption

Water-soluble vitamins are absorbed with water and enter the bloodstream directly from the small intestine. Most water-soluble vitamins are absorbed in the duodenum and jejunum, although vitamin B_{12} is absorbed in the ileum. Water-soluble vitamins are not stored in the body, and excess amounts are excreted, so it's important to consume adequate amounts of them every day. Note that even though most water-soluble vitamins aren't stored, dietary excesses can still be harmful.

THE TAKE-HOME MESSAGE Fat-soluble vitamins—A, D, E, and K—are not as bioavailable as water-soluble vitamins. They need dietary fat to be absorbed and are stored in the body. Because they are stored, overconsumption of fat-soluble vitamins can be toxic. The water-soluble B and C vitamins are absorbed with water. Excess water-soluble vitamins are excreted through the urine, and generally aren't stored.

What Are Antioxidants?

Antioxidants (*anti* = against, *oxidants* = oxygen-containing substances) are a group of compounds that include vitamins E and C, the mineral selenium, **flavonoids** (colorful pigments found in fruits and vegetables), and **carotenoids** (such as beta-carotene, zeaxanthin, lutein, and lycopene). Just as their name implies, antioxidants counteract the **oxidation** that takes place in cells. Recall that oxidation reactions are essential chemical reactions that are part of metabolism, such as energy production (discussed in Chapter 8). However, in some reactions, oxidation can be damaging, such as when free radicals are formed.

During oxidation, harmful oxygen-containing **free radicals**—molecules with an unpaired electron, which makes them very unstable—are created as by-products of the body's metabolic reactions. Free radicals can also result from exposure to chemicals in the environment (such as cigarette smoke and air pollution) or from the damaging effects of the sun's ultraviolet rays. The unpaired electron in free radicals enables them to damage cells by altering cell structure, body proteins, and even DNA.[2]

To become more stable, free radicals are continually searching for an electron to steal from another molecule. Once the theft occurs, a new free radical is created, and it becomes a thief in pursuit of another molecule to attack. A free radical can also become stable by depositing its unpaired electron onto another molecule.

antioxidants Substances that neutralize harmful oxygen-containing free radicals that can cause cell damage. Vitamins A, C, and E and beta-carotene are antioxidants.

flavonoids Food pigments that act as antioxidants and may help reduce the risk of chronic diseases; flavonoids are found in many fruits, vegetables, tea, and wine.

carotenoids A group of yellow, red, and orange pigments found in plants; three of them are precursors to vitamin A. The body stores carotenoids in the liver and in fat cells.

oxidation A chemical reaction in which oxygen combines with other substances, resulting in the loss of an electron.

free radicals Unstable molecules that contain an unpaired electron; free radicals can damage the cells of the body and possibly contribute to the increased risk of chronic diseases.

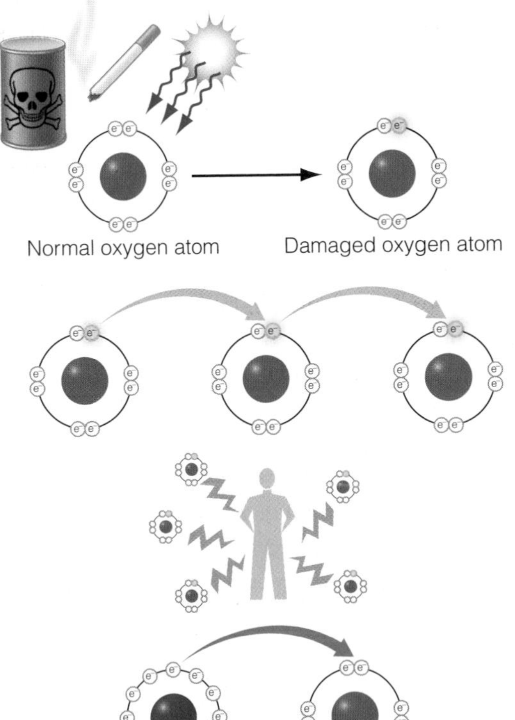

Normal oxygen atom
Damaged oxygen atom
Antioxidant
Repaired oxygen molecule
a Normal reactions in the body, and stressors such as chemicals in the environment, smoking, and ultraviolet light create free radicals.
b Free radicals have an unpaired electron that seeks an electron from another compound, causing a chain reaction of oxidation.
c Free radicals lead to oxidative stress. This accelerates the aging process and increases the risk of heart disease, cancer, diabetes, arthritis, macular degeneration, Parkinson's disease, and Alzheimer's disease.
d Antioxidants, such as vitamin E, neutralize free radicals by "lending" an electron to stabilize damaged atoms.

▲ **Figure 9.3 Antioxidants Neutralize Free Radicals**

a Normal vision and the ability to clearly see the world around you is often taken for granted.

b People with age-related macular degeneration (AMD) have difficulty seeing things directly in front of them.

c Cataracts cause vision to become cloudy.

▲ **Figure 9.4 Normal and Impaired Vision**

Source: National Institutes of Health, National Eye Institute.

This causes the molecule that takes on the electron to become a new free radical. **Figure 9.3** illustrates free radicals in action in the body.

Antioxidants are part of the body's natural defense system to neutralize free radicals and stop them from damaging cells. If free radicals accumulate faster than the body can neutralize them, causing a condition known as **oxidative stress,** their damaging effects can contribute to various chronic diseases and conditions, including heart disease, cancer, aging, diabetes mellitus, arthritis, Parkinson's disease, and Alzheimer's disease.[3]

Free radicals can also damage eyes, contributing to **age-related macular degeneration (AMD)** and cataracts. Over 1.75 million Americans have AMD that results from damage to the macula, a tiny area of the eye that is needed for central vision (the ability to see things that are directly in front of you). The macula is shown in the eye illustrated in the vitamin A section on page 344. AMD can make activities such as reading, driving, and watching television impossible (**Figure 9.4**). AMD is the most common cause of blindness in Americans 60 years of age and older.[4] A study conducted by the National Eye Institute (NEI) found that supplements containing large amounts of antioxidants (vitamin C, vitamin E, and beta-carotene) along with the minerals zinc and copper were effective in reducing the risk of AMD as well as the loss of vision in individuals with advanced stages of AMD.[5]

Some studies have also suggested that specific antioxidants—namely vitamins C and E and the carotenoids lutein and zeaxanthin—may help lower the risk of cataracts.[6] More than half of all Americans have experienced cataracts by the time they reach 80 years of age, and many undergo surgery to remove them. A **cataract** is a common

oxidative stress A condition whereby free radicals are being produced in the body faster than they are neutralized.

age-related macular degeneration (AMD) A disease that affects the macula of the retina, causing blurry vision and potentially blindness.

cataract A common eye disorder that occurs when the lens of the eye becomes cloudy.

eye condition among older adults in which the lens of the eye becomes cloudy, resulting in blurred vision, as shown in Figure 9.4c. NEI recommends consuming antioxidant- and carotenoid-rich vegetables and fruits, such as citrus fruits, broccoli, and dark green leafy vegetables, for the health of the eyes.[7]

There is no question that antioxidants play an important role in the body and that diets high in antioxidant-rich fruits, vegetables, and whole grains are associated with lower incidences of some diseases. However, these foods also contain other protective compounds. For example, **phytochemicals** (*phyto* = plant), naturally occurring plant compounds that give fruits and vegetables their vibrant colors, have many beneficial functions in the body, such as acting as antioxidants, stimulating the immune system, and interacting with hormones that may help prevent certain cancers.[8, 9] Carotenoids and flavonoids are considered phytochemicals that have antioxidant properties. Table 9.2 emphasizes the importance of a colorful diet so as to consume an abundance of phytochemicals.

The big question that remains is if antioxidant *supplements* provide the same health protection as antioxidants consumed in foods. Studies are currently under way exploring the role of antioxidant supplements in fighting disease. At this time, the American Heart Association, National Cancer Institute, and United States Preventive Services Task Force do not advocate taking supplements to reduce the risk of specific diseases, but encourage eating a phytochemical- and antioxidant-rich, well-balanced diet.[10, 11] See Health Connection: Nutrition and Cancer Prevention for more information on the cancer-fighting benefits of antioxidants.

THE TAKE-HOME MESSAGE Antioxidants, such as vitamins E and C, the mineral selenium, flavonoids, and carotenoids, help counteract the damaging effects of oxygen-containing molecules called free radicals. If free radicals accumulate faster than the body can neutralize them, the damaging effects of oxidative stress can contribute to chronic diseases and conditions. Fruits, vegetables, and whole grains are excellent sources of antioxidants.

phytochemicals Naturally occurring substances in fruits, vegetables, and whole grains that protect against certain chronic diseases.

TABLE 9.2 The Phytochemical Color Guide

The National Cancer Institute recommends eating a variety of colorful fruits and vegetables daily to provide your body with valuable vitamins, minerals, fiber, and disease-fighting phytochemicals. Whole grains also have phytochemicals and have been added to this list.

Color	Phytochemical	Found In
Red	Anthocyanins	Apples, beets, cabbage, cherries, cranberries, red cabbage, red onions, red beans
Yellow/ Orange	Beta-carotene	Apricots, butternut squash, cantaloupe, carrots, mangoes, peaches, pumpkin, sweet potatoes
	Flavonoids	Apricots, clementines, grapefruits, lemons, papaya, pears, pineapple, yellow raisins
White	Alliums/allicin	Chives, garlic, leeks, onions, scallions
Green	Lutein, zeaxanthin	Broccoli, collard greens, honeydew melon, kale, kiwi, lettuce, mustard greens, peas, spinach
	Indoles	Arugula, broccoli, bok choy, brussels sprouts, cabbage, cauliflower, kale, Swiss chard, turnips
Blue/Purple	Anthocyanins	Blackberries, black currants, elderberries, purple grapes
	Phenolics	Eggplant, plums, prunes, raisins
Brown	Beta-gluton, lignans, phenols, plant sterols, phytoestrogens, saponins, tocotrienols	Barley, brown rice, oats, oatmeal, whole grains, whole-grain cereals, whole wheat

Source: Adapted from Fruits and Veggies–More Matters. 2012. Available at www.fruitsandveggiesmorematters.org.

Health Connection

Nutrition and Cancer Prevention

What Is Cancer?

The term **cancer** is used to identify a group of more than 100 diseases characterized by uncontrolled growth and spread of abnormal cells.[1] The most common type for both men and women is lung cancer, with skin, breast, prostate, and colorectal cancers also occurring in large numbers. The types differ not only in where they occur in the body (see Table 1), but also in their causes, treatments, and prognoses. Carcinomas—cancers of epithelial cells that line the internal and external cavities of the body, including the glands—represent almost 80 to 90 percent of all cancers in adults. Sarcomas, or cancers of the connective tissue, occur in bone and muscle. Lymphoma, including both Hodgkin's disease and non-Hodgkin's lymphoma, is the third most frequently diagnosed cancer in children. Leukemia differs from the other types of cancer in that it does not result in a tumor. It is an aggressive cancer of the white blood cells formed in the bone marrow.

TABLE 1 Types of Cancer

Type of Cancer	Description
Carcinoma	Cancer of the epithelial cells; includes cancers of various glandular tissue, including breast, thyroid, and skin
Sarcoma	Cancer of connective tissue, such as bone or muscle
Leukemia	Cancer associated with the blood or blood-forming tissues
Lymphoma	Cancer of the lymph nodes or other lymph tissues

Cancer is responsible for 22.8 percent of all deaths in the United States, making it the second leading cause of death, behind heart disease.[2] Even though the death rate from cancer has declined slightly since 2004, an estimated 577,190 Americans died of cancer in 2012, or 1,500 per day. About one-third of these cancer deaths in 2012 were related to overweight or obesity, physical inactivity, and poor diet.[3]

1 Hormones and growth factors stimulate the cell to grow. Nutrients are needed for parts of the cell to develop. Vitamin A can arrest the cell cycle at this time.

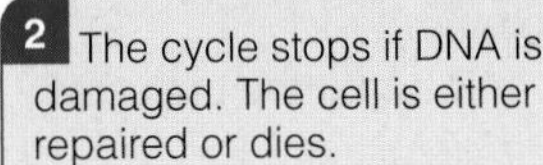

2 The cycle stops if DNA is damaged. The cell is either repaired or dies.

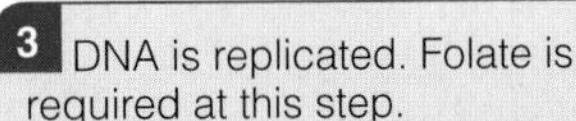

3 DNA is replicated. Folate is required at this step.

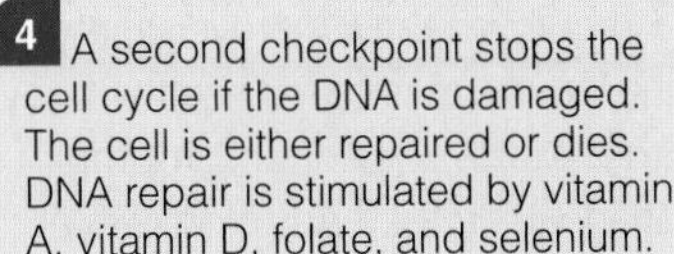

4 A second checkpoint stops the cell cycle if the DNA is damaged. The cell is either repaired or dies. DNA repair is stimulated by vitamin A, vitamin D, folate, and selenium.

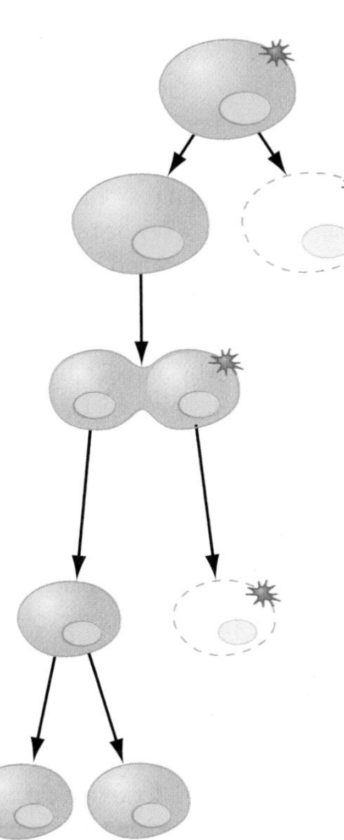

5 A final checkpoint before the cell divides into two identical daughter cells ensures each daughter cell has the correct DNA.

▲ **Figure 1 Normal Cell Growth and Division**
Normally, damaged or mutated cells are repaired or die off to prevent them from producing more damaged cells. Various nutrients are involved as part of the process.

Carcinogenesis: The Cancer Process

Most cancers take years to develop, as abnormal cells need time to grow, reproduce, and spread. The normal cell cycle is controlled by specific **protooncogenes,** which turn the cell replication cycle on and off, and suppressor genes, which stop any mutated cells from replicating. Cancer develops when a lack of control by these genes allows mutated cells to replicate, divide, and grow.

The process of cancer development, or **carcinogenesis,** generally occurs in three stages: initiation, promotion, and progression. Normally, cell damage is repaired before abnormal cells begin to accumulate (see **Figure 1**) or the cell dies before it proliferates, because there are checkpoints along the various stages of cell division that help maintain the integrity of DNA. The initiation stage begins when a cell is exposed to a **carcinogen,** or cancer-causing agent,

cancer A general term for a large group of diseases characterized by uncontrolled growth and spread of abnormal cells.

protooncogenes Specialized genes that turn on and off cell division.

carcinogenesis The process of cancer development.

carcinogen Cancer-causing substance, including tobacco smoke, air and water pollution, ultraviolet radiation, and various chemicals.

that damages the DNA. **Cancer initiators** include a variety of environmental factors such as hormones, viruses, ultraviolet light, or smoke; or dietary factors such as alcohol, excess kilocalories, and excess dietary fat. This stage of cancer development is usually short lived because the damaged DNA is either repaired quickly or carcinogenesis progresses to the next stage, called cancer promotion.

Once the mutation is initiated, a **cancer promoter,** such as the hormone estrogen or alcohol, stimulates the damaged cells to divide and multiply in the promotion stage. As the mass of cells, or tumor, grows, it can disrupt surrounding tissues and even develop its own network of blood vessels to obtain nutrients (see **Figure 2**).

A tumor may take years to develop. Once the tumor has developed, in the progression stage a **cancer progressor** changes the cancerous cells from a benign (harmless) tumor to a more aggressive, malignant cancer that can spread, or **metastasize,** throughout the body.

1 During the **initiation** stage, DNA is altered and a damaged cell is produced.

2 In the **promotion** stage, damaged cells reproduce and form a tumor.

3 During the **progression** stage, the tumor continues to grow and may spread to nearby tissues or other areas of the body.

▲ **Figure 2 The Stages of Carcinogenesis**

The Role of Diet in Cancer Risk and Progression

Dietary factors can influence the development of cancer cells at the initiation, promotion, and progression stages.

cancer initiator A carcinogen that initiates the mutation in DNA; these mutations cause the cell to respond abnormally to physiological controls.

cancer promoter A substance that induces a cell to divide and grow rapidly, and reduces the time that enzymes have to repair any damage or mutation; examples of cancer promoters are dietary fats, alcohol, and estrogen.

cancer progressor A compound that stimulates cancer cell proliferation and causes cancer cells to invade healthy tissue and spread to other sites; hormones are an example of a substance that stimulates cancer progression.

metastasize To spread or grow into other parts of the body, as in reference to cancer cells.

Foods that Can Lower Cancer Risk

Plant-based foods have a significant impact on reducing cancer risk.[4] Nonstarchy vegetables and fruits are associated with reductions in lung, mouth and esophageal, stomach, and colon cancer.[5] Bladder cancer rates in men have been reduced with a higher intake of cruciferous vegetables, such as cauliflower, broccoli, and brussels sprouts; and eating more tomatoes may reduce the risk of developing prostate cancer.[6] These foods are high in phytochemicals, antioxidants, and dietary fiber, and low in energy density, all of which are likely to yield protective effects.

Some specific vitamins and minerals can also help lower cancer risk. Retinoids (vitamin A), vitamin D, folate, and the mineral selenium can help repair DNA in the initiation stage and can stop the development of cancer by inhibiting the progression of damaged cells. Vitamins C and E and selenium may help prevent cancer from spreading to nearby tissues. Omega-3 fatty acids may help to reduce cancer cell growth.

Other nutrients, such as vitamin D, may inhibit the proliferation of cancer cells and stimulate cell differentiation. This research is in the early stages, however, and no conclusive evidence has been presented to show a cause-and-effect relationship.

Fiber helps dilute waste products, which may contain cancer-promoting agents, in the intestinal tract and quickly move these out of the body, reducing exposure to these cells. Also, the healthy bacteria that live in the colon feast on the fiber, creating a by-product that may also help in the fight against cancer, especially colorectal cancer. Fiber-containing fruits and vegetables are also low in kilocalories and high in bulk, so they improve satiety. Thus, a fiber-rich diet can help individuals maintain a healthy body weight. Evidence also suggests that excessive alcohol consumption increases liver, mouth, esophageal, breast, and colon cancer.

There is epidemiological evidence that certain nutrients may retard the progress of cancer development, although the exact mechanism is still unknown.[7] These key nutrients, including the antioxidant vitamins A, C, and E, may protect DNA from the initial damage.

Foods that Can Raise Cancer Risk

Some foods may increase the risk of developing cancer. For example, red meat, especially when grilled, is associated with an increased risk of stomach, pancreatic, colon, and kidney cancer.

When the saturated fat in meat hits a hot surface, such as a frying pan or charcoal briquettes, it forms benzopyrene, a probable carcinogen, which is absorbed into the meat. Nitrates and nitrites, used as preservatives in processed meats, including bacon, ham, and sandwich meats, can be converted to another class of carcinogens known as nitrosamines and may increase cancer risk.

Physical Activity, Obesity, and Cancer Risk

Maintaining a healthy weight throughout life may be one of the most important ways to protect against cancer. Among U.S. adults 50 years of age or older, an estimated 14 percent of the cancer deaths in men and 20 percent in women can be attributed to overweight and obesity. Although the mechanism is still unknown, the increased levels of hormones and insulin in overweight individuals may be the link.[8]

Routine physical activity reduces the risk of several types of cancer, in part by helping maintain a healthy weight. The exercise does not have to be intense to be effective. In the California Teachers Study, women who had never used hormone replacement therapy during their lifetime and who participated in moderate exercise had a greater reduction in colon cancer risk than women who reported more strenuous physical activity.[9] The reason exercise reduces cancer risk is still not clear. However, the benefits may be due to a reduction in chronic inflammation, stimulating the immune system, or reducing obesity.[10]

Overconsumption of energy-dense foods can increase risk of obesity and thus cancer risk. An energy-dense diet, especially one high in dietary fat, may contribute to obesity, especially in sedentary individuals.[11] Dietary fat intake does not cause breast cancer, but weight gain later in life may. A healthy weight and physical activity will reduce the risk of developing breast, colon, rectal, endometrial, esophageal, and kidney cancer. Obesity increases the risk for thyroid, cervical, and prostate cancers.

Dietary and Lifestyle Recommendations

In 2007, a review of over 7,000 research studies and input from hundreds of scientists worldwide culminated in publication of a landmark report entitled *Food, Nutrition, Physical Activity, and the Prevention of Cancer: A Global Perspective.*[12] This report identified the nutritional and lifestyle factors that may modify the risk of developing cancer (see Table 2 on page 332).

The best advice for reducing the risk of cancer is to consume a varied, healthy, plant-based diet, limit saturated fat and sugar intake, maintain a healthy weight, avoid tobacco, limit alcohol intake, and lead an active lifestyle. Because many cancers take years, if not decades, to develop after the initial DNA damage, the sooner healthy changes are made, the more likely they are to help individuals avoid cancer later in life.

The Future of Cancer and Nutrition Research

There are several promising areas of research that explore the relationship between nutrition and cancer. For example, there seem to be connections between lycopene and vitamin E and the reduced risk for prostate cancer and evidence for the protective effects of calcium against colon cancer. The effects of new policies regarding promotion of energy-dense foods aimed at children, and fast-food restaurants, are also on the research agenda.

TABLE 2 Recommendations for Reducing Cancer Risk	
Recommendations	**Personal Health Goals**
Be as lean as possible within the normal range of body weight	■ Ensure that body weight through childhood and adolescent growth projects toward the lower end of the normal BMI range at age 21 ■ Maintain body weight within the normal range from age 21 ■ Avoid weight gain and increases in waist circumference throughout adulthood
Be physically active as part of everyday life	■ Be moderately physically active, equivalent to brisk walking, for at least 30 minutes every day ■ As fitness improves, aim for 60 minutes or more of moderate, or 30 minutes or more of vigorous, physical activity every day ■ Limit sedentary habits such as watching television
Limit consumption of energy-dense foods and avoid sugary drinks	■ Consume energy-dense foods sparingly ■ Avoid sugary drinks ■ Avoid fast foods, or consume only sparingly
Eat mostly foods of plant origin	■ Eat at least five portions/servings (at least 400 g or 14 oz) of a variety of fruits and nonstarchy vegetables every day ■ Eat relatively unprocessed cereals (grains) and/or legumes with every meal ■ Limit refined starch foods ■ People who consume starchy roots or tubers as staples need to also consume sufficient nonstarchy vegetables, fruits, and legumes
Limit intake of red meat and avoid processed meat	■ People who eat red meat should consume less than 500 g (18 oz) a week and avoid processed meats
Limit alcoholic drinks	■ If alcoholic drinks are consumed, limit consumption to no more than two drinks a day for men and one drink a day for women
Limit consumption of salt	■ Avoid salt-preserved, salted, or salty foods; preserve foods without using salt ■ Limit consumption of processed foods with added salt to ensure an intake of less than 6 g (2.4 g sodium) a day
Avoid moldy cereals (grains) or legumes	■ Do not eat moldy cereals (grains) or legumes
Aim to meet nutritional needs through diet alone	■ Dietary supplements are not recommended for cancer prevention

References

1. World Cancer Research Fund and the American Institute for Cancer Research. 2007. *Food, Nutrition, Physical Activity, and the Prevention of Cancer: A Global Perspective.* Washington, DC: American Institute for Cancer Research.
2. American Cancer Society. 2012. *Cancer Statistics.* Available at www.cancer.org/docroot/STT/stt_0.asp. Accessed April 2012.
3. Ibid.
4. Saxe, G. A., J. M. Major, L. Westerberg, S. Khandrika, and T. M. Downs. 2008. Biological Mediators of Effect of Diet and Stress Reduction on Prostate Cancer. *Integrative Cancer Therapy* 7:130–138.
5. Ibid.
6. American Cancer Society. 2012. *Cancer Statistics.*
7. Saxe. 2008. Biological Mediators.
8. Calle, E. E., C. Rodriguez, K. Walker-Thurmond, and M. J. Thun. 2003. Overweight, Obesity, and Mortality from Cancer in a Prospectively Studied Cohort of U.S. Adults. *New England Journal of Medicine* 348:1625–1638.
9. Mai, P. L., J. Sullivan-Halley, G. Ursin, D. O. Stram, D. Deapen, D. Villaluna, P. L. Horn-Ross, et al. 2007. Physical Activity and Colon Cancer Risk among Women in the California Teachers Study. *Cancer Epidemiological Biomarkers and Prevention* 16:517–525.
10. Harriss, D. J., N. T. Cable, K. George, T. Reilly, A. G. Renehan, and N. Haboubi. 2007. Physical Activity Before and After Diagnosis of Colorectal Cancer: Disease Risk, Clinical Outcomes, Response Pathways and Biomarkers. *Sports Medicine* 37:947–960.
11. Holmes, M. D. and W. C. Willett. 2004. Does Diet Affect Breast Cancer Risk? *Breast Cancer Research* 6:170–176.
12. World Cancer Research Fund and the American Institute for Cancer Research. 2007. *Food, Nutrition, Physical Activity, and the Prevention of Cancer: A Global Perspective.* Washington, DC: American Institute for Cancer Research.

What's the Best Source of Vitamins?

Whole foods, including fruits, vegetables, and whole grains, remain the best way to meet vitamin needs: They provide more than just vitamins because they are also rich in disease-fighting phytochemicals, antioxidants, and fiber. The *Dietary Guidelines for Americans* recommends eating a wide variety of foods from each food group, with ample amounts of vitamin-rich fruits, vegetables, whole grains, and dairy foods. **Figure 9.5** illustrates each food group and the vitamins it contributes to the diet.

Table 9.3 on page 334 shows the estimated intake for each nutrient that a 2,000-kilocalorie diet based on the *Dietary Guidelines* will provide. As shown in the table, vitamins D and E are the only nutrients that may be a challenge to get enough of.[12] However, adding some margarine on toast, a few nuts to yogurt, and a little salad dressing on a dinner salad will increase overall intake. Refer to the Table Tips for vitamin E (on page 356) for more suggestions.

Vitamins Can Be Destroyed during Cooking or Storage

How you prepare and store fresh foods once you obtain them can affect their nutritional content. Water-soluble vitamins can be destroyed by exposure to air, ultraviolet (UV) light, water, changes in pH, or heat. In fact, vegetables and fruits begin to lose their vitamins almost immediately after being harvested, and some preparation and storage methods can accelerate vitamin loss. Though the fat-soluble vitamins tend to be more stable than water-soluble vitamins, some food preparation techniques can cause the loss of these vitamins as well.

Exposure to Oxygen

Air—or, more specifically, exposure to oxygen—can destroy the water-soluble vitamins and the fat-soluble vitamins A, E, and K. Thus, fresh vegetables and fruits should be stored in airtight, covered containers and used soon after being purchased.

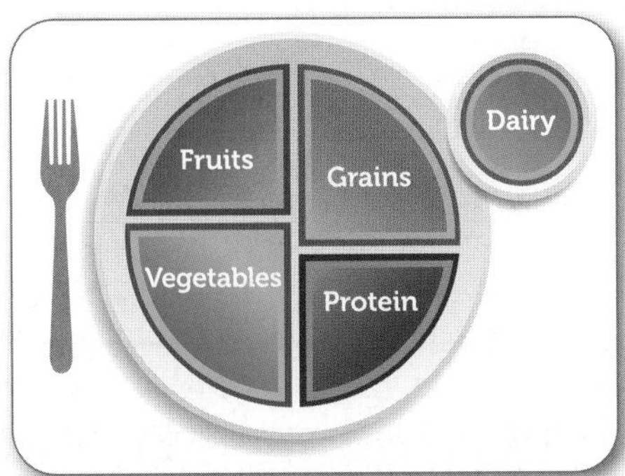

Vegetables	Fruits	Grains	Protein	Dairy
Folate Vitamin A Vitamin C Vitamin E	Folate Vitamin C	Folic acid Niacin Vitamin B_6 Vitamin B_{12} (if fortified) Riboflavin Thiamin	Niacin Thiamin Vitamin B_6 Vitamin B_{12}	Riboflavin Vitamin A Vitamin B_{12} Vitamin D

▲ **Figure 9.5 Vitamins Found Widely in the Food Groups**
Eating a wide variety of foods from all food groups will ensure that you meet your vitamin needs.

TABLE TIPS

Preserve Your Vitamins!

Cook vegetables in a small amount of already boiling water—not cold water brought to a boil. Use any leftover cooking liquid as a soup or gravy base.

Don't rinse rice before cooking it or pasta after cooking it. You'll wash away water-soluble vitamins.

Microwave or stir-fry vegetables instead of boiling or frying them. These methods reduce the amount of time vegetables are exposed to heat and therefore the amount of vitamins that are lost.

Store produce in a refrigerator and eat it soon after purchasing.

Cut vegetables and fruits in larger pieces to reduce the surface area exposed to oxygen. Prepare vegetables close to the time that they are going to be cooked and/or served.

Source: Adapted from U.S. Department of Agriculture Food and Nutrition Services. 2002. *Chapter 5, Quality Meals in Building Blocks for Fun and Healthy Meals—A Menu Planner for the Child and Adult Care Food Program.* USDA Team Nutrition Resources. Available at www.fns.usda.gov/tn/Resources/buildingblocks.html. Accessed July 2008.

TABLE 9.3 Meeting the Dietary Reference Intakes with Healthy Food Choices

Nutrient	Estimated Vitamin Intake Based on 2,000 Kilocalories*	Institute of Medicine Recommendations, Nutrient RDA/AI
Vitamin A, μg RAE	851	700–900
Vitamin D, IU	258	600
Vitamin E, mg	8.3	15.0
Vitamin K, μg	140	90–120
Thiamin, mg	1.8	1.1–1.2
Riboflavin, mg	2.2	1.1–1.3
Niacin, mg	23.0	14.0–16.0
Vitamin B_6, mg	2.3	1.3–1.7
Vitamin B_{12}, μg	6.5	2.4
Folate, μg	628	400
Vitamin C, mg	126	75–90
Choline, mg	340	425–550

*The highest intake level for young adult men or women is stated.

Note: RDA = Recommended Dietary Allowance; AI = Adequate Intakes; RAE = retinol activity equivalents; mg = milligrams; μg = micrograms

Source: U.S. Department of Agriculture. 2010. *Report of the Dietary Guidelines Advisory Committee on the Dietary Guidelines for Americans, 2010.* Available at www.cnpp.usda.gov/DGAs2010-DGACReport.htm; Food and Nutrition Board, Institute of Medicine, National Academies. *Dietary Reference Intakes Series.* Available at www.iom.edu/Reports.aspx. Accessed November 2012.

Exposure to Light

Light, especially ultraviolet light (UV), can destroy vitamins, including the water-soluble vitamin riboflavin. Foods stored in glass containers, such as milk or grains, or sun-dried fruits and vegetables, can lose vitamins. For example, up to 80 percent of the riboflavin content of milk in glass containers can be destroyed by sunlight.[13] This is the reason milk is sold in opaque or cardboard containers. The traditional methods of sun-drying fruits and vegetables destroy susceptible vitamins such as beta-carotene and vitamin C. However, new advances in solar drying have shown some promise.[14]

Exposure to Water

Water-soluble vitamins will leach out of foods when soaked or cooked in liquids, so cooking foods in as little water as possible is recommended to retain those vitamins.[15] The water should be boiling when vegetables are cooked even if you use a steamer basket. The boiling water inactivates the enzymes naturally found in the food that oxidize the vitamin, changing it to a form that is not metabolically active. For instance, potatoes are a good source of vitamin C but they also contain an enzyme, ascorbic oxidase, that changes the chemical structure of vitamin C to an inactive form. Potatoes added to boiling water retain more vitamin C than if they were added to cold water and brought to a boil.

Changes in pH

Changes in pH can destroy some vitamins, especially thiamin and vitamin C. Most vitamins are stable in acid, but adding ingredients such as baking soda to foods increases the pH and destroys pH-sensitive vitamins. For instance, adding baking soda to shorten the cooking time of beans or other legumes destroys the thiamin content.

Cooking foods in the microwave allows for a shorter cooking time, which means fewer vitamins are lost.

Exposure to Heat

Heat, especially prolonged heat from cooking, will also destroy water-soluble vitamins, especially vitamin C. Because they are exposed to less heat, vegetables cooked by microwaving, steaming, or stir-frying can have approximately one-and-a-half times more vitamin C after cooking than if they were boiled, which involves longer heat exposure.[16] Whereas heat reduces the vitamin content of foods, cooler temperatures help preserve them. For this reason, produce should be stored in the refrigerator rather than on a counter or in a pantry. A package of fresh spinach left at room temperature will lose over half of its folate, a B vitamin, after four days. Keeping the spinach in the refrigerator delays that loss until eight days.[17] See the Table Tips for more ways to preserve the vitamins in foods.

Some Foods Are Fortified with Vitamins

When you pour a glass of orange juice, you know that you are getting a significant intake of vitamin C. However, depending on the brand of orange juice, you may also be meeting the recommendations for vitamin E and vitamin D—two nutrients that are not naturally found in oranges. This is due to the process called fortification. **Fortified foods** are becoming more popular with the American consumer. For example, sales of foods fortified with one popular nutrient, omega-3 fatty acids, approached $4 billion in 2010.[18]

Food fortification is the voluntary addition of nutrients by manufacturers to enhance the nutrient quality of the food and to prevent or correct dietary deficiencies. Vitamins and minerals are the most commonly used nutrients in fortified foods, but fiber, amino acids, essential fatty acids, and other bioactive ingredients are also sometimes added. Based on current Food and Drug Administration (FDA) regulations, all 13 vitamins and 20 minerals can be added to foods.[19]

Enrichment of foods is a form of fortification. Foods that are enriched, such as rice, bread, flour, pasta, and other refined grains, have levels of nutrients added to bring the nutritional value back to their original state before the grain was processed. The nutrients that are required by law to be added to refined grains include four water-soluble B vitamins (thiamin, riboflavin, niacin, and folate) and the mineral iron.

Fortified Foods Can Help Ensure Adequate Intake for Some Individuals

Fortified foods can be a valuable option for individuals whose diet falls short of some nutrients. For instance, an adult on a very low-kilocalorie diet may not be getting adequate vitamins and minerals from food and would benefit from fortified cereals. Strict vegans or individuals who are lactose intolerant and do not consume dairy products would benefit from drinking vitamin D– and calcium–fortified soy milk. Older adults who are inactive and thus have lower kilocalorie needs may choose fortified foods to add vitamin E to their limited dietary selections. Women in their childbearing years may look to folic acid–fortified cereals to help them meet their daily needs for this B vitamin.

Fortified Foods Can Contribute to Health Risks

Because overconsumption of a vitamin or mineral can result in nutrient toxicity, individuals who consume high amounts of some fortified foods may be at risk for

fortified foods Foods with added vitamins and minerals; fortified foods often contain nutrients that are not naturally present in the food or in higher amounts than the food contains naturally.

health problems. If a heavily fortified food, like some cereals, snack bars, and beverages, claims to contain "100% of the vitamins needed daily," then eating several servings of the food or a combination of several fortified foods is similar to taking several multivitamin supplements. Individuals are more likely to overconsume vitamins from fortified foods than from whole foods.

Fortified foods can also do a disservice in the diet if they displace other vitamin- and mineral-rich foods. For example, a sugary orange drink that has vitamin C added to it should not replace vitamin C–rich orange juice. While the vitamin C content of the two beverages may be the same, the orange-flavored drink doesn't compare well with the juice when it comes to providing other nutrients and phytochemicals. As you can see in **Figure 9.6**, the orange drink is basically orange-flavored water sweetened heavily with added sugar and fortified with vitamin C. Even though the sugar content is similar for each beverage, the orange-flavored drink is sweetened with corn syrup whereas the pure orange juice is sweetened naturally with sugars found in the orange.

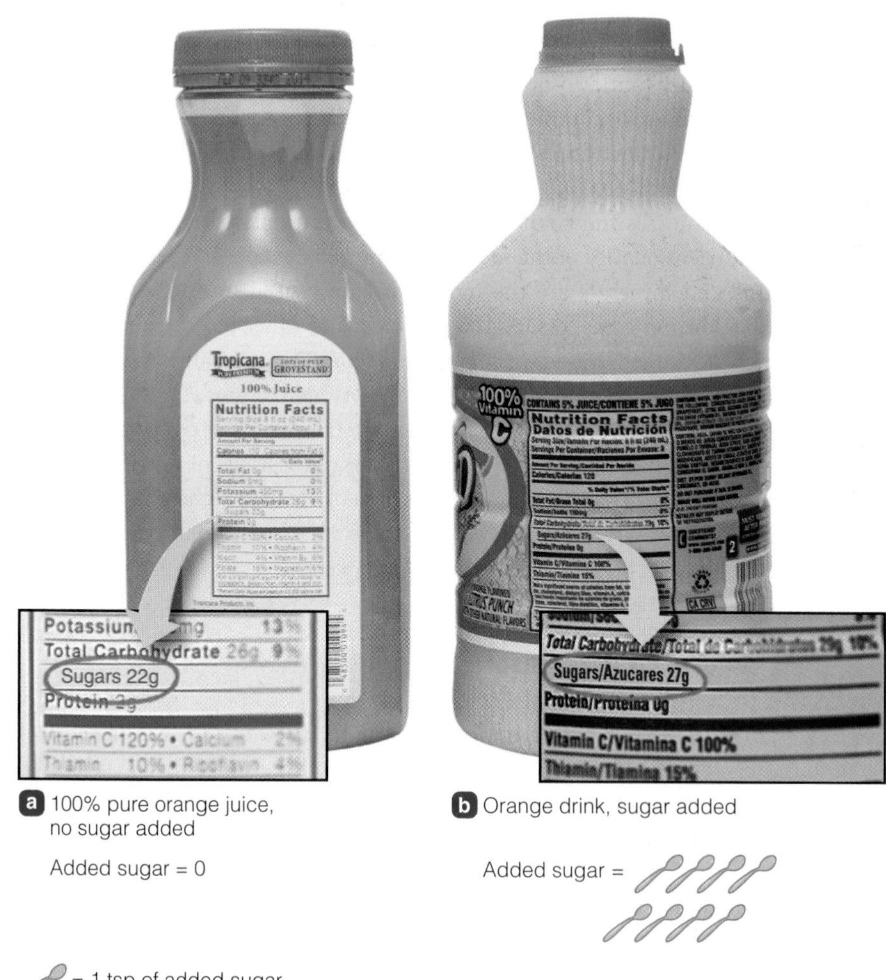

▲ **Figure 9.6 The Nutritional Value of Juices versus Fruit Drinks**
While both of these beverages are a good source of vitamin C, they are worlds apart in nutrient content. Pure orange juice **(a)** is also an excellent source of the mineral potassium and doesn't contain any added sugar. Orange drink **(b)** is basically sugar water fortified with vitamin C. A glass of it contains the equivalent of 8 teaspoons of added sugar.

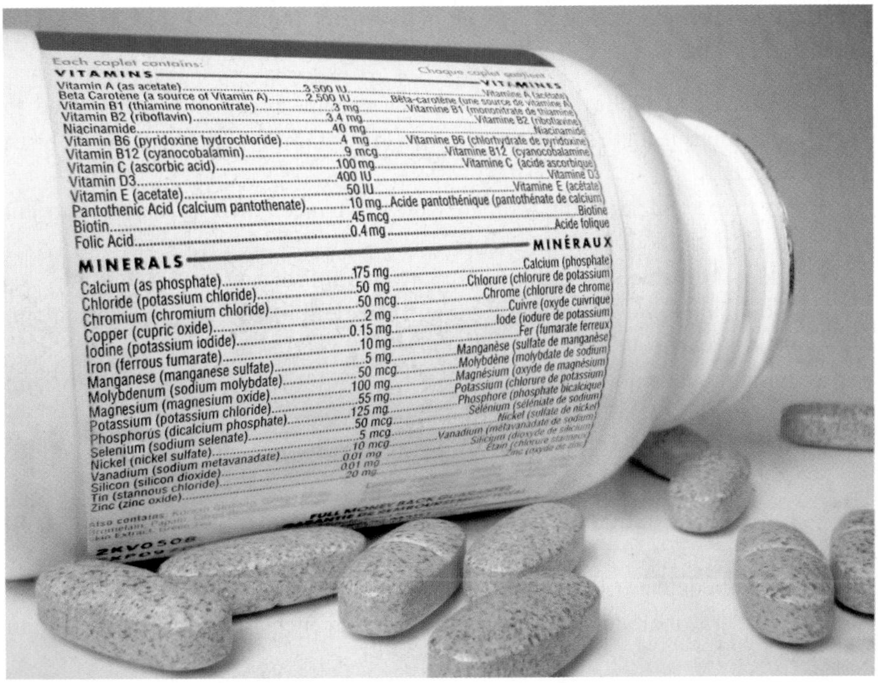

Supplements should be used with caution, and should not substitute for a consuming a healthy diet.

Vitamins Are Popular Dietary Supplements

As with sales of fortified foods, U.S. sales of supplements have increased markedly in the last several decades. An estimated 40 percent of Americans spend over $1 billion a year on vitamin and mineral supplements, and these supplements are the third most popular over-the-counter drug category that Americans buy.[20]

Vitamin Supplements Are Not a Substitute for Healthy Eating

Consumers often choose supplements because they are unwilling to improve their diets. However, supplements should never be used to replace a healthy diet. The Academy of Nutrition and Dietetics maintains that an unhealthy diet of nonnutritious foods cannot be transformed into a healthy diet by simply ingesting a daily supplement. There is little scientific evidence to promote the use of dietary supplements in place of eating a healthy, balanced diet. Remember that disease-fighting phytochemicals, fiber, and other substances that the body needs are all missing from a bottle of supplements.

Further, supplement use may have adverse side effects. In fact, most of the reported problems associated with vitamin toxicity are related to supplement use, and consuming fortified foods in addition to a supplement can also cause the overconsumption of nutrients. Any individual who is considering taking supplements should consult a credible source of nutrition information, such as a Registered Dietitian, before purchasing or consuming supplements.

Supplements May Be Helpful for Some Individuals

Whereas many healthy individuals do not need to consume supplements, some supplements are useful for people who cannot meet their nutrient needs through a regular, varied diet. Among those who may benefit from taking a dietary supplement are:[21]

- Women of childbearing age who may become pregnant, as they need to consume adequate synthetic folic acid (a B vitamin) to prevent certain birth defects
- Pregnant and lactating women who can't meet their increased nutrient needs with foods
- Older individuals, who need adequate amounts of synthetic vitamin B_{12}
- Individuals who do not drink enough milk and/or do not have adequate sun exposure to meet their vitamin D needs
- Individuals on low-kilocalorie diets that limit the amount of vitamins and minerals they can consume through food
- Strict vegetarians, who have limited dietary options for vitamins D and B_{12} and other nutrients
- Individuals with food allergies or lactose intolerance that limit food choices
- Individuals who abuse alcohol, have medical conditions such as intestinal disorders, or are taking medications that may increase their need for certain vitamins
- Individuals who are food insecure and those who are eliminating food groups from their diet
- Infants who are breast-fed should receive 400 IU of vitamin D daily unless they are also consuming at least 1 quart of vitamin D–fortified formula daily. Children age 1 and older should receive 400 IU of vitamin D daily if they consume less than 1 quart of milk per day. Adolescents who consume less than 400 IU of vitamin D daily from their diet would also benefit from a supplement.

Supplements can interact or interfere with certain medications, so individuals should consult a doctor before consuming a supplement if they are taking prescription medications.

The U.S. Pharmocopeia Verified Mark

Supplements Are Not Regulated

Another factor to keep in mind regarding the use of dietary supplements (including vitamins, minerals, and herbs) is that they are not stringently regulated by the FDA. In fact, the individuals most responsible for regulating these substances are their manufacturers. Unlike drugs, dietary supplements—unless they contain a new ingredient—do not need approval from the FDA before they can be marketed to the public, and the FDA cannot remove a supplement from the marketplace unless it has been shown to be unsafe or harmful to the consumer.[22]

There is an organization that provides some guidance for consumers when it comes to labeling dietary supplements. The **U.S. Pharmacopoeia (USP)** is a nonprofit organization that sets standards for dietary supplements.[23] Though it does *not* endorse or validate health claims made by the supplement manufacturers, it will test the supplement to ensure that it:

- Contains the ingredients in the amounts stated on the label
- Will disintegrate and dissolve in a reasonable amount of time in the body for proper absorption
- Is free of contaminants
- Has been manufactured using safe and sanitary procedures

U.S. Pharmacopeia (USP) A nonprofit organization that sets purity and reliability standards for dietary supplements.

Supplement manufacturers can voluntarily submit their products to the USP's staff of scientists for review. Products that meet the preceding criteria can display the USP seal on their labels.

For individuals who choose to use supplements, the best place to start when picking a supplement is to carefully read the label. The FDA does have strict guidelines for the information that must appear on any supplement label. For example, the term "high potency" can only be used if at least two-thirds of the nutrients in the supplement contain at least 100 percent of the daily value. The label must also clearly identify the contents of the bottle. While a supplement may have the USP seal of approval for quality and purity, it doesn't have the FDA's approval, even if it makes a claim. Supplements must contain a panel that lists the serving size, the number of capsules or tablets in the bottle, the amount of the vitamin in each capsule, and the percentage of the daily value. All the ingredients must also be listed.

THE TAKE-HOME MESSAGE A well-balanced diet that provides adequate kilocalories can meet many individuals' daily vitamin needs. Vitamins in foods can be destroyed or lost by exposure to air, water, UV light, changes in pH, and heat. Vitamins, especially fat-soluble vitamins, can be toxic if taken in megadose amounts. As long as they are consuming an adequate, balanced diet, fortified foods and supplements are unnecessary for most healthy people.

Putting It All Together

Vitamins A, D, E, and K—the fat-soluble vitamins—are typically found in the lipid portion of foods. These vitamins are insoluble in water and require bile and the formation of micelles for absorption. Once absorbed into the small intestine, fat-soluble vitamins are packaged along with the other dietary lipids into chylomicrons for transport throughout the body. Chylomicron remnants, which still contain the fat-soluble vitamins, are taken up by the liver, where they are stored for use in the future. When cells need the vitamins, a specialized protein transports each vitamin through the blood.

Because fat-soluble vitamins are easily stored, they do not need to be consumed daily. This makes it easier to maintain blood levels of each vitamin when the diet varies from day to day. However, with the exception of vitamin K, storing fat-soluble vitamins poses a greater risk of the levels becoming toxic.

The sources of each fat-soluble vitamin, the basic function it performs in the body, the symptoms of deficiencies and toxicity, and the recommended intakes are listed in Table 9.4 and discussed in detail on the following pages. Take the Self-Assessment to see if your diet is rich in foods containing these vitamins.

TABLE 9.4 Food Sources, Functions, Symptoms of Deficiencies and Toxicity, and the Recommended Intakes of the Fat-Soluble Vitamins

Fat-Soluble Vitamin	Food Sources	Physiological Function	Deficiency Symptoms	Toxicity Symptoms	Adult RDA/AI
Vitamin A	■ Beef liver ■ Fortified dairy products	Vision, protein synthesis, growth, immune function, bone health	Night blindness, xerophthalmia, keratinization	Compromised bone health; birth defects during pregnancy	Males: 900 μg RAE/day Females: 700 μg RAE/day
Beta-carotenes	■ Sweet potatoes ■ Carrots ■ Squash				
Vitamin D	■ Fatty fish such as salmon, tuna, sardines ■ Fortified foods, such as dairy products, orange juice, and cereals	Calcium balance, bone health, cell differentiation, immune system	Rickets and osteomalacia	Hypercalcemia	Males and females: 15 μg/day
Vitamin E	■ Vegetable and seed oils ■ Nuts, seeds ■ Fortified cereals ■ Green leafy vegetables	Antioxidant, health of cell membranes, heart health	Hemolysis of RBCs	Nerve problems, muscle weakness, and uncontrolled movement of body parts	Males and females: 15 mg alpha-tocopherol/day
Vitamin K	■ Green leafy vegetables ■ Soybeans ■ Canola and soybean oils ■ Beef liver	Carboxylation, blood clotting, and bone health	Excessive bleeding	None known	Males: 120 μg/day Females: 90 μg/day

Self-Assessment

Are You Getting Enough Fat-Soluble Vitamins in Your Diet?

Take this brief self-assessment to see if your diet contains enough food sources of the four fat-soluble vitamins.

1 Do you eat at least 1 cup of deep yellow or orange vegetables, such as carrots and sweet potatoes, or dark green vegetables, such as spinach, every day?

Yes ☐ **No** ☐

2 Do you consume at least 2 glasses (8 ounces each) of milk daily?

Yes ☐ **No** ☐

3 Do you eat a tablespoon of vegetable oil, such as corn or olive oil, daily? (Tip: Salad dressings, unless they are fat free, count!)

Yes ☐ **No** ☐

4 Do you eat at least 1 cup of leafy green vegetables in your salad and/or put lettuce in your sandwich every day?

Yes ☐ **No** ☐

Answers

If you answered yes to all four questions, your diet is close to meeting your fat-soluble vitamin needs! If you answered no to any one of the questions, your diet needs some fine-tuning. Deep orange and dark green vegetables are excellent sources of vitamin A, and milk is an excellent choice for vitamin D. Adding small amounts of vegetable oils to a vitamin K–rich leafy green salad will improve the vitamin E content.

Nutrition in Practice: Abbey

Abbey's mom is a cosmetologist, so she knows the effect of sunlight exposure and its impact on the aging of skin. Even though she grew up in Wisconsin, her mother lathered her up with a sunscreen with SPF of 30 every day before leaving for school or going outside to play, and always dressed her in hats and light cotton, long-sleeved shirts and pants in the summer. To Abbey, putting on sunsreen and covering her skin from hat to toe before leaving the house is as routine as brushing her teeth.

For her college admission, Abbey needed to get a complete physical. When taking a family history, the doctor uncovered that her mom has osteomalacia. When the doctor got her blood laboratory report back, he called Abbey to tell her that her blood level of vitamin D was on the low side of normal and suggested she visit a dietitian.

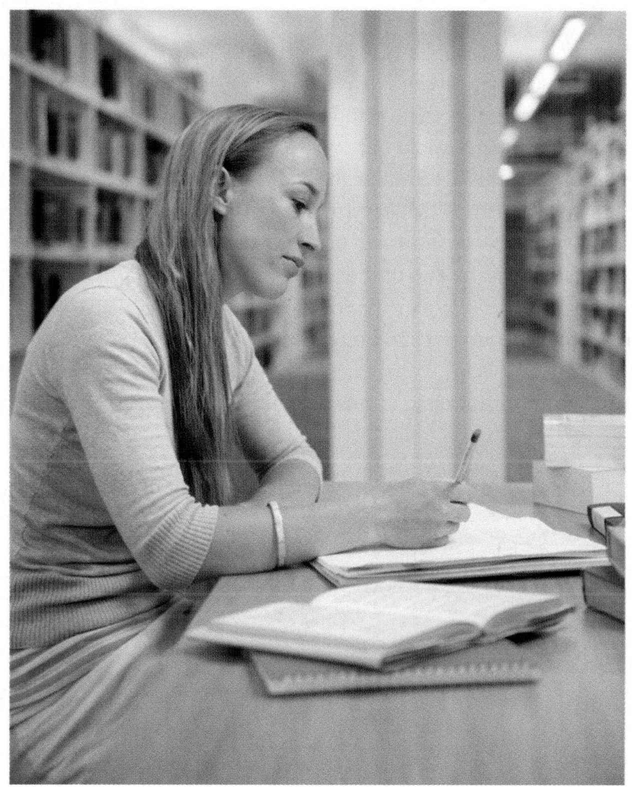

Abbey's Stats:

- □ Age: 17
- □ Height: 5 feet 5 inches
- □ Weight: 128 pounds

Critical Thinking Questions

1. What symptoms might Abbey expect to have if her levels of vitamin D continue to decline?
2. Why does Abbey's avoidance of sunlight increase her potential deficiency of vitamin D?
3. Based on her food record, why do you think that she is deficient in vitamin D?

Dietitian's Observation and Plan for Abbey:

- □ Discuss the need to add vitamin D–fortified foods to her diet to meet her daily needs. Explain why cheese is a good source of calcium, but it does not contain vitamin D.
- □ Abbey agrees to eat cereal with skim milk for breakfast prior to leaving for school, having a vitamin D–fortified yogurt as a daily afternoon snack, and to consume a large glass of skim milk with dinner.

A month later, Abbey returns to the dietitian. Because she often eats dinner with her friends at the local pizzeria, she is having a difficult time routinely having a glass of milk with dinner. The dietitian recommends that Abbey consume a glass of milk or a mug of hot cocoa made with milk daily when she gets home in the evening.

Abbey's Food Log

Food/Beverage	Time Consumed	Hunger Rating*	Location
Nothing	6 am	3	
Bagel with cream cheese	9:30 am	5	High school cafeteria
Turkey and Swiss cheese sandwich, chips, cola	12:30 pm	5	High school cafeteria
Cheese and crackers	3:30 pm	3	Kitchen
Pizza, 2 slices	6:30 pm	4	With friends in a restaurant

*Hunger Rating (1–5): 1 = not hungry; 5 = super hungry

Exploring **Vitamin A**

What Is Vitamin A?

The term vitamin A refers to a family of fat-soluble **retinoids** that include **retinol, retinal,** and **retinoic acid** (**Figure 9.7**). These compounds are similar in their chemical structure. They each contain a ring with a polyunsaturated fatty acid tail. Attached at the end of the fatty acid tail is either an alcohol group (retinol), an aldehyde group (retinal), or an acid group (retinoic acid). Whereas retinol, retinal, and retinoic acid all participate in essential functions in the body, retinol, the alcohol form, is the most usable. In foods, vitamin A is found as retinol or as a **retinyl ester,** which has an ester group attached at the fatty acid tail. The body also stores vitamin A as a retinyl ester in the liver. Retinol can be reversibly

Form found in animal foods and stored in body

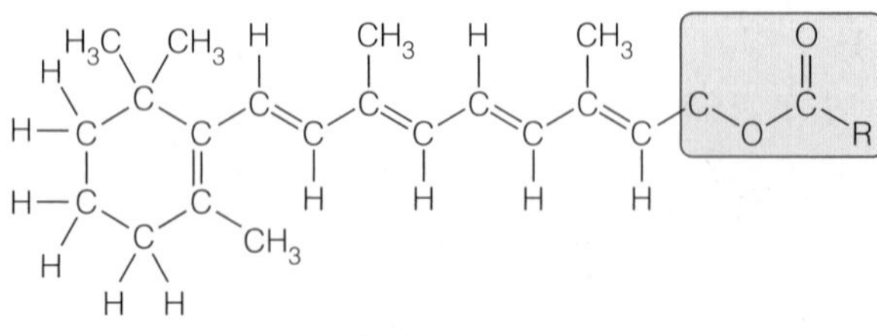

Retinyl ester

Form found in plants

Beta-carotene

Splits into 2 retinal

Retinol (alcohol form)
• Reproduction

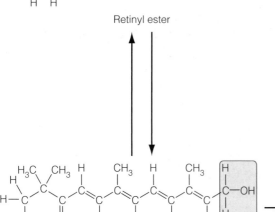

Retinal (aldehyde form)
• Vision

Retinoic acid
• Regulates growth

▲ **Figure 9.7 The Conversion of the Three Vitamin A Compounds**
Retinyl esters, found in foods and the form of vitamin A stored in the liver, are converted to retinol (alcohol). Retinol can be transformed to retinal (aldehyde) and then to retinoic acid. Beta-carotene is split during digestion to yield two molecules of retinal.

converted to retinal, the aldehyde form. Retinal can be transformed into the acidic form called retinoic acid, but the process is irreversible.

Retinoids are preformed vitamin A, which means they are in a form that the body can readily use. Preformed sources of vitamin A are found primarily in animal foods.

On the right side of Figure 9.7 is the structure of one of the family of provitamin A compounds called **carotenoids.** The provitamin A compounds found in plants are precursors to retinol in the body. Three such compounds—**beta-carotene** (β-carotene), beta-cryptoxanthin (β-cryptoxanthin), and alpha-carotene (α-carotene)—are the most common carotenoids, the yellow-red pigments that give carrots, butternut squash, and cantaloupe their vibrant, deep orange color. For vegans, these carotenoids are the only dietary source of vitamin A. Almost 25 to 35 percent of the dietary vitamin A consumed by adults in the United States comes from carotenoids, especially beta-carotene.[24]

Vitamin A Absorption and Transport

All forms of preformed vitamin A are absorbed by active transport in the small intestine with the help of bile salts and micelles. The rate of absorption of preformed vitamin A is high, ranging from 70 to 90 percent as long as your diet contains some fat. Beta-carotene, in contrast, is absorbed via passive diffusion at a much lower rate of 5 percent to up to 60 percent.[25] Fat in the diet enhances the absorption of vitamin A, but reduces absorption in the presence of diarrhea or an infection in the GI tract. Beta-carotene absorption is reduced with high fiber intakes and improved when foods are cooked. For example, the amount of beta-carotene absorbed from cooked carrots is much higher than that from raw carrots.

Most forms of vitamin A are packaged as a chylomicron along with other dietary lipids, and absorbed into the lymph fluid. Retinoic acid doesn't need a chylomicron, but rather is attached to a protein called albumin and absorbed into the portal vein. Carotenes are converted to vitamin A in the intestine before absorption.

Vitamin A is stored in the liver until needed by the body. Retinol binding protein transports the retinol from storage through the bloodstream to the receptor sites located on the cells.

Vitamin A is difficult to excrete from the body. When the liver becomes saturated with vitamin A, some is excreted through the bile to prevent toxicity.

Metabolic Functions of Vitamin A

Each form of retinoid plays a specific role in the body. Retinal (the aldehyde form) participates in vision. The hormonelike action of retinoic acid (the acid form) is essential for growth and development of cells, including bone development. Retinol (the alcohol form) supports reproduction and a healthy immune system. In addition to these critical roles, vitamin A may help prevent cancer.

Vitamin A in Vision

One of the most well-known functions of vitamin A is the role it plays in vision. Light that passes into the eyes and hits the retina will be translated into visual images with the help of two vitamin A–dependent proteins, **rhodopsin** and

retinoids The term used to describe the family of preformed vitamin A compounds.

retinol The alcohol form of preformed vitamin A.

retinal The aldehyde form of preformed vitamin A.

retinoic acid The acid form of preformed vitamin A.

retinyl ester The ester form of preformed vitamin A found in foods and stored in the body.

carotenoids The family of provitamin compounds that includes beta-carotene.

beta-carotene One of the provitamin A carotenoids.

rhodopsin A compound found in the rods of the eye that is needed for night vision. It is comprised of *cis*-retinal and the protein opsin.

continued

iodopsin. These proteins are found in the tips of light-absorbing cells in the retina called **rods** and **cones,** respectively. Rhodopsin, which contains *cis*-retinal (the aldehyde form of vitamin A), absorbs the light entering the rods. The light changes the shape of *cis*-retinal to *trans*-retinal, detaching it from the protein opsin. This change in shape is referred to as **bleaching.** When rhodopsin is bleached, it transmits a signal through the optic nerve to the part of the brain involved in vision.

After rhodopsin is bleached, most of the *trans*-retinal returns to its *cis* shape. This form is now able to bind with opsin, which regenerates rhodopsin and the eye's light-absorbing capabilities. This reaction is illustrated in **Figure 9.8.**

Walking into a dark building after being in the sun without sunglasses may require taking time to adjust to the dimmer light. This adjustment period occurs because the reformation of *trans*- to *cis*-retinal takes time. Fortunately, there is a pool of vitamin A in the retina to help with this conversion.

In order for vitamin A to participate in the visual cycle, it must first be metabolized in the retina. Retinol attaches to **retinol binding protein (RBP)** and is transported through the blood to the eye. Once inside the retina, retinol is converted to retinal before moving into the photoreceptor cells of the rods.

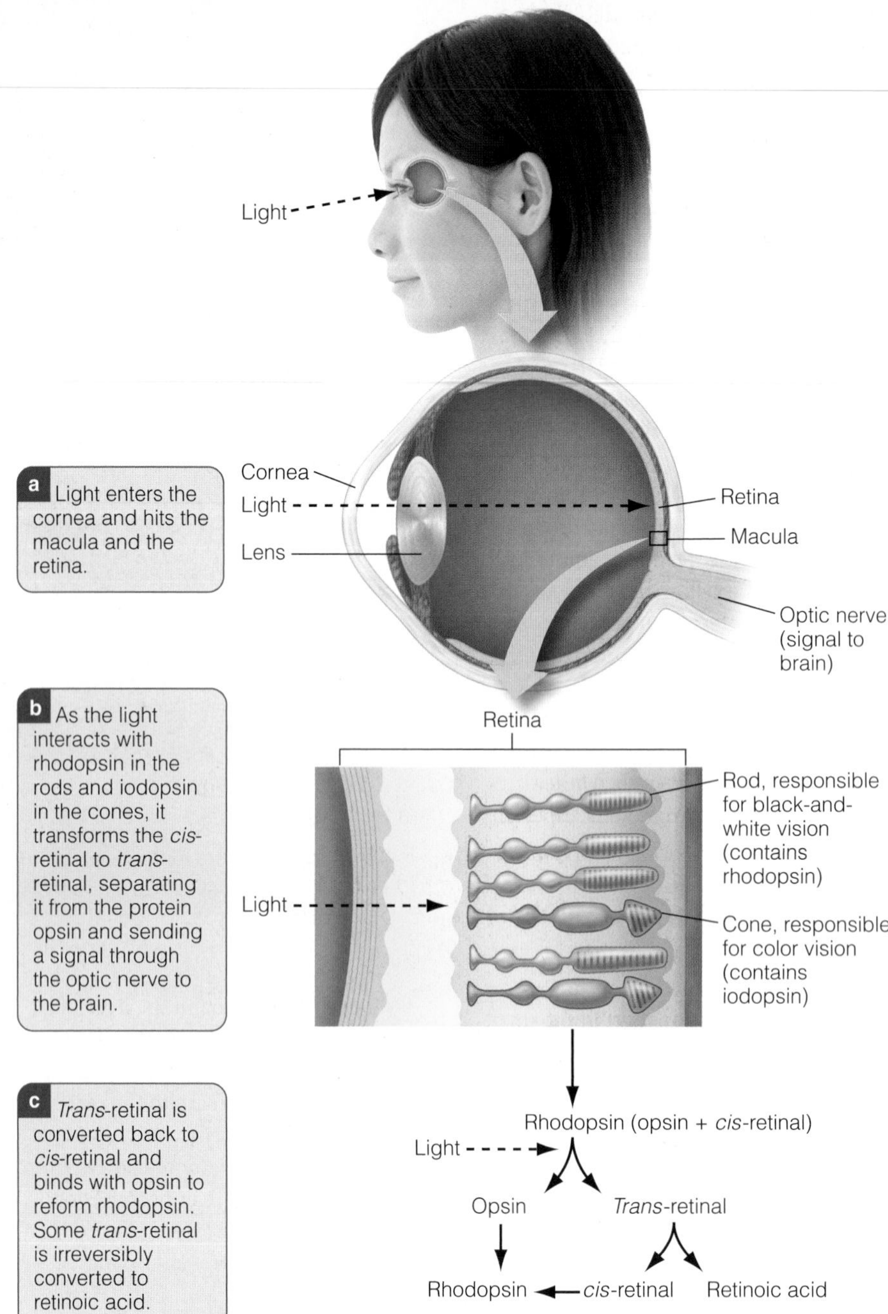
Light
a Light enters the cornea and hits the macula and the retina.
Cornea
Light
Lens
Retina
Macula
Optic nerve (signal to brain)
b As the light interacts with rhodopsin in the rods and iodopsin in the cones, it transforms the *cis*-retinal to *trans*-retinal, separating it from the protein opsin and sending a signal through the optic nerve to the brain.
Retina
Light
Rod, responsible for black-and-white vision (contains rhodopsin)
Cone, responsible for color vision (contains iodopsin)
c *Trans*-retinal is converted back to *cis*-retinal and binds with opsin to reform rhodopsin. Some *trans*-retinal is irreversibly converted to retinoic acid.
Rhodopsin (opsin + *cis*-retinal)
Light
Opsin
Trans-retinal
Rhodopsin
cis-retinal
Retinoic acid

▲ **Figure 9.8 Retinal and Its Role in Vision**

iodopsin The compound found in the cones of the eye that is needed for color vision.

rods Light-absorbing cells responsible for black-and-white vision and night vision.

cones Light-absorbing cells responsible for color vision.

bleaching When light enters the eye and interacts with rhodopsin, splitting it into *trans*-retinal and opsin.

retinol binding protein (RBP) A protein made in the liver that transports retinol through the blood to the cells.

epithelial cells Cells that line the cavities in the body and cover flat surfaces such as the skin.

cell division The process of dividing one cell into two separate cells with the same genetic material.

cell differentiation The process of a less specialized immature cell becoming a specialized mature cell.

Vitamin A in Protein Synthesis and Cell Differentiation

Vitamin A is important for keeping the epithelial cells moist and structurally sound. **Epithelial cells** in the skin protect the body from damage from the sun. The epithelial cells that line the lungs, intestinal tract, eyes, and urinary tract are round, moist, lined with cilia, and secrete a thick mucus. The mucus coats the cells and protects them from bacteria and viruses that can infiltrate the body and cause infection. Vitamin A deficiency can cause these cells to become flattened, hard, and unable to produce mucus (**Figure 9.9**). Vitamin A also works with the immune system to create white blood cells (*lymphocytes*) and antibodies that fight foreign invaders should they enter the bloodstream.

Vitamin A stimulates **cell division** and **cell differentiation** of the epithelial cells as they grow and develop. Retinoic acid prompts gene expression, a process that uses genetic information to make the proteins needed to begin cell division. As cells divide and cluster together, changes occur that cause them to become different from their initiating cells. This differentiation determines what cells become in the body. For immature skin cells to differentiate into mature skin cells, for example, vitamin A acts as a signal to turn on the genes to create the proteins needed to make healthy skin.

This role of vitamin A is one reason dermatologists prescribe retinoid-containing medications, such as Retin-A or Accutane, to treat acne. Retin-A is a topical medication that works by enhancing the turnover of skin cells and inhibiting the formation of acne. Accutane is a medication taken orally that manipulates cell differentiation through gene expression of acne-producing cells to alter their development in the skin.[26, 27]

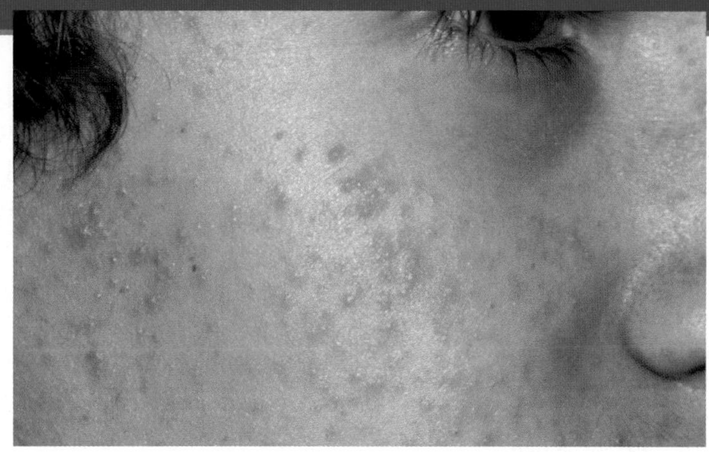

Vitamin A derivatives can help treat acne.

Vitamin A in Growth and Reproduction

In addition to its role in cell differentiation, vitamin A plays several critical roles in growth and reproduction. Both retinol and retinoic acid participate in growth, although the mechanism is still unknown. What is known is that without vitamin A, embryonic and fetal development is impaired, especially in the development of the limbs, heart, eyes, and ears.[28] Children fail to grow when their diets lack vitamin A, but when either retinol or retinoic acid are given, growth is enhanced.

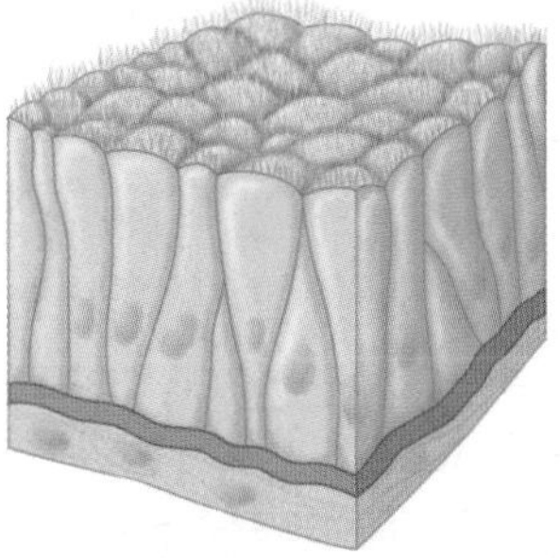

a Healthy epithelial cells are rounded, moist, and contain mucus-secreting cells and cilia lining the surface.

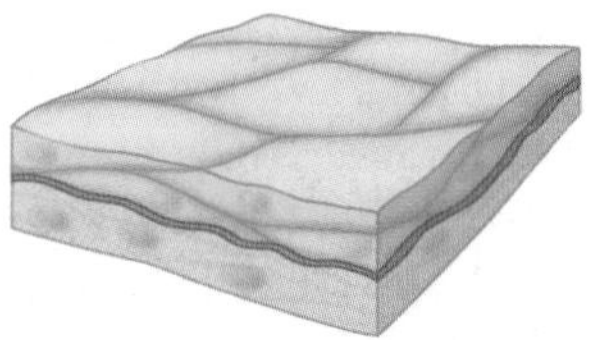

b A vitamin A deficiency can lead to unhealthy epithelial cells that are flat, hard, and unable to produce mucus.

▲ **Figure 9.9 Healthy and Vitamin A–Deficient Epithelial Cells**

Retinol, but not retinoic acid, is essential for reproduction. Normal levels of retinol are required for sperm production in males and normal menstrual cycles in females.

Vitamin A and Bone Health

All three forms of vitamin A may help regulate the cells involved in bone growth. Too much vitamin A stimulates bone resorption—breaking down bone—and inhibits bone formation, which can negatively affect healthy bones and may be a risk factor for developing osteoporosis.[29] Both excessive intake and insufficient intake of vitamin A have negative impacts on bone density. Research from the Nurses' Health Study reports retinol intakes less than 510 μg RAE (1,700 IU) and more than 2,030 μg RAE (6,700 IU) per day may increase fracture risk (beta-carotene has no effect).[30] A diet closer to 600 to 850 μg RAE (2,000 to 2,800 IU) per day of vitamin A is most likely to improve the bone mineral density of elderly men and women.[31]

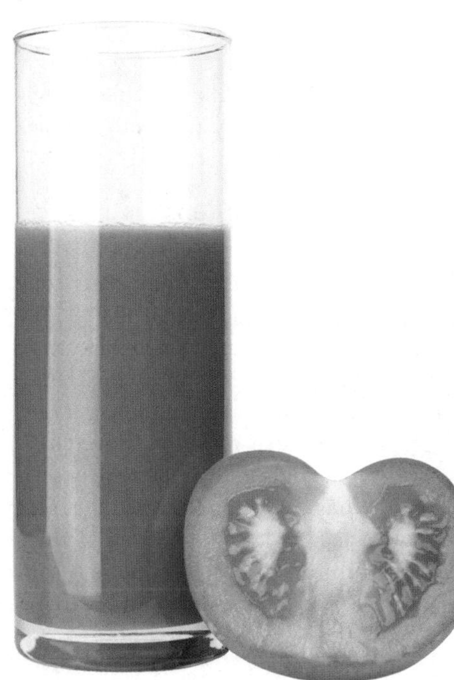

The carotenoid lycopene, found in tomatoes and tomato products, functions as an antioxidant in the body.

Carotenoids as Antioxidants

Provitamin A compounds are able to quench free radical reactions and protect cells from damage. Lycopene, which is the form of carotenoid that gives red tomatoes their dark red color, is especially effective in quenching free radicals. Two other carotenoids, lutein and zeaxanthin (found in corn and dark green leafy vegetables), protect the eyes from free radical damage.[32]

Daily Needs

The Recommended Dietary Allowance (RDA) for vitamin A is based on maintaining sufficient storage of the vitamin in the liver. Vitamin A in foods and supplements

continued

can be measured in two ways: in micrograms (μg) of **retinol activity equivalents (RAE)** and in **international units (IU).**

Because retinol is the most usable form of vitamin A and because provitamin A carotenoids can be converted to retinol, the preferred way to measure vitamin A in foods is to include all forms as RAE. However, some vitamin supplements and food labels show the older measure, IU, on their products. (Note: 1 μg RAE is the equivalent of 3.3 IU.) The Calculation Corner provides more detail on the conversion from IU to micrograms RAE.

Adult females need 700 μg RAE (2,310 IU) of vitamin A daily, whereas adult males need 900 μg RAE (3,000 IU) daily. This is the average amount needed to maintain adequate stores in the body.[33] A daily recommendation for beta-carotene hasn't been established, but the Institute of Medicine suggests consuming 3 to 6 milligrams of beta-carotene every day from foods.[34] This can easily be obtained by consuming five or more servings of fruits and vegetables. This amount of beta-carotene will also provide about 50 percent of the recommended vitamin A intake. Hence, eating beta-carotene-rich foods will add not only antioxidants to the diet, but also vitamin A.

Vegetarians who eat no animal foods, including vitamin A–rich milk and eggs, need to be especially conscientious about eating carotenoids and beta-carotene-rich foods to meet their daily vitamin A needs.

Calculation Corner

Converting International Units for Vitamin A

International units (IU) are a system of measurement of the biologic activity or potency of a substance, such as a vitamin, that produces a particular effect. Because each vitamin differs in potency per milligram, the conversion factors from IU to milligrams will also differ.

(a) Vitamin A is measured in retinol activity equivalents, or RAE. Use the following conversion factors to determine the micrograms retinol activity equivalents (μg RAE) found in 1 IU:

1 IU retinol is the biological equivalent of 0.3 μg retinol or 0.3 μg RAE or 0.6 μg beta-carotene

Example: A vitamin supplement contains 25,000 IU of retinol. How many μg RAE does it contain?

Answer: 0.3 μg × 25,000 IU = 7,500 μg RAE

(b) The requirements for vitamin A are expressed as RAE. To determine the amount of RAE in micrograms in a meal, you have to convert the various forms of vitamin A equivalents. For example:

1 μg RAE = 1 μg retinol and 12 μg beta-carotene.

The first step is to divide the amount of beta-carotene by 12 to convert to RAE. Next, add that number to the preformed vitamin A in the meal.

Example: If a meal contains 500 μg retinol and 1,800 μg beta-carotene, how many μg RAE does the meal contain?

Answer: 500 μg retinol + (1,800 μg beta-carotene ÷ 12) = 650 μg RAE

Food Sources

Milk, cereals, cheese, egg yolks, and organ meats (such as liver) are the most popular sources of preformed vitamin A in the U.S. diet. Liver is especially abundant in vitamin A. For example, 1 ounce of beef liver contains 2 milligrams of retinol, or more than 100 percent of the RDA of vitamin A for adults.

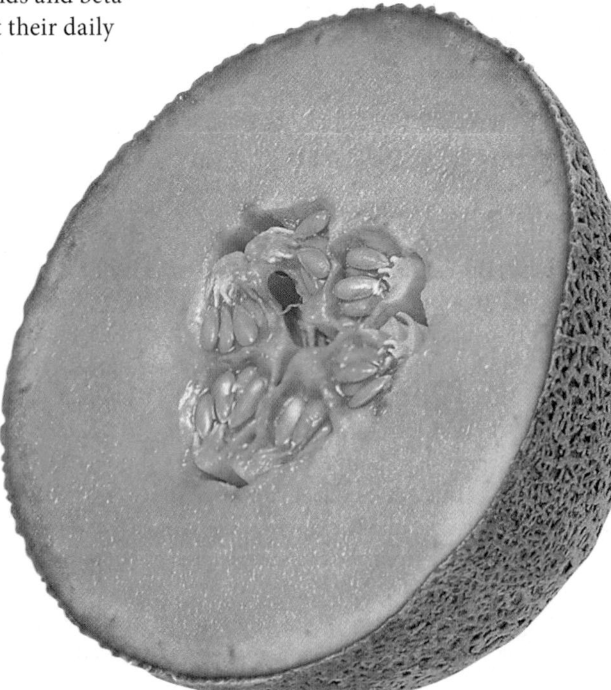

Carrots, spinach, and sweet potatoes are American favorites for provitamin A carotenoids, including beta-carotene. Similar to vitamin A and other fat-soluble vitamins, carotenoids are absorbed more efficiently when fat is present in the GI tract. Adding as little as 1 tablespoon of vegetable oil to the diet daily can increase the absorption of carotenoids by as much as 25 percent.[35]

Figure 9.10 shows the vitamin A content in μg RAE, and includes both retinoid- and carotenoid-rich sources.

Too Much Vitamin A

Because 90 percent of vitamin A is stored in the liver, chronic daily consumption of more than 30,000 micrograms of preformed vitamin A (more than 300 times the RDA for adults) can lead to **hypervitaminosis A** (*hyper* = over, *osis* = condition), an extremely serious condition in which the liver accumulates toxic levels of vitamin A. Hypervitaminosis A can lead to deterioration and scarring of the liver and even death. To prevent toxicity, the tolerable upper

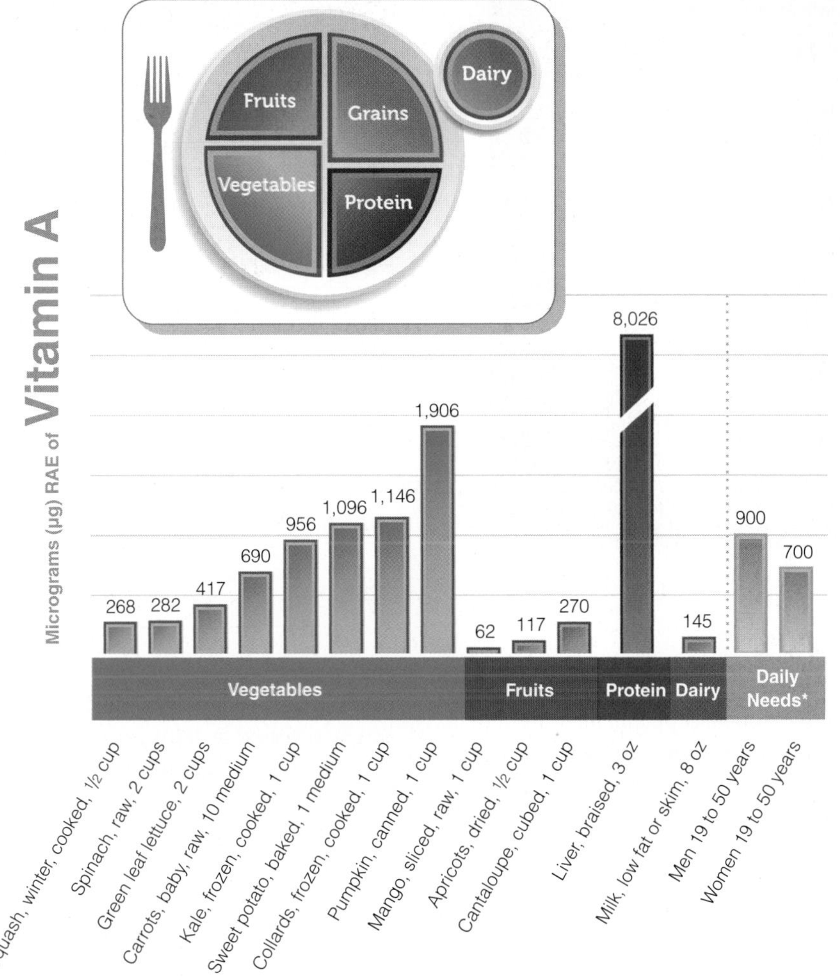

▲ **Figure 9.10 Food Sources of Vitamin A**

intake level (UL) of preformed vitamin A for adults has been set at 3,000 µg (10,000 IU) daily.[36]

Vitamin A Toxicity

Vitamin A toxicity is caused by ingesting too much preformed vitamin A, not carotenoids. Consuming more than 15,000 µg of preformed vitamin A at one time or over a short period of time can lead to nausea, vomiting, headaches, dizziness, and blurred vision. Overconsumption of preformed vitamin A is usually due to taking supplements and is less likely to occur from overeating vitamin A in foods.

Higher intake of preformed vitamin A during pregnancy, particularly in the first trimester, can cause birth defects in the face and skull and damage the child's central nervous system. All women of childbearing age who are using retinoids for acne or other skin conditions should take the proper steps to avoid becoming pregnant.[37]

Vitamin A and Osteoporosis

While vitamin A is needed for bone health, some research suggests that consuming too much may lead to **osteoporosis,** which in turn increases the risk of fractures. Osteoporosis-related hip fractures appear to be prevalent in Swedes and Norwegians, who tend to have high consumption of vitamin A–rich cod-liver oil and specialty dairy products that have been heavily fortified with vitamin A.[38]

Additional studies involving both women and men have shown similar associations between high vitamin A intake and increased risk of fractures. As little as 1,500 micrograms (3,000 IU) of retinol, which is slightly more than twice the RDA recommended for women, can be unhealthy for bones.[39] This amount can be quickly reached when taking a supplement and eating a diet rich in vitamin A–fortified foods. The Daily Value [DV] for vitamin A used in the Nutrition Facts panel on food labels is 5,000 IU. Recall from Chapter 2 that the DV used on food labels are based on older recommendations, not the current recommended intakes. Consuming a serving of a food that provides a large percentage of the DV for vitamin A may mean consuming more than the upper limit.

Overconsuming Carotenoids

The upper levels apply only to preformed vitamin A from foods, fortified foods, and supplements. Provitamin A carotenoids in foods are not toxic and do not pose serious health problems. The body has a built-in safeguard to prevent provitamin A carotenoids from contributing to vitamin A toxicity, birth defects, or bone damage. If individuals consume more carotenoids than needed to meet vitamin A needs, the body will decrease their conversion to retinol. Extra amounts of carotenoids are stored in the liver and in the subcutaneous fat.

Eating too many carotenoids can, however, cause the nonthreatening

retinol activity equivalents (RAE) The unit of measure used to describe the total amount of all forms of preformed vitamin A and provitamin A carotenoids in food.

international units (IU) A system of measurement of a biologically active ingredient such as a vitamin that produces a certain effect.

hypervitaminosis A The serious condition in which the liver accumulates toxic levels of vitamin A.

osteoporosis A condition in which bones become brittle and porous, making them fragile due to depletion of calcium and bone proteins.

continued

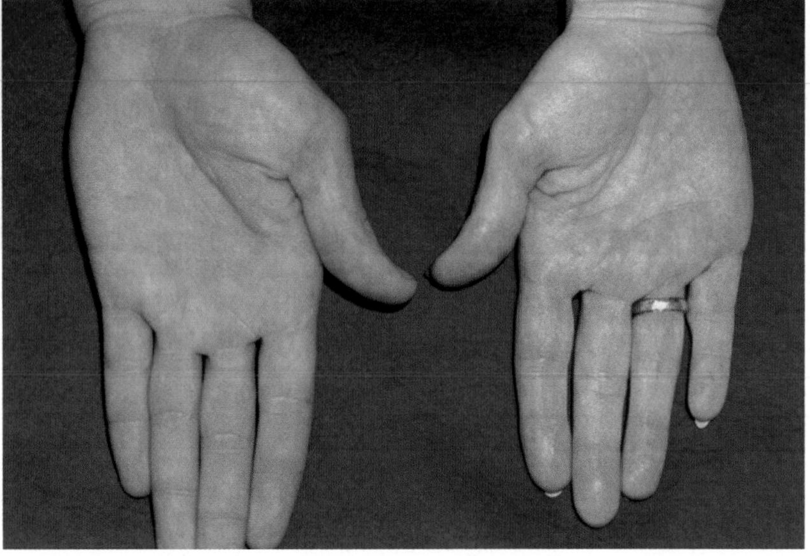

The hand on the right exhibits the orange-tinged skin characteristic of carotenodermia.

TABLE TIPS

Score an A

Dunk baby carrots in a tablespoon of low-fat ranch dressing for a healthy snack.

Keep dried apricots in your backpack for a sweet treat.

Add baby spinach to a lunchtime salad.

Bake sweet potatoes rather than white potatoes at dinner.

Buy frozen mango chunks for a ready-to-thaw beta-carotene-rich addition to cottage cheese or yogurt.

condition **carotenodermia** (*carotene* = carotene, *dermia* = skin), which results in orange-tinged skin, particularly in the palms of the hands and soles of the feet. Because these areas are cushioned with fat, they become more concentrated with the pigments and more visibly orange in color (right hand in photo). Cutting back on carotenoid-rich foods will reverse carotenodermia.

Overconsuming Beta-Carotene Supplements

Although a diet abundant in carotenoid-rich foods is not dangerous, carotenoid supplements may be. In a study of adult male smokers, those who consumed beta-carotene supplements were shown to have significantly higher rates of lung cancer than those who didn't take the supplements. While some earlier studies suggested alcohol may contribute to the effects of beta-carotene supplements on lung cancer risk, more recent research shows consistent evidence that beta-carotene supplements alone increase a smoker's risk of lung cancer and mortality.[40]

carotenodermia The presence of excess carotene in the blood resulting in an orange color to the skin due to excessive intake of carrots or other carotene-rich vegetables.

night blindness The inability to see in dim light or at night due to a deficiency of retinal in the retina.

xerophthalmia Permanent damage to the cornea causing blindness due to a prolonged vitamin A deficiency.

keratinization The accumulation of the protein keratin in epithelial cells, forming hard, dry cells unable to secrete mucus due to vitamin A deficiency.

Too Little Vitamin A

Vitamin A deficiency is uncommon in the United States but is a serious problem in developing countries. Signs of vitamin A deficiency, such as vision problems and increased infections, begin to develop after the liver stores of vitamin A are depleted.

Vitamin A Deficiency and Blindness

If the diet is deficient in vitamin A, an insufficient pool of retinal in the retina can result in **night blindness,** or the inability to see in the dark. Individuals with night blindness have difficulty seeing at dusk, because they can't adjust from daylight to dark, and may not be able to drive a car during this time of the day. If diagnosed early, night blindness can be reversed by taking vitamin A.

A prolonged vitamin A deficiency can lead to complete blindness. A severe deficiency of vitamin A results in dryness and permanent damage to the cornea, a condition called **xerophthalmia** (*xero* = dry, *ophthalm* = eye). Up to 10 million children, mostly in developing countries, suffer from xerophthalmia annually, and as many as 500,000 of these children go blind every year because they don't consume enough vitamin A. Vitamin A deficiency is the number-one cause of preventable blindness in children.[41]

Vitamin A Deficiency and Immunity

Keratinization of the epithelial tissues will form throughout the body with vitamin A deficiency. The epithelial cells secrete keratin that creates a hard, dry epithelial cell, which is unable to secrete the protective layer of mucus. Without mucus, the cells are unable to function properly, creating an environment susceptible to infection, especially in the nasal passages and the intestinal, urinary, and respiratory tracts. Keratinization also occurs in the skin.

Exploring Vitamin D

What Is Vitamin D?

Vitamin D (**calciferol**) is called the "sunshine vitamin" because it is derived from the reaction between ultraviolet (UV) rays and a form of cholesterol found in the skin. Exposure to sunlight can synthesize up to 100 percent of the vitamin D the body needs.[42] For this reason, vitamin D is often considered a conditionally essential nutrient. However, it still fits the criteria of a vitamin because a deficiency of this compound can cause symptoms that are cured once adequate intake is restored. Because of its function, vitamin D is also considered a **prohormone** that is activated inside the body. Vitamin D is found in two forms. **Cholecalciferol** or **vitamin D_3** is the form produced in the skin and found in animal foods. **Ergocalciferol** or **vitamin D_2** is found in plants and dietary supplements.

Ergocalciferol and cholecalciferol differ chemically in the structure of their side chains, as illustrated in **Figure 9.11**. Ergocalciferol or D_2 contains a double bond in the side chain between carbons 22 and 23 and a methyl group on carbon 24. Cholecalciferol or D_3 has a single bond in the place of the double bond and a hydrogen on carbon 24. Even though their structure is different, it does not affect their ability to function in the body.

Vitamin D Metabolism

Whether from food or sunlight, vitamin D enters the body in an inactive form. In the skin, a compound called **7-dehydrocholesterol** or **provitamin D_3** (which is made in the liver from cholesterol) is converted to **previtamin D_3** or **precalciferol** when UV rays hit the skin (see **Figure 9.12**). Precalciferol is changed to cholecalciferol, which slowly diffuses through the skin into the blood attached to a protein called **vitamin D_3 binding protein (DBP).** Cholecalciferol is then taken up by the liver to begin the activation process.

Once cholecalciferol reaches the liver, a two-step activation process begins. First, liver enzymes add a hydroxyl group on the twenty-fifth carbon of cholecalciferol, forming **25-hydroxycholecalciferol** (see step 3 in Figure 9.12). This newly formed compound circulates in the blood transported by DBP. In the kidneys a second hydroxyl group

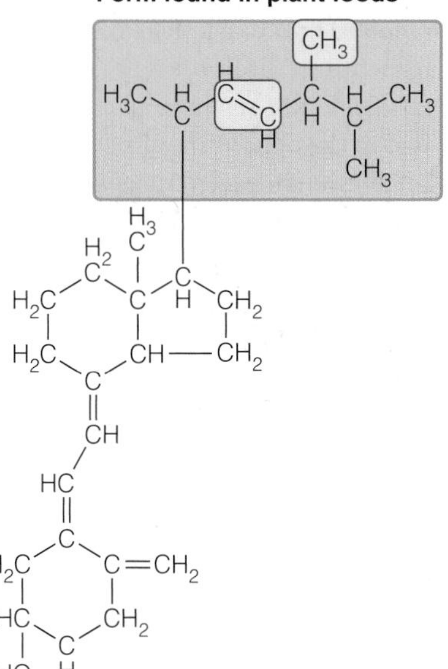

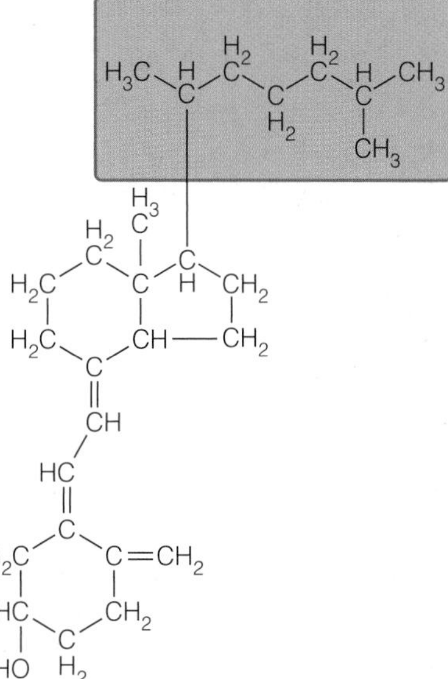

▲ **Figure 9.11 The Chemical Structure of Vitamin D**
Vitamin D is found in the ergocalciferol (vitamin D_2) form in plants and the cholecalciferol (vitamin D_3) form in animal foods.

calciferol The family of vitamin D compounds.

prohormone A physiologically inactive precursor to a hormone.

cholecalciferol (vitamin D_3) The form of vitamin D found in animal foods and formed from precalciferol in the skin. This is the form absorbed through the skin into the blood.

ergocalciferol (vitamin D_2) The form of vitamin D found in plants and dietary supplements.

7-dehydrocholesterol (provitamin D_3) The compound in the skin that is converted to precalciferol by UV light from the sun; synthesized in the liver from cholesterol.

previtamin D_3 (precalciferol) The compound that is formed from 7-dehydrocholesterol when sunlight hits the skin.

vitamin D_3 binding protein (DBP) A protein made in the liver that transports vitamin D through the blood to the cells.

25-hydroxycholecalciferol The compound formed in the liver by adding a hydroxyl group to the 25th carbon of cholecalciferol.

continued

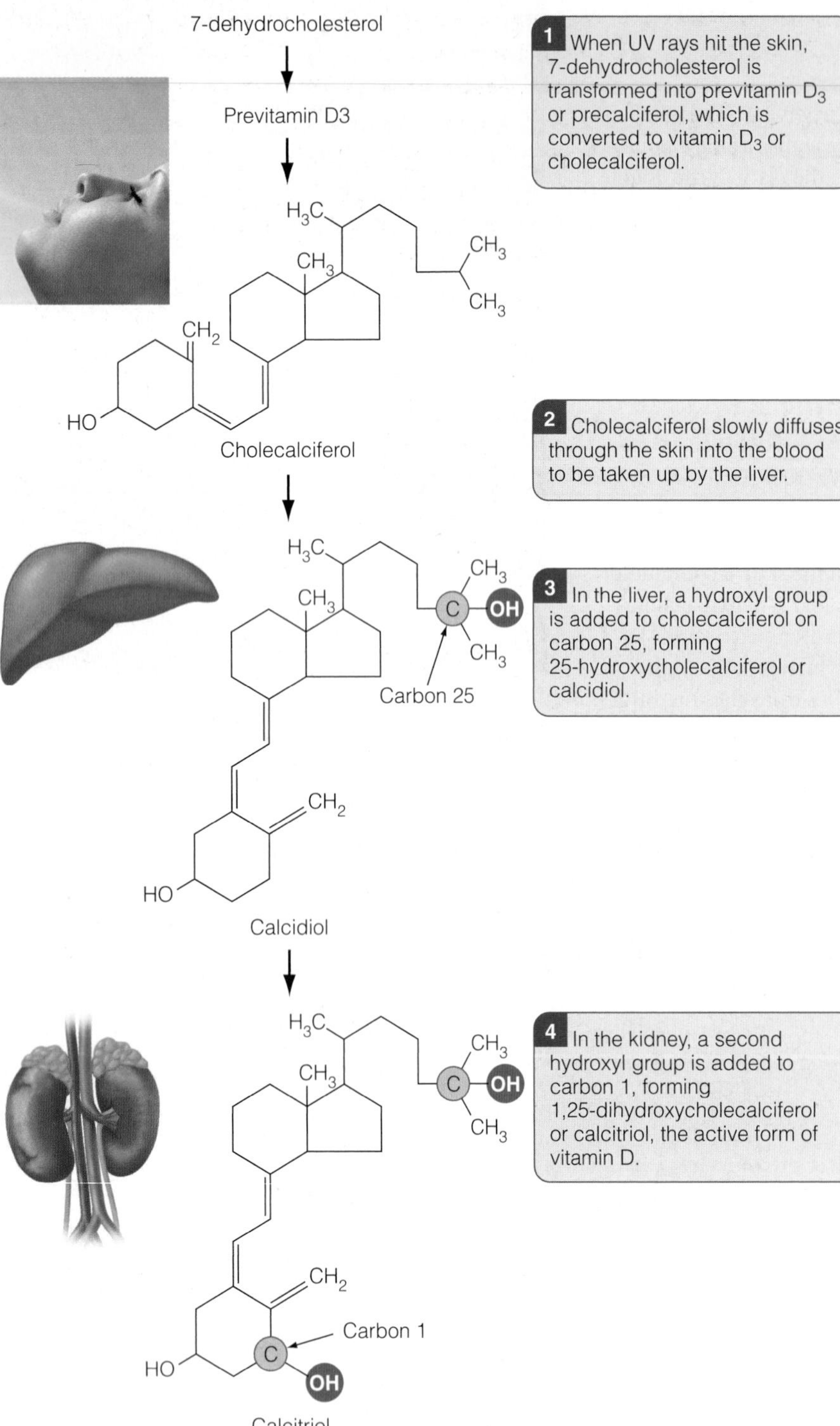
7-dehydrocholesterol
Previtamin D3
1 When UV rays hit the skin, 7-dehydrocholesterol is transformed into previtamin D3 or precalciferol, which is converted to vitamin D3 or cholecalciferol.
H3C
CH3
CH3
CH3
CH2
HO
Cholecalciferol
2 Cholecalciferol slowly diffuses through the skin into the blood to be taken up by the liver.
H3C
CH3
CH3
C
OH
CH3
Carbon 25
3 In the liver, a hydroxyl group is added to cholecalciferol on carbon 25, forming 25-hydroxycholecalciferol or calcidiol.
CH2
HO
Calcidiol
H3C
CH3
CH3
C
OH
CH3
4 In the kidney, a second hydroxyl group is added to carbon 1, forming 1,25-dihydroxycholecalciferol or calcitriol, the active form of vitamin D.
CH2
Carbon 1
C
HO
OH
Calcitriol

▲ **Figure 9.12 The Metabolism of Vitamin D**

is added on the first carbon, forming **1,25-dihydroxycholecalciferol.** This is the active form of vitamin D, also called **calcitriol** (see step 4 in Figure 9.12), that leaves the kidney and enters the cells.

Vitamin D_2 and vitamin D_3 consumed in the diet are absorbed into the small intestine as part of a micelle along with other dietary lipids. Each is repackaged into a chylomicron and circulates through the lymph system before arriving at the liver for storage.

Blood calcium levels influence the metabolism of vitamin D (see **Figure 9.13**). When blood calcium levels drop, **parathyroid hormone (PTH)** is secreted from the parathyroid gland and travels to the kidney to activate vitamin D or 25-hydroxycholecalciferol. This boost in the levels of active vitamin D enhances the intestinal absorption of calcium, increases the amount of calcium reabsorbed through the kidneys, and mobilizes calcium from the bone. The result is that blood calcium levels return to normal.

Metabolic Functions of Vitamin D

Vitamin D regulates two important bone minerals, calcium and phosphorus. Vitamin D also participates in several other functions, including cell differentiation, stimulation of the immune system, blood pressure regulation, and insulin secretion.

The Role of Vitamin D in Bone Growth

Calcitriol functions as a hormone to stimulate the absorption of calcium and phosphorus in the intestinal tract. It also functions to maintain a healthy ratio of calcium and phosphorus levels in the blood to promote uptake of these two minerals in the bone. As calcium levels in the blood rise, more calcium is deposited in the bone. Vitamin D controls the interaction between *osteoblasts* and *osteoclasts,* the two specialized bone cells involved in remodeling bone. Because of its role in regulating calcium and phosphorus, vitamin D helps to build and maintain bone mass.

Vitamin D May Prevent Some Cancers

Research studies have shown that the incidence of breast, colon, and prostate cancers is greater among individuals living in sun-poor areas of the world than among those living in sunny regions. Vitamin D helps regulate the growth and differentiation of certain cells.

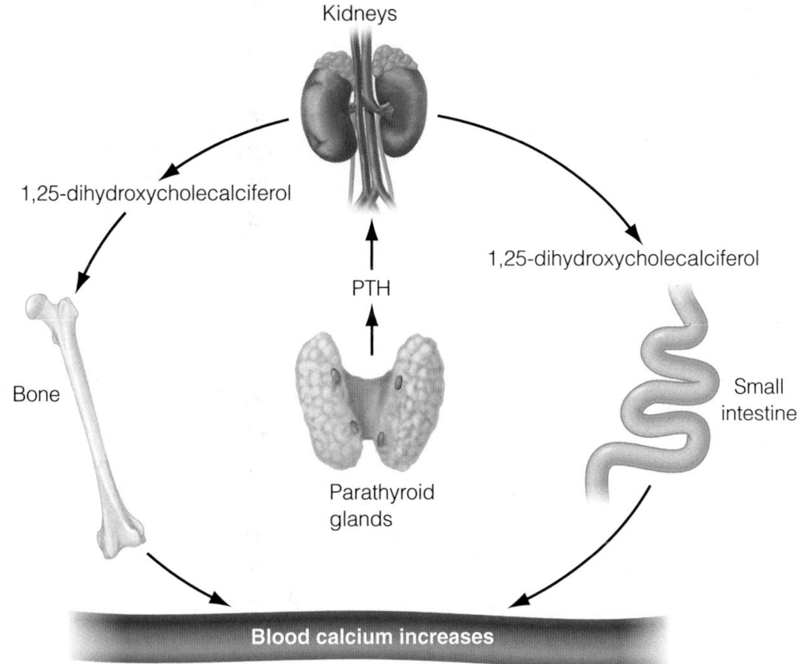

▲ **Figure 9.13 The Relationship of Blood Calcium to Parathyroid Hormone and Vitamin D**
Low blood levels of calcium stimulate the parathyroid glands to release parathyroid hormone (PTH). PTH stimulates the kidneys to increase the amount of active vitamin D, which in turn increases calcium absorption from the intestines, stimulates the reabsorption of calcium through the kidneys, and releases calcium from the bone. These actions help raise blood calcium back to normal levels.

Researchers speculate that a deficiency of vitamin D in the body may reduce the proliferation of healthy cells and allow cancer cells to flourish.[43]

Vitamin D May Prevent Diabetes

Vitamin D may also help reduce the risk of diabetes mellitus. Those with type 2 diabetes mellitus often have low blood levels of vitamin D. One study revealed that insulin resistance, or the inability of the cells to use insulin in the blood, was more pronounced in people with low levels of vitamin D in the blood.[44]

Vitamin D May Regulate the Immune System

The active form of vitamin D may reduce the risk of developing certain autoimmune disorders, such as inflammatory bowel syndrome (which is not the same thing as irritable bowel syndrome). Most cells in the immune system, such as T cells and macrophages, have a receptor for vitamin D. The role of vitamin D is still not understood, but some researchers suggest that it may affect the function of the immune system and inhibit the development of autoimmunity.[45]

Vitamin D May Help Regulate Blood Pressure

Vitamin D reduces hypertension by acting on the gene that regulates the renin-angiotensin system, the system that regulates blood pressure.[46] Vitamin D appears to reduce the activity of this gene, which results in less renin being produced. Renin is an enzyme that balances sodium and potassium levels in the blood, which controls blood pressure (we will discuss the relationship of renin to hypertension in Chapter 11). Further evidence for the role of vitamin D in regulating blood pressure is the fact that blood pressure readings tend to be higher during the winter, when people are exposed to less sunlight, than in the summer. People with mild hypertension may be able to lower their blood pressure by spending a little time in the sun.

Daily Needs

Not everyone can rely on the sun to meet his or her daily vitamin D needs. There are a number of limiting factors that influence vitamin D synthesis from sun: melanin content of the skin, whether it is cloudy or smoggy, and use of sunscreen. There is new positive evidence, however, that even during the winter months sun exposure is strong enough to synthesize adequate vitamin D in the skin.[47]

Individuals with darker skin, such as African Americans, have a higher amount of the skin pigment melanin, which reduces vitamin D production from sunlight. To derive the same amount of vitamin D as people with less melanin, these individuals need a longer period of sun exposure. A cloudy day can reduce the synthesis of vitamin D by 50 percent, and by 60 percent if it is smoggy or you sit in the shade.[48] And the use of sunscreen can block the body's ability to synthesize vitamin D by more than 95 percent.[49] Because of these variables involving sun exposure, daily vitamin D needs are based on the amount in foods and are not based on the synthesis of vitamin D in the skin from exposure to sunlight.

1,25-dihydroxycholecalciferol The active form of vitamin D, also called calcitriol, that is formed in the kidney by adding a second hydroxyl group on the first carbon to 25-dihydroxycholecalciferol.

calcitriol The active form of vitamin D, also referred to as 1,25-dihydroxycholecalciferol.

parathyroid hormone (PTH) The hormone secreted from the parathyroid glands that activates vitamin D formation in the kidney.

continued

The RDA for adults is 15 to 20 micrograms (600 to 800 IU) of vitamin D daily, depending on your age. These recommendations are listed in both micrograms and international units.[50] Learn how to convert micrograms to IUs in the Calculation Corner.

The RDA for children has been set at 15 micrograms (600 IU) of vitamin D per day for children ages one to thirteen. This is an increase in vitamin D from 5 micrograms due to newly reported research suggesting that the previous RDA was too low. Vitamin D supplementation as high as 2,000 IUs is safe for children.[51]

When reading labels to assess the amount of vitamin D in foods, keep in mind that the Daily Value (DV) on the Nutrition Facts panel is set at 400 IU, a recommendation based on the older RDA for vitamin D. This means the amount of vitamin D in a serving of a packaged food does not reflect the new, higher recommendations for children and adults.[52]

Food Sources

One of the easiest ways to get vitamin D from food is to drink fortified milk, which provides 100 IU, or 2.5 micrograms, of vitamin D per 8 fluid ounces. Other than fortified milk, breakfast cereals, yogurt, and fatty fish (such as sardines and salmon), very few foods provide ample amounts of vitamin D (see **Figure 9.14**). With this scarcity of naturally occurring food sources, it isn't surprising that many Americans are not meeting their daily vitamin D needs.[53]

Calculation Corner

Converting International Units for Vitamin D

Vitamin D content in dietary supplements and fortified foods is often listed in international units (IU), while vitamin D found in food is measured in μg cholecalciferol. Use the following conversion factor to determine the μg cholecalciferol in 1 IU.

1 IU of cholecalciferol is equivalent to 0.025 μg cholecalciferol

Example: A vitamin supplement contains 1,000 IU of cholecalciferol. How many μg cholecalciferol does it contain?

Answer: 0.025 μg cholecalciferol $\times$ 1,000 IU $=$ 25 μg cholecalciferol

Too Much Vitamin D

The tolerable upper limit (UL) for vitamin D has been set at 100 micrograms (4,000 IU) for individuals nine years or older. This upper limit is over six times higher than the recommended daily amount. Consuming too much vitamin D can cause loss of appetite, nausea, vomiting, and constipation.

As with the other fat-soluble vitamins, excess amounts of vitamin D are stored in the adipocytes, and an accumulation can reach toxic levels, causing **hypervitaminosis D.** This condition causes overabsorption of calcium from the intestines as well as calcium loss from bones. When both of these symptoms occur, blood calcium levels can become dangerously high.

A chronically high amount of calcium in the blood, or **hypercalcemia** (*hyper* = over, *calc* = calcium, *emia* = blood), can cause damaging calcium deposits in the tissues of the kidneys, lungs, blood vessels, and heart. Excess vitamin D can also affect the nervous system and cause severe depression.[54]

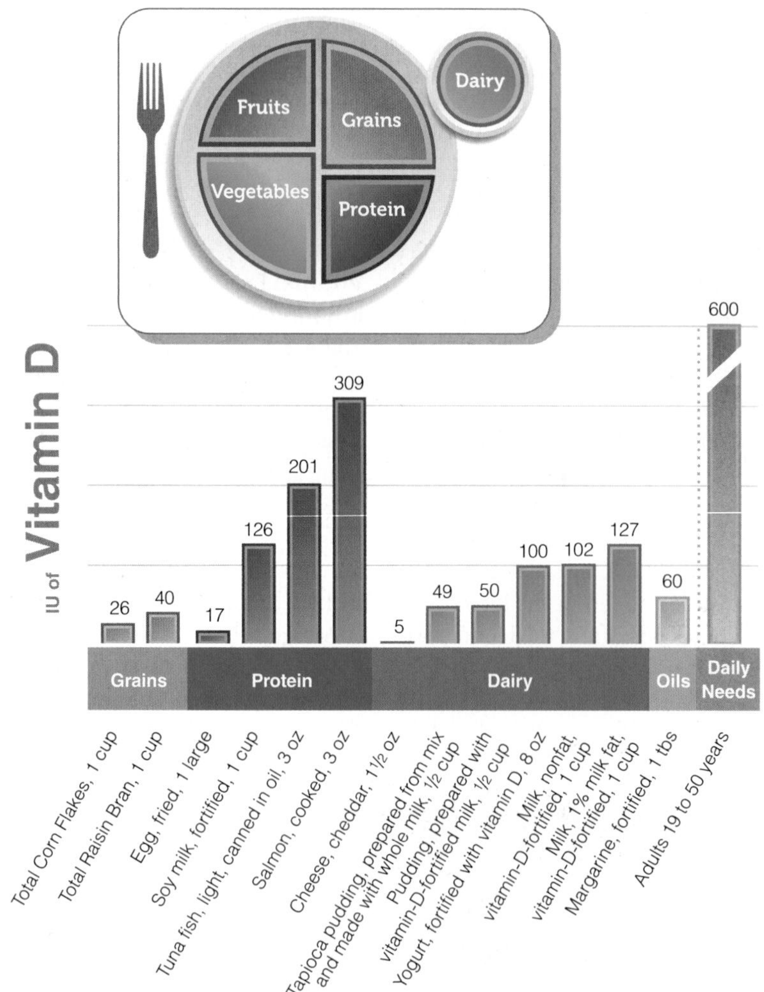

▲ **Figure 9.14 Food Sources of Vitamin D**

Hypervitaminosis D rarely occurs as a result of consuming too much vitamin D from foods, even fortified foods. The only exception is fish oils, specifically cod-liver oil, which provides 34 micrograms (1,360 IU) of vitamin D per tablespoon. Luckily, the less-than-pleasant taste of cod-liver oil is a safeguard against overconsumption. A more likely culprit behind hypervitaminosis D is the overuse of vitamin D supplements.

Sun worshippers don't have to worry about hypervitaminosis D from the sun (although they should be concerned about the risk of skin cancer). Overexposing the skin to UV rays eventually destroys the inactive form of vitamin D in the skin, causing the body to shut down production of vitamin D.

Too Little Vitamin D

Vitamin D deficiencies are increasing worldwide, most likely due to individuals' misunderstanding of the critical role of sunshine as a source of vitamin D. **Rickets** is one of the consequences of a lack of sunshine and insufficient dietary intake of vitamin D in children. The bones of children with rickets aren't adequately mineralized with calcium and phosphorus, and this causes them to weaken. Because of their "soft bones," these children cannot hold up their own body weight, and often develop bowed legs.[55] Babies with rickets also have a delayed closure of the anterior fontanelle or "soft spot" in the skull.[56, 57]

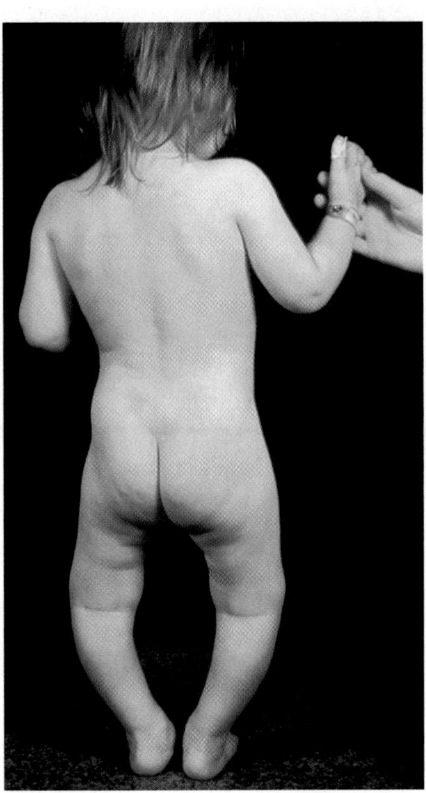

Rickets can cause bowed legs in children.

Since fortification of milk with vitamin D beginning in the 1930s, rickets has been considered a rare disease among children in the United States. However, the disease has resurfaced as a public health concern. In the late 1990s, a review of hospital records in Georgia suggested that as many as five out of every 1 million children between 6 months and 5 years of age in that state were hospitalized with vitamin D–related rickets.[58] Similarly, more than 20 percent of over 300 adolescents at a Boston-based hospital clinic were recently found to be deficient in vitamin D.[59] Whether the increase in rickets is due to a rise in the incidence of rickets or an increased awareness is not clear. The majority of cases of rickets in the United States have been reported in solely breast-fed African-American infants. In Canada, the incidence of rickets was reported as 2.9 per 100,000 infants, almost all of whom were breast-fed.[60] Because the vitamin D content of breast milk is affected by the vitamin D status of the mother, the American Academy of Pediatrics recommends that all breast-fed infants receive a supplement of 10 micrograms (400 IU) per day until they are also consuming 32 ounces of vitamin D–fortified formula or whole milk daily.[61]

The *Dietary Guidelines for Americans, 2010* and the Academy of Pediatrics recommends that all children 2 years and older drink low-fat milk to promote bone health. A National Health and Nutrition Examination Survey (NHANES) of children ages 2 to 19 years of age conducted in 2007–2008 reported that an average of 70 percent of children are drinking milk daily, most of which was 2 percent milk. Children should be encouraged to drink low-fat milk to lower caloric intake but at the same time consume a good source of vitamin D and calcium.[62]

Increased concern over skin cancer may be a factor in the rise of rickets among American children. Skin cancer is the most common form of cancer in the United States, and childhood sun exposure appears to increase the risk of skin cancer in later years. Because of this, organizations such as the Centers for Disease Control and the American Cancer Society have run campaigns that recommend limiting exposure to ultraviolet light. People are encouraged to use sunscreen, wear protective clothing when outdoors, and minimize activities in the sun. The American Association of Pediatricians also recommends that infants younger than 6 months not be exposed to direct sunlight. With less exposure to UV light, many children aren't able to synthesize vitamin D in adequate amounts to meet their needs, thereby increasing their risk of developing rickets. The increased use of child day-care facilities, which may limit outdoor activities during the day, may also play a role in this increased prevalence of rickets.

hypervitaminosis D A condition resulting from excessive amounts of vitamin D in the body.

hypercalcemia A chronically high amount of calcium in the blood.

rickets A vitamin D deficiency in children resulting in soft bones.

continued

Other Vitamin D Deficiency Disorders

Osteomalacia is the adult equivalent of rickets and can cause muscle and bone weakness and pain. The bones can't mineralize properly because there isn't enough calcium and phosphorus available in the blood. Although there may be adequate amounts of these minerals in the diet, the deficiency of vitamin D hampers their absorption.

Vitamin D deficiency and its subsequent effect on decreased calcium absorption can lead to osteoporosis, a condition in which the bones can mineralize properly, but there isn't enough calcium in the diet to maximize the bone density or mass.

Muscle weakness and pain is also associated with low levels of serum vitamin D concentrations. One study found that a vitamin D supplement of 20 micrograms (800 IU) per day plus calcium was more effective in increasing muscle strength and reducing the number of falls reported by elderly women than just calcium alone.[63]

osteomalacia The adult equivalent of rickets, causing muscle and bone weakness, and pain.

TABLE TIPS

Ways to Get Vitamin D

Use vitamin D–fortified low-fat milk, not cream, in hot or iced coffee.
Buy vitamin D–fortified low-fat yogurts and have one daily as a snack. Top it with a vitamin D–fortified cereal for another boost of D.
Start the morning with vitamin D–fortified cereal, and cover it with plenty of low-fat or skim milk.
Flake canned salmon over a lunchtime salad.
Make instant hot cocoa with hot milk rather than water.
Drink vitamin D–fortified orange juice with breakfast.

Exploring Vitamin E

VITAMIN E

What Is Vitamin E?

There are eight different forms of naturally occurring vitamin E, but one form, **alpha-tocopherol (α-tocopherol),** is most active in the body (**Figure 9.15**). The synthetic form of vitamin E found in dietary supplements is only half as active as the natural form. Alpha-tocopherol is the only form of vitamin E that is reflected in the Dietary Reference Intakes.

Vitamin E Absorption and Transport

Vitamin E is absorbed with the aid of bile salts and micelles into the cells of the small intestinal lining. Once absorbed, vitamin E is transported as part of a chylomicron through the lymph fluid into the blood, where it eventually arrives at the liver. Some researchers have suggested that vitamin E is transported through the cells of the small intestine attached to a protein, but so far a transport protein

Vitamin E (alpha-tocopherol)

▲ **Figure 9.15 The Structure of Alpha-Tocopherol**
There are eight different types of vitamin E compounds (or tocopherols), but alpha-tocopherol is the most active and is the form reflected in the Dietary Reference Intakes.

has not been discovered. More than 90 percent of the vitamin E is stored in the adipose tissue. Excess vitamin E is excreted through the bile, urine, feces, and the pores in the skin.

Metabolic Functions of Vitamin E

Vitamin E is sometimes referred to as the vitamin in search of a disease to cure. For almost 40 years after its discovery, scientists searched unsuccessfully for a curative role for vitamin E. They now have shifted their focus and begun valuing the vitamin's importance as an effective antioxidant and in maintaining healthy cell membranes. Vitamin E also plays an important function in blood clotting. The role of vitamin E in preventing cardiovascular disease is still unclear. Even though vitamin E was thought to show promise in preventing other diseases such as cancer or cataracts, researchers have not been able to provide conclusive evidence supporting this.

Vitamin E as an Antioxidant

Vitamin E's nutritional claim to fame is its role as a powerful antioxidant, particularly in cell membranes. Recall from Chapter 5 that phospholipids are critical components of cell membranes. Many phospholipids contain unsaturated fatty acids, which are vulnerable to the damaging effects of free radicals. Vitamin E is unique in its ability to neutralize free radicals before they can harm cell membranes (see **Figure 9.16**). The hydrogen ions in vitamin E quickly react with the free radical and stop the chain reaction. In doing so, vitamin E itself is altered and loses its antioxidant abilities.

Oxidation of the LDL cholesterol carrier in the blood is also harmful, as it contributes to the buildup of artery-clogging plaque. Antioxidants, including vitamin E, help protect the LDL cholesterol carrier from being oxidized and reduce the risk of atherosclerosis in the arteries.[64]

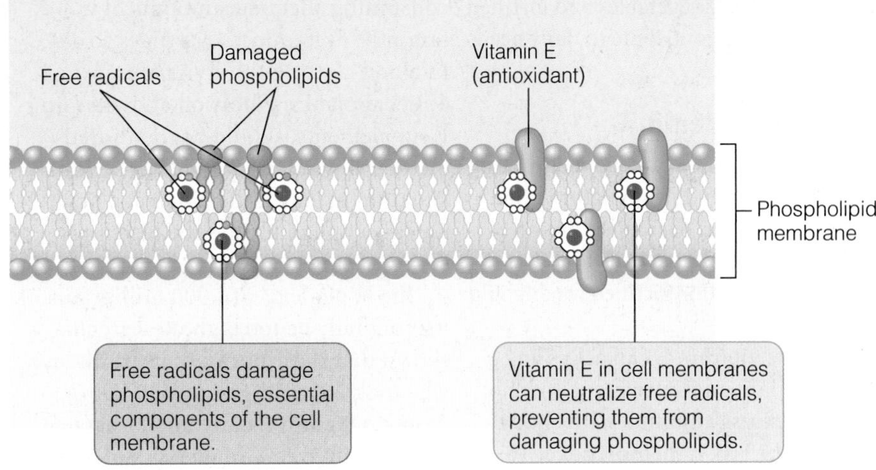

Free radicals
Damaged phospholipids
Vitamin E (antioxidant)
Phospholipid membrane
Free radicals damage phospholipids, essential components of the cell membrane.
Vitamin E in cell membranes can neutralize free radicals, preventing them from damaging phospholipids.

▲ Figure 9.16 **Vitamin E as an Antioxidant in Cell Membranes**

Vitamin E as an Anticoagulant

Vitamin E is an anticoagulant (*anti* = against, *coagulant* = causes clotting), which means that it inhibits platelets from unnecessarily clumping together and creating a damaging clot in the bloodstream. Vitamin E also alters the stickiness of the cells that line the lymph and blood vessels. This reduces plaque buildup that clogs the passageways, reducing the risk of having a heart attack or stroke. Although this function clearly helps maintain the health of the cardiovascular system, studies are still under way to assess if the long-term use of vitamin E supplements could play a protective role against heart disease.

Daily Needs

Adults should consume 15 milligrams (22.4 IU) of vitamin E daily (see the Calculation Corner to learn how to convert vitamin E in milligrams to international units) as an Adequate Intake (AI). Because alpha-tocopherol is the most active form of vitamin E in the body, vitamin E requirements are presented in alpha-tocopherol equivalents. Researchers speculate that healthy Americans are not consuming adequate amounts of vitamin E.[65]

Food Sources

Vegetable oils (and foods that contain them), avocados, nuts, and seeds are good food sources of vitamin E. The *Dietary Guidelines for Americans* specifically recommend consuming vegetable oils daily to meet vitamin E needs.

alpha-tocopherol (α-tocopherol) The most active form of vitamin E in the body.

continued

Some green leafy vegetables and fortified cereals can also contribute to daily needs (see **Figure 9.17**).

Too Much Vitamin E

There isn't any known risk of consuming too much vitamin E from natural food sources. However, overconsumption of the synthetic form that is found in supplements and/or fortified foods could pose risks.

Because vitamin E can act as an anticoagulant and interfere with blood clotting, excess amounts in the body increase the risk of **hemorrhage.** To prevent hemorrhage, the upper limit from supplements and/or fortified foods is 1,000 milligrams for adults. This applies only to healthy individuals consuming adequate amounts of vitamin K. (Vitamin K also plays a role in blood clotting.) Individuals taking anticoagulant medication and vitamin E supplements, should be monitored by their physician to avoid the serious situation in which the blood can't clot quickly enough to stop the bleeding from a wound.

The upper level of 1,000 milligrams may actually be too high. Research has shown that those at risk of heart disease who took 265 milligrams (400 IU) or more of vitamin E daily for at least one year had an overall higher risk of dying. One theory is that too much vitamin E may disrupt the balance of other antioxidants in the body, causing more harm than good.[66]

hemorrhage Excessive bleeding or loss of blood.

Too Little Vitamin E

Though rare, a chronic vitamin E deficiency can cause nerve problems, muscle weakness, and uncontrolled movement of body parts. Because vitamin E is an antioxidant and is found in the membranes of red blood cells, a deficiency can also increase the susceptibility of cell membranes to damage by free radicals. Individuals who can't absorb fat properly may fall short of their vitamin E needs.

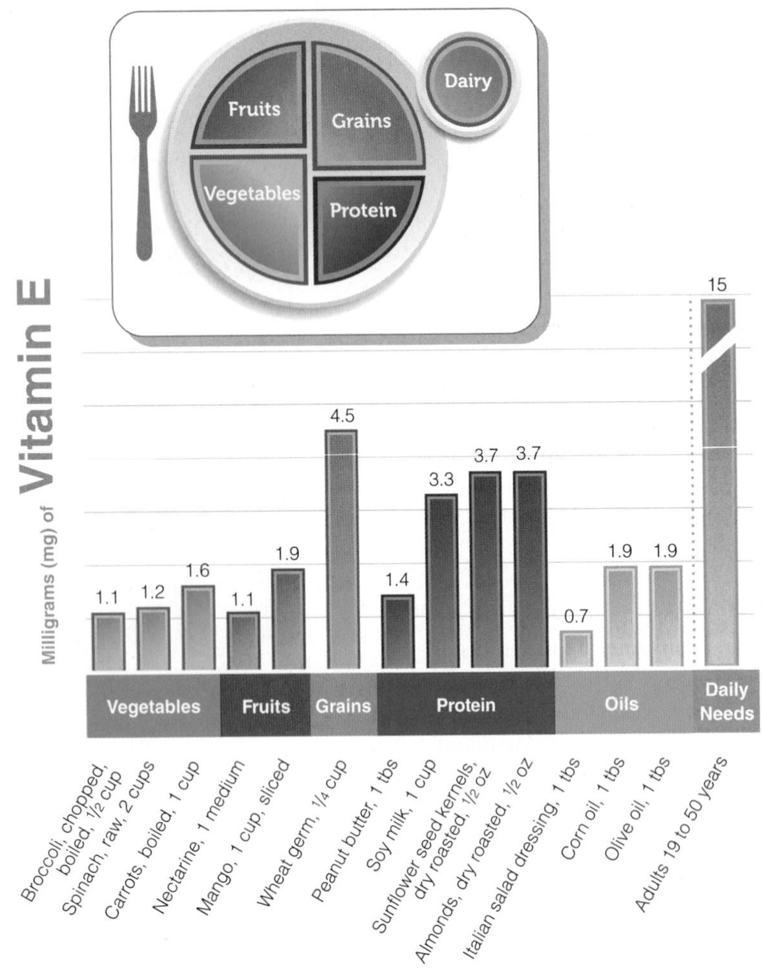

▲ **Figure 9.17 Food Sources of Vitamin E**

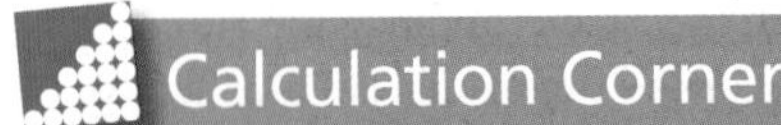

Converting International Units for Vitamin E

Vitamin E content in dietary supplements and fortified foods is often listed in international units (IU), while vitamin E found naturally in food is measured in milligrams of alpha-tocopherol (mg α-tocopherol). Use the following conversion factors to determine the alpha-tocopherol equivalents in mg α-tocopherol found in 1 IU.

1 IU of alpha-tocopherol is equivalent to 0.67 mg alpha-tocopherol

1 IU of alpha-tocopherol is equivalent to 0.45 mg of synthetic alpha-tocopherol

Example: A vitamin supplement contains 400 IU of alpha-tocopherol. How many mg α-tocopherol does it contain?

Answer: 0.67 mg × 400 IU = 268 mg α-tocopherol

or

0.45 mg × 400 IU = 180 mg α-tocopherol (synthetic α-tocopherol)

TABLE TIPS
Enjoying Your Es

- Add fresh spinach and broccoli to salad.
- Add a slice of avocado, or use guacamole as a spread, on sandwiches.
- Spread peanut butter on apple slices.
- Top low-fat yogurt with wheat germ.
- Pack a handful of almonds in a zip-closed bag for a snack.

Exploring Vitamin K

What Is Vitamin K?

Vitamin K is found naturally in two forms. Some plants manufacture **phylloquinone,** or **vitamin K_1.** This is the primary source of vitamin K in the diet. In animals, bacteria that reside naturally in the colon synthesize **menaquinone,** also referred to as **vitamin K_2.** A third form of vitamin K, called **menadione,** or **vitamin K_3,** is synthetic and formulated for use in animal feed and vitamin supplements (**Figure 9.18**).

Vitamin K Absorption and Transport

About 80 percent of dietary vitamin K is absorbed, mostly in the jejunum. In contrast, only 10 percent of the vitamin K produced by bacteria in the large intestine is absorbed. Both forms of vitamin K are incorporated into chylomicrons and transported to the liver, where they are stored for future use. When the diet is deficient in vitamin K, the storage forms are transported by the lipoproteins VLDL, LDL, and HDL.

Excess vitamin K is excreted, mostly bound to bile. It can also be eliminated through the urine. Vitamin K is stored in small amounts, mostly in the liver.

Metabolic Functions of Vitamin K

Vitamin K is so named because of its role in *koagulation*, the Danish word for **coagulation,** or blood clotting.[67] It also functions as a cofactor in several key roles in the body, and is essential for strengthening the bones.

Vitamin K Promotes Blood Clotting

A series of reactions, referred to as a cascade, must happen before the blood coagulates and forms a blood clot (**Figure 9.19**). At seven steps in the cascade, a carboxyl group is added to a protein, which enables the protein to bind calcium ions, a process that is essential for more than just coagulation. The reaction, called **carboxylation** (see the Chemistry Boost for an illustration), is catalyzed by a carboxylase enzyme that is dependent on vitamin K as a coenzyme. Four of these vitamin K–dependent

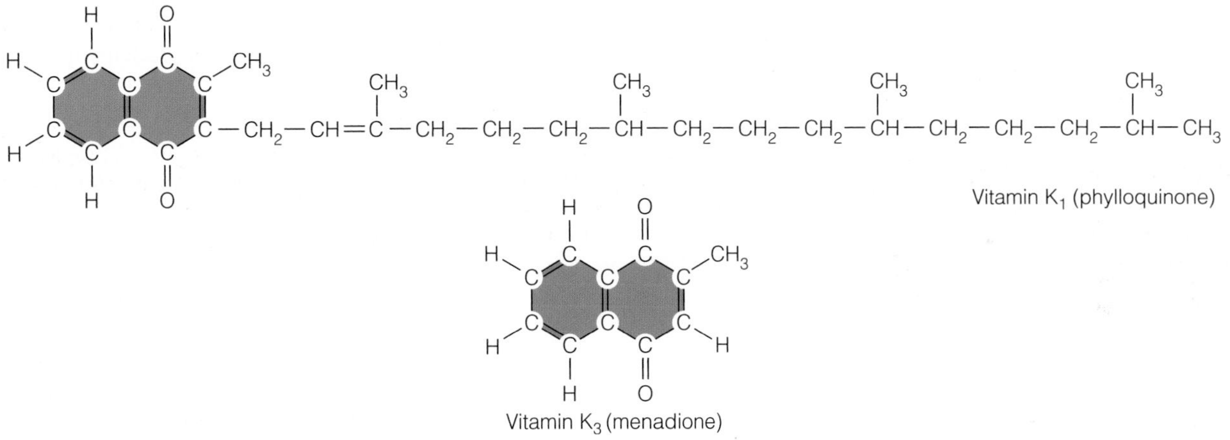

Vitamin K_1 (phylloquinone)

Vitamin K_3 (menadione)

▲ **Figure 9.18 The Structure of Vitamin K**
Vitamin K occurs naturally in plants as phylloquinone. Menadione is the synthetic form of vitamin K.

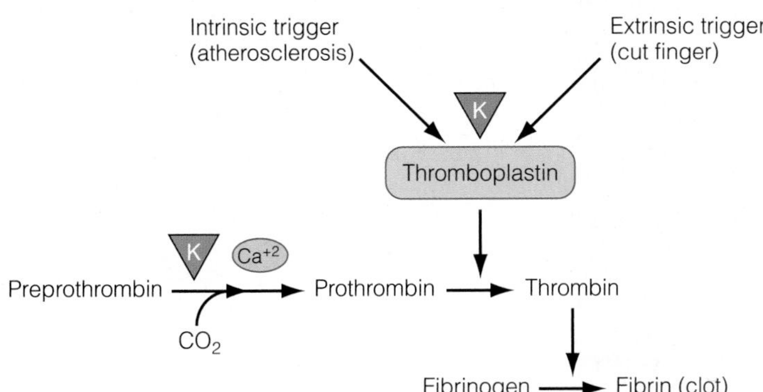

▲ **Figure 9.19 The Role of Vitamin K in Blood Clotting**
Vitamin K is a coenzyme involved in carboxylation reactions of several proteins during blood clotting.

phylloquinone (vitamin K_1) The form of vitamin K found in plants.

menaquinone (vitamin K_2) The form of vitamin K produced by bacteria in the colon.

menadione (vitamin K_3) The synthetic form of vitamin K used in animal feed and dietary supplements.

coagulation The process of blood clotting.

carboxylation The chemical reaction in which a carboxyl group is added to a molecule.

continued

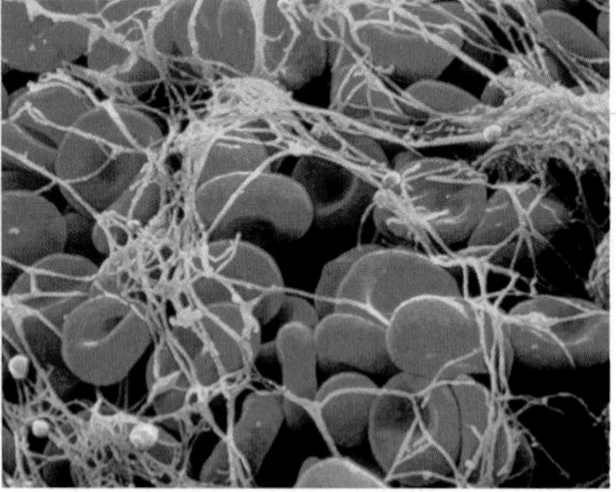

▲ Figure 9.20 **Vitamin K Promotes Blood Clotting**
Vitamin K is best known for its role in healthy blood clotting (SEM, magnified x1,900).

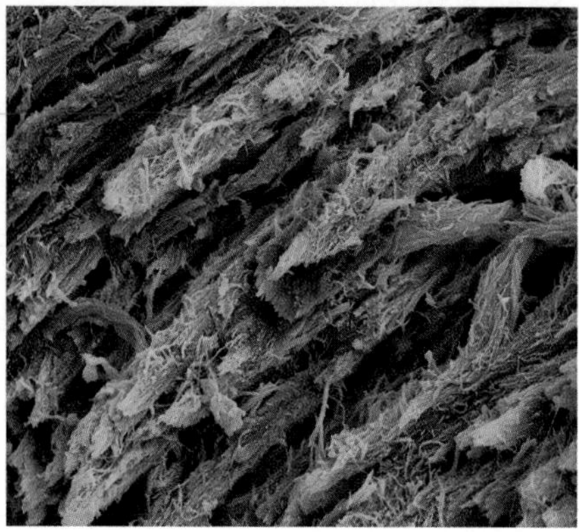

Bone matrix, (colored SEM, magnified x2,000).

proteins are known as **clotting factors:** II (prothrombin), VII, IX, and X. Once calcium is bound to the clotting factors, the clotting process continues with the conversion of prothrombin to thrombin. Thrombin converts fibrinogen to fibrin, the actual blood clot (**Figure 9.20**). As soon as vitamin K has completed its role in activating the carboxylase enzyme, it is released and the enzyme must be activated again. Without vitamin K, a simple nick or cut could quickly result in hemorrhage.

Anticoagulants (anticlotting medications) such as Coumadin (also known as **warfarin**) decrease vitamin K activity, resulting in thinner blood. Severe liver disease will also result in lower blood levels of the vitamin K–dependent clotting factors and increase the risk of hemorrhage.

Vitamin K Promotes Strong Bones

Vitamin K participates in the carboxylation of other proteins. Two of these proteins are essential components in bone formation: *osteocalcin* and *matrix Gla protein*. Osteocalcin is a type of Gla protein secreted by bone-forming osteoblasts. Matrix Gla protein is found in the bone matrix, blood vessels, and cartilage. The carboxylation of osteocalcin and matrix Gla protein is necessary for calcium ions to bind to the bone matrix, which strengthens the bone and improves bone mass.[68] Matrix Gla protein may also provide protection against atherosclerosis.[69]

clotting factors Substances involved in the process of blood clotting, such as prothrombin and fibrinogen.

warfarin An anticoagulant drug given to prevent blood from clotting.

Daily Needs

Currently, the amount of vitamin K made from bacteria in the intestinal tract that contributes to meeting daily needs is not known. Because of this, it is hard to determine an Estimated Average Requirement (EAR), so an Adequate Intake (AI) is reported instead. Therefore, the AI for dietary vitamin K is based on the average amount consumed by healthy Americans.[70] Adult women need 90 micrograms (1,000 IU) of vitamin K per day, and men need 120 micrograms (1,300 IU) daily.

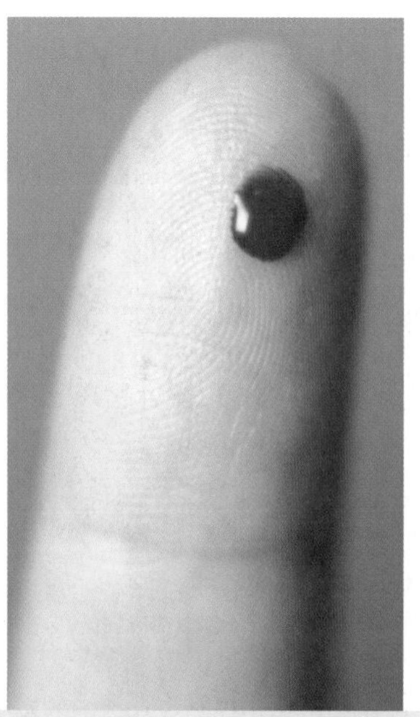

Food Sources

To meet vitamin K needs, think green. Green vegetables like broccoli, asparagus, spinach, salad greens, brussels sprouts, and green cabbage are all rich in vitamin K. Vegetable oils and margarine are the second largest source of vitamin K in the diet (see **Figure 9.21**). A green salad with oil-and-vinegar dressing at lunch and three-quarters of a cup of broccoli at dinner will meet an individual's vitamin K needs for the entire day.

Too Much or Too Little

There are no known adverse effects of consuming too much vitamin K from foods or supplements, so an upper intake level hasn't been set for healthy people.

Individuals taking anticoagulant medications such as Coumadin need to maintain a consistent intake of vitamin K. This medication decreases the activity of vitamin K and prolongs the time it takes for blood to clot. If individuals taking Coumadin suddenly increase the vitamin K in their diets, the vitamin can override the effect of the drug, enabling the blood to clot too quickly. In contrast, a sudden decline in dietary vitamin K can enhance the effectiveness of the drug and increase the risk of bleeding.[71]

Chemistry Boost

Carboxylation Reactions

Carboxylation is a chemical reaction that occurs when a carboxyl group (COOH) is added to a protein, such as during the blood-clotting reaction. As illustrated, the glutamic acid molecule is converted to carboxyglutamic acid with the aid of vitamin K. The carboxyl group in this illustration is shown as COO^-.

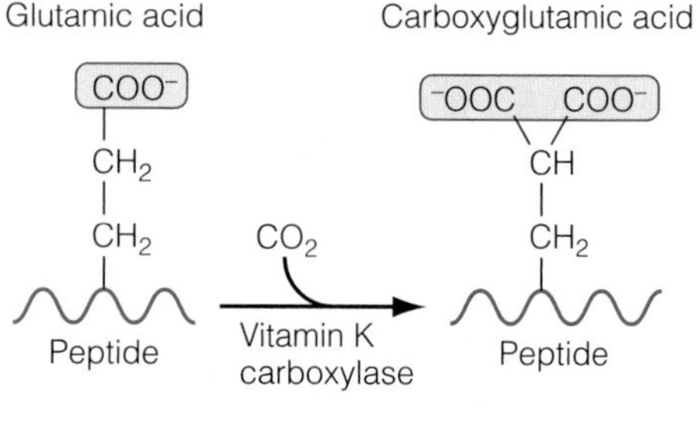

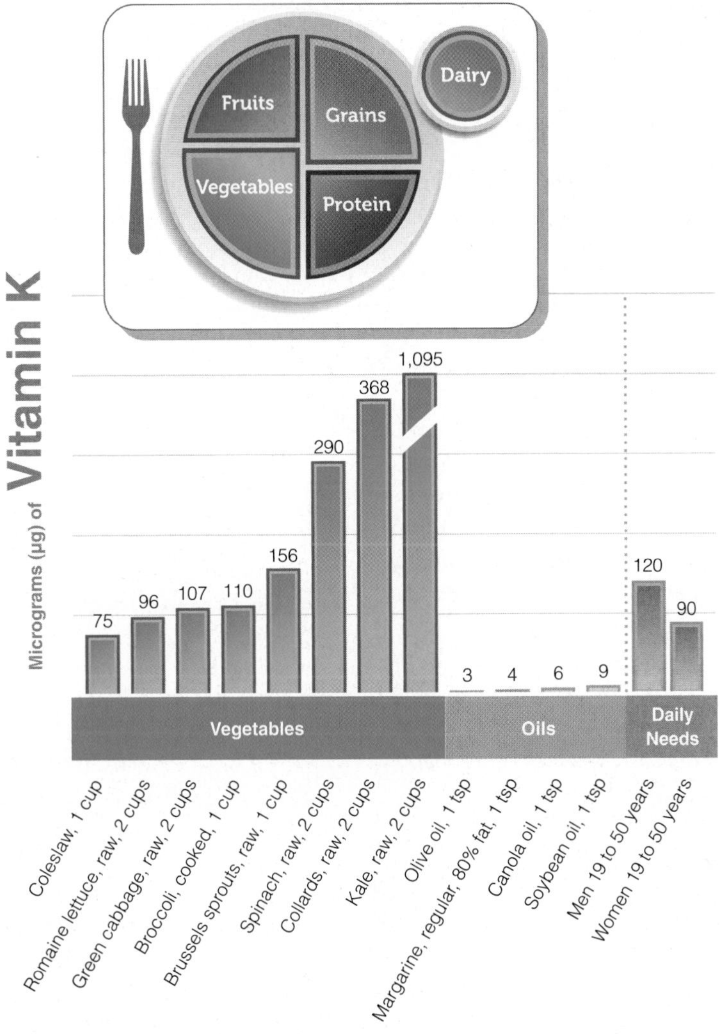

▲ **Figure 9.21 Food Sources of Vitamin K**

TABLE TIPS

Getting Your Ks

Have a green salad daily.

Cook with soybean oil.

Add shredded green cabbage to salad, or top a salad with a scoop of coleslaw.

Add a small amount of margarine to steamed spinach. Both will provide some vitamin K.

Dunk raw broccoli florets in salad dressing for two sources of vitamin K.

Babies are born with low levels of vitamin K in their bodies. This is because little vitamin K passes through the placenta and newborns have sterile intestinal tracts with few bacteria to produce vitamin K. In addition, breast milk is low in vitamin K. For this reason, newborns are routinely given vitamin K soon after birth, either as an injection or by mouth, to enable blood clotting until the bacteria in the intestinal tract can begin to produce vitamin K.[72]

A vitamin K deficiency severe enough to affect blood clotting is extremely rare in healthy individuals.[73] People with conditions such as gallbladder disease, which reduces the absorption of fat and fat-soluble vitamins in the intestinal tract, may be at risk for not meeting their vitamin K needs.

Even though the exact mechanism is unknown, a chronic dietary deficiency of vitamin K may be a factor in increased hip fractures in older men and women. A diet rich in phylloquinone (vitamin K_1) has been shown to improve bone mineral content in older women.[74]

Visual Chapter Summary

1 Vitamins Are Essential Organic Compounds

Vitamins are essential, organic compounds the body requires in small amounts for normal metabolic functions. There are 13 different vitamins found naturally in foods, added to foods through fortification, or concentrated in dietary supplements. These 13 vitamins are classified as either water-soluble or fat-soluble. The water-soluble vitamins include the B-complex vitamins and vitamin C. The fat-soluble vitamins are vitamins A, D, E, and K.

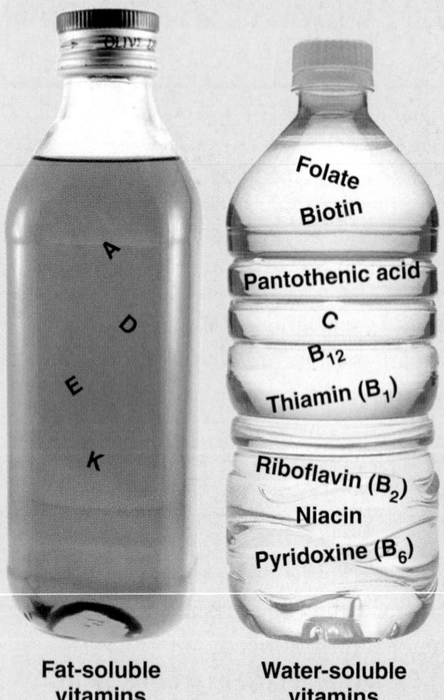

Fat-soluble vitamins

Water-soluble vitamins

2 Vitamins Differ in Their Absorption and Storage

Vitamins are often attached to proteins in food and must be released in the stomach to be absorbed. Once freed, fat-soluble vitamins are transported as part of micelles and absorbed through the lymph system as part of chylomicrons. Fat-soluble vitamins are stored in the body and need fat to be absorbed. Water-soluble vitamins are absorbed with water and typically aren't stored in the body for extended periods.

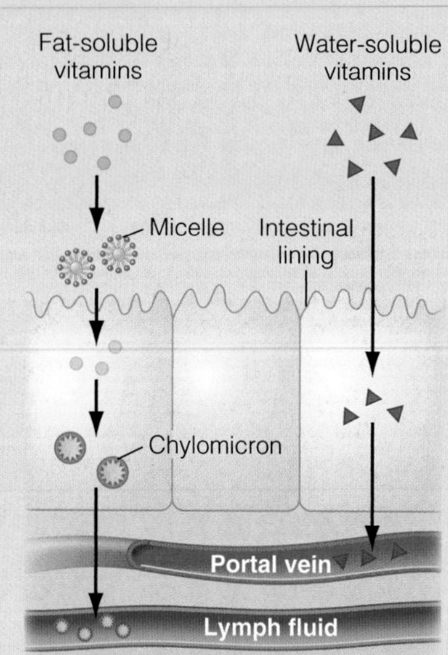

3 Antioxidants Suppress Free Radicals

Antioxidants, such as vitamins E and C and beta-carotene, neutralize harmful oxygen-containing molecules called free radicals that can damage cells by lending them an electron. Free radicals can contribute to chronic diseases such as cancer and heart disease and accelerate the aging process. Diets abundant in antioxidant-rich fruits, vegetables, and whole grains are associated with a lower incidence of many diseases.

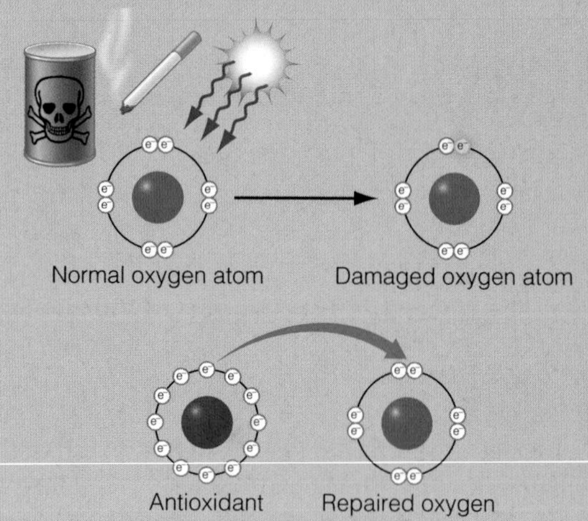

4 Vitamins Are Found in Every Food Group

Whole foods, including fruits, vegetables, whole grains, legumes, dairy, and meats, provide phytochemicals, antioxidants, and fiber in addition to vitamins. Food preparation techniques can cause the loss of vitamins. Fortified foods and vitamin supplements can help individuals with inadequate diets meet their nutrient needs. However, supplements should never replace a healthy diet. The U.S. Pharmacopoeia (USP) seal on a supplement label indicates that the supplement has been tested and meets the criteria for purity and accuracy. It does not ensure safety.

Vegetables	Fruits	Grains	Protein	Dairy
Folate	Folate	Folic acid	Niacin	Riboflavin
Vitamin A	Vitamin C	Niacin	Thiamin	Vitamin A
Vitamin C		Vitamin B_6	Vitamin B_6	Vitamin B_{12}
Vitamin E		Vitamin B_{12} (if fortified)	Vitamin B_{12}	Vitamin D
		Riboflavin		
		Thiamin		

5 Vitamin A

Vitamin A refers to a family of retinoids, which include retinol, retinal, and retinoic acid. Retinol is most usable in the body. Retinal is essential for eye health and vision. The retinoids are also essential for cell growth and development, reproduction, and a healthy immune system. Three carotenoids, alpha-carotene, beta-carotene, and beta-cryptoxanthin, are provitamins that can be converted to vitamin A in the body; beta-carotene is the most commonly consumed. Vitamin A is stored in the liver until needed, and is not easily excreted from the body.

Most of the dietary, preformed vitamin A consumed (70 to 90 percent) is absorbed; absorption occurs via active transport in the small intestine. Beta-carotene is absorbed at a much lower rate. Vitamin A in foods is measured in retinol activity equivalents (RAE). Preformed vitamin A is found in milk, cereals, cheese, egg yolks, and organ meats, especially liver. Provitamin A sources include carrots, spinach, and sweet potatoes.

Vitamin A deficiencies can result in vision problems and increased infections. Toxic amounts of vitamin A can compromise bone health and can lead to birth defects during pregnancy.

6 Vitamin D

The active form of vitamin D is calcitriol. Although vitamin D (the "sunshine vitamin") can be made in the body with the help of ultraviolet rays from the sun, some individuals are not exposed to enough sunlight to meet their needs. Vitamin D regulates blood calcium, enhances the absorption of calcium and phosphorus from the small intestine, and maintains healthy bones. It may also help regulate blood pressure and the immune system, and it may prevent diabetes and some cancers.

Milk and fortified yogurts are excellent food sources of vitamin D. A deficiency of vitamin D can cause rickets in children and osteomalacia in adults. Hypervitaminosis D can result in hypercalcemia, affect the nervous system and cause severe depression.

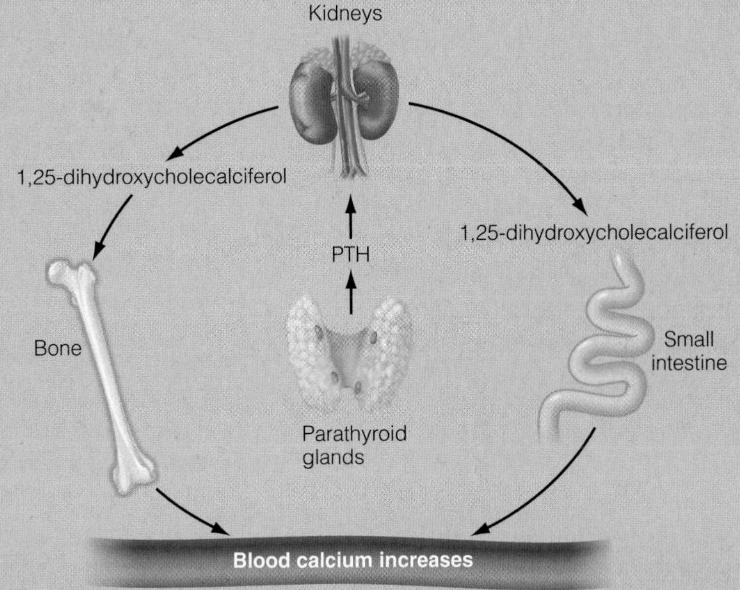

7 Vitamin E

Alpha-tocopherol is the most active form of vitamin E in the body. Vitamin E is an antioxidant that protects the cells' membranes. It plays an important role as an anticoagulant and may help prevent the oxidation of LDL cholesterol.

Vegetable oils, avocados, nuts, and seeds are good sources of vitamin E. Green leafy vegetables and fortified cereals also contribute to daily intake. The recommended intake for vitamin E is presented in alpha-tocopherol equivalents.

Too little vitamin E, although rare, may result in nerve problems, muscle weakness, and increase susceptibility to free radical damage. Excess amounts of vitamin E from supplements may cause hemorrhage.

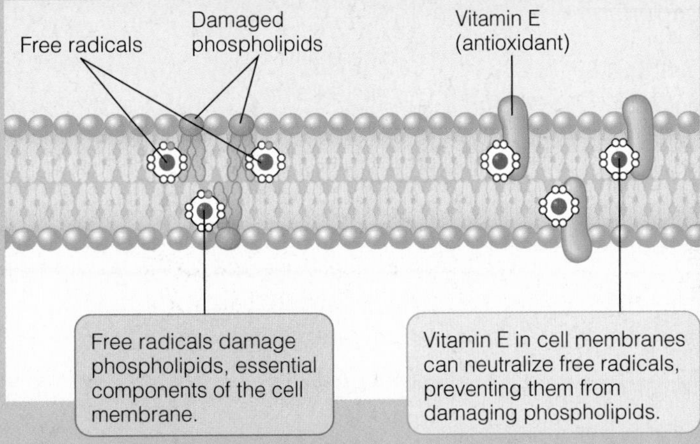

Free radicals
Damaged phospholipids
Vitamin E (antioxidant)
Free radicals damage phospholipids, essential components of the cell membrane.
Vitamin E in cell membranes can neutralize free radicals, preventing them from damaging phospholipids.

8 Vitamin K

Vitamin K is a fat-soluble vitamin found naturally as phylloquinone in plants, and as menaquinone (manufactured by bacteria) in the colons of animals. Vitamin K is a coenzyme for the carboxylation of factors involved in blood clotting and two proteins involved in bone formation. Dietary sources include leafy greens, vegetable oils, and margarine. A deficiency of vitamin K may result in hemorrhage and bone fractures. Individuals taking anticoagulant medications need to carefully monitor their vitamin K intake. There are no known toxicity problems.

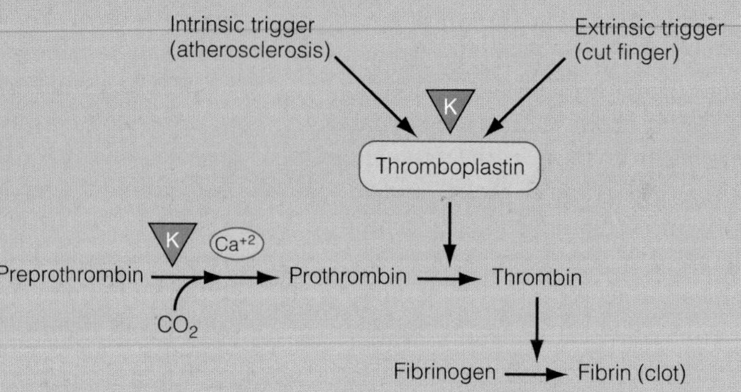

9 Fat-Soluble Vitamins May Reduce Cancer Risk

Cancer is a disease caused by the uncontrolled reproduction of damaged cells. Carcinogens, or cancer-causing substances, damage cells by altering their DNA. Genetic, environmental, and lifestyle factors all play a role in cancer risk, but lifestyle factors have the most influence. Dietary factors that reduce the risk for cancer include consumption of abundant amounts of fruits, vegetables, and whole grains; these provide antioxidants, phytochemicals, and fiber that may have a protective effect.

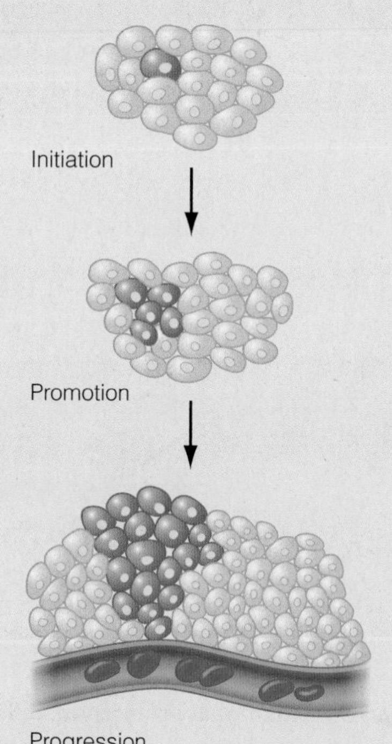

Terms to Know

- retinoids
- retinol
- retinal
- retinoic acid
- beta-carotene
- retinol binding protein (RBP)
- retinol activity equivalents (RAE)
- hypervitaminosis A
- carotenoids
- carotenodermia
- night blindness
- xeropthalmia
- keratinization
- calciferol
- cholecalciferol (vitamin D_2)
- ergocalciferol (vitamin D_3)
- previtamin D_3 (precalciferol)
- 25-hydroxycholecalciferol
- 1,25-dihydroxycholecaliciferol
- calcitriol
- parathyroid hormone (PTH)
- hypervitaminosis D
- hypercalcemia
- rickets
- osteomalacia
- alpha-tocopherol (α-tocopherol)
- phylloquinone (vitamin K_1)
- menoquinone (vitamin K_2)
- menadione (vitamin K_3)
- protooncogenes
- carcinogenesis

MasteringNutrition™

Build your knowledge—and confidence!—in the Study Area of MasteringNutrition with a variety of study tools.

Check Your Understanding

1. Vitamins are
   a. essential nutrients needed in large amounts to prevent disease.
   b. classified as either water-soluble or fat-soluble nutrients.
   c. defined as inorganic nutrients.
   d. easily made by the body from leftover glucose.
2. Vitamins can be destroyed by
   a. cold.
   b. ultraviolet light.
   c. acid pH.
   d. all of the above.
3. An individual who does not produce enough bile will have difficulty absorbing
   a. thiamin (B_1).
   b. vitamin A.
   c. folate.
   d. pantothenic acid.
4. A megadose of a vitamin
   a. occurs when you eat too much of one particular food.
   b. is necessary to prevent a variety of diseases.
   c. is defined as 10 times the RDA.
   d. is safe because all vitamins are easily excreted from the body.
5. Which of the following are considered antioxidants?

a. vitamin E and beta-carotene
b. vitamin D and vitamin K
c. vitamin E and vitamin K
d. vitamin A and vitamin D

6. The most usable form of vitamin A in the body is
   a. retinol.
   b. retinal.
   c. retinoic acid.
   d. retinoids.
7. Vitamin D
   a. is not toxic if consumed in amounts greater than the RDA.
   b. is made in the skin from 1,25-dihydroxyvitamin D_3 and ultraviolet light.
   c. is found in whole milk, but not in skim milk.
   d. is all of the above.
8. The role of vitamin E in the body is to
   a. prevent oxidative damage to cell membranes.
   b. serve as a coenzyme.
   c. enhance the absorption of calcium and phosphorus.
   d. participate in blood clotting.
9. Vitamin K is necessary for the synthesis of
   a. glycogen.
   b. rhodopsin.
   c. prothrombin.
   d. cholecalciferol.
10. Important lifestyle factors that impact an individual's cancer risk include
   a. consuming a healthy diet that includes adequate amounts of fruits, vegetables, and whole grains.
   b. maintaining a healthy body weight and being physically active.
   c. avoiding carcinogens such as tobacco smoke and air pollution.
   d. all of the above.

Answers

1. (b) Vitamins are classified by their solubility, as either fat-soluble or water-soluble nutrients. They are organic nutrients needed in small amounts in the diet because the body cannot synthesize sufficient amounts to maintain health.
2. (b) Some vitamins, especially water-soluble vitamins, are destroyed by exposure to heat (such as during cooking) but not to cold temperatures, ultraviolet light, and an alkaline pH.
3. (b) Fat-soluble vitamins such as vitamin A are absorbed along with dietary fat, which requires bile for the process. Thiamin, folate, and pantothenic acid are water-soluble vitamins and do not need bile for absorption.
4. (c) A megadose of a vitamin is defined as 10 times or more of the RDA. Megadose levels can only be achieved by taking a supplement and can be harmful even if the vitamin is water-soluble.
5. (a) Both vitamin E and beta-carotene function as antioxidants in the body. Vitamins A, D, and K perform other essential functions, but are not antioxidants.
6. (a) Retinol is the most usable form of vitamin A in the body. Retinoids include all three forms of preformed vitamin A: retinol, retinal, and retinoic acid.
7. (b) Vitamin D is a fat-soluble vitamin stored in the liver. It can be toxic if ingested in supplemental form in amounts greater than the RDA. The active form of vitamin D is 1,25-dihydroxyvitamin D_3 and 7-dehydrocholesterol is the compound in the skin that is converted to vitamin D from sunlight. Both whole and skim milk are usually fortified with vitamin D.
8. (a) Vitamin E functions as an antioxidant to prevent oxidative damage to cell membranes. Water-soluble vitamins usually serve as coenzymes, active vitamin D enhances the absorption of calcium and phosphorus, and vitamin K participates in blood clotting.
9. (c) Vitamin K is necessary for the synthesis of prothrombin, a protein that is involved in blood clotting. Rhodopsin is formed with retinal (vitamin A), and cholecalciferol is the active form of vitamin D in the body. Glycogen is the stored form of glucose found in muscles and liver.
10. (d) Consuming a healthy diet that is rich in cancer-fighting phytochemicals and fiber, being physically active and controlling your weight, and eliminating environmental carcinogens such as smoking are all important lifestyle factors that reduce cancer risk.

Answers to Myths and Misconceptions

1. **False.** Although vitamins perform numerous essential functions in the body, they do not provide energy. Only the macronutrients (carbohydrates, protein, and fat) and alcohol provide kilocalories.
2. **True.** Fat-soluble vitamins are often found in foods that contain fat. For example, vitamin E is found in vegetable oils and vitamin A is found in egg yolks. However, some fat-soluble vitamins are also found in fortified foods that are low in fat, such as fortified cereals.
3. **False.** Overconsumption of vitamin supplements can result in intakes above the tolerable upper limits. Such high intakes can in turn lead to harmful toxicity symptoms.
4. **True.** Healthy individuals can meet their vitamin requirements by consuming an adequate, balanced diet. However, some individuals, such as those with a specific vitamin deficiency, strict vegans, or those with dietary restrictions, may benefit from taking a dietary supplement.
5. **False.** Cooking foods in a microwave will help retain more vitamins because of the reduced cooking time and exposure to heat. Foods prepared in a microwave oven also require very little cooking water; this prevents leaching of water-soluble vitamins.
6. **True.** Deep orange vegetables and some green vegetables are good sources of the vitamin A precursor beta-carotene, which is converted to vitamin A in the body.

7. **True.** In the skin is a compound called 7-dehydrocholesterol, which is converted to a previtamin D form when the ultraviolet rays of the sun alter its structure.
8. **False.** Vitamin K actually helps blood clot, as it participates in the synthesis of several proteins involved in the blood-clotting cascade.
9. **False.** The main role of vitamin E is as an antioxidant that helps protect cell membranes. However, the fat-soluble vitamins D and K are involved in bone health.
10. **False.** Antioxidants serve several beneficial functions in the body, but there is no magic pill for aging.

Web Resources

- To learn more about the importance of fruits and vegetables to vitamin intake, visit www.fruitsandveggiesmorematters.org
- To learn more about the role of alternative therapies and dietary supplements in health and disease prevention, visit www.complementarynutrition.org
- To find out the latest recommendations for vitamins, visit http://ods.od.nih.gov/Health_Information/Vitamin_and_Mineral_Supplement_Fact_Sheets.aspx
- For more information about how diet can impact cancer risk, visit the Diet and Cancer page at the American Cancer Society Prevention and Early Detection page: www.cancer.org/docroot/PED/content/PED_3_2X_Common_Questions_About_Diet_and_Cancer.asp

References

1. Rosenfeld, L. 1997. Vitamine-Vitamin. The Early Years of Discovery. *Clinical Chemistry* 43:680–685.
2. Droge, W. 2002. Free Radicals in the Physiological Control of Cell Function. *Physiology Review* 82:47–95.
3. Ibid.
4. National Eye Institute, National Institutes of Health. 2004. *Age-Related Macular Degeneration: What You Should Know.* Updated June 2004. Available at www.nei.nih.gov/health/maculardegen/nei_wysk_amd.PDF. Accessed April 2012.
5. Age-Related Eye Disease Study Research Group. 2001. A Randomized, Placebo-Controlled, Clinical Trial of High-Dose Supplementation with Vitamins C and E, Beta-Carotene, and Zinc for Age-Related Macular Degeneration and Vision Loss: AREDS Report No. 8. *Archives of Ophthalmology* 119:1417–1436.
6. Mares, J. A., T. L. La Rowe, and B. A. Blodi. 2004. Doctor, What Vitamins Should I Take for My Eyes? *Archives of Ophthalmology* 122:628–635.
7. The National Eye Institute, National Institutes of Health. 2004. *Cataract: What You Should Know.* Available at www.nei.nih.gov/health/cataract/webcataract.pdf. Accessed April 2012.
8. Craig, W. J. 1997. Phytochemicals: Guardians of Our Health. *Journal of the American Dietetic Association* 97:S199–S204.
9. Riccioni, G., B. Mancini, E. Di Ilio, T. Bucciarelli, and N. D'Orazio. 2008. Protective Effect of Lycopene in Cardiovascular Disease. *European Review for Medical and Pharmacological Sciences* 12:183–190.
10. Kris-Etherton, P., A. H. Lichtenstein, B. V. Howard, D. Steinberg, and J. L. Witztum. 2004. Antioxidant Vitamin Supplements and Cardiovascular Disease. *Circulation* 110:637–641.
11. U.S. Department of Agriculture, U. S. Department of Health and Human Services. 2010. *Dietary Guidelines for Americans, 2010.* 7th ed. Washington, DC: U.S. Government Printing Office.
12. Ibid.
13. Shils, M. E., M. Shike, A. C. Ross, B. Caballero, and R. J. Cousins. 2006. *Modern Nutrition in Health and Disease.* 10th ed. Philadelphia: Lippincott Williams & Wilkins.
14. Santos, P. H. S. and M. A. Silva. 2008. Retention of Vitamin C in Drying Processes of Fruits and Vegetables—A Review. *Drying Technology—An International Journal* 26:1421–1437.
15. Athar, N., A. Hardacre, G. Taylor, S. Clark, R. Harding, and J. McLaughlin. 2006. Vitamin Retention in Extruded Food Products. *Journal of Food Composition and Analysis* 19:379–383.
16. Lee, S. K. and A. A. Kader. 2000. Preharvest and Postharvest Factors Influencing Vitamin C Content of Horticultural Crops. *Postharvest Biology and Technology* 20:207–220.
17. Pandrangi, S. and L. E. LaBorde. 2004. Retention of Folate, Carotenoid and Other Quality Characteristics in Commercially Packaged Fresh Spinach. *Journal of Food Science* 69:C702–C707.
18. Packaged Facts Project. 2011. *Omega-3 Ingredient Market to Grow 40% by 2015.* Available at www.packagedfacts.com. Accessed April 2012.
19. Institute of Medicine, Food and Nutrition Board. 2003. *Dietary Reference Intakes: Guiding Principles for Nutrition Labeling and Fortification.* Washington, DC: The National Academies Press.
20. Packaged Facts. 2002. *The U.S. Market for Fortified Foods: Expanding the Boundaries.* Available at www.marketresearch.com. Accessed April 2012.
21. Balluz, L. S., S. M. Kieszak, R. M. Philen, and J. Mulinare. 2000. Vitamin and Mineral Supplement Use in the United States. *Archives of Family Medicine* 9:258–262.
22. Food and Drug Administration. 2004. *FDA Announces Major Initiatives for Dietary Supplements.* Available at www.fda.gov/NewsEvents/Newsroom/PressAnnouncements/2004/ucm108369.htm. Accessed April 2012.
23. United States Pharmacopoeia. 2008. *USP's Dietary Supplement Verification Program.* Available at www.uspverified.org/index.html. Accessed April 2012.
24. Institute of Medicine, Food and Nutrition Board. 2001. *Dietary Reference Intakes: Vitamin A, Vitamin K, Arsenic, Boron, Chromium, Copper, Iodine, Iron, Manganese, Molybdenum, Nickel, Silicon, Vanadium, and Zinc.* Washington, DC: The National Academies Press.
25. Gropper, S. S., J. L. Smith, and J. L. Groff. 2009. *Advanced Nutrition and Metabolism.* 5th ed. Belmont, CA: Wadsworth.
26. Akhavan, A. and S. Bershad, 2003. Topical Acne Drugs: Review of Clinical Properties, Systemic Exposure, and Safety. *American Journal of Clinical Dermatology,* 4:473–492.
27. Bershad, S. V. 2001. The Modern Age of Acne Therapy: A Review of Current Treatment Options. *Mount Sinai Journal of Medicine* 68:279–286.
28. Institute of Medicine, Food and Nutrition Board. 2001. *Dietary Reference Intakes: Vitamin A, Vitamin K, Arsenic, Boron, Chromium, Copper, Iodine, Iron, Manganese, Molybdenum, Nickel, Silicon, Vanadium, and Zinc.*
29. de Souza, G. P. and L. G. Martini. 2004. Vitamin A Supplementation and Risk of Skeletal Fracture. *Nutrition Reviews* 62:65–67.
30. Feskanich, D., V. Singh, W. C. Willett, and G. A. Colditz. 2002. Vitamin A Intake and Hip Fractures Among Postmenopausal Women. *Journal of the American Medical Association* 287:47–54.
31. Promislow, J. H., D. Goodman-Guren, D. J. Slymen, and E. Barrett-Connor. 2002. Retinol Intake and Bone Mineral Density in the Elderly: The Rancho Bernardo Study. *Journal of Bone Mineral Research* 17:1359–1362.
32. Ross, A. C. 2006. Vitamin A and Carotenoids. In M. E. Shils, M. Shike, A. C. Ross, B. Caballero, and R. J. Cousins, eds. *Modern Nutrition in Health and Disease.* 10th ed. Philadelphia: Lippincott Williams & Wilkins.
33. Institute of Medicine, Food and Nutrition Board. 2001. *Dietary Reference Intakes: Vitamin A, Vitamin K, Arsenic, Boron, Chromium, Copper, Iodine, Iron, Manganese, Molybdenum, Nickel, Silicon, Vanadium, and Zinc.*

34. Ibid.
35. Brown, M. J., M. G Ferruzzi, M. L. Nguyen, D. A. Cooper, A. L. Eldridge, S. J. Swartz, and W. S. White. 2004. Carotenoid Bioavailability Is Higher from Salads Ingested with Full-fat than with Fat-reduced Salad Dressings as Measured with Electrochemical Detection 1'2'3. *American Journal of Clinical Nutrition* 80:396–403.
36. Institute of Medicine, Food and Nutrition Board. 2001. *Dietary Reference Intakes: Vitamin A, Vitamin K, Arsenic, Boron, Chromium, Copper, Iodine, Iron, Manganese, Molybdenum, Nickel, Silicon, Vanadium, and Zinc.*
37. Ibid.
38. Brinkley, N. and D. Krueger. 2000. Hypervitaminosis A and Bone. *Nutrition Reviews* 58:138–144.
39. Feskanich, D. 2002. Vitamin A Intake and Hip Fractures Among Postmenopausal Women. *Journal of the American Medical Association* 287:47–54.
40. Virtamo, J., P. Pietinen, J. K. Huttunen, P. Korhonen, N. Malila, M. J. Virtanen, D. Albanes, P. R. Taylor, and P. Albert. 2003. Incidence of Cancer and Mortality Following Alpha-Tocopherol and Beta-Carotene Supplementation: A Postintervention Follow-up. *Journal of the American Medical Association* 290:476–485.
41. World Health Organization. 2004. *Nutrition, Micronutrient Deficiencies.* Available at www.who.int/nutrition/topics/vad/en. Accessed April 2012.
42. Institute of Medicine, Food and Nutrition Board. 2010. *Dietary Reference Intakes for Calcium and Vitamin D.* Washington, DC: The National Academies Press.
43. Ibid.
44. Chiu, K. C., A. Chu, V. L. W. Go, and M. F. Saad. 2004. Hypovitaminosis D Is Associated with Insulin Resistance and Cell Dysfunction. *American Journal of Clinical Nutrition* 79:820–825.
45. Cantorna, M. T., Y. Zhu, M. Froicu, and A. Wittke. 2004. Vitamin D Status, 1,25-dihydroxyvitamin D_3, and the Immune System. *American Journal of Clinical Nutrition* 80:1717S–1720S.
46. Li, Y. C. 2003. Vitamin D Regulation of the Renin-Angiotensin System. *Journal of Cellular Biochemistry* 88:327–331.
47. Institute of Medicine, Food and Nutrition Board. 2010. *Dietary Reference Intakes for Calcium and Vitamin D.*
48. Holick, M. F., and T. C. Chen. 2008. Vitamin D Deficiency: A Worldwide Problem with Health Consequences. *American Journal of Clinical Nutrition* 87:1080S–1086S.
49. Institute of Medicine, Food and Nutrition Board. 2010. *Dietary Reference Intakes for Calcium and Vitamin D.*
50. Ibid.
51. Ibid.
52. Ibid.
53. Ibid.
54. Ibid.
55. Weisberg, P., K. S. Scanlon, R. Li, and M. E. Cogswell. 2004. Nutritional Rickets among Children in the United States: Review of Cases Reported between 1986 and 2003. *American Journal of Clinical Nutrition* 80:1697S–1705S.
56. Wagner, C. L., and F. R. Greer. 2008. Prevention of Rickets and Vitamin D Deficiency in Infants, Children, and Adolescents. *Pediatrics* 122:1142–1152.
57. Rajah, J., J. A. Jubeh, A. Haq, A. Shalash, and H. Parsons. 2008. Nutritional Rickets and Z Scores for Height in the United Arab Emirates: To D or Not to D? *Pediatrics International* 50:424–428.
58. Centers for Disease Control and Prevention. 2001. Severe Malnutrition among Young Children—Georgia, January 1997–June 1999. *Morbidity and Mortality Weekly Report.* Available at www.cdc.gov/mmwr/preview/mmwrhtml/mm5012a3.htm. Accessed April 2012.
59. Gordon, C. M., K. C. DePeter, H. A. Feldman, E. Grace, and S. J. Emans. 2004. Prevalence of Vitamin D Deficiency among Healthy Adolescents. *Archives of Pediatric and Adolescent Medicine* 158:531–537.
60. Ward, L. M., I. Gaboury, M. Ladhani, and S. Zlotkin. 2007. Vitamin D–Deficiency Rickets among Children in Canada. CMAJ 177:161–166.
61. Wagner, C. L. and F. R. Greer. 2008. Prevention of Rickets and Vitamin D Deficiency in Infants, Children, and Adolescents. *Pediatrics* 122:1142–1152.
62. Kit, B. K., M. D. Carroll, and C. L. Ogden. 2011. *Low-Fat Milk Consumption Among Children and Adolescents in the United States, 2007–2008.* Available at www.cdc.gov/nchs/data/databriefs/db75.pdf. Accessed April 2012.
63. Venning, G. 2005. Recent Developments in Vitamin D Deficiency and Muscle Weakness among Elderly People. *British Medical Journal* 330:524–526.
64. National Institutes of Health, Office of Dietary Supplements. 2007. *Vitamin E.* Available at http://ods.od.nih.gov/factsheets/vitamine.asp. Accessed April 2012.
65. Ibid.
66. Miller, E. R., R. Pastor-Barriso, D. Dalal, R. A. Riemersma, L. J. Appel, and E. Guallar. 2005. Meta-Analysis: High-Dosage Vitamin E Supplementation May Increase All-Cause Mortality. *Annals of Internal Medicine* 142:37–46.
67. Almquist, H. J. 1975. The History of Vitamin K. *The American Journal of Clinical Nutrition* 28:656–659.
68. Bolton-Smith, C., M. E. McMurdo, C. R. Paterson, P. A. Mole, J. M. Harvey, S. Fenton, C. J. Prynne, et al. 2007. Two-Year Randomized Controlled Trial of Vitamin K_1 (Phylloquinone) and Vitamin D_3 Plus Calcium on the Bone Health of Older Women. *Journal of Bone and Mineral Research* 22:509–519.
69. O'Donnell, C. J., M. K. Shea, P. A. Price, D. R. Gagnon, P. W. F. Wilson, M. G. Larson, D. P. Kiel, et al. 2006. Matrix Gla Protein is Associated with Risk Factors for Atherosclerosis but Not with Coronary Artery Calcification. *Arteriosclerosis, Thrombosis, and Vascular Biology* 26:2769–2774.
70. Institute of Medicine. 2006. *Dietary Reference Intakes: The Essential Guide to Nutrient Requirements.* Washington, DC: The National Academies Press.
71. National Institutes of Health. 2003. *Coumadin and Vitamin K.* Available at http://ods.od.nih.gov/factsheets/cc/coumadin1.pdf. Accessed April 2012.
72. American Academy of Pediatrics, Committee on Fetus and Newborn. 2003. Controversies Concerning Vitamin K and the Newborn. *Pediatrics* 112:191–192.
73. Institute of Medicine. 2006. *Dietary Reference Intakes: The Essential Guide to Nutrient Requirements.*
74. Booth, S. L., L. Martini, J. W. Peterson, E. Saltzman, G. E. Dallal, and R. J. Wood. 2003. Dietary Phylloquinone Depletion and Repletion in Older Women. *Journal of Nutrition* 133:2565–2569.

10 Water-Soluble Vitamins

Chapter Objectives

After reading this chapter, you will be able to:

1. Describe the role water-soluble vitamins play in activating enzymes.
2. Describe the metabolic functions, best food sources, the recommended dietary allowance, and the impact on the body of too much or too little thiamin.
3. Describe the metabolic functions, best food sources, the recommended dietary allowance, and the impact on the body of too much or too little riboflavin.
4. Describe the metabolic functions, best food sources, the recommended dietary allowance, and the impact on the body of too much or too little niacin.
5. Describe the metabolic functions, best food sources, the recommended dietary allowance, and the impact on the body of too much or too little pantothenic acid.
6. Describe the metabolic functions, best food sources, the recommended dietary allowance, and the impact on the body of too much or too little biotin.
7. Describe the metabolic functions, best food sources, the recommended dietary allowance, and the impact on the body of too much or too little vitamin B_6.
8. Describe the metabolic functions, best food sources, the recommended dietary allowance, and the impact on the body of too much or too little folate.
9. Describe the metabolic functions, best food sources, the recommended dietary allowance, and the impact on the body of too much or too little vitamin B_{12}.
10. Describe the metabolic functions, best food sources, the recommended dietary allowance, and the impact on the body of too much or too little vitamin C.
11. Explain the role that vitamin B_6, folate, and vitamin B_{12} may play in reducing the risk of coronary heart disease.
12. Describe the functions of compounds that have vitamin-like biological roles but are not classified as vitamins.

1. All water-soluble vitamins are destroyed during cooking. T/F
2. Biotin and pantothenic acid are lesser known versions of vitamin C. T/F
3. The primary role of the B vitamins is to provide energy. T/F
4. The body can make plenty of niacin from the amino acid tryptophan. T/F
5. Consuming too much vitamin B_6 can cause nerve damage. T/F
6. Older adults are likely to absorb less vitamin B_{12} than younger adults. T/F
7. Folate reduces the risk of certain birth defects. T/F
8. It is difficult to obtain enough pantothenic acid from foods. T/F
9. Eating raw egg whites inhibits the absorption of biotin. T/F
10. Taking vitamin C supplements will prevent the common cold. T/F

See page 406 for answers to these Myths and Misconceptions.

In the previous chapter you were introduced to the organic micronutrients called vitamins and learned specifically about the four fat-soluble vitamins A, D, E, and K. This chapter describes the nine water-soluble vitamins, the roles they play in the body, the best food sources, how much you need on a daily basis, and the risks associated with consuming excessive amounts or not enough. We'll also look at how these vitamins work together to facilitate metabolism and other body processes.

What Are Water-Soluble Vitamins?

There are nine water-soluble vitamins: eight of them are B-complex vitamins and the ninth is vitamin C. When initially discovered in the early 1900s, the "water-soluble B" was thought to be one vitamin. After years of research, it became apparent that this was not a single substance but rather many vitamins—thiamin, riboflavin, niacin, vitamin B_6, folate, vitamin B_{12}, pantothenic acid, and biotin—known collectively as the B vitamins.

Water-soluble vitamins are different from fat-soluble vitamins in that they dissolve in water, are generally not stored in the body, and are often excreted through the urine. Another distinction from fat-soluble vitamins is that most water-soluble vitamins are not toxic, though there are exceptions when megadose levels are ingested.

Many water-soluble vitamins are easily destroyed by heat, light, pH, or oxidation. Vitamin C and folate deteriorate during cooking; vitamin B_{12} and riboflavin are destroyed by ultraviolet light; and thiamin, or B_1, is easily destroyed in an alkaline pH. All of the water-soluble vitamins leach when foods containing the vitamins are soaked in water.

In general, all the water-soluble vitamins are absorbed, transported, and stored in the same way. In foods, water-soluble vitamins are usually attached to proteins and require hydrolysis during digestion to free the vitamin for absorption (**Figure 10.1**). Once digestion has released the vitamins, they are absorbed through the small intestine by passive diffusion when the diet contains large amounts and by active transport when intakes are low. The absorbed vitamins are then transported through the portal vein to the liver.

The Primary Functions of Water-Soluble Vitamins

Although vitamins don't provide kilocalories and thus aren't a source of energy, the B vitamins share a role as **coenzymes** in energy production. Water-soluble vitamins are also involved in blood formation, maintaining a healthy nervous system, and, in the case of vitamin C, act as an antioxidant in the body.

The B Vitamins Act as Coenzymes in Many Metabolic Processes

coenzymes Substances, often vitamins, that bind to an enzyme to facilitate enzyme activity; the coenzyme is not permanently altered by the chemical reaction.

As coenzymes, vitamins bind to the active site of an enzyme to catalyze the enzyme to either build new compounds or break compounds apart (**Figure 10.2**). In fact, the primary function of the water-soluble vitamins is activating enzymes in the

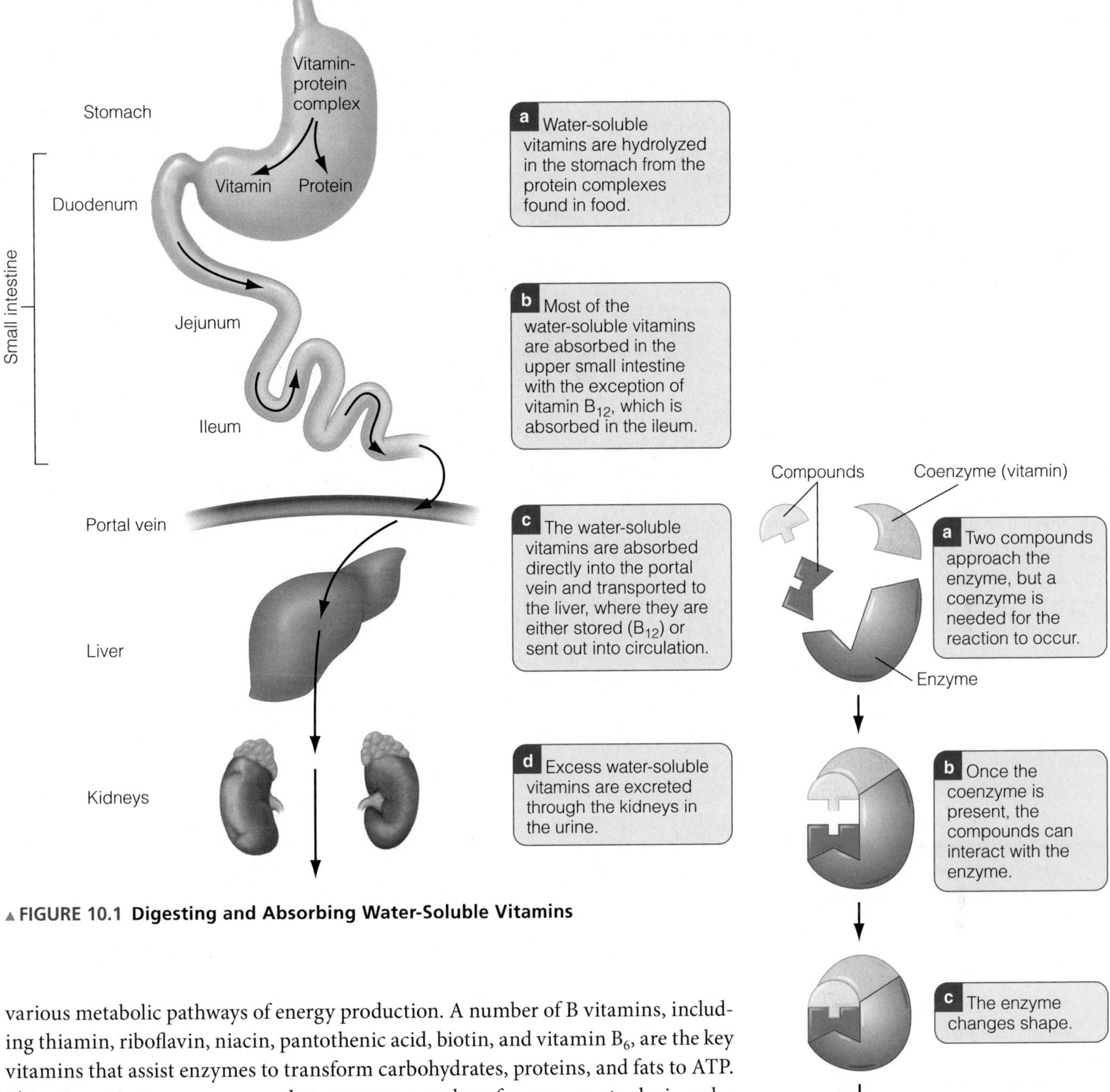

Stomach
Vitamin-protein complex
Vitamin
Protein
Duodenum
Small intestine
Jejunum
Ileum
Portal vein
Liver
Kidneys
a Water-soluble vitamins are hydrolyzed in the stomach from the protein complexes found in food.
b Most of the water-soluble vitamins are absorbed in the upper small intestine with the exception of vitamin B_{12}, which is absorbed in the ileum.
c The water-soluble vitamins are absorbed directly into the portal vein and transported to the liver, where they are either stored (B_{12}) or sent out into circulation.
d Excess water-soluble vitamins are excreted through the kidneys in the urine.
Compounds
Coenzyme (vitamin)
Enzyme
a Two compounds approach the enzyme, but a coenzyme is needed for the reaction to occur.
b Once the coenzyme is present, the compounds can interact with the enzyme.
c The enzyme changes shape.
d The reaction occurs, and the product is released.
Product

▲ **FIGURE 10.1 Digesting and Absorbing Water-Soluble Vitamins**

▲ **FIGURE 10.2 B Vitamins Function as Coenzymes**

various metabolic pathways of energy production. A number of B vitamins, including thiamin, riboflavin, niacin, pantothenic acid, biotin, and vitamin B_6, are the key vitamins that assist enzymes to transform carbohydrates, proteins, and fats to ATP. Thiamin activates an enzyme that removes a carbon from pyruvate during glycolysis. Vitamin B_6 acts as a coenzyme in all transamination reactions. Folate and vitamin B_{12} also assist enzymes in producing energy, but in a lesser role. Without the B vitamins, energy production would come to a halt.

Water-Soluble Vitamins in Noncoenzymatic Roles

The function of the water-soluble vitamins doesn't end with the B vitamins' roles as coenzymes. Vitamin C acts as an antioxidant and helps neutralize free radicals. Thiamin is necessary for nerve function, and niacin participates in protein synthesis. Folate and vitamin B_{12} function in the formation of red blood cells, a process called **hemopoiesis**, and the replenishment of cells. And several of the B vitamins play a role in heart health (see Examining the Evidence: Do B Vitamins Improve Heart Health?).

hemopoiesis The formation of red blood cells.

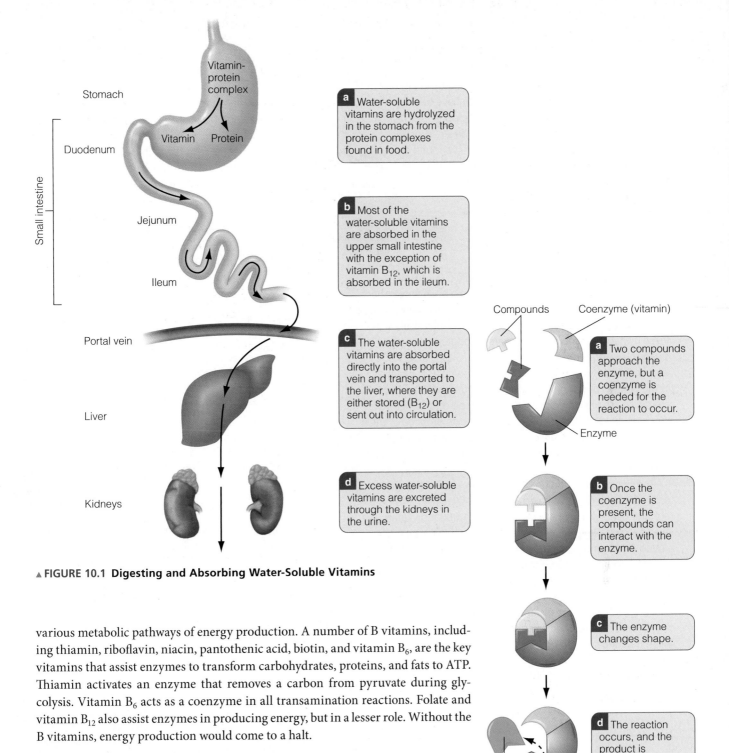

EXAMINING THE EVIDENCE Do B Vitamins Improve Heart Health?

In the late 1970s, researchers noticed that individuals with a very rare genetic disorder, whereby they have too much of the amino acid homocysteine in their blood, suffer from a higher than average incidence of heart disease.[1] Since then, approximately 80 research studies have found an association between high levels of homocysteine and the increased risk for heart disease. Exactly how this amino acid contributes to heart disease isn't known: Excessive amounts of homocysteine may injure the arteries, decrease the flexibility of the blood vessels, or increase the likelihood of clots forming in the blood. Because vitamin B_6, folate, and vitamin B_{12} are all involved in metabolizing homocysteine in the body, researchers began studying the effect of these vitamins on this amino acid.[2]

Numerous studies have suggested that low blood levels of these B vitamins, especially folate, are associated with an increased level of homocysteine in the body. Supplements of B vitamins show some promise in reducing homocysteine levels in the blood. For example, studies reported that folate supplements lowered homocysteine levels by 25 percent. When folate was combined with vitamin B_{12}, homocysteine dropped another 7 percent. Other combinations of B vitamins are being tested for their effect on homocysteine levels, including vitamin B_6 and riboflavin.

The mandatory addition of folic acid to enriched grains and grain products to prevent certain birth defects may also be fighting heart disease. In a study of over 1,000 individuals, the average blood level of folate was higher and the level of the amino acid homocysteine lower after the implementation of the folic acid enrichment program than such levels noted before the program began.[3]

The key question, though, is whether reducing homocysteine levels lowers the incidence of heart attacks or death from heart disease. Studies are currently under way to determine if taking supplements of these B vitamins will lower this risk. Some have shown promise in vitamin supplementation reducing heart attacks,[4] while others have not.[5]

In addition to cardiovascular disease, recent research has also shown a decline in cognitive function in elderly people when homocysteine levels are high and B vitamin intakes are low.[6] Data from the Framingham Study found people with the highest homocysteine levels were most likely to develop dementia compared to those with lower levels of the protein. At this point, a benefit of taking B vitamin supplements to reduce the risk of dementia or cognitive impairment has yet to be reported.[7] Until more is known, individuals should eat a diet that is naturally rich in these B vitamins.

References

1. Finklestein, J. D. 2000. Homocysteine: A History in Progress. *Nutrition Reviews* 58:193–204.
2. Appel, L. J., E. R. Miller, S. H. Jee, R. Stolzenberg-Solomon, P. Lin, T. Erglinger, M. R. Nadeau, and J. Selhub. 2000. Effect of Dietary Patterns on Serum Homocysteine: Results of a Randomized Controlled Feeding Study. *Circulation* 102:852–857.
3. Jacques, P. F., J. Selhub, A. G. Bostom, P. W. F. Wilson, and I. H. Rosenberg. 1999. The Effects of Folic Acid Fortification on Plasma Folate and Total Homocysteine Concentrations. *New England Journal of Medicine* 340:1449–1454.
4. Schnyder, G., M. Roffi, Y. Flammer, R. Pin, and O. M. Hess. 2002. Effect of Homocysteine-Lowering Therapy with Folic Acid, Vitamin B_{12}, and Vitamin B_6 on Clinical Outcome after Percutaneous Coronary Intervention. The Swiss Heart Study: A Randomized Controlled Trial. *Journal of the American Medical Association* 288:973–979.
5. Albert, C. M., N. R. Cook, J. M. Gaziano, E. Zaharris, J. MacFadyen, E. Danielson, J. E. Buring, and J. E. Manson. 2008. Effect of Folic Acid and B Vitamins on Risk of Cardiovascular Events and Total Mortality among Women at High Risk for Cardiovascular Disease: A Randomized Trial. *New England Journal of Medicine* 299:2027–2036.
6. Tucker, K. L., N. Qiao, T. Scott, I. Rosenberg, and S. Avron, III. 2005. High Homocysteine and Low B Vitamins Predict Cognitive Decline in Aging Men: The Veterans Affairs Normative Aging Study. *American Journal of Clinical Nutrition* 82:627–635.
7. Smith, A. D. 2008. The Worldwide Challenge of the Dementias: A Role for B Vitamins and Homocysteine? *Food Nutrition Bulletin* 29:S143–S172.

THE TAKE-HOME MESSAGE There are nine water-soluble vitamins: eight B-complex vitamins and vitamin C. All water-soluble vitamins dissolve in water, are generally not stored in the body, and are excreted through the urine. Water-soluble vitamins are absorbed in the small intestine and transported through the portal vein to the liver. Water-soluble vitamins in foods can be lost or destroyed by exposure to air, water, and heat. The B-complex vitamins function as coenzymes in energy production. Some B vitamins are also involved in nerve health, blood formation, protein synthesis, and heart health. Vitamin C acts as an antioxidant.

Exploring **Thiamin (Vitamin B_1)**

What Is Thiamin (B_1)?

Thiamin, or vitamin B_1, was the first B vitamin to be discovered. The path to its discovery began in the 1890s in East Asia. A Dutch doctor, Christiann Eijkman, noticed that chickens and pigeons that ate polished rice (rice with the nutrient- and thiamin-rich outer layer and germ stripped away) developed **polyneuritis** (*poly* = many, *neur* = nerves, *itis* = inflammation). This debilitating nerve condition resulted in the birds not being able to fly or stand up. Eijkman noted that polyneuritis was also a symptom of beriberi, a similar disease that had been observed in humans.

a Thiamin is composed of a nitrogen containing amine ring and a thiazole ring that contains sulfur.

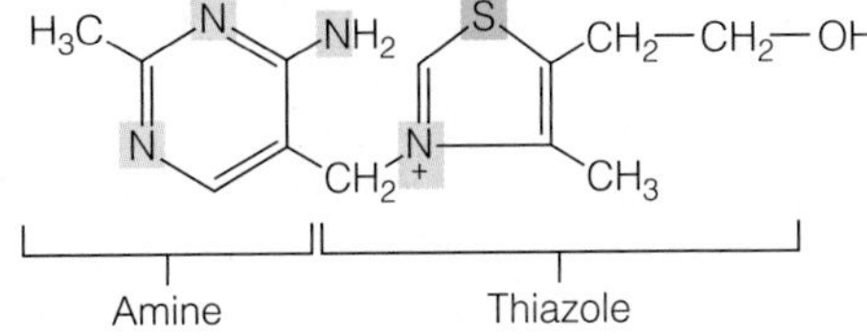

b The active form of thiamin called thiamin pyrophosphate (TPP) has two phosphate groups added to thiamin.

H_3C N NH_2 S CH_2—CH_2—O—P(=O)(OH)—O—P(=O)(OH)—O^- N CH_2 N+ CH_3

Phosphate groups

Thiamin pyrophosphate

▲ **FIGURE 10.3 The Structures of Thiamin and Thiamin Pyrophosphate**

When Eijkman changed the birds' diet to unpolished rice, with the outer layer and germ intact, the birds were cured.[1] Though Eijkman realized that the unpolished rice eliminated the symptoms, he didn't know why. Later, in 1911, Casimir Funk, a Polish biochemist, identified thiamin as the curative factor in the unpolished rice.

The thiamin molecule (**Figure 10.3**) contains an amine ring, which contains nitrogen, and a thiazole ring that contains sulfur. The amine ring was the basis for initially naming this compound a *vitamine* (the *e* was later dropped). Dietary forms of thiamin are converted to the active coenzyme form, **thiamin pyrophosphate (TPP)**, in the body by adding two phosphate groups to the molecule.

Thiamin is one of the vitamins that are sensitive to changes in pH. The practice of using baking soda during cooking (to cook beans faster, for example) destroys thiamin and its ability to function. The basic solution breaks the bond between the rings and the central carbon. Using more acid-based foods, such as tomatoes, when cooking thiamin-rich foods protects the vitamin from destruction.

Thiamin is absorbed in the small intestine, mostly in the jejunum, primarily by passive diffusion. At lower intakes, thiamin is absorbed by active transport. It is transported through the blood and excreted through the urine.

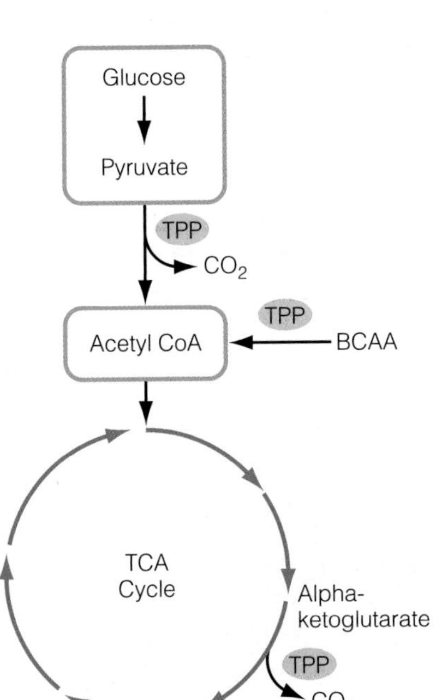

a Thiamin pyrophosphate (TPP) activates the enzyme decarboxylase that removes a carbon from pyruvate, forming carbon dioxide and acetyl CoA during glycolysis.

b TPP participates in the combustion of the branched-chain amino acid (BCAA) to acetyl CoA.

c TPP activates the enzyme that removes a carbon from alpha-ketoglutarate, forming carbon dioxide and succinyl CoA in the TCA cycle.

▲ **FIGURE 10.4 The Function of Thiamin Pyrophosphate in Energy Metabolism**

Functions of Thiamin

Thiamin participates in the production of ATP in several different reactions, most of which involve carbohydrates. The coenzyme TPP activates an enzyme (called a *decarboxylase*) that removes a carbon from pyruvate (a three-carbon molecule) to form acetyl CoA (a two-carbon molecule) and carbon dioxide (**Figure 10.4**).

polyneuritis Inflammation of the peripheral nerves.

thiamin pyrophosphate (TPP) The coenzyme form of thiamin with two phosphate groups as part of the molecule.

continued

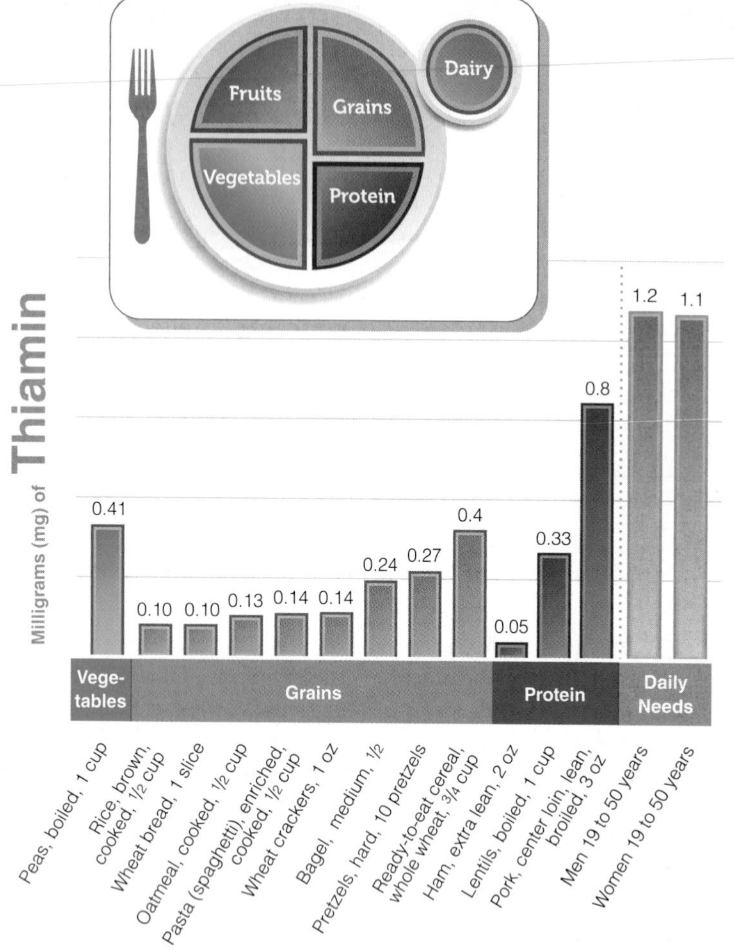

▲ **FIGURE 10.5 Food Sources of Thiamin**

A similar TPP-dependent enzyme converts alpha-ketoglutarate (a five-carbon molecule) to succinyl CoA (a four-carbon molecule) in the TCA cycle.

Thiamin pyrophosphate is also essential for protein metabolism. Thiamin assists in converting three branched-chain amino acids—leucine, isoleucine, and valine—into acetyl CoA to enter the TCA cycle. Without thiamin, energy production from glucose and amino acids would be impossible.

Thiamin is also used in the pathway to synthesize sugars called pentoses that are needed as the starting material for DNA and RNA. This same pathway forms NADPH, a form of niacin needed for fat synthesis.

In addition, thiamin plays a noncoenzyme role in the functioning of the nervous system, contributing to the transmission of nerve impulses. Although the actual mechanism is unclear, thiamin may participate in the manufacture of specific chemicals involved in conducting nerve signals.

beriberi The thiamin deficiency that results in weakness; the name translates to "I can not."

peripheral neuropathy Damage to the peripheral nerves causing pain, numbness, and tingling in the feet and hands, and muscle weakness.

Daily Needs

The RDA for thiamin for adults is 1.1 milligrams for women and 1.2 milligrams for men. Currently, adult American men consume close to 2 milligrams of thiamin daily, whereas women, on average, consume approximately 1.2 milligrams daily, so both groups are meeting their daily needs.[2] These requirements may be greater for those who ingest more kilocalories, especially from carbohydrates.

Food Sources

Enriched and whole-grain foods, such as bread and bread products, ready-to-eat cereals, pasta, rice, nuts, and combined foods such as sandwiches, are the biggest contributors of thiamin in the American diet. Lean pork is the most nutrient-dense source of naturally occurring thiamin. A medium-sized bowl of thiamin-fortified ready-to-eat cereal in the morning and a sandwich at lunch will meet the daily thiamin requirement (see **Figure 10.5**).

Too Much or Too Little

There are no known toxicity symptoms from consuming too much thiamin. For this reason no tolerable upper level has been set.

The disease that occurs in humans who are deficient in thiamin is **beriberi**, which means "I can not." General symptoms of beriberi include loss of appetite, weight loss, memory loss, confusion, muscle weakness, and **peripheral neuropathy**. Beriberi can be classified as "wet" or "dry." Wet beriberi is characterized by edema and congestive heart failure, while dry beriberi victims show signs of muscle wasting without edema and nerve degeneration.

Thiamin deficiencies result from insufficient dietary intake, malabsorption, alcoholism, or prolonged diarrhea. A deficiency of thiamin can also occur when there is an increased need and insufficient thiamin is consumed, such as during pregnancy and lactation.

In the United States, refined grains are enriched with thiamin, so instances of beriberi are rare. Individuals in poor countries with an inadequate food supply, who rely heavily on refined grains that are not enriched, are more

susceptible to a thiamin deficiency and to the symptoms associated with beriberi.

Americans, however, are not completely immune to thiamin deficiencies. Those who chronically abuse alcohol tend to have a poor diet that is probably deficient in thiamin. Alcohol consumption also interferes with the absorption of the small amounts of thiamin that may be in the diet, accelerating its loss from the body. Alcoholics may find themselves battling a thiamin deficiency, and chronic alcohol abuse can lead to an advanced form of thiamin deficiency called Wernicke-Korsakoff syndrome (see Chapter 7). Wernicke-Korsakoff syndrome is a progressively damaging brain disorder that can cause mental confusion and memory loss, difficulty seeing clearly, low blood pressure, uncontrolled movement of the arms and legs, and even coma. Although some of these symptoms can be reversed after the person is medically treated with thiamin, some of the memory loss may be permanent.[3]

TABLE TIPS

Thrive on Thiamin

- Sprinkle cereal on yogurt.
- Toss pasta with peas. Both foods will boost thiamin intake.
- Add cooked rice to soups.
- Have a sandwich made with whole grains and lean meats.
- Enjoy oatmeal for breakfast.

Exploring Riboflavin (Vitamin B_2)

What Is Riboflavin (B_2)?

Riboflavin, also known as vitamin B_2, is a water-soluble compound composed of a side chain and a ring structure. The structures of riboflavin and its two coenzyme forms are illustrated in **Figure 10.6**. **Flavin mononucleotide (FMN)** is composed of three rings plus a sugar alcohol,

flavin mononucleotide (FMN) A coenzyme form of riboflavin, which functions in the electron transport chain.

a Riboflavin contains a 3-ring structure with a side chain attached.

H$_3$C CH$_3$ OH OH OH N N—CH$_2$—CH—CH—CH—CH$_2$OH O= N N H O

Riboflavin

b The two active forms of riboflavin: FMN has one pyrophosphate added to the riboflavin molecule. FAD has an AMP molecule plus a second pyrophosphate.

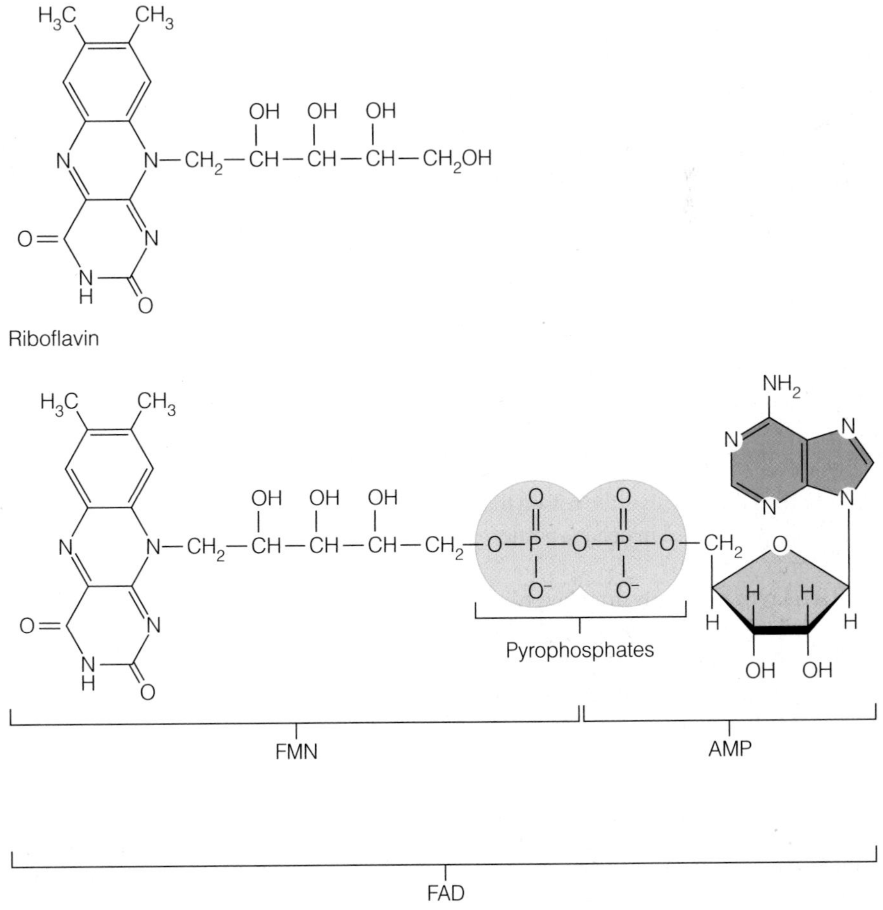

H$_3$C CH$_3$ OH OH OH N N—CH$_2$—CH—CH—CH—CH$_2$—O—P—O—P—O—CH$_2$ O O O$^-$ O$^-$ NH$_2$ N N N N O H H H H OH OH O= N N H O

Pyrophosphates

FMN

AMP

FAD

▲ **FIGURE 10.6 The Structures of Riboflavin and the Coenzyme Forms FAD and FMN**

continued

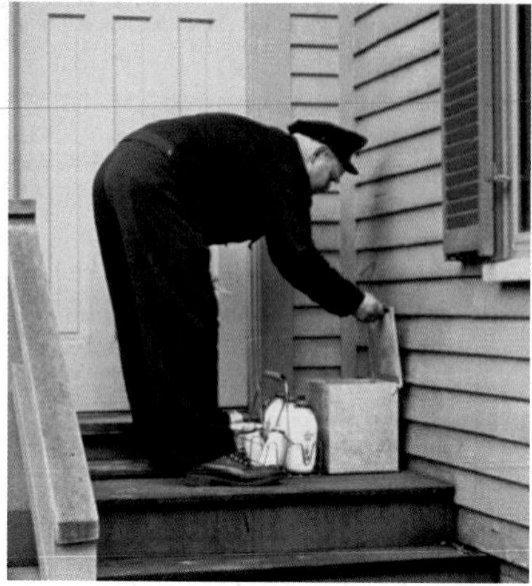

shown as a straight chain in Figure 10.6. Attached is one pyrophosphate. **Flavin adenine dinucleotide (FAD)** combines FMN plus an addition pyrophosphate, and adenine and a five-carbon sugar referred to as AMP. Both coenzyme forms are active in the body.

Riboflavin is fairly stable during cooking except in the presence of ultraviolet light. Not so long ago, milk, a source of abundant riboflavin, made its way to a household not via the grocery store cooler, but by way of a daily visit from a milkman. At each delivery, the milkman placed the clear glass milk bottles inside a covered "milk box" outside the home. The box helped protect the light-sensitive riboflavin in the milk from being destroyed by sunlight. Today, some dairy farmers sell milk in glass bottles, touting the improved taste and environmental benefits of using reusable bottles rather than opaque plastic containers. However, what they don't advertise is that the sunlight that reaches milk in glass containers destroys much of its riboflavin. In fact, in just 30 minutes, UV can destroy over 30 percent of the riboflavin in glass-bottled milk.[4] This is the reason that most milk is packaged in opaque bottles or cardboard containers.

Riboflavin is usually attached to proteins in food and must be released during digestion. Hydrochloric acid denatures the protein, which frees the riboflavin to be absorbed by active transport in the small intestine.

Functions of Riboflavin

Riboflavin participates in energy metabolism mostly through oxidation-reduction reactions. Both FMN and FAD have the ability to accept hydrogen ions in metabolic reactions. For example, in the conversion of carbohydrates and proteins into energy, hydrogen ions are transferred to FAD in the TCA cycle, which reduces it to $FADH_2$ (**Figure 10.7**). The $FADH_2$ transports the electrons to the electron transport chain to produce ATP. In addition to riboflavin's function in converting carbohydrates and proteins into energy, it also participates as $FADH_2$ in beta-oxidation, which converts fatty acids into ATP. FAD is also involved in oxidation-reduction reactions that protect cells from oxidative stress (see the Chemistry Boost on page 376 on oxidation-reduction reactions).[5]

Riboflavin enhances the functions of other B vitamins, such as niacin, folate, and vitamin B_6. For instance, riboflavin as FAD helps convert folate to its active form and aids in the reaction that converts the amino acid tryptophan to niacin, and FMN is essential to convert vitamin B_6 to its coenzyme form.[6] Because riboflavin is involved in the metabolism of several other vitamins, a severe riboflavin deficiency may affect many enzyme systems.

Daily Needs

The recommended daily intake of riboflavin for adult males is 1.3 milligrams and 1.1 milligrams for females. The average intake of riboflavin for adult males in the U.S. is about 2 milligrams per day, and adult females in the U.S. consume about 1.5 milligrams per day. This is well above the RDA.

Food Sources

Milk and yogurt are the most popular sources of riboflavin in the diets of American adults, followed by enriched cereals and grains (see **Figure 10.8**). A breakfast of cereal and milk and a lunchtime pita sandwich and yogurt will meet riboflavin needs for the day. For those individuals who follow a gluten-free diet, riboflavin needs can be met by consuming gluten-free grains such as quinoa, rice, or oats.

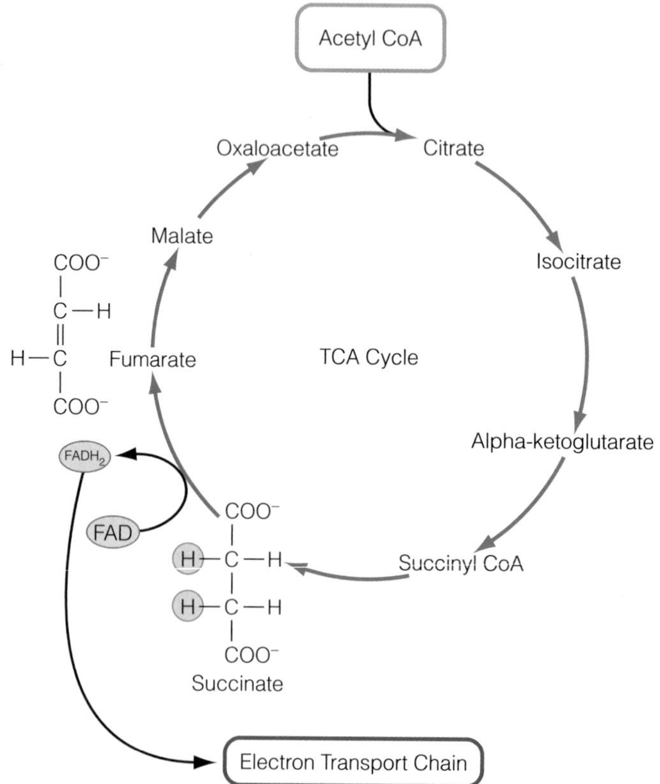

▲ **FIGURE 10.7 The Role of FAD in the TCA Cycle**
The riboflavin coenzyme FAD participates in the removal of hydrogen atoms from succinate to form fumarate and $FADH_2$ in the TCA cycle.

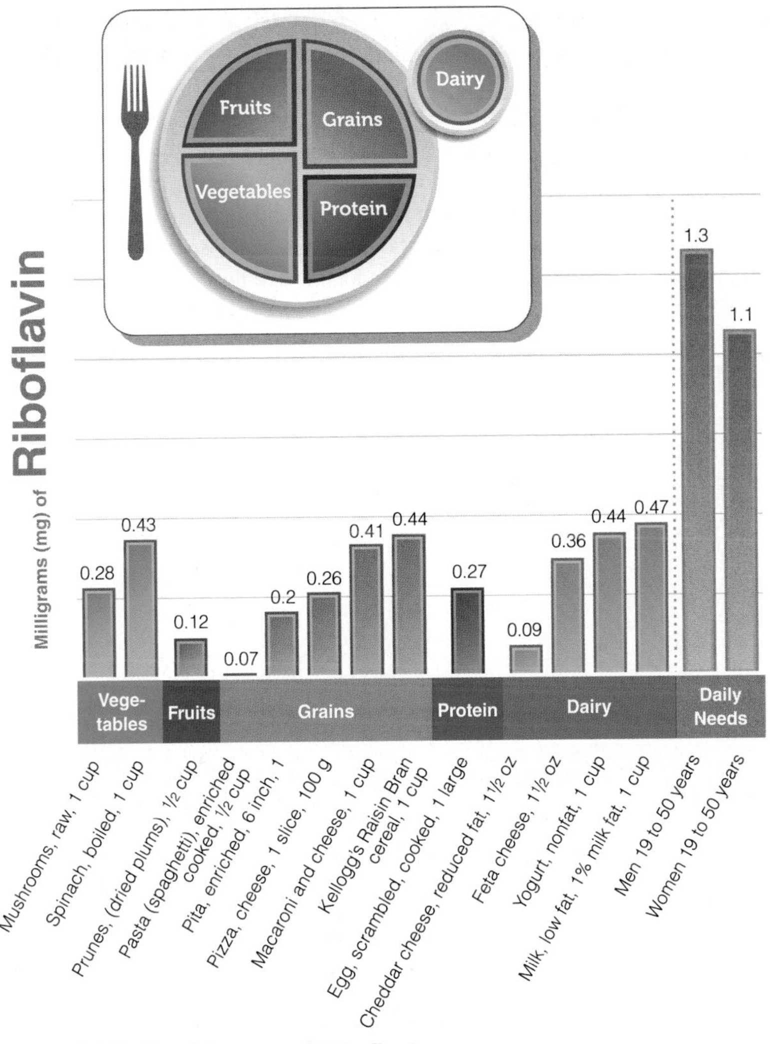

▲ FIGURE 10.8 **Food Sources of Riboflavin**

a Cheilosis

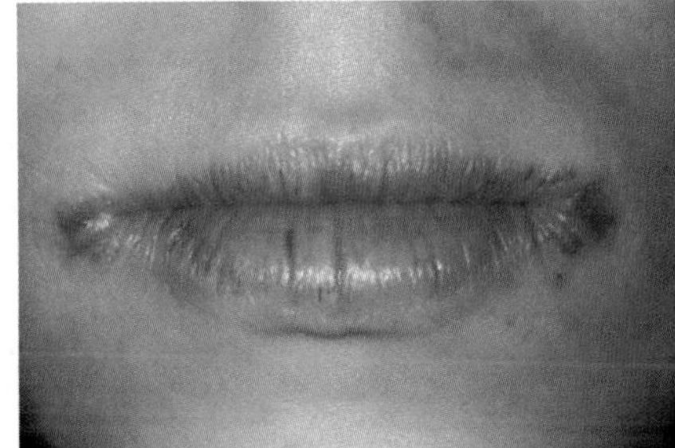

b Glossitis

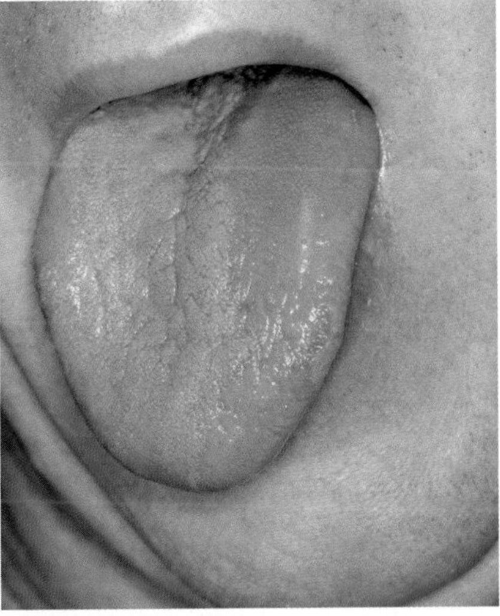

▲ FIGURE 10.9 **The Symptoms of Ariboflavinosis**
The symptoms of a deficiency of many of the B vitamins (including ariboflavinosis) include (a) cheilosis and (b) glossitis.

Too Much or Too Little

The body tightly controls the metabolism of riboflavin. About 95 percent of riboflavin is absorbed, and excessive amounts are excreted in urine. In fact, because riboflavin is a bright yellow compound, consuming large amounts through supplements will turn urine as yellow as a school bus. While this isn't dangerous to health, it isn't beneficial either. No tolerable upper level for riboflavin has been determined.

Ariboflavinosis is the name for riboflavin deficiency (**Figure 10.9**). The term covers a host of symptoms in which the cells in the tissues that line the throat, mouth, tongue, and lips become inflamed or swollen. Symptoms include a sore throat, an irritated lining of the inside of the mouth (**stomatitis**), an inflamed tongue (**glossitis**) that may appear shiny and purplish red, and cracked or sore lips (**cheilosis**) with cracks at the corners of the mouth. In older adults,

flavin adenine dinucleotide (FAD) A coenzyme form of riboflavin that functions as an electron carrier in energy metabolism.

ariboflavinosis A deficiency of riboflavin characterized by cheilosis, stomatitis, and glossitis.

stomatitis Inflammation of the mucous lining of the mouth.

glossitis Inflammation of the tongue.

cheilosis A non-inflammatory condition of the lips characterized by chapping and fissuring.

continued

RIBOFLAVIN

TABLE TIPS
Raise Your Riboflavin

- Have a glass of low-fat milk with meals.
- A yogurt snack is a riboflavin snack.
- Pizza is a good source of riboflavin.
- Enriched pasta will enrich the meal with riboflavin.
- Macaroni and cheese provides a double source of riboflavin—the pasta and the cheese.
- Spinach, almonds, Crimini mushrooms, asparagus, and eggs are gluten- and dairy-free sources of riboflavin.

a deficiency of riboflavin reduces the conversion of vitamin B_6 to its active form and is reversed when riboflavin supplements are given.[7, 8, 9] Riboflavin deficiencies also alter iron metabolism and the synthesis of hemoglobin.[10]

Chemistry Boost

Oxidation-Reduction Reactions

Oxidation-reduction reactions, also called redox reactions, are a family of chemical reactions in which electrons are transferred from one molecule to another for transport. The **oxidation reaction** and the **reduction reaction** always occur in pairs, and you can't have one without the other. In an oxidation reaction, an electron is lost from one molecule and gained by another molecule in a reduction reaction.

FAD and FMN are major electron carriers in oxidation-reduction reactions during the TCA cycle. The oxidized form is FAD and the reduced form is $FADH_2$. The oxidation-reduction reaction is illustrated as follows:

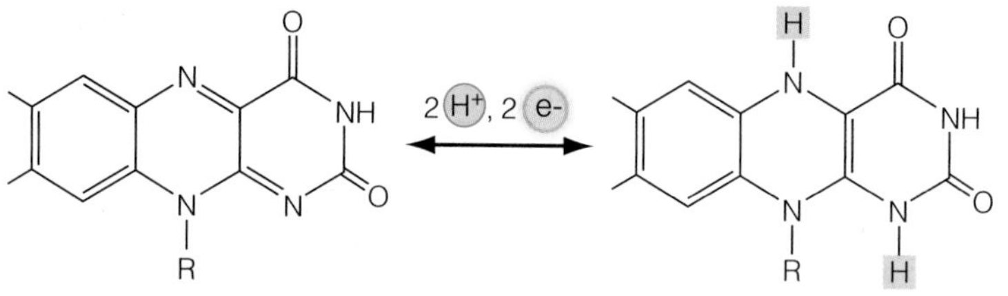

FAD ⟷ ($2H^+$, 2 e-) $FADH_2$

During the TCA cycle, compounds release hydrogen ions during oxidation, which are grabbed by FAD to form $FADH_2$.

The reduced form ($FADH_2$) carries the electrons to the electron transport chain, where they are released and FAD is reformed to grab more hydrogen ions. The released hydrogen ions combine with oxygen to form water.

Here is an example of this oxidation-reduction reaction:

$$\text{succinate} + \text{FAD} \rightarrow \text{fumarate} + \text{FADH}_2$$

The oxidized form of flavin mononucleotide is FMN and the reduced form is $FMNH_2$. Other water-soluble vitamins such as niacin (NAD^+) and vitamin C also play important roles in oxidation-reduction reactions.

oxidation reaction A reaction in which an atom loses an electron.

reduction reaction A reaction in which an atom gains an electron.

NIACIN

Exploring Niacin (Vitamin B_3)

What Is Niacin (B_3)?

Niacin, or vitamin B_3, is the generic term for **nicotinic acid** and **nicotinamide**, which are the two active forms of niacin derived from food (**Figure 10.10**). Both forms are converted to the active coenzymes **nicotinamide adenine dinucleotide (NAD^+)** and **nicotinamide adenine dinucleotide phosphate ($NADP^+$)** in the liver. These coenzymes play an essential role in energy metabolism.

The niacin found in plant foods, such as wheat or corn, is much less bioavailable than niacin from meat and dairy products. Niacin in corn, for example, is bound to a protein that is difficult to absorb. Soaking corn in alkaline lime water, as is done in some Meso-American cultures before using it to make tortillas, helps release the vitamin and improve its bioavailability.[11] This practice is not recommended, however, because the alkalinity increases the pH, which destroys the other B vitamins present in corn.

Most of the niacin in foods is absorbed by simple diffusion in the small intestine. It circulates through the blood to the liver, where it is converted to NAD^+ and $NADP^+$.

Functions of Niacin

NAD^+ and $NADP^+$ are key to the metabolism of glucose, protein, fat, and alcohol. These coenzymes participate in both

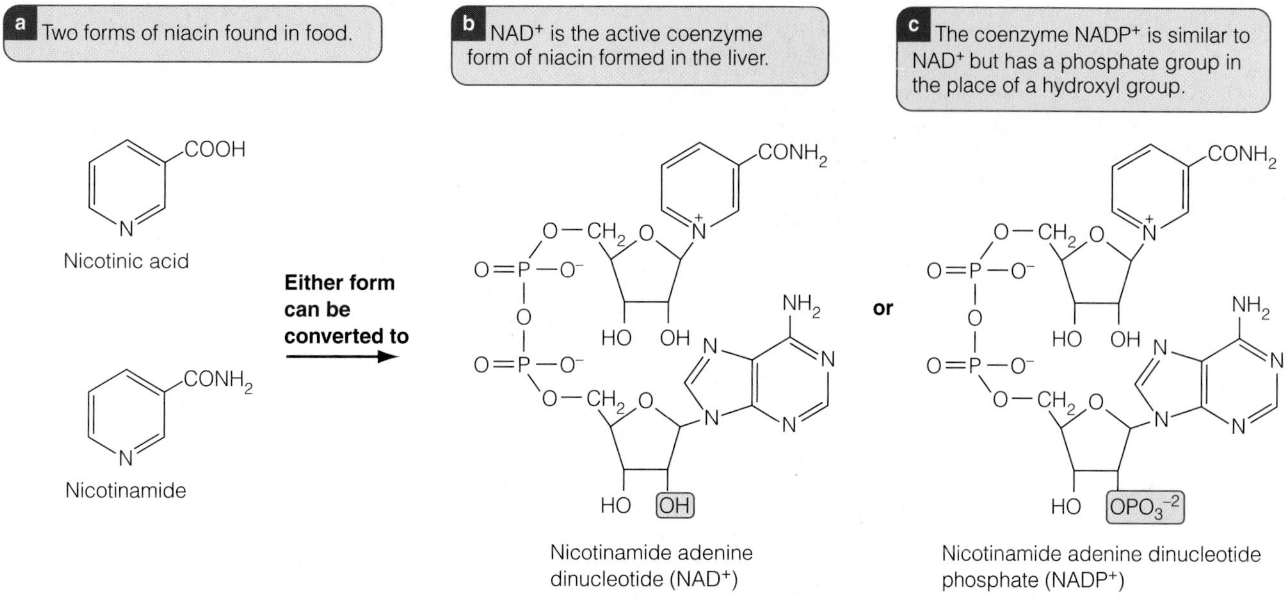

a Two forms of niacin found in food.

b NAD^+ is the active coenzyme form of niacin formed in the liver.

c The coenzyme $NADP^+$ is similar to NAD^+ but has a phosphate group in the place of a hydroxyl group.

COOH

Nicotinic acid

$CONH_2$

Nicotinamide

Either form can be converted to

$CONH_2$ $O=P-O^-$ $O-CH_2$ O HO OH NH_2 N HO OH

Nicotinamide adenine dinucleotide (NAD^+)

or

$CONH_2$ $O=P-O^-$ $O-CH_2$ O HO OH NH_2 N HO OPO_3^{-2}

Nicotinamide adenine dinucleotide phosphate ($NADP^+$)

▲ **FIGURE 10.10 The Structures of Niacin and Its Coenzyme Forms NAD^+ and $NADP^+$**

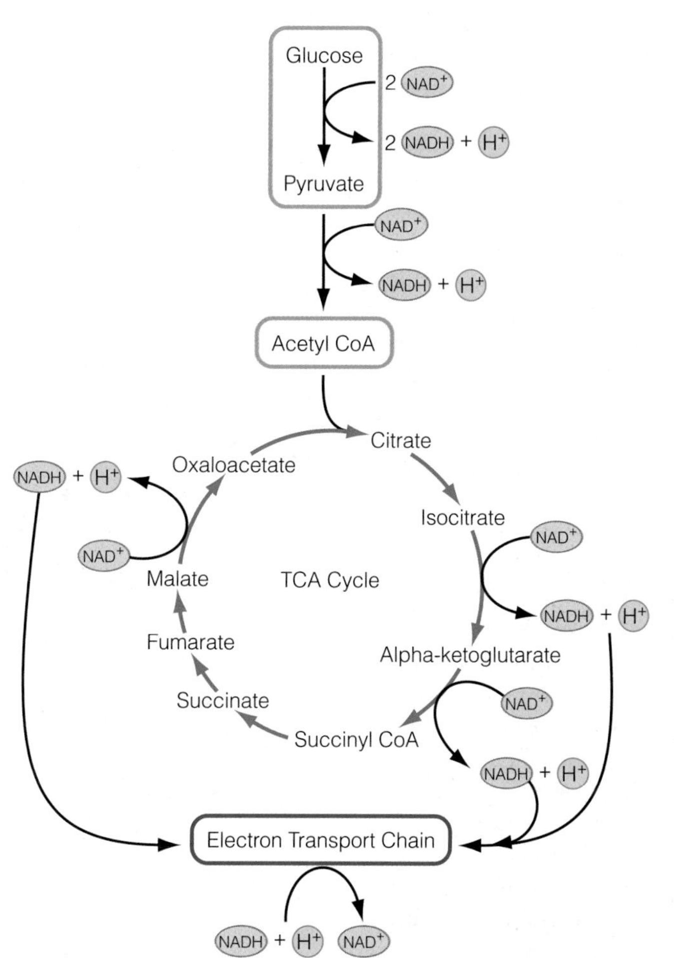

▲ **FIGURE 10.11 Niacin Functions as NAD^+ in Energy Metabolism**
The coenzyme form of niacin, NAD^+, participates in oxidation-reduction reactions in glycolysis, transporting H^+ atoms to the electron transport chain.

oxidation-reduction reactions. NAD^+ functions mostly in catabolic energy-producing reactions (**Figure 10.11**)—for instance, in fatty acid oxidation. In this reaction, NAD^+ is reduced to $NADH^+$, which carries the H^+ to the electron transport chain. There, it combines with oxygen to form water and ATP.

$NADP^+$ can act in both oxidation and reduction reactions. In reduction reactions, this coenzyme form of niacin can synthesize compounds such as fat and cholesterol. Niacin also aids in vitamin C and folate metabolism.

Niacin is needed to keep skin cells healthy and the digestive system functioning properly. Niacin in the form of nicotinic acid (not nicotinamide) has been used since 1955 to lower the total amount of cholesterol in the blood, by lowering Lp(a) lipoprotein, the LDL

nicotinic acid A form of niacin found in foods and sometimes prescribed to lower LDL cholesterol.

nicotinamide A form of niacin that is found in food and as a topical cream in treating acne.

nicotinamide adenine dinucleotide (NAD^+) A coenzyme form of niacin that functions as an electron carrier and can be reduced to NADH during metabolism.

nicotinamide adenine dinucleotide phosphate ($NADP^+$) A coenzyme form of niacin that functions as an electron carrier and can be reduced to NADPH during metabolism.

continued

cholesterol carrier. It can also lower high levels of fat (triglycerides) in the blood and simultaneously raise the level of the HDL cholesterol carrier.[12]

When nicotinic acid is used to treat high blood cholesterol, it is considered a pharmacological dose or drug. The two to four grams per day often prescribed by a physician is more than 40 times the upper level of 35 milligrams per day for niacin. For this reason, individuals should *never* consume high amounts of niacin unless they are monitored by a physician.

Daily Needs

While niacin is found in many foods, it can also be synthesized in the body from the amino acid tryptophan. For this reason, daily niacin needs are measured in **niacin equivalents (NE)**. It is estimated that 60 milligrams of tryptophan can be converted to 1 milligram of niacin or 1 milligram NE. This conversion depends on the B vitamins riboflavin and vitamin B_6, and the mineral iron. The Calculation Corner illustrates how to calculate niacin equivalents from tryptophan.

The recommended daily amount of niacin for adults is 14 milligrams NE for women and 16 milligrams NE for men, an amount set to prevent the deficiency disease pellagra. American adults, on average, far exceed their daily niacin needs.[13]

Food Sources

Niacin used by the body comes from two sources: preformed niacin found in food and niacin formed from excess amounts of the amino acid tryptophan. Preformed niacin is found in meat, fish, poultry, enriched whole-grain breads and bread products, and fortified cereals (see **Figure 10.12**). Protein-rich foods,

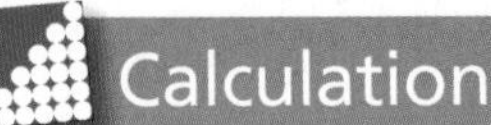

Calculation Corner

Niacin Equivalents

The recommendation for niacin is expressed in milligrams of niacin equivalents (mg NE) that reflect either the amount of preformed niacin in foods or the amount that can be formed from a food's content of the amino acid tryptophan.

Calculating mg NE from a meal can be completed by two different methods.

(a) If you know the amount of preformed niacin in milligrams (mg) and the amount of tryptophan in grams (g) in the meal, then use this formula to calculate the total amount of niacin equivalents in the meal:

$$(\text{tryptophan} \times 1{,}000 \div 60) + \text{preformed niacin} = \text{mg NE}$$

In this formula, the amount of tryptophan must be converted from grams to milligrams (tryptophan × 1,000) and then divided by 60 (60 mg of tryptophan can be converted into 1 mg of niacin). Then add the preformed niacin found in the meal for the total milligrams of niacin.

Example: A breakfast contains 0.02 g of tryptophan and 7.0 mg of preformed niacin. How many mg NE does the meal contain?

Answer: (0.02 g tryptophan × 1,000 ÷ 60) + 7.0 mg niacin = 7.3 mg NE

(b) If you only know the total amount of protein in the meal, but not the tryptophan content, you must estimate the amount of tryptophan. Total protein in a meal is approximately 1.1 percent tryptophan. This formula uses the 1.1 percentage to calculate mg NE:

$$(0.011 \times \text{g of protein}) \times 1{,}000 \div 60 + \text{preformed niacin} = \text{mg NE}$$

Example: A breakfast contains 8 g of protein and 3 mg of preformed niacin. How many mg NE does the meal contain?

Answer: (0.011 × 8 g protein) × 1,000 ÷ 60 + 3 mg preformed niacin = 4.5 mg NE

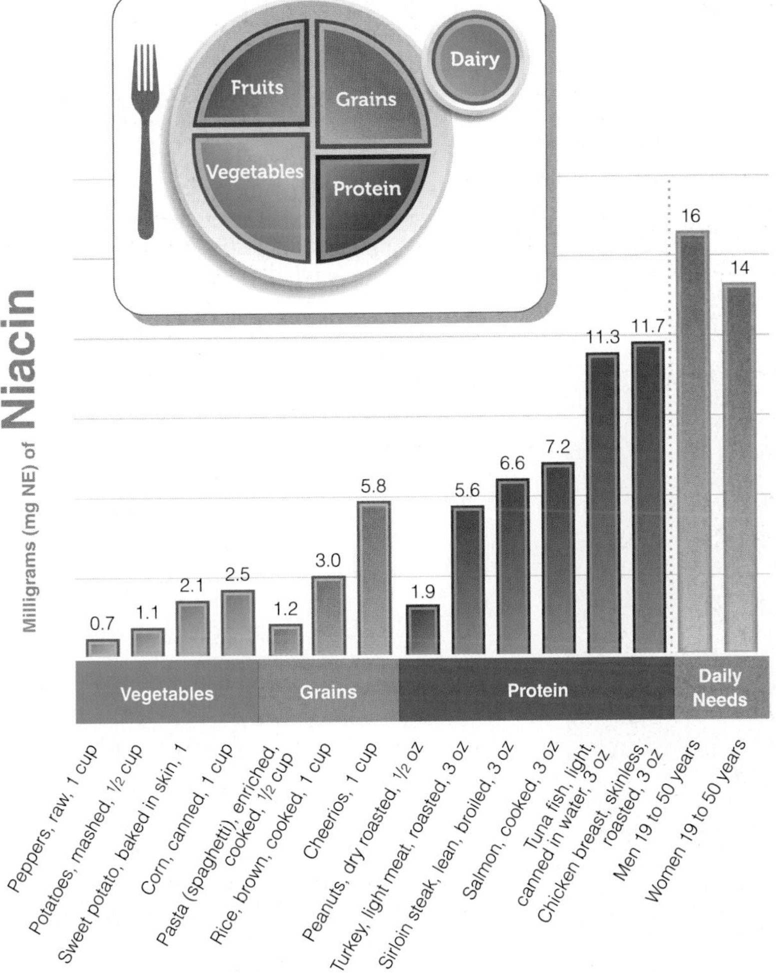

▲ **FIGURE 10.12 Food Sources of Niacin**

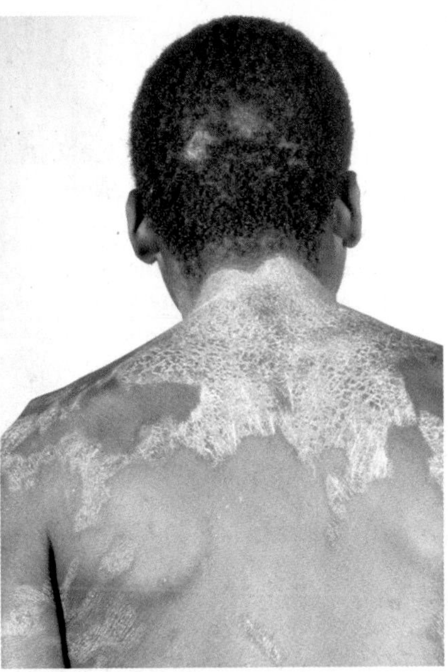

▲ **FIGURE 10.13 Dermatitis Can Result from Pellagra**

particularly animal foods such as meat, are also good sources of tryptophan. However, if an individual is falling short of both dietary protein and niacin, tryptophan will first be used to make protein, at the expense of niacin needs in the body.[14]

Unlike some B vitamins, niacin is stable in foods and is not destroyed by heat or ultraviolet light. Because niacin is water soluble, it can leach if food is cooked or soaked in water.

Too Much or Too Little

As with most water-soluble vitamins, there isn't any known danger of consuming too much niacin from foods. However, overconsuming niacin (more than one gram per day) by taking supplements or eating too many overly fortified foods can cause flushing, a reddish coloring of the face, arms, and chest. Excess niacin can also cause nausea, heartburn, and vomiting, be toxic to the liver, and raise blood glucose levels. The upper level for niacin for adults is 35 milligrams. This upper level applies only to healthy individuals; it may be too high for those with certain medical conditions, such as diabetes mellitus and liver disease.[15]

Too little niacin in the diet can result in the deficiency disease **pellagra** (**Figure 10.13**). In the early 1900s, pellagra was widespread among the poor living in the southern United States, where people relied on corn—which contains little available niacin and no tryptophan—as a dietary staple. The symptoms of pellagra—*dermatitis, dementia,* and *diarrhea*—led to its being known as the disease of the three Ds. A fourth D, *death,* was also often associated with the disease.

Once fortified cereal grains became available, pellagra disappeared as a widespread disease in the United States. The niacin in fortified grains and protein-rich diets was later identified as the curative factor. Although no longer common in the United States, pellagra does occur among individuals who abuse alcohol and have a very poor diet.

TABLE TIPS

Need More Niacin?

- Have a serving of enriched cereal in the morning.
- Dip niacin-rich peppers in hummus.
- Enjoy a lean chicken breast at dinner.
- Snack on peanuts.
- Put tuna fish flakes on salad.

niacin equivalents (NE) A measurement that reflects the amount of niacin and tryptophan in foods that can be used to synthesize niacin.

pellagra A disease resulting from a deficiency of niacin or tryptophan.

Exploring **Pantothenic Acid**

What Is Pantothenic Acid?

Pantothenic acid makes up part of the metabolic compound *acetyl CoA (coenzyme A),* the gateway molecule in energy metabolism (**Figure 10.14**). This essential B vitamin is absorbed in the small intestine by active transport when intake is low, and by passive diffusion at higher intakes. Once absorbed, pantothenic acid is circulated through the blood to the liver. The vitamin itself is not stored, but high levels of acetyl CoA are found in the liver, kidney, adrenal glands, and brain.[16]

$HO{-}CH_2{-}C(CH_3)(H_3C){-}CH(OH){-}C(=O){-}NH{-}CH_2{-}CH_2{-}C(=O){-}O^-$

Pantothenic acid

Is a component of

$CH_2{-}O{-}P(=O)(O^-){-}O{-}P(=O)(O^-){-}O{-}CH_2{-}C(CH_3)(H_3C){-}CH(OH){-}C(=O){-}NH{-}CH_2{-}CH_2{-}C(=O){-}NH{-}CH_2{-}CH_2{-}SH$

Adenine

$O{=}P(O^-){-}O^-$; OH

Coenzyme A

▲ **FIGURE 10.14 The Structures of Pantothenic Acid and Coenzyme A**
Pantothenic acid is part of coenzyme A, which combines with the amino acid cysteine to become acetyl CoA, the gateway molecule for all nutrients to enter the TCA cycle during energy metabolism.

TABLE TIPS

A Plethora of Pantothenic Acid

Sprinkle a tablespoon of brewer's yeast on cooked oatmeal in the morning.

Add colorful kale, avocado, and tomatoes to salad greens.

Enjoy a three-bean salad with the midday meal.

Include nuts and seeds, such as peanuts and sunflower seeds, among regular snack foods.

Substitute sweet potatoes for baked potatoes at dinner.

Functions of Pantothenic Acid

As part of acetyl CoA, pantothenic acid functions in numerous reactions that are essential to metabolism. Coenzyme A is needed in fat metabolism both to synthesize fatty acids and to convert them to energy. Pantothenic acid participates in carbohydrate metabolism in the conversion of pyruvate to acetyl CoA, and in protein metabolism by converting some amino acids to intermediate substrates in the TCA cycle (see **Figure 10.15**). Pantothenic acid is also used in the synthesis of cholesterol, steroid hormones, and the neurotransmitter acetylcholine.[17]

Daily Needs

The adequate intake (AI) for pantothenic acid has been set at 5 milligrams per day for both adult males and females. This recommendation is based on the amount needed to replace the amount excreted in the urine.

Food Sources

Pantothenic acid gets its name from the Greek word

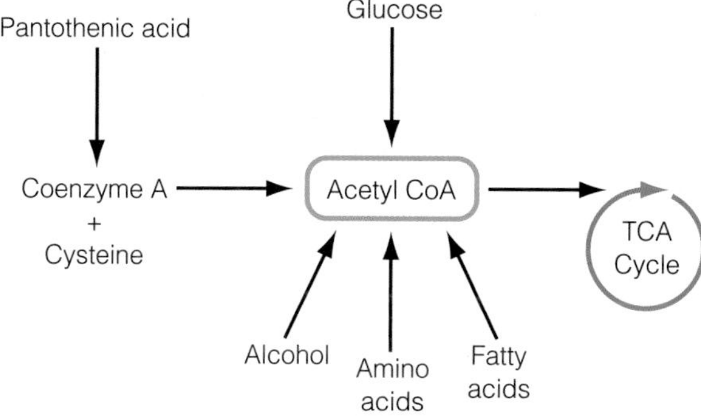

▲ **FIGURE 10.15 Pantothenic Acid and Energy Metabolism**
As part of coenzyme A, pantothenic acid participates in energy metabolism through its role in forming acetyl CoA.

pantothen, which means "everywhere," because it is found in almost every food. The highest amounts are found in whole-grain cereals, nuts and legumes, peanut butter, meat, milk, and eggs. Pantothenic acid can be destroyed by heat, so refined grains and foods that are processed, such as frozen or canned vegetables, fish, and meat, are lower in pantothenic acid than their fresh counterparts.

Too Much or Too Little

Like many of the other B vitamins, there are no known adverse effects from consuming too much pantothenic acid, and therefore no tolerable upper level has been established.

Although a pantothenic acid deficiency is rare, individuals who fall short of their need may experience fatigue, nausea, vomiting, numbness, muscle cramps, and difficulty walking.

During World War II, prisoners of war in Asia experienced "burning feet" syndrome. The symptoms ranged from heat sensations and tingling on the soles of their feet to a painful burning intense enough to disrupt sleep. Their diet consisted predominantly of nutrient-poor polished rice. A doctor in India who was studying an identical phenomenon in his patients discovered that when he gave them supplements of pantothenic acid, the condition stopped.[18] In both situations, the syndrome was later attributed to a diet deficient in pantothenic acid.

Exploring **Biotin**

What Is Biotin?

In 1914, doctors discovered that adding raw egg white to a balanced diet resulted in dermatitis and hair loss, depression, and nausea. The condition, referred to as *egg white injury,* was caused by the binding of the vitamin biotin with **avidin**, a protein found in egg whites. Avidin can bind up to four molecules of biotin, which renders the vitamin unavailable for absorption. The problem only occurs when raw eggs are consumed, as cooking eggs denatures the avidin and prevents it from binding to biotin.

Biotin is made up of sulfur-containing double rings and a side chain (**Figure 10.16**). During digestion, the protease enzyme **biotinidase** releases biotin from food in the small intestine, allowing the free biotin to be absorbed by active transport. Once absorbed into the portal vein, biotin is taken up by the liver and stored in small amounts.

Functions of Biotin

Biotin functions as a coenzyme for enzymes that add carbon dioxide to compounds involved in energy metabolism. As illustrated in **Figure 10.17**, biotin acts as a coenzyme in the synthesis of fatty acids from acetate formed from acetyl CoA; it replenishes oxaloacetate from pyruvate, which is important in the TCA cycle and in gluconeogenesis; it aids in the metabolism of the amino acid leucine; and it helps convert some amino acids into compounds that can be used in the TCA

▲ **FIGURE 10.16 The Chemical Structure of Biotin**
A molecule of biotin contains both nitrogen and sulfur as part of its structure.

avidin A protein in raw egg whites that binds biotin.

biotinidase An enzyme in the small intestine that releases biotin from food to allow it to be absorbed.

continued

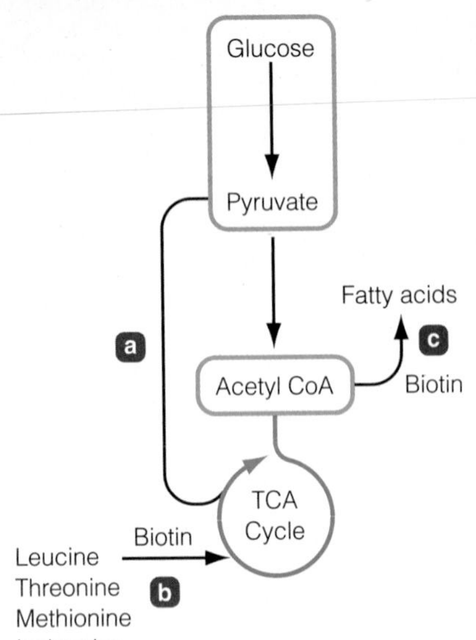

a Biotin helps add a CO_2 to pyruvate to form oxaloacetate, a compound in the TCA cycle. This is a key step in gluconeogenesis.

b Biotin helps break down leucine, threonine, methionine, and isoleucine to be used in the production of energy through the TCA cycle.

c Biotin plays a key role in synthesizing fatty acids from acetyl CoA.

▲ **FIGURE 10.17 The Role of Biotin as a Coenzyme in Energy Metabolism**

cycle. Thus, without adequate biotin, energy metabolism would be impaired.

Biotin also may play a role in DNA replication and the transcription of genes. In fact, over 2,000 genes depend on biotin.[19] The exact mechanisms of biotin's role are still unclear.

Biotin plays a noncoenzyme role in cell development and growth. For this reason, some refer to biotin as the "beauty vitamin" in that it helps maintain healthy hair and nails.

Daily Needs

The adequate intake of biotin has been set at 30 micrograms per day for both adult males and females. However, compared with the other B vitamins, much less data is available on which to base the daily need for biotin. This is one reason that the Nutrition Facts panel used in food labeling lists the Daily Value for biotin at 300 micrograms, or ten times the AI. This is unusual because the Daily Value for most other water-soluble vitamins is much lower.

Food Sources

Even a small amount of peanuts (¼ cup) provides more than 60 percent of the daily requirement for biotin. Other biotin-rich food sources include yeast, egg yolks, whole grains, liver and other organ meats, and fish.

Too Much or Too Little

There is little evidence that consuming too much biotin can have toxic side effects, even at doses as high as 200 milligrams per day.[20] For this reason, a tolerable upper level has not been set.

Some biotin is synthesized by bacteria in the intestinal tract, which may be a reason deficiencies are rare. However, whether the biotin produced by bacteria is absorbed remains unknown.

Though deficiencies of biotin are rare, they can occur if an individual eats more than 12 raw egg whites per day over a prolonged period of time. Biotin deficiencies may also occur in patients receiving total parenteral nutrition (feeding intravenously when the GI tract is not functioning, such as after surgery) that lacks biotin. Other circumstances in which biotin may be lacking include conditions that impair absorption such as Crohn's disease or ulcerative colitis, and in some individuals with rare genetic disorders, such as a lack of biotinidase, the digestive enzyme that hydrolyzes biotin from protein.[21]

Symptoms of a biotin deficiency include dermatitis, especially around the eyes, nose, and mouth, conjunctivitis, hair loss, and alterations in the central nervous system resulting in lethargy, hallucinations, and depression.

Biotin enhances cell development, promoting the health of hair and nails.

TABLE TIPS

Boundless Biotin

- Spread a tablespoon of peanut butter on whole-wheat toast at breakfast.
- Add a chopped hard-boiled egg to a green salad for lunch.
- Choose walnuts and almonds as a mid-morning or midafternoon snack.
- Mix fresh raspberries and strawberries with yogurt.
- Bake salmon or halibut for a fresh fish dinner.

Exploring Vitamin B_6

What Is Vitamin B_6?

Vitamin B_6 is a collective name for several related compounds, including **pyridoxine**, the major form found in plant foods and used in supplements and fortified foods.[22] Two other forms, **pyridoxal** and **pyridoxamine**, are found in animal food sources such as chicken and meat (**Figure 10.18**).

The bioavailability of vitamin B_6 is about 75 percent, and all forms are absorbed in the small intestine by passive diffusion. Once absorbed, the vitamin is attached to albumin and transported to the liver. The liver activates the vitamin by adding a phosphate group to form **pyridoxal phosphate (PLP)**. This active form of B_6 is stored in the body, mostly in the muscle, with a smaller amount stored in the liver.

Functions of Vitamin B_6

Vitamin B_6 acts as a coenzyme for more than 100 enzymes. Most of these enzymes are involved in protein metabolism. Vitamin B_6 also is a key player in glucose metabolism and red blood cell synthesis, and it interacts with other nutrients, including riboflavin, niacin, and zinc.

Vitamin B_6 and Amino Acid Metabolism

Almost every amino acid needs PLP during its metabolism. For example, PLP is needed during transamination to create nonessential amino acids (**Figure 10.19**). Because of this role, without vitamin B_6 all amino acids would become essential. Vitamin B_6 also helps convert the amino acid tryptophan to niacin.[23]

Vitamin B_6 and Carbohydrate Metabolism

Vitamin B_6 has a double role in the metabolism of carbohydrates. The PLP coenzyme participates in glycogenolysis in the muscle, thus enabling the body to tap into its glycogen stores for energy. Its second role is to activate enzymes involved in gluconeogenesis to produce glucose from noncarbohydrate compounds.

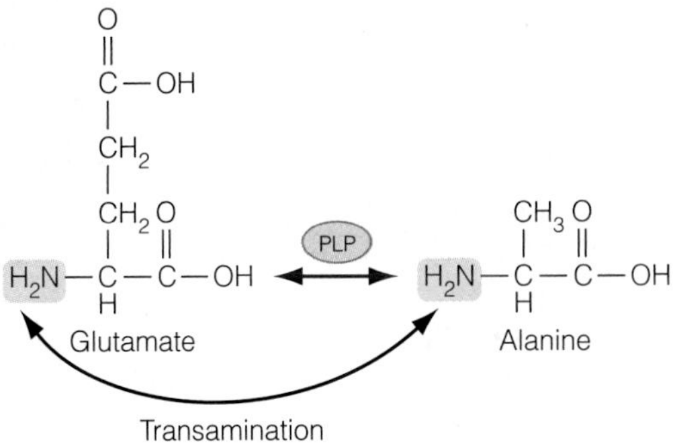

▲ **FIGURE 10.19 Vitamin B_6 Assists in Transamination**
PLP helps transfer an amine group to form a new amino acid.

Vitamin B_6 may also participate in fat metabolism, although the role is still unclear.

Other Functions of B_6

Vitamin B_6 is needed to make the oxygen-carrying hemoglobin in the red

pyridoxine The alcohol form of vitamin B_6.

pyridoxal The aldehyde form of vitamin B_6.

pyridoxamine The amine form of vitamin B_6.

pyridoxal phosphate (PLP) The active coenzyme form of vitamin B_6.

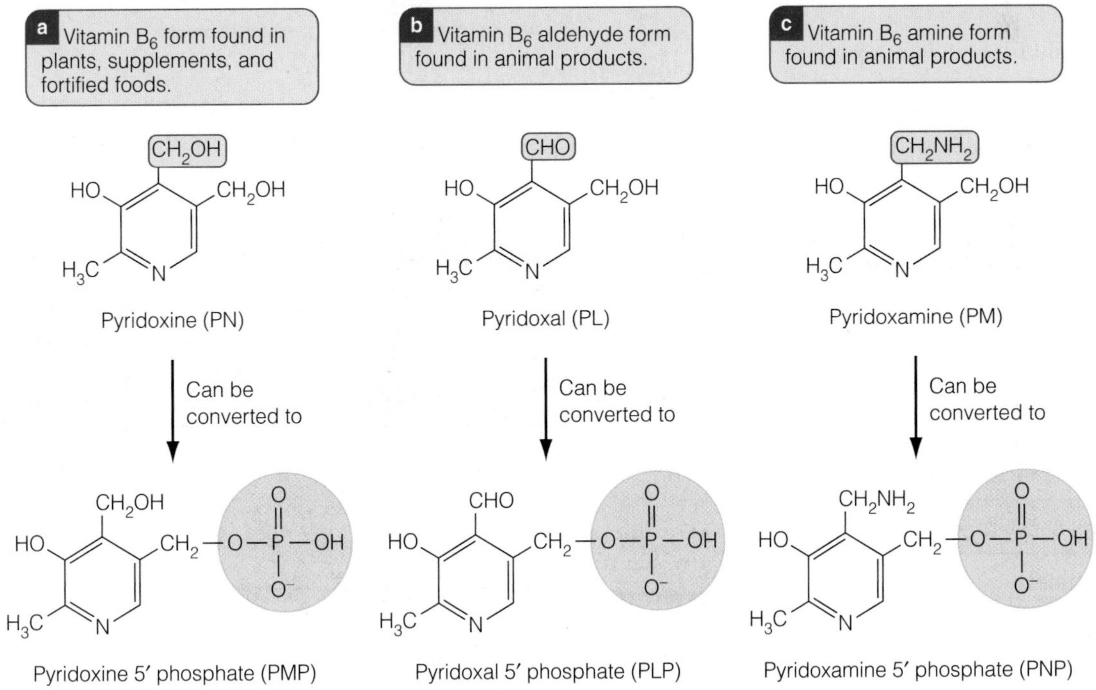

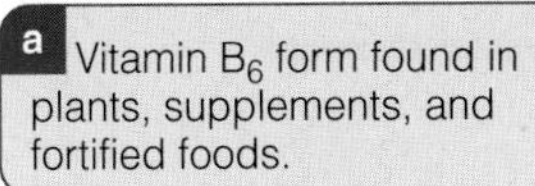

▲ **FIGURE 10.18 The Structures of the Various Forms of Vitamin B_6**

continued

blood cells and to keep the immune and nervous systems healthy.[24] Vitamin B_6 activates the enzyme responsible for the first step in the synthesis of hemoglobin.

Recent research indicates that vitamin B_6, along with folate and vitamin B_{12}, may help reduce the risk of heart disease. See Examining the Evidence: Do B Vitamins Improve Heart Health? on page 370 for more information.

Vitamin B_6 is routinely prescribed to reduce nausea and vomiting during pregnancy. Some double-blind studies have reported that an intake of 30 milligrams of vitamin B_6 daily was helpful in reducing morning sickness; other studies have reported no benefit.[25]

Daily Needs

Adult women need 1.3 to 1.5 milligrams and men need 1.3 to 1.7 milligrams of vitamin B_6 daily, depending on their age.

Food Sources

Vitamin B_6 is found in a wide variety of foods, including ready-to-eat cereals, meat, fish, poultry, many vegetables and fruits, nuts, peanut butter, and other legumes (see **Figure 10.20**). Because of the widespread availability of vitamin B_6, Americans on average easily meet their daily needs.

Too Much or Too Little

Because vitamin B_6 is stored in the body, excess intake can be toxic. To protect against potential nerve damage, a tolerable upper limit of 100 milligrams per day has been set for adults over the age of 18.

It is extremely difficult to consume a dangerous level of vitamin B_6 from food alone. However, taking vitamin B_6 in supplement form can be harmful. Over the years, vitamin B_6 has been touted to aid a variety of ailments, including carpal tunnel syndrome and premenstrual syndrome (PMS), and individuals may take a supplement to try to relieve these conditions. However, research studies have failed to show any significant clinical benefit in taking vitamin B_6 supplements for either of these syndromes.

Taking large amounts of vitamin B_6 through supplements may be associated with a variety of ill effects, including nerve damage. Individuals taking as little as 200 milligrams and as much as 6,000 milligrams of vitamin B_6 daily for two months experienced difficulty walking and tingling sensations in their legs and feet. These symptoms

TABLE TIPS

Boost Vitamin B_6

- Have a stuffed baked potato with steamed broccoli and grilled chicken for lunch.
- Grab a banana for a midmorning snack.
- Add cooked barley to soup.
- Snack on prunes.
- Add kidney beans to chili or salad.

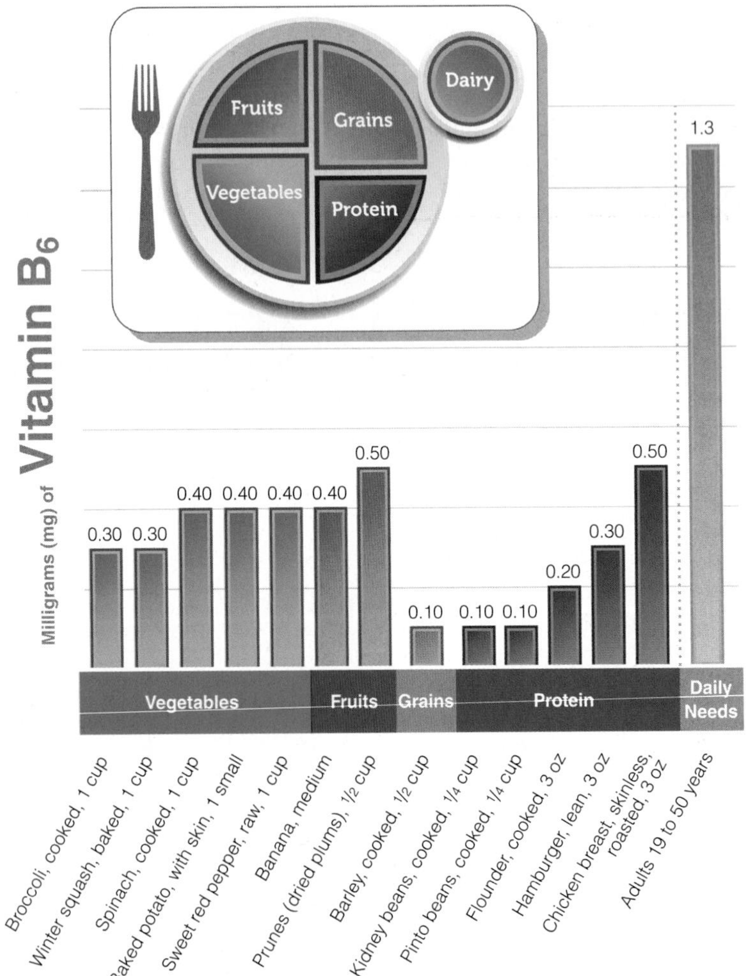

▲ **FIGURE 10.20 Food Sources of Vitamin B_6**

subside once supplement consumption stops.[26]

The telltale signs of a vitamin B_6 deficiency are a sore tongue, inflammation of the skin, depression, confusion, and **microcytic hypochromic anemia**. This type of anemia results in small (microcytic) red blood cells that look pale (hypochromic) in comparison with healthy red blood cells.

Those who consume too much alcohol are more likely to fall short of their vitamin B_6 needs. Not only does alcohol deplete the body of vitamin B_6, but those suffering from alcoholism are likely to have an unbalanced, unvaried diet.

microcytic hypochromic anemia A form of anemia in which red blood cells are small and pale in color due to lack of hemoglobin synthesis due to vitamin B_6 deficiency.

Exploring Folate

What Is Folate?

The naturally occurring form of folate is found in many foods, while the synthetic form, **folic acid**, is added to foods and found in supplements. (Actually, a very small amount of folic acid can occur naturally in foods. But, for practical purposes, in this book folic acid refers to the synthetic variety.) Compared to folate, folic acid is a simpler molecule. It is also easier to absorb than the natural form (more bioavailable), but once absorbed, both forms perform equally well. The synthetic form is more stable.[27]

There are three parts to the molecular structure of folate (**Figure 10.21**): *pteridine* (pronounced ter-e-deen), *para-aminobenzoic acid* or PABA, and at least one glutamate. Most folate found in foods is in **polyglutamate** form, which means it has at least three glutamate molecules.

Before folate can be absorbed, all but one of the glutamates must be removed from the side chain to form **monoglutamate** (one glutamate) during digestion (**Figure 10.22**). Once inside the intestinal cell, four hydrogen atoms (tetra) and a methyl group (CH_3) are added to the monoglutamate, creating **5-methyltetrahydrofolate (5-methyl THF)**. This is the form of folate that is transported through the circulation to the liver. A small amount of folate is stored in the liver, but the majority is excreted in the urine. For folate to be active in the body, the methyl group from 5-methyl THF must be removed to form active tetrahydrofolate (THF), as shown in Figure 10.21.

Folate-rich foods can lose folate when exposed to heat and light, making raw foods more abundant in folate than cooked foods. The bioavailability of folate can vary, and some foods, including beans, legumes, and cabbage, contain inhibitors of the enzymes that remove the glutamates during digestion. This reduces the absorption of folate.[28]

a Folate found in foods is composed of pteridine, PABA, and a glutamate molecule.

Pteridine

PABA

Glutamate

b Folate accepts four hydrogen atoms to become tetrahydrofolate (THF), the active coenzyme form of folate.

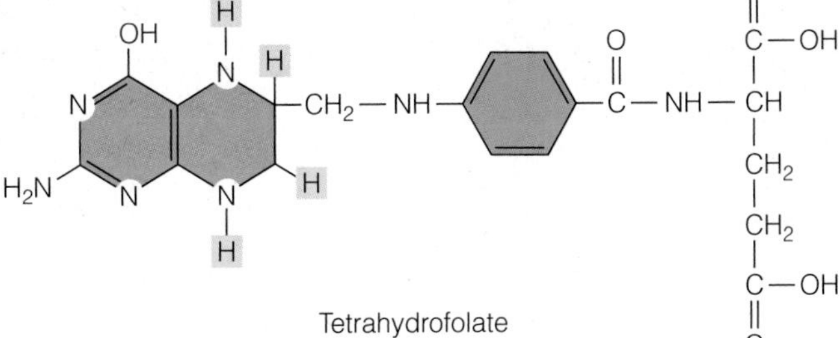

▲ **FIGURE 10.21 The Structures of Folate and Its Coenzyme Form**

Functions of Folate

The role of folate in the body is to transfer single-carbon compounds, such as

folic acid The form of folate often used in vitamin supplements and fortification of foods.

polyglutamate A form of folate that naturally occurs in foods.

monoglutamate The form of folate absorbed through the cells of the small intestine.

5-methyltetrahydrofolate (5-methyl THF) The most active form of folate.

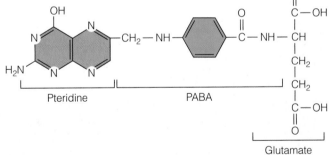

continued

a methyl group (CH_3), to other compounds. This function is necessary to form new compounds.

Amino Acid Synthesis

The transfer of single-carbon compounds is essential for the synthesis of several nonessential amino acids, such as converting homocysteine to methionine in DNA metabolism. To convert homocysteine to methionine, the first step of a two-step process in DNA synthesis, 5-methyl folate is required. If the synthesis of DNA is disrupted, the body's ability to create and maintain new cells is impaired. For this reason, folate plays many important roles, from preventing birth defects to fighting cancer and heart disease. Folate also helps the body use amino acids and is needed to help red blood cells divide and increase in adequate numbers.

Neural Tube Development

Folate plays an extremely important role during pregnancy, particularly in the first few weeks after conception, often before the mother knows she is pregnant. Fetal growth and development is characterized by rapid cell division, and a folate deficiency during pregnancy can result in **neural tube defects**. The neural tube forms the baby's spine, brain, and skull. If the neural tube doesn't develop properly, two common birth defects, **anencephaly** and **spina bifida**, can occur. In anencephaly, the brain doesn't completely form, so the baby can't function and dies soon after birth. In spina bifida (**Figure 10.23**), the baby's spinal cord and backbone aren't properly developed, causing learning and physical disabilities, such as the inability to walk.[29] Increased folic acid consumption by the mother reduces the risk of these birth defects by 50 to 70 percent if begun at least a month prior to conception and continued during the early part of pregnancy.[30]

Research studies to date suggest that synthetic folic acid has a stronger protective effect than food folate. Since 1998, the FDA has mandated that folic acid be added to all enriched grains and

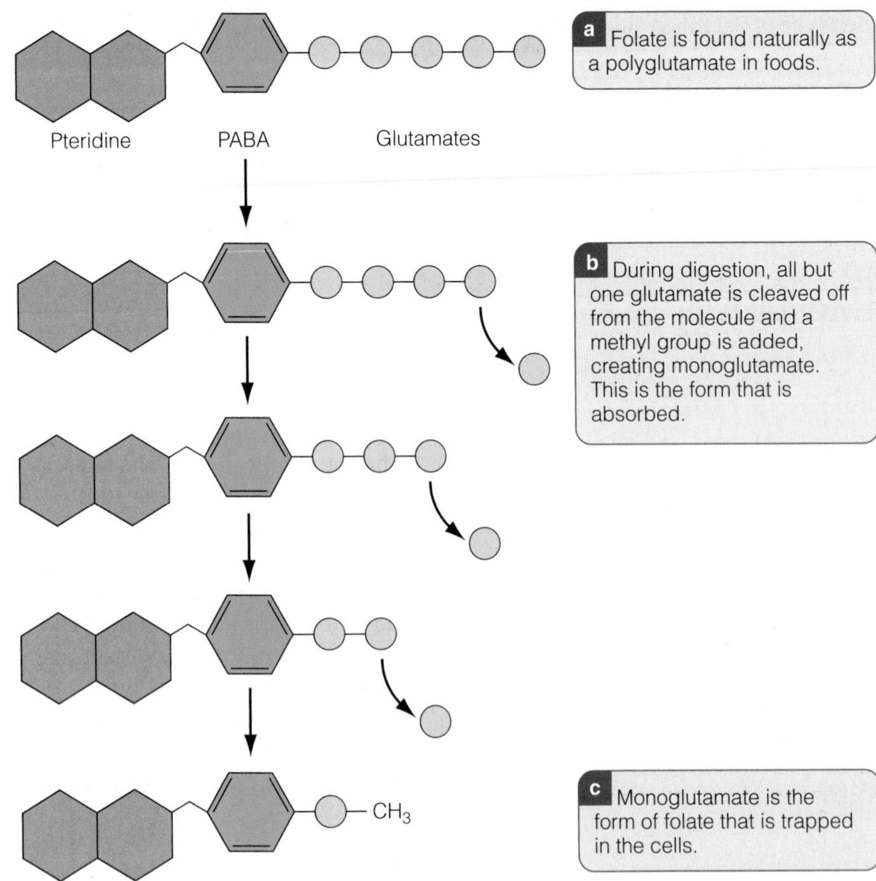

Pteridine
PABA
Glutamates
a Folate is found naturally as a polyglutamate in foods.
b During digestion, all but one glutamate is cleaved off from the molecule and a methyl group is added, creating monoglutamate. This is the form that is absorbed.
CH_3
c Monoglutamate is the form of folate that is trapped in the cells.

▲ **FIGURE 10.22 The Digestion of Folate**

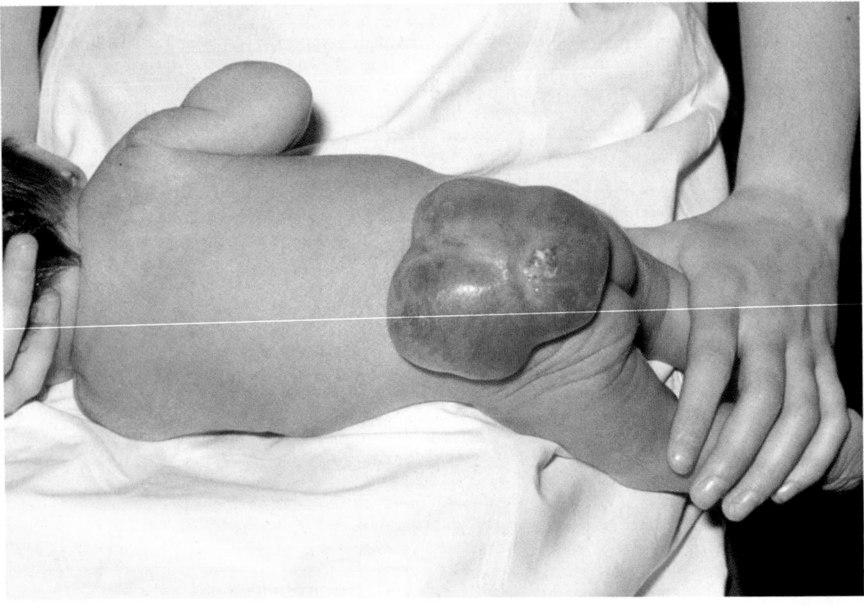

▲ **FIGURE 10.23 An Infant with Spina Bifida**

neural tube defects Any major birth defect of the central nervous system, including the brain, caused by failure of the neural tube to properly close during fetal development.

anencephaly A neural tube defect that results in the absence of major parts of the brain and spinal cord.

spina bifida A serious birth defect in which the spinal cord is malformed and lacks the protective membrane coat.

dietary folate equivalents (DFE) A measurement used to express the amount of folate in a food or supplement.

cereal products. This enrichment program has reduced the incidence of neural tube defects by over 25 percent.[31]

Folate and Cancer

Inadequate amounts of folate in the body can disrupt the cell's DNA and prevent repair, potentially triggering the development of cancer.[32] In particular, folate has been shown to help reduce the risk of colon cancer. Studies show that men and women taking a multivitamin supplement or otherwise consuming their recommended amounts of folate have a lower risk of developing colon cancer. Other studies report an association between diets low in folate and an increased risk of breast and pancreatic cancers.

Daily Needs

Synthetic folic acid is absorbed 1.7 times more efficiently than folate that is found naturally in foods.[33] Because of this, folate needs are measured in **dietary folate equivalents (DFE)**. Most adults should consume 400 micrograms DFE of folate daily.

The Nutrition Facts panel on food labels doesn't make a distinction between folate and dietary folate equivalents. The Calculation Corner describes how to convert folic acid measurements on food labels to DFE.

Women who are planning to become pregnant should consume 400 micrograms of folic acid daily from fortified foods or supplements, along with a diet high in naturally occurring folate. Women with a family history of neural tube defects should, under the guidance of their physicians, take even larger amounts.[34] Because 50 percent of pregnancies in the United States are unplanned, any woman who may become pregnant is advised to follow these same recommendations.

Food Sources

Because folic acid is required by law to be added to enriched cereals and grains, pastas, breads, rice, and flours can be rich sources of the vitamin. The best natural food sources of folate are dark green leafy vegetables such as spinach, broccoli, and asparagus. (This is easy to remember if you know that the term folate is derived from the Latin name *folium,* or foliage). In addition, legumes (dried peas and beans), seeds, and liver are all good sources of this vitamin (see **Figure 10.24**).

Calculation Corner

Dietary Folate Equivalents

The RDA for folate is expressed in dietary folate equivalents (DFE) to account for the differences between the absorption of naturally occurring folate and the synthetic folate used in fortified foods and supplements. Folate found naturally in foods is only half as bioavailable as folate found in supplements or fortified foods. To adjust for this difference in bioavailability, one DFE is equal to 1 microgram (μg) of naturally occurring folate or 0.6 μg of folic acid. To convert the micrograms of folic acid found on a food label to DFE, multiply the amount listed on the label by the constant 1.7.

Example: A ready-to-eat cereal label shows that a serving contains 25 percent of the Daily Value for folate. The Daily Value uses 400 μg as the standard value. To find the folate in micrograms in a serving of cereal, multiply 400 μg $\times$ 0.25 = 100 μg of folate.

Next, multiply 100 μg of folate $\times$ 1.7 to determine the dietary folate equivalents:

Answer: 100 μg $\times$ 1.7 = 170 μg DFE

Remember, the RDA for folate is 400 μg DFE.

continued

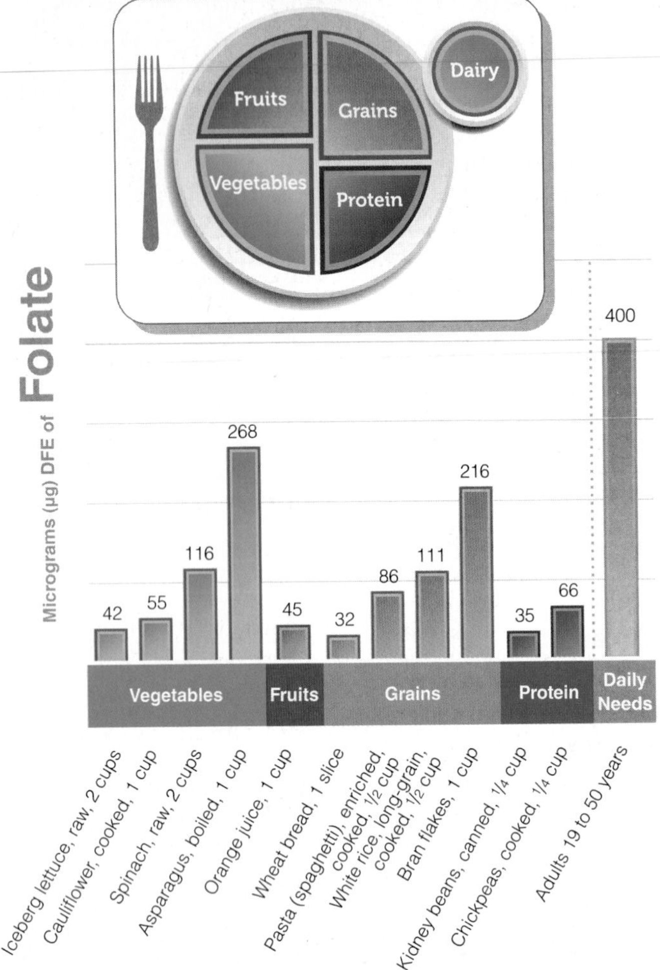

▲ **FIGURE 10.24 Food Sources of Folate**

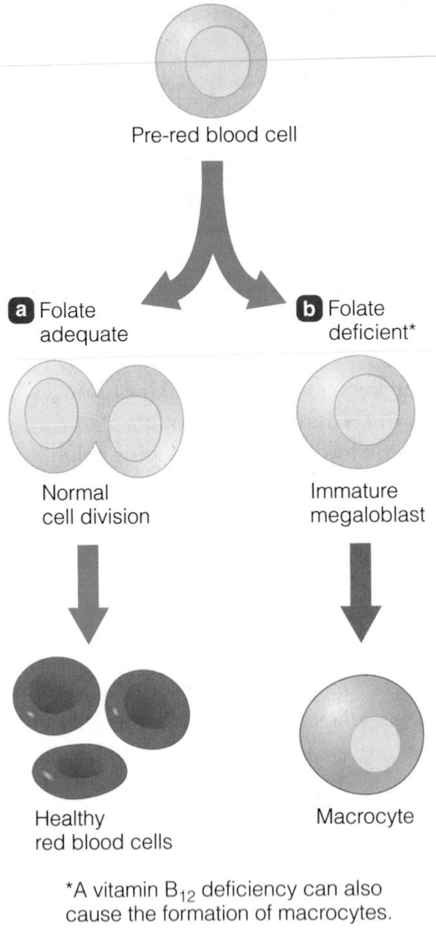

Pre-red blood cell

a Folate adequate

b Folate deficient*

Normal cell division

Immature megaloblast

Healthy red blood cells

Macrocyte

*A vitamin B_{12} deficiency can also cause the formation of macrocytes.

▲ **FIGURE 10.25 Altered Red Blood Cells with Folate Deficiency**
Folate is required for normal cell division. If the diet is deficient in folate, macrocytes are formed.

Too Much or Too Little

There is no danger in consuming excessive amounts of naturally occurring folate in foods. However, consuming too much folic acid, either through supplements or fortified foods, can be harmful for individuals who are deficient in vitamin B_{12}.

A vitamin B_{12} deficiency can cause anemia and, more dangerous, crippling and irreversible nerve damage. Too much folate in the diet masks the symptoms of B_{12} deficiency anemia. Though the folate can correct anemia, the nerve damage due to the vitamin B_{12} deficiency persists. This delays a proper diagnosis and corrective therapy with vitamin B_{12}. By the time the person is given the vitamin B_{12}, irreversible nerve damage may have occurred.[35]

A folate deficiency results in abnormally large and immature red blood cells known as **megaloblasts** (*megalo* = large). These cells develop into abnormally large red blood cells called **macrocytes**, which have a diminished oxygen-carrying capacity. Eventually, **macrocytic anemia** causes a person to feel tired, weak, and irritable and to experience shortness of breath. Because folate needs vitamin B_{12} to produce healthy red blood cells, a deficiency of either vitamin can lead to macrocytic anemia (**Figure 10.25**).

An upper level of 1,000 micrograms has been set for folic acid from enriched and fortified foods and supplements (not naturally occurring folate in foods) to safeguard those who may be unknowingly deficient in vitamin B_{12}. Over-the-counter prenatal vitamins can contain as much as 800 micrograms of folic acid.

megaloblasts Large, immature red blood cells.

macrocytes Large cells such as a red blood cell.

macrocytic anemia A form of anemia characterized by large, immature red blood cells.

TABLE TIPS

Fulfill Folate Needs

Have a bowl of fortified cereal in the morning.

Add chickpeas to a tossed green salad at lunch.

Add layers of fresh spinach leaves to your sandwich.

Have a handful of enriched crackers as a late-afternoon snack.

Exploring Vitamin B_{12}

What Is Vitamin B_{12}?

The family of compounds referred to as vitamin B_{12} is also called **cobalamin** because it contains the metal cobalt. In **Figure 10.26**, two forms of vitamin B_{12} are illustrated: cyanocobalamin, the form of vitamin B_{12} found in foods, and methylcobalamin, the active form of vitamin B_{12}. Both forms contain cobalt (highlighted in orange in Figure 10.26), but cyanocobalamin also contains a cyanide, illustrated as CN.[36] Methylcobalamin is similar in structure, except the cyanide is replaced with a methyl group.

In the stomach, vitamin B_{12} is released from food by the action of pepsin and hydrochloric acid during digestion, and then attaches to a transport protein secreted from the salivary glands called **R protein**, which carries vitamin B_{12} into the small intestine. Another type of protein called **intrinsic factor (IF)** is secreted from the parietal cells in the stomach (**Figure 10.27**) and travels in the chyme into the intestine. Pancreatic proteases hydrolyze the vitamin B_{12}–R protein complex, releasing vitamin B_{12} to bind with intrinsic factor. This newly formed complex travels to the ileum, where a specific receptor site recognizes the intrinsic factor and absorbs the vitamin B_{12}–IF complex by endocytosis into the cell. Inside the intestinal cell, IF is degraded, releasing B_{12} to bind to another protein carrier called **transcobalamin** for transport throughout the blood.

Vitamin B_{12} is stored mostly in the liver and excreted through the bile and the urine. Unlike the other

cobalamin The vitamin involved in energy metabolism and the conversion of homocysteine to methionine; another name for vitamin B_{12}.

R protein The protein secreted from the salivary glands that binds vitamin B_{12} in the stomach and transports it into the small intestine during digestion.

intrinsic factor (IF) A glycoprotein secreted by the stomach that helps in the absorption of vitamin B_{12}.

transcobalamin The protein that transports vitamin B_{12} in the blood.

a **Cyanocobalamin** is the form of vitamin B_{12} found in foods. It contains an atom of cobalt and an atom of cyanide (shaded blue).

b **Methylcobalamin** is the active form of vitamin B_{12}. The cyanide has been replaced with a methyl group (shaded blue).

▲ **FIGURE 10.26 The Structure of Vitamin B_{12}**

continued

water-soluble vitamins, the body stores plenty of vitamin B_{12}, so symptoms of a deficiency can take years to develop.[37]

Functions of Vitamin B_{12}

Vitamin B_{12} functions as two coenzymes, **methylcobalamin** and **deoxyadenosylcobalamin**. Methylcobalamin is used to convert homocysteine to the amino acid methionine, which in turn provides the methyl group used in DNA and RNA synthesis. Without adequate vitamin B_{12}, homocysteine levels accumulate, which is considered a risk factor for cardiovascular disease, and DNA synthesis is slowed, which results in macrocytic anemia.

The vitamin B_{12} coenzyme deoxyadenosylcobalamin helps form succinyl CoA during the TCA cycle. Thus, vitamin B_{12} plays an essential role in using nutrients for energy.

The relationship between vitamin B_{12} and folate is an important one to emphasize: Vitamin B_{12} activates folate and in turn becomes active itself. Recall in the discussion on folate that for folate to be converted from the inactive 5-methyl THF, vitamin B_{12} must first cleave off the methyl group. The vitamin B_{12}-plus-methyl group is now active itself (**Figure 10.28**).

Like folate, vitamin B_{12} plays an important role in keeping cells, particularly red blood cells, healthy. It is also one of the three B vitamins that collectively could be heart healthy (see the Examining the Evidence feature on page 370). The maintenance of the **myelin sheath** that protects nerve fibers also depends on vitamin B_{12}, and vitamin B_{12} stimulates osteoblast activity for healthy bone.[38]

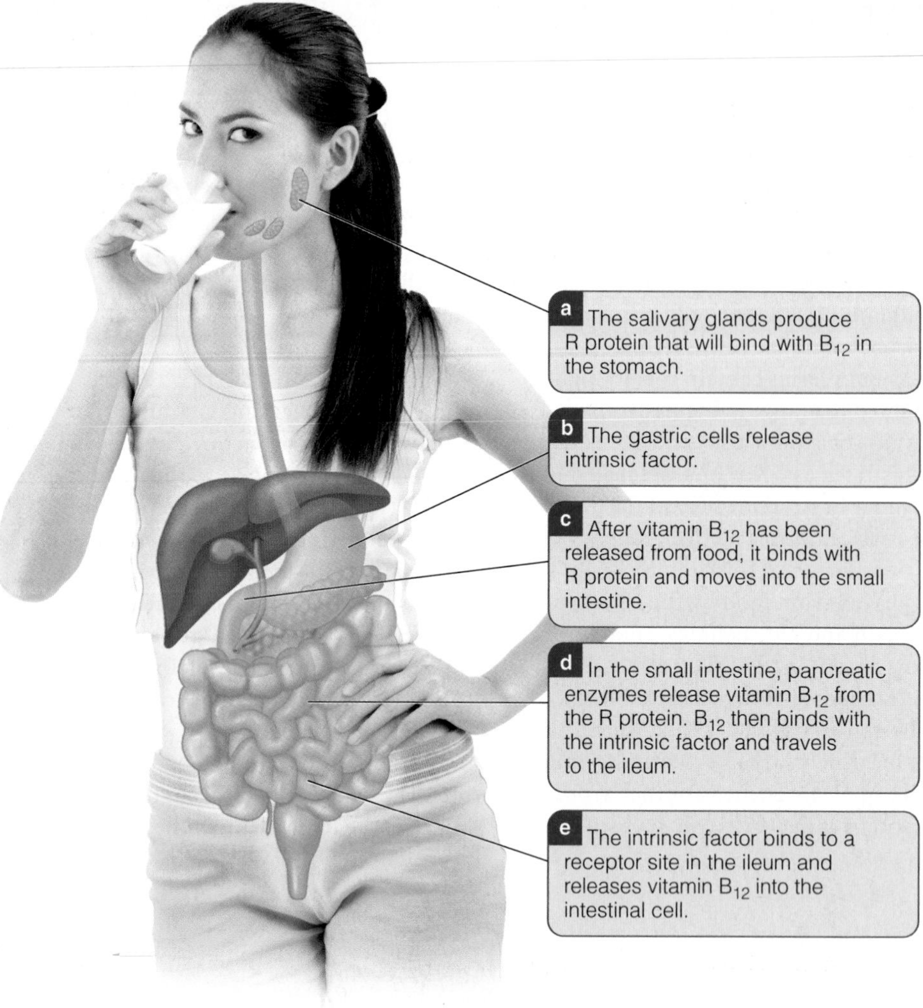

a The salivary glands produce R protein that will bind with B_{12} in the stomach.
b The gastric cells release intrinsic factor.
c After vitamin B_{12} has been released from food, it binds with R protein and moves into the small intestine.
d In the small intestine, pancreatic enzymes release vitamin B_{12} from the R protein. B_{12} then binds with the intrinsic factor and travels to the ileum.
e The intrinsic factor binds to a receptor site in the ileum and releases vitamin B_{12} into the intestinal cell.

▲ **FIGURE 10.27 The Absorption of Vitamin B_{12}**

Daily Needs

Adults need 2.4 micrograms of vitamin B_{12} daily. Nonvegetarian American adults, on average, consume over 4 micrograms daily through animal foods.

The body's ability to absorb naturally occurring vitamin B_{12} diminishes with age. This decline appears to be due to a reduction in hydrochloric acid in the stomach, which is needed to activate pepsinogen to pepsin. Pepsin is the enzyme that hydrolyzes the bonds that bind the B_{12} to the proteins in food. If the bonds aren't broken, the vitamin can't be released. This condition, called **atrophic gastritis**, is experienced by up to 30 percent of individuals over the age of 50.

With less acid present, the bacteria normally found in the intestines aren't properly destroyed and so tend to overgrow. These abundant bacteria feed on vitamin B_{12}, diminishing the amount of the vitamin that may be available for absorption. Luckily, the synthetic form of vitamin B_{12} used in fortified foods and supplements isn't bound to a protein and doesn't depend on hydrochloric acid secretions to be absorbed. Because the synthetic

methylcobalamin The coenzyme form of vitamin B_{12} that converts homocysteine to methionine.

deoxyadenosylcobalamin The coenzyme form of vitamin B_{12} that converts intermediate substances in the TCA cycle.

myelin sheath The tissue that surrounds and protects the nerves.

atrophic gastritis Chronic inflammation of the stomach.

pernicious anemia A form of anemia caused by a lack of intrinsic factor needed for absorption of vitamin B_{12}, forming large, immature red blood cells.

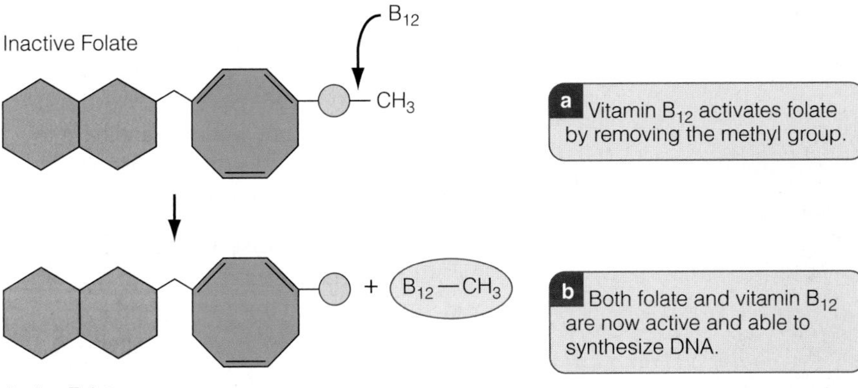

▲ **FIGURE 10.28 Vitamin B_{12} Activates Folate**

variety is a more reliable source, individuals over the age of 50 should meet their vitamin B_{12} needs primarily from fortified foods or a supplement.

Other factors contributing to malabsorption include a lack of sufficient intrinsic factor, gastric bypass surgery, or a lack of pancreatic enzymes needed to hydrolyze the B_{12}–R protein complex in the small intestine. Individuals who are unable to absorb vitamin B_{12} due to a deficiency in intrinsic factor often develop **pernicious anemia** (*perni-cious* = harmful). Not surprisingly, the pernicious anemia associated with the inability to absorb vitamin B_{12} occurs in about 2 percent of individuals over the age of 60.[39] Individuals with this condition must be given regular injections of vitamin B_{12}, which delivers the vitamin directly into the muscle and blood, bypassing the intestine.

Food Sources

Naturally occurring vitamin B_{12} is found only in foods from animal sources, such as meat, fish, poultry, and dairy products. A varied diet that includes the minimum recommended servings of these food groups will easily meet daily needs (see **Figure 10.29**).

Using a microwave to cook vitamin B_{12}–rich foods may reduce the amount of the vitamin by as much as 30 to 40 percent.[40] It appears that vitamin B_{12} is the one exception when it comes to using a microwave to retain vitamins.

Synthetic vitamin B_{12} is found in fortified soy milk and some ready-to-eat cereals, which are ideal sources for older adults and strict vegetarians who avoid all animal foods.

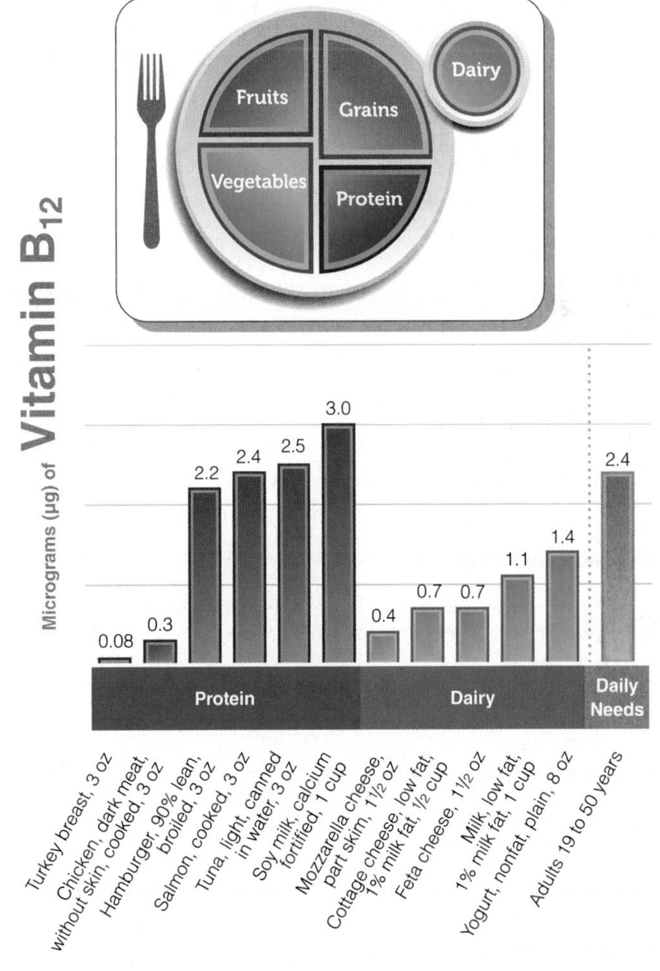

▲ **FIGURE 10.29 Food Sources of Vitamin B_{12}**

continued

Nutrition in Practice: Leland

Leland Yang has been a vegan for about 20 years. He feels that he has done a terrific job of sticking to his diet even though he travels monthly to corporate meetings across the United States. Lately, he has noticed a tingling in his legs. In fact, sometimes it feels as though his toes "fall asleep" as they became numb. Leland went to his doctor and described his symptoms. A tad perplexed, the doctor ordered blood tests for Leland and discovered that he is deficient in vitamin B_{12}, which is essential for a healthy nervous system. The doctor suggested that he speak with a dietitian.

Leland's Stats:

- □ Age: 52
- □ Height: 5 feet 10 inches
- □ Weight: 150 pounds

Critical Thinking Questions

1. Why would a deficiency in vitamin B_{12} cause Leland's symptoms?
2. Based on his food record, why do you think Leland is deficient in this specific vitamin?
3. What foods would Leland have to add to his diet to meet his daily need of this vitamin?

Dietitian's Observation and Plan for Leland:

- □ Discussed the need to add a synthetic source of vitamin B_{12} to his diet in order to meet his daily needs as a vegan and because he is over the age of 50.
- □ Advised adding a serving of a whole-grain cereal that is fortified with 100% of the daily value for vitamin B_{12}, either at breakfast or as a snack along with his afternoon trail mix snack.
- □ Suggested taking a vitamin B_{12} supplement.

Two weeks later, Leland returned for a follow-up visit with the dietitian. Because of his travel schedule he is having difficulty obtaining a vitamin B_{12}–fortified cereal at hotels when he travels. The dietitian recommended that he take a vitamin B_{12} supplement to make sure that he would be able to meet his vitamin B_{12} need daily, as well as continue with a healthy, well-balanced diet.

Leland's Food Log:

Food/Beverage	Time Consumed	Hunger Rating*	Location
Whole-wheat bread with peanut butter, orange juice	6 am	5	Kitchen
Handful of almonds		3	
Hummus in a whole-wheat pita stuffed with lettuce and tomato	12:30 pm	5	Lunch room
Banana, soy yogurt, green tea			
Trail mix	3 pm	3	Office
Tofu stir-fry on brown rice, dinner roll with margarine, lemon sorbet, water	6:30 pm	4	In dining hall

*Hunger Rating (1–5): 1 = not hungry; 5 = super hungry

Too Much or Too Little

At present, there are no known risks of consuming too much vitamin B_{12} from foods, fortified foods, or supplements, and no upper level has been set. This may be due to reduced absorption of the vitamin at higher intakes. For healthy individuals, there is no known benefit from taking B_{12} supplements if the diet provides adequate amounts of the vitamin.

Because vitamin B_{12} and folate work closely together to make healthy red blood cells, a vitamin B_{12} deficiency can cause macrocytic anemia, the same type of anemia caused by a folate deficiency. In macrocytic anemia due to a vitamin B_{12} deficiency, there is enough folate available for red blood cells to divide but the folate is trapped as 5-methyl THF and can't be utilized properly. In fact, in most cases of macrocytic anemia the true cause is more likely a B_{12} deficiency than a folate deficiency.

Because pernicious anemia is a type of macrocytic anemia, its initial symptoms are the same as those seen in a folate deficiency: fatigue and shortness of breath. Because vitamin B_{12} is needed to protect nerve cells, including those in the brain and spine, one long-term consequence of pernicious anemia is nerve damage, which may be indicated by tingling and numbness in the arms and legs and problems walking. If diagnosed early enough, these symptoms can be reversed with treatments of vitamin B_{12}.

TABLE TIPS

Bolster Vitamin B_{12}

- Enjoy heart-healthy fish at least twice a week.
- Sprinkle steamed vegetables with reduced-fat shredded cheese.
- Drink milk or fortified soy milk.
- Try a cottage cheese-and-fruit snack in the afternoon.
- Enjoy a grilled chicken breast on a bun for lunch.

Exploring Vitamin C

What Is Vitamin C?

Vitamin C, also known as **ascorbic acid**, is probably more widely known to the public than any other nutrient. Whereas almost all mammals, can synthesize vitamin C, humans lack the necessary enzyme to convert glucose to vitamin C in the cells, and must rely on food to meet their daily needs.[41] The structure of vitamin C is similar to glucose in that it's a six-carbon molecule (**Figure 10.30**).

Vitamin C is absorbed in the small intestine mostly by active transport. Higher intakes are absorbed by simple diffusion in the stomach and small intestine. As the intake of vitamin C increases, the amount absorbed decreases. In fact, the intestine absorbs less than 50 percent of vitamin C when the intake is one gram or greater. Additionally, more vitamin C is excreted through the kidneys when intake is high.

Once absorbed into the portal vein, vitamin C is transported to the liver. The cells take up vitamin C assisted by glucose transport proteins. Vitamin C is not stored.

Ascorbic acid

[Structure: HO–C=C(–HO)–CH(–O–)–C(=O); side chain HO—CH—CH_2OH]

▲ **FIGURE 10.30 The Structure of Ascorbic Acid**
The hydrogen atoms of ascorbic acid are easily donated to free radicals.

Functions of Vitamin C

Vitamin C plays a complex role in most of the biological systems in the body. For instance, vitamin C is necessary for the synthesis of collagen and tyrosine. It also participates in neurotransmitter synthesis, as an antioxidant, and in the absorption of iron. It differs from the B vitamins in that it does not act as a coenzyme; however, vitamin C does assist with some reactions.

Vitamin C and Collagen Synthesis

Vitamin C participates in a number of hydroxylation reactions (adding OH groups). In particular, vitamin C enables hydroxylation reactions to make the fibrous protein **collagen**, the most abundant protein in the body. Collagen formation happens in several steps. First the three strands of collagen that contain the amino acids glycine and proline are assembled and twisted together to form a ropelike structure called *procollagen*. The rope is formed when hydroxyl groups are substituted for a hydrogen ion in the proline, forming hydroxyproline. Next, hydroxyl groups are substituted for the hydrogen ion in each lysine, forming hydroxylysine. The hydroxylation reaction is catalyzed by an iron-containing enzyme that must first be activated (**Figure 10.31**). Recall that enzymes must be restored or activated after they

ascorbic acid The active form of vitamin C.

collagen A protein found in connective tissue, including bones, teeth, skin, cartilage, and tendons.

continued

participate in a chemical reaction. In this case, the iron portion of the enzyme that hydroxylates collagen must be reduced to reactivate the enzyme. Vitamin C acts as the reducing agent, changing the iron (Fe^{+3}) in the enzyme back to its reduced form (Fe^{+2}). By donating the hydrogen to the inactive enzyme, vitamin C is destroyed and can't be reused in the next reaction. Because collagen gives strength to connective tissue and acts as a glue that keeps cells together (including in the skin, bones, teeth, cartilage, tendons, and blood vessels),[42] a vitamin C–deficient diet would affect the entire body.

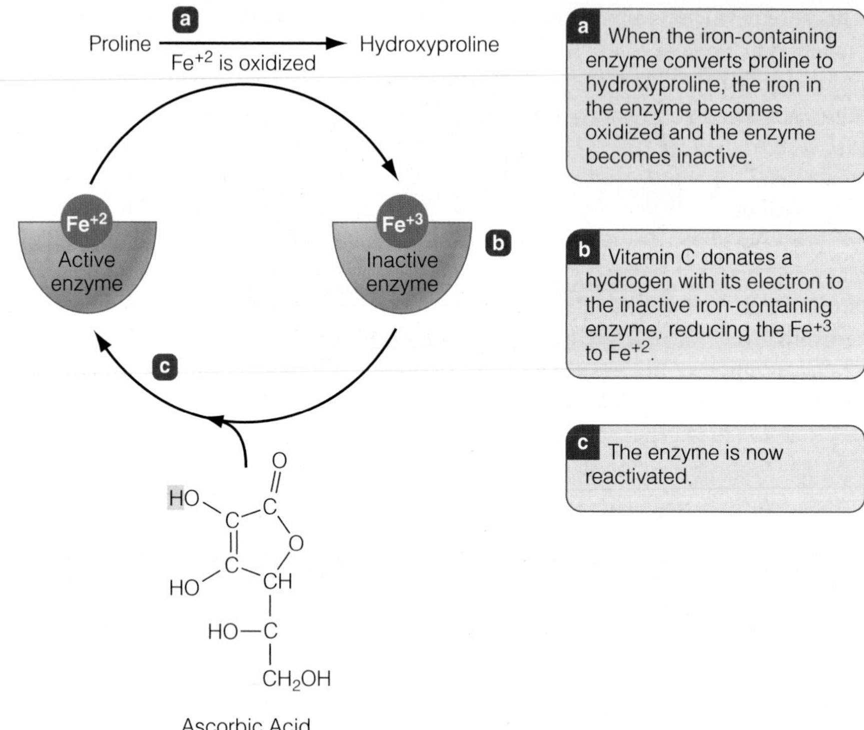

a
Proline
Hydroxyproline
Fe^{+2} is oxidized
Fe^{+2}
Active enzyme
Fe^{+3}
Inactive enzyme
b
c
HO
HO
HO—C
CH_2OH
Ascorbic Acid
a When the iron-containing enzyme converts proline to hydroxyproline, the iron in the enzyme becomes oxidized and the enzyme becomes inactive.
b Vitamin C donates a hydrogen with its electron to the inactive iron-containing enzyme, reducing the Fe^{+3} to Fe^{+2}.
c The enzyme is now reactivated.

▲ **FIGURE 10.31 The Role of Vitamin C in Collagen Formation**

Vitamin C as an Antioxidant

Like beta-carotene and vitamin E, vitamin C acts as an antioxidant that may help reduce the risk of chronic diseases such as heart disease and cancer. As you learned in Chapter 9, a free radical contains an unpaired electron. If the molecule is *oxidized* it has a positive charge when electrons are removed; a *reduced* molecule has a negative charge from an abundance of electrons. Vitamin C can donate or accept electrons to balance a free radical or change the charge in oxidation-reduction reactions.[43]

Vitamin C and Iron Absorption

Vitamin C enhances the absorption from plant foods of nonheme iron (iron not found in red blood cells). When individuals consume vitamin C with nonheme iron, it acts as a reducing agent, which improves the absorption of that form of iron.[44] This is also true for other minerals such as copper and chromium.

Vitamin C and the Immune System

Vitamin C helps maintain a healthy immune system by enabling the body to make white blood cells, like the ones shown in the photo. These blood cells fight infections, and this immune-boosting role has fostered the belief that high doses of vitamin C can cure the common cold. Examining the Evidence: Does Vitamin C Prevent the Common Cold? on page 396 takes a look at this theory.

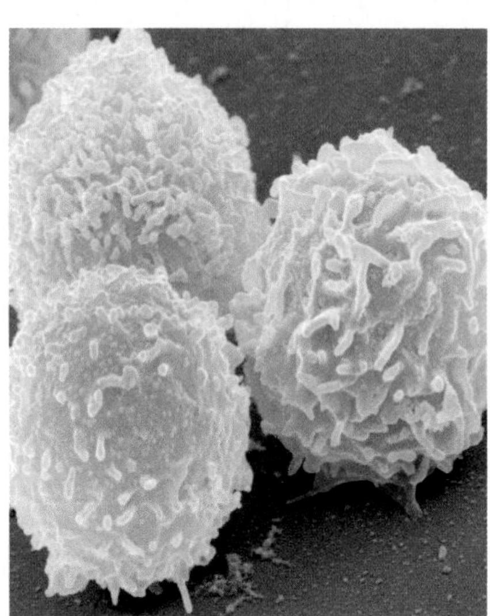

White blood cells

Vitamin C and Stress

Vitamin C may reduce the body's response to stress. When the body responds to a stressful situation, the hypothalamus begins a cascade of reactions, starting with stimulating the pituitary gland to secrete stress hormones. In turn, the pituitary hormones direct the adrenal glands to synthesize and secrete cortisol into the blood. The cells of the adrenal glands contain high levels of vitamin C, which are released along with cortisol.[45] It's this relationship between the stress response and vitamin C that prompts researchers to study the possibility of a link between vitamin C and stress in humans despite a lack of direct evidence for such a link.

Other Functions of Vitamin C

Vitamin C also participates in other important reactions in the body. Vitamin C donates an electron in the conversion of tryptophan and tyrosine to two neurotransmitters, serotonin and norepinephrine. Vitamin C is also essential in the synthesis of thyroxine (the hormone produced by the thyroid gland), converts cholesterol to bile, and helps break down histamine, the component behind the inflammation seen in many allergic reactions.[46]

Daily Needs

Women need to consume 75 milligrams of vitamin C daily, and men need to consume 90 milligrams daily to meet their needs. Smoking accelerates the

hemochromatosis A blood disorder characterized by the retention of an excessive amount of iron.

scurvy A disease caused by a deficiency of vitamin C and characterized by bleeding gums and a skin rash.

breakdown and elimination of vitamin C from the body, so all individuals who smoke need to consume an additional 35 milligrams of vitamin C every day to make up for these losses.[47]

Food Sources

Americans meet about 90 percent of their vitamin C needs by consuming fruits and vegetables, with orange and grapefruit juice being the most popular sources in the diet. One serving of either juice will just about meet an adult's daily needs. Tomatoes, peppers, potatoes, broccoli, oranges, and cantaloupe are also excellent sources (see **Figure 10.32**). Meats, dairy, grains, and legumes are considered poor sources of the vitamin.

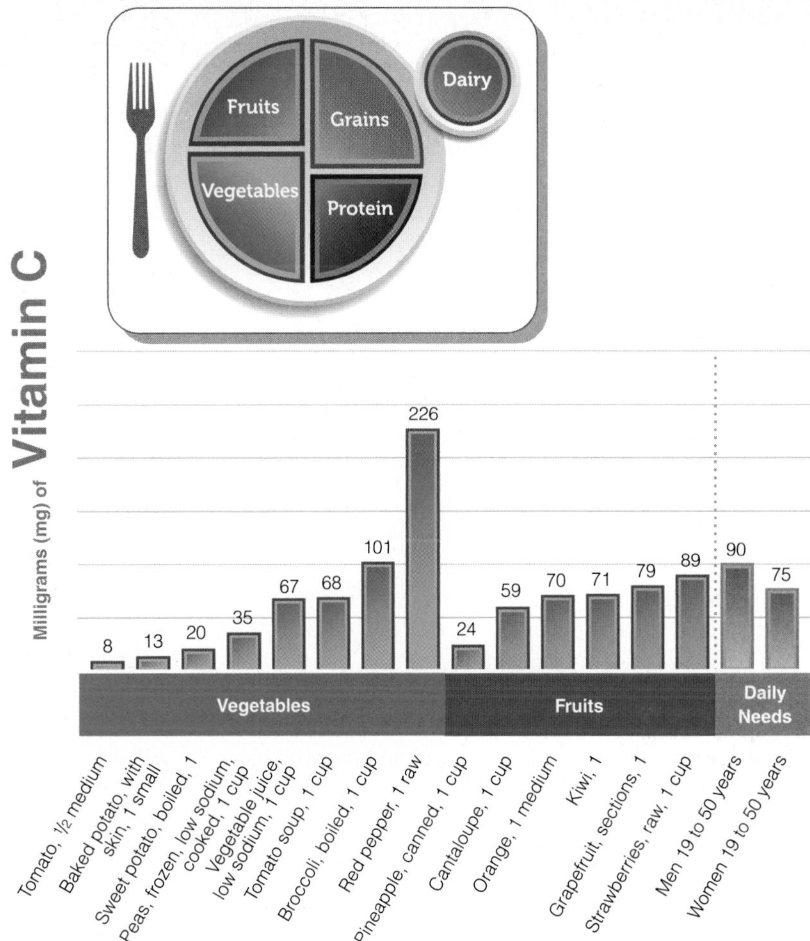

▲ **FIGURE 10.32 Foods Sources of Vitamin C**

Too Much or Too Little

Although excessive amounts of vitamin C aren't known to be toxic, consuming over 3,000 milligrams daily through the use of supplements has been shown to cause nausea, stomach cramps, and diarrhea. To avoid the intestinal discomfort that excessive amounts of the vitamin can cause, the upper level for vitamin C for adults is set at 2,000 milligrams. Too much vitamin C can also lead to the formation of kidney stones in individuals with a history of kidney disease or gout. In addition, vitamin C supplementation can result in false positives or false negatives in some medical tests.

Because vitamin C helps to absorb the form of iron found in plant foods, those with a rare disorder called **hemochromatosis,** which causes the body to store too much iron, should avoid excessive amounts of vitamin C. Iron toxicity is extremely dangerous and can damage many organs, including the liver and heart.

For centuries, **scurvy**, the disease of a vitamin C deficiency, was the affliction of sailors on long voyages. After many weeks at sea, sailors would run out of vitamin C–rich produce and then develop the telltale symptoms: swollen and bleeding gums (**Figure 10.33**), a rough rash on the skin, coiled or curly arm hairs, and wounds that wouldn't heal.

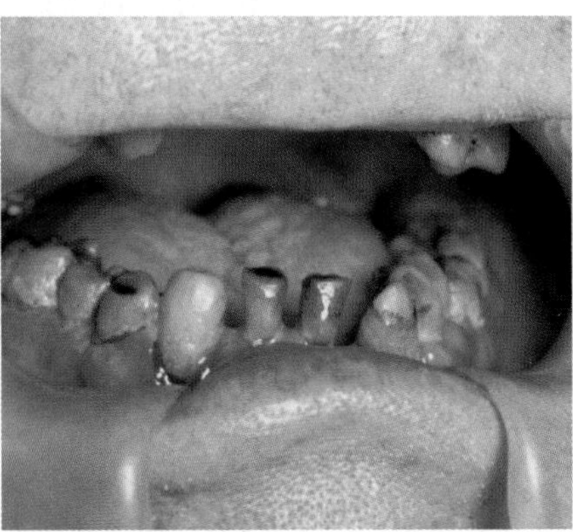

▲ **FIGURE 10.33 Gum Disease Can Result from Scurvy**

Scurvy rarely occurs today. Scurvy that is seen in the twenty-first century is associated with poverty, especially in young children.[48] Adult males are more susceptible than adult females, possibly due to nutritional ignorance, lower intakes of fruits and vegetables, poor access to groceries, reclusiveness, or alcoholism.[49] Scurvy can be prevented by as little as 10 milligrams of vitamin C per day, or the amount found in a slice of a fresh orange.

TABLE TIPS

Juicy Ways to Get Vitamin C

- Have a least one citrus fruit (such as an orange or grapefruit) daily.
- Put sliced tomatoes on sandwiches.
- Enjoy a fruit cup for dessert.
- Drink low-sodium vegetable juice for an afternoon refresher.
- Add strawberries to low-fat frozen yogurt.

EXAMINING THE EVIDENCE

Does Vitamin C Prevent the Common Cold?

More than 200 viruses can cause the common cold, and colds are the leading cause of doctor visits in the United States. Americans will suffer a billion colds this year alone.[1] Symptoms often last for up to two weeks, and students miss over 22 million school days every year battling the common cold.[2]

The Truth about Catching a Cold

Contrary to popular belief, you can't catch a cold from being outside without a coat or hat on a cold day. Rather, the only way to catch a cold is to come into contact with a cold virus. Contact can be direct, such as by hugging or shaking hands with someone who is carrying the virus, or indirect, such as by touching an object like a keyboard or telephone contaminated with a cold virus. After you touch a contaminated object, the next time you touch your nose or rub your eyes, you transfer these germs from your hands into your body. You can also catch a cold virus by inhaling virus-carrying droplets from a cough or sneeze of someone with the cold.

The increased frequency of colds during the fall and winter is likely due to people spending more time indoors in the close quarters of classrooms, dorm rooms, and the workplace, which makes the sharing of germs easier. The low humidity of the winter air can also cause mucous membranes to be drier and more permeable to the invasion of these viruses. In addition, the most common cold viruses survive longer when the weather is colder and the humidity is low.

Vitamin C and the Common Cold

In the 1970s, a scientist named Linus Pauling theorized that consuming at least 1,000 milligrams of vitamin C daily would prevent the common cold.[3] Since that initial theory was published, the reported research has been mixed. Several studies have suggested that vitamin C in doses larger than 1 gram per day may help reduce the duration and severity of a cold in some individuals once the cold is contracted. This may be due to the antihistamine effect that vitamin C can have in the body when taken at large doses.[4] However, a meta-analysis of the relationship of vitamin C to preventing the common cold found no benefit in either preventing the common cold or reducing the duration or severity.[5] In special circumstances, such as ultramarathon athletes using vitamin C prior to extreme exercise[6] or in people with other illnesses,[7] vitamin C supplementation may have some benefit. In addition, people who appear to benefit from vitamin C supplements are those who have a low intake of dietary vitamin C or are under severe acute stress. The published research study designs differ and therefore caution should be used in promoting the use of vitamin C to prevent the common cold until conclusive research has been produced.

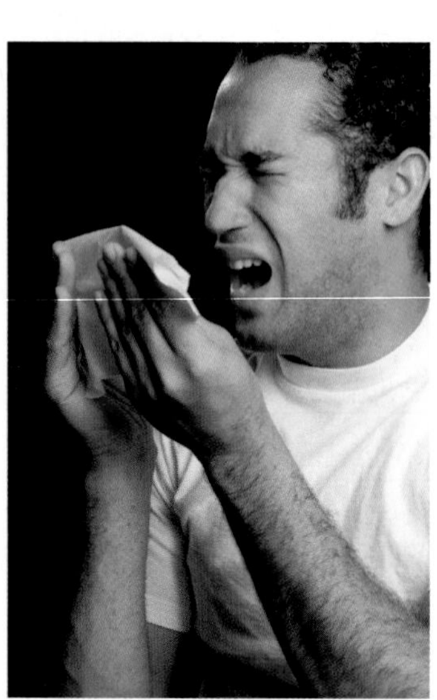

Other Cold Remedies: The Jury Is Still Out

Recently, other dietary substances, such as the herb echinacea and the mineral zinc, have emerged as popular treatment strategies for the common cold. Echinacea was used centuries ago by some Native American populations to treat coughs and sore throats. Recent studies have shown that the herb comes up short in preventing or affecting the duration or severity of a cold and may contribute to side effects such as a rash and intestinal discomfort.[8] The results of a recent review of over 300 studies using echinacea were inconclusive, and more research needs to be done.[9]

Studies of zinc have also had mixed results. In a randomized, double-blind, placebo-controlled study, individuals who received 13 milligrams of zinc gluconate in lozenge form had fewer days of cold symptoms than the placebo group.[10] Similar results have been reported with zinc acetate.[11] Caution should be exercised, however, because chronic intake of zinc supplements can actually suppress the immune system.[12] Zinc and its role in the immune system will be covered in the chapter on trace minerals.

What You Can Do

One of the best ways to reduce your chances of catching a cold is to wash your hands frequently with soap and water. This will lower the likelihood of transmitting germs from hands to mouth, nose, or eyes. One study found that children who washed their hands four times a day had over 20 percent fewer sick days from school than those who washed their hands less frequently. When soap and water aren't available, gel sanitizers or disposable alcohol-containing hand wipes can be an effective alternative.[13] Covering the mouth and nose during coughing or sneezing and then immediately washing the hands will help prevent the spread of germs to other people and objects.

Finally, the Centers for Disease Control recommends the following steps to take if you do get a cold:

- Get plenty of rest.
- Drink plenty of fluids. (Chicken soup and juices are considered fluids.)
- Gargle with warm salt water or use throat lozenges for a sore throat.

- Dab petroleum jelly on a raw nose to relieve irritation.
- Take aspirin* or acetaminophen (Tylenol) for headache or fever.

References

1. National Institute of Allergy and Infectious Diseases, National Institutes of Health. 2007. *The Common Cold.* Available at www.niaid.nih.gov/topics/commoncold/pages/default.aspx. Accessed November 2012.
2. Centers for Disease Control. 2004. *Stopping Germs at Home, Work and School.* Available at www.cdc.gov. Accessed May 2012.
3. Pauling, L. 1971. The Significance of the Evidence about Ascorbic Acid and the Common Cold. *Proceedings from the National Academy of Science* 68:2678–2681.
4. Hemila, H. and Z. S. Herman. 1995. Vitamin C and the Common Cold: A Retrospective Analysis of Chalmer's Review. *Journal of the American College of Nutrition* 14:116–123.
5. Douglas, R. M. and H. Hemila. 2005. Vitamin C for Preventing and Treating the Common Cold. *PLoS Medicine* 2:e168.
6. Peters, E. M., J. M. Goetzsche, B. Grobbelaar, and T. D. Noakes. 1993. Vitamin C Supplementation Reduces the Incidence of Postrace Symptoms of Upper-Respiratory-Tract Infection in Ultramarathon Runners. *American Journal of Clinical Nutrition* 57:170–174.
7. Sasazuki, S., S. Sasaki, Y. Tsubono, S. Okubo, M. Hayashi, and S. Tsugane. 2006. Effect of Vitamin C on Common Cold: Randomized Controlled Trial. *European Journal of Clinical Nutrition* 60:9–17.
8. Turner, R. B., R. Bauer, K. Woelkart, T. C. Haulsey, and D. Gangemie. 2005. An Evaluation of *Echinacea angustifolia* in Experimental Rhinovirus Infections. *New England Journal of Medicine* 353:341–348.
9. Caruso, T. J. and J. M. Gwaltney. 2005. Treatment of the Common Cold with Echinacea: A Structured Review. *Clinical Infectious Diseases* 40:807–810.
10. Mossad, S. B., M. L. Macknin, S. V. Mendendorp, and P. Mason. 1996. Zinc Gluconate Lozenges for Treating the Common Cold. A Randomized Double-Blind, Placebo-Controlled Study. *Annals of Internal Medicine* 125:81–88.
11. Prasad, A. S., F. W. Beck, B. Bao, D. Snell, and J. T. Fitzgerald. 2008. Duration and Severity of Symptoms and Levels of Plasma Interleukin-1 Receptor Antagonist, Soluble Tumor Necrosis Factor Receptor, and Adhesion Molecules in Patients with Common Cold Treated with Zinc Acetate. *The Journal of Infectious Disease* 197:795–802.
12. Institute of Medicine. 2006. *Dietary Reference Intakes: The Essential Guide to Nutrient Requirements.* Washington, DC: The National Academies Press.
13. National Institute of Allergy and Infectious Diseases, National Institutes of Health. 2007. *The Common Cold.*

*The American Academy of Pediatrics recommends that children and teenagers avoid consuming aspirin or medicine containing aspirin when they have a viral illness, as it can lead to a rare but serious illness called Reye's syndrome. This syndrome can cause brain damage or death.

Self-Assessment

Are You Getting Enough Water-Soluble Vitamins in Your Diet?

Take this brief self-assessment to see if your diet is rich in the water-soluble B vitamins and vitamin C.

1. Do you consume at least ½ cup of enriched rice or pasta daily?

   Yes ☐ **No** ☐
2. Do you eat at least 1 cup of a fortified, ready-to-eat cereal or hot cereal every day?

   Yes ☐ **No** ☐
3. Do you have at least one slice of bread, a bagel, or a muffin daily?

   Yes ☐ **No** ☐
4. Do you enjoy a citrus fruit or fruit juice, such as an orange, a grapefruit, or orange juice every day?

   Yes ☐ **No** ☐
5. Do you have at least one cup of vegetables throughout your day?

   Yes ☐ **No** ☐

Answer

If you answered "yes" to all of these questions, you are eating a healthy diet with abundant vitamin B and vitamin C! Rice, pasta, cereals, and bread and bread products are all excellent sources of B vitamins, and citrus fruits are rich in vitamin C. In fact, all vegetables can contribute to meeting daily vitamin C needs. If you answered "no" more often than "yes," read on to learn how to add more Bs and C to your diet.

What Are Other Vitamin-Like Compounds?

Some compounds may not be classified as a vitamin by strict definition but are still essential to overall health. These compounds are often synthesized in adequate amounts in the body but may become essential under certain circumstances, such as during illness or chronic disease. The vitamin-like compounds include choline, carnitine, lipoic acid, and inositol.

Choline Helps Protect the Liver

Choline is a conditionally essential nutrient that the body needs for healthy cells and nerves. Choline is a nitrogen-containing compound that is often grouped with the family of B vitamins but by strict definition it is not classified as a vitamin. Although the body can synthesize choline from the amino acid methionine, it isn't able to synthesize enough of it to meet the body's needs.[50]

Choline serves a number of uses in the body. It is part of the phospholipid that makes up cell membranes; it functions in liver metabolism; it is a precursor for the neurotransmitter acetylcholine and thus participates in nerve transmission; it assists in the transport of lipids as part of the VLDL; and it plays a key role in fetal development.[51, 52]

To be safe, the current recommendation of 425 milligrams for women and 550 milligrams for men is based on the amount needed to guard against liver damage. Choline is so widely available in foods, especially milk, liver, eggs, and peanuts, that it is unlikely intake would ever fall short. However, too much choline from supplements can cause sweating and vomiting as well as hypotension (*hypo* = low), or low blood pressure. Too much choline can also cause a person to emit an unpleasant fishy odor as the body tries to get rid of the excess. The tolerable upper level (UL) of 3,500 milligrams for choline has been set to prevent blood pressure from dropping too low.

Carnitine, Lipoic Acid, and Inositol

Carnitine, lipoic acid, and inositol, all vitamin-like substances, are needed for overall health and important body functions. Unlike choline, however, they are not essential nutrients because the body can synthesize them in adequate amounts without the need to consume them in foods. Deficiency symptoms are not known to occur in humans.

Carnitine (*carnus* = flesh), which is synthesized from the amino acids lysine and methionine, is needed to properly utilize fat. It is abundant in foods from animal sources, such as meat and dairy products. Although there is no research to support the claim, carnitine supplements are sometimes advertised to promote weight loss and help athletes improve their performance.[53]

Similar to many B vitamins, **lipoic acid** helps cells generate energy. In fact, when it was discovered, it was initially thought to be a vitamin.[54] The body synthesizes adequate amounts of lipoic acid from short-chain fatty acids and it is found in a variety of plant and animal foods. In addition to its role in energy metabolism, lipoic acid is also being studied for its potential role as an antioxidant that could help reduce the risk of certain chronic diseases, such as diabetes mellitus and cataracts.[55]

Lastly, **inositol** is needed to keep cell membranes healthy. As with the other important vitamin-like substances, healthy individuals can synthesize enough inositol from glucose or consume sufficient amounts in plant sources to meet their needs, so supplements are not necessary. Inositol can be ingested from plant sources, or synthesized from glucose.

choline A vitamin-like substance that is a precursor for the neurotransmitter acetylcholine, which is essential for healthy nerves.

carnitine A vitamin-like substance used to transport fatty acids across the mitochondrial membrane to properly utilize fat.

lipoic acid A vitamin-like substance used in energy production; it may also act as an antioxidant.

inositol A water-soluble compound synthesized in the body that maintains healthy cell membranes.

THE TAKE-HOME MESSAGE Choline is an essential nutrient that is needed for the integrity of cell membranes, nerve transmission, lipid transport, and liver health. Carnitine, lipoic acid, and inositol are needed for important body functions and overall health, but are not essential nutrients.

Putting It All Together

Table 10.1 summarizes the nine water-soluble vitamins, their active coenzyme forms, major functions in the body, major food sources, and the toxicity and deficiency symptoms and diseases that result when the vitamins are consumed in inadequate amounts. How do water-soluble vitamins fit with the other essential nutrients you have learned about thus far? Water-soluble vitamins mainly function as catalysts for reactions involved in energy metabolism (**Figure 10.34**). Six of the

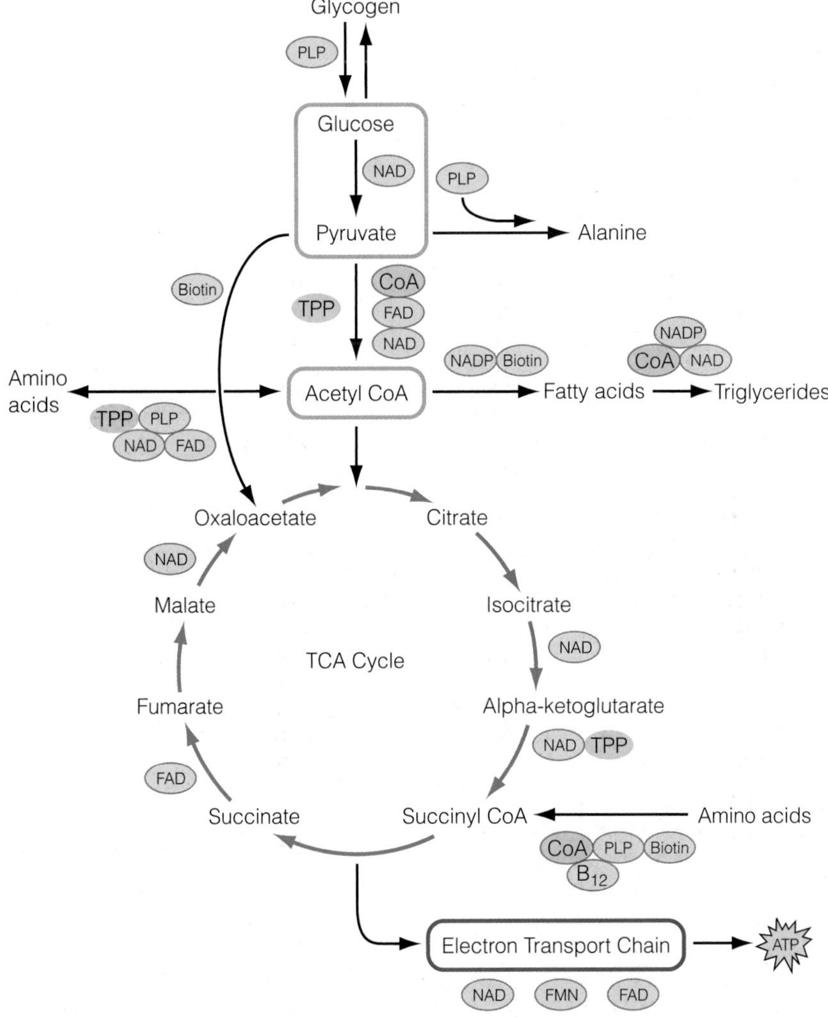

▲ **FIGURE 10.34 B Vitamins Function in Energy Metabolism**
Legend: TPP = thiamin pyrophosphate
NAD = nicotinamide adenine dinucleotide (niacin)
NADP = nicotinamide adenine dinucleotide (niacin)
FAD = flavin adenine dinucleotide (riboflavin)
FMN = flavin mononucleotide (riboflavin)
PLP = pyridoxal phosphate (B_6)
CoA = coenzyme A (pantothenic acid)
Biotin = biotin
B_{12} = vitamin B_{12}
THF = tetrahydrofolate (folate)

TABLE 10.1 Food Sources, Functions, Symptoms of Deficiencies and Toxicity, and the Recommended Intakes of the Water-Soluble Vitamins

Vitamin	RDA/AI (19 years+)	Major Functions	Deficiency/ Disease Symptoms	Active Form	Toxicity Symptoms/UL	Major Food Sources
Thiamin (B_1)	Males: 1.2 mg/day Females: 1.1 mg/day	Coenzyme in: ■ Carbohydrate metabolism ■ BCAA metabolism	Beriberi; characterized by nerve damage	TPP	None known	Pork, enriched and fortified foods, whole grains
Riboflavin (B_2)	Males: 1.3 mg/day Females: 1.1 mg/day	Coenzyme in oxidation-reduction reactions ■ Carbohydrate metabolism ■ Fat metabolism	Ariboflavinosis; characterized by inflammation of the mouth and tongue	FAD, FMN	None known	Milk, enriched and fortified foods, whole grains
Niacin (B_3)	Males: 16 mg/day Females: 14 mg/day	Coenzyme in oxidation-reduction reactions ■ Carbohydrate metabolism ■ Fat metabolism ■ DNA	Pellagra; characterized by dermatitis, diarrhea, and dementia	NAD, NADP	Flushing, blurred vision, liver dysfunction, and glucose intolerance UL: 35 mg/day	Lean meats, enriched and fortified grains and cereals
Pantothenic Acid	Males and females: 5 mg/day	Part of coenzyme A used in energy metabolism	Symptoms include fatigue, nausea, vomiting, numbness, muscle cramps, and difficulty walking	Coenzyme A	None known	Widespread in foods, including whole-grain cereals, nuts and legumes, peanut butter, meat, milk, and eggs
Biotin	Males and females: 30 μg/day	■ Energy metabolism ■ Fat synthesis ■ Glycogenesis ■ Amino acid metabolism	Symptoms include dermatitis, conjunctivitis, depression, and hair loss	Biotin	None known	Peanuts, yeast, egg yolks, grains, liver and other organ meats, and fish; also produced by bacteria in the GI tract
Vitamin B_6	Males and females: 1.3 mg/day	■ Protein metabolism ■ Homocysteine metabolism ■ Glycogenolysis	Microcytic hypochromic anemia; characterized by fatigue, paleness of skin, shortness of breath, dizziness, and lack of appetite	PLP	Sore tongue, dermatitis, depression, confusion, irritability, headaches, and nerve damage UL: 100 mg/day	Fortified cereals, meat, fish, poultry, many vegetables and fruits, nuts, peanut butter, and other legumes
Folate	Males and females: 400 μg/day Pregnant women and women of childbearing age who may become pregnant: 600 μg/day	■ DNA and red blood cell formation ■ Homocysteine metabolism	Macrocytic anemia; characterized by fatigue, headache, glossitis, and GI tract symptoms such as diarrhea	THF	Masks vitamin B_{12} deficiency UL: 1,000 μg/day	Dark green leafy vegetables, enriched pasta, rice, breads and cereals, legumes

TABLE 10.1 Food Sources, Functions, Symptoms of Deficiencies and Toxicity, and the Recommended Intakes of the Water-Soluble Vitamins *continued*

Vitamin	RDA/AI (19 years+)	Major Functions	Deficiency/ Disease Symptoms	Active Form	Toxicity Symptoms/UL	Major Food Sources
Vitamin B_{12}	Males and females: 2.4 μg/day	■ Synthesis of new cells, especially red blood cells ■ Health of nerve tissue ■ Activates folate ■ Catabolism of amino acids and fatty acids in energy metabolism	Pernicious anemia; characterized by fatigue, glossitis, and nerve damage as indicated by tingling and numbness in the hands and feet	Methylcobalamin	None known	Animal products, including lean meats, fish, poultry, eggs, and cheese, and fortified foods
Vitamin C	Males: 90 mg/day Females: 75 mg/day	■ Collagen formation ■ Antioxidant ■ Iron absorption ■ Immune system	Scurvy; characterized by bleeding gums, pinpoint hemorrhages, joint pain	Ascorbic acid	Nausea, diarrhea, fatigue, insomnia UL: 2,000 mg/day	Citrus fruit, tomatoes, peppers, potatoes, broccoli, and cantaloupe

B vitamins—thiamin, riboflavin, niacin, pantothenic acid, biotin, and vitamin B_6—participate as coenzymes that activate enzymes in glycogenolysis, glycolysis, the TCA cycle, and the electron transport chain. Without these coenzymes, we would be unable to utilize the carbohydrates, fats, and proteins we consume daily. Vitamin B_6, folate, and vitamin B_{12} assist in protein metabolism and DNA/RNA synthesis. Together with fat-soluble vitamins and healthy fats, vitamin C has antioxidant properties that help protect the body from disease. The DRIs for each of these vitamins, whether an AI or RDA, must be met consistently to avoid deficiencies. If one or more of these vitamins is missing in the diet, normal body functions are impossible, and susceptibility to disease increases. A diet rich in whole grains, fruits, and vegetables and adequate in lean dairy foods and meats, poultry, fish, plant proteins, and healthy oils can help provide these essential nutrients in the proper balance for good health.

Visual Chapter Summary

1 Water-Soluble Vitamins Act as Coenzymes in Metabolic Processes

The B-complex vitamins thiamin, riboflavin, niacin, vitamin B_6, pantothenic acid, and biotin function as coenzymes in the conversion of carbohydrates, proteins, and fats to energy; in fatty acid, cholesterol, and protein synthesis; and in glycogenolysis and gluconeogenesis. Vitamins catalyze enzyme activity when they bind to the active site of an enzyme.

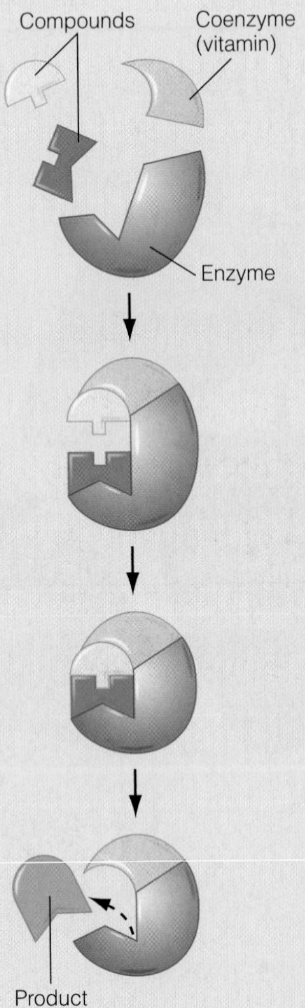

2 Thiamin (B_1)

Thiamin in the active form of TPP functions in glycolysis and the TCA cycle. Thiamin also participates in nerve transmission. The best sources of thiamin are lean pork, enriched and whole-grain foods, ready-to-eat cereals, pasta, rice, and nuts. The thiamin RDA for adults is 1.1 mg for women and 1.2 mg for men. There are no known toxicity problems for thiamin. A deficiency of thiamin can result in beriberi. Chronic alcohol abuse can lead to an advanced form of thiamin deficiency called Wernicke-Korsakoff syndrome.

Phosphate groups

Thiamin pyrophosphate

3 Riboflavin (B_2)

The riboflavin coenzymes FMN and FAD transfer hydrogen ions in oxidation-reduction reactions during energy metabolism. Riboflavin also enhances the function of niacin, folate, vitamin B_{12}, and iron metabolism in hemoglobin formation. Milk and yogurt are the most popular sources of riboflavin. The riboflavin RDA for adults is 1.1 mg for women and 1.3 mg for men. Excess amounts are excreted in urine and there are no known toxicity symptoms. A deficiency in riboflavin results in ariboflavinosis.

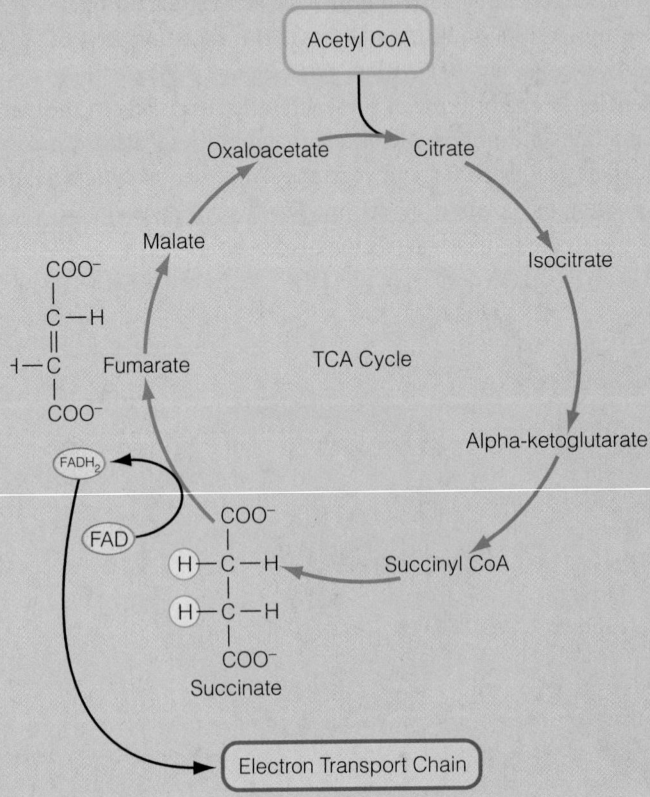

4 Niacin (B_3)

Niacin is also called nicotinic acid and nicotinamide. The active coenzyme forms, nicotinamide adenine dinucleotide (NAD^+) and nicotinamide adenine dinucleotide phosphate ($NADP^+$), are involved in the catabolism of carbohydrates, fats, and proteins in energy metabolism. Niacin in larger doses has been shown to lower blood cholesterol levels; when used for this purpose it is considered a drug. Niacin is found in a variety of foods, including meat, fish, poultry, fortified cereals, and enriched breads.

Niacin is also formed from leftover tryptophan. The niacin RDA for adults is 14 mg NE for women and 16 mg NE for men. There is no danger of consuming too much niacin although overconsumption of niacin supplements can cause flushing. A deficiency of niacin results in pellagra.

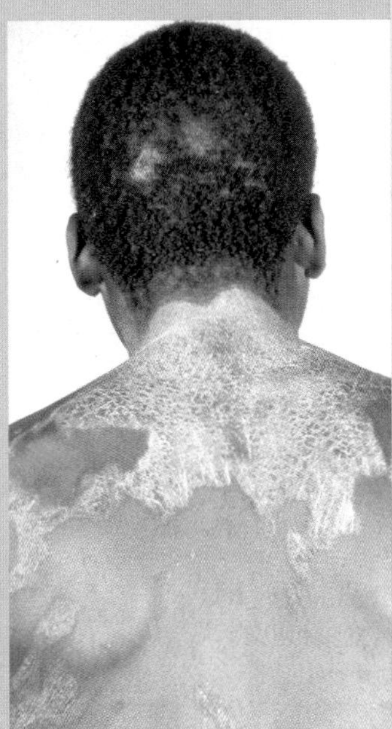

5 Pantothenic Acid

Pantothenic acid, as part of coenzyme A, helps synthesize acetyl CoA, the gateway molecule in energy metabolism. Coenzyme A is needed for fat synthesis and fat catabolism, the conversion of pyruvate to acetyl CoA, and converting some amino acids to substrates in the TCA cycle. Pantothenic acid is found in a wide variety of foods, including whole-grain cereals, nuts and legumes, peanut butter, milk, meat, and eggs. The adequate intake (AI) for pantothenic acid is 5 mg for both adult females and males. There are no known adverse affects from consuming too much pantothenic acid from foods and deficiencies are rare.

Pantothenic acid

Is a component of

Adenine

Coenzyme A

6 Biotin

Biotin is a coenzyme for enzymes that add carbon dioxide to compounds during energy metabolism. Biotin is necessary for the synthesis of fatty acids, and it participates in gluconeogenesis and in the metabolism of amino acids. Biotin may play a role in DNA replication and transcription. Food sources of biotin include peanuts, yeast, egg yolks, grains, fish, and liver. The adequate intake (AI) of biotin has been set at 30 micrograms for both adult females and males. There is little evidence that biotin is toxic. Deficiencies of biotin are rare except when large amounts of raw eggs are consumed. Avidin in raw egg whites binds biotin in the intestinal tract and prevents it from being absorbed. Some humans have a rare genetic disorder in which they lack the enzyme biotinidase, which breaks biotin away from protein in foods during digestion.

7 Vitamin B_6

Vitamn $B_{6,}$ also known as pyridoxine, pyridoxal, and pyridoxamine, acts as a coenzyme for over 100 enzymes. Most of these enzymes are involved in protein metabolism. Vitamin B_6 is also a key player in glycogenolysis and red blood cell synthesis, and interacts with other nutrients including riboflavin, niacin, and zinc. The active form of vitamin B_6 is pyridoxal phosphate (PLP). Vitamin B_6 is found in meat, fish, poultry, legumes, bananas, and fortified cereals. Adult women need 1.3 to 1.5 milligrams and men need 1.3 to 1.7 milligrams of B_6 depending on their age. The vitamin is stored in the body and consuming toxic amounts from supplements may cause neurological damage. A deficiency of vitamin B_6 can result in microcytic hypochromic anemia, depression, and inflammation of the skin. Drinking too much alcohol can deplete the body of vitamin $B_{6.}$

Glutamate ⟷ (PLP) ⟷ Alanine

Transamination

8 Folate

Folate is naturally found in foods, but is more easily absorbed as the synthetic form, folic acid, found mostly in fortified foods and supplements. The active form of folate is called tetrahydrofolate, or THF. Its role in metabolism is transferring single-carbon compounds, such as a methyl group, to other compounds. This function of folate is critical to cell division. Folate may also prevent some cancers. Folate is found in fortified foods, leafy green vegetables, enriched pasta, rice, breads, and cereals. Adults should consume 400 micrograms DFE of folate daily. Consuming too much folate can obscure a vitamin B_{12} deficiency. A deficiency of folate results in macrocytic anemia. Babies born to mothers who are deficient in folate have a higher risk of neural tube defects such as anencephaly and spina bifida.

Tetrahydrofolate

9 Vitamin B_{12}

Vitamin B_{12} is a family of compounds also referred to as cobalamin. To be absorbed, vitamin B_{12} requires the aid of R protein from the salivary glands and intrinsic factor from the stomach. It is transported through the blood attached to a protein carrier called transcobalamin. Vitamin B_{12} functions as two different coenzymes involved in DNA and RNA synthesis, the conversion of homocysteine to methionine, and in utilizing fats and proteins for energy. Vitamin B_{12} also activates folate by removing the methyl group from folate, which in turn activates vitamin B_{12}. Vitamin B_{12} is found naturally in animal foods and the synthetic form is used in fortified soy milk and some cereals. Adults need 2.4 micrograms daily. There are no known toxicity risks of consuming too much vitamin B_{12}. A deficiency of vitamin B_{12} causes macrocytic anemia. A prolonged vitamin B_{12} deficiency can cause nerve damage.

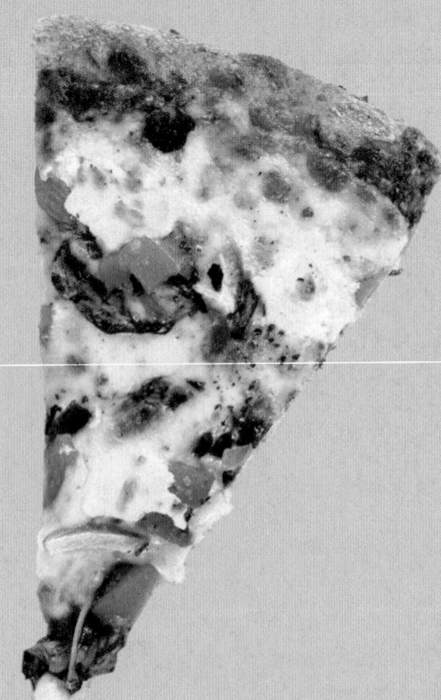

10 Vitamin C

Vitamin C, also known as ascorbic acid, assists in the formation of collagen necessary for healthy bones, teeth, skin, and blood vessels. As an antioxidant, vitamin C reduces free radical damage and supports a healthy immune system. Vitamin C also improves the absorption of nonheme iron. Vitamin C is found in a wide variety of fruits and vegetables, including citrus fruits, tomatoes, potatoes, and broccoli. Adult women should ingest 75 milligrams and adult men need 90 milligrams of vitamin C daily. Excessive amounts, such as from supplements, can cause intestinal discomfort. Vitamin C doesn't prevent the common cold but may reduce the duration and severity of a cold in some people. A deficiency of vitamin C results in scurvy.

Ascorbic acid

11 Other Vitamin-Like Compounds Are Not Essential

Choline is a conditionally essential nutrient that the body needs for healthy cells and nerves. Carnitine, lipoic acid, and inositol are vitamin-like compounds that are used for important body functions and overall health. They are not considered essential because they can be synthesized in sufficient amounts in the body.

Terms to Know

- hemopoiesis
- polyneuritis
- beriberi
- thiamin pyrophosphate (TPP)
- peripheral neuropathy
- flavin adenine dinucleotide (FAD)
- flavin mononucleotide (FMN)
- ariboflavinosis
- glossitis
- stomatitis
- cheilosis
- oxidation reaction
- reduction reaction
- nicotinic acid
- nicotinamide adenine dinucleotide (NAD^+)
- nicotinamide adenine dinucleotide phosphate ($NADP^+$)
- pellagra
- niacin equivalents (NE)
- pantothenic acid
- avidin
- biotinidase
- pyridoxine
- pyridoxal
- pyridoxamine
- pyridoxal phosphate (PLP)
- microcytic hypochromic anemia
- folic acid
- polyglutamate
- monoglutamate
- methyltetrahydrofolate (5-methyl THF)
- neural tube defects
- anencephaly
- spinal bifida
- dietary folate equivalents (DFE)
- megaloblasts
- macrocytes
- macrocytic anemia
- choline
- lipoic acid

MasteringNutrition™

Build your knowledge—and confidence—in the Study Area of MasteringNutrition with a variety of study tools.

Check Your Understanding

1. The primary function of the B-complex vitamins is
   a. as a source of energy.
   b. as a coenzyme.
   c. as an antioxidant.
   d. to synthesize DNA.
2. The coenzyme that functions in the transfer of hydrogen atoms is
   a. pantothenic acid.
   b. vitamin B_6.
   c. riboflavin.
   d. biotin.
3. A deficiency of thiamin can cause
   a. rickets.
   b. beriberi.
   c. scurvy.
   d. osteomalacia.
4. Folic acid can reduce the risk of
   a. acne.
   b. neural tube defects.
   c. night blindness.
   d. pellagra.
5. The vitamin that is part of the structure of acetyl CoA is
   a. biotin.
   b. thiamin.
   c. pantothenic acid.
   d. niacin.
6. The body requires more of this water-soluble vitamin than any other.
   a. vitamin B_6
   b. niacin
   c. riboflavin
   d. vitamin B_{12}
7. The vitamin involved as a coenzyme in more than 100 enzymes, most of which are amino acid reactions, is
   a. riboflavin.
   b. pantothenic acid.
   c. vitamin B_6.
   d. biotin.
8. Vitamin B_{12} is essential for the health and function of
   a. nerve cells.
   b. epithelial cells.
   c. eye tissue.
   d. none of the above.
9. A lack of intrinsic factor is associated with
   a. pernicious anemia.
   b. spina bifida.
   c. neural tube defects.
   d. microcytic hypochromic anemia.
10. Vitamin C functions in the body as
    a. a cofactor in collagen synthesis.
    b. an antioxidant.
    c. a reducing agent.
    d. all of the above.

Answers

1. (b) The primary function of the B-complex vitamins is to activate enzymes involved in a variety of chemical reactions. B-complex vitamins are not a source of energy but do act as coenzymes in energy

metabolism. Unlike vitamin C, the B-complex vitamins are not antioxidants. Even though some of the B-complex vitamins are involved in DNA synthesis, it is not their primary function.

2. (c) Riboflavin, in the form of FAD and FMN, transfers hydrogen atoms during energy metabolism. Pantothenic acid is part of coenzyme A, which forms acetyl CoA; vitamin B_6 is a coenzyme for protein metabolism; and biotin is a coenzyme for carboxylase enzymes.
3. (b) A thiamin deficiency results in beriberi. Rickets and osteomalacia are caused by a lack of vitamin D and scurvy results from a vitamin C deficiency.
4. (b) Folic acid reduces the risk of birth defects such as neural tube defects. Vitamin A can reduce acne and night blindness, while niacin can prevent pellagra.
5. (c) Pantothenic acid is part of coenzyme A, which forms acetyl CoA. Biotin, thiamin, and niacin all function as coenzymes.
6. (b) The dietary requirement for niacin is 16 milligrams per day for males and 14 milligrams for females, compared with 1.3 milligrams of vitamin B_6 for both males and females, 1.3 milligrams or 1.1 milligrams of riboflavin for males or females, respectively, and 2.4 micrograms per day of vitamin B_{12} for both genders.
7. (c) Vitamin B_6 activates more than 100 enzymes involved in protein metabolism. Riboflavin, pantothenic acid, and biotin are all involved in energy metabolism.
8. (a) Vitamin B_{12} is essential for the health and function of nerve cells. Vitamin A is essential for epithelial cells and eye tissue.
9. (a) A lack of intrinsic factor causes the malabsorption of vitamin B_{12}, which results in pernicious anemia. Spina bifida and neural tube defects are the result of a folate deficiency. Microcytic hypochromic anemia is caused by a deficiency of vitamin B_6.
10. (d) Vitamin C functions in the body as a cofactor in collagen synthesis, as an antioxidant, and as a reducing agent.

Answers to Myths and Misconceptions

1. **False.** Some water-soluble vitamins, such as vitamin C and folate, are easily destroyed by heat. But others, including niacin and vitamin B_6, are stable in cooking. However, all water-soluble vitamins leach into water, so drier cooking methods will help retain more of these vitamins.
2. **False.** Biotin and pantothenic acid are both B vitamins involved in energy production, not forms of vitamin C.
3. **False.** Vitamins do not provide energy. However, the B-complex vitamins are essential to energy production in that they are involved in numerous metabolic processes.
4. **False.** Niacin can be made from excess tryptophan, but the amount of niacin synthesized is insufficient to meet the body's needs.
5. **True.** Very large doses of vitamin B_6 (from as low as 500 milligrams) can cause sensory neuropathy, which causes pain, numbness, and tingling in the feet and hands.
6. **True.** Older adults may produce less hydrochloric acid and intrinsic factor than younger adults, which can hinder their ability to absorb adequate amounts of vitamin B_{12}.
7. **True.** Adequate folate intake before and during the early months of pregnancy can lower the risk of neural tube defects, including spina bifida and anencephaly.
8. **False.** A dietary deficiency of pantothenic acid is rare because this B vitamin is widespread throughout the food supply. Excellent sources include chicken, beef, egg yolk, and vegetables such as broccoli, tomatoes, and mushrooms.
9. **True.** The protein avidin, found in egg whites, can bind biotin and prevent it from being absorbed. Cooking the egg denatures the avidin and prevents this problem.
10. **False.** There is no clear evidence that vitamin C supplements prevent the common cold, though they may reduce the severity of cold symptoms in some people in some situations.

Web Resources

- To learn more about vitamin and mineral supplements, visit http://ods.od.nih.gov/Health_Information/Vitamin_and_Mineral_Supplement_Fact_Sheets.aspx
- For tips on how to include more fruits and vegetables in your diet, visit www.cdc.gov/nccdphp/dnpao/index.html
- For more information on cooking with microwave ovens to preserve vitamins, visit www.foodscience.csiro.au/micwave1.htm

References

1. Rosenfeld, L. 1997. Vitamine-Vitamin: The Early Years of Discovery. *Clinical Chemistry* 43:680–685.
2. Institute of Medicine, Food and Nutrition Board. 1998. *Dietary Reference Intakes: Thiamin, Riboflavin, Niacin, Vitamin B_6, Folate, Vitamin B_{12}, Pantothenic Acid, Biotin, and Choline*. Washington, DC: The National Academies Press.
3. National Institute of Neurological Disorders and Stroke (NINDS). 2007. *NINDS Wernicke-Korsakoff Syndrome Information Page*. Available at www.ninds.nih.gov/disorders/wernicke_korsakoff/wernicke-korsakoff.htm. Accessed May 2012.
4. Herreid, E. O., B. Ruskin, G. L. Clark, and T. B. Parks. 1952. Ascorbic Acid and Riboflavin Destruction and Flavor Development in Milk Exposed to the Sun in Amber, Clear, Paper, and Ruby Bottles. *Journal of Dairy Science* 35:772–778.
5. Institute of Medicine, Food and Nutrition Board. 1998. *Dietary Reference Intakes: Thiamin, Riboflavin, Niacin, Vitamin B_6, Folate, Vitamin B_{12}, Pantothenic Acid, Biotin, and Choline*.
6. McCormick, D. B. 1989. Two Interconnected B Vitamins: Riboflavin and Pyridoxine. *Physiology Review* 69:1170–1198.
7. Madigan, S. M., F. Tracy, H. McNulty, J. Eaton-Evans, J. Coulter, H. McCartney, and J. J. Strain. 1998. Riboflavin and Vitamin B_6 Intakes and Status and Biochemical

Response to Riboflavin Supplementation in Free-Living Elderly People. *American Journal of Clinical Nutrition* 68:389–395.
8. Lowik, M. R., H. van den Berg, C. Kistemaker, H. A. Brants, and J. H. Brussaard. 1994. Interrelationships between Riboflavin and Vitamin B_6 among Elderly People. *International Journal of Vitamin Nutrition Research* 64:198–203.
9. Powers, H. J. 1995. Riboflavin-Iron Interactions with Particular Emphasis on the Gastrointestinal Tract. *Proceedings of the Nutrition Society* 54:509–517.
10. Institute of Medicine. 2006. *Dietary Reference Intakes: The Essential Guide to Nutrient Requirements.* Washington, DC: The National Academies Press.
11. Squibb, R. L., J. E. Braham, G. Abboyave, and K. S. Scrimshaw. 1958. A Comparison of the Effect of Raw Corn and Tortillas (Lime-Treated Corn) with Niacin, Tryptophan or Beans on the Growth and Muscle Niacin of Rats. *Journal of Nutrition* 67:351–361.
12. Canner, P. L., K. G. Berge, N. K. Wenger, J. Stamler, L. Friedman, R. J. Prineas, and W. Friedewald. 1986. Fifteen-Year Mortality in Coronary Drug Project Patients: Long-Term Benefit with Niacin. *Journal of the American College of Cardiology* 8:1245–1255.
13. Institute of Medicine, Foods and Nutrition Board. 1998. *Dietary Reference Intakes: Thiamin, Riboflavin, Niacin, Vitamin B_6, Folate, Vitamin B_{12}, Pantothenic Acid, Biotin, and Choline.*
14. Bourgeois, C., D. Cervantes-Laurean, and J. Moss. 2006. Niacin. In M. E. Shils, A. C. Ross, B. Caballero, and R. J. Cousins, eds. *Modern Nutrition in Health and Disease.* 10th ed. Baltimore: Lippincott Williams & Wilkins.
15. Institute of Medicine, Food and Nutrition Board. 1998. *Dietary Reference Intakes: Thiamin, Riboflavin, Niacin, Vitamin B_6, Folate, Vitamin B_{12}, Pantothenic Acid, Biotin, and Choline.*
16. Trumbo, P. R. 2006. Pantothenic Acid. In *Modern Nutrition in Health and Disease.* 10th ed.
17. Tahiliani, A. G., and C. J. Beinlilch. 1991. Pantothenic Acid in Health and Disease. *Vitamins and Hormones* 46:165–228.
18. Glusman, M. 1947. The Syndrome of "Burning Feet" (Nutritional Melagia) as a Manifestation of Nutritional Deficiency. *American Journal of Medicine* 3:211–223.
19. Gropper, S. S., J. L Smith, and J. L. Groff. 2009. *Advanced Nutrition and Human Metabolism.* 5th ed. Belmont, CA: Wadsworth.
20. Institute of Medicine. 2006. *Dietary Reference Intakes: The Essential Guide to Nutrient Requirements.*
21. U. S. National Library of Medicine. 2008. *Genetics Home Reference. Your Guide to Understanding Genetic Disorders.* Available at http://ghr.nlm.nih.gov/ Accessed May 2012.
22. Institute of Medicine, Food and Nutrition Board. 1998. *Dietary Reference Intakes: Thiamin, Riboflavin, Niacin, Vitamin B_6, Folate, Vitamin B_{12}, Pantothenic Acid, Biotin, and Choline.*
23. Mackey, A. M., S. R. Davis, and J. F. Gregory. 2006. Vitamin B_6. In *Modern Nutrition in Health and Disease.* 10th ed.
24. Ibid.
25. Koren G. and C. Maltepe. 2006. Preventing Recurrence of Severe Morning Sickness. Canadian Family Physician 52:1545–1546.
26. Schaumburg, H., J. Kaplan, A. Windebran, N. Vick, S. Rasmus, D. Pleasure, and M. J. Brown. 1983. Sensory Neuropathy from Pyridoxine Abuse. *New England Journal of Medicine* 309:445–448.
27. Neuhouser, M. L., S. A. A. Beresford, D. E. Hickok, and E. R. Monsen. 1998. Absorption of Dietary and Supplemental Folate in Women with Prior Pregnancies with Neural Tube Defects and Controls. *Journal of the American College of Nutrition* 17:625–630.
28. Ibid.
29. Centers for Disease Control and Prevention. 2007. *Folic Acid.* Available at www.cdc.gov/ncbddd/folicacid. Accessed May 2012.
30. Ibid.
31. Ibid.
32. Ulrich, C. M. 2007. Folate and Cancer Prevention: A Closer Look at a Complex Picture. *American Journal of Clinical Nutrition.* 86:271–273.
33. Institute of Medicine, Food and Nutrition Board. 1998. *Dietary Reference Intakes: Thiamin, Riboflavin, Niacin, Vitamin B_6, Folate, Vitamin B_{12}, Pantothenic Acid, Biotin, and Choline.*
34. National Institutes of Health, Office of Dietary Supplements. 2004. *Dietary Supplement Fact Sheet: Folate.* Available at http://ods.od.nih.gov/factsheets/folate.asp. Accessed May 2012.
35. Institute of Medicine, Food and Nutrition Board. 1998. *Dietary Reference Intakes: Thiamin, Riboflavin, Niacin, Vitamin B_6, Folate, Vitamin B_{12}, Pantothenic Acid, Biotin, and Choline.*
36. National Institutes of Health, Office of Dietary Supplements. 2004. *Dietary Supplement Fact Sheet: Vitamin B_{12}.* Available at http://ods.od.nih.gov/factsheets/VitaminB12-HealthProfessional. Accessed November 2012.
37. Ibid.
38. Tucker, K. L., M. T. Hannan, P. F. Jacques, J. Selhub, I. Rosenberg, P. W. Wilson, and D. P. Kiel. 2002. Low Plasma Vitamin B_{12} Is Associated with Lower BMD: The Framingham Osteoporosis Study. *American Society for Bone and Mineral Research* 17:S174.
39. Tahiliani, A. G., and C. J. Beinlilch. 1991. Pantothenic Acid.
40. Watanabe, F., K. Abe, T. Fujita, M. Goto, M. Hiemori, and Y. Nakano. 1998. Effects of Microwave Heating on the Loss of Vitamin B_{12} in Foods. *Journal of Agricultural Food Chemistry* 46:206–210.
41. Iqbal, L., A. Khan, and M. Khattak. 2004. Biological Significance of Ascorbic Acid (Vitamin C) in Human Health. *Pakistan Journal of Nutrition* 3:5–13.
42. Ibid.
43. Padayatty, S. J., A. Katz, Y. Wang, P. Eck, O. Kwon, J. Lee, S. Chen, et al. 2003. Vitamin C as an Antioxidant: Evaluation of Its Role in Disease Prevention. *Journal of the American College of Nutrition* 22:18–35.
44. Iqbal, L., et al. 2004. Biological Significance of Ascorbic Acid.
45. Padayatty, S., J. Doppman, R. Chang, Y. Wang, J. Gill, D. A. Papanicolaou, and M. Levine. 2007. Human Adrenal Glands Secrete Vitamin C in Response to Adrenocorticotropic Hormone. *American Journal of Clinical Nutrition* 86:145–149.
46. Iqbal, L., et al. 2004. Biological Significance of Ascorbic Acid.
47. Institute of Medicine, Food and Nutrition Board. 1998. *Dietary Reference Intakes: Thiamin, Riboflavin, Niacin, Vitamin B_6, Folate, Vitamin B_{12}, Pantothenic Acid, Biotin, and Choline.*
48. Hirschmann, J. V. and G. J. Raugi. 1999. Adult Scurvy. *Journal of the American Academy of Dermatology* 41:895–910.
49. Weinstein, M., P. Babyn, and S. Zlotkin. 2001. An Orange a Day Keeps the Doctor Away: Scurvy in the Year 2000. *Pediatrics* 108:e55.
50. Zeisel, S. H., K. A. Da Costa, P. D. Franklin, E. A. Alexander, J. T. Lamont, N. F. Sheard, and A. Beiser. 1991. Choline, an Essential Nutrient for Humans. *Federation of American Societies for Experimental Biology* 5:2093–2098.
51. Fischer, L. M., K. A. Da Costa, L. Kwock, P. W. Stewart, T. S. Lu, S. P. Stabler, R. H. Allen, and S. H. Ziesel. 2007. Sex and Menopausal Status Influence Human Dietary Requirements for the Nutrient Choline. *American Journal of Clinical Nutrition* 85:1275–1285.
52. Caudill, M. 2010. Pre- and Postnatal Health: Evidence of Increased Choline Needs. *Journal of the American Dietetic Association* 110:1198–206.
53. National Institutes of Health, Office of Dietary Supplements. 2006. *Carnitine.* Available at http://ods.od.nih.gov/factsheets/carnitine.asp. Accessed May 2012.
54. Packer, L., E. H. Witt, and H. J. Tritschler. 1994. Alpha-Lipoic Acid as a Biological Antioxidant. *Free Radical Biology and Medicine* 19:227–250.
55. Smith, A. R., S. V. Shenvi, M. Widlansky, J. H. Suh, and T. M. Hagen. 2004. Lipoic Acid as a Potential Therapy for Chronic Diseases Associated with Oxidative Stress. *Current Medicinal Chemistry* 11:1135–1146.

11 Water

Chapter Objectives

After reading this chapter, you will be able to:

1. Explain why water is so important and describe the functions of water in the body.
2. Describe the various processes that maintain water balance in the body.
3. Describe the roles of water, sodium, hormones, and enzymes in the development of hypertension.
4. Describe the daily recommended intake for water consumption.
5. Explain the effects of diuretics, such as caffeine and alcohol, on the balance of body water.
6. Differentiate between dehydration and water intoxication, and describe the symptoms of each.

1. The body can survive for weeks without food and water. T/F
2. A morning mug of coffee counts toward daily water needs. T/F
3. Daily consumption of at least 8 cups of water is essential for health. T/F
4. Drinking large amounts of water will help flush wastes from the body. T/F
5. Drinking extra water leads to weight loss. T/F
6. Exercise often leads to dehydration. T/F
7. Sodium should be eliminated from the diet to prevent fluid retention. T/F
8. Eating bananas reduces hypertension. T/F
9. Drinking alcohol causes dehydration. T/F
10. Enhanced waters are healthier than plain water. T/F

See page 432 for answers to these Myths and Misconceptions.

Everyone needs water to live. But exactly why is this the case, and how much water do you really need? In this chapter, we will explore the essential functions that water plays in the body, as well as the mechanisms that keep fluids and other substances in a healthy balance. We will also find out how to make sure that you are meeting your daily needs and, equally important, how to avoid consuming toxic amounts of water.

Why Is Water Essential to Life?

Water (H_2O) is the most abundant substance in the body and, as such, is the most important. You could survive for weeks without food, but only for a few days without water.

The average healthy adult body is composed of about 45 to 75 percent water. The distribution of this water depends on an individual's age, gender, and the composition of fat and muscle in the body (**Figure 11.1**). Because muscle tissue is approximately 65 percent water, while fat tissue contains only 10 to 40 percent, some individuals have less body water than others.[1] Males have a higher percentage of muscle mass and a lower percentage of fat tissue than females of the same age, and therefore males have more body water. For the same reason, muscular athletes have a higher percentage of body water than sedentary individuals. Body water also decreases with age, so older individuals have less than younger individuals. A newborn infant averages about 75 percent of body weight as water, while an older adult only has about 45 percent body water.[2]

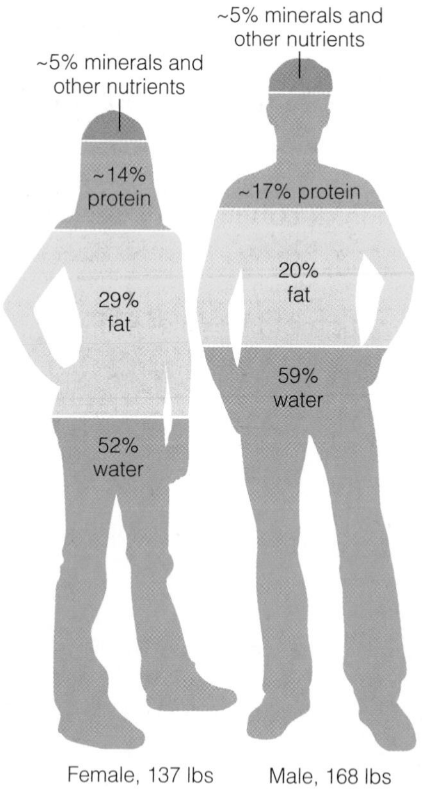

~5% minerals and other nutrients
~14% protein
29% fat
52% water
Female, 137 lbs

~5% minerals and other nutrients
~17% protein
20% fat
59% water
Male, 168 lbs

▲ **Figure 11.1 The Composition of the Body**
Water is the predominant body component for both men and women.

The Functions of Water in the Body

Water is a **polar** molecule, which means it has a neutral electrical charge because the negative charge on the hydrogen atoms and the positive charge on the oxygen molecules balance each other (**Figure 11.2**). Its polarity allows water to attract other charged molecules and maintain acid-base balance in the body.

Water's polar quality enables it to play a role as a medium in which other substances can dissolve. As part of blood and other fluids, water transports nutrients, waste products, and other substances between cells and tissues. Water also helps maintain a constant body temperature; lubricates and protects joints and other areas; and enables chemical reactions, including those that provide the body with energy, and enables acid-base balance to take place within the cells. Without water, metabolism would grind to a halt.

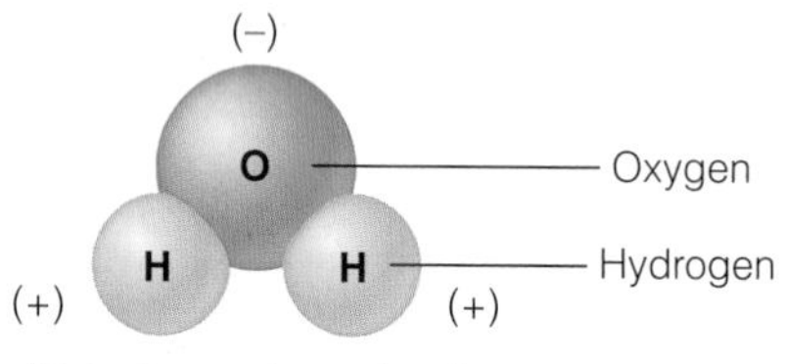

▲ **Figure 11.2 Water Is a Polar Molecule**
The oxygen atom of water has a partial negative charge and the hydrogen atoms have a partial positive charge, making the overall charge of a molecule of water neutral.

Water Is the Universal Solvent and Transport Medium

Water is commonly known as a universal **solvent,** a liquid in which substances dissolve. Its polarity allows it to attract charged particles into a solution, and dissolve a variety of other polar substances, including proteins, glucose, and some minerals. As illustrated in **Figure 11.3**, the positive and negative charges of water attract the

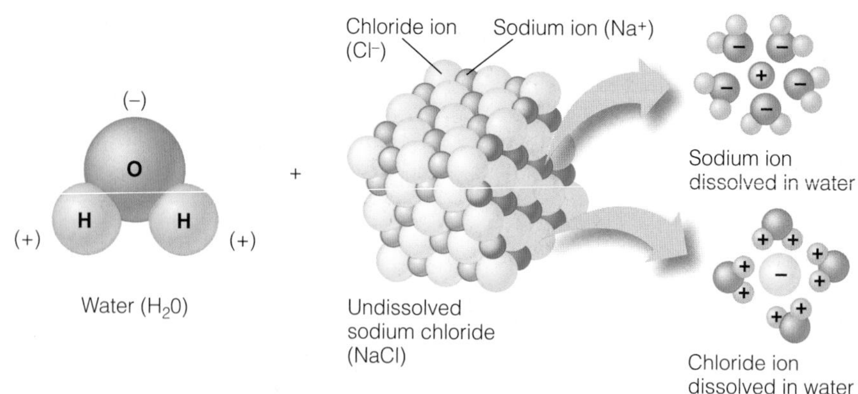

▲ **Figure 11.3 Water Is a Universal Solvent**
Water is a universal solvent that can dissolve salts such as sodium chloride (NaCl). The negatively charged Cl^- is attracted to the positive charge of the hydrogen ions (H^+) and the positive charge of Na^+ is attracted to the negative charge of oxygen (O^-). Thus, the water slowly dissolves the salt.

polar Having a pair of equal and opposite charges; water is a polar molecule because oxygen has a negative charge and hydrogen has a positive charge.

solvent A liquid in which substances dissolve to form a new solution. Water is called the universal solvent because it can dissolve a variety of substances, including minerals and glucose.

positive and negative charges of table salt, called sodium chloride (Na^+Cl^-). The result is that salt dissolves in water. Compounds that are not polar, such as lipids, are not attracted to water and thus do not dissolve.

Water's function as a solvent is critically important in digestion. For example, about 7,000 milliliters of watery gastric juices dissolve digested nutrients. Water also helps transport dissolved nutrients and other substances throughout the body. Blood is made up of water (about 83 percent) and red blood cells, and the water in blood allows it to transport oxygen, nutrients, and hormones to the cells. Water also helps transport waste products away from cells to be excreted in urine and stool.

Water is vital for many body functions, but it is not stored in the body, so adequate amounts must be consumed daily.

Water Helps Maintain Body Temperature

Water is a heat buffer similar to the coolant fluid in a car. In the blood, water absorbs, carries, and ultimately releases heat to keep the body from overheating. It absorbs heat from the body's internal core and carries it to the skin for release. Water works well as a coolant because it has a high **specific heat,** a measurement of the amount of energy required to raise 1 gram of water 1 degree Celsius (1°C). This characteristic allows water to absorb and hold onto heat with very little change in temperature.

If the body's core gets too hot, this cooling mechanism is not enough to maintain a safe temperature. A jog on a hot summer day, for example, can generate an enormous amount of internal heat and would likely tax the heat-absorbing capacity of the body's water. In this case, water transfers the heat to the skin to reduce the heat load. As the core temperature increases, the hypothalamus is triggered and dilates the blood vessels, increasing the flow of warmed blood to the skin's surface. At the same time, the rising skin temperature activates the three million sweat glands to release additional water and salts through the pores of the skin. The increasing heat breaks apart the hydrogen bonds of the water, and transforms it from a liquid (*sweat*) to a vapor. As the sweat evaporates from the surface of the skin, heat dissipates and cools the skin (**Figure 11.4**), leaving the salt behind. The cooled blood returns to the muscle. The water in sweat that drips off your body releases very little heat.

Water Is a Lubricant and a Protective Cushion, and Provides Structure to Muscle Cells

Water acts as a lubricant for joints and sensitive eye tissue. It lubricates and moistens food in the mouth as part of saliva, and is part of the mucus that lubricates the intestinal tract. Water is the main component of the fluid that bathes certain organs, including the brain, and thus acts as a cushion to protect organs from injury during a fall or other trauma. During pregnancy, a developing fetus is surrounded by a sac of watery amniotic fluid, which helps protect it from physical harm.

Water also provides a structural component to cells, much like air in a balloon. Without water, a cell would be limp and shriveled. Athletes experience the structural features of water when the muscle feels full following a carbohydrate-loading diet. This is because glycogen is surrounded by water when it is stored in muscle cells. For every molecule of glucose within the glycogen structure, 2.7 grams of water are attached, adding bulk and structure to the muscle cells.[3]

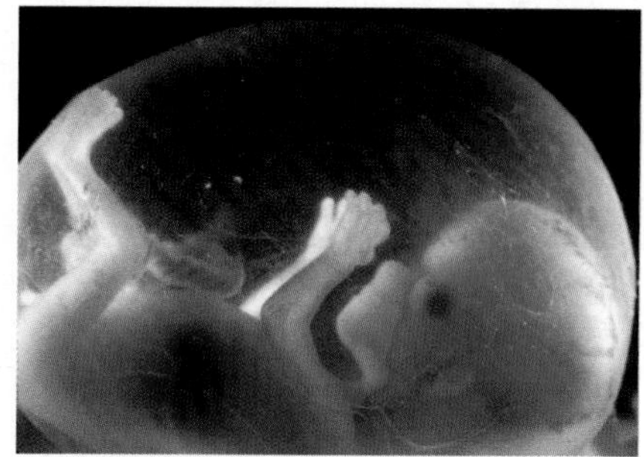

A developing fetus is cushioned in a sac of watery amniotic fluid to protect it from physical harm during pregnancy.

Water Participates in Hydrolysis and Condensation Reactions

Water is essential for most chemical reactions in the body. During digestion, carbohydrates, proteins, and fats require water to hydrolyze the bonds that hold these molecules together. For example, when sucrose is digested (refer to Chapter 4), hydrolysis adds a hydrogen ion to fructose and a hydroxyl group to glucose; then each

specific heat A measurement of the energy required to raise a gram of a substance, such as water, 1 degree Celsius.

▸ **Figure 11.4 Water Helps Regulate Body Temperature**
Water transports heat from the body's core to the skin for release.

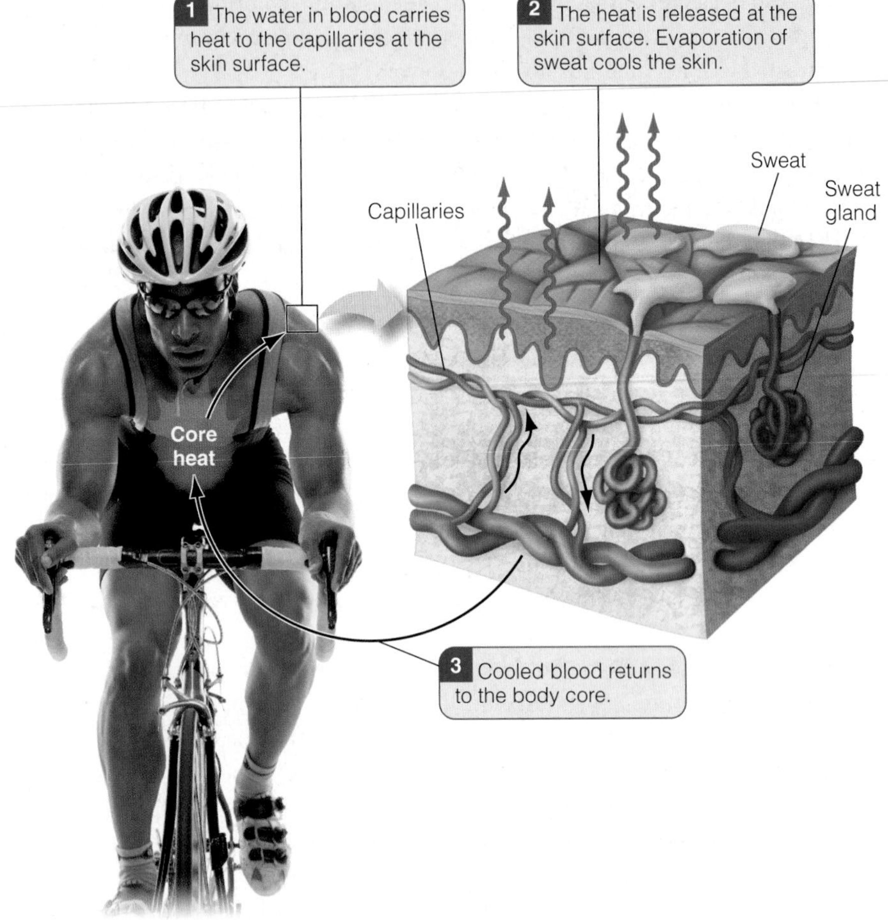

1 The water in blood carries heat to the capillaries at the skin surface.
2 The heat is released at the skin surface. Evaporation of sweat cools the skin.
Sweat
Sweat gland
Capillaries
Core heat
3 Cooled blood returns to the body core.

monosaccharide is absorbed. When smaller molecules are combined through condensation, such as when excess glucose is stored as glycogen in the liver and muscle, the opposite occurs. In this case, a water molecule is released from every bond that is formed.

Water Plays a Role in Acid-Base Balance

Acid-base balance is essential to maintain homeostasis in the body. As you learned in Chapter 3, a normal pH in human blood ranges from 7.35 to 7.45, which reflects the amount of hydrogen ions present—more hydrogen ions means a lower, more acidic pH. Because water is polar, it can be used to reduce or increase the pH levels by either breaking down or forming carbonic acid. In other words, water can act as either an acid or a base. These reactions are described in the Chemistry Boost.

THE TAKE-HOME MESSAGE The body is more than 45 percent water. Muscle tissue has more water than fat tissue, therefore men have more body water than women and younger individuals have more body water than older individuals. Water is polar and therefore interacts with other nutrients and serves as an acid-base buffer in the body. Water is a universal solvent that helps transport oxygen and nutrients throughout the body, absorbs and releases heat to regulate body temperature, acts as a lubricant through saliva and mucus, and provides a protective cushion for the brain and other organs. Water adds structure to cells and participates in chemical reactions, including hydrolysis and condensation.

acid-base balance The mechanisms used to maintain body fluids close to a neutral pH so the body can function properly.

Chemistry Boost

Water and Acid-Base Balance

When water dissociates, it tends to break up into H^+ and OH^- (hydroxide) ions. One hydrogen atom breaks its bond with oxygen, leaves behind its electron, and becomes positively charged. (Recall that a positively charged hydrogen atom is called a hydrogen ion.) The other hydrogen remains attached to the oxygen molecule. Oxygen retains both of its original electrons and now has an extra electron from the hydrogen, which gives the molecule a negative charge. The OH^- molecule is called a hydroxide ion.

$$H_2O \leftrightarrow H^+ + OH^-$$

When a solution has more H^+ than OH^- ions, it is acidic. When the solution has more OH^- than H^+ ions, it is basic (refer to the pH scale in Chapter 3).

Water can regulate acid-base balance by forming or breaking down carbonic acid (H_2CO_3). This buffering action is reversible, as illustrated in the following two reactions:

(a) During exercise, carbon dioxide is produced as a by-product of energy metabolism. Carbon dioxide is a gas that quickly dissolves in water, forming carbonic acid (H_2CO_3). If the reaction continues, carbonic acid can be further reduced to hydrogen (H^+) and bicarbonate ions (HCO_3^-). The increase in H^+ results in a decrease in pH and makes the environment more acidic.

$$H_2O + CO_2 \rightarrow H_2CO_3 \rightarrow H^+ + HCO_3^-$$

(b) The reaction can be reversed and act as a buffer to neutralize excess hydrogen ions. In this reaction, H^+ ions formed during energy metabolism (recall from Chapter 8 that H^+ are formed during glycolysis and the TCA cycle) combine with bicarbonate (HCO_3^-) to form water and carbon dioxide. This increases the pH and makes the environment more alkaline.

$$H^+ + HCO_3^- \rightarrow H_2CO_3 \rightarrow H_2O + CO_2$$

How Is Water Balance Maintained?

The amount of water in the fluid compartments in the body is tightly regulated. Maintaining fluid balance, or homeostasis, is necessary for normal reactions to take place within the cells. The body maintains this delicate balance by adapting to changes in water intake and water loss. When the amount of water consumed is equal to the amount excreted, the body is in **water balance.**

Sources of Body Water Include Beverages and Food

The first aspect of being in water balance is consuming enough water. The largest source of body water comes from beverages such as tap or bottled water, milk, juices, coffee, and soft drinks. An additional source of water comes from foods, especially from fruits and vegetables, which contain more water by weight than do grains. All foods contain some water.

In addition to the water ingested through beverages and foods, water is generated during metabolism, referred to as **metabolic water.** For example, condensation reactions, such as those that occur during energy metabolism, yield a small amount of water. One hundred grams of carbohydrate can yield almost 55 grams of metabolic water by the time they have been catabolized to ATP. In addition, the water that was joined with glucose during glycogenesis is later released when glycogen is hydrolyzed to produce glucose.

Food and beverages are a source of water for the body.

water balance A state of equilibrium when the intake of water equals the amount of water excreted.

metabolic water Water that is formed in the body as a result of metabolic reactions. Condensation reactions are an example of a chemical reaction that results in the production of water.

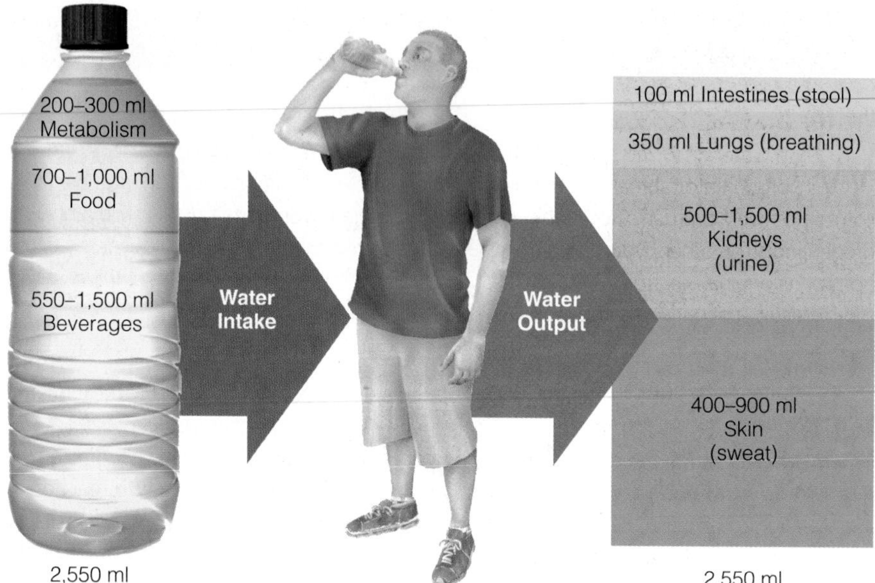

▲ **Figure 11.5 Sources of Body Water and Routes of Excretion**
Most of the body's water comes from foods and beverages and a small amount is generated during metabolism. Water is lost from the body through the urine, stool, sweat, and exhaled breath. The amount of water consumed and generated is balanced with the amount excreted each day.

The intake of water from fluids, food, and metabolism contributes to the total average intake of 2,550 milliliters daily (about 2 quarts). **Figure 11.5** illustrates the sources of water in the body and the routes of excretion.

Water Is Excreted through the Kidneys, Large Intestine, Lungs, and Skin

To maintain water balance, water is excreted through urine and sweat, and as water vapor through the lungs. The majority of fluid lost is through the kidneys, which produce approximately 1,500 milliliters of urine each day. The more water ingested, the more urine produced. The opposite is also true. The less water an adult consumes, or if a greater amount of water is lost through other means such as through sweat, the less urine is produced. About 100 milliliters of water is also lost through intestinal fluids in the stool. This amount can vary depending on the dietary intake of plant fibers and whether an individual is experiencing diarrhea. Excess water loss through diarrhea and vomiting can amount to as much as 1,500 to 5,000 milliliters and can result in **dehydration.** (Dehydration will be discussed in detail later in the chapter.)

Water that evaporates during exhalation and water lost through the skin as the body releases heat constitute **insensible water loss,** which takes place throughout the day, generally without being noticed. Exhaled air, which contains small water droplets, releases about 200 to 400 milliliters of water per day. This amount increases in an arid climate and with the heavier breathing that occurs during physical activity.[4]

Insensible water loss doesn't include the water lost in sweat. The amount of water lost during sweating varies greatly and depends upon many environmental factors, such as the temperature, the humidity, the wind, the sun's intensity, clothing worn, and the amount of physical activity. For example, if you jump rope in the noontime sun on a summer day wearing a heavy coat, you could lose almost 2,000

dehydration The excessive loss of body fluids; usually caused by lack of fluid intake, diarrhea, vomiting, or excessive sweating.

insensible water loss The loss of body water that goes unnoticed, such as by exhalation during breathing and the evaporation of water through the skin.

to 3,000 milliliters of water per hour as sweat.[5] In contrast, you would lose only about 50 milliliters of water per hour as sweat if you sat under a shady tree on a dry, cool day wearing a light tee shirt and slacks.

Water Is Balanced between Fluid Compartments

The body's fluids are located within cells, called **intracellular fluid (ICF),** or located outside the cells, called **extracellular fluid (ECF).** Each compartment contains specific components. ICF contains potassium, proteins, and various organic acids. ECF is primarily composed of sodium chloride and sodium bicarbonate solutions.

There are two types of extracellular fluids: interstitial fluids and intravascular fluids. **Interstitial fluids** bathe the outside of cells, but do not circulate throughout the body. **Intravascular fluids** are found in the blood and the lymph vessels, and circulate throughout the body. Interstitial fluid makes up about 75 percent of the ECF and acts as an area of exchange between the blood fluids and the cells (**Figure 11.6**).

The fluids found in the ECF and ICF are not static—they move between compartments easily. Water must first pass through the cell membranes. The cell membranes control the concentration of intracellular and extracellular fluids and also allow minerals to flow between the intracellular fluid compartments.

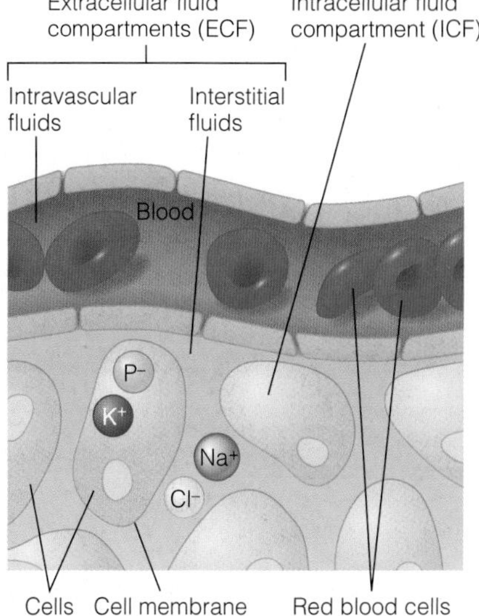

▲ **Figure 11.6 The Intracellular and Extracellular Fluid Compartments**
Water is a key component of the fluid both inside (intracellular) and outside (extracellullar) of cells. Potassium (K^+) is the major electrolyte found in the ICF and sodium (Na^+) is the major electrolyte located in the ECF.

Electrolytes Participate in Fluid Balance

Some minerals act as **electrolytes** (*electro* = electricity, *lytes* = soluble), or charged ions that conduct electrical current. If they have a positive charge they are classified as **cations,** while negatively charged ions are called **anions.** Sodium (Na^+) and chloride (Cl^-) are the main electrolytes in the ECF, while potassium (K^+) and phosphate (P^-) are the major ions inside the cell. Electrolytes help maintain water balance between compartments by "pulling" water into and out of blood and cells, a process referred to as **osmosis.** While the minerals sodium, potassium, phosphate, magnesium, calcium, and chloride all function as electrolytes in the body, sodium has the greatest effect on fluid balance. Sodium and potassium also influence fluid balance in the sodium-potassium pump.

Osmosis

Shifts in fluid from the ICF to the ECF are solely due to osmosis (*osmos* = pushing), a powerful factor influencing water balance between cell compartments. Water diffuses by osmosis through cell membranes by moving from a dilute or low concentration of particles or electrolytes (also called *solutes)* on one side of the membrane to a high concentration of electrolytes on the other side of the membrane. To put it another way, electrolytes attract water. Cell membranes are **selectively permeable,** which means they allow some substances, such as water, to pass freely while other substances, such as salts, are restricted.

The osmotic pressure inside a cell is based on the **osmolality,** or concentration of particles in a solution, and controls the directional flow of water. The difference between the osmolality (or number of solutes) on each side of the permeable membrane is called the **osmotic gradient.** As the osmolality on one side the membrane increases, the osmotic gradient increases, and water is drawn across the membrane to the electrolytes. The membrane swells under the pressure of the increase in water (osmotic pressure). This increase in osmotic pressure prevents water from flowing away from the concentrated side of the membrane until balance has been restored between the fluid compartments. For example, heavy sweating during work or exercise outdoors results in a greater loss of water than electrolytes from the blood (ECF) (sweat is 75 percent water), which shifts the osmolality of the ECF to a higher

intracellular fluid (ICF) The fluid found in the cytoplasm within the cells; it represents the largest fluid compartment in the body.

extracellular fluid (ECF) The water found outside the cell, including the intravascular fluid and the interstitial fluid.

interstitial fluid The fluid that surrounds cells. It is the main component of extracellular fluid.

intravascular fluid The fluid found inside the blood vessels and the lymph fluid.

electrolytes Ions such as sodium, potassium, chloride, and calcium in the blood and within the cells that are able to conduct electrical current when they are dissolved in body water.

cations Positively charged ions.

anions Negatively charged ions.

osmosis The diffusion of water or any solvent across a semipermeable cell membrane from a weak concentration of solutes to a more concentrated solute.

selectively permeable Describes the feature of cell membranes that allows some substances to cross the membrane more easily than other substances.

osmolality A measurement of the concentration of solutes per kilogram of solvent in a solution.

osmotic gradient The difference in concentration between two solutions on each side of the permeable cell membrane.

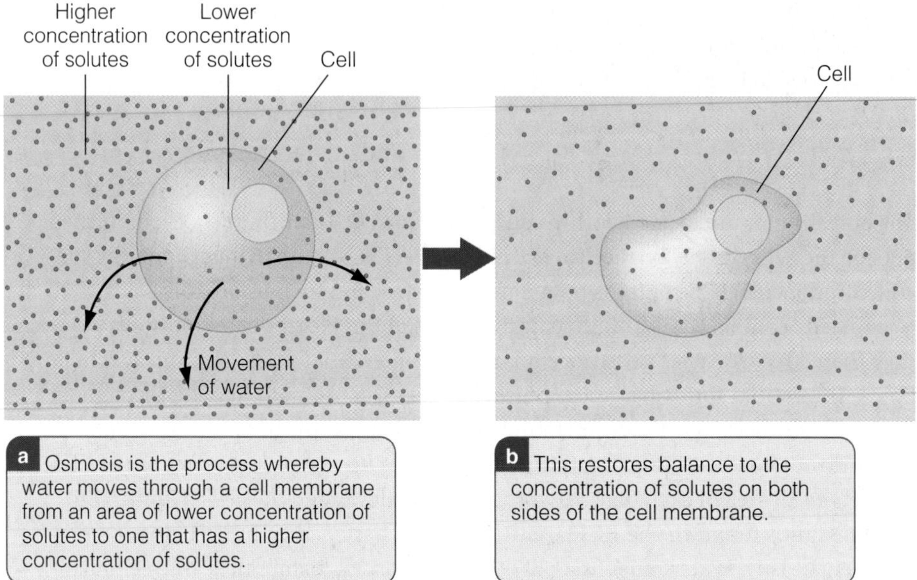

Higher concentration of solutes
Lower concentration of solutes
Cell
Movement of water
Cell
a Osmosis is the process whereby water moves through a cell membrane from an area of lower concentration of solutes to one that has a higher concentration of solutes.
b This restores balance to the concentration of solutes on both sides of the cell membrane.

▶ **Figure 11.7 Osmosis**

osmotic gradient compared with the ICF. That is, there is a greater concentration of solutes to water in the ECF than the ICF. As the osmolality increases in the ECF, water is drawn from the ICF into the ECF and increases the osmotic pressure in the ECF until balance is achieved. The opposite is also true. If you drink a large amount of water quickly, the water in the ECF dilutes the concentration of the solutes compared with the ICF and reduces the osmotic pressure in the ECF, allowing the flow of water from the ECF into the ICF. If the concentration of solutes to water is similar on either side of the membrane, water reaches equilibrium (**Figure 11.7**). Osmosis only affects the movement of water between compartments, not the solutes themselves. The concentration of solutes within the two fluid compartments is controlled by the mechanism referred to as the sodium-potassium pump.

The Sodium-Potassium Pump

The mechanism that maintains the normal electrolyte concentrations and therefore controls the fluid volume within the cell is called the **sodium-potassium pump** (see **Figure 11.8**). This pump works by actively transporting sodium ions out of the ICF in exchange for potassium ions. Sodium is normally higher in the ECF than the ICF. Because of these differences in concentrations, sodium tends to leak into the cell and potassium leaks out of the cell. As sodium enters the ICF, water diffuses across the cell membrane into the cell to balance the sodium ions. In other words, where sodium ions go, water will follow. As water moves inside the cell, the cell swells, causing an increase in osmotic pressure. In healthy cells, to prevent the cell from bursting, the sodium-potassium pump transports three sodium (Na^+) ions out of the cell and exchanges them for two potassium (K^+) ions that move inside the cell. The pump results in a net loss of ions, which creates an electrical and chemical gradient that drives water out of the cell, and reduces the swelling.

The sodium-potassium pump is found in every cell, but plays an especially important role in the electrical conduction in nerve and muscle cells and in the absorption of nutrients. The transport of ions by the sodium-potassium pump creates an osmotic gradient, and changes the electrical charge that causes the nerve to transmit a signal or the muscle to contract. The sodium-potassium pump is also the driving force behind the absorption of as much as two liters of consumed fluid each day, plus the water secreted into the GI tract in gastric juices. As sodium ions move back across the cell membrane, they are joined by glucose and amino acids to be

sodium-potassium pump A protein located in the cell membrane that actively transports sodium out of the cell in exchange for potassium ions.

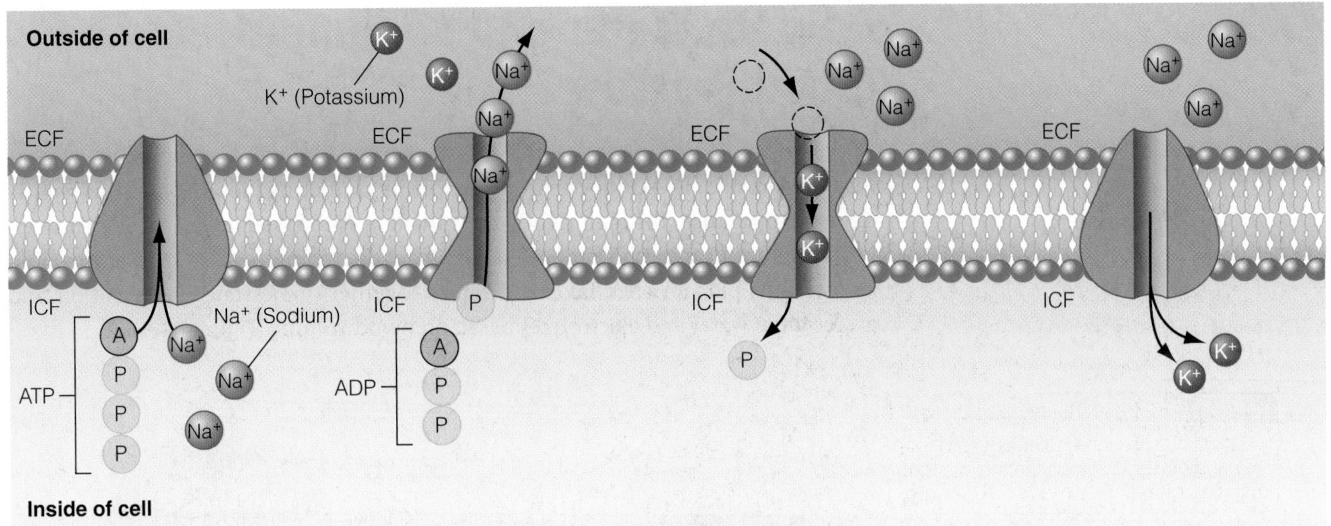

1 Inside the cell three Na^+ ions and ATP bind to the surface of the protein channel of the sodium-potassium pump.

2 The ATP is hydrolyzed into ADP and P providing the energy needed to change the shape of the protein. The change in shape forces the Na^+ ions outside of the cell. A phosphate remains attached to the protein.

3 Once the Na^+ ions have been released, the pump binds two K^+ ions in the ECF and releases the phosphate inside the cell.

4 The pump changes back to its original shape and releases the two K^+ ions inside the cell. The pump is then ready to go again.

▲ **Figure 11.8 The Sodium-Potassium Pump**
The sodium-potassium pump is a protein in the cell membrane that transports sodium ions out of a cell while moving potassium ions inside the cell. This active transport of Na^+ and K^+ ions requires energy. For every three sodium ions pumped out of the cell, two potassium ions are transported into the cell.

absorbed inside the cell. Hence, the change in electrical charge drives the absorption of various nutrients into the villi.

Proteins Regulate Fluid Balance

Protein plays a major role in keeping water dispersed evenly between the ECF and the ICF (refer again to Chapter 6). This is especially true for the protein albumin. As the concentration of albumin rises in the blood, water is drawn out of the interstitial fluid into the blood by osmosis. If your diet is severely low in protein, the blood levels of albumin drop, causing an accumulation of water in the interstitial spaces and swelling of the body tissues. Adequate protein intake is essential to fluid balance.

THE TAKE-HOME MESSAGE Water balance is achieved when the amount of water consumed and produced by the body via food, beverages, and metabolism equals the amount excreted through the kidneys, skin, lungs, and feces. Body water is contained in either the intracellular or extracellular fluid compartments. Most body water is intracellular and located inside of cells. Extracellular fluid either bathes the outside of the cells (interstitial) or is found in the blood (intravascular). Osmosis is the process of water moving from an area of higher concentration to lower concentration across a cell membrane. The sodium-potassium pump helps maintain electrolyte and fluid balance inside and outside of cells. Albumin in the blood helps maintain fluid balance between the interstitial fluid and the blood.

How Do Water and Sodium Affect Blood Pressure?

If the body retains too much fluid, blood volume—and therefore blood pressure—is likely to rise. The kidneys play a key role in regulating blood volume, as well as electrolyte balance, through tightly controlled hormonal signals. Three hormones, including antidiuretic hormone (ADH, also called *vasopressin*), angiotensin, and aldosterone, plus an enzyme called renin, together orchestrate the retention and excretion of water and electrolytes based on blood volume (**Figure 11.9**).

1a In the brain, the hypothalamus detects high concentrations of salt in the blood and stimulates the pituitary gland.

1b The pituitary gland releases ADH, which travels to the kidneys.

1c ADH stimulates kidneys to reabsorb more water, which increases blood volume and blood pressure.

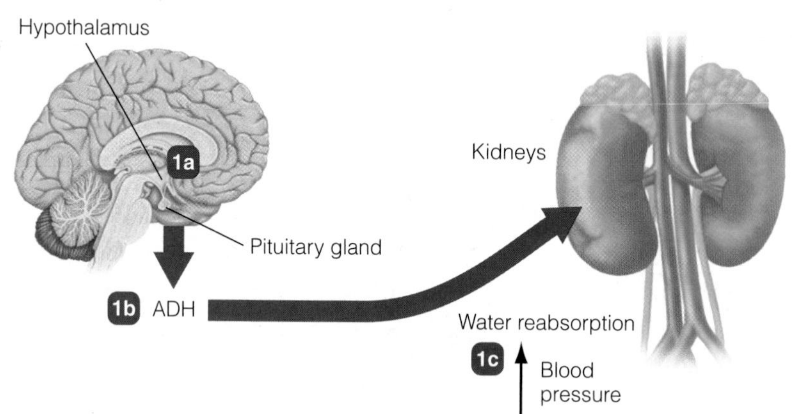

2a The kidneys sense a drop in blood volume and release the enzyme renin.

2b Renin activates the protein angiotensinogen to angiotensin I.

2c The lungs convert angiotensin I to angiotensin II.

2d Angiotensin II is a vasoconstrictor and causes the blood vessels to contract, which increases blood pressure.

2e Angiotensin II stimulates the adrenal glands to release aldosterone.

2f Aldosterone signals the kidneys to reabsorb more sodium, which increases blood volume and blood pressure.

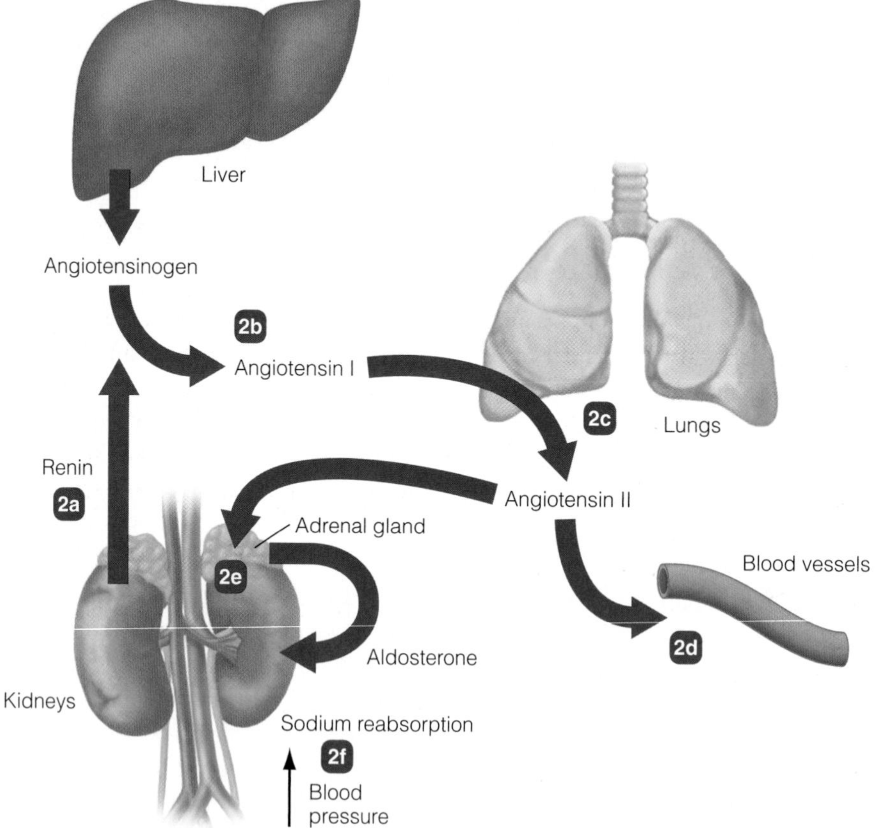

▲ **Figure 11.9 Blood Volume Regulates Blood Pressure**
Blood pressure is controlled by two hormones: antidiuretic hormone (ADH) secreted from the pituitary glands (1a–1c) and aldosterone released from the adrenal glands (2a–2f)..

ADH Helps Stimulate Fluid Intake and Reduce Urine Output

When blood volume drops, the hypothalamus detects a decrease in blood pressure and an increase in the concentration of salts (osmolality). This stimulates the **thirst mechanism** and fluid intake. At the same time you begin to feel thirsty, the hypothalamus stimulates the pituitary gland to release **antidiuretic hormone (ADH).** ADH travels through the blood to the kidneys and stimulates the reabsorption of water, which reduces urine production. Together, the intake of water and the reduced urine output restore blood volume and return osmolality to normal levels.

Renin Helps the Body Reabsorb Water and Salts

The enzyme **renin,** secreted by the kidneys, is released when blood pressure falls or sodium concentration is reduced. This enzyme splits off a protein called **angiotensin I** from the protein **angiotensinogen** produced by the liver and found in the blood. As the blood flows into the lungs, the angiotensin I is swiftly converted into **angiotensin II,** which has both short-term and long-term effects on blood pressure.

Angiotensin II is a powerful *vasoconstrictor* (*vaso* = vessel, *constrictor* = tightening) that narrows the blood vessels and raises blood pressure. This short-term reaction can prevent severe blood loss from hemorrhage or after an injury.

The long-term blood pressure control of angiotensin II relates to its action on the kidneys. First, it directly stimulates the kidneys to reabsorb water and salts to increase blood volume and blood pressure. Secondly, angiotensin II stimulates the adrenal glands to release aldosterone. These long-term effects take hours or days to affect blood pressure.

Aldosterone Helps Stimulate Sodium Reabsorption

The renin-angiotensin system adapts to changes in dietary sodium intake. If you consume very little sodium, osmolality drops in the ECF. Fluid automatically shifts from the blood to the interstitial fluid, causing a decrease in blood volume and blood pressure. Under these circumstances, angiotensin II would trigger the adrenal glands to release **aldosterone,** which signals the kidney to retain more sodium; this indirectly leads to water being retained. The opposite would be true if you consumed a very large amount of sodium; the renin-angiotensin system would lead to the kidneys excreting the excess.

The mechanisms involved in controlling blood pressure are directly related to blood volume and sodium concentrations in the ECF. This explains the need for controlling dietary sodium and remaining hydrated, especially for individuals with high blood pressure. Any factors that interfere with these control mechanisms can lead to chronic high blood pressure, or hypertension.

THE TAKE-HOME MESSAGE In response to changes in blood volume and osmolality, the body takes action to maintain homeostasis and return blood pressure to normal. The hormones antidiuretic hormone (ADH) and aldosterone direct the kidneys to reabsorb water and sodium. The enzyme renin increases sodium retention, and angiotensin II is a vasoconstrictor. These control mechanisms adjust to changes in dietary sodium and fluid intake to prevent hypertension.

thirst mechanism A complex interaction between the brain and the hypothalamus triggered by a loss of body water; the interaction leads to a feeling of thirst.

antidiuretic hormone (ADH) A hormone secreted by the pituitary gland when blood volumes are low; ADH reduces the amount of water excreted through the kidneys, constricts the blood vessels, and raises blood pressure; also known as vasopressin.

renin An enzyme secreted by the kidneys that participates in the renin-angiotensin system; renin increases blood volume, vasoconstriction of the blood vessels, and blood pressure.

angiotensin I and II The active protein in the blood that causes *vasoconstriction* in the blood vessels and triggers the release of aldosterone from the adrenal glands, which raises blood pressure.

angiotensinogen A precursor protein produced in the liver and found in the blood; it is converted to the active form called angiotensin.

aldosterone A hormone secreted from the adrenal glands in response to reduced blood volume; aldosterone signals the kidneys to reabsorb sodium, which increases blood volume and blood pressure.

How Much Water Do You Need and What Are the Best Sources?

Your daily water requirements may be different from those of your grandparents, parents, siblings, and even the classmate sitting next to you. The amount of water a person needs depends on physical activity, environmental factors such as air temperature and humidity, and diet.

The current recommendation for daily water consumption is based on the reported total water intake (from both beverages and food) of healthy Americans.[6] Currently, healthy female adults consume about 12 cups of water daily, whereas men consume about 16 cups of water daily. About 80 percent of this intake is from beverages and the other 20 percent comes from foods. Therefore, adult women should ingest about 9 cups (~80 percent of 12 cups) and adult males approximately 13 cups (~80 percent of 16 cups) of beverages daily. People who are very active have higher water requirements because they lose more water by sweating. These beverage guidelines are illustrated in **Figure 11.10**.

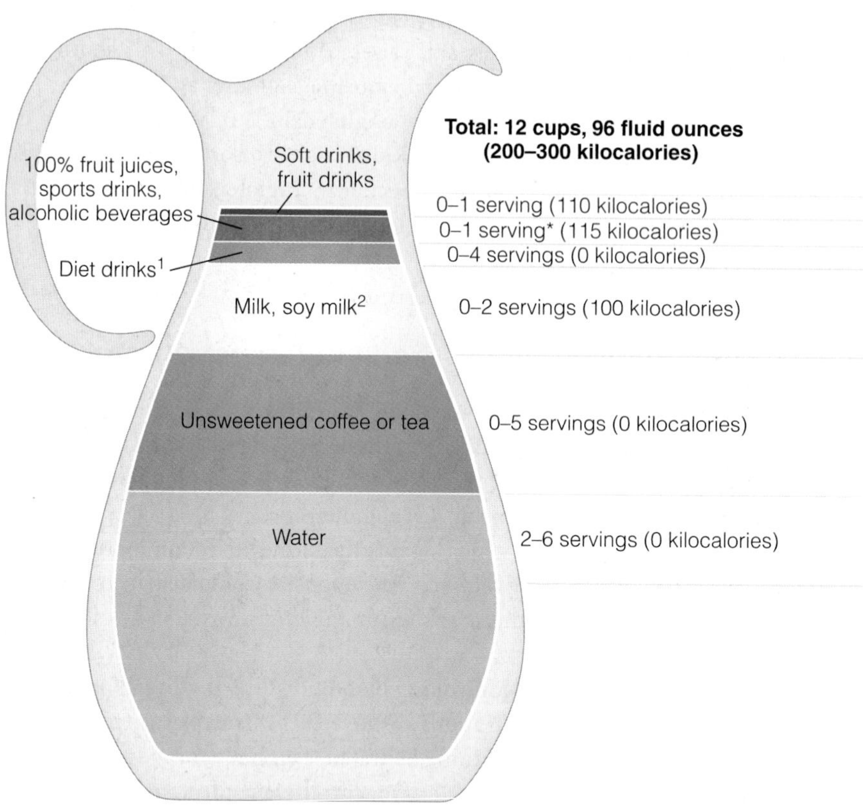

▲ **Figure 11.10 Daily Beverage Recommendations**
The acceptable beverage patterns for an adult female on a 2,200-kilocalorie daily intake.
Source: B. M. Popkin, L. E. Armstrong, G. M. Bray, B. Caballero, B. Frei, and W. C. Willett, "A New Proposed Guidance System for Beverage Consumption in the United States," *American Journal of Clinical Nutrition* 83 (2006): 529–542.

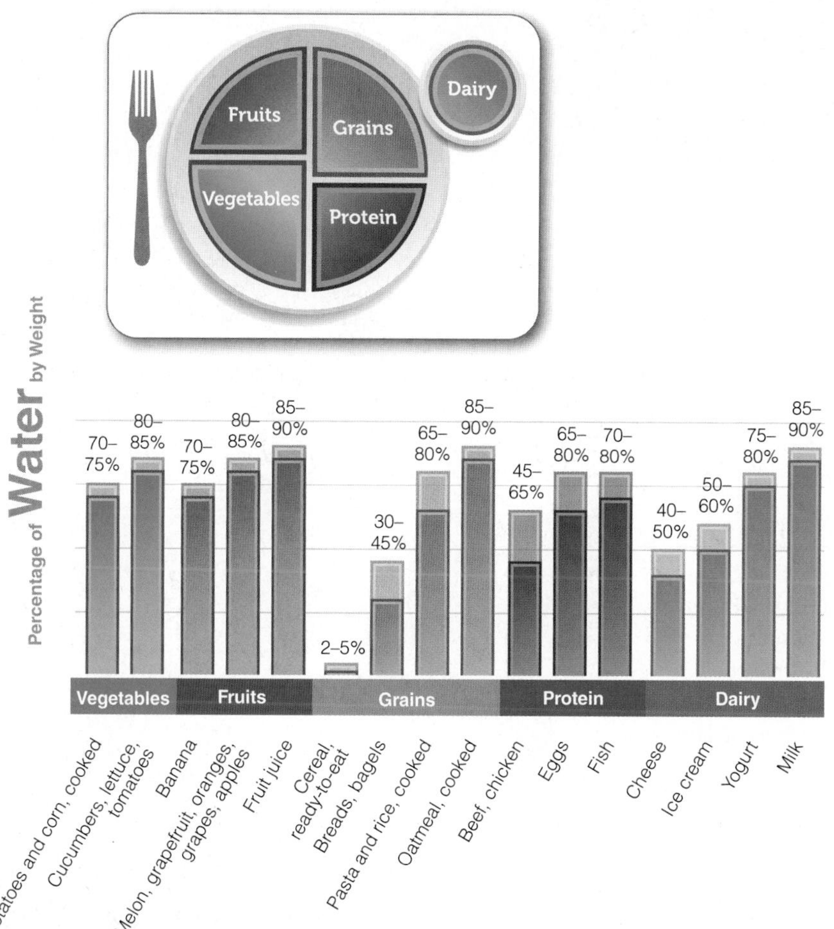

▲ **Figure 11.11 Water Content of Foods**

Source: A. Grandjean and S. Campbell, *Hydration: Fluids for Life* (Washington, DC: ILSI Press, 2004), available at www.ilsi.org.

If that sounds like a lot, keep in mind that a well-balanced, 2,200-kilocalorie diet that includes beverages at all meals and snacks provides about 12 cups of water.[7] Drinking bottled or tap water, milk, and juices throughout the day can help meet the body's needs. (Spotlight: Is Bottled Water Better than Tap Water? discusses the differences and similarities between tap water and bottled water.)

Most foods can also contribute to daily water needs (see **Figure 11.11**). Fruits and vegetables, such as watermelon, grapes, and lettuce, which can be more than 70 percent water by weight, rank as the best food sources of water. Even dry grain products, like bagels and bread, provide some water.

THE TAKE-HOME MESSAGE Daily water needs vary according to an individual's physical activity level, environment, and diet. Adult women should consume about 12 cups of water (9 cups from beverages; 3 cups from foods) daily, whereas adult men should consume about 16 cups (13 cups from beverages; 3 cups from foods) daily. Those who are very active need more water to avoid dehydration.

TABLE TIPS

Bottoms Up

Drink low-fat or skim milk with each meal to help meet both calcium and fluid needs.

Freeze grapes for a juicy and refreshing snack.

Add a vegetable soup to lunch for a fluid-packed meal.

Spoon slightly thawed frozen strawberries onto low-fat vanilla ice cream for a cool sweet treat. Look for packaged berries in the frozen food section of the supermarket.

Add a slice of fresh lemon or lime to a glass of water to make it even more refreshing.

SPOTLIGHT

Is Bottled Water Better than Tap Water?

What items do you *have* to have when you walk out the door in the morning? Your keys? Your student ID? Your wallet? What about a bottle of water? Would you never leave home without it? Are you one of the many individuals who drink *only* bottled water? If you are, you're certainly not alone. But is bottled water really better or safer than tap water?

Although many people drink bottled water in the belief that it is "pure," the reality is that drinking 100 percent *pure* water is impossible. Whether you fill your reusable water bottle from the tap or purchase bottled water, the water will contain some impurities. However, this does not mean that the water is unsafe for most individuals to drink. (Note that individuals with a weakened immune system, such as those with HIV/AIDS, undergoing chemotherapy, and/or taking steroids, should speak with their health care provider prior to drinking any water. These individuals may need to take precautions such as boiling their water—no matter the source—before consuming it.[1])

The sources of any water will vary from faucet to faucet and bottle to bottle, making it virtually impossible to make a direct comparison. There are some basic points to understand about each type, though. Let's look at how tap and bottled water compare in terms of regulation, cost, and safety.

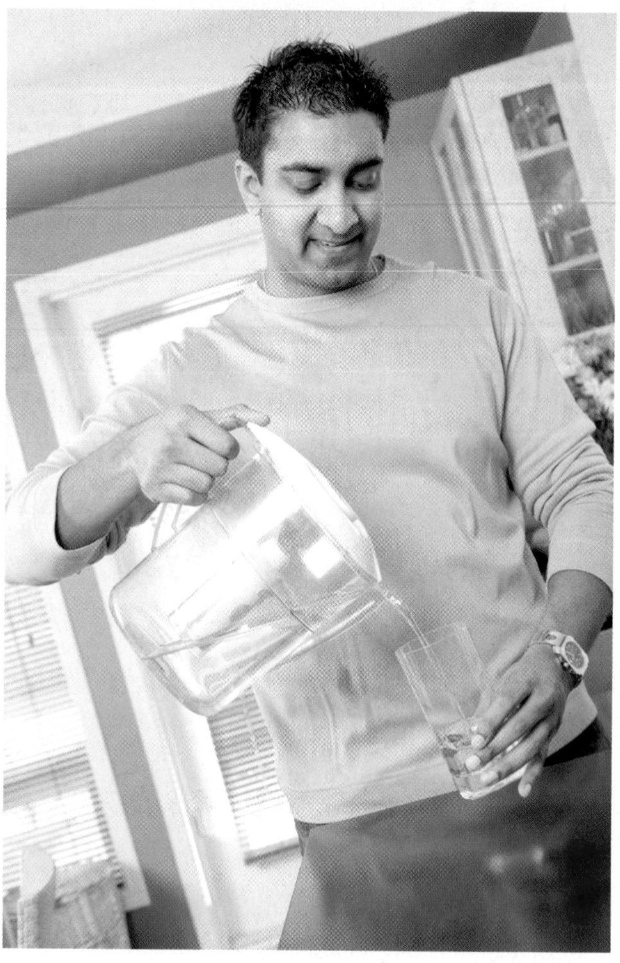

The Benefits of Tap Water

Tap water in the United States is clean, safe, and cheap. Most Americans obtain their drinking water from a community water system. The source of this municipal water can be underground wells or springs, rivers, lakes, or reservoirs. Regardless of the source, all municipal water is sent to a treatment plant where dirt and debris are filtered out, bacteria are killed, and other contaminants are removed. The Environmental Protection Agency (EPA) oversees the safety of public drinking water with national standards that set limits for more than 80 naturally occurring and man-made contaminants that may find their way into drinking water. Hundreds of billions of dollars have been invested in these treatment systems to ensure that the public water is safe to drink.[2]

Each year, the community water suppliers must provide an annual report about the quality and source of tap water. In fact, many of these regional reports can be accessed online at www.epa.gov. Even with these precautions, some individuals, who may not like the taste of their tap water or who have health concerns, use an in-home water treatment device to further filter their water. Filter devices can range from a less costly pitcher or device mounted on the kitchen faucet to a more costly, larger system that treats all the water that enters the home. Depending upon the device, it can filter contaminants such as bacteria, viruses, lead, nitrates, and pesticides. Whatever the device used, it is important that it be maintained regularly to ensure that it is working effectively.

You may have heard the terms "hard" or "soft" water used to describe tap water. The "hardness" refers to the amount of metals—specifically, calcium and magnesium—in the water. The higher the amount, the harder the water. There aren't any health concerns from drinking hard water. In fact, there may be a benefit, as hard water may contribute small amounts of these minerals to your daily diet. Whether your water is hard or soft is less important than meeting your daily needs for enough water.

American tap water also has a positive impact on the nation's dental health. About two-thirds of Americans who drink from public systems are getting fluoride in their water.[3] Fluoridation of water has been shown to reduce the incidence of dental caries by strengthening tooth enamel.

Lastly, tap water costs less than a penny a gallon, making it a very affordable way to stay hydrated.

The Truth about Bottled Water

Bottled water is second only to carbonated soft drinks in popularity among Americans. Per capita consumption of bottled water doubled in the last decade, and 8.82 billion gallons of plain water were sold in 2009 alone. However, the trend appears to be slowing. Recent environmental concerns about bottled water, which include increased energy consumption, greenhouse gas emissions, waste, and the environmental effect of water extraction,[4] may be affecting sales, which grew only 9 percent in 2007 compared with 16 percent in 2006.[5] Even though the growth is slowed, sales are still increasing yearly, with 3.5% growth in 2010 and 4.1% growth in 2011.[6]

Bottled water that is sold through interstate commerce is regulated by the FDA. Thus, as with other food products, manufacturers must adhere to specific FDA regulations, such as standards of identity. In other words, if the label on the bottle states that it is "spring water," the manufacturer must derive the water from a very specific source (see Table 1).

Interestingly, some bottled water may actually come from a municipal water source. This bottled water must also adhere to a standard of quality set forth by the FDA, which specifies the maximum amount of contaminants that can be in the water for it still to be considered safe for consumption.[7] The FDA bases its standards for bottled water sold interstate on the EPA's standards for public drinking water. However, water that is bottled and sold within the same state is not regulated by the FDA.[8]

The price of bottled water can be hefty, ranging from $1 to $4 a gallon. An individual who spends $1.50 per bottle of water and buys two bottles daily would spend more than $20 per week and more than $80 per month buying bottled water. Over the course of a nine-month school year, that amounts to more than $750 for a beverage that you can get for free from a water fountain. Finally, many bottled waters are not fluoridated, so relying on bottled water as a primary water source can shortchange dental health.[9]

Another costly bottled beverage option is the newer "designer" drinks such as vitamin waters and enhanced waters. These drinks often advertise health benefits beyond just keeping you hydrated. Sold under brand names such as Aquafina Alive and Dasani Plus, they have been "enhanced" or fortified with additional compounds such as vitamins, sugar, caffeine, and protein, though most Americans typically consume enough or even too much of these nutrients in their diet. These designer waters can cost more than $2.50 for a 20-ounce bottle—more than $10 a gallon!

The FDA requires that the ingredients added to enhanced water or vitamin water beverages must be identified on the ingredient list on the label. Read Examining the Evidence: Enhanced Water: What Are We Really Drinking? for more information on these products. Sparkling water is treated as a soft drink, including what information is required on the label. If the product claims to be "very low sodium," it must use the statement "not a significant source of sodium" on the label.[10]

The Environmental Cost of Bottled Water

The waste management of plastic water bottles has become a national problem. Almost 30 billion plastic bottles are sold each year in the United States, but only two out of every ten of these bottles are recycled.[11] The rest end up in landfills. Not only are the landfills growing, but the cost of producing plastic water bottles is also high. Researchers estimate that the energy equivalent of more than 17 million barrels of oil are used to produce the plastic water bottles Americans use each year, or enough energy to fuel a million cars for a year.[12]

TABLE 1 Sources of Bottled Water

Bottled water is labeled according to its source or how it is treated prior to bottling.

Mineral water	Water that is derived from an underground source that contains a specific amount of naturally occurring minerals and trace elements. These minerals and elements cannot be added to the water after it has been bottled.
Spring water	Water that is obtained from underground water that flows naturally to the surface. The water is collected at the spring, or at the site of a well purposefully drilled to obtain this water.
Sparkling water	Spring water that has carbon dioxide gas added before it is bottled. Also called seltzer water or club soda. Note: This is technically considered a soft drink, not a bottled water. Sparkling water does not have to adhere to FDA regulations for bottled water.
Distilled water	Water that has been boiled and processed to remove most, but not all, contaminants.
Flavored water	Water that has a flavor such as lemon or lime added. It may also contain added sugars and kilocalories.
Vitamin water	Water that has vitamins added to it. Such water may also contain added sugars and kilocalories.

Sources: A. Bullers, "Bottled Water: Better Than Tap?" *FDA Consumer* (2002), Food and Drug Administration; Center for Science in the Public Interest, "Water, Water . . . Everywhere." *Nutrition Action Health Letter* (June 2000).

TABLE 2 Bottled vs Tap Water: A Summary

	Bottled Water	Tap Water
Cost to Consumers	■ About \$1.00–\$4.00 per gallon	■ About \$0.003 per gallon
Safety	■ Bottled water is generally safe. ■ Some bottled water is not tested for contaminants. ■ Only bottled water sold across state lines is regulated by the FDA. ■ Bottled water not sold across state lines is regulated by state and local guidelines.	■ Municipal water is regulated by EPA, state, and local regulations for contaminants. ■ EPA guidelines require that the public have access to water quality reports and that it be notified if water quality is outside established bounds.
Benefits to Consumers	■ The packaging of bottled water may make it more convenient than tap water. ■ Bottled water may taste better than tap water.	■ Tap water is available at the faucet. ■ Tap water often contains fluoride, which helps to prevent tooth decay. ■ Tap water is much cheaper than bottled water. ■ Much less energy is required to produce tap water, and much less waste is generated by using a cup or reusable container rather than disposable plastic bottles.

Although refilling and reusing the bottles from bottled water may seem like an environmentally friendly and cost-effective idea, the practice is not advised. The plastic containers cannot withstand repeated washing and the plastic can actually break down, causing chemicals to leach into the water. Sturdier water bottles that are designed for reuse must be thoroughly cleaned with hot soapy water after each use to kill germs.

The bottom line is that both tap water and bottled water can be safe to drink, and the choice is likely to come down to personal preference, costs, and concern about environmental impacts. Table 2 summarizes the similarities and differences between the two types of water.

References

1. Grandjean, A. C., K. J. Reimers, and M. E. Buyckx. 2003. Hydration: Issues for the 21st Century. *Nutrition Reviews* 61:261–271.
2. Sheng, H. 2000. Body Fluids and Water Balance. In *Biochemical and Physiological Aspects of Human Nutrition*. Philadelphia: W. B. Saunders.
3. Institute of Medicine. 2004. *Dietary Reference Intakes: Water, Potassium, Sodium, Chloride, and Sulfate*. Washington, DC: The National Academies Press.
4. Gies, E. 2008. *Rising Sales of Bottled Water Trigger Strong Reaction from U.S. Conservationists*. Available at www.nytimes.com/2008/03/19/business/worldbusiness/19iht-rbogbottle.html. Accessed November 2012.
5. Environmental Leader. 2007. *Bottled Water Manufacturers Face Uncertain Future*. Available at www.environmentalleader.com/2007/10/08/bottled-water-manufacturers-face-uncertain-future. Accessed May 2012.
6. Beverage Marketing Corporation. 2011. *Bottled Water Recovers Somewhat from Recessionary Years, New Report from Beverage Marketing Corporation Shows*. Available at www.beveragemarketing.com/?section=pressreleases. Accessed May 2012.
7. Grandjean, A., and S. Campbell. 2004. *Hydration: Fluids for Life*. Available at www.ilsi.org. Accessed May 2012.
8. Ibid.
9. Marieb, E. N., and K. Hoehn. 2007. *Human Anatomy and Physiology*. 7th ed. San Francisco: Pearson/Benjamin Cummings.
10. FDA. 2012. *Carbonated Soft Drinks: What You Should Know*. Available at www.fda.gov. Accessed May 2012.
11. Earth 911.com. 2012. 360: Recycling Plastic Bottles. Available at http://earth911.com/news/2009/06/08/360-recycling-plastic-bottles. Accessed November 2012.
12. The United States Conference of Mayors. 2008. Supporting Municipal Water Systems. Available at www.usmayors.org/resolutions/76th_conference/environment_07.asp. Accessed November 2012.

EXAMINING THE EVIDENCE

Enhanced Water: What Are We Really Drinking?

Although bottled water has become increasingly popular in the last few decades, it seems to be losing ground to a new type of bottled beverage: enhanced waters, which often advertise health benefits beyond just hydration.

The name "enhanced water" generally refers to any type of bottled water that has added ingredients to improve its taste and increase nutrient content. These beverages, which are sold under brand names such as Aquafina Alive, Propel, Fruit$_2$O, and Dasani Plus, have been fortified with vitamins, fiber, caffeine, herbs, protein, and sometimes even oxygen. Some contain as many kilocalories as a soft drink, while others are similar in mineral content to a sports drink. Some enhanced waters are presented as energy boosters because they contain caffeine, while others, like Fruit$_2$O Relax, claim to calm and relax nerves. Still other products boast improved mental acuity, elevated mood, or other functional benefits. The accompanying table compares some of the more popular brands.

Do enhanced waters provide any health benefits? In one study, when people without folate deficiency and normal homocysteine levels consumed mineral water fortified with folic acid, vitamins B_6, B_{12}, and D, and calcium, their folate status was enhanced and their homocysteine levels dropped.[1] Other results indicated that calcium used to fortify the enhanced water was bioavailable.[2] But that's not the whole picture.[3] Results reported from the Iowa Women's Health Study suggest that the use of multivitamin supplements, which include vitamins often found in enhanced waters, increased total mortality risk.[4] Whereas some results are promising, other results raise concerns. The bottom line is that these bottled waters are not meant to replace fruits and vegetables or balanced meals in the diet.

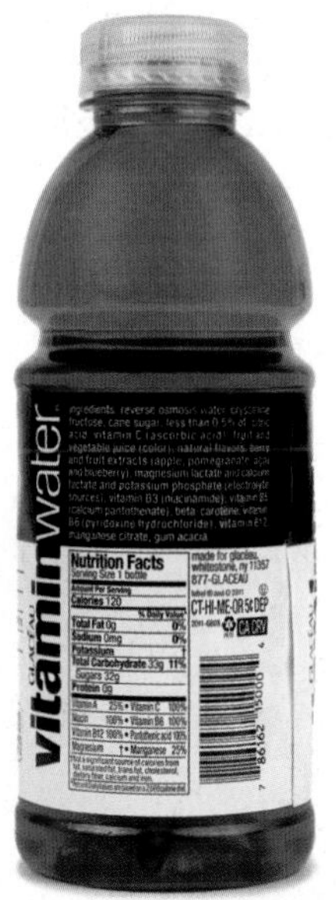

Enhanced waters cost about $1.49 for a 20-ounce bottle that may provide 100 percent of one or more vitamins. A generic multivitamin pill costs approximately 10 cents a day for 100 percent or more of 13 vitamins and minerals. Thus, vitamin water costs about 15 times what a daily multivitamin does and provides fewer nutrients.

The Nutrient Content of Enhanced Waters

Bottled Beverage	Serving Size	Kilocalories	Sweeteners	Added Nutrients
Dasani Plus	8 oz	0	Artificial sweeteners acesulfame potassium, sucralose	Guarana, ginseng, chromium, B vitamins
Fruit$_2$O Energy	8 oz	0	Acesulfame potassium, sucralose	Caffeine, B vitamins
Fruit$_2$O Relax	8 oz	0	Acesulfame potassium, sucralose	Chamomile, hibiscus, B vitamins
Propel Invigorating	8 oz	20	5 gm sugar	Caffeine, B vitamins
Skinny Water	16.9 oz	10	None	Super CitriMax and ChromeMate, calcium
SoBe Life Water	8 oz	50	13 gm sugar	Vitamin E, vitamin C, and B vitamins
Special K_2O Protein Water	16 oz	50	Acesulfame potassium, sucralose	Fiber, calcium, whey protein, niacin, vitamin B_6, vitamin B_{12}
Vitaminwater Defense	8 oz	50	13 gm sugar	Zinc, four B vitamins, vitamin C, electrolytes
Vitaminwater Energy	8 oz	40	13 gm sugar	Vitamins C, E, and A, B vitamins, caffeine, guarana, ginseng
Vitaminwater XXX	8 oz	50	13 gm sugar	Vitamin C and B vitamins plus 50 mg of acai-blueberry-pomegranate extract

References

1. Tapola, N. S., H. M. Karvonen, L. K. Niskanen, and E. S. Karkkinen. 2004. Mineral Water Fortified with Folic Acid, Vitamins B_6, B_{12}, D, and Calcium Improves Folate Status and Decreases Plasma Homocysteine Concentration in Men and Women. *European Journal of Clinical Nutrition* 58:376–385.
2. Coiro, V., G. Zanardi, J. G. Saccani, P. Rubino, G. Manfredi, and P. Chiodera. 2008. High-Calcium Mineral Water as a Calcium Supplementing Measure for Post-Thyroidectomy Hypocalcemia. *Minerva Endocrinologica* 33:7–13.
3. Harvard School of Public Health. 2012. *Enhanced Water "Unequivocally Harmful to Health," Says HSPH Nutrition Expert.* Available at www.hsph.harvard.edu/news/features/coverage-in-the-media/nutrition-news-willett-vitamin-water-unhealthy. Accessed May 2012.
4. Mursu, J., K. Robien, L. J. Harnack, K. Park, and D. R. Jacobs. 2011. Less Is More: Dietary Supplements and Mortality Rates in Older Women. The Iowa Women's Health Study. *Archives of Internal Medicine* 171:1625–1633.

A cup of coffee gives you a "pick me up" without causing dehydration.

Do Diuretics Like Caffeine and Alcohol Affect Water Balance?

Beverages such as alcoholic drinks, regular coffee, and tea contribute significantly to total water intake, but alcohol and caffeine are also considered **diuretics,** and contribute to water loss. Overconsumption of some of these substances can upset fluid balance.

Caffeine Does Not Cause Significant Loss of Body Water

Caffeine is a mild diuretic that blocks the action of ADH in the kidneys. However, researchers have not been able to confirm that this mild diuretic actually results in dehydration. In fact, caffeine doesn't cause a significant loss of body water over the course of a day compared with noncaffeinated beverages. Individuals who routinely consume caffeinated beverages actually develop a tolerance for its diuretic effect and experience less water loss over time.[8, 9] Although caffeine may have other detrimental effects on the body, such as jitteriness and insomnia, moderate intakes of caffeinated beverages don't appear to have a significant negative effect on hydration.

Alcohol Can Be Dehydrating

Similar to caffeine, alcohol interferes with water balance by inhibiting ADH, which can induce urination as quickly as 20 minutes after alcohol is consumed. Unlike caffeine, alcohol can be dehydrating. The water lost affects the concentrations of electrolytes in the body, especially potassium, which affects metabolism. This may be partly responsible for the thirst, lightheadedness, and dry mouth that are often part of a hangover. Older drinkers appear to overcome this suppression of ADH faster and resist dehydration better than do younger drinkers. Reducing the amount of alcohol consumed and drinking water after consuming alcohol can help prevent dehydration. (For more on alcohol, see Chapter 7.)

diuretics Substances that increase the production and secretion of urine; they are often used as antihypertensive drugs.

Diuretic Medications Can Help Treat Hypertension

Pharmaceutical diuretics are often prescribed as a first line of treatment for hypertension. These drugs promote diuresis (increased excretion of urine) by inhibiting the reabsorption of sodium. As you've already learned, if the kidney excretes more sodium, water loss will also increase. This action reduces blood volume, which lowers blood pressure.

Some types of diuretics also increase potassium loss. This is because the increase in sodium loss from the ECF into the urine stimulates aldosterone and the sodium-potassium pump, which increases sodium reabsorption in exchange for potassium. This increase in potassium loss increases the risk of **hypokalemia.** A small drop in potassium levels usually doesn't cause symptoms, but moderate to larger drops cause lower blood pressure, muscle weakness and cramps, and constipation. Patients taking diuretics are closely monitored by their doctors to prevent electrolyte imbalances. They are encouraged to eat potassium-rich foods such as bananas, peanut butter, and tomatoes. In some cases, potassium supplements may be prescribed.

THE TAKE-HOME MESSAGE Moderate caffeine intake does not affect fluid balance. Alcohol reduces the effects of ADH and can cause dehydration. Pharmaceutical diuretics are prescribed to reduce hypertension but may cause electrolyte imbalances.

What Are the Effects of Too Much or Too Little Water?

Although water is an essential nutrient, it can also be harmful if consumed in excess. And, just as with other nutrients, consuming too little can lead to adverse symptoms and conditions.

Consuming Too Much Water Can Cause Hyponatremia

Water intoxication is rare because healthy individuals who consume a balanced diet will just produce more urine to eliminate excess water. However, drinking fluids too fast without adequate sodium replacement depletes sodium and increases the rate of urine production. When too much water enters the cells, the tissues swell with the excess fluid and the concentration of sodium in the extracellular fluid drops, resulting in **hyponatremia** (*hypo* = under, *natrium* = sodium, *emia* = blood).

In April 2002, 28-year-old Cynthia Lucero was running the Boston Marathon. About five miles from the finish line, Lucero began to feel wobbly and mentioned to a friend that she felt dehydrated even though she had been consuming fluids throughout her run. She suddenly collapsed and was taken to a nearby hospital. She died the next day, due to swelling of the brain brought on by hyponatremia caused by overconsumption of fluids.[10, 11] The condition doesn't just occur among endurance athletes. In January 2007, a woman named Jennifer Strange collapsed after competing in a California radio contest to see who could drink the most water without using the restroom. She was found dead in her home a few hours after completing the contest.

Drinking adequate fluid replaces water lost from sweating during exercise and prevents dehydration.

hypokalemia A dangerously low level of blood potassium.

water intoxication A potentially dangerous medical condition that results from drinking too much water too quickly, also known as *hyperhydration*; can lead to hyponatremia and possible death.

hyponatremia A dangerously low level of sodium in the blood that can result from water intoxication or a lack of sodium during heavy exercise.

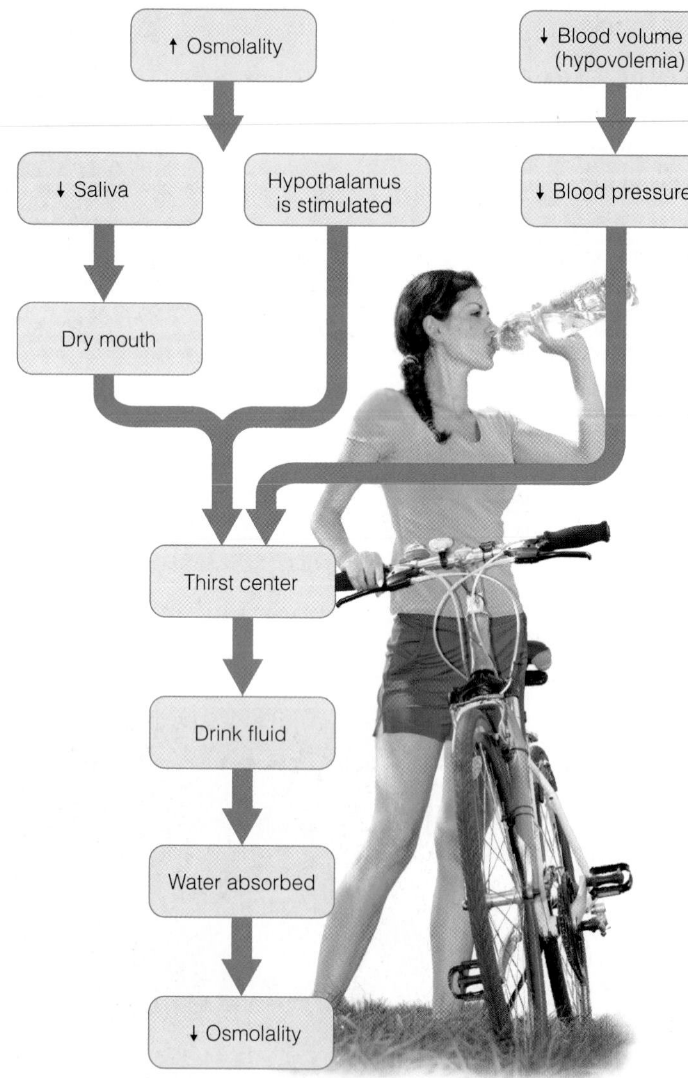

▲ **Figure 11.12 The Thirst Mechanism**
The thirst mechanism is stimulated when solutes in the blood become more concentrated. The thirst center in the hypothalamus stimulates a sensation of thirst, which in turn stimulates water consumption and returns the blood osmolality to normal.

Symptoms of the swelling in the brain that occurs as a result of water intoxication include fatigue, confusion, and disorientation.[12] Mistakenly treating these symptoms by consuming more fluids will only make matters worse.

The seriousness of overhydration has prompted the USA Track & Field Association to revise its hydration guidelines for long-distance and marathon runners to avoid hyponatremia. Chapter 16 provides these guidelines and shows you how to calculate how much fluid you need during exercise.

Consuming Too Little Water Is a Common Problem

While overhydration can have dire effects on the body, inadequate water intake, or dehydration, occurs much more frequently and can be just as harmful. Dehydration can be the result of either not drinking enough water, or losing excessive amounts of water as a result of diarrhea, vomiting, high fever, or the use of diuretics. Dehydration can result from as little as a 2 percent loss of body water and can trigger a loss of short-term and long-term memory, lower attention span and cognition, and reduced ability to maintain core temperature. It can also increase the risk of urinary tract infections and fatigue.

For some populations, such as children, the elderly, and athletes, the consequences of dehydration can be severe. In the elderly, for example, dehydration has been misdiagnosed as dementia.[13] Even a 1 to 2 percent loss of body water can impair an athlete's cardiovascular and thermoregulatory response and reduce the athlete's capacity for exercise. See Table 11.1 for common signs of dehydration.

The Thirst Mechanism Signals Dehydration

Thirst, which is usually perceived after mild dehydration has begun, is often the first physical sign of dehydration. The resultant urge to drink plays an important role in preventing further dehydration and restoring water balance in the body.

Figure 11.12 illustrates the reactions that occur as part of the thirst mechanism. When water is lost from the body, reduced blood volume (also called **hypovolemia**; *hypo* = reduced, *vol* = volume, *emia* = blood) can occur. Less circulating blood can lead to reduced blood pressure and, if severe enough, hypotension. Together, hypovolemia and hypotension can reduce cardiac output, impair digestion, and may cause fainting or blacking out.

When an individual is dehydrated, water is depleted from the ECF and the ICF, but not necessarily in equal proportions. Initially, water loss is from the ECF, which becomes more concentrated in solutes. This increase in concentration draws water from the ICF into the ECF in an attempt to maintain homeostasis and water balance. At this stage, the water balance in the ECF is maintained, but causes ICF dehydration. If both sodium and water are lost, then the ECF (remember that sodium is the major electrolyte in the ECF) is mostly affected. Less fluid is excreted through the skin,

hypovolemia A low blood volume.

lungs, and kidneys in an attempt to adapt to the change in fluid. These adaptations are important to reduce the effects on blood volume and the concentration of solutes, but they do not return fluid levels to normal. Fluids must be consumed to restore blood volume.

Just quenching thirst will not typically provide enough fluids to remedy dehydration. This isn't a concern for moderately active individuals eating a balanced diet, as fluids from beverages and food throughout the day will eventually restore water balance.[14] However, elderly people, and individuals who are very physically active or who have vigorous jobs, such as fire fighters, are at higher risk of dehydration if they don't take in enough fluid, or they lose body water copiously through sweating. These individuals need to take additional steps to ensure that they are properly hydrated.

TABLE 11.1 Signs of Dehydration

Mild Dehydration	Moderate Dehydration	Severe Dehydration
Dry lips and mouth Thirst Inside of mouth slightly dry Low urine output; concentrated urine appears dark yellow	Thirst Very dry mouth Sunken eyes Sunken fontanelles (the soft spots on an infant's head) Tenting (skin doesn't bounce back readily when pinched and lifted slightly)	All signs of moderate dehydration Rapid and weak pulse Cold hands and feet Rapid breathing Blue lips Lethargic, comatose

Monitor Water Intake to Avoid Overhydration and Dehydration

One way to monitor hydration is the cornerstone method, which involves measuring body weight before and after long bouts of vigorous physical activity or labor and noting changes. If a person weighs less after an activity than before, the weight change is due to loss of body water, and that water must be replenished. The general recommendation is that for every pound of weight lost in water, 16 fluid ounces (2 cups) of water should be consumed. Alternatively, if a weight gain is noted, overhydration is likely, and less fluid should be consumed before the next activity.

Urine color can also be used to assess hydration. Individuals who are dehydrated produce less urine due to the release of ADH. The urine that is produced is more concentrated, as it contains a higher proportion of compounds to the smaller volume of water. This causes the urine to be darker in color.[15] The National Athletic Trainers Association has created a chart to help individuals assess if they are drinking enough fluids to offset the amount of water lost through sweating (see **Figure 11.13**).[16] Individuals who are very physically active and who notice that the color of their urine darkens during the day, to the point where it resembles the shade of a yield sign or darker, likely need to increase their fluid intake. (Note: Other factors, such as consuming excessive amounts of the B vitamin riboflavin, and certain medications, can also affect the color of urine.)

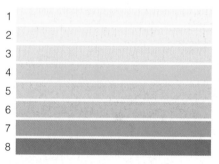

▲ **Figure 11.13 Urine Color Guide**
Clear or light yellow urine indicates adequate hydration. Dark urine (color 7 or darker) indicates dehydration and the need to consume more fluids.

Putting It All Together

Water is the universal solvent, and the main component of the fluids in which all reactions involving the energy-producing nutrients (carbohydrates, proteins, and fats) take place in the body. The nutrients, vitamins, and minerals that aid in these chemical reactions work in conjunction with water to meet metabolic needs. Consuming a wide variety of foods from all food groups, with an emphasis on maintaining sufficient fluid intake, is the best diet prescription to meet the body's needs for carbohydrates, proteins, fat, vitamins, minerals, and water.

Visual Chapter Summary

1 Water Is the Most Abundant Nutrient in the Body

Water (H_2O) is the most abundant substance in the body and makes up about 45 to 75 percent of body weight.

Water is a polar molecule, which makes it an excellent solvent. It is a key component of all body fluids, including blood, lymph, and the fluid inside and around cells, and is part of amniotic fluid. Water contributes to digestive juices and exports products through the intestinal cells; transports oxygen, nutrients, and hormones to the cells; and transports waste products to be excreted in urine and stool.

Water helps maintain body temperature, acts as a lubricant for joints and sensitive eye tissue, moistens food through the action of saliva, is part of mucus that lubricates the intestinal tract, and bathes organs, including the brain. Water is essential for most chemical reactions in the body.

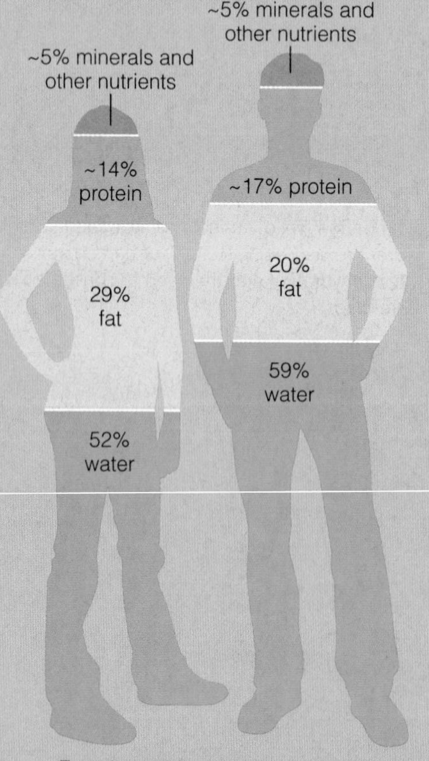

2 Water Balance Is Maintained through Ingestion and Excretion and between Fluid Compartments

When the amount of water consumed in foods and beverages, and produced as metabolic water, is equal to the amount excreted, the body is in water balance. Water is excreted through urine and sweat, and as water vapor through the lungs.

Body water is either inside cells (intracellular fluid, ICF) or outside the cells (extracellular fluid, ECF). Extracellular fluid is comprised of interstitial fluid, found immediately outside and between the cells, and intravascular fluid, found in blood and lymph. Osmosis and the sodium-potassium pump influence water balance between the ICF and the ECF.

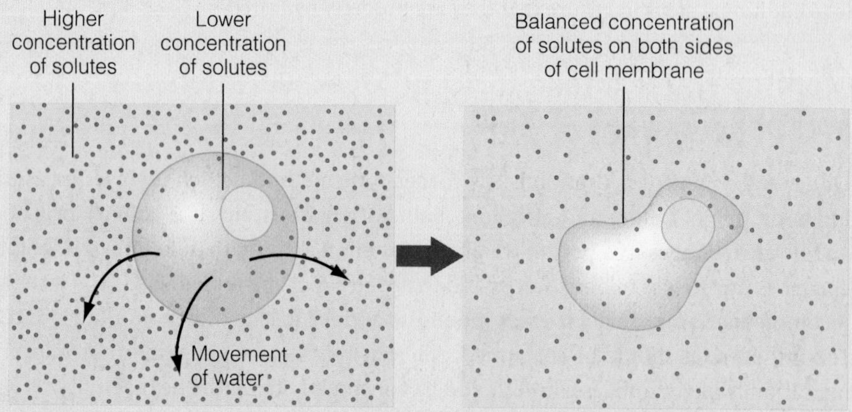

3 Water, Sodium, and Hormones Affect Blood Pressure

The kidneys, hypothalamus, pituitary gland, lungs, adrenal glands, and liver all play a role in maintaining blood volume. The hypothalamus detects a drop in blood volume and signals the pituitary gland to release ADH, which increases the absorption of water through the kidneys. The kidneys also react to reduced blood volume by releasing the enzyme renin to convert a liver protein to angiotensin. This protein stimulates the adrenal gland to release the hormone aldosterone, which stimulates the kidneys to reabsorb sodium. The result is a return of blood volume to normal.

The mechanisms involved in blood pressure regulation directly relate to the sodium concentrations in the ECF. Low intakes of sodium decrease the osmolality in the ECF which stimulates the renin-angiotensin system. If sodium intake is high, the renin-angiotensin system is reduced and the excess sodium is excreted. Any factors that alter this control mechanism can result in chronic hypertension.

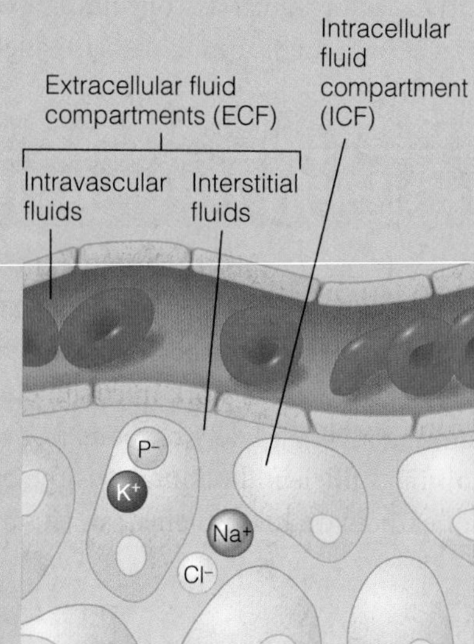

4 Daily Water Recommendations Are Based on Water Balance

The current daily water recommendations are based on the reported total water intake (from both beverages and food) of healthy Americans. Adult women should ingest about 9 cups (~80 percent of 12 total cups of water), and adult males, approximately 13 cups (~80 percent of 16 total cups of water) of beverages daily. People who are very active and sweat a lot have higher water requirements. The majority of water intake comes from beverages (about 500 to 1,500 milliliters) and food (700 to 1,000 milliliters). Metabolic water produces about 200 to 300 milliliters per day. Water is lost through the urine (500 to 1,500 milliliters), the lungs as water vapor (350 milliliters), the feces (150 milliliters), and sweat (400 to 900 milliliters). All foods contain some water. Cooked hot cereals and fruits and vegetables are robust sources of water.

5 Diuretics Can Cause Dehydration

Caffeinated beverages such as coffee, tea, and soft drinks contribute to daily water needs. Caffeine is a mild diuretic but doesn't cause a significant loss of body water compared with noncaffeinated beverages. Individuals who routinely consume caffeine develop a tolerance to its diuretic effect and experience less water loss over time. Alcohol interferes with water balance by inhibiting ADH.

6 Consuming Too Much or Too Little Water Can Be Lethal

Consuming too much water, a condition called water intoxication, is rare but can be lethal. Drinking fluids too fast without adequate sodium replacement depletes sodium, increases urine production, and results in hyponatremia. This condition can cause fatigue, muscle weakness, confusion, convulsions, and even death.

Dehydration occurs when there is an insufficient amount of water in the body due to reduced fluid intake or to excessive loss due to diarrhea, vomiting, high fever, or the use of diuretics. Dehydration triggers short-term and long-term memory loss, lowers attention span and cognition, reduces the ability to maintain core temperature, and can increase the risk of urinary tract infections and fatigue.

Thirst is often the first sign of dehydration. When water is lost from the body, hypovolemia, or reduced blood volume, can result. The thirst mechanism, which is controlled by the hypothalamus and ADH, stimulates fluid consumption to return fluid levels to normal. Urine color can be used to monitor hydration.

Terms to Know

- metabolic water
- insensible water loss
- intracellular fluid (ICF)
- extracellular fluid (ECF)
- interstitial fluid
- intravascular fluid
- electrolytes
- renin
- aldosterone
- osmosis
- sodium-potassium pump
- diuretic
- water intoxication
- hyponatremia
- dehydration
- hypovolemia

MasteringNutrition™

Build your knowledge—and confidence—in the Study Area of MasteringNutrition with a variety of study tools.

Check Your Understanding

1. Which of the following is a function that water performs in the body?
   a. provides energy to the muscles
   b. helps transport waste products for excretion
   c. acts as an antioxidant
   d. participates in the synthesis of proteins
2. Most of the excess body water is lost daily in
   a. exhaled water vapor.
   b. fecal matter.
   c. urine.
   d. sweat.
3. The sodium-potassium pump functions to pump
   a. sodium ions out of the cell and potassium ions into the cell.
   b. sodium ions into the cell and potassium ions out of the cell.
   c. sodium and potassium ions into the cell.
   d. sodium and potassium ions in both directions in and out of the cell.
4. Hypovolemia is the result of
   a. drinking too much water too quickly.
   b. hypernatremia.
   c. dehydration.
   d. all of the above.
5. The fluid in the blood is an example of
   a. intracellular fluid.
   b. extracellular fluid.
   c. intravascular fluid.
   d. both b and c.
6. The hormone that signals the kidneys to reabsorb sodium is called
   a. antidiuretic hormone.
   b. aldosterone.
   c. angiotensin.
   d. renin.
7. The thirst mechanism is stimulated by
   a. an increase in blood volume.
   b. an increase in blood pressure.
   c. an increase in the concentration of solutes in the blood.
   d. a decrease in the concentration of solutes in the blood.
8. The purpose of sweating is to
   a. regulate body temperature.
   b. excrete waste products.
   c. excrete sodium ions.
   d. maintain potassium balance.
9. All bottled water is regulated by the FDA.
   a. True
   b. False
10. Hypokalemia is defined as
    a. low levels of sodium in the blood.
    b. low blood volume.
    c. high potassium levels in the blood.
    d. low levels of potassium in the blood.

Answers

1. (b) Water picks up waste products from cells and transports them to the kidneys to be excreted in the urine. Water participates in chemical reactions that provide energy but does not provide energy itself, nor does it act as an antioxidant or help synthesize proteins.
2. (c) The majority of fluid lost is through the kidneys, which produce approximately 1,500 milliliters of urine each day. Exhaled air and lung vapor excrete about 200 to 400 milliliters of water per day, and about 100 milliliters of water is lost through intestinal fluids in the stool. The amount of water lost through the skin as sweat varies depending on environmental temperatures and physical activity.
3. (a) The sodium-potassium pump pumps sodium ions out of the cell and potassium ions into the cell. This helps pull water into compartments to maintain fluid balance.
4. (c) Hypovolemia is the result of reduced blood volume usually due to dehydration or excessive blood loss. Drinking too much water too quickly can result in water intoxication. Hypernatremia, or excess levels of sodium in the blood, would increase blood volume rather than reduce blood volume.
5. (d) Extracellular fluid is the fluid outside the cell and includes the intravascular fluid, which is in the blood and the capillaries, and interstitial fluid, found between the cells. Intracellular fluid is located inside the cells.
6. (b) The hormone aldosterone signals the kidneys to reabsorb sodium. Antidiuretic hormone signals the kidneys to reabsorb water. Angiotensin is a vasoconstrictor and renin is an enzyme.
7. (c) The thirst mechanism is stimulated by an increase in the concentration of solutes in the blood. Consuming fluids will dilute the solute concentration, increase blood volume, and increase blood pressure, all of which decrease the sensation of thirst.
8. (a) Sweating releases heat from the body and helps regulate body temperature. Whereas sweat does contain waste products and sodium ions, excretion of these is not the main function of sweating.
9. (b) False. The FDA only regulates bottled water that is sold through interstate commerce. Bottled water that is produced and sold within the same state is not regulated by the FDA.
10. (d) Hypokalemia is a low level of potassium in the blood; hyperkalemia denotes high blood potassium levels. Hyponatremia refers to low levels of sodium in the blood, and hypovolemia means decreased blood volume.

Answers to Myths and Misconceptions

1. **False.** You may be able to survive weeks without food but you can't live for more than a few days without water.
2. **True.** Your morning cup of java does contribute to daily water needs,

even though it may contain caffeine, a diuretic.

3. **True.** Depending on age, gender, and body composition, a minimum of eight glasses of water per day may be necessary to maintain a healthy level of body water. The recommended intake for adult women is 9 cups per day and 13 cups for men.
4. **False.** Water does transport waste products for excretion from the body, but drinking large amounts will not increase that function and may cause overhydration and hyponatremia, which is a dangerous condition.
5. **False.** Water participates in energy metabolism but does not directly contribute to weight loss.
6. **True.** It is easy to become dehydrated during exercise because of excess sweating, especially in warm, humid environments. Drinking plenty of fluid before, during, and after a workout is key to maintaining hydration.
7. **False.** Sodium is an essential nutrient and should never be eliminated from the diet. A balanced diet and adequate fluid intake will prevent fluid retention.
8. **True.** Potassium-rich foods can play a role in reducing hypertension. Potassium works together with sodium to regulate fluid balance and reduce blood pressure.
9. **True.** Alcohol is a diuretic and excess consumption can cause dehydration.
10. **False.** Enhanced waters such as vitamin waters contain additional kilocalories. To improve fluid intake, plain water is just as healthy and much cheaper.

Web Resources

- For more information on high blood pressure, visit Your Guide to Lowering High Blood Pressure at www.nhlbi.nih.gov/hbp/index.html
- For more information on current research related to hydration during exercise, visit the Gatorade Sports Science Institute at www.gssiweb.com
- For more information on the FDA regulations and bottled water, visit www.fda.gov/ForConsumers/ConsumerUpdates/ucm203620.htm

References

1. Institute of Medicine. 2004. *Dietary Reference Intakes: Water, Potassium, Sodium, Chloride, and Sulfate.* Washington, DC: The National Academies Press.
2. Marieb, E. N., and K. Hoehn. 2007. *Human Anatomy and Physiology.* 7th ed. San Francisco: Pearson/Benjamin Cummings.
3. McArdle, W. D., F. I. Katch, and V. L. Katch. 2009. *Sports and Exercise Nutrition.* 3rd ed. Baltimore: Lippincott Williams & Wilkins.
4. Passe, D., M. Horn, J. Stofan, C. Horswill, and R. Murray. 2007. Voluntary Dehydration in Runners Despite Favorable Conditions for Fluid Intake. *International Journal of Sport Nutrition and Exercise Metabolism* 17:284–295.
5. McArdle, W. D., et al. 2009. *Sports and Exercise Nutrition.*
6. Grandjean, A., and S. Campbell. 2004. *Hydration: Fluids for Life.* Available at www.ilsi.org. Accessed May 2012.
7. Institute of Medicine. 2004. *Dietary Reference Intakes: Water, Potassium, Sodium, Chloride, and Sulfate.*
8. Armstrong, L. E., A. C. Pumerantz, M. W. Roti, D. A. Judelson, G. Watson, J. C. Dias, B. Sokmen, et al. 2005. Fluid, Electrolyte, and Renal Indices of Hydration During 11 Days of Controlled Caffeine Consumption. *International Journal of Sport Nutrition and Exercise Metabolism* 15:252–265.
9. Maughan, R. J., and J. Griffin. 2003. Caffeine Ingestion and Fluid Balance: A Review. *Journal of Human Nutrition and Dietetics* 16:411–420.
10. Arnold, D. 2002. To the End, Marathon Was at Center of Student's Life. *The Boston Globe.* Boston. Available at www.remembercynthia.com/BostonGlobe.htm. Accessed August 2008.
11. Smith, S. 2002. Marathon Runner's Death Linked to Excessive Fluid Intake. *The Boston Globe.* Boston. Available at www.remembercynthia.com/Hyponatremia_BostonGlobe.htm. Accessed May 2012.
12. Grandjean, A. C., K. J. Reimers, and M. E. Buyckx. 2003. Hydration: Issues for the 21st Century. *Nutrition Reviews* 61:261–271.
13. Sentongo, T. A. 2004. The Use of Oral Rehydration Solutions in Children and Adults. *Gastroenterology Reports* 6:307–313.
14. Institute of Medicine. 2004. *Dietary Reference Intakes: Water, Potassium, Sodium, Chloride, and Sulfate.*
15. Ibid.
16. Casa, D. J., L. E. Armstrong, S. K. Hillman, S. J. Montain, R. C. Reiff, B. S. E. Rich, W. O. Roberts, and J. A. Stone. 2000. National Athletic Trainers Association Position Statement: Fluid Replacement for Athletes. *Journal of Athletic Training* 35:212–224.

12 Major Minerals

Chapter Objectives

After reading this chapter, you will be able to:

1. Describe the differences between the major and trace minerals and the factors that affect their bioavailability, absorption, and retention.
2. List the functions, food sources, and the toxicity and deficiency symptoms associated with sodium.
3. List the functions, food sources, and the toxicity and deficiency symptoms associated with chloride.
4. Explain the role of sodium in the development of hypertension and the role of minerals in maintaining normal blood pressure.
5. List the functions, food sources, and the toxicity and deficiency symptoms associated with potassium.
6. List the functions, food sources, and the toxicity and deficiency symptoms associated with calcium.
7. Compare the roles of minerals in the development of healthy bone tissue and osteoporosis, and outline the factors that influence the risk of developing the disease.
8. List the functions, food sources, and the toxicity and deficiency symptoms associated with phosphorus.
9. List the functions, food sources, and the toxicity and deficiency symptoms associated with magnesium.
10. List the functions, food sources, and daily needs associated with sulfate.

1. The very best way to ensure an adequate intake of minerals is to take supplements. T/F
2. Minerals are simpler molecules than vitamins. T/F
3. Hypertension is a preventable condition. T/F
4. Minerals are more bioavailable in plant foods than in animal foods. T/F
5. Eating more fruit can improve bone density. T/F
6. A diet rich in potassium can help lower blood pressure. T/F
7. Most dietary sodium comes from salt added to foods during cooking. T/F
8. A serving of milk will provide about a third of an adult's daily calcium needs. T/F
9. Consuming too much phosphorus interferes with calcium absorption. T/F
10. Sulfur is not an essential nutrient. T/F

See page 470 for answers to these Myths and Misconceptions.

What do a cast-iron skillet, the salt on an icy road, and the copper pipes used in plumbing all have in common? They contain some of the same minerals that play essential roles in the body. From iron to sodium to copper, these substances occur as part of the earthen world around you and are necessary for your day-to-day functioning.

In this chapter, we will explore the roles that the major minerals play in the body. We will discuss the average person's daily needs for each mineral and, equally important, how to avoid consuming toxic amounts. The trace minerals will be covered in Chapter 13.

What Are Minerals?

Only 14 of the 92 known **minerals** are essential to body function. Minerals, like vitamins, can be part of enyzmes to help chemical reactions take place in cells, work with the immune system, participate in muscle contraction, and keep the heart beating. In short, minerals are essential to overall health and well-being.

minerals Inorganic elements essential to the nutrition of humans.

major minerals Minerals needed in amounts greater than 100 milligrams per day. These include sodium, chloride, potassium, calcium, phosphorus, magnesium, and sulfur.

trace minerals Minerals needed in amounts less than 20 milligrams daily. These include iron, zinc, selenium, fluoride, chromium, copper, manganese, and molybdenum.

Minerals are classified into two groups. The **major minerals,** or macrominerals, are *major* because humans need to consume them in amounts greater than 100 milligrams per day (daily needs for some major minerals exceed 1,000 milligrams per day), and there are at least 5 grams of the mineral in the body (**Figure 12.1**). Calcium is considered a major mineral because adults need to eat at least 1,000 milligrams per day, and the body contains approximately 1,000 grams of calcium. Other major minerals include sodium, chloride, potassium, phosphorus, magnesium, and sulfur.

The second group, the **trace minerals,** are also known as microminerals because they are needed in amounts less than 20 milligrams per day, and the body contains less than 5 grams total. Iron is an example of a trace mineral; the average adult male needs about 8 milligrams per day and has a total of about 3 to 4 grams in his body. Other trace minerals include zinc, copper, selenium, chromium, iodide, manganese, molybdenum, and fluoride.

* Based on a 154-pound person

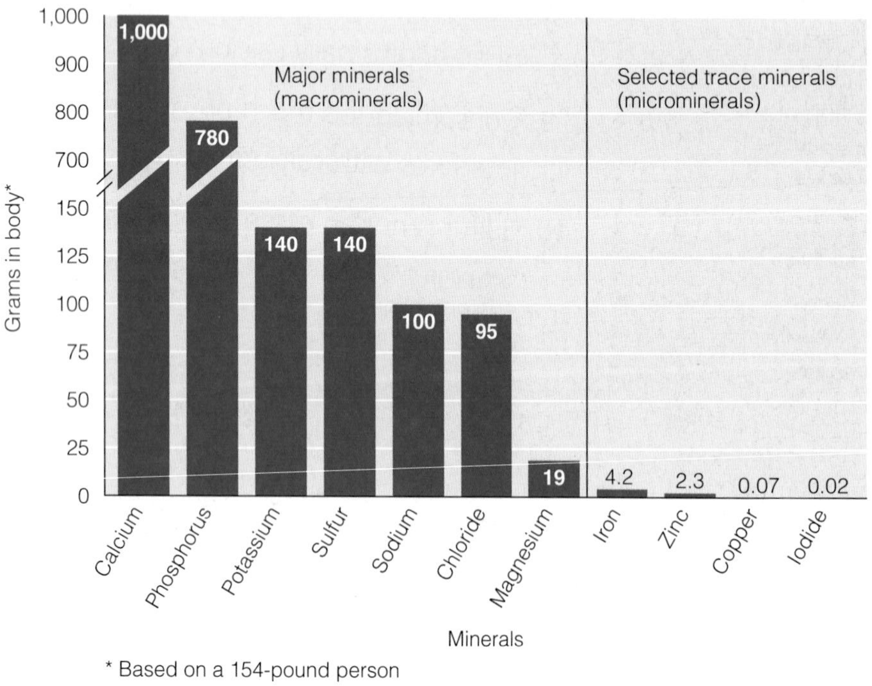

▲ **Figure 12.1 The Minerals in Your Body**
Major minerals are present in larger amounts than trace minerals in the human body. However, all are equally important to health.

Minerals Are Inorganic Elements Needed by the Body

Minerals do not contain carbon, and are therefore classified as inorganic. Unlike vitamins, single molecules of minerals contain only atoms of the same element, such as calcium (Ca), iron (Fe), or other essential minerals, in the form of inorganic salts, including sodium chloride, or NaCl (see **Figure 12.2**). Molecules of vitamins are more complex and contain other elements.

Minerals are also different from vitamins in that minerals are very stable in food; that is, they tend to be water insoluble and are not destroyed by heat, acid, oxygen, or ultraviolet light.[1] Vitamins are much less stable in cooking, and the water-soluble vitamins can easily leach into cooking water (see Chapter 9). The only exception to this is the mineral potassium, which, similar to water-soluble vitamins, may leach.

When mineral salts dissolve in body water, they separate (or *dissociate*) into individually charged particles, or ions. Minerals found in the body are most often found as individual ions or as inorganic compounds.

Minerals differ from the macronutrients in that they remain intact during digestion and generally don't change their shape or structure when performing their biological functions. Thus, the potassium in bananas has the same ion charge as the potassium inside muscle cells.

a Na^+, an example of an inorganic nutrient

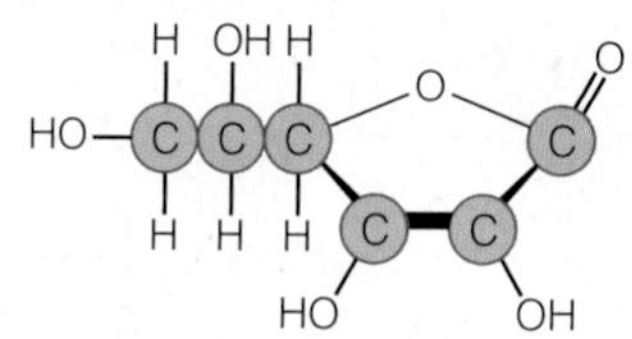

b Vitamin C, an example of an organic nutrient

▲ **Figure 12.2 The Structure of an Inorganic Versus an Organic Nutrient**
(a) Minerals are inorganic, so their molecular structure consists solely of the mineral itself, or in combination with another mineral.
(b) Organic nutrients, including carbohydrates, proteins, lipids, and vitamins, contain carbon, hydrogen, and oxygen. Vitamin B_6 also contains nitrogen.

Minerals Vary in Their Bioavailability

Eating a meal that contains a food high in a particular mineral does not mean the body will absorb that mineral during digestion. Recall that the degree to which a nutrient is absorbed and ultimately available to be used in the body is called its bioavailability.

The **bioavailability** of minerals is affected by several factors. For example, nutritional status, or the amount of the mineral stored in the body, will influence how much is absorbed. If you are deficient in a mineral, such as calcium, you will absorb a greater percentage of that mineral from food. Similarly, if your body has an adequate amount of a mineral, it will absorb less of it from food. Because some minerals can be toxic in high amounts, this ability to adjust the amount absorbed helps prevent the body from accumulating excessive amounts.

Minerals also often compete with each other for absorption in the GI tract. Some minerals, such as calcium, magnesium, iron, copper, and zinc, are absorbed in their ionic state. These minerals have the same ionic charge, so they vie for the same protein carriers during absorption. Too much of one mineral, such as calcium, Ca^{+2}, can cause a decrease in the absorption and metabolism of another mineral, such as magnesium, Mg^{+2}, leading to an imbalance.[2, 3] Thus, bioavailability of each mineral depends on the amount of both minerals in the intestinal tract at the time of absorption.[4] This is one reason why most people should avoid taking single-mineral supplements.

The bioavailability of minerals can also be reduced if the minerals are attached to **binders** such as oxalates (acids found in vegetables) or phytates (acids found in grains and legumes). The acid-mineral complex passes through the intestinal tract unabsorbed and thus eliminated in the stool. An example of this is the oxalate that binds with the calcium in spinach. Spinach is technically high in calcium, but the vegetable is actually a poor calcium source because the oxalates render most of the mineral unavailable for absorption. In fact, an individual will absorb only about one-tenth the amount of calcium from spinach as from milk.[5] In some cases, cooking a food, such as legumes that contain phytates, can help increase the bioavailability of its minerals by breaking down the bonds between the minerals and the binders.[6]

Polyphenols in tea and coffee also bind and inhibit the body's absorption of minerals, such as iron, reducing bioavailability.[7, 8] Drinking a different beverage with a meal, such as juice, milk, or water, would be a better choice than coffee or tea to improve mineral absorption.

bioavailability The degree to which a nutrient is absorbed from foods and used in the body.

binders Compounds such as oxalates and phytates that bind to minerals in foods and reduce their bioavailability.

Oxalates found in spinach bind to calcium, reducing the amount of calcium the body is able to absorb.

Some nutrients improve the bioavailability of minerals. Vitamin C enhances the absorption of iron from plant foods. Animal protein from meat, fish, and poultry enhances zinc absorption, and calcium, phosphorus, and magnesium absorption are enhanced by vitamin D. A summary of the factors that affect the bioavailability of minerals is presented in Table 12.1.

Minerals Serve Numerous Functions

In addition to the roles of some minerals in fluid and electrolyte balance, minerals frequently work together to perform other important functions in the body, such as forming blood (iron and copper), building healthy bones (calcium, phosphorus, magnesium, and fluoride), and maintaining a healthy immune system (zinc).[9] Minerals can also be part of enzymes, participate in energy production, and play an invaluable role in structural growth.

The body maintains a tight control over mineral balance. The GI tract and the kidneys help to closely regulate water and electrolyte balance (refer to Chapter 11). To maintain homeostasis, minerals found in the gastric juices and in sloughed-off intestinal cells are either excreted through the feces or reabsorbed through the large intestine. The kidneys respond to changing levels of minerals by excreting excess minerals or reabsorbing the minerals when needs are greater. For example, when sodium levels in blood are low, the kidneys reabsorb sodium and excrete potassium to balance positive ions in the body. These controls ensure that a sufficient amount of each mineral is available to perform normal muscle contraction, transmit nerve impulses, sustain heart function, and maintain healthy blood.

Minerals Help Maintain Fluid Balance

The electrically charged minerals are essential to balance fluid outside the cell (extracellular) with fluid inside the cell (intracellular), that is, to maintain fluid balance. The sodium and chloride located mainly outside of cells, and the potassium (with the help of calcium, magnesium, and sulfur) located mostly inside cells, all play key roles in maintaining fluid balance. Without these minerals, cells could swell and burst from taking in too much fluid, or shrink from dehydration.

cofactors Similar to a coenzyme, a substance that binds to an enzyme to help catalyze a reaction. The term cofactor generally refers to a metal ion, while a coenzyme is usually an organic molecule such as a vitamin.

TABLE 12.1 Factors That Affect the Bioavailability of Minerals

Factors That Increase Bioavailability	Factors That Reduce Bioavailability
Deficiency in a mineral increases absorption	Binders, such as oxalates found in some vegetables
Cooking increases the bioavailability of minerals in legumes	Phytates found in grains
Vitamin C increases the absorption of some minerals such as iron	Polyphenols in tea and coffee
Vitamin D increases the absorption of calcium, phosphorus, and magnesium	Supplementation of single minerals affects absorption of competing minerals

Minerals Participate as Cofactors

Minerals are similar to many vitamins in that they can act as **cofactors** in important enzyme systems. Mineral cofactors may be loosely or tightly bound to an enzyme, and once a reaction is complete, the mineral is released. For example, the mineral selenium acts as a cofactor for the complex antioxidant enzyme system glutathione peroxidase. This system reduces free radical formation and repairs the damage already done by free radicals. Without the mineral selenium, glutathione peroxidase would be unable to convert free radicals to less harmful substances, and the effect would be oxidative tissue damage that could result in cardiovascular disease and cancer. Other metabolic processes such as energy production, muscle contraction, and nerve transmission also require minerals as cofactors.

Minerals Make Up Bones and Teeth

The major minerals calcium, phosphorus, and magnesium, along with the trace mineral fluoride, make up the crystalline structure that gives strength to bones and teeth. In fact, **hydroxyapatite** crystals make up about 60 percent of bone mass. The hydroxyapatite minerals attach to the protein collagen during bone formation and accumulate during **mineralization.** Inadequate buildup of hydroxyapatite crystals during bone formation, or too much withdrawal of the minerals during adulthood, leads to weakened and brittle bones, similar to the way using too few bolts and girders during construction will lead to an unsafe skyscraper.

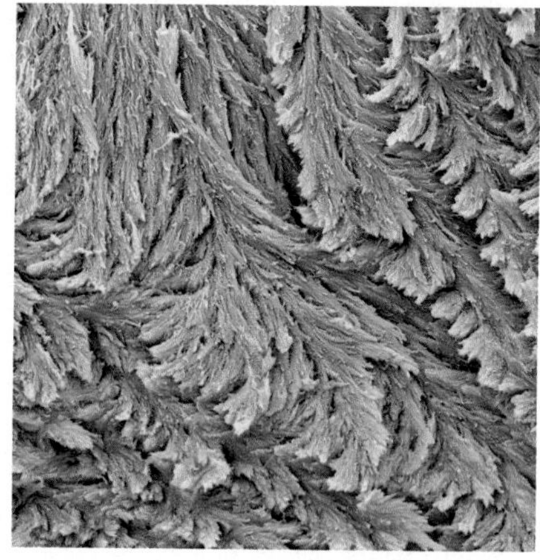

Hydroxyapatite crystals in the outer layer of bone

Minerals Can Be Toxic

Like some fat-soluble vitamins, minerals can be toxic if ingested in high amounts. However, mineral toxicity from an excess dietary intake is rare in healthy individuals because the amounts found in foods are not that high, and most Americans do not generally exceed the UL for minerals. Also, the body can adapt its absorption or excretion of many minerals according to its needs. In other words, the small intestine can reduce absorption of a particular mineral if the body already contains an adequate amount, and the kidneys can filter excess minerals from the blood and excrete them through the urine.

However, ingesting more than the UL of a mineral, such as by taking large amounts of supplements, may lead to illness and even death. Excessive levels of magnesium in the blood can result in heart problems or an inability to breathe,[10] while excessive amounts of calcium may cause nausea, vomiting, loss of appetite, increased urination, kidney toxicity, confusion, and irregular heart rhythm.[11] Although mineral toxicity is more likely to occur in individuals with certain conditions, such as acute or chronic kidney failure, even in healthy people ingesting excessive amounts of minerals will lead to unwanted side effects.

Though minerals have much in common with each other and work together to support numerous body functions, they are each important for individual reasons, and we will explore these in greater detail. In the following pages, we will discuss the functions, daily needs, food sources, and deficiency and toxicity issues for each of the major minerals.

THE TAKE-HOME MESSAGE Minerals are inorganic nutrients classified as either major or trace based on the amount found in the body and the amount needed daily. The bioavailability of minerals can vary based on an individual's nutrient status and whether the mineral is bound with other substances in food or ingested together. Minerals play a vital role in numerous physiological functions: in bone and blood health, in fluid balance, as cofactors in energy production and muscle contraction, and in nerve transmission. Because most people do not ingest overly high amounts of minerals in foods, and because the body can adjust its absorption and excretion of minerals, mineral toxicity is rare in healthy individuals; however, toxicity can occur by ingesting high doses of minerals through supplementation.

hydroxyapatite The crystalline salt structure that provides strength in bones and teeth. Calcium and phosphorus are the main minerals found in the structure.

mineralization The process of adding minerals, including calcium and phosphorus, to the collagen matrix in the bone, which makes the bone strong and rigid.

Exploring Sodium

What Is Sodium?

Sodium is a positively charged mineral (cation) found usually combined with chloride as table salt (NaCl). Table salt accounts for about 90 percent of the sodium you consume and approximately 40 percent of the weight of table salt is sodium. Thus, in 6 grams (1 teaspoon) of table salt, approximately 2.4 grams are sodium.

In the body, **sodium (Na^+)** is a major electrolyte and cation found primarily in the blood and extracellular fluid surrounding the cells. Because of its location in these two compartments, it plays a key role in regulating blood volume. The rest of the body's sodium is located on the surface of the hydroxyapatite crystals in bones, in nerve tissue, and in muscle tissue.

Absorption, Transport, and Excretion

When you ingest table salt, fluid from the lining of the stomach breaks the bonds between the sodium and chloride ions and the ions mix with the digestive juices. Once the two ions dissociate they can both be absorbed.

Most sodium (95 to 100 percent) is absorbed throughout the small intestine, though a small amount (up to 5 percent) passes through the intestinal tract and is excreted in the feces. Once absorbed, sodium moves freely throughout the blood until it is filtered by the kidney and excreted through the urine.

The amount of sodium in the blood is maintained at a precise level by the kidneys. To maintain sodium balance, the amount eaten must equal the amount lost. If blood sodium levels drop, the hormone angiotensin II stimulates the adrenal glands to secrete the hormone aldosterone, which in turn stimulates the kidneys to reabsorb more sodium, returning the blood levels to normal (see Chapter 11 to review this process). Likewise, when the blood levels of sodium are too high, angiotensin II is reduced and the adrenal glands stop releasing aldosterone, allowing the kidneys to excrete the excess sodium in the urine (**Figure 12.3**). The kidneys also reabsorb sodium in exchange for H^+ when the pH is too acidic, thereby restoring acid-base balance.

A small amount of sodium is also lost through daily perspiration. The amount of sodium lost through the skin depends upon the rate of sweating, the amount of sodium consumed (the more sodium in the diet, the higher the loss through sweat), and the intensity of heat in the environment. As you become more acclimated to environmental heat, you lose less sodium over time.

Functions of Sodium

Sodium plays an important role in regulating fluid balance. In addition, sodium plays a role in transmission of nerve impulses, muscle contractions, and transport of nutrients. Sodium also affects the taste of food and is used to preserve food.

Sodium Helps Regulate Fluid Balance

The volume of fluid in the extracellular compartment is determined by the amount of electrolytes, including sodium, that are present. Any shift in the concentration of electrolyte concentration in any fluid compartment affects the amount of fluid present.

As soon as dietary sodium is absorbed, it is quickly distributed throughout the circulation, increasing the concentration of Na^+ in the blood. This, in turn, stimulates the hypothalamus, which activates the thirst mechanism and triggers the release of ADH from the pituitary gland. The result is that you drink more water and excrete less urine, thereby helping to restore the balance between sodium and fluid in the body.

When Sodium Levels Are Low

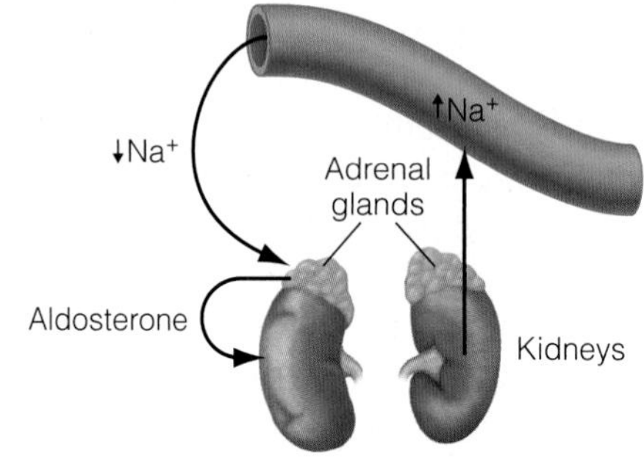

a When sodium levels in the blood are low, aldosterone is released from the adrenal glands, which triggers the kidneys to reabsorb sodium into the blood.

When Sodium Levels Are High

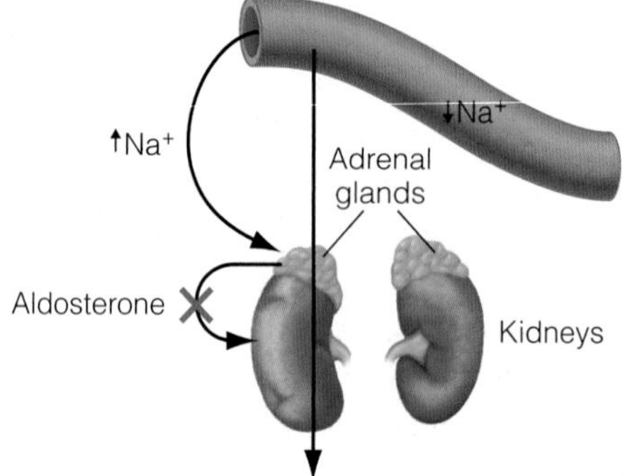

b When sodium levels in the blood are high, the adrenal glands stop secreting aldosterone, and the kidneys excrete the excess sodium through the urine. This lowers the levels of sodium in the blood.

▲ Figure 12.3 **Sodium Balance Is Maintained by the Kidneys**

sodium (Na^+) The major cation in the extracellular fluid.

Sodium Transmits Nerve Impulses and Participates in Muscle Contraction

Sodium works with potassium to help transmit all nerve impulses, including those that signal muscles to contract. This mechanism is called the sodium-potassium pump (refer again to Chapter 11). Both sodium and potassium are positively charged cations, with sodium outside the cell and potassium inside the cell. When sodium is transported by the sodium-potassium pump through the membrane into a nerve cell, the cell becomes more positively charged, which triggers a signal along the nerves to the muscle cells. The muscle is then stimulated to contract.

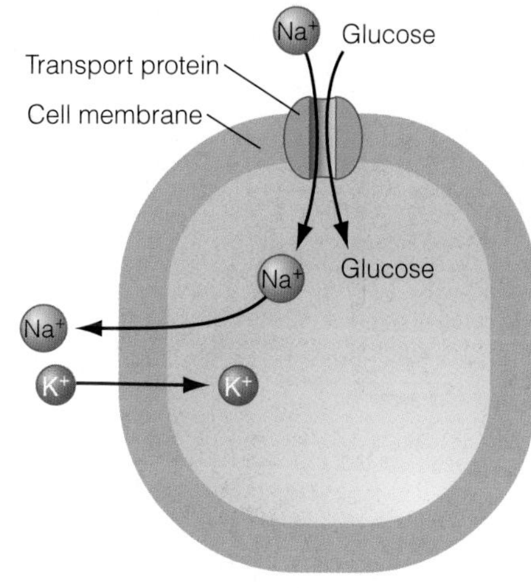

▲ **Figure 12.4 Sodium Helps Transport Some Nutrients**
Sodium binds to the same carrier molecule that transports glucose, galactose, and some amino acids across the cell membrane.

Sodium Helps Transport Some Nutrients

Sodium plays an important role in transporting nutrients such as glucose, galactose, and amino acids across cell membranes. Some of the protein carriers that transport glucose and amino acids through the body also have a site where Na^+ binds (**Figure 12.4**). As Na^+ moves across the cell membrane through the protein carrier, it draws the other nutrients attached to the carrier inside the cell.

Sodium Preserves Food and Enhances Flavor

Sodium is frequently added to foods (as sodium chloride) to enhance flavor and preserve freshness. In breads, sodium serves multiple functions beyond enhancing flavor: It is added to yeast breads to prevent the yeast from overexpanding the dough. It is also used to reduce the growth of bacteria and mold in many bread products and luncheon meats. Sodium in other forms, such as sodium phosphate, sodium carbonate, and sodium bicarbonate (baking soda), are food additives and preservatives that perform similar functions in other foods. Monosodium glutamate (MSG) is a form of sodium commonly added to Asian cuisines to intensify the flavor of foods.

Daily Needs

Many people know that a diet too high in sodium is often linked to one of the nation's biggest health problems: high blood pressure (see Health Connection: Controlling Hypertension).[12] Fewer people know that consuming too much sodium can also contribute to calcium-deficiency osteoporosis,[13] fluid retention, weight gain, stomach ulcers, and stomach cancer.[14] On the other hand, too little sodium can reduce blood volume. So how much sodium do we really need each day?

The daily minimum amount of sodium needed for normal body function is 180 milligrams, or about enough to cover the face of a penny (less than 1/16 th of a teaspoon).[15] However, planning a balanced diet with such a small amount of sodium is virtually impossible, so the DRI committee set an AI recommendation at a more realistic level: 1,500 milligrams daily (about ¼ of a teaspoon) for adults up to 51 years of age (see **Figure 12.5**).[16] This sodium recommendation, which is about eight times the minimum amount needed, is set to accommodate a variety of foods from all the food groups so individuals can meet all their other nutrient needs. It also allows for increased needs of moderately active individuals, who lose more sodium in sweat, and those who are not adjusted to the environmental temperature. Those who are very physically active or not acclimated to heat will likely need to consume a higher amount of sodium. Americans currently consume more than double the recommended amount, or over 3,400 milligrams, of sodium (about ½ of a teaspoon) daily, on average.[17]

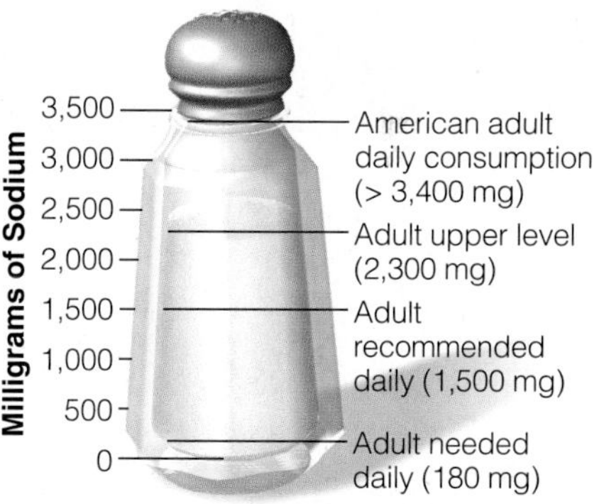

▲ **Figure 12.5 Recommended Intake of Sodium**

Food Sources

The vast majority of dietary sodium, a hefty 77 percent in American diets, comes from processed foods such as canned goods (particularly soups), cured meats, and frozen or packaged meals. Comparing the amount of sodium in a fresh tomato (11 milligrams) to the amount found in a cup of canned tomatoes (355 milligrams) quickly illustrates just how much sodium is added by manufacturers during processing. Some sauces and condiments, such as soy sauce (900 milligrams/tablespoon) or ketchup (190 milligrams/tablespoon), also contribute hefty amounts of sodium.[18]

continued

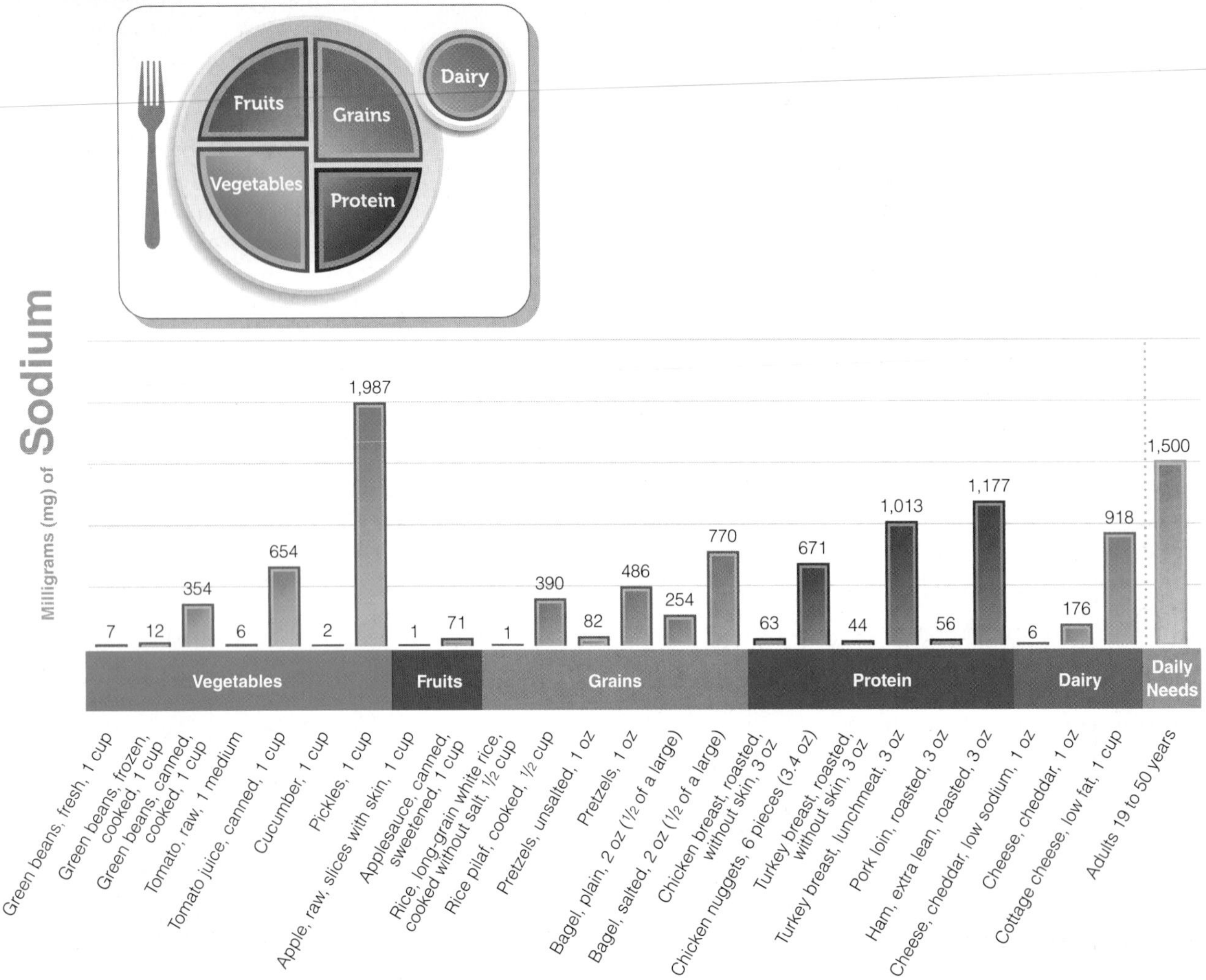

Fruits
Grains
Dairy
Vegetables
Protein

Milligrams (mg) of **Sodium**

Vegetables	Green beans, fresh, 1 cup	7
Vegetables	Green beans, frozen, cooked, 1 cup	12
Vegetables	Green beans, canned, cooked, 1 cup	354
Vegetables	Tomato, raw, 1 medium	6
Vegetables	Tomato juice, canned, 1 cup	654
Vegetables	Cucumber, 1 cup	2
Vegetables	Pickles, 1 cup	1,987
Fruits	Apple, raw, slices with skin, 1 cup	1
Fruits	Applesauce, canned, sweetened, 1 cup	71
Grains	Rice, long-grain white rice, cooked without salt, ½ cup	1
Grains	Rice pilaf, cooked, ½ cup	390
Grains	Pretzels, unsalted, 1 oz	82
Grains	Pretzels, 1 oz	486
Grains	Bagel, plain, 2 oz (½ of a large)	254
Grains	Bagel, salted, 2 oz (½ of a large)	770
Protein	Chicken breast, roasted, without skin, 3 oz	63
Protein	Chicken nuggets, 6 pieces (3.4 oz)	671
Protein	Turkey breast, roasted, without skin, 3 oz	44
Protein	Turkey breast, lunchmeat, 3 oz	1,013
Protein	Pork loin, roasted, 3 oz	56
Protein	Ham, extra lean, roasted, 3 oz	1,177
Dairy	Cheese, cheddar, low sodium, 1 oz	6
Dairy	Cheese, cheddar, 1 oz	176
Dairy	Cottage cheese, low fat, 1 cup	918
Daily Needs	Adults 19 to 50 years	1,500

▲ **Figure 12.6 Sodium Content of Selected Processed and Natural Foods**

About 12 percent of Americans' sodium consumption is from eating foods that naturally contain sodium (see **Figure 12.6**). For example, rice rolls made with seaweed are naturally high in sodium (240 milligrams per serving) because of the high salt concentration in the seaweed. Another 5 percent of sodium intake is from salt that's added during cooking, and 6 percent is from salt used to season foods at the table.

Too Much Sodium

Given that the body excretes excess dietary sodium, do you need to worry about eating too much? The short answer is, absolutely. Researchers have established that there is a direct relationship between sodium intake and elevated blood pressure (or **hypertension**), particularly in individuals who are salt sensitive.

hypertension High blood pressure.

Certain segments of the population are more likely to be salt sensitive, including elderly individuals, people with diabetes or chronic kidney disease, and African-Americans.[19] Whereas about 35 percent of Caucasians appear to be salt sensitive, African-Americans have a much higher rate of 75 percent. Overall, about 50 percent of individuals with hypertension react to salt intake. However, in general, as a person's intake of sodium increases, so does their blood pressure,[20] and reducing dietary sodium may improve blood pressure regardless of race or salt sensitivity.

Health Connection

Controlling Hypertension

What Is Hypertension?

To understand hypertension, you need to know that blood pressure is a measure of the force that blood exerts against the walls of arteries. With every beat, the heart pumps blood into the arteries, and thus to all areas of the body. Blood pressure is highest at the moment of the heart beat (measured as **systolic pressure**) and lower when the heart is at rest between beats (measured as **diastolic pressure**). An individual's blood pressure is expressed as a reading of systolic pressure over diastolic pressure. Blood pressure of less than 120/80 mm Hg (millimeters of mercury) is considered normal. A blood pressure reading of 90/60 mm Hg is usually considered low, although it varies from one person to the next.

Hypertension is simply high blood pressure, and it doesn't happen overnight; it develops over time, in stages. The first stage, prehypertension, occurs as blood pressure begins to rise above normal—that is, systolic blood pressure falls within 120 mm Hg to 139 mm Hg or the diastolic reading reaches 80 to 89 mm Hg.[1] Someone with prehypertension is about 2.5 times more likely to develop cardiovascular disease than someone with normal blood pressure.

If prehypertension is left untreated, it can advance to Stage 1 hypertension, which is characterized by a systolic pressure between 140 mm Hg and 159 mm Hg or a diastolic pressure of 90 mm Hg to 99 mm Hg. The most severe hypertension is Stage 2, which occurs when the systolic pressure rises to 160 mm Hg or higher and the diastolic pressure is 100 mm Hg or higher. Both numbers are important, but after age 50 the most common form of hypertension is when the systolic blood pressure is high and the diastolic pressure is within normal range.

Hypertension is an increasing problem in the United States. In fact, if you were sitting in a room with three other adults, there is a good chance that one of you would have this condition. Whereas blood pressure rises naturally with age, due in part to the increased stiffness of the arteries,[2] untreated hypertension can result in serious medical problems, including increasing the risk of heart disease, stroke, and kidney damage.[3]

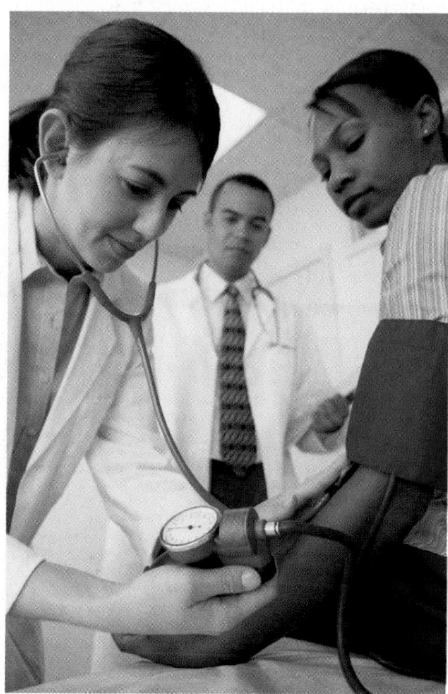

Having your blood pressure checked regularly is the only way to make sure you aren't developing high blood pressure.

Why Is Hypertension Called a "Silent Killer"?

Hypertension is referred to as the "silent killer" because there are no visible symptoms and people can be unaware that they have it. The only way to be sure that blood pressure levels are within normal range is to have your blood pressure checked regularly.

Individuals with chronic high blood pressure eventually develop thicker and stiffer arterial walls, which contributes to atherosclerosis. The heart becomes enlarged and weakened as it has to work harder to pump enough oxygen- and nutrient-laden blood throughout the body. This can lead to fatigue, shortness of breath, and possibly heart attack. Hypertension can also damage the arteries leading to the brain, kidneys, and legs, which increases the risk of stroke, kidney failure, and partial leg amputation.

Can You Control Your Risk of Hypertension?

Various factors increase the chances of developing hypertension, some of which you can control and others you cannot.

Factors You Cannot Control

Family history, the aging process, and race can all impact the likelihood that a person will develop high blood pressure. If your parents, siblings, or grandparents have or had hypertension, you are at a higher risk of developing the condition. Typically, the risk of hypertension increases after the age of 35 for men, and women generally experience increased risk after menopause. Hypertension is more prevalent, and tends to occur earlier and be more severe, in African-Americans than in Caucasians.[4]

Factors You Can Control

The good news is that there are more risk factors that you *can* control than those you can't, including diet, alcohol consumption, body weight, and physical activity.

Eating a balanced diet is a proven strategy to lower blood pressure. A large research study, called DASH (Dietary Approaches to Stop Hypertension), followed 456 healthy men and women, 22 years of age and older, on three different diets. One diet was a typical American diet: low in fruits, vegetables, and dairy products and high in

systolic pressure The pressure within the arteries during a heart beat.

diastolic pressure The pressure within the arteries between heart beats.

continued

fat, saturated fat, and cholesterol. The second diet was rich in just fruits and vegetables, and the third, the DASH diet, was a balanced diet that was lower in fat, saturated fat, cholesterol, and sweets, and high in whole grains, fruits, vegetables, and low-fat dairy products. In fact, the *Dietary Guidelines for Americans* and Choose MyPlate recommend the DASH diet as one of the best plans to meet their recommendations. Table 1 illustrates the DASH eating plan.[5]

The study found that subjects who followed the DASH diet experienced a significant reduction in blood pressure compared with those who followed the other two diets. Because all three diets in the study contained approximately 3,000 milligrams of sodium per day, researchers were unable to attribute the lowered blood pressure experienced by the DASH diet followers to a reduction in sodium intake. Rather, the researchers concluded that the blood pressure–lowering effect of the DASH diet was due to its abundance of fruits and vegetables, which provide healthy doses of potassium and magnesium, and because of its numerous servings of dairy foods, which are rich in calcium. The study concluded that dietary potassium, magnesium, and calcium can all play a role in lowering blood pressure.[6] Recent research suggests that the increase in fruits and vegetables also contributes powerful antioxidants that reduce oxidative stress, and thus lower blood pressure.[7]

A follow-up to the DASH study, called the DASH-Sodium study, went one step further and investigated whether reducing the amount of dietary sodium in each of the three diets could also help lower blood pressure. Not surprisingly, it did. While the result of this study showed that reducing dietary sodium from about 3,300 milligrams to 2,400 milligrams daily lowered blood pressure, the biggest reduction occurred when sodium intake was limited to only 1,500 milligrams daily. This study not only reinforced sodium's role in blood pressure but also showed that the DASH diet, along with a reduction of sodium, is the best dietary combination to fight hypertension.[8]

Can the DASH diet be improved? The authors of the Optimal Macronutrient Intake Trial to Prevent Heart Disease (OMNIHeart Trial) asked this question. These researchers compared the benefits of shifting the carbohydrate intake in healthy diets such as DASH to either protein (about half of which was plant protein) or unsaturated fat (mostly monounsaturated oils) for systolic and diastolic blood pressure. The results of eating 10 percent more protein and 10 percent more kilocalories from monounsaturated fat reduced systolic blood pressure by an additional 1.4 mm Hg over the DASH diet.[9]

The researchers concluded that all three diets (the DASH diet, as well as both the higher protein and higher monounsaturated fat versions of the OMNI diet) lowered blood pressure and thus cardiovascular risk.

In addition to improving eating patterns, limiting alcohol consumption can reduce the risk of developing hypertension. Studies have shown that individuals who regularly had three to six drinks daily (recall from Chapter 7 that a drink equals 12 ounces of beer, 5 ounces of wine, or $1^1/_2$ ounces of distilled alcohol) and then reduced their alcohol consumption by 67 percent, on average, were able to reduce their systolic pressure by over 3 mm Hg and their diastolic pressure by 2 mm Hg.[10]

Attaining a healthy body weight can also markedly reduce the risk for hypertension. Individuals who are obese are twice as likely to have hypertension as those at a healthy weight. Even modest weight loss can have an impact. Losing as little as 10 pounds can reduce a person's blood pressure, and may actually prevent hypertension in overweight individuals even if they haven't yet reached a healthy weight. Additional weight loss can have an even more dramatic effect on blood pressure.

Lastly, engaging in regular physical activity, in addition to its other health benefits, can also help lower blood pressure. In fact, regular aerobic exercise can lower blood pressure even if weight loss hasn't occurred. Moderate-intensity exercise, such as a brisk, 30-minute walk, at least five days a week is sufficient to reduce blood pressure, regardless of age.[11] However, increasing exercise intensity above moderate levels has not been found to lower blood pressure.

The research on high blood pressure is clear: Diet and lifestyle changes help

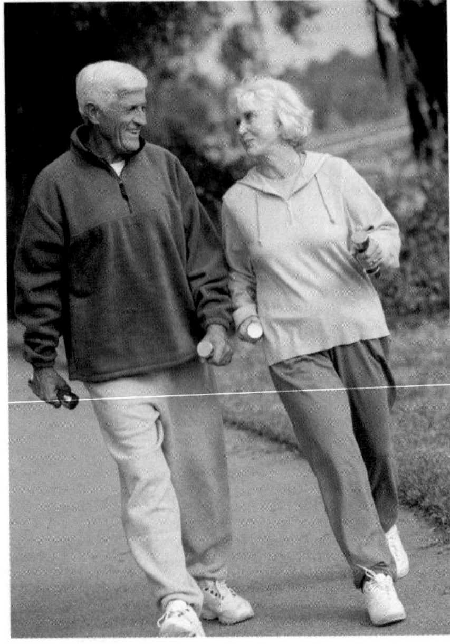

Diet, alcohol consumption, body weight, and physical activity are all factors that you can control that influence blood pressure.

TABLE 1 Dietary Approaches to Stop Hypertension (DASH) Eating Plan Based on a 2,100-Kilocalorie Diet

Food Group	Servings	Serving Size	Importance to the Diet
Grains	7–8/day	1 slice of bread ½ cup dry cereal ½ cup cooked pasta, rice, or cereal	Major source of energy and fiber
Vegetables	4–5/day	1 cup raw leafy vegetables ½ cup cooked vegetables 6 oz vegetable juice	Rich sources of potassium, magnesium, and fiber
Fruits	4–5/day	6 oz fruit juice 1 medium fruit ¼ cup dried fruit ½ cup fresh, frozen, or canned fruit	Important sources of potassium, magnesium, and fiber
Low-fat or fat-free dairy	2–3/day	8 fl oz milk 1 cup yogurt 1½ oz cheese	Major sources of calcium and protein
Meat, poultry, and fish	≤2/day	3 oz cooked meat, poultry, or fish	Rich sources of protein and magnesium
Nuts, seeds, and dry beans and peas	4–5/week	1½ oz or ⅓ cup nuts ½ oz or 2 tbs seeds ½ cup cooked dried beans or peas	Rich sources of energy, potassium, magnesium, protein, and fiber
Fats and oils	2–3/day	1 tsp soft margarine 1 tbs low-fat mayonnaise 2 tbs light salad dressing 1 tsp vegetable oil	Adds satiety, but remember the DASH diet has only 27% of energy as fat
Sweets	5/week	1 tbs sugar 1 tbs jelly or jam ½ oz or 5 jelly beans 8 oz sugared lemonade	Sweets should be low in fat

Source: Adapted from M. M. Windhauser, D. B. Bernst, N. M. Karanja, S. W. Crawford, S. E. Redican, J. F. Swain, J. M. Karimbakas, et al., "Translating the Dietary Approaches to Stop Hypertension Diet from Research to Practice: Dietary and Behavior Change Techniques," *Journal of the American Dietetic Association* 99 (1999): S90–S95.

continued

Health Connection (continued)

TABLE 2 Take Charge of Your Blood Pressure!

If You	By	Your Systolic Blood Pressure* May Be Reduced By
Reduce your sodium intake	Keeping dietary sodium consumption to no more than 2,400 mg daily	8–14 mm Hg
Follow the DASH diet	Consuming a heart-healthy diet that is abundant in fruits, vegetables, and low-fat dairy products; 58% carbohydrate, 15% protein, and 27% fat	8–14 mm Hg
Lose excess body weight	Consuming only an amount of kilocalories that allows you to maintain a normal, healthy body weight	5–20 mm Hg for every 22 lbs of weight loss
Stay physically active	Participating in aerobic exercise (such as brisk walking) 30 minutes per day most days of the week	4–9 mm Hg
Drink alcohol only in moderation	Limiting consumption to no more than 2 drinks daily for men and 1 drink daily for women	2–4 mm Hg

*Controlling the systolic pressure is more difficult than controlling the diastolic pressure, especially for individuals 50 years of age and older. Therefore, it is the primary focus for lowering blood pressure. Typically, as systolic pressure goes down with diet and lifestyle changes, the diastolic pressure will, also.

Data from A. V. Chobanian, et al., "The Seventh Report of the Joint National Committee on Prevention, Detection, Evaluation, and Treatment of High Blood Pressure," *Journal of the American Medical Association* 289 (2003): 2560–2572.

reduce blood pressure and help prevent hypertension. Table 2 summarizes what you can do to control your blood pressure and reduce your risk of developing hypertension.

References

1. Rosamond, W., K. Flegal, K. Furie, A. Go, K. Greenlund, N. Haase, S. M. Hailpern, et al. 2008. Heart Disease and Stroke Statistics—2008 Update: A Report from the American Heart Association Statistics Committee and Stroke Statistics Subcommittee. *Circulation* 117: e25–e146.
2. Franklin, S. S., W. Gustin, N. D. Wong, M. G. Larson, M. A. Weber, W. B. Kannel, and D. Levy. 1997. Hemodynamic Patterns of Age-Related Changes in Blood Pressure. *Circulation* 96:308–315.
3. American Heart Association. 2012. *About High Blood Pressure.* Available from www.americanheart.org.
4. Ibid.
5. Windhauser, M. M., D. B. Bernst, N. M. Karanja, S. W. Crawford, S. E. Redican, J. F. Swain, J. M. Karimbakas, et al. 1999. Translating the Dietary Approaches to Stop Hypertension Diet from Research to Practice: Dietary and Behavior Change Techniques. *Journal of the American Dietetic Association* 99:S90–S95.
6. Harsha, D. W., W. P. Lin, E. Obarzanek, N. M. Karanja, T. J. Moore, and B. Caballero. 1999. Dietary Approaches to Stop Hypertension: A Summary of Study Results. *Journal of the American Dietetic Association* 99:S35–S39.
7. Lopes, H. F., K. L. Martin, K. Nashar, J. D. Marrow, T. L. Goodfriend, and B. M. Egan. 2003. DASH Diet Lowers Blood Pressure and Lipid-Induced Oxidative Stress in Obesity. *Hypertension* 41:422–430.
8. Svetkey, L. P., F. M. Sacks, E. Obarzanek, W. M. Vollmer, L. J. Appel, P. Lin, N. M. Karanja, et al. 1999. The DASH Diet, Sodium Intake and Blood Pressure Trial (DASH-Sodium): Rationale and Design. *Journal of the American Dietetic Association* 99:S96–S104.
9. Appel, L. J., F. M. Sacks, V. J. Carey, E. Obarzanek, J. F. Swain, E. R. Miller, P. R. Conlin, et al. 2005. Effects of Protein, Monounsaturated Fat, and Carbohydrate Intake on Blood Pressure and Serum Lipids: Results of the OMNIHeart Randomized Trial. *Journal of the American Medical Association* 294:2455–2464.
10. Fuchs, F. D., L. E. Chambless, P. K. Whelton, J. Nieto, and G. Heiss. 2001. Alcohol Consumption and the Incidence of Hypertension: The Atherosclerosis Risk in Communities Study. *Hypertension* 37:1242–1250.
11. Choudhury, A. and G. Y. H. Lip. 2005. Exercise and Hypertension. *Journal of Human Hypertension* 19:585–587.

High blood pressure increases the risk for heart disease, stroke, and kidney disease. Unfortunately, many Americans will develop hypertension sometime during their life. The upper level for sodium for adults is set at 2,300 milligrams, or about 1 teaspoon of table salt, in order to help reduce the risk. The current *Dietary Guidelines for Americans* also recommend that sodium intake should be limited (see Chapter 2).

The DASH (Dietary Approaches to Stop Hypertension) diet plan and the newer version called the OMNI (Optimal Macronutrient Intake) diet have both been shown to reduce hypertension. Both plans focus on consuming fruits, vegetables, low-fat or nonfat dairy products, lean meats, whole grains, and legumes.

If your diet is too high in sodium, and the kidneys do not excrete enough to maintain sodium balance, a condition called **hypernatremia** (*hyper* = too much, *natrium* = sodium, *emia* =

hypernatremia Excessive amounts of sodium in the blood.

hypertonic Having a high solute concentration.

blood) can result. When the extracellular fluid becomes **hypertonic** (too concentrated in solutes), water will move from intracellular fluid to the extracellular fluid until a balance of concentrated ions has been restored. Thus, changes in the concentration outside the cell will affect the concentration of water inside the cell. In addition, if the kidneys are functioning correctly, less fluid will be excreted in the urine and the thirst mechanism will be stimulated.

Consuming too much sodium may also affect bone health.[21, 22] In both human and animal studies, research has shown that sodium in the urine correlates to reduced reabsorption of calcium by the kidneys. This lack of reabsorption leads to greater calcium loss in the urine and may contribute to bone loss, especially in postmenopausal women.[23]

Reducing Sodium Intake

Because the majority of sodium comes from processed foods, and a fair amount comes from the salt that you add to your foods, cutting back on these two sources is the best way to lower dietary intake. One way to scale back sodium intake in processed foods is to read labels carefully. However, even this can be a challenge if you're not well versed in label terms.

"Low sodium," for instance, means there is less than 140 milligrams of sodium per serving, while "sodium free" means the product may contain up to 5 milligrams per serving. "Reduced sodium" means only that the sodium content of the "regular" version has been reduced by 25 percent, and "light in sodium" means it has been reduced by 50 percent. A regular version of a product like soy sauce may have 1,000 milligrams of sodium in 1 tablespoon, while 1 tablespoon of light soy sauce contains 500 milligrams, or 33 percent of the AI. Note that even though the product's sodium has been reduced, it is still considered high in sodium.

While reading nutrition labels is helpful to control sodium intake, using the Daily Values as a guide can result in consuming higher than recommended sodium levels. The Daily Values, designed as a general idea of how the nutrients in the food fit into an overall diet, are based on older reference values and are not as current as the DRIs. The Daily Value for sodium is based on 2,400 milligrams of sodium per day, which is higher than both the AI (1,500 milligrams) and the UL (2,300 milligrams) for sodium. For example, the sodium content for a beef hot dog with a bun is approximately 1,400 milligrams, or 58 percent of the Daily Value. However, that one hot dog would satisfy the AI for sodium for the day. If you ate two hot dogs, your sodium intake would be 2,800 milligrams, which is greater than the UL.

The best way to reduce sodium intake is to limit consumption of processed foods and bypass the saltshaker at the table. If you do purchase processed foods, buy only products labeled as "low sodium" or "sodium free." When cooking, season foods with a variety of herbs or other flavorings such as black pepper, Tabasco sauce, lemon juice, or a no-salt seasoning blend instead of salt.

TABLE TIPS

Shake the Salt Habit

Dilute canned soups by combining a can of regular vegetable soup and a can of low-sodium vegetable soup for soup with less sodium. Add cooked, frozen vegetables for an even healthier meal.

Limit deli meats to no more than 3 ounces on your sandwich, and pile on naturally low-sodium tomatoes, lettuce, cucumbers, and shredded cabbage.

Choose low-sodium dried fruits (apricots and raisins) and unsalted walnut pieces or almonds for a sweet or crunchy snack.

Skip salty french fries and enjoy a sodium-free baked potato instead.

Use olive oil and vinegar instead of salad dressing on your salad, or dilute regular salad dressing with an equal portion of vinegar to cut the sodium content.

Too Little Sodium

Dietary sodium deficiency is rare in healthy individuals who consume a balanced diet. However, individuals who

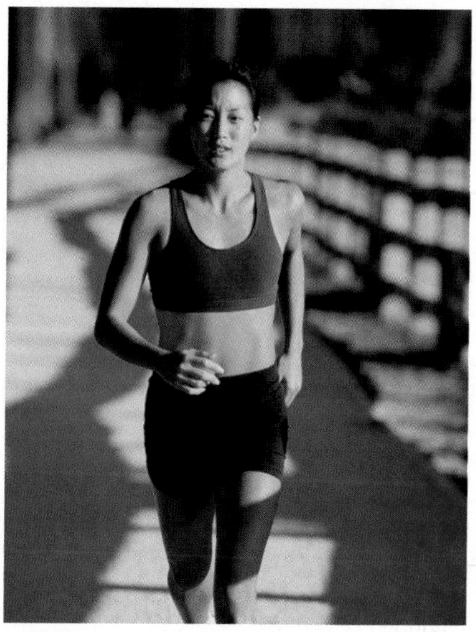

continued

consume too much water in a short amount of time, such as marathon runners or military trainees, risk diluting sodium and other electrolytes in the excessive volume of body fluid (referred to as **hypotonic**), which can result in **hyponatremia** (*hypo* = under, *natrium* = sodium, *emia* = blood), a condition that can be fatal. Symptoms include headache, muscle weakness, fatigue, and seizures that can eventually lead to coma and death.

Too little sodium can also result when excessive amounts of the mineral are lost through the kidneys, such as with the use of diuretics. Diuretics also inhibit sodium reabsorption and can cause hyponatremia.[24]

hypotonic Having a low solute concentration.

hyponatremia Abnormally low levels of sodium in the blood.

Exploring Chloride

What Is Chloride?

Chloride (Cl^-) is an anion almost always found attached to sodium as sodium chloride in foods. Within the body, this major electrolyte is found mostly in the blood (approximately 88 percent), with the remainder (approximately 12 percent) found in the intracellular fluid and as part of hydrochloric acid in the stomach. Chloride should not be confused with chlorine, a powerful disinfectant that is poisonous when inhaled or ingested.

When chloride is ingested as table salt, it dissociates in the stomach, mixes with the digestive juices, and is absorbed through the small intestine. Chloride is excreted through the urine, although small amounts of chloride can be lost in the feces and through the skin.

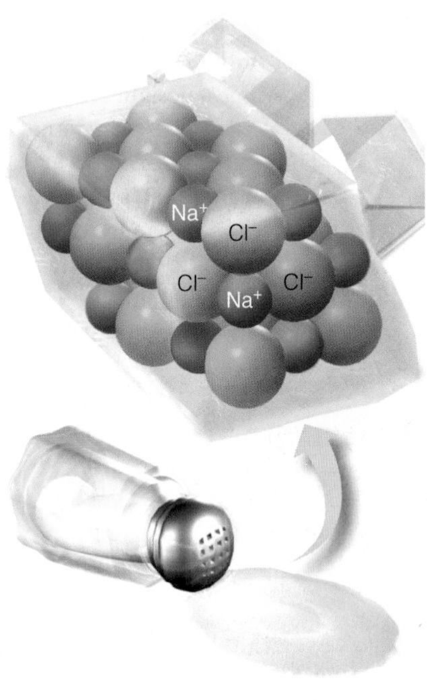

Functions of Chloride

The negative charge of Cl^- balances the positive charge of Na^+ in the extracellular fluid to maintain fluid balance. Chloride assists in the removal of CO_2 from the blood, helping maintain a normal pH range, and participates in digestion as part of hydrochloric acid (HCl).

Daily Needs

The AI for chloride is set at about 2,300 milligrams a day for adults aged 19 to 50. Due to their high salt intake, Americans in general consume well above this requirement. In fact, on average, Americans consume an estimated 3,400 milligrams to just over 7,000 milligrams of dietary chloride daily.[25]

Food Sources

Table salt accounts for almost all the chloride you ingest daily. Approximately 60 percent of the weight of table salt is chloride. Thus, in 6 grams (1 teaspoon) of table salt, approximately 3.8 grams are chloride. In addition to processed foods that contain sodium chloride, chloride is also found naturally in seaweed, tomatoes, olives, lettuce, celery, and rye. Chloride is also part of potassium chloride, the main ingredient in salt substitutes.

Too Much or Too Little

Because sodium chloride is the major source of chloride in the diet, the upper level for adults for chloride is set at 3,600 milligrams to coincide with the upper level for sodium.[26]

Chloride toxicity is rare. However, athletes who become extremely dehydrated may experience **hyperchloremia,** or hyperconcentration of chloride in the blood. The best way to avoid this condition is to drink sufficient fluid and electrolytes when exercising in extreme heat.

Though chloride deficiency rarely occurs in healthy individuals, a serious bout of vomiting and/or diarrhea can cause excessive loss of chloride as part of hydrochloric acid. Some diuretics can cause an increase in chloride excretion in the urine, resulting in low chloride levels in the blood, or **hypochloremia.** The symptoms of hypochloremia include shallow breathing, muscle weakness, muscle spasms, and twitching.

chloride (Cl^-) Major anion in the extracellular fluid.

hyperchloremia Abnormally high level of chloride in the blood.

hypochloremia Abnormally low level of chloride in the blood.

Exploring Potassium

What Is Potassium?

Potassium (K^+) is the major cation found in the intracellular fluid (ICF). About 85 percent of consumed potassium is absorbed throughout the small intestine and colon. The kidney maintains potassium balance by excreting excess potassium through the urine and minor amounts through the sweat.

Functions of Potassium

Potassium is essential for cellular and electrical function of all cells, tissues, and organs in the human body. Together with other minerals, potassium participates in fluid and pH balance, conducts electrical impulses in the body (which helps maintain a regular heart beat), and plays a key role in skeletal and smooth muscle contraction, making it important for normal digestive and muscular function.

Potassium Helps Maintain Fluid Balance and Acts as a Blood Buffer

Over 95 percent of the potassium in the body is found within cells. Together with sodium and chloride, potassium helps maintain fluid balance. Water can flow freely from the extracellular to the intracellular fluid, depending on the concentration of electrolytes on either side of the cell membrane (see Chapter 11). Potassium ions also help maintain blood pH and acid-base balance.

Most products marketed as salt substitutes contain potassium chloride.

Potassium Helps with Nerve Impulse Conduction and Muscle Contraction

As mentioned earlier, potassium, together with sodium, plays a key role in the contraction of muscles, including the heart, and the conduction of nerve impulses. When potassium is exchanged for sodium in the sodium-potassium pump, it generates an electrical current and allows the nerve impulse to conduct. The nerve impulse generates muscle contractions and regulates your heart beat.

Potassium Can Help Lower High Blood Pressure

A diet that is plentiful in potassium has been shown to help lower blood pressure, especially in salt-sensitive individuals who respond more intensely to sodium's blood pressure–raising capabilities. Potassium causes the kidneys to excrete excess sodium from the body, and keeping sodium levels low can help lower blood pressure. The DASH diet that was discussed earlier in relation to reducing high blood pressure is abundant in potassium-rich fruits and vegetables. Further, substituting potassium chloride for sodium chloride when seasoning foods during cooking or at the table has been found to reduce systolic blood pressure.[27]

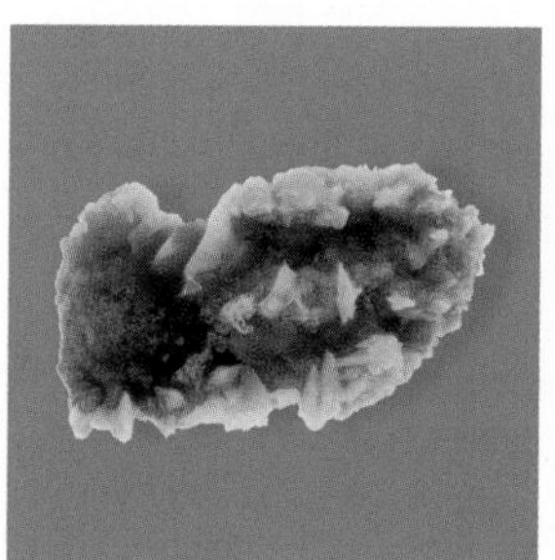
Kidney stone

Potassium Plays a Role in Bone Health and Reduces Kidney Stones

Because potassium acts as a buffer in the blood, it helps keep the bone-strengthening minerals calcium and phosphorus from being lost from the bones and kidneys. Numerous studies suggest that having plenty of potassium in the diet helps increase bone density, and thus bone strength.[28] Consuming potassium-rich foods may reduce the amount of calcium excreted and improve bone health.[29]

Potassium also may be beneficial in reducing kidney stones. Individuals with unusually high levels of calcium in the urine are at a higher risk of developing kidney stones. Increasing dietary potassium through fruits and vegetables or potassium supplements, such as potassium citrate, reduces the amount of calcium excreted in the urine. Potassium attaches to the calcium and prevents the formation of mineral crystals that can form kidney stones.[30]

Potassium Balance in the Body

After it enters the blood, dietary potassium is quickly taken up into the cells. When there is excess potassium in the blood, the kidneys excrete more potassium in the urine. The kidneys control the level of potassium in the same way that they control sodium. When the blood levels of potassium are low, the kidneys reabsorb potassium and return the blood levels to normal. The difference between the maintenance of potassium and sodium blood levels is that the hormone aldosterone is stimulated when blood K^+ is high and Na^+ is low, resulting in potassium excretion and sodium reabsorption. In other words, the release of aldosterone causes potassium to be lost from the body, while sodium is retained.

Daily Needs

An AI of 4,700 milligrams has been established for potassium for all adults. This amount is recommended to help

potassium (K^+) Main cation in the intracellular fluid.

continued

those with sodium sensitivity reduce their risk of high blood pressure. This AI also lowers the risk of developing kidney stones and preserves bone health. A UL for potassium has not been established because there is no evidence that high levels of dietary potassium cause detrimental effects.

Because Americans fall short of their servings of fruits and vegetables, adult females consume only about 2,200 to 2,500 milligrams of potassium daily, and adult males consume only 3,300 to 3,400 milligrams daily.[31]

Food Sources

Fruits and vegetables, especially bananas, watermelon, potatoes, leafy green vegetables, and sweet potatoes, are excellent sources of potassium. The *Dietary Guidelines for Americans* recommend consuming an abundance of fruits and vegetables to meet potassium needs. Seven servings, or about four cups, of fruit and vegetables is the minimum amount recommended daily for adults aged 19 and older. Lean meat, low-fat dairy products, and nuts are also good sources of potassium in the diet (see **Figure 12.7**).

Too Much or Too Little

There is little danger of consuming too much potassium from foods, and excess amounts are excreted in the urine. However, consuming too much from supplements or salt substitutes can cause **hyperkalemia** (*kalemia* = potassium in blood) for some people. Hyperkalemia can cause irregular heart beats, damage the heart, and even be life-threatening.

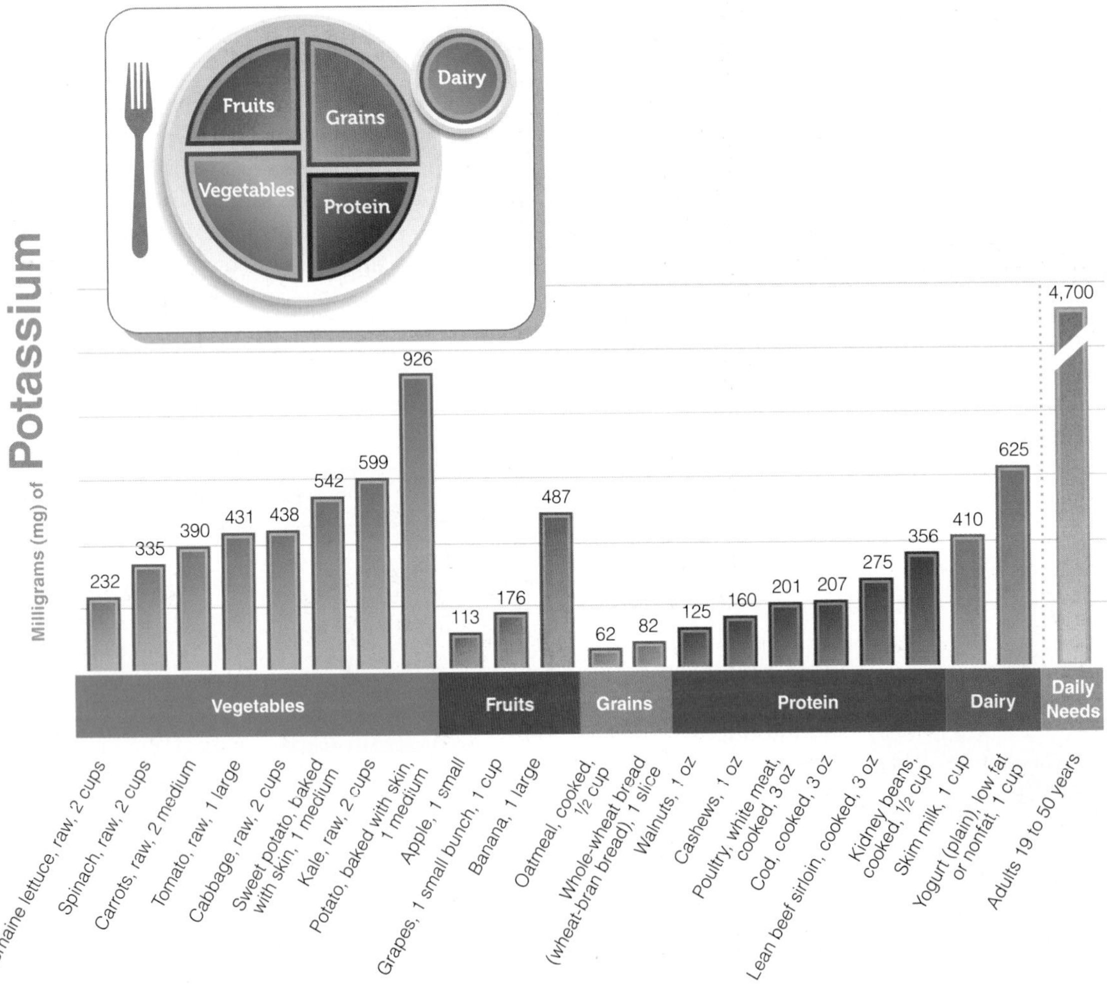

Fruits | Grains | Dairy | Vegetables | Protein

Milligrams (mg) of Potassium

		Milligrams (mg) of Potassium
Vegetables	Romaine lettuce, raw, 2 cups	232
Vegetables	Spinach, raw, 2 cups	335
Vegetables	Carrots, raw, 2 medium	390
Vegetables	Tomato, raw, 1 large	431
Vegetables	Cabbage, raw, 2 cups	438
Vegetables	Sweet potato, baked with skin, 1 medium	542
Vegetables	Kale, raw, 2 cups	599
Vegetables	Potato, baked with skin, 1 medium	926
Fruits	Apple, 1 small	113
Fruits	Grapes, 1 small bunch, 1 cup	176
Fruits	Banana, 1 large	487
Grains	Oatmeal, cooked, ½ cup	62
Grains	Whole-wheat bread (wheat-bran bread), 1 slice	82
Protein	Walnuts, 1 oz	125
Protein	Cashews, 1 oz	160
Protein	Poultry, white meat, cooked, 3 oz	201
Protein	Cod, cooked, 3 oz	207
Protein	Lean beef sirloin, cooked, 3 oz	275
Protein	Kidney beans, cooked, ½ cup	356
Dairy	Skim milk, 1 cup	410
Dairy	Yogurt (plain), low fat or nonfat, 1 cup	625
Daily Needs	Adults 19 to 50 years	4,700

▲ **Figure 12.7 Sources of Potassium in Selected Foods**

TABLE TIPS

Potassium Pointers

Enjoy a 6-ounce glass of a citrus juice, such as orange or grapefruit, at breakfast to boost potassium intake.

Add leafy greens, such as spinach, to your lunchtime sandwich.

Add a spoonful of chopped nuts, such as walnuts or almonds, to yogurt.

Choose bean soup to go with a sandwich.

Bake a regular or sweet potato to increase potassium at dinner.

Those at a higher risk for hyperkalemia include individuals with impaired kidneys, such as people with type 1 diabetes mellitus, those with kidney disease, and individuals taking medications for heart disease or diuretics that cause the kidneys to block the excretion of potassium. These individuals may also need to consume less dietary potassium than the recommended daily amount as advised by their health care professional.

Although a deficiency of dietary potassium is rare, too little potassium can cause **hypokalemia.** This may occur during bouts of vomiting and/or diarrhea, and has been observed in individuals who suffer with anorexia nervosa or bulimia nervosa. Hypokalemia can cause muscle weakness, cramps, glucose intolerance, and, in severe situations, irregular heart beats and paralysis.[32] Even a moderately low intake of potassium, without developing hypokalemia, can increase the risk of developing high blood pressure, kidney stones, and loss of bone mass.

hyperkalemia Abnormally high levels of potassium in the blood.

hypokalemia Abnormally low levels of potassium in the blood.

Exploring Calcium

What Is Calcium?

Calcium (Ca^{+2}) is one of the most abundant divalent cations (two positive charges) in nature and is found in everything from pearls to eggshells. Calcium is also the most abundant mineral in the body. Over 99 percent of the body's calcium is located in the bones and teeth.[33]

Bioavailability and Absorption

The bioavailability of calcium in various foods can be influenced by other food components. For example, vitamin D and lactose each improve the absorption of calcium, so vitamin D-fortified milk is a good source of absorbable calcium. Protein intake may also influence the absorption of calcium from a meal. Low protein intake reduces the amount of calcium absorbed through the intestines, and high protein intake increases the amount of calcium excreted in the urine.[34, 35] On the other hand, oxalates and phytates found in foods that contain calcium, such as spinach (contains oxalates) or whole-wheat bread (contains phytates), reduce the bioavailability of calcium (**Figure 12.8**).[36]

A person who is deficient in calcium will absorb more of the mineral from foods than someone whose body has an adequate amount. However, the more calcium consumed at one time, the lower the rate of absorption. Therefore, consuming a calcium-containing food in smaller and more frequent portions, such as one 8-ounce glass of milk with breakfast and another with lunch, rather than a 16-ounce glass with dinner, will increase the amount of calcium you absorb overall.

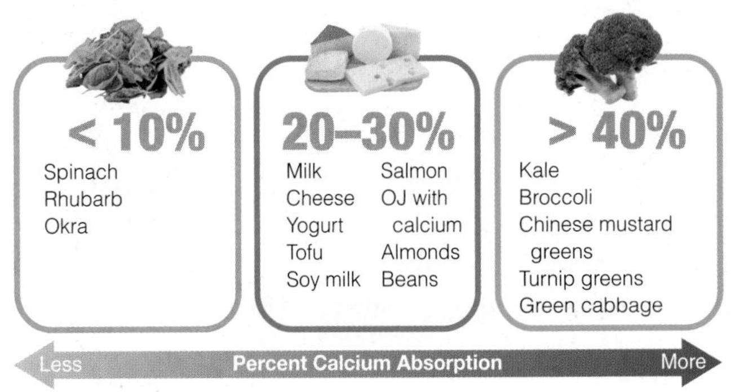

▲ **Figure 12.8 Bioavailability of Calcium**

Hormones Regulate Calcium Balance

The amount of calcium in the body is tightly controlled by hormones that respond to changes in blood calcium levels. When blood calcium levels are low (see **Figure 12.9**), the parathyroid gland releases parathyroid hormone (PTH), which responds by stimulating the kidneys to convert more vitamin D to its active form, calcitriol. Together, calcitriol

calcium (Ca^{+2}) One of the most abundant divalent cations found in nature and in the body.

continued

and PTH increase blood levels of calcium by increasing the amount of calcium absorbed through the intestinal tract, reducing the amount of calcium excreted through the kidneys, and releasing calcium from bone.

Another hormone, **calcitonin,** decreases blood calcium levels after a calcium-rich meal by stimulating the uptake of calcium into the bone. Calcitonin may also reduce the activation of vitamin D, thus reducing the amount of calcium absorbed through the small intestine. The action of calcitonin results in less calcium being absorbed, more calcium being deposited into the bone, and more calcium being excreted through the urine. The end result is normal levels of calcium in the blood and increased calcium levels in bones.[37]

Functions of Calcium

Most people are probably aware that calcium is essential for building strong bones and teeth. But that's not the only function of calcium in the body. An optimal level of dietary intake of calcium is also essential for contracting muscles, sending and receiving nerve impulses, releasing hormones, blood clotting, and maintaining a normal heart beat. Calcium also helps lower blood pressure and may even reduce the risk of developing colon cancer, kidney stones, and obesity.

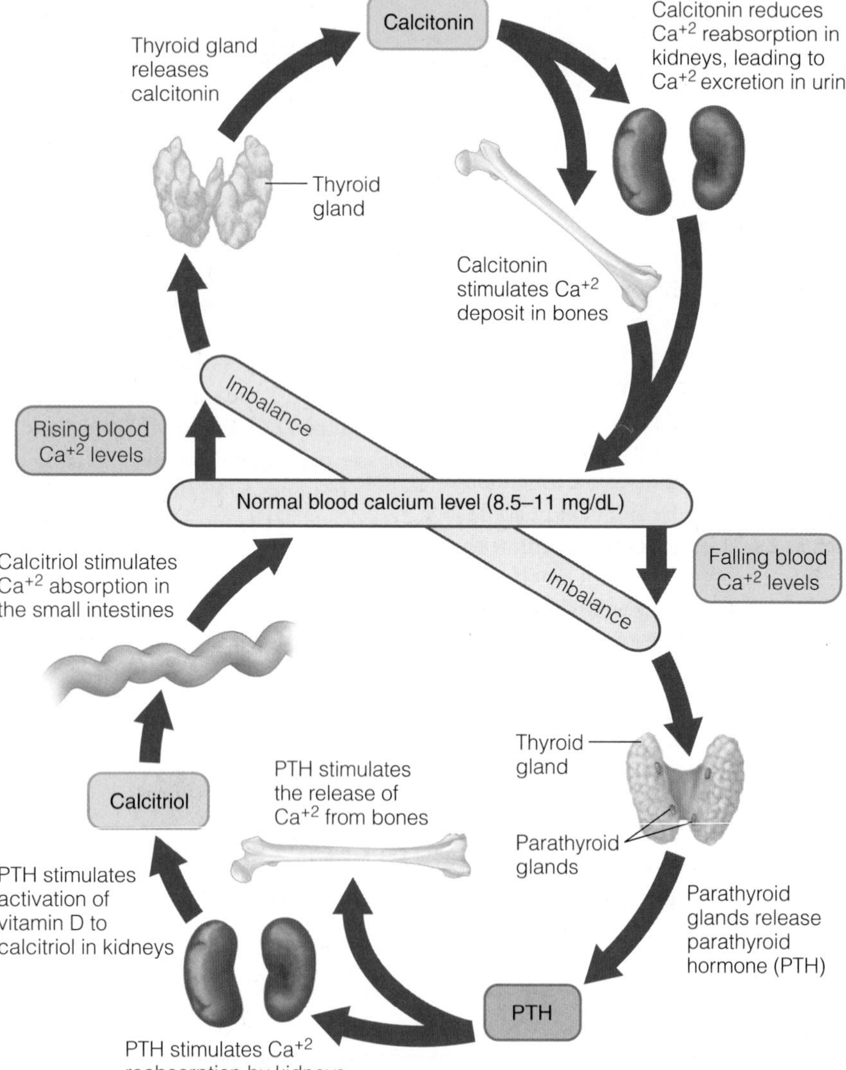

▲ **Figure 12.9 Hormones Maintain Calcium Homeostasis**

Calcium Helps Build Strong Bones and Teeth

Calcium is the primary mineral in the hydroxyapatite crystals that provide strength and structure to the bones and the enamel on teeth.[38]

The skeleton is made up of two types of bone (see **Figure 12.10**): **cortical bone,** which is the compact, dense bone that makes up the surface of bone tissue, and **trabecular bone,** which is the spongy interior portion. The trabecular bone has a high rate of turnover and is sensitive to changes in dietary calcium intake. It provides a reserve of calcium that can be used to raise blood levels when the diet is deficient in calcium.

Calcium Plays a Role in Muscles, Nerves, and Blood

The 1 percent of calcium that's not in the bones or teeth is in the extracellular fluid and in the intracellular components in the

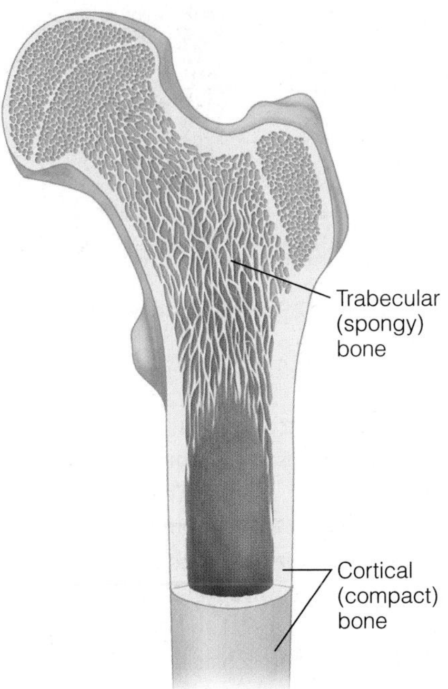

▲ Figure 12.10 **Trabecular and Cortical Bone**

muscles and other tissues. When a muscle is stimulated by nerve impulses, calcium ions flow into the cell through a calcium channel and bind to proteins in the cell. This binding initiates a chain of events that results in the muscle contraction.

Calcium in the blood stimulates the release of hormones, activates enzymes, and helps the nervous system transmit messages. For example, calcium stimulates the enzyme that breaks down glycogen to provide energy for muscles to contract. Blood calcium must be maintained at a constant level for the body to function properly.

Calcium is also needed to dilate and contract the blood vessels and help blood to clot. Calcium ions bind to the seven clotting factors that are vitamin K dependent, resulting in the formation of blood clots after an injury.

Calcium May Help Lower High Blood Pressure and Prevent Colon Cancer

Studies have shown that a heart-healthy diet rich in calcium, potassium, and magnesium can help lower blood pressure. The DASH diet contains three daily servings of low-fat dairy foods, the minimum amount recommended to obtain this protective effect.[39, 40]

A diet with plenty of calcium has also been shown to help reduce the risk of developing benign tumors in the colon that may eventually lead to cancer. Calcium may protect the lining of the colon from damaging bile acids and cancer-promoting substances.[41]

Calcium May Reduce the Risk of Kidney Stones

The majority of the more than 2 million kidney stones that Americans suffer every year consist mainly of calcium oxalate. Although health professionals in the past often warned those who suffer with kidney stones to minimize their dietary calcium, this advice has since been reversed, as research has shown that a balanced diet, along with adequate (but not excessive) amounts of calcium, may actually reduce the risk of developing kidney stones.[42, 43] Calcium binds with the oxalates in foods in the intestines and prevents their absorption. With fewer oxalates filtering through the kidneys, fewer stones are formed.

Calcium May Reduce the Risk of Obesity

Some preliminary research suggests that low-calcium diets may trigger several responses that increase the risk for obesity.[44, 45, 46] When calcium intake is inadequate, the active form of vitamin D, calcitriol, increases in the body to enhance dietary calcium absorption. PTH is also increased, which causes less calcium to be lost from the body. These hormone responses also cause a shift of calcium into fat cells, which stimulates fat production and storage. The opposite also appears to be true: When the diet is high in calcium, less calcitriol is produced, resulting in less calcium stored in fat cells and more fat being burned for energy. In addition, preliminary results suggest that high dietary calcium intake may increase the amount of fat excreted in the feces as well as increase core body temperature.[47, 48] However, calcium is not a magic pill in the battle against obesity and clearly

more research is needed to confirm this relationship.

Daily Needs

The AI for calcium is 1,000 to 1,100 milligrams of calcium daily, depending on your age. Most Americans 20 years of age and older are consuming less than 800 milligrams of calcium daily.[49]

Food Sources

Americans get the majority of their calcium from dairy products, with an average of 55 percent of their intake coming from

calcitonin A hormone secreted by the thyroid gland that lowers blood calcium levels.

cortical bone The hard outer layer of bone.

trabecular bone The inner structure of bone, also known as spongy bone because of its appearance. This portion of bone is often lost in osteoporosis.

continued

these sources. An 8-ounce glass of nonfat milk, 1 cup of nonfat yogurt, or 1½ ounces of hard cheese each provides 300 milligrams of calcium. Three servings (or about 3 cups) of low-fat dairy foods will just about meet many adults' daily needs. Note that selecting low-fat and nonfat dairy products, such as skim milk and nonfat yogurt, is key to minimizing saturated fat intake.

In general, Americans are not meeting the recommendations for dairy suggested by the *Dietary Guidelines for Americans*. You can use the Self-Assessment to estimate your calcium intake and find out if you are getting enough of this important mineral in your diet.

Dairy is not the only excellent source of calcium. Bok choy, broccoli, canned salmon with bones (the calcium is in the bones), and tofu that is processed with calcium can also add calcium to the diet. Calcium-fortified foods, such as juices and cereals, are also excellent sources (see **Figure 12.11**).

Too Much or Too Little

The upper limit for calcium is 2,500 milligrams daily to avoid **hypercalcemia,** or too much calcium in the blood, subsequent impaired kidneys, and calcium deposits in the body. Too much dietary calcium can also cause constipation and interfere with the absorption of other minerals, such as iron, zinc, magnesium, and phosphorus.

If the diet is low in calcium, the mineral will be pulled from bone for the sake of maintaining a constant level in the blood. When blood calcium levels fall below normal, **hypocalcemia** results. A chronic deficiency of dietary calcium can lead to less dense, weakened, and brittle bones (see **Figure 12.12**) and increased risk for osteoporosis and bone fractures. See Health Connection: Building a Stronger Bone for more about the importance of forming and maintaining healthy bone.

Calcium Supplements

Some individuals, based on their diet, medical history, or both, are advised by their health care provider to take a calcium supplement. The calcium in these supplements is part of a compound, typically either calcium carbonate or calcium citrate. Calcium carbonate tends to be the least expensive and the most common form of calcium purchased. It is most effective when consumed with a meal, as the acidic juices in the stomach help with its absorption.[50] Calcium citrate can be taken any time throughout the day, as it doesn't need the help of acidic juices to be absorbed. Calcium citrate usually works best for those ages 50 and older who may produce less stomach acid as they age.[51]

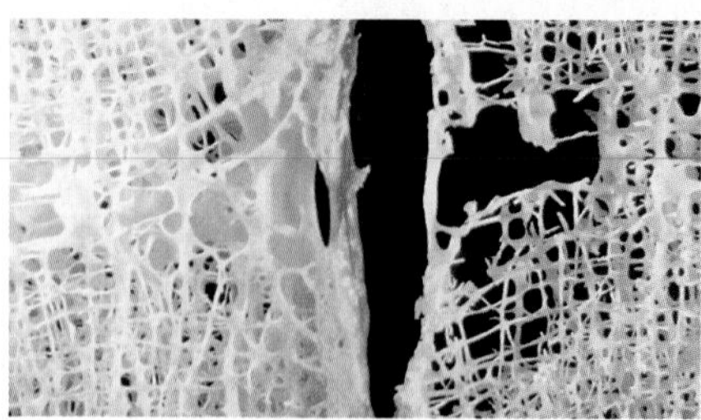

▲ **Figure 12.12 Normal and Abnormal Bone**
Healthy bone (left) vs. weakened bone (right)

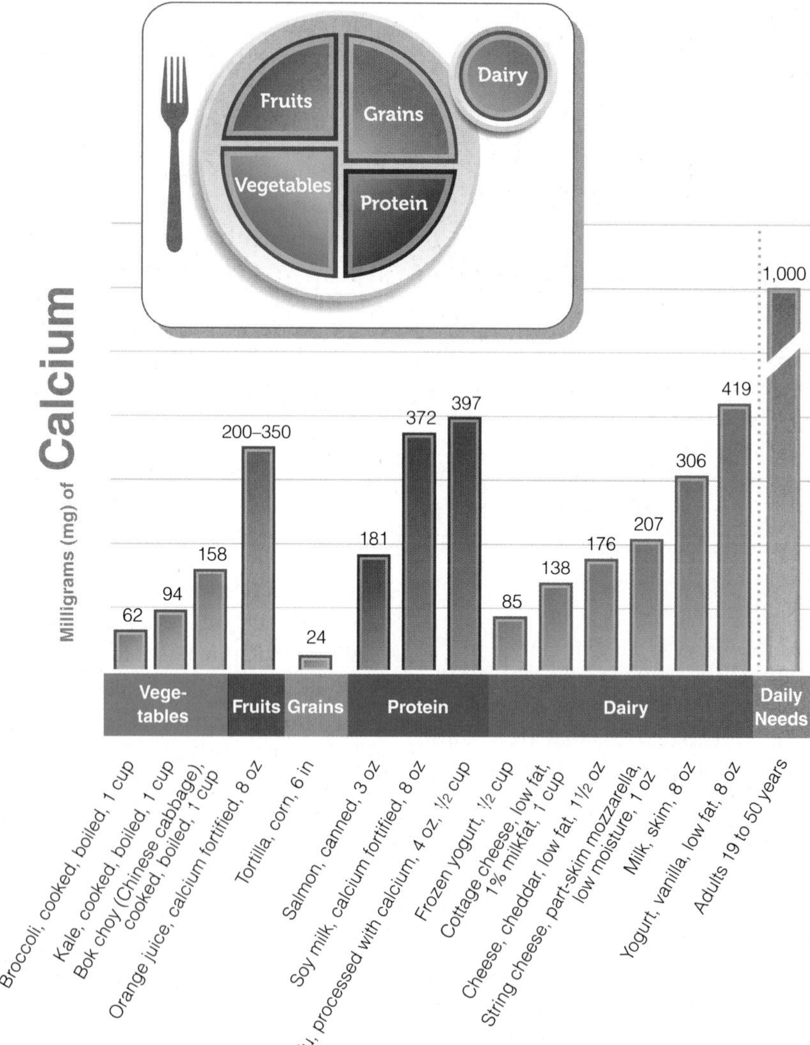

▲ **Figure 12.11 Calcium Content of Selected Foods**

hypercalcemia Abnormally high levels of calcium in the blood.

hypocalcemia Abnormally low levels of calcium in the blood.

Health Connection

Building a Stronger Bone

What Are Strong Bones and Why Are They So Important?

Strong, healthy bones are those with a high **bone mineral density (BMD).** BMD is the density of hydroxyapatite crystals within the trabecular bone and cortical bone. Stronger bones have a higher density than weaker bone. Weak and brittle bones can lead to osteoporosis, one of the biggest physical problems experienced by Older adults in the United States. Older adults with this condition experience a myriad of health problems, from bone breaks and fractures to reduced mobility and diminished quality of life. Unfortunately, by the time an older adult finds out he or she has osteoporosis, little can be done, because an individual's lifelong bone health is largely determined during childhood, adolescence, and early adulthood, when the person is accumulating peak bone mass. This means that, during your college years, you are building up the bone health you'll need for a healthy older age.

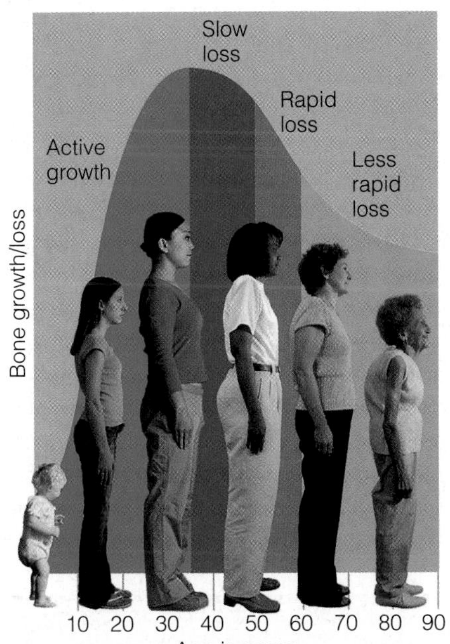

▲ **Figure 1 Change in Bone Mass As You Age**
In your early years, more bone is added than lost in your body. In their mid-30s, women begin to slowly lose bone mass until menopause, when the rate of loss is accelerated for several years. Bone loss continues after age 60 but at a slower rate.

You can think of bone mass as being like a retirement account. The more you save when you are young and preserve throughout your adulthood, the more you will have for your later years. Conversely, if you don't save enough early in life, you may end up with little to fall back on when you need it. If children don't reach their maximum bone mass by young adulthood, they will not have adequate bone mass stored for their later years. If an adult doesn't have a healthy diet and lifestyle that includes regular exercise, he or she may experience accelerated bone loss after age 30.

When Does Bone Growth Occur?

Bones are dynamic, living tissues that are constantly being broken down and reformed. Specialized cells called osteoclasts work to remove older layers of bones, while osteoblasts continuously form new bone. Although this process occurs throughout the life span, the majority of bone growth and buildup of bone mass occurs during childhood, adolescence, and early adulthood, when the osteoblasts are more active than the osteoclasts. During these life stages, more bone mass is added than is lost in the body. Although growth of bone length typically ceases during the teenage years, bone mass will continue to accumulate into the early years of young adulthood. The maximum bone mass an adult will accrue, referred to as **peak bone mass,** usually occurs when a person is in his or her 20s. Some additional bone mass can be added when an individual is in his or her 30s.

After peak bone mass is reached, the loss of bone mass begins to slowly exceed the rate at which new bone is added.[1] Starting in their mid-30s, women begin to slowly lose bone mass until menopause, when the rate of loss accelerates for several years (see **Figure 1**). Bone loss continues in women after age 60, but at a slower rate. Bone loss also occurs in men as they age.

If you are fortunate enough to have elders, such as grandparents, in your life, you may have heard them comment that they are "shrinking as they age." Of course, they aren't really shrinking. But they may be losing height as the vertebrae in their backbone collapse, causing curvature of the spine, which affects their posture (see **Figure 2**).[2] This outward sign means that their backbone has lost bone mass over the years, and has become unsturdy to the point that it can't hold up their body weight. As older individuals begin to hunch over, they can lose as much as a foot in height.[3]

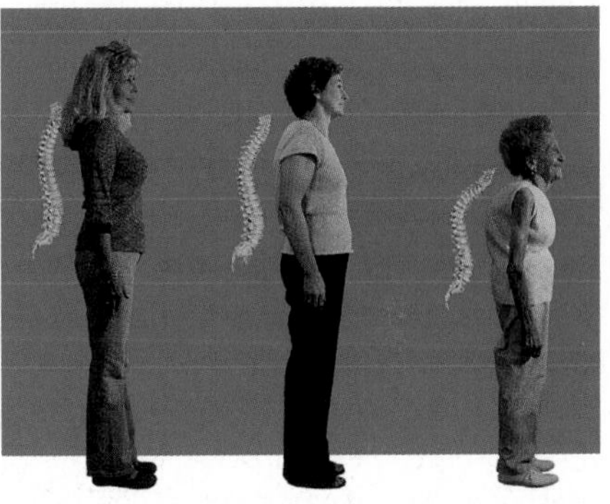

▲ **Figure 2 Deterioration of the Vertebrae**
Weakened bones in the vertebrae cause the spine to collapse over time, resulting in the "shrinking" effect experienced by some older adults.

What Is Osteoporosis?

As bones lose mineral mass they become porous and **osteoporosis** (*osteo* = bone, *porosis* =

bone mineral density (BMD) The amount of minerals, in particular calcium, per volume in an individual's bone.

peak bone mass The genetically determined maximum amount of bone mass an individual can build up.

osteoporosis A condition whereby the bones are less dense, increasing the risk of fractures.

continued

porous) can develop. There are two main classifications of osteoporosis. **Type I osteoporosis** is associated with a decrease in estrogen levels during menopause and is present in 5 to 20 percent of American women aged 50 to 75 years. The lower levels of estrogen in a postmenopausal woman's body cause a reduction in bone mineral density. This, in turn, leads to weak and brittle bones. Type I osteoporosis is often associated with fractures of the spine, hip, wrist, or forearm. Because Type I osteoporosis is usually related to a drop in estrogen levels at menopause, it is more likely to occur in women than in men.

Type II osteoporosis, or age-related osteoporosis, occurs when the breakdown of bone outpaces the rebuilding of bone over time. Type II osteoporosis is mostly associated with leg and spinal fractures, and occurs in both men and women. Note that older women can have both types of osteoporosis simultaneously.[4]

The weakened, fragile bones associated with both types of osteoporosis are prone to fractures. A minor stumble while walking can result in a fall that breaks a hip, ankle, or arm bone. Shopping, showering, dressing, and even brushing one's teeth become challenges for many older people with osteoporosis.

Hip fractures can be devastating because they often render a person immobile, which quickly affects quality of life. Feelings of helplessness and depression often ensue. Up to two-thirds of all individuals with hip fractures are never able to regain the quality of life they had prior to the injury, and about 20 percent will die within a year due to complications from the injury. By the year 2020, an estimated more than 61 million Americans will either have or be at risk for hip fractures due to osteoporosis, and even more will be at risk for fractures of other bones.[5]

How Do We Measure Bone Density?

Bone density tests for adults compare an individual's bone mineral density with that of a healthy 30-year-old. The most accurate tool is a dual-energy X-ray absorptiometry, or DEXA, test, which is a fast and easy test that uses two beams of low-energy X-ray radiation (see **Figure 3**). DEXA can measure bone loss of as little as 2 percent per year. In a DEXA scan, strong, dense bones allow less of the X-ray beam to pass through them. The amounts of each X-ray beam that are blocked by bone and soft tissue are compared with each other. The data from a DEXA is presented as a T-score, which is compared with the ideal or peak bone mineral density of a healthy 30-year-old adult. A healthy normal bone will have a T-score of +1 to –1, whereas a low T-score between –1 and –2.5 indicates **osteopenia** (*penia* = poverty), signaling low bone mass. A very low score, less than –2.5, indicates osteoporosis.

Type I osteoporosis Osteoporosis that results from lowered estrogen levels women experience during menopause. This type of osteoporosis is characterized by rapid bone loss.

Type II osteoporosis Osteoporosis that occurs in both men and women; characterized by the slow loss of bone mass over time due to aging.

osteopenia A condition in which the bone mineral density is lower than normal but not low enough to be classified as osteoporosis.

What Factors Influence Bone Mass?

As with hypertension, diabetes, and other chronic conditions, there are choices you can make today to lessen your likelihood of experiencing weakened bones or osteoporosis in the future. Among the factors that matter most are diet, exercise, and the use of drugs (including nicotine) and alcohol.

The Role of Diet

Calcium intake during childhood and adolescence is strongly related to higher bone mineral density in older men and women. Adequate vitamin D intake is also important, as vitamin D promotes the absorption of calcium and is essential to attain peak bone mass.

Adequate intake of the minerals magnesium and potassium has also been associated with increased bone health. One study found that the bone mineral density in the neck of the femur (or thigh bone) was higher in women who had consumed high amounts of fruit (a good source of both magnesium and potassium) in their childhood than in women who had consumed medium or low amounts.[6] Diets rich in vitamin K reduce the risk of hip fractures, probably due to a reduction in bone turnover, although vitamin K doesn't appear to improve bone mineral density.[7] Consuming adequate levels of omega-3 fatty acids also has a positive effect in achieving peak bone mass.[8] The

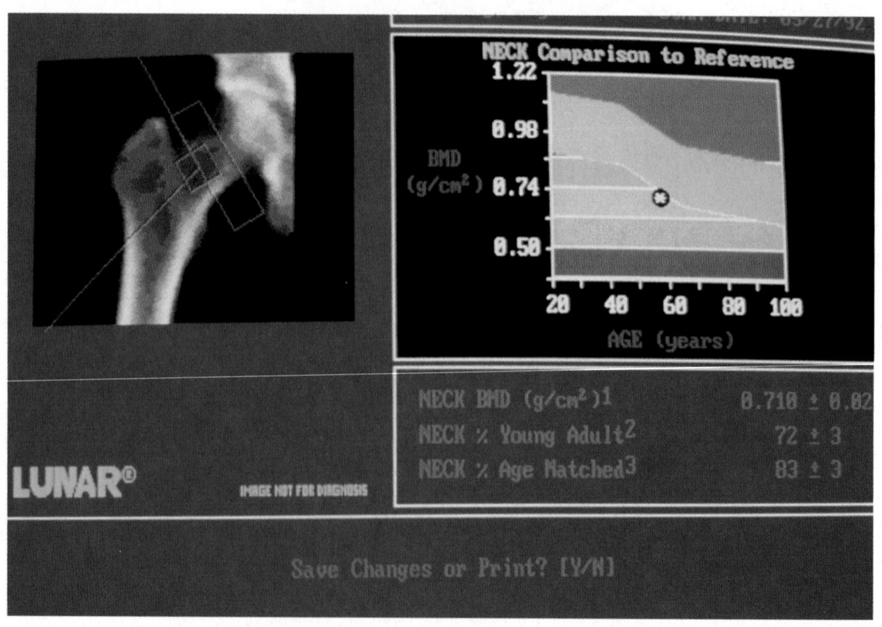

▲ **Figure 3 Dual-Energy X-Ray Absorptiometry**
A DEXA scan is the most accurate way to measure bone mineral density.

sodium-osteoporosis link is still unclear. A healthy diet that meets the current recommendations for calcium and sodium is adequate for the health and maintenance of bone.

One dietary habit that may have a negative impact on bone mineral density is the regular consumption of carbonated beverages. Several observational studies have shown a relationship between low bone mineral density and an increase in fracture rates in teenagers who consume higher amounts of soda and other carbonated beverages. The bone mineral density in the heels of females aged 12 to 15 was inversely related to the amount of carbonated beverages they consumed. However, no relationship was observed in boys the same age.[9] A similar study reported a relationship between carbonated beverage intake and risk of fracture.[10] However, this relationship has not been substantiated with experimental studies.[11] Researchers theorize that the correlation between carbonated beverage intake and poor bone health may have more to do with the displacement of milk in the diet than with the carbonated beverages themselves.

The role of protein in osteoporosis remains controversial. Protein positively correlates with an increase in bone density, but high protein intakes combined with lower intakes of calcium increase urinary calcium loss. It appears from the current research that protein should not be detrimental to bone density if both protein and calcium are present in the recommended levels.

Although food is the best source of nutrients to develop and maintain healthy bones, some individuals are advised to take a supplement by their health care provider. However, supplements that contain high doses of nutrients other than calcium have been shown to have adverse effects on bone health. For example, high doses of vitamin A supplements in the form of retinol can significantly increase the risk of hip fracture in older individuals.[12]

Taking high doses of vitamin C for bone health has produced mixed results. In some studies, vitamin C intakes of 100 milligrams to 125 milligrams have improved bone mineral density and reduced the risk of hip fractures in postmenopausal women. However, higher intakes of vitamin C (greater than 2,000 milligrams) may increase the risk of fracture, as well as the risk of developing kidney stones, although more research is required to support these findings.[13]

Exercise Improves Bone Mass

Weight-bearing exercises help maintain bone and increase bone mass. High-impact exercise, such as hiking or weight training, has been found to be an inexpensive, safe, and effective means to improve bone mineral density, prevent osteoporosis, and reduce the risk of falls and fractures. High-impact physical activity has been shown to increase the growth and the mineral content of the bones in girls and adolescent females.[14, 15] However, to achieve this benefit, the diet must also contain an adequate amount of calcium and kilocalories.

These same increases in bone mineral density are reported in premenopausal women over the age of 18 who have stopped growing in height but can still improve bone mineral density.[16] After menopause, the benefits of weight-bearing exercise show increases in not only bone mineral density but also overall muscle strength.[17] The muscle action of pulling on the bone stimulates the osteoblasts to build more bone.

Exercise only improves bone strength in the bones that are impacted by the exercise.[18] For example, weight training the lower body will not improve the upper arms or bones of the wrist, where many older women sustain fractures.

Intensity is also important to consider when choosing an exercise to improve bone mineral density. For example, high-intensity walking at a pace of more than 4 miles per hour (rather than a leisurely stroll at about 2 miles per hour) increases the stress on the muscle and bone and results in an increase in the bone mineral density of the hip.[19] Choose exercises that you enjoy but that provide the intensity required to improve both the mineral density of the bone and overall muscular strength.

Body Weight Impacts Bone Mass

Body weight also has an impact on achieving peak bone mass. Women who are slightly heavier than their normal-weight counterparts have higher bone mineral density, especially in the spine and the hip. However, when an individual loses weight, the effect may be detrimental to their bone. During moderate weight loss, bones appear to maintain mineral density, especially when there is adequate calcium in the diet.[20] However, when the weight loss is severe, such as in young women diagnosed with anorexia nervosa, the loss of bone mineral density is significant.[21] The key to maintaining healthy bone mass appears to be losing weight slowly and eating adequate amounts of calcium and kilocalories.

The Effects of Smoking on Bone Mass

Bone mineral density is significantly reduced in people who smoke.[22, 23] Postmenopausal women who reportedly smoked prior to menopause were found to have significantly lower bone mineral density scores than women who never smoked. Though the mechanism related to smoking and its impact on bone mineral density and fracture risk is not completely understood, several theories have been suggested. First, smokers have lower levels of parathyroid hormone and calcitriol, suggesting that more calcium is removed from the bone. Women who smoke also have lower body weights, which could account for less estrogen, less protective body fat (important during a fall), and reduced load on bones (load improves bone density). Regardless of the mechanism, the risk of fracture in smokers has been reported to be 35 percent higher compared with nonsmokers.[24] Similar effects of smoking have also been reported in men.[25] The good news is that stopping smoking causes bone mineral density to improve.[26]

continued

The Impact of Alcohol on Bone Mass

Excessive alcohol intake has been associated with osteoporosis[27] and related fractures. This is due in part to the malnourishment often seen in chronic alcoholics, which may include insufficient calcium intake. In addition, alcohol may reduce vitamin D metabolism and alter osteoblast activity, thereby interfering with calcium absorption and bone formation, and produce a hormonal imbalance affecting parathyroid hormone, estrogen, and testosterone.

Not all research reports a negative relationship of alcohol to bone health.[28] In a recent study of moderate drinkers, the results suggested that social drinking or moderate alcohol intake may have a positive impact on bone mineral density. Researchers reported that alcohol intake of about 1 to 3 glasses of wine per day in elderly women correlated with higher bone mineral density. Two possible mechanisms have been proposed for the improved bone mineral density found with moderate alcohol consumption. First, calcitonin production may be stimulated, which has been shown to improve bone mineral density in the spine. Second, moderate alcohol intake may stimulate higher estrogen levels. More research is needed to clarify the impact of alcohol consumption on bone health.

A Recipe for Healthy Bones

To improve and maintain bone mineral density, consume a diet adequate in calcium and kilocalories, maintain a healthy body weight, participate in weight-bearing exercise, don't smoke, and, if you drink alcohol, do so only in moderation.

References

1. National Institutes of Health. Osteoporosis and Related Bone Diseases National Resource Center. 2007. *Osteoporosis Overview.* Available from www.niams.nih.gov/bone/hi/overview.pdf. Accessed May 2012.
2. Forsmo, S., H. M. Hvam, M. L. Rea, S. E. Lilleeng, B. Schei, and A. Langhammer. 2007. Height Loss, Forearm Bone Density and Bone Loss in Menopausal Women: A 15-Year Prospective Study. The Nord-Trøndelag Health Study, Norway. *Osteoporosis International* 18:1261–1269.
3. Patlak, M. 2001. Bone Builders: The Discoveries Behind Preventing and Treating Osteoporosis. *The FASEB Journal* 15:1677.
4. National Institutes of Health. 2007. *Osteoporosis Overview.*
5. National Osteoporosis Foundation Advocacy. 2007. *America's Bone Health: The State of Osteoporosis and Low Bone Mass.* Available from www.nof.org. Accessed November 2012.
6. New, S. A., S. P. Robins, M. K. Campbell, J. C. Martin, M. J. Garton, C. Bolton-Smith, D. A. Grubb, et al. 2000. Dietary Influences on Bone Mass and Bone Metabolism: Further Evidence of a Positive Link Between Fruit and Vegetable Consumption and Bone Health? *American Journal of Clinical Nutrition* 71:142–151.
7. Booth, S. L., K. L. Tucker, H. Chen, M. T. Hannan, D. R. Gagnon, L. A. Cupples, P. W. Wilson, et al. 2000. Dietary Vitamin K Intakes Are Associated with Hip Fracture but Not with Bone Mineral Density in Elderly Men and Women. *American Journal of Clinical Nutrition* 71:1201–1208.
8. Högström, M., P. Nordstrom, and A. Nordstrom. 2007. n-3 Fatty Acids Are Positively Associated with Peak Bone Mineral Density and Bone Accrual in Healthy Men: The NO2 Study. *American Journal of Clinical Nutrition* 85:803–807.
9. McGartland, C., P. J. Robson, L. Murray, G. Cran, M. J. Savage, D. Watkins, M. Rooney, and C. Boreham. 2003. Carbonated Soft Drink Consumption and Bone Mineral Density in Adolescence: The Northern Ireland Young Hearts Project. *Journal of Bone and Mineral Metabolism* 18:1563–1569.
10. Wyshak, G. 2000. Teenaged Girls, Carbonated Beverage Consumption, and Bone Fractures. *Archives of Pediatric Adolescent Medicine* 154:610–613.
11. Heaney, R. P. 2001. Carbonated Beverages and Urinary Calcium Excretion. *American Journal of Clinical Nutrition* 74:343–347.
12. Feskanich, D., V. Singh, W. C. Willet, and G. A. Colditz. 2002. Vitamin A Intake and Hip Fractures Among Postmenopausal Women. *Journal of the American Medical Association* 287:47–54.
13. Leveille, S. G., A. Z. LaCroix, T. D. Koepsell, S. A. Beresford, G. Van Bell, and D. M. Buchner. 1997. Dietary Vitamin C and Bone Mineral Density in Postmenopausal Women in Washington State, USA. *Journal of Epidemiology and Community Health* 51:479–485.
14. Nichols, J. F., M. J. Rauh, M. T. Barrack, and H. S. Barkai. 2007. Bone Mineral Density in Female High School Athletes: Interactions of Menstrual Function and Type of Mechanical Loading. *Bone* 41:371–377.
15. Janz, K. F., J. M. Gilmore, S. M. Levy, E. M. Letuchy, T. L. Burns, and T. J. Beck. 2007. Physical Activity and Femoral Neck Bone Strength during Childhood: The Iowa Bone Development Study. *Bone* 41:216–222.
16. Aki, V., A. Vainionpaa, R. Korpelainen, J. Leppaluoto, and T. Jamsa. 2005. Effects of High-Impact Exercise on Bone Mineral Density: A Randomized Controlled Trial in Premenopausal Women. *Osteoporosis International* 16:191–197.
17. Engelke, K., W. Kemmler, D. Lauber, C. Beeskow, R. Pintag, and W. A. Kalender. 2006. Exercise Maintains Bone Density at Spine and Hip EFOPS: A 3-year Longitudinal Study in Early Postmenopausal Women. *Osteoporosis International* 17:133–142.
18. Ducher, G., N. Tournaire, A. Meddahi-Pelle, C. L. Benhamou, and D. Courteix. 2006. Short-Term and Long-Term Site-Specific Effects of Tennis Playing on Trabecular and Cortical Bone at the Distal Radius. *Journal of Bone and Mineral Metabolism* 24:484–490.
19. Borer, K. T., K. Fogleman, M. Gross, J. M. LaNew, and D. Dengel. 2007. Walking Intensity for Postmenopausal Bone Mineral Preservation and Accrual. *Bone* 41:713–721.
20. Riedt, C. S., Y. Schlussel, N. von Thun, H. Ambia-Sobhan, T. Stahl, M. P. Field, R. M. Sherrell, and S. A. Shapses. 2007. Premenopausal Overweight Women Do Not Lose Bone During Moderate Weight Loss with Adequate or Higher Calcium Intake. *American Journal of Clinical Nutrition* 85:972–980.
21. Diamanti, A., C. Bizzarri, M. Gambarara, A. Calce, F. Montecchi, M. Cappa, G. Biaco, and M. Castro. 2007. Bone Mineral Density in Adolescent Girls with Early Onset of Anorexia Nervosa. *Clinical Nutrition* 26:329–334.
22. Lorentzon, M., D. Mellstrom, E. Haug, and C. Ohlsson. 2007. Smoking Is Associated with Lower Bone Mineral Density and Reduced Cortical Thickness in Young Men. *Journal of Clinical Endocrinology & Metabolism* 92:497–503.
23. Demirbag, D., F. Ozdemir, and M. Ture. 2006. Effects of Coffee Consumption and Smoking Habit on Bone Mineral Density. *Rheumatology International* 26:530–535.
24. Baron, J. A., B. Y. Farahmand, E. Weiderpass, K. Michaellsson, A. Alberts, I. Persson, and S. Ljunghall. 2001. Cigarette Smoking, Alcohol Consumption, and Risk of Hip Fracture in Women. *Archives of Internal Medicine* 161:983–988.
25. Lorentzon, M., et al. 2007. Smoking Is Associated with Lower Bone Mineral Density.
26. Oncken, C., K. Prestwood, A. Kleppinger, Y. Wang, J. Cooney, and L. Raisz. 2006. Impact of Smoking Cessation on Bone Mineral Density in Postmenopausal Women. *Journal of Women's Health* 15:1141–1150.
27. Ganry, O., C. Baudoin, and P. Fardellone. 2000. Effect of Alcohol Intake on Bone Mineral Density in Elderly Women: The EPIDOS Study. *American Journal of Epidemiology* 151:773–780.
28. Rapuri, P. B., J. C. Gallagher, K. E. Blahorn, and K. L. Ryschon. 2000. Alcohol Intake and Bone Metabolism in Elderly Women. *American Journal of Clinical Nutrition* 72:1206–1213.

Nutrition in Practice: Martha

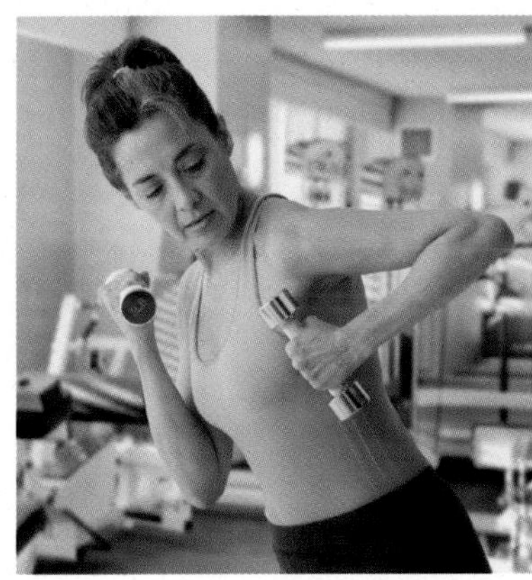

Because Martha is postmenopausal, her doctor wanted to do a bone density scan at her last annual physical. Approximately, two weeks after the test, the nurse practitioner (NP) called and told Martha that her T-score was "on the lower side." Martha was surprised to hear this, as she walks 4 miles daily and lifts weights three times a week, and considers herself in good shape. The NP recommended that Martha meet with a registered dietitian (RD) to make sure that she was consuming adequate amounts of calcium in her diet. Martha is hesitant to talk to a RD because she is afraid that the dietitian is going to ask her to take a calcium supplement. Martha will do *anything* to avoid swallowing pills. The NP convinces Martha to make an appointment with the RD.

Martha's Stats:

- Age: 54
- Height: 5 feet 5 inches
- Weight: 138 pounds
- BMI: 23

Critical Thinking Questions

1. How much calcium should Martha be consuming daily?
2. Based on her food log, approximately how much calcium is Martha consuming?
3. How can Martha add more calcium-rich foods at her meals and snacks to meet her daily needs?

Dietitian's Observation and Plan for Martha:

- Discuss the need to consume at least 3 servings of low fat dairy plus a serving of a calcium-fortified food to meet the 1,200 mg of calcium needed daily.
- Substitute a string cheese for the banana as a snack before her morning walk.
- Prepare the oatmeal with skim milk rather than water and switch to calcium-fortified orange juice in the morning.
- Remove an ounce of turkey from and add 1.5 ounces of low fat cheddar cheese to her lunchtime sandwich.
- Replace her evening snack with a blender smoothie that contains 8 ounces of yogurt, fruit, a splash of skim milk, and ice.

Two weeks later, Martha returns for a follow-up visit with the dietitian. She has made all of the changes that the RD recommended but doesn't like the evening smoothie. She complains that the smoothie is "too watery." The RD recommends that she use frozen berries rather than the fresh variety and eliminate the ice. Both of these changes will allow the smoothie to be cold and thick without it getting "too watery."

Martha's Food Log

Food/Beverage	Time Consumed	Hunger Rating*	Location
Banana (before her morning walk)	6 am	4	Kitchen
Oatmeal made with water, orange juice, and tea with lemon and sugar	7:30 am	5	Kitchen
Turkey sandwich with lettuce, small salad with Italian dressing, berries	12 pm	5	Employee's lunch room
Chicken, small baked potato, handful of broccoli	6:30 pm	5	Kitchen
½ pint of frozen yogurt	8 pm	3	Watching TV

*Hunger Rating (1-5): 1 = not hungry 5 = super hungry

Calcium from unrefined oyster shell, bone meal, or dolomite (a rock rich in calcium) may contain lead and other toxic metals. Supplements from these sources should state on the label that they are "purified" or carry the USP symbol to ensure purity.

Regardless of the form, all calcium, whether from supplements or from fortified or naturally occurring foods, should be consumed in doses of 500 milligrams or less, as this is the maximum that the body can absorb efficiently at one time. In other words, if a person has been advised to take 1,000 milligrams of calcium daily, 500 milligrams should be consumed in the morning and the other 500 milligrams in the afternoon or evening.[52] Because calcium can interfere with and reduce the absorption of iron, a calcium supplement shouldn't be taken at the same time of day as an iron supplement.

Calcium supplements can sometimes cause constipation and flatulence (gas), especially when taken in large amounts. Increasing the amount of

CALCIUM

Self-Assessment

Estimating Your Calcium Intake

Complete the table below to estimate the total amount of calcium you consumed yesterday. Then, compare it to the AI listed in the text. Are you meeting your calcium needs?

Product	Number of Servings	Calcium Content per Serving	Total Amount of Calcium (mg)
Milk, 8 oz		300 mg	
Fortified orange juice, 8 oz		300 mg	
Fortified cereals, snacks (no milk added)		100 mg	
Fortified cereal with 4 oz milk		250 mg	
Yogurt, 8 oz		400 mg	
Cheese, 1 oz		200 mg	
Legumes, 1 cup		225 mg	
Leafy green vegetables, 1 cup cooked (low-oxalate vegetables such as kale and collard greens)		185 mg	
Total mg calcium			

Adapted from the International Osteoporosis Foundation, www.iofbonehealth.org.

fiber in the diet helps avoid these less-than-pleasurable side effects. As with any mineral supplement, be cautious about adding a calcium supplement to your diet if you are already consuming plenty of low-fat dairy foods and/or calcium-fortified foods.

TABLE TIPS

Calcium Counts

Use skim or low-fat milk on your morning cereal.

Spoon a few chunks of tofu onto a salad bar lunch for extra calcium.

Use low-fat pudding or yogurt to satisfy a sweet tooth.

Top calcium-rich pizza with more calcium from vegetables such as broccoli and raw leafy greens.

Spread nonfat or low-fat ricotta cheese on toast for a snack.

Drink calcium-fortified orange juice with your morning cereal.

PHOSPHORUS

Exploring **Phosphorus**

What Is Phosphorus?

Phosphorus is the second most abundant mineral in the body. The majority of phosphorus—about 85 percent—is found in bone tissue bound with calcium. The remainder is in the muscle, cell membranes, and extracellular fluids.

About 70 percent of the phosphorus in the diet is absorbed through the small intestine. Foods that contain the binder phytate reduce the absorption of phosphorus, whereas vitamin D enhances its bioavailability. Other minerals, including magnesium, calcium, and aluminum, decrease the absorption of phosphorus. These three minerals are often found in antacids and can be used to reduce high blood levels of phosphorus.[53]

phosphorus The second most abundant mineral in the body.

Parathyroid hormone (PTH) controls phosphorus metabolism in the same way it manages calcium metabolism. When blood levels of phosphorus are low, PTH stimulates the resorption of the mineral from the bone to raise blood levels. Unlike calcium, however, PTH also stimulates the kidneys to

excrete phosphorus through the urine. Most phosphorus is excreted in the urine and the rest is lost in the feces.

Functions of Phosphorus

Phosphorus plays a role in the health of bones and teeth. It also helps provide the structure for cell membranes, participates in metabolism, acts as an acid-base buffer, and is part of DNA and RNA.

Phosphorus Is Needed for Bones and Teeth and Is an Important Component of Cells

Together with calcium, phosphorus plays a key role in the formation of the crystalline structure called hydroxyapatite that gives the bones and teeth their strength. The concentration of phosphorus as the salt calcium phosphate in bone is about fifty percent as much as calcium.

Phosphorus is also part of phospholipids (see **Figure 12.13**), which give cell membranes their structure. Phospholipids act as a barrier to keep specific substances out of the cells while letting others in.

Phosphorus Is Needed during Metabolism

Phosphorus is part of the adenosine triphosphate (ATP) molecule and thus helps store energy generated from the metabolism of carbohydrates, protein, and fat for later use. Phosphorus is also part of creatine phosphate, which is found in muscle. Creatine phosphate can provide phosphorus to ADP when cells require more energy.

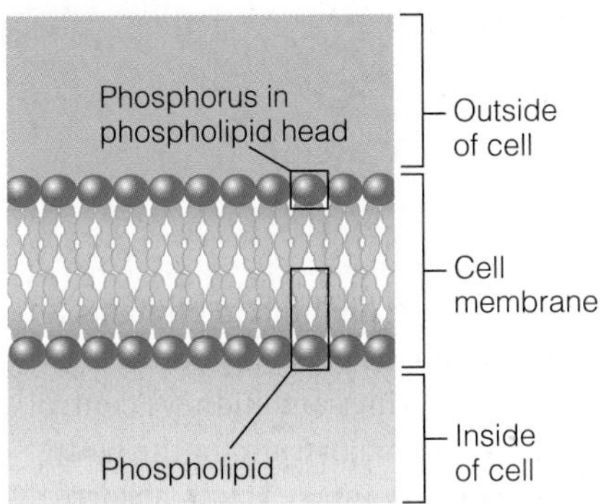

▲ **Figure 12.13 Phosphorus Forms Phospholipids**
Phosphorus makes up part of the phospholipids found in cell membranes.

Phosphorus Acts as a Buffer and Is Part of the DNA and RNA of Every Cell

If the blood becomes too acidic or too basic, phosphorus can act as a buffer. Within the cells, phosphorus in the form of phosphate can bind excess hydrogen ions, thus increasing the pH. Blood pH must always stay within a very narrow range to prevent damage to tissues.

Another major function of phosphorus is that it is incorporated into the backbone of DNA and RNA molecules.

Daily Needs

The RDA for adult males and females has been set at 700 milligrams of phosphorus daily. Americans, on average, consume more than 1,000 milligrams of phosphorus daily.

Food Sources

A balanced, varied diet will easily provide an adequate amount of phosphorus (see **Figure 12.14**). Foods from animal sources such as meat, fish, poultry, and dairy products are excellent sources of phosphorus. Plant seeds such as beans, peas, nuts, and cereal grains contain phosphorus in the

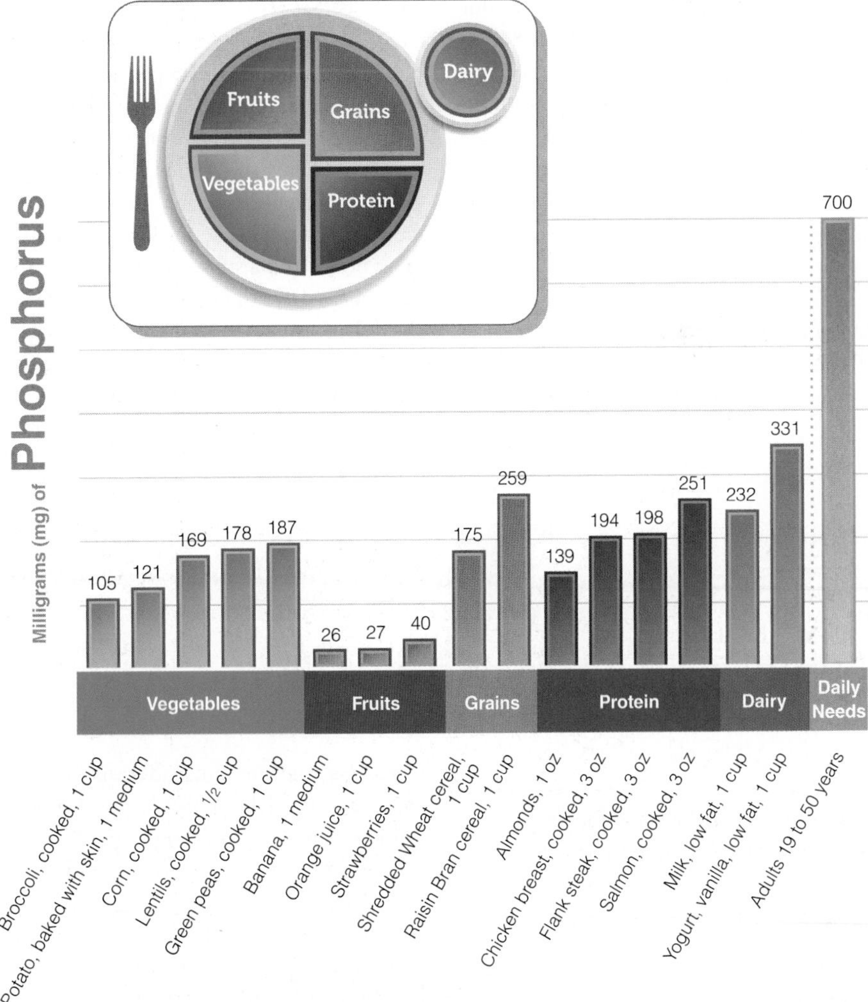

▲ **Figure 12.14 Sources of Dietary Phosphorus**

continued

form of phytates, which are only about 50 percent bioavailable. Soft drinks and colas, which contain the additive phosphoric acid, are another common food source of phosphorus. However, these beverages should be limited in the diet due to their high refined sugar content.

hyperphosphatemia Abnormally high level of phosphorus in the blood.

hypophosphatemia Abnormally low level of phosphorus in the blood.

Too Much or Too Little

Typically, consuming too much dietary phosphorus and its subsequent effect, **hyperphosphatemia,** is only an issue for individuals with kidney problems who cannot excrete excess phosphorus. Consistently high phosphorus and low calcium intake can cause the loss of calcium from bones and a subsequent decrease in bone mass. Loss of bone mass increases the risk of osteoporosis. Hyperphosphatemia can also lead to depositing calcium (also known as calcification) in soft tissues such as the arteries and kidneys. To protect against this, the upper level for phosphorus has been set at 4,000 milligrams daily for adults aged 19 to 50 and 3,000 milligrams for those 50 years of age and older.

Too little phosphorus in the diet can cause dangerously low blood levels, a condition called **hypophosphatemia,** and result in muscle weakness, bone pain, rickets, confusion, and, at the extreme, death. Because phosphorus is so abundant in the diet, however, a deficiency is very rare. In fact, a person would have to be in a state of near starvation before experiencing a phosphorus deficiency.

TABLE TIPS

Balance Phosphorus with Calcium

Substitute sodas with refreshing lemonade to quench your thirst.

Blend together calcium-fortified orange juice and slightly thawed frozen strawberries for a refreshing smoothie.

Skip the butter and sprinkle chopped unsalted peanuts over calcium-rich steamed vegetables for a crunchy topping.

Dip raw broccoli florets into a nonfat sour cream–based dip for a snack.

Stir-fry chicken breast with calcium-rich vegetables for a balanced ratio of phosphorus to calcium.

Exploring Magnesium

What Is Magnesium?

Magnesium (Mg^{+2}) is the fourth most abundant divalent cation in the body. About 60 percent of the body's magnesium is found in bones, 25 percent in muscle, and the remainder inside various other cells. A mere 1 percent is found in the blood—though, like blood calcium, this amount must be maintained at a constant level.

magnesium (Mg^{+2}) A major divalent cation in the body.

The bioavailability of magnesium in a typical diet is about fifty percent. Diets that are high in fiber and whole grains, which are high in phytates, lower magnesium absorption.

The intestines and kidneys control the levels of magnesium in the body. When dietary intake is low, absorption of magnesium through the small intestine increases and the kidneys excrete less.

Functions of Magnesium

Magnesium plays many roles in metabolism, including the synthesis of DNA, RNA, and protein. Magnesium also aids in the transmission of nerve impulses and has an impact on the health of muscles, bones, and the heart, blood sugar, and blood pressure.

Magnesium Is Needed for Metabolism and to Maintain Healthy Muscles, Nerves, Bones, and Heart

Magnesium is associated with more than 300 enzymatic reactions in the body, including many associated with the metabolism of carbohydrates, proteins, and fats, and the phosphorylation of ADP to ATP.

Magnesium is used during the synthesis of DNA, RNA, and body proteins during the transcription, translation, and replication phases. Magnesium also plays a vital role in bone metabolism and cell membrane synthesis.

Magnesium helps muscles, including the heart muscle, and nerves to function properly. It is also needed to help maintain healthy bones and a regular heart beat.

Magnesium May Help Lower High Blood Pressure and Reduce the Risk of Diabetes Mellitus

Magnesium is another abundant mineral in the DASH diet, though the actual role of magnesium in blood pressure has not yet been identified.

Some studies suggest that a diet abundant in magnesium may help decrease the risk of type 2 diabetes.[54] Low blood levels of magnesium, which often occurs in individuals with type 2 diabetes, may impair the release of insulin, one of the hormones that regulate blood glucose. This may lead to elevated blood glucose levels in those with preexisting diabetes and those at risk for type 2 diabetes.[55]

Daily Needs

The RDA for adult females aged 19 and older ranges from 310 milligrams to 320 milligrams of magnesium, whereas men of the same age need 400 milligrams to 420 milligrams of magnesium daily.

Currently, many Americans fall short of the recommended intake of magnesium. Females consume only about 70 percent of their RDA, or about 220 milligrams daily, on average. Males consume approximately 320 milligrams daily, on average, or approximately 80 percent of the amount recommended. Because older adults tend to consume fewer calories, and thus less dietary magnesium, they are at an even higher risk of falling short of their needs.

Food Sources

The biggest contributors of magnesium in Americans' diets are green leafy vegetables, whole grains, nuts, legumes, and fruits. Milk, yogurt, meat, and eggs are also good sources (see **Figure 12.15**). A peanut butter sandwich on whole-wheat bread, along with a glass of low-fat milk and a banana, will provide more than 200 milligrams, or about half of an adult's daily needs. Because the majority of the magnesium in bread products is in the bran and germ of the grain kernel, products made with refined grains such as white flour are poor magnesium sources. Finally, beverages such as

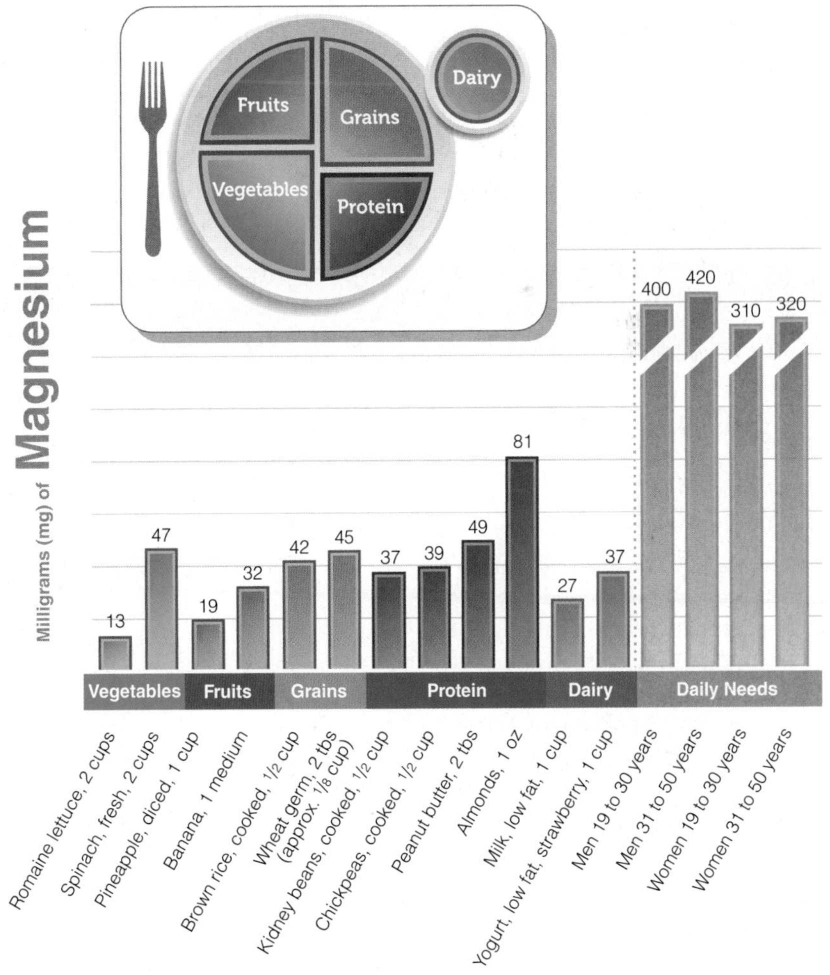

▲ **Figure 12.15 Food Sources of Magnesium in Selected Foods**

continued

coffee, tea, and cocoa also contain some magnesium.

Too Much or Too Little

There is no known risk in consuming too much magnesium from food sources. However, consuming large amounts from supplements has been shown to cause intestinal problems such as diarrhea, cramps, and nausea. In fact, some laxatives (such as milk of magnesia) contain magnesium because of its known cathartic effect. The upper level for magnesium from supplements, not foods, is set at 350 milligrams for adults. This level is to prevent diarrhea, the first symptom that typically arises when too much magnesium is consumed.

Even though many Americans don't meet their dietary magnesium needs, deficiencies are rare in healthy individuals because the kidneys compensate for low magnesium intake by excreting less of it. However, some medications may cause magnesium deficiency. Certain diuretics can cause the body to lose too much magnesium, and some antibiotics, such as tetracycline, can inhibit the absorption of magnesium, both of which can lead to a deficiency. Individuals with poorly controlled diabetes or who abuse alcohol can experience excessive losses of magnesium in the urine, which could also cause a deficiency. A severe magnesium deficiency can cause muscle weakness, seizures, fatigue, depression, and irregular heart beats.

TABLE TIPS

More Magnesium

Sprinkle chopped almonds over whole-grain cereal in the morning for two crunchy sources of magnesium.

Add baby spinach to a salad.

Add rinsed, canned black beans to salsa for a vegetable dip with added magnesium.

Spread peanut butter on whole-wheat crackers for a satisfying afternoon snack.

Try precooked brown rice for an easy way to add whole grains.

Exploring Sulfate

What Is Sulfate?

Sulfate (SO_4) is the oxidized form of the mineral sulfur that is found in plants and occurs naturally in drinking water. In the body, sulfur is usually found as part of other compounds, mostly proteins. It is also part of two important B vitamins, thiamin and biotin.

Sulfate is absorbed throughout the GI tract, including the stomach, small intestine, and colon. About 80 percent of the sulfate you eat is absorbed, and the excess excreted in the urine. Sulfate is found in the body's tissues as part of keratin, especially in hair, skin, and nails.

sulfate (SO_4) The oxidized form of the mineral sulfur.

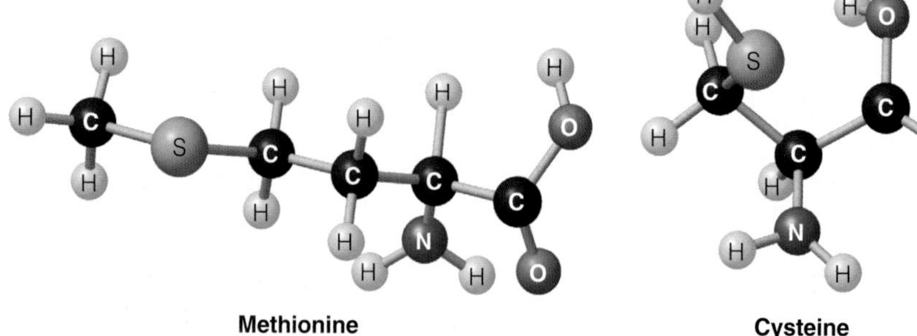

▲ **Figure 12.16 Sulfur Is Part of Some Amino Acids**

Functions of Sulfate

The amino acids methionine and cysteine both contain sulfur. These two amino acids are incorporated into body proteins and help give proteins their three-dimensional shape (**Figure 12.16**). This enables the proteins to perform effectively as enzymes and hormones and provide structure to the body.

Sulfur-based substances, called sulfites, are used as preservatives by food manufacturers. They help prevent

food spoilage and discoloration in foods such as dried fruits. Sulfites occur naturally in wine due to the fermentation process, and are added to prevent oxidation. People who are sensitive to sulfites may experience headache, sneezing, swelling of the throat, or hives and should avoid sulfite-containing foods and beverages.

Daily Needs

There is insufficient data to determine an EAR, an RDA, an AI, or even a UL for sulfate. The amount of sulfate most Americans consume has been estimated from consumption data on the sulfur-containing amino acids.

Food Sources

About 65 percent of dietary sulfate comes from foods that contain methionine, cysteine, glutathione, and taurine. A varied diet that contains meat, poultry, fish, eggs, legumes, dairy foods, fruits, and vegetables will provide good sources of sulfate.

Beverages including beer, wine, and some juices that are made from municipal water supplies also contain sulfate. As much as 1.3 grams of sulfate per day may come from drinking water due to contamination from groundwater, pipes, and harmless bacteria.[56] Some dietary supplements may also add to total sulfate intake. For example, chondroitin sulfate and glucosamine are popular supplements for osteoarthritis and joint problems.

Too Much or Too Little

Although a UL has not been established, a possible link has been suggested between high levels of sulfate and ulcerative colitis. Bacteria in the colons of people with this condition appear to convert some of the sulfite-containing compounds into by-products that promote the disease.[57]

Most people eat sufficient protein to provide adequate amounts of sulfur-containing amino acids. There are no known toxicity or deficiency symptoms for sulfate.

Putting It All Together

Minerals round out the list of essential nutrients the body needs to maintain good health. An overview of the minerals, which includes their functions and food sources, is presented in Table 12.2.

All nutrients work together to meet energy needs and keep the body functioning properly. Water is the universal solvent and the main component of the fluids in which all reactions involving the energy-producing nutrients (carbohydrates, protein, and fats) take place in the body. Vitamins and minerals aid in these chemical reactions.

Currently, Americans, on average, are meeting many of their nutrient needs, but could improve their intake of some nutrients. Consuming a wide variety of foods from all the food groups, with an emphasis on whole grains, whole fruits, and vegetables, along with adequate amounts of lean dairy and meat, poultry, and plenty of fluids, is the best diet prescription to meet your needs for carbohydrates, protein, fat, vitamins, minerals, and water.

TABLE 12.2 Food Sources, Functions, Symptoms of Deficiencies and Toxicity, and the Recommended Intakes of the Major Minerals

Trace Mineral	Function	Adult AI or RDA	Daily Tolerable Upper Level	Excellent Food Sources	Deficiency Symptoms and Outcomes	Toxicity Symptoms and Outcomes
Sodium (Na)	■ Major cation outside the cell ■ Regulates body water and blood pressure	1,500 mg/day	2,300 mg/day	Processed foods, seaweed, table salt	■ Headache ■ Nausea and vomiting ■ Fatigue ■ Disorientation	■ Edema ■ Hypertension
Chloride (Cl)	■ Part of HCl ■ Participates in acid-base balance	2,300 mg/day	3,600 mg/day	Processed foods, seaweed, table salt, and rye	■ Rare that symptoms occur unless related to loss of sodium	■ Vomiting
Potassium (K)	■ Major cation inside the cell ■ Regulates body water and blood pressure	4,700 mg/day	None established	Fruits and vegetables, meat, dairy, and nuts	■ Muscle weakness and cramps ■ Glucose intolerance ■ Irregular heartbeat and paralysis	■ Irregular heart beat and heart damage
Calcium (Ca)	■ Formation of bones and teeth ■ Muscle contraction and relaxation ■ Blood clotting ■ Heart and nerve function	1,000 mg/day	2,500 mg/day	Milk and dairy products, leafy greens, broccoli, salmon, sardines, legumes, calcium-fortified orange juice	■ Bone loss (osteoporosis) ■ Bone fractures	■ Constipation ■ Impaired kidneys ■ Calcium deposits in tissues
Phosphorus (P)	■ Formation of bones and teeth ■ Part of the ATP energy molecule ■ Transport of lipids ■ Acid-base balance	700 mg/day	4,000 mg/day	Meat, fish, poultry, eggs, cereals	■ Muscle weakness ■ Bone pain (osteoporosis)	■ Decrease in bone mass ■ Calcium deposits in tissues
Magnesium (Mg)	■ Participates in muscle contraction and nerve conduction	Women: 310 mg/day Men: 400 mg/day	350 mg/day (from supplements only; all adults)	Green leafy vegetables, whole grains, nuts, legumes, dairy, and fruits	■ Weakness and fatigue ■ Confusion and seizures ■ Depression ■ Irregular heart beats	■ Diarrhea, cramps, and nausea (from supplements, not food)
Sulfur (S)	■ Part of keratin found in hair and skin ■ Formation of collagen ■ Participates in acid-base balance and cellular respiration	None established	None established	All protein-containing foods such as meat, fish, poultry, eggs, legumes, nuts, and dairy	■ None known	■ May promote ulcerative colitis

Visual Chapter Summary

1 Major and Trace Minerals Are Essential Inorganic Nutrients

Major and trace minerals are essential inorganic nutrients found in foods. Major minerals are required in amounts greater than 100 milligrams per day; trace minerals are needed in less than 20 milligrams per day. The body contains more major minerals than trace minerals (at least 5 grams of each major mineral and less than 5 grams of each trace mineral). The major minerals include sodium, chloride, calcium, phosphorus, potassium, magnesium, and sulfur. The trace minerals include iron, zinc, copper, selenium, chromium, iodide, manganese, molybdenum, and fluoride.

The bioavailability of minerals is reduced by binders in foods, including phytates, found in grains, and oxalates, found in some vegetables. The absorption can also be influenced by an individual's current mineral status, the amount of the mineral consumed at one time, and competition with other minerals that have the same ionic state in the GI tract. The kidney regulates mineral levels in the blood by excreting more or less of the mineral as needed.

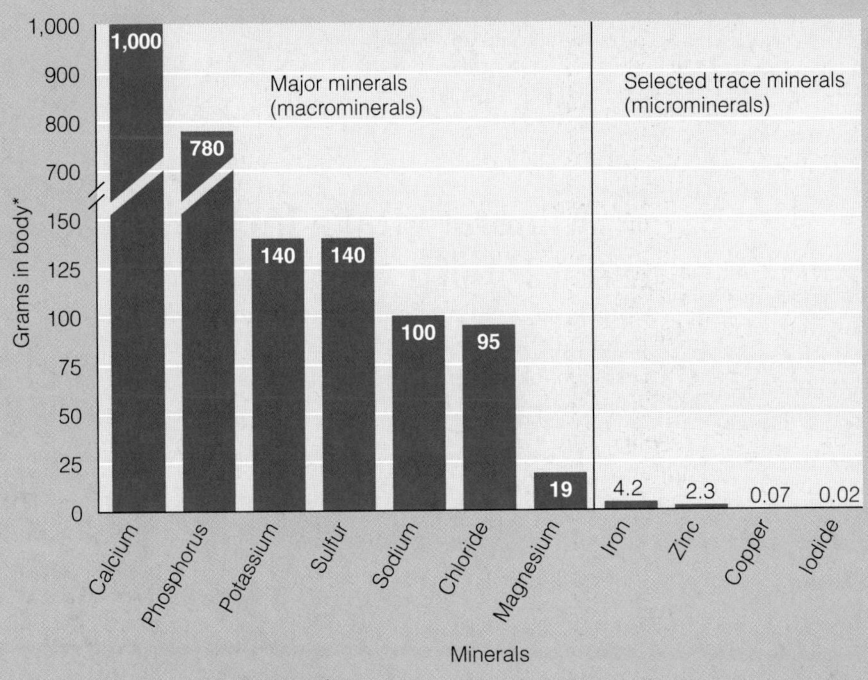

* Based on a 154-pound person

2 Sodium

Sodium plays an important role in balancing the fluid between blood and cells, transmits nerve impulses, participates in muscle contraction, and transports some nutrients across cell membranes. Sodium also is used to preserve food and enhance food flavors. Americans currently consume more than double the amount of sodium recommended daily, predominantly as sodium chloride (table salt). Processed foods are the major source of sodium in the diet. Too much sodium can cause hypertension, hypernatremia, and bone loss. Too little sodium results in hyponatremia. Symptoms include headache, muscle weakness, fatigue, and even seizures.

When Sodium Levels Are Low

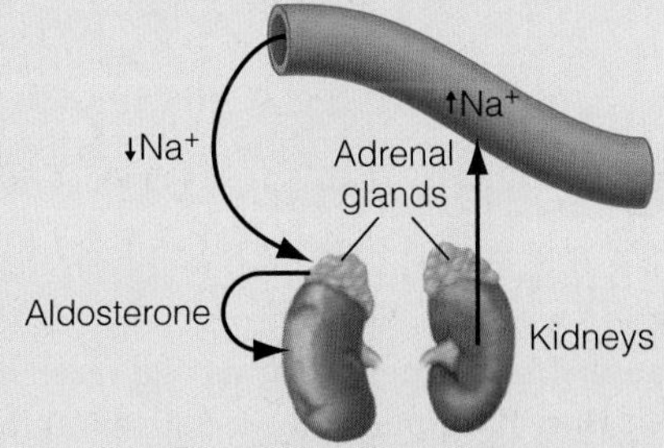

When Sodium Levels Are High

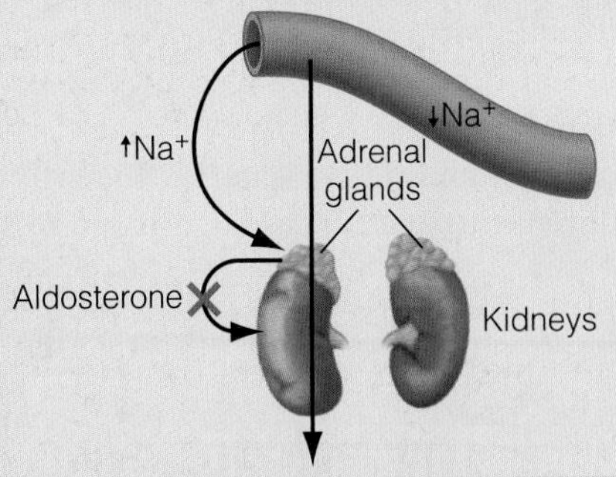

3 Chloride

The anion chloride works with sodium to maintain fluid balance. Chloride also assists in maintaining pH balance in the blood and is part of hydrochloric acid in the stomach. Table salt accounts for almost all the chloride you consume. Chloride toxicity is rare but hyperchloremia can occur due to extreme dehydration. Deficiencies are also rare and are generally caused by extreme vomiting and diarrhea, resulting in hypochloremia. Symptoms include shallow breathing, muscle weakness, spasms, and twitching.

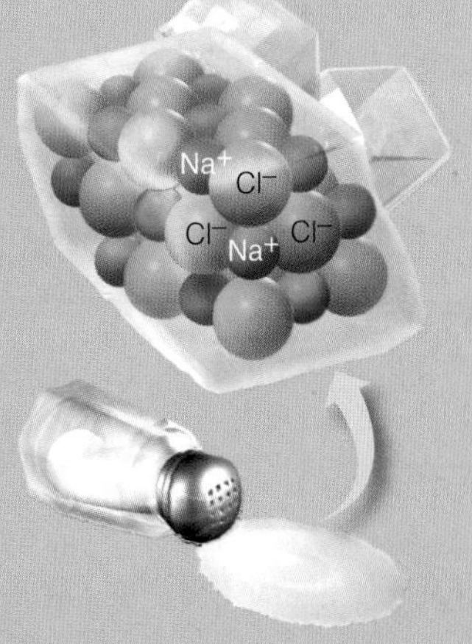

4 Minerals Including Sodium Can Influence Blood Pressure

Reducing dietary sodium and following the DASH diet, which is abundant in foods rich in potassium, magnesium, and calcium, can help lower blood pressure. Losing excess weight, being physically active, and limiting alcohol can also lower blood pressure.

5 Potassium

Potassium functions in muscle contraction and nerve impulse conduction; it can lower blood pressure, maintain bone health, help maintain fluid balance, act as a blood buffer, and may prevent kidney stones. The current recommendations to increase fruits and vegetables in the diet will help meet potassium needs. Too much potassium from supplements results in hyperkalemia, whereas too little causes hypokalemia.

6 Calcium

Calcium, along with phosphorus, provides bones and teeth with strength and structure. Calcium also participates in muscle contraction, sending and receiving nerve impulses, releasing hormones, blood clotting, and maintaining a normal heartbeat. It may also prevent colon cancer and reduce the risk of kidney stones. Dairy foods can be a good source of both calcium and phosphorus. Too much calcium causes hypercalcemia and may cause kidney stones or constipation. It may also interfere with the absorption of iron, zinc, magnesium, and phosphorus. Too little calcium causes hypocalcemia and can lead to osteoporosis and bone fractures.

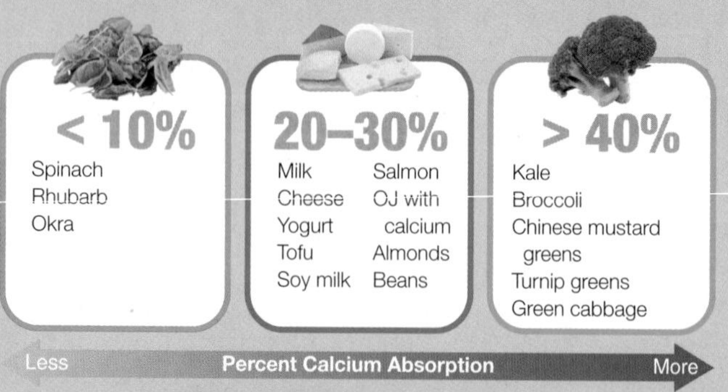

7 Mineral Intake Influences Bone Health

Osteoporosis is a condition characterized by frail bones. A chronic deficiency of dietary calcium and/or vitamin D, excess alcohol consumption, and smoking can all increase the risk of osteoporosis.

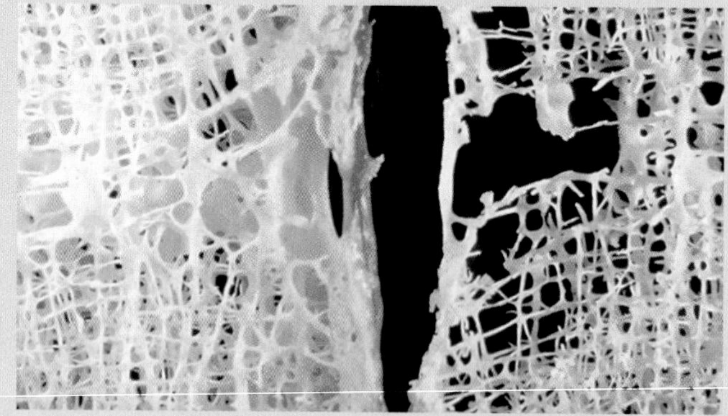

8 Phosphorus

Phosphorus is a major component of bones and teeth. It functions as a component of ATP, as part of phospholipids, as an acid-base buffer, and as part of DNA and RNA. Phosphorus is abundant in meat, fish, poultry, and dairy products. Consuming too much phosphorus results in hyperphosphatemia, which can cause calcification of the soft tissues. Too little phosphorus causes hypophosphatemia and muscle weakness, bone pain, confusion, and, in children, rickets.

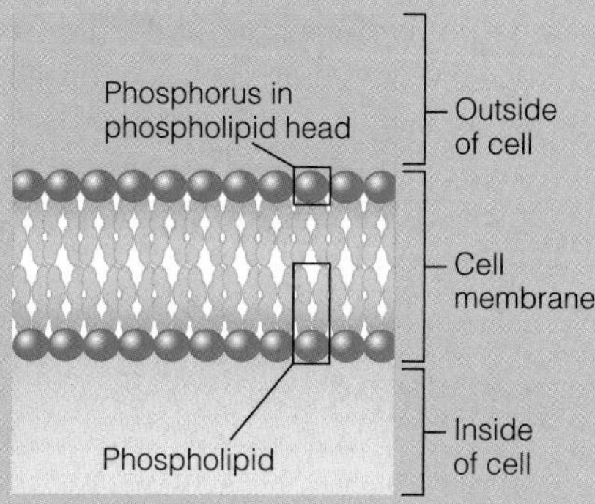

9 Magnesium

Magnesium is part of more than 300 enzymes controlling metabolism, heart function, and bone structure. Magnesium is abundant in leafy green vegetables, legumes, and beverages such as coffee and tea. Too much magnesium from taking supplements can cause intestinal problems such as diarrhea, cramps, and nausea. Deficiencies of magnesium are rare but the use of some medications can result in a magnesium deficiency and cause muscle weakness, seizures, fatigue, depression, and irregular heart beats.

10 Sulfate

In the body, sulfate, the oxidized form of the mineral sulfur, provides shape to proteins and is part of the vitamins thiamin and biotin. Sulfate is part of some amino acids and is used as a preservative in processed foods. The best food sources of sulfate are meats, chicken, and fish, and it can also be found in beverages such as beer and wine. Too much sulfate may relate to ulcerative colitis.

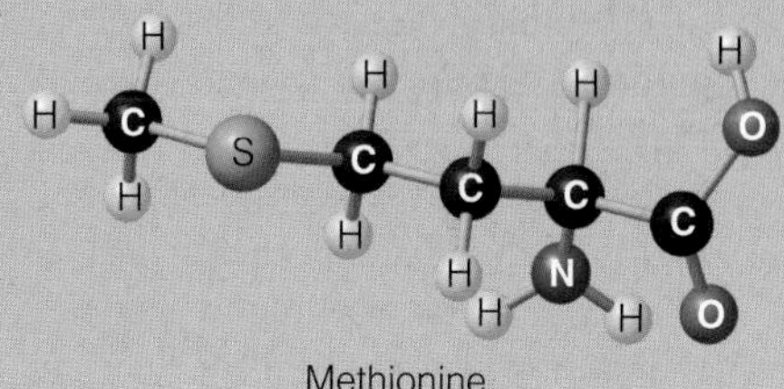

Terms to Know

- major minerals
- trace minerals
- bioavailability
- binders
- cofactors
- hydroxyapatite
- hypertension
- hypernatremia
- hypertonic
- hypotonic
- hyponatremia
- hypercholoremia
- hypochloremia
- hyperkalemia
- hypokalemia
- calcitonin
- cortical bone
- trabecular bone
- hypercalcemia
- hypocalcemia
- peak bone mass
- osteoporosis
- hyperphosphatemia
- hypophosphatemia

MasteringNutrition™

Build your knowledge—and confidence—in the Study Area of MasteringNutrition with a variety of study tools.

Check Your Understanding

1. The bioavailability of minerals is reduced by
   a. phytates.
   b. ascorbic acid.
   c. having a deficiency in the mineral.
   d. vitamin D.
2. In the body, minerals can
   a. help maintain fluid balance.
   b. be part of enzymes.
   c. work with the immune system.
   d. do all of the above.
3. The daily recommendation for sodium intake for adults up to age 51 is
   a. 3,400 milligrams.
   b. 2,300 milligrams.
   c. 1,500 milligrams.
   d. 180 milligrams.
4. Hypokalemia is due to a lack of sufficient ______________ in the blood.
   a. potassium
   b. phosphorus
   c. calcium
   d. sodium
5. The major anion found in the extracellular fluid is
   a. potassium.
   b. phosphorus.
   c. sulfate.
   d. chloride.
6. Blood levels of calcium can be increased by
   a. increased excretion of calcium in the urine.
   b. increased absorption of calcium through the small intestine.
   c. increased secretion of PTH.
   d. all of the above.
7. Phosphorus is necessary
   a. to maintain magnesium balance.
   b. to promote blood clotting.
   c. to provide energy as part of ATP.
   d. for all of the above.
8. The majority of magnesium is in the
   a. blood.
   b. bones.
   c. muscle cells.
   d. extracellular fluid.

9. Which of the following minerals does not have an RDA, AI, or UL recommendation?
   a. sulfur
   b. magnesium
   c. calcium
   d. sodium
10. Fluid balance is maintained by which of the following minerals?
   a. magnesium and sulfur
   b. potassium and phosphorus
   c. calcium and chloride
   d. sodium and potassium

Answers

1. (a) The bioavailability of minerals is reduced by binders in food, including phytates found in grains.
2. (d) Although you need only small amounts of minerals in your diet, they play enormously important roles in the body, such as helping to maintain fluid balance, being part of enzymes, and working to keep the immune system healthy.
3. (c) The AI for sodium for adults up to 51 years of age is 1,500 milligrams. The upper level for sodium daily is 2,300 milligrams, whereas the absolute minimum is 180 milligrams per day.
4. (a) Hypokalemia is defined as a below-normal level of potassium in the blood. The term for low phosphorus levels in the blood is hypophosphatemia; hypocalcemia is a low level of calcium; hyponatremia is a low level of sodium in the blood.
5. (d) Chloride is the major anion in the extracellular fluid. Potassium is a major cation inside cells. Phosphorus is a major component of bones and teeth, and sulfur helps give shape to proteins.
6. (b) Calcium blood levels can be raised by increasing the amount absorbed through the small intestine. Parathyroid hormone (PTH) lowers the level of calcium in the blood by stimulating the kidney to excrete more calcium in the urine.
7. (c) Phosphorus is a necessary mineral because it is part of the energy molecule ATP.
8. (b) More than half of the magnesium in the body is found in bone. Less than 1 percent is found in extracellular fluid, such as the blood.
9. (a) There is not enough data to determine an RDA, AI, or UL for sulfur. Calcium and sodium have established AIs, while magnesium has enough data for an RDA.
10. (d) Sodium and potassium are the major cations responsible for maintaining fluid balance. Magnesium, chloride, phosphorus, calcium, and sulfur play a variety of other key roles in the body.

Answers to Myths and Misconceptions

1. **False.** Consuming a diet rich in fruits, vegetables, lean meats, and low-fat dairy products provides ample intake of minerals without the need to take a supplement.
2. **True.** Minerals are single inorganic elements, often found in salt form or as electrically charged ions, whereas vitamins are complex molecules that contain carbon, hydrogen, oxygen, and, in some cases, nitrogen and sulfur.
3. **True.** For most people, following a diet rich in fruits and vegetables, moderating alcohol intake, and participating in aerobic exercise can reduce the risk of developing hypertension.
4. **False.** Both plant and animal products are bioavailable mineral sources.
5. **False.** Eating foods abundant in bioavailable calcium will improve bone density. Fruits are typically not high in calcium.
6. **True.** The DASH diet, which is high in potassium-rich fruits and vegetables, has been shown to lower blood pressure.
7. **False.** Most of the sodium Americans eat is from processed foods.
8. **True.** One serving of milk contains about 300 milligrams of calcium. The AI for adults aged 19 to 50 is 1,000 milligrams of calcium daily.
9. **True.** An excess of phosphorus may interfere with calcium absorption. However, if calcium intake is adequate, this will not cause a problem.
10. **False.** Sulfur plays a key role in shaping proteins and in the vitamins thiamin and biotin, and is essential to overall health. It is therefore an essential nutrient.

Web Resources

- For more on the DASH diet, visit DASH for Health at www.dashforhealth.com
- For more on osteoporosis, visit the National Osteoporosis Foundation at www.nof.org
- For more on high blood pressure, visit www.nhlbi.nih.gov/hbp/index.html

References

1. Viadel, B., R. Barbera, and R. Farre. 2006. Calcium, Iron and Zinc Uptakes by Caco-2 Cells from White Beans and Effect of Cooking. *International Journal of Food Sciences and Nutrition* 57:190–197.
2. Olivares, M., F. Pizarro, and M. Ruz. 2007. New Insights About Iron Bioavailability: Inhibition by Zinc. *Nutrition* 23:292–295.
3. Arredondo, M., R. Martinez, M. T. Nunez, M. Rus, and M. Olivares. 2006. Inhibition of Iron and Copper Uptake by Iron, Copper and Zinc. *Biological Research* 39:95–102.
4. Olivares, M., et al. 2007. New Insights About Iron Bioavailability.
5. Institute of Medicine. 2006. *Dietary Reference Intakes: The Essential Guide to Nutrient Requirements*. J. Otten, J. Hellwig, and L. Meyers, eds. Washington, DC: The National Academies Press.
6. Viadel, B., et al. 2006. Calcium, Iron and Zinc Uptakes.
7. Yang, C. S. and J. D. Landau. 2000. Effects of Tea Consumption on Nutrition and Health. *Journal of Nutrition* 130:2409–2412.
8. Morck, T. A., S. R. Lynch, and J. D. Cook. 1983. Inhibition of Food Iron Absorption by Coffee. *American Journal of Clinical Nutrition* 37:416–420.
9. Stipanuk, M. H. 2000. *Biochemical and Physiological Aspects of Human Nutrition*. Philadelphia: W. B. Saunders.
10. Institute of Medicine. 2006. *Dietary Reference Intakes*.
11. Olivares, M., et al. 2007. New Insights About Iron Bioavailability.
12. Matkovic, V., J. Z. Llich, L. C. Hsieh, M. A. Tzagournis, B. J. Lagger, and P. K. Goel.

1995. Urinary Calcium, Sodium, and Bone Mass of Young Females. *American Journal of Clinical Nutrition* 62:417–425.
13. Ibid.
14. Tsugane, S., S. Sasazuki, M. Kobayashi, and S. Sasaki. 2004. Salt and Salted Food Intake and Subsequent Risk of Gastric Cancer Among Middle-Aged Japanese Men and Women. *British Journal of Cancer* 90:128–134.
15. Stipanuk, M. H. 2000. *Biochemical and Physiological Aspects of Human Nutrition.*
16. Institute of Medicine. 2006. *Dietary Reference Intakes.*
17. Ibid.
18. Ibid.
19. Institute of Medicine. 2005. *Dietary Reference Intakes for Water, Potassium, Sodium, Chloride, and Sulfate.* Washington, DC: The National Academies Press.
20. American Heart Association. 2012. *About High Blood Pressure.* Available from www.americanheart.org. Accessed May 2012.
21. Jones, G., T. Beard, V. Parameswaran, T. Greenway, and R. von Witt. 1997. A Population-Based Study of the Relationship Between Salt Intake, Bone Resorption, and Bone Mass. *European Journal of Clinical Nutrition* 51:561–565.
22. Sellmeyer, D. E., M. Schloetter, and A. Sebastian. 2002. Potassium Citrate Prevents Increased Urine Calcium Excretion and Bone Resorption Induced by a High Sodium Chloride Diet. *Journal of Clinical Endocrinology & Metabolism* 87:2008–2012.
23. Matkovic, V., et al. 1995. Urinary Calcium, Sodium, and Bone Mass of Young Females.
24. Institute of Medicine. 2006. *Dietary Reference Intakes.*
25. Ibid.
26. Institute of Medicine. 2005. *Dietary Reference Intakes for Water, Potassium, Sodium, Chloride, and Sulfate.*
27. The China Salt Substitute Study Collaborative Group. 2007. Salt Substitution: A Low-Cost Strategy for Blood Pressure Control Among Rural Chinese. A Randomized, Controlled Trial. *Journal of Hypertension* 25:2011–2018.
28. New, S. A., S. P. Robins, M. K. Campbell, J. C. Martin, M. J. Garton, C. Bolton-Smith, D. A. Grubb, et al. 2000. Dietary Influences on Bone Mass and Bone Metabolism: Further Evidence of a Positive Link Between Fruit and Vegetable Consumption and Bone Health? *American Journal of Clinical Nutrition* 71:142–151.
29. Sellmeyer, D. E., et al. 2002. Potassium Citrate Prevents Increased Urine Calcium Excretion.
30. Curhan, G. C., W. C. Willett, E. B. Rimm, and M. J. Stampfer. 1993. A Prospective Study of Dietary Calcium and Other Nutrients and the Risk of Symptomatic Kidney Stones. *New England Journal of Medicine* 328:833–838.
31. Institute of Medicine. 2006. *Dietary Reference Intakes.*
32. Sheng, H. 2000. Body Fluids and Water Balance. In *Biochemical and Physiological Aspects of Human Nutrition.* W. B. Saunders: Philadelphia.
33. Institute of Medicine. 1997. *Dietary Reference Intakes: Calcium, Phosphorus, Magnesium, Vitamin D, and Fluoride.* Washington, DC: The National Academies Press.
34. Kerstetter, J. E., K. O. O'Brien, and K. L. Insogna. 1998. Dietary Protein Affects Calcium Absorption. *American Journal of Clinical Nutrition* 68:859–865.
35. Kerstetter, J. E., M. E. Mitnick, C. M. Gundberg, D. M. Caseria, A. F. Ellison, T. O. Carpenter, and K. L. Insogna. 1999. Changes in Bone Turnover in Young Women Consuming Different Levels of Dietary Protein. *Journal of Clinical Endocrinology & Metabolism* 84:1052–1055.
36. Weaver, C. M., R. P. Heaney, B. R. Martin, and M. L. Fitzsimmons. 1991. Human Calcium Absorption from Whole Wheat Product. *Journal of Nutrition* 121:1769–1775.
37. Stipanuk, M. H. 2000. *Biochemical and Physiological Aspects of Human Nutrition.*
38. Ibid.
39. Miller, G. D., G. D. DiRienzo, M. E. Reusser, and D. A. McCarron. 2000. Benefits of Dairy Product Consumption on Blood Pressure in Humans: A Summary of the Biomedical Literature. *Journal of the American College of Nutrition* 19:147S–164S.
40. Miller, E. R., T. P. Erlinger, and L. J. Appel. 2006. The Effects of Macro-Nutrients on Blood Pressure and Lipids: An Overview of the DASH and OmniHeart Trials. *Current Atherosclerosis Reports* 8:460–465.
41. Baron, J. A., M. Beach, J. S. Mandel, R. U. van Stolk, R. W. Haile, R. S. Sandler, R. Rothstein, et al. 1999. Calcium Supplements for the Prevention of Colorectal Adenomas. *New England Journal of Medicine* 340:101–107.
42. Curhan, G. C., et al. 1993. A Prospective Study of Dietary Calcium.
43. Borghi, L., R. Schianchi, T. Meschi, A. Guerra, U. Maggiore, and A. Novarini. 2002. Comparison of Two Diets for the Prevention of Recurrent Stones in Idiopathic Hypercalciuria. *New England Journal of Medicine* 346:77–84.
44. Khashayar, S. and N. M. Maalouf. 2005. Dietary Calcium, Obesity and Hypertension—The End of the Road? *Journal of Clinical Endocrinology & Metabolism* 90.
45. Poddar, K. H., K. W. Hosig, S. M. Nichols-Richardson, E. S. Anderson, W. G. Herbert, and S. E. Duncan. 2009. Low-Fat Dairy Intake and Body Weight and Composition Changes in College Students. *Journal of the American Dietetic Association* 109:1433–1438
46. Ochner, C. N. and M. R. Lowe. 2007. Self-Reported Changes in Dietary Calcium and Energy Intake Predict Weight Regain following a Weight Loss Diet in Obese Women. *Journal of Nutrition* 137:2324–2328.
47. Schrager, S. 2005. Dietary Calcium Intake and Obesity. *Journal of the American Board of Family Practice* 18:205–210.
48. Boon, N., G. B. J. Hul, J. H. C. H. Stegen, W. E. M. Sluijsmans, C. Valle, D. Langin, N. Viguerie, and W. H. M. Saris. 2007. An Intervention Study of the Effects of Calcium Intake on Faecal Fat Excretion, Energy Metabolism, and Adipose Tissue mRNA Expression of Lipid-Metabolism Related Proteins. *International Journal of Obesity* 31:1704–1712.
49. Institute of Medicine. 2006. *Dietary Reference Intakes.*
50. Stipanuk, M. H. 2000. *Biochemical and Physiological Aspects of Human Nutrition.*
51. Straub, D. 2007. Calcium Supplementation in Clinical Practice: A Review of Forms, Doses, and Indications. *Nutrition in Clinical Practice: Official Publication of the American Society for Parenteral and Enteral Nutrition* 22:286–296.
52. Ibid.
53. Gropper, S. S., J. L. Smith, and J. L. Groff. 2005. *Advanced Nutrition and Human Metabolism.* 4th ed. Belmont, CA: Thomson Wadsworth.
54. Larsson, S. C. and A. Wolk. 2007. Magnesium Intake and Risk of Type 2 Diabetes: A Meta-Analysis. *Journal of Internal Medicine* 262:208–214.
55. Sharma, A., S. Dabla, R. P. Agrawal, H. Barjatya, D. K. Kochar, and R. P. Kothari. 2007. Serum Magnesium: An Early Predictor of Course and Complications of Diabetes Mellitus. *Journal of the Indian Medical Association* 105:16–20.
56. Institute of Medicine. 2006. *Dietary Reference Intakes.*
57. Pitcher, M. C. L., E. R. Beatty, G. R. Gibson, and J. H. Cummings. 1996. Methionine Derivatives Diminish Sulphide Damage to Colonocytes—Implications for Ulcerative Colitis. *Gut* 39:77–81.

13 Trace Minerals

Chapter Objectives

After reading this chapter, you will be able to:

1. Describe the characteristics and functions of trace minerals in the body.
2. Describe mechanisms of iron absorption and transport, key functions, recommended intakes, food sources, and toxicity and deficiency symptoms associated with iron.
3. Describe the key functions, recommended intakes, food sources, and toxicity and deficiency symptoms associated with copper.
4. Describe the key functions, recommended intakes, food sources, and toxicity and deficiency symptoms associated with zinc.
5. Describe the key functions, recommended intakes, food sources, and toxicity and deficiency symptoms associated with selenium.
6. Describe the key functions, recommended intakes, food sources, and toxicity and deficiency symptoms associated with fluoride.
7. Describe the key functions, recommended intakes, food sources, and toxicity and deficiency symptoms associated with chromium.
8. Describe the key functions, recommended intakes, food sources, and toxicity and deficiency symptoms associated with iodine.
9. Describe the key functions, recommended intakes, food sources, and toxicity and deficiency symptoms associated with molybdenum.
10. Describe the key functions, recommended intakes, food sources, and toxicity and deficiency symptoms associated with manganese.
11. Describe the potential roles, deficiency symptoms, food sources, and potential toxicity associated with arsenic, boron, nickel, silicon, and vanadium.

1. Trace minerals are called trace because food contains such small amounts. T/F
2. Meat is the primary source of iron in the American diet. T/F
3. Taking iron supplements can cause a copper deficiency. T/F
4. Zinc can cure the common cold. T/F
5. Consuming too much selenium can cause vomiting and diarrhea. T/F
6. Most bottled waters contain fluoride. T/F
7. Chromium can help weight lifters build bigger muscles. T/F
8. Iodized salt is the only reliable source of iodine. T/F
9. Cinnamon is a good source of manganese. T/F
10. Consuming leafy green vegetables will ensure a diet rich in molybdenum. T/F

See page 507 for answers to these Myths and Misconceptions.

Thus far you've learned that minerals are inorganic molecules required by the body that must be consumed in the diet. We discussed the major minerals in Chapter 12 and their structural and functional roles in your body. In this chapter, we'll examine the important functions and unique qualities of the trace minerals. We'll also discuss the amounts needed in the diet, the absorption and transport of each, and the best foods from which to obtain them.

What Are Trace Minerals and Why Do You Need Them?

Iron, zinc, selenium, fluoride, chromium, copper, iodine, manganese, and molybdenum are known as the **trace minerals** (or microminerals). They are needed by the body in much smaller amounts than the major minerals. Collectively, less than 5 grams of trace minerals are found in the body,[1] and even though the daily dietary need for each is less than 20 milligrams, they are just as necessary for health as other nutrients are.

Similar to the major minerals, trace minerals are found in both plant and animal foods, but the best food sources are whole grains, legumes, dairy, meat, and seafood. The trace mineral amount found in a given plant food depends partly on the mineral content in the soil in which the food was grown. In addition, processing removes trace minerals found in the bran and germ of grains. For this reason, whole grains contain more trace minerals than do refined grains. Trace minerals found in all foods are stable in cooking.

Bioavailability of Trace Minerals Can Vary

Like the major minerals, the bioavailability of trace minerals can vary according to an individual's nutritional status, other foods that are eaten, and the form of the mineral.

Trace minerals often compete with each other for absorption in the GI tract. Some trace minerals, such as iron, copper, and zinc are absorbed in their ionic state. These minerals have the same ionic charge ($^{+}2$) and use the same protein carriers during absorption. Too much of one mineral, such as iron, Fe^{+2}, can cause a decrease in the absorption and metabolism of another mineral, such as copper, Cu^{+2}, leading to an imbalance.[2, 3] Thus, bioavailability of each mineral depends on the amount of both minerals in the intestinal tract at the time of absorption.[4] This is one reason why most people should avoid taking single-mineral supplements. Trace minerals also need very little digestion to be absorbed. Some trace minerals, such as iron, are recycled in the body and can be used repeatedly.

Most Trace Minerals Function as Cofactors

Several trace minerals function as cofactors. This function is similar to that of coenzymes, in that trace minerals are part of an enzyme complex. The enzymes that trace minerals such as manganese and molybdenum attach to and activate are referred to as **metalloenzymes.**

trace minerals Minerals required in amounts smaller than 100 milligrams per day that are essential to health; also called microminerals.

metalloenzymes Active enzymes that contain one or more metal ions that are essential for their biological activity.

Other essential roles of trace minerals include helping hormones function, for example, iodine is a component of the thyroid hormone thyroxine. Trace minerals, including iron, maintain the health of red blood cells and some trace minerals, such as fluoride, are part of the structure of bones and teeth. Other trace minerals, including copper and selenium, are important components of antioxidant enzymes.

Trace Mineral Deficiencies and Toxicity Are Hard To Determine

Because trace minerals are found in short supply in the body, symptoms of deficiency are hard to identify, and deficiencies are often overlooked. This fact also makes it difficult to establish recommended intakes, including tolerable upper limits to prevent toxicity.

In this chapter each individual trace mineral will be covered in detail, beginning with iron.

THE TAKE-HOME MESSAGE Trace minerals are inorganic nutrients that are needed in small amounts in the body. Their bioavailability is affected by the amount in the body, and whether the mineral competes with other substances for absorption. Trace minerals help hormones function, maintain red blood cells, are part of the structure of bones and teeth, and act as cofactors.

The ingredients of this sandwich are good sources of trace minerals: The whole-wheat bread contributes zinc, copper, chromium, iodine, and manganese to your diet, while a few slices of low-fat turkey adds iron, zinc, and selenium. Top off your sandwich with manganese-rich leafy greens and cranberries packed with selenium to make this a meal brimming with a variety of essential trace minerals.

Exploring Iron

IRON

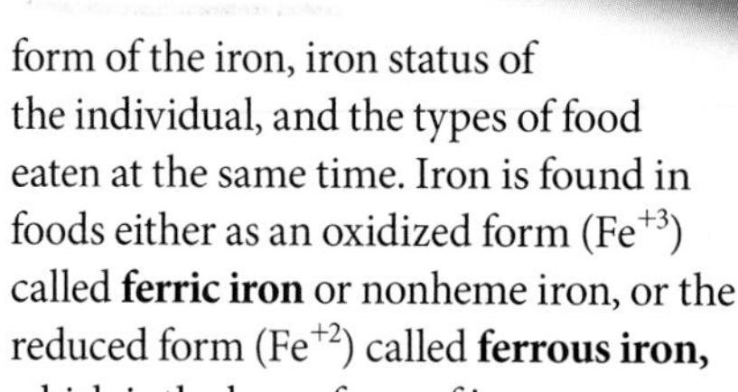

What Is Iron?

Iron (Fe) is the most abundant mineral on Earth, and the most abundant trace mineral in the body. A 130-pound female has over 2,300 milligrams (2.3 grams) of iron—about the weight of a dime—in her body, whereas a 165-pound male has 4,000 milligrams (4.0 grams)—slightly less than the weight of two dimes.[5] Iron deficiency is the most common nutrient deficiency around the world, and iron-deficiency anemia is common in women of childbearing age and children, particularly in the developing world, but also in the United States.

Heme and Nonheme Iron

Two forms of iron are found in foods: **heme iron** and **nonheme iron.** Heme iron is part of the proteins **hemoglobin** (in red blood cells) and **myoglobin** (in muscle cells), and part of cytochromes in the electron transport chain. It is therefore found in animal foods such as meat, poultry, and fish. Nonheme iron is found in plant foods such as grains and vegetables and comprises more than 80 percent of the iron consumed in foods (100 percent for vegans). It is also the form of iron used to enrich breads and fortify cereals.

Iron Bioavailability

The bioavailability of iron is influenced by several factors, including the molecular form of the iron, iron status of the individual, and the types of food eaten at the same time. Iron is found in foods either as an oxidized form (Fe^{+3}) called **ferric iron** or nonheme iron, or the reduced form (Fe^{+2}) called **ferrous iron,** which is the heme form of iron.

Heme iron is two to three times more bioavailable than nonheme iron. Nonheme iron is often bound to acids, such as oxalates in leafy vegetables or polyphenols in tea and coffee, which makes it more difficult to absorb. A serving of cooked spinach, for example, contains approximately 6 milligrams of nonheme iron, but less than 1 percent is absorbed because of the oxalates in the spinach. The polyphenols in tea or coffee can reduce the absorption of nonheme iron in a meal by as much as 70 percent.[6]

There are ways in which nonheme iron bioavailability can be improved. For example, adding vitamin C to a meal that contains nonheme iron can enhance its rate of absorption. In the intestinal tract, vitamin C donates an electron to the ferric form, which reduces it to the more bioavailable ferrous form. As little as 25 milligrams of vitamin C—the amount in about one-quarter cup of orange juice—can double the amount of nonheme iron absorbed from a meal and 50 milligrams of vitamin C can increase the amount absorbed by about sixfold.

Another way to enhance nonheme iron absorption from foods is to eat meat, fish, or poultry at the same meal as the nonheme iron source; this is referred to as the MFP factor (**m**eat, **f**ish, and **p**oultry). The peptides in these animal-derived foods are thought to be the enhancing factors. The meat in a turkey sandwich will help enhance the absorption of the nonheme iron in whole-wheat bread (see Table 13.1).

Let's look more closely at the mechanisms that affect iron absorption.

Iron Absorption and Transport

The absorption-transport mechanism of iron (**Figure 13.1**) is tightly controlled, which helps regulate the amount of iron absorbed into the body and prevent iron toxicity. Once the iron is absorbed into the blood, only 1 to 2 grams is lost daily from the body except through blood loss.

Iron must cross two cell membranes in the small intestine, the brush border

heme iron Iron found as part of a heme group found in hemoglobin in the blood, myoglobin in muscles, and in the mitochondria as part of the cytochromes.

nonheme iron Iron that is not attached to heme.

hemoglobin The oxygen-carrying, heme-containing protein found in red blood cells.

myoglobin The oxygen-carrying, heme-containing protein found in muscle cells.

ferric iron The oxidized form of iron (Fe^{+3}).

ferrous iron The reduced form of iron (Fe^{+2}).

ferritin A protein that stores iron in the intestine.

hemosiderin A protein that stores iron in the body.

Chemistry Boost

The Oxidation and Reduction of Iron

Iron can exist in two valence states: ferrous (Fe^{+2}) and ferric (Fe^{+3}). Ferric (Fe^{+3}) iron is *reduced* to ferrous (Fe^{+2}) iron, meaning it has gained electrons and has a more negative oxidation number ($^{+}2$ versus $^{+}3$). The opposite is true when ferrous iron is oxidized to ferric iron; it loses an electron and the oxidation number increases.

$$Fe^{+2} \leftrightarrow Fe^{+3} + e^{-}$$

Recall that:

When a substance is oxidized, it . . .	When a substance is reduced, it . . .
Loses electrons	Gains electrons
Has a more positive oxidation number	Attains a more negative oxidation number
Is the reducing agent	Is the oxidizing agent

TABLE 13.1 Factors that Influence Iron Absorption	
Enhance Iron Absorption	**Decrease Iron Absorption**
■ Sufficient hydrochloric acid in the stomach ■ The form of iron in the food; heme iron is more easily absorbed than nonheme iron ■ Increased need for iron (blood loss, pregnancy, growth) ■ Vitamin C in the small intestine at the same time ■ Presence of MFP factor (meat, fish, poultry)	■ Phytates in cereal grains (dietary fiber) ■ Oxalates ■ Polyphenols (tea or coffee) ■ Reduced hydrochloric acid in stomach ■ Excess use of antacids ■ Excess minerals such as calcium, zinc, and magnesium

and the basolateral membrane, before it is absorbed into the portal vein. Heme iron crosses the brush border of the enterocyte attached to a protein carrier. Once inside the enterocyte, the enzyme *heme oxygenase* releases the ferrous iron (Fe^{+2}) from hemoglobin.[7] If the body does not need the iron immediately, ferrous iron is oxidized to the ferric form and binds to the protein **ferritin,** which acts as a temporary storage form of iron in the intestine. Once ferritin becomes saturated with iron, additional iron can be attached to another protein called **hemosiderin** for storage. If not needed by the body, this iron remains stored until the intestinal cells are sloughed off and excreted through the feces.

Nonheme iron is absorbed less efficiently than heme iron. Nonheme iron must first be released during digestion and reduced to ferrous iron (Fe^{+2}) by stomach acids and pepsin to improve its absorption rate across the brush border. Both the ferrous (Fe^{+2}) and ferric (Fe^{+3}) forms of iron from nonheme sources are absorbed across the brush border attached to a transport protein. Nonheme iron is also affected by the alkaline environment of the small intestine, which renders it less soluble and thus less bioavailable. Similar to heme iron, once inside the enterocyte, nonheme iron is stored attached to ferritin until needed or excreted as intestinal cells are sloughed off. Any nonheme iron that remains bound to food or other compounds in the intestinal tract remains unabsorbed and is excreted in the feces.

When the body needs iron, the ferritin releases the ferric (Fe^{+3}) iron, which is again reduced to the ferrous (Fe^{+2}) form.

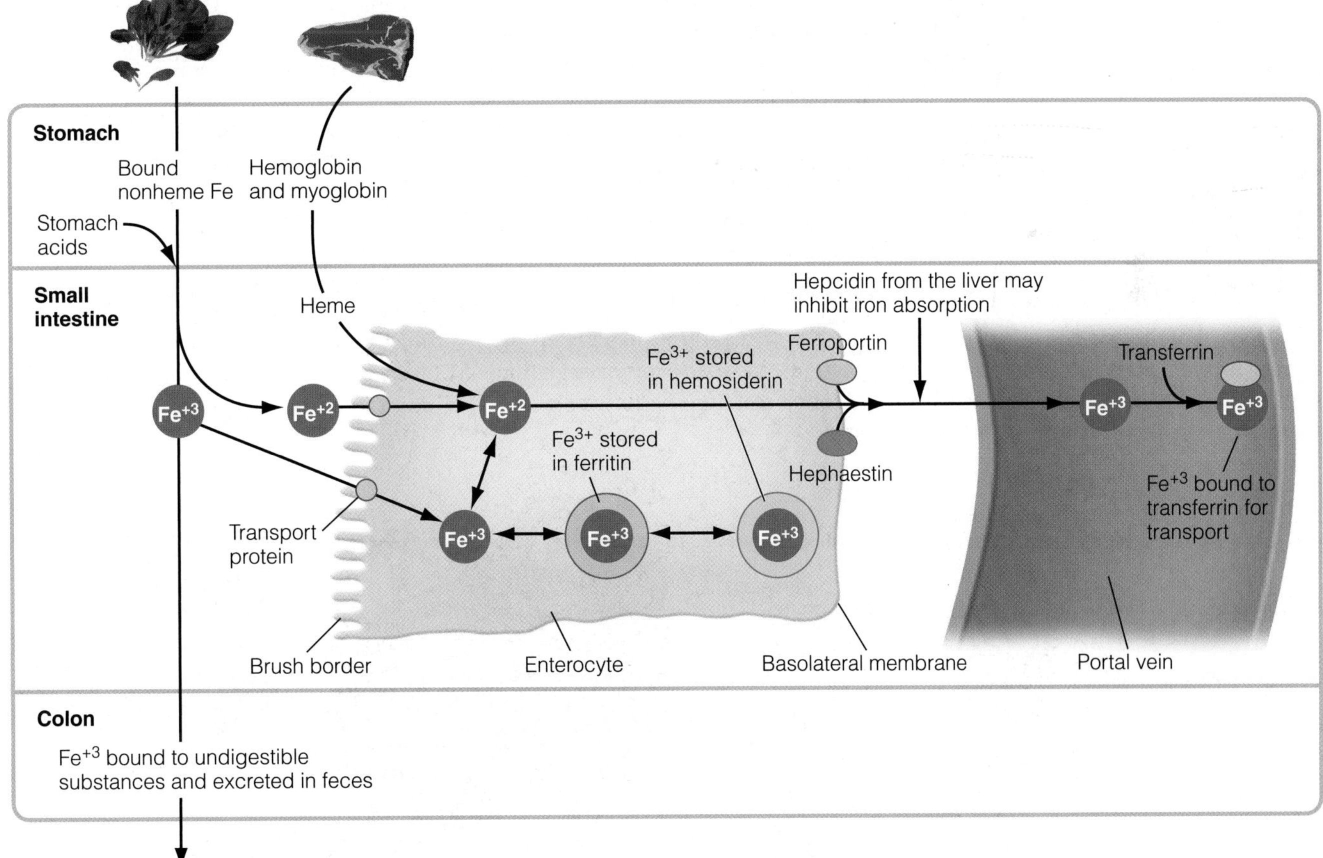

▲ **Figure 13.1 The Absorption and Transport of Iron**

Iron is absorbed into the enterocyte and attached to ferritin in the enterocyte. When the body requires iron, it is released from ferritin, attached to ferroportin, oxidized to ferric iron by hephaestin, and transported through the blood attached to transferrin. The liver hormone hepcidin controls the process.

continued

Ferrous iron attaches to **ferroportin,** a protein that transports the iron across the basolateral membrane into the portal vein. Once ferroportin crosses the basolateral membrane, it releases the ferrous iron (Fe^{+2}). Ferrous iron is once again oxidized to ferric iron (Fe^{+3}) by a copper-containing enzyme called **hephaestin** and attaches to a protein carrier in the blood called **transferrin,** which transports the iron throughout the body.[8]

Hormonal Regulation of Iron Absorption

A hormone produced by the liver called **hepcidin** controls iron absorption.[9] When iron stores are high, the liver produces more hepcidin, which inhibits ferroportin from transporting iron across the basolateral membrane—in a sense, trapping the iron in the enterocyte. When iron stores are low, hepcidin levels are decreased, which allows ferroportin to actively transport iron out of the enterocyte into the portal blood.

Stored Iron Affects Iron Absorption

Iron status influences the amount of ferritin produced in the intestinal tract. Thus, if the iron stores in the body are low, less ferritin is produced, to allow more iron to be absorbed directly into the bloodstream. In other words, the lower the stores, the greater the percentage of iron absorbed. If the body contains adequate iron stores, it will absorb an average of 14 to 18 percent of the iron consumed in the average mixed diet. When iron stores are high, the amount of iron absorbed can be as low as 5 percent of the iron consumed, because more ferritin is produced to block iron from absorption and to store the iron in the intestinal cells. The iron stored in the iron pool is usually excreted in the feces as the intestinal cells slough off. This mechanism, referred to as a mucosal block, prevents excess iron from entering the blood and causing iron toxicity. In some cases, such as when iron is overconsumed in supplements, this protective feature is overwhelmed and too much iron is absorbed, causing iron overload.

Iron Recycling

As a key component of blood, iron is highly valuable to the body and is treated accordingly. The amount of iron absorbed is not sufficient to meet the body's daily iron needs; therefore, approximately 95 percent of the iron in the body is recycled and reused.[10] In blood, the iron found in the heme portion of hemoglobin is broken down in the liver and spleen, with 20 to 25 milligrams of iron salvaged per day. This iron is then used for synthesizing new red blood cells in the bone marrow, incorporated into iron-containing enzymes, or stored as ferritin for use later. Very little iron is excreted or shed in hair, skin, and sloughed-off intestinal cells. In fact, most iron loss is due to bleeding.

Functions of Iron

Iron plays a major role in a variety of key functions. It participates in oxidation-reduction reactions because of its ability to be changed from its ferrous (Fe^{+2}) to ferric (Fe^{+3}) forms and back again.

Hemoglobin and Myoglobin Transport Oxygen

Approximately two-thirds of the iron in the body is in hemoglobin and myoglobin (**Figure 13.2**). The heme in hemoglobin binds with oxygen from the lungs and transports it to the tissues for their use. Hemoglobin also picks up a small amount of carbon dioxide waste products from the cells and transports them back to the lungs to be exhaled.

Similarly, iron is part of the protein myoglobin that transports and stores oxygen in the muscles. Heme in myoglobin accepts oxygen from hemoglobin and transports it to the muscle and heart muscle cells. Myoglobin also transports the carbon dioxide produced in the muscle and heart muscle cells to hemoglobin in the blood for excretion. In other words, myoglobin in the muscle works with hemoglobin in the blood in the exchange of oxygen and carbon dioxide.

Iron Participates in Energy Metabolism

Iron performs as a cofactor in enzymes involved in energy metabolism. Recall from Chapter 8 that electrons produced during glycolysis and in the TCA cycle are delivered to the electron transport chain by nicotinamide adenine dinucleotide plus hydrogen and flavin adenine dinucleotide ($NADH^+ + H^+$ and $FADH_2$). Iron-containing cytochromes in the mitochondria carry the electrons to

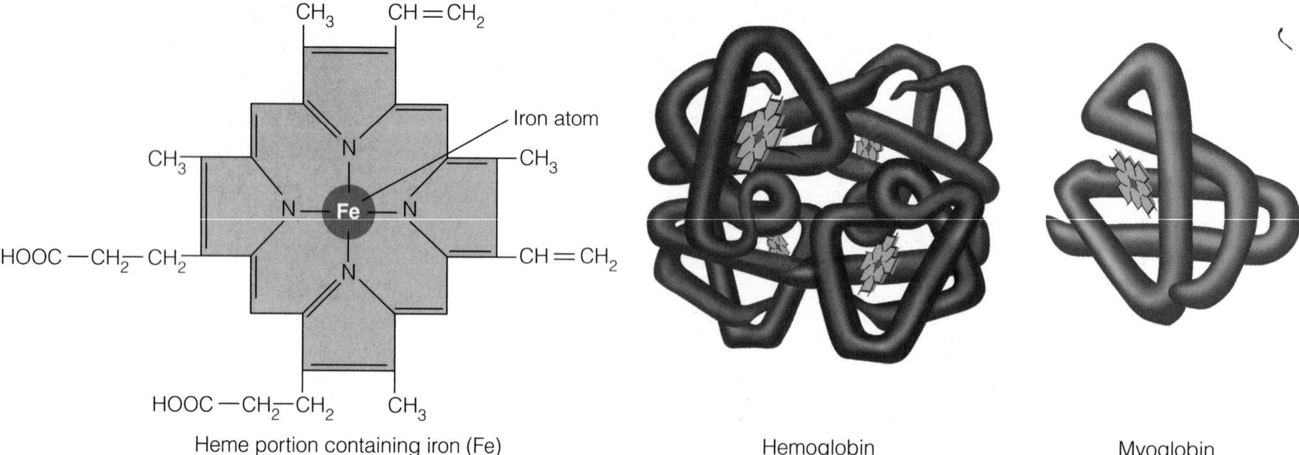

▲ **Figure 13.2 Iron-Containing Hemoglobin and Myoglobin**
Iron is part of the heme in hemoglobin and myoglobin.

oxygen to eventually produce ATP, carbon dioxide, and water. Iron also participates in the conversion of citrate to isocitrate in the TCA cycle. In iron-deficiency anemia, both of these functions are diminished, which leads to fatigue.

Iron Is Important for Immune Function

Iron is necessary for the production of the lymphocytes and macrophages that help fight infection, and macrophages may store iron to prevent pathogens from using the mineral to multiply.[11] Iron is also a cofactor for several key enzymes involved in protecting cell membranes from free radical damage.

Iron Is Needed for Brain Function

In the brain, iron helps enzymes that are involved in the synthesis of neurotransmitters, including dopamine, epinephrine, norepinephrine, and serotonin, which send messages to the rest of the body.[12] A deficiency of iron in children can impact cognitive development and their ability to learn and retain information. Studies have shown that children with iron-deficiency anemia in their early years can have persistent, decreased cognitive ability during their later school years.[13]

Daily Needs

Adult females, aged 19 to 50, need 18 milligrams daily to cover the iron lost during menstruation. After menopause, usually around age 50, a woman's daily iron needs drop to 8 milligrams because she is no longer losing blood monthly. Adult males need 8 milligrams of dietary iron daily. The recommendations for women and men take into account a typical American diet, which includes both heme and nonheme iron sources. The dietary iron needs of vegetarians are 1.8 times higher than those of nonvegetarians due to the lower bioavailability of the nonheme iron found in plant foods.[14]

Adult men consume more than twice their recommended iron needs—over 16 milligrams, on average, daily. Adult premenopausal women consume only about 70 percent of their daily need, or approximately 13 milligrams, on average. Postmenopausal women consume slightly over 12 milligrams of iron daily, so, like men, they are more than meeting their needs.

Food Sources

About half of Americans' dietary iron intake comes from iron-enriched bread and other grain foods such as cereals (see **Figure 13.3**). Meat, fish, poultry, and egg yolks are rich sources of efficiently absorbed heme iron; however, this form of iron contributes only 12 percent of the dietary needs of males and females. Cooking foods in iron pans and skillets can also increase their nonheme iron content, as foods absorb iron from cookware.[15]

Too Much Iron

Consuming too much iron from supplements can cause constipation, nausea, vomiting, and diarrhea. The upper level for iron for adults is set at 45 milligrams daily, as this level is slightly less than the amount known to cause these intestinal symptoms. This upper level doesn't apply to, and is too high for, individuals with liver disease or other diseases that can affect iron stores in the body, such as certain genetic disorders.

Iron Poisoning in Children

In the United States the accidental consumption of supplements containing iron is the leading cause of poisoning deaths in children under age 6. Ingestion of as little as 200 milligrams has been shown to be fatal. Children who swallow iron supplements can experience symptoms such as nausea, vomiting, and diarrhea within minutes. Intestinal bleeding can also occur, which can lead to shock, coma, and even death. The FDA has mandated that a warning statement about the risk of iron poisoning in small children be put on every iron supplement label and that pills that contain 30 milligrams or more of iron must be individually wrapped.[16]

Iron Overload

Undetected excessive storing of iron in the body over several years is called *iron overload* and can damage a person's tissues and organs, including the heart, kidneys, liver, and nervous system. **Hemochromatosis,** a genetic disorder in which individuals absorb too much dietary iron, can cause iron overload. Though this condition

ferroportin A protein found on the basolateral surface of the enterocyte that transports iron out of the enterocyte into the portal vein.

hephaestin A copper-containing enzyme that catalyzes the conversion of ferrous to ferric iron before attaching to transferrin for transport.

transferrin An iron-transporting protein.

hepcidin A hormone produced in the liver that regulates the absorption and transport of iron.

hemochromatosis A genetic disorder that causes the body to store excessive amounts of iron.

continued

TABLE TIPS

Enhance Your Iron Intake

Enjoy an iron-enriched whole-grain cereal along with a glass of vitamin C–rich orange juice to boost the nonheme iron absorption in cereal.

Add plenty of salsa (vitamin C) to bean burritos to enhance the absorption of the nonheme iron in both the beans and the flour tortilla.

Stuff a baked potato (nonheme iron, vitamin C) with shredded cooked chicken (heme iron) and broccoli (vitamin C) and top it with melted low-fat cheese for a quick and iron-rich dinner.

Eat a small box of raisins (nonheme iron) and a clementine or tangerine (vitamin C) as a sweet snack that's abundant in iron.

Add chickpeas (nonheme iron) to salad greens (vitamin C). Don't forget the tomato wedges for another source of iron-enhancing vitamin C.

is congenital, its symptoms often don't manifest until adulthood. If not diagnosed and treated early enough, organ damage can occur. Individuals with hemochromatosis need to avoid iron supplements throughout their lives, as well as large amounts of vitamin C supplements, which enhance iron absorption.

Other Effects of Too Much Iron

Some studies suggest that iron can stimulate free radical production in the body, which can damage the arteries leading to the heart and may contribute to heart disease. It has also been suggested that iron's role in free radical production may increase the risk of cancer. Though this association is not definite, unless you are medically diagnosed with iron deficiency, it doesn't make any sense to consume excessive amounts of iron.

Too Little Iron

If the diet is deficient in iron, body stores will be slowly depleted so as to keep blood hemoglobin in a normal range. Iron-deficiency anemia occurs when body stores are so depleted that blood hemoglobin levels decrease. Red blood cells contain less heme and become small and pale. This will diminish the delivery of oxygen through the body, causing fatigue and weakness. Individuals with iron-deficiency anemia are also more susceptible to and have a reduced ability to fight infections.[17] Health Connection: Preventing Iron-Deficiency Anemia provides more information on this deficiency.

Because of their increased iron needs, pregnant women, menstruating women and teenaged girls, especially those with heavy blood losses, and preterm or low birth weight infants, as well as older infants and toddlers, are often not meeting their iron needs and are at risk of becoming deficient.[18]

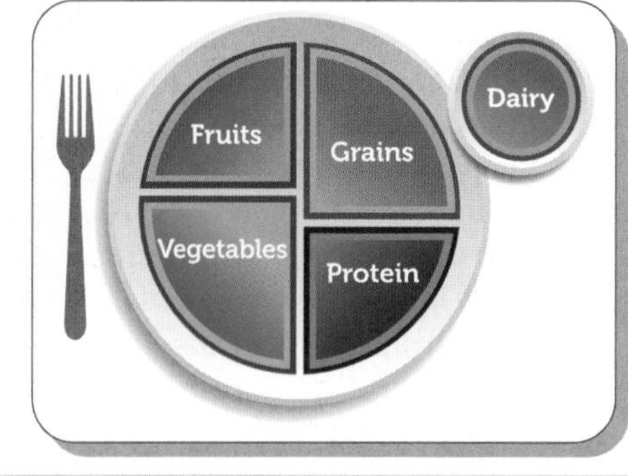

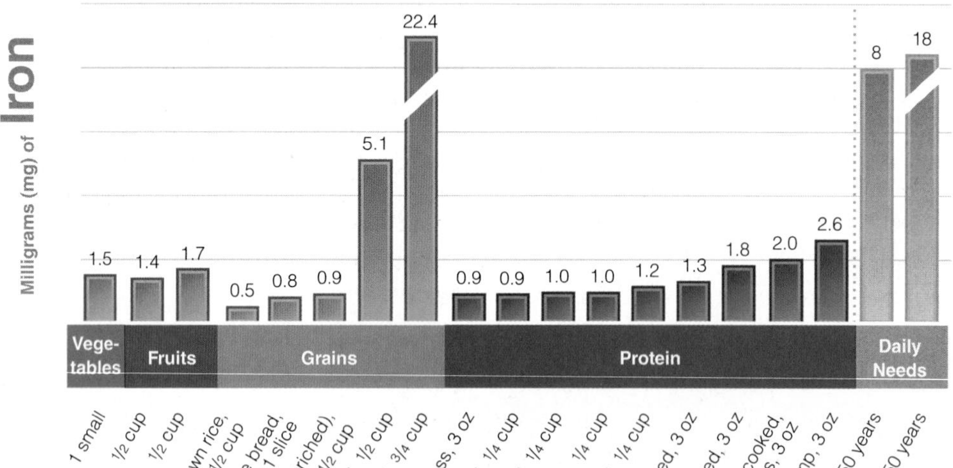

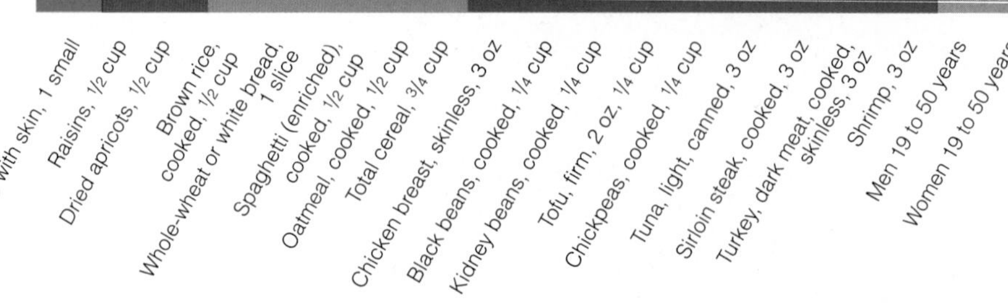

▲ **Figure 13.3 Food Sources of Iron**

Nutrition in Practice: Diane

During her senior year at high school, Diane has been experiencing fainting spells, and according to her mother, she becomes short of breath prior to the faint. Diane's nails have become brittle, and she always seems to look "pale." At the pediatrician's office, the nurse drew some of Diane's blood and the doctor ordered a complete blood count (CBC) from the lab. The blood test revealed that she had iron-deficiency anemia. While the doctor recommended that Diane take an iron supplement, her mother wanted her to meet with a Registered Dietitian (RD) to make sure that her diet contained iron-rich foods, especially since she will be leaving for college in a month.

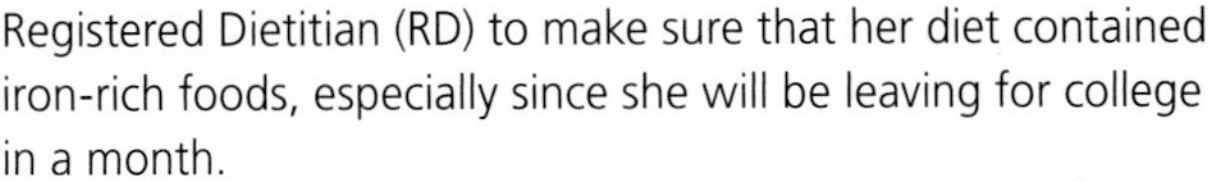

Diane's Stats:

- Age: 18
- Height: 5 feet 0 inches
- Weight: 98 pounds
- BMI: 19.1

Critical Thinking Questions

1. How much iron should Diane be consuming daily?
2. Based on her food log, how can Diane add more heme and nonheme iron-rich foods at her meals and snacks to meet her daily needs?
3. Which iron-rich food group is Diane likely falling short of in her diet?
4. What other foods can be added to her meals and snacks that would improve her body's absorption of nonheme iron?

Dietitian's Observation and Plan for Diane:

- Discuss the difference between heme and nonheme iron in the diet.
- Add whole-grain cereal and a source of vitamin C such as berries to her morning yogurt.
- Snack on nuts and dried fruits instead of candy in the morning.
- Need to consume at least 5 to 6 ounces of protein foods in the diet to increase her daily iron consumption. Change her lunchtime sandwich to include 2 to 3 ounces of protein foods such as turkey and lean roast beef.
- Add a salad and/or vegetables with dinner to increase her vitamin C intake at dinner.
- Drink some vitamin C–rich orange or grapefruit juice along with her evening popcorn snack.

Two weeks later, Diane returns for a follow-up visit with the dietitian. She has made all of the dietary changes, but is concerned about her ability to consume this diet once she gets to college. She plans to be on the college's unlimited meal plan for her freshman year. The RD gives Diane suggestions for her college meals, and they devise a list of the snacks that she can safely store in her dorm room. Diane makes an appointment to meet with the RD for another diet assessment when she comes home for her Thanksgiving break.

Diane's Food Log

Food/Beverage	Time Consumed	Hunger Rating*	Location
Yogurt	7 am	3	Kitchen
Candy bar	11:30 am	5	High school
Cream cheese and jelly sandwich, milk	1:30 pm	5	High school cafeteria
Chocolate chip cookies and milk	4 pm	4	Kitchen, studying
Pork chop and rice	6:30 pm	5	Kitchen
Popcorn	10 pm	3	Bedroom, surfing Internet

*Hunger Rating (1–5): 1 = not hungry; 5 = super hungry

Health Connection

Preventing Iron-Deficiency Anemia

Do you donate blood more than two to four times a year? Are you a female of childbearing age, a vegetarian, or just don't eat right? If you answered *yes* to any one of these questions, you may be at risk of developing an iron deficiency. Unfortunately, you are not alone. An estimated 20 percent of women, 3 percent of men, and 50 percent of all pregnant women are iron deficient.[1] Being iron deficient, however, does not mean you have iron-deficiency anemia.

What Is Iron-Deficiency Anemia?

As the name suggests, **iron-deficiency anemia,** which is the most common form of anemia, results from insufficient iron in the body. Women, who have smaller stores of iron and who lose more blood (due to menstruation) than men, are at a higher risk. In men and postmenopausal women, iron deficiency is often the result of blood loss due to ulcers, increased use of aspirin, and specific cancers such as colon, esophagus, and stomach cancer.

Anemia develops slowly when the normal levels of stored iron have been depleted and the number of red blood cells falls below normal. As the iron stores are decreasing, the bone marrow gradually produces fewer red blood cells. When the reserves of iron are depleted, there are fewer and abnormally smaller red blood cells.

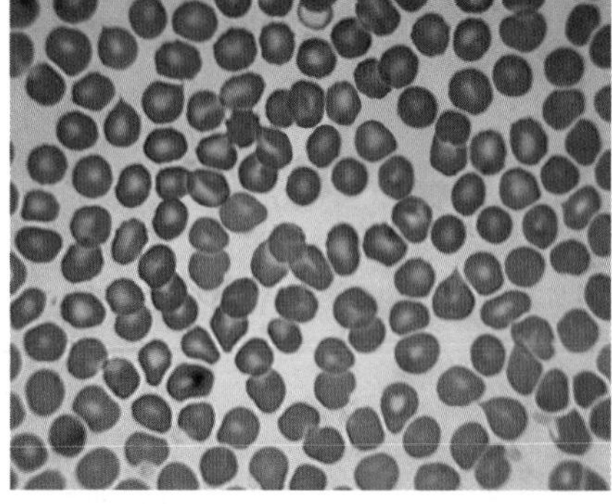

a Normal healthy red blood cells

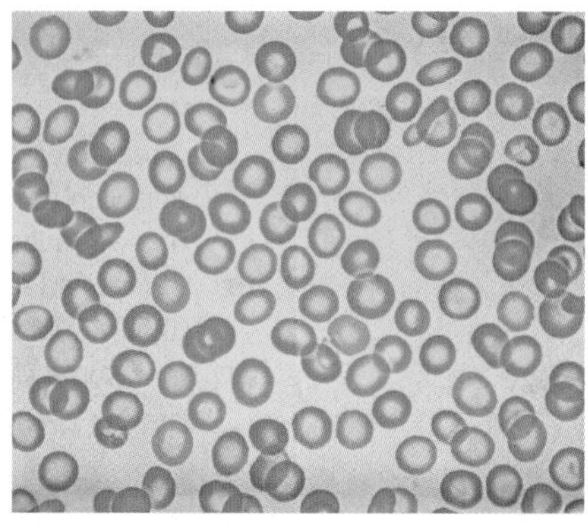

b Microcytic red blood cells affected by anemia

Normal and Microcytic Red Blood Cells

Microcytic red blood cells affected by anemia are small and pale in color compared with normal red blood cells due to lower heme concentration.

Signs and Symptoms of Iron-Deficiency Anemia

Mild iron-deficiency anemia may go unnoticed. The most common symptoms include fatigue, especially during physical exertion, due to the lack of red blood cells and, thus, the inability to carry sufficient oxygen to the muscle cells. Other possible signs may include pale skin color, irritability, shortness of breath, sore tongue, brittle nails, headache in the frontal lobe, a blue tinge to the whites of the eyes, and decreased appetite (especially in children).[2] In young children, a mild iron-deficiency anemia can result in intellectual impairment that is irreversible even after adding iron supplements to the diet.[3] Mild iron-deficiency anemia during pregnancy may cause premature births, low birth weight, and even maternal mortality.

Individuals who have been diagnosed with iron-deficiency anemia may also practice *pica*, a condition characterized by eating clay and other nonfood items, including burnt matches and rubber bands.[4] Pica may exacerbate iron-deficiency anemia because the nonfood substances reduce the bioavailability of iron.

iron-deficiency anemia A type of anemia due to a lack of dietary iron or excessive loss of blood.

total iron-binding capacity (TIBC) A blood test that measures the amount of iron that transferrin can bind. A higher TIBC indicates iron-deficiency anemia.

Testing for Iron-Deficiency Anemia

If you suspect you might have iron-deficiency anemia, a variety of simple blood tests can provide the correct diagnosis. Blood tests show a normal or low hemoglobin level, abnormal number, shape, or size of red blood cells, and the level of iron stored in the body.

A complete blood count, or CBC, measures the hemoglobin level in the blood. A normal range for hemoglobin is 11.1 to 15.0 grams per deciliter. Anemia is diagnosed if the test reveals a hemoglobin level below 11.1. A CBC also determines the hematocrit, or the ratio of red blood cells to fluid in the blood. A normal hematocrit is between 32 and 43 percent red blood cells. If the tests reveal lower than normal hemoglobin, hematocrit, or both, the individual is diagnosed with anemia.

The CBC provides critical information on the size of red blood cells that helps confirm the type of anemia. The mean cell volume measurement classifies the anemia as *microcytic* (small) anemia, *normocytic* (normal) anemia, or *macrocytic* (large) anemia. In iron-deficiency anemia, the red blood cells are usually smaller than normal, or *microcytic* (see Figure).

Another test can be conducted to measure serum iron. This test directly measures the amount of iron in the blood, but it doesn't accurately reflect the stores of iron. To estimate iron stores, the **total iron-binding capacity (TIBC),** or transferrin levels, are measured. If iron-deficiency anemia exists, the total iron-binding capacity and the ability to transport more iron will be high.

Treatment for Iron-Deficiency Anemia

Iron supplements are usually necessary to correct iron-deficiency anemia and restore the iron reserves. Oral iron supplements in the ferrous, or Fe^{+2}, form, sold as ferrous sulfate, ferrous gluconate, or ferrous fumarate, are the most easily absorbed.[5] These supplements, taken for several weeks or even months, are best taken with orange juice or another vitamin C–rich substance to improve iron absorption. Recall that vitamin C makes iron more bioavailable. Avoid taking iron supplements with milk or antacids, which may interfere with the absorption of iron.

References

1. Centers for Disease Control and Prevention. 2012. *Anemia or Iron Deficiency.* Available at www.cdc.gov/nchs/fastats/anemia.htm. Accessed May 2012.
2. National Institutes of Health. 2011. *Iron-Deficiency Anemia.* Available at www.nlm.nih.gov/medlineplus/ency/article/000584.htm. Accessed November 2012.
3. Bryan, J., S. Osendarp, D. Hughes, E. Calvaresi, K. Baghurst, and J. W. van Klinken. 2004. Nutrients for Cognitive Development in School-Aged Children. *Nutrition Reviews* 62:295–306.
4. Singhi, S., R. Ravishanker, P. Singhi, and R. Nath. 2003. Low Plasma Zinc and Iron in Pica. *Indian Journal of Pediatrics* 70:139–143.
5. Maghsudlu, M., S. Nasizadeh, G. R. Toogeh, T. Zandieh, S. Parandoush, and M. Rezayani. 2008. Short-Term Ferrous Sulfate Supplementation in Female Blood Donors. *Transfusion* 48:1192–1197.

Exploring Copper

What Is Copper?

Copper (Cu) may bring to mind ancient tools, great sculptures, or American pennies (although pennies are no longer made of solid copper), but it is also associated with several key body functions.

Copper is found in two different forms in the body: the oxidized form called **cupric** (Cu^{+2}) and the reduced form called **cuprous** (Cu^{+}).

Copper Absorption and Transport

Copper is absorbed mostly in the small intestine. As with iron, the absorption of copper is based on the body's need for the mineral and the ability to free copper from food complexes during digestion with the aid of hydrochloric acid and the digestive enzyme pepsin in the stomach.

The absorption mechanisms for copper are not clear. However, it appears that once copper is free, it is reduced to the cupric (Cu^{+}) state by enzymes on the surface of the enterocyte and then absorbed across the brush border mostly by active transport. After crossing the brush border, copper is either used by the enterocyte, stored attached to a zinc-containing protein called metallothionein, or transported across the basolateral membrane into the blood.

The bioavailability of copper can be enhanced by amino acids, especially

cupric The oxidized form of copper (Cu^{+2}).

cuprous The reduced form of copper (Cu^{+}).

continued

those that contain sulfur. However, phytates in legumes and cereals can reduce the bioavailability of copper, similar to iron. Excess zinc can also reduce the biovailability of copper because zinc stimulates more metallothionein, which binds copper in the enterocyte. Iron, molybdenum, calcium, and phosphorus also reduce the absorption of copper.

Absorbed copper crosses the basolateral membrane and attaches to the protein albumin to be transported through the portal vein to the liver. In the liver, copper is incorporated into another protein called **ceruloplasmin.** Very little copper, about 100 milligrams, is stored in the body. Most excess copper is excreted through the feces as part of bile.

Functions of Copper

Copper is part of several metalloenzymes and proteins. Many of these proteins are essential for oxidation reactions and reducing damage by free radicals. Copper-containing ceruloplasmin is the enzyme mentioned earlier that oxidizes iron from the ferrous form (Fe^{+2}) to the ferric form (Fe^{+3}) (**Figure 13.4**). If the diet is deficient in copper, the amount of copper-containing enzymes hephaestin and ceruloplasmin are reduced and iron accumulates in the intestinal cell rather than being attached to and transported by transferrin. A copper deficiency can thus result in iron-deficiency anemia.[19]

As part of the cytochromes, copper assists in energy production in the electron transport chain. And as part of the enzyme lysyl oxidase, copper links the proteins collagen and elastin together in connective tissue. Superoxide dismutase is a copper-containing enzyme that protects cells from free radical damage.

In addition, copper also helps synthesize melanin (the dark pigment found in skin) and plays an important role as a cofactor in blood clotting in immune response.[20]

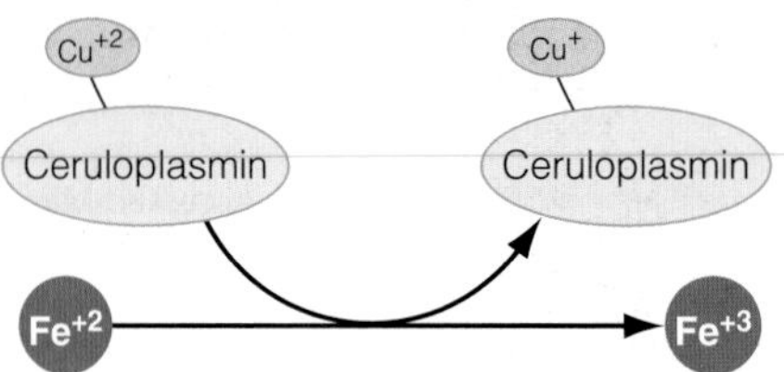

▲ **Figure 13.4 Ceruloplasmin Oxidizes Iron**
The copper-containing protein ceruloplasmin oxidizes ferrous iron (Fe^{+2}) to ferric iron (Fe^{+3}) before iron can bind to transferrin for transport in the blood.

Daily Needs

Adult women and men need 900 micrograms of copper daily. U.S. women consume 1,000 to 1,100 micrograms, whereas men consume 1,300 to 1,500 micrograms daily, on average.

Food Sources

Organ meats (such as liver), seafood, nuts, and seeds are abundant in copper. Bran cereals, whole-grain products, and cocoa are also good sources (see **Figure 13.5**). Whereas potatoes, milk, and chicken are low in copper, they are consumed in such abundant amounts that they contribute a fair amount of copper to Americans' diets.

Too Much or Too Little

Excessive intakes of copper supplements can cause stomach pain and cramps,

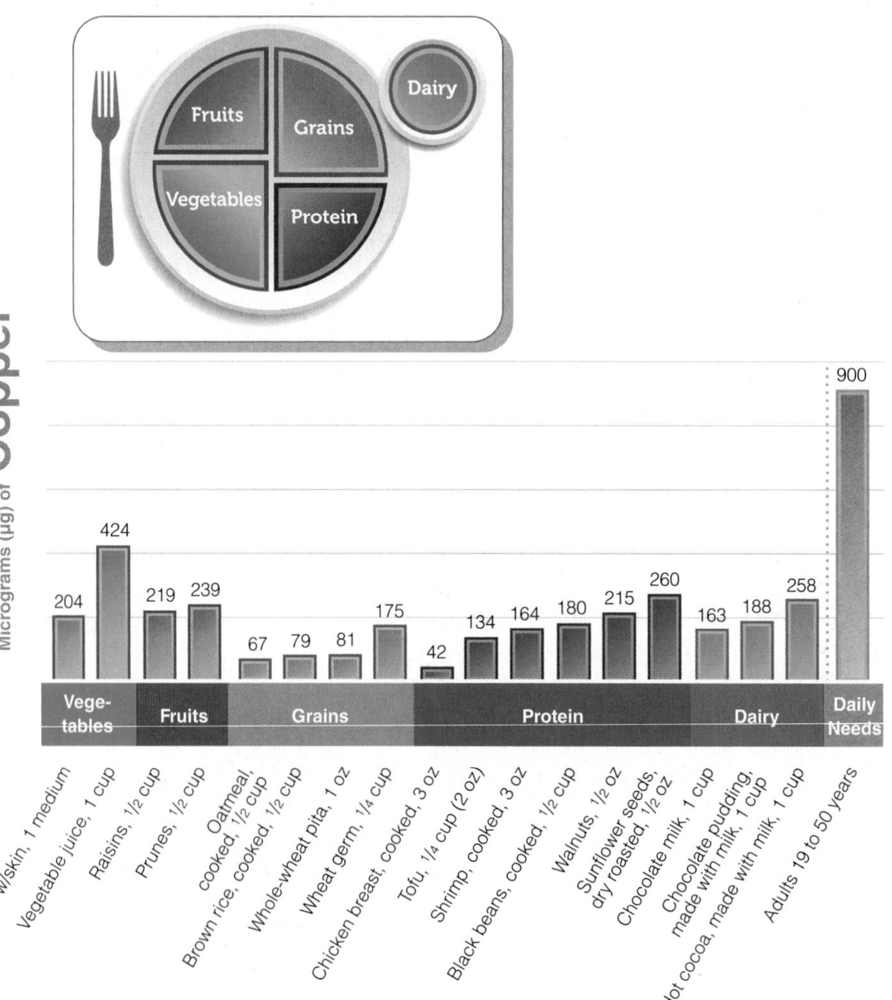

▲ **Figure 13.5 Food Sources of Copper**

ceruloplasmin A protein found in the blood that transports copper.

Menkes' disease A genetic disorder that interferes with copper absorption.

Wilson's disease A rare genetic disorder that results in accumulation of copper in the body.

nausea, diarrhea, vomiting, and even liver damage. The upper level for copper for adults is set at 10,000 micrograms daily.

Copper deficiency is rare in the United States. Its symptoms resemble those of iron deficiency: fatigue and weakness. It has occurred in premature babies fed milk formulas, in malnourished infants fed cow's milk, and in individuals given intravenous feedings that lacked adequate amounts of copper.

Two genetic diseases affect copper metabolism. A rare genetic disorder, **Menkes' disease,** is a copper transport disorder. Copper accumulates in the kidney, brain, and liver and can cause developmental problems, osteoporosis, cardiovascular disease, and death. Another genetic disease, called **Wilson's disease,** prevents the body from excreting copper through the bile. An accumulation of copper in the brain and liver results in severe liver and brain damage if left untreated.

TABLE TIPS

Counting Copper

Make hot cocoa with milk, rather than water, for two sources (cocoa and milk) of copper.

Mix raisins with brown rice at dinner.

Top chocolate pudding with a sprinkling of crushed walnuts for a dessert that is both sweet and crunchy.

Choose sunflower seeds for an afternoon snack.

Ladle black beans and salsa into a whole-wheat pita. Top with reduced-fat Cheddar cheese. Zap it in the microwave for a Mexican lunch with a copper kick.

COPPER

Exploring **Zinc**

ZINC

What Is Zinc?

Zinc (Zn^{+2}) is found in very small amounts in almost every cell of the body, but mostly in bone and muscle. It is involved in the function of more than 100 metalloenzymes, including those used for protein synthesis. As important as it is, it was not recognized as an essential nutrient until 1974.

Zinc Absorption and Transport

Like iron and copper, the absorption of zinc is controlled at the small intestine (**Figure 13.6**). Once it has been absorbed into the intestinal cell, it is bound to a protein called **metallothionine,** which stores zinc and temporarily prevents it from being absorbed into the portal vein. The body produces more metallothionine when zinc stores are high, to prevent toxicity, and less when zinc is deficient. If the zinc isn't needed, it diffuses into the lumen of the small intestine and is excreted through the feces. When it is needed, zinc stored in enterocytes is released from metallothionine and attaches to a transport protein for absorption across the basolateral membrane. The zinc is then released to attach to albumin for transport through the portal vein to the liver.

Zinc absorption can be reduced when high levels of nonheme iron are present in the intestinal tract. The use of iron supplements may be a factor in zinc status and diets high in fiber and phytates also reduce zinc absorption. Consuming animal protein improves zinc absorption.

Zinc Recycling

Zinc is found in the intestine as part of the pancreatic digestive juices. Because these juices are repeatedly excreted into and reabsorbed by the small intestine, zinc is recycled back to the pancreas to be reused. The zinc that is not recycled is excreted through the feces. Zinc can also be excreted in small amounts through the urine, sweat, and sloughed-off skin and hair.

Functions of Zinc

Zinc plays a role in growth and development, in the immune system, and in the healing of wounds. It also influences taste and can help fight macular degeneration.

Zinc Is Needed for DNA Synthesis

Zinc is necessary for DNA and RNA synthesis. Zinc helps regulate gene expression by turning genes on and off and controlling transcription.[21] Delayed growth and maturation in children is a characteristic of zinc deficiency.

metallothionine A metal-binding protein rich in sulfur-containing amino acids that transports ions.

continued

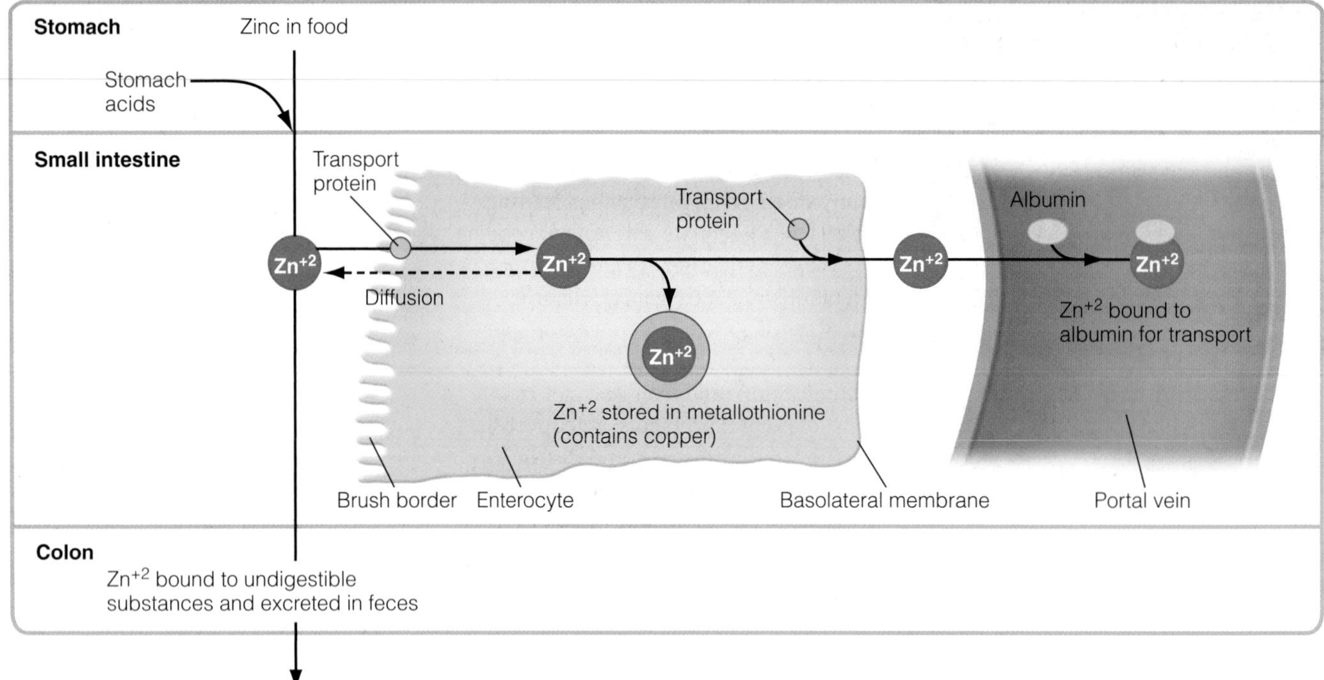

▲ **Figure 13.6 Zinc Absorption**
Zinc is absorbed into the enterocyte and attached to metallothionine for storage. When the body needs more zinc, it is released from metallothionine, transported across the basolateral membrane, and attached to albumin for transport through the body.

Zinc Supports the Immune System

Zinc affects a variety of key factors involved in maintaining a healthy immune system. For example, zinc is a component of thymic hormone, which controls and facilitates the maturation of lymphocytes and killer macrophages. Zinc also acts as an antioxidant and stabilizes cell membranes to provide a barrier to infection.[22] Without sufficient zinc, cell membranes become more susceptible to damage by free radicals and oxidation. Zinc helps reduce the inflammation that can accompany skin wounds, and helps wounds heal by being part of enzymes and proteins that repair skin cells and enhance their proliferation.[23]

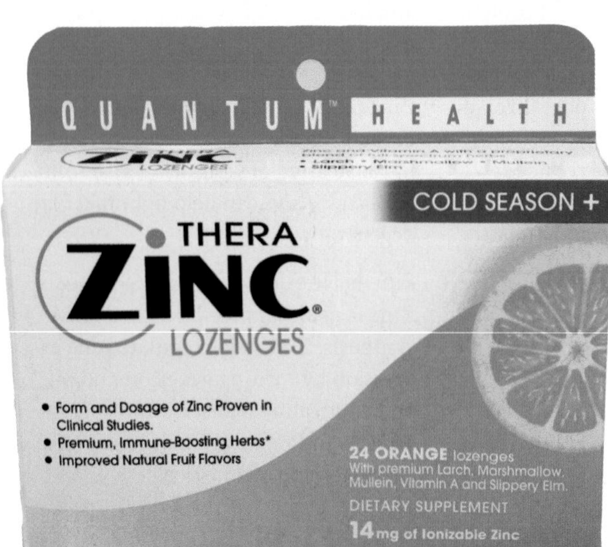

Recent research suggests that zinc lozenges and nasal gels may help reduce the severity and duration of cold symptoms.

Zinc lozenges are sometimes advertised to help reduce the severity and duration of the common cold. Whereas early research found little benefit to using them,[24] more recent research from Finland suggests zinc lozenges or syrup, if taken within 24 hours of the first sign of the sniffles, reduce the severity and duration of the common cold.[25] Zinc gluconate used as a nasal gel may also show promise, as it has lessened the duration[26] and the severity of cold symptoms in some cases.[27] Though the mechanism is still unclear, researchers suggest that zinc gels may reduce the duration of colds by blocking the viral infection at the site where cold viruses enter the body—the nasal passage. But not everyone is convinced. Possible side effects of the use of zinc nasal gels or lozenges include loss of smell, bad taste in the mouth, and nausea. More research is needed to understand the dosage and possible side effects before any recommendations can be made.

Zinc Improves Taste Perception

Zinc activates areas of the brain that perceive taste and smell. Its importance to appetite was first demonstrated in 1972 when researchers showed that taste disorders responded to zinc supplementation. Zinc also influences taste preferences and may be linked to anorexia, which responds to zinc treatment.[28]

Zinc May Prevent Age-Related Macular Degeneration

Research studies show that zinc may play a role in reducing the risk of age-related macular degeneration (AMD), a condition that hampers central vision. Zinc may work with an enzyme in the eyes that's needed to properly use vitamin A for vision. Zinc may also help mobilize vitamin A from the liver to ensure adequate blood levels of this vitamin. Supplements that contain antioxidants along with zinc have been shown to reduce the risk of AMD. (For more information about the causes and treatment of AMD, see Chapter 9.)

Daily Needs

Adult men need 11 milligrams of zinc daily, whereas women need 8 milligrams daily. American adults, on average, are meeting their zinc needs. Men are consuming from 11 milligrams to over 14 milligrams daily and women are consuming 8 to 9 milligrams of zinc daily, on average.

Vegetarians, especially strict vegetarians, can have as much as a 50 percent higher need for zinc. Phytates in plant foods such as grains and legumes, which are staples of vegan diets, can bind with zinc, reducing its absorption in the intestinal tract.

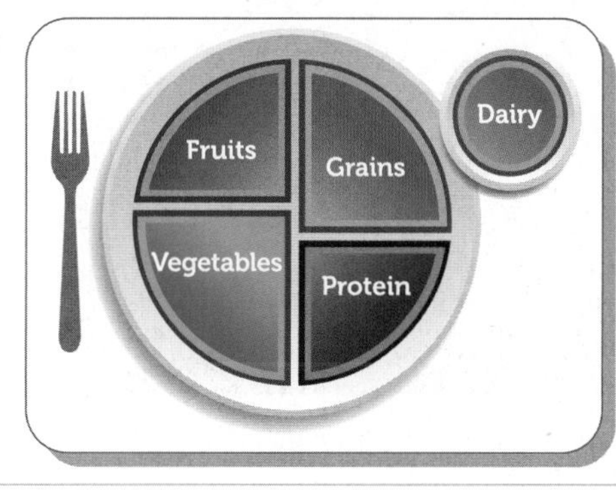

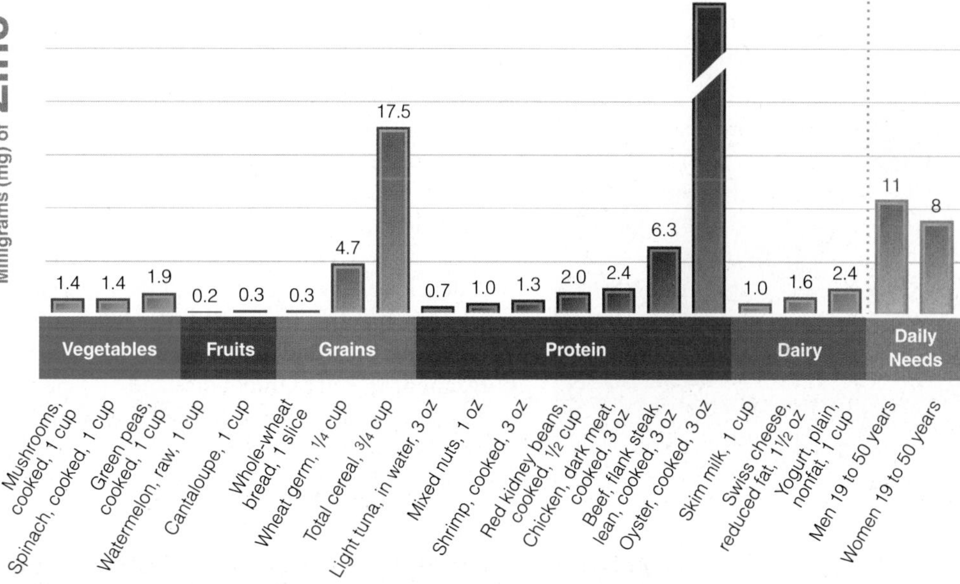

▲ **Figure 13.7 Food Sources of Zinc**

Food Sources

Red meat, some seafood, and whole grains are excellent sources of zinc (see **Figure 13.7**). The dark meat in chicken and turkey is higher in zinc than the white meat. Because zinc is found in the germ and bran portion of grains, refined grains have as much as 80 percent less zinc than whole grains. This is yet another reason to favor whole-grain products over those made with refined grains.

Too Much or Too Little

The upper level for zinc in food and/or supplements for adults is set at 40 milligrams daily. Consuming too much zinc, as little as 50 milligrams, can cause stomach pains, nausea, vomiting, and diarrhea. Approximately 60 milligrams of zinc daily has been shown to lower body levels of copper by competing for absorption in the intestinal tract.

continued

This is an excellent example of how the overconsumption of one mineral can compromise the benefits of another. Excessive amounts, such as 300 milligrams of zinc daily, have been shown to suppress the immune system and lower HDL ("good") cholesterol.

A zinc deficiency can result from too much iron, which can interfere with zinc transport. The transport protein, transferrin, transports both zinc and iron. In an iron overload, transferrin becomes saturated with iron, which reduces the sites available for zinc transport. Iron transport will also be impaired if transferrin is saturated with zinc.

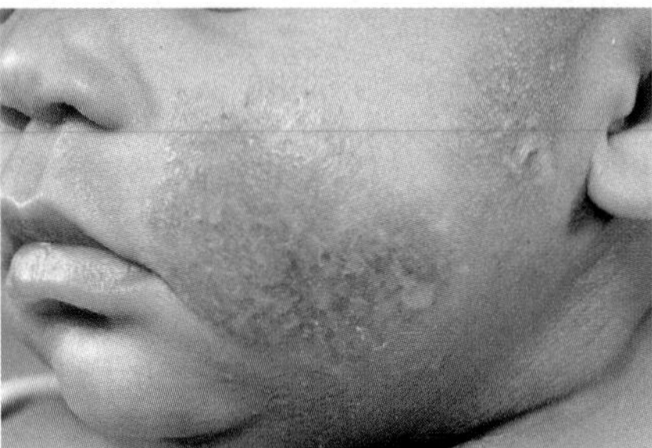

Skin rash is one of the symptoms of zinc deficiency.

A deficiency of zinc can cause hair loss, loss of appetite, impaired taste of foods, diarrhea, and delayed sexual maturation, as well as impotence and skin rashes. Because zinc is needed during development, a deficiency can slow and impair growth. Classic studies of groups of people in the Middle East showed that people who consumed a diet mainly of unleavened bread, which is high in zinc-binding phytates, experienced impaired growth and dwarfism.[29] Impaired growth may be partially reversed if zinc is restored in the diet.

TABLE TIPS

Improve Zinc Intake

Enjoy a tuna fish sandwich on whole-wheat bread at lunch for a double serving (fish and bread) of zinc.

Add kidney beans to a soup or salad.

Pack a small handful of mixed nuts and raisins in a zip-closed bag for a snack on the run.

Make oatmeal with milk for two servings of zinc in one bowl.

Add cooked green peas to casseroles, stews, soups, and salads.

Exploring Selenium

What Is Selenium?

The mineral selenium (Se) is a component of a class of proteins called **selenoproteins,** many of which are enzymes. Most dietary selenium is in the form of **selenomethionine.** Unlike iron and zinc, selenium absorption is based on the individual's needs. In fact, more than 85 percent of dietary selenium is absorbed mostly in the duodenum by passive diffusion.[30] Once absorbed, selenium is stored as selenomethionine or selenoprotein in a variety of tissues, including the liver, muscles, kidneys, and bone (**Figure 13.8**). Homeostasis of selenium is maintained by the kidneys, which excrete excess amounts through the urine.

selenoproteins Proteins that contain selenomethionine.

selenomethionine An amino acid that contains selenium rather than sulfur.

Functions of Selenium

Selenium plays a critical role in thyroid function and helps fight cancer via its antioxidant properties.

Selenium Is Required by the Thyroid

Three selenium-containing enzymes help regulate thyroid hormones in the body. These enzymes activate and deactivate thyroid hormone to maintain balance, and promote normal development and growth by regulating the thyroid gland.

Selenium Plays an Antioxidant Role and May Help Fight Cancer

Selenoproteins, such as glutathione peroxidase, function as antioxidants that protect the cells from free radical damage. Research studies have suggested that deaths from cancers, such as lung, colon, and prostate cancers, are lower in groups of people who consume more selenium.[31] Selenium's antioxidant capabilities, and its ability to potentially slow the growth of tumors, are thought to be the mechanism behind its anticancer effects.[32] The FDA allows a Qualified Health Claim on food labels and dietary supplements that states, "Selenium may

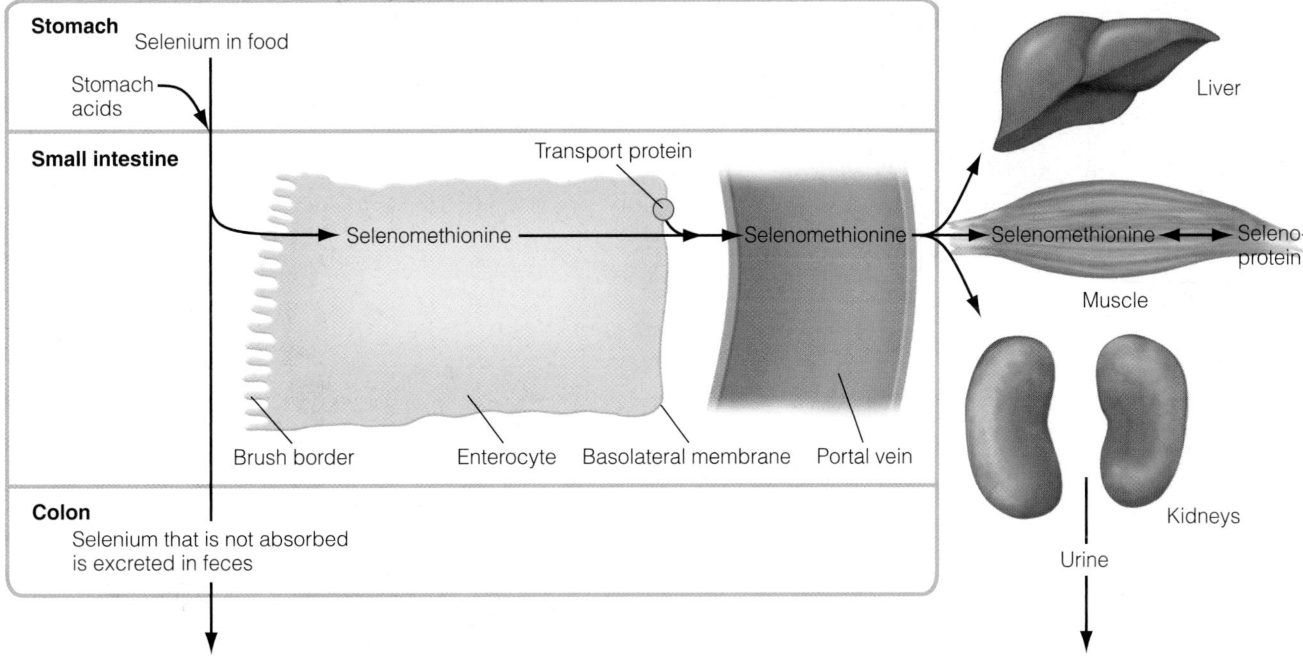

▲ **Figure 13.8 Metabolism of Selenium**
Selenium is easily absorbed, transported, and stored in the body, mostly as selenomethionine.

reduce the risk of certain cancers but the evidence is limited and not conclusive to date."[33]

Daily Needs

Adult females and males need 55 micrograms of selenium daily. American adults are more than meeting their needs—they consume about 80 to 160 micrograms daily, on average. The RDA is set to maintain optimal activity of the enzyme glutathione peroxidase. Most manufacturers do not include selenium on food labels unless the food has been fortified with the mineral. In this case, the label uses 70 micrograms as the standard for the percent Daily Value.

Food Sources

Nuts, meat, seafood, cereal, grains, dairy foods, and fruits and vegetables can all contribute to dietary selenium (see **Figure 13.9**). However, the amount of selenium in foods depends upon the soil where the plants were grown and the animals grazed. For example, wheat grown in selenium-rich soil can have more than a tenfold higher amount of the mineral than wheat grown in selenium-poor soil.

Too Much or Too Little

Too much selenium can cause toxicity and a condition called **selenosis.** A person with selenosis will have brittle nails and hair, both of which may fall out. Other symptoms include stomach and intestinal discomfort, a skin rash, garlicky breath, fatigue, and damage to the nervous system. A chronic intake of as little as 1 to 3 milligrams per day can result in toxicity. Thus, the upper level for selenium for adults is set at 400 micrograms daily to prevent the loss and brittleness of nails and hair.

Though rare in the United States, a selenium deficiency can cause **Keshan disease,** which damages the heart. This disease typically only occurs in children who live in rural areas that have selenium-poor soil. However, some researchers speculate that selenium deficiency alone may not cause

TABLE TIPS

Seeking Out Selenium

Top a toasted whole-wheat bagel with a slice of reduced-fat Cheddar cheese for a hot way to start the day.

Spread peanut butter on whole-wheat crackers. Top each cracker with a slice of banana.

Top dinner pasta with broccoli for a selenium-smart meal.

Zap sliced apples, sprinkled with a little apple juice and cinnamon, in the microwave and top with vanilla yogurt for a tasty snack.

Spoon a serving of low-fat cottage cheese into a bowl and top with canned sliced peaches and almonds for a fabulous dessert.

selenosis The presence of toxic levels of selenium.

Keshan disease A disease related to a deficiency of selenium.

continued

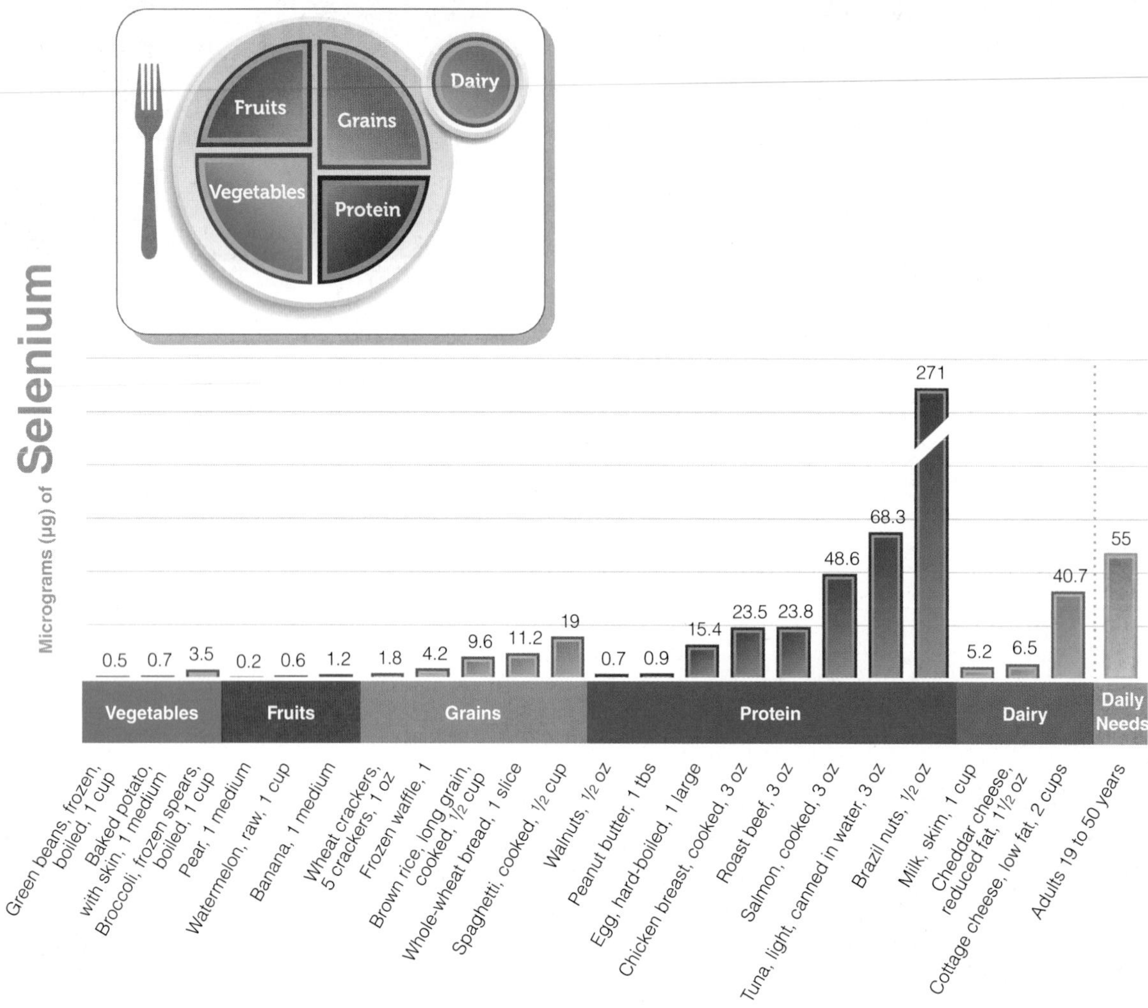

▲ **Figure 13.9 Food Sources of Selenium**

Keshan disease, but the selenium-deficient individual may also be exposed to a virus, which, together with the selenium deficiency, leads to the damaged heart.[34]

Some reports suggest that selenium deficiencies may result in changes in thyroid hormone.[35] For example, there is a higher incidence of thyroiditis, such as the autoimmune thyroid disease called Hashimoto's, in individuals with lower levels of selenium.[36] This may be due to a decrease in activity of enzymes that require selenium as a cofactor within thyroid cells.

Exploring **Fluoride**

What Is Fluoride?

Fluoride (F^-) is the safe ion form of fluorine, a poisonous gas. Fluoride is not classified as essential because the body does not require it for normal growth and development. However, it plays a critical role in developing strong teeth that are resistant to decay.

Fluoride is found naturally in plants and animals, and often added to the water supply. Almost all the fluoride consumed in the diet is absorbed in the small intestine and taken up by the bones and developing teeth.

fluoroapatite The crystalline structure that results when hydroxyapatite has been changed by exposure of the tooth to fluoride.

Functions of Fluoride

The best known function of fluoride is its role in maintaining healthy teeth. Fluoride forms **fluoroapatite**

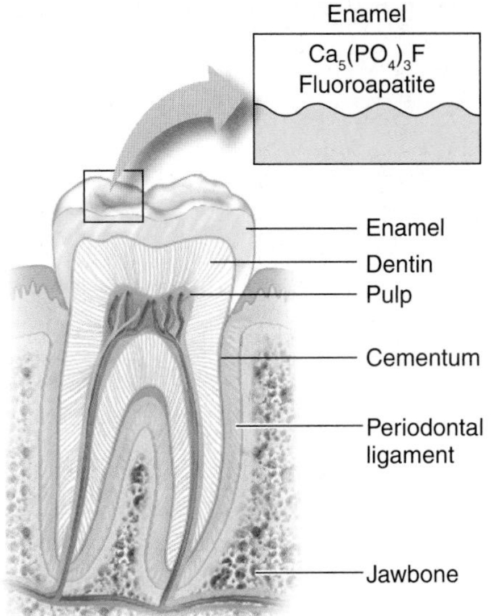

▲ **Figure 13.10 Structure of Fluoroapatite in Teeth**

by replacing the OH in hydroxyapatite crystals with fluoride. Fluoroapatite helps harden the outer layer of the tooth (the *enamel*) and makes the tooth more resistant to damage (see **Figure 13.10**). Over time, acids produced by bacteria in the mouth, and from acidic foods and beverages, erode tooth enamel. Continual exposure of the teeth to these acids, especially during tooth formation, or if fluoride is lacking, can result in dental caries.

Fluoride from food, beverages, and dental products, such as toothpaste, can repair enamel that has already started to erode. Fluoride also interferes with the ability of the bacteria to metabolize carbohydrates, thus reducing the amount of acid they produce, and provides a protective barrier between the tooth and the destructive acids. Fluoride in the saliva continually bathes the teeth's surface, which helps remineralize the hydroxyapatite structure of the tooth and reduce the effect of the bacteria.[37] Consuming adequate amounts of fluoride is extremely important during infancy and childhood, when teeth are developing, and for maintenance of healthy teeth throughout life.

In the 1930s, scientists noticed lower rates of dental caries among individuals whose community water systems contained significant amounts of fluoride. Studies confirmed that the fluoride was the protective factor in the water. Since 1945, most communities have fluoridated their water, and today 67 percent of Americans live in communities that have a fluoridated water supply. The increase in access to fluoridated water is the major reason there has been a decline in dental caries in the United States, and fluoridation of water is considered one of the ten greatest public health advances of the twentieth century.[38]

Fluoride also helps maintain strong bones by stimulating the osteoblasts. Fluoride in combination with calcium and vitamin D may increase bone mineral density and reduce the incidence of osteoporosis.

Daily Needs

Adult men should consume 3.8 milligrams and adult women 3.1 milligrams of fluoride daily to meet their needs. If tap water is fluoridated at 0.7 milligrams per liter, an individual would have to consume at least 15 cups of water daily, through either beverages or cooking, to meet fluoride needs (1 liter = 4.2 cups).

Currently, adults consume 1.4 to 3.4 milligrams of fluoride daily if they are living in communities with fluoridated water. The number drops to only 0.3 to 1.0 milligram consumed daily if the water isn't fluoridated.[39] In 2010, more than 73.9 percent of people were drinking fluoridated water.[40] This is close to the *Healthy People 2020* goal that 79.6 percent of people consume water that has the optimum level of fluoride recommended for preventing tooth decay.[41]

continued

Food Sources

Foods in general are not a good source of fluoride. The best sources are fluoridated water and beverages and foods made with this water, such as coffee, tea, and soups. Another source of fluoride can be juices made from concentrate using fluoridated tap water (remember, not all tap water contains fluoride). Water and processed beverages such as soft drinks account for up to 75 percent of Americans' fluoride intake. Tea is also a good source of fluoride, as tea leaves accumulate fluoride. Because the decaffeination process involves the use of mineral water, which is naturally high in fluoride, decaffeinated tea has twice the amount of fluoride as the caffeinated variety.[42]

Most bottled waters sold in the United States have less than the optimal amount of fluoride. It is difficult to determine the fluoride content of many bottled waters because currently, fluoride amounts only have to be listed on the label if fluoride has been specifically added. Consumers need to check the label to see if the bottled water they purchase contains added fluoride.

Too Much or Too Little

Because of fluoride's protective qualities, too little exposure to or consumption of fluoride increases the risk of dental caries.

Having some fluoride is important for healthy teeth, but too much can cause **fluorosis,** a condition whereby the teeth become mottled (pitted) and develop white patches or stains on the surface (see **Figure 13.11**). Fluorosis creates teeth that are extremely resistant to caries but cosmetically unappealing.

Fluorosis occurs when teeth are forming, so only infants and children up to 8 years of age are at risk. Once teeth break through the gums, fluorosis can't occur. Fluorosis results from overfluoridation of water, swallowing toothpaste, or excessive use of dental products that contain fluoride. Some research suggests that fluorosis may be reversible, but more studies are needed to determine this.

Skeletal fluorosis can occur in bones when a person consumes at least 10 milligrams of fluoride daily for 10 or more years. This is a rare situation that may happen when water is mistakenly overfluoridated. Skeletal fluorosis can cause bone concentrations of fluoride that are up to five times higher than normal and result in stiffness or pain in joints, osteoporosis, and calcification of the ligaments.

fluorosis A condition caused by excess amounts of fluoride, resulting in mottling of the teeth.

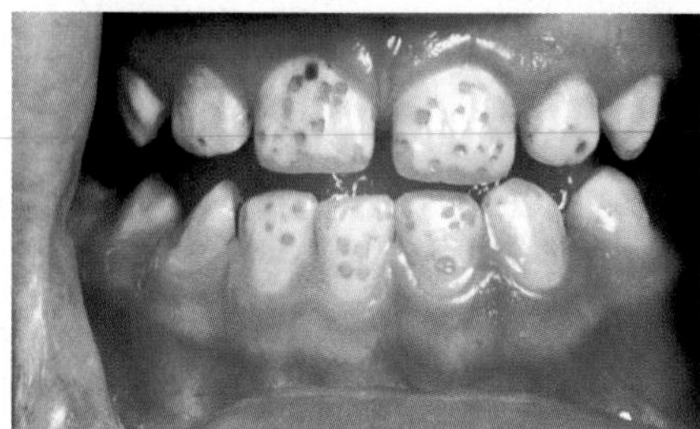

▲ **Figure 13.11 Fluorosis**
Teeth pitted by fluorosis.

The upper level for adults has been set at 10 milligrams to reduce the risk of fluorosis in the bones. Note, however, that the upper level for infants and children is much lower, to prevent fluorosis in teeth. Infants in their first 6 months of age should ingest no more than 0.7 milligrams per day or 0.9 milligrams per day for infants 7 to 12 months old. Children from 1 to 3 years of age should not ingest more than 1.3 milligrams per day or 2.2 milligrams per day for children ages 4 to 8.

TABLE TIPS

Fabulous Ways to Get Fluoride

Pour orange juice into ice cube trays and pop a couple of frozen cubes into a glass of tap water for a refreshing and flavorful beverage.

Use tap water when making coffee, tea, or juice from concentrate, and for food preparation.

Brew a mug of flavored decaffeinated tea, such as French vanilla or gingerbread, to keep you warm while you're hitting the books.

Two Points of View

Does Drinking Unfluoridated Water Affect Dental Health?

Two experts give their perspectives on the role of fluoridated water in dental health.

Howard Pollick, BDS, MPH
School of Dentistry, University of California, San Francisco

Dr. Howard Pollick, BDS, MPH, is a graduate of the Dental School, University of Manchester, England and the School of Public Health at UC Berkeley. A full-time clinical professor in the Department of Preventive and Restorative Dental Sciences of the School of Dentistry at the University of California, San Francisco, Dr. Pollick is a diplomate of the American Board of Dental Public Health, an American Dental Association (ADA) expert spokesperson on fluoridation, Chair of the Fluoridation Advisory Committee for the California Dental Association Foundation, and a past chair of the Oral Health Section of the American Public Health Association.

Q: Is there a concern that drinking unfluoridated bottled water, instead of tap water, on a regular basis could be a detriment to healthy teeth?

A: Because the use of bottled water has increased and because the majority of commercial bottled water is low in fluoride, there is the potential for an increase in dental caries.[1, 2] To encourage bottled water manufacturers to provide optimally fluoridated water, the ADA has introduced a certification program for foods and beverages that are beneficial to oral health, including fluoridated bottled water.[3] The CDC has further information on their website.[4]

Q: What evidence is there to support your position?

A: Evidence is limited because there have not been sufficient well-designed studies. In 1993, a U.S. study found that 35 percent of people drinking bottled water were doing so primarily as a substitute for the consumption of other beverages.[5] If bottled water is being consumed rather than sugar beverages, then this could reduce the risk for tooth decay. However, in South Australia, where rainwater is collected by about 80 percent of rural households and about 30 percent of metropolitan households, a study has found an increase in tooth decay among children using rainwater and bottled water. Cross-sectional results of a longitudinal study of caries experience in South Australian children found that children with 100 percent lifetime consumption of nonpublic water (rainwater and bottled water) had 52.7 percent higher deciduous caries scores than children with zero percent lifetime consumption of nonpublic water. After controlling for socioeconomic characteristics, the effect of consumption

Hardy Limeback, BSc, PhD, DDS
Professor, Faculty of Dentistry, University of Toronto

Hardy Limeback, BSc, PhD, DDS, is a professor in the University of Toronto's Faculty of Dentistry. He was a member of the Canadian Dental Association Council of Education and the Consumer Products Recognition Committee. He is an executive board member of the International Society for Fluoride Research and the Associate Editor of *Fluoride*.

Q: Is there a concern that drinking unfluoridated bottled water, instead of tap water, on a regular basis could be a detriment to healthy teeth?

A: "Unfluoridated" bottled water may or may not contain fluoride naturally. In Canada, all bottled water must list fluoride ion content as part of the basic labelling information. The following additional information must be on the label of spring and mineral water: dissolved mineral salt content, a statement indicating whether ozone or fluoride has been added, and a statement relating the geographic location of the underground source of the water. If children with developing teeth drink bottled spring water with more than the recommended level of fluoride on a daily basis, dental fluorosis will result. If adults drink spring water with too much natural fluoride, skeletal fluorosis can result. At the opposite end, there are concerns that drinking "pure" water without fluoride somehow makes the teeth more susceptible to decay. That is because it has always been assumed that fluoride needs to be ingested to make the teeth more resistant to decay. If fluoride works to prevent dental decay it works topically, after the teeth appear in the mouth. This is now well established. Fluoride is not a nutrient. It is not a coenzyme nor is it essential for normal development. In fact it is a potent inhibitor of many essential human enzymes. Dental decay is not a fluoride-deficiency disease.

Q: What evidence is there to support your position?

A: Over the last 20 years, dental researchers have shown that fluoride does not affect the resistance of the teeth to dental decay through systemic ingestion. In 2001, the CDC carried out a review that states, "Fluoride works primarily after teeth have erupted, especially when small amounts are maintained constantly in the mouth, specifically in dental plaque and saliva."[10]

At the same time, evidence is mounting that fluoridation of tap water no longer protects against decay. There

of nonpublic water on caries experience in the deciduous dentition remained significant.[6]

Additionally, in 2006, the FDA's Center for Food Safety and Applied Nutrition issued a Health Claim Notification for Fluoridated Water and Reduced Risk of Dental Caries. Labels on bottled water with 0.6 to 1.0 mg/L fluoride may claim "Drinking fluoridated water may reduce the risk of [dental caries or tooth decay]." In addition, the health claim is not intended for use on bottled water products specifically marketed for use by infants.[7]

Q: What is the most important issue consumers need to know about their water intake?

A: From a dental health perspective, consumers should inform their dentist about their use of bottled water. The ADA recommends that dentists ask their patients about bottled water use and advise them about the possible removal of fluoride by some home water treatment systems. Further, the ADA and the CDC recommend labeling of bottled water with the fluoride concentration of the product.[8, 9]

are several recent studies where it has been difficult to show any benefit of fluoridation at 1.0 parts per million (ppm) to permanent teeth. Many countries no longer fluoridate their drinking water. Most countries that still fluoridate have set the maximum fluoride level at 1.5 ppm and have lowered the recommended "optimum" fluoride level (to 0.7 ppm or less) over the concern that even at 1.0 ppm (the previous "optimum" level) there is evidence of too much dental fluorosis in the communities.

Q: What is the most important issue consumers need to know about their water intake?

A: Water is essential for good health. Humans need to consume plenty of water for adequate hydration of tissues, proper kidney function, and to rid the body [of] harmful metabolites. When fluoride is added to drinking water (or occurs naturally in high amounts), water intake has to be carefully monitored. The risk is too much fluoride ingestion. This is particularly crucial for children whose teeth are still forming. Since all forms of dental fluorosis permanently alter the tooth structure, often requiring extensive dental work, it is very important to balance the water intake needs of growing children with the potential for fluoride toxicity. The American Dental Association released a warning in 2006 stating that fluoridated tap water should not be used to reconstitute infant formula in order to reduce the risk of dental fluorosis. For adults, where it is recommended that they drink the equivalent of eight glasses or more of water each day, there is a real concern that the consumption of fluoride from tap water exceeds the upper level. Currently, the upper level set by the US EPA is about 4 mg/day (or 1 liter of 4 ppm fluoride in drinking water). In 2006, the National Academy of Science Subcommittee on Fluoride in Drinking Water recommended that this be lowered. The EPA has yet to act on those recommendations.

References

1. Broffitt, B., S. M. Levy, J. J. Warren, and J. E. Cavanaugh. 2007. An Investigation of Bottled Water Use and Caries in the Mixed Dentition. *Journal of Public Health Dentistry* 67:151–158.
2. Armfield, J. M. and A. J. Spencer. 2004. Consumption of Nonpublic Water: Implications for Children's Caries Experience. *Community Dentistry and Oral Epidemiology* 32:283–296.
3. American Dental Association. 2008. *New ADA Program Tags Smile Healthy Products.* Available at www.ada.org/prof/resources/pubs/adanews/adanewsarticle.asp?articleid=2851. Accessed May 2012.
4. Centers for Disease Control and Prevention. 2011. *Bottled Water and Fluoride.* Available at www.cdc.gov/fluoridation/fact_sheets/bottled_water.htm. Accessed May 2012.
5. Hurd, R. E. 1993. Consumer Attitude Survey on Water Quality Issues. Denver, CO: American Water Works Association Research Foundation.
6. Armfield, J. M. and A. J. Spencer. 2004. Consumption of Nonpublic Water: Implications for Children's Caries Experience.
7. Food and Drug Administration. Center for Food Safety and Applied Nutrition. 2008. *Health Claim Notification for Fluoridated Water and Reduced Risk of Dental Caries.* Available at www.fda.gov/Food/LabelingNutrition/LabelClaims/FDAModernizationActFDAMAClaims/ucm073602.htm. Accessed May 2012.
8. American Dental Association. 2002. *ADA Policy on Bottled Water, Home Water Treatment Systems and Fluoride Exposure.* Available at www.ada.org/2085.aspx. Accessed November 2012.
9. Centers for Disease Control and Prevention (CDC). 2001. *Recommendations for Using Fluoride to Prevent and Control Dental Caries in the United States.* Available at www.cdc.gov/fluoridation/fact_sheets/fl_caries.htm. Accessed May 2012.
10. Centers for Disease Control and Prevention. 2001. Recommendations for Using Fluoride to Prevent and Control Dental Caries in the United States. MMWR Recommendations and Reports 50(RR14):1–42. Available at www.cdc.gov/mmwr/preview/mmwrhtml/rr5014a1.htm. Accessed October 2012.

Exploring Chromium

What Is Chromium?

Chromium (Cr) is the most recent mineral to be found necessary in humans. Researchers became interested in chromium as a factor in the metabolism of glucose in the 1950s. Twenty years later, it was identified as an essential mineral.[43] Chromium is found in two ionic forms: **Trivalent chromium** (Cr^{+3}) is the active form of chromium found in food and **hexavalent chromium** (Cr^{+6}) is a toxic, carcinogenic form of the mineral produced from industrial waste.

Very little chromium is absorbed (less than 2.5 percent).[44] Once absorbed, the mineral is stored in a variety of tissues, including the liver, muscle, and spleen. Chromium can be excreted in the urine, especially when the diet is high in simple sugars.[45]

Functions of Chromium

Chromium plays an essential role in how the body makes use of insulin. It also has an impact on prediabetes, metabolic syndrome, and weight.

Chromium Helps Insulin in the Body

The main function of chromium is to increase insulin's effectiveness in cells. The role of chromium in this mechanism is not clearly understood, but it has been suggested that once insulin binds to the insulin receptor on the surface of the cells, chromium moves inside the cell and stimulates the transport of glucose across the cell membrane.[46] Chromium may also improve insulin's effects on the metabolism and storage of carbohydrates, fats, and protein in the body.

Because it works with insulin, some researchers believe that chromium may help individuals who have diabetes mellitus or prediabetes (glucose intolerance) to improve their blood glucose control. One small study suggests that a chromium supplement may reduce the risk of insulin resistance, and therefore, favorably affect the handling of glucose in the body. Improving the body's sensitivity to insulin and maintaining a normal blood glucose level can possibly lower the incidence of type 2 diabetes in individuals at risk.[47] However, a large research study has yet to be reported that might confirm this theory.

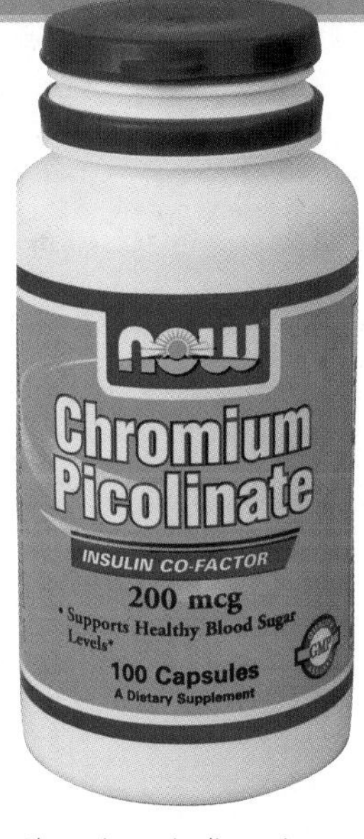

Chromium picolinate is often marketed as a weight loss supplement; however, little scientific evidence supports this use.

Chromium May Prevent or Improve Metabolic Syndrome

Individuals with insulin resistance may not develop diabetes but could develop other health-related problems including metabolic syndrome, which comprises a cluster of risk factors including obesity, high lipid levels in the blood, hypertension, and hyperglycemia. Additionally, insulin resistance has been associated with cardiovascular disease.[48] Because chromium reduces insulin resistance, some researchers suggest that chromium supplements, particularly those that contain niacin, might reduce the symptoms of metabolic syndrome as well as lower blood sugar. Nutrigenomics could shed some light on these mechanisms and lead to new dietary strategies to prevent these insulin-resistance disorders.[49]

Based on this research, the FDA has allowed a Qualified Health Claim on chromium supplements. However, the supplement label must state that the evidence regarding the relationship between chromium supplements and either insulin resistance or type 2 diabetes is not certain at this time.[50]

Chromium Does Not Improve Body Composition

Although advertisements have sometimes touted chromium supplements as an aid to losing weight and building lean muscle, research doesn't support the claim. A review of over 20 research studies found no benefits from taking up to 1,000 micrograms of chromium daily.[51] In one specific study, ingesting a combination of chromium picolinate and conjugated linoleic acid for three months did not improve the weight and body composition of overweight young women.[52]

Daily Needs

Adult men aged 19 to 50 need 30 to 35 micrograms of chromium daily, whereas women need 20 to 25 micrograms daily, on average, depending upon their age. American men consume an estimated 33 micrograms of chromium from foods, and women consume 25 micrograms, on average, daily.[53]

Food Sources

Many foods contain chromium, but the amount varies and is influenced by the amount of chromium in the soil. Whole grains are good sources of chromium, while refined grains contain much less. Meat, fish, and poultry and some fruits and vegetables can also provide chromium, whereas dairy foods are low in the mineral (see **Figure 13.12**).

trivalent chromium The oxidative form of chromium (Cr^{+3}) found in food.

hexavalent chromium The oxidative form of chromium (Cr^{+6}) that is toxic.

continued

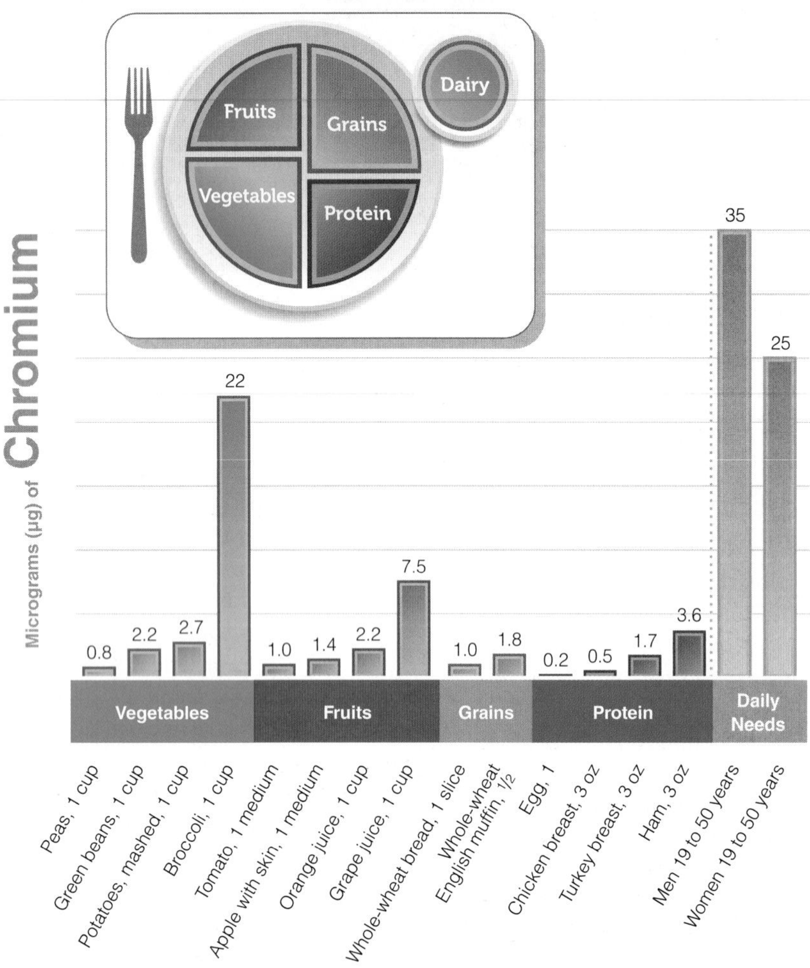

▲ **Figure 13.12 Food Sources of Chromium**

Too Much or Too Little

Excess chromium, such as from supplements, may reduce the absorption, transport, and utilization of iron by binding to transferrin.[54] However, there are no known risks in humans from consuming excessive amounts of chromium from food or supplements, so no upper level has been set.

A chromium deficiency is very rare in the United States. Individuals who have a chromium deficiency show signs similar to those observed in diabetics, such as elevated blood glucose, and in people with cardiovascular disease, such as elevated fatty acids in the blood.[55] When a chromium deficiency has been shown to exist in individuals with type 2 diabetes, they experienced lower blood glucose levels and less insulin resistance when they were given chromium supplements. However, it is not clear if individuals with diabetes who do not have a chromium deficiency would benefit by taking a supplement.

TABLE TIPS

Cram in the Chromium

Toast a whole-wheat English muffin and top it with a slice of lean ham for a chromium-laden breakfast.

Add broccoli florets to salad for a chromium-packed lunch.

Try an afternoon glass of cold grape juice for a refreshing break. Add an apple for a double dose of chromium.

Combine mashed potatoes and peas for a sweet and starchy addition to dinner.

Split a firm banana in half, lengthwise, and spread a small amount of peanut butter on each side.

Exploring Iodine

What Is Iodine?

Iodine (I) in the ionic form **iodide** (I^-) is an essential mineral. Like the fluoridation of community drinking water, the iodization of salt was a significant advance for public health in the United States. Prior to the 1920s, many Americans suffered from the iodine deficiency disease, **goiter** (**Figure 13.13**). Once salt manufacturers began adding iodine to their product, incidence of the disease dropped. Today, rates of the disease are very low in the United States, though not in other parts of the world.

▶ **Figure 13.13 Goiter**
Goiter refers to the enlarged thyroid gland caused by an iodine deficiency.

Functions of Iodine

Iodine is essential for the thyroid, a butterfly-shaped gland that wraps around the trachea. The thyroid *traps* iodine to make some essential hormones. Approximately 60 percent of thyroid hormones are comprised of iodine. The thyroid gland converts iodide to *tetraiodothyronine,* also referred to as T_4, or **thyroxine.** One of the iodide ions is removed from T_4 to form *triiodothyronine,* or T_3. The amount of T_4 produced by the thyroid is much greater than the amount of T_3, but T_3 is more potent. Both of these active thyroid hormones are released from the thyroid gland into the blood.

The powerful thyroid hormones affect the majority of cells. They help regulate metabolic rate, reproduction, and nerve, muscle, and heart function. Thyroid hormones also control the rate of energy production in the TCA cycle. Children need thyroid hormones for normal growth of bones and brain development.[56]

The metabolism of the thyroid gland and the production of thyroxine is controlled by the hypothalamus. When the blood level of T_4 (thyroxine) is reduced, the hypothalamus responds by releasing **thyroxine-releasing hormone (TRH),** which stimulates the pituitary gland to produce **thyroxine-stimulating hormone (TSH).** TSH stimulates the thyroid to trap more iodide ions from the blood to produce more T_4. When the blood levels of T_4 rise, the hypothalamus shuts off the production of TRH and TSH to maintain thyroid hormone homeostasis. When the diet is low in iodine, the blood levels of iodide ions will become low and T_4 synthesis decreased, stimulating the process all over again (**Figure 13.14**).

Daily Needs

Adult men and women need only 150 micrograms of iodine daily to meet their needs, an amount easily met by consuming seafood and iodized salt. In fact, Americans currently consume 230 to 410 micrograms of iodine daily, on average, depending upon their age and gender.

Food Sources

The amount of iodine that occurs naturally in foods is typically low, approximately 3 to 75 micrograms in a serving, and is influenced by the amount of iodine in the soil, water, and fertilizers used to grow foods. Fish can provide higher amounts of iodine, as they concentrate it from seawater (**Figure 13.15**). Iodized salt provides 400 micrograms of iodine per teaspoon. Note that not all salt has added iodine. Kosher salt, for example, has no additives, including iodine. Processed foods that use iodized salt or iodine-containing preservatives are also a source.

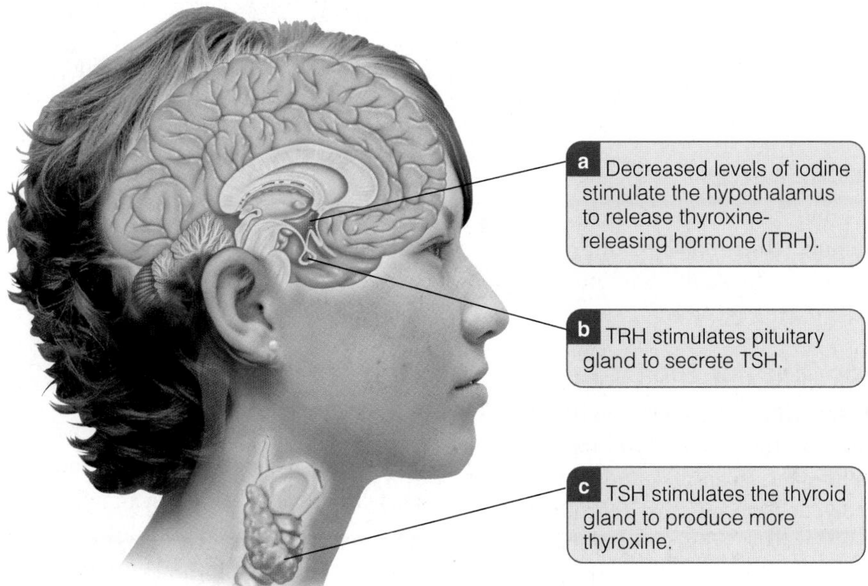

a Decreased levels of iodine stimulate the hypothalamus to release thyroxine-releasing hormone (TRH).
b TRH stimulates pituitary gland to secrete TSH.
c TSH stimulates the thyroid gland to produce more thyroxine.

▲ **Figure 13.14 The Thyroid Gland Produces the Hormone Thyroxine**

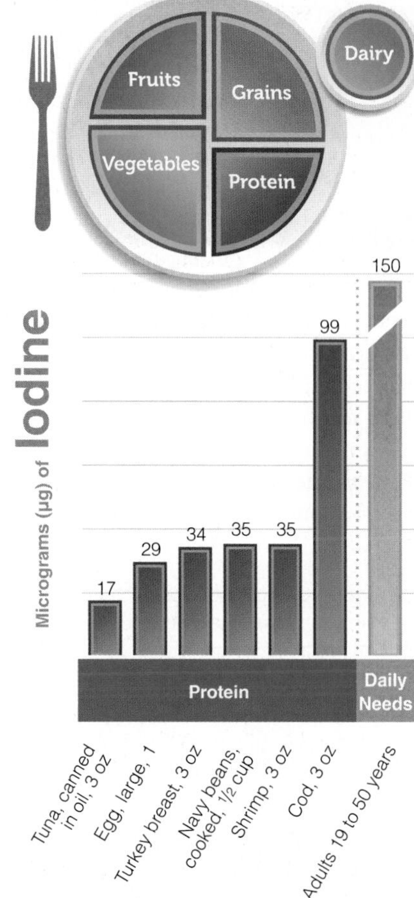

▲ **Figure 13.15 Food Sources of Iodine**

Too Much or Too Little

An early sign of iodine deficiency is the enlarged thyroid gland known as *simple goiter.*[57] A goiter epidemic in the midwestern United States prompted the campaign for mandatory iodization of salt.

iodide The ion form of iodine in the body (I^-).

goiter The enlargement of the thyroid gland, mostly due to iodine deficiency.

thyroxine The less active form of thyroid hormone, also known as *tetraiodothyronine* (T_4).

thyroxine-releasing hormone (TRH) A hormone secreted by the hypothalamus that stimulates the pituitary gland to release thyroxine-stimulating hormone (TSH).

thyroxine-stimulating hormone (TSH) A hormone released by the pituitary that stimulates the thyroid gland to trap more iodine to produce more thyroid hormone (T_4 and T_3).

continued

The campaign was successful, and the use of iodized salt spread rapidly throughout the United States.

Consuming naturally occurring substances called **goitrogens,** found in foods such as rutabagas, cabbage, soybeans, and peanuts, can also result in a secondary deficiency and goiter if a person is iodine deficient. These antithyroid compounds reduce the absorption of iodide ions by the thyroid gland and decrease the amount of thyroid hormone released into the blood.

goitrogens Substances in food that reduce the utilization of iodine by the thyroid gland, resulting in goiter.

cretinism A condition caused by a deficiency of thyroid hormone during prenatal development, resulting in abnormal mental and physical development in children.

A deficiency of iodine during the early stages of fetal development can damage the brain of the developing baby, causing mental retardation. If the iodine deficiency is severe, **cretinism,** also known as *congenital hypothyroidism* (*congenital* = born with, *hypo* = under, *ism* = condition), can occur (**Figure 13.16**). Individuals with cretinism can experience abnormal sexual development, mental retardation, and dwarfism. Early detection of an iodine deficiency and treatment in women of childbearing age is critical to avoid irreversible damage in their offspring.

Consuming too much iodine can challenge the thyroid, impairing its function and reducing the synthesis and release of thyroxine. The result is similar to an iodine deficiency. Because of this, the upper level for adults for iodine is 1,100 micrograms. Pregnant women should avoid ingesting too much iodine from iodized salt and prenatal supplements to prevent fetal damage.

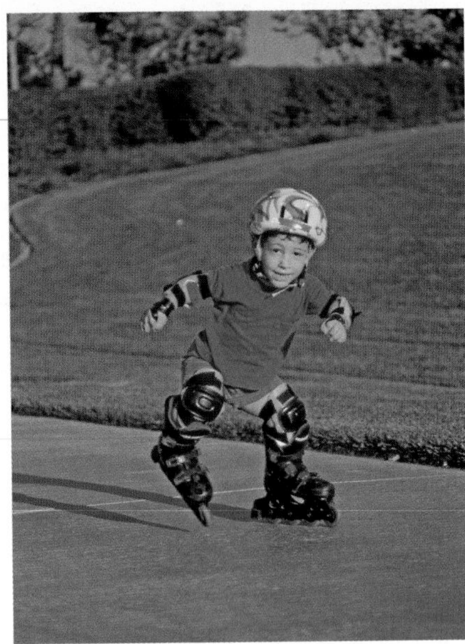

▲ **Figure 13.16 Cretinism**
Cretinism can result in a child born to a mother who was iodine deficient during the first few months of pregnancy when fetal development is the most active. The child can be born with stunted mental and physical development.

Exploring **Molybdenum**

What Is Molybdenum?

Molybdenum (Mo) is part of several metalloenzymes involved in the metabolism of certain amino acids and oxidation-reduction reactions. For example, molybdenum is a cofactor for sulfate oxidase, the mitochondrial enzyme that converts sulfite (SO_3^{-2}) to sulfate (SO_4^{-2}) in the metabolism of methionine and cysteine.

Daily Needs

The RDA for adult men and women is set at 45 micrograms of molybdenum daily. American women currently consume 76 micrograms and men consume 109 micrograms of molybdenum daily, on average.

Food Sources

Legumes are excellent sources of molybdenum. Other molybdenum-rich foods include grains, nuts, dairy products, and leafy green vegetables.[58]

Too Much or Too Little

There is limited research on the adverse effects of too much dietary molybdenum in humans. In animal studies, too much molybdenum can cause reproductive problems and kidney disorders. Because of this finding in animals, the upper level for molybdenum in humans has been set at 2 milligrams for adults.

A deficiency of molybdenum has not been seen in healthy individuals. However, a deficiency was observed in an individual who was fed intravenously using a molybdenum-deficient formula for years and developed symptoms that included rapid heartbeat, headaches, and night blindness.

Exploring **Manganese**

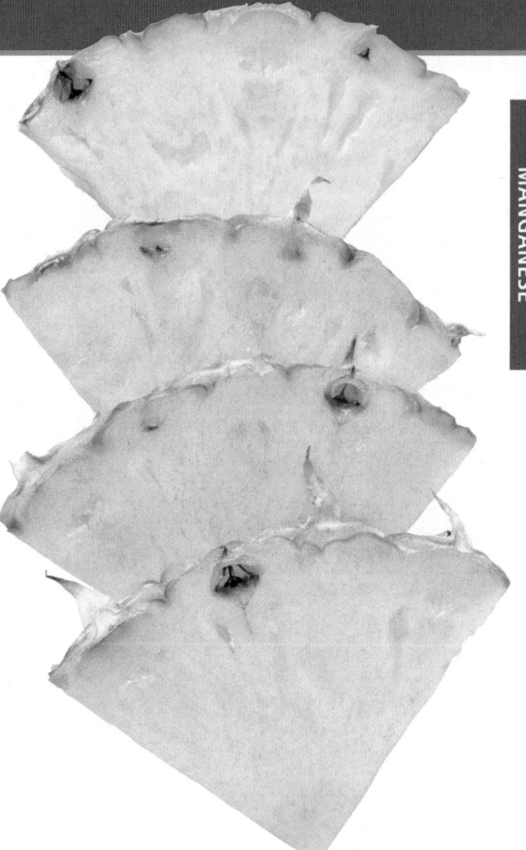

What Is Manganese?

Manganese (Mn) is a trace mineral that is either part of, or activates, many enzymes in the body. Much of the manganese in the body is found in bones and the accessory organs of the digestive tract, including the liver and pancreas.

Functions of Manganese

This mineral acts as a cofactor for a variety of metalloenzymes involved in the metabolism of carbohydrates, fats, and amino acids. For example, in glycolysis, the conversion of pyruvate to oxaloacetate in the TCA cycle requires manganese. Manganese participates in the formation of the bone matrix and helps build cartilage that supports the joints.

Daily Needs

The AI for manganese for adult women has been set at 1.8 milligrams, and at 2.3 milligrams for men. Americans are easily meeting their manganese needs. Adult women consume over 2 milligrams of manganese daily, and adult men consume over 2.8 milligrams daily, on average, from the foods in their diet.[59]

Food Sources

Manganese is prevalent in plant foods. Whole grains, nuts, legumes, tea, vegetables, and fruits such as pineapples, strawberries, and bananas are all robust sources of manganese (**Figure 13.17**). A teaspoon of ground cinnamon provides just under 0.5 milligram of manganese.

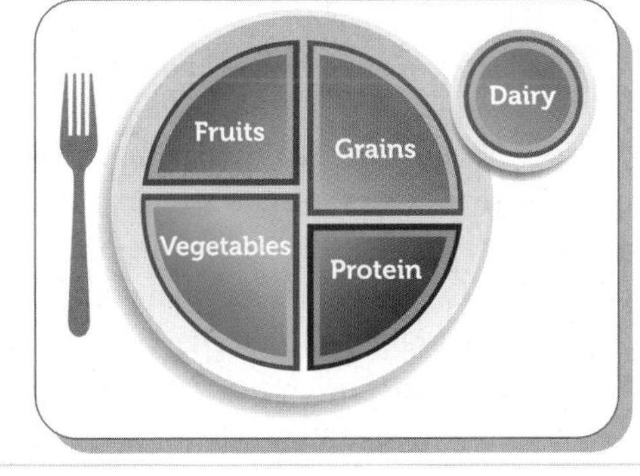

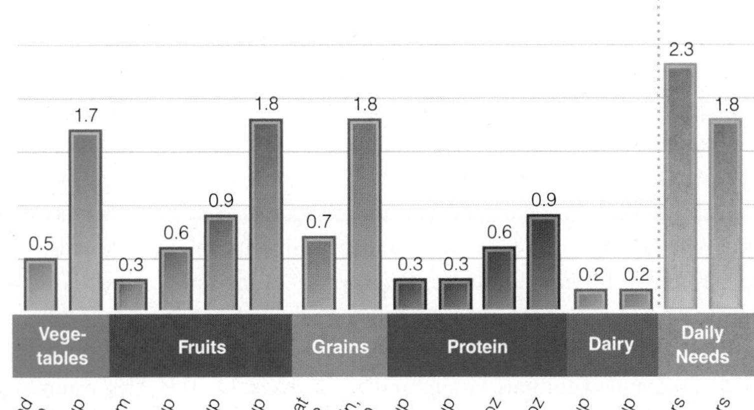

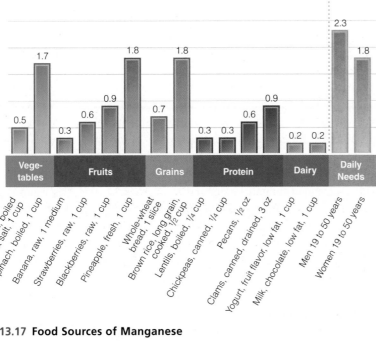

▲ **Figure 13.17 Food Sources of Manganese**

Too Much or Too Little

Manganese toxicity generally only occurs upon exposure to environmental pollutants, such as in manganese mining, battery manufacturing, and steel production.[60] For example, it has been reported in welders in the United States who inhaled manganese in the welding fumes due to lack of ventilation.[61] Toxicity can damage the nervous system and result in symptoms that resemble Parkinson's disease.[62]

While toxicity is usually due to environmental pollutants, there have been reports of toxicity resulting from dietary intake. Manganese is found naturally in soil and under certain circumstances naturally high levels can be found in ground water. A study of children in Canada who drank tap water with high levels of manganese showed lower IQ scores.[63] Most sources of water contain low levels (less than 10 μg/liter) of manganese. The Environmental Protection Agency (EPA) recommends that drinking water have no more than 50 μg/

continued

liter.[64] In addition, to protect against this toxicity, the tolerable upper level for dietary intake of manganese has been set at 11 milligrams daily.

A deficiency of manganese is rare in healthy individuals who consume a balanced diet. However, as with some other minerals, phytates can reduce the absorption of manganese. Excessive intake of other minerals from dietary supplements, including iron and calcium, may also reduce manganese absorption. Consuming a diet deficient in manganese can cause a rash and scaly skin.[65]

TABLE TIPS

Managing Manganese

Sprinkle whole-wheat toast with a dusting of cinnamon.

Combine cooked brown rice, canned and rinsed lentils, and chickpeas for dinner in a snap.

Spoon vanilla yogurt over canned crushed pineapples and sliced bananas for a tropical snack.

Arsenic, Boron, Nickel, Silicon, and Vanadium: Are They Important to Health?

A few other minerals exist in the body, but their nutritional importance in humans has not yet been established. These minerals include arsenic, boron, nickel, silicon, and vanadium. Whereas limited research suggests that these may have a function in animals, there isn't enough data to confirm an essential role in humans.[66]

Arsenic may be needed in the metabolism of a specific amino acid in rats. A deficiency may impair growth and reproduction in other animals. The best food sources of arsenic are dairy products, meat, poultry, fish, grains, and cereal products. There are no adverse toxicity effects in humans from the organic form of arsenic found in foods. The inorganic form is poisonous for humans.

A deficiency of boron may be associated with reproductive abnormalities in certain fish and frogs, which suggests a possible role in normal development in other animals. Grape juice, legumes, potatoes, pecans, peanut butter, apples, and milk are all good food sources of boron. No known adverse effect from boron has been reported from foods. Some research suggests that high amounts of boron may cause reproductive and developmental problems in animals. Because of this, the upper limit for human adults has been set at 20 mg daily, which is more than 10 times the amount American adults consume daily, on average.

Nickel may be needed by specific enzymes in the human body. It is considered an essential mineral in animals. Grains and grain products, vegetables, legumes, nuts, and chocolate are good sources of nickel. No known toxicity of nickel has been shown in humans when consuming a normal diet. In rats, high exposure to nickel salts can cause toxicity, with symptoms such as lethargy, irregular breathing, and a lower than normal weight gain. Because of this, the upper limit for adults is set at 1 mg daily for nickel salts.

Silicon may be needed for bone formation in animals. Grains, grain products, and vegetables are good sources of silicon. There is no known risk of silicon toxicity to animals from food sources.

Vanadium has insulin-like actions in animals. A deficiency of vanadium increases the risk of miscarriage. Vanadium can be purchased in supplement form, but mushrooms, shellfish, parsley, and black pepper are good food sources. There is no known risk of vanadium toxicity in humans by consuming foods. Too much vanadium has been shown to cause kidney damage in animals. Because of the known toxicity in animals, the upper limit for adults is set at 1.8 mg daily.

Putting It All Together

In their roles as cofactors, antioxidants, and parts of other compounds, trace minerals help perform numerous essential functions in the body (see Table 13.2). Trace minerals regulate the utilization of protein and carbohydrate for energy production. Without the proper amounts of trace minerals, the body would be unable to produce healthy red blood cells, fight infection, prevent oxidative damage to cells, and grow and develop properly. Like the other micronutrients, they are needed by the body in much smaller amounts than proteins, lipids, carbohydrate, or water. But as with all nutrients, insufficient amounts will lead to deficiency symptoms and, eventually, negative health effects. A varied diet that is robust in fruits, vegetables, and whole grains, as well as some animal products, will provide adequate amounts of all nutrients. As Table 13.3 shows, Americans are meeting many of their nutrient needs, but could improve their intake of some nutrients.

TABLE 13.2 Trace Minerals: Functions, Recommendations, Sources, Deficiency and Toxicity Symptoms, and Nutrient Interactions

Trace Mineral	Function	Adult AI or RDA	Daily Tolerable Upper Level	Excellent Food Sources	Deficiency Symptoms and Outcomes	Toxicity Symptoms and Outcomes	Interaction with Other Nutrients
Iron (Fe)	■ Major component of hemoglobin and myoglobin; carries oxygen and carbon dioxide ■ Part of cytochromes ■ Enhances immune system	Women: 18 mg/day Men: 8 mg/day	45 mg	Meat, fish, poultry, enriched and fortified breads and cereals	■ Fatigue ■ Microcytic anemia ■ Poor immune function ■ Growth retardation in infants	■ Vomiting, nausea, diarrhea, constipation ■ Organ damage, including the kidney and liver	■ Zinc ■ Calcium ■ Ascorbic acid
Copper (Cu)	■ A component of several metalloenzymes ■ Enzymes involved in iron metabolism ■ Connective tissue enzymes ■ Antioxidant enzymes	900 μg/day	10,000 μg	Cocoa, whole grains, legumes, and shellfish	■ Anemia ■ Impaired immune function ■ Impaired growth and development	■ Vomiting, abdominal pain, nausea, diarrhea ■ Liver damage	■ Zinc ■ Iron
Zinc (Zn)	■ Cofactor for several metalloenzymes ■ DNA and RNA synthesis ■ Part of the enzyme superoxide dismutase	Women: 8 mg/day Men: 11 mg/day	40 mg	Seafood, meat, whole grains	■ Skin rash and hair loss ■ Diarrhea ■ Loss of taste and smell ■ Depressed growth and development	■ Nausea, vomiting, cramps, diarrhea ■ Loss of appetite ■ Headaches ■ Impaired immune function	■ Iron ■ Calcium and phosphorus ■ Copper ■ Folate ■ Protein ■ Phytates

(continued)

TABLE 13.2 Trace Minerals: Functions, Recommendations, Sources, Deficiency and Toxicity Symptoms, and Nutrient Interactions *continued*

Trace Mineral	Function	Adult AI or RDA	Daily Tolerable Upper Level	Excellent Food Sources	Deficiency Symptoms and Outcomes	Toxicity Symptoms and Outcomes	Interaction with Other Nutrients
Selenium (Se)	■ A component of antioxidant enzymes	55 μg/day	400 μg	Meat, seafood, fish, eggs, whole grains	■ Muscle weakness and pain ■ May trigger Keshan disease	■ Brittle hair and nails ■ Skin rash ■ Garlic breath odor ■ Fatigue ■ Irritability	Unknown
Fluoride (F)	■ Part of fluoroapatite, which makes teeth stronger ■ Enhances bone formation	Women: 3 mg/day Men: 4 mg/day	10 mg	Fluoridated water, tea, seaweed	■ Increased susceptibility to dental caries	■ Fluorosis in teeth and skeletal fluorosis	■ Calcium
Chromium (Cr)	■ Improves insulin response	Women: 20–25 μg/day Men: 30–35 μg/day	Data insufficient to establish a UL	Pork, egg yolks, whole grains, nuts	■ Elevated postmeal blood glucose	■ Unconfirmed toxicity effects	■ Vitamin C ■ Phytates ■ Simple sugars
Iodine (I)	■ Component of the thyroid hormone thyroxine	150 μg/day	1,100 μg	Iodized salt, seafood, dairy products	■ Goiter ■ Cretinism	■ Thyroiditis ■ Goiter ■ Hypothyroidism and hyperthyroidism	Unknown
Molybdenum (Mo)	■ Cofactor for a variety of metalloenzymes	45 μg/day	2,000 μg	Legumes, nuts, leafy vegetables, dairy, cereals	Unknown in humans	Unknown in humans	Unknown
Manganese (Mn)	■ Cofactor for metalloenyzmes involved in carbohydrate metabolism	Women: 1.8 mg/day Men: 2.3 mg/day	11 mg	Beans, oats, nuts, tea	Unknown in humans	■ Abnormal central nervous system effects	■ Calcium ■ Iron ■ Phytates

TABLE 13.3 Putting It All Together: Making Better Nutrient Choices

American Adults Typically Consume Enough	But Could Improve Their Dietary Choices to Include More
Saturated fat	Unsaturated fat in place of saturated fat
Carbohydrates	Fiber-rich foods and fewer added sugars
Vitamins A, E, and K	Vitamin D if not exposed to adequate sunlight
B vitamins and vitamin C	Synthetic folic acid (premenopausal women only)
	Synthetic vitamin B_{12} (individuals 51+ years only; vegans)
Sodium, phosphorus, zinc, selenium, chromium, copper, iodine, manganese, molybdenum	Potassium, calcium, magnesium, iron (premenopausal women only; vegans), zinc (vegans), fluoride (if not consuming fluoridated water)
Fluids with added sugar	Fluids (water)

Visual Chapter Summary

1 Trace Minerals Are Essential Inorganic Nutrients

Trace minerals are inorganic elements the body needs in small amounts. The bioavailability and absorption of trace minerals are affected by soil content, nutrient status, and the composition of the diet. The bioavailability of trace minerals depends on the individual's nutrient status, other foods eaten at the same time, and the form of the mineral. Once absorbed, several trace minerals, including iron and zinc, are recycled repeatedly for use in the body. For this reason, toxicity can be a concern. Trace minerals function as cofactors that activate metalloenzymes and provide structure to the body; they help hormones function; and they are part of proteins such as hemoglobin.

2 Iron

Iron absorption is tightly controlled and depends on the iron status of the individual, the form of iron in the food, and the types of foods eaten together. Iron is stored as ferritin or hemosiderin and transported attached to transferrin. Iron functions as part of the oxygen-carrying transport proteins—hemoglobin in the red blood cells and myoglobin in the muscles. As part of cytochromes in the electron transport chain, iron is involved in energy production.

The RDA for iron is 18 milligrams per day for menstruating women and 8 milligrams per day for men and postmenopausal women. Heme iron is found in meat, poultry, and fish. Nonheme iron is found in plant foods, such as grains and vegetables. Nonheme iron is the predominant source of iron in the diet but isn't absorbed as readily as is heme iron.

Iron toxicity can lead to hemochromatosis and possibly death. Iron deficiency is the most common nutrient deficiency in the world. A deficiency of iron in children can impact their ability to learn and retain information. Iron-deficiency anemia can cause fatigue and weakness.

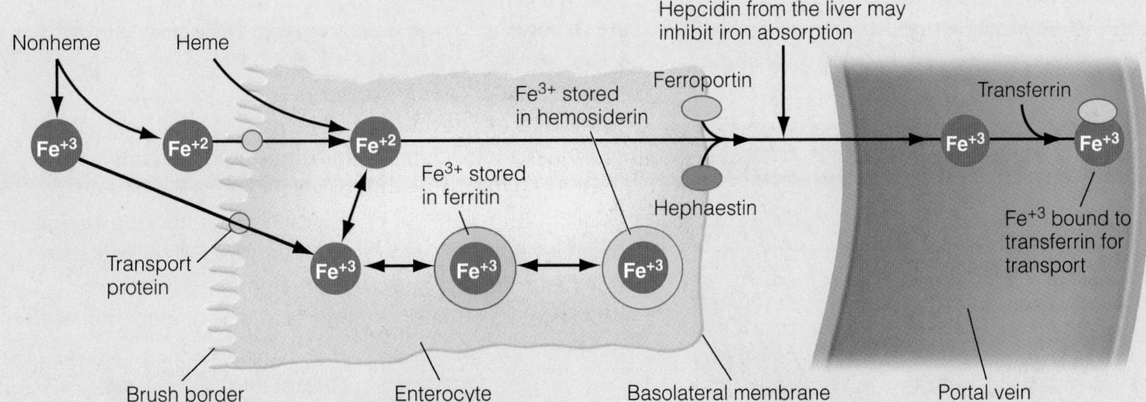

3 Copper

Copper status is regulated by absorption in the small intestine. Copper is absorbed attached to albumin. Very little copper is stored and most is excreted in the urine. Copper is part of the protein ceruloplasmin, which converts ferrous iron to ferric iron. Copper is thus necessary for the synthesis of hemoglobin and red blood cells. Copper is a cofactor for metalloenzymes involved in energy production and in the synthesis of connective tissue. Copper is part of the superoxide dismutase enzyme, which reduces free radical damage in cells.

The AI for copper is 900 micrograms for adults. Copper is found in a variety of foods, especially seafood, nuts, and seeds. Some genetic diseases result in the accumulation of copper and cause tissue damage and even death if left untreated.

A deficiency of copper results in anemia and weakened bones and connective tissue.

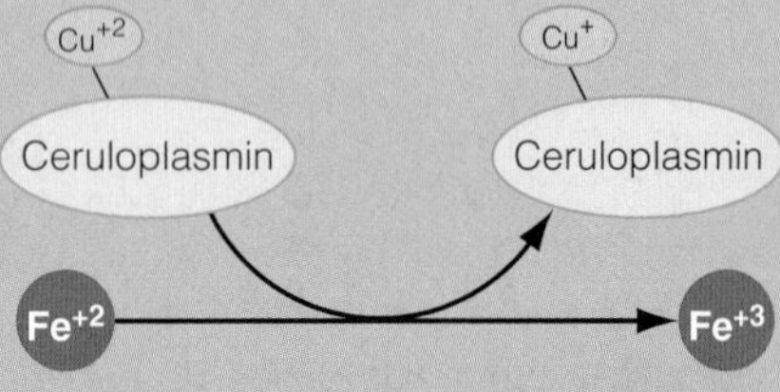

4 Zinc

Zinc plays a role in the structure of RNA and DNA, in taste acuity, and in helping prevent age-related macular degeneration (AMD). Zinc does not fight the common cold but zinc lozenges or gels used in nasal passages may reduce the duration of a cold.

The RDA for zinc is 11 mg per day for adult males and 8 mg per day for adult females. Meat, fish, and whole grains are good sources of zinc.

Consuming too much zinc can cause vomiting and diarrhea, suppress the immune system, and lower HDL cholesterol. Eating too little can impair growth, cause loss of hair and loss of appetite, and delay sexual maturation.

5 Selenium

Selenium is a component of a group of proteins called selenoproteins, which act as antioxidants in the body and may help fight cancer. Selenium also regulates thyroid function.

Adults need 55 micrograms of selenium per day. All food groups contribute selenium, including nuts, meat, and seafood.

Toxicity of selenium results in brittle teeth and fingernails, garlic odor in the breath, gastrointestinal problems, and damage to the nervous system. A deficiency of selenium can lead to Keshan disease, which damages the heart. Selenium deficiency may also result in changes in thyroid hormone production.

6 Fluoride

Fluoride is not an essential nutrient, but it helps maintain the structure of bones and teeth and helps prevent dental caries.

Adult males should consume 3.8 mg and women 3.1 milligrams of fluoride daily. The primary dietary source of fluoride is a fluoridated water supply and the consumption of foods and beverages prepared using fluoridated water.

In children, consumption of too much fluoride during tooth development can result in fluorosis. In adults, too much fluoride can cause skeletal fluorosis, which results in joint stiffness or pain, osteoporosis, and calcification of the ligaments.

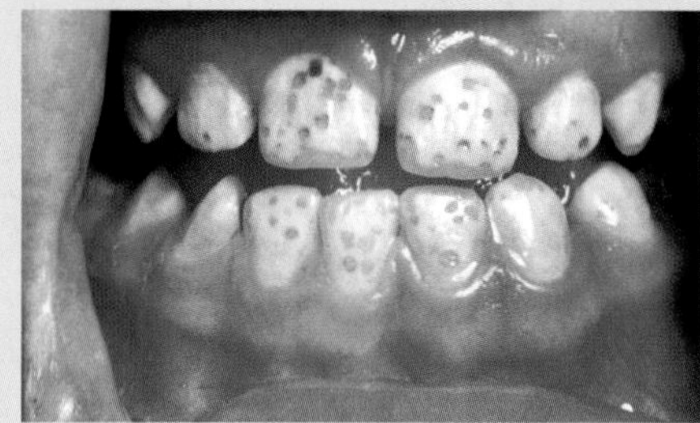

7 Chromium

Chromium helps insulin function, may improve the metabolism and storage of carbohydrates, fats, and protein, may reduce prediabetes, and may improve metabolic syndrome. It has not been proven to enhance weight loss or build muscle mass during exercise. Adult men need 30 to 35 micrograms of chromium daily and women need 20 to 25 micrograms daily. Many plant foods contain chromium, depending on the soil levels. Chromium toxicity by taking supplements interferes with iron metabolism. Deficiencies of chromium are very rare in the United States.

8 Iodine

Iodine is essential to make the thyroid hormones T_3 and T_4, which help regulate metabolic rate and stimulate growth and development. Adult men and women need only 150 micrograms of iodine daily. Iodine is found mostly in iodized salt, seafood, including shellfish, and dairy products. A deficiency of iodine during pregnancy causes mental retardation and cretinism in the offspring. A deficiency of iodine during adulthood causes simple goiter, which is characterized by an enlarged thyroid gland. Iodine toxicity causes both hypothyroidism and hyperthyroidism.

9 Molybdenum

Molybdenum is a cofactor for enzymes that synthesize proteins, including DNA and RNA. The RDA for adult men and women is 45 micrograms daily. Molybdenum is found in legumes, whole grains, and nuts. A deficiency of molybdenum causes cardiovascular problems and headaches. Molybdenum does not appear to be toxic in humans.

10 Manganese

Manganese assists enzymes involved in energy metabolism, and functions in synthesis of bone and as an antioxidant. The AI for manganese is 2.3 milligrams for men and 1.8 milligrams for women daily. Manganese is found in legumes, nuts, and whole grains. A deficiency of manganese causes poor growth, weak bones, and dry skin. Manganese is generally not toxic except due to environmental contamination.

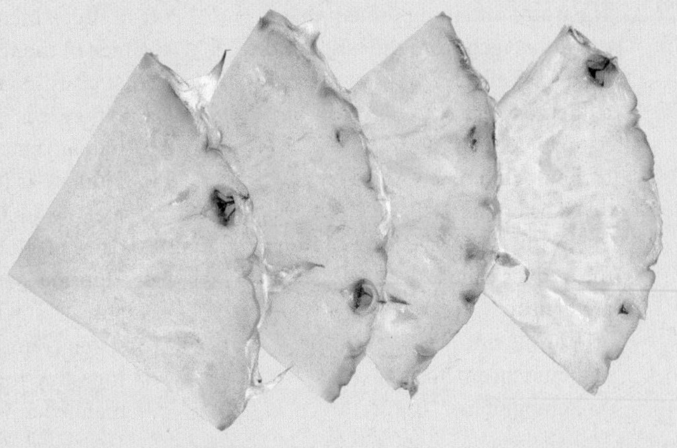

11 Other Minerals: Arsenic, Boron, Nickel, Silicon, and Vanadium

Other minerals, including arsenic, boron, nickel, silicon, and vanadium, may play a role in maintaining health. More research is needed to understand the role each of these trace minerals plays in the human body.

Terms to Know

- trace minerals
- metalloenzymes
- heme iron
- nonheme iron
- hemoglobin
- myoglobin
- ferric iron
- ferrous iron
- ferritin
- hemosiderin
- ferroportin
- transferrin
- hemochromatosis
- iron-deficiency anemia
- cupric
- cuprous
- ceruloplasmin
- metallothionine
- selenoproteins
- selenomethionine
- selenosis
- fluoroapatite
- fluorosis
- iodide
- goiter
- thyroxine
- thyroxine-releasing hormone (TRH)
- thyroxine-stimulating hormone (TSH)
- goitrogens
- cretinism

MasteringNutrition™

Build your knowledge—and confidence—in the Study Area of MasteringNutrition with a variety of study tools.

Check Your Understanding

1. The bioavailability of trace minerals is affected by
   a. the time of day you consume foods containing trace minerals.
   b. the form of the trace mineral.
   c. the protein content of your diet.
   d. the fat content of your diet.
2. The iron-containing protein that carries oxygen from the lungs to the tissues is called
   a. hemosiderin.
   b. myoglobin.
   c. hemoglobin.
   d. transferrin.
3. The primary storage form of iron in the body is called
   a. ferritin.
   b. transferrin.
   c. hemochromatosis.
   d. hemoglobin.
4. Copper is transported through the circulation by the blood protein called
   a. transferrin.
   b. albumin.
   c. hemoglobin.
   d. myoglobin.
5. A zinc deficiency may result in which of the following conditions?
   a. cretinism
   b. dental caries
   c. stunted growth
   d. the inability to reduce ferrous iron to ferric iron
6. Selenium may help prevent cancer due to its role as
   a. a toxin.
   b. an enzyme.
   c. an antioxidant.
   d. a supplement.
7. Which of the following statements is true regarding fluoride?
   a. Fluoride is considered an essential nutrient.
   b. Fluoride is found mostly in animal products such as meat and dairy products.
   c. Fluoride is part of the hydroxyapatite crystal that makes your teeth stronger and resistant to decay.
   d. Ingesting more than the recommended amount of fluoride increases your susceptibility to tooth decay.
8. Chromium increases the effectiveness of which hormone?
   a. thyroid-stimulating hormone
   b. insulin
   c. antidiuretic hormone (ADH)
   d. glucagon
9. The amount of manganese absorbed in the body is increased by
   a. a good source of phytates in the meal.
   b. the use of calcium supplements.
   c. the use of iron supplements.
   d. eating a manganese-rich diet.
10. The enlarged thyroid gland that is symptomatic of goiter is caused by
   a. iron deficiency.
   b. zinc deficiency
   c. iodine deficiency.
   d. selenium deficiency.

Answers

1. (b) The bioavailability of trace minerals in the food you consume can vary depending on the form of the mineral, your nutrient status, and the foods you chose to eat. The protein and fat content of the food does not influence trace mineral bioavailability, nor does the time of day the food is eaten.

2. (c) Hemoglobin is the iron-containing protein in red blood cells that carries oxygen. Hemoglobin exchanges oxygen with myoglobin, another protein found in muscle. Hemosiderin is the stored form of iron and transferrin is the protein that transports iron throughout the body.
3. (a) Ferritin is the primary storage form of iron in the body. Transferrin is the protein that transports iron. Hemochromatosis is a hereditary disorder in which the body absorbs and stores too much iron. Hemoglobin is found in red blood cells and contains heme.
4. (b) Albumin is the blood protein that transports copper. Transferrin transports iron, and hemoglobin and myoglobin are iron-containing proteins that participate in oxygen and carbon dioxide exchange.
5. (c) Zinc plays a significant role in growth and cell division. A deficiency of this trace mineral results in stunted growth. A deficiency of iodine during pregnancy results in cretinism. Fluoride makes the tooth enamel resistant to dental caries and copper functions as a cofactor to reduce ferrous iron to ferric iron.
6. (c) As part of selenoproteins, selenium functions as an antioxidant that protects cells from free radical damage.
7. (c). Fluoride, which is not considered an essential nutrient because the body doesn't require it for normal growth and development, makes up part of the hydroxyapatite crystal that strengthens tooth structure and helps the tooth resist decay. It is found mostly in fluoridated water, tea, and seaweed. Consuming too much fluoride can cause fluorosis, a discoloration of the teeth.
8. (b) Chromium increases insulin's effectiveness in cells. Iodine is needed to make thyroid hormones; ADH is the hormone that directs kidneys to minimize water loss and concentrate urine; and glucagon is the hormone that has the opposite effect to insulin, stimulating the release of glucose into the blood.
9. (d) Tissue levels of manganese are related to the amount present in your diet, thus eating a manganese-rich diet improves the amount of manganese absorbed. Phytates in food bind or inhibit the absorption of manganese, and other minerals in supplement form, such as iron and calcium supplements, decrease the absorption of manganese.
10. (c) Iodine deficiency results in goiter. Zinc deficiencies alter taste sensitivity; iron deficiencies cause microcytic anemia; and a deficiency of selenium may cause Keshan disease.

Answers to Myths and Misconceptions

1. **False.** Trace minerals are called *trace* because they are needed in small dietary amounts (less than 100 milligrams per day) and are found in small amounts in the body (less than 5 grams).
2. **False.** Although meat and seafood are rich sources of iron in the American diet, they are not the only sources. Enrichment and fortification processes make many bread products and cereals good sources of iron, as are some vegetables. Animal products contain heme iron, which is more bioavailable than the nonheme iron found in plant foods. Whole grains contain phytates and some vegetables contain oxalates, which reduce the bioavailability of nonheme iron.
3. **False.** Even though iron competes with other minerals, including zinc and copper, for binding to a transport protein in the small intestine, iron supplements do not appear to affect copper absorption or cause copper deficiency. Iron supplements do significantly reduce zinc absorption and could result in a zinc deficiency.
4. **False.** Zinc lozenges and gels do not prevent or cure the common cold. Some studies have reported that zinc lozenges or nasal gels may reduce the severity and duration of cold symptoms.
5. **True.** Excess selenium intake from dietary supplements is toxic. The symptoms include vomiting, diarrhea, fatigue, and hair loss.
6. **False.** Most bottled water sold in the United States does not contain fluoride. However, most tap water in the United States has been fluoridated.
7. **False.** Chromium supplementation does not appear to increase protein synthesis or have a beneficial effect on body composition or muscle mass.
8. **True.** While iodine is found in saltwater fish and in small amounts in dairy products, the only reliable source of iodine is iodized salt. Plants can be a good source of iodine, but only if they are grown in iodine-rich soil.
9. **True.** Two teaspoons of cinnamon contain 0.76 milligrams of manganese, or about 38 percent of the AI.
10. **False.** Vegetables are generally low in molybdenum. Other plant-based products such as legumes, nuts, and grains are considered good food sources of this trace mineral.

Web Resources

- To find out if your community water is fluoridated and how much fluoride is added, visit the Centers for Disease Control and Prevention's website, My Water's Fluoride, at http://apps.nccd.cdc.gov/MWF/Index.asp
- For more information on trace minerals, visit the U.S. Department of Health and Human Services' website at www.healthfinder.org
- For more information on iron and the symptoms associated with iron deficiency and iron overload, visit the Iron Overload Diseases Association at www.ironoverload.org
- Visit the American Cancer Society website for more information on selenium's role in cancer prevention at www.cancer.org.
- For more information on thyroid health, visit the American Thyroid Association at www.thyroid.org.

- For more information on the importance of minerals and mineral supplements visit MedlinePlus, a service of the U. S. National Library of Medicine and National Institutes of Health, at www.nlm.nih.gov/medlineplus.

References

1. Institute of Medicine. 2001. *Dietary Reference Intakes: Vitamin A, Vitamin K, Arsenic, Boron, Chromium, Copper, Iodine, Iron, Manganese, Molybdenum, Nickel, Silicon, Vanadium, and Zinc.* Washington, DC: The National Academies Press.
2. Olivares, M., F. Pizarro, and M. Ruz. 2007. New Insights About Iron Bioavailability Inhibition by Zinc. *Nutrition* 23:292–295.
3. Arredondo, M., R. Martinez, M. T. Nunez, M. Rus, and M. Olivares. 2006. Inhibition of Iron and Copper Uptake by Iron, Copper and Zinc. *Biological Research* 39:95–102.
4. Olivares, M., et al. 2007. New Insights About Iron Bioavailability.
5. Ibid.
6. Zijp, I. M., O. Korver, and L. B. M. Tijburg. 2000. Effect of Tea and Other Dietary Factors on Iron Absorption. *Critical Reviews in Food Science and Nutrition* 40:371–398.
7. Donovan, A., C. N. Roy, and N. C. Andrews. 2006. The Ins and Outs of Iron Homeostasis. *Physiology* 21:115–123.
8. Fuqua, B. K., C. D. Vulpe, and G. J. Anderson. 2012. Intestinal Iron Absorption. *Journal of Trace Elements in Medicine and Biology* 26:115-119.
9. Ganz, T. 2004. Hepcidin in Iron Metabolism. *Current Opinion in Hematology* 11:251–254.
10. Ibid.
11. Kuvibidila, S., and B. S. Baliga. 2002. Role of Iron in Immunity and Infection. In *Nutrition and Immune Function.* P. C. Calder, C. J. Field, and H. S. Gill, eds. New York: CABI Publishing.
12. Beard, J. 2003. Iron Deficiency Alters Brain Development and Functioning. *Journal of Nutrition* 133:1468S–1472S.
13. Black, M. M. 2003. Micronutrient Deficiencies and Cognitive Function. *Journal of Nutrition* 133:3927S–3931S.
14. Institute of Medicine. 2006. *Dietary Reference Intakes: The Essential Guide to Nutrient Requirements.* J. J. Otten, J. P. Helwig, and L. D. Meyers, eds. Washington, DC: The National Academies Press.
15. Britton, H. C. and C. E. Nossamn. 1986. Iron Content of Food Cooked in Iron Utensils. *Journal of the American Dietetic Association* 86:897–901.
16. Juurlink, D. N., M. Tenenbein, G. Koren, and D. A. Redelmeier. 2003. Iron Poisoning in Young Children: Association with the Birth of a Sibling. *Canadian Medical Association Journal* 168:1539–1542.
17. Ahluwalia, N., J. Sun, D. Krause, A. Mastro, and G. Handte. 2004. Immune Function Is Impaired in Iron-Deficient, Homebound, Older Women. *American Journal of Clinical Nutrition* 79:516–521.
18. Centers for Disease Control and Prevention. 2010. *Hemochromatosis (Iron Storage Disease).* Available at www.cdc.gov/ncbddd/hemochromatosis/index.html. Accessed May 2012.
19. Chen, H., G. Huang, T. Su, H. Gao, Z. K. Attieh, A. T. McKie, G. J. Anderson, and C. D. Vulpe. 2006. Decreased Hephaestin Activity in the Intestine of Copper-Deficient Mice Causes Iron Deficiency. *Journal of Nutrition* 136:1236–1241.
20. Turnlund, J. R. 2006. Copper. In *Modern Nutrition in Health and Disease.* M. E. Shils, M. Shike, A. C. Ross, B. Caballero, and R. J. Cousins, eds. Philadelphia: Lippincott Williams & Wilkins.
21. Institute of Medicine. 2001. *Dietary Reference Intakes: Vitamin A.*
22. Shankar, A. H. and A. S. Prasad. 1998. Zinc and Immune Function: The Biological Basis of Altered Resistance to Infection. *American Journal of Clinical Nutrition* 68:447S–463S.
23. Ibs, K. and L. Rink. 2003. Zinc-Altered Immune Function. *Journal of Nutrition* 133:1452S–1456S.
24. Farr, B. M. and J. M. Gwaltney. 1987. The Problems of Taste in Placebo Matching: An Evaluation of Zinc Gluconate for the Common Cold. *Journal of Chronic Disease* 40:875–879.
25. Singh, M. and R. R. Das. 2011. Zinc for the Common Cold. *Cochrane Database Systematic Review* 16:CD001364.
26. Hulisz, D. 2004. Efficacy of Zinc Against Common Cold Viruses: An Overview. *Journal of the American Pharmacology Association* 44:594–603.
27. Zafer, K., N. Bayram, and T. Atik. 2007. Effect of Zinc Sulfate on Common Cold in Children: Randomized, Double Blind Study. *Pediatrics International* 49:842–847.
28. Birmingham, C. L. and S. Gritzner. 2006. How Does Zinc Supplementation Benefit Anorexia Nervosa? *Eating and Weight Disorders* 11:e109–e111.
29. King, J. C. and R. J. Cousins. 2006. Zinc. In *Modern Nutrition in Health and Disease.* M. E. Shils, M. Shike, A. C. Ross, B. Caballero, and R. J. Cousins, eds. Philadelphia: Lippincott Williams & Wilkins.
30. Burk, R. F. and O. A. Levander. 2006. Selenium. In *Modern Nutrition in Health and Disease.* M. E. Shils, M. Shike, A. C. Ross, B. Caballero, and R. J. Cousins, eds. Philadelphia: Lippincott Williams & Wilkins.
31. Coombs, G. F. 2005. Current Evidence and Research Needs to Support a Health Claim for Selenium and Cancer Prevention. *Journal of Nutrition* 135:343–347.
32. Li, H., M. J. Stampfer, E. L. Giovannucci, J. S. Morris, W. C. Willett, M. Gaziano, and J. Ma. 2004. A Prospective Study on Plasma Selenium Levels and Prostate Cancer Risk. *Journal of the National Cancer Institute* 96:696–703.
33. FDA. 2012. *Summary of Qualified Health Claims Subject to Enforcement Discretion.* Available at www.fda.gov/Food/Labeling Nutrition/LabelClaims/Qualified HealthClaims/ucm073992.htm#selenium. Accessed May 2012.
34. Beck, M. A., O. A. Levander, and O. Handy. 2003. Selenium Deficiency and Viral Infection. *Journal of Nutrition* 133:1463S–1467S.
35. Turker, O., K. Kumanlioglu, I. Karapolat, and I. Dogan. 2006. Selenium Treatment in Autoimmune Thyroiditis: 9 Month Follow-Up with Variable Doses. *Journal of Endocrinology* 290:151–156.
36. Gartner, R., B. C. H. Gasnier, J. W. Dietrich, B. Krebs, and M. W. A. Angstwurm. 2002. Selenium Supplementation in Patients with Autoimmune Thyroiditis Decreases Thyroid Peroxidase Antibodies Concentrations. *Journal of Clinical Endocrinology and Metabolism* 87:1687–1691.
37. American Dental Association. *2005 Fluoridation Facts.* Available at www.ada.org/sections/newsAndEvents/pdfs/fluoridation_facts.pdf. Accessed May 2012.
38. Centers for Disease Control and Prevention. 2011. *Dental Fluorosis.* Available at www.cdc.gov/fluoridation/safety/dental_fluorosis.htm. Accessed May 2012.
39. Institute of Medicine. 2006. *Dietary Reference Intakes: The Essential Guide to Nutrient Requirements.*
40. Centers for Disease Control and Prevention. 2012. *Community Water Fluoridation. Fact Sheet.* Available at www.cdc.gov/fluoridation/fact_sheets/index.htm. Accessed May 2012.
41. Centers for Disease Control and Prevention. 2012. *Fluoridation Basics.* Available at www.cdc.gov/fluoridation/benefits/background.htm. Accessed May 2012.
42. Centers for Disease Control and Prevention. 2012. *Community Water Fluoridation.*
43. Mertz, W. 1993. Chromium in Human Nutrition: A Review. *Journal of Nutrition* 123:626–633.
44. Institute of Medicine. 2006. *Dietary Reference Intakes: The Essential Guide to Nutrient Requirements.*
45. Ibid.
46. Chen, G., P. Liu, and G. R. Pattar. 2006. Chromium Activates Glucose Transporter 4 Trafficking and Enhances Insulin-Stimulated Glucose Transport in 3T3-L1 Adipocytes via a Cholesterol-Dependent Mechanism. *Molecular Endocrinology* 20:857–870.
47. Ibid.
48. Hummel, M., E. Standl, and O. Schnell. 2007. Chromium in Metabolic and Cardiovascular Disease. *Hormone and Metabolic Research* 39:743–751.
49. Lau, F. C., M. Bagchi, C. K. Sen, and D. Bagchi. 2008. Nutrigenomic Basis of Beneficial Effects of Chromium (III) on Obesity and Diabetes. *Molecular and Cellular Biochemistry* 317:1–10.

50. Cefalu, W. T. and F. B. Hu. 2004. Role of Chromium in Human Health and in Diabetes. *Diabetes Care* 27:2741–2751.
51. Diaz, M. L., B. A. Watkins, Y. Li., R. A. Anderson, and W. W. Campbell. 2008. Chromium Picolinate and Conjugated Linoleic Acid Do Not Synergistically Influence Diet- and Exercise-Induced Changes in Body Composition and Health Indexes in Overweight Women. *Journal of Nutritional Biochemistry* 19:61–68.
52. Lukaski, H. C., W. A. Siders, and J. G. Penland. 2007. Chromium Picolinate Supplementation in Women: Effects on Body Weight, Composition, and Iron Status. *Nutrition* 23:187–195.
53. Institute of Medicine. 2006. *Dietary Reference Intakes: The Essential Guide to Nutrient Requirements.*
54. Lukaski, H. C., et al. 2007. Chromium Picolinate Supplementation.
55. Roussel, A. M., M. Andriollo-Sanchez, M. Ferry, N. A. Bryden, and R. A. Anderson. 2007. Food Chromium Content, Dietary Chromium Intake and Related Biological Variables in French Free-Living Elderly. *British Journal of Nutrition* 98:326–331.
56. Dunn, J. T. 2006. Iodine. In *Modern Nutrition in Health and Disease.* M. E. Shils, M. Shike, A. C. Ross, B. Caballero, and R. J. Cousins, eds. Philadelphia: Lippincott Williams & Wilkins.
57. Institute of Medicine. 2001. *Dietary Reference Intakes: Vitamin A.*
58. Ibid.
59. Ibid.
60. Santamaria, A. B. 2008. Manganese Exposure, Essentiality and Toxicity. *Indian Journal of Medical Research* 128:484–500.
61. Antonini, J. M., A. B. Santamaria, N. T. Jenkins, E. Albini, and R. Lucchini. 2006. Fate of Manganese Associated with the Inhalation of Welding Fumes: Potential Neurological Effects. *Neurotoxicology* 27:304–310.
62. Barceloux, D. G. 1999. Manganese. *Clinical Toxicology* 37:293–307.
63. Bouchard, M. F., S. Sebastien, B. Barbeau, M. Legrand, M. Brodeur, T. Bouffard, E. Limoges, et al. 2010. Intellectual Impairment in School-Age Children Exposed to Manganese from Drinking Water. *Environmental Health Perspective* 119:138–143.
64. Environmental Protection Agency. 2007. *Drinking Water Contaminants.* Available at http://water.epa.gov/drink/contaminants/index.cfm. Accessed May 2012.
65. Friedman, B. J., J. H. Freeland-Graves, C. W. Bales, et al. 1987. Manganese Balance and Clinical Observations in Young Men Fed a Manganese-Deficient Diet. *Journal of Nutrition* 117:133–143.
66. Institute of Medicine. 2001. *Dietary Reference Intakes: Vitamin A.*

14 Energy Balance and Body Composition

Chapter Objectives

After reading this chapter, you will be able to:

1. Define the terms energy balance, positive energy balance, and negative energy balance as they relate to body weight.
2. Explain the factors that contribute to total daily energy expenditure (TDEE), including basal metabolic rate (BMR), thermic effect of food (TEF), thermic effect of exercise (TEE), and adaptive thermogenesis.
3. Calculate BMR and estimated energy requirement (EER) using equations and physical activity factors.
4. Define the term body composition, and explain the methods used to assess lean body mass and body fat.
5. Define the term healthy body weight and explain the limitations of the various methods used to estimate a healthy body weight.
6. Explain how body fat and fat distribution can affect health.

1. Exercise isn't necessary to lose weight. T/F
2. Being skinny is always healthier than being overweight. T/F
3. Men burn more kilocalories than women. T/F
4. BMI can be used to determine if you are at a healthy weight, overweight, or obese. T/F
5. Storing fat around the hips is as unhealthy as storing it around the waist. T/F
6. Body composition is the same thing as body weight. T/F
7. Eating an excess 100 kilocalories per day will result in a weight gain of a pound a week. T/F
8. Skinfold calipers are the most accurate way to measure body composition. T/F
9. Women should aim for less than 5 percent body fat. T/F
10. Overweight people are more likely to experience sleep apnea. T/F

See page 534 for answers to these Myths and Misconceptions.

Flip through a magazine, watch a little television, or spend some time online, and before long you'll find someone talking about body fat and cutting kilocalories to lose weight. In fact, body weight and how to achieve weight loss comprise one of the most frequently covered health stories in the media. Do you count every kilocalorie you eat? Do you wonder if your current weight is a healthy one?

In this chapter, we'll discuss the concept of energy balance, the methods used to assess energy intake and energy expenditure, and the factors that influence body weight and body composition.

What Is Energy Balance and Why Is It Important?

The concept of **energy balance** can be boiled down to five simple words: energy in versus energy out. In short, the amount of energy (in the form of kilocalories) consumed needs to equal the amount expended so that the body does not store the excess kilocalories as fat or break down stored fat for energy. This energy balance equation is one of the most important factors influencing body weight and body composition.

An Energy Imbalance Results in Weight Gain or Loss

Body weight remains constant when the energy equation is balanced. If energy intake is greater than the amount of energy expended, the body is in a state of **positive energy balance** (**Figure 14.1**). In this situation, weight gain can occur from an increase in muscle mass, an increase in adipose tissue, or both. Positive energy balance is essential during growth periods such as pregnancy, infancy, childhood, and adolescence. Strength training requires a positive energy balance to increase muscle mass, and when the body is in a state of repair following surgery or an illness. However, nonpregnant, healthy adults will experience an unhealthy weight gain if they are in a regular state of positive energy balance. Even a small but chronic positive energy balance can result in weight gain over time. For every 3,500 excess kilocalories consumed, about a pound of body weight is gained. So if an individual takes in 100 excess kilocalories per day, he or she will gain a little less than one pound after one month, and about 10 pounds after one year. Most likely this weight gain will be stored as fat in the adipose tissue.

A **negative energy balance** occurs when the amount of energy ingested doesn't meet the energy output. Negative energy balance occurs if food intake is reduced, if more kilocalories are expended through exercise than consumed in foods, or both. When less energy is consumed, energy needs are met by mobilizing energy reserves such as stored fat. The result of a negative energy balance is usually weight loss, mostly from adipose tissue. However, some of the weight loss may reflect a decrease in muscle mass, stored glycogen, and water.

The energy balance equation appears to be quite simple. If we would simply consume the same number of kilocalories as we expend, we could maintain a healthful body weight. However, energy balance is more complex than it seems.

energy balance The state at which energy (kilocalorie) intake from food and beverages is equal to energy (kilocalorie) output from BMR and physical activity.

positive energy balance The state in which energy intake is greater than energy expenditure. Over time, this results in weight gain.

negative energy balance The state in which energy intake is less than energy expenditure. Over time, this results in weight loss.

Food and Beverages Provide Energy In

As you learned in earlier chapters, the kilocalories that make up energy intake come from the carbohydrates, proteins, fats, and alcohol found in foods and beverages.

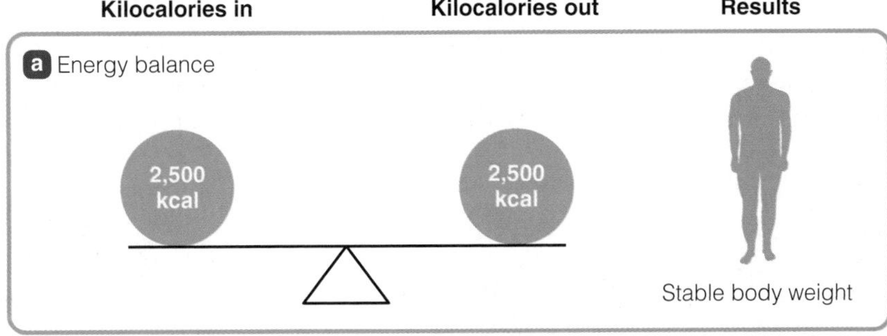

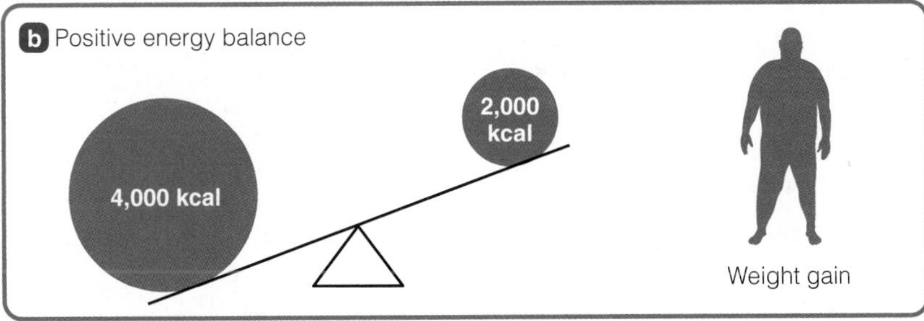

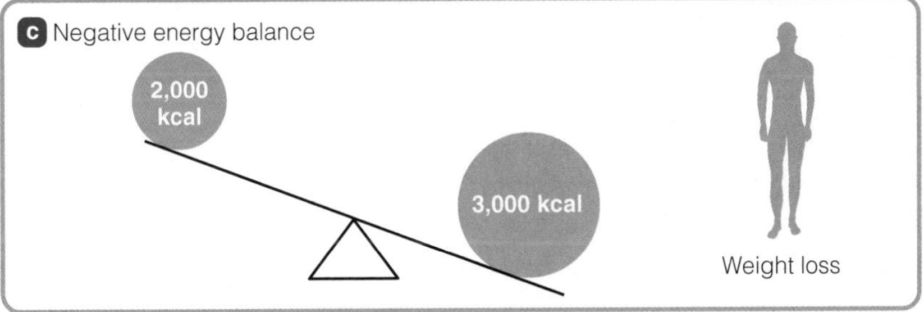

▲ **Figure 14.1 The Concept of Energy Balance**
A chronic state of positive or negative energy balance will result in a change in body weight.

The number of kilocalories found in a given food or beverage can be determined in one of two ways: either in a lab using a **bomb calorimeter,** or by calculating the grams of carbohydrate, fat, protein, and alcohol in the food.

A bomb calorimeter (**Figure 14.2**) determines the amount of energy in a food by burning the food and measuring the amount of heat produced. The energy released when the chemical bonds in the food are broken raises the temperature of the water in the calorimeter. Because one kilocalorie is the heat required to raise the temperature of one kilogram of water one degree Celsius, the rise in water temperature indicates the amount of kilocalories in the food.

The burning of food also releases carbon and hydrogen, which combine with oxygen to form carbon dioxide and water. Hence, measuring the amount of oxygen consumed during combustion in the calorimeter provides an indirect measurement of the energy content of a food.

The body is not as efficient as a bomb calorimeter and does not completely digest or metabolize the kilocalories it consumes. The energy that isn't oxidized to yield carbon dioxide and water is stored as either glycogen or body fat. The kilocalorie values obtained from a bomb calorimeter must be adapted to reflect the inefficiency of the body. These corrected values are called **physiological fuel values** and reflect the kilocalories actually transformed into energy in the body. These are the caloric values presented in food composition tables and databases.

Because bomb calorimeters are available only in laboratories, most individuals who want to estimate energy intake use nutrition analysis software or food

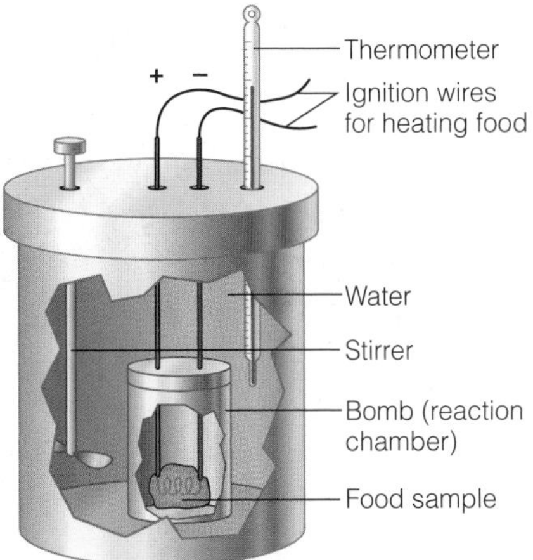

▲ **Figure 14.2 A Bomb Calorimeter Measures Energy in Foods**
A bomb calorimeter directly measures the kilocalorie content of food by measuring the heat released during combustion.

bomb calorimeter An instrument used to measure the amount of heat released from food during combustion; the amount of heat produced is directly related to the amount of kilocalories in a given food.

physiological fuel values The real energy value of foods that are digested and absorbed; they are adjusted from the results of bomb calorimetry because of the inefficiency of the body.

composition tables to calculate the kilocalories contained in foods. These resources provide the kilocalorie content of a given food as calculated by multiplying the grams of macronutrient in the food by the kilocalories contained in each gram (see the Calculation Corner).

Calculation Corner

Calculating the Energy Content of a Meal

Calculate the total energy content of this breakfast meal using the fuel values of 4 kilocalories per gram for carbohydrates and protein, and 9 kilocalories per gram for fat.

Food	Carbohydrate (g)	Protein (g)	Fat (g)		Kilocalories
½ cup cooked oatmeal	12	3	0	=	_______
½ cup nonfat milk	6	4	0	=	_______
½ cup orange juice	12	0	0	=	_______
2 slices whole-wheat toast	30	6	2	=	_______
1 tbs margarine	0	0	10	=	_______
8 fl oz coffee	0	0	0	=	_______
Total kilocalories				=	_______

(a) Complete the table by calculating the total kilocalories for each food. Multiply the fuel value of each macronutrient by the number of grams found in each food. For example, 1/2 cup of cooked oatmeal would be calculated as follows:

Total kcal = (12 g carbohydrate × 4 kcal/g) + (3 g protein × 4 kcal/g) + (0 g fat × 9 kcal/g)

Total kcal = 60 kcal

(b) After you have calculated the total kilocalories for each food, add the kilocalories for each food together to determine the total kilocalories for the meal.

Body Processes and Physical Activity Result in Energy Out

The other side of the energy equation is the expenditure of energy. Differences in *basal metabolism*, the *thermic effect of food* (TEF), *the thermic effect of exercise* (TEE), and *adaptive thermogenesis* mean that the energy needed throughout the day will vary for every individual. Knowing your energy expenditure provides the basis for either establishing energy balance to maintain weight or creating an energy imbalance to gain or lose weight.

THE TAKE-HOME MESSAGE Energy balance is the relationship between energy intake and energy expenditure. In positive energy balance, more kilocalories are consumed than expended, resulting in weight gain. In negative energy balance, more kilocalories are expended than consumed, resulting in weight loss.

How Is Total Daily Energy Expenditure Calculated?

total daily energy expenditure (TDEE) The total kilocalories needed to meet daily energy requirements; based on basal metabolism, physical activity, the thermic effect of food, and adaptive thermogenesis.

The number of kilocalories necessary to balance the energy in with the energy out, called the **total daily energy expenditure (TDEE),** has several components.

Basal and Resting Metabolic Rate Contribute to TDEE

The energy needed to fuel the body's vital functions, such as pumping blood, expanding the lungs, and brain function, is known as its **basal metabolism** and is expressed as a **basal metabolic rate (BMR).** This is the amount of energy spent to meet the body's basic physiological needs when it's at physical, emotional, and digestive rest, but not asleep—in other words, the minimum amount of energy needed to keep your awake, resting body alive. If you sit on the couch to watch television, you aren't engaged in any physical activity but your body is still active at a cellular level and requires energy for its basic functions.

Approximately 60 percent of your total daily energy kilocalories is determined by BMR (**Figure 14.3**). The factor that most affects BMR is **lean body mass (LBM).** Lean body mass is defined as the muscle, bone, and other nonfat tissue that makes up your body weight. Because lean body mass is more active tissue than body fat, it burns kilocalories at a higher rate than stored fat, even at rest. Thus, the more lean body mass you have, the greater your BMR—about 70 percent of your BMR is attributable to the metabolic activity of your LBM. Additional factors such as age, gender, body size, genes, ethnicity, emotional and physical stress, thyroid hormone levels, nutritional state, and environmental temperature, as well as caffeine and nicotine intake, affect BMR. Table 14.1 on page 516 explains each of these factors.

BMR, which is determined by an indirect measurement of the amount of oxygen consumed, is measured when a person is awake and cellular activity is the lowest. To get an accurate BMR measurement, your sympathetic nervous system cannot be stimulated. This is the reason a person's BMR is usually measured in a laboratory setting in the morning while the person lies motionless in a controlled (no shivering or sweating) environment after a 12-hour overnight fast. Neither the digestion of food nor physical activity (which both require energy) is factored into the BMR.

Because such precise circumstances are needed to measure BMR, it is a challenge to obtain. For this reason, the **resting metabolic rate (RMR)** is often used instead. The RMR is the amount of energy used by the body, measured when the person is lying calmly after only a 3- to 4-hour fasting period. The RMR is about 6 percent higher than the BMR, as it reflects increases in energy expenditure related to any recent food intake or physical activity.

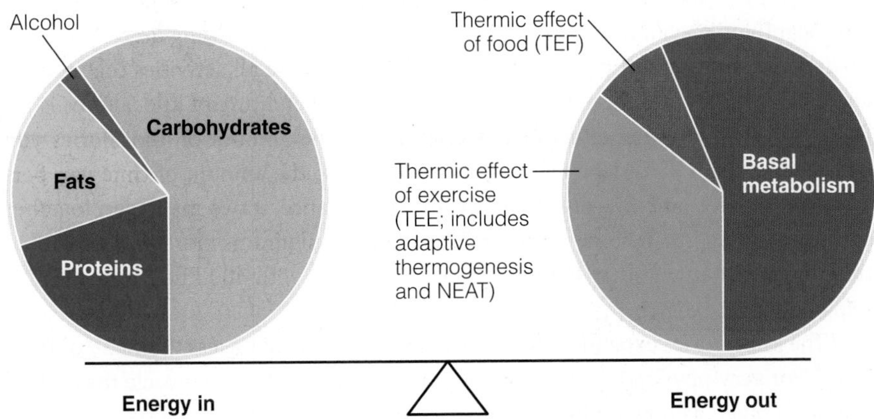

▲ **Figure 14.3 Requirements for the Total Daily Energy Expenditure**
The amount of total energy expended during a 24-hour period is comprised of an individual's basal metabolism, the thermic effect of exercise or physical activity, and the thermic effect of foods. A sedentary individual will expend a larger percentage of energy from basal metabolism compared with an active person who would have a greater need for energy to fuel physical activity.

basal metabolism The amount of energy expended by the body to meet its basic physiological needs, including muscle tone and heart and brain function.

basal metabolic rate (BMR) The measure of basal metabolism taken when the body is at rest in a warm, quiet environment, after a 12-hour fast; expressed as kilocalories per kilogram of body weight per hour.

lean body mass (LBM) Total body weight minus the fat mass; it consists of water, bones, vital organs, and muscle. LBM is the metabolically active tissue in the body.

resting metabolic rate (RMR) The measure of the amount of energy expended by the body at rest and after approximately a 3- to 4-hour fasting period. This rate is about 6 percent higher than BMR.

TABLE 14.1 Factors That Affect Basal Metabolism

Factor	Explanation
Lean body mass	Lean body mass, which is mostly muscle mass, is more metabolically active than fat tissue, so more kilocalories are needed to maintain it. Athletes who have a large percentage of lean body mass due to their increased muscle mass will have a higher BMR than individuals who aren't athletic.
Age	For adults, BMR declines about 1 to 2 percent per decade after the early adult years but it increases by 15 percent during pregnancy. For children, BMR increases during times of rapid growth such as infancy and adolescence.
Gender	Women have less lean body mass, and typically have a higher percentage of body fat than men. This results in women having a BMR up to 10 percent lower than men's. Women also tend to have a smaller body size. (See below.)
Body size	Taller individuals will have a higher BMR due to increased surface area compared with shorter individuals. More surface area means more heat lost from the body, which causes the metabolism rate to increase to maintain the body's temperature.
Genes	Research suggests that genes may affect BMR, as individuals within families have similar metabolic rates.
Ethnicity	African-Americans have BMRs that are about 10 percent lower than those of Caucasians.
Stress	Hormones such as epinephrine, which are released during emotional stress, increase BMR. Physiological stress on the body caused by injury, fever, burns, and infections also causes the release of hormones that raise BMR. Heat loss from the body through wounds, as well as the response of the immune system during infection, increase BMR.
Hormones	An increase in thyroid hormone increases BMR, whereas too little of this hormone lowers BMR. Hormone fluctuations during a woman's menstrual cycle lower BMR during the phase before ovulation.
Starvation	Starvation and fasting for more than about 48 hours lower BMR.
Environmental temperature	Being very cold or very hot can increase BMR. The change is minimal if clothing or air temperature are adjusted.
Caffeine	Caffeine can raise BMR, but only slightly when consumed regularly in moderate amounts.
Drugs	Nicotine may increase BMR.* Stimulant drugs such as amphetamine and ephedrine increase BMR.

*Note: Smoking is not a weight-management strategy. Some people may think that replacing snacks with cigarettes helps them stay slim, but the health risks associated with smoking, such as lung cancer, heart disease, and stroke, make it a foolish habit. Anyone concerned about weight gain when quitting smoking can minimize the chances of this with exercise.

Data from Food and Nutrition Board, National Institute of Medicine, *Dietary Reference Intakes: The Essential Guide to Nutrient Requirements* (Washington, DC: The National Academies Press, 2006).

Energy Is Used for Physical Activity or Exercise

While BMR accounts for the largest proportion of energy expenditure, the heat produced by contracting muscle during physical activity or exercise can contribute significantly to the amount of energy expended each day. Walking across campus, vacuuming your home, or pulling weeds in the garden are all activities that require energy above the minimum needed for BMR. This expenditure of kilocalories is referred to as the **thermic effect of exercise (TEE).** The amount of kilocalories you need each day for TEE depends on the activity itself, the amount of time you perform the activity, and how much you weigh. For instance, if two males run together at the same pace for an hour, but one male weighs 10 kilograms more than the other, the heavier male will burn 496 kilocalories compared with 400 kilocalories for his lighter running partner.

The kilocalories expended for TEE for sedentary people is less than half of their BMR. For very physically active individuals who have a greater muscle mass, TEE can be as much as double their BMR. In short, the more physical activity an individual incorporates into a daily routine, the more kilocalories he can consume to maintain energy balance. For example, two females who weigh the same and are similar in age both have a BMR of 1,200 kilocalories. One female is sedentary and her TEE is only 600 kilocalories, while the second female has a much higher TEE of 2,000 kilocalories because of her physically active lifestyle. Based on her TEE,

thermic effect of exercise (TEE) This refers to the increase in muscle contraction that occurs during physical activity, which produces heat and contributes to the total daily energy expenditure.

non-exercise activity thermogenesis (NEAT) The energy expended for all activities not related to sleeping, eating, or exercise, including fidgeting, performing work-related activities, and playing.

thermic effect of food (TEF) The amount of energy expended by the body to digest, absorb, transport, metabolize, and store energy-yielding nutrients from foods.

the sedentary female can only consume 1,800 kilocalories per day (BMR + TEE) to maintain energy balance and not gain weight. In contrast, because of her higher TEE, the physically active female must eat 3,200 kilocalories per day to meet her energy requirements and not lose weight. Further, the amount of energy expended during physical activity goes beyond the activity itself. Exercise causes a small increase in energy expenditure for some time after the activity has stopped because of the recovery and adaptation the body undergoes following the exercise.[1]

In addition to the energy required to walk, talk, run, and climb stairs, TEE also includes the cost of energy to maintain posture and body position. This form of energy expenditure is called **non-exercise activity thermogenesis,** or **NEAT.** NEAT also includes the energy expended for fidgeting and other activities we don't normally consider exercise. NEAT may play a key role in energy balance. Adults who fidget or are hyperactive tend to burn more kilocalories than people who are more placid.[2] While sitting in front of a computer all day does expend kilocalories, the amount is minimal.[3] Read Examining the Evidence: What Is NEAT about Fidgeting? for more information on the influence of NEAT on energy expenditure.

Once you crawl out of bed in the morning, the kilocalories you expend to stretch, take a shower, and get dressed are classified as TEE.

Energy Used for Digestion and Absorption Is Called the Thermic Effect of Food (TEF)

In addition to BMR and TEE, kilocalories are needed to digest and absorb the foods you eat, called the **thermic effect of food (TEF).** The body uses energy to process the macronutrients and extract kilocalories from foods. Immediately after eating and for several hours after a meal, energy expenditure increases to provide ATP for peristalsis, digestion, absorption, and transport of nutrients. Approximately 10 percent of the kilocalories in food consumed is used for TEF. In other words, about 10 kilocalories in a 100-kilocalorie cookie will be used to process the cookie. This concept is similar to that of gross versus net salary. Although an individual receives a gross salary, taxes and deductions will result in his ultimately receiving less than that amount. Likewise due to TEF, the gross kilocalories found in a food are slightly more than the net amount available for BMR and physical activity.

The type of nutrients consumed will influence the TEF. For instance, a meal high in protein has the highest thermic effect (approximately 20 to 30 percent), probably because of the synthesis of body proteins after a protein meal. Carbohydrates have a greater TEF (5 to 10 percent) than fat (0 to 3 percent), most likely due to the energy cost to convert glucose into glycogen. The energy cost of converting fat into stored triglycerides is minimal. Other factors that influence the TEF, such as composition of a meal, alcohol intake, age, and athletic training status, are presented in Table 14.2 on page 520. A trained athlete appears to be able to digest and absorb food with fewer kilocalories TEF than the untrained. An obese individual also has a lower TEF, but the reason is most likely related to an inefficient or impaired TEF. Note that the amount of kilocalories used for TEF is small compared with the amount expended by BMR and physical activity.

The process of digesting and absorbing foods requires energy called the thermic effect of food.

Energy Is Used for Adaptive Thermogenesis

Energy can also be expended by producing heat (**thermogenesis**). *Adaptive thermogenesis* is the body's regulation of heat production, influenced by environmental changes such as stress, temperature, or diet, which result in a change in metabolism. Shivering when the temperature drops is an example of adaptive thermogenesis.

Experts are still not sure how adaptive thermogenesis relates to total daily energy expenditure. The ability to regulate how much heat is produced from food

thermogenesis The generation of heat from the basal metabolism, digestion of food, and physical activity that provides necessary warmth; *adaptive thermogenesis* and *non-exercise activity thermogenesis (NEAT)* are other terms used to describe specific aspects of the generation of heat.

EXAMINING THE EVIDENCE

What Is NEAT About Fidgeting?

Fidgeting is one aspect of the energy expenditure referred to as NEAT, or non-exercise activity thermogenesis.[1] The term NEAT, coined by cardiologist Dr. James A. Levine, is a component of TEE that refers to the energy we expend for everything we do while awake except eating or participating in structured exercise such as jogging, aerobics, or power walking. NEAT includes walking to work, dancing, gardening, and, yes, even fidgeting.

As a nation, the less often we move, the more obese we become.[2] Research has reported a strong correlation between a drop in NEAT and an increase in weight gain, specifically body fat.[3] Studies report that lean people who are sedentary stand and move 152 minutes longer per day than obese individuals do. And obese subjects sit 164 minutes per day (over 2.5 hours) more than lean subjects. In other words, people who are classified as obese have low NEAT.[4] Sitting, it would seem, increases your risk of obesity and all of the health risks associated with excess weight.

The amount of kilocalories burned by NEAT activities can vary substantially between individuals. Levine and colleagues report that NEAT can vary by almost 2,000 kilocalories per day.[5] What accounts for these large differences in daily energy expenditure? Let's examine the evidence.

Your Occupation Impacts NEAT

The advancement of technology has reduced NEAT by limiting the physical activity of jobs in the workplace. According to current research, working in a sedentary occupation is the main factor contributing to lower NEAT.[6] Among employed workers, men with sedentary jobs (secretaries, motor vehicle operators) were 22 percent less active and women were 30 percent less active than those with more active professions, such as farm or construction workers.[7] If you compare this to steps taken per day, a desk-bound man or woman takes only 5,000 to 6,000 steps a day. That compares with about 18,000 steps a day for the average man and 14,000 for the average woman in an Amish farming community.[8]

In controlled studies of sedentary adults, changes in the work environment that encourage NEAT, such as fidgeting and standing, have been shown to reduce weight gain. For example, standing rather than sitting is an example of passive work that burns more kilocalories. The figure illustrates the differences of energy expenditure in standing versus sitting during work. For those who find it difficult to stand during the workday, sitting on a therapy ball, which requires the individual to contract core muscles, may be another passive means to increase energy expenditure.[9]

Walking slowly at the rate of about 1 mile per hour while working at your desk increases energy expenditure by about 200 kilocalories per hour compared to sitting at your desk.

Research is currently being conducted in a variety of office settings on the feasibility of using walking stations in the workplace, and the impact these stations may have on body composition, cognitive function, and job productivity. The use of walking desks should increase NEAT energy expenditure and may improve overall health in the workplace.

Leisure Time and NEAT

Labor-saving devices and technology make it possible to squelch much leisure-time NEAT through the use of riding lawnmowers, electronically programmed vacuum cleaners, bread machines, microwave ovens, electric hammers, and handheld video games.[10, 11] Consider your leisure-time hours after work or school and on the weekends. Do you surf the Internet or watch television for hours until bedtime, just

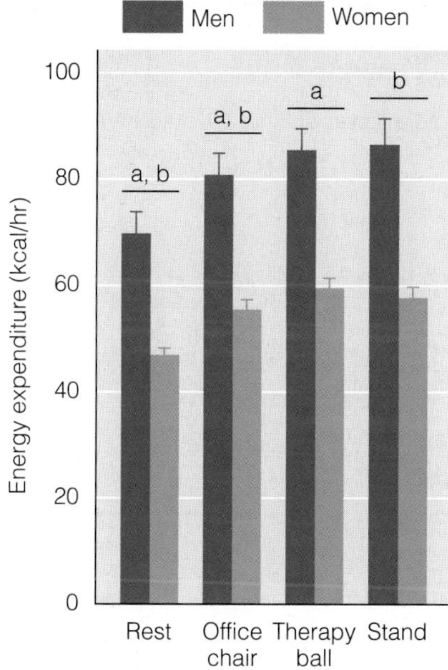

Energy expenditure in males and females expressed as kilocalories per hour during rest, office chair, therapy ball, and standing postures. Data are mean ± S.E.; $p < 0.05$ for means with the same letter.

Source: Beers, E. A., J. N. Roemmich, L. H. Epstein, and P. J. Horvath. 2008. Increasing Passive Energy Expenditure During Clerical Work. *European Journal of Applied Physiology* 103:353–360. Copyright © by Springer. Reprinted with permission of Springer Science+Business Media.

moving the mouse or using the remote control? If this were your routine after work, the average energy expenditure for that sedentary activity would be about 70 kilocalories per hour.[12] What if you cleaned house, walked your dog after dinner, or worked in the garden as an alternative? Instead of 70 kilocalories per hour, you could burn 200 to 400 kilocalories per hour. This change in NEAT could potentially increase the amount of energy you burn by more than 800 kilocalories per day.

NEAT Changes with Food Intake

Research suggests that when you eat too much, NEAT increases or when you eat too little, NEAT decreases. This was illustrated in a study that overfed non-obese subjects 1,000 kilocalories per day for eight weeks. As expected, the subjects gained between 1.4 kilograms and 7.2 kilograms of weight. What was unexpected was that there was also an increase in NEAT, including changes in posture, fidgeting, and daily activities. The increase in NEAT seemed to be a factor in those who gained less weight than the others. The researchers concluded that the increase in NEAT helped resist additional weight gain even when subjects overate.[13]

Move and Walk More to Prevent Obesity

Even if you engage in regular structured exercise, your overall daily energy expenditure may be relatively low if you spend the rest of your time sitting. The secret to increasing your NEAT and burning more kilocalories during the day, especially during work hours, is to get up out of the chair and move more. Find ways to work simple movements into your day—tap your feet, pace while you talk on the phone, stand while you read, get up and walk to a coworker's desk instead of emailing. Any additional NEAT activities will help minimize the potential health risks of a chair-sitting lifestyle. See the Fitness Tips for helpful suggestions.

FITNESS TIPS

Increase Your NEAT

- Find a friend at work to walk with at lunch.
- Stand or pace while talking on the telephone.
- Put on your headset and listen to your favorite music while you walk during your morning break.
- Set your NEAT goal to stand at least 2.5 hours per day.
- Fold laundry while watching your favorite TV show.
- Take the stairs instead of riding the elevator or escalator.
- If you drive to work or school, park farther from the building.
- Buy a pedometer to measure your steps; aim for 10,000 per day.

Adapted from J. Levine and S. Yeager, *Move a Little, Lose a Lot: New N.E.A.T. Science Reveals How to Be Thinner, Happier, and Smarter* (New York: Crown Publishers, 2009).

References

1. Levine, J. A. 2012. Non-Exercise Activity Thermogenesis (NEAT). *Best Practices in Research Clinical Endocrinology Metabolism* 16:679–702.
2. Lanningham-Foster, L., L. J. Nysee, and J. A. Levine. 2003. Labor Saved, Calories Lost: The Energetic Impact of Domestic Labor-Saving Devices. *Obesity Research* 11:1178–1181.
3. Levine, J. A., N. L. Eberhardt, and M. D. Jensen. 1999. Role of Non-Exercise Activity Thermogenesis in Resistance to Fat Gain in Humans. *Science* 283:212–214.
4. Levine, J. A., L. M. Lanningham-Foster, S. K. McCrady, et al. 2005. Inter-Individual Variation in Posture Allocation: Possible Role in Human Obesity. *Science* 307:584–586.
5. Ibid.
6. Levine, J. A., W. M. W. Vander, J. O. Hill, and R. C. Klesges. 2006. Non-Exercise Activity Thermogenesis: The Crouching Tiger Hidden Dragon of Societal Weight Gain. *Arteriosclerosis, Thrombosis, and Vascular Biology* 26:729–736.
7. Van Domelen, D. R., A. Koster, P. Caserotti, R. J. Brychta, K. Y. Chen, J. J. McClain, R. P. Trojano, et al. 2011. Employment and Physical Activity in the U. S. *American Journal of Preventive Medicine* 41:136–145.
8. Bassett, D. R., P. L. Schneider, and G. E. Huntington. 2004. Physical Activity in an Old Order Amish Community. *Medicine & Science in Sports & Exercise* 36:79–85.
9. Beers, E. A., J. N. Roemmich, L. H. Epstein, and P. J. Horvath. 2008. Increasing Passive Energy Expenditure During Clerical Work. *European Journal of Applied Physiology* 103:353–360.
10. Hayes, M., M. Chustek, S. Heshka, Z. Wang, A. Pietrobelli, and S. B. Heymsfield. 2005. Low Physical Activity Levels of Modern *Homo sapiens* among Free-Ranging Mammals. *International Journal of Obesity* 29:151–156.
11. Lanningham-Foster, et al. 2003. Labor Saved, Calories Lost.
12. ChooseMyPlate. 2012. *How Many Calories Does Physical Activity Use?* Available at www.choosemyplate.gov/food-groups/physicalactivity_calories_used_table.html. Accessed June 2012.
13. Levine, J. A., et al. 1999. Role of Non-Activity Thermogenesis.

TABLE 14.2 Factors That Influence the Thermic Effect of Food

Factor	Effects on the Thermic Effect of Food
Type of macronutrient	Fat has the least effect on TEF; protein has the greatest effect.
Meal composition	Consuming all three macronutrients together produces a lower TEF than would be produced by protein or carbohydrates separately.
Fiber content	A high-fiber meal produces a lower TEF.
Age	TEF declines as we age.
Environmental temperature	Consuming a meal in a cold environment increases TEF.
Alcohol	Alcohol consumption increases TEF but reduces TEF if alcohol is consumed in a cold environment.
Intense exercise	TEF is higher following intense exercise.
Training status	Individuals who are trained athletes have a lower TEF than untrained individuals.
Obesity	Obese individuals have a lower TEF than normal-weight individuals.

Data from J. Kang, *Bioenergetics Primer for Exercise Science* (Champaign, IL: Human Kinetics, Inc., 2008).

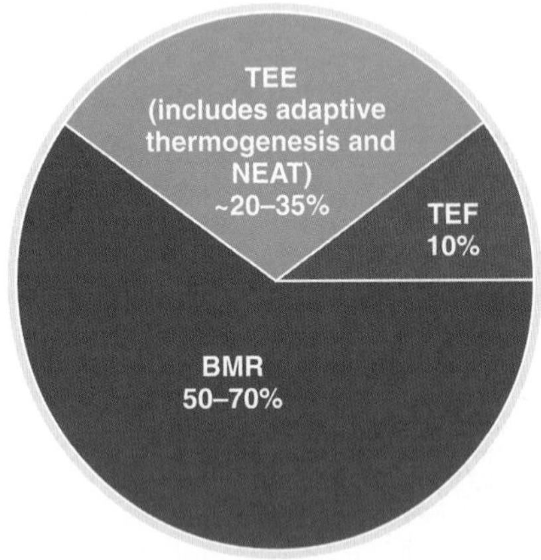

▲ **Figure 14.4 The Factors Involved in Energy Balance**
The thermic effect of food, along with basal metabolism, physical activity, and adaptive thermogenesis account for the energy-out side of the energy balance equation. The protein, carbohydrate, fat, and alcohol found in foods and beverages provide energy intake.

energy rather than storing the kilocalories in fat tissue may be partly responsible for weight gain in overweight individuals versus their lighter peers. Some researchers believe adaptive thermogenesis explains why two people can have the same diet and exercise patterns but have completely different body compositions.

Figure 14.4 summarizes the factors that contribute to your daily energy expenditure.

THE TAKE-HOME MESSAGE About 60 percent of total daily energy expenditure (TDEE) is attributable to basal metabolic rate (BMR), the amount of energy spent to meet the body's basic physiological needs when it is at rest. The metabolic activity of lean body mass accounts for about 70 percent of BMR. In addition to BMR, TDEE includes the thermic effect of food (TEF), or the energy spent to digest and absorb nutrients from food, and the thermic effect of exercise (TEE), or the energy spent on physical activities. The thermic effect of exercise includes non-exercise activity thermogenesis (NEAT). Adaptive thermogenesis, another component of TEE, regulates the amount of heat produced when food is metabolized and may be responsible for reducing energy expenditure when food intake is reduced.

How Do We Measure Energy Expenditure?

Have you ever wondered how many kilocalories you burn walking to class or washing your car? Or how resting metabolic rate is calculated? Several methods have been developed to measure energy expenditure. Some of these methods require the skills of a trained technician using expensive equipment. Other methods involve simple equations and a calculator.

Direct and Indirect Calorimetry Measure Energy Expenditure

An individual's energy expenditure can be measured by *direct calorimetry* or *indirect calorimetry.* Both methods quantify the amount of energy produced during rest and physical activity.

Direct calorimetry measures the amount of heat the body generates and can be determined using a metabolic chamber in a specialized laboratory. Briefly, a metabolic chamber is an airtight room designed with the comforts an individual would need for normal daily living such as a bed, chair, TV, telephone, treadmill for exercise, and bathroom. The temperature and relative humidity in the room are controlled and the oxygen and carbon dioxide concentrations of the air supply and exhaust are measured for 24 hours. The concept is similar to the bomb calorimeter, but rather than measuring the amount of heat generated by burning food, this method measures the change in water temperature caused by heat that dissipates from a body sitting in an airtight chamber. Although this method provides a precise answer to the question of how many kilocalories an individual expends, for most people its use is too expensive and impractical.

The more practical and less expensive approach is to use an indirect measurement, called **indirect calorimetry,** to estimate the amount of energy expended. Indirect measurements sample the amount of oxygen consumed and carbon dioxide produced during exercise and for a specific amount of time. Metabolic calculations can then be done to determine energy expenditure. **Figure 14.5** illustrates two examples of indirect calorimetry: On the right is an example of indirect calorimetry during exercise using a metabolic cart often found in exercise science labs. On the left is an example of measuring energy expenditure at rest.

Simple Calculations Are Used to Estimate Energy Expenditure

Recall Table 2.2 from Chapter 2, which helped *estimate* energy needs for a 24-hour period using indirect calorimetry. This table was derived from the DRIs' estimated

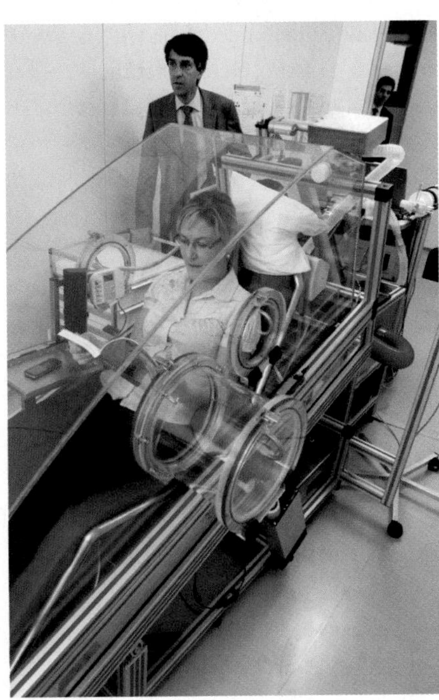

(a) Measuring metabolic rate at rest

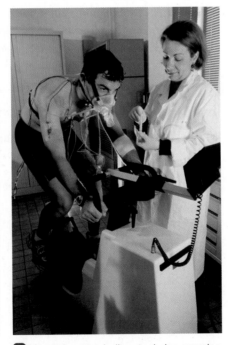

(b) Measuring metabolic rate during exercise

▲ **Figure 14.5 A Metabolic Cart Indirectly Measures Energy Expenditure**
A metabolic cart measures the amount of oxygen consumed and carbon dioxide produced at rest (a) or during exercise (b). This information can then be used to indirectly calculate an individual's energy expenditure.

direct calorimetry A direct measurement of the energy expended by the body obtained by assessing heat loss.

indirect calorimetry An indirect measurement of energy expenditure obtained by measuring the amount of oxygen consumed and carbon dioxide produced.

TABLE 14.3 Physical Activity Factors for Men and Women

Physical Activity Level	Physical Activity Factor for Men	Physical Activity Factor for Women
Sedentary	1.00	1.00
Low level of activity (walking approximately 2 miles per day at 3 to 4 miles per hour)	1.11	1.12
Active (walking approximately 7 miles per day at 3 to 4 miles per hour)	1.25	1.27
Very active (walking approximately 17 miles per day at 3 to 4 miles per hour)	1.45	1.48

Data from Food and Nutrition Board, National Institute of Medicine, *Dietary Reference Intakes: The Essential Guide to Nutrient Requirements* (Washington, DC: The National Academies Press, 2006).

energy requirement. The **estimated energy requirement (EER)** is the average kilocalorie intake that is estimated to maintain energy balance based on a person's gender, age, height, body weight, and level of physical activity. The physical activity levels are separated into categories ranging from sedentary to very active, as shown in Table 14.3, and can be used along with a person's specific gender, age, height, and weight to compute individualized estimated energy requirements. One such calculation used by the DRI committee to estimate EER is presented in the Calculation Corner.[4] You can obtain an even more precise EER by assessing every minute of movement and physical activity that you do throughout the day and, based on this, calculating the energy that you expend.

Another calculation often used is the Harris-Benedict equation, which also calculates RMR based on gender, age, height, and weight, and applies an activity factor to determine total daily energy expenditure. The drawback to this equation is that it does not include lean body mass, so it may not be accurate for individuals who are very muscular (for whom it will underestimate kilocalorie needs) or who are very fat (for whom it will overestimate kilocalorie needs). In those circumstances, other calculations, such as the Mifflin-St. Jeor equation, may be used in clinical settings.

FITNESS TIPS

Achieve Energy Balance

Track the number of kilocalories you consume in one day, and compare it to the estimated number of kilocalories you expend. Are you most often in positive, or negative, energy balance?

Take steps to increase muscle mass, such as by weight training. This will help increase your metabolic rate.

Keep a diary to calculate how much energy you expend each day doing normal, everyday tasks.

Calculate your BMI and measure your waist circumference. Are you within the healthy range to reduce the risk of developing certain diseases?

Identify your favorite exercise that you can engage in at least 30 minutes a day most days of the week to avoid too much sedentary time.

Calculation Corner

What's Your Estimated Energy Requirement (EER)?

You can estimate your energy requirement for kilocalories using this two-step calculation:

1. First, complete the information below.
   a. My age is ________.
   b. My physical activity during the day based on Table 14.3 is ________.
   c. My weight in pounds is ________ divided by 2.2 = ________ kilograms.
   d. My height in inches is ________ divided by 39.4 = ________ meters.
2. Using your answers from each part of step 1, complete the following calculation based on your gender and age.
   Males, 19+ years old, use this calculation:
   EER = [662 − (9.53 × ____)] + ____ × [(15.91 × ____) + (539.6 × ____)]
   (a) (b) (c) (d)
   Females, 19+ years old, use this calculation:
   EER = [354 − (6.91 × ____)] + ____ × [(9.36 × ____) + (726 × ____)]
   (a) (b) (c) (d)

estimated energy requirement (EER) The average kilocalorie intake that is estimated to maintain energy balance based on a person's gender, age, height, body weight, and level of physical activity.

THE TAKE-HOME MESSAGE Energy expenditure can be measured by direct calorimetry using a metabolic chamber or by indirect calorimetry using a metabolic cart. Simple calculations can also be used to estimate energy expenditure using age, height, weight, and physical activity.

What Is Body Composition and How Is It Assessed?

Body tissues include bone, skin, muscle, fat, organs, and blood, which are comprised of the same basic nutrients: water, protein, minerals, and fat. The ratio of fat tissue to lean body mass is called **body composition.** This ratio, stated as a *percent body fat,* is particularly important for the sake of measuring health risks associated with too much body fat. It's essential to know what your body mass is composed of so as to take the necessary steps to achieve a healthy body weight and control health risks.

Most Body Fat Is Stored in Adipose Tissue

Two types of fat make up total body fat: **essential fat,** which includes the fat found in the bone marrow, heart, lungs, liver, spleen, kidneys, intestines, muscles, and central nervous system; and stored fat, found in **adipose tissue,** or fat cells. Essential fat is just that—essential for the body to function. Women have four times (12 percent) more essential fat than men (3 percent) because of the fat deposits in breast tissue and surrounding the uterus, related to pregnancy and lactation. Whereas every cell contains some fat, most body fat is the storage fat found in adipose tissue.

Excess stored fat can be found as **subcutaneous fat** under the skin or as **visceral fat** around the internal organs. Subcutaneous and visceral fat insulate the body from cold temperatures and help protect and cushion the internal organs (**Figure 14.6**). Men and women store subcutaneous fat slightly differently, with men more likely

body composition The ratio of fat to lean tissue (muscle, bone, and organs) in the body; usually expressed as percent body fat.

essential fat A component of body fat that is necessary for health and normal body functions; includes the fat stored in bone marrow, heart, lungs, liver, spleen, kidneys, intestines, muscles, and lipid-rich tissues of the central nervous system is essential fat.

adipose tissue Connective tissue that is the main storage site for fat in the body.

subcutaneous fat The fat located under the skin and between the muscles.

visceral fat The body fat associated with the internal organs and stored in the abdominal area.

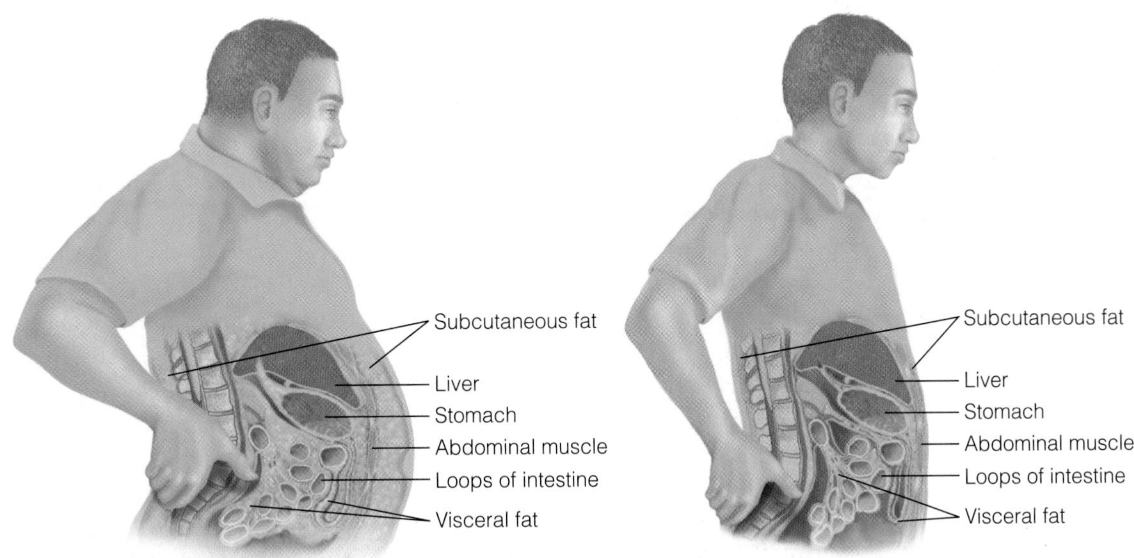

▲ **Figure 14.6 Visceral and Subcutaneous Fat Storage in the Body**
Visceral fat stored around the organs of the abdomen is more likely to lead to health problems than is subcutaneous fat sandwiched between the muscle and skin.

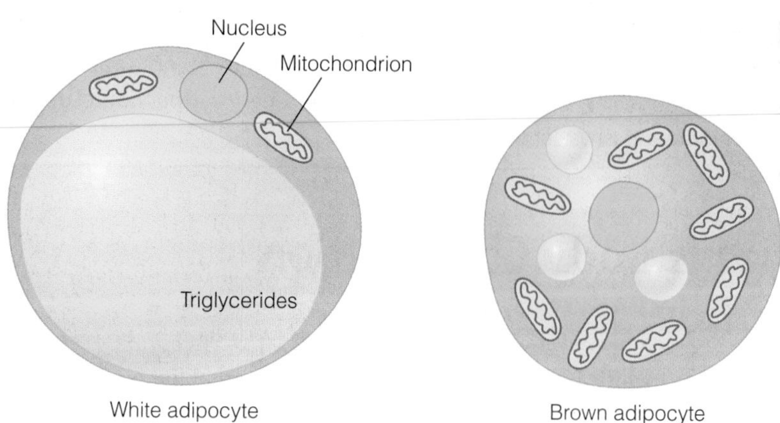

▲ **Figure 14.7 White Adipocyte and Brown Adipocyte**
Brown adipose tissue has significantly more mitochondria and less stored triglycerides than white adipose tissue.

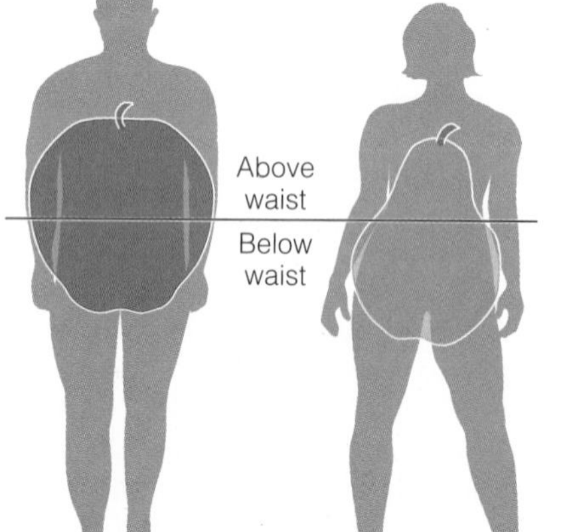

▲ **Figure 14.8 Android and Gynoid Fat Distribution Patterns**
Men and women store subcutaneous fat differently. Men tend to store it in the abdomen, buttocks, and thighs—often referred to as "apple-shaped" fat distribution —while women tend to store subcutaneous fat in the breasts, buttocks, abdomen and arms for more of a "pear-shaped" appearance.

to accumulate it in the belly, hips, and thighs, and women more apt to store it in the breasts, neck, and upper arms, as well as in the hips and thighs.

Adipose tissues will release fat to be used as fuel when the body is in negative energy balance. An adipocyte shrinks as more fat is hydrolyzed from storage, and overall body weight is lost. When the body is in positive energy balance, fat accumulates in adipose tissue, the fat cells expand in size, and weight gain occurs.

Adipose tissue is described as *white fat* because of its creamy, white appearance. Another type of adipose tissue, called **brown adipose tissue (BAT),** is made up of specialized fat cells that contain more mitochondria and are rich in blood (**Figure 14.7**). While white adipose tissue is used as a storage depot for excess kilocalories, the function of BAT is to generate heat. Found primarily in infants, BAT protects infants from heat loss and cold. Recent research suggests that adults, especially older adults, have more BAT than once thought. Studies have shown that the more BAT an adult has, the lower their body mass index, suggesting that this active tissue plays an important role in adult metabolism.[5] This may be due to the fact that brown adipose tissue converts kilocalories into heat rather than storing them in the adipocyte.

Body Fat Distribution Affects Health

How much fat you carry isn't the only determinant of health risk—where you carry it also matters. Storing excess fat around the waist versus carrying it around the hips and thighs has been shown to increase the risk of heart disease, diabetes, and hypertension.[6] **Central obesity** (also known as *android obesity*) is due to storing too much visceral and subcutaneous fat in the abdomen (**Figure 14.8**). This is sometimes referred to as an "apple-shaped" fat distribution pattern and is more common in men than in women. **Gynoid obesity** is due to excess subcutaneous fat stored in the lower part of the body around the thighs and buttocks. This "pear-shaped" fat distribution pattern is more frequently found in women than in men.

Because visceral fat is located near the liver, it is believed that fatty acids released from the fat storage area travel to the liver and can lead to insulin resistance, high levels of fat, low levels of the good HDL cholesterol, and high levels of LDL cholesterol in the blood, which all increase the risk of heart disease and diabetes. Insulin resistance also increases the risk for hypertension. Men, postmenopausal women, and obese people tend to have more visceral fat than young adults and lean individuals.

brown adipose tissue (BAT) A type of adipose tissue, found primarily in infants, that produces body heat; it gets its name from the large number of mitochondria and capillaries responsible for the brown color.

central obesity An excess storage of visceral fat in the abdominal area, indicated by a waist circumference greater than 40 inches in males and 35 inches in females; central obesity increases the risk of heart disease, diabetes, and hypertension. Also referred to as *android obesity*.

gynoid obesity An excessive storage of body fat in the thighs and hips of the lower body.

TABLE 14.4 Body Composition Reference Standards for Adult Men and Women

	Men	Women
Essential fat	3 percent of total body fat	12 percent of total body fat
Desirable fatness for good health	10 to 20 percent body fat	16 to 26 percent body fat
Overfat	More than 25 percent body fat	More than 30 percent body fat

Data from W. D. McArdle, F. I. Katch, and V. L. Katch, *Sports and Exercise Nutrition*, 3rd ed. (Baltimore: Lippincott Williams & Wilkins, 2008).

Body Fat Levels Affect Health

Carrying either too much or too little body fat can affect body functions and impair health. Everyone needs to have a certain amount of body fat to meet basic needs, but excess amounts of body fat can impact overall health. For this reason, specific body composition standards have been developed over the years from a variety of research to help individuals avoid health risk (Table 14.4). These body fat ranges, which can be measured using a variety of indirect methods, are based on epidemiological studies of the general population of Americans.

Body Composition Is Assessed Indirectly

There are several indirect measurements used to estimate the percentage of body fat and lean body mass in the body. The most popular indirect techniques are found in laboratory settings and include hydrostatic weighing, air displacement, dual-energy X-ray absorptiometry (DEXA), bioelectrical impedance, and skinfold measurement (Table 14.5).

Percent Body Fat

Because fat mass has a lower density than either muscles or bones, it is possible to estimate body fat percentage from body volume. **Hydrostatic weighing** and **air displacement plethysmography** are two methods that use body volume to measure percent body fat. Hydrostatic weighing is based on the principle that an object immersed in water is buoyed up by a force equal to the weight of the fluid displaced by the object. In other words, if the density of an object is greater than the density of water, the object will sink. If the density of the object is less than water, the object will float. We can use this principle to determine body composition by measuring the difference in body weight in air compared with under water. With a 2 to 3 percent margin of error, hydrostatic weighing is considered one of the most accurate assessment tools. The BodPod, an air displacement plethysmography device that measures air rather than water displacement, is similarly accurate within 3 percent. Both hydrostatic weighing and the BodPod have pros and cons. While both are accurate, hydrostatic weighing takes longer; some people find it difficult to be submersed under water; and the equipment is usually only found in research facilities. The BodPod, on the other hand, is faster and it only requires you to sit quietly in a chamber. See the Calculation Corner on page 527 for the equation used to determine body composition from either of these body volume methods.

Dual-energy X-ray absorptiometry (DEXA) is the most accurate method of determining body composition; its margin of error is only 1 to 4 percent. This noninvasive method uses two low-energy X-ray beams: One detects all tissues and the

hydrostatic weighing A method used to assess body volume by underwater weighing.

air displacement plethysmography A procedure used to estimate body volume based on the amount of air displaced.

dual-energy X-ray absorptiometry (DEXA) A method that uses two low-energy X-rays to measure body density and bone mass.

TABLE 14.5 Ways to Measure Percentage of Body Fat

▲ **Hydrostatic Weighing**
How It Is Done: A person is weighed on land and also suspended in a water tank. This is done to determine the density of the body. Fat is less dense and weighs less than muscle mass and this will be reflected when the person is weighed in the water. The difference of a person's weight in water and on land is then used to calculate the percentage of body fat.
Cost: $$
Accuracy: 2–3% margin of error

Air Displacement Plethysmography ▶ Using a BodPod
How It Is Done: A person's body volume is determined by measuring air displacement. The person sits in a special chamber (called the BodPod) and the air displacement in the chamber is measured. From this measurement, the percentage of body fat can be estimated.
Cost: $$$
Accuracy: 2–3% margin of error

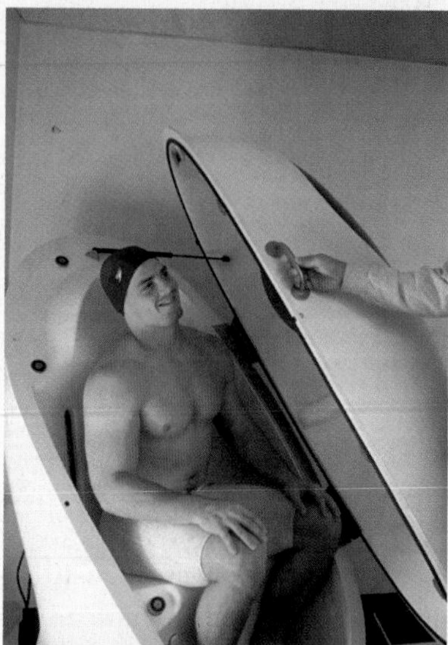

◀ **Dual-Energy X-Ray Absorptiometry (DEXA)**
How It Is Done: Beams of X-ray energy from two different sources are used to measure bone, fat, and lean tissue. The type of tissue that the beams pass through will absorb different amounts of energy. The percentage of body fat can be determined from the difference between the two readings.
Cost: $$$
Accuracy: 1–4% margin of error

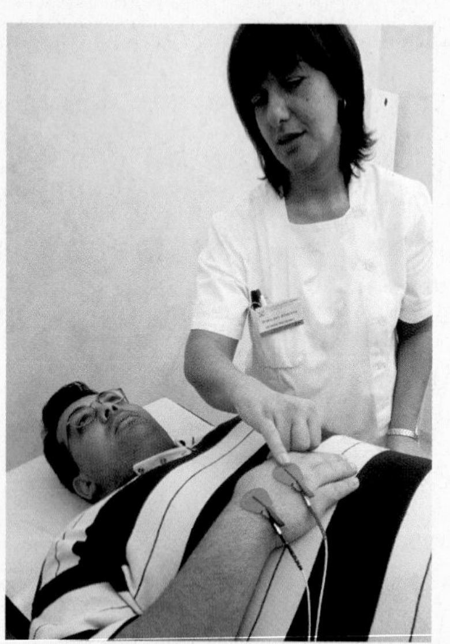

▲ **Bioelectrical Impedance (BIA)**
How It Is Done: An electric current flows through the body and its resistance is measured. Lean tissue is highly conductive and less resistant than fat mass. Based on the current flow, the volume of lean tissue can be estimated. From this information, the percentage of body fat can be determined.
Cost: $
Accuracy: 3–4% margin of error

Skinfold Thickness Measurements ▶
How It Is Done: Calipers are used to measure the thickness of fat that is located just under the skin in the arm, in the back, on the upper thigh, and in the waist area. From these measurements, percent body fat can be determined.
Cost: $
Accuracy: 3–4% margin of error

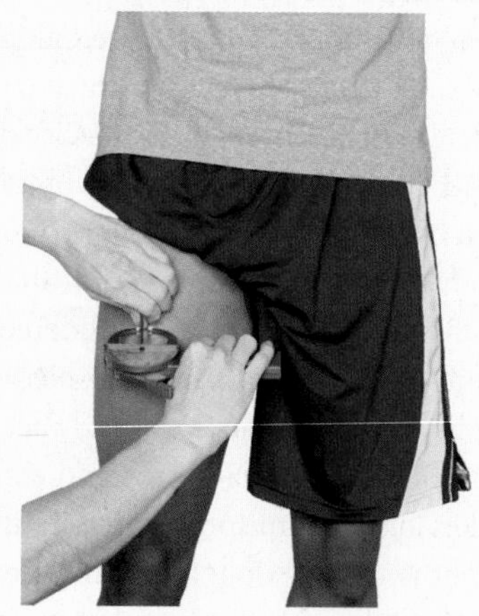

$ = very affordable
$$ = less affordable
$$$ = expensive

other detects only lean body mass. The computer calculates the difference to determine the percentage of body fat.

Bioelectrical impedance analysis (BIA) measures the resistance to a low-energy current as it travels through muscle and body fat. The current travels more quickly through lean body mass, which is high in body water and electrolytes, than through fat tissue. The resistance of the fat tissue is used to calculate body composition. BIA is not as accurate as body density tests and can be affected by age, hydration status, and consuming food and alcohol prior to the test.

Anthropometric (relating to body measurement) techniques are the simplest methods available and involve using a **skinfold caliper** to measure fat in various body locations. The metal calipers are used to pinch the subcutaneous fat at selected sites on the body. A trained technician grasps the skin and fat between the thumb and forefinger and pulls it gently away from the muscle. The caliper exerts a constant pressure while measuring the skinfold thickness in millimeters. These values are then used to calculate percent body fat. When conducted by a trained technician, skinfold caliper tests are fairly accurate.

Calculation Corner

Body Volume and Density

The body volume determined by either hydrostatic weighing or air displacement is mathematically converted to density and then to percentage body fat using this equation:

Body density = body weight (kg)/body volume (L)

Percent body fat = (495/body density) – 450

Example: The body volume of an 83-kilogram male (182.6 pounds) was determined from hydrostatic weighing to be 79.4 L. Dividing body weight by body volume yields a body density of 1.0453. Body density can then be used to determine percent body fat as follows:

(495/1.0453) – 450 = 23.5% body fat

Waist Circumference

Because abdominal fat can be particularly detrimental to health, measuring a person's **waist circumference** can quickly reveal whether he or she is at increased risk (Figure 14.9). A woman with a waist measurement of more than 35 inches or a man with a belly that's more than 40 inches around is at a higher health risk than people with slimmer middles. Carrying extra fat around the waist can increase health risks even if you are not overweight. In other words, a person who may be at a healthy weight based on their height, but who has excess fat around the middle, is at a higher health risk.

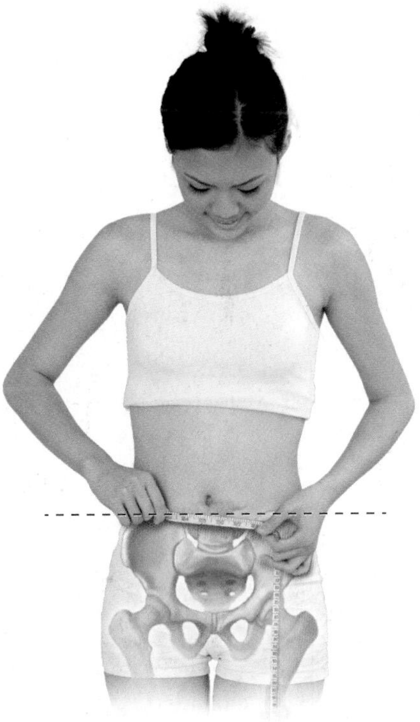

▲ **Figure 14.9 Measuring Waist Circumference**
The waist circumference measurement is taken at the celiac crest (top of the hip bone), as shown by the dashed line.

THE TAKE-HOME MESSAGE The body is composed of lean and fat tissue. Adipose tissue is classified as essential fat or fat that is stored as either subcutaneous or visceral fat. How much fat a person has and the placement of that fat can increase the risk of heart disease, diabetes, and hypertension, especially if the fat is distributed in the abdomen. Hydrostatic weighing, air displacement plethysmography, dual-energy X-ray absorptiometry, (DEXA), bioelectrical impedance analysis (BIA), and skinfold measurements are all techniques used to determine body composition. Measuring waist circumference can determine whether an individual has excess fat around the middle, which can increase the risk of several chronic diseases.

How Do We Estimate a Healthy Body Weight?

The terms body weight and body composition are not synonymous. Body weight is defined as the total mass of a person expressed in either pounds (lb) or kilograms (kg). As you just learned, body composition is the percentage of body weight that is composed of fat and lean body mass. Even though the terms *body weight* and

bioelectrical impedance analysis (BIA) A method used to assess the percentage of body fat by using a low-level electrical current; body fat resists or impedes the current, whereas water and muscle mass conduct electricity.

skinfold caliper A tool used to measure the thickness of subcutaneous fat.

waist circumference Measurement taken at the top of the hip bone; used to determine the pattern of obesity.

body composition do not measure the same component, they are often used interchangeably in the popular media.

Two common methods used to help individuals estimate whether their own percent body fat falls within a healthy range are height-weight tables and body mass index (BMI). These reference standards are indirect estimates of body composition, and therefore somewhat imprecise, but they can be used as a rough guide to a healthy body weight for most people.

Height and Weight Tables Can Provide a Healthy Weight Range

Height-weight tables have been used since the 1940s in large-scale studies that were designed to investigate the relationship between weight and disease. The most commonly used version was developed by the Metropolitan Life Insurance Company. The company published the Desirable Weights for Men and Women table in 1959 based on data collected from millions of policyholders. The most recent version of the table was published in 1999 and provides a recommended desirable weight range for a given height based on gender and frame size.

Several factors make the data used in these tables problematic. For example, the data does not represent the American population as a whole. The tables were originally designed with data from 25-to 59-year-olds, which means they may underrepresent older adults and individuals younger than 25 years of age. The original data were not standardized by the researchers. For instance, subjects self-reported their height and weight; the weights were measured at different times of the year; and there was no standard procedure regarding wearing shoes or clothing when taking the height and weight measurements. Lastly, the tables were constructed with the assumption that weight is associated with body fat. Today, height-weight tables are used mostly by insurance companies to determine mortality rates. Most health experts use body mass index rather than height-weight tables to determine healthy weight.

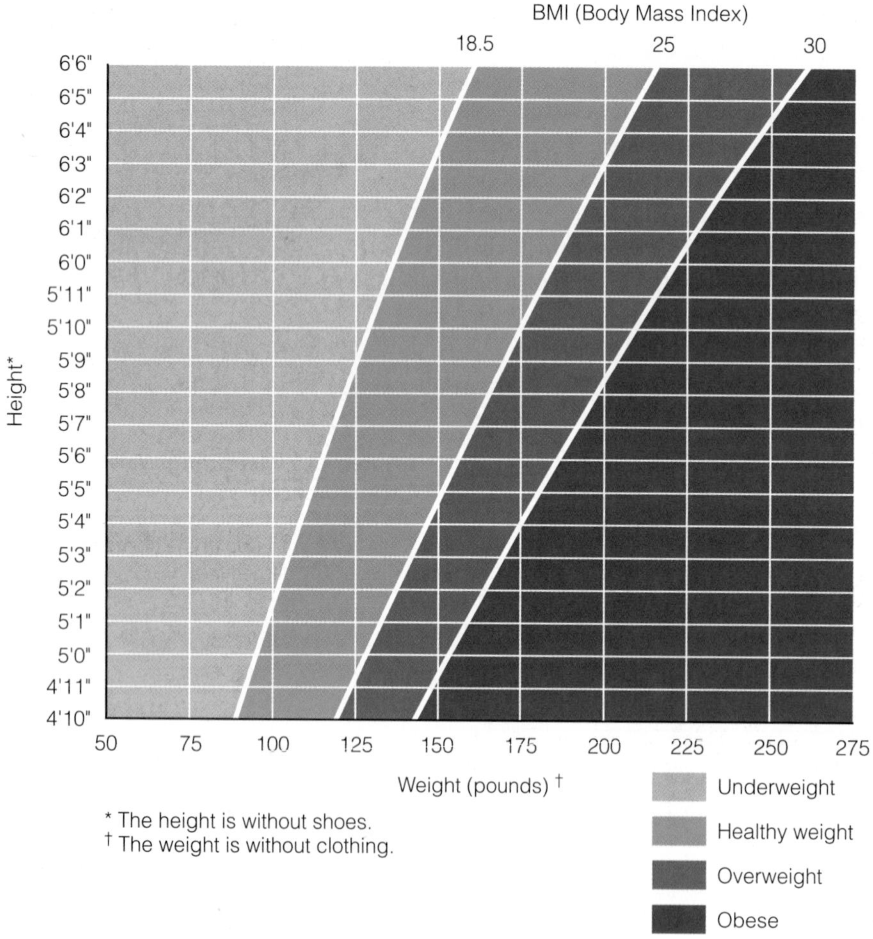

▲ **Figure 14.10 What's Your BMI?**
A BMI between 18.5 and 24.9 is considered healthy. A BMI over 25 is considered overweight, and a BMI over 30 is obese. A BMI under 18.5 is considered underweight, and can also be unhealthy.

Body Mass Index Is a Useful Indicator of Healthy Weight for Most People

Body mass index (BMI) (Figure 14.10) is a convenient method of calculating body weight in relationship to height, and is a useful screening tool to determine an individual's risk of disease. It is calculated using either of the following formulas:

Calculation Corner

Converting BMI to Percent Body Fat

Now that you have learned how to calculate body mass index (BMI), how does this number correlate to the amount of stored body fat? Several researchers have presented equations that show a correlation between BMI and percent body fat in adults. One equation published in the *British Journal of Nutrition* was used to predict percent body fat from BMI.[1] The results of this research showed that the formulas, which are age and gender specific, can predict valid estimates of body fat comparable to prediction errors obtained from skinfold thickness measurements or BIA. The prediction equations do, however, overestimate percent body fat in obese individuals. Follow these steps to practice using these prediction equations.

1. If you are a female, use this formula: 1.2 (BMI) + 0.23 (age(y)) – 5.4

For example, a 21-year-old female with a BMI of 25 would calculate percent body fat as follows:

1.2 (25) + 0.23 (21) – 5.4 = 30 + 4.83 – 5.4 = 29.43 percent body fat

2. A male would use this formula: 1.2(BMI) + 0.23(age(y)) – 16.2

For example, a 31-year-old male with a BMI of 21 would calculate percent body fat as follows:

1.2 (21) + 0.23 (31) – 16.2 = 25.2 + 7.13 – 16.2 = 16.13 percent body fat

Now, using your own BMI, complete the calculation for percent body fat.

Note that these calculations do not consider ethnicity. The BMI–body fat relationship varies between different ethnic groups[2] and should be used in conjunction with other measurements such as waist circumference and percent body fat to provide a true picture of a healthy body weight.

References

1. Deurenbert, P., J. A. Weststrate, and J. C. Seidell. 1991. Body–Mass Index as a Measure of Body Fatness: Age- and Sex-Specific Prediction Formulas. *British Journal of Nutrition* 65:105–114.
2. Luke, Amy. 2009. Ethnicity and the BMI-Body Fat Relationship. *British Journal of Nutrition* 102:485–487.

$$\text{BMI} = \frac{\text{body weight (in kilograms)}}{\text{height}^2 \text{ (in meters)}}$$

or

$$\text{BMI} = \frac{\text{body weight (in pounds)} \times 703}{\text{height}^2 \text{ (in inches)}}$$

A BMI of 18.5 to 24.9 is considered a **healthy weight** based on height. A BMI between 25 and 29.9 is considered **overweight,** and a BMI above 30 is considered **obese.** As the BMI increases above 25, the risk of dying from diseases increases, although research shows that the risk is modest until a person reaches a BMI of 30.[7] Obese individuals have a 50 to 100 percent higher risk of dying prematurely than those at a healthy weight.[8] Because BMI has been shown to correlate with health risks associated with excess body fat, an equation can be used to estimate body fat percentage from BMI (see the Calculation Corner).

While BMI can be useful in determining disease risks, it is important to note that BMI is not a *direct* measure of the percentage of body fat, and it doesn't specify if body weight is predominantly muscle or fat.[9] Therefore, athletes and people with a high percentage of muscle mass may have a BMI over 25, yet have a low percentage of body fat. Although these individuals are overweight based on their BMI, they are not "overfat" and unhealthy, and their muscular weight doesn't increase their health risk. In contrast, an older adult may be in a healthy weight range, but steadily

body mass index (BMI) A calculation of body weight in relationship to height.

healthy weight A body weight in relationship to height that doesn't increase the risk of developing any weight-related health problems or diseases. A BMI between 18.5 and 24.9 is considered healthy.

overweight A body weight that increases risk of developing weight-related health problems; defined as having a BMI between 25 and 29.9.

obese A condition of excess body weight due to an abnormal accumulation of stored body fat; a BMI of 30 or more is considered obese.

lose weight due to an unbalanced diet or poor health. This chronic weight loss is a sign of loss of muscle mass and the depletion of nutrient stores in the body, which increases health risks even though the BMI seems healthy. Also, because height is factored into the BMI, individuals who are very short—less than 5 feet—may have a high BMI, but, similar to athletes, may not be unhealthy.[10]

Combining indirect measurements is one way to get a better estimate of body composition. For example, a person who has both a BMI greater than 25 and a large waist circumference is considered at a higher risk for health problems than if he or she only had a high BMI but a low waist circumference (**Figure 14.11**).

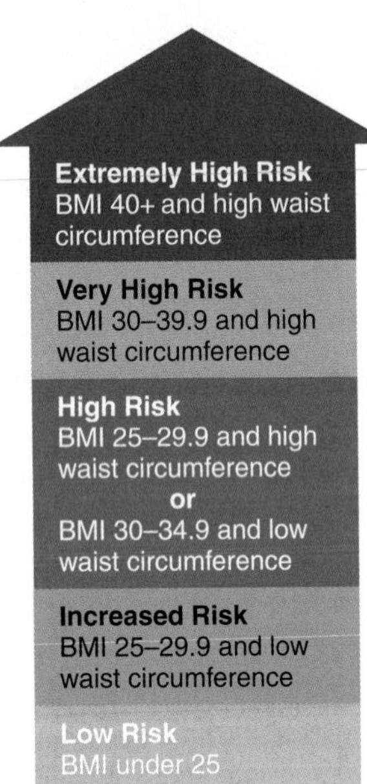

Extremely High Risk
BMI 40+ and high waist circumference
Very High Risk
BMI 30–39.9 and high waist circumference
High Risk
BMI 25–29.9 and high waist circumference
or
BMI 30–34.9 and low waist circumference
Increased Risk
BMI 25–29.9 and low waist circumference
Low Risk
BMI under 25

▲ **Figure 14.11 Using BMI and Waist Circumference to Determine Health Risk**
Considering both BMI and waist circumference can give you a good idea of total risk levels for several chronic diseases.

THE TAKE-HOME MESSAGE Height and weight tables and BMI are used to screen for overweight and obesity. Height-weight tables do not necessarily indicate a healthy weight for everyone. The body mass index (BMI) is a calculation of the ratio of weight to height and can be used to assess health risks. It is not a direct measure of body fat and may be inaccurate for frail individuals or those with large muscle mass.

What Are the Health Risks Associated with Body Weight and Body Composition?

Weighing too much or too little can both be harmful to health. Underweight adults, particularly older adults, can experience serious health risks, and an increased rate of obesity is directly related to higher rates of several chronic diseases among Americans.[11] Obesity is strongly correlated to several leading causes of death, including heart disease, type 2 diabetes, and cancer.

Body weight can be a predictor for health risk because of its relationship to body composition. In general, heavier people tend to have a higher percentage of body fat. The higher the percent of body weight as body fat, the greater the health risks. For example, results from a recent study suggest that there is a significant rise in heart rate as adipose tissue accumulates, which may indicate an increased risk of hypertension.[12] Age was also found to be a factor in this study. Obese individuals aged 21 to 30 had heart rates similar to their non-obese peers (an average of 1.1 beats per minute higher), while obese individuals aged 51 to 60 had an average heart rate almost 7 beats per minute higher than their non-obese peers.

Being Underweight Increases Health Risks

Whereas some individuals have a BMI below 21 but are healthy, for others, a low body weight is symptomatic of malnutrition, substance abuse, or disease. A BMI of less than 18.5 is considered **underweight** and is associated with a higher risk of anemia, osteoporosis and bone fractures, heart irregularities, and amenorrhea (loss of menstruation in women). Underweight and significant weight loss are also correlated to depression and anxiety. The inability to fight off infection, trouble regulating body temperature, decreased muscle strength, and even an increase in the risk of prematurely dying are all associated with being underweight.

Certain diseases, such as cancer, inflammatory bowel disease, and celiac disease, can cause malabsorption and result in weight loss, leading to being underweight. Other inadvertent causes of underweight include certain medications,

underweight Weighing too little for your height; defined as a BMI less than 18.5.

such as some antidepressants; osteoporosis; and blood pressure drugs, all of which can decrease appetite. Smoking and substance abuse can also lead to unhealthy weight loss.

Being Overweight Increases Health Risks

Overweight and obese people have an increased risk for having heart disease, and the risk increases as BMI increases. Obesity can lead to congestive heart failure due to the inability of the heart to pump enough blood through the blood vessels. Other conditions correlated to body weight and percent body fat include a greater chance of developing hypertension, stroke, and hyperlipidemia. More than 80 percent of people with type 2 diabetes are overweight. Metabolic syndrome, a condition named for a group of risk factors associated with overweight and obesity, is seen more often in individuals who have android obesity. Excess weight raises the chance of developing a variety of cancers, including colon, breast, endometrial, and gallbladder cancer. Obesity correlates to osteoarthritis, a condition in which the tissue that protects the joints of the knees, hips, and lower back wears away. And finally, the risk of gallstones, sleep apnea, and reproductive problems increases with body weights above the standards established for health.[13]

In Chapter 15 you will learn more about the relationship of weight to health and the safe methods used to achieve and maintain a healthy weight to reduce the risk of developing these diseases.

THE TAKE-HOME MESSAGE A BMI less than 18.5 is considered underweight and is associated with anemia, osteoporosis and bone fractures, heart irregularities, amenorrhea, depression, anxiety, depressed immune system, trouble regulating body temperature, and decreased muscle strength. A BMI greater than 25 is associated with an increased risk of heart disease, cancer, type 2 diabetes, metabolic syndrome, osteoarthritis, gallstones, sleep apnea, and reproductive disorders.

Putting It All Together

Foods rich in complex carbohydrates such as whole grains, vegetables, and fruits that provide fiber, vitamins, and minerals are generally lower in kilocalories and higher in bulk. Consuming a wide variety of foods whose kilocalorie content equals the amount of total daily energy expended will maintain a balanced energy equation. Lean meats, poultry, and fish, calcium-rich dairy foods, and healthy oils should be included to provide protein, minerals, vitamins, and essential fats. A well-balanced diet including all food groups like this enables you to meet your nutrient and energy needs and should be combined with adequate amounts of daily physical activity to maintain a healthy body weight.

Visual Chapter Summary

1 Energy Balance Is Achieved When Energy In Equals Energy Out

Energy balance is the relationship between energy consumed and energy expended. Body weight remains constant when energy intake equals energy expenditure. When more energy is consumed than expended, the body is in positive energy balance and weight gain occurs. When the intake of kilocalories falls short of energy needs or you expend more energy than you consume, the body is in negative energy balance and weight loss occurs.

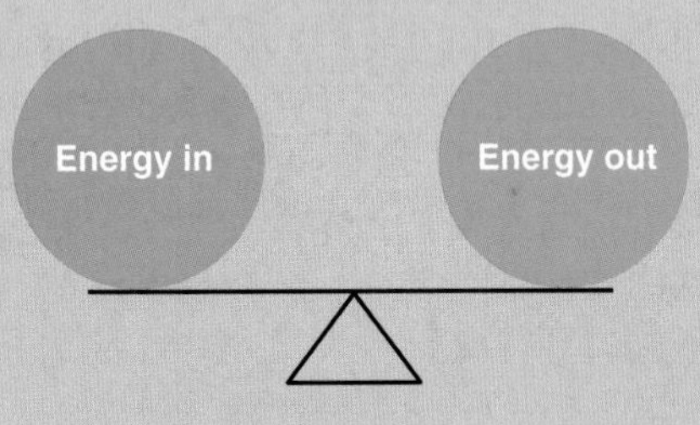

Energy balance

2 Three Factors Contribute to TDEE

Total daily energy expenditure is based on basal metabolic rate (BMR), the thermic effect of food (TEF), and the thermic effect of exercise (TEE), or physical activities.

The BMR is influenced mainly by lean body mass, and is also affected by age, gender, body size, genes, ethnicity, emotional and physical stress, thyroid hormone levels, nutritional state, and environmental temperature.

The thermic effect of exercise (TEE) includes the energy required to walk, talk, run, exercise, and maintain posture while standing and sitting. One component of TEE, non-exercise activity thermogenesis, or NEAT, is the energy used for all activity that is not structured exercise, including unconscious muscle activity. Adaptive thermogenesis adds to TDEE by producing heat in response to environmental changes such as stress, temperature changes, or diet.

The thermic effect of food—energy used to process macronutrients and extract kilocalories from foods—has a small but positive impact on total daily energy expenditure.

Total Daily Energy Expenditure (TDEE)

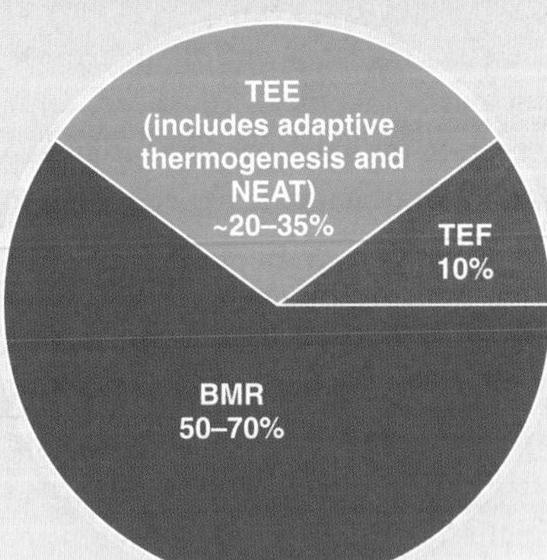

3 Energy Expenditure Can Be Measured Directly or Indirectly

Energy expenditure can be measured directly with a metabolic chamber or indirectly based on oxygen consumed and carbon dioxide produced during activity. The estimated energy requirement (EER) can be calculated using an individual's age, weight, height, and physical activity level.

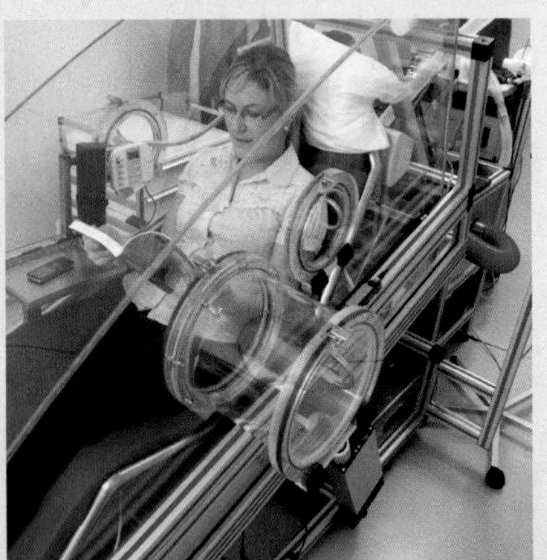

4 Body Composition Is Comprised of Lean Body Mass and Fat

Body composition refers to the ratio of fat to lean body mass and is measured as a percent body fat. Total body fat is comprised of essential fat, found in bone marrow, organs, muscles, and the central nervous system, and storage fat, found in adipose tissue. Stored fat can be visceral, located around the organs, or subcutaneous, located just beneath the skin. White adipose tissue is primarily a storage tissue; brown adipose tissue contains more mitochondria, is rich in blood, and generates heat.

The most accurate instrument to measure body composition is dual-energy X-ray absorptiometry (DEXA). Body composition is also estimated from body volume using hydrostatic weighing and air displacement plethysmography. Bioelectrical impedance analysis measures resistance by body fat; skinfold calipers estimate subcutaneous fat; and waist circumference measures android obesity.

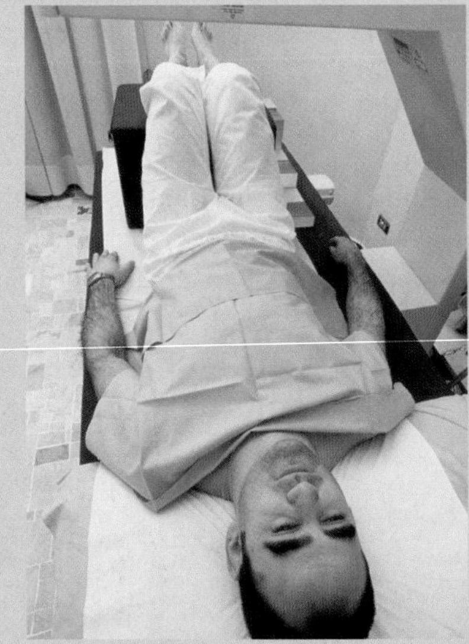

5 Ranges of Healthy Body Weight Are Estimated Using BMI

Reference standards have been developed as indirect measurements of a healthy body weight. Body mass index (BMI) is a calculation of body weight related to height and is correlated with disease risk. A BMI of 18.5 to 24.9 is considered healthy. A BMI from 25 to 29.9 is considered overweight and a BMI of 30 or greater is considered obese. A BMI lower than 18.5 is considered underweight.

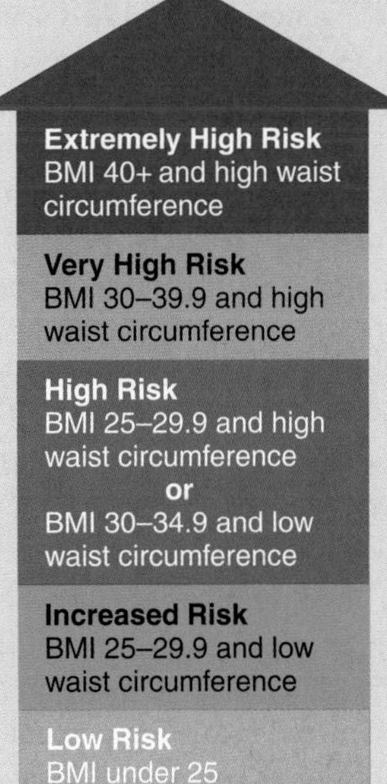

Extremely High Risk
BMI 40+ and high waist circumference
Very High Risk
BMI 30–39.9 and high waist circumference
High Risk
BMI 25–29.9 and high waist circumference
or
BMI 30–34.9 and low waist circumference
Increased Risk
BMI 25–29.9 and low waist circumference
Low Risk
BMI under 25

6 There Are Health Risks Associated with Body Fat and Fat Distribution

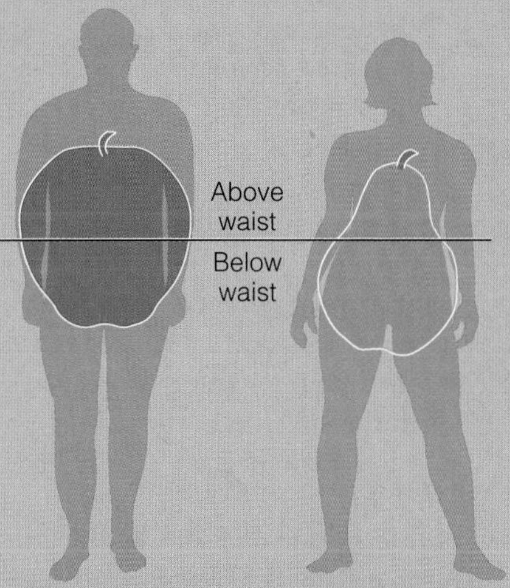

Overweight and obesity increases the individual's risk of heart disease, hypertension, stroke, and hyperlipidemia. Other factors, including type 2 diabetes, metabolic syndrome, osteoarthritis, and certain cancers, are also associated with overweight and obesity, and the risk increases as BMI increases.

The placement of body fat also affects overall health. Storing excess fat around the waist has been shown to increase the risk of heart disease, diabetes, and hypertension. The more visceral fat stored around the abdomen located near the liver, the greater the risk of insulin resistance, hyperlipidemia, and low levels of HDL cholesterol, all of which increase the risk of heart disease and diabetes.

Too little body fat can affect body functions and impair health. A BMI of less than 18.5 is considered underweight and may be a sign of malnutrition.

Terms to Know

- positive energy balance
- negative energy balance
- bomb calorimeter
- total daily energy expenditure (TDEE)
- basal metabolic rate (BMR)
- thermic effect of food (TEF)
- thermic effect of exercise (TEE)
- estimated energy requirement (EER)
- resting metabolic rate (RMR)
- lean body mass (LBM)
- non-exercise activity thermogenesis (NEAT)
- thermogenesis
- essential fat
- visceral fat
- subcutaneous fat
- body composition
- brown adipose tissue (BAT)
- central (android) obesity
- gynoid obesity
- body mass index (BMI)
- hydrostatic weighing
- air displacement plethysmography
- dual-energy X-ray absorptiometry (DEXA)
- bioelectrical impedance analysis (BIA)
- skinfold caliper
- waist circumference
- overweight
- obese
- underweight

MasteringNutrition™

Build your knowledge—and confidence—in the Study Area of MasteringNutrition with a variety of study tools.

Check Your Understanding

1. An individual who is regularly in negative energy balance will most likely
   a. lose weight.
   b. gain weight.
   c. maintain current body weight.
   d. burn more muscle weight than fat weight.
2. Kyle has a BMI of 27. He is considered
   a. underweight.
   b. overweight.
   c. at a healthy weight.
   d. obese.

3. Central or android obesity refers to
   a. the excess accumulation of fat around the hips and thighs.
   b. the excess accumulation of fat in the abdomen.
   c. the excess accumulation of fat in the arms and legs.
   d. the excess accumulation of subcutaneous fat.
4. The basal metabolic rate (BMR) refers to
   a. the amount of energy expended during physical activity.
   b. the amount of energy expended during digestion.
   c. the amount of energy consumed daily.
   d. the amount of energy expended to meet basic physiological needs that enable the organs and cells to function.
5. Fat surrounding the vital organs within the abdomen is called
   a. subcutaneous fat.
   b. visceral fat.
   c. brown adipose tissue.
   d. cellulite.
6. The method that uses the fact that lean tissue is denser than water to measure body composition is called
   a. air displacement plethysmography.
   b. bioelectrical impedance analysis.
   c. dual-energy X-ray absorptiometry.
   d. hydrostatic weighing.
7. For most adults, BMR accounts for ______________ percent of the total daily energy expenditure.
   a. 15
   b. 30
   c. 50
   d. 60
8. Which of the following statements is true?
   a. Lean body mass is more metabolically active than fat tissue.
   b. Women generally have less essential fat than men.
   c. Nicotine depresses the BMR.
   d. African-Americans have BMRs that are about 10 percent higher than Caucasians.
9. Will's breakfast contains 525 kilocalories. How many kilocalories will he expend (TEF) to process this meal?
   a. 5 to 10 kilocalories
   b. 50 to 100 kilocalories
   c. 125 to 140 kilocalories
   d. 150 to 175 kilocalories
10. Will weighs 180 pounds. How many kilocalories does he need to ingest to support his BMR for 24 hours?
   a. 1,562 kilocalories
   b. 1,795 kilocalories
   c. 1,968 kilocalories
   d. 2,049 kilocalories

Answers

1. (a) Negative energy balance means the amount of energy intake is less than the energy output. If maintained over time, negative energy balance will most likely result in weight loss.
2. (b) Because Kyle's BMI falls between 25 and 29.9, he is considered overweight. If his BMI was under 18.5, he would be underweight, whereas a BMI of 18.5 to 24.9 would put him in the healthy weight category. A BMI of 30 or higher is considered obese.
3. (b) Central obesity refers to the accumulation of excess fat in the stomach area and can be determined by measuring a person's waist circumference. Central obesity increases the risk of heart disease, diabetes, and hypertension. Excess accumulation of fat around the hips and thighs is called gynoid obesity.
4. (d) BMR refers to the minimum amount of energy needed to maintain cellular functions and keep blood circulating and lungs breathing. The amount of energy expended during physical activity is not factored into the BMR. The energy cost of digesting, absorbing, and processing food is called the thermic effect of food (TEF) and is also not part of BMR. The amount of energy consumed is part of the energy intake and doesn't factor into the BMR.
5. (b) Fat deposits that surround the vital organs within the abdomen are called visceral fat. Subcutaneous fat is sandwiched between the muscle and skin in various locations throughout the body. Brown adipose tissue is found in infants and children (and in adults in small amounts) and produces heat rather than storing excess fat. Cellulite is subcutaneous fat trapped in the connective tissue under the skin.
6. (d) Hydrostatic weighing is the method used to measure body composition based on the fact that lean tissue is denser than water. Air displacement plethysmography is based on the amount of air the body displaces. Bioelectrical impedance measures the resistance of a current by body fat, and dual-energy X-ray absorptiometry measures body fat by passing X-rays through fat-free mass and fat mass.
7. (d) For most adults, BMR accounts for approximately 60 percent of the total daily energy expenditure. The more active you are, the less influence the BMR has on the total daily energy expenditure.
8. (a) Lean body mass is more metabolically active than fat tissue and requires more kilocalories to maintain. Women have four times as much essential fat as men. Nicotine raises the BMR and African-Americans have lower BMRs than Caucasians.
9. (b) The thermic effect of food costs approximately 10 percent of the total kilocalories to process a normal mixed meal. Ten percent of 525 kilocalories equals 52 kilocalories.
10. (c) Using the simple calculation for males of 1.0 kcals/kg × 24 hours computes to 1,968 kilocalories for Will's BMR.

Answers to Myths and Misconceptions

1. **True.** Technically, exercise isn't necessary to produce a negative energy balance. It is, however, the best approach to prevent a drop in basal metabolism, and to promote health benefits.
2. **False.** Having a BMI of less than 18.5 indicates a state of underweight. Being underweight increases the risk of serious health

consequences, including anemia, heart irregularities, osteoporosis, amenorrhea, depression, and anxiety.

3. **True.** Males have a higher BMR than females mostly because they have more muscle mass and lower levels of essential fat. This higher BMR results in higher energy expenditure.
4. **True.** The *Dietary Guidelines for Americans* recommend using weight for height or body mass index calculations to estimate whether you are at a healthy weight.
5. **False.** Android obesity, or storing excess fat around the abdomen, puts an individual at higher risk for cardiovascular disease and diabetes than gynoid obesity, which is the storage of excess fat around the hips.
6. **False.** Body weight measures the amount of total body fat plus lean body mass, but does not assess the amounts of each, while body composition indicates the ratios of body fat to total body weight and lean body mass to total body weight.
7. **False.** If you eat an extra 100 kilocalories per day for a week, that is equal to 700 additional kilocalories, not the 3,500 kilocalories needed to gain a pound.
8. **False.** The most accurate techniques for measuring body composition are the densitometry measurements, including underwater hydrostatic weighing, air displacement plethysmography, and DEXA scans. However, skinfold calipers are often the least expensive and most practical method for individuals measuring body composition in a gym or recreation center, rather than at a lab.
9. **False.** A percent body fat of less than 25 for a male and 30 for a female would be considered normal. A woman should have at least 12 percent body fat to maintain normal functions, while a man can have as little as 3 percent body fat and still maintain normal body functions.
10. **True.** Overweight individuals have an increased risk of developing sleep apnea, which interrupts sleep.

Web Resources

- For more on overweight and obesity, visit the Centers for Disease Control and Prevention at www.cdc.gov/nccdphp/dnpa/obesity/index.htm
- For more information on assessing body composition and health risks, visit the National Heart, Lung and Blood Institute at www.nhlbi.nih.gov/health/public/heart/obesity/lose_wt/risk.htm

References

1. Beers, E. A., J. N. Roemmich, L. H. Epstein, and P. J. Horvath. 2008. Increasing Passive Energy Expenditure During Clerical Work. *European Journal of Applied Physiology* 103:353–360.
2. Levine, J. A., N. L. Eberhardt, and M. D. Jensen. 1999. Leptin Responses to Overfeeding: Relationship with Body Fat and Non-Exercise Activity Thermogenesis. *Journal of Clinical Endocrinology & Metabolism* 84:2751–2754.
3. Beers, E. A., et al. 2008. Increasing Passive Energy Expenditure.
4. Food and Nutrition Board. 2005. *Dietary Reference Intakes for Energy, Carbohydrate, Fiber, Fat, Fatty Acids, Cholesterol, Protein, and Amino Acids (Macronutrients)*. Washington, DC: National Academies Press.
5. Cyress, A. M., S. Lehman, G. Williams, I. Tal, D. Rodman, A. B. Goldfine, F. C. Kuo, et al. 2009. Identification and Importance of Brown Adipose Tissue in Adult Humans. *New England Journal of Medicine* 360:1509–1517.
6. National Institutes of Health. 2000. *Clinical Guidelines on the Identification, Evaluation, and Treatment of Overweight and Obesity in Adults*. Available at www.nhlbi.nih.gov/guidelines/obesity/prctgd_c.pdf. Accessed June 2012.
7. Ibid.
8. Ibid.
9. Centers for Disease Control and Prevention. *Body Mass Index: Considerations for Practioners*. Available at www.cdc.gov/obesity/downloads/BMIforPactitioners.pdf. Accessed June 2012.
10. National Institutes of Health. 2000. *Clinical Guidelines on the Identification, Evaluation, and Treatment of Overweight and Obesity in Adults*.
11. Centers for Disease Control and Prevention. 2008. *Assessing Your Weight*. Available at www.cdc.gov/nccdphp/dnpa/healthyweight/assessing. Accessed June 2012.
12. Shekharappa, R., J. S. Smilee, P. T. Mallikarjuan, K. J. Vadavathi, and M. P. Iayarajan. 2011. Correlation Between Body Mass Index and Cardiovascular Parameters in Obese and Non-Obese in Different Age Groups. *International Journal of Biological and Medical Research* 2:551–555.
13. Centers for Disease Control and Prevention. 2008. *The Health Effects of Overweight and Obesity*. Available at www.cdc.gov/nccdphp/dnpa/healthyweight/effects/index.htm. Accessed June 2012.

15 Weight Management and Disordered Eating

Chapter Objectives

After reading this chapter, you will be able to:

1. Define the terms underweight, overweight, obesity, and extreme obesity.
2. Describe the role of hyperplasia and hypertrophy of adipocytes in the development of obesity.
3. Define the terms appetite, hunger, and satiety, and describe the physiological factors involved in regulating food intake.
4. Discuss the role of genetics and the environment in the development of underweight, overweight, and obesity.
5. Describe the role of diet and exercise in achieving a reasonable rate of weight loss.
6. Design a food and exercise plan that will help maintain a healthy weight.
7. Describe the role of diet and exercise in achieving a healthy weight gain.
8. List the criteria used to diagnose eating disorders, including anorexia nervosa and bulimia nervosa, describe other disordered eating patterns, including night eating syndrome and binge eating, and discuss the treatment options for disordered eating.

1. Healthy weight loss occurs only with at least 2 hours of daily exercise. T/F
2. The body stops synthesizing fat cells after adolescence. T/F
3. Grazing throughout the day helps curb appetite and control body weight. T/F
4. Losing even 10 pounds can improve health. T/F
5. Genetics and the environment both affect body weight. T/F
6. Eating *more* vegetables and fruits can help an individual lose weight. T/F
7. Obesity is the result of eating too much and exercising too little. T/F
8. The nutrient that has the most effect on satiety is fat. T/F
9. Disordered eating and eating disorders are the same thing. T/F
10. Eating disorders can be fatal. T/F

See page 577 for answers to these Myths and Misconceptions.

In the last two decades, rates of overweight and obesity have exploded in the United States. In the early 1960s, fewer than 32 percent of Americans were overweight. Today, about 67 percent of Americans are overweight, and more than 33 percent of adults (about 72 million people) and 17 percent of children are obese.[1, 2] Not surprisingly, as more and more individuals cross the threshold into being overweight, the topic has garnered much interest in popular culture. In fact, in 2011, obesity was ranked among the top five health stories in the media.[3]

Despite its prevalence, people do not enjoy being overweight, and regularly spend large amounts of money in search of a "cure." Americans currently spend over $60 billion[4]—the highest amount ever—on everything from over-the-counter diet pills to books, magazines, online support groups, and commercial dieting centers to help shed their excess weight. Unfortunately, none of these diets are having much success, and the cost to the U.S. health care system has been estimated at over $190 billion to treat the medical complications associated with being overweight.[5]

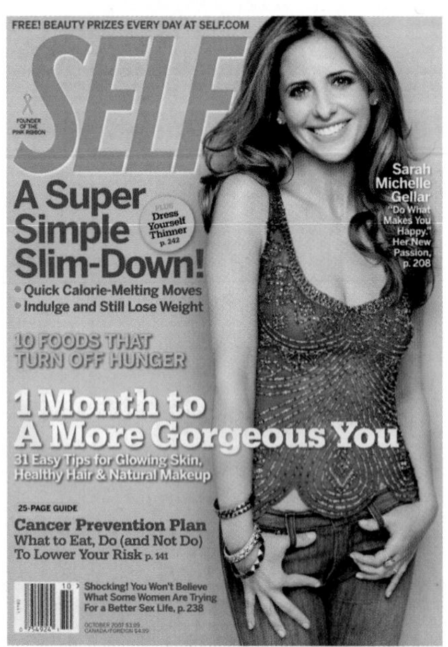

Weight management is such a hot topic in the United States that it is frequently covered by the mainstream media.

Despite the large dollar outlay spent in an attempt to lose weight, rates of overweight and obesity are still high. As you learned in Chapter 2, there has been encouraging news in the last several years that the rapid increase has leveled off and rates seem to have stabilized. The challenge now is to drive those rates down.

In this chapter, you will learn the truth about weight gain among college students and adults, as well as the overall rates of overweight and obesity in the United States, the keys to successful weight management, and healthy strategies for weight loss. We will also discuss the disordered eating patterns that sometimes occur among young women and men.

Why Is Weight Management Important?

Weight management means maintaining body weight within a healthy range. As you learned in Chapter 14, a healthy weight is a body weight that doesn't increase the risk of developing any weight-related health problems or diseases (Table 15.1).[6] In contrast, being underweight or overweight can lead to numerous diseases and conditions. Underweight individuals, particularly undernourished older adults, are at risk for low body protein and fat stores and a depressed immune system, which makes it more difficult to fight infections. Injuries, wounds, and illnesses that would normally improve in healthy individuals can cause serious medical complications, including death, in underweight individuals.[7]

Being overweight can increase the risk of hypertension, stroke, heart disease, gallbladder disease, type 2 diabetes, osteoarthritis, joint stress, sleep apnea, and some cancers, including endometrial, breast, and colon cancer. Being overweight is also a stepping stone for developing obesity, and potentially even **severe obesity** (Table 15.2). Carrying extra body weight is so detrimental to health that for overweight individuals, losing as little as 10 to 20 pounds results in health benefits.[8]

Heart disease and diabetes are two of the most serious conditions associated with overweight and obesity. Overweight people tend to have high blood levels of both triglycerides and LDL cholesterol, and less HDL cholesterol, which is an

TABLE 15.1 Definitions of Underweight, Overweight, and Obesity in Adults

Classification	BMI (kg/m^2)
Underweight	< 18.5
Normal weight	18.5–24.9
Overweight	25–29.9 (also defined as being 10 to 15 pounds above a healthy weight)
Obesity	30–39.9
Severe Obesity	> 40

TABLE 15.2 Ways to Classify Obesity

Obesity Is Classified By . . .	
Percent of body fat	Women: > 32%
	Men: > 25%
Distribution of body fat	Excess subcutaneous and visceral fat stored in the upper body (abdomen and waist); referred to as central or android obesity
	Excess subcutaneous fat stored in the lower body (hips, buttocks, thighs); referred to as gynoid obesity
Body mass index (BMI)	Women: > 30
	Men: > 25

unhealthy combination for the heart. The insulin resistance that can develop over time in overweight individuals causes the pancreas to work harder to produce more insulin, and can eventually cause the organ to stop producing insulin altogether, leading to diabetes. Does this mean obesity itself is a disease? Read the Two Points of View on page 540 for the perspective of two experts.

Beyond the physical effects of carrying too much body weight, obese and overweight individuals are often at a social, educational, and economic disadvantage. Overweight people suffer more discrimination and are more likely to be denied job promotions and raises than normal-weight individuals.[9] Obese females are less likely to be accepted into college, especially higher-ranked schools. Social situations, such as attending movies or sporting events, and travel on buses and airplanes may be limited for obese individuals due to restrictive seat sizes. These prejudices and limitations can result in lower self-esteem. Additionally, popular perceptions of laziness or weakness about overweight individuals can further affect their feelings of self-confidence and self-worth. Images of slender models as the ideal in advertising and other media help perpetuate the notion that overweight individuals are less desirable.

People often feel fat when they look in the mirror regardless of their body weight.

The psychological effects of obesity and even underweight can be just as destructive to an individual's health as the physical problems. Obese and overweight people are less likely to exercise because they are embarrassed to change in the locker room or work out at a gym. Obese people have higher rates of suicide than slim people and are more likely to use alcohol and drugs when compared with their normal-weight peers. And underweight people tend to have higher rates of depression.

To address all of these health concerns, two of the *Healthy People 2020* national health objectives aim to increase the proportion of adult Americans who are at a healthy weight by 10 percent and reduce the number of adult Americans, children, and adolescents who are obese by 10 percent.[10]

THE TAKE-HOME MESSAGE Weight management means maintaining a healthy weight (BMI 18.5 to 24.9) to reduce the risk of specific health problems. Being either overweight (BMI 25 to 29.9) or underweight (BMI less than 18.5) can be unhealthy. Heart disease and diabetes are two of the most consequential health effects of being overweight or obese. Social and psychological effects of obesity and underweight include discrimination, low self-esteem, depression, suicide, and alcohol and drug problems. *Healthy People 2020* aims to increase the percentage of adults who are at a healthy weight by 10 percent and reduce the number of adults, children, and adolescents who are obese by 10 percent.

weight management Maintaining a healthy body weight; defined as having a BMI of 18.5 to 24.9.

severe obesity Having a BMI of 40 or above; also defined as 120 percent of ideal body weight for females and 124 percent for males.

Two Points of View

Is Obesity a Disease?

Two experts discuss whether obesity should be considered a disease and the implications for using the term.

J. Michael Gonzalez-Campoy, MD, PhD, Face

Medical Director/CEO, Minnesota Center for Obesity, Metabolism and Endocrinology

Dr. J. Michael Gonzalez-Campoy is medical director and CEO of the Minnesota Center for Obesity, Metabolism and Endocrinology. He is a recognized international expert on diabetes and obesity and a proponent of adiposopathy as a treatment target. He coined the term *bariatric endocrinology* to formalize the concept that obesity is a treatable endocrine disease. Dr. Gonzalez-Campoy is a past member of the board of directors of the American Association of Clinical Endocrinologists (AACE), and past member of the Board of Trustees of the American College of Endocrinology (ACE).

Q: Does obesity fit the classic definition of a disease?

A: A disease is anything that takes away from health. Obesity is a disease because it may cause physical complications, metabolic derangements (adiposopathy), and psychological problems. The physical complications of obesity include the need to expend excess calories moving excessive body mass, sleep apnea, gastroesophageal reflux, urinary incontinence, and degenerative osteoarthritis, among others. Metabolic derangements include cholelithiasis [gallstones], insulin resistance, hypertension, type 2 diabetes mellitus, dyslipidemia [abnormal concentrations of blood lipoproteins], atherosclerosis, gout, polycystic ovarian syndrome, infertility, male hypogonadism, breast cancer, and uterine cancer. In association with obesity, psychological problems include eating disorders like bulimia and binge eating, low self-esteem, and depression. Those with an elevated body mass index (BMI) who do not currently have any of the above complications of obesity, are best considered not to have any of these problems *yet.* In 2010 AACE held a state of the science conference on pathogenic adipose tissue, and in 2011 AACE recognized obesity as a disease, putting in place a campaign to implement effective treatments for it.

Q: What evidence supports your opinion?

A: From actuarial tables we know that as the BMI increases, the incidence and risk of premature death also increases. Clearly the incidence of the complications of obesity is higher as the BMI increases. In addition to this, the Centers for Disease Control and Prevention has published epidemiological data that clearly documents an increase

Glenn Gaesser, PhD

Director, Healthy Lifestyles Research Center at Arizona State University
Professor of Exercise and Wellness at Arizona State University

Glenn Gaesser, PhD, is a professor of exercise and wellness, director of the Healthy Lifestyles Research Center at Arizona State University, and a fellow of the American College of Sports Medicine. He has written and lectured extensively on the subjects of exercise, diet, and obesity. He is the author of *Big Fat Lies: The Truth About Your Weight and Your Health* (Gurze, 2002).

Q: Does obesity fit the classic definition of a disease?

A: Obesity is currently defined as having a body mass index (BMI) of 30 or greater. By this definition, obesity does not fit the classic definition of a disease. Disease is generally defined as a condition that impairs normal functioning and is typically manifested by distinguishing signs and symptoms. There are millions of men and women with BMIs greater than 30 who have quite normal body function and who have no discernable signs and/or symptoms of health problems. For them, being "obese" is normal and healthy, and does not pose a threat. Indeed, using BMI cut-points to define obesity, or even what constitutes "normal" or "overweight," is archaic and should be discontinued.

Q: What evidence supports your opinion?

A: A report published in the *Archives of Internal Medicine* in 2008 showed that approximately one-third of men and women surveyed were "metabolically healthy," which is defined as having no more than one of the classic cardiometabolic risk markers (i.e., elevated blood pressure, elevated triglycerides, low HDL cholesterol, elevated glucose, insulin resistance, or systemic inflammation). A number of researchers have used similar criteria to characterize a "healthy obese" population. For these individuals, having a BMI greater than 30 is "normal" and should in no way be considered a disease. Furthermore, a great many studies show that, for certain established diseases, obesity may be preferred to having a so-called "normal" BMI. In chronic heart failure, for example, mortality rates are lower in obese persons than persons in the "normal" BMI range—in other words, obesity is protective. Finally, it has been shown that "obese" persons who have moderate-to-high levels of cardiovascular fitness resulting from regular in the percent of the population that has obesity over the past 25 years. Along with this increase in obesity there has been a parallel increase in new cases of diabetes mellitus. So with increasing BMI for an individual there is an increased risk of personal medical problems. And for society, the more people we have who are obese, the higher the burden of obesity-related complications. Finally, emerging data that the medical treatment of obesity decreases the risk of obesity complications, is adding to established data of risk reduction with the weight loss that follows bariatric surgery.

Q: How would the treatment options change if obesity were classified as a disease?

A: Overweight and obesity have diagnostic codes in the *International Classification of Diseases-9* (ICD-9) manual. However, obesity was not considered a disease when Medicare first created a list of diseases that it would cover. In many states there are laws that make the payment by the government for obesity medications illegal. Many third-party payers think obesity is a character flaw and the consequence of personal irresponsibility. Thus, many patients are not able to have access to the care they need. When obesity is universally considered a disease—not just in the ICD-9 manual, but also by third-party payers—patients will have access to the medical care they need, including lifestyle counseling, medical nutrition therapy, pharmacotherapy, and surgery, if appropriate. The research and development of obesity medications will improve when we all agree that obesity is a disease.

Q: In your opinion, would fewer Americans be obese if it were called a disease?

A: In my opinion calling obesity a disease is not going to change the causes of the obesity epidemic. We must focus on public health campaigns and breed a generation of healthy children for the obesity epidemic to subside. Agreeing that obesity is a disease will allow the third-party payer system to change. This in turn will improve access to care for patients who already have health problems from obesity. In the end, when we treat obesity as a disease, we will significantly delay or prevent the chronic complications that go along with it. Americans stand to save billions in health-care dollars that would have gone to treat the complications of obesity when they invest in the treatment of obesity itself.

exercise have *lower* mortality rates than their thinner counterparts who are unfit. This shows that in terms of longevity it is more important to be fit than it is to be thin.

Q: How would the treatment options change if obesity were classified as a disease?

A: If obesity were classified as a disease, I think that a significant number of large people would be unjustly stigmatized and unnecessarily "treated." For a "metabolically healthy" obese person, what needs to be treated? Having a BMI greater than 30 may be perfectly normal for them. The rationale for classifying obesity as a disease is based on the assumption that obese persons are at increased risk of cardiometabolic disease and premature death. However, many so-called weight-related health problems can be treated with exercise and a healthy diet, independent of weight change. For example, high blood pressure, insulin resistance, blood lipid abnormalities, and systemic inflammation can all be improved, if not entirely remedied, by exercise and diet, even if weight loss does not occur. In fact, several studies on overweight and obese persons show that exercise may improve cardiometabolic profile even in persons who experience a *gain* in body fat. This strongly suggests that body fat is not the underlying cause of many health problems linked to obesity.

Q: In your opinion, would fewer Americans be obese if it were called a disease?

A: Calling obesity a disease would have little, if any, impact on the number of persons considered obese by BMI criteria. Body weight and body fat are determined by a combination of genetics and lifestyle, with genetics playing the greater role. Improving diet and/or increasing physical activity levels have relatively little effect on BMI, perhaps reducing it by no more than about 1 BMI unit, on average. However, improving diet and increasing physical activity greatly improves health, and should be encouraged without emphasis on weight loss itself. Calling obesity a disease—and thus providing even greater rationale for weight loss—might actually make things worse. Weight loss is frequently followed by weight regain, often leading to a life of weight cycling. Weight cycling itself has been reported to increase risk for many of the health problems associated with obesity. Thus continued focus on shedding pounds may ultimately worsen, rather than improve, the health of persons for whom weight loss "treatment" is prescribed. We should be mindful of the words of former *New England Journal of Medicine* editors Kassirer and Angell, that "the cure for obesity may be worse than the condition."

How Do Fat Cells Form and Expand?

People become obese for two reasons: (1) because fat cells (adipocytes) can expand to store more fat in a process known as **hypertrophy**, and (2) because once a fat cell fills to capacity, it stimulates the production of more fat cells in a process known as **hyperplasia**. The excess cells build up into excess fat tissue, which is stored throughout the body (**Figure 15.1**).

The Number of Fat Cells in the Body Never Decreases

The average non-obese adult's body contains approximately 30 billion to 50 billion adipocytes, each of which holds between 0.4 and 0.5 micrograms of fat. Overweight or obese adults most likely have the same number of adipocytes as normal weight adults but their fat cells are much larger, between 0.6 to 1.2 micrograms of fat. There is evidence that when the fat cells reach their maximum size, additional fat cells may be synthesized (hyperplasia). When an overweight or obese adult loses weight, the size of the fat cell shrinks, but the number of cells does not. After weight loss, the smaller fat cells remain and can easily be filled up again when energy intake is greater than energy output. Although hyperplasia appears to slow with age,[11] the growth and production of fat cells continues throughout life. Every year about 10 percent of fat cells die and are replaced by new ones. The result is that once you create new fat cells as a child, that number of fat cells remain with you for life.[12] Whether additional fat cells are formed as an adult and what turns on hyperplasia is still not clear.

The pounds of body fat can be calculated based on the number and size of the adipocytes. Practice these calculations in the Calculation Corner.

Calculation Corner

Number and Size of Fat Cells

The average adult has 30×10^9 fat cells, with each fat cell containing approximately 0.4 micrograms of fat. How many pounds of body fat would an average adult's body contain? Remember that 1,000 micrograms = 1 mg; 1,000 mg = 1 g; 1,000 g = 1 kg.

Answer:

$$30 \times 10^9 = 30{,}000{,}000{,}000 \text{ fat cells} \times 0.4\ \mu g \text{ of fat per cell}$$
$$= 12{,}000{,}000{,}000\ \mu g \text{ of fat}$$

$$12{,}000{,}000{,}000\ \mu g = 12 \text{ kg} \times 2.2 \text{ lb} = 26.4 \text{ lbs of body fat}$$

In an adult male weighing 150 pounds (68 kg), 26 lbs of body fat (12 kg) would equal 17 percent body fat.

$$26 \text{ lbs}/150 \text{ lbs} = 0.17 \times 100 = 17\%$$

How would the percentage of body fat change if the fat cell number were 40×10^9? Or if the fat cell size were 0.5 μg?

The Size of Fat Cells Grows and Shrinks

The size of fat cells is regulated by the enzyme lipoprotein lipase (LPL), which is made in the adipose tissue and lies on the surface of the adipocyte. As you learned in Chapter 5, LPL increases lipogenesis, or the accumulation of fat in the adipocyte. Another enzyme, called hormone-sensitive lipase (HSL), plays the opposite role in fat metabolism. HSL stimulates lipolysis, or the hydrolysis of triglycerides inside the adipocyte, and frees the fatty acids, which are then released into the bloodstream. It

hypertrophy An increase in size; in adipocytes, hypertrophy refers to the increase in size of the cells.

hyperplasia An increase in the number of cells due to cell division.

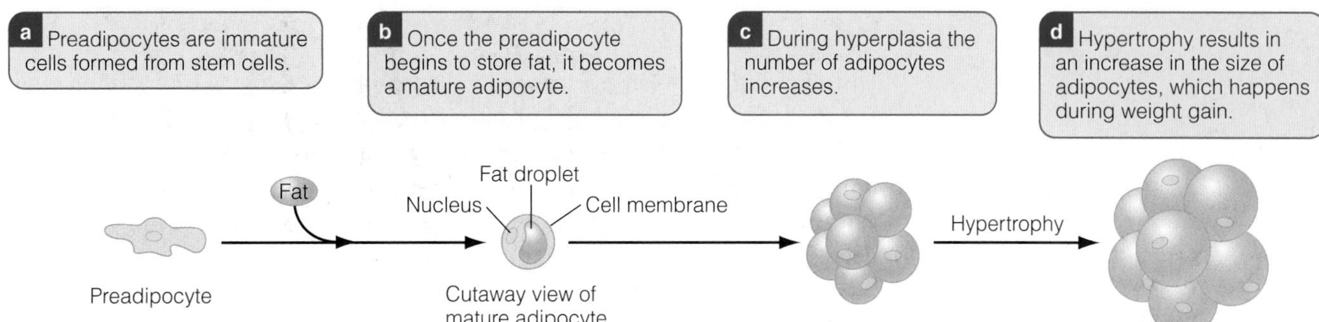

a Preadipocytes are immature cells formed from stem cells.
b Once the preadipocyte begins to store fat, it becomes a mature adipocyte.
c During hyperplasia the number of adipocytes increases.
d Hypertrophy results in an increase in the size of adipocytes, which happens during weight gain.
Fat
Fat droplet
Nucleus
Cell membrane
Hypertrophy
Preadipocyte
Cutaway view of mature adipocyte

▲ **Figure 15.1 The Formation of Adipocytes**

is the balance between fat being broken down (lipolysis) or synthesized (lipogenesis) that affects the size of the adipocyte. This is similar to a savings account—as you save money, the balance grows until you take it out and the balance shrinks. The activity of LPL and HSL differs in overfat and lean individuals.[13] Heavier people have a much more efficient activity rate of LPL, especially after eating. This makes it much easier to store energy from the meal. The activity of LPL increases following weight loss, which makes it much easier to regain lost weight.

Differences in LPL activity are also noted between genders. In men, LPL is more active in the visceral, abdominal fat cells than in females, but females have higher LPL activity rates in the hips and thighs than do males. This is probably the reason women deposit more fat in the lower body and why adipose tissue in these areas is more stable and takes longer to be oxidized. Overall, women oxidize more fat for fuel during exercise than men and although the reason is still unclear, a male's LPL activity is higher following exercise than a female's.

THE TAKE-HOME MESSAGE The average adult body contains 30 billion to 50 billion adipocytes. Once adipocytes are formed, they can increase or decrease in size as fat storage needs change, but they can never decrease in number. Every year 10 percent of fat cells die and are replaced. The enzymes lipoprotein lipase and hormone-sensitive lipase influence the balance between lipolysis and lipogenesis.

How Is Food Intake Regulated?

Why do you feel hungry? There are a variety of factors that influence not only how much we eat, but the type of food we choose to eat. These factors include strong physiological and psychological influences that go beyond the need for energy.

Hunger and Satiety Affect the Desire to Eat and Stop Eating

Two strong physiological factors, hunger and satiety, affect the amount of food individuals consume. **Hunger** is the physical sensation associated with the need or intense desire for food. Physiological signals such as low blood sugar or an empty stomach trigger hunger and searching for food. Once eating begins, hunger will subside as the feeling of fullness, or **satiety**, sets in. **Satiation** and hunger are both controlled by hormones produced in the brain and the gastrointestinal tract. These hormonal signals control short-term eating and determine how long eating lasts, how much is eaten, and the length of time between eating episodes.[14] The greater the satiation, the longer the time between eating.

hunger A strong sensation indicating a physiological need for food.

satiety The feeling of satiation or "fullness" produced by the consumption of food.

satiation The state of being satisfactorily full, which inhibits the ability to eat more food.

Appetite Often Triggers Eating for Unnecessary Reasons

Distinguishing between true hunger and **appetite**, the desire to eat based on other factors, can be difficult. Appetite is often stimulated even when we are satiated. The desire to eat may be triggered by the smell, taste, texture, or color of a specific food, or by external cues such as time of day, social occasions, or other people. Appetite can also be triggered by learned behavior, and by emotions such as stress, fear, and depression.

The Brain and Hormones Control Feeding

In the brain, two regions of the hypothalamus control the trigger mechanisms that stimulate hunger and satiation: the *ventromedial nucleus* and the *lateral hypothalamus* (**Figure 15.2**). These regions receive signals from both inside and outside the brain.

Satiation

Satiety is triggered in the ventromedial nucleus in response to a variety of physiological cues. After a meal, the stomach becomes distended, sending signals from stretch receptors in the lining of the stomach to the brain to suppress hunger. As protein, fatty acids, and monosaccharides reach the small intestine, two hormones, cholecystokinin (CCK) and peptide YY (PYY), are released, sending feedback to

appetite The desire to eat food whether or not there is hunger; a taste for particular foods and cravings in reaction to cues such as the sight, smell, or thought of food.

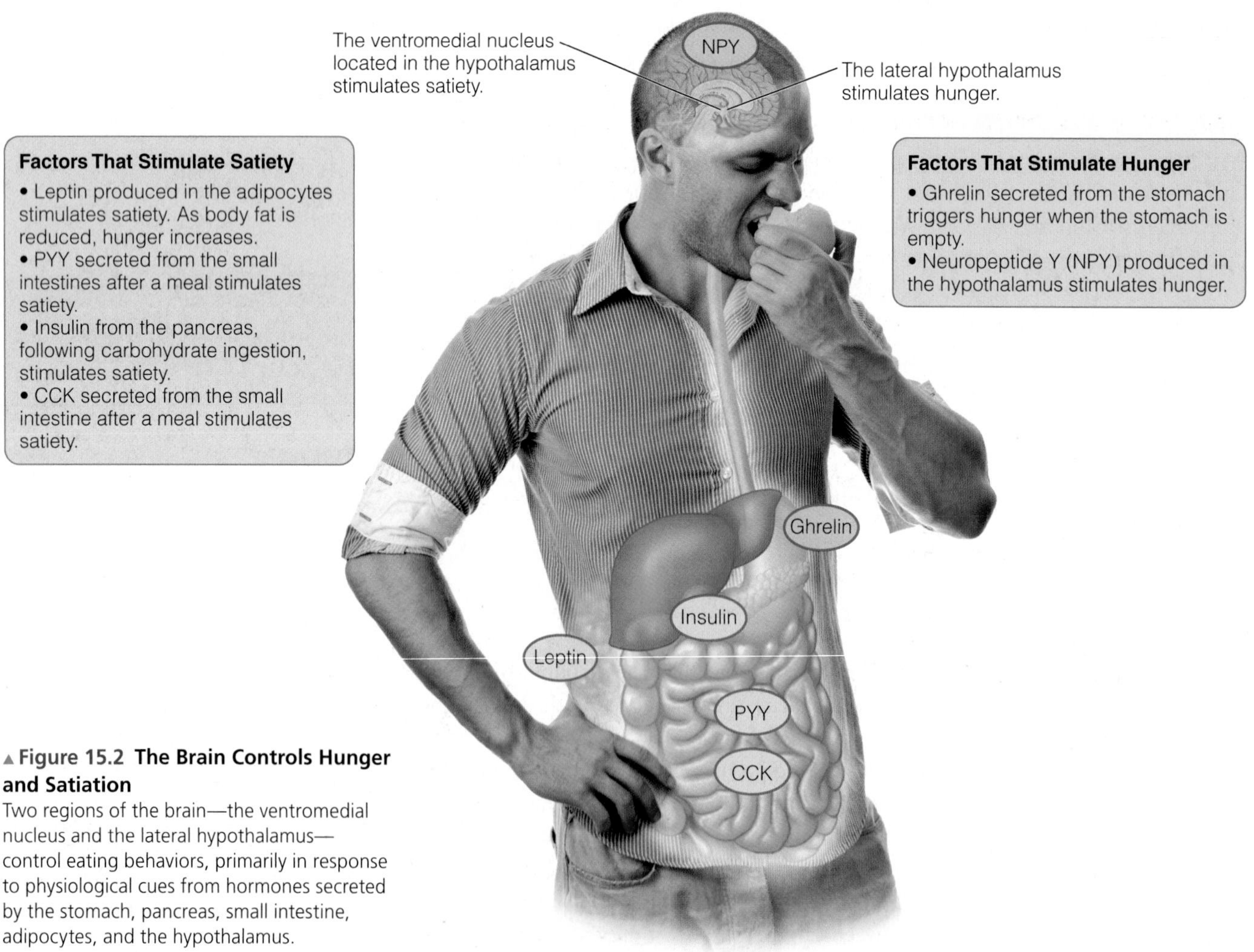

The ventromedial nucleus located in the hypothalamus stimulates satiety.
NPY
The lateral hypothalamus stimulates hunger.
Factors That Stimulate Satiety
• Leptin produced in the adipocytes stimulates satiety. As body fat is reduced, hunger increases.
• PYY secreted from the small intestines after a meal stimulates satiety.
• Insulin from the pancreas, following carbohydrate ingestion, stimulates satiety.
• CCK secreted from the small intestine after a meal stimulates satiety.
Factors That Stimulate Hunger
• Ghrelin secreted from the stomach triggers hunger when the stomach is empty.
• Neuropeptide Y (NPY) produced in the hypothalamus stimulates hunger.
Ghrelin
Insulin
Leptin
PYY
CCK

▲ **Figure 15.2 The Brain Controls Hunger and Satiation**
Two regions of the brain—the ventromedial nucleus and the lateral hypothalamus—control eating behaviors, primarily in response to physiological cues from hormones secreted by the stomach, pancreas, small intestine, adipocytes, and the hypothalamus.

the hypothalamus to increase satiety and decrease hunger.[15] Once these nutrients are absorbed, the hormone insulin is released, which also results in a decrease in hunger.[16]

Other hormones, including leptin produced in adipose tissue, influence hunger and satiety. The production of leptin is controlled by the obese gene (*ob*) and increases in amount as the fat stores increase. Leptin is a satiety signal. It acts on receptors found in the hypothalamus to decrease hunger and food intake, probably by inhibiting neuropeptide Y (NPY), a hormone that stimulates hunger. At the same time, leptin creates a negative energy balance by raising the body temperature, which in turn increases energy expenditure and stimulates the oxidation of fatty acids in the liver and muscles. Thus, leptin regulates the amount of fat stored in the adipose tissue.[17] Leptin may also be partly responsible for regaining lost body fat. When adipocytes shrink during weight loss, leptin levels drop. This reduction in leptin stimulates hunger and may drive the body to eat more to reestablish fat stores.

Not only does weight loss affect leptin levels, but intake of certain vitamins and minerals has been shown to lower leptin concentrations and affect hunger levels. For example, zinc supplements have been reported to lower leptin in obese individuals and may be responsible for overeating.[18] On the other hand, ingesting too little vitamin A and C also appears to inhibit leptin secretion.[19] The mechanism of vitamin and mineral intake effect on the hormone leptin is still unclear.

In addition to the influence of hormones, certain macronutrients, especially protein, influence satiety and reduce the intake of food. Researchers have reported that protein intake ranging from 15 to 30 percent of total kilocalorie intake significantly reduces food intake.[20]

Hunger

While the ventromedial nucleus affects satiety, the lateral hypothalamus controls hunger. The lateral hypothalamus is stimulated by the hormone ghrelin, which is produced in the gastric cells. Ghrelin has the opposite effect of leptin—it stimulates hunger. Ghrelin concentrations rise in the blood before a meal and ghrelin travels through the blood to the hypothalamus, where it activates neuropeptide Y and stimulates hunger.

The production of ghrelin changes throughout the day. More ghrelin is produced between meals, during sleep, or when you fast. This increase in ghrelin production signals the hypothalamus that the body needs energy. Ghrelin levels drop following a meal, especially one that contains high amounts of carbohydrate and/or kilocalories. This drop in ghrelin levels signals satiety and decreases the urge to eat.

Lean individuals tend to have higher levels of ghrelin than individuals with more body fat, especially in the morning hours. The fact that ghrelin levels increase when an individual is on a low-kilocalorie diet may be one reason people on weight-reduction diets are hungry and find it difficult to lose weight.[21]

In an ideal world, the physiological mechanisms would keep the body in perfect energy balance. Individuals would eat when they were hungry and stop once they were satiated. The reality is that many people override these mechanisms and end up in energy imbalance. Eating in the absence of hunger may be a behavioral trait through which obesity-promoting genes can cause positive energy balance. Factors like genetics and the environment also affect the energy balance equation.

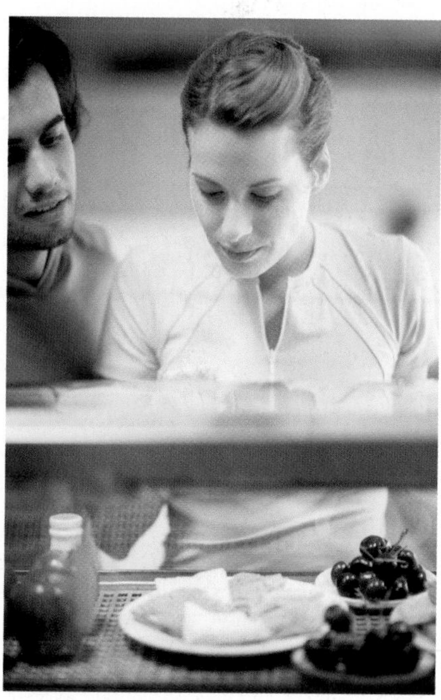

Hunger is stimulated by circulating hormones and signals from your intestinal tract.

THE TAKE-HOME MESSAGE Food intake is controlled by hunger, satiety, and appetite. Hunger is a strong physiological need for food and satiety is the physiological response to food intake, resulting in satisfaction. Hunger and satiety are controlled by the hypothalamus and regulated by neuropeptides, hormones, and neural signals from the gastrointestinal tract and adipocytes. Appetite is the desire for food controlled by psychological factors. The hormones leptin and ghrelin play key roles in triggering hunger and satiety, with ghrelin triggering hunger and leptin triggering satiation.

How Do Genetics and Environment Influence Obesity and Weight Management?

People who share genes will often have similar body weights.

Most health professionals now agree that obesity arises from the interaction of multiple genes (not just a single gene) with the environment, making weight management and the prevention of obesity challenging.[22] The relationship of genes to obesity was first demonstrated in studies on separated identical twins raised in different home environments who have similar weight gain and body fat distribution.[23] On the other hand, our genetic code has not changed in the last few decades, since the obesity epidemic began. Therefore the environment in which we work and live must have a strong effect on weight. This relationship is referred to as a **gene–environment interaction**. The question is, which is stronger, nature or nurture?

Two new areas of study, nutrigenomics and epigenetics, may hold the answer to this question. The science of nutrigenomics, first introduced in Chapter 1, has identified specific genes that are involved in the body's response to certain nutrients such as dietary fat, and can pinpoint the variation in the gene that may be responsible for the body's response. However, even with identical twins that have the same genetic makeup, the response to overeating or restricting kilocalories varies.

Researchers are still unclear what mechanism causes genes and nutrients to interact. This is where epigenetics comes into play. Epigenetic mechanisms may integrate the signals from your genes with environmental signals and change the way the genes behave in response to food intake.

Genetics Can Influence Hunger, Satiety, and Insulin Response

There are currently more than 40 genetic variants that are associated with obesity.[24] Some of these genes influence how you store body fat, hunger and satiety patterns, and food intake.[25] The possibility of genes affecting hunger suggests that genetic differences in the level or the functioning of some hormones can influence a person's body weight and appetite.[26]

Earlier in the chapter, you learned that the hypothalamus regulates hunger and satiety by responding to signals from the adipocytes, the pancreas, the stomach, and the small intestine. These signals are conveyed to the brain by the hormones leptin, insulin, CCK, peptide YY, and ghrelin. The hypothalamus then instructs you to eat more or eat less. Multiple genes are involved in the way the body receives and responds to the signals, and even small changes in each gene can turn the gene "on" or "off." These small changes are called single-nucleotide polymorphisms, referred to as SNPs, or "snips." Each SNP represents a change in the building blocks of DNA, or a copy error. For example, in a gene with a SNP, a length of DNA might have the nucleotide thymine (T) in place of the nucleotide cytosine (C), which changes the way the gene behaves. This is similar to dialing a telephone number with one wrong digit. Most SNPs have no effect whatsoever on body weight, but some play an important role in how individuals respond to food intake.

gene–environment interaction The interaction of genetics and environmental factors that increases the risk of obesity in susceptible individuals.

There are SNPs of specific genes that affect eating behavior. For example, a SNP of the ghrelin gene may cause high levels of ghrelin (remember, ghrelin stimulates hunger) to be released, which may cause some people to overeat and become obese.[27] Individuals who are genetically prone to a leptin deficiency (remember, leptin suppresses appetite) become massively obese, yet when they are given leptin, their appetite decreases and their weight falls to within a healthy range.[28] Ironically, many obese people have adequate amounts of leptin, but the brain has developed a resistance to it, rendering its appetite control ineffective.[29] For these individuals, other mechanisms prevent leptin from functioning as a regulator of appetite.

The adipocytes also secrete another hormone called **adiponectin**, which controls the body's response to insulin. The levels of this hormone are higher in lean people but are low in obese individuals and type 2 diabetics. This difference may be explained by a single-nucleotide polymorphism of the adiponectin gene and may explain why obesity increases the risk for diabetes.

Some individuals also respond differently to their environment, suggesting that genetic differences can maintain obesity. When excessive amounts of food are available, some people store more fat, and in environments where food is scarce, they lose less fat compared with others.[30]

Genetics may also affect thermogenesis, which in turn impacts how kilocalories are expended in the body. Genes may cause different rates of thermogenesis in brown adipose tissue and in non-exercise activity thermogenesis (NEAT). When some individuals overeat, they burn rather than store excess kilocalories and are thus better able to manage their energy balance.[31] Many overweight individuals don't appear to have this compensatory mechanism.

Some researchers have described a genetic "**set point**" that determines body weight. This theory holds that the body fights to remain at a specific body weight and opposes attempts at weight loss. The body may even enable very easy weight gain when weight is lost in order to get back to this "set point." In other words, a person's weight remains fairly constant because the body "has a mind of its own." Given that the weight of Americans has disproportionately increased over the last few decades relative to previous decades, this theory either isn't true or the set point can be overridden.[32]

If a person's lifestyle stays the same, his or her weight should remain fairly stable. However, if the environment shifts to make it easier to gain weight, the body will also shift, but it will shift upward. For example, rats, who should genetically be able to maintain a healthy body weight, have been shown to overeat and become fat when given access to unlimited fatty foods and sweets.[33]

Research comparing the Pima Indians in Arizona to their ancestors in Mexico reveals that the environment can impact weight-susceptible populations. The Arizona Pima Indians share ancestry with the Mexican Pima Indians who migrated from a remote location in the northwestern part of Mexico. The original population of Mexican Pima Indians passed their genetic heritage on to their Arizona descendants, but not their lifestyle. The traditional Mexican Pimas lived a physically active lifestyle and ate a diet both rich in complex carbohydrates and lower in animal fats than that of the "Americanized" Pimas living in Arizona, who had a more sedentary lifestyle and consumed a fatty diet. Mexican Pimas had, on average, a BMI of about 25, compared with Arizona Pimas who had, on average, a BMI of over 33.[34, 35] The traditional Pimas had a better chance of avoiding obesity because they lived in a healthier environment. This suggests that even if you have a genetic predisposition to being overweight, it's not a done deal. If you are determined to make healthy dietary choices and engage in regular physical activity, you can overcome your genes.

adiponectin A hormone produced in the adipocytes that controls the body's response to insulin and may be involved in reducing the risk of obesity and type 2 diabetes.

set point A weight-control theory that states each individual has a genetically established body weight. Any deviation from this point will stimulate changes in body metabolism to reestablish the normal weight.

Self-Assessment

Does Your Environment Impact Your Energy Balance?

1. Do you eat out at least once a day?

   Yes ☐ **No** ☐

2. Do you often buy snacks at convenience stores or vending machines?

   Yes ☐ **No** ☐

3. Do you buy the supersized portions of fast foods or snacks?

   Yes ☐ **No** ☐

4. When you order pizza, do you have it delivered?

   Yes ☐ **No** ☐

5. Do you drive around the parking lot to get the closest parking space to the entrance?

   Yes ☐ **No** ☐

6. Do you get off at the subway or bus stop that is nearest to your destination?

   Yes ☐ **No** ☐

7. Do you take the elevator when stairs are available in a building?

   Yes ☐ **No** ☐

Answer

All of the above habits contribute to an obesity-promoting environment. If you answered "yes" to three or more, you should think about how you can improve your lifestyle habits.

Environmental Factors Can Increase Appetite and Decrease Physical Activity

Many stimuli in the environment can drive appetite. In addition to aromas and certain venues such as movie theaters, events such as holidays and sporting events, people, including friends and family, and even the convenience of obtaining food can all encourage eating in the absence of hunger.

Over the past few decades, the environment around us has changed in ways that have made it easier to incur a positive energy imbalance and gain weight. An environment in which people can easily and cheaply obtain endless amounts of energy-dense food may be one of the biggest culprits in the current obesity epidemic. To explain how these two factors interact with each other, researchers have used the analogy that genes load the gun but an obesity-promoting environment pulls the trigger.[36] Environmental factors that seem particularly important include lack of time, an abundant food supply and portion distortion, and lack of physical activity. Take the Self-Assessment: Does Your Environment Impact Your Energy Balance? to reflect upon your environment and whether it may impact the lifestyle decisions you make throughout the day.

Lack of Time

One environmental factor influencing the weight of Americans is that we're not eating at home as much. Research shows that adults spend more time traveling to work and devote more of their daily hours to work than in previous decades.[37] This longer workday means there is less time to devote to everyday activities, such as food preparation. Today, almost a third of Americans' daily kilocalories come from ready-to-eat foods that are not prepared at home.[38] Between 1972 and 1995, the prevalence of eating out in the United States increased by almost 90 percent, a trend that is expected to increase steadily to the year 2020.[39] To accommodate this demand, the number of eateries in the United States has almost doubled, to nearly 900,000 food service establishments, during the last three decades.[40]

Dining out frequently is associated with a higher BMI. Research has shown that women who dine out five or more times weekly consume close to 300 kilocalories more on dining-out days than do women who eat at home.[41] The top foods selected when eating out, especially among college-aged diners, are energy-dense french fries and hamburgers.[42] Less-energy-dense, waist-friendly vegetables, fruits, and salads didn't even make the top choices on the list. For many people, dining out often is harming their diet by making energy-dense foods too readily available and displacing less-energy-dense vegetables and fruits.

Periods of economic decline and high unemployment, although financially stressful, can actually be beneficial when it comes to improving people's body weight. One of the first cost-cutting measures in many households is to dine out less and eat at home more, which often helps cut kilocalorie intake. In one 2009 survey, 47 percent of respondents indicated that eating out less was one way they planned to reduce spending in the wake of the 2008 recession.[43] According to the National Restaurant Association, in March 2008, 55 percent of restaurants nationwide showed a drop in business compared with March 2007.[44]

Research has shown that women who dine out five or more times weekly consume close to 300 kilocalories more on dining-out days than do women who eat at home.

An Abundant Food Supply and Portion Distortion

In the United States food is easy to get, there's a lot to choose from, and portion sizes are generous. All of these factors are associated with consuming too many kilocalories.[45]

Years ago, people went to a bookstore for the sole purpose of buying a book. Now they go to a bookstore to sip a vanilla latte and nibble on biscotti while they ponder which book to buy. Americans can grab breakfast at a hamburger drive-through, lunch at a museum, a sub sandwich at many gas stations, and a three-course meal of nachos, pizza, and ice cream at a movie theatre.

This access to a variety of foods is problematic for weight-conscious individuals. The appeal of a food diminishes as it continues to be eaten (that is, the first bite will taste the best and each subsequent bite loses some of that initial pleasure), but having a variety of foods available allows the eater to move on to another food once boredom sets in.[46] The more good-tasting foods that are available, the more a person will eat. For example, during that three-course meal at the movie theatre, once you're tired of the nachos, you can move on to the pizza, and when that loses its appeal, you can dig into the ice cream. If the pizza and ice cream weren't available, you would have stopped after the nachos and consumed fewer kilocalories.

Portion sizes of french fries have more than doubled from the past. Choose the smaller size to reduce the ingestion of kilocalories.

As you learned from Chapter 2, the portion sizes of many foods, such as french fries and sodas, have doubled, if not tripled, compared with the portions listed on food labels. Consumers perceive "supersized" portions as bargains because they often cost only slightly more than the regular size. Research shows that people tend to eat more of a food, and thus more kilocalories, when larger portions are served.[47] In other words, when served a supersized soft drink, a person will consume more, if not all, of it even though a smaller drink would have provided the same level of satisfaction.

At home, the size of the serving bowl or package of food influences the amount that ends up on the plate. Serving from a large bowl or package has been shown to increase the serving size by more than 20 percent.[48] This means that you are more likely to scoop out (and eat) a bigger serving of ice cream from a half-gallon container than from a pint container. To make matters worse, most people don't compensate for these extra kilocalories by reducing the portions at the next meal.[49]

Lack of Physical Activity

Americans are not only eating about 300 more kilocalories daily (and have been since 1985), they are also expending less energy during their entire day.[50] The increase in "kilocalories in" and decrease in "kilocalories out" is a recipe for a positive energy imbalance and weight gain. Compared with years past, Americans are expending less energy both at work and in the little leisure time that they have.

When your great-grandparents went to work in the morning in the 1940s, chances are good they headed out to the fields or off to the factory. Your parents and older siblings, though, are more likely to head to an office and sit in front of a computer, and you will probably sit at a desk for much of your workday. This shift in work from jobs that required manual labor to jobs that are sedentary has been shown to increase the risk of becoming overweight or obese.[51] One study found that men who sit for more than six hours during their workday are at higher risk of being overweight than those who sit for less than an hour daily.[52] Technology in the workplace now allows us to communicate with everyone without having to leave our desks. This means that people no longer have to get up and walk to see the colleague down the hall or the client across town.

Researchers estimate that a 145-pound person expends 3.9 kilocalories for each minute of walking, compared with 1.8 kilocalories per minute sitting. Thus, walking 10 minutes during each workday to communicate in person with coworkers would expend 10,000 kilocalories annually, yet only about 5,000 kilocalories would be expended if the person sat in the office sending e-mails or calling colleagues on the phone. Over the course of a year, these extra 5,000 kilocalories not expended could add up to over a pound of body weight. After five years in the workforce, there would be around five extra pounds of body weight sitting in the chair.

As technology continues to advance and allows for less energy expenditure during the day, *planned* physical activity at another time of day must make up

Increased amounts of "screen time" are contributing to decreased amounts of physical activity.

the difference. Unfortunately, more than 20 percent of Americans report no daily leisure-time physical activity, due partly to the fact that leisure and social activities have also become more sedentary.[53] Research shows that those aged 2 to 18 years old spend over 5 hours daily, on average, on a combination of "screen time" activities. These include watching TV, playing video games, and non-work/school–related computer time—even though experts have suggested limiting screen time to 2 hours daily.

With less energy being expended during both work and play, weight gain is becoming easier and the need for weight loss even greater. Combine this with an environment that is conducive to eating and it's not difficult to see why many people are becoming overweight or obese. Many Americans have to begin making conscious diet and lifestyle changes that will help them lose weight, or at the very least, prevent further weight gain.

THE TAKE-HOME MESSAGE Genetic influences, including the blood levels of leptin and ghrelin, play a role in obesity and weight management. Several current environmental factors—which provide easy access to a variety of energy-dense foods and at the same time decrease energy expenditure—encourage obesity.

How Can You Lose Weight Healthfully?

Although the easiest way to avoid having to lose weight is to not gain weight in the first place, for those looking to shed pounds, healthy weight loss is an attainable goal. There are more than 3,000 diet books on the market, written by everyone from popular TV show therapists to celebrity advisers and self-proclaimed experts with credible credentials. Many of these books promise quick, dramatic results. The reality is that few are based on legitimate science (see Examining the Evidence: What Are the Latest Trends in Popular Diets? for more on how the various diet plans compare). The real key to weight loss is a commitment to adopting healthy diet and lifestyle habits, and maintaining them over time.

Strive for a Reasonable Rate of Weight Loss

According to the National Institutes of Health, overweight individuals should aim to lose about 10 percent of their body weight over a six-month period.[54] This means that the goal for an overweight, 180-pound person would be to shed 18 pounds in half a year, which would be about 3 pounds a month or ¾ pound weekly. Because a person must have an energy deficit of approximately 3,500 kilocalories to lose a pound of fat, a deficit of 250 to 500 kilocalories daily will result in a reasonable weight loss of about ½ to 1 pound weekly. Any diet that promises quicker weight-loss results is likely to restrict kilocalories to the point of falling short of nutrient needs. Practice calculating the amount of reasonable weight loss you can expect in the Calculation Corner.

Though there is no single diet approach that has been universally embraced, many health experts agree that a person needs to modify three areas of life for successful, long-term weight loss. These three areas are diet, physical activity, and behavior (see **Figure 15.3** on page 553).

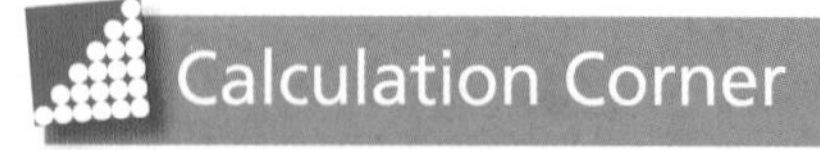

Calculation Corner

Calculating Percentage of Weight Loss

If an overweight individual weighs 237 pounds at the beginning of a weight-loss program, what would he or she weigh after six months if the recommendations for healthy weight loss were followed?

Answer: The individual's initial weight minus 10 percent

$237 \text{ lbs} - (237 \times 0.10) = 213.3 \text{ lbs}$

Remember that Kilocalories Count

When it comes to losing weight, two important words need to be remembered: kilocalories count—no matter where they come from. Because an energy imbalance of too many kilocalories in and not enough kilocalories out causes weight gain,

EXAMINING THE EVIDENCE

What Are the Latest Trends in Popular Diets?

Americans spend over $60 billion annually on weight-loss programs, products, and pills and are more than willing to keep reaching into their wallets for the next quick diet fix.[1] Although it may seem that there is a new fad diet around every corner, many of these diets have actually been around for years.

Whether it's the low-carbohydrate, high-protein and high-fat diets of the 1970s (Dr. Atkins' Diet Revolution), the very high-carbohydrate and very low-fat diets of the 1980s and 1990s (Pritikin diets and Dr. Ornish's diet), or the return to the low-carbohydrate, high-protein and high-fat diets in the early 2000s (Dr. Atkins' New Diet Revolution, South Beach), they all have one thing in common: Kilocalories are reduced by either manipulating the amount of carbohydrate, protein, and fat consumed or reducing portion sizes. The table below presents the classification of these diets.

After four decades of clashing popular diets, does one dietary approach emerge as the clear winner in the battle of the bulge? The answer is no. Researchers who analyzed close to 200 weight-loss studies using a variety of these diets concluded that it's the kilocalories, not the composition of the diet, that count when it comes to losing weight.[2] In fact, a study comparing the Atkins, Ornish, Weight Watchers, and Zone diets showed that no matter what diet the individuals followed, they

Distinguishing Among Popular Diets

Dietary Approach	Weight Loss Claim	What You Eat	Pros	Cons	Examples
Very low kilocalorie	Severely limiting kcals burns fat and reduces body weight	400 to 800 kcals per day; liquid meals containing vitamins, electrolytes, minerals, and essential fatty acids; high in protein (up to 125 g/day)	Quick weight loss of 15–20% in 12–16 weeks; improves glycemic control in type 2 diabetics; reduced hypertension and hyperlipidemia	Numerous side effects: fatigue, hypotension, headaches, dizziness, constipation and gallstones in long-term use; loss of lean body tissue; regain 50% of weight lost in one year	■ Medifast ■ Cabbage Soup Diet ■ Cookie Diet
Balanced, reduced kilocalorie	Moderate reduction of kcals promotes weight loss at a healthy rate	1,200 to 1,800 kcals per day; balanced 45–65% carbohydrate, 20–30% fat and 10–35% protein; wide variety of foods; portions are controlled	Average weight loss of 1 to 2 pounds per week; approach balances reduced food intake by portion sizes and exercise, which helps maintain lean body mass; behavior modification	Low adherence rates; some programs require prepackaged foods	■ Jenny Craig ■ Weight Watchers ■ Nutrisystem ■ The Biggest Loser Diet
Restricted carbohydrate, high protein	Insulin promotes fat storage; low glycemic foods are more satisfying, which limits total food intake	Less than 100 gm carbohydrate per day; excludes most fruits, grains, starchy vegetables, and legumes; allows meat, limited dairy, and fats	Hunger is controlled; weight loss; improved glycemic control; may improve HDL and triglycerides	Reduced glycogen, loss of lean body tissue and electrolytes; side effects include fatigue, headaches, dizziness, and constipation; nutritional deficiencies	■ Atkins Diet ■ South Beach Diet ■ Belly Fat Cure
High carbohydrate, low fat	When fat is restricted, fewer kcals are consumed	< 20% fat, > 55% carbohydrate; low-energy-dense plant foods: fruits, vegetables, whole grains; low or void of animal foods; limited nuts and seeds	Significant weight loss due to low kcal intake; allows you to eat more	Low adherence rates; limited food options, may have poor nutrient absorption due to low fat intake and high fiber	■ Ornish Diet ■ Pritikin Program ■ Pasta Diet

all lost about the same amount of weight, on average, by the end of one year.[3]

A very interesting point emerged from this study: People who were most diligent about adhering to the diet—no matter which one—experienced the most weight loss. However, over 20 percent of the dieters called it quits only two months into the study and more than 40 percent of them dropped out after one year. The highest dropout rates occurred among followers of the Atkins or Ornish diets. The researchers speculate that the rigidity and lack of variety of foods in these extreme diets caused the higher dropout rates.

Red Flags for Diet Hype

Marketers often make sensational claims about fad diets and weight-loss products. These red flags can often tell you if a diet is questionable.

It's the Carbohydrates, Not the Kilocalories, That Make You Fat!

Some diet ads claim you can eat as much protein and fat as you want as long as you keep away from carbohydrates. These diets claim that consumption of pasta, breads, rice, and many fruits and vegetables should be limited, but fatty meats such as ribs, salami, bologna, and poultry with skin, as well as butter, bacon, and cheeses should be on the menu often.

Diets that severely limit carbohydrates (less than 100 grams) eliminate so many foods, as well as sweets and treats, that it is impossible for a person not to consume at least 500 fewer kilocalories daily. This will theoretically produce about one pound of weight loss per week.[4] Curtailing the carbohydrates will likely also curtail dietary fat.[5] This is because cutting out the bagel (carbs) also means cutting out the butter or cream cheese that's slathered on top. Also, the monotonous nature of these diets causes people to become "bored" with eating, so they stop.

However, a diet high in saturated fat and low in fiber and phytochemicals is a recipe for heart disease, cancer, constipation, elevated blood cholesterol levels, and deficiencies in many vitamins and minerals, such as vitamins A, E, and B_6, folate, calcium, iron, zinc, and potassium.[6] Besides being potentially unhealthy, such a restricted diet is difficult to adhere to for an extended period of time.

Lose Ten Pounds in One Week!

Many diets guarantee rapid weight loss. The 4- to 7-pound weight loss during the first week of a restricted diet is due to loss of body water that results from two physiological processes. First, because the reduced amount of carbohydrates can't support the body's need for glucose, stored glycogen in the liver and muscle will be broken down. Each gram of glycogen removed from storage causes the loss of 2 grams of water with it. Because the body stores about 500 grams of glycogen, it can lose approximately 2 pounds of water weight during the first week of a low-carbohydrate diet. Secondly, ketone bodies generated by the breakdown of fat for energy are lost from the body through the kidneys. This will also cause the body to lose sodium. As you learned in Chapter 11, where sodium goes, water follows. Thus, the ketone bodies that cause sodium loss will also cause water loss.[7]

Note that it would be impossible for the body to lose more than a few pounds of *fat* in one week. To lose just one pound of body fat in a week requires a negative energy balance of 3,500 kilocalories per week, or 500 kilocalories per day. For 10 pounds of fat, that would equal a deficit of 35,000 kilocalories for seven days, or 5,000 kilocalories per day. This is a reduction of more than double the amount of kilocalories most people consume in a day.

Although water weight may be lost during the first week on a diet, the rate of weight loss after that is determined by the energy imbalance in the body. This is true for any kilocalorie-reducing diet. As soon as carbohydrates are added back to the diet, the body will retain water and some water weight will come back on. When it comes to shedding weight, quick loss usually means quick regain.

Celebrity-Endorsed Miracle Weight-Loss Products with a Money-Back Guarantee!

Just because a celebrity tries to sell a product doesn't mean that the product works. It just means that the celebrity is being paid to do what he or she does best: act. The Federal Trade Commission (FTC) has charged many firms that sell dubious products with public deception. One such company, Enforma Natural Products, Inc., was fined $10 million.[8] Forget about getting your money back. The FTC has received numerous complaints from dissatisfied customers who have unsuccessfully tried to get a refund. The more miraculous the claim, the more likely you are to lose money, not weight.

Naturally Occurring Plants, Herbs, and Other Substances Will Result in Weight Loss Without Risk!

"Natural" substances, such as guar gum, glucomannan, chitosan, and bitter orange are not necessarily safer or more effective for weight loss. Glucomannan is a compound found in the root of the starchy konjac plant, and guar gum is a type of dietary fiber found in a specific bean. Both are ineffective in weight loss. Chitosan is produced from a substance found in shellfish. Though the claim is that these substances decrease the absorption of fat in the body, research doesn't back up the claim. Bitter orange is a plant that is being touted as a substitute for ephedra (see the medications listed in the Health Connection: Extreme Measures for Extreme Obesity on page 563), yet the research is not definitive on its ability to stimulate weight loss.[9]

Guar gum has been shown to cause diarrhea, flatulence, and gastrointestinal disturbances. Chitosan may cause nausea and flatulence.[10] Bitter orange can increase blood pressure and interfere with the metabolism of other drugs in the body.[11] Naturally occurring substances are not necessarily safe to consume, and there's no evidence that they help with weight loss.

References

1. PRWeb. 2011. U. S. Weight Loss Market Worth $60.9 Billion. Available at www.prweb.com/releases/2011/5/prweb8393658.htm. Accessed June 2012.
2. Freedman, M., J. King, and E. Kennedy. 2001. Popular Diets: A Scientific Review. *Obesity Research* 9:1S–40S.
3. Dansinger, M., J. Gleason, J. Griffith, H. Selker, and E. Schaefer. 2005. Comparison of the Atkins, Ornish, Weight Watchers, and Zone Diets for Weight Loss and Heart Disease Risk Reduction. *Journal of the American Medical Association* 293:43–53.
4. Yudkin, J. and M. Carey. 1960. The Treatment of Obesity by the "Highfat" Diet: The Inevitability of Calories. *The Lancet* 2:939–941.
5. Ornish, D. 2004. Was Dr. Atkins Right? *Journal of the American Dietetic Association* 104:537–542.
6. Denke, M. 2001. Metabolic Effects of High-Protein, Low-Carbohydrate Diets. *The American Journal of Cardiology* 88:59–61.
7. Ibid.
8. Federal Trade Commission. 2000. Marketers of "The Enforma System" Settle FTC Charges of Deceptive Advertising for Their Weight-Loss Products. Available at www.quackwatch.org/02ConsumerProtection/FTCActions/enforma.html. Accessed June 2012.
9. Dwyer, J., D. Allison, and P. Coates. 2005. Dietary Supplements in Weight Reduction. *Journal of the American Dietetic Association* 105:S80–S86.
10. Pittler, M. and E. Ernst. 2004. Dietary Supplements for Body-Weight Reduction: A Systematic Review. *American Journal of Clinical Nutrition* 79:529–536.
11. Dwyer, J., et al. 2005. Dietary Supplements in Weight Reduction.

reversing the imbalance will cause the opposite. That is, taking in fewer kilocalories and burning off more will result in weight loss. The dietary goal then, is to reduce the number of kilocalories consumed in foods. This can be done in several ways: by choosing lower-kilocalorie foods, by eating less food overall, or a combination of both.

However, cutting back too drastically on kilocalories is a culprit behind many failed weight-loss attempts. If a person skips meals or isn't satiated at each meal because of skimpy portions, the person will experience hunger between meals and be more inclined to snack on energy-dense foods. Thus a key factor for success during the weight-loss process is for the person to eat a healthy, balanced diet that provides fewer kilocalories, but is also *satisfying*. One strategy that many find helpful is to eat several small, nutritious meals throughout the day rather than the typical three large meals. Eating more frequent meals will keep a person from getting too hungry and overeating at one sitting, while keeping meals small and nutrient dense will ensure adequate nutrient intake without an overconsumption of kilocalories. Note that eating several small meals is not the same thing as *grazing*.

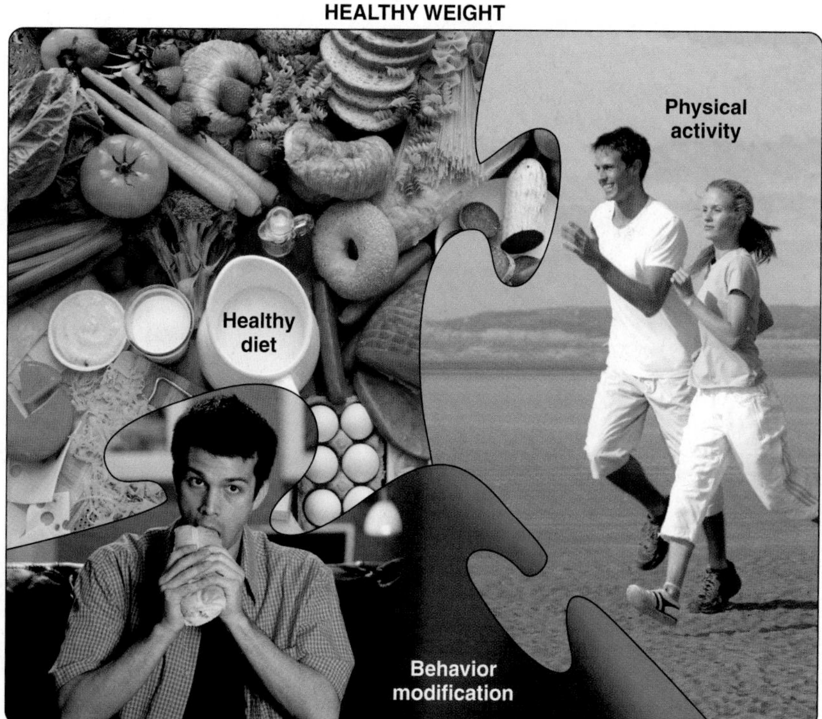

▲ **Figure 15.3 Three Pieces of the Long-Term Weight-Loss Puzzle**
Diet, physical activity, and behavior modification are the three keys to long-term weight management.

Grazing involves constant eating or nibbling throughout the day without allowing for feelings of hunger or satiation. This mindless eating behavior results in overconsumption of kilocalories and is considered a high-risk behavior for weight gain.[55]

Eat More Vegetables, Fruit, and Fiber

Research suggests that the volume (or bulk) of food consumed at a meal is very important. People tend to eat the same amount of food regardless of its energy density—that is, the amount of kilocalories in the meal.[56] In other words, a meal or snack needs to be of sufficient size (high in volume or bulk) in order to feel full or satisfying. As you learned in Chapter 4, it is very easy to overeat energy-dense, low-volume foods such as candy, which can easily fill you *out* before they fill *up*. In other words, you'll consume excess kilocalories before you become satiated. The reverse of this—consuming high-volume, low-energy-density, watery vegetables and fruits at meals and snacks—is associated with increased satiety and reduced feelings of hunger and kilocalorie intake—all helpful in weight management.[57] Try calculating the energy density of foods in the Calculation Corner.

In fact, consuming a large, high-volume, low-energy-density salad at the beginning of a meal can reduce the kilocalories eaten at that meal by over 10 percent.[58] Adding vegetables to sandwiches and soups will increase both the volume of food consumed and meal satisfaction and help displace higher kilocalorie items (**Figure 15.4**). Feeling full after eating a sandwich loaded with vegetables reduces the consumption of energy-dense potato chips. This is important because you don't need to eliminate chips from your diet if you enjoy them. Any food—from chocolate

Change low-volume...

3/4 cup chicken broth: **29** calories
1/2 cup chicken (white meat): **106** calories
1 cup noodles: **212** calories

347 total calories

2 slices whole-wheat bread: **138** calories
4 oz ham: **125** calories
2 oz American cheese: **213** calories

476 total calories

...to high volume

3/4 cup chicken broth: 29 calories
1/2 cup chicken (white meat): 106 calories
1/2 cup noodles: 106 calories
1/2 cup mixed vegetables: 59 calories
300
total calories
2 slices whole wheat-bread: 138 calories
2 oz ham: 63 calories
1 oz American cheese: 106 calories
2 slices tomato: 7 calories
2 leaves Romaine lettuce: 10 calories
324
total calories

▲ **Figure 15.4 Adding Volume to Meals**
Adding high-volume foods like fruits and vegetables to sandwiches, soups, and meals can add to satiety and displace foods higher in kilocalories, two factors that can improve weight management.

Calculation Corner

Calculating Energy Density

Energy density of foods can be calculated and compared using the method described by Barbara Rolls, PhD.[1] The calculation is done by dividing the kilocalories in a serving of food by the weight in grams of a serving of the food. Try calculating the energy density from the labels of two different foods to determine which one is more energy dense.

a Ben & Jerry's Chubby Hubby Ice Cream

Nutrition Facts

Serving Size ½ cup (111g)
Servings per Container 4

Amount Per Serving	
Calories 340	Calories from Fat 180
	% Daily Value*
Total Fat 20g	31%
Saturated Fat 10g	50%
Trans Fat 0g	
Cholesterol 55g	18%
Sodium 140mg	6%
Total Carbohydrate 33g	11%
Dietary Fiber 1g	4%
Sugars 25g	
Protein 7g	
Vitamin A 10% •	Vitamin C 0%
Calcium 10% •	Iron 4%

* Percent Daily Values are based on a 2,000 calorie diet. Your daily values may be higher or lower depending on your calorie needs

b Frozen Broccoli Florets

Nutrition Facts

Serving Size 1 cup (85g)
Servings Per Container 3

Amount Per Serving	
Calories 25	Calories from Fat 0
	% Daily Value*
Total Fat 0g	0%
Saturated Fat 0g	0%
Trans Fat 0g	
Cholesterol 0mg	0%
Sodium 10mg	0%
Total Carbohydrate 5g	2%
Dietary Fiber 3g	12%
Sugars 1g	
Protein 3g	
Vitamin A 15% •	Vitamin C 60%
Calcium 2% •	Iron 2%

* Percent Daily Values are based on a 2,000 calorie diet. Your daily values may be higher or lower depending on your calorie needs

1. To calculate the energy density of Chubby Hubby ice cream, divide the kilocalories by the weight in grams.
2. Now calculate the energy density of the frozen broccoli florets using the label information:

Answer: Chubby Hubby: 340 kcals/111 g = 3.1
Frozen broccoli florets: 25 kcals/85 g = 0.3

Reference

1. Rolls, B. J. and E. A. Bell. 2000. Dietary Approaches to the Treatment of Obesity. *Medical Clinics of North America* 84:401–418.

to chips—can be modest in kilocalories if eaten in modest amounts. Table 15.3 provides examples of low-, moderate-, and high-energy-density foods.

Fiber also contributes to the bulk of vegetables and fruits and their ability to prolong satiety.[59] Overweight individuals have been shown to consume less dietary fiber and fruit than normal-weight people.[60] For these reasons, high-fiber foods are a key part of a weight-loss diet. The Table Tips provide easy ways to add these foods to your diet.

Add Some Protein and Fat to Meals

Because protein has the most dramatic effect on satiety, high-protein diets tend to reduce hunger and can help in weight loss.[61] Because fat slows the movement of food out of the stomach into the intestines, it can also prolong satiety. Therefore,

TABLE TIPS

Eat More to Weigh Less

Eat more whole fruit and drink less juice at breakfast. The orange will have more fiber and bulk than the OJ.

Make the vegetable portions on your dinner plate twice the size of the meat portion.

Have a side salad with low-fat dressing with a lunchtime sandwich instead of a snack bag of chips.

Order your next pizza with less pepperoni and more peppers, onions, and tomatoes. A veggie pizza can have 25 percent fewer kilocalories and about 50 percent less fat and saturated fat than a meat pie.

Cook up a whole-wheat-blend pasta instead of enriched pasta for your next Italian dinner. Ladle on plenty of tomato sauce and don't forget the big tossed salad as the appetizer.

TABLE 15.3 The Energy Density of Foods

▲ Low
These foods provide 0.7 to 1.5 kilocalories per gram and are high in water and fiber. Examples include most vegetables and fruits—tomatoes, cantaloupe, strawberries, broccoli, cauliflower, broth-based soups, fat-free yogurt, and cottage cheese.

▲ Medium
These foods have 1.5 to 4 kilocalories per gram and contain less water. They include bagels, hard-cooked eggs, dried fruits, lean sirloin steak, hummus, whole-wheat bread, and part-skim mozzarella cheese.

▲ High
These foods provide 4 to 9 kilocalories per gram, are low in moisture, and include chips, cookies, crackers, cakes, pastries, butter, oil, and bacon.

Adapted from Centers for Disease Control and Prevention, *Can Eating Fruits and Vegetables Help People to Manage Their Weight?* 2005. Available at www.cdc.gov/nccdphp/dnpa/nutrition/pdf/rtp_practitioner_10_07.pdf. Accessed June 2012.

adding some lean protein and healthy fat at all meals and even with snacks can help reduce hunger. This is not to say that carbohydrates should be severely restricted or eliminated; rather, it reinforces the basic fact that all macronutrients are necessary in the correct proportions.

Keep in mind also that adding high-saturated-fat foods such as whole milk, whole-milk cheese, fatty cuts of meat, and butter to the diet comes at the expense of cardiovascular health. A better bet would be to add lean meat, skinless chicken, fish, nuts, and oils, which are kinder to both a person's waist and heart. (Note: Unsaturated fat still contains 9 kilocalories per gram, so excessive amounts of nuts and oils, even though these are heart healthy, can quickly add excess kilocalories to the diet.)

Use MyPlate as a Weight-Loss Guide

Meals that contain a high volume of fruits and vegetables, whole grains, some lean protein, and modest amounts of fat are a smart combination for weight loss, so a diet that contains all five food groups can be used to lose weight. Most importantly, this type of diet is well balanced and will meet daily nutrient needs.

Reducing the intake of kilocalories a little at a time can add up to healthy weight loss. A 180-pound, overweight person who consumes 2,800 kilocalories daily can reduce his or her intake to 2,400 to 2,600 kilocalories, incurring a kilocalorie deficit of 200–400 kilocalories daily. He or she will then lose 10 pounds in about three months. Small changes, like switching from full-fat to nonfat dairy products or replacing an afternoon soda with a glass of water, will contribute to this kilocalorie reduction. Following the recommendations at ChooseMyPlate.gov to eat a variety of foods, but replacing higher kilocalorie foods with lower kilocalorie options within each food group, will result in a satisfying diet and weight loss.

Emphasizing high-volume, nutrient-dense foods will help ensure adequate nutrient intake and can be a boon to weight loss. Look at the difference between the foods shown in **Figure 15.5**. The snack and dinner on the left are low in volume, but high

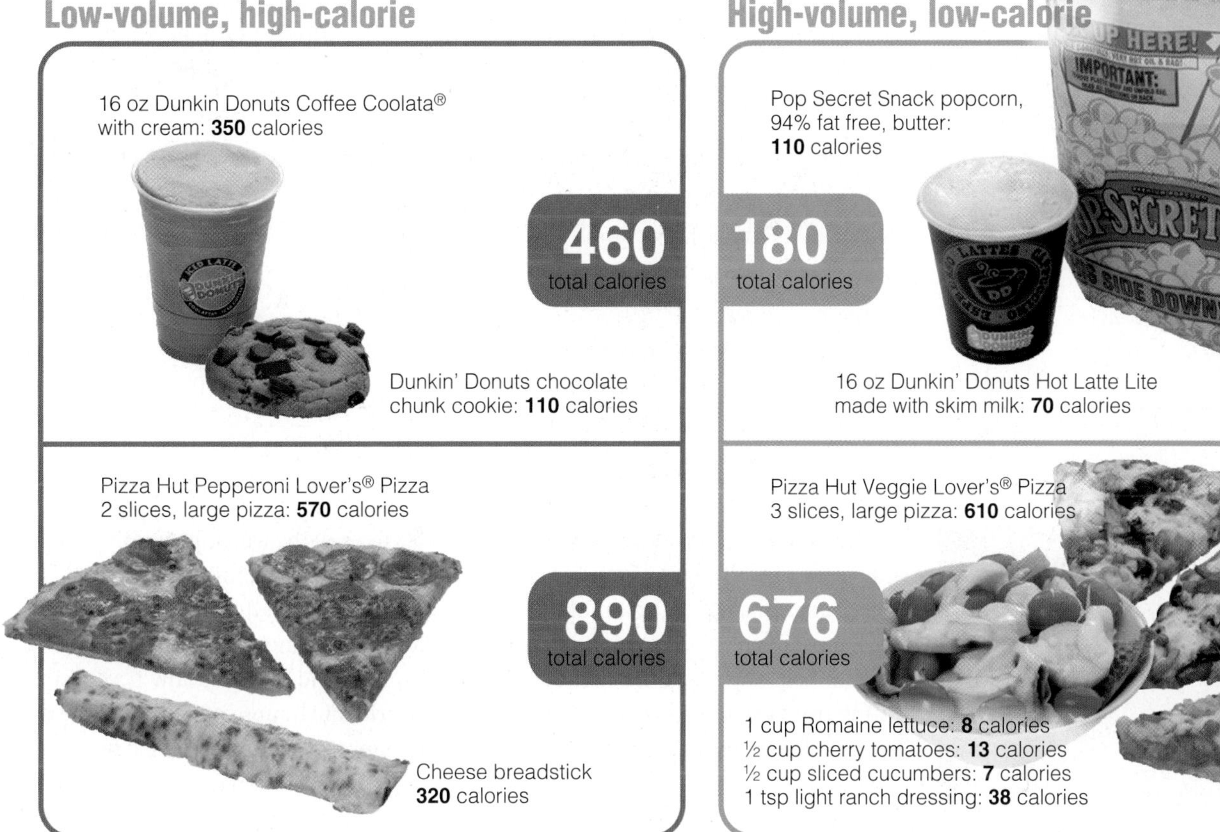

▲ **Figure 15.5 The Volume of Food**
Low-volume, high-kilocalorie foods can be much less satisfying than higher volume, lower kilocalorie foods.

in kilocalories. The foods on the right are high in volume but have almost 500 fewer kilocalories combined. These higher volume foods will be more satisfying for fewer kilocalories.

Increase Physical Activity to Lose Weight

Regular physical activity can not only add to the daily energy deficit needed for weight loss, but can also displace sedentary activity such as watching television, which often leads to mindless snacking on energy-dense foods.[62] Going for a walk and expending kilocalories rather than watching a movie while snacking on a bag of tortilla chips will provide kilocaloric benefits beyond the exercise alone. Establishing an exercise program that incorporates cardiorespiratory and strength-training activities will have even greater benefits, one of which is the increased metabolic rate that occurs with an increase in muscle mass. Increased metabolic rate means the body expends more energy at rest, which can help with weight loss.

Individuals are advised to devote 60 to 90 minutes daily to moderate-intensity activities to aid in weight loss and prevent weight gain.[63] Moderately intense physical activity would be the equivalent of walking 3.5 miles per hour (Table 15.4).

Over time, expending more kilocalories will help lower the overall amount of body fat. Note, however, that individuals cannot control which fat deposits are reduced. Therefore, focusing exercise on a particular part of the body, such as the thighs, will not lead to localized fat loss. In other words, "spot reducing" does not work.

TABLE 15.4 Kilocalories Used during Activities

Moderate Physical Activity	Approximate Kilocalories/Hour for a 154-lb Person*	Vigorous Physical Activity	Approximate Kilocalories/Hour for a 154-lb Person*
Hiking	370	Running/jogging (5 mph)	590
Light gardening/yard work	330	Bicycling (> 10 mph)	590
Dancing	330	Swimming (slow freestyle laps)	510
Golf (walking and carrying clubs)	330	Aerobics	480
Bicycling (< 10 mph)	290	Walking (4.5 mph)	460
Walking (3.5 mph)	280	Heavy yard work (chopping wood)	440
Weight lifting (general light workout)	220	Weight lifting (vigorous effort)	440
Stretching	180	Basketball (vigorous)	440

*Calories burned per hour will be higher for persons who weigh more than 154 lbs (70 kg) and lower for persons who weigh less.

Adapted from Centers for Disease Control and Prevention, *Dietary Guidelines for Americans, 2005.*

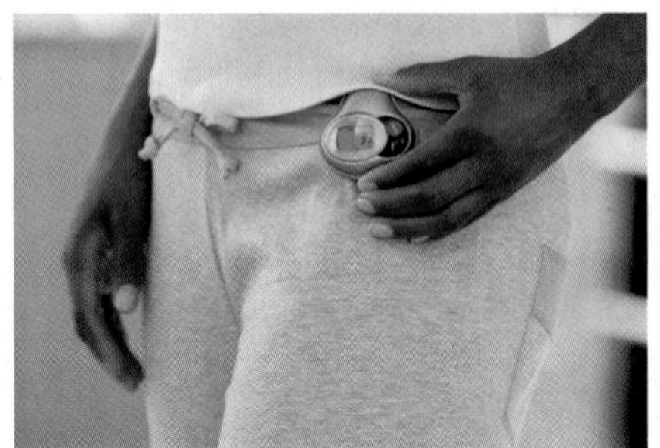

Wearing a pedometer, like the one shown here, can help you track your steps. Remember to aim for 10,000 steps per day.

Research suggests that accumulating 10,000 steps daily, which generally is the equivalent of walking 5 miles, can help reduce the risk of becoming overweight.[64] Americans, on average, accumulate only 900 to 3,000 steps daily.[65] To reach 10,000 steps, most people need to make a conscious effort to keep moving. Using a pedometer can help you track the number of steps you take and let you know if you are hitting this target, or if you need to get up and move much more often. The Fitness Tips provide more suggestions on how to expend more energy during the day.

FITNESS TIPS

Get UP and MOVE

Skip the text messages and walk to visit your friends on campus.

Don't go to the closest coffee shop for your morning latte; walk to the java joint that is a few blocks farther away.

Take a five-minute walk at least twice a day. A little jolt of exercise can help break the monotony of studying and work off some stress.

Accomplish two goals at once by cleaning your dorm room or apartment. A 150-pound person will burn about 4 kilocalories for every minute spent cleaning. Scrub, sweep, or vacuum for 30 minutes and you could work off about 120 kilocalories.

Offer to walk your neighbor's pet daily.

Break Bad Habits

Many incoming college freshmen worry more about gaining weight—the "freshman 15"—than about how they'll manage the combination of their course load and new-found freedom. The term "freshman 15" was coined to describe a gain in weight that some college students experience during their first year away from home. However, little data supports the theory. Several new studies have reported that freshman weight gain is actually less than 5 pounds for most college students. A small study at Rutgers State University reported an average gain of only 2.86 pounds during the first year of college.[66] Similar results were reported from a Dartmouth College study, which found weight gains in both men (a gain of 3.5 pounds) and women (a gain of 4.0 pounds), but not the legendary 15 pounds (though still higher than the rate of weight gain for an average American adult). Most of the weight gain occurred during the first semester and was maintained over the entire school year.[67] The reality seems to be that freshmen students eat less and exercise more than common perceptions allow; however, they do tend to consume higher amounts of "junk" food, eat fewer whole foods, and drink more alcohol than they did while living at home.[68] But for freshmen who do gain weight, research suggests that it is more likely due to a decrease in physical activity than an increase in kilocalorie intake.[69] As with adults, freshman weight gain can be prevented by breaking the chain of behaviors leading to poor diet and exercise habits.

Behavior modification focuses on changing the eating behaviors that contribute to weight gain or impede weight loss. Several behavior modification techniques can be used to identify and change poor eating behaviors. These techniques used to identify weight gain behaviors include self-monitoring the behaviors by keeping a food log, controlling environmental cues that trigger eating when not hungry, and learning how to better manage stress.[70] Understanding the habits and emotions that drive your eating and exercise patterns is a key element of behavior modification. Once you have identified the less-than-healthy behaviors resulting in weight gain, you can replace them with new behaviors that promote weight loss and weight management.

A food log allows individuals to track the kinds of foods they eat during the day, when and where they eat them, their moods, and their hunger ratings. Based on this information, people can restructure their environment, how they respond to their environment, or both to minimize or eliminate the eating behaviors that interfere with their weight management.

If you were to keep a food record, a typical day's log may be similar to the one in **Figure 15.6.** You might have habits that are common to people who struggle with their weight. These include skipping breakfast daily, which causes people to be very hungry in the late morning and increases impulsive snacking on energy-dense, low-nutrition foods from vending machines. A study of overweight women who typically skipped breakfast showed that once they started consuming cereal for breakfast, they indulged in less impulsive snacking.[71] Eating a bowl of high-fiber whole-grain cereal with skim milk (approximately 200 kilocalories) will likely appease morning hunger and help you bypass an 11 a.m. vending machine snack of 270-kilocalorie cookies and a 210-kilocalorie sports drink. This one behavior change would not only save a person 280 kilocalories in the morning, but reduce added sugar intake and add more nutrition to daily food intake. Additionally, adding a less-energy-dense salad at lunch could help increase satiety and displace at least one of the energy-dense cookies that people often grab with a sandwich.

Food Log

For: Hannah

Date: Monday, September 6

Food and drink	Time eaten	What I ate/ Where I ate it	Hunger level*	Mood †
Breakfast		Skipped it	3	G
Snack	11 a.m.	Oreo cookies, PowerAde from vending machine during morning class.	5	E
Lunch	1:30 p.m.	Ham and cheese sandwich, 2 large M&M cookies in student union cafeteria.	4	B
Snack				
Dinner	6:30 p.m.	Hamburger, french fries, salad at kitchen table	4	F
Snack	7 p.m. to 10 p.m.	Large bag of tortilla chips and entire bag of Pepperidge Farm Milano cookies while studying at kitchen table	1	I

*Hunger levels (1–5): 1 = not hungry; 5 = super hungry

† **Moods:**
A = Happy; B = Content; C = Bored; D = Depressed; E = Rushed; F = Stressed; G = Tired; H = Lonely; I = Anxious; J = Angry

▲ **Figure 15.6 Food Log**
Keeping track of when, where, and what you eat, as well as why you ate it, can yield some surprising information. Do you think you sometimes eat out of boredom or stress, rather than because you're hungry?

behavior modification Changing behaviors to improve health outcomes. In the case of weight management, it involves identifying and altering eating patterns that contribute to weight gain or impede weight loss.

Nutrition in Practice: Victor

After his first year at college, Victor became concerned about his weight gain. He felt sluggish compared to a year ago. In fact, he even lost interest in playing pickup basketball with his friends. In an effort to increase his energy levels, he started going to the gym several times a week. When he got on the scale at the gym, he was shocked to learn that he hadn't gained the dreadful "freshman 15" but rather a more horrifying "freshman 20!" He had never struggled with weight in high school, but he knows he has been eating bigger meals at college than at home because the food is good and he is on a unlimited food plan. When Victor discovered that his college employs a Registered Dietitian who counsels both the faculty and students, he decided to make an appointment.

Victor's Stats:

- ☐ Age: 19
- ☐ Height: 5 feet 9 inches
- ☐ Weight: 185 pounds
- ☐ BMI: 27.3

Critical Thinking Questions

1. What would be a healthy weight for Victor?
2. Based on his food log, which waist-friendly food groups are inadequate in his diet?
3. What beverage recommendations would you make based on his food log?

Dietitian's Observation and Plan for Victor:

- ☐ Discuss the need to cut back on some excess kilocalories in his diet without causing him to be hungry during the day. To achieve this goal, he needs to add more low-energy-dense fruits, vegetables, and beverages to his meals and snacks to help him feel satiated and displace higher kilocalorie items at his meals and snacks.
- ☐ For breakfast have a whole-wheat bagel and a small amount of cream cheese and take a piece of fruit for his mid-morning snack rather than the scone.
- ☐ Replace the fries at lunch with a salad with low-kilocalorie dressing.
- ☐ Substitute a small low-fat frozen yogurt topped with fresh fruit for the large ice cream in the afternoon.
- ☐ Substitute a piece of fruit for the potato chips in the evening.
- ☐ Order a latte with skim milk instead of the higher kilocalorie mid-morning mocha coffee at the coffee shop.
- ☐ Drink water or noncaloric beverages at all meals.

Two weeks later, Victor returns for a follow-up visit with the dietitian. He has lost a pound of weight and is excited! He has added more fruits and vegetables to his diet, and surprisingly, feels full. He no longer drinks sugary beverages during the day. The RD works with Victor to choose leaner sources of protein at lunch and dinner. Victor agrees to try the turkey or veggie burger at lunch and grilled chicken at dinner. He makes another appointment to see the RD in two weeks.

Victor's Food Log

Food/Beverage	Time Consumed	Hunger Rating*	Location
Bacon and eggs with toast and butter	7 am	3	Dining hall
Coffee (Mocha Supreme) and scone	10:30 am	2	Coffee shop
Cheeseburger, fries, large cola	1:30 pm	5	Dining hall
Soft-serve ice cream, large, chocolate with fudge	4 pm	4	Dining hall
Fried chicken, mashed potatoes, corn, large cola	6:30 pm	3	Dining hall
Potato chips	10 pm	1	Study

*Hunger Rating (1–5): 1 = not hungry; 5 = super hungry

Stress-induced eating associated with studying can be modified by a change in environment—for example, by going to the campus library, where eating is prohibited. In fact, removing access to snacks altogether is an excellent environmental change—once snacks are "out of sight" they are more likely to be "out of mind."

Exercising before or after studying would be a healthier way to relieve stress than eating a bag of snacks. The Table Tips list some additional healthy behaviors that can easily be incorporated into your life.

THE TAKE-HOME MESSAGE For successful, long-term weight loss, people need to reduce their daily kilocalorie intake, increase their physical activity, and change their behavior. Adding low-energy-density, high-volume vegetables, fruit, and fiber along with some lean protein and healthy oils to the diet can help increase satiety and reduce unplanned snacking. Incorporating approximately 60 to 90 minutes of physical activity daily can facilitate weight loss. Changing unhealthy habits by restructuring the environment to minimize or eliminate unhealthy eating can also help shed extra pounds.

TABLE TIPS

Adopt Some Healthy Habits

Don't eat out of boredom or stress; go for a jog instead.

Food shop with a full stomach and a grocery list. Walking around aimlessly while hungry means you are more likely to grab items on a whim.

The next time you pass a difficult course or get that long-awaited raise, celebrate without a plate. Replace the traditional restaurant dinner with a no-kilocalorie reward such as a new music download or a weekend hike.

Declare a vending machine–free day at least once a week, save money, and stop the impulsive snacking. On that day, pack two pieces of fruit as satisfying snacks.

How Can Weight Loss Be Maintained?

Losing weight is only half the battle. You or someone you know may be familiar with the typical fad diet experience: the triumphant rush associated with dropping 10 pounds of weight, the disappointment that sets in when 15 pounds are regained, then a new round of hope when 10 of them are re-shed. The ability to maintain weight loss over time is a challenge. Several factors can sabotage long-term maintenance of weight loss. These include weight cycling and the energy gap.

Weight Cycling Can Lead to Health Problems

Studies have indicated that an estimated 90 to 95 percent of individuals who lose weight regain it within several years.[72] This fluctuation is known as **weight cycling**, and some research suggests that it can lead to problems such as hypertension, gallbladder disease, and elevated blood cholesterol levels, not to mention depression and feelings of frustration.[73] Weight cycling often occurs when weight is lost quickly through a restrictive fad diet. Once the goal weight is reached, a person on one of these diets usually returns to the way he or she was eating before the diet. Because the weight was lost quickly, the body's metabolism may have slowed to compensate for the reduction in energy intake, thus making it easier for the weight to come back once pre-diet eating is resumed.

Recent research suggests that weight cycling may be on the wane. A study of 800 people who lost weight showed that they were able to keep off at least 30 pounds for five years. These people were successful losers because they adopted healthier habits to lose weight, and maintained those habits after they reached their weight goal.[74] They commonly limited the intake of fatty foods, monitored their kilocalorie intake, and ate nearly five times a day, on average. (For many people, eating more frequent, smaller meals allows them to avoid becoming ravenous and overeating at the next meal.) The majority of them weighed themselves weekly and maintained a high level of daily physical activity, expending the energy equivalent of walking 4 miles a day.[75] This suggests that weight loss can be maintained as long as the individual doesn't revert to the unhealthy habits that caused the excess weight in the first place.

One way to help the body adjust to its new lower weight is to increase exercise. Increasing exercise can enhance lean muscle mass, which in turn helps prevent a drop in basal metabolism. At the same time making gradual changes in energy intake will help avoid a drastic increase in body weight.

weight cycling The repeated gain and loss of body weight.

Physical Activity Helps Reduce the Energy Gap Problem

Individuals who lose weight often experience an "**energy gap**." After weight loss, a person will have lower overall energy needs, as there is less body weight to maintain. The energy gap is the difference in daily kilocalories that are needed for weight maintenance before and after weight loss.[76] Researchers have estimated that the energy gap is about 8 kilocalories per pound of lost weight.[77] For example, someone who lost 30 pounds would need approximately 240 fewer kilocalories a day to maintain the new, lower body weight.

Physical activity can help close this energy gap. The person can eat 240 fewer kilocalories, expend this amount of kilocalories through added physical activity, or do a combination of both. Because the environment we live in seems to encourage eating more than discourage it, researchers believe that increasing daily physical activity is likely the easier way to close the energy gap.[78] *Adding* something (physical activity) to one's lifestyle is often easier than *removing* something (kilocalories). Thus, the recommendation is to engage in 60 to 90 minutes of moderate physical activity daily in order to maintain weight loss.[79]

Note that formerly obese individuals who've lost weight will still have more adipocytes (hyperplastic obesity) than lean individuals, and will always have a propensity for weight gain. Their metabolism is much more efficient in restoring fat deposits, and the large number of adipocytes that shrank during weight loss are still there, ready to restore excess energy stores.

Some individuals are candidates for extreme treatment including weight loss medications and bariatric surgery to help them shed their unhealthy excess weight. Health Connection: Extreme Measures for Extreme Obesity discusses treatment options for those with BMIs of greater than 40.

THE TAKE-HOME MESSAGE People who lose weight are most likely to keep it off if they maintain the positive diet and lifestyle habits that helped them lose the weight. Setting realistic weight-loss goals will prevent the false hope syndrome often associated with trying to achieve goal weights too quickly. Exercise will improve muscle mass, prevent a decline in basal metabolism, and help overcome plateaus often associated with weight loss. Eating less and/or exercising more will help close the energy gap that occurs after weight loss.

What Is the Healthiest Way to Gain Weight?

For people who are underweight, weight gain can be as challenging and frustrating as losing weight is for an overweight individual. The major difference is that the thin person rarely gets sympathy from others.

Like overweight individuals, those who are underweight experience an energy imbalance. In their case, however, they consume fewer kilocalories than they expend each day. Because those who wish to gain weight want to add muscle mass, rather than large amounts of fat, the challenge is to eat sufficient energy to meet their basal metabolic needs plus provide fuel for the exercise needed to stimulate muscle synthesis.

People who want to gain weight need to do the opposite of those who are trying to lose weight—they need to make each bite more energy dense. Adding at least 500 kilocalories to their daily energy intake will enable them to add about a pound of extra body weight weekly.

energy gap The difference between the numbers of kilocalories needed to maintain weight before and after weight loss.

Health Connection

Extreme Measures for Extreme Obesity

For most people, the best path to a healthy body weight is to commit to improving their diet and exercising more. However, for some individuals, these measures are not enough to attain adequate weight loss. In fact, those who are extremely obese are at such a high risk for conditions such as heart disease and stroke, and even of dying, that a much more aggressive weight-loss treatment may be necessary. Extreme treatments for the extremely obese include a very low-kilocalorie diet, medications, and/or surgery.

Very Low-Kilocalorie Diets

On her television show in 1988, a very petite Oprah Winfrey beamed after having lost 67 pounds in less than a year using a **very low-kilocalorie diet**, specifically one comprised primarily of liquid protein. Her protein-rich diet provided fewer than 800 kilocalories per day, was very low in carbohydrates, and had minimal amounts of fat. It, and others like it, are designed to help individuals at high risk of disease drop a substantial amount of weight in a short amount of time. However, they are not a long-term solution. After consuming the diet for 12 to 16 weeks, the dieter is switched over to a well-balanced, low-kilocalorie diet.

Very low-kilocalorie diets have to be supplemented with vitamins and minerals and must be medically supervised by a doctor, as they can cause dangerous electrolyte imbalances as well as gallstones, constipation, fatigue, hair loss, and other side effects.[1] The National Institutes of Health doesn't recommend very low-kilocalorie diets because well-balanced low-kilocalorie diets are just as effective in producing a similar amount of weight loss after one year, and are less dangerous.[2]

After all that effort, Oprah ultimately regretted her very low-kilocalorie diet. "I had literally starved myself for four months—not a morsel of food—to get into a pair of size 10 Calvin Klein jeans," claims Oprah. "Two hours after that show, I started eating to celebrate—of course, within two days those jeans no longer fit!"[3] Oprah has continued to struggle with her weight for the next two decades. In 2005, Oprah reached her goal weight of 160 pounds and was convinced she knew how to maintain her new weight. Two years later her life started to become "unbalanced," which resulted in weight gain once again. By 2009, she had regained 40 pounds, putting her back up to the 200-pound mark.

Weight-Loss Medications

Some prescription medications can help a person lose weight by either suppressing the appetite or inhibiting the absorption of fat in the intestinal tract. The biggest risks associated with taking such drugs are often the potential side effects; because of this, they are almost always available only by prescription and must be taken under the care of a health care provider.

In the 1980s Oprah Winfrey reached her goal weight by consuming a very low-kilocalorie, liquid protein diet. She has since regained and lost the weight several times, and often publicly discusses the challenges of maintaining weight loss.

One appetite suppressant is the drug sibutramine (trade name Meridia), which reduces hunger and increases thermogenesis. The increased thermogenesis results in increased energy expenditure. However, the drug can also increase a person's heart rate and blood pressure, and therefore may not be appropriate for those who have hypertension, which tends to occur often in overweight individuals.

The fat-absorption-inhibitor orlistat (trade name Xenical) is a prescription medication that inhibits an intestinal enzyme needed to break down fat. If fat isn't broken down, the fat (and kilocalories) will not be absorbed by the body. Up to about a third of the dietary fat in a meal will be blocked and expelled in the stool. Orlistat needs to be taken at each meal and should be used with a diet that provides no more than about 30 percent of its kilocalories from fat. Because fat is lost in the stool, the drug can cause oily and more frequent stools, flatulence, and oily discharge.[4] Ironically, these side effects may help an individual adhere to a low-fat diet, as these effects are more pronounced if a high-fat meal is consumed.

A reduced-strength version of orlistat (brand named Alli) is approved as an over-the-counter medication for overweight adults 18 years and older. Alli, combined with a low-kilocalorie, low-fat diet and regular exercise, aids in modest weight loss. Because of the recent reports of rare, but serious, cases of liver damage in individuals using Xenical and Alli, both of these drugs must now carry warnings on their labels.[5]

Sometimes the side effects of weight-loss medications can be so serious that the medication must be withdrawn from the market. For instance, the FDA has prohibited the sale of supplements that contain ephedra

very low-kilocalorie diet A diet of fewer than 800 kilocalories per day. These diets are high in protein, very low in (or devoid of) carbohydrates, and have a minimal amount of fat. Also referred to as a *protein-sparing modified fast.*

(also called Ma huang), the plant source for ephedrine. Ephedrine has been shown to cause chest pains, palpitations, hypertension, and an accelerated heart rate. In 2003, baseball player Steve Bechler died at age 23 after taking a weight-loss supplement containing ephedrine during spring training. Ephedrine was determined to have contributed to his death.[6]

Bariatric Surgery

Bariatric surgery has been shown to be an effective means of weight loss for moderately to severely obese people compared with low-kilocalorie diets and medication.[7] The term bariatric surgery refers to different procedures that either reduce the absorption of kilocalories or restrict food intake. A type of bariatric surgery that results in malabsorption of kilocalories is called gastric bypass surgery. The procedure restricts the size of the stomach and reroutes the food past the upper section of the small intestine or duodenum where most of the kilocalories and nutrients are absorbed. A restrictive procedure, such as gastric banding, helps you lose weight by reducing the size of the stomach to hold only about ¼ cup of food.

bariatric surgery A surgical procedure that promotes weight loss by limiting the amount of food that can be eaten or absorbed.

gastric bypass surgery A type of bariatric surgery that reduces the functional volume of the stomach to minimize the amount of food eaten. Such surgeries are sometimes used to treat extreme obesity.

Gastric Bypass Surgery

The most common form of bariatric surgery is **gastric bypass surgery**. This surgical technique was developed in the middle of the twentieth century and quickly grew in popularity. The first gastric bypass surgery was performed in 1967 by Dr. Edward Mason, a surgeon at the University of Iowa.[8] By 1998, approximately 13,000 obese patients each year underwent gastric bypass to reduce the size of their stomachs. Ten years later that number had increased to over 190,000—more than a 1,400 percent increase.[9] During gastric bypass surgery, the stomach is reduced in size by making a small pouch at the top of the stomach with surgical staples (see the figure). The stomach pouch is connected to the jejunum, bypassing the rest of the stomach and the upper small intestine. This reduces the size of the stomach so that it holds less than ¼ cup of food. Consumed food leaves the small stomach pouch through a surgically added intestinal loop that attaches directly to the small intestine. After the surgery, individuals need to consume small, frequent meals because the stomach pouch can only expand to a maximum of about 5 ounces, the size of a woman's fist. Bypass patients not only eat less because of their smaller stomachs, but have higher levels of

FOOD BANK
FOR NEW YORK CITY
Al Roker, NBC's *Today Show* weatherman, lost approximately 140 pounds after gastric bypass surgery.

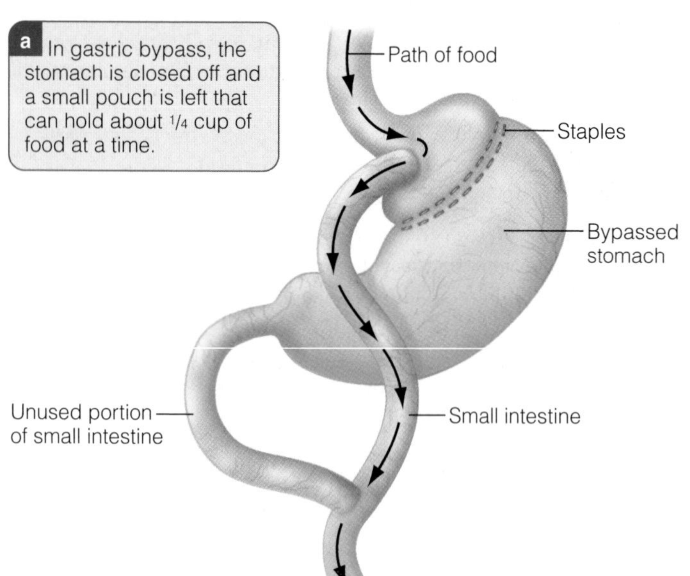
a In gastric bypass, the stomach is closed off and a small pouch is left that can hold about 1/4 cup of food at a time.
Path of food
Staples
Bypassed stomach
Unused portion of small intestine
Small intestine

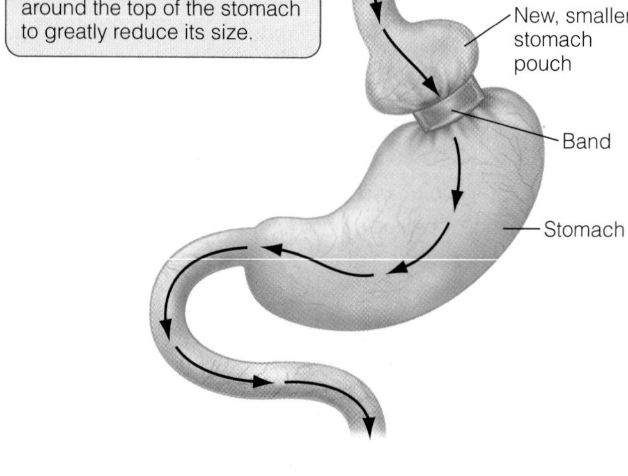
b In gastric banding, a silicone band is placed around the top of the stomach to greatly reduce its size.
Path of food
New, smaller stomach pouch
Band
Stomach

Bariatric surgery restricts food intake and promotes malabsorption.

satiety and lower levels of hunger after the surgery. This loss of appetite is thought to be due to lower levels of ghrelin associated with the loss of stomach area.[10]

Because food is rerouted past the majority of the stomach and the duodenum, individuals can experience deficiencies of vitamin B_{12}, iron, and calcium. Recall from Chapter 10 that vitamin B_{12} needs intrinsic factor (IF) secreted from the gastric cells to be absorbed, which is missing after surgery. Iron and calcium are typically absorbed in the upper part of the small intestine, which is now bypassed. Vitamin B_{12} injections or supplements must be taken because of these deficiencies.

Gastric Banding Surgery

A type of gastric surgery that's becoming more popular is a reversible procedure (unlike the permanent gastric bypass surgery), **gastric banding**, in which a silicone band is placed around the top of the stomach to create a small pouch with a very narrow opening at the bottom for the food to pass through. This delays the emptying of the stomach contents so that a person will feel fuller longer. The doctor can adjust the opening of the pouch by inflating or deflating the band.

Research reports that most people who have bariatric surgery begin to lose weight quickly following the surgery. The estimated weight loss is approximately 50 percent of the excess weight. Thus, if an individual is 100 pounds overweight, the surgery should result in a loss of 50 pounds. In a meta-analysis of 22,094 patients who had gastric surgery, the average percentage of excess weight loss was 61.2 percent. People who underwent gastric bypass surgery lost more weight (61.6 percent) than did those who chose gastric banding (47.5 percent). Other benefits of gastric surgery included the reduction of diabetes in 76.8 percent of patients, improved hyperlipidemia in more than 70 percent of patients, and the elimination of hypertension (in 61.7 percent) and sleep apnea (in 85.7 percent).[11]

Although dramatic amounts of weight loss can occur, there are also risks involved. About 10 percent of those undergoing gastric bypass surgery experience complications such as gallstones, ulcers, and bleeding in the stomach and intestines. Approximately 1 to 2 percent die.[12] After surgery, individuals need to be monitored long term by their doctor and nutrition professionals to ensure that they remain healthy and meet their nutritional needs.

Liposuction Is Cosmetic

Another form of surgery, **liposuction**, is less about health and more about physical appearance. During liposuction, a doctor removes subcutaneous fat from the abdomen, hips, or thighs (and sometimes other areas of the body) by suctioning it out with a penlike instrument. People often undergo liposuction to get rid of **cellulite**, which isn't a medical term, but refers to fat cells that give skin a dimpled appearance. Complications such as infections, scars, and swelling can arise after liposuction.

Liposuction is effective in removing fatty deposits from specific areas of the body but won't help you drop any weight. Fat that was removed from your thighs is permanently gone, but the remaining fat cells can still expand and new fat cells can form.[13] You may notice beautifully sculpted thighs only to find the fat in your upper arms increasing in size.

Liposuction is a surgical procedure that removes subcutaneous fat. Unlike gastric banding or bypass surgeries, liposuction is purely cosmetic and does not result in health benefits.

gastric banding A type of gastric surgery that uses a silicone band to reduce the size of the stomach so that less food is needed to feel full.

liposuction The surgical removal of subcutaneous fat. Usually performed on the abdomen, hips, and thighs, and/or other areas of the body.

cellulite A nonmedical term that refers to fat cells under the skin that give it a ripplelike appearance. Contrary to popular belief, cellulite is no different from other fat in the body.

References

1. United States Department of Health and Human Services, National Institutes of Health. 2008. *Very Low-Calorie Diets.* Available at www.win.niddk.nih.gov/publications/low_calorie.htm. Accessed June 2012.
2. National Heart, Lung, and Blood Institute. 1998. *Clinical Guidelines on the Identification, Evaluation, and Treatment of Overweight and Obesity in Adults.* Available at www.nhlbi.nih.gov/guidelines/obesity/ob_gdlns.htm. Accessed June 2012.
3. Mariant, M. 2005. Oprah Regrets Her 1988 Liquid Diet. *USA Today* (November). Available at www.usatoday.com/life/people/2005-11-16-oprah-liquid-diet_x.htm. Accessed June 2012.
4. DeWald, T., L. Khaodhiar, M. Donahue, and G. Blackburn. 2006. Pharmacological and Surgical Treatments for Obesity. *American Heart Journal* 151:604–624.
5. Food and Drug Administration. 2010. *FDA Drug Safety Communication: Completed Safety Review of Xenical/Alli (Orlistat) and Severe Liver Injury.* Available at www.fda.gov/Drugs/DrugSafety/PostmarketDrugSafetyInformationforPatientsandProviders/ucm213038.htm. Accessed June 2012.
6. FDA. 2004. *FDA Issues Regulation Prohibiting Sale of Dietary Supplements Containing Ephedrine Alkaloids and Reiterates Its Advice That Consumers Stop Using These Products.* Available at www.fda.gov/NewsEvents/Newsroom/PressAnnouncements/2004/ucm108242.htm. Accessed November 2012.
7. Picot, J., J. Jones, J. L. Colquitt, E. Gospodarevskaya, E. Loveman, L. Baxter, and A. J. Clegg. 2009. The Clinical Effectiveness and Cost-Effectiveness of Bariatric (Weight Loss) Surgery for Obesity: A Systematic Review and Economic Evaluation. *Health Technology Assessment* 13:1–190.
8. Twoop Timeline. 2006. *Gastric Bypass Surgery.* Available at www.twoop.com/medicine/archives/2005/10/gastric_bypass_surgery.html. Accessed June 2012.
9. Health Grades. 2011. *Health Grades 2011: Bariatric Trends in American Hospitals.* Available at www.healthgrades.com/business/img/HealthGradesBariatricSurgeryTrendsAmerHospReport2011.pdf. Accessed June 2012.

10. Crookes, P. 2006. Surgical Treatment of Morbid Obesity. *Annual Review of Medicine* 57:243–264.
11. Buchwald, H., Y. Avidor, E. Braunwald, M. D. Jensen, W. Pories, K. Fahrbach, and K. Schoelles. 2004. Bariatric Surgery: A Systematic Review and Meta-Analysis. *Journal of the American Medical Association* 292:1724–1737.
12. Crookes, P. 2006. Surgical Treatment of Morbid Obesity.
13. Hernandez, T. L., J. M. Kittelson, C. K. Law, L. L. Ketch, N. R. Stob, R. C. Lindstrom, A. Scherzinger, et al. 2011. Fat Redistribution Following Suction Lipectomy: Defense of Body Fat and Patterns of Restoration. *Obesity* 19:1388–1395.

Of course, someone who wants to gain weight should not just load up on high-fat, high-kilocalorie foods. The quality of the extra kilocalories is very important. Snacking on an extra 500 kilocalories of jellybeans will add 500 kilocalories of sugar and little nutrient value. Rather, these individuals should make energy-dense, nutritious choices from a variety of foods within each food group. For example, instead of eating a slice of toast in the morning, they should choose a whole-grain waffle. In a salad bar lunch, adding coleslaw will provide 10 times the kilocalories of plain cabbage. **Figure 15.7** contrasts more- and less-energy-dense foods within each food group. Eating larger portion sizes at meals and energy-dense snacks during the day will also add kilocalories. The Table Tips provide easy and portable snack ideas.

Regular exercise and resistance training will stimulate muscle growth and help avoid excess fat storage. Remember that it takes time to gain weight and build sufficient muscle mass. Be patient and continue to choose healthy foods until you reach your goal weight.

TABLE TIPS

Healthy Snacks for Healthy Weight Gain

Stash an 8-ounce container of 100 percent fruit juice (about 100 kilocalories) in your bag, plus one of the 150-kilocalorie snacks listed below for a quick 250-kilocalorie snack (food and juice combined) between meals.

Graham crackers, 5 crackers (2½″ square)

Mixed nuts, 1 oz

Fig bars, 2-oz package

Pudding, individual serving sizes, 4 oz

Peanut butter on whole-wheat crackers (1 tbs peanut butter on 6 crackers)

THE TAKE-HOME MESSAGE People who want to gain weight need to consume additional kilocalories through energy-dense foods so that they take in more energy than they expend. Adding nutrient-dense snacks between meals and increasing portion sizes during meals are easy ways to increase the number of kilocalories consumed. Add resistance exercise to build muscle mass and avoid excess fat storage.

What Is Disordered Eating, What Are the Warning Signs, and How Is It Treated?

Attaining a healthy weight, whether it means gaining or losing a few pounds, is a worthwhile goal that can result in lowered risk of disease and a more productive life. However, patterns of eating that involve severe kilocalorie restriction, binge eating, purging, or other abnormal behaviors can be severely damaging to health. Whereas disordered eating and eating disorders are sometimes thought of as psychological rather than nutrition-related topics, it's important to be aware of them and recognize their symptoms.

The term **disordered eating** is used to describe a variety of eating patterns considered abnormal and potentially harmful. Refusing to eat, compulsive eating, binge eating, restrictive eating, vomiting after eating, and abusing diet pills, laxatives, or diuretics are all examples of disordered eating behaviors. **Eating disorders**, in contrast, are diagnosed when a person meets specific criteria that

disordered eating Abnormal and potentially harmful eating behaviors that do not meet specific criteria for anorexia nervosa and bulimia nervosa or binge eating disorder.

eating disorders Psychological illnesses that involve specific abnormal eating behaviors: anorexia nervosa (self-starvation) and bulimia nervosa (bingeing and purging).

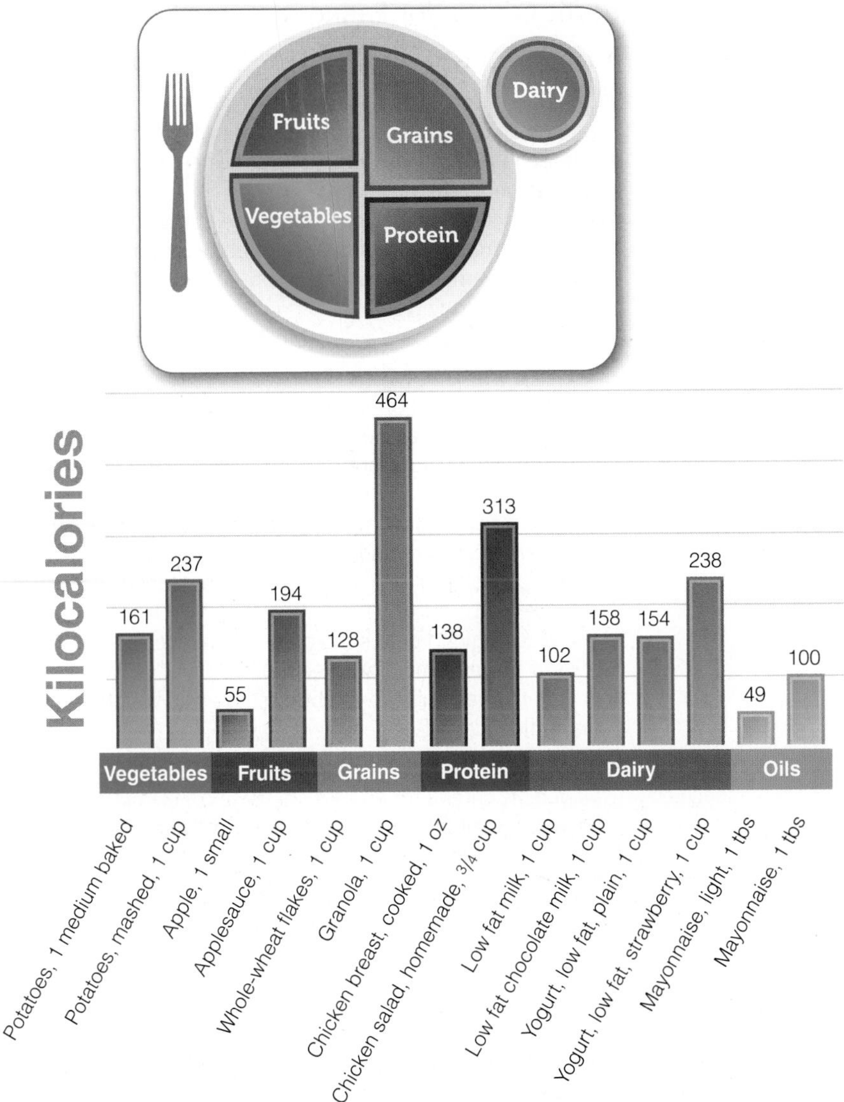

▲ **Figure 15.7 More- and Less-Energy-Dense Food Choices, by Food Group**
Choosing more energy-dense, but still nutritious, foods can help those who are underweight gain weight.

include disordered eating behaviors as well as other factors (see Table 15.5). It is possible for someone to have disordered eating without having an actual eating disorder.

In the United States, approximately 11 million people struggle with eating disorders.[80] Adolescent and young adult females in predominantly white upper-middle- and middle-class families are the population with highest prevalence. However, eating disorders and disordered eating among males, minorities, and other age groups are increasing.[81, 82] Anyone can develop an eating disorder, regardless of gender, age, race, ethnicity, or social status.

Societal pressure to be thin and have a "perfect" figure is one factor that likely affects rates of disordered eating among girls and women. Images of models and celebrities with abnormally low body weights are portrayed as ideal, which frequently leads to body dissatisfaction among "normal" people. Thinness is too often associated with beauty, success, and happiness, and therefore many people believe that they cannot be beautiful, successful, or happy unless they are thin. Many females

TABLE 15.5 Diagnostic Criteria for Eating Disorders

Eating Disorder	Diagnostic Criteria
Anorexia nervosa	■ Consistent body weight under the minimally normal weight for age and height (less than 85% of expected) ■ Intense fear of gaining weight or becoming fat, even though underweight ■ Disturbance in the way one's body weight or shape is experienced, excessive influence of body weight or shape on self-esteem, or denial of the seriousness of the current low body weight ■ In females, absence of at least three consecutive menstrual cycles
Bulimia nervosa	■ Recurrent episodes of binge eating, which is characterized by eating larger than normal amounts of food in a short period of time, and a lack of control over eating during the binge ■ Recurrent purging in order to prevent weight gain, such as by self-induced vomiting; misuse of laxatives, diuretics, enemas, or other medications; fasting; or excessive exercise ■ The bingeing and purging occurs, on average, at least twice a week for three months ■ Persistent overconcern with body shape and weight, which may influence self-esteem
Eating disorder not otherwise specified	■ Disordered eating behaviors that do not meet the full diagnostic criteria for anorexia nervosa or bulimia nervosa, including binge eating disorder* and night eating syndrome.

*Separate diagnostic criteria for binge eating disorder have been proposed for the Fifth Edition of the DSM.

Adapted from American Psychiatric Association, *Diagnostic and Statistical Manual of Mental Disorders*, 4th ed., Text Revision (Washington, DC: American Psychiatric Association, 2000).

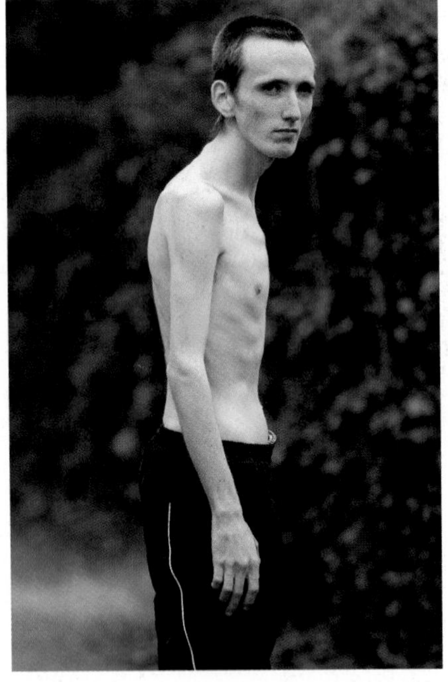

Although the highest rates of disordered eating patterns occur among females, males are not immune. Adolescents in particular can feel pressure to achieve a certain body image.

will try to achieve this perfect figure at any cost, including plastic surgery, liposuction, and engaging in disordered eating behaviors.

About 10 percent of all eating disorders occur in men. This may be an underestimate though, as many men, as well as women, feel ashamed or embarrassed and may hide their problem. In fact, the prevalence of eating disorders among both males and females is probably higher than reported. Researchers have found that men diagnosed with eating disorders have higher rates of other psychiatric illness like depression and anxiety disorders compared with men who do not have eating disorders.[83]

There are several different types of eating disorders, including anorexia nervosa, bulimia nervosa, and binge eating disorder. Each type of eating disorder has specific diagnostic criteria that make the eating disorder unique. Night eating syndrome is a form of eating disorder that is not described with specific diagnostic criteria in the *Diagnostic and Statistical Manual* of the American Psychiatric Association.

Anorexia Nervosa Results from Severe Kilocalorie Restriction

anorexia nervosa An eating disorder in which people intentionally starve themselves, causing extreme weight loss.

Anorexia nervosa is a serious, potentially life-threatening eating disorder that is characterized by self-starvation and excessive weight loss. People who suffer from anorexia nervosa have an intense fear of gaining weight or being "fat." This fear causes them to control their food intake by restricting the amount of food they consume, resulting in significant weight loss.

Many people with anorexia nervosa have a fear of eating certain foods, such as those that contain fat and sugar, or all foods. They believe that these foods will make them "fat," regardless of how little of them they eat. A distorted sense of body image is also present because sufferers usually see themselves as fat even though they are underweight. This misperception of body size contributes to the behavior of restricting food intake in order to lose (more) weight. For instance, someone with anorexia nervosa might eat only a piece of fruit and a small container of yogurt during an entire day. Some may also exercise excessively as a means of controlling their weight. You can read more about the concept of body image in Spotlight: A Closer Look at Body Image.

Numerous health consequences can occur with anorexia nervosa and some can be fatal. One of the most serious health effects is an electrolyte imbalance, specifically low blood potassium, which can occur if someone with anorexia also engages in episodes of purging. An electrolyte imbalance can lead to an irregular heart rhythm. Low blood potassium is the most fatal health effect among people who have an eating disorder. Additionally, due to their extreme lack of body fat, internal body temperature drops and individuals with this disorder feel cold even when it is hot outside. In an effort to regulate body temperature, their body may begin to grow **lanugo** (downy hair), particularly on the face and arms.

The body of a person with anorexia nervosa is not getting enough nutrients. As a result, the body's processes begin to slow or shut down in an effort to conserve energy for its most vital functions. The person may begin to experience a decrease in heart rate and blood pressure, overall weakness and fatigue, hair loss, and a disruption of hormones resulting in amenorrhea (cessation of menstruation in women). The digestive process also slows down, which often results in constipation, bloating, and delayed gastric emptying. Dehydration, iron deficiency, and osteoporosis can also result from inadequate nutrient intake.

Bulimia Nervosa Involves Cycles of Binge Eating and Purging

Bulimia nervosa is another type of eating disorder that can be life-threatening. During times of binge eating, the person lacks control over eating and consumes larger than normal amounts of food in a short period of time. Following the binge, the person counters the excess food consumption with some type of purging. Many people assume that bulimics purge by vomiting, but self-induced vomiting is only one form. Purging can be described as any behavior that assists in "getting rid" of food to prevent weight gain or to promote weight loss. This can include vigorous exercise, abuse of diet pills, laxatives, or diuretics, and strict dieting or fasting.

As with anorexia nervosa, people with bulimia nervosa often suffer from depression and have low self-esteem. They may feel shame and guilt about their eating behaviors, and may try to hide their eating problems from others. Those who have bulimia nervosa are overly concerned with body shape and weight, but usually do not have the same distorted body image as someone with anorexia nervosa.

People with bulimia nervosa often eat in secret.

Most of the health consequences that occur with bulimia nervosa are associated with self-induced vomiting, such as tears in the esophagus, swollen parotid glands (the salivary glands located on each side of the face in front of the ears), tooth decay and gum disease (due to stomach acid), and broken blood vessels in the eyes (due to pressure from vomiting). One sign of bulimia nervosa is often scar tissue on the knuckles of a person's fingers, which forms from their being frequently

lanugo Very fine, soft hair on the face and arms of people with anorexia nervosa.

bulimia nervosa An eating disorder characterized by consuming large quantities of food and then purging through vomiting, laxative and diuretic use, and/or excessive physical exercise.

A Closer Look at Body Image

Body image refers to the way that you perceive and what you believe about your physical appearance, whether you are looking in the mirror or picturing yourself in your mind.[1] Most people think of body image as being about body weight and shape, but it actually refers to any physical attribute such as skin color, hair texture, or height.

Body image can be further defined as having positive or negative characteristics. People with a positive body image view themselves as they truly are (no distortion) and overall feel comfortable and confident in and about their body. They engage in healthy eating and exercise behaviors and don't spend a lot of time worrying about weight, dieting, or changing their looks using extreme measures. They accept their body and don't define their self-worth based on physical appearances.[2] In contrast, those with a negative body image often have distorted views of the way they look and may view their shape as other than it actually is. This is especially true of people with anorexia nervosa. Additionally, they are ashamed, uncomfortable, or self-conscious about their physical appearance and spend a large amount of time focusing on their weight or aspects of their appearance that they perceive as unattractive.[3] A negative body image can contribute to the development or continuation of unhealthy behaviors, like disordered eating, in many individuals.

What Is Body Dysmorphic Disorder?

Body dysmorphic disorder (BDD) is a mental illness in which a person's preoccupation with minor or imaginary physical flaws causes significant distress or impairment in work, school, or other areas of functioning. BDD is estimated to affect slightly more than 2 percent of the U.S. population and frequently occurs along with other psychiatric disorders, such as obsessive-compulsive disorder, anorexia nervosa, and clinical depression.[4]

Muscle dysmorphia, also referred to as "bigorexia" or "reverse anorexia," is a specific type of BDD that typically occurs in males who have a well-defined muscular build but view themselves as being small or weak.[5] Symptoms of muscle dysmorphia include extreme exercise (especially weight lifting) and attention to diet, anxiety when missing a workout, constant mirror checking, use of anabolic steroids to enhance muscle mass, and neglecting family, friends, or work in order to exercise. Media influence on men and their muscle mass and size is thought to be a major contributing factor in the increasing prevalence of muscle dysmorphia. Anyone with these symptoms should seek professional help and treatment, as symptoms can get worse over time.

body dysmorphic disorder (BDD) A mental illness in which a person is excessively concerned about and preoccupied by a perceived defect in his or her body.

How Can You Attain a Positive Body Image?

Many factors can influence your body image, including family, friends, peers, media, and culture. We live in a society where certain images are labeled "ideal," yet are not achievable by most. Nonetheless, we strive to get the "perfect" body through any means necessary. Comparing our bodies with those of friends, models, and celebrities that we view as more attractive only leads to lowered self-esteem and feeling "not good enough."

The following are strategies to help you attain a positive body image:[6]

- Know and accept what determines your physical characteristics (genetics, stage of life, nutritional intake, activity levels).
- Eat normally by responding to hunger and fullness cues.
- Avoid comparing yourself to others, especially models and celebrities.
- Recognize that you are a whole person and not just individual parts.
- Respect yourself and others.

References

1. National Eating Disorders Association. 2012. *Learn Basic Terms and Information on a Variety of Eating Disorder Topics.* Available at www.nationaleatingdisorders.org/information-resources/general-information.php. Accessed June 2012.
2. National Eating Disorders Association. 2005. *Handout on Body Image.* Available at www.nationaleatingdisorders.org/nedaDir/files/documents/handouts/BodyImag.pdf. Accessed June 2012.
3. Ibid.
4. Koran, L. M., E. Abujaoude, M. D. Large, and R. T. Serpe. 2008. The Prevalence of Body Dysmorphic Disorder in the United States Adult Population. *CNS Spectrums* 13:316–322.
5. Mosley, P. E. 2009. Bigorexia: Bodybuilding and Muscle Dysmorphia. *European Eating Disorder Review* 17:191–198.
6. National Eating Disorders Association. 2005. *Handout on Body Image.*

used to induce vomiting. Electrolyte imbalance can occur with bulimia nervosa and can be fatal. People with bulimia nervosa may experience dehydration and constipation due to frequent episodes of binge eating and purging.

Laxative abuse can cause serious medical complications, depending on the type, amount, and length of time the person has used them. Laxatives used repeatedly can cause constipation, dehydration due to fluid loss in the intestines, electrolyte imbalances, fluid retention, bloody stools, and impaired bowel function.

Binge Eating Disorder Involves Compulsive Overeating

Binge eating disorder is characterized by recurrent episodes of binge eating without purging. People who have binge eating disorder eat without regard to physiological cues. They may eat for emotional reasons, which results in an out-of-control feeling while eating and physical and psychological discomfort after eating. Many people who struggle with this type of eating disorder will often eat in secret and feel ashamed about their behaviors.

The health effects of binge eating disorder are most commonly those that are associated with obesity because most people who struggle with binge eating disorder are of normal or heavier-than-average weight. Health effects may include high blood pressure, high cholesterol levels, heart disease, type 2 diabetes, and gallbladder disease.

Binge eating disorder has specific signs and symptoms; however, it does not have its own diagnostic criteria like anorexia nervosa and bulimia nervosa. Because it still requires treatment, it falls into the diagnostic category of "Eating Disorders Not Otherwise Specified." Other behaviors in this category include purging without bingeing, restrictive eating by people who are in a normal weight range despite having significant weight loss, bingeing and purging but not frequently enough to meet criteria for bulimia, and chewing and spitting out food instead of swallowing it.

Night Eating Syndrome Is a Type of Eating, Sleeping, and Mood Disorder

Night eating syndrome is described as an abnormal eating pattern in which a person consumes the majority of daily kilocalories after the evening meal, as well as wakes up during the night, possibly even several times, to eat. In addition, the person typically does not have an appetite during the morning hours and consumes very little throughout the day. One study found that people with night eating syndrome consume 56 percent of their 24-hour kilocalorie intake between the hours of 8:00 p.m. and 6:00 a.m. This study also found that people with night eating syndrome generally do not binge eat with each awakening; rather, they eat smaller portions of food on several occasions throughout the night.[84] This disorder does not correlate to BMI or obesity; people of all weights and sizes can develop night eating syndrome.[85, 86]

Night eating syndrome appears to be a unique combination of disordered eating, a sleep disorder, and a mood disorder. Research has shown that night eating syndrome is associated with low self-esteem, depression, reduced daytime hunger, and less weight loss among obese patients.[87] Stress also appears to be a contributing factor in the development and continuation of night eating syndrome.[88] Someone may feel guilty, ashamed, or embarrassed while they are eating during the night, as well as the next morning. Night eating occurs mostly during the weekend and is most common in young adults between the ages of 18 and 30.[89]

People with night eating syndrome may consume more than half their day's kilocalories between 8 p.m. and 6 a.m.

Self-Assessment

Are You at Risk for an Eating Disorder?

Mark the following statements True or False to help you find out.

1. I constantly think about eating, weight, and body size.
   True ☐ **False** ☐
2. I'm terrified about being overweight.
   True ☐ **False** ☐
3. I binge eat and can't stop until I feel sick.
   True ☐ **False** ☐
4. I weigh myself several times each day.
   True ☐ **False** ☐
5. I exercise too much or get very rigid about my exercise plan.
   True ☐ **False** ☐
6. I have taken laxatives or forced myself to vomit after eating.
   True ☐ **False** ☐
7. I believe food controls my life.
   True ☐ **False** ☐
8. I feel extremely guilty after eating.
   True ☐ **False** ☐
9. I eat when I am nervous, anxious, lonely, or depressed.
   True ☐ **False** ☐
10. I believe my weight controls what I do.
    True ☐ **False** ☐

Analysis

These statements are designed to help you identify potentially problematic eating behavior. These statements do *not* tell you if you have an eating disorder. Look carefully at any statement you marked as True and decide if this behavior prevents you from enjoying life or makes you unhealthy. Changing these behaviors should be done gradually, making small changes one at a time. Contact your student health services center or your health care provider if you suspect you need help.

Different Eating Disorders Have Some Traits and Signs in Common

A common trait of people with eating disorders is perfectionism. Unrealistic standards can produce a sense of failure and lowered self-worth. Many people who struggle with eating disorders are trying to gain some control in their lives. When external factors feel out of control, the person with an eating disorder gets a sense of security from being able to control personal food and weight issues. They may withdraw from social interactions because food is often present and they do not feel comfortable eating around others. Depression and low self-esteem also exist among many people who have eating disorders.

Most college students today know someone with an eating disorder, but may not know how to help them. Learning about eating disorders can help individuals understand why a friend or loved one can have destructive eating behaviors and be seemingly unaware of the damage, pain, or danger they can cause. Everyone should be aware of the warning signs of disordered eating behaviors so they can potentially identify them in friends and loved ones (Table 15.6).

If you are concerned about someone, find a good time and place to gently express your concerns without criticism or judgment. Realize that you may be rejected or your friend may deny the problem. Be supportive and let the person know that you are available if they want to talk to you at another time. You should also realize that there are many things that you cannot do to help a loved one or friend get better. You cannot force an anorexic to eat, keep a bulimic from purging, or make a binge eater stop overeating. It is up to the individual to decide when he or she is ready to deal with the issues in life that led to the eating disorder.

Eating Disorders Can Be Treated

The most effective treatment for eating disorders is a multidisciplinary team approach including psychological, medical, and nutrition professionals. All members of the team must be knowledgeable and experienced with eating disorders because it is a complex area; some health care professionals do not feel comfortable treating eating disorders. A physician or other medical professional should closely monitor anyone who struggles with an eating disorder, as some eating disorders can be life-threatening. In severe cases, a physician may require the patient to be hospitalized as part of the treatment. A psychologist can help the person deal with emotional and other psychological issues that may be contributing to the eating disorder.

A Registered Dietitian can help someone with an eating disorder establish normal eating behaviors. Some nutritional approaches to eating disorders include identifying binge triggers, safe and unsafe foods, and hunger and fullness cues. Food journals are often helpful to identify eating patterns, food choices, moods, disordered eating triggers, eating cues, and timing of meals and snacks. Meal plans are also used in some instances to ensure adequate kilocalorie and nutrient intake among those with anorexia nervosa, and to help avoid overeating among those with bulimia nervosa or binge eating disorder.

Most people can recover from an eating disorder and may not have to struggle with it for the rest of their lives. When treatment is sought in the early stages, there is a better chance that the person will recover fully and have a shorter recovery process than someone who begins treatment after many years. Some people continue to have the desire to engage in disordered eating behaviors; however, they are able to refrain from actually doing these behaviors. Unfortunately, some individuals may never fully recover from an eating disorder. Caregivers must recognize that recovery is a process that often takes years and has no "quick fix."

TABLE 15.6 Warning Signs for Eating Disorders

Symptom	Explanation/Example
Weight is below 85% of ideal body weight	Refusal to accept and maintain body weight (even if it is within normal range)
Exercises excessively	Often exercises daily for long periods of time to burn kilocalories and prevent weight gain. May skip work or class to exercise.
Preoccupation with food, weight, and diet	Constantly worries about amount and type of food eaten. May weigh himself or herself daily or several times per day.
Distorted body image	Does not see himself/herself as he or she truly is. May comment on being fat even if underweight.
Refusing to eat	Will avoid food in order to lose weight or prevent weight gain. May avoid only certain foods, such as those with fat and sugar.
Loss of menstrual period	Periods become irregular or completely absent
Diet pill use or laxative use	Evidence of pill bottles, boxes, or packaging
Changes in mood	May become more withdrawn, depressed, or anxious, especially around food
Hair loss	Hair becomes thinner and falls out in large quantities
Avoids eating around others	Wants to eat alone. Makes excuses to avoid eating with others.

THE TAKE-HOME MESSAGE Disordered eating is characterized by an abnormal eating pattern. Eating disorders include disordered eating behaviors and other specific diagnostic criteria. Approximately 11 million people in the United States struggle with eating disorders, including females, males, minorities, and predominantly upper- and middle-class individuals of all age groups. Eating disorders include anorexia nervosa, bulimia nervosa, binge eating or compulsive overeating, and night eating syndrome. Eating disorders are most effectively treated with a multidisciplinary team of psychologists, physicians, and Registered Dietitians. A full recovery takes time but is possible, especially if the disorder is treated in the early stages.

Putting It All Together

Choosing foods rich in complex carbohydrates, lean proteins, and healthy fats can provide the energy necessary to fuel daily activities while at the same time maintain a healthy body weight. Vitamins, such as the B vitamins, and certain minerals, including iron, participate in the chemical reactions that enable cells to obtain and use the energy during metabolism especially when on a weight loss program. Foods that are more energy dense can contribute to unwanted weight gain if the kilocalories ingested exceed the kilocalories expended.

Avoid unwanted weight gain by controlling portion sizes and eating a healthy diet based on all five food groups, expending more energy through daily physical activity, and changing your environment to break the chain of behaviors that may compromise body weight and, ultimately, health. A diet rich in protein and high-volume, low-density foods including fruits, vegetables, and whole grains, and small amounts of heart-healthy fats such as lean meat, skinless chicken, fish, and nuts will help control hunger and appetite.

Visual Chapter Summary

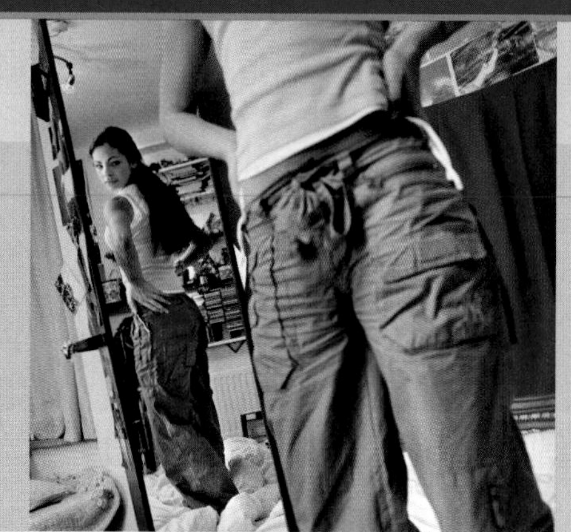

1 Healthy Body Weight Is Defined By Body Mass Index

The terms used to describe individual body weights are based on body mass index. Underweight is defined as a BMI < 18.5; normal weight is a BMI ranging between 18.5 and 24.9; overweight ranges from a BMI of 25 to 29.9; obesity is considered to be a BMI greater than 30 and extreme obesity a BMI greater than 40.

2 Fat Cells Form, Expand, and Shrink

Fat cells can increase in size to store more fat (hypertrophy) and new fat cells can be produced (hyperplasia) to replace old cells and and to create additional cells once existing ones fill to capacity. During weight loss, fat cells shrink but are not destroyed.

The enzymes lipoprotein lipase and hormone-sensitive lipase influence the balance between lipolysis and lipogenesis. LPL activity is greater in obese individuals and in women.

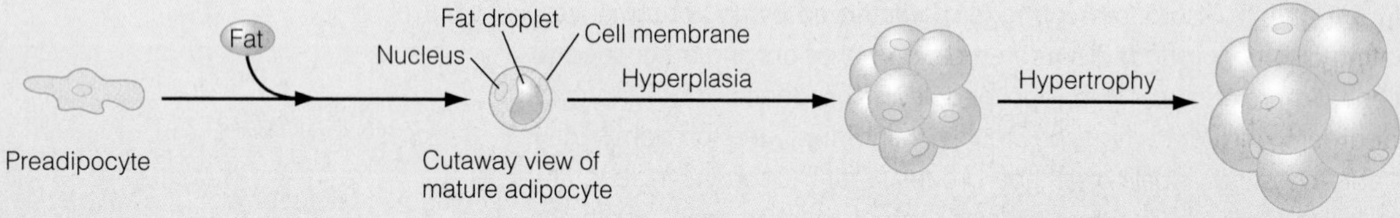

3 Food Intake Is Regulated By the Hypothalamus

Food intake is regulated by the physiological responses known as hunger and satiety. Hunger prompts the body to eat and subsides soon after eating begins. Satiety determines the length of time between meals or snacks.

Hunger is controlled by the lateral hypothalamus and satiety is controlled by the ventromedial nucleus of the hypothalamus. Both areas of the brain respond to hormonal and neural signals from the GI tract. Certain hormones, including neuropeptide Y from the hypothalamus and ghrelin from the stomach stimulate hunger. Other hormones, including cholecystokinin and peptide YY from the small intestine, insulin from the pancreas, and leptin from adipose tissue, increase satiety. A meal higher in fiber and volume increases satiety. Foods high in protein are the most satiating.

Appetite is a nonphysiological desire for food and can be affected by psychological factors or the sight, smell, taste, and thought of food, as well as emotions, environment, and social settings.

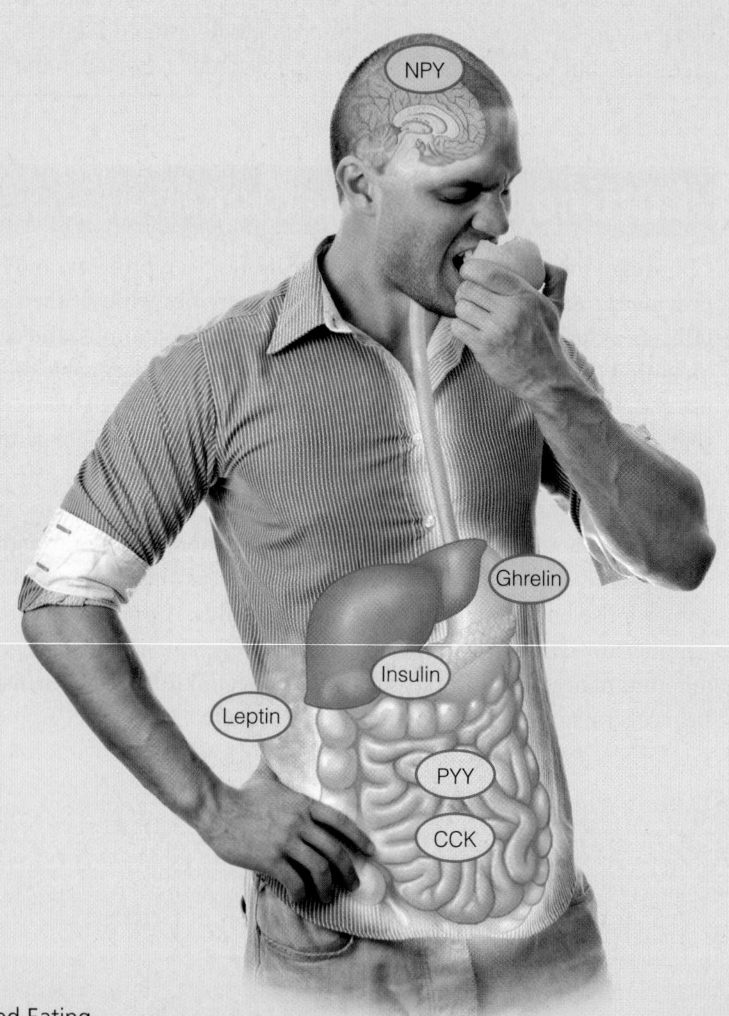

4 Genetics and Environment Both Influence Obesity and Weight Management

An individual's genetic makeup can influence the predisposition or risk of becoming obese. Single-nucleotide polymorphisms of multiple genes influence the secretion of appetite control hormones such as ghrelin and leptin. Genetic makeup also influences thermogenesis for maintaining a specific weight.

A gene–environment interaction in which genetically prone individuals have easy access to a variety of large portions of food and an environment that encourages a sedentary lifestyle, promotes obesity. Eating too much and moving too little add to the risk of obesity.

5 A Healthful Way to Lose Weight Includes Eating Less and Exercising More

A healthy, reasonable rate of weight loss is losing 10 percent of body weight over a six-month period. Losing weight rapidly can cause a person to fall short of meeting nutrient needs. Many fad diets promise quick results but can be unhealthy for the long term.

Expending more kilocalories than consumed is the key to weight loss. Eating more low-energy-density, high-volume foods, such as vegetables and fruit, improves satiation, which results in fewer kilocalories consumed. Because protein has the most dramatic effect on satiety, eating high-protein lean meats, chicken, and fish at meals can help reduce hunger between meals. Because fat slows the movement of food out of the stomach into the intestines, it can also prolong satiety.

Routine physical activity and exercise can add to the daily energy deficit needed for weight loss. To aid in weight loss, overweight individuals should partake in 60 to 90 minutes of moderate-intensity exercise daily and continue at least this amount of activity daily to maintain the weight loss.

6 Behavior Modification Helps Maintain a Healthy Weight

Individuals who wish to maintain long-term weight loss must permanently change the eating behaviors that contributed to weight gain or impeded weight loss. Self-monitoring of these behaviors by keeping a food record, controlling environmental cues that trigger eating when not hungry, and learning how to better manage stress are all behavior modification techniques that can be used by individuals who eat "out of habit" and in response to their environment.

7 Eat More Nutrient-Dense Foods and Exercise to Gain Weight Healthily

Individuals who wish to gain weight must increase kilocalorie intake and exercise to build muscle mass. Consuming larger portions at mealtimes and energy-dense snacks between meals can help with weight gain.

8 Disordered Eating and Eating Disorders Have Common Traits and Treatments

Disordered eating describes a variety of abnormal eating patterns, such as restrictive eating, binge eating, vomiting after eating, and abusing laxatives or diet pills. Eating disorders are diagnosed by meeting specific criteria that include disordered eating behaviors.

Anorexia nervosa is characterized by self-starvation and excessive weight loss. Bulimia nervosa involves repeated cycles of binge eating and purging. Binge eating disorders are characterized by binge eating without purging. Night eating syndrome is described as excessive kilocalorie intake in the evening and waking up during the night to eat.

The most effective treatment for eating disorders involves a multidisciplinary team approach including psychological, nutrition, and medical professionals.

Terms to Know

- hypertrophy
- hyperplasia
- hunger
- satiety
- appetite
- set point
- gene–environment interaction
- behavior modification
- disordered eating
- eating disorder
- anorexia nervosa
- bulimia nervosa

MasteringNutrition™

Build your knowledge—and confidence—in the Study Area of MasteringNutrition with a variety of study tools.

Check Your Understanding

1. The physiological need for food is called
   a. hunger.
   b. satiety.
   c. appetite.
   d. hyperplasia.
2. The section of the hypothalamus that controls hunger is called the
   a. ventromedial nucleus.
   b. lateral hypothalamus.
   c. hippocampus.
   d. pituitary gland.
3. When an individual loses body fat
   a. there is a decrease in the number of adipocytes due to hyperplasia.
   b. there is a decrease in the size of the fat cells due to hypertrophy.
   c. there is no change in the adipocytes, but subcutaneous fat is lost.
   d. the adipocytes shrink but the number of cells stays the same.
4. A rate of sustainable, healthy weight loss is ½ to 1 pound per week.
   a. True
   b. False
5. After a large meal of pasta and tomato sauce, the stomach is distended. Which hormone is released because of the distention of the stomach?
   a. cholecystokinin
   b. insulin
   c. ghrelin
   d. leptin
6. Which of the following can increase the risk of becoming overweight?
   a. having a parent who is obese
   b. consuming more meals at home than dining out
   c. reducing the amounts of "screen time" during the day
   d. decreasing the size of your food portions at meals
7. What is the best dietary approach to losing weight?
   a. eliminate all carbohydrates from the diet
   b. reduce kilocalorie intake and increase energy expenditure through physical activity
   c. consume foods high in both protein and fat to stimulate satiety
   d. limit fat intake to less than 5 grams per day
8. Mary Ellen was obese and lost 30 pounds during the last year by eating a well-balanced, kilocalorie-reduced diet and being physically active daily. To maintain her weight loss, she should continue to eat a healthy diet, monitor her eating behaviors, and
   a. accumulate 30 minutes of physical activity three times a week.
   b. accumulate 45 minutes of physical activity three times a week.
   c. accumulate at least 60 minutes of physical activity daily.
   d. accumulate more than 2 hours of physical activity daily.
9. Eating disorders include all of the following except
   a. bulimia nervosa.
   b. night eating syndrome.
   c. anorexia nervosa.
   d. daytime eating syndrome.
10. Lanugo, or downy hair growth, is common in what type of eating disorder?
    a. anorexia nervosa
    b. bulimia nervosa
    c. binge eating disorder
    d. night eating syndrome

Answers

1. (a) The physiological need for food is called hunger. Satiety is the feeling of fullness or satisfaction that sets in after eating begins, while appetite is defined as the desire for a food even in the absence of hunger.

Hyperplasia is an increase in the number of fat cells.

2. (b) The lateral hypothalamus controls hunger, while the ventromedial nucleus is responsible for satiation. The hippocampus is a structure involved in memory consolidation. The pituitary gland, located beneath the hypothalamus, secretes many hormones important to homeostasis; it is not technically part of the brain.
3. (d) When the body loses fat, the adipocyte shrinks in size but the number of fat cells remains constant. Adipocytes are the specialized cells that make up all adipose tissue, including subcutaneous fat. Hyperplasia is an increase in fat cells when the old cells have become saturated with fat and hypertrophy is the increase in the size of the adipocyte as it stores more fat.
4. (a) The average person can healthfully lose about ½ to 1 pound per week.
5. (a) A distended stomach causes the release of cholecystokinin, which is associated with the feeling of satiation and the ending of eating. Insulin will be released once this carbohydrate-heavy meal is digested and absorbed into the blood. Ghrelin is released from the stomach when it is empty, and stimulates feeding. Leptin is secreted from the adipocyte and stimulates hunger when the fat cell shrinks.
6. (a) Having a parent who is overweight and/or obese may indicate you have a genetic predisposition to becoming overweight. Increasing your regular physical activity by reducing screen time, eating more meals at home, and reducing food portions are methods that will reduce your risk of becoming overweight.
7. (b) The best approach to losing weight is to reduce the total amount of kilocalories by reducing the amount of food consumed and increasing energy expenditure through physical activity. Consuming a diet that eliminated carbohydrates or contained high-protein, high-fat foods or less than 5 grams of fat per day would be unbalanced in nutrient content and could result in malnutrition.
8. (c) If Mary Ellen would like to keep the weight off, she should try to accumulate at least 60 to 90 minutes of physical activity daily.
9. (d) All of these terms except daytime eating syndrome are considered a form of eating disorder. Night eating syndrome is a combination of disordered eating and a sleep and mood disorder, and it has been proposed for inclusion in the next edition of the *Diagnostic and Statistical Manual* of the American Psychiatric Association.
10. (a) The downy hair that grows on the face and arms to help regulate body temperature occurs in people with anorexia nervosa.

Answers to Myths and Misconceptions

1. **False.** While the recommendation for weight loss is to accumulate at least 60 to 90 minutes of daily physical activity, the bottom line is that for weight loss to occur, more energy must be expended than is consumed. This can be accomplished by consuming less, exercising more, or a combination of both.
2. **False.** The bodies of individuals who fill up existing fat cells will synthesize new fat cells, regardless of age. Ten percent of fat cells are replaced with new cells every 10 years.
3. **False.** Grazing is considered a high-risk behavior for weight management because the foods that are typically chosen are low in protein and not satiating. Individuals may also consume higher amounts of kilocalories by eating mindlessly rather than consuming planned, smaller meals.
4. **True.** Weight loss of as little as 10 pounds can improve health if an individual is overweight.
5. **True.** Nature and nurture both play a role in regulating body weight. Nature (genes) often sets the stage, while nurture (environment and personal behavior) directly affects weight management.
6. **True.** Increasing the volume of food and the fiber content of meals by eating *more* vegetables and fruits can improve appetite control, reducing kilocalorie intake and thus helping attain weight loss.
7. **True.** At its most basic, weight gain occurs because of a positive energy balance. However, genetics and the environment play strong roles.
8. **False.** Of all the nutrients, protein has the most powerful effect on satiety.
9. **False.** Disordered eating describes a variety of eating patterns considered abnormal and potentially harmful. Eating disorders are diagnosed by meeting specific criteria that include disordered eating behaviors as well as other factors. It is possible for someone to have disordered eating without having an actual eating disorder.
10. **True.** The long-term starvation of anorexia nervosa and consistent purging of bulimia nervosa (which can lead to electrolyte imbalance) can be fatal.

Web Resources

- For more on overweight and obesity, visit the Centers for Disease Control and Prevention at www.cdc.gov/nccdphp/dnpa/obesity/index.htm
- For more information on weight control and physical activity, visit the Weight-control Information Network (WIN) at http://win.niddk.nih.gov/index.htm
- For more weight-loss shopping tips, recipes, and menu makeovers, visit the USDA's Nutrition and Weight Management website at www.nutrition.gov
- For more information on gastric bypass surgery, visit the American

Society for Metabolic and Bariatric Surgery at www.asbs.org

- For more information on eating disorders and their prevention and treatment, visit the National Eating Disorders Association at www.nationaleatingdisorders.org

References

1. Centers for Disease Control and Prevention. 2011. *Obesity: Halting the Epidemic by Making Health Easier.* Available at www.cdc.gov/NCCDPHP/publications/AAG/obesity.htm. Accessed June 2012.
2. Manson, J., P. Skerrett, P. Greenland, and T. Van Itallie. 2004. The Escalating Pandemics of Obesity and Sedentary Lifestyle: A Call to Action for Clinicians. *Archives of Internal Medicine* 164:249–258.
3. WebMD. 2011. *Top Ten Health News Stories of 2011.* Available at www.webmd.com/diet/features/webmds-top-health-stories-of-2011. Accessed June 2012.
4. PRWeb. 2011. *U. S. Weight Loss Market Worth $60.9 Billion.* Available at www.prweb.com/releases/2011/5/prweb8393658.htm. Accessed June 2012.
5. Begley, Sharon. 2012. The Costs of Obesity. *Huffpost Healthy Living.* Available at www.huffingtonpost.com/2012/04/30/obesity-costs-dollars-cents_n_1463763.html. Accessed June 2012.
6. Weight-control Information Network. 2004. *Do You Know the Health Risks of Being Overweight?* Updated April 2010. Available at http://win.niddk.nih.gov/publications/health_risks.htm. Accessed June 2012.
7. National Institutes of Health. 1998. *Clinical Guidelines on the Identification, Evaluation, and Treatment of Overweight and Obesity in Adults.* Available at www.nhlbi.nih.gov/guidelines/obesity/ob_gdlns.htm. Accessed June 2012.
8. Hammond, K. 2004. Dietary and Clinical Assessment. In L. Mahan and S. Escott-Stump, eds. *Krause's Food, Nutrition, and Diet Therapy.* 11th ed. Philadelphia: Saunders.
9. Hunte, H. E. R. and D. R. Williams. 2008. The Association between Perceived Discrimination and Obesity in a Population-Based Multiracial and Multiethnic Adult Sample. *American Journal of Public Health* 98:1–8.
10. U.S. Department of Health and Human Services. 2012. *Healthy People 2020.* Available at www.healthypeople.gov/2020/about/default.aspx. Accessed June 2012.
11. Spalding, K. L., E. Arner, P. O. Westermark, S. Bernard, B. A. Buchholz, O. Bergmann, L. Blomqvist, et al. 2008. Dynamics of Fat Cell Turnover in Humans. *Nature* 453:783–787.
12. Ibid.
13. Perreault, L., J. M. Lavely, J. M. Kittelson, and T. J. Horton. 2004. Gender Differences in Lipoprotein Lipase Activity after Acute Exercise. *Obesity Research* 12:241–249.
14. Mattes, R., J. Hollis, D. Hayes, and A. Stunkard. 2005. Appetite: Measurement and Manipulations Misgivings. *Journal of the American Dietetic Association* 105:S87–S97.
15. Ibid.
16. Smith, G. 2006. Controls of Food Intake. In M. Shils, et al., eds. *Modern Nutrition in Health and Disease.* 10th ed. Philadelphia: Lippincott Williams & Wilkins.
17. Rosenbaum, M., M. Sy, K. Pavlovich, R. L. Leibel, and J. Hirsch. 2008. Leptin Reverses Weight-Loss-Induced Changes in Regional Neural Activity Responses to Visual Food Stimuli. *Journal of Clinical Investigations* 118:2583–2591.
18. Garcia, O. P., D. Ronquillo, M. del Carmen, M. Camacho, K. Z. Long, and J. L. Rosado. 2012. Zinc, Vitamin A, and Vitamin C Status Are Associated with Leptin Concentrations and Obesity in Mexican Women: Results from a Cross-Sectional Study. *Nutrition and Metabolism* 9:59–79.
19. Ibid.
20. Astrup, A. 2005. The Satiating Power of Protein—A Key to Obesity Prevention? *American Journal of Clinical Nutrition* 82:1–2.
21. Huda, M. S. B., T. Dovey, S. P. Wong, P. J. English, J. Halford, P. McCulloch, J. Cleator, et al. 2009. Ghrelin Restores 'Lean-Type' Hunger and Energy Expenditure Profiles in Morbidly Obese Subjects but Has No Effect on Postgastrectomy Subjects. *International Journal of Obesity.* 33:317–325.
22. Heber, D. 2010. An Integrative View of Obesity. *American Journal of Clinical Nutrition* 91:280S–283S.
23. Hill, J., V. Catenacci, and H. Wyatt. 2006. Obesity: Etiology. In M. Shils, et al., eds. *Modern Nutrition in Health and Disease.* 10th ed. Philadelphia: Lippincott Williams & Wilkins.
24. Herrera, B. M., S. Keildson, and C. M. Lindgren. 2011. Genetics and Epigenetics of Obesity. *Maturitas* 69:41–49.
25. O'Rahilly, S. O. and I. S. Forooqui. 2008. Human Obesity as a Heritable Disorder of the Central Control of Energy Balance: Inheritance and Human Obesity. *International Journal of Obesity* 32:S55–S61.
26. Center for Genomics and Public Health. 2004. *Obesity and Current Topics in Genetics.* Updated November 2007. Available at www.cdc.gov/genomics/resources/diseases/obesity/obesedit.htm. Accessed November 2012.
27. Hill, J., et al. 2006. Obesity: Etiology.
28. Bray, G. and C. Champagne. 2005. Beyond Energy Balance: There Is More to Obesity than Kilocalories. *Journal of the American Dietetic Association* 105:S17–S23.
29. Brodsky, I. 2006. Hormones and Growth Factors. 2006. In M. Shils, et al., eds. *Modern Nutrition in Health and Disease.* 10th ed. Philadelphia: Lippincott Williams & Wilkins.
30. Office of Genetics and Disease Prevention Public Health Perspectives. 2006. *Obesity and Genetics: What We Know, What We Don't Know and What It Means.* Updated November 2007. Available at www.cdc.gov/genomics/resources/diseases/obesity/obesknow.htm. Accessed November 2012.
31. Hill, J., et al. 2006. Obesity: Etiology.
32. Ibid.
33. Gale, S., T. Van Itallie, and I. Faust. 1981. Effects of Palatable Diets on Body Weight and Adipose Tissue Cellularity in the Adult Obese Female Zucker Rat (*fa/fa*). *Metabolism* 30:105–110.
34. Ravussin, E., M. Valencia, J. Esparza, P. Bennett, and L. Schulz. 1994. Effects of a Traditional Lifestyle on Obesity in Pima Indians. *Diabetes Care* 17:1067–1074.
35. Wang, S. and K. Brownell. 2005. Public Policy and Obesity: The Need to Marry Science with Advocacy. *Psychiatric Clinics of North America* 28:235–252.
36. Loos, R. and T. Rankinen. 2005. Gene-Diet Interactions on Body Weight Changes. *Journal of the American Dietetic Association* 105:S29–S34.
37. The Keystone Group. 2009. *The Keystone Forums on Away-from-Home Food, Opportunities for Preventing Weight Gain and Obesity.* Available at https://keystone.org/images/keystone-center/spp-documents/2011/Forum_on_Away-From-Home_Foods/forum_report_final_5-30-06.pdf. Accessed November 2012.
38. Ibid.
39. Wang, S., et al. 2005. Public Policy and Obesity.
40. The Keystone Group. 2009. *The Keystone Forums.*
41. Clemens, L., D. Slawson, and R. Klesges. 1999. The Effect of Eating Out on Quality of Diet in Premenopausal Women. *Journal of the American Dietetic Association* 99:442–444.
42. Larson, N., D. Neumark-Sztainer, M. N. Laska, and M. Story. 2011. Young Adults and Eating Away from Home: Associations with Dietary Intake Patterns and Weight Status Differ by Choice of Restaurant. *Journal of the American Dietetic Association* 111:1696–1703.
43. Reuters. 2009. *Workers Say Spending Less on Eating Out: Survey.* Available at http://uk.reuters.com/article/economyNews/idUKTRE51M7AQ20090223. Accessed June 2012.
44. Shaw, T. 2009. Economy's Chill Puts Ice on Eating Out. *The Denver Post.* Available at www.denverpost.com/food/ci_9533052. Accessed June 2012.
45. Meyers, A., A. Stunkard, and M. Coll. 1980. Food Accessibility and Food Choice. *Archives of General Psychiatry* 37:1133–1135.
46. Rolls, B. 1986. Sensory-Specific Satiety. *Nutrition Reviews* 44:93–101.
47. Rolls, B. 2003. The Supersizing of America. *Nutrition Today* 38:42–53.
48. Wansink, B. 1996. Can Package Size Accelerate Usage Volume? *Journal of Marketing* 60:1–14.

49. Rolls, B., L. Roe, and J. Meengs. 2006. Larger Portion Sizes Lead to a Sustained Increase in Energy Intake over 2 Days. *Journal of the American Dietetic Association* 106:543–549.
50. Putnam, J., J. Allshouse, and L. Kantor. 2002. U.S. Per Capita Food Supply Trends: More Calories, Refined Carbohydrates, and Fats. Economic Research Service, USDA. *Food Review* 25:2–15.
51. French, S., M. Story, and R. Jeffery. 2001. Environmental Influences on Eating and Physical Activity. *Annual Reviews of Public Health* 22:309–335.
52. Mummery, W., G. Schofield, R. Steele, E. Eakin, and W. Brown. 2005. Occupational Sitting Time and Overweight and Obesity in Australian Workers. *American Journal of Preventive Medicine* 29:91–97.
53. French, S., et al. 2001. Environmental Influences on Eating.
54. National Institutes of Health. 1998. *Clinical Guidelines on the Identification, Evaluation, and Treatment of Overweight and Obesity in Adults.*
55. Colles, S. L., J. B. Dixon, and P. E. O'Brien. 2008. Grazing and Loss of Control Related to Eating: Two High-Risk Factors following Bariatric Surgery. *Obesity* 16:615–622.
56. Lissner, L., D. Levitsky, B. Strupp, H. Kalkwarf, and D. Roe. 1987. Dietary Fat and the Regulation of Energy Intake in Human Subjects. *American Journal of Clinical Nutrition* 46:886–892.
57. Tohill, B., J. Seymour, M. Serdula, L. Kettel-Khan, and B. Rolls. 2004. What Epidemiologic Studies Tell Us about the Relationship between Fruit and Vegetable Consumption and Body Weight. *Nutrition Reviews* 62:365–374.
58. Rolls, B., E. Bell, and E. Thorwart. 1999. Water Incorporated into a Food but Not Served with a Food Decreases Energy Intake in Lean Women. *American Journal of Clinical Nutrition* 70:448–455.
59. Burton-Freeman, B. 2000. Dietary Fiber and Energy Regulation. *Journal of Nutrition* 130:272S–275S.
60. Davis, J., V. Hodges, and B. Gillham. 2006. Normal-Weight Adults Consume More Fiber and Fruit than Their Age- and Height-Matched Overweight/Obese Counterparts. *Journal of the American Dietetic Association* 106:833–840.
61. Mattes, R., et al. 2005. Appetite: Measurement and Manipulations Misgivings.
62. Keim, N., C. Blanton, and M. Kretsch. 2004. America's Obesity Epidemic: Measuring Physical Activity to Promote an Active Lifestyle. *Journal of the American Dietetic Association* 104:1398–1409.
63. Saries, W., S. Blair, M. van Baak, et al. 2003. How Much Physical Activity Is Enough to Prevent Unhealthy Weight Gain? Outcome of the IASO Stock Conference and Consensus Statement. *Obesity Reviews* 4:101–114.
64. Jakicic, J. and A. Otto. 2005. Physical Activity Consideration for the Treatment and Prevention of Obesity. *American Journal of Clinical Nutrition* 82:226S–229S.
65. Shape Up America! 2006. *10,000 Steps.* Available at www.shapeup.org/resources/10000steps_2006fs.pdf. Accessed November 2012.
66. Hoffman, D., P. Policastro, V. Quick, and S. K. Lee. 2006. Changes in Body Weight and Fat Mass of Men and Women in the First Year of College: A Study of the "Freshman 15." *Journal of American College Health* 55:41–45.
67. Holm-Denoma, J. M., T. E. Joiner, K. D. Vohs, and T. F. Heatherton. 2008. The "Freshman Fifteen" (the "Freshman Five" Actually): Predictors and Possible Explanations. *Health Psychology* 27:S3–S9.
68. Ibid.
69. Jung, M. E., S. R. Bray, and K. A. M. Ginis. 2008. Behavior Change and the Freshman 15: Tracking Physical Activity and Dietary Patterns in 1st Year University Women. *Journal of American College Health* 56:523–530.
70. Poston, W. and J. Foreyt. 2000. Successful Management of the Obese Patient. *American Family Physician* 61:3615–3622.
71. Rosenbaum, M., R. Leibel, and J. Hirsch. 1997. Obesity. *New England Journal of Medicine* 337:396–407.
72. Ibid.
73. National Institute of Diabetes and Digestive and Kidney Diseases. 2006. *Weight Cycling.* Available at http://win.niddk.nih.gov/publications/cycling.htm. Accessed June 2012.
74. Klem, M. L., R. R. Wing, M. T. McGuire, H. M. Seagle, and J. O. Hill. 1997. A Descriptive Study of Individuals Successful at Long-Term Maintenance of Substantial Weight Loss. *American Journal of Clinical Nutrition* 66:239–246.
75. Ibid.
76. Hill, J., H. Wyatt, G. Reed, and J. Peters. 2003. Obesity and the Environment: Where Do We Go from Here? *Science* 299:853–855.
77. Hill, J., H. Thompson, and H. Wyatt. 2005. Weight Maintenance: What's Missing? *Journal of the American Dietetic Association* 105:S63–S66.
78. Ibid.
79. U.S. Department of Health and Human Services. 2005. *Report of the Dietary Guidelines Advisory Committee on the* Dietary Guidelines for Americans, 2005. Available at www.health.gov/DietaryGuidelines/dga2005/report. Accessed June 2012.
80. National Eating Disorder Association. 2008. *Statistics: Eating Disorders and Their Precursors.* Available at www.nationaleatingdisorders.org. Accessed June 2012.
81. Hrabosky, J. I. and C. M. Grilo. 2007. Body Image and Eating Disordered Behavior in a Community Sample of Black and Hispanic Women. *Eating Behaviors* 8:106–114.
82. Ricciardelli, L. A., M. P. McCabe, R. J. Williams, and J. K. Thompson. 2007. The Role of Ethnicity and Culture in Body Image and Disordered Eating Among Males. *Clinical Psychology Reviews* 27:582–606.
83. Woodside, D. B., P. E. Garfinkel, E. Lin, P. Goering, A. S. Kaplan, D. S. Goldbloom, and S. H. Kennedy. 2001. Comparisons of Men with Full or Partial Eating Disorders, Men without Eating Disorders, and Women with Eating Disorders in the Community. *American Journal of Psychiatry* 158:570–574.
84. Birketvedt, G. S., J. Florholmen, J. Sundsfjord, B. Osterud, D. Dinges, W. Bilker, and A. Stunkard. 1999. Behavioral and Neuroendocrine Characteristics of the Night Eating Syndrome. *Journal of the American Medical Association* 282:657–663.
85. Marshall, H. M., K. C. Allison, J. P. O'Reardon, G. Birketvedt, and A. J. Stunkard. 2004. Night Eating Syndrome among Nonobese Persons. *International Journal of Eating Disorders* 35:217–222.
86. Striegel-Moore, R. H., D. L. Franko, D. Thompson, S. Affenito, and H. C. Kraemer. 2006. Night Eating Prevalence and Demographic Correlates. *Obesity* 14:139–147.
87. Gluck, M., A. Geliebter, and T. Satov. 2001. Night Eating Syndrome Is Associated with Depression, Low Self-Esteem, Reduced Daytime Hunger, and Less Weight Loss in Obese Outpatients. *Obesity Research* 9:264–267.
88. Birketvedt, G. S., J. Sundsfjord, and J. R. Florholmen. 2002. Hypothalamic-Pituitary-Adrenal Axis in the Night Eating Syndrome. *American Journal of Physiology, Endocrinology, and Metabolism* 282:E366–E369.
89. Striegel-Moore, R. H., et al. 2006. Night Eating Prevalence and Demographic Correlates.

16 Nutrition and Fitness

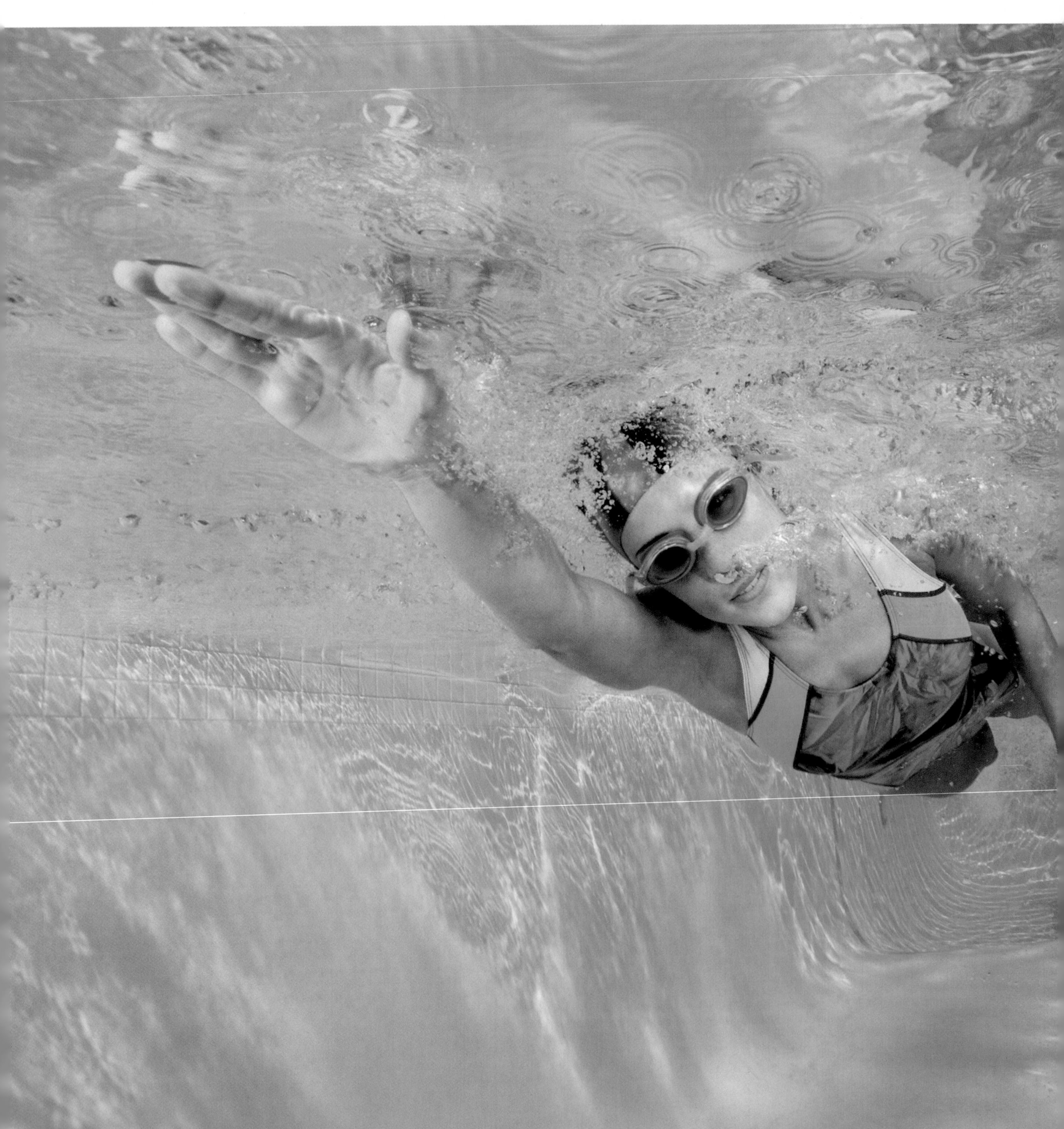

Chapter Objectives

After reading this chapter, you will be able to:

1. List and describe the five basic components of fitness.
2. Explain the main features of a successful fitness program.
3. Describe the role of carbohydrate, fat, and protein in exercise.
4. Discuss optimal foods to consume before, during, and after exercise.
5. Describe the importance of vitamins and minerals for physical fitness.
6. Explain the relationship between fluid intake and fitness.
7. Discuss issues surrounding the use of dietary supplements and ergogenic aids in fitness programs.

1. Most people in the United States are physically fit. T/F
2. As little as 60 minutes of physical activity per week will provide health benefits. T/F
3. Carbohydrate, fat, and protein provide energy during exercise. T/F
4. Low- to moderate-intensity exercise uses more fat than carbohydrate for fuel. T/F
5. Athletes should eat immediately after training. T/F
6. Vitamin and mineral supplements always improve athletic performance. T/F
7. Many athletes are at risk for iron deficiency. T/F
8. Everyone who exercises should consume sports drinks. T/F
9. You can never drink too much water. T/F
10. The NCAA classifies caffeine as a banned substance when consumed in high amounts. T/F

See page 618 for answers to these Myths and Misconceptions.

Whether you are a weekend warrior, walking for fitness, or a triathlete, your eating habits are just as important to your fitness and athletic performance as the exercise itself. Your body is like a car: It requires fuel to make it move. If you are driving in a car race, you will make sure that you have enough gas to make it through the competition. Similar to the gas in a car, nutrients from food provide the energy needed to move the body, especially during exercise. The more you move, the more energy is required. Nutrients are also needed to help the body recover after exercise so that you receive the benefits of the activity and have energy to repeat the activity. Fueling your body with the proper balance of nutrients is necessary to achieve optimal fitness levels and optimal athletic performance.

In this chapter, we will explore the components and health benefits of physical fitness, the role the various nutrients play in physical activity, and how nutrition relates to physical fitness and athletic performance. You do not have to be a competitive or trained athlete to find the information in this chapter beneficial. It is intended for anyone seeking to understand the relationship between nutrition and physical fitness and apply that knowledge to their personal lifestyle.

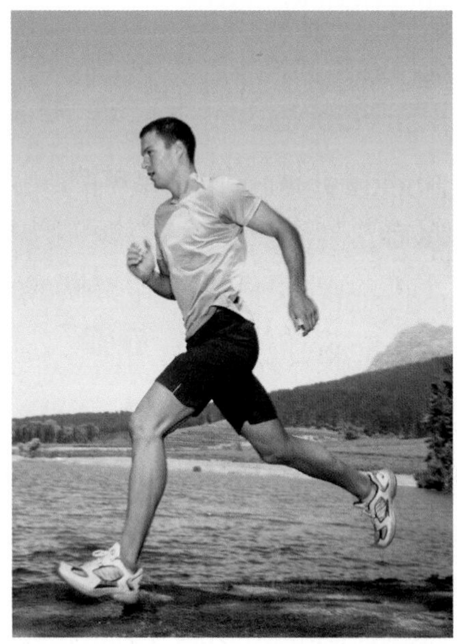

Running is a great way to improve cardiorespiratory fitness.

What Is Physical Fitness and Why Is It Important?

Most of us strive to be physically fit. But what does the term mean? Can you carry a heavy bag of groceries up a flight of steps without becoming winded, lift a heavy box from a shelf without straining a muscle, or feel invigorated after a long bike ride on the weekends? And are you at a healthy body weight? If the answer is yes to these questions, you match the definition of being physically fit. **Physical fitness** can be defined as good health or physical condition, primarily as the result of exercise and proper nutrition.

What does it take to achieve physical fitness? Do you have to participate in a specific exercise or can you become physically fit by being active? These two terms—exercise and physical activity—are often used interchangeably, but technically they are not the same thing. **Physical activity** refers to body movement that expends energy (kilocalories). Activities such as gardening, walking the dog, and playing with children can all be regarded as physical activity. **Exercise** is formalized training or structured physical activity, like step aerobics, running, or weight lifting. However, for our purposes in this chapter, the terms exercise and physical activity will be used interchangeably.

Along with consuming a healthy diet, being physically active is one of the two critically important components of overall health and fitness. You cannot achieve optimal fitness if you ignore either of these areas.

physical fitness The ability to perform physical activities requiring cardiorespiratory endurance, muscle endurance, strength, and/or flexibility; physical fitness is acquired through physical activity and adequate nutrition.

physical activity Voluntary movement that results in energy expenditure.

exercise Any type of structured or planned physical activity.

cardiorespiratory endurance The body's ability to sustain prolonged exercise.

muscular strength The greatest amount of force exerted by the muscle at one time.

muscular endurance The ability of the muscle to produce prolonged effort.

Physical Fitness Has Five Components

Cardiorespiratory endurance, muscular strength, muscular endurance, flexibility, and body composition are the five basic components of physical fitness. All five components contribute to physical fitness.

Cardiorespiratory endurance is the ability to sustain cardiorespiratory exercise, such as running and biking, for an extended length of time. This requires that the heart, blood, and lungs provide enough oxygen and nutrients to the working muscles to avoid fatigue. Someone who can run a mile without being too out of breath to talk has good cardiorespiratory endurance. Someone who is out of breath after climbing one flight of stairs, on the other hand, does not.

Muscular strength is the ability to produce force for a brief period of time, while **muscular endurance** is the ability to exert force over a long period of time without fatigue. Together muscular strength and endurance produce muscular fitness. Increasing muscle strength and endurance is best achieved with **resistance training.** You probably associate muscle strength with bodybuilders or weight lifters, and it is true that these people train to be particularly strong. However, other athletes, such as cheerleaders and ballet dancers, also work hard to strengthen their muscles. Consider the strength it takes to lift another person above the head. Holding a person over the head for several minutes shows exceptional muscular endurance.

Flexibility is the range of motion around a joint. Improved flexibility is achieved with stretching. Athletic performance, joint function, and muscular function are all enhanced with improved flexibility. In addition, improved flexibility reduces the likelihood of injury. A gymnast exhibits high flexibility when performing stunts and dance routines. In contrast, people with low flexibility may not be able to bend over and touch their toes from a standing or sitting position.

Finally, **body composition** is the proportion of muscle, fat, water, and other tissues in the body. Collectively, these make up total body weight. Body composition can change without total body weight changing, because muscle takes up less space per pound than body fat. This is why an individual can lose inches without noticing a drop in body weight. Contrary to popular belief, body fat does not "turn into" muscle nor does muscle "turn into" body fat. Both muscle and fat can be lost with weight loss or increased with weight gain, but neither directly converts into the other.

Physical Fitness Provides Numerous Health Benefits

It is common knowledge that eating a balanced diet and exercising regularly helps maintain good health. It is also clear that even modest amounts of exercise will provide health benefits, and the more you exercise, the more fit you'll be. However, despite the fact that the benefits of exercise are well known and well documented, over half of adults living in the United States do not meet the recommendations for regular physical activity.[1]

How does physical activity maintain good health? It reduces the risk of developing chronic diseases like type 2 diabetes mellitus, some forms of cancer, and cardiovascular disease. Physical activity improves body composition, bone health, and immune function. Being physically fit also enhances mental well-being, increases the likelihood of restful sleep, and helps reduce stress. Table 16.1 lists some of the numerous health benefits that result from being physically active on a regular basis. Individuals have to be cautious, however, not to **overexercise** and increase the risk of injury.

To improve the health of American adults and children through regular physical activity, the U.S. Department of Health and Human Services developed the *2008 Physical Activity Guidelines for Americans.* This publication gives information and guidance on the types and amounts of physical activity that provide substantial health benefits for Americans aged 6 years and older. The recommendations are based on a review of scientific research on the benefits of physical activity, and conclude with the main idea that regular physical activity over time can produce long-term health benefits.[2]

THE TAKE-HOME MESSAGE Physical fitness is the state of being in good physical condition through proper nutrition and regular physical activity. The five components of physical fitness are cardiorespiratory endurance, muscular strength, muscular endurance, flexibility, and body composition. To achieve optimal fitness, all five components must be considered. The numerous health benefits of physical

resistance training Exercising with weights to build, strengthen, and tone muscle to improve or maintain overall fitness; also called strength training.

flexibility Ability to move joints freely through a full and normal range of motion.

body composition The relative proportions of muscle, fat, water, and other tissues in the body.

overexercise Excessive physical activity without adequate rest periods for proper recovery.

TABLE 16.1 The Benefits of Physical Fitness

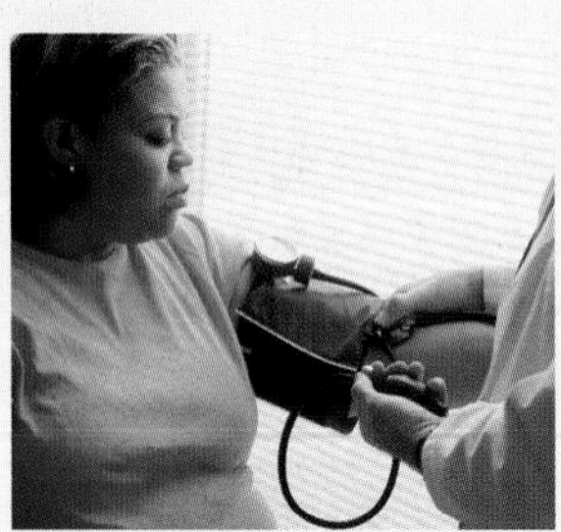

▲ **Reduced Risk of Cardiovascular Disease**
How It Works: Research has shown that moderate physical activity lowers blood pressure.[1] In addition, exercise is positively associated with high-density lipoprotein cholesterol (HDL).[2]

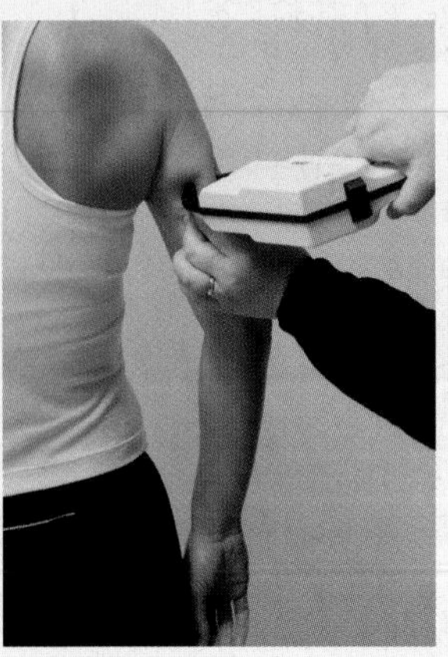

▲ **Improved Body Composition**
How It Works: Individuals with moderate cardiorespiratory fitness have less total fat and abdominal fat compared with people with low cardiorespiratory fitness.[3]

▲ **Reduced Risk of Type 2 Diabetes**
How It Works: Exercise helps control blood glucose levels by increasing insulin sensitivity.[4] This not only reduces risk for type 2 diabetes, but also improves blood glucose control for those who have been diagnosed with type 2 diabetes.

▲ **Reduced Risk of Some Forms of Cancer**
How It Works: Increased physical activity has been associated with a reduced risk of colon, breast, endometrial, and lung cancers. This reduced risk is likely the result of a reduction in overall body weight and other hormonal and metabolic mechanisms.[5]

Source: 1. Whelton, S. P., A. Chin, X. Xin, and J. He. 2002. Effect of Aerobic Exercise on Blood Pressure: A Meta-Analysis of Randomized, Controlled Trials. *Annals of Internal Medicine* 136:493–503.
2. Alhassan, S., K. A. Reese, J. Mahurin, E. P. Plaisance, B. D. Hilson, J. C. Garner, S. O. Wee, and P. W. Grandjean. 2006. Blood Lipid Responses to Plant Stanol Ester Supplementation and Aerobic Exercise Training. *Metabolism* 55:541–549.
3. Janssen, I., P. T. Katzmarzyk, R. Ross, A. S. Leon, J. S. Skinner, D. C. Rao, J. H. Wilmore, et al. 2004. Fitness Alters the Associations of BMI and Waist Circumference with Total and Abdominal Fat. *Obesity* 12:525–537.
4. O'Donovan, G., E. M. Kearney, A. M. Nevill, K. Woolf-May, and S. R. Bird. 2005. The Effects of 24 Weeks of Moderate- or High-Intensity Exercise on Insulin Resistance. *European Journal of Applied Physiology* 95:522–528.
5. US Department of Health and Human Services. Physical Activity Guidelines Advisory Committee Report, 2008 [Internet]. Washington (DC): ODPHP Publication No. U0049. 2008 Available from www.health.gov/paguidelines/Report/pdf/CommitteeReport.pdf. Accessed June 2012.

activity include reduced risk of several chronic diseases, including type 2 diabetes and cardiovascular disease; improved body composition, bone health, and immune function; more restful sleep; and reduced stress.

What Does a Successful Physical Fitness Program Look Like?

Physical fitness programs generally incorporate activities that are based on the five components of fitness, including aerobic exercise, resistance training, and stretching. A successful fitness program should be tailored to meet the needs of the individual and performed consistently so that any gains in physical fitness are not lost. It is also important to incorporate activities that are enjoyable so that they are more likely to become a regular part of one's lifestyle. Someone who hates to jog, for example, is not likely to be consistent about going for a daily run.

TABLE 16.1 The Benefits of Physical Fitness *continued*

▲ **Improved Bone Health**
How It Works: Bone density has been shown to improve with weight-bearing exercise and resistance training, thereby reducing the risk for osteoporosis.[6, 7, 8]

▲ **Improved Immune System**
How It Works: Regular exercise can enhance the immune system, which may result in fewer colds and other infectious diseases.[9]

▲ **Improved Mental Well-Being**
How It Works: Regular exercise protects against the onset of depression and anxiety disorders, reduces symptoms in people diagnosed with depression and anxiety, delays the incidence of dementia, and overall enhances mental well-being.[10]

▲ **Improved Sleep**
How It Works: People who engage in regular exercise often have better quality of sleep. This is especially true for older adults.[11]

6. Kato, T., T. Terashima, T. Yamashita, Y. Hatanaka, A. Honda, and Y. Umemura. 2006. Effect of Low-Repetition Jump Training on Bone Mineral Density in Young Women. *Journal of Applied Physiology* 100:839–843.
7.Daly, R. M., D. W. Dunstan, N. Owen, D. Jolley, J. E. Shaw, and P. Z. Zimmet. 2005. Does High-Intensity Resistance Training Maintain Bone Mass during Moderate Weight Loss in Older Overweight Adults with Type 2 Diabetes? *Osteoporosis International* 16:1703–1712.
8. Yung, P. S., Y. M. Lai, P. Y. Tung, H. T. Tsui, C. K. Wong, V. W. Hung, and L. Qin. 2005. Effects of Weight-Bearing and Nonweight-Bearing Exercises on Bone Properties Using Calcaneal Quantitative Ultrasound. *British Journal of Sports Medicine* 39:547–551.
9. Karacabey, K., O. Saygin, R. Ozmerdivenli, E. Zorba, A. Godekmerdan, and V. Bulut. 2005. The Effects of Exercise on the Immune System and Stress Hormones in Sportswomen. *Neuroendocrinology Letters* 26:361–366.
10. U.S. Department of Health and Human Services. *Physical Activity Guidelines Advisory Committee Report*, 2008 [Internet]. Washington (DC): ODPHP Publication No. U0049. 2008 Available from www.health.gov/paguidelines/Report/pdf/CommitteeReport.pdf. Accessed June 2012.
11 Tworoger, S. S., Y. Yasui, M. V. Vitiello, R. S. Schwartz, C. M. Ulrich, E. J. Aiello, M. L. Irwin, et al. 2003. Effects of a Yearlong Moderate-Intensity Exercise and a Stretching Intervention on Sleep Quality in Postmenopausal Women. *Sleep* 26:830–836.

Cardiorespiratory Exercise Improves Cardiorespiratory Endurance and Body Composition

Cardiorespiratory exercise, such as high-impact aerobics, stair climbing, and brisk walking, often involves continuous activities that use large muscle groups (abdomen, legs, and buttocks). This type of exercise is predominantly aerobic because it uses oxygen. During cardiorespiratory exercise, the heart beats faster and more oxygen-carrying blood is delivered to tissues.

How does this work? As exercise begins, the body requires more oxygen to break down nutrients for energy, so it increases blood flow (volume) to the working muscles. It accomplishes this by increasing heart rate and **stroke volume.** The body also redistributes blood from internal organs to maximize the volume of blood that is delivered to the muscles.

An individual's level of cardiorespiratory fitness can be measured by the maximum amount of oxygen his muscles can consume during exercise, or **VO_2max.** A person who is more physically fit has a higher VO_2max and can

stroke volume The amount of blood pumped by the heart with each heart beat.

VO_2max The maximum amount of oxygen (ml) a person uses in one minute per kilogram of body weight.

exercise at a higher intensity without fatigue than someone who is not as fit. A trained athlete, for example, might have a VO_2max of 50 to 80 milliliters per kilogram per minute (ml/kg/min), while a sedentary, unfit individual might have a VO_2max of 25 to 30 ml/kg/min.[3] Two of the highest VO_2max ever recorded were for two cross-country skiers, a male and a female, who measured 94 and 77 ml/kg/min, respectively.[4]

Cardiorespiratory conditioning, which includes making gradual increases in exercise intensity, will help increase VO_2max, and therefore improve cardiorespiratory endurance and overall physical fitness. In addition, cardiorespiratory exercise can help individuals maintain a healthy body weight and improve body composition by reducing body fat. (You will learn later in this chapter how aerobic exercise "burns" fat for energy.) Cardiorespiratory exercise also reduces stress, and lowers the risk of heart disease by maintaining normal cholesterol levels and lowering heart rate and blood pressure. As the heart becomes a more efficient pump, it does not have to work as hard with each beat.

Strength Training Improves Muscle Strength, Muscle Endurance, and Body Composition

Strength (or resistance) training is designed to increase muscle mass, strength, and endurance. Maintaining adequate muscle mass and strength is important for everyone. Contrary to common belief, resistance training does not necessarily lead to large, bulky muscles. Many females, as well as males, use resistance training to define their muscles and improve their physical appearance and body composition.

In general, individuals should perform a low number of repetitions using heavy weights to increase muscle strength. To increase muscular endurance, perform a high number of repetitions using lighter weights. Heavier weights can also be used to improve muscular endurance by allowing short rest intervals between repetition sets.

Rest periods between sets of an exercise and between workouts are important to avoid overworking muscles and increasing risk of injury. Muscle that is not adequately rested may break down and not recover, leading to a loss of muscle mass. The amount of rest recommended during a workout depends on a person's fitness goals and level of **conditioning.** If increasing strength is the goal, long rest periods of 2 to 3 minutes between sets are best. If the goal is to increase muscular endurance, shorter rest periods of 30 seconds or less are recommended.

The general guideline for rest periods between workouts is two days, or a total of 48 hours, between workouts that use the same muscle groups. However, strength training can be performed daily as long as different muscles are used on consecutive days. For example, you can perform upper body strength training on one day, working your biceps, triceps, and pectoral muscles, and on the following day do leg lifts, squats, and lunges to work your lower body muscles.

Improving flexibility can help reduce muscle soreness and lower the risk of injury.

cardiorespiratory conditioning Improvements in the delivery of oxygen to working muscles as a result of aerobic activity.

conditioning The process of improving physical fitness through repeated activity.

Stretching Improves Flexibility

Most people associate flexibility with gymnasts or dancers, but everyone can benefit from being more flexible and enjoying a full range of motion. Improving flexibility can reduce muscle soreness and the risk of injury, as well as improve balance, posture, and circulation of blood and nutrients throughout the body. Stretching, such as through yoga, is the most common exercise used to improve flexibility.

The FITT Principle Can Be Used to Design a Fitness Program

FITT is an acronym for *frequency, intensity, time,* and *type*. The FITT principle provides an easy way to design a successful physical fitness regimen or conditioning program.

Frequency is how often an individual performs the activity, such as the number of times per week. **Intensity** refers to the degree of difficulty at which the activity is performed. Common terms used to describe intensity are low, moderate, and vigorous (high). One measure of intensity for cardiorespiratory exercise is **rating of perceived exertion (RPE),** in which the person performing the activity self-assesses the level of intensity. The RPE is based on your current level of fitness and your perception of how hard you are working. The scale ranges from 1 (rest) to 10 (maximal exertion). A range of 5 to 7 on the RPE scale (somewhat hard to hard) is recommended for most adults to achieve fitness. A more precise method of measuring intensity is using your **target heart rate.** Your target heart rate is the range (given in percentages of maximal heart rate) that your heart rate should fall within to ensure that you are training aerobically. For example, a target heart rate of 60 percent would be considered low intensity compared to a target heart rate of 80 percent, which is considered high intensity. The Calculation Corner illustrates how to calculate your target heart rate. For weight training, intensity is referred to as **repetition maximum (RM).** For example, 1 RM is the maximum amount of weight that can

Calculation Corner

Target Heart Rate

Target heart rate can be useful in determining the intensity level of cardiorespiratory exercise. One method used to calculate your target heart rate (THR) begins with calculating an estimate of your maximal heart rate (HRmax). Use the following formula to calculate an estimated HRmax.

206.9 – (age in years × 0.67) = estimated HRmax

Before you can calculate your THR, you must first decide the intensity level at which you wish to exercise. Use the following as a guideline:

- Light/low intensity = 55% to 64% of HRmax
- Moderate intensity = 65% to 84% of HRmax
- High intensity = 85% to 95% of HRmax

Now, multiply your estimated HRmax by the desired intensity level to determine your target heart rate.

THR = HRmax × intensity level

Example: John, a 45-year-old office manager, wants to know what his target heart rate should be as he begins his new training program.

1. Calculate John's estimated HRmax:

   206.9 – (45 × 0.67) = 177 estimated HRmax

2. Multiply John's estimated HRmax × intensity at 65% and 84% to determine his THR.

   177 × 0.65 = 115 THR

   177 × 0.84 = 149 THR

John's THR for moderate intensity is between 114 and 148 bpm. John can adjust his THR based on his RPE.

Data from Bushman, B., Ed. 2011. ACSM's Complete Guide to Fitness & Health.

intensity The level of difficulty of an activity.

rating of perceived exertion (RPE) A subjective measure of the intensity level of an activity using a numerical scale.

target heart rate A heart rate in beats per minute (expressed as a percentage of maximum heart rate) achieved during exercise that indicates the level of intensity at which fitness levels can increase.

repetition maximum (RM) The maximum amount of weight that can be lifted for a specified number of repetitions.

FITNESS TIPS

Get Moving!

Schedule physical activity into your day, just like you would schedule a meeting, class, or work.

Find activities that you enjoy. Make exercise something you look forward to, so that you're more likely to keep it up.

Ask a friend or coworker to exercise with you. Many people are more likely to exercise if they have a partner to motivate them.

Track your exercise in a log or journal so you see how much you are getting and note improvement over time.

Take advantage of activities that are offered at your college or university, including club sports, intramurals, group fitness classes, and personal training sessions.

Be adventurous and try new activities. If you're used to jogging or going to the gym, try hiking or racquetball. Mixing up your routine will help prevent boredom.

be lifted once. Time, or **duration,** is how long the activity is performed, such as a 30-minute run. And lastly, type means the specific activity performed.

The frequency, intensity, time (duration), and types of exercise that are right for a person depend partly on what goal the individual is trying to achieve. For individuals seeking health benefits, the *2008 Physical Activity Guidelines* state that as little as 60 minutes a week of moderate-intensity activity offers some health benefits. However, a total amount of 150 minutes (2 hours and 30 minutes) a week of moderate-intensity aerobic activity provides substantial health benefits for adults by reducing the risk of many chronic diseases. To gain additional health benefits, such as a lower risk of colon and breast cancer, up to 300 minutes (5 hours) per week of moderate-intensity physical activity is recommended. Additionally, resistance training at a moderate or high intensity and that involves all major muscle groups should be performed two or more days a week.

Do you feel like you don't have the time to exercise? This is a common barrier that keeps many people from engaging in regular physical activity. The good news is that aerobic activity can be performed in sessions as short as 10 minutes to get some health benefits. Of course, the more activity performed, the greater the benefits. Taking advantage of short periods of time during the day for a brisk 10-minute (or longer) walk will help you meet the recommendations for physical activity.

Engaging in more vigorous-intensity activities, such as jogging or fast-paced swimming, for longer duration will result in even greater health benefits. Individuals striving to maintain body weight and prevent gradual weight gain should participate in approximately 60 minutes of moderate- to vigorous-intensity activity on most days of the week, and avoid consuming excess kilocalories. Those striving to lose weight should participate in at least 60 to 90 minutes of daily moderate-intensity physical activity and adjust kilocalorie intake so that more kilocalories are expended than are consumed.

The Physical Activity Pyramid is another tool that can be used as a guide to meeting physical activity needs. It is designed to show examples of activities and how often they should be performed for optimal health and physical fitness (**Figure 16.1**). People with diabetes mellitus, high blood pressure, heart disease, and other chronic diseases should consult with a health care provider before participating in any exercise program, especially one to be performed at a vigorous intensity.

Individuals seeking improved physical fitness in addition to health benefits can follow the general recommendations outlined by the American College of Sports Medicine. These guidelines for cardiorespiratory endurance, muscular fitness, and flexibility for healthy adults are summarized in Table 16.2 using the FITT principle.

duration The length of time that an activity is performed.

TABLE 16.2 Using FITT to Improve Fitness

	Cardiorespiratory Fitness	Muscular Fitness	Flexibility
Frequency	3–5 days per week	2–3 days per week	2–3 days per week
Intensity	64–95% of maximum heart rate	60–80% of 1 RM	To the point of feeling tightness or slight discomfort
Time	20–60 minutes per day (150 minutes per week), continuous or intermittent (minimum of 10-minute bouts)	8–10 different exercises performed in 2–4 sets, 8–12 repetitions	2–4 repetitions for each muscle group; hold static stretch for 10–30 seconds
Type	Brisk walking, jogging, biking, step aerobics	Free weights, machines with stacked weights, resistance bands	Stretching, yoga

Data from American College of Sports Medicine, "Position Stand: Quantity and Quality of Exercise for Developing and Maintaining Cardiorespiratory, Musculoskeletal, and Neuromotor Fitness in Apparently Healthy Adults: Guidance for Prescribing Exercise," *Medicine & Science in Sports & Exercise* 43 no. 7 (2011).

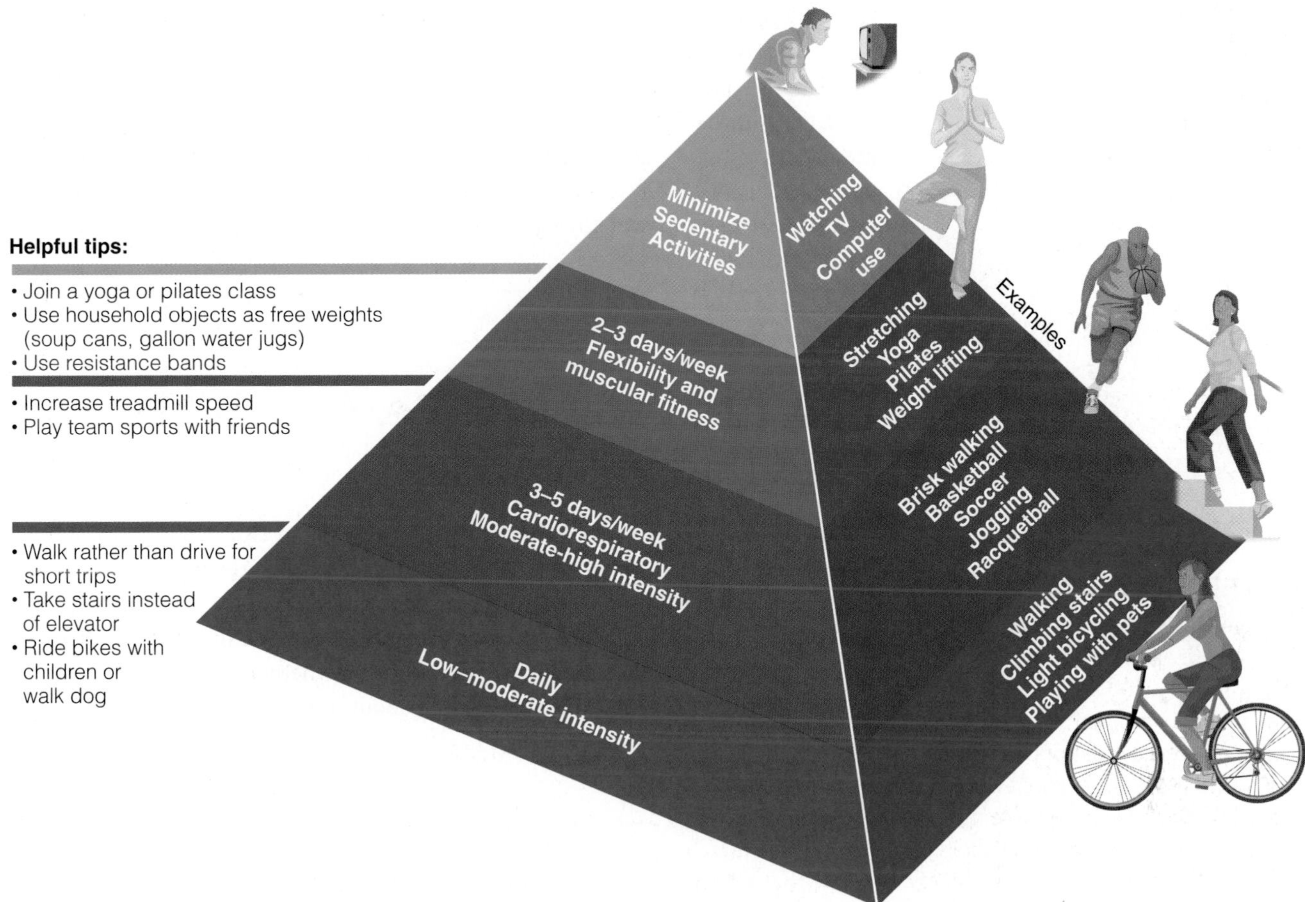
Helpful tips:
• Join a yoga or pilates class
• Use household objects as free weights (soup cans, gallon water jugs)
• Use resistance bands
• Increase treadmill speed
• Play team sports with friends
• Walk rather than drive for short trips
• Take stairs instead of elevator
• Ride bikes with children or walk dog
Minimize Sedentary Activities
2–3 days/week Flexibility and muscular fitness
3–5 days/week Cardiorespiratory Moderate-high intensity
Daily Low–moderate intensity
Watching TV Computer use
Stretching Yoga Pilates Weight lifting
Brisk walking Basketball Soccer Jogging Racquetball
Walking Climbing stairs Light bicycling Playing with pets
Examples

▲ **Figure 16.1 Physical Activity Pyramid**

The Progressive Overload Principle Can Help Improve Fitness Over Time

During conditioning, the body gradually adapts to the activities that are being performed. Over time, if the activity is kept exactly the same, the body doesn't have to work as hard and fitness levels will plateau as a result. To continue to improve fitness levels, the body must be challenged by performing different workout regimens on a regular basis. This can be done using the **progressive overload principle.** Modifying one or more elements of the FITT principle will challenge the body in different ways so that the level of fitness improves. For example, someone trying to improve cardiorespiratory endurance might gradually increase the duration of a run. To increase muscle strength, an individual might gradually increase the amount of weight being lifted.

As the body responds to the work it is being asked to do, physical fitness will be enhanced. The muscles will increase in size (**hypertrophy**), endurance, and strength, and the body will enjoy increased cardiorespiratory endurance and improved flexibility. However, if conditioning is executed improperly or nutrient intake is inadequate for physical activity, muscles can lose mass (**atrophy**), endurance, and strength, and cardiorespiratory fitness levels will suffer negative effects.

progressive overload principle A gradual increase in exercise demands resulting from modifications to the frequency, intensity, time, or type of activity.

hypertrophy To grow larger in size.

atrophy To shrink in size.

THE TAKE-HOME MESSAGE Cardiorespiratory exercise improves cardiorespiratory endurance and body composition. Strength training can improve muscle strength and endurance as well as body composition. Stretching can enhance flexibility. An effective conditioning program can be designed using the FITT principle, which stands for frequency, intensity, time, and type of activity. The *2008 Physical Activity Guidelines* state that most people should aim for at least 60 minutes of moderate activity per week for some health benefits, while greater amounts of exercise are needed for substantial health benefits, weight loss, and to improve physical fitness. Applying the progressive overload principle to workouts will help individuals achieve optimal fitness levels.

How Are Carbohydrate, Fat, and Protein Used During Exercise?

Food meets our nutrient needs for physical activity in two ways. Food supplies the energy, particularly from carbohydrate and fat, that the body needs to perform an activity. And food provides nutrients, predominantly from carbohydrate and protein, that help the body recover properly so that it can repeat the activity. The type of food used to supply energy depends on whether the physical activity is anaerobic or aerobic, reactions you learned about in Chapter 8. Let's review these energy-producing reactions.

Chemistry Boost

ATP

Energy, in the form of ATP, is produced in the body's cells by a series of chemical reactions. The amount of ATP that is stored in the cells is limited and therefore must be made continuously during metabolism. ATP is hydrolyzed to ADP to release energy for muscle contraction. Creatine phosphate donates a phosphate to ADP to reform small amounts of ATP during exercise but is limited in supply. At rest, creatine phosphate is reformed and ready to participate in ATP synthesis during exercise.

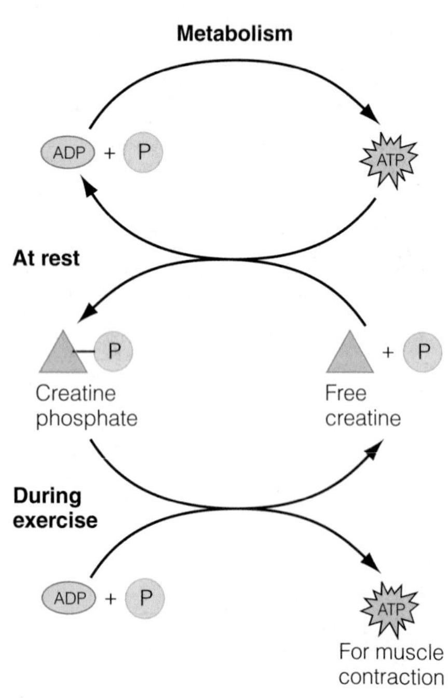

Anaerobic Energy Production during Exercise

Recall that all body actions require energy in the form of adenosine triphosphate (ATP) produced either aerobically (requiring oxygen) or anaerobically (without oxygen) from macronutrients in foods. While much of the energy production during cardiorespiratory exercise is aerobic, anaerobic energy production is typically utilized for quick, intense activities that require strength, such as lifting weights; agility and speed, such as sprinting; or a sudden burst of power, such as jumping for a slam dunk during a basketball game.

During the first few seconds of physical activity the body relies heavily on anaerobic energy production from ATP and creatine phosphate (PCr) found in muscle cells (see the Chemistry Boost). Most anaerobic activities are fueled by the ATP found in the muscle (about 2 to 3 seconds) and rely on creatine phosphate to resynthesize ATP (about another 7 to 8 seconds) in addition to small amounts of ATP produced during glycolysis.

Energy is released from ATP when the bond connecting the end phosphate is hydrolyzed from the ATP molecule, leaving adenosine diphosphate (ADP) (**Figure 16.2**). ADP is regenerated to ATP in the mitochondria of the cell when creatine phosphate donates a phosphate molecule. Creatine phosphate is a quick source of phosphate with a dual role in energy production. Energy is directly produced when the phosphate group is removed from the creatine phosphate molecule. This is an example of a catabolic reaction releasing energy. Energy is indirectly produced because the released phosphate group is donated to ADP, which regenerates ATP, and sets up another round of energy production.

The body produces a small amount of creatine from foods, including meat and fish, or creatine can be supplied to the body directly from dietary supplements. With the help of the liver and kidneys, creatine is converted to creatine phosphate and stored in skeletal muscle and other tissues, including the cardiac muscle and brain. The amount of creatine phosphate stored in the muscles is

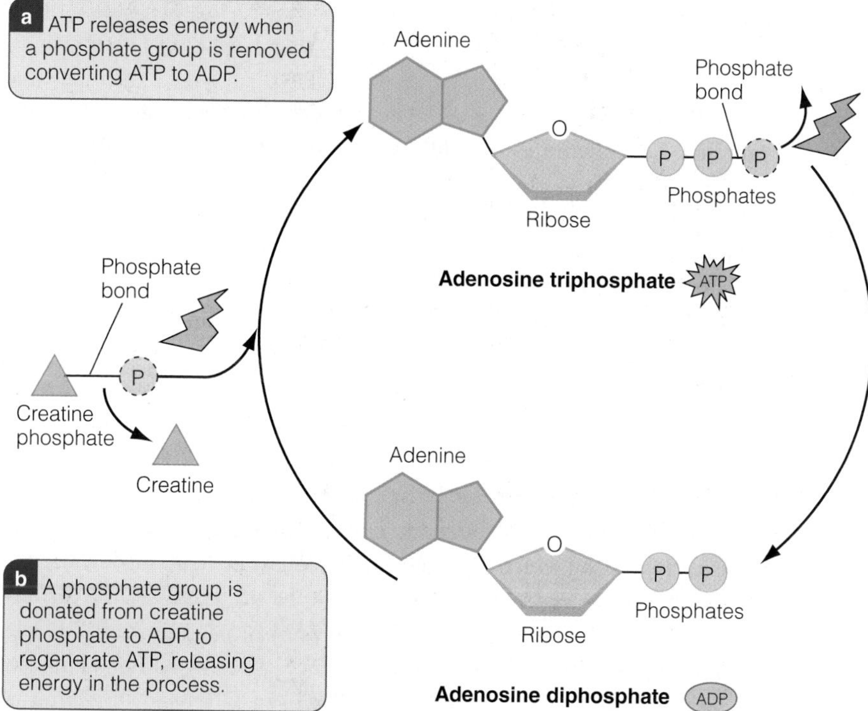

▲ **Figure 16.2 Anaerobic Energy Metabolism**
During anaerobic metabolism, energy is released from the breakdown of ATP and creatine phosphate.

limited and becomes depleted after up to 10 seconds of maximum-intensity activity. Creatine phosphate is regenerated when the muscle cell is at rest, such as between sprints or in between sets during weight training, to prepare for the next exercise effort.

Aerobic Energy Production during Exercise

Just like creatine phosphate, the amount of ATP in cells is limited and can support only a few seconds of intense exercise, such as is needed to perform a 100-meter sprint. When the ATP and creatine phosphate stores are unable to meet sustained energy demands, breathing becomes heavier and oxygen intake increases. At this point the pace of exercise slows down and the body begins to rely more on aerobic production of ATP because the amount needed to support the quick bursts or sprints cannot be generated fast enough by anaerobic energy production. With oxygen in the cell, pyruvate formed from glucose during glycolysis is converted into acetyl CoA and is metabolized through aerobic metabolism to produce ATP.

The body relies on a mixture of carbohydrate, fat, and protein for energy during exercise, but the type and amount of these nutrients that is used depends on the intensity and duration of the exercise, the body's nutritional status, and the level of physical fitness. Remember that carbohydrate contributes to both anaerobic and aerobic energy production and fat contributes to the aerobic generation of ATP. Protein can be used for energy production when kilocalorie needs haven't been met. In exercise metabolism, the body prefers to use protein to promote muscle growth and recovery.

Carbohydrate Is the Primary Energy Source during High-Intensity Exercise

Carbohydrate is the predominant fuel used during high-intensity, short-duration, anaerobic exercise. Carbohydrate provides energy to the working muscle either through blood glucose, stored glycogen in the muscles and the liver, or the consumption of dietary carbohydrates (**Figure 16.3**). In adults, the amount of glycogen stored in the muscles ranges from about 200 grams to 500 grams. In addition, the liver stores around 60 to 120 grams of glycogen, which can be converted into glucose through glycogenolysis and released into the blood. The amount of glycogen that each person stores depends on many factors, including the person's nutritional intake and fitness levels.

The body stores about 2,600 kilocalories of energy as glycogen, of which 2,000 kilocalories can be used. The rate at which glycogen stores are utilized depends on the intensity and duration of the exercise. If the exercise is high intensity, short duration, glycogen stores are depleted in about 20 minutes compared with low-intensity, long-duration exercise during which glycogen stores can last up to 90 minutes.

Glucose derived from stored muscle glycogen is the preferred source for energy during exercise; however, liver glycogen stores are just as important. Muscle cells first rely on glycogen stored in the muscles for energy during activity, but also blood glucose formed from the breakdown of liver glycogen. Glycogen stored in the liver is converted into glucose and delivered to the bloodstream to maintain normal blood glucose levels, both during periods of activity and at rest. Liver glycogen is

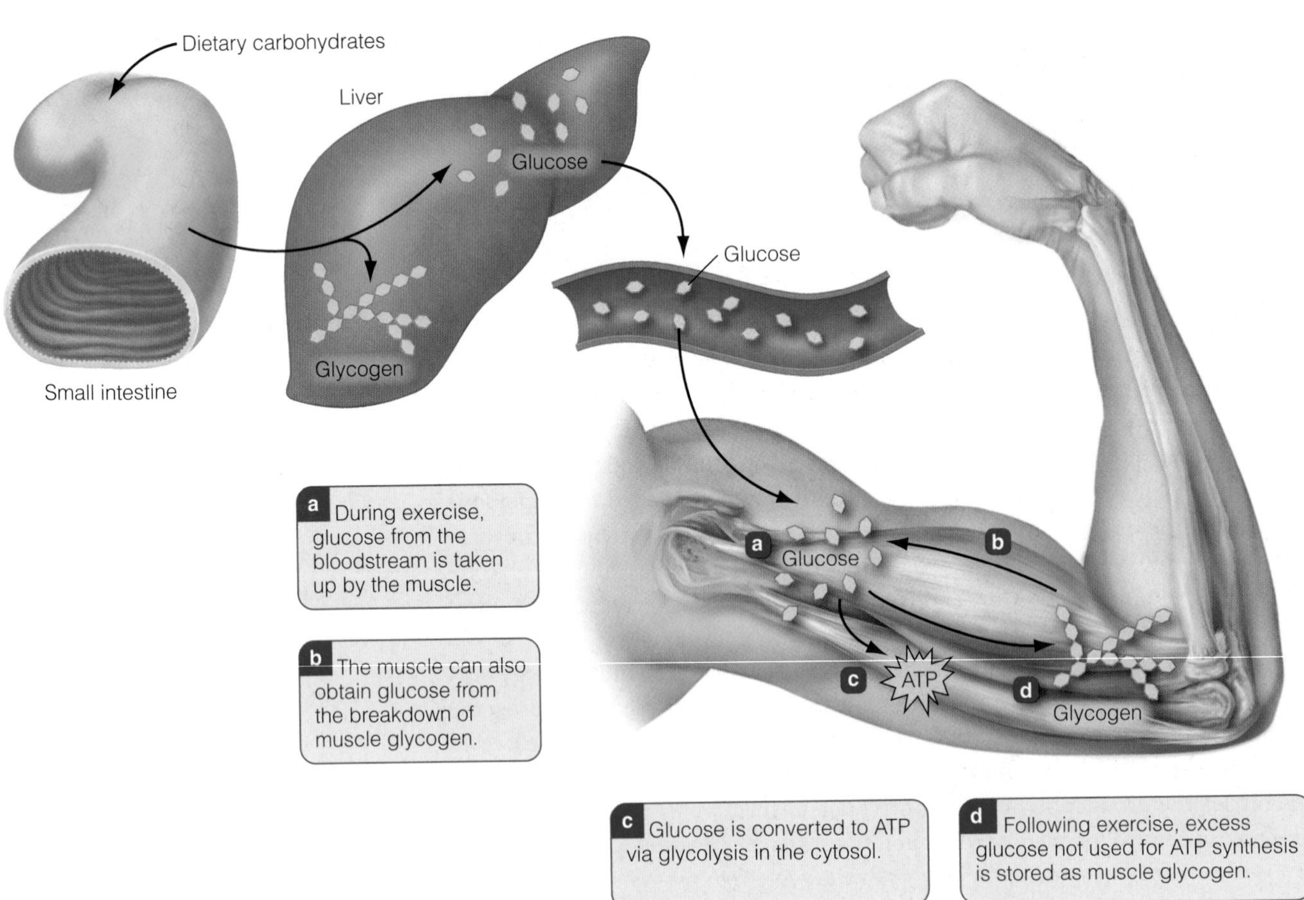

Dietary carbohydrates
Liver
Glucose
Glucose
Glycogen
Small intestine
a During exercise, glucose from the bloodstream is taken up by the muscle.
b The muscle can also obtain glucose from the breakdown of muscle glycogen.
a
Glucose
b
c
ATP
d
Glycogen
c Glucose is converted to ATP via glycolysis in the cytosol.
d Following exercise, excess glucose not used for ATP synthesis is stored as muscle glycogen.

▲ **Figure 16.3 Glucose Utilization during Exercise**

depleted faster when a person's muscle glycogen stores are suboptimal at the start of exercise.

Whereas muscle and liver glycogen provide glucose for the muscle cells during activity, blood glucose is also the energy source for the brain. If the brain does not receive the glucose to meet its energy needs, individuals may feel a lack of coordination or lack of concentration—two things no one wants to experience, especially during exercise or a sport competition.

Recall that during anaerobic metabolism, pyruvate formed during glycolysis is reduced to lactate when the mitochondria lack sufficient oxygen to transform pyruvate into acetyl CoA. When lactate is produced at a low rate, as during aerobic metabolism, muscles can effectively clear it from the blood and use it as an energy source. For example, during low-intensity exercise, the body is able to oxidize the lactate that is produced by the muscle during glycolysis and therefore it does not accumulate in the working muscle tissue. The body also shuttles excess lactate to other tissues, such as the brain, heart, and liver, to prevent excessive accumulation in the muscle. Lactate from the muscle diffuses into the blood, is picked up by the liver, and enters the Cori cycle. In the Cori cycle (see Figure 8.8 in Chapter 8), lactate undergoes gluconeogenesis, is converted back to glucose, and is returned to the bloodstream to be used for energy again.

As exercise intensity increases, the energy demands are greater than the amount of ATP the cell can produce aerobically using available oxygen. As a result, more hydrogen ions are rapidly generated as glucose is anaerobically metabolized to pyruvate. These excess hydrogen ions combine with pyruvate to form lactate, which diffuses quickly into the blood. As exercise intensity continues, the levels of lactate and hydrogen ions increase as the body attempts to produce enough ATP to meet energy demands. The increase in hydrogen ions may negatively affect exercise performance due to a reduction in pH in the muscle cell. The good news is that the ability of the muscles to effectively use and shuttle lactate to other tissues improves with training. For many years, lactate "buildup" in muscles was thought to be a cause of muscle fatigue, but now scientists are finding that lactate can also be an important fuel during exercise.[5]

Intensity Affects the Use of Glucose and Glycogen

Muscles use glucose for energy no matter how intense the exercise. However, research shows that as the intensity of exercise increases, the use of glucose and glycogen for energy also increases.[6] Carbohydrates are the preferred energy source at high intensity levels because, unlike fat and protein, carbohydrate is efficiently oxidized for energy as the intensity of activity increases. At very high intensities, carbohydrates supply most of the energy in the form of muscle glycogen. Although carbohydrates are not the main energy source during prolonged low- to moderate-intensity exercise, they still provide some energy for the working muscles.

Duration Affects the Use of Glucose and Glycogen

In addition to intensity, the duration of exercise also affects the source and amount of carbohydrate used to fuel physical activity. At the start of low- to moderate-intensity exercise, stored muscle glycogen is the main source of energy. As muscle glycogen stores diminish, the liver also contributes its glycogen to be converted to glucose for energy and to prevent hypoglycemia.

During prolonged exercise, the body relies more on blood glucose (generated from stored liver glycogen) and less on muscle glycogen as its carbohydrate source of energy. In addition to affecting the source of carbohydrate, duration also affects how much carbohydrate is used. After about 20 minutes, as low- to

SPOTLIGHT Carbohydrate Loading

The goal of carbohydrate loading, which begins about a week before an endurance event, is to maximize the storage capacity of muscle glycogen. Increasing the amount of stored muscle glycogen can improve an athlete's endurance performance by providing the energy to fuel activity at an optimal pace for a longer period of time.

Not all athletes or physically active people will have improved performance with carbohydrate loading, however. The people who are likely to benefit the most from this strategy are those who participate in endurance events or exercise that lasts more than 90 minutes. Examples of endurance events include marathons, triathlons, cross-country skiing, and long-distance cycling and swimming. Individuals who exercise or train for less than 90 minutes should follow the standard recommendations for carbohydrate intake for athletes to ensure adequate muscle glycogen stores. Research has also shown that women are less likely than men to have improved performance with carbohydrate loading because women oxidize significantly more fat and less carbohydrate and protein during endurance exercise compared with men.[1]

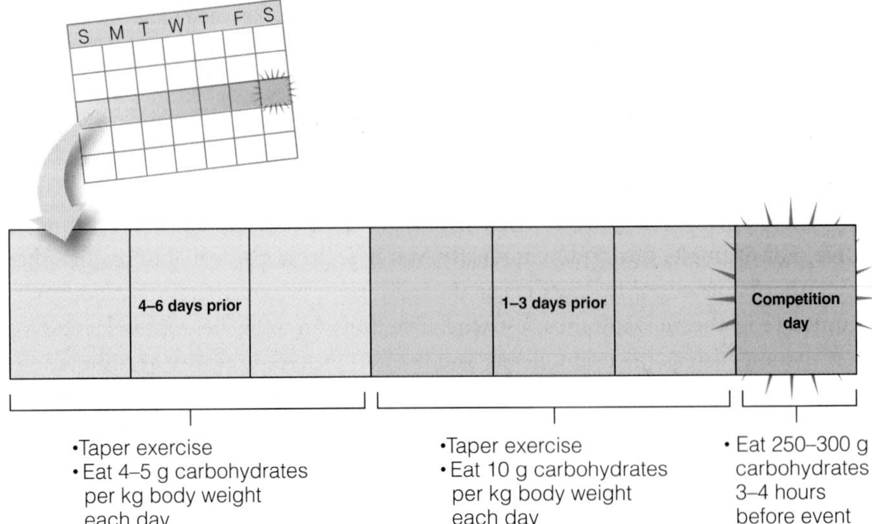
S M T W T F S
4–6 days prior
1–3 days prior
Competition day
•Taper exercise
•Eat 4–5 g carbohydrates per kg body weight each day
•Taper exercise
•Eat 10 g carbohydrates per kg body weight each day
• Eat 250–300 g carbohydrates 3–4 hours before event

Carbohydrate loading involves tapering exercise and gradually increasing carbohydrate intake the week before a competitive event. On the day of the competition, a high-carb meal is eaten 3 to 4 hours before the event begins.

So how do athletes start carbohydrate loading? When this concept was first developed, athletes began by training very hard for three to four days in addition to eating a low-carbohydrate diet (less than 5 to 10 percent of total kilocalories). This period was called the depletion phase and was thought to be necessary to increase glycogen stores during the next phase, called the loading phase. The loading phase involved three to four days of minimal or no training while eating a diet high in carbohydrates. This resulted in higher muscle glycogen stores and better endurance performance.

Many people found the depletion phase hard to endure and would often experience irritability, hypoglycemia, and fatigue.

moderate-intensity exercise continues, muscles rely less on glycogen and glucose and more on fat for fuel (more on this in a later discussion). Remember that the body will always use glycogen for energy during exercise, and if the intensity and duration of the exercise last long enough, muscle and liver glycogen stores become depleted and the activity can no longer be sustained. Many endurance runners refer to this as "hitting the wall."

Conditioning Affects the Use of Glucose and Glycogen

Research has shown that the amount of glycogen that the muscles can hold can be affected by training.[7, 8] When muscles are well trained, they have the ability to store 20 to 50 percent more glycogen than untrained muscles. More stored glycogen means more fuel for working muscles to use, which means individuals can exercise for a longer period of time and increase endurance. Just eating a high-carbohydrate meal before competition will not improve performance; individuals need to train their muscles *and* eat a high-carbohydrate diet regularly to maximize the effect.

In fact, today, many endurance athletes have modified this training strategy to exclude the depletion phase. Research has shown that depleting muscle glycogen stores is not necessary to increase the amount of stored muscle glycogen. However, there will be greater increases in muscle glycogen by initially depleting muscle glycogen stores.[2]

To begin a modified carbohydrate-loading regimen, athletes taper exercise about seven days prior to the event by doing a little less activity each day. This is often the hardest recommendation to follow because many athletes feel that they will be out of shape if they stop training before competition. But tapering exercise is necessary to increase muscle glycogen; otherwise, the body will continue to burn glycogen for fuel rather than storing it to be used for energy during the upcoming event. One study showed that athletes can decrease training by 70 percent about one week prior to an endurance event without negatively affecting performance.[3]

In addition to tapering exercise, carbohydrate loading involves eating a high-carbohydrate diet that provides about 4 to 5 grams of carbohydrate per kilogram of body weight for the first three to four days. During the last three days of tapering exercise, carbohydrate intake is increased to 10 grams per kilogram of body weight. Lastly, a meal that is high in carbohydrate (providing about 250 to 300 grams), moderate in protein, and low in fat should be consumed about 3 to 4 hours prior to the start of the event to further maximize glycogen stores.

Despite the emphasis on carbohydrate, athletes need to be sure not to compromise intake of protein and fat. They still need to include at least 0.8 grams of protein per kilogram of body weight (some athletes may require more protein) in their training diet, as well as about 20 to 25 percent of kilocalories coming from fat, preferably unsaturated fats.

The table below is a sample one-day menu that might be used the day before an event. This menu is high in carbohydrate, adequate in protein, and low in fat.

References

1. Tarnopolsky, M. A., S. A. Atkinson, S. M. Phillips, and J. D. MacDougall. 1995. Carbohydrate Loading and Metabolism during Exercise in Men and Women. *Journal of Applied Physiology* 78:1360–1368.
2. Goforth, W. H., D. Laurent, W. K. Prusaczyk, K. E. Schneider, K. F. Peterson, and G. I. Shulman. 2003. Effects of Depletion Exercise and Light Training on Muscle Glycogen Super-compensation in Men. *American Journal of Physiology–Endocrinology and Metabolism* 285:E1304–E1311.
3. Houmard, J. A., D. L. Costill, J. B. Mitchell, S. H. Park, R. C. Hickner, and J. N. Roemmich. 1990. Reduced Training Maintains Performance in Distance Runners. *International Journal of Sports Medicine* 11:46–52.

Sample Carbohydrate-Loading Menu

Breakfast	Lunch	Dinner	Snack
1 cup orange juice ½ cup Grape-Nuts cereal 1 medium banana 1 cup 2% milk 1 English muffin 1 tbs jelly	2 slices oatmeal bread 3 oz turkey breast with lettuce, tomato 8 oz apple juice 1 cup frozen yogurt	3 cups spaghetti (6 oz uncooked) 1 cup tomato sauce 2 oz ground turkey ¼ loaf multigrain bread (4 oz)	1 cup vanilla yogurt 6 fig bars
750 kilocalories	*750 kilocalories*	*1,300 kilocalories*	*500 kilocalories*
85% carbohydrates	*65% carbohydrates*	*70% carbohydrates*	*80% carbohydrates*
Total: 3,300 kilocalories: 75% carbohydrates (610 g), 15% protein (125 g), 10% fat (40 g)			

How Much Carbohydrate Is Needed for Exercise?

Recall that most adults require that 45 to 65 percent of their daily energy intake come from carbohydrates. As we've already learned, the amount of carbohydrate needed to fuel physical activity depends greatly on the duration of the activity. Glycogen stores are continuously being depleted and replenished. For those who exercise often, eating carbohydrate-rich foods on a regular basis is important to provide the muscles with adequate glycogen. When glycogen stores are inadequate, the muscles have only a limited amount of energy available to support activity, which has been shown to reduce athletic performance and promote fatigue.[9,10] Keep in mind that the glycogen storage capacity of both the muscles and the liver is limited. Once the muscles and liver have stored all of the glycogen possible, any excess glucose will be converted into fatty acids and stored in the form of body fat.

Carbohydrate loading is one training strategy that athletes use to build up muscle glycogen stores before a competition. See Spotlight: Carbohydrate Loading for an explanation of this strategy.

carbohydrate loading A diet and training strategy that maximizes glycogen stores in the body before an endurance event.

The best types of carbohydrates to eat during and immediately after exercise are simple carbohydrates, such as sports drinks, bars and gels, bananas, bagels, or corn flakes, because they are absorbed and enter the bloodstream quickly, and therefore can be used immediately for energy (glucose) or to replenish glycogen stores. Complex carbohydrates like whole-grain rice and pasta, oatmeal, and whole wheat are ideal to eat a couple of hours before exercise because they take longer to digest than simple carbohydrates and enter the bloodstream much more slowly, thereby providing a sustained source of energy. Remember, however, that complex carbohydrates are generally high in fiber, and too much fiber can cause bloating, gas, and diarrhea.

Fat Is the Primary Energy Source during Low- to Moderate-Intensity Exercise

Fat is supplied to muscles as an energy source in two forms: fatty acids stored in muscle tissue and free fatty acids in the blood derived from those stored in adipose tissue. Fatty acids in the muscle directly supply energy to the muscles, so they are used for energy during exercise before the fatty acids in adipose tissue. Recall from Chapter 8 that when the body breaks down stored body fat for energy (lypolysis), triglycerides in adipose tissue are first hydrolyzed into fatty acids and glycerol, and then released into the bloodstream. Circulating free fatty acids are taken up by the muscles and go through beta-oxidation inside the mitochondria to produce energy. Glycerol is taken up by the liver, where it is converted into glucose through gluconeogenesis to help maintain blood glucose levels and provide energy (see **Figure 16.4**).

a The breakdown of triglycerides in the adipose tissue yields free fatty acids and glycerol which diffuses into the bloodstream.

b Free fatty acids and glycerol are also hydrolyzed from adipose tissue in the muscle.

c Free fatty acids and glycerol are taken up by the muscle cell for energy. Glycerol may also enter the liver and produce glucose through gluconeogenesis. The glucose formed diffuses into the bloodstream.

d The free fatty acids undergo aerobic oxidation in the muscle cell to produce ATP. Glycerol is anaerobically transformed to pyruvate, which is converted into ATP through aerobic metabolism.

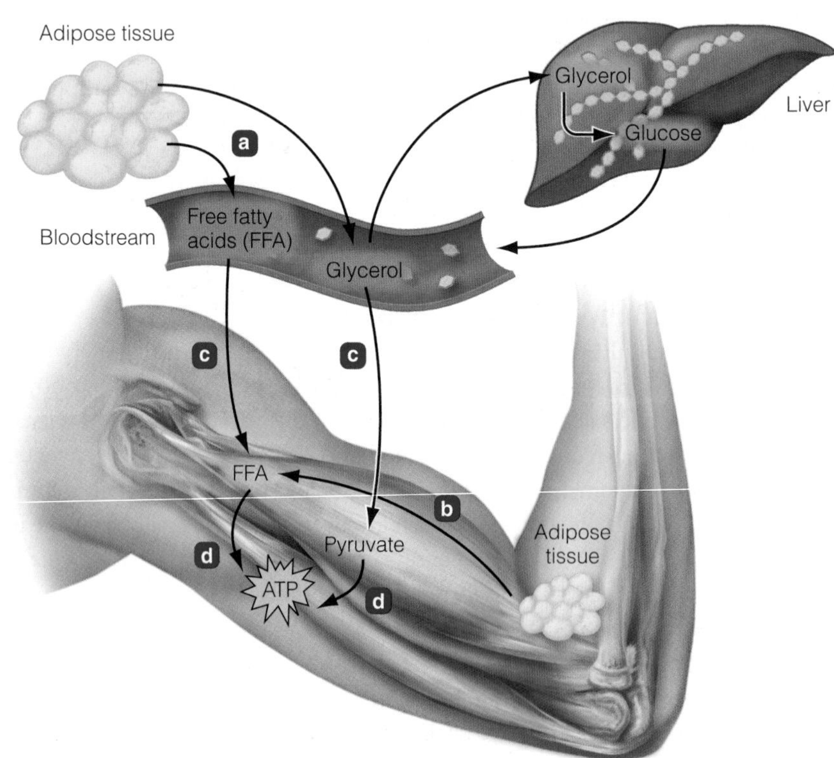

▲ **Figure 16.4 Fatty Acid and Glycerol Utilization during Exercise**

There are advantages to storing excess energy as fat rather than carbohydrate and protein. Fat is a more concentrated source of energy because it provides more than twice the kilocalories of carbohydrate or protein; this is because, unlike glycogen and protein, stored fat does not contain water. In addition, greater amounts of energy can be stored as fat because, while glycogen stores are limited, the capacity of fat cells is unlimited.

Intensity Affects the Use of Fat

Just as with carbohydrates, fat is used for energy during rest and aerobic exercise. The exercise intensity affects the source and amount of fat used. Recall that fatty acids require oxygen to be converted into energy (beta-oxidation). Therefore, the availability of oxygen is one of the most important factors for determining what nutrient the muscles use the most for energy.

During low- to moderate-intensity exercise, sufficient oxygen is available to oxidize fat efficiently enough to keep up with the demand for energy. Fat supplies nearly all of the energy required during low- to moderate-intensity activity, relative to the amount of carbohydrate and protein that is used **(Figure 16.5)**. At low-intensity exercise, the body uses mostly free fatty acids in the blood (released from adipose tissue), rather than fatty acids stored in muscle, for energy. During moderate-intensity exercise, the body begins to use more fatty acids from muscle triglycerides and less fatty acids released from adipose tissue. At the same time, more muscle glycogen is used and contributes to about half of total energy.

As exercise intensity increases and greater demands are placed on the cardiorespiratory system, the availability of oxygen declines. With less oxygen, fatty acids cannot be converted into energy fast enough to meet the demand. Because glucose oxidation is more efficient than fat oxidation at higher intensities, muscles begin to rely less on fat and more on glucose for fuel. Does this mean that individuals who are trying to lose weight and body fat should reduce the intensity of their workout? Examining the Evidence: What Is the Truth about the Fat-Burning Zone? discusses this issue.

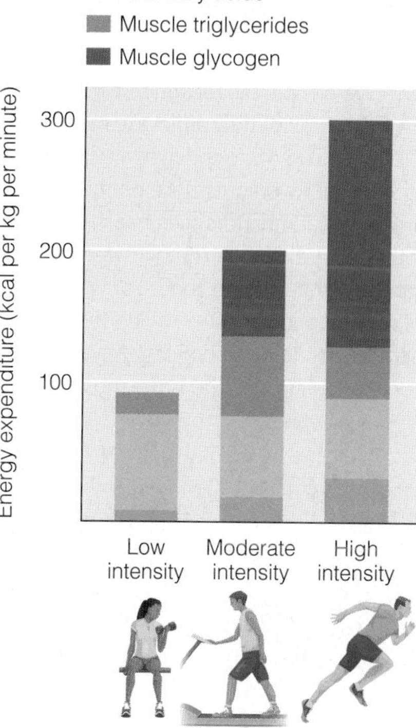

▲ **Figure 16.5 Energy Use during Varying Intensities of Exercise**
The body prefers to use carbohydrate and fat for energy during exercise. The intensity of the exercise will determine how much of these are used.
Data from J. A. Romijn, et al., "Regulation of Endogenous Fat and Carbohydrate Metabolism in Relation to Exercise Intensity and Duration," *American Journal of Physiology–Endocrinology and Metabolism* 265 (September 1993): E380–E391.

Duration Affects the Use of Fat

In general, the use of fat for energy increases throughout the duration of low- to moderate-intensity exercise. During the first 15 to 20 minutes of exercise, fat utilization by the muscles increases at a slow rate due to the time required to oxidize fat for energy. During this time, free fatty acids in the bloodstream are taken up by the muscles and used for energy, which causes blood levels to drop. This in turn stimulates an increase in lypolysis, by way of the hormone epinephrine, and more fatty acids are hydrolyzed from adipose tissue and released into the bloodstream to provide (more) energy for the working muscles.

Once the duration of moderate-intensity activity exceeds 20 minutes, the level of fatty acids in the bloodstream becomes greater than normal as the body continues to use and release stored fat for energy. Because of this increase in blood levels, the body increases its use of fatty acids for energy.

Conditioning Affects the Use of Fat

An individual's level of conditioning can affect how much fat the body will use for energy. Endurance training results in an increase in the amount of fatty acids stored in the muscles, which can increase the amount of fat used for energy because it directly supplies fuel to the muscles. Training also causes muscle cells to produce new and larger mitochondria, which oxidize fatty acids to produce ATP. Lastly, training is thought to increase enzymes that aid in fatty acid oxidation. For these reasons, muscles that are well trained will use more fat for energy than muscles that are not

EXAMINING THE EVIDENCE What Is The Truth About the Fat-Burning Zone?

Many people recognize the importance of exercise, especially of the cardiovascular system, for weight loss. They head off to the gym and jump on an exercise machine to start their workout. Once on the machine, they hook up to a device that monitors their heart rate, which lets them know if they are working at 65 to 73 percent of maximum heart rate, called the fat-burning zone—or working at more than 73 percent of maximum heart rate—called the "cardio" zone. Because many people seek to lose body fat, they exercise in the fat-burning zone, believing that this is the most effective way to lose weight. After all, it is true that the body will burn more fat at lower intensities and will burn more carbohydrate as the intensity increases. So, is staying in the fat-burning zone the best advice to follow if you are trying to lose weight? The simple answer is no. Let's look at some calculations to better understand why.

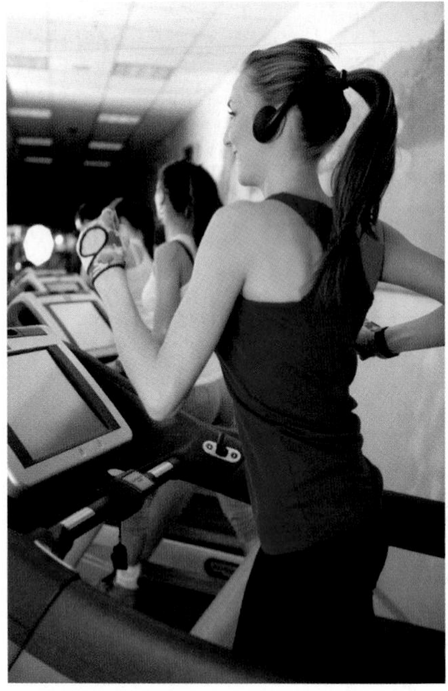

Exercising in the "fat-burning" or "cardio" zone are both effective methods to burn kilocalories and reduce body weight.

If you are trying to lose weight, you need to burn more kilocalories than you consume. Working out is an excellent way to do this, but you need to be aware of how many kilocalories you are burning, and aim to work off as many as possible. In the fat-burning zone at 65 percent of maximum heart rate, a moderately fit person will burn an average of 220 kilocalories during 30 minutes of exercise. At this same intensity, fat supplies about 50 percent of the total kilocalories burned for energy. This means that the person is burning an average of 110 fat kilocalories (50 percent of 220). As the intensity increases to about 85 percent of maximum heart rate, this same person burns an average of 330 kilocalories during 30 minutes of exercise, with fat supplying only about 33 percent of the total kilocalories burned. Guess what? The person still burns the same number of fat kilocalories (33 percent of 330, or 110), but is burning more total kilocalories (330 kilocalories) at the higher intensity, which will help meet his or her weight-loss goal sooner than exercising at a lower intensity (burning only 220 kilocalories). The bottom line is, you don't need to stay in the fat-burning zone to effectively lose body fat. You just need to expend more kilocalories than you take in so that there is an overall kilocalorie deficit.

If you prefer not to exercise at a high intensity, there is an advantage to exercising at a lower intensity. If you have time for a long workout, you can probably exercise at a lower intensity for a longer period of time without getting tired. In other words, if you are jogging at 6 mph (high intensity), you may get tired after you cover 3 miles. However, if you are walking briskly at 4 mph (lower intensity), you may be able to cover 4 miles because you aren't as fatigued. Walking the extra 30 minutes and covering that extra mile will allow you to expend more overall kilocalories during your workout (330 kilocalories for 30 minutes of jogging versus 440 kilocalories for 60 minutes of walking). But if you have a busy lifestyle and feel pressed for time to exercise, don't be afraid to go beyond the fat-burning zone to get the most out of your workout and effectively lose weight.

as well trained. Because they use more fat and less glycogen, conditioned individuals have the potential to increase endurance by "sparing" glycogen stores for later use.

Recall that the body requires more oxygen to convert fatty acids into energy than it does to convert glucose into energy. This need for more oxygen creates more stress for the cardiovascular system. Conditioning the body through regular exercise results in the ability of the heart and lungs to deliver oxygen to working muscles more efficiently at higher intensity, thus the oxidation of fatty acids for energy is greater.

The Amount of Fat Needed for Exercise

Dietary recommendations for fat intake are generally the same for active people as for the average adult population, with 25 to 30 percent of kilocalories coming from fat.[11] Remember from Chapter 5 that high intakes of saturated and *trans* fats have been linked to high cholesterol levels and heart disease. Physically active people sometimes assume that because they're in shape, they don't have to worry about these diseases. While it is true that physical activity grants some protection against heart disease, athletes and other fit people can also have high cholesterol, heart attacks, and strokes. Everyone, regardless of activity level, should limit saturated fat to no more than 10 percent of total kilocalories and consume primarily unsaturated fats in foods to meet the body's need for dietary fat.[12]

Some athletes, such as endurance runners and those in sports where low body weight is important, such as gymnasts and figure skaters, may feel they can benefit from a very low-fat diet (less than 20 percent). Though consuming too much dietary fat is a concern, limiting fat intake too much is also undesirable. Consuming less than adequate amounts of fat is more likely to result in inadequate consumption of kilocalories, essential fatty acids, and fat-soluble vitamins, which can negatively affect exercise performance.[13, 14]

Weight training increases muscle mass, which contributes to increased use of fat for energy.

Protein Is Primarily Needed to Build and Repair Muscle

Protein is the nutrient most commonly associated with muscle and its relationship to physical activity, especially strength training. Recall from Chapter 6 that dietary and body proteins are broken down into amino acids and then reassembled into the various proteins that perform specific functions in the body, referred to as protein turnover. When protein synthesis occurs more often than breakdown, conditions are favorable for increases in muscle protein, which can translate to more muscle mass, strength, and endurance.

Exercise affects protein turnover by increasing the level of cortisol, a hormone associated with muscle protein breakdown during physiological stress, in the body. Nutritionally, protein synthesis can be achieved by consuming adequate dietary protein, in addition to carbohydrate and fat, because the amino acids and other nutrients are critical in promoting muscle growth (hypertrophy) and recovery after exercise. Protein synthesis is necessary to maintain or improve performance.

The Body Can Use Protein for Energy

Just as during rest, the body prefers to use carbohydrate and fat as its main energy sources during exercise. All active people use small amounts of protein for energy, but greater amounts are used when kilocalorie intake and carbohydrate stores are insufficient.

When dietary and body proteins are used for energy, they are broken down into amino acids that are then released into the bloodstream. The amino acids are carried to the liver where they get converted into glucose, which supplies the working muscles with energy. Remember that once amino acids are transformed to glucose, they must be used for energy. If not, they are converted into fatty acids and stored as body fat.

If the body has to use a significant amount of protein for energy, that protein is not available to perform its vital functions and the rate of protein breakdown exceeds protein synthesis. Muscle atrophy is a likely consequence of protein breakdown when dietary intakes are inadequate to support physical activity. This commonly occurs in athletes who are trying to lose weight, those who need to "make weight" for a specific sport like wrestling, or in individuals who unintentionally do not eat enough to compensate for nutrients expended during physical activity.

How Much Protein Is Needed for Exercise?

Many athletes and people who exercise assume that they need substantially more protein than people who do not exercise. Although it is true that those who are fit and physically active need more protein than those who are sedentary, their need is not significantly higher. The RDA for protein for most healthy adults, including recreational exercisers, is 0.8 grams per kilogram of body weight per day. Most people, including athletes, exceed this amount, with intake ranging from 0.9 to 2.3 grams per kilogram of body weight.

Recreational exercisers can meet their need for protein with a balanced diet. The increased protein needs of competitive and elite athletes, as well as bodybuilders, can also be met with a balanced diet. Endurance athletes are advised to consume 1.2 to 1.4 grams of protein per kilogram of body weight daily. People who primarily participate in resistance and strength activities may need to consume as much as 1.6 to 1.7 grams per kilogram of body weight daily.[15]

THE TAKE-HOME MESSAGE Carbohydrate and fat are the primary sources of fuel during exercise. Carbohydrates provide energy in the form of blood glucose and muscle and liver glycogen, and are the main energy source during high-intensity exercise. Fat is the main energy source during rest and low-intensity exercise. Protein provides amino acids that are necessary to promote muscle growth and repair muscle breakdown caused by exercise.

How Does the Timing of Meals Affect Fitness and Athletic Performance?

The timing of meals and snacks before, during, and after exercise or athletic performance has a significant impact on energy levels and recovery time. The breakdown of muscle protein that can result from inadequate total energy and/or carbohydrate intake can lead to loss of muscle mass and strength, and lack of energy, which can negatively affect exercise performance.

One of the most important considerations about eating before exercise is allowing sufficient time for the food to digest so that it doesn't negatively affect performance by causing cramps, bloating, or other discomforts. In general, larger meals (those that make you feel quite full) may take 3 to 4 hours to digest, whereas smaller meals (those that make you feel satisfied but not overly full) may take only 2 to 3 hours to digest. A liquid supplement or small snack may take about 30 minutes to 1 hour for digestion. These are general guidelines and may not apply to everyone, so individuals should experiment with their own eating and exercise schedule well before a workout or competition to know how long to wait before starting an activity.

For exercise lasting longer than 1 hour, food intake during exercise is important in order to maintain a blood supply of glucose. Carbohydrate intake should begin shortly after the start of exercise and continue at 15- to 20-minute intervals throughout. For long-lasting endurance activities, a total of 30 to 60 grams of carbohydrate should be consumed per hour to prevent early fatigue. Sports drinks and gels are one way to take in carbohydrate immediately before or during activity, but foods such as crackers and sports bars are also commonly eaten.

Consuming the appropriate foods after exercise is important to support muscle recovery. During exercise, especially strength training, muscles are under a great deal of stress, which can result in overstretching and tearing of proteins and potential inflammation. After exercise, the body is in a catabolic (breaking down) state: Muscle and liver glycogen stores are low or depleted, muscle protein is broken down, and the immune system is suppressed.

Foods eaten after exercise will affect how fast the body recovers, which in turn may affect how soon it is ready for the next workout or training session. This is especially important for competitive athletes who may train more than once per day.

Optimal Foods Before Exercise

A pre-exercise meal should contain adequate amounts of carbohydrate to maximize muscle and liver glycogen stores and maintain normal blood glucose levels. In general, the pre-exercise meal should contain 1 to 4.5 grams of carbohydrate per kilogram of body weight and be consumed 1 to 4 hours prior to exercise.

Consuming carbohydrate immediately before exercise (about 15 to 30 minutes prior to the start) provides an advantage because it gives muscles an immediate source of energy (glucose) and spares glycogen stores, which allows for exercise for a longer duration or at a higher intensity without the body becoming tired as quickly.[16, 17] Carbohydrate intake prior to the start of exercise can also help reduce muscle damage by causing the release of insulin, which promotes muscle protein synthesis.

A pre-exercise meal must contain adequate amounts of carbohydrate.

Just as the body needs a continuous supply of carbohydrate, it also needs moderate amounts of protein throughout the day. Timing protein intake around activity will have a significant impact on muscle preservation, growth, and recovery. The consumption of both protein *and* carbohydrate before exercise benefits the body by producing a greater increase in muscle glycogen synthesis than the consumption of carbohydrate alone. With more glycogen in the muscles and proper training, endurance will increase. Another benefit of consuming both protein and carbohydrate before exercise is that it results in greater protein synthesis after the exercise is over, compared with either protein or carbohydrate alone.[18] The making of new body proteins, including muscles, is necessary for optimal fitness and muscle preservation, repair, and growth.

Foods with a higher fat content take longer to digest than foods that are higher in carbohydrate and protein, and can lead to feelings of sluggishness or discomfort, which can impair performance. For this reason, high-fat foods should generally be avoided several hours before exercise. Of course this is a general guideline, and not all active people who consume higher fat foods before exercise experience difficulty.

Optimal Foods During Exercise

As mentioned earlier, sports drinks, bars, and gels provide easily digested carbohydrates that are optimal during sport performance. Glucose, sucrose, and maltodextrin are the best forms of carbohydrate to consume during exercise because the body absorbs them more quickly than other forms. Fructose, the sugar found in fruit and fruit juice, should generally be avoided because it may cause gastrointestinal problems or stomach discomfort.

Many sports drinks and gels contain only carbohydrate and electrolytes, while some also contain protein. For endurance athletes, consuming both carbohydrate and protein during exercise has been shown to improve net protein balance at rest as well as during exercise and postexercise recovery.[19] This net balance will, in turn, have a positive effect on muscle maintenance and growth.

Sports drinks can be a good source of carbohydrate during exercise.

Optimal Foods After Exercise

Consuming carbohydrate after exercise will help replenish muscle and liver glycogen stores and stimulate muscle protein synthesis. The muscles are most receptive to storing new glycogen within the first 30 to 45 minutes after the end of exercise, so this is a crucial time period in which to provide the body with carbohydrate.[20] Consuming carbohydrate up to 2 hours after the end of exercise will still promote muscle glycogen storage, but not as efficiently. Waiting longer than 2 hours will result in even less glycogen stored. Research shows that consuming carbohydrate immediately after exercise also results in a more positive body protein balance.[21]

Consuming protein and carbohydrate after exercise results in increased muscle protein synthesis. In addition, protein intake immediately after exercise rather than several hours later results in greater muscle protein synthesis. Research studies have shown that the addition of protein to carbohydrate intake causes an even greater increase in glycogen synthesis than either carbohydrate or protein alone, and therefore both nutrients should be consumed both before and after exercise.[22, 23]

Clearly, the body recovers more quickly after exercise when carbohydrate and protein are consumed in proper amounts before, during, and after exercise. Studies have shown that consumption of carbohydrate and protein in a ratio of approximately 3:1 (in grams) is ideal to promote muscle glycogen synthesis, protein synthesis, and faster recovery time.[24]

What is the best way to get these two nutrients? Whey protein (such as in milk) is the preferred protein source because it is rapidly absorbed and contains all of the essential amino acids that the body needs. Most athletes and regular exercisers prefer to consume a liquid supplement that contains carbohydrate and protein rather than solid foods immediately after exercising. Commercial shakes and drinks are one option, but they can be expensive. A cheaper alternative is low-fat chocolate milk, which will provide adequate amounts of carbohydrate and protein to assist in recovery.[25] A liquid supplement or small snack consumed after exercise should be followed by a high-carbohydrate, moderate-protein, low-fat meal within the next 2 hours for optimum recovery.

Low-fat chocolate milk is a low-cost option to provide the whey protein and carbohydrate that help with muscle and glycogen synthesis after exercise.

Competitive athletes should always experiment with timing nutrient intake and consuming new foods and beverages during practice and not on the day of competition. Finding out that a particular food doesn't agree with you a few hours before an important race or event could be an unpleasant surprise.

The importance of carbohydrate and protein for recovery is clear. What about fat? Some people who load up on high-fat foods after a workout or competition experience fatigue that often results in less-than-optimal performance during the next workout.

THE TAKE-HOME MESSAGE Consuming the right balance of nutrients at the right time can improve exercise performance and recovery time. Certain foods are better consumed before, during, and after exercise for optimal results. Higher fat foods should generally be avoided before exercise, while carbohydrate and protein are important for energy and recovery before, during, and after exercise.

What Vitamins and Minerals Are Important for Fitness?

In addition to several other important functions, vitamins and minerals play a major role in the metabolism of carbohydrate, fat, and protein for energy during exercise. Some also act as antioxidants and help protect cells from the oxidative stress that can occur with exercise.

Antioxidants Can Help Protect Cells from Damage Caused by Exercise

Muscles use more oxygen during exercise than at rest. As a result, the body increases production of free radicals that damage cells, especially during intense, prolonged exercise. Antioxidants, such as vitamins E and C, are known to protect cells from the damage of free radicals. Vitamin C also assists in the production of collagen, which provides most of the structure of connective tissues like bone, tendons, and ligaments. This, in turn, can reduce the likelihood of developing strains, sprains, and fractures that may occur as a result of exercise.

Whereas adequate intake of vitamins E and C through nutrient-rich foods has been linked to good health, which in turn can positively affect exercise and training, research has not shown that the use of vitamin E or C supplements above the RDA improves athletic performance, nor that it decreases oxidative stress in highly trained athletes.[26, 27]

Deficiencies of Some Minerals Can Be of Concern for Highly Active People

In addition to their important roles in normal body functions and health, minerals are essential to physical fitness and athletic performance. In general, active people do not need more minerals than less active individuals. However, iron and calcium should be given special attention by some active people who may be at risk for deficiencies.

Iron

Iron is important to exercise because it is necessary for energy metabolism and transporting oxygen within muscle cells and throughout the body. Iron is a structural component of hemoglobin and myoglobin, two proteins that carry and store oxygen in the blood and muscle, respectively. If iron levels are low, hemoglobin levels can also fall, diminishing the blood's ability to carry oxygen to the cells. If this occurs during exercise, the result can be early fatigue. (Individuals can also feel tired if iron levels are low and they are not exercising.) Iron supplementation can improve aerobic performance for people with depleted iron stores.[28]

When iron levels are severely diminished, anemia can occur. Athletes and physically fit people are prone to iron-deficiency anemia for many reasons, including poor dietary intake or increased iron losses. Women can lose a lot of iron during menstruation, depending on their iron status and menstrual blood flow. This is one reason why female athletes are at a greater risk for iron-deficiency anemia than male athletes. Long-distance runners and athletes in sports where they must "make weight" have been noted to be at higher risk for iron-deficiency anemia. Athletes in other sports such as basketball, tennis, softball, and swimming also have been shown to have suboptimal iron status.[29, 30]

Some people experience decreased levels of hemoglobin because of training, especially when the training is quite strenuous. During exercise, blood volume increases and concentrations of hemoglobin in the blood decrease. This is often referred to as **sports anemia,** or pseudoanemia, and is not the same as iron-deficiency anemia. Iron-deficiency anemia typically has to be treated with iron supplementation. Sports anemia can be corrected on its own because the body can adapt to training and produce more red blood cells, which restores normal hemoglobin levels.

sports anemia Low concentrations of hemoglobin in the blood; results from an increase in blood volume during strenuous exercise.

Another effect of exercise on iron is intravascular hemolysis (*hemo* = blood, *lysis* = breaking down), the bursting of red blood cells. Also called "foot strike hemolysis," this condition occurs when feet repeatedly hit a hard surface (the ground) during running, causing red blood cells to burst and release iron. The iron is recycled by the body and not lost, and therefore does not typically contribute to iron deficiency.

All individuals, whether they exercise or not, can maintain iron status by consuming adequate amounts of iron-rich foods, and supplements if necessary. However, many female athletes do not consume enough iron to meet their needs, which often leads to low iron levels. This is especially true for female athletes who exhibit disordered eating patterns; see Health Connection: What Is the Female Athlete Triad? for more information. Some vegetarian athletes are especially susceptible to iron deficiency and need to plan their diets appropriately so they consume adequate amounts of foods plentiful in iron.

Calcium

Most people know about the importance of calcium to maintain bone health. Some people, including athletes, are particularly susceptible to broken bones and fractures. Having adequate calcium in the diet can reduce one's risk for these types of injuries. In addition, calcium affects both skeletal and heart muscle contraction, and hormone and neurotransmitter activity during exercise. It also assists in blood clotting in response to a cut or other minor hemorrhage, which may occur during exercise or competition.

Calcium is lost in sweat; the more individuals sweat, the more calcium they lose. One study concluded that bone loss is related to dietary calcium, and that exercise can increase bone mineral content (the mass of all minerals in bone) only when calcium intake is sufficient to compensate for what is lost through sweating.[31]

While adequate calcium intake is essential, calcium supplements are not recommended unless intake from food and beverages does not meet the RDA. Choosing foods that are high in calcium, including fortified foods, can ensure that all individuals, including athletes, meet their needs for calcium.

Choose broccoli as a pizza topping to increase your calcium intake.

Vitamin and Mineral Supplements Are Generally Not Necessary

Many athletes mistakenly believe that vitamins and minerals themselves supply energy, or that consuming extra vitamins and minerals can enhance performance. Studies have shown that multivitamin and mineral supplements are the supplements most commonly used by college athletes.[32, 33] Can vitamin and mineral supplements really improve athletic performance? The answer is: not unless the body is already deficient in the nutrient. For people who consume enough vitamins and minerals in their diet, taking more than the RDA will not result in improved performance during exercise.[34]

Active people generally do not need more vitamins than sedentary people because vitamins can be used repeatedly in metabolic reactions. Everyone, not just athletes, should obtain vitamins and minerals through foods before considering the use of supplements. As long as individuals consume adequate amounts of kilocalories by eating a wide variety of nutrient-dense foods, they are likely to meet vitamin and mineral requirements; thus, it is probably a waste of money to use vitamin and mineral supplements. In addition, excess intakes of some vitamins and minerals, especially from supplements, can be harmful (see Chapters 9, 10, 12, and 13). Anyone, including athletes, should consult with a physician or a Registered Dietitian before taking dietary supplements.

Health Connection

The Female Athlete Triad

Christy Henrich joined the U.S. gymnastics team in 1986 weighing 95 pounds at 4 feet, 11 inches tall. Shortly after joining the team, Christy succeeded as a gymnast, but after a judge told her she needed to lose weight, she developed anorexia nervosa. Sadly, her weight plummeted to 47 pounds, and she died from multiple organ failure at the age of 22.

The anorexia that Christy battled is one part of the **female athlete triad,** a combination of disordered eating, amenorrhea, and osteoporosis. Female athletes are often pressured to reach or maintain an unrealistically low body weight and/or level of body fat. This pressure contributes to the development of disordered eating, which helps to initiate the triad. The major concern with this disorder is that it not only reduces the performance of the athlete but may have serious medical and psychological consequences later in life.

Disordered Eating

Athletes who have disordered eating may engage in abnormal, and often harmful, eating behaviors in order to lose weight or maintain a low body weight. At one extreme are those who fulfill the diagnostic criteria for anorexia nervosa or bulimia nervosa. At the other end are those who unintentionally take in fewer kilocalories than they need. They may appear to be eating a healthy diet—one that would be adequate for a sedentary individual—but their kilocalorie needs are higher due to their level of physical activity.

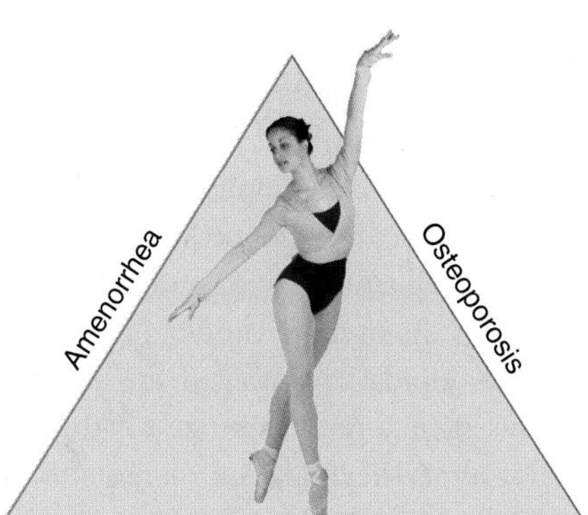

Female athletes for whom body size or appearance is an issue, such as dancers, gymnasts, and skaters, are often particularly vulnerable to the female athlete triad.

Many athletes mistakenly believe that losing weight by any method enhances performance and that disordered eating is harmless. Disordered eating can occur in athletes (both male and female) in all types of sports, but it is most common among athletes in sports where appearance is important, such as figure skating, gymnastics, and ballet, and sports in which individuals strive to maintain a low body weight, such as wrestling, rowing, and horse racing.

Amenorrhea

Amenorrhea, the absence of at least three consecutive menstrual cycles, is the most recognizable component of the triad. This menstrual disorder is caused by a failure to consume enough energy to compensate for the "energy cost" of the exercise. Unfortunately, many females welcome the convenience of not menstruating and do not report it; however, this may put them at risk for reduced bone mass and increased rate of bone loss caused by decreased levels of estrogen in the body.

Osteoporosis

Osteoporosis is the loss of bone mineral density and the inadequate formation of bone. Premature osteoporosis, which is perpetuated by poor nutrition and amenorrhea, puts the athlete at risk for stress fractures and hip and vertebral fractures, as well as the loss of bone mass that may be irreplaceable.

Signs and Treatment

All individuals, including friends, teachers, and coaches, involved with these athletes should be aware of the warning signs because the triad components are very often not recognized, not reported, or are denied. Warning signs include menstrual changes, weight changes, disordered eating patterns, cardiac arrhythmia, depression, or stress fractures. Those working with such athletes should provide a training environment in which athletes are not pressured to lose weight, and should be able to recommend appropriate nutritional, medical, and/or psychological resources if needed. Treatment of an athlete with this disorder is multidisciplinary, and needs to involve cooperation among the athlete's physician, dietician, psychologist, coach or trainer, family, and friends.

female athlete triad A syndrome of the three interrelated conditions occurring in some physically active females: low energy availability (often from disordered eating), amenorrhea, and decreased bone density or osteoporosis.

amenorrhea Absence of menstruation for at least three consecutive cycles.

THE TAKE-HOME MESSAGE Vitamins and minerals play important roles in metabolism, and vitamins E and C can act as antioxidants. Some athletes need to pay special attention to their intakes of iron and calcium. Iron is important because of its role in transporting oxygen in blood and muscle. Iron deficiency is prevalent among athletes, especially females and vegetarians. Calcium intake is important for bone health and muscle contraction. Adequate amounts of all nutrients can be consumed in foods, so supplements are not usually necessary.

How Does Fluid Intake Affect Fitness?

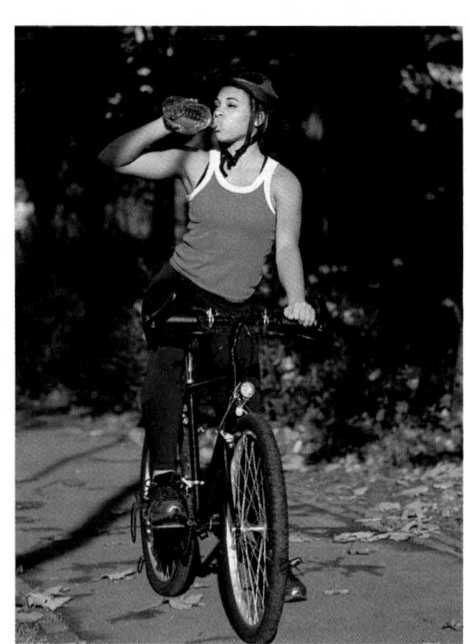

Staying hydrated during physical activity is important to maintain electrolyte balance and help regulate body temperature.

As basic as it sounds, water is one of the most important nutrients during physical activity. Drinking too little fluid, or losing too much fluid and electrolytes through sweating, causes physiological changes that can negatively affect exercise performance and health. Early fatigue or weakness can occur when the body doesn't have sufficient amounts of water. Consuming adequate fluids on a regular basis, as well as monitoring fluid losses during physical activity, are key to maintaining optimal performance and preventing **dehydration** (also called *hypohydration*) and electrolyte imbalance.

Fluid and Electrolyte Balance and Body Temperature Are Affected by Exercise

During physical activity, the body loses more water via sweat and exhalation of water vapor than when it's less active. This lost water needs to be replaced during and after exercise to maintain normal fluid balance.

Electrolytes are also lost during exercise. Sodium and chloride and, to a lesser extent, potassium are contained in sweat. An electrolyte imbalance can cause heat cramps, as well as nausea, lowered blood pressure, and edema in the hands and feet, all of which can hinder performance. When electrolyte losses are within the range of normal daily dietary intake, they can easily be replaced by consuming foods rich in sodium, chloride, and potassium within 24 hours after exercise. Electrolytes can also be replaced by beverages that contain them, such as sports drinks, if preferred or if food is not available.

During exercise, sweat releases the heat generated by the breakdown of nutrients to keep body temperature normal. The amount of fluid lost through sweating varies from person to person. Some people sweat heavily, while others may sweat very little. Regardless of how much you sweat, it is important that you don't allow your body to lose too much fluid without replacing it with water or other beverages.

Exercising in hot, humid weather results in more fluid being lost in breathing, which will increase the body's need for fluids. However, if the air is very humid (that is, it contains a lot of water), sweat may not evaporate off the skin, and the body can't cool down. This can cause **hyperthermia,** and increase the risk of heat exhaustion or heat stroke. One significant warning sign of heat stroke is a complete lack of sweating. This happens when an individual is extremely dehydrated and cannot produce sweat, which prevents the release of heat and causes body temperature to rise. Other warning signs of heat exhaustion and heat stroke are shown in Table 16.3.

Many athletes and other active people may not realize that they can be at risk for **hypothermia,** which is just as serious as hyperthermia. Cold weather, especially if wet, can contribute to hypothermia when a person is exercising for a long period of time. Someone who is running at a slow pace in cold weather may produce very

dehydration Loss of water in the body as a result of inadequate fluid intake or excess fluid loss, such as through sweating; also called *hypohydration*.

hyperthermia A rise in body temperature above normal.

hypothermia A drop in body temperature to below normal.

TABLE 16.3 Warning Signs of Heat Exhaustion and Heat Stroke

Heat Exhaustion	Heat Stroke
Profuse sweating	Red, hot, and dry skin (no sweating)
Fatigue	Rapid, strong pulse
Thirst	Rapid, shallow breathing
Muscle cramps	Throbbing headache
Headache	Dizziness
Dizziness or light-headedness	Nausea
Weakness	Extreme confusion
Nausea and vomiting	Unconsciousness
Cool, moist skin	Extremely high body temperature (above 103°F [39.4°C], orally)

little heat, causing the body temperature to fall. Keep in mind that the body still sweats when exercising in cold weather, so meeting fluid needs is still important. Wearing adequate clothing and drinking fluids at least at room temperature or warmer will help prevent hypothermia.

Fluids Are Needed Before, During, and After Exercise

Many active people are aware that it's important to stay hydrated during exercise, but the need for water doesn't begin with the first sit-up or lap around the track. Meeting fluid needs before and after activity is important to maintain fluid and electrolyte balance and optimize performance.

Recall from Chapter 11 that most healthy adult women need 9 cups of water daily, while most healthy adult men need about 13 cups. This is a general guideline to follow for adequate hydration. Another way to determine estimated daily fluid needs is to divide body weight by 2. This reveals the number of ounces of fluid (8 ounces = 1 cup) needed daily, not including the additional needs associated with exercising.

Pre-exercise hydration is essential to replace sweat losses. As you learned in Chapter 11, you can determine fluid needs during exercise by weighing yourself both before and after an activity. Because the amount of weight that is lost is mainly due to losses in body water, you should consume 16 to 24 fluid ounces (about 2 to 3 cups) of fluid for every pound of body weight lost.[35] The American College of Sports Medicine has specific recommendations for how much fluid to drink before and during exercise. See Table 16.4 for these recommendations.

Some Beverages Are Better than Others

Beverages like tea, coffee, soft drinks, fruit juice, and, of course, water contribute to daily fluid needs. But what is the best type of fluid for preventing dehydration prior to and during activity? What about for rehydrating your body after activity? For these purposes, not all beverages are equal.

Sports drinks are popular in the fitness world and are often marketed as tasty beverages to all groups of people, not just athletes. They typically contain 6 to 8 percent carbohydrate as well as sodium and potassium, two electrolytes that are critical in muscle contraction and maintaining fluid balance. One purpose of sports drinks is to replace fluid and electrolytes that are lost through sweating, which is vital to prevent or treat muscle cramps associated with exercise. Sports drinks have

TABLE 16.4 ACSM Hydration Recommendations	
When?	**How Much Fluid?**
4 hours before exercise	16–20 fl oz (2–2½ cups)
10 to 15 minutes before exercise	8–12 fl oz (1–1½ cups)
At 15- to 20-minute intervals when exercising less than 60 minutes	3–8 fl oz (⅜–1 cup)
At 15- to 20-minute intervals when exercising more than 60 minutes	3–8 fl oz (⅜–1 cup) sports beverage (5–8 percent carbohydrate with electrolytes)
After exercise for every pound of body weight lost	20–24 fl oz (2½–3 cups)

been shown to be superior to water for rehydration, mostly because their flavor causes people to drink more than they would of just plain water.[36]

Sports drinks also provide additional carbohydrate to prevent glycogen depletion. This is beneficial during long endurance events or exercise when glycogen stores may be running low. Consuming a sports drink during exercise provides glucose, which can be used as an immediate energy source and prevent further decline in muscle glycogen stores. The amount of carbohydrate in sports drinks (6 to 8 percent) is formulated for optimal absorption, which makes it preferred over other beverages, such as soft drinks and fruit juice, with higher concentrations and different types of carbohydrate.

However, not everyone needs sports drinks in order to stay adequately hydrated. For exercise that lasts less than 60 minutes, water can sufficiently replace fluids lost through sweating and food consumption following exercise can adequately replace electrolytes. Sports drink consumption can be beneficial for some people who exercise for less than one hour. But generally, a sports drink is most beneficial when physical activity lasts longer than 60 minutes, because fluids, electrolytes, and/or glucose are inevitably lost in greater amounts and need to be replenished to avoid fatigue and other negative effects on performance.[37] Sports beverages provide approximately 60 kilocalories for each 8-ounce cup, so remember that they can be a source of unwanted extra kilocalories.

Other beverages may be suboptimal for hydration during physical activity. Fruit juice and juice drinks contain a larger concentration of carbohydrate and do not hydrate the body as quickly as beverages with a lower concentration of carbohydrate (like sports drinks). Carbonated drinks contain a large amount of water; however, the air bubbles from the carbonation can cause stomach bloating and may limit the amount of fluid consumed. In addition, fructose (the type of carbohydrate provided by carbonated soft drinks) is not as well absorbed as the glucose or sucrose that is found in sports drinks.

Though alcohol may seem like an unlikely choice for rehydration, some people may drink alcoholic beverages, such as beer, in order to quench thirst. But because alcohol is a diuretic, it can actually contribute to dehydration. Alcohol during performance can also impair judgment and reasoning, which can lead to injuries for both the exerciser and those nearby.

Caffeinated beverages, such as coffee, energy drinks, and some soft drinks, contribute to the DRI for water but are not optimal sources for meeting fluid needs for physical activity. Caffeine, a diuretic, should only be consumed in moderate amounts (less than about 300 milligrams, or the amount found in three 8-ounce cups of coffee, per day), because excessive intake can cause increased heart rate, nausea, vomiting, excessive urination, restlessness, anxiety, and difficulty sleeping.[38] However, recall from Chapter 11 that caffeine will not contribute to dehydration in individuals who regularly consume it.

Fluids such as milk and fruit and vegetable juices can help meet daily water needs. Whole fruits and many other foods are also good sources of water.

Consuming Too Little or Too Much Fluid Can Be Harmful

As the body loses fluid during physical activity, it will send signals of thirst to stimulate fluid consumption. However, by the time an individual feels thirsty, he or she may already be dehydrated. **Figure 16.6** shows the effect of dehydration on exercise performance. As shown in the figure, thirst is not a good indicator of fluid needs for most athletes and physically active people. Athletes need to know the warning signs of dehydration so they can respond by drinking adequate fluids and prevent health consequences and impaired exercise performance.

Becoming dehydrated over a short period of time, such as during a single exercise session or sports competition, can result in **acute dehydration.** Acute dehydration most commonly occurs if an individual is not adequately hydrated before beginning a hard exercise session, especially if that person has been sick, if it is extremely hot and humid, or if the temperature is significantly different from what the person is used to. To prevent acute dehydration, follow a regimented hydration

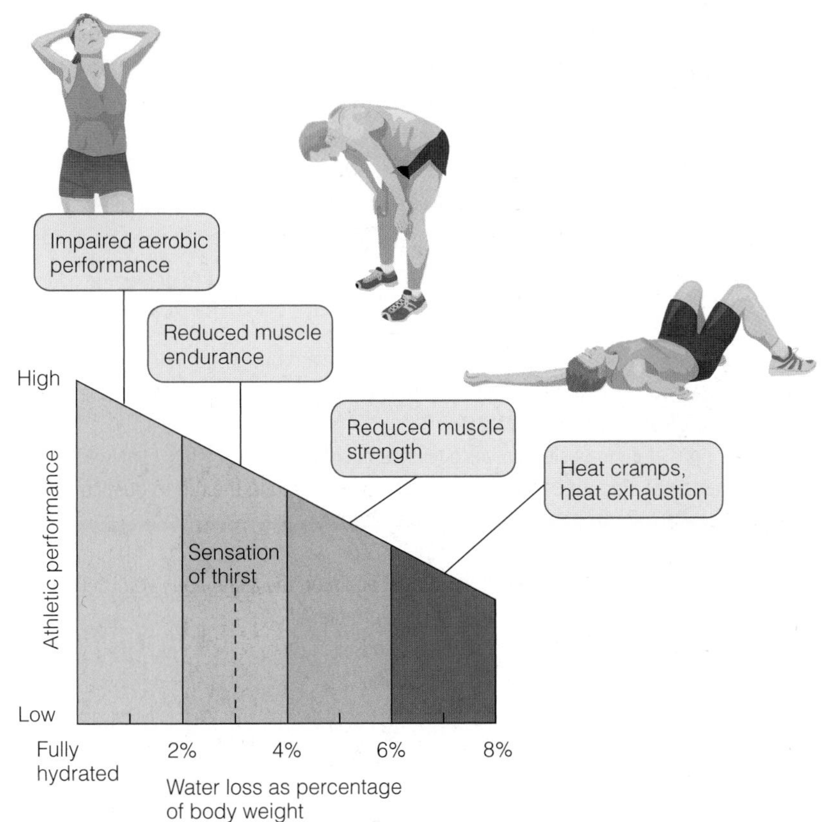

▲ **Figure 16.6 Effects of Dehydration on Exercise Performance**
Failing to stay hydrated during exercise or competition can result in fatigue and cramps and, in extreme cases, heat exhaustion. Because the thirst mechanism doesn't kick in until after dehydration has begun, replacing fluids throughout physical activity is important.
Source: Adapted from E. Burke and J. Berning, *Training Nutrition* (Travers City, MI: Cooper Publishing Group, 1996).

acute dehydration Dehydration that sets in after a short period of time.

Self-Assessment

Are You Meeting Your Fitness Recommendations and Eating for Exercise?

Now that you know how to plan an effective fitness strategy and eat for optimal fitness and performance, think about your current dietary and exercise habits. Take this brief assessment to find out if your daily habits are as healthful as they could be:

1. Do you participate in at least 60 minutes of moderately intense physical activity during the week?

   Yes ☐ **No** ☐

2. Do you participate in strength training 2 to 3 times per week?

   Yes ☐ **No** ☐

3. Do you drink 6 to 12 ounces of fluid every 15 to 20 minutes during exercise?

   Yes ☐ **No** ☐

4. Do you drink a sports beverage after moderate or high-intensity exercise lasting longer than 1 hour?

   Yes ☐ **No** ☐

5. Do you consume carbohydrate and protein within 30 to 45 minutes after stopping exercise?

   Yes ☐ **No** ☐

Answer

If you answered "yes" to all of the questions, you are well on your way to optimal fitness. Participating in regular exercise, including aerobic exercise and strength training, helps you maintain optimal health and improves your level of fitness. Eating and drinking adequate nutrients also improves fitness. If you answered "no" to any of the questions, review this chapter to learn more on fitness and eating for exercise.

schedule using water or sports drinks to hydrate before, during, and after exercise sessions or competition.

Chronic dehydration refers to being inadequately hydrated over an extended period of time, such as during several sports practices or games. The most common warning signs of chronic dehydration include fatigue, muscle soreness, poor recovery from a workout, headaches, and nausea. Very dark urine and infrequent bathroom trips (less than every 3 or 4 hours) can be signs of chronic dehydration. As with acute dehydration, following a regimented hydration schedule throughout the day will help prevent chronic dehydration.

When speaking of hydration and physical activity, we are usually concerned about consuming *enough* fluids so that we do not become dehydrated. However, consuming too much fluid can also be harmful. Taking in too much water without sufficient electrolytes can dilute the blood and result in **hyponatremia.** Symptoms of severe hyponatremia may include rapid weight gain, bloated stomach, nausea, vomiting, swollen hands and feet, headache, dizziness, confusion, disorientation, and lack of coordination. Hyponatremia is more likely to occur in those who participate in endurance sports or prolonged exercise periods (greater than 4 hours), in which fluid and sodium loss is more likely.

Drinking as much fluid as possible and "staying ahead of thirst" has been the recommendation for hydration among long-distance runners for quite some time. However, due to growing concern about overhydration and hyponatremia, USA Track & Field (USATF) revised its hydration guidelines to lower the risk of hyponatremia among long-distance runners. The USATF recommends consuming 100 percent of fluids lost due to sweat while exercising, and to be sensitive to the onset of thirst as the signal to drink, rather than "staying ahead of thirst."

If you are a distance runner, see the Calculation Corner for a hydration test to determine your fluid needs during long-distance races.[39] Keep in mind that you

Calculation Corner

Fluid Needs

The next time you take a 1-hour training run, use the following process to determine your fluid needs.

1. Make sure that you are properly hydrated before the workout. Your urine should be clear.
2. Do a warm-up run to the point where you start to sweat, then stop. Urinate if necessary.
3. Weigh yourself on an accurate scale.
4. Run for 1 hour at an intensity similar to your targeted race.
5. Drink a measured amount of a beverage of your choice during the run to quench your thirst. Be sure to keep track of how much you drink.
6. Do not urinate during the run.
7. After you have finished the run, weigh yourself again on the same scale you used in step 3.
8. Calculate your fluid needs using the following formula:
   - **a.** Enter your body weight from step 3 in pounds ________
   - **b.** Enter your body weight from step 7 in pounds ________
   - **c.** Subtract b. from a. ________
   - **d.** Convert the pounds of weight in c. to fluid ounces by multiplying by 15.3 ________
   - **e.** Enter the amount of fluid you consumed during the run in ounces ________
   - **f.** Add e. to d. ________

The final figure is the number of ounces of fluid that you must consume per hour to remain well hydrated.

Source: "USATF Self-Testing Program for Optimal Hydration," by Douglas Casa, from USA Track and Field Website, 2007.

chronic dehydration Dehydration over a long period of time.

hyponatremia Dangerously low levels of sodium in the blood.

should perform this hydration test well before a competition or event, and perform the test again if your level of fitness improves or if the climate changes from when you initially determined your fluid needs.

THE TAKE-HOME MESSAGE Being adequately hydrated before, during, and after exercise is important to sustain fluid and electrolyte balance and a normal body temperature. Inadequate hydration can impair performance. Water is the preferred beverage for hydration, but sports drinks can be beneficial during moderate- or vigorous-intensity exercise. Overhydration can be just as important to avoid as dehydration, but is more likely to occur among people engaging in endurance sports or prolonged exercise.

Can Dietary Supplements Contribute to Fitness?

Competitive athletes are always looking for an edge, and many turn to supplements in the hope of improving their performance. Supplement manufacturers may claim that their products enhance immunity, boost metabolism, improve memory, or provide some other physical enhancement. Because the Food and Drug Administration does not strictly regulate dietary supplements, the manufacturers do not have to prove the validity of these claims or the safety or efficacy of their products. As a result, many athletes risk their health and, in some cases, eligibility for competition by taking supplements that can be ineffective or even dangerous.

Dietary Supplements and Ergogenic Aids May Improve Performance, but Can Have Side Effects

The term **ergogenic aid** describes any substance used to improve athletic performance, including dietary supplements. Although the makers of dietary supplements do not have to prove their products' effectiveness, researchers have examined several supplements and their effects on athletic performance. Studies have indicated that some dietary supplements have a positive effect on performance, while others do not. Further, some ergogenic aids cause serious side effects.

Athletes sometimes take supplements, such as creatine phosphate or caffeine, to enhance their performance. Supplements are not strictly regulated by the FDA, so their quality and effectiveness can vary widely.

Creatine

Creatine is one of the most well-known dietary supplements in the fitness industry today. In the early 1990s, research revealed that creatine supplementation increased creatine stores in the muscles (in the form of creatine phosphate), which increased the amount of ATP generated and improved performance during high-intensity, short-duration exercise.[40]

However, the data on whether creatine supplements enhance performance is mixed. Studies have supported the hypothesis that creatine supplementation improves athletic performance in high-intensity, short-duration activities such as weight training, when the body relies on anaerobic energy metabolism. In addition, creatine supplementation has been shown to increase muscle strength and muscle mass. But research has shown

ergogenic aid A substance, such as a dietary supplement, used to enhance athletic performance.

mixed results in creatine supplementation improving sprint-running performance, with some studies showing improvement and others showing no benefit.[41, 42]

To date, creatine has not been found to have negative effects on blood pressure, or kidney or liver function among healthy people.[43, 44] Anyone considering taking creatine supplements should check with a health care provider first.

Caffeine

Caffeine used to be considered by athletes mostly in the context of its effect on hydration. Today, caffeine has gained popularity as an ergogenic aid among athletes, trainers, and coaches. Caffeine may decrease perception of effort by stimulating the central nervous system, directly affect the breakdown of muscle glycogen, and increase the availability of fatty acids during exercise, therefore sparing glycogen stores.

Studies on the effects of caffeine on exercise have shown that caffeine enhances athletic performance, mostly during endurance events.[45, 46] However, research has not shown that caffeine provides any benefit during short-duration activities, such as sprinting.[47]

Caffeine is considered a banned substance by some athletic associations when consumed in high amounts. For example, the National Collegiate Athletic Association (NCAA) classifies caffeine as a banned substance when urine concentrations exceed 15 micrograms per milliliter. For most people, this would be the equivalent of drinking 4 or 5 cups of coffee within one hour.

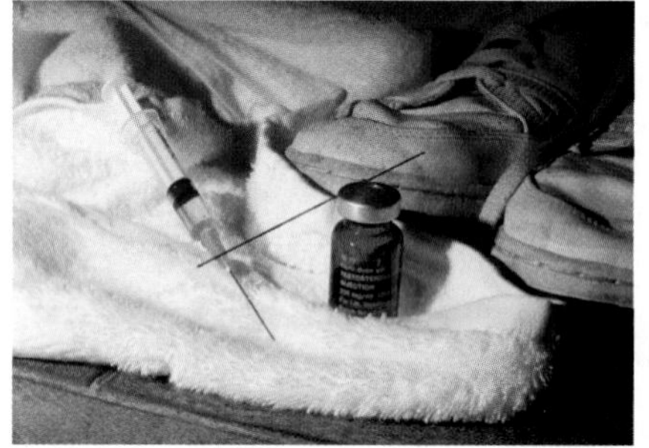

Anabolic steroids are sometimes used by athletes seeking to bulk up. Because they are testosterone based, they can have unique harmful effects on the body for men and women.

Anabolic Steroids

Anabolic steroids (*anabolic* = to stimulate growth) are testosterone-based substances designed to mimic the bodybuilding characteristics of testosterone. There are two primary effects of anabolic steroids. The anabolic effect, which is the one users are seeking, promotes protein growth and muscle development, which leads to bigger muscles and greater strength. Most athletes want to be stronger and will often turn to anabolic steroids to build muscle to a level beyond what is naturally possible.

The other effect, which is undesirable, is the androgenic. Taking in testosterone causes the body to decrease its own production of the hormone, leading to a hormone imbalance. In men, this can cause shrinkage of the testicles, decreased sperm production, impotence, painful urination, severe acne (especially on the back), and changes in hair growth (an increase in facial hair and a decrease in hair on the head). Men may also experience psychiatric side effects such as extreme mood swings and aggressiveness, which can lead to violence.

Women who use anabolic steroids also experience androgenic effects. Like men, women may experience severe acne, increased facial and body hair, and loss of hair on the head. Additionally, women may experience a lower voice, increased aggressiveness, amenorrhea, and increased sex drive.

Abusing anabolic steroids, whether to improve performance or physical appearance, can lead to severe health consequences such as liver and kidney tumors, liver cancer, high blood pressure, trembling, and increases in LDL cholesterol. Although anabolic steroids can increase muscle mass and strength, their use among collegiate and professional athletes is prohibited.

Growth Hormone

Growth hormone is a hormone-based substance—similar to anabolic steroids—used by some athletes to gain a competitive edge. Growth hormone has been promoted with claims of increasing muscle mass and strength and decreasing body fat, thereby improving performance. Some competitive athletes use growth hormone instead of anabolic steroids to build muscles because they believe it is less likely to be detected through current drug testing methods.

Growth hormone is naturally produced by the pituitary gland to stimulate growth in children. Synthetic, or man-made, growth hormone was originally created for children with growth hormone deficiency to enable them to reach their full height. It targets numerous tissues, including bones, skeletal muscle, fat cells, immune cells, and liver cells. Growth hormone increases protein synthesis by increasing amino acid transport across cell membranes, causing an increase in muscle mass but not strength. This increased muscle mass without added strength could actually impair performance by reducing power, speed, and endurance. Growth hormone also decreases glycogen synthesis and the use of glucose for energy, causing an increase in fat breakdown and the use of fatty acids for energy. This, in turn, can decrease body fat.

Little research exists on the effectiveness of growth hormone in improving fitness and athletic performance, and the results of studies that have been done are mixed. Growth hormone has been shown to reduce body fat and increase fat-free mass in well-trained adults.[48, 49] However, other studies show that it does not improve muscle strength or lean body mass in healthy adult athletes or the elderly.[50, 51] It also appears to have no positive effect on cardiovascular performance in adults with growth hormone deficiency.[52]

Abuse of growth hormone can have serious health effects, including the development of diabetes, atherosclerosis (hardening of the arteries), and hypertension. Excess growth hormone as a result of supplement abuse can also cause **acromegaly,** a condition in which tissues, bones, and internal organs grow abnormally large.

The man on the right, who is more than eight feet tall, has acromegaly caused by a tumor on his pituitary gland. Growth hormone abuse can also cause acromegaly in specific tissues, bones, or organs of the body.

Erythropoietin and Blood Doping

Erythropoietin is a hormone produced by the kidneys when there is a decrease in blood oxygen levels. The hormone travels to the bone marrow and stimulates the formation of red blood cells. Synthetic versions of erythropoietin are used as ergogenic aids because increasing the number of red blood cells increases the oxygen-carrying capacity of the blood. This results in the athlete being able to train at a higher intensity without becoming fatigued as quickly, thereby having the potential to improve performance and overall physical fitness.[53] Despite its popularity among competitive athletes, synthetic erythropoietin is a banned substance in most athletic organizations.

Before synthetic erythropoietin was discovered, the most common way to increase the oxygen-carrying capacity of the blood was blood doping. Blood doping, or red blood cell reinfusion, involves removing 250 to 500 milliliters of an athlete's own blood, extracting the red blood cells, and storing them for a few weeks prior to competition. The stored red blood cells are reinfused as the competition day approaches, so that the athlete has a higher than normal number of blood cells in his or her body. This results in an increase in the amount of oxygen in the blood, which can increase aerobic endurance.

Synthetic erythropoietin and blood doping can be dangerous because they increase blood viscosity (thickness). If the blood becomes too thick, it moves slowly and can clog capillaries. If this occurs in the brain, it results in a stroke. If there is a blood clot in the vessels of the heart, it causes a heart attack. Both of these can be life-threatening events. Erythropoietin may also cause sudden death during sleep, which is believed to have been a contributing factor in numerous deaths among professional European cyclists in recent years.

Sports Bars and Shakes May Provide Benefits

Sports bars and shakes are not defined as dietary supplements by the FDA because they are more like food and contain one or more macronutrients. However, people

acromegaly A condition in which tissues, bones, and internal organs grow abnormally large; can be caused by abuse of growth hormone supplements, or by a hormonal disorder in which the pituitary gland produces too much growth hormone.

Sports bars and shakes should supplement, not replace, whole, nutritious foods.

often refer to these items as supplements because they are typically eaten in addition to whole-food meals and snacks.

The main energy source in most commercial sports bars and shakes is carbohydrate, with protein and fat contributing smaller amounts of energy. The ratio of the macronutrients in these foods varies depending on the purpose. Bars and shakes that are intended to provide energy for and recovery from exercise have a greater proportion of carbohydrates. Those that are promoted for muscle protein synthesis typically contain more protein than carbohydrate and fat. Bars and shakes that are high in protein are often used by vegetarians and some athletes who need additional sources of protein in their diet. Most bars and shakes also contain a variety of vitamins and minerals. These vitamins and minerals may not be necessary for individuals who consume regular, balanced meals or take a daily multivitamin.

Sports bars and shakes can be convenient for some individuals, but they are often expensive. An energy bar may be trendy and easy to stash in a book bag, but an old-fashioned peanut butter sandwich on whole-grain bread would cost less and be just as easy to carry. Overall, it is best to limit intakes of commercial sports bars and shakes so that they don't become a substitute for whole, nutritious foods.

THE TAKE-HOME MESSAGE Dietary supplements and ergogenic aids, such as creatine, caffeine, anabolic steroids, growth hormone, erythropoietin, and blood doping, may enhance performance, but can have serious health effects. Sports bars and shakes are convenient sources of energy, but are often more expensive than whole foods and should only be included as a minor part of an overall healthy diet.

Putting It All Together

Being physically active is as important to overall health as consuming adequate amounts of the macro- and micronutrients that you read about in previous chapters. Using ChooseMyPlate to make nutrient-dense food choices and understanding which foods provide the most energy will help you consume adequate energy for exercise without consuming too many kilocalories. Consuming adequate fluid is an important goal for everyone, and athletes need to be particularly aware of their hydration levels during exercise and competition.

You can use the *2008 Physical Activity Guidelines,* the FITT principle, and the Physical Activity Pyramid to help develop a conditioning program to meet your health and fitness goals. Incorporating even modest amounts of physical activity into your day will help provide some of the same benefits as a healthful diet. Maintaining a healthy weight will help reduce the risk of obesity and diabetes, and physical fitness can also ensure that "good" blood cholesterol levels are normal, which will also reduce the risk for heart disease.

Visual Chapter Summary

1 Physical Fitness Includes Five Components for Health

Physical fitness, defined as good health or physical condition, includes five basic components: cardiorespiratory endurance, muscular strength, muscular endurance, flexibility, and body composition.

2 A Successful Physical Fitness Program Uses FITT Principles

Fitness programs generally incorporate activities that are based on the five components of fitness, including aerobic exercise, resistance training, and stretching. A successful fitness program should be tailored to meet the needs of the individual and performed consistently so that any gains in fitness are maintained.

FITT is an acronym for frequency (how often), intensity (degree of difficulty or effort), time (how long), and type (specific activity). Rating of perceived exertion (RPE) is used to measure intensity for cardiorespiratory exercise, while repetition maximum (RM) measures intensity for weight training.

Minimize Sedentary Activities

2–3 days/week
Flexibility and muscular fitness

3–5 days/week
Cardiorespiratory
Moderate-high intensity

Daily
Low–moderate intensity

3 Carbohydrate, Fat, and Protein Fuel Exercise

Carbohydrate, fat, and protein are all used by the body during exercise. The source of energy needed to fuel exercise depends on the intensity and duration of the activity, and an individual's current fitness level.

The body relies heavily on anaerobic energy from ATP and creatine phosphate (PCr) during the first few minutes of exercise. As exercise continues, the body relies on aerobic production of ATP mainly from carbohydrate and fat, obtained from blood glucose and stored glycogen, and fatty acids stored in muscle tissue and free fatty acids in the blood derived from lipolysis. Fat supplies nearly all of the energy required during rest and low- to moderate-intensity activity.

Protein primarily functions to maintain, build, and repair tissues, including muscle tissue. As long as the diet is adequate in total kilocalories, carbohydrate, and fat, only small amounts of protein are used for energy during exercise.

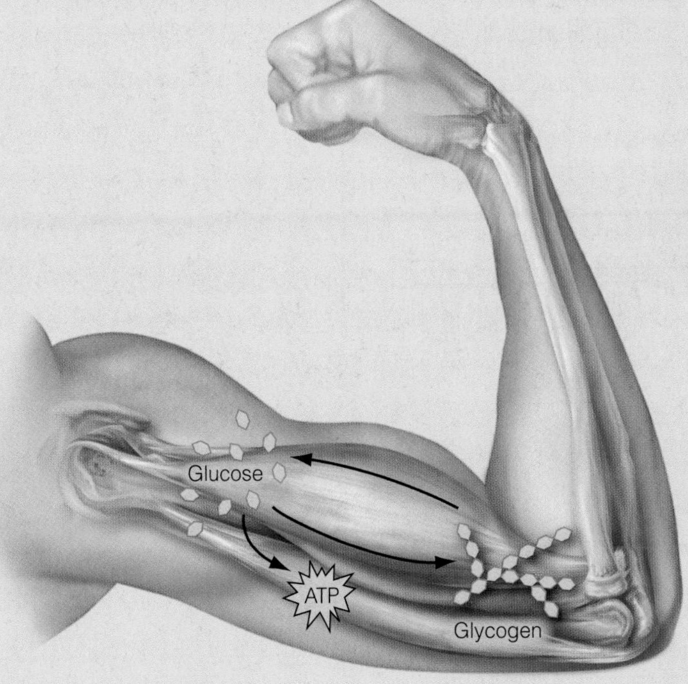

4 Timing of Meals Affects Fitness Performance

The timing of meals before, during, and after exercise impacts energy levels and recovery time. Consuming both protein and carbohydrate 1 to 4 hours before exercise produces a greater increase in muscle glycogen synthesis, promotes greater endurance, and results in greater protein synthesis after exercise is over. Consuming carbohydrate 15 to 30 minutes prior to the start of exercise gives muscles an immediate source of energy, spares glycogen stores, and protects muscles from damage.

Within the first 30 to 45 minutes post-exercise, carbohydrate helps replenish glycogen stores and stimulates muscle protein synthesis. Protein and carbohydrate after exercise results in increased muscle protein synthesis, with protein intake immediately following exercise resulting in greater muscle protein synthesis.

5 Vitamins and Minerals Assist in Energy Metabolism

Vitamins and minerals assist in energy metabolism and are necessary for fitness. Athletes do not have greater needs for vitamins and minerals than nonathletes, and intakes of vitamins and minerals above the RDA do not improve athletic performance. Supplements containing vitamins and minerals are not necessary when adequate amounts are obtained through consuming a variety of foods.

Female and vegetarian athletes are at greater risk of developing iron deficiency and should consume iron-rich foods regularly. Athletes also need to be sure their calcium intake is adequate to help reduce their risk of bone fractures during physical activity.

6 Fluid Intake Affects Fitness and Performance

Being adequately hydrated before, during, and after exercise helps maintain fluid and electrolyte balance and normal body temperature. Water is the best fluid for hydration during exercise, though sports drinks can be beneficial for moderate- to vigorous-intensity exercise. Dehydration and overhydration should both be avoided because they can be harmful to health.

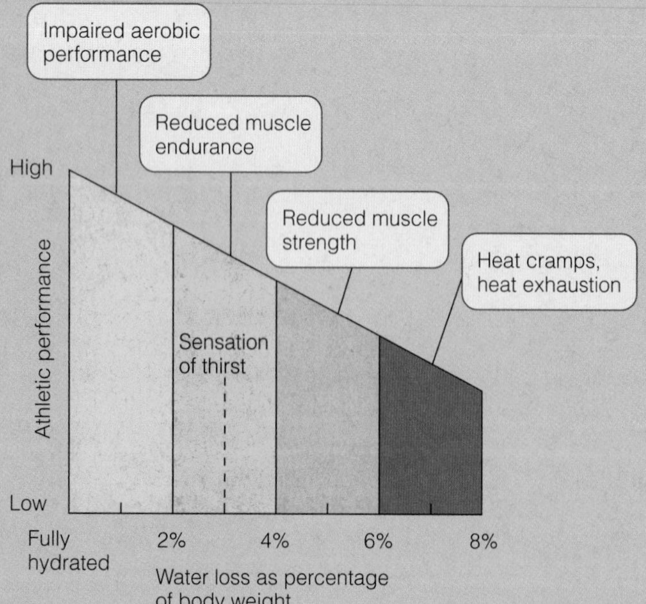

7 Some Dietary Supplements Can Contribute to Fitness

Dietary supplements and ergogenic aids are not strictly regulated for their safety and efficacy; those who choose to use them may be placing their health, and possibly their eligibility for competition, at risk. Some dietary supplements, such as creatine and caffeine, are used as ergogenic aids to improve athletic performance. Creatine has been shown to increase muscle strength and mass. Caffeine has been shown to improve endurance performance, but has not shown any benefit in activities of short duration.

Nondietary ergogenic aids are used to enhance muscle size and strength or enhance endurance. Anabolic steroids can increase muscle mass and strength, but will also cause undesirable androgenic side effects for both men and women. Growth hormone may increase muscle mass and decrease body fat, but also has serious health effects. Synthetic erythropoietin and blood doping can improve endurance, but can also thicken the blood, which may lead to a stroke or heart attack.

Terms to Know

- physical fitness
- cardiorespiratory endurance
- muscular strength
- muscular endurance
- resistance training
- flexibility
- body composition
- overexercise
- stroke volume
- VO_2max
- intensity
- repetition maximum (RM)
- rating of perceived exertion (RPE)
- duration
- progressive overload principle
- hypertrophy
- atrophy
- dehydration
- hyponatremia
- sports anemia
- amenorrhea
- hyperthermia
- hypothermia
- ergogenic aid
- acromegaly

MasteringNutrition™

Build your knowledge—and confidence—in the Study Area of MasteringNutrition with a variety of study tools.

Check Your Understanding

1. Which of the following is one of the five components of physical fitness?
   a. hydration
   b. cardiorespiratory endurance
   c. stress
   d. body mass index
2. Gradually increasing the exercise demands on the body is called
   a. cardiorespiratory endurance.
   b. VO_2 max.
   c. progressive overload.
   d. hypertrophy.
3. Well-trained muscles have the ability to store
   a. an unlimited amount of glycogen.
   b. up to 200 grams of glycogen.
   c. up to 300 grams of glycogen.
   d. up to 400 grams of glycogen.
4. The body obtains most of its energy from ______________ during low-intensity activity.
   a. muscle glycogen
   b. liver glycogen
   c. muscle protein
   d. fatty acids
5. Under what conditions will the body use significant amounts of protein for energy during exercise?
   a. inadequate kilocalorie and fluid intake
   b. inadequate carbohydrate and protein stores
   c. inadequate protein stores and fluid intake
   d. inadequate kilocalorie intake and carbohydrate stores
6. A pregame meal should be
   a. high in carbohydrate, low in fat.
   b. high in carbohydrate and high in fat.
   c. low in carbohydrate, high in fat.
   d. low in protein, high in fat.
7. A condition that occurs when too much water is consumed or too much sodium is lost in sweating, resulting in abnormally low levels of sodium in the blood, is called
   a. acute dehydration.
   b. chronic dehydration.
   c. hyponatremia.
   d. hypothermia.
8. A commercial sports drink might be beneficial because it
   a. provides electrolytes and carbohydrates, and contributes to hydration.
   b. is marketed to everyone, not just athletes.
   c. typically contains 12 to 16 percent carbohydrate.
   d. hydrates better than fruit juice and soft drinks.
9. An appropriate exercise recovery beverage would be
   a. a soft drink.
   b. coffee.
   c. low-fat chocolate milk.
   d. orange juice.
10. Acromegaly can be caused by abuse of which ergogenic aid?
    a. creatine
    b. growth hormone
    c. anabolic steroids
    d. erythropoietin

Answers

1. (b) Cardiorespiratory endurance, along with muscular strength, muscular endurance, body composition, and flexibility, are the five basic components of physical fitness. Hydration, stress, and body mass index are not components of physical fitness.
2. (c) The progressive overload principle allows an individual to improve his or her performance as the body adapts to increasingly difficult physical activity. Cardiorespiratory endurance is one aspect of physical fitness. VO_2 max is the maximum amount of oxygen a person uses in one minute, and hypertrophy is the building of new muscle mass.
3. (d) Muscles that are well trained have the ability to store about 20 to 50 percent more glycogen than normal, or up to 400 grams; however, the storage capacity of all muscle glycogen is limited.
4. (d) Fatty acids are the main source of energy during low-intensity activity. As the intensity increases, the body will use fewer fatty acids and more glycogen for energy.
5. (d) The body will use larger amounts of protein for energy if overall kilocalorie intake is inadequate and if carbohydrate stores are low. Fluid intake will not affect the use of protein for energy during exercise.
6. (a) A meal before a game or workout should be high in carbohydrate to maximize glycogen stores and low in fat to prevent feelings of fatigue or discomfort.
7. (c) Hyponatremia occurs when blood levels of sodium become abnormally low as a result of drinking too much water or not replacing sodium lost through sweating. Long-distance runners are at higher risk for developing hyponatremia. Acute and chronic dehydration are both

outcomes of consuming too little water. Hypothermia is a drop in body temperature to below normal.

8. (a) Sports drinks supply fluids to rehydrate the body during and after exercise, electrolytes to replace those lost during sweating, and carbohydrate, which acts as an immediate source of energy that can potentially improve performance. Sports drinks typically contain 6 to 8 percent carbohydrate, which makes them a better beverage for hydration than drinks that contain more carbohydrate, such as fruit juice and soft drinks.
9. (c) Low-fat chocolate milk is a good exercise recovery beverage because it contains an appropriate ratio of carbohydrate and protein that is necessary for optimal recovery. Soft drinks, coffee, and orange juice will provide the body with fluids, but lack other nutrients that are ideal for recovery after exercise.
10. (b) Abusing growth hormone causes acromegaly, a disease in which tissues, bones, and internal organs grow abnormally large in size.

Answers to Myths and Misconceptions

1. **False.** Fewer than half of all Americans meet recommendations for physical activity.
2. **True.** According to the *2008 Physical Activity Guidelines*, as little as 60 minutes of physical activity per week will bestow health benefits, including improved bone health and lowered risk of certain diseases.
3. **True.** The body does use carbohydrate, fat, and protein for energy during exercise, but the amount of each that is used partly depends on the intensity of the exercise.
4. **True.** The body prefers to use fat as its primary fuel source during low- to moderate-intensity exercise.
5. **True.** Consumption of nutrients immediately after stopping exercise will improve recovery.
6. **False.** Taking vitamin and/or mineral supplements is only beneficial if an individual is deficient in vitamins or minerals.
7. **True.** Female and vegetarian athletes in particular are at higher risk for iron deficiency.
8. **False.** Sports drinks are generally beneficial only when exercise lasts for longer than 1 hour.
9. **False.** Overhydration can dilute the blood and alter the body's delicate fluid and electrolyte balance.
10. **True.** In fact, just a few cups of coffee can supply excessive amounts of caffeine.

Web Resources

- For more information on The President's Council on Fitness, Sports, and Nutrition, visit www.fitness.gov
- For more information on exercise presented by the American Council on Exercise, visit www.acefitness.org
- For more information from the American College of Sports Medicine, www.acsm.org
- For more information on nutrition and fitness, visit the Academy of Nutrition and Dietetics, www.eatright.org
- For more information from the Sports, Cardiovascular, and Wellness Nutrition: A Dietetic Practice Group of the Academy of Nutrition and Dietetics, visit www.scandpg.org
- For more information on the National Collegiate Athletic Association, visit www.ncaa.org

References

1. Centers for Disease Control and Prevention. 2007. Prevalence of Physical Activity Among Adults—United States, 2001–2005. *Morbidity and Mortality Weekly Report* 56:1209–1212.
2. U.S. Department of Health and Human Services. 2008. *Physical Activity Guidelines for Americans.* Available at www.health.gov/paguidelines/guidelines/default.aspx#toc. Accessed June 2012.
3. Wilmore, J. H. and D. L. Costill. 2005. *Physiology of Sport and Exercise.* 3rd ed. Champaign, IL: Human Kinetics.
4. Astrand, P. and K. Rodahl. 1986. *The Textbook of Work Physiology: Physiological Bases of Exercise.* 3rd ed. New York: McGraw-Hill.
5. Brooks, G. 2002. Lactate Shuttles in Nature. *Biochemical Society Transactions* 30:258–264.
6. Romijn, J. A., E. F. Coyle, L. S. Sidossis, A. Gastaldelli, J. F. Horowitz, E. Endert, and R. R. Wolfe. 1993. Regulation of Endogenous Fat and Carbohydrate Metabolism in Relation to Exercise Intensity and Duration. *American Journal of Physiology–Endocrinology and Metabolism* 265:E380–E391.
7. Costill, D., R. Thomas, R. Robergs, D. Pascoe, C. Lambert, S. Barr, and W. Fink. 1991. Adaptations to Swimming Training: Influence of Training Volume. *Medicine & Science in Sports & Exercise* 23:371–377.
8. Sherman, W., M. Peden, and D. Wright. 1991. Carbohydrate Feeding 1 Hour Before Exercise Improves Cycling Performance. *American Journal of Clinical Nutrition* 54:866–870.
9. Coyle, E. F., A. R. Coggan, M. K. Hemmert, and J. L. Ivy. 1986. Muscle Glycogen Utilization during Prolonged Strenuous Exercise When Fed Carbohydrate. *Journal of Applied Physiology* 61:165–172.
10. Hargreaves, M. 2004. Muscle Glycogen and Metabolic Regulation. *Proceedings of the Nutrition Society* 63:217–220.
11. American College of Sports Medicine, American Dietetic Association, and Dietitians of Canada. 2000. Nutrition and Athletic Performance Joint Position Statement. *Medicine & Science in Sports & Exercise* 32:2130–2145.
12. Ibid.
13. Brownell, K. D., S. N. Steen, and J. H. Wilmore. 1987. Weight Regulation Practices in Athletes: Analysis of Metabolic and Health Effects. *Medicine & Science in Sports & Exercise* 19:546–556.
14. Horvath, P. J., C. K. Eagen, S. D. Ryer-Calvin, and D. R. Pendergast. 2000. The Effects of Varying Dietary Fat on the Nutrient Intake in Male and Female Runners. *Journal of the American College of Nutrition* 19:42–51.
15. American College of Sports Medicine, et al. 2000. Nutrition and Athletic Performance Joint Position Statement.
16. Yaspelkis, B. B., J. G. Patterson, P. A. Anderla, Z. Ding, and J. L. Ivy. 1993. Carbohydrate Supplementation Spares Muscle Glycogen during Variable-Intensity Exercise. *Journal of Applied Physiology* 75:1477–1485.
17. Coyle, E. F., J. M. Hagberg, B. F. Hurley, W. H. Martin, A. A. Ehsani, and J. O. Holloszy. 1983. Carbohydrate Feeding during Prolonged Strenuous Exercise Can Delay Fatigue. *Journal of Applied Physiology* 55:230–235.
18. Miller, S. L., K. D. Tipton, D. L. Chinkes, S. E. Wolf, and R. R. Wolfe. 2003. Independent and Combined Effects of Amino Acids and Glucose After Resistance Exercise. *Medicine & Science in Sports & Exercise* 35:449–455.

19. Koopman, R., D. L. Pannemans, A. E. Jeukendrup, A. P. Gijsen, J. M. Senden, D. Halliday, W. H. Saris, et al. 2004. Combined Ingestion of Protein and Carbohydrate Improves Protein Balance during Ultra-Endurance Exercise. *American Journal of Physiology–Endocrinology and Metabolism* 287:E712–E720.
20. Ivy, J. L., A. L. Katz, C. L. Cutler, W. M. Sherman, and E. F. Coyle. 1988. Muscle Glycogen Synthesis After Exercise: Effect of Time of Carbohydrate Ingestion. *Journal of Applied Physiology* 64:1480–1485.
21. Roy, B. D., M. A. Tarnopolsky, J. D. MacDougall, J. Fowles, and K. E. Yarasheski. 1997. Effect of Glucose Supplement Timing on Protein Metabolism After Resistance Training. *Journal of Applied Physiology* 82:1882–1888.
22. Rasmussen, B. B., K. D. Tipton, S. L. Miller, S. E. Wolf, and R. R. Wolfe. 2000. An Oral Essential Amino Acid-Carbohydrate Supplement Enhances Muscle Protein Anabolism After Resistance Exercise. *Journal of Applied Physiology* 88:386–392.
23. Zawadzki, K. M., B. B. Yaspelkis, and J. L. Ivy. 1992. Carbohydrate-Protein Complex Increases the Rate of Muscle Glycogen Storage After Exercise. *Journal of Applied Physiology* 72:1854–1859.
24. Zawadzki, K. M., et al. 1992. Carbohydrate-Protein Complex; Ivy, J. L., H. W. Goforth, B. M. Damon, T. R. McCauley, E. C. Parsons, and T. B. Price. 2002. Early Postexercise Muscle Glycogen Recovery Is Enhanced with a Carbohydrate-Protein Supplement. *Journal of Applied Physiology* 93:1337–1344.
25. Karp, J. R., J. D. Johnston, S. Tecklenburg, T. D. Mickleborough, A. D. Fly, and J. M. Stager. 2006. Chocolate Milk as a Post-Exercise Recovery Aid. *International Journal of Sport Nutrition and Exercise Metabolism* 16:78–91.
26. McAnulty, S. R., L. S. McAnulty, D. C. Nieman, J. D. Morrow, L. A. Shooter, S. Holmes, C. Heward, and D. A. Henson. 2005. Effect of Alpha-Tocopherol Supplementation on Plasma Homocysteine and Oxidative Stress in Highly Trained Athletes Before and After Exhaustive Exercise. *Journal of Nutritional Biochemistry* 16:530–537.
27. Nieman, D. C., D. A. Henson, S. R. McAnulty, L. S. McAnulty, N. S. Swick, A. C. Utter, D. M. Vinci, et al. 2002. Influence of Vitamin C Supplementation on Oxidative and Immune Changes After an Ultra-Marathon. *Journal of Applied Physiology* 92:1970–1977.
28. Dubnov, G. and N. W. Constantini. 2004. Prevalence of Iron Depletion and Anemia in Top-Level Basketball Players. *International Journal of Sport Nutrition and Exercise Metabolism* 14:30–37.
29. Gropper, S. S., D. Glessing, K. Dunham, and J. M. Barksdale. 2006. Iron Status of Female Collegiate Athletes Involved in Different Sports. *Biological Trace Element Research* 109:1–14.
30. Dubnov, G., et al., 2004. Prevalence of Iron Depletion.
31. Klesges, R. C., K. D. Ward, M. L. Shelton, W. B. Applegate, E. D. Cantler, G. M. Palmieri, K. Harmon, and J. Davis. 1996. Changes in Bone Mineral Content in Male Athletes: Mechanisms of Action and Intervention Effects. *Journal of the American Medical Association* 276:226–230.
32. Krumbach, C. J., D. R. Ellis, and J. A. Driskell. 1999. A Report of Vitamin and Mineral Supplement Use Among University Athletes in a Division I Institution. *International Journal of Sport Nutrition and Exercise Metabolism* 9:416–425.
33. Herbold, N. H., B. K. Visconti, S. Frates, and L. Bandini. 2004. Traditional and Nontraditional Supplement Use by Collegiate Female Varsity Athletes. *International Journal of Sport Nutrition and Exercise Metabolism* 14: 586–593.
34. Singh, A., F. M. Moses, and P. A. Deuster. 1992. Chronic Multivitamin-Mineral Supplementation Does Not Enhance Physical Performance. *Medicine & Science in Sports & Exercise* 24:726–732.
35. Rosenbloom, C., ed. 2000. *Sports Nutrition: A Practice Manual for the Professional Working with Active People.* Chicago: IL: The American Dietetic Association
36. Wilk, B. and O. Bar-Or. 1996. Effect of Drink Flavor and NaCl on Voluntary Drinking and Hydration in Boys Exercising in the Heat. *Journal of Applied Physiology* 80:1112–1117.
37. American College of Sports Medicine. 1996. Position Stand on Exercise and Fluid Replacement. *Medicine & Science in Sports & Exercise* 28:i–vii.
38. McGee, W. 2005. *Caffeine in the Diet.* National Institutes of Health Medline Plus Medical Encyclopedia. Available at www.nlm.nih.gov/medlineplus/ency/article/002445.htm. Accessed June 2012.
39. USA Track & Field. Press Release April 19, 2003. *USATF Announces Major Change in Hydration Guidelines.* Available at www.usatf.org/news/showRelease.asp?article=/news/releases/2003-04-19-2.xml. Accessed June 2012.
40. Greenhaff, P. L., A. Casey, A. H. Short, R. Harris, K. Söderlund, and E. Hultman. 1993. Influence of Oral Creatine Supplementation on Muscle Torque during Repeated Bouts of Maximal Voluntary Exercise in Man. *Clinical Science* 84:565–571.
41. Vandenberghe, K., M. Goris, P. Van Hecke, M. Van Leemputte, L. Vangerven, and P. Hespel. 1997. Long-Term Creatine Intake Is Beneficial to Muscle Performance during Resistance Training. *Journal of Applied Physiology* 83:2055–2063.
42. Kreider, R. B., M. Ferreira, M. Wilson, P. Grindstaff, S. Plisk, J. Reinardy, E. Cantler, and A. L. Almada. 1998. Effects of Creatine Supplementation on Body Composition, Strength, and Sprint Performance. *Medicine & Science in Sports & Exercise* 30:73–82.
43. Mayhew, D. L., J. L. Mayhew, and J. S. Ware. 2002. Effects of Long-Term Creatine Supplementation on Liver and Kidney Functions in American College Football Players. *International Journal of Sport Nutrition and Exercise Metabolism* 12:453–460.
44. Kreider, R. B., C. Melton, C. J. Rasmussen, M. Greenwood, S. Lancaster, E. C. Cantler, P. Milnor, and A. L. Almada. 2003. Long-Term Creatine Supplementation Does Not Significantly Affect Clinical Markers of Health in Athletes. *Molecular and Cellular Biochemistry* 244:95–104.
45. Wiles, J. D., S. R. Bird, J. Hopkins, and M. Riley. 1992. Effect of Caffeinated Coffee on Running Speed, Respiratory Factors, Blood Lactate, and Perceived Exertion during 1500-Meter Treadmill Running. *British Journal of Sports Medicine* 26:116–120.
46. Spriet, L. L., D. A. MacLean, D. J. Dyck, E. Hultman, G. Cederblad, and T. E. Graham. 1992. Caffeine Ingestion and Muscle Metabolism during Prolonged Exercise in Humans. *American Journal of Physiology–Endocrinology and Metabolism* 262:E891–E898.
47. Paton, C. D., W. G. Hopkins, and L. Vollebregt. 2001. Little Effect of Caffeine Ingestion on Repeated Sprints in Team-Sport Athletes. *Medicine & Science in Sports & Exercise* 33:822–825.
48. Crist, D. M., G. T. Peake, P. A. Egan, and D. L. Waters. 1988. Body Composition Responses to Exogenous GH during Training in Highly Conditioned Adults. *Journal of Applied Physiology* 65:579–584.
49. Foss, M. and S. Keteyian. 1998. *Physiological Basis for Exercise and Sport.* 6th ed. Boston: McGraw-Hill, 498.
50. Deyssig, R., H. Frisch, W. Blum, and T. Waldorf. 1993. Effect of Growth Hormone Treatment on Hormonal Parameters, Body Composition, and Strength in Athletes. *Acta Endocrinologica* 128:313–318.
51. Lange, K., J. Andersen, N. Beyer, F. Isaksson, B. Larsson, M. Rasmussen, A. Juul, et al. 2002. GH Administration Changes Myosin Heavy Chain Isoforms in Skeletal Muscle but Does Not Augment Muscle Strength or Hypertrophy, Either Alone or Combined with Resistance Exercise Training in Healthy Elderly Men. *Journal of Clinical Endocrinology & Metabolism* 87:513–523.
52. Woodhouse, L. J., S. L. Asa, S. G. Thomas, and S. Ezzat. 1999. Measures of Submaximal Aerobic Performance Evaluate and Predict Functional Response to Growth Hormone (GH) Treatment of GH-Deficient Adults. *Journal of Clinical Endocrinology & Metabolism* 84:4570–4577.
53. Ekblom, B. and B. Berglund. 1991. Effect of Erythropoietin Administration on Maximal Aerobic Power. *Scandinavian Journal of Medicine and Science in Sports* 1:88–93.

17 Life Cycle Nutrition

Pregnancy through Infancy

Chapter Objectives

After reading this chapter, you will be able to:

1. Describe the stages of pregnancy and some possible risks to fetal development.
2. Discuss the key diet and lifestyle factors associated with a successful pregnancy.
3. Identify key nutrient needs for women and potential complications in the first trimester of pregnancy.
4. Identify key nutrient needs for women and potential complications in the second trimester of pregnancy.
5. Identify key nutrient needs for women and potential complications in the third trimester of pregnancy.
6. List special concerns of younger, older, and low-income mothers-to-be.
7. Describe the benefits of breast-feeding.
8. Explain why formula is a healthy alternative to breast milk.
9. Discuss the nutritional needs of infants.
10. Explain when and how solid foods may be introduced to infants.

1. A father's health has no impact on the health of a developing fetus. T/F
2. Drinking red wine is fine during pregnancy. T/F
3. Morning sickness only happens between 8 a.m. and noon during the first trimester. T/F
4. Pregnant women shouldn't exercise. T/F
5. Formula is better for babies than breast milk. T/F
6. Breast milk helps boost a baby's immune system. T/F
7. Chubby babies should be put on diets. T/F
8. Infants never need supplements. T/F
9. Commercially sold baby food is always less healthy than homemade. T/F
10. Raw carrots are a great way for an infant to get vitamin A. T/F

See page 663 for answers to these Myths and Misconceptions.

When a woman is pregnant, her body facilitates the division, growth, and specialization of millions of new cells in her developing child. The raw materials for this rapid growth are provided by the nutrients she consumes in foods. Her diet, then, must not only maintain her own health, but also foster and maintain the health of her baby.

Even before a woman becomes pregnant, she can do a variety of things to give her baby the best chance for a healthy beginning to life. In fact, before conception the father's nutrition and lifestyle can also have a positive impact on the pregnancy.

In this chapter, we will explore the specific nutrient requirements that a pregnant woman needs to ensure a healthy pregnancy. We'll also explore the diet and lifestyle factors in both the mother and father that can help ensure successful conception and healthy fetal development, as well as the nutritional needs and concerns of infants in their first year of life. Let's begin by reviewing the stages of pregnancy and the mechanisms that allow the developing child to obtain nutrients from the mother.

What Are the Critical Periods of Prenatal Development?

A full-term pregnancy averages 38 weeks from **conception** to birth, and is divided into three roughly equal 13-week trimesters (*tri* = three, *mester* = month). Prenatal development is divided into the embryonic and fetal periods. Many important physiological changes occur during the first weeks of pregnancy, even before a woman knows she is pregnant.

The Placenta Plays a Key Role

The initial two weeks after conception is called the preembryo period, during which the fertilized egg, or **zygote,** travels down the fallopian tube to embed itself in the lining of the woman's uterus (**Figure 17.1**). Once attached, the zygote immediately begins obtaining nutrients from the mother. This enables both the fertilized egg (soon to be called an **embryo**) and the placenta to develop. The **placenta** is the site of common tissue between the mother and the embryo where nutrients, oxygen, and waste products are exchanged through the **umbilical cord** (**Figure 17.2**). Although maternal and fetal blood do not actually mix, due to the double lining of cells in the placenta, this tissue allows the embryo to make use of the mother's mature organ systems to perform physiological functions for it while it is developing.

The placenta prevents the passage of red blood cells, bacteria, and many large proteins from mother to fetus. However, potentially harmful substances, such as alcohol and drugs, can cross the placenta to the fetus. The placenta also releases hormones required to support the physiological changes of pregnancy, including the hormones that trigger labor and delivery.

Eight weeks after conception, the developing embryo is called a **fetus.** As the fetus develops, the mother's diet and lifestyle habits continue to be critical in supporting and nurturing it.

conception The moment when a sperm fertilizes an egg.

zygote A fertilized egg during the first two weeks after conception.

embryo A fertilized egg during the third through the eighth week of pregnancy.

placenta The organ that allows nutrients, oxygen, and waste products to be exchanged between a mother and fetus.

umbilical cord The cord connecting the fetus to the placenta.

fetus A developing embryo that is at least eight weeks old.

critical periods Developmental stages during which cells and tissue rapidly grow and differentiate to form body structures.

Critical Periods Impact Fetal Development

Growth and development of the embryo and fetus follow predetermined paths. Cells multiply, differentiate, and establish functional tissues and organs during various **critical periods** in the first trimester of pregnancy (**Figure 17.3**). These periods of rapid cellular activity are highly vulnerable to nutritional deficiencies, toxins, and other potentially harmful factors (or *insults*).

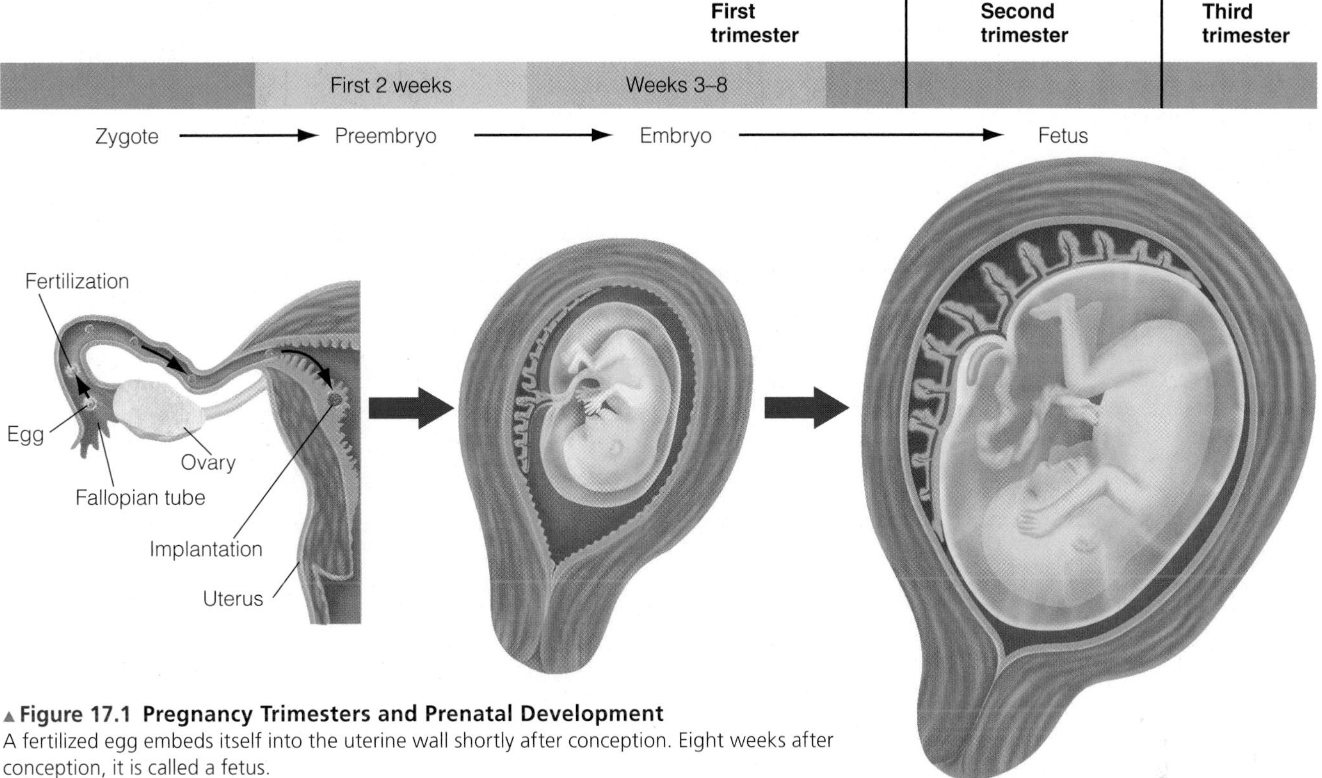

▲ **Figure 17.1 Pregnancy Trimesters and Prenatal Development**
A fertilized egg embeds itself into the uterine wall shortly after conception. Eight weeks after conception, it is called a fetus.

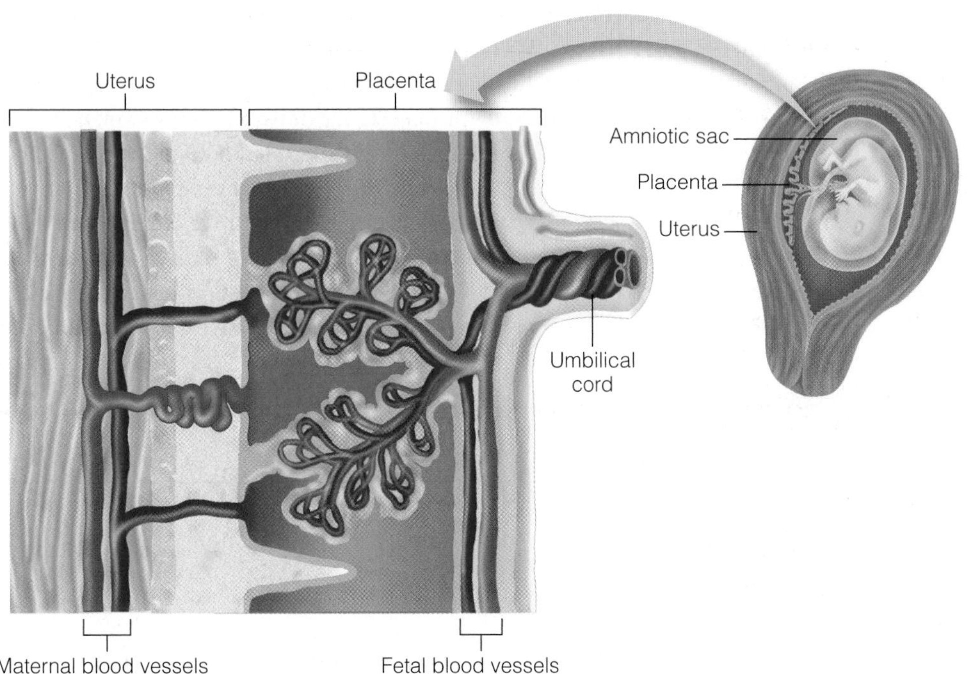

▲ **Figure 17.2 The Placenta**
The placenta is the site of common tissue between the mother and the embryo where nutrients, oxygen, and waste products are exchanged through the umbilical cord. The maternal blood vessels exchange nutrients and oxygen with the fetal vessels, and the fetal vessels deliver waste products for the maternal blood to carry away for excretion. Note that while substances diffuse between the two circulatory systems, no mixing of maternal and fetal blood occurs.

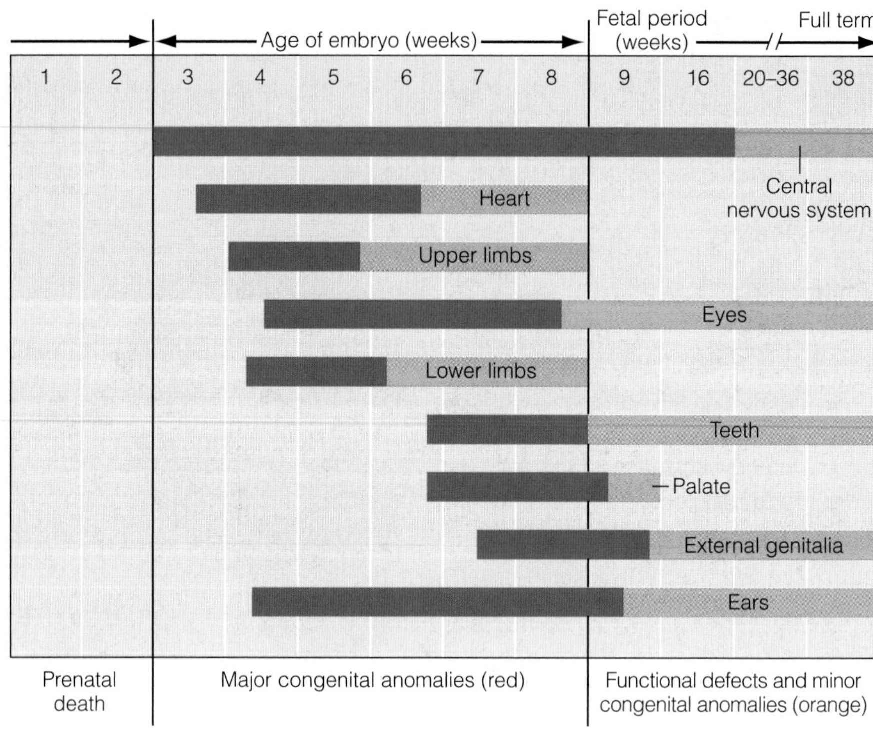

▲ **Figure 17.3 Prenatal Development**
The damage caused by toxins or lack of nutrients during pregnancy can vary according to the stage of fetal development. Damage done during critical periods may be irreversible.

The harm that results from the influence of a toxin or deficiency during a critical period is often irreversible, and can impact future developmental stages. For example, persons conceived during periods of famine have a higher cumulative incidence of heart disease, and the disease occurs at an earlier age (see Table 17.1). Both micronutrient and macronutrient malnutrition may contribute to the onset of heart disease.[1] Suboptimal fetal growth may set an individual up for, or have programming effects on, hypertension, impaired glucose tolerance, and lipid metabolism later in life. Inadequate iron intake in early pregnancy during the critical period for the central nervous system may cause poor cognitive development.[2]

In contrast, optimal maternal nutrition during critical periods of pregnancy may prevent or delay a child's risk of chronic diseases, such as heart disease and diabetes, later in life. There is growing evidence that maternal nutrition can alter

TABLE 17.1 Increased Risks from Exposure to Famine during Gestation

First Trimester	Second Trimester	Third Trimester
Glucose intolerance	Glucose intolerance	Glucose intolerance
Blood lipid profile associated with atherosclerosis	Kidney disease	
Coronary heart disease	Obstructive lung disease	
Stress sensitivity		
Obesity (women only)		
Breast cancer		

Data from "The Dutch Famine and its Long-Term Consequences for Adult Health" by T. Roseboom, S. de Rooj, and R Painter. EARLY HUMAN DEVELOPMENT.

how genes are expressed, and adverse events during critical periods of gestation can persist into adulthood.[3] This phenomenon is part of an emerging area of research into **metabolic or fetal programming.** The relationship between maternal nutrition, metabolic programming, and adult-onset chronic disease is supported by studies that show that inadequate nutrient intake during pregnancy predisposes the child to metabolic diseases in adulthood.[4] These impacts may even affect the child's future children.

THE TAKE-HOME MESSAGE A healthy pregnancy lasts about 38 weeks and is divided into three trimesters. The placenta is the site through which oxygen, nutrients, and waste products are exchanged, though the maternal and fetal blood supplies do not mix. Toxins, insufficient nutrients, and other harmful factors can cause irreversible damage to the fetus, especially during critical periods. Metabolic programming for future risk of disease begins early and varies with exposure during different critical periods.

What Nutrients and Behaviors Are Most Important for a Healthy Pregnancy?

Some dietary and lifestyle changes that a woman should make during a pregnancy are obvious. For instance, many people know that women who smoke or drink alcohol while pregnant are gambling with their child's health. However, in order to support a healthy pregnancy, some changes should be adopted pre-conception. In addition, a father-to-be's pre-conception diet and behaviors can impact the health of a prospective pregnancy.

Prospective Fathers Should Adopt a Healthy Lifestyle

To improve the outcome of a pregnancy, both women and men need to consider dietary and lifestyle changes. Men take note: A man's lifestyle and diet habits may affect his fertility. Smoking, alcohol and drug abuse, and obesity have been associated with decreased production and function of sperm.[5,6] In contrast, zinc and folate have both been associated with the production of healthy sperm, and antioxidants—such as vitamins E and C and carotenoids—may help protect sperm from damage by free radicals.[7]

Men should consume a well-balanced diet that contains adequate amounts of fruits and vegetables (for antioxidants and folate), as well as whole grains, lean meats and dairy foods, legumes, and nuts (for zinc).[8] Stopping smoking, abstaining from alcohol or drinking only in moderation, and striving for a healthy body weight are all beneficial. A healthy baby is the product of two healthy parents, so fathers-to-be who make appropriate diet and lifestyle changes prior to conception help ensure the health of their offspring.

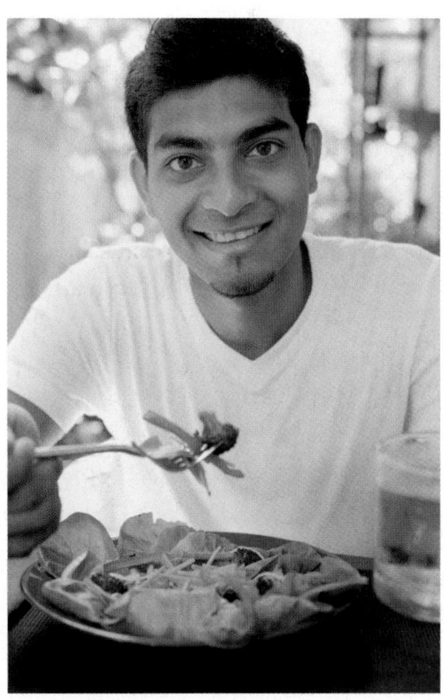

Prospective fathers need to be aware of their diet habits prior to conception.

Before and During Pregnancy, Mothers Should Adopt a Healthy Lifestyle

Anyone who has run a marathon, or known someone who has, knows that a tremendous amount of effort and diligence goes into training for the event. The commitment doesn't begin on the day of the race, but as far as a year in advance. In fact, the more time and effort the runner puts into preparing for the race, the better the results are likely to be.

metabolic or fetal programming The process by which the prenatal environment interacts with genetic and other factors to produce permanent change.

Ask any woman who has had a baby and she will tell you that planning for, carrying, and delivering a healthy child was the marathon of her life. Attaining a healthy weight, eating a healthy diet, and changing unhealthy lifestyle habits are extremely important parts of prepregnancy and pregnancy.

Attain a Healthy Weight

Women who want to get pregnant should strive for a healthy weight *before* conception. Women who begin pregnancy at a healthy weight are likely to conceive more easily, have an uncomplicated pregnancy, and have an easier time nursing the baby.[9]

In contrast, overweight or obese women may have a harder time getting pregnant, possibly due to irregular menstrual cycles. When they do become pregnant, they are at increased risk of hypertension and gestational diabetes.[10] They also have a greater chance of requiring an induced labor or a cesarean section.[11] Hypertension during pregnancy increases the risk of dying for both mother and baby.[12,13,14] Children born to overweight or obese women are at greater risk of being born larger than normal, and of having more difficulties breathing, a slower heart rate, and potential heart defects and certain birth defects. These babies are also at a higher risk of developing childhood obesity,[15] and later in life, heart disease and diabetes.[16]

Overweight or obese women should consider shedding some excess weight prior to conception to improve the chances of a healthier pregnancy and baby. Once an overweight or obese woman becomes pregnant, she should focus on moderating her weight gain, rather than trying to lose weight. A woman, whether at a healthy weight, overweight, or obese, should never try to lose weight during pregnancy.

Underweight women also need to strive for a healthy weight before getting pregnant. A woman who is underweight has a lighter weight placenta, which can interfere with her body's ability to deliver nutrients to the fetus. With less nutrition available, there is an increased risk of delivering a **low birth weight** baby weighing less than 5 ½ pounds. A low birth weight baby is usually premature, and is at a higher risk of health problems, including developmental disabilities, lung disease, and dying within the first year of life, than an infant born at a healthy weight.

Underweight mothers are also at higher risk for delivering **small for gestational age (SGA)** babies, who are born full term but weigh less than the 10th percentile of weight for gestational age. Although some babies are small because of genetics (their parents are small), most SGA babies are small because of fetal growth problems that occur during pregnancy. The fetus may not have received the nutrients and oxygen needed for proper growth and development of organs and tissues.

Get Plenty of Folic Acid

Folic acid is needed to create new cells and help the baby grow and develop properly. Consuming the DRI of folic acid beginning one month prior to conception and continuing through the early weeks of pregnancy has been shown to reduce the risk of neural tube birth defects (such as anencephaly and spina bifida, discussed in Chapter 10) in infants. These birth defects originate during a critical period for development of the nervous system, typically three to four weeks after conception—a time when few women even know that they are pregnant. For this reason, women who are capable of becoming pregnant and planning to conceive should consume 400 micrograms of folic acid daily through supplements or fortified foods (see Chapter 10). Women who have previously delivered a baby with a neural tube defect should consult with their health care provider, as they may benefit from an even higher dose of the vitamin.

low birth weight Describes a baby weighing less than 5 ½ pounds at birth.

small for gestational age (SGA) Term for babies who weigh less than the 10th percentile of weight for gestational age.

TABLE 17.2 Fish Intake during Pregnancy

Pregnant and nursing women and women of childbearing age who may become pregnant should follow these guidelines for eating fish.

Do Not Eat	Limit	Enjoy
Shark Swordfish King mackerel Tilefish (golden bass or golden snapper)	Albacore (white) tuna to no more than 6 oz weekly Locally caught fish from nearby lakes, rivers, and coastal areas. Check local advisories regarding its safety before consuming it. If no advice is available for a particular species, eat up to 6 oz weekly. Don't consume any other fish during that week.	Up to 12 oz weekly of fish with low levels of methylmercury, such as: Canned light tuna Cod Catfish Crab Pollack Salmon Scallops Shrimp

Moderate Fish Consumption

Recall from Chapter 5 that the Food and Drug Administration (FDA) recommends that women of childbearing age who may become pregnant, those pregnant and nursing, and young children should avoid certain fish that may contain high amounts of the toxin *methylmercury*. This form of mercury can harm the nervous system of the developing fetus, especially during the first trimester of pregnancy. All fish contain some methylmercury; Table 17.2 summarizes the fish consumption guidelines for prepregnant, pregnant, and lactating women.

Consume Only a Moderate Amount of Caffeine

Some studies have investigated whether caffeine consumption affects a woman's fertility. Research suggests that consuming 500 milligrams or more of caffeine daily may delay conception.[17] Though the mechanism by which caffeine affects fertility is unknown, to be safe, women who are trying to get pregnant should consume less than 200 milligrams of caffeine per day, and women who are already pregnant should limit their intake to no more than 150 milligrams per day. This means limiting coffee, tea, and soda to a cup or two a day—or better yet, switching to decaffeinated versions of these drinks. See Table 17.3 for the caffeine content in several common dietary sources.

During pregnancy, the caffeine that a woman drinks in her coffee or soda can be passed on to her baby (as can anything else she consumes). Because the fetus cannot break down caffeine, it may linger in his or her body longer than in the mother's. For these reasons, questions have been raised regarding the safety of caffeine consumption during pregnancy. Research studies to date support that caffeine intake of less than 150 milligrams daily, or the amount in 12 ounces of coffee, doesn't increase the risk of miscarriage or birth defects during pregnancy. However, research has also shown that women who consumed 200 milligrams or more of caffeine daily (two or more cups of regular coffee or five 12-ounce cans of caffeinated soda) had twice the miscarriage risk of women who consumed no caffeine. The increased risk appeared to be due to the caffeine itself, rather than other chemicals in coffee, as caffeine intake from noncoffee sources such as caffeinated soda, tea, and hot chocolate showed a similar increased risk of miscarriage. Researchers suggest that caffeine may interfere with cell development and decrease placental blood flow.[18] Smoking or drinking alcohol in addition to consuming too much caffeine further increases the risk of miscarriage.

TABLE 17.3 Common Sources of Caffeine

Beverage	Caffeine (mg)
Coffee (8 oz)	
Brewed, drip	85
Brewed, decaffeinated	3
Espresso (1 oz)	40
Tea (8 oz)	
Brewed	40
Iced	25
Soft drinks (8 oz)	24
Energy drinks (8 oz)	80
Hot cocoa (8 oz)	6
Chocolate milk (8 oz)	5
Milk chocolate (1 oz)	6

Data from National Toxicology Program, Department of Health and Human Services, http://ntp.niehs.nih.gov; International Food Information Council (IFIC), www.foodinsight.org.

Smoking during pregnancy can seriously harm the fetus.

Avoid Cigarettes

Cigarette smoking increases the risk of infertility, making conception more difficult.[19] When a smoker does conceive and continues to smoke during her pregnancy, her infant will weigh a half pound less, on average, than infants of nonsmokers and will be at an increased risk of being born prematurely or dying. Prenatal exposure to smoke can increase the risk of **sudden infant death syndrome (SIDS)** and may stunt the infant's growth and reduce future intellectual and behavioral performance.[20] Though there are thousands of substances in cigarettes and cigarette smoke that can harm the fetus, carbon monoxide and nicotine are particularly dangerous because they reduce the amount of oxygen that reaches the baby, thus intensifying adverse effects.

Pregnant women who smoke often weigh less and gain less weight during pregnancy than nonsmokers, which can contribute to a low birth weight baby. Women who smoke do not necessarily consume fewer kilocalories, but may have an increased metabolic rate. The higher metabolic rate of the pregnant smoker burns kilocalories before the baby can use them. This robs the baby of the kilocalories needed to develop properly and contributes to a lower birth weight.[21]

Even secondhand smoke can affect the health of a mom-to-be and her infant. Exposure to passive smoke can affect the infant's ability to grow properly.[22] Thus, pregnant women and new mothers should avoid work, home, or social environments where they are exposed to secondhand smoke.

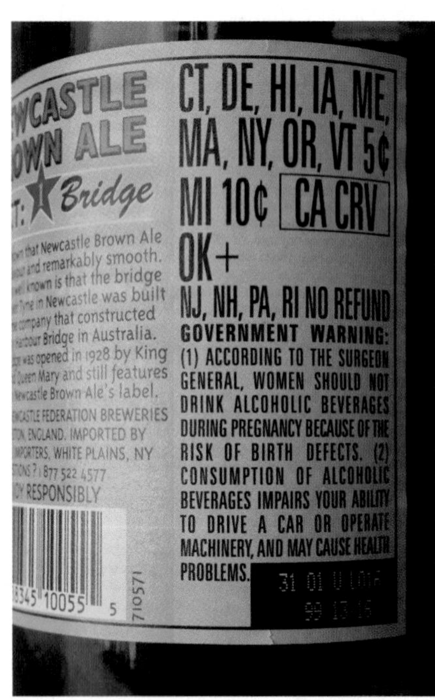

As with smoking, drinking alcohol during pregnancy exposes the fetus to potentially toxic substances. Alcohol labels and cigarette packages are required by law to display the Surgeon General's warning about these dangers.

sudden infant death syndrome (SIDS) The unexplained death of an infant at less than 1 year of age.

botanicals A part of a plant, such as its root, that is believed to have medicinal or therapeutic attributes.

Don't Drink Alcohol

Because alcohol can affect a baby within weeks after conception, before a woman is aware that she is pregnant, the Surgeon General recommends that all women who may become pregnant abstain from alcohol.[23] As you read in Chapter 7, drinking alcohol during pregnancy can lead to fetal alcohol spectrum disorders (FASDs) in the baby. Children exposed to even low levels of alcohol during pregnancy can be born with learning and behavioral disabilities. Because there is no known safe level of alcohol consumption, pregnant women need to abstain completely to eliminate the chance of having a baby with these disorders.

Avoid Illicit Drugs

Smoking marijuana can reduce fertility in both males and females. When used during pregnancy, illicit drugs can increase the risk of miscarriage, preterm labor, a low birth weight baby, and birth defects, which means that the estimated 4.5 percent of pregnant women who use marijuana, cocaine, Ecstasy, and heroin are putting their unborn children at major risk.[24] After birth, the baby may experience drug withdrawal symptoms, such as excessive crying, trembling, and seizures, as well as long-term health problems such as heart defects and behavioral and learning problems.

Women who use these substances should speak with their health care provider about how to stop their habits. They can also visit the National Drug and Alcohol Treatment Referral Routing Service at www.niaaa.nih.gov or phone 1-800-662-HELP (4357).

Avoid Botanicals

Whereas many pregnant women won't even consider taking over-the-counter drugs without clearance from their health care provider, they often don't have the same level of caution when it comes to taking botanical products. **Botanicals** are plants (including herbs) or parts of a plant that are believed to have medicinal effects. Because these products are perceived to be "natural," people often assume they can take them without risk. Many people even consider them safer than over-the-counter drugs. In fact, this isn't always true, and in some cases, botanicals can be harmful or even dangerous.

Blue cohosh, for example, is an herb that is sometimes used to induce labor, but has been associated with seizures, strokes,[25] and heart attacks[26] in newborns. In addition to blue cohosh, other supplements, such as juniper, pennyroyal, goldenseal, and thuja, as well as teas such as raspberry tea, may also cause contractions of the uterus, which can lead to a miscarriage or premature labor.

Green tea, believed by many to be healthy due to its antioxidant content, contains a compound that inhibits folic acid, and may therefore increase risk of neural tube defects.[27, 28] Pregnant women should avoid green tea for this reason. In fact, the American Academy of Pediatrics (AAP) recommends that pregnant women limit herbal teas in general to two 8-ounce cups daily and choose teas contained in filter bags (rather than loose leaf).[29, 30]

Few research studies have been conducted on the safety and effectiveness of botanical products during pregnancy. Pregnant women should assume that all herbs and botanical supplements are unsafe and should always check with their health care provider before consuming them.

Manage Chronic Conditions

Chronic conditions such as diabetes, hypertension, and phenylketonuria (PKU) can have a negative effect on the outcome of a pregnancy and therefore must be successfully managed *before* a woman conceives.

Women with diabetes mellitus may not be aware that the disorder increases the risk of maternal and fetal complications. High blood glucose levels during the first two months of pregnancy are associated with congenital abnormalities in the newborn, such as malformations of the pelvis, central nervous system, and heart. A higher rate of miscarriages may occur. Optimal blood glucose control can help ensure a successful pregnancy. Medications used by women with diabetes should be evaluated before conception, as drugs commonly used to treat diabetes and its complications may be contraindicated or not recommended during pregnancy.[31]

Women with preexisting, or chronic, high blood pressure are more likely to have certain complications during pregnancy than those with normal blood pressure. High blood pressure can harm the mother's kidneys and other organs, and it can cause low birth weight and early delivery.

Women with PKU can have healthy children as long as they are aware of and maintain strict adherence to their low-phenylalanine diet throughout their pregnancy. Women with poorly controlled PKU during a pregnancy put their baby at risk for delayed development, mental retardation, poor growth, heart defects, and other structural birth defects.

Women with chronic diseases who are contemplating pregnancy would benefit from prepregnancy counseling. Dietary counseling is important before and throughout pregnancy and the postpartum (after delivery) period.

THE TAKE-HOME MESSAGE Good nutrition and healthy lifestyle habits are important for both men and women before conception. Smoking, alcohol abuse, and obesity are associated with decreased production and function of sperm. Conception is easier for women when they are at a healthy weight. Women should consume adequate amounts of folic acid prior to getting pregnant and continue to take it during pregnancy. Women should also avoid fish that may contain high amounts of methylmercury, and consume caffeine only in moderation. Smoking, drinking alcohol, taking recreational drugs, and taking botanicals should be avoided. All preexisting medical conditions should be addressed prior to conception. Proper nutrition and a healthy lifestyle can prevent birth defects and may reduce future health risks.

Self-Assessment

Are You Ready for a Healthy Pregnancy?

Both men and women should have healthy habits before becoming parents. Take the following self-assessment to see if you need some diet and lifestyle fine-tuning before trying to get pregnant.

For Both Men and Women

1. Are you overweight?
   Yes ☐ **No** ☐
2. Do you smoke?
   Yes ☐ **No** ☐
3. Do you abuse alcohol?
   Yes ☐ **No** ☐
4. Do you use any illicit drugs such as marijuana, cocaine, and/or Ecstasy?
   Yes ☐ **No** ☐

Additional Questions for Women Only

1. Do you drink alcohol?
   Yes ☐ **No** ☐
2. Do you take herbs or use herbal teas?
   Yes ☐ **No** ☐
3. Do you drink more than 12 ounces of caffeinated coffee or energy drinks or four cans of caffeinated soft drinks daily?
   Yes ☐ **No** ☐
4. Do you eat albacore tuna, swordfish, mackerel, tilefish, and/or shark?
   Yes ☐ **No** ☐
5. Do you consume less than 400 micrograms of folic acid daily?
   Yes ☐ **No** ☐

Answers

If you answered yes to any of these questions, review the previous section to find out how these diet and lifestyle habits can impact a pregnancy.

What Nutrients and Behaviors Are Important in the First Trimester?

During the first trimester, the fetus achieves numerous developmental milestones: Organs are beginning to develop and function. The liver begins to form red blood cells, the heart begins beating, the limbs are taking shape, and the brain is growing rapidly. In fact at this time, the head is much larger than the body to accommodate the rapidly developing brain. In spite of all this activity, the fetus still weighs just a half ounce and measures only about three inches long. It has a *lot* more growing to do before being born.

Physiological Changes Occur in the Mother

The mother's body is also changing rapidly. Her breasts may be tender, and she may start to experience several "side effects" of pregnancy, such as a newly heightened sense of taste or smell, and seemingly random food cravings. She may also experience "morning sickness," or nausea, which is so common that women and health care professionals often use it as an initial sign of possible pregnancy.[32]

Morning Sickness

One of the biggest myths of pregnancy is that morning sickness occurs in the morning. Ask any of the 80 percent of women who experience nausea and vomiting during pregnancy, and many will tell you that they certainly wished their symptoms ended by noon. However, it can occur at any time of the day. Morning sickness usually begins during the first trimester and often ends by the twentieth week of pregnancy, although about 10 percent of women experience it longer.[33] The causes of morning sickness are unknown, but lower blood sugar during early pregnancy or fluctuating hormone levels, particularly the increase in estrogen, may play a role.[34] Estrogen heightens a woman's perception of odors (experts sometimes refer to this as the "radar nose" of pregnancy), which leads to nausea and can trigger vomiting.[35] The presence of *Helicobacter pylori* bacteria in the digestive tract has also been associated with morning sickness.[36] Emotional stress or traveling can aggravate the problem.

Though there are no known dietary deficiencies that cause morning sickness or diet changes that can prevent it, some women find relief in eating small, frequent meals that are high in carbohydrates such as pasta, rice, and crackers, and avoiding an empty stomach. Salty foods such as potato chips combined with sour and tart beverages such as lemonade have been shown to help.[37] Vitamin B_6 may also reduce the nausea and vomiting. Because there is an upper limit for vitamin B_6 intake, pregnant women should consult their health care professional before increasing it.

Ginger has also been shown to help, which explains why some pregnant women find relief in drinking ginger ale. However, ginger root may inhibit a specific enzyme in the body, causing potentially adverse effects, including interfering with blood clotting.[38] As with vitamin B_6, pregnant women should not consume ginger supplements or extracts without first consulting their health care provider.

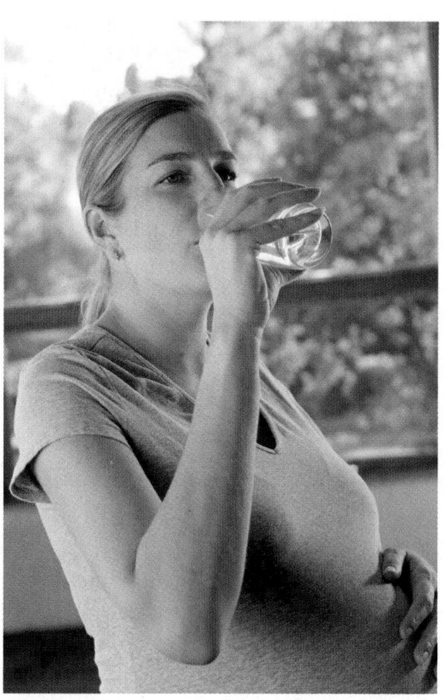

Ginger ale can help alleviate morning sickness for some women.

Though morning sickness is uncomfortable, it usually does not harm the health of the woman or her fetus. However, in rare cases (less than 1 percent of pregnancies) some women experience the more severe **hyperemesis gravidarum** (*hyper* = overstimulated, *emesis* = vomiting, *gravida* = pregnant), which can cause serious complications, such as dehydration, electrolyte imbalances, and weight loss. Women with hyperemesis gravidarum often have to be hospitalized for treatment.

The loss of appetite that often accompanies nausea can be harmful if it causes the mother to reduce her intake of nutritious foods. Whereas avoiding coffee, tea, or fried or spicy foods (common aversions for pregnant women) is fine, limiting consumption of fruits, vegetables, or whole grains may lead to malnutrition. When the fetus does not receive adequate nutrients during pregnancy, overall tissue and organ growth is limited.

hyperemesis gravidarum Excessive vomiting during pregnancy that can lead to dehydration and loss of electrolytes.

Cravings

While some pregnant women have an aversion to certain foods, other women can have cravings for specific foods. Chocolate, citrus fruits, pickles, chips, and ice cream are foods that women commonly report craving when they are pregnant.[39] Research has not found a physiological explanation for these cravings; for example, women who crave ice cream are not necessarily deficient in calcium. There is no harm in occasionally indulging food cravings in moderation.

There is potential harm, though, when women crave and consume nonfood substances. **Pica** is the abnormal, compulsive intake of nonedible items such as laundry starch, burnt matches, cornstarch, clay, dirt, paint chips, or baking soda. Pica is more common in African-American women and those with a family history of this type of eating. Pica has been associated with low blood levels of iron, which has led to the theory that these women are seeking out nonfood substances that contain this mineral.[40] However, other research suggests that pica *causes* the iron deficiency seen in these women.[41] Consuming nonfood substances can lead to the ingestion of toxic compounds, such as lead, that could lead to lead poisoning and other ill effects in both the mother and the baby.[42]

Set Goals for Adequate Weight Gain

Healthy women gain, on average, 27.5 pounds during pregnancy (**Figure 17.4**).[43] The fetus comprises about a third of the total weight gained, and the rest is maternal tissues. Not coincidentally, this is the approximate amount of weight that is needed to support the growth of the baby. Because a woman's prepregnancy weight can impact the health of the growing baby, women at a healthy weight (with a BMI between 18.5 and 24.9) should gain 25 to 35 pounds, whereas underweight or overweight women have slightly different goals (see Table 17.4). These recommendations are based on striking a balance between the baby's and the mother's health. Healthy weight gain provides for adequate growth so that the baby will reach a healthy weight of about 6.5 to 8.5 pounds, yet does not increase the risk of complications during delivery or cause excess weight gain for the mother.[44] Gaining excess weight will make it more difficult to lose the weight once the baby is born and increases the likelihood of the mother remaining overweight many years after delivery.[45]

After 11 weeks of development, the fetus is just over an inch in length. Pregnant women typically gain only about two pounds in the first trimester. This means

TABLE 17.4 Recommended Weight Gain during Pregnancy

Body Mass Index (BMI)	Recommended Weight Gain (in Pounds)
<18.5	28–40
18.5–24.9	25–35
25–29.9	15–25
>30.0	11–20

Source: WEIGHT GAIN DURING PREGNANCY; REEXAMINING THE GUIDELINES, a report of the Institute of Medicine. Copyright © 2009 by the National Academy of Sciences, Courtesy of the National Academies Press, Washington, D.C. Reprinted with permission.

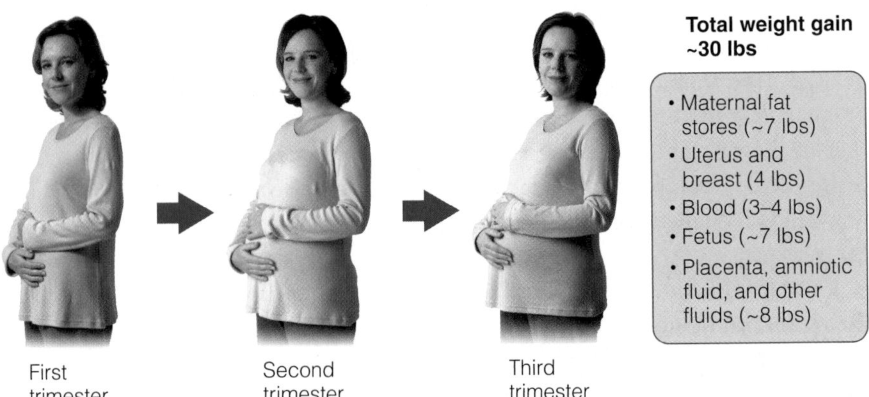

▲ **Figure 17.4 Components of Weight Gain during Pregnancy**
Healthy-weight women gain 25 to 35 pounds, on average, during pregnancy.

pica Eating nonfood substances such as dirt and clay.

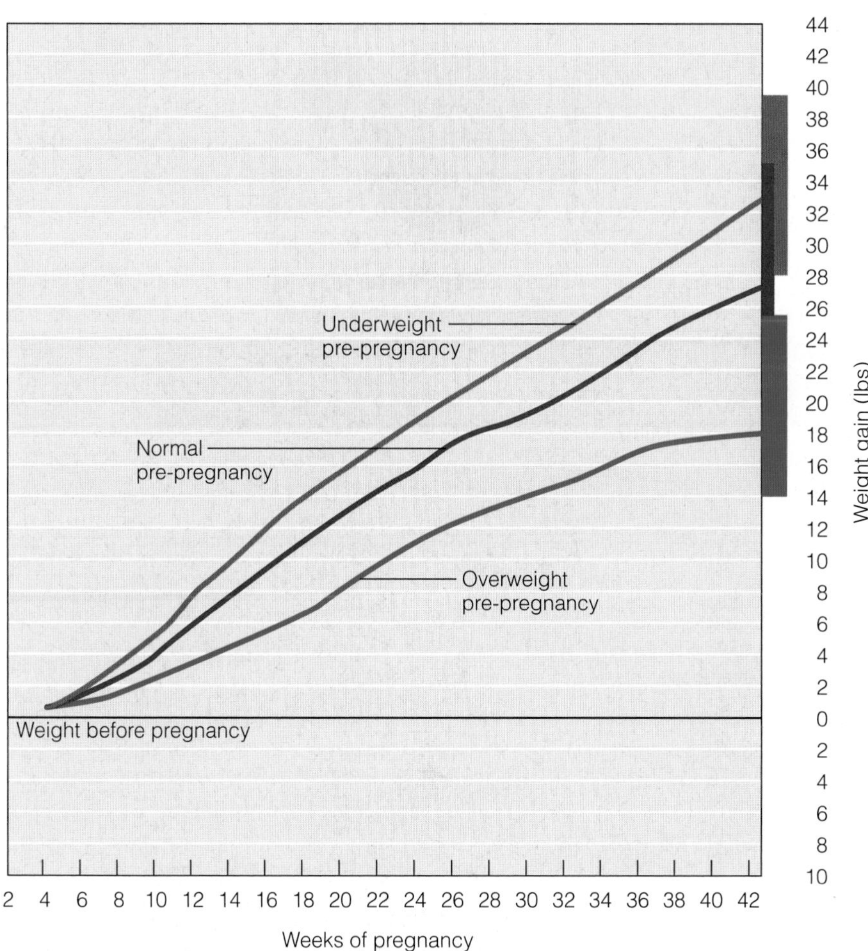

◂ **Figure 17.5 Patterns of Weight Gain** A chart such as this is often used to monitor the rate of weight gain during pregnancy. To use the chart, find the number of weeks pregnant. Go up the line until you reach your weight gain and mark an "x" there. Your weight gain should follow a pattern similar to that shown on the chart. Pregnant women should chart their weight gain every two to four weeks.

Source: Parent Link Centre, Alberta Children's Services. www.parentlinkalberta.ca/publish/474.htm. Accessed June 2012.

that they would need about 100 additional kilocalories during this early stage of pregnancy. However, a pregnant woman does have an increased need for certain nutrients immediately after conception. The fact that she needs more of some nutrients, but not many more kilocalories, creates a potential dietary dilemma.

Patterns of weight gain, that is, the rate of weight gained per week of pregnancy after the first trimester as well as total weight gain, influence the outcome of the pregnancy. **Figure 17.5** shows healthy patterns of weight gain during pregnancy. Differences in the physiological response to pregnancy account for variations in weight gain. The recommended pattern of weight gain serves as a target and to identify women who should be evaluated for insufficient or excessive gain.

Ensure Adequate Nutrient Intake

In the first trimester, a pregnant woman needs up to 50 percent more of certain nutrients—including folate, iron, zinc, copper, and calcium—than before she was pregnant (**Figure 17.6**). How does a mom-to-be increase her intake of these nutrients without taking in more kilocalories? She has to carefully choose nutrient-dense foods and may need a prenatal supplement.

Folate

The DRI for folate is 400 micrograms daily. If a woman is conscientious about taking folic acid prior to conception and continues to take a supplement and/or

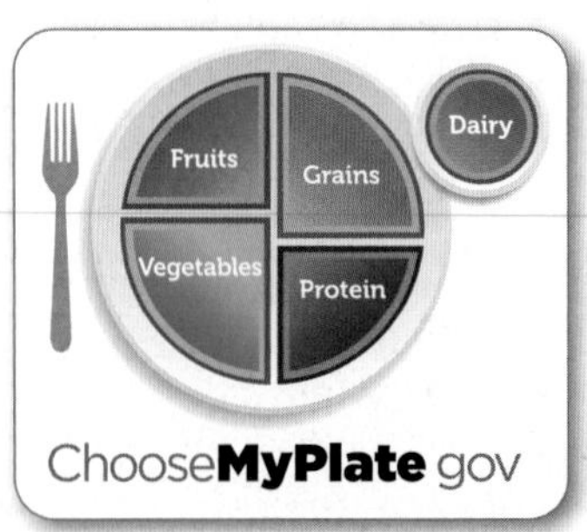

Vegetables	Fruits	Grains	Protein	Dairy	Oils
2.5 cups	2 cups	6 oz eq	5.5 oz eq	3 cups	6 tsp

Nutrient	Recommended DRI for Nonpregnant Women Age 19–50 Years	Recommended Nutrient Intake During Pregnancy
Protein	46 g	71 g
Carbohydrates	130 g	175 g (minimum)
Linoleic acid	12 g	13 g
Alpha-linolenic acid	1.1 g	1.4 g
Dietary folate equivalents	400 µg	600 µg*
Thiamin	1.1 mg	1.4 mg
Riboflavin	1.1 mg	1.4 mg
Niacin equivalents	14 mg	18 mg
Vitamin B_6	1.3–1.5 mg	1.9 mg
Vitamin B_{12}	2.4 µg	2.6 µg
Vitamin C	75 mg	85 mg
Vitamin E	15 mg	15 mg
Vitamin A	700 µg	770 µg
Vitamin D	15 µg	15 µg
Calcium	1,000 mg	1,000 mg
Magnesium	310–320 mg	350–360 mg
Copper	900 µg	1,000 µg
Iron	18 mg	27 mg†
Phosphorus	700 mg	700 mg
Zinc	8 mg	11 mg
Calories	**2,000–2,200‡**	**§**

* Supplemented and/or fortified foods are recommended.
† A supplement is recommended.
‡ Varies depending upon activity level and weight.
§ Doesn't increase until second and third trimester.

▲ **Figure 17.6 Nutrient Needs during Pregnancy**
A balanced 2,000-kilocalorie diet can meet most of a pregnant woman's increased nutrient needs even before she adds kilocalories in her second and third trimesters.

consume folic acid–fortified foods, she should be able to meet her increased needs for this vitamin. Foods high in folate include green leafy vegetables, citrus fruits and juices, and whole-grain products.

Iron

A pregnant woman's increased iron needs are not as easy to meet. Even though a woman loses less iron during pregnancy because she's not menstruating, and she absorbs up to three times more iron from foods than before she was pregnant, she still needs to increase her dietary intake for several reasons. She needs extra iron to make additional red blood cells, which increase her oxygen-carrying capacity and help replace the blood lost during delivery. A woman also needs extra iron to prevent anemia, a condition associated with premature delivery and an increased risk of dying for both mother and baby.[46] Finally, iron is essential for fetal growth and development, and for the growth of the placenta.[47]

Although meat, fish, poultry, and enriched grains supply iron, the amount recommended during pregnancy is unlikely to be met from food alone, so a supplement is often needed.[48] Many women are prescribed a prenatal supplement to help meet their iron and other increased nutrient needs. Foods that contain substances that inhibit iron absorption, including milk products (calcium), high-fiber foods (phytate), and coffee and tea (polyphenolic compounds), should not be consumed with iron-rich supplements.

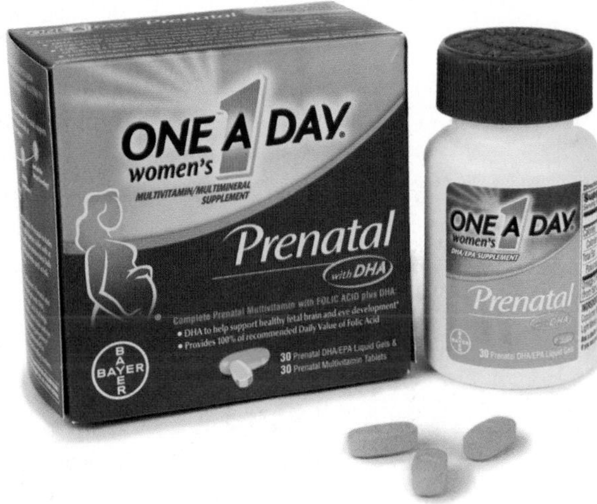

Prenatal supplements can help pregnant women meet their increased needs for iron, folic acid, and other essential nutrients.

Zinc and Copper

Because iron can interfere with the absorption of other minerals, a woman taking more than 30 milligrams of iron daily should also take 15 milligrams of zinc and 2 milligrams of copper to prevent a deficiency of these minerals.[49] Zinc is needed in protein metabolism and in the synthesis of DNA so that cells can replicate and differentiate. Copper, as part of enzymes, is needed in the production of energy, the synthesis of connective tissues, and in the transport and use of iron.

Calcium

A pregnant woman absorbs more calcium from foods during pregnancy to offset the amount of calcium needed by the growing fetus, but she still needs to meet her daily needs to preserve bone mass and to prevent osteoporosis later in life. Currently, more than half of women of childbearing age fail to get the correct number of MyPlate-recommended servings from the dairy, fruit, and vegetable groups, putting them at risk of not meeting many nutrient needs, including calcium.[50]

One way to ensure adequate calcium intake during pregnancy is to consume nutrient-dense milk, rather than nutritionally empty sodas. Milk contains vitamin D, calcium, and protein, all of which are needed by the mother and the growing baby. Regular sodas, on the other hand, contain kilocalories, sugar, and not much else, and may take the place of nutrient-dense foods, thus are not a good choice for women during this nutritionally critical period.

Vitamin D

Another nutrient important for bone health, vitamin D, is also frequently underconsumed, and there is a high prevalence of low circulating serum vitamin D concentrations among women of childbearing age. Insufficient vitamin D during pregnancy leads to poor absorption and use of calcium, which in turn hampers fetal bone formation. Infants born to mothers with vitamin D deficiency tend to be small, have poorly calcified bones and abnormal tooth enamel, and experience low blood calcium levels.[51] Vitamin D deficiency during pregnancy may affect chronic disease susceptibility soon after birth, as well as later in life.[52,53] To avoid vitamin D deficiency, consumption of vitamin D–rich foods and sensible sun exposure are encouraged.

Other Nutrients

Other nutrients are also of concern during the first trimester, and throughout pregnancy, especially if the mother is a vegetarian or vegan. Pregnant women, especially vegetarians, should be mindful about meeting their need for alpha-linolenic acid, an essential fatty acid found in nuts, soybeans, and canola oil. Essential fatty acids are needed in the development of cell membranes and so are important in the formation of new tissues, particularly those of the central nervous system.[54] Choline is important during pregnancy and when nursing the baby. Choline is needed for healthy cells to divide and grow, especially in the brain.[55] Vegans who don't consume any animal products need to make sure that they are getting a reliable source of vitamin B_{12}. Vegans also have higher zinc and iron needs even when they aren't pregnant, so a supplement will also ensure that they meet their needs for these minerals.

Overconsumption of Some Nutrients

While it's important that pregnant women meet their nutrient needs, it is equally important that they not consume too much of some nutrients. Too much vitamin A can be toxic and increase the risk of birth defects, especially when taken during the first trimester (see Chapter 9). Women who take a supplement should consume no more than 5,000 IU (1,500 micrograms RAE) of preformed vitamin A daily, which is 100 percent of the Daily Value (DV) listed on the Nutrition Facts Panel. Vitamin D can also be toxic in high amounts, and supplements should only be consumed under the supervision of a woman's health care provider.

Sugar Substitutes

Even though diet sodas usually don't contain kilocalories, they are likely to contain sugar substitutes. During pregnancy, sugar substitutes may be used in moderation along with a balanced, nutrient-rich meal plan. Products that contain the sugar substitutes aspartame (Equal), sucralose (Splenda), acesulfame-K (Sunett), and saccharin (Sweet 'N Low) have been deemed safe to consume within the FDA's level of acceptable daily intake.[56] Women with PKU, however, should avoid using aspartame.

Foodborne Illness Is a Concern

During pregnancy, a woman's immune system is weakened and the fetus's immune system is undeveloped, both of which set the stage for potential difficulties in fighting off pathogens that can cross the placenta. The bacterium *Listeria monocytogenes,* for example, may cause miscarriages, premature labor, low birth weight, developmental problems, and even infant death.

Some foods, like raw meats and fish, are more likely to carry pathogens and should be handled with care or avoided during pregnancy. Pregnant women should also avoid undercooked meat, fish, or poultry; unpasteurized milk, cheese, and juices; and raw sprouts. You will learn more about foodborne pathogens, including *Listeria monocytogenes,* and how to safeguard your foods in Chapter 20.

Food that may carry pathogens, such as the raw fish of sashimi, should be avoided by pregnant women for their own safety and the safety of their fetus.

THE TAKE-HOME MESSAGE Many women experience morning sickness and cravings during the first trimester. Women should gain from 25 to 35 pounds during pregnancy, depending upon their prepregnancy weight. The needs for many nutrients increase during pregnancy, but, other than iron, most can be met with a balanced diet. For pregnant women to obtain the iron they need, a supplement is often prescribed. Pregnant women should avoid excess amounts of preformed vitamin A and vitamin D and use sugar substitutes in moderation. They should also avoid raw or undercooked foods that may contain pathogens.

What Nutrients and Behaviors Are Important in the Second Trimester?

For many pregnant women, the nausea and fatigue of the first trimester subside during the second trimester, and appetite begins to increase. The baby is growing rapidly: Blood cells are forming in the baby's bone marrow, the body grows bigger than the head, the ears become prominent, the eyes blink, and the lips suck. The fetus weighs just under 2 pounds and is about 13 inches long by the end of this trimester.

The mother's body is also changing as her amniotic fluid and blood volume increase, her breasts get larger, and she stores more fat. During this period of growth, the mother should focus on consuming adequate kilocalories and nutrients, exercise if possible, and be aware of potential complications.

▲ **Figure 17.7 Adding Kilocalories and Nutrients**
The extra kilocalorie and nutrient needs of the second and third trimesters can be met with nutrient-dense diet additions.

Consume Adequate Kilocalories, Carbohydrate, and Protein

During the second and third trimesters, the mother's kilocalorie needs increase, and she should gain slightly less than a pound per week until delivery. She should consume an additional 340 kilocalories daily during the second trimester. This is the equivalent of adding two servings from the grain group and a serving each from the meat, vegetable, and fruit groups. A whole-wheat English muffin topped with peanut butter, accompanied by baby carrots (340 kilocalories total; **Figure 17.7**), fits these requirements, as do many other food combinations (see the Table Tips for some suggestions). This combination of food groups provides plentiful essential fatty acids, carbohydrates, fiber, calcium, zinc, iron, and protein—the nutrients that a woman needs more of during pregnancy.

Pregnant women need a minimum of 175 grams of carbohydrates per day (versus 130 grams for nonpregnant women) to supply the amount of glucose required for both the developing brain and the energy needs of the fetus, and to prevent ketosis. This amount is easily provided in a typical balanced diet. A pregnant woman's protein needs also increase by about 35 percent, to about 71 grams daily, during the second and third trimesters.

Get Enough Exercise

Daily exercise during pregnancy can help improve sleep, lower the risk of hypertension and diabetes, prevent backaches, help relieve constipation, shorten labor, and allow women to return more quickly to their prepregnancy weight after delivery. Exercise may also provide an emotional boost by reducing stress, depression, and anxiety.[57] The American College of Obstetricians and Gynecologists recommends 30 minutes or more of moderate exercise on most, if not all, days of the week, as long as the woman doesn't have any medical issues or complications.[58] Pregnant women should check with their health care provider before exercising to see if it is appropriate.

Low-impact activities such as walking, swimming, and stationary cycling are best because they pose less risk of injury for both mother and baby. As long as there are no complications, even jogging may be permitted. In contrast, high-impact activities, such as downhill skiing and basketball, could injure the baby and cause joint injuries for the mother (Table 17.5). Exercising moms-to-be should take special care to avoid a significant increase in their body core temperature, and to drink plenty of fluids to avoid dehydration.[59] Pregnant women should also avoid saunas,

TABLE TIPS

340 Snacks

Create a "340 snack" with just three to five ingredients. Start with a whole or enriched grain. Complement it with servings from the protein, low-fat dairy, vegetable, or fruit food groups.

Spread 3 tablespoons of low-fat cream cheese on 2 brown rice cakes topped with a sliced banana for a 340-calorie pick me up.

Add ¼ cup granola cereal and ½ cup mixed berries to 1 cup low-fat yogurt for a 340-kilocalorie refreshing yogurt parfait.

Stuff 1 whole-wheat tortilla with ½ cup refried beans, 2 tablespoons salsa, ¼ cup shredded Cheddar cheese, and ¼ cup shredded lettuce for a 340-kilocalorie burrito to wrap up your afternoon.

TABLE 17.5 Safe and Unsafe Exercises during Pregnancy

Safe Activities	Unsafe Activities (Contact Sports and High-Impact Activities)
Walking	Hockey (field and ice)
Stationary cycling	Basketball
Low-impact aerobics	Football
Swimming	Soccer
Dancing	Gymnastics
Jogging	Horseback riding
	Skating
	Skiing (snow and water)
	Vigorous racquet sport
	Weight lifting

Adapted from American College of Obstetrics and Gynecology. 2011. *Exercise during Pregnancy.* Available at www.acog.org/~/media/For%20Patients/faq119.pdf?dmc=1&ts=20120409T2228386423. Accessed April 2012.

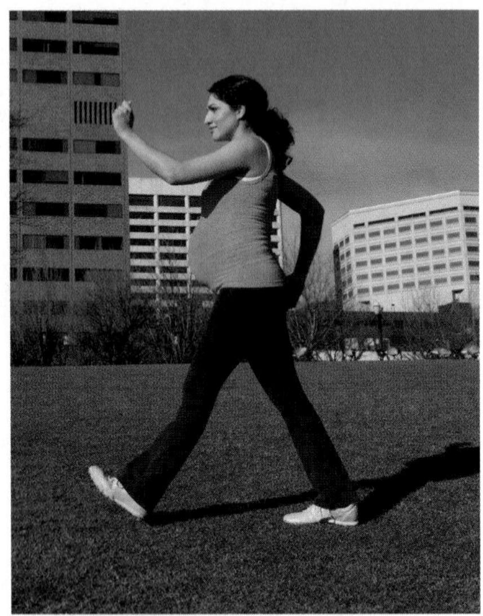

Walking is one form of exercise that is safe for both mother and baby, and helps reduce the risk of diabetes.

gestational diabetes Diabetes that occurs in women during pregnancy.

macrosomia Term for a large newborn, weighing more than 8 pounds, 13 ounces.

jaundice A yellowish coloring of the skin due to the presence of bile pigments in the blood.

hot tubs, and steam rooms. High body temperature may cause the mother's blood pressure to fall, which can deprive the fetus of adequate oxygen and nutrients. Research also suggests that the use of a hot tub during early pregnancy may increase the risk of neural tube defects and miscarriage.[60,61]

Be Alert to Potential Complications: Gestational Diabetes and Hypertension

Women may develop complications during pregnancy that can endanger their health and the health of their child. Potential complications include gestational diabetes and hypertension.

Gestational Diabetes

Sometimes a pregnant woman develops high blood glucose levels during her pregnancy and is diagnosed with **gestational diabetes** (*gestation* = pregnancy). This type of diabetes occurs in about 7 percent of pregnancies in the United States and manifests after approximately the twentieth week.[62] A pregnant woman should be tested for gestational diabetes during her second trimester.

Though the cause of gestational diabetes is still unknown, the hormones from the placenta appear to lead to insulin resistance in the mother, which in turn causes hyperglycemia. This elevated blood glucose crosses the placenta, stimulating the baby's pancreas to make more insulin, which leads to the storage of excess glucose as fat and can result in **macrosomia** (*macro* = large, *somia* = body), or a large baby.[63] A larger than normal baby may be at risk of injury to its shoulders during delivery or may increase the risk of a cesarean delivery.[64]

Gestational diabetes also increases the risk of the baby developing **jaundice,** breathing problems, and birth defects.[65] Because the baby is producing extra insulin during pregnancy, this hormone is elevated after birth, causing a rapid drop in blood glucose levels, which can cause hypoglycemia.[66]

Although this type of diabetes usually doesn't continue after the baby is born, women with gestational diabetes and their babies are at higher risk of developing type 2 diabetes, as well as hypertension and being overweight later on in life.[67]

Certain factors can increase a woman's risk for gestational diabetes:

- Being overweight
- Being over 25 years old
- Having a history of higher-than-normal blood glucose levels
- Having a family history of diabetes
- Being of Hispanic, African-American, Native American, or Pacific Islander descent
- Having previously given birth to a very large baby (> 9 pounds) or a stillborn baby
- Having had gestational diabetes in the past

According to the National Institute of Child Health and Human Development, if a woman has two or more of these risk factors, she is at high risk for developing gestational diabetes and should be tested earlier, during the first trimester of her pregnancy.[68] Having one risk factor indicates average risk, while having no risk factors indicates low risk.[69] Eating healthfully, maintaining a healthy weight, and exercising regularly can help reduce the risk of developing diabetes during pregnancy.

To achieve normal maternal blood glucose levels, women with gestational diabetes should receive nutritional counseling, by a Registered Dietitian when possible.

Because gestational diabetes is a major risk factor for future maternal diabetes, it presents a "teachable moment" during which women can be alerted to take action to decrease risk.

Hypertension

Hypertension during pregnancy can damage the woman's kidneys and other organs and increase the risk of low birth weight and premature delivery.[70] It occurs in about 8 percent of pregnancies in the United States.[71] Though some women have hypertension prior to conceiving, others develop it during their pregnancy.

Pregnancy-induced hypertension includes three categories of high blood pressure: **gestational hypertension, preeclampsia,** and **eclampsia,** each progressively more medically serious. Gestational hypertension is more likely to occur halfway through pregnancy and be a sign of preeclampsia. Preeclampsia (also known as *toxemia*) occurs when the pregnant woman has hypertension and severe edema, and her urine contains protein, which is a signal of damage to her kidneys.[72] Though some swelling or edema in a woman's feet and ankles is normal during pregnancy, the dramatic edema seen in preeclampsia is visible in her face and hands and can cause weight gain of more than 2 pounds a week.[73]

The cause of preeclampsia is not known, but it is dangerous to the baby because less oxygen- and nutrient-rich blood reaches the placenta.[74] Women who have hypertension prior to pregnancy or develop it during pregnancy, are overweight, under the age of 20 or over the age of 40, are carrying more than one baby, or have diabetes are at higher risk of developing preeclampsia.[75] If left untreated, preeclampsia can lead to eclampsia, which can cause seizures in the mother and is a major cause of death of women during pregnancy.[76]

The only cure for preeclampsia and eclampsia is to deliver the baby. However, delivery too early (before 32 weeks) is unsafe for the baby. Bed rest, medications, and hospitalization are used to treat preeclampsia until the baby can be safely born.[77] Calcium supplements had been postulated to prevent preeclampsia, but research doesn't support this claim, especially if the mother's diet is adequate in calcium.[78,79] Some research suggests that antioxidants, specifically vitamins C and E, may reduce the risk, but more research is needed.[80]

THE TAKE-HOME MESSAGE Pregnant women should consume an additional 340 kilocalories daily during the second trimester. A varied selection of nutrient-dense foods will easily meet increased kilocalorie needs. Exercise can provide numerous benefits during pregnancy. Some women develop gestational diabetes and pregnancy-induced high blood pressure and need to be closely monitored by a health care professional.

FITNESS TIPS

Exercising While Pregnant

Consult your health care provider before beginning or continuing an exercise program.

Begin slowly to avoid excessive fatigue and shortness of breath.

In warm weather, exercise in the early morning or evening to avoid becoming overheated.

Drink plenty of fluids to stay hydrated.

Report any problems or unusual symptoms such as chest pains, contractions, dizziness, headaches, calf swelling, blurred vision, vaginal discharge or bleeding, and/or abdominal pain immediately to your health care provider.

U.S. Department of Health and Human Services. 2009. *Tips for Pregnancy: Fit for Two.* Available at http://win.niddk.nih.gov/publications/PDFs/fitfortwo.pdf.

What Nutrients and Behaviors Are Important in the Third Trimester?

By the end of the last trimester, a pregnant woman should be taking in an extra 450 daily kilocalories and continuing to gain about 1 pound per week. (Adding a banana to the English muffin with peanut butter and carrot will increase this snack to about 450 kilocalories. Check out the Table Tips for some more suggestions.) She is likely to have a harder time getting around due to her expanding body. Climbing stairs may literally take her breath away and finding a comfortable sleeping position could take some maneuvering. At the end of the third trimester, the baby will weigh approximately 7 pounds.

pregnancy-induced hypertension High-blood pressure resulting from pregnancy; includes *gestational hypertension, preeclampsia,* and *eclampsia.*

gestational hypertension Hypertension occurring during pregnancy in a woman without prior history of high blood pressure.

preeclampsia Serious medical condition developed late in pregnancy in which hypertension, severe edema, and protein loss occur.

eclampsia Seizures or coma in a woman with preeclampsia.

TABLE TIPS

Going from 340 to 450

What nutrient-dense foods could accompany a sandwich and a cup of milk? Consider adding an apple or banana to the snack.

A small handful of chopped nuts can top a yogurt parfait.

Orange wedges go well with a burrito.

Melt a slice of cheese on a veggie burger.

Garnish a green salad with an ounce of whole-grain croutons.

A refreshing tall fruit-yogurt-wheat germ smoothie totaling 450 kilocalories may be slowly sipped to extend the pleasure. It can also be consumed in divided doses.

As the growing baby exerts pressure on the mother's intestines and stomach, she may experience heartburn. Hormonal changes may also slow the movement of food through the GI tract, and increase the likelihood of stomach contents refluxing back into the esophagus, also causing heartburn. To minimize heartburn, pregnant women should eat frequent, small meals rather than fewer, larger meals, and avoid foods that may irritate the esophagus, such as spicy or highly seasoned foods. They also shouldn't lie down immediately after meals, and they should elevate their heads during sleep to minimize reflux.[81]

Constipation is very common near the end of pregnancy. The slower movement of food through the GI tract, coupled with a tendency for less physical activity due to the awkward distribution of body weight, reduces regularity and causes a more sluggish stool. The high amount of iron in prenatal supplements can also contribute to constipation.[82] Exercise and consuming fiber-rich foods such as bran cereals, beans, whole grains, fruits, and vegetables, along with plenty of fluids, can help prevent or alleviate constipation.

THE TAKE-HOME MESSAGE During the third trimester, a woman needs an additional 450 kilocalories per day and should continue gaining about a pound per week. Heartburn and constipation commonly occur during the third trimester. Regular exercise, increasing fiber in the diet, and consuming plenty of fluids can help reduce constipation.

What Special Concerns Might Younger, Older, or Low-Income Mothers-to-Be Face?

Pregnancy and childbirth stress the body of a mother-to-be no matter what her age, but women younger or older than the physically optimal childbearing age range of 20 to 25 may face additional challenges. In particular, women who become pregnant during their teenaged years and women over the age of 35 are at higher risk for certain complications.

Teenaged Mothers May Face Nutritional Challenges

More than 410,000 babies are born to girls under age 20 in the United States annually.[83] Because a teenaged girl's body is still growing, she has higher nutrient needs than does an adult woman. In addition, adolescents are more likely to eat on the run, skip meals, eat less-nutrient-dense snacks, and consume inadequate amounts of whole grains, fruits, vegetables, and low-fat or fat-free dairy products. Add this unbalanced diet to the increased needs of pregnancy, and pregnant teens are likely falling short of many of their nutrient requirements, especially iron, folic acid, and calcium, and potentially even kilocalories.

A pregnant teen's inadequate diet can mean not only a low birth weight or SGA baby, but her own diminished health status. Teens who deliver infants with normal birth weight appear to do so by lowering their own resting energy needs and ceasing linear growth, compared with nonpregnant girls who continue to grow.[84] Hence pregnancy during adolescence results in weight loss and depletion of fat and lean body mass.[85]

Nutrition in Practice: Susan

Susan was thrilled when she learned she was pregnant. Eager to start her family, she had recently given up cigarette smoking and started exercising regularly, walking after work every day and going on weekend bike rides and hiking trips with her husband. During her first prenatal visit, her physician referred Susan to a Registered Dietitian for nutritional counseling and since then she has been following an individualized vegan meal plan. Despite suffering from morning sickness through the first two trimesters, Susan has continued to work full time. During her second trimester, Susan's physician prescribed a prenatal supplement, citing concern about Susan's vegan diet and her not obtaining adequate nutrition due to morning sickness. At her most recent prenatal visit, Susan told her doctor that she had recently started experiencing heartburn after supper and occasional constipation, and the doctor referred her to the RD for another consultation.

Susan's Stats:

- □ Age: 27
- □ Height: 5 feet 6 inches
- □ Weight (pre-conception): 148 pounds
  Weight (34 weeks): 169 pounds
- □ BMI (pre-conception): 24

Critical Thinking Questions

1. Which foods in Susan's log are rich in these nutrients: fiber, vitamin B_{12}, folate, iron, zinc, and calcium?
2. How can Susan avoid or minimize heartburn and constipation?

Dietitian's Observation and Plan for Susan:

- □ Discuss the importance of optimal nutrient intake to maintain the recommended weight gain pattern during pregnancy.
- □ To minimize heartburn, continue eating frequent, small meals, and avoid foods that may irritate the esophagus, such as spicy or highly seasoned foods. Discourage Susan from lying down immediately after meals and recommend keeping her head elevated during sleep.
- □ Discuss the reasons why constipation is common near the end of pregnancy, and advise Susan to continue with regular exercise. Also recommend drinking plenty of fluids and consuming fiber-rich foods such as bran cereals, beans, whole grains, fruits, and vegetables, along with plenty of fluids.

Susan follows the RD's suggestions for preventing heartburn and constipation and finds she is experiencing symptoms much less frequently. Susan hopes to breast-feed her baby, so two weeks before her due date, Susan returns for a follow-up appointment with the dietitian to discuss her nutrient needs once she starts breast-feeding. The dietitian advises Susan that she will have increased fluid needs while she is breast-feeding, so she will need to drink about 13 cups of fluids daily. Because she will need an additional 330–400 kilocalories from nutrient-dense foods, similar to her nutrient needs during the third trimester of her pregnancy, she can maintain her present meal plan.

Susan's Food Log

Food/Beverage	Time Consumed	Hunger Rating*	Location
Fortified whole-grain cereal topped with blueberries and fortified soy milk; decaffeinated coffee with sugar substitute	6:30 a.m.	2	In kitchen at home
Whole-grain English muffin topped with peanut butter and shredded carrots; soy milk	9:30 a.m.	4	Staff break room
Black beans and brown rice with broccoli and carrots; spinach salad with vinaigrette dressing; diet soda	12:30 p.m.	5	Staff break room
Banana	3 p.m.	2	In the car driving to gym
Soy milk	4 p.m.	4	In the car on the way home
Vegetarian lentil soup; whole-wheat pasta topped with mushroom sauce and soy cheese; soy milk	6:30 p.m.	3	In the dining room at home
Soy yogurt sprinkled with wheat germ, raisins, and nuts	9 p.m.	2	In front of the TV at home

***Hunger Rating (1–5);** 1 = not hungry; 5 = super hungry

Due to additional steps and fertility treatments taken to ensure pregnancy, older mothers often deliver multiples—twins, triplets, or quads.

Teenaged mothers are also more likely to develop pregnancy-induced hypertension and iron-deficiency anemia and deliver premature babies, putting the baby at risk for health problems. They are more likely to engage in unhealthy lifestyle habits such as smoking, drinking alcohol, and taking illicit drugs, all of which can compromise the baby's health,[86] and are less likely to receive adequate prenatal care.

Older Mothers May Have Special Concerns

At the other end of the age spectrum are women who delay pregnancy until their later childbearing years. The number of women who fall into this category has increased significantly in the last two decades: Since 1990, the number of births to women over age 35 has risen 40 percent. Today, births to mothers over age 35 represent over 35 percent of overall births in the United States.[87]

Though most women in this age group experience normal, healthy pregnancies, they are at higher risk for certain complications, beginning with the ability to conceive. Fertility typically begins to decline in women starting in their early 30s, so getting pregnant may take longer. These women are also at higher risk of developing diabetes and high blood pressure during pregnancy, and their babies are more likely to have Down syndrome or other developmental disabilities.

Older mothers should try to achieve a healthy body weight prior to conception, avoid smoking, eat a balanced diet before and during pregnancy, and consume adequate amounts of folic acid. As with all pregnant women, they should limit their caffeine intake and avoid alcohol and illicit drugs. See Table 17.6 for a summary of factors that relate to high-risk pregnancy.

Low-Income Mothers May Need Food Assistance

Adequate nutrition during pregnancy is critical for the health of both the mother and child. The government program Special Supplemental Nutrition Program for Women, Infants, and Children (WIC) is designed to ensure that pregnant women and mothers with young children have access to nutrition information

TABLE 17.6 Factors Associated with High-Risk Pregnancy

Factor	Conditions Associated with Increased Risk
Lifestyle	Smoking, alcohol and drug abuse
	Use of botanicals, supplements
Age	Adolescent, over age 35
Weight	Prepregnancy: underweight, obese
	During pregnancy: insufficient or excessive weight gain
Health	Chronic diseases (diabetes, hypertension, medications)
	Previous history (baby born with neural tube defect)
	Gestational diabetes, pregnancy-induced hypertension
Food intake	Environmental contaminants (methylmercury, pica)
	Insufficient or excessive kilocalorie intake
	Nutrient deficiencies (folic acid, iron, calcium, vitamin D, B_{12})
	Foodborne illness
Socioeconomic status	Poverty, limited food supply, low educational level

and nutritious foods during the most critical years of growth and development. WIC provides supplemental foods, health care referrals, and nutrition education for low-income pregnant and postpartum women, and children up to age 5 who are at nutritional risk.[88] Supplemental foods include iron-fortified infant formula and infant cereal, iron-fortified adult cereal, vitamin C–rich fruit or vegetable juice, eggs, milk, cheese, peanut butter, dried beans/peas, tuna fish, and carrots.[89] The program improved the nutritional status of nearly 9 million WIC participants in 2012.[90]

Evaluation studies have shown that the WIC program has been playing an important role in improving birth outcomes and containing health care costs. It reduces the incidences of iron-deficiency anemia in women during pregnancy and after delivery, and helps improve babies' birth weights. It also leads to fewer premature births, fewer infant deaths, and increased prenatal care. Every dollar spent on prenatal WIC participation for low-income women saves between $1.77 and $3.13 in health care costs within the first 60 days after birth.[91]

THE TAKE-HOME MESSAGE Teens who become pregnant are at higher risk of developing hypertension and delivering a premature and low birth weight baby. Because a teen is still growing, she will likely have a hard time meeting both her own nutrient needs and her baby's, unless she is diligent about eating a well-balanced diet. Women over age 35 may have a harder time conceiving, and are at higher risk for high blood pressure and diabetes during pregnancy, and have higher rates of babies born with developmental disabilities. The Special Supplemental Nutrition Program for Women, Infants, and Children (WIC) is a government-funded program that provides food assistance for nutritionally at-risk mothers during pregnancy, and for at-risk children through the first five years of life.

What Are the Benefits and Nutrient Needs of Breast-Feeding?

A woman who has just given birth begins a period of **lactation,** that is, her body produces milk to nourish her new infant. The infant's suckling at the mother's nipple stimulates milk production. Signals sent from the nipple to the hypothalamus in the mother's brain prompt the pituitary gland to release two hormones: prolactin and oxytocin. Prolactin causes milk to be produced in the breast, while oxytocin triggers a **letdown response,** which releases milk so the infant can receive it through the nipple[92] (see **Figure 17.8**).

The adage "breast is best" when nourishing an infant is still true. Through **breast-feeding,** or nursing, mothers provide food that is uniquely tailored to meet their infant's nutritional needs in an easily digestible form. Breast-feeding also provides many other advantages for both the mother and the baby.

Breast-Feeding Provides Physical, Emotional, and Financial Benefits for Mothers

Breast-feeding not only provides optimal nutrition and immunological benefits for the baby, it helps improve the health of the mother and can be cheaper, safer, and more convenient than bottle-feeding. The health and emotional benefits can last for years after infancy.

lactation The production of milk in a woman's body after childbirth, and the period during which it occurs.

letdown response The release of milk from the mother's breast to feed a nursing baby.

breast-feeding The act of feeding an infant milk from a woman's breast.

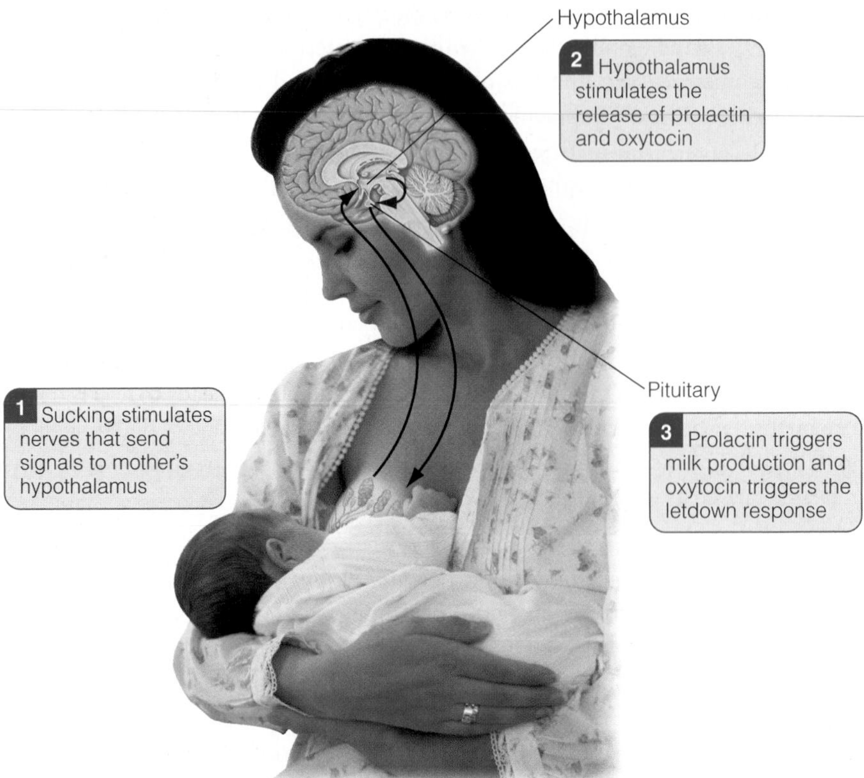
Hypothalamus
2 Hypothalamus stimulates the release of prolactin and oxytocin
Pituitary
1 Sucking stimulates nerves that send signals to mother's hypothalamus
3 Prolactin triggers milk production and oxytocin triggers the letdown response

▸ **Figure 17.8 The Letdown Response**

Pregnancy Recovery and the Risk of Some Chronic Diseases

In addition to stimulating the release of breast milk, the hormone oxytocin stimulates contractions in the uterus, which helps the organ return to its prepregnancy size and shape. Breast-feeding also reduces blood loss in the mother after delivery.[93] It may help some women return to their prepregnancy weight and manage their postpregnancy weight.

Women in their 20s who breast-feed for up to two years may reduce the risk of breast and ovarian cancer. Breast-feeding has also been shown to reduce the risk of hip fractures later in life, increase bone density, and reduce the risk of type 2 diabetes.[94]

Expense and Convenience

A new mother who uses formula rather than breast-feeding her baby will spend an estimated $1,500 for the first year's worth of formula alone. An estimated cost associated with breast-feeding comes to about $600 for the first year,[95, 96] primarily from buying the extra food a woman needs to eat to produce her infant's milk. In other words, making breast milk is cheaper than buying formula. One study concluded that the national cost of not breast-feeding infants in their first year of life is as much as $13 billion dollars.[97]

There are other costs associated with formula-feeding beyond the price of the product. For instance, infants fed solely on commercial formula have higher health care costs in the first year of life. In addition, there is the cost to produce, package, and ship formula throughout the United States. There are also environmental costs associated with the 550 million formula cans and 800,000 pounds of paper packaging and waste that are disposed of in landfills each year, and costs associated with the energy needed to properly clean the feeding bottles.[98] For the family, the environment, and society as a whole, breast-feeding uses fewer resources than formula-feeding.

Feeding from the breast is more convenient than bottle-feeding because the milk is always sterile and at the right temperature, and there is no need to prepare bottles. The mother also doesn't need to prepare the milk before feeding, and she has less cleanup to do afterward.

The intimacy of breast-feeding promotes bonding between mother and child.

Stress Reduction and Bonding

Recent research suggests that exclusive breast-feeding is associated with a mother's reduced reactivity to psychological stress.[99] In addition, the close interaction between mother and child during nursing promotes a unique bonding experience. The physical contact helps the baby feel safe, secure, and emotionally attached to the mother.[100]

Breast-Feeding Provides Nutritional and Health Benefits for Infants

There are more than 200 compounds in breast milk that benefit infants. Numerous research studies indicate that breast-feeding provides nutritional and health advantages that can last years beyond infancy.[101] It is one of the most important strategies for improving an infant's long-term health prospects.

Best for an Infant's Unique Nutrition Needs

The nutritional composition of breast milk changes as an infant grows. Right after birth, a new mother produces a carotenoid-rich, yellowish fluid called **colostrum** that has little fat but a lot of protein, vitamin A, and minerals. Colostrum also contains immune factors that help protect the infant from infections, particularly in the digestive tract.

Four to seven days later, actual breast milk begins to flow. Breast milk is high in lactose, fat, and B vitamins, and lower in fat-soluble vitamins, sodium, and other minerals. These nutrients are proportionally balanced to enhance their absorption.[102] Breast milk is low in protein so as not to stress an infant's immature kidneys with excessive amounts of nitrogen waste products. The protein is also mostly in the form of alpha-lactalbumin, which is easier for the infant to digest.[103] The nutrient composition of breast milk continues to change as the baby grows and his or her needs change.[104] By the time an infant has breast-fed for six months, the mother's milk will contain less protein than it did during the first month.[105]

Although breast-feeding is the recommended method of infant feeding and provides infants with necessary nutrients and immune factors, breast milk alone does not provide infants with an adequate intake of vitamin D. The American Academy of Pediatrics (AAP) now recommends that all infants have a minimum intake of 400 IU of vitamin D per day, beginning during the first two months of life and continuing throughout childhood. Breast milk typically contains a vitamin D concentration of 25 IU per liter or less.[106] Breast-fed infants, even if they are supplemented with vitamin D–fortified formula, should be supplemented with vitamin D drops. It is unlikely that breast-fed infants would consume enough formula per day to supply 400 IU of vitamin D.

Protection against Infections, Allergies, and Chronic Diseases

Breast milk provides the infant with a disease-fighting boost until the baby's own immune system matures. Research supports that breast-feeding decreases the risk and severity of diarrhea and other intestinal disorders, respiratory infections, meningitis, ear infections, and urinary tract infections.[107]

colostrum The fluid that is expressed from the mother's breast after birth and before the development of breast milk.

One protein in breast milk, lactoferrin, protects the infant against bacteria, viruses, fungi, and inflammation by binding with iron and making it unavailable to bacteria that need it to flourish.[108] Lactoferrin also inhibits the ability of bacteria to stick to the walls of the intestines, which impedes their growth and reproduction.

Breast milk provides other beneficial compounds, such as antioxidants, hormones, enzymes, and growth factors that play a role in the development of the infant and protect the baby from pathogens, inflammation, diseases, and allergies.[109] Some research suggests that breast milk may also protect against sudden infant death syndrome (SIDS), asthma, leukemia, heart disease, and diabetes mellitus.[110]

Reduced Childhood Obesity Risk

Breast-feeding, especially if continued beyond six months, may help reduce the risk of childhood obesity. The reason for this isn't clear, but could be associated with the tendency of breast-fed infants to gain less weight during the first year of life than formula-fed infants. The lower weight gain may be due to breast-fed infants having more control over when they start and stop eating than their bottle-fed counterparts.[111] If a caregiver controls how much food is consumed, rather than the child's internal cues, the result could be chronic overfeeding.[112,113]

Brain Development

Lastly, breast milk may help infants with intellectual development. Breast milk is rich in two unsaturated fatty acids, docosahexaenoic acid (DHA) and arachidonic acid (AA), which are important for the development of vision and the central nervous system, particularly the brain (see Chapter 5). Research suggests that breast-fed infants may have greater cognitive function, measured by IQ and academic success in school, than formula-fed babies, which may be due in part to these two fatty acids.[114,115]

Breast-Feeding Is Recommended by Experts

Because of all of the benefits, AAP and the Academy of Nutrition and Dietetics recommend that women exclusively breast-feed for the first six months and then use a combination of appropriate foods and breast-feeding during at least the first year. Currently, 76.9 percent of American women initiate breast-feeding when their infants are born, which is below the goal of 81.9 percent set for the nation in *Healthy People 2020.*[116,117] However, only 47.2 percent still breast-feed their infants at six months and only 25.5 percent continue until the baby is one year of age.[118] This falls short of the national goal of 60.6 percent of infants to be breast-feeding at six months and at least 34.1 percent to remain nursing at age 1.[119]

The breast-fed infant doesn't always have to consume breast milk directly from the breast. Milk can be expressed with a breast pump, refrigerated, and fed to the baby in a bottle by another caregiver at another time. This allows the mother to work outside the home or enjoy a few hours "off duty." Expressed breast milk needs to be used within 24 hours, or it can be stored in the freezer for three to six months. Spotlight: Breast-Feeding at Work Can Work addresses the dilemma of moms who want to breast-feed but who also want or need to return to work.

Breast-Feeding Mothers Have Special Nutrient and Lifestyle Needs

During the first six months of breast-feeding, the mother produces about three-fourths liter of breast milk daily. In the second six months, she produces a little over half a liter daily. During this period, her body needs additional amounts of fluid and nutrients.

SPOTLIGHT

Breast-Feeding at Work Can Work

For many women, the decision to breast-feed their infants is an easy one. The bigger challenge is how to juggle breast-feeding with returning to work or school.

Many women feel uncomfortable about breast-feeding or pumping breast milk outside the home, especially at their place of employment. Consider that about 50 percent of mothers with babies 1 year of age or younger are employed, and you can see that this reluctance is a big issue.[1] And the hesitation isn't just one-sided: Research shows that most companies don't offer support for working breast-feeding mothers, even though employer support for breast-feeding can extend the duration of a mother nursing her baby, which would benefit both mothers and babies.[2] The reality is that many women have to choose between breast-feeding and a paycheck.

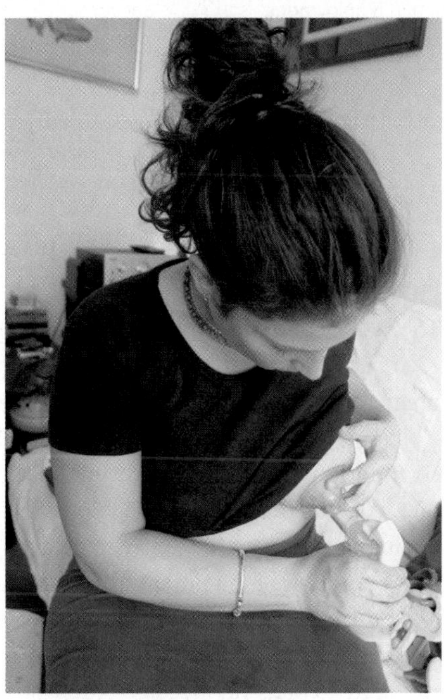

Women can express breast milk using a breast pump and store the milk in the refrigerator or freezer for later use.

But this may be slowly changing. In 1998, the state of Minnesota mandated that its companies aid and support breast-feeding moms. From 1998 to 2002, the percentage of women still breast-feeding at six months more than doubled within the state.[3] Currently, 24 states in the United States have laws to support breast-feeding in the workplace.[4]

Amendment to Section 4207 of the Patient Protection and Affordable Care Act (also known as Health Care Reform) requires employers to provide reasonable break time and a private, non-bathroom place for nursing mothers to express breast milk during the workday, for one year after the child's birth. The new requirements became effective when the Affordable Care Act was signed into law on March 23, 2010. The law does not preempt state laws that provide greater protections to employees.[5]

Worksite support is not only healthy for the infant but, in many ways, healthy for the corporate bottom line. Employers may be able to influence the duration of breast-feeding and so improve the health of both mother and baby. Because breast-fed infants are sick less often than formula-fed babies, annual health care costs are approximately $400 lower for breast-fed than for non-breast-fed babies.[6] Employees who are able to breast-feed are also happier, miss fewer work days (whether for their own illness or to tend to a sick infant), are more productive, and show greater loyalty to the employer.[7] In fact, a company's commitment to supporting breast-feeding women can be used as a recruitment tool when seeking new workers. It is estimated that each $1 invested in a corporate breast-feeding program saves the company $3.[8]

Skilled lactation support and workplace policies can enable many mothers to plan to breast-feed on return to work.[9] Women who return to work while lactating need only minimal worksite resources to accommodate their breast-feeding. First, they need adequate break times throughout the day and access to a private, comfortable room with an electrical outlet in order to pump their breast milk. They also need a sink in which to wash their hands and the pumping equipment, and a refrigerator for storing the milk.[10]

Some companies have gone beyond these minimum requirements. For example, Johnson & Johnson initiated a companywide breast-feeding program called Nurture Space. Employees who are new mothers, or their spouses or partners, receive a lactation education kit that includes an instructional DVD, a breast-feeding guide, and other educational materials. They also receive a discount on a portable breast pump and free telephone consultations with a certified lactation consultant. At many Johnson & Johnson corporate locations there are Nurture Space rooms where breast-feeding mothers can comfortably express their milk during the workday.

References

1. Centers for Disease Control and Prevention. 2011. *Breast Feeding. Promotion and Support.* Available at www.cdc.gov/breastfeeding/promotion/employment.htm. Accessed April 2012.
2. Slusser, W., L. Lange, V. Dickson, C. Hawkes, and R. Cohen. 2004. Breast Milk Expression in the Workplace: A Look at Frequency and Time. *Journal of Human Lactation* 20:164–169.
3. Johnson, M. 2008. Letter to the Editor: Twentieth Anniversary Issue. *Journal of Human Lactation* 22:14–15.
4. National Conference of State Legislatures. 2011. *State Summary of Breast-Feeding Laws.* Available at www.ncsl.org/issues-research/health/breastfeeding-state-laws.aspx. Accessed April 2012.
5. U.S. Breast-Feeding Committee. 2011. *Workplace Support in Federal Law.* Available at www.usbreastfeeding.org/Employment/WorkplaceSupport/WorkplaceSupportinFederalLaw/tabid/175/Default.aspx. Accessed June 2012.
6. U.S. Breast-Feeding Committee. 2002. *Workplace Breast-Feeding Support.* Available at www.usbreastfeeding.org/Portals/0/Publications/Workplace-2002-USBC.pdf. Accessed April 2012.

(continued)

(continued)

7. Abdulwadud, O. A. and M. E. Snow. 2007. Interventions in the Workplace to Support Breast-Feeding for Women in Employment. *Cochrane Database of Systematic Reviews*. Issue 3. Article No. CD006177.
8. U.S. Breast-Feeding Committee. 2010. *Workplace Accommodations to Support and Protect Breast-Feeding*. Available at www.usbreastfeeding.org/Portals/0/Publications/Workplace-Background-2010-USBC.pdf. Accessed November 2012.
9. Kosmala-Anderson, J. and L. M. Wallace. 2006. Breast-Feeding Works: The Role of Employers in Supporting Women Who Wish to Breast-Feed and Work in Four Organizations in England. *Journal of Public Health* 28:183–191.
10. U.S. Breast-Feeding Committee. 2010. *Workplace Accommodations to Support and Protect Breast-Feeding*.

Fluid and Nutrient Requirements

To meet her increased fluid needs, a breast-feeding woman should drink about 13 cups of water and beverages daily. Recall from Chapter 11 that most healthy non-pregnant women need 9 cups of water daily.

A breast-feeding woman also needs 500 extra kilocalories daily during the first six months of lactating. However, not all of these kilocalories have to come from the diet. Approximately 170 kilocalories are mobilized daily from fat that was stored during pregnancy. Only 330 extra kilocalories need to come from foods. This use of fat stores allows for a potential weight loss of about 2 pounds a month.

During the second six months of breast-feeding, less energy is available from stored body fat, so a lactating woman needs to consume about 400 extra kilocalories daily to meet her needs.[120] Interestingly, these amounts of extra kilocalories are comparable to the needs of pregnant women during the second and third trimesters. Although a breast-feeding woman's dietary carbohydrate requirements increase slightly—along with a slightly higher need for some vitamins and minerals—a well-balanced diet similar to the one she consumed during pregnancy will meet her needs. Lactating women who are vegans should make sure that they consume adequate amounts of vitamin B_{12} and zinc.

Lifestyle Habits

Anything that goes into a breast-feeding mother's body can potentially pass into her breast milk, and ultimately to her baby. Illicit drugs, such as cocaine, heroin, and marijuana, for example, can be transferred to a breast-fed infant and cause harm. Methylmercury, which a mother can overconsume if she eats certain fish, can also be harmful, so nursing mothers should adhere to the FDA's guidelines about fish to minimize the infant's exposure (refer to Table 17.2 on page 627).

Nursing women should limit coffee consumption and avoid alcohol and smoking. Caffeine can interfere with a baby's sleep and cause crankiness, so coffee consumption should be limited to two to three 8-ounce cups daily. Nursing women should also avoid alcohol, because it can appear in breast milk and inhibit milk production. They should not smoke, because nicotine can be passed on in breast milk and smoking is associated with a decrease in milk production and smaller weight gains in the baby.[121]

Breast milk can reflect the foods a mother eats and cause problems for the baby. For example, babies can become fussy if the mother has consumed certain spicy or gassy foods. The mother can abstain from that food, wait a few days, and then try it again. If the infant reacts the same way, it's best to stop eating that food while nursing.

Children with a strong family history of food allergy may benefit from breast-feeding. To keep possible food allergens out of breast milk, however, mothers may choose to exclude common offending foods from their diet, such as cow's milk, eggs, fish, peanuts, or tree nuts that could cause an allergic reaction in the baby. Delayed exposure to these foods may prolong the baby's allergy-free period.[122] However, mothers need to keep in mind that highly restrictive diets tend to be low in kilocalories and can severely limit nutrient intake. To ensure adequate nourishment, nursing mothers are encouraged to work with a Registered Dietitian in planning healthful meals.

THE TAKE-HOME MESSAGE Breast-feeding can help mothers return to their pre-pregnancy weight and reduce the risk of certain cancers, osteoporosis, and type 2 diabetes. It is the least expensive and most convenient way to nourish an infant, and helps the mother and baby bond. Human milk is rich in nutrients, antibodies, and compounds that can protect the baby against infections, allergies, and chronic diseases, and may enhance the child's cognitive development. Women are advised to breast-feed exclusively for the first six months, and then breast-feed to supplement solid food for the first year. A mother needs to increase her fluid and nutrient intake to help her body produce breast milk. Nursing mothers should limit caffeine consumption and avoid illicit drugs, alcohol, smoking, and food allergens.

When Is Formula a Healthy Alternative to Breast Milk?

If an infant isn't going to be breast-fed, the only other healthy option is formula. Formula is designed to match the energy-nutrient composition of breast milk. For some women, formula-feeding is a personal preference. For others it is necessary, as breast-feeding may not be possible due to illness or other circumstances.

Some Woman May Not Be Able to Breast-Feed

Some health conditions or lifestyle choices make breast-feeding unsafe for an infant. Women who are infected with HIV (human immunodeficiency virus), the virus that causes AIDS, should not breast-feed, as this virus can be transmitted to the child through breast milk. Women who have AIDS (acquired immune deficiency syndrome), human T cell leukemia, or active tuberculosis, who are receiving chemotherapy and/or radiation, or who use illegal drugs should also not breast-feed for the same reason.

In some circumstances, however, breast-feeding is the better option in spite of the dangers. For HIV-infected women living in countries where there is inadequate food, an unsafe food and water supply, and/or frequent incidences of nutritional deficiencies and infectious diseases, the benefits of breast milk may outweigh the risks of HIV infection for the baby.[123]

An infant born with a genetic disorder called galactosemia can't metabolize lactose and shouldn't be breast-fed.[124]

Lastly, any woman taking prescribed medications should check with her health care provider to ensure that they are safe to consume while breast-feeding.

Infant formula is available in several forms and varies in cost and ingredients. Infant formula is highly regulated by the FDA, so any formula on the market in the United States can be considered safe.

Formula Can Be a Healthy Alternative to Breast-Feeding

The best alternative to breast-feeding is to feed an infant with a commercially made formula. Formula is developed to be as similar as possible to breast milk (see Table 17.7), so formula-fed infants can grow and develop normally. The FDA regulates all infant formulas sold in the United States and has set specific requirements for the nutrients that the formula must contain.

TABLE 17.7 Nutritional Similarities between Infant Formula and Breast Milk

Nutrient	Amount in Breast Milk	Amount in Formula
Protein (g/100ml)	1.8	1.4
Fat (g/100 ml)	4	4.8
Carbohydrate (g/100 ml)	7	7.3
Sodium (mg/100 ml)	1.3	0.7
Calcium (mg/100 ml)	22	53
Phosphorus (mg/100 ml)	14	38
Iron (mg/ 100 ml)	0.03	0.1
Zinc (mg/ 100 ml)	3.2	5.1
Vitamin D (IU/100 ml)	4	41

Formula is typically made from cow's milk that has been altered to improve its nutrient content and digestibility. Soy protein–based formulas are free of cow's protein and lactose and can be used for infants who can't tolerate cow's milk protein–based formula or who are in vegan families. **Hypoallergenic infant formulas** are also available for infants who can't consume cow's milk or soy formulas. The AAP recommends that all formula-fed infants consume iron-fortified formulas to reduce the risk of iron deficiency during infancy.[125]

Cow's milk itself should not be fed to infants, as it won't meet the nutritional needs of the baby. It contains too much protein, mainly in the form of casein, which is difficult for the infant to digest.[126] Cow's milk, even whole milk, is too low in fat and linoleic acid, and too high in sodium and potassium.[127] Also, the iron in cow's milk is poorly absorbed, and can cause intestinal blood loss in infants, which will cause iron loss and, possibly, anemia.[128] Feeding infants cow's milk can also increase their risk of developing an allergy to cow's milk.[129]

Commercially made infant formulas can be purchased as powder, as a concentrated liquid, or in ready-to-use forms. Powdered formula is the cheapest, while the ready-to-use form tends to be the most expensive. Care should be taken to mix the powdered or concentrated liquid with the correct amount of water so the formula will not be too diluted or too concentrated.

If the infant doesn't finish the bottle, the formula should be discarded, rather than saved for another feeding. The bacteria in the infant's mouth can contaminate the formula, and multiply to levels that could be harmful even if the formula is reheated. Constant reheating of the formula also destroys some of the heat-sensitive nutrients.[130] Formula should not be left out at room temperature for more than two hours, as bacteria can multiply to unhealthy levels.

Infants should not be allowed to sleep with a bottle containing sugary liquids (milk, formula, fruit juice, soda, and other sweetened drinks), as this practice can lead to **nursing bottle tooth decay** (see **Figure 17.9**) and ear infections. Liquids from bottles tend to pool in the mouth during sleep. The normal bacteria in the mouth change the sugar to an acid, which gradually dissolves the immature enamel and allows tooth decay to occur.[131,132]

In addition, drinking from the bottle while lying down prevents liquid from fully draining from the eustachian tubes. The liquid buildup increases the risk of ear infections.[133] The American Academy of Pediatric Dentistry recommends avoiding putting infants to sleep with bottles and sweetened pacifiers. To prevent tooth decay, parents can massage and cleanse infant gums with a soft cloth after each feeding.[134]

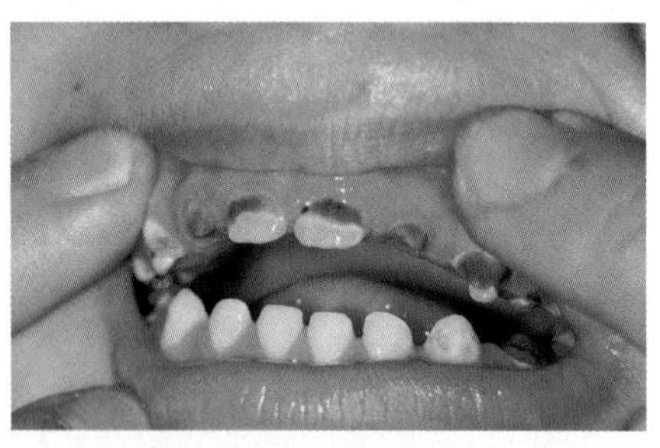

▲ **Figure 17.9 Nursing Bottle Tooth Decay** When infants are given a bottle shortly before sleep, the sugary beverage can pool in the mouth and dissolve immature tooth enamel.

THE TAKE-HOME MESSAGE If a woman doesn't breast-feed, formula is the only healthy option. Commercially made formulas are modified from soy or cow's milk, and patterned after human breast milk. Cow's milk should not be given before age 1, as it is too high in protein and some minerals and too low in fat. Powdered and concentrated formulas need to be mixed carefully so they are not too diluted or concentrated for the baby's digestive system. Tooth decay and ear infections can be prevented by avoiding bedtime bottle feedings.

hypoallergenic infant formulas Specially developed formulas for infants who have food allergies and cannot tolerate regular formula.

nursing bottle tooth decay Tooth decay from prolonged tooth contact with formula, milk, fruit juice, or other sugar-rich liquid offered to an infant in a bottle.

What Are an Infant's Nutrient Needs and Why Are They So High?

Parents and caregivers can be confident that breast milk and commercial formulas are meeting their infants' unique nutritional needs. Nevertheless, they will benefit from knowing exactly what those nutrient needs are and why they are so high.

Infants Grow at an Accelerated Rate

During **infancy,** or the first year of life, a child experiences a tremendous amount of growth. In fact, an infant doubles his or her birth weight by about 6 months of age, and triples it by the age of 12 months. Length doubles around the end of the first year as well. Consider this growth rate in adult terms: An individual who weighs 100 pounds on January first would weigh 200 pounds by the end of June, and 300 pounds by New Year's Eve! An adult would have to eat an enormous amount of food every day to actually make this happen, but for infants, this is a normal growth rate.

Infants are doing much more than getting heavier and longer. Cognitive and social developments are also under way. As time goes by, infant communication skills go beyond crying, and at around 3 months of age a baby usually starts to smile. Preferences become clearer, too: for particular people (such as the mom), for specific activities (getting kisses or being held), and for certain foods (such as mashed bananas).[135]

An infant should reach certain stages of physical development within a distinct time frame. Not growing as expected may be a sign that something is wrong. Parents, caregivers, and health care providers need to be alert to infants who miss developmental milestones and then look more deeply into the situation. The child may not be receiving sufficient nutrition (see **Figure 17.10**). Perhaps an infant has a poor appetite, and the new mom has no idea that the child should be eating more frequently. Maybe an infant is having digestive problems, and the day-care provider does not mention the frequency of dirty diapers.

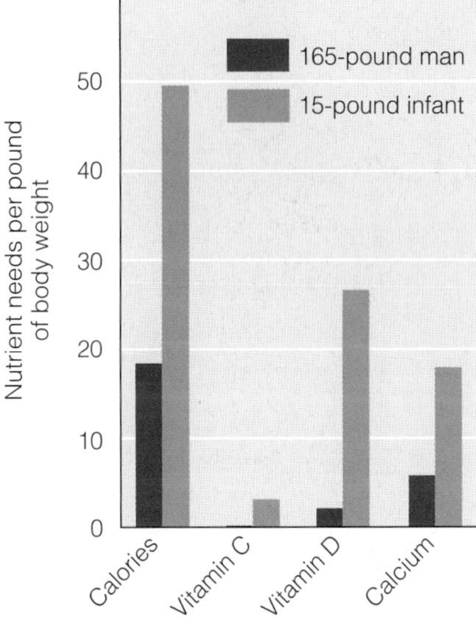

▲ **Figure 17.10 Nutrient Needs per Pound of Body Weight**
Nutrient recommendations for a 5-month-old infant and an adult male compared on the basis of body weight.
Data from USDA, *Dietary Reference Intakes: Recommended Intakes for Individuals*, www.usda.gov.

Optimal infant nutrition is sometimes hindered by circumstance. In less developed countries where poverty is the norm and food is scarce, problems such as protein-energy malnutrition (see Chapter 6) are common. Even in developed countries, problems with poor infant nutrition may affect growth. For example, iron-deficiency anemia (see Chapter 13) is sometimes seen in infants when caregivers substitute juice or cow's milk for breast milk or formula.[136] Or, if a breast-fed infant does not begin consuming iron in solid foods by 4 to 6 months of age, the iron storage runs out, paving the way for anemia.

An infant who does not receive adequate nutrition (whether in quantity or quality) may have difficulty reaching developmental **milestones** (**Figure 17.11**). Think of these as checkpoints of physical, social, and cognitive development. Because most parents do not know the specific nutrient needs of their infant, it's important that they monitor these checkpoints to ensure that they are providing the right amount and type of nourishment.

If a child doesn't reach the appropriate milestones, he or she may eventually develop a condition called *failure to thrive (FTT).* A child with FTT is delayed in physical growth or size or does not gain enough weight. Poor appetite, poor diet, or a medical problem that has not yet been diagnosed can all cause FTT. Sometimes, FTT results from inappropriate care or neglect. Caregivers and health care providers need to be aware of the signs of this condition and watch for those signs in their children and patients.

In addition to milestones, parents and health care providers can use **growth charts** to track physical development progress. Typically, measures of head circumference, length, weight, and weight for length are used to assess growth. These measures are taken at each wellness check visit to the health care provider, about once a month for the first year. The information obtained from the measurements is plotted on a growth chart, placing the child into a **percentile.** Percentiles rank the infant with regard to other infants of the same age in a reference group. For example, a 4-month-old who is in the 25th percentile for weight for that age weighs less than

infancy The age range from birth to 12 months.

milestones Objectives or significant events that occur during development.

growth charts Series of percentile curves that illustrate the distribution of selected body measurements in U.S. children.

percentile The most commonly used clinical indicator to assess the size and growth patterns of children in the United States. An individual child is ranked according to the percentage of the reference population he or she equals or exceeds.

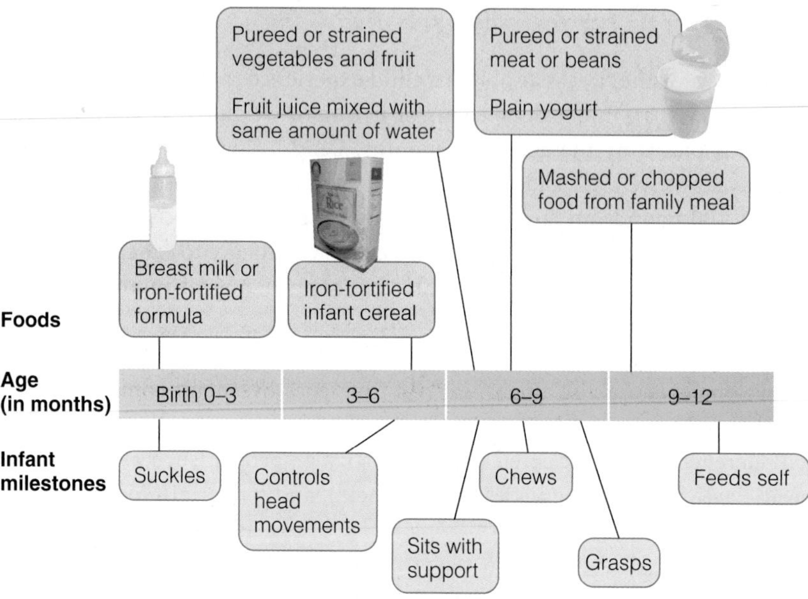

▲ **Figure 17.11 Foods and Milestones for Baby's First Year**
During the first year after birth, an infant's diet will progress from breast milk or formula to age-appropriate versions of family meals.

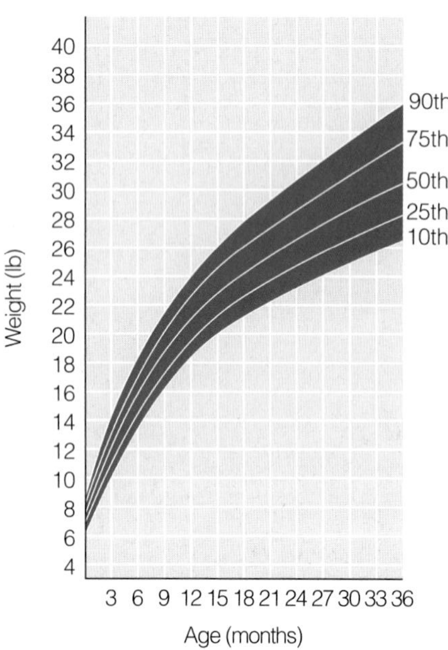

▲ **Figure 17.12 Growth Chart**
Growth charts can help determine if a child is growing at a healthy rate for her age.

75 percent of 4-month-olds and weighs the same as or more than 25 percent[137] (see **Figure 17.12**). Regular checkups enable health care providers to identify and address any inconsistencies in patterns of growth.

Infants Have Specific Kilocalorie, Iron, and Other Nutrient Needs

Though one size does not fit all, there are certain guidelines to follow to meet an infant's nutrient needs. An average of 108 kilocalories per kilogram of body weight is recommended for the first six months of life.[138] Again, imagine a similar proportion of kilocalories at the scale of an adult who weighs 150 pounds (68 kilograms)—it would work out to 7,344 (68 kg × 108) kilocalories per day. That would be more than twice the kilocalories required by an elite Olympic athlete!

Carbohydrate, protein, and fat needs all change within the first year of life. Infants up to 6 months of age should consume 60 grams of carbohydrate per day, which increases to 95 grams per day at 7 to 12 months. Infants need 9.1 grams of protein per day during the first six months of life, which increases to 11 grams daily in the second six months. (The DRIs for infants are listed on the inside front cover of this textbook.) Limiting fat at this stage of the life cycle should be avoided, as it could negatively impact growth. In fact, healthy babies should never be put on weight-loss diets, as this can have a severely negative impact on their physical or mental development.

Three nutrients must be added to an infant's diet: vitamin K, vitamin D, and iron. All newborns should receive an injection of vitamin K to ensure that their blood will clot. This is necessary because infants are born with a sterile gut, and some vitamin K is produced from intestinal bacteria.[139]

The amount of vitamin D in breast milk is not enough to prevent rickets, so infants should also receive 400 IU of vitamin D drops daily beginning during the first two months of life. Infants exclusively fed vitamin D–fortified formula would not require additional vitamin D. Once they reach age 1, they can drink vitamin D–fortified milk at meals; however, if food intake does not offer adequate vitamin D, they may still need

Calculation Corner

Determining Kilocalorie and Fat Content of Breast Milk

The daily energy needs of infants 0 to 6 months are typically met with a liter of breast milk. One liter of breast milk provides 60 grams of carbohydrate, 9.1 grams of protein, and 31 grams of fat.

Approximately how many kilocalories are found in a liter of breast milk?

60 g carbohydrate × 4 kcal/g = 240 kcal

9.1 g of protein × 4 kcal/g = 36.4 kcal

31 g of fat × 9 kcal/g = 279 kcal

Answer: A liter of breast milk provides approximately 555 kilocalories.

The fat in breast milk contributes what proportion of the kilocalories?

Answer: From the above calculations, 279 kilocalories come from fat.

279 kcal from fat ÷ 555 total kcal = 50.3 × 100 = 50%

Answer: Fat represents 50 percent of the total kilocalories found in breast milk.

---

supplementation. Exposure of the infant's skin to sunlight to obtain vitamin D is not recommended because it can cause sunburns and increases the risk of skin cancer.[140]

Iron-rich foods, such as enriched cereals, should be introduced at around 6 months, as the infant's stores of iron are depleted at about this time. Premature infants, who have lower iron stores because they were born early, may need iron supplementation before age 6 months.[141]

Because vitamin B_{12} is naturally found only in animal foods, supplementation may be recommended if the infant is being breast-fed by a strictly vegan mother. If the child's water supply is nonfluoridated, or if bottled water is used for mixing formula, a fluoride supplement may also be necessary.[142]

An infant's fluid needs generally are met with breast milk or formula. Extra fluid is only necessary in hot climates or to rehydrate following episodes of diarrhea, fever, or vomiting, when the body loses fluid and electrolytes. Extra fluid should still be limited even in these circumstances, as filling up on water might keep a baby from being hungry for nutrient-rich breast milk or formula.[143]

Beverages such as apple juice are a popular component of infant diets. In fact, 100 percent juice is considered one of the major sources of infants' kilocalories.[144] However, though juice provides some nutrients, it may provide so many kilocalories that the infant will prefer to drink rather than to eat food, and displace necessary nutrients. Juices should be given only in moderation, and only 100 percent juice, not juice drinks, should be used.

THE TAKE-HOME MESSAGE Infants grow at a dramatic rate during the first year of life. Caregivers and health care providers can monitor infant growth by making sure the child achieves appropriate developmental milestones and by using growth charts. Nutrient needs during the first year of life are substantial, and supplements may be needed in some circumstances.

When Are Solid Foods Safe?

Often, proud parents can hardly wait to show off how their baby is eating "real food." It is an exciting time, because eating **solid foods** represents maturing skills in the baby. Typically, solid foods are introduced at around 4 to 6 months of

solid foods Foods other than breast milk or formula given to an infant, usually around 4 to 6 months of age.

age.[145] However, parents should not suddenly decide to serve their baby steak! The infant must be nutritionally, physiologically, and physically ready to eat solid foods.

Solid Foods May Be Introduced Once Certain Milestones Are Met

First, the infant needs to be nutritionally ready for solid foods. Common sense tells us that as babies get bigger in size, they need more nutrients. Thus, an older, larger infant has higher nutrient needs than a younger, smaller one. Though breast milk can technically still provide most nutrients, introducing solid foods will further meet the infant's needs and help him or her develop feeding skills.

The infant also needs to be physiologically ready; that is, body systems need to be able to process solid foods. At birth, and in early infancy, the GI tract and organs such as the kidneys cannot process solid foods. In addition, introducing solid foods too early may increase a child's risk of allergic reactions to common allergy-causing foods.

Even when an infant is nutritionally and physiologically ready for solid foods, he or she still needs to be physically ready. Physical readiness is specific to the individual child and depends on whether he or she has met the necessary developmental milestones. To determine physical readiness, the following questions must be answered:

- Has the **tongue-thrust reflex** faded? The tongue-thrust reflex protects infants against choking. The tongue automatically pushes outward when a substance is placed on it. The reflex fades at around 4 to 6 months of age.
- Does the infant have head and neck control? Without such control, the infant is at greater risk for choking on solids.
- Does the infant swallow with ease?
- Is the infant able to sit with support?
- Does the infant have the ability to turn his or her head to indicate "I'm full!"?

When the answers to all of these questions is "yes," it is safe and realistic to begin offering solid foods. If the answer to any question is "no," parents and caregivers should wait until the infant does develop the appropriate skills.[146]

Solid Foods Should Be Introduced Gradually

Solid foods like rice cereal and oatmeal can be introduced to infants between 4 and 6 months of age.

Once an infant is ready for solids, foods should be introduced gradually to make sure the child isn't allergic or intolerant. The best practice is to introduce only one new food per week.[147,148] Parents and caregivers should be mindful of how the infant reacts to a new food. If she or he develops hives or a rash, or starts sneezing or vomiting, the food may be the culprit. The least allergy-causing food—rice cereal—is a great first food. It is best offered to the infant when it is heavily diluted with breast milk or formula so there is a familiar taste mixed in with the new taste. This will promote the infant's acceptance of the new food. Whole cow's milk shouldn't be given to an infant until after 1 year of age.

After several days to a week of feeding the infant rice cereal (assuming there has been no negative reaction), a next step is to introduce other single-grain cereals, such as barley or oats. Once all of these have been fed to the infant without difficulty, then multigrain cereals (rice, barley, and oats) can be offered.

The next step is to offer pureed vegetables, so that the infant will become familiar with the more bitter taste of these foods; then fruits in the same manner; then meats. All of these foods should be introduced one at a time.

tongue-thrust reflex A forceful protrusion of the tongue in response to an oral stimulus, such as a spoon.

Phasing in solid foods should take place over a period of several months. The food should initially be served pureed. As the infant's chewing and swallowing skills improve with practice, pureed foods can be replaced with soft, cooked foods. Refer again to Figure 17.10, which shows the progression in the infant's diet from breast milk or formula to age-appropriate versions of family meals. Parents and caregivers should offer a given food more than once, over several days, to give the infant the opportunity to accept the food.[149]

Many parents wonder if they should make homemade baby food. This is an admirable idea, and gives the child exposure to fresh, unprocessed meals. However, many store-bought baby foods are of high quality and comparable to homemade. While some companies opt to add sugar, salt, or other less-desirable ingredients, others use organic produce or no preservatives or additives. One benefit of homemade food that everyone might agree upon is the financial savings—there are no added costs for fancy packaging and labels. The choice to use homemade or commercial baby food is up to the parent or caregiver.

Some Foods Are Dangerous and Should Be Avoided

Not surprisingly, many foods are not appropriate for a baby. Some foods, like hot dog rounds or raw carrot slices, present a choking hazard and need to be cut into very small pieces or avoided altogether. Because infants have few teeth, foods should have a soft texture so they do not require excessive chewing; ideally, foods with texture should easily melt in the mouth, like a cracker. No matter what they are eating, infants should always be supervised.

Parents and caregivers should avoid feeding infants common allergens, such as chocolate, cheese, fish, strawberries, egg whites, cow's milk, and peanuts. Reactions may range from a very mild tingling sensation in the mouth or swelling of the tongue and the throat to difficulty breathing, hives, vomiting, abdominal cramps, diarrhea, a drop in blood pressure, and loss of consciousness or death. (See Health Connection: A Taste Could Be Dangerous: Food Allergies for an explanation of the mechanism of allergic reactions.) Waiting a few months until the infant's digestive system has matured—when the child becomes at least a year old—is a smart way to keep the infant safe.[150]

Though some cultures and families have used honey-dipped pacifiers to calm infants for generations, this is a dangerous practice and should never be done. Honey has been known to carry spores of *Clostridium botulinum*, which can lead to a fatal disease called **botulism.** Infants with botulism become lethargic, feed poorly, and suffer from constipation. They have a weak cry and poor muscle tone. Untreated symptoms may cause paralysis of the arms, legs, trunk, and respiratory muscles. The resulting respiratory failure is what makes this disease potentially deadly. Older children and adults can consume honey without these concerns because their mature intestinal tracts are not susceptible to the spores.[151]

Herbal tea may also pose a risk to infants. Even though the label says "natural," that does not always mean it is safe, because herbal remedies are not regulated. Many herbs are not well researched, and the effectiveness and potential dangers are not always known.[152]

Parents and caregivers also need to think before adding seasonings to their infants' foods. Added salt, sugar, and butter are acquired tastes—that is, infants are not born with a desire for them. Restaurants, processed foods, and our own habits have taught us to think that food only tastes "right" if it is salty, sweet, or buttery. Infants do not care if something is bland, and there is no nutritional benefit to enhancing the taste of foods with additional flavors for them. At this stage of the life cycle, infants can learn to find the natural flavors in whole foods to be satisfying, without added kilocalories, fat, or sodium.

botulism A rare but serious paralytic illness caused by the bacterium *Clostridium botulinum*.

Health Connection

A Taste Could Be Dangerous: Food Allergies

One-year-old Adam was playing in the sandbox at the neighborhood playground, when his babysitter pulled a peanut butter cookie from her backpack. She broke off a small bite of the cookie and handed it to Adam, knowing that he must be hungry for his afternoon snack.

After a minute of chewing, Adam started to wheeze and have difficulty breathing. Then he vomited. The sitter quickly used her cell phone to call for emergency help. She gave the rest of the cookie to one of the paramedics who rushed Adam to the hospital. Unbeknownst to the sitter, Adam had developed a food allergy to peanuts.

A **food allergy** is an abnormal physical reaction of the immune system in response to the consumption of a particular food allergen. **Food allergens** are proteins that are not broken down during cooking or by the body's gastric juices and enzymes during digestion. Because they are not degraded, they enter the body intact, and can cause an adverse reaction by the immune system if the allergen is perceived as a foreign invader.

A food allergy reaction occurs in two stages, the "sensitization stage" followed by the actual response, or "allergic reaction stage." In the first stage (see the figure on the next page) the food allergens don't produce a reaction but rather sensitize or introduce themselves to the person's immune system. In response to the initial introduction of the food allergens, the immune system creates an army of antibodies that enter the blood. The antibodies attach to **mast cells** found in connective tissues, setting the stage for a potential future allergic reaction.

food allergy An abnormal reaction by the immune system to a particular food.

food allergens Proteins that are not broken down by cooking or digestion and enter the body intact, causing an adverse reaction by the immune system.

mast cells Cells in connective tissue to which antibodies attach, setting the stage for potential future allergic reactions.

anaphylactic reactions Severe, life-threatening physiological reactions that cause constriction of the airways in the lungs, which inhibits the ability to breathe.

food intolerance Adverse reaction to a food that does not involve an immune response.

The reaction stage occurs when a person eats the food allergens for the second and subsequent times. After they are consumed, the food allergens come in contact with the mast cells. The mast cells release chemicals such as heparin and histamine that trigger reactions in the body. The areas in the body that manifest a food allergy reaction are the areas where mast cells are prevalent, such as under the skin and mucosa. In very sensitive individuals, even minute exposure to a food allergen—just one peanut, for example—can trigger an allergic reaction.[1] Reactions appear quickly after eating the food. In fact, an itchiness in the mouth may occur as soon as the food touches the tongue, and skin reactions and difficulty breathing may develop within minutes. After the food reaches the stomach and begins to be digested, vomiting and/or diarrhea may result. When they enter the blood, the food allergens can cause a drop in blood pressure.

Individuals with allergies or their caretakers often carry a syringe injector of epinephrine (adrenaline) to be self-administered in severe reactions and help treat these symptoms. Epinephrine constricts blood vessels, relaxes the muscles in the lungs to help with breathing, and decreases swelling and hives.

Eggs, cow's milk, and peanuts are the most common sources of food allergens in children. These and other common allergens, such as strawberries, chocolate, and fish, should be avoided for infants in order to prevent sensitization and subsequent allergic responses. In adults, shellfish, peanuts, tree nuts, fish, wheat, soy, and eggs are the most common sources of food allergens. These foods comprise 90 percent of those that cause reactions to food allergens. Some children will outgrow their reactions to milk, and up to 20 percent of them will outgrow a peanut allergy.[2] In contrast, adults are rarely able to rid themselves of a food allergy once it is established.

The number of young people who had a food or digestive allergy increased 18 percent between 1997 and 2007, according to the Centers for Disease Control and Prevention.[3] Approximately 3 million U.S. children and teenagers under age 18—nearly 4 percent of that age group—were reported to have such an allergy in the previous 12 months.[4] In the United States, food allergies are the cause of 2,000 admittances to the hospital, approximately 30,000 **anaphylactic reactions** (*ana* = without, no, *phylaxis* = protection), which are severe, life-threatening allergic reactions, and almost 200 deaths annually.[5] An anaphylactic reaction can cause vomiting and constriction or narrowing of the airways in the lungs, which inhibits breathing.

Note that a food allergy is different from a **food intolerance.** The symptoms of a food intolerance may mimic a food allergy, but a food intolerance does not involve the immune system.

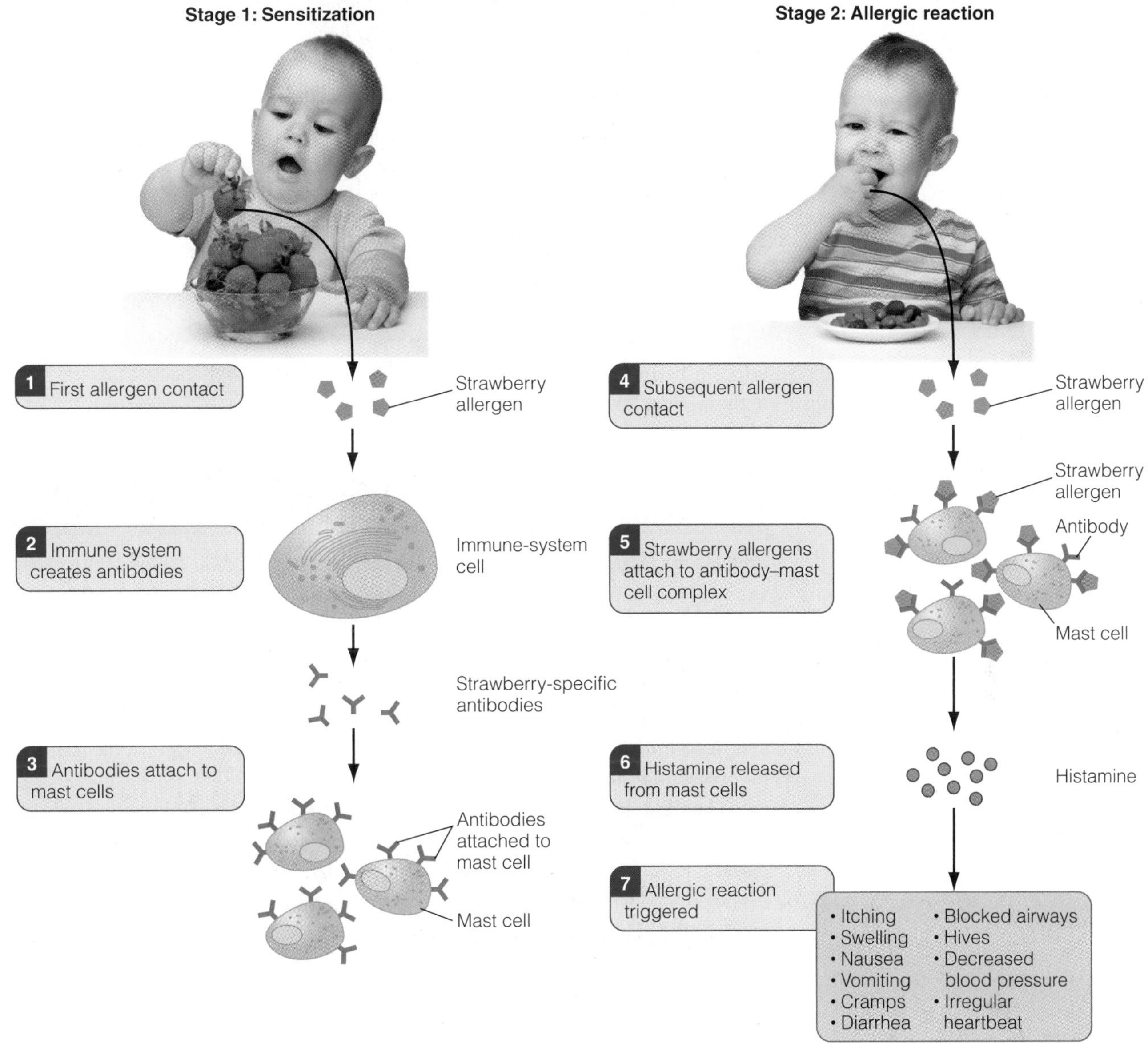

Reactions to Allergens
The reaction stage occurs when a person eats the food allergens for the second and subsequent times.

The FDA requires that virtually all food ingredients be listed on the food label, and that the food label state whether the product contains protein from any of the eight major foods known to cause an allergic reaction: milk, eggs, fish, shellfish, tree nuts, peanuts, soy, and wheat.[6] The FDA is continually working with food manufacturers and consumer groups to improve public education about food allergies and the seriousness of anaphylactic reactions, in particular for the most common sources of food allergies.[7]

References

1. National Institute of Allergy and Infectious Diseases. 2012. *Food Allergy: An Overview.* Available at www.niaid.nih.gov/topics/foodallergy/documents/foodallergy.pdf. Accessed April 2012.
2. The Food Allergy and Anaphylaxis Network. 2012. *Common Food Allergens.* Available at www.foodallergy.org/page/common-food-allergens-index. Accessed April 2012.
3. Centers for Disease Control and Prevention. 2009. *Food Allergy Among U.S. Children: Trends in Prevalence and Hospitalizations.* Available at www.cdc.gov/nchs/data/databriefs/db10.pdf. Accessed April 2012.
4. Ibid.
5. Long, A. 2002. The Nuts and Bolts of Peanut Allergy. *New England Journal of Medicine* 346:1320–1322.
6. Food and Drug Administration. 2009. *Food Allergen Labeling and Consumer Protection Act of 2004* (Title II of Public Law 108–282). Report to the Committee on Health, Education, Labor, and Pensions, United States Senate, and the Committee on Energy and Commerce, United States House of Representatives. Available at www.fda.gov/food/labelingnutrition/FoodAllergensLabeling/GuidanceCompliance RegulatoryInformation/ucm106187.htm. Accessed April 2012.
7. Food and Drug Administration. 2005. *Compliance Policy Guide. Section 555.250. Statement of Policy for Labeling and Preventing Cross-Contact of Common Food Allergens.* Available at www.fda.gov/ICECI/ComplianceManuals/CompliancePolicyGuidance Manual/ucm074552.htm. Accessed April 2012.

Do babies need fiber to keep them "regular" like adults? Though fiber is useful for many reasons, too much can actually be harmful to an infant because it can pull nutrients through the GI tract before they have a chance to be absorbed. At this time, no recommendations have been established for fiber during the first year of life. As the infant gets older, more fiber is suitable.

THE TAKE-HOME MESSAGE An infant must be physically and physiologically ready before being introduced to solid foods. Solid foods should be introduced gradually and cautiously. Foods that may be choking hazards should be avoided, and children should always be supervised while eating. Common food allergens, honey, and herbal tea should be avoided for the first year, and seasonings such as salt, sugar, and butter should not be added to an infant's foods. Parents and caregivers must educate themselves about foods that are appropriate and those that are not in order to keep the infant safe and healthy.

Putting It All Together

Pregnancy, lactation, and infancy are periods of the life cycle during which women and babies have unique nutrient needs. Women need to refer to the DRIs for pregnancy and lactation (listed on the inside front cover of this textbook) to make sure they consume adequate kilocalories, protein, iron, and folate for both their own health and that of their developing baby. Babies have high nutrient and kilocalorie needs during their first year to sustain their rapid growth and development. **Figure 17.13** summarizes the nutritional and lifestyle guidelines for babies and their parents.

The lifestyle habits mentioned in earlier chapters—like smoking and drinking too much alcohol—that have been shown to lead to chronic diseases such as heart disease, cancer, and cirrhosis are also unhealthy during pregnancy and lactation. Both men and women should adopt healthier lifestyles before pregnancy in order to increase the likelihood of having a healthy baby.

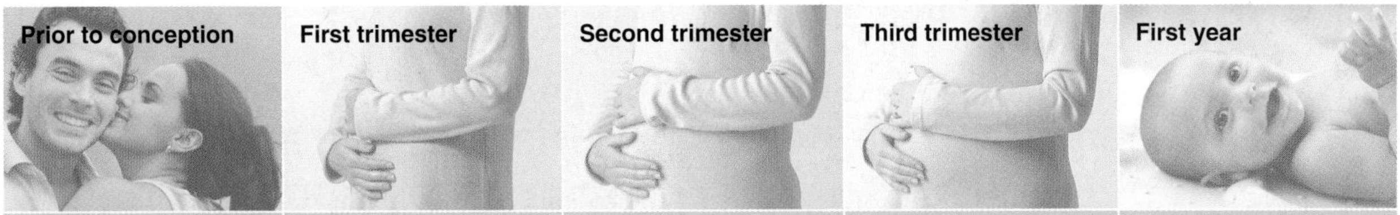

	Prior to conception	First trimester	Second trimester	Third trimester	First year
Father	• Stop smoking • Limit alcohol • Maintain a healthy weight • Consume a balanced diet				
Mother	• Consume a balanced diet • Maintain a healthy weight • Add folic acid to diet • Limit caffeine • Avoid certain fish with high levels of methylmercury • Avoid alcohol, herbs, illicit drugs, and smoking • Exercise regularly	• Consume a balanced diet • Continue getting folic acid • Take an iron-rich supplement • Limit caffeine • Avoid too much vitamin A • Avoid foodborne illness • Continue exercising	• Consume a balanced diet with adequate calories for growth • Continue exercising	• Consume a balanced diet with adequate calories for growth • Eat frequent small meals if more comfortable • Choose high-fiber foods • Drink plenty of fluids • Continue nonimpact exercises	• Consume a balanced diet with adequate calories and fluids for breast-feeding • Nursing mothers should avoid illicit drugs, smoking, and alcohol • Limit caffeine • Avoid certain fish with high levels of methylmercury
Baby					• Supplement diet with vitamins K and D and sources of iron or iron-fortified foods • Avoid common food allergens, honey, and herbal tea • Consume breast milk or formula as primary source of calories • Do not start drinking cow's milk until after this year • Introduce solid foods gradually and one at a time • Avoid too much fiber and excessive amounts of juice

▲ **Figure 17.13 Summary of Nutritional Guidelines**
Nutritional guidelines for both parents and infants are shown above.

Visual Chapter Summary

1 There Are Several Critical Periods of Prenatal Development

An average healthy pregnancy lasts about 38 weeks and is divided into three 13-week trimesters. The initial two weeks after conception is called the pre-embryo stage when the zygote implants into the uterine wall. It gradually develops into an embryo during weeks three through eight. This is the critical period when major congenital anomalies can occur. After eight weeks, the embryo is called a fetus. It is during this critical period of development that nutrients, oxygen, and waste products are exchanged between the mother and fetus, through the placenta. Some toxins and other substances from the mother can cross the placenta and harm the developing embryo and the fetus.

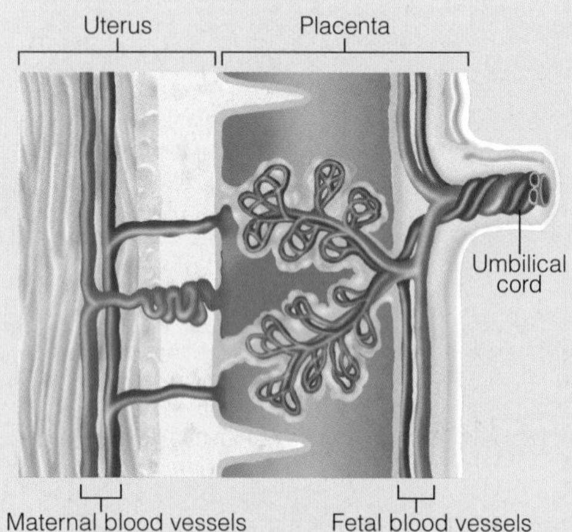

2 Nutrient Intake and Healthy Behaviors Are Important for a Healthy Pregnancy

Both the father and the mother should make healthy diet and lifestyle changes prior to pregnancy. For healthy sperm, men should stop smoking, abstain from alcohol or drink only in moderation, strive for a healthy body weight, and consume a well-balanced diet. Prior to pregnancy, women should also abstain from alcohol, smoking, and caffeine, and strive for a healthy weight. In addition, women should consume adequate amounts of folic acid to reduce the risk of neural tube defects. During pregnancy, women should abstain from alcohol, herbs, and illicit drugs. Pregnant women should avoid fish that contain high amounts of methylmercury and consume caffeine only in moderation.

Exercise during pregnancy can help improve sleep, lower the risk of hypertension and diabetes, prevent backaches, help relieve constipation, shorten labor, and reduce stress and depression. Low-impact activities such as walking, swimming, and stationary cycling are recommended to prevent injury to both mother and baby.

3 Specific Nutrients Are Important during the First Trimester

A woman's needs for many nutrients, including folate, iron, zinc, copper, and calcium, increase up to 50 percent during pregnancy. With the exception of iron, for which a prenatal supplement is usually needed, most nutrient requirements can be met with a balanced diet. Care should be taken to avoid consuming too much preformed vitamin A and vitamin D, which can cause birth defects. Sufficient carbohydrates, protein, alpha-linolenic acid, and choline are necessary throughout pregnancy. About 100 additional kilocalories are needed to gain two to three pounds in the first trimester. Awareness of food safety is also important, as bacteria such as *Listeria monocytogenes* may cause miscarriages, premature labor, delivery of a low birth weight infant, developmental problems, or even infant death.

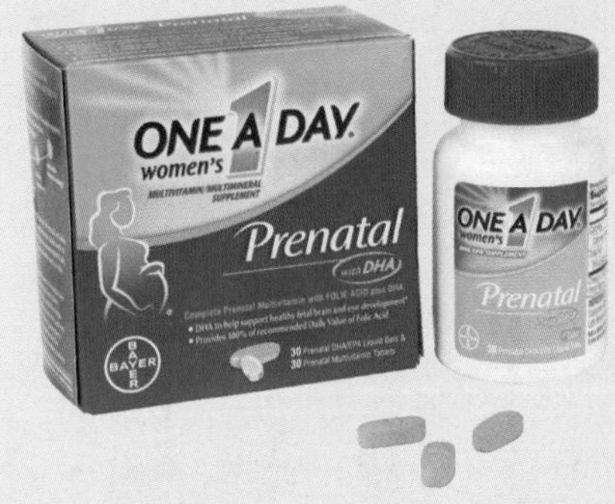

4 Additional Carbohydrates and Protein Are Important during the Second Trimester

Many pregnant women find that the nausea and fatigue of the first trimester diminish during the second trimester, and appetite begins to increase. The mother's kilocalorie needs also increase. A pregnant woman should consume an additional 340 kilocalories daily during the second trimester and should gain around a pound per week. Pregnant women need about 175 grams of carbohydrate and 71 grams of protein. These needs can be met with a balanced diet. The risk of gestational diabetes and hypertension can be reduced during the second trimester with a healthy diet, daily exercise, and managing body weight.

5 Healthy Eating Behaviors and Weight Gain Are Important Considerations during the Third Trimester

By the end of the last trimester, a pregnant woman should be taking in an extra 450 kilocalories daily and continue to gain about 1 pound per week. The slower movement of food through the GI tract can contribute to heartburn and constipation. Reduced physical activity and iron supplementation can also contribute to constipation. To minimize heartburn, pregnant women should eat smaller but frequent meals, eliminate spicy foods that may irritate the esophagus, and avoid lying down immediately after meals. Exercise and consuming fiber-rich foods, along with plenty of fluids, can help prevent or alleviate constipation.

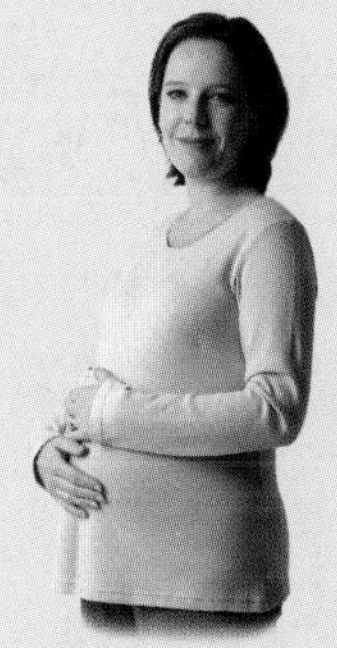

Third trimester

Total weight gain ~30 lbs

- Maternal fat stores (~7 lbs)
- Uterus and breast (4 lbs)
- Blood (3–4 lbs)
- Fetus (~7 lbs)
- Placenta, amniotic fluid, and other fluids (~8 lbs)

6 Younger, Older, or Low-Income Mothers-to-Be Face Special Challenges

Women younger or older than the physically optimal childbearing age range of 20 to 25 may face additional challenges during pregnancy. Teenage mothers are at risk for pregnancy-induced hypertension, iron-deficiency anemia, and delivering premature and low birth weight babies. Older women are at risk of developing diabetes and high blood pressure. Their infants are more likely to have Down syndrome or other disabilities. Low income women are at greater risk of iron-deficiency anemia and premature and low birth weight infants.

7 Breast-Feeding Benefits Both Mother and Child

Breast-feeding is the gold standard for feeding an infant. It provides physical, emotional, and financial benefits and convenience for the mother and nutritional and health benefits for the infant. Breast milk is rich in nutrients, antibodies, and other compounds that provide the infant with a disease-fighting boost until the baby's own immune system matures. Because of all the benefits, women are encouraged to exclusively breast-feed for the first six months. Breast-feeding mothers need to consume 330 to 400 extra kilocalories daily to produce breast milk.

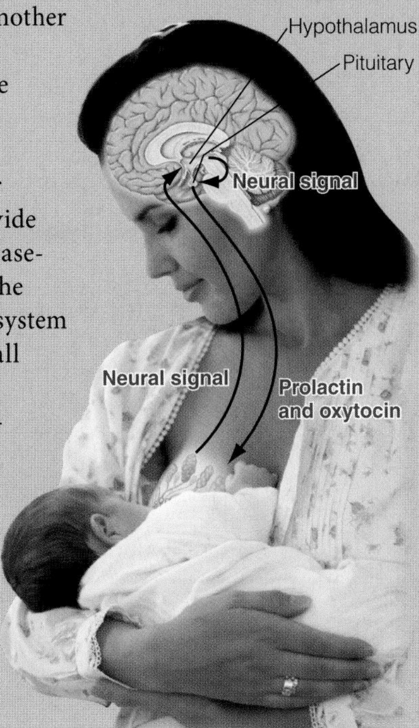

8 Formula Can Be a Healthy Alternative to Breast Milk

If an infant isn't breast-fed, the only healthy alternative is commercially made formula. Commercially made formulas are modified from soy or cow's milk, and patterned after human breast milk. For some women, formula-feeding is a personal preference. For others it is necessary, since breast-feeding may not be possible due to illness or other circumstances. Tooth decay and ear infections can be prevented by avoiding bedtime bottle feedings when infants are placed in bed with a bottle.

9 Infants Have Specific Nutrient Needs

An infant doubles his or her birth weight by around 6 months of age, and triples it by 12 months. Poor infant nutrition (whether in quality or quantity) will likely prevent ideal growth and the ability of the child to meet milestones on time. Infants need approximately 108 kilocalories per kilogram of body weight during the first six months of life. All infants should receive a vitamin K injection at birth, and breast-fed infants need vitamin D supplements. Infants older than 6 months need to begin taking in iron through food sources, as their stored iron supply is depleted around this time.

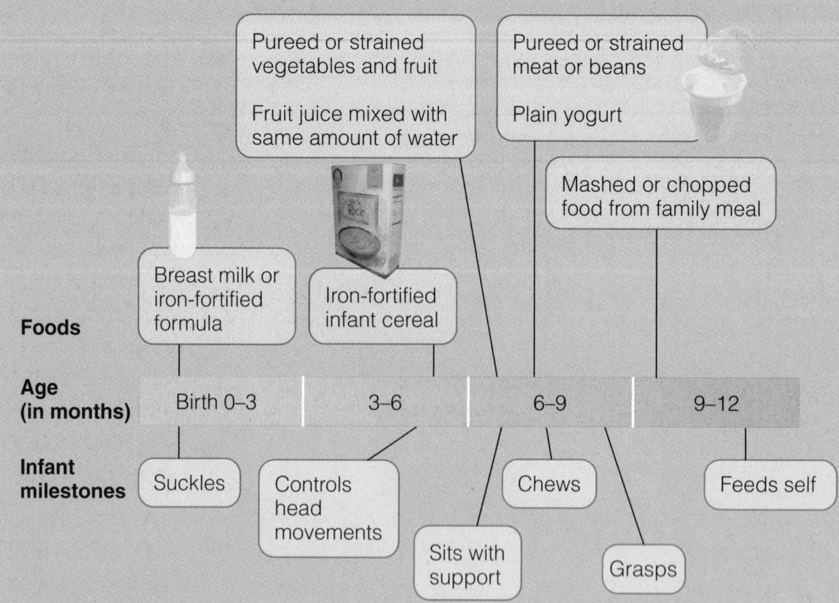

10 Solid Foods Should Be Introduced Gradually after Certain Milestones Are Reached

An infant is ready to begin eating solid foods if the infant's birth weight has doubled, the infant has the ability to sit with support and can control his or her head and neck, the infant's tongue-thrust reflex has faded, and his or her swallowing skills are mature. Once an infant is ready for solids, foods should be introduced gradually to make sure the child isn't allergic or intolerant. The best suggestion is to introduce only one new food per week.

Terms To Know

- embryo
- placenta
- fetus
- pica
- gestational diabetes
- pregnancy-induced hypertension
- lactation
- letdown response
- colostrum
- nursing bottle tooth decay

MasteringNutrition™

Build your knowledge—and confidence—in the Study Area of MasteringNutrition with a variety of study tools.

Check Your Understanding

1. To prevent neural tube birth defects, a woman should start taking 400 micrograms of folic acid
   a. during the first trimester.
   b. during the second trimester.
   c. at least one month prior to conception and during the early weeks of pregnancy.
   d. during the last trimester.
2. The production and function of sperm in males may decrease because of
   a. antioxidants.
   b. zinc.

c. folate.
d. obesity.

3. The definition of a low birth weight baby is one who is born weighing less than
   a. 5 ½ pounds.
   b. 6½ pounds.
   c. 7½ pounds.
   d. 8½ pounds.
4. Mary Ellen is pregnant and going out to a seafood restaurant for dinner. She should not order
   a. flounder.
   b. shrimp.
   c. swordfish.
   d. lobster.
5. A woman at a healthy weight should gain ______________ pounds during pregnancy.
   a. 15 to 25
   b. 20 to 30
   c. 25 to 35
   d. 30 to 40
6. During pregnancy, a woman's need for many nutrients increases. Which mineral requirement is unlikely to be met through her diet alone?
   a. iron
   b. potassium
   c. sodium
   d. calcium
7. During the second trimester of pregnancy, a woman should increase her daily kilocalorie intake by
   a. 340 kilocalories.
   b. 400 kilocalories.
   c. 440 kilocalories.
   d. 500 kilocalories.
8. Breast-feeding can have which of the following benefits for both mother and child?
   a. relief of intestinal disorders
   b. reduced risk of type 2 diabetes
   c. fewer respiratory infections
   d. less chance of meningitis
9. Andy is a healthy, 3-month-old baby boy who is being breast-fed by his mother. Which of the following nutrients needs to be added to his diet?
   a. vitamin D
   b. potassium
   c. vitamin C
   d. calcium
10. Six-month-old Cathy is ready for solid foods. The first food that should be introduced in her diet is
    a. oatmeal.
    b. rice cereal.
    c. pureed vegetables.
    d. cow's milk.

Answers

1. (c) To reduce the risk of these birth defects, folic acid should be consumed prior to conception and continue during the early weeks of pregnancy.
2. (d) Obesity, along with smoking and alcohol abuse, is associated with the decreased production and functioning of sperm. Zinc and folate help produce healthy sperm, while antioxidants, in particular vitamins E and C and carotenoids, may help protect sperm.
3. (a) A baby born weighing less than 5½ pounds is considered a low birth weight baby.
4. (c) The swordfish is off-limits during pregnancy because of its high methylmercury content.
5. (c) A woman at a healthy weight should gain 25 to 35 pounds during pregnancy.
6. (a) Because a pregnant woman's increased iron needs cannot be easily met through the diet, she will likely need a prescribed prenatal supplement. She can get the potassium, sodium, and calcium she needs through a well-balanced diet.
7. (a) A pregnant woman needs 340 extra kilocalories daily during the second trimester to meet her needs. During the third trimester, she needs an extra 450 kilocalories every day. She doesn't need additional daily kilocalories during the first trimester, but does have additional nutrient needs, so she should be sure to eat nutrient-dense foods.
8. (b) Breast-feeding reduces the risk of type 2 diabetes in both the mother and child. The other benefits—fewer intestinal disorders and respiratory infections, and lower risk of meningitis—accrue to the nursing child.
9. (a) While breast milk is an ideal food for baby Andy, it doesn't contain enough vitamin D, so he should receive daily drops in his diet.
10. (b) Cooked rice cereal is the perfect choice as it is the least likely to cause an allergic reaction. If Cathy tolerates the rice cereal well, oatmeal could be the next grain added to her diet. Pureed vegetables could follow. Milk shouldn't be introduced into Cathy's diet until she turns 1 year of age.

Answers to Myths and Misconceptions

1. **False.** Fathers need to eat healthy diets and avoid certain substances prior to conception to help produce a healthy baby.
2. **False.** Any type of alcohol, including red wine, can harm a growing fetus.
3. **False.** Though it's called morning sickness, nausea during the first trimester can happen at any time of day.
4. **False.** Physical activity can be good for mothers-to-be, though some activities need to be avoided.
5. **False.** Formula can be a healthy alternative, but breast milk is best for a baby.
6. **True.** Antibodies in breast milk are passed from the mother to the baby, which can bolster an infant's immune system.
7. **False.** Infants should never be put on a weight-loss diet. Babies need kilocalories and fat to support their rapid growth and development.
8. **False.** Most infants receive an injection of vitamin K at birth, and supplemental vitamin D is needed in an infant's diet.
9. **False.** While homemade baby food may taste better, commercially prepared versions are tightly regulated and just as nutritious.
10. **False.** Although they're a good source of vitamin A, raw carrots are a potential choking hazard for an infant.

Web Resources

- For more information on meal planning during pregnancy and lactation, visit ChooseMyPlate for pregnant and breast-feeding women at www.choosemyplate.gov/pregnancy-breastfeeding/pregnancy-nutritional-needs.html
- For more information on breast-feeding, visit the La Leche League International website at www.llli.org
- For more information on children and their dietary needs, visit the American Academy of Pediatrics at www.aap.org
- To obtain growth charts and guidelines for their use, visit www.cdc.gov/nchs/nhanes.htm
- For more information on food allergies, visit the Food Allergy and Anaphylaxis Network at www.foodallergy.org

References

1. Painter, R. C., S. R. de Rooij, P. M. Bossuyt, T. A. Simmers, C. Osmond, D. J. Barker, et al. 2006. Early Onset of Coronary Artery Disease after Prenatal Exposure to the Dutch Famine. *American Journal of Clinical Nutrition* 84:322–327.
2. Szajewska, H., M. Ruszczynski, and A. Chmielewska. 2010. Effects of Iron Supplementation in Nonanemic Pregnant Women, Infants, and Young Children on the Mental Performance and Psychomotor Development of Children: A Systematic Review of Randomized Controlled Trials. *American Journal of Clinical Nutrition* 91:1684–1690.
3. Tarry-Adkins, J. L. and S. E. Ozanne. 2011. Mechanisms of Early Life Programming: Current Knowledge and Future Directions. *American Journal of Clinical Nutrition* 94(6 Suppl):1765S–1771S.
4. Stover, P. J. and M. A. Caudill. 2008. Genetic and Epigenetic Contributions to Human Nutrition and Health: Managing Genome-Diet Interactions. *Journal of the American Dietetic Association* 108:1480–1487.
5. Wong, W., C. Thomas, J. Merkus, G. Zielhuis, and R. Steegers-Theunissen. 2000. Male Factor Subfertility: Possible Causes and the Impact of Nutritional Factors. *Fertility and Sterility* 73:435–442.
6. Sharpe, R. M. 2010. Environmental/Lifestyle Effects on Spermatogenesis. *Philosophical Transaction of the Royal Society Biological Sciences* 365:1697–1712.
7. Young, S. S., B. Eskenazi, F. M. Marchetti, G. Block, and A. Wyrobek. 2008. The Association of Folate, Zinc and Antioxidant Intake with Sperm Aneuploidy in Healthy Non-Smoking Men. *Human Reproduction* 23:1014–1022.
8. Wong, et al. 2000. Male Factor Subfertility; Young, et al. 2008. The Association of Folate, Zinc and Antioxidant Intake with Sperm Aneuploidy.
9. Kaiser, L. and L. Allen. 2008. Position of the American Dietetic Association: Nutrition and Lifestyle for a Healthy Pregnancy Outcome. *Journal of the American Dietetic Association* 108:553–561.
10. Pandey, S. and S. Bhattacharya. 2010. Impact of Obesity on Gynecology. *Women's Health* 6:107–117.
11. Kaiser, et al. 2008. Position of the American Dietetic Association; Ramachenderan, J., J. Bradford, and M. Mclean. 2008. Maternal Obesity and Pregnancy Complications: A Review. *Australian and New Zealand Journal of Obstetrics and Gynaecology* 48:228–235.
12. Chobanian, A., G. Bakris, H. Black, W. Cushman, L. Green, J. Izzo, et al. 2003. Seventh Report of the Joint National Committee on Prevention, Detection, Evaluation, and Treatment of High Blood Pressure. *Hypertension* 42:1206–1252.
13. Ramachenderan, et al. 2008. Maternal Obesity and Pregnancy Complications.
14. Institute of Medicine. 1990. *Nutrition during Pregnancy*. Washington, DC: The National Academies Press.
15. Kaiser, et al. 2008. Position of the American Dietetic Association.
16. Tam, W. H., R. C. Ma, X. Yang, A. M. Li, G. T. C. Ko, A. P. S. Kang, et al. 2010. Glucose Intolerance and Cardiometabolic Risk in Adolescents Exposed to Maternal Gestational Diabetes. *Diabetes Care* 122:1229–1234.
17. Homan, G. F., M. Davies, and R. J. Norman. 2007. The Impact of Lifestyle Factors on Reproductive Performance in the General Population and Those Undergoing Infertility Treatment: A Review. *Human Reproduction Update* 13:209–223.
18. Weng, X., R. Odouli, and D. K. Li. 2008. Maternal Caffeine Consumption during Pregnancy and the Risk of Miscarriage: A Prospective Cohort Study. *American Journal of Obstetrics & Gynecology* 198:279.e1–279.e8.
19. U.S. Department of Health and Human Services. 2004. *The Health Consequences of Smoking: A Report of the Surgeon General*. Atlanta: Centers for Disease Control and Prevention, National Center for Chronic Disease Prevention and Health Promotion, Office on Smoking and Health.
20. U.S. Department of Health and Human Services. 2004. *The Health Consequences of Smoking.*
21. Institute of Medicine. 1990. *Nutrition during Pregnancy.*
22. Kaiser, et al. 2008. Position of the American Dietetic Association.
23. U.S. Department of Health and Human Services. 2005. U.S. Surgeon General Releases Advisory on Alcohol Use in Pregnancy. Available at www.surgeongeneral.gov/news/2005/02/sg02222005.html. Accessed November 2012.
24. American College of Obstetricians and Gynecologists. 2008. *At-Risk Drinking and Illicit Drug Use: Ethical Issues in Obstetric and Gynecologic Practice*, American College of Obstetricians and Gynecologists Committee Opinion, Number 442. Available at www.acog.org/Resources_And_Publications/Committee_Opinions/Committee_on_Ethics/At_Risk_Drinking_and_Illicit_Drug_Use_Ethical_Issues_in_Obstetric_and_Gynecologic_Practice. Accessed April 2012.
25. Dog, T. L. 2009. The Use of Botanicals During Pregnancy and Lactation. *Alternative Therapies* 15:54–58.
26. Jones, T. and T. Lawson. 1998. Profound Neonatal Congestive Heart Failure Caused by Maternal Consumption of Blue Cohosh Herbal Medication. *Journal of Pediatrics* 132:550–552.
27. Ye, R., A. Ren, L. Zhang, Z. Li, J. Liu, L. Pei, et al. 2011. Tea Drinking as a Risk Factor for Neural Tube Defects in Northern China. *Epidemiology* 22:491–496.
28. Navarro-Peran, E., J. Cabezas-Herrera, F. Garcia-Canovas, M. Durrant, R. Thorneley, and J. Rodríguez-Lopez. 2005. The Antifolate Activity of Tea Catechins. *Cancer Research* 65:2059–2064.
29. Broussard, C. S., C. Louik, M. A. Honein, A. A. Mitchell, and the National Birth Defects Prevention Study. 2010. Herbal Use Before and During Pregnancy. *American Journal of Obstetrics and Gynecology* 202:443.e1–443.e6.
30. Kleinman, R., ed. 2008. *Pediatric Nutrition Handbook*. 6th ed. Elk Grove Village, IL: American Academy of Pediatrics.
31. American Diabetes Association. 2004. Preconception Care of Women with Diabetes (Position Statement). *Diabetes Care* 27(Suppl. 1): S76–S78.
32. Chan, R. L., A. F. Olshan, D. A. Savitz, A. H. Herring, J. L. Daniels, H. B. Peterson, et al. 2011. Maternal Influences on Nausea and Vomiting in Early Pregnancy. *Maternal and Child Health Journal* 15:122–127.
33. Ibid.
34. King, T. L. and P. A. Murphy. 2009. Evidence-Based Approaches to Managing Nausea and Vomiting in Early Pregnancy. *Journal of Midwifery and Women's Health* 54:430–444.
35. Erick, M. 1994. Battling Morning (Noon and Night) Sickness. *Journal of the American Dietetic Association* 94:147–148.
36. Strong, T. 2001. Alternative Therapies of Morning Sickness. *Clinical Obstetrics and Gynecology* 44:653–660;
37. Erick. 1994. Battling Morning (Noon and Night) Sickness.
38. King, et al. 2009. Evidence-Based Approaches to Managing Nausea and Vomiting in Early Pregnancy.

39. Kaiser, et al. 2008. Position of the American Dietetic Association.
40. Thihalolipava, S., B. M. Candalla, and J. Ehrlich. 2012. Examining Pica in NYC Pregnant Women with Elevated Blood Lead Levels. *Maternal and Child Health Journal* (Epub ahead of print.) Available from www.springerlink.com/content/f21128461441h738. Accessed April 2012.
41. Bakhireva, L. N., A. S. Rowland, B. N. Young, S. Cano, S. T. Phela, K. Artyushkova, et al. 2012. Sources of Potential Lead Exposure Among Pregnant Women in New Mexico. *Maternal and Child Health Journal* (Epub ahead of print.) Available from www.springerlink.com/content/a60675321l860514. Accessed April 2012.
42. Kaiser, et al. 2008. Position of the American Dietetic Association.
43. Institute of Medicine. 1990. *Nutrition during Pregnancy.*
44. Institute of Medicine. 2009. Weight Gain during Pregnancy: Reexamining the Guidelines. Available at www.iom.edu/Reports/2009/Weight-gain-during-pregnancy-reexamining-the-guidelines.aspx. Accessed April 2012.
45. Smith, S. A., T. Hulsey, and W. Goodnight. 2008. Effects of Obesity on Pregnancy. *Journal of Obstetric, Gynecologic, & Neonatal Nursing* 37:176–184.
46. Institute of Medicine. 1990. *Nutrition during Pregnancy*; Kaiser, et al. 2008. Position of the American Dietetic Association.
47. Institute of Medicine. 1990. *Nutrition during Pregnancy.*
48. Ibid.
49. Kaiser, et al. 2008. Position of the American Dietetic Association.
50. Young, B. E., T. J. McNanley, E. M. Cooper, A. W. McIntyre, F. Witter, Z. L. Harris, and K. O. O'Brien. 2012. Maternal Vitamin D Status and Calcium Intake Interact to Affect Fetal Skeletal Growth in Utero in Pregnant Adolescents. *American Journal of Clinical Nutrition*. 95:1103–1112.
51. Brannon, P. M. and M. F Picciano. 2011. Vitamin D in Pregnancy and Lactation in Humans. *Annual Review of Nutrition* 31:89–115.
52. McGrath, J. 2001. Does "Imprinting" with Low Prenatal Vitamin D Contribute to the Risk of Various Adult Disorders? *Medical Hypotheses* 56:367–371.
53. Wagner, C. L., S. N. Taylor, A. Dawodu, D. D. Johnson, and B. W. Hollis. 2012. Vitamin D and Its Role During Pregnancy in Attaining Optimal Health of Mother and Fetus. *Nutrients* 4:208–230.
54. Eijsden, M. V., G. Hornstra, M. F. van der Wal, T. G. M. Vrijkotte, and G. J. Bonse. 2008. Maternal n–3, n–6, and *Trans* Fatty Acid Profile Early in Pregnancy and Term Birth Weight: A Prospective Cohort Study. *American Journal of Clinical Nutrition* 87:887–895.
55. Jiang, X., J. Yan, A. A. West, C. A. Perry, O. V. Malysheva, S. Devapatla, et al. 2012. Maternal Choline Intake Alters the Epigenetic State of Fetal Cortiosl-Regulating Genes in Humans. *Federation of American Societies of Experimental Biology Journal* 26:1995–2007.
56. Duffy, V. and M. Sigman-Grant. 2004. Position of the American Dietetic Association: Use of Nutritive and Nonnutritive Sweeteners. *Journal of the American Dietetic Association* 104:255–275.
57. American College of Obstetricians and Gynecologists. 2010. Exercise during Pregnancy. Available at www.acog.org/~/media/For%20Patients/faq119.pdf?dmc[equals]1&ts[equals]20120408T0033520544. Accessed April 2012.
58. American College of Obstetricians and Gynecologists. Committee Obstetric Practice. 2002. ACOG Committee Opinion No. 267, Exercise during Pregnancy and the Postpartum Period. *Obstetrics & Gynecology* 99:171–173.
59. Wang, T.W., and B. S. Apgar. 1998. Exercise During Pregnancy. *American Family Physician* 57:1846-1852.
60. Milunsky, A., M. Ulcickas, K. J. Rothman, W. Willet, S. S. Jick, and H. Jick. 1992. Maternal Heat Exposure and Neural Tube Defect. *Journal of the American Medical Association* 268:882–885.
61. Li, D. K., T. Janevic, R. Odouli, and L. Liu. 2004. Hot Tub Use during Pregnancy and the Risk of Miscarriage. *American Journal of Epidemiology* 158:931–937.
62. Kaiser, et al. 2008. Position of the American Dietetic Association.
63. American Diabetes Association. 2012.*Gestational Diabetes.* Available at www.diabetes.org/diabetes-basics/gestational. Accessed April 2012.
64. German Institute for Quality and Efficiency in Health Care. 2011. *Gestational Diabetes: Does a Routine Examination Help to Avoid Complications for Mother and Child?* Available at www.ncbi.nlm.nih.gov/pubmedhealth/PMH0010399. Accessed April 2012.
65. American Diabetes Association. 2012. *Gestational Diabetes.*
66. American Diabetes Association. 2012. *Gestational Diabetes.*
67. Ibid.
68. American Diabetes Association. 2012. Standards of Medical Care in Diabetes. *Diabetes Care* 35:S4–S10.
69. American Diabetes Association. 2012. *Gestational Diabetes.*
70. Chobanian, et al. 2003. Seventh Report of the Joint National Committee on Prevention, Detection, Evaluation, and Treatment of High Blood Pressure; American College of Obstetricians and Gynecologists. 2011. *High Blood Pressure during Pregnancy.* Available at www.acog.org/~/media/For%20Patients/faq034.pdf?dmc[equals]1&ts=20120408T0131589597. Accessed April 2012.
71. Kaiser, et al. 2008. Position of the American Dietetic Association; American College of Obstetricians and Gynecologists. 2011. *High Blood Pressure during Pregnancy.*
72. Chobanian, et al. 2003. Seventh Report of the Joint National Committee on Prevention, Detection, Evaluation, and Treatment of High Blood Pressure; American Academy of Family Physicians. 2010. *Pregnancy-induced Hypertension.* Available at http://familydoctor.org/familydoctor/en/diseases-conditions/pregnancy-induced-hypertension.html. Accessed April 2012.
73. Ibid.; U.S. National Library of Medicine. 2010. *Medical Encyclopedia: Eclampsia.* Available at www.nlm.nih.gov/medlineplus/ency/article/000899.htm. Accessed April 2012.
74. American Academy of Family Physicians. 2010. *Pregnancy-induced Hypertension.*
75. Kaiser, et al. 2008. Position of the American Dietetic Association; American College of Obstetricians and Gynecologists. 2011. *High Blood Pressure during Pregnancy.*
76. Ibid.
77. Chobanian, et al. 2003. Seventh Report of the Joint National Committee on Prevention, Detection, Evaluation, and Treatment of High Blood Pressure.
78. Solomon, C. and E. Seely. 2004. Preeclampsia: Searching for the Cause. *New England Journal of Medicine* 350:641–642.
79. Roberts, J., J. Balk, L. Bodnar, J. Belizan, E. Bergel, and A. Martinez. 2003. Nutrient Involvement in Preeclampsia. *Journal of Nutrition* 133:1684S–1692S.
80. Kaiser, et al. 2008. Position of the American Dietetic Association; Roberts, et al. 2003. Nutrient Involvement in Preeclampsia.
81. Kaiser, et al. 2008. Position of the American Dietetic Association.
82. Ibid.
83. Centers for Disease Control and Prevention. 2011. *Teen Birth Rates Declined Again in 2009.* Available from www.cdc.gov/Features/dsTeenPregnancy. Accessed April 2012.
84. Casanueva, E., M. E. Rosello-Soberon, L. M. De-Regil, M. C. Arguelles, and M. I. Cespedes. 2006. Adolescents with Adequate Birth Weight Newborns Diminish Energy Expenditure and Cease Growth. *Journal of Nutrition* 136:2498–2501.
85. Rah, J. H., O. Christian, A. A. Shamim, U. T. Arju, A. B. Labrique, and R. Mahbubur. 2008. Pregnancy and Lactation Hinder Growth and Nutritional Status of Adolescent Girls in Rural Bangladesh. *Journal of Nutrition* 138:1505–1511.
86. Rees, J. and B. Worthington-Roberts. 1994. Position of the American Dietetic Association: Nutrition Care for Pregnant Adolescents. *Journal of the American Dietetic Association* 94:449–450.
87. Centers for Disease Control and Prevention. 2012. *Three Decades of Twin Births in the United States, 1980–2009.* Available at www.cdc.gov/nchs/data/databriefs/db80.htm#agedistribution. Accessed April 2012.
88. Position of the American Dietetic Association. 2006. Child and Adolescent Food and Nutrition Programs. *Journal of the American Dietetic Association* 106:1467–1475.

89. Food and Nutrition Service. 2012. WIC Food Packages—Regulatory Requirements for WIC-Eligible Foods. Available at www.fns.usda.gov/wic/benefitsandservices/foodpkgregs.htm. Accessed April 2012.
90. Food and Nutrition Service. 2012. *WIC Program: Total Participation.* Available from www.fns.usda.gov/pd/26wifypart.htm. Accessed November 2012.
91. Food and Nutrition Service. 2012. *About WIC: How WIC Helps.* Available at www.fns.usda.gov/wic/aboutwic/howwichelps.htm. Accessed April 2012.
92. Picciano, M. F. and S. S. McDonald. 2006. Lactation. In Shils, M. E., M. Shike, A. C. Ross, B. Caballero, and R. J. Cousins. *Modern Nutrition in Health and Disease.* 10th ed. Philadelphia: Lippincott Williams & Wilkins.
93. U.S. Department of Health and Human Services (HSS). 2000. *HHS Blueprint for Action on Breast-Feeding.* Available at www.womenshealth.gov/breastfeeding/government-in-action/hhs-blueprints-and-policy-statements. Accessed April 2012.
94. Ibid.
95. U.S. Department of Health and Human Services. 2011. The Surgeon General's Call to Action to Support Breastfeeding. Washington, DC: U.S. Department of Health and Human Services, Office of the Surgeon General. Available at www.surgeongeneral.gov/library/calls/breastfeeding/index.html. Accessed November 2012.
96. Labbok, M. and E. Taylor. 2008. Achieving Exclusive Breastfeeding in the United States: Findings and Recommendations. Washington, DC: United States Breastfeeding Committee. Available at www.usbreastfeeding.org/Portals/0/Publications/Barriers-EBF-2008-USBC.pdf. Accessed April 2012.
97. Batrick, M. and A. Reinhold. 2010. The Burden of Suboptimal Breast-Feeding in the United States. *Pediatrics* 125:e1048–e1056.
98. Ibid.
99. Kim, P., R. Feldman, L. C. Mayes, V. Eicher, N. Thompson, J. F. Leckman, et al. 2011. Breastfeeding, Brain Activation to Own In fant Cry, and Maternal Sensitivity. *Journal of Child Psychology and Psychiatry* 52:907–915.
100. U.S. Department of Health and Human Services. 2011. The Surgeon General's Call to Action to Support Breastfeeding.
101. National Research Council. 1991. *Nutrition During Lactation.* Washington, DC: The National Academies Press, 1991.
102. James, D. and R. Lessen. 2009. Position of the American Dietetic Association: Promoting and Supporting Breast-Feeding. *Journal of the American Dietetic Association* 109:1926–1942.
103. U.S. Department of Health and Human Services. 2000. *HHS Blueprint for Action on Breast-Feeding*; James, et al. 2009. Position of the American Dietetic Association: Promoting and Supporting Breast-Feeding.
104. Ibid.
105. Picciano, et al. 2006. Lactation.
106. Casey, C. F., D. Slawson, and L. R. Neal. 2010. Vitamin D Supplementation in Infants, Children, and Adolescents. *American Family Physician.* 81:745–748.
107. James, et al. 2009. Position of the American Dietetic Association: Promoting and Supporting Breast-Feeding.
108. Bidlack, W. and W. Wang. 2006. Designing Functional Foods. In Shils, M. *Modern Nutrition in Health and Disease.* Philadelphia: Lippincott Williams & Wilkins.
109. Picciano, et al. 2006. Lactation.
110. James, et al. 2009. Position of the American Dietetic Association: Promoting and Supporting Breast-Feeding; Lawrence, R. M. and R. A. Lawrence. 2011. Breastfeeding: More Than Just Good Nutrition. *Pediatrics in Review* 32:267–280.
111. U.S. Department of Health and Human Services. 2000. *HHS Blueprint for Action on Breast-Feeding;* Owen, C. G., R. M. Martin, P. H. Whincup, G. D. Smith, and D. G. Cook. 2005. Effect of Infant Feeding on the Risk of Obesity across the Life Course: A Quantitative Review of Published Evidence. *Pediatrics* 115:1367–1377.
112. Ibid.; Lawrence, et al. 2011. Breastfeeding: More Than Just Good Nutrition.
113. Ibid.; Owen, et al. 2005. Effect of Infant Feeding on the Risk of Obesity Course.
114. James, et al. 2009. Position of the American Dietetic Association: Promoting and Supporting Breast-Feeding.
115. Oddy, W. H., J. Li, A. J. O. Whitehouse, S. R. Zubrick, and E. Malacova. 2011. Breastfeeding Duration and Academic Achievement at 10 Years. *Pediatrics* 127:e137–e145.
116. Centers for Disease Control and Prevention. 2012. *Breastfeeding Among U.S. Children Born 2000–2009, CDC National Immunization Survey.* Available at www.cdc.gov/breastfeeding/data/NIS_data/index.htm. Accessed November 2012.
117. Department of Health and Human Services. 2010. *Healthy People 2020.* Maternal, Infant, and Child Health. Available at www.healthypeople.gov/2020/topicsobjectives2020/overview.aspx?topicid=26. Accessed April 2012.
118. Centers for Disease Control and Prevention. 2012. *Breastfeeding Among U.S. Children.*
119. Centers for Disease Control and Prevention. 2012. *Breastfeeding Report Card—United States, 2012.* Available at www.cdc.gov/breastfeeding/data/reportcard.htm. Accessed November 2012.
120. Institute of Medicine. *Nutrition during Lactation.*
121. Ward, R., B. Bates, W. Benitz, D. Burchfield, J. Ring, J. Walls, and P. Walson. 2001. The Transfer of Drugs and Other Chemicals into Human Milk. American Academy of Pediatrics Committee on Drugs. *Pediatrics* 108:776–784.
122. National Institute for Health and Clinical Excellence. 2011. Food Allergy in Children and Young People. Diagnosis and Assessment of Food Allergy in Children and Young People in Primary Care and Community Settings NICE Clinical Guidelines, No. 116. Available at www.ncbi.nlm.nih.gov/pubmedhealth/PMH0033575. Accessed April 2012.
123. U.S. Department of Health and Human Services. 2000. *HHS Blueprint for Action on Breast-Feeding.*
124. Ibid.; Lawrence, et al. 2011. Breastfeeding: More Than Just Good Nutrition.
125. Baker, R. D., F. R. Greer, and Committee on Nutrition. 2010. Diagnosis and Prevention of Iron Deficiency and Iron-Deficiency Anemia in Infants and Young Children (0–3 Years of Age). *Pediatrics* 126:1040–1050.
126. Udall, J. and R. Suskind. 1999. Cow's Milk versus Formula in Older Infants: Consequences for Human Nutrition. *Acta Paediatrica. Supplementum* 430:61–70.
127. Ibid.; Heird, W. and A. Cooper. 2006. Infancy and Childhood. In Shils, M. *Modern Nutrition in Health and Disease.* Philadelphia: Lippincott Williams & Wilkins.
128. Ibid.
129. Caffarelli, C., F. Baldi, B. Bendandi, L. Calzone M. Marani, and P. Pasquinelli. 2010. Cow's Milk Protein Allergy in Children: A Practical Guide. *Italian Journal of Pediatrics* 36:5.
130. Food and Drug Administration. 2005. *Food Safety for Moms-to-Be Once Baby Arrives.* Available at www.fda.gov/food/resourcesforyou/healtheducators/ucm089629.htm. Accessed April 2012.
131. Palmer, C. A. 2003. *Diet and Nutrition in Oral Health.* Upper Saddle River, NJ: Prentice-Hall.
132. American Dental Association. 2012. *Baby Bottle Tooth Decay.* Available at www.ada.org/3034.aspx. Accessed April 2012.
133. Nainar, S. M. and S. M. Hashim. 2004. Role of Infant Feeding Practices on the Dental Health of Children. *Clinical Pediatrics* 43:129–133.
134. American Academy of Pediatric Dentistry. 2011. *Policy on Early Childhood Caries (ECC): Classifications, Consequences, and Preventive Strategies.* Available at www.aapd.org/media/Policies_Guidelines/P_ECCClassifications.pdf. Accessed April 2012.
135. Stettler, N., J. Bhatia, A. Parish, and V. A. Stallings. 2011. Feeding Healthy Infants, Children, and Adolescents. In Kliegman, R. M., R. E. Behrman, H. B. Jenson, and B. F. Stanton, eds. *Nelson Textbook of Pediatrics.*19th ed. Philadelphia: Saunders Elsevier.
136. Bogen, D. L., A. K. Duggan, G. J. Dover, and M. H. Wilson. 2000. Screening for Iron-Deficiency Anemia by Dietary History in a High-Risk Population. *Pediatrics* 105:1254–1259.
137. National Center for Health Statistics. 2010. *CDC Growth Charts: United States.* Available at www.cdc.gov/growthcharts. Accessed April 2012.
138. Institute of Medicine. Food and Nutrition Board. 2005. *Dietary Reference Intakes for*

Energy, Carbohydrate, Fiber, Fat, Fatty Acids, Cholesterol, Protein, and Amino Acids. Washington, DC: The National Academies Press.

139. Lawrence, et al. 2011. Breastfeeding: More Than Just Good Nutrition.
140. Ibid.
141. Ibid.
142. Institute of Medicine. Food and Nutrition Board. 2005. *Dietary Reference Intakes for Energy, Carbohydrate, Fiber, Fat, Fatty Acids, Cholesterol, Protein, and Amino Acids.*
143. Stettler, et al. 2011. Feeding Healthy Infants, Children, and Adolescents.
144. Briefel, R., L. M. Kalb, E. Condon, D. M. Deming, N. A. Clusen, M. K. Fox, et al. 2010. The Feeding Infants and Toddlers Study 2008: Study Design and Methods. *Journal of the American Dietetic Association* 110:S16–S26.
145. American Heart Association, S. Gidding, B. Dennison, L. Birch, S. Daniels, M. Gilman, A. Lichtenstein, et al. 2006. Dietary Recommendations for Children and Adolescents: A Guide for Practitioners. *Pediatrics* 117:544–559.
146. Neelon, S. E. B. and M. Briley. 2011. Position of the American Dietetic Association: Benchmarks for Nutrition Programs in Child Care Settings. *Journal of the American Dietetic Association* 111:607–615.
147. Ibid.
148. Butte, N., K. Cobb, J. Dwyer, L. Graney, W. Heird, and K. Rickard. 2004. The Start Healthy Feeding Guidelines for Infants and Toddlers. *Journal of the American Dietetic Association* 104:442–454.
149. Butte, et al. 2004. The Start Healthy Feeding Guidelines.
150. The Food Allergy and Anaphylaxis Network. 2012. Available at www.foodallergy.org. Accessed April 2012.
151. Centers for Disease Control and Prevention. 2010. *Botulism.* Available at www.cdc.gov/nczved/divisions/dfbmd/diseases/botulism/#what. Accessed April 2012.
152. March of Dimes. 2009. *Drugs, Herbs, and Dietary Supplements.* Available at www.marchofdimes.com/pregnancy/alcohol_drugsherbs.html. Accessed April 2012.

18 Life Cycle Nutrition
Toddlers through Adolescence

Chapter Objectives

After reading this chapter, you will be able to:

1. Describe the nutrient needs of toddlers and preschoolers.
2. Discuss how parents can influence young children's food preferences.
3. Describe the nutrient needs of school-aged children.
4. Identify the nutrition-related issues facing school-aged children, including obesity and type 2 diabetes.
5. Describe the nutritional needs of adolescents.
6. Discuss the nutritional issues that affect adolescents including eating disorders among teenagers.

1. Toddlers grow at the same rate as infants. T/F
2. Toddlers and preschoolers are often too busy to eat. T/F
3. Children can receive all the nutrients they need by drinking milk. T/F
4. Iron deficiency in young children is caused by eating too much chicken. T/F
5. Once a child refuses a food, there is no point in offering it again. T/F
6. Young children often go on food "jags." T/F
7. The rise in childhood obesity is due entirely to fast food. T/F
8. Lunches served under the National School Lunch Program have to follow certain nutritional regulations. T/F
9. As long as teens drink diet soda, they don't have to worry about negative health effects. T/F
10. Most teens consume adequate amounts of calcium and iron. T/F

See page 697 for answers to these Myths and Misconceptions.

Toddlers live busy lives. The world is full of interesting things to explore and do, so sitting down at a table to eat isn't high on their list of priorities. In addition, their stomachs are still small, so a few bites of fruit, a handful of cereal, and a cup of milk may be enough to satisfy them before they are squirming in their seats, looking for the next adventure.

Just when parents think they've got a handle on good nutrition and eating habits for their toddlers, they find the toddler is no more and they have a young child heading off to kindergarten. During the elementary school years, providing healthy nutrition for a child begins to change dramatically and parents need to develop a whole new set of skills and knowledge. And so it goes through adolescence. As children grow, their nutritional needs change, sometimes because of physical changes and sometimes because of social and emotional changes. In this chapter, we'll explore the unique nutrition needs of toddlers, preschoolers, school-aged children, and adolescents as they grow and change.

What Are the Nutritional Needs of Toddlers and Preschoolers?

Using child-sized dishes at mealtimes can help caregivers monitor portion sizes.

There are two distinct age categories during early childhood: **toddlers** (1- to 3-year-olds) and **preschoolers** (aged 3 to 5 years). Toddlers and preschoolers are still growing at a rapid rate, but their growth rates have slowed significantly compared with those of infants. During the second year of life, the average weight gain is about 3 to 5 pounds, and the average height or length gain is about 3 to 5 inches a year.[1] As a result of this slowed growth, the nutritional needs and appetites of toddlers diminish, relative to the needs of infants.

Whereas parents spend their child's first year tending to the infant's constant desire for food, they often spend the toddler and preschool years trying to make sure their busy child takes enough time to eat.[2] Toddlers and preschoolers need the same nutrients as older people, but they need them in different amounts due to their lower energy needs (kilocalories per kilogram of body weight), smaller appetites, and smaller stomachs. Toddlers and preschoolers tend not to eat much food at one sitting, so they need to eat frequently in order to keep up with their nutrient needs. Thus they should get many of their kilocalories from small meals and snacks eaten throughout the day.

As a toddler's appetite diminishes, caregivers may grow concerned that the child isn't eating enough. As long as parents monitor growth and stay alert for anything that seems suspicious (such as changes in the child's energy level; diarrhea; nausea; vomiting; or changes in the quality of the child's hair, skin, or nails), it is likely that the child's food intake will be sufficient. The chart shown in **Figure 18.1** is used to measure the growth of children at different intervals to determine an individual's rate of growth compared with standard growth curves for age and gender. Growth charts can be used to assess whether a child is developing at a rate comparable to other children of the same age and gender. In general, sudden changes in growth below the 10th percentile or above the 80th percentile may be cause for concern. See the Calculation Corner to practice reading a growth chart.

Young Children Need to Eat Frequent, Small Meals and Nutrient-Dense Foods

Toddlers are extremely active. Just watching them move from activity to activity would exhaust most adults. Because toddlers are always on the go, they need between 1,000 and 1,600 kilocalories per day. And as toddlers tend to eat in small quantities, to get the right amounts of macronutrients and micronutrients, they need to eat nutrient-dense meals and snacks. Meals and snacks should therefore

toddlers Children aged 1 to 3 years old.

preschoolers Children aged 3 to 5 years old.

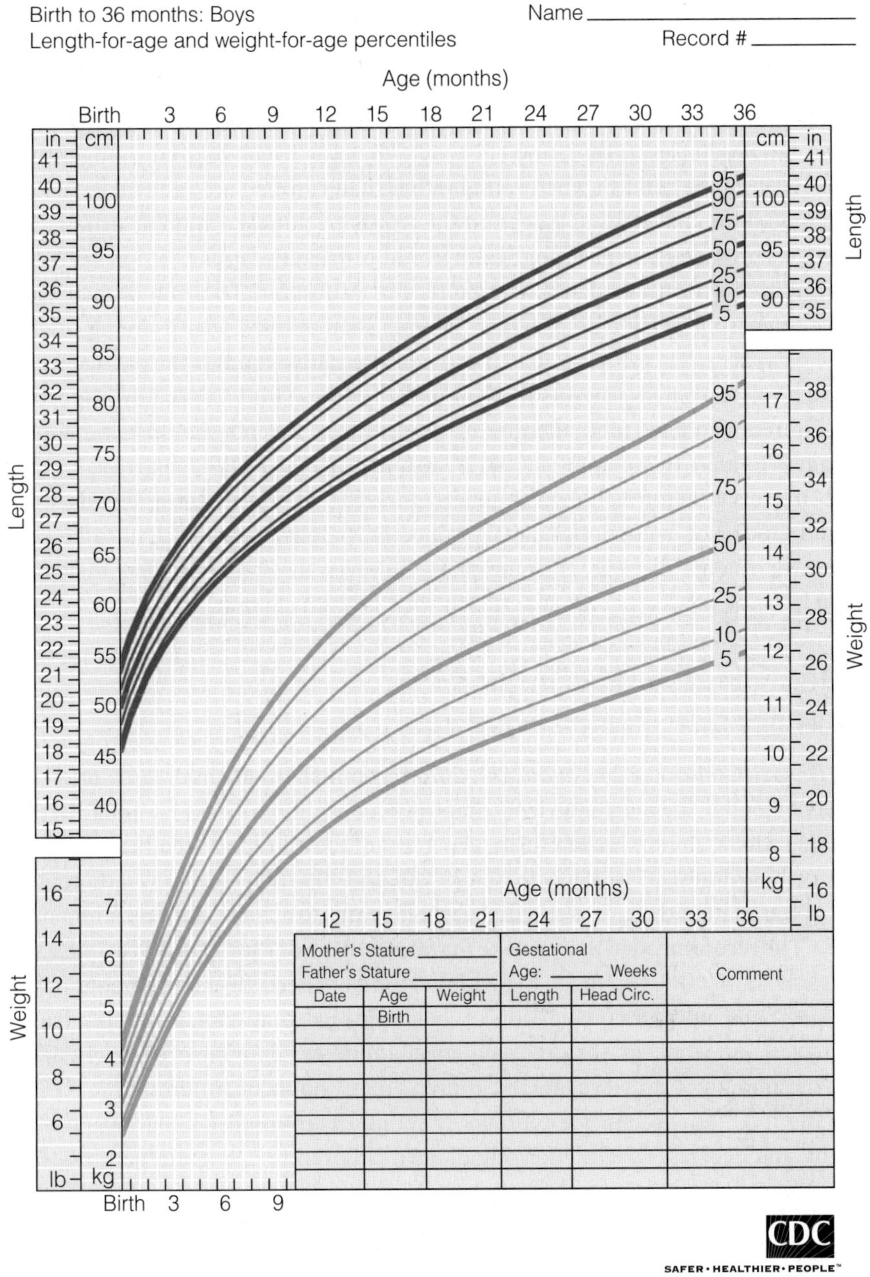

Birth to 36 months: Boys
Length-for-age and weight-for-age percentiles

Name ______________________
Record # __________

Age (months)

Mother's Stature ________
Father's Stature ________

Gestational Age: ______ Weeks

Date	Age	Weight	Length	Head Circ.	Comment
	Birth				

CDC
SAFER · HEALTHIER · PEOPLE™

◂ **Figure 18.1 Growth Chart**
Growth charts can be used to assess whether a child is developing at a rate comparable to other children of the same age and gender.

Source: Developed by the National Center for Health Statistics in collaboration with the National Center for Chronic Disease Prevention and Health Promotion (2000). Available at www.cdc.gov/growthcharts. Accessed July 2012.

Calculation Corner

Reading Growth Charts

Reading a growth chart is essential to monitor a child's growth patterns. Follow the steps below to determine the percentile of Marcus, a male who weighs 16 pounds and is 26 inches tall at 6 months of age.

Step 1. Select the appropriate chart for age and gender.

Step 2. Locate Marcus's age at the bottom of the chart.

Step 3. Locate Marcus's weight along the side of the chart.

Step 4. Mark where Marcus's age and weight meet.

Step 5. Locate Marcus's height in inches along the side of the chart.

Step 6. Mark where Marcus's age and height meet.

At what percentile is Marcus for both weight and length?

Answer: Marcus is at the 25th percentile for both weight and length. This means that 75 percent of the population falls above and 25 percent below.

consist of small portions of meat and beans, fruits, vegetables, milk, and whole grains instead of items like chicken nuggets, french fries, sugary drinks, cookies, and crackers, which are nutrient poor and high in kilocalories.[3] (The Daily Food Plans for Preschoolers and Kids, discussed later in this chapter, can be used to determine specific numbers of servings for young children.)

Parents must be mindful about portion sizes for young children and avoid pushing children to eat more than they need. One way to help ensure proper portion sizes is to use child-sized plates and cups, which are usually a smaller size more appropriate for the quantity of food a child can fit into his or her stomach. The rule of thumb is to serve one tablespoon of food per year of age. A two-year-old, for example, would require two tablespoons of food. Of course, caregivers looking after children with larger or smaller appetites need to tailor portion sizes to each child's individual needs.

TABLE TIPS

Prepare Tasty Treats for Toddlers

Fresh pear, peach, or plum, peeled and cut into very small bites

Mini bagel (not toasted, cut into small bites)

Whole-grain pumpkin or bran muffin

Natural applesauce (no added sugar)

Yogurt with sliced bananas

Remember: Young children should always be supervised while eating!

Whenever young children are given solid foods, it is important that the food not pose a choking hazard. All foods should be cut into bite-sized pieces. The American Academy of Pediatrics recommends keeping hot dogs, nuts and seeds, chunks of meat or cheese, whole grapes, hard candy, popcorn, chunks of peanut butter, raw vegetables, raisins, and chewing gum away from children younger than age 4.[4] Having the child sit when eating rather than running around will lessen the likelihood of food becoming lodged in the windpipe during a stumble or fall. The Table Tips provide some ideas for healthy, toddler-friendly snacks.

Children who attend day care often receive a substantial portion of their daily kilocalories from a day-care provider. Parents should know what is being offered at the day-care site so as to be able to provide alternative foods if the day-care provider's meals and snacks are insufficient or unhealthy. This is especially important for children who have food allergies or intolerances. Parents should ask day-care providers to alert them about special occasions, such as birthday parties, so they can bring in a treat for their own child if their child is allergic to certain foods. Even if children do not have special dietary concerns, parents have the right to be firm about what their child eats. In some cases, however, day-care providers may offer menu items or snacks that are superior to what is given at home.

Young Children Need Adequate Carbohydrate, Protein, and Fat

The *Dietary Guidelines for Americans, 2010* recommend that children be offered a variety of foods. The macronutrient composition of children's diets is similar to that of young adults. Approximately 45 to 65 percent of the kilocalories daily are to come from carbohydrates, 25 to 35 percent from fats, and 10 to 30 percent from protein.

At least half of the grains should be whole grains to achieve fiber recommendations.[5] The recommended daily intake for fiber is 19 grams for 1- to 3-year-olds and 25 grams for 4- to 8-year-olds. Like adults, toddlers need fiber to promote bowel regularity and prevent constipation. A balanced diet that contains whole fruits, vegetables, and whole grains can easily meet a toddler's daily fiber needs. In addition, the amount of added sugars in children's diets should be minimized.

The RDA for protein for toddlers is set at 1.1 grams per kilogram of body weight, and decreases slightly for school-aged children to 0.95 gram per kilogram of body weight.[6] Adequate carbohydrate intake has a protein-sparing effect. Protein can be used for growth and tissue repair rather than for energy.

The recommendation for total dietary fats is 30 to 35 percent of total kilocalories for children 2 to 3 years old, and decreases to 25 to 35 percent for children over age 4. Dietary fat contributes to normal development of the brain and nerve cells. Fats are used for the synthesis of myelin, a substance that insulates nerve cells and aids in nerve conduction. Some neurons are fully myelinated at birth, such as those in the motor cortex that control the ability of infants to suck. Intensive myelination continues as infants fine-tune their vision, hearing, language, emotions, and physical capabilities. Most of the dietary fats should be polyunsaturated and monounsaturated fats, such as from fish, nuts, and vegetable oils. Intakes of solid fats should be limited, as they have a high content of saturated and/or *trans* fatty acids, which are usually solid at room temperature.[7]

Young Children Need to Consume Enough Calcium and Iron

Iron and calcium are particularly important to young children's development. During this period, calcium supports rapid growth of bones, and iron is needed to prevent developmental delays.

Calcium Needs

Toddlers need calcium to develop healthy bones. Children between 1 and 3 years of age should consume 700 milligrams of calcium per day, and children aged 4 and 5 should consume 1,000 milligrams.[8] They can easily meet their needs with two to four 8-ounce glasses of milk daily; each glass provides 300 milligrams of calcium.

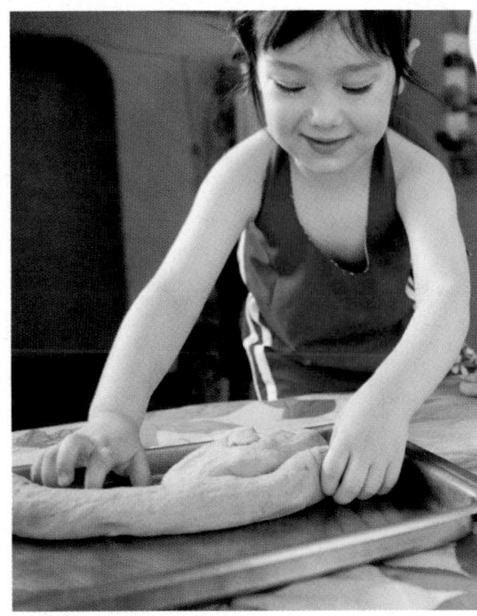

Having kids help in the kitchen is one way to get them excited about trying new foods and eating healthy meals.

Iron Needs

During periods of rapid growth, young children are at particular risk for iron deficiency, which can lead to developmental delays such as diminished mental, motor, and behavioral functioning.[9] Children who suffer from iron-deficiency anemia as infants are more likely to have to repeat a grade in school, have reduced math achievement and written expression, and show differences in motor function, spatial memory, and selective recall.[10] A review of studies investigating iron deficiency in children with attention deficit/hyperactivity disorder (ADHD) found that children with the most severe iron deficiencies were also the most inattentive, impulsive, and hyperactive.[11] Longitudinal studies indicate that anemic children diagnosed in infancy continue to be developmentally delayed after 10 years of follow-up.[12]

Iron deficiency is the most common nutrient deficiency among young children. In the United States, an estimated 7 percent of children between the ages of 1 and 2 experience iron deficiency. Worldwide, iron deficiency affects about 2 billion people, and young children and their mothers are the most commonly and severely affected.[13]

Often, the culprit behind iron deficiency in children in the United States is an overly milk-heavy diet. The foods of infancy—breast milk, iron-fortified formula, and baby cereals—are good sources of iron. As children start eating more adult foods, they require a variety of iron-rich foods to maintain their iron status. If children get too large a percentage of their kilocalories from iron-poor cow's milk, iron-rich foods may be displaced.[14] Parents and caregivers must include good sources of iron, such as lean meats, beans, and iron-fortified cereals, in toddlers' diets. The Table Tips list kid-friendly ways to enjoy foods that have plenty of iron.

Although iron deficiency is a real concern, iron toxicity can also occur in small children. Iron toxicity is a leading cause of death in children under age 6. Because so little iron is excreted from the body, it can build up to toxic levels in the tissues and organs. Children have died from ingesting as little as 200 milligrams of iron.[15] To protect children from accidental iron poisoning, the FDA requires warning labels on iron-containing drugs and dietary supplements.[16] Chapter 13 discusses how the body's protective mechanism attempts to prevent excess iron from entering the blood and causing iron toxicity.

TABLE TIPS

Create Kid-Friendly, Iron-Rich Foods

Stir raisins into warm cereal, or provide a small box of raisins for a snack.

Add cooked chickpeas to tossed salads for an iron boost.

Tote a baggy of an enriched breakfast cereal on car trips and errands for an iron-rich snack.

Use iron-enriched pastas such as macaroni or spaghetti. Toss in some lean meatballs for a double dose of iron.

Mix enriched rice with dinnertime veggies for a nutrient-dense meal.

Lead Poisoning

An equally serious problem is that iron deficiency is significantly associated with low-level lead poisoning in this age group, as demonstrated by a study of 3,650 children, aged 9 to 48 months.[17] Approximately 4 percent of American children have elevated blood lead levels due to consuming paint chips or small pieces of metal, soil, and even water.[18] Children who live in older homes that have lead pipes or faucets are at risk of consuming lead in their drinking water. Inhaling lead dust from paint or swallowing lead can affect any of the body's organs, but the nervous system is most vulnerable.

Young Children Need to Consume Enough Vitamin D

The American Academy of Pediatricians has recently recommended that children aged 1 to 8 should consume 10 micrograms (400 IU) of vitamin D daily.[19] Vitamin D is found in fortified milk, egg yolk, and certain types of fish. Consuming 2 cups of milk daily will meet only half of this recommendation, so vitamin D–fortified cereals and/or a supplement are needed.

Young Children Need Nutrient-Dense Food

A toddler's or preschooler's daily fluid recommendations are based on the child's weight. For example, a 7-pound child needs about 2 cups of fluid per day; a 21-pound child needs 5 cups; and a 44-pound child needs 8 cups. However, drinking too much fluid may displace nutrient-dense solid foods and important nutrients such as iron (for a child with a milk-heavy diet) or fiber (for a child who gets "fruit" from juice rather than actual whole fruit). To ensure adequate amounts of nutrient-dense foods, caregivers need to monitor a child's beverage intake and provide water, milk, and a limited amount of 100 percent juice, while avoiding soda and sugary drinks.

Young Children Can Grow Healthfully on Vegetarian Diets

Young children can grow and develop normally on a vegetarian diet, as long as their dietary patterns are well planned. Vegetarian diets are rich in whole grains, vegetables, and fruits, the very foods that are encouraged for the general population. Because vegetarian foods are high in fiber, however, the amount of foods needed to meet nutrient requirements may exceed what young children can eat. Their small stomachs cannot hold too much food at one time. Young children may eat several times throughout the day to get enough food to meet their energy and nutrient needs. Good sources of calcium, iron, and zinc should be emphasized for vegetarian children. A reliable source of vitamin B_{12} is important for vegan children.[20]

THE TAKE-HOME MESSAGE Toddlers grow at a much slower rate than infants, and have reduced appetites. Adults should be sure to offer children appropriate portion sizes. Caregivers need to be sure that toddlers get adequate amounts of kilocalories, carbohydrates, proteins, fats, calcium, iron, vitamin D, and fiber, and avoid lead. Caregivers also need to monitor a child's beverage intake and provide water, milk, and 100 percent juice while avoiding soda and sugary drinks. Caregivers feeding toddlers a vegetarian diet need to emphasize good sources of calcium, iron, and zinc and a reliable source of vitamin B_{12}.

How Can Adults Influence Young Children's Eating Habits?

As a young child grows and develops increasingly independent feeding skills (see Table 18.1), the variety of healthy food choices in his or her diet should increase. Because eating habits form early in life, parents can help their children establish lifelong appreciation for a variety of nutrient-dense foods. If a child's first encounter with cooked peas results in all the peas ending up on the floor, this doesn't mean that peas should be permanently off the menu. Research shows that a child may need to be exposed to a food 10 times or more before accepting it.[21] Parents also must not remove healthy foods, like broccoli or brussels sprouts, from a child's diet because they themselves don't like them. Children will often adapt to the foods made available to them.

TABLE 18.1 Food Skills of Young Children

Age	Developmental Feeding Skill
1–2	Child uses the big muscles of the arm and can tear and snap vegetables, help scrub, drink from a cup, and help feed self.
3	Child uses the medium muscles of the hand and can help pour, mix, shake, and spread foods. Child can crack nuts with supervision and feed self independently.
4	Child uses the small muscles of the fingers and can peel, juice, crack raw eggs, and use all utensils and napkins.
5	Child uses eye-hand coordination and can measure, cut with supervision, grind, and grate.

Shaping Early Food Preferences

According to Ellyn Satter, an expert on child feeding and nutrition, there is a division of responsibility when it comes to control of feeding. The adult is responsible for what the child is offered to eat, as well as when and where the food is offered. The child, however, is responsible for whether he or she eats, and how much.[22] Food issues and power struggles can occur when adults think that their job is not only to provide the food but also to make sure that the child eats it. Often, parents encourage their children to "clean their plates," even though the children may have indicated that they are finished eating. This is a risky habit that encourages overconsumption of kilocalories, which can ultimately lead to obesity. Children should be allowed to stop eating once they are full.

Small children can sometimes seem to have very narrow food preferences. Parents may think, "My child only eats chicken nuggets and fries," or "She hates vegetables." Though it's true that toddlers often demonstrate picky eating, parents should not give up on encouraging them to try and to accept new foods.

Parents have tremendous influence over shaping their children's food preferences. One way to help small children accept a varied diet is to eat a varied diet yourself. Research suggests that adults' vegetable consumption should serve as a "model" for younger diners.[23,24] That is, adults should load up their own plates with a variety of vegetables, and snack on items like carrot sticks and apple slices between meals, so that children will be more likely to follow suit. Children often mimic adults' behaviors, including the unhealthy ones. A mom who only drinks diet soda for dinner, or a dad who insists that his 3-year-old eat asparagus but never puts it on his own plate, may send confusing messages. Involving children in the food shopping, menu selection, and preparation of meals is another way to encourage them to enjoy a variety of foods.

food jags When a child will only eat the same food meal after meal.

Trying New Foods

Whereas picky eating involves not wanting to try new foods, **food jags** are a child's tendency to want to eat only a limited selection of foods. This behavior of getting "stuck" on a small selection of foods is quite common and normal in young children. Luckily, food jags are usually temporary. A child who only wants to eat pretzels and oranges, or refuses to eat anything green, will likely emerge from the phase within a few days or weeks.

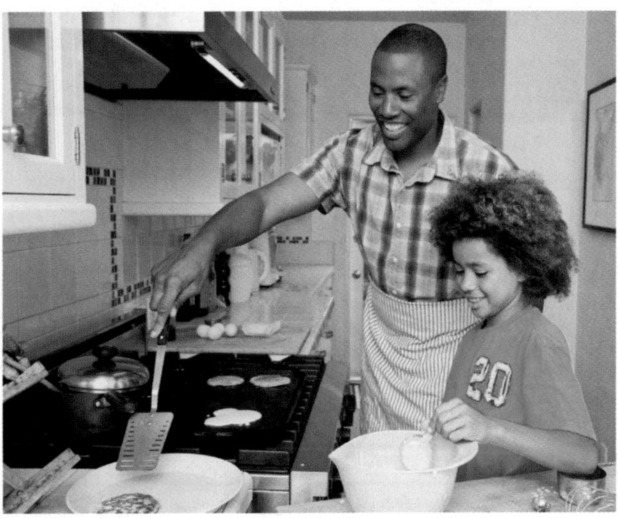

Encourage children to enjoy a variety of healthy foods by involving them in preparing the family meal.

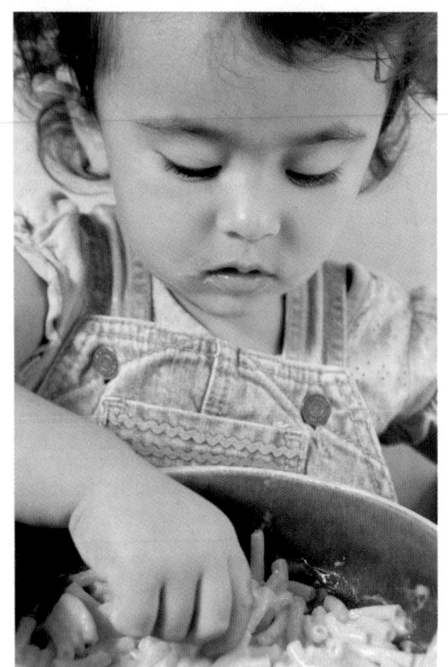

Food jags, such as wanting to only eat one food (like macaroni and cheese), or avoiding certain foods, are common among toddlers.

If a parent or caregiver senses that the food jag is not going away, then it might be more serious than the natural tendency for a child to assert some independence. At that point, it is helpful to pay careful attention to what the child is eating as well as what he or she is avoiding. Is the child really "eating only goldfish crackers" or is the parent forgetting that the child is also drinking milk and eating green beans and orange slices when they are offered? A parent or caregiver can keep a food diary of everything the child eats and drinks for a few days to help identify any major problems. Sharing concerns (and the food diary) with the child's health care provider and asking for advice may prevent serious nutrient deficiencies in the long run.

In some cases, indulging the food jag may be a means to an end. For example, if a child really does stay stuck on something like pasta, a parent or caregiver can offer a variety of foods within that category (for example, serving different shapes of pasta, introducing whole-grain versions, or using nutrient-dense accompanying ingredients). Another, braver tactic is to gradually wean the child from a particular food. Parents and caregivers must remember that they have ultimate authority. Though this should not be license to have dinner-table wars, it does mean that the adult needs to control the situation in a healthy manner for the sake of the child.

MyPlate for Preschoolers is a tool that can help adults plan a healthy diet for this age group (see the Web Resources section at the end of this chapter).

THE TAKE-HOME MESSAGE Although adults are responsible for what a child is offered to eat, the child is responsible for whether and how much he or she eats. Toddlers and preschoolers will stop eating when full, and shouldn't be forced to clean their plates. Caregivers should be good role models when it comes to getting children to try new foods. New foods may need to be offered 10 times or more before they are accepted. Food jags are normal and usually temporary.

What Are the Nutritional Needs of School-Aged Children?

School-aged children, usually considered those between the ages of 6 and 12, still have plenty of growing to do, and the quality of their diet impacts their growth. See Table 18.2 for the range of kilocalorie needs for children in this age group. During the school years, gross and fine motor skills become more refined,

school-aged children Children between the ages of 6 and 12.

TABLE 18.2 Kilocalorie Needs for Children and Adolescents

		Activity Level*		
Age	**Gender**	**Sedentary**	**Moderately Active**	**Active**
2–3 years (toddlers)	Male and female	1,000	1,000–1,400	1,000–1,400
4–8 years (preschoolers and school aged)	Female	1,200	1,400–1,600	1,400–1,800
4–8 years (preschoolers and school aged)	Male	1,400	1,400–1,600	1,600–2,000
9–13 years (school aged)	Female	1,600	1,600–2,000	1,800–2,200
9–13 years (school aged)	Male	1,800	1,800–2,200	2,000–2,600
14–18 years (adolescent)	Female	1,800	2,000	2,400
14–18 years (adolescent)	Male	2,200	2,400–2,800	2,800–3,200

*Note: These levels are based on Estimated Energy Requirements (EER) from the Institute of Medicine (IOM) Dietary Reference Intakes macronutrients report, 2002, calculated by gender, age, and activity level for reference-sized individuals. "Reference size," as determined by the IOM, is based on median height and weight for ages up to 18 years.

Source: HHS/USDA, 2010, *Dietary Guidelines for Americans, 2010.*

Cut back on kid's sweet treats

1. Serve small portions
2. Offer healthy drinks
3. Use the check-out lane that does not display candy
4. Chose not to offer sweets as rewards
5. Make fruit the everyday dessert
6. Make food fun
7. Encourage kids to invent new snacks
8. Play detective in the cereal aisle
9. Make treats "treats," not everyday foods
10. If kids don't eat their meal, they don't need sweet "extras"

Be a healthy role model for children

1. Show by example
2. Go food shopping together
3. Get creative in the kitchen
4. Offer the same foods for everyone
5. Reward with attention, not food
6. Focus on each other at the table
7. Listen to your child
8. Limit screen time
9. Encourage physical activity
10. Be a good food role model

▲ **Figure 18.2 Tips and Daily Food Plans from ChooseMyPlate.gov**
Adapted from USDA, "10 Tips Nutrition Education Series," 2011. Available at www.choosemyplate.gov/healthy-eating-tips/ten-tips.html.

and children's growth rates are steady until the adolescent growth spurt. The average annual growth is 7 pounds and 2.5 inches.[25]

Due to the routine of school and being away from home, school-aged children do not eat as many times throughout the day as do toddlers and preschoolers. This schedule, however, is appropriate for them. School-aged children have a greater capacity to consume more food, are better able to maintain their blood glucose longer, and tend to be less hungry between meals and snacks. Families, caregivers, and schools contribute to the nutritional needs of children. They can help in ensuring that children are making healthy food choices, getting regular exercise, and maintaining healthy body weights.

MyPlate Can Help Guide Food Choices

Because most parents are not nutrition experts, the idea of trying to meet all of the nutrient needs of children can be overwhelming and confusing. Fortunately, user-friendly versions of the Daily Food Plans and the new 10 Tips Nutrition Education System (see **Figure 18.2**) available at ChooseMyPlate.gov can help parents guide their children's choices. The Super Tracker creates a meal plan that shows what and

Nutrition in Practice: Max

Three-year-old Max has a very active life. He wakes up early in the morning. He enjoys his breakfast of banana chunks and some whole-grain cereal at the kitchen table. After a few bites of food and a sip of milk, he becomes distracted by the noise outside the window. He runs to see a neighbor mowing the grass. He asks to go outside and play with the family dog, Burt. Together they find all the puddles of water left by yesterday's rain shower. By noon, his father suggests that it's time to go to the kitchen and get something to eat, but Max isn't interested. There's too much to see, do, and explore before he has to lie down for his afternoon nap. It's not until his father starts calling for a pizza delivery later in the afternoon that Max suddenly becomes hungry.

Max's father, a single parent, has discovered that meal preparation is more challenging than he anticipated. He is worried that Max may be missing some essential nutrients from his diet, but he is not sure how to get his son to slow down and eat when he should. And since pizza has become a frequent menu item, the pizza parlor phone number is now on "speed dial." Max's father decides to seek the help of a Registered Dietitian for advice.

Max's Stats:

- Age: 3
- Height: 3 feet 1 inch
- Weight: 32 pounds

Critical Thinking Questions

1. What advice do you have for Max's father concerning feeding a toddler?
2. What do you think is the best strategy for ensuring that a toddler like Max gets adequate nutrition without putting him at risk for obesity?

Dietitian's Observation and Plan for Max:

- Discuss the importance of optimal nutrient intake to maintain the recommended growth pattern during childhood.
- Offer a variety of foods to help Max get the nutrients he needs from every food group.
- Encourage Max to participate in preparing family meals.
- Participate in family physical activities. Regular exercise helps in preventing obesity.

The Registered Dietitian gave Max's father several strategies to improve Max's nutrient intake. During breakfast, Max now eats a fortified cereal with milk. At lunch Max's father pops a whole-wheat English muffin into the toaster and spreads it with peanut butter topped with shredded carrots—Max's favorite. He takes Max to a local farmers' market and lets him choose some of the ingredients for their week's meals. Then, when preparing the evening meal, he gets Max involved washing vegetables and helping to assemble a salad.

Max's Food Log

Food/Beverage	Time Consumed	Hunger Rating*	Location
Whole grain cereal with milk and banana chunks	6:30 a.m.	5	Kitchen table
Pizza and cola	6 p.m.	5	Kitchen table

*Hunger Rating (1–5): 1 = not hungry; 5 = super hungry

how much the child should eat to meet his or her needs. It also provides ideas to help with meal planning (see **Figure 18.3**) as well as tips for making healthy foods fun for children.

The portions of the ChooseMyPlate.gov website about children encourage kids to:

- *Be physically active every day.*
- *Choose healthier foods from each group.* Every food group has foods that should be eaten more often than others. Choices from the vegetables, fruits, grains, protein, and dairy groups should be varied.

◂**Figure 18.3 The USDA's Super Tracker Offers Personalized Plans and Food Trackers**
The USDA's Super Tracker is an online diet and physical activity tool that helps you plan, assess, and analyze your daily food intake and activities.
Source: www.choosemyplate.gov.

- *Eat more of some food groups than others.* The sizes of the food groups as highlighted in MyPlate indicate suggested relative proportions.
- *Eat foods from every food group every day.* The different colors of the food groups shown in MyPlate represent the five different food groups (and don't forget healthy oils).
- *Make the right choices for you.* ChooseMyPlate.gov gives everyone in the family personal ideas on how to eat better and exercise more.
- *Take it one step at a time.* Start with one new, good thing a day, and continue to add another new one every day.

Children who have special health-related issues or chronic diseases may not necessarily be able to follow the Daily Food Plans for Preschoolers and for Kids. For example, children with autism may become especially fixated on specific foods or be reluctant to try new foods. Overcoming these issues generally requires intervention and support from professionals who work with children with special needs, such as a health care provider or a Registered Dietitian.

School Lunches Contribute to Children's Nutritional Status

The National School Lunch Program (NSLP) provides nutritionally balanced, low-cost or free lunches to more than 30.5 million children each school day.[26] The NSLP meals are designed to meet certain nutrient guidelines, including minimum levels for kilocalories, protein, calcium, iron, vitamin A, and vitamin C. The percentage of kilocalories from total fat is set at 30 percent and saturated fat at 10 percent. Table 18.3 also presents recommended levels for other nutrients. For some children, the food that they eat at school is the healthiest meal—perhaps the only meal—they eat all day.

TABLE 18.3 Minimum Nutrient and Kilocalorie Levels for School Lunches (School Week Averages)

Nutrients and Energy Allowances	Minimum Requirements* Preschool	Grades K–6	Grades 7–12
Energy allowances (kilocalories)	517	664	825
Total fat (g)†	17 g	22 g	28 g
Saturated fat (g)‡	6 g	7 g	9 g
RDA for protein (g)	7 g	10 g	16 g
RDA for calcium (mg)	267 mg	286 mg	400 mg
RDA for iron (mg)	3.3 mg	3.5 mg	4.5 mg
RDA for vitamin A (RE)	150 RE	224 RE	300 RE
RDA for vitamin C (mg)	14 mg	15 mg	18 mg

Source: USDA Food and Nutrition Service. Available at www.fns.usda.gov/cnd/menu/menu.planning.NSLP.htm. Accessed April 2012.

*Based on the enhanced menu approach, maximizing low-fat alternatives and increasing kilocalorie intake of fruits, vegetables, and grains/breads. Alternative menu planning options are available, including optional grade K–3 enhanced menu planning.

†Total fat not to exceed 30 percent of total kilocalories; grams of fat will vary depending on the actual level of kilocalories offered.

‡Saturated fat to be less than 10 percent of total kilocalories; grams of fat will vary depending on the actual level of kilocalories offered.

TABLE TIPS

Tips for Packing School Lunches

Get children interested in packing their lunches by having them pick out a fun lunch box or decorate a brown paper bag with stickers.

Involve the child in planning lunches and then shopping for the items.

Make a lunch calendar and go over which days kids will eat at school and which days they'll pack their lunch.

Invite children to pack their own lunch. Be sure to give them options, like leftovers or a choice of healthy ingredients.

Select new foods that kids will like and ask them if there are new items they want to try.

Be mindful of what kids are actually eating and what they might be leaving behind or throwing away. If, for example, the apple keeps coming back day after day, it's time to try an orange.

Imagine that you are a school food service director running a school cafeteria. On the one hand, you are running a business. You need to make money for payroll, to keep the ovens heated, to purchase dishes on which to serve the food and soap for the dishwasher, and so forth. On the other hand, you have hungry customers with distinct preferences and dislikes. Finally, as the school food service director, you must meet the nutritional requirements set by the USDA so that you are able to serve the children who need a lower priced or free meal. The USDA donates certain foods, which keeps prices down, but you have to stick to the regulations in order to receive these foods. You may also have competition from nearby fast-food restaurants or vending machines.

In order to serve healthy school lunches, the director has to plan a balanced meal, using a variety of food groups, in the right portions, depending on the age of the student. Many times, healthy substitutions can be made that will improve the quality of the meal. School lunch standards include maximum levels for the percent of kilocalories from fat and other nutrients (Table 18.4).

The National School Lunch Program provides breakfast and noontime meals for millions of school-aged children.

If children are not eating school lunches, parents and caregivers may provide a healthy substitute. Given money to purchase lunch, children may select foods that are less nutrient-dense. A lunch of candy bars and soda will short-change the child by approximately one-third of his or her nutrition for the day. Rather, it makes nutritional sense for the parent *and* the child to use MyPlate as a guide to put together a mutually agreeable, healthy, and appealing lunch for the child to take to school. When the child is invested in the planning, the lunch has a better chance of being eaten. Without the input and buy-in of the child, the healthy lunch may end up being swapped for unhealthy foods—or worse, tossed in the garbage. The Table Tips can help provide some useful ideas to improve the likelihood that a child will actually eat the lunch that he or she helped pack.

TABLE 18.4 Food and Beverages That Meet Recommended School Standards

Preferred Foods for All Students (Tiers 1 and 2)	
Tier 1 Foods	
Recommended for students of all grade levels during the school day, and include fresh or minimally processed foods such as fruits, vegetables, whole grains, and nonfat dairy products. Limited to:	
■ 200 kilocalories or less per portion ■ No more than 35% of total kilocalories from fat ■ Less than 10% of total kilocalories from saturated fats ■ Zero *trans* fat ■ 35% or less of kilocalories from total sugars, except for yogurt with no more than 30 g of total sugars, per 8-oz portion as packaged ■ Sodium content of 200 mg or less per portion as packaged	■ Individual fruits: apples, pears, oranges ■ Fruit cups packed in juice or water ■ Vegetables: baby carrots, broccoli ■ Dehydrated or dried fruits ■ 100% fruit juice or low-sodium 100% vegetable juice ■ Whole-grain, low-sugar cereals ■ 100% whole-grain mini bagels ■ 8-oz servings of low-fat fruit-flavored yogurt with < 30 grams of sugar per serving
Tier 1 Beverages	
Low in kilocalories and sugar, nutrient dense, and caffeine free, with the exception of trace amounts of naturally occurring caffeine substances	■ Water without flavoring, additives, or carbonation ■ Low-fat (1%) and nonfat milk in 8-oz portions ■ 100% juice in 4-oz portions as packaged for elementary/middle school and 8 oz (2 servings) for high school
Tier 2 Foods	
Designed only for high school students after the end of the school day and do not necessarily provide a serving of fruits, vegetables, whole grains, or low-fat or nonfat dairy; however, they do meet the food composition recommendations for kilocalories, fat, sugar, and sodium	■ Same as Tier 1 above ■ May also include processed foods such as certain baked potato chips, whole-wheat crackers, animal cracker cookies, graham crackers, and pretzels
Tier 2 Beverages	
These are Tier 1 beverages that are sold after school and are low in kilocalories and sugar, nutrient dense, and caffeine free, with the exception of trace amounts of naturally occurring caffeine substances	■ Same as Tier 1 above

Source: Reprinted with permission from "Nutrition Standards for Foods in Schools: Leading the Way toward Healthier Youth," 2007, by the National Academy of Sciences. Courtesy of the National Academies Press, Washington, D.C.

The Importance of Breakfast

In addition to serving lunches, some schools also have school breakfast programs. Research has shown that eating breakfast may be associated with healthier body weight in children and adolescents. Breakfast may positively benefit cognitive function (especially memory), academic performance, school attendance rates, psychosocial function, and mood.[27] If a child is hungry during the midmorning hours it will impact his or her learning during this time period.

The habit of skipping breakfast is often seen in children and adolescents who are overweight or obese, with a possible relationship to dieting and disordered eating. Those who miss breakfast are less likely to engage in physical activity.[28]

If children don't have time to eat breakfast at home and aren't receiving a school breakfast, caregivers can provide nutritious morning meals that can be eaten on the way to school. See the Table Tips for some on-the-go breakfast ideas.

TABLE TIPS

Breakfast on the Go

Mix some dry, unsweetened, whole-grain cereal with an individual-sized container of low-fat yogurt. Throw in some banana slices, berries, or dried fruit to make it even more nutritious.

Sprinkle reduced-fat cheese on a corn tortilla and melt it in the oven or microwave. Add some salsa and corn and roll it up into a portable tortilla tube.

Spread a thin layer of natural peanut butter or all-fruit preserves on a toasted whole-wheat waffle, and pair it with a travel cup of skim milk.

Does the School Lunch Program Need to Be Improved?

School lunch programs deal with a captive audience of 53 million kids every day and contribute a lot of nutrition to school-aged children. Whether they are from high-income or low-income families, all students can eat lunch in schools. Subsidies enable low-income children to pay less or eat meals for free, so school lunch programs feed kids who may not have much else to eat.

What Are Some Benefits of the School Lunch Program?

National studies done by USDA have shown that children who eat meals at school have a better overall nutritional profile than children who do not. The school meals in a recent study surpassed the RDAs recommended by the USDA. Children who participate in school lunch programs have lower intake of sugars than children who do not participate, and they are more likely to have a healthy body weight. Those who don't eat a school lunch are more likely to eat something from home or a vending machine, and some of those choices may be higher in fat or sugar. In addition, the program is a real security blanket for many low-income youth who may not have many other food choices outside of school.[1]

But this is not only a food assistance program. It helps protect children from excess weight gain, because they are eating well-balanced food instead of junk food. Students who eat school meals are more likely to consume vegetables and more milk products, not only in school but also during a 24-hour period. From their meals at school, they learn how to eat correctly.[2]

Where Does the Food in the School Lunch Program Come From?

Most schools obtain the food that goes into typical school lunch programs from the USDA commodity program, a federal program that makes surplus commodity goods available to schools for free. In this program, the government contracts with farmers and agrees to buy all their surplus food. They make a list of available items for schools to view, and schools that participate in the school lunch program can obtain these foods for free. There are about 100 choices available, but they vary from state to state. Commodity foods make up about 20 percent of the food used in school lunch programs and include grains, brown rice, fruits, vegetables, low-fat cheese, and lean meat.

Schools can take the commodity food in its raw state, or send it to a manufacturer to have it further processed. That dual approach has brought problems. Under the commodity program, school lunch services have gotten into the fast-food approach to cooking. Many schools no longer make foods from scratch. They might get whole turkeys, but instead of cooking the turkey and slicing it, they contract the cooking out to an outside firm and it gets turned into turkey nuggets. The idea is to save on labor costs, but it really compromises good nutrition. There are numerous nutritious commodity foods that would have positive health impacts on kids but that are hardly ever served in schools, such as brown rice, lentils, and bulgur wheat.

Another 75 to 80 percent of foods are purchased from distributors who are associated with national suppliers but are local to a particular school. A school lets the distributor know exactly what food it wants and the specifications for that food. Schools can get water-packed canned fruit, for example, instead of fruit packed in heavy syrup. Schools can also work with distributors and suppliers to create the foods they seek. For example, they can buy pizza that has a whole-wheat crust and low-fat cheese. These companies have worked with the school lunch program to create products for the school market.

But schools also obtain foods from food vendors, often the same ones who supply foods to restaurants. Foods from these companies tend to be higher up on the processed end of the food chain—processed meat, or applesauce instead of apples. In general, when schools purchase food, they've been going in the direction of getting things they think the kids will like—a lot of fast-food, processed foods—and not thinking about broader health concerns or introducing kids to new foods.

In addition to the commodity foods, schools can have fresh produce coming from local produce distributors or even local farmers. There are 300 to 400 school districts that are purchasing produce from local growers. That's especially true for school districts with year-round growing seasons.[3]

How Can the School Lunch Program Be Improved?

One of the great successes of the school lunch program is providing needed kilocalories to children who are poor. Eating a nutritious meal at school is more than just kilocalories, however. By making strategic changes in the types of foods served and adding nutrition to the school curriculum, the rate of childhood obesity may be reduced and the overall health of children of all ages may be improved.

School meals have been carefully evaluated with one goal in mind: to provide students with healthy, nutritious meals. At the same time, school lunch services reflect a general trend in children's food choices. Similar to adults, each child is different with different tastes. The challenge is to provide healthier options that consist of whole, unprocessed foods that kids will eat and enjoy while staying within budget using the commodity program. One example is to provide fruits and vegetables in "salad" bars, such as a potato or pasta bar with fresh vegetable toppings. To reduce waste and improve the efficiency of school food budgets, schools could adopt the "offer rather than serve" option where students can opt out of certain foods. And finally schools could schedule recess before lunch to combat the "hurry and eat" approach most students practice. Student appetites are better after they exercise, and they drink more fluid and waste less food. This leads to increased nutrient intake.

A second strategy is to add nutrition education to the curriculum to encourage children to make better health choices outside of school or at home. The more students understand about food and its relationship to their health, the more likely they are to choose the healthier choices offered in a school meal program. One place to start is to use the school meal program as a model for teaching kids about nutrition and how food is grown and produced. Teachers can take field trips to educate students on the foods available to them locally, set up school gardens to raise fresh produce, and get students involved in choosing and preparing foods at home.

Meals offered through the school lunch program can improve if everyone—including school administrators, food service staff, teachers, parents and the children themselves—accepts the challenges.

References

1. USDA Food and Nutrition Service. 2012. *Healthy Meals, Healthy Schools, Healthy Kids.* Available at www.fns.usda.gov/cga/factsheets/school_meals.pdf. Accessed June 2012.
2. Gundersen, C., B. Kreider, and J. Pepper. 2012. The Impact of the National School Lunch Program on Child Health: A Nonparametric Bounds Analysis. *Journal of Econometrics* 166:79–91.
3. USDA Food and Nutrition Service. 2009. *Schools/Child Nutrition Commodity Programs.* Available at www.fns.usda.gov/fdd/programs/schcnp/pfs-schcnp.pdf. Accessed June 2012.

Promoting Fruit and Vegetable Consumption Matters

To increase the nutritive content of the American diet, *Healthy People 2020* encourages people aged 2 years or older to eat at least two daily servings of fruit and at least three daily servings of vegetables, with emphasis on dark green, red, and orange vegetables.[29] The Centers for Disease Control and Prevention (CDC) and the Fruits & Veggies—More Matters program promote simple ways to increase fruit and vegetable consumption.[30] Parents can help set healthy eating habits early in their children's lives by planning meals that incorporate more fruits and vegetables in the family's diet. Suggestions on increasing fruit and vegetable consumption are detailed in Table 18.5.

Children with Food Allergy and Intolerance

Approximately 12 percent of children are reported to have a food allergy. Food allergy is an abnormal response to a food triggered by the body's immune system. In contrast, food intolerance is a digestive system response in which no antibodies are produced.[31] Symptoms of food allergy may include swelling, nausea, coughing, vomiting, drop in blood pressure, breathing difficulty, blackouts, and even death. Tree nuts and peanuts are the leading causes of deadly allergic reactions called anaphylaxis. Because peanut allergies can be dangerous for kids who have them, "peanut-free" zones are being established in schools across the country. In addition to the cafeterias, care must be exercised in multiple locations and events at the school, such as classroom parties and bake sales. Children may not have to eat peanuts or peanut-containing foods to have an allergic reaction. They may have had contact with peanuts by touching peanuts, using a peanut-containing skin care product, or breathing in peanut dust, such as when in close proximity to other people eating peanuts.[32]

TABLE 18.5 TASTE: Increasing Fruits and Vegetables in the Family Meal	
T: Try something new at every eating occasion	■ Add shredded carrots to casseroles, chili, lasagna, meatloaf, or soup. ■ Drop berries into cereal, pancakes, or yogurt. ■ Make fruit smoothies and veggie burritos. ■ Use leftover veggies for salad, or add them to a can of soup. ■ Keep grab-and-go snacks handy, such as boxes of raisins, dried-fruit trail mix, or frozen 100% fruit bars. Cherry tomatoes and carrot sticks with hummus can be a tasty and refreshing veggie treat.
A: All forms of fruits and veggies count!	■ Consider fresh, frozen, 100% juice, canned, and dried. ■ Cook fruits and veggies in different ways, including steamed, slow-cooked, sautéed, stir-fried, grilled, and microwaved.
S: Shop smart	■ Fresh produce in season is more affordable. Look for specials. ■ Clean and cut up the produce, so it will be ready to use. ■ At a restaurant, substitute vegetables for high-fat side orders.
T: Turn it into a family activity	■ Kids skewer a shish-kabob or make pizza. ■ Farmer's markets can be a fun trip for kids.
E: Explore the bountiful variety	■ Use salad bars or buffets to try new flavors. ■ On a shopping trip, kids pick out a new produce item for the family meal.

Source: Table adapted from "T.A.S.T.E. Tips and Information for Moms" from Fruits & Veggies—More Matters website, September 6, 2012.

There are no drugs or treatments available that prevent food allergies. For children with food allergies, the only way to avoid allergic reactions is to avoid allergenic foods. It is important to carefully read the list of ingredients on the label of prepared foods to be eaten. Many allergens, such as peanuts, eggs, and milk, may appear in prepared foods in which one would not normally expect them. Since 2006, the Food and Drug Administration (FDA) has required U.S. food manufacturers to list the ingredients of prepared foods. In addition, they must use plain language to disclose whether their products contain (or may contain) any of the top eight allergenic foods—eggs, milk, peanuts, tree nuts, soy, wheat, shellfish, and fish.[33] Nutritional counseling can provide guidance on how best to avoid allergenic foods in planning nutritious meals.

THE TAKE-HOME MESSAGE MyPlate addresses the nutritional needs of school-aged children. School meals provide nourishment for many children at breakfast and lunch. These meals may benefit children's cognitive function, academic performance, school attendance rates, psychosocial function, and mood. For children who do not eat school breakfasts or lunches, parents and caregivers need to provide a healthy alternative. Due to the danger of food allergies, care must be taken to avoid consumption and contact with food allergens.

What Nutrition-Related Issues May Affect School-Aged Children?

School-aged children become increasingly independent of their parents in many ways. For example, they develop self-care skills such as tying their own shoes or buckling their own seat belts. In spite of this increasing independence, parents and caregivers remain in charge of children's health and welfare, and they must keep several nutrition-related issues in mind. These include obesity, type 2 diabetes, and dental hygiene. At this point in the life cycle, children are learning habits that they may keep for life, so encouraging a healthy lifestyle is essential. Parents and caregivers should capitalize on their role-model status, as children are watching and learning from the habits and actions of adults.

School-Aged Children Are Experiencing Higher Rates of Obesity

In recent decades, there has been an increase in overweight and obesity among school-aged children. Over one-third of U.S. children and adolescents are currently overweight or obese.[34] (See **Figure 18.4**.) Based on the BMI-for-age growth charts, children are considered overweight when they have a BMI greater than or equal to the 95th percentile. Children with a BMI greater than or equal to the 85th percentile but less than the 95th percentile are considered at risk for overweight.

The use of BMI to determine overweight and obesity in children is controversial. BMI is not a diagnostic tool. It is used only for screening. For example, a child may have a high BMI for age and sex, but to determine if excess fat is a problem, further assessments are required. These assessments might include body composition measurements, evaluations of diet, physical activity, and family history, and other appropriate health screenings.[35]

A combination of factors contributes to the increase in **childhood obesity.** Genetics and environment both play big roles. Among children under age 3, the strongest predictor of adulthood obesity is parental obesity. In fact, the risk of becoming an obese adult is 50 percent if one parent is obese and 80 percent if both parents are obese.[36] One reason for this increased risk might be prenatal overnutrition. Increased nutrients might cross the placenta and change appetite, endocrine function, or energy metabolism. [37]

Only a small percentage of overweight or obesity in children can be attributed to genetic or hormonal defects. For example, Prader-Willi syndrome, Turner syndrome, and hypothyroidism are genetic or hormonal defects that lead to child obesity, but these disorders are very rare.[38] One factor is certain: The rise in obesity is linked with environmental factors that often lead to overconsumption of kilocalories and participation in too little physical activity.

Overconsumption of Kilocalories

Children are taking in excess kilocalories from several sources. For instance, they can grab nutritionally empty, sugar- and kilocalorie-heavy sodas and candy from

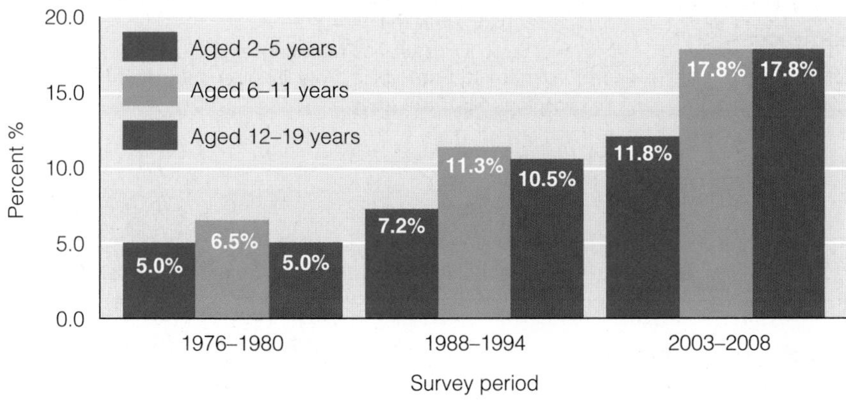

▲ **Figure 18.4 Increase in Overweight among U.S. Children and Adolescents**

Note: Overweight is defined as a BMI greater than or equal to the gender- and weight-specific 95th percentile from the CDC 2000 Growth Charts.

Data from NCHS Health E-Stat: Prevalence of Overweight Among Children and Adolescents: United States, 2003-2004. Available at www.cdc.gov/nchs/data/hestat/overweight/overweight_child_03.htm. Accessed April 2012.

childhood obesity The condition of a child's having too much body weight for his or her height. Rates of childhood obesity in the United States are increasing.

EXAMINING THE EVIDENCE

Does Sugar Cause ADHD?

Many young children are diagnosed with behavior-related conditions such as **attention deficit/hyperactivity disorder (ADHD)** (sometimes still called attention deficit disorder, or ADD). ADHD is a condition—generally identified in early childhood—in which children are inattentive, hyperactive, and impulsive.[1] Children with ADHD have difficulty controlling their behavior. An estimated 3 to 5 percent of children (about 2 million) in the United States have ADHD. Given the characteristics of the condition, it can be difficult and frustrating to manage for parents, caregivers, and teachers. Parents often wonder if dietary factors, like sugar intake or food additives, are responsible for their children's behavior.

Although the myth that sugar contributes to ADHD persists, there is no research to support this. In one study, children whose mothers felt they were sugar sensitive were given aspartame as a substitute for sugar. Half of the mothers were told their children were given sugar, half that their children were given aspartame. The mothers who thought their children had received sugar rated them as more hyperactive than the other children and were more critical of their behavior.[2]

attention deficit/hyperactivity disorder (ADHD) (previously known as attention deficit disorder, or ADD) A condition in which an individual may be easily distracted, have difficulty listening and following directions, difficulty focusing and sustaining attention, difficulty concentrating and staying on task, and/or inconsistent performance in school.

Currently, the Academy of Nutrition and Dietetics has concluded that sugar doesn't have an effect on behavior or learning. The American Academy of Pediatrics has also confirmed that there is no evidence that ADHD is caused by eating too much sugar, or by food additives, allergies, or immunizations.[3]

With so many children and families affected by ADHD, more theories about the cause of ADHD have emerged in recent years. There have been studies citing a possible connection between cigarette and alcohol use during pregnancy and increased risk for the child to have ADHD. Other studies have noted a higher risk of ADHD with high levels of lead in the bodies of preschoolers. Attention disorders often run in families, so there are likely to be genetic influences.[4]

There is a range of treatments for ADHD. Medication, psychotherapy, and behavioral therapies, as well as diet restrictions, are among the many methods used to address the condition. Parents of children with ADHD may want to consult with a dietitian to help their child with nutritional issues, such as underweight due to side effects of medications that decrease appetite. Disruptive mealtimes may also be a concern (if untreated). Organizations such as the National Institute of Mental Health (www.nimh.nih.gov) and the American Academy of Child and Adolescent Psychiatry (www.aacap.org/index.ww) provide information for families with children who have ADHD.

References

1. National Institute of Mental Health. 2004. *Attention Deficit Hyperactivity Disorder.* Available at www.ncbi.nlm.nih.gov/pubmedhealth/PMH0002518. Accessed April 17, 2012.
2. Ibid.
3. Position of the American Dietetic Association. 2004. Use of Nutritive and Nonnutritive Sweeteners. *Journal of the American Dietetic Association* 104:255–275.
4. Wallis, D., H. F. Russell, and M. Muenke. 2008. Review: Genetics of Attention Deficit/Hyperactivity Disorder. *Journal of Pediatric Psychology.* 33:1085–1099.

vending machines, sometimes even in their school's hallway or cafeteria. Snacks can add many kilocalories to a child's day, especially if a child has a habit of munching on fat- and sugar-laden items like chips or cookies while watching television at home. The use of sugary sodas and sports beverages among school-aged children has increased, and these beverages often replace the water, nutrient-dense milk, and (occasional) 100 percent fruit juice that would better provide the fluid they need without the empty kilocalories.

While excess sugar and sweets may make weight management a challenge for children and parents, research doesn't support the idea that sugar makes a child's behavior a challenge. Nevertheless, many parents believe that excess sugar and sweets can lead to hyperactive behavior in their children. Examining the Evidence: Does Sugar Cause ADHD? discusses this further.

Another key factor leading to increased kilocalorie intake is that food is everywhere, including in places where it was previously unavailable, such as at gas stations, in libraries, and in bookshops. Finally, food portions at restaurants and at home are bigger than they used to be.[39]

While children tend to enjoy high-kilocalorie foods and eat them in significant quantities, they often avoid lower kilocalorie, healthful foods like fruits and vegetables. High-fat french fries and potato chips are the favorite vegetables of many school-aged children. Though these foods are technically considered vegetables, they contain too much fat and too many kilocalories to make the grade nutritionally. The 2004 NHANES reported that over the preceding five years the consumption of fried potatoes had increased 18 percent in the United States, while vegetable consumption had decreased by over 43 percent.[40] In fact, more recent research reports that over 90 percent of children do not meet the recommendations for vegetable intake.[41]

Underparticipation in Physical Activity

Multiple factors also contribute to the decreased level of physical activity seen in recent years. The combined amount of screen time a child spends in front of a television or computer, or playing video games, is now significant. Research shows that 8- to 18-year-olds spend more than 3 hours watching TV daily. The amount increases to an average of 4.5 hours daily when TV time is combined with videos, DVDs, and movies. Children in the United States spend slightly more than 1 hour daily on the computer, with about 49 minutes daily of video games (boys are more likely to play than girls).[42] Children often have TV sets and computers in their bedrooms, likely promoting even more screen time. Children are also watching television ads that encourage consumption of unhealthy, fatty foods and snacking while watching TV.[43] In addition to their tendency to spend more time in front of TV and computer screens, children are getting less physical activity while at school and during other parts of their day. Seventy-five percent of 9- to 13-year-olds ride in a car for trips of less than a mile, and only 1 percent ride a bike.[44]

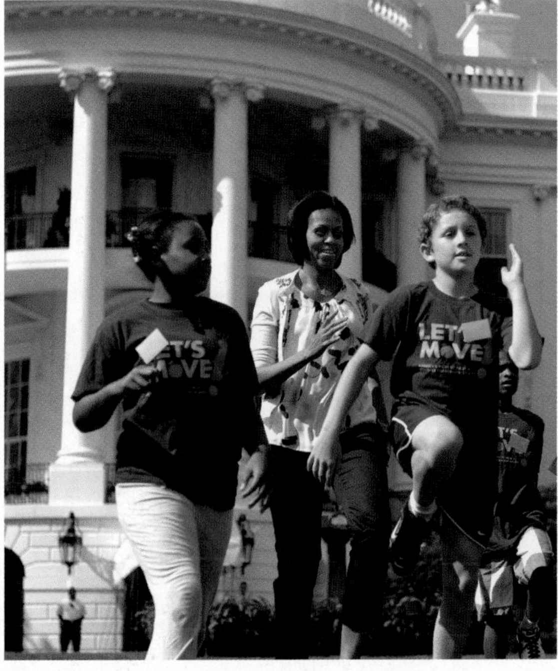

Let's Move! is a comprehensive initiative, launched by First Lady Michelle Obama, that encourages children to increase their physical activity.

Other Environmental Factors

As children age, outside influences like peers, advertising, and the media can impact their food intake. As early as preschool, peers influence a child. By observing what other children are eating, children may want to try something out of the ordinary. However, it is equally likely that children may reject healthy meals, such as those provided at school lunch, because the lunches are unpopular with their peers.[45] Even portion sizes may become more affected by environmental influences. This is important because portion sizes play an important role in the amount of food and kilocalories consumed at a meal (see Chapter 2).

One of the more significant environmental influences on children's food choices is media because of the amount of time that children spend in front of television screens. Researchers have found wide discrepancies between what health experts recommend children eat and what marketing on television promotes as desirable to eat. Advertisements shown during children's Saturday morning television programming seldom encourage eating the foods that food and nutrition professionals recommend children eat more of, such as fruits, vegetables, low-fat dairy products, and whole grains. Instead, most advertisements promote foods high in fat, sugars, or sodium, or low in nutrients.[46]

Risk Reduction

The American Association of Pediatrics (AAP) has been focusing on preventing childhood obesity, with its associated comorbid conditions in childhood and likelihood of persistence into adulthood. Parental obesity and steep weight gain during early childhood help to identify children who might benefit from preventive measures. To reduce their children's risk of becoming overweight or obese, parents and caregivers need to be sure that children receive adequate nutrients without overloading on kilocalories, sugar, and fat, and that they participate in plenty of physical activity. The AAP recommends that parents and caregivers serve as role models when it comes to healthy eating and offer children healthy snacks such as vegetables, fruits, low-fat dairy products, and whole grains coupled with physical activity. How do we get children to enjoy vegetables? In addition to providing well-prepared, fresh, and tasty vegetables, caregivers should give strong verbal encouragement, at school, at home, and in the community, to help children obtain their recommended servings.[47] To encourage physical activity, screen time should be limited to no more than 2 hours daily.[48]

Treatment of Overweight or Obesity

Treatment goals for overweight children are to promote a healthy lifestyle and maintain weight, rather than attempt weight loss. Because children are still growing in height, maintaining weight while they continue to grow reduces the degree of overweight.[49] Encouraging overweight children to participate in regular physical activity helps them achieve the treatment goals.

Increased Rates of Childhood Obesity May Lead to Increased Rates of Type 2 Diabetes

One result of increased obesity among children is an associated increase in rates of type 2 diabetes. As you learned in Chapter 4, this previously adult-onset disease has now become a childhood-onset disease as well. There is a connection between type 2 diabetes and overweight in adults, and a similar connection for children (see Health Connection: Health Effects of Childhood Obesity).

Children should be encouraged to eat fresh fruit and vegetables whenever possible.

What can families do to prevent type 2 diabetes? To start, identify those at highest risk. If a family's father and grandfather have it, then paying close attention to the children's health is essential. Decreasing a child's risk factors, such as being overweight or sedentary, ought to be on the "to do" list as well. If a child is diagnosed with type 2 diabetes, early intervention and treatment are a must. The sooner the family learns what the child needs to eat and how to manage all other aspects of the disease, the better off the child will be.

For children who have type 2 diabetes, family support and encouragement are essential to their ability to successfully manage the disease. The entire family should consider eating in the same fashion as the child, because managing type 2 diabetes

Health Connection

Health Effects of Childhood Obesity

Obese children and adolescents are more likely to have high cholesterol or high blood pressure; both are risk factors for cardiovascular disease. In a sample of 5- to 17-year-olds, 70 percent of obese youth had at least one risk factor for cardiovascular disease. Obese children and adolescents are also more likely to have prediabetes, a condition in which blood glucose levels indicate a high risk for development of type 2 diabetes.[1] They are at greater risk for bone and joint problems, sleep apnea, and social and psychological problems such as stigmatization and poor self-esteem.

As they become adults, obese children and adolescents are likely to remain obese and are therefore at greater risk for adult health problems such as heart disease, type 2 diabetes, stroke, several types of cancer, and osteoarthritis. Overweight and obesity are associated with increased risk for certain types of cancer, including cancer of the breast, colon, endometrium, kidney, pancreas, gallbladder, thyroid, ovary, and prostate, as well as multiple myeloma and Hodgkin's lymphoma.[2]

Diabetes among Youth

Type 2 diabetes, once known as "adult onset" diabetes, is increasingly being diagnosed in youth. The SEARCH for Diabetes in Youth Study, funded by the CDC and the National Institutes of Health, is assessing the burden of diabetes among American children and adolescents under age 20. Researchers found that 19,000 had type 2 diabetes, an increase of 21 percent among American youth from 2001–2009. The proportion of youth with type 2 diabetes was highest among Native American and non-Hispanic black youth.[3] Increasing diabetes rates is of grave concern, because these youth will live with diabetes most of their lives and may develop diabetes-related complications, such as heart and kidney disease, nerve damage, and vision problems, at a much younger age. Researchers noted that the risk of early-onset type 2 diabetes is heavily impacted by exposure to maternal diabetes or obesity in the womb. The cycle of obesity creates a transgenerational problem, as the offspring of women who are obese or who have type 2 diabetes during pregnancy are more likely to develop diabetes early in life.

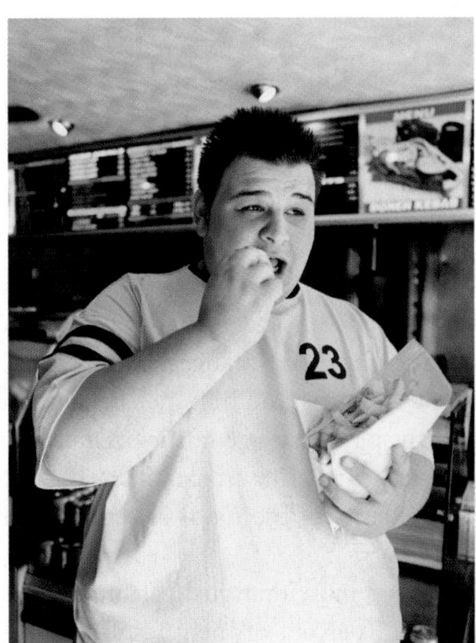

Prevention

Promoting healthy lifestyle habits, including healthy eating and regular physical activity, can reduce the risk of obesity and its related diseases. The dietary and physical activity behaviors of children and adolescents are influenced by many sectors of society; these factors include families, communities, schools, child-care sites, health care providers, faith-based institutions, governmental agencies, media, and food and beverage producers, as well as entertainment industries. Schools play a critical role by establishing a safe and supportive environment with policies and practices that promote healthy lifestyle behaviors. Schools also provide opportunities for students to learn about and practice healthy eating and physical activity behaviors.[4]

References

1. Centers for Disease Control and Prevention. 2011. *National Diabetes Fact Sheet: National Estimates and General Information on Diabetes and Prediabetes in the United States, 2011.* Available from www.cdc.gov/diabetes/pubs/pdf/ndfs_2011.pdf. Accessed June 2012.
2. Centers for Disease Control and Prevention. 2012. *Childhood Obesity Facts.* Available at www.cdc.gov/healthyyouth/obesity/facts.htm. Accessed June 2012.
3. American Diabetes Association. June 9, 2012. *Press Release: Diabetes Rates Increase Significantly Among American Youth.* Available at www.diabetes.org/for-media/2012/sci-sessions-SEARCH.html. Accessed June 2012.
4. Centers for Disease Control and Prevention. 2012. *Childhood Obesity Facts.*

involves moderation, variety, and balance. Physical activity is also a major part of managing this disease, and everyone can take part in this as well. Taking a family walk or bike ride after dinner instead of turning on the TV, or enjoying weekend games of basketball or tennis, are excellent ways to teach the importance of exercise. The child is more likely to feel supported and succeed with keeping diabetes under control if everyone in the family is educated about what to do to help.

School-Aged Children Should Practice Good Dental Hygiene

The potential for tooth decay begins as soon as the teeth start to emerge from the gums, so parents and caregivers must encourage tooth-friendly dental practices as early as possible. Unfortunately, school-aged children frequently do not practice adequate dental hygiene habits, and dental caries usually result. In 2011, the Centers for Disease Control and Prevention (CDC) reported that tooth decay affects more than one-fourth of U.S. children aged 2 to 5 years.[50]

In addition to regular brushing and flossing, the American Dental Association recommends that "infants and young children should be provided with a balanced diet in accordance with the *Dietary Guidelines for Americans.*" Eating healthy foods makes a difference in the health of teeth. Children's consumption of juice drinks, soft drinks, milk, and starches should be limited, as these may bathe the teeth in sugar and lead to dental caries.[51]

THE TAKE-HOME MESSAGE Increasing obesity rates are contributing to rising rates of type 2 diabetes in school-aged children. Parents and caregivers need to be sure children limit their empty-kilocalorie and sugar intake and get enough physical activity. They can model the behaviors they wish to promote. In addition to regular physical activities, the entire family can share in meals that promote the concepts of moderation, variety, and balance. Children should practice good dental hygiene to prevent dental caries.

What Are the Nutritional Needs of Adolescents?

Adolescence is the stage of the life cycle between ages 9 and 19. With adolescence come many hormonal, physical, and emotional changes. Among the physical changes are a rapid **growth spurt,** and, for girls, the first menstrual period, or **menarche.** Growth must be supported with appropriate quantities of nutrients. Adequate kilocalories (energy), protein, calcium, and iron are particularly important at this stage. The greatest concern is the quality of the foods selected in order to support optimal adolescent growth.

The growth spurt of adolescence involves more than just getting taller. While height increases (adolescents attain about 15 percent of their adult height during this stage), weight also increases (they attain about 50 percent of their ideal adult weight), and bones grow significantly. Increases in lean muscle mass and body fat stores are also part of the spurt.

As with younger age groups, rates of overweight and obesity are increasing among adolescents. Results from the 2009–2010 National Health and Nutrition Examination Survey (NHANES) show that the percentage of overweight adolescents aged 12 to 19 increased from 11 to 17 percent.[52]

adolescence The developmental period between childhood and early adulthood (approximately ages 9 through 19).

growth spurt A rapid increase in height and weight.

menarche The onset of menstruation.

The consequences of the trend toward greater rates of overweight and obesity are particularly significant for girls. Adolescent girls who take in too much fat and/or too little fiber may experience menarche earlier than other girls, especially if they are inactive.[53] More than half of young people in grades 9 to 12 do not regularly engage in vigorous physical activity. Daily participation in high school physical education classes dropped from 42 percent in 1991 to 18 percent in 2009.[54]

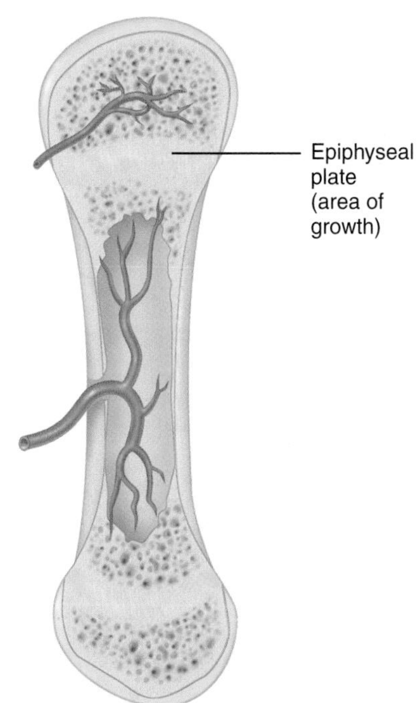

▲ **Figure 18.5 Epiphyseal Plate in Long Bone**

Adolescent bone growth takes place along the epiphyseal plate. Once the plates close, lengthening of the bone stops.

Adolescents Need Calcium for Bone Development

Adolescents experience rapid bone growth, and inadequate calcium intake can harm this process. Almost half of **peak bone mass** is accumulated during adolescence. Most of the growth occurs in the **epiphyseal plate** (Figure 18.5), the area of tissue near the end of the long bones. The growth plate determines the future length and shape of the mature bone. At some point during adolescence, bone growth is complete. The plates close and are replaced by solid bone.[55] For this reason, adolescence is the last chance to maximize the potential of the bone, and calcium and vitamin D intakes influence that potential. Inadequate calcium intake is one factor that can lead to low peak bone mass and is considered a risk factor for osteoporosis.[56] The AI for calcium increases from 1,000 milligrams for children aged 4 to 8 to 1,300 milligrams for those aged 9 to 18. The AI for vitamin D is now at 600 IU for children and adolescents.

Research supports the role of adequate calcium intake for bone health. One study followed females for seven years and looked at their bone health. Results (at the age of 15 to 18 years old) indicated that subjects' hip and forearm bone density was increased in those who had been given calcium supplements or dairy products rather than a placebo.[57] Another study asked boys aged 13 to 17 years to consume an additional three servings per day of either 1 percent milk or unfortified juice. The boys in the milk group had significantly greater increases in bone mineral density than those in the juice group.[58]

Inadequate calcium intake among adolescents is not uncommon. The Nationwide Food Consumption Survey (NFCS) reported that calcium intake by adolescent boys 12 to 19 years of age averaged 1,125 milligrams per day, whereas the same survey showed that average calcium intake by adolescent girls was only 814 milligrams per day, far below the 1,300 milligrams recommended.[59] One reason for this trend is teens' increased preference for sugar-laden soft drinks instead of milk or calcium-fortified soy milk. One study found that about the average daily consumption of regular (kilocalorie-containing) soft drinks by boys aged 13 to 18 is two 12-ounce cans and by girls one and one-half cans.[60] Sodas and other empty-kilocalorie beverages, such as energy drinks and sports drinks, may taste good and be popular with peers, but are missing the calcium that is so crucial for developing bones. Even nonkilocalorie diet sodas are undesirable because they are likely displacing other nutrient-dense fluids in the diet. The Calculation Corner on page 692 shows how to determine how much of a teen's daily calcium requirement is fulfilled by a glass of milk.

Adolescents Need Iron for Muscle Growth

Adolescents need additional iron to support muscle growth and increased blood volume. Adolescent girls also need more iron to support the onset of menstruation. The RDA for girls aged 14 to 18 is 15 milligrams per day, whereas for boys of the same age it is only 11 milligrams per day. These higher recommendations are based on the amount of dietary iron needed to maintain adequate iron stores. Iron needs are highest during growth spurts and after the onset of menstruation.

peak bone mass The maximum bone mass achieved.

epiphyseal plate The growth plate of the bone. In puberty, growth in this area leads to increases in height.

Calculation Corner

Adolescent Calcium Needs

Teens need an adequate intake of calcium to support bone growth.

Approximately how much calcium is found in an 8-ounce serving of milk containing 30 percent of the Daily Value for calcium? Refer to the Daily Values for Food Labels in the inside back cover of the textbook.

Daily Value of calcium = 1,000 mg

$0.30 \times 1{,}000 \text{ mg} = 300 \text{ mg}$

Answer: Eight ounces of milk contains 300 milligrams of calcium.

The Adequate Intake (AI) for calcium is 1,300 milligrams of calcium per day for teens. An 8-ounce serving of milk contributes what proportion of a teen's calcium need?

From the above calculations, 300 milligrams come from an 8-ounce serving.

$300 \text{ mg calcium} \div 1{,}300 \text{ mg calcium recommended} = 0.23 \times 100 = 23\%$

Answer: One 8-ounce serving represents 23 percent of a teen's daily recommended intake for calcium.

Unfortunately, females at this age often have an inadequate iron intake, especially if they diet or restrict their food intake. In the NHANES III study, iron deficiency was found in over 14 percent of the girls aged 15 to 18 years and 12 percent of the boys aged 11 to 14 years.[61] Iron deficiency existed in both males and females and in teens of all races and socioeconomic levels.[62] Teens who limit enriched grains, lean meats, and legumes in their diet run the risk of failing to meet their daily iron needs. The symptoms of weakness, fatigue, and short attention span that some teens experience might be due to low iron intake. Iron deficiency can also result in poor appetite, increased susceptibility to infection, and irritability. Iron-deficiency anemia is characterized by additional symptoms of paleness, exhaustion, and rapid heart rate. Hemoglobin level is used to identify iron-deficiency anemia. Iron supplementation would be prescribed to replenish iron stores.[63]

TABLE TIPS

Teen Table Tips

Encourage teens to read labels on soda to find out how many kilocalories are in a serving.

Talk to teens about real-life stories of people using weight-loss pills, or other quick fixes to lose weight rather than eating in a healthy way to get results.

Direct teens to credible websites for information, such as http://kidshealth.org/teen/food_fitness.

Be a role model! Eat well, get enough rest, exercise, be realistic about dieting, and don't smoke.

Teach teens to look for healthy options, such as salads and granola bars, at fast-food restaurants and in vending machines so they can make their own food choices without compromising health.

THE TAKE-HOME MESSAGE Adolescence brings many changes, including rapid physical growth. Calcium and iron intake are particularly important during this period to ensure adequate bone and muscle growth, and support increased blood volume. Increased consumption of soft drinks and decreased milk consumption can compromise bone health. Increased consumption of enriched or whole grains, lean meats, and legumes among teens may improve their iron stores.

What Nutritional Issues Affect Adolescents?

Adolescence is a time of dramatic social and emotional growth as well as physical growth. Some nutrition-related issues during adolescence may be an indirect result of the social and emotional growth that is occurring. Adolescents experience a strong desire for independence and individuality. For example, they may earn their own money through a part-time job, as well as have their own transportation. They will likely want to make their own food choices, which may be less nutritious than what they were previously served at home. Even if they do not have their own money or transportation, many adolescents exhibit a level of defiance toward authority that may be manifested at the table.

Teen eating habits are often influenced by peers and social settings.

Outside Influences Play a Role

Adolescence is a vulnerable time in one's development as a person. Peers, media, and other nonparent role models exert tremendous influence on adolescents. To fit in, teens may feel pressured by popular classmates. They see television personalities who reportedly achieved dramatic weight loss, and want to do the same. However, their favorite celebrities may have a diet of cigarettes, caffeine, and alcohol. These glamorous individuals with unhealthy habits are not only famous, but likely rich, thin, and attractive—three qualities desirable to most teens, who live for the moment and think the "future" means next weekend. As a result, teens willingly adopt damaging habits in order to emulate the magic transformations they see in the media. Unfortunately, these habits are not only unhealthy but can also contribute to low self-esteem when the outcomes are not as dramatic as expected.

Researchers have found that eating family meals is associated with better nutritional intake and more healthful eating patterns among teens.[64] Family meal patterns during adolescence predict diet quality and meal patterns during early young adulthood. Dietary habits established early tend to be stable. Family meals were significantly related to greater intakes of healthful foods and nutrients that are often consumed in low amounts by young adults. Eating dinner together can have a positive effect on the character and social development, communication skills, family bond, and culinary skills of family members.[65]

Adolescents Are Sometimes at Risk for Disordered Eating

As discussed in Chapter 15, poor body image can exist in both males and females and may lead to eating disorders. Disordered eating behaviors are more prevalent among adolescent girls than adolescent boys. If an eating disorder is not detected or is left untreated, there can be numerous physical and emotional consequences later. Because adolescents don't necessarily consider the long-term consequences of their actions, the threat of these consequences may not be enough to prevent disordered eating. A recent study reported that family meals played a protective role in reducing the risk of disordered eating, suggesting a need for interventions aimed at promoting family meals.[66] Teens who are able to successfully overcome an eating disorder may require the long-term support of a team of professionals dedicated to this area of work as well as support from their family members and friends. Interventions can increase the adaptability and coping skills of teens and family members to prevent eating disorders.[67]

Teens grapple with trying to fit in and must adjust to new bodies, new thoughts, new situations, and new experiences. All of this, along with the typical adolescent feeling of immortality, may encourage an adolescent to engage in risky tactics to reach a desired weight. Teens can sometimes adopt a variety of unhealthy habits, including eating very little food, skipping meals, smoking cigarettes, using diet pills, self-inducing vomiting, or using laxatives or diuretics, all of which can lead to disordered eating. A longitudinal study found that teenaged girls' use of diet pills nearly doubled from 8 to 14 percent over a five-year period. Almost 22 percent of teenaged girls have resorted to diet pills, laxatives, vomiting, or skipping meals. The rate for teenaged boys was half that of the girls.[68]

In contrast to girls who want to lose weight, many adolescent boys yearn to "pump up" to be bigger or heavier. They are more prone to using nutritional supplements that promise more muscles.[69]

A study found that, compared with teens who did not use any weight-control methods, adolescents who engaged in unhealthful behaviors to control their weight exhibited a slightly higher body mass index and a greater risk for being overweight, binge eating, or extreme dieting five years later.[70] In essence, the teen ends up with two problems: the feeling of failure, as well as the health consequences associated with the risky tactic used to try to change his or her weight.

In addition to body image issues, alcohol and drug use can adversely affect dietary intake of energy and nutrients. Eating healthfully becomes less important to the teen who abuses alcohol or drugs.

Teens with a nutrition-related health risk can benefit from nutrition assessment and counseling. Parents can play a key role in helping their children build a positive body image, avoid unhealthy weight control behaviors, and engage in healthy eating and physical activity behaviors.[71]

THE TAKE-HOME MESSAGE Adolescents want to have control over their food and lifestyle decisions. Peers and media also exert a strong influence. Adolescents are sometimes at risk of developing disordered eating patterns due to poor body image, emotional issues, or peer pressure. Because adolescents often live in the here and now, they may not think about the long-term health consequences of poor diet and lifestyle habits they adopt during their teen years.

Putting It All Together

Childhood and adolescence are periods of growth and development. Early exposure to a variety of healthful foods helps to promote lifelong good eating habits. Parents and caregivers can help encourage children to lead active lifestyles. Overweight and obesity among children and adolescents may be avoided with more healthful food choices and regular physical activity. The adolescent growth spurt requires increased intake of foods rich in calcium and iron. Adolescence is also a period of social and emotional growth. Teens' search for personal identity and independence can result in behaviors with long-term consequences.

Visual Chapter Summary

1 The Needs of Toddlers and Preschoolers Are Met with Small, Nutrient-Dense Meals

Toddlers and preschoolers need frequent, small, nutrient-dense meals and snacks to consume adequate amounts of kilocalories and nutrients to fuel their busy lifestyles. Young children need enough calcium, vitamin D, and fiber to ensure healthy bone growth and bowel regularity. Milk, water, and diluted juices are better beverage choices than sweetened, flavored drinks.

2 Adults Influence Young Children's Eating Habits

Young children may be picky eaters and go on food jags, but these behaviors are normal and usually temporary. Caregivers should allow children to participate in food preparation and to choose the foods they eat from among several healthy options. New foods may need to be offered up to 10 times before the child accepts them. Caregivers also should act as role models and help children form lifelong healthy eating habits by adopting such habits themselves.

3 The Nutritional Needs of School-Aged Children Can Be Guided by MyPlate

The quality of the diet impacts the growth of school-aged children. Children have the capacity to eat more, maintain blood glucose levels longer, and are less hungry between meals.

Children who bring lunch from home should be involved in the planning and preparation of the lunch so they are more likely to consume it. Research supports that an adequate breakfast can impact a child's energy levels and mental performance throughout the day.

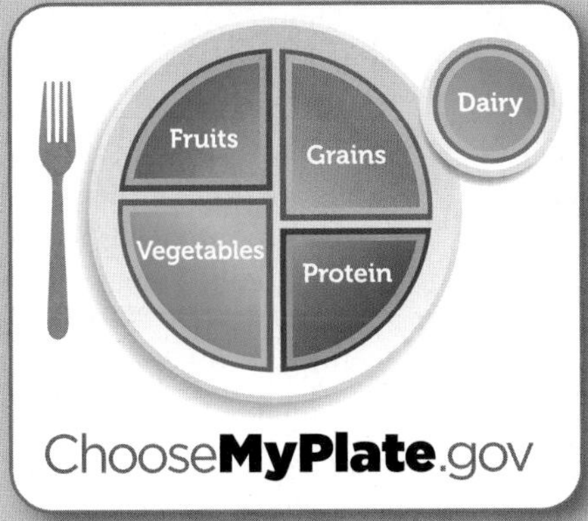

4 Obesity and Type 2 Diabetes May Affect School-Aged Children

Obesity and type 2 diabetes are occurring at higher rates in children. Genetic and environmental factors, including poor dietary choices and not enough exercise, are key sources of this problem.

There is no conclusive evidence that sugar causes hyperactivity or ADHD in children. However, some caregivers claim that making certain dietary changes helps improve their child's behavior.

5 Nutritional Needs of Adolescents Are Based on Hormonal and Physical Changes

Rates of overweight and obesity are increasing among adolescents. Adolescent girls who take in too much fat and/or too little fiber may experience menarche earlier than other girls.

Adolescents experience rapid bone growth, and adequate calcium intake supports this process. Overconsumption of soda may interfere with calcium intake if it displaces milk in the diet. Adequate iron intake is important for growth of lean muscle and blood volume. Girls' need for dietary iron increases after the onset of menstruation. Dieting or limiting enriched grains, lean meats, and legumes can lead to inadequate iron intake.

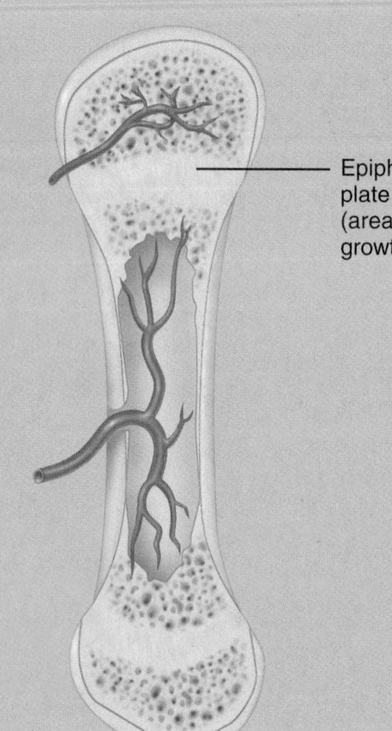

6 Nutritional Issues That Affect Adolescents Are Due to Social and Emotional Changes

Adolescents are heavily influenced by peers, media, and other nonparental role models, which may lead them to adopt unhealthy eating and lifestyle habits, such as skipping meals, choosing unhealthy foods, dieting, or smoking. Adolescents are sometimes at risk of developing disordered eating patterns due to poor body image, emotional issues, or peer pressure.

Terms to Know

- toddlers
- preschoolers
- food jags
- school-aged children
- childhood obesity
- adolescence
- growth spurt
- menarche
- peak bone mass
- epiphyseal plate

MasteringNutrition™

Build your knowledge—and confidence—in the Study Area of MasteringNutrition at with a variety of study tools.

Check Your Understanding

1. When feeding toddlers and preschoolers, what is the rule of thumb for portion size?
   a. one tablespoon per year of age
   b. two tablespoons per year of age
   c. three tablespoons per year of age
   d. four tablespoons per year of age
2. Children living in older homes may be at higher risk for
   a. iron toxicity.
   b. calcium toxicity.
   c. vitamin D toxicity
   d. lead toxicity.
3. In order to foster healthy eating habits in children, caregivers should
   a. serve them only the foods they like.
   b. offer them a limited variety of foods.
   c. insist that they eat everything on their plate.
   d. allow them to stop eating when they are full.
4. MyPlate illustrates the ______________ food groups that are the building blocks of a healthy diet.
   a. four
   b. five
   c. seven
   d. ten
5. Children are considered overweight if they have a BMI greater than or equal to the ______________ percentile.
   a. 65th
   b. 75th
   c. 85th
   d. 95th
6. The American Academy of Pediatrics recommends that screen time be limited to no more than ______________ daily.
   a. 1 hour
   b. 2 hours
   c. 3 hours
   d. 4 hours

7. There appears to be a relationship between the rise in childhood obesity and the increase in
   a. childhood cancers.
   b. eating disorders.
   c. type 2 diabetes in children.
   d. childhood cavities.
8. Which mineral supports healthy bone development and is particularly important during adolescence?
   a. calcium
   b. iron
   c. zinc
   d. copper
9. The need for iron increases during adolescence to support muscle growth and ______________.
   a. blood formation
   b. bone development
   c. heart health
   d. kidney function
10. A recent study reported that ______________ play(s) a protective role in reducing the risk of disordered eating.
    a. social engagement
    b. restful sleep
    c. family meals
    d. regular physical activity

Answers

1. (a) The rule of thumb is one tablespoon per year of age. Because young children have reduced appetites, they should not be pushed to eat more than they need.
2. (d) Plumbing and faucets in older homes may contain lead that can leach into a child's drinking water, increasing the risk for lead poisoning. Iron toxicity is a concern in young children, but isn't more likely in children living in older homes.
3. (d) Caregivers should allow young children to stop eating when they are full. Forcing children to clean their plate may result in food struggles or overeating. Children should be offered a wide variety of foods, not just the things they like.
4. (b) MyPlate illustrates these five food groups: vegetables, fruits, grains, dairy, and protein foods. They are the building blocks for a healthy diet using a familiar image—a place setting for a meal.
5. (d) Children with a BMI greater than or equal to the 95th percentile are considered overweight.
6. (b) To allow time for physical activity, the American Academy of Pediatrics recommends that screen time be limited to no more than 2 hours daily.
7. (c) Rates of type 2 diabetes among children have risen along with rates of overweight and obesity.
8. (a) Adolescents need adequate amounts of calcium to support their growing bones.
9. (a) The need for iron is increased in adolescent girls to promote blood formation as they start to menstruate.
10. (c) Family meals have been reported to play a protective role in reducing the risk of disordered eating, suggesting a need for interventions aimed at promoting family meals.

Answers to Myths and Misconceptions

1. **False.** Toddlers' growth slows down significantly compared with infants'. During the second year of life, a toddler may gain 3 to 5 pounds.
2. **True.** Between the ages of 1 and 4, small children are extremely active and sometimes forget to eat.
3. **False.** Milk is a source of important nutrients; however, it doesn't provide all the nutrients that growing children need. A variety of other foods are also needed to provide key nutrients for proper growth and development.
4. **False.** Iron deficiency is often caused by a limited diet that relies too heavily on milk or other iron-poor food sources.
5. **False.** Parents and caregivers may need to offer foods numerous times before a child accepts the food.
6. **True.** Young children often refuse foods of a certain color, texture, or taste. Alternatively, they may get hooked on a particular food and eat only that item for a while.
7. **False.** Though high-fat, high-sugar foods often found in fast-food restaurants are part of the problem, that's only half the story. Too little exercise and too much screen time also contribute.
8. **True.** The school lunch and school breakfast programs must meet specific requirements in order to receive funding from the USDA.
9. **False.** Sodas, including diet sodas, are nutritionally empty beverages, and the teenage years are a nutritionally critical period.
10. **False.** Inadequate calcium and iron intakes are common among adolescents. Teens tend to prefer sugar-sweetened soft drinks over calcium-rich milk. Teens need iron to support muscle growth and increased blood volume. Adolescent girls also need more iron to support the onset of menstruation.

Web Resources

- For more information on nutrition for preschoolers, visit www.choosemyplate.gov/preschoolers.html
- For more information on nutrition during the younger years, visit www.cdc.gov/healthyyouth/nutrition/facts.htm
- For more information on children's and teens' health, visit http://kidshealth.org
- For more about ADHD, visit www.ncbi.nlm.nih.gov/pubmedhealth/PMH0002518
- To learn about practical tools for keeping kids at a healthy weight, visit We Can! at www.nhlbi.nih.gov/health/public/heart/obesity/wecan/index.htm
- For more about the USDA's School Lunch Program, visit www.fns.usda.gov/cnd/lunch
- For more information on increasing fruit and vegetable consumption, visit Fruits & Veggies—More Matters, at www.fruitsandveggiesmorematters.org

References

1. National Center for Health Statistics. 2000. *2000 CDC Growth Charts for the United States: Methods and Development.* U.S. Vital and Health Statistics, Health Resources Administration. Washington, DC: U.S. Government Printing Office. Available at www.cdc.gov/growthcharts/2000growthchart-us.pdf. Accessed April 2012.
2. American Academy of Pediatrics. n.d. *Promoting Healthy Nutrition.* Available at http://brightfutures.aap.org/pdfs/Health_Promotion_Information_Sheets/healthynutrition.pdf. Accessed April 2012.
3. Siega-Riz, A. M., D. M. Deming, K. C. Reidy, M. K. Fox, E. Condon, and R. R. Briefel. 2010. Food Consumption Patterns of Infants and Toddlers: Where Are We Now? *Journal of the American Dietetic Association* 110:S38–S51.
4. American Academy of Pediatrics. *Age-Related Safety Sheets: 6–12 Months.* 2012. Available at www.healthychildren.org/English/tips-tools/Pages/Safety-for-Your-Child-6-to-12-Months.aspx. Accessed April 2012.
5. HHS/USDA. 2010. *Dietary Guidelines for Americans, 2010.* Available at www.health.gov/dietaryguidelines/dga2010/dietaryguidelines2010.pdf. Accessed April 2012; Institute of Medicine. 2005. *Dietary Reference Intakes for Energy, Carbohydrate, Fiber, Fat, Fatty Acids, Cholesterol, Protein, and Amino Acids (Macronutrients).* Washington, DC: National Academies Press.
6. Institute of Medicine. 2005. *Dietary Reference Intakes for Energy, Carbohydrate, Fiber, Fat, Fatty Acids, Cholesterol, Protein, and Amino Acids (Macronutrients).*
7. Ibid.; HHS/USDA. 2010. *Dietary Guidelines for Americans, 2010.*
8. Institute of Medicine. 2010. *Dietary Reference Intakes for Calcium and Vitamin D.* Washington, DC: National Academies Press. Available at www.iom.edu/reports/2010/dietary-reference-intakes-for-calcium-and-vitamin-D.aspx. Accessed April 2012.
9. Killip, S., J. M. Bennett, and M. D. Chambers. 2007. Iron-Deficiency Anemia. *American Family Physician* 75:671–678.
10. Millichap, J. G. and M. M. Yee. 2012. The Diet Factor in Attention Deficit/Hyperactivity Disorder. *Pediatrics* 129:330–339.
11. Ibid.
12. U.S. Preventive Services Task Force. 2006. *Screening for Iron-Deficiency Anemia—Including Iron Supplementation for Children and Pregnant Women: Recommendation Statement.* Publication No. AHRQ 06-0589. Available at www.uspreventiveservicestaskforce.org/uspstf06/ironsc/ironrs.htm. Accessed April 2012.
13. World Health Organization. 2002. *World Health Report 2002: Reducing Risks, Promoting Healthy Lives.* Available at www.who.int/whr/2002. Accessed April 2012.
14. Siega-Riz, et al. 2010. Food Consumption Patterns of Infants and Toddlers.
15. Corbett, J. V. 1995. Accidental Poisoning with Iron Supplements. *MCN: The American Journal of Maternal Child Nursing* 20:234.
16. U.S. Food and Drug Administration. 2011. *Code of Federal Regulations Title 21. Sec. 101.17 Food Labeling Warning, Notice, and safe Handling Statements.* Available at www.accessdata.fda.gov/scripts/cdrh/cfdocs/cfcfr/CFRSearch.cfm?fr=101.17. Accessed April 2012.
17. Wright, R. O., S.-W. Tsaih, J. Schwartz, R. J. Wright, and H. Hu. 2003. Association between Iron Deficiency and Blood Lead Level in a Longitudinal Analysis of Children Followed in an Urban Primary Care Clinic. *Journal of Pediatrics* 142:9–14.
18. Agency for Toxic Substances and Disease Registry. 2007. *Fact Sheet: Lead.* Available at www.atsdr.cdc.gov/tfacts13.pdf. Accessed April 2012.
19. Institute of Medicine. 2011. *Dietary Reference Intakes for Calcium and Vitamin D.*
20. Craig, W. J. and A. R. Mangels. 2009. Position of the American Dietetic Association: Vegetarian Diets. *Journal of the American Dietetic Association* 109:1266–1282.
21. Wardle, J., M.-L. Herrera, L. Cooke, and E. L. Gibson. 2003. Modifying Children's Food Preferences: The Effects of Exposure and Reward on Acceptance of an Unfamiliar Vegetable. *European Journal of Clinical Nutrition* 57:341–348.
22. Satter, E. 2012. *Ellyn Satter's Division of Responsibility in Feeding.* Available at www.ellynsatter.com/ellyn-satters-division-of-responsibility-in-feeding-i-80.html. Accessed April 2012.
23. Neelon, S. E. B. and M. Briley. 2011. Position of the American Dietetic Association: Benchmarks for Nutrition Programs in Child Care Settings. *Journal of the American Dietetic Association* 111:607–615.
24. Haire-Joshu, D., M. B. Elliot, N. M. Caito, K. Hessler, M. S. Nanney, N. Hale, T. K. Boehmer, et al. 2008. High 5 for Kids: The Impact of a Home Visiting Program on Fruit and Vegetable Intake of Parents and Their Preschool Children. *Preventive Medicine* 47:77–82.
25. Kliegman, R. M., B. F. Stanton, J. St. Geme, N. F. Schor, and R. E. Behrman. 2011. *Nelson Textbook of Pediatrics.* 19th ed. Philadelphia: W. B. Saunders.
26. U.S. Department of Agriculture, Food and Nutrition Service. 2011. *National School Lunch Program.* Available at www.fns.usda.gov/cnd/lunch/AboutLunch/NSLPFactsheet.pdf. Accessed April 2012.
27. Rampersaud, G. C., M. A. Pereira, B. L. Girard, J. Adams, and J. D. Metzl. 2005. Breakfast Habits, Nutritional Status, Body Weight, and Academic Performance in Children and Adolescents. *Journal of the American Dietetic Association* 105:743–760.
28. Ibid.
29. Healthy People 2020. 2012. Nutrition and Weight Status Objectives. Available at www.healthypeople.gov/2020/topics objectives2020/objectiveslist.aspx?topicid=29. Accessed April 2012.
30. Blanck, H. M., C. Gillespie, J. E. Kimmons, J. D. Seymour, and M. K. Serdula. 2008. Trends in Fruit and Vegetable Consumption among U.S. Men and Women, 1994–2005. *Preventing Chronic Disease* 5:2.
31. Boyce, J. A., A. Assa'ad, A. W. Burks, S. M. Jones, H. A. Sampson, R. A. Wood, et al. 2010. Guidelines for the Diagnosis and Management of Food Allergy in the United States: Report of the NIAID-Sponsored Expert Panel. *Journal of Allergy and Clinical Immunology* 126:S1–S58.
32. National Institutes of Health. 2011. Food Allergies. *MedlinePlus Magazine* 6:24–25.
33. Food and Drug Administration. 2006. *Guidance for Industry: Questions and Answers Regarding Food Allergens, Including the Food Allergen Labeling and Consumer Protection Act of 2004.* Available at www.fda.gov/downloads/Food/GuidanceComplianceRegulatoryInformation/GuidanceDocuments/FoodLabelingNutrition/UCM301394.pdf. Accessed June 2012.
34. Ogden, C. L., M. D. Carroll, B. K. Kit, and K. M. Flegal. 2012. Prevalence of Obesity and Trends in Body Mass Index Among U.S. Children and Adolescents, 1999–2010. *Journal of the American Medical Association* 307:483–490.
35. Centers for Disease Control and Prevention. 2011. *Healthy Weight: About BMI for Children and Teens.* Available at www.cdc.gov/healthyweight/assessing/bmi/childrens_bmi/about_childrens_bmi.html. Accessed April 2012.
36. American Academy of Child and Adolescent Psychiatry. 2011. *Facts for Families: Obesity in Children and Teens.* Available at www.aacap.org/galleries/FactsForFamilies/79_obesity_in_children_and_teens.pdf. Accessed April 2012.
37. Axmaker, L. 2009. *Childhood Obesity – The AAP Weighs In.* Available at www.sfmc.net/PDF/Healthy-Rewards/20301-95Childhood Obesity-TheAA.pdf. Accessed April 2012.
38. Mullen, M. C. and J. Shield. 2004. *Childhood and Adolescent Overweight: The Health Professional's Guide to Identification, Treatment, and Prevention.* Chicago: American Dietetic Association.
39. National Institutes of Health. 2012. *We Can: Ways to Enhance Children's Activity and Nutrition. A National Obesity-Prevention Program.* Available at www.nhlbi.nih.gov/health/public/heart/obesity/wecan/index.htm. Accessed April 2012.
40. Ibid.
41. Langevin, D. D., C. Kwiatkowski, G. McKay, J. O'Sullivan Maillet, R. Touger-Decker, J. K. Smith, et al. 2007. Evaluation of Diet Quality and Weight Status of Children from a Low Socioeconomic Urban Environment

Supports "At Risk" Classification. *Journal of the American Dietetic Association* 107:1973–1977.

42. Roberts, D. F., U. G. Foehr, and V. Rideout. 2005. *Generation M: Media in the Lives of 8–18-Year-Olds*. Henry J. Kaiser Family Foundation. Available at www.kff.org/entmedia/upload/Generation-M-Media-in-the-Lives-of-8-18-Year-Olds-Report.pdf. Accessed January 2009.
43. Mendoza, J. A., F. J. Zimmerman, and D. A. Christakis. 2007. Television Viewing, Computer Use, Obesity, and Adiposity in U.S. Preschool Children. *International Journal of Behavioral Nutrition and Physical Activity* 4:44.
44. Centers for Disease Control and Prevention. 2002. *Exploratory Research Report. Life's First Great Crossroad: Tweens Make Choices that Affect Their Lives Forever.* Available at www.cdc.gov/youthcampaign/research/PDF/LifesFirstCrossroads.pdf. Accessed April 2012.
45. Samour, P. Q. and K. King, eds. 2012. *Handbook of Pediatric Nutrition*. 4th ed. Sudbury, MA: Jones and Bartlett Publishers, Inc.
46. Batada, A., M. D. Seitz, M. G. Wootan, and M. Story. 2008. Nine Out of 10 Food Advertisements Shown during Saturday Morning Children's Television Programming Are for Foods High in Fat, Sodium, or Added Sugars, or Low in Nutrients. *Journal of the American Dietetic Association* 108:673–678.
47. Perry, C., D. B. Bishop, G. L. Taylor, M. Davis, M. Story, C. Gray, et al. 2004. A Randomized School Trial of Environmental Strategies to Encourage Fruit and Vegetable Consumption among Children. *Health Education & Behavior* 31:65–76.
48. American Academy of Pediatrics. Committee on Nutrition. 2003. Prevention of Pediatric Overweight and Obesity. *Pediatrics* 112:424–430.
49. Perry, C., et al. 2004. A Randomized School Trial of Environmental Strategies to Encourage Fruit and Vegetable Consumption among Children; Mullen, M. C., et al. 2004. *Childhood and Adolescent Overweight.*
50. Centers for Disease Control and Prevention. 2011. *Preventing Cavities, Gum Disease, Tooth Loss, and Oral Cancers at a Glance 2011.* Available at www.cdc.gov/chronicdisease/resources/publications/AAG/doh.htm. Accessed June 2012.
51. American Dental Association. 2000. *Position Statement on Early Childhood Caries.* Available at www.ada.org/2057.aspx. Accessed June 2012.
52. Ogden, et al. 2012. Prevalence of Obesity and Trends in Body Mass Index.
53. Must, A., E. N. Naumova, S. M. Phillips, M. Blum, B. Dawson-Hughes, and W. M. Rand. 2005. Childhood Overweight and Maturational Timing in the Development of Adult Overweight and Fatness: The Newton Girls Study and Its Follow-Up. *Pediatrics* 116:620–627.
54. Centers for Disease Control and Prevention. 2011. School Health Guidelines to Promote Healthy Eating and Physical Activity. *Morbidity and Mortality Weekly Report* 60:5.
55. Institute of Medicine. 2011. *Dietary Reference Intakes for Calcium and Vitamin D*; KidsHealth.org. 2010. *Growth Plate Injuries.* Available from http://kidshealth.org/parent/medical/bones/growth_plate_injuries.html. Accessed April 2012.
56. Institute of Medicine. 2011. *Dietary Reference Intakes for Calcium and Vitamin D.*
57. Atkinson, S. A., G. P. McCabe, C. M. Weaver, S. A. Abrams, and K. O. O'Brien. 2008. Are Current Calcium Recommendations for Adolescents Higher than Needed to Achieve Optimal Peak Bone Mass? The Controversy. *Journal of Nutrition* 138:1182–1186.
58. Volek, J. S., et al. 2003. Increasing Fluid Milk Favorably Affects Bone Mineral Density Responses to Resistance Training in Adolescent Boys. *Journal of the American Dietetic Association* 103:1353–1356.
59. Forshee, R. A., P. A. Anderson, and M. L. Storey. 2006. Changes in Calcium Intake and Association with Beverage Consumption and Demographics: Comparing Data from CSFII 1994–1996, 1998 and NHANES 1999–2002. *Journal of the American College of Nutrition* 25:108–116.
60. Center for Science in the Public Interest. 2005. *Liquid Candy.* Available at www.cspinet.org/new/pdf/liquid_candy_final_w_new_supplement.pdf. Accessed June 2012.
61. Alaimo, K. 1994. *Dietary Intake of Vitamins, Minerals and Fiber of Persons Ages 2 Months and Over in the United States.* Third National Health and Nutrition Examination Survey Phase 1, 1988–1991: Advance Data from Vital and Health Statistics, No. 258. Hyattsville, MD: National Center for Health Statistics.
62. Ibid.
63. Killip, et al. 2007. Iron-Deficiency Anemia.
64. Larson, N. I., D. Neumark-Sztainer, P. J. Hannan, and M. Story. 2007. Family Meals during Adolescence Are Associated with Higher Diet Quality and Healthful Meal. *Journal of the American Dietetic Association* 107:1502–1510.
65. Halas-Liang, M. 2011. Parenting Food Choices Through Family Meals as a Way to Meet the Dietary Guidelines for Americans. *On the Cutting Edge* 32:15–18.
66. Neumark-Sztainer, D., M. E. Eisenberg, J. A. Fulkerson, M. Story, and N. I. Larson. 2008. Family Meals and Disordered Eating in Adolescents: Longitudinal Findings from Project EAT. *Archives of Pediatrics and Adolescent Medicine* 162:17–22.
67. Berge, J. M., K. Loth, C. Hanson, J. Croll-Lambert, and D. Neumark-Sztainer. 2011. Family Life Cycle Transitions and the Onset of Eating Disorders: A Prospective Grounded Theory Approach. *Journal of Clinical Nursing* 21:1355–1363.
68. Neumark-Sztainer, D., M. Wall, J. Guo, M. Story, J. Haines, and M. Eisenberg. 2006. Obesity, Disordered Eating, and Eating Disorders in a Longitudinal Study of Adolescents: How Do Dieters Fare 5 Years Later? *Journal of the American Dietetic Association* 106:559–568.
69. Vertalino, M., M. E. Eisenberg, M. Story, and D. Neumark-Sztainer. 2007. Participation in Weight-Related Sports Is Associated with Higher Use of Unhealthful Weight Control Behaviors and Steroid Use. *Journal of the American Dietetic Association* 107:434–440.
70. Neumark-Sztainer, D., et al. 2006. Obesity, Disordered Eating, and Eating Disorders in a Longitudinal Study of Adolescents.
71. Ibid.

19 Life Cycle Nutrition
Older Adults

Chapter Objectives

After reading this chapter, you will be able to:

1. Describe the demographics of aging in America and explain why Americans are living longer.
2. Describe common changes that occur as a result of aging.
3. Summarize the nutrient needs of older adults.
4. Discuss some of the nutrition-related health concerns common to old age.
5. Describe the social, economic, and psychological factors that can affect the health of older Americans.

1. Chronic disease is an inevitable part of aging. T/F
2. Heart disease is the number-one cause of death among Americans. T/F
3. A lack of dietary fiber leads many older adults to suffer from constipation. T/F
4. The population of those 65 years and older is declining. T/F
5. Many older individuals are more susceptible to diabetes due to a lack of vitamin D. T/F
6. Too much vitamin A can increase the risk of bone fractures. T/F
7. Herbal supplements are rarely used by older adults. T/F
8. Older adults need fewer daily kilocalories than when they were younger. T/F
9. Food insecurity among elders is a nonissue in the United States. T/F
10. Alcohol abuse is extremely rare among older adults. T/F

See page 729 for answers to these Myths and Misconceptions.

For most people, the adult years between the ages of 20 and 65 are a period of homeostasis and optimally functioning body systems. After about age 65, body functions begin to slow and degenerate and older adulthood begins. The experience of aging is unique for everyone, and changes in functions do not occur at the same rate or to the same degree in any two people.

Although the older years should be a positive time of life, the development of chronic disease and disability can impose heavy health and economic burdens on a person and greatly diminish quality of life. Although the risk of disease and disability increases with age, poor health is not inevitable.

In this chapter we'll discuss the physical, economic, and emotional aspects of aging, and the nutrient needs of older adults. We'll also examine the most common dietary challenges older adults face, and ways to minimize health risks and promote a healthier older age.

What Are the Demographics of Aging in America?

Although the potential **life span** of the human body hasn't changed much (it's currently around 120 years) over the last century, the average age to which we are living has increased significantly. In fact, from 1900 to 2008, **life expectancy** at birth increased from 46 to 76 years for men and from 48 to 81 years for women.[1] This **longevity,** or duration of life, is affected by numerous factors, including lifestyle, genetics, and the environment.[2] Older Americans today not only live longer than their predecessors, but also have lower rates of disability, higher levels of education, and a lower incidence of poverty.[3]

In spite of this good news, coming up with a definition of the process of **aging** is not straightforward. Aging can have a positive connotation, as in "aging wine" or "aging cheese"; some things get better with age. In humans, aging is a natural, yet complex, process associated with physical and psychological changes that, over time, lead to death. **Senescence** is another term for growing old and is defined as a process that begins at conception and ends at death.

America's Population Is Getting Older and More Diverse

Given the rise in life expectancy, it isn't surprising that the United States' population is aging at a rapid rate. The large group of baby boomers born after World War II (between 1946 and 1964) are reaching their 60s, and those at the front end of this group, who began turning age 65 in 2011, are expected to be in the fastest growing segment of the population over the next decade. In 2010, the population of people aged 65 and older numbered 40.3 million. This means that about one in seven people, or 13 percent of the population, is an older American. By 2030, the number of Americans aged 65 and older will be more than 74 million, and they'll comprise roughly 20 percent of the U.S. population. By 2050, this number will rise to over 88.5 million (**Figure 19.1**). The 85-and-older population is projected to increase from 5.5 million in 2010 to 19 million by 2050.[4]

As the United States as a whole grows more diverse, so does the population aged 65 and older. By the year 2050, the percentage of older Americans who are white is expected to drop by about 10 percent, while the percentages of older Americans who are black and Asian are expected to rise by 12 percent and 3 percent, respectively **(Figure 19.2)**. Although not shown as a separate group in Figure 19.2, the number of Hispanics aged 65 and older is projected to experience the sharpest population growth, tripling as a proportion of the population by 2030. Fully 42 percent of the population of Americans aged 65 and older will be of minority status in 2050.[5] Health professionals working with this age group will need to respect the variations in food habits, attitudes toward health, and differences in family roles

life span The maximum age to which members of a species can live.

life expectancy The average length of life for a population of individuals.

longevity The duration of an individual's life.

aging Changes that accumulate over time, ultimately leading to death.

senescence Another term for aging.

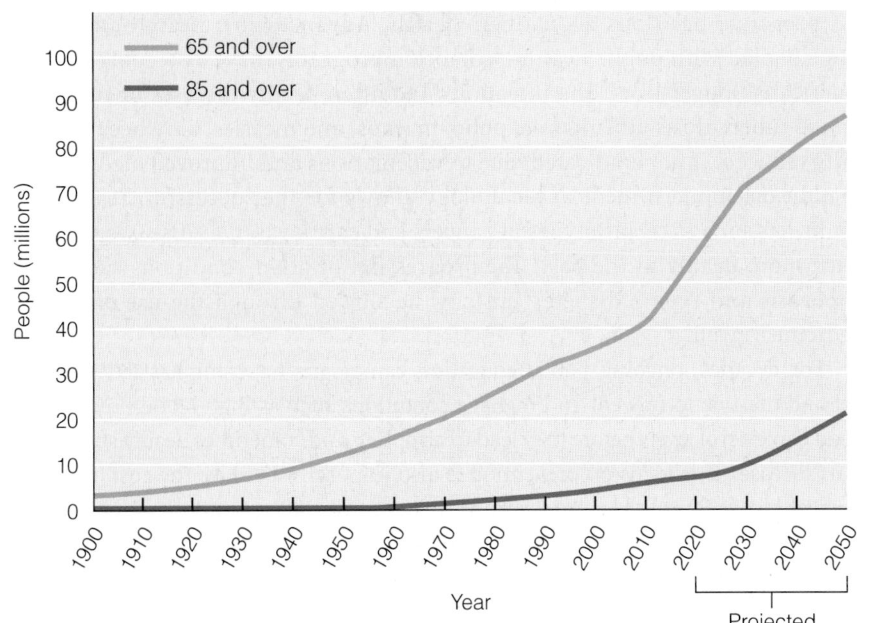

◀ **Figure 19.1 The Aging Population**
The number of older adults in the United States is expected to increase dramatically over the next several decades.
Data from www.agingstats.gov.

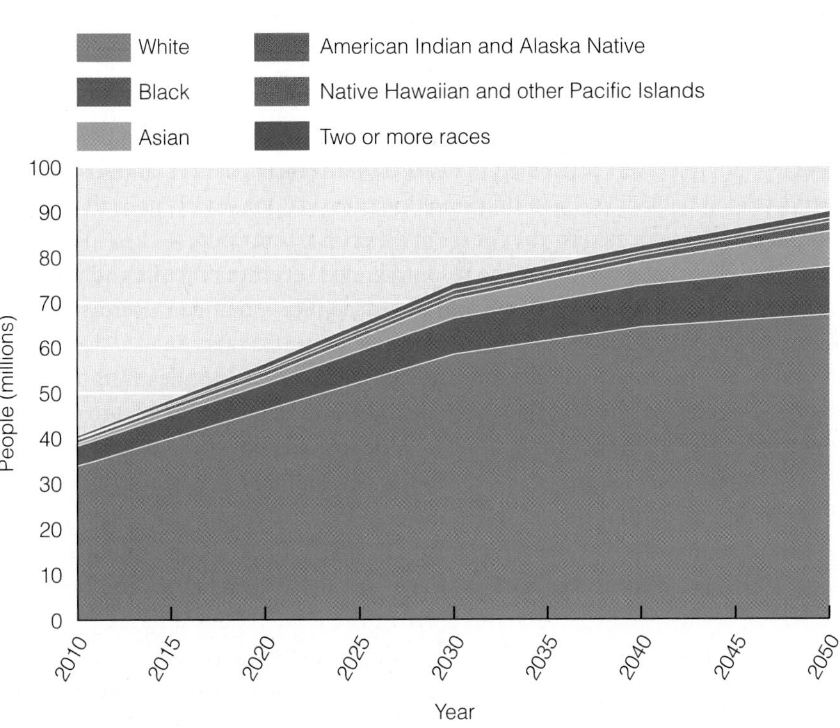

◀ **Figure 19.2 Projected U.S. Population Aged 65 and Over by Race: 2010–2050**
America's aging population will become more racially and ethnically diverse over the next several decades.
Note: Unless otherwise specified, data refer to the population who reported a race alone. Populations for each race group include both Hispanics and non-Hispanics, as Hispanics may be of any race.
Source: U.S. Census Bureau. 2010. *The Next Four Decades: The Older Population in the United States: 2010 to 2050*. Available at www.census.gov/prod/2010pubs/p25-1138.pdf. Accessed July 2012.

resulting from a racially and ethnically diverse population. Having an understanding of how race and ethnicity affect nutrient needs and the development of chronic disease is critical to successfully creating and delivering health and nutrition messages that are appropriate for diverse peoples.

Improved Health Care and Disease Prevention Are Lengthening the Life Span

The increase in the number of older Americans can be attributed to several factors. For example, baby boomers have access to the vast amount of health information that is available via the Internet and are using it to make informed and proactive decisions about their health. Advances in research and health care, coupled with public health–promotion programs, have also contributed to Americans' longer lives. The infectious and often deadly diseases of the 1900s, such as tuberculosis, pneumonia, polio, mumps, and measles, have been dramatically reduced, if not eradicated, due to vaccinations and improved medical care. In addition, modern medical technology allows for the successful treatment of conditions such as certain types of cancers and cardiovascular diseases that were much more deadly in the past. The progression of other conditions such as osteoporosis and type 2 diabetes can now be slowed through the use of modern medicine as well.

For decades, ongoing public education campaigns have emphasized a healthy diet and lifestyle to prevent and manage conditions such as high blood pressure and blood cholesterol levels before they lead to crippling and sometimes deadly strokes and heart disease. This focus on prevention is also important because the cost of providing health care for an older American is three to five times greater than for someone younger than 65. Efforts by older adults to improve their health will help limit the escalation in health care costs and reduce the proportion of the nation's income spent on health care.[6]

Smoking, Poor Diet, and Physical Inactivity Contribute to Leading Causes of Death

According to the CDC, in 2008 over 50 percent of the deaths among persons aged 65 years and older were attributed to diseases of the heart, cancer, and stroke.[7] Poor health-related behaviors, including smoking, physical inactivity, poor diet, and alcohol misuse, practiced over the course of a lifetime, contribute to these diseases. In contrast, a diet that emphasizes the recommended servings of fruits and vegetables can supply beneficial antioxidants and phytochemicals that can decrease the risk of several chronic diseases. Limiting saturated and *trans* fats can also decrease the risk for heart disease, which remains the number-one cause of death in the United States. The rates of physical inactivity in the United States continue to rise, contributing to the increase in the number of people who are overweight and obese. Having excess body weight is a factor in the development of chronic diseases such as heart disease, cancer, stroke, and diabetes.

The Centers for Disease Control State of Aging and Health Report (also known as the National Report Card) assesses the health status and health behaviors of adults aged 65 years and older in the United States. Based on *Healthy People 2010*, key indicators of older adult health help guide policy makers in developing strategies to improve the mental and physical health of Americans in their later years (see Spotlight: Key Indicators of Older Adult Health).[8] Older adults are encouraged to adopt healthier behaviors and obtain regular health screening to reduce the risk for many chronic diseases. These preventive health behaviors would help improve the quality of life, reduce health disparities, and save on health care dollars.

THE TAKE-HOME MESSAGE Life span is the maximum age to which members of a species can live, and longevity is the duration of an individual's life. Life expectancy has increased markedly in the United States over the last century. The U.S. population is living longer due to improved health care, disease prevention, and increased access to health information. The leading causes of death among older adults are heart disease, cancer, and stroke.

SPOTLIGHT Key Indicators of Older Adult Health

The Centers for Disease Control and Prevention use data on the following indicators to assess the health status and behaviors of U.S. adults aged 65 and older. Results are published in its report, *The State of Aging and Health in America*:

Health Status
Physically Unhealthy Days
Frequent Mental Distress
Oral Health: Complete Tooth Loss
Disability

Health Behaviors
No Leisure-Time Physical Activity
Eating ≥ 5 Fruits and Vegetables Daily
Obesity
Current Smoking

Preventive Care and Screening
Flu Vaccine in Past Year
Ever Had Pneumonia Vaccine
Mammogram within Past 2 Years
Colorectal Cancer Screening
Up-to-date on Select Preventive Services—Men
Up-to-date on Select Preventive Services—Women
Cholesterol Checked in Past 5 Years

Injuries
Hip Fracture Hospitalizations—Men
Hip Fracture Hospitalizations—Women

Source: Centers for Disease Control. (n.d.). *State of Aging and Health in America*. Available from http://apps.nccd.cdc.gov/SAHA/Default/IndicatorMenu.aspx. Accessed June 2012.

What Changes Occur as Part of the Aging Process?

Most age-related changes are gradual and accumulate over time, and there is considerable variation in how older adults are affected by them. The rate at which individuals change depends on the genes they inherit, the environment in which they live, and the lifestyle they follow. Genetics will determine the rate at which cells are maintained and repaired and can influence development of a number of chronic diseases, such as cardiovascular disease and cancer. Environmental factors such as oxidative stress, caused by excessive sun exposure or cigarette smoking, can cause cellular damage and lead to cell mutation or death.

Lifestyle factors, including stress levels, can contribute to the aging process by making a person more susceptible to illness. Stress can have many sources—including pressures at work, school, or home—and if prolonged can increase the level of the hormone cortisol. High cortisol levels can lead to increases in body weight, decreased immune function, and an increased inflammatory response. Other lifestyle choices, like what foods to eat and how much exercise to participate in, affect the rate of aging. A diet that is high in saturated fats and low in antioxidants and fiber can accelerate the aging process. Regular weight-bearing, flexibility, and cardiovascular exercise can keep muscles strong and limber, while a sedentary routine can lead to atrophy and poor physical condition. Regular exercise throughout adulthood is largely the reason why some older adults can run marathons at 70 years of age.

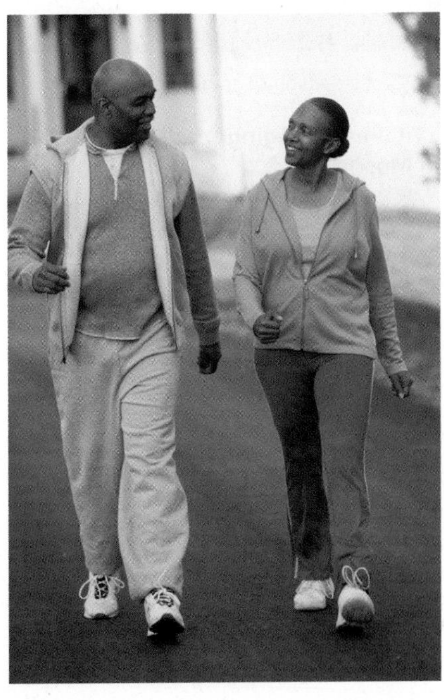

The number-one physical activity among older Americans is walking. Gardening is second most prevalent, followed by bicycling. Don't know what to get your grandparents for a birthday gift? Consider a pair of walking shoes.

The **physiologic age** of a person can vary greatly from that person's **chronologic age,** and can reflect a wide range of changes that affect not only physical appearance but also body function and response to daily living. Overall, the changes that occur through aging involve a general slowing down of all organ systems due to a gradual decline in cellular activity. This slowing limits normal functions and makes individuals more susceptible to death and disease. Being aware of the most

physiologic age A person's age estimated in terms of body health, function, and life expectancy.

chronologic age A person's age in number of years of life.

important physiological changes that occur with age can help individuals understand the implications of these changes for nutritional needs.

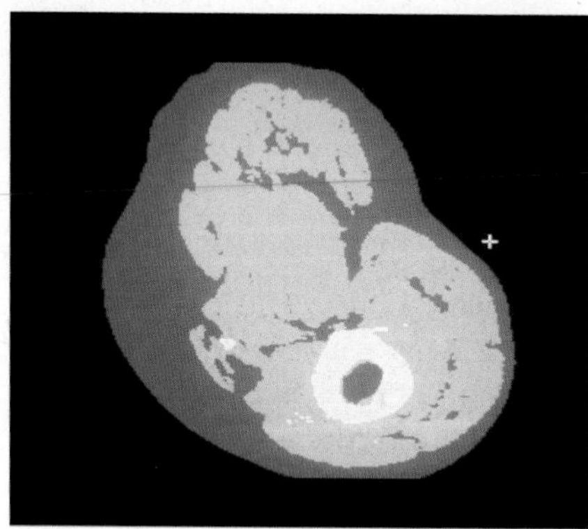

a Cross-section of a young adult's thigh

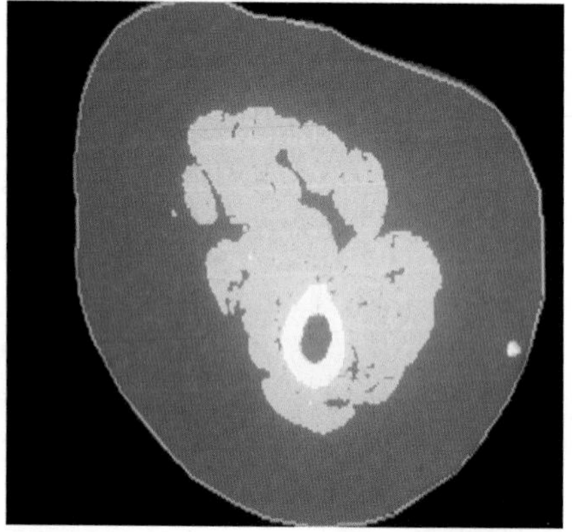

b Cross-section of an older adult's thigh

▲ **Figure 19.3 Aging Leads to Decrease in Muscle Mass**
Note the proportionally reduced muscle area (in yellow) of the older, sedentary adult in the bottom image compared with that of a younger, more active adult. Most people lose a significant amount of muscle as they age, which could be prevented by engaging in regular physical activity.

Weight and Body Composition Change

Aging leads to changes in body composition that can affect overall health and nutrition status. Older adults commonly gain weight, and fat deposits in the abdominal area increase. As with younger age groups, the combination of dietary excess, poor food choices, and physical inactivity has led to the increased incidence of overweight and obesity in older adults. Currently, over two-thirds of Americans over the age of 65 are classified as overweight and approximately one-third are classified as obese.[9] Although the risk of death associated with obesity itself is lower in older adults, obesity increases the risk for cardiovascular disease, stroke, diabetes, cancer, and other health complications that reduce the quality of life.

Unintentional weight loss and low body weight may occur among some older adults. Chronic inadequate food intake may result in malnutrition, reducing resistance to infections, as well as other adverse health outcomes, such as frailty, loss of independence, and functional decline.[10]

Even if body weight is in a healthy range, aging leads to decreases in lean tissue and muscle mass (**Figure 19.3**). **Sarcopenia,** or reduced muscle mass and function, is caused by changes in muscle and nerve tissue that result from decreased physical activity. Day-to-day activities become more difficult, putting older adults at higher risk for falls and fractures. Loss of muscle tissue also reduces the ability to breathe deeply and reduces gastrointestinal activity. Although everyone experiences these changes to some degree, regular physical activity can slow or minimize the effects. Through optimal nutrition and regular physical activity, aging individuals are better able to preserve physical function as well as their independence and quality of life.

Our Immune Function Decreases as We Age

Inflammation is the immune system's normal response to infection or injury. As a person ages, the function of the immune system and its ability to fight off infection and disease decrease. Age-related changes in immune function leave older adults at risk for a host of inflammatory diseases. Low-level inflammation is linked to chronic, age-related diseases, including rheumatoid arthritis, atherosclerosis, osteoporosis, and type 2 diabetes.

A decrease in immune function may be partially due to inadequate dietary intake, which contributes to the development of nutritional deficiencies. The immune response depends on an adequate nutritional intake to supply the materials necessary for cell differentiation and synthesis of immune factors. It is not uncommon for older adults to be deficient in zinc, iron, beta-carotene, folic acid, and vitamins B_6, B_{12}, C, D, and E.[11] Deficiency of key nutrients such as these in conjunction with advanced age can decrease the body's ability to fight infections and disease.

Our Sensory Abilities Decline as We Age

In older age there is a progressive decline in the senses of vision, hearing, taste, and smell that becomes more severe in persons over the age of 70. This decline in sensory abilities can result in decreased food and nutrient intake. For example, poor vision can make shopping for food and preparing meals more difficult. Hearing loss can lead to social isolation and solitary eating, which in turn may limit a person's interest in food.

sarcopenia Age-related progressive loss of muscle mass, muscle strength, and function.

A decline in the sense of smell may have an even greater impact on an individual's interest in food.[12] Older people with a diminished sense of smell have a reduced interest in cooking and consuming a variety of foods. Research has shown that in retirement homes where the residents are offered flavorful foods, consumption increases.[13] Assisting older adults in maintaining an adequate and varied diet through the use of highly seasoned foods can help offset nutritional deficiencies and make meals enjoyable.

Gastrointestinal Changes Occur as We Age

As a person ages, a number of changes occur within the gastrointestinal tract and its accessory organs that affect the chewing and digestion of foods and the absorption of nutrients. One major change is that saliva production may decrease, especially in people who take medications. Decreased saliva production makes swallowing more difficult (a condition known as dysphagia) and may reduce taste perception. A lack of saliva also increases the risk of tooth decay and periodontal disease. Many elderly people may be missing teeth or wearing dentures, which can make chewing difficult, limit food choices, and contribute to poor nutrition.

Changes in digestive secretions and motility of the stomach also occur. Production of hydrochloric acid and pepsin declines, which can result in decreased absorption of certain nutrients. This reduction in secretions can contribute to the development of atrophic gastritis, which affects protein digestion, and can interfere with the absorption of iron, calcium, vitamin B_6, vitamin B_{12}, and folate.[14] A decline in gastrointestinal motility can contribute to constipation, gas, and bloating. A decline in physical activity, a low-fiber diet, and low fluid intake will exacerbate these problems. Stomach emptying may also slow, reducing hunger and thus food and nutrient intake.

Our Brain Function Also Changes as We Age

As people age, they change psychologically as well as biologically. An aging brain—and everything that entails, from the annoying inconveniences of age-related memory loss to more serious conditions like Alzheimer's disease and dementia—was once equated with neuron failure. Improved technology such as higher resolution magnetic resonance imaging (MRI) has generated a wealth of information about the physical changes in the aging brain. Scientists no longer hold the longstanding belief that vast numbers of brain cells are lost with age. Instead, studies have demonstrated brain cell growth throughout the life span.

The aging brain is far more resilient than was previously believed. Age-related changes in cognitive function vary considerably across individuals and across cognitive domains, with some cognitive functions appearing more susceptible than others to the effects of aging. Research seeks to understand normal, aging-related cognitive deficits toward the goal of using the brain's regenerative potential to restore function lost to injury or neurodegenerative disease.[15]

Cognitive ability affects both immediate and long-term health status. Older adults with impaired cognitive function are more likely to lose self-care abilities, including self-feeding. Inadequate food and fluid intake can result in further decline in health and function.

THE TAKE-HOME MESSAGE Among the notable physiologic effects of aging are changes in weight and body composition, including an increase in fat mass relative to muscle tissue. Weight loss occurring among older adults may result in malnutrition, reducing elders' resistance to infections. Immune function decreases, partly as a result of nutrient deficiencies, and the senses of vision, hearing, taste, and smell also diminish, lessening the enjoyment of food. Older adults may also experience gastrointestinal difficulties, such as reduced saliva production and slower GI motility. With impaired cognitive function, older adults may experience inadequate food and fluid intake. Optimal nutrition can prevent further decline in health and preserve function.

What Are the Nutrient Needs of Older Adults?

Gender, health status, diet, and level of physical activity can all influence an older individual's nutrient needs. The *Dietary Guidelines for Americans, 2010* recognizes that people over the age of 50 are a specific population that requires special consideration. The Dietary Reference Intakes for Older Adults takes these differences into account; nutrient recommendations have been designed to address the needs of males and females 51 years of age and older. Additionally, Steps to a HealthierUS, a U.S. Department of Health and Human Services initiative, encourages Americans to live longer, better, healthier lives by eating a nutritious diet, underscoring the importance of prevention in successful aging. **Figure 19.4** provides a graphic representation of the nutritional needs of older adults. The key feature of a nutritious diet during aging is that older adults need to get adequate amounts of protein, complex carbohydrates, vitamins, and minerals, but take in fewer kilocalories.

MyPlate for Older Adults

Illustration by Betsy Hayes ©2011 Tufts University http://now.tufts.edu/articles/eat-well-age-well

▸ **Figure 19.4 Older Adults Benefit from Good Nutrition and Physical Activity**
Older adults need to focus on nutrient-dense foods that contain adequate fiber, calcium, vitamin B_{12}, and vitamin D. With a declining metabolic rate, they require fewer kilocalories. Food choices should emphasize complex carbohydrates, lean protein foods, and healthy fats. They also need to ensure adequate fluid intake and regularly engage in physical activity.

Calculation Corner

Estimating Energy Expenditure Using the Harris-Benedict Equation

Sue, a 70-year-old retired nurse, has slowed down in her activities. She continues to walk 2 miles a day. She is 5 feet 7 inches (170.2 cm) tall and maintains her weight at 154 pounds (70 kg). Use the Harris-Benedict Equation below to determine her Estimated Energy Expenditure (EER). Sue was active at the same body weight when she was 30. How has her EER changed?

Answer:

1. Use the Harris-Benedict Equation for Females to calculate Sue's RMR:

   RMR = 655.1 + (9.6 × weight in kg) + (1.8 × height in cm) – (4.7 × age in years)

   655.1 + (9.6 × 70 kg) + (1.8 × 170.2 cm) – (4.7 × 70) = 1,304.46 kcalories

   655.1 + 672 + 306.36 – 329 = 1,304.46

2. Next, apply the activity factor to determine total daily energy expenditure:

   Sedentary: 1.00; Low level of activity: 1.12; Active: 1.27; Very Active: 1.48

   1,304.46 × 1.12 = 1,461 kcalories

3. Now put the equations together to calculate her EER at age 30:

   655.1 + (9.6 × 70 kg) + (1.8 × 170.2 cm) – (4.7 × 30) = 1,492.46 kcalories

   1,492.46 × 1.27 activity factor = 1,895 kcalories

Compared with her needs at age 30, Sue now requires 434 fewer kcalories. Most vitamin and mineral requirements remain the same or have increased. Lower energy needs means that Sue must select nutrient-dense foods with fewer kilocalories to maintain her body weight.

Older Adults Need Fewer Kilocalories, Not Less Nutrition

Because a person's metabolic rate naturally declines with age, older adults need fewer kilocalories. The decline in their metabolism is a combination of the natural loss of muscle mass (recall that muscle mass requires more energy to be maintained than fat mass) and the tendency for less daily physical activity. This decline amounts to approximately 10 daily kilocalories per year of age for men and 7 daily kilocalories per year of age for women.[16] (See the Calculation Corner for one way of estimating energy expenditure.) In other words, a man at age 60 needs 300 fewer daily kilocalories—about the amount in a turkey sandwich—than he needed at age 30. Some research has even suggested that at 80 years of age, kilocalorie intake may be reduced by as much as 1,000 kilocalories daily in some men and by 600 kilocalories daily in some women compared with their needs when they were in their 20s.[17] Examining the Evidence: Does Kilocalorie Restriction Extend Life? explores the possible ramifications of decreased kilocalorie intake.

Though kilocalorie needs may be reduced, the need for many nutrients and phytochemicals is not. In fact, the requirement for some nutrients actually increases in older adults, making nutrient-dense food selections even more important. Because phytochemicals, especially antioxidants, have possible roles in helping to reduce the risk of certain cancers, heart disease, cataracts, and age-related macular degeneration, foods need to be both nutrient dense and phytochemical dense. The Table Tips give some guidelines for healthy eating for older adults.

TABLE TIPS

Healthy Eating for Older Adults

Eat a fiber-rich diet by including 2 servings of fruits, 3 servings of vegetables, and 3 servings of whole grains every day. Other fiber-rich foods include legumes, dried beans, and 100% bran cereals.

Drink enough fluids by including six to eight (8-ounce) glasses of fluid every day.

Consume calcium- and vitamin D–rich foods, including low-fat milk, yogurt, greens, canned salmon with bones, dried beans and peas, and tofu.

Eat protein-rich foods by including lean meats, dried beans, peas, and tofu.

Focus on a plant-based diet—research reveals that a variety of nutrient-dense fruits and vegetables provide antioxidants and phytochemicals that may protect cells against free radicals.

Older Adults Need Adequate Protein

According to the DRIs for older adults, protein requirements (as grams per kilogram of body weight) do not change with age. However, because overall kilocalorie

EXAMINING THE EVIDENCE

Does Kilocalorie Restriction Extend Life?

When an individual reaches the age of 100, he or she earns the moniker of centenarian. In the last several decades, the number of people reaching this milestone has increased around the world. Researchers are actively gathering information about where these people live, how they live, and what they eat to gain a better understanding of the aging process and the factors that contribute to longevity. One finding to date is that centenarians follow nutritionally dense diets and eat whole unprocessed foods, vegetables, and fish, and they eat several small meals over the course of the day as opposed to consuming three large meals. Smaller amounts of food equals fewer kilocalories. Does this mean that kilocalorie restriction leads to a longer life? Numerous researchers are exploring this concept.

The benefits of consuming small amounts of food throughout the day have been supported in recent research on kilocaloric restriction in rats. Studies have shown that a kilocalorie-restricted diet can extend the lives of underfed rats up to 50 percent longer than those of rats given an unlimited supply of food.[1] Human studies on kilocaloric restriction have been limited; however, centenarians have been shown to follow the "less is more" philosophy when it comes to eating, and regularly eat to the point where they are only 80 percent full.

Kilocalorie restriction may be one of the reasons Okinawans live long and healthy lives.

Populations with large numbers of centenarians have been the subject of epidemiological studies, with the most notable and longest running study being conducted on the Japanese island of Okinawa. In Okinawa there are more centenarians per capita than anywhere else in the world, which prompted a research study to examine their habits. The Okinawa Centenarian Study examined over 900 Okinawan centenarians and numerous other elderly in their 70s, 80s, and 90s in order to identify factors associated with their increased life span.[2] The findings suggested that genetics and lifestyle habits explain why Okinawans remain healthy far into their senior years. Low kilocaloric intake was first reported in Okinawans in 1967[3] and researchers hypothesized that kilocaloric restriction was partly responsible for their long and healthy life.

This observation is consistent with the free radical theory of aging, which states that damage from free radicals generated from metabolizing food into energy damages vital body molecules, including DNA. Accumulated damage then accelerates the aging process. Additionally, the Okinawan diet is high in green leafy and yellow root vegetables, sweet potatoes, and soy, supplemented with fish. This type of diet is very high in antioxidant vitamins, which may be a contributor to the inhabitants' extended life span.[4] The health benefits that have been linked to the Okinawan diet are many and include decreased mortality from diseases of the heart and cancer as well as increased functional and cognitive capacity at older ages versus Americans.[5]

While research in this area continues, scientists maintain that the best diet for long life and health is one that meets the DRIs for adequate nutrients without exceeding energy requirements. Because kilocalorie-restricted diets are less likely to provide all the nutrients the body needs to function, they are not currently advised. Individuals are encouraged to seek the advice of a Registered Dietitian in establishing a meal plan to meet personal nutrition goals.

References

1. Omodei, D. and L. Fontana. 2011. Calorie Restriction and Prevention of Age-Associated Chronic Disease. *Federation of European Biochemical Societies Letters* 585:1537–1542.
2. Willcox, B. J., K. Yano, R. Chen, D. C. Willcox, B. L. Rodriguez, K. H. Masaki, T. Donlon, et al. 2004. How Much Should We Eat? The Association between Energy Intake and Mortality in a 36-Year Follow-Up Study of Japanese-American Men. *The Journals of Gerontology, Biological Sciences, and Medical Sciences* 59:789–795.
3. Willcox, D. C., B. J. Willcox, H. Todoriki, J. D. Curb, and M. Suzuki. 2006. Caloric Restriction and Human Longevity: What Can We Learn from the Okinawans? *Biogerontology* 7:173–177.
4. Ibid.
5. Ibid.

needs decline, individuals must obtain a relatively higher proportion of kilocalories from protein-rich foods. For healthy older people, the RDA is 0.8 grams per kilogram of body weight, or about 56 grams for men and 46 grams for women. This equals roughly 10 to 35 percent of kilocalories and should include foods that provide all the essential amino acids. Protein is essential for reducing the loss of lean tissue and muscle and helping to prevent excessive loss of bone. In addition, older people who are ill or have suffered trauma will need a higher protein intake to assist in tissue repair and wound healing, and to improve immune function.

Older Adults Should Consume More Complex Carbohydrate

Carbohydrate intake for older adults remains at 45 to 65 percent of total daily kilocalories, just as for younger adults. The emphasis should be on complex carbohydrates, particularly those that are higher in nutrient density. Foods high in complex carbohydrate contain more fiber than simple sugars, which can help prevent constipation, and thus diverticulosis, and decrease the risk of diabetes. Because kilocalorie needs and fiber intake decline with increasing age, the AI for fiber is 30 grams per day for men over the age of 50 years, and 21 grams per day for women over 50. Therefore, older adults need to eat not only nutrient-dense but also high-fiber foods, such as whole grains, fruits, and vegetables, at each meal. Over 70 percent of Americans over age 50, on average, do not meet their daily fiber needs.[18]

Older Adults Should Continue to Moderate Fat Intake

High dietary fat intake, particularly saturated fats and *trans* fats, has been clearly shown to increase the risk for cardiovascular disease and certain types of cancers. In addition, because fat is kilocalorie dense, it can contribute to becoming overweight or obese. Healthy older people should aim for a diet that has 20 to 35 percent of kilocalories from fat, with 5 to 10 percent from omega-6 fatty acids and 0.6 to 1.2 percent from omega-3 fatty acids. Diets should be as low as possible in *trans* fatty acids, as no DRI has been established for this nutrient. Total cholesterol intake should be no more than 300 milligrams per day.

However, as for younger adults, fat should not be eliminated from the diet. Fat is necessary for the absorption of fat-soluble vitamins and provides essential fatty acids. The consumption of fatty fish that are high in omega-3 fatty acids has been shown to positively affect heart health. Severe fat restriction in the elderly may produce negative nutritional consequences.

Older Adults Need to Watch Intake of Vitamins A, D, and B_{12}

Though the recommended daily amount of vitamin A doesn't change for those over age 50, there is a concern that, because it can accumulate to toxic amounts in the body, consuming preformed vitamin A in excess of the RDA may increase the risk of osteoporosis and fractures (see Chapter 9). Older adults should be cautious when choosing supplements and fortified foods so as to avoid overconsuming preformed vitamin A.[19] The vitamin A precursor, beta-carotene, is not of concern and actually offers the added bonus of acting as an antioxidant in the body.

The skin's ability to make vitamin D from sunlight declines with age. Further, the intestines and kidneys lose some ability to absorb and convert vitamin D into its active form.[20] Because of these changes, the need for dietary vitamin D doubles at age 50 and triples at age 70. Recall that vitamin D is needed to properly use calcium and phosphorus to strengthen bones, and inadequate amounts of this vitamin can increase the risk of osteoporosis. Vitamin D also plays a role in maintaining adequate insulin levels. Preliminary evidence suggests that vitamin D supplementation may help to reduce high blood sugar levels as well as increase insulin levels in people with type 2 diabetes. Vitamin D has also been shown to increase the anticancer properties of the immune system and survival in people with cardiovascular disease, and is involved in blood pressure regulation.[21] Older adults need to make sure that they consume vitamin D–fortified dairy products, and many, especially those who have difficulty tolerating lactose as they age, would also benefit from a supplement (Table 19.1).

The RDA for vitamin B_{12} is the same for younger and older adults; however, because the stomach produces less acidic digestive juices as it ages, up to 30 percent of people over the age of 50 cannot absorb the form of vitamin B_{12} that naturally occurs in foods. They can, however, absorb the synthetic variety found in fortified foods and supplements, and these sources should be added to their diet to meet their needs. Vitamin B_{12}, along with adequate amounts of folate and vitamin B_6, may also help lower homocysteine. High amounts of homocysteine may increase the risk of heart disease. The American Heart Association does not support B vitamin supplementation for delaying cardiovascular disease at this time.[22]

TABLE 19.1 Dietary Changes for Older Adults

Recommended Change	Rationale	Examples
Increase intake of nutrient-dense foods	A lower metabolic rate reduces daily kilocalorie needs	Choose foods in each food group that are low in added sugar and saturated fat
Consume adequate fiber	A decreased energy intake decreases fiber requirements	Choose whole-wheat bread, whole-grain cereals, brown rice, vegetables, and whole fruit
Increase intake of water and nutrient-dense fluids	Decreased ability of kidneys to concentrate urine and decreased thirst mechanism can both increase risk of dehydration	Drink low-fat or skim milk and water with and between meals; limit sugary, low-nutrient soft drinks
Increase intake of foods high in beta-carotene to meet vitamin A needs and avoid vitamin A supplements and heavily fortified foods	Higher excess amounts of stored preformed vitamin A in the body can increase fracture risk	Choose carrots, cantaloupe, potatoes, broccoli, and winter squash
Increase intake of vitamin D–fortified foods	Lower ability to make the active form of vitamin D decreases the absorption of calcium and phosphorus and increases the risk of osteoporosis	Choose vitamin D–fortified milk, yogurt, and cereals. Add a supplement if needed.
Increase intake of synthetic form of vitamin B_{12}	Decreased acidic stomach juices will lessen the absorption of vitamin B_{12} in foods	Choose vitamin B_{12}–fortified cereals and soy milk. Add a supplement if needed.
Increase intake of iron-rich foods	The prevalence of anemia increases with age	Choose lean meat, fish, and poultry. Enjoy enriched grains and cereals along with vitamin C–rich foods (such as citrus fruits) to enhance absorption.
Increase intake of zinc-rich foods	A zinc deficiency can suppress immune system and appetite	Choose fortified cereals, lean meats, poultry, legumes, and nuts
Increase intake of calcium-rich foods	Aging increases the risk of osteoporosis and dietary calcium deficiency	Consume 3 servings of dairy foods daily, plus a serving of a calcium-fortified food. Add a supplement if needed.

Older Adults Need to Be Sure to Get Enough Iron, Zinc, and Calcium

Iron deficiency is common in older adults, and over 10 percent of adults 65 years of age and older, and over 20 percent of those 85 or more years old, experience iron-deficiency anemia.[23] Though iron deficiency can occur from intestinal blood loss, an estimated one-third of the anemia in older adults is attributed to inadequate iron consumption alone and/or in combination with diets deficient in folate and vitamin B_{12}.[24] Iron deficiency can lead to fatigue, decreased physical activity, and an impaired immune system. Though women over age 50 need less dietary iron than they did in their younger years (due to the end of menstruation), eating iron-rich foods is still important (see Table 19.1).

Zinc is also needed for a healthy immune system, in particular in the production of white blood cells that fight infection. Zinc plays a role in taste, and a deficiency can depress one's appetite and lessen the desire to eat nutritious foods. Zinc deficiency may occur from inadequate zinc intake or absorption. About 25 percent of older Americans are not meeting their daily dietary zinc needs, and would benefit from adding more foods rich in zinc or fortified with zinc to their diets. If unable to obtain the recommended amount of zinc from food, zinc supplements may fulfill their daily needs.[25]

Lastly, the need for calcium increases 20 percent, to 1,200 milligrams daily for those over the age of 50. More than 70 percent of older Americans are falling short of their dietary calcium needs, which increases their risk of weak bones and fractures.[26] An estimated 10 million Americans over age 50 have osteoporosis and another 34 million are at risk of developing it.[27] Older adults should consume at least three servings of dairy foods, plus a serving of a calcium-fortified food or a supplement, daily (see Chapter 12).

Older Adults May Benefit from Nutritional Supplements

The use of nutritional supplements with the intention of preventing deficiencies, improving health, and delaying age-related chronic disease is a common practice among older adults. However, research on whether nutritional supplements provide true health benefits is mixed, and there is only limited scientific support for the health-related efficacy of multivitamin and/or mineral supplements for older adults.

Some findings regarding stroke, depression, and macular degeneration are encouraging. Preliminary research suggests that antioxidant supplements have benefits for age-related macular degeneration, and selenium has benefits for cancer prevention. The strongest support is for the health benefits of vitamin D and calcium supplements when intake of these nutrients is not optimal.[28] Clear health benefits have also been shown with modest increases in consumption of fatty fish or fish oil supplements, including a reduction in the risk of sudden cardiac death. In addition, there is evidence that high-dose fish oil supplements may lower serum triglyceride levels.[29]

Dietary consumption of vitamins D and E, calcium, and magnesium tend to be low in seniors, and vitamin and mineral supplementation can improve intakes of vitamins E, D, B_6, folic acid, and calcium. But seniors tend to exceed the Tolerable Upper Limit with supplementation of niacin, folic acid, and vitamin A. As a consequence of the mixed research results, whether to take a vitamin-mineral supplement, and which one to take, is confusing to many older adults.

The beta-carotene found in many fruits and vegetables is a good source of vitamin A for seniors, as it won't contribute to vitamin A toxicity.

TABLE 19.2 Checklist for Talking about Nutritional Supplements

Questions about Nutritional Supplements to Ask a Health Care Provider
Can I obtain the same nutrients in adequate amounts from food?
Is taking a nutritional supplement an important part of my total diet?
Are there any precautions or warnings I should know about (for example, is there an amount or "upper limit" I should not go above)?
Are there any known side effects (such as loss of appetite, nausea, or headaches)? Do they apply to me?
Are there any foods, medicines (prescription or over the counter), or other supplements I should avoid while taking this product?
If I am scheduled for surgery, should I be concerned about the nutritional supplements I am taking?

Adapted from U.S. Food and Drug Administration. 2011. *Dietary Supplements: Tips for Older Dietary Supplement Users.* Available at www.fda.gov/Food/DietarySupplements/ConsumerInformation/ucm110493.htm. Accessed May 2012.

Conflicting reports in the media add to the confusion. Older adults who use nutritional supplements to foster better nutritional and health status need to read labels carefully. Moreover, they need to consult their health care provider to ensure appropriate nutritional supplement use. Using a checklist like the one in Table 19.2 can help an individual have an effective conversation about nutritional supplements with a health care provider.

Older Adults Need to Stay Hydrated

Consuming adequate amounts of fluid is important for older adults, especially those over 85 years of age.[30] Illness and medications can affect a kidney's ability to function properly. Changes in the kidneys may affect an elderly person's ability to concentrate urine and hold onto water. Dehydration occurs more readily because older people's thirst mechanism also becomes blunted. Certain medications may cause the body to lose water and/or further desensitize the thirst mechanism.[31]

Though older adults have the same fluid requirements as younger people, the desire to avoid frequent trips to the bathroom, especially when they are away from home, often causes them to deliberately consume less fluid. The incidence of urinary incontinence (the loss of bladder control) also increases with age due to prostate problems in men and weakened bladder muscles in many women after pregnancy. This may further reduce the enthusiasm to consume fluids during the day. Dehydration can also lead to constipation, another common condition in older adults, as the stool becomes hard and compacted in the colon. Because of the need for nutrient-dense foods, there is little room in an older adult's diet for sugar-laden soft drinks that are high in kilocalories and low in nutrients. Water and low-fat or skim milk are better beverages with which to meet their fluid needs and avoid dehydration.

Older Adults Should Eat Right for Good Health and Disease Prevention

According to the World Health Organization (WHO), the best dietary strategy for aging adults to maintain good health and to prevent chronic diseases is to consume a varied, nutrient- and phytochemical-dense, heart-healthy diet.[32] This is the same dietary advice that is recommended in the *Dietary Guidelines for Americans.*

The majority of older Americans aren't heeding this advice. The prevalence of malnutrition is estimated to be 23 percent among older Americans, with another 46 percent considered at risk of malnutrition. An estimated 30 to 60 percent of older adults are undernourished, with energy intakes less than two-thirds of the recommended dietary allowance (RDA).[33] When the diets of Americans 65 years of age and older were assessed in 2012 for compliance with the *Dietary Guidelines for Americans*, only 19 percent of those studied had diets that could be rated as "good." More than 65 percent of older Americans were eating diets that needed improvement and 13 percent were consuming diets rated as "poor."[34] In fact, this research showed that less than 30 percent of those studied consumed the recommended servings from the fruit and milk groups, which reduces their dietary sources of phytochemicals, fiber, calcium, and vitamin D. Many older adults have inadequate servings of vegetables and whole grains, limiting dietary sources of zinc, iron, folate, and antioxidants.[35] The diets of many older adults have also been shown to be too high in saturated fat, cholesterol, and sodium.[36] Table 19.3 on page 716 summarizes the many diseases and conditions that a healthy diet can affect.

Regular physical activity can help older adults stay physically, mentally, and socially healthy.

Older Adults Should Stay Physically Active in Spite of Physical and Mental Challenges

Even with the physical changes that accompany aging, no one is too old to exercise. Physical activity is not a luxury for older adults, it's a necessity. Routine physical activity can help lower the risk of heart disease, colon and breast cancer, diabetes, hypertension, osteoporosis, arthritis, and obesity. It can help maintain healthy bones, muscles, and joints, and reduce anxiety, stress, and depression. Routine exercise improves sleep, flexibility, and range of motion, and can help postpone the decline in cognitive ability that naturally occurs in aging.[37] Older adults in good physical shape are able to live independently longer, reducing the need for assistance with everyday functions.

Despite the many health benefits of being physically active, only 16 percent of those aged 64 to 74 and 12 percent of those 75 years of age and older engage in at least 30 minutes of moderate activity five days a week. Lifestyle activities such as working in the garden, mowing the lawn, raking leaves, and even dancing will all provide health benefits. Older adults would also benefit from strength-training activities such as lifting weights and calisthenics at least twice a week to help maintain muscle strength.[38]

THE TAKE-HOME MESSAGE Older adults need fewer kilocalories but not less nutrition as they age. Meals should be nutrient dense and intake of empty kilocalories should be decreased. Adequate carbohydrate (including fiber) and protein intake are essential, and fat consumption should continue to be moderate. Fruits and vegetables should be emphasized to ensure sufficient intake of beneficial antioxidants and phytochemicals. Some vitamin and mineral consumption, including vitamins A, D, and B_{12} and the minerals iron, zinc, and calcium, should be particularly monitored to ensure adequate intake. Fluid needs are also important to prevent dehydration and constipation. Older adults should remember to eat right and stay physically active to maintain their health.

TABLE 19.3 Eating Right to Fight Age-Related Diseases and Conditions

A varied, plant-based diet with plenty of phytochemicals, fiber, and essential nutrients is the best diet defense against the conditions and chronic diseases associated with aging.

Condition/Disease	Disease-Fighting Compounds
Alzheimer's disease, Parkinson's disease	Antioxidants, vitamins E and C, and carotenoids
Anemia	Iron Folate Vitamin B_{12}
Cancer (colon, prostate, breast)	Fiber in whole grains, fruits, vegetables Phytochemicals (phenols, indoles, lycopene, beta-carotene)
Cataracts, age-related macular degeneration	Vitamins C and E Phytochemicals (lycopene, lutein, zeaxanthin) Zinc
Constipation, diverticulosis	Fiber
Heart disease	Vitamins B_6, B_{12}, and folate Omega-3 fatty acids Soluble fiber Phytochemicals in whole grains
Hypertension, stroke	Calcium Magnesium Potassium
Impaired immune response	Iron Zinc Vitamin B_6
Obesity	Fiber as part of low-kilocalorie, high-satiety fruits and vegetables
Osteoporosis	Calcium Vitamins D and K
Type 2 diabetes	Chromium Fiber Vitamin D Phytochemicals

What Are Some Nutrition-Related Health Concerns of Older Adults?

Aging is often associated with significant health problems. Decreased mobility due to arthritis, vision disorders, and dementia are among the various, nutrition-related health issues that older adults may face.

Decreased Mobility Affects Most Older Adults

Physical disability is very common among the elderly: 16 to 22 percent of adults 65 to 84 years of age, and 27 percent of adults 85 years and older, report difficulty with the activities of daily living, such as carrying groceries, reaching over their heads, and stooping.[39] Over half of adults aged 70 and older need help with daily activities, including preparing and eating nutritionally balanced meals.[40]

Some of this loss of function can be attributed to sarcopenia. However, the most common cause of disability is **arthritis** (*arthr* = joint, *itis* = inflammation), which affects 59 percent of all older adults. Arthritis can cause pain, stiffness, and swelling in joints, muscles, tendons, ligaments, and bones. Getting out of bed, trying to open a jar of mustard, or climbing stairs can all be challenging for anyone with arthritis. There are over 100 types of arthritis; *osteoarthritis* and *rheumatoid arthritis* most commonly occur in older adults. Osteoporosis can also affect mobility in aging adults.

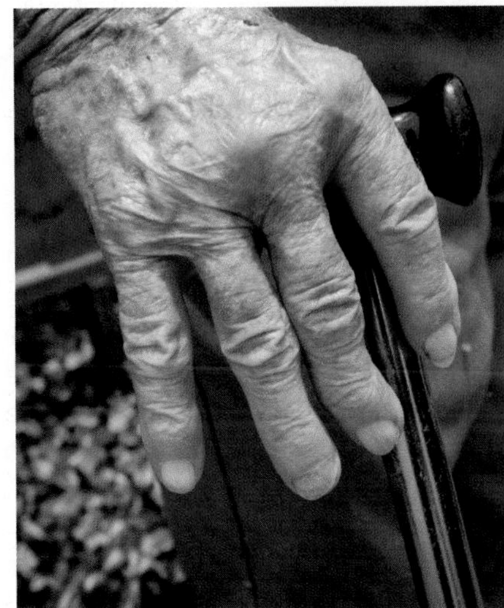

▲ **Figure 19.5 Effects of Osteoarthritis**
Osteoarthritis can affect any joint. When multiple hand joints become affected, pain, swelling, and stiffness make routine tasks difficult to accomplish. Studies show that people who actively manage their osteoarthritis have less pain and function better.

Osteoarthritis

An estimated 27 million Americans suffer from osteoarthritis. More than half of adults aged 65 and older have this type of arthritis in at least one joint.[41] Osteoarthritis occurs when the cartilage, which covers the ends of the bones at the joints, wears down, causing the bones to rub together (see **Figure 19.5**). This constant friction causes swelling, loss of motion, and pain. Osteoarthritis commonly occurs in the fingers, neck, lower back, knees, and hips. Exercises that increase flexibility, keep joints limber, and improve the range of motion can help maintain mobility in people with osteoarthritis. Losing excess weight will also help relieve some of the stress at the hip and knee joints that bear the weight of the body.[42, 43]

Research has shown that the dietary supplements glucosamine and chondroitin sulfate, which are naturally found in cartilage, may provide some pain relief for individuals with mild to moderate knee pain due to osteoarthritis. It doesn't appear to help those with severe knee pain.[44] Individuals with osteoarthritis should speak with their health care provider to find out if they might benefit from using this supplement. For safety's sake, they should also discuss the use of all supplements, including herbs, with a health care provider prior to consuming them. Health Connection: Drug, Food, and Herb Interactions discusses the potentially harmful interactions between certain herbs, nutrients, and drugs.

Rheumatoid Arthritis

Rheumatoid arthritis, which occurs in about 2 million U.S. adults, is an inflammatory disease of the joints.[45] Research suggests that numerous compounds in a Mediterranean-type diet, which is rich in fish, vegetables, and olive oil, may help protect against or manage rheumatoid arthritis. The omega-3 fatty acids in fish have anti-inflammatory effects and may help reduce the stiffness and joint tenderness of rheumatoid arthritis.[46] The current recommendation to eat two fish meals weekly to protect against heart disease may also be helpful for those who suffer from this type of arthritis. Compounds in cooked vegetables have been shown to possibly lower the risk of rheumatoid arthritis, and the fatty acids in olive oil may also help reduce the inflammation.[47]

Routine exercise can help those who suffer from arthritis. Exercise can help reduce joint pain and stiffness, and increase range of motion. It can also build muscles and increase flexibility. Swimming, aquatic exercises, and walking can all help older adults with arthritis.

Gout

Gout is increasingly becoming a health problem for older adults. In 2011, roughly 32 million adults were at risk of developing the disease.[48] Studies show that fatter waistlines and hypertension are largely to blame for the increased incidence of

arthritis Inflammation in the joints that can cause pain, stiffness, and swelling in joints, muscles, tendons, ligaments, and bones.

Health Connection

Drug, Food, and Herb Interactions

Recent studies, including the third National Health and Nutrition Examination Survey, indicate that as those in the elderly population have become more involved in their health care, their use of nonvitamin and nonmineral supplements such as herbs has increased.[1] There is concern, however, that herbal supplements are being used in combination with prescription and over-the-counter medications, creating the potential for negative supplement-drug interactions. A growing concern among many physicians is that some herbal remedies such as ginkgo biloba and garlic may increase the risk of bleeding after surgery. St. John's wort, when combined with prescription antidepressant medications, may also produce negative effects.

In addition to drug-herb interactions, prescription drugs can also interact with other prescription and over-the-counter drugs. About 80 percent of older adults take both prescription and nonprescription medications at the same time, but use more than one pharmacy or order their medications online or through the mail, so they run the risk of unknowingly ingesting incompatible substances. This is a key reason why individuals must *always* discuss the drugs, herbs, and supplements they are taking with their pharmacist or health care provider.

Food can also interact with medications in several ways. For example, it can delay, decrease, or increase the absorption of a drug. The calcium in milk products, for instance, can bind with tetracycline (an antibiotic), decreasing its absorption.

Potential Side Effects of Selected Herbs and Supplements

Herb/Nutrient	Purported Use	Potential Side Effects	Drug Interactions
Black cohosh	Reduce hot flashes and other menopausal symptoms	Possible headache and stomach discomfort	May exert estrogen activity and affect breast tissue
Calcium	Prevent osteoporosis	Constipation; calcium deposits in body	Decreases the absorption of tetracycline, thyroid medication, iron, zinc, and magnesium
Coenzyme Q-10	Hypertension, diabetes mellitus, congestive heart failure	Nausea, vomiting	Tricyclic antidepressants may decrease action of CoQ-10
DHEA	To treat atherosclerosis, hyperglycemia, and cancer	Irregular heart beat, insomnia, restlessness, aggressiveness	Corticosteroids, hormone replacement therapy
Dong Quai root	Relieve menopausal symptoms	Excessive bleeding due to blood thinning	Blood-thinning drugs and aspirin. Enhances the blood-thinning actions of vitamin E, garlic, and ginkgo biloba.
Echinacea	Treat the common cold	Skin inflammation in sensitive individuals	May decrease effectiveness of immune-suppressing drugs (cyclosporine, corticosteroids)
Evening primrose oil	Help with chronic fatigue syndrome	Mild stomach and intestinal discomfort; headaches	May interfere with drugs used in epilepsy (phenothiazines)
Fish oil	Reduce the risk of heart disease	Excessive amounts could raise both blood glucose and LDL cholesterol levels, increase the risk of excessive bleeding, and cause a fishy aftertaste in mouth	Blood-thinning drugs and aspirin

Data from A. Fragakis, *The Health Professional's Guide to Popular Dietary Supplements*, 3rd ed. (Chicago: American Dietetic Association, 2007); L. Skidmore-Roth, *Mosby's Handbook of Herbs and Natural Supplements*, 4th ed. (St. Louis, MO: Mosby Elsevier, 2009); C. Brown, "Overview of Drug Interactions," *U.S. Pharmacist* 25 (2008): e1–e16; J. Maskalyk, "Grapefruit Juice: Potential Drug Interactions," *Canadian Medical Association Journal* 167 (2002): 279–280; U.S. Food and Drug Administration. 2011. *Dietary Supplements: Tips for Older Dietary Supplement Users*. Available at www.fda.gov/food/dietarysupplements/ConsumerInformation/ucm110493.htm. Accessed May 2012.

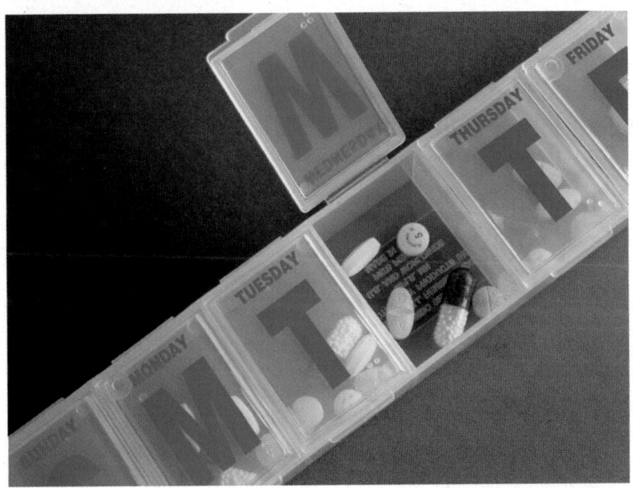

Daily pill containers like this one are often used by older adults to remind them to take various medications.

For this reason, tetracycline shouldn't be taken with milk or calcium-fortified foods. In contrast, grapefruit and grapefruit juice will increase the absorption of calcium channel–blocking agents, which are a type of medication often used to treat heart disease. Drugs can also interfere with the metabolism of certain substances in foods. The compound tyramine, which is abundant in aged cheese, smoked fish, yogurt, and red wine, is metabolized by an enzyme called monoamine oxidase. Certain medications called monoamine oxidase inhibitors, which may be prescribed to treat depression, prevent tyramine from being properly metabolized. High levels of tyramine in the blood can result in dangerously high blood pressure.

See the accompanying table for a list of potential interactions.

Reference

1. Wold, R. S., S. T. Lopez, C. L. Yau, L. M. Butler, S. L. Pareo-Tubbeh, D. L. Waters, et al. 2005. Increasing Trends in Elderly Persons' Use of Nonvitamin, Nonmineral Dietary Supplements and Concurrent Use of Medications. *Journal of the American Dietetic Association* 105:54–63.

Herb/Nutrient	Purported Use	Potential Side Effects	Drug Interactions
Garlic, garlic supplements	Lower blood cholesterol levels	Possible stomach and intestinal discomfort	Blood-thinning drugs and aspirin. Enhances the blood-thinning actions of vitamin E and ginkgo biloba.
Ginkgo biloba	Reduce memory loss, dementia	Possible stomach and intestinal discomfort	Blood-thinning drugs and aspirin. Enhances the blood-thinning actions of vitamin E and garlic.
Ginseng	Reduce fatigue, stress	None known at this time	May interfere with MAO inhibitors, diabetes medication, heart medication (digoxin), blood-thinning drugs, and aspirin. Enhances the blood-thinning actions of vitamin E, garlic, and ginkgo biloba.
Grapefruit, grapefruit juice	Source of vitamin C	None known at this time	Potentiates certain heart medications (calcium channel–blocking agents), corticosteroids, immunosuppressants
Hawthorn	Hypertension, congestive heart failure	Increased risk of bleeding	Blood-thinning drugs
Kava kava	Reduce anxiety, stress	Possible stomach and intestinal discomfort	Potentiates the effects of alcohol and antianxiety medications
St. John's wort	Reduce depression	Excessive amounts may cause an allergic reaction in some individuals	Avoid when taking antidepressants. Can decrease the effect of certain heart medications (digoxin), oral contraceptives, and cyclosporine.
Vitamin E	Reduce the risk of heart disease	Excessive amounts can interfere with blood clotting, increasing the risk of hemorrhage	Blood-thinning drugs
Vitamin K	Help blood clot	None known at this time	Blood-thinning drugs

gout, and the risk increases with age. In gout, excess uric acid forms crystals in the joints and causes pain and inflammation. Excess uric acid builds up when purine, a nitrogen-containing substance, is metabolized and either too much uric acid is produced or too little is excreted by the kidneys.

Obesity, hypertension, diabetes, kidney disease, excessive alcohol intake, and a family history of gout are risk factors.[49] Although soft drinks contain low levels of purine, they contain large amounts of fructose, which is the only carbohydrate known to increase uric acid levels. In contrast, diet soda is not associated with the risk of gout.[50]

Weight control, regular exercise, limiting alcohol, and eating a heart-healthy diet while avoiding foods that are high in purine (meats and seafood) and sugar could help decrease the severity or frequency of gout attacks. Higher consumption of dairy foods is associated with a decrease in risk.[51]

Osteoporosis

The bone disease osteoporosis can also affect the mobility of older adults. From calcium deficiency, other nutrient deficiencies, and other contributing factors (see Chapter 12), an adult's declining bone density can result in osteoporosis and the possibility of spontaneous fractures. Thinning and hardening of the vertebrae also occur, making the spine more rigid. This results in a reduction in height and makes bending, reaching, and walking difficult. Older adults who suffer falls and fractures are often forced to walk with a walker for assistance or become confined to a wheelchair, making living independently and cooking and preparing healthy meals difficult. Osteoporosis treatments include the recommended amounts of calcium and vitamin D from food or supplements, weight-bearing exercise, and medication.

Eye Disease Is a Concern for Many Older Adults

Vision disorders are also prevalent in older age. As described in Chapter 9, age-related macular degeneration is the most common cause of blindness in older Americans. Macular degeneration is a result of oxidative damage to the macula, the area of the retina that distinguishes fine detail. Deterioration of this area can make it more difficult to see and can eventually result in blindness.

Cataracts are another reason for declining vision and are caused by the formation of cloudy spots on the lens of the eye. The lens of the eye lies behind the iris and pupil and works much like a camera lens, focusing light on the retina where the image is recorded. The lens is made mostly of water and protein and the protein is arranged in a way that keeps the lens clear and allows light to pass through. As a person ages, some of the protein may clump together and form a cataract, which starts to cloud a small area of the lens.[52] Cataracts are so common in the elderly that they are thought to be a normal part of the aging process. The chance of developing a cataract in those over the age of 70 is more than 50 percent. Some evidence suggests that ethnic ancestry influences the likelihood of developing cataracts. Cataracts are the leading cause of treatable vision loss among black Americans aged 40 and over, and it is the number-one cause of low vision among Americans of Latino, African, and European descent.[53]

Both cataracts and age-related macular degeneration have a nutrition etiology. The development of cataracts has been linked to diets low in vitamins C and E and carotenoids. Thus, adequate intake of antioxidants and phytochemicals in the form of fruits and vegetables may slow or prevent the development of these diseases.[54]

cataracts Clumps of protein that form on the lens of the eye, clouding vision.

Alzheimer's Disease Is a Serious Problem for Some Older Adults

Although it's normal for older adults to experience some cognitive changes, such as taking longer to learn new information, a more serious mental decline can be cause for concern. Some adults begin to forget where they live, become increasingly disoriented, have difficulty speaking, and/or become emotionally unstable. These individuals may be experiencing **dementia** due to changes in brain function, which interferes with their ability to remember, speak, and "be themselves." The most common form of dementia in older adults is **Alzheimer's disease.** This irreversible disease slowly damages the brain tissues and can progress over the years to severe brain damage. An estimated 5.4 million Americans have Alzheimer's disease, with approximately 13 percent of adults showing signs of it as early as age 65.[55]

Neurons (nerve cells) are destroyed by Alzheimer's disease. Signals that form memories and thoughts travel through a nerve cell as a tiny electrical charge. Nerve cells connect to one another at synapses. When a charge reaches a synapse, it triggers the release of chemicals called neurotransmitters. The neurotransmitters travel across the synapse, carrying signals to neurons. Alzheimer's disease disrupts both the way electrical charges travel within nerve cells and the activity of neurotransmitters. Alzheimer's disease leads to nerve cell death and tissue loss throughout the brain. With fewer nerve cells and synapses, the brain shrinks, affecting its functions. Scientists are working hard to identify the causes of cell death in the Alzheimer's brain as well as determine strategies to slow its progression. The "Brain Tour" presents details on Alzheimer's disease: www.alz.org/braintour.

Scientists are investigating a gene called ApoE4 that appears to make people more prone to developing Alzheimer's. This gene is also associated with inflammation in atherosclerosis.[56] Though the mechanism isn't clear, research suggests that free radicals and inflammation may contribute to the brain damage observed in Alzheimer's disease and that antioxidants, such as vitamins E and C, and selenium, may help slow its progression.[57] However, rigorous trials of supplements have not shown them to be consistently beneficial, including for those who already have Alzheimer's disease.[58]

A diet adequate in the B vitamins folate, B_6, and B_{12}, which may help lower homocysteine levels in the body, could also play a role.[59] A high blood level of homocysteine may damage the blood vessels in the brain, affecting its function. Consuming adequate amounts of these vitamins may help prevent the damage. Diets that support heart health also support the health of the brain.

Some research suggests that the anti-inflammatory activities of omega-3 fatty acids may reduce the risk of Alzheimer's disease. Omega-3 supplementation in patients with mild to moderate Alzheimer's disease is related to fewer depressive symptoms. Higher dietary intake and circulating levels of omega-3 have also been related to a reduced risk for dementia and slower cognitive decline.[60, 61]

Other types of supplements have been studied as well. The herb ginkgo biloba had been purported to improve memory. However, the results of the Gingko Evaluation of Memory (GEM) Study failed to show benefit in preventing dementia in the elderly with normal cognition or mild cognitive impairment.[62]

Physical and mental inactivity, smoking, obesity, diabetes, hypertension, and depression (each modifiable by behavioral intervention) have been shown to be risk factors for the development of Alzheimer's disease. Researchers estimated that 25 percent improvement in these conditions among the general population would prevent as many as 16.5 percent of Alzheimer's disease cases in the United States.[63]

Elders with dementia are likely to need full-time care and shouldn't be allowed to take walks, jogs, or bike rides alone. However, accompanying an elder during any

dementia A disorder of the brain that interferes with a person's memory, learning, and mental stability.

Alzheimer's disease A type of dementia.

of these activities is a great way for two people to get some exercise. Although those with dementia experience mental deterioration, they should be encouraged to stay active as long as possible to prevent physical deterioration.

THE TAKE-HOME MESSAGE Older adults face various health concerns that can have an impact on nutrition needs or that can be affected by nutrition. Decreased mobility caused by arthritis, gout, and osteoporosis is common in older age. Glucosamine and chondroitin sulfate supplements may help with the pain of arthritis, and nutritional changes can help control the symptoms of gout. Vision disorders, including macular degeneration and cataracts, are also common. Risk of developing both diseases may be reduced by a diet that includes foods rich in antioxidants and phytochemicals. Alzheimer's disease and other forms of dementia are serious problems that affect some older adults. Some evidence indicates that foods rich in B vitamins and omega-3 fatty acids can help reduce the risk of these brain diseases. It is important to help elders with dementia maintain their mental and physical activity levels in order to prevent cognitive and physical deterioration.

What Socioeconomic and Psychological Issues Affect the Nutrition of Older Adults?

Along with the physical problems that affect an older adult's nutritional status, various economic, social, and psychological factors can have a potentially negative impact as well. For example, older adults often experience a reduction in income due to retirement and may find that they have to choose between filling their prescriptions or buying food. For individuals with inadequate financial resources, conditions like food insecurity can result.

Food Insecurity Has Nutritional Impacts

Income levels tend to decrease with age. In 2010, 16 percent of persons over age 65 lived below the poverty level (in 2010, the poverty rates for individuals and couples over the age of 65 were $10,458 and $13,194, respectively).[64] Minority groups within the population aged 65 and over had higher poverty rates: 18.2 percent of blacks and 18.0 percent of Hispanics, compared with 6.9 percent of whites. The median income for all persons aged 65 and older was $13,716 in 2010, with whites earning $14,575, blacks earning $9,322, and Hispanics $9,845.[65] In light of these numbers, it's not surprising that almost 8 percent of American households with elders experience **food insecurity,** or the routine lack of sufficient food to feed those living there.[66] Research has shown that elders who consistently experience food insecurity not only have more than double the risk of not meeting their daily nutritional needs, but also tend to be in only fair to poor health.[67] Limited finances aren't always the cause of food insecurity. Some elders may be able to afford food but lack the physical means to obtain it, prepare it, or consume it (due to health issues such as tooth loss).[68]

In order to help community advocates identify older adults potentially at risk for food insecurity, the American Academy of Family Physicians and other organizations created the Nutrition Screening Initiative (NSI). The NSI is designed to promote routine screening of older persons in both community and institutional settings through a network of dietitians, public health nutritionists, community workers, and physicians (see the Self-Assessment).[69]

food insecurity The chronic lack of sufficient food to nutritiously feed oneself.

Community Resources Exist for Older Adults

Programs such as Meals On Wheels provide hot meals to older adults who cannot leave their home.

Government-supported food assistance programs that are available to the larger population, such as food stamps, also serve older adults; however, there are also federally funded food assistance programs specifically for older adults. These programs are funded under the 1965 Older Americans Act to provide support and services to individuals aged 60 and older.[70] The Act brought federal support to **Meals On Wheels,** making it one of the most significant volunteer programs in the country. Having the Meals On Wheels driver stop in daily assures that older adults receive nourishment and remain safe in their homes.[71] The goals of the Older Americans Act are to help seniors maintain good health, an adequate quality of life, and an acceptable level of independence.

In addition to Meals On Wheels, the Older Americans Act funds the Elderly Nutrition Program (ENP), which provides **congregate meals**—hot meals served at specified sites in the community, such as churches, synagogues, and senior centers. This guarantees that older adults receive a nutritious daily meal and provides an opportunity for them to socialize. Often, transportation to these meals is also available. The program brings consistency and quality to senior center programs.

Self-Assessment

Are You at Nutritional Risk?

Circle the number in the right-hand column for the statements that apply to you (or someone you know, if you are taking the assessment for a friend or relative). Add up the circled numbers to determine your score.

Statement	
I have an illness or condition that has made me change the kind and/or amount of food I eat.	2
I eat fewer than two meals per day.	3
I eat few fruits or vegetables or milk products.	2
I have three or more drinks of beer, liquor, or wine almost every day.	2
I have tooth or mouth problems that make it hard for me to eat.	2
I don't always have enough money to buy food.	4
I eat alone most of the time.	1
I take three or more different prescribed or over-the-counter drugs a day.	1
Without wanting to, I have lost or gained 10 pounds in the last six months.	2
I am not always physically able to shop, cook, and/or feed myself.	2
Total	____

Answer

If your score is

0–2 Good! Your diet and lifestyle don't appear to put you at risk of not meeting your nutritional needs.

3–5 You are at moderate nutritional risk. Your local office on aging, senior citizens' center, or health department can help you improve your nutritional health.

6 or over You are at high nutritional risk. Bring this checklist the next time you see your doctor, dietitian, or other qualified health or social service professional. Ask for help to improve your nutritional health.

Source: "Determine Your Nutritional Health" by the Nutrition Screening Initiative. Copyright © 1991 the Nutrition Screening Initative. Reprinted with permission.

Meals On Wheels A program that delivers nutritious meals to homebound older adults.

congregate meals Low- or no-cost meals served at churches, synagogues, or other community sites where older adults can receive a nutritious meal and socialize.

Young people in the community can help make sure that older adults are familiar with and take advantage of the numerous services available to them. Consider "adopting" a senior neighbor or family member and, if necessary, help him or her locate these services.

Psychological and Emotional Conditions Can Affect Nutritional Health

Whereas many seniors live happy, fulfilled lives, some individuals can be affected by grief, depression, and loneliness as they lose family or friends, learn to live alone, or adjust to new environments, such as living with family or in an assisted living facility. If their emotional health deteriorates, they sometimes resort to drugs and alcohol to cope.

Depression and Grief

Up to 20 percent of older adults can suffer from depression, ranging from mild to major depressive disorders.[72] The loss of significant others and friends as well as chronic pain and concerns about their own health can add to feelings of grief, sadness, and isolation. Depression can interfere with an older adult's motivation to eat, be physically active, and socialize—all of which can impact mental and physical health.

Family and friends need to be aware of the changes in elders' eating and lifestyle habits. Younger adults need to help elders reconnect with their communities after a loss and adjust to a new lifestyle. As mentioned, neighbors can "adopt an elder" who may be living alone and coordinate regular visits and delivery of meals. A quick visit by several supportive friends over the course of a month can go a long way to help seniors stay healthy.

Alcohol Abuse

As they age, adults become more sensitive to the intoxicating effects of alcohol. This is due in part to the decline of body water. Individuals with a lower percentage of body water will have a higher blood alcohol concentration (BAC) and thus feel its effects sooner. The beer that an individual could manage easily at a younger age may have a narcotic effect at age 75.[73] Prescription and nonprescription medications (on average, people over age 65 are taking two to seven prescription medications daily[74]) can interact with alcohol by intensifying its effects; alcohol can diminish the effects of medication; or both effects can occur. For example, someone who is taking anticoagulants to reduce the risk of blood clots may interfere with the drugs' effectiveness if he or she chronically consumes alcohol.[75]

An elderly person's increased alcohol consumption could be a way of self-medicating. Chronic health problems, loss of friends and loved ones, or financial stress could make alcohol an appealing sedative to temporarily ease discomfort or depression. The same as at any age, though, consuming alcohol only makes things worse. Heavy drinking can exacerbate depression, which can lead to more drinking.[76] Also, because alcohol impairs one's judgment and interferes with coordination and reaction time, elders who have been drinking are at a higher risk for stumbling, falling, and fracturing bones.

Health care providers sometimes misdiagnose alcohol abuse in elders as the forgetfulness and disorientation associated with "normal aging."[77] **Figure 19.6** lists the red flags from the National Institute of Aging that may signal alcohol abuse in an older adult. Because of the numerous potential interactions with alcohol, the National Institute on Alcohol Abuse and Alcoholism recommends that adults over 65 who choose to drink should consume no more than one alcoholic drink daily.[78]

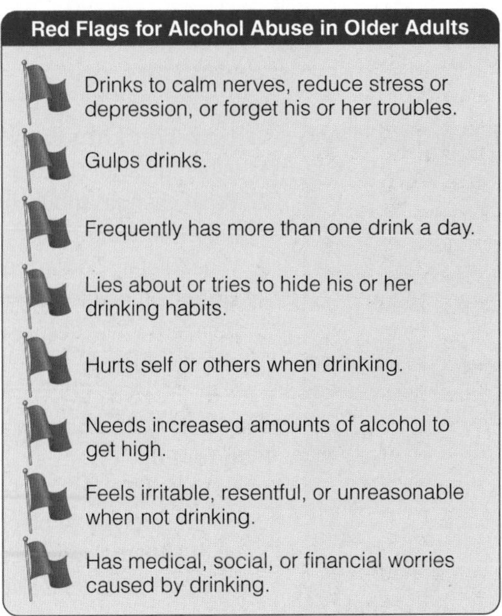

Red Flags for Alcohol Abuse in Older Adults
Drinks to calm nerves, reduce stress or depression, or forget his or her troubles.
Gulps drinks.
Frequently has more than one drink a day.
Lies about or tries to hide his or her drinking habits.
Hurts self or others when drinking.
Needs increased amounts of alcohol to get high.
Feels irritable, resentful, or unreasonable when not drinking.
Has medical, social, or financial worries caused by drinking.

▲ **Figure 19.6 Red Flags for Alcohol Abuse in Older Adults**
Adapted from National Institute on Aging. 2012. *Alcohol Use In Older People*. Available at www.nia.nih.gov/health/publication/alcohol-use-older-people. Accessed May 2012.

THE TAKE-HOME MESSAGE Financial challenges (potentially leading to food insecurity), emotional and psychological conditions (including grief, loneliness, and depression), and alcohol abuse can impair the abilities of older adults to maintain healthy diets and lifestyles. Alcohol can also interfere with the actions of numerous prescription drugs. Many community resources exist to help elders cope with their life challenges. The Older Americans Act has been particularly effective at providing nutritional support to seniors.

Putting It All Together

The U.S. population is aging at an unprecedented rate and older adults are the fastest growing population group. The physiological processes of aging are inevitable and include loss of muscle mass, decline in sensory perceptions, and impaired ability to absorb nutrients. A nutritious diet and physical activity throughout the life span contribute to successful aging and can help an older adult maintain independence. Although kilocalorie needs decline, older adults need to base their diet on the same nutrient-dense foods as all other individuals, including whole grains, lean proteins, low-fat dairy products, dried beans, fruits, vegetables, adequate fiber, and adequate fluid. Loss of loved ones and social isolation coupled with decreased income can lead to depression, alcohol abuse, and nutritional risk. By maintaining an active life that includes social activities, a healthy diet, and physical activity, a high quality of life can be maintained.

Nutrition in Practice: Ed

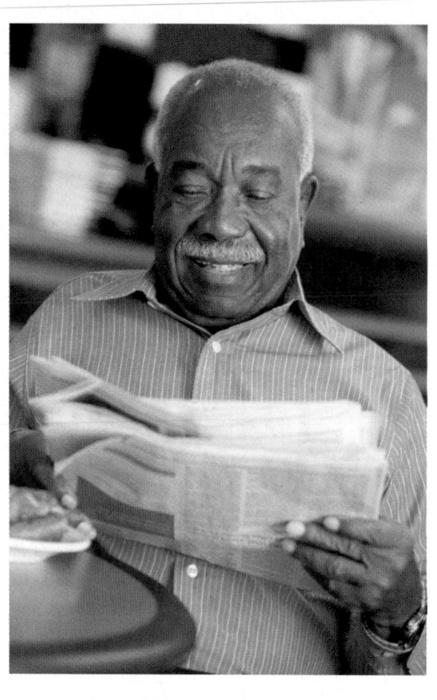

Ed recently retired at age 66. Although he grew up on a diet rich in saturated fats from eggs, cheese, and dairy, he has avoided these foods since his father survived a heart attack. Ed now consumes a largely plant-based diet of fruits, vegetables, legumes, and whole grains. However, Ed also has a sweet tooth, frequently dines out, and often enjoys a well-done steak. He was physically active during his school years, but became sedentary after college. He now goes for daily walks with his wife Ellie after dinner. During inclement weather, they go to the Y to strength-train and walk on the treadmill for 30 minutes. Despite watching his diet and exercising, Ed continues to carry 30 extra pounds. His fasting blood glucose is 120 mg/dl and cholesterol is 230 mg/dl. Blood pressure is 135/88. His family history reveals diabetes, heart-related diseases, osteoporosis, arthritis, and low thyroid. Ed suspects that he, too, is at risk for heart disease, but isn't sure that dietary changes at this point will make much of a difference. He decides to seek advice from his Registered Dietitian.

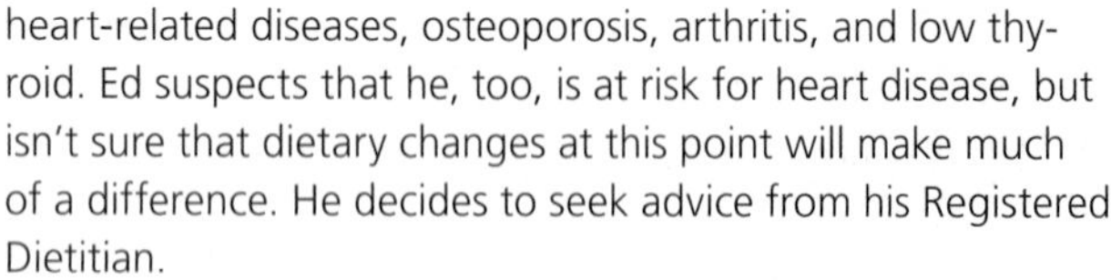

Ed's Stats:

- □ Age: 66
- □ Height: 5 feet 10 inches
- □ Weight: 200 pounds
- □ BMI: 28.7
- □ Fasting Blood Glucose: 120 mg/dl
- □ Total Cholesterol: 230 mg/dl
- □ Blood Pressure: 135/88 mm Hg

Critical Thinking Questions

1. What behaviors is Ed doing right?
2. What changes should he make to improve his health?
3. What dietary advice would you give to Ed to help him to obtain the nutrients he needs while decreasing his risk for chronic disease?

Dietitian's Observation and Plan for Ed:

- □ His BMI of 28.7 places Ed in the overweight category. A blood glucose reading of 120 m/dl indicates prediabetes. His blood pressure is slightly elevated. The dietitian can work with Ed in establishing an individualized meal and exercise plan for reducing blood glucose, serum cholesterol, and body weight.
- □ A plant-based meal plan consisting of fruits, vegetables, legumes, and whole grains tends to be heart healthy. The meal plan includes a specified number of servings from each food group and distributed throughout the day, matching Ed's food preferences and lifestyle.
- □ Dining out can be challenging for individuals on any meal plan. Portion sizes tend to exceed those normally recommended. The dietitian can provide strategies for making heart-healthy food selections and controlling portions, while incorporating some favorite foods. Although Ed can still enjoy an occasional lean steak at his favorite restaurant, he may be sharing an entrée or have extra food to take home.
- □ Ed can benefit from a regularly scheduled exercise program. Physical activity will help him reduce the risk factors—elevated blood glucose, cholesterol, and blood pressure—associated with diabetes and heart disease. Exercise physiologists at the Y can monitor Ed's blood pressure as well as his progress in the exercise program.

Ed's Food Log

Food/Beverage	Time Consumed	Hunger Rating*	Location
Fortified whole-grain cereal topped with blueberries and fortified nonfat milk; coffee with sugar	6:30 a.m.	2	In the kitchen
Black beans and brown rice with broccoli and carrots; spinach salad with vinaigrette dressing; coffee with sugar	12:30 p.m.	5	In the kitchen
Banana	3 p.m.	2	In front of the TV after an afternoon walk
Well-done rib-eye steak; green salad with vinaigrette; baked potato with sour cream and chives; glass of red wine; chocolate crème brule for dessert; coffee with sugar	6:30 p.m.	3	At Ed's favorite steakhouse with friends

***Hunger Rating (1–5):** 1 = not hungry; 5 = super hungry

Visual Chapter Summary

1 The Demographics of Aging in America Are Changing

Improved health care, public health initiatives, and widespread access to health information have helped lead to a longer life expectancy for Americans. The average life expectancy for men in the United States is 75 years and for women 80 years. By 2030, people aged 65 and older will comprise about 20 percent of the U.S. population. America's older population is also becoming increasingly racially and ethnically diverse.

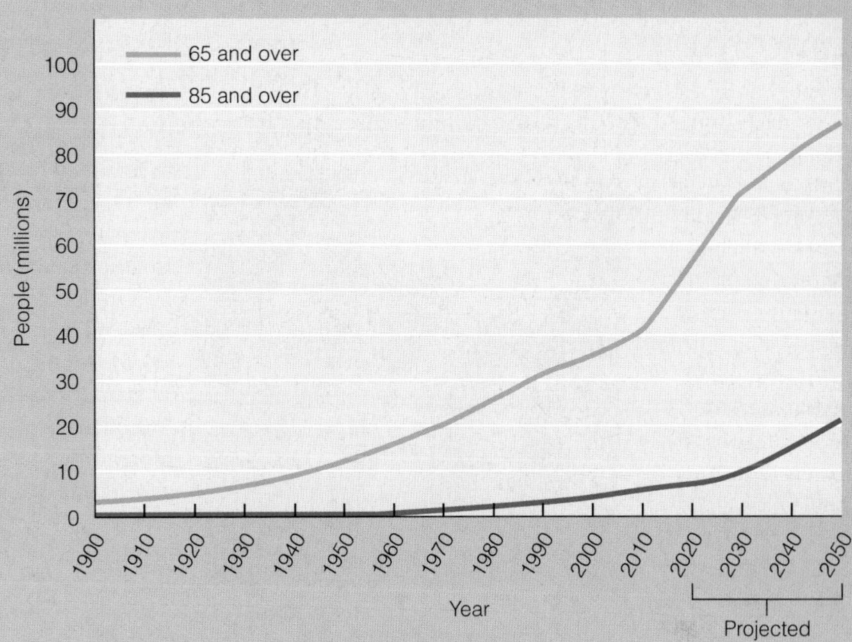

2 Physical and Cognitive Changes Occur as Part of the Aging Process

The majority of age-related changes are gradual and accumulate over time. Physiological effects of aging include changes in body composition, including reduced muscle mass (sarcopenia) and increased body fat; a decrease in immune function; declining sensory abilities; gastrointestinal changes; and changes in brain function. These changes can have a negative influence on the desire to eat and on the body's ability to extract nutrients from food.

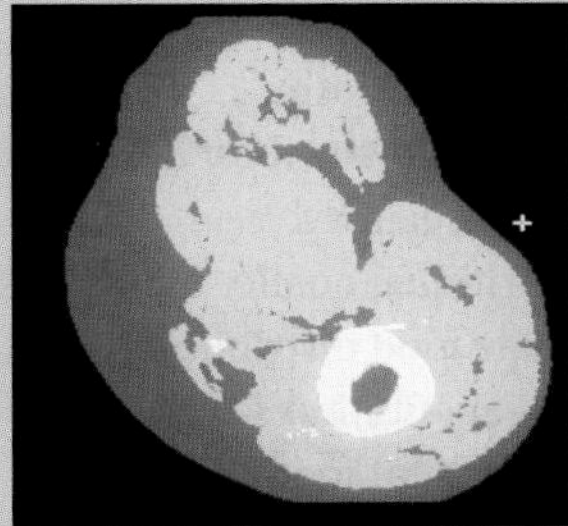
Young adult's thigh

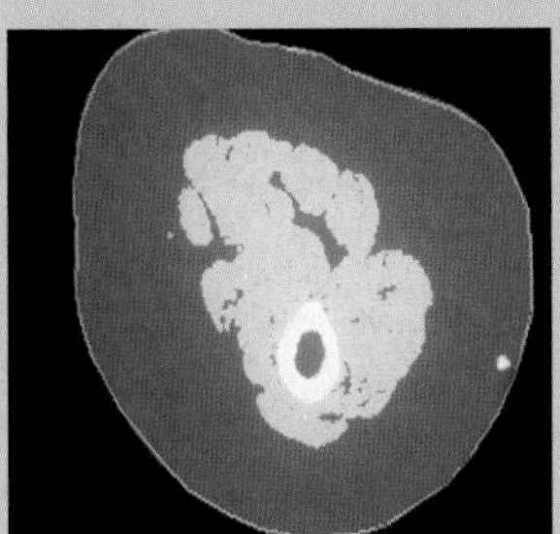
Older adult's thigh

3 The Nutrient Needs Change for Older Adults

Metabolism slows with age, so older adults need fewer kilocalories than their younger counterparts. Older adults should ensure that they get an adequate intake of high-quality lean protein, complex carbohydrates, and unsaturated fat, and that they consume enough fluid, vitamins D and B_{12}, and the minerals iron, calcium, and zinc. Vitamin D requirements double at age 50 and triple at age 70.

Staying physically active can help lower the risk of heart disease, colon and breast cancer, diabetes, hypertension, osteoporosis, arthritis, and obesity. It can help maintain healthy bones, muscles, and joints, and reduce anxiety, stress, and depression, improve sleep, flexibility, and range of motion, and postpone the decline in cognitive ability.

4 Older Adults Have a Variety of Nutrition-Related Health Concerns

Over 6.8 million U.S. elders report difficulty with activities of daily living due to decreased mobility. More than 50 percent of all older adults are affected by some form of arthritis, including osteoarthritis, rheumatoid arthritis, and gout. Other nutrition-related health issues include osteoporosis, dementia, and eye problems such as macular degeneration and cataracts

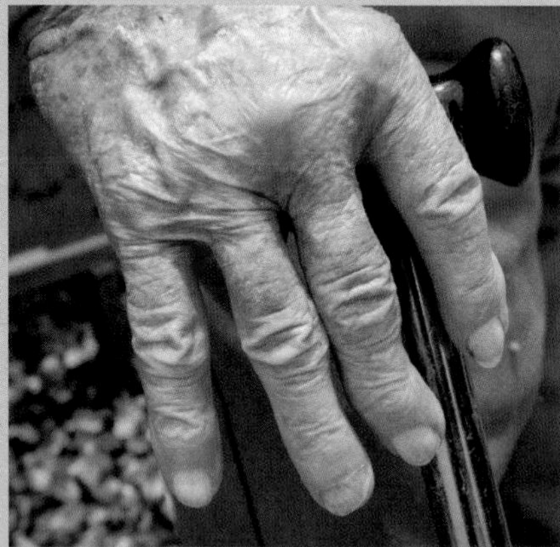

5 Socioeconomic and Psychological Issues Can Affect the Nutritional Health of Older Adults

Older adults sometimes suffer from food insecurity due to financial hardship or physical disabilities. Loss of loved ones coupled with social isolation can lead to depression and grief in older adults. This may lead to a decreased motivation to eat as well as an increased reliance on alcohol.

Terms to Know

- aging
- senescence
- life span
- life expectancy
- longevity
- physiologic age
- chronologic age
- sarcopenia
- arthritis
- cataracts
- dementia
- Alzheimer's disease
- food insecurity
- Meals On Wheels
- congregate meals

MasteringNutrition™

Build your knowledge—and confidence—in the Study Area of MasteringNutrition with a variety of study tools.

Check Your Understanding

1. Which of the following refers to the loss of muscle that occurs with aging?
   a. senescence
   b. sarcopenia
   c. osteoarthritis
   d. dysphagia
2. Which of the following factors has contributed to the increased longevity of older Americans?
   a. decline in infant mortality
   b. rising health care costs
   c. advances in medical research
   d. increased incidence of dementia
3. With increasing age, the kidneys lose some ability to convert ____ into its active form.
   a. vitamin A
   b. vitamin B_{12}
   c. vitamin D
   d. vitamin K
4. Constipation in older adults can be a result of
   a. decreased GI motility.
   b. insufficient vitamin B_{12}.
   c. excessive fiber.
   d. too much fluid.
5. Older adults may benefit from adding zinc to their diet to
   a. help with weight loss.
   b. boost the immune system.
   c. promote bone growth.
   d. increase muscle mass.
6. Alzheimer's disease
   a. is an inevitable part of aging.
   b. is caused by a high-fat diet.
   c. leads to loss of memory.
   d. leads to thinning of the bones.
7. The risk of developing osteoporosis can be reduced by
   a. eating a diet high in fruits and vegetables.
   b. drinking plenty of fluids.
   c. engaging in weight-bearing exercise.
   d. taking vitamin supplements.
8. The need for both ________ increases with age.
   a. water and lead
   b. calcium and vitamin D
   c. protein and lipids
   d. vitamin K and biotin
9. Which of the following best describes food insecurity?
   a. poor nutritional quality of food
   b. inadequate food distribution
   c. concerns about food safety
   d. lack of sufficient food
10. Congregate meals are
    a. meals delivered to the homes of older adults who are homebound.
    b. frozen meals that adults can purchase at the supermarket.
    c. hot meals that are served at specified sites in the community.
    d. meals served to members of churches or synagogues.

Answers

1. (b) Sarcopenia refers to a loss of muscle mass that occurs with aging. Senescence is the scientific term for the physical changes that occur with age. Osteoarthritis is an inflammation of the joints, and dysphagia is difficulty swallowing.
2. (c) Advances in medical research are a key reason for increased longevity. Infant mortality rates, though relevant to overall life expectancy, are not a direct factor in the longevity of older adults. Rising health care costs and the incidence of dementia are also irrelevant.
3. (c) Vitamin D is converted into its active form by the kidneys.
4. (a) As people age, GI motility slows, leading to problems with constipation. Vitamin B_{12} absorption decreases with age, but this does not affect GI motility. A high-fiber, high-fluid diet will help relieve constipation, not cause it.
5. (b) Adequate zinc is needed for a healthy immune system. Zinc has nothing to do with losing weight, promoting bone growth, or increasing muscle mass.
6. (c) Alzheimer's causes a loss of memory. Although the exact mechanism for its development is unknown, it does not cause thinning of the bones and is not linked to a high-fat diet, nor is it inevitable.
7. (c) Osteoporosis can be slowed by engaging in regular weight-bearing exercise. A diet rich in calcium and vitamin D and low in sodium can also slow its progression.
8. (b) The need for both vitamin D and calcium is increased in older adults. Protein, fat, and water needs don't change with aging. Lead is a toxin and should never be consumed. Vitamin K and biotin are necessary for health, but are not needed in higher amounts by older adults.
9. (d) Food insecurity refers to the routine lack of sufficient food. It does not describe problems with the distribution, safety, or nutritional quality of food.
10. (c) Congregate meals are meals served to older adults at specific sites in a community. Although those sites may be churches, synagogues, or senior centers, participants do not need to be members. Meals served to older adults who are homebound are typically part of the Meals On Wheels program. The supermarket contains a variety of frozen meals that can be purchased by adults of all ages.

Answers to Myths and Misconceptions

1. **False.** Chronic disease development is not inevitable. A lifetime of healthy eating and physical activity is the best prevention.
2. **True.** Heart disease remains the number-one cause of death in the United States.
3. **True.** A slowed gastrointestinal system in conjunction with low fluid and fiber intakes can lead to constipation in older adults.
4. **False.** The number of adults over the age of 65 continues to rise.
5. **True.** Vitamin D helps maintain adequate insulin levels and may act to lower blood sugar levels.
6. **True.** Vitamin A is stored in the body and too much can increase the risk for osteoporosis and fractures.
7. **False.** The use of herbal supplements and alternative treatments continues to increase.
8. **True.** Because a person's metabolism slows naturally with age, older adults need less food energy (kilocalories) than their younger counterparts.
9. **False.** Financial circumstances or reduced mobility can cause older adults to experience food insecurity, often for the first time in their lives.
10. **False.** Older adults sometimes turn to alcohol to deal with discomfort, loneliness, or boredom.

Web Resources

- For more general health information for older adults, visit www.cdc.gov/aging/aginginfo/index.htm
- For more information on herbs and interactions, visit the National Center for Complementary and Alternative Medicine, National Institutes of Health, at http://nccam.nih.gov
- For more information on Meals On Wheels, visit www.mowaa.org
- For information on legislative updates related to congregate meals and resources on diseases, elder rights, and nutrition, visit the Administration on Aging, part of the Administration for Community Living at www.aoa.gov
- For information on good nutrition for all ages, visit the Academy of Nutrition and Dietetics (formerly the American Dietetic Association) at www.eatright.org

References

1. U. S. Census Bureau. 2012. *Table 105. Life Expectancy at Birth, by Sex, Age, and Race.* Available at www.census.gov/compendia/statab/2012/tables/12s0105.pdf. Accessed June 2012.
2. Stibich, Mark. 2007. *Human Life Span.* Available at http://longevity.about.com/od/longevity101/g/life_span.htm. Accessed April 30, 2012.
3. U.S. Census Bureau. 2011. *Census Bureau Releases Comprehensive Analysis of Fast-Growing 90-and-Older Population.* Available at www.census.gov/newsroom/releases/archives/aging_population/cb11-194.html. Accessed April 2012.
4. U.S. Census Bureau. 2008. *An Older and More Diverse Nation by Midcentury.* Available at www.census.gov/newsroom/releases/archives/population/cb08-123.html. Accessed April 2012.
5. Vincent, G. K. and V. A. Velkoff. 2010. The Next Four Decades: The Older Population in the United States: 2010 to 2050. *Current Population Reports* P25–1138. Washington, DC: U.S. Census Bureau. Available at www.census.gov/prod/2010pubs/p25-1138.pdf. Accessed April 30, 2012; Center for Elders and the Court. n.d. *Demographics of the Aging Population.* Available at www.eldersandcourts.org/Aging.aspx. Accessed May 11, 2012; Fritz, C. 2005. *Older Minorities: A Demographic Profile.* Available at www.prcdc.org/files/Older_Minorities.pdf. Accessed May 2012.
6. Ibid.
7. Heron, M. 2012. *Deaths: Leading Causes for 2008.* Available at www.cdc.gov/nchs/data/nvsr/nvsr60/nvsr60_06.pdf. Accessed June 2012.

8. Centers for Disease Control. n.d. *State of Aging and Health in America.* Available from http://apps.nccd.cdc.gov/SAHA/Default/IndicatorMenu.aspx. Accessed June 2012.
9. Ogden, C. L., M. D. Carroll, M. A. McDowell, and K. M. Flegal. 2012. Prevalence of Obesity in the United States, 2009–2010. NCHS Data Brief no. 82. Hyattsville, MD: National Center for Health Statistics. Available at www.cdc.gov/nchs/data/databriefs/db82.pdf. Accessed May 2012.
10. Martin, C. T., J. Kayser-Jones, N. A. Stotts, C. Porter, and E. S. Froelichter. 2007. Risk for Low Weight in Community Dwelling Adults. *Clinical Nurse Specialist* 21:203–211.
11. Kurczmarski, M. and D. Weddle. 2005. Position Paper of the American Dietetic Association: Nutrition Across the Spectrum of Aging. *Journal of the American Dietetic Association* 105:616–633; Heffner, K. 2011. Neuroendocrine Effects of Stress on Immunity in the Elderly: Implications for Inflammatory Disease. *Immunology and Allergy Clinics of North America* 31:95–108.
12. Kurczmarski, M. and D. Weddle. 2005. Position Paper of the American Dietetic Association: Nutrition Across the Spectrum of Aging.
13. Ibid.
14. Ibid.
15. Glisky, E. 2007. Changes in Cognitive Function in Human Aging. In Riddle, D. R., ed. *Brain Aging: Models, Methods, and Mechanisms.* Boca Raton, FL: CRC Press. Available at www.ncbi.nlm.nih.gov/books/NBK3885. Accessed May 2012.
16. Institute of Medicine. 2005. *Dietary Reference Intakes for Energy, Carbohydrates, Fiber, Fat, Protein, and Amino Acids.* Washington, DC: National Academies Press.
17. Kurczmarski, M., et al. 2005. Position Paper of the American Dietetic Association: Nutrition Across the Spectrum of Aging; Wakimoto, P. and G. Block. 2001. Dietary Intake, Dietary Patterns, and Changes with Age: An Epidemiological Perspective. *Journals of Gerontology Series A: Biological Sciences and Medical Sciences* 56A:65–80.
18. Bernstein, M. and A. S. Luggen. 2009. *Nutrition for the Older Adult.* Burlington, MA: Jones and Bartlett Learning; Sieber, C. 2010. *Nutrient Needs of the Older Adult.* Available at www.nestle.com/Common/Nestle Documents/Documents/R_and_D/News/ESPEN-2010-NNI-Symposium-Proceedings.pdf. Accessed November 2012.
19. Sebastian, R. S., L. E. Cleveland, J. D. Goldman, and A. J. Moshfegh. 2007. Older Adults Who Use Vitamin/Mineral Supplements Differ From Non-Users in Nutrient Intake Adequacy and Dietary Attitudes. *Journal of the American Dietetic Association* 107:1322–1332.
20. Bales, C. and C. Ritchie. 2006. The Elderly. In M. Shils, M. Shike, A. Ross, B. Caballero, and R. Cousins, eds. *Modern Nutrition in Health and Disease,* 10th ed. Philadelphia: Lippincott Williams & Wilkins.
21. Vitamin D Council. n.d. *Vitamin D Research.* Available at www.vitamindcouncil.org/about-vitamin-d/how-to-get-your-vitamin-d/vitamin-d-supplementation. Accessed May 2012.
22. Office of Dietary Supplements. 2011. *Dietary Supplement Fact Sheet: Vitamin B_{12}.* Available from http://ods.od.nih.gov/factsheets/VitaminB12-HealthProfessional. Accessed June 2012.
23. Kurczmarski, M., et al. 2005. Position Paper of the American Dietetic Association: Nutrition Across the Spectrum of Aging; Lands, R. H. 2009. Anemia in the Elderly. *Clinical Geriatrics* 17:25–28. Available at www.clinicalgeriatrics.com/articles/Anemia-Elderly. Accessed May 2012.
24. Ibid.
25. Institute of Medicine. Dietary Reference Intakes for Energy.
26. Sareh, P., M. Sourwine, C. D. Rochester, and N. I. Steinle. 2011. Vitamin D and Calcium: Implications for Healthy Aging. *Clinical Geriatrics* 19:29–34.
27. National Osteoporosis Foundation. 2011. *Fast Facts.* Available at www.nof.org/learn/basics. Accessed June 2012.
28. Sebastian, R. S., et al. 2007. Older Adults Who Use Vitamin/Mineral Supplements.
29. U.S. Food and Drug Administration. 2011. *Dietary Supplements: Tips for Older Dietary Supplement Users.* Available at www.fda.gov/Food/DietarySupplements/Consumer Information/ucm110493.htm. Accessed May 2012.
30. Kurczmarski, M., et al. 2005. Position Paper of the American Dietetic Association: Nutrition Across the Spectrum of Aging.
31. Ibid.
32. World Health Organization. 2002. *Keep Fit for Life: Meeting the Nutritional Needs of Older Persons.* Geneva, Switzerland: WHO. Available at www.who.int/nutrition/publications/olderpersons/en/index.html. Accessed December 2008.
33. Juan, W., M. Lino, and P. Basiotis. 2004. Quality of Diet of Older Americans. *Nutrition Insight* 29. U.S. Department of Agriculture, Center for Nutrition Policy and Promotion. Available at www.cnpp.usda.gov/Publications/NutritionInsights/Insight29.pdf. Accessed May 2012.
34. Loreck, E., R. Chimakurthi, and N. I. Steinle. 2012. Nutritional Assessment of the Geriatric Patient: A Comprehensive Approach Toward Evaluating and Managing Nutrition. *Clinical Geriatrics* 20:20–26.
35. Cooke, A., and J. Friday. 2005. *Pyramid Servings Intakes in the United States 1999–2002: CNRG Table Set 3.0.* Community Nutrition Research Group, Agricultural Research Service, U.S. Department of Agriculture. Available awww.ars.usda.gov/Services/docs.htm?docid=8503. Accessed May 2012.
36. Juan, W., et al. 2004. Quality of Diet of Older Americans; Cooke, A., et al. 2005. *Pyramid Servings Intakes in the United States 1999–2002: CNRG Table Set 3.0.*
37. World Health Organization. 2002. *Keep Fit for Life.*
38. Agency for Healthcare Research and Quality and the Centers for Disease Control and Prevention. 2002. *Physical Activity and Older Americans: Benefits and Strategies.* Available at www.ahrq.gov/ppip/activity.htm. Accessed May 2012.
39. Centers for Disease Control. 2011. *Health, United States.* Available from www.cdc.gov/nchs/data/hus/2011/145.pdf. Accessed July 2012.
40. Ibid.
41. Centers for Disease Control. 2011. *Osteoarthritis.* Available from www.cdc.gov/arthritis/basics/osteoarthritis.htm. Accessed July 2012.
42. National Institute of Arthritis and Musculoskeletal and Skin Diseases. 2010. *Osteoarthritis.* Available at www.niams.nih.gov/Health_Info/Osteoarthritis/default.asp. Accessed May 2012.
43. Bijlsma, J. W., F. Berenbaum, and F. P. Lafeber. 2011. Osteoarthritis: An Update with Relevance for Clinical Practice. *The Lancet* 377:2115–2126.
44. Sawitzke, A. D., H. Shi, M. F. Finco, D. D. Dunlop, C. L. Harris, N. G. Singer, et al. 2010. Clinical Efficacy and Safety of Glucosamine, Chondroitin Sulfate, Their Combination, Celecoxib or Placebo Taken to Treat Osteoarthritis of the Knee: 2-year Results from GAIT. *Annals of the Rheumatic Diseases* 69:1459–1464.
45. National Institute of Arthritis and Musculoskeletal and Skin Diseases. 2004. *Rheumatoid Arthritis.* Available at www.niams.nih.gov/Health_Info/Rheumatic_Disease/default.asp. Accessed May 4, 2012.
46. Choi, H. 2005. Dietary Risk Factors for Rheumatic Diseases. *Current Opinion in Rheumatology* 17:141–146.
47. Lahiri, M., C. Morgan, D. P. M. Symmons, and I. N. Bruce. 2012. Modifiable Risk Factors for RA: Prevention Better than Cure? *Rheumatology* 51:499–512.
48. Splete, H. 2011. A Fifth of American Adults Are at Risk for Gout. *Family Practice News.* Available at www.internalmedicinenews.com/fileadmin/content_pdf/fpn/archive_pdf/vol41iss1/70038_main.pdf. Accessed June 2012.
49. Fletcher, J. 2012. *Gout Growing in U.S., Mostly in Men and Seniors.* Available at www.agingcare.com/News/gout-growing-in-men-and-seniors-147424.htm. Accessed May 2012.
50. Choi, H. K. and G. Curhan. 2008. Soft Drinks, Fructose Consumption, and the Risk of Gout in Men: Prospective Cohort Study. *British Medical Journal* 338:309–318.
51. Choi, H. K., K. Atkinson, E. W. Karlson, W. Willett, and G. Curhan. 2004. Purine-Rich Foods, Dairy and Protein Intake, and the Risk of Gout in Men. *New England Journal of Medicine* 350:1093–1103.
52. National Eye Institute. 2009. *Cataracts.* Available at www.nei.nih.gov/health/

cataract/cataract_facts.asp. Accessed May 2012.

53. Lighthouse International. 2012. *Reducing Risk of Cataract*. Available at www.lighthouse.org/eye-health/prevention/reducing-risk-of-cataract. Accessed May 2012.
54. Kurczmarski, M., et al. 2005. Position Paper of the American Dietetic Association: Nutrition Across the Spectrum of Aging.
55. Alzheimer Association. 2012. *Alzheimer's Disease Facts and Figures*. Available from www.alz.org/downloads/facts_figures_2012.pdf. Accessed July 2012.
56. Bell, R. D., E. A. Winkler, I. Singh, A. P. Sagare, R. Deane, Z. Wu, et al. 2012. Apolipoprotein E Controls Cerebrovascular Integrity via Cyclophilin. *Nature* 10:819–828.
57. Martin, A. 2003. Antioxidant Vitamins E and C and Risk of Alzheimer's Disease. *Nutrition Reviews* 61: 69–79.
58. Galasko, D. R., E. Peskind, C. M. Clark, J. F. Quinn, J. M. Ringman, G. A. Jicha, et al. 2012. Antioxidants for Alzheimer Disease: A Randomized Clinical Trial with Cerebrospinal Fluid Biomarker Measures. *Archives of Neurology* 69:836–841.
59. Nourhashemi, F., S. Gillette-Guyonnet, S. Andrieu, A. Ghisolfi, P. Ousset, H. Grandjean, A. Grand, J. Pous, B.Vellas, and J. Albarede. 2000. Alzheimer Disease: Protective Factors. *American Journal of Clinical Nutrition* 71: 643S–649S.
60. Tan, Z. S., W. S. Harris, A. S. Beiser, R. Au, J. J. Himali, S. Debette, et al. 2012. Red Blood Cell Omega-3 Fatty Acid Levels and Markers of Accelerated Brain Aging. *Neurology* 78:658–664
61. Gu, Y., N. Schupf, S. A. Cosentino, J. A. Luchsinger, and H. Scarmeas. 2012. Nutrient Intake and Plasma [Beta]-Amyloid. *Neurology* 78:1832–1840.
62. DeKosky, S. T., J. D. Williamson, A. L. Fitzpatrick, R. A. Kronmal, D. G. Ives, J. A. Saxton, et al. 2008. Gingko Biloba for the Prevention of Dementia. *Journal of the American Medical Association* 300:2253–2262.
63. Barnes, D. E. and K. Yaffe. 2011. The Projected Effect of Risk Factor Reduction on Alzheimer's Disease Prevalence. *Lancet Neurology* 10:819–828.
64. Short, K. 2011. *The Research Supplemental Poverty Measure: 2010*. Available from www.census.gov/prod/2011pubs/p60-241.pdf. Accessed July 2012.
65. Employee Benefit Research Institute. 2011. *Income Statistics of the Population Aged 55 and Over*. Available at www.ebri.org/pdf/publications/books/databook/DB.Chapter%2006.pdf. Accessed May 2012; Wu, K. B. 2010. *Income, Poverty, and Health Insurance Coverage of Older Americans, 2010*. Available at www.aarp.org/content/dam/aarp/research/public_policy_institute/econ_sec/2011/fs232v2.pdf. Accessed May 2012.
66. Coleman-Jensen, A., M. Nord, M. Andrews, and S. Carlson. 2011. *Household Food Security in the United States, 2010*. Economic Research Service. Available at www.ers.usda.gov/publications/err125. Accessed May 2012.
67. Johnson, M. A., J. T. Dwyer, G. L. Jensen, J. W. Miller, J. R. Speakman, P. Starke-Reed, et al. 2011. Challenges and New Opportunities for Clinical Nutrition Interventions in the Aged. *Journal of Nutrition* 141:535–541.
68. Seligman, H. K., B. A. Laraia, and M. B. Kushel. 2010. Food Insecurity Is Associated with Chronic Disease among Low-Income NHANES Participants. *Journal of Nutrition* 140:304–310.
69. Sinnett, S. S., R. Bengle, A. Brown, A. P. Glass, M. A. Johnson, and J. S. Lee. 2010. The Validity of Nutrition Screening Initiative DETERMINE Checklist Responses in Older Georgians. *Journal of Nutrition for the Elderly* 29:393–409.
70. Administration on Aging. 2012. *Reauthorization of the Older Americans Act*. Available at http://aoa.gov/AoARoot/AoA_Programs/OAA/Reauthorization/docs/OAAreauth_summaries_stakehldrs.pdf. Accessed May 2012.
71. Meals On Wheels Association of America. 2012. Available at www.mowaa.org. Accessed May 2012.
72. American Psychological Association. *Mental and Behavioral Health and Older Americans*. Available at www.apa.org/about/gr/issues/aging/mental-health.aspx. Accessed May 2012.
73. National Institute on Alcohol Abuse and Alcoholism. Updated 2007. *Helping Patients Who Drink Too Much: A Clinician's Guide*. Available at http://pubs.niaaa.nih.gov/publications/Practitioner/CliniciansGuide2005/guide.pdf. Accessed May 2011.
74. National Institute on Aging. 2012. *Alcohol Use In Older People*. Available at www.nia.nih.gov/health/publication/alcohol-use-older-people. Accessed May 2012; U.S. Department of Health and Human Services. 2011. *Medication Review May Benefit Home Health Care Patients*. Available at http://healthfinder.gov/news/newsstory.aspx?docID=659205. Accessed May 2012.
75. National Institute on Alcohol Abuse and Alcoholism. Updated 2007. *Helping Patients Who Drink Too Much*.
76. Ibid.
77. National Institute on Aging. 2012. *Alcohol Use In Older People*.
78. National Institute on Alcohol Abuse and Alcoholism. Updated 2007. *Helping Patients Who Drink Too Much*.

20 Food Safety, Technology and Availability

Chapter Objectives

After reading this chapter you will be able to:

1. Distinguish between foodborne infection and foodborne intoxication and provide an example of each.
2. Summarize strategies to prevent foodborne illness in the home, and when traveling.
3. Describe how the food supply is protected in the United States.
4. Explain the role of food additives, hormones, antibiotics, and pesticides in food production and safety.
5. Discuss biotechnology and the controversy over genetic engineering.
6. Describe what constitutes a sustainable food system.
7. Explain what information is available to help you be informed about food choices.

1. Contaminated foods always smell bad. T/F
2. Hand washing is more effective in preventing food contamination than using a hand sanitizer. T/F
3. A kitchen sponge is a prime environment for the breeding and spread of bacteria. T/F
4. Freezing foods kills bacteria. T/F
5. Leftovers that have been stored in the fridge for a week will still be safe to eat. T/F
6. As long as the expiration date hasn't passed, packaged food is always safe to eat. T/F
7. Food additives must demonstrate a "zero risk" of cancer to human beings in order to meet FDA approval. T/F
8. Pesticides can be washed off of produce with plain water. T/F
9. Organic foods can sometimes contain synthetic pesticides. T/F
10. Genetically engineered foods often contain genes from nonplant organisms. T/F

See page 789 for answers to these Myths and Misconceptions.

Most people don't think a lot about where food comes from before it appears on the supermarket shelf. Have you considered, for example, where the ingredients in your morning cereal and orange juice originated or what measures were taken to protect their safety? No matter what you are eating, it likely started out on a farm. Getting food safely from farms to your plate requires several steps and a huge amount of human and natural resources. These steps comprise a food system, and include all of the processes and resources involved in growing, harvesting, processing, packaging, transporting, marketing, and consuming food (see **Figure 20.1**). Risks to both food safety and availability occur at each step in the food system.

Although consumers in the United States enjoy a relatively safe food supply, continued advances in food production and distribution, new food sources, and the growing volume of food imports make it ever more difficult to protect our food supply from unintentional or deliberate contamination. Food contamination occurs when food contains pathogens or levels of toxic substances that make the food unfit for consumption. In the United States the FDA (Food and Drug Administration), USDA, and other government agencies monitor and regulate the food supply to help ensure that foods remain free of contamination and safe to consume. However, despite well-intended efforts, not all food is safe to consume. In this chapter we will learn more about how contaminants enter our food system and what safety standards are in place to prevent that from happening. Consumers can learn to protect themselves from food contamination by following the simple recommendations presented.

The most common cause of food contamination that results in foodborne illness is by pathogens, disease-causing organisms found in food under certain conditions. The CDC (Centers for Disease Control) estimated that 1 in 6 Americans suffered some degree of foodborne illness caused by pathogens in 2011.[1] Contamination of food by natural or chemical toxins may also cause foodborne illness. Some consumers also question the safety of the intentional use of food additives and preservation techniques such as irradiation. This chapter addresses these concerns and provides information about the safety standards that are in place to protect consumers.

Although you may have access to enough safe and healthy food now, your children or your children's children may not have the same access. The world's population continues to increase, yet the natural resources needed to grow, produce, and distribute safe food are limited. This tension between a growing population and limited natural

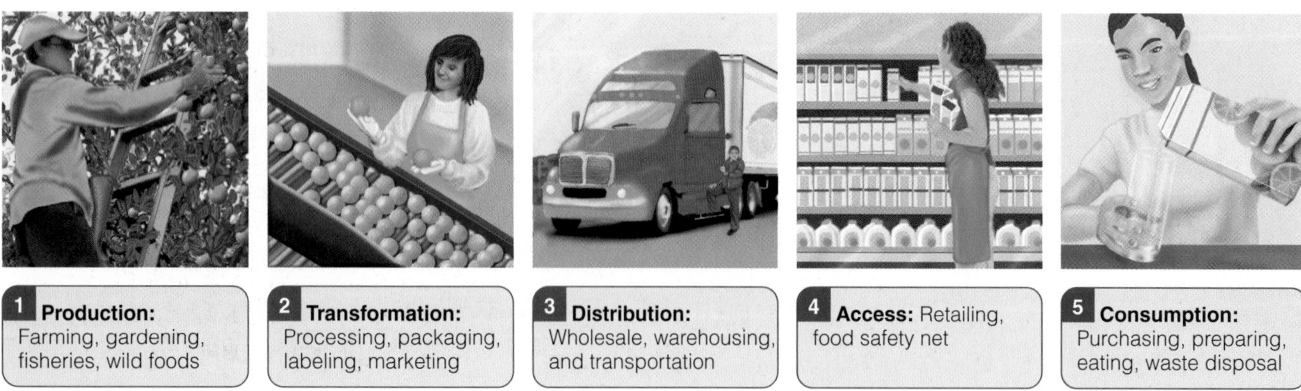

▲ **Figure 20.1 The Food System**
There are several steps involved in processing food from the beginning stages of production to the consumer.

resources has led to changes in the food system that not all consumers embrace. For example, some farmers give antibiotics and hormones to livestock and treat crops with pesticides in order to increase production, but these practices may lead to unintended changes to the end product or the environment. Methods that reduce energy use and waste may enhance the sustainability of food systems. This chapter closes with a discussion about issues related to the sustainability of food systems and how consumers may be interested in making choices that increase the probability that safe food will continue to be available for generations to come.

How Common Are Foodborne Illnesses and What Causes Them?

Foodborne illness continues to be a major preventable public health threat even in industrialized countries. In the United States **foodborne illness** causes 1 in 6 Americans (or 48 million people) to become ill every year, and about 128,000 are hospitalized.[2] These illnesses most commonly result in distressing gastrointestinal symptoms such as cramps, diarrhea, and vomiting, but in extreme circumstances can result in death. Approximately 3,000 Americans die of foodborne disease every year.[3]

The goal of preventing foodborne illness is shared by individuals; food producers, manufacturers, and processors; and several government agencies. Efforts to prevent foodborne illnesses have led to extensive **food safety** practices and guidelines. Several government agencies work together to ensure the safety of foods from the farm to the table, and in the home, consumers can minimize the risk of contaminating foods by following specific storage and preparation guidelines.

The FDA recognizes that advances in production and distribution, new food sources, and the growing volume of food imports present challenges to maintaining a safe food supply. Prior to the advent of convenience foods like bagged lettuce, a contaminated head of lettuce might have affected only one family. Now, however, a contaminated head of lettuce may be processed with thousands of other heads and placed into bags that end up in thousands of homes. This could lead to large outbreaks of illness, making the source difficult to pinpoint.[4] Prevention of such outbreaks remains a public health priority for governmental agencies. The *Healthy People 2020* document and the 2010 *Dietary Guidelines for Americans* both highlight areas of concern related to food safety, with specific objectives aimed at improving safe food practices and decreasing foodborne illness outbreaks.

Foodborne Illness Is Caused by Pathogens and Toxins

Foodborne illness is caused by consuming contaminated food that results in either an infection or intoxication. *Foodborne infection* is caused by consuming foods or beverages that are contaminated with disease-causing organisms, also known as **pathogens.** Once ingested, the pathogens may grow in the intestinal tract of humans and cause illness. Pathogens that can make humans ill include some (but not all) bacteria, viruses, molds, parasites, and prions (Table 20.1).

Foodborne intoxications are caused by eating foods contaminated with a toxin. **Toxins** can be naturally part of a plant or seafood, can be the result of a chemical contamination, or, more commonly, are produced by harmful pathogens. Some but not all bacteria, including *Clostridium botulinum, Staphylococcus aureus,*

foodborne illness Sickness caused by consuming pathogen- or toxin-containing food or beverages. Also known as foodborne disease or food poisoning.

food safety Guidelines and procedures that help keep foods free from contaminants and safe to eat.

pathogens Collective term for disease-causing organisms. Pathogens include microorganisms (viruses, bacteria) and parasites, and are the most common source of foodborne illness.

toxins Poisons that can be produced by living organisms.

TABLE 20.1 Pathogens That Cause Foodborne Illness

Microbe	Where You Find It	How You Can Get It	What You May Experience
Viruses			
Noroviruses	In the stool or vomit of infected individuals	Fecal-to-oral transmission; eating ready-to-eat foods or drinking liquids contaminated by an infected person; eating contaminated shellfish; touching contaminated objects and then putting hands in mouth	Watery diarrhea, nausea, vomiting, flulike symptoms; possible fever. Symptoms can appear 24–48 hours after onset, last 24–60 hours, and are typically not serious.
Hepatitis A (HAV)	In the stool of infected individuals	Fecal-to-oral transmission; eating raw produce irrigated with contaminated water; eating raw or undercooked foods that have not been properly reheated; drinking contaminated water	Diarrhea, dark urine, jaundice, flulike symptoms that can appear 30 days after incubation, and can last 2 weeks to 3 months.
Bacteria			
Campylobacter jejuni	Intestinal tracts of animals and birds, unpasteurized milk, untreated water, and sewage	Drinking contaminated water or raw milk; eating raw or undercooked meat, poultry, or shellfish	Fever, headache, and muscle pain followed by diarrhea (sometimes bloody), abdominal pain, and nausea; appears 2 to 5 days after eating; may last 7 to 10 days; Guillain-Barré syndrome may occur
Clostridium botulinum	Widely distributed in nature in soil, water, on plants, and in the intestinal tracts of animals and fish. Grows only in environments with little or no oxygen.	Eating improperly canned foods, garlic in oil, vacuum-packaged and tightly wrapped food	Bacteria produce a toxin that causes illness by affecting the nervous system. Symptoms usually appear after 18 to 36 hours. May experience double vision, droopy eyelids, trouble speaking and swallowing, and difficulty breathing. Fatal in 3 to 10 days if not treated.
Clostridium perfringens	Soil, dust, sewage, and intestinal tracts of animals and humans. Grows only in little or no oxygen.	Called "the cafeteria germ" because many outbreaks result from eating food left for long periods in steam tables or at room temperature. Bacteria are destroyed by cooking, but some spores may survive.	Bacteria produce toxin that causes illness. Diarrhea and gas pains may appear 8 to 24 hours after eating; usually last about 1 day, but less severe symptoms may persist for 1 to 2 weeks.
Escherichia coli O157:H7	Intestinal tracts of some mammals, unpasteurized milk, unchlorinated water. One of several strains of *E. coli* that can cause human illness.	Drinking contaminated water, unpasteurized apple juice or cider, or unpasteurized milk; eating raw or rare ground beef or uncooked fruits and vegetables	Diarrhea or bloody diarrhea, abdominal cramps, nausea, and weakness. Can begin 2 to 5 days after food is eaten, lasting about 8 days. Small children and elderly adults may develop hemolytic uremic syndrome (HUS) that causes acute kidney failure. A similar illness, thrombotic thrombocytopenic purpura (TTP), may occur in adults.
Enterotoxigenic *Escherichia coli* (major cause of traveler's diarrhea)	Intestinal tracts of some mammals and unpasteurized dairy products. More common in developing countries.	Fecal-to-oral transmission; consuming stool-contaminated water and foods from unsanitary water supplies and food establishments	Diarrhea, nausea, vomiting, stomach cramping, bloating, fever, and weakness

TABLE 20.1 Pathogens That Cause Foodborne Illness *continued*

Microbe	Where You Find It	How You Can Get It	What You May Experience
Listeria monocytogenes	Intestinal tracts of humans and animals, milk, soil, leafy vegetables; can grow slowly at refrigerator temperatures	Eating ready-to-eat foods such as hot dogs, luncheon meats, cold cuts, fermented or dry sausage, other deli-style meat and poultry, or soft cheeses; drinking unpasteurized milk	Fever, chills, headache, backache, sometimes upset stomach, abdominal pain and diarrhea; may take up to 3 weeks to become ill; may later develop more serious illness in high-risk individuals
Salmonella (over 2,300 types)	Intestinal tracts and feces of animals; *Salmonella enteritidis* in eggs	Eating raw or undercooked eggs, poultry, and meat, unpasteurized milk and dairy products, and seafood; can also be spread by infected food handlers	Stomach pain, diarrhea, nausea, chills, fever, and headache usually appear 8 to 72 hours after eating. May last 1 to 2 days.
Shigella (over 30 types)	Human intestinal tract; rarely found in other animals	Fecal-to-oral transmission by consuming contaminated food and water. Most outbreaks result from eating food, especially salads, prepared and handled by workers with poor personal hygiene.	Disease referred to as "shigellosis" or bacillary dysentery. Diarrhea containing blood and mucus, fever, abdominal cramps, chills, and vomiting begin 12 to 50 hours from ingestion of bacteria; can last a few days to 2 weeks.
Staphylococcus aureus	On humans (skin, infected cuts, pimples, noses, and throats)	Consuming foods that were contaminated by being improperly handled. Bacteria multiply rapidly at room temperature.	Bacteria produce a toxin that causes illness. Severe nausea, abdominal cramps, vomiting, and diarrhea occur 1 to 6 hours after eating; recovery within 2 to 3 days.
Parasites			
Cryptosporidium parvum	In the intestines of humans and animals	Fecal-to-oral transmission; drinking contaminated water; eating contaminated produce	Stomach pains, diarrhea, cramps, fever, and vomiting
Cyclospora cayetanensis	Human stool	Fecal-to-oral transmission; drinking contaminated water; eating contaminated produce	Diarrhea, flatulence, stomach cramps, vomiting, fatigue
Giardia lamblia	In the intestines of humans and animals	Fecal-to-oral transmission; drinking contaminated water; eating contaminated produce	Diarrhea, stomach pains, flatulence
Trichinella spiralis	In undercooked or raw meats containing *Trichinella* worms	Raw or undercooked contaminated meat, usually pork or game meats	Nausea, vomiting, diarrhea, fever, aching joints and muscles

Source: Centers for Disease Control and Prevention (CDC). 2004. *Diagnosis and Management of Foodborne Illness: A Primer for Physicians*; CDC. 2012. *Norovirus: Food Handlers*; CDC. 2003. *Viral Hepatitis A*; CDC. 2004. *Traveler's Diarrhea*; MMWR Recommendations and Reports 50 (January 2001): 1–69; CDC. 2004. *Parasitic Disease Information*. All available at www.cdc.gov. Food Safety and Inspection Service. 2006. *Foodborne Illness: What Consumers Need to Know*; Food Safety and Inspection Service. 2001. *Parasites and Foodborne Illness*. Both available at www.fsis.usda.gov.

Clostridium perfringens, and *Bacillus cereus*, produce toxins that cause intoxication. Viruses and parasites do not cause foodborne intoxication. Foodborne intoxications generally produce fairly severe gastrointestinal symptoms and in some cases may even result in death.

Pathogens may be present in the raw ingredients of the food or may contaminate the food at any stage of the food system. For example, fruit flies have been shown to transfer *Escherichia coli* O157:H7 to apples under laboratory conditions.[5] *Escherichia coli* as well as several other disease-causing pathogens are found in the intestinal tract and fecal matter of humans or animals. Food may become contaminated with these pathogens if it comes into contact with fecal matter, and individuals can become infected by putting food or hands that have been in contact with fecal matter into their mouths. This is a common route of transmission of foodborne illness and is called the **fecal-to-oral transmission** route.

Even when a contaminated food is eaten, it may not result in foodborne illness. Many pathogens are killed in the mouth by antimicrobial enzymes and in the stomach by hydrochloric acid. In addition, the potential for a pathogen to cause illness depends on the amount that is consumed, the potency, and the nutritional and immune status of the person who consumes it. Pathogens that survive the natural defense systems of the body undergo an *incubation period* before the symptoms of illness begin. Depending on the type and number of pathogens swallowed, the delay can range from hours to days (refer to Table 20.1 for a description of incubation periods). It is during this incubation period that the pathogens pass through the stomach into the intestine, where they attach to the intestinal walls and begin multiplying and cause illness.

Bacterial infections can be diagnosed by specific laboratory tests for the causative organism through the culturing of stool samples in the laboratory. Parasites can be identified by examining stool samples under a microscope. Viruses are more difficult to identify under a microscope due to their small size, and they are difficult to culture. To identify viruses, scientists test stool samples for genetic markers that indicate whether or not a particular virus is present.[6]

In the United States the most common foodborne infections are caused by noroviruses, *Salmonella* (bacterium), *Clostridium perfringens* (bacterium), *Campylobacter* (bacterium), and *Staphylococcus aureus* (bacterium that produces a toxin).[7] Together these pathogens accounted for 91 percent of all domestically acquired cases of foodborne illness in the United States in 2011. **Norovirus** is currently responsible for more than half of all foodborne illness in the United States, making it the single most common cause of foodborne disease in this country. The differences between different foodborne disease–causing pathogens will be discussed next.

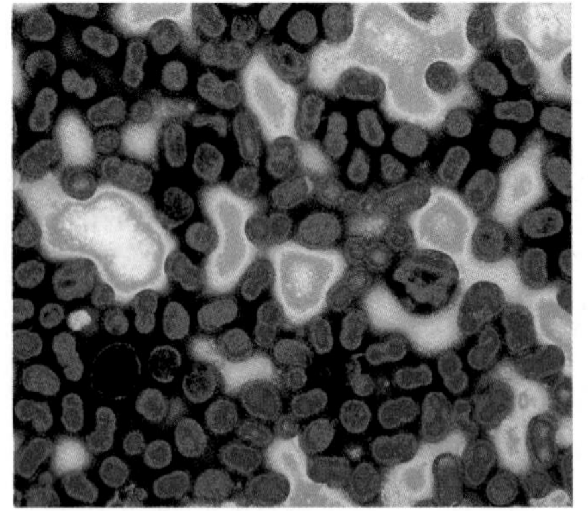

Viruses, such as the hepatitis A virus, need a host to survive and multiply.

Viruses

The term **virus** denotes a microscopic infectious agent that contains chromosomes that carry genetic information (DNA or RNA) for its own replication. Viruses must have a living **host,** such as a plant or an animal, to survive. When an individual eats a contaminated plant or animal as food, the pathogen can invade the cells of the stomach and intestinal walls. The virus can then cause the cells' genetic material to start producing more viruses, ultimately leading to illness.[8]

Bacteria

Bacteria are very small living organisms that lack a cell nucleus. Thousands of types of bacteria are naturally present in our environment. If you were to swab your kitchen sink right now and look at the results under a microscope, you would find that there are about 16 million bacteria living on each square centimeter (less than half an inch) of the sink. Whereas viruses need a host to survive, bacteria can flourish on both living and nonliving surfaces, and can multiply on sponges, dishtowels, cutting boards and countertops, and in sinks. Given the right conditions, a single bacterium divides rapidly enough to produce colonies of billions of bacteria over the course of just one day.

Not all bacteria cause disease in humans, and some that live in the human gut are even beneficial for health.[9] The human gut harbors 500 to 1,000 different types of bacteria; some of these produce small amounts of vitamins such as vitamin K and biotin, others aid in digestion of some nutrients, and still others help maintain the integrity of the lining of the gut. Harmful bacteria that enter the gut compete

fecal-to-oral transmission The spread of pathogens by putting something in the mouth, such as hands or food, that has been in contact with infected stool.

norovirus The most common type of virus that causes foodborne illness. They can cause gastroenteritis, or the "stomach flu."

virus A microscopic organism that carries genetic information for its own replication; a virus can infect a host and cause illness.

host A living plant or animal (including a human) that a virus infects for the sake of reproducing.

bacteria Single-celled microorganisms without an organized nucleus. Some are benign or beneficial to humans, while others can cause disease.

for resources with the beneficial bacteria and, depending on the amount of bacteria, the type of bacteria, and the condition of the human host, may result in illness.

Contamination of food by some types of bacteria causes it to spoil, while contamination of food by other types of bacteria may cause foodborne illness. Bacteria that cause food to spoil result in the deterioration of the quality of food but may or may not introduce pathogens that cause foodborne illness. Though most individuals will not become seriously ill after eating spoiled foods, these items can cause nausea and shouldn't be eaten. In contrast to spoiled foods, contaminated foods that contain bacterial pathogens may look and smell perfectly fine. It is not safe to eat food just because it "looks fine" or "smells OK."

Bacteria may be present on products when they're purchased at the grocery store, even when recommended procedures are followed. Raw meat, poultry, seafood, and eggs can all pick up and harbor bacteria during processing. Produce is not sterile either, and is often eaten raw—lettuce, tomatoes, sprouts, and melons may carry pathogenic bacteria. Although they can grow in just about any food, bacteria grow particularly well on foods high in protein, such as meat, dairy foods, and beans. Even ready-to-eat foods that have been cooked can become cross-contaminated with bacteria from raw products or poor personal hygiene of food handlers.

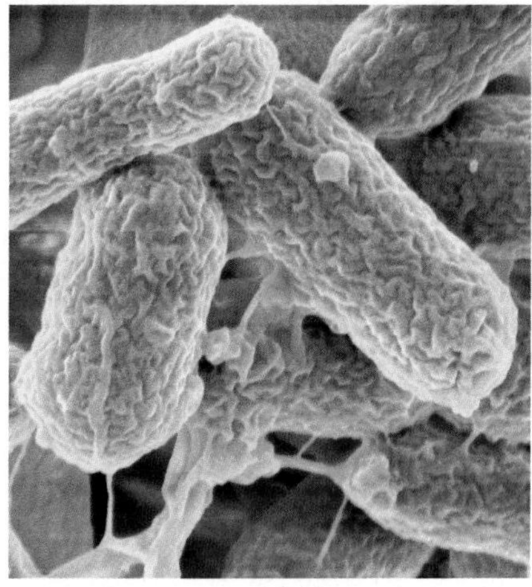

E. coli O157:H7 is the strain that causes most foodborne illness. Most other forms of *E. coli* are harmless.

One type of foodborne bacterium that is of particular concern is *Escherichia coli* O157:H7. Although most strains of *E. coli* are benign, *E. coli* O157:H7 infection results in severe, even life-threatening illness for some individuals. *E. coli* O157:H7 infections can result in **hemolytic uremic syndrome** (*hemo* = blood, *lyti* = destroyed, *uremic* = too much urea in blood), which results in the destruction of red blood cells and damage to and eventual failure of the kidneys.[10] Contaminated ground beef has been the culprit behind most cases of foodborne illness caused by *E. coli* O157:H7. Because bacteria live in the gastrointestinal tracts of healthy cattle, they can easily come into contact with the meat of the animal during the slaughtering process and then get mixed in when the beef is being ground. *E. coli* is destroyed by heat, and most outbreaks have occurred because consumers or food service workers undercooked the meat.

Foods that were not previously recognized as potential sources of *E. coli* have emerged as such in the past decade. These include unpasteurized fruit and vegetable juices, sprouts, and bagged lettuce. Bagged spinach was recalled in 2006 after it was announced by the FDA that products from Natural Selections in California were contaminated with *E. coli* O157:H7. The products were distributed throughout Alaska, Oregon, Washington, and Idaho, and it took several months for the FDA to allow bagged spinach back on the market.

Molds

Molds are multicellular fungi that form a filamentous growth and thrive on damp surfaces. Spores give mold the color you see, and when airborne they spread very easily. Some molds cause allergic reactions and respiratory problems, while a number of molds grow on foods such as breads, cheeses, and fruits. Not all molds are detrimental; some are used to make certain cheeses like Roquefort, blue, Gorgonzola, and Brie. Molds flourish in foods such as breads made without preservatives, because they prefer warmer temperatures and thrive at room temperature. Molds also grow on fruits and vegetables and will grow in the refrigerator in jams, jellies, and even cured, salty meats, given enough time.

Some molds in the right conditions produce mycotoxins that can lead to food intoxication if ingested. One example of this is aflatoxin, a cancer-causing poison, which is sometimes found on moldy peanuts. To avoid mold growth in peanuts and other legumes, store them in a dry environment; avoid eating any legumes that have

hemolytic uremic syndrome A rare condition that can be caused by *E. coli* O157:H7 and results in the destruction of red blood cells and kidney failure. Very young children and the elderly are at a higher risk of developing this syndrome.

molds Microscopic fungi that live on plant and animal matter. Some can produce mycotoxins which are harmful.

an off color. Many countries monitor foods for aflatoxin due to its potent disease-causing effects. However, because of their visibility, molds are easy to identify and food that is moldy should be discarded. Cooking and freezing stop mold growth but do not kill the toxins present.[11]

Parasites

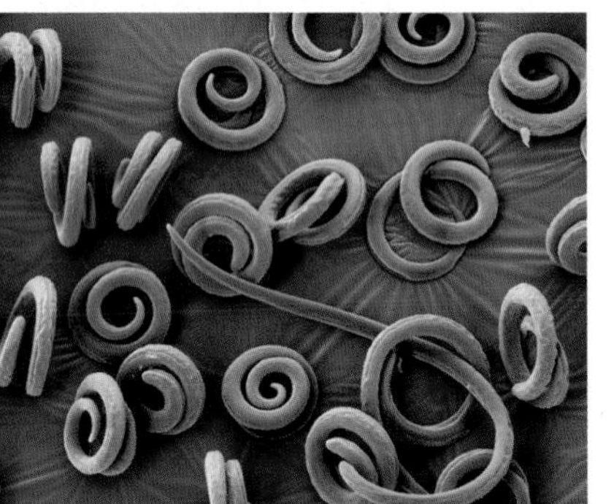

The parasitic roundworm *Trichinella spiralis*.

Parasites are small living organisms, occasionally in the egg or larval phase, that, like viruses, take their nourishment from hosts. They can be found in food and water and are often transmitted through the fecal-to-oral route.[12] The most common parasitic illness outbreaks in the United States have been caused by just a few types: *Cryptosporidium parvum, Cyclospora cayetanensis, Giardia lamblia*, and *Trichinella spiralis*. However, foodborne illness caused by parasites is much less common in the United States than is illness caused by other types of pathogens.[13]

Both *Cryptosporidium parvum* and *Cyclospora cayetanensis* can be found in contaminated water or food sources, while *Giardia lamblia* is one of the most common sources of waterborne illness. Hikers who drink unfiltered water from streams or lakes often become infected with the *Giardia* parasite. *Trichinella spiralis* (see photo) is an intestinal worm whose larvae (hatched eggs) can travel from the digestive tract to the muscles of the body. See Table 20.1 for a summary of these parasites and the foodborne illnesses they cause.

Prions

A **prion** is an infectious agent composed of misfolded protein. Prions are responsible for diseases known as spongiform encephalopathies, such as bovine spongiform encephalopathy (BSE, or mad cow disease) in cattle and Creutzfeldt-Jakob disease (CJD) in humans. All known prion diseases affect the structure of brain and neural tissue and are untreatable. Cattle and other ruminant animals can be infected by consuming feed that contains prion-containing tissues of infected animals. Humans can be infected by consuming meat (muscle) or brain tissue of infected livestock.

Great Britain experienced an outbreak of BSE in the 1990s that resulted in cross-contamination of prion disease to humans. Since that time, the United States has taken specific steps to protect the public against beef contaminated with BSE. First and foremost, ruminant animals such as cattle and sheep, meat and meat products from ruminant animals, and animal feed that contains animal protein derived from countries that are at risk for BSE can no longer be imported into the United States. Also, feed for ruminant animals that is sold in North America is banned from containing any ruminant protein. This type of feed has been identified as a major route of BSE transmission. Sick or lame cattle and specific tissues of cattle, such as the small intestines and spinal cord tissue, which have the greatest risk of containing the BSE agent, are banned from the food supply. And lastly, techniques previously used when slaughtering cattle and separating the meat, which likely increased the potential for the animal's meat to become contaminated, have been prohibited.[14]

BSE is not irradicated, but the incidence of infection is sporadic and rare. Though approximately 150 people died of CJD after becoming infected from eating contaminated livestock in Great Britain in the 1990s, no human has ever been infected with CJD by eating infected meat in the United States. Since 2003 there have been only four cases of BSE reported in the U.S. cattle supply, including the most recent report of a dairy cow in California being infected with BSE in 2012. In a press briefing, the USDA's chief veterinary officer said the cow's meat did not enter the food supply and the carcass was destroyed, so the risk to human health was minimal.[15]

parasites Organisms that live on or in another organism. Parasites obtain their nourishment from their hosts.

prions Short for proteinaceous infectious particle. Self-reproducing protein particles that cause degenerative brain diseases.

Some Illnesses Are Caused by Natural Toxins

Many toxins that occur in plants and animals function as natural pesticides and assist in fending off predators. In many cases, these natural toxins are present in amounts too small to harm humans, but there are instances in which the toxins found in plant and animal foods can make a person seriously ill.

Marine Toxins

In addition to the pathogenic microbes that can be found in raw or undercooked seafood, naturally occurring **marine toxins** can cause illness if fish or other seafood is not cooked thoroughly. In fact, some of these toxins are not destroyed by cooking.

Spoiled finfish, such as tuna and mackerel, can cause **scombrotoxic fish poisoning,** in which the spoilage bacteria break down proteins in the fish and generate histamine, which in turn can accumulate to harmful levels. Consuming fish that contain large amounts of histamine can cause symptoms such as diarrhea, flushing, sweating, and vomiting within 2 minutes to 2 hours.[16]

Large, predatory reef fish, such as barracuda and grouper, can sometimes be infected with ciguatoxins, which when eaten can cause **ciguatera poisoning.** In this case, toxins travel through the food chain and **bioaccumulate** in larger species (see **Figure 20.2**). Ciguatoxins originate in microscopic sea organisms called dinoflagellates, which are eaten by small tropical fish, which in turn are eaten by larger fish. When people consume the larger fish, the consumption of the accumulated concentrations of toxin can result in illness.[17] In addition to experiencing various gastrointestinal discomforts, individuals infected with ciguatera may have temperature sensation reversal in their mouth when they eat.[18] For example, hot liquids and hot foods feel cold, and vice versa.

Marine **neurotoxins** (*neuro* = nerve, *toxin* = toxic), can contaminate certain shellfish, such as mussels, clams, scallops, oysters, crabs, and lobsters, that typically live in the coastal waters of New England and the Pacific states. Neurotoxins are also produced by a particular reddish-brown-colored dinoflagellate. These reddish-brown dinoflagellates can become so abundant that the ocean appears to have red streaks, also known as red tides. Eating shellfish contaminated with neurotoxins can lead to **paralytic shellfish poisoning.** Symptoms include mild numbness or tingling in the face, arms, and legs, as well as headaches and dizziness. In severe cases muscle paralysis, the inability to breathe, and death could result.[19]

marine toxins Chemicals that occur naturally and contaminate some fish.

scombrotoxic fish poisoning A condition caused by consuming spoiled fish that contain large amounts of histamines. Also referred to as histamine fish poisoning.

ciguatera poisoning A condition caused by marine toxins that are produced by dinoflagellates and have bioaccumulated in fish that the affected person consumes.

bioaccumulate To build up the levels of a substance or chemical in an organism over time, so that the concentration of the chemical is higher than would be found naturally in the environment.

neurotoxins Toxins that affect the nerves and can cause symptoms including mild numbness or tingling in the face, arms, and legs, as well as headaches and dizziness. Severe cases of neurotoxicity could result in death.

paralytic shellfish poisoning A condition caused by a reddish-brown-colored dinoflagellate that contains neurotoxins.

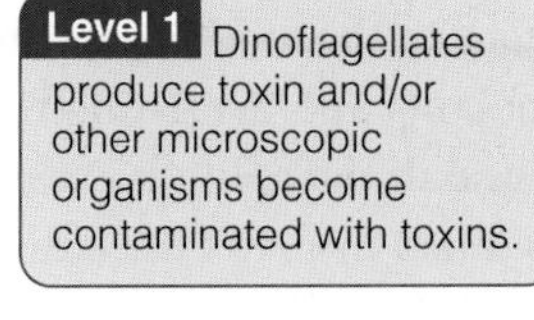

Level 1 Dinoflagellates produce toxin and/or other microscopic organisms become contaminated with toxins.

Level 2 Small fish eat the dinoflagellates. Over time, the toxins accumulate and become more concentrated in their bodies.

Level 3 Large, predatory fish consume the smaller contaminated fish, which increases their toxin concentration.

Level 4 Fishermen catch the larger fish for human consumption.

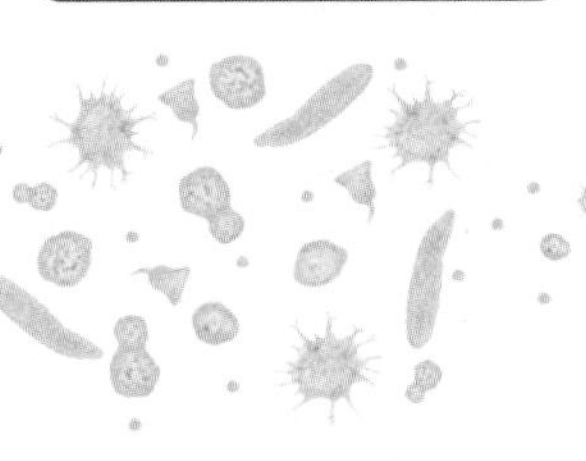

Increasing accumulation of biotoxins equals bioaccumulation

▲ **Figure 20.2 Bioaccumulation of Toxins**

Toxins in Other Foods

Many plant foods naturally contain toxins in small amounts, and don't generally present problems when eaten in reasonable portions; however, consuming them in very large amounts could be harmful. Potatoes that have been exposed to light can develop a green tinge on the surface, which indicates that they contain increased amounts of **solanine,** a toxin that can cause fever, diarrhea, paralysis, and shock. Peeling potatoes and removing the green layer will ensure that the potato can be safely eaten. Eating 2 to 5 milligrams of solanine per kilogram of body weight will result in symptoms and eating 3 to 6 milligrams of solanine per kilogram of body weight may result in death.[20] The amount of solanine in potatoes is very small, on the order of about 0.2 milligrams per gram of potato. Eating approximately 1 pound of green potatoes would likely make a 100-pound person ill. Wild lima beans contain high amounts of *cyanogenic glycosides*, which can be converted to the poison cyanide. The variety of lima beans sold commercially has minimal, non-threatening amounts of this substance, so it is safe to eat. Cassava, a root vegetable, also contains cyanogenic glycosides and has been known to cause cyanide poisoning in people who regularly eat raw or unprocessed cassava. Raw soybeans contain amylase inhibitors, which are inactivated when the beans are cooked or fermented. Cruciferous vegetables such as cabbage and broccoli contain small quantities of *goitrogens*, compounds that interfere with the function of the thyroid gland when eaten raw and in excessive quantities.[21] However, even people with thyroid disease seem to be able to tolerate intakes of up to 1 serving of raw cruciferous vegetables a day. Although some natural foods may contain toxic substances, the risk of actual harm is small.

However, other foods contain toxins that are harmful even in trace amounts, and so should be avoided altogether. Certain wild mushrooms, for example, are poisonous; they contain toxins that can cause nausea, vomiting, liver damage, and death.

Chemical Agents Sometimes Cause Foodborne Illness

Consumers are becoming increasingly concerned about environmental damage caused by industrial and household chemicals. Traces of these substances can travel through the food chain and be ingested by people, posing numerous risks to health. Awareness of the potential environmental and health risks caused by these chemicals has led to a search for less dangerous alternatives.

Polychlorinated Biphenyls (PCBs)

Polychlorinated biphenyls (PCBs) are chemicals that occur in the food supply due to industrial pollution. These chemicals were used as coolants and insulating fluids for transformers and capacitors, as flame retardants, and in the manufacture of plasticizers, waxes, and paper. Production of PCBs was banned in 1979 due to their high toxicity and persistence in the environment.[22]

Exposure to PCBs can cause cancer and have other adverse effects in animals, and may be **carcinogenic** (*carcin* = cancer, *genic* = forming) in humans. PCB exposure in adults can cause skin conditions such as acne and rashes as well as liver damage. It is of particular concern for pregnant and lactating women because prenatal exposure and consumption of contaminated breast milk can damage a child's nervous system and cause learning defects. Also, because young children are smaller, exposure to PCBs will have a proportionately greater effect on them than would the same level of exposure in adults.[23]

Although PCBs are no longer manufactured in the United States, they do not degrade and can therefore still make their way into the environment through

solanine Toxin found in potato surfaces exposed to light that can cause fever, diarrhea, and shock if consumed in large amounts.

polychlorinated biphenyls (PCBs) Synthetic chemicals that have been shown to cause cancer and other adverse effects on the immune, reproductive, nervous, and endocrine systems in animals. PCBs may cause cancer in humans.

carcinogenic Causing cancer.

releases from hazardous waste sites, the burning of commercial or municipal waste, and the improper disposal of consumer products, such as old television sets and electrical fixtures and devices.[24] PCBs have been shown to contaminate the sediments in rivers and lakes. Because PCBs don't degrade, they bioaccumulate in small organisms and fish and travel up the food chain when eaten by larger fish. When humans eat fish that have PCBs in their flesh they can be ingesting potentially harmful levels, which is the major chemical risk associated with eating fish.[25]

The EPA began regulating PCBs in drinking water in 1992, and the agency is working to lower the amount of PCBs in the environment.[26] Although the FDA routinely monitors PCB levels in the food supply, the toxin can be found in nonregulated food sources, such as locally caught fish. Consumers should therefore research and adhere to local fish consumption advisories.[27] See the Table Tips for the EPA website that lists current advisories, as well as tips to minimize exposure to toxins and chemical agents in foods.

Methylmercury

Mercury occurs naturally, but is also produced as an industrial by-product or pollutant. An airborne form of mercury can accumulate on the surface of streams and oceans and be transformed by the bacteria in the water into the toxic form of methylmercury. As fish either absorb the methylmercury from the water or eat smaller fish that contain methylmercury, they can bioaccumulate the substance to high levels. Larger fish, including shark, swordfish, king mackerel, and tilefish, contain high levels of mercury, so the FDA and EPA recommend that women who are or may become pregnant, women who are nursing, and young children should avoid consuming these fish.[28]

TABLE TIPS

Avoid Toxins and Chemical Agents in Fish and Seafood

Keep fish, especially finfish, such as fresh tuna, mackerel, grouper, and mahi mahi, chilled in the refrigerator to prevent spoilage and the formation of histamine toxins.

Never consume finfish or shellfish that is sold as bait, as these do not meet food safety regulations.

Observe all fish consumption advisories. To learn if an advisory is in place for the fish in your area, visit the EPA's Fish and Wildlife Consumption website at www.epa.gov/waterscience/fish/states.htm.

If you fish recreationally, always check with the local or state health department for specific advice based on the local waters to avoid eating PCB-containing fish.

Eat a variety of types of fish to minimize the exposure to a particular toxin.

Adapted from Centers for Disease Control and Prevention. 2002. *Marine Toxins.* Available at www.cdc.gov/ncidod/dbmd/diseaseinfo/marinetoxins_g.htm; Agency for Toxic Substances and Disease Registry. Updated 2003. *ToxFAQ for Polychlorinated Biphenyls (PCBs).* Available at www.atsdr.cdc.gov/toxfaqs/tf.asp?id=140&tid=26; Environmental Protection Agency Persistent Bioaccumulative and Toxic (PBT) Chemical Program. n.d. *PBTs and You.* Available at www.epa.gov/oppt/pbt/pubs/pbtsandyou.htm. Accessed December 2008.

Some People Are at Higher Risk for Foodborne Illness

Some individuals are at greater risk of contracting a foodborne disease than others. Older adults, young children, pregnant women, and those with a compromised immune system are more susceptible to contracting foodborne illness and suffering complications than the rest of the population. Shifting population demographics mean more and more Americans are at risk for foodborne illness. For example, about 15 percent of the U.S. population is currently 62 years of age or older. The number of Americans 62 years of age and older is projected to reach 19 percent by the year 2030.[29] In addition to age, any condition that weakens a person's immune system, such as HIV, AIDS, cancer, or diabetes, can increase his or her risk of contracting foodborne illness.[30]

The hormonal shifts that occur during pregnancy can affect a pregnant woman's immune system, making her more vulnerable to a potentially life-threatening illness caused by the bacterium *Listeria monocytogenes.* Infection with *Listeria* can result in miscarriage (see Health Connection: The Lowdown on *Listeria*). Certain deli meats, undercooked frankfurters, and ready-to-eat foods are associated with listeriosis.

In older adults, age-related deterioration of the immune system increases the risk for foodborne illness. In addition, the level of gastric juice produced by the stomach declines with age, resulting in fewer foodborne pathogens being destroyed during digestion and greater risk of gastrointestinal infections and their complications. This puts the elderly at higher risk of dying of **gastroenteritis,** which is a severe complication of foodborne illness.[31] Individuals in institutional settings (such as nursing homes, hospitals, schools, and on cruise ships), where groups of people eat foods from the same source, are also at higher risk of foodborne illness. Improper handling of foods and poor hygiene practices of food service workers are often the causes of foodborne disease outbreaks in institutional settings.

gastroenteritis Inflammation of the stomach and intestines.

Health Connection

The Lowdown on *Listeria*

Listeriosis, the illness caused by the bacterium *Listeria monocytogenes,* seriously affects approximately 2,500 individuals annually, with pregnant women being 20 times more likely than other people to become infected. *Listeria* can reach the fetus through the placenta, be transmitted to the developing baby, and lead to severe illness, premature delivery, miscarriage, and stillbirth. Older adults and those with a weakened immune system are also at risk for becoming very sick or even dying.

Animals can harbor *Listeria,* which leads to contamination of meat and dairy foods. Pasteurization will kill *Listeria*, so unpasteurized soft cheeses, such as Camembert, Brie, and blue cheeses, carry a higher risk of containing *Listeria*. Compared with hard cheeses such as Parmesan, these soft cheeses are less acidic and contain more moisture, two conditions that enhance bacterial growth. Even though cooking can also destroy *Listeria*, the lower cooking temperature used during the processing of soft cheeses isn't high enough to destroy this bacterium.

Soft cheese can be contaminated with *Listeria*.

Because contamination can occur after processing, many outbreaks have been associated with foods such as hot dogs, deli-style luncheon meats, Brie cheese, salami, and paté. *Listeria* can also continue to multiply at refrigerated temperatures.

The following tips can help pregnant women and other higher risk individuals reduce their likelihood of contracting *Listeria:*

- Reheat ready-to-eat luncheon meats, cold cuts, fermented and dry sausage, deli-style meat and poultry products, and hot dogs until they are steamy hot to kill any existing bacteria before you eat them.
- Wash your hands with hot, soapy water after touching these types of ready-to-eat foods, or any foods, for that matter. Thoroughly wash cutting boards, dishes, and utensils to avoid cross-contamination.
- Avoid soft cheeses such as feta, Brie, Camembert, blue-veined (blue) cheese, and Mexican-style cheeses unless they are made with pasteurized milk. (Read the ingredients list to see if pasteurized milk was used.) You can safely eat hard cheeses, semi-soft cheese such as mozzarella, pasteurized processed cheeses, cream cheese, and cottage cheese.
- Avoid unpasteurized milk and foods made from unpasteurized milk.
- Avoid refrigerated smoked seafood such as smoked salmon (lox or nova style), trout, whitefish, cod, tuna, or mackerel unless they are used in an entrée such as a heated casserole. You can safely eat canned fish and shelf-stable smoked seafood.
- Avoid refrigerated paté or meat spreads. You can safely eat canned or shelf-stable varieties.
- Eat precooked or ready-to-eat perishable items before the expiration date on the food label.

Source: Centers for Disease Control (CDC). 2011. Listeria *(Listeriosis).* Available at www.cdc.gov/listeria; USDA. 2012. *Fact Sheets: Protect Your Baby and Yourself from Listeriosis.* Available at www.fsis.usda.gov/Fact_Sheets/Protect_Your_Baby/index.asp. Accessed August 2012.

For a healthy person, infection with foodborne illness generally results in acute symptoms, such as diarrhea and vomiting, that require only supportive care. However, for young children, older adults, and immunocompromised persons, foodborne illness can result in septicemia, renal failure, or death. In pregnant women, foodborne illness can result in miscarriage or stillbirth.

THE TAKE-HOME MESSAGE Foodborne illness is a serious public health problem. Many disease-bearing pathogens are present in the environment and can contaminate the water and food supply. Foodborne illness is caused by consuming pathogens in contaminated food or drinks. Viruses and bacteria are the most common causes in the United States, although parasites and prions can also cause some foodborne illness. Toxins can occur naturally in foods and are also introduced as a result of chemical contamination of the environment. Chemicals such as polychlorinated biphenyls (PCBs) and methylmercury have been shown to bioaccumulate in fish as a result of environmental contamination. Certain populations, including the elderly, children, pregnant women, and those with compromised immune systems, are at higher risk of contracting foodborne illness and suffering complications.

What Strategies Can Be Used to Prevent Foodborne Illness?

One of the best ways to prevent foodborne illness is to keep the pathogens that cause it from flourishing in foods. For example, in order for bacteria to thrive and multiply, they must have the proper conditions. These include 1) a source of nutrients (including glucose, amino acids, or vitamins and/or minerals), 2) moisture, 3) a pH above 4.6 (considered low acidity), 4) temperatures in the range of 40 to 140 degrees Fahrenheit, and 5) time (at least 20 minutes) to multiply.[32] Protein- and nutrient-rich animal foods, such as raw and undercooked meat, poultry, seafood, eggs, and unpasteurized milk, are the most common types of foods that provide conditions for rapid bacterial growth.

Bacteria thrive in moist environments, such as in raw chicken that is sitting in its juices. Dry foods, such as uncooked rice, sugar, flour, and cereals, do not usually support bacterial growth until they are hydrated with a liquid. However, these foods can be contaminated by infected utensils or hands. For example, if a person with infected hands takes a handful of cereal directly out of the box, this will transfer bacteria onto the food. Although the bacteria may not multiply, they will survive, and, once eaten, the moist environment of the GI tract will provide the optimal conditions for growth, eventually resulting in foodborne illness.

Bacteria don't thrive in acidic foods (pH less than 4.6) such as vinegar and citrus fruits, so these foods seldom provide the conditions necessary for growth. However, animal protein has a higher pH and provides the right conditions for bacteria to flourish.

Bacteria multiply most abundantly between the temperatures of about 40°F and 140°F. At body temperature, or 98.6°F, bacteria can divide and double within 30 minutes, and multiply to millions in about 12 hours.[33] Because bacteria need such a short time period to multiply, it is important to realize that perishable food, such as raw meat, left at room temperature for an extended period can become a feast for bacterial growth.

Consumers can take various measures when consuming and handling food to reduce the risk of foodborne illness. These include preventing the growth of bacteria and destroying any pathogens that may be present. This can be done through the consistent practice of proper food consumption, handling, and storage strategies at home and while traveling.

Practice Food Safety at Home

An easy way to remember the important points of home food safety is by focusing on the "Core Four" of the Fight BAC! campaign of the nonprofit Partnership for Food Safety Education: Cleaning, Combating cross-contamination (or separating), Cooking, and Chilling (**Figure 20.3**).[34] You will learn more about the Partnership for Food Safety Education later in this chapter.

▲ **Figure 20.3 Fight BAC!**
The Fight BAC! symbol sums up the "Core Four" of keeping food safe in the kitchen: clean, combat cross-contamination (separate meats from ready-to-eat foods), cook thoroughly, and chill to a cold enough temperature.

TABLE TIPS

Wash Your Hands!

After using the toilet
After changing a diaper
After touching animals
Before and after food preparation, especially when handling raw meat or poultry
After blowing your nose
After coughing or sneezing into your hands
Before and after treating wounds
After handling garbage
Before inserting or removing contact lenses

Proper hand washing:

Wet hands with warm, running water and apply liquid soap or use clean bar soap. Lather well.
Rub hands together vigorously for at least 20 seconds (recite the alphabet twice or sing "Happy Birthday" twice).
Scrub all surfaces, including the backs of hands, wrists, between fingers, and under fingernails.
Rinse well.
Dry hands with a clean or disposable towel.
Use a towel to turn off the faucet, and if in a public restroom use a clean towel to open the door as well.

Source: Mayo Clinic. 2008. *Hand Washing: An Easy Way to Prevent Infection.* Available at www.mayoclinic.com/health/hand-washing/HQ00407. Accessed August 2008.

Clean Hands and Produce

Cleaning is one of the simplest ways to reduce the chances of microbial contamination, and proper hand washing is one of the most important overall strategies for preventing foodborne illness. If everyone practiced proper hand washing techniques, the incidences of foodborne illness could decrease by about half.[35] The Table Tips summarize proper hand washing techniques.

Proper hand washing refers to washing hands *thoroughly,* as well as washing hands *regularly.* This last part, regular washing, is where many people fall short. Germs accumulate on hands from a variety of sources throughout the day, and if hands are not regularly washed, these germs can infect the body after being passed into the mouth, nose, and eyes. Individuals also spread the germs to others by touching surfaces such as doorknobs. In a study conducted at Utah State University, over 100 participants were videotaped to observe their food handling practices. After reviewing the video, the researchers found that only 2 percent of the participants had washed their hands correctly, with warm soapy water and plenty of agitation and time. Though warm tap water isn't hot enough to kill microbes, it is superior to cold water for removing dirt, oil, and germs from hands. The researchers also found that the average time the participants spent washing their hands was a mere 7 seconds, rather than the recommended minimum of 20 seconds.[36]

In instances where hand washing is not an option, such as when traveling or eating on the run, using disposable wipes or hand gel sanitizers can be an excellent alternative. Only the alcohol-based products are effective in killing germs. The CDC recommends choosing products that contain at least 60 percent alcohol.[37] Individuals should keep hand sanitizers in the car, purse, desk drawer, and backpack so that proper hand hygiene can be practiced at all times. Office workers in particular can benefit from regular use of hand sanitizer. Studies conducted in the workplace have identified an astounding 25,127 germs per square inch on the average office phone, 3,295 germs per square inch on computer keyboards, and 1,676 germs per square inch on the average computer mouse![38]

In addition to hands, anything that touches food, such as knives, utensils, and countertops, should be thoroughly cleaned between each use. Cutting boards should be placed in the dishwasher or scrubbed with hot soapy water and rinsed after each use. Nonporous cutting boards made of plastic, marble, and tempered glass are easier to keep clean than the more porous wooden cutting boards or wooden surfaces. Cracked cutting boards should be discarded, as they can harbor pathogenic microbes and lead to cross-contamination. Kitchen sinks and cutting boards should be regularly sanitized by filling the sink with hot water and adding one teaspoon of bleach per quart of water. Let the board sit in the sanitizing liquid for a few minutes to kill the microbes, then rinse it thoroughly.

A kitchen sponge is an ideal environment for bacteria because it provides the ideal temperature, moisture, and nutrients (food particles). Household kitchen sponges and dishcloths have been shown to harbor more fecal bacteria than toilet seats.[39] Consequently, sponges and dishcloths need to be washed often in the hot cycle of the washing machine, preferably with bleach in addition to the soap. They can also be soaked in a bleach solution along with the cutting boards, run through the dishwasher (including the dry cycle), or placed in the microwave for one minute at its highest setting.

The countertop sponge may very well be the most contaminated item in your kitchen. Food scraps, moisture, and room temperature can lead to a thriving bacterial colony on this common cleaning item.

All fruits and vegetables should be thoroughly washed under cold running tap water before eating. Even foods like cantaloupe, which doesn't have an edible peel or rind, have been known to carry *Salmonella,* and the microbe can be transferred from the peel or rind to the fruit by the knife used to cut it open. Washing the fruit with a vegetable brush will help remove any dirt or microbes on its surface. Fruit should be washed *before* placing it on the countertop or cutting board to avoid picking up and spreading germs from the countertop.

Combat Cross-Contamination

Produce, especially if it's going to be eaten raw, should never come in contact with raw meat, poultry, or fish during the food preparation process. If these items do come in contact, they could **cross-contaminate** each other, meaning that microbes could be spread from one item to the other. Because raw meat, poultry, and fish contain microbes, they should be kept separate from ready-to-eat foods such as fruits and vegetables during food preparation and stored separately in the refrigerator. Uncooked meats, fish, and poultry should either be cleaned and frozen or stored in airtight containers on the bottom shelf of the refrigerator. This will prevent any drippings containing microbes from coming in contact with cooked foods or raw fruits and vegetables. When purchasing groceries, raw meats should be bagged separately from produce. One additional tip is to place shopping bags on the kitchen floor for unpacking, rather than on the countertop where they could potentially leave germs.

Marinades that are used to tenderize and flavor meats, poultry, or fish should never be used as a basting or serving sauce. The basting brush can transfer microbes, so unless the marinade is boiled for several minutes to kill any pathogens, foodborne illness is a risk. A better bet would be to discard the used marinade and create a fresh batch to use as the sauce.

The knife and cutting board used to cut and prepare raw meat, poultry, or fish should not be used to slice vegetables or bread unless both have been thoroughly cleaned with hot soapy water. Ideally, separate cutting boards should be kept on hand for meat and nonmeat foods. All plates and bowls that have contained raw meats, poultry, and fish should be thoroughly washed before using them again. For example, at a barbecue, the plate that held the raw hamburgers should *never* be used to serve the cooked burgers unless it has been thoroughly washed between each use.

Another common source of cross-contamination occurs when soiled dishtowels are used to dry clean dishes or utensils. A towel that was used to wipe up raw

cross-contaminate The transfer of pathogens from a food, utensil, cutting board, kitchen surface, and/or hands to another food or object.

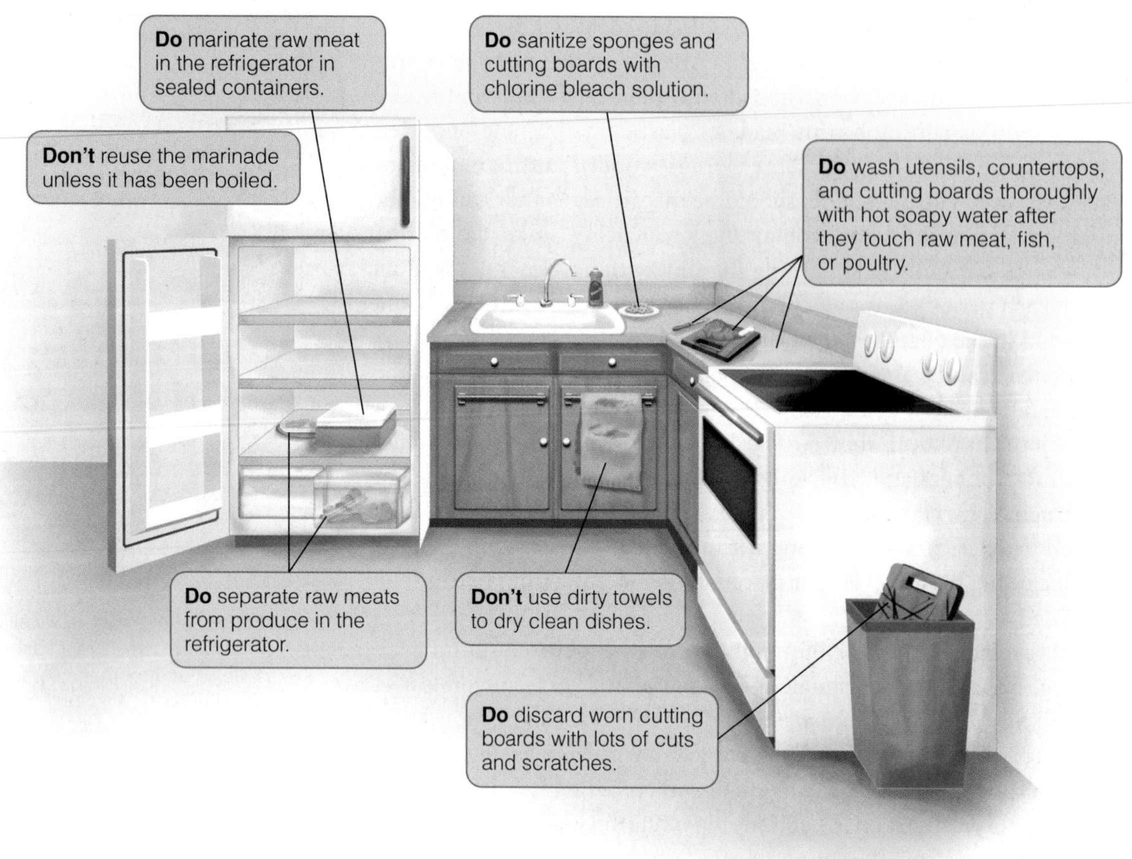

▲ **Figure 20.4 The Do's and Don'ts of Avoiding Cross-Contamination**

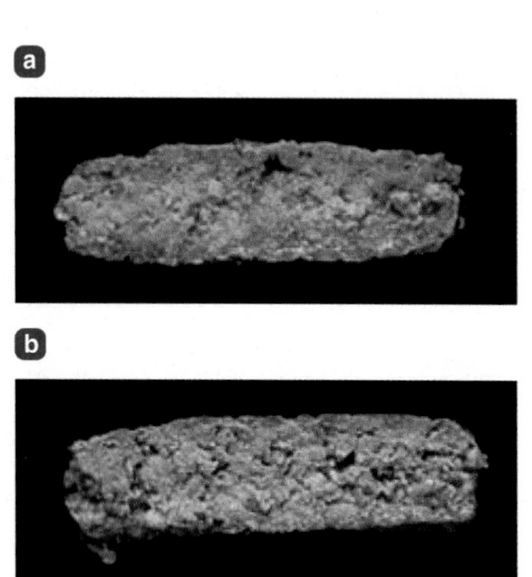

▲ **Figure 20.5 Cook Meats Thoroughly to Kill Pathogens**
A hamburger needs to reach an internal temperature of 160°F to ensure that all foodborne pathogens are killed. Color is not an indication of "doneness."

meat juices or your hands can transfer those microbes to your clean dishes or utensils. You could easily coat those clean surfaces with a layer of germs. **Figure 20.4** summarizes some of the ways to combat cross-contamination in the kitchen.

Cook Foods Thoroughly

A common food safety misconception is that meat that looks brown is fully cooked. Look at the two hamburger patties in **Figure 20.5**. The brown patty on the bottom might look as thoroughly cooked as the pinker patty above, but it's actually not. Ground meat (beef, pork, veal, and lamb) must reach an internal temperature of 160°F to kill pathogens known to cause illness. Because meat can lose its pink color before it is safe to eat, color is not a reliable way to determine if meat is thoroughly cooked. There are also some lean varieties of beef that can remain pink even though they have reached an internal temperature of 160°F, high enough to kill any potential pathogens.

The color of beef is largely determined by **myoglobin,** a protein that provides the purplish-red pigment in meat (and poultry). The denaturing of this protein is what causes meat to turn from pink to brown during cooking. However, if the meat starts out brown, this color change won't occur. Thus, a burger could look "done" when it may still be raw in places. Research has shown that hamburgers can look "well done" while only having reached an internal temperature of approximately 135°F.[40]

myoglobin A protein that provides the purplish-red color in meat and poultry.

Poultry color can also be misleading because it can remain pink after thorough cooking. This is caused by a chemical reaction that occurs in the poultry from gases

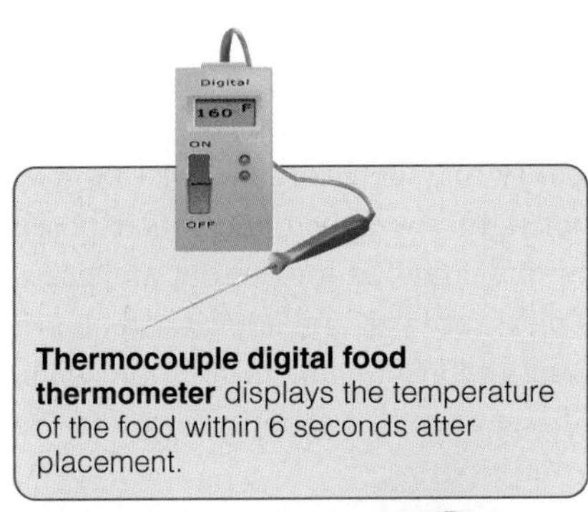

Thermocouple digital food thermometer displays the temperature of the food within 6 seconds after placement.

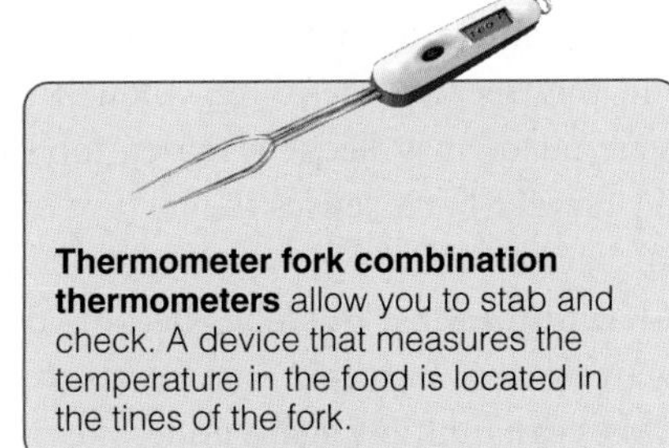

Thermometer fork combination thermometers allow you to stab and check. A device that measures the temperature in the food is located in the tines of the fork.

Thermistor digital food thermometers take approximately 10 seconds to display the temperature of the food on the dial.

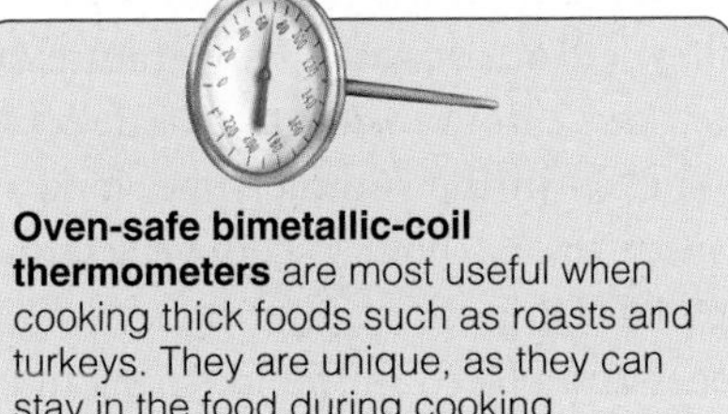

Oven-safe bimetallic-coil thermometers are most useful when cooking thick foods such as roasts and turkeys. They are unique, as they can stay in the food during cooking.

▲ **Figure 20.6 Food Thermometers**
There are several types of food thermometers available for measuring the internal temperature of cooked foods. The thermometer should be inserted at least one-half inch deep into the food, and should be washed thoroughly after each use, and before insertion into any food.

in the oven that give the meat a pink tinge. Because younger birds have thin skins, the gases can react with their flesh more easily and make the meat look pinker than that of older birds. Also, nitrates and nitrites added to some poultry as a preservative can give poultry a pink tinge (see the discussion of food additives later in the chapter).[41]

The only way to determine if food has reached an internal temperature high enough to kill pathogens is to use a food thermometer. **Figure 20.6** shows several types of food thermometers available for use when cooking. Table 20.2 provides a list of the internal temperatures that foods should reach to ensure that they are safe to eat.

TABLE 20.2 Safe Food Temperatures

If You Are Cooking (Food)	The Food Thermometer Should Reach (°F)*
Ground Meat and Meat Mixtures	
Beef, pork, veal, lamb	160
Turkey, chicken	165
Fresh Beef, Veal, Lamb	
Medium	160
Well Done	170
Poultry	
Chicken, turkey, whole or parts	165
Duck and goose	165
Fresh Pork	
Medium	160
Well done	170
Ham, raw	160
Ham, precooked (to reheat)	140
Eggs and Egg Dishes	
Eggs	Cook until yolk and white are firm
Egg dishes	160
Leftovers and Casseroles	165

*The thermometer should be placed in the thickest part of the food item.

Source: USDA Food Safety and Inspection Service. 2012. *Appliances and Thermometers.* Available at http://www.fsis.usda.gov/Fact_Sheets/Appliances_&_Thermometers_Fact_Sheets/index.asp.

Chill Foods at a Low Enough Temperature

Proper chilling and refrigeration of foods is essential to inhibit the growth of pathogens. But just how low must the temperature be? Foodborne bacteria multiply most rapidly in temperatures between 40°F and 140°F (or 5°C to 60°C), a range known as the "**danger zone.**" To keep foods out of the danger zone, hot foods must be kept *hot*, above 140°F, and cold foods need to be served *cold*, below 40°F, or even lower (see **Figure 20.7**). This means that when cooked foods like lasagna are on a buffet table, they should be sitting on a hot plate or other heat source that keeps their temperature above 140°F, while cold prepared foods such as potato salad should be sitting on ice that will keep them chilled and at 40°F or below at all times.[42]

Refrigerating foods for storage is another key aspect of keeping them chilled and inhibiting the growth and reproduction of pathogenic microbes. With the exception of the *Listeria* bacterium, cold temperatures will *slow down* microbes' ability to multiply to dangerous levels; note that chilling does not kill them or completely stop their growth. To ensure that the growth of microbes on foods is controlled, refrigerator temperatures should be set at or below 40°F. The only way to know if the temperature in a refrigerator or freezer is low enough is to use a thermometer. Refrigerator and freezer thermometers can be purchased for several dollars at most grocery and discount stores, yet fewer than 65 percent of Americans

danger zone The range of temperatures between 40°F and 140°F at which foodborne bacteria will multiply most rapidly. Room temperature falls within the danger zone.

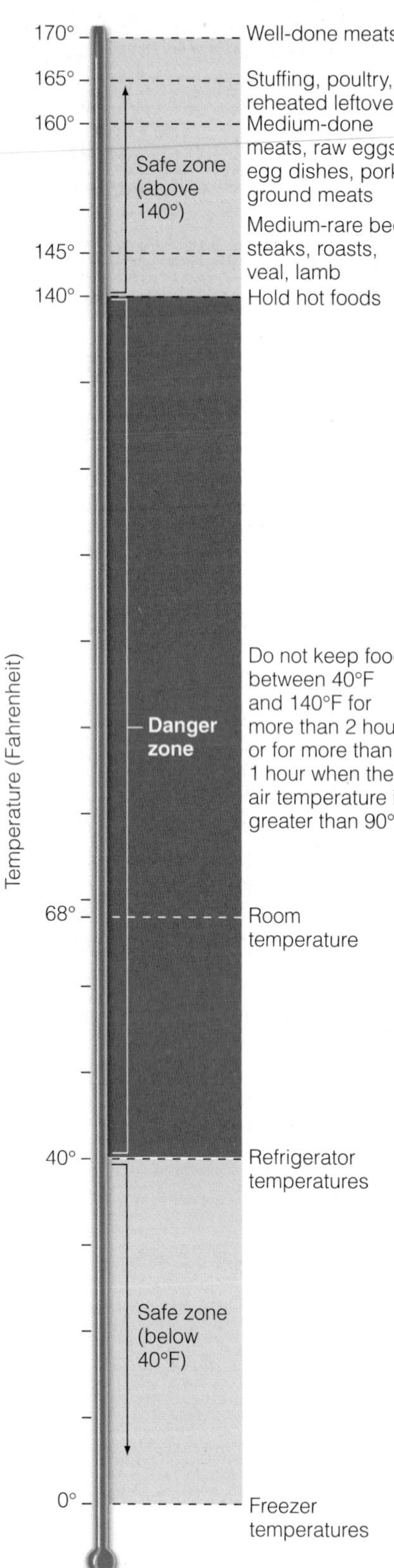

▲ **Figure 20.7 The Danger Zone**
Bacteria multiply rapidly in the "danger zone," between temperatures of 40°F and 140°F.

use a refrigerator thermometer. An estimated 20 percent of Americans' refrigerators aren't cold enough to keep foods safe.[43]

The temperature for the freezer should be set at 0°F or below. Food will stay safe in the freezer indefinitely, though its quality may deteriorate. (For example, "freezer burn" may occur if frozen food is not tightly wrapped and gets exposed to air. Freezer burn causes the texture of food to change, as it dries out and accumulates ice crystals. This will result in a less pleasant taste and appearance, but it isn't harmful.) Most microbes become dormant and are unable to multiply when they are frozen, but they aren't destroyed. Therefore, when food is defrosted the microbes can multiply again under the right conditions.

Two hours is the critical time to remember. Perishables such as raw meat and poultry left out at room temperature (a temperature within the danger zone) for more than 2 hours will not be safe to eat. In temperatures above 90°F, such as in the kitchen in the summertime, foods shouldn't be left out at room temperature for more than 1 hour.[44] Leftovers should be refrigerated within 2 hours of being prepared. Large roasts and pots of soup or stews should be divided into smaller batches and placed in shallow pans in order to cool down more quickly in the refrigerator. If these items have been left in the danger zone for too long or have been mishandled, bacteria can not only grow, but also produce toxins that are heat resistant. These toxins won't be destroyed even if the food is cooked to a proper internal temperature, and could cause illness if consumed.[45]

Once food is refrigerated it shouldn't be held for more than a few days, even when kept at the proper temperature. The rule of thumb is that leftovers can be in the refrigerator at 40°F or below for no more than four days. Just as there are the "4Cs" of food safety, after *four* days in the refrigerator, leftovers are ready *for* disposal. Raw meats, poultry, and seafood can be kept for a maximum of two days in the refrigerator. A good food safety strategy is the acronym FIFO, which means "first in, first out." In other words, use food first that has been in the refrigerator the longest. Table 20.3 lists the storage times for various foods. If you are unsure about the safety of a food, remember this rhyme: *When in doubt, throw it out.*

Minimizing the risk for developing a foodborne illness requires a conscious effort to clean, cook, chill, and avoid cross-contamination to keep foods safe. Think about how many of these strategies you use in your own kitchen and use the Self-Assessment on page 752 to help identify areas in which you may need to improve your food safety habits.

Practice Food Safety While Traveling

Travelers should follow food safety procedures to reduce the risk of illness while traveling abroad. One type of *E. coli,* enterotoxigenic (*entero* = intestines, *toxi* = toxin, *genic* = forming) *E. coli,* is a common cause of **traveler's diarrhea.** Each year, up to 50 percent of international travelers have their trips interrupted by unpleasant intestinal side effects. Traveler's diarrhea is primarily caused by consuming contaminated food, water, or ice. People visiting countries where proper sanitation is in question, including some developing countries in Latin America, Africa, the Middle East, and Asia, are at a higher risk of contracting it.[46] See the Table Tips for suggestions on how to avoid traveler's diarrhea and other forms of foodborne disease while traveling.

THE TAKE-HOME MESSAGE Proper food handling and storage strategies, particularly cleaning, preventing cross-contamination, cooking to recommended temperatures, and chilling at recommended temperatures, can help reduce the risk of foodborne illness. Anything that comes in contact with foods, including hands,

TABLE 20.3 Safe Storage of Perishable Foods

Product	Storage Time After Purchase*	
For Raw Foods		
Poultry	1 or 2 days	
Beef, veal, pork, and lamb	3 to 5 days	
Ground meat and ground poultry	1 or 2 days	
Fresh variety meats (liver, tongue, brain, kidneys, heart, intestines)	1 or 2 days	
Cured ham, cook-before-eating	5 to 7 days	
Sausage from pork, beef, or turkey, uncooked	1 or 2 days	
Eggs	3 to 5 weeks	
	Unopened, After Purchase*	**After Opening***
For Processed Product Sealed at Plant		
Cooked poultry	3 to 4 days	3 to 4 days
Cooked sausage	3 to 4 days	3 to 4 days
Sausage, hard/dry, shelf-stable	6 weeks/pantry	3 weeks
Corned beef, uncooked, in pouch with pickling juices	5 to 7 days	3 to 4 days
Vacuum-packed dinners, commercial brand with USDA seal	2 weeks	3 to 4 days
Bacon	2 weeks	1 week
Hot dogs	2 weeks	1 week
Luncheon meat	2 weeks	3 to 5 days
Ham, fully cooked, whole	7 days	3 days
Ham, canned, labeled "keep refrigerated"	9 months	3 to 4 days
Ham, canned, shelf-stable	2 years/pantry	3 to 5 days
Canned meat and poultry, shelf-stable	2 to 5 years/pantry	3 to 4 days
Leftovers		3 to 4 days

*Based on refrigerator home storage (at 41°F or below) unless otherwise stated.

Source: Food Safety and Inspection Service. 2005. *Keep Foods Safe! Food Safety Basics.* Available at www.fsis.usda.gov/Fact_Sheets/Keep_Food_Safe_Food_Safety_Basics/index.asp.

should be thoroughly washed, and produce should always be washed before eating it. Fruits and vegetables need to be kept separate from raw meats, poultry, and fish, and from any utensils that touch them. Checking the internal temperature of cooked food with a food thermometer is the only accurate way to tell if it is safe to eat. Perishables should be properly and promptly chilled to minimize the growth of bacteria. Raw meat, poultry, and seafood should be used within two days. Leftovers that are refrigerated should be discarded after four days. Extra caution is needed when traveling abroad to avoid foodborne illness. Countries including those in Latin America, Africa, the Middle East, and Asia may have different standards for food and water safety than those in the United States.

TABLE TIPS

Avoiding Foodborne Illness While Traveling

If you are traveling abroad, look up the country you're visiting on the Centers for Disease Control's (CDC's) National Center for Infectious Diseases Travelers' Health Destination website at www.cdc.gov/travel/destinat.htm to find out about any specific health advisories for that area.

Do not eat raw or undercooked meat or seafood.

Do not consume raw fruits and vegetables unless you wash and peel them. Thoroughly cooked fruits and vegetables should be safe to eat.

Do not consume foods or beverages from street vendors or restaurants that appear to be unsanitary.

Do not drink tap water or use ice made from tap water unless it has been boiled first or treated with iodine or chlorine. Bottled water should be safe.

Do not consume unpasteurized milk or other unpasteurized dairy foods.

Source: Centers for Disease Control, Division of Bacterial and Mycotic Diseases. Updated 2004. *Travelers' Diarrhea.* Available at www.cdc.gov/ncidod/dbmd/diseaseinfo/travelersdiarrhea_g.htm.

traveler's diarrhea A common pathogen-induced intestinal disorder experienced by some travelers who visit areas with unsanitary conditions.

Self-Assessment

How Do Your Food Safety Habits Stack Up?

Take the following quiz to find out.

How Often Do You	Always	Sometimes	Never
Wash your hands before preparing food?			
Scrub your fruits and vegetables under cold, running water before eating them?			
Use an insulated pouch with an ice pack to carry your perishable lunches and snacks, such as meat-filled sandwiches and/or yogurt and cheese?			
Wash your hands after using the bathroom?			
Throw out refrigerated leftovers after four days?			
Chop raw vegetables on a clean chopping board rather than the one you just used for raw meat, fish, or poultry?			
Use a thermometer to determine if the meat or poultry you are cooking is done?			

Answer

If you answered "Always" to all of the above you are practicing superior food safety skills. If you didn't, there's more you can do to reduce your chances of contracting a foodborne illness.

How Is the Food Supply Protected?

The sources of our foods have changed dramatically over the years, and families rarely grow their own food or purchase it directly from a farm. Food from all over the country and the world is available in grocery stores. Keeping this vast and diverse food supply safe is the responsibility of farmers, food manufacturers, and several government agencies. In this section, we'll look at the food safety implications of our food system and the technologies available to expand and monitor our food supply. These include regulations as well as processes that occur from farm to table such as food preservation techniques, product dating, and irradiation. We'll start by looking at the government agencies that monitor our food supply, and then look at the contribution that food manufacturers make.

Several Government Agencies and Programs Protect the Food Supply

The current system for overseeing the safety of the food supply began in 1906 when Congress charged the USDA with responsibility for monitoring the safety of our nation's food. Today, several federal agencies share responsibility for food safety in the United States.[47] Table 20.4 lists these agencies and summarizes the roles they

TABLE 20.4 Agencies that Oversee the Food Supply

Agency	Responsible For
USDA Food Safety and Inspection Service (FSIS)	Ensuring safe and accurately labeled meat, poultry, and eggs
Food and Drug Administration (FDA)	Ensuring the safety of all other foods besides meat, poultry, and eggs
Environmental Protection Agency (EPA)	Protecting you and the environment from harmful pesticides
Animal and Plant Health Inspection Service (APHIS)	Protecting against plant and animal pests and disease

Source: Food and Drug Administration and the U.S. Department of Agriculture. 2000. *A Description of the U.S. Food Safety System*. Available at www.fsis.usda.gov/OA/codex/system.htm.

each play in safeguarding foods. The **Food Safety Initiative (FSI),** begun in 1997, coordinates the research, inspection, outbreak response, and educational activities of the various government agencies. The goal of the FSI is to make sure that government agencies work collaboratively. Rates of foodborne illness caused by several pathogens including *Shigella, Yersinia*, STEC (Shiga toxin–producing *E. coli*), *E. coli* O157:H7, *Campylobacter*, and *Listeria* were approximately 25 percent lower in 2010 than they were in 1999, a trend likely attributable to the joint efforts of these organizations.[48]

An example of collaboration among government agencies is FoodNet (www.cdc.gov/foodnet), which is a combined effort among the Centers for Disease Control and Prevention (CDC), the United States Department of Agriculture (USDA), the Food and Drug Administration (FDA), and ten state health departments. The program consists of active surveillance for foodborne diseases and related studies designed to help public health officials understand the epidemiology of foodborne diseases in the United States. The objectives of the program include determining the burden of foodborne illness in the United States, monitoring trends over time, assessing the incidence of foodborne illness and its relation to specific foods and settings, and developing interventions to reduce the overall burden of foodborne illness.

The CDC coordinates another program called PulseNet (www.cdc.gov/pulsenet), which is a national network of public health and food regulatory agency laboratories, including those at the CDC, USDA/FSIS, and the FDA, designed to identify and contain foodborne illness outbreaks. PulseNet participants perform molecular subtyping called **DNA fingerprinting** on foodborne disease–causing bacteria. DNA fingerprinting can be used to identify strains of organisms such as *Escherichia coli* O157:H7 at the DNA level. These "fingerprints" are submitted electronically to a database at the CDC and the information is available on demand to participants. Finding similar strains of a bacterium in both a person and a food suggests a common source and potential connection.[49] If similar patterns emerge at the same time in different states, this could indicate a potential outbreak. Once a suspicious foodborne illness outbreak is reported, several government agencies work together to contain the disease.

The *E. coli* outbreak in spinach that occurred in the fall of 2006 is one example of how multiple government agencies work together to identify and contain an outbreak. The CDC, through its monitoring and surveillance programs, detected an outbreak of illness due to *E. coli* O157:H7 and immediately alerted the FDA. DNA fingerprinting was used by PulseNet to determine that all infected individuals had consumed the same strain of *E. coli*, and to trace the strain to bagged raw spinach grown in California. The fingerprinting also allowed the agencies to link

Food Safety Initiative (FSI) Coordinates the research, surveillance, inspection, outbreak response, and educational activities of the various government agencies that work together to safeguard food.

DNA fingerprinting A technique in which bacterial DNA "gene patterns" (or "fingerprints") are detected and analyzed to distinguish between different strains of a bacterium.

the tainted food to reported illnesses in 26 states. Once the source of the outbreak was confirmed, the CDC issued an official health alert about the outbreak, and the FDA advised consumers to stop eating raw spinach. Before the outbreak was over, more than 200 people were infected, and more than half of them were hospitalized. Three individuals died and 31 developed hemolytic uremic syndrome from the outbreak. However, through the collaborative efforts and swift action of these federal and state agencies, the outbreak was contained in a short period of time and its impact was minimized.[50]

In an effort to improve the safety of the U.S. food supply, the FDA published its Food Protection Plan in November 2007 as a forward-oriented concept for identifying potential hazards before they result in an outbreak.[51] Creation of the plan was prompted by changes in demographic and consumption patterns, the globalization of the food supply, and the emergence of new threats and communication issues. The plan has a three-pronged approach that includes prevention, intervention, and response, and addresses the product life cycle in an attempt to prevent contaminated food from ever reaching consumers.

The FDA and USDA have adopted a food safety program called Hazard Analysis and Critical Control Points (HACCP) that is used to identify and control foodborne hazards that may occur in all stages of the food production process.[52] The HACCP approach was first conceived in the 1960s when the U.S. National Aeronautics and Space Administration (NASA) asked a private food manufacturer to design the foods for space flights. HACCP includes seven principles that focus on the analysis of potential hazards associated with foods and the identification of critical control points in the production of a food so that preventive measures can be put in place to minimize risks. For example, procedures for monitoring temperatures throughout a food's production need to be in place. Manufacturers also apply food preservation techniques to some foods to make them safer for consumers. These techniques will be discussed later in the chapter.

Once food arrives at retail and food service establishments such as grocery stores and restaurants, retailers must ensure that they are in compliance with FDA regulations. The Food Code is a reference document published by the FDA that local, state, and federal regulators use as a model for the development of their own food safety rules and to be consistent with national food regulatory policy. The Food Code provides practical, science-based guidance, including HACCP guidelines, and provisions to help purveyors minimize foodborne illness.[53]

Consumer food safety education is available through the Partnership for Food Safety Education (PFSE), a program designed to educate the public about safe food handling after purchase. Fight BAC! is one of the many consumer campaigns run by this program and is specifically geared toward educating children on food safety issues.

From the farmer to the consumer, everyone involved in the production and preparation of food plays a role in making sure the food we eat is safe. The **farm-to-table continuum** is a visual tool that shows how farmers, food manufacturers, transporters of food, retailers, and you, the consumer, can help ensure a safe food supply. **Figure 20.8** shows the steps in this continuum.

Food Manufacturers Use Preservation Techniques to Destroy Contaminants

In addition to government efforts to help prevent foodborne illness, food manufacturers also work to safeguard food. Food processing, preservation techniques, and irradiation help destroy contaminants and/or maintain a food's color and freshness.

farm-to-table continuum Illustrates the roles that farmers, food manufacturers, food transporters, retailers, and consumers play in ensuring that the food supply, from the farm to the plate, remains safe.

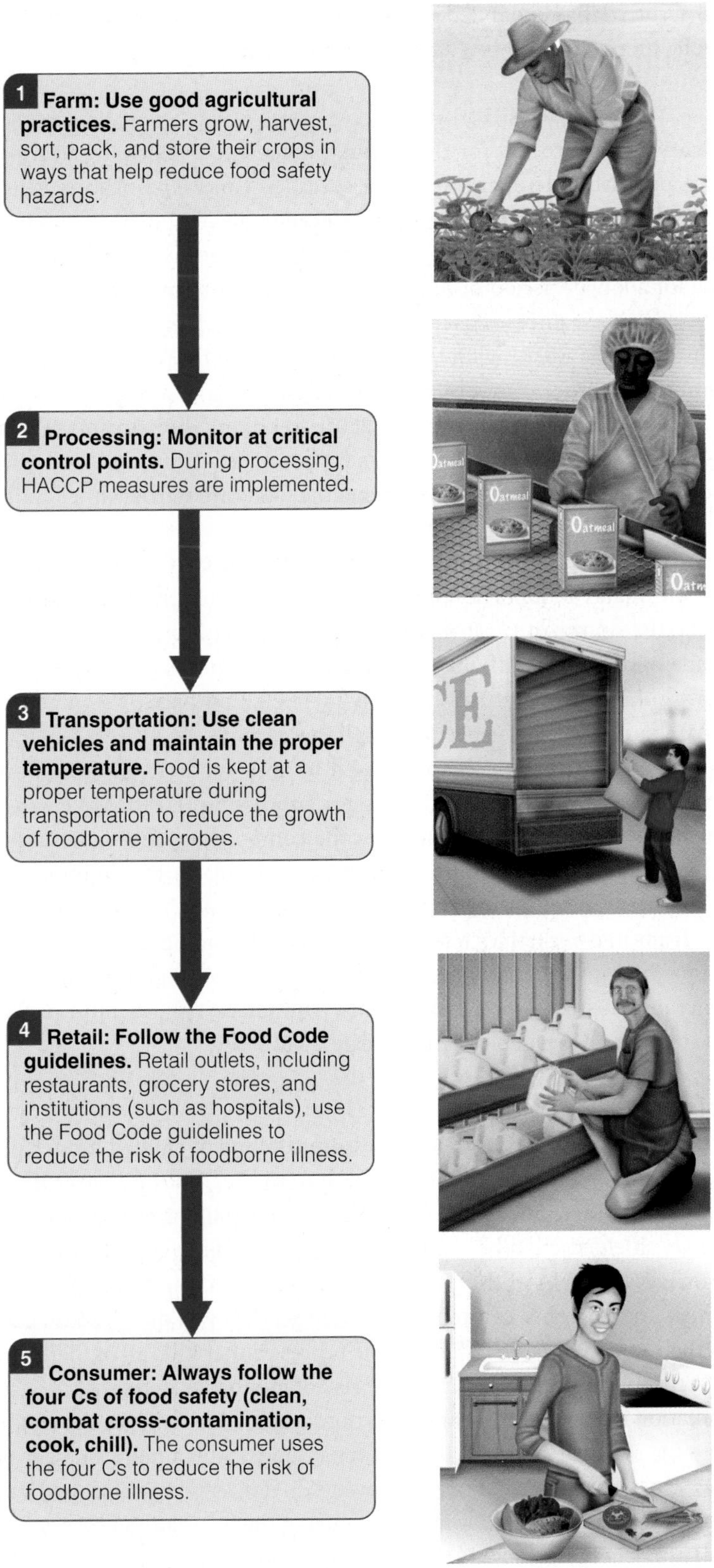

1 Farm: Use good agricultural practices. Farmers grow, harvest, sort, pack, and store their crops in ways that help reduce food safety hazards.

2 Processing: Monitor at critical control points. During processing, HACCP measures are implemented.

3 Transportation: Use clean vehicles and maintain the proper temperature. Food is kept at a proper temperature during transportation to reduce the growth of foodborne microbes.

4 Retail: Follow the Food Code guidelines. Retail outlets, including restaurants, grocery stores, and institutions (such as hospitals), use the Food Code guidelines to reduce the risk of foodborne illness.

5 Consumer: Always follow the four Cs of food safety (clean, combat cross-contamination, cook, chill). The consumer uses the four Cs to reduce the risk of foodborne illness.

◂ Figure 20.8 The Farm-to-Table Continuum Every step in the farm-to-table continuum plays an important role in reducing microbes and the spread of foodborne illness.

Product dating and coding can help determine if a food is still safe to eat and can be useful when identifying recalled products.

Food preservation methods, some of which have been in use for thousands of years, include heating, canning, pickling, salting, drying, and freezing, and food manufacturers and consumers continue to use these methods to keep foods safe. At the same time, manufacturers' use of newer techniques such as irradiation and

food preservation The treatment of foods to reduce deterioration and spoilage, and help prevent the multiplication of pathogens that can cause foodborne illness.

chemical additives has expanded as consumers demand fast and convenient foods, new flavors, increased shelf life, and improved textures.

Pasteurization and Canning

Pasteurization is a process for destroying pathogenic bacteria by heating liquid foods to a prescribed temperature for a specified time. The process kills *E. coli* O157:H7, *Salmonella,* and *Listeria monocytogenes,* all of which can be present in raw milk. Pasteurization improves the quality of dairy products and keeps all products fresh for a longer period of time. In addition to dairy products, pasteurization is required for some juices like fresh apple juice and other foods. Unpasteurized juices must display a warning on the label to alert consumers.[54]

Canning is a process in which foods are packed into airtight containers and then heated to temperatures of 240°F to 250°F to kill microorganisms. The amount of exposure time to heat varies by the type of food, its acidity, and its density. Processing conditions are chosen to ensure that the foods are sterile while retaining the most nutrients.[55]

Commercial canning is regulated by the FDA and HACCP procedures, which virtually eliminates foodborne illness. However, improperly home-canned products can be the source of *Clostridium botulinum,* a foodborne bacterium that can survive in environments without air and that creates **spores** that are not destroyed at normal cooking temperatures (refer to Table 20.2 on page 749). A temperature higher than boiling (212°F) is needed to kill these spores.[56]

Two newer preservation methods used to keep foods fresh are modified atmosphere packing (MAP) and high-pressure processing (HPP). **MAP** is a process during which the manufacturer modifies the composition of the air surrounding the food in a package. The modification process decreases the amount of oxygen present in order to delay the decay of fresh produce. MAP is used in foods such as packaged fruits and vegetables to extend their shelf life and preserve their quality.[57] **HPP** is a method in which foods are exposed to pulses of high pressure, which destroys microorganisms. Foods such as jams, fruit juices, fish, vacuum-packed meat products, fruits, and vegetables can be treated with HPP.[58]

Irradiation

Similar to pasteurization of milk and pressure cooking of canned foods, foods can be treated with ionizing radiation to kill pathogenic bacteria and parasites. During the process of **irradiation,** foods are subjected to a radiant energy source within a protective, shielded chamber called an *irradiator.* The energy from the radiant waves damages the DNA of the pathogens, causing defects in their genetic instructions. Unless the microbes can repair the damage, they will die. Because pathogens differ in their sensitivity to irradiation, the process either kills all of them or greatly reduces their numbers, thus reducing the risk of foodborne disease.[59]

Irradiation is a cold process and does not significantly increase the temperature or change the physical characteristics of most foods, which helps prevent nutrient loss. Also, just as foods cooked in a microwave do not retain microwaves, irradiated foods do not retain the energy waves used during the irradiation process.[60] Most of the irradiating energy passes through the food and the packaging without leaving any residue behind.[61]

Irradiation destroys bacteria such as *Campylobacter, E. coli* O157:H7, and *Salmonella* and helps control insects and parasites.[62] It does not destroy viruses, such as norovirus and hepatitis A, or the prion particles associated with mad cow disease (BSE). The nucleic acid of viruses is too small to be destroyed and prions do not have nucleic acid, which makes them resistant to irradiation at the doses approved by the FDA for foods. Irradiation can also stop the ripening process in some fruits

pasteurization The process of heating liquids or food at high temperatures to destroy foodborne pathogens.

canning The process of packing food in airtight containers and heating them to a temperature high enough to kill bacteria.

spores Hardy reproductive structures that are produced by certain bacteria and fungi.

modified atmosphere packaging (MAP) A food preservation technique that changes the composition of the air surrounding the food in a package to extend its shelf life.

high-pressure processing (HPP) A method used to pasteurize foods by exposing the items to pulses of high pressure, which destroys the microorganisms that are present.

irradiation A process in which foods are placed in a shielded chamber, called an *irradiator,* and subjected to a radiant energy source. This kills specific pathogens in food by breaking up the cells' DNA.

and vegetables and reduce the number of food spoilage bacteria. Irradiated strawberries can last up to three weeks in the refrigerator, compared with only a few days for untreated berries.[63]

Food irradiation has been studied and tested for more than 50 years and remains the most researched food-related technology ever approved in the United States.[64] Irradiation has been used for years to sterilize surgical instruments and implants and to destroy disease-promoting microbes in foods served to hospital patients who have weakened immune systems. However, the use of irradiation in foods is not widespread due to consumer concerns and the expense of building the facilities.[65]

Since 1986, all irradiated products must carry the international "radura" symbol, along with the phrase "treated by irradiation" or "treated with radiation" on the package (**Figure 20.9**). If a product such as sausage contains irradiated meat or poultry, these items must be listed as "irradiated pork" or "irradiated chicken" on the food label.[66] A label is not required if a minor ingredient, such as a spice, has been irradiated and used in the product.

Irradiation cannot be used with all foods. It causes undesirable flavor changes in dairy products, egg whites tend to become milky and liquid, fatty meats may develop an odor, and it causes tissue softening in some fruits such as peaches, nectarines, and grapefruits. Foods that are currently approved for irradiation in the United States include fruits and vegetables, herbs and spices, fresh meat, pork, and poultry, wheat flour, and white potatoes.[67]

Although irradiation has many advantages, it doesn't guarantee that a food is free from all pathogens, and some foods such as steak tartare (a dish that contains raw ground beef) should still not be eaten raw, even if they have been irradiated. Irradiation complements but does not replace the need for proper food handling practices by food growers, processors, and consumers.

Product Dating Can Help Determine Peak Quality

Food product expiration dates on almost all food products, with the exception of certain poultry, baby food products, and infant formulas, are provided voluntarily by food manufacturers and are not required by federal law. However, currently more than 20 states require some form of mandatory food product dating.

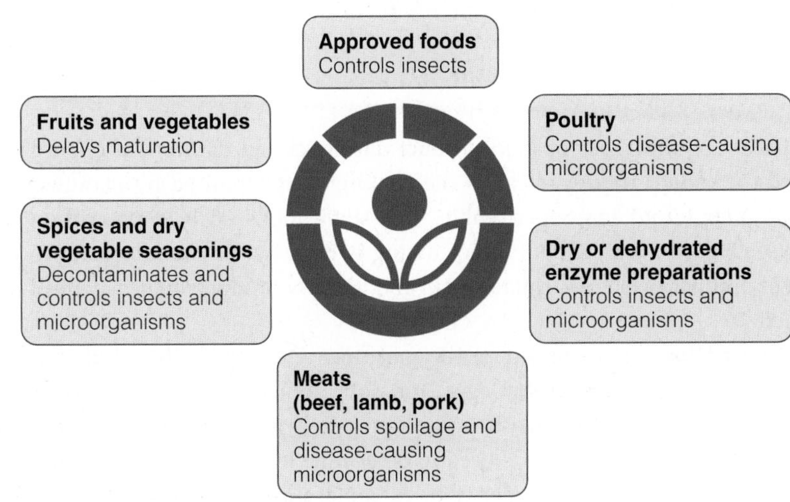

▲ **Figure 20.9 FDA-Approved Uses of Irradiation**
The international radura symbol must appear on all irradiated foods.

a Closed food product dating refers to the coded packing numbers that you often see on nonperishable foods such as canned soups.

b Open food product dating must contain a calendar date and is used on perishable food items along with information on how to use the date.

▲ **Figure 20.10 Closed and Open Food Product Dating**

There are two types of food product dating: closed dating and open dating. **Closed** (or **coded**) **dating** refers to the packing numbers used by manufacturers that are often found on nonperishable, shelf-stable foods, such as cans of soup and fruit (see **Figure 20.10**). This type of dating is used by the manufacturer to keep track of product inventory, rotate stock, and identify products that may need to be recalled.[68]

Open dating is more useful for the consumer and is typically found on perishable items such as meat, poultry, eggs, and dairy foods. Open dating must include at least a month and a day, and if the product is shelf-stable or frozen, the year must also be included. Open dating is used to determine if a product is at its peak quality but does not refer to food safety. For example, a carton of yogurt that has been mishandled and not refrigerated for several hours may be unsafe to eat even though the date on the container hasn't passed.

closed or **"coded" dating** Refers to the packing numbers that are decodable only by manufacturers and are often found on nonperishable, shelf-stable foods.

open dating Typically found on perishable items such as meat, poultry, eggs, and dairy foods; must contain a calendar date.

Open-dated products must also contain a phrase next to the date that tells the consumer how to interpret it. If there is "Sell By" next to the date, the product should be purchased on or before that date. This date takes into consideration additional time for storage and use at home, so if the food is bought by the "Sell By" date it can still be eaten at a later date. If there is "Best if Used By" or "Use By" next to it, the date shows how long the manufacturer thinks a food will be of optimal quality. This does not necessarily mean that the product should not be used after the suggested date, as these dates refer to product quality, not safety.[69]

The Safety of the Water Supply Is Regulated

The Environmental Protection Agency (EPA) is the government body responsible for ensuring that consumers have a safe water supply; the Safe Drinking Water Act (SWDA) is the principal federal statute that affords that protection. Health-based standards are set by the EPA to protect the nation's drinking water from unsafe amounts of contaminants. In most cases the EPA delegates to the states responsibility for ensuring that the health standards are met. Every year each state must produce an annual report on whether water systems within the state are meeting drinking water standards. The EPA collects and stores this information in a database called the Safe Drinking Water Information System (SDWIS). If there is an immediate threat to your health due to the violation of a drinking water standard, SDWA requires that your water agency notify you promptly through the media.[70, 71]

THE TAKE-HOME MESSAGE Several government agencies, including the FDA and USDA, share responsibility for food safety in the United States. HACCP is a food safety program used by the FDA, the USDA, and the food industry to identify and control hazards that may occur in any part of the food system. Manufacturers may use other techniques such as pasteurization, canning, and irradiation to preserve food and destroy contamination. The FDA has approved the use of irradiation in the U.S. food supply even though some consumers have concerns about the safety of irradiated foods.

What Role Do Food Additives, Hormones, Antibiotics, and Pesticides Play in Food Production and Safety?

Food manufacturers use various types of **food additives** for many different reasons. Commonly used additives include preservatives (such as antioxidants and sulfites), nutrients, and flavor enhancers (such as MSG). Food producers also give food-producing animals hormones and antibiotics to improve the health and food yield of these animals, but they may cause unintentional side effects in consumers.[72] Other food producers use pesticides on plants to boost production.

Preservatives Prevent Spoilage and Increase Shelf Life

Most food additives are **preservatives** that are added to foods to prevent spoilage (usually by destroying microbes) and increase shelf life. The most common antimicrobial preservatives are salt and sugar. Salt has been used for centuries, particularly in meat and fish, to create a dry environment in which bacteria cannot multiply. Most (65 percent) of the salt consumed in the United States comes from

food additives Substances added to food that affect its quality, flavor, freshness, and/or safety.

preservatives Substances that extend the shelf life of a product by retarding chemical, physical, or microbiological changes.

processed and prepared foods that you find in grocery and convenience stores.[73] Sugar is used for the same preserving effect in products such as canned and frozen fruits and condiments.

Nitrites and **nitrates** are ionic salts, chemical compounds that result from the bonding of a positively charged ion to a negatively charged ion, that are added to foods to prevent microbial growth and are used in cured meats such as hot dogs and hams to prevent the growth of *Clostridium botulinum*. These are the chemicals that give these foods their pink color. The use of these salts has been controversial due to the fact that they form carcinogenic nitrosamines in the digestive tract of animals.[74]

The addition of antioxidants to foods can prevent an off taste or off color in a product that's vulnerable to damage by oxidation. Currently two vitamins are approved for use as food additives due to their actions as antioxidants: vitamin E and vitamin C. Vitamin E is added to oils and cereals to prevent the fats in them from becoming rancid, and vitamin C is often added to cut fruit to prevent premature browning. Butylated hydroxyanisole (BHA) and butylated hydroxytoluene (BHT) are two chemical antioxidants that are also used as preservatives. In some but not all experimental trials with animals, feeding high amounts of BHT and BHA caused increased risk of some cancers, but in other studies feeding animals high amounts of BHT and BHA caused decreased risk of some cancers.[75] There is little evidence to suggest that the low doses of BHT and BHA used as preservatives are harmful for humans, and these ingredients are on the FDA's **GRAS (generally recognized as safe)** list.

Sulfites are a group of antioxidants that are used as preservatives to help prevent the oxidation and browning of some foods and to inhibit the growth of microbes.[76] Sulfites are often found in dried fruits and vegetables, packaged and prepared potatoes, wine, beer, bottled lemon and lime juice, and pickled foods.[77]

For most people sulfites pose no risk, but there are people who experience adverse reactions. Individuals who are sensitive to sulfites may experience symptoms ranging from chest tightness, difficulty breathing, and hives to the more serious and potentially fatal anaphylactic shock. Studies suggest that the sulfur dioxide in the sulfites appears to cause these symptoms.[78] People at highest risk for negative reactions include people who suffer from asthma, those who are taking steroids, and those who have extremely sensitive airways.

Due to the risk of adverse reactions in people who are sulfite sensitive, the FDA has prohibited the use of sulfites on fruits and vegetables that are served raw, such as in a salad bar, or are advertised as "fresh." The FDA requires that foods containing sulfite additives or ingredients treated with sulfites must declare "added sulfites" in the ingredients list on the label. Food sold in bulk, such as dried fruit treated with sulfites, must display the ingredients on a sign near the food. Because sulfites destroy the B vitamin thiamin, the FDA prohibits their use in enriched grain products and other foods that are good sources of the vitamin.[79]

nitrites and **nitrates** Substances that can be added to foods to function as a preservative and to give meats such as hot dogs and luncheon meats a pink color.

generally recognized as safe (GRAS) A designation given by the FDA to substances intentionally added to food, indicating that the substance is considered safe by experts and is exempted from further testing.

sulfites Preservatives used to help prevent foods from turning brown and to inhibit the growth of microbes. Often used in wine and dried fruit products.

Additives Are Used to Enhance Food Quality and Appeal

Food manufacturers also use additives to increase the quality or appeal of their products. Some additives improve food texture and consistency. Others enhance the nutrient content, color, or flavor of food. Table 20.5 lists some commonly used non-perservative additives and their functions in foods.

Additives to Enhance Texture and Consistency

Food additives can enhance the texture and consistency of food in a number of ways. Gums and pectins are used to improve consistency and texture and are often added to thicken yogurts and puddings. Emulsifiers improve the stability, consistency, and homogeneity of high-fat products like mayonnaise and ice cream. Lecithin is an example of an emulsifier that is added to some salad dressings. Leavening agents such as yeast or baking powder are added to breads to incorporate gases into dough that cause them to rise. Anti-caking agents such as sodium aluminosilicate and calcium carbonate prevent products like powdered sugar that are crystalline in nature from absorbing moisture and lumping. Humectants such as propylene glycol are added to increase moisture in products so that they stay fresh.

Additives to Improve Nutrient Content

Additives can be used to enhance a product's nutritional content, such as when refined grains are enriched with added B vitamins (folic acid, thiamin, niacin, and riboflavin) and iron. In some cases, such additions are mandated. This was the case in 1996, when the FDA published regulations requiring the addition of folic acid to enriched breads, cereal, and other grain products in order to help decrease the risk of neural tube defects in newborns.

Additives to Improve Visual Appeal

Additives can also enhance the color of foods. There are two main categories that make up the FDA's list of permitted colors. "Certifiable" color additives are man-made and are derived primarily from petroleum and coal sources. You can recognize these types of additives by the following prefixes: FD&C, D&C, or Ext. An example is FD&C Yellow, which is often found in cereals and baked goods. The second main category of color additives is obtained largely from plant, animal, or mineral sources. Examples include caramel color and grape color extract.

Adverse physical or allergic reactions to color additives are rare, although FD&C Yellow No. 5 may cause itching and hives in some people. This additive is found in beverages, desserts, and processed vegetables and is required to be listed on food labels.

MSG to Enhance Flavor

Monosodium glutamate (MSG) is the sodium salt of glutamic acid, a nonessential amino acid, and is often used as a flavor enhancer in Asian foods, canned vegetables and soups, and processed meats. Consumers can buy it in a form that is similar in texture to salt. Although it doesn't have a strong taste of its own, it enhances sweet, salty, sour, and bitter tastes.

monosodium glutamate (MSG) The sodium salt of glutamic acid, used as a flavor enhancer.

TABLE 20.5 Commonly Used Food Additives

Additive(s)	Function(s)	Found In
Alginates, carrageenan, glyceride, guar gum, lecithin, mono- and diglycerides, methyl cellulose, pectin, sodium aluminosilicate	Impart/maintain desired consistency	Baked goods, cake mixes, coconut, ice cream, processed cheese, salad dressings, table salt
Ascorbic acid (vitamin C), calcium carbonate, folic acid, thiamine (B_1), iron, niacin, pyridoxine (B_6), riboflavin (B_2), vitamins A and D, zinc oxide	Improve/maintain nutritive value	Biscuits, bread, breakfast cereals, desserts, flour, gelatin, iodized margarine, milk, pasta, salt
Ascorbic acid, benzoates, butylated hydroxyanisole (BHA), butylated hydroxytoluene (BHT), citric acid, propionic acid and its salts, sodium nitrite	Maintain palatability and wholesomeness	Bread, cake mixes, cheese, crackers, frozen and dried fruit, lard, margarine, meat, potato chips
Citric acid, fumaric acid, lactic acid, phosphoric acid, sodium bicarbonate, tartrates, yeast	Produce light texture and control acidity/alkalinity	Butter, cakes, cookies, chocolates, crackers, quick breads, soft drinks
Annatto, aspartame, caramel, cloves, FD&C Red No. 40, FD&C Blue No. 1, fructose, ginger, limonene, MSG, saccharin, turmeric	Enhance flavor or provide desired color	Baked goods, cheeses, confections, gum, spice cake, gingerbread, jams, soft drinks, soup, yogurt

Source: FDA. n.d. *Food Additives Status List*. Available at www.fda.gov/food/foodingredientspackaging/foodadditives/foodadditivelistings/ucm091048.htm.

After an extensive review, the FDA classified MSG as GRAS and confirmed that MSG is safe to consume in the amounts typically used in processed foods and cooking (a typical meal that contains MSG has less than 0.5 gram). However, when consumed in large quantities such as 3 or more grams at a time, it may cause short-term reactions in people who are sensitive to it.[80] These reactions, which are called the **MSG symptom complex,** can include numbness, a burning sensation, facial pressure or tightness, chest pain, rapid heart beat, and drowsiness. In addition, people with asthma may have difficulty breathing after consuming MSG. For these reasons, the FDA requires that all foods containing MSG declare this ingredient on the food label.

Food Additives Are Closely Regulated by the FDA

Food additives are under strict regulation by the FDA, with consumer safety a top priority. The Federal Food, Drug and Cosmetic Act of 1938 gave the FDA authority to regulate food and food ingredients, including the use of food additives. The 1958 Food Additives Amendment further mandated that manufacturers document a food additive's safety and obtain FDA approval before using it in a food.[81]

Two categories of food additives were exempted from this amendment. The first category includes substances that were known to be safe before 1958 and were given **prior-sanctioned** status. For example, because nitrates were used to preserve meats before 1958, they have prior-sanctioned status, but *only* for their use in meats. They can't be used in other foods, such as vegetables, without FDA approval.[82] The second category includes substances that have a long history of being safe for consumption, such as salt, sugar, and spices, or have extensive research documenting that they are safe to consume, such as vitamins and MSG. These additives are exempt from FDA approval because they are "generally recognized as safe" (GRAS).[83]

The FDA continually monitors both prior-sanctioned additives and those with GRAS status to ensure that current research continues to support their safety. To remain on the GRAS list, an additive must not have been found to be carcinogenic in animals or humans. The 1958 Food Additive Amendment also included the **DeLaney Clause,** which was created to protect consumers from additives found to be carcinogenic. The clause states that no substances that have been shown to cause cancer in animals or humans at any dosage may be added to foods. However, with the present increases in technology and the ability to detect substances at very low levels, the clause is considered outdated. To address this issue the FDA deems additives safe if lifetime use presents no more than a one-in-a-million risk of cancer in human beings. If an additive is suddenly called into question, the FDA can prohibit its use or require that the food manufacturer conduct additional studies to ensure its safety.[84]

Even with these safeguards in place, some additives, such as MSG and sulfites, may cause adverse reactions in some people, and should be avoided by those who are sensitive to them.

Some Food Additives Are Unintentional

The food additives discussed in the preceding sections are all **intentional food additives** used to improve the quality of food products. However, **unintentional food additives** may sometimes be indirectly added to a food. For example, very small amounts of substances used during packaging or processing may inadvertently end up in the food. The safety of packaging must therefore be determined by manufacturers to ensure that packing substances aren't harmful to the consumer. Unintentional additives may also include chemicals from processing or traces of

MSG symptom complex A series of reactions such as numbness, burning sensation, facial pressure or tightness, chest pain, rapid heart beat, and drowsiness that can occur in some individuals after consuming MSG.

prior-sanctioned Substances that the FDA had determined were safe for use in foods prior to the 1958 Food Additives Amendment.

DeLaney Clause Clause in the Food Additives Amendment mandating that additives shown to cause cancer at any level must be removed from the marketplace.

intentional food additives Substances added intentionally to foods to improve food quality.

unintentional food additives Substances that enter into foods unintentionally during manufacturing or processing.

compounds provided to food-producing animals. For example, dioxins used during the manufacture of bleached paper such as coffee filters may end up in coffee and other foods and beverages. Dioxins can accumulate in the food chain and are carcinogenic to animals. The FDA requires that dioxin levels in products be so low as to present no health risks to people.[85]

Hormones and Antibiotics Are Provided to Food-Producing Animals to Enhance the Food Supply

Hormones and antiobiotics are two classes of compounds that are sometimes used to improve the health or output of food-producing animals. The use of these substances is intentional but changes in the final food product due to their presence are not and are a subject of consumer controversy and concern.

Bovine Growth Hormone

Bovine growth hormone (BGH), also known as bovine somatotropin, is produced naturally by cows. Some dairy farmers and ranchers treat their cattle with the naturally occurring form of BGH in order to produce animals that are leaner and produce more milk. Scientists can also produce a synthetic version of the hormone, **recombinant bovine somatotropin (rbST),** and cows injected with this form can produce up to 25 percent more milk than untreated cows.[86]

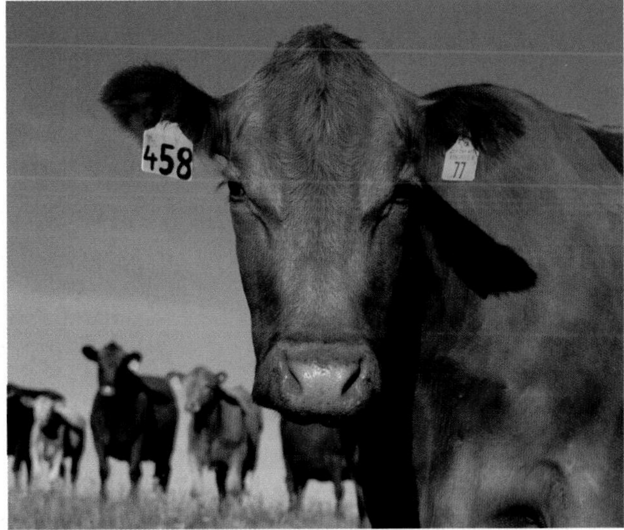

Natural bovine growth hormone or its synthetic version, are sometimes injected into cows to increase milk production.

Consumer groups and Health Canada (the FDA equivalent in Canada) have questioned the long-term safety of rbST. Traces of both the synthetic and natural form of BGH remain in the meat and milk of cows. Also of concern is that milk from rBGH-treated cows has higher levels of IGF-1, a hormone that normally helps some types of cells to grow.[87] The FDA's extensive review of the safety of the use of rbST has found no evidence that it poses any long-term health threat to humans.[88] However, consumer pressure due to concerns over the long-term safety of rbST has led to a decrease in the percent of milk produced in the United States from cows treated with rbST.

Other steroid hormones are sometimes used to increase the amount of weight that cattle gain and the amount of meat they produce, and to increase milk production in dairy cows. The FDA has approved the use of these hormones in cattle, as they have been shown to be safe at their approved level of use and not a health concern to consumers.[89]

Antibiotics

Antibiotics are sometimes given to livestock and are generally used for three purposes: (1) to treat animals that are sick; (2) to prevent disease; and (3) to promote growth. When antibiotics are used properly in the treatment of sick animals and to prevent the spread of disease they are used for a relatively short period of time. However, when used to promote growth and increase the amount of meat and milk produced, they are used over a long period of time. Low-dose antibiotics are routinely put in animal feed to stimulate weight gain, but the long-term use can contribute to the creation of **antibiotic-resistant bacteria.**[90]

Pathogenic bacteria such as *Campylobacter, E. coli* O157:H7, and *Salmonella* are commonly found in the gastrointestinal tracts of animals without making them sick. However, the long-term use of antibiotics in animals can result in antibiotic-resistant bacteria strains in their intestinal tracts. This practice poses a human

bovine growth hormone (BGH) A hormone that is essential for normal growth and development in cattle.

recombinant bovine somatotropin (rbST) A synthetically made hormone identical to a cow's natural growth hormone, somatotropin, that stimulates milk production. Also known as rbGH (recombinant bovine growth hormone).

antibiotics Drugs that kill or slow the growth of bacteria.

antibiotic-resistant bacteria Bacteria that have developed a resistance to an antibiotic such that they are no longer affected by antibiotic medication.

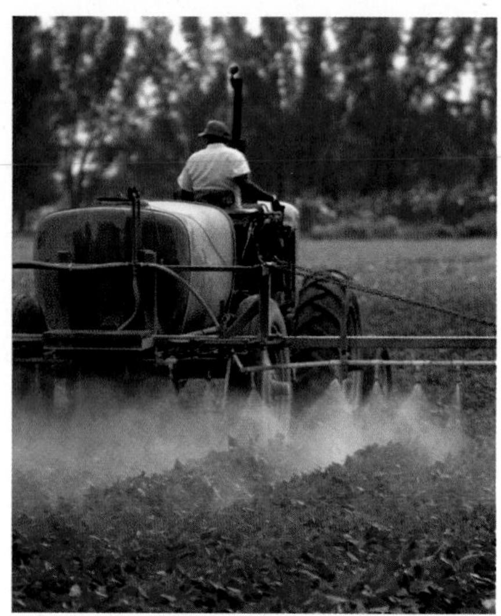

Farmers use pesticides on food crops to diminish the damage from pests.

health risk if a person contracts a foodborne infection from the resistant bacteria and is treated with the same antibiotic used to treat the animals. The antibiotic will not be effective in treating the illness because resistance to the medicine has developed through its chronic use in the animals.

An example of antibiotic resistance posing a risk to human health occurred as a result of the discovery that the antibiotic fluoroquinolone could be used to successfully treat *Campylobacter,* which is commonly found in chickens. In 1995 the antibiotic began to be used regularly in poultry as a treatment and as a preventive. After a period of chronic use, the bacteria developed a resistance to the medicine. This resulted in *Campylobacter*-induced foodborne illness in humans whose infections were resistant to treatments with fluoroquinolone.[91]

The chronic intake of antibiotics can create additional strains of organisms that are resistant and cause the "overgrowth" of other bacteria in the animal. These surviving bacteria can flourish and multiply to high levels and treatment with typical antibiotics to control these surviving, resistant bacteria may be unsuccessful. This perpetuates the need for a higher dose of medication and/or a longer treatment period.

Pesticides Are Widely Used in Agriculture to Improve Food Production

Pesticides are used to prevent plant disease and insect infestations and can be applied to crops in the fields or after harvest. These chemicals play an important role in food production by controlling threats to the food supply. Despite the beneficial role that they play in assuring consumers a wide variety of foods, concerns about pesticides in food persist. A year-long study in 1998 of the role of pesticides in U.S. agriculture concluded that a variety of pesticide technologies, including chemical methods, can be used to produce safe, productive, and profitable crops.[92]

Types of Pesticides

Several different types of pests can diminish or destroy crop yields, including weeds, insects, microorganisms (bacteria, viruses), fungi (mold), and rodents (rats and mice). **Herbicides** are a type of pesticide used to kill weeds, **insecticides** kill insects, **antimicrobials** are used on microorganisms, **fungicides** are used to destroy mold, and **rodenticides** poison and kill rodents. Each one of these pesticides is designed to target and destroy a specific type of pest.

Pesticides can be biologically or chemically based. Biologically based pesticides, such as biopesticides and sex pheromones, use material from animals, plants, bacteria, and some minerals and are typically less toxic than chemical pesticides.[93] Unlike chemical pesticides, biopesticides only harm a specific pest, and thus are not harmful to birds and other animals that may come into contact with them. For example, baking soda can be diluted with water and sprayed on plants to inhibit the growth of fungi without risk to animals or humans. Insect sex pheromones can be used to interfere with the reproduction of insects known to harm plants.

Chemically based **organophosphates** make up about half of all insecticides in the United States and are used on fruits, nuts, vegetables, corn, wheat, and other crops, as well as on commercial and residential lawns and plants. They are also used to help control mosquitoes and termites.[94] These pesticides kill pests by affecting their nervous systems. The EPA has recently reviewed the safety of organophosphates and concluded that they do not pose a health risk based on current human exposure in food and water.[95]

Antimicrobials, a special type of chemical pesticide that includes disinfectants and sanitizers, are used to destroy and control the spread of microorganisms on

pesticides Substances that kill or repel pests such as insects, weeds, microorganisms, rodents, or fungi.

herbicides Substances that are used to kill and control weeds.

insecticides Pesticides used to kill insects.

antimicrobials Substances or a combination of substances, such as disinfectants and sanitizers, that kill or inhibit the growth of microorganisms.

fungicides Chemicals used to kill mold.

rodenticides Poisons used to kill rats, mice, and other rodents.

organophosphates A group of synthetic pesticides that adversely affect the nervous systems of pests.

surfaces or objects, such as walls, countertops, and floors.[96] Sanitizers are often used in addition to washing with soap and water in food processing plants and in restaurants. Waterless, alcohol-based hand gels that are useful against pathogens are approved by the FDA for use in health care settings but are not approved for use in food service and retail establishments. Alcohol-based hand gels do not kill all types of pathogens, though using an antimicrobial hand gel is better than nothing when water and soap are not available for hand washing.[97]

The Risks of Pesticides

Chemically based pesticides are not without risks and because they are strong chemicals, they can cause unintended harm to animals, the environment, and even humans. Residues of these chemicals remain on fruits and vegetables that reach consumers, and infants and young children are particularly susceptible to their hazards. Research has shown that some pesticides, depending upon their level of toxicity and how much is consumed, may cause serious health problems, such as cancer, birth defects, and nerve damage.[98]

To address these issues, *Healthy People 2020* includes an objective focused on reducing the number of health care visits related to pesticide exposure per year and advocates a reduction in the use of certain potentially dangerous pesticides.[99] In addition, the American Medical Association has urged the U.S. government to improve public education, workplace training, science-based research, and the ongoing surveillance of pesticide usage.[100] In order to protect public health and the environment, the types of pesticides and how often they can be used, as well as the amount of residue that can remain on foods when they reach consumers, are heavily regulated in the United States.

EPA, USDA, and FDA Regulate Pesticides

The EPA requires extensive test data from pesticide producers demonstrating that pesticide products can be used with "a reasonable certainty of no harm." To determine this, the EPA uses a four-step human health **risk assessment** that includes hazard identification, dose-response assessment, exposure assessment, and risk characterization (see **Figure 20.11**).

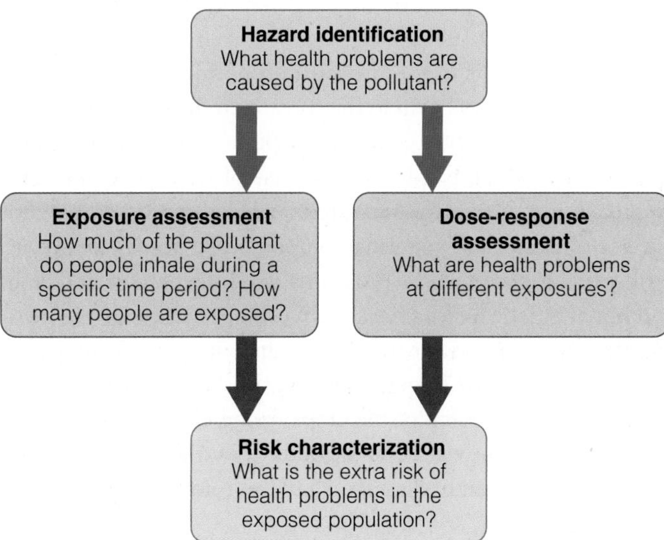

▲ **Figure 20.11 EPA's 4-Step Risk Assessment Process**
This four-step process is used by the EPA to assess risk of pesticides to humans.
Adapted from Environmental Protection Agency. 1991. *Risk Assessment for Toxic Air Pollutants: A Citizen's Guide.* Available at www.epa.gov/ttn/atw/3_90_024.html.

risk assessment The process of determining the potential human health risks posed by exposure to substances such as pesticides.

The first step, hazard identification, identifies the potential hazards or ill effects that may develop after exposure to a specific pesticide. Tests looking at a wide range of side effects, from eye and skin irritations to more serious health effects such as cancer, are often performed on laboratory animals.

Because "the dose makes the poison," the second step, dose-response assessment, determines the dose levels at which adverse effects occur in animals and then uses this information to calculate a potentially equal dose in humans.

The third step, exposure assessment, determines all the ways that a person could typically be exposed to that specific pesticide. Most foods are grown with the use of pesticides, so one route of exposure is through eating food. Some pesticides applied to farmland make their way into drinking water supplies, which is another route of exposure. Exposure could also occur through inhalation or absorption through the skin when using household disinfectants or gardening pesticides around the home. The EPA has a separate program for assessing occupational risk and the level of exposure that pesticide applicators and vegetable and fruit pickers face due to the nature of their jobs.

The fourth and last step, risk characterization, is the process of combining the hazard, dose-response, and exposure assessments to determine the pesticide's overall risk. Using the conclusions of a risk assessment, the EPA can make an informed decision regarding whether to approve a pesticide or chemical for use freely or with restrictions.[101]

Acceptable tolerance levels are set using a margin of safety due to the potential differences that exist between the effects of a pesticide on animals and its effect on humans, as well as differences among humans. A safety factor of tenfold or less, depending on the evidence, is added to protect the most vulnerable groups, such as infants and children, for whom the same amount of pesticide provides a larger dose per unit of body weight than for adults.[102] Thus, much effort goes into ensuring that the food supply is safe, yet affordable, so that consumers obtain foods that are nutrient dense while being exposed to a minimum amount of pesticide.

In addition to the EPA, the USDA and the FDA are also involved in regulating pesticides. The EPA is charged with approving pesticides for their specific usages, regulating how much of the pesticide can be used, and establishing acceptable tolerance levels. The USDA enforces the tolerance levels for meat, poultry, and eggs, and the FDA enforces tolerance levels for all other foods.[103]

Alternatives to Pesticides

The goal of this approach is to use the most economical methods to control pests while causing the least risk of harm to the consumer, the crops, or the environment. One method that some growers use to manage pests in their crops is **integrated pest management (IPM),** which emphasizes the use of natural toxins. Growers using the IPM approach use preventive measures, such as rotating crops, choosing pest-resistant strains of plants, and planting nonfood crops nearby to lure away pests.[104] When an infestation occurs, IPM programs use information about the life cycle of pests and nonsynthetic alternatives, such as biopesticides or the introduction of natural predators (specific insects that eat the unwanted pests), to limit damage. As a last resort, IPM growers use targeted spraying of chemical pesticides.

Currently, about 70 percent of the crops in the United States are grown using some form of IPM.[105] However, because foods grown using IPM methods are not thus labeled, consumers cannot distinguish them from foods grown with the use of synthetic pesticides.

acceptable tolerance levels The maximum amount of pesticide residue that is allowed in or on foods.

integrated pest management (IPM) Alternative to pesticides that uses the most economical and the least harmful methods of pest control to minimize risk to consumers, crops, and the environment.

Minimizing Pesticides in the Diet

More than 80 percent of the pesticide residue remaining on the skins of fruits and vegetables can be removed simply by washing them with clean, running water and scrubbing them with a vegetable brush. A study conducted by the University of California found that there was no difference in the amount of residue removed when the fruit was washed with plain water or with a commercial produce wash.[106] Peeling the skin from fruits and vegetables can help reduce pesticide residues and harmful microbes, but it also eliminates some of the fiber and micronutrients. For leafy vegetables such as cabbage and lettuce, the outer leaves can be removed and discarded to minimize risk. Consumers should also be aware that because of the strict pesticide guidelines in place in the United States, the amount of pesticide residue on fruits and vegetables should be below the EPA acceptable tolerance levels even *before* they reach the market.

Eating a variety of produce from a variety of locations will also minimize the consumption of any one type of pesticide. Although people who eat more fruits and vegetables potentially increase their exposure to pesticides, they still typically have a lower risk of cancer than those who eat fewer fruits and vegetables.[107] Locally grown produce may contain fewer pesticides than shipped produce because it does not contain those applied to extend shelf life. See **Figure 20.12** for a summary of strategies to minimize pesticides in the diet.

THE TAKE-HOME MESSAGE Food additives have long been used for food preservation and are often used by modern manufacturers to preserve foods, enhance their color or flavor, or add to their nutrient content. Antioxidants, sulfites, and MSG are examples of additives used to preserve foods and enhance flavor. Growth hormone is often given to dairy cows to increase milk production. Animal feed containing low doses of antibiotics has been used to increase the growth of cattle, poultry, and pigs, but can lead to antibiotic-resistant strains of bacteria. All compounds intentionally added to foods or provided to food-producing animals are strictly regulated by the FDA, but some compounds may be added unintentionally during processing or cause adverse reactions in sensitive individuals. All intentional food additives must be listed on food labels. Pesticides are used to destroy or mitigate pests and are strictly regulated by several government agencies. Programs are in place to reduce their use and to find safer alternatives. Consumers can minimize exposure to plant pesticides by washing produce under running tap water before consuming it, buying from producers that practice IPM, and eating a wide variety of foods.

Wash: Thoroughly wash and scrub all fresh fruits and vegetables under running water to dislodge bacteria and some of the pesticide residue. Running water is more effective for this purpose than soaking the fruit and vegetables.

Peel and trim: Peeling fruits and vegetables and discarding the outer leaves of leafy vegetables helps reduce pesticides. Trimming the visible fat from meat and the fatty skin from poultry and fish helps reduce some of the pesticide residue that remains in the fatty tissue of the animal.

Eat a variety of foods: Eating a variety of foods reduces the chance of being overexposed to any particular pesticide.

◂ **Figure 20.12 Reducing Pesticides in Foods**

What Is Biotechnology and Why Is It Used?

Traditional methods for breeding a plant or animal with new characteristics have been practiced for thousands of years. Historically, farmers have crossbred plants by trial and error, crossing two plants to produce a hybrid offspring with the desired combination of characteristics. This process is called **plant breeding.** Today's apples are an example of a plant food that has resulted from generations of deliberate crossbreeding. For thousands of years, humans crossbred different versions of the apple tree to produce more desirable offspring. For example, if one tree produced large apples with thinner skins, and another produced smaller, sour apples with thicker skins, an ancient apple farmer might have bred the two in the hope of producing a tree with large, fleshy, hardy fruit. The initial hybrids contain qualities from both parents, and it usually takes dozens of additional crosses and many years to separate the desirable traits from the less desirable ones. The ultimate result, though, is that modern apples look nothing like their small, sour ancestors.

The apples of today are larger and sweeter than their ancestors, thanks to hundreds of years of selective breeding.

In the last two centuries, as scientists understood more about the workings of DNA and how to manipulate it, the process of breeding for particular characteristics has become faster and more controlled. Today, scientists use **biotechnology** to modify the actual **genomes** of plants and animals to create desired characteristics with great precision. American farmers routinely use selectively bred, genetically modified plants to create disease-resistant crops that produce larger, hardier fruits and vegetables and increase overall crop yields. The production of foods using plant or animal products that have been modified genetically helps to keep food costs low and availability high. In fact, the majority of fruits and vegetables on the market today are a product of genetic modification.[108]

Genetic Engineering Is the Latest Form of Biotechnology

Genetic engineering (GE) allows scientists to alter the genetic makeup of an organism by manipulating DNA sequences. In genetic engineering, or bioengineering, an exact gene or genes from the DNA sequence of an organism are isolated and inserted into the DNA of another species of organism to create the genetically modified product (**Figure 20.13**).

This cutting and splicing of genes into the genome of another cell is called recombinant DNA (rDNA) technology. Organisms that have been genetically engineered to contain both original and foreign genes are called **genetically modified organisms (GMOs).** These GMOs are used to grow genetically engineered (GE) plants that produce GE foods.

Farmers in the United States have adopted genetically engineered crops widely since their introduction in 1996. Soybeans and cotton genetically engineered with herbicide-resistant traits have been the most widely accepted crops. According to the USDA's National Agricultural Statistics Service (NASS), in 2012 88 percent of the corn, 93 percent of the soybeans, and 94 percent of the cotton planted in the United States were genetically engineered varieties.[109]

plant breeding A type of biotechnology in which two plants are crossbred to produce offspring with desired traits from both.

biotechnology The manipulation of living organisms or their components to develop or manufacture useful products.

genome The total genetic information of an organism stored in the DNA of its chromosomes.

genetic engineering (GE) A biological technique that isolates and manipulates the genes of organisms to produce a targeted, modified product.

genetically modified organisms (GMOs) Organisms that have been genetically engineered to contain both original and foreign genes.

Genetic Engineering Can Produce More and Better Foods

The economic benefits of GE foods are substantial. Proponents believe that these foods can be good for the environment by helping to feed countries that have an

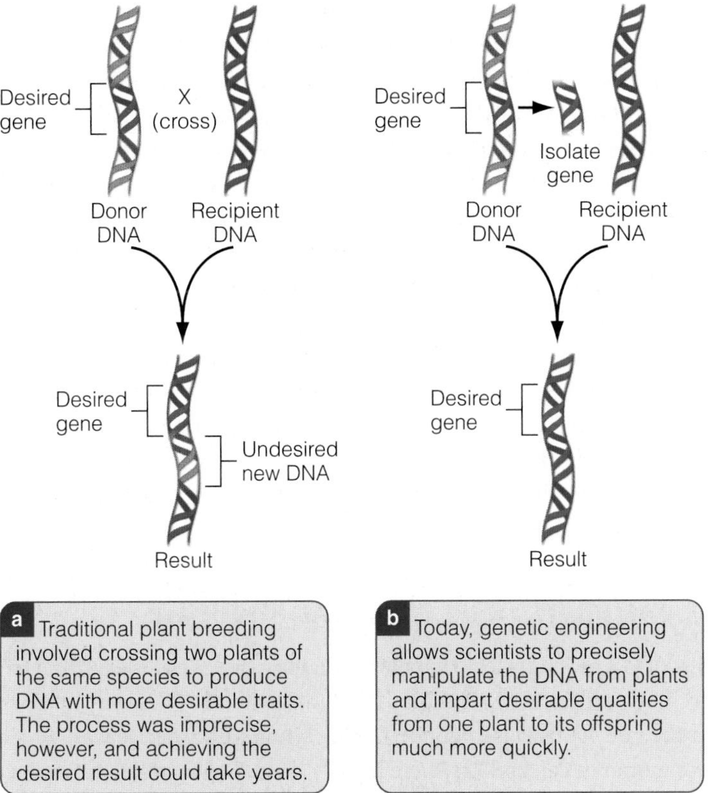
Desired gene
X (cross)
Donor DNA
Recipient DNA
Desired gene
Undesired new DNA
Result
Desired gene
Isolate gene
Donor DNA
Recipient DNA
Desired gene
Result
a Traditional plant breeding involved crossing two plants of the same species to produce DNA with more desirable traits. The process was imprecise, however, and achieving the desired result could take years.
b Today, genetic engineering allows scientists to precisely manipulate the DNA from plants and impart desirable qualities from one plant to its offspring much more quickly.

▲ **Figure 20.13 Plant Breeding versus Genetic Engineering**

inadequate food supply, improving the quality and quantity of foods available year round, and creating new uses for plants in industries such as pharmaceuticals and manufacturing.

The original purpose of GE plants was to reduce the amount of pesticides used on food crops by engineering the plants themselves to be more resistant to pests. This would benefit both the health of consumers and the environment.[110] For example, the bacterium *Bacillus thuringiensis* (*Bt*), which is found naturally in soil, produces a toxin that is poisonous to certain pests but not to humans or animals. When the gene for this toxin is inserted into a crop plant, the plant becomes resistant to these pests.[111] Some corn crops in the United States contain the *Bt* gene, which makes them resistant to some insect pests (see **Figure 20.14**). Because chemical insecticides are not necessary, many benign insects are spared, and insect **biodiversity** is retained. Almost 15 percent of corn and cotton harvested in the United States in 2012 were varieties genetically engineered to contain the *Bt* gene.[112]

▲ **Figure 20.14 European Corn Borer Caterpillar** *Bt* corn has been genetically engineered to produce a protein that is toxic to the larva of the European corn borer, the most damaging insect pest of corn in North America.

Another goal of the first-generation GE products was to use this technology to improve a crop's tolerance to herbicides. With an herbicide-resistant version of a desired crop, a farmer can spray herbicide over a field to kill a variety of weeds without harming the crop.[113] According to the USDA, approximately 93 percent of soybeans have been genetically modified to be herbicide resistant.[114]

The second generation of GE products to hit the market was designed for increased shelf life and improved nutrient composition.[115] Tomatoes that stay firm and ripe longer were among the first genetically engineered foods to be sold to consumers. An example of genetically altering a plant to improve its nutrient profile is "golden rice." This rice has gene segments from a bacterium and a daffodil that

biodiversity The variability among living organisms on the Earth, including the variability within and between species and within and between ecosystems.

▲ **Figure 20.15 Genetically Engineered Golden Rice**
"Golden rice" is rich in both beta-carotene and iron, and is a product of genetic engineering.

encode the rice grain to make beta-carotene and to concentrate the levels of iron (see **Figure 20.15**). If planted by farmers and accepted by consumers in southeast Asia, "golden rice" could help eliminate the epidemic of vitamin A and iron deficiency in Asia and worldwide.[116] Another example is genetically modified, high-oleic-acid soybeans, which produce oil that is less prone to becoming rancid and thus is more stable when used for frying foods.

Genetic research has progressed to third-generation GE products that hold promise in the pharmaceutical, environmental, and industrial arenas. In fact, the first GE product created for commercial use was human insulin (needed by diabetics) produced by genetically engineered *E. coli*.[117] In addition to bacteria, plants can be genetically modified to create substances with numerous medical uses, such as vaccines, antibiotics, anti-clotting drugs, hormones, and substitutes for certain blood substances.[118] Scientists are currently experimenting with the concept of "growing" vaccines for measles, hepatitis B, and norovirus in produce.[119] Using common foods to produce and deliver medicine is a promising area of current research in biotechnology.

Some Consumers Have Concerns about GE Foods

Opponents of GE products fear that biotechnology can cause everything from harm to monarch butterflies to the creation of "Frankenfoods." A study at Cornell University in the late 1990s raised concerns that when milkweed leaves, which are the sole diet of monarch caterpillars, were heavily dusted with pollen from *Bt* corn, and then *exclusively* fed to monarch butterfly caterpillars, many of them died. Critics of this finding said that this experiment didn't mimic a "real-life" setting. Most milkweed doesn't grow close enough to cornfields to collect significant amounts of corn pollen, especially since this heavy pollen typically doesn't travel far from its place of origin. Hence, it is unlikely that monarch caterpillars would feed primarily on milkweed that contains such an enormous amount of GE corn pollen.[120] After conducting extensive research coordinated by the USDA, researchers concluded that the monarch butterflies' exposure to GE corn pollen in a natural setting is minimal and so is not likely to be dangerous to these butterflies.[121, 122]

Opponents of GE foods point out that there are some risks involved in cutting and splicing specific genes. Some of these include the introduction of allergens, disruption of the ecosystem, and introduction of resistant weeds, as well as ethical dilemmas. Proponents of GE foods respond that these fears are not based on evidence that can justify the concerns.

Genetic engineering is more tightly regulated than any other technology, so there are safeguards in place to halt or prevent undesirable outcomes. The principal risk appears to be the introduction of a known food allergen into a GE product. Under the FDA's new biotech policy, companies must tell consumers on the food label when a product includes a gene from one of the common allergy-causing foods, unless it can show that the protein produced by the added gene does not cause allergies.[123] The following eight foods account for 90 percent of all food allergies: milk, eggs, peanuts, tree nuts, fish, shellfish, soy, and wheat.[124]

Other concerns have arisen about the production of plant toxins, changes in the nutrient content and substances in foods, and the production of unsafe animal feed. Table 20.6 lists the safeguards that are in place to address these issues.

GE Foods Are Highly Regulated in the United States

GE foods in the United States are regulated by the same three government agencies that regulate pesticides: the FDA, USDA, and EPA. The FDA ensures that GE

TABLE 20.6 Concerns and Regulations for GE Foods

Concern	FDA Regulation
Undesirable genetic modification	To avoid the creation of undesirable products, all genes used must not have prior evidence of encoding any harmful substances. The genes must also be stably inserted into the plant in order to avoid any rearranging of genetic information that would produce an undesirable substance.
Introduction of allergens	GE foods must be monitored for food allergens. Protein encoded from common allergen food sources (such as milk, eggs, fish, tree nuts, and legumes) should be presumed to be allergens and should be labeled as such on the GE food.
Excessive level of toxins	GE foods should not contain natural toxins at levels that are higher than those found naturally in plants.
Changes in nutrients	All GE foods should be monitored to assess unintentional changes in the nutrient levels in the plants and their ability to be utilized in the human body as compared with their conventional counterparts.
Creation of new substances	If the genes that are introduced into plants encode substances that are different in structure and function than those normally found in foods, these substances would need to be approved by the FDA, as would any other food additive. However, if these substances are GRAS or "substantially equivalent" to substances that already exist in foods, they do not need the FDA's premarket approval.
Unsafe animal feeds	Because a single plant may be the predominant food source in an animal feed, all GE animal feeds must meet the same strict safety standards that are in place for food that is grown for humans.

Source: FDA. 2012. *Genetically Engineered Plants for Food and Feed.* www.fda.gov/Food/Biotechnology/default.htm.

foods are safe to eat and labeled if they contain a suspected allergen. The USDA ensures that the plants are safe to grow, while the EPA makes certain that the gene for any pesticide, such as that for *Bt* toxin, inserted into a plant is safe and won't have adverse environmental effects. Though these agencies work together to ensure the safety of GE foods, the FDA has the overall authority to remove any GE food that doesn't meet the same high safety standards that are set for its conventionally grown equivalent.[125]

The FDA must review and approve all GE products before they are allowed on the market. As part of this process, the FDA mandates that the developers of GE foods conduct extensive tests to ensure the safety of those foods. After testing is completed, the developer is required to send the FDA a report of the information pertaining to the product. The FDA will review the documentation and seek additional information as warranted. Once all FDA guidelines are satisfied, the food will be considered safe and will be allowed to enter the market. More than 50 GE foods, including canola oil, corn, cottonseed oil, potatoes, soybeans, squash, and tomatoes, have been evaluated by the FDA and are considered as safe as their conventional counterparts.[126]

Most consumers want genetically engineered foods to be labeled; however, the FDA has concluded that because there isn't any scientific evidence that GE foods differ from their conventionally grown counterparts, labeling isn't warranted.[127] This position is shared by the American Medical Association and the Society of Toxicology.[128] Canada follows the United States in this regard. If a manufacturer chooses to voluntarily label a product it may state that the product has been "genetically engineered." Mandatory labeling of GE foods is required in Europe, Japan, Australia, and New Zealand.[129]

Consumer acceptance of GE foods is increasing as a result of such foods becoming more common, their putative health benefits, and improved quality. In a survey of approximately 1,000 American adults conducted in January 2004, almost 60 percent felt that biotechnology would benefit themselves and their families in the future. Interestingly, over 60 percent of the consumers surveyed said that food safety issues, such as food handling/preparation, packaging, or disease/contamination, were their primary concern, compared with 1 percent who identified concerns over biotechnology as their top concern. The majority of consumers also stated that they would be likely to use GE produce that was modified to protect against insect damage, required less pesticide application during growing, or had improved taste or freshness.[130]

THE TAKE-HOME MESSAGE Traditional plant breeding and modern genetic engineering are types of biotechnology that alter an organism's genetic makeup to create a new plant or animal with more desirable traits. Genetically engineered crops can be developed to be pest resistant, to provide additional nutrients, and to enhance flavor and quality. GE products are heavily regulated to minimize undesirable genetic modifications, the introduction of disease, and unfavorable nutrient changes in food, as well as to reduce the risk of creating potential food allergens and unsafe feed for animals. Labeling is not mandatory for GE foods in the U.S.

What Is a Sustainable Food System?

"Eat Green" and "Eat Sustainably" are common phrases used in the media to talk about feeding the world's growing population on limited resources, but few Americans actually know what these phrases mean. According to a recent survey, more than half of American adults are not familiar with the concept of producing food sustainably.[131]

Sustainable means to be able to be maintained indefinitely. A sustainable food system is one that will survive over the long term. To maintain a sustainable food system, the natural resources used to produce, transport, and distribute food are conserved instead of being destroyed or depleted. Minimal natural resources, such as soil and water, are depleted to grow food, and minimal energy is used to transport food to consumers. A sustainable diet contains foods that are produced in ways that are ecologically neutral.

According to a 2002 article from *Environmental Health Perspectives*, America's current industrialized agriculture system is using resources including topsoil, fossil fuel, and water at unsustainable rates. We are also degrading the environment, reducing biodiversity, and polluting the air and water.

The Academy of Nutrition and Dietetics (formerly the American Dietetic Association) developed a model that provides a useful way to think about the factors that contribute to a sustainable food system.[132] Sustainability involves every sector in the food system and is influenced by many factors.

As shown in **Figure 20.16**, natural and human resources are the inputs of any food system. In a model that promotes sustainability, natural resources must be conserved and protected as foods are produced. The foods produced should be healthy, culturally and socially acceptable, affordable, and sustainable for future generations. Individuals producing the foods must be treated with respect. All aspects of the system must be economically viable for all participants so that people can afford to buy food and farmers and other workers can afford to provide food.

sustainable Referring to a method of resource use that can be maintained indefinitely because it does not deplete or permanently damage the resource.

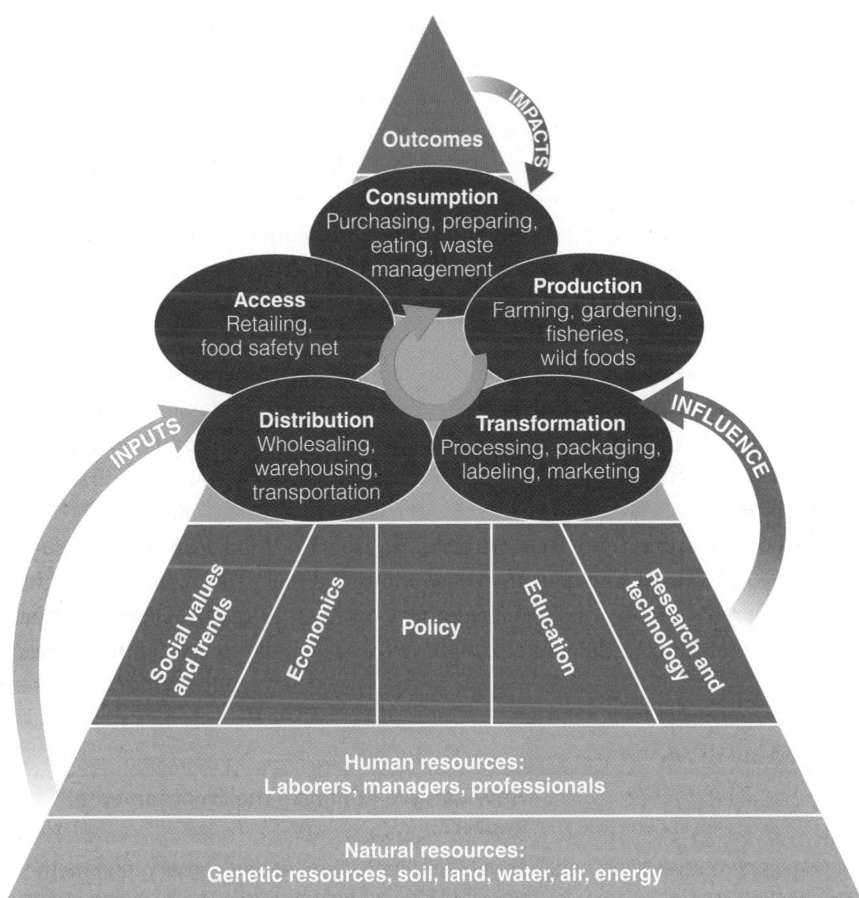

▲ **Figure 20.16 Sustainable Food Systems Model**

Source: A. H. Harmon and B. L. Gerald, "Position of the American Dietetic Association: Food and Nutrition Professionals Can Implement Practices to Conserve Natural Resources and Support Ecological Sustainability," *Journal of the American Dietetic Association* 107 (2007): 1033–1043.

The next higher level of the model consists of external factors that influence the use of human and natural resources, including social and cultural values and trends, economic factors, local, federal, and international policy, education, and research and technology. All of these factors are constantly changing as new trends, financial resources, and research emerge.

The resources that contribute to a sustainable food system and the influences on that system interact with the continuing cycle of production, transformation, distribution, and access, which produces outcomes for both consumers and the environment. In a sustainable food system, outcomes include preservation of the resources used in addition to production of adequate foods.

Before you can understand what it takes to manage the natural resources involved in food production sustainably, you need to have a grasp of how unsustainable agricultural practices affect the environment. From the water required for irrigation to the fuel needed to run the tractors to the animal wastes produced in feedlots, the processes of growing, harvesting, and transporting food products require the use and potential depletion and contamination of natural resources.

Food Production Requires Both Internal and External Resources

Notice that numerous natural resources are used when growing crops and raising animals for food. These natural resources can be divided into two categories. Some natural resources can be classified as internal because they are used to produce foods. Other natural resources can be classified as external because they are used to move food products from the farm to the consumer. Both internal and external resources share a common characteristic: When they are used to produce crops and raise animals, they generate natural and man-made by-products that affect the environment. Table 20.7 describes several of the challenges associated with using internal resources, including land and water, to produce food, and various strategies that can be employed to protect the environment.

External resources, or those not used in the actual growing of the food, also contribute to the environmental costs of food production. For example, the use of fossil fuels to grow, process, and transport food contributes to the release of *carbon dioxide gas emissions*. The carbon dioxide and other gases released when fossil fuels are burned for energy are referred to as greenhouse gases, as these gases absorb and trap heat in the air and re-radiate that heat downward. It is estimated that global temperatures could increase by 35 to 39 degrees Fahrenheit by 2100 due to these greenhouse gases.[133]

Carbon emissions associated with the transport of food from farm to supermarket are substantial, and consumers use additional fuel to drive to the supermarket and to prepare food at home. The lettuce, oranges, or cantaloupes that appear in supermarkets during the winter may have traveled 1,400 to 2,400 miles to reach

TABLE 20.7 Environmental Effects of Food Production

The Effect	The Challenge	How Can We Minimize the Environmental Impact?
Land overuse	Excessive use of farming equipment, overtilling, and livestock overgrazing can all damage soil.	Proper land management and conservation methods of tilling can help preserve the land and replenish soil nutrients.
Soil erosion	Wind and rain can cause more than 1.5 billion tons of nutrient-rich topsoil to be blown and washed away each year. When fertile topsoil is lost, crop yield declines.	Proper crop covering and shielding from wind as well as proper tillage of the soil can dramatically reduce erosion.
Water depletion	Irrigation accounts for 80 percent of water consumption in the United States; hence, excessive irrigation can deplete naturally occurring groundwater.	Precision farming and the conscious reduction of overwatering can help preserve water.
Water runoff	After a rainfall (or watering of crops), the water runoff from farms can spread pesticides from crops and pathogens in animal manure to other fields, surface water, and downfield rivers and streams, contaminating these ecosystems.	Basins can be installed to collect the runoff water to prevent contamination prior to discharge to streams and rivers.
Airborne emissions	Emissions of ammonia and nitrogen (see below) in manure are released into the air. The ammonia released from these airborne emissions can settle on water surfaces, killing fish and encouraging the growth of toxic algae, both of which disrupt the natural ecosystem.	The proper handling of manure (see below) mitigates this problem.
Nitrate production	The production of nitrates from the nitrogen in manure can pollute surface water and groundwater that is used as drinking water.	Proper collection, stockpiling, and disposal of manure to minimize the leaching of nitrates into runoff and groundwater, as proposed in the latest EPA regulations, will help concentrated animal feeding operations (CAFOs) to safely manage manure.

Data from A. H. Harmon and B. L. Gerald, "Position of the American Dietetic Association: Food and Nutrition Professionals Can Implement Practices to Conserve Natural Resources and Support Ecological Sustainability," *Journal of the American Dietetic Association* 107 (2007): 1033–1043; Department of Agriculture Economic Research Service. 2004. *Irrigation and Water Use.* Available at www.ers.usda.gov/topics/farm-practices-management/irrigation-water-use.aspx. Accessed November 2012; U.S. Environmental Protection Agency. 2009. *Ag 101: Crop Production.* Available at www.epa.gov/oecaagct/ag101/cropmajor.html. Accessed January 2010; U.S. Environmental Protection Agency. 2009. *Ag 101: Beef Production.* Available at www.epa.gov/oecaagct/ag101/beef.html. Accessed January 2010.

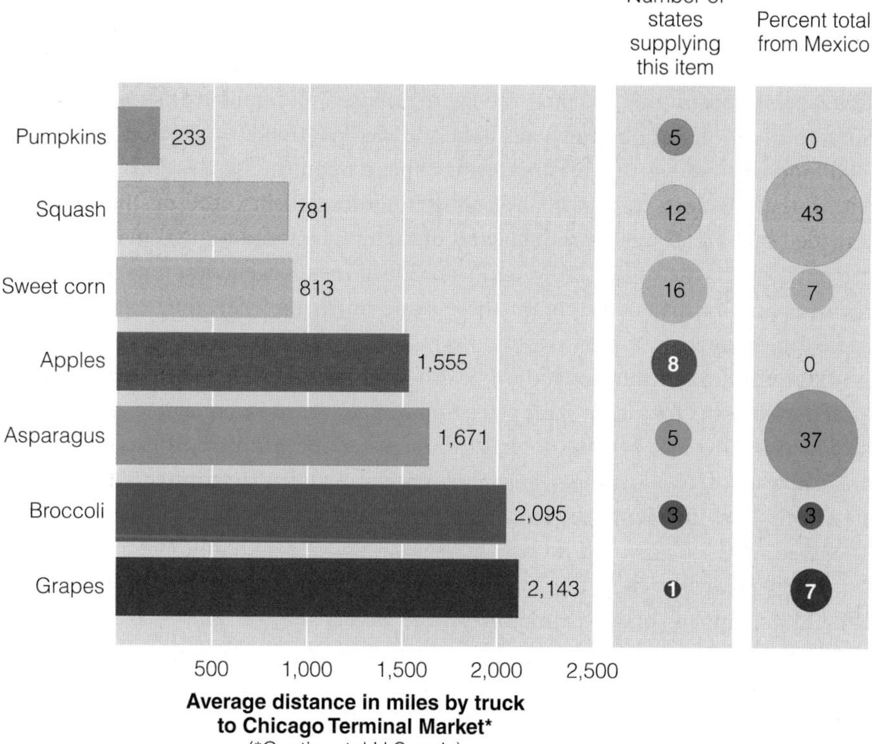

▲ **Figure 20.17 How Far Did Your Food Travel?**
You might be surprised to learn just how far some of your food travels to get to your local supermarket.

Adapted from R. Pirog, et al., "Food, Fuel, and Freeways: An Iowa Perspective on How Far Food Travels, Fuel Usage, and Greenhouse Gas Emissions," Leopold Center for Sustainable Agriculture (2002). Available at www.leopold.iastate.edu/pubs-and-papers/2001-06-food-fuel-freeways.

consumers.[134] Produce trucked from various states and from Mexico to Chicago has traveled an average of slightly over 1,500 miles, which is more than a 20 percent increase since the early 1980s (see **Figure 20.17**).[135] The amount of fossil fuel used to transport that produce all those miles, coupled with the increase in carbon dioxide gas emissions into the air from burning that fuel, has enormous environmental costs.[136] A study conducted in Iowa showed that produce made available from national sources and shipped in from various distances used 4 to 17 times more fuel and released 5 to 17 times more carbon dioxide gas emissions than produce that was locally produced.[137]

Natural resources aside, these fuel costs are factored into the price of the food, so they affect consumers' financial resources. An estimated 12 percent of your food dollars goes toward the cost of getting food from the farm to your plate. And as the price of oil increases, the price that you pay for food will also increase.[138] Thus, the farther your food has to travel, the more resources will be used, which not only has a negative effect on the environment, but also is a drain on your wallet. For these reasons, many people are trying to buy more and more of their food from locally grown sources.

Preserving Natural Resources Is the First Step toward Sustainability

Abuse of any of the natural resources required to grow foods can prevent sustainability. Soil, biodiversity, energy, and water are the key natural resources that must be preserved in a sustainable food system.

The Soil Food Web

More than 99 percent of the food you eat is produced on land, compared with less than one percent that comes from the sea. All land crops are dependent upon the thin layer of topsoil that sits atop the Earth's crust.[139] It's not surprising, then, that numerous experts are concerned about soil degradation.[140] In **Figure 20.18**, the "soil food web" shows that all organisms depend upon the Earth's soil. Organisms within the soil, such as bacteria and other microorganisms, feed on the nutrients provided by animal waste products and decaying plant and animal matter. Plants use nutrients in the soil to grow, and to produce fruit, vegetables, nuts, and seeds. Humans and animals later obtain these same nutrients when they eat the plants and plant products.

Just as all organisms depend on healthy soil for survival, healthy soil depends on the organisms to anchor it in place and to keep it well oxygenated. Plant roots help hold soil in place, which protects it from water and wind erosion, and they also break up the soil to allow the dispersal of oxygen. As topsoil is formed and regenerated from decaying plants, organisms, animals, and rocks, a perfect, perpetual web is formed.

Problems arise when the topsoil can't be regenerated and/or is less fertile. When this happens plants cannot grow, the web is severed, and nourishment for all—the animals, microorganisms, plants, and you—suffers.[141] The natural process of regenerating one inch of nutrient-rich topsoil takes more than 500 years.[142] Improper agricultural practices that facilitate erosion of soil faster than it can be regenerated disrupt the entire web and food system.[143]

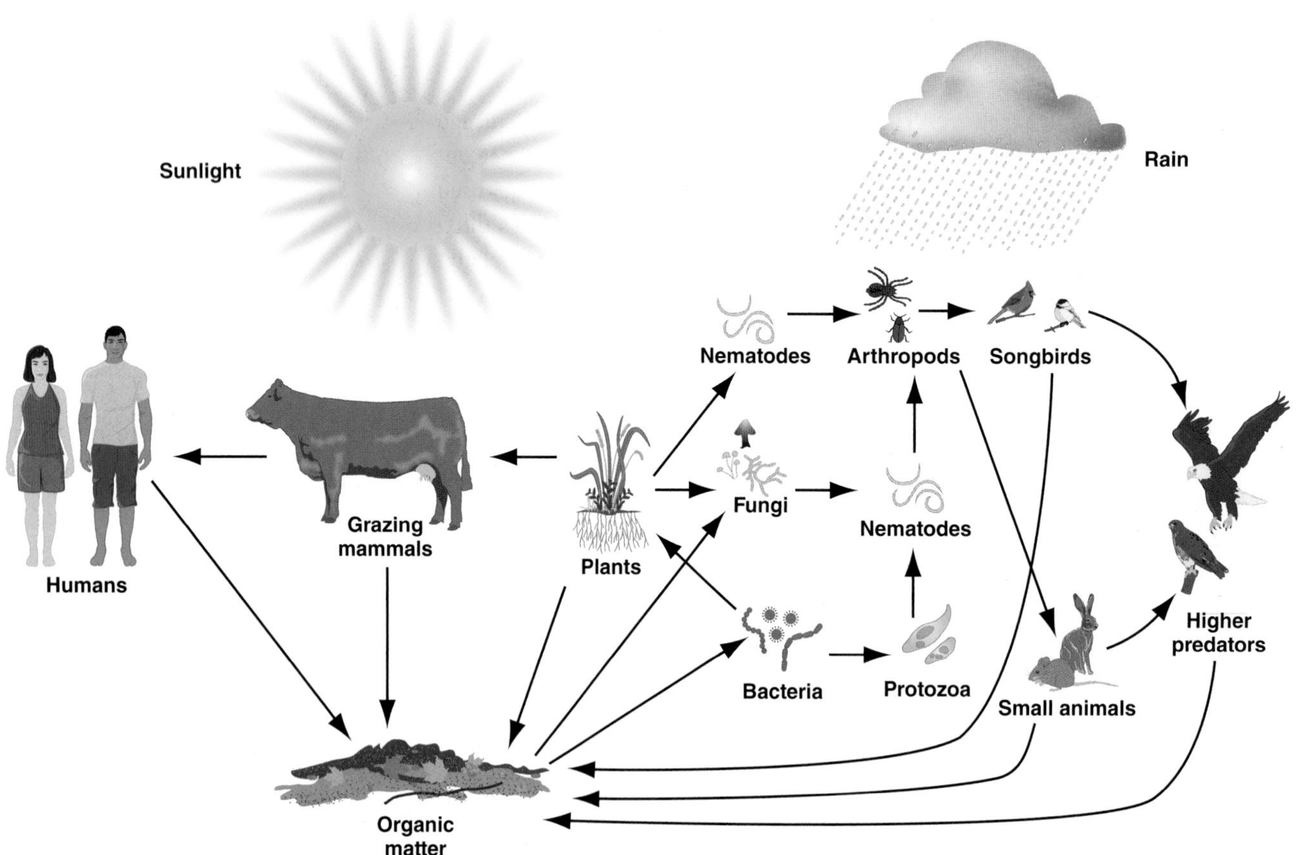

▲ **Figure 20.18 The Soil Food Web**

Source: Bureau of Land Management. n.d. *The Soil Food Web.* Available at www.blm.gov/nstc/soil/foodweb/index.html. Accessed May 2010.

The Importance of Biodiversity

As you can deduce from the soil web, achieving and maintaining biodiversity is an important part of a sustainable food system, and the extinction of even one member of the web can have dramatic consequences. For example, the rapid decline in the honeybee population in the United States since 2006, termed *colony collapse disorder,* has impacted the pollination, and therefore availability, of fruits, vegetables, and tree nuts (consider that an estimated 30 percent of the foods that you eat need pollination to flourish).[144] Lack of biodiversity among aquatic systems is also a potential problem. More than 70 percent of commercial fisheries are overharvested, endangering the existence of more than 30 percent of native fish in North America.[145] As biodiversity is reduced, the variety and nutritional quality of foods available may also be reduced.[146]

Energy

Research suggests that almost 16 percent of the total energy consumption in the United States is used in the production, processing, transport, and preparation of our food.[147] The use of fossil fuel is costly and the release of carbon dioxide from the burning of it harms the environment. A sustainable food system can both reduce the reliance on fossil fuel and reduce pollution.

More energy (as well as land and water) is required to produce a meat-based diet than to produce a plant-based diet.[148] Every pound of animal protein generated from livestock requires approximately 6 pounds of plant protein in the form of feed.[149] Allowing livestock to graze on pasture rather than feeding them a grain diet would cut the amount of fuel needed to produce and transport feed grain in half.[150]

Producing chemical fertilizers and pesticides for crops also requires large amounts of fossil fuels.[151] Avoiding these chemicals and using natural fertilizers, such as animal manure, not only cuts the use of fossil fuel, but also can make soil more fertile.[152] Research also shows that crop rotation and other aspects of organic farming result in less soil erosion than nonorganic methods.[153]

Water

According to the EPA, since the 1950s, the population in America has nearly doubled and our water consumption has more than tripled.[154] The average American uses 100 gallons—about 1,600 full glasses—of water each day.[155] By 2013, it is estimated that more than 35 states will experience water shortages.[156]

This heightened demand for water is a danger not only to the environment but also to your health. You need water to survive; therefore, conserving water now to ensure a healthy supply in the future makes sense. There are several steps you and/or your family can take to conserve water. Installing water-efficient appliances, including washing machines and dishwashers, helps cut down on water used for daily chores. If all households installed water-efficient appliances, the United States would save more than 3 trillion gallons annually.[157] Low-flow toilets and showerheads can also help save water, as can turning off the tap while washing dishes or brushing your teeth. When it comes to individual water conservation, think of saving water one gallon at a time.

Locally Grown Food Requires Fewer Natural Resources

Because of the environmental and financial costs associated with shipping foods over long distances, some people are choosing to become **locavores** and attempt to eat locally grown food whenever possible. Locavores try to frequent local farms, farmers' markets, and roadside stands rather than buy similar foods at supermarkets. It may be very difficult for locavores to consume 100 percent of their diet from local sources year round. For example, although Vermonters have access to fresh dairy foods 365

locavore A person who eats locally grown food whenever possible.

days a year, robust fruit and vegetable crops are hard to find under a foot of snow in the dead of winter. Depending on where they live, many locavores try to eat foods grown locally and then supplement with foods from the supermarket. Farmers' markets are an important resource for people who value food grown locally; see Spotlight: Farmers' Markets to understand more about how these markets work.

The movement for "eating locally" has gained momentum for numerous reasons. Among these is that most people perceive locally grown foods as tasting better. A locally grown summer tomato, for example, is usually much more flavorful than one that has been shipped in a refrigerated truck for 2,000 miles. Eating locally also has environmental benefits, because the less your food travels, the less energy is being used to get it to you.

In addition, local, small farms are typically run by farmers who not only farm the land but also live on it. They harvest foods at peak ripeness, tend to use little packaging, and travel fewer miles to distribute their goods, all of which can potentially reduce negative effects on the environment. The "food miles" saved can be eye-opening. Table 20.8 shows the distance travelled for the ingredients in a meal that were obtained locally or from conventional sources. A meal consisting of foods obtained at a local supermarket can travel as much as 60 times the miles of the same meal made from locally grown foods. Home gardening can reduce food miles to food steps. Spotlight: You as a Sustainable Farmer on page 780 explains how to grow your own vegetables even if you don't have a backyard.

Many large supermarkets now sell locally grown produce. This combining of locally grown foods with conventionally grown foods allows consumers to do "one-stop shopping" rather than have to drive to farmers' markets, farm stands, or **community-supported agriculture (CSA)** pickups in addition to the supermarket. Corporate America is also making it easier to eat locally. Some large corporations and industrial complexes have weekly farmers' markets on their premises. Employees can shop for locally grown foods during the day and head home with the fixings for dinner.[158] The USDA recently awarded more than $5 million in grants to support local food connections between farmers and consumers, even in large cities, with its "Know Your Farmer, Know Your Food" initiative.[159]

Some individuals wrongfully assume that locally grown food is the same as sustainably grown food. A *sustainable diet* contains foods that meet your nutrient and health needs but can be produced for a long time without negatively impacting the environment.[160] Buying food from small local farms doesn't guarantee that the foods were grown in a sustainable way, nor does being from a distant farm mean that those farmers didn't practice sustainable agriculture.

TABLE 20.8 Food Miles in a Meal

Food Item	Local Source	Distance Traveled from Local Source	Conventional Source	Distance Traveled through Conventional Channels*
Chuck roast	Local grass-fed beef farm	75 miles	Colorado	675 miles
Potatoes	Farmers' market	10–15 miles	Idaho	1,300 miles
Carrots	Backyard garden	40 feet	California	1,700 miles
Green beans	Backyard garden	40 feet	California	1,700 miles

*Distance is approximate to Chicago, IL.

community-supported agriculture (CSA) An arrangement where individuals pay a fee to support a local farm, and in exchange receive a weekly or biweekly box of fresh produce from the farm.

SPOTLIGHT Farmers' Markets

According to the USDA, farmers' markets are an integral part of the urban–farm linkage and their growth has continued to rise. The number of farmers' markets nationwide has increased from 1,755 in 1994 to 7,864 in 2012.[1] The USDA estimates that these markets generate approximately $1 billion in consumer spending each year. Most of this growth, a boon to local communities' economies, can be attributed to consumer interest in obtaining fresh products directly from the farm. In many cases consumers have the opportunity to personally interact with the farmer who grows the produce.

The USDA, in conjunction with the Agricultural Marketing Service (AMS), provides technical support to managers of farmers' markets by hosting conferences and training sessions throughout the country to present research findings and information on marketing strategies with agricultural producers, Extension economists, state Department of Agriculture personnel, and other parties interested in supporting direct farm marketing venues. Many farmers' markets accept WIC (Women, Infants, and Children) program food voucher coupons and provide nutrition education and food preparation demonstrations in conjunction with local and state health departments.

The USDA's AMS has also formed the Farmers Market Consortium, which is a public/private sector partnership dedicated to helping farmers' markets by sharing information about funding and resources available to them. The consortium publishes a Farmers Market Resource Guide that provides a centralized repository of information about federal and private resources that support farmers' markets. The USDA also publishes a National Farmers Market Directory that organizes farmers' markets by state and includes contact information, dates, and times of operation.

Farmers' markets provide fresh produce to the consumer.

Produce sold at farmers' markets is available according to the season; although adapting to eating seasonally can be an adjustment, it is one that is more environmentally friendly because produce is not transported long distances for sale.

Farmers' markets vary by what can be sold but generally a product must be grown or raised or made (baked, canned, and so on) by the farm selling it. "Local" is also usually understood to mean food that comes from independent farmers and producers rather than from large corporations.

Costs at farmers' markets vary and sometimes produce may be more expensive than at a grocery store. Food bought in the conventional system where pesticides are used and the food is transported thousands of miles and stored in warehouses is heavily subsidized at all stages of production and produces costs not reflected in the purchase price. These costs include depleted fossil fuel reserves for fertilizer, cultivation, and transportation; water pollution from pesticide runoff; and the contribution of emissions to global warming.

Some products sold at farmers' markets are certified organic, while others use integrated pest management (IPM) or use organic methods but are not USDA certified. Farmers sell directly to consumers for a number of reasons and those who do generally care for their land and use sustainable growing practices to keep it healthy.

Farmers' markets are good for the local economy, the health of the land, and the health of the people. The USDA's farmers' market locator tells you where to find a farmers' market near you: http://search.ams.usda.gov/farmersmarkets.

Reference

1. USDA. Agricultural Marketing Service. 2012. Farmers Markets and Direct-to-Consumer Marketing. Available at www.ams.usda.gov. Accessed November 2012.

THE TAKE-HOME MESSAGE A sustainable food system is one that will survive over the long term. To maintain a sustainable food system, the natural resources used to produce, transport, and distribute the food are conserved instead of being destroyed or depleted. Minimal natural resources such as soil and water are depleted to grow the food and minimal energy is used to transport food to consumers. A sustainable diet contains foods that are produced in a way that is ecologically neutral. Natural resources are used internally to produce foods and externally to move foods from producers to consumers. Buying locally grown food is one way to reduce the use of external natural resources in food systems.

SPOTLIGHT You as a Sustainable Farmer: Growing Vegetables in a Container

You might think you need a yard, a hoe, and a shovel to have a garden, but this isn't necessarily the case. Edible plants can grow in all kinds of environments and containers, and for those living in dorms or apartments, a sunny window sill, a balcony, or your front step will provide enough space to create your own garden. All you need are a container, potting soil, water, a plant, and sunlight. In fact, there are even advantages to growing plants in containers rather than in the ground. There won't be any weeds to pull, and you'll have fewer pests to damage your plants. Your garden is also transportable so you can move it if you need to.

Growing plants in a container garden can provide healthy, nutritious vegetables for your dinner table.

The Container

Most any container, such as a ceramic pot, planter box, one- to five-gallon tubs, or even the plastic trash container under your desk, will do. The size of the container will depend on what you want to grow (see table). Drainage is key to growing a hearty plant. So, your container must have two important elements: 1) 1/4-inch drilled holes, evenly spaced along the bottom of the container, and 2) an inch-thick layer of coarse gravel, pebbles, or broken pieces of a clay pot in the bottom of the container. This layer will allow excess water to drain from the plant.

The Potting Mixture

In place of soil, potting mixtures, which may be a combination of several compounds such as sawdust, peat moss, and vermiculite (a mineral that puffs up when exposed to heat such as from the sun), can be purchased at most garden centers, many hardware stores, and even online. The amount of potting mixture that you need will depend on the type of vegetables you want to grow and the size of your container (see table).

The Plant

Many of the vegetables that grow in a backyard garden will also sprout quite nicely in a container garden. The table provides a list of the easier-to-grow vegetables for first-time gardeners that are ideal for containers. Transplants (small plants that you transfer to the container) can be purchased at garden centers, farmers' markets, local farm stands, and even some supermarkets. When these transplants become available in your area, it is time to begin your vegetable garden.

Fertilizing

Because the rejuvenating, nutrient-rich soil of a backyard is missing in a container garden, you will need to routinely fertilize your plants. You can purchase a powdered fertilizer at your local supermarket, garden center, or hardware store and dilute it with water as directed on the package. Pour this diluted

Vegetables: From Plant to Plate

Vegetable	Minimum Container Size	Number of Plants	Amount of Sunlight	Approximate Number of Days to Harvest
Cabbage	1 gallon	1 plant	Partial shade	48–53
Cucumbers	1 gallon	2 plants	Full sun	46–66
Green beans	1 gallon	2–3 plants	Full sun	37–58
Lettuce	1 gallon	4–6 plants	Partial shade	41–56
Peppers	2 gallon	2 plants	Full sun	82–112
Tomatoes	3 gallon	1 plant	Full sun	84–124

Adapted from S. Cotner and J. Masabni. 2009. Vegetable Gardening in Containers. AgriLife Extension, Texas A&M System. Available at http://repository.tamu.edu/bitstream/handle/1969.1/87590/pdf_2695.pdf?sequence=1. Accessed April 2010; Iowa State University Extension. 2005. *Container Vegetable Gardening*. Available at www.extension.iastate.edu/publications/pm870b.pdf. Accessed April 2010.

nourishment around the plant once a week or every other week.

Watering

Container plants tend to dry out more quickly than plants grown in outdoor gardens. Depending on the plant, you may need to water daily. Avoid waiting until the soil is completely dried out. Pour enough water so that some liquid will drain out the bottom of the container. (Put a foil pan under your plant if you are growing it inside your home to catch any excess water.) Avoid overwatering, which can be as damaging to a growing plant as underwatering. If your plant becomes waterlogged, the roots won't be able to "breathe" and receive the oxygen the plant needs to grow. You'll end up with root rot.

Harvesting

This is the fun part, as you get to eat your bounty. The table gives you a ballpark idea of how long it will take from planting your vegetables until you can enjoy them on your plate.

What Can You Do to Ensure the Foods You Eat Are Safe and Sustainable?

Many factors, including decisions made by food workers at all points in the food system as well as decisions made by policy makers, affect the safety and quality of foods that are available to you. At the end of the day, though, you get to choose which food products you buy and consume. Knowing and understanding the terms found on food labels or posted near foods can help you select the healthiest and most environmentally friendly options.

Know The Label Terms that Indicate How Animal Foods Are Produced

Both the FDA and USDA are the consumer watchdogs for food labeling, and labeling of animal food products is essential when it comes to determining how the animals were fed, housed, and treated. The label terms for meat and poultry are determined and defined by the USDA. The following list includes terms often found on prepackaged meat products:[161]

- *Certified.* Indicates that the USDA has evaluated a meat product for class, grade, or other quality characteristics (for example, "Certified Angus Beef").
- *Fresh Poultry.* Poultry that has never had an internal temperature below 26°F.
- *Free Range.* Producers must demonstrate that the animal has been allowed access to the outdoors.
- *Kosher.* Meat and poultry products that were prepared under the supervision of a rabbi.
- *Natural.* The food contains no artificial ingredient or added color and is only minimally processed; that is, using processes that do not fundamentally alter the raw product. The label must explain the use of the term natural (such as "no added colorings or artificial ingredients").
- *No Hormones (pork or poultry).* Hormones are not allowed in raising hogs or poultry. Therefore, the claim "no hormones added" cannot be used on the labels of pork or poultry unless it is followed by a statement that says, "Federal regulations prohibit the use of hormones."
- *No Hormones (beef).* The phrase "no hormones administered" may be approved for use on the label of beef products if no hormones have been used in raising the animals.
- *No Antibiotics.* May be used on labels for meat or poultry products if the animals were raised without antibiotics.

In addition to these common terms, the use of the term "organic" is appearing on increasing numbers of products on supermarket shelves.

Understand the Meaning of the Term Organic

Organic food production involves growing crops without the use of most synthetic pesticides, synthetic fertilizers, bioengineering, or irradiation. Only antibiotic-free or growth hormone–free animals can be used to produce organic meat, poultry, eggs, and dairy foods.[162] Organic food production is more ecologically sound than other methods, and many consumers perceive organic foods to be healthier than their nonorganic counterparts. Consequently, consumer demand for organic products is increasing, growing to $28.6 billion (4 percent of total food sales) in 2010, compared with $6.1 billion (1.2 percent of total food sales) in 2000.[163]

The Organic Foods Production Act and the National Organic Standards (NOS) developed in 2002 by the USDA are intended to assure consumers that the organic foods they purchase are produced, processed, and certified consistent with national standards. Before the NOS were in place, over 50 organizations and state agencies had their own unique sets of organic standards and guidelines.[164] The NOS implemented under the USDA's National Organic Program provide specific criteria that food producers must meet during production, handling, and processing in order to label their products *organic*. These standards define substances both approved for and prohibited from use in organic food production. For example, organic foods cannot be grown using sewage sludge, and the farming and processing operations that produce and handle foods labeled as organic must be certified by a USDA-accredited inspector.[165]

Consumers who purchase organically grown and processed foods should not assume that they are pesticide free. Organically grown crops may come into contact with chemicals due to drift from wind and rainwater. Also, though organic farmers use IPM, and grow more disease- and pest-resistant plants, they can also use synthetic pesticides and biopesticides to control weeds and insects. The National Organic Program has created the National List of Allowed and Prohibited Substances that identifies substances that can and cannot be used in organic crop production. The list contains natural (biological) and synthetic substances that are allowed as well as natural substances that are prohibited. Included on the list of allowed substances are several synthetic pesticides, such as insecticidal soaps, microbials, botanicals, and minerals, while some natural substances, such as ash from the burning of manure, are prohibited from use in organic farming.[166]

▲ **Figure 20.19 The USDA Organic Seal** Foods that are labeled or advertised with the USDA Organic Seal must contain at least 95 percent organic ingredients.

The USDA contends that there is no credible evidence to suggest that organic fruits and vegetables are safer or nutritionally superior to those grown in a conventional manner.[167] In addition, the Organic Trade Association confirms that there currently isn't conclusive evidence that organic foods are more nutritious than conventionally grown foods.[168] Organic food differs from conventionally grown produce only in the way it is grown, handled, and processed. Microbial contaminants that cause foodborne illness can be found in organic foods as well as in conventional foods. Nevertheless, organic foods may cost more than those that are conventionally grown.

Labeling of organic foods is strictly regulated and consumers can identify organically produced foods by looking for the USDA Organic Seal (**Figure 20.19**). Foods that display this seal or otherwise state that they are organic must contain at least 95 percent organic ingredients. There are other label claims and standards for foods that are 100 percent organic or made with organic ingredients. The labeling requirements are based on the percentage of a product's ingredients that are organic. See Table 20.9 for the standards that organic label claims must meet.

organic Being free of chemical-based pesticides, synthetic fertilizers, irradiation, and bioengineering. A USDA-accredited certifying inspector must certify organic foods.

TABLE 20.9 Various Levels of Organic

If the label says ▶

"Organic" and/or displays the USDA Organic seal

Then: The food contains at least 95 percent organic ingredients.

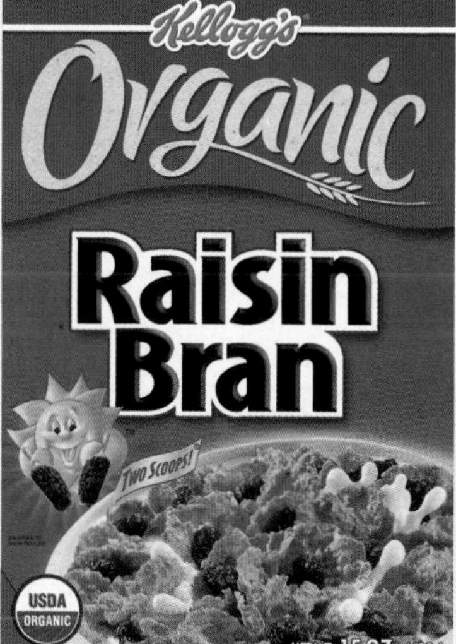

▲ If the label says

"100% Organic"

Then: The food must be composed entirely of organic ingredients. *Note:* These foods cannot contain sulfites and must declare the certifying agent. The USDA Organic seal may be displayed.

◀ If the label says

"Made with Organic Ingredients"

Then: The food contains at least 70 percent organic ingredients.

◀ If the label says

nothing about organic claims

Then: The food contains less than 70 percent organic ingredients.

THE TAKE-HOME MESSAGE Labeling terms can provide information that can help you select safe and sustainable foods. Organic foods are grown without the use of some chemical pesticides, synthetic fertilizers, sewage sludge, hormones, bioengineering, or irradiation. The National Organic Standards provide specific criteria and guidelines for the production, handling, processing, and labeling of organic foods, as well as mandatory certification by an accredited inspector. Organic foods may cost more than conventionally grown foods, and there is no conclusive evidence that they are more nutritious than conventionally grown foods.

Two Points of View

Can Organic Go Large Scale?

As organic foods become more popular, more supermarket and discount chains are offering them. Does the buying and selling of organic foods on a national scale defeat the purpose? What does "organic" mean to most people? We ask two experts in the field.

Bob Scowcroft

Cofounder, Organic Farming Research Foundation

Bob Scowcroft cofounded the Organic Farming Research Foundation, based in Santa Cruz, California in 1990. He retired from the Executive Director position in 2011. The nonprofit group's mission is to sponsor research related to organic farming practices, to disseminate research results to organic farmers and to growers interested in adopting organic production systems, and to educate the public and decision makers about organic farming issues.

Q: What is the definition of "organic" and how is organic food regulated?

A: There is a definition I really like from the early days of constructing organic regulations. It says that an organic production system is one that avoids or excludes the use of synthetically compounded fertilizers, pesticides, growth-regulating hormones, and livestock feed additives. It also says, to the maximum extent feasible, that organic farming systems rely on alternative growing methods, such as crop rotation, mechanical cultivation, and biological pest control, to maintain soil production, supply plant nutrients, and control pests.

The USDA is responsible for enforcing national organic standards, and more recently they have begun to do so. Many states have also become engaged in enforcing their organic regulations as well. Within North America, the Ag Census reports that there are over 14,000 farmers who are certified organic with another 8,000 claiming organic systems in place on their small farms. Plus we now have independent, professional inspectors who are well trained and can report organic farmers and/or businesses if they're in violation.

Q: Why are organic foods becoming more popular, and how has this affected their availability?

A: The primary reason is the growing public concern surrounding the industrial factory farmed system that produces conventional foods. Increased media attention on pesticide food contaminations and the overuse of antibiotic drugs in our meat and poultry supply has encouraged an ever increasing group of consumers to purchase organically labeled products. As of 2011, organic is about 4.5 percent of our food economy. [In 2010] total sales of

Mark Kastel

Cofounder and Director, Organic Integrity Project, the Cornucopia Institute

Mark Kastel is cofounder of The Cornucopia Institute, a progressive farm policy research group based in Wisconsin. His professional experience includes political consulting and lobbying on behalf of family farm groups and business development work benefiting family-scale farmers. He has also been a certified organic grower.

Q: What is the definition of "organic" and how is organic food regulated?

A: Since 2002, when the USDA finally implemented the Organic Food Production Act, there has been only one legal definition for organic food in the United States. No one can legally produce food to a lower standard. There is also a prohibition against saying you're producing food to a higher standard.

Unfortunately, there is debate over the interpretation of the standards. Large corporate agribusiness concerns have now invested in organics. Interpretation and lack of enforcement are definitely hot topics. A premier issue for us right now is industrial dairy farms producing organic milk. Some of these farms have 8,000 to 10,000 animals or more in feedlot-like conditions. This is contradictory to the intent and spirit of the law.

Q: Why are organic foods becoming more popular, and how has this affected their availability?

A: There are two reasons for the growing popularity. The first is that multiple food scares have woken up a lot of consumers who are really interested in providing healthy, safe food for their families. Whether it's the relationship between antibiotic use in livestock and resistant bacteria, pathogens in our environment and food supply, toxic and carcinogenic chemical residue on our food, or hormones not thoroughly tested on humans, consumers have a wide list of concerns almost universally addressed by organic production.

The other reason is that people who are living an increasingly frenzied lifestyle are finding additional meaning in their lives through a connection to food. That connection has historically been an important part of the human race. It's only since the Industrial Revolution that most of our population is disconnected from food production. And only in the last 75 years has it moved away from being a local enterprise, with food shipped from far away, organic foods in the United States was reported to be $27 billion. A significant portion of that growth has been generated by traditional supermarkets and "big-box" stores.

Some in the organic world aren't comfortable with large corporations opening up organic divisions to meet supermarket and box store demand. But there's a positive side to this development. Introducing organically labeled products through more mainstream channels allows "us" to introduce organic to an economic strata that has never before had the opportunity to purchase organic food at a competitive price. I believe that this has in turn facilitated the growth in smaller organic farms and correspondingly farmer's markets. Which, in turn, has led to new interest in the buying local movement.

Q: Is it possible to grow and distribute truly organic foods on a national scale? Why or why not?

A: It's possible, but it's complex. It depends on how well a specific product ships, and its shelf life. That's why you see some organic products—nuts, apples, bagged salads—available now on a national scale. In other cases, the infrastructure to make it work just isn't there. That's the case with most meat and poultry. To get truly national distribution, you need regional distribution networks that are certified organic, you need producers to feed into those networks, and you need products that ship well. I do see certain critical components that may well be unsustainable within a large-scale food system. One example, the energy needed to ship food long distances will remain volatile.

Q: How will the landscape of organic foods change in the future?

A: I think it will be tumultuously positive. Sadly, there are more food safety issues out there, and those will mean another big wave of consumers moving to purchase organic products. Some people in the organic movement will question that growth again. But both perspectives are right. You'll be able to get the freshest local salads from one of the thousands of producers at farmers markets if you wish, but you can also get organic tomato paste (as one example) from big-brand companies selling in a box store, too.

all wrapped in plastic. Organic food is an opportunity not only to protect your family from harmful substances or provide for them an improved level of nutrition, but to also restore this connection.

Q: Is it possible to grow and distribute truly organic foods on a national scale? Why or why not?

A: From a technical standpoint, the answer is "Yes." The definition of organic is about the production method. And in some cases, large scale might be appropriate. If almonds or macadamia nuts can only be grown in one environment, you're going to need a wider distribution.

But it's not organic to concentrate livestock on a factory farm in Colorado and ship their food—grain, hay, soybeans—in from around the world from hundreds of sources. From a philosophical standpoint, shipping that feed isn't organic and then shipping the milk all over the country isn't organic. There's supposed to be this intrinsic relationship between the livestock and the land, and the livestock and the people. This all gets broken when you do it from a distance. A farm like that might be certified organic, but it's certainly not a sustainable system.

Q: How will the landscape of organic foods change in the future?

A: More and more people are finding meaning between their food and the land. They start with their concerns over health and safety of food, like maybe their milk. Then they start to read labels on their food and pay attention to where it comes from. Food scares, like the nationwide *E. coli* spinach recall in 2006, have also really upped the interest in farmers' markets and local food.

Changes are also coming in how organic food is sold. Half of all organic food is now sold in traditional supermarkets. The jury is out whether this extreme growth we're experiencing is going to be good or bad for organics. If the integrity can be maintained, consumers and farmers will win. It will create more and more opportunity on a local and regional level for people to connect with their food and each other.

Putting It All Together

Americans have access to one of the safest food supplies in the world. However, it is still possible for our food to be affected by biological or chemical contamination. The risk of foodborne illness can be decreased by proper food selection, preparation, and storage. Consumers can use the information on food labels to make more informed choices about whether the foods have been grown using techniques that have less environmental impact. Other methods, such as genetic engineering, hold promise for increasing crop yields and improving the nutrient content of foods.

Visual Chapter Summary

1 Foodborne Illness Is Caused by Pathogens and Toxins

Pathogens (viruses, bacteria, molds, parasites, and prions) are the primary causes of foodborne infection. Toxins produced by pathogens or present in food, either naturally or through chemical contamination, can cause foodborne intoxication. Noroviruses are the single largest cause of foodborne illness.

The most common bacteria that cause foodborne illness are *Campylobacter*, *E. coli* O157:H7, and *Salmonella*. Marine toxins and chemical contaminants, such as PCBs and methylmercury, can bioaccumulate to toxic levels in fish.

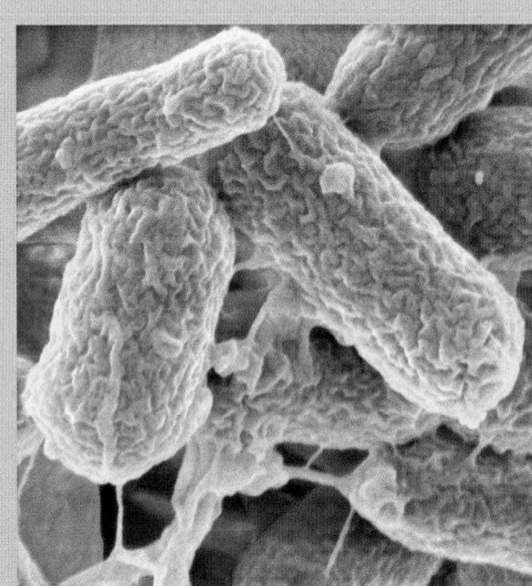

2 Proper Food Handling Can Prevent Foodborne Illness

Proper food handling techniques during four critical steps—cleaning, combating cross-contamination, cooking, and chilling—can help reduce the risk of foodborne illness. Foodborne bacteria multiply most rapidly in temperatures between 40°F and 140°F (or 5°C to 60°C), a range known as the danger zone. Cold foods should be stored and served below 40°F, and hot foods must be kept above 140°F. Extra caution is needed when traveling abroad, particularly in developing countries, to avoid foodborne illness. As a general guideline to avoid foodborne illness while traveling, do not eat raw produce unless you wash and peel it first, and avoid drinking tap water or using ice made from tap water unless the water is boiled or treated with iodine or chlorine first.

3 Everyone Plays a Role in Protecting Our Food Supply

Everyone, from the farmer to the consumer, plays an important role in food safety. Through the coordinated effort of the Food Safety Initiative, numerous U.S. government agencies work together to safeguard America's food supply against foodborne illness. Hazard Analysis and Critical Control Point (HACCP) procedures are used by both the FDA and USDA to identify and control foodborne hazards that occur in all stages of the food system. Food manufacturers use techniques such as pasteurization, canning, and irradiaton to help keep food safe for extended periods of time. Food irradiation exposes a food item to a radiant energy source that kills or greatly reduces some pathogens.

4 Food Additives, Chemical Enhancers, and Pesticides Play a Role in Food Production and Safety

Food additives are used as preservatives, antioxidants, flavoring, coloring, and leavening agents; to maintain a food's consistency; and to add nutrients. Pesticides are substances that allow crop plants to flourish by killing or repelling damaging pests. Natural biopesticides and antimicrobials are less toxic than chemical pesticides such as organophosphates. Integrated pest management (IPM) is used by many farmers and is designed to use the most economical methods to control pests with the least risk of harm to the consumer, the crops, and the environment.

5 Biotechnology Is Used to Alter the Genetic Makeup of Plants

Biotechnology, such as plant breeding and genetic engineering, is the application of biological techniques to alter the genetic makeup of living cells in order to create a desired trait in an organism. Plant breeding creates disease-resistant crops and increases the yield of crops.

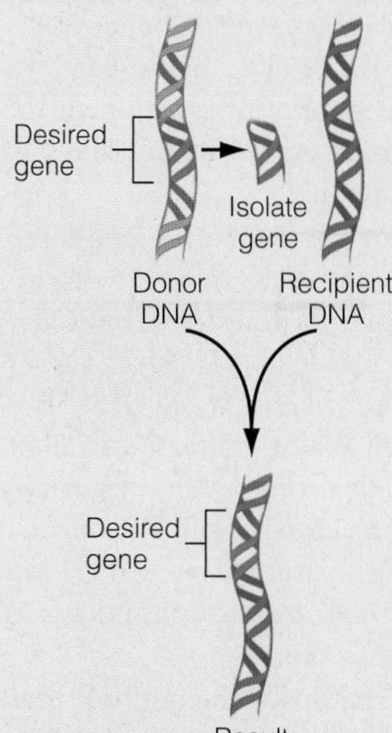

Genetic engineering is a more precise technique in which a specific gene or genes are inserted into the DNA of another cell to create a genetically modified product. Genetic engineering is done to improve crop yields and reduce the use of pesticides. It may have other environmental, industrial, and biological benefits. Genetically engineered foods are heavily regulated in the United States.

6 A Sustainable Food System Conserves Natural Resources

Sustainability involves every sector in the food system. Sustainable food systems need to be naturally or ecologically sound, socially acceptable and humane, and economical. Factors that influence and impact the food system include social values and trends, economics, policy, education, and research and technology. Soil, biodiversity, energy, and water are key natural resources that must be preserved. Local, federal, and international food and agriculture policies that encourage practices that preserve natural resources are needed before current food systems can become more sustainable.

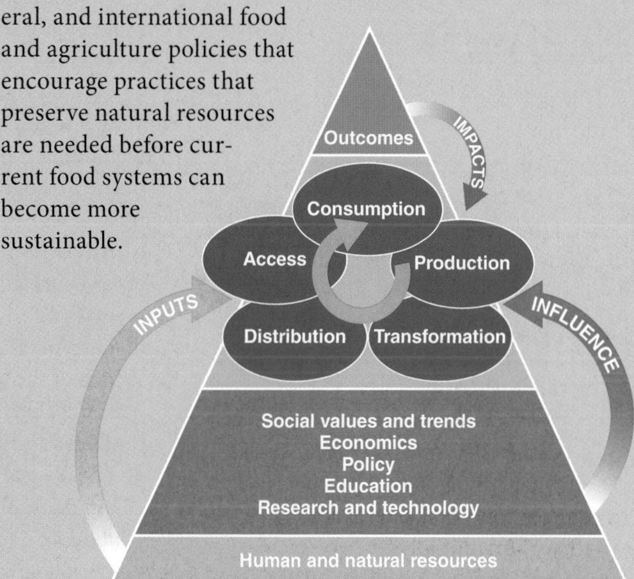

7 Be an Informed Food Consumer

Many factors may influence the foods that are available to you, but ultimately, you choose the foods you purchase and consume. It is up to you to recognize and understand label terms that indicate how foods are produced. Organic foods are grown without the use of some synthetic pesticides, synthetic fertilizers, bioengineering, and irradiation. All foods advertised as "organic" must meet specific standards and be certified by a USDA-accredited inspector. Organic foods are not necessarily more healthy, safe, or nutritious than conventionally grown foods.

Terms to Know

- foodborne illness
- pathogens
- norovirus
- toxins
- virus
- host
- fungi
- molds
- parasites
- prions
- marine toxins
- bioaccumulate
- polychlorinated biphenyls (PCBs)
- gastroenteritis
- cross-contaminate
- danger zone
- Food Safety Initiative (FSI)
- farm-to-table continuum
- food preservation
- pasteurization
- canning
- spores
- modified atmosphere packaging (MAP)
- high-pressure processing (HPP)
- irradiation
- food additives
- preservatives
- nitrates
- nitrites
- sulfites
- monosodium glutamate (MSG)
- generally recognized as safe (GRAS)
- DeLaney Clause
- bovine growth hormone (BGH)
- antibiotics
- antibiotic-resistant bacteria
- pesticides
- herbicides
- insecticides
- antimicrobials
- fungicides
- integrated pest management (IPM)
- plant breeding
- biotechnology
- genetic engineering
- genetically modified organisms (GMOs)
- sustainable
- biodiversity
- locavore
- community-supported agriculture (CSA)
- organic

MasteringNutrition™

Build your knowledge—and confidence—in the Study Area of MasteringNutrition with a variety of study tools.

Check Your Understanding

1. Which of the following produce toxins that may cause foodborne illness?
   a. parasites
   b. viruses
   c. bacteria
   d. food additives
2. Which of the following pathogens is the most common cause of foodborne infection in the United States?
   a. *Clostridium botulinum*
   b. norovirus
   c. *Trichinella spiralis*
   d. *Escherichia coli* O157:H7
3. At what temperature, known as the danger zone, do bacteria readily thrive and multiply?
   a. any temperature above 40°F
   b. between 20°F and 120°F
   c. between 40°F and 140°F
   d. any temperature below 140°F
4. Which of the following food additives is on the FDA's GRAS list, is often added to enhance the flavor of savory foods, and causes adverse reactions among some individuals?
   a. nitrites
   b. sulfites
   c. monosodium glutamate
   d. vitamin E
5. Which of the following is the most likely source of mercury intoxication?
   a. green potatoes
   b. sardines
   c. large predatory fish
   d. unpasteurized milk
6. Which two government agencies oversee the safety of the majority of foods in the United States?
   a. United States Department of Agriculture (USDA) and Environmental Protection Agency (EPA)
   b. Centers for Disease Control and Prevention (CDC) and USDA
   c. USDA and Food and Drug Administration (FDA)
   d. FDA and EPA
7. Which of the following sets of four steps is part of the Fight BAC! campaign?
   a. cutting, cleaning, chopping, and chilling
   b. cleaning, combating cross-contamination, cutting, and chilling
   c. clearing, combating cross-contamination, cutting, and chilling
   d. cleaning, combating cross-contamination, cooking, and chilling
8. Which of the following preservation techniques destroys specific foodborne pathogens by breaking up the cells' DNA?
   a. irradiation
   b. pasteurization
   c. canning
   d. high-pressure processing
9. Which of the following is a justified reason for buying food grown and produced locally?
   a. Locally grown food is more nutrient dense than non–locally grown food.
   b. Locally grown foods are organic foods.
   c. Locally grown foods are free from pesticides.
   d. Locally grown foods use fewer natural resources than do non–locally grown foods.
10. A frozen chicken enchilada that has the USDA Organic seal on its label means which of the following?
    a. One hundred percent of the ingredients in the product are organic.
    b. No pesticides were used to grow the corn from which the tortillas were made.
    c. The chickens in the enchilada were grown without using antibiotics or growth hormones.
    d. The organic enchilada is better for you because it is nutritionally superior to a nonorganic chicken enchilada.

Answers

1. (c) Bacteria. Bacteria are the only pathogens that produce toxins and cause illness due to foodborne intoxication. Some but not all parasites, viruses, and bacteria cause illness due to foodborne infection. Food additives are common in food and should not cause illness. Food additives are either approved by the FDA prior to their use or have GRAS or prior-sanctioned status based on a history of safe consumption.
2. (b) Norovirus. Half of all foodborne illness is caused by infection due to the norovirus. Illnesses due to *Clostridium botulinum*, *Trichinella spiralis*, and *Escherichia coli* O157:H7 are much less common. *Clostridium botulinum* is a bacterium that causes foodborne intoxication, *Trichinella spiralis* is a parasite, and *Escherichia coli* O157:H7 is a bacterium that causes infection.
3. (c) Bacteria thrive and multiply best between the temperatures of 40°F and 140°F. Bacteria can grow or multiply on any living or nonliving surface or object, but also need a source of nutrients, moisture, time, and a pH above about 4.6 to thrive.
4. (c) Monosodium glutamate. Food additives are approved by the FDA for a number of different reasons. Monosodium glutamate is a flavor enhancer and has GRAS status, but some people, including those with asthma, may experience symptoms such as numbness, a burning sensation, facial pressure or tightness, chest pain, and rapid heart beat after consuming MSG. Nitrites and sulfites and vitamin E are additives that help preserve food.
5. (c) Large predatory fish are the most common source of methylmercury. Predatory fish bioaccumulate methylmercury at high levels by absorbing it from polluted water and eating smaller fish that also contain it. Mercury poisoning can damage the central nervous system, and the FDA and EPA recommend that women who are pregnant or

nursing and young children avoid consumption of these types of fish. Potatoes turn green after having been exposed to sunlight and may contain a toxin known as solanine. Unpasteurized milk may be a source of pathogens but is not a likely source of mercury.

6. (c) The USDA and FDA oversee the safety of most foods in the U.S. Neither the CDC nor the EPA has direct regulatory oversight of the food supply.
7. (d) To prevent foodborne illness, it's important to employ proper food handling strategies when cleaning, combating cross-contamination, cooking, and chilling the foods in your meal.
8. (a) Irradiation involves using radiation to damage the DNA of pathogens. Pasteurization and canning both use high temperatures to kill pathogens, while high-pressure processing employs pulses of high pressure.
9. (d) Locally grown food requires fewer external natural resources in the form of fossil fuels from farm to your fork. However, just because a food is grown locally does not mean that it is grown organically or otherwise differently from foods that are grown further from your home.
10. (c) The USDA Organic seal indicates that 95 percent of the ingredients in a food are grown organically and that food-producing animals used in the product were grown without the use of hormones or antibiotics. Some, but not all, pesticides may be used by organic farmers. There is little evidence that organically grown foods are more nutritious or safer for you than foods grown using conventional methods.

Answers to Myths and Misconceptions

1. **False.** A food may contain disease-causing bacteria or other contaminants, yet look and smell perfectly fine.
2. **False.** Hand sanitizer will kill most disease-causing pathogens, as will soap and water. It is not necessary to wash your hands with soap and water if you use hand sanitizer.
3. **True.** A kitchen sponge provides the perfect medium for bacterial growth: moisture, nutrients, and room temperature.
4. **False.** Freezing doesn't kill bacteria but puts them in a dormant state. Once thawed, some bacteria can continue to grow and reproduce.
5. **False.** Leftovers should be thrown out if they're not consumed within three to five days.
6. **False.** Package dates refer to food quality, not safety.
7. **False.** The FDA deems food additives safe if they present a "negligible risk" of cancer to human beings with lifetime use.
8. **True.** A good scrub with cold, running water and a vegetable brush can remove most pesticide residue, and many germs, from produce.
9. **True.** Some synthetic pesticides have been approved for use on organic crops.
10. **True.** For example, a bacterial gene inserted into plant DNA has been used to develop insect-resistant varieties of corn, potatoes, and soybeans.

Web Resources

- For food safety education, visit www.fightbac.org
- For foodborne illness fact sheets, visit www.fsis.usda.gov/fact_sheets/Foodborne_Illness_&_Disease_Fact_Sheets/index.asp
- For more information on organic foods, visit www.ams.usda.gov/nop/indexIE.htm
- For information on biotechnology, visit www.fda.gov/Food/Biotechnology/default.htm

References

1. Centers for Disease Control and Prevention. 2011. *CDC Estimates of Foodborne Illness in the United States.* Available at www.cdc.gov/foodborneburden/2011-foodborne-estimates.html. Accessed May 2012.
2. Ibid.
3. Ibid.
4. Food and Drug Administration. 2007. *Food Protection Plan.* Available at www.fda.gov/oc/initiatives/advance/food/plan.html. Accessed November 2008.
5. Center for Food Safety and Applied Nutrition. 2001. *Chapter IV: Outbreaks Associated with Fresh and Fresh-Cut Produce. Incidence, Growth, and Survival of Pathogens in Fresh and Fresh-Cut Produce.* Available at www.fda.gov/Food/ScienceResearch/ResearchAreas/SafePracticesforFoodProcesses/ucm091265.htm. Accessed May 2012.
6. Centers for Disease Control and Prevention. 2012. *Foodborne Illness, Foodborne Disease, (Sometimes Called "Food Poisoning").* Available at www.cdc.gov/foodsafety/facts.html. Accessed November 2012.
7. Centers for Disease Control and Prevention. 2011. *CDC Estimates of Foodborne Illness in the United States.*
8. Center for Food Safety and Applied Nutrition. Updated 2011. Food Safety A to Z Reference Guide: U-V-W: Virus. Available at www.fda.gov/Food/ResourcesForYou/StudentsTeachers/ScienceandTheFoodSupply/ucm215850.htm. Accessed November 2012.
9. Sears, C. L. 2005. A Dynamic Partnership: Celebrating Our Gut Flora. *Anaerobe* 11:247–251.
10. Centers for Disease Control and Prevention. Updated 2012. *E. coli (Escherichia coli).* Available at www.cdc.gov/ecoli/general/index.html. Accessed November 2012.
11. United States Department of Agriculture. 2005. *Fact Sheet: Molds on Foods: Are They Dangerous?* Available at www.fsis.usda.gov/fact_sheets/Molds_On_Food/index.asp. Accessed November 2008.
12. Food Safety and Inspection Service. 2001. *Parasites and Foodborne Illness.* Available at www.fsis.usda.gov/Fact_Sheets/Parasites_and_Foodborne_Illness/index.asp. Accessed November 2008.
13. Gerald, B. J. and J. E. Perkin. 2003. Position of the American Dietetic Association: Food and Water Safety. *Journal of the American Dietetic Association* 103:1203–1218.
14. U.S. Department of Agriculture. 2012. *Hot Issues: BSE.* Available at www.aphis.usda.gov/animal_health/animal_diseases/bse/index.shtml. Accessed November 2012.
15. USDA. 2012. Statement by USDA Chief Veterinary Officer John Clifford Regarding a Detection of Bovine Spongiform Encephalopathy (BSE) in the United States. Release No. 0132.12, April 24, 2012. Available at www.usda.gov/wps/portal/usda/usdahome?contentidonly=true&contentid=2012/04/0132.xml. Accessed August 2012.

16. Centers for Disease Control and Prevention. 2005. *Marine Toxins.* Available at www.cdc.gov/ncidod/dbmd/diseaseinfo/marinetoxins_g.htm. Accessed November 2008.
17. Ibid.
18. Ibid.
19. Ibid.
20. National Toxicology Program, Department of Health and Human Services. 2005. *Executive Summary of Chaconine and Solanine.* Available at http://ntp-server.niehs.nih.gov/index.cfm?objectid=6F5E930D-F1F6-975E7037ACA48ABB25F4. Accessed August 2012.
21. Taylor, S. 2006. Food Additives, Contaminants, and Natural Toxicants and Their Risk Assessment. In Shils, M., M. Shike, A. Ross, B. Caballero, and R. Cousins. *Modern Nutrition in Health and Disease.* 10th ed. Philadelphia: Lippincott Williams & Wilkins.
22. U.S. Environmental Protection Agency. 2012. *Polychlorinated Biphenyls (PCBs).* Available at www.epa.gov/epawaste/hazard/tsd/pcbs/pubs/about.htm. Accessed November 2012.
23. Agency for Toxic Substances and Disease Registry. Updated 2007. *ToxFAQ for Polychlorinated Biphenyls (PCBs).* Available at www.atsdr.cdc.gov/toxfaqs/tf.asp?id=140&tid=26. Accessed November 2012.
24. U.S. Environmental Protection Agency. 2008. *Polychlorinated Biphenyls (PCBs).*
25. Ibid.
26. Environmental Protection Agency. 2006. *Consumer Fact Sheet on PCBs.* Available http://water.epa.gov/drink/contaminants/basicinformation/historical/upload/Archived-Consumer-Fact-Sheet-on-Polychlorinated-Biphenyls.pdf. Accessed November 2012.
27. Gerald. 2003. Position of the American Dietetic Association: Food and Water Safety; U.S. Environmental Protection Agency. 2008. *Polychlorinated Biphenyls (PCBs).*
28. Department of Health and Human Services and Environmental Protection Agency. 2004. *What You Need to Know about Mercury in Fish and Shellfish.* Available at www.fda.gov/Food/ResourcesForYou/Consumers/ucm110591.htm. Accessed November 2012.
29. Administration on Aging, U.S. Department of Health and Human Services. 2011. *A Profile of Older Americans 2010.* Available at www.aoa.gov/aoaroot/aging_statistics/Profile/2010/docs/2010profile.pdf. Accessed August 2012.
30. Gerald. 2003. Position of the American Dietetic Association: Food and Water Safety.
31. Buzby, J. C. 2003. Older Adults at Risk of Complications from Microbial Foodborne Illness. *FoodReview* 25:30–35.
32. United States Department of Agriculture Food Safety and Inspection Service. 2011. *Fact Sheets: Safe Food Handling.* Available at www.fsis.usda.gov/fact_sheets/danger_zone/index.asp. Accessed June 2012.
33. USFDA. 2007. *Teacher's Guide for Middle Level Science Classrooms. Science and Our Food Supply.* Available at www.fda.gov/food/resourcesforyou/studentsteachers/scienceandthefoodsupply/ucm181842.htm#main. Accessed August 2012.
34. Partnership for Food Safety Education. 2010. *Safe Food Handling: The Core Four Practices.* Available at www.fightbac.org/safe-food-handling. Accessed March 2012.
35. Center for Food Safety and Applied Nutrition. 2007. *Food Safety A to Z Reference Guide: Handwashing.* www.fda.gov/Food/ResourcesForYou/StudentsTeachers/ScienceandTheFoodSupply/ucm215837.htm. Accessed November 2012.
36. Food Safety and Inspection Service. 2003. *The Food Safety Educator: Special Conference Issue: Thinking Globally, Working Locally.* Available at www.fsis.usda.gov/OA/educator/educator8-1.htm. Accessed November 2012.
37. CDC. 2012. Handwashing: Clean Hands Save Lives. Available at www.cdc.gov/handwashing. Accessed November 2012.
38. BBC News. 2004. Lifting the Lid on Computer Filth. Available at http://news.bbc.co.uk/2/hi/health/3505414.stm. Accessed November 2012.
39. Food Safety and Inspection Service. 2003. *The Food Safety Educator.*
40. Agriculture Research Service, Food Safety and Inspection Service. 1998. *Premature Browning of Cooked Ground Beef.* Available at www.fsis.usda.gov/OPHS/prebrown.htm. Accessed November 2008.
41. Food Safety and Inspection Service. 2008. *The Color of Meat and Poultry.* Available at www.fsis.usda.gov/Fact_Sheets/Color_of_Meat_&_Poultry/index.asp. Accessed November 2008.
42. Food and Drug Administration. 2005. *Food Code.* Available at www.fda.gov/Food/FoodSafety/RetailFoodProtection/FoodCode/default.htm. Accessed November 2012.
43. American Dietetic Association. 2001. *Survey Reveals Americans Need a Refrigeration Refresher.* Available at http://homefoodsafety.org/media-releases-apr6-2001. Accessed November 2012; Partnership for Food Safety Education. 2006. *Fridge Fact Sheet.* Available at www.fightbac.org.
44. Food Safety and Inspection Service. 2006. *How Temperatures Affect Food.* Available at www.fsis.usda.gov/Fact_Sheets/How_Temperatures_Affect_Food/index.asp. Accessed November 2008.
45. Ibid.
46. Centers for Disease Control, Division of Bacterial and Mycotic Diseases. Updated 2006. *Travelers' Diarrhea.* Available at www.cdc.gov/ncidod/dbmd/diseaseinfo/travelersdiarrhea_g.htm. Accessed November 2012.
47. Food and Drug Administration and U.S. Department of Agriculture. 2000. *A Description of the U.S. Food Safety System.* Available at www.fsis.usda.gov/OA/codex/system.htm. Accessed November 2008.
48. Centers for Disease Control and Prevention (CDC). 2011. Vital Signs: Incidence and Trends of Infection with Pathogens Transmitted Commonly Through Food. 1996–2010. *Morbidity and Mortality Weekly Report* 60:749–755.
49. Centers for Disease Control. 2008. *PulseNet: The National Molecular Subtyping Network for Foodborne Disease Surveillance.* Available at www.cdc.gov/pulsenet. Accessed November 2008.
50. Bracket, R. 2006. Statement before the Committee on Health, Education, Labor and Pensions, United States Senate. Available at www.fda.gov/NewsEvents/Testimony/ucm110926.htm. Accessed November 2012; Food and Drug Administration. 2006. *Nationwide* E. coli *O157:H7 Outbreak: Questions and Answers.* Available at www.fda.gov. Accessed November 2008.
51. Food and Drug Administration. 2007. *Food Protection Plan.*
52. Food and Drug Administration. 2001. HACCP: A State-of-the-Art Approach to Food Safety. *FDA Backgrounder.* Available at www.fda.gov. Accessed November 2008.
53. Food and Drug Administration. 2005. *Food Code.*
54. Center for Food Safety and Applied Nutrition. 1998. Updated 2001. *What Consumers Need to Know about Juice Safety.* Available at www.fda.gov/Food/ResourcesForYou/Consumers/ucm110526.htm. Accessed November 2012.
55. FoodReference.com. n.d. *About Canned Food.* Available at www.foodreference.com/html/artcanninghistory.html. Accessed November 2008.
56. Tauxe, R. B. 2001. Food Safety and Irradiation: Protecting the Public from Foodborne Infections. Centers for Disease Control and Prevention, Emerging Infectious Diseases. Available at wwwnc.cdc.gov/eid/article/7/7/01-7706_article.htm. Accessed November 2012.
57. Center for Food Safety and Applied Nutrition. 2001. *Analysis and Evaluation of Preventive Control Measures for the Control and Reduction/Elimination of Microbial Hazards on Fresh and Fresh-Cut Produce.* Available www.fda.gov/Food/ScienceResearch/ResearchAreas/SafePracticesforFoodProcesses/ucm090977.htm. Accessed November 2012.
58. Finley, J., D. Deming, and R. Smith. 2006. Food Processing: Nutrition, Safety, and Quality. In Shils, M., M. Shike, A. Ross, B. Caballero, and R. Cousins. *Modern Nutrition in Health and Disease.* 10th ed. Philadelphia: Lippincott Williams & Wilkins.
59. Tauxe. 2001. Food Safety and Irradiation; Food and Drug Administration. 2000. *Food Irradiation: A Safe Measure.* Available at www.fda.gov/opacom/catalog/irradbro.html. Accessed November 2008.
60. Food and Drug Administration. 2000. *Food Irradiation.*

61. Tauxe. 2001. Food Safety and Irradiation; Emmert, K., V. Duffy, and R. Earl. 2000. Position of the American Dietetic Association: Food Irradiation. *Journal of the American Dietetic Association* 100:246–253.
62. Tauxe. 2001. Food Safety and Irradiation; Food and Drug Administration. 2000. *Food Irradiation.*
63. Food and Drug Administration. 2000. *Food Irradiation.*
64. Emmert, et al. 2000. Position of the American Dietetic Association: Food Irradiation.
65. Iowa State University. 2006. *Food Irradiation—What Is It?* Available at www.extension.iastate.edu/foodsafety/irradiation. Accessed November 2008.
66. Food Safety and Inspection Service. 2005. *Irradiation of Raw Meat and Poultry: Questions and Answers.* Available at www.fsis.usda.gov/Fact_Sheets/Irradiation_and_Food_Safety/index.asp. Accessed November 2008; Tauxe. 2001. Food Safety and Irradiation.
67. Centers for Disease Control and Prevention. 2005. *Frequently Asked Questions about Food Irradiation.* Available at www.cdc.gov/ncidod/dbmd/diseaseinfo/foodirradiation.htm. Accessed November 2008.
68. Lewis, C. 2002. Food Freshness and "Smart" Packaging. *FDA Consumer* 36:25–29.
69. Food Safety and Inspection Service. Updated 2007. *Focus On: Food Product Dating.* Available at www.fsis.usda.gov/Fact_Sheets/Food_Product_Dating/index.asp. Accessed November 2008.
70. Environmental Protection Agency. 2008. *It's Your Drinking Water: Get to Know It and Protect It!* Available at http://www.epa.gov/ogwdw/consumer/pdf/itsyours.pdf. Accessed November 2012.
71. Environmental Protection Agency. 2008. *Safe Drinking Water Act (SDWA). Regulations and Guidance.* Available at www.epa.gov/ogwdw000/regs.html. Accessed November 2008.
72. Gerald. 2003. Position of the American Dietetic Association: Food and Water Safety.
73. Centers for Disease Control and Prevention (CDC). 2012. Vital Signs: Food Categories Contributing the Most to Sodium Consumption—United States, 2007–2008. *Morbidity and Mortality Weekly Report* 6:62–98.
74. Mirvish, S. S., J. Haorah, L. Zhou, M. L. Clapper, K. L. Harrison, and A. C. Povey. 2002. Total N-Nitroso Compounds and Their Precursors in Hot Dogs and in the Gastrointestinal Tract and Feces of Rats and Mice: Possible Etiologic Agents for Colon Cancer. *Journal of Nutrition* 132(Suppl):3526S–3529S.
75. National Toxicology Program, Health and Human Services. 2011. *12th Report on Carcinogens.* Available at http://ntp.niehs.nih.gov/?objectid=03C9AF75-E1BF-FF40DBA9EC0928DF8B15. Accessed May 2012.
76. Center for Food Safety and Applied Nutrition. 2000. *Sulfites: An Important Food Safety Issue.* Available at www.cfsan.fda.gov/~dms/fssulfit.html. Accessed November 2008.
77. International Food Information Council. 1997. *Everything You Need to Know about Asthma and Food.* Available at http://www.foodinsight.org/Content/6/Everything-You-Need-to-Know-About-Asthma-Food.pdf. Accessed November 2012.
78. Papazian, R. 1996. Sulfites: Safe for Most, Dangerous for Some. Center for Food Safety and Applied Nutrition. Available at www.tequestafamilypractice.com/articles/Sulfite_Allergy.pdf. Accessed November 2012.
79. Center for Food Safety and Applied Nutrition. 2000. *Sulfites.*
80. Ibid.
81. FDA. n.d. *Food Additives Status List.* Available at www.fda.gov/food/foodingredientspackaging/foodadditives/foodadditivelistings/ucm091048.htm. Accessed November 2012.
82. Rados, C. 2004. GRAS: Time-Tested and Trusted Food Ingredients. *FDA Consumer.* Available at www.fda.gov/Food/FoodIngredientsPackaging/GenerallyRecognizedasSafeGRAS/default.htm. Accessed November 2012.
83. FDA. n.d. *Food Additives Status List.*
84. Rados. 2004. GRAS.
85. Food and Drug Administration. 2008. *Questions and Answers about Dioxins.* Available at www.fda.gov/Food/FoodSafety/FoodContaminantsAdulteration/ChemicalContaminants/DioxinsPCBs/ucm077524.htm. Accessed November 2012.
86. Center for Veterinary Medicine. 1999. *Report on the Food and Drug Administration's Review of the Safety of Recombinant Bovine Somatotropin.* Available at www.fda.gov/AnimalVeterinary/SafetyHealth/ProductSafetyInformation/ucm130321.htm. Accessed November 2012.
87. American Cancer Society. 2011. *Learn About Cancer: Recombinant Bovine Growth Hormone.* Available at www.cancer.org/cancer/cancercauses/othercarcinogens/athome/recombinant-bovine-growth-hormone. Accessed June 2012.
88. Center for Veterinary Medicine. 2002. *The Use of Steroid Hormones for Growth Promotion in Food-Producing Animals.* Available at www.fda.gov/AnimalVeterinary/NewsEvents/FDAVeterinarianNewsletter/ucm110712.htm. Accessed November 2012.
89. Ibid.
90. Centers for Disease Control and Prevention. 2005. *Frequently Asked Questions about NARMS.* Available at www.cdc.gov/ncidod/dbmd/diseaseinfo/files/foodborne_illness_FAQ.pdf. Accessed November 2012.
91. Ibid.
92. Committee on the Future Role of Pesticides in U.S. Agriculture. Board on Agriculture and Natural Resources. Board on Environmental Studies and Toxicology. National Research Council. 2000. *The Future Role of Pesticides in U.S. Agriculture.* Washington, DC: The National Academies Press.
93. U.S. Environmental Protection Agency. 2008. *About Pesticides: What Is a Pesticide?* Available at www.epa.gov/pesticides/about/index.htm. Accessed November 2008.
94. Ibid.
95. U.S. Environmental Protection Agency. 2006. *Organophosphate Pesticides (OP) Cumulative Assessment: 2006 Update.* Available at www.epa.gov/oppsrrd1/cumulative/2006-op. Accessed November 2012.
96. U.S. Environmental Protection Agency. Updated 2006. *Pesticides: Topical and Chemical Fact Sheets—Antimicrobial Pesticide Products.* Available at www.epa.gov/pesticides/factsheets/antimic.htm. Accessed November 2008.
97. Food and Drug Administration. 2003. *Hand Hygiene in Retail and Food Service Establishments.* Available at www.fda.gov/Food/FoodSafety/RetailFoodProtection/IndustryandRegulatoryAssistanceandTrainingResources/ucm135577.htm. Accessed November 2012.
98. U.S. Environmental Protection Agency. 2012. *Pesticides and Safety. Health Problems Pesticides May Pose.* Available at www.epa.gov/opp00001/food/risks.htm. Accessed September 2012.
99. U.S. Department of Health and Human Services. 2012. *Healthy People 2020: Environmental Health Objectives.* Available at www.healthypeople.gov/2020/topicsobjectives2020/overview.aspx?topicid=12. Accessed November 2012.
100. American Medical Association. Updated 2003. *Report 4 of the Council on Scientific Affairs (I-94).* Available at www.ama-assn.org/ama1/pub/upload/mm/443/csai-94.pdf. Accessed November 2008.
101. U.S. Environmental Protection Agency. 2007. *Pesticides: Topical and Chemical Fact Sheets—Assessing Health Risks from Pesticides.* Available at www.epa.gov/pesticides/factsheets/riskassess.htm. Accessed November 2008.
102. U.S. Environmental Protection Agency. Updated 2006. *Pesticides: Regulating Pesticides—Laws.* Available at www.epa.gov/pesticides/regulating/laws.htm. Accessed November 2008.
103. U.S. Environmental Protection Agency. Updated 2006. *Pesticides and Food: How the Government Regulates Pesticides.* Available at www.epa.gov/pesticides/food/govt.htm. Accessed November 2008; U.S. Environmental Protection Agency. Updated 2006. *Pesticides: Regulating Pesticides—Laws.*
104. U.S. Environmental Protection Agency. Updated 2006. *Pesticides: Topical and Chemical Fact Sheets—Integrated Pest Management (IPM) and Food Production.*

Available at www.epa.gov/pesticides/fact sheets/ipm.htm. Accessed November 2008.
105. International Food Information Council. 2006. *Agriculture and Food Production.* Available at www.foodinsight.org. Accessed November 2008.
106. Krieger, R. I., P. Brutsche-Keiper, H. R. Crosby, and A. D. Krieger. 2003. Reduction of Pesticide Residues of Fruit Using Water Only or Plus Fit Fruit and Vegetable Wash. *Bulletin of Environmental Contamination and Toxicology* 70:213–218.
107. American Cancer Society. 2000. *The Environment and Cancer Risk.* Available at www .cancer.org. Accessed November 2008.
108. Gregar, J. L. 2000. Biotechnology: Mobilizing Dietitians to Be a Resource. *Journal of the American Dietetic Association* 100:1306–1308.
109. Economic Research Service. 2012. *Adoption of Genetically Engineered Crops in the U.S.* Available at www.ers.usda.gov/data -products/adoption-of-genetically -engineered-crops-in-the-us.aspx. Accessed November 2012.
110. McCullum, C. 2000. Food Biotechnology in the New Millennium: Promises, Realities, and Challenges. *Journal of the American Dietetic Association* 100:1311–1315; Bren, L. 2003. Genetic Engineering: The Future of Foods. *FDA Consumer* 37:28–34.
111. McCullum. 2000. Food Biotechnology.
112. Economic Research Service. 2012. *Adoption of Genetically Engineered Crops in the U.S.*
113. Gregar. 2000. Biotechnology.
114. Economic Research Service. 2012. *Adoption of Genetically Engineered Crops in the U.S.*
115. Shoemaker, R., D. D. Johnson, and E. Golan. 2003. Consumers and the Future of Biotech Foods in the United States. *Amber Waves.* Available at www.ers.usda.gov/ Amberwaves/November03/Features/future ofbiotech.htm. Accessed November 2008.
116. McCullum. 2000. Food Biotechnology.
117. Gregar. 2000. Biotechnology.
118. American Dietetic Association. 1995. Biotechnology and the Future of Food. *Journal of the American Dietetic Association* 95:1429–1432.
119. Ibid.
120. Bren. 2003. Genetic Engineering: The Future of Foods; Shoemaker, et al. 2003. Consumers and the Future of Biotech Foods.
121. United States Department of Agriculture. 2007. *Q&A:* Bt *Corn and Monarch Butterflies.* Available at www.ars.usda.gov/is/br/ btcorn. Accessed November 2012.
122. Jones, L. 1999. Genetically Modified Foods. *British Medical Journal* 318:581–584.
123. Maryanski, J. H. 1997. Bioengineered Foods: Will They Cause Allergic Reactions? Center for Food Safety and Applied Nutrition. Available atwww.fda.gov/Food/ Biotechnology/default.htm. Accessed November 2012; American Medical Association. 2005. *Report 10 of the Council on Scientific Affairs (I-94). Genetically Modified Crops and Foods.* Available at www.ama-assn.org/resources/doc/csaph/ a12-csaph2-bioengineeredfoods.pdf. Accessed November 2012;Thompson, L. 2000. Are Bioengineered Foods Safe? *FDA Consumer* 34:18–23.
124. U.S. Food and Drug Administration. 2012. *Have Food Allergies? Read the Label.* Available at www.fda.gov/ForConsumers/ ConsumerUpdates/ucm254504.htm. Accessed June 2012.
125. Thompson, L. 2000. Are Bioengineered Foods Safe?
126. Formanek, R. 2001. Proposed Rules Issued for Bioengineered Foods. *FDA Consumer* 35:9–11.
127. Thompson, L. 2000. Are Bioengineered Foods Safe?
128. American Medical Association. 2005. *Report 10 of the Council on Scientific Affairs*; Society of Toxicology. 2002. *Society of Toxicology Position Paper: The Safety of Genetically Modified Foods Produced through Biotechnology.* Available at www.toxicology. org. Accessed December 2006.
129. Thompson, L. 2000. Are Bioengineered Foods Safe?
130. International Food Information Council. 2006. *Support for Food Biotechnology Stable Despite News on Unrelated Food Safety Issues.* Available at www.foodinsight.org. Accessed December 2006.
131. International Food Information Council. 2009. *Sustainable Agriculture: Can Biotechnology Play a Role?* Available at www.foodin sight.org. Accessed February 2010.
132. Harmon. 2007. Position of the American Dietetic Association: Food and Nutrition Professionals Can Implement Practices to Conserve Natural Resources and Support Ecological Sustainability. *Journal of the American Dietetic Association* 107:1033–1038.
133. National Oceanic and Atmospheric Administration, National Climatic Data Center. 2008. *Global Warming Frequently Asked Questions.* Available at www.ncdc.noaa.gov/ oa/climate/globalwarming.html#q1. Accessed January 2010.
134. Harmon. 2007. Position of the American Dietetic Association: Food and Nutrition Professionals Can Implement Practices; Pirog, R., T. Van Pelt, K. Enshayan, and E. Cook. 2001. *Food, Fuel, and Freeways: An Iowa Perspective on How Far Food Travels, Fuel Usage, and Greenhouse Gas Emissions.* Leopold Center for Sustainable Agriculture. Available at www.leopold.iastate.edu/pubs -and-papers/2001-06-food-fuel-freeways. Accessed November 2012.
135. Pirog, et al. 2001. *Food, Fuel, and Freeways*; Tompkins County Relocalization Project. 2005. Implications of Fossil Fuel Dependence for the Food System. *Energy Bulletin.* Available at www.resilience.org. Accessed January 2010.
136. Pirog, et al. 2001. *Food, Fuel, and Freeways.*
137. Ibid.
138. Tompkins County Relocalization Project. 2005. Implications of Fossil Fuel Dependence for the Food System; Hendrickson, J. 1996. Energy Use in the U.S. Food System: A Summary of Existing Research and Analysis. Center for Integrated Agricultural Systems, UW-Madison. Available at www. cias.wisc.edu/wp-content/uploads/2008/07/ energyuse.pdf. Accessed January 2010.
139. Brown, L. 2008. *Plan B 3.0. Mobilizing to Save Civilization.* New York: W.W. Norton & Company.
140. Pimentel, D., and M. Pimentel. 2003. Sustainability of Meat-Based and Plant-Based Diets and the Environment. *Journal of the American Dietetic Association* 78:660S–663S.
141. Howard, A. 1940. *The Agricultural Testament.* London: Oxford University Press.
142. Environmental Protection Agency. 2009. *What on Earth Is Soil?* Available at www .epa.gov/gmpo/edresources/soil.html. Accessed February 2010.
143. Tagtow. 2009. Healthy Land, Healthy Food and Healthy Eaters. Available at www .uwyo.edu/winwyoming/pubs/healthy land%20healthyfood%20healthyeaters.pdf. Accessed September 2012.
144. United States Department of Agriculture. 2010. *Colony Collapse Disorder Progress Report.* Available at www.ars.usda.gov/is/br/ ccd/ccdprogressreport2010.pdf. Accessed July 2012.
145. United Nations Food and Agriculture Organization. 2006. *The State of World Fisheries and Aquaculture.* Available at www.fao.org/docrep/009/A0699e/ A0699E05.htm. Accessed February 2010; Hilborn, R., T. Quinn, D. Schindler, and D. Rogers. 2003. Biocomplexity and Fisheries Sustainability. *Proceedings of the National Academy of Sciences of the USA* 100:4. Available at www.pnas.org/con tent/100/11/6564.full. Accessed February 2010.
146. Tagtow. 2009. Healthy Land, Healthy Food and Healthy Eaters.
147. Hendrickson, M. and H. James. 2008. Does the World Need U.S. Farmers Even If Americans Don't? *Journal of Agricultural and Environmental Ethics* 21:311–328.
148. Pimentel, et al. 2003. Sustainability of Meat-Based and Plant-Based Diets; Harmon. 2007. Position of the American Dietetic Association: Food and Nutrition Professionals Can Implement Practices.
149. Pimentel, et al. 2003. Sustainability of Meat-Based and Plant-Based Diets.
150. Ibid.
151. Heller, Martin C. and Gregory A. Keoleian. 2000. *Life Cycle-Based Sustainability Indicators for Assessment of the U.S. Food System.* Ann Arbor, MI: Center for Sustainable Systems, University of Michigan, 42.
152. Harmon. 2007. Position of the American Dietetic Association: Food and Nutrition Professionals Can Implement Practices.
153. Pimentel, D., P. Hepperly, J. Hanson, D. Douds, and R. Seidel. 2005. Environmental, Energetic, and Economic Comparisons of Organic and Conventional Farming Systems. *BioScience* 55:573–582.

154. EPA. 2010. *Watersense.* Available at www.epa.gov/watersense. Accessed November 2012.
155. Ibid.
156. Ibid.
157. Ibid.
158. Harmon. 2007. Position of the American Dietetic Association: Food and Nutrition Professionals Can Implement Practices.
159. United States Department of Agriculture. 2009. *USDA Awards More than $5 Million in Grants to Support Local Food Initiatives.* Available at www.csrees.usda.gov/newsroom/news/2009news/11181_cfp.html. Accessed January 2010.
160. Harmon. 2007. Position of the American Dietetic Association: Food and Nutrition Professionals Can Implement Practices; Herremans, I. and R. Reid. 2002. Developing Awareness of the Sustainability Concept. *Journal of Environmental Education* 34:16–20; Brundtland, G. 1987. *Our Common Future.* New York: Oxford University Press; Herrin, M. and J. D. Gussow. 1989. Designing a Sustainable Regional Diet. *Journal of Nutrition Education* 21:270–275.
161. USDA. 2006. *Meat and Poultry Labeling Terms.* www.fsis.usda.gov/Fact_Sheets/Meat_&_Poultry_Labeling_Terms/index.asp. Accessed February 2010.
162. Agricultural Marketing Service, National Organic Program. 2008. *Organic Food Standards and Labels: The Facts.* Available at www.ams.usda.gov/AMSv1.0/nop. Accessed November 2012.
163. Organic Trade Association. 2011. *U.S. Organic Industry Overview.* Available at www.ota.com/pics/documents/2011OrganicIndustrySurvey.pdf. Accessed August 2012.
164. International Food Information Council. 2003. *USDA Launches Organic Standards.* Available at www.foodinsight.org. Accessed November 2008.
165. Agricultural Marketing Service, National Organic Program. 2008. *Organic Food Standards.*
166. Agency for Toxic Substances and Disease Registry. Updated 2007. *ToxFAQ for Polychlorinated Biphenyls (PCBs).*
167. Dangour, A. D., K. Lock, A. Hayter, A. Aikenhead, E. Allen, and R. Uauy. 2010. Nutrition-Related Health Effects of Organic Foods: A Systematic Review. *American Journal of Clinical Nutrition* 92:203–210.
168. Organic Trade Association. 2005. *The Past, Present and Future of the Organic Industry.* Available at www.ota.com/pics/documents/Forecasting2005.pdf. Accessed December 2008.

21 Hunger at Home and Abroad

Chapter Objectives

After reading this chapter, you will be able to:

1. Summarize the extent of hunger in the United States and around the world.
2. Discuss the factors that give rise to hunger in the United States.
3. Describe the causes of hunger worldwide.
4. Identify populations that are at greatest risk for malnutrition.
5. Describe the physiological consequences of hunger.
6. Explain several ways to reduce hunger.

1. Hunger exists in every country in the world—including the United States. T/F
2. About one-seventh of the world's population does not have enough to eat. T/F
3. If you have a job, you will never experience food insecurity. T/F
4. Depression among mothers has been associated with food insecurity. T/F
5. Farmers already grow enough food to feed everyone on the planet today. T/F
6. Earthquakes can cause food shortages. T/F
7. Once you reach a certain age, you don't need to worry about malnutrition. T/F
8. Fortifying foods is a good idea, but it doesn't really affect malnutrition. T/F
9. You can't be obese and food insecure at the same time. T/F
10. The world's hunger problems would be solved if we just got food to everyone. T/F

See page 817 for answers to these Myths and Misconceptions.

We all know what "I'm hungry" feels like. After a long day working, a grumbling or gnawing in the stomach, a feeling of fatigue, or maybe light-headedness are all signs that tell us we need to eat. How many of us, however, know what it is like to be hungry day in and day out, never to feel truly full, or to lose weight though we don't want to?

Who are the people in the United States and the rest of the world who are hungry? What are the effects of chronic hunger? And, once we understand the causes and scope of this problem, what can we do about it? Can one person's actions really help people who are hungry? In this chapter, we'll explore the conditions of hunger and malnutrition, their causes and effects, and potential solutions in the United States and around the world.

How Prevalent Is Chronic Hunger?

The majority of people in the United States enjoy a high level of **food security:** they have the financial resources to access adequate amounts of healthy food on a regular basis. They probably describe hunger as the uneasy or painful physical sensation caused by a short-term lack of food. However, the term hunger as used in this chapter refers to more than just a growling stomach before dinner. According to the USDA definition, **hunger** is a physiological condition that can result from food insecurity. **Food insecurity** describes "household-level economic and social conditions of uncertain access to adequate food."[1] The USDA Economic Research Service uses labels to convey the severity of food insecurity in the United States (Table 21.1).[2]

Food insecurity is common among older adults, who may suffer from decreased mobility in addition to inadequate financial resources. Older adults may also suffer from *food insufficiency* when they occasionally or persistently have too little food. Other populations, including individuals and families in rural and urban regions, experience *food poverty*: inconsistent access to food due to financial constraints or geographic circumstances.[3]

The Census Bureau conducts an annual survey of food security, in which it asks questions about anxiety over the household food budget, the quantity and quality of food eaten, and the instances of reduced food intake. The survey is regarded as a reliable indicator for assessing the well-being of households as well as

TABLE 21.1 Ranges of Food Security

General Category	Level of Food Security	Description of Conditions in the Household
Food Security	High food security	No reported indications of food-access problems or limitations.
	Marginal food security	One or two reported indications—typically of anxiety over food sufficiency or shortage of food in the house. Little or no indication of changes in diets or food intake.
Food Insecurity	Low food security	Reports of reduced quality, variety, or desirability of diet. Little or no indication of reduced food intake.
	Very low food security	Reports of multiple indications of disrupted eating patterns and reduced food intake.

Source: Adapted from USDA Economic Research Service. 2006. Available at www.ers.usda.gov/topics/food-nutrition-assistance/foodsecurity-in-the-us/definitions-of-food-security.aspx. Accessed November 2012.

food security The degree to which an individual has regular access to adequate amounts of healthy foods.

hunger An individual-level physiological condition that may result from food insecurity.

food insecurity A household-level economic and social condition of uncertain access to adequate food.

measuring progress toward the *Healthy People 2020* goal of reducing food insecurity to 6 percent of U.S. households.[4]

In 2011, the USDA found that 14.9 percent of American households were food insecure at least some time during the year, including 5.7 percent with very low food security.[5] About 50.1 million people in the United States lived in food-insecure households in 2011, with 12.1 million adults living in households with very low food security and 8.6 million children living in food-insecure households in which children, along with adults, were food insecure.[6] The number of people in the worst-off households, those classified as "very low food security," rose from 5.4 percent in 2010 to 5.7 percent in 2011, which may indicate that the conditions for the poorest Americans are declining.

In addition, black and Hispanic households experienced food insecurity at higher rates than the national average, with 25.1 percent and 26.2 percent experiencing food insecurity, respectively. About 37 percent of single women heading up a household with children experienced food insecurity. Between 2009 and 2011, the five states with the highest food insecurity rates were Mississippi, Texas, Arkansas, Alabama, and Georgia.[7] (**Figure 21.1**)

Worldwide, the numbers are even higher. The United Nations Food and Agriculture Organization, which measures undernutrition, estimated that for the years 2006 to 2008, approximately 850 million people worldwide, or 13 percent of the world's population, were undernourished.[8] The rising costs of food, fuel, and fertilizer contributed to the increase; food prices, for example, rose 52 percent between 2007 and 2008.[9] Hunger and food insecurity exist despite the fact that current global food production exceeds the needs of the population. World agriculture produces 17 percent more kilocalories per person today than it did 30 years ago, which is enough to provide everyone in the world with at least 2,700 kilocalories per day.[10]

Thanks to agricultural advances, the world's farmers can grow plenty of food. However, distribution problems and other factors keep some people from getting enough to stave off hunger.

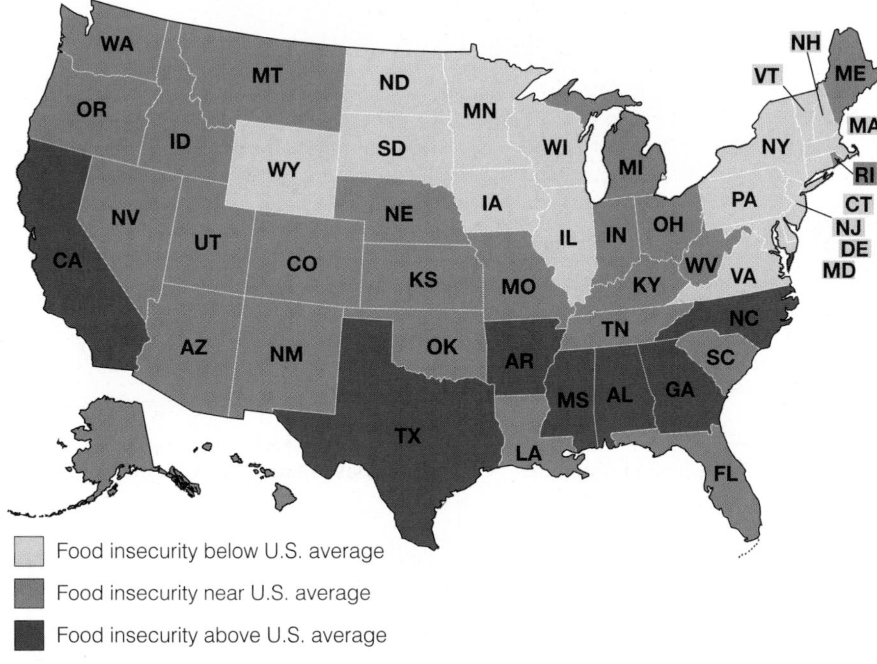

▲ **Figure 21.1 Hunger in the United States**
Though some areas of the United States have higher rates of food insecurity and/or hunger, these conditions can happen anywhere. In this map, data for three years, 2009–2011, were combined to provide more reliable statistics at the state level.

Source: USDA Economic Research Service. Updated 2012. *Food Security in the U.S.: Key Statistics and Graphics.* Available at www.ers.usda.gov/topics/food-nutrition-assistance/food-security-in-the-us/key-statistics-graphics.aspx. Accessed November 2012.

Hunger exists in every country around the world. In the United States, which is a **developed country**, hunger most frequently results from individual economic hardship and poverty. In **developing** and **least developed** countries—collectively referred to as the developing world—poverty is also a factor, but situations such as war, civil unrest, and famine can also come into play.

More people live in developing than in developed countries. Of a global population of 7 billion people, approximately 1 billion live in developed countries (see **Figure 21.2**). The other 6 billion live in the developing world, where they have a lower standard of living and lack many goods and services. The World Bank estimates that there were 925 million undernourished people in the world in 2010,[11] and in 2008, the World Bank reported that there were an estimated 1,345 million poor people in developing countries living on $1.25 a day or less.[12] See Spotlight: A Look at the Numbers: The State of Hunger around the World for more data about global rates of hunger.

developed country A country that is advanced in multiple areas, such as income per capita, life expectancy, rate of literacy, industrial capability, technological sophistication, and economic productivity.

developing country A country that is growing in multiple areas, such as income per capita, life expectancy, rate of literacy, industrial capability, technological sophistication, and economic productivity.

least developed country A country that shows little growth in multiple areas, such as income per capita, life expectancy, rate of literacy, industrial capability, technological sophistication, and economic productivity.

THE TAKE-HOME MESSAGE Hunger is an individual physiological condition that may result from food insecurity. Food insecurity is the limited or uncertain access to foods of sufficient quality or quantity to live an active, healthy life and is divided into the subcategories of *low food security* and *very low food security.* Hunger and food insecurity are experienced by people in the United States and around the world, and are usually due to poverty, civil unrest, or other circumstances.

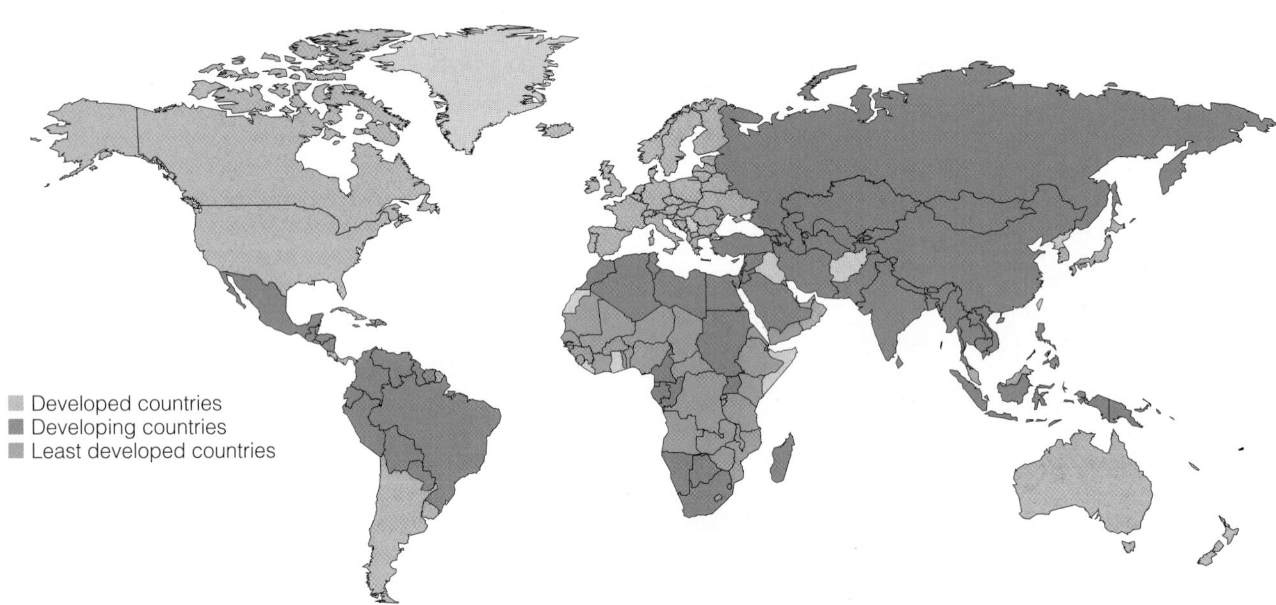

Examples of Developed Countries	Examples of Developing Countries	Examples of Least Developed Countries
United States	China	Ethiopia
Canada	India	Sudan
Japan	Mexico	Angola
Australia	Brazil	Haiti
New Zealand	Mongolia	Sierra Leone
Most Western European nations	Saudi Arabia	Yemen

▲ **Figure 21.2 Hunger in Developed, Developing, and Least Developed Countries Around the World**
Hunger is a global problem. In developed countries, such as the United States, Canada, and the countries of Western Europe, people often experience hunger due to disability, periods of unemployment, and poverty. In least developed countries, like many in central Africa, war, civil conflict, and natural disasters can lead to chronic hunger.

A Look at the Numbers: The State of Hunger around the World

Hunger is not a local or regional problem, but a global problem. Around the world:

- More than 1.4 billion people live below the international poverty line, earning less than $1.25 per day.[1]
- About 1 billion people regularly drink contaminated water.[2]
- An estimated 250,000 to 500,000 vitamin A–deficient children become blind every year, half of them dying within 12 months of losing their sight.[3]
- In the developing world every second pregnant woman and about 40 percent of preschool children are estimated to be anemic.[4]
- Low birth weight is a major determinant of mortality, morbidity, and disability in infancy and childhood and also has a long-term impact on health outcomes in adult life. In the developing world the low birth weight rate is 30 percent.[5]

References

1. World Hunger Education Service. 2012. *World Hunger and Poverty Facts and Statistics.* Available at www.worldhunger.org/articles/Learn/world%20hunger%20facts%202002.htm#Hunger_concepts_and_definition. Accessed June 2012.
2. WHO. The Health and Environment Linkages Initiative (HELI). 2012. *Water, Health and Ecosystems.* Available at www.who.int/heli/risks/water/water/en. Accessed June 2012.
3. World Health Organization. 2008. *Micronutrient Deficiencies.* Available at www.who.int/nutrition/topics/vad/en/index.html. Accessed June 2012.
4. Ibid.
5. World Health Organization. 2012. *Feto-Maternal Nutrition and Low Birth Weight.* Available at www.who.int/nutrition/topics/feto_maternal/en/index.html. Accessed June 2012.

What Factors Contribute to Hunger in the United States?

Although the United States is the wealthiest nation in the world, and the farmers grow sufficient food to feed every person, many people in this country cannot afford to buy meat and vegetables at a grocery store or dine out at a local restaurant. Hunger is a very real problem across the United States, in inner cities, the suburbs, and in rural areas. Various factors contribute to this problem, starting with poverty.

Poverty Leads to Food Insecurity

Poverty is the principal cause of food insecurity in the United States. For people living in the inner cities, poverty can be a result of adverse cultural and behavioral factors that limit opportunities for employment. The revitalization of city centers can also make life too expensive for many poor residents, forcing them to move to suburban areas where housing is cheaper but jobs may still not be available. In rural areas, household income and education levels are generally lower and unemployment rates higher than in cities.[13] Many low-income families must choose between paying the rent and buying groceries—a tough decision, especially when there are young children in the home.

Hunger and poverty are the result of a complex interaction of factors that warrants a closer look.

Poverty and Hunger

The U.S. Census Bureau calculates the number of people living in poverty using poverty thresholds, which are defined according to strict guidelines. The Census estimated that for 2010, about 15.3 percent of the United States population lived at or below the poverty threshold, including 15.7 million children.[14] For a married

poverty Lacking the means to provide for material or comfort needs.

In the United States, poor single parents and their children can experience food insecurity due to unemployment, low wages, or other circumstances that lead to financial hardship.

couple, or a single mother plus a child, poverty means a household income below $15,504 per year. A family of four would be impoverished with an income below $22,811.[15]

Factors that lead to poverty include unemployment, lack of resources needed to get and keep a job (such as a car, a working telephone, and a permanent address), medical issues, and poor financial choices. Whatever the cause, poverty is often difficult to overcome. Lack of education or training, poor health, limited or no access to credit, and other obstacles can lock someone into circumstances with few prospects. In addition, people are often unaware of the resources available to assist them and do not know where to go or whom to ask for help.

According to the USDA, those at the greatest risk of being food insecure are living in households with these life situations:[16]

- Household is headed by a single woman
- Household members are in a minority group
- Household income is below the poverty level
- There are children in the household
- Household is located in the inner city

These circumstances can contribute to poverty by producing additional disadvantages, such as increased exposure to crime and fewer employment opportunities. Lack of child care or expensive child-care arrangements impose additional stress and can drain an already-tight budget. Single mothers may feel "trapped" with very few employment options or the freedom to explore additional career paths because of obligations to their children. Single mothers with dependent children are more likely to experience times without adequate amounts of food than are families headed by a married couple.[17]

In today's competitive work environment, people without job skills typically have a harder time securing employment than those who are highly educated or who have specialized skills. Consequently, it's not surprising that an individual's education level affects food insecurity—those without a high school diploma are more than twice as likely to experience food insecurity as are those who have graduated from high school. Even employed individuals with advanced education may experience hunger if they are laid off, are unemployed for an extended period, or are unable to relocate for a job.

Additionally, people can sometimes be steadily employed in a low-wage full-time job, seasonal jobs, or in several part-time jobs, and still experience hunger. In fact, in 2008, about 8.9 million adults were classified among the **working poor**. Though they had jobs, they still had incomes below the poverty line.[18] High housing and utility costs can consume most of the household budget and leave little money for food. Individuals in these households may be living "paycheck to paycheck." An unexpected expense, such as an illness or a costly auto repair, can force them and their families to choose between paying the bills and consuming a healthy, adequate diet.

Illness and Disability Can Also Lead to Hunger

Adults who are chronically ill or disabled are less likely to earn a steady income and are therefore at risk of having a poor diet. Nutritionally compromised individuals tend to be less productive at work and at increased risk for further illnesses. They may also lack the money or health care coverage to obtain proper medical care to improve their health. Having a chronic illness and routinely missing work to visit a physician can significantly reduce a paycheck, and thus available funds for food.

working poor Individuals or families who are steadily employed but still experience poverty due to low wages or high dependent expenses.

Drug abuse and alcohol abuse are also common causes of poverty and hunger, and, in extreme situations, homelessness. According to Substance Abuse and Mental Health Services Administration estimates, in 2003, 38 percent of homeless people were dependent on alcohol and 26 percent abused other drugs.[19] These individuals typically find it difficult to get and keep steady employment and to shop for and prepare nutritious food.

Mental illness can also contribute to or cause poverty, malnutrition, and hunger in the United States. According to the National Coalition for the Homeless, some 20 to 25 percent of individuals who are homeless are also mentally ill.[20] Mentally ill people, often including the homeless, can be difficult to reach, counsel, or help. They may be forced to rely on charity, church meals, or public assistance programs for most of their food. People who suffer from mental illness, such as anxiety disorders, phobias, depression, paranoia, schizophrenia, or some eating disorders, lose interest in eating or have decreased access to cooking facilities. Depression among mothers, particularly those in low-income families, has been associated with food insecurity in households.[21] Children living in these homes are more likely to routinely go without food or to rely on unhealthy diets, such as food from fast-food restaurants, and they are more likely to have mental health problems themselves.[22]

THE TAKE-HOME MESSAGE Factors that contribute to hunger in the United States include poverty, unemployment, and illness. Food insecurity and hunger are particularly prevalent in households headed by a single mother, minorities, the poor, those living in inner cities, and among those with unstable or seasonal professions.

What Factors Contribute to Hunger around the World?

Hunger in the developing world is often caused by a complex set of factors. Once again, poverty lies at the heart of the problem; however, war, political unrest, agricultural challenges, disease, or natural disasters can also cause food insecurity for large numbers of people, particularly in Asian and African nations (**Figure 21.3**).

Discrimination and Inequality Promote Poverty

In many poor countries, discrimination and inequality exist at both the national and local levels. For example, at the national level, control over land and other assets is often unequal, so that even increased crop yields do not decrease food insecurity. Very few people in these countries own their own land, and a plentiful crop will primarily benefit the landowner, not the farm laborer. Women, especially, suffer from discrimination. The Hunger Project found that while women produce 50 percent of the world's food, they own only 1 percent of the land.[23]

Cultural practices may also compromise access to food at the local or household level. In some cultures and within some families, the amount of food available to an individual is influenced by gender, control of income, education, birth order, and age.[24] Gender inequity is a serious problem worldwide. In many cultures women and girls are viewed as less valuable than men and boys, and they therefore receive less food and education. In sub-Saharan Africa the ratio of boys' to girls' enrollment in primary and secondary schools is eight to one.[25] Accordingly, two-thirds

Self-Assessment

Are You at Risk for Hunger?

Take the quiz below to find out if you are at risk for hunger.
In the past 12 months:

1. Have you ever run out of money to buy food?
   Yes ☐ **No** ☐
2. Have you ever eaten less than you felt you should because there was not enough money to buy food or enough food to eat?
   Yes ☐ **No** ☐
3. Have you ever completely depleted your food supply because there was not enough money to buy replacement groceries?
   Yes ☐ **No** ☐
4. Have you ever gone to bed hungry because there was not enough food to eat?
   Yes ☐ **No** ☐
5. Have you ever skipped meals because there was not enough money to buy food?
   Yes ☐ **No** ☐
6. Have you ever relied on a limited number of foods to feed yourself because you were running out of money to buy food?
   Yes ☐ **No** ☐

Answers

If you have no "Yes" replies, you are food secure. If there are one to three "Yes" replies, you are at risk for food insecurity. If there are four or more "Yes" replies, you are likely in the low or very low food security category.

Source: Adapted from The Community Childhood Hunger Identification Project Survey. 1995; R. E. Kleinman, et al. "Hunger in Children in the United States: Potential Behavioral and Emotional Correlates," *Pediatrics* 101 (1998): 3–10.

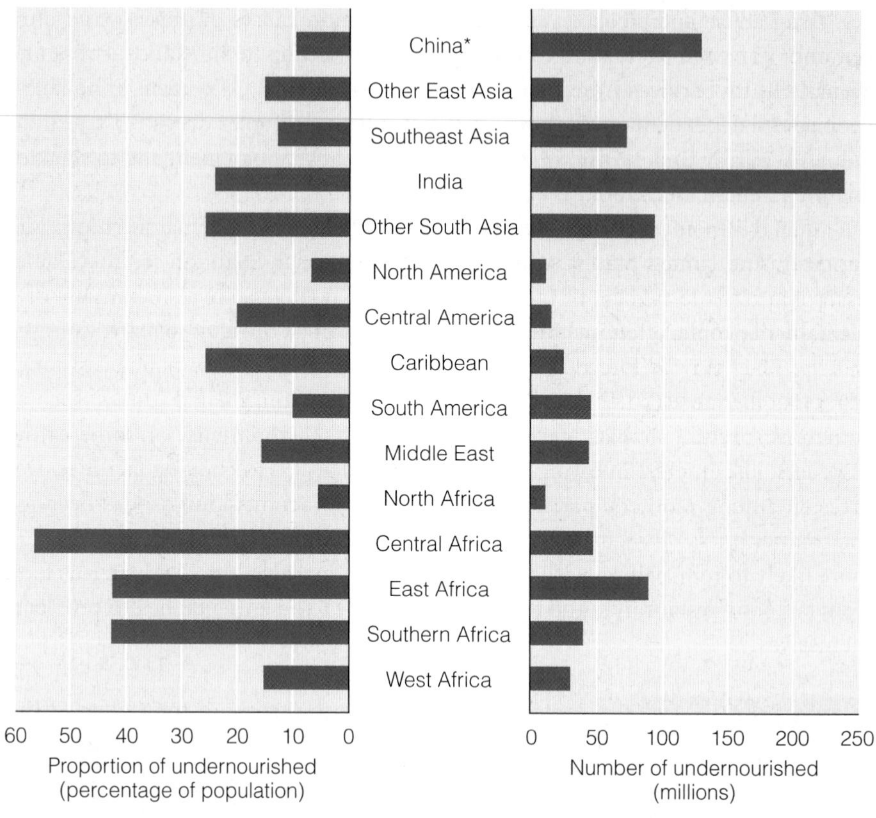

▲ **Figure 21.3 Number and Proportion of Undernourished People**
Many developing and least developed nations have high rates of food insecurity.

of the almost 900 million illiterate adults in the world are women. It is estimated that 70 percent of the 1.2 billion people who live in extreme poverty are female.[26]

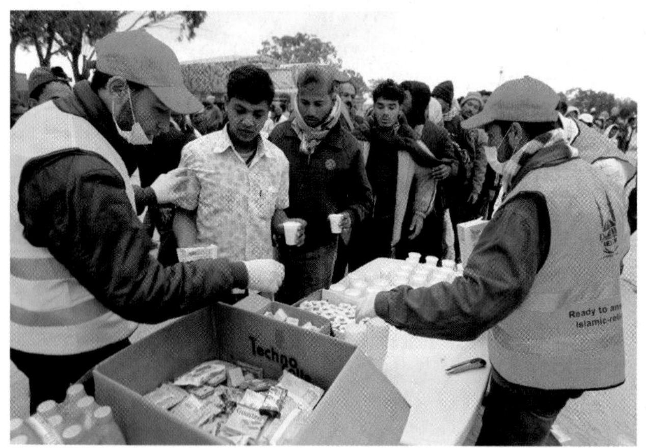

Many hunger relief programs work to provide food aid to needy nations. However, successfully delivering the food to those who need it is often challenging.

Political Sanctions and Armed Conflicts Disrupt the Food Supply

Political **sanctions** and agricultural embargoes create food shortages by decreasing access to agricultural supplies, fuel, or crops. Shortages of these crucial items often hurt the average citizen more than the government they are meant to target.

One country or group of countries may use sanctions to postpone or replace military action and force political change on another government. Other goals for sanctions include restoring democracy, condemning human rights abuses, and punishing groups that protect terrorists or international criminals. Sanctions often result in harm to innocent people and can create or intensify a cycle of chronic food shortages. Higher prices for fuel, food, and other essentials may deprive average citizens of clean drinking water and food. Sanctions also contribute to a failing economy by decreasing household income. If the imposed sanction lowers the demand for certain products by blocking their import by other countries, businesses and workers that rely on this trade will suffer negative economic effects. All of these factors can lead to widespread food shortages that, if left unchecked, may cause a collapse in food production and distribution and, ultimately, famine.[27]

sanctions Boycotts or trade embargoes used by one country or international group to apply political pressure on another.

Armed conflict is another serious problem. According to the World Food Programme, armed conflicts are a major cause of world hunger.[28] War and civil and political unrest cause hunger because of the disruption to agriculture, food distribution, and normal community activities. During the past two decades, the world has experienced an increase in regional conflicts. Examples include ethnic warfare, terrorism, and internal struggles for resources in countries such as Colombia, Ethiopia, Rwanda, Somalia, Sierra Leone, Congo, and Sudan. During wars and regional conflicts, government money is often diverted from nutrition and food distribution programs and redirected toward weapons and military support. Conflicts have caused a rise in global hunger and overwhelmed the efforts of humanitarian agencies. Political turbulence can compromise humanitarian food distribution, making it difficult for food aid to reach the people in need. In some cases, assistance programs and aid workers may have to abandon war-torn areas and curtail their relief efforts.

Natural Disasters and Depleted Resources Limit Food Production

Natural disasters such as droughts, floods, storms, earthquakes, crop diseases, and insect plagues can create food and water shortages in any country. However, in American communities, relief programs are in place to help affected populations. In the developing world, the impact of natural disasters can completely devastate communities. Lack of communication and transportation systems, inadequate funding for relief programs, an inability to relocate populations from disaster-prone areas, and the incapacity to make homes and farms less vulnerable to destructive weather forces can all contribute to the problem.

Drought is the leading cause of severe food shortages in the developing world. When drought conditions exist or access to safe and clean drinking water is limited, **famine** and undernutrition result. This is particularly true in rural areas where people depend on agriculture for both food and income. Similarly, lack of water can force livestock owners to slaughter part of their herd or sell animals at "distress sales."[29]

Floods and excessive rain can also destroy food crops, and are major causes of food shortage. For example, in India, more than 70 percent of the annual rainfall occurs during the three months of monsoon season. Farmers must contend with water scarcity for nine months of the year only to be faced with crop failure later if monsoon rains are overly heavy.

The depletion of natural resources also causes reduced food production. Specific agricultural practices such as misuse of fertilizers, pesticides, and water may increase the yield in the short term, but inhibit production in the long term.[30] When the population of a poor country expands and food is in short supply, critical decisions are often made concerning the use of water, forest resources, and land. These choices often pit the needs of the people against concerns for the environment, threatening limited resources even more. Thus, a long-term investment in preserving natural resources could help reduce poverty and hunger.

Shortsighted farming techniques can take a heavy toll on crops and farmland.

Overpopulation Leads to Food Scarcity

The projected world population is 7.8 billion people by 2020, and 9.7 billion by 2050.[31] Most of this growth is taking place in less developed regions, where the population is expected to rise from 5.4 billion people in 2007 to 8.3 billion people in 2050.[32] Whenever rapid population growth occurs in areas that are strained for

famine A severe shortage of food caused by weather-related crop destruction, poor agricultural practices, pestilence, war, or other factors.

food production, the resulting **overpopulation** can take a toll on the local people's nutritional status.

People in the developing world tend to have more children due to poor health conditions. Because the infant and child death rate is so high, many children do not live to reach adulthood. Therefore, parents have more children to ensure that some of their offspring will survive into adolescence. Large families are needed to work on farms to help generate income and to support older family members later in life.[33] This tendency contributes to the cycle of poverty and hunger because the economy cannot sustain such rapid population growth. The World Bank promotes gender equality and development to break this cycle, ensuring that girls and women in particular receive a basic education.[34]

THE TAKE-HOME MESSAGE Factors that give rise to hunger around the world include poverty, discrimination, political sanctions and conflicts, poor agricultural practices, and overpopulation.

Which Populations Are at Greatest Risk for Malnutrition?

Infants, children, and pregnant and lactating women are at higher risk for malnutrition than are other groups. Malnourished women are more likely to be ill, have smaller babies, and die at a younger age. Furthermore, whenever infant and child mortality rates are high, birth rates are also high as women tend to try to have more babies when they fear losing them. This, of course, perpetuates the cycle of malnutrition and death.[35] Finally, the ill and elderly populations are also at greater risk for malnutrition.

Pregnant and Lactating Women Are At Risk for Malnutrition

As you know from Chapter 17, nutrient requirements increase during pregnancy and lactation. Adequate nutrition during pregnancy greatly enhances the likelihood of having a healthy, full-term, normal-weight infant. Additionally, a healthy pregnancy increases the chances of the mother being able to lactate and breast-feed successfully.

Pregnant women need extra kilocalories and nutrients—in particular, protein, vitamins, and minerals—to support a healthy pregnancy. In general, during the first six months of a pregnancy, the majority of the additional kilocalories are used to nourish the mother as her body undergoes the changes necessary to support a pregnancy. During the last three months of a pregnancy, the majority of extra kilocalories are needed by the growing infant to supply the infant's reserves of protein, fat, and various micronutrients.[36] Improperly nourished pregnant women often give birth to malnourished infants.

Because human breast milk is the ideal nourishment for infants, women in the developing world are encouraged to breast-feed their babies. The global recommendation is for women to nurse their babies for the first six months and to continue nursing with supplemental foods into the child's second year of life.[37] One exception to this recommendation applies to women who are HIV positive, many of whom live in the poorest countries. Mothers with HIV risk passing the virus to their infants through breast milk, and therefore should be encouraged to use formula or a noninfected wet nurse to feed their babies instead of nursing children

overpopulation When a region has more people than its natural resources can support.

themselves. However, because many HIV-positive women live in poverty and can't afford these alternatives, they may still choose to breast-feed their children. In these cases, the benefits of providing the nutrients in the breast milk outweigh the risks of passing the HIV infection on to the baby.

Infants and Children Are Susceptible to Malnutrition

Infants are particularly susceptible to malnutrition because they are growing rapidly, have high nutrient requirements (per unit of body weight), and may be cared for by mothers who are malnourished themselves. Infants are dependent on their caregivers to give them adequate breast milk or formula.

After 6 months of age infants require solid food in addition to breast milk, which puts them at increased risk for malnutrition if food supplies are limited. As an infant transitions from an all–breast milk diet to a diet of breast milk plus solid foods, she or he is also at risk for improper weaning, which can lead to diminished growth during the first year of life and the potential for severe malnutrition during the second year of life.[38] In other cases babies are given foods that are inappropriate, such as foods that are too high in protein or are difficult for an infant to chew.[39] During the sixth to twelfth months of life, children may be more likely to be exposed to contaminated food and water, which may cause diarrhea and dehydration. When infants begin to crawl and walk, their risk of exposure to and thus infection by bacteria and parasites increases. Some parasitic infestations cause nutritional deficiencies directly. For example, hookworms suck blood from the lining of the gut, causing iron deficiency.

The risk of malnutrition continues from infancy into early childhood and may result from food shortages within the family or chronic disease. For example, children who are ill or malnourished have poor appetites—their normal hunger sensations are diminished. In some children maldigestion and malabsorption exacerbate the problem by increasing the loss of nutrients.

AIDS has orphaned an estimated 13 million children worldwide, especially in sub-Saharan Africa and Asia. An estimated 34 million people in the world had HIV/AIDS in 2010, including 3.4 million children under age 15.[40] Most of these children are born to mothers with HIV or obtain the virus during infancy (via childbirth or breast-feeding). This situation increases the likelihood of a child's being malnourished.[41] The loss of one or both parents from disease may also lead to decreased family income and a greater risk of malnourishment.

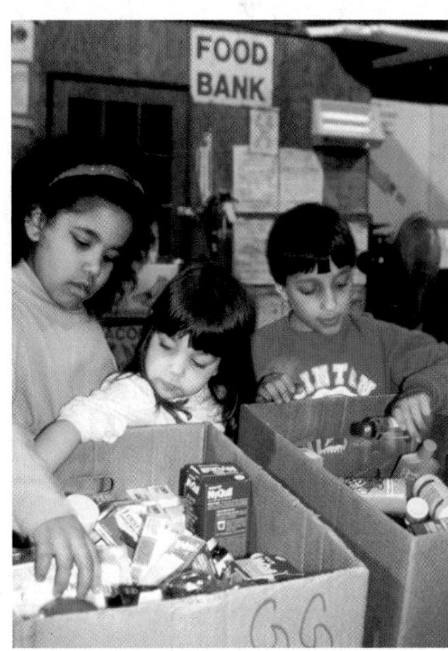

Everyone—from children to adults—can experience hunger, but we can also all help with efforts to reduce it.

The Ill and the Elderly Also May Suffer from Undernourishment

People who are chronically ill may have malabsorption problems that worsen their nutritional status. Liver and kidney disease can impair the body's ability to process and use some nutrients. Some cancer patients and many people with AIDS experience anorexia, which further complicates their treatment and their ability to eat.

Although older adults need fewer kilocalories due to a decrease in their metabolic rate and lower levels of physical activity, they have higher requirements for several minerals and vitamins. Older people may be at risk for nutrient deficiencies because of a decreased sense of taste and smell, immobility, malabsorption, or chronic illnesses. They are also at more risk for disease and disability due to an aging immune system than are younger individuals. Loneliness, isolation, poverty, missing teeth, confusion, or disinterest in cooking and eating also contribute to malnutrition. Many elderly people in developing countries are undernourished,

TABLE 21.2 Comparing Two Shopping Lists

Meal	Low-Cost Shopping List	Cost	Healthy Shopping List	Cost
Breakfast	Dozen large eggs	$2.79	Cereal, 10 oz	$3.24
	Bacon, 12 oz	$2.39	Skim milk, 1 gallon	$3.99
	Fruit punch, 1 gallon	$2.78	Orange juice, 1 gallon	$5.58
Snack	Potato chips, 1 lb	$3.99	All-natural popcorn, 1 lb	$5.31
Lunch	Bologna, 1 lb	$2.89	Solid white tuna, 1 lb	$3.44
	White bread, 1 lb	$3.69	Whole-wheat bread 1 lb	$3.79
Dinner	Pasta sauce with meat, 1 lb	$3.39	Chicken breast, 1 lb	$5.99
	Pasta, 1 lb	$1.50	Broccoli, 1 lb	$1.89
Dessert	Ice cream, ½ gallon	$5.89	Strawberries, 2 lbs	$6.98
Total		$29.31		$40.21

Note: Sample prices are from one Phoenix, AZ supermarket, 2008.

Table adapted from "Grocery Store Price Comparisons: 2008-Fresh Fruits & Vegetables" from QShopOnline, www.qshoponline.com/QSOnline/comparisons_2008.htm. Accessed June 2012.

emaciated, and anemic. In addition, most elderly people, whether in the United States or in other countries, live on a fixed income or have no income at all and must depend on family members to provide for them. In such cases, food is often stretched, and meals are smaller or are skipped altogether. All of these factors contribute to an increased rate of food insecurity and hunger in the older adult population.

Ironically, obesity among those who are food insecure is common. High-fat, high-kilocalorie diets are more affordable than diets based on lean meats, fish, vegetables, and fruits. There is a clear link in women between food insecurity and overweight and obesity. Research suggests that mothers often restrict their food intake during periods of food insufficiency to protect their children from hunger. These chronic ups and downs of food intake can contribute to obesity.[42]

People on limited incomes often shop for cheap foods because they can buy more. However, low-cost foods are often low-quality foods lacking nutrition. Fruit punch, for example, is about half the price of orange juice, and it is nutritionally inferior to orange juice. For those living on a limited budget, filling their cupboards with food, even if it is less nutrient-dense food, takes precedence over choosing foods with nutritional value. Table 21.2 illustrates how less-nutritious foods can be less expensive, and therefore more appealing, to those with severe financial constraints. As you have learned from previous chapters, a diet high in empty kilocalories and low in nutrient-dense foods can increase the risk of obesity *and* malnutrition.

THE TAKE-HOME MESSAGE Pregnant and lactating women, infants and children, and the ill and elderly are particularly vulnerable to the effects of malnutrition. People who are obese can also suffer from malnutrition.

What Are the Effects of Chronic Hunger?

The effects of hunger can range from acute and reversible to chronic and irreversible. All human beings have an essential need for water and nutritious and adequate food in order to be healthy. When food or water is not available or is in limited supply, symptoms of nutrient deficiencies and emaciation will become apparent. If the lack of food continues, it can prompt a downward health spiral that is hard to reverse (**Figure 21.4**).

In times of reduced kilocaloric intake, such as in times of fasting, famine, serious disease, or severe malnutrition, the body attempts to conserve energy and preserve body tissues by lowering basal metabolism. Over an extended period of time, however, the body needs to find a new source of energy and begins to break down its own tissue. This results in the reduction of stored fat and ultimately the deterioration of internal organs and muscle mass. In prolonged starvation, adults can lose up to 50 percent of their body weight. The greatest amount of deterioration occurs in the intestinal tract and the liver; the loss is moderate in the heart and kidneys; and the least damage occurs in the brain and nervous system.[43]

Let's look at some individual effects of chronic hunger and malnutrition.

Lack of food
Fatigue, apathy, no ambition
Weight loss
Compromised health and disease
Anemia
Decreased growth
Malabsorption in GI tract
Loss of muscle mass

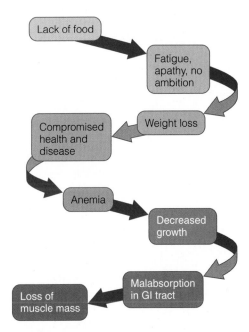

▲ **Figure 21.4 Downward Spiral of Hunger and Malnutrition**
Lack of food can lead to numerous other symptoms that compound the problem of hunger.

Children Suffer Impaired Growth and Development

If a child does not receive adequate kilocalories and nutrients while growing, his or her development will be affected. A child is likely to experience both physical and mental problems, including insufficient weight gain, improper muscle development, lowered resistance to infection, **growth stunting**, and impaired brain development (**Figure 21.5**).[44] The bodies of children who are undernourished compensate for a lack of food by decreasing physical and mental growth. Children are more likely to show behavioral, emotional, and academic problems if they come from families that experience hunger and food insufficiency rather than

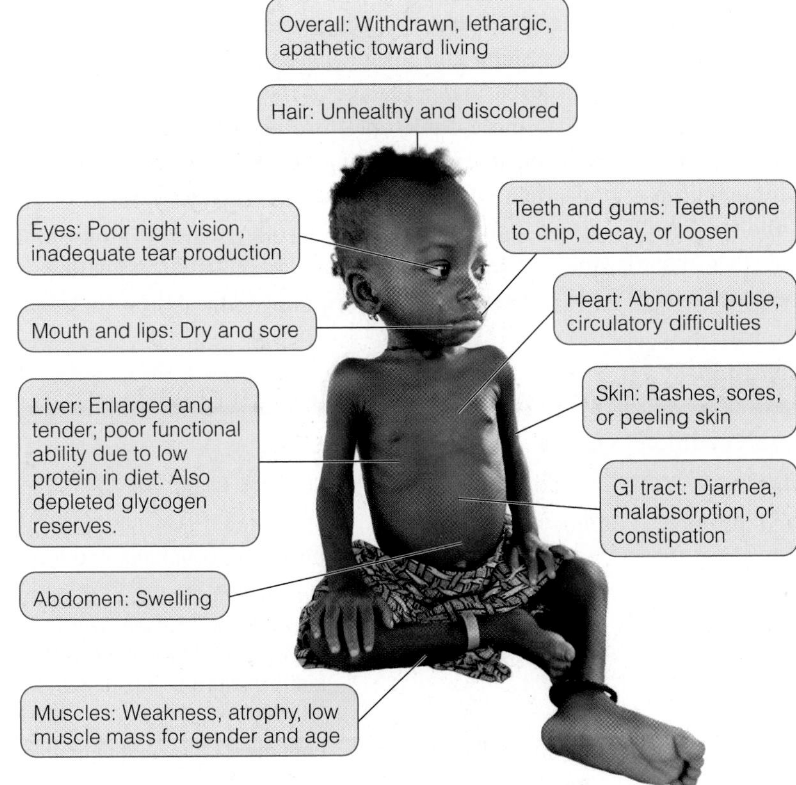

▲ **Figure 21.5 Symptoms of Starvation**
As hunger persists, physical symptoms set in and lead to further complications.

growth stunting Impaired growth and development primarily manifested in early childhood and including malnutrition during fetal development. Once growth stunting occurs, it is usually permanent.

from families that do not report hunger experiences.[45] In particular, long-term undernutrition is associated with increased anxiety, irritability, attention problems, and school absence and tardiness rates.[46, 47]

If hunger persists or occurs at early, crucial times of brain development, cognitive development is impaired.[48] Slowed brain growth could result in permanent lower intelligence and hindered learning ability. As a result, malnourished children may have a difficult time completing an elementary education, which has a measurable impact on income-earning ability later in life. Research demonstrates that underweight and malnourished children complete fewer years of school compared with well-nourished children.[49]

Even if the children are healthy enough to regularly attend school, hunger and malnutrition impair cognitive development.[50] Malnourished children also tend to be fatigued, inattentive, and unresponsive to their learning environment. Peers, teachers, and adult caregivers may neglect a child who does not respond to or interact with others.

Malnourished children grow poorly; globally, an estimated 225 million children experience height stunting. Deficiencies of energy, protein, iron, and zinc, as well as prolonged infection, have been implicated as causes. Approximately 195 million children under 5 years old in the developing world, or about one in three, are physically stunted (decreased height for age), and about 13 percent of children under 5 years old in the developing world suffer from physical **wasting** (decreased weight for age).[51] Growth stunting has also been associated with long-term detrimental effects on physical work capacity and fertility.[52]

Weakened Immunity Results in Disease

A malnourished individual has a weakened immune system, which increases his or her vulnerability to various infections. Fever, parasitic disease, pneumonia, measles, typhoid, cholera, and malaria are examples of conditions that can occur because of weakened immune systems and chronic malnutrition.

In 2011, 6.9 million children under the age of five died.[53] The World Health Organization estimates that more than one-third of all childhood deaths in developing countries are associated with chronic hunger and malnutrition. The most common causes of death in post-neonatal children (that is, those who survive birth and the first 28 days of life) are pneumonia or other acute respiratory infection, diarrhea, malaria, and measles, all of which have malnutrition as an underlying contributing factor.[54] Table 21.3 summarizes the ramifications of these illnesses.

TABLE 21.3 Common Illnesses in Malnourished Children

Disease/Condition	Cause	Effect
Diarrhea	Pathogenic infections	Severe dehydration
Acute respiratory illness	Virus or bacteria	Pneumonia, bronchitis, colds, fast breathing, coughing, and fever
Malaria	Parasite (transmitted by a mosquito)	Flu, weakness, sweating, shivering, shaking, nausea, liver failure, infected red blood cells, and kidney failure or bleeding in the kidneys
Measles	Respiratory illness caused by a highly contagious virus, transmitted by airborne droplets	Pneumonia, brain inflammation, infection, diarrhea, and seizures

wasting The diminishment of muscle and fat tissue caused by extremely low energy intake from too little food and therefore too little energy; sometimes referred to as *acute malnutrition.*

TABLE 21.4 Most Common Vitamin and Mineral Deficiencies among the Malnourished

Vitamin or Mineral	Effects of Deficiency	Incidence
Vitamin A	Eye disease, blindness	Vitamin A deficiency is the leading cause of preventable blindness in children in developing countries.
Iron	Iron-deficiency anemia	Extremely common worldwide. Anemia is most common among 7- to 12-month-old infants; toddlers and young children (< 8 years of age); women of reproductive age; and anyone who has lost large amounts of blood.
Iodine	Goiter, cretinism	Iodine deficiency is the world's most prevalent, yet easily preventable, cause of brain damage. Up to 790 million people (13% of the world's population) have some form of iodine deficiency, goiter, or mental impairment caused by lack of iodine.
Folate	Macrocytic anemia	Folate deficiency is common among women of reproductive age; individuals with limited diets and reduced vegetable consumption; individuals who abuse alcohol; and obese individuals.
Vitamin B_{12}	Pernicious anemia	B_{12} deficiency is common among elderly men and women (> 50 years of age); African-American adults; individuals who have malabsorption syndromes; and vegetarians who don't take enough B_{12} supplementation.

Diarrhea—caused by viruses, parasites, and other harmful microorganisms—can result in severe dehydration (loss of fluids and electrolytes). The gastrointestinal infections that cause diarrhea kill around 2.2 million people globally each year, mostly children in developing countries. The use of contaminated water is a major cause of diarrhea.[55]

Vitamin and mineral deficiencies and their resulting diseases are also serious concerns for people living in developing countries as well as for the impoverished in the United States. For example, more than 2 billion people, or more than one-third of the world's population, live with vitamin A, iron, or iodine deficiency. These micronutrient deficiencies are sometimes referred to as "hidden hunger." Table 21.4 lists the most common vitamin and mineral deficiencies observed in those who are malnourished.

Infant and Child Mortality Rates Increase

Malnutrition is part of a vicious cycle that passes hunger and illness from one generation to the next. Unfortunately, many young women experience undernutrition during their own infancy and childhood. Girls who were low birth weight babies or were undernourished and ill during the first five years of life may be physically stunted and less able to support a healthy pregnancy when they become adults. The infants born to malnourished women are more likely to be malnourished themselves, to experience chronic illness, and to have an increased risk of premature death.

THE TAKE-HOME MESSAGE The effects of chronic malnutrition are devastating and can produce irreversible damage, depending on the stage of life. If malnutrition occurs during adulthood, the body will try to conserve nutrients and preserve its own organs, but eventually there could be irreversible organ damage. Physical effects of malnutrition in infants and children include stunted growth, impaired mental development and immunity, and higher likelihood of disease.

How Can We Reduce Hunger?

In the United States, hunger relief efforts exist at many levels. At the local level, individuals, families, churches, and community relief agencies seek out and assist people who have insufficient resources. Examples of assistance include hot meals and free food provided by local shelters and food banks, as well as education and job training provided by local and state governments, nonprofit organizations, and faith-based organizations. Some hunger relief efforts are undertaken at the corporate and governmental level. These organizations provide food aid and create economic opportunity for people who want to improve their lives. See Spotlight: Food Assistance Programs in the United States for examples of programs that exist to help combat hunger in the United States.

In addition to the human (person-to-person) help provided by people and organizations, technology is also playing a role in alleviating malnutrition. As research and development provide new ways to pack more nutrition into food crops, hunger may be reduced. Enriched crops will ultimately benefit hungry people by providing some of the common nutrients that are in low supply in current crops. The following discussion looks at a number of possible solutions to the problem of hunger around the world.

Improve Agriculture, Water Usage, and Sanitation

Agriculture plays an important role in the economy and food security of most developing countries. The long-term solution to hunger requires balancing the number of people in a country with the amount of food that can be locally produced. In countries where more than 34 percent of the population is undernourished, almost 70 percent of the people rely on agriculture for their employment.[56] Increasing a country's capacity to feed its population by developing manageable systems for producing food benefits the worker, the landowner, and the community. Crop sales generate income that travels through the economic system; this can significantly decrease poverty and help reduce hunger.

Agricultural Practices and Techniques

Biotechnology, specifically the production of genetically modified foods, can create crops with increased yields and pest resistance. Some staple crops, such as corn and rice, can be bioengineered to contain nutrients or precursors, like the beta-carotene in "golden rice," to help alleviate common deficiencies. ("Golden rice" is helping to alleviate vitamin A deficiency, which is the leading cause of blindness worldwide.) Biotechnology can also improve the quality of plant foods by improving the taste or shelf life of fruits and vegetables.

Better land management, appropriate crop selection, and biotechnology can all help eliminate hunger.

On the other end of the spectrum, many farmers are turning to organic farming. In organic farming, farmers do not use GMOs, or chemical pesticides or fertilizers, which means they maintain biodiversity and reduce pollution.[57] When they thus balance the soil, the crops growing there tend to become healthier, and more disease resistant. While the yield from an organic farm may be lower than that of an industrial farm, the mineral content in organic foods tends to be higher, and organically grown plants tend to be more drought resistant.

Proper land management and appropriate crop selection can also help increase agricultural production. For example, in many countries productive land that could be used for food

Food Assistance Programs in the United States

The USDA spent over $103 billion in 2011 on numerous food assistance programs to feed Americans in need.[1] Some of the main programs are reviewed below.

- The federally subsidized Supplemental Nutrition Assistance Program (SNAP) (formerly called the Food Stamp Program) puts food on the table for close to 45 million people a month.[2] Individuals who are eligible for food stamps can use coupons to purchase specified foods, such as fruit, vegetables, cereals, meats, and dairy products, at their local authorized supermarket. (Items such as alcohol, tobacco products, and household items are not covered.)
- The Special Supplemental Nutrition Program for Women, Infants, and Children (WIC) helps safeguard the health of low-income women, infants, and children up to age 5 years. Specifically, the program provides nutritious food to at-risk women and children to supplement their diets. The program also emphasizes nutrition education and offers referrals to health care professionals.

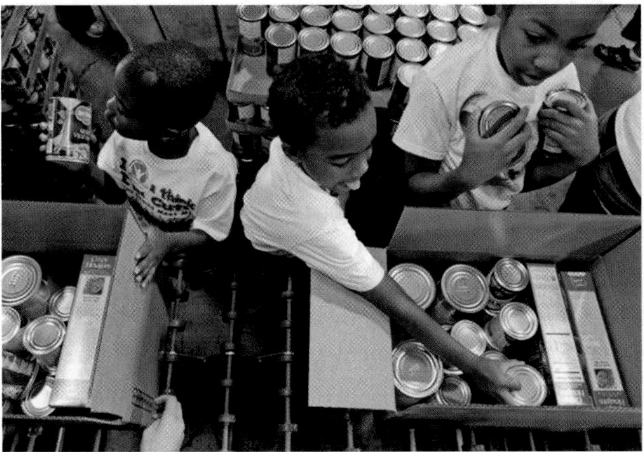

- Under the National School Lunch Program, over 31 million school children a year receive free or reduced-price lunches.[3] A subsidized breakfast is sometimes also available at schools.
- The Summer Food Service Program is a federal program that combines a meal or feeding program with a summer activity program for children. It is available to communities based on income criteria.
- The Child and Adult Care Food Program provides nutritious meals to low-income children and senior adults who receive day care or adult care outside the home. There are income guidelines and specific menu requirements for program participation.
- Congregate meals for the elderly and Meals On Wheels are two types of programs for the elderly (recall that you read about these in Chapter 19) that provide meals at a community site or delivered to the home.
- Additional programs are available for low-income Native Americans or for individuals living on a reservation or members of a federally recognized tribe. Some communities also have special feeding or church programs for new immigrants, guest workers, or children of immigrants. College towns often sponsor special programs for international students and their families.

References

1. USDA. 2012. *The Food Assistance Landscape: FY 2011 Annual Report.* Available at www.ers.usda.gov/media/376910/eib93_1_.pdf. Accessed November 2012..
2. Ibid.
3. Ibid.

crops is frequently used for nonnutritive crops, such as tobacco or flowers. This is done to generate income through crop sales to industrialized nations. If some of this land were used instead to raise food crops for domestic consumption, such as high-protein beans, vegetables, grains, seeds, nuts, or fruit, instead of export crops, hunger could be reduced.[58] This argument applies to raising meat, as well. If farmers raised crops instead of animals for consumption, they could, generally speaking, feed more people.

Land ownership is directly related to food security and is a way of motivating farmers to make better decisions regarding irrigation, crop rotation, land fallowing (plowed, but unplanted, land), and appropriate soil management.[59] Land ownership is part of a long-term solution to a very complex problem. Part of this problem is that land ownership is not evenly distributed across most populations, and some landowners grow nonfood crops, such as tobacco, rather than crops that might feed local people. It is unlikely that this situation will change without *land reform,* in which governments create rules to reallocate land to landless people. In some countries there are grassroots programs under way that provide access to land for women and their families for the purpose of growing food and planting gardens.

Water and Sanitation

Providing safe water is critical in reducing hunger. Global freshwater consumption continues to rise at more than twice the rate of population growth, creating health problems associated with lack of access to safe water and sanitation. Progress is being made to improve drinking water sources through programs that build wells and piped connections to dwellings; still, over 780 million people use unsafe drinking water sources, and 2.5 billion people (37 percent of the developing world's population) do not have improved sanitation facilities.[60]

The World Health Organization estimates that 88 percent of all diarrheal illnesses in the world are attributable to inadequate water or sanitation.[61] The consequences of unsanitary conditions are enormous. Entire communities are often at risk for health problems from drinking contaminated water. A person who has diarrhea is at increased risk for malnutrition.[62]

Poor access to sufficient quantities of water is closely related to ecosystem conditions. About one-third of the world's population lives in countries with moderate to high water stress, and problems of water scarcity are increasing, due in part to ecosystem depletion and contamination. Two out of every three persons on the globe may be living in water-stressed conditions by the year 2025 if the present global consumption patterns continue.[63] Water ecosystems are vital to the replenishment and purification of water resources, but development and land use have greatly affected the sustainability of many such systems.

Some innovative solutions are being proposed to alleviate the world's water problems. For example, in Tanzania, solar energy is being used to thermally purify the water supply. Water is poured into plastic jugs that are placed on black-covered roofs and allowed to heat for several hours. Once the temperature of the water exceeds 50°C, it becomes safe to drink. The solar heat and UV rays effectively destroy common waterborne bacteria such as those that cause cholera, typhoid, and dysentery.[64]

Preserving the health of both freshwater and coastal ecosystems is necessary and vital to the health and well-being of an increasing proportion of the world's population. Solutions to water management and protection include efforts at a number of levels. At the ecosystem level, protection of natural watersheds is necessary to ensure that the natural filtration and purification mechanisms will continue. Integrated water management is another solution that includes the allocation of water resources on a shared and managed basis to governments, tourism, fisheries, and industries. Finally, water needs to be protected from contamination at all levels. This includes conservation and safe filtration and use at the household level, along with development and implementation of water monitoring and controls at the local, national, and global levels.[65]

Access to clean drinking water is just as important as adequate nutrition for human health.

Fortify Foods to Raise Nutrient Levels

Globally the most common micronutrient deficiencies include iodine, iron, and vitamin A. The fortification of staple foods with nutrients can help to alleviate these deficiencies. For food fortification to work, the staple foods must be shelf-stable, affordable, and consistently available in the food supply. Rice, cereals, flours, salt, and even sugar are examples of foods that can be successfully fortified.

Because food fortification is inexpensive, as well as enormously beneficial, fortification programs are being developed and implemented worldwide. Countries all across the globe fortify foods such as salt, flour, oil, sugar, and soy sauce with iron, iodine, and vitamin A.[66]

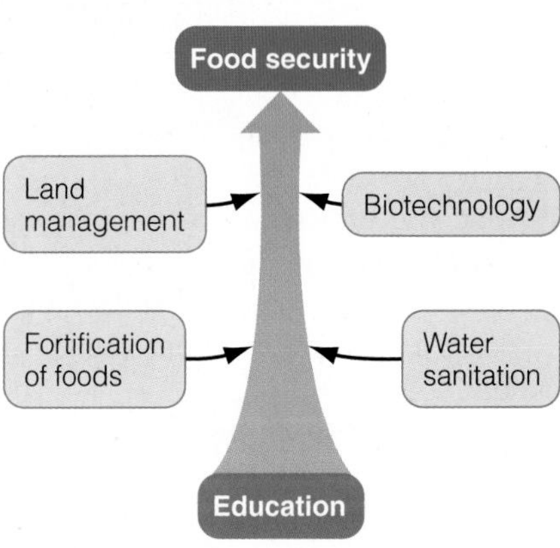

▲ **Figure 21.6 Factors in Food Security**

Promote Education

Education plays an important role in ensuring food security (see **Figure 21.6**). Educated people are more likely to have economic opportunities, and be less likely to fall into the cycle of poverty. Literacy and education also build self-esteem and self-confidence, two qualities that help people overcome life's challenges.

Education also reduces poverty in other ways. For example, one study found that societies with a more educated population enjoyed:[67]

- Higher earning potential
- Improved sanitation
- More small businesses and rural enterprises
- Lower rates of infant mortality and improved child welfare
- Higher likelihood of technological advancement

The type and format of education varies depending on the needs of the people. To help solve hunger problems, education in the developing world ought to focus on including women and girls, and on literacy, technical knowledge, agricultural skills, horticulture, health education, and the development of natural resources. A focus on agricultural education can help improve knowledge and skills and promote increased agricultural production. Educating women is of particular importance: It has been shown that population growth slows when women are educated.[68]

Generally, educators in the developed world should focus on land management, the importance of land reform, biotechnology, improved crop yields, boosting nutrient levels within crops, and continued development of drought-resistant and insect-repelling plants.

THE TAKE-HOME MESSAGE Reducing or eliminating hunger benefits everyone. Local charities and community groups, corporations, and governments can provide aid and organize programs to alleviate hunger. Biotechnology and food fortification are two strategies that help provide healthier, hardier food crops with additional nutrients. Education of the world's population is also important, along with proper land management and proper crop selection.

Putting It All Together

For most Americans, food choice involves selecting nutrient-dense foods from a variety of food groups that provide sufficient amounts of protein, carbohydrate, fat, vitamins, minerals, and water, without overloading on kilocalories, unhealthy fats, salt, and sugar. Food insecurity is a major problem in the United States, and hunger and malnutrition cause major problems worldwide.

For many people around the world, safe, nutritious food and clean water are difficult to obtain. For particularly vulnerable populations, including the poor, children, the sick and elderly, and citizens of impoverished or war-torn areas, gaining reliable access to food and clean water is the most important challenge to overcome.

As the global population continues to increase, a greater emphasis will need to be placed on sustainable agricultural practices and integrated resource management. The effects of improper land and water usage coupled with increases in energy costs can have negative impacts on the health of Americans as well as people around the world.

SPOTLIGHT Hunger among Us (and How You Can Help!)

Food insecurity may be closer than you think. In fact, you may have friends, relatives, or neighbors who've experienced hunger sometime in their lives.

Here's a true account of one young man's experience with hunger.

I grew up poor. My mother, who was single, worked two jobs to support us AND pay her way through college. I was never hungry then, but when I got to college I realized how little wiggle room there can be in a food budget!

It was my first week at LSU in Baton Rouge. We started classes a few days before Labor Day weekend, then got a four-day break before classes really went into full swing the following Tuesday. I was enrolled in the 3-squares-a-day university meal plan, but the program ran Monday through Friday only. The dining halls weren't open until after the Labor Day weekend anyway. My mom had given me as much money as she could spare at the time—$20.00. Since I did not have cooking facilities at the dormitory, I was forced to go "out" to eat, and pay for the public transportation to get to places to eat, for the first three days of class.

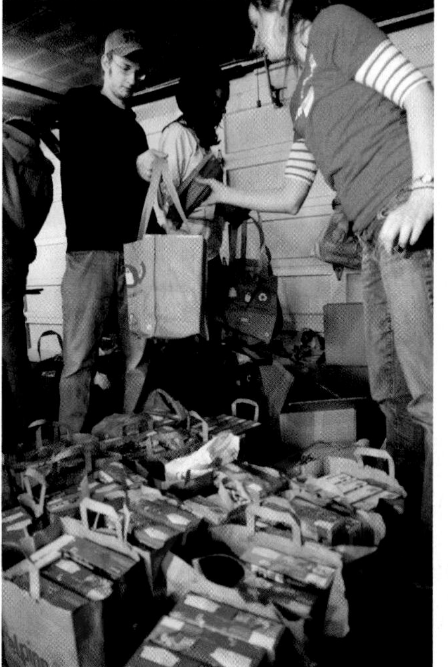

Then the worst happened. My mother was going to pick me up on Thursday evening to bring me back home to New Orleans for the weekend. But Thursday morning her car got stolen. She had to spend all of her money on the insurance deductible, and didn't have any extra to get me a bus ticket home. I was stuck on campus, and everyone I knew there had already left for the extended weekend. I had no money, no job to earn money, no food, and the dining halls were closed.

I lived on Celestial Seasonings herbal tea and Ovaltine (made with water, and appropriated from my roommate) for four days. I was a wreck because I was so hungry. I couldn't concentrate on anything, I had no patience at all, and I lost over 10 pounds, which I really could not afford to lose since I weighed about 115 pounds at the time.

The good part is that this situation was only temporary for me. I skipped my first class on Tuesday morning to go eat a mammoth breakfast at the dining hall. But this sort of catch-22 situation can, and does, happen to people everywhere. For most, it isn't a temporary situation at all.

You'd think that this would never happen to someone like me—I'm a middle-class college student. It certainly opened my eyes to what numerous Americans have to face every day. It also made me understand the problems my mother was facing when she was in nursing school when I was little and couldn't chip in at all.

I would have gone to a food bank if I had known about them then. Please, PLEASE volunteer your time at your local shelters, and donate food and money whenever you are able to. The next person that has to go to a food bank might be me, or you!

In addition to the many food assistance programs available, people occasionally also use a **food pantry** or **emergency kitchen** to supplement the various food assistance programs.

America's Second Harvest, the largest hunger relief organization in the United States, was started to help individuals who are routinely without food. The mission of this organization is to eradicate hunger and ensure that no American goes to bed hungry. America's Second Harvest not only distributes 1.8 billion pounds of excess and donated food and grocery items annually, but it also works to increase public awareness of hunger as well as being an advocate for those who are hungry.

America's Second Harvest has over 200 food banks and a food rescue organization that serves every county in the United States. These food banks collect surplus food from national food companies and other large donors and store it in a centralized location. Volunteers travel to these food banks and gather and transport the donated foods to local food pantries. Volunteers and workers at a food rescue organization "rescue" prepared food, such as ready-to-eat surplus items from banquets, company and college cafeterias, and restaurants, that would otherwise go to waste. Sometimes food rescue centers are located in the same building as food banks.

When it comes to fighting hunger in America, everyone needs to pitch in. You can help your needy neighbors in three ways: give funds, give food, and give time. Funds can be donated online at www.secondharvest.org. You can donate food by hosting a food drive. Finally, you can volunteer your time by helping out in your local community, perhaps by tutoring children on healthy eating practices, repackaging donated food, stocking shelves at a local food pantry, or transporting food to the hungry.

To find out where you can help, visit the America's Second Harvest website and search for opportunities using the Volunteer Match service (www.secondharvest.org).

food pantry Community food assistance location where food is provided to needy individuals and families.

emergency kitchen A kitchen or a commercial food service that prepares for natural disasters, emergencies, or terrorist attacks.

Visual Chapter Summary

1 Chronic Hunger Is Prevalent Throughout the World

Hunger is a physiological condition that can result from food insecurity. The USDA divides food insecurity into two subcategories: *low food security* and *very low food security.* Despite abundant food production, many people in the United States and around the world suffer from chronic hunger and food insecurity. Less than one-sixth of the world's population lives in developed nations that have a high standard of living. Many of the world's residents live in developing or least developed countries and have access to fewer resources.

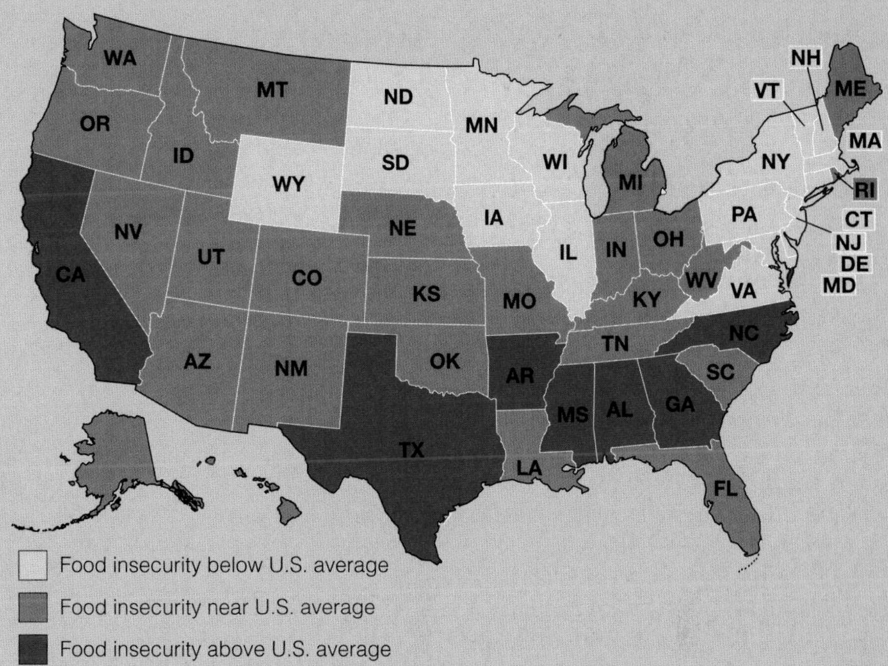

2 Several Factors Contribute to Hunger in the United States

In the United States, hunger often occurs in rural areas, inner cities, and suburbs. Causes include poverty, disease or disability, lack of education, and inadequate wages. Mental illness and/or drug and alcohol abuse sometimes lead to homelessness, which in turn often results in hunger.

3 Various Factors Contribute to Hunger around the World

Political sanctions, armed conflicts, crop failure, wasteful agricultural practices, and overpopulation factor into rates of hunger in many countries. When a country's economy is dependent on agriculture, natural disasters such as droughts, floods, diseases, and insect infestations can have a dire impact on food production and levels of hunger.

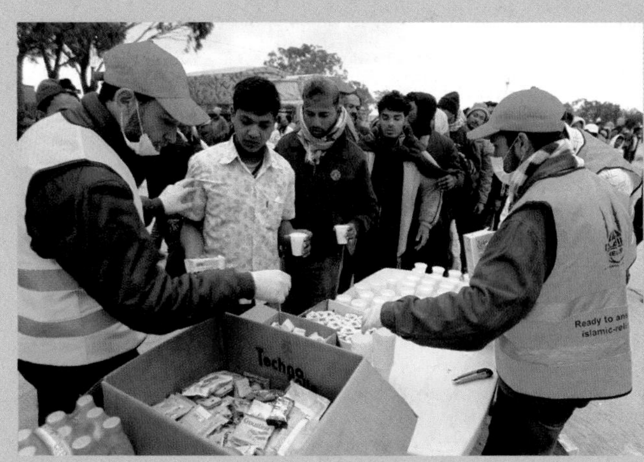

4 Pregnant and Lactating Women, Children, the Ill, and Older Adults Are at Greatest Risk for Malnutrition

Pregnant and lactating women have higher kilocalorie and nutrient needs. If they are improperly nourished, their infants may be, too. Infants and children in general have high nutrient needs because they are growing rapidly. They are dependent on their caregivers for food, making them more susceptible to food insecurity. Chronically ill people may have malabsorption problems. Older adults may be at risk for malnutrition because of higher needs for several micronutrients, decreased senses of smell and taste, chronic illness, compromised immunity, and lack of mobility.

5 Chronic Hunger Damages Your Health

Effects of chronic hunger include stunted growth, wasting, impaired immune function, infections, anemia, and nutrient deficiencies. A nutrient deficiency can lead to serious, permanent health damage in both children and adults.

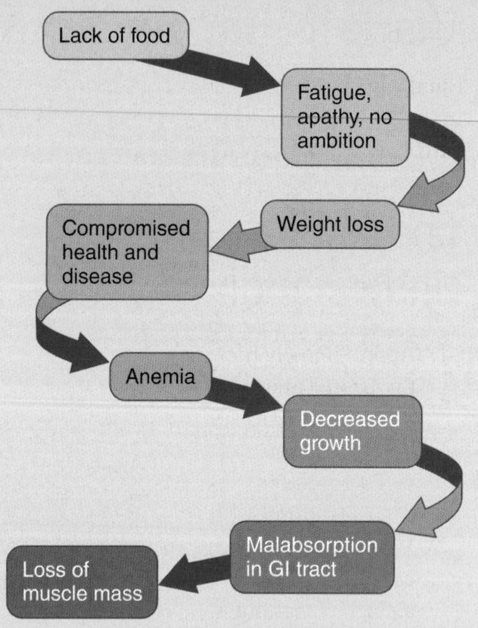

6 Providing Greater Food Resources Can Reduce Hunger

Biotechnology and food fortification are helping to reduce hunger worldwide by providing larger and more nutrient-dense food crops. Because deficiencies of iron, iodine, and vitamin A are most common, these are the nutrients most often used to fortify foods.

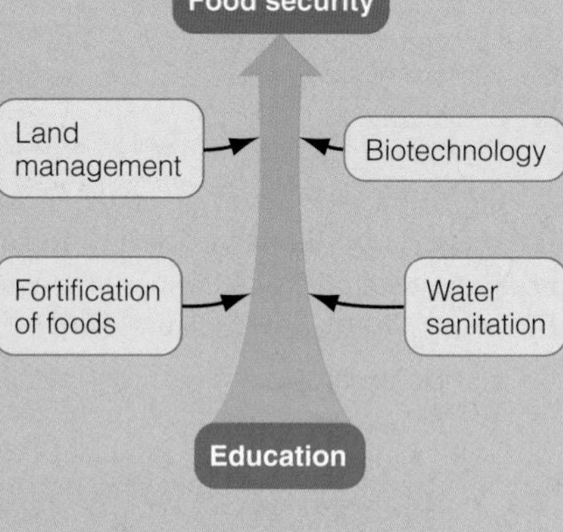

Community and faith-based organizations can help ease hunger by providing free food and meals and assistance programs to help people overcome poverty and food insecurity. Corporations and governments can invest in biotechnologies and education programs that provide more nutrient-dense foods and increase economic opportunity.

Food assistance programs such as the Supplemental Nutrition Assistance Program, WIC, and the National School Lunch Program, among others, provide assistance to those who experience food insecurity in the United States. Local and national organizations, such as America's Second Harvest, provide opportunities and food for those in their communities who are food insecure.

Terms to Know

- hunger
- food insecurity
- poverty
- developed country
- developing country
- least developed country
- working poor
- famine
- overpopulation
- growth stunting
- wasting
- food pantry
- emergency kitchen

MasteringNutrition™

Build your knowledge—and confidence—in the Study Area of MasteringNutrition with a variety of study tools.

Check Your Understanding

1. Approximately how many people in the United States are food insecure?
   a. 11.3 million
   b. 14.8 million
   c. 50.1 million
   d. 16.2 million
2. Which of the following is a leading cause of famine?
   a. lack of technology
   b. lack of education
   c. natural disaster
   d. underpopulation
3. Which of the following states in the United States had one of the highest food insecurity rates between 2009 and 2011?
   a. Missouri
   b. Michigan
   c. North Dakota
   d. Mississippi
4. What does "hidden hunger" refer to?
   a. malnutrition in poor countries that no one knows about
   b. micronutrient deficiencies in the diet
   c. hunger in rich countries that people can't see
   d. lack of protein in the diet
5. Which of the following groups are especially vulnerable to illness?
   a. infants and young children
   b. adolescents
   c. adult men
   d. adult women
6. What is the projected world population for 2050?
   a. 7.8 billion
   b. 9.7 billion
   c. 6 billion
   d. 6.2 billion
7. A lack of which micronutrient has been implicated in causing blindness in children?
   a. vitamin K
   b. iodine
   c. iron
   d. vitamin A
8. Who are the "working poor"?
   a. workers classified as low income by the United States Department of Labor
   b. workers who have no steady employment
   c. workers who are employed but have incomes that fall below the poverty line
   d. workers who earn minimum wage
9. Which nutrients are most likely to be used to fortify food?
   a. vitamins D, E, and K
   b. sodium, potassium, and chloride
   c. magnesium, phosphorus, and sulfur
   d. iron, iodine, and vitamin A
10. How many people are killed each year by gastrointestinal infections that cause diarrhea?
    a. about 5.5 million
    b. about 800,000
    c. about 2.2 million
    d. about 3.2 million

Answers

1. (c) About 50.1 million people in the United States lived in food-insecure households in 2011.
2. (c) Natural disasters, such as drought, are a leading cause of famine. Lack of education would only be an indirect cause, at best. Biotechnology and underpopulation bear no relation to famine.
3. (d) Between 2009 and 2011, the five states with the highest food insecurity rates were Mississippi, Texas, Arkansas, Alabama, and Georgia.
4. (b) Hidden hunger refers to micronutrient deficiencies, such as of vitamin A, iron, or iodine. This condition affects over 2 billion people in the world.
5. (a) Infants and young children have immature immune systems. Adolescents and adults have mature immune systems that are stronger and function better.
6. (b) The projected world population for 2050 is 9.7 billion.
7. (d) Vitamin A is implicated in preventable blindness.
8. (c) The working poor include individuals who are employed yet still have incomes below the official poverty line.
9. (d) Iron, iodine, and vitamin A are frequently used to fortify food because deficiencies of them are linked to many common and serious illnesses.
10. (c) About 2.2 million people are killed each year by the gastrointestinal infections that cause diarrhea.

Answers to Myths and Misconceptions

1. **True.** While hunger may be more severe in developing countries, it occurs all over the globe.
2. **True.** Over 850 million people, or 13% of the world's population are hungry.
3. **False.** Even those who have jobs sometimes experience food insecurity.
4. **True.** Depression among mothers, particularly those in low-income families, has been associated with food insecurity in households.
5. **True.** The world's agricultural producers grow enough food to nourish every man, woman, and child on the planet. The challenge is distributing their products evenly.
6. **True.** Natural disasters such as droughts, floods, storms, earthquakes, crop diseases, and insect plagues can create food and water shortages in any country.
7. **False.** Malnutrition can occur in anyone. Those at greatest risk include pregnant and lactating women, infants and children, and the ill and elderly.
8. **False.** Fortifying foods can provide numerous nutrients that some populations wouldn't otherwise obtain.

9. **False.** There is a clear link in women between food insecurity and overweight and obesity.
10. **False.** While getting food to hungry people is a short-term solution, the hunger issue is more complex. Reducing hunger over the long term involves improving agriculture, water use and sanitation, and education.

Web Resources

- To learn more about one organization that is fighting global poverty, visit CARE at www.care.org
- To find out how the Food and Agriculture Organization of the United Nations leads international efforts to defeat hunger, visit www.fao.org
- To learn more about an international children's group, visit the UNICEF website at www.unicef.org
- For more about the World Health Organization, visit www.who.org
- To learn more about how biotechnology is impacting food production in developing countries, visit www.sustaintech.org

References

1. USDA. 2011. *Food Security in the United States: Definitions of Hunger and Food Security.* Available at www.ers.usda.gov/topics/food-nutrition-assistance/food-security-in-the-us/definitions-of-food-security.aspx. Accessed November 2012.
2. Ibid.
3. Food Bank for New York City. 2011.*Food Poverty in NYC.* Available at www.foodbanknyc.org/food-poverty-in-nyc. Accessed June 2012.
4. Healthy People.gov. 2012. *Nutrition and Weight Status.* Available at www.healthypeople.gov/2020/topicsobjectives2020/overview.aspx?topicid=29. Accessed November 2012.
5. USDA. Economic Research Service. 2012. *Household Food Security in the United States in 2011.* Available at www.ers.usda.gov/media/884525/err141.pdf. Accessed November 2012.
6. Ibid.
7. Ibid.
8. Food and Agriculture Organization of the United Nations. 2008. *Hunger on the Rise.* Available at www.fao.org/newsroom/en/news/2008/1000923. Accessed June 2012.
9. Ibid.
10. World Hunger Education Service. 2012. *World Hunger and Poverty Facts and Statistics. Does the World Produce Enough Food to Feed Everyone?* Available at www.worldhunger.org/articles/Learn/world%20hunger%20facts%202002.htm#Does_the_world_produce_enough_food_to_feed_everyone. Accessed June 2012.
11. Ibid.
12. Ibid.
13. USDA. Economic Research Service. 2012. *Data Sets.* Available at www.ers.usda.gov/StateFacts/us.htm#PIE. Accessed June 2012.
14. U.S. Census Bureau. 2012. Poverty Status in the Past 12 Months. Available at http://factfinder2.census.gov/faces/nav/jsf/pages/index.xhtml. Accessed June 2012.
15. United States Census Bureau. 2011. *Poverty: Poverty Thresholds.* Available at www.census.gov/hhes/www/poverty/data/threshld/index.html. Accessed November 2012.
16. USDA. Updated 2011. *Food Security in the United States..*
17. Ibid.
18. U.S. Department of Labor, Bureau of Labor Statistics. 2010. *A Profile of the Working Poor, 2008.* Available at www.bls.gov/cps/cpswp2008.pdf. Accessed June 2012.
19. National Coalition for the Homeless. 2009. *Substance Abuse and Homelessness.* Available at www.nationalhomeless.org/factsheets/addiction.pdf. Accessed June 2012.
20. National Coalition for the Homeless. 2006. *Mental Illness and Homelessness.* Available at www.nationalhomeless.org/publications/facts/Mental_Illness.pdf. Accessed June 2012.
21. Whitaker, R. C., S. M. Phillips, and S. M. Orzel. 2006. Food Insecurity and the Risks of Depression and Anxiety in Mothers and Behavior Problems in their Preschool-Aged Children. *PEDIATRICS* 118: e859–e868. Available at www.pediatricsdigest.mobi/content/118/3/e859.full. Accessed June 2012.
22. Ibid.
23. The Hunger Project. 2008. *Factsheet: Women Farmers and Food Security.* Available at www.thp.org/learn_more/speeches_reports/research/factsheet_on_women_farmers. Accessed November 2012.
24. Smith, L. C. and L. Haddad. 2000. *Explaining Child Malnutrition in Developing Countries: A Cross-Country Analysis.* Washington, DC: International Food Policy Research Institute. Available at www.ifpri.org/publication/explaining-child-malnutrition-developing-countries-0. Accessed June 2012.
25. UNESCO. 2012. *Key Messages and Data on Girls' and Women's Education and Literacy.* Available at www.unesco.org/new/fileadmin/MULTIMEDIA/HQ/ED/pdf/globalpartners-key-messages.pdf. Accessed June 2012.
26. United Nations Association of the United States of America and the Business Council for the United Nations. 2006. *Millennium Development Goals.* Available at www.un.org/millenniumgoals. Accessed June 2012.
27. Petrescu, Ioana M. 2010. *The Humanitarian Impact of Economic Sanctions.* Available at www.publicpolicy.umd.edu/ioana-petrescu. Accessed November 2012.
28. World Food Programme. 2012. *Hunger. What Causes Hunger?* Available at www.wfp.org/hunger/causes. Accessed June 2012.
29. Ibid.
30. Mission 2014: Feeding the World. *Ineffective/Inadequate Agricultural Practices.* Available at http://12.000.scripts.mit.edu/mission2014/problems/ineffectiveinadequate-agricultural-practices. Accessed June 2012.
31. United Nations, Department for Economic and Social Affairs. Population Division, Population Estimates and Projects Section. 2011. *World Population Prospects. Annual Population 2011–2100—Both Sexes.* Available at http://esa.un.org/unpd/wpp/index.htm. Accessed November 2012.
32. Ibid.
33. Scott, B., E. W. Counts, M. Medora, and C. Woolery. 1998. The Dietitian's Role in Ending World Hunger: As Citizen and Health Professional. *Topics in Clinical Nutrition* 13:31–45.
34. The World Bank. 2011. *Getting to Equal: How Educating Every Girl Can Help Break the Cycle of Poverty.* Available at http://go.worldbank.org/03WKKO0LV0. Accessed June 2012.
35. Raivio, K. 1990. How Does Infant Mortality Affect Birth Rates? *Duodecim* 106:1187–1189. (Article in Finnish) Available at www.ncbi.nlm.nih.gov/pubmed/1670537. Accessed June 2012.
36. King, F. S. and A. Burgess. 1993. *Nutrition for Developing Countries.* 2nd ed. Oxford, England: Oxford Medical Publications, Oxford University Press.
37. World Health Organization. 2002. *The Optimal Duration of Exclusive Breast-Feeding: A Systematic Review.* Geneva: World Health Organization.
38. King, et al. 1993. *Nutrition for Developing Countries.*
39. Beers, M., R. Porter, T. Jones, J. Kaplan, and M. Berkwits, eds. 2006. Infant Nutrition. In *The Merck Manual of Diagnosis and Therapy, Section 19—Pediatrics, Chapter 256: Health Management in Normal Newborns, Infants, and Children.* Available at www.merck.com/mmpe/sec01.html. Accessed June 2012.
40. UNICEF. Childinfo. Updated 2012. *Statistics by Area. HIV/AIDS.* www.childinfo.org/hiv_aids.html. Accessed June 2012.
41. Struble, M. B., Aomari, L. L. 2003. Position of the American Dietetic Association: Addressing World Hunger, Malnutrition, and Food Insecurity. *Journal of the American Dietetic Association* 103:1046-57.
42. Food Research and Action Center. 2011. *Food Insecurity and Obesity: Understanding the Connections.* Available at http://frac.org/pdf/

frac_brief_understanding_the_connections .pdf. Accessed November 2012.

43. Beers, M., R. Porter, T. Jones, J. Kaplan, and M. Berkwits, eds. 2006. Starvation. In *The Merck Manual of Diagnosis and Therapy, Section 1—Nutritional Disorders, Chapter 2: Malnutrition Topics.* Available at www.einet .net/review/23319-608153/THE_MERCK_ MANUAL_Sec_1_Ch_2_Malnutrition.htm. Accessed June 2012.
44. World Food Programme. 2012. *Hunger. What Is Malnutrition?* Available at www .wfp.org/hunger/malnutrition. Accessed June 2012.
45. Kleinman, R. E., et al. 1998. Hunger in Children in the United States: Potential Behavioral and Emotional Correlates. *Pediatrics* 101:3–10.
46. Scanlon, K. S. 1989. (Thesis) Activity and Behavior Changes of Marginally Malnourished Mexican Pre-Schoolers. Storrs, CT: University of Connecticut.
47. Mora, J. O. 1979. Nutritional Supplementation, Early Stimulation, and Child Development. In J. Brozek, ed. *Behavioral Effects of Energy and Protein Deficits.* Bethesda, MD: U.S. Department of Health, Education, and Welfare (NIH).
48. Uvin, P. 1994. The State of World Hunger. In P. Uvin, ed. *The Hunger Report, 1993.* Langhorne, PA: Gordon and Breach Science Publishers.
49. U.S. Department of Health and Human Services. 2011. *2011 HHS Poverty Guidelines.* Available at http://aspe.hhs.gov/ poverty/11poverty.shtml. Accessed June 2012.
50. WHO. 2012. *Nutrition. Micronutrient Deficiencies. Iron-Deficiency Anaemia.* Available at www.who.int/nutrition/topics/ida/en/ index.html. Accessed June 2012.
51. United Nations Children's Fund (UNICEF). 2009. *Tracking Progress on Child and Maternal Nutrition: A Survival and Development Priority.* Available at www.unicef.org/ publications/files/Tracking_Progress_ on_Child_and_Maternal_Nutrition_ EN_110309.pdf. Accessed November 2012.
52. Martorell, R., J. Rivera, and H. Kaplowitz. 1992. Consequences of Stunting in Early Childhood for Adult Body Size in Rural Guatemala. *Annales Nestlé* 48:85–92*th* .
53. World Health Organization. Media Centre. 2012. *Children: Reducing Mortality.* Available at www.who.int/mediacentre/factsheets/fs178/ en/index.html. Accessed November 2012.
54. Ibid.
55. World Health Organization. 2012. *Water Sanitation Health. Water-Related Diseases. Diarrhoea.* Available at www.who.int/ water_sanitation_health/diseases/diarrhoea/ en. Accessed June 2012.
56. Food and Agriculture Organization. 2006. *The State of Food Insecurity in the World, 2006.* Available at www.fao.org/docrep/009/ a0750e/a0750e00.HTM. Accessed June 2012.
57. IFOAM. 2009. *Environmental Benefits of Organic Agriculture.* Available at www.ifoam. org/growing_organic/1_arguments_for_oa/ environmental_benefits/environmental_benefits_main_page.html. Accessed June 2012.
58. Lappe, F. and J. Collins. 1998. *World Hunger: Twelve Myths.* 2nd ed. New York: Grove Press.
59. Ibid.
60. WHO/UNICEF. 2012. *Water, Sanitation and Hygiene.* Available at www.unicef.org/wash. Accessed June 2012.
61. WHO. Media Centre. 2009. Reducing Childhood Deaths from Diarrhoea. New Release. Available at www.who.int/ mediacentre/news/releases/2009/childhood_ deaths_diarrhoea_20091014/en/index.html. Accessed November 2012.
62. WHO. Media Centre. 2009. *Diarrhoeal Disease. Fact Sheet no. 330.* Available at www .who.int/mediacentre/factsheets/fs330/en/ index.html. Accessed June 2012.
63. United Nations. International Decade for Action 'Water for Life' 2005–2015. 2012. *Water Scarcity.* Available at www.un.org/ waterforlifedecade/scarcity.shtml. Accessed June 2012.
64. BBC News, Africa. 2006. *Using the Sun to Sterilize Water.* Available at http://news.bbc .co.uk/2/hi/africa/4786216.stm. Accessed June 2012.
65. The Health and Environment Linkages Initiative. 2008. *Water, Health, and Ecosystems.* Available at www.who.int/heli/risks/water/ water/en. Accessed June 2012.
66. Global Alliance for Improved Nutrition. 1996. *Why Food Fortification?* Available at www.gainhealth.org/programs/gain -national-food-fortification-program. Accessed June 2012.
67. Cleland, J. G., and J. K. Van Ginneken. 1988. Maternal Education and Child Survival in Developing Countries: The Search for Pathways of Influence. *Social Science and Medicine* 27:1357–1368.
68. Population Reference Bureau. 2012. *Human Population: Women. Factors Affecting Family Size.* Available at www.prb.org/educators/ teachersguides/humanpopulation/women .aspx. Accessed June 2012.

Appendices

Appendix A Metabolism Pathways and Biochemical Structures

When learning about the science of nutrition, it is important to understand basic principles of metabolism and to know the molecular structures of important nutrients and molecules. Chapter 8 of the text provides a detailed discussion of the major metabolic processes that occur within the body. This appendix gives additional information and detail on several metabolism pathways and biochemical structures of importance.

Metabolism Pathways

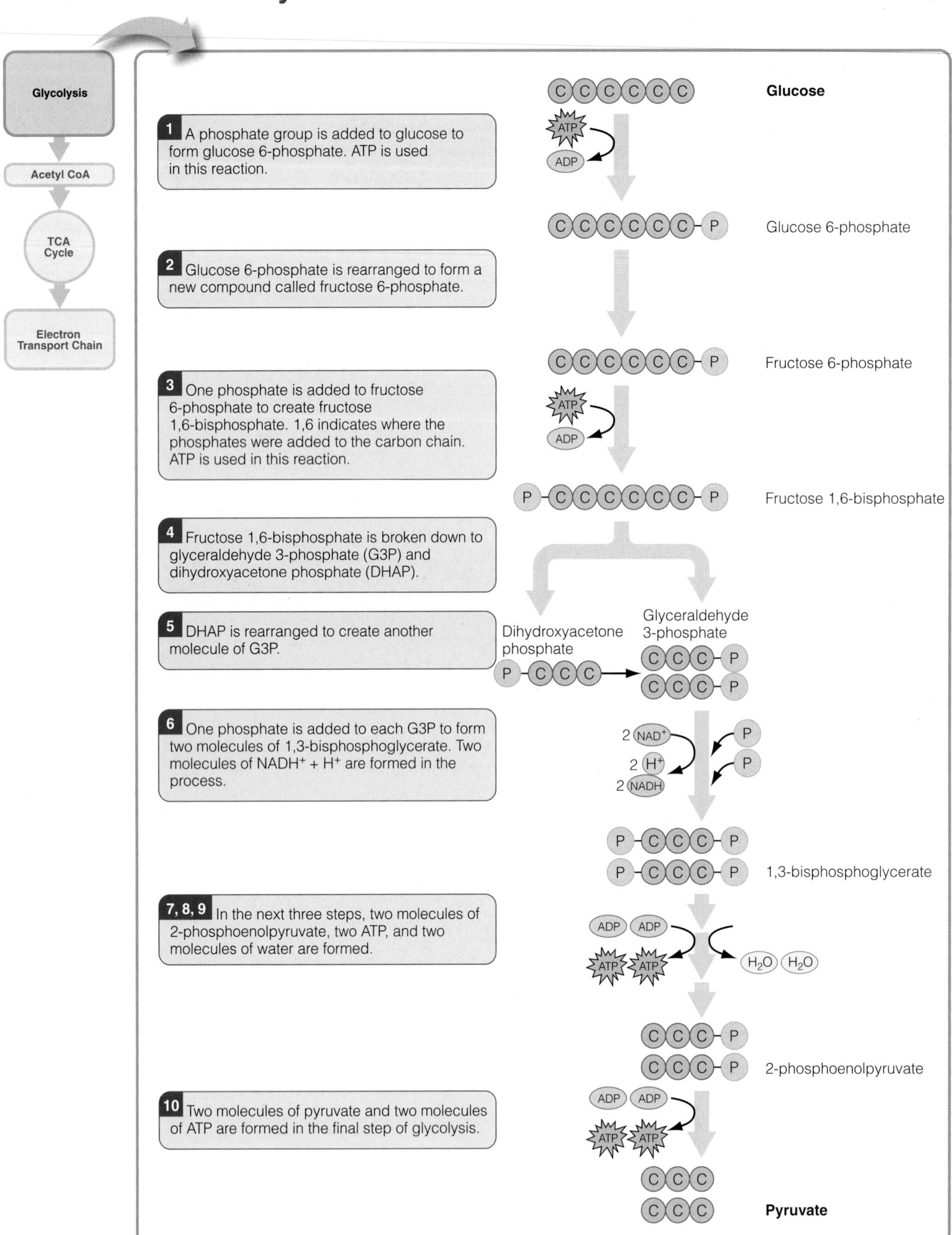

Glycolysis
Acetyl CoA
TCA Cycle
Electron Transport Chain
1 A phosphate group is added to glucose to form glucose 6-phosphate. ATP is used in this reaction.
2 Glucose 6-phosphate is rearranged to form a new compound called fructose 6-phosphate.
3 One phosphate is added to fructose 6-phosphate to create fructose 1,6-bisphosphate. 1,6 indicates where the phosphates were added to the carbon chain. ATP is used in this reaction.
4 Fructose 1,6-bisphosphate is broken down to glyceraldehyde 3-phosphate (G3P) and dihydroxyacetone phosphate (DHAP).
5 DHAP is rearranged to create another molecule of G3P.
6 One phosphate is added to each G3P to form two molecules of 1,3-bisphosphoglycerate. Two molecules of NADH⁺ + H⁺ are formed in the process.
7, 8, 9 In the next three steps, two molecules of 2-phosphoenolpyruvate, two ATP, and two molecules of water are formed.
10 Two molecules of pyruvate and two molecules of ATP are formed in the final step of glycolysis.
Glucose
ATP
ADP
Glucose 6-phosphate
Fructose 6-phosphate
Fructose 1,6-bisphosphate
Dihydroxyacetone phosphate
Glyceraldehyde 3-phosphate
2 NAD⁺
2 H⁺
2 NADH
1,3-bisphosphoglycerate
H₂O
2-phosphoenolpyruvate
Pyruvate

▲ **Figure A.1** Glycolysis Pathway.

Glycolysis
Acetyl CoA
TCA Cycle
Electron Transport Chain
1 Two molecules of pyruvate each lose a carbon and gain a molecule of coenzyme A.
2 Coenzyme A attaches to the remaining two carbons to form acetyl CoA.
2 Pyruvate
2 H^+
2 NADH 2 NAD^+
Lactate
CoA CoA
2 NAD^+
CO_2 CO_2
2 H^+
2 NADH
2 Acetyl CoA

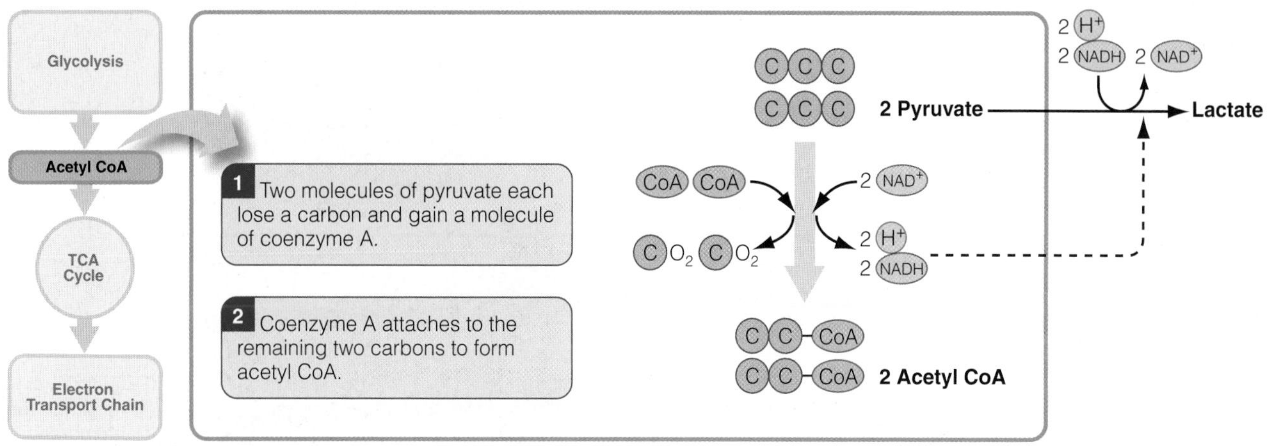

▲ **Figure A.2** Acetyl CoA Pathway.

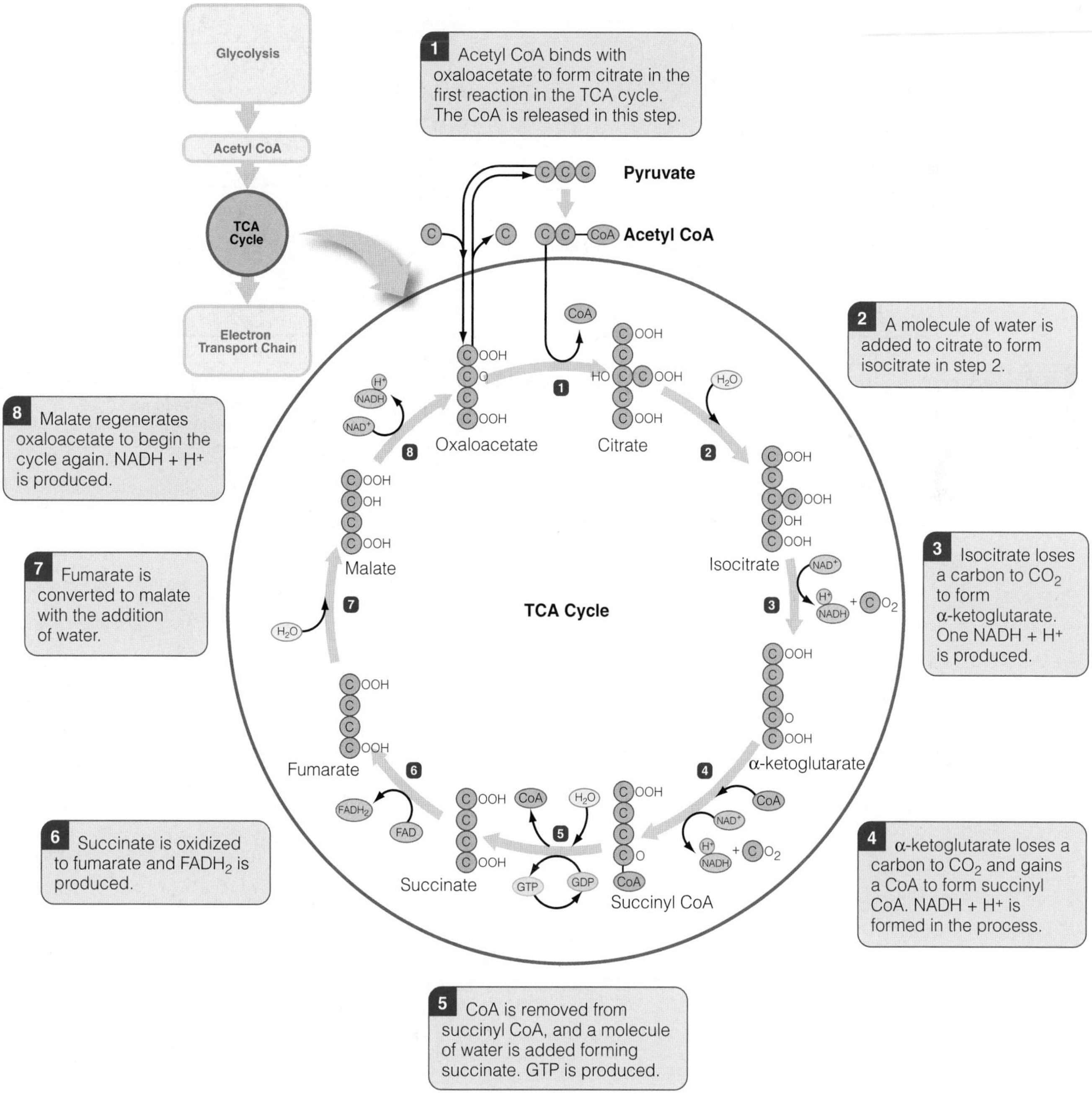

Glycolysis
Acetyl CoA
TCA Cycle
Electron Transport Chain
1 Acetyl CoA binds with oxaloacetate to form citrate in the first reaction in the TCA cycle. The CoA is released in this step.
Pyruvate
Acetyl CoA
2 A molecule of water is added to citrate to form isocitrate in step 2.
3 Isocitrate loses a carbon to CO_2 to form α-ketoglutarate. One NADH + H+ is produced.
4 α-ketoglutarate loses a carbon to CO_2 and gains a CoA to form succinyl CoA. NADH + H+ is formed in the process.
5 CoA is removed from succinyl CoA, and a molecule of water is added forming succinate. GTP is produced.
6 Succinate is oxidized to fumarate and $FADH_2$ is produced.
7 Fumarate is converted to malate with the addition of water.
8 Malate regenerates oxaloacetate to begin the cycle again. NADH + H+ is produced.
TCA Cycle
Oxaloacetate
Citrate
Isocitrate
α-ketoglutarate
Succinyl CoA
Succinate
Fumarate
Malate
CoA
H_2O
NAD^+
NADH
H^+
CO_2
GTP
GDP
FAD
$FADH_2$

▲ **Figure A.3** TCA cycle.

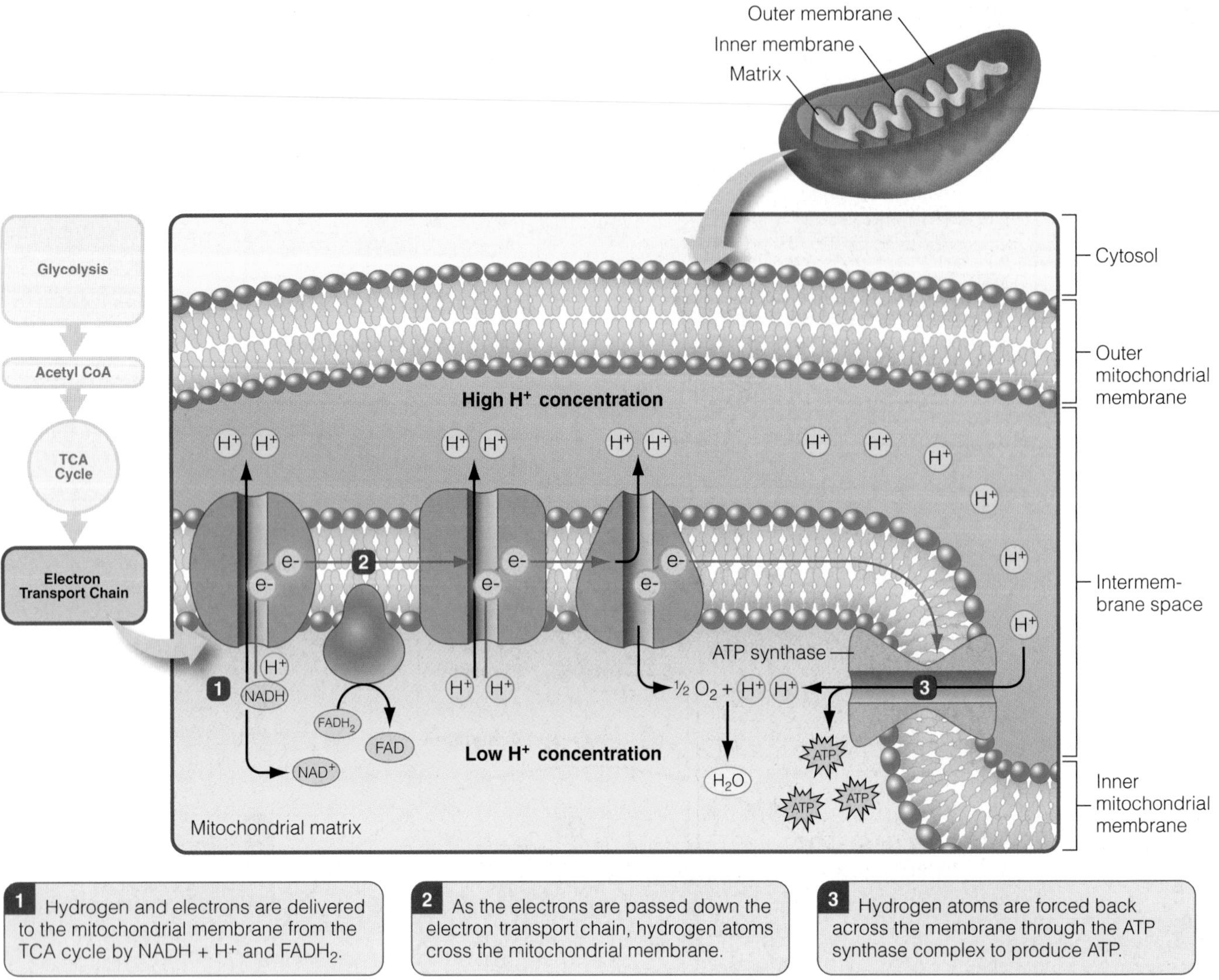

1 Hydrogen and electrons are delivered to the mitochondrial membrane from the TCA cycle by NADH + H+ and $FADH_2$.

2 As the electrons are passed down the electron transport chain, hydrogen atoms cross the mitochondrial membrane.

3 Hydrogen atoms are forced back across the membrane through the ATP synthase complex to produce ATP.

▲ **Figure A.4** Electron transport chain.

a **Sources of energy use and production in the different metabolic pathways**

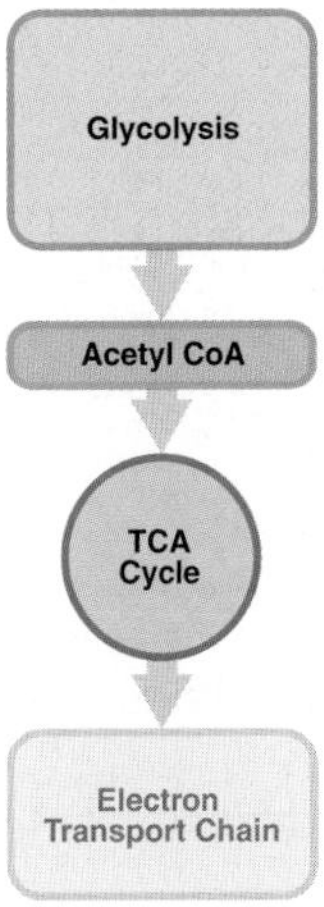

Glycolysis → Acetyl CoA → TCA Cycle → Electron Transport Chain

	Metabolic reaction	Reaction by-product	Number used	Number produced	Net usage/ production
Glycolysis	Glucose → Fructose 1,6-biphosphate	ATP	2		−2 ATP
	Glyceraldehyde 3-phosphate → 1,3-bisphosphoglyceric acid	NADH + H^+		2	2 NADH + H^+
	1,3-bisphosphoglyceric acid → Pyruvic acid	ATP		4	4 ATP
Acetyl CoA	Pyruvic acid → Acetyl CoA	NADH + H^+		2	2 NADH + H^+ via electron transport chain
TCA Cycle	Isocitrate → Succinyl CoA	NADH + H^+		4	4 NADH + H^+ via electron transport chain
	Succinyl CoA → Succinate	GTP		2	2 GTP
	Succinate → Fumarate	$FADH_2$		2	2 $FADH_2$ via electron transport chain
	Malate → Oxaloacetate	NADH + H^+		2	2 NADH + H^+ via electron transport chain

b **Energy balance sheet for glucose oxidation**

Reaction by-product	Number produced	Number of ATP produced per product	Net usage/ production
ATP	4 − 2 = 2	1	2 × 1 = 2 ATP
NADH + H^+ from glycolysis	2	2 to 3	2 × 2 = 4 or 2 × 3 = 6 ATP
NADH + H^+ from TCA cycle	8	3	8 × 3 = 24 ATP
GTP	2	1	2 × 1 = 2 ATP
$FADH_2$ via electron transport chain	2	2	2 × 2 = 4 ATP
Balance of energy from the oxidation of one unit of glucose: 36 to 38 ATP			

▲ **Figure A.5** Products of metabolic pathways.

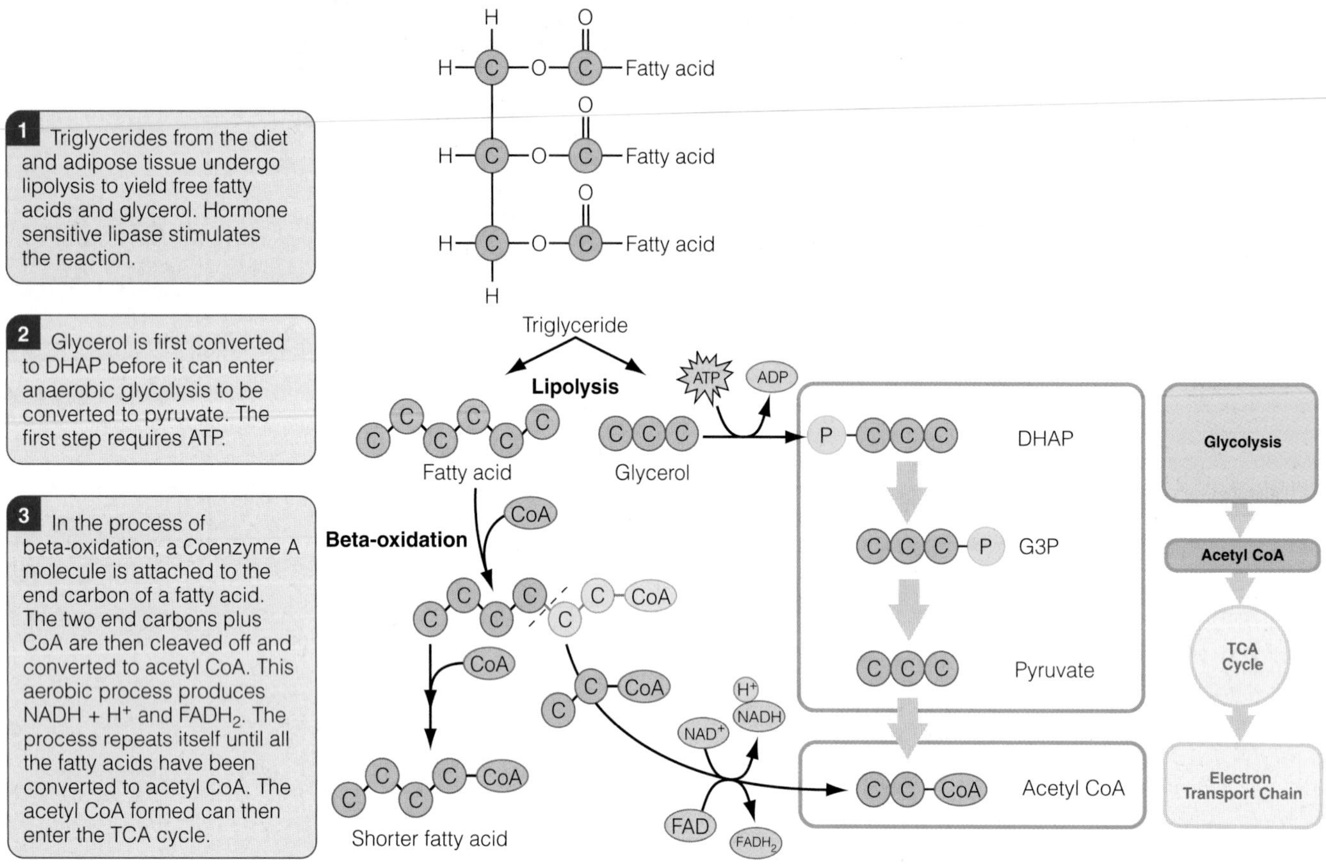

1 Triglycerides from the diet and adipose tissue undergo lipolysis to yield free fatty acids and glycerol. Hormone sensitive lipase stimulates the reaction.
2 Glycerol is first converted to DHAP before it can enter anaerobic glycolysis to be converted to pyruvate. The first step requires ATP.
3 In the process of beta-oxidation, a Coenzyme A molecule is attached to the end carbon of a fatty acid. The two end carbons plus CoA are then cleaved off and converted to acetyl CoA. This aerobic process produces NADH + H+ and FADH2. The process repeats itself until all the fatty acids have been converted to acetyl CoA. The acetyl CoA formed can then enter the TCA cycle.
Fatty acid
Fatty acid
Fatty acid
Triglyceride
Lipolysis
ATP
ADP
Fatty acid
Glycerol
DHAP
G3P
Pyruvate
Acetyl CoA
Beta-oxidation
CoA
Shorter fatty acid
H+
NADH
NAD+
FAD
FADH2
Glycolysis
Acetyl CoA
TCA Cycle
Electron Transport Chain

▲ **Figure A.6** using fat for energy.

Glycolysis
Acetyl CoA
TCA Cycle
Electron Transport Chain
Acetyl CoA
Acetyl CoA
H2O
Ketogenesis
CoA CoA
OOH
Acetoacetate
H+
NADH
NAD+
OH
OOH
Beta-hydroxybutyrate
O2
Acetone
1 Ketone bodies are produced in the mitochondria of the liver through ketogenesis from excess acetyl CoA.
2 Acetoacetate can be reduced to beta-hydroxybutyrate using NADH + H+ producing NAD+, or it can form acetone after a carbon is removed creating carbon dioxide.

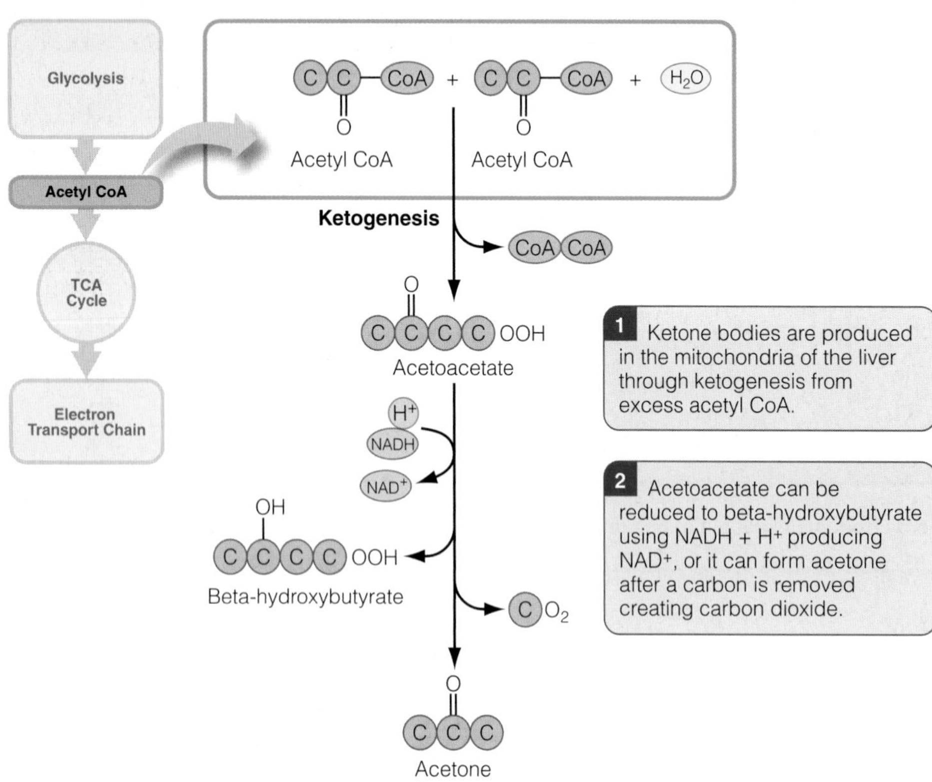

▲ **Figure A.7** Ketone bodies.

Biochemical Structures

Amino Acid Structures

Amino acids all have the same basic core but differ in their side chains. The following amino acids have been classified according to their specific type of side chain.

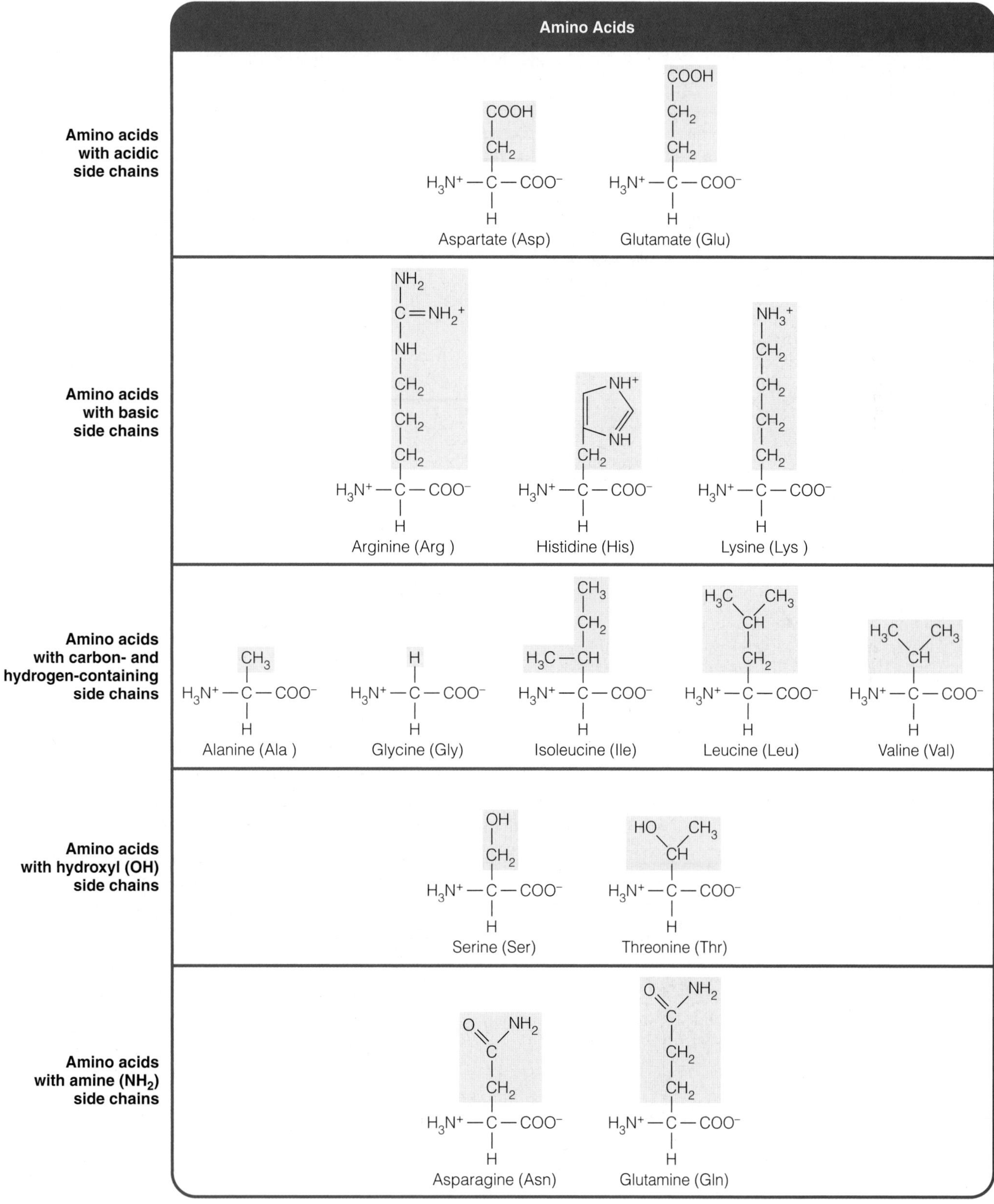

▲ **Figure A.8** Amino Acid Structures.

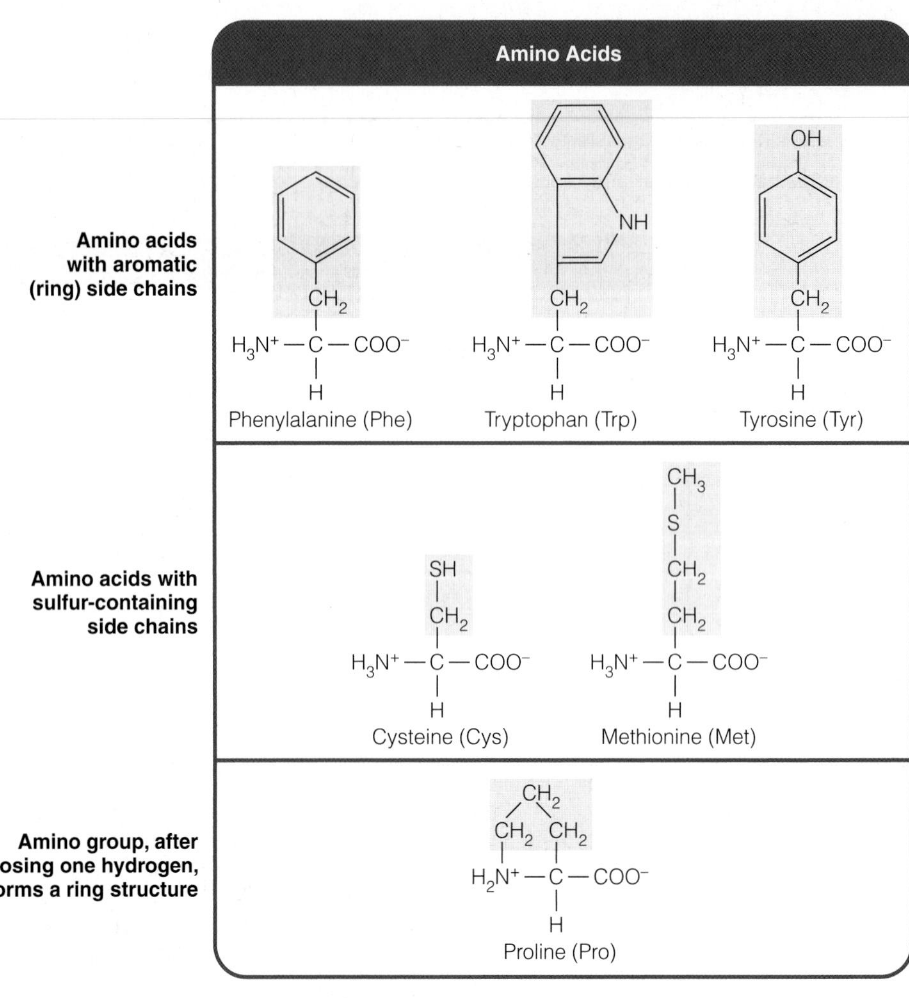

▲ **Figure A.8** Amino Acid Structures. *(Continued)*

Vitamin Structures and Coenzyme Derivatives

Many vitamins have common names (for example, vitamin C, vitamin E) as well as scientific designations (for example, ascorbic acid and α-tocopherol). Most vitamins are found in more than one chemical form. Many of the vitamins illustrated here have an active coenzyme form; review both the vitamin and coenzyme structures and see if you can locate the "core vitamin" structure within each of the coenzymes. The vitamins found in food or supplements are not always in the precise chemical form needed for metabolic activity, and therefore the body often has to modify the vitamin in one way or another. For example, many of the B vitamins are phosphorylated, meaning that they have a phosphate group attached.

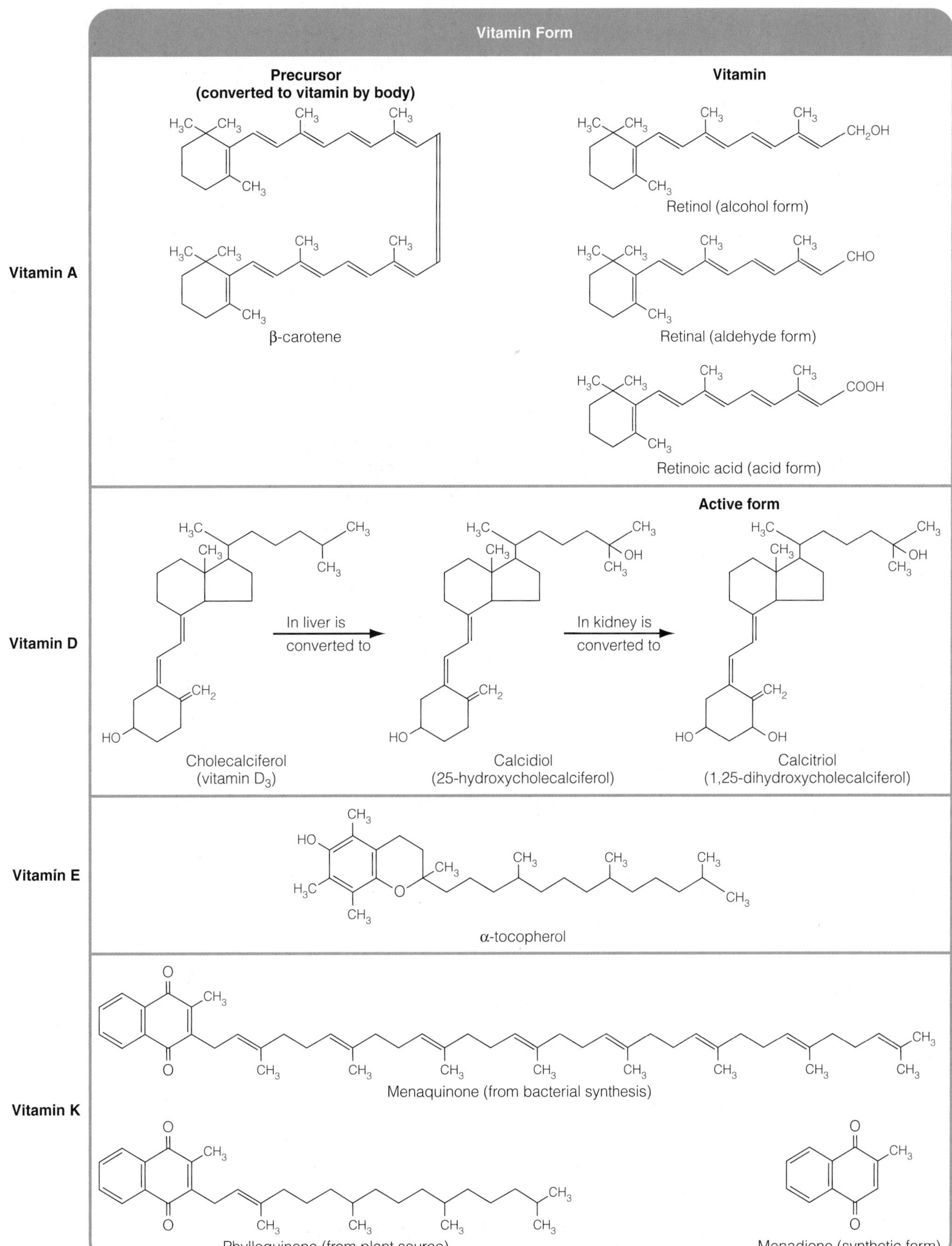

▲ **Figure A.9** Fat-Soluble Vitamins.

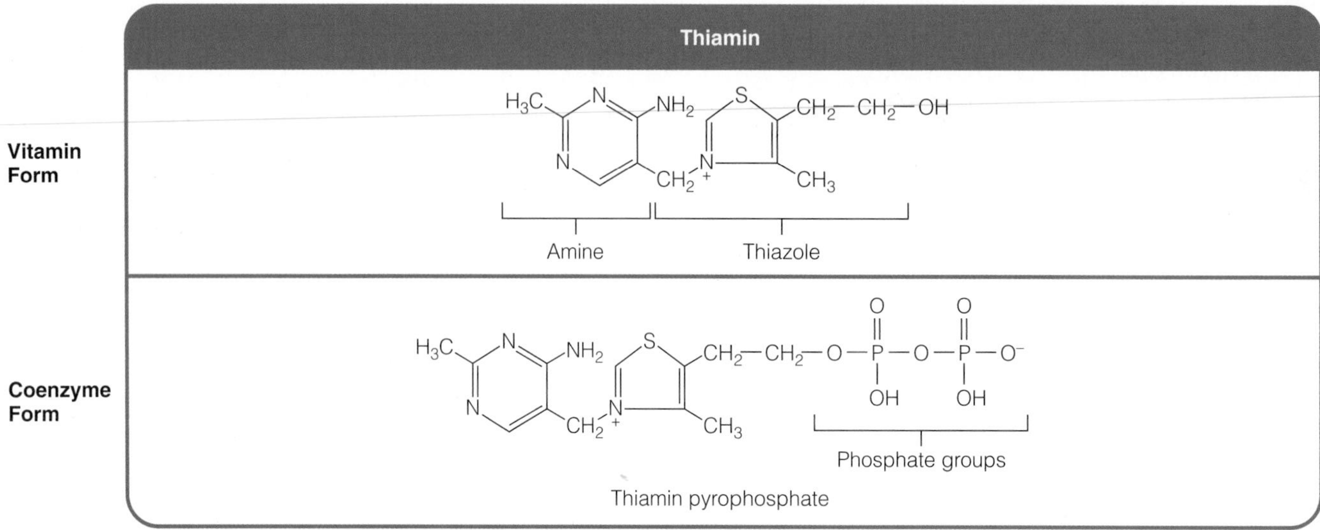

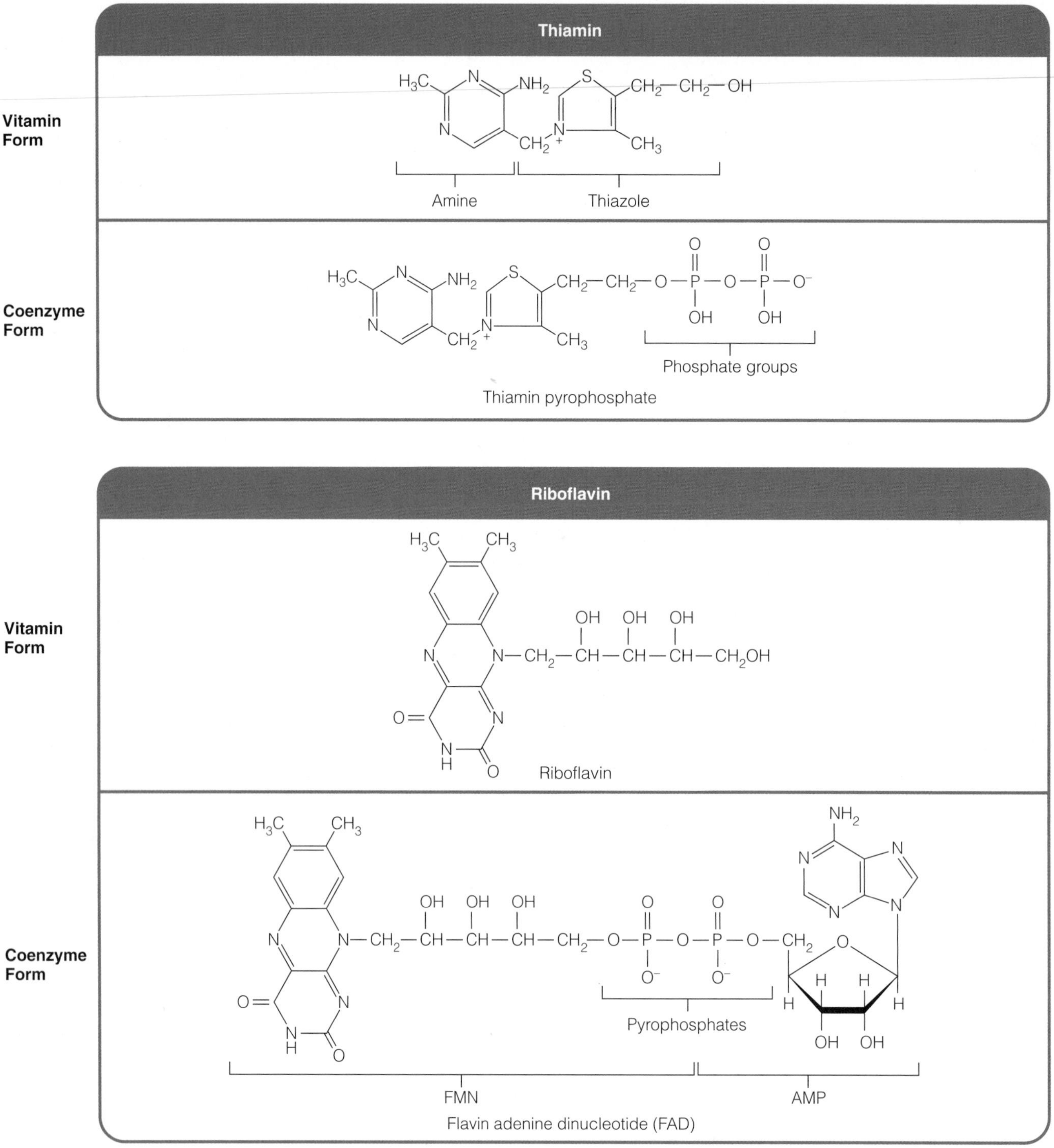

Thiamin
Vitamin Form
Amine
Thiazole
Coenzyme Form
Phosphate groups
Thiamin pyrophosphate
Riboflavin
Vitamin Form
Riboflavin
Coenzyme Form
Pyrophosphates
FMN
AMP
Flavin adenine dinucleotide (FAD)

▲ **Figure A.10** Water-Soluble Vitamins and Their Coenzymes.

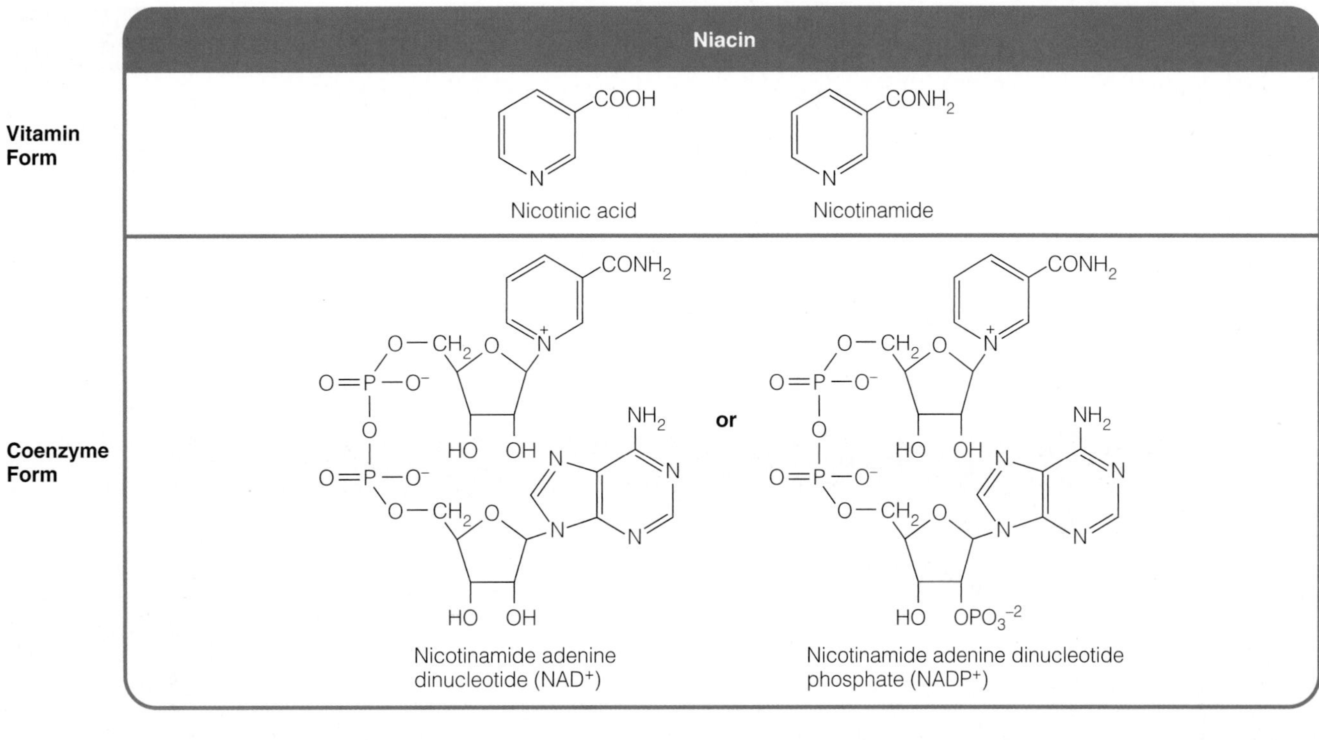

Pantothenic acid

Vitamin Form

$HO-CH_2-C(CH_3)(H_3C)-CH(OH)-C(=O)-NH-CH_2-CH_2-C(=O)-O^-$

Pantothenic acid

Coenzyme Form

$CH_2-O-P(=O)(O^-)-O-P(=O)(O^-)-O-CH_2-C(CH_3)(H_3C)-CH(OH)-C(=O)-NH-CH_2-CH_2-C(=O)-NH-CH_2-CH_2-SH$

Adenine

H H H H

O OH

$O=P-O^-$

O^-

Coenzyme A

▲ **Figure A.10** Water-Soluble Vitamins and Their Coenzymes. *(Continued)*

Biotin

Vitamin Form

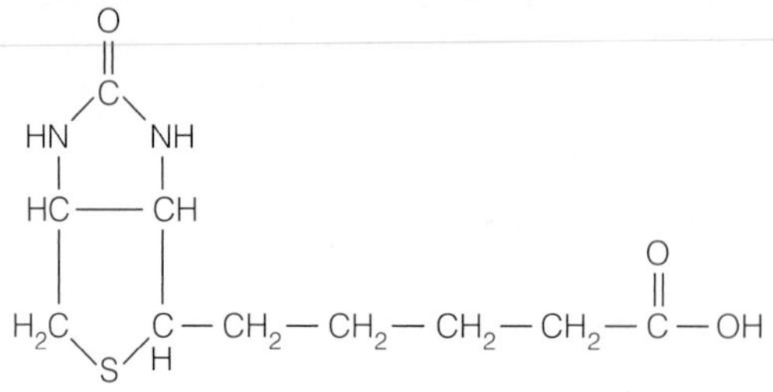

Vitamin B_6

Vitamin Form

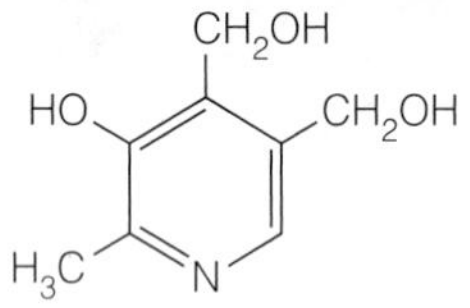

Pyridoxine (PN)

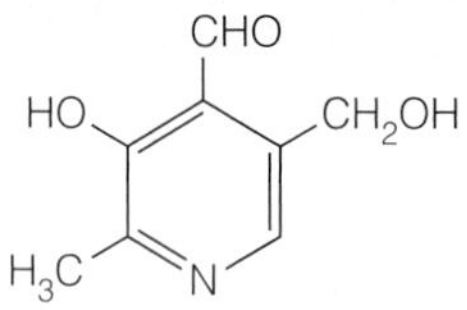

Pyridoxal (PL)

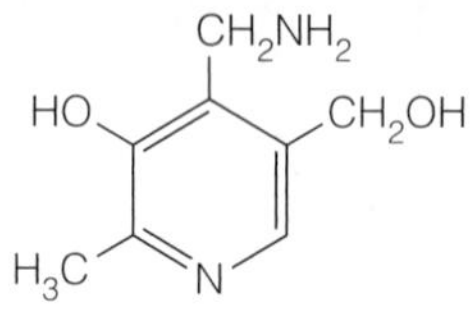

Pyridoxamine (PM)

Coenzyme Form

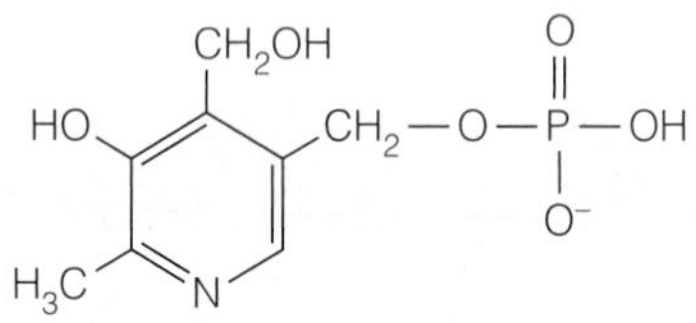

Pyridoxine 5′ phosphate (PMP)

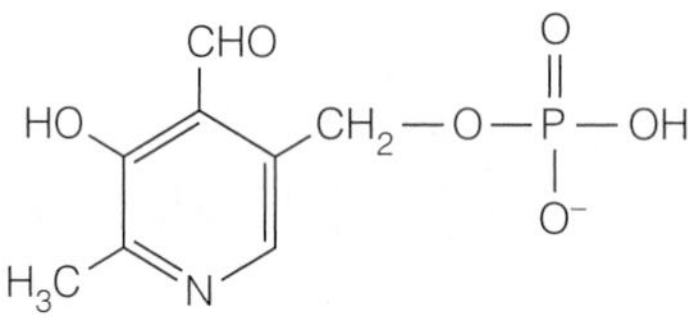

Pyridoxal 5′ phosphate (PLP)

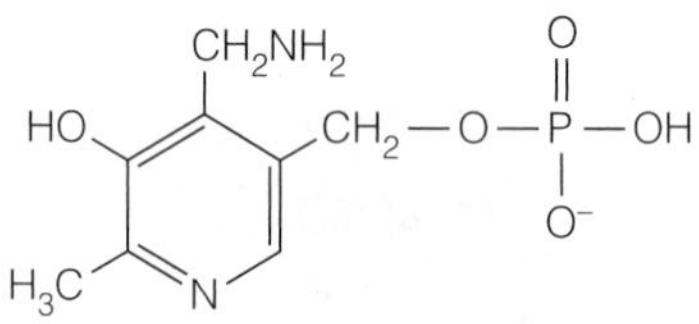

Pyridoxamine 5′ phosphate (PNP)

Folate

Vitamin Form

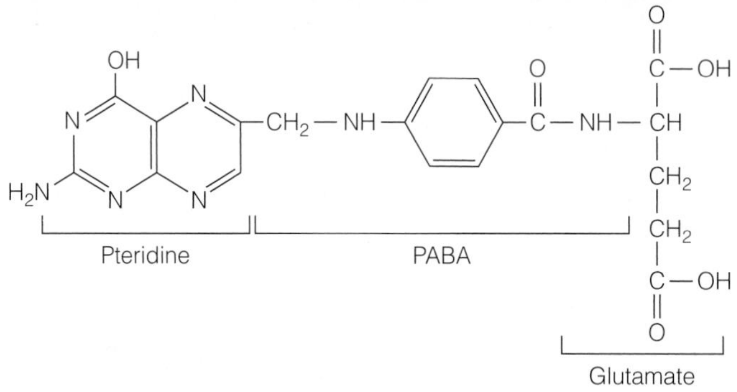

Coenzyme Form

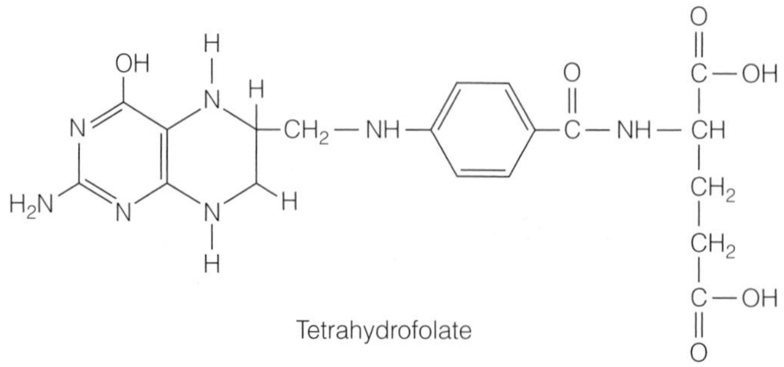

Tetrahydrofolate

▲ **Figure A.10** Water-Soluble Vitamins and Their Coenzymes. *(Continued)*

Vitamin B_{12}

Vitamin Form

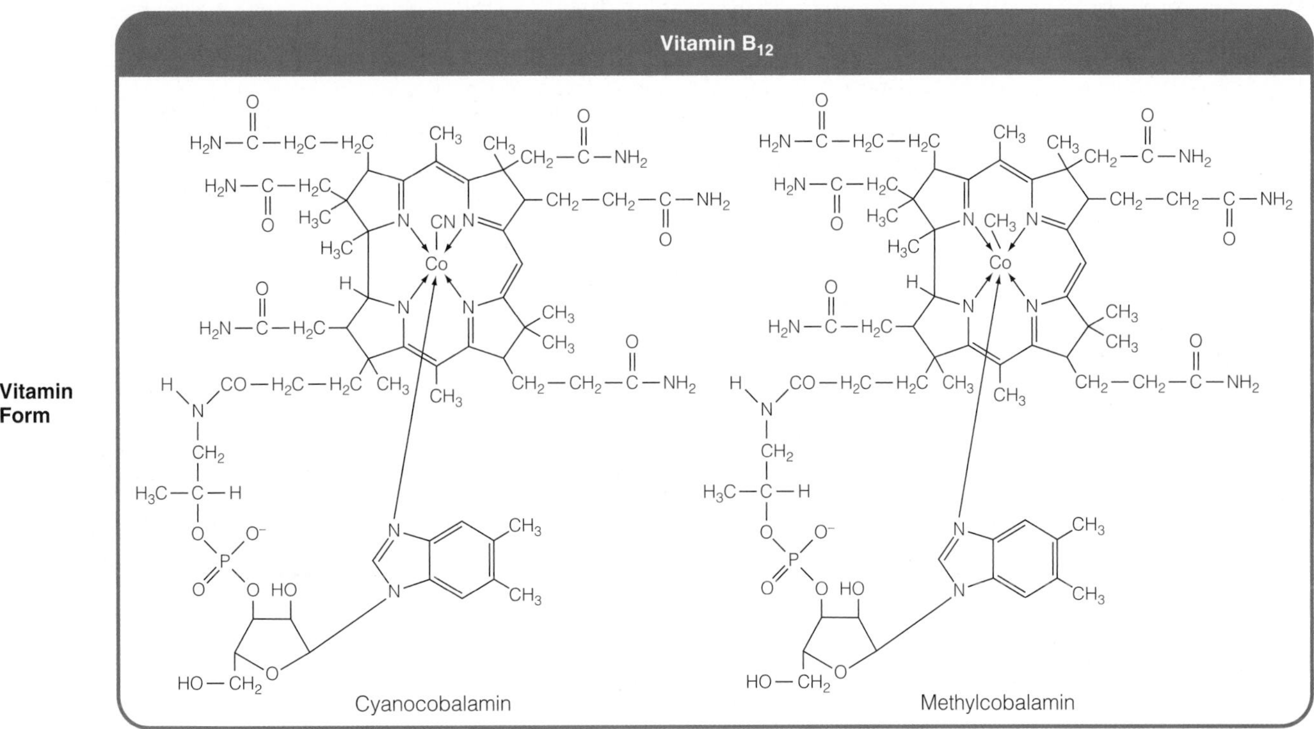

Vitamin C

Vitamin Form

$$\text{Ascorbic acid} \underset{\text{Reduction } (+2H^+)}{\overset{\text{Oxidation } (-2H^+)}{\rightleftharpoons}} \text{Dehydroascorbic acid}$$

Ascorbic acid

Dehydroascorbic acid

Choline

Vitamin Form

$$H_3C-{}^{+}N(CH_3)_2-CH_2-CH_2OH$$

▲ **Figure A.10** Water-Soluble Vitamins and Their Coenzymes. *(Continued)*

Calculation and Conversion Aids

Commonly Used Metric Units

millimeter (mm): one-thousandth of a meter (0.001)
centimeter (cm) : one-hundredth of a meter (0.01)
kilometer (km) : one-thousand times a meter (1,000)
kilogram (kg) : one-thousand times a gram (1,000)
milligram (mg) : one-thousandth of a gram (0.001)
microgram (μg) : one-millionth of a gram (0.000001)
milliliter (ml) : one-thousandth of a liter (0.001)

Conversion Factors

Use the following table to convert U.S. measurements to metric equivalents:

Original Unit	Multiply By	To Get
ounces avdp	28.3495	grams
ounces	0.0625	pounds
pounds	0.4536	kilograms
pounds	16	ounces
grams	0.0353	ounces
grams	0.0022	pounds
kilograms	2.2046	pounds
liters	1.8162	pints (dry)
liters	2.1134	pints (liquid)
liters	0.9081	quarts (dry)
liters	1.0567	quarts (liquid)
liters	0.2642	gallons (U.S.)
pints (dry)	0.5506	liters
pints (liquid)	0.4732	liters
quarts (dry)	1.1012	liters
quarts (liquid)	0.9463	liters
gallons (U.S.)	3.7854	liters
millimeters	0.0394	inches
centimeters	0.3937	inches
centimeters	0.0328	feet
inches	25.4000	millimeters
Inches	2.5400	centimeters
Inches	0.0254	meters
feet	0.3048	meters
meters	3.2808	feet
meters	1.0936	yards
cubic feet	0.0283	cubic meters
cubic meters	35.3147	cubic feet
cubic meters	1.3079	cubic yards
cubic yards	0.7646	cubic meters

International Units

Some vitamin supplements may report vitamin content as International Units (IU).

To convert IU to:

- Micrograms of vitamin D (cholecalciferol), multiply the IU value by 0.025.
- Milligrams of vitamin E (alpha-tocopherol), multiply the IU value by 0.67 if vitamin E is from natural sources. Multiply the IU value by 0.45 if vitamin E is from synthetic sources.
- Vitamin A: 1 IU = 0.3 μg retinol or 0.3 μg RAE or 0.6 μg beta-carotene

Retinol Activity Equivalents

Retinol activity equivalents (RAE) are a standardized unit of measure for vitamin A. RAE account for the various differences in bioavailability from sources of vitamin A. Many supplements will report vitamin A content in IU, as shown above, or in retinol equivalents (RE).

1 μg RAE = 1 μg retinol
12 μg beta-carotene

To calculate RAE from the RE value of vitamin carotenoids in foods, divide RE by 2. Divide the amount of beta-carotene by 12 to convert to RAE.

For vitamin A supplements and foods fortified with vitamin A, 1 RE = 1 RAE.

Folate

Folate is measured as dietary folate equivalents (DFE). DFE account for the different factors affecting bioavailability of folate sources.

1 μg DFE = 1 μg food folate
0.6 μg folate from fortified foods
0.5 μg folate supplement taken on an empty stomach
0.6 μg folate as a supplement consumed with a meal

To convert micrograms of synthetic folate, such as that found in supplements or fortified foods, to DFE:

$$\mu g \text{ synthetic folate} \times 1.7 = \mu g \text{ DFE}$$

For naturally occurring food folate, such as spinach, each microgram of folate equals 1 microgram DFE:

$$\mu g \text{ folate} = \mu g \text{ DFE}$$

Niacin

Niacin is measured as niacin equivalents (mg NE). NE reflects the amount of preformed niacin in foods or the amount that can be formed from a food's content of the amino acid niacin.

To calculate mg NE from a meal:

If you know the tryptophan and preformed niacin in a meal: (tryptophan × 1,000 ÷ 60) + preformed niacin = mg NE

If you know the total amount of protein in a meal but not the tryptophan content: (0.011 × g of protein) × 1,000 ÷ 60 + preformed niacin = mg NE

Length: U.S. and Metric Equivalents

¼ inch	= 0.6 centimeters
1 inch	= 2.5 centimeters
1 foot	= 0.3048 meter
	30.48 centimeters
1 yard	= 0.9144 meter
1 millimeter	= 0.03937 inch
1 centimeter	= 0.3937 inch
1 decimeter	= 3.937 inches
1 meter	= 39.37 inches
	1.094 yards
1 micrometer	= 0.00003937 inch

Weights and Measures

Food Measurement Equivalencies from U.S. to Metric

Capacity

⅕ teaspoon	= 1 milliliter
¼ teaspoon	= 1.23 milliliters
½ teaspoon	= 2.5 milliliters
1 teaspoon	= 5 milliliters
1 tablespoon	= 15 milliliters
1 fluid ounce	= 30 milliliters
¼ cup	= 59 milliliters
⅓ cup	= 79 milliliters
½ cup	= 118 milliliters
1 cup	= 237 milliliters
1 pint (2 cups)	= 473 milliliters
1 quart (4 cups)	= 0.95 liter
1 liter (1.06 quarts)	= 1,000 milliliters
1 gallon (4 quarts)	= 3.79 liters

Weight

0.035 ounce	= 1 gram
1 ounce	= 28 grams
¼ pound (4 ounces)	= 113 grams
1 pound (16 ounces)	= 454 grams
2.2 pounds (35 ounces)	= 1 kilogram

U.S. Food Measurement Equivalents

3 teaspoons	= 1 tablespoon
½ tablespoon	= 1½ teaspoons
2 tablespoons	= ⅛ cup
4 tablespoons	= ¼ cup
5 tablespoons + 1 teaspoon	= ⅓ cup
8 tablespoons	= ½ cup
10 tablespoons + 2 teaspoons	= ⅔ cup
12 tablespoons	= ¾ cup
16 tablespoons	= 1 cup
2 cups	= 1 pint
4 cups	= 1 quart
2 pints	= 1 quart
4 quarts	= 1 gallon

Volumes and Capacities

1 cup	= 8 fluid ounces
	½ liquid pint
1 milliliter	= 0.061 cubic inch
1 liter	= 1.057 liquid quarts
	0.908 dry quart
	61.024 cubic inches
1 U.S. gallon	= 231 cubic inches
	3.785 liters
	0.833 British gallon
	128 U.S. fluid ounces
1 British Imperial gallon	= 277.42 cubic inches
	1.201 U.S. gallons
	4.546 liters
	160 British fluid ounces
1 U.S. ounce, liquid or fluid	= 1.805 cubic inches
	29.574 milliliters
	1.041 British fluid ounces
1 pint, dry	= 33.600 cubic inches
	0.551 liter
1 pint, liquid	= 28.875 cubic inches
	0.473 liter
1 U.S. quart, dry	= 67.201 cubic inches
	1.101 liters
1 U.S. quart, liquid	= 57.75 cubic inches
	0.946 liter
1 British quart	= 69.355 cubic inches
	1.032 U.S. quarts, dry
	1.201 U.S. quarts, liquid

Energy Units

1 kilocalorie (kcal) = 4.2 kilojoules
1 megajoule (MJ) = 239 kilocalories
1 kilojoule (kJ) = 0.24 kcal
1 gram carbohydrate = 4 kcals
1 gram fat = 9 kcals
1 gram protein = 4 kcals

Temperature Standards

	°Fahrenheit	°Celsius
Body temperature	98.6°	37°
Comfortable room temperature	65–75°	18–24°
Boiling point of water	212°	100°
Freezing point of water	32°	0°

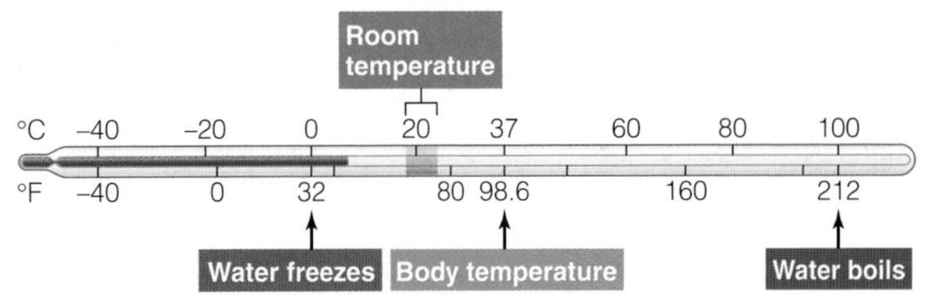

Temperature Scales

To Convert Fahrenheit to Celsius

[(°F – 32) × 5]/9

1. Subtract 32 from °F
2. Multiply (°F – 32) by 5, then divide by 9

To Convert Celsius to Fahrenheit

[(°C × 9)/5] + 32

1. Multiply °C by 9, then divide by 5
2. Add 32 to (°C × 9/5)

Appendix C U.S. Exchange Lists for Meal Planning

Starch List

1 starch choice = 15 g carbohydrate, 0–3 g protein, 0–1 g fat, and 80 cal

Icon Key

☺ = More than 3 g of dietary fiber per serving.

! = Extra fat, or prepared with added fat. (Count as 1 starch + 1 fat.)

ǃ = 480 mg or more of sodium per serving.

Food	Serving Size
Bread	
Bagel, 4 oz	¼ (1 oz)
! Biscuit, 2½" across	1
Bread	
☺ reduced-calorie	2 slices (1½ oz)
white, whole-grain, pumpernickel, rye, unfrosted raisin	1 slice (1 oz)
Chapatti, small, 6" across	1
! Cornbread, 1¾" cube	1 (1½ oz)
English muffin	½
Hot dog bun or hamburger bun	½ (1 oz)
Naan, 8" by 2"	¼
Pancake, 4" across, ¼" thick	1
Pita, 6" across	½
Roll, plain small	1 (1 oz)
! Stuffing, bread	⅓ cup
! Taco shell, 5" across	2
Tortilla	
Corn, 6" across	1
Flour, 6" across	1
Flour, 10" across	⅓ tortilla
! Waffle, 4"-square or 4" across	1
Cereals and Grains	
Barley, cooked	⅓ cup
Bran, dry	
☺ oat	¼ c
☺ wheat	½ c
☺ Bulgur (cooked)	½ c
Cereals	½ c
☺ bran	½ c
cooked (oats, oatmeal)	½ c
puffed	1½ c
shredded wheat, plain	½ c
sugar-coated	½ c
unsweetened, ready-to-eat	¾ c
Couscous	⅓ c
Granola	
low-fat	¼ c
! regular	¼ c
Grits, cooked	½ c
Kasha	½ c
Millet, cooked	⅓ c
Muesli	¼ c
Pasta, cooked	⅓ c
Polenta, cooked	⅓ c
Quinoa, cooked	⅓ c
Rice, white or brown, cooked	⅓ c
Tabbouleh (tabouli), prepared	½ c
Wheat germ, dry	3 tbs
Wild rice, cooked	½ c
Starchy Vegetables	
Cassava	⅓ c
Corn	½ c
on cob, large	½ cob (5 oz)
☺ Hominy, canned	¾ c
☺ Mixed vegetables with corn, peas, or pasta	1 c
☺ Parsnips	½ c
☺ Peas, green	½ c
Plantain, ripe	⅓ c
Potato	
baked with skin	¼ large (3 oz)
boiled, all kinds	½ c or ½ medium (3 oz)
! mashed, with milk and fat	½ c
French fried (oven-baked)	1 cup (2 oz)
☺ Pumpkin, canned, no sugar added	1 c
Spaghetti/pasta sauce	½ c
☺ Squash, winter (acorn, butternut)	1 c
☺ Succotash	½ c
Yam, sweet potato, plain	½ c
Crackers and Snacks	
Animal crackers	8
Crackers	
! round-butter type	6
saltine-type	6
! sandwich-style, cheese or peanut butter filling	3
! whole-wheat regular	2–5 (¾ oz)
☺ whole-wheat lower fat or crispbreads	2–5 (¾ oz)

Food	Serving Size
Graham crackers, 2½" square	3
Matzoh	¾ oz
Melba toast, about 2" by 4" piece	4 pieces
Oyster crackers	20
Crackers and Snacks	
Popcorn	3 c
! ☺ with butter	3 c
☺ no fat added	3 c
☺ lower fat	3 c
Pretzels	¾ oz
Rice cakes, 4" across	2
Snack chips	
fat-free or baked (tortilla, potato), baked pita chips	15–20 (¾ oz)
! regular (tortilla, potato)	9–13 (¾ oz)
Beans, Peas, and Lentils	
(Count as 1 starch + 1 lean meat)	
☺ Baked beans	⅓ c
☺ Beans, cooked (black, garbanzo, kidney, lima, navy, pinto, white)	½ c
☺ Lentils, cooked (brown, green, yellow)	½ c
☺ Peas, cooked (black-eyed, split)	½ c
▮ ☺ Refried beans, canned	½ c

Fruit List

1 fruit choice = 15 g carbohydrate, 0 g protein, 0 g fat, and 60 cal

Weight includes skin, core, seeds, and rind.

Icon Key

☺ = More than 3 g of dietary fiber per serving.

! = Extra fat, or prepared with added fat.

▮ = 480 mg or more of sodium per serving.

Food	Serving Size
Apples	
unpeeled, small	1 (4 oz)
dried	4 rings
Applesauce, unsweetened	½ c
Apricots	
canned	½ c
dried	8 halves
☺ fresh	4 whole (5½ oz)
Banana, extra small	1 (4 oz)
☺ Blackberries	¾ c
Blueberries	¾ c
Cantaloupe, small	⅓ melon or 1 c cubed (11 oz)
Cherries	
sweet, canned	½ c
sweet, fresh	12 (3 oz)
Dates	3
Dried fruits (blueberries, cherries, cranberries, mixed fruit, raisins)	2 tbs
Figs	
dried	1½
☺ fresh	1½ large or 2 medium (3½ oz)
Fruit cocktail	½ c
Grapefruit	
large	½ (11 oz)
sections, canned	¾ c
Grapes, small	17 (3 oz)
Honeydew melon	1 slice or 1 c cubed (10 oz)
☺ Kiwi	1 (3½ oz)
Mandarin oranges, canned	¾ c
Mango, small	½ fruit (5½ oz) or ½ c
Nectarine, small	1 (5 oz)
☺ Orange, small	1 (6½ oz)
Papaya	½ fruit or 1 c cubed (8 oz)
Peaches	
canned	½ c
fresh, medium	1 (6 oz)
Pears	
canned	½ c
fresh, large	½ (4 oz)
Pineapple	
canned	½ c
fresh	¾ c
Plums	
canned	½ c
dried (prunes)	3
small	2 (5 oz)
☺ Raspberries	1 c
☺ Strawberries	1¼ c whole berries
☺ Tangerines, small	2 (8 oz)
Watermelon	1 slice or 1¼ c cubes (13½ oz)

Food	Serving Size
Fruit Juice	
Apple juice/cider	½ c
Fruit juice blends, 100% juice	⅓ c
Grape juice	⅓ c
Grapefruit juice	½ c
Orange juice	½ c
Pineapple juice	½ c
Prune juice	⅓ c

Milk and Yogurts

1 milk choice = 12 g carbohydrate and 8 g protein

Food	Serving Size	Count As
Fat-Free or Low-Fat (1%)		
(0–3 g fat per serving, 100 calories per serving)		
Milk, buttermilk, acidophilus milk, Lactaid	1 c	1 fat-free milk
Evaporated milk	½ c	1 fat-free milk
Yogurt, plain or flavored with an artificial sweetener	¾ c (6 oz)	1 fat-free milk
Reduced-Fat (2%)		
(5 g fat per serving, 120 calories per serving)		
Milk, acidophilus milk, kefir, Lactaid	1 c	1 reduced-fat milk
Yogurt, plain	¾ c (6 oz)	1 reduced-fat milk
Whole		
(8 g fat per serving, 160 calories per serving)		
Milk, buttermilk, goat's milk	1 c	1 whole milk
Evaporated milk	½ c	1 whole milk
Yogurt, plain	8 oz	1 whole milk
Dairy-Like Foods		
Chocolate milk		
fat-free	1 c	1 fat-free milk + 1 carbohydrate
whole	1 c	1 whole milk + 1 carbohydrate
Eggnog, whole milk	½ c	1 carbohydrate + 2 fats
Rice drink		
flavored, low-fat	1 c	2 carbohydrates
plain, fat-free	1 c	1 carbohydrate
Smoothies, flavored, regular	10 oz	1 fat-free milk + 2½ carbohydrates
Soy milk		
light	1 c	1 carbohydrate + ½ fat
regular, plain	1 c	1 carbohydrate + 1 fat
Yogurt		
and juice blends	1 c	1 fat-free milk + 1 carbohydrate
low carbohydrate (less than 6 g carbohydrate per choice)	¾ c (6 oz)	½ fat-free milk
with fruit, low-fat	¾ c (6 oz)	1 fat-free milk + 1 carbohydrate

Sweets, Desserts, and Other Carbohydrates List

1 other carbohydrate choice = 15 g carbohydrate and variable protein, fat, and calories.

Icon Key

▮ = 480 mg or more of sodium per serving.

Food	Serving Size	Count As
Beverages, Soda, and Energy/Sports Drinks		
Cranberry juice cocktail	½ c	1 carbohydrate
Energy drink	1 can (8.3 oz)	2 carbohydrates
Fruit drink or lemonade	1 c (8 oz)	2 carbohydrates
Hot chocolate		
regular	1 envelope added to 8 oz water	1 carbohydrate + 1 fat
sugar-free or light	1 envelope added to 8 oz water	1 carbohydrate
Soft drink (soda), regular	1 can (12 oz)	2½ carbohydrates
Sports drink	1 cup (8 oz)	1 carbohydrate
Brownies, Cake, Cookies, Gelatin, Pie, and Pudding		
Brownie, small, unfrosted	1¼" square ⅞", high (about 1 oz)	1 carbohydrate + 1 fat
Cake		
angel food, unfrosted	1½ of cake (about 2 oz)	2 carbohydrates
frosted	2" square (about 2 oz)	2 carbohydrates + 1 fat
unfrosted	2" square (about 2 oz)	1 carbohydrate + 1 fat
Cookies		
chocolate chip	2 cookies (2¼" across)	1 carbohydrate + 2 fats
gingersnap	3 cookies	1 carbohydrate
sandwich, with creme filling	2 small (about ⅔ oz)	1 carbohydrate + 1 fat
sugar-free	3 small or 1 large (¾ oz–1 oz)	1 carbohydrate + 1–2 fats
vanilla wafer	5 cookies	1 carbohydrate + 1 fat
Cupcake, frosted	1 small (about 1¾ oz)	2 carbohydrates + 1–1½ fats
Fruit cobbler	½ c (3½ oz)	3 carbohydrates + 1 fat
Gelatin, regular	½ c	1 carbohydrate
Pie		
commercially prepared fruit, 2 crusts	⅙ of 8" pie	3 carbohydrates + 2 fats
pumpkin or custard	⅛ of 8" pie	1½ carbohydrates + 1½ fats
Pudding		
regular (made with reduced-fat milk)	½ c	2 carbohydrates
sugar-free, or sugar-free and fat-free (made with fat-free milk)	½ c	1 carbohydrate
Candy, Spreads, Sweets, Sweeteners, Syrups, and Toppings		
Candy bar, chocolate/peanut	2 "fun size" bars (1 oz)	1½ carbohydrates + 1½ fats
Candy, hard	3 pieces	1 carbohydrate
Chocolate "kisses"	5 pieces	1 carbohydrate + 1 fat
Coffee creamer		
dry, flavored	4 tsp	½ carbohydrate + ½ fat
liquid, flavored	2 tbs	1 carbohydrate

Food	Serving Size	Count As
Fruit snacks, chewy (pureed fruit concentrate)	1 roll (¾ oz)	1 carbohydrate
Fruit spreads, 100% fruit	1½ tbs	1 carbohydrate
Honey	1 tbs	1 carbohydrate
Jam or jelly, regular	1 tbs	1 carbohydrate
Sugar	1 tbs	1 carbohydrate
Syrup		
chocolate	2 tbs	2 carbohydrates
light (pancake type)	2 tbs	1 carbohydrate
regular (pancake type)	1 tbs	1 carbohydrate
Condiments and Sauces		
Barbeque sauce	3 tbs	1 carbohydrate
Cranberry sauce, jellied	¼ c	1½ carbohydrates
Gravy, canned or bottled	½ c	½ carbohydrate + ½ fat
Salad dressing, fat-free, low-fat, cream-based	3 tbs	1 carbohydrate
Sweet and sour sauce	3 tbs	1 carbohydrate
Doughnuts, Muffins, Pastries, and Sweet Breads		
Banana nut bread	1" slice (1 oz)	2 carbohydrates + 1 fat
Doughnut		
cake, plain	1 medium, (1½ oz)	1½ carbohydrates + 2 fats
yeast type, glazed	3¾" across (2 oz)	2 carbohydrates + 2 fats
Muffin (4 oz)	¼ muffin (1 oz)	1 carbohydrate + ½ fat
Sweet roll or Danish	1 (2½ oz)	2½ carbohydrates + 2 fats
Frozen Bars, Frozen Dessert, Frozen Yogurt, and Ice Cream		
Frozen pops	1	½ carbohydrate
Fruit juice bars, frozen, 100% juice	1 bar (3 oz)	1 carbohydrate
Ice cream		
fat-free	½ c	1½ carbohydrates
light	½ c	1 carbohydrate + 1 fat
no sugar added	½ c	1 carbohydrate + 1 fat
regular	½ c	1 carbohydrate + 2 fats
Sherbet, sorbet	½ c	2 carbohydrates
Yogurt, frozen		
fat-free	⅓ c	1 carbohydrate
regular	½ c	1 carbohydrate + 0–1 fat
Granola Bars, Meal Replacement Bars/Shakes, and Trail Mix		
Granola or snack bar, regular or low-fat	1 bar (1 oz)	1½ carbohydrates
Meal replacement bar	1 bar (1⅓ oz)	1½ carbohydrates + 0–1 fat
Meal replacement bar	1 bar (2 oz)	2 carbohydrates + 1 fat
Meal replacement shake, reduced-calorie	1 can (10–11 oz)	1½ carbohydrates + 0–1 fat
Trail mix		
candy/nut-based	1 oz	1 carbohydrates + 2 fats
dried-fruit-based	1 oz	1 carbohydrate + 1 fat

Nonstarchy Vegetable List

1 vegetable choice = 5 g carbohydrate, 2 g protein, 0 g fat, 25 cal

Icon Key

☺ = More than 3 g of dietary fiber per serving.

▮ = 480 mg or more of sodium per serving.

- Amaranth or Chinese spinach
- Artichoke
- Artichoke hearts
- Asparagus
- Baby corn
- Bamboo shoots
- Beans (green, wax, Italian)
- Bean sprouts
- Beets
- ▮ Borscht
- Broccoli
- ☺ Brussels sprouts
- Cabbage (green, bok choy, Chinese)
- ☺ Carrots
- Cauliflower
- Celery
- ☺ Chayote
- Coleslaw, packaged, no dressing
- Cucumber
- Eggplant
- Gourds (bitter, bottle, luffa, bitter melon)
- Green onions or scallions
- Greens (collard, kale, mustard, turnip)
- Hearts of palm
- Jicama
- Kohlrabi
- Leeks
- Mixed vegetables (without corn, peas, or pasta)
- Mung bean sprouts
- Mushrooms, all kinds, fresh
- Okra
- Onions
- Oriental radish or daikon
- Pea pods
- ☺ Peppers (all varieties)
- Radishes
- Rutabaga
- ▮ Sauerkraut
- Soybean sprouts
- Spinach
- Squash (summer, crookneck, zucchini)
- Sugar pea snaps
- ☺ Swiss chard
- Tomato
- Tomatoes, canned
- ▮ Tomato sauce
- ▮ Tomato/vegetable juice
- Turnips
- Water chestnuts
- Yard-long beans

Meat and Meat Substitutes List

Icon Key

! = Extra fat, or prepared with added fat. (Add an additional fat choice to this food.)

▮ = 480 mg or more of sodium per serving (based on the sodium content of a typical 3 oz serving of meat, unless 1 or 2 is the normal serving size).

Food	Amount
Lean Meats and Meat Substitutes	
(1 lean meat choice = 7 g protein, 0–3 g fat, 45 calories)	
Beef: Select or Choice grades trimmed of fat: ground round, roast (chuck, rib, rump), round, sirloin, steak (cubed, flank, porterhouse, T-bone), tenderloin	1 oz
▮ Beef jerky	1 oz
Cheeses with 3 g of fat or less per oz	1 oz
Cottage cheese	¼ cup
Egg substitutes, plain	¼ cup
Egg whites	2
Fish, fresh or frozen, plain: catfish, cod, flounder, haddock, halibut, orange roughy, salmon, tilapia, trout, tuna	1 oz
▮ *Fish, smoked:* herring or salmon (lox)	1 oz
Game: buffalo, ostrich, rabbit, venison	1 oz
▮ Hot dog with 3 g of fat or less per oz (8 dogs per 14 oz package) (*Note: May be high in carbohydrate.*)	1
Lamb: chop, leg, or roast	1 oz
Organ meats: heart, kidney, liver (*Note: May be high in cholesterol)*	1 oz
Oysters, fresh or frozen	6 medium

Pork, lean
- ▮ Canadian bacon ... 1 oz
- rib or loin chop/roast, ham, tenderloin ... 1 oz

Poultry without skin: Cornish hen, chicken, domestic duck or goose (well drained of fat), turkey ... 1 oz

Processed sandwich meats with 3 g of fat or less per oz: chipped beef, deli thin-sliced meats, turkey ham, turkey kielbasa, turkey pastrami ... 1 oz

Salmon, canned ... 1 oz

Sardines, canned ... 2 medium

▮ Sausage with 3 g or less fat per oz ... 1 oz

Shellfish: clams, crab, imitation shellfish, lobster, scallops, shrimp ... 1 oz

Tuna, canned in water or oil, drained ... 1 oz

Veal: Lean chop, roast ... 1 oz

Medium-Fat Meat and Meat Substitutes

(1 medium-fat meat choice = 7 g protein, 4–7 g fat, and 130 calories)

Beef: corned beef, ground beef, meatloaf, Prime grades trimmed of fat (prime rib), short ribs, tongue ... 1 oz

Cheeses with 4–7 g of fat per oz: feta, mozzarella, pasteurized processed cheese spread, reduced-fat cheeses, string ... 1 oz

Egg (*Note: High in cholesterol, limit to 3 per week.*) ... 1

Fish, any fried product ... 1 oz

Lamb: ground, rib roast ... 1 oz

Pork: cutlet, shoulder roast ... 1 oz

Poultry: chicken with skin; dove, pheasant, wild duck, or goose; fried chicken; ground turkey ... 1 oz

Ricotta cheese ... 2 oz or ¼ c

▮ Sausage with 4–7 g fat per oz ... 1 oz

Veal: Cutlet (no breading) ... 1 oz

High-Fat Meat and Meat Substitutes[a]

(1 high-fat meat choice = 7 g protein, 8+ g fat, 150 calories)

Bacon
- ▮ pork ... 2 slices (16 slices per lb or 1 oz each, before cooking)
- ▮ turkey ... 3 slices (½ oz each before cooking)

Cheese, regular: American, bleu, brie, cheddar, hard goat, Monterey Jack, queso, Swiss ... 1 oz

▮ ! *Hot dog:* beef, pork, or combination (10 per lb-sized package) ... 1

▮ *Hot dog:* turkey or chicken (10 per lb-sized package) ... 1

Pork: ground, sausage, spareribs ... 1 oz

Processed sandwich meats with 8 g of fat or more per oz: bologna, pastrami, hard salami ... 1 oz

▮ *Sausage with 8 g of fat or more per oz:* bratwurst, chorizo, Italian, knockwurst, Polish, smoked, summer ... 1 oz

[a]These foods are high in saturated fat, cholesterol, and calories, and may raise blood cholesterol levels if eaten on a regular basis. Try to eat 3 or fewer servings from this group per week.

Plant-Based Proteins

Because carbohydrate and fat content varies among plant-based proteins, you should read the food label.

Icon Key

☺ =More than 3 g of dietary fiber per serving; 7g protein; calories vary.

▮ = 480 mg or more of sodium per serving (based on the sodium content of a typical 3-oz serving of meat, unless 1 or 2 oz is the normal serving size).

	Food	Amount	Count As
	"Bacon" strips, soy-based	3 strips	1 medium-fat meat
☺	Baked beans	⅓ c	1 starch + 1 lean meat
☺	*Beans, cooked:* black, garbanzo, kidney, lima, navy, pinto, white	½ c	1 starch + 1 lean meat
☺	"Beef" or "sausage" crumbles, soy-based	2 oz	½ carbohydrate + 1 lean meat
	"Chicken" nuggets, soy-based	2 nuggets (1½ oz)	½ carbohydrate + 1 medium-fat meat
☺	Edamame	½ c	½ carbohydrate + 1 lean meat
	Falafel (spiced chickpea and wheat patties)	3 patties (about 2 inches across)	1 carbohydrate + 1 high-fat meat
	Hot dog, soy-based	1 (1½ oz)	½ carbohydrate + 1 lean meat
☺	Hummus	⅓ c	1 carbohydrate + 1 high-fat meat

☺ Lentils, brown, green, or yellow	½ c	1 carbohydrate + 1 lean meat
☺ Meatless burger, soy-based	3 oz	½ carbohydrate + 2 lean meats
☺ Meatless burger, vegetable- and starch-based	1 patty (about 2½ oz)	1 carbohydrate + 2 lean meats
Nut spreads: almond butter, cashew butter, peanut butter, soy nut butter	1 tbs	1 high-fat meat
☺ *Peas, cooked:* black-eyed and split peas	½ c	1 starch + 1 lean meat
▮☺ Refried beans, canned	½ c	1 starch + 1 lean meat
"Sausage" patties, soy-based	1 (1½ oz)	1 medium-fat meat
Soy nuts, unsalted	¾ oz	½ carbohydrate + 1 medium-fat meat
Tempeh	¼ cup	1 medium-fat meat
Tofu	4 oz (½ cup)	1 medium-fat meat
Tofu, light	4 oz (½ cup)	1 lean meat

Fat List

1 fat choice = 5 g fat, 45 cal

Icon Key

▮ = 480 mg or more of sodium per serving.

Food	Serving Size
Unsaturated Fats—Monounsaturated Fats	
Avocado, medium	2 tbs (1 oz)
Nut butters (trans fat-free): almond butter, cashew butter, peanut butter (smooth or crunchy)	1½ tsp
Nuts	
almonds	6 nuts
Brazil	2 nuts
cashews	6 nuts
filberts (hazelnuts)	5 nuts
macadamia	3 nuts
mixed (50% peanuts)	6 nuts
peanuts	10 nuts
pecans	4 halves
pistachios	16 nuts
Oil: canola, olive, peanut	1 tsp
Olives	
black (ripe)	8 large
green, stuffed	10 large
Polyunsaturated Fats	
Margarine: lower-fat spread (30% to 50% vegetable oil, *trans* fat-free)	1 tbs
Margarine: stick, tub (*trans* fat-free), or squeeze (*trans* fat-free)	1 tsp
Mayonnaise	
reduced-fat	1 tbs
regular	1 tsp
Mayonnaise-style salad dressing	
reduced-fat	1 tbs
regular	2 tsp
Nuts	
Pignolia (pine nuts)	1 tbs
walnuts, English	4 halves
Oil: corn, cottonseed, flaxseed, grape seed, safflower, soybean, sunflower	1 tsp
Oil: made from soybean and canola oil—Enova	1 tsp
Plant stanol esters	
light	1 tbs
regular	2 tsp
Salad dressing	
▮ reduced-fat (*Note: May be high in carbohydrate.*)	2 tbs
▮ regular	1 tbs
Seeds	1 tbs
flaxseed, whole	1 tbs
pumpkin, sunflower	1 tbs
sesame seeds	1 tbs
Tahini or sesame paste	2 tsp
Saturated Fats	
Bacon, cooked, regular or turkey	1 slice
Butter	
reduced-fat	1 tbs
stick	1 tsp
whipped	2 tsp
Butter blends made with oil	
reduced-fat or light	1 tbs
regular	1½ tsp
Chitterlings, boiled	2 tbs (½ oz)
Coconut, sweetened, shredded	2 tbs
Coconut milk	
light	⅓ c
regular	1½ tbs
Cream	
half and half	2 tbs
heavy	1 tbs

light . . . . 1½ tbs
whipped . . . . 2 tbs
whipped, pressurized . . . . ¼ c
Cream cheese
reduced-fat . . . . 1½ tbs (¾ oz)
regular . . . . 1 tbs (½ oz)
Lard. . . . . 1 tsp

Oil: coconut, palm, palm kernel . . . . . . 1 tsp
Salt pork . . . . ¼ oz
Shortening, solid . . . . 1 tsp
Sour cream
reduced-fat or light . . . . 3 tbs
regular . . . . 2 tbs

Free Foods List

A *free food* is any food or drink that has less than 20 calories and 5 g or less of carbohydrate per serving. Foods with a serving size listed should be limited to three servings per day. Foods listed without a serving size can be eaten as often as you like.

Icon Key

▮ = 480 mg or more of sodium per serving.

Food	Serving Size
Low Carbohydrate Foods	
Cabbage, raw	½ c
Candy, hard (regular or sugar-free)	1 piece
Carrots, cauliflower, or green beans, cooked	¼ c
Cranberries, sweetened with sugar substitute	½ c
Cucumber, sliced	½ c
Gelatin	
dessert, sugar-free	
unflavored	
Gum	
Jam or jelly, light or no sugar added	2 tsp
Rhubarb, sweetened with sugar substitute	½ c
Salad greens	
Sugar substitutes (artificial sweeteners)	
Syrup, sugar-free	2 tbs
Modified Fat Foods with Carbohydrate	
Cream cheese, fat-free	1 tbs (½ oz)
Creamers	
nondairy, liquid	1 tbs
nondairy, powdered	2 tsp
Margarine spread	
fat-free	1 tbs
reduced-fat	1 tsp
Mayonnaise	
fat-free	1 tbs
reduced-fat	1 tsp
Mayonnaise-style salad dressing	
fat-free	1 tbs
reduced-fat	1 tsp
Salad dressing	
fat-free or low-fat	1 tbs
fat-free, Italian	2 tbs
Sour cream, fat-free, reduced-fat	1 tbs
Whipped topping	
light or fat-free	2 tbs
regular	1 tbs
Condiments	
Barbecue sauce	2 tsp
Catsup (ketchup)	1 tbs
Honey mustard	1 tbs
Horseradish	
Lemon juice	
Miso	1½ tsp
Mustard	
Parmesan cheese, freshly grated	1 tbs
Pickle relish	1 tbs
Pickles	
▮ dill	1½ medium
sweet, bread and butter	2 slices
sweet, gherkin	¾ oz
Salsa	¼ c
▮ Soy sauce, regular or light	1 tbs
Sweet and sour sauce	2 tsp
Sweet chili sauce	2 tsp
Taco sauce	1 tbs
Vinegar	
Yogurt, any type	2 tbs

Drinks/Mixes

Any food on this list—without serving size listed—can be consumed in any moderate amount.

Icon Key

ı = 480 mg or more of sodium per serving.

- ı Bouillon, broth, consommé
- Bouillon or broth, low sodium
- Carbonated or mineral water
- Club soda
- Cocoa powder, unsweetened (1 tbs)
- Coffee, unsweetened or with sugar substitute
- Diet soft drinks, sugar-free
- Drink mixes, sugar-free
- Tea, unsweetened or with sugar substitute
- Tonic water, diet
- Water
- Water, flavored, carbohydrate free

Seasonings

Any food on this list can be consumed in any moderate amount.

- Flavoring extracts (for example, vanilla, almond, peppermint)
- Garlic
- Herbs, fresh or dried
- Nonstick cooking spray
- Pimento
- Spices
- Hot pepper sauce
- Wine, used in cooking
- Worcestershire sauce

Combination Foods List

Icon Key

☺ = More than 3 g of dietary fiber per serving.

ı = 600 mg or more of sodium per serving (for combination food main dishes/meals).

Food	Serving Size	Count As
Entrées		
ı Casserole type (tuna noodle, lasagna, spaghetti with meatballs, chili with beans, macaroni and cheese)	1 c (8 oz)	2 carbohydrates + 2 medium-fat meats
ı Stews (beef/other meats and vegetables)	1 c (8 oz)	1 carbohydrate + 1 medium-fat meat + 0–3 fats
Tuna salad or chicken salad	½ c (3½ oz)	½ carbohydrate + 2 lean meats + 1 fat
Frozen Meals/Entrées		
ı ☺ Burrito (beef and bean)	1 (5 oz)	3 carbohydrates + 1 lean meat + 2 fats
ı Dinner-type meal	generally 14–17 oz	3 carbohydrates + 3 medium-fat meats + 3 fats
ı Entrée or meal with less than 340 calories	about 8–11 oz	2–3 carbohydrates + 1–2 lean meats
Pizza		
ı cheese/vegetarian thin crust	¼ of 12" (4½ to 5 oz)	2 carbohydrates + 2 medium-fat meats
ı meat topping, thin crust	¼ of 12" (5 oz)	2 carbohydrates + 2 medium-fat meats, + 1½ fats
ı Pocket sandwich	1 (4½ oz)	3 carbohydrates + 1 lean meat + 1–2 fats
ı Pot pie	1 (7 oz)	2½ carbohydrates + 1 medium-fat meat + 3 fats
Salads (Deli-Style)		
Coleslaw	½ c	1 carbohydrate + 1½ fats
Macaroni/pasta salad	½ c	2 carbohydrates + 3 fats
ı Potato salad	½ c	1½ carbohydrates + 1–2 fats
Soups		
ı Bean, lentil, or split pea	1 cup	1 carbohydrate + 1 lean meat
ı Chowder (made with milk)	1 c (8 oz)	1 carbohydrate + 1 lean meat + 1½ fats
ı Cream (made with water)	1 c (8 oz)	1 carbohydrate + 1 fat

Food	Serving Size	Exchanges per Serving
▮ Instant	6 oz prepared	1 carbohydrate
▮ with beans or lentils	8 oz prepared	2½ carbohydrates + 1 lean meat
▮ Miso soup	1 c.	½ carbohydrate + 1 fat
▮ Oriental noodle	1 c.	2 carbohydrates + 2 fats
Rice (congee)	1 c.	1 carbohydrate
▮ Tomato (made with water)	1 c (8 oz)	1 carbohydrate
▮ Vegetable beef, chicken noodle, or other broth-type	1 c (8 oz)	1 carbohydrate

Fast Foods List[a]

Icon Key

☺ = More than 3 g of dietary fiber per serving.

! = Extra fat, or prepared with added fat.

▮ = 600 mg or more sodium per serving (for fast food main dishes/meals).

Food	Serving Size	Exchanges per Serving
Breakfast Sandwiches		
▮ Egg, cheese, meat, English muffin	1 sandwich	2 carbohydrates + 2 medium-fat meats
▮ Sausage biscuit sandwich	1 sandwich	2 carbohydrates + 2 high-fat meats + 3½ fats
Main Dishes/Entrees		
▮☺ Burrito (beef and beans)	1 (about 8 oz)	3 carbohydrates + 3 medium-fat meats + 3 fats
▮ Chicken breast, breaded and fried	1 (about 5 oz)	1 carbohydrate + 4 medium-fat meats
Chicken drumstick, breaded and fried	1 (about 2 oz)	2 medium-fat meats
▮ Chicken nuggets	6 (about 3½ oz)	1 carbohydrate + 2 medium-fat meats + 1 fat
▮ Chicken thigh, breaded and fried	1 (about 4 oz)	½ carbohydrate + 3 medium-fat meats + 1½ fats
▮ Chicken wings, hot	6 (5 oz)	5 medium-fat meats + 1½ fats
Oriental		
▮ Beef/chicken/shrimp with vegetables in sauce	1 c (about 5 oz)	1 carbohydrate + 1 lean meat + 1 fat
▮ Egg roll, meat	1 (about 3 oz)	1 carbohydrate + 1 lean meat + 1 fat
Fried rice, meatless	½ c.	1½ carbohydrates + 1½ fats
▮ Meat and sweet sauce (orange chicken)	1 c	3 carbohydrates + 3 medium-fat meats + 2 fats
▮☺ Noodles and vegetables in sauce (chow mein, lo mein)	1 c	2 carbohydrates + 1 fat
Pizza		
▮ Cheese, pepperoni, regular crust	⅛ of 14" (about 4 oz)	2½ carbohydrates + 1 medium-fat meat + 1½ fats
▮ Cheese/vegetarian, thin crust	¼ of 12" (about 6 oz)	2½ carbohydrates + 2 medium-fat meats + 1½ fats
Sandwiches		
▮ Chicken sandwich, grilled	1	3 carbohydrates + 4 lean meats
▮ Chicken sandwich, crispy	1	3½ carbohydrates + 3 medium-fat meats + 1 fat
Fish sandwich with tartar sauce	1	2½ carbohydrates + 2 medium-fat meats + 2 fats
Hamburger		
▮ large with cheese	1	2½ carbohydrates + 4 medium-fat meats + 1 fat
regular	1	2 carbohydrates + 1 medium-fat meat + 1 fat
▮ Hot dog with bun	1	1 carbohydrate + 1 high-fat meat + 1 fat
Submarine sandwich		
▮ less than 6 grams fat	6" sub	3 carbohydrates + 2 lean meats
▮ regular	6" sub	3½ carbohydrates + 2 medium-fat meats + 1 fat
Taco, hard or soft shell (meat and cheese)	1 small	1 carbohydrate + 1 medium-fat meat + 1½ fats

[a]The choices in the Fast Foods list are not specific fast food meals or items, but are estimates based on popular foods. You can get specific nutrition information for almost every fast food or restaurant chain. Ask the restaurant or check its website for nutrition information about your favorite fast foods.

Salads		
❙ ☺ Salad, main dish (grilled chicken type, no dressing or croutons)	Salad	1 carbohydrate + 4 lean meats
Salad, side, no dressing or cheese	Small (about 5 oz)	1 vegetable
Sides/Appetizers		
❙ French fries, restaurant style	Small	3 carbohydrates + 3 fats
Medium		4 carbohydrates + 4 fats
Large		5 carbohydrates + 6 fats
❙ Nachos with cheese	Small (about 4½ oz)	2½ carbohydrates + 4 fats
❙ Onion rings	1 serving (about 3 oz)	2½ carbohydrates + 3 fats
Desserts		
Milkshake, any flavor	12 oz	6 carbohydrates + 2 fats
Soft-serve ice cream cone	1 small	2½ carbohydrates + 1 fat

Alcohol List

In general, 1 alcohol choice (½ oz absolute alcohol) has about 100 calories.

Alcoholic Beverage	Serving Size	Count As
Beer		
light (4.2%)	12 fl. oz.	1 alcohol equivalent + ½ carbohydrate
regular (4.9%)	12 fl. oz.	1 alcohol equivalent + 1 carbohydrate
Distilled spirits: vodka, rum, gin, whiskey, 80 or 86 proof	1½ fl. oz.	1 alcohol equivalent
Liqueur, coffee (53 proof)	1 fl. oz	1 alcohol equivalent + 1 carbohydrate
Sake	1 fl. oz	½ alcohol equivalent
Wine		
dessert (sherry)	3½ fl. oz.	1 alcohol equivalent + 1 carbohydrate
dry, red or white (10%)	5 fl. oz	1 alcohol equivalent

Academic Journals

International Journal of Sport Nutrition and Exercise Metabolism
www.humankinetics.com/IJSNEM

Journal of Nutrition
www.nutrition.org

Nutrition Research
www.journals.elsevierhealth.com/periodicals/NTR

Nutrition
www.journals.elsevierhealth.com/periodicals/NUT

Nutrition Reviews
www.ingentaconnect.com/content/ilsi/nure

Obesity
www.nature.com/oby/index.html

International Journal of Obesity
www.nature.com/ijo

Journal of the American Medical Association
http://jama.ama-assn.org

New England Journal of Medicine
http://content.nejm.org

American Journal of Clinical Nutrition
www.ajcn.org

Journal of the Academy of Nutrition and Dietetics
www.adajournal.org

Aging

Administration on Aging
www.aoa.gov

American Association of Retired Persons (AARP)
www.aarp.org

Health and Age
Sponsored by the Novartis Foundation for Gerontology & The Web-Based Health Education Foundation
www.healthandage.com

National Council on Aging
www.ncoa.org

International Osteoporosis Foundation
www.iofbonehealth.org

National Institute on Aging
www.nia.nih.gov

Osteoporosis and Related Bone Diseases National Resource Center
www.osteo.org

American Geriatrics Society
www.americangeriatrics.org

National Osteoporosis Foundation
www.nof.org

Alcohol and Drug Abuse

National Institute on Drug Abuse
www.nida.nih.gov

National Institute on Alcohol Abuse and Alcoholism
www.niaaa.nih.gov

Alcoholics Anonymous
www.alcoholics-anonymous.org

Narcotics Anonymous
www.na.org

National Council on Alcoholism and Drug Dependence
www.ncadd.org

National Clearinghouse for Alcohol and Drug Information
http://ncadi.samhsa.gov

Canadian Government

Health Canada
www.hc-sc.gc.ca

Canadian Council of Food and Nutrition
www.nin.ca

Agricultural and Agri-Food Canada
www.arg.gc.ca

Canadian Food Inspection Agency
www.inspection.gc.ca/english/toce.shtml

Canadian Institute for Health Information
www.cihi.ca

Canadian Public Health Association
www.cpha.ca

Canadian Nutrition and Professional Organizations

Dietitians of Canada, Canadian Dietetic Association
www.dietitians.ca

Canadian Diabetes Association
www.diabetes.ca

National Eating Disorder Information Centre
www.nedic.ca

Canadian Paediatric Society
www.cps.ca

Disordered Eating/ Eating Disorders

American Psychiatric Association
www.psych.org

Harvard Eating Disorders Center
www.mclean.harvard.edu/patient/child/edc.php

National Institute of Mental Health
www.nimh.nih.gov

National Association of Anorexia Nervosa and Associated Disorders (ANAD)
www.anad.org

National Eating Disorders Association
www.nationaleatingdisorders.org

Eating Disorder Referral and Information Center
www.edreferral.com

Overeaters Anonymous
www.oa.org

Exercise, Physical Activity, and Sports

American College of Sports Medicine (ACSM)
www.acsm.org

American Physical Therapy Association (APTA)
www.apta.org

Gatorade Sports Science Institute (GSSI)
www.gssiweb.com

National Coalition for Promoting Physical Activity (NCPPA)
www.ncppa.org

Sports, Cardiovascular, and Wellness Nutrition (SCAN)
www.scandpg.org

President's Council on Physical Fitness and Sports
www.fitness.gov

American Council on Exercise
www.acefitness.org

IDEA Health & Fitness Association
www.ideafit.com

Food Safety

Food Marketing Institute
www.fmi.org

Agency for Toxic Substances and Disease Registry (ATSDR)
www.atsdr.cdc.gov

Food Allergy and Anaphylaxis Network
www.foodallergy.org

Foodsafety.gov
www.foodsafety.gov

The USDA Food Safety and Inspection Service
www.fsis.usda.gov

Consumer Reports
www.consumerreports.org

Center for Science in the Public Interest: Food Safety
www.cspinet.org/foodsafety/index.html

Center for Food Safety and Applied Nutrition
www.fda.gov/Food/FoodSafety

Food Safety Project
www.extension.iastate.edu/foodsafety

Organic Consumers Association
www.organicconsumers.org

Infancy and Childhood

Administration for Children and Families
www.acf.hhs.gov

The American Academy of Pediatrics
www.aap.org

Kidshealth: The Nemours Foundation
www.kidshealth.org

National Center for Education in Maternal and Child Health
www.ncemch.org

Birth Defects Research for Children, Inc.
www.birthdefects.org

USDA/ARS Children's Nutrition Research Center at Baylor College of Medicine
www.kidsnutrition.org

Centers for Disease Control—Healthy Youth
www.cdc.gov/healthyyouth

International Agencies

UNICEF
www.unicef.org

World Health Organization
www.who.int/en

The Stockholm Convention on Persistent Organic Pollutants
www.pops.int

Food and Agricultural Organization of the United Nations
www.fao.org

International Food Information Council
www.ific.org

Pregnancy and Lactation

San Diego County Breastfeeding Coalition
www.breastfeeding.org

National Alliance for Breastfeeding Advocacy
www.naba-breastfeeding.org

American College of Obstetricians and Gynecologists
www.acog.org

La Leche League
www.lalecheleague.org

National Organization on Fetal Alcohol Syndrome
www.nofas.org

March of Dimes Birth Defects Foundation
http://modimes.org

Professional Nutrition Organizations

Academy of Nutrition and Dietetics (AND)
www.eatright.org

American Dental Association
www.ada.org

American Heart Association
www.americanheart.org

The American Society for Nutrition (ASN)
www.nutrition.org

Dietitians in Integrative and Functional Medicine
www.complementarynutrition.org

The Institute for Functional Medicine
www.functionalmedicine.org

North American Association for the Study of Obesity (NAASO)
www.naaso.org

The Society for Nutrition Education
www.sne.org

American College of Nutrition
www.americancollegeofnutrition.org

American Obesity Association
www.obesity.org

American Council on Science and Health
www.acsh.org

American Diabetes Association
www.diabetes.org

Institute of Food Technologists
www.ift.org

ILSI Human Nutrition Institute
www.ilsi.org

Trade Organizations

American Meat Institute
www.meatami.com

National Dairy Council
www.nationaldairycouncil.org

United Fresh Fruit and Vegetable Association
www.uffva.org

U.S.A. Rice Federation
www.usarice.com

U.S. Government

The USDA National Organic Program
Agricultural Marketing Service

www.ams.usda.gov

U.S. Department of Health and Human Services
www.hhs.gov

Food and Drug Administration (FDA)
www.fda.gov

Environmental Protection Agency
www.epa.gov

Federal Trade Commission
www.ftc.gov

Office of Dietary Supplements
National Institutes of Health
http://dietary-supplements.info.nih.gov

Nutrient Data Laboratory
Beltsville Human Nutrition Research Center,
Agricultural Research Service
www.ars.usda.gov/nutrientdata

National Digestive Diseases Information Clearinghouse
http://digestive.niddk.nih.gov

The National Cancer Institute
www.cancer.gov

The National Eye Institute
www.nei.nih.gov

The National Heart, Lung, and Blood Institute
www.nhlbi.nih.gov/index.htm

National Institute of Diabetes and Digestive
and Kidney Diseases
www.niddk.nih.gov

National Center for Complementary
and Alternative Medicine
http://nccam.nih.gov

U.S. Department of Agriculture (USDA)
www.usda.gov

Centers for Disease Control and Prevention (CDC)
www.cdc.gov

National Institutes of Health (NIH)
www.nih.gov

Food and Nutrition Information Center
Agricultural Research Service, USDA
www.nal.usda.gov/fnic

National Institute of Allergy and Infectious Diseases
www.niaid.nih.gov

Weight and Health Management

North American Association for the Study
of Obesity (NAASO)
www.obesityresearch.org

The Vegetarian Resource Group
www.vrg.org

American Obesity Association
www.obesity.org

Anemia Lifeline
www.anemia.com

The Arc
www.thearc.org

Bottled Water Web
www.bottledwaterweb.com

Food and Nutrition
Institute of Medicine
www.iom.edu/Global/Topics/Food-Nutrition.aspx

The Calorie Control Council
www.caloriecontrol.org

TOPS (Take Off Pounds Sensibly)
www.tops.org

Shape Up America!
www.shapeup.org

World Hunger

Center on Hunger, Poverty, and Nutrition Policy
http://nutrition.tufts.edu

Freedom from Hunger
www.freefromhunger.org

Oxfam International
www.oxfam.org

WorldWatch Institute
www.worldwatch.org

The Hunger Project
www.thp.org

U.S. Agency for International Development
www.usaid.gov

Feeding America
www.feedingamerica.org

Food First
www.foodfirst.org

Glossary

1,25-dihydroxycholecalciferol The active form of vitamin D, also called calcitriol, that is formed in the kidney by adding a second hydroxyl group on the first carbon to 25-dihydroxycholecalciferol.

25-hydroxycholecalciferol The compound formed in the liver by adding a hydroxyl group to the 25th carbon of cholecalciferol.

5-methyltetrahydrofolate (5-methyl THF) The most active form of folate.

7-dehydrocholesterol (provitamin D_3) The compound in the skin that is converted to precalciferol by UV light from the sun; synthesized in the liver from cholesterol.

A

absorption The process of moving nutrients from the GI tract into the circulatory system.

absorptive state The period after you eat when the stomach and small intestines are full and anabolic reactions exceed catabolic reactions.

Acceptable Macronutrient Distribution Ranges (AMDRs) A healthy range of intakes for the energy-containing nutrients—carbohydrates, proteins, and fats—expressed as a percentage of total daily energy. The AMDRs for adults are 45 to 65 percent carbohydrates, 10 to 35 percent protein, and 20 to 35 percent fat.

acceptable tolerance levels The maximum amount of pesticide residue that is allowed in or on foods.

accessory organs Organs that participate in digestion but are not considered part of the GI tract. They include the liver, pancreas, and gallbladder.

acetaldehyde One of the first compounds produced in the metabolism of ethanol. Eventually, acetaldehyde is converted to carbon dioxide and water and excreted.

acetaldehyde dehydrogenase (ALDH). The enzyme that converts acetaldehyde to acetate; this is the second step in oxidizing ethanol in the liver.

acetyl CoA A two-carbon compound formed when pantothenic acid combines with acetate.

acid-base balance The mechanisms used to maintain body fluids close to a neutral pH so the body can function properly.

acidosis A condition in which the blood is more acidic than normal, generally due to excessive hydrogen ions.

acromegaly A condition in which tissues, bones, and internal organs grow abnormally large; can be caused by abuse of growth hormone supplements, or by a hormonal disorder in which the pituitary gland produces too much growth hormone.

active transport The process of absorbing nutrients with the help of a carrier molecule and energy expenditure.

acute Describes a sudden onset of symptoms or disease.

acute dehydration Dehydration that sets in after a short period of time.

added sugars Sugars that are added to processed foods and sweets.

adenosine diphosphate (ADP) A nucleotide composed of adenine, ribose, and two phosphate molecules; it is formed when one phosphate molecule is removed from ATP.

adenosine triphosphate (ATP) A high-energy molecule composed of adenine, ribose, and three phosphate molecules; cells use this to fuel all biological processes.

Adequate Intake (AI) The *approximate* daily amount of a nutrient that is sufficient to meet the needs of similar individuals within a population group. The Food and Nutrition Board uses AIs for nutrients that do not have enough scientific evidence to calculate an RDA.

adipocytes Cells in adipose tissue that store fat; also known as fat cells.

adiponectin A hormone produced in the adipocytes that controls the body's response to insulin and may be involved in reducing the risk of obesity and type 2 diabetes.

adipose tissue Connective tissue that is the main storage site for fat in the body.

adolescence The developmental period between childhood and early adulthood (approximately ages 9 through 19).

age-related macular degeneration (AMD) A disease that affects the macula of the retina, causing blurry vision and potentially blindness.

aging Changes that accumulate over time; in living organisms, many of these changes render the organism more likely to die.

air displacement plethysmography A procedure used to estimate body volume based on the amount of air displaced.

albumin A protein produced in the liver and found in the blood that helps maintain fluid balance.

alcohol A chemical class of organic substances that contain one or more hydroxyl groups attached to carbons. Examples include ethanol, glycerol, and methanol. Ethanol is often referred to as "alcohol."

alcohol abuse Continuing to consume alcohol even though the behavior has created social, legal, and/or health problems.

alcohol dehydrogenase (ADH) One of the alcohol-metabolizing enzymes, found in the stomach and the liver, that converts ethanol to acetaldehyde.

alcohol liver disease A degenerative liver condition that occurs in three stages: (1) fatty liver, (2) alcoholic hepatitis, and (3) cirrhosis.

alcohol poisoning When the BAC rises to the point that a person's central nervous system is affected and his or her breathing and heart rate are interrupted.

alcohol tolerance When the body adjusts to long-term alcohol use by becoming less sensitive to the alcohol. More alcohol needs to be consumed in order to get the same euphoric effect.

alcoholic hepatitis Stage 2 of alcohol liver disease, in which the liver becomes inflamed.

alcoholism A chronic disease characterized by craving for and elevated tolerance to alcohol, inability to control alcohol intake, and dependency on alcohol to prevent withdrawal symptoms; also referred to as *alcohol dependence*.

aldosterone A hormone secreted from the adrenal glands in response to reduced blood volume; aldosterone signals the kidneys to reabsorb sodium, which increases blood volume and blood pressure.

alkalosis A condition in which the blood has a lower hydrogen ion concentration and a higher pH than is generally considered normal.

allergen A substance, such as wheat, that causes an allergic reaction.

alpha-ketoglutarate A compound that participates in the formation of nonessential amino acids during transamination.

alpha-linolenic acid A polyunsaturated essential fatty acid; part of the omega-3 fatty acid family.

alpha-tocopherol (a-tocopherol) The most active form of vitamin E in the body.

Alzheimer's disease A type of dementia.

amenorrhea Absence of menstruation.

amine group The nitrogen-containing part (NH_2) connected to the carbon of an amino acid.

amino acid pools Limited supplies of amino acids that accumulate in the blood and cells; amino acids are pulled from the pools and used to build new proteins.

amino acid score The composition of essential amino acids in a protein compared with a standard, usually egg protein.

amino acids The building blocks of protein. There are 20 different amino acids composed of carbon, hydrogen, oxygen, and nitrogen.

amylopectin A branched chain of polysaccharides found in starch.

amylose A straight chain of polysaccharides found in starch.

anabolic reactions Metabolic reactions that combine smaller compounds into larger molecules.

anaphylactic reactions Severe, life-threatening physiological reactions that cause constriction of the airways in the lungs, which inhibits the ability to breathe.

anencephaly A neural tube defect that results in the absence of major parts of the brain and spinal cord.

angiotensin I and II The active protein in the blood that causes *vasoconstriction* in the blood vessels and triggers the release of aldosterone from the adrenal glands, which raises blood pressure.

angiotensinogen A precursor protein produced in the liver and found in the blood; it is converted to the active form called angiotensin.

anions Negatively charged ions.

anorexia nervosa An eating disorder in which people intentionally starve themselves, causing extreme weight loss.

antibiotic-resistant bacteria Bacteria that have developed a resistance to an antibiotic such that they are no longer affected by antibiotic medication.

antibiotics Drugs that kill or slow the growth of bacteria.

antibodies Proteins that bind to and neutralize pathogens as part of the body's immune response.

antidiuretic hormone (ADH) A hormone secreted by the pituitary gland when blood volumes are low; ADH reduces the amount of water excreted through the kidneys, constricts the blood vessels, and raises blood pressure; also known as *vasopressin*.

antimicrobials Substances or a combination of substances, such as disinfectants and sanitizers, that control the spread of bacteria and viruses on nonliving surfaces or objects.

antioxidants Substances that neutralize harmful oxygen-containing free radicals that can cause cell damage. Vitamins A, C, and E and beta-carotene are antioxidants.

anus The opening of the rectum, or end of the GI tract.

appetite The desire to eat food whether or not there is hunger; a taste for particular foods and cravings in reaction to cues such as the sight, smell, or thought of food.

arachidonic acid An omega-6 fatty acid formed from linoleic acid; it is used to synthesize the eicosanoids, including leukotrienes, prostaglandins, and thromboxanes.

ariboflavinosis A deficiency of riboflavin characterized by cheilosis, stomatitis, and glossitis.

arthritis Inflammation in the joints that can cause pain, stiffness, and swelling in joints, muscles, tendons, ligaments, and bones.

ascorbic acid The active form of vitamin C.

atherosclerosis Narrowing of the coronary arteries due to buildup of debris along the artery walls.

atrophic gastritis Chronic inflammation of the stomach.

atrophy To shrink in size.

attention deficit/hyperactivity disorder (ADHD) (previously known as attention deficit disorder, or ADD) A condition in which an individual may be easily distracted, have difficulty listening and following directions, difficulty focusing and sustaining attention, difficulty concentrating and staying on task, and/or inconsistent performance in school.

avidin A protein in raw egg whites that binds biotin.

B

balance The diet principle of providing the correct proportion of nutrients to maintain health and prevent disease.

bariatric surgery A surgical procedure that promotes weight loss by limiting the amount of food that can be eaten or absorbed.

basal metabolic rate (BMR) The measure of basal metabolism taken when the body is at rest in a warm, quiet environment, after a 12-hour fast; expressed as kilocalories per kilogram of body weight per hour.

basal metabolism The amount of energy expended by the body to meet its basic physiological needs, including heart rate, muscle tone, and brain function.

behavior modification Changing behaviors to improve health outcomes. In the case of weight management, it involves identifying and altering eating patterns that contribute to weight gain or impede weight loss.

beriberi The thiamin deficiency that results in weakness; the name translates to "I can not."

beta-carotene One of the provitamin A carotenoids.

beta-oxidation A series of metabolic reactions in which fatty acids are oxidized to acetyl CoA; also called *fatty acid oxidation*.

bicarbonate A negatively charged alkali ion produced from bicarbonate salts; during digestion, bicarbonate ions are released from the pancreas to neutralize HCl in the duodenum.

bile A secretion produced in the liver and stored in the gallbladder. It is released through the common bile duct into the duodenum to digest dietary fat.

binders Compounds such as oxalates and phytates that bind to minerals in foods and reduce their bioavailability.

binge drinking The consumption of five or more alcoholic drinks by men, or four or more drinks by women, in about two hours.

bioaccumulate A substance or chemical builds up in an organism over time, so that the concentration of the chemical is higher than would be found naturally in the environment.

bioavailability The degree to which a nutrient is absorbed from foods and used in the body.

biodiversity The variability among living organisms on the Earth, including the variability within and between species and within and between ecosystems.

bioelectrical impedance analysis (BIA) A method used to assess the percentage of body fat by using a low-level electrical current; body fat resists or impedes the current, whereas water and muscle mass conduct electricity.

biological value The percentage of absorbed amino acids that are efficiently used to synthesize proteins.

biotechnology The application of biological techniques to living cells, which alters their genetic makeup.

biotinidase An enzyme in the small intestine that releases biotin from food to allow it to be absorbed.

blackouts Periods of time when an intoxicated person cannot recall part or all of an event.

bleaching When light enters the eye and interacts with rhodopsin, splitting it into *trans*-retinal and opsin.

blood alcohol concentration (BAC) The amount of alcohol in the blood. BAC is measured in grams of alcohol per deciliter of blood, usually expressed as a percentage.

blood lipid profile A measurement of blood lipids used to assess cardiovascular risk.

body composition The ratio of fat to lean tissue (muscle, bone, and organs) in the body; usually expressed as percent body fat.

body dysmorphic disorder (BDD) A mental illness in which a person is excessively concerned about and preoccupied by a perceived defect in his or her body.

body mass index (BMI) A calculation of body weight in relationship to height; used to determine whether an individual is underweight, at a healthy weight, or overweight or obese. A BMI between 18.5 and 24.9 is considered healthy.

bolus A soft mass of chewed food.

bomb calorimeter An instrument used to measure the amount of heat released from food during combustion; the amount of heat produced is directly related to the amount of kilocalories in a given food.

bone mineral density (BMD) The amount of minerals, in particular calcium, per volume in an individual's bone.

borborygmus Grumbling of the stomach caused by air pockets formed as food is pushed through the GI tract.

botanicals A part of a plant, such as its root, that is believed to have medicinal or therapeutic attributes.

botulism A rare but serious paralytic illness caused by the bacterium *Clostridium botulinum*.

bovine growth hormone (BGH) A hormone that is essential for normal growth and development in cattle.

bran The indigestible outer shell of the grain kernel.

breast-feeding The act of feeding an infant milk from a woman's breast.

brown adipose tissue (BAT) A type of adipose tissue, found primarily in infants, that produces body heat; it gets its name from the large number of mitochondria and capillaries responsible for the brown color.

buffers Substances that help maintain the proper pH in a solution by attracting or donating hydrogen ions.

bulimia nervosa An eating disorder characterized by consuming large quantities of food and then purging through vomiting, laxative and diuretic use, and/or excessive physical exercise.

C

calciferol The family of vitamin D compounds.

calcitonin A hormone secreted by the thyroid gland that lowers blood calcium levels.

calcitriol The active form of vitamin D, also referred to as 1,25-dihydroxycholecalciferol.

calcium (Ca^{+2}) One of the most abundant divalent cations found in nature and in the body.

cancer A general term for a large group of diseases characterized by uncontrolled growth and spread of abnormal cells.

cancer initiator A carcinogen that initiates the mutation in DNA; these mutations cause the cell to respond abnormally to physiological controls.

cancer progressor A compound that stimulates cancer cell proliferation and causes cancer cells to invade healthy tissue and spread to other sites; hormones are an example of a substance that stimulates cancer progression.

cancer promoter A substance that induces a cell to divide and grow rapidly, and reduces the time that enzymes have to repair any damage or mutation; examples of cancer promoters are dietary fats, alcohol, and estrogen.

canning The process of heating food to a temperature high enough to kill bacteria and then packing the food in airtight containers.

carbohydrate loading A diet and training strategy that maximizes glycogen stores in the body before an endurance event.

carboxyl or acid group The organic group attached to an amino acid that is composed of one carbon, one hydrogen, and two oxygen atoms (COOH).

carboxylation The chemical reaction in which a carboxyl group is added to a molecule.

carcinogen Cancer-causing substance, including tobacco smoke, air and water pollution, ultraviolet radiation, and various chemicals.

carcinogenesis The process of cancer development.

carcinogenic Causing cancer.

cardiac arrhythmia A disturbance in the beating and rhythm of the heart; can be caused by excessive alcohol consumption.

cardiac myopathy Condition in which the heart becomes thin and weak and is unable to pump blood throughout the body; also called disease of the heart muscle.

cardiorespiratory conditioning Improvements in the delivery of oxygen to working muscles as a result of aerobic activity.

cardiorespiratory endurance The body's ability to sustain prolonged exercise.

carnitine A vitamin-like substance used to transport fatty acids across the mitochondrial membrane to properly utilize fat.

carotenodermia The presence of excess carotene in the blood resulting in an orange color to the skin due to excessive intake of carrots or other carotene-rich vegetables.

carotenoids A group of yellow, red, and orange pigments found in plants; three of them are precursors to vitamin A including beta carotene. The body stores carotenoids in the liver and in fat cells.

catabolic reactions Metabolic reactions that break large compounds into smaller molecules.

catalysts Substances that aid and speed up reactions without being changed, damaged, or used up in the process.

cataract A common eye disorder that occurs when the lens of the eye becomes cloudy.

cataracts Clumps of protein that form on the lens of the eye, clouding vision.

cations Positively charged ions.

celiac disease Genetic disease that causes damage to the small intestine when gluten-containing foods are eaten.

cell differentiation The process of a less specialized immature cell becoming a specialized mature cell.

cell division The process of dividing one cell into two separate cells with the same genetic material.

cellulite A nonmedical term that refers to fat cells under the skin that give it a ripplelike appearance. Contrary to popular belief, cellulite is no different from other fat in the body.

cellulose A nondigestible polysaccharide found in plant cell walls.

central obesity An excess storage of visceral fat in the abdominal area, indicated by a waist circumference greater than 40 inches in males and 35 inches in females; central obesity increases the risk of heart disease, diabetes, and hypertension. Also referred to as *android obesity*.

ceruloplasmin A protein found in the blood that transports copper.

cheilosis A non-inflammatory condition of the lips characterized by chapping and fissuring.

chemical digestion Breaking down food through enzymatic reactions.

chief cells Specialized cells in the stomach that secrete an inactive protein-digesting enzyme called pepsinogen.

childhood obesity The condition of a child's having too much body weight for his or her height. Rates of childhood obesity in the United States are increasing.

chloride (Cl^2) Major anion in the extracellular fluid.

chlorophyll The green pigment in plants that absorbs energy from sunlight to begin the process of photosynthesis.

cholecalciferol (vitamin D_3) The form of vitamin D found in animal foods and formed from precalciferol in the skin. This is the form absorbed through the skin into the blood.

cholecystokinin (CCK) A hormone released by the duodenum that stimulates the gallbladder to release bile.

cholesterol A common sterol found in animal products and made in the liver from saturated fatty acids; cholesterol is found in cell membranes and is used to make a variety of hormones.

choline A vitamin-like substance that is a precursor for the neurotransmitter acetylcholine, which is essential for healthy nerves. A component of the phospholipid lecithin.

chronic Describes a symptom or condition that lasts over a long period of time.

chronic dehydration Dehydration over a long period of time.

chronologic age A person's age in number of years of life.

chylomicron A type of lipoprotein that carries digested fat and other lipids through the lymph system into the blood.

chyme The semi-liquid, partially digested food mass that leaves the stomach and enters the small intestine.

ciguatera poisoning A condition caused by marine toxins produced by dinoflagellates (microscopic sea organisms). Small fish eat dinoflagellates and larger fish consume the small fish. The toxins then bioaccumulate in the fish.

cirrhosis Stage 3 of alcohol liver disease, in which liver cells die and are replaced by scar tissue.

cis The configuration of a fatty acid in which the carbon chains on each side of the double bond are on the same side.

closed or "coded" dating Refers to the packing numbers that are decodable only by manufacturers and are often found on nonperishable, shelf-stable foods.

clotting factors Substances involved in the process of blood clotting, such as prothrombin and fibrinogen.

coagulation The process of blood clotting.

cobalamin The vitamin involved in energy metabolism and the conversion of homocysteine to methionine; another name for vitamin B_{12}.

coenzymes Substances, often vitamins, that bind to an enzyme to facilitate enzyme activity; the coenzyme is not permanently altered by the chemical reaction.

cofactors Similar to a coenzyme, a substance that binds to an enzyme to help catalyze a reaction. The term cofactor generally refers to a metal ion, while a coenzyme is usually an organic molecule such as a vitamin.

collagen A protein found in connective tissue, including bones, teeth, skin, cartilage, and tendons.

colostrum The fluid that is expressed from the mother's breast after birth and before the development of breast milk.

community-supported agriculture (CSA) An arrangement where individuals pay a fee to support a local farm, and in exchange receive a weekly or biweekly box of fresh produce from the farm.

complete protein A protein that provides all the essential amino acids, along with some nonessential amino acids. Soy protein and protein from animal sources are complete proteins.

complex carbohydrates A category of carbohydrates that contain many sugar units combined. A polysaccharide is a complex carbohydrate.

conception The moment when a sperm fertilizes an egg.

condensation A chemical reaction in which two molecules combine to form a larger molecule, and water is released.

conditionally essential [amino acids] Those nonessential amino acids, such as tyrosine and glycine, that become essential (and must be consumed in the diet) when the body cannot make them.

conditioning The process of improving physical fitness through repeated activity.

cones Light-absorbing cells responsible for color vision.

congeners Fermentation by-products or additives in alcohol that may contribute to hangover symptoms.

congregate meals Low- or no-cost meals served at churches, synagogues, or other community sites where older adults can receive a nutritious meal and socialize.

consensus Agreed-upon conclusion of a group of experts based on a collection of information.

constipation The infrequent passage of dry, hardened stools.

control group In experimental research, the group that does not receive the treatment but may be given a placebo instead; used as a standard for comparison.

Cori cycle A series of metabolic reactions in liver cells that convert lactate to glucose; also called *gluconeogenesis*.

cortical bone The hard outer layer of bone.

cortisol A hormone produced by the adrenal cortex that stimulates gluconeogenesis and lipolysis.

C-reactive protein (CRP) A protein found in the blood that is released from the cells during inflammation; used as a marker for the presence of atherosclerosis.

creatine phosphate (PCr) A compound that provides a reserve of phosphate to regenerate ADP to ATP.

cretinism A condition caused by a deficiency of thyroid hormone during prenatal development, resulting in abnormal mental and physical development in children.

critical periods Developmental stages during which cells and tissue rapidly grow and differentiate to form body structures.

Crohn's disease A form of ulcerative colitis in which ulcers form throughout the GI tract and not just in the colon.

cross-contaminate The transfer of pathogens from a food, utensil, cutting board, kitchen surface, and/or hands to another food or object.

crypts Glands at the base of the villi; they contain stem cells that manufacture young cells to replace the cells of the villi when they die.

cupric The oxidized form of copper (Cu^{2+}).

cuprous The reduced form of copper (Cu^{+}).

cytochromes Protein complexes that move electrons down the electron transport chain; they contain the minerals iron and copper.

cytokines Substances that damage liver cells and lead to scarring.

cytosol The fluid portion of the cell where anaerobic metabolism takes place.

D

Daily Values (DVs) Reference values developed by the Food and Drug Administration and used on nutrition labels to describe the amount of a nutrient provided in one serving of the food.

danger zone The range of temperatures between 40°F and 140°F at which foodborne bacteria will multiply most rapidly. Room temperature falls within the danger zone.

deamination The removal of the amine group from an amino acid when amino acids are used for energy, fat synthesis, or gluconeogenesis.

dehydration Loss of water in the body as a result of inadequate fluid intake or excess fluid loss, such as through sweating; also called *hypohydration*.

dehydration The excessive loss of body fluids; usually caused by lack of fluid intake, diarrhea, vomiting, or excessive sweating.

DeLaney Clause Clause in the Food Additives Amendment mandating that additives shown to cause cancer at any level must be removed from the marketplace.

dementia A disorder of the brain that interferes with a person's memory, learning, and mental stability.

denature Altering a protein's shape, generally the secondary, tertiary, or quaternary structure, which changes its function; the chains of amino acids remain linked together by peptide bonds.

dental caries Tooth decay.

deoxyadenosylcobalamin The coenzyme form of vitamin B_{12} that converts intermediate substances in the TCA cycle.

developed country A country that is advanced in multiple areas, such as income per capita, life expectancy, rate of literacy, industrial capability, technological sophistication, and economic productivity.

developing country A country that is growing in multiple areas, such as income per capita, life expectancy, rate of literacy, industrial capability, technological sophistication, and economic productivity.

diabetes mellitus A medical condition whereby an individual either doesn't have enough insulin or is resistant to the insulin available, resulting in a rise in blood glucose levels. Diabetes mellitus is often called diabetes.

diarrhea The abnormally frequent passage of watery stools.

diastolic pressure The pressure within the arteries between heart beats.

dietary folate equivalents (DFE) A measurement used to express the amount of folate in a food or supplement.

Dietary Guidelines for Americans Guidelines published every five years by the Department of Health and Human Services and the United States Department of Agriculture that provide dietary and lifestyle advice to healthy individuals aged 2 and older to maintain good health and prevent chronic diseases. They are the basis for the federal food and nutrition education programs.

Dietary Reference Intakes (DRIs) Reference values for nutrients developed by the Food and Nutrition Board of the Institute of Medicine, used to plan and evaluate the diets of healthy people in the United States and Canada. It includes the Estimated Average Requirement (EAR), the Recommended Dietary Allowance (RDA), the Adequate Intake (AI), and the Tolerable Upper Intake Level (UL).

digestion A process that breaks down food into individual molecules small enough to be absorbed through the intestinal wall.

diglyceride A remnant of fat digestion that consists of a glycerol with two attached fatty acids; also the form of fat used as an emulsifier in food production.

dipeptide A protein chain made up of two amino acids joined together by a peptide bond.

direct calorimetry A direct measurement of the energy expended by the body obtained by assessing heat loss.

disaccharide Simple sugar that consists of two sugar units combined. There are three disaccharides: sucrose, lactose, and maltose.

disordered eating Abnormal and potentially harmful eating behaviors that do not meet specific criteria for anorexia nervosa and bulimia nervosa or binge eating disorder.

distillation The evaporation and then collection of a liquid by condensation. Liquors are made using distillation.

diuretics Substances that increase the production and secretion of urine; they are often used as antihypertensive drugs.

diverticula Small bulges at weak spots in the colon wall.

diverticulitis Infection of the diverticula.

diverticulosis The existence of diverticula in the lining of the large intestine or colon.

DNA fingerprinting A technique in which bacterial DNA "gene patterns" (or "fingerprints") are detected and analyzed to distinguish between different strains of a bacterium.

double-blind placebo-controlled study An experimental study in which neither the researchers nor the subjects in the study are aware of who is receiving the treatment or the placebo.

dual-energy X-ray absorptiometry (DEXA) A method that uses two low-energy X-rays to measure body density and bone mass.

duration The length of time that an activity is performed.

E

eating disorders Psychological illnesses that involve specific abnormal eating behaviors: anorexia nervosa (self-starvation) and bulimia nervosa (bingeing and purging).

eclampsia Seizures or coma in a woman with preeclampsia.

edema The accumulation of excess water in the spaces surrounding the cells, which causes swelling of the body tissue.

eicosanoids Hormonelike substances in the body. Prostaglandins, thromboxanes, and leukotrienes are all eicosanoids.

eicosapentaenoic acid (EPA) and **docosahexaenoic acid (DHA)** EPA (C20:5n–3) and DHA (C22:6n–3) are omega-3 fatty acids that are synthesized in the body and found in cold-water fish. These compounds may be beneficial in reducing heart disease.

electrolytes Ions such as sodium, potassium, chloride, and calcium in the blood and within the cells that are able to conduct electrical current when they are dissolved in body water.

electron transport chain The final stage of energy metabolism when electrons are transferred from one complex to another, resulting in the formation of ATP and water.

elimination Excretion of undigested and unabsorbed food through the feces.

elongation The phase of protein synthesis in which the polypeptide chain grows longer by adding amino acids.

embryo A fertilized egg during the third through the eighth week of pregnancy.

emergency kitchen A kitchen or a commercial food service that prepares for natural disasters, emergencies, or terrorist attacks.

empty calories Kilocalories that provide little nutrition, such as those found in candy.

emulsifier A compound that keeps two incompatible substances, such as oil and water, mixed together.

emulsify To break large fat globules into smaller droplets.

endocytosis A type of active transport in which the cell membrane forms an indentation, engulfing the substance to be absorbed.

endosperm The starchy inner portion of a cereal grain.

endotoxins Damaging products produced by intestinal bacteria that travel in the blood to the liver and initiate the release of cytokines.

energy The capacity to do work.

energy balance The state at which energy (kilocalorie) intake from food and beverages is equal to energy (kilocalorie) output from BMR and physical activity.

energy density A measurement of the kilocalories in a food compared with the weight (grams) of the food.

energy gap The difference between the numbers of kilocalories needed to maintain weight before and after weight loss.

energy-yielding nutrients The three nutrients that provide energy to the body to fuel physiological functions: carbohydrates, lipids, and protein.

enriched grains Refined grain foods that have folic acid, thiamin, niacin, riboflavin, and iron added.

enterocytes Absorptive epithelial cells that line the walls of the small intestine.

enterogastrones A group of GI tract hormones, produced in the stomach and small intestine, that controls gastric motility and secretions.

enterohepatic circulation The process of recycling bile from the large intestine back to the liver to be reused during fat digestion.

enzymes Substances, mostly proteins, that increase the rate of chemical changes or catalyze chemical reactions; also called biological catalysts.

epidemiological research Research that studies the variables that influence health in a population; it is often observational.

epiglottis Cartilage at the back of the tongue that closes off the trachea during swallowing.

epinephrine A hormone produced by the adrenal glands that signals the liver cells to release glucose; also referred to as the "fight-or-flight" hormone.

epiphyseal plate The growth plate of the bone. In puberty, growth in this area leads to increases in height.

epithelial cells Cells that line the cavities in the body and cover flat surfaces such as the skin.

ergocalciferol (vitamin D_2) The form of vitamin D found in plants and dietary supplements.

ergogenic aid A substance, such as a dietary supplement, used to enhance athletic performance.

esophagus Tube that connects the mouth to the stomach.

essential [amino acids] The nine amino acids that the body cannot synthesize; they must be obtained through dietary sources.

essential [nutrients] Nutrients that must be consumed from foods because they cannot be made in the body in sufficient quantities to meet its needs and support health.

essential fat A component of body fat that is necessary for health and normal body functions; the fat stored in bone marrow, heart, lungs, liver, spleen, kidneys, intestines, muscles, and lipid-rich tissues of the central nervous system is essential fat.

essential fatty acids The two polyunsaturated fatty acids that the body cannot make and therefore must be eaten in foods: linoleic acid and alpha-linolenic acid.

Estimated Average Requirement (EAR) The average daily amount of a nutrient needed by 50 percent of the individuals in a similar age and gender group.

estimated energy requirement (EER) The average kilocalorie intake that is estimated to maintain energy balance based on a person's gender, age, height, body weight, and level of physical activity.

estrogen The hormone responsible for female sex characteristics.

ethanol The type of alcohol, specifically *ethyl alcohol* (C_2H_5OH), found in alcoholic beverages such as wine, beer, and liquor.

exchange lists A diet planning tool that groups foods together based on their carbohydrate, protein, and fat content. One food on the list can be exchanged for another food on the same list.

exercise Any type of structured or planned physical activity.

experimental group In experimental research, the group of participants given a specific treatment, such as a drug, as part of the study.

experimental research Research involving at least two groups of subjects receiving different treatments.

extracellular fluid (ECF) The water found outside the cell, including the intravascular fluid and the interstitial fluid.

F

facilitated diffusion The process of absorbing nutrients with the help of a carrier molecule.

famine A severe shortage of food caused by weather-related crop destruction, poor agricultural practices, pestilence, war, or other factors.

farm-to-table continuum Illustrates the roles that farmers, food manufacturers, food transporters, retailers, and consumers play in ensuring that the food supply, from the farm to the plate, remains safe.

fat substitutes Substances that replace added fat in foods; they provide the creamy properties of fat for fewer kilocalories and total fat grams.

fat-soluble vitamins Vitamins that dissolve in fat and can be stored in the body.

fatty acid The most basic unit of triglycerides and phospholipids; fatty acids consist of even numbers of carbon chains ranging from two to 80 carbons in length.

fatty liver Stage 1 of alcohol liver disease, in which fat begins to build up in the liver cells.

fecal-to-oral transmission The spread of pathogens by putting something in the mouth, such as hands or food, that has been in contact with infected stool. Poor hygiene, such as not washing hands after using the bathroom, can be a cause of this contamination.

ferment To metabolize sugar into carbon dioxide and other gases.

fermentation The process by which yeast converts sugars in grains or fruits into ethanol and carbon dioxide.

ferric iron The oxidized form of iron (Fe^{+3}).

ferritin A protein that stores iron.

ferroportin A protein found on the basolateral surface of the enterocyte that transports iron out of the enterocyte into the portal vein.

ferrous iron The reduced form of iron (Fe^{+2}).

fetal alcohol spectrum disorders (FASDs) A range of conditions that can occur in children who are exposed to alcohol in utero.

fetal alcohol syndrome (FAS) The most severe of the fetal alcohol spectrum disorders (FASDs); children with FAS will display physical, mental, and behavioral abnormalities.

fetus A developing embryo that is at least eight weeks old.

fiber A nondigestible carbohydrate that provides structural support to the cell walls in plants.

flatulence Production of excessive gas in the stomach or the intestines.

flavin adenine dinucleotide (FAD) A coenzyme form of riboflavin that functions as an electron carrier in energy metabolism.

flavin mononucleotide (FMN) A coenzyme form of riboflavin, which functions in the electron transport chain.

flavonoids Food pigments also called phytochemicals, that act as antioxidants and neutralize free radicals and may help reduce the risk of chronic diseases; flavonoids are found in many fruits, vegetables, nuts, seeds, tea, and wine.

flavoproteins Protein complexes that move electrons down the electron transport chain; they contain the B vitamin riboflavin.

flexibility Ability to move joints freely through a full and normal range of motion.

fluid balance The difference between the amount of water taken into the body and the amount of water excreted.

fluoroapatite The crystalline structure that results when hydroxyapatite has been changed by exposure of the tooth to fluoride.

fluorosis A condition caused by excess amounts of fluoride, resulting in mottling of the teeth.

folic acid The form of folate often used in vitamin supplements and fortification of foods.

food additives Substances added to food that affect its quality, flavor, freshness, and/or safety.

food allergens Proteins that are not broken down by cooking or digestion and enter the body intact, causing an adverse reaction by the immune system.

food allergy An abnormal reaction by the immune system to a particular food.

food guidance systems Visual diagrams that provide a variety of food recommendations to help a person create a well-balanced diet.

food insecurity A household-level economic and social condition of uncertain access to adequate food.

food intolerance Adverse reaction to a food that does not involve an immune response.

food jags When a child will only eat the same food meal after meal.

food pantry Community food assistance location where food is provided to needy individuals and families.

food preservation The treatment of foods to reduce deterioration and spoilage, and help prevent the multiplication of pathogens that can cause foodborne illness.

food safety Guidelines and procedures that help keep foods free from contaminants and safe to eat.

Food Safety Initiative (FSI) Coordinates the research, surveillance, inspection, outbreak response, and educational activities of the various government agencies that work together to safeguard food.

food security The degree to which an individual has regular access to adequate amounts of healthy foods.

foodborne infection An illness caused by the ingestion of food contaminated with harmful pathogens. Also known as *foodborne disease* or *food poisoning*.

fortified foods Foods with added vitamins and minerals; fortified foods often contain nutrients that are not naturally present in the food or in higher amounts than the food contains naturally.

free radicals Unstable molecules that contain an unpaired electron; free radicals can damage the cells of the body and possibly contribute to the increased risk of chronic diseases.

fructose The sweetest of all the monosaccharides; also known as fruit sugar or levulose.

functional fiber The nondigestible polysaccharides that are added to foods because of a specific desired effect on human health.

functional foods Foods that may provide additional health benefits beyond the basic nutrient value.

fungicides Chemicals used to kill mold.

G

galactose A monosaccharide that links with glucose to create the sugar found in dairy foods.

galactosemia The genetic disorder characterized by high levels of galactose in the blood due to the inability to convert galactose to glucose.

gallbladder A pear-shaped organ located behind the liver. The gallbladder stores bile produced by the liver and secretes the bile through the common bile duct into the small intestine.

gallstones Stones formed from cholesterol in the gallbladder or bile duct.

gastric banding A type of gastric surgery that uses a silicone band to reduce the size of the stomach so that less food is needed to feel full.

gastric bypass surgeries A type of bariatric surgery that reduces the functional volume of the stomach to minimize the amount of food eaten. Such surgeries are sometimes used to treat extreme obesity.

gastric inhibitory peptide (GIP) A hormone produced by the small intestine that slows the release of chyme from the stomach.

gastric pits Indentations or small pits in the stomach lining where the gastric glands are located; gastric glands produce gastric juices.

gastrin A stomach hormone released after eating a meal that stimulates the release of hydrochloric acid.

gastritis Inflammation of the lining in the stomach.

gastroenteritis Inflammation of the lining of the stomach and intestines; also known as *stomach flu*.

gastroesophageal reflux disease (GERD) The backward flow of stomach contents into the esophagus due to improper functioning of the LES, resulting in heartburn.

gastrointestinal (GI) tract A long tube comprised of the organs of the digestive tract. It extends from the mouth through the esophagus, stomach, and small and large intestines to the anus.

gene The basic biological unit in a segment of DNA that contributes to the function of a specific protein.

gene–environment interaction The interaction of genetics and environmental factors that increases the risk of obesity in susceptible individuals.

gene expression The processing of genetic information to create a specific protein.

generally recognized as safe (GRAS) A designation given to substances intentionally added to food by the FDA that indicates the substance is considered safe by experts and is exempted from further testing.

genetic engineering (GE) A biological technique that isolates and manipulates the genes of organisms to produce a targeted, modified product.

genetically modified A cell that has its genetic makeup altered.

genetically modified organisms (GMOs) Organisms that have been genetically engineered to contain both original and foreign genes.

genome The total genetic information of an organism stored in the DNA of its chromosomes.

germ The vitamin-rich embryo, or seed, of a grain.

gestational diabetes Diabetes that occurs in women during pregnancy.

gestational hypertension Hypertension occurring during pregnancy in a woman without prior history of high blood pressure.

ghrelin A hormone produced in the stomach that stimulates hunger.

glossitis Inflammation of the tongue.

glucagon The hormone secreted from the alpha cells of the pancreas that stimulates glycogenolysis and gluconeogenesis to increase blood levels of glucose.

glucogenic amino acids Amino acids that can be used to form glucose through gluconeogenesis.

gluconeogenesis The formation of glucose from noncarbohydrate sources such as glucogenic amino acids, pyruvate, lactate, and glycerol.

glucose The most abundant carbohydrate in nature and the primary energy source for the body.

glycemic index A rating scale of the likelihood of foods to increase the levels of blood glucose and insulin.

glycemic load The amount of carbohydrate in a food multiplied by the amount of the glycemic index of that food.

glycerol The three-carbon backbone of a triglyceride.

glycocalyx Substance on the microvilli that contains protein- and carbohydrate-digesting enzymes.

glycogen The storage form of glucose in animals, including humans.

glycogen storage disease A genetic disorder characterized by the inability to break down glycogen due to the lack of glucose 6-phosphatase.

glycogenesis The process of assembling excess glucose into glycogen in the liver and muscle cells.

glycogenolysis The hydrolysis of glycogen to release glucose.

glycolysis The breakdown of glucose; for each molecule of glucose, two molecules of pyruvate and two ATP molecules are produced.

glycosidic bond A bond that forms when two sugar molecules are joined together during condensation.

goblet cells Cells throughout the GI tract that secrete mucus.

goiter The enlargement of the thyroid gland, mostly due to iodine deficiency.

goitrogens Substances in food that reduce the utilization of iodine by the thyroid gland, resulting in goiter.

growth charts Series of percentile curves that illustrate the distribution of selected body measurements in U.S. children.

growth hormone A hormone that regulates glucose metabolism by increasing glycogenolysis and lipolysis.

growth spurt A rapid increase in height and weight.

growth stunting Impaired growth and development primarily manifested in early childhood and including malnutrition during fetal development. Once growth stunting occurs, it is usually permanent.

gynoid obesity An excessive storage of body fat in the thighs and hips of the lower body.

H

hangover A collective term for the unpleasant symptoms, such as a headache and dizziness, that occur after drinking an excessive amount of alcohol; many of the symptoms are caused by high levels of acetaldehyde in the blood.

health claims Claims on food labels that describe a relationship between a food, food component, dietary ingredient, or dietary supplement and a disease or health-related condition.

Healthy People 2020 A set of disease prevention and health promotion objectives for Americans to meet during the second decade of the twenty-first century.

healthy weight A body weight in relationship to height that doesn't increase the risk of developing any weight-related health problems or diseases.

heart attack Permanent damage to the heart muscle that results from a sudden lack of oxygen-rich blood; also called a *myocardial infarction (MI).*

heme iron Iron found as part of a heme group found in hemoglobin in the blood, myoglobin in muscles, and in the mitochondria as part of the cytochromes.

hemochromatosis A genetic disorder that causes the body to store excessive amounts of iron.

hemoglobin The oxygen-carrying, heme-containing protein found in red blood cells.

hemolytic uremic syndrome A rare condition that can be caused by *E. coli* O157:H7 and results in the destruction of red blood cells and kidney failure. Very young children and the elderly are at a higher risk of developing this syndrome.

hemopoiesis The formation of red blood cells.

hemorrhage Excessive bleeding or loss of blood.

hemorrhoid Swelling in the veins of the rectum and anus.

hemosiderin A protein that stores iron in the body.

hepatic portal vein A large vein that connects the intestinal tract to the liver and transports newly absorbed nutrients.

hepatic vein The vein that carries the blood received from the hepatic portal vein away from the liver.

hepcidin A hormone produced in the liver that regulates the absorption and transport of iron.

hephaestin A copper-containing enzyme that catalyzes the conversion of ferrous to ferric iron before attaching to transferrin for transport.

herbicides Substances that are used to kill and control weeds.

hexavalent chromium The oxidative form of chromium (Cr^{+6}) that is toxic.

hexose A sugar that contains six carbons; glucose, galactose, and fructose are all hexoses.

high-density lipoproteins (HDLs) Lipoproteins that remove cholesterol from the tissues and deliver it to the liver to be used as part of bile and/or to be excreted from the body. Because of this, HDL is known as the "good" cholesterol.

high-pressure processing (HPP) A method used to pasteurize foods by exposing the items to pulses of high pressure, which destroys the microorganisms that are present.

homocystinuria A genetic disorder characterized by the inability to metabolize the essential amino acid methionine.

hormone A substance, usually protein- or lipid-based, that initiates or directs a specific action. Insulin, glucagons, ADH, and estrogen are examples of hormones in the body.

hormone-sensitive lipase The enzyme that catalyzes lipolysis of triglycerides.

host A living plant or animal (including a human) that a virus infects for the sake of reproducing.

hunger A strong sensation indicating a physiological need for food.

hydrochloric acid (HCl) A strong acid produced in the stomach that aids in digestion.

hydrogenation Adding hydrogen to an unsaturated fatty acid to make it more saturated and solid at room temperature.

hydrolysis A chemical reaction that breaks the bond between two molecules with water. A hydroxyl group is added to one molecule and a hydrogen ion is added to the other molecule.

hydrophobic "Water fearing." In nutrition, the term refers to compounds that are not soluble in water.

hydrostatic weighing A method used to assess body volume by underwater weighing.

hydroxyapatite The crystalline salt structure that provides strength in bones and teeth. Calcium and phosphorus are the main minerals found in the structure.

hypercalcemia Abnormally high levels of calcium in the blood.

hyperchloremia Abnormally high level of chloride in the blood.

hyperemesis gravidarum Excessive vomiting during pregnancy that can lead to dehydration and loss of electrolytes.

hyperkalemia Abnormally high levels of potassium in the blood.

hypernatremia Excessive amounts of sodium in the blood.

hyperphenylalanemia Elevated levels of blood phenylalanine due to a lack of the enzyme phenylalanine hydroxylase.

hyperphosphatemia Abnormally high level of phosphorus in the blood.

hyperplasia An increase in the number of cells due to cell division.

hypertension High blood pressure; defined as a systolic blood pressure higher than 140 mm Hg and/or a diastolic blood pressure greater than 90 mm Hg.

hyperthermia A rise in body temperature above normal.

hypertonic A solution that has a higher concentration of solutes.

hypertriglyceridemia The presence of high levels of triglycerides in the blood. Defined as triglyceride levels between 400 and 1,000 milligrams per deciliter.

hypertrophy To grow larger in size.

hypervitaminosis A condition resulting from the presence of excessive amounts of vitamins in the body; also referred to as *vitamin toxicity.*

hypervitaminosis A The serious condition in which the liver accumulates toxic levels of vitamin A.

hypervitaminosis D A condition resulting from excessive amounts of vitamin D in the body.

hypoallergenic infant formulas Specially developed formulas for infants who have food allergies and cannot tolerate regular formula.

hypocalcemia Abnormally low levels of calcium in the blood.

hypochloremia Abnormally low level of chloride in the blood.

hypoglycemia A blood glucose level that drops to lower than 70 mg/dl.

hypokalemia Abnormally low levels of potassium in the blood.

hyponatremia A dangerously low level of sodium in the blood that can result from water intoxication or a lack of sodium during heavy exercise.

hypophosphatemia Abnormally low level of phosphorus in the blood.

hypothermia A drop in body temperature to below normal.

hypothesis An idea or explanation proposed by scientists based on observations or known facts.

hypotonic A solution that has a lower concentration of solutes.

hypovolemia A low blood volume.

I

ileocecal valve The sphincter that separates the small intestine from the large intestine.

immunity The state of having built up antibodies to a particular foreign substance so that when particles of the substance enter the body, they are destroyed by the antibodies.

impaired glucose tolerance A condition whereby a fasting blood glucose level is higher than normal, but not high enough to be classified as having diabetes mellitus. Also called *prediabetes.*

inborn errors of metabolism Genetic conditions in which an individual lacks an enzyme that controls a specific metabolic pathway, resulting in the buildup of toxins.

incomplete protein A protein that is low in one or more of the essential amino acids. Proteins from plant sources tend to be incomplete.

indirect calorimetry An indirect measurement of energy expenditure obtained by measuring the amount of oxygen consumed and carbon dioxide produced.

infancy The age range from birth to 12 months.

inorganic Describing compounds that do not contain carbon.

inositol A water-soluble compound synthesized in the body that maintains healthy cell membranes.

insecticides Pesticides used to kill insects.

insensible water loss The loss of body water that goes unnoticed, such as by exhalation during breathing and the evaporation of water through the skin.

insoluble fiber A type of fiber that isn't dissolved in water or fermented by intestinal bacteria.

insulin The hormone secreted from the beta cells of the pancreas that stimulates the uptake of glucose from the blood into the cells.

insulin resistance The inability of the cells to respond to insulin.

integrated pest management (IPM) Alternative to pesticides that uses the most economical and the least harmful methods of pest control to minimize risk to consumers, crops, and the environment.

intensity The level of difficulty of an activity.

intentional food additives Substances added intentionally to foods to improve food quality.

interesterification The process that food manufacturers use to rearrange the fatty acids on the triglyceride molecule to improve the consistency and usefulness of processed food.

international units (IU) A system of measurement of a biologically active ingredient such as a vitamin that produces a certain effect.

interstitial fluid The fluid that surrounds cells. It is the main component of extracellular fluid.

intracellular fluid (ICF) The fluid found in the cytoplasm within the cells; it represents the largest fluid compartment in the body.

intravascular fluid The fluid found inside the blood vessels and the lymph fluid.

intrinsic factor (IF) A glycoprotein secreted by the stomach that helps in the absorption of vitamin B_{12}.

iodide The ion form of iodine in the body (I^-).

iodopsin The compound found in the cones of the eye that is needed for color vision.

iron-deficiency anemia A type of anemia due to a lack of dietary iron or excessive loss of blood.

irradiation A process in which foods are placed in a shielded chamber, called an *irradiator,* and subjected to a radiant energy source. This kills specific pathogens in food by breaking up the cells' DNA.

irritable bowel syndrome (IBS) An intestinal disorder resulting in abdominal discomfort, pain, diarrhea, constipation, and bloating; the cause is unknown.

isoflavones Naturally occurring phytoestrogens, or weak plant estrogens, that function in a similar fashion to the hormone estrogen in the human body.

J

jaundice A yellowish coloring of the skin due to the presence of bile pigments in the blood.

K

keratinization The accumulation of the protein keratin in epithelial cells, forming hard, dry cells unable to secrete mucus due to vitamin A deficiency.

Keshan disease A disease caused by a deficiency of selenium.

ketoacidosis A form of metabolic acidosis, or pH imbalance due to excess acid, that occurs when excess ketone bodies are present in the blood; most often seen in individuals with untreated type 1 diabetes., which can result in coma or death.

ketogenesis The formation of ketone bodies from excess acetyl CoA.

ketogenic Describing molecules that can be transformed into ketone bodies.

ketone bodies The by-products of the incomplete breakdown of fat.

ketosis The condition of increased ketone bodies in the blood.

kilocalorie The amount of energy required to raise the temperature of 1 kilogram of water 1 degree centigrade; used to express the measurement of energy in foods; 1 kilocalorie is equal to 1,000 calories.

kwashiorkor A state of PEM where there is a severe deficiency of dietary protein.

L

laboratory experiment A scientific experiment conducted in a laboratory. Some laboratory experiments involve animals.

lactate A three-carbon compound generated from pyruvate when mitochondria lack sufficient oxygen.

lactation The production of milk in a woman's body after childbirth, and the period during which it occurs.

lactose intolerant When maldigestion of lactose results in symptoms such as nausea, cramps, bloating, flatulence, and diarrhea.

lactose maldigestion The inability to digest lactose due to low levels of the enzyme lactase.

lactose A disaccharide composed of glucose and galactose; also known as milk sugar.

lanugo Very fine, soft hair on the face and arms of people with anorexia nervosa.

large intestine The lowest portion of the GI tract, where water and electrolytes are absorbed and waste is eliminated.

lean body mass (LBM) Total body weight minus the fat mass; it consists of water, bones, vital organs, and muscle. LBM is the metabolically active tissue in the body.

least developed country A country that shows little growth in multiple areas, such as income per capita, life expectancy, rate of literacy, industrial capability, technological sophistication, and economic productivity.

lecithin A phospholipid made in the body that is integral in the structure of cell membranes; also known as phosphatidylcholine.

letdown The release of milk from the mother's breast to feed the baby.

licensed dietitian (LD) An individual who has met specified educational and experience criteria deemed by a state licensing board necessary to be considered an expert in the field of nutrition. An RD would meet all the qualifications to be an LD.

life expectancy The average length of life for a population of individuals.

life span The maximum age to which members of a species can live.

lignin A noncarbohydrate form of dietary fiber that binds to cellulose fibers to harden and strengthen the cell walls of plants.

limiting amino acid An essential amino acid that is in the shortest supply, relative to the body's needs, in an incomplete protein.

linoleic acid A polyunsaturated essential fatty acid; part of the omega-6 fatty acid family.

lipases A group of lipid-digesting enzymes.

lipid A category of carbon, hydrogen, and oxygen compounds that are insoluble in water.

lipogenesis The process that converts excess glucose into fat for storage.

lipoic acid A vitamin-like substance used in energy production; it may also act as an antioxidant.

lipoprotein Capsule-shaped transport carrier that enables fat and cholesterol to travel through the lymph and blood.

lipoprotein lipase (LPL) An enzyme that hydrolyzes triglycerides in lipoproteins into three fatty acids and glycerol.

liposuction The surgical removal of subcutaneous fat. Usually performed on the abdomen, hips, and thighs, and/or other areas of the body.

liver The largest organ in the body, located in the upper abdomen. This organ aids digestion by secreting bile.

locavore A person who eats locally grown food whenever possible.

long-chain fatty acids Fatty acids with a chain of 12 carbons or more.

longevity The duration of an individual's life.

low birth weight A baby weighing less than 5 1/2 pounds at birth.

low-density lipoproteins (LDLs) Lipoproteins that deposit cholesterol in the walls of the arteries. Because this can lead to heart disease, LDL is referred to as the "bad" cholesterol.

lower esophageal sphincter (LES) The muscular ring located between the base of the esophagus and the stomach.

Lp(a) protein A lipoprotein containing LDL cholesterol found in the blood; this lipoprotein has been correlated to increased risk of heart disease.

lymph fluid Fluid that circulates through the body in lymph vessels and eventually enters the bloodstream.

lymphatic system A system of interconnected spaces and vessels between the tissues and organs that contains lymph and circulates fat-soluble nutrients throughout the body.

M

macrocytes Large cells such as a red blood cell.

macrocytic anemia A form of anemia characterized by large, immature red blood cells.

macronutrients Organic nutrients, including the energy-containing carbohydrates, lipids, proteins, and water that the body needs in large amounts.

macrosomia A large newborn, weighing more than 8 pounds, 13 ounces.

magnesium (Mg^{+2}) A major divalent cation in the body.

major minerals Minerals found in the body in amounts greater than 5 grams and needed in amounts greater than 100 milligrams per day. These include sodium, chloride, potassium, calcium, phosphorus, magnesium, and sulfur.

malabsorption A problem associated with the lack of absorption of nutrients through the intestinal tract.

malnourished A condition that results when the body does not receive the right amount of essential nutrients to maintain health; overnourished and undernourished are forms of malnutrition.

malnutrition The long-term outcome of consuming a diet that is either lacking in the essential nutrients or contains excess energy; an imbalance of nutrients in the diet.

maltose A disaccharide composed of two glucose units joined together.

maple syrup urine disease (MSUD) A genetic disorder characterized by the inability to metabolize branched-chain amino acids; symptoms include a maple syrup smell in the urine.

marasmus A state of PEM where there is a severe deficiency of kilocalories, which perpetuates wasting; also called *starvation*.

marine toxins Chemicals that occur naturally and contaminate some fish.

mast cells Cells in connective tissue to which antibodies attach, setting the stage for potential future allergic reactions.

mastication Chewing food.

Meals On Wheels A program that delivers nutritious meals to homebound older adults.

mechanical digestion Breaking down food by chewing, grinding, squeezing, and moving food through the GI tract by peristalsis and segmentation.

medical nutrition therapy The integration of nutrition counseling and dietary changes, based on individual medical and health needs, to treat a patient's medical condition.

medium-chain fatty acids Fatty acids with a chain of six to 10 carbons.

megadose An amount of a vitamin or mineral that's at least 10 times the amount recommended in the DRI.

megaloblasts Large, immature red blood cells.

menadione (vitamin K_3) The synthetic form of vitamin K used in animal feed and dietary supplements.

menaquinone (vitamin K_2) The form of vitamin K produced by bacteria in the colon.

menarche The onset of menstruation.

Menkes' disease A genetic disorder that interferes with copper absorption.

messenger RNA (mRNA) A type of RNA that copies the genetic information from the DNA and carries it from the nucleus to the ribosomes in the cell.

metabolic or fetal programming The process by which the prenatal environment interacts with genetic and other factors to produce permanent change.

metabolic pathway A sequence of reactions that convert compounds from one form to another.

metabolic water Water that is formed in the body as a result of metabolic reactions. Condensation reactions are an example of a chemical reaction that results in the production of water.

metabolism The sum of all chemical reactions in the body.

metalloenzymes Active enzymes that contain one or more metal ions that are essential for their biological activity.

metallothionine A metal-binding protein rich in sulfur-containing amino acids that transports ions.

metastasize To spread or grow into other parts of the body, as in reference to cancer cells.

methylcobalamin The coenzyme form of vitamin B_{12} that converts homocysteine to methionine.

micelle Transport carrier in the small intestine that enables fatty acids and other compounds to be absorbed.

microcytic hypochromic anemia A form of anemia in which red blood cells are small and pale in color due to lack of hemoglobin synthesis due to vitamin B_6 deficiency.

micronutrients Essential nutrients the body needs in smaller amounts: vitamins and minerals.

microsomal ethanol oxidizing system (MEOS) The second metabolic pathway for oxidizing ethanol, used at higher intakes of alcohol; it also participates in metabolizing drugs.

microsomes Small vesicles in the cytoplasm of liver cells where oxidative metabolism of alcohol takes place.

microvilli Tiny projections on the villi in the small intestine.

milestones Objectives or significant events that occur during development.

mineralization The process of adding minerals, including calcium and phosphorus, to the collagen matrix in the bone, which makes the bone strong and rigid.

minerals Inorganic elements essential to the nutrition of humans.

mitochondrion A cellular organelle that produces energy from carbohydrates, proteins, and fats; *pl.* mitochondria.

moderate drinking According to the *Dietary Guidelines for Americans,* up to one drink per day for women and up to two drinks a day for men.

moderation The diet principle of providing reasonable but not excessive amounts of foods and nutrients.

modified atmosphere packaging (MAP) A food preservation technique that changes the composition of the air surrounding the food in a package to extend its shelf life.

molds Microscopic fungi that live on plant and animal matter. Some can produce mycotoxins which are harmful.

monoglutamate The form of folate absorbed through the cells of the small intestine.

monoglyceride A remnant of fat digestion that consists of a glycerol with only one fatty acid attached to one of the three carbons.

monosaccharide Simple sugar that consists of a single sugar unit. There are three monosaccharides: glucose, fructose, and galactose.

monosodium glutamate (MSG) A flavor enhancer.

monounsaturated fatty acid (MUFA) A fatty acid that has one double bond.

MSG symptom complex A series of reactions such as numbness, burning sensation, facial pressure or tightness, chest pain, rapid heart beat, and drowsiness that can occur in some individuals after consuming MSG.

mucus Secretion produced throughout the GI tract that moistens and lubricates food and protects membranes.

muscular endurance The ability of the muscle to produce prolonged effort.

muscular strength The greatest amount of force exerted by the muscle at one time.

myelin sheath The tissue that surrounds and protects the nerves.

myoglobin The oxygen-carrying, heme-containing protein that contains heme found in muscle cells.

MyPlate A food guidance system that illustrates the recommendations in the *Dietary Guidelines for Americans* and the Dietary Reference Intakes (DRIs) nutrient goals.

N

naturally occurring sugars Sugars such as fructose and lactose that are found naturally in foods.

negative energy balance The state in which energy intake is less than energy expenditure. Over time, this results in weight loss.

neural tube defects Any major birth defect of the central nervous system, including the brain, caused by failure of the neural tube to properly close during fetal development.

neurotoxins Toxins that affect the nerves and can cause symptoms including mild numbness or tingling in the face, arms, and legs, as well as headaches and dizziness. Severe cases of neurotoxicity could result in death.

niacin equivalents (NE) A measurement that reflects the amount of niacin and tryptophan in foods that can be used to synthesize niacin.

nicotinamide adenine dinucleotide (NAD^+) A coenzyme form of niacin that functions as an electron carrier and can be reduced to NADH during metabolism.

nicotinamide adenine dinucleotide phosphate ($NADP^+$) A coenzyme form of niacin that functions as an electron carrier and can be reduced to NADPH during metabolism.

nicotinamide A form of niacin that is found in food and as a topical cream in treating acne.

nicotinic acid A form of niacin found in foods and sometimes prescribed to lower LDL cholesterol.

night blindness The inability to see in dim light or at night due to a deficiency of retinal in the retina.

nitrites and nitrates Substances that can be added to foods to function as a preservative and to give meats such as hot dogs and luncheon meats a pink color.

nitrogen balance The difference between nitrogen intake and nitrogen excretion.

nonessential [amino acids] The 11 amino acids the body can synthesize and that therefore do not need to be consumed in the diet.

nonessential nutrients Nutrients that can be made in sufficient quantities in the body to meet the body's requirements and support health.

non-exercise activity thermogenesis (NEAT) The energy expended for all activities not related to sleeping, eating, or exercise, including fidgeting, performing work-related activities, and playing.

nonheme iron Iron that is not attached to heme.

norepinephrine A hormone produced by the adrenal glands that stimulates glycogenolysis and gluconeogenesis.

normal blood pressure A systolic blood pressure less than 120 mm Hg (the top number) and a diastolic blood pressure less than 80 mm Hg (the bottom number). Referred to as 120/80.

noroviruses The most common type of virus that causes foodborne illness. They can cause gastroenteritis, or the "stomach flu." Also known as *Norwalk-like viruses.*

nursing bottle tooth decay Tooth decay from prolonged tooth contact with formula, milk, fruit juice, or other sugar-rich liquid offered to an infant in a bottle.

nutrient content claims Claims on the food label that describe the level or amount of a nutrient in the food. Terms such as *free, high, reduced,* or *lite* are examples of nutrient content claims.

nutrient density A measurement of the nutrients in a food compared with the kilocalorie content; nutrient-dense foods are high in nutrients and low in kilocalories.

nutrient requirements The amounts of specific nutrients needed to prevent malnutrition or deficiency; reflected in the DRIs.

nutrients Compounds in foods that sustain body processes. There are six classes of nutrients: carbohydrates, fats (lipids), proteins, vitamins, minerals, and water.

nutrition The science that studies how nutrients and compounds in foods nourish the body and affect body functions and overall health.

Nutrition Facts panel The area on the food label that provides a list of specific nutrients obtained in one serving of the food.

nutritional genomics A field of study of the relationship between genes, gene expression, and nutrition.

nutritionist A generic term with no recognized legal or professional meaning. Some people may call themselves a nutritionist without having any credible training in nutrition.

O

obese A condition of excess body weight due to an abnormal accumulation of stored body fat; a BMI of 30 or more is considered obese.

obesity For adults, having a BMI greater than 30.

observational research Research that involves systematically observing subjects to see if there is a relationship to certain outcomes.

oils Fats that are liquid at room temperature.

oligosaccharides Three to ten units of monosaccharides combined.

omega-3 fatty acid A family of polyunsaturated fatty acids with the first double bond located at the third carbon from the omega end.

omega-6 fatty acid A family of polyunsaturated fatty acids with the first double bond located at the sixth carbon from the omega end.

open dating Typically found on perishable items such as meat, poultry, eggs, and dairy foods; must contain a calendar date.

organic Describing compounds that contain carbon or carbon–carbon bonds. Also describes foods free of chemical-based pesticides, synthetic fertilizers, irradiation, and bioengineering. A USDA-accredited certifying inspector must certify organic foods

organophosphates A group of synthetic pesticides that adversely affect the nervous systems of pests. They are currently being re-reviewed by the EPA to ensure their safety.

osmolality A measurement of the concentration of solutes per kilogram of solvent in a solution.

osmosis The diffusion of water or any solvent across a semipermeable cell membrane from a weak concentration of solutes to a more concentrated solute.

osmotic gradient The difference in concentration between two solutions on each side of the permeable cell membrane.

osteomalacia The adult equivalent of rickets, causing muscle and bone weakness, and pain.

osteopenia A condition in which the bone mineral density is lower than normal but not low enough to be classified as osteoporosis.

osteoporosis A condition in which bones become brittle and porous, making them fragile due to depletion of calcium and bone proteins.

overexercise Excessive physical activity that can last several hours a day without adequate rest periods for proper recovery.

overnourished The condition of having consumed excess energy or nutrients.

overnutrition The state of consuming excess nutrients or energy.

overpopulation When a region has more people than its natural resources can support.

overweight For adults, having a BMI greater than 25.

oxaloacetate The starting molecule for the TCA cycle.

oxidation A chemical reaction in which oxygen combines with other substances, resulting in the loss of an electron.

oxidation reaction A reaction in which an atom loses an electron.

oxidative stress A condition whereby free radicals are being produced in the body faster than they are neutralized.

P

pancreas A large gland located behind the stomach that releases digestive enzymes after a meal. The pancreas also secretes the hormones insulin and glucagon, which control blood glucose.

paralytic shellfish poisoning A condition caused by a reddish-brown-colored dinoflagellate that contains neurotoxins.

parasites Organisms that live on or in another organism. Parasites obtain their nourishment from their hosts.

parathyroid hormone (PTH) The hormone secreted from the parathyroid glands that activates vitamin D formation in the kidney.

parietal cells Specialized cells in the stomach that secrete the gastric juices hydrochloric acid and intrinsic factor.

passive diffusion The process of absorbing nutrients freely across the cell membrane.

pasteurization The process of heating liquids or food at high temperatures to destroy foodborne pathogens.

pathogens Collective term for disease-causing organisms. Pathogens include microorganisms (viruses, bacteria) and parasites, and are the most common source of foodborne illness.

peak bone mass The genetically determined maximum amount of bone mass an individual can build up. The maximum bone mass achieved.

peer-reviewed journal A journal in which scientists publish research findings, after the findings have gone through a rigorous review process by other scientists.

pellagra A disease resulting from a deficiency of niacin or tryptophan.

pepsin The active protease that begins the digestion of proteins in the stomach.

pepsinogen The inactive precursor of pepsin; pepsinogen is stored in the gastric cells and is converted to pepsin by hydrochloric acid.

peptide A protein chain made up of fewer than 50 amino acids.

peptide bonds The bonds that connect amino acids, created when the acid group of one amino acid is joined with the nitrogen-containing amine group of another amino acid through condensation.

peptide YY A hormone produced in the small intestine that reduces hunger.

percentile The most commonly used clinical indicator to assess the size and growth patterns of children in the United States. An individual child is ranked according to the percentage of the reference population he or she equals or exceeds.

peripheral neuropathy Damage to the peripheral nerves causing pain, numbness, and tingling in the feet and hands, and muscle weakness.

peristalsis The forward, rhythmic motion that moves food through the digestive system. Peristalsis is a form of mechanical digestion because it influences motion, but it does not add chemical secretions.

pernicious anemia A form of anemia caused by a lack of intrinsic factor needed for absorption of vitamin B_{12}, forming large, immature red blood cells.

pesticides Substances that kill or repel pests such as insects, weeds, microorganisms, rodents, or fungi.

pH A measurement of the concentration of hydrogen ions in the body fluid. The measurement that indicates the acidity or alkalinity of a solution.

pharynx The area of the GI tract between the mouth and the esophagus; also called the throat.

phenylketonuria (PKU) A genetic disorder characterized by the inability to metabolize the essential amino acid phenylalanine.

phospholipids A category of lipids that consist of two fatty acids and a phosphorus group attached to a glycerol backbone. Lecithin is an example of a phospholipid found in food and in the body.

phosphorus The second most abundant mineral in the body.

photosynthesis A process by which plants create carbohydrates using the energy from sunlight.

phylloquinone (vitamin K_1) The form of vitamin K found in plants.

physical activity Voluntary movement that results in energy expenditure.

physical fitness The ability to perform physical activities requiring cardiorespiratory endurance, muscle endurance, strength, and/or flexibility; physical fitness is acquired through physical activity and adequate nutrition.

physiologic age A person's age estimated in terms of body health, function, and life expectancy.

physiological fuel values The real energy value of foods that are digested and absorbed; they are adjusted from the results of bomb calorimetry because of the inefficiency of the body.

phytochemicals Naturally occurring substances in fruits, vegetables, and whole grains that protect against certain chronic diseases.

phytostanols A type of plant sterol similar in structure to cholesterol.

phytosterols Naturally occurring sterols found in plants.

pica Eating nonfood substances such as dirt and clay.

placebo An inactive substance, such as a sugar pill, administered to a control group during an experiment.

placenta The organ that allows nutrients, oxygen, and waste products to be exchanged between a mother and fetus.

plant breeding A type of biotechnology in which two plants are crossbred to produce offspring with desired traits from both.

plaque The hardened buildup of cholesterol-laden foam cells, platelets, cellular waste products, and calcium in the arteries that results in atherosclerosis.

polar Having a pair of equal and opposite charges; water is a polar molecule because oxygen has a negative charge and hydrogen has a positive charge.

polychlorinated biphenyls (PCBs) Synthetic chemicals that have been shown to cause cancer and other adverse effects on the immune, reproductive, nervous, and endocrine systems in animals. PCBs may cause cancer in humans.

polydipsia The symptom of excessive thirst, common in diabetes mellitus.

polyglutamate A form of folate that naturally occurs in foods.

polyneuritis Inflammation of the peripheral nerves.

polypeptide A protein chain consisting of ten to more than a hundred amino acids joined together by peptide bonds.

polyphagia The symptom of an excessive desire to eat, common in diabetes mellitus.

polysaccharides Many sugar units combined. Starch, glycogen, and fiber are all polysaccharides.

polyunsaturated fatty acid (PUFA) A fatty acid with two or more double bonds.

polyuria The symptom of excessive urination, common in diabetes mellitus.

portion The quantity of a food usually eaten at one sitting.

positive energy balance The state in which energy intake is greater than energy expenditure. Over time, this results in weight gain.

postabsorptive state The period when you haven't eaten for more than four hours and the stomach and intestines are empty. Energy needs are met by the breakdown of stores.

potassium (K^+) Main cation in the intracellular fluid.

poverty Lacking the means to provide for material or comfort needs.

preeclampsia Serious medical condition developed late in pregnancy in which hypertension, severe edema, and protein loss occur.

preformed vitamins Vitamins found in food.

pregnancy-induced hypertension High-blood pressure resulting from pregnancy; includes *gestational hypertension, preeclampsia,* and *eclampsia.*

preschoolers Children aged 3 to 5 years old.

preservatives Substances that extend the shelf life of a product by retarding chemical, physical, or microbiological changes.

previtamin D_3 (precalciferol) The compound that is formed from 7-dehydrocholesterol when sunlight hits the skin.

primary malnutrition A state of being malnourished due to lack of consuming essential nutrients.

primary structure The first stage of protein synthesis after transcription when the amino acids have been linked together with a peptide bond to form a simple linear chain.

prions Short for proteinaceous infectious particle. Self-reproducing protein particles that cause degenerative brain diseases.

prior-sanctioned Substances that the FDA had determined were safe for use in foods prior to the 1958 Food Additives Amendment.

probiotics Live microorganisms, which, when administered in adequate amounts, confer a health benefit on the host.

progressive overload principle A gradual increase in exercise demands resulting from modifications to the frequency, intensity, time, or type of activity.

prohormone A physiologically inactive precursor to a hormone.

proof A measure of the amount of ethanol contained in alcoholic beverages.

proportionality The relationship of one entity to another. Vegetables and fruits should be consumed in a higher proportion than dairy and protein foods in the diet.

proteases A classification of enzymes that catalyze the hydrolysis of protein.

protein digestibility corrected amino acid score (PDCAAS) A score measured as a percentage that takes into account both digestibility and amino acid score and provides a good indication of the quality of a protein.

protein turnover The continual process of degrading and synthesizing protein.

protein-energy malnutrition (PEM) A lack of sufficient dietary protein and/or kilocalories.

proteins Large molecules, made up of chains of amino acids, that are found in all living cells; the sequence of amino acids is determined by the DNA.

protooncogenes Specialized genes that turn on and off cell division.

provitamin A vitamin precursor that is converted to a vitamin in the body.

public health nutritionists Individuals who may have an undergraduate degree in nutrition but who are not Registered Dietitians.

pyridoxal phosphate (PLP) The active coenzyme form of vitamin B_6.

pyridoxal The aldehyde form of vitamin B_6.

pyridoxamine The amine form of vitamin B_6.

pyridoxine The alcohol form of vitamin B_6.

pyruvate A three-carbon molecule formed from the oxidation of glucose during glycolysis.

Q

quackery The promotion and selling of health products and services of questionable validity. A quack is a person who promotes these products and services in order to make money.

quaternary structure The fourth geometric pattern of a protein; formed when two or more polypeptide chains cluster together, forming a final ball-like structure.

R

R protein The protein secreted from the salivary glands that binds vitamin B_{12} in the stomach and transports it into the small intestine during digestion.

rancidity The spoiling of fats through oxidation.

rating of perceived exertion (RPE) A subjective measure of the intensity level of an activity using a numerical scale.

recombinant bovine somatotropin (rbST) A synthetically made hormone identical to a cow's natural growth hormone, somatotropin, that stimulates milk production. Also known as rbGH (recombinant bovine growth hormone).

Recommended Dietary Allowance (RDA) The recommended daily amount of a nutrient that meets the needs of nearly all individuals (97 to 98 percent) in a similar age and gender group. The RDA is set higher than the EAR.

rectum Final 8-inch portion of the large intestine.

reduction reaction A reaction in which an atom gains an electron.

refined grains Grain foods that are made with only the endosperm of the kernel. The bran and germ have been removed during milling.

Registered Dietitian (RD) A health professional who is a food and nutrition expert; RDs obtain a college degree in nutrition from an Academy of Nutrition and Dietetics–accredited program, and pass a national exam to become a Registered Dietitian.

remineralization Replacing the lost minerals in a decayed lesion or dental caries on a tooth.

renin An enzyme secreted by the kidneys that participates in the renin-angiotensin system; renin increases blood volume, vasoconstriction of the blood vessels, and blood pressure.

repetition maximum (RM) The maximum amount of weight that can be lifted for a specified number of repetitions.

resistance training Exercising with weights to build, strengthen, and tone muscle to improve or maintain overall fitness; also called strength training.

resistant starch A type of starch that is not digested in the GI tract but has important health benefits in the large intestine.

resting metabolic rate (RMR) The measure of the amount of energy expended by the body at rest and after approximately a 3- to 4-hour fasting period. This rate is about 6 percent higher than BMR.

retinal The aldehyde form of preformed vitamin A.

retinoic acid The acid form of preformed vitamin A.

retinoids The term used to describe the family of preformed vitamin A compounds.

retinol The alcohol form of preformed vitamin A.

retinol activity equivalents (RAE) The unit of measure used to describe the total amount of all forms of preformed vitamin A and provitamin A carotenoids in food.

retinol binding protein (RBP) A protein made in the liver that transports retinol through the blood to the cells.

retinyl ester The ester form of preformed vitamin A found in foods and stored in the body.

rhodopsin A compound found in the rods of the eye that is needed for night vision. It is comprised of *cis*-retinal and the protein opsin.

rickets A vitamin D deficiency in children resulting in soft bones.

risk assessment The process of determining the potential human health risks posed by exposure to substances such as pesticides.

rodenticides Poisons used to kill rats, mice, and other rodents.

rods Light-absorbing cells responsible for black-and-white vision and night vision.

S

saliva Secretion from the salivary glands that softens and lubricates food, and begins the chemical breakdown of starch.

salivary amylase A digestive enzyme that begins breaking down carbohydrate (starch) in the mouth; other important enzymes during carbohydrate digestion include pancreatic amylase, maltase, sucrase, and lactase.

salivary glands Cluster of glands located underneath and behind the tongue that release saliva in response to the sight, smell, and taste of food.

sanctions Boycotts or trade embargoes used by one country or international group to apply political pressure on another.

sarcopenia Age-related progressive loss of muscle mass, muscle strength, and function.

satiation The state of being satisfactorily full, which inhibits the ability to eat more food.

satiety The feeling of satiation or "fullness" produced by the consumption of food.

saturated fatty acid A fatty acid in which all of the carbons are bound with hydrogen.

school-aged children Children between the ages of 6 and 12.

scientific method A process used by scientists to gather and test information for the sake of generating sound research findings.

scombrotoxic fish poisoning A condition caused by consuming spoiled fish that contain large amounts of histamines. Also referred to as *histamine fish poisoning.*

scurvy A disease caused by a deficiency of vitamin C and characterized by bleeding gums and a skin rash.

secondary malnutrition A state of being malnourished due to interference with nutrient absorption and metabolism.

secondary structure The geometric shape of a protein caused by the hydrogen ions of amino acids linking together with the amine group, causing the straight chain to fold and twist.

secretin A hormone secreted from the duodenum that stimulates the stomach to release pepsin, the liver to make bile, and the pancreas to release digestive juices.

segmentation Muscular contractions of the small intestine that move food back and forth, breaking the mixture into smaller and smaller pieces and combining it with digestive juices.

selectively permeable Describes the feature of cell membranes that allows some substances to cross the membrane more easily than other substances.

selenomethionine An amino acid that contains methionine rather than sulfur.

selenoproteins Proteins that contain selenomethionine.

selenosis The presence of toxic levels of selenium.

senescence Another term for aging.

serving size A recommended portion of food that is used as a standard reference on food labels.

set point A weight-control theory that states each individual has a genetically established body weight. Any deviation from this point will stimulate changes in body metabolism to reestablish the normal weight.

severe obesity Having a BMI of 40 or above; also defined as 120 percent of ideal body weight for females and 124 percent for males.

short-chain fatty acid A fatty acid with a chain of two to four carbons.

sickle-cell anemia A blood disorder caused by a genetic defect in the development of hemoglobin. Sickle-cell anemia causes the red blood cells to distort into a sickle shape and can damage organs and tissues.

side chain The part of an amino acid that provides it with its unique qualities; also referred to as the R group.

simple carbohydrates Carbohydrates that consist of one sugar unit (monosaccharides) or two sugar units (disaccharides).

skinfold caliper A tool used to measure the thickness of subcutaneous fat.

small for gestational age (SGA) Babies who weigh less than the 10th percentile of weight for gestational age.

small intestine The long coiled chamber that is the major site of digestion of food and the absorption of nutrients.

social drinking Moderate drinking of alcoholic beverages during social settings within safe limits.

sodium (Na^+) The major cation in the extracellular fluid.

sodium-potassium pump A protein located in the cell membrane that actively transports sodium out of the cell in exchange for potassium ions.

solanine Toxin found in potato surfaces exposed to light that can cause fever, diarrhea, and shock if consumed in large amounts.

solid foods Foods other than breast milk or formula given to an infant, usually around 4 to 6 months of age.

solubility The ability to dissolve into another substance.

soluble fiber A type of fiber that dissolves in water and is fermented by intestinal bacteria. Many soluble fibers are viscous and have thickening properties.

solvent A liquid in which substances dissolve to form a new solution. Water is called the universal solvent because it can dissolve a variety of substances, including minerals and glucose.

specific heat A measurement of the energy required to raise a gram of a substance, such as water, 1 degree Celsius.

sphincter A circular ring of muscle that opens and closes in response to nerve input.

spina bifida A serious birth defect in which the spinal cord is malformed and lacks the protective membrane coat.

spores Hardy reproductive structures that are produced by certain bacteria. Some bacterial spores can survive boiling temperature (212°F).

sports anemia Low concentrations of hemoglobin in the blood; results from an increase in blood volume during strenuous exercise.

starch The storage form of glucose in plants.

sterols A category of lipids that contains four connecting rings of carbon and hydrogen. Cholesterol is the most common sterol.

stomach A J-shaped muscular organ that mixes and churns food with digestive juices and acid to form chyme.

stomatitis Inflammation of the mucous lining of the mouth.

stool Waste produced in the large intestine; also called *feces*.

stroke volume The amount of blood pumped by the heart with each heart beat.

stroke A condition caused by a lack of oxygen to the brain that could result in paralysis and possibly death.

structure/function claims Claims on the label that describe the role of a nutrient or dietary compound that is proposed to influence the structure or function of the human body. For example, "Calcium builds strong bones" is a structure/function claim.

subcutaneous fat The fat located under the skin and between the muscles.

substrate A substance or compound that is altered by an enzyme.

sucrose A disaccharide composed of glucose and fructose; also known as table sugar.

sudden infant death syndrome (SIDS) The unexplained death of an infant at less than 1 year of age.

sugar substitutes Alternatives to table sugar that sweeten foods for fewer kilocalories.

sulfate (SO_4) The oxidized form of the mineral sulfur.

sulfites Preservatives used to help prevent foods from turning brown and to inhibit the growth of microbes. Often used in wine and dried fruit products.

systolic pressure The pressure within the arteries during a heart beat.

T

target heart rate A heart rate in beats per minute (expressed as a percentage of maximum heart rate) achieved during exercise that indicates the level of intensity at which fitness levels can increase.

tertiary structure The third geometric shape of a protein; occurs when the side chains of the amino acids, most often containing sulfur, form bridges, causing the protein to form even stronger bonds than in the secondary structure; these bonds form loops, bends, and folds in the molecule.

thermic effect of exercise (TEE) This refers to the increase in muscle contraction that occurs during physical activity, which produces heat and contributes to the total daily energy expenditure.

thermic effect of food (TEF) The amount of energy expended by the body to digest, absorb, transport, metabolize, and store energy-yielding nutrients from foods.

thermogenesis The generation of heat from the basal metabolism, digestion of food, and physical activity that provides necessary warmth; *adaptive thermogenesis* and *non-exercise activity thermogenesis (NEAT)* are other terms used to describe the generation of heat.

thiamin pyrophosphate (TPP) The coenzyme form of thiamin with two phosphate groups as part of the molecule.

thirst mechanism A complex interaction between the brain and the hypothalamus triggered by a loss of body water; the interaction leads to a feeling of thirst.

thyroxine The less active form of thyroid hormone, also known as *tetraiodothyronine* (T_4).

thyroxine-releasing hormone (TRH) A hormone secreted by the hypothalamus that stimulates the pituitary gland to release thyroxine-stimulating hormone (TSH).

thyroxine-stimulating hormone (TSH) A hormone released by the pituitary that stimulates the thyroid gland to trap more iodine to produce more thyroid hormone (T_4 and T_3).

toddlers Children aged 1 to 3 years old.

Tolerable Upper Intake Level (UL) The maximum daily amount of a nutrient considered safe in a group of similar individuals.

tongue-thrust reflex A forceful protrusion of the tongue in response to an oral stimulus, such as a spoon.

total daily energy expenditure (TDEE) The total kilocalories needed to meet daily energy requirements; based on basal metabolism, physical activity, the thermic effect of food, and adaptive thermogenesis.

total iron-binding capacity (TIBC) A blood test that measures the amount of iron that transferrin can bind. A higher TIBC indicates iron-deficiency anemia.

toxicity The accumulation of a substance to a harmful level.

toxins Poisons that can be produced by living organisms.

trabecular bone The inner structure of bone, also known as spongy bone because of its appearance. This portion of bone is often lost in osteoporosis.

trace minerals Minerals found in the body in amounts less than 5 grams and needed in amounts less than 20 milligrams daily. These include iron, zinc, selenium, fluoride, chromium, copper, manganese, and molybdenum.

trans The configuration of a fatty acid in which the carbon chains are on opposite sides of the double bond.

***trans* fat** Substance that contains mostly *trans* fatty acids, a result of hydrogenating an unsaturated fatty acid, causing a reconfiguring of some of its double bonds. A small amount of *trans* fatty acid occurs naturally in foods from animal sources.

transamination The transfer of an amino group from one amino acid to a keto acid to form a new nonessential amino acid.

transcobalamin The protein that transports vitamin B_{12} in the blood.

transcription The first stage in protein synthesis, in which the DNA sequence is copied from the gene and transferred to messenger RNA.

transfer RNA (tRNA) A type of RNA that transfers a specific amino acid to a growing polypeptide chain in the ribosomes during the processes of translation and elongation.

transferrin An iron-transporting protein.

translation The second phase of protein synthesis; the process of converting the information in mRNA to an amino acid sequence in the ribosomes.

transport The process of moving absorbed nutrients throughout the body through the circulatory and lymph systems.

transport proteins Proteins that carry lipids (fat and cholesterol), oxygen, waste products, minerals, and vitamins through your blood to your various organs and tissues. Proteins can also act as channels through which some substances enter your cells.

traveler's diarrhea A common pathogen-induced intestinal disorder experienced by some travelers who visit areas with unsanitary conditions.

tricarboxylic acid cycle (TCA) A cycle of aerobic chemical reactions in the mitochondria that oxidize glucose, amino acids, and fatty acids, producing hydrogen ions to be used in the electron transport chain, some ATP, and by-products carbon dioxide and water.

triglycerides A type of lipid commonly found in foods and the body; also known as fat. Triglycerides consist of three fatty acids attached to a glycerol backbone.

tripeptide A protein chain made up of three amino acids joined together by peptide bonds.

trivalent chromium The oxidative form of chromium (Cr^{+3}).

Type I osteoporosis Osteoporosis that results from lowered estrogen levels women experience during menopause. This type of osteoporosis is characterized by rapid bone loss.

Type II osteoporosis Osteoporosis that occurs in both men and women; characterized by the slow loss of bone mass over time due to aging.

U

U.S. Pharmacopeia (USP) A nonprofit organization that sets purity and reliability standards for dietary supplements.

ulcer A sore or erosion of the stomach or intestinal lining.

ulcerative colitis A chronic inflammation of the colon or large intestine that results in ulcers forming in the lining of the colon.

umbilical cord The cord connecting the fetus to the placenta.

undernourished A condition in which the individual lacks sufficient energy or is deficient in quality or quantity of essential nutrients.

undernutrition A state of inadequate nutrition whereby a person's nutrient and/or energy needs aren't met through the diet.

underweight Weighing too little for your height; defined as a BMI less than 18.5.

unintentional food additives Substances that enter into foods unintentionally during manufacturing or processing.

unsaturated fatty acid A fatty acid in which there are one or more double bonds between carbons.

upper esophageal sphincter The muscular ring located at the top of the esophagus.

urea A nitrogen-containing waste product of protein metabolism that is mainly excreted through the urine via the kidneys.

V

variety The diet principle of consuming a mixture of different food groups and foods within each group.

vegetarian A person who avoids eating animal foods. Some vegetarians only avoid meat, fish, and poultry, while others (vegans) avoid all animal products, including milk, eggs, and cheese.

very low-density lipoproteins (VLDLs) Lipoproteins that deliver fat made in the liver to the tissues. VLDL remnants are converted into LDLs.

very low-kilocalorie diet A diet of fewer than 800 kilocalories per day. These diets are high in protein, very low in (or devoid of) carbohydrates, and have a minimal amount of fat. Also referred to as a *protein-sparing modified fast*.

villi Small, fingerlike projections that line the interior of the small intestine.

virus A microscopic organism that carries genetic information for its own replication; a virus can infect a host and cause illness.

visceral fat The body fat associated with the internal organs and stored in the abdominal area.

vitamin D_3 binding protein (DBP) A protein made in the liver that transports vitamin D through the blood to the cells.

vitamins Thirteen essential, organic micronutrients that are needed by the body for normal functions, such as regulating metabolism and assisting in energy production, growth, reproduction, and overall health.

VO_{2max} The maximum amount of oxygen (mL) a person uses in one minute per kilogram of body weight.

W

waist circumference Measurement taken at the top of the hip bone; used to determine the pattern of obesity.

warfarin An anticoagulant drug given to prevent blood from clotting.

wasting The diminishment of muscle and fat tissue caused by extremely low energy intake from too little food and therefore too little energy; sometimes referred to as *acute malnutrition*.

water balance A state of equilibrium when the intake of water equals the amount of water excreted.

water intoxication A potentially dangerous medical condition that results from drinking too much water too quickly, also known as *hyperhydration*; can lead to hyponatremia and possible death.

water-soluble vitamins Vitamins that dissolve in water; they generally cannot be stored in the body and must be consumed daily.

weight cycling The repeated gain and loss of body weight.

weight management Maintaining a healthy body weight; defined as having a BMI of 18.5 to 24.9.

Wernicke-Korsakoff syndrome A severe brain disorder associated with chronic excessive alcohol consumption; symptoms include vision changes, loss of muscle coordination, and loss of memory; the cause is a thiamin deficiency.

whole grains Grain foods that are made with the entire edible grain kernel: the bran, the endosperm, and the germ.

Wilson's disease A rare genetic disorder that results in accumulation of copper in the body.

working poor Individuals or families who are steadily employed but still experience poverty due to low wages or high dependent expenses.

X

xerophthalmia Permanent damage to the cornea causing blindness due to a prolonged vitamin A deficiency.

Z

zoochemicals Nonnutritive animal compounds that play a role in fighting chronic diseases.

zygote A fertilized egg during the first two weeks after conception.

Index

Page references followed by *fig* indicate an illustrated figure; followed by *t* indicate a table.

A

D

E

G

N

O

P

U

V

W

X

Y

Z

Credits

Photo Credits

p. iv, Brand X/AGE Fotostock; p. v, top right: Radius Images/Alamy; **p. v, bottom:** Robert George Young/Photographer's Choice/Getty Images; **p. vi, top:** Stockstudios/Shutterstock; **p. vi, bottom left:** Ranplett/iStockphoto; **p. vi, bottom right:** Fuse/Jupiter Images; **p. vii:** Suzannah Skelton/iStockphoto; **p. viii, top left:** Comstock/Jupiter Images; **p. viii, center right:** Steve Hix/Somos/Thinkstock; **p. ix, top:** Asia Images Group Pte Ltd/Alamy; **p. ix, bottom:** Jacker5000/iStockphoto; **p. x, top left:** Jupiterimages/liquidlibrary/Thinkstock; **p. x, top right:** Laura Dwight/PhotoEdit; **p. x, bottom:** BananaStock/Jupiter Images; **p. xi:** Creatas/Jupiter Image; **p. xii, top:** Foodcollection/Getty Images; **p. xii, bottom:** Ariel Skelley/Thinkstock; **p. xiii, top right:** Smileus/Shutterstock; **p. xiii, bottom left:** Numboes/iStockphoto; **p. xiv:** Mike Flippo/Shutterstock, **p. xv:** Stephen Beaudet/Corbis Flirt/Alamy; **p. xvi:** Elenathewise/Fotolia; **p. xvii:** Elenathewise/Fotolia; **p. xix, top:** Joan Salge Blake; **p. xix, bottom:** Tom Schmidt/Fine Photo; **p. xx:** Stella L Volpe.

Chapter 1 **p. 2–3, Chapter Opener:** Ersler Dmitry/Shutterstock; **p. 4, bottom left:** Blend Images Photography/Veer Inc.; **p. 5, top right:** Foodfolio/Alamy; **p. 5, bottom right:** Corbis Super RF/Alamy; **p. 5, top center:** Dorling Kindersley, Inc.; **p. 5, center right:** Steve Casimiro/Photodisc/Getty Images; **p. 6, top left:** Taylor S. Kennedy/National Geographic/Getty Images; **p. 6, bottom left:** Steve Smith/Purestock/SuperStock; **p. 7, top right:** Pearson Education/Pearson Science; **p. 7, center right:** Pearson Education/Pearson Science; **p. 7, bottom right:** Pearson Education/Pearson Science; **p. 8, bottom left:** Barry Gregg/Corbis; **p. 8, top left:** Photodisc/Getty Images; **p. 8, center left:** Michael Krinke/iStockphoto; **p. 10, top left:** Peter Bernik/Shutterstock.com; **p. 12, center left:** Darqué/Photocuisine/Age Fotostock; **p. 12, bottom left:** D. Hurst/Alamy; **p. 13, top right:** Purestock/Getty Images; **p. 14, bottom left:** Pearson Education/Pearson Science; **p. 14, bottom center:** Bill Aron/PhotoEdit, Inc.; **p. 15, bottom right:** Evgeniya Uvarova/Shutterstock; **p. 16, top right:** Biophoto Associates/Photo Researchers, Inc.; **p. 20, top left:** PE HE Benjamin Cummings; **p. 22, top left:** Auremar/Fotolia; **p. 28, top left:** Dr. Tim Evans/Photo Researchers, Inc.; **p. 29, bottom right:** Midosemsem/Fotolia; **p. 30, top right:** Photodisc/Getty Images; **p. 30, bottom right:** Peter Bernik/Shutterstock.com; **p. 30, top left:** Blend Images Photography/Veer Inc.; **p. 31, top right:** Auremar/Fotolia

Chapter 2 **p. 36–37, Chapter Opener:** Rob Meinychuk/AGE Fotostock **p. 38, center left:** Dorling Kindersley, Inc.; **p. 39, center left:** Kristin Piljay/Pearson Education/Pearson Science; **p. 39, bottom left:** Kristin Piljay/Pearson Education/Pearson Science; **p. 39, center:** Kristin Piljay/Pearson Education/Pearson Science; **p. 39, bottom center:** Kristin Piljay/Pearson Education/Pearson Science; **p. 40, top right:** Kristin Piljay/Pearson Education/Pearson Science; **p. 40, bottom right:** Pearson Education/Pearson Science; **p. 42, bottom right:** lunamarina/Fotolia; **p. 42, bottom left:** Daemys/iStockphoto; **p. 42, top left:** Masterfile; **p. 44, top right:** U.S. Department of Agriculture; **p. 49, bottom right:** Peter Cavanagh/Alamy; **p. 55, top left:** Richard Megna/Fundamental Photographs; **p. 55, center left:** Richard Megna/Fundamental Photographs; **p. 55, center left:** Richard Megna/Fundamental Photographs; **p. 55, bottom left:** Richard Megna/Fundamental Photographs; **p. 57, top right:** Radius Images/Alamy; **p. 60, top center:** Pearson Education/Pearson Science; **p. 60, center:** Pearson Education/Pearson Science; **p. 62, bottom center:** Pearson Education/Pearson Science; **p. 62, bottom left:** Pearson Education/Pearson Science; **p. 62, bottom right:** Pearson Education/Pearson Science; **p. 63, bottom right:** Kristin Piljay/Pearson Education/Pearson Science; **p. 64, center:** Pearson Education/Pearson Science; **p. 64, center left:** Pearson Education/Pearson Science; **p. 64, center right:** Pearson Education/Pearson Science; **p. 66, top left:** Pearson Education/Pearson Science; **p. 68, top left:** Dorling Kindersley, Inc.; **p. 68, bottom left:** Pearson Education/PH College; **p. 69, center left:** Peter Cavanagh/Alamy

Chapter 3 **p. 72–73, Chapter Opener:** John Anthony Rizzo/Getty Images; **p. 75, center:** Tom Grill/Corbis; **p. 76, top center:** Japack/Age Fotostock; **p. 77, top right:** Corbis; **p. 77, center right:** Corbis; **p. 79, top center:** David Musher/Photo Researchers, Inc.; **p. 79, center:** Steve Gschmeissner/Photo Researchers, Inc; **p. 79, bottom center:** Don W. Fawcett/Photo Researchers; **p. 79, top left:** Maridav/Shutterstock; **p. 81, top right:** Tom Grill/Corbis; **p. 82, top left:** Tom Grill/Corbis; **p. 83, bottom left:** Red Chopsticks/Age Fotostock; **p. 85, bottom left:** John Lund/Tiffany Schoepp/Blend Images/Corbis; **p. 94, top left:** Images-USA/Alamy; **p. 95, center right:** Dr. E. Walker/Science Photo Library/Photo Researchers, Inc.; **p. 95, bottom right:** Southern Illinois University/Photo Researchers, Inc.; **p. 96, top center:** Kristin Piljay/Pearson Education; **p. 98, center left:** Cristovao/Shutterstock; **p. 99, bottom right:** David Musher/Photo Researchers, Inc.; **p. 101, top center:** BananaStock/Age Fotostock; **p. 102, bottom center:** Robert George Young/Photographer's Choice/Getty Images; **p. 102, top right:** wavebreakmedia ltd/Shutterstock; **p. 103, bottom left:** Koki Iino/Getty Images; **p. 104, bottom left:** Tom Grill/Corbis; **p. 105, bottom left:** John Lund/Tiffany Schoepp/Blend Images/Corbis; **p. 106:** David Musher/Photo Researchers, Inc.

Chapter 4 **p. 108–109, Chapter Opener:** papkin/Shutterstock; **p. 115, top left:** Felicia Martinez/PhotoEdit, Inc.; **p. 116, top left:** Barbro Bergfeldt/Fotolia; **p. 116, center left:** Anna/Fotolia; **p. 117, top right:** Foodcollection/Getty Images; **p. 118, center left:** Kristin Piljay/Pearson Education; **p. 119, center:** KO Studio/Shutterstock; **p. 123, center left:** Yuri Arcurs/Shutterstock; **p. 123, bottom left:** Flashon Studio/Shutterstock; **p. 125, top right:** Valentyn Volkov/Shutterstock; **p. 125, center right:** dragon_fang/Shutterstock; **p. 127, top center:** Moodboard Premium/Glow Images, Inc.; **p. 128, bottom center:** Photo Researchers, Inc/Pearson; **p. 133, top left:** Supri Suharjoto/Shutterstock; **p. 134, top left:** Elenathewise/Fotolia; **p. 135, bottom right:** Comstock/Jupiter Images; **p. 140, top left:** Pearson Education; **p. 140, top center:** Pearson Education; **p. 141, top center:** D. Hurst/Alamy; **p. 142, top left:** Ingram Publishing/Alamy; **p. 142, top center:** Pearson Education/Pearson Science; **p. 143, top right:** Michael Newman/PhotoEdit, Inc.; **p. 148, center left:** Pearson Education; **p. 148, bottom left:** Kristin Piljay/Pearson Education; **p. 151, bottom right:** PhotoLink/Photodisc/Getty Images; **p. 152, center:** Pearson Education; **p. 152, center right:** Pearson Education

Chapter 5 **p. 156–157, Chapter Opener:** Michael Paul/StockFood Creative/Getty Images; **p. 159, top right:** Ryan McVay/Lifesize/Getty Images; **p. 162, top left:** Gemenacom/Fotolia; **p. 165, top right:** Chas/Shutterstock; **p. 167, center:** Comstock Images/Jupiter Images; **p. 173, top center:** David M. Phillips/Photo Researchers, Inc; **p. 175, top left:** Pearson Education/Pearson Science; **p. 175, top right:** Pearson Education/Pearson Science; **p. 178, bottom left:** ERIC SCHRADER/Pearson; **p. 179, bottom left:** Helen Sessions/Alamy; **p. 180, bottom left:** Dianne McFadden/Shutterstock; **p. 183, top left:** Kristin Piljay/Pearson Education; **p. 183, top center:** Kristin Piljay/Pearson Education; **p. 183, top center:** Kristin Piljay/Pearson Education; **p. 183, top right:** Kristin Piljay/Pearson Education; **p. 183, top right:** Kristin Piljay/Pearson Education; **p. 184, bottom left:** Brand X Pictures/Age Fotostock; **p. 184, top center:** Doug Perrine/Nature Picture Library; **p. 187, top center:** Shebeko/Shutterstock; **p. 190, top left:** Kristin Piljay/Pearson; **p. 191, top center:** Stockbyte/Getty Images; **p. 194, bottom center:** Ligia Botero/Photodisc/Getty Images; **p. 195, center:** Serghei Starus/iStockphoto; **p. 196, bottom left:** Kristin Piljay/Pearson; **p. 197, center:** Comstock/Jupiter Images; **p. 201, bottom right:** Photos.com; **p. 201, top right:** Shebeko/Shutterstock

Chapter 6 **p. 206–207, Chapter Opener:** Food and Drink/SuperStock; **p. 208, center left:** Proles Productions/Age Fotostock; **p. 212, center left:** SoFood/Alamy; **p. 214, center:** John Lund/Tiffany Schoepp/Blend Images/Corbis; **p. 216, top left:** Oliver Meckes/Nicole Ottawa/Pearson; **p. 219, center right:** PhotoAlto/Alamy; **p. 220, center left:** Dr. P. Marazzi/Science Photo Library/Photo Researchers Inc.; **p. 222, top left:** JUERGEN BERGER/Photo Researchers/Pearson; **p. 224, center right:** Ruth Jenkinson/Dorling Kindersley, Inc.; **p. 224, bottom right:** Brian Yarvin Photography/Photo Researchers, Inc; **p. 224, bottom right:** Monkey Business Images/Shutterstock; **p. 225, center right:** Elke Dennis/Shutterstock; **p. 226, bottom left:** Kristin Piljay/Pearson Education; **p. 227, top right:** Macdaddy/Dreamstime/Pearson; **p. 228, center:** Philip Dowell/Dorling Kindersley, Inc.; **p. 228, center:** Lehner/iStockphoto; **p. 228, center right:** Kristin Piljay/Pearson; **p. 228, center left:** Lim ChewHow/Shutterstock; **p. 229, center left:** Clive Streeter and Patrick McLeavy/Dorling Kindersley, Inc.; **p. 229, center:** Akalong Suitsuit/Fotolia; **p. 229, center right:** Kristin Piljay/Pearson; **p. 229, center:** stockstudios/Shutterstock; **p. 230, bottom left:** Elena Elisseeva/Shutterstock; **p. 232, top right:** Brand X/Age Fotostock; **p. 232, left:** Elenathewise/Fotolia; **p. 233, top right:** Brand X/Age Fotostock; **p. 233, top left:** Brand X/Age Fotostock; **p. 234, center:** Igor Dutina/iStockphoto; **p. 234, bottom right:** Alasdair Thomson/iStockphoto; **p. 238, center:** Kristin Piljay/Pearson; **p. 238, center right:** Kristin Piljay/Pearson; **p. 239, center left:** Kristin Piljay/Pearson; **p. 243:** DAI KUROKAWA/EPA/Newscom; **p. 244, top center:** michaeljung/Shutterstock; **p. 245:** Farah Abdi Warsame/AP Images; **p. 246, bottom right:** PhotoAlto/Alamy; **p. 247, bottom right:** Brand X Pictures/Getty Images; **p. 247, bottom left:** DAI KUROKAWA/EPA/Newscom; **p. 247, center right:** Elena Elisseeva/Shutterstock; **p. 247, top left:** Monkey Business Images/Shutterstock

Chapter 7 **p. 250–251, Chapter Opener:** Vstock LLC/Getty Images; **p. 253, bottom right:** Syracuse Newspapers/Jim Commentucci/The Image Works; **p. 254, center left:** Pearson Education/Pearson Science; **p. 255, top right:** yukata/Fotolia; **p. 255, center right:** Foodcollection/Getty Images; **p. 255, bottom center:** Pearson Education/Pearson Science; **p. 255, bottom right:** Pearson Education/Pearson Science; **p. 255, center:** johnfoto18/Shutterstock; **p. 257, bottom center:** ol_vic/Shutterstock; **p. 259, top center:** Digital Vision/Getty Images; **p. 260, top left:** FoodPix/Photos.com; **p. 262, bottom center:** Corbis; **p. 262, top left:** Jim Varney/Photo Researchers, Inc.; **p. 264, bottom left:** David R. Frazier/Photolibrary, Inc./Alamy; **p. 265, center right:** Fuse/Jupiter Images; **p. 266, top left:** Ruth C. Enge/Pearson Education/Pearson Science; **p. 266, top center:** James C. Fell/Pearson Education/Pearson Science; **p. 267, bottom right:** Image Source/Corbis RF; **p. 269, center left:** Joe Koshellek/MCT/Newscom; **p. 271, bottom left:** Richard Megna/Fundamental Photographs, NYC; **p. 271, bottom right:** Richard Megna/Fundamental Photographs, NYC; **p. 272, center:** Dusanzidar/Dreamstime; **p. 272, center right:** Unpict/Fotolia; **p. 272, center right:** Danny Hooks/Fotolia; **p. 272, bottom right:** AmpFotoStudio.com/Fotolia; **p. 272, center:** Pali Rao/peepo/iStockphoto; **p. 272, top center:** Antonio Muñoz Palomares/iStockphoto; **p. 272, bottom center:** iofoto/Shutterstock; **p. 272, top right:** Joy Brown/Shutterstock; **p. 274, top right:** Arthur Glauberman/Photo Researchers, Inc; **p. 275, top center:** Pearson Education/Pearson Science; **p. 277, bottom center:** Fetal Alcohol & Drug Unit (FAS); **p. 279, bottom right:** Corbis; **p. 279, bottom left:** Digital Vision/Getty Images; **p. 280, bottom left:** Image Source/Corbis RF; **p. 280, top:** yukata/Fotolia; **p. 280, center right:** Joe Koshellek/MCT/Newscom

Chapter 8 **p. 284–285, Chapter Opener:** Sorbis/Shutterstock; **p. 287, center right:** BloomImage/Corbis; **p. 290, bottom left:** Kristin Piljay/Pearson Education; **p. 296, bottom:** Don Mason/Blend Images/Alamy; **p. 306, top center:** Rudchenko Liliia/Shutterstock; **p. 308, top center:** April_89/Fotolia; **p. 308, center:** Sniegirova Mariia/Shutterstock.com; **p. 312, center right:** Chris Rout/Alamy; **p. 313, top left:** Abbott Laboratories; **p. 314, top center:** JIM KAPUT/Pearson Education/Pearson Science; **p. 314, top left:** Ruth Debusk/Pearson Education/Pearson Science; **p. 317, top left:** Rudchenko Liliia/Shutterstock; **p. 317, top right:** Abbott Laboratories

Chapter 9 **p. 320–321, Chapter Opener:** Andi Berger/Shutterstock; **p. 323, bottom right:** Stockbyte/Getty Images; **p. 323, bottom center:** Mtsyri/Shutterstock; **p. 325:** Best View Stock/Alamy; **p. 327, top right:** National Eye Institute; **p. 327, center right:** National Eye Institute; **p. 327, bottom right:** National Eye Institute; **p. 329, bottom left:** Best View Stock/Alamy; **p. 331, bottom left:** Brand X/Age Fotostock; **p. 331, center right:** Brand X/Age Fotostock; **p. 331, top right:** JupiterImages/liquidlibrary/Thinkstock; **p. 332, bottom right:** Brand X/Age Fotostock; **p. 335, top right:** Pearson Education/Pearson Science; **p. 336, center:** Kristin Piljay/Pearson Science; **p. 337, top left:** Gravßa Victoria/Shutterstock; **p. 338, center left:** U.S. Pharmacopeial Convention; **p. 341, top right:** Frank and Helena/Cultura/Glow Images, Inc.; **p. 342, top right:** Elena Schweitzer/Shutterstock; **p. 343, top right:** Sarsmis/Shutterstock; **p. 344, top center:** Digital Vision/Getty Images; **p. 345, top right:** Dr. P. Marazzi/Photo Researchers, inc.; **p. 345, bottom left:** Timmary/Shutterstock; **p. 346, bottom center:** Brand X/Age Fotostock America, Inc; **p. 348, top left:** James Stevenson/Photo Researchers; **p. 349, top right:** GustoImages/Photo Researchers, Inc.; **p. 350, top left:** Seth Joel/Photographer's Choice/Getty Images; **p. 351, bottom left:** John Smith/Photolibrary/Getty Images; **p. 353, top center:** Michael Littlejohn/Prentice Hall, Inc; **p. 353, bottom left:** Biophoto Associates/Photo Researchers, Inc.; **p. 354, top left:** Jacek Chabraszewski/Fotolia; **p. 355, center:** Ian O'Leary/Dorling Kindersley, Inc., Ltd; **p. 355, bottom right:** Rachel Epstein/PhotoEdit, Inc.; **p. 358, top left:** Dee Breger/Photo Researchers, Inc.; **p. 358, bottom center:** Cristina Pedrazzini/Photo Researchers, Inc.; **p. 358, top center:** SPL/Photo Researchers, Inc.; **p. 359, bottom left:** Brand X/Age Fotostock; **p. 359, top right:** Brand X/Age Fotostock; **p. 360, center left:** Stockbyte/Getty Images; **p. 360, left:** Mtsyri/Shutterstock; **p. 361, bottom left:** Sarsmis/Shutterstock

Chapter 10 **p. 366–367, Chapter Opener:** TOHRU MINOWA/Age Fotostock; **p. 370, top center:** Martin Carlsson/CarlssonInc/iStockphoto; **p. 371, center left:** Isabelle Rozenbaum/Age Fotostock; **p. 372, bottom right:** Joe Gough/Fotolia; **p. 374, top left:** Ralph Morse//Time Life Pictures/Getty Images; **p. 375, bottom left:** JJAVA/Fotolia; **p. 375, top right:** Biophoto Associates/Photo Researchers, Inc.; **p. 375, center right:** SPL/Photo Researchers, Inc.; **p. 378, bottom left:** D. Hurst/Alamy; **p. 378, top left:** Elena Elisseeva/Shutterstock; **p. 379, top right:** Dr. M.A. Ansary/Photo Researchers; **p. 380, center left:** Smileus/Shutterstock; **p. 381, top right:** Justin Lightley/Photographer's Choice/Getty Images; **p. 382, center right:** Richard Semik/Shutterstock; **p. 382, bottom left:** MaxPhotographer/Shutterstock; **p. 384, top right:** FoodCollection/Photolibrary/Getty Images; **p. 386, bottom right:** Biophoto Associates/Photo Researchers/Getty Images; **p. 387, top right:** BRAND X PICTURES/Age Fotostock; **p. 387, bottom left:** Tim Ridley/Dorling Kindersley, Inc., Ltd; **p. 389, top right:** AmpFotoStudio/Shutterstock; **p. 390, top center:** Apple's Eyes Studio/Shutterstock; **p. 391, center left:** Kristin Piljay/Pearson Science; **p. 392, top center:** Tetra Images/Alamy; **p. 393, top left:** 28/Ocean/Corbis; **p. 393, center right:** Edyta Pawlowska/Shutterstock; **p. 394, center:** SPL/Photo Researchers, Inc.; **p. 395, bottom center:** St. Mary's Hospital Medical School/Photo Researchers, Inc; **p. 396, center right:** Antagain/iStockphoto; **p. 396, bottom left:** Jason Stitt/Shutterstock.com; **p. 401, bottom left:** Brand X/Age Fotostock; **p. 401, center right:** Brand X/Age Fotostock; **p. 403, bottom left:** Dr. M.A. Ansary/Photo Researchers; **p. 403, bottom right:** MaxPhotographer/Shutterstock; **p. 404, bottom center:** Vasko Miokovic/iStockphoto; **p. 405:** AmpFotoStudio/Shutterstock

Chapter 11 **p. 408–409, Chapter Opener:** Hugh Whitaker/Age Fotostock; **p. 411, bottom right:** Claude Edelmann/Photo Researchers; **p. 411, top right:** Steve Hix/Somos/Thinkstock; **p. 412, top center:** Radius Images/Alamy; **p. 413, bottom right:** bit24/Fotolia; **p. 422, top right:** Wave Royalty Free/Alamy; **p. 423, center right:** Dynamic Graphics Group/Jupiter Images; **p. 425, top right:** Kristin Piljay/Pearson Education, Inc.; **p. 426, center left:** Lucianne Pashley/Age Fotostock; **p. 427, center right:** Dave & Les Jacobs/Blend Images/Getty Images; **p. 428, top center:** Monika Wisniewska/Shutterstock; **p. 431, top right:** Lucianne Pashley/Age Fotostock; **p. 431, center right:** Stephen Beaudet/Corbis Flirt/Alamy; **p. 431, bottom left:** bit24/Fotolia

Chapter 12 **p. 434–435, Chapter Opener:** John E. Kelly/FoodPix/Getty Images; **p. 438, top left:** Keko64/Shutterstock; **p. 439, top right:** Eye of Science/Photo Researchers, Inc.; **p. 441, center right:** Richard Megna/Fundamental Photographs; **p. 441, bottom center:** Kristin Piljay/Pearson Education, Inc.; **p. 442, bottom right:** Corbis Premium RF/Alamy; **p. 443, bottom center:** John Lund/Tiffany Schoepp/Blend Images/Getty Images; **p. 444, bottom right:** Stockbyte/Getty Images; **p. 444, center left:** Comstock/Jupiter Images;

p. 447, bottom right: Scott Thomas/Getty Images; **p. 447, center:** Kristin Piljay/Pearson Education, Inc.; **p. 447, top center:** Kristin Piljay/Pearson Education, Inc.; **p. 449, bottom center:** Steve Sant/Alamy; **p. 449, top right:** Nick Emm/Alamy; **p. 449, bottom left:** Kristin Piljay/Pearson Education, Inc.; **p. 450, top left:** Joe Gough/Shutterstock; **p. 451, bottom right:** Motorlka/Fotolia; **p. 451, bottom left:** Smit/Shutterstock; **p. 451, bottom center:** Elena Schweitzer/Shutterstock; **p. 452, top right:** BRAND X PICTURES/Age Fotostock; **p. 453, bottom right:** D.Hurst/Alamy; **p. 453, top right:** Lehner/iStockphoto; **p. 454, top right:** Michael Klein/Peter Arnold/Getty Images; **p. 454, top left:** Kristin Piljay/Pearson Education, Inc.; **p. 455, center left:** Office of the Surgeon General; **p. 455, center right:** Office of the Surgeon General; **p. 456, bottom right:** Catherine Ursillo/Photo Researchers, Inc.; **p. 457, top center:** Stockbyte/Getty Images; **p. 459, top center:** Jose Luis Pelaez/Blend Images/Getty Images; **p. 460, bottom right:** Nitr/Shutterstock; **p. 461, top right:** Aprilphoto/Dreamstime; **p. 462, top left:** Vaivirga/Fotolia; **p. 463, top center:** Ian O'Leary/Dorling Kindersley, Inc., Inc.; **p. 464, top left:** BananaStock/Jupiter Images; **p. 465, top left:** Larry Korb/Shutterstock; **p. 468, center right:** Motorlka/Fotolia; **p. 468, center right:** Michael Klein/Peter Arnold/Getty Images; **p. 468, top right:** Suzannah Skelton/iStockphoto; **p. 468, center left:** Smit/Shutterstock; **p. 468, center:** Elena Schweitzer/Shutterstock; **p. 468, top left:** Keko64/Shutterstock **p. 469, top right:** Ingram Publishing/Alamy

Chapter 13 **p. 472–473, Chapter Opener:** travellinglight/Alamy; **p. 475, bottom left:** Nayashkova Olga/Shutterstock; **p. 476, top center:** Food Features/Alamy; **p. 479, bottom left:** helenlbuxton/Fotolia; **p. 479, center right:** C Squared Studios/Photodisc/Getty Images; **p. 480, top right:** dehooks/iStockphoto; **p. 481, top center:** PhotoAlto/Sigrid Olsson/Jupiter Images; **p. 482, top center:** Ric Grave/Photo Researchers, Inc.; **p. 482, center:** Joaquin Carrillo Farga/Photo Researchers, Inc.; **p. 483, bottom left:** SednevaAnna/iStockphoto; **p. 485, top left:** Foodcollection/Getty Images; **p. 486, bottom left:** Kristin Piljay/Pearson Education, Inc.; **p. 487, bottom left:** Jon Edwards Photography/Bon Appetit/Alamy; **p. 488, top center:** Medical-on-Line/Alamy; **p. 488, center left:** al62/Fotolia; **p. 488, bottom right:** Image Source/Jupiter Images; **p. 489, bottom center:** Ross Hailey/MCT/Newscom; **p. 491, bottom center:** Gabe Palmer/Alamy; **p. 491, top right:** Don Farrall/Photodisc/Getty Images; **p. 492, bottom left:** John A Rizzo/Age Fotostock; **p. 492, top right:** National Institute of Dental Research; **p. 493, top left:** Pearson; **p. 493, top center:** Pearson; **p. 495, center left:** Foodcollection.com/Alamy; **p. 495, top center:** Pearson; **p. 496, bottom right:** Mike Goldwater/Alamy; **p. 497, bottom left:** Corbis; **p. 498, top left:** Richard Megna/Fundamental Photographs; **p. 498, bottom left:** marco mayer/Shutterstock; **p. 498, top right:** Myrleen Ferguson Cate/PhotoEdit, Inc.; **p. 498, center right:** Anna Hoychuk/Shutterstock; **p. 499, top right:** Foodcollection/Getty Images; **p. 500, top left:** Viktor/Fotolia; **p. 503, top right:** FoodCollection/SuperStock; **p. 504, top right:** Jon Edwards Photography/Bon Appetit/Alamy; **p. 504, bottom left:** Foodcollection/Getty Images; **p. 504, bottom right:** National Institute of Dental Research; **p. 505, center right:** Mike Goldwater/Alamy; **p. 505, bottom right:** Foodcollection/Getty Images; **p. 505, center left:** Sally Scott/Shutterstock; **p. 505, bottom left:** Max/Shutterstock; **p. 506:** Anna Hoychuk/Shutterstock

Chapter 14 **p. 510–511, Chapter Opener:** Erik Isakson/Getty Images; **p. 517, center right:** Michael Newman/PhotoEdit, Inc.; **p. 517, top right:** Cultura Limited/SuperStock; **p. 518, bottom left:** TIMOTHY A. CLARY/AFP/Getty Images/Newscom; **p. 521, bottom left:** Ruben Sprich/Reuters/Landov; **p. 521, bottom center:** Philippe Psaila/Photo Researchers, Inc; **p. 526, top left:** David Madison/Getty Images; **p. 526, top right:** Joe Traver/Time Life Pictures/Getty Images; **p. 526, bottom right:** Elena Dorfman/Pearson Education; **p. 526, center:** Mauro Fermariello/Photo Researchers, Inc.; **p. 526, bottom left:** Mauro Fermariello/Photo Researchers, Inc; **p. 527, center right:** Inmagine/Alamy; **p. 532, bottom left:** Ruben Sprich/Reuters/Landov; **p. 532, bottom right:** Mauro Fermariello/Photo Researchers, Inc.

Chapter 15 **p. 536–537, Chapter Opener:** Purestock/Getty Images; **p. 538, top:** Bill Aron/PhotoEdit, Inc.; **p. 539, center right:** BananaStock/Jupiter Images; **p. 540, top left:** Michael Gonzalez-Campoy/Pearson Science; **p. 540, top center:** Glenn Gaesser/Pearson Education; **p. 544, bottom center:** Dmitri Maruta/Alamy; **p. 545, bottom right:** Laurence Mouton/PhotoAlto/Alamy; **p. 546, top left:** Ilene MacDonald/Alamy; **p. 548, bottom left:** Inmagine Asia/Inmagine Asia/Age Fotostock; **p. 549, top right:** Kristin Piljay/Pearson Education, Inc.; **p. 550, top left:** GlowImages/Alamy; **p. 552, top, right:** Evan Vucci/AP Images; **p. 553, center right:** Image Source/Alamy; **p. 553, center:** Comstock Images/Comstock/Jupiter Images; **p. 553, center:** Morgan Lane Photography/Shutterstock; **p. 554, center left:** U.S. Department of Health and Human Services; **p. 554, center right:** U.S. Department of Health and Human Services; **p. 554, bottom left:** U.S. Department of Health and Human Services; **p. 554, bottom right:** U.S. Department of Health and Human Services; **p. 556, top center:** Photolibrary/Alamy; **p. 556, top right:** Foodcollection RF/Getty Images; **p. 556, top left:** Radius Images/JupiterImages; **p. 557, top left:** Richard Megna/Fundamental Photographs; **p. 557, top right:** Richard Megna/Fundamental Photographs; **p. 557, center left:** Richard Megna/Fundamental Photographs; **p. 557, center right:** Richard Megna/Fundamental Photographs; **p. 558, center left:** Ruth Jenkinson/Dorling Kindersley, Inc.; **p. 560, top center:** Carlos E. Santa Maria/Shutterstock; **p. 563, top right:** CHARLES BENNET/AP Images; **p. 564, top right:** Peter Kramer/AP Images; **p. 565, top right:** LIU JIN/AFP/Newscom; **p. 568, center left:** Nick Obank/Barcroft Media/Landov; **p. 569, center right:** Fuse/Jupiter Images; **p. 570, top right:** Lucas Allen White/Shutterstock; **p. 571, bottom right:** D.Hurst/Alamy; **p. 574, bottom right:** Dmitri Maruta/Alamy; **p. 574, top:** BananaStock/Jupiter Images; **p. 575, top right:** Ilene MacDonald/Alamy; **p. 575, bottom right:** Image Source/Alamy; **p. 575, bottom right:** Richard Megna/Fundamental Photographs; **p. 575, bottom center:** Comstock Images/Comstock/Jupiter Images; **p. 575, center:** Morgan Lane Photography/Shutterstock; **p. 575, bottom left:** Inmagine Asia/Inmagine Asia/Age Fotostock; **p. 576, top right:** Fuse/Jupiter Images

Chapter 16 **p. 580–581, Chapter Opener:** Erik Isakson/The Image Bank/Getty Images; **p. 582, center left:** Dan Dalton/Digital Vision/Getty Images; **p. 584, top left:** Jose Luis Pelaez Inc/Blend Images/Alamy; **p. 584, top right:** Dex Image/Alamy; **p. 584, top center:** Arpad/Fotolia; **p. 584, top center:** Tamara Lackey/Getty Images; **p. 585, top left:** Tetra Images/Getty Images; **p. 585, top center:** Ryan McVay/Photodisc/Getty Images; **p. 585, top center:** Stockbyte/Getty Images; **p. 585, top right:** Stockbyte/Getty Images; **p. 586, center left:** Creatas/Jupiter Images; **p. 598, center left:** webphotographeer/iStockphoto; **p. 599, top right:** Stockbroker/MBI/Alamy; **p. 601, bottom right:** Kristin Piljay/Pearson Education; **p. 601, center right:** Elena Gaak/Shutterstock; **p. 602, center left:** Kayte Deioma/PhotoEdit, Inc.; **p. 604, center left:** Vasko Miokovic/iStockphoto; **p. 605, bottom left:** Fuse/Getty Images; **p. 606, center left:** Image Source/Jupiter Images; **p. 609, top right:** siegi/fotolia; **p. 611, bottom right:** Kristin Piljay/Pearson Education, Inc.; **p. 612, center left:** SPL/Photo Researchers, Inc.; **p. 613, top right:** Marcelo Sayao/EPA/Newscom; **p. 614, top left:** Kristin Piljay/Pearson Education, Inc.; **p. 615, top left:** Dan Dalton/Digital Vision/Getty Images; **p. 616, top right:** Stockbroker/MBI/Alamy; **p. 616, bottom right:** Kristin Piljay/Pearson Education, Inc.; **p. 616, top left:** Elena Gaak/Shutterstock

Chapter 17 **p. 620–621, Chapter Opener:** Image Source/Getty Images; **p. 625, center right:** Asia Images Group Pte Ltd/Alamy; **p. 628, top left:** dalaprod/Fotolia; **p. 628, center left:** Kristin Piljay/Pearson Education; **p. 631, bottom right:** BlueMoon Stock/SuperStock; **p. 632, bottom center:** Andy Crawford/Dorling Kindersley, Inc.; **p. 632, bottom center:** Andy Crawford/Dorling Kindersley, Inc.; **p. 632, bottom center:** Andy Crawford/Dorling Kindersley, Inc.; **p. 635, top right:** Kristin Piljay/Pearson Education, Inc.; **p. 636, bottom left:** Eiichi Onodera/Emi Kimata/JupiterImages; **p. 637, top right:** Richard Megna/Fundamental Photographs; **p. 638, center left:** Blend Images/SuperStock; **p. 641, top center:** Monkey Business/Fotolia; **p. 642, top left:** ZUMA Press/Newscom; **p. 644, top center:** Ariel Skelley/Cusp/Corbis; **p. 645, top right:** It Stock Free/Age Fotostock; **p. 647, top center:** Sally and Richard Greenhill/Alamy; **p. 649, bottom right:** Kayte Deioma/PhotoEdit, Inc.; **p. 650, center left:** Dr. Martin S. Spiller, DMD; **p. 654, bottom left:** Laura Dwight/PhotoEdit, Inc.; **p. 656, bottom right:** Brand X/Age Fotostock; **p. 657, top left:** Serhiy Kobyakov/Shutterstock; **p. 657, top right:** Serhiy Kobyakov/Shutterstock; **p. 659, top center:** Andy Crawford/Dorling Kindersley, Inc.; **p. 659, top center:** Andy Crawford/Dorling Kindersley, Inc.; **p. 659, top center:** Andy Crawford/Dorling Kindersley, Inc.; **p. 659, top left:** MedioImages/Photodisc/Getty Images; **p. 659, top right:** American Images Inc/Photodisc/Getty Images; **p. 660, bottom right:** Kristin Piljay/Pearson Education, Inc.; **p. 660, top right:** Blend Images/SuperStock; **p. 661, bottom right:** Ariel

Skelley/Cusp/Corbis; **p. 661, center right:** Andy Crawford/Dorling Kindersley, Inc.; **p. 661, top left:** Richard Megna/Fundamental Photographs; **p. 661, bottom left:** ZUMA Press/Newscom; **p. 662, left:** Kayte Deioma/PhotoEdit, Inc.; **p. 662, bottom:** Laura Dwight/PhotoEdit, Inc.

Chapter 18 **p. 668–669, Chapter Opener:** Tom Stewart/Age Fotostock; **p. 670, center left:** Simon Brown/Dorling Kindersley, Inc.; **p. 673, top right:** Huntstock/Creatas/Jupiter Images; **p. 675, bottom right:** Ronnie Kaufman/Larry Hirshowitz/Blend Images/Alamy; **p. 676, top left:** Skip Nall/Alamy; **p. 677, top left:** Gengberg/Dreamstime; **p. 677, center right:** Wavebreakmedia/Dreamstime; **p. 678, top center:** Zdenek Rosenthaler/Shutterstock.com; **p. 679, top left:** U.S. Department of Agriculture; **p. 680, bottom left:** Mike Booth/Alamy; **p. 682, bottom left:** Mike Flippo/Shutterstock; **p. 686, top center:** picturesbyrob/Alamy; **p. 687, bottom right:** Tim Sloan/AFP/Getty Images/Newscom; **p. 688, bottom left:** Marnie Burkhart/Fancy/Alamy; **p. 689, bottom left:** Digital Vision/Getty Images; **p. 693, top right:** Chris Rout/Bubbles Photolibrary/Alamy; **p. 695, top left:** N. Aubrier/Age Fotostock; **p. 695, bottom right:** picturesbyrob/Alamy; **p. 695, top right:** Wavebreakmedia/Dreamstime; **p. 696, top right:** Chris Rout/Bubbles Photolibrary/Alamy

Chapter 19 **p. 700–701, Chapter Opener:** Image Source; **p. 705, center right:** Ariel Skelley/Thinkstock; **p. 706, top left:** USDA/USDA Ag. Research Center; **p. 706, top left:** USDA/USDA Ag. Research Center; **p. 708, bottom right:** Tufts University; **p. 710, center left:** Chris Willson/Alamy; **p. 713, bottom right:** Altrendo Images/Stockbyte/Getty Images; **p. 715, top right:** FancyVeerSet1/Fancy/Alamy; **p. 717, top right:** GalinaSt/Fotolia; **p. 719, top left:** Michael P. Gadomski/Photo Researchers, Inc.; **p. 723, top right:** Tina Manley/Alamy; **p. 726, top center:** Monkey Business Images/Shutterstock; **p. 727, bottom right:** FancyVeerSet1/Fancy/Alamy; **p. 727, bottom left:** USDA/USDA Ag. Research Center; **p. 727, center left:** USDA/Agricultural Research Service; **p. 728, right:** Tina Manley/North America/Alamy; **p. 728, top center:** GalinaSt/Fotolia

Chapter 20 **p. 732–733, Chapter Opener:** Philippe Desenrck/Photolibrary/Getty Images; **p. 738:** PHANIE/Photo Researchers, Inc.; **p. 739:** Dr. Gary Gaugler/Photo Researchers, Inc.; **p. 740:** Eye of Science/Photo Researchers, Inc.; **p. 744:** Jacek Chabraszewski/Shutterstock; **p. 747:** Piga & Catalano/Age Fotostock; **p. 748, center left:** United States Department of Agriculture; **p. 748, bottom left:** United States Department of Agriculture; **p. 757:** United States Department of Agriculture; **p. 758, top:** Kristin Piljay/Pearson Education/Pearson Science; **p. 758, center:** Kristin Piljay/Pearson Education/Pearson Science; **p. 763:** Sam Wirzba/Agstockusa/Age Fotostock; **p. 764:** Illene MacDonald/PhotoEdit, Inc., Inc.; **p. 768:** Smileus/Shutterstock; **p. 769, bottom:** Scott Camazine/Photo Researchers, Inc.; **p. 770:** Joel Nito/AFP/Getty Images; **p. 779:** Marvin Dembinsky Photo Associates/Alamy; **p. 779:** United States Department of Agriculture; **p. 780:** Marina Nabatova/Shutterstock; **p. 782:** United States Department of Agriculture; **p. 783, top left:** Pearson Education/Pearson Science; **p. 783, top right:** Pearson Education/Pearson Science; **p. 783, bottom left:** Pearson Education/Pearson Science; **p. 783, bottom right:** Pearson Education/Pearson Science; **p. 784, left:** Pearson Education/Pearson Science; **p. 784, right:** Pearson Education/Pearson Science; **p. 786, bottom left:** Kristin Piljay/Pearson Education/Pearson Science; **p. 786, bottom center:** Kristin Piljay/Pearson Education/Pearson Science; **p. 786, top left:** Dr. Gary Gaugler/Photo Researchers, Inc.; **p. 786, bottom right:** Illene MacDonald/PhotoEdit, Inc.; **p. 787:** United States Department of Agriculture

Chapter 21 **p. 794–795, Chapter Opener:** John Lamparski/WireImage/Getty Images; **p. 797, top:** Lulu/Fotolia; **p. 800:** Jane Alexander/Photofusion Picture Library/Alamy; **p. 802:** Mohamed Messara/Landov; **p. 803:** Mike Boyatt/Agstockusa; **p. 805:** Jeff Greenberg/PhotoEdit, Inc.; **p. 807:** Jean-Marc Giboux/Getty Images; **p. 810:** Alain Evrard/Robert Harding World Imagery; **p. 811:** ZUMA Press/Newscom; **p. 812:** Boris Roessler/dpa/picture-alliance/Newscom; **p. 814:** ZUMA Press/Newscom; **p. 815, bottom left:** Jane Alexander/Photofusion Picture Library/Alamy; **p. 815, bottom right:** Mohamed Messara/Landov; **p. 816:** Jeff Greenberg/PhotoEdit, Inc.

Tolerable Upper Intake Levels (ULs*)

	Vitamins							
Life Stage Group	Vitamin A (μg/d)[a]	Vitamin C (mg/d)	Vitamin D (μg/d)	Vitamin E (mg/d)[b,c]	Niacin (mg/d)[c]	Vitamin B_6 (mg/d)	Folate (μg/d)[c]	Choline (g/d)
Infants								
0–6 mo	600	ND[d]	25	ND	ND	ND	ND	ND
6–12 mo	600	ND	38	ND	ND	ND	ND	ND
Children								
1–3 y	600	400	63	200	10	30	300	1.0
4–8 y	900	650	75	300	15	40	400	1.0
Males								
9–13 y	1,700	1,200	100	600	20	60	600	2.0
14–18 y	2,800	1,800	100	800	30	80	800	3.0
19–30 y	3,000	2,000	100	1,000	35	100	1,000	3.5
31–50 y	3,000	2,000	100	1,000	35	100	1,000	3.5
51–70 y	3,000	2,000	100	1,000	35	100	1,000	3.5
>70 y	3,000	2,000	100	1,000	35	100	1,000	3.5
Females								
9–13 y	1,700	1,200	100	600	20	60	600	2.0
14–18 y	2,800	1,800	100	800	30	80	800	3.0
19–30 y	3,000	2,000	100	1,000	35	100	1,000	3.5
31–50 y	3,000	2,000	100	1,000	35	100	1,000	3.5
51–70 y	3,000	2,000	100	1,000	35	100	1,000	3.5
>70 y	3,000	2,000	100	1,000	35	100	1,000	3.5
Pregnancy								
≤18 y	2,800	1,800	100	800	30	80	800	3.0
19–50 y	3,000	2,000	100	1,000	35	100	1,000	3.5
Lactation								
≤18 y	2,800	1,800	100	800	30	80	800	3.0
19–50 y	3,000	2,000	100	1,000	35	100	1,000	3.5

Data from: Reprinted with permission from the Dietary Reference Intakes series. Copyright 1997, 1998, 2000, 2001, 2005, 2011 by the National Academies of Sciences, courtesy of the National Academies Press, Washington, D.C. These reports may be accessed via www.nap.edu.

[a] As preformed vitamin A only.

[b] As α-tocopherol; applies to any form of supplemental α-tocopherol.

[c] The ULs for vitamin E, niacin, and folate apply to synthetic forms obtained from supplements, fortified foods, or a combination of the two.

[d] ND = Not determinable due to lack of data of adverse effects in this age group and concern with regard to lack of ability to handle excess amounts. Source of intake should be from food only to prevent high levels of intake.

Note: A Tolerable Upper Intake Level (UL) is the highest level of daily nutrient intake that is likely to pose no risk of adverse health effects to almost all individuals in the general population. Unless otherwise specified, the UL represents total intake from food, water, and supplements. Due to a lack of suitable data, ULs could not be established for vitamin K, thiamin, riboflavin, vitamin B_{12}, pantothenic acid, biotin, and carotenoids. In the absence of a UL, extra caution may be warranted in consuming levels above recommended intakes. Members of the general population should be advised not to routinely exceed the UL. The UL is not meant to apply to individuals who are treated with the nutrient under medical supervision or to individuals with predisposing conditions that modify their sensitivity to the nutrient.

Tolerable Upper Intake Levels (ULs*)

Life Stage Group	Elements															
	Boron (mg/d)	Calcium (mg/d)	Copper (µg/d)	Fluoride (mg/d)	Iodine (µg/d)	Iron (mg/d)	Magnesium (mg/d)[e]	Manganese (mg/d)	Molybdenum (µg/d)	Nickel (mg/d)	Phosphorus (g/d)	Selenium (µg/d)	Vanadium (mg/d)[f]	Zinc (mg/d)	Sodium (g/d)	Chloride (g/d)
Infants																
0–6 mo	ND[d]	1,000	ND	0.7	ND	40	ND	ND	ND	ND	ND	45	ND	4	ND	ND
6–12 mo	ND	1,500	ND	0.9	ND	40	ND	ND	ND	ND	ND	60	ND	5	ND	ND
Children																
1–3 y	3	2,500	1,000	1.3	200	40	65	2	300	0.2	3	90	ND	7	1.5	2.3
4–8 y	6	2,500	3,000	2.2	300	40	110	3	600	0.3	3	150	ND	12	1.9	2.9
Males																
9–13 y	11	3,000	5,000	10	600	40	350	6	1,100	0.6	4	280	ND	23	2.2	3.4
14–18 y	17	3,000	8,000	10	900	45	350	9	1,700	1.0	4	400	ND	34	2.3	3.6
19–30 y	20	2,500	10,000	10	1,100	45	350	11	2,000	1.0	4	400	1.8	40	2.3	3.6
31–50 y	20	2,500	10,000	10	1,100	45	350	11	2,000	1.0	4	400	1.8	40	2.3	3.6
51–70 y	20	2,000	10,000	10	1,100	45	350	11	2,000	1.0	4	400	1.8	40	2.3	3.6
>70 y	20	2,000	10,000	10	1,100	45	350	11	2,000	1.0	3	400	1.8	40	2.3	3.6
Females																
9–13 y	11	3,000	5,000	10	600	40	350	6	1,100	0.6	4	280	ND	23	2.2	3.4
14–18 y	17	3,000	8,000	10	900	45	350	9	1,700	1.0	4	400	ND	34	2.3	3.6
19–30 y	20	2,500	10,000	10	1,100	45	350	11	2,000	1.0	4	400	1.8	40	2.3	3.6
31–50 y	20	2,500	10,000	10	1,100	45	350	11	2,000	1.0	4	400	1.8	40	2.3	3.6
51–70 y	20	2,000	10,000	10	1,100	45	350	11	2,000	1.0	4	400	1.8	40	2.3	3.6
>70 y	20	2,000	10,000	10	1,100	45	350	11	2,000	1.0	3	400	1.8	40	2.3	3.6
Pregnancy																
≤18 y	17	3,000	8,000	10	900	45	350	9	1,700	1.0	3.5	400	ND	34	2.3	3.6
19–50 y	20	2,500	10,000	10	1,100	45	350	11	2,000	1.0	3.5	400	ND	40	2.3	3.6
Lactation																
≤18 y	17	3,000	8,000	10	900	45	350	9	1,700	1.0	4	400	ND	34	2.3	3.6
19–50 y	20	2,500	10,000	10	1,100	45	350	11	2,000	1.0	4	400	ND	40	2.3	3.6

Data from: Reprinted with permission from the Dietary Reference Intakes series. Copyright 1997, 1998, 2000, 2001, 2005, 2011 by the National Academies of Sciences, courtesy of the National Academies Press, Washington, D.C. These reports may be accessed via www.nap.edu.

[d] ND = Not determinable due to lack of data of adverse effects in this age group and concern with regard to lack of ability to handle excess amounts. Source of intake should be from food only to prevent high levels of intake.

[e] The ULs for magnesium represent intake from a pharmacological agent only and do not include intake from food and water.

[f] Although vanadium in food has not been shown to cause adverse effects in humans, there is no justification for adding vanadium to food, and vanadium supplements should be used with caution. The UL is based on adverse effects in laboratory animals, and this data could be used to set a UL for adults but not children and adolescents.

Note: A Tolerable Upper Intake Level (UL) is the highest level of daily nutrient intake that is likely to pose no risk of adverse health effects to almost all individuals in the general population. Unless otherwise specified, the UL represents total intake from food, water, and supplements. Due to a lack of suitable data, ULs could not be established for vitamin K, thiamin, riboflavin, vitamin B_{12}, pantothenic acid, biotin, and carotenoids. In the absence of a UL, extra caution may be warranted in consuming levels above recommended intakes. Members of the general population should be advised not to routinely exceed the UL. The UL is not meant to apply to individuals who are treated with the nutrient under medical supervision or to individuals with predisposing conditions that modify their sensitivity to the nutrient.